34,50

P9-BYO-328

The First 80 Years

The Christian Science Monitor
1908–1988

The First 80 Years

The Christian Science Monitor®   1908–1988

The Christian Science Publishing Society · Boston, Massachusetts · USA

Books from
THE
CHRISTIAN
SCIENCE
MONITOR.

© Copyright 1988 The Christian Science Publishing Society.
All rights reserved.

Printed in the United States of America

No portion of this work may be reprinted or transmitted in any form without express prior written permission from the publisher, except for brief portions or
samples used as review material.

ISBN 0-87510-194-1

Contents

1970–1988

Introduction

In Jules Verne's classic novel, Phileas Fogg traveled around the world in 80 days, sampling the diversity of the cultures he encountered. So, too, the reader can travel through this collection of 80 years of *The Christian Science Monitor* to glimpse the rich variety of deeds and events spanning the years since the Monitor's first issue on Nov. 25, 1908.

Our purpose here is not to celebrate a birthday, but to mark the progress of our civilization, as well as this newspaper, through a single window into each year. The Monitor, unlike many other newspapers, is not a "front page" publication. It seeks to provide significant information with sufficient background and perspective to increase understanding—and that cannot be accomplished on a front page alone. The paper's identity is realized through all its pages, its photos, its national and international news coverage, its editorials, and its features on the arts, the home, and the whole fabric of the human scene.

80 years ago Mary Baker Eddy founded the Monitor as a central and crowning element of the Christian Science Church, which she had established some years earlier. Her injunction to church leaders in 1908 was that the paper must be started "without fail," and that "the Cause demands that it be issued now."

But it was not to be an organ of church news; neither was it to proselytize or preach. Its mission, in the words of the paper's first editor, Archibald McLellan, was "to publish the real news of the world in a clean, wholesome manner, devoid of the sensational methods employed by so many newspapers." And it was to include one special column each day for religious material.

In an editorial in the Monitor's first issue, Mrs. Eddy sounded the keynote for its editors. She wrote that the object of the Monitor was "to injure no man, but to bless all mankind." In other words, the Monitor was to be an unselfish publication, for the benefit of the world and not just for the church.

Today the Monitor remains a newspaper devoted to public service, aiming to enlighten, elevate, and educate the reader. As the recipient of five Pulitzer Prizes and countless other awards, it has sought constantly to uplift journalistic standards. And if it sometimes missed the mark itself, it has often been in the vanguard of newspaper excellence.

The pages assembled here were not necessarily selected to represent the best work of the Monitor during a given year. Chosen as records of each year's most memorable event, they reflect the work of many editors through many eras. Some of them may seem quaint: Styles change in newspapering just as they do in clothes, and today's Monitor editors very likely would have treated some of the events differently.

Not even every significant event has been included in this book. The reader will note that many occurrences considered important—armed conflicts, wars of independence, catastophic natural phenomenon,—have not been included. This is not to suggest that these events are inconsequential. It is simply that the scope of this book does not allow an exhaustive historical chronicle.

Yet because these pages remain a true register of those events, we trust you will enjoy traveling with us—without benefit of Phileas Fogg and his various vehicles—through 80 years of our collective history.

Katherine W. Fanning
Editor
The Christian Science Monitor

Editorial

(Extract from the leading Editorial in Vol. 1, No. 1, of *The Christian Science Monitor*, November 25, 1908)

SOMETHING IN A NAME

I have given the name to all the Christian Science periodicals. The first was *The Christian Science Journal*, designed to put on record the divine Science of Truth; the second I entitled *Sentinel*, intended to hold guard over Truth, Life, and Love; the third, *Der Herold der Christian Science*, to proclaim the universal activity and availability of Truth; the next I named *Monitor*, to spread undivided the Science that operates unspent. The object of the *Monitor* is to injure no man, but to bless all mankind.

Mary Baker Eddy

Editors of the *Monitor*

ARCHIBALD McLELLAN
November 25, 1908–June 8, 1914

FREDERICK DIXON
June 8, 1914–Jan. 30, 1922

DEWITT JOHN
May 15, 1964–Sept. 30, 1970

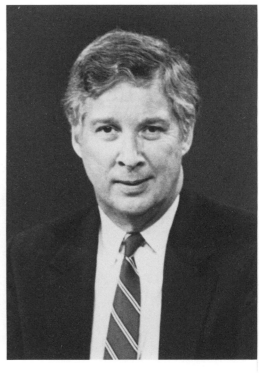

JOHN HUGHES
October 1, 1970–May 31, 1979

WILLIS J. ABBOTT
January 30, 1922–April 1927

ROSCOE DRUMMOND
January 21, 1934–Dec. 1, 1939

ERWIN D. CANHAM
December 1, 1939–May 15, 1964

EARL W. FOELL
June 1, 1979–June 1, 1983

KATHERINE FANNING
June 1, 1983–Present

Over the years, the *Monitor* has received thousands of letters from readers. Many were written by some of this century's most influential thinkers and leaders both at home and abroad.

The following is a sampling of what these prominent individuals have had to say about the newspaper.

Calvin Coolidge: ". . . I want to take this opportunity of expressing to you my sincere appreciation of the support which you have given me. If opportunity offers, I hope that you will express to your associates my personal thanks for the fairness and courtesy which the Monitor has always shown." (In a letter to Willis J. Abbott written from the White House on Nov. 7, 1924. Mr. Abbott was a staff member of the Monitor.)

Fiorello H. La Guardia (then mayor of New York): "*The Christian Science Monitor* is the greatest paper in the United States—you can put that in your headlines!"

Wendell Willkie (presidential candidate): "*The Christian Science Monitor* is one of the greatest newspapers of the world. I admire and read its editorial page. I know of no newspaper more consistently both wise and right."

Thomas E. Dewey (then Governor of New York): "I have the warmest regard for *The Christian Science Monitor*, which is truly a great newspaper. In the course of many conversations with experienced and responsible newspaper men I have never met one who did not look upon *The Christian Science Monitor* as a model newspaper. There could be no higher testimony to the value and distinction of the Monitor than the respect and admiration of the people of your own craft. You have truly earned your high reputation for painstaking accuracy and fairness in all public issues. You have shown how a paper can maintain jealously that reputation, avoiding the lurid and the sensational, and yet be supremely readable. These accomplishments are reached only by a high degree of professional skill and earnest journalistic conscience."

Winston Churchill: ". . . (the Manchester Guardian) . . . seems to me to occupy in this country something like the distinguished position that *The Christian Science Monitor* does in the United States—a position of singular distinction in British journalism."

Dwight D. Eisenhower: "For half a century, true to the highest standards of responsible reporting, the *Monitor* has grown in service to a wide community. With freedom, fairness, and sensitivity, it has recorded the events of our day and written with clarity of its judgements for the morrow. In its pages are found the facts and opinions upon which intelligent decisions can be firmly based."

Lowell Thomas (commentator): "The *Monitor* is one of the world's great newspapers. I shout that from the housetops at every opportunity."

John F. Kennedy: "I think that the able and excellent editorial comment and news coverage given this whole problem of Indo-China's independence in the *Monitor* has had an important effect on opinion here in Congress."

Eleanor Roosevelt: "I am familiar with *The Christian Science Monitor* and it seems to me one of the best and most valuable newspapers that we have in this country."

Franklin D. Roosevelt: "The constructive service which *The Christian Science Monitor* has consistently rendered to better understanding between nations is widely appreciated in all parts of the world . . . The preservation of peace needs the devoted support of newspapers throughout the world, and it is encouraging to find The Christian Science Monitor devoting itself further to the enlargement of understanding between the English-speaking peoples . . ."

Walter Lippmann: "There is no more scrupulously objective newspaper dealing with international affairs than the *Monitor*."

First Issue of
The Christian Science Monitor

THE CHRISTIAN SCIENCE MONITOR

STOCK EDITION. BOSTON, MASS., WEDNESDAY, NOVEMBER 25, 1908.—VOL. I., NO. 1. PRICE TWO CENTS.

CARNEGIE DOES NOT WANT TO BE TARIFF WITNESS

Steel Magnate Says He Has Served His Time in Matters and Views Are Well Known.

71 YEARS OLD TODAY

Chairman Payne of Ways and Means Committee Makes Public Correspondence With Multi-Millionaire.

WASHINGTON, Nov. 25—In a letter to Chairman Payne of the House ways and means committee, Andrew Carnegie, who is celebrating his 71st birthday in New York today, declined to appear as a witness at the present tariff hearing. He says:

"I have served my full time in Washington upon tariff matters, and beg to be excused from further service in that direction. I am no longer in business and in my "Century" article I have said all that I have to say upon that subject. Manufacturers will appear before you from whom you can obtain required details.

"Reading the comment upon my article by various distinguished gentlemen in Washington, as published yesterday, I see they have not read the article itself, but only a few striking extracts separated from the context.

"When you read it, you will discover that my faith in protection wherever it is proved to be necessary, is as strong as ever, and that I continue also to believe that the surest way to secure needed protection is to reduce protective duties from time to time, and finally abolish them when no longer needed.

"Pursuing this policy, our party has already reduced its duties upon steel rails from $28 to $7, and other duties in greater or less degree. The McKinley tariff, which made great reductions, is a case in point. It would prove false to its history and its pledges if it failed now. In the most critical times, the protective policy has received indispensable aid from patriotic Democrats in Congress as I have shown. This is as it should be. Duties upon imports should cease to be a party question. Only what is best for the common country should be thought of.

"I attach supreme importance to the maintenance of present duties upon the articles used chiefly by the rich, not from the protective, but from the revenue point of view. Special attention is required in the revenue needs of the country these days to meet increased expenditures, and, as far as I know, none can be obtained with so little pressure upon the people, as the two hundred and odd million now flowing into the treasury from such articles.

"Yours, as a true protectionist,
(Signed) "ANDREW CARNEGIE."

Chairman Payne said in his reply to Mr. Carnegie:

"Your letter of the 24th instant received. I regret that you decline to come before the committee, as we are anxious to get all information possible upon this schedule, as upon all other schedules of the tariff act. You were invited because we thought you could give, in answer to questions, further information than that contained in your article. We are seeking all the information possible and every intelligent source, and welcome the attendance of any citizen, whatever his views may be upon the question of tariff rates. Of course, the committee, in adjusting rates, must be governed by the facts presented."

SHIP RELIEF IS SAFE AT LUZON

MANILA, Nov. 25—The hospital ship Relief is safe and is proceeding to Manila under her own steam after a series of experiences which for a time threatened her safety.

Leaving Guam in the midst of a howling gale, the storm increased in strength until on the 18th the vessel tossed so that her engines became disabled. Her captain laid her head to the waves and ordered temporary repairs made.

While these were in progress fire broke out in the hold, but it was soon extinguished. The engineers finally managed to fix things so that a start could be made, although caution had to be observed and speed curtailed.

The Relief was reported today off southern Luzon and will reach the harbor tonight or tomorrow.

CALL TROOPS TO QUELL STUDENTS

ROME, Nov. 25—Troops had to be called to aid the police in suppressing an anti-Austrian student demonstration this afternoon. Hundreds of arrests have been made. The students planned a meeting at the university. By order of the police, the university was closed, but the meeting was held nevertheless.

Many incendiary speeches denunciatory of Austria were made and finally the students started to march in a body to the Austrian legation. The police interfered, and with the military dispersed the mob. The Austrian ambassador has protested against the public burning of the Austrian flag and the government is expected to apologize.

A dozen members of the chamber of deputies have announced that they will interpolate Foreign Minister Tittoni regarding Italy's attitude on the Balkan situation. They will demand that it be openly anti-Austrian.

THANKSGIVING SERVICE.

The First Church of Christ, Scientist, The Mother Church, at Falmouth, Norway and St. Paul streets, Boston, will hold its regular Thanksgiving service tomorrow at 10:45 a. m. The subject is "Thanksgiving."

CONSTRUCTION WORK RAPIDLY PROGRESSES ON GREAT DAM ACROSS THE CHARLES RIVER BASIN

Lock and Sluices Completed and Machinery Installed in New Lock-House on Boston Side of Stream.

LOCK IN OPERATION

LOCKS AND SLUICES IN CHARLES RIVER DAM.
Upper Picture Shows Small Lock for Motor Boats and the Eight Sluices—Lower Picture Shows the Main 45-Foot Lock Open, with Scherzer Drawbridge Uplifted.

Sufficient progress has been made on the Charles river dam to warrant the statement that the work will be in a very satisfactory condition before severe weather compels a partial cessation of work on this enormous piece of construction.

Arthur I. Plaisted, electrical engineer for the Charles river basin commission, who is temporarily in charge of the locks, has furnished a reporter of The Monitor some interesting information as to the progress of the undertaking.

The lower lock house is well along and practically inclosed; the interior finish alone remains to be done. The upper house is nearing completion; the roof is going on at present.

The work of driving piles for the harbor wall is in progress, as well as the banking up of earth on both sides of the shut-off dam.

The concreting is nearly finished, with the exception of the banking of the harbor wall, and this work can be continued even in quite severe weather, during the warmer portion of the day, provided the work is enclosed in a "special form" or canvas covering.

Largest Lock Gates in America.

The huge lock gates which the commission has installed are the first of this type to be used in America and are notable specimens of engineering skill. They are also the largest lock gates in America. This same type, known as the "sliding gate," will be used in the Panama enterprise.

These gates are operated by electricity and slide back and forth much like a freight-car door, with the rail, however, in this case, underneath and three feet below the bed of the dock.

When the lock is open the gates are back under the lock house, the outer edge is flush with the walls of the lock. At the inner end of each gate is a trolley which takes its power from a wire running in line with the gate the whole width of the inclosure.

The gates are filled with steam radiators, connected by flexible pipes with the steam boilers in the lock house. Thus provision is made against the formation of ice about the gates. The channel for the gate is 90 feet long and the lock is 45 feet wide.

Two Centrifugal Pumps.

There are two centrifugal pumps at the lock, both electrically driven, which may be used for emptying it in case it is necessary to make repairs or clean it out. These two pumps have a total capacity of about 26,000,000 gallons per day, and would empty the lock in about six hours.

The drawbridge is a Scherzer rolling-lift bridge, a patented type of bascule bridge which has been successfully used in other places. It consists of two leaves, giving a total width of roadway of 85 feet. It has a clear span of 52 feet. In each leaf of the bridge there are about 380,000 pounds of ballast, made up of concrete and scrap iron.

Four of the huge stone piers which are to support the new bridge, just below the Scherzer bridge and close to the downstream side of the dam, are nearly finished. This bridge will be for the sole use of the Boston Elevated Railway.

Finished Within a Month.

The engineer and his assistants are busy moving all electrical appliances from the temporary quarters to the permanent operating tower, a fine structure of stone and brick, which will be practically finished with all the apparatus installed in about a month. This tower is located on the Boston side of the river at the foot of Leverett street, near the site once occupied by the end of the old Craigie bridge.

CITY WINS $5000 IN LAND CASE

Judgment Is Entered in Case of Property Purchased From Cemetery Trustee and Superintendent.

Judgment for $5000 for the plaintiff was entered in the superior court today in the suit of the city of Boston against William J. Fallon and James H. Morton. The amount represents part of the profit made in the sale of land, owned by Morton, who was superintendent of Mt. Hope cemetery, to the city. At the time of the sale Mr. Fallon, a brother-in-law of Morton, was one of the cemetery trustees.

The fact that Morton owned the land was known to the city, but it was not known that Fallon, a member of the board of trustees that voted to purchase the land, was interested in the deal. Fallon and Morton shared the profit, amounting to $9420. Fallon's share was $4710. There was some doubt as to whether the city could recover against Morton, who had not concealed the fact that he owned the property.

The city, by agreement reached after a conference between counsel representing the city and Fallon and Morton, formally entered suit against both men and agreed to accept $5000 in settlement of its claim. The money has been paid to the city.

The action was the result of the recent expose of land deals by the finance commission. Ex-Assistant District Attorney Sughrue, counsel for the commission, laid bare the facts at a public hearing and immediately the law department of the city took steps to get back part of the profit made. John D. McLaughlin, assistant corporation counsel, had charge of the matter for the city.

SARDINIA BEACHED BECAUSE OF FIRE

Liner Burned Just Outside Malta While on Her Way From Liverpool—Many Lives Lost.

MALTA, Nov. 25—Many lives, the number of which cannot be ascertained for five hours, were lost when the Papayanni-Elierman liner was destroyed by fire outside of this harbor today. The steamer, which plies between Liverpool, Malta and Alexandria, had on board some 200 passengers, 25 or 30 of whom were English, and carried a crew of 44. Many of the passengers are missing and several of them are undoubtedly penned in the smoking hull, which lies on the shore off the harbor entrance, while others were drowned when they jumped overboard to escape the flames which enveloped the vessel.

The Sardinia left Malta early today for Alexandria, carrying in addition to the passengers and crew, a large cargo of merchandise She had hardly cleared the harbor entrance when smoke was observed issuing from the cargo hold. The crew was summoned to fire quarters and a detachment sent below. Almost before they had disappeared below decks, the forward hatch seemed to explode and in an instant the vessel was ablaze from stern to stem.

In the neighborhood of 100 passengers, including most of the British, are among the missing, although there is still a possibility that some of these have been picked up and landed elsewhere. Levantins and Greeks made up the majority of the passengers on the Sardinia, and these acted half crazed when the disaster happened, utterly defying discipline.

This hampered the crew both in fighting the fire and in trying to get the lifeboats and rafts overboard.

Up to mid-afternoon 50 bodies had been brought ashore from the wreck.

The survivors are scattered among so many rescuing boats that it will be impossible to secure any facts about the death list until all return to port.

BOSTON LIBRARY IS GIVEN A RARE BOOK COLLECTION

Mrs. Louise Chandler Moulton and Philip Bourke Marston Volumes Include Many Autograph Copies.

The Boston Public Library has been enriched by the gift of the library of the late Mrs. Louise Chandler Moulton, including also that of Philip Bourke Marston, who gave his library to Mrs. Moulton.

The principal value of this rare collection of books lies in the fact that many of them are "association copies," volumes presented to either Mrs. Moulton or Mr. Marston by the authors. Many of the books are autographed and some contain a personal sentiment. Among them are Swinburne's "Atlanta in Calydon," the London edition of 1865, an autograph copy of Christina Rossetti's "The Prince's Progress," and many American first editions.

NO DEMOCRACY, ZUEBLIN SAYS

Second Lecture in Course on "The American Municipality" Deals With the Training of the Citizen.

Prof. Charles Zueblin gave today his second lecture in his Wednesday course on "The American Municipality" at 6 Marlborough street, his subject being "The Training of the Citizen."

While Mr. Zueblin believes in democracy and the realization of its ideal so far as possible, he says we must not flatter ourselves that we have reached it. In training the citizen we must not lose sight of things as they are.

He took the given characteristics of democracy, namely: liberty, equality and fraternity, and said we do not have them today in their ideal state, but adds that if we cannot have them in all things, we can have them in the essential things.

Mr. Zueblin then pointed out how these characteristics may be realized at the present time. He said the laboring man is in great need of liberty, the liberty to work in that to which he is adapted. Equality of citizenship is needed. If we must have discrimination it should be as to the individual and not as to the class. Every one who gives good to the democracy should have a part in it and take it. There is much opportunity for fraternity in the associations of men and women to promote our civic welfare.

37,000 TURKEYS FOR HOME MARKET

In the transportation of Thanksgiving turkeys Boston this year has received the best service in its history. One train of 26 freight cars brought 37,000 turkeys from Cincinnati in 50 hours, the largest shipment of poultry ever made to the Boston market. Heretofore when fast time has been made with similar loads the goods have come by express.

ASK INJUNCTION AGAINST CHELSEA SHOE WORKERS

Walton V. Logan Alleges Union Men Interferred With Employes at Factory After Strike Was Declared.

NAMES EIGHT MEN

Walton & Logan, shoe manufacturers in Lynn and Chelsea, brought a bill in the supreme court today against Benjamin Baker and eight other members of the Shoe Workers' nion of Chelsea seeking an injunction to restrain the defendants from interfering with their employees and with persons entering and leaving their factory in Chelsea.

The lasters and the edgeworkers in the factory in Lynn went out last month on a sympathetic strike owing to the installation of a labor saving device in the plant of another manufacturer. The complainants had to close their shop in Lynn. Subsequently the union men left at the Chelsea shop.

As a result of an adverfising for help about 500 to 800 persons were secured by the company, from a third to a half of the normal number. Members of the shoe workers' union in Chelsea were charged with interfering with persons working in the shop.

Judge Loring issued an order of notice returnable Friday.

FIREMAN SAVES ENTIRE FAMILY

Brave Rescuer Swung From Roof 70 Feet Above Sidewalk in New York to Aid Seven Persons.

NEW YORK, Nov. 25—Lowering himself over the cornice of a five-story tenement house and hanging 70 feet above the sidewalk, Frank Semple, a fireman, today by desperate efforts prevented David Lynch, his wife and five children from leaping from the window to escape the flames.

Semple had seized a rope and reached the roof through the adjoining tenement. Fastening the rope to a chimney he lowered himself just in time to save the family. Later they were taken in safety from the burning building.

SAVES CHILDREN AND WIFE AT FIRE

Quick wit and curage enabled Thomas Starr, living on Sagamore sreet, Revere, to rescue his family, consisting of his wife and two small children, from their burning home early today. The cottage which the Starr's occupied and another unoccupied house which stood nearby were destroyed. The origin of the fire is unknown.

BROCKTON CHURCH DEDICATION NEAR

BROCKTON, Nov. 25—The cornerstone of the new First Baptist church will be laid with impressive ceremonies at the sit of the new edifice, corner of Warren avenue and West Elm street, tomorrow. The Rev. Arthur C. Archibald pastor will preside at the exercises, in the old edifice. There will be an organ prelude and doxology, followed by invocation by the Rev. A. T. Ringold. There will be addresses by the Rev. Alan Hudson, the Rev. Dr. Albert Marion Hyde, and the Rev. Julian S. Wadsworth, all of this city, and the dedicatory address itself by the Rev. Edward Holyoke of Providence.

George W. Jeffry, superintendent of the Sunday School, will preside at the filling of the cornerstone and prayer will be offered by the Rev. Oscar D. Thomas.

SPEAKER'S CLUB FOR HARVARD MEN

Fifty Harvard students interested in public speaking have just organized a speakers' club. Prof. Irving L. Winter '86 inoutlining the purpose of the club proposed that topics of local interest be discussed and that part of the work of the meetings be prepared ahead.

Prof. George P. Baker '87 suggested that public meetings be held as often as possible, and that critic be present to give advice.

A committee of graduates with Professor Winter as adviser was appointed to consider the various suggestions and call the next meeting.

Mills Again on Full Time.

GREAT BARRINGTON, Nov. 25—The Monument cotton mills, which have been running on short time for several months, are being operated this week in full. Four hundred hands are employed. The Rising paper mill, employing 350 hands, is also on full time after running on a short-time schedule for a year or more.

UNVEIL STATUE OF GEN. SHERIDAN AT WASHINGTON

Salute of 17 Guns Fired in Honor of Civil War Hero When Son Pulls Aside Covering of Memorial.

NOTED MEN PRESENT

WASHINGTON, Nov. 25—While a battery of field artillery boomed forth the 17 guns of a general's salute, 2d-Lieut. P. H. Sheridan Jr., this afternoon pulled the rope unveiling the bronze memorial statue of his father, Gen. "Phil" Sheridan, of civil war fame, in the presence of the President, Secretary of War Wright and a host of civil and military notables and citizens.

All the regular soldiers, sailors and marines stationed near Washington and the district national guard participated in the ceremonies, together with the Marine band. They formed an imposing parade that was later reviewed by the President and chief of staff, Gen. J. Franklin Bell.

Secretary of War Wright presided, in the capacity of chairman ex-officio of the statue commission. He made a short address, lauding the exploits and patriotism of the dashing cavalry commander. General Wright fought on the other side in the historic conflict, and his remarks were of all the more interest for that reason.

President Roosevelt made the principal address. Gen. Horace Porter of New York also spoke. The Right Rev. P. I. O'Connell, rector of the Catholic University, offered the invocation, and the recently elected Bishop of Washington, the Rev. Alfred Harding of the Episcopal church, pronounced the benediction.

NIGHT SCHOOLS FOR DES MOINES

Success of Plan Last Year Causes Educational Board to Resume Sessions This Season.

DES MOINES, Ia., Nov. 25—Free public night schools, which were tried in Des Moines last year, proved so successful that the school board has voted to open two buildings in East and West Des Moines for the work this year. The greatest interest is taken in the classes for teaching the English language to foreign born settlers. Fully 75 of these men and women, youths and girls, ranging in age from 15 to 70, gather nightly to pore over their primers and spelling books.

GOV. GUILD MAKES GOETTING ADVISER

Col. August H. Goetting of Springfield was today appointed councillor from the western Massachusetts district by Gov. Curtis Guild, Jr., to complete the term of the late Franklin W. Russell of Pittsfield.

Colonel Goetting is one of the most prominent Republicans in the state and at the recent election was chosen councillor to succeed the late Mr. Russell. Colonel Goetting was for many years chairman of the Republican State Committee, and has several times been mentioned in connection with the candidacy for Lieutenant-Governor.

NEW FACTORY SOON TO START

BROCKTON, Nov. 25—George E. Keith, president of the George E. Keith Corporation, announces that he expects machinery for the manufacture of women's shoes, at East Weymouth, will be installed soon and that the firm will be doing business in the new factory before Christmas. Several hundred employees will be needed.

The corporation has purchased a large tract of land on which it may erect homes for the workmen.

THANKSGIVING DAY FORECAST

WASHINGTON, Nov. 25—The weather bureau predicts for Thanksgiving day cloudy and unsettled conditions in the east and south, with continued warm weather east of the rocky mountains.

The following is the forecast for Boston and New England:

For Boston and vicinity: Cloudy tonight; Thursday, occasional rain; light easterly to southerly winds.

For New England: Rain tonight in north portions, cloudy in south.

High tide 12:06 a. m. and 12:20 p. m.

SALVED WOOL SOLD FOR $75,000.

The wool salved from the Leyland and Cunard docks in East Boston after the fire of July 8 has been sold at auction by the Underwriters' Salvage Company for $75,000.

EXPERT REVIEWS CONDITIONS IN THE DISTURBED BALKAN COUNTRIES

Interesting Phase of Economic Duel Between England and Germany Discussed.

LANDMARK HISTORY

Installment Stories of Situation in Near-Far East Presented for Readers of The Christian Science Monitor.

The Christian Science Monitor has arranged to have a comprehensive review of the past and present conditions existing in the Balkan peninsula and a discussion of the future prospects presented to its readers in installments from the pen of a close student of the situation in this near Eastern country. The first installment is given below.

It has been aptly said apropos of recent events in the Balkan peninsula that they mark but another phase of the economic duel between England and Germany.

Since the treaty of Berlin in 1878, all international problems, and more especially the Eastern question, have undergone a radical change, a change due to the all-pervading influence of modern Germany's rise to the rank of a foremost industrial and commercial power. It had been a time-honored diplomatic axiom that the rivalry between England and Russia from Constantinople to Pekin was fixed and permanent. Owing to this antagonism Austria's old interests and England's later ones had become nearly identical. This triangular relationship culminated at the Congress of Berlin when Russia's designs were completely defeated through the Anglo-Austrian entente.

Germany was "the honest broker" on that occasion, but still a broker with an eye to business. For although Bismarck remarked that the Eastern question was not worth the bones of a Pomeranian grenadier, his imperial successor at the helm thought otherwise. He deliberately wedged himself between Russia and England and thereby accomplished two objects. He supplanted English influence at Constantinople and insensibly made Austria's Eastern policy subservient to her own. It was presumably understood that at an opportune moment Turkey could and should be induced to join the Triple Alliance. This would have given the Emperor absolute predominance from the mouth of the Rhine to the mouth of the Euphrates. The final capping was to be the completion of the Bagdad railway, capable of transporting Prussian soldiers to the very gates of India. Needless to say, the prospect opened immense vistas of conquest, both to the man of the mailed lst and the fanatical Moslem soldier. It wasc haracteristic of this arrangement that Germany claimed farthest Turkey for herself, while she left European Turkey to be absorbed by Austria. It also accounts for Germany's apparently disinterested attitude towards the Macedonian medley, otherwise incomprehensible.

During the Boer war England was in imminent danger from a most powerful European combination. Germany, France, and Russia were about to coerce England and force peace on her. What broke up this nascent coalition which might have changed the face of the globe, is still a matter of conjecture. Not so the conclusions England drew therefrom and the measures she adopted to prevent a repetition of the attempt. That fiasco was the starting point of King Edward's "League of Peace," which has now resulted in the

CONTINUED ON PAGE TWO.

172 DEMOCRATS 219 REPUBLICANS IN NEXT HOUSE

Taft Followers Lose Four While Bryan Contingent Wins Six New Representatives in Congress.

INDIANA CHANGES

WASHINGTON, Nov. 25—The new House of Representatives of the 61st Congress which meets on the first Monday in December will be composed of 219 Republicans and 172 Democrats, a total of 391, according to the temporary roll which has been completed. The total in the last House was 289, of whom 223 were Republicans and 166 Democrats. The result is a net loss of four from the Republican side and a net gain of six on the Democratic side, the discrepancy being due to present vacancies. All told, the Democrats gained 17 districts and the Republicans 12.

The most marked advance made by the Democrats was in Indiana, the home of Mr. Bryan's running mate, Mr. Kern. Of the entire 13 members constituting the Indiana delegation, only two will be Republicans in the next Congress, whereas in the present Congress there are eight Republicans from that state. Colorado will not send so many Democrats as Indiana, owing to her smaller population, but that state recorded even a greater revolution in that, whereas all three members of the present delegation are now Republican, in the next House all will be Democratic. Mr. Bryan's own state of Nebraska added two to the Democratic column in the House, making an equal division of the six members from that state. Of the other Democratic gains, Ohio recorded three, Illinois one and Kentucky one.

The most striking accretions of the Republicans were made in North Carolina, where three members were taken from the Democratic column, and in Oklahoma, where there was a gain of two. Missouri and Pennsylvania also switched two members each from the Democratic to the Republican side, and New Jersey, Rhode Island and Wisconsin each supplied one of the Republican additions. Otherwise than as herein noted, the various state delegations will remain as at present.

The states which will be solidly Democratic are: Alabama, Arkansas, Colorado, Florida, Georgia, Louisiana, Mississippi, Nevada, South Carolina, Texas, and those which will be solidly Republican, California, Connecticut, Delaware, Idaho, Kansas, Maine, Michigan, Montana, New Hampshire, North Dakota, Oregon, Rhode Island, South Dakota, Utah, Vermont, Washington, West Virginia, Wyoming.

New York will have in the next, as it has in the present house, 26 Republicans and 11 Democrats. Maryland 3 and 3, but with a swap in districts; Virginia 9 to 1 in favor of the Democrats, as in the past; Tennessee 8 to 2, as now; Minnesota 8 Republicans and 1 Democrat; Massachusetts, 11 Republicans to 3 Democrats, the present proportion; Iowa 10 to 1 in favor of the Republicans, but with a change as to the district represented by a Democrat.

LARGE HALL AT CAPITAL WANTED

Auditorium for National Conventions and Social Functions at Washington Favored by Well-Known Men.

WASHINGTON, Nov. 25—There is general interest here in the plans for a great auditorium for the use of national conventions and for the holding of inaugural balls and other large functions which is to be constructed in Washington if the ideas of a committee of well-known men are carried out. Robert Bacon of New York, assistant secretary of state, heads the list of projectors, which includes C. C. Glover, president of the Riggs National Bank; George E. Hamilton, president of the Capital Traction Company, and Gen. Henry C. Corbin (retired). Secretary Root, John R. McLean and others may be connected later with the project, which contemplates the formation of a corporation with $1,500,000 capital.

The auditorium, when completed, will seat 12,000 persons, and will be so arranged that it can be used for almost any purpose. At present the national capital is sadly in need of a large hall, especially for convention uses and for the inaugural balls. Usually the inaugural balls are given in the Pension Building, which is quite inadequate for the purpose, and which cannot be used without the permission of Congress. The building project is just now in the hands of a committee of 12, which is to be increased to 50, and it is hoped the organization of the company and collection of subscriptions may be so expedited that the auditorium will be ready for use by March 4.

ANNUAL GAIN SET AT $10,000,000

Freight Revenues to Profit This Much by New Rates, Declares Western Traffic Manager.

LOS ANGELES, Calif., Nov. 25—Ten million dollars a year will be added to the freight revenues of the railroads by the increase in westbound transcontinental freight rates which become effective January 1, according to the estimate of Fred P. Gregson, traffic manager of the Associated Jobbers of Los Angeles.

Mr. Gregson has received a press proof of the new tariff, which is issued by the Transcontinental Freight Bureau.

"The increase in rates is not nearly as bad as I feared it would be," said Mr. Gregson, after going through the tariff.

"There are a great many changes in rates—in fact, I think about 75 per cent of all the rates have been changed. I have not discovered any great discriminations in the increases that have been made, however.

"One item which might work a hardship on our foundrymen and some manufacturers is the rate on certain kinds of iron, which has been raised from 75 to 80 cents and on which the rate is the same on the unfinished as on the finished product.

"Live poultry in carload lots is raised from $2.00 to $2.20 a hundred weight. Boots and shoes are raised from $2.50 to $2.75, plaster from $7 to $8 a ton, while hardware and structural iron men are touched up all along the line. Plumbers' supplies, building hardware, drugs and chemicals, glassware, electrical machinery and many other items are raised."

New Home Ready for The Monitor

The practical completion of the extension of the Christian Science Publishing Society's building, which is to be the home of The Christian Science Monitor, was reached today, just nine weeks from the time work was begun. The work of tearing down and removing the apartment houses which formerly occupied the site was begun in the last week in August, but the actual work on the construction of the new building did not start till Sept. 16. During this time two shifts of men have been employed and some night work was performed.

The architect of the building is Solon Spencer Beman of Chicago, one of the best-known men in his profession in the country. Mr. Beman has been represented here by C. C. Moody of Chicago as superintendent of construction.

The extension, 80x60 feet, is a thoroughly fireproof steel structure, no wood being used in its construction except for casements of inside doors and windows and finishing purposes, and consists of a basement and two stories.

The exterior is of rusticated Bedford limestone and the architecture is in perfect harmony with and a continuation of the lines of the main building. The style may be classed as that of the modern type of bank building.

The extension, which faces on St. Paul street, is set back from the roadway some 20 feet, thus affording ample room for a wide sidewalk, granite curbing and ornamental fence, and increasing the opportunity for light.

The mechanical department comprises a battery of two Goss presses, a quad and a straight line machine, eight Mergenthaler linotype machines together with the modern stereotyping and mailing room facilities.

It is estimated that 70,000 copies can be printed hourly and that each mailing machine will wrap, strap, address and bundle 4,000 copies per hour, the equivalent of the work required of 10 persons for the same time.

A special feature of the building is the spectator's gallery located on a large landing on the stairs half way between the basement and the first floor. This is inclosed in plate glass and affords a complete view of the press room and the working of the big presses and mailing machines.

THE HOME OF THE CHRISTIAN SCIENCE PUBLISHING SOCIETY
SEPTEMBER 22
OCTOBER 17
OCTOBER 31
NOVEMBER 7
OCTOBER 10
OCTOBER 24

SCENES INCIDENT TO THE ERECTION OF THE PUBLISHING HOUSE EXTENSION WHERE THE CHRISTIAN SCIENCE MONITOR IS EDITED AND PRINTED.

CANADIAN CITY IS WORKING FOR BETTER DOCKS

Victoria (B. C.) Board of Trade Seeks to Develop Vancouver Island and Win Ocean Trade.

EXPECT NEW LINERS

VICTORIA, B. C., Nov. 25—The board of trade here is inaugurating an aggressive campaign for the improvement of the docking facilities at Esquimalt, and for the greater development of Vancouver Island. Esquimalt possesses undoubted advantages with respect to the Pacific carrying trade, and in view of the Canadian Pacific Railway's announced intention to transfer its large Atlantic liners to its Pacific service, and of the probable entrance upon the island of the Grand Trunk Pacific, the need has become apparent for larger docks at this point.

Fifteen years ago there was but one line of small steamers plying to the Orient, but this trade has developed until several lines are now engaged in it. The intention is to interest the Canadian government to construct a large modern graving dock at Esquimalt for the accommodation of foreign merchant ships, as the present dock has proved inadequate for the larger vessels now in use.

As this is especially Canada's growing time, the merchants of its most westerly port naturally desire that their city, as well as Vancouver Island, shall be prepared to cope with and to profit by the rapidly increasing ocean trade of the Pacific, a large part of which passes their very doors.

FIRST TAFT BABY BORN.

Marshwood, a little hamlet just outside of Scranton, Pa., has suddenly become famous through the birth of William Taft Snyder. The happy father received the following telegram from the President-elect:

"My Dear Sir: I write to thank you for having named your baby after me, and express the hope that he may have a long and prosperous life. Sincerely yours, William H. Taft."

FISHING TRUST BY ENGLISHMEN IS NEW VENTURE

Capitalists Combine to Promote Salmon and Deep-Sea Fisheries Along Coast of British Columbia.

VICTORIA, B. C., Nov. 25—A company of English capitalists is being promoted to engage in various industries in British Columbia, one of which will be the salmon and deep sea fisheries along its coast. It will be known as the Canadian Pacific Trading and Development syndicate, with headquarters at Prince Rupert, the western terminal of the Grand Trunk Pacific Railway. Experiments have been made in shipping whole salmon to England by cold storage, the results of which have been eminently successful. Salmon shipped in this way have been pronounced by fish dealers to be equal to the best Scotch salmon for smoking purposes, and, with the exception of the fresh Scotch salmon, superior to all other salmon which is placed on the English market. The company have a large smoking plant and also intend entering the smoked salmon trade.

This company will maintain a fleet of small fishing steamers, and a large fast steel steamer to collect the fish from the various stations which are to be established at Graham and Moresby islands of the Queen Charlotte group, and at other points from the Naas to the east coast of Vancouver Island. Half a million dollars will be expended during the coming year in developing the industries of the province. If sufficient fishing labor cannot be obtained in British Columbia it is the intention to bring practical fishermen with their families from Great Britain to settle on the Canadian Pacific coast.

It is believed that the market for these fish is practially unlimited. In concluding a recent interview the company's representative said: "I have been greatly impressed with what I have seen of the resources of British Columbia. I have been over the world a good deal, and no country has indications of future prosperity greater than this. I feel almost certain that within 20 years or less British Columbia will be the greatest mineral producing area, and among the wealthiest countries of the world in its rich resources."

CAN INTERCEPT WIRELESS NOTES

Italian Scientists Experimenting in Normandy, However, Claim Own Messages Cannot Be Tampered With.

PARIS, Nov. 25—If the claims of Bellini and Tosi, two Italian scientists who have been experimenting with wireless telegraphy on the coast of Normandy with the French government's consent, are correct, then the use of their system will give immense advantage to the government which secures it. The Italian experimenters claim to have been able to intercept wireless messages in transit from every English station and from ships at sea. They further claim that their own messages cannot be tampered with and that they have solved the problem of independent wireless telegraphy.

The result claimed was said to be attained by two rectangular aerials fixed at right angles and so attached to the apparatus for reception and transmission as to permit the transmission of unequal currents. By a law of mechanics these two electro-magnetic currents unite and produce an electro-magnetic field, and the Hertzian rays are projected in a single vertical plane which can be alternated instantly by means of the Bobine device. It is claimed to be able to determine by triangulation the exact position of ships at sea in distress, the position and speed of a hostile squadron and the reading of secret exchanges between friendly fleets and armies.

LODGE GETS BIBLE.

A copy of the "Breeches" Bible, published in London in 1599, said to be the book on which George Washington was obligated as a Master Mason, has been restored to Lodge of Antiquity, 1, Q. R., A. F. and A. M., the oldest Masonic lodge in Canada, to which it originally belonged.

COLISEUM TO BE BUILT FOR 14,000 PEOPLE

Des Moines, Ia., Building Will Be Commenced When Necessary Hundred Thousand Dollars Is Raised.

SITE ON RIVER FRONT

DES MOINES, Ia., Nov. 25—A coliseum building seating 14,000 people is practically assured for Des Moines by the response to popular subscriptions for stock in the enterprise. Over $75,000 has been pledged, and work will start when the $100,000 mark is reached. A site has been leased on the river front. Such a building has been desired for several years by the business interests to entertain conventions, exhibits, national gatherings and political meetings.

PLENTY OF ROOM OVERHEAD.

Get away from the big mob of little men, and come on up. Nobody has yet managed to fill out the space between here and the stars. There's nothing but room overhead. Competition is intense only down below. The hardest struggle is the beginning. The outset of life is the biggest trial. The start takes more time than the race.—Herbert Kaufman, in Chicago Record-Herald.

DICTATES OF FASHION.

The most extraordinary thing about fashion, says the Rome "Moda," is that it works miracles at will. One season slimness is the rule, the next rotundity is preferred. And the elegant woman obeys without the slightest trouble.

NAVY EXPERT GIVES VIEWS

Commander A. L. Key, U. S. N., whose famous letter criticising the design of some of the new American battleships, particularly the North Dakota, led to the President calling the Newport naval conference, is in command of the new scout cruiser Salem, registered at the Boston navy yard.

Both the North Dakota and the Salem were built at the Fore River yards in Quincy. Commander Key was on duty at the shipyard from the time the Salem was begun until he took command of her last July so his criticisms on battleship construction are based on personal observation.

On his arrival in Boston Commander Key said that he was highly pleased with the results of the conference. He welcomed it mainly as affording the opening wedge for public criticism and intelligent interest in the American navy. That the people of this country are too confident that their ships are the finest afloat and that they take too much for granted in their designs was one of his complaints. "What we need," he said, "is to arouse the people to intelligent criticism of our warships; not fault finding, but fair-minded discussion of their good points and their defects. I do not think our ships are the only ones that have faults, but I do think that such meetings as that held at Newport will aid greatly in making our ships better able to fight.

"It is time that the seagoing officers who sail and fight our warships had a hand in their designing, and I think that the time has come when they will. The conference passed a resolution seeking to have a board of competent seagoing officers pass upon all future plans. Either that course will be followed or else there will be a yearly conference after the idea of that at Newport to take up general discussion and criticism of warship plans."

REVIEWS CONDITIONS IN THE BALKANS

CONTINUED FROM PAGE ONE.

new triple entente between England, France, and Russia.

Russia's defeat in the far East by England's partner forced her to face the situation nearer home, and she had no choice but to come to terms with either the old or the new rival. She chose the former, France's friend.

The immediate consequence was the only event that was apt to detach Turkey from Germany—the abolition of the old regime by the Young Turkish party under the tacit auspices of England and France.

In the midst of this ultra modern struggle between the giants among the nations, it is curious to note interests directly descended from mediaeval conditions and aspirations. There is no stranger contrast than the ambitions based on the "historic rights" dating back four centuries of the Balkan peoples and the commercial and strategic interests of the great powers in the Levant.

If we follow the landmarks of Balkan history, we can trace, in the midst of increasing din and confusion, the birth and growth of a nation which has just attained to manhood—a nation of the Balkan and for the Balkan.

The work left unfinished by the Romans, the welding together of the peoples south of the Danube, was slowly progressing in the alternate expansion and concentration of the Bulgarian people when the Turkish conquest obliterated all outward signs of Slave progress in the Balkans. The nationalization of the latter will be the work of their maturer years.

The conditions surrounding and shaping their rise were passing strange and their struggle—the Balkan Kultur-Kampf—is the only independent factor in a country where all vital interests are controlled by the rivalry of the great powers.

If the general situation in the Balkans today is but a reflection of Anglo-German relations, the Bulgarian declaration of independence is a landmark pointing back to Roman times when the masters of the world abandoned the task the Bulgars have undertaken.

It also points ahead to a time when the balance of Europe and world power will be a trick forgotten in the bustle of the world's true work.

The confusion of tongues and nationalities in the Balkans is not remarkable from a racial point of view, for there are peoples whose make-up is considerably more mixed. The remarkable feature is the complete absence of unification of interests, customs, and political, social, religious views and aspirations. Before inquiring into the causes of this peculiarity, it is necessary to state that a Greek, for instance, may become a Bulgar, or a Bulgar a Greek merely by transferring his allegiance from the Greek Patriarch to the Bulgarian Exarch and vice versa. This is a means of self-preservation daily resorted to, in the murderous "Kultur-Kampf" of Macedonia. The only exception is the Albanian, who has rigidly preserved his racial individuality and remains an Albanian, whether he be Roman Catholic, Moslem, or Greek orthodox. The creed has become the pivot of all Balkan relations and with it goes the language as its vehicle.

This will become clear when we see that the Greek is not pure Greek nor the Bulgarian a Bulger, and even the Serb not a pure Slav; that the Roumanian has nothing of the Roman but the name, and that of the latter's speech he caught but an echo; that the European Turk far from being a Mongolian is largely descended from Georgian, Circassian, Armenian, Greek and Slavic female slaves and renegade soldiers.

Blanchard, King & Co.

HOLIDAY GOODS

Imported Brass and Leather Novelties.
Choice Neckwear.
Full Dress Requisites.

250 Boylston St., Boston

Union Underwear

The comfort of Underwear is to be unconscious of it.

Yale and Holmes Brands have very important features not found in any other make.

Men's Unions retail $1.00 to $15.00 each. Ladies' Unions in Holmes Brand have Patented Changeable Gores. Doubles the life of the garment. Retail $2.75 to $15.00 each.

Send for samples and descriptive booklet, and give name of your dealer.

Holmes Knitting Co. MALDEN —MASS.—
Boston Office, 67 Chauncey St., Room 35

$3.25 Postpaid in U. S. Soft Inside and Out

The Pillow Shoe

For woman's wear. *Absolute comfort.* A beautiful hand turned shoe; no breaking in required. Soft, flexible, durable and dressy. The sole oak leather, the whole top genuine vici kid, soft and pliable. *Rubber heels, no linings to wrinkle or chafe.* We guarantee to fit you perfectly. *Absolute comfort and satisfaction or money cheerfully refunded.* Write today for our free illustrated booklet and special self-measurement blank. Address SUFFOLK SHOE COMPANY
184 Summer St., Dept. C, Boston, Mass

High Grade Employees
— FOR —
MERCANTILE HOUSES and HOTELS

References Investigated. Also FIRST CLASS POSITIONS SECURED

Mercantile Reference and Bond Asso'n.
387 WASHINGTON ST., BOSTON
Est. 1885 'Phone Main 6595

Brandon Hall
Beacon Street
Brookline

Furnished or unfurnished apartments, any number rooms desired.

Modern in every respect.

ARTHUR L. RACE, Proprietor.

CHICKERING HALL

Thursday evening, Dec. 3, at 8.15. Pianoforte recital by

JULIAN PASCAL

HELEN ALLEN HUNT, contralto, assisting artist.

Seats $1.50, $1.00 and 50 cents, on sale at the hall.

Athletic Events of the Day — College Football Rules

HARVARD TAUGHT OLD AND NEW GAME THIS YEAR

First Year Since New Rules Were Made That Crimson Knew and Was Able to Play New Game.

TEAM PLAY STRONG

This year has been the first time since the new game of football was introduced that Harvard has turned out a team thoroughly drilled in the new as well as the old style of play. The new rules, which were made in 1905, were so radically different from the old ones that the systems which had been used in the old game could not be successfully applied to the new one, and while the head coaches of the other larger colleges were busy making plans to utilize the possibilities opened up by the new rules, Harvard was using her time in building up an offence and defence along the old lines. As a result, when the teams came to face Dartmouth and Yale they suffered defeat. During the three years previous to the time when Coach Haughton took hold of the eleven, Harvard suffered three defeats at the hands of Yale, one by the Carlisle Indians, and one defeat and a tie by Dartmouth.

A marked change has been apparent in the development of the 1908 eleven. The players were first taught the finest details regarding individual play, and after they had mastered this to the satisfaction of the coaches they were taught team play, both offensive and defensive, much attention being given to the forward pass and the onside kick. In one game this year Harvard has tried the forward pass and the onside more times than during the whole season of 1906, and her victory over Dartmouth was directly due to the mixing of forward passes with the line-plunging attack of former years. Little use was made of these plays in the Yale game, as that team had been coached to break them up, and the Harvard quarterback saw the wisdom of not trying them, especially after a score had been made.

The material at hand when the season opened was not very encouraging to the coaches. Only four of last year's men were candidates for the team and the new men had had little or no practice of varsity character. By hard work and ability to teach green men, they succeeded in developing one of the best teams Harvard has ever turned out, and one that could face Yale with the confidence born of the knowledge that it knew the game as it is played today. The successful football team's excellence depends upon the individual ability of each player being moulded into a smooth, well-running team of eleven men, and it was with this end in view that the coaches turned their attention during the preliminary season.

This year's team more nearly resembled Ben Dibblee's team of 1898 than any other Harvard eleven. With the exception of Fish and Burr, there was not a man who was first choice for the Yale game of last year. The team showed the same spirit and aggressiveness as was apparent in '98 and the members sacrificed their individual ability in order that the team might be a unit in all its plays.

As individuals the members of the team developed into players of more than average ability. Captain Burr turned out to be one of the best guards and punters ever trained at Cambridge. Fish developed into one of the best tackles that ever played the game, and the coaching which he received in the handling of forward passes and his ability to execute their teaching made him a star in that department. Cutler, who had had practically no experience at quarter, was taken in hand last September by Coach Daly and developed into one of the best of the year. While the other men were all of more than the average type, their greatest value to the team was in their ability and willingness to work together as one in the interests of the eleven as a whole and not for their individual advancement.

It is with such individuals as composed this year's Harvard team, aided by the proper system of coaching, that successful results are accomplished on the football field and with a continuation of the present force of coaches at Cambridge and a good supply of such desirable candidates trying for the team, it would seem as if the future should bring to Harvard her share of victories over Yale on the gridiron.

THANKSGIVING ENDS FOOTBALL.

Justice Weaver of the Iowa supreme court, at Des Moines, Ia., in writing an opinion relative to the contract of a teacher of athletics in the Johnson County schools, has defined the football season to be that part of the school year ending with Thanksgiving Day. The judge wrote: "The remainder of the year of the university student may be devoted to the study of football, but the football season proper ends appropriately with a general thanksgiving."

EXPECT NO GREAT CHANGE IN RULES

Yachting Department of A. C. A. Not Expected to Make Radical Changes in Motor Boat Racing.

While at first it was thought that the announcement made by the Automobile Club of America that its yachting department was to assume charge of motor-boat racing would result in radical changes being made in the present rules, it begins to look as if such would not be the case.

In discussing the proposed change H. S. Gamble, secretary of the National Association of Engine and Boat Manufacturers, says:

"There is no need for any alarm whatever as to the club in question becoming the dominating factor in the motorboat sport of the country. It is simply a matter of international character. The representative clubs of Europe have formed what they term a congress known as the International Association Yachting-Automobile. From what information I have been able to gather on the subject it seems that this congress is so composed that they are 'it,' in so far as international matters go, and they have asked the A. C. A. to become a representative of that body in this country. Under this state of affairs all challenges for any foreign event must be made through the A. C. A. and in challenges for any foreign trophy held in this country all foreign clubs or representative clubs of any country send their challenges through the A. C. A. So far as I can learn, if a foreign club should challenge for the Harmsworth trophy now held by the Motor Boat Club of America and that club should receive the challenge through the A. C. A. and question the latter body's right in the matter, that is when the challenge is sent to them (A. C. A.) and not direct to the holding club, and the holding club should refuse to accept the club's challenge, why naturally if the A. C. A. was backed up by this foreign congress there would be no race; consequently in due time the trophy would revert to the trustees who have control of the trophy. There is quite a little feeling in the matter in some circles, notably the American Power Boat Association and the Motor Boat Club of America, and the only way to prove the standing of the A. C. A. and the power vested in that body by this foreign congress is to make a test case of it, which will no doubt be done when a challenge is received, if one should be forthcoming, from England for the Harmsworth trophy.

"The A. C. A. have no intention whatever of controlling the sport in this country, and in so far as I know they will have nothing to do for the present or in the near future, if at all, with the sport in this country outside that of an international character. Whether the A. C. A. will prove a factor in the international affairs of racing is something for the future to determine. As you are no doubt aware, a convention of motor boat owners is to be held during the national show in New York and it is more than probable that a national body will be the outcome of this convention who will endeavor to put the sport in the position it should be."

ROWING BOOM LOOKED FOR

Flooding of the Charles River Basin Expected to Increase Interest in Rowing There.

Now that the Charles River basin has been flooded by the building of the dam at East Cambridge, it is expected that there will be a great increase in the amount of rowing done there. While there have always been a number of rowing enthusiasts who have made use of the river, there were many others who would have liked to row but could not get out at the right time to take advantage of the tide.

Great interest is now being taken in rowing at Harvard, and this assures the presence of a large number of shells on the river every day during term time. Evenings will undoubtedly see many business men taking exercise there after work.

It will not take much of the coming season for people to learn what splendid conditions have been created by the flooding of the basin, and as soon as they do they will not be slow in taking advantage of them. Interest which has been on the decline among the various rowing clubs during the past few years on account of the condition of the river, will now revive, and the regattas to be held next year should see a large number of contestants entered.

INCENTIVE FOR MOTOR RACING.

The "London Times" protests against the motor road racing which prevails in England. That paper says: "There has never been any adequate justification of motor racing on the highway, except the practical lessons of construction. Now that this justification has been very largely removed, the sole remaining incentive of motor road racing is shown to be that passion for excessive speed which is the cause of the worst motoring offences."

ROWING EVENTS OPEN TO WORLD'S PROFESSIONALS

England to Hold Handicap Sculling Races on Thames Course Next July — Big Prizes Offered.

COMMITTEES CHOSEN

LONDON, Nov. 25—There is now no doubt regarding the revival of professional rowing contests in this country next year. For some weeks plans have been discussed and those interested in the sport have worked hard to make the movement a success, with the result that enough money has already been pledged to assure the carrying out of an extensive program. A big handicap open to the world for a purse of $2500 has already been decided upon, and enough more money is in hand to insure the holding of minor races.

The plans call for the holding of a $500 handicap for United Kingdom scullers on April 19, and to be continued until the winners are declared.

The international handicap for $2500 will be rowed the latter part of July. Colonial and foreign entries will have to be made not later than May 1. Those residing in the United Kingdom will have one month's grace, and for them entries close June 1. The committee wants time to look up the entries from abroad.

It was decided at a recent meeting of the committee that the heats and finals should be decided over the full championship course from Putney to Mortlake or vice versa, and that the prize money should be divided, $1250 for first, $500 for second and the remaining $750 to be divided at the discretion of the committee among the other competitors.

The committee in charge of the regatta is Guy Nickalls and G. E. B. Kennedy, the ex-champions; H. S. Blackstaffe, the present Olympic champion; W. G. East, the king's bargemaster, who was formerly a professional sculler; Thomas Sullivan, ex-champion of England and trainer of George Towns; R. H. Forster, the old college oarsman, and V. M. Mansell of the "Sportsman."

All entries for this event should be addressed in care of the "Sportsman," London, Eng., and the entrance fee which must accompany the entry is one guinea, or $5.25.

It is now time for the scullers of the United States to get their boats ready and begin to exercise on the road if they are contemplating a trip to this city.

NEW YORK BALL TEAMS IN SOUTH.

NEW YORK, Nov. 25—Both the National and American baseball teams of this city will play games in the South next spring on their return North from their training grounds. The Nationals are to train in Marlin Springs, Tex., and will play a couple of games with the Detroit Americans in San Antonio. The Americans will play three games with the Richmond (Va.) team April 10, 11 and 12.

SEATTLE GETS TRACK MEET.

SEATTLE, Wash., Nov. 25—Resolutions were passed at the last annual meeting of the A. A. U. to hold the next outdoor championships in this city next August in conjunction with the Alaskan-Yukon Exposition. As these resolutions have been referred to the championship committee, which has full power to name the place, the committee is going ahead with its plans. A stadium and special track and field for the various events are in course of preparation. All standard A. A. U. championships will be provided for. There will be both salt and fresh water for aquatic sports of every kind, includ- bring to Harvard her share of victories war canoe race.

PRACTISING FOR CLASS SERIES IN BASKETBALL

Teams Representing Harvard Classes to Have Contests in December—Varsity Practice After Christmas.

E. S. ALLEN CAPTAIN

The outlook for a good basketball team at Harvard this year is quite bright. The varsity team will not be called out until after the Christmas holidays, but practice will begin next week for the class team candidates. A series of contests is to be held for the championship of the college, all four classes entering. Matches will begin about December 8 and be concluded previous to the Christmas recess.

Of last year's team E. S. Allen, '09; P. Brooks, '09; S. Brown, '10; G. G. Browne, '10; E. S. Currie, '09; H. Fish, '10, and F. W. Scribner, '10, are eligible again this year, only C. Almy, '08, and O. A. Wyman, '08, having left college. Good material will be furnished by the members of last year's freshman team, and of these E. P. Miller, forward; H. T. Weber, guard, and F. Wellmann, centre, will make the competition fast.

No coach has as yet been appointed for the team as the question of the employing of a professional has not yet been decided upon by the athletic council, but if one is engaged, it will probably be D. J. Prior, who played on last year's Brown team.

E. S. Allen, '09, of Cincinnati, O., is captain this year. He was captain of his freshman team and has played right forward on the varsity for the past two years. He is 20 years old, 5 feet 11½ inches tall and weighs 165 pounds. He has won a number of prizes in broad jumping and was a member of his class football team.

The athletic committee has approved the following schedule for the varsity team:

Jan. 12, Technology at Cambridge.
Jan. 16, Princeton at Princeton.
Jan. 23, Brown at Cambridge.
Jan. 29, Tufts at Cambridge.
Feb. 6, Brown at Cambridge.
Feb. 12, Yale at Cambridge.
Feb. 20, Dartmouth at Cambridge.
Feb. 26, Yale at New Haven.

On account of the fact that the athletic committee would allow the team to play only half as many games as last year, West Point, Wesleyan, Andover, Williams and Holy Cross have not been given matches this winter.

NEW CUP OFFERED FOR DORY RACES

NEW YORK, Nov. 25—Negotiations are now being carried on by the New Yacht Club to promote an international race here next summer in which dories from Holland will meet American.

A new cup will be offered by the New York Athletic Club yachtsmen and others for this international contest and during the winter the matter will be laid officially before the Royal Yacht Club committee in Holland. It is the general belief of those who are interested in organizing the race for next season that the three Royal Yacht clubs of Holland will combine to send over at least one boat, although three are allowed.

Last summer George G. Fry's dory Tautog, entered by the American Yacht Club, raced in Holland and won the silver trophy. It is a beautiful representation of an old Dutch full rigged ship with fifteen little old men in silver on the deck and every detail of the rigging admirably designed. It is not a perpetual prize, but was won outright by Mr. Fry.

U. S. TO HAVE 200,000,000.

WASHINGTON, Nov. 25—Prof. J. L. Snyder, of the Michigan Agricultural College, in an address here, predicted that 40 years from now there would be 200,000,000 population in the United States, and that the tendency now was toward segregation into classes.

CAPTAIN E. S. ALLEN,

Harvard Basketball Team.

SKATING RACES FOR THIS WINTER

NEW YORK, Nov. 25—There are a number of speed skating-races to be held in this city this winter, and every afternoon the ice at the St. Nicholas Skating Rink is filled with fast men preparing for them. The Eastern Skating Association has awarded to the St. Nicholas Skating Association the sanction to hold a series of races on Dec. 19, and a program of three races has already been arranged as follows: A half-mile handicap, one mile novice race and a two-mile handicap. This will be preliminary to the races for the metropolitan championships in January and the Eastern championship series in February.

Notes From the Field of Sports.

Harvard is certainly fortunate in having a man who is as capable of coaching end players as is David Campbell, captain of the 1901 eleven. One of the best ends ever turned out at any college, he has the ability to teach a candidate the fine points of the play. For the last two years he has come to Cambridge from the middle west for this purpose.

It is to be hoped that those students who took such an interest in the football mass meetings at the Harvard Union this year will follow it up with meetings in the interests of the rest of the athletic contests of the year.

Quarterback Balenti of the Carlisle Indian football team certainly proved to be a worthy successor to Hudson and the other famous goal-kickers who have helped make the Indians famous on the football field. His kicking was responsible for winning the navy game.

This year was the third in succession that Andover defeated Exeter at football and every one of the victories can be traced to the fact that Andover played the new game while Exeter stuck to the old style. Until the Exeter coaches realize that the old style of game cannot be depended upon to gain ten yards in four downs, there will be little prospect of their turning out winning teams.

Brown will lose a very valuable football player next year by the graduation of John Mayhew, captain of this year's eleven. Mayhew has been ranked as one of the best half-backs in the country and his place will be a hard one to fill.

It will be interesting to see how Danzig, the first baseman which the Boston Americans sent out to Portland, Ore., last spring for development, turns out next spring, as Manager McCready of the Portland team claims that he is now one of the best men playing that position. If he is as good as reported, he will certainly fit in very nicely as first base was one of the weakest spots on the Boston American team last season.

Now that Longboat is a full-fledged professional runner it is to be hoped that he will do as his trainers want. No man ever showed more promise at over 10 miles than he did when he won the B. A. A. Marathon race in 1906.

The Automobile Club of France is to hold its big race of 1909 at Angers instead of Dieppe. It is expected that the new course will furnish a better chance for high speed with less danger than was possible on the old course. The new course extends through the province of Anjou.

YALE BASKETBALL DATES.

Yale's basketball schedule for this year has been given out and includes all of the leading colleges. As was the case last year no southern trip will be taken during the Easter recess. The dates announced are as follows:

Dec. 5, College of the City of New York at New York; Dec. 9, Manhattan at New York; Dec. 12, Fordham at New York; Jan. 9, Wesleyan at Middletown; Jan. 13, Princeton at New Haven; Jan. 16, Dartmouth at Boston; Jan. 20, alumni at New Haven; Jan. 23, Princeton at Princeton; Jan. 27, Trinity at Hartford; Jan. 30, Brooklyn Polytechnic Institute at Brooklyn; Feb. 3, University of Pennsylvania at New Haven; Feb. 5, Pratt Institute at Brooklyn; Feb. 6, West Point at West Point; Feb. 12, Harvard at Cambridge; Feb. 13, Brown at Providence; Feb. 17, Columbia at New Haven; Feb. 20, University of Pennsylvania at Philadelphia; Feb. 23, Columbia at New Haven.

TUFTS SCHEDULE FOR BASKET BALL

Two trips to New York are scheduled for the Tufts basketball team this year. On the first trip the five will play Manhattan Jan. 22, Pratt Institute, Jan. 23 and Fordham, Jan. 24. The games scheduled for the second trip are Hamilton at Clinton, Feb. 4 and Cornell at Ithaca, Feb. 6. The full schedule follows:

Jan. 7—M. I. T. at Tufts.
Jan. 9—Brown at Providence.
Jan. 13—Dartmouth at Tufts.
Jan. 22—Manhattan at New York.
Jan. 23—Pratt Institute at New York.
Jan. 24—Fordham at New York.
Jan. 26—Holy Cross at Worcester.
Jan. 29—Harvard at Cambridge.
Feb. 4—Hamilton at Clinton, N. Y.
Feb. 5—Open.
Feb. 6—Cornell at Ithaca, N. Y.
Feb. 10—Holy Cross at Tufts.
Feb. 13—M. I. T. at Tufts.
Feb. 19—Hamilton at Tufts.
Feb. 25—Williams at Tufts.

"The Car That Is Seen and Not Heard."

Stevens-Duryea

Imitated but Not Equalled.

The Car that gives the most mileage on gasoline.
The Car with the hill-climbing record.
The Car with less weight per H. P. than others.
The Car that gives the most mileage on tires.
The Car that gives the least trouble.
In fact, THE CAR.

The J. W. Bowman Co. 911 Boylston Street

Manufactured by Stevens-Duryea Co., Chicopee Falls, Mass. | Members Association of Licensed Automobile Manufacturers.

A WHITE STEAMER FOR $2000

Not since 1904 have we made a car priced at so low a figure as $2000. The White —"the car in a class by itself"—has thus been brought within the range of a larger number of purchasers than has been the case in recent years.

The new $2000 White car, known as our Model "O," has none of the attributes of the "cheap machine." It is simply a "smaller edition" of our $4000 car. The new Model "O" is rated at 20 steam horse-power, which means that it can do the work of gasoline cars rated at much higher figures. The wheel-base is 104 inches; the tires, both front and rear, are 32 x 3 1-2 inches. The car is regularly fitted with a straight-line five-passenger body. The frame is of heat-treated pressed steel. The front axle is a one-piece forging of I-beam cross section.

The nature of the steam engine is such that the engine of small power has all the desirable attributes of the engine of high power. In other words, as the weights of our small car and of our large car are proportionate to the power of their respective engines, the small car can do anything that our large car can do.

To summarize the features of our new Model "O" car—it is noiseless, odorless, smokeless and absolutely free from vibration. All speeds from zero to maximum are obtained by throttle control alone. The speed of the car responds instantly to the throttle; the engine can never be stalled. The directions for driving are summed up in the phrase, "Just open the throttle and steer." It starts from the seat—"no cranking." It is the ideal moderate priced machine. It is the best for the man who wishes to drive and take care of his own car. It is the result of our nine years of experience in building the White Steam Car—the only machine which finds a ready market in every portion of the globe.

WRITE FOR CIRCULAR GIVING FULL DETAILS OF THIS CAR

THE WHITE COMPANY
CLEVELAND, OHIO

NEW YORK CITY, Broadway at 62d Street
BOSTON, 320 Newbury Street
PHILADELPHIA, 629-33 North Broad Street
PITTSBURG, 138-148 Beatty Street
CLEVELAND, 407 Rockwell Avenue
CHICAGO, 240 Michigan Avenue
SAN FRANCISCO, Market Street at Van Ness Avenue
ATLANTA, 120-122 Marietta Street

LITERATURE IN THE PHILIPPINES IS IMPROVING

Native Spirit Longing for Independence Is Reflected in Journalism and Dramatic Productions.

RIZAL IS THE HERO

MANILA, Nov. 25—Filipino literature, as yet hardly more than in a nascent state, is showing a vigorous development and already bears the imprint of the longing of the native spirit for independent nationality. The influence of the American occupation of the islands, while not always friendly toward the primitive attempts at journalism and dramatic production—nor inexcusably hostile, in many instances—has proved a stimulus in the long run to the growth of a literary spirit indigenous to the archipelago.

Literary enterprise was not fostered among the natives by the Spanish government authorities. Quite the reverse. Had not Rizal wielded a facile and eloquent pen, peradventure he had not faced the firing squad upon the Luneta. The official canonization of Rizal as a hero by the American civil government and the removal of the ban from his writings gave the signal for the bringing together of a great mass of writings by, about and concerning this estimable, if visionary, young native. Every incident concerning Jose Rizal, no matter how lacking in real significance, was dwelt upon with all the circumstantiality of historical importance. Further, every trace of writings by Filipinos during the Spanish regime was brought together in the pathetic attempt to formulate at once a literature expressive of the aspirations of the people.

The breaking down of the Spanish censorship in 1898 was interpreted as heralding a degree of freedom akin to license, and too literal an application of this idea was severely reprehended in various instances. Nevertheless, much encouragement has been extended by the government and by the American public here to the production of dramas and other literature not especially aimed at the overthrow of American control.

The literary enterprises of the Filipinos find expression in three general forms, namely, newspapers and periodicals, plays and books. The newspapers are most in evidence and display signs of much activity. El Renacimiento, a daily paper printed jointly in Spanish and Tagalog, has prospered so well, materially, that it recently has been able to undertake an English edition. Its circulation is something immense, it being said that there is hardly a native in the islands who is not more or less under its influence. Its policy—one of hostility toward the Americanization of the islands—has brought it in contact with the authorities forcefully once or twice, but this seems to have increased rather than to have diminished its vogue. The success and influence of this newspaper makes it a type of its class which includes a dozen or so newspapers in Manila, printed in Spanish and Tagalog, and bearing more or less fanciful names.

Allow Freedom in Native Plays.

Even greater freedom of thought has been voiced in the native dramas than in the native newspapers, if that is possible and considerable leniency has been exercised by the government in regard to utterances considered inimical to good order. With the actual suppression of one or two plays actually seditious in tone and hidden meaning, if not in actual language, a more reasonable class of productions has come into being, and that "the play's the thing" as a medium for reaching the native of the ordinary class is evidenced by the crowds that almost nightly pack the big bamboo theaters in Manila suburbs and the outlying towns.

Books in the native tongue of necessity have been largely translations from other languages. A Tagalog version of Schiller's "William Tell" has been put out recently, the translation having been made by Rizal when he was a student in Germany, more than a score of years ago. This is but the beginning of a library of standard works that is to be put in popular form for the edification of the Filipino public by the Libreria Manila Filatelica. Two novels also have been published recently in Tagalog by the same house, one being named "Pinaglahuan," by Faustine Aguilar, and the other "Anino nang Kapahon," by Francisco Laksamana. Besides these, quite a list of novels in Tagalog have been put out in the past eight years, at prices that put them within the reach of the poorest natives, who read them avidly.

CHARLES J. MOORE
Consulting Mining Engineer
El Mar Apartments, Suite No. 12, 1116 East 13th Ave., Denver, Colorado.
Tel., York 873—Code Bedford McNeill. Also at Goldfield, Nevada.

DEWEY'S SIMPLOFILLER PERFECT
Fountain Pen
Simplest to fill. No leaky and sweating joints. Pleasing holiday gift. Prices $1.50, $2.00, $2.50, $3.00, $3.50, $4.00, $5.00. Guaranteed. Sent on approval. Write for catalogue and prices to solicitors.
EDSON E. DEWEY,
8 Cypress Apartments, Brookline, Mass.
Telephone 1467-4.

ROOSEVELT MAY WIN MORE FAME ON AFRICAN TRIP

Shooting of Bird or Beast Unknown to Science Would Give the President Added Laurels.

GETS EXPERT ADVICE

WASHINGTON, Nov. 25—What a certificate of distinction it would be for President Roosevelt—or ex-President Roosevelt, is he would be then—if he should bring down a beast or bird not known to the zoologists or ornithologists, while away on his African hunt! Yet this he is very likely to do if he follows the advice brought him by Sir Harry Johnston, the intrepid little English explorer who won knighthood from Queen Victoria in recognition of his feats in the dark continent.

It is likely that the President will not fail to avail himself of the English sportsman's knowledge of that strange country.

From Mombassa, the old Portuguese seaport, where the Roosevelt party will entrain, the railroad leads through a rich forest country, abounding in game, but rather too well-known to the conventional sporting world to engage more than the passing interest of one who wishes to write his name with that of Nimrod.

After that the track leads up into a country where "there is rock to the right, and rock to the left, and low, lean thorn between," with scrub growth that besets the traveler's way. This is not very promising but from this the road leads to the Athi plains, great table-lands, veldt for the most part, high enough to be cool, and shading off into the inscrutable desert on the north. There is good shooting here, but it is not far enough off the beaten track to suit the requirements. However, President Roosevelt understands that a perfect feast of adventure and exploration awaits him if he detrains somewhere in this veldt region and roams to the north of the railroad track, where he will find Mt. Kenya, a huge volcanic cone, its gaunt flank shrouded in perpetual snow, its foot surrounded by marvelous forests, untracked and almost unexplored.

There, in that trackless wilderness, pristine and unspoiled, is the chance of the sportsman's life to shoot something altogether new and uncatalogued. Only very recently some hardy hunters, pushing upward to that country, shot a gigantic black forest boar, hitherto absolutely unknown to naturalists.

Then, if Mr. Roosevelt desires to continue on an ideal trip, he may return to the railroad and take train for the Nanchi plateau, bordering the northern end of Lake Victoria Nyanza. This country literally swarms with game of all descriptions. Mt. Elgon, an extinct volcano, rises out of the center of a miniature Yellowstone park, with geysers, mud terraces, and all manner of natural wonder. He may hunt there as long as he lists and then push along to the native kingdom of Buganda, one of the states of Uganda.

Buganda does not boast of any very ferocious beasts, but it has quite a distinguished line to offer in the way of birds. Here is the whale-headed stork, something sure to please the adventurous sportsman alert for something new.

From Buganda the trail to the boundary of the Congo state will lead to the Mount Ruwenzori region, a wonderful place, where near the equator may be seen a mountain 18,000 feet high, snow-capped the year around. More forests and more unexplored veldt, and more than all else, more strange animals. It is the huntsman's happy hunting grounds, replete with new game. It is where Sir Harry added the okapi to his credit and to the zoologists' lists. President Roosevelt may be fortunate enough to slay a specimen of this animal. It is somewhat after the general plan of the giraffe, but smaller, and dissimilar in some other points. Quite likely there are other beasts, altogether strange to the present written lore, awaiting the ex-presidential rifle.

Thence, after satisfying his thirst for game shooting and photographing, Mr. Roosevelt could proceed up along through the Unyoro country to Lake Albert, then down the Nile to Khartoum and thence to Cairo, being joined by Mrs. Roosevelt possibly at historic Khartoum.

VOCATION BUREAU FOR YOUNG PEOPLE

At the Civic Service House Where Information and Expert Counsel Is Given Free to Applicants.

"To aid young people in choosing an occupation, preparing themselves for it, finding an opening in the chosen field, and building up a career of efficiency and success," is the mission of the vocation bureau of the Civic Service House, 112 Salem street.

In addition to offering counsel by experts free to all applicants, the director, Meyer Bloomfield, has arranged a series of Sunday evening talks by successful men upon the qualifications for entrance into the various professions in which they are leaders. Next Sunday evening's talk will be by David A. Ellis, member of the Boston school board, upon the profession of law.

SATRAPY TO USURP POWER OF NEW CHINESE RULER IS FOUGHT

Missionary and Legation Circles Regard Prince Ching's Firm Stand as Hopeful Sign.

INTRIGUE AT COURT

PEKIN, Nov. 25—Prince Ching's firm stand against the organizing of a satrapy to gain control of the Chinese government during the minority of the young sovereign is regarded in missionary and legation circles—where questions of Chinese statecraft are better understood, perhaps, that they are by the run of Europeans—as one of the most hopeful signs of the new order of things. Prince Ching is a decided liberal, whose influence was used, as far as compatible with his personal safety, to protect the foreigners in 1900, the yearn known in local annals as "Boxer year."

Ching was one of the inner ring of the Empress Dowager's advisers immediately after the affair of 1898, which practically dethroned Kwang Hsu; but this fact is not cherished against him by those familiar with the needs of Chinese diplomacy. His action in shutting the door against the possibility of any new dowager securing such power as did his imperial mistress in 1898 is looked on as the most significant comment upon the regime which he supported on that occasion.

Ching is a Manchu and is bound by the oaths of his clan and in loyalty to his ancestors to support the Manchu dynasty, which, had it toppled in 1898, might well have been supplanted by a Chinese dynasty, to restore which some odd millions of subjects of the big teakwood throne have pledged and organized themselves. To make it even more of an object to the present regime to yield the unwelcome foreigner a decorous modicum of protection, Kang Yu-wei, the "pretender"—if such the aspirant to the throne of his ancestors may be called—is himself closely in touch with foreign thought and feeling, and doubtless, should some stroke of good fortune waft him upon that throne, would people the Forbidden City with foreign advisers if not foreign protectors.

Furthermore, the eventual "restoration" of the imperial scepter to Chinese hands has a patient, resourceful, vigilant and inscrutable ally in the person of Viceroy Yuan, grand councillor, commander-in-chief of the land and naval forces, without whom hardly an act in the domestic economy of the empire has been executed during the past four years. Yuan has risen to incredible heights, for a Chinese under a Manchu dynasty, and rumor hints that in case of an overturn he would not scruple to snatch the scepter in hands strengthened by his personal control of an important portion of the army. He is on the best of terms with foreign governments, for in 1898, in spite of the direct behests of the Dowager that he immediately wage a war of extermination against all foreigners in his province—Shan-tung—he gathered the foreigners together and sent them, under strong guard, to the British consulate at Che-fu, and posted guards to protect all foreign houses and stations in his jurisdiction.

Yuan and Ching regard each other with secret vigilance, and neither cares to give the other's faction the advantage of incurring for his own the ill will of the terrible "outside barbarians."

Still another cogent argument in favor of respectful treatment of the resident foreigner is the huge German fortress which frowns upon the Chienmen, or the Emperor's gate, and from which the sacred Forbidden City could be reduced to a scrap heap in scarcely more than an hour should it come to hostilities. All the foreign nations have perfected an inter-working series of defences for their legations, but the Kaiser, in reprisal for the shooting of his minister, reared a stronghold that virtually commands all Pekin.

LEARN POLITICS THE FIRST THING

Immigrants Who Settle in Northwest Quickly Recognize Power of Ballot—Defeat One Candidate.

WASHINGTON, Nov. 25—Newly arrived immigrants who settle in the Northwest are apt pupils in politics, if reports received by the Department of Commerce and Labor may be believed.

Under recent legislation, foreign-born residents of Wisconsin, Michigan and the Dakotas, as well as several other states, were allowed to vote at the last election upon their swearing to their intention of becoming naturalized. All these affidavits find their way to Washington and are filed away in the archives of the division of naturalization.

As an evidence of the interest taken in the presidential election this year, the returns from some localities showed four or five times the volume of business in October that they did for any previous month of the year.

That the aliens are quick to realize the possibilities of the ballot was shown by the defeat of one county clerk who had not handled the business of making new citizens to the satisfaction of the incoming Norwegians. He was beaten by foreigners who had never voted before.

FRESH AIR FOR LONDON POOR

LONDON, Nov. 25—The London fresh air fund, which was originated by C. Arthur Pearson, has completed another season's work on behalf of the many thousands of little waifs and strays who are compelled to pass their lives amid the squalor and dirt of the slums in the east end of London and those of the great industrial centers in the provinces.

The accounts for the season have been made up, and an examination of them brings out the following interesting figures:

Income	£12,050
Expenditures	11,351
Balance	608

The children were given the following holidays:

	One day.	Two weeks
London	106,890	2000
Provincial	128,400	1645
Total	235,290	3645

The number of children sent into the country for one day this summer shows an increase of nearly 2000 as compared with the number for last year. Of the 106,890 London children who were sent for a day's outing, 66,720 spent the day at Loughton, 14,270 at Greenwich park, 6,800 at Hampstead, while 19,100 went in small parties to various other places.

Altogether since the fund was inaugurated in 1892 a total of 2,075,855 children have been sent for a day in the country, while 3,645 have been enabled to have a fortnight holiday amid rural scenes or at the seaside. Every summer special outings for cripples are organized, and these form one of the most touching aspects of the fund's work. The cost per child for a day's outing is ninepence, while 10 shillings pays for a fortnight's holidays.

There are many things we cannot afford to get for less than their full price—Henry F. Cope.

TO CURE MISHAPS ON RAILWAYS

Fagan Looks for Time When Superintendent Can Remove Railway Employes for Incompetency.

James O. Fagan, the traveler, philosopher, scholar and critic of present methods of railroad management, works for the Boston and Maine railroad as a tower signalman, because its gives him a living and time to study and write. Notwithstanding his free lance characteristics he is a friends of the president of the road.

Mr. Fagan expresses himself freely on the causes and cures of railroad accidents. As many already know, his recent magazine articles on live railroad topics have won him a lectureship at Harvard.

Mr. Fagan says that his study of the causes of preventable accidents began when he heard a railway superintendent say that he hoped to live to see the day when a superintendent could remove an engineer or a trainman whom he believed to be unfit for his place. He calls attention to the responsibilities of crossing tenders, upon whose attention to duty so many lives depend, but who, he said, never receive a single word of instruction concerning that duty.

In speaking of railroad accidents that are due to carelessness of employees, Mr. Fagan says that most of them could be traced to lack of attention, the psychology of which he discussed. The great frequency of railway accidents in America, he says, is an American characteristic, for which the public was in part to blame. The problem is how to connect the preventable accident with its cause in the railway man's mind. Railway managements, he says, should treat their employes more like men and less like instruments; should take them more into their confidence and make them feel that their interests are identical with those of the management.

TO EQUIP BOSTON HEAVY ARTILLERY

War Department Will Supply Outfit of Instruments Similar to Those Used by Regulars.

Word has just been received at the armory of the First Massachusetts Heavy Artillery that the war department next spring will supply the regiment with a full equipment of such instruments as are used by the regular army at seacoast defences

The apparatus consists of the following: Depression position finder, fire commander's board, plotting board mortar, mortar quadrant, plotting boards, azimuth instruments, range boards, gun deflection boards, mortar deflection board, wind component indicators, sets forward rulers, prediction scales, time range boards.

For some time the war department has been working out the details of the law enacted by the last Congress at the suggestion of Representative Peters, under which $25,000 was appropriated for equipping coast artillery militia armories with apparatus to enable the militia to practise at seacoast defnce during the intervals between the encampments and maneuvers.

FISHERMEN AT NEWFOUNDLAND ARE PEACEFUL

Captain Perry of Revenue Cutter Gresham Reports Satisfactory Relations Existing at Island.

DISPUTES DROPPED

That the relations at present between the American fishermen who invade the waters of Newfoundland and the government of that island are the most satisfactory for many years, is the report which Captain Perry, in command of the revenue cutter Gresham, brings to Boston from the Bay of Islands, from which he has just returned after a six weeks' cruise.

The animated disputes which in years past have occurred over the fisheries privilege, apparently have been disposed of by the Newfoundland government which has evinced a desire to meet the Americans halfway, and in spite of the modus vivendi which exists and provides that American vessels going to Newfoundland short handed, shall not employ Newfoundland crews except on the high seas, has but little effect on the American vessels. The American skippers seem to be perfectly willing to conform to the local restrictions and pay their duty of $75 per cargo and employ the Newfoundland crews.

Captain Perry states that although there have been but few American schooners in the northern waters up to the time he left there, every indication points to a general move to Newfoundland waters within a short time. The outlook for good catches is very reassuring and will doubtless be taken advantage of by the American fishermen.

During the stay of the Gresham in Newfoundland waters several of the officers made hunting trips and returned with several large caribou. They were given every possible attention by the government officials and were allowed to do all the shooting they cared to.

Some men think the only way to preserve the landmarks is to sit on the fence.—Henry F. Cope.

PLANS FOR NEW OPERA HOUSE

Eben D. Jordan Will Lay Cornerstone to Huntington Avenue Building on November 30.

The laying of the corner stone of the Boston Opera House on Huntington avenue will take Nov. 30, at 3 o'clock, and it is expected that the directors of the Metropolitan Opera House in New York will be present.

The stone will be laid by Eben D. Jordan, president of the Boston Opera Company. Governor Guild and Mayor Hibbard will speak.

Beneath the stone will be placed a bronze box containing a list of the stockholders up to the evening of Thanksgiving Day, phonographic records of the voices of America's greatest contemporary singers, music by American composers, musical programs and the newspapers of the day.

MISSION COLLEGES DOING GOOD WORK

Secretary Barton of the American Board of Missions at Boston says that the American colleges at Aintab, in northern Syria, known as the Central Turkey College, and at Smyrna where the International College is, with similar institutions at Constantinople, Marsovan, Harpoot, Tarsus and Beirut, with their various preparatory schools all over the country, have had more to do in preparing the Ottoman Empire for the most sweeping yet bloodless revolution ever recorded in history, than all other influences combined.

Dispatches just received from various parts of the Ottoman Empire by the American board reveal a wide-spread interest in education upon the part of the people of that country. This interest is not confined to any one race, but characterizes Armenians, Greeks and Mohammedans alike. Central Turkey College, for instance, whose president, Dr. John E. Merrill, is just now in Boston, reports an increase in students of 15 per cent, with every department crowded.

The International College, at Smyrna, whose president is the Rev. Alexander MacLachlan, has over 300 students in attendance, in spite of the fact that an increase of 20 per cent has recently been made in the tuition demanded.

Charles Frohman has obtained a new comedy, "Penelope," by Somerset Maugham. The play will be produced at the Comedy theatre, London, in January.

PRESIDENT IS PREPARING HIS MESSAGE

Communication at Opening of Second Session of Sixtieth Congress Will Be a Notable One.

REVIEW OF HIS WORK

Has Discussed the Subject Matter Only With His Successor and a Few Intimate Friends.

WASHINGTON, Nov. 25—President Roosevelt's message to the second session of the 60th Congress, will doubtless prove a notable state paper. While there will be short special messages on particular subjects between Dec. 7, when Congress meets, and March 4, when it expires by constitutional limitation, this will probably be the last formal communication which President Roosevelt will indict. It will be, in a sense, his farewell address to the American people.

Contrary to his usual custom, President Roosevelt is discussing his message with nobody except President-elect Taft and one or two very intimate friends. It has been written out, much of it in the President's own hand. Parts of it were written during the summer at Oyster Bay.

It is understood that the message will review the seven and three quarters years of his administration, recounting what he has been able to accomplish in the line of constructive legislation, and then passing to the difficulties and problems which will be handed down to his successor. These subjects will be handled on broad general lines, rather than with reference to specific recommendations to the session just beginning.

GOVERNMENT BY COMMISSION.

Quincy, the home of the Adams family, is one of the Massachusetts cities that are inclined to favor the plan of government by commission. A number of New England cities will divest themselves of their mayors and boards of aldermen and councilmen within the next two years. But we know as yet of no Connecticut city that is proposing to make the change.—Hartford Times.

Concerning Fitness

IF THERE BE any one characteristic of the Arts of today that stands out prominently it is **Simplicity**. In Painting, in Sculpture, in Architecture, in Music, this tendency toward the direct and the simple is evident. Nor have the lesser Arts been stragglers in the movement toward **Perfection**. The cabinet-maker, the binder of books, the worker in silver and gold, the weaver, the printer and the spinner, each has done his part to make like progress in his art.

Of all the Arts, none has taken greater or more noticeable strides than Interior Decoration. It has come home to us that the furniture, the coverings of the walls, the hangings, should harmonize with the nature of the house.

Each room, in fact, should express, in a form adapted to its particular uses, the **Character** of the design of the building. If it be colonial, the furniture, the wall papers, the dishes, the table linen may also be colonial. Or, if the building be English, then the furniture may be of English design. There is, however, the danger of being too literal. It is the **Appearance** of the work that should govern the selection of details which must always be adapted and modified to meet the requirements not only of the day, but the house, and even of the room. And upon the ability to appreciate the subtleness of particular problems, rests the real value of the Interior Decorator.

To be a judge of **Fitness** is not given to many. Study and experience will not suffice. There must be a certain sense of **Proportion** and **Balance**. If then, this be rare, the value is surely something. To the architect himself, the confidence that his design will be carried out with faithfulness and sympathy must bring a sense of pleasure as well as relief.

We beg leave to invite your inspection of that part of our store which is known as the Upholstery Department. Here it is our desire to carry out, in the details left to our charge, the **Thought** that the architect has embodied in his building. Not only the curtains, rugs, wall hangings, but even the table service—the linen and the china—may be left to our care. Designs will be made for each detail of the furnishing and submitted to the architect for his approval.

We believe that we have already achieved considerable success, and are sure that the feeling of confidence that our careful co-operation with the architect has always inspired, is of permanent value—not only to us, but also to our clients.

We would appreciate the favor of being asked further to show our ability.

Most Respectfully,

SHEPARD NORWELL COMPANY

BOSTON, MASS.

A. Towell & Co. 24 Winter St. is recognized as Headquarters for Holiday Gifts

Suggestions for Holiday Gifts
NECKWEAR | CANES
SHIRTS | HANDKERCHIEFS
GLOVES | BAGS
HOSIERY | TOILET OUTFITS
WAISTCOATS | JEWELRY, ETC.
J. T. DYER
Haberdasher and Hatter
34 BOYLSTON STREET

Going to Philadelphia?
STOP AT THE
NEW HOTEL HANOVER
ARCH and 12th STREETS
American plan, $2.50 per day and up.
European plan, $1.00 per day and up.
WILLIAM C. RICHARDSON, Prop.

THE MONITOR IN THE HOME INSURES CLEAN READING.

Holiday Goods
—IN—
Pocket Knives,
Razors, Scissors,
Cases of Scissors
Dressing Cases, Toilet Sets, Opera and Field Glasses, Fine Purses and Pocketbooks, Elegant Carving Knives, Silver Fruit Knives, Cameras,
And a multitude of beautiful articles specially suitable for HOLIDAY GIFTS.
SKATES
Dame, Stoddard & Co.
374 WASHINGTON ST.
Opposite Bromfield St., Boston.

6

CONGRESS WILL NOT CONSIDER MANY REFORMS

Long List of Important Matters Are Still in the Transition Stage in the Lower Branch.

SUPPLY BILLS LEAD

Party Chiefs Disposed to Discourage Agitation of Subjects Outside of Regular Routine.

WASHINGTON, Nov. 25—In addition to the regular supply bills Congress will have before it, in the various stages of legislative progress, the following matters, many of which have been the subject of special recommendation from the White House:

Child labor regulation under the powers of the so-called commerce clause of the constitution. The Beveridge bill will come up for a vote in the Senate in December, according to an agreement made last winter.

Regulation of the powers of injunction as applied to labor and other disputes.

Amendments of the interstate commerce law to legalize traffic agreements and provide for a supervision of security issues.

Amendment of the anti-trust law to exempt proper combinations from its penalties, and to bring improper combinations under government inspection.

Postal savings banks.

Creation of an official permanent deep-waterways commission.

Inheritance tax.

Compulsory investigation of industrial disputes.

Legislation for the betterment of the condition of the farmer along lines to be recommended by the "country life" commission.

Regulation by government supervision of the telegraph and telephone business, in accordance with suggestions to be made by Labor Commissioner Neill in response to the Senate's resolution of May 28, 1908.

Purchase of the White Mountain and Southern Appalachian forests for a governmental reserve.

Removal of the duty on wood pulp and pulp wood.

Government regulation of mineral and coal deposits under public lands.

Navy reorganization.

Parcels post.

Ship subsidy.

Bills covering practically all the topics have been introduced. In a few instances they have even been considered in committee and recommended. The anti-trust bill was the subject of hearings before the House judiciary committee. The ship subsidy bill passed the House and reposes in the House committee on postoffices and postroads. The Appalachian forest reserve bill was adversely reported from the House judiciary committee and reposes in the House agricultural committee.

It may be stated with entire frankness that most of the foregoing topics will stand no chance in the lawmaking operations of the coming Congress. The Republican leaders are disposed to hold the work of the session to the passage of the supply bills as closely as possible, and to discourage agitation of any other subjects.

EIFFEL TOWER AS WIRELESS DEPOT

With Scanty Appliances Station in Paris Receives Messages From a Distance of 2500 Kilometres.

A new and extremely powerful radiotelegraph station is in course of construction, in which the Eiffel tower is employed for the support of the antennae. The power of the transmission apparatus in use at the present time is only rated 10 kilowatts. The energy is now furnished by one of the Paris electricity companies; it is an alternating current of 42 periods, at a tension of 3,000 volts. This pressure is reduced to 220 volts by a transformer, installed in close proximity to the tower. The current passes over a circuit which comprises the manipulator, an adjustable induction coil and the primary of a transformer.

In spite of the scanty appliances which the station has had at its disposal hitherto, some remarkable results have been obtained. Messages have been received from a distance of nearly 2,500 kilometres, and during the existence of the Moroccan disturbances the service rendered was much appreciated.

It has therefore been decided to arrange for a permanent installation at high power, in lieu of the present one. The new station will be subterranean and the energy developed will exceed 10 horsepower.

URGES AID FOR MISSIONS ABROAD

Discussion Proves Feature of Campaign Meetings of the Laymen's Missionary Movement.

A feature of the campaign of the laymen's massionary movement meetings in Boston was the consideration of the sum that the churches of this country should give to foreign missions. J. Campbell White, who presided at the meeting, said:

"Foreign missions are the best investment a man can make. For each missionary in the field the average expense of the total expenditures by the board is $1717. This includes the expense of 100,000 native workers. We ought to be giving $50,000,000 a year toward missions. Up to date there has been a greater readiness among men to give life than money. There are more than 1,000,000,000 people in non-Christian lands, and nine tenths of them have not had an intelligent opportunity of accepting Christianity."

It was decided that the campaigners' conferences of the movement had established 12 points with regard to the missionary problem, the most important of which were:

The pastor is the most important single factor in the missionary life of the congregation.

Absolutely essential is the cooperation of a group of strong laymen whose chief responsibility through the year shall be the promotion of missionary intelligence and the organization of thorough methods of missionary finance.

Public education is indispensable if the best results are to be secured.

The next step is a thoroughly organized canvass of, the entire church membership for individual subscriptions.

The one most important condition of success in this enterprise is prayer. It is not primarily a financial movement, but a spiritual uprising.

STEEL PLANT WILL DOUBLE DULUTH'S POPULATION

United States Steel Corporation Is Investing $20,000,000 to Develop Plants in This Great Railroad Center.

TRADE INCREASING

DULUTH, Minn., Nov. 25—Duluth has many great and beautiful temples dedicated to learning and commerce and pleasure, with more and greater ones planned and in course of construction. The United States Steel Corporation is investing $20,000,000 in a steel plant in Duluth. This will almost double the city's population. Other large manufacturing concerns are flourishing here, and from Duluth commercial men travel in every direction, for this city's geographical location has made it a great distributing center. The Wisconsin Central railroad is burrowing its way into the city, under one of its principal streets, at an expense for its Duluth terminal of $3,000,000, and the Soo Line is crowding time to get here. Seven other large railroads and several smaller ones are already here.

Duluth has been facetiously spoken of as a city 15 miles long and two blocks wide. A serious description, and one which would do the city justice, would be a word painting of great beauty, and would tell of churches and schools and homes, more beautifully monumental than most cities of Duluth's population can boast: of parks and drives and natural scenic attractions which are proving a very valuable asset.

"The Zenith City of the Unsalted Seas" has grown, within a few years, into a manufacturing and railroad center of extended renown—a port from which and to which mighty ships of commerce go and come, bringing and taking a greater tonnage in freight than any other port in the world, save only New York can account for, and which is reaching out in every direction for more commerce, and for better facilities and more modern and up-to-date methods of carrying on its great industries, not forgetting the more important part of providing well for the spiritual and the social, religious and material welfare of her citizens.

One of the city's most pleasing and beautiful improvements is the creation of a civic center, in which the federal government, the county of St. Louis and the municipality of Duluth are interested. This civic center will have grouped in it the new St. Louis county court house, now nearing completion at a cost of $1,000,000, the new federal building to replace the one already outgrown, and the new City Hall. The site is a grand one, overlooking the busy harbor, and the plans of the architects reveal, or present an inspiring picture, and one which should have an uplifting influence on the people of this city.

Within the past year the new Y. M. C. A. building costing nearly $300,000 was completed and occupied, and the corner stone of the new Y. W. C. A., to cost $150,000, was laid. These buildings occupy prominent corners and stand as substantial monuments to the whole-souled generosity of the public.

GRAND OPERA SCHOOL PLANNED

In connection with the new opera house to be erected in this city, there has been organized a school for grand opera, and already two scholarships have been received, one from Miss Geraldine Farrar and the other from David Bispham. The value of the scholarships is $500 and entitles the recipient to free tuition in the new school for one year.

In her letter transmitting the scholarship Miss Farrar pays tribute to the generosity of Eben D. Jordan in his connection with the projected school, and expresses her opinion that the school will fill a long-felt want among the students of operatic music in America. The opportunities offered by the new school, she feels, will furnish American women with the possibilities of acquiring at home that which hitherto they have had to fight for abroad.

Under the projected scheme for the operatic school, not only can the education be received here, but the singers can make their debut in the new opera house without waiting for foreign approval.

FAIRBANKS PREFERS FARMING

INDIANAPOLIS, Nov. 25—Vice-President Fairbanks will give up law and devote all this time to his large landed interests in Illinois after his retirement from office on March 4.

Though Mr. Fairbanks has been in politics actively since 1886, he has maintained his offices and occasionally has appeared in the trial of cases in court. Since he was elected to the Senate, however, he has been more of a consulting attorney than an active practitioner. The fact that he has vacated his offices and moved his library to his residence is construed to mean that he may retire from the active practice of law permanently.

EXHAUSTED DEER WILLING CAPTIVE

Pursued by Dogs, It Runs Close to Mail Wagon in Berkshire Town, Seeking Protection of Carrier.

A deer ran close to the mail wagon of Edward Cassidy when near the home of H. P. Bliss in Sheffield and willingly gave itself into the custody of the mail carrier, who drove off the dogs.

The several dogs which followed close upon the trail of the frightened and almost exhausted deer had evidently followed their coveted prey many miles, for the deer, though nearly full grown and very fleet of foot, was almost ready to drop from sheer exhaustion when Uncle Sam's mail distributor happened along.

Since the law protecting deer from hunters at all seasons has been in effect they have been exceptionally numerous throughout southern Berkshire and have frequently been seen in village streets as well as with herds of cattle, but this is the first time that one has been captured alone in the open.—Berkshire Courier.

AID FOR GERMAN UNEMPLOYED

BERLIN, Nov. 25—Unanimous action by the labor unions of Germany is expected to result in governmental aid being given to the unemployed at once. The problem in the empire is most serious. It is declared by the labor leaders who today presented the result of their investigations to the ministry, that already more than one third of their total membership are out of work and have no means of support.

The authorities agree that the situation is more serious than in a generation, and the Berlin authorities are about to inaugurate extensive public improvements to provide work for the involuntarily idle.

This will be but a "drop in the bucket," however, and the plan now proposed is for the German government to carry into effect extensive plans for national improvements which were tentatively approved some time ago.

Hardly a day passes without reductions in the number of working hours or the dismissal of large numbers of laborers, somewhere, and often in many places at once, throughout the empire.

The depression is attributed mainly to the "backwash" from the recent hard times in America and to the crushing pressure of taxation upon industries of every class in Germany.

DEEP INTEREST IN RIVER WORK

BREMEN, Germany, Nov. 25—The deepening of the lower river Weser, Bremen's waterway to the sea, and the extension of harbor constructions have created an intense and lively commercial interest among the whole body of merchants. The traffic has so increased that the harbor facilities, made at an expense of many millions, have become insufficient for the business, and the port must again be enlarged.

Bremen was the first port of the continent that undertook to establish a regular steamship service with the United States. From that small beginning in 1847, 60 years ago, it has constantly increased its shipping and trade until during last year, 1907, Bremen ships carried over 225,000,000 emigrants and more than $52,000,000 worth of merchandise to the United States, and brought back to Bremen from the United States $154,000,000 worth of merchandise, including 460,000 metric tons of raw cotton, valued at $124,000,000

The first ship of the North German Lloyd Steamship Company from this port arrived in New York on July 4, 1858, with 100 tons of freight and one first-cabin passenger; now the gross tonnage of its merchant fleet exceeds that of the navy of the United States. Bremen has, besides the North German Lloyd, more than 100 river steamers and coasting vessels and nearly another hundred large ocean-going vessels. It was largely this steamship company that extended Bremen's commerce in India, China and Australia and greatly participated in increasing the figures of the imports and exports of this port.

DRESSES TURKEY FOR PRFSIDENT

WESTERLY, R. I., Nov. 25—The Rhode Island turkey which Horace Vose will send to the President, according to his annual custom, to grace the table of the White House on Thanksgiving Day, went on the block yesterday and will be shipped to Washington today. It is the best of a lot of chestnut-fed birds which have been selected and specially reared as candidates for the distinction. The bird weighs 26 pounds.

President Grant was the first occupant of the White House to receive a Thanksgiving turkey from Vose, and each year since then the gift has been renewed.

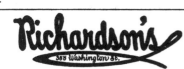

NEW CANADIAN RAILROAD WILL AID NORTHWEST

Grand Trunk Pacific, Transcontinental System Will Open Up Unsettled Districts Near Prince Rupert.

BOOM IS EXPECTED

VICTORIA, B. C., Nov. 25—The building of the Grand Trunk Pacific, the new Canadian transcontinental railway system, is ever a live topic in northwestern Canada, whose settlement has progressed far in advance of proper railway facilities. This road will not only minister to the needs of many districts already settled, but will open up for settlement large areas of new country.

The announcement is made that the survey of Prince Rupert, the western terminal of the road, is being rapidly completed, and it is expected that the city lots will be auctioned off about the first of May, when a rush for the best properties is anticipated.

The government of British Columbia is sharing with the railway the work of preparing the city for its coming inhabitants, and is expending large sums in sewer construction and in preparation of streets and sidewalks. There will probably be tremendous activity in building operations at this point during the coming summer.

OLD DEED FILED IN BOSTON.

A deed executed in the second year of the reign of George II., of England, has been filed at the registry of deeds in Boston. It conveys three and one-half acres of woodland in Dorchester from Obadiah Swift to John Robinson.

NEW $10,000,000 TUNNEL WILL EASE TRAFFIC CONGESTION IN BIG CITY

Washington Street Tube Offers Solution to Transportation Problem in Boston Business Section.

SOON TO BE READY

With the opening of the new $10,000,000 Washington street tunnel for underground trains the street transportation service of Boston undergoes a sweeping transformation. The elevated trains heretofore running through the heart of the city by way of the old subway under Tremont street are diverted to the new tunnel which is 5,676 feet long, thus making Washington street the trunk line for that kind of service throughout the city. Their place is taken in the old subway by through lines of surface cars, running in from Tremont street and Shawmut avenue, on the south, and continuing to the North Station, at the northerly outlet, where they swing around a loop and return on their courses. At the North Station the trains of the new tunnel and the through cars of the old subway stop at common station, where transfers can be made by walking up or down stairs.

In this way, for the first time, the city gets the advantage of two underground services instead of one, north and south, under the congested section of the city. At the same time, surface cars from the northern suburbs continue to run into the old subway and loop back from the heart of the city at Scollay square; while, similarly, surface cars from the south and west run in as far as Park street station, where they also loop back. Each of these loops allows a transfer with the surface cars on the "through" tracks by crossing a station platform. Cars running east from the city, under the harbor through the East Boston tunnel, although starting from Scollay square as heretofore, will connect with the new Washington street tunnel service one block from their starting point, where the new tunnel dips under the tube running to East Boston.

Speed and safety are increased for the elevated trains in taking the new route. In the tunnel they have almost a straight line from one side of the business section to the other, whereas the old subway, built originally for surface cars only, compelled the heavy elevated equipment to wind around tortuous curves and to dip abruptly through a sub-subway that involves double curves both horizontally and vertically. Passengers as well as trainmen will be glad of the smooth, straight stretches of track in the new rapid transit route, the longer and roomier platforms and the escalators between low-level stations and the street.

Opening the new tunnel is only a step in the rapid transit developments now under way here. The next move will be the opening of the elevated extension southward from the present terminal at Dudley street to Forest Hills square, two miles beyond. That change

CONTINUED ON PAGE SEVEN.

Richardson's
388 Washington St.

Overcoat Needs

of the business man, young man or student with expensive tastes are better anticipated than ever before.

In every garment made by ALFRED BENJAMIN & CO. you see the thoroughbred lines and exclusive fabrics that you would look for at a high-class tailor's.

But the price——that is just where we know we can interest you. We want you to know us, and see our new Overcoat models for winter wear.

$20—$25—$30—$35

This is distinctly "A Shop for Men" conducted on principles that appeal to the good tastes and economical tendencies of the shrewest buyers.

Charles B. Hubbell, Manager

You eliminate all element of chance or uncertainty if your contract calls for an

Estey Pipe Organ

The quality is of the same highest grade as that maintained by the Estey Organ Company since the inception of the business in 1846, the continued excellence of which has resulted in making the Estey Organ the accepted world's standard.

Your correspondence is respectfully solicited.

Estey Organ Co.

Boston, 120 Boylston Street
St. Louis, 1116 Olive Street
New York, 7 West 29th Street
Atlanta, 93 Peachtree Street
Philadelphia, 1118 Chestnut Street
London, Eng., Oxford Street

FACTORIES, BRATTLEBORO, VT.

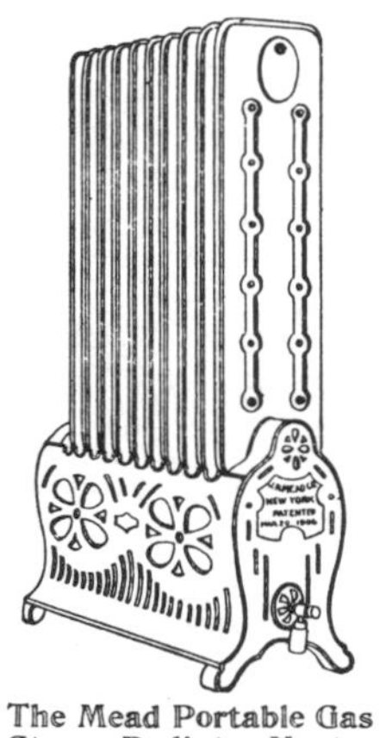

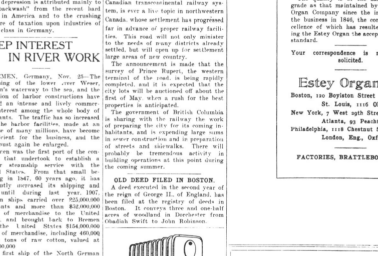

The Mead Portable Gas Steam Radiator Heater

STEAM HEAT WITHOUT PIPING OR BOILER. GAS FOR FUEL.

Write us for descriptive catalog of our full line of Gas Heating Appliances and Odorless Gas Logs.

The J. H. Mead Company
242 FOURTH AVE., NEW YORK CITY
Factory GRAND RAPIDS, MICH.

The Cobb-Eastman Company

OUR IDEAL
Perfection through earnest efforts

OUR AIM
Success following our Ideal

OUR DESIRE
Your Consideration and Patronage

Our Ideal will only be Realized by Sincerity. We have stopped the buying and selling of other men's products, for their first consideration is Profit and Trade. Our aim is Excellence, through honest business methods.

Fine Furniture and Woodwork
Decorations
Fabrics Wall Papers

372-378 BOYLSTON STREET
BOSTON, MASSACHUSETTS

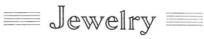

For Attractive, Reliable and Reasonable-Priced

Jewelry

Watches | CALL AND SEE STOCK AT | Silverware

SAWYER'S, 10 Summer Street, Boston, Mass.

The Children's Star
THE BEST CHRISTMAS GIFT
A Juvenile Magazine Shorn of Error.
$1.50 a Year. Send for Sample Copy.
The Sherman, Washington, D. C.

M'Cann's Tours de Luxe to Florida, Cuba, West Indies, California.
Europe and Old Mexico
Write for booklet "S." Railroad and steamship tickets everywhere.
M'CANN'S TOURS, 1328 BROADWAY, N.Y.

DAVIS BECOMES PEAT EXPERT FOR GOVERNMENT

Former University of Michigan Specialist Has Written Comprehensive Treatise on Subject.

WILL TEST SAMPLES

HOUGHTON, Mich., Nov. 25—Steady depletion of the world's coal resources will force upon the nations the development of other kinds of fuel, and peat promises to stand prominently in the foreground. It is capable of comparatively rapid growth and can be developed in marshes that it would be impossible or expensive to reclaim for other purposes.

Charles A. Davis, formerly connected with the University of Michigan, who prepared for the Michigan geological Survey papers on "Marl" and "Material for Cement" and later specialized on peat, has been appointed to the newly created position of "peat expert" by the United States geological survey.

Mr. Davis' specialization on peat for the Michigan geological survey led him to prepare the most exhaustive and thorough treatise on this subject that has ever been written. It has served to bring the peat resources of Michigan prominently before the world, and because of the adaptability of the soil of certain districts in Michigan to peat growth, this industry promises to become one of steadily increasing importance in the state.

The appointment of Mr. Davis to the position in the United States Geological survey came from men who were unknown to him until he began, under temporary appointments a year ago, to make reports upon peat culture. The appointment is therefore based wholly upon merit.

In his new position as "peat expert" in the United States geological survey, one of his first steps will be the testing of large samples of peat in the latest types of producer-gas engines. He will also follow the discoveries of Caro and Frank in the production of ammonium sulphate from peat by the use of superheated steam to break up the nitrogen compounds in the peat. These compounds are then converted into ammonia so that the commercial product can be readily saved.

Arrangements have been made for cooperative work between the University of Michigan and the United States geological survey, by which the latter will make some important investigations in the Michigan lower peninsular coal measures. These investigations and tests are to be specifically along the line of gas making, looking into the possibility of extending the known measures of coals suitable for the manufacture of illuminating gas.

They will be conducted under the immediate direction of the University of Michigan at Ann Arbor, which will furnish the plant and the necessary assistants. The United States geological survey will provide the engineering-chemist and the field force to procure the samples.

Perry Barker, who has had extensive experience in combustion tests of fuels and in chemical analyses for the United States geological survey, has been assigned as engineering-chemist in this work.

The work for the University of Michigan will be under the direction of Alfred H. White, Jr., professor of chemical engineering.

NEWS ITEMS FROM GREATER BOSTON

Attempts are being made today to raise the ferryboat Revere, which sank at the East Boston ferry repair slip yesterday. It is supposed the accident was due to an open seacock or a disconnected delivery pipe. The boat was the oldest in the service of the city, having been in constant use 34 years.

Caleb Chase, senior member of Chase & Sanborn Company, expired today at his Brookline home, 1546 Beacon street. He was born in Harwich, Cape Cod, in 1831, where he was educated and received his early training in the mercantile business. Since becoming a prominent factor in the coffee business Mr. Chase has proved a generous benefactor to his native town.

In a statement issued by the finance commission on the matter of their recent report on the municipal music expenditures, the commission denies that it suggested, or even intimated, that the musicians should be paid a wage of but $1.50 per day. They declare the first recommendations relative to the reduction of expenses in the music department could be carried out without working any hardship to the musicians.

Captain Barrett of the steamer Old Colony, bound from New York to Boston, has reported here that the big gas buoy located on Stone Horse Shoals in Vineyard Sound, has gone adrift and was sighted off Nobska Point, many miles from its original location.

It has been definitely settled that Dr. Richard C. Maclaurin, the newly elected president of the Massachusetts Institute of Technology, will take up his duties here the latter part of May.

Boston's new $10,000,000 tunnel under Washington street, will be officially inspected by the Rapid Transit Commission today. It is expected that the tunnel will be opened to the public the first week in December.

Arthur Bissell W. K. Cowan

BISSELL-COWAN PIANO COMPANY

Factors in Chicago for

American Piano Company

Manufacturers of

Standard Instruments

Including the production of

Messrs.

Wm. Knabe & Company

Chickering & Sons

Haines Bros.

Marshall & Wendell and others

Also Player-Pianos from these eminent sources

This organization of piano-forte makers marks an epoch in the piano industry, providing a combination of skill and resources heretofore unknown, and resulting in advantages to the public which make investigation of these instruments imperative on the part of intending purchasers.

203-207 Michigan Avenue

The Fine Arts Building - - Chicago, Illinois

WILL MAKE REPORT ON OUR RESOURCES

State Commission of Conservation to Review Natural Possibilities — Traffic Improvements Planned.

What Massachusetts contains in the way of undeveloped water power, forest lands and timber, and other natural resources, will be known definitely for the first time when the new state commission of conservation makes its report to Governor Guild early in the coming year. Prof. George F. Swain of the Massachusetts Institute of Technology is the engineering expert on the new commission, and State Forester Rane is the member qualified to give special assistance with reference to the forestry considerations. This first work of the commission will be little more than a general round-up of possibilities and availabilities. If there is positive work to be undertaken for systematic development of resources, that will be dealt with later. Prof. Swain contributes to the state commission the advantage gained from his experience with the national commission of conservation, to which he was one of the original appointees. The national body is engaged in much the same work for the country as a whole as the state commission for Massachusetts, and its report will go to Congress at the coming session.

Development of the resources of Massachusetts, as hinted at in the appointment of this commission, was an idea uppermost with Governor Guild much of the time while he was beginning the work of his administration. The feeling had been growing that something needed to be done to keep Massachusetts in the front rank of industrial and commercial progress, and the commission of conservation was named to piece out the work not covered by the commission on commerce and industry and the commission for metropolitan improvement, both named by Governor Guild for general progressive study and recommendation in the fields which their names suggest.

So far the Commission on Commerce and Industry, although having the broadest kind of authority and range as to subjects of inquiry and study, has made no report except that on the Boston & Maine-New Haven merger.

The Metropolitan Improvement Commission is now preparing to send in a very important report on the railroad facilities in the Boston district. It will make some suggestion for a more productive use of terminals, particularly whereby goods coming in from or to a certain railroad may be handled at any waterfront terminal irrespective of ownership.

Another section of this report will suggest routes for developing boulevards or highways, circling Boston in an inner and outer series, to allow intercommunication among the suburbs without necessitating a journey through the congested part of the city. For the boulevard work the commission has had the assistance of Arthur A. Shurtleff, while William R. Wadsworth, C. E., of the Insttiute of Technology, has been giving his aid in working out the problem of railroad terminals.

FOR INDUSTRIAL NIGHT SCHOOLS

Boston Educator Favors Institution in Address at Meeting of National Society in Atlanta.

ATLANTA, Ga., Nov. 25—Charles H. Morse, secretary and executive officer of the Massachusetts Commission on Industrial Education, in addressing the annual meeting of the National Society for the Promotion of Industrial Education, recently on the subject of evening industrial schools, said in part:

"We in Massachusetts have the feeling that both evening and day industrial schools should be developed, each class to cover a distince field and fill distinct needs. My theme today is, however, evening industrial schools.

"The need of evening industrial schools manifests itself in a number of ways: By the result of argument from existing conditions, by canvass among the people of a community, but most forcibly of all by the number who register as pupils in evening industrial schools when such are established. The pupils in such schools vary in age from extreme youth, 14 or 15 years, to persons of even advanced middle age, but they practically all have the same qualification that they left school at or near the age limit of compulsory day school attendance. Moreover, the great majority have a distinct idea of acquiring knowledge along some special line of industrial work which they have already entered upon, and either wish to broaden their knowledge of what they are already engaged upon or they wish to inform themselves concerning some field which they see ahead of them, and in which they feel they would be better off."

NOVEL GIFT MADE TO Y. M. C. A.

Auburn Association Must Keep Out of Debt in Future, According to Condition Made by Benefactor.

AUBURN, N. Y., Nov. 25—A gift to the Y. M. C. A., practically binding the association to keep out of debt, was the novel form of benefaction recently announced by Miss Caroline Willard of Auburn. She agreed to liquidate the association's present indebtedness and make repairs to the building, at a total expense of about $11,000, on condition that the organization hereafter shall not incur debts that it cannot meet readily.

About a year ago there was opened in this city a magnificent building devoted to the advancement of women. It was the gift of Mrs. Eliza W Osborne, who for many years has devoted her energies to the cause of the enfranchisement of her sex. Closely following this came the announcement that the Hon. Thomas Mott Osborne, a son of the donor of the Woman's Union building, was about to construct a new theater to be called the Jefferson, in honor of the distinguished American actor.

The beautiful structure nearly is ready for dedication. The auditorium is constructed on the megaphone plan and the architects believe that the slightest sound on the stage may be heard as distinctly in the rear of the house as in the front. The Jefferson will be one of the handsomest playhouses in the United States, and it is safe to assume that it will be devoted to such attractions as will serve to have their influence for good upon the public.

15-30 H. P.

THE IDEAL TOWN CAR

The... Stearns

Best STOCK Car of the World

30-60 H. P.

THE IDEAL TOURING CAR

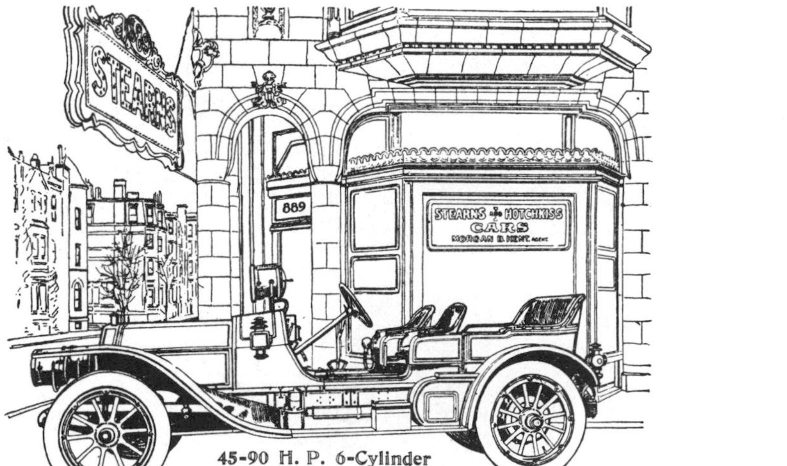

45-90 H. P. 6-Cylinder Stearns Runabout

30--60 Horse-Power	Limousine Body . . .	$5750
	Touring Car Body . .	4600
	Toy Tonneau	4600

15--30 Horse-Power	Touring Car Body . .	$3200
	Runabout Body . . .	3200
	Landaulet Body . . .	3800

The Stearns

AT BRIARCLIFF—Defeated every American and nine foreign Cars.
AT FORT GEORGE HILL—Won First, Second, Third and Fourth.
IN SEVEN HILL CLIMBS—In all parts of the United States—It won.
AT BRIGHTON BEACH—It won the 50-mile Stock Car, and 6-Cylinder, 5-mile races.

ARRANGE FOR A DEMONSTRATION

MORGAN B. KENT, 889 Boylston St., Boston

Telephone 534 Back Bay

TRY TO PROTECT GIRLS STUDYING MUSIC ABROAD

Americans and Foreigners Join Efforts to Better Conditions for the Young Students.

BERLIN, Nov. 25—At present one is hearing and reading much of the kindly efforts of Americans, as well as foreigners, to ameliorate the condition of American music students, more especially girls, in Europe. It certainly seems to one looking from the standpoint of a somewhat lengthy experience with this problem, that the same amount of energy could be more profitably employed in cultivating a more rational view of the whole matter in the thoughts of Americans in general, American mothers in particular.

One cannot help wondering at the calm optimism with which girls of 18 or younger are sent to countries of which they do not even know the language, still less the morals, to find boarding places for themselves, to choose their own companionship, unguided, unguarded, frequently unadvised. Many of these girls have been carefully brought up in the home circle, so carefully indeed that any knowledge of the world and its ways has been scrupulously kept from them. In this condition, suddenly placed in a strange city, lonely and homesick, believing that they must stay and accomplish that for which they have come in spite of every untoward circumstance, is it strange that they grasp eagerly at any diversion, at any companionship offered, and that finally many of them are ashamed to go back to their native towns, because of abject failure?

Success the Spark.

Those who succeed musically, who fan the spark of genius with which they start into a bright flame, do so often at a sacrifice of comfort, of natural spontaneous poyousness, which is far out of proportion to the results. What is it all for? Why are households separated, and lonely hearts on both sides of the Atlantic? (For in the rare cases when girls are not sent alone, they are accompanied by mothers obliged to make the tremendous sacrifice of separation from husband and home, sometimes for years.) Why is it? Because so far our American people, as a nation, demand something with a foreign stamp.

Because it is better? No, rather because it is "different." We have just as good teachers of piano, violin and vocal music in the United States as can be found in Europe. Indeed, many of those in Europe today are American citizens, and would joyfully return to their native—or adopted—land to teach, if a field were provided for their efforts; but they, too, because of so-called public opinion, are obliged to live in Europe in order to have the necessary "prestige" to teach Americans, who cross the ocean to study with them.

It is a farce! As Americans we are in many ways so well satisfied that we are blinded to the absurd. We swagger through countries which were ages old in cultivation when our own beautiful land was still unknown, find fault with all other constitutions and institutions, claim our own as "God's," boldly announce that it is the greatest and best in every particular, and then refuse at home to accept our own products unless they are stamped "made in Germany," or France, as the case may be.

Laugh at Americans.

No wonder European nations laugh at us! They do, constantly. Germany is glad to have our teachers, our singers, our players. Nearly every opera house has one or more representatives. The "directors" like Americans, for they have good voices, and, as a rule, do earnest, serious work. Surely this ability should not be driven from its natural environment by lack of appreciation. It is a pleasure to see that thought along these lines is being stirred in all directions at present, as evidenced by the organization of opera classes in different American cities, the desire to promote an interest in a higher class of music, and to show that we have native material.

Guard Home Talent.

Of that there is not the slightest doubt. The great point is to cultivate that material at home. Mothers, keep your daughters near you, if not in the house, at least safely protected while they are studying for concert or operatic stage. Put them where a sense of self-respect will demand the same conduct which you would expect of them at home. Much of the wrongdoing and wrong-going in foreign lands is comprised in the often-heard remark, "No one knows me here." The whole question is much more than simply one of music, it is the preservation of womanliness and morality, the high standard of womanhood of which America has always been so justly proud. Like nearly every other moral or ethical question it must begin with the mothers, with an awakening to present conditions, and a united effort to change them.

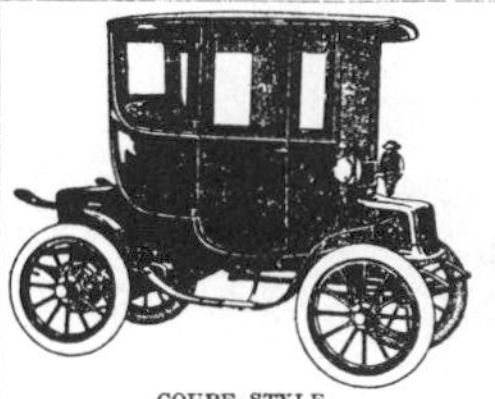

Electric Carriages......

COUPE STYLE

The harmony of line and perfection of finish in Rauch & Lang cars appeal to those who demand the best. The comfortable quarters are upholstered and fitted with every device known to convenience.

Absolute safety is assured by the patented "R. & L." safety lock and electric brake control. The car is built to satisfy the critical purchaser of fine carriages. Used under all weather conditions, and driven by any member of the family.

Any particular car will be demonstrated to you personally by any of the agencies located in the principal cities of the United States. Six models and twelve styles from which to select.

Catalogue for the asking.

The Rauch & Lang Carriage Co.

2197 West 25th Street, CLEVELAND, O.

Peerless Rubber Mfg. Company

MANUFACTURERS OF HIGH GRADE

Mechanical Rubber Goods

Air Brake Hose Water Hose Steam Hose

Pneumatic Tool Hose

Rubber Belting Rubber Mats and Matting

Rubber Sheet Floor Covering

SOLE MANUFACTURERS OF THE CELEBRATED

Rainbow Packing and Peerless Piston Packing

WRITE FOR CATALOGUE.

Peerless Rubber Mfg. Company

16 Warren Street, New York

PENNSYLVANIA MAKING PLANS TO PURIFY RIVERS

Systematic Campaign Inaugurated for Elimination of Sewage From Different Streams in State.

WORK UNDER WAY

HARRISBURG, Pa., Nov. 25—The state of Pennsylvania has seriously undertaken the task of restoring its rivers and tributary streams to their primitive condition of purity.

This laudable result is to be brought about by means of a systematic campaign for the elimination of the raw sewage of cities and towns and the polluting drainage of mills and factories.

When it is considered that four cities of more than 100,000 population, 16 cities of from 20,000 to 100,000 population, 24 cities of from 10,000 to 20,000 population and more than 3,000 towns or villages of less than 10,000 population are using the streams of this state as open sewers, and that the peculiar local conditions in each of these more than 3,000 communities must be dealt with individually for the accomplishment of the desired result, the greatness of the task may be apprehended.

When it is considered further that 7,000,000 people are dependent for their water supply for domestic and commercial purposes on the streams into which these 3,000 cities and villages drain their sewage, the importance of the clean water campaign inaugurated by the government of Pennsylvania becomes likewise apparent.

Drastic legislation was regarded as necessary to accomplish the overcoming of municipal practices that had been in vogue for several hundred years. The state could not directly compel cities and towns to install sewage disposal plants, because the money necessary for such improvements could be extended only by authority of the voters of the several communities or their representatives in the city and borough councils. But a way was found. The Legislature of 1905 enacted that no municipality nor manufacturing plant could "extend" its sewer system without a permit from the State Department of Health, and that the State health commissioner, with the approval of the Governor and the attorney general, might specify the conditions on which such permits should be granted. Thus, as the natural growth of each community compels its authorities to ask permission to build additional sewers, the state is empowered to deny that essential permission until a practical plan for the disposal of their sewage has been accepted by the petitioners.

The intelligent consideration employed in the application of this law, through Dr. Samuel G. Dixon, commissioner of health, and his chief sanitary engineer, F. Herbert Snow, has done much to allay the fears at first entertained as to the advisability of clothing state officials with arbitrary power over the affairs of municipalities. Care has been taken in every instance to adjust the requirements to the financial ability of the city or town.

Although it is less than three years since the law went into effect, 110 cities and towns have been directed to install sewage disposal plants within specified periods, the work in many instances being well under way, and seven cities and towns have completed the installation and have sewage disposal plants in full operation. The conditions in hundreds of other communities are being studied by the engineers of the department, with a view to the adoption of plans for each place. Thus, though comparatively speaking only a start has been made, the practicability of the method has been established and the way opened for more rapid progress in future years toward the elimination of sewage contamination from the waters of Pennsylvania.

Meanwhile, that the people shall not have to await the necessarily slow process of sewage disposal in order to have clean water, the State is pushing the establishment of filtration plants as rapidly as possible. A companion act to that affecting sewage gives the department of health jurisdiction over municipal and private water plants, with power to compel filtration where the sources of supply are found to be impure. Under this law approximately 50 cities and towns and private companies have provided, or are preparing to provide, adequate sand or mechanical filtration for the water furnished to their people, and this requirement will be extended throughout the State as fast as the facts are ascertained to warrant such action.

Philadelphia, Pittsburg, Harrisburg, Reading, McKeesport and other important cities already have successful filter plants, and the small communities are rapidly falling into line for clean water

BALLOON-FRIGHTENED NEGROES.

The balloon Yankee, after a sail of 450 miles from St. Louis dropped into a field full of negroes, causing consternation among them. They thought it was a supernatural visitor and many fled in panic

VIEW OF SOUTH BROAD STREET IN PHILADELPHIA WHICH IS CALLED OFFICIAL BUSINESS CENTER

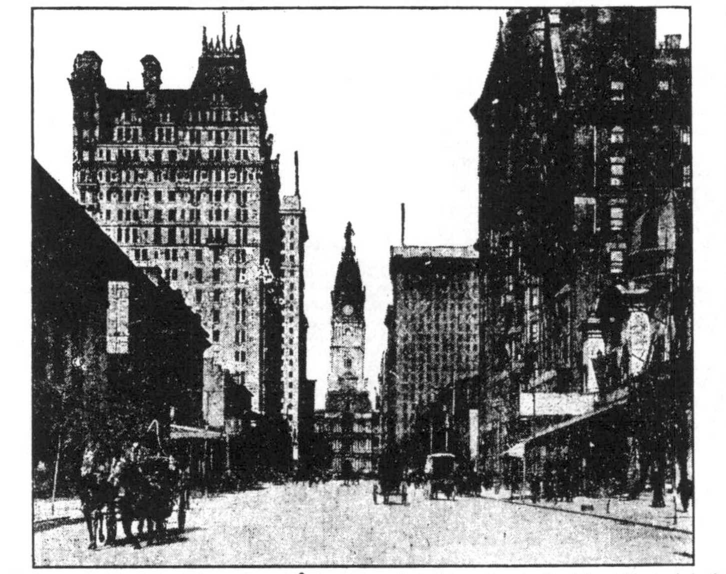

The lower end of South Broad street, shown in this picture, may be called the official center of Philadelphia. City hall is the building with the clock tower standing at the end of the thoroughfare. On the right, a short distance toward the foreground, is the North American building, a plain but imposing structure, Hotel Walton being the one still nearer, with the conical shaped towers. Broad Street Theatre is in the right foreground. On the left, in the middle distance, the building with the ornamental towers is the Bellevue-Stratford hotel.

SAYS GROWTH IN NORTHWEST IS MARVELOUS

Great Northern Railway Company Official Strongly Impressed With Prosperity and Development.

TRUSTS FAVORED

NEW YORK, Nov. 25—E. T. Nichols, third vice-president of the Great Northern Railway Company, returned from his trip of inspection over the system, which he made with James J. Hill, is vividly impressed with the prosperity and development of the growing towns in the far Northwest.

"I knew that the Pacific coast towns were going ahead," said Mr. Nichols, "but I had no idea of the extent of the improvement shown. It is six years since I visited Seattle, Tacoma and Vancouver, and the progress made in that short period was simply astounding to me.

"From Seattle to the Canadian boundary, along Puget Sound, six years ago the country was covered with thick forests. Much of this forest land has now been cleared and transformed into farms that are unsurpassed in the Northwest. The fruit crops raised there are remarkable. I learned of farmers who were obtaining as high as $2,000 an acre from their crops.

"All this farming territory naturally aids in the growth of the towns. The country is rich and the lumber industry appears to be flourishing in spite of the setback it received within the last year.

"What especially attracted our attention was the type of homes of the general public. They were family homes that spoke of prosperity and were far above the average of homes in other parts of the country.

"There was no sign of a boom. The growth was natural and healthy.

"There was no evidence of any feeling against corporations such as is prevalent in the Middle West. On the contrary, the general public displayed their appreciation for the development of the transcontinental railroads and regarded them as factors which had done much to create their prosperity."

NEW $10,000,000 TUBE

CONTINUED FROM PAGE FIVE.

will come about June 1. By that time changes in stations all along the line will have been made possible eight-car trains instead of those of five or six cars, the present limit.

Next summer another section of elevated trackage is due to be completed. This will be for heavy, semi-convertible surface cars, however, virtually extending the present through tracks of the old subway from the North station across the Charles river to East Cambridge, where an incline will provide easy connection with surface tracks to Harvard square and to Somerville.

In addition, two wholly new subways are now about to be constructed. One will start at Harvard square, Cambridge, and bring various lines of surface cars from that point to a loop under the present Park street station of the old subway. Another will extend from the Park street subway station under Boston Common and Back Bay streets to the Boston shore of the Charles River basin, connecting with the surface tracks near the junction of Beacon street and Commonwealth avenue. Neither of these new projects can be ready for use before the end of three years, but work on the preliminaries is already far advanced. With the new work now coming into use they will go far to give adequate transit to the ever-increasing population of Boston and its suburbs.

RUSSIAN WILL BE TAUGHT THIS YEAR AT UNIVERSITY OF MICHIGAN

Increasing Trade Relations Force Language Course —Fossil Specimens Added to Museum.

PROF. MEADER BACK

ANN ARBOR, Mich., Nov. 25—Something new in language work was inaugurated at the University of Michigan this fall, when a course in Russian language was added to the curriculum. The rapidly increasing trade relations between Russia and the United States, the demand for American engineers and diplomatic officers in Russia, the unusual interest with which Americans have been following the struggle of the Russians for political and religious freedom, the riches to be found in Russian literature, and the rapidly increasing part which the Russian language is playing in the development of the science of languages, are the causes advanced for the inauguration of the course.

Professor Meader, of the Russian department, has returned from an extended European tour, and brought back a hundred rare Russian volumes.

Many interesting specimens of vertebrae fossils have been added to the college museum as the result of the scientific expedition which Prof. Ermine Cowles Case, M.S., Ph.D., of the geological department of the University of Michigan, led into the desert region of Texas recently. This expedition was sent out by the American Museum of Natural History in New York, with a view of enlarging its collections, which are the largest of the kind in the world.

About 900 pounds of bones were secured, some of which are quite new to science. Among the skeletons reclaimed is a great finback lizard, several feet long, and carrying on its back a curious thin fin. This creature has enormous tusks with which to seize its prey. Other discoveries were of small reptiles and amphibians, encased in scale and plate armor. As these forms appear to have been the natural prey of the great finback lizard, their armor was doubtless developed as a defence against this attack. Another skeleton secured in part is that of the ship-lizard, Naosaurus, so called because the spines upon its back and had cross bars like the yard-arms of a ship. Another skeleton belongs to the great eight-foot amphibian, Eryops, whose skull was two or three feet long, and who had jaws armed with sharp teeth and tusks. This animal was to the Permian lakes what the alligator and crocodile are to the warm southern waters today.

Reports submitted to the board of regents show an enrollment in the University of Michigan of 5188 students. This does not include those registered in the summer session Of the students in the literary department 39 per cent are women.

WOMEN IN A NEW PLAN TO DO GOOD

New York Group Organizes a "Committee on Bumps" to Learn How to Serve City Government.

NEW YORK, Nov. 25—A "committee on bumps" is the extraordinary title of a group of women who are conferring with William D. Allen, secretary of the Bureau of Municipal Research, for ways and means to do good in the metropolis. At a recent meeting of the Woman's Forum, held in the rooms of the League for Political Education, Mr. Allen addressed the club on civic lawlessness, and took occasion to rebuke the members for their own lack of responsibility.

"You are all lawless," he told them. "Not a woman here but is responsible in a measure for the ramshackle tenements and conditions that overwork the young."

As the women sat up in astonishment at this arraignment, Mr. Allen told them why being a "Lady Bountiful" or a "Pippa" passing with a song where crime was rife, was not performing the whole duty of a good woman. He told them of Glencoe, Ill., where the people put bumps at the street crossings to stop the speeding of automobiles, and asked them if they did not think they could help good government by establishing some bumps that would prevent lawlessness from speeding in the highways of New York.

The Forum promptly voted to appoint a committee on "bumps," with their president, Miss Helen Varick Boswell, as chairman. The committee will confer with the Bureau for Municipal Research to learn how to be of service in good government.

MASONS GET OLD BIBLE.

A copy of the famous Breeches Bible, published in London in 1599, on which George Washington was obligated as a Master Mason, was restored recently to a Montreal Masonic lodge.

SURG.-GEN. RIXEY WANTS 2 SHIPS

Naval Chief Sees Need of Vessels Like Relief to Form Nucleus of a Floating Hospital.

WASHINGTON, D. C., Nov. 25—Surgeon-General P. M. Rixey of the navy has so high an opinion of the hospital ship Relief as an adjunct to the battleship fleet on its long cruise that he is asking for two more such ships to form a nucleus of a floating hospital base in case of war. The Relief, which came into considerable prominence about a year ago on account of the contention over the assignment of Surgeon Stokes to command, has had a picturesque career and was the theatre of very effective work during not only the Spanish war, but later in the Philippine insurrection and the North China campaign. In the last episode it formed a moving link between the American army hospital in China and the American base hospital in Nagasaki.

Surgeon-General Rixey's plan calls for an appropriation of $3,000,000 to build the two additional ships. He recognizes the possibility of adapting passenger ships to this service, but argues that this conversion would require time and that the possession by the navy of three floating hospitals, with a capacity of 300 patients each, would tide over the critical juncture.

The surgeon-general holds that the presence of the Relief with the fleet on its world tour has been responsible in no small measure for the splendid efficiency of the fleet, contributing as much to that end as the presence of the supply and repair ships. The health of the naval force afloat, in spite of the greatly increased numbers, has been unusually good during the present voyage.

When a man gets to arguing with his conscience you may be sure his appetites are busy.—Henry F. Cope.

FINDS BUSINESS IS IMPROVING

Providence "Board of Trade Journal" Voices Renewed Confidence in Industrial World.

PROVIDENCE, Nov. 25—Preceding 10 columns of specific statements, showing a general feeling of optimism in every line of industry in the state of Rhode Island, the Providence "Board of Trade Journal" today, in a special prosperity number, says:

"A renewed confidence in business. The consensus of the opinions of leading manufacturers of the state, irrespective of the form of the industry, is to that effect. In the industrial line this applies with considerable force; the reports from the textile field are of the same tenor, and the jewelry manufacturers claim increased orders and demands for their product. The commercial field has also felt the change of attitude toward business; and from these various branches of activity the "Board of Trade Journal" has received very optimistic reports.

RUN WITH FULL FORCE.

The Union Buffalo cotton mills, of Union, S. C., which operated more spindles and looms than any other textile corporation in the South, have orders to run each of their three plants to the fullest capacity.

HEROIC ACT SAVES WOMAN

Going to a Fire Driver Parker Sends Apparatus Into Pole to Prevent Running Down Woman.

BROCKTON, Nov. 25—Driver Parker of the Brockton fire department performed a heroic act in preventing a collision with a woman while going to a fire.

It was necessary for Parker to spin the wagon sharply around the corner of Belmont street. A woman stepped into the street at almost the same instant. Parker threw himself against the reins and crashed the pair of horses and the wagon against the pole on which fire box 64, which had sounded, is fastened, bringing one of the horses to the ground, lacerated about the flank. The driver was thrown headforemost from his seat.

He landed on the back of the nigh horse and escaped without injury.

HE QUIETLY FADED AWAY.

"I suppose," said the poor but otherwise truthful young man, cautiously feeling his way, "that you wouldn't be satisfied with love in a cottage?"

"Why not?" queried the fair maid. "I'm sure I'd rather marry the right man with an income of only $10,000 a year than a millionaire I didn't love."

And having sense enough to see through the hole in a doughnut, the young man quietly faded away.—Exchange.

FIRE ENGINES OUT OF SERVICE

High Pressure System in New York Will Do Away With Many Steamers the Coming Season.

As a result of a sweeping order to the New York Fire Department which went into effect recently twenty-five steamers were cut out of service. This is in the high pressure district of the water supply, and the hose tenders or hose wagons will be given preference. So marked has been the success of the new system that it is predicted that after this winter engines will cease to roll in the high pressure district. Possibly one may respond at an easy jog to each alarm.

FINDER RETURNS LOST CHECK

Frank Ellis of Brockton, Mass., recently found on the street a letter containing a check for $48,856. He restored his find to the sender, a local manufacturing concern, and received a reward of $5.

The letter was lost on the way to the postoffice, trampled under foot by passers by, and finally kicked into the gutter. Although the check was not negotiable, its return to those who had started it on its way to a New York firm in payment of a bill saved much trouble.

Chandler & Co.

151 TREMONT STREET, BOSTON

Successful Specializing in the Department of

Dresses, Gowns and Costumes

THE FINISHED DRESS in its multitude of styles, THE FINISHED GOWN in variety for every occasion, and the FINISHED COSTUME for every formal function are now to be found in hundreds of models, ready for immediate wear in Chandler & Co.'s entirely new and finely appointed modern department.

The absolute necessity of the modern society woman for gowns befitting the various occasions of her daily life, the needs of thousands going away during the winter season, the parade of dresses at fashionable hotels and the demands of evening and afternoon functions in the home, have all combined to require a multiplicity of dresses for the individual.

This department places at the buyer's disposal at any and all times the most beautiful of dresses, the most elaborate of costumes, and the most stylish of gowns, designed by the great designers of Paris, made from the finest imported materials, with workmanship of the highest order, at prices one-third to one-half those which the same garments would cost if made to order.

The House Beautiful

The beauty and charm of AMERICAN HOME INTERIORS have now become as much a matter of design, color and execution as is the architecture.

By use of inexpensive materials in the hands of a skilled decorator, the interiors of modest homes, as well as palatial residences, are transformed into BEAUTY and COMELINESS.

Our facilities and methods give us opportunity for SPECIALIZATION, so that our patrons' every requirement is treated as an individual problem.

Oriental Rugs — Those who have made a study of Oriental Rugs will appreciate the worth of our collection. NEVER have we been in a position to offer such excellent specimens of genuine ORIENTAL RUGS at prices so reasonable.

Seamless Rugs — Beautiful in design and of fast vegetable color, we are exhibiting an exclusive line of Imported SEAMLESS RUGS from Europe and India. We make to order in special designs, sizes up to 33 feet in width at prices upward from 60 cents per square foot.

Furniture — For the lover of the rare and beautiful in furniture, we present an array of specimens and sketches of exquisite ORIGINAL PIECES with CHOICE REPRODUCTIONS in *every style of every period.*

Wall Coverings — Distinctive WALL COVERINGS in harmony with your home cost but little more than those of ordinary degree, and by our patented processes we are enabled to offer *Economy* in addition to *Exclusive Treatment* and *Design.*

We invite correspondence and inspection of our stock and methods, offering sketches, samples of fabrics and estimates to the prospective customer.

ALLEN, HALL & CO. 384 BOYLSTON ST. 390 BOSTON
Allen, Hall & Co. Building.

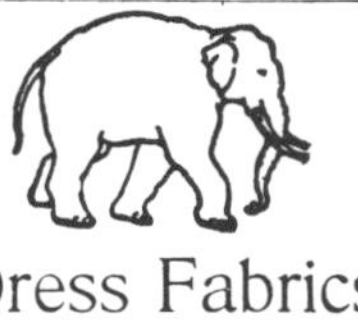

Dress Fabrics

New and Most Attractive Importations

Fine Broadcloths, English Serges, Kamil Cloth

Heavy and Light Weight Chuddahs, Velveteens in New Colorings, Liberty Silks and Satins, Gauzes and Chiffons.

And Many Other Delicate Materials for Evening Wear.

DAVIS
East India House
273 BOYLSTON STREET

AIM OF WORKERS FOR CHARITY ON THANKSGIVING

Permanent Benefit is Desired Rather Than Public Feast Given Promiscuously to the Poor.

ITS SPIRIT DEFINED

In dealing with the problems of modern life, poverty, sickness and crime, a noticeable change has been made in methods of healing and reform. Where a few years ago it seemed that the public could satisfy its conscience by occasionally, as on such a day as Thanksgiving, pouring out a liberal donation from its treasury to the miserable and unfortunate, it is now generally felt that discretion should leaven generosity, and intelligent persons are unwilling to give blindly for the sake of salving their uneasiness as to the happiness of others.

That promiscuous giving failed to reach the desired ends of relief to the needy is shown by the investigations of such highly organized social machinery as the associated charities in the great cities of the country. Usually the associated charities are, as in Boston, not relief organizations, but information and distributive bureaus for the relief work of churches and philanthropies of wealthy societies and also for the state and city funds set aside for the unfortunate.

Miss Alice L. Higgins, general secretary for the Associated Charities of Boston, tells the writer that it is an interesting story in the records of the society and not merely a story but an actual fact that not long ago an old woman who lived alone in the North End with no companion but a cat; received as a Thanksgiving donation from various sources, all ignorant of one another's kindly deed, seven turkeys with the accessories of a dinner. Thus charity was cheated of its object and made farcical and wasteful.

"The Associated Charities of Boston," says Miss Higgins, "as an organization and as individual members, does think of this day with peculiar interest and sentiment.

"It is so much more than a feast day, Thanksgiving rightly conceived, it is so much more than just a chance for the poor to be greedy and the wealthy to pour out indulgences to that greed, that to so interpret the day, or to allow the poor and uneducated to think we so interpret it, is to miss a great opportunity for enlightening the newcomers into America, the poor immigrants and the newcomers into the civic or national consciousness, those men and women who are beginning to think broadly and understand themselves as social units.

"We of the Associated Charities do not like to think of the individual as the social unit, but rather of the family as such. The family is the natural nucleus around which all happiness and permanent success must cluster. If a man gets away from family, he is pretty sure to become a vagrant, and vagrancy is one of the great problems to be dealt with in America.

"I speak of vagrancy," said Miss Higgins, "because it is one of the great problems of social life, and also because this very spirit of Thanksgiving may help to perpetuate it, if not rightly directed. What right have we to conceive of the poor as a class, huddle them together and label them as such? What right have we to bring great concourses of the poor together to eat in some great hall and then go into the galleries and stare at them through opera glasses while they eat at the expense of the public?

"To whom shall such beneficiaries be grateful? Will the eating of a banquet spread for them in such a spirit make them at all understand the meaning of the harvest home of the nation and its day of thanks. If the personnel of the company of diners at such feasts in public halls today were analyzed, it would be found that many of the men are vagrants, and probably have already been given money for drink by charitably minded on the streets. These will go out from the dinner penniless and without work, but they have served to make a festive spectacle to gratify the charitable. What of their needs for tomorrow—have the charitable no further duty?

"It seems as though the real need of the vagrant who eats at a public Thanksgiving dinner should be more vitally understood on such a day as this when busy persons stop to think of others. The poor man alone in the world needs a little more study, he should be investigated. If he has a family in Dakota or Texas, he should be returned to that family, even though that will cost a great deal more than giving him a dinner.

"Therefore, I feel that the methods of the Associated Charities in Boston and other large cities vindicate themselves for the quiet, unobtrusive way in which they meet this great festival. It should not be thought that we in Boston are not interested in Thanksgiving because we do not spread a public dinner for thousands. The Associated Charities of Boston have 16 sections which cover the city. There are 16 salaried district secretaries. Besides this organized force, there are 800 volunteer workers in the city, each of whom has an average of four families to visit. Not all of these families are in actual need, but many are temporarily in need of guidance and assistance from a more intelligent and perhaps more wealthy friend.

"More than 3000 families are in touch with the Associated Charities of Boston at this season, and these are constantly changing, those who are helped rising to the plane of self-sufficiency and becoming helpers in their turn. None is so good to the poor as the poor, for each understands the actual needs of his neighbors. Also none is so aristocratic as the poor, for the class spirit is strong among them and the effort to maintain caste and rise from stage to stage is very noticeable.

"We do not ask the poor family we assist to entertain a homeless person, but often a family will do that, or ask permission to help us in that way. The family group averages about seven persons, and it is the effort of the friendly visitor to make this a family festival and to further see that any stragglers from a family that can be brought home on this day shall partake of the Thanksgiving. It is a day on which we have a singular opportunity to reach the poor immigrants and teach them something of the national spirit. The younger generation gets its first lesson from this day, perhaps, in those traditions which are a part of our American consciousness.

"It is difficult to aid others by wholesale," concluded Miss Higgins. "It is almost an impossibility to arouse any interest or love in that way. Similarly, it is difficult to help the isolated person. Such should be restored to the family relation. In family groups the greatest happiness is experienced and the healthiest ambition and truest national pride aroused. For that reason, we hope that the gatherings around the family tables today all over the country will result in an all-the-year-round benefit to all who partake of the feast."

LIFE ON MARS MAY BE SHOWN

Professor Wood of Johns Hopkins University Working on a Telescope That May Tell Planet Secrets.

BALTIMORE, Nov. 25—A mercury telescope, by which it is hoped that life, if it exists, may be seen on the planet Mars, has been worked out by Professor R. W. Wood of Johns Hopkins University. In detailing his discovery Dr. Wood says:

"The fundamental principle of the new telescope is that a liquid surface, such as mercury, when set in rotation, becomes concave, assuming the form of a perfect paraboloid, which is the form of surface best adapted to telescope mirrors. The mirror already constructed has a diameter of 20 inches and consists of a shallow circular basin filled with mercury and mounted on a vertical shaft and set in motion by an electric motor. Star images smaller than a pin hole have been obtained with the mirror rotating at such speed that its focal length was 15 feet. A slight disturbance, due to periodic variations in the velocity, remains, which probably can be overcome by altering the construction of the mounting of the mirror.

"If the 20-inch instrument can be made to give perfect definition, which appears to be extremely probable, the construction of a much larger one will be undertaken. One of the great advantages of the mercury mirror is that the focal length can be made as long or as short as one pleases by altering the speed of rotation."

Professor Wood said that a mirror 15 or 20 feet in diameter mounted in the tropics at the bottom of a deep pit might enable people to observe details on Mars and the other planets which cannot be seen with smaller instruments.

RAISE ORANGES ON TEXAS FARMS

AUSTIN, Texas, Nov. 25—The growing of oranges on a commercial basis is marking a new epoch in the development of Bee county, and this year's crop promises to be greater than ever before.

Bee county is the home of the original Dugat orange. This tree, by the way, is now more than 23 years old; it is still bearing fruit, and it is the mother of more than 100,000 trees planted all the way from Florida to California. Oranges were grown until two years ago either for ornamental purposes or for the pleasure of having them, but now it is a business.

VALUE OF GOOD ROADS.

The railroads do not pay any particular attention to the condition of the country roads. They take the wheat, corn and other farm products at the railway station and the producer gets the value, or market price, of the shipment. If the farmers of the nation are paying one million dollars a day more than they should in the cost of carrying their products to the shipping point, it requires no expert to show that if they had good roads they would be receiving one million dollars a day more for their products than they are now receiving, or about three dollars a year for every man, woman and child in the nation. Every cent saved in the cost of transportation is a cent added to the price the farmer receives for his products. The addition of $250,000,000 a year to the income of the American farmers would mean a great strengthening of the purchasing power of the agricultural class and a marked increase of agricultural assets. In addition to this direct gain, the good road adds a value to every acre of farm land in the nation, a growth in value that would much more than cover the cost of establishing and maintaining good roads. No farmer can lose on any investment he may make in improving the highways.—Omaha Bee.

POPULARITY OF BASEBALL GAINS IN THE ORIENT

American National Game Is Becoming Bond Between the People of the Occident and the East.

JAPANESE BEATEN

TOKIO, Nov. 25—The victory of the American baseball team over the Japanese team of Waseda University is taken with equanimity by the Japanese who did not expect to beat the Americans at the latter's national game. It is believed that the contest will lead to the development of the game in Japan and a series of contests, possibly a league.

There is abundant material here in the Orient for excellent baseball teams. The Japanese themselves an active and athletic people, taking readily to foreign methods of exhibiting their craft and skill, are continually embracing new systems of physical culture which they readily assimilate with their own. At every Oriental port where any Americans reside there are baseball and football teams which play off league series vying in interest with the cricket matches of the British. According to the stories related by the officers and men of the U. S. Navy the Philippines are a veritable hot-bed for the propagation of the great American game. Every department, bureau, office and division in the insular civil service has its team of players, nearly every company, troop and battery in the military arm is represented, not to mention the headquarters and all-army star aggregations, balltossers from the quartermasters' corrals, officers' teams and those representing the different ships and navy yards of the floating service.

The Filipinos themselves are making great progress in learning the intricacies of the game, and as a good percentage of them are either left-handed or ambidextrous the number of "south-paw twirlers" is something amazing and their curves are truly bewildering. Baseball is one of the few American institutions to which the Filipino took at first sight, and they have received a great deal of instruction from their American neighbors. It is no uncommon thing for an excited group of urchins to hail a passing dignitary of the government with the demand that he adjudicate a disputed point of the game, somewhat after this fashion:

"Hi, senor, this boy out—no?"

Baseball is becoming a bond between the Occident and the Orient, because, unlike the more aristocratic sports of the Europeans, it is a game that can be mastered by the Asiatics.

Good Enough for GOOD FLOORS

and pretty enough to use for interior decorative work and on all sorts of furniture. It was the wear-resisting qualities of the varnish that suggested the name.

PATTON'S SOLE-PROOF FLOOR COATINGS

They withstand hard usage to a remarkable degree, and they are as pretty as they are tough.

With a Sole-Proof Graining Outfit, even an amateur can reproduce all sorts of natural wood-grain effects.

Sole-Proof Floor Coatings are sold in 10 colors by reputable retailers whose business existence depends upon the quality of their wares.

Free Sample—Write for beautiful color card and booklet, and if you enclose 10c in stamps to cover packing and postage, we will send free sample can—enough to finish a chair.

PATTON PAINT COMPANY,
341 LAKE ST., MILWAUKEE, WIS.

Silk Petticoats $3.65

These petticoats are actually worth $5.00, but we are making a special feature of them at this price. We also make petticoats to measure from $5.00 to $10.00. We give a guarantee for satisfactory wear with every skirt. All our silks and satins are retailed at wholesale prices. Mail orders receive prompt attention.

The Ideal Silk Store
29 Temple Place
Boston, Mass.

Over Emerson's Take Elevator H. M. NASH.

The Worry of Buying Gifts

That would not bear the stamp of sameness is easily obviated, as our objets d'art are in a class by themselves.

Jewelry, Antiques, Linen, Laces, Brass, Copper, Bronzes, Wood Toys. HANDICRAFT OF RUSSIAN PEASANTS.

Russian Importing Co.
429 Boylston St., Boston.

BIG INCREASE IN SHIPBUILDING

Admiral Bowles Gives Encouraging Statistics, but Does Not See Bright Opening for Incoming Year.

A total of 1457 vessels, of 614,216 gross tons, was the output of the shipbuilding plants of the United States for the fiscal year ending June, 1908, according to a statement just made by Rear Admiral Francis T. Bowles, (U. S. N., retired) president of the society of Naval Architects and Marine Engineers. These figures show an increase of 300 vessels over the previous year.

Admiral Bowles further states that the present year does not open so favorably, and adds:

"The outlook for a good year would be much brighter if the shadow of so-called high finance had not fallen upon some of the largest and strongest of our coastwise and steamship lines. The combination under one control of the steamship services of our Atlantic seaboard has left a heritage of embarrassment for which the industry itself is in no way responsible."

Admiral Bowles declares that there is reason to hope that Congress will pass an ocean mail bill, and adds that President-elect Taft has ever been an earnest advocate of the cause of American shipbuilding.

MANY LEAVE BROOKLYN.

Ten thousand more people leave Brooklyn every day than return to it, according to the count made by the public service commission.

The Royal

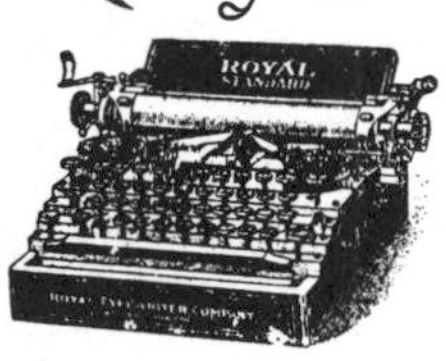
ROYAL
STANDARD

Standard Typewriter $65.00

HONESTLY MADE
HONESTLY PRICED

You can pay more, but you cannot buy more.

Royal Typewriter Co.
268 DEVONSHIRE ST., BOSTON, MASS

Allan F. McIntyre
Dealer

Machinery, Boilers, Rails, and Spiral riveted water pipe, valves, fittings, etc., for Irrigation, Town supply, Mines, Hydro-Electric plants, etc.

MONADNOCK BLDG.,
CHICAGO, ILLS., U. S. A.

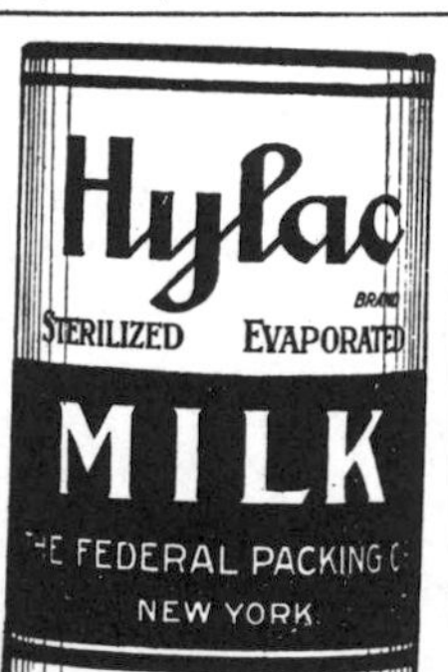
Hylac
BRAND
STERILIZED EVAPORATED
MILK
THE FEDERAL PACKING Co
NEW YORK

Hylac Milk

is the richest and purest of cows' milk, produced on model dairy farms under the most perfect conditions.

Hylac Milk

is given the consistency of rich dairy cream by the *Hylac* process of evaporation in vacuum.

Hylac Milk

comes in the new *Hylac* solderless, sanitary tins which insure the contents indefinitely in any temperature.

Hylac Milk

in the pantry means *convenience, economy, superiority.*

Six cents in stamps for a sample tin of HYLAC.

Federal Packing Co.
103 HUDSON ST., NEW YORK, N. Y.

NATURAL VENTILATION
WITH OUR
AIR PUMP
PURE AIR

Autoforce Ventilating System
53 DEVONSHIRE STREET,
BOSTON.

Crane's Linen Lawn

Good stationery—of what does it consist?

First, honesty; second, attractiveness; third, appropriateness; fourth, style.

For one hundred years the Crane mills at Dalton have been the leading makers of fine writing papers. Today no writing papers so fully define the phrase "good stationery" as Crane's Writing Papers, identified by the water-mark.

Obtainable at all stores where good stationery is sold.

Eaton, Crane & Pike Company
SOLE MANUFACTURING AGENTS.

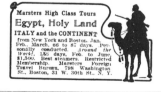

Marsters High Class Tours
Egypt, Holy Land
ITALY and the CONTINENT
from New York and Boston, Jan., Feb., March, 66 to 87 days. Personally conducted. *Around the World*, 133 days, Feb. to June, $1,500. Best steamers. Restricted Membership. Marsters Foreign Travel Bureau, 798 Washington St., Boston, 31 W. 30th St., N. Y.

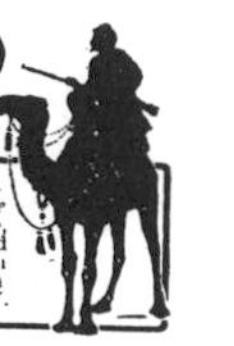

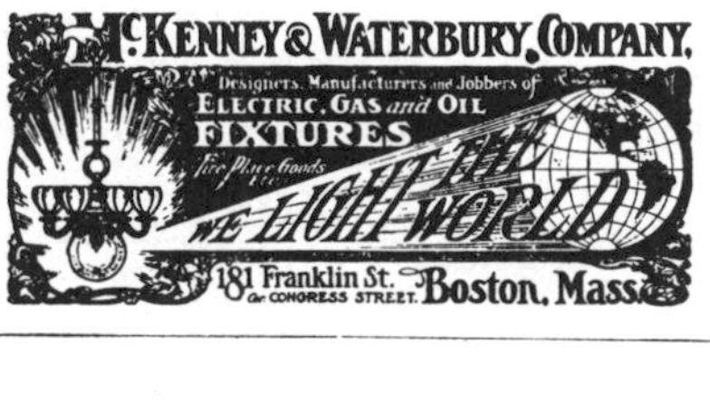
McKENNEY & WATERBURY COMPANY.
Designers, Manufacturers and Jobbers of
ELECTRIC, GAS and OIL
FIXTURES
WE LIGHT THE WORLD
181 Franklin St.
Cor. CONGRESS STREET.
Boston, Mass.

Boston Elevated

To Our Patrons:

The use of the Washington Street tunnel will greatly augment the facilities for transportation and its kindred conveniences which our system already provides, but the removal of the elevated trains from the subway to this tunnel (required by law) will necessarily involve many changes, both with respect to the elevated trains themselves and to the routes of surface cars. These changes will be of great advantage to the majority of our patrons, but during the transitition period there will be undoubtedly some annoying incidents. The officials of the Company will do everything feasible to make things run smoothly, but the Company asks the cooperation of its patrons, and a further share of that consideration with which they have favored the Company in the past, and which the Company has been glad to reciprocate. When the changes have been made, and both passengers and employes have become accustomed to them, fafacilities will be much superior to those now existing.

Changes

After the withdrawal of elevated trains from the subway, and during its alteration for the use of surface cars, which will take several days, it will be necessary to discontinue the service between Pleasant Street and Boylston Street. Surface cars will be run on tracks hitherto used by elevated trains between Boylston Street and the North Station. Passengers wishing to go beyond the North Station should transfer at that point to elevated trains either for Charlestown or for Atlantic Avenue.

Boston Elevated Railway Co.

THAYER, M'NEIL & HODGKINS
Footwear
FOR MEN AND WOMEN

Possesses a charm of individuality and exclusiveness not to be found in any other shoes.

Every day a great many people visit our store for the first time.

All of them have worn shoes for a long time, yet, because they never before have worn *our* shoes, they hold the opinion that all shoes of a given price are much alike. Our shoes *form a class*—of their own—by themselves. A distinct class in tangible, wearable, durable, reliable *leather quality*. Viewed in any light they are the best "money-worth" obtainable. Will you let us prove it to you?

THAYER, M'NEIL & HODGKINS

47 *Temple Place* 15 *West Street*

Are Your Stocks, Bonds AND Valuable Papers Insured?

Absolute Protection, which is better than mere insurance and at a small fraction of the cost, can be secured at the

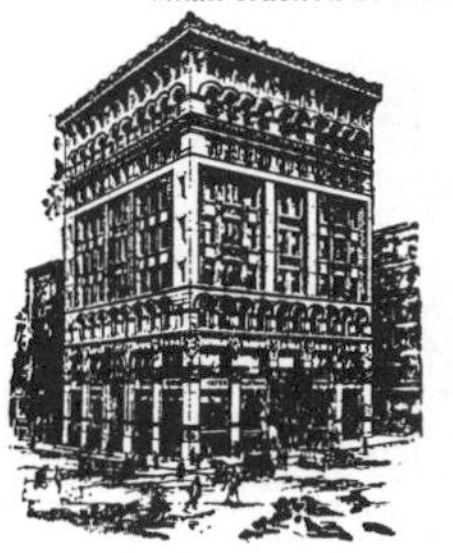

New Safe Deposit Vaults
OF THE
INTERNATIONAL TRUST COMPANY

With all the latest safeguards, improvements, and accommodations, in its own Fireproof Building, specially constructed for the purpose.

Attractive Reading, Writing, and Waiting Rooms.

Exclusive and Perfectly Appointed Accommodations for Ladies.

Its NEW and ATTRACTIVE Banking Rooms furnish unexcelled accommodations and facilities for all departments of its business.

SPECIAL ACCOMMODATIONS for ladies' accounts.

Interest allowed on deposits subject to check, and special rates on time deposits.

Accounts invited.

INTERNATIONAL TRUST COMPANY
MILK, DEVONSHIRE AND ARCH STREETS, BOSTON, MASS.

Capital, $1,000,000.00 Surplus (Earned) $4,000,000.00

Was Hood's Milk
on
Your Table
This Morning?

THE COLLVER TOURS
(Exceptional and Exclusive.)

$2350 Round the World $2750

MEDITERRANEAN, TRANS-SIBERIA AND SOUTH AMERICA.

The Boston Travel Society Old World Journeys

Round the world, January and February departures, four months' journeys, $1325 to $1500. European educational journeys. Mention the itinerary desired.

The Collver Tours Company, Boylston and Berkeley Streets BOSTON.

CAUSE FOR THANKSGIVING IN MEXICO

Material Progress of the Country Within the Current Decade Shown by Comparison of Figures.

LEADERSHIP OF DIAZ

MEXICO CITY, Nov. 25.—In material prosperity Mexico and the United States have much in common to be grateful for on any day of the year, as well as on Thanksgiving Day.

The threatening mining legislation designed to shut Americans out from mining investments in this country was quashed by the federal government. Though financial depression like a cloud settled down upon this republic last autumn, this autumn finds the cloud gradually disappearing. Despite the so-called hard times, there has been a steady increase in all lines during 1908 as compared with 1901 and 1904, the figures for 1908 being approximate.

On a certain occasion President Diaz called the United States "Mexico's big brother." Speaking to him one Thanksgiving day, he asked the writer about the significance of the occasion. He then remarked that Mexico ought to have a Thanksgiving day also, for it had much to be grateful for.

Following are a few of the comparative figures that tell the story of national progress:

	1901.	1908.
Schools	9,491	18,000
Pupils	718,715	1,500,000
Foreign trade	$340,000,000	$515,000,000
Balance in favor of Mexico	10,000,000	45,000,000
Federal, state and municipal revenues	94,564,867	150,000,000
Debt	262,000,000	270,000,000
Banks, capital	65,150,000	95,000,000
Railroad passengers	12,000,000	25,000,000
Railroad freight (tons)	8,000,000	18,000,000
Railroad revenues	40,000,000	70,000,000
Shipping entries and exits	14,789	30,000
Shipping passengers	12,000	100,000
Mines, production (est.)	100,000,000	155,000,000
Agricultural products	314,914,377	550,000,000
Real property	850,000,000	2,000,000,000

In 1876, when President Diaz came into power, the population of this country was 8,000,000, and it is 20,000,000 today. The government revenues then were $15,000,000 a year against $100,000,000 today. About $40,000,000 in silver was the amount of foreign capital invested. Now Americans have invested in this country $800,000,000, Britishers $350,000,000, and other nationalities $200,000,000, making a gold investment of $1,350,000,000. The value of city property, then $150,000,000, is now in the neighborhood of $2,000,000,000. Real estate in the City of Mexico, valued then at 10 cents a square meter, is held now at $20 per square meter.

There was no coal mined then and seven years ago not one kilogram of coal was produced in the country. This year the coal fields cover 300,000 acres, and the yield is something like 5,000,000 tons this year.

General Diaz found 500 kilometers of railroad, where now there are 35,000 kilometers; 10,000 kilometers of telegraph, now 100,000 kilometers; 700 post-offices, now 3,500.

The coinage in this country in 1876 was about $20,000,000, but for 1908 the gold coined will be about $33,000,000, silver about $98,000,000, copper and nickel $40,000,000, making a total coinage this year of $181,000,000.

In 1876 Mexico imported $50,000 worth of cotton. Today Mexico has 150 factories consuming 70,000,000 pounds annually, or one third of what is now actually imported every year from the United States.

The sugar crop 32 years ago was 40,000 tons, but today it is 120,000 tons per annum.

The federal appropriation this year for schools is about $3,000,000, or a per capita of $65, whereas in the United States the per capita is $28 (silver).

General Diaz 33 years ago found the country almost hopelessly in debt, her bonds shrunken to half their value, and no bidders, and in a remarkably short period of time brought about an equilibrium. Today the bonds of Mexico command the highest price in Latin America, the nearest approach being the Argentine Republic. The interest on the bonded debt is paid punctually, and while the gross debt of Mexico has increased, it has been largely due to the immense scheme of public improvements, including $150,000,000 for port improvements, and $100,000,000 for federal buildings now under construction, to say nothing of possibly $500,000,000 which the railroads of the country have already cost in subventions and other aids.

Although the United States is unique among the nations of the world in the visible manifestation of Thanksgiving day, Mexico has indeed great cause for gratitude also. To see a nation like the United States, springing in 130 years from a population of 3,000,000 to 80,000,000, on its knees on Thanksgiving day is a sight unique among the nations of the world. It is a scene of sacred significance—a touch of silence on mills and factories, shops and farms and 150 Christian denominations opening their doors for special services.

Under the far-flung flag of unsetting stars, all round the planet, Americans observe Thanksgiving day, and nowhere more gratefully than in Mexico, favored in the possession of a ruler whom President McKinley once declared to be "the greatest in the world." As a nation builder, President Diaz has had few, if any, equals and no superiors in the history of the world.

STUDENTS PLAN WEEK OF EVENTS AT THANKSGIVING

Many Entertainments Then at University of Pennsylvania — Football Game With Cornell.

GAY JUNIOR WEEK

PHILADELPHIA, Nov. 25—Social life at the University of Pennsylvania reaches its maximum point of activity with the incoming of Thanksgiving week. Junior week at the college is then in full sway, beginning with Theater Night on the Monday before Thanksgiving. Blocks of several hundred seats have been reserved for the students and songs and dances appropriate to such an assemblage are scattered throughout the play of the mimic world.

On Wednesday evening the Bellevue Stratford is the scene of a concert given by the combined musical clubs of Cornell and Pennsylvania.

The annual Thanksgiving day battle between the two universities takes place the next day when both Pennsylvania and Cornell play their final football game of the season. After the overwhelming defeat of Michigan by Pennsylvania, there seems to be no doubt here as to the outcome of the game.

Thanksgiving evening a fraternity dance will be held in Houston Club and fraternities throughout the university give teas on Friday afternoon. In the evening of that day the Junior Ball will be held in the gymnasium. This, with the one exception of the Senior's day ball, is the most important social function of the year, attended by the best of Philadelphia society. As a final wind-up of the week the Army-Navy game, drawing crowds from all over the country, is played Saturday afternoon on Franklin Field.

THANKSGIVING MOTHER HONORED

People of Newport, N. H., Pay Tribute to Woman Whose Personal Appeal Won Recognition of Day.

NEWPORT, N. H., Nov. 25—In the Thanksgiving season the people of this town take pride in the fact that the woman whose influence brought the holiday to national recognition was born in Newport—Mrs. Sarah J. Hale. She was born here October 24, 1788.

Her father held a commission in the revolutionary army, and both her parents were of Puritan descent. She taught school from 1804 until 1813 when she was married to David Hale, also of Newport.

The death of her husband in 1822 left her with five young children and with scanty means for their support.

In 1828 she became editor of the newly established Ladies' Magazine, which in 1837 was united with Godey's Ladies' Book.

She wrote many books and gave much time and thought to benevolent, educational and patriotic undertakings.

She was one of the founders and first president of the Seamen's Aid Society.

She removed from Boston to Philadelphia in 1841 and in that city established in 1837 the Ladies' Medical Missionary Society.

After many years of effort she succeeded in having Thanksgiving day generally observed, President Lincoln, in 1864, responding to her direct personal appeal. In every succeeding year during her lifetime she was accustomed to repeat the appeal and always with the same result.

She passed away in Philadelphia, April 30, 1879.

THANKSGIVING REPORT COMING

Secretary Wilson Discloses Fact That Farm Crop Values Will Be About $8,000,000,000.

WASHINGTON, Nov. 25—The secretary of agriculture is preparing to spring a "Thanksgiving Annual Report." It is learned that while the industrial and monetary sections of the country were suffering from a panic, the farmer has been prospered more than ever in the history of the nation.

Mr. Wilson has disclosed the fact that the total value of the farm crops this year will be approximately $8,000,000,000 as compared with $7,500,000,000 a year ago.

AUTO FOR EVERY THOUSAND.

Careful calculation of the production of automobiles in America next year places the output of all the factories close to 75,000 cars. This total product, valued at approximately $120,000,000, will be built by 253 manufacturers: this means that a car will be marketed for about every 1,000 of population in the country and that the cars will average $1,500 in price.

This flux of automobiles into the American market will amount to half as many cars as have been acquired since the sale of automobiles began, the number already owned by private concerns being about 150,000 cars.

THANKSGIVING DAY MEANING IN OLD COLONY

Conditional Gratitude to Providence Voted at Town Meeting by Connecticut Settlers in 1705

HARVEST IS MENTAL

In the "Outlook" some years ago appeared the story of "A Delayed Thanksgiving." From the records of a Connecticut town, as quoted, it appears that a town meeting held "Oct. 29, 1705," voted to postpone Thanksgiving for a week from the first Thursday in November, concluding with the statement: "Our present circumstances being such that it cannot with conveniency be attended on that day."

A descendant of the clerk who made the record remembered hearing an explanation of the conditions darkly hinted at when the town meeting voted to defer the observance of a day of gratitude.

Up from New York a sloop was making its way loaded with supplies. On board were some casks of molasses, quite necessary if the good housekeepers were to make pies. Was it contrary winds that delayed the vessel, then it was the work of Providence. The sloop being delayed, the delivery of the molasses was delayed, and the making of the pies consequently delayed. Evidently Thanksgiving to Providence could not "with convenience be attended." This at least was the view of the people of Colchester, "in His Majesty's Colony of Connecticut, in New England," over 200 years ago.

Recalls Ancient Hebrew Custom.

Anciently, the Hebrew people observed "the feast of ingathering at the year's end," when the fruits of labor had been gathered in from the fields. And the custom of celebrating "Harvest Home" is a reminder of that ancient "Feast of Tabernacles." When the forefathers of our land appointed a day for recognition of God by thanksgiving, they probably could not foresee the changes we now know, the incredible increase of population crowding our cities, whose dwellers are generations away from the work of the fields and the gathering of the fruits of the earth. To the city dweller Thanksgiving day may mean only the cessation of business so that he may attend a football game. He does not know the thankful prayer in the heart of the man who has brought his harvest home to crown the long year's toil and waiting.

There are those who make their prayers with conditions, saying to their God, "If Thou wilt give me my heart's desire, then will I praise Thee and be thankful." Sometimes they say, "I have not had what I wanted this year, so I have no reason to be thankful." They are like the men in Colchester town; their Thanksgiving is conditional.

When We Are Really Grateful.

But when an understanding of real being dawns upon the consciousness of man, he finds gratitude spontaneous. This gratitude is just love overflowing to God because of what He is. Every day has some of the fruitage of being in it. Every day some harvested blessing from Divine Love is brought home to the life. This continual Thanksgiving brings peace to the mind and blesses the heart with contentment. It is well known to the Christian Scientist, who attends the services of the national Thanksgiving Day with peculiar happiness. To him it is not the one only day in the year for thanking God; for every testimonial meeting is a thanksgiving service; so he comes to it prepared by 52 rehearsals, and uses its opportunity to express to others his sense that "the earth is full of the goodness of the Lord."

A STUPID TRADITION.

It remained for the president of Bryn Mawr College to make the best condensed account of hazing which has been heard for many a day. She is Miss M. Cary Thomas, and in her address to the students she declared hazing to be "unlovely, ungenerous, childish and vulgar." She also said that while "this survival of savagery" ought to be stamped out of men's colleges, it "is really a social crime for women students without any such stupid traditions behind them."—Hartford Times.

Dorothy Vernon

The American Perfume

THIS exquisitely dainty perfume in a glass stopper two-ounce bottle, put up in a handsome embossed box, makes an ideal gift—one that will delight the heart of every woman of refined tastes.

Dorothy Vernon is an American perfume of rare and distinctive fragrance. Its odor is delightful, refined, subtle and satisfying. It is equal to the choicest foreign perfumes, while the absence of import duty lowers its cost to American women 65 per cent.

Dorothy Vernon Perfume is sold by most good dealers at $1.00 for the two-ounce package. Dorothy Vernon Toilet Water and Sachet Powder come in the same odor.

If your dealer cannot supply you, send the price—$1.00—with his name and address, to us, and we will express you the two-ounce Xmas package prepaid.

The
Jennings Co., Perfumers
Dept. S. C., Grand Rapids, Mich.

THANKSGIVING

From The Christian Science Sentinel

ETERNAL God of Life and Truth and Love,
I thank Thee who hast to my soul conveyed
A consciousness of spiritual birth.
To see Thy face, mine eye is turned above
That I may catch a clear, diviner sense
To use in aid of mortals on the earth.

Bert Poole.

PRAISE SERVICE IN CHURCHES ON THANKSGIVING

Christian Scientists Will Find Really Great Feast of the Day in Their Devotional Exercises.

RECALL BLESSINGS

Tomorrow, in Christian Science churches throughout the United States, as in churches of other denominations, will be found large companies of men and women giving part of this oldest American holiday to a definite manifestation of the true spirit in which the day originally was set apart.

Gladness and good cheer have characterized the anniversary ever since Governor Bradford, in 1621, appointed a day for public praise and prayer after the Pilgrims' first harvest. But to any thoughtful individual present at a large Christian Science Thanksgiving service it must be apparent that something has given these latter people a larger measure of joy and gratitude than ordinarily is observed. Eagerly as they enter into the pleasures of family reunions and the common festivities, it is often said that to those participating therein the services in the Christian Science churches are the really great feast of the day.

This service is always among the most inspiring and joyous of the year. After the reading of an appropriate lesson, which is the same for all the Christian Science churches, comprising selections from the Bible and correlative passages from the Christian Science textbook, remarks suitable to the occasion are made by many of those present. Usually as many as can find opportunity in the half hour given to this part of the service arise and speak of some experience which has brightened or perhaps transformed their lives.

So definite and tangible are the blessings acknowledged, and so profoundly impressive are many of the testimonies of healing and of difficulties overcome that often strangers are convinced that the divine Love, Wisdom and Power taught and demonstrated by the Master today are saving men from sin, disease and even death, and that Christian Scientists have found how to avail themselves of such salvation.

WILL TAKE MARINES' PLACES.

Six hundred apprentices from the naval training station will be called upon about Dec. 10, some of them to go to the Pacific stations and some to go to the battleships and cruisers of the Atlantic fleet. They will take the places to some extent of the marines, who have been ordered removed from the war vessels by President Roosevelt.

SALVATION ARMY MAKES PLANS FOR MANY THANKSGIVING DAY FESTIVITIES

Permanent Influences for Good Often Acquired Over Persons to Whom Relief Is Extended.

HUMANITY HELPED

Many individuals disposed to help their fellow-men, upon seeing the Salvation Army workers collecting funds for their great holiday dinners, have asked the question: "Does this really help to uplift humanity? Does it lead to lasting benefit to those so fed?"

Officers of the Salvation Army assert that this conspicuous feature of their work is an imoprtant one in a practical way. Col. Adam Gifford, head of the Salvation Army in New England, when questioned along this line at his headquarters in the People's Palace, replied:

"Do we find a permanent work growing out of the Thanksgiving investigations? Most certainly. The Thanksgiving investigation is only an incident of the daily visiting of the poor. But permanent relief has resulted from this special inquiry. I can give you an example or two: An old woman was found by our officers, living alone with no one to help her. Sympathetic inquiry following temporary relief developed the fact that she had two sons in the regular army of the United States. We made inquiry by letter until we located these men. Our letters came back to us endorsed by the comments of all the United States army officers who had helped to locate these men, and with the statement from the district paymaster that by the consent of the men a percentageof their pay would be stopped out of their envelope each month and forwarded direct from the paymaster to the mother so long as she lives. Thus the old and enfeebled woman was taken off our relief roll, and was made to feel the independence of proper care from her own kin. The men themselves were given an opportunity to respect themselves in the proper execution of filial devotion. There was a triple permanent result.

"Another case was that of a man about 85, who lived with a son upward of 60. The son could do something for himself but could not earn enough to care for his father. By paying $150 to a home for aged men we were able to get the old man accepted for the remainder of his life and he lived for five years in this pleasant place a spiritual, happy old age. He was over 90 when he passed away, beloved by the entire household.

"There are lonely men in the great cities of the country who are in need even though it be because of their own sins and weakness. We help these men, too. The Salvation Army does not ask how they came to be in a helpless condition, how they came to be drunkards, how they came to be out of work, nor what church they attend. It asks only the question 'Are you in need?' Now there are men as weak as water, who will promise and break their promises, who will keep sober for a while and then drink again. When we help these our critics say we give indiscriminately to vagrants.

"But that also is not a just criticism, for we never give to any one without following up the gift with personal interest and personal effort to restore the recipient to his right relation with society. We do not always succeed at once, sometimes these cases get away from us, and wander to another city. But sooner or later the Army in one city or another gets them again and very likely will permanently redeem them.

"It is said that we are sentimental," continued Colonel Gifford. "Well, we do endeavor to put sentiment into this great work. There is a great deal of satisfaction in doing a great practical work, a satisfaction in seeing a need and relieving it, and relieving it permanently. But we feel that we have a right to the warm sentiment of love which always follows the helpful contact of one human heart with another, and we know that nothing but this sentiment of love will go down to the depths and take hold of a man and patiently, persistently, and wisely help him to his feet, support him there and finally enable him to stand alone.

DECISIONS OF TWO JUDGES.

A Western judge, sitting in chambers, seeing from the piles of papers in the lawyers' hands that the first case was likely to be hotly contested, asked: "What is the amount in question?" "Two dollars," said the plaintiff's counsel. "I'll pay it," said the judge, handing over the money. "Call the next case." He had not the patience of Sir William Grant, who, after listening for two days to the arguments of counsel as to the construction of a certain act, quietly observed when they had done, "That act has been repealed."

JORDAN MARSH CO

Remember: *Buying goods here is a safe investment, GUARANTEED BY THE REPUTATION OF THIS GREAT MERCANTILE INSTITUTION—the foremost retail house in New England.*

We give prompt and careful attention to the filling of all mail and telephone orders.

Rare Display of Fashionable Furs

Coats, Muffs and Scarfs of the Highest Grade Skins At Prices Made Possible Through Our Early Buying

At the close of each winter the trappers and traders of the Northwest bring the finest pelts to the various fur-trading centers of that section. Our buyer was on the ground this year at the most favorable time to get the very pick of the furs as they were brought in. Most of these we had made up in our own factories, which fact, combined with our early buying of tremendous quantities, enables us to offer

Second Floor

Qualities and Values Impossible to Equal Elsewhere

Women's Coats of Caracul, Pony and Other Stylish Furs

CARACUL COATS—Women's caracul coats, 44 inches long, shawl collar of same, fine glossy skins. Special value. Price.. 75.00

CARACUL COATS—Women's caracul coats, 40 inches long, Leipsic dye, lynx collar and cuffs. Price.................. 125.00

CARACUL COATS—Women's 50-inch caracul coats, beautiful glossy skins. Leipsic dye, lynx collar and cuffs. Price... 150.00

RUSSIAN PONY COATS—Women's full length black Russian pony coats, shawl collar of same fine quality skins. Price.... 80.00

RUSSIAN PONY COATS—Women's brown Russian pony coats, shawl collar of blended Australian opossum, 48 in. long. Price.. 90.00

MUSKRAT COATS—Women's long natural muskrat coats, shawl collar of same, brocaded satin lined. Price.................. 115.00

SQUIRREL COATS—Women's blended squirrel coats, fine quality skins, brocaded satin lined. Prices.. 115.00 to 145.00

RACCOON COATS—Women's raccoon coats, fine quality skins. Price 75.00

OPOSSUM COATS—Women's Australian opossum coats, full sweep. Price 50.00

225.00 Bengaline Silk Opera Coats at 150.00
Only three of these; shown in tan, wisteria and taupe; squirrel lined; shawl collar of pointed fox or of pointed lynx.

300.00 Bengaline Silk Opera Coat at 200.00
Lined with squirrel, made with shawl collar of chinchilla; an exceptionally beautiful model and a rare value.

Lynx Furs have advanced in price 80 per cent. and American Sable 30 per cent. since Spring. We bought freely of both when prices were lowest and have on hand a sufficient quantity to last some time. We therefore have not advanced our prices and offer to our patrons Lynx and American Sable muffs and scarfs at less than the present cost of these skins.

AMERICAN SABLE MUFFS—Good quality skins, 5 stripes. Price 25.00

AMERICAN SABLE MUFFS of dark American sable, made with 7 stripes. Price 50.00

AMERICAN SABLE MUFFS—Dark eastern muffs, 8 stripes. Prices .... 100.00 to 150.00

LYNX MUFFS—Glossy skins, pillow or rug shape. Prices .... 25.00 to 90.00

Scarfs and collars to match.................. 20.00 to 90.00

AMERICAN SABLE SCARF—American sable throw scarf, 3 stripes, finished with tails and paws. Price.................. 35.00

AMERICAN SABLE STOLES—Trimmed with heads and tails, various styles. Prices.............. 85.00 to 200.00

BEAVER SETS—Consisting of pillow muff and throw scarf. Price 35.00

FOX SETS—Isabella and sable fox sets, consisting of a collar and pillow rug muff. Prices............ 17.50 to 40.00

MARTEN MUFFS—Pillow shape. Prices......... 12.00 to 50.00

Rug shape, tail trimmed, at.................. 35.00

Scarfs to match, priced from.................. 12.00 and 15.00

Shawl collars, specially priced at.................. 22.50

SQUIRREL SETS—Natural squirrel, clear skins, pillow muff and throw scarf. Price.................. 15.00

Pointed Lynx Set, Special at . . . 140.00
Rug Muff trimmed with heads and tails, finished with shirred lining; collar to match, trimmed with head and white tipped tails.

Black Lynx Set, Special at . . . 160.00
Animal shape muff, collar rimmed with heads and tails, both muff and collar lined with Skinner satin. A beautiful set.

Latest News of the Financial and Business World

PENNSYLVANIA SHOWS GRADUAL IMPROVEMENT

Big Railroad Is Recovering Its Business, Although Not So Rapidly as Had Been Hoped For.

SURPLUS IN SIGHT

That many investors consider Pennsylvania railroad stock almost as safe as an ordinary bond is indicated by the price at which the stock has been selling. For although the stock is said to have been earning 8 per cent this year, there is no talk of increasing the dividend beyond the 6 per cent rate. At 130 the stock yields the investor 4.61 per cent. As a money earner and safe investment Pennsylvania has been for many years regarded as a desirable investment. The company operated 3858 miles of track, of which 1705 are owned and the remaining 2153 are operated under lease or as agent.

The Pennsylvania always has been under conservative management, and when the directors some time ago decided to make 6 per cent the regular rate of dividend they took into consideration vast improvements that were to be made, for while bond issues are needed for the greater part of work under way and to be undertaken, provision must be made for meeting the interest on the bonds as well as for the principal.

Business has been improving slowly on the company's lines probably because they traverse a field that felt the business depression more than any other section of the country. The decrease in the company's earnings of nearly $1,000,000 last August was the largest for any single month of the year, and the decreases have been growing steadily smaller since then. This is due both to the cutting down of expenses and to the fact that there are fewer idle cars and locomotives now than there were last summer. Business is showing a betterment all along the line, but the improvement has not been as rapid as had been hoped for by many. If the total loss of business for the year does not exceed $8,400,000, as estimated, stockholders probably will be very well satisfied.

Fixed charges will be increased this year to the extent of about $2,000,000 by reason of a year's interest on the $60,000,000 notes of March 15, 1907, eight months' interest on the $40,000,000 consolidated mortgage 4s issued last May, and several thousand more for last year's equipment trusts and the assumption of bonds of several subsidiary roads. However, not all of the rentals of the Pennsylvania are on a fixed basis, so that in dull times these charges are not as great as at other times when business is brisk. A large part of the rentals are contingent on the net earnings of the leased lines. In the year 1907 the rentals amounted to $4,877,000 and for the 12 months ended June 30 they were less than $3,500,000.

The 6 per cent dividend distribution this year will call for $18,875,000, as against $21,900,000 in 1907. It is estimated that the surplus after dividends will be about $7,000,000 to use for improvements, sinking funds and other expenses of the kind. The balance in 1907 was $11,675,000.

EUROPE BIDS FOR ARGENTINE TRADE

FRANKFORT, Ger., Nov. 25—Industrial countries in Europe are reaching out trade lines to take advantage of the continued and growing prosperity of the Argentine Republic. Various new steamship lines to Argentine are planned or are in course of organization. Among these are a line from Sweden and one from Denmark, which are to transport Scandinavian emigrants and products. Holland has decided to grant a subvention for a new steamship line to South American countries. Austria is about to recognize her steamship service to that part of America, and Russia is contemplating the establishment of direct steamship connection with South America.

Shipping and merchant-marine interests have been suffering for some time past, which causes parties concerned therein to look up and seize other opportunities for employment and to reduce losses. It is this fact which brings new competitors into Argentine's foreign trade.

The Faneuil Hall National Bank

of Boston.

Capital	$1,000,000
Surplus	500,000
Undivided profits	135,666

CHARLES E. MORRISON..President
G. W. FISKE ....Vice-President
T. G. HILER ....Cashier
H. P. SANBORN ....Asst. Cashier

Directors

CHARLES E. MORRISON
HENRY D. YERXA
GEORGE H. LAWRENCE
GEORGE S. WRIGHT
EDWARD A. RICH
WALTER S. GLIDDEN
G. W. FISKE
J. C. F. SLAYTON
J. H. FLETCHER
CYRUS S. HAPGOOD
EDWARD McLELLAN
ROBT. W. WILLIAMSON
T. G. HILER

BUSINESS OUTLOOK FOR 1909

PROSPECTS for business for 1909 are good. The crops of 1908 were excellent, confidence among commercial interests is rapidly being restored and everything points to a return of normal prosperity in commercial and industrial lines.

It has been pointed out frequently during the past months of commercial inactivity that business was being conducted largely on a "hand-to-mouth" basis. Manufacturers were not making any greater quantities of their products than orders called for and wholesalers and retailers were not buying any more goods than necessary to supply the immediate wants of their customers. The consequence is that stocks of merchandise and all manufactured products are very low, generally speaking.

The fear of future disaster which was responsible for this condition is now giving way to a feeling of confidence. Business is being resumed all over the country and, although the year 1909 may not see the great volume of business that was witnessed just before the panic of 1907, a great betterment in most industrial and commercial lines is the general prediction.

Upon the extent of this business improvement depends the restoration of many industrial companies' dividends that either were reduced or passed in 1908.

No change was made in the United States Steel Corporation dividend rates during the period of depression and it is fair to assume that with the earnings of this company constantly increasing larger dividend disbursements may follow. The corporation expects to show a fair surplus this year after charges and dividends but it is expected that appropriations for new construction will be small.

An increase of the dividend rate of the Corn Products Refining company is not expected as it is spending several million dollars for additions and recently borrowed $1,000,000. It is paying 4 per cent on the preferred stock at present.

A resumption of dividends on the preferred stock of the Republic Iron & Steel company is expected some time next year if the iron and steel industry continues to improve. The company could have paid 7 per cent on the preferred stock in 1908 but the directors were obliged to pass the dividend as the mortgage bond agreement provided that net current assets of not less than $6,500,000 be maintained.

The American Smelting & Refining company is said to have been earning more than its present dividends but an increase in the rate on the common stock is not expected soon.

The net profits of the Standard Oil company are reported to be nearly 100 per cent greater than the dividends. Owing to the litigation in which the company is involved an increase in the rate is not expected.

Although the statement of the Allis Chalmers company shows about 4 per cent profit on the preferred stock it is thought that it will be at least a year before dividends are paid.

The American Can company is said to have been doing an excellent business by reason of the large fruit crop but no increase in the dividend on the preferred stock is anticipated.

According to C. M. Schwab a resumption of dividends on the preferred stock of the Bethlehem Steel Corporation is not expected for two years as it is desired to accumulate a good working capital before making any dividend disbursements.

A resumption of dividends on the stock of the Westinghouse Electric & Manufacturing company may not be expected for at least two years as it is desired to place the company on a strong financial basis before paying dividends.

No change has been made in the dividend rate of the United States Rubber company and if earnings continue at the present rate no change may be expected.

More than enough has been earned by the American Sugar Refining company to pay the present dividends but an increase in the rate is improbable.

Before the dividends of either the Amalgamated or Anaconda Copper company are increased it is the purpose o fthese companies to increase the surplus.

If the business revival continues as much as hoped for, especially among mining companies, a resumption of dividends by the Chicago Pneumatic Tool company is likely.

There is no talk of dividends on the sotkc of the American Steel Foundries Company. The earnings of the company have been rather small during the past year.

There is talk of an increase in the common dividend rate of the National Lead Company, owing to very much improved business conditions.

There is little prospect of a declaration of an initial dividend on the common stock of the Colorado Iron & Fuel Company.

No dividends have been paid by the Lackawanna Steel Company since its organization and until it has increased its working capital a disbursement to tsockholders is not probable.

ALASKA TRADE GROWS BRISK

Return of Prosperity to United States Causes Similar Revival in Land Rich in Resources.

SITKA, Nov. 25—The return of prosperous conditions to the United States is paralleled by a similar revival of all lines of exploitation in Alaska. When Secretary Seward consummated the trade by which the vast wilderness of Alaska passed under American domination in 1867 he was censured by many for buying "a barren, worthless, God-forsaken region." That such it is not is testified by the wonderful riches that have been taken out of this land since its cession to the United States.

The only revenue that Russia derived from Alaska was the rich fur trade which the Viceroy of Baranof carried on in behalf of his imperial master—and himself. After his death this trade languished until the future of the country seemed indeed hopeless, and Alaska lay a profitless burden upon the back of the Russian government.

Ignorant of the vast mineral wealth, without another despot to send to wring the animal wealth from hills and rivers, the Czar's government turned eagerly to the United States as a possible purchaser of the province. The Washington administration, not then blunted to a sense of gratitude toward imperial Russia for its helpful attitude during our civil war, agreed to take the country at a price that seemed to Secretary Seward's critics fabulous.

Seward's prophecy that it would take the American people a generation to become reconciled to the purchase and indorse his policy has been fulfilled, and the approbation of the people has been given with a promptitude unusual in history.

APPLES PLENTY IN THE MARKETS

Supply Is Kept Close to Demand and Prices Rule High in New York City at the Present Time.

NEW YORK, Nov. 25—Plenty of apples of good quality are coming to market, but the available supply for the consumer is being kept close to the demand, and as a rule high prices are demanded, particularly for the best grades, declare trade experts. Overstocking of the market is prevented by withdrawal of a large proportion of selected apples which are going into cold storage to be held until mid-winter, when yet higher prices will be expected.

In one week about 90,000 barrels of apples came to the market. The finest have beenc oming in boxes, showing careful selection, packing and handling, and many of these are going into the refrigerators. From all of the recent receipts the best stock has been chosen for the more pretentious shops and for holding. Dealers are particularly anxious to get the choice grades from the Ben Davis and Spitzenberg stocks. There is also a marked demand for Kings.

BULLDOG IS POPULAR.

The bulldog has the distinction of being popular as well as expensive, according to "Fry's Magazine," which says: "Not long ago £1000 each was paid for two champions who went to America; while £200 or £300 is not at all an unusual price for a good one."

NO WAR-PAINT FOR BATTLESHIPS

Change at Present Time Might Result in Suspicion of Motives for Adopting New Color.

WASHINGTON, Nov. 25—If the American battleship fleet, now stopping temporarily in the Philippines, should have its white sides painted in the new drab color adopted for the American navy the word would at once go around that it was a war measure.

If the change were to be made while the ships are at Manila it would probably be taken as a direct menace to Japan; and if it occurred at any point in the Mediterranean, there would be rumors of trouble with some European power.

For this reason, acting Secretary of the Navy Newberry has directed that the battleships shall retain their peaceful dress of white until they reach their home ports.

The new drab color has been selected with a view of making the ships as inconspicuous as possible while at sea.

WIRELESS SYSTEM FOR THE PACIFIC

Capitalists Interested in Phosphate Islands Subscribe for Stock of New Telegraph Company.

TAHITI, Nov. 25—A system of wireless telegraphy is proposed for establishment among the scattered islands of the Pacific ocean. United States Consul J. D. Dreber says that capitalists interested in extensive phosphate operations on various islands are identified with the movement.

Y. M. C. A. WORK RECOGNIZED

BILLINGS, Mont., Nov. 25—(Special)—A check for $1,000 has been contributed by the Chicago, Burlington & Quincy railroad company to the Y. M. C. A. of Billings in recognition of the good work being done by the organization. The money, in the form of a voucher, was received by the association from Second Vice-President Daniel Willard. The officers were highly gratified at the receipt of the letter.

PRAISE FOR ADMIRAL SPERRY.

It is fortunate that we should have in command of the fleet visiting Japan so accomplished and able an officer as Rear Admiral Charles S. Sperry. He has no superior in the navy of the United States, or in any other navy, for that matter. At the last Hague conference his intellectual ability, his thorough knowledge of his profession, of international law and of technical details concerning the navies and the harbors of other nations placed him in the lead among the representatives of great navies, and his countrymen were proud to have as their representative so able and well equipped an officer. The ability with which Admiral Sperry is handling his fleet, the courtesy and good sense he is showing in his intercourse with foreigners, will add still further to the esteem in which he is held at home and abroad as an able sea officer, well equipped in all that concerns his profession, and a high minded and dignified representative of his country.—Army and Navy Journal.

FERTILIZER MEN WILL FORM MERGER

Herman Schmidtmann, Phosphate King of Germany, Will Be an Officer of Company.

NEW YORK, Nov. 25—Representatives of many fertilizer companies, principally in the South, held a meeting here lately to perfect plans for the merger of the companies into a concern with $25,000,000 preferred and $25,000,000 common stock. Most of the terms of the merger were agreed upon and it is probable that articles of incorporation will be filed in New Jersey in a few days.

One of the men interested in the merger said that Herman Schmidtmann, whom he characterized as the "phosphate king" of Germany, would be an officer of the company, and that several foreign companies would enter the combination. In this city the principal parties in interest are Lewisohn Bros. and the Tennessee Copper Company, which they control.

INDUSTRY AND FINANCE.

It is announced that within 10 days the Detroit Furnace Company will be reopened and operated at full capacity after being closed for nearly a year.

Increased activity is reported at the Pullman shops. The steel car plant started on a large order from the Harriman system.

It is considered unlikely that a complete report of the monetary commission will be ready for Congress for at least two years.

The Walkill Transit Company, which operates a trolley line at Middletown, N. Y., will advance wages of conductors and motormen beginning Thanksgiving day.

The New York Stock Exchange gave notice that the preferred stock of National Railroad Company of Mexico has been stricken from the list.

Haverhill (Mass.) 4 per cent 10-year bonds amounting to $58,000 were awarded Perry, Coffin & Burr at 103.55. They are dated April 1, 1908, payable April 1, 1918.

The West Pittston (Pa.) school district has sold $47,000 4½ per cent semi-annual 5-30-year optional bonds to the Union Savings & Trust Company of Pittsson for a premium of $357.20.

The Southern Pacific Company has applied to the New York Stock Exchange to list $74,866,400 additional common stock to be issued from time to time in exchange for preferred stock. According to representatives of the company the listing is in the nature of a formality to place the company in a position to exchange the common for preferred shares in case the holders of the latter should desire to exercise their conversion privilege.

The preferred stock is convertible into common at par at option of holders before July 1, 1910. The common stock was authorized long ago in sufficient amounts to cover the preferred, but the listing of it had been delayed until this time.

It is stated, however, that this action does not supersede any other plan which the management may have in view for the retirement of the preferred shares.

DIVIDENDS.

The Jackson Company declared a dividend of $30 a share payable Dec. 1 to stock of record Nov. 23.

The Great Falls Manufacturing Company has declared a dividend of 6 per cent payable Dec. 1 to stock of record Nov. 23.

TRADE OFTEN PROMOTED BY GOLDEN RULE

Preeminence of England and Germany in Exports Aided by Regard for the Wishes of Customers.

GIVE SQUARE DEAL

WASHINGTON, Nov. 25—It is coming to be pretty well established by the the department of commerce and labor consular reports that the application of the "square deal" by manufacturers and shippers in the development of foreign trade yields rich results.

The plain facts of the matter are that sincerity, honesty and the golden rule have played a part in the preeminence which England and Germany have acquired in trade with foreign countries. As a result, their commercial operations go far to meet the needs of all parties concerned in the distribution of the world's products. At least, that is the inference given by Consul Pierre Paul Demers of Barranquilla, Colombia, in an interesting statement of possibilities for American trade in his territory.

"The American," he says, "as a rule exports when he has time and considers the foreign market his dumping ground. He is only a novice in the art of packing and shipping and will invariably disregard the instructions of his foreign customer. He has been in the habit of doing up his merchandise in a certain way for the domestic market, and it is hard to persuade him to do it otherwise.

"The chances are that his letters of instructions will be glanced at and filed, and the shipping clerks allowed to proceed in their usual manner. It is the existence of such conditions, be it only in a few exceptional cases, that constitutes a serious obstacle to the growth of our foreign commerce."

The German and English manufacturers, according to Consul Demers, by reason of being largely dependent on the export trade, are more punctilious. Invariably, he says, they send their very best canvassers all over the world, and offer to the fullest extent guarantees and inducements as regards credit, and they make it a specialty to cater to demands and tastes peculiar to the locality.

NEWS OF THE STREET.

The report is current that the directors of the Sloss-Sheffield Steel & Iron Company have decided to restore the dividend on the common stock to a 5 per cent basis when they take action on the matter early next year. It also is reported that they may declare a dividend of ¾ of 1 per cent to reimburse the shareholders for the reduction of ¼ of 1 per cent that was made for three quarterly periods during the present year. Following the usual custom, the directors will declare the full dividend of 7 per cent on the preferred stock in qarterly instalments before any disbursement is ordered on the common stock. Recent advices from the Birmingham district state that a few days ago all previous records of the Sloss-Sheffield Company in the matter of production in a single day were broken by the Lady furnace in Sheffield, when 270 tons of iron were made.

The very low stage of water in several rivers that traverse the coal territories of the central West has brought about activity in coal mining at many places in Illinois, Kentucky, Ohio and West Virginia. At a number of places coal veins are exposed that are being worked day and night with all the resources that are at hand.

At several places along the Ohio and Mississippi rivers the low water stage has not only exposed rich coal veins, but has brought the water below the levels of a number of coal laden boats and barges that were sunk many years ago. Last week 700,000 bushels of prime Pittsburg coal was taken from the wreckage of barges sunk in an accident at Hickman, Ky., 16 years ago.

The three big battleships recently launched in Great Britain, Bellerophon, Temeraire and Superb, will consume 3,650,000 pounds of American lake and electrolytic copper, and 1,000,000 pounds will be required for each of the three big battleships whose keels are to be laid at once in England, according to the "Boston Financial News." For account of the men-of-war on the stocks of Continental Europe, 19,000,000 pounds of lake and electrolytic copper will be needed within a year. The mercantile marine contracts under way in European yards will consume 57,000,000 pounds of copper within a year.

Although work is slack at domestic shipyards, the tonnage under contract will call for the consumption of 6,000,000 pounds of lake, electrolytic and casting copper within a year. The navy yards, ordnance works and the mint are consuming annually about 12,000,000 pounds of copper. The ship repairing plants on both oceans and along the Great Lakes are working up about 10,000,000 pounds of copper a year in various forms of bronze and brass.

There has been considerable buying of precious and base metals during the past two weeks. Consumers for some time past have been delaying purchasing their stocks until they were assured that the business revival would be permanent and transactions in metals have been of the hand-to-mouth variety. Notwithstanding the heavy purchasing of the recent past it is said that most of the orders were for immediate delivery and that there is a good future for all metals.

Pig iron producers say they have enough orders on their books to keep things going at the present monthly output for several months. Some of the largest mills report that they are operating about 65 per cent of capacity. It is also reported that a good deal of important business is about to be signed up by the constructional engineering corporations. This will bring about heavy purchases of iron and steel.

It is reported by some of the big copper consumers that they are working about 65 per cent of capacity. Sheet and rod copper and brass are quite active. Trade is better in cast and spun copper and brass wares than was expected some time ago. Electrolytic works within the zone of this city are said to be shipping about 80,000,000 pounds of copper a month.

Old Colony Trust Company

MAIN OFFICE, AMES BUILDING.
BRANCH OFFICE, 52 TEMPLE PLACE

Complete banking facilities and Safe Deposit Vaults at each office.

Capital - $1,500,000
Surplus - $5,500,000

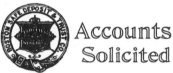

Accounts Solicited

This company solicits your account, whether it is large or small. Its officers will welcome an opportunity to talk over banking matters and discuss the special advantages offered by this institution, whether an account is opened or not.

Interest paid on daily balances subject to check.

Boston Safe Deposit & Trust Co.

87 MILK STREET, BOSTON

Capital $1,000,000 Surplus (Earned) $2,000,000

The National Shawmut Bank

OF BOSTON, MASS.

Shawmut Bank Building, 40 Water St.

Capital and Surplus	$ 8,000,000
Assets	$100,000,000

The Largest Financial Institution in New England

ACCEPTS SMALL ACCOUNTS and gives to them the same careful attention as to larger ones.

PAYS INTEREST on personal, trustee, and inactive non-borrowing accounts subject to check.

GUARANTEES THE SECURITY of its deposits by its capital and surplus of $8,000,000.00 and further stockholders' liability of $3,500,000.00.

OFFERS TO CUSTOMERS every accommodation consistent with sound and conservative banking.

ESTABLISHED 1886

The Services

of our long-established, well-equipped brokerage office are hereby extended to all those desiring to purchase, sell or exchange all classes of REAL ESTATE.

Frank L. Fisher Co.

440 Columbus Ave.

NEW YORK.

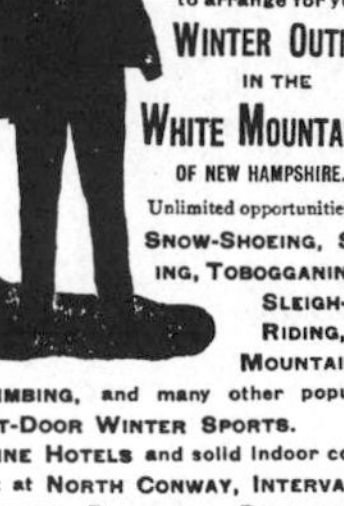

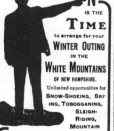

NOW IS THE TIME to arrange for your WINTER OUTING IN THE WHITE MOUNTAINS OF NEW HAMPSHIRE.

Unlimited opportunities for SNOW-SHOEING, SKI-ING, TOBOGGANING, SLEIGH-RIDING, MOUNTAIN CLIMBING, and many other popular OUT-DOOR WINTER SPORTS.

FINE HOTELS and solid indoor comfort at NORTH CONWAY, INTERVALE, JACKSON, PLYMOUTH, BETHLEHEM, LITTLETON, FRANCONIA, TWIN MOUNTAIN, FABYAN, BRETTON WOODS, LANCASTER, GORHAM.

Further information supplied by C. M. BURT, G.P.A., BOSTON, MASS.

BOSTON AND MAINE RAILROAD

Grand Central Hotel

Superior Ave. and Spring St.
CLEVELAND, OHIO

One hundred rooms, steam heat, baths, elevator. Rates reasonable. No bar.

Strikes Like the Human Finger

And that secures the real human expression

The Melville Clark Apollo Player Piano

Is the only player in the world in which *every one of the 88 pneumatic fingers*, covering the entire keyboard of a 7 1-3 octave piano, *strikes the piano key on top* in front of the key fulcrum. *A direct stroke.* This is *the touch that secures a genuinely human expression.* Each one of these 88 *pneumatic fingers is hinged as the human hand is hinged* at the wrist.

No 65 note player can achieve the musical results possible on this 88-note Apollo player of 7 1-3 octaves, because a 65-note or a 5 1-2 octave player cannot play the great musical compositions as they were written without being transposed or otherwise mutilated.

The Apollo plays all standard 58, 65 and 88-note music rolls and is the best player in the world.

Send for handsomely illustrated catalogue to the manufacturers.

MELVILLE CLARK PIANO COMPANY,

Steinway Building, Chicago.

GEO. H. CHAMPLIN & CO., Agents,
181 Tremont St., Boston, Mass.

Frederic Hinckley Edward F. Woods

HINCKLEY & WOODS INSURANCE
32 KILBY ST.
BOSTON

FIRE LIABILITY, AUTOMOBILE, BURGLARY AND EVERY DESCRIPTION OF INSURANCE AT LOWEST RATES.

Telephones 1465, 1466, 1467 & 4085, Main.

Contributions on Topics of Interest by Subscribers are Solicited

THE HOME FORUM

A Page of Interest to All . . . the Family . . .

Birds in Winter

ARE you a bird lover? Have you spent many happy hours of pleasant summer days studying their habits? Have you felt a pang of sorrow when on a warm autumn day you have seen them gathering in companies in some park tree or country hedge, holding a chorus or a council? Of course you knew, if you are a bird lover, that that was the signal for their departure to a warmer clime for the winter. Have you watched for the first robin and announced with joy that you had seen one and so you knew that spring is come?

Perhaps you have never realized that about one seventh of all the birds do not migrate at all. They are the hardy little sparrows. No winter day is too cold for them, no more than the hottest day of summer is too warm for them. There is not a day in the year when you cannot find one of this great family of birds when you take your walk.

Some people despise the sparrow and speak of it as though it was a little pest. Farmers will often tell you that it destroys a great deal of the crop seed, dispossesses more valuable birds, and really has no virtues. But the sparrow eats the seeds of the weed crop, too, and helps to keep down the undesirable vegetation. He is in many ways a very desirable little citizen.

The English sparrow was brought to Brooklyn in 1851 by naturalists who wished to experiment and see if this bird would not rid the shade trees of a destructive worm. This the sparrows very shortly accomplished both for Brooklyn and New York, and every one loved the sparrow at that time and put seeds out for it and made little bird houses in their gardens for fear the climate would prove too severe.

But the sparrow needed no such coddling. He showed that he could thrive where other birds would starve. He is as cheerful in the intensest cold weather as in the heat of summer. As for giving him a house in the garden, that is quite too thoughtful. Mr. Sparrow takes a home almost anywhere. He will live in the cornices, the eves, the tops of pillars, the vines, the deserted nests of other birds. He is fearless, intrepid, inquisitive, hardy, determined. He does not wait to be made welcome, he takes up his residence and stays. He has great families of birdlings, and the sparrow has multiplied in the land in the past fifty years beyond all scientific expectation.

It has been conceded by the wise men who know, and experiment with birds so that they will be sure they know, that the country will never be rid of sparrows. They are here to stay. Therefore, it seems unkind to speak of them as pests, and rowdies, and bird nuisances. These sparrows do not kill other birds, though they dispute with them and crowd themselves into every interesting place. The native birds have to learn the lesson of standing for their own rights and taking the world as cheerfully as the sparrow.

One reason why the sparrows thrive where other birds are destroyed is because of their protective coloring. You have perhaps been surprised sometimes by a sparrow's hopping near you, because until he hopped you did not know he was there. He has dull brown and gray streaked feathers, much the color of the hedges and the trees, and if he keeps his saucy chirping still, he can go his way unobserved where a brightly colored songster would be likely to invite destruction from some one who wished to own his feathers. Protective coloring is a method for all weaker forms of life to preserve themselves. Thus you will observe the squirrel and the lizard and the toad color themselves, according to the places they live.

Often when you think there are no birds around, you will be able to bring a perfect swarm of them by scattering seeds or crumbs and standing a little apart. Down from the brown trees and out from the bushes they will come with a swoop and a hop, hop, hop! When you go into the park on a winter's day it is a very pleasant diversion to coax them around you. Have with you a piece of stale bread or some canary seed. You will soon see how tame the sparrows will grow.

It is possible to accustom the birds to coming about your window by sprinkling seeds on the window sill occasionally. If you have never tried it, you will be surprised to see how much comradeship there is in the visits of the birds for their breakfast. They will usually sing and chirp, and their funny, saucy manners are very engaging. Some people try to drive them away from their vines and trees, because they profess to be disturbed by their chatter. But that is rather a foolish way to feel about such little comrades.

Observe this. There are many different kinds of sparrows. The tribe I have been speaking of is the English sparrow, but if you keep a sharp lookout you will see that there are other kinds who have the same general coloring, with a slightly different marking, who have the same way of flying, consisting of short swoops, rather heavy and labored, and not at all like the graceful flight of the swallow, for example.

Keep your eyes open for the song sparrow. He is the most cheerful little neighbor and one who will become quite a regular visitor if you encourage him. He has fine dark streaks on his light breast which seem to form a darker spot in the center. He has a pretty song and one which is most enjoyable because it remains with us when all the other songsters have fled before the snow storms.

The song of this sparrow has been described by a bird lover thus: "It begins with a full round note, three times repeated, then dashes off into a sweet, short, lively intricate strain that almost trips itself in its hasty utterance. He has a repertoire of six different melodies, and few birds can rival him in musical ecstacy."

Is not this a bird worth wooing in the dull winter months? Scatter the seed for him and you will fetch him sooner or later, for he has a sharp eye for feeding places. He will not be dislodged by the English sparrow, his cousin, but will boldly hop toward him and without fighting drive him away. He doesn't even scold, he just Is, and holds the field. And after he has won his place on the roof of your piazza, or on a broad sunny window ledge, he will give you a pretty payment in melody for your remembrance of him.

WOMAN IN THE SOUTHLAND WHO DOES GOOD WORK

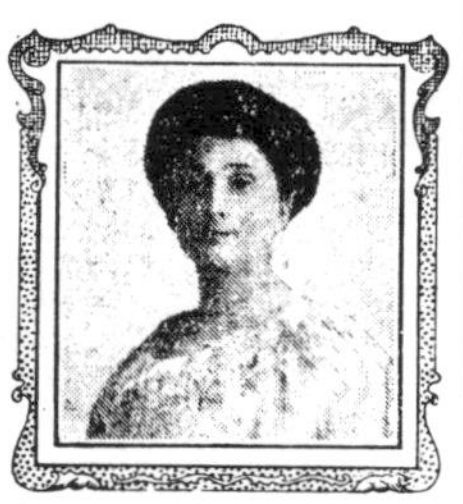

Mrs. Joseph B. Dibrell.

DURING the coming session of the state Legislature in Texas the politicians will have a new factor to deal with in the attempt of the women of the Lone Star state to effect certain reforms, which it is conceded will hasten the approach of a more clean government and the realization of better citizenship.

Foremost among the cultured and brilliant women of Texas who have thrown themselves into the reform movement with great zest is Mrs. Joseph B. Dibrell, wife of ex-Senator Dibrell of Sequin.

The success of the reform movement in Texas, which has been persistently urged by the women of the state, is in no small way, due to the activities of Mrs. Dibrell, who has long been known as an earnest worker for municipal reform and all that aids in the making of better citizenship and the uplifting of the home and the sacred duties of the wife and mother.

Endowed with wealth, health and unlimited enthusiasm, Mrs. Dibrell has long been a prominent figure among the women of her state, and at the coming session of the Texas Legislature she will take the leadership of the reform movement on the part of the organized women's clubs of the state.

A great lover of art, Mrs. Dibrell has recently purchased the beautiful estate of the late Elizabeth Ney, sculptor, collector and art connoisseur, and this she is planning to turn into an art museum, to be thrown open to the lovers of art, much the same as Mrs. John L. Gardner opens her Venetian palace at various times during the year. Mrs. Dibrell conceived the idea of her art museum from a visit to Mrs. Gardner's palace last summer, while attending the convention of the Federation of Women's Clubs in this city.

"THE LAST ENEMY"

BEN HAWORTH-BOOTH.

My barque is hastening onward to a bourne
Of summer seas; and soon the boatswain may
Pipe me the signal at the close of day
Or 'neath the opening eyelids of the morn.

The storm upon my window wakens me;
Upon the clamorous night my spirit peers,
Where leafless boughs and lonely glimmering meres
Reach forward to the fog-enfolded sea.

On such a night as this 'tis hard to tell
Thine heart that on the darkness and the deep
One Hand alone doth guide and guard and keep;
'Tis hard, but it is true—and all is well.

On such a night I used to deem, of yore,
'Twere fearful to depart, to wander forth
Upon the howling tempest of the north,
Over the frozen fields and shuddering shore;

To pass away upon the wild night air—
A formless fear, a sightless, senseless thing!
'Twas terrible! but now the morn doth bring
A wisdom far more wise, a faith more fair.

We are the sons of Life—not sons of death—
And in His great design all, all is well;
Can mourning mummeries or the funeral bell
Prove that we perish with the passing breath?

There dies indeed the noisome taint of earth
That Truth has not destroyed—but naught beside—
The sin, the selfishness, the pain, the pride;
But life lives on, and faith attains new birth.

CHANGES IN DRESS IN PAST CENTURY

Perhaps one of the most interesting (and amusing) instances of feminine fidelity where fashion is concerned is that which is brought to light as we turn over the pages of modes for the last century, roughly speaking, writes Mrs. Evan Nepean in the Queen. It is almost impossible to imagine a greater number of changes in dress than those which took place from the beginning of 1800 until the present day. And yet, through them all, the Greek key pattern appeared and disappeared and reappeared in the most delightful way, and the ladies whose attire was furthest removed from any suspicion of classic drapery revelled in it with the greatest ardor of all! One would have imagined oneself most likely to find it in the Napoleonic period, in the days of the Directoire; but no. And I suppose we should be wearing it most of all just at present, or, shall we say, a year back, and doubtless we should have done so, but for the fact that we had nearly done it to death a little while before—nearly, not quite. I am inclined to rank the Greek key pattern as nearest to immortality in the world of dress.

IN THE MIDST OF ICEBERGS.

The captain of the ship Erskine M. Phelps had a thrilling experience in threading his way among icebergs recently on a voyage around Cape Horn. Altogether 75 bergs were counted, some of immense height and others almost awash. The latter were the most dangerous, as it was hard to keep track of

The Christian Science Monitor

Published daily, except Sunday, by
The Christian Science Publishing Society
Falmouth and St. Paul Streets, Boston, Mass., U. S. A.

Publishers of "The Christian Science Journal," "Christian Science Sentinel," "Der Herold der Christian Science," and other publications pertaining to Christian Science.

Application made for entry as second class matter.

TERMS

Single copies, 2 cents. By carrier in the Greater Boston newspaper district, 12 cents the week.

SUBSCRIPTIONS BY MAIL, PREPAID

In the United States, Canada and Mexico:
Daily, six months..........$3.00
Daily, one year.............. 5.00
In all other countries:
Daily, six months........... 4.50
Daily, one year............. 8.00

All checks, money orders, etc., should be made payable to The Christian Science Publishing Society, Boston, Mass., U. S. A.

The Christian Science Monitor will be found for sale at all newsstands in New England, and in Christian Science Reading Rooms throughout the world.

All articles for publication should be addressed to the Managing Editor.

No attention will be paid to unsigned communications and no manuscript will be returned unless accompanied by postage.

Rates for advertising will be furnished upon application to the Business Department.

Owing to the limited space devoted to advertising in The National Edition of The Christian Science Monitor, reservations must be made one week in advance of day of issue.

Telephone........Back Bay 4330
Five Trunk Lines.

PHILIPPINE HOUSEKEEPING IS EASY

American women who are accustomed to the cares of much housekeeping will appreciate the easy manner in which domestic work is done in the Philippines. The more pretentious Philippine houses are those occupied by Americans. They are mostly beautiful and attractive and withal simple in style and furnishing. The floors are hardwood and uncarpeted. The walls are unplastered and painted white or left the natural color. The furniture is of bamboo or rattan or the Austrian bent wood, and house furnishing can be made both artistic and comfortable.

Sometimes the walls are decorated with large plaid mats woven of soft grasses in every conceivable shape. These mats make artistic backgrounds for collections of native hats or baskets. The windows are made of translucent shells, many dozens of which are set in a single frame. These frames slide back on runners so that it is possible to open up nearly the entire side of a house when desired.

Housekeeping in such a house is, consequently, quite a small task. There is no dread of spring or autumn house-cleaning. Houses in the Philippines are cleaned daily as thoroughly as the average American home is cleaned twice a year by dint of the hardest kind of scrubbing, washing and sweeping. The servants slide over the floors with a floor cloth under each foot, polishing the floors with oil. Little dusting is needed and it requires but a few moments every morning to put things in tidy shape. It is a clean country, little clothing is worn and the family washing is a small expense.

GOOD NEWSPAPERS MEAN GOOD GOVERNMENT

If we want responsible government we must have responsible newspapers. If the two previous points are proved this one follows logically as a matter of course. If we are governed by public opinion, and the newspapers make public opinion, our government will necessarily be good or bad, according as the newspapers are good or bad. "A good tree cannot bring forth evil fruit, neither can a corrupt tree bring forth good fruit."—President Hadley, Yale University.

AN INVENTION THAT WILL PLEASE THE LADIES

Womankind everywhere will be thankful to the man who has invented an electric hair dryer. This little machine may be held in the hand as conveniently almost as a hand mirror. It is made of aluminum and weighs 2¾ pounds. When in operation it drives a strong current of either cold or warm air by the simple turning of a key. Turned one notch, a strong current of cold air is forced out of the tube. Turned two notches, the air becomes warm. The turning of the key to the second notch switches in a resistance, and the current of air flowing through this resistance generates the heat which warms it. Like all other electric household articles, it is connected to a convenient electric lamp socket by an electric cord.

IN HER KINGDOM

GRACEFUL may seem the fairy form,
With youth, and health, and beauty warm,
Gliding along the airy dance,
Imparting joy at every glance.
And lovely, too, when o'er the strings
Her hand of music woman flings,
While dewey eyes are upward thrown,
As if from heaven to claim the tone.
But never in her varied sphere,
Is woman to the heart more dear
Than when her homely task she plies,
With cheerful duty in her eyes;
And every lowly path well trod,
Looks meekly upward to her God.

—Caroline Gilman.

A Mexican Bronze Cast That Weighs About Four Tons

After the close of the International Fair in New Orleans some twenty years ago, the Mexican government ordered that the Mexican pavilion at that exhibition, with all of its valuable contents, be sent to Mexico City. In this collection were many strange castings of Aztec gods. A fire destroyed the pavilion before it could be removed and nearly all of its contents were lost, but what remained were shipped to Mexico. The ship on which the remnants were loaded, however, sunk near Vera Cruz. A casting weighing four tons, of bronze, strange to say, and one other, were the only ones recovered from the wreck. The great casting is safe at last in the Mexican Military Museum.

Working Out Our Problem.

REV. G. A. KRATZER.
(Reprinted from "Christian Science Sentinel.")

MANY students of Christian Science, as well as Christian people generally, make a mistake in attempting too much at the start, or rather in not rightly selecting the phase or manifestation of error over which they attempt to demonstrate at the beginning. Error as a whole presents many problems to be solved, and no young student of Christianity is competent to work on them all at the same time, and find success in his efforts. He must choose among the problems, working them one at a time, although it is true that the solving of any one problem contributes to the solution of all the rest.

The most frequent mistake made by many who are trying to be Christian Scientists is in attempting to demonstrate peace without before they have demonstrated peace within. They think they must solve the world's problems, or their church's problems, or at least the problems of their family or friends, in order to solve their own. The scientific order of demonstration is the exact reverse. A man must cast the beam out of his own eye before he can see clearly to cast the mote out of his brother's eye. We must be sufficiently acquainted with God, good, and sufficiently grounded in our consciousness of Him, sufficiently able to dwell "in the secret place of the most High," so that in our own consciousness we have become largely impervious to the darts of error, before we are strongly enough placed in good to be of very much service to other people. If we have not a firm inward hold on peace and harmony, we shall not do much toward imparting these qualities to other people or to outward situations.

Beginners in Christian Science need to follow the example of Jesus. Before he entered upon his ministry, he went apart for 40 days into the wilderness to pray. He saw that each should have his own consciousness closely and firmly and unalterably united with God, good, before undertaking the problems of the world. During these 40 days there were sick to be healed, there were evils to be cast out, there were wrongs to be righted, but for the time Jesus paid no attention to them; he was giving his entire attention to getting so firmly placed and grounded in the abiding consciousness of God, good, that he would be able to attack these evils all the more successfully later on, and without being himself overthrown in the process.

We do not need to make a physical journey into a material desert in order to follow the example of Jesus in this particular. It is sufficient to withdraw our thoughts from other people's problems for a time, so that we may give our entire attention to the solution of our own—become sufficiently acquainted with God so that we shall be permanently at peace within, even while the storms of error rage all around us. When we have demonstrated such inward and abiding peace that feelings of anger, jealousy, envy, resentment, self-pity, brooding over wrongs, and the like, are not stirred into activity by the conduct of others, then we have gotten into a position to be of real service in overcoming the errors in our family, in the church, and in the world at large. Of course, such a demonstration is a matter of degree. Probably there are very few who have reached such a height of spiritual attainment that inharmonious feelings are not at times aroused into momentary activity; but we must have become sufficiently assimilated to God, sufficiently habituated in the abiding consciousness of good, sufficiently alert with regard to error, so that we promptly put out these intruders upon harmonious consciousness instead of admitting and cherishing them, before we can be very helpful to others.

While we are passing through the advancing periods of understanding, the human sense may be subject to more or less of disquietude and unrest. There will be "days" when all will appear bright and clear. Then other problems will arise, which we are not able to solve for a time, and we may pass through a period of "night." Then we succeed in solving or overcoming these difficulties of understanding or experience, and come into a brighter and fuller "day." Finally, we arrive at the goal of complete understanding, where we know the truth, and know that we know it, and feel scientifically confident that we can abide in the consciousness of Truth and protect ourselves from coming under the domination of error. While there is much that we have not demonstrated, yet we feel that we understand God, understand His universe, and understand ourselves, and that we have sufficient hold on the truth so that we can make our way forward gradually to a complete demonstration of that which we know to be true, without let or hindrance from error.

When we have attained this consciousness, we have reached the day of rest,—not a period of idleness, by any means, but rather a period of activity in demonstration of the truth. Like God, we are able to "rest in action" (Science and Health, p. 519). We work vigorously for our own advancement and the advancement of others. While doing so, we are confronted with all sorts of errors, but they do not disturb the harmony of our consciousness while we are overcoming them. We are strong enough in the truth so that they cannot disturb us. So we are in perfect repose, even while we are actively working. This period of repose, this day of rest, is our Sabbath day. We should "remember the Sabbath day, to keep it holy;" that is, our consciousness should rest in God, we should not allow inharmonious, annoying, unholy thoughts and feelings to enter. We should keep our consciousness pure and clear, and our Sabbath day, our spiritual consciousness, having been attained, should endure forever.

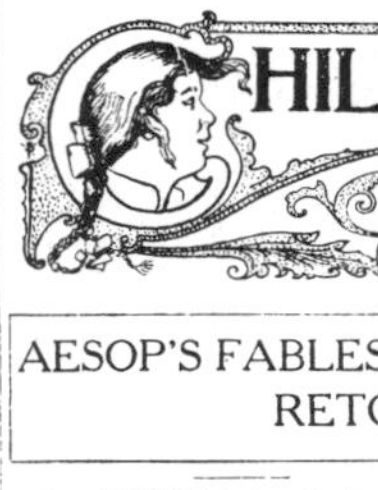

CHILDRENS DEPARTMENT

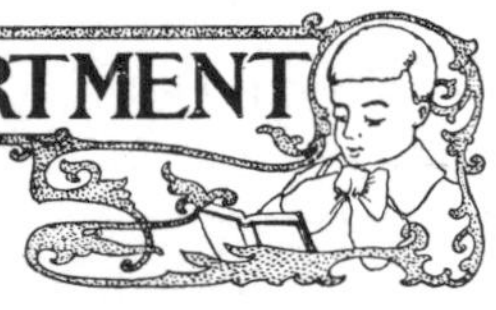

LET US BE MERRY

"Excuse me," said the old lady as she entered the store. "How long have you been in the drug business?"

"About ten years, madam."

"Then, you must know it pretty well?"

"Well, I think I do."

"That's good. All I want just now is a two-cent postage stamp."

"You seem overheated, my lad," said the kindly gentleman behind the scenes in the melodrama theater.

"Yes, sir," responded the youngster. "I've the hottest part in the show."

"What do you do?"

"Why, I have to get away up in the flies and tear up paper for the storm in the blizzard scene."

"Most people," said the thoughtful thinker, "take life seriously."

"Well," replied the light thinker, "there is no reason why they should not. It is a serious thing to take life."

Oh, sir, please, I have swallowed a pin," exclaimed a servant maid running into her employer's study. "Never mind, Mary, never mind," said her employer, soothingly, "here's another."

Minister (to elderly female crofter)—I'm sorry to hear your potatoes are very bad this year, Janet.

E. F. C.—Deed they are, sir, but I've reason to be thankful to Providence that other folks are as badly off as myself.

AESOP'S FABLES RETOLD

A FATHER had a family of sons who were perpetually quarreling among themselves. When he failed to heal their disputes by his exhortations, he determined to give them a practical illustration of the evils of disunion; and for this purpose he one day told them to bring him a bundle of sticks. When they had done so, he placed the faggot into the hands of each of them in succession, and ordered them to break it in pieces. They each tried with all their strength, and were not able to do it. He next unclosed the faggot, and took the sticks separately one by one, and again put them into their hands, on which they broke them easily. He then addressed them in these words: "My sons, if you are of one mind, and unite to assist each other, you will be as this faggot, uninjured by all the attempts of your enemies; but if you are divided among yourselves, you will be broken as easily as these sticks."

Do you detect the moral in this fable? It is wisely drawn, but too narrow in its application. The children of God are all of one family and they should be of one mind in every good work. We should not try to exalt either ourselves or our families, but make our willing service bend to the good of all.

THE ART DIVINE

So quietly doth Friendship stroll
Along the paths of men,
So surely doth her keen, pure soul
Reach out beyond our ken
And feel the need in every heart
That cries for light and love,
Her ministry becomes an art
All other arts above.

Thus you and I all unawares
Are drawn from earth's far ways
To help each other lift the cares
That throng this mortal maze.
We know not why we meet, or part,
Except we see the plans
That underlie her subtle art,
But Friendship understands.

—Jeannette A. Becker.

HARDWARE PUZZLE

R	C	S	H	S
E	I	L	C	A
W	A	N	I	M
L	R	E	M	G
O	T	L	O	B

Find 12 articles found in a hardware shop. You may move from square to square, up, down and slanting, but you must not skip. You may use the same letter twice.

A SWARM OF BEES

B hopeful, B happy, B cheerful, B kind, B busy of body, B modest of mind, B earnest, B truthful, B firm and B fair, of all Miss B havior B sure and B ware.

B think ere you stumble for what may B fall, B true to yourself and B faithful to all. B brave too. B ware of sins that B set. B sure that one sin will another B get.

B watchful, B ready, B open, B frank, B polite to all whatever the rank. B just and B generous, B honest, B wise, B mindful of time and B certain it flies.

B prudent, B liberal, of order B fond. Buy what you need B fore Buying B yond.

B prompt and B dutiful, still B polite. B grateful, B cautious of those who B tray. B loved thou shalt B.—Home Notes.

CHARADE

The shepherds worshipped me long ago,
But cooks now use me, as you know.
A simple word of Saxon tongue,
But Germans often do me wrong.
Now, keep my third and do not scoff;
With me you cannot be far off.
My whole a temple most sublime
And built in good Agrippa's time.

"When I came of age," said Mr. Softleigh, "I promised mother that I'd never marry till I found the right girl." "I'm very sorry, Mr. Softleigh, but you're the wrong man."

Science and Health
With Key to the Scriptures

The Text Book of Christian Science

By MARY BAKER G. EDDY.

A complete list of Mrs. Eddy's Works on Christian Science with descriptions and prices will be sent upon application.

Address ALLISON V. STEWART, Publisher, Falmouth and St. Paul Streets, Boston, Mass.

THE CHRISTIAN SCIENCE MONITOR

"First the blade, then the ear, then the full grain in the ear."

EDITORIAL

Boston, Mass., Wednesday, November 25, 1908.

Something In a Name

By Mary Baker G. Eddy

The gentleman, Mr. Frank Bell, has caught my thunder; therefore he will not object to the lightning which accompanies it.

I have given the name to all the Christian Science periodicals. The first was THE CHRISTIAN SCIENCE JOURNAL, designed to put on record the divine Science of Truth; the second I entitled SENTINEL, intended to hold guard over Truth, Life and Love; the third, DER HEROLD DER CHRISTIAN SCIENCE, to proclaim the universal activity and availability of Truth; the next I named MONITOR, to spread undivided the Science that operates unspent. The object of THE MONITOR is to injure no man, but to bless all mankind.

HARRISBURG, PA., Nov. 2, 1908.

Rev. Mary Baker G. Eddy, Brookline, Mass.

Dear Leader—As a newspaper man I thank you for THE CHRISTIAN SCIENCE MONITOR in prospect, and I feel sure that such will be the sentiment of hundreds of newspaper workers all over the land when THE MONITOR in fact shall have demonstrated the feasibility of clean journalism.

A definition of "monitor" is, "One who advises," and I foresee that when this CHRISTIAN SCIENCE MONITOR shall have proved that there is such a thing as newspaper success along non-sensational lines, there will follow a widespread readjustment of news policies, for which I am sure none will be more truly thankful than an army of honest, conscientious toilers in the ranks of newspaperdom.

Gratefully yours, FRANK BELL,
Managing Editor Harrisburg Telegraph.

A Word of Appreciation

It is fitting that the editorial columns of the first issue of THE CHRISTIAN SCIENCE MONITOR should carry a tribute to the Rev. Mary Baker G. Eddy, discoverer and pioneer of Christian Science.

Brought into being with her approval, THE MONITOR plainly shows that, after nearly 43 years of consistent pioneering and untiring leadership, Mrs. Eddy is still foremost in progress.

Her pioneer work in the re-establishment of spiritual healing as taught and proved by Christ Jesus is revolutionizing human thought as regards disease and sin.

Her pioneer work in the rehabilitation of primitive Christianity is bearing fruit in a worldwide religious reform, demanding that those who declare the Christ as their Saviour shall give evidence of their faith by their works.

As the discoverer and founder of Christian Science, Mrs. Eddy started in 1883 a monthly publication called "The Christian Science Journal," the first periodical to circulate a current literature that healed. Mrs. Eddy's ideal, even then, was a "newspaper edited and published by Christian Scientists." (Miscellaneous Writings, page 4.)

Recognizing that her message was inherently cosmopolitan—to all mankind and to all peoples—she established in 1903 "Der Herold der Christian Science," a monthly magazine in the German language.

When the weekly paper, the "Christian Science Sentinel," was published in 1898, she was again a pioneer, advancing a step nearer her purpose to have a newspaper which purpose today, after 25 years of patient preparation, finds fuller expression in THE CHRISTIAN SCIENCE MONITOR.

Christian Scientists are not unduly enthusiastic nor apart from fact when they claim that Mrs. Eddy's life is proof both of her inspired mission and her personal integrity.

She is marvelous because of her spiritual scientific understanding of God, her consecration to Principle, and her patience in demonstration. It is just as characteristic of her to wait 25 years for "a newspaper edited and published by Christian Scientists," as it is for her to have such a newspaper at the end of 25 years.

She is profound because she is simple—direct in logic, sturdy in argument, steadfast in conviction, impersonal in the great religious activities which have made her the world's benefactor.

Looking without prejudice upon Mrs. Eddy's achievements—a reformed medical system, a healing literature, a spiritualized philosophy, a scientific Christianity, the signs everywhere of man thinking, Mind dominate and matter dethroned—witnessing, too, the insistent retirement from public notice of the human personality that has done these things, it is inconceivable that Mrs. Eddy could be actuated by anything less than a deep conviction of Truth and a sincere desire to help humanity.

Eminent as a woman, eminent as a religious reformer, Mrs. Eddy is uniquely eminent as an author. Pioneer there as elsewhere, she is the originator of a noble literature, the aim of which is to elevate the human consciousness to an understanding of the allness of good and the nothingness of evil.

As the student of the art of sculpture must gain dominion over the clay before he can set forth his ideals in a manner acceptable to the connoisseur, so Mrs. Eddy has been obliged to struggle long with words and phrases of original material meaning before she could express her spiritual concepts in a way which the literary critic would pronounce workmanlike.

Her first purpose was not to write prettily but to get her message to the public. Much of her recent labor has been to improve the literary setting of this message. To-day her great work, "Science and Health with Key to the Scriptures," is a study in appropriate literary expression. It marks Mrs. Eddy not only an original thinker in the domain of metaphysics but a stylist of marked and notable characteristics.

Christian Science, as taught by Mrs. Eddy, is before the world to be judged by what it does. All may not be willing to strive for the ideal of perfection which she places as the goal of human endeavor; but we are convinced that no one, who perceives ever so slightly what Mrs. Eddy means by Christian Science, will quarrel with her or with her teachings.

It seems to be in the regular order of things that if Mr. Whitelaw Reid is desirous of returning to America, and Mr. George von L. Meyer is desirous of going to the Court of St. James, such an arrangement may be brought about as will enable Mr. Reid to step from the British ambassadorship into the cabinet, probably as secretary of state.

The Importance of the Unimportant

What a man is doing may not indicate what he would like to do, therefore by his vocation you may not always judge the man. He may be working under discipline, guided by the direction of wiser minds, controlled by the demands of an organization. Ruskin suggested that a man's tastes would reveal what he was. Get acquainted with a man's unfulfilled desires and you may know what he is becoming. If it is the unspoken prayer in the heart that decides the tendency of his life, then it is important for a man's welfare that he alertly guard "the imagination of the heart." The dreamy current of unguided thought which wanders in the mind of an idle man is usually supposed to be of no importance. The passing from mind to mind of suggestions unmoral, or frankly immoral, is considered uninfluential pastime. The perusal of writings where the transient flashing of wit is supposed to compensate for the salacious inferences is defended. But as well say that the *ignis fatuus* that glimmers over the marsh compensates for its malarial breath. In whatever way they find entrance to a man's mind it is true that "evil communications corrupt good manners." Furthermore it is manners that express the man.

The explanation of the success which follows effort in Christian Science is often sought. Critics say that will-power, personal magnetism, concentration of mental energies, strength of determination, account for results; but they are all wrong. Interesting demonstrations are made by children, for themselves and others. In the child is not found controlling personal magnetism, but rather simplicity and limpid purity of thought. And it is not the humanly measured strength of thought in the Christian Scientist, but the purity and rightness of his thought which accounts for his success. By right-thinking a man is brought into affiliation with the active good controlling the universe. The pure in heart not only shall see, but do see God.

Under the discipline of Christian Science teaching men awake to see the importance of what they had considered unimportant. They had lazily accepted the verdict of critics against other men, they had entertained causeless prejudices, they had fed little fires of resentment within and hated honest men without cause, and felt that they were doing no wrong since all this was concealed in the realm of thought. Also they had been open to the influence of the panic fear of others, hospitable to the expressed anxiety and prophecy of evil in current talk, and wholly unaware of the influence on their lives of such mental conditions. When the light of truth comes there is a complete reforming of the habits, tastes and desires. Ideal conditions are not reached at once, and no one should unkindly judge the Christian Scientist who is in process. All that makes for righteousness, mercy, and good will he considers important. You must judge him by his aims—by his prayers, if you will.

One Thousand Miles Nearer To Central America

The idea of constructing a ship canal across the Florida peninsula is far from being a new one, although it has been revived and brought into prominence lately by a discussion in a convention of the Gulf Coast Inland Waterways Association held at Columbus, Ga. It is as old, almost, as the idea of a canal across the isthmus of Panama.

It has long been felt by those who have been enthusiastic in their advocacy and support of the Panama canal project that if this great waterway is to be as valuable as it ought to be to our Eastern seaports it can only be made so by the construction of the Florida canal. The latter would place the commerce of the Atlantic states 1,000 miles closer to the republics of Central America than it is now, and reduce to an equal degree the distance between the Atlantic seaports and the Pacific, on the completion of the Panama canal.

Very little cutting, comparatively, would have to be done in order to make a waterway across the Florida peninsula above the Everglades. It would be necessary in the first place to make a connection between the Atlantic and Lake Okeechobee at a point, perhaps, just north of Fort Worth, and, in the second place, a connection between Lake Okeechobee and the Caloosahatchie river.

The \$50,000,000 which it is estimated the canal would cost would be expended mainly in deepening the present watercourses and in dredging. The gulf terminus of the canal would in all probability be at Fort Myers, or, more properly, Punta Rassa. The carrying out of this project would be a boon to the export trade of the country.

England's Fear of an Invasion Unwarranted

At a time when the people of Germany are almost a unit in condemning the attitude of their Emperor toward their neighbors, and particularly toward England, it is regrettable that Lord Roberts should, by his declarations in the House of Lords, fan the dying embers of international bitterness into new life.

In telling the peers what the Kaiser might do, in the matter of invading England, he leaves the unhappy impression on the British mind that this is the thing which the former will do at the earliest opportunity, unless certain precautions are taken to prevent him from doing it. He fails to take cognizance of the fact that the Kaiser has quite recently been shorn of much of his personal power, and that even though he might now have the disposition to make war upon England he lacks the ability to do so.

The German people are desirous of living in peace with their neighbors. They have seldom gone to war unless under the very greatest provocation. They have much in common with the English people, with whom they are on the friendliest terms. Aside from all other considerations, it would not be to their interest, and they know it, to engage in a strife which might result in sweeping their great and growing commerce from the seas.

It is high time that the war lords in England were being silenced also. The English and the German peoples are perfectly content to live in peace, if only the professional fighters of both countries will permit them to do so.

There does not appear to be any reason why the New England states should not get together for mutual and general advancement. They are already bound together sentimentally; they might just as well be bound together practically. And there need be no sectionalism in the alliance.

Did Bret Harte Know the California of '49?

It has been charged of late that Kipling in the earliest and the best, because the most natural, of his writings—in the sketches that gave us at once most pleasure and most instruction—did not paint the true India. It has been charged of late that Lafcadio Hearn, in those pictures of the Orient that have charmed two hemispheres, did not paint the real Japan. And now comes Professor Josiah Royce of Harvard with the startling declaration that Bret Harte, whom thinking Americans are more and more disposed to regard as the most distinctively and originally native of all our writers, did not paint the real California of the '49 period. Says the professor:

> **As a Californian I can say that not one childhood memory of mine suggests any social incident or situation that in the faintest degree gives meaning or confirmation to Bret Harte's stories. But it is also true that Bret Harte never saw the mines in '49 and '50, and that years later he collected the chance material of his stories from hearsay. It is also true that the social order which he depicts is an order that never was on land or sea, and that his tales are based upon a deliberately false romantic method.**

Unfortunately for Professor Royce all the evidence is against him. It is true that Bret Harte was not in California in 1849 or 1850, but he was in California in 1856 when the civilization introduced by the "Argonauts" was beginning to make itself felt, and all through the period of which '49 and '50 were simply the beginning. Those who worked with pick and shovel in those days, in the gulches and canyons of the Sierra Nevada have since testified to the marvelous accuracy of Bret Harte's descriptions and portraitures. Some who were adventurers, gamblers and saloonkeepers in the gold fields during the '50s have borne like testimony in later years. The files of newspapers of the period testify to the fidelity of Bret Harte's art to truth. The civilization which the Forty-Niners brought to California was only an exaggerated form of the civilization in the river towns of Illinois and Missouri—the states which did more than any others to people California at that day—for years before and after the outbreak of the California gold fever, and Mark Twain, John Hay and scores of other observers and writers have testified to this.

The best testimony of all, however, is that conditions, situations and episodes, like unto those painted by Bret Harte, modified only by the changes that have affected every quarter of the country and every class of people in the country, have since existed and developed in other mining camps from Virginia City to Leadville, from Butte to Cripple Creek.

The fact that Professor Royce's childhood memory does not suggest any of the incidents or the situations observed, pictured and immortalized by Bret Harte, should have no weight even with Professor Royce himself. No doubt many thousands of things have occurred round about him even in his manhood hours of which he has taken no note. As a learned professor he ought to know, and in all probability does know, that it does not follow from the fact that we fail to see things or to be impressed by them that these things have no existence, and are not visible to others.

When the People Hoard Their Dollars

One of the many peculiar phases of the recent financial and commercial depression was what might be called the rejection by the people of the subsidiary coin.

That is to say, when the money panic came the average person held on as long as possible to his whole dollars, whether paper or silver. As a consequence the demand for halves, quarters, dimes and nickels fell off amazingly.

When the depression began there was about \$3,000,000 of subsidiary coin in the United States treasury, but during the next seven months this amount was increased to \$24,500,000, or at the rate of over \$3,000,000 per month. However, notwithstanding the presidential campaign and the doleful predictions made by partisans on every side as to what would happen unless their particular candidates were elected, the demand for "small change" began to make itself felt once more in Washington, and since then fully \$10,000,000 of the amount accumulated has found its way back into its legitimate channels, a fact that indicates the return of public confidence.

The people are once more "breaking" their dollars. They are beginning, in other words, to see that there was no cause for the "panic"—no cause for the "depression"—no reality to their fear beyond that which they themselves gave to it. Nothing has changed but the human sense of things. Belief brought on the panic. Understanding is destroying its effects.

New England Conference Unique and Important

The conference of governors and governors-elect of the New England states, which has just closed in this city, was in many respects one of the most unique and important gatherings held in the country during recent years. There have been state conferences in the past, it is true, but their purpose has been sectional in a political sense, or, in an economic sense, antagonistic to other divisions of the Union. Disagreeable memories are associated with most of them, painful memories with some of them.

In the present instance, however, the object has been purely to conserve and promote the interests of one section without infringing in the least upon the interests of other sections. Indeed, the purpose was broad and patriotic, in that the conference was not striving to do for New England anything that it would not be glad to have the rest of the country take a hand in.

Many facts were brought out which are of vital importance to New England and its people. But this was by no means all. The discussions which took place in the conference contain food for national reflection, and the gathering may be pronounced one of national importance in so far as it will assist in concentrating the thought of the country upon the paramount question of conserving and developing our natural resources.

We have it from one who must be classed as a student of eminent scientists, if not an eminent scientist himself, and who has written to a New York contemporary on the subject, that geology, anthropology, and prehistoric archeology all go to prove that there is a maximum and a minimum period for the existence of man upon the earth, viz.—from 20,000 to 100,000 years. There is here, it may be noticed by the careful reader, a margin of 80,000 years, which is a very liberal one indeed, considering that the sciences which get the credit for fixing the maximum and minimum periods of man's existence are popularly reputed to be exact.

1909-1929

THE CHRISTIAN SCIENCE MONITOR

LAST EDITION. BOSTON, MASS., THURSDAY, MARCH 4, 1909—VOL. I., NO. 83. PRICE TWO CENTS.

Taft Inaugurated President Today

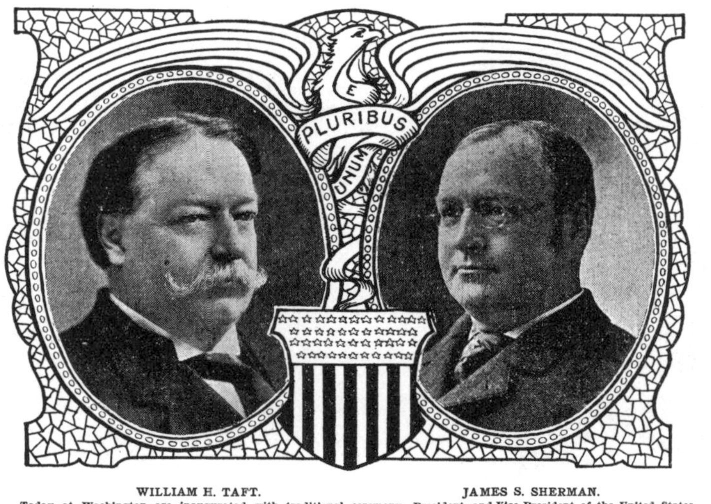

WILLIAM H. TAFT. JAMES S. SHERMAN.

Today at Washington are inaugurated with traditional ceremony, President and Vice-President of the United States.

NATION'S NEW RULER TAKES FORMAL OATH OF OFFICE AT CAPITOL IN WASHINGTON

Sun Breaks Through Over Capital City, and Forenoon's Isolation Both as to Rail and Wire Communication Is Relieved—Original Program Goes Through.

WASHINGTON—President William Howard Taft of Ohio and Vice-President James S. Sherman of New York formally assumed the reins of government of the United States at 12:55 p. m. today.

The new administration was born amid scenes of turmoil, so far as the elements are concerned, that have never been equalled in the history of the republic on inauguration day.

But it was launched with enthusiasm, so far as the people themselves are concerned, that eclipsed any demonstration that in the past marked the fourth of March, and the blizzard was defied by thousands upon thousands of patriots who cared little so long as they could have a part in welcoming the 27th President in a fitting manner.

The ceremony was performed in the Senate chamber owing to the storm, which continued all morning. Crowds in the streets took their inning out in cheering for the outgoing and incoming Presidents. "What's the matter with Taft, he's all right," boomed out again and again, interspersed with "Hurrah for Teddy, he's all right," and men, women and children joined in the vocal tribute to the chief men of the day.

shook him warmly by the hand, and the incoming official, after a hasty glance at the crowded chamber, turned and faced the man he was to succeed. The oath of

The signal for the first real cheering of the day was sounded from a 10-inch gun in the navy yard a mile away in response from a message flashed from the dome of the Capitol conveying the information that the President had been sworn in. The boom of the gun was taken up by every noise-producing instrument in the District of Columbia and for 15 minutes the deep notes of steam whistles, the shriek of tin horns, the whirl of rattles and the yip-yip-yip of cheering thousands created an uproar that was at least outward evidence that the Taft administration was welcome to all.

Roosevelt and Taft Leave the White House

The day was the worst in the memory of the oldest inhabitant. The storm, which began in rain, had changed to a blizzard during the night and when day dawned decorations and poorly-constructed reviewing stands were in many cases laid low, trains and surface railways were blocked, and wire communication cut off.

All trains were late and hardly a wheel was turning on the trolley cars. As a matter of fact almost 1500 incoming strangers had spent the night in the big union station and when day broke they were still far away from their lodgings. Not until after 11 o'clock was there a break in the gloomy, overhanging skies.

At 10:45 a. m. President Roosevelt and the President-elect left the White House in the executive carriage. Two secret service men sat on the box and the windows of the carriage were all up so that no one was able to catch a glimpse of the occupants. They were driven rapidly to the Capitol and were hurried at once to the President's room, in the rear of the Senate chamber, where President Roosevelt got down to the last work of his administration, signing a number of bills as they were brought over from Congress.

In the meanwhile those who had tickets admitting them to the capitol buildings were being ushered to the places reserved for them. Vice-President-elect James S. Sherman was early on the ground, accompanied by the members of his family. He went into the House first and later went across to the Senate and took refuge from the curiosity seekers in the Vice-President's room, where he remained until noon. Inasmuch as the Vice-President was the first to take the oath, the crowd who had credentials permitting them to see the show packed the various galleries and the space that had been set aside for them. In the executive galleries were the Taft, Fairbanks and Sherman families and they were the center of attraction, until the actual ceremonies began.

Chief Justice Fuller Enters Senate Chamber

In order that there would be plenty of room for all entitled to be present on the floor the senators were grouped on the right of the center aisle of the chamber. At 11.45 the first of the participants, the justices of the supreme cour in their black robes and headed by Chi Justice Fuller, filed in and were seat They were quickly followed by the members of the diplomatic corps and then came the House of Representatives, most of the members resplendent in the blackest of frock coats and the whitest of linen. Governors of states and officialdom in every branch folowed, and, almost before they had settled back in their places there was a sound of cheering from the corridors and through the main portals came President Roosevelt and President-elect Taft, arm in arm. They were escorted down the aisle to the two chairs reserved for them by the stated committee, Senators Knox, Lodge and Bacon, and Representatives Burke, Young and Gaines. As the two distinguished gentlemen proceeded down the aisle they were cheered to the echo by galleries and floor.

(Continued on Page Five.)

TAX COMMISSIONER CONSIDERS COURSE IN ASSESSORS' CASE

Latest Developments Show Considerable Doubt as to the Future Action in the Two Towns.

ASK FOR THE LAW

Claim Is Made That E. R. Searles Should Have Been Assessed for Ten Million Dollars.

Latest developments show considerable doubt as to the future course of State Tax Commissioner W. D. T. Trefry in prevailing upon the assessors of the town of Methuen and the city of Malden to increase the value of estates in their municipalities.

In Methuen it is the Searles case that is prominent. Here it is claimed that Edward P. Searles, formerly of Great Barrington, was assessed for $80,000 of personal property when the state officials claim he should be assessed for $10,000,000.

The matter was referred to the attorney-general as to the meaning of the new law under which the duties of the new supervisors of assessors are defined. It was one of these supervisors that brought up the Searles case and it was heralded as being the first of a series that would mean the bringing to light of a large amount of personal property that heretofore had escaped taxation.

While the state tax commissioner has received no formal opinion from the attorney-general as to what the new law means, the two officials have had several conferences over the subject and the tax commissioner is led to believe that he would not have any great likelihood of success if he attempted to prosecute the Searles case or the Malden case under it.

At the same time the state tax commissioner declines to say what he will do in the matter. It is a fact that he referred to the situation in his annual report recently submitted to the Legislature so that there is a basis for the General Court to take action to remedy the uncertain situation that exists.

The matter is likely to be called to the attention of the committee on taxation and both the tax commissioner and the attorney-general will be called in to explain just what the loophole in the present law is in which they fear they may fail this time if they undertake a test case. Then the committee and the Legislature will decide whether it is advisable to amend the law and close this loophole.

YALE HONORS HER NOTED ALUMNUS

NEW HAVEN, Conn.—Yale is today honoring her most distinguished son, William Howard Taft, and is celebrating in a fitting manner his inauguration as President of the United States.

The Yale News, the official organ of the university, issued a supplement in honor of the event, containing several articles on the President. In an article under the head of "Taft as a Student," Prof. Edward S. Dana gives the class record of the new President and his remarkable ability as a student. "Always prominent among the 78 men," reads the article, "his able mind gave him at once a rank among the few highest scholars of his class and whose force of character made his influence felt among all his fellows."

In an article under the caption of "Taft as a Classmate," Ernest C. Johnson tells of the President's popularity among his fellow students and his participation in all their sports.

A parade of the students and graduates was planned to take place late today.

TAX RATE DIFFERENCE CITED.

City Auditor Mitchell announced today that the difference in the tax rates by the mayor's budget and the City Council budget is 75 cents on each $1000.

MEXICANS SEND "BIG STICK."

EL PASO, Tex.—A handsomely carved "big stick" from Mexcian admirers to President Roosevelt passed through the Custom House here Wednesday.

Wright Brothers Voted Gold Medals by House

WASHINGTON — Orville and Wilbur Wright, the Ohio aeroplanists, by authority of a resolution passed by the House last Wednesday afternoon, will each receive a gold medal from the government as a mark of recognition and appreciation of their services in inventing the Wright aeroplane and for their "courage in aerial navigation."

The measure has already passed the Senate. It carries an appropriation of not to exceed $400 for the two medals, the designing of which is left to the secretary of war.

"I Want to Make Good," Declares President Taft To His Brothers of Yale

WASHINGTON — "I feel in all my bones and nerves the disposition to 'make good,'" declared President-elect Taft on Wednesday night in addressing about 700 Yale alumni at their smoker. "I hope with nerve to be able to stand just criticism and to improve by it and not to 'care a durn' for unjust criticism.

"Many circumstances have worked together to place me where I am," he said. "I am about to enter upon one of the most perilous journeys any man in our country can enter upon.

"Great obstacles can be met by the observance of common sense, courage, the sense of proportion and the absence of swell-headism, which principles are inculcated at Yale. The disposition to meet each difficulty as it arises will accomplish what ought to be done.

"A man ought not to put himself in the attitude of fearing these difficulties, but have the courage to meet them as they come. That is my hope. If is proves otherwise then I will not have 'made good.'"

THE inaugural addresses of President Taft and Vice-President Sherman will be found on Page 6 of today's Christian Science Monitor.

HOW ROOSEVELT SPENT HIS LAST DAY AS PRESIDENT

WASHINGTON—Men who have been 50 years at the White House have no recollection of scenes such as were witnessed there Wednesday during the closing hours of President Roosevelt's administration. It is estimated that between 10 a. m. and 2 p. m. at least 2500 visitors came to say goodby to the chief executive.

President stood the test with the hardihood and joyousness that made his greetings to every man or woman more pleasant than usual. During all this time he stopped at intervals to sign bills coming in from Congr or to attach his name to photographs brought to him.

The President signed the District of Columbia, the fortifications, the army and the naval appropriation bills and the Brownsville bill, which rmits the discharged negro soldiers of the 25th infantry to reenlist in the army upon establishing their innocence.

President Roosevelt spent a busy afternoon. He shook hands with the White House Republican Glee Club of Columbus, Ohio, at 2:30 o'clock, and listened to songs by its members. Later he received Governor Draper of Massachusetts, Governor Hughes of New York, Governor Hadley of Missouri, and Governor Pothier of Rhode Island, with their respective staffs.

Among those received by appointment were the members of the interstate commerce commission. The President exchanged with each member cordial personal greetings. Chairman Knapp, speaking for the commission, said that the country was indebted to the President's persistent efforts and commanding influence for notable measures of regulation.

In response, the President said that "you have done the work while I have seemed to get the credit for it. I have tried to be a decent President for a decent people."

Quite early in the evening he received his old friends from Oyster Bay, and at the same time he received the friends and neighbors of Vice President-elect Sherman. After this he shook hands with the famous Hamilton Club of Chicago.

Soon after 6 o'clock the President left his office for the last time. His work there is done and what work he did today was executed in the President's room at the Capitol. The most affecting of all the farewells at the White House was when the President called all the clerks, messengers and other attaches of his executive staff into his office just before he left them. He made a few remarks, telling them how greatly he appreciated the way they had assisted him in the seven years of his administration. Both he and they, he declared, had worked in common for the welfare of the nation and both had done their best. He wished them all farewell and good luck. Then he shook hands with each of them. A number of the White House attaches were remembered by the President with personal gifts. The last Roosevelt dinner in the White House was served at 8 o'clock with 14 persons present, constituting members of the families of the retiring and incoming Presidents. Mr. and Mrs. Taft were the principal guests. None of the Roosevelt children was present, and the Taft children spent the night at the Boardman residence.

Miss Ethel Roosevelt left Washington Wednesday for Oyster Bay. Quentin Roosevelt will remain at school, in Alexandria, Va., until the close of the school year.

THEODORE ROOSEVELT'S FAREWELL---
"I've tried to be a decent President for a decent people"

Points From President Taft's Inaugural Address

ROOSEVELT REFORMS — Pledges himself to the maintenance and enforcement of the reforms initiated by President Roosevelt.

TARIFF—Revision of the tariff is of pressing importance and a bill must be drawn in accordance with the ante-election promises of the party in power, and passed as promptly as possible. He will call an extra session of Congress and recommends that no other legislation be attempted.

DEFICIT — Points out that there will be a national deficit of $100,000,000, and urges that the new tariff bill be so framed as to restore the balance and provide ample revenue hereafter. If duties prove insufficient, he recommends new kinds of taxation, particularly a graduated inheritance tax.

ARMY AND NAVY — Demands an adequate army and a strong navy as the best conservators of our peace with other nations. Our international policy is to promote peace, but in the controversies likely to arise in the Orient, growing out of the open door and other issues, the United States can only maintain her interests and secure respect to her demands if able to back them up by something besides verbal protest and diplomatic note.

TREATY RIGHTS — The President should have power to enforce treaty rights of Asiatic or other aliens in federal courts and not run the risk of war by being obliged to explain that these things are under state or city control.

MONEY AND BANKS — Promises that new administration will reform monetary and banking laws so as to secure greater elasticity and allow the giving of aid in case of financial stress.

POSTAL SAVINGS BANKS—Urges incoming Congress to enact a proper postal savings bank bill.

MAIL SUBSIDIES—Hopes that establishment of new steamship lines to South America and the Orient may be encouraged by mail subsidies.

PANAMA CANAL—Insists that lock type is most feasible for Panama canal and says he will devote all energy possible to pushing the work on the plans adopted.

SOUTHERN POLICY—Disclaims intent to change electoral vote of South, but hopes to promote ever increasing sectional good feeling. Says danger of control by ignorant electorate in South has passed and that the negro must base hope for future status on his own industry and self-restraint. The federal government will not interfere with the South in the regulation of its domestic affairs. Executive will, however, exercise a careful discretion in the matter of making negro appointments.

INJUNCTION AND BOYCOTT — Pledges himself to promote further legislation to make railroads responsible for the personal safety of employees. Declares for the right of issuance of the temporary injunction and declares boycott an instrument of tyranny.

STREETS OF NATION'S CAPITAL THRONGED BY THOUSANDS

WASHINGTON—The streets of Washington Wednesday night were thronged with thousands of eager sightseers who in expectancy of the great event of the morrow, paraded back and forth, exchanging greetings and welcoming old friends. Everywhere the spirit of the celebration reigned and everybody was ready and waiting for that greatest of all American pageants, the inauguration of a President.

Congress had a busy day, cleaning up the odds and ends of legislation, while both President Roosevelt and President-elect Taft, harbored under the same roof, were equally busy receiving callers and making the final arrangements for the inaugural ceremony.

Hosts gathered here from all parts of the country, awaiting the spectacle, when Mr. Taft will be inducted into the highest office in the gift of the people.

Pennsylvania avenue Wednesday night, along its mile and a quarter length from the Capitol to the treasury, looked picturesque. The asphalt reflected in its glistening surface long golden shadows from the festooned arches above. The finishing touches in the decorative scheme of the magnificent court of honor were finished and the final rehearsal of the orchestra for the inaugural ball at the pension office building was held. Pennsylvania avenue was cleared of all vehicles, street cars and pedestrians at 9 o'clock this morning by an order issued by the superintendent of police.

The rush of visitors from all parts of the country continued unabated and the city is in the usual pre-inaugural state of congestion. It is estimated that fully 200,000 people are already here and each incoming train and boat adds its quota to the visiting throng.

British Press Today Warmly Praises the Outgoing President

LONDON—The London morning papers today (Thursday) publish long editorials, articles of appreciation and portraits of the incoming and outgoing Presidents of the United States. The tributes to President Roosevelt are of the most enthusiastic character. They rank him in the great line with Washington, Lincoln and Grant, as the most fascinating personality in the two hemispheres, only rivalled in that respect by the Emperor of Germany, his government marking the consolidation of America's position as a world power, as the Morning Post says, "without attacks on the rights or interests of other nations."

BANK GUARANTY BILL WILL PASS

Bryan's Famous Measure Is Recommended by Nebraska House for Passage by the Legislature.

LINCOLN, Neb.—William J. Bryan's bank deposit guaranty bill was recommended to pass the House, and the bill will be pushed through both branches of the Legislature. No bank with less than $10,000 capital can be chartered, and the capital required is proportioned to population. Interest on deposits is restricted to 4 per cent, and no bank is permitted to advertise the guaranty deposit feature, save on its stationery and a placard hung in its window.

Within 60 days after the bill becomes a law, an assessment of one half of 1 per cent on average daily deposits for six months is to be levied. On January and July of next year assessments of one quarter of 1 per cent are to be levied. After that semi-annual assessments of one twentieth of 1 per cent must be paid when the fund falls below one half of 1 per cent of total deposits in the banks. Depositors of a failed bank are to get their money on proof of claims not later than 60 days.

TOPEKA, Kan.—The House and Senate voted to concur in the second conference report on the bank guaranty law, and the bill will become a law as soon as it is signed by the Governor. Trust companies are not permitted to come under the provisions of the law. New banks must exist a year before being permitted to become guaranty banks and savings deposits are protected when not in excess of $100 for each individual depositor.

NEW HAVEN SEEKS TO ACQUIRE ROADS

ALBANY—The second district public service commission today authorized the New York & Stamford Railway Company, a subsidiary company of the New York, New Haven & Hartford Railroad Company, to issue a mortgage of $2,000,000 covering bonds to the Union Trust Company of New Haven Conn. Application was made to the commission by the New Haven for authority to purchase the stock of the New York & Portchester Railroad Company and the New York, Westchester & Boston Railroad Company.

JUDGE HEARS KING COUNSEL

Judge William Schofield of the superior court this afternoon again heard counsel on the bill of exceptions filed in the case of C. F. King, the financier now serving a sentence in prison for larceny. The hearing is to get the exceptions into proper form for consideration by the supreme court.

SAVE TEN ON LIGHTER.

NEW YORK—The police patrol tug of the Brooklyn department succeeded in passing lines to the stranded steam lighter which grounded off Coney Island Wednesday night and towed her safely to a dock. There were 10 men on the lighter.

U. S. S. GERANIUM TO BE SOLD.

BATH, Me.—The U. S. lighthouse tender Geranium is about to be sold at auction. The Geranium was built at Newburg, N. Y., in 1863, and was formerly the U. S. S. John A. Dix.

PRISONERS SAVE GUARD AT A FIRE

SAN FRANCISCO—Fire was discovered in a jute warehouse of San Quentin prison Wednesday, and only after hard fighting by officials, convicts, the fire department of San Rafael and fire boats from San Francisco were other buildings saved.

One hundred convicts and 20 guards fought the flames. The prisoners made no efforts to escape and did good work, several rescuing a guard who fell into the fire. A Gatling gun was saved by several prisoners. The loss is estimated at $50,000.

FATAL FIRE IN BROOKLYN.

NEW YORK—A woman and son perished in a fire that destroyed a tenement house in Seventh avenue, Brooklyn, today.

CREW IS RESCUED IN BREECHES BUOY

EASTPORT, L. I.—In a sea that was pounding the stranded schooner Merry to pieces on the sand bar off this port, Captain Farrow, Captain Denison and 30 of the schooner's crew and members of the Merritt-Chapman Wrecking Company were rescued in a breeches buoy today by the Moriches life saving crew. The men went aboard the schooner Wednesday with the intention of making attempt to float her at high tide. Before Captain Farrow, the last man to leave the vessel, had been hauled through the breakers, the ship had begun to break up. The Merry has been stranded for two weeks. She was bound from Boston for Newport News.

FREIGHT RATES UPHELD.

The railroad commissioners today decided against Reis & Company who complained that the freight rates charged between Springfield and Boston for interurban shipments were unreasonable.

BROOKLINE HOLDS CAUCUSES TODAY

Citizens' caucuses are to be held in Brookline this afternoon and evening, from 4:15 to 10 o'clock, for the nomination of town officers. The town meeting will be held March 16. Beside the five present members of the board of selectmen, who are all candidates for reelection, four others seek the office, Lyman J. Clark, Frank B. Connor, James L. Quinn and Ambrose E. Pratt. There are two candidates for town auditor, Francis L. Muldowney and Paul M. Hubbard.

The town meeting will vote "yes" or "no" on the questions of license, police vacations, pensions for teachers and a plan to protect forest lands from fire.

PERSIAN CONSUL GENERAL

WASHINGTON—H. H. Topakyan has been appointed consul general of Persia at New York city. Mr. Topakyan is a well known business man of this city. He was Persian commissioner and director of the Persian and Ottoman exhibits at the World's Fair in Chicago in 1892.

CHURCH CENTENARY CLOSES.

More than 800 parishioners and friends of Park Street Church attended the reception and banquet in Ford Hall Wednesday evening which marked the close of the week of festivities with which that church has observed its centennial.

CANTON RIVER BOATS BURN.

VICTORIA, B. C.—One thousand Chinese perished as the result of a fire on a number of flower boats upon the Canton river.

Ambassadors Resign Their Posts

WASHINGTON—The resignations of all of the ambassadors and ministers in the diplomatic service of the United States have been received at the state department in accordance with precedent. This is a formal procedure incident to a change of administration and leaves the incoming President free to rearrange the service.

Ambassador Francis, at Vienna, and Ambassador Griscom, at Rome, propose to retire from the diplomatic service as soon as possible after March 4.

THE CHRISTIAN SCIENCE MONITOR

LAST EDITION. BOSTON, MASS., MONDAY, JULY 26, 1909—VOL. I., NO. 202. PRICE TWO CENTS.

DEADLOCK MAY KILL ALL POSSIBILITY OF TARIFF LEGISLATION

Although Situation May Clear in a Day or So It Promises Now to Protract Session of Congress Into August.

NO CHANGE TODAY

Senator Aldrich Is Said to Be Sincere in His Statement That Free Hides Would Never Pass the Senate.

WASHINGTON—The tariff situation may clear up today or tomorrow, or during the week, but there are elements in the situation that point very strongly to the possibility that the deadlock now on between the two houses may protract the work of the conferees and carry the tariff session of Congress well into August.

Indeed, the possibility is equally great that there may be no tariff legislation at all, although leaders in both Houses are as yet unwilling to face such an alternative.

Senator Aldrich continues to claim, and probably with a good deal of truth, that if he should yield to the House and the President in the matter of free hides it would be impossible to carry the conference report through the Senate. He says there are seven Republican senators from the range states of the Rocky mountains who are unalterably opposed to free hides, and says they will vote against any conference report providing for them.

This will be sufficient strength to defeat the conference report in the Senate, according to Mr. Aldrich, because he says the 10 insurgent senators cannot be depended upon to come to his relief, even if what the President demands is granted. These insurgents continue to be hostile. They do not even warm up to the President, claiming that he has not asked for enough in the way of reductions, and since the Aldrich majority in the Senate is only about 14 votes, it is easy to see that if the 10 insurgents and the seven range senators vote against the report the Senate will be in the position of defeating the tariff bill.

In the House the outlook is just as cheerless. Chairman Payne says he will not sign a conference report which does not give free hides and provide for reductions in the leather schedule. Any conference report sent to the House without his signature will probably be defeated in that body.

What, then, are the conferees to do? Anybody giving a satisfactory answer to this question will earn the everlasting gratitude of the President and Chairman Payne on the one side, and of Senator Alurich and the stand-patters on the other.

Neither side wants to defeat the bill. The effect of such a course on the Republican party in the next campaign would be disastrous, and the President, as a good party man, does not want to do

(Continued on Page Four, Column Five.)

CHILDREN ENJOY NAHANT OUTING

Three Hundred Youngsters From Various Churches Today on Randidge Fund Excursion.

Three hundred children and attendants today are enjoying an outing at Nahant on the Randidge fund excursion, which left Otis wharf this morning under the auspices of the City Missionary Society.

Several different churches were represented, among them churches in Dorchester, Roxbury, Jamaica Plain and the city proper. The children were all well and neatly dressed, and behaved well on the pier. They had arrrived a half-hour early, and while they were on the wharf waiting for the boat the boys spent their time in organizing baseball nines and arranging games, while the girls arranged for races and games of their own.

William A. O'Brien and W. Stanwood Field have charge of the excursions for the school board.

The delegation of 150 children from Emmanuel Church on Walnut street was under the care of Miss Miller and that of Boylston Church, Boylston and Amory streets, Jamaica Plain, under the charge of Mrs. Howe and Mrs. William Picken. Eliot Church on Kenilworth street, Roxbury, sent 60 children, with Miss Gillis, Miss Leavatt and Mrs. Duffy as attendants, and the Congregational Church at Uphams Corner, Dorchester, sent 75, under Miss Briggs and Miss Stanley.

TAFT TO SEE WRIGHT FLY.

WASHINGTON—President Taft announced thi safternoon that he will go out to Ft. Myer this evening to watch the first official trial of the Wright aeroplane. He will travel in the White House automobile from the Chevy Chase golf links.

MONITORIALS

BY

Nixon Waterman.

THE WAY TO HER HEART.

("There is one way women could get the ballot all over the world in 18 months. That way would be for every woman to take an oath not to marry until woman's suffrage was granted." —Mrs. O. H. P. Belmont.)

As lovers do, in speech and song,
He begged her name the day.
With admiration deep and strong
He wooed her ardently and long,
But still she answered, "Nay."

He brought her jewels, good to see,
And precious gems galore,
And cried, "Now, will you marry me,
Oh, fairest of the fair?" But she
Refused him as before.

Again he told his heart's desire:
"My dear!" cried he, "I'll mow
The lawn and build the kitchen fire
And do such chores as you require!"
She, sighing, answered, "No."

Said he: "Your life shall be a dream
Of beauty and delight
I'll bring you chocolates and cream!"
(That should have won her, it would seem,
But still it didn't, quite.)

Full eighteen months did he devote
To toil, then, one glad day,
Poor, worn and in a ragged coat,
He brought to her the right to vote
And then she answered, "Yea!"

AND THEN HE LEFT.

"Do you fancy," asked he, "that a fellow like me
Could make you contented and happy?"
Her answer: "Well, yes, perhaps so, unless
He was too nearly like you," crushed Chappy.

No doubt England will call her fleet of flying warships her aero-dreadnautical navy.

HYMEN AND HISTORY.

He must be married who, in books, our nation's life relates,
For only married men can tell of their United States.
And let me here inquire: Would their happiness increase
If all our Michiganders chose to marry Portuguese?

The big, bread-insuring crop of the northwestern states is nearly ready to harvest and the happy farmers as they view it are humming "In this wheat by and by."

HEARD AT THE MILL.

Spindle—How do you feel after your encounter with me?

Wool—Worsted.

The true story of the scenes about Tangier would make a thrilling book. It should be bound, of course, in Morocco.

It would be a fine compliment if the civilized nations of the earth would suspend the hammer and clatter incident to the building of their many "Dreadnoughts during the first week of September while the international peace congress holds its eighteenth annual meeting at Stockholm.

WHAT THE NEIGHBORS SAY.

"In spite of his wealth, Miss Myllion's suitor must be an everyday sort of man."

"Why do you think so?"

"I notice that he calls seven times a week."

MATRIMONIAL SECRET.

There's many a husband does, alack!
Strange things he ne'er confesses:
Sometimes a man (behind her back)
Will "hook" his own wife's dresses!

HOT AND COLD.

The lover thinks his sweetheart nice
But till he knows he's got her;
Whene'er he tries to break the ice
He's always in hot water.

In inviting the "warring elements" of Congress to dine with him President Taft affirms his belief in the truth of the saying: "There is no trouble so large that it cannot be covered by a tablecloth."

TWO POINTS OF VIEW.

"Do you think the hammock season has a tendency to increase courting among the young people?"

"On the contrary, I think it suspends it."

INTERNATIONAL REFORM.

The time has come when things that plague
Can all be fixed without fierce spats:
Let's take our troubles to The Hague;
We've had enough "Kilkenny Cats."

AMERICA TO SEE MRS. PANKHURST

NEW YORK—Mrs. Emeline Pankhurst, leader of the militant suffragettes of England, is coming to America soon, according to announcement today by Mrs. Harriet Stanton Blatch, president of the Equal Suffrage Society and the League for Self-Supporting Women. She will begin her American campaign at a reception to be given her in Carnegie Hall, and will visit several other cities in America.

Holds School Attendance Record With Perfect Score For Dozen Years in Melrose

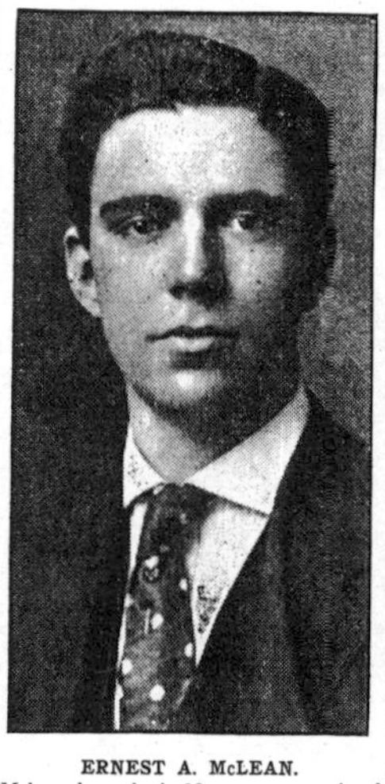

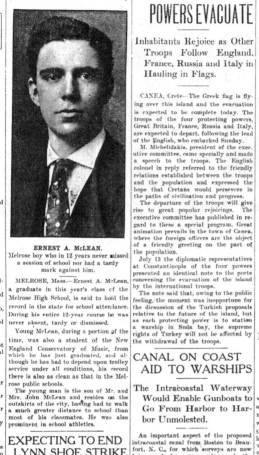

ERNEST A. McLEAN.

Melrose boy who in 12 years never missed a session of school nor had a tardy mark against him.

MELROSE, Mass.—Ernest A. McLean, a graduate in this year's class of the Melrose High School, is said to hold the record in the state for school attendance. During his entire 12-year course he was never absent, tardy or dismissed.

Young McLean, during a portion of the time, was also a student of the New England Conservatory of Music, from which he has just graduated, and although he has had to depend upon trolley service under all conditions, his record there is also as clean as that in the Melrose public schools.

The young man is the son of Mr. and Mrs. John McLean and resides on the outskirts of the city, having had to walk a much greater distance to school than most of his classmates. He was also prominent in school athletics.

EXPECTING TO END LYNN SHOE STRIKE

LYNN, Mass.—The packing room employees union executive board expects to present plans of a piece work system or wage scale to the firms of V. K. & A. H. Jones, Joseph Caunt & Sons, and James Phelan today, following the admission of the factory owners that such plans would be given consideration.

LOWER TAX RATES FOR WINCHESTER

WINCHESTER, Mass.—In addit on to a reduction of $1.20 in the tax rate (from $17.40 to $16.20), the assessors report a gain in personal valuation of $456,150, and of real $497,000.

The total valuation of the town is: Personal $2,352,800 and real $10,078,150.

CRETE FLYING FLAG OF GREECE AS THE POWERS EVACUATE

Inhabitants Rejoice as Other Troops Follow England, France, Russia and Italy in Hauling in Flags.

CANEA, Crete—The Greek flag is flying over this island and the evacuation is expected to be complete today. The troops of the four protecting powers, Great Britain, France, Russia and Italy, are expected to depart, following the lead of the English, who embarked Sunday.

M. Michelidakis, president of the executive committee, came specially and made a speech to the troops. The English colonel in reply referred to the friendly relations established between the troops and the population and expressed the hope that Cretans would persevere in the paths of civilization and progress.

The departure of the troops will give rise to great popular rejoicings. The executive committee has published in regard to these a special program. Great animation prevails in the town of Canea, where the foreign officers are the object of a friendly greeting on the part of the population.

July 13 the diplomatic representatives at Constantinople of the four powers presented an identical note to the porte concerning the evacuation of the island by the international troops.

The note said that, owing to the public feeling, the moment was inopportune for the discussion of the Turkish proposals relative to the future of the island, but as each protecting power is to station a warship in Suda bay, the supreme rights of Turkey will not be affected by the withdrawal of the troops.

CANAL ON COAST AID TO WARSHIPS

The Intracoastal Waterway Would Enable Gunboats to Go From Harbor to Harbor Unmolested.

An important aspect of the proposed intracoastal canal from Boston to Beaufort, N. C., for which surveys are now being made by army engineers, is the comparative safety it will afford to the movement of gunboats, submarines, torpedo boats and other small craft.

In time of war this movement could be carried on from harbor to harbor without being molested by a possible blockading fleet. At no time would the vessels in transit be outside of the three-mile limit.

The completion of the Cape Cod canal is destined in time to have a wide military influence. Then, a ship leaving Norfolk, Va., would pass through Chesapeake bay to the Delaware river, thence by canal across New Jersey to the Raritan river, New York bay, the East river, Long Island sound, Buzzards bay, the Cape Cod canal to Boston. The saving in time and the reduction of the dangers to shipping are counted to offset the cost of the work—about $13,000,000.

BLERIOT TODAY IS AWARDED PRIZE FOR FIRST AERIAL SAIL ACROSS ENGLISH CHANNEL

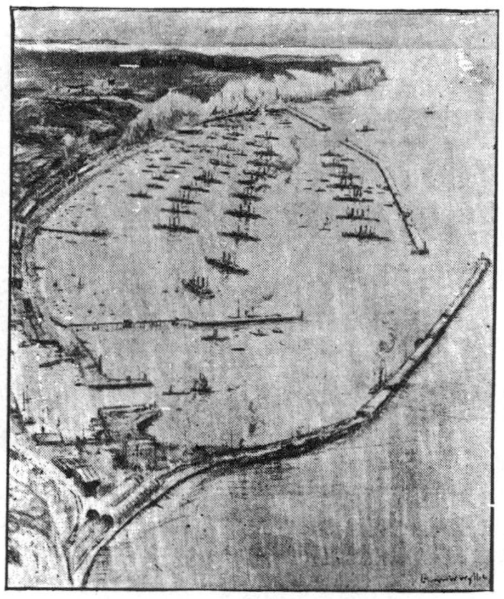

(Drawn by Charles Wyllie for the London Sphere.)

DOVER, ENG., NEAR WHICH BLERIOT LANDED.

The Northfall meadow in which the aeronaut alighted is behind the famous chalk cliffs, shown fronting the promontory in the background. The improved harbor and breakwater are in the middle ground.

Half Million Greet Him in London and Great Crowd Honors Aeronaut Who Arouses Wild Enthusiasm.

LONDON—London gave a tremendous welcome to Louis Bleriot, the French aeronaut who crossed the English channel in his monoplane Sunday morning, when 500,000 people met him today at the station and another 500,000 cheered him on his way to the Savoy Hotel, where the daring aeronaut was the guest of honor at a luncheon and received a prize.

Hundreds of notable figures in England joined in the vast throng and submitted to all sorts of inconveniences just to get a glimpse of the aeronaut who in 30 minutes accomplished a feat that has immortalized his name.

Bleriot was completely overcome by the intensity of enthusiasm and the display in his honor. He declared that the honors shown him compensated him a hundredfold for the fortune he has spent in mastering aviation.

The Daily Mail's £1000 prize was formally turned over to Bleriot when he reached the Savoy Hotel. The presentation speech was made by Lord Northcliffe, amid scenes which for enthusiasm have seldom been equaled.

According to present arrangements,

(Continued on Page Four, Column One.)

Immediate Results Due To Bleriot's Aerial Feat Include Prize and Orders

THE direct results of Louis Bleriot's aerial navigation of the English channel are today noticeable as follows:

Baron Deforest of London has offered a prize of $20,000 to the first British aeronaut to cross the channel in a British-built aeroplane in record time.

Foreign governments are in a rush to secure French aerial machines. The Spanish government has ordered a French built airship of 141,280 cubic feet. In January last the Belgian government commissioned a 249,580 cubic foot gas capacity frameless French dirigible.

Russia, besides the Bayard-Clement, has just taken delivery of a Lebaudy airship built at Moisson. The Austrian military authorities intend to procure a vessel of the French semi-rigid type in addition to the Parseval type of airship already ordered in Germany.

Private subscriptions are being made in London to purchase airships for the government, the latter having pleaded that it could not afford extensive experiments in this line. A $5000 subscription was received today from Waldorf Astor.

TALKS ON WIRELESS 'PHONE TODAY OVER THE CHARLES RIVER

The Apparatus Invented by A. Frederick Collins of Newark, N. J., Proves to Be Practicable.

EXPLAINS ITS USE

Dr. Axel Kopp of Copenhagen, in Charge, Declares Method Outclasses Telegraph System in Simplicity.

A successful experiment at "wireless telephoning" across the Charles river was made this afternoon by A. Frederick Collins of Newark, N. J., to show Massachusetts capitalists the practicality of the device which is intended ultimately to supplant the old method.

Among those who were present at the experiment were J. W. Long, George Eliot, Frank Florence, W. R. DeGrucey, Clarence H. Kelsea, Henry Skilton, H. S. Osborne, Emery Low and George A. Smith.

The apparatus was a conductivity of 25-volts resistance. The electrical waves were carried through the water over a distance of about a quarter of a mile. It is the first time that experiments of this nature have been carried on in Massachusetts. The apparatus is of simple construction, being identical on either side of the river.

The electrical waves were received at each end by plates of copper and zinc a yard square. Dr. Axel C. S. L. Kopp of Copenhagen, who took part in the experiments, said that the telephone was not yet perfected, but that the experiments that are now being carried on gave promise that in a short time the wireless telephone would be perfected and would be a competitor of wireless telegraphy. He also said that if he had had a larger voltage resistance the experiments this afternoon would have been a great deal more successful than they were.

Dr. Kopp claims that the wireless telephone is more practical than the wireless telegraph because it does not require an expert to operate it. He gave as an instance the following:

"In case of war if an operator of a wireless telegraph station was unable to attend to his instrument there would be no one able to send important messages. In the case of the wireless telephone any one can operate it. It is easily moved from place to place and it is expected when it is perfected, to be superior to all other methods of communication."

SHIRLEY OPENING POSTPONED.

SHIRLEY, Mass.—The opening of the new state industrial school for boys, which was to have taken place today, has been postponed until next Saturday. The grounds are still in a condition of incompletion and the trustees deemed it wise to postpone the event to allow a general cleaning.

Citizens of Salem Tomorrow Will Present Rich Silver Service to the Scout Cruiser Namesake

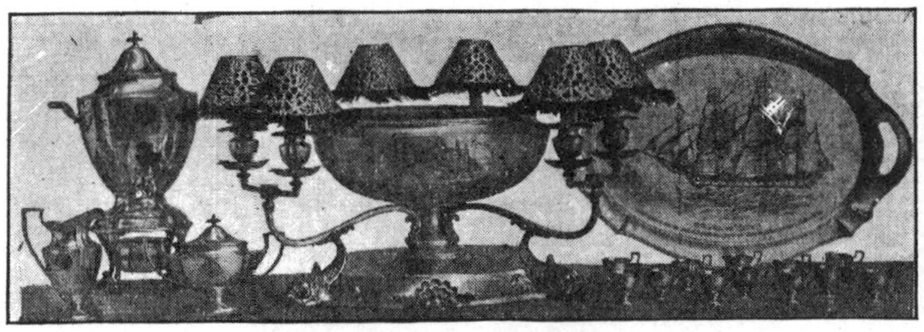

GIFT OF SALEM PEOPLE TO THEIR WARSHIP.

This silver set was purchased from a fund raised by a popular subscription of ten cents each. It proved to be immensely popular.

MALDEN EXPECTS LOWER TAX RATE

The tax rate in Malden, which will be announced this week, is expected to be greatly reduced this year owing to rigid research by the present assessors of Malden. The rate, it is understood, will be in the neighborhood of $17, against the rate last year of $19.50.

A year ago a finance commission was appointed by Mayor Richards to investigate the city's financial condition. As a result the assessors were asked for their resignations on account of allowing over $2,000,000 of personal property and real estate to escape their notice.

NAGEL TO LEAVE CHICAGO.

CHICAGO—The secretary of commerce and labor, Mr. Nagel, will return to Washington early in the week.

Bursting Bombs, the Glare of Red Fire, Aquatic Parade and Concert Will Usher in the Merry-Making.

SALEM, Mass.—Old Home week observance starts here tonight with an illumination at the Willows and Juniper point. Promptly at 8 o'clock three big bombs will be set off, and this will be the signal for the burning of red fire, great quantities of which will be lighted at Fort Lee. This display will be visible all along the North Shore. Beside the fireworks there will be a parade in which

(Continued on Page Five, Column Four.)

REFINED SUGAR PRICE RAISED.

NEW YORK—All grades of refined sugar were advanced 10 cents a hundred pounds today.

FITCHBURG POWER RIGHT CURTAILED

FITCHBURG, Mass.—Aldermen who are investigating say that the state gas and electric light commissioners established a precedent for Massachusetts when they revised the franchise granted by the board of aldermen to the Connecticut River Transmission Company, cutting out clauses providing for pole locations in streets not on the direct transmission line and prohibiting the power concern from running its wires close to industrial establishments

The Fitchburg Gas & Electric Light Company is due to handle every bit of power sold in Fitchburg. It will deliver the power over locations which the aldermen will be asked to grant. In the original franchise the transmission company was given permission to run a line by several mills and factories.

OFF TO APPROVE NEW TOWER PLAN

U. S. Architect Leaves Boston to Present His Favor of Custom House Change to Secretary MacVeagh.

Supervising Architect J. K. Taylor left Boston today for Washington, where he will send in his approval of the plans for the proposed custom house tower to Secretary of the Treasury Franklin MacVeagh. Mr. Taylor will also recommend to the treasury chief the temporary quarters for the custom house during the time of the repairs to the present building.

When asked for information relative to the site of the temporary quarters, Mr. Taylor said that he could not speak for publication until he had filed a report in Washington.

There is every reason to believe, however, that the Washington official favors the R. H. Stearns Building on Tremont street.

NEW CITY RECORD URGED BY MAYOR

Mayor Hibbard, in a communication to the board of aldermen today urged the establishment of the City Record, a municipal publication, as soon as practically possible.

On the advice of Corporation Counsel Babson the mayor says that unless the city newspaper is established before Sept. 10 no contract that requires advertisement can legally be made by the city.

To meet this situation the mayor transmitted an order establishing the paper to be published weekly at the selling price of $1 a year or 5 cents a copy. The rates for advertising are left by the mayor to be fixed later.

Mayor Hibbard also sent in an order transferring $5000 from the reserve fund to start the paper. The orders were referred to the committee on public improvements.

OPEN MUSHROOM EXHIBITION TODAY

Edible and Non-Edible Varieties Are Shown at Display of the Boston Mycological Club on State Street.

Many interesting varieties of mushrooms will be shown this afternoon at the weekly exhibition of the Boston Mycological Club in the Merchants National Bank building, 28 State street.

These exhibitions are of an educational nature, and are intended to instruct the general public to distinguish between edible and non-edible mushrooms. The public is invited to attend the exhibitions, which will be open from now on every Monday from 12 noon until 3 p. m., until Oct. 1.

These exhibitions, which are in charge of Miss J. F. Conant, consist of the best specimens obtained during the week by the club. Last week's products are somewhat smaller than usual. The edible varieties are labeled with white cards, non-edible with red cards and those the nature of which has not been definitely determined with green cards.

Among the best specimens on exhibition this week are a fine bunch of clilocybe nulpiceps, a large white variety of hyrophorus, a bright yellow variety found in swamps, agaricus campetris and the ordinary meadow mushrooms, which variety is most familiar for table consumption.

TRAGEDY IN WESTPORT.

NEW BEDFORD, Mass.—Robert M. Fanning, a well-known resident of Westport, slew his wife, Tina Hall Fanning, at about 1 o'clock this morning near their home and later came to the central police station in this city where, after handing to an officer a letter expressing regret for what had happened and requesting good care for his infant daughter, he committed suicide by shooting. Mrs. Fanning was the daughter of George Hall, a wealthy and prominent citizen of Westport.

THE CHRISTIAN SCIENCE MONITOR

LAST EDITION. BOSTON, MASS., SATURDAY, MAY 7, 1910—VOL. II., NO. 137. PRICE TWO CENTS.

HUGE PARK SQUARE REALTY PROJECT IS GIVEN OUT IN DETAIL

Development of 17 Acres of Property Worth $4,500,000 One of Largest American City Enterprises.

STREETS APPROVED

Plan to Take Land on St. James Avenue to Give 100-Foot Approach Is Being Considered.

The proposed development of the old Park square railroad station property is expected to prove one of the most notable real estate projects that has ever been put through in any large American city. It will open up approximately 17 acres in Boston's business section which have lain idle since the Boston & Providence railroad moved into the South Station terminal.

This land is now assessed for $4,500,000, but it is impossible to estimate the probable increase in real estate values in the vicinity that would naturally follow the pending improvements.

Final permission of both the Boston street commissioners and the mayor has now been obtained for the cutting of a 70-foot thoroughfare lengthwise through the entire tract. This will be known as Stuart street extension, and will run from Clarendon street to Columbus avenue near its junction with Ferdinand street.

Only the mayor's approval is now needed to authorize construction of another wide highway, to be called Arlington street extension, from opposite Ferdinand street northerly to Providence street, whence it will turn and run to Park square. Arlington street extension will probably eventually be prolonged, after demolition of intervening buildings, so as to run through to Arlington and Boylston streets.

Plans have also been considered for the taking of some $1,180,000 assessed value of land on the south side of St. James avenue and its extension as a 100-foot avenue to Park square. This would relieve the congestion at the Public Garden entrance to the subway, but the cost, especially in view of the damage to Westminster Chambers and adjoining properties, would be exceedingly heavy.

It had been the intention, in the event of the widening of St. James avenue, to rely on an act of 1904, permitting such landtaking. Some question as to the constitutionality of that act has just been raised, however, in the recent opinion given by the Massachusetts supreme court to the Legislature with reference to the feasibility of a North-South station tunnel boulevard. However, if a pending amendment to the state constitution is adopted, it is probable that any constitutional objections to this St. James avenue taking will be removed.

It is probable that actual work on the Stuart-Arlington street extensions will begin within 60 days. The expense, amounting to slightly under $100,000, will be borne by the Park Square Real Estate Trust.

Following the completion of these streets it is expected that several commodious buildings will be erected. The money, for some of them at least, will be furnished by the trust, although no definite plans as to what the buildings will be have as yet been made.

The situation up to the present is that the New Haven railroad has placed the property in the hands of four trustees with full powers for its development on broad lines. A most adequate carrying-out of the plan would seem assured, not only from its railroad backing, but also from the fact that the trustees are men of exceptional business experience and caliber. These trustees, as appointed by the trust deed of last year, are Moses Williams, Amory A. Lawrence, Alfred Bowditch and Laurence Minot.

The trust deed also authorized an issue, already outstanding, of $5,200,000 certificates, all of which is held by the New Haven road in formal payment for the property. Further future issues of shares and the putting out of not exceeding $4,000,000 notes or bonds are provided for.

A public offering of the outstanding shares, now owned entirely by the New Haven, will probably be made.

Advantages to Be Gained By Opening Park Square Realty for Investment

PROJECT will open up 17 acres of downtown Boston property which has long lain idle.

Two streets will be extended to give access to land that is to be developend.

Land is now assessed for $4,500,000, but its improvement will greatly increase values.

Bonds of $5,200,000 are outstanding and will be offered to public later.

Work on the extension of the streets will begin within 60 days.

The New King of England

His Majesty George V. successor to Edward VII.

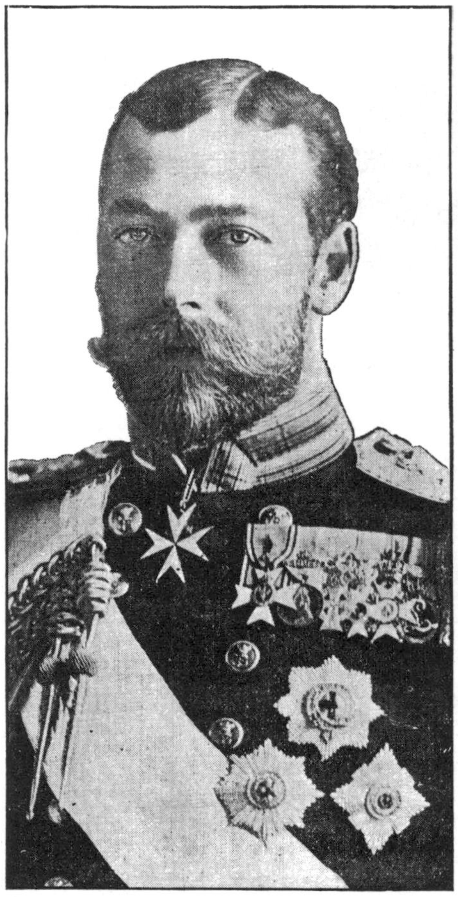

The Late King Edward

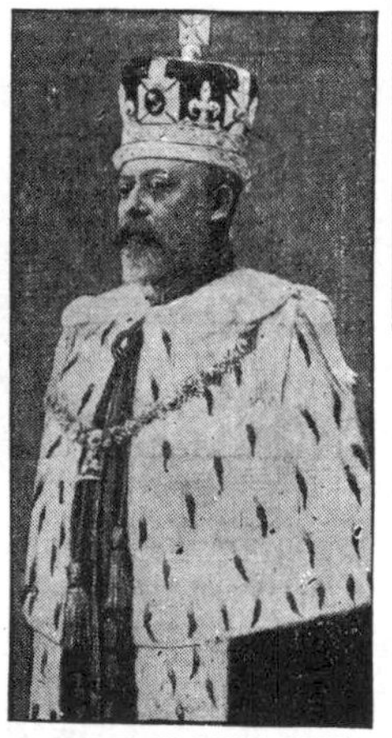

MONARCH IN ROYAL ROBES.
As Prince of Wales he won hearts of all Americans during his visit here in 1860.

The New Queen of England

Mary Victoria who succeeds Queen Alexandra.

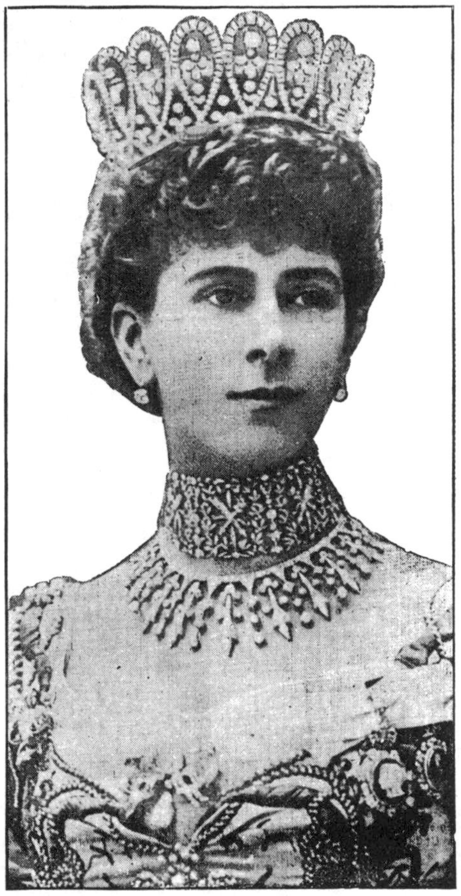

COSTA RICA RELIEF WORK CONTINUING WITH ALL RAPIDITY

SAN JUAN DEL SUR, Nicaragua—Relief work at the scene of the earthquake in Cartago is continuing as rapidly as Costa Rica can bring aid to the city. The authorities are making every effort to care for those rendered destitute by the earthquake, which left scarcely a house standing.

Martial law has been declared in the town to prevent disorder. The survivors are being removed to San Jose, 14 miles distant.

SAN JOSE, Costa Rica—Latest estimates of Wednesday's earthquake place casualties at 2000. Thousands were injured. Food and clothing are lacking.

Cartago was affected most and 1000 persons probably perished there. The town was destroyed. Only a few buildings in the suburbs still stand and the survivors, homeless, are hungry.

The entire interior of Costa Rica suffered. Paraiso and Pacaca, mentioned in Friday's despatches, were almost obliterated. Hundreds perished in these cities.

President Gonzales Viquez and President-elect Ricardo Jiminez with nurses and soldiers, are in the destroyed cities.

The property loss is variously estimated at from $25,000,000 to $50,000,000.

PANAMA—Advices received here from the province of Cartago in Costa Rica state that the earthquake shocks of Wednesday night affected the towns along the railroad line from Cartago to Port Limon.

The American National Red Cross will receive contributions for the earthquake victims at Cartago, Costa Rica. Donations should be sent to the treasurer of the American National Red Cross in Washington or to Gardiner M. Lane, 44 State street, Boston.

HIGH STATE TAX IS PREDICTED.

The state tax this year will be between $5,500,000 and $6,000,000, according to Representative Norman H. White of Brookline, House chairman of the ways and means committee, the subcommittee of the Legislature which handles the state's finances. The state tax last year was $4,500,000. The high mark thus far is $5,500,000, established in 1908.

FIELD DAY FOR KEENE DAUGHTERS

KEENE, N. H.—Keene members and friends of the Daughters of the American Revolution will hold a field day at Concord and Lexington, Mass., on Tuesday, May 10.

CHANGE OF ENGLISH RULE ALTERS TOUR OF EX-PRESIDENT

STOCKHOLM, Sweden—The European entertainment of Theodore Roosevelt will be considerably curtailed as the result of the change of sovereigns in Great Britain.

Out of courtesy Mr. Roosevelt has cancelled all programs arranged for him at Berlin and at London, as well as here, and his visits to the three capitals will probably be of a very simple character.

Mr. Roosevelt and his party will leave here tomorrow afternoon for Berlin, unless the program is altered later today.

Mr. Roosevelt does not yet know what change will be made in his plans for his visits to Berlin and London.

He and his wife visited three museums today and he reviewed a cavalry drill this afternoon. This evening a municipal dinner will be given in his honor.

LONDON—The change of sovereigns will mean the abandonment of the principal functions of ex-President Roosevelt's tour. The official receptions and the embassy entertainments will be cancelled, and the presentation of the freedom of the city and the luncheon at the Guildhall will probably be given up. If Mr. Roosevelt's visit to England is carried out it will be shorn of all display.

BERLIN—Emperor William of Germany, nephew of the late King of England, is expected to go to London. This may result in a cancellation of Mr. Roosevelt's visit to Berlin May 9-15.

MEN CONFIDENT OF STRIKE ENDING

PROVIDENCE, R. I.—Encouraged by the conference between representatives of the building trades council and officials of the J. W. Bishop Company, who have charge of the work of constructing the Greystone mills near North Providence, the 1000 building laborers who have been on strike there since the first of the month feel confident that their grievances will be amicably adjusted today.

The men want an increase in pay and a shorter working day.

BIGGER FALL RIVER DIVIDEND.

FALL RIVER, Mass.—The statement of the dividends of local corporations for the second quarter of 1910, just issued from the office of G. M. Haffards & Co., shows a total of $442,650 on a capitalization of $27,105,000, an average of 1.68 per cent, an increase over that of the like quarter in 1909.

HAIL GEORGE V. KING OF BRITISH DOMAINS IN CEREMONY TODAY

Erstwhile Prince of Wales Is Sworn Before the Privy Council in Throne Room of St. James Palace.

ACCEPTS HIS TRUST

First Proclamation of New Monarch Is for All Officially to Proceed With Their Regular Duties.

LONDON—King George V. was formally administered the oath of office as the reigning monarch in succession to the late King Edward from the quadrangle of St. James Palace at 4 o'clock this afternoon.

The privy council met at the palace in accordance with the time-honored custom and formally declared King Edward deceased. Immediately afterward the government leaders visited King George who had driven to the palace and was in an adjoining room. The lord chancellor advanced and administered the dual oaths of office affecting England and Scotland, which were responded to amid a silence that was impressive.

The new ruler at once announced that he would ascend the throne as King George V. The heir apparent, Prince Edward Albert, then stepped forward and the oath of succession was administered to him, following the ancient ritual of the British throne.

The new King in his speech of acceptance, if such it might be called, made several touching allusions to the father of whom he had just been bereft and to the trying circumstances under which he was being called to the throne.

The ceremony of swearing the new King was begun by the firing of the royal salute of 101 guns, which was concluded just as the King finished his speech.

The administering of the oath and the speech of the King were to have been followed by the reading of the royal proclamation from the quadrangle of the palace, the proclamation having been prepared by the privy council. Owing to the lateness of the hour, however, the proclamation was postponed until Monday morning at 9 o'clock. This proclamation reads as follows:

"Whereas it has pleased Almighty God to call in his mercy our late sovereign, King Edward, of blessed and glorious memory, from whose decease the imperial crown of Great Britain and Ireland solely and rightfully comes to the high and mighty Prince George;

"We, therefore, as lords of the spiritual and temporal realm, being here assisted by these members of his late majesty's privy council, with numbers of other principal gentlemen of quality, and with the lord mayor, aldermen and citizens of London, hereby with one voice consent, and with tongue and heart publish and proclaim that the high and mighty Prince George, now by the death of our late sovereign of happy memory, becomes our only rightful liege lord, George V. by the grace of God, of the United Kingdom of Great Britain and Ireland and of the British dominions beyond the seas King, defender of the faith, and Emperor of India, toward whom we acknowledge all faith and constant obedience, and with all hearty and humble affection beseeching God, through whom kings and queens reign, to bless the royal King George V. with long and happy years to reign over us.

"Given at the court of St. James on this the seventh day of May, 1910."

A fanfare from the heralds followed,

(Continued on Page Eleven, Column One.)

HERE IS ANALYTICAL STUDY BY A HARVARD PROFESSOR

Frederick C. de Sumichrast, Former President of the Victorian Club of Boston, Tells About the Complex Problems Confronting New King of England.

Prof. Frederick C. de Sumichrast of Harvard University, a native of England, today said:

"King George V. was aware that some day he, in his turn, would have to undertake the grave duties of ruler of the British empire. The need for his doing so has arisen with startling suddenness, and the new sovereign is confronted with some problems that demand, for their safe solution, the highest statesmanship and the greatest prudence. In the forefront is the complicated situation in Great Britain.

"The ministry which is now in power is admittedly a weak one, the slave of conflicting interests and claims put forward with fierce intensity by the Radicals, the socialists, the Laborites, the Irish. This is a serious handicap for the new ruler; he is at once plunged into a difficult crisis which has already aroused violent political passions.

"The Liberal ministry looks, as a last resort, to the creation of a practically infinite number of peers to overcome the adverse majority in the present House of Lords. It is in the highest degree unlikely that King Edward would ever have consented to applying so heroic a remedy, although he did favor the reforms indicated by Lord Rosebery, but it is still more improbable that his successor will allow himself to be thus made use of. He will then find himself in opposition to his titular advisers, who will go to the country on the cry of royal hostility to democracy.

"On the other hand, he will have the great majority of the people with him, and an election run on the lines suggested will almost surely result in a bad defeat for the Asquith cabinet. But the problem of the Lords is not the only domestic difficulty which has to be faced.

"The contest between tariff reform and the perpetuation of a form of free trade which places Great Britain at a disadvantage not only with foreign countries but even with her own colonies, that contest has to be fought out, and the new King cannot remain a merely passive spectator, for, even within the broad limits of his constitutional prerogative, he can exercise a powerful influence on the policy of the country. The chances are that, having not long since traveled through the length and breadth of the empire and seen conditions for himself and not through the eyes of partizans, he will incline to the policy of tariff reform.

"Another problem is the perennial Irish question which is closely related ot the question of redistribution of seats. That some form of home rule, which shall preserve intact the union, will ere long be granted to the Irish is much more than probable. The study of the problem, the better acquaintance with the working of autonomy in the great component states of the empire, which are none the less very loyal, will surely tend to dissipate some of the fear felt by the adversaries of home rule. The new King has given no indication of his views in this regard, but views, and clear-cut ones, he must have in the near future, even if he has none now.

"It is one of the burdens of power that the man who is entrusted with it must be prepared to decide and to say why he so decides.

"Then there are other problems within the empire, no longer merely domestic but distinctly imperial. It was most important that the first Parliament of the Union of South Africa should be opened by the heir to the throne, in view of the impossibility of this function being discharged by the sovereign himself. Now, of course, some arrangement will have to be devised to satisfy the British and Dutch in South Africa, and to smooth some of the many difficulties which the union is intended to remove. It is not Viscount Gladstone who can accomplish that task; the King's own sense and ability will have to come into play.

"India presents another complex case. The recent changes made in the constitution of the Governor-General's council, which have turned it into a sort of Indian imperial Parliament, and the other changes in the making up and powers of the provincial councils, have inaugurated a new era in the mode of ruling that immense dependency with its 300,000,000 inhabitants. The new King has been in India; he is a student and may have formed clear opinions of his own on this all-important point.

"Then he has the European problems to face. The entente cordiale with France was brought about by his father who had special advantages in this respect, advantages which George V. does not possess. It is not enough to create; one must maintain. King Edward maintained the entente and made it firmer; his son and successor has that task before him.

"The analogous relations with the other great powers are not so firmly settled: Russia may renew aspirations which the Japanese war crushed for a time, and these aspirations may reawaken the Russian scare which has of recent years been replaced by the dread of war with Germany. Here again are

(Continued on Page Eleven, Column Four).

TEACHERS IN BUSY PROGRAM ON FINAL DAY OF CONVENTION

Reports, Attendance on Lectures at Museum and Reception Are on Art Instructors' List for Day.

'PURE DESIGN' TALK

Election of Arthur D. Dean as President and of Other Officers Is Decided at the Morning Session.

A business meeting, a series of lectures at the Museum of Fine Arts and a reception at the Normal Art School are scheduled for the teachers attending the convention of the Eastern Art and Manual Training Teachers Association today, the final day of the convention.

Dr. Denman W. Ross of Harvard University, the first speaker at this morning's meeting, read a paper on "The Study of Pure Design," in which he preached a delightful sermon on "Order," not only in the study and execution of pure design but in daily life as well.

John J. Enneking, the Boston painter, speaking on "Manual Training from the Artist's Point of View," told of the training of an artist and laid emphasis on certain ideals for which the art student should strive.

He pointed out that success in painting depends entirely on the individual. The teacher can instruct him in the various theories of expression, the mere grammar of art, but he cannot teach him art itself.

Mr. Enneking recommended that art students keep in mind the favorite motto of the Japanese artists: "First style, then system, then character."

At the business meeting held at 10 o'clock at the Art Museum the following officers were elected: President, Arthur D. Dean, Albany, N. Y.; vice-president, Walter R. Perry, Brooklyn, N. Y.; recording secretary, Miss Eva E. Struble, Newark, N. J.; corresponding secretary, Ada B. Williams, Cleveland, O.; editor, F. H. Daniels, Newton.

The secretary reported that 155 active members and 157 associate members had joined the association during the convention. It was voted that the association become a chapter of the American Federation of Art.

CHINESE PRINCE THANKS MR. TAFT

WASHINGTON—President Taft has received a telegram of farewell from Prince Tsai Tao of China who is now on his way to Europe. The telegram is as follows:

Mr. President: As I am bidding farewell to the American shores, I desire to thank you with all my heart for the magnificent reception given me by the government and people of the United States in every place that I have visited. I shall carry away with me to my own country all the memories of my stay in the United States. Long may heaven bless you with health and happiness.

(Signed) TSAI TAO.

FIFTY ARE SAVED FROM A STEAMER

The steamer Normandy sank off St. Johns, N. F., today, but all on board were rescued, according to information received by the marine department of the Boston Chamber of Commerce.

It is said that the Normandy was on her way to ply the lakes, and that there were 50 passengers on board.

GOVERNMENT RESTS HEINZE CASE.

NEW YORK—Following the testimony of Expert Accountant John P. Fernsler in the trial of F. A. Heinze for the alleged misapplication of funds of the Mercantile National Bank in 1907 in the United States circuit court, the government rested its case.

SOUTH END TO ASK MORE CARS.

The railroad commissioners will give a hearing Thursday on the petition of the South End Improvement Association for a relocation of the cars running between Grove Hall and the Park street subway, via Blue Hill avenue and Dudley street.

The Little Prayer of King Edward VII. as Taught Him When a Boy by Mother

O ALMIGHTY GOD, I thank Thee for all the mercies which Thou hast given me this day. Take me this night under the shadow of Thy wing and grant that I may rise again in health and safety, for Thou only canst protect me. Bless dear papa, mama, my brother and sisters, and make me a good boy through Jesus Christ, our Lord.—Evening prayer of Prince of Wales as taught him about 1851 by his mother, Queen Victoria.

THE CHRISTIAN SCIENCE MONITOR

LAST EDITION — BOSTON, MASS., TUESDAY, MAY 16, 1911—VOL. III., NO. 145 — PRICE TWO CENTS

EXPERT CHASE SAYS SINKING FUND INQUIRY STARTED BY HAMLIN

Appears Before the Committee on Ways and Means of the Legislature to Answer Statements of Mr. Stevens.

HAS DATA WITH HIM

Says That When the Examination Began He Had Not Expected to Find "Crude Mathematical Mistakes."

Claiming that he started his investigation of the sinking funds of the state at the request of Charles S. Hamlin at the time he was Democratic candidate for Governor and pointing out an alleged mistake of $110,000, Harvey S. Chase appeared before the legislative joint committee on ways and means again today for another hearing on the recent investigation made of the state treasurer's department by Mr. Chase at the direction of Governor Foss. State Treasurer Elmer A. Stevens was present also.

Today's hearing was given for the express purpose of allowing Mr. Chase to reply to criticisms of his report made before the committee by Treasurer Stevens at a former hearing. In asking for another opportunity to be heard in defense of his report, Mr. Chase claimed that the remarks of the treasurer had impaired his reputation as an efficient business man.

Mr. Chase brought with him to the committee room today several large charts and other data with the aid of which, he said, he expected to refute Mr. Stevens' argument that the system of computing sinking funds now in vogue in the treasury department is superior to that proposed by Mr. Chase.

Mr. Chase declared that the attack of Treasurer Stevens had been unprovoked and wholly unexpected by him, but maintained that the theory and argument of the latter were based upon fallacy.

"When we began the examination," said Mr. Chase, "we did not expect to find crude mathematical mistakes. We were greatly surprised when we found the first of them, which was in the computations relating to one of the direct debt sinking funds, as follows:

"In order to familiarize ourselves with Mr. Stevens' methods and to verify his sinking fund calculations, we picked out one sinking fund—the war loan—and computed it ourselves according to the treasurer's method. We came out at the end with a deficiency of $17,000 in the fund, whereas the treasurer's figures on his clerk's working sheets showed a surplus of $93,000 in the same fund—a difference of $110,000 (the sum of these two amounts).

"We examined our figures carefully. I spent three hours one Saturday night at my office going over them myself. We could find no inaccuracies. On Monday morning I went with Mr. Tuttle to the treasurer's office and asked the clerk for the original computations on this sinking fund. These were given to us and we took them to the auditor's office, where a room had been placed at our disposal at the beginning of the whole investigation where we examined the clerk's figures and soon found the trouble. Instead of adding 1 per cent to the

(Continued on Page Four, Column Four.)

NEWTON TO RAISE TEN THOUSAND FOR PLAYGROUND

Aiming to complete the $10,000 fund needed to increase the playground facilities of Newton, a committee of 21 members of the Waban Improvement Society will commence a canvass this week.

It is proposed to purchase land for playground purposes in the Waban section of the city. The movement has the indorsement of Mayor Hatfield.

FREE SCHOLARSHIPS IN TECHNOLOGY BILL CUTS GRANT $20,000

Richard C. Maclaurin, President of Institute, Points Out Objection to Measure Before Governor.

CITES SCHOOL NEEDS

Indicates That $100,000 Yearly From the State Is Required to Provide Expansion to Meet Demands.

Special attention is called by Richard C. Maclaurin, president of the Institute of Technology, in a statement given to The Christian Science Monitor today to the fact that the institute will in reality receive only $80,000 state aid under the provisions of the bill now before the Governor, granting $100,000 subsidy annually to the institute, with the requirement that two students from each state senatorial district be given free scholarships.

There will be 80 such free scholarships, valued at a total of $20,000 annually.

President Maclaurin's statement follows:

A resolve of the Legislature grant-

(Continued on Page Five, Column Four.)

PLAN TO MAKE ROOM FOR THE ADDITIONAL HIGH SCHOOL PUPILS

With the prospect of having about 14,000 pupils in Boston's high schools in September the school committee with the aid of the schoolhouse commissioners will start at once to work out a plan for providing accommodations for the several hundred increase over last year.

At the meeting of the committee Monday evening it was estimated that a bill carrying at least $120,000 will have to be passed in order to provide the necessary accommodations and a new school will probably have to be erected.

On receiving the report of W. Stanford Field, director of the evening and continuation schools, the committee decided to take up the question of keeping out of the evening high schools the hundreds of students who enter annually and then drop out. Mr. Field's report states that last year 4000 of these pupils left the evening high schools the first month, while several hundred others attended only occasionally.

He pointed out that those who entered and then discontinued the attendance prevented many others from gaining entrance at the beginning of the year when the accommodations were restricted.

HOUSE VOTES INQUIRY INTO AFFAIRS OF U. S. STEEL CORPORATION

WASHINGTON—A sweeping investigation of the United States Steel Corporation was ordered today when Representative Stanley's resolution passed the House unanimously.

The debate on the resolution was marked by a discussion of the supreme court decision in the Standard Oil Company by Representative Borland (Dem., Mo.).

Democrats of the House are seeking today for some way to minimize the effect of the action of Representative Anderson of Ohio, also a

(Continued on Page Two, Column Seven.)

In remailing your copies of the Monitor to others the following postage schedule will be helpful . . . .

Issues of 12 to 16 pages require postage 1c
Issues of 18 to 32 pages require postage 2c
Issues of 32 to 48 pages require postage 3c
Issues containing 60 pages require postage 4c
Issues containing 68 pages require postage 4c
Issues containing 96 pages require postage 6c

AMENDMENT URGED TO TRUST LAW, DUE TO THE OIL DECISION

Senate Progressives Meet and Agree to Ask Congress to Remove Loophole Left by Use of Qualifying Word.

OLD RULE REVERSED

Combination Held to Be Monopoly in "Unreasonable" Restraint of Trade Allowed Half Year Grace.

WASHINGTON—At an informal conference of Senate progressives today it was decided to urge an amendment to the Sherman anti-trust law as a result of the Standard Oil decision, reading as follows:

"No combination in restraint of trade shall be regarded as reasonable within the terms of this act."

It is the view of the progressives that writing by the court of the word "reasonable" before "restraint of trade" has afforded a loophole for the escape of big monopolies.

When President Taft and his cabinet assemble today they will immediately take up the decision handed

(Continued on Page Two, Column One.)

STANDARD TO OBEY DECREE BUT GO RIGHT ON SAYS ITS COUNSEL

NEW YORK—The Standard Oil Company will obey the decree of the supreme court. This was the statement today of M. F. Elliot, chief counsel for the company.

"Not having yet seen the opinion of the court in full," he said, "it is impossible to make any long statement. The full opinion must be read and studied by my associates and myself before it can be intelligently dealt with.

"It may now be said, however, that the Standard Oil Company will obey the decree of the court and that all the companies embraced in the court's decree will carry on their business as usual under the direction of their own officers and through their own corporate organization."

CHICAGO—Alfred B. Eddy, general counsel of the Standard in Chicago, said today:

"The Standard company of New Jersey has wittingly or unwittingly violated a law which is not understood even by its framers. The immediate danger of today's decision, it appears to me, lies in the fact that hundreds of thousands of people will read only the yellow press opinions on the effects of the decision, instead of reading the decision itself.

"The business of the Standard Oil Company will go on as usual, although conditions will be made to comply with the statute law and the decisions affecting it. With the provisions of the Sherman law clearly understood, the Standard Oil Company will be able to go forward with a certainty and a precision that it has not known for many years.

"It now remains for the managers of this great business organization to meet the changed conditions through reorganization."

FENWAY LAND BILL IN HANDS OF GOV. FOSS

The Boston News Bureau says today:

The Fenway lands bill providing for the extension of Boylston street and the further opening up of these lands, has passed both branches of the Legislature and is now in the hands of Governor Foss.

The Governor has always been a believer in the development of these Fenway lands and long ago invested several hundred thousand dollars in them at less than the assessed valuation.

The only question that can now arise concerning the Governor's action on the bill is as to whether he will let it become law without his signature. Of course Mr. Foss never had any idea of being Governor when he put his money into Back Bay lands. He was then, as now, simply a believer in the port of Boston.

The bill providing for a street across the Back Bay Fens to connect Huntington avenue with Audubon road became a law without Governor Foss' signature Monday, the time limit having expired.

GOV. DIX URGES INCOME TAX.

ALBANY, N. Y.—Governor Dix sent a letter today to Speaker Frisbie of the Assembly urging the House to take action on the pending income tax amendment to the United States constitution.

U. S. SUPREME COURT THAT DECIDED BIG CASE

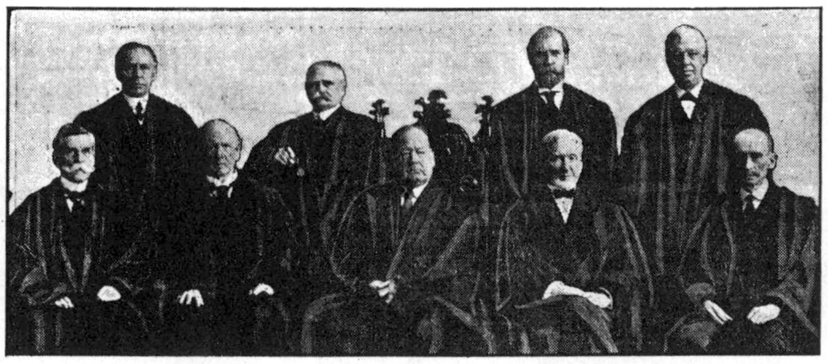

(Copyright by Harris & Ewing, Washington, D. C.)

Top row—Justices Van Devanter, Lurton, Hughes and Lamar. Second row—Justices Holmes and Harlan, Chief Justice White, Justices McKenna and Day.

LYNN SHOE FACTORY OWNERS FAVOR PLAN TO ABOLISH STRIKES

LYNN, Mass.—"To make Lynn the banner shoe city of the world" was the sentiment at the continued meeting of the Lynn Shoe Manufacturers Association here today.

A committee was appointed to consider the articles of the peace agreement offered by the labor unions whereby it is hoped to avoid all lockouts and strikes in the future.

Among the manufacturers and workers a desire is evidenced for the signing of some agreement whereby all disputes will be left either to state or to local arbitration, the men continuing at work, and the differences in wages to be adjusted from the date of the beginning of the dispute. In this way there will not be the great loss in wages that now obtains in the case of lockouts and strikes.

The election of officers by the manufacturers association was again deferred and will be taken up at the next meeting. The A. M. Creighton Company signed an agreement today with seven labor unions whereby there will be no differences for the ensuing year. A similar agreement was signed Monday by Brophey Brothers.

HOUSE SUSTAINS GOV. FOSS' VETO ON LIVING COST REPORT

By a vote of 188 to 23 the House today sustained Governor Foss' veto of the bill providing for the printing of additional copies of the report of the state commission on the cost of living.

Following the roll call on this question the House adjourned, having finished its calendar for the day.

This is the first time that the House calendar has been finished at the morning session.

In the debate on the question of sustaining the Governor's veto Representative Washburn of Worcester, speaking in support of the veto, called the attention of the House to the political at-

(Continued on Page Two, Column Three.)

S. J. ELDER CALLS OIL DECISION WHOLESOME

Samuel J. Elder of Boston, who was one of the American representatives at the Newfoundland fisheries conference at The Hague, in discussing the Standard Oil decision said today:

"I think the decision will have a wholesome effect. It was practically unanimous and Justice Harlan's dissent does not detract from the force of the opinion as to restraint of trade.

"It is now clearly shown to the country that undue or unreasonable restraint of trade is within the prohibition of the act.

"The decision has long been discounted in financial circles and is not likely to cause disturbance. The uncertainty, however, as to what the decision would be has delayed important undertakings and developments. These projects undoubtedly will now be prosecuted with vigor."

Dana Malone, former attorney-general of Massachusetts, said that such a decision had been expected for a long time and that it would have a salutary effect. It is of the utmost importance to business, he pointed out, that the question should be settled.

Melville M. Bigelow, dean of the Boston University law school, said that the questions involved were so great that he would not presume to form an opinion till he had read the decision.

Former Gov. John D. Long said: "This decision will have an exceedingly favorable effect on the business of the country at large. It has long been discounted by the more astute business men, but nevertheless the final decision cannot fail to have a salutary effect."

Lyman B. Greenleaf, president of the Boston stock exchange: "The decision has long been anticipated by stock brokers, and the result, if anything, will be to stimulate the market. In my opinion the corporations will adjust themselves to the change which this precedent involves, and that the general result will work good all the way round."

W. J. Garland, assistant United States district attorney, said that he had not read the full decision, but that he considered it an epoch-making one. In his opinion, however, the Standard Oil Company will combine its business in some manner even though the present organization has been found to be illegal.

"The Standard Oil decision," said Louis A. Chandler, "emphasizes the fact of the general centralization of power in the federal government, where it properly belongs, following the recent decision by the same court in the federal corporation tax cases.

"The individual states have not enforced and evidently will not enforce the laws on their statute books which were designed to curb the rapacious exercise of the money power.

"It has remained for the strong central

(Continued on Page Two, Column Two.)

AVIATOR M'CURDY BOSTON VISITOR

J. A. D. McCurdy, the aviator, was in Boston Monday and made a visit to Marblehead to look over the aeroplane plant of the Burgess Company & Curtis.

Charles K. Hamilton's biplane has been repaired at the factory and will be taken to Squantum aviation field probably on Thursday where Mr. Hamilton will test it. The machine damaged by W. Starling Burgess during a flight two weeks ago is nearly ready for use again.

SPRINGFIELD FIRE PUT OUT AFTER $100,000 LOSS

SPRINGFIELD, Mass.—Fire that broke out in the L. J. Ball Company's grocery store on State street about noon today destroyed that building and two adjoining structures before it was brought under control about 1:30 p. m.

The buildings and contents, whose value is estimated at $100,000, are a total loss.

There were many rescues of people caught by rapidly spreading flames. Five bakers in the Call building were forced to make their escape by ladders, while a woman was carried from the top floor of the Estabrook building.

LOOKS FOR HARBOR BILL REPORT SOON

Senator Brown said this afternoon that his bill for an appropriation of $9,000,000 for the development of Boston harbor would be reported favorably, probably on Wednesday by the committee on metropolitan affairs.

The committee is considering substituting it for the original harbor proposition which called for the expenditure of $3,000,000, to be used for developing the Commonwealth property in East Boston only.

OHIO BRIBERY REPORT READY.

COLUMBUS, O.—A report by the grand jury investigating alleged bribery in the General Assembly is expected late this afternoon. It is known that a number of indictments have been found.

ZEPPELIN PASSENGER AIRSHIP DESTROYED AT DUESSELDORF

DUESSELDORF—The Zeppelin passenger-carrying airship Deutschland II. was destroyed here today.

The big dirigible was being taken from the shed preparatory to a flight to Frankfurt, with a number of passengers.

Just as the airship cleared the shed a gust of wind drove her back against the entrance. Several of the balloonettes burst and destroyed her equilibrium. The wind again lifted her and dropped her on the roof of the shed, a total wreck.

NEW YORK—Copies of the new official map of Canada, received at the Aero Club here indicate that in winning the James Gordon Bennett trophy last year, Alan R. Hawley established a new world's record for a continuous balloon flight. The America II. was credited with 1172 miles, but the new map shows it traveled 1207 miles, eclipsing the mark made by Count de La-aulx of 1192 miles, more than 10 years ago.

The Aero Club moved Monday from the Engineers building, in Thirty-ninth street, to the club's new home at the southeast corner of Forty-first street and Madison avenue.

RHEIMS—The world's speed records, with and without a passenger, were broken here Monday in monoplane flights. A speed of more than 160 kilometers (99.5 miles) an hour was attained in the first flight by Henry Weymann, an American, who started from Mourmelon with Count Robillard as a passenger.

Later Lieutenant Fequant in a new monoplane, with Lieutenant Biey acting as observation officer, made a flight over the same course. He completed the distance in 10m. 20s., attaining a speed of 162 kilometers (100.7 miles) an hour.

HARTFORD, Conn.—This city announced today exhibitions of flying by men from the Wright camp for May 29 and 30. The Connecticut Fair Association will conduct the meet. An intercity flight may be attempted to Springfield.

NEW HAVEN, Conn.—It is now expected that Glenn H. Curtiss will be here on Saturday to take part in the Yale Aero Club's meet. J. A. D. McCurdy will make attempts on Friday and Saturday to operate a wireless instrument from his machine and to send messages to New York.

KINGSTON, N. Y.—The balloon piloted by Leo Stevens, which ascended here, landed in the Green Pond woods, near Erving, Mass.

PHILADELPHIA—The aeroplane of Tom Sopwith was partially wrecked at the Point Breeze race track.

CHICAGO—The Aero Club of Chicago has raised $60,000 of $100,000 needed for a meet to be held from Aug. 12 to 18 at Grant Park.

STREET BOARD SAYS PARK SQUARE CHANGES WILL COST $2,184,370

Salem D. Charles, chairman of the board of street commissioners, submitted the report of the board for the estimated total cost of the proposed Park square improvements to the mayor today, setting $2,184,370 as the total estimated cost and $831,214.69 as the estimated benefits to the property holders in the vicinity.

The estimated cost includes widening and changing the grade and construction of Providence street, the extension of Arlington street from Boylston to Providence street, the widening of St. James avenue from Berkeley street to Copley square and the widening of Ferdinand street from Columbus avenue to Castle square.

Included in the report is the estimated cost of widening Pleasant street from Park square to Broadway. The report says in this connection:

"No detailed plans were available at the time you asked for the figures and consequently the work had to be delayed.

(Continued on Page Two, Column Four.)

OIL TRUST DECISION SENDS PRICES UP IN SECURITIES MARKETS

Considerable Irregularity on Account of Profit Taking, but Stocks Make Good Advance.

BUSINESS IS HEAVY

Fluctuations Are Numerous but There Is No Appearance of a Heavy Liquidation Anywhere.

The full text of the Standard Oil case decision may be found on pages 6, 7 and 8.

It was evident that the United States supreme court decision in the Standard Oil case was favorably regarded in the securities markets from the manner in which stocks advanced in both New York and London at the opening today.

Higher London prices for American securities foreshadowed a strong opening in New York and in this respect traders were not disappointed.

Standard Oil opened on the New York curb with sales at 679 to 675. It is now 675 to 680. The market closed yesterday at 675 to 680. The last sale being 679¾. There was considerable excitement on the curb.

The financial interests of Wall street gave considerable importance to the statement contained in the decision that corporations whose operations are "not unreasonably restrictive of competition" are not affected.

It was pointed out that the general belief had been that a decision adverse to the Standard Oil Company would be

(Continued on Page 14, Column 1.)

NEW MOVE TO PUNISH LABOR LEADERS FOR ALLEGED CONTEMPT

WASHINGTON—A commission was appointed today by Justice Daniel Wright of the District of Columbia supreme court, to determine whether Samuel Gompers, John Mitchell and Frank Morrison, the labor leaders, were guilty of contempt and upon their decision he will base further action in the case.

Justice Wright named as members of the commission J. J. Darlington, Daniel Davenport and James M. Beck, all three of whom were counsel against the labor leaders in the original contempt proceedings.

Justice Wright is proceeding on the instructions of the supreme court of the United States in the decision Monday, which set aside the jail sentences, but clearly indicated that it did so without prejudice. According to the view of Justice Wright the supreme court left open the possibility of Justice Wright himself ordering contempt proceedings against the three men for failure to obey an injunction issued by him.

It was held that the court dismissed the jail sentences on the ground that the action was brought by the Bucks Stove & Range Company and that in such event only a fine could be assessed. The inference was left that if the court itself had taken the initiative the result would have been different.

Justice Wright's order authorizes the commission to investigate the entire proceedings in which the labor leaders were sentenced and institute contempt proceedings if they deem the facts warrant such action under the direction of the supreme court.

Justice Wright said he ordered the investigation "to the end that the authority of the court may be established, vindicated and sustained."

DIAZ'S RESIGNATION REPORTED SENT TO MEXICAN CONGRESS

NEW YORK—A despatch from Mexico City says that it is stated upon highest authority there that the resignation of President Diaz has actually been written to take effect immediately.

The resignation is said to be in the hands of a special committee of the national Congress, but has not yet been accepted.

JUAREZ, Mexico—"Mexico will do everything in its power to bring about peace. The only thing that can block

(Continued on Page Two, Column Six.)

THE CHRISTIAN SCIENCE MONITOR

LAST EDITION — BOSTON, MASS., TUESDAY, OCTOBER 31, 1911—VOL. III., NO. 286 — PRICE TWO CENTS

CAMPAIGN MANAGERS FORECAST A VICTORY FOR MR. FROTHINGHAM

Supporters of Lieutenant-Governor Base Their Calculations for Election on Figures Used by Democrats

NO FIGURE IS SET

Candidates on State Ticket Prepare for Rallies to Be Held in Brockton, Taunton and Other Places

Campaign managers for Lieutenant-Governor Frothingham today forecast his election as Governor next Tuesday, basing their calculations on figures of probable results of the voting as estimated by leading Democrats.

In arriving at this conclusion the Republican leaders used the figures given for 18 large cities of the state, including Boston. Even if there were no change in all the other cities and towns of the state in the vote for Governor from that of last year, it is claimed that Mr. Frothingham will gain enough in these 18 cities to insure his victory.

No attempt was made to estimate how much Mr. Frothingham will probably win by.

Charles S. Baxter, campaign manager for Lieutenant-Governor Frothingham, in telling how he and his associates figured a victory for the Republican gubernatorial candidate, said: "We took figures given out by Democrats residing in these 18 cities. These Democrats were asked to state what they thought would be the result of the balloting for Governor in their cities only. Invariably the reply was that Mr. Foss will fall below what he received last year, and that Mr. Frothingham would gain over Governor Draper's vote of last year.

"They told us how much they thought the change would be and we used their figures in our estimates. They didn't agree with our figures in many cases. Mr. Frothingham's strength was underestimated, we thought, but we preferred to take the Democratic figures.

"In Boston, for instance, we asked several Democrats for their opinions of the conditions here. The result of the replies showed that these men as a whole believed that Mr. Foss will run 8000 votes behind his vote of last year. At that time he carried the city over Governor Draper by 28,000.

"While the average Democratic figures we received as estimates for this year was 20,000, we feel quite certain that the Governor cannot possibly get more than a 15,000 majority over Mr. Frothingham.

"In our estimate, however, we use the Democratic figures and give Mr. Foss credit for 20,000 majority.

"Many Republicans are figuring how the Democrats can claim a 20,000 majority for Mr. Foss when Mayor Fitzgerald running against Mr. Frothingham a few years ago for mayor of Boston received only about 8000 majority."

Continuing their tour of the large cities of eastern Massachusetts, which is the plan laid out for the closing days of the campaign, Lieutenant-Governor Frothingham and other Republican leaders will speak in Brockton and Taunton this evening. Mr. Frothingham will devote today to preparing for his speeches tonight, selecting such topics as may be used with effect in these cities.

Thirteen rallies arranged under the direction of the Republican state committee will be held in other parts of the state this evening. Leading Republicans have been assigned to speak at all of them.

The Brockton rally tonight will be held in Canton hall and the local Republican committee is planning to bring out a big audience. In addition to the Lieutenant-Governor, Robert Luce, Speaker Walker and Congressman Good of Iowa are the scheduled orators of the evening.

City hall, Taunton, is to be the scene

(Continued on page four, column three)

VOTE FOR MAYOR AT LOS ANGELES PRIMARY ELECTION

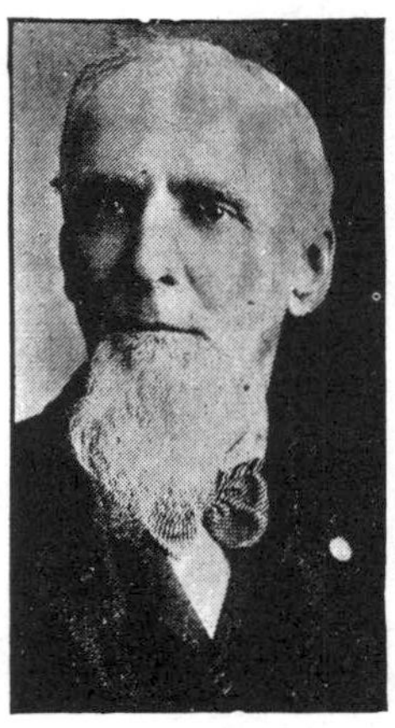

MAYOR GEORGE ALEXANDER

LOS ANGELES, Cal.—After an active campaign the municipal primary for the nomination of candidates for mayor is being held here today. Under the law any candidate receiving a majority of all votes cast at a primary is elected and need not be voted upon at the general election.

It is conceded that the mayoralty contest is between George Alexander, Republican incumbent, and Job Harriman, Socialist and one of the attorneys for James B. McNamara. Mushel and Gregory are the other candidates.

The constitutional amendment granting women the right of suffrage was not passed in time to permit them to vote in today's primary, but they will be eligible for the general election.

MANY REFERENDUMS TO BE ACTED ON AT THE STATE ELECTION

In addition to balloting for the regular candidates for office at the state election Nov. 7 all the voters of the state will be asked to answer one or more referendum questions. Some of these involve amendments to the state constitution and are of interest to the state at large; others have to do purely with local matters.

Throughout the state the ballots will ask for a statement as to whether the voter favors amending the state consitution so as to legalize the use of voting machines at elections in Massachusetts. A resolve for such an amendment has twice passed the Legislature and now the question comes before the people in the form of a referendum.

With these machines in use the voter will register his choice of candidates by the push-button method, thus doing away with the paper ballot. The machine counts automatically and shows the total vote cast for each candidate. It has been claimed by many favoring the scheme that had the machines been in use during the recent election in Maine there would have been no conflict over the returns.

Another proposed amendment to the state constitution on which all the voters will be asked to register their opinion increases the power of the Legislature to authorize the taking of land and property for laying out, widening or relocating highways or streets by the commonwealth, or by a county, a city or a town. With this amendment the Legislature could authorize by special act the taking of more land and property "than are needed for the actual construction of such highway or street."

There is a proviso, however, to the effect "that the land and property authorized to be taken are specified in the act and no more in extent than would be sufficient for suitable building lots

(Continued on page four, column one)

TRIED TO BUILD UP THE STATE INDUSTRIES SAYS GOVERNOR FOSS

Chief Executive at Lawrence Declares That No Man in Massachusetts Has More at Stake Than He Has

SPEAKS ON TARIFF

Asserts That President Taft Knows That His Party Faces Defeat and Therefore Publicly Admits It

Characterizing as ridiculous the campaign declarations of his opponent that business ruin would follow his reelection, Governor Foss addressed a large gathering of Lawrence voters at the Franklin house this noon. "Why should I endeavor to destroy the business industries of Massachusetts when I have spent my whole life in business life in building them up?" said the Governor in opening. "I have tried to bring about conditions that would keep our industries here instead of driving them to other parts of the country.

"No man in Massachusetts has more at stake in her business success than I have. I have built mills and factories employing thousands of people, and have shown my love for Massachusetts by refusing to do as so many others have done—remove nearer the source of my raw material.

"I made up my mind to keep the industry here in Massachusetts and fight for better tariff conditions. Does that look as though I would endeavor to bring about conditions that would result in ruin and disaster?

"I have sought to so modify conditions that our few remaining industries would not be driven from the state by adverse tariff laws. Where is the big furniture industry that employed thousands in Cambridge and Charlestown and Boston a little over a score of years ago? Driven from Massachusetts by a tariff policy that refused to let us get our raw material from a source only 150 miles away. Driven to Michigan, and today every Massachusetts furniture dealer has to make his pilgrimages half across the continent when he desires to stock up.

"The cost of living is increasing because a Republican President vetoed the measures of relief that the Democrats and the progressive Republicans forced through Congress in response to the public sentiment which is nation wide.

"Today that President, after a trip of 14,000 miles through the country, after meeting and touching elbows with millions of his fellow countrymen and having their views expressed to him after he has made his explanations and apologies for his action, is forced to admit that defeat will greet the Repub-

(Continued on page four, column two)

TURKS RETAKE TWO TRIPOLI FORTS AND FORCE ITALIANS BACK

(By the United Press)

CONSTANTINOPLE—Turkish troops with their Arab allies have retaken two forts at Tripoli and forced the Italians to entrench themselves within the city, after abandoning large quantities of guns, rifles, ammunition and provisions, according to a telegram from Rahmi Bey, the deputy for Saloniki, who is now at Tripoli. It says:

"The Italians were unable to resist the fierce assaults of the Arabs and were compelled to retreat.

"The Italians still hold three forts. The Arabs display remarkable heroism and hope to recapture the city."

The message is undated.

The government today notified foreign ambassadors that all pourparlers looking to mediation between Turkey and Italy have been broken off.

(By the United Press)

TRIESTE—Italy has seized and occupied the Turkish islands of Rhodes and Lesbos, according to despatches received here from Milan. This is presumed to be a part of the naval demonstration threatened against Turkey in retaliation for its recent successes in Tripoli. It is highly offensive to Austria.

(By the United Press)

VIENNA—With far from encouraging reports on the situation in Tripoli, Italy today is facing new crises in Austria's attitude toward naval maneuvers in Turkish waters and the imminence of anti-militarist and anti-monarchist uprising within her own borders.

African news is still meager, owing to the Italian control of the cables, but it seems certain that the Turks have reoccupied the outskirts of the city of

(Continued on page four, column six)

Regent of the Bay State D. A. R. Who Is Presiding at the Annual Convention

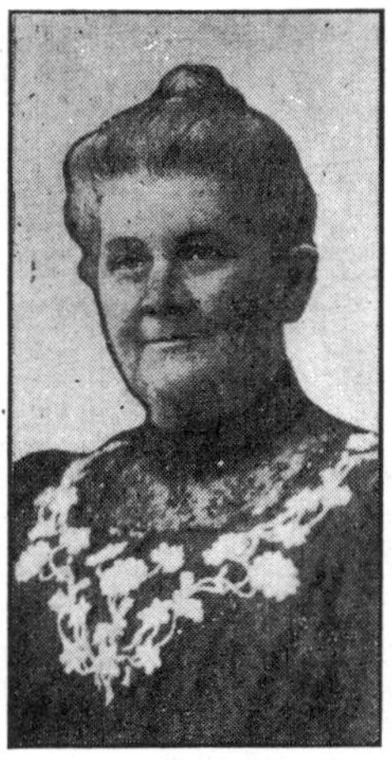

MRS. JAMES G. DUNNING

D. A. R. URGES A ROOM FOR MASSACHUSETTS IN NATIONAL BUILDING

A Massachusetts room in the Memorial Continental building in Washington to be furnished by the Massachusetts organization, Daughters of the American Revolution, will be the principal subject of discussion at the afternoon session of the annual D. A. R. convention in Kings chapel today.

The Continental building was built by the national organization two years ago and certain of the rooms have been furnished by various states with furniture, pictures and decorations appropriate to the state which gives its name to the room. The proposition before the delegates this afternoon is expected to be unanimously approved.

Mrs. James G. Dunning of Springfield, state regent, presided in the morning session, which was given over to the hearing of regents' and committee reports. There were about 200 delegates present.

TAMMANY CHARGED WITH SELLING PLACES ON JUDICIAL TICKET

Three Investigations Are Started in New York City on the Eve of the County Election

NEW YORK—On the eve of the county elections Tammany Hall is facing a situation which its opponents declare is going to develop the greatest political scandals in years and proof that Tammany Hall has been selling places on the judicial ticket.

Three legal investigations were instituted today into the Brooklyn judiciary mixup, and from the three, opponents of Tammany say, will come some startling exposures. John Doe proceedings have been started here by District Attorney Whitman, before Judge Rosalsky, an inquiry was started in Queen's court by Assistant District Attorney DeWitt and

(Continued on page four, column five)

SENATOR LODGE FOR ACTION ON PASSPORT VIOLATION BY RUSSIA

Tells Boston Jews Who Protest to Him Against Discrimination That Something Should Be Done

NOW INTOLERABLE

Statesman Indicates It Is His Belief That United States Should Compel Adherence to Treaty or Abrogate It

Senator Lodge in a reply to an appeal made by Boston Hebrews says something ought to be done at once about Russia's discrimination against American passports. He says the situation is intolerable and intimates that either the United States should make Russia treat Ameri-

(Continued on page ten, column three)

Boston Civic Worker and One of Foremost in Move to Nullify Russian Pact

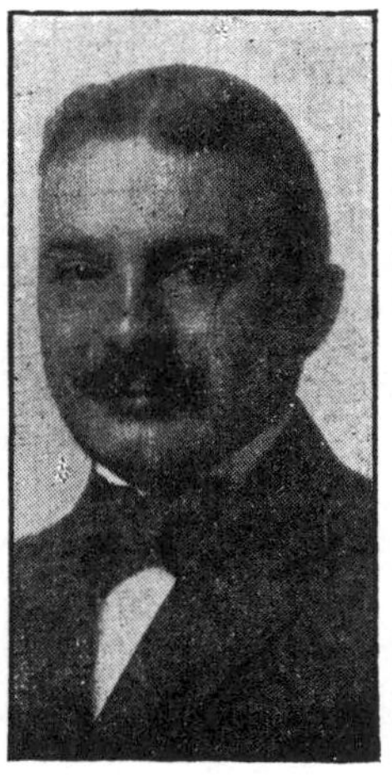

MAX MITCHELL

SOUTH STATION WORK OF EXTENSION BEGUN

Preparations were begun today for the moving of the ticket department of the New York, New Haven & Hartford, which are now in New Haven, to a suite of offices on the fifth floor of the South station. Extensive changes are now in progress and shelves and storage spaces are being provided in the new offices, which are connected.

These offices are beside those of the advertising agent, all forming a part of the general passenger department. In order to accomplish this change the janitors have been given another room.

The station master's old office on the midway floor of the station is now vacant and the station master installed on the next floor above, where larger quarters are available. Two passenger elevators will go in the space previously occupied by the station master.

The new elevators are intended for accommodation of the offices in the new extension. The postoffice, which also needs larger quarters, will be installed between track 1 and the baggage room, where a large space is now available.

START CAMPAIGN FOR FREIGHT TUBE UNDER HARBOR URGES MAYOR

"The freight terminals of Boston are as congested as they can be," said Mayor Fitzgerald today, "and there seems to be no way of remedying the situation for a year or more."

This condition is due to the Legislature, he said, in that it refused to pass the bill enabling the New Haven road to build its tunnel beneath the harbor. The mayor further said that he had placed the matter before the New Haven road and that the executives had stated that the rejection of their tunnel plan had made a delay in their plans, and that there was no way of transfering freight readily from the north to the south side of the city. The tunnel would enable them to establish a large freight terminal near the South station accessible by Northern avenue and Summer street extension.

The mayor stated that Boston had about reached its limits in the transportation of freight across the city and that it takes two or three times as long as it should, and that this was making it impossible to compete with other cities.

The Chamber of Commerce, the marketmen, and shippers, according to the mayor, should get together and make it plain to the Legislature next year that the needs of the city require the passage of a bill that will make possible the New Haven tunnel beneath the harbor.

MR. WICKERSHAM NOW ARGUINC TRUST'S PLAN

NEW YORK—In addressing the United States circuit court this afternoon on the reorganization plan of the tobacco trust Attorney-General Wickersham's manner in beginning was by no means unfriendly toward the company's plan. The attorney-general rarely spoke, however, in defense of the company's plan.

He called special attention to the fact that under it the control of the American and subsidiary companies would be transferred from the common to the preferred stockholders.

Mr. Wickersham asserted that mutual ownership of securities under the tobacco plan was practically unavoidable and that there were several precedents for such ownership as in the dissolution of the Northern Securities Company. He said, however, that as an abstract proposition he was not in favor of such ownership.

He said that he had to confess considerable sympathy for the independents who appeared before the court in this case and considerable surprise over the indignation expressed by counsel for the company on the attitude of the independents. Delancey Nicoll preceded Mr. Wickersham in an argument for the trust plan.

Mr. Nicoll went on to say that he and his associates had been met at every turn by objections from the attorney-general and intimated that many of the drastic features of the company's plan were largely a result of Mr. Wickersham's objections.

Judge Noyes interrupted Mr. Nicoll with frequent questions. Mr. Nicoll made a strong argument in favor of distributing the stocks of the subsidiary companies to the same stockholders. He declared that there would be active competition between the Lorillard, Liggett & Meyers and Reynolds companies in spite of the proposed plan for the ownership of securities.

PITTSBURGH KEEPING PRESIDENT BUSY ON HIS TRIP TO THAT CITY

PITTSBURGH—President Taft found a busy day mapped out for him on his arrival here this morning and with the ardor of those in the party considerably dampened by his utterances just before leaving Chicago which were accepted by some as a forecast of his own defeat in 1912.

Mr. Taft was first taken to Forbes field where he watched the "first aid" teams under the auspices of the Red Cross Society show the uses of the various life-saving devices used to rescue miners. The President presented medals to the teams which a committee selected as being the most prfect in the work.

Following this a parade of nearly 20,000 miners was reviewed by the President and he was then escorted to the Hotel Schenley for luncheon.

From there he goes to the wharf where Mrs. Alice Longworth is scheduled to name the little New Orleans, a replica of the first steamboat of the same name to navigate the Ohio and Mississippi rivers. The original New Orleans was built in 1811 by Nicholas J. Roosevelt, uncle of Theodore Roosevelt.

A dinner will be served for the President in the Soldiers' and Sailors' Memorial hall tonight by the members of the

(Continued on page five, column five)

RECORD ATTENDANCE AT WAKEFIELD NIGHT SCHOOL DUE TO LAW

WAKEFIELD, Mass.—The evening schools of this town opened Monday night with an enrolment of 100 pupils, and about 200 more are expected tonight and Thursday.

The unusually large registration is due to the effect on the factory and mill employees of the new law which compels the attendance of illiterates under 21 instead of 18 years.

The regular night school is in charge of Ross Vardon, principal of the Greenwood school, and the assisting teachers are Miss Mildred Ruggles of the Franklin school, Miss Eleanor Emerson, formerly principal of the Hurd school; Miss Grace Tenney and Miss Joyce Fielder of Reading.

A special class in sewing, independent of the regular night school, will be opened tonight, and more than 50 girls have registered. The teachers are Miss Nellie Wilkins of Everett, Miss Luna Bigelow of Boston and Miss Lucy Cox of Malden.

EARLY SHOPPING CAMPAIGN

The early Christmas shopping campaign of the retail trade board of the Chamber of Commerce is about to begin. The committee has laid out a plan calculated to produce better results than those of the last two years.

REBELS RECAPTURE MOST OF HANKOW IN FIGHT BEING WAGED

Forts Drive Gunboats Off, Then Revolutionary Force Crosses River and Makes Troops Retire to Suburbs

EDICTS YIELD ALL

Throne Promises Amnesty, Full Constitution, a New Cabinet Without Nobles, and End of Manchu Rights

(By the United Press)

SHANGHAI, China—Reports by wireless from the foreign warships off Hankow make it plain that though the rebels have driven the imperialists from the city proper, the battle is still continuing in the outskirts. No quarter is being shown on either side.

The rebels, it appears, drove the imperial warships from their position in the Yangtse between Hankow and Wuchang by a fire from the forts on the Wuchang side, which they held. The flotilla, compelled to drop down the river out of range, left the way clear for the rebels to recross to Hankow free from the cross-fire which drove them from Hankow on the day of its recapture by the imperial troops.

The recent rebel defeat resulting in the loss of Hankow was not serious. They were outnumbered, and finding their position difficult to hold, fell back upon Wuchang. Reinforced and resupplied with ammunition, there they resumed the struggle.

Instead of entrenching themselves in Hankow, the imperialists had been looting and burning the city. In spite of the fire from the imperialists the rebels recrossed the stream and engaged the troops at close quarters.

(By the United Press)

PEKING—Edicts continue to issue in the first person from the throne, all giving way to the demands of the National Assembly, guided by Yuan Shih Kai. The rebels are even praised in one edict for aiding in bringing about the reforms now granted and many of the Emperor's relatives are condemned. It is also announced that Manchu officeholders must go and that pensions to Manchus will be cut off.

These edicts have caused disaffection in the rank of the Manchus and the throne has no longer solid support in that quarter. Many Manchus and Chinese are seeking protection from each other in the foreign legations, which are guarded carefully.

(By the United Press)

HANKOW, China—Fighting has been resumed between the revolutionists and imperial troops here. The imperialists tried to rush the rebels' position at Wuchang, but were repulsed with heavy loss. The battle continues. One thousand rebels and 300 imperialists have been killed since Friday.

Rebel soldiers boarded a British ship looking for Manchu citizens. The commander of the ship summoned the naval guard of foreign marines and the rebels were driven back to the shore.

The rebels are operating the Hunan mint and making quantities of dollar coins daily. The new revolutionary paper is being redeemed immediately on presentation.

WASHINGTON—The provisional republic of Kwantung, recently declared at a meeting of the citizens of Canton, has fallen, according to state department advices. The loyalty of the troops to the viceroy is reported to be the chief cause of failure. Although Canton is reported quiet the situation in that city and in Nanking is said to be threatening.

(Special to the Monitor)

LONDON—As the senior officer in Chinese waters Vice-Admiral Sir Arthur Leigh Winslowe takes command of the foreign blue-jackets of all nationalities in any action on land or sea that it may be necessary to take. Sir Arthur has been 46 years in the navy, starting his career in 1865 and attaining the rank of vice-admiral in 1908, when he was one of the lords of the admiralty. Since last year he has filled the position of commander-in-chief of the China squadron.

Sir Arthur Winslowe was present as a spectator at the storming of Port Arthur and Wei-hai-Wei during the war between China and Japan. In 1882 he served in the Egyptian war, taking part in the battle of Tel-el-Kebir. The admiral also commanded the Ophir when King George and Queen Mary, as duke and duchess of York, went to Australia and South Africa.

REAL ESTATE MEN VISIT MAYOR

A committee from the Massachusetts Real Estate Exchange called on the mayor today to ask that the place of telephone operator at the exchange to answer questions in regard to real estate be made permanent. A girl has been there temporarily for the last four or five months. The mayor said that it would cost the city $500 a year.

¶ Clean printing is by no means unessential to clean journalism. The Monitor is cleanly printed. Its readers are glad to share it with others because it bears the stamp of cleanliness . . . . .

POSTAGE REQUIRED FOR MAILING TODAY'S PAPER

In United States......... 2c — To Foreign Countries...... 3c

CARPATHIA ALONE HAS SURVIVORS OF LOST LINER TITANIC

Hope That Virginian and Parisian Had Picked Up Passengers Leaves as Two Vessels Are Heard From

NUMBER SAVED 866

From 1100 to 1300 Reported Lost When Great Ship Founders Four Hours After Crashing Into Iceberg

NEW YORK—Hope for the safety of passengers of the Titanic which foundered early Monday morning on the Grand Banks of Newfoundland, other than those reported by wireless from the Cunarder Carpathia en route to this city, was practically abandoned this afternoon.

Latest reports placed only 866 persons and they chiefly women and children on the Carpathia, while even the officials of the White Star line admitted there was practically no hope for the remaining 1100 to 1300 passengers and crew.

Up until 2 o'clock there had been a glimmering hope that in addition to the Carpathia other vessels that had rushed to the scene on receipt of the wireless appeal for aid had been in time to make rescues. Rumor had the Allan liner Virginian and the Parisian taking off some. But this hope faded when word was received from the two vessels that they had reached the scene too late.

The Carpathia will land at New York late Thursday afternoon according to a wireless received there today by William Loeb, collector of the port.

James F. Curtis, assistant secretary of the treasury has ordered that the customs regulations be waived that the landing of the passengers be facilitated.

NEW YORK—The Cunard line announces the Carpathia will reach this port Thursday evening or early Friday morning with over 800 survivors from the Titanic. The following message was also made public:

"7:55 a. m., New York time, latitude 41.45 north, longitude 50.20 west. I am proceeding to New York unless otherwise ordered with about 800. After having consulted with Mr. Ismay and considering the circumstances with so much ice about consider New York best. Large number icebergs and 20 miles of field ice with bergs among them.

"Rostrom, commanding Carpathia."

MONTREAL—Captain Gambell of the Virginian reported to the Allan line agents here that his rescue trip had been fruitless.

"We arrived too late to rescue any one," says Gambell, "and we are proceeding to Liverpool."

HALIFAX, N. S.—The Sable island wireless reports: "We are now in communication with the Parisian. She has no Titanic's passengers aboard."

NEW YORK—Officials of the White Star line Monday night at 8 o'clock announced they had received a wireless message from the steamship Olympic stating that the Titanic, which struck an iceberg 10:25 p. m. Sunday, sank at 2:20 a. m. Monday in 41.16 degrees north latitude, 50.14 degrees west longitude, and that all her boats containing 866 persons, mostly women and children, had been accounted for. There were 2160 passengers and crew aboard.

The passengers authentically accounted for are aboard the Carpathia now bound for New York which reached the scene of disaster at daybreak Monday. The steamships Parisian and Virginian were also at the scene of the disaster. The Anchor line steamer California may also have information about survivors.

A wireless from St. John, N. B., says the Allan liner Virginian is headed for that port.

A wireless picked up early today from the Olympic at Cape Race, N. F., confirms the report that the Carpathia, with 866 survivors of the Titanic, mostly women and children, is being rushed to New York. The message concludes:

"Grave fears are felt for the safety of the balance of the passengers and crew.

At 8:20 a. m. Vice-President Franklin

(Continued on page five, column one)

¶ EVERYWHERE THE MONITOR GOES ITS BENEFICIAL INFLUENCE IS FELT. BY PASSING YOUR COPY ALONG YOU ARE CONTRIBUTING YOUR SHARE IN THIS GOOD WORK

POSTAGE REQUIRED FOR MAILING TODAY'S PAPER
In United States..........1c
To Foreign Countries......2c

PARTIAL LIST OF SURVIVORS OF THE TITANIC AS VERIFIED

A

Astor, Mrs. John; Amadill, Miss GlorJacob and maid. getta.
Abbott, Mrs. Rose. Anderson, Harry.
Abelson, Hanna. Andrews, Miss Cornelia.
Allison, Master, and nurse Angle, Wm., and wife
Allen, Miss E. W.

B

Balls, Ada R. Brayton, George.
Becker, Miss Ruth. Becker, Mrs. Allen.
Becker, Richard. Becker, Miss Mary.
Benthams, Miss Lillian. Beule, Edward.
Bishop, Mrs. D. A. Buyhl, Miss Dagnan.
Burns, Miss G. M. Bayton, Mrs. George
Bystrom, Karolina. A.
Bassino, Miss A. Brown, Miss Edith.
Barrett, Carl B. Bowen, Miss.
Bessette, Miss. Beckwith, R. T., and
Blank, Henry. wife.
Baxter, Mrs. James. Bucknell, Mrs. S. W.,
Bonnell, Miss Caroline. and maid.
Bass, Miss K. Barkworth, O. H.
Buys, Miss Margaret. Bowerman, Elsie.
Brown, Mrs. J. J.

C

Carter, William E., Charles, William F.
wife and maid. Croft, Miss Miller M.
Christie, M. J. Chaffee, Mrs. H. L.
Clark, Mrs. Ada. Christy, Mrs. Alice.
Collier, Miss Marjorie. Collier, Mrs. Stuart.
Caldwell, Mrs. Sylvan. Collier, Mrs. Charlotte.
Cameron, Miss. Caldwell, Albert.
Chibnace, Mrs. B. Calderbeed, F. P.
Cander, Mrs. Church- Cardeza, Mrs. J. W.
ill. and maid.
Clarke, Mrs. William Cardeza, T. D. M.,
M., and manservant.
Cassebere, Mrs. D. D. Chevre, Paul.
Chandanson, Miss Cherry, Miss Gladys.
Victorine. Chambers, N. C., and
Cavendish, Mrs. Tur- wife.
rell, and maid.

D

Davidson, Miss Mary. Drachensted, Alfred
Doling, Elsie. Davis, Miss Mary.
Driscoll, B. Doling, Mrs. Ada.
Davies, Miss Agnes. Drew, Mrs. Lulu.
Durante, Leonora A. Davies, John.
Davidson, Mrs. Devilliers, Mrs. B.
Thornton. Daniel, Robert W.
Douglas, Mrs. F. C. Deane, Mrs. Ethel.
Douglas, Mrs. Wal- Dodge, Mrs. Washington.
ter. ington.
Dodge, Dr. Washing- Duvant, Miss Florentine.
ton, wife and son.
Daniel, Miss Sarah.

E

Ellis, Miss. Encarnacion, Rendardo.
Emnock, Phillip.
Endres, Miss Caroline.

F

Fantini, Mrs. Mark. Fortune, Miss Alice.
Faunthope, Mrs. Eliz- Fortune, Mrs.
abeth. Flynn, J. I.
Francatelli, Miss. Frauenthal, Dr.
Flegenheim, Miss Henry and wife.
Antoinette. Frolicher, Mrs.
Fortune, Miss Mabel. Marguerite.
Former, Miss
Elaine.

G

Genovese, Orgene. Gibson, Miss D.
Gerrcia, Mrs. Marcy. Goldenberg, E. L.
Gracie, Col. Archi- and wife.
bald. Greenfield, Mrs.L.D.
Graham, Mrs. Wil- Gibson, Mrs. L.
liam. Gordon, Sir Cosmo
Googlt, James. Duff.
Graham, Mr. Gordon, Lady.
Graham, Mrs. M. E. Guraide, Miss Ethel.

H

Hart, Miss Eva. Healy, Miss Nora.
Harper, Miss Nancy. Hanson, Miss Jennie.
Hewlett, Miss Mary. Hanson, Miss J.
Harris, George. Hocking, Eliza.
Hold, Miss Annie. Hamaninian, W.
Hocking, Miss Nellie. Harris, Mrs. L. Y. B.
Homer, Henry. Halverson, Mrs. Alex-
Hays, Mrs. Charles M. ander.
Hegeboom,Mrs.J.C. Hoyt, F. M., and
Hawkeford, W. J. wife.
Harper, H. S., wife Harder, Miss Annie.
and man servant Hippach, Mrs. Ida S.
Haven, H. Hippach, Mrs. Jean
Hart, Mrs. Esther.

I

Ismay, J. Bruce.

J

Jackson, Mrs. Amy.

K

Keen, Miss Nora. Kenchen, Miss Emil.
Kelly, Miss Fannie. Kennyman, F. A.

L

Lavory, Miss Bertha. Lenore, Mrs. Elizabeth.
Leach, Jessie W.
Lauch, Mrs. Alex- Leader, Mrs. A.
ander. Linkkanca, Miss
Lehman, Miss Anna.
Bertha. Linse, Mrs. Ernest H.
Longley, Miss G. F. Linse, Miss Mary C.
Lawebe, Miss Juliet. Lindstrom, Mrs. J.
Laroche, Miss Louise.

M

Mange, Miss Paula. Marshall, Mr.
Marvin, Mrs. D. W. Marshall, Mrs.
Maisny, Miss Ruberta.Mullingtere, Mrs.
Mellcord, Madame. Elizabeth and
Mallett, Madame. children.
Marshall, Miss Kate Mellet, Andrio.
McDearmont, Miss McGowan,Miss Anne.
Lella. Mellors, John.

Nasraelle, Miss Ninahan, Mrs.
Adelia. Ninahan, Mrs. Daisy.
Newson, Miss Helen. Nye, Mrs. Elizabeth

O

O'Connell, Robert. Ormond, Flennan.
O'Quick, Miss Jane. nie.
O'Quick, Miss Phyl- Oathy, E. C.
lis. Oathy, Miss Helen R.
O'Quick, Miss Win- Ovies, S.
Oxenham, Percy J.

P

Pallis, Signor Emilio. Pearman, Mrs. Jane.
Parsch, Mrs. L. Pirrie, Lord, designer
Pensky, Miss Rosie. of Titanic.
Phillips, Miss Alice. Peuchen, Maj. Arthur.
Potter, Mrs. Thomas,Padro, Julian.
Jr. Portaslupp, Mrs.
Panhart, Miss Ninette. Em-
ile.

Rogers, Miss Eliza. Ryerson, Miss Emily
Riddale, Mrs. Lacy. B.
Ranouf, Miss Lizzie Ryerson, Mrs Arthur.
Rosenbaum, Miss. Ryerson, John.
Roimans, C. Rothschild, Mrs.
Rogers, Selina. Rhelms, Mrs. George.
Rother, Countess of. Richards, Miss Emily.
Robert, Mrs. Edna S. Richards, W. Jr.
maid. Richards, Mr.
Renago, Mrs. M. J. Ruy, Miss Emile.
Renault, Miss Annie.

S

Skellery, Miss Wil- Snyder, John, and
liam. wife.
Stone, Mrs. George N. Silverthorne, Mr.
Segresser, Mrs.Emma Simonlus, Col. Al-
Silby, Mrs. Wm. B. fonso, president of

Smith, Mrs. Lucien P., the Swiss Bankver-
Somrine, Mrs. L. ein.
Soubet, Paul. Sincook, Miss Maud
Spedden, J. O., and Smith, Mrs. Marion.
wife. Silvana, A. L.
Shelell, Robert D. Salsman, A. L.
Serdeala, Miss Au- Stengel, C. E. H. E.,
gusta. and wife.
Seward, Frederick. Spencer, W. A., wife
Sloper, William T. and maid.
Swift, Mrs. F. J.

T

Tucker, Mrs., and Thayer, J. B.
maid. Tucker, G. M., Jr.
Taussig, Ruth. Trout, Miss Edna S.
Thorne, G., and wife. Thayer, Mrs. J. B.
Taylor, E. S., and Thayer, J. B., Jr.
wife. Trout, Mrs. Jessie.

W

Washington, Mr. stone.
West, Mrs. and two West, Miss Mary.
children. Ward, Miss Anna.
Weis, Mrs. Matilda. Williams, Richard M.
Moore, Miss Florence. Williams, N. H.
Webber, Miss Susan. Warner, Mrs. F. M.
Watt, Miss Bessie Winton, Miss Hendea A.
Webb, Mrs. A. den A.
Wells, Mr. Widener, Mrs. George
Wright,Miss Marion P.
Watt, Miss Bertha. Williams, Charles.
Wells, Miss Williams, Duane.
Willard, Miss Con-

Y

Young, Miss Marie.

The list of survivors contains names not in the passenger list. These are probably of persons who boarded the Titanic at Cherbourg or are names misspelled in the sending.

BOSTON PASSENGERS ACCOUNTED FOR AND THOSE NOT REPORTED

Boston residents on the Titanic and accounted for were:

A. W. Newell, president of the Fourth National Bank, and his daughters.

Percival W. White of the firm of Nelson D. White & Co., cotton manufacturers, Winchendon.

Mrs. J. M. Brown of Acton and her sister, Mrs. E. D. Appleton.

Mrs. Walter G. Stephenson of Haverford, Pa., who was a Mrs Eustis of Beacon street.

Mrs. J. Bradley Cummings, wife of J. Bradley Cummings, formerly of this city but now of New York.

Mrs. Jacques Futrelle.

Miss Elizabeth M. Eustis of 1026 Beacon street probably figures as Miss Ellis, there being no such name on the first or second-cabin list.

UNACCOUNTED FOR

Clarence Moore of Washington and Beverly Farms.

Herbert H. Hilliard and Timothy J. McCarthy, lawyers for Jordan Marsh Company, George Q. Clifford, president of the Helcher Last Co. of Stoughton.

Jacques Futrelle, the author, of Scituate.

Mr. and Mrs. E. N. Kimball, president of Hallett & Davis Piano Co.

Walter C. Porter of Worcester, connected with the Porter Last Co.

Dr. Thomas F. Myles.

GREYLOCK MOUNTAIN DEVELOPMENT BILLS UP FOR DISCUSSION

Three bills for the development of the Greylock mountain reservation in Berkshire county were up for discussion today before the legislative committee on harbors and public lands.

These bills cover recommendations of the Greylock commission established by an act of the Legislature in 1898. One is for an appropriation of $5000 for the erection of seven iron towers on sites in the reservation. Another is for an appropriation of $1000 for a survey of the lands and the third is for an appropriation of $1000 for markers to define the outside lines of the reservation.

In urging that the appropriation for the erection of the towers be made the commissioners pointed out that without these towers visitors to the reservation are unable to get a proper view of the grounds. They further said that the establishment of these towers would in a great measure prevent forest fires since there would be many points from which observations could be made.

The Greylock reservation contains 8160 acres and lies in the towns of Williamstown, New Ashford, Cheshire, Adams and the city of North Adams.

A caucus of House Republicans has been called for tomorrow afternoon to receive the congress redistricting map fixed up by the committee appointed at the meeting of Republicans who object to the bill passed by the Senate.

TECH STUDENTS START PROM WEEK WITH BOOK RUSH

Junior "prom" week at Technology began at noon today with the annual Tech rush which is a violent effort on the part of several hundred students to get the first copy of the Technique, the annual publication, followed by a general scramble for each of the 99 copies remaining. E. B. Goodell '15 of Montclair, N. J., and M. J. Smith '13 of Cassadaga, N. Y., were both winners in the annual Technique rush which was held by the Technology students this noon. Both men pulled the book out of the window at the same time.

The first 20 copies have been numbered in gold and President MacLaurin has placed his signature on the fly leaf of each. The first four books and the twentieth are of the de luxe edition and the men securing these will have the price of the book refunded to them.

FIVE CANDIDATES FOR SCHOLARSHIP

Five candidates for the Rotch traveling scholarship, established by Benjamin S. Rotch, are being examined in French and construction today at the office of Clarence H. Blackall, 20 Beacon street, secretary of the Boston Society of Architects. The examinations are held at 10 a. m. and 2 p. m.

ST. JOHNS MAYOR HERE

W. J. Ellis, mayor of St. Johns, Newfoundland, is in Boston today as the guest of Mayor Fitzgerald. He went on an automobile tour about the city this afternoon with Louis K. Rourke, commissioner of public works.

BAY STATE HOUSE VOTES 116 TO 94 FOR FEDERAL INCOME TAX

Resolution Ratifying Amendment to Constitution Wins After Subject Is Fully Debated by Representatives

OPPONENT IS ACTIVE

Strong Arguments Are Made Against Proposition by Mr. Pope Who Contends Fundamental Idea Is Illegal

On a roll-call vote by 116 to 94 the House agreed today to the resolution ratifying the income tax amendment proposed for the United States constitution.

Representative Sanborn of Lawrence said that history had shown that a government in order to exist must have unlimited powers of taxation and he pointed out that in a time of war several of the usual sources of revenue might fail. Representative Silvester of Worcester also spoke in favor of the amendment.

Mr. Pope called such a tax unconstitutional. He said it would give Congress the power to levy a tax on every man, woman and child in the country.

Another objection advanced by Mr. Pope was that the amendment would allow the government to tax the incomes on state, city and town bonds, which, he said, would be hostile to the credit of some states and municipalities.

One of the chief arguments for the tax, he said, was that it would permit a reduction of the tariff, but although the national government has received $70,000,000 from a new corporation tax in the last three years, there has been no hint of a reduction in the tariff.

From the Massachusetts standpoint, he said, there can be no argument in favor of the federal income tax—what it really means is that Massachusetts' wealth shall be subject to the onslaughts of the western and southern states, and will permit them to obtain for themselves a part of the money which should be paid into the state treasury. Evidence of this is given in the fact that there are before Congress bills asking an aggregate of more than $100,000,000 for the construction of federal highways in southern and western states.

Mr. Cogswell of Lynn defended the amendment, saying that its purpose is to remedy conditions which permit one third of all the wealth of the nation to be in the hands of only 51 men, as statistics show to be the fact. It is the only method which has ever been devised of adequately reaching the wealth of the nation.

Mr. Meaney of Blackstone quoted President Taft as favoring the amendment, and Mr. Pope replied that the President stated that he favored it only in "time of dire distress."

Mr. Curtin of Brookline said that some of the friends of the amendment should point out wherein it will benefit the citizens and industries of Massachusetts. From his own study, he said, he believed the proposition an economic fallacy.

MANITOU IN FROM ANTWERP AFTER A GOOD PASSAGE

The Red Star line steamer Manitou, Capt. A. E. Tribe, arrived here today from Antwerp. She brought 36 cabin passengers and 3400 tons of general cargo. She left Antwerp April 4 and encountered favorable conditions all the way.

Only nine out of the 36 passengers were citizens and included Mr. and Mrs. Gustave Vanhoutte of Woonsocket, R. I. Miss Marie Gordon of Smargom, Russia, came over to join her father in this city. Jnanendra N. Sharman of Calcutta, was also a passenger. He has made several years study of Sanskrit at Munich, and is on his way to the University of Wisconsin for a further study.

Edourard Renger of Zeskov, Russia, who has recently graduated from the University of Aachen, at Aachen, Germany, is here to assist a Russian mining expert at Massachusetts Institute of Technology.

Plaster relief of Abraham Lincoln made in class as part of regular work

Casts of persons living in neighborhood made by members of settlement classes

SPECIMENS OF LINCOLN HOUSE WORK

EXHIBIT OF CLASS WORK IS OPENED AT LINCOLN HOUSE

Class work is exhibited today at the Lincoln house, 80 Emerald street, at the annual display. An exhibition of folk dancing will be given for evening visitors.

The exhibit includes work done in clay modeling, drawing and design, cooking, needlework, millinery, basket weaving and wood sloyd. In an exhibit of plaster casts made in the advanced evening class which has been meeting twice a week there are two heads of a boy and one of a girl, done from persons in the neighborhood who posed for the artists.

The relief of Lincoln is to be placed over the front entrance. It has been possible this year to do more with this kind of work than formerly on account of the complete equipment which was installed some months ago.

Joseph Dianchi made the heads of the boys and Miss Alice Shepherd made the head of the girl.

Membership in Lincoln house is open to men, women and children in the South End, the dues ranging from 25 cents to $1 a year. Any group of Leighborhood residents who wish to form a club for any good purpose may have the free use of a room for meetings by joining the house. In summer months the roof garden supplies the place of most clubs.

Besides industrial classes and social clubs Lincoln house also has athletic teams which use the large gymnasium for basket ball and other games. The gymnasium, as well as the baths and bowling alleys, is never closed except for repairs.

On alternate Thursday evenings house dances are given. The last party this season will be on April 30. The other Thursday evenings are utilized for free lectures. Lectures are also given in the winter months on Sunday afternoons and last season were on such subjects as "Attempted Improvements in Factories," "Recent Progress in Cities" and "Working Women and the State."

The closing exercises tomorrow afternoon at 4:15 o'clock will include a play, "The Toy Shop," by the children and the other members are now busy with rehearsals for plays which are to be given for the public in May. Preparation is also being made for the part in which H. Blackall, 20 Beacon street, will Lincoln House children are to take when the inter-settlement pageant is given in Franklin park on May 30.

The work of Lincoln house is directed by John D. Adams, assisted by Harry Lyon and Miss Grace T. Wills. The house next door is used as a home for the women residents and there are also many volunteer teachers and leaders who come in once a week from the various colleges.

AMERICAN WOMAN CROSSES CHANNEL IN AEROPLANE FLIGHT

(By the United Press)

LONDON—It was announced here this afternoon that Miss Harriet Quimby of America, had flown across the English channel after having been known in England as a Mrs. Griffith and in France as Madame Afenir. It is supposed that she wished to conceal her identity for some purpose in connection with her literary work.

Miss Harriet Quimby continued on her way as far as Boulogne. There she encountered a dense fog, and after circling over the city was forced to descend. She decided to await the arrival of a mechanician to overhaul her machine, and then to begin a return trip to England.

In crossing the channel Miss Quimby kept an altitude of about 4000 feet and steered by compass. She made Boulogne without mishap and landed safely.

(By the United Press)

NEW YORK—It was made known today that Miss Harriett Quimby, the American girl who was reported to have flown across the English channel in an aeroplane, had been known in France for some time. She was expected to return to this country early in May in connection with her work as aviation editor of a weekly publication.

CONVENTION OF DEMOCRATS IN CHICAGO SPLITS

CHICAGO—Two sets of delegates will appear at the Democratic state convention at Peoria on Friday from Cook county demanding to be seated as a result of the split at the county convention on Monday.

For more than three hours 25 militiamen, unarmed, held possession of the seventh regiment armory while two rival forces, the Hearst-Harrison faction and the followers of Roger C. Sullivan, national committeeman, disputed the right of each other to enter the armory.

Repeated demands were made by Commissioner Czarnecki, delegated by Judge Owens of the county court to open the convention, that the door be unbarred. The militia refused and Judge Owens in person went to the armory and demanded admittance. He, too, was refused. Then the police were ordered by Judge Owens to break in the doors.

The Hearst-Harrison precinct committeemen who had been standing in line wearing badges inscribed "Harmony" entered the building.

Not a man of the Sullivan forces was present. Instead, they and the Democrats known as Dunne men held a convention at another hall.

BALLOT COMMISSION DECIDES AGAINST THE USE OF THE CIRCLE

Absence of George Fred Williams' Name Leaves Group of Candidates for Delegates-at-Large Incomplete

MR. VAHEY SUES

Asks Court for Writ of Mandamus Forbidding Secretary of State to Place Circle on Ballots

No circle will appear at the head of the Democratic state committee group of candidates for delegates-at-large on the presidential preference primary ballot, the Massachusetts ballot law commission deciding this afternoon that this is not a complete group, the name of George Fred Williams having been taken from the group and no substitution having been made by the Democratic state committee.

It was decided that circles should be placed on the presidential preferential primary bill at the heads of complete groups of candidates for delegates-at-large. The decision was averse to the petition of Thomas P. Riley, chairman of the Democratic state committee, who asked that the circle be placed at the top of the group of seven names of candidates known as the Democratic state committee' slate, which was headed by Dr. John W. Coughlin of Fall River. The decision was given after three hearings on the question by the commission.

Before the decision was announced a writ of mandamus was filed today in the supreme court asking that Albert P. Langtry, secretary of state, be ordered not to place a circle on the ticket at the head of the incomplete group of candidates for delegates known as the Democratic state committee slate, thus enabling an elector to vote the whole party ticket by placing a cross in the circle. The petition was filed by James H. Vahey, one of the candidates named, and the announcement was made at the hearing before the Massachusetts ballot law commission on the question as to whether this circle should be placed at the head of the group.

Mr. Vahey made the announcement in his final arguments against using the circle, saying that he had been late in acting because the ballots were being printed and he wished to save his rights and consequently did not wait for the decision of the ballot law commission. If the ballot law commission decided against the use of the circle, he said, he would withdraw his petition, but if it favored the circle he would press the petition.

Final arguments were made by David A. Shaw, representing the Democratic state committee, who said that he was willing to rest his case on the history and adoption of the primary law as provided by the statutes in 1897. Frank J. Donahue and Mr. Vahey argued against him.

MAYOR ASKS COUNCIL TO EXPEND $55,000 IN RESOILING COMMON

Mayor Fitzgerald sent a special message to the city council this afternoon urging that $55,000 of the income of the Parkman fund be appropriated for the resoiling of Boston Common. Accompanying the message was a letter from D. Henry Sullivan, superintendent of public grounds, in which he said that if more money is not forthcoming immediately he would have to suspend work by Thursday.

Little change in Mayor Fitzgerald's 1912 budget have been made by the committee on appropriations, which sent the budget back to the council today for action. Its total is $14,460,444.

The largest items are $4,448,700 for the public works department, $2,216,000 for the police department and $1,000,000 for the fire department.

The council will try this afternoon to elect a city clerk to succeed the late John T. Priest, and the supporters of James Donovan of ward 9, former president of the Democratic city committee, say that he will be elected on the first ballot. Other members of the council expect a deadlock.

Wilfred J. Doyle, assistant city clerk, is likely to be a compromise candidate in case of a deadlock, it is said.

OIL RECEIVERS APPOINTED

MUSKOGEE, Ok.— Receivers were appointed for the Central Fuel Oil Company in the federal court here on Monday upon the application of the Bankers Trust company of New York, holder of a $6,000,000 mortgage against the general company.

THE CHRISTIAN SCIENCE MONITOR

LAST EDITION — BOSTON, MASS., WEDNESDAY, NOVEMBER 6, 1912—VOL. IV., NO. 292 — PRICE TWO CENTS

PORTE APPEAL TO POWERS UNHEEDED

SIR EDWARD GREY TELLS COMMONS OF BALKAN SITUATION

Declares That Both Belligerents Must Ask for Intervention Before Action by Other Nations Is Possible

TURKS NOT READY

Total Unpreparedness Made Evident by Latest News of Retreat on Way to Suburbs of Capital

BULGARS SUPPLIED

Captured From the Retreating Divisions Sufficient Provisions to Make Continued Pursuit Possible

HEROISM DISPLAYED

{Special Cable to the Monitor from its European Bureau

LONDON—Politically, the situation in the Balkans was admirably summed up last night by Sir Edward Grey in the House of Commons. The powers, he declared, were not disposed to dispute the rights of the Balkan states to formulate when they pleased terms on which they were prepared to conclude peace. It was true that an appeal had been made by the Porte to the great powers, but it would be a very delicate matter for the powers to interfere between two belligerents, unless they did so at the request of both. This probably expresses all that at the moment it is definitely possible to say on the political question, nor until terms of the allies are disclosed can anything very definite be known.

Bulgarian cavalry have been seen off Lake Derkos, right under the northern flank of the Tchataldja lines. Their presence is a sign of the intense daring of General Savoff's advance. If it is anything more than a mere cavalry reconnaissance it shows that news of the two days halt of the Bulgarian staff made use of by the Reichpost correspondent to disseminate, was a blind.

It is quite possible that the force which was seen were partizans engaged in the supposed blowing up of the aqueduct of the capital. Interruption of this water supply, it may as well be said at once, is not material. If true it will doubtless prove of the greatest inconvenience to the European colony in Constantinople. But there is plenty of water of a sort for the use of the troops and natives.

A great deal of ingenuity has been devoted to proving that the Bulgarians could not possibly continue their advance for want of food. As a matter of fact enormous stores were captured at Kirk Kilisse from which there is an available railway to Baba Eske. This railway is not shown on the maps as it was only opened by the Turks after the declaration of war. It is believed that these stores amounted to three months' supplies and on them no doubt the Bulgarian advance has been carried on. Had it not been for this and other captures the Bulgarian advance would necessarily have been much slower.

All along the road from the magazines at Jamboli to Adrianople mile after mile of commandeered carts drawn by powerful white oxen are pouring munitions steadily into the besieging camp. The rate at which these wagons move is not more than 10 miles a day so that the position of the Bulgarians may easily be realized if they had been compelled to rely upon their own transport. It is possible, though not very likely, that a loop line has been constructed right around Adrianople. But even if this were the case, there would probably still

(Continued on page six, column four)

GOV. FOSS NAMES NEW OFFICIALS

Nominations sent to the Governor's council at their noon meeting today by Governor Foss include the following: Charles H. Mace to be associate medical examiner for Hampshire county vice Dr. Lyman, Clarence P. Curley of Provincetown to be medical examiner for Barnstable county, Moses S. Case of Marblehead to be trial justice of Essex county Francis H. Rowley of Brookline to be special police officer upon the recommendation of the Society for the Prevention of Cruelty to Children, and Charles E. Rogerson of Milton to be trustee of the Massachusetts homeopathic hospital vice Erastus T. Colburn.

Particular attention is called to the war news published on the authority of the European Bureau of The Christian Science Monitor. These despatches are sent us by the Bureau as quickly as the news is verified.

Other despatches carried in these columns from the scene of war are published on the authority of the United Press Associations.

FURTHER BULGAR SUCCESS REPORTED

(By the United Press)

PARIS—The Bulgarians completely routed the Turks at Chorlu and Sarai during the night, according to a despatch received today from Sofia. The despatch said the road to Constantinople is now practically open.

(By the United Press)

LONDON—Bulgarians defeated the Turks between Sarai and Chorlu, according to a report here today. The victors were hastening to join the attack on the Thataldja forts, Constantinople's last defenses. The Turkish authorities in Salonika, it was said, were disagreed whether or not to surrender to the Greeks.

BRIDGE REPAIRS CAUSE CHANGE IN CAR SERVICE

Repairs, which the city is making to Harvard bridge, necessitate changes in the trolley car service principally affecting Cambridge. On and after Thursday the Boston Elevated regular outbound service will be operated over Harvard bridge, as usual, and the inbound through service will be run via Brookline street, Cottage Farm and Commonwealth avenue.

A shuttle car will be operated between Central square, Cambridge, and the Cambridge end of the Harvard bridge.

During the bridge repairs, passengers boarding outbound Harvard bridge or shuttle cars in Cambridge may, upon request at the time of payment of fare, receive a transfer to the Cambridge subway at Central square station to inbound trains, and outbound transfers obtained at Central square station from the Cambridge subway trains will be honored as far as the Cambridge end of Harvard bridge on inbound cars from Central square, routed via Massachusetts avenue.

Passengers boarding outbound Harvard bridge or shuttle cars in Cambridge may, upon request at the time of payment of fare, receive a transfer good at Central square to Pearl street for the regular through service now temporarily diverted via Brookline street bridge.

INDICTED MEN GAVE $5000 BAIL IN COURT TODAY

Horatio W. Heath, general manager, and George H. Swift, director, of the Consolidated Rendering Company, charged with others with maintaining a combination in restraint of trade, refused to enter a plea before Judge Morton in the United States district court today, on the indictments recently found against them. Each was held in $5000 bail, furnished by the National Sureties Company as surety. Counsel was given three weeks in which to determine whether he would file demurrers to the indictments.

FRENCH BULL DOG SHOW DEC. 3 AND 4

With 196 special prizes offered in addition to the regular blue, red and yellow ribons in each of the 45 classes, there is sure to be a record entry for the seventh annual specialty show of the French Bull Dog Club of New England which will be held in Horticultural hall Dec. 3 and 4.

Chief of these prizes are the $100 gold dog offered by the club to the best puppy dog, the Dreamwold plate, the Noswal trophy, the Lawson bowl and the Champion Gamin's Riquet cup for the dog taking winners at most shows, beginning with the Monmouth County Kennel show of 1912 and ending with the French Bull Dog Club of America specialty show of 1914.

BOULDER MOVED FOR PARK TABLET

SALEM, Mass.—Eight horses attached to a big dray passed through the city yesterday with the eight-ton boulder to be used as the base on which a bronze tablet will be placed at Ledge Hill park, in North Salem, to commemorate the fact that this park, some 40 acres in extent, was bequeathed to the city by the late Dr. William Mack and his sister, Miss Esther C. Mack.

The boulder was hauled three miles from The Willows, where, according to scientists, it has rested near old Ft. Lee, ever since the glacial period.

PLEA FOR PORT PACT IS MADE BEFORE THE EXECUTIVE COUNCIL

Representatives of Chamber of Commerce Present Arguments for Reclaiming of Commonwealth Pier

READY TO WORK

Directors Prepared to Begin Actual Port Development Work as Soon as Decision Is Made on Contract

Representatives of the Boston Chamber of Commerce stated the position of the chamber in favor of approving the contract between the Old Colony, and New Haven roads and the port directors for the cancellation of the lease of the Commonwealth pier before the public meeting of the Governor's council today.

Senator George H. Tinkham and George F. Harriman, engineer, intimated that those interested in port development were requested to be present. Joseph B. Russell, president of the chamber, presented the official vote of that body in favor of approving the contract. George S. Smith, former president; William C. Brewer, chairman of the chamber committee on maritime affairs, and John Lowell, chairman of the committee on transportation, also appeared as representatives of the chamber in favor of approving the contract.

Once more the directors of the port stand ready to start work on the dredging and preliminary work on the pier at the moment the council decides in favor of the contract.

The directors of the Hamburg-American line are sailing today from New York on the Kaiserin Auguste Victoria for Hamburg at 3 o'clock. This will give sufficient opportunity for Hugh Bancroft, chairman of the directors, to communicate to the Hamburg-American officials the decision of the council, should it prove favorable, before they leave this country to make their report in Europe.

The vote of the council is expected by the commercial interests of the port to be favorable as it is not considered possible that the members would delay any longer the fruition of one of the most important steps for the development of the port that has come to it for many decades. Popular demand for favorable action is pointed out by many business men as an irresistible factor.

MANY PLOTS FOR MELROSE PARKS

Plans for the extension of the Melrose park system, by the purchase of additional land, containing more than 100,000 square feet, have been made by the Melrose park commission, approved by the mayor, and will soon come before the board of aldermen for an appropriation.

The property in question includes the purchase of the Benson ice house on the Main street end of the pond, upon which the city, through former Alderman J. C. F. Slayton, holds an option of $6500. An adjoining lot of land containing 16,528 square feet, another parcel containing 12,592 square feet on the Melrose street side, will give to the city all of the land on the north and east shores, with the exception of the boat house property, two buildings on Main street and four houses on Crystal street.

In addition, the plan calls for the purchase of the Boston Ice Company property on the Tremont street side of the pond, containing 68,461 square feet of land and a strip containing 7130 square feet belonging to the Fells Ice Company.

IRON WORKERS STRIKE TODAY

NORRISTOWN, Pa.—Twelve hundred employees of the Alan Wood Iron & Steel Company of Conshohocken struck today when refused a 10 per cent wage increase.

LENGTH OF TRUNKS SUBJECT OF INQUIRY OF INTEREST HERE

Boston Trunk, Whip, Wardrobe Manufacturers to Protest Before Interstate Commerce Board Examiner

AGAINST NEW RULE

Protestants Declare Railroad Regulation for Excess Charge Would Compel Them to Go Out of Trade

Boston trunk, wardrobe, whip and other manufacturers will be represented at the hearing on the proposed rule of the railroads limiting the length of trunks that may be carried, to be held in Washington before Special Examiner Marshall tomorrow by J. C. Lincoln of the Merchants Association of New Work, who is to testify in behalf of New England interests.

Representatives of railroad traffic associations, merchant travelers and the theatrical profession will appear before the examiner to present their testimony. The rule in question limits the length of trunks that may be carried free as baggage to 45 inches, and prohibits the carriage as baggage of trunks more than 70 inches in length.

The railroads of the country gave notice of the proposed change in baggage rules early in the spring, saying that they would go into effect July 1 of this year. When the proposal became public, protests were filed with the interstate commerce commission, alleging various grounds why the proposed new rules should not be permitted to become effective, the protestants asking for a hearing, and the suspension of the new rule, pending the result of the hearing.

The commission accordingly suspended the proposed baggage rules, and have already held one hearing, at which several of the protestants appeared. This was before Chairman Prouty. Other parties wanted to be heard, and another hearing was accordingly set for Thursday, before Special Examiner Marshall.

The record shows that the protestants include, among others, the whip-makers of the country, manufacturers of clothing, millinery and hats, manufacturers of shaped steel and members of the theatrical profession.

The latter were the first to ask the commission for relief from the alleged burdensome rule. Many of them, in letters on file with the commission, declare that they will be obliged to go out of business if the rules are put into effect. Among these are a harpist, another requires paraphernalia which will not go into a 45-inch trunk, and still others carry special scenery which has been transported as baggage under the railroad rules. The proposed new rule provides for a charge equal to 10 pounds of excess baggage for each inch in the length of a trunk in excess of 45 inches. The protestants say that the excess charges will be so great as to prevent them from making a livelihood with their present salaries.

A manufacturer of millinery, illustrating the effect of the proposed rule, says that it costs a salesman $8 or $9 per week excess charges under present rules, for one trunk, and that this charge would be increased to at least $18 per week, if the new rules are allowed to become effective. "Large hats require large trunks," this complainant says. "The cost of carrying these large trunks is heavy enough now, and if the new rule becomes effective, it will impose an added cost that will eventually fall upon the consumer."

The clothing and garment makers declare that their salesmen are of necessity equipped with large-sized wardrobe trunks, and that the enforcement of the new rule will entail great additional expense to them. The hat makers say also that their traveling men carry specially made trunks in excess of the proposed minimum length.

CLEAN JOURNALISM HAS THE LOYAL SUPPORT OF AN EVER-GROWING NUMBER OF FRIENDS IN ALL PARTS OF THE WORLD—MANY OF THESE FRIENDS HAD THEIR FIRST INTRODUCTION TO CLEAN JOURNALISM THROUGH THE KINDNESS OF MONITOR READERS, WHO DAILY PASS THEIR COPIES ALONG. WHY NOT MAKE A NEW FRIEND FOR CLEAN JOURNALISM?

POSTAGE REQUIRED FOR MAILING TODAY'S PAPER
In United States..........2c — To Foreign Countries.......3c

WOODROW WILSON GAINING AS RETURNS ARE REVISED

WOODROW WILSON

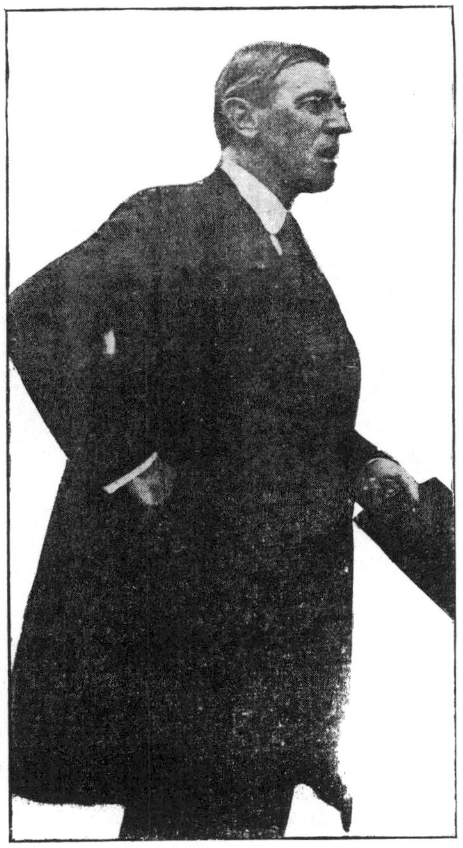

DEMOCRATS CLAIM THIRTY-EIGHT STATES FOR THEIR CANDIDATE

Rhode Island, New Hampshire and Probably Iowa Latest to Join Ranks of Others Which Changed

WYOMING DISPUTED

Victors Count on 412 Votes in Electoral College With 99 for Col. Roosevelt and 20 for the President

NEW YORK — Further gains for Woodrow Wilson were recorded as the belated returns came in today, and this afternoon, the President-elect was credited with 412 votes in the electoral college. In addition there was a strong trend to Mr. Wilson in the rural returns from Illinois, with the Democrats claiming that state would yet add its 29 votes to the Wilson column.

During the day Rhode Island and New Hampshire were shifted from Mr. Taft's column to Mr. Wilson. This gave the Democrats a clean sweep in New England with the exception of Vermont, which went for Mr. Taft.

Colonel Roosevelt was definitely credited with 99 electoral votes, but his managers insisted that he would also have the five votes of South Dakota, as yet credited to Mr. Taft, who is given 20 votes in all.

The Democrats claimed Wyoming, but the figures were not yet conclusive, and Wyoming remained in Mr. Taft's column, Mr. Taft being credited with 20 electoral votes.

Mr. Wilson has carried the following 38 states: Alabama, Arizona, Arkansas, California, Colorado, Connecticut, Delaware, Florida, Georgia, Indiana, Iowa, Kentucky, Louisiana, Maryland, Maine, Massachusetts, Minnesota, Mississippi, Missouri, Montana, Nebraska, Nevada, New Hampshire, New Jersey, New Mexico, New York, North Carolina, North Dakota, Ohio, Oklahoma, Oregon, Rhode Island, South Carolina, Tennessee, Texas, Virginia, West Virginia, Wisconsin.

(Other news on the national election will be found on page 8).

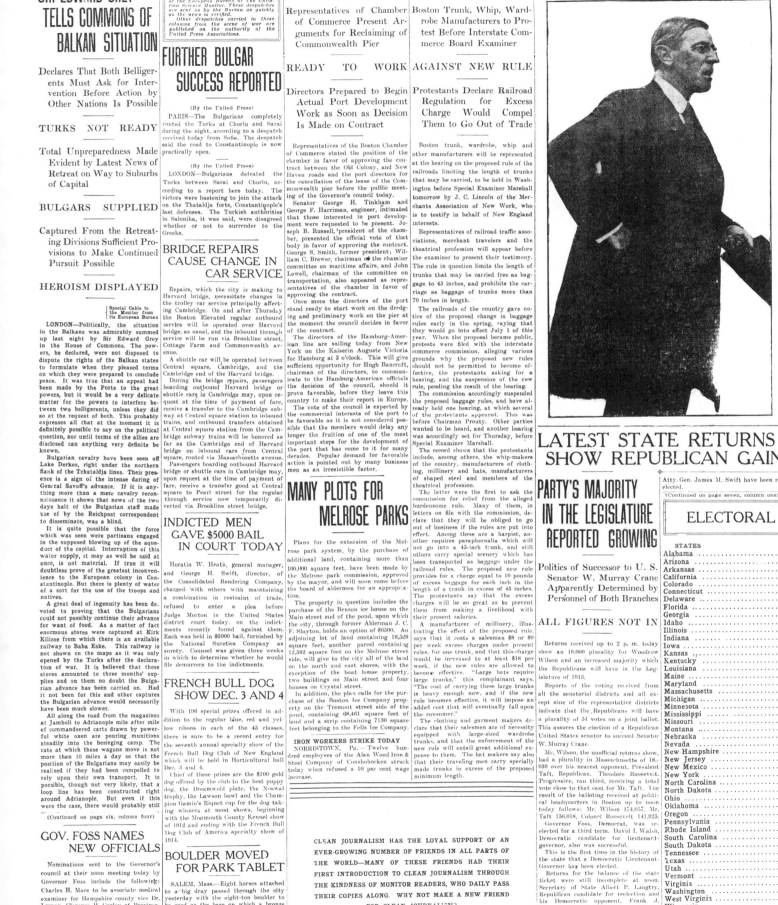

LATEST STATE RETURNS SHOW REPUBLICAN GAIN

PARTY'S MAJORITY IN THE LEGISLATURE REPORTED GROWING

Politics of Successor to U. S. Senator W. Murray Crane Apparently Determined by Personnel of Both Branches

ALL FIGURES NOT IN

Returns received up to 2 p. m. today show an 18,000 plurality for Woodrow Wilson and an increased majority which the Republicans will have in the Legislature of 1913.

Reports of the voting received from all the senatorial districts and all except nine of the representative districts indicate that the Republicans will have a plurality of 51 votes on a joint ballot. This assures the election of a Republican United States senator to succeed Senator W. Murray Crane.

Mr. Wilson, the unofficial returns show, had a plurality in Massachusetts of 18,039 over his nearest opponent, President Taft, Republican. Theodore Roosevelt, Progressive, ran third, receiving a total vote close to that cast for Mr. Taft. The result of the balloting received at political headquarters in Boston up to noon today follows: Mr. Wilson 174,057, Mr. Taft 156,018, Colonel Roosevelt 141,925.

Governor Foss, Democrat, was reelected for a third term. David I. Walsh, Democratic candidate for lieutenant-governor, also was successful.

This is the first time in the history of the state that a Democratic Lieutenant-Governor has been elected.

Returns for the balance of the state ticket were still incomplete at noon. Secretary of State Albert P. Langtry, Republican candidate for reelection and his Democratic opponent, Frank J. Donahue, were running close with the latter slightly in the lead. At the Democratic state committee headquarters it was said this noon that Mr. Donahue would win by about 2000 votes.

The contests for the three other places on the state ticket also are close, although the political leaders generally believe that Treasurer Elmer A. Stevens, Auditor John E. White and Atty. Gen. James M. Swift have been reelected.

(Continued on page seven, column one)

ELECTORAL VOTE RESULT

STATES	Number of Electors	Wilson	Taft	Roosevelt
Alabama	12	12	..	..
Arizona	3	3	..	..
Arkansas	9	9	..	..
California	13	13	..	..
Colorado	6	6	..	..
Connecticut	7	7	..	..
Delaware	3	3	..	..
Florida	6	6	..	..
Georgia	14	14	..	..
Idaho	4	..	4	..
Illinois	29	..	..	29
Indiana	15	15	..	..
Iowa	13	13	..	..
Kansas	10	..	..	10
Kentucky	13	13	..	..
Louisiana	10	10	..	..
Maine	6	6	..	..
Maryland	8	8	..	..
Massachusetts	18	18	..	..
Michigan	15	..	..	15
Minnesota	12	12	..	..
Mississippi	10	10	..	..
Missouri	18	18	..	..
Montana	4	4	..	..
Nebraska	8	8	..	..
Nevada	3	3	..	..
New Hampshire	4	4	..	..
New Jersey	14	14	..	..
New Mexico	3	3	..	..
New York	45	45	..	..
North Carolina	12	12	..	..
North Dakota	5	5	..	..
Ohio	24	24	..	..
Oklahoma	10	10	..	..
Oregon	5	5	..	..
Pennsylvania	38	..	..	38
Rhode Island	5	5	..	..
South Carolina	9	9	..	..
South Dakota	5	..	5	..
Tennessee	12	12	..	..
Texas	20	20	..	..
Utah	4	..	4	..
Vermont	4	..	4	..
Virginia	12	12	..	..
Washington	7	..	..	7
West Virginia	8	8	..	..
Wisconsin	13	13	..	..
Wyoming	3	..	3	..
Totals	531	412	20	99
Necessary to a choice	266	..	..	..

WILSON 412
ROOSEVELT 99
TAFT 20

(There may be changes in some of the states where the vote is incomplete, but the comparative results will be practically the same as the above table.)

THE CHRISTIAN SCIENCE MONITOR

INTERNATIONAL EDITION {Copyright 1913 By The Christian Science Publishing Society} BOSTON, MASS., TUESDAY, OCTOBER 28, 1913—VOL. V., NO. 284 PRICE TWO CENTS

SCOTS GREYS ESCORT ROYAL COUPLE

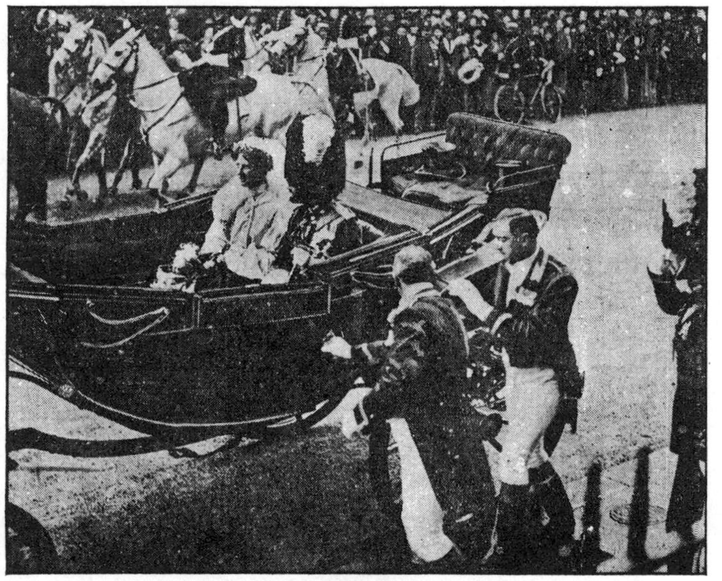

(Copyright by London News Agency)

Prince and Princess Arthur arriving at 15 Portman square, London, the residence of bride's mother

(Special to the Monitor)

LONDON—Londoners took a keen interest in the wedding of Prince Arthur of Connaught and the Duchess of Fife which, as stated by cable, took place recently at the Chapel Royal, St. James palace.

An hour before the ceremony was due to commence more than 20,000 people lined that part of the Mall which runs between Buckingham palace and the garden entrance to St. James palace, and large crowds gathered also at various places on the route from the palace to the residence of the princess royal in Portman square.

The ceremony in the chapel was simple. The King, who gave the bride away, stood near her during the service as also did the princess royal. The archbishop of Canterbury in his address said that in that memorable place at the center of British home life, they were performing a ceremony wherein all the land rejoiced. From a full heart they with tens of thousands outside bade godspeed to bride and bridegroom.

After the benediction bride and bridegroom left the chapel to the strains of Mendelssohn's wedding march. After the usual formalities the bride and bridegroom held a reception in the throne room and then returned to Portman square, the journey being made in an open state landau. A detachment of the Scots Greys preceded the royal couple who were greeted with cheers all along the route.

INTERNAL HOME RULE PROPOSED FOR ULSTERMEN

Sir Edward Grey Says Government Is Prepared to Give Province Control of Education, Police and Appointments

SPEAKS AT BERWICK

Special Cable to the Monitor from its European Bureau

LONDON—Speaking yesterday at Berwick, Sir Edward Grey made a notable contribution toward the home rule controversy. After declaring that the government would insist on the principle of the bill and that if violence was exerted against it, it would be met by violence, he explained that it was a part of the inevitable great devolution scheme for giving home rule in turn to Scotland and England. At the same time he declared that short of sacrificing the absolute principle of the bill the government were prepared to go to almost any length to secure settlement by consent.

If, he explained, Ulster was seriously afraid of what would happen under the new bill, the government was prepared to give her local autonomy; in other words a sort of home rule within home rule by permitting her to have control within the province of education, poliee and administrative appointments.

Sir Edward spoke with the greatest earnestness and declared that the government was absolutely serious in its offer, that if their opponents in Ulster were equally serious arrangements might be hoped for, only each must give the other credit for the same seriousness.

The phrase "home rule within home rule" is capable, of course, of extraordinary latitude, and it is possible that it has fallen to Sir Edward Grey to make the first proposal on lines advocated by the prime minister on which settlement may be found possible. In any case it is the first attempt at a constructive policy by a leading minister since the publication of Lord Loreburn's famous letter, and probably the proposal will play a great part in the negotiations of the next few months.

MILK DEALERS HEAR BOSTON MAN

CHICAGO—At the sixth annual convention of the International Milk Dealers Association held here Monday, C. H. Hood, president of H. P. Hood & Sons, wholesale and retail milk dealers of Boston, spoke on "Problem of Handling and Distributing Milk for a Large City."

HOME PROBLEMS ON FARMS TO TO BE SOLVED

North Dakota Agricultural Association Plans Departure in State Work and Woman Expert Is to Have Charge of Undertaking

COOPERATION IS ASKED

FARGO, N. D.—Director Thomas P. Cooper of the united experiment station and the better farming association in this state has developed a new idea. He is arranging with the women to work out the problems of the farm home, the arrangement of the farm kitchen, the installation of modern conveniences and other things of this nature.

North Dakota is the first of all the United States to attempt to solve this problem. Miss Mildred M. Vietch, a North Dakota girl, is the woman selected for the work and she is the first to engage in this line in the entire country says the Forum. In carrying out the ideas of Director Cooper she is a pioneer in the movement that may mean much for the farmers' wives of this country.

The farm women have to do more with less conveniences than the women in cities and towns. There are many conveniences that may be added to the farm homes at a very slight cost. It will be the purpose of the field woman of the better farming movement to place these facts before the farmers and their wives and to illustrate definitely how they may be installed in any particular home and under the peculiar conditions that may prevail.

GIOLITTI VICTORY OUTLOOK IN ITALY

Special Cable to the Monitor from its European Bureau

LONDON—Reports of the Italian elections are as yet only fragmentary, but they portend a large majority for Signor Giolitti.

GREATER PARIS PLANS GOING BEFORE MUNICIPAL COUNCIL

Extending Boundaries to Cover Territory Six Times Larger Is Proposition of Prefect Delanney, Who Would Demolish Fortifications, Give Broad Avenues

Special Cable to the Monitor from its European Bureau

LONDON—A scheme originated by M. Delanney, prefect of the Seine, is to be submitted to the Paris municipal council.

This proposal is to form a greater Paris some six times larger than the present city. The inner fortifications are to be removed and arrangements made to extend the municipal boundaries so as to administer the whole area together. Houses in the central quarters round St. Lazare railway station and in other parts of Paris will be removed, with the object of relieving congestion.

Following the example of Haussmann, broad avenues and gardens will be established, linking up the suburbs with the city. The proposal includes also final demolition of the fortifications as proposed some time ago.

ENGRAVING BUREAU VAULTS IMBEDDED IN LIVE WIRES

WASHINGTON—Construction work is in progress on the five vaults in the new building of the bureau of engraving and printing, at Fourteenth and B streets southwest. The estimated cost of construction will be approximately $110,000. Wire will form a network outside of all the vaults, of six-inch squares, and the wire will be charged with electricity for protection. The vaults are to be provided with the most modern safety time locks.

The largest of the vaults will be the one intended for the storing of engraving plates. The vault is to be located in the basement of the north court in the main building, between the third and fourth wings, as they are arranged beginning at the south end of the building. This vault will be 50 feet by 100 feet and 20 feet in height.

The postage stamp vault will be in the east end of the second wing basement, and will measure 45x50 feet, with a height of 18 feet. The vault for the internal revenue stamps will be in the basement of the main building just off the third wing, 45x56 feet in size, and 18 feet high.

The miscellaneous currency vault will be located in the basement of the main building, just off the second wing. It will measure 27x37 feet.

The second floor will be provided with the treasurer's vault, where bullion is to be deposited, says the Herald. This will be 25x47 feet, with a height of 17 feet.

MR. BRYAN IS IN FAVOR OF "NAVAL HOLIDAY" PLANS

WASHINGTON—William J. Bryan, secretary of state, Monday gave cordial approval to Secretary Daniels' statement that if other naval powers agreed to suspend naval construction for a stated period, or, as Winston Churchill put it, "take a naval holiday," the United States also would gladly do so.

A similar idea was embedded in Secretary Bryan's original proposal to the world powers for a universal peace pact, but was abandoned when it became evident that strong opposition would follow.

LONDON P. & O. SERVICE OFFICERS QUIT THEIR WORK

About Thirty Men Make Demand for Better Pay and Ask Other Concessions

Special Cable to the Monitor from its European Bureau

LONDON—Some 30 officers of the P. & O. service have ceased work, demanding better pay and other concessions. The officers are members of the merchant service guild and the secretary of the steamship company declares that the directors at present intend to take no further steps unless the officers discharge themelves.

Owing to the demand for berths on the large liners it is considered that the company will find no difficulty in replacing the officers should they resign.

SPAIN'S PREMIER SELECTS MINISTRY WITH DIFFICULTY

Special Cable to the Monitor from its European Bureau

LONDON—Senor Dato has succeeded in forming a Conservative ministry in Madrid. The refusal of Senor Maura to assist him and his departure from the capital made the task of the new premier particularly difficult. It is understood that the new cabinet will carry on the policy of the Liberals respecting the French entente.

BRITAIN'S POSTAL HEAD PROFITED BY TRIP TO AMERICA

Special Cable to the Monitor from its European Bureau

LONDON—Herbert Samuel, postmaster general, has returned from Canada and the United States.

In the course of an interview he declared that he had gained valuable information regarding telephone systems.

FILIPINOS' JOBS ARE CONFIRMED

WASHINGTON—The Senate Monday confirmed President Wilson's nominations of four native Filipinos to the Philippine commission, one of whom is to be secretary of finance and justice for the islands.

Senator Borah had given notice that he would block confirmation unless satisfactory assurances were given that the nominees were in favor of freedom on the islands.

MRS. PANKHURST'S LECTURE CANCELED

INDIANAPOLIS, Ind.—Mrs. Emmeline Pankhurst will not address the Woman's Franchise League of Indiana in this city, as had been planned. The engagement was canceled on Monday by the league officials.

The reason given was that Mrs. Pankhurst requested that she be permitted to take up a collection in addition to the stipulated sum which she had first agreed to accept for addressing the league.

CIVIC SOCIETIES FORM FEDERATION

NEW YORK—Civic organizations of New York formed a federation on Monday at a meeting of their representatives at the City Club. The object of the federation is "to enable the federated associations to act together for the promotion of community interests of a nonpolitical character."

PITTSBURGH MEN TO EXTEND TRADE BY TROLLEY TRIPS

Commercial Club Plans to Spend Day in Visiting Nearby Towns and Cities in Special Cars

PITTSBURGH—Innovations in extending trade and developing business have been inaugurated by the Pittsburgh Commercial Club. By trolley, the first pilgrimage is to be made Nov. 1. One day will be required to visit the business men of Butler, Evans City, Harmony, Zelienople and Ellwood City.

Two cars of the Harmony route will be in action and at the disposal of the club to journey to places where the aggregate population is more than 30,000. A tentative schedule provides the time to be spent at each point as follows: Evans City, 45 minutes; Butler, four hours and 45 minutes; Zelienople-Harmony, one hour, and Ellwood City four hours and 45 minutes, says the Gazette Times.

A. C. Terry is chairman of the committee in charge. One of the cars to be used will be the special parlor car operated by the trolley line. It is equipped with a motion picture apparatus which will be utilized in the various towns. Meals will be served at Butler and Ellwood City.

POWERS TO BACK UNITED STATES' MEXICAN POLICY

American Government to Lead All Nations in Single, Concerted Course of Action Toward the Southern Republic

GREAT BRITAIN ACTS

WASHINGTON—It is the talk in official circles here today that the powers, led by the United States, will adopt a concerted policy toward Mexico.

Reports from the British foreign office that Great Britain would do nothing in the Mexican situation, now that the election had been held in the southern republic, without consultation with the United States, added strength to the report that the American government plans a note to the powers.

Secretary Bryan, when shown despatches from London which asserted that Great Britain's recognition of Provisional President Huerta was given to extend only until the elections, stated that such had been the understanding here all the time.

It was the general belief in official

(Continued on page seven, column two)

WORLD PEACE AIM IS TO BE STUDIED BY TORONTO CLUB

University's International Polity Considers Means of Settling Disputes Without War

TORONTO, Ont.—The International Polity Club of the University of Toronto has been formed to encourage the study of international relations and problems relating to the economic futility of armed aggression, and to consider means of settling disputes without war. The membership is open to the faculty, graduates and undergraduates of the University, says the Globe. The following officers were appointed: Honorary presidents, Norman Angell and President Falconer; president, Main Johnson; vice-presidents, Professor G. Jackson and Craig McKay; secretary and treasurer, P. Goforth; joint secretary and treasurer, H. J. Duncan.

President Falconer declares himself such a strong believer in democracy that he always believed a nation could trust the people with anything that was reasonable. He held that the more thinking people there were all over the world the larger would be the consensus of opinion which would render impossible certain things that once were. President Falconer pointed out that the club was non-partizan, and all shades of political opinion might belong to it.

PANAMA CANAL EFFECT IS THEME AT MOBILE CONGRESS

Various Speakers Tell of Future in the Light of New Waterway—President Wilson Sees Emancipation From Outside Control Coming for Pan-America

MOBILE, Ala.—The Panama canal was the theme of speeches before the Southern Commercial Congress today. Memorial services were to be held in many of Mobile's churches at noon, at which prominent speakers were to eulogize Senator John Tyler Morgan, called "the father of the Panama idea."

In the regular sessions of the congress, Col. D. C. Collier, president of the Panama-Pacific exposition, spoke on the Panama canal and the great Southwest; John H. Haslam, chairman of the royal commission on agricultural credit, Saskatchewan province, on Canada's interest in the waterway; Senator Ransdell of Louisiana, on the canal's effect on American river and harbor improvements; Senator Jacintho Ferreira de Cunah, consul-general of Brazil, on commercial relations of South American nations with the United States, and Commissioner of Agriculture E. J. Watson of South Carolina, on what the commerce of the Panama canal means to the South.

Expectations of increased business from those interested in manufacturing and business as a result of the canal was expressed in addresses by Col. Harvie Jordon, president of the Tennessee Coal & Iron Company; Bradford Knapp, in charge of the department of agriculture's special farmers' cooperative demonstration work; Julian S. Carr, of Durham, N. C.; J. Rice Smith, of Richmond, Va.; Representative Hobson, of Alabama, and John M. Parker, honorary president of the Southern Commercial Congress. Five minute "free forum" talks by delegates followed each set speech.

Tonight Secretary of State Bryan was scheduled to lead discussion of the Panama Canal from the standpoint of South and Central America. Director John Barrett, of the Pan-American Union, the minister to Panama, the Peruvian minister, and the minister from Bolivia were also scheduled to speak.

Modern woman and her fields of usefulness, was the theme of discussions at the opening sessions of the woman's auxiliary of the congress. Mrs. O'Neal, wife of the Governor of Alabama, welcomed the delegates. Prominent speakers outlined woman's work in patriotic societies. These speakers represented the D. A. R., United Daughters of the Confederacy, Colonial Dames and the Daughters of the War of 1812. Mrs. Pennybacker, president of the General Federation of Women's Clubs, discussed

(Continued on page seven, column one)

EXPERT SOUGHT AS CURATOR AT ZOO

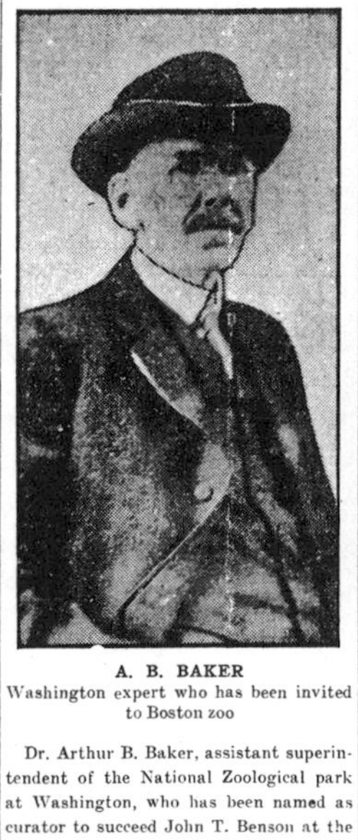

A. B. BAKER
Washington expert who has been invited to Boston zoo

Dr. Arthur B. Baker, assistant superintendent of the National Zoological park at Washington, who has been named as curator to succeed John T. Benson at the Boston zoo, accompanied D. Henry Sullivan, chairman of the park commissioners, in a visit to the zoo yesterday at Franklin park and to meet other city officials. Mr. Baker will be in Boston for about a week. Before he returns it is expected he will have made known his attitude in regard to the acceptance of the position.

UNITED STATES BUYS RADIUM

WASHINGTON—The bureau of standards of the department of commerce has bought $2100 worth of radium for establishing a standard for the United States. The first lot, worth $600, arrived on Monday.

NEW BATTLESHIP TEXAS IS FAST IN HER TRIALS

Most Powerful Dreadnought Afloat Exceeds Contract Speed by 1 1-4 Knots an Hour

ROCKLAND, Me.—Following the repairing of the engine which interrupted her standardization trial on Thursday the superdreadnought Texas, the most powerful battleship afloat, left to resume her builders' trials.

The trials were entirely satisfactory to the builders and government officials. The fastest run over the mile course was at the rate of 22.28 knots, exceeding by more than 1¼ knots the speed required by the contract.

The Texas made three runs over the mile course at 21-knot speed and five at the best speed attainable. It is expected the battleship will go to sea immediately for the four-hour official acceptance test, during which she must average better than 21 knots to meet the contract requirements.

The other trials will be held while the warship is on her way back to Newport News.

JAMES LARKIN IS SENTENCED FOR SEDITION

Dublin Strike Leader Found Not Guilty of Inciting to Riot or of Larceny, Makes James Connolly Leader

ACTS WHILE IN PRISON

Temporary Transfer of His Authority Announced Before Trial, When Priests' Charge of Proselytizing Is Denied

Special Cable to the Monitor from its European Bureau

LONDON—The Monitor's correspondent in Dublin telegraphs that the trial of James Larkin before Justice Madden was begun and completed yesterday. The jury returned a verdict of guilty on the first charge of sedition; not guilty on the second and third charges of inciting to riot and larceny.

The accused, addressing the court, declared that the evidence was based on that of one witness in a crowd of 8000 people and that the shorthand writer's notes were entirely incorrect.

The judge, in passing sentence, declared that the prisoner had brought terrible responsibility upon himself and that he must go to prison for seven months.

The Monitor correspondent, describing the scene in court, declares that the statements in the papers that Larkin lounged into court late are entirely incorrect. He arrived very hurriedly barely a moment after the court had assembled and had evidently no intention of keeping it waiting. He was evidently perfectly prepared for sentence and had already made arrangements for handing over the temporary leadership of the movement to James Connolly.

On the eve of the trial there was a great meeting of some 5000 to 6000 people in Phoenix park, where Larkin was greeted with immense applause. It was here he announced that from the following day Connolly would temporarily succeed to leadership, and defended his position regarding the deportation of children, declaring that he had never said a word against archbishops, or allowed a child to be proselytized, and that priests who had made statements to the contrary knew they were saying what was not true.

His remarks about children being taken to other homes, and about the action of the Ancient Order of Hibernians in opposing this were received with loud applause.

Another speaker at the meeting was Mr. Williams, London representative of the Railway Transport Federation. He contradicted the statement made in the Freemans Journal that Mr. Sedden had been sent into Dublin to settle the dispute over the heads of Larkin and his colleagues. The statement represented, be insisted, a deliberate attempt to drive a wedge between the men and their leaders, and he called on them to resist an attack which was being made upon the very essence of trades unionism.

The remaining speakers were emphatic in their condemnation of those who had opposed the removal of the children to homes where they could be properly cared for, and denounced the mob which, in some instances, actually attacked parents and took away their children from them.

Yesterday evening two bombs were exploded inside a street near the quays by a couple of boys who were seen to place them and light matches.

U. S. SENDS INQUIRY ABOUT MRS. RAND

WASHINGTON—Former Gov. Henry T. Gage of California has telegraphed to the state department asking that the government use its good offices in behalf of his daughter, Mrs. Lucille Rand, who has been arrested at Kingstown, Ire., on a charge of kidnaping. Mr. Gage said his daughter was a humanitarian worker, and had drawn herself into difficulty while seeking homes for starving children of Dublin strikers.

His request was transmitted to Ambassador Page at London.

To students, teachers and those in public and private life as well, each issue of the Monitor represents a fund of useful, needed information of a kind that is inspiring and constructive as well. To pass your copy along to another reflects credit upon the giver and the paper alike.

POSTAGE REQUIRED FOR MAILING TODAY'S PAPER
In United States....2c In England..........1½d In Germany..........5pf

THE CHRISTIAN SCIENCE MONITOR

LAST EDITION | Copyright 1914 By The Christian Science Publishing Society | BOSTON, MASS., MONDAY, JUNE 29, 1914—VOL. VI., NO. 182 | PRICE TWO CENTS

BOSTON BACKS CITIES' PLAN TO FORM ALLIANCE

Defensive and Offensive Union of Municipalities Is Planned to Represent People's Interests With Service Corporations

BUREAU ADVOCATED

Mayor Blankenburg of Philadelphia Has Already Secured Backing of Chicago, New York and Cleveland Mayors

Mayor Curley today announced his intention of participating in a defensive and offensive alliance of the cities of the country to deal with large public utility corporations. The alliance is being formed under the auspices of Mayor Blankenburg of Philadelphia. Mayor Carter Harrison of Chicago, Mayor Mitchel of New York and Mayor Baker of Cleveland have already enlisted.

The alliance is sending letters to the mayors of every city, and a nation-wide conference will be held next autumn. While this conference is being held, Philadelphia will be conducting a campaign before the public service commission for a lower schedule of rates for electric light and power.

The plan calls for the formation of a bureau of public utilities research, which shall equip itself to give to the cities able assistance in the same manner in which large utility companies give aid to smaller ones.

Just now the city of Boston is contending with the Edison Electric Illuminating Company over the question of what is a fair price per lamp for the lighting of the city's streets. Under ar-

(Continued on page seven, column one)

SETTLEMENT ANNEX RISES STEADILY

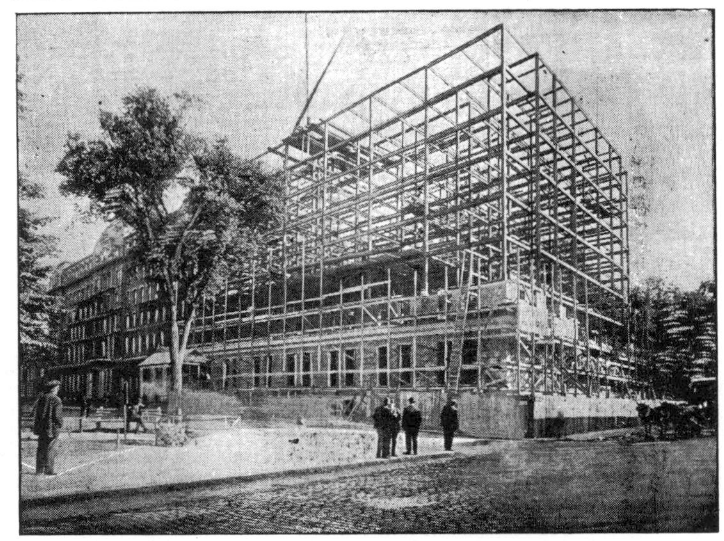

View of new Franklin Square house addition, looking from Washington street

With all of the steel structural work completed to the top on the new $250,000 annex to the Franklin Square House at Washington, Newton and James streets, workmen are now busily engaged in putting up the brick walls. The walls are today about half way to the top of the nine-story structure. Three floors also have been constructed and work on the others is progressing.

As yet no definite date for the dedication has been set, but it is expected that the new annex will be completed by Oct. 15 and that it will be opened by Nov. 1. Accommodations will be provided at the Franklin Square House with the completion of the annex for about 750 girls.

SUPERINTENDENCY CANDIDATES TAKE EXAMINATIONS

Examination of candidates for positions as superintendents in state superintendency unions are being conducted today and will be continued tomorrow at the State House. For the purpose of supplying them with adequate school supervision the towns of the state having a valuation under $2,500,000 have been formed into groups, each group employing one superintendent of schools for the entire district. There are 75 such unions. These include 239 towns. The number of towns in each group varies from two to six and the number of schools ranges from 17 to 54. A minimum salary of $1500 has been fixed.

A candidate for a union superintendency must first pass a state examination and hold a state certificate. If he is successful in obtaining a position, he is assured a tenure of three years. Capable and competent men are as a rule either continued in office from term to term or graduated to more important places in the cities and towns around Boston.

STATE AWARDS GARDEN PRIZES

Diplomas from the state were presented by Wilfrid Wheeler, secretary of agriculture, to the six prize winners in the corn and potatoes contests at the State House today.

The winners have just returned from a trip through Maine under the guidance of Prof. O. A. Morton of the state agricultural college, who has charge of the boys' and girls' club work. After the presentation the boys went to Arlington to inspect the market gardens there.

HOUSE PASSES COTTON SALES BILL

WASHINGTON—By 84 to 21, the House this afternoon passed the Lever "cotton futures" bill, regulating speculation in cotton on exchanges.

VERACRUZ REPORTS REVOLT

VERACRUZ—Revolt of 1000 Huerta troops at Queretaro and their desertion to the Villistas was reported here today by refugees who arrived from Mexico City.

FEDERAL GOOD ROADS BILL IS ABOUT TO BE REPORTED

Senate Postoffice Committee Expected to Approve Modified Bourne Plan With Loan Fund of $500,000,000 and Government Payment of One Half Maintenance

WASHINGTON—The Senate postoffice committee has practically agreed to report a modification of the Bourne billion dollar good roads bill in place of the Shackleford $25,000,000 a year plan which passed the House. The Bourne plan maps out a billion dollar expenditure in 50 years, the government to borrow the money on 3 per cent bonds and loan it to the states at 4 per cent, the difference being used to liquidate the debt. Four per cent a year, half of it by the federal government, is provided for upkeep.

In brief, the plan is for the states to build their roads on United States credit and the United States will pay half for maintenance.

The Senate will cut the Bourne figures in two, making the total amount for 50 years $500,000,000, but will increase the allowance for maintenance. Investigation convinces the senators that not more than this can be expended wisely, as much difficulty is experienced now getting contractors to build roads. Maryland, it is seen, is compelled to let road contracts to New York and New England firms.

It is likely that $2,000,000 will be provided by the United States for maintenance the first year, an equal amount to be spent by the states, the amount doubling the second year and increasing annually in proportion as the road mileage increases.

The states will determine where roads shall be built but the federal inspector must approve the construction before federal funds may be used for upkeep. Provision is made to see that roads are built for farmers, not wholly for automobiles.

ARCHITECT FOR BOYS' CLUB SOUGHT

Selection of an architect for the proposed $60,000 clubhouse for the Roxbury Boys Club and Institute of Industry is to be made as soon as possible. A meeting of the committee is to be held tomorrow evening in the store of Victor Heath. Two architects have submitted plans.

It is the intention to have the structure admirably equipped for both instruction and recreation purposes.

A site centrally located on Dudley, near the Dudley street terminal, was bought recently.

NEBRASKA TO GO ON MILITIA CRUISE

Tomorrow morning the United States battleship Rhode Island will steam away from the Charlestown navy yard for a summer militia cruise with militiamen aboard. She has been thoroughly overhauled during her stay here. The Rhode Island goes first to Fortress Monroe, Va., picking up militiamen at Newport News.

Three torpedoboat destroyers, the Patterson, Trippe and the Ammen, were today floated into the large drydock No. 2 at the navy yard, where they will be scraped and painted below water level.

LEGISLATORS DECIDE TO WORK LONGER HOURS

Members of Lower House Will Hasten Final Adjournment by Continuing Daily Sessions Till 5 in the Evening

BRIDGE MUST BIDE TIME

An order introduced by Representative Channing Cox of Boston, that the House sit from 10 in the morning until 6 p. m. for the balance of this session was discussed. He said that if the House worked expeditiously for the rest of this week, it might be possible to finish the session then.

Mr. Haines of Medford objected. He said that if the House sits until 6 many members cannot get trains for home until 7 or 8 o'clock; proper consideration of legislation will suffer on account of extreme length of daily meetings, and questions should not be rushed through in order to prorogue a few days sooner.

Mr. Cox then amended his motion to read from 10 until 5 o'clock, and by a voice vote the order was adopted.

Another order introduced by Mr. Cox that this week shall be deemed the last week of the session was adopted without debate.

Mr. Haines of Medford attempted to have the Wellington bridge bill discharged from the calendar. When asked by Mr. Washburn for some reason he said the Wellington bridge was an important highway between Somerville and Medford and it was of the highest importance that the bridge be repaired at once.

Mr. Hays of Boston said: "The gentleman from Medford has been on his feet for 20 minutes protesting against rushing matters and now he is trying to cram this down our throats. I would like to read the bill."

Mr. Haines finally withdrew his motion

MOTION PICTURES TO DISPLAY BAY STATE CARE OF FORESTS

Motion pictures are being planned by Frank W. Rane, state forester, as a medium of education in the forestry work of the state. They will show the different methods and processes used by the forest rangers in the development of state forests and when shown in Massachusetts will be accompanied by an explanatory talk by the state forester or one of his assistants. These pictures of men and apparatus at work will also be shown at the Panama-Pacific exposition.

Governor Walsh has been invited by Mr. Rane to attend the state forestry field day to be held July 7 on the estate of Gen. Charles Francis Adams, in Lincoln. Steps in the development of forestry will be exemplified on different portions of the 600-acre estate by Mr. Rane and his division superintendents, together with the various methods of spraying with high, low and hand power machines.

Plantation in woodland of larch, Scotch pine and hemlock, neglected woodland, woodland thinning and tracts of land with a pure stand of evergreen from which all hard woods have been removed and old growth of pine, one of the finest remaining groups will be shown. The tramp will be about three miles long. Samples of barks and fire prevention equipment on a private estate will be displayed.

Selectmen in towns through the state where the same conditions prevail will be invited to attend

SALEM BEGINS PREPARATIONS TO REBUILD CITY

Committee Votes $5000 to Start 200 Men at Work at Once Cleaning Up Section so That Reconstruction May Begin

INQUIRY BEING HELD

SALEM, Mass.—Five thousand dollars was voted by the general relief committee today to start 200 men at work tomorrow morning on the clean up work preparatory to rebuilding the burned sections of this city.

Eugene Fabens, chairman of the committee, asked for and received $5000 to supply furnishing for some of the houses, while the city council at its meeting appropriated $15,000 to provide temporary housing for the refugees.

Confidence in the ability of the citizens to rehabilitate the city was indicated in the opening of bids for $100,000 as a temporary loan in anticipation of taxes which was awarded to the Old Colony Trust at the low rate of 2.5 per cent.

With this encouragement the city council took up a discussion of plans for the rebuilding of the city and decided that next week action would be taken on a scheme for laying out the streets broader and straighter than they were before.

At the relief committee meeting Acting Adj.-Gen. Charles H. Cole explained how the control of the city would gradually be turned over to the citizens beginning tomorrow, when 40 civilians will be substituted for soldiers, thereby being afforded an opportunity to earn a day's pay.

The first move toward rehabilitation of commercial Salem will be made by the Korn Leather Company, which plans to resume operations at once. This will be the first of the destroyed factories to start up. Machinery will be moved over from Peabody with which to work, and as many men as possible will be given employment.

The state police, in addition to con-

(Continued on page six, column four)

INQUIRY INTO UNEMPLOYMENT IS PETITIONED

State Senate to Consider Whether It Will Concur With the House in Investigating the Situation of Labor Conditions

RESOLVE IS OFFERED

Proposition Put Forward by Morrison I. Swift Awaits Action by the Legislature—Committee Hearings Are Advocated

Investigation of the reasons for unemployment in Massachusetts is provided in a resolve which the legislative committee on rules has recommended should be admitted for consideration at the present session of the Legislature.

The resolve is today in the Senate clerk's office awaiting a vote as to whether the Senate will concur with the House in suspending joint rule number 12 so that the resolve may be admitted. If admitted the resolve will be referred to the committee on labor for a public hearing and report.

Introduced on petition of Morrison I. Swift, the resolve provides as follows: Resolved, That the state board of labor and industries be directed to investigate the problem of unemployment within this commonwealth and the measures that have been taken in other states and countries for its solution, and to endeavor to devise plans for the solution of the problem here by the public provision of work or by other methods or both.

The board may give public hearings if it deems them necessary, and shall have authority to administer oaths and to require the attendance of persons and the production of papers and books respecting all matters pertaining to the subject of the inquiry.

The board may employ such necessary clerical or other assistance, and may incur such other reasonable expenses, in the performance of its duties, as may be approved by the Governor and council.

The board shall report the results of its investigations and its recommendations to the next General Court, together with bills embodying them, not later than January 10, 1915.

MOTHER CHURCH ADDS TO RELIEF WORK FOR SALEM

Collections Taken at Sunday Services Will Be Used by Committee to Aid the Needy

The collections taken at The First Church of Christ, Scientist, in Boston, at morning and evening services on Sunday, together with contributions coming from other sources, will be used by the Christian Science relief committee for all those who are in need as a result of the Salem fire.

Cash contributions may be sent to Adam H. Dickey, 103 Falmouth street, Boston, or to Elmer E. Chain, 16 Lynde street, Salem. Clothing and other supplies may be sent direct to First Church of Christ, Scientist, 16 Lynde street, Salem, Mass.

The Salem Christian Science Church relief committee has a supply station in their church building which is just outside the fire zone. As this committee has a wide acquaintance among those who suffered loss by fire it will be able to tender efficient aid.

FEDERAL INCOME TAX LAW HELD CONSTITUTIONAL

DETROIT, Mich.—Constitutionality of the new federal income tax law was upheld today in a decision rendered by Judge Arthur J. Tuttle in the United States district court here. This is the first court ruling on the law.

The validity of the act was questioned by John F. and Horace E. Dodge, Detroit manufacturers. Appeal will be made to the United States supreme court.

BRIDGE ENGINEER RESIGNS PLACE

Fred H. Fay, division engineer of the bridge and ferry division of the public works department of the city, has handed in his resignation to take effect July 1. Mr. Fay leaves to enter private business with Prof. Charles M. Spoffard of the Institute of Technology, and Sturgis Thorndike, formerly with the public works department. The salary was $5000.

Samuel E. Tinkham, of the sanitary engineering department is to act in Mr. Fay's place, which will not be filled immediately owing to lack of work for the division.

SOMERVILLE MAN IS WINNER OF THE SHELDON FELLOWSHIP

Rufus Stickney Tucker of 32 Powder House boulevard, Somerville, has been awarded the Sheldon traveling fellowship at Harvard University for this year. This is considered to be the highest honor which can be bestowed upon a Harvard student, and is awarded annually to a graduate student, who has the initiative of selecting his own subject for research work.

Mr. Tucker is to study the effect of land taxes and will sail for England tomorrow on the steamer Cymric from Boston. He has specialized in the Harvard graduate school for three years in the department of economics, studying particularly public finances.

A native of Somerville, Mr. Tucker received his education in the public schools there, graduating from the Somerville Latin school in 1907. He received his A. B. degree from Harvard in 1911 and in 1912 won his A. M. degree. He was given a Ph. D. degree at commencement this month.

The past year he has been an assistant instructor in economics at Harvard and Radcliffe.

From Liverpool Mr. Tucker will go to Glasgow for a month. After brief study in London, he will continue his work on the continent until August, 1915, when he expects to return to Boston.

OFFICIALS OPEN THEIR OFFICES IN CITY HALL ANNEX

Occupation of the new city hall annex by the first of the city departments formerly located in rented quarters began today. The public buildings department is taking up its headquarters on the ninth floor, the board of health moves into its rooms on the eleventh floor tomorrow and the registrar's office, that of the sealer of weights and measures, and the election commission's offices at 100 Summer street are to be deserted for the new building this week.

It is expected that all the departments now occupying the outside quarters that have cost the city $50,000 annually will be in the annex by Sept. 1.

MONITOR INDEX FOR TODAY

Business and finance........... Pages 14-15
- Stock market quotations
- Dividends declared
- Produce prices
- Weather report

Editorial .... Page 18
- Another test for Austria-Hungary
- Pan-American precedents making
- College graduates see visions
- The over-ocean flight

Fashions and household .... Page 8
- Housedress woman can don quickly.
- Doing one's best for inadequate pay

General news—
- Federal good roads bill.................... 1
- Cities plan utilities alliance............ 1
- Salem plans rebuilding.................... 1
- Legislative proceedings.................. 1
- Heir to Austrian throne and wife shot 1
- Turkey opens railway line............ 2
- World airship rules urged............. 2
- Salvation Army congress in London.... 2
- World trade board has problem....... 3
- Armament topic of peace meeting 3
- Albania complications seen........... 3
- Congress proceedings 4
- Carranza asks more time 5
- Minimum wage hearing 6
- City Fourth of July plans 7
- Army and navy orders................. 9

Special Articles—
- Champaign-Urbana woman's club..... 9
- Portsmouth, O., gets costly bridge..... 5
- Monitorials 7

Sporting .... Page 16
- Pacific coast tennis
- Major league baseball
- English lawn tennis

The Home Forum.................. Page 17
- Divine Mind's ideas good only
- Ruins of Ft. San Lorenzo, Panama

POSTAGE REQUIRED FOR MAILING COPIES OF THE MONITOR

Up to 16 pages,	in United States, 1c;	to Foreign Countries, 2c
Up to 24 pages,	in United States, 2c;	to Foreign Countries, 3c
Up to 32 pages,	in United States, 2c;	to Foreign Countries, 4c
Up to 40 pages,	in United States, 3c;	to Foreign Countries, 5c
Up to 48 pages,	in United States, 3c;	to Foreign Countries, 6c

OPERA CHORUS RETURNS FROM PARIS SEASON

Singers Express Satisfaction With Artistic Outcome of Their Trip —Members of Staff of Company on Cincinnati

SHIP BRINGS TOURISTS

Returning from a successful 10-week engagement in Paris, 24 members of the Boston opera chorus arrived in Boston today as passengers of the Hamburg-American liner Cincinnati from Hamburg and English channel ports. Twelve other passengers aboard the liner also were connected with the opera company.

The singers all expressed gratification at a successful season in the French capital. The American members of the chorus were twice glad—once for the good outcome of their trip, and once for a sight again of their native shores.

Ralph Lyford, chorus director and assistant conductor of the opera company, with Mrs. Lyford, Benjamin Nielsen, connected with the scenery department, and Mrs. Nielsen, and Taddeo Wronski, the bass, accompanied by his wife were among those returning. Messrs. Lyford and Wronski brought with them plans for opening in Boston a studio of dramatic art.

Passengers on the Cincinnati numbered 363, of whom 81 traveled in the saloon, 80 second class, 39 third class and 163 steerage. The liner had a favorable trip, though forced to anchor this morning outside of the harbor for about an hour.

HEIR TO THRONE OF AUSTRIA AND HIS WIFE SHOT

Archduke Franz Ferdinand and Archduchess Attacked by Servian Student in Streets of Bosnian Capital During Visit

BOMB ALSO IS THROWN

Late Archduke One of Firmest Adherents of Church of Rome in Europe and Originator of a Plan for Great Slav Division

Special Cable to the Monitor from its European Bureau

VIENNA—The capital of Bosnia was yesterday the scene of another of those terrible incidents in the history of the house of Hapsburg. The heir to the throne of Austria and his wife were fatally shot in the streets of Serajevo by a Servian student, Princip. The first shot struck the archduke, and the second the archduchess, who was endeavoring to cover him.

The maneuvers of the Bosnian army had brought the archduke to Serajevo. On Sunday morning he left the barracks at 10 o'clock to drive to the town hall. On his way a bomb was thrown at him by a printer named Gabrinovitch.

He appears to have warded it off with his arm with the result that it fell into the roadway where an explosion inflicted a few scratches on the attendants in the following carriage.

Having satisfied himself that practically no one was injured the archduke drove to the town hall. He was received by the burgomaster and town council, but before the former could commence his speech the archduke interfered with the remark that he had come to visit the capital of Bosnia and had been greeted by a bomb thrown at him in the street. After this he directed the burgomaster to proceed.

Drive to Girls' School

On completion of the ceremony he and the archduchess reentered their carriages and drove to the girls' high school. After stopping the motor here he proceeded and had just reached the junction of Franz Josef Strasse and Rudolf Strasse when Princip fired his fatal shots. The motor was hurried to Konak to obtain medical help, but it was then too late.

What the effects of the tragedy will be, is at present impossible to say. The new heir to the throne, Archduke Karl Franz Josef, is a young man who served in the seventh dragoon regiment. Very little is known of his opinions and it is improbable that he has developed any very strong views.

The late archduke, on the contrary, was a soldier whose influence in the army was immense and who was also a convinced supporter of the Jesuits. He was indeed one of the firmest adherents of the church of Rome in Europe. Politically he was known to have conceived plans for the formation of an enormous Slav division of the empire which would have converted the dual monarchy into a triple one. This and his notorious antipathy to Pan-Servianism had caused him to be regarded in Belgrade with considerable disfavor.

Act May Be Political

The crime of Serajevo may have been an anarchist one, but it is equally likely to have been purely political. The harsh policy adopted toward the Servian kingdom and the determination to build up Albania at its expense has indeed been regarded largely as inspired by him.

He was again no particular friend of the Italian alliance and to him were attributed those difficulties between the two kingdoms which clouded the last years of Count Aehrenthal's ministry. For this reason the pistol shot of Princip will be regarded perhaps differently on the Vatican and on the Quirinal. In both there will be the same detestation of the crime, but while the pope will have lost a powerful friend, the King will have lost a lukewarm ally.

It is in Rome, perhaps, even more than in Vienna, that the loss of the archduke will be felt. He was essentially a pope's man and his organization of Christian Socialists in Austria was his reply to the effort to form anti-Romanist organizations in the country. In Germany the Kaiser loses principally a strong ally whilst, at the same time, the one man who would have been most formidable in holding together the German elements of the dual monarchy disappears.

Already it is said the days of the Austrian empire are numbered and that the German provinces will gravitate inevitably toward Berlin. This has often been said before, but it remains to be seen whether this time there is any more truth in these rumors of disintegration than in the past.

MESSAGE SENT TO EMPEROR

WASHINGTON—Upon receipt of a telegram from the American ambassador at Vienna reporting the shooting of Archduke Ferdinand of Austria, and his wife, President Wilson sent a message of condolence to Emperor Franz Jose-

THE CHRISTIAN SCIENCE MONITOR

LAST EDITION | Copyright 1914 By The Christian Science Publishing Society | BOSTON, MASS., WEDNESDAY, DECEMBER 9, 1914—VOL. VII., NO. 12 * PRICE TWO CENTS

GAINS MADE BY NO LICENSE IN CITY ELECTIONS

Temperance Advances in Worcester, Lawrence and Lowell Among Features of Balloting in 21 Cities Tuesday

HEAVY VOTE GENERAL

Revere Elects Arthur B. Curtis as Its First Mayor, While Voters of Attleboro Bestow Honor on Harold E. Sweet

Another gain for temperance was registered at the municipal elections held in 21 Massachusetts cities yesterday. While no city changed from license to no-license, as happened in the case of Northampton a week ago, there was a net gain for no-license of 2765 votes.

Some notable changes were made in the voting on the license question. The license majority in Worcester, for instance, dropped from 4772 to 2372. In Lawrence it fell off an even 2000 votes and at Lowell the no-license forces lowered the "yes" majority by 1081 votes.

Both the new cities increased the "no" majorities they had given last year as towns, Attleboro raising its majority for no-license from 653 to 1235 and Revere from 321 to 368.

Medford's "no" majority jumped from 1248 to 2018, and Everett's went from 1536 to 1998.

Revere and Attleboro held their first elections as cities.

Revere elected Arthur B. Curtis as its first mayor. Attleboro chose Harold E. Sweet.

Losses Are Few

The falling off of the "no" majorities in some of the cities was relatively small in most instances. The drop of 1607 in the Newton no-license majority was not regarded as significant. The voting there was very light because of lack of important contests, about 1800 less attending the polls than in 1913. The absentees are believed to have been largely no-license voters.

Lynn, Taunton, Gloucester and Haverhill gave larger majorities for license than they did a year ago, the increases ranging from 134 in the case of Gloucester to 485 in the case of Lynn. In the latter city, the license majority was raised from 36 in 1913 to 521.

Totals for the various changes in majorities yesterday show a gain of 1155 in "yes" majorities and a loss of 5612 in "yes" majorities as compared with a loss of 3553, including the 1607 in Newton, in "no" majorities. The net result was a gain of 2765 for the "no" voters.

Republicans Win

In general the Republican candidates for election were more successful than their Democratic opponents in cities where the voting was according to partizan lines. A conspicuous case was that of Woburn, where the Republicans wrested control of the mayoralty and the aldermanic chamber from the Democrats.

Harold P. Johnson was chosen mayor of Woburn over James H. Kelley, Democrat, by a plurality of 225. C. C. Clarke, independent, received 235 votes.

Other Woburn officials elected follow:

Aldermen-at-large—Thomas H. Cannon, D.; Edward H. Cummings, R.; Ellis H. Marshall, R.; James McGovern, R.; Walter R. Merchant, R.; Frank C. Nichols, R.; Arthur F. Ray, R.; Moses W. True, Ind.

Ward aldermen—Ward 1, Thomas H. McGowan, D.; ward 2, Harry Petersen, R.; ward 3, Joseph B. Devlin, D.; ward 4, Benjamin C. Rix, Ind.; ward 5, John P. Lynch, D., R.; ward 6, Winthrop M. Dearborn, R.; ward 7, Frank H. Graham, R., D.

School committee—Fred J. Brown, R., D.; Frank Kimball, R. D., Elizabeth W. Barker, R. D.

Contest in Lawrence

In the contest for mayor of Lawrence between two former mayors, John P. Kane won over William P. White by a vote of 5474 to 5177. The heaviest vote in the history of the city was cast.

John A. Flanagan won the contest for director of public property and Robert S. Maloney was elected director of health and charities. The school committee places went to Thomas M. Jordan and Michael A. Landers.

Lynn also cast the largest vote in its history, reelecting Mayor George H. Newhall for two years over John H. Cogswell by a vote of 8914 to 8083.

Frank A. Turnbull, commissioner of finance, was defeated by Roy F. Bergengren by a majority of 1809, while George H. McPhetres, commissioner of streets and highways, was reelected over H. H. Moore by a majority of 7289.

The Rev. C. Thurston Chase and S. Walter McDonough were elected to the school committee.

On a referendum the voters rejected the proposed "two platoon" system for the fire department by a vote of 11,295 to 4653.

Harold E. Sweet won the election for mayor of Attleboro over James A. Leedham, Jr., by a vote of 2326 to 804. The proposition to give the firemen one day

(Continued on page nine, column two)

GOVERNOR NAMES NEW JUSTICE OF SUPREME COURT

James B. Carroll of Springfield Proposed to Executive Council to Fill Vacancy on Bench

Among several important appointments Governor Walsh sends to the executive council at its regular session this afternoon is that of James B. Carroll of Springfield as a member of the superior court bench to succeed Justice Edward Peter Pierce of Brookline, named for the vacancy on the bench of the supreme judicial court.

The Governor named John F. Tobin of Quincy as a member of the board of labor and industries to succeed John Golden of Fall River, resigned. Mr. Tobin was educated in the public schools of Canada and worked as a shoe worker there until 1881, when he went to Rochester, N. Y. There he worked until 1895. In that year he was elected president of the Boot and Shoe Workers Union of the United States and Canada. He then moved to Boston and established the headquarters of the organization here and since has continued as head.

Other appointments are: John J. Tobin of Boston, member of the board of registration in pharmacy; John A. Fennessey of Boston, trustee of the Boston state hospital.

Other nominations were William G. Maguire of Boston to be clerk of the East Boston district court and Francis X. Reilly of Westboro to be clerk of the first district court of eastern Worcester.

Just before Mr. Carroll's name was sent in to succeed Judge Pierce the Governor received a delegation from the state branch of the American Federation of Labor urging him to retain Mr. Carroll as head of the industrial accident board. The delegation consisted of Edward S. Alden of Holyoke and Martin T. Joyce of Boston. There was also present a delegation from the Boston Central Labor Union: Representative Lewis F. Sullivan and Michael J. Murphy, deputy fire prevention commissioner.

RIVERS CONGRESS HEARS DEFENSE OF LEGISLATION

Senator Ransdell Says Federal Appropriations Are Not Dictated by Politics

WASHINGTON—Before 1000 delegates and visitors to the National Rivers and Harbors congress which opened today, Senator Ransdell, president of the organization, replied to charges that federal appropriations for rivers and harbors are dictated by political interests and favoritism.

The Louisiana senator said that to assert that river and harbor bills were full of appropriations for unworthy purposes was "a slanderous accusation" and denied that the congress was a "lobby."

Senator Fletcher also referred in caustic terms to the critics of river and harbor appropriations. Secretary of State Bryan made a brief welcoming address.

PRESIDENT WILSON IN CHAIR AT RED CROSS MEETING

WASHINGTON—With women knitting for Belgian soldiers and President Wilson presiding at the afternoon session, the tenth annual meeting of the American Red Cross Society was held today.

Reports submitted showed that $966,100 has been contributed for European relief and that 432,600 pounds of absorbent cotton and 579,000 yards of absorbent gauze have been sent by the society to Europe.

"There is undoubtedly much destitution in many parts of Mexico," said Counsellor Lansing of the state department in his report, "but because of the disturbed conditions the administration of relief in most parts of the country is practically impossible."

Dr. P. P. Jacobs of New York, who is directing the Red Cross Christmas seals campaign, reported that the sales this year will far exceed those of 1913, which amounted to 45,000,000.

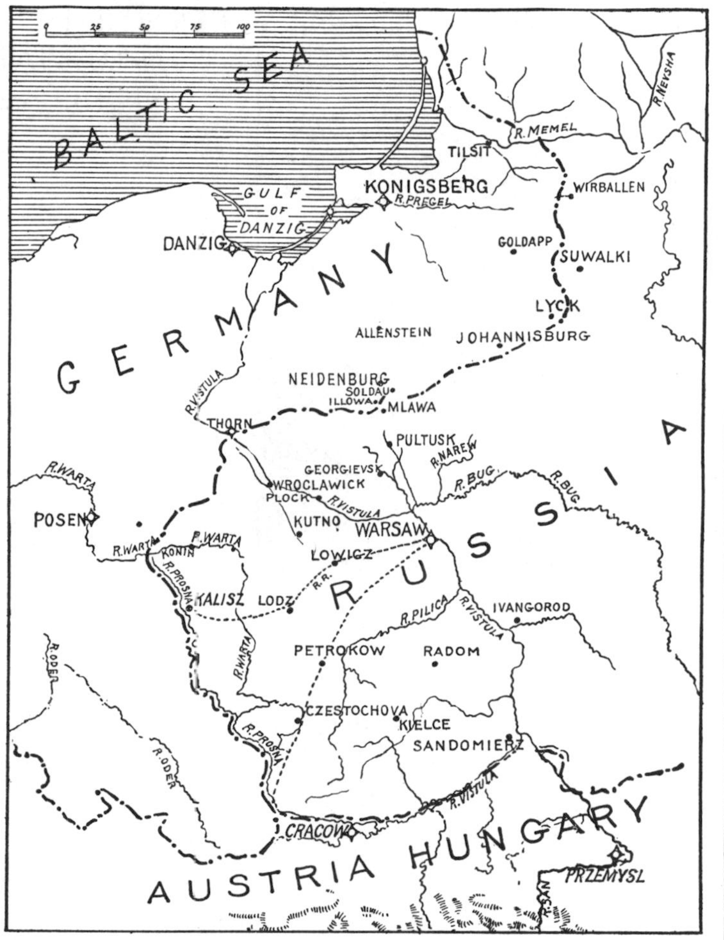

Scene of Russo-German operations, showing position of Lodz, Cracow and Warsaw

MR. WALSH URGES ENTHUSIASM FOR FARM INDUSTRY

Massachusetts Executive Says Great Markets Invite State to Become Leader in Agriculture, the Bedrock of All Business

WORCESTER, Mass—Gov. David I. Walsh advocates the appointment of a state commissioner of agriculture to devote all his time to the interests of the farmer. In an address before the Massachusetts state grange Tuesday he urged the members to show greater enthusiasm in the advancement of the business of farming and in seeking fair and favorable legislation.

"Industries may come and business enterprises of various sorts may come," he said in part, "but in the last analysis the bed rock on which all business is built is agriculture. It is the business above all others which the nation and the state should encourage.

"I want to see Massachusetts not only provide an education for the children of the public schools, but for every man, woman and child outside the public schools.

"It is a shame that we are not able to so develop and advance this business, with these great markets at our doors, that Massachusetts shall become the leading agricultural commonwealth in the nation. We need some enthusiasm in handling this matter. If there were more shown in regard to it, there would not be a single fair proposition in the interests of agriculture that would not pass the Legislature and be signed by the Governor."

MONITOR INDEX FOR TODAY

PEACE LEADER IS TOURING SCHOOLS OF NEW ENGLAND

Dr. James L. Tryon Also to Speak Before Societies and Clubs in Behalf of Movement

Dr. James L. Tryon, secretary of the New England department of the American Peace Society is in Maine this week on a speaking trip to preparatory schools, colleges and peace societies. Dr. Tryon left Boston Sunday, giving a lecture at Exeter, N. H., on his way to Maine. A lecture was given in Portland yesterday and he speaks in Lewiston today to the students of Bates College at the morning chapel exercises on "Germany in War Times."

An address is scheduled under the auspices of Bates College on "The European War and the Way to Peace" this evening. A stereopticon lecture on "One Hundred Years of Peace" will be delivered at the Jordan high school tomorrow morning and will be followed by the same address at the Edward Little high school in Auburn. Dr. Tryon will address the Orono Woman's Club Friday night and spend Saturday and Sunday in Bangor.

"World Federation and Police" is the subject of the talk to be given to the students of the University of Maine at Orono to which he returns next Monday morning. Dr. Tryon speaks that evening to the Y. M. C. A. of Augusta, and Tuesday to the Maine State Grange, which meets in Lewiston, ending his trip with a second address in Portland.

DELAYED FRUITER LIMON ARRIVES

United States mail was delayed three days, and a big cargo of ripening fruit was brought in by the United Fruit Company's steamer Limon, Capt. Benjamin Terfry, which was three days late in arriving from Havana, Cuba. The vessel arrived at Long wharf today, after encountering gales at sea. Seven days were taken by the banana boat to come from Havana, a trip usually done in four to five days. There were no passengers on the vessel. In cargo were 30,090 stems bananas, 100 boxes oranges, 26 crates grapefruit, 279 crates tomatoes and three crates peppers.

SHAH OF PERSIA TELLS OF CORDIAL RELATIONS

Special Cable to the Monitor from its European Bureau

LONDON, Dec. 8—At the opening of the Mejliss yesterday by the Shah of Persia the neutrality of Persia was referred to in a speech from the throne as also the cordial relations with all the powers

PARIS REPORTS MORE ACTIVITY IN YSER REGION

Official Communique Claims Some Gains in the Argonne, Which Berlin Headquarters Report Says Are Without Foundation

Special Cable to the Monitor from its European Bureau

PARIS, Dec. 8, 5 p. m.—An official communique reports that the Germans yesterday showed greater activity than on Sunday but in the Yser region and about Ypres the French artillery replied successfully.

Referring to the capture of Vermelles the communique states that this possession had for two months been the scene of a determined struggle. The Germans gained a footing there on Oct. 16 and in the fighting Oct. 21 to 25 succeeded in driving the French from the locality. After Oct. 25, however, sapping and mining operations brought the French steadily back to the edge of the forest, and on Dec. 1 they carried the park and the chateau.

Artillery battles have occurred on the Aisne and in the Champagne, the French heavy artillery dispersing several gatherings of Germans. In the Argonne the French, the report says, have gained some ground on the forest of La Grurie and to the northwest of Pont-a-Mousson in La Pretre wood.

Dec. 9—An official announcement states the Germans made a valiant attack at Veloi, south of Ypres, but were repulsed whilst the struggles in the forests of the Argonne and east of the Seine still continue vigorously.

BERLIN, Dec. 8, 6 p. m.—Headquarters report that the condition of the roads on the coast of Flanders has greatly hampered the movements of the German troops. North of Arras, the Germans have made some slight progress. Reports of French advance in the Argonne are stated to be without foundation, the Germans on the contrary gaining ground slowly but continuously. A French attack on the positions north of Nancy was repulsed yesterday, the report declares.

TRANSFERS ORDERED AT A NEW POINT

Orders were issued by the public service commission today that the Boston Elevated Railway Company issue transfer at the junction of Harvard and Commonwealth avenues to passengers on cars inbound on Commonwealth avenue to inbound Harvard avenue cars and vice versa, excepting passengers boarding in the Boylston street subway.

BARON KATO SAYS TIES WITH ALLIES GROW STRONGER

Japanese Foreign Minister Thanks United States for Work Done at Berlin Embassy

Special Cable to the Monitor from its European Bureau

TOKIO, Dec. 9—In the course of a speech delivered by Baron Kato, the foreign minister, in the Japanese Diet, yesterday, the speaker stated with satisfaction that the relations between Japan and the powers which are in common with Japan in a state of war, have grown more intimate than ever.

Various questions raised between Japan and China in connection with the attack on Kiao-chau, he said, have been on the whole settled satisfactorily. Referring to the success of the naval and military operations at Tsing-tao, Baron Kato expressed high appreciation of the loyal assistance rendered by the British land and naval forces.

Regarding the action in the Pacific, the imperial government had, he said, despatched a squadron to the German South Sea islands which are now under military occupation. Previous to the rupture of diplomatic relations with Germany, the German government, Baron Kato stated, detained many Japanese in different parts of the country, even imprisoning some on pretext of protecting the Japanese, the protests of Japanese representatives in Berlin against the treatment being ignored and a request for permisssion to visit the places where the Japanese were interned being refused. The Japanese government having requested the United States government to protect the Japanese embassy in Berlin and Japanese interests in Germany, the United States government consented and as a result a great majority of the Japanese have been released.

"We deeply appreciate," Baron Kato continued, "and are sincerely grateful to the United States for their good will." Regarding China the Japanese government hoped nothing would disturb peace and order, its maintenance being of the greatest importance.

DR. ANNA H. SHAW ENTERTAINED BY BACK BAY WOMEN

Dr. Anna Howard Shaw, president of the National American Women's Suffrage Association, who arrived in Boston yesterday for a two-days' visit, will spend most of her time during the next year speaking for equal suffrage in the states where the vote will probably be the issue next fall. The first of February she goes South for three months. The national organization will concentrate its work for suffrage in the South, especially on Alabama.

Dr. Shaw was given an informal reception at the home of Mrs. Robert Gould Shaw yesterday afternoon, 151 Commonwealth avenue. Mrs. Wirt Dexter, and Mrs. Robert Gould Shaw received with Dr. Shaw. Mrs. Harry Russell, Mrs. Joseph Fay and Mrs. James A. Parker assisted. Dr. Shaw spoke in the Arlington town hall last night. She will speak at an afternoon reception at the home of Mrs. Robert Gould Shaw Jr., in Brookline, tomorrow afternoon, after which she will return to New York.

RULES FOR STATE BANKS PROBLEM OF RESERVE BOARD

WASHINGTON—The federal reserve board held its conference Tuesday with representatives of state banks and trust companies to discuss regulations for their entrance to the federal system but failed to reach a point where definite rules to govern their admission could be outlined.

The committee of state bankers, appointed by the American Bankers Association, later announced its inability to solve the problem for the present. The board probably will take it up with the governors of the 12 reserve banks Thursday and with the federal advisory council.

Bankers here tentatively offered one idea which did not meet with great favor among board members. They proposed that state banks and trust companies be permitted to quit the federal system without the process of liquidation now required.

The bankers pointed out that hardships might be imposed upon state institutions through the power of the board by law to make regulations to govern the operation of all member banks, and that in such case no remedy would be left to them but liquidation.

MYRON T. HERRICK GREETED BY MANY

NEW YORK—Myron T. Herrick, former ambassador to Paris, returned home today on the French liner Rochambeau. A big delegation from Cleveland, 400 members of the Ohio Society in New York, and several score French-Americans, headed by the French consul, were at the dock to meet him.

He returned as a private citizen, but the bearer of the Grand Cross of the Legion of Honor, conferred upon him by wireless from France. Commander Dumont of the Rochambeau formally decorated Mr. Herrick in the salon of the ship yesterday.

GERMANS SAID TO BE PURSUING RUSSIAN ARMY

Berlin Official Statement Declares the Kaiser's Forces Are Following Up Lodz Victory East and Southeast of the City

PRISONERS ARE TAKEN

Petrograd Intimates Capture of Point in Stating Town Had Lost Military Importance and Defense Not Now So Urgent

Special Cable to the Monitor from its European Bureau

BERLIN, Dec. 8, 6 p. m.—Headquarters report that in Poland the Germans are pursuing the retreating Russians east and southeast of Lodz. Besides the large losses already reported the Russians, it is stated, have lost 1500 prisoners with 16 cannon and ammunition carts.

PETROGRAD, Dec. 8—An official statement announces that Austrian and German forces have been observed north and south of Cracow. Intermingling of the forces, the report states, is because the Austrians are no longer capable of independent action.

During the fighting in the latter part of November, Lodz acquired considerable military importance but the German offensive on the Lodz-Lovicz line having failed the question of the defense of Lodz is no longer so urgent.

The defense of this large city, the report continues, drawing the bombardment of the Germans, presents many military difficulties, giving the Russian front an abnormal contour and embarrassing communications with the rear.

It may be expected, the report concludes, that with a lull on the left bank of the Vistula the Russian line near Lodz will be reformed.

AMSTERDAM, Dec. 9—From Budapest it is officially announced the Russians, who had entered the district of Saros and Zemplin, are retreating, the Austrian troops being in Galician territory at several points. Two or three Hungarian communes only, the report adds, are in Russian hands.

AUSTRIAN FORCES REGROUPING, SAYS OFFICIAL REPORT

Special Cable to the Monitor from its European Bureau

AMSTERDAM, Dec 9—An official Austrian report states that the regrouping of the Austrian forces continues according to plans, the Serbian attempts to interfere with the movements having been repulsed with severe losss. The Austrian offensive movement south of Belgrade, the report adds, progresses favorably, 14 officers and some 400 men having been captured.

NISH, Dec. 8—Fighting on the northeastern front continued on Dec. 5. According to an official statement the Serbians, who had resumed the offensive, were successful along the whole line, especially on the left wing, where the Austrians were compelled to retire in disorder and the Serbians captured in the pursuit six officers and 1810 prisoners, two mountain howitzers, five mountain guns, four machine guns and stores.

NOMINATED BY THE PRESIDENT

WASHINGTON—The President today nominated:

To be associate justice of the supreme court of the District of Columbia, Frederick L. Siddons of Washington.

To be third judge of the circuit court of the first circuit of the territory of Hawaii, Thomas B. Stuart of Honolulu.

To be United States attorneys: John D. Lynn of Rochester, N. Y., western district of New York; John A. Fain of Lawton, Okla., western district of Oklahoma.

To be United States marshal: Ewing C. Bland of Kansas City, Mo., western district of Missouri.

Brigadier-general to be major-general: Frederick Funston.

PITTSFIELD BOYS ARE NOMINATED

Special to the Monitor from its Washington Bureau

WASHINGTON — Representative Treadway today nominated the following Massachusetts boys as candidates for West Point Military Academy: Principal, William C. Cuggan of Pittsfield; alternates Clinton S. Merry and T. Ackley Gaylord of Pittsfield.

For the Navy Academy: Principal, William E. Hilbert, Holyoke; alternates, Paul G. Neal, Williamstown; Alfred E. Robinson, Hinsdale, and Thomas M. A. Dillon of Pittsfield. The West Point examination will be in March and the Annapolis examination in February or April.

THE CHRISTIAN SCIENCE MONITOR

LAST EDITION { Copyright 1915 } { By The Christian Science Publishing Society }   BOSTON, MASS., THURSDAY, MAY 13, 1915—VOL. VII., NO. 143   PRICE TWO CENTS

NOTE OF U. S. TO GERMANY TO BE SENT TODAY

Document Stating Policy in Reference to the Sinking of the Lusitania Will Be Given Out for Publication Tomorrow

NATION UNANIMOUS

President Gets Many Messages From All Parts of Country Indorsing His Course — He Will Go to New York

Special to The Christian Science Monitor from its Washington Bureau

WASHINGTON—President Wilson finished the American note to Germany this morning and left the White House at 10:15 for an automobile ride. It was understood that the note would go forward by cable immediately, probably via Italy. It will be published in the Friday morning newspapers.

Secretary Bryan said that the note would go forward during the day and probably would be delivered to the German foreign office Friday morning. It is between 1000 and 1500 words long, he said.

Telegrams continue to arrive at the White House from all parts of the country, almost unanimously expressing a purpose to "stand by the President."

The President plans to go to New York for the naval review, as previously arranged, probably leaving Washington Friday night and returning the following Wednesday night or Thursday morning. He is to attend the city committee luncheon Monday and will review the fleet Tuesday as it passes out to sea.

Referring to the President's note to Germany, whilst it is perfectly possible to forecast the terms of the document, and whilst this has been very generally done, we feel compelled to adhere to the request of the President not to give publicity to partial statements of such documents of vital importance, until the full terms are published.

On the occasion of the note sent to the British government some months ago, the President was personally and officially embarrassed by the publication of forecasts which were so partial as not only to prove entirely inadequate but positively inaccurate. The situation so created was humiliating for the President and embarrassing to the government, and both the President and the government should be protected from a repetition of it.

GERMANY CANCELS ALL NOTICES OF WARNING

WASHINGTON—The German embassy last night notified by letter and telegraph newspapers in all of the larger cities of the United States to discontinue the publication of its advertisement warning Americans against transatlantic travel on belligerent ships. The message to the newspapers follows:

"Please cancel without fail imperial German embassy advertisement ordered to appear again next Saturday, May 15."

THE PRESIDENT HEARS FROM PROFESSOR TAFT

WASHINGTON—President Wilson received a letter from Prof. W. H. Taft yesterday expressing confidence in his ability to handle the situation growing out of the sinking of the Lusitania. The President has written a reply to Professor Taft thanking him warmly. Professor Taft in his letter expressed his views on what should be done in the present situation. While the letter was not made public, it was understood that Professor Taft and the President are in substantial accord on the subject.

(Continued on page nine, column two)

MONITOR INDEX FOR TODAY

MAP SHOWS GERMAN SOUTHWEST AFRICA AND ITS CAPITAL WINDHOEK.

GERMAN CAPITAL IN S. W. AFRICA IN BRITISH HANDS

Special Cable to The Christian Science Monitor from its European Bureau

CAPE TOWN, Thursday—An official statement announces the entry of General Botha into Windhoek, the capital of German Southwest Africa, without opposition, yesterday, the Union Jack being hoisted at the Rathaus.

Some 3000 Europeans and 12,000 natives were in the town.

CONVENTION OF PROHIBITIONISTS OF STATE OPENS

State Chairman Bingham Pledges Party to Be True to Responsibilities as First Session Is Called to Order in Ford Hall

Pledging the Massachusetts Prohibition party to be true to its responsibilities this year in view of its increased prominence in the state which is now the focal point of prohibition activities, Solon W. Bingham, state chairman, today opened the annual convention of the party at Kingsley hall, Ford building. In attendance were 150 delegates.

The convention will name the party's candidate for Governor of Massachusetts, and adopt a platform. William Shaw of Ballardvale, treasurer of the United Society of Christian Endeavor, is practically the only candidate mentioned for the gubernatorial nomination among the delegates today. It was expected he would receive the nomination. Many present wore Shaw buttons.

It was said by one official of the party this forenoon that the gubernatorial candidate in all probability would be the only one decided upon today, the remainder of the state ticket being left to the decision of the executive committee.

Following the reading of the formal call of the convention by Acting Secretary Wilbur D. Moon, prayer was offered by Frank Curtis and then State Chairman Bingham introduced Howard E. Kershner of Boston as the temporary chairman.

Says Prohibition Is Coming

Declaring that the tide is setting in the direction of prohibition and that now is the time in which to keep the issue clear by placing the party ticket before the voters, Mr. Kershner delivered a lengthy address before the convention. The speaker formerly was a Kansan. He said in part:

As an adopted son of Massachusetts I join my heart and hand with yours for a fight to the last ditch for prohibition here even as we now have in Kansas. And then joining the interests of the 48 states of this great empire separated by 3000 miles, together we will work, the sturdy Puritan New England

WATER WORKS MEN CHOOSE N. Y.

CINCINNATI—New York was chosen as the next convention city at the annual convention of the American Waterworks Association.

RESPONSIBILITY FOR LUSITANIA LOSS DISCUSSED

In Official Circles in Britain Situation Is Considered and Explanation Given — Steamer Unarmed During the War

Special Cable to The Christian Science Monitor from its European Bureau

LONDON, Thursday—Regarding the German government's statement that the responsibility for the Lusitania's sinking rests with the British government which, through its plan of starving the German civilian population, compelled Germany to resort to retaliatory measures, official circles point out that in December last Von Tirpitz foreshadowed in an interview with the Associated Press a submarine blockade of Great Britain and on Jan. 30 and Feb. 1, respectively, a merchant ship and a hospital ship were torpedoed.

Feb. 4, the German government declared its intention of instituting a general submarine blockade of Great Britain and Ireland with the avowed purpose of cutting off supplies, the blockade being put into effect Feb. 18.

As already stated, a merchant vessel had been torpedoed at the end of January. Before February 4 no vessel carrying food supplies for Germany had been stopped by the British government except when there was reason to believe the supplies were intended for the use of armed forces of the enemy or the enemy government.

The British government had informed the state department on Jan. 29 that they were bound to place in prize courts foodstuffs on the Wilhelmina, which was going to a German port in view of the government control of foodstuffs in Germany, the cargo being destined for an enemy government and, therefore, liable to capture.

The decision of the British government to carry out these measures was due to the instituting of the submarine blockade by the German government. This, added to other infractions of international law by Germany, led to the British reprisals which differ from the German action in that the British government scrupulously respect the lives of non-combatants traveling in German vessels.

The latter do not even enforce the recognized penalty of confiscation for a breach of blockade whereas the German policy is to sink enemy and neutral vessels at sight, totally disregarding the lives of non-combatants and neutral property.

As to the German statement that despite their offer to stop the submarine war if the starvation plan was given up, Great Britain had taken even more stringent blockade measures, the reply is that it is not understood from the reply of the German government that they were prepared to abandon the policy of sinking British merchant vessels by submarines.

The Germans refuse to abandon the using of mines for offensive purposes on the high seas on any conditions. They have committed various other infractions of international law such as strewing the high seas and trade routes with mines and British and neutral vessels will continue to run danger from this source whether Germany abandons the submarine blockade or not.

Since the employment of submarines, contrary to international law, the Germans have also used asphyxiating gases and poisoned wells in South Africa. As to the German representation that the British merchant vessels are generally armed and repeatedly ram submarines, it is replied that it is scarcely surprising that such vessels knowing their liability to be sunk without warning should take measures for self-defense.

Regarding the Lusitania, she was not armed on her last voyage and has not been armed during the whole war.

Regarding Germany's attempt to justify the Lusitania's sinking by the fact that she had arms and munitions on board, it is pointed out that the presence of contraband on a neutral vessel does render her liable to capture but not to destruction with the loss of a large portion of the crew and passengers.

Every enemy vessel is a fair prize but there is no real provision, not to speak of the dictates of humanity, to justify what can only be described as murder because a vessel carried contraband.

As to the German argument that after repeated official and unofficial warnings, the British government were responsible for the loss of life as they considered themselves able to declare the vessel ran no risk and thus lightheartedly assumed responsibility for human lives on board the steamer which owing to its armament and cargo was liable to destruction, the reply is that the British government never declared the boat ran no risk.

The fact that the Germans issued a warning shows that the crime was premeditated and that they had no more right to murder the passengers after warning than before.

In conclusion it is pointed out that in spite of attempts to put the blame on Great Britain the fact remains that it was a German torpedo fired from a German submarine that sank the vessel causing the loss of over 1000 lives.

ITALY ORDERS GERMANS BARRED FROM STEAMERS

Teutonic Allies Also Are Excluded Under an Order Just Announced in Boston

Citizens of Germany, Austria-Hungary and Turkey are now barred from the steamers of all the Italian lines, according to orders from Italy received by Charles V. Dasey, local agent for these lines in Boston. All persons descended from citizens of these countries, even if naturalized citizens of the United States or other countries, are also barred from the vessels of Italy. No exceptions are made in these rules favoring nurses or others on similar missions.

The agents here say this is the result of the sinking of the Lusitania. Up to this time women, children and men past the fighting age could secure passage even when intending to travel into Germany. This order resulted in several persons in Boston being forced to give up their tickets.

NEW YORK—Representatives of the big Italian steamship lines today said they had received instructions that hereafter they should refuse passage to women and children of German, Austrian or Turkish nationality and even naturalized Americans formerly of those countries.

RUSSIANS DRIVE GERMANS OUT OF SHAVLI DISTRICT

Petrograd Announces Opponents' Advance in West Galicia Checked—Vienna Tells Gains

Special Cable to The Christian Science Monitor from its European Bureau

PETROGRAD, Thursday—The general staff report in the Shavli district the Russians continued to press the Germans successfully, driving them from Shavli to the southwest. On the left of the Vistula, south of Sochaczew, in mid-Poland, the Russian infantry crossed the Bzura Tuesday night capturing a group of German trenches after a bayonet fight and taking several dozen prisoners. The German efforts to attack the Russian reconstruction of troops south of Skierniewice and Rawa were repulsed.

In West Galicia, the Russians, in the direction of North Lutowiska on the Carpathian front near Smolnik, continued retirement to previously assigned positions, the hostile offensive being checked by the Russian counter-attacks. Towards the Uzsok pass and Stryj, the Austrian attacks were repulsed with heavy Austrian losses.

Near Rozianka, east of Uzsok, a hostile mine exploded near the Russian trenches and an attack followed. A determined Russian counter-attack compelled an Austrian flight in disorder.

In East Galicia, in the Jaworik range region, the Russians completed their success by an energetic offensive. During the past few days the Austro-Germans at this point suffered heavily, leaving over 5000 on the field.

In the transdniester region, on the Czernowitz-Obertyn front, for a distance of over 40 miles, the Russians took the offensive and progressed very successfully.

The Russians captured numerous prisoners, over 5000 on Monday, alone, six guns, eight machine-guns and much booty being also taken. The Austrians retiring hastily evacuated the whole of the left bank of the Dneister, being ejected also from Zaleszczeki.

VIENNA, Thursday—An official communique states that the defeat of the Russians' third army right armies is increasing in magnitude. The Russian troops with trains are flying in disorder towards Jaroslau, Przemysl and Chyrow. Strong Russian columns are flying from the Sanok and Lisko region eastwards, being attacked from the south by the Austrians advancing via Baligrod and Poland.

In a further pursuit the Austrians crossed the Lower Wislok, capturing Rzeszow. Dynow, Sanok and Lisko are in Austrian hands.

Owing to the extraordinary Austrian successes in West and Central Galicia, the Russians' Carpathian front, east of the Uzsok pass, is also beginning to waver, the Austro-Germans troops attacking on the entire front. The Russians near Turka, and in the Orawa and Opor valleys are retreating.

North of the Vistula, the Austro-Germans have advanced across the Nida, while in southeast Galicia, strong Russian forces have crossed the Dneister toward Horodenka, the Austrians evacuating Zaleszczyki.

BERLIN, May 13—Headquarters report on the Bzura, a Russian battalion which attempted to cross the Bzura was annihilated. In Galicia, the Russian pursuit continues. A battalion of the fourth Prussian regiment of the guard captured 14 officers, including a colonel, 4500 men, many guns and a machine-gun company, with teams and baggage.

Allied troops crossed the San between Sanok and Dynow and reached further north, to the Rzeszow and Miliec district. The Germans fighting on both sides of Stryj have ejected the Russians from their positions.

DETROIT CARMEN STRIKE

DETROIT, Mich.—Twenty-two hundred motormen and conductors of the Detroit Street Railway Company went on strike at 6 a. m. today. The company made no effort to run cars.

Map shows French and Belgian territory where present extensive operations are in progress

BEHAVIOR OF TEUTON TROOPS IN BELGIUM SEEN

British Committee Appointed to Consider Evidence Collected for Government Makes Report

Special Cable to The Christian Science Monitor from its European Bureau

LONDON, Thursday—The report of the committee appointed by the prime minister in December last to consider and report on the evidence collected for the British government as to the behavior of German troops in Belgium is published.

The committee consists of Sir Frederick Pollock, K. C., Sir Edward Clarke, K. C., Sir Kenelm Digby, K. C., Sir Alfred Hopkinson, K. C., Mr. H. A. L. Fisher and Mr. Harold Cox, with Lord Bryce as chairman.

Summarizing its conclusions the committee declares:

It will be seen that the committee has come to a definite conclusion on each of the heads under which the evidence has been classified:

It is proved:

First—That there were in many parts of Belgium deliberate and systematically organized massacres of the civil population, accompanied by many isolated outrages.

Second—That in the conduct of the war generally innocent civilians, both men and women, were killed in large numbers, women attacked and children slain.

Third—That looting, house burning and the wanton destruction of property were ordered and countenanced by the officers of the German army, that elaborate provision had been made for systematic incendiarism at the very outbreak of war, and that the burning and destruction were frequently where no military necessity could be alleged, being indeed part of a system of general terrorization.

Fourth—That the rules and usages of war were frequently broken, particularly by the using of civilians, including women and children, as a shield for advancing forces exposed to fire, to a less degree by killing the wounded and prisoners and in the frequent abuse of the Red Cross and the white flag.

Sensible as they are of the gravity of these conclusions, the committee conceives it would be doing less than its duty if it failed to record them as fully established by the evidence. Deplorable conditions prevailed over many parts of Belgium on a scale unparalleled in any war between civilized nations during the last three centuries.

The report makes an official document of 61 printed pages, or upward of 30,000 words. It states that 1200 witnesses have been examined, the depositions being taken by examiners of legal knowledge and experience, though without authority to administer an oath. The committee also submits extracts from a number of diaries taken from the Germans, chiefly German soldiers, and in many cases officers.

DYE SITUATION IN U. S. IS HELD LESS SERIOUS

Newark Manufacturer Declares Textile Mills Do Not Necessarily Face a Shutdown

Special Cable to The Christian Science Monitor from its Eastern Bureau

NEW YORK—"While it is unquestionably true that there is a serious shortage of dyestuffs in the United States at this time, there is also not the slightest danger that the textile industries, or any of the allied industrial activities depending largely upon dyes for their processes will be hampered to the point of shutting down," said Eugene Merz, of the firm of Heller & Merz, of Newark, N. J.

Mr. Merz is recognized in the United States not only as an authority on dyes and dye making, but as a member of one of the pioneer American firms engaged in producing domestic dyes. To a Christian Science Monitor representative who interviewed him at the big plant on Hamburg place, Newark, Mr. Merz said emphatically:

"There are more angles of view on this one question than on any diplomatic subject I have ever heard of. One may obtain every shade of opinion between no dyes with an immediate suspension of all textile industries, to one asserting there is no shortage and that the whole thing is a bugaboo. The truth of the situation is difficult to arrive at, but by no means impossible, and I think a great part of the outcry is instigated from selfish or political motives on the part of those interested.

"I am well aware that the government at Washington is concerned over the dyestuff situation in this country, and I think it may well be, for to some considerable extent at least our government during many years has been the architect of the situation that now confronts us, in that it took no measures to encourage an industry that has struggled for 25 years to get itself upon a sure productive footing, but on the contrary acted with certain home interests in discouraging the American manufacturer of dyes."

"Then you believe there is a political phase to the present situation?" Mr. Merz was asked.

"If by a political phase you mean that the tariff enters into the matter, I must say yes," he replied. "During years this tariff on dyes and raw chemical materials for their preparation has been a recurrent issue. With every change in the tariff there has been the concerted attempt to reduce the duty on the finished product, and to raise the rate on the raw materials. Where the American manufacturer has been granted a living protection rate for his encouragement the duty on the product has been automatically absorbed by the European manufacturer.

"As an example, some few years ago we bought a certain chemical from an English firm and paid the duty. Then the rate was raised and immediately the shipments instead of coming to us C. I. F. began to arrive F. O. B. New York. In order to keep his customers the English firm took care of the duty. When the situation was reversed, on another

(Continued on page ten, column two)

FRENCH REPORT SEVERE ACTIONS NORTH OF ARRAS

Paris Communique Asserts Germans Delivered Fruitless Counter-Attacks With Reinforcements—Big Teuton Loss

TOWNS BOMBARDED

Berlin Admits French Still Hold German Trenches, but Declares Attempt to Retake Hartmannsweilerkopf Points Fail

Special Cable to The Christian Science Monitor from its European Bureau

PARIS, Thursday—The latest official communique reports the continuance of severe fighting north of Arras, the Germans delivering fruitless counter-attacks Tuesday night, with reinforcements.

The Germans experienced particularly severe losses in an attack against Neuville St. Vaast.

A second attack between Carency and Ablain was also repulsed and a third attack, starting from Ablain, also completely failed. The French progressed, Wednesday morning, in the woods, east of Carency, and carried three successive lines of trenches bordering the wood to the north of Carency.

The French then penetrated into the wood, being thus very close to the last communication remaining open to the defenders of the position, finally capturing another part of the village, taking 400 prisoners.

Wednesday, the French attacked a portion of Neuville St. Vaast, still held by the Germans, capturing several groups of houses.

The total prisoners captured by the French since Saturday is 4000.

Elsewhere, the French attacks near Berry-au-Bac, Beausejour and between Marie Therese and Bagatelle.

Wednesday—An official communique states that in the sector north of Arras, the French maintained all their gains except in front of Loos, where a night counter attack enabled the Germans to retake part of the ground captured during the day.

On the remainder of the front there were artillery combats.

BERLIN, Thursday—Headquarters report that hostile airmen bombarded Bruges Tuesday without causing any military damage.

East of Ypres the Germans carried an important height.

Dunkirk was bombarded by the Germans Tuesday and east of Dixmude the Germans shot down a British aeroplane.

Between Carency and Neuville, north of Arras, the French still hold the German trenches captured lately, but all of the French attempts to break through the German line Tuesday failed.

French attacks were specially directed against the positions east and southeast of Vermelles, Lorette height, Ablain and Carency and the German positions north and northeast of Arras, all the attacks breaking down with heavy French losses.

A French attempt to retake Hartmannsweilerkopf has collapsed. After strong artillery preparations, the French chasseurs Alpins reached a blockhouse on the ridge but were immediately ejected.

BRITISH PLAN TO INTERN ALIENS OF HOSTILE COUNTRIES

Special Cable to The Christian Science Monitor from its European Bureau

LONDON, Thursday — Anti-German demonstrations continued yesterday throughout England, being especially violent in London and at Southend, where a recent Zeppelin raid occurred. At the latter place the military were called out.

The question of dealing with the situation is under consideration by the government.

Wednesday—In the House of Commons this afternoon Mr. Asquith said the government were carefully considering the practicability of segregation and internment of aliens of hostile countries on a more comprehensive scale.

He hoped to make a more definite statement tomorrow.

JOHANNESBURG, Thursday — Anti-German disturbances last night resulted in extensive damage to numerous warehouses, hotels and shops.

THIRD GERMAN ATTACK FAILS

Special Cable to The Christian Science Monitor from its European Bureau

LONDON, Thursday—Sir John French reports that the British repulsed another German attack Tuesday evening south of the Menin road, this being the third costly failure experienced by the Germans there Tuesday. Elsewhere there is no change.

FEDERAL BUILDING BEGUN

LAWTON, Okla.—Government contractors began work recently on the Lawton Federal Building and the Dry Land Farming Building at Lawton. The former building is to cost near $200,000 and the latter near $10,000, says the Dallas News.

THE CHRISTIAN SCIENCE MONITOR

LAST EDITION | Copyright 1916 By The Christian Science Publishing Society | BOSTON, MASS., SATURDAY, SEPTEMBER 9, 1916—VOL. VIII., NO. 243 | PRICE TWO CENTS

OFFICIAL NEWS OF THE WAR FROM CAPITALS

As far as the official news available is concerned the position in southern Rumania remains somewhat obscure. According to the official statement from Sofia the Bulgarians and Germans are advancing from Turtukai along the right bank of the Danube in the direction of Silistria, whilst at the other end of the Dobrudja line they have occupied Dobric Baltjik, Kavarna and Kali Akra. Unofficial advices by way of London report the gathering of large Russo-Rumanian forces to stem the Bulgarian advance along the Black sea coast, and although there is, as yet, no official confirmation of this movement, a vigorous attack on the German-Bulgarian right wing is generally regarded as the obvious Russo-Rumanian counter move. An attack in force on the German-Bulgarian right wing would render any further advance of the invaders along the Danube in the highest degree risky.

In the Transylvanian theater the Rumanians continue to make progress, and Vienna admits an Austro-Hungarian retirement west of Csik Szereda, about 50 miles north of Kronstadt.

On the eastern front Petrograd claims further advances in the Gnota Lipa region; whilst on the western front both London and Paris report the general situation unchanged.

Special Cable to The Christian Science Monitor from its European Bureau

BERLIN, Germany, Saturday—The German official report issued yesterday follows:

Eastern war theater: There was nothing new to report on the front of Prince Leopold.

Front of Archduke Charles: On the Zlota Lipa, southeast of Brzezany and on the Najaromka, repeated Russian

(Continued on page five, column one)

STATE CONTROL OF FOOD URGED AT BIRMINGHAM

Special Cable to The Christian Science Monitor from its European Bureau

BIRMINGHAM, England, Saturday—Yesterday's sitting of the Trade Union Congress was engaged mainly on non-contentious business. The largest questions discussed were the rising price of food and the Chinese peril involved in the employment of Chinese on British ships.

J. Hill, Boiler Makers, member of the parliamentary committee, moved a resolution stating the congress viewed with alarm the enormous increase in food prices, expressing profound astonishment and indignation that since the increased price was largely due to the actions of ship owners and others in charging enormous rates for transport, the government had not completely taken over the control of shipping, railways and all transport to ensure for the people wholesome food and the general necessities of life at the lowest charges and calling upon the government immediately to do so, to control home food products and to fix maximum prices for food and other commodities.

Mr. Hill said the government had asked labor that the iron law of supply and demand should not be applied regarding labor and the vast majority of trade unionists at once expressed their agreement. In these circumstances it was a confession of incompetence for the government to allow supply and demand to operate unrestrictedly in the matter of the necessities which labor was compelled to buy. He felt nothing more could be done to put pressure on the government but Mr. Bramley proposed organizing protest meetings all over the country, while Mr. Bromley, Locomotive Union, proposed they should adjourn the congress, charter a special train and go up to Parliament to interview Mr. Asquith.

The question of employment of Chinamen was brought up by sailors' representatives. One speaker explained that Chinese were filtering from ports to inland towns, and Chinese laundries were being set up. Repatriation of Chinamen was demanded, the demand being supported by startling reports of evil doings in Chinese dens in Liverpool and London. The motion for repatriation of all Chinese, not of British nationality, was agreed to.

Disapproval of the present system of labor exchanges was shown in many speeches, and the Amalgamated Society of Carpenters and Joiners proposed a scheme of remodeling the exchanges. Havelock Wilson proposed the motion should be dropped, declaring labor exchanges were an entirely useless system, and that in well-organized trades employers came to union offices to get men. The congress sympathized with this attitude, and the scheme was defeated.

Trade Union Extensions

Special Cable to The Christian Science Monitor from its European Bureau

BIRMINGHAM, England, Saturday—At the trade union congress today resolutions on the subject of workers' housing and extension of the trade union movement in the Dominions were passed. J. Turner also proposed a resolution seeking development of the cooperative movement and that plans should be prepared for the successful development of productive distribution and banking activities of cooperative movements.

WHAT TAKING OF TURTUKAI GIVES CENTRAL GROUP

So-Called Fortress Is but Series of Dugouts and Earthworks, Constituting Bridgehead

Special Cable to The Christian Science Monitor from its European Bureau

LONDON, England—Regarding Rumania's entry into the war it should be clearly realized that Rumania has £20,000,000 or £30,000,000 worth of securities in Germany and that German banks may endeavor to dispose of these securities in the United States in view of the announcement by the Rumanian government that they are compelled to suspend all government securities and state loan coupons in possesion of the Austro-Hungarian and German holders, also all shares and bonds with their warrants and dividends, and as was explained to a representative of The Christian Science Monitor recently, people in the United States purchasing such securities will run the serious risk of holding unnegotiable paper.

Meanwhile the capture of Turtukai, in Rumanian pronounciation, or Tutrakan in Bulgarian, is being much discussed and The Christian Science Monitor representative learns from a most reliable source that the report of the capture of 20,000 prisoners is a gross exaggeration since as a matter of fact

(Continued on page five, column two)

ALLIES TO MAKE NO CHANGE IN BLACKLIST PLAN

Lord Robert Cecil Emphatically Declares Policy to Continue—Is War Measure, No Connection With After-War Program

Special Cable to The Christian Science Monitor from its European Bureau

LONDON, England, Saturday—The continued agitation in the United States over the blacklist, as indicated in American correspondents' telegrams to the British press, puzzles many authorities here. They find alleged grounds of the agitation inexplicable and incline to regard it as a vamped up agitation.

While Lord Robert Cecil does not take the latter position, he confessed yesterday in an interview that the telegrams in the press puzzled him. The apparent confusion of the blacklist with the Paris conference, he said, was curious, as the one had nothing to do with the other.

Regarding retaliatory legislation in the United States, he hesitated to express an opinion, as the telegrams did not make it clear how much of the

(Continued on page two, column one)

GERMANY CONFIDENT IN FACING FUTURE

Special Cable to The Christian Science Monitor from its European Bureau

BERLIN, Germany—The Germania, in an article which the Koelnische Zeitung attributes to a Center party deputy present at the meeting, says the secret conference between the chancellor and the party leaders left the final impression that, despite the hard necessity of facing the third winter of the war, Germany can contemplate future developments with confidence. Her supply of men in adequate, as is proved by her decision not to extend the landsturm service.

Though the harvest will not be a record one, it will be better than last year's so that the food supply will be about the same, if distribution is adequately organized.

A Berlin telegram to the Frankfurter Zeitung makes a point of declaring nothing was said at the conference concerning the military, political or financial situation that could not easily be published, and emphasizes the fact that the chancellor was most confident.

SPANISH CORTES TO BE REOPENED AT EARLY DATE

Financial Questions to Come Up First—El Liberal Resents Censor's Action in Deleting Anti-Austro-German Article

Special Cable to The Christian Science Monitor from its European Bureau

MADRID, Spain, Saturday—The premier has announced it is likely the Cortes will be reopened on Sept. 20 and that in any case it would be postponed only a few days beyond that date. Usually Parliament does not reassemble until late in October. It is further announced that the first business taken up will be the budget and some bills put forward by Senor Alba, the minister of finance, after which projected legislation on war profits will be considered.

El Liberal in the issue following that in which the censor came down so heavily upon it explains that the two-column article blacked out by the government at the last moment was written by an eminent and most careful impartial writer, Gomez Carrillo, and it asks if the government has decided to regard as an attack upon Spain's neutrality anything that might be said against Austria and Germany and if with this in view it is determined to make a display of severity against newspapers friendly to the Allies, adding that for itself it will not submit to such arbitrariness nor play at such a game.

Next to this bold statement is a letter from Gomez Carrillo saying that when a year ago he wrote such things no official resentment was shown and asking if the neutrality of Spain or the meaning of the words has changed. He says he has not the vanity to believe that he compromises the neutrality of Spain, but only without passion wishes to speak the truth gathered from documents in which it is shown that Germany has made of the war a horrible thing which not only dishonors herself but shames humanity. He concludes: If to say that is a sin, to think it is a duty.

In the next column to these declarations is given without comment telegraphed news of the sinking of another Spanish steamer by a German submarine.

This affair of El Liberal creates intense interest and the general feeling is that it would be entirely wrong to assume that because of the government's scrupulous care for neutrality at the present moment it is more kindly disposed to the Central Powers, but that the probability is that exactly the opposite is the case and existing circumstances are very difficult.

Germanophiles are extremely active.

SWISS NEGOTIATIONS WITH GERMANY ENDED

Special Cable to The Christian Science Monitor from its European Bureau

BERNE, Switzerland—Swiss papers announce negotiations with the German delegation have been successfully concluded. Germany has made considerable concessions and withdrawn the main demand, namely, delivery of purchases by her agents of goods in return for coal and iron. The compensation system has been replaced on a new basis satisfactory to both parties and deliveries on both sides will be made in future rather by the government than private individuals, so as to establish better control.

An official announcement will not be made until the Swiss federal council has heard a report of the negotiations.

INTENSE ARTILLERY DUEL IN THE BALKANS

Special Cable to The Christian Science Monitor from its European Bureau

PARIS, France, Friday—A violent artillery duel on the Struma front and in the Lake Doiran and Betesh mountains region is reported.

MONITOR INDEX FOR TODAY

PRESIDENT WILSON GOES TO SHADOW LAWN

ATLANTIC CITY, N. J.—President Wilson left Atlantic City for Shadow Lawn early today, well pleased with the reception accorded him by the National American Woman's Suffrage Association.

For their part, the suffragists were openly delighted with the things the President told them. It was the first political national convention the President ever addressed, but suffrage leaders united today in declaring he made a fine impression.

GOVERNOR CALLS SPECIAL SESSION OF LEGISLATURE

Members of Two Branches to Assemble Next Tuesday Following Decision That Suffolk Apportionment Is Unconstitutional

Governor McCall issued a proclamation this morning convening an extraordinary session of the Legislature on Tuesday, Sept. 12, for the settlement of the reapportionment problem and to meet situations growing out of the presence of Massachusetts militiamen on the Mexican border. Little more than an hour later the reapportionment board met in city hall to attempt to rectify their report on the reapportionment of representative seats for Suffolk county, held invalid by the decision of the state supreme court, handed down yesterday.

Upon assembling in their respective chambers on Tuesday next, the House and Senate will meet in joint convention, and the Governor at noon will submit his legislative program to the joint convention in the form of an address similar to the procedure of inauguration day.

The Governor will outline a legislative program to provide such compensation for the Massachusetts militiamen at the front as will enable them to properly care for their dependents and to allow them to cast their votes at the state elections for federal officials, and to straighten the Suffolk county representative apportionment tangle. Legislation will also be proposed to provide transportation back home for such Massachusetts militiamen as are discharged at the border.

The vote of the executive council this morning was as follows:

"Voted, That in the opinion of the Governor and council an exigency has arisen whereby it is imperative that the General Court be called together in special session, and that the Governor be hereby advised and authorized to issue a proclamation calling the General Court into special session on the 12th day of September, 1916, at 11 o'clock a. m."

The proclamation reads as follows:

"Whereas the Constitution of the commonwealth provides that 'the Governor, with advice of council, shall have full power and authority,' during the recess of the General Court, 'to call it together sooner than the time to which it may be adjourned or prorogued if the welfare of the commonwealth shall require the same,' and

"Whereas it is not apparent that our Massachusetts soldiers at the border will be returned to the commonwealth before the November election, and consequently they may be deprived of the right of suffrage, and

"Whereas the welfare of the commonwealth requires that provision be made to allow them to vote for such candidates as the Legislature under our constitution may have power to authorize them to vote for, and also that legislation be passed making possible the appropriation of money by the commonwealth and its various cities and towns which in conjunction with any provisions made by the na-

(Continued on page six, column one)

EVANS LEADING AT HAVERFORD

MERION CRICKET CLUB, Haverford, Pa.—Charles Evans, Jr., Edgewater, national open golf champion, was 3 up on R. A. Gardner, Hinsdale, the amateur title-holder, at the end of the first round of their 36-hole match for the 1916 amateur golf championship of the United States today.

FRENCH FINANCIAL AFFAIRS

Special Cable to The Christian Science Monitor from its European Bureau

PARIS, France—M. Ribot, finance minister, yesterday handed to the budget committee a bill for provisional credits of f.8,347,000,000 for the last quarter of 1916, which makes a total credit of f.61,000,000,000 voted since the loan began. He touched on the subject of payments being made abroad and referred to the recent arrangements made between France and England for the regulation of sterling exchange and concluded by announcing that he would lay the bill before the Chamber authorizing the issue of a new loan on Tuesday.

NEW CANADIAN WAR LOAN

Special to The Christian Science Monitor

OTTAWA, Ont.—The new Canadian war loan of $100,000,000 of 15-year 5 per cent bonds at 97½ will be offered to the public next Tuesday.

REPUBLICANS CLAIMING BIG GAINS IN MAINE

Marked Impression Made by Mr. Hughes—Democrats Remain Confident—Views of Leaders on Both Sides

By the United Press

AUGUSTA, Me.—The voice of the campaign spellbinder is resounding throughout Maine today. Judging from predictions by both Republican and Democratic leaders, sifted down, the Republicans are expecting a victory but not a complete one. The Democrats are still claiming everything, and the confident tone of the Republican leaders falters just a trifle when one of the senatorial races is mentioned, and a couple of the congressional fights are questioned.

Republican leaders today were unanimous in declaring that the presence on the battle ground of nominee Charles E. Hughes has worked tremendously in favor of a Republican vote. First of all, the candidate has not been in such fighting trim as now at any time on his transcontinental campaign tour, just closing. He is at the climax of his power in campaign oratory, and even Democrats concede that he has made a good impression here. Maine Republicans have been overjoyed at the sudden switch of the Republican nominee from ambiguity, from generalities of criticism to direct, forceful assault upon the Democratic citadel.

Those of the Governor's party assert that the heckling which Mr. Hughes received at Nashville stimulated him to renewed efforts and hardened his determination to hustle. Two weeks ago, Republican leaders here admitted today, they were considerably doubtful as to the outcome. In the interval a flood of oratory probably unparalleled in politics has been loosed on Maine voters. The Democrats sent five cabinet members to preach the gospel of Wilsonian Democracy. They hurled senators and congressmen without end at the voters. Tonight one of the most popular of Democracy's orators, Senator Ollie M. James, winds up the administration's fight at Lewiston. For the Republicans, Mr. Hughes says his final word at Rockland. Theodore Roosevelt has spoken. So have Senator Harding, who was chairman of the Chicago convention; Lodge and Borah, and Raymond Robins, who was chairman of the Progressive national convention. President Samuel Gompers of the American Federation of Labor has been doing effective work for Wilson in assailing Hughes' labor record.

A birdseye view of Maine politics shows, according to leaders on both sides, about the following:

Gubernatorial race: Carl T. Milliken is opposing Governor Curtis. Republicans insist he has the better chance because of the sudden impetus given the Republican campaign through the appearance here of Mr. Hughes. The Democrats insist that Mr. Curtis has earned reelection and will obtain it. General opinion among plain voters is that Mr. Milliken has a trifle the better of it today.

Senatorial race: Two seats are open. Bert M. Fernald, a former Governor, is opposing Kenneth C. M. Sills, a professor, for the short term vacancy made by the passing away of Senator Burleigh. Public opinion gives Mr. Fernald a shade the better of the fight, but it will be close. For the long term Fred Hale, son of Maine's famous senator, is opposing Senator Charles F. Robinson. The fight between these two is probably the most bitter of all the Maine contests. Mr. Johnson is a vice-president of the Free Trade League and represents exactly the Wilson policies and the Wilson democracy. The Democratic national committee has done yeoman work to aid Mr. Johnson and would regard his defeat of Mr. Hale as a victory in Maine, even if other nominees failed, because he has been the center of the Maine contest. Up until Mr. Hughes' appearance in the state with Mr. Hale, the Republican nominee has appeared everywhere with Mr. Hughes since York Harbor. General opinion gave him slight chance to defeat Mr. Johnson, but it was admitted today that he

(Continued on page eight, column three)

BRITISH MACHINES ATTACK AERODROME

Special Cable to The Christian Science Monitor from its European Bureau

LONDON, England Friday—The admiralty announces an attack was carried out yesterday afternoon by naval aeroplanes on the enemy aerodrome at St. Denis Westrem. Many bombs were dropped effectively. One machine failed to return. A naval aeroplane successfully brought down a hostile kite balloon near Ostend. The attack was carried out under a most heavy anti-aircraft fire but the pilot safely returned.

FRENCH LOAN ANNOUNCEMENT

Special Cable to The Christian Science Monitor from its European Bureau

LONDON, England, Saturday—The French loan announcement confirms the expectation current in London financial circles for the past week and accounts for the recent steady improvement in London-Paris rate of exchange which yesterday was quoted at 27 francs 97½ centimes. There is as yet no official indication of a portion of the French loan being issued in London.

RHODE ISLAND STARTS A NEW CLEAN-UP DAY

It Proposes to Take Down All Advertising Signs on Public Highways of the State

Special to The Christian Science Monitor

PROVIDENCE, R. I.—The state board of public roads has appointed Saturday, Oct. 14, as "Clean-up day," and is organizing a campaign to remove from the public highways all advertising signs tacked or placed upon any tree, fence or pole, on the public right of way. This campaign is announced as the result of a consultation held Tuesday by the members of the roads board and Col. Edward S. Cornell, secretary of the National Highways Protective Association.

A statute enacted by the General Assembly at its session last spring gives anyone the right to tear down and destroy all signs of an advertising nature, hung upon the public right of way. This does not include, of course, billboards or other signs erected upon private property. Since the enactment of this law, practically nothing has been done to enforce its provisions and remove the thousands of signs about the state.

The roads board is sending to all of the local improvement associations, and the town councils, throughout the state, a letter explaining the move-

(Continued on page four, column one)

PROHIBITIONISTS CONDEMN BOTH BIG PARTIES

Hanly and Landrith on Special Train Tour Urge Temperance People to Vote for Men Who Will Express Their Ideals

Special to The Christian Science Monitor from its Western Bureau

ROCK ISLAND, Ill.—The first day's run of the Prohibition "presidential special" proved encouraging for the national tour of the party's candidates, which turns north and toward the Pacific coast today. Attendance at 12 cities in Illinois and one in Iowa yesterday proved substantial in the aggregate. It is estimated that former Governor J. Frank Hanly of Indiana and Dr. Ira Landrith of Tennessee talked to upwards of 3000 persons during the day. In several small towns school was dismissed and the children thronged with their elders around the rear platform of the special. Several of the small farming communities in central Illinois gave the temperance campaigners a more generous attendance than the cities. Women formed half the day meetings. The night sessions here and in Moline and Davenport, totaling 750 persons, were 80 per cent men. Due attention was given the women voters by the speakers.

The character of the speaking was on such a high plane as to earn very favorable comment. Governor Hanly showed himself, as a prohibition orator, a powerful and convincing talker. He is an earnest speaker of the so-called old school. His running mate exhibits a quick adaptability and humor interspersed with southern stories. Together the pair make a great team. They appealed to their auditors as forceful and capable. The first day of the national tour sets prohibition oratory on a new plane, dignified, well reasoned, pleasing. It will set a standard for local prohibition orators throughout the country. Efforts yes-

(Continued on page eight, column four)

GROUNDS FOUND FOR CONSPIRACY CHARGE

Special to The Christian Science Monitor from its Eastern Bureau

NEW YORK, N. Y.—In Salem, the county seat of Washington county, an investigation has been started by District-Attorney Wyman H. Bascom to discover whether there was a conspiracy among those persons whom Thomas Mott Osborne holds responsible for the attempt to remove him as warden of Sing Sing prison.

Mr. Osborne returned to the prison some time ago after obtaining exoneration of the charges brought against him. He and his friends have been diligently seeking into the causes for the attempt to cast discredit upon his administration of the prison, and it is said that the evidence gathered is now sufficient to warrant an inquiry by the district attorney.

LANDS OPENED TO PUBLIC IN AUGUST

WASHINGTON, D. C.—More than 1,124,000 acres were designated in August as nonirrigable and rendered subject to entry under the provisions of the enlarged homestead act as follows: In California, 429,300 acres, located in 11 counties; in Kansas, 3100 acres in western part; in New Mexico, 152,700 acres, in eastern and central parts; in South Dakota, 11,600 acres in western part; in Washington, 633 acres, all within the diminished Colville Indian reservation; in Wyoming, 526,400 acres in the northern and eastern parts.

CANADIANS DENY THEY ENGAGED IN LOBBY WORK

Sir Joseph Pope States He Discussed Fishery Question With Mr. Lansing and Asked That Action Be Deferred

Special to The Christian Science Monitor

OTTAWA, Ont.—Charges to the effect that a Canadian lobby at Washington caused the elimination of the Chamberlain amendment regarding the north Pacific fishery dispute, are denied by Sir Joseph Pope, Canadian representative to Washington on this question.

"I went to Washington in my official capacity as undersecretary for external affairs at the request of the government," said Sir Joseph. "While there I had two interviews with Mr. Lansing, secretary of state, and discussed the north Pacific fishery question. I proposed to Mr. Lansing that immediate action, as contemplated by the Chamberlain amendment, be deferred to give opportunity for joint investigation and an amicable solution of the problem. This has apparently been done.

"While in Washington, outside of a call at the British embassy that was the extent of my activity on the part of the Canadian government in connection with fishing interests. I never solicited the aid of a member of either the Senate or the House of Representatives, nor was I at the Capitol. That was the extent of the Canadian lobby."

From Sir Robert Borden's office there was also a denial of a Canadian lobby at Washington. There it was stated that the Canadian representative was instructed only to ask that action be deferred until both countries had an opportunity to investigate the question at issue. This was granted.

Investigation Ordered

Foreign Lobby Activities to Be Subject of Committee Inquiry

WASHINGTON, D. C.—A resolution by Senator Curtis of Kansas, directing the Senate lobby committee to investigate the activities of the alleged foreign lobby opposing the retaliatory provision of the revenue bill against Canadian fisheries, was passed yesterday by the Senate.

The resolution was adopted after the Senate had disposed of a similar resolution by referring it to a committee. The new resolution adopted provides for a report at the next session of Congress.

Senator Reed, Democrat, a member of the lobby committee, said he believed it was high time for the American government to show other nations that it regarded as offensive any efforts to influence legislation in Congress.

SYMPATHETIC STRIKE ACTION MAY BE TAKEN

NEW YORK, N. Y.—A contest for the preservation of unionism in New York was forecasted today when the Central Federated Union, representing approximately 750,000 men and women of all trades, appointed a committee with power to call a general sympathetic strike if such action is necessary to aid the striking employees of the traction companies.

The action of the federated union was taken after an all night session at the labor temple. The traction companies were assailed for their attempt to destroy the Amalgamated Association of Street and Electric Railway Employees.

The second day of the strike of unionized employees in New York's subway and on elevated railway and surface car lines brought little interruption to service.

Theodore P. Shonts, president of the Interborough Rapid Transit Company and the New York Railways Company, offered to take back all striking New York Railways Company employees (surface car motormen and conductors) who resigned from the union by today. Strike breakers, he declared, would be put in the places of all those employees who do not accept his offer.

Union officials asserted that 3000 elevated railway and subway employees were out, but made no claims that service was being hampered. On the New York Railway's surface lines, however, they asserted that service was being seriously interrupted.

BAKERS STANDARDIZE TEN-CENT BREAD

CHICAGO, Ill.—Recommendations to all bakers of the United States that the 5-cent loaf of bread be abandoned and the 10-cent loaf standardized were made after considerable discussion at the closing session of the executive committee of the National Association of Master Bakers yesterday. They urged that the recommendations be put into effect immediately.

Economic waste incident to the manufacture of the 5-cent loaf was emphasized as a reason for its discontinuance. Saving in manufacture, improvement in quality and standardization are urged in favor of the 10-cent loaf. It is also recommended that where local conditions make it necessary, a smaller loaf may be maintained with a price consistent with the cost of manufacture.

THE CHRISTIAN SCIENCE MONITOR

INTERNATIONAL EDITION { Copyright 1916 By The Christian Science Publishing Society } BOSTON, MASS., SATURDAY, NOVEMBER 11, 1916—VOL. VIII., NO. 297 PRICE TWO CENTS

OFFICIAL NEWS OF THE WAR FROM CAPITALS

After a long period of inactivity in that region, the Germans, yesterday, launched a vigorous offensive against the Russian positions on the eastern front, north of Volhynia. Berlin reports that the attack extended over a front of about 2½ miles, in the district of Skrobowa, about 12 miles northeast of Baranovichi, north of the Pinsk marshes, and resulted in the Russians being driven back to their second line trenches beyond the Skrobowa brook. The official German communique also claims the capture of nearly 4000 prisoners and a considerable quantity of war material.

Petrograd admits the retirement north of Volhynia, but reports a steady advance in the Dobrudja, where the Russians, now fighting for the recapture of the "bridgehead" of the Danube causeway at Tchernavoda have taken the village of Dunarea some two miles west of that town. As the Danube at this point runs due north and south, this has led to the assumption that Field Marshal von Mackensen's forces had in fact crossed the Danube, although this movement had never been before disclosed. As was explained, however, at the time that von Mackensen took Tchernavoda on his march north, Tchernavoda is a considerable distance from the actual bed of the river, which here flows through vast stretches of swamp lands. Across these the railway from Constanza runs on a great causeway, the distance between Tchernavoda and Fetesci on the opposite bank of the river being about 12½ miles. The village of Dunarea is thus well on the right bank of the river.

Determined fighting still continues on the Transylvanian frontier but the general position remains practically unchanged.

There is no news of importance from the remaining theaters.

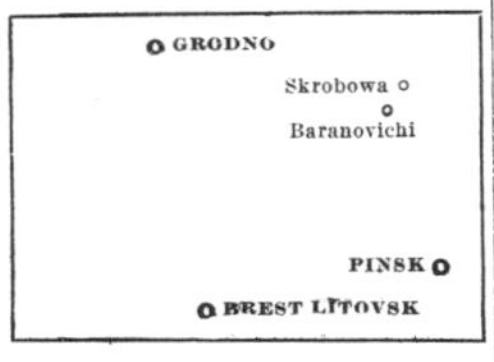

Diagram of region north of Pinsk marshes shows Skrobowa, where new German offensive has begun.

Special Cable to The Christian Science Monitor from its European Bureau

BERLIN, Germany (Saturday)—Yesterday's official statement says:

Brandenburg troops and Infantry Regiment 401, under the leadership of Major-General von Wyna, stormed several Russian defensive lines over a front of about four kilometers in the district of Skrobowa, and threw back the Russians beyond Skrowoba brook. Our losses were small, while the Russians suffered heavy sanguinary losses. Our opponents lost as prisoners 49 officers and 3880 men. The booty is 27 machine guns and 12 mine throwers. The Russians suffered a heavy defeat.

In the Somme sector hostile local attacks were delivered without success near Eaucourt l'Abbaye, Gueudecourt and Lesboeufs and at Pressoire.

Stronger French forces advanced on both sides of Sailly. They were repulsed in part by hand-to-hand fighting.

Front of Archduke Charles Francis: Our attacks in the Georgeny Mountains have progressed favorably. The ground which had been lost on Nov. 4 in the engagement in progress there

(Continued on page twelve, column one)

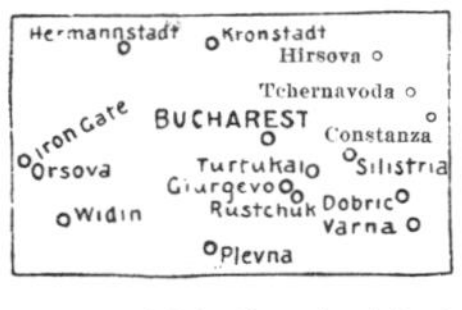

Diagram of Dobrudja region indicates Tchernavoda, where contest is being waged between Russo-Rumanian and German-Bulgarian forces.

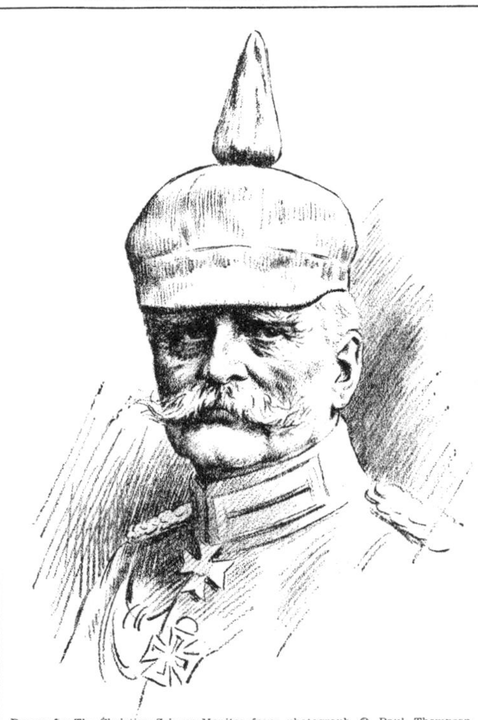

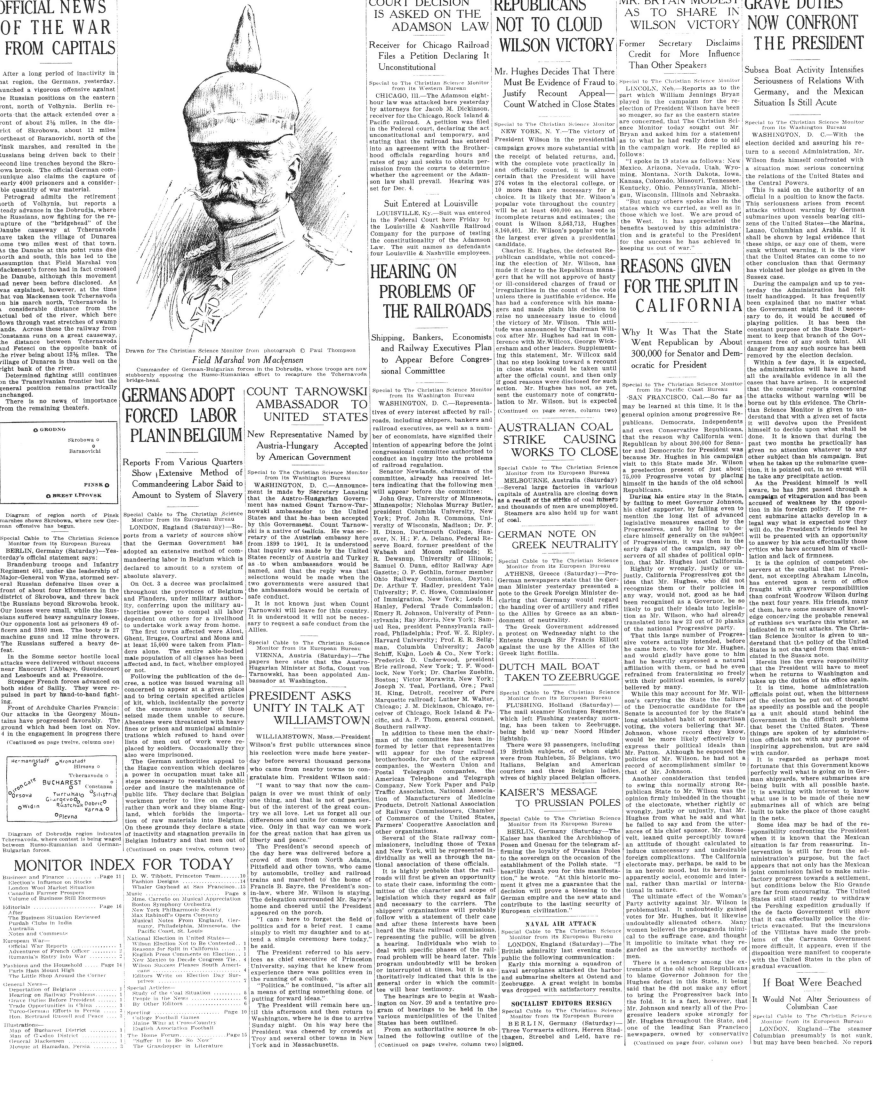

Drawn for The Christian Science Monitor from photograph © Paul Thompson

Field Marshal von Mackensen

Commander of German-Bulgarian forces in the Dobrudja, whose troops are now stubbornly opposing the Russo-Rumanian effort to recapture the Tchernavoda bridge-head.

GERMANS ADOPT FORCED LABOR PLAN IN BELGIUM

Reports From Various Quarters Show Extensive Method of Commandeering Labor Said to Amount to System of Slavery

Special Cable to The Christian Science Monitor from its European Bureau

LONDON, England (Saturday)—Reports from a variety of sources show that the German Government has adopted an extensive method of commandeering labor in Belgium which is declared to amount to a system of absolute slavery.

On Oct. 3 a decree was proclaimed throughout the provinces of Belgium and Flanders, under military authority, conferring upon the military authorities power to compel all labor dependent on others for a livelihood to undertake work away from home.

The first towns affected were Alost, Ghent, Bruges, Courtrai and Mons and at least 15,000 were taken from Flanders alone. The entire able-bodied male population of all classes has been affected and, in fact, whether employed or not.

Following the publication of the decree, a notice was issued warning all concerned to appear at a given place and to bring certain specified articles of kit, which, incidentally the poverty of the enormous number of those seized made them unable to secure. Absentees were threatened with heavy fines or prison and municipal administrations which refused to hand over lists of men out of work were replaced by soldiers. Occasionally they also were imprisoned.

The German authorities appeal to the Hague convention which declares a power in occupation must take all steps necessary to reestablish public order and insure the maintenance of public life. They declare that Belgian workmen prefer to live on charity rather than work and they blame England, which forbids the importation of raw materials into Belgium. On these grounds they declare a state of inactivity and stagnation prevails in Belgian industry and that men out of

(Continued on page twelve, column two)

COUNT TARNOWSKI AMBASSADOR TO UNITED STATES

New Representative Named by Austria-Hungary Accepted by American Government

Special to The Christian Science Monitor from its Washington Bureau

WASHINGTON, D. C.—Announcement is made by Secretary Lansing that the Austro-Hungarian Government has named Count Tarnow-Tarnowski ambassador to the United States and that he has been accepted by this Government. Count Tarnowski is a native of Galicia. He was secretary of the Austrian embassy here from 1899 to 1901. It is understood that inquiry was made by the United States recently of Austria and Turkey as to when ambassadors would be named, and that the reply was that selections would be made when the two governments were assured that the ambassadors would be certain of safe conduct.

It is not known just when Count Tarnowski will leave for this country. It is understood it will not be necessary to request a safe conduct from the Allies.

Special Cable to The Christian Science Monitor from its European Bureau

VIENNA, Austria (Saturday)—The papers here state that the Austro-Hugarian Minister at Sofia, Count von Tarnowski, has been appointed Ambassador at Washington.

PRESIDENT ASKS UNITY IN TALK AT WILLIAMSTOWN

WILLIAMSTOWN, Mass.—President Wilson's first public utterances since his reelection were made here yesterday before several thousand persons who came from nearby towns to congratulate him. President Wilson said:

"I want to say that now the campaign is over we must think of only one thing, and that is not of parties, but of the interest of the great country we all love. Let us forget all our differences and unite for common service. Only in that way can we work for the great nation that has given us liberty and peace."

The President's second speech of the day here was delivered before a crowd of men from North Adams, Pittsfield and other towns, who came by automobile, trolley and railroad trains and marched to the home of Francis B. Sayre, the President's son-in-law, where Mr. Wilson is staying. The delegation surrounded Mr. Sayre's home and cheered until the President appeared on the porch.

"I came here to forget the field of politics and for a brief rest. I came simply to visit my daughter and to attend a simple ceremony here today," he said.

The President referred to his services as chief executive of Princeton University, saying that he knew from experience there was politics even in the running of a college.

"Politics," he continued, "is after all a means of getting something done, of putting forward ideas."

The President will remain here until this afternoon and then return to Washington, where he is due to arrive Sunday night. On his way here the President was cheered by crowds at Troy and several other towns in New York and in Massachusetts.

MONITOR INDEX FOR TODAY

COURT DECISION IS ASKED ON THE ADAMSON LAW

Receiver for Chicago Railroad Files a Petition Declaring It Unconstitutional

Special to The Christian Science Monitor from its Western Bureau

CHICAGO, Ill.—The Adamson eight-hour law was attacked here yesterday by attorneys for Jacob M. Dickinson, receiver for the Chicago, Rock Island & Pacific railroad. A petition was filed in the Federal court, declaring the act unconstitutional and temporary, and stating that the railroad has entered into an agreement with the Brotherhood officials regarding hours and rates of pay and seeks to obtain permission from the courts to determine whether the agreement or the Adamson law shall prevail. Hearing was set for Dec. 4.

Suit Entered at Louisville

LOUISVILLE, Ky.—Suit was entered in the Federal Court here Friday by the Louisville & Nashville Railroad Company for the purpose of testing the constitutionality of the Adamson Law. The suit names as defendants four Louisville & Nashville employees.

HEARING ON PROBLEMS OF THE RAILROADS

Shipping, Bankers, Economists and Railway Executives Plan to Appear Before Congressional Committtee

Special to The Christian Science Monitor from its Washington Bureau

WASHINGTON, D. C.—Representatives of every interest affected by railroads, including shippers, bankers and railroad executives, as well as a number of economists, have signified their intention of appearing before the joint congressional committee authorized to conduct an inquiry into the problems of railroad regulation.

Senator Newlands, chairman of the committee, already has received letters indicating that the following men will appear before the committee:

John Gray, University of Minnesota, Minneapolis; Nicholas Murray Butler, president Columbia University, New York; Prof. John R. Commons, University of Wisconsin, Madison; Dr. F. H. Dixon, Dartmouth College, Hanover, N. H.; F. A. Delano, Federal Reserve Board, former president of the Wabash and Monon railroads; E. R. Dewsnup, University of Illinois; Samuel O. Dunn, editor Railway Age Gazette; O. P. Gothlin, former member Ohio Railway Commission, Dayton; Dr. Arthur T. Hadley, president Yale University; F. C. Howe, Commissioner of Immigration, New York; Louis H. Hanley, Federal Trade Commission; Emery R. Johnson, University of Pennsylvania; Ray Morris, New York; Samuel Rea, president Pennsylvania railroad, Philadelphia; Prof. W. Z. Ripley, Harvard University; Prof. E. R. Seligman, Columbia University; Jacob Schiff, Kuhn, Loeb & Co., New York; Frederick D. Underwood, president Erie railroad, New York; T. F. Woodlock, New York; Dr. Charles Zueblin, Boston; Victor Morawitz, New York; Joseph N. Teal, Portland, Ore.; Paul H. King, Detroit, receiver of Pere Marquette railroad; Luther M. Walter, Chicago; J. M. Dickinson, Chicago, receiver of Chicago, Rock Island & Pacific, and A. P. Thom, general counsel, Southern railway.

In addition to these men the chairman of the committee has been informed by letter that representatives will appear for the four railroad brotherhoods, for each of the express companies, the Western Union and Postal Telegraph companies, the American Telephone and Telegraph Company, New York Paper and Pulp Traffic Association, National Association of Manufacturers of Medicine Products, Detroit National Association of Railway Commissioners, Chamber of Commerce of the United States, Farmers' Cooperative Association and other organizations.

Several of the State railway commissioners, including those of Texas and New York, will be represented individually as well as through the national association of these officials.

It is highly probable that the railroads will first be given an opportunity to state their case, informing the committee of the character and scope of legislation which they regard as fair and necessary to the carriers. The shippers' organizations will probably follow with a statement of their case and after these interests have been heard the State railroad commissions, representing the public, will be given a hearing. Individuals who wish to deal with specific phases of the railroad problem will be heard later. This program undoubtedly will be broken or interrupted at times, but it is authoritatively indicated that this is the general order in which the committee will hear testimony.

The hearings are to begin at Washington on Nov. 20 and a tentative program of hearings to be held in the various municipalities of the United States has been outlined.

From an authoritative source is obtained the following outline of the

(Continued on page twelve, column two)

REPUBLICANS NOT TO CLOUD WILSON VICTORY

Mr. Hughes Decides That There Must Be Evidence of Fraud to Justify Recount Appeal—Count Watched in Close States

Special to The Christian Science Monitor

NEW YORK, N. Y.—The victory of President Wilson in the presidential campaign grows more substantial with the receipt of belated returns, and, with the complete vote practically in and officially counted, it is almost certain that the President will have 276 votes in the electoral college, or 10 more than are necessary for a choice. It is likely that Mr. Wilson's popular vote throughout the country will be at least 400,000 as, based on incomplete returns and estimates; the count is Wilson 8,563,713, Hughes 8,160,401. Mr. Wilson's popular vote is the largest ever given a presidential candidate.

Charles E. Hughes, the defeated Republican candidate, while not conceding the election of Mr. Wilson, has made it clear to the Republican managers that he will not approve of hasty or ill-considered charges of fraud or irregularities in the count of the vote unless there is justifiable evidence. He has had a conference with his managers and made plain his decision to raise no unnecessary issue to cloud the victory of Mr. Wilson. This attitude was announced by Chairman Willcox after Mr. Hughes had sat in conference with Mr. Willcox, George Wickersham and other leaders. Supplementing this statement, Mr. Willcox said that no step looking toward a recount in close states would be taken until after the official count, and then only if good reasons were disclosed for such action. Mr. Hughes has not, as yet, sent the customary note of congratulation to Mr. Wilson, but is expected

(Continued on page seven, column two)

AUSTRALIAN COAL STRIKE CAUSING WORKS TO CLOSE

Special Cable to The Christian Science Monitor from its European Bureau

MELBOURNE, Australia (Saturday)—Several large factories in various capitals of Australia are closing down as a result of the strike of coal miners and thousands of men are unemployed.

Steamers are also held up for want of coal.

GERMAN NOTE ON GREEK NEUTRALITY

Special Cable to The Christian Science Monitor from its European Bureau

ATHENS, Greece (Saturday)—Pro-German newspapers state that the German Minister yesterday presented a note to the Greek Foreign Minister declaring that Germany would regard the handing over of artillery and rifles to the Allies by Greece as an abandonment of neutrality.

The Greek Government addressed a protest on Wednesday night to the Entente through Sir Francis Elliott against the use by the Allies of the Greek light flotilla.

DUTCH MAIL BOAT TAKEN TO ZEEBRUGGE

Special Cable to The Christian Science Monitor from its European Bureau

FLUSHING, Holland (Saturday)—The mail steamer Koningen Regentes, which left Flushing yesterday morning, has been taken to Zeebrugge, being held up near Noord Hinder lightship.

There were 93 passengers, including 19 British subjects, of whom eight were from Ruhleben, 25 Belgians, two Italians, Belgian and American couriers and three Belgian ladies, wives of highly placed Belgian officers.

KAISER'S MESSAGE TO PRUSSIAN POLES

Special Cable to The Christian Science Monitor from its European Bureau

BERLIN, Germany (Saturday—The Kaiser has thanked the Archbishop of Posen and Gnesau for the telegram affirming the loyalty of Prussian Poles to the sovereign on the occasion of the establishment of the Polish state. "I heartily thank you for this manifestation," he wrote. "At this historic moment it gives me a guarantee that the decision will prove a blessing to the German empire and the new state and contribute to the lasting security of European civilization."

NAVAL AIR ATTACK

Special Cable to The Christian Science Monitor from its European Bureau

LONDON, England (Saturday)—The British admiralty last evening made public the following communication:

Early this morning a squadron of naval aeroplanes attacked the harbor and submarine shelters at Ostend and Zeebrugge. A great weight in bombs was dropped with satisfactory results.

SOCIALIST EDITORS RESIGN

Special Cable to The Christian Science Monitor from its European Bureau

BERLIN, Germany (Saturday)—Three Vorwaerts editors, Herren Stadthagen, Streebel and Leid, have resigned.

MR. BRYAN MODEST AS TO SHARE IN WILSON VICTORY

Former Secretary Disclaims Credit for More Influence Than Other Speakers

Special to The Christian Science Monitor

LINCOLN, Neb.—Reports as to the part which William Jennings Bryan played in the campaign for the reelection of President Wilson have been so meager, so far as the eastern states are concerned, that The Christian Science Monitor today sought out Mr. Bryan and asked him for a statement as to what he had really done to aid in the campaign work. He replied as follows:

"I spoke in 19 states as follows: New Mexico, Arizona, Nevada, Utah, Wyoming, Montana, North Dakota, Iowa, Kansas, Colorado, Missouri, Tennessee, Kentucky, Ohio, Pennsylvania, Michigan, Wisconsin, Illinois and Nebraska.

"But many others spoke also in the states which we carried, as well as in those which we lost. We are proud of the West. It has appreciated the benefits bestowed by this administration and is grateful to the President for the success he has achieved in keeping us out of war."

REASONS GIVEN FOR THE SPLIT IN CALIFORNIA

Why It Was That the State Went Republican by About 300,000 for Senator and Democratic for President

Special to The Christian Science Monitor from its Pacific Coast Bureau

SAN FRANCISCO, Cal.—So far as may be learned at this time, it is the general opinion among progressive Republicans, Democrats, Independents and even Conservative Republicans, that the reason why California went Republican by about 300,000 for Senator and Democratic for President was because Mr. Hughes in his campaign visit to this State made Mr. Wilson a preelection present of just about 75,000 Progressive votes by placing himself in the hands of the old school Republicans.

During his entire stay in the State, by failing to meet Governor Johnson, his chief supporter, by failing even to mention the long list of advanced legislative measures enacted by the Progressives, and by failing to declare himself generally on the subject of Progressivism, it was then in the early days of the campaign, say observers of all shades of political opinion, that Mr. Hughes lost California.

Rightly or wrongly, justly or unjustly, California Progressives got the idea that Mr. Hughes, who did not recognize them or their policies in any way, would not, good as he had been recognized as a Governor, be so likely to put their ideals into legislation as Mr. Wilson, who had already translated into law 22 out of 30 planks of the national Progressive party.

That this large number of Progressive voters actually intended, before he came here, to vote for Mr. Hughes, and would gladly have gone to him had he heartily expressed a natural affiliation with them, or had he even refrained from fraternizing so freely with their political enemies, is surely believed by many.

While this may account for Mr. Wilson's carrying the State the failure of the Democratic candidate for the Senate is accounted for by the State's long established habit of nonpartisan voting, the voters believing that Mr. Johnson, whose record they know, would be more likely effectively to express their political ideals than Mr. Patton. Although he espoused the policies of Mr. Wilson, he had not a record of accomplishment similar to that of Mr. Johnson.

Another consideration that tended to swing this normally strong Republican State to Mr. Wilson was the opinion firmly imbedded in the thought of the electorate, whether rightly or wrongly, justly or unjustly, that Mr. Hughes from what he said and what he failed to say and from the utterances of his chief sponsor, Mr. Roosevelt, leaned quite perceptibly toward an attitude of thought calculated to induce unnecessary and undesirable foreign complications. The California electorate may, perhaps, be said to be in an heroic mood, but its heroism is apparently social, economic and internal, rather than martial or international in nature.

The ultimate effect of the Woman's Party activity against Mr. Wilson is problematical. It undoubtedly gained votes for Mr. Hughes, but it likewise undoubtedly alienated others. Many women believed the propaganda inimical to the suffrage case, and thought it impolitic to imitate what they regarded as the unworthy methods of men.

There is a tendency among the extremists of the old school Republicans to blame Governor Johnson for the Hughes defeat in this State, it being said that he did not make any effort to bring the Progressives back into the fold. It is a fact, however, that Mr. Johnson and nearly all of the Progressive leaders spoke strongly for Mr. Hughes throughout the State, and one of the leading San Francisco newspapers, owned by conservative

(Continued on page four, column one)

GRAVE DUTIES NOW CONFRONT THE PRESIDENT

Subsea Boat Activity Intensifies Seriousness of Relations With Germany, and the Mexican Situation Is Still Acute

Special to The Christian Science Monitor from its Washington Bureau

WASHINGTON, D. C.—With the election decided and assuring his return to a second Administration, Mr. Wilson finds himself confronted with a situation most serious concerning the relations of the United States and the Central Powers.

This is said on the authority of an official in a position to know the facts. This seriousness arises from recent attacks without warning by German submarines upon vessels bearing citizens of the United States—the Marina, Lanao, Columbian and Arabia. If it shall be shown by legal evidence that these ships, or any one of them, were sunk without warning, it is the view that the United States can come to no other conclusion than that Germany has violated her pledge as given in the Sussex case.

During the campaign and up to yesterday the Administration had felt itself handicapped. It has frequently been explained that no matter what the Government might find it necessary to do, it would be accused of playing politics. It has been the constant purpose of the State Department to keep that branch of the Government free of any such taint. All danger from any such source has been removed by the election decision.

Within a few days, it is expected, the administration will have in hand all the available evidence in all the cases that have arisen. It is expected that the consular reports concerning the attacks without warning will be borne out by this evidence. The Christian Science Monitor is given to understand that with a given set of facts it will devolve upon the President himself to decide upon what shall be done. It is known that during the past two months he practically has given no attention whatever to any other subject than his campaign. But when he takes up the submarine question, it is pointed out, in no event will he take any precipitate action.

As the President himself is well aware, he has just passed through a campaign of vituperation and has been accused of weakness by the opposition in his foreign policy. If the recent submarine attacks develop in a legal way what is expected now they will do, the President's friends feel he will be presented with an opportunity to answer by his acts effectually those critics who have accused him of vacillation and lack of firmness.

It is the opinion of competent observers at the capital that no President, not excepting Abraham Lincoln, has entered upon a term of office fraught with graver responsibilities than confront Woodrow Wilson during the next four years. His friends, many of them, have some measure of knowledge concerning the probable renewal of ruthless sea warfare this winter, as indicated in recent attacks. The Christian Science Monitor is given to understand that the policy of the United States is not changed from that enunciated in the Sussex note.

Herein lies the grave responsibility that the President will have to meet when he returns to Washington and takes up the duties of his office again.

It is time, home administration officials point out, when the bitterness of the election be put out of thought as speedily as possible and the people as a unit should stand behind the Government in the difficult problems that beset the United States. These things are spoken of by administration officials not with any purpose of inspiring apprehension, but are said with candor.

It is regarded as perhaps most fortunate that this Government knows perfectly well what is going on in German shipyards, where submarines are being built with all possible haste. It is awaiting with interest to know what use is to be made of these new submarines all of which are being built to take the place of those caught in the nets.

Some idea may be had of the responsibility confronting the President when it is known that the Mexican situation is far from reassuring. Intervention is still far from the administration's purpose, but the fact appears that not only has the Mexican joint commission failed to make satisfactory progress towards a settlement, but conditions below the Rio Grande are far from encouraging. The United States still stand ready to withdraw the Pershing expedition gradually if the de facto Government will show that it can effectually police the districts evacuated. But the incursions of the Villistas have made the problems of the Carranza Government more difficult, it appears, even if the disposition were manifest to cooperate with the United States in the plan of gradual evacuation.

If Boat Were Beached

It Would Not Alter Seriousness of Columbian Case

Special Cable to The Christian Science Monitor from its European Bureau

LONDON, England—The steamer Columbian presumably is not sunk, but may have been beached. No report

THE CHRISTIAN SCIENCE MONITOR

LAST EDITION | Copyright 1917 By The Christian Science Publishing Society | BOSTON, MASS., FRIDAY, MARCH 16, 1917—VOL. IX, NO. 92 | * | PRICE TWO CENTS

CABINET MAY ACT TO AVERT RAILWAY STRIKE

Brotherhoods and Managers Indicate Readiness to Take Up Further Discussion if President Should Express Desire

Special to The Christian Science Monitor from its Washington Bureau

WASHINGTON, D. C.—It was expected that President Wilson would make known today what steps he is to take in the effort to avoid a strike on the railroads but no announcement was forthcoming.

A meeting of the Cabinet was called for 2:30 o'clock and it is anticipated that the situation will be discussed at that meeting and a decision reached as to what means can be used to assure the uninterrupted, continuance of traffic.

It was announced at the White House that a letter received from New York during the morning from both the brotherhood men and from the managers indicated that they are willing to take up further discussion and the feeling prevailed that both sides were waiting for the President to speak.

The fact has added strength to the generally prevailing conviction that the brotherhoods have taken advantage in the present national crisis to force their personal cause. Brotherhood members at the Union Station in Washington say they have received no strike order and that they were not even asked to vote on the strike question. Furthermore they declare the strike order of last fall is not now in force.

In some quarters there is a feeling that if the President should speak at this moment firmly on the strike question and make the fact evident to the world that either side in the controversy that stands in the way of an amicable settlement of the question at issue, will be held by the people of the country as morally guilty of treason at this juncture, a settlement could be reached, because neither side would desire to incur the odium that would result.

No statement has been authorized by the White House, and all officials professed to be ignorant of what the President might intend to do. Some thought that, having appealed again and again to both sides to adjust their differences, there was no step left for him to take. Others believed he certainly would make some move before the hour set for the strike.

The President is known to regard a strike as inconceivable in view of the international crisis, the already congested condition of freight traffic and the ever rising cost of food. Apparently, however, he feels that he practically is powerless unless as it becomes necessary for him to adopt measures to keep the mails moving.

After a telephone conference with Secretary Wilson of the Labor Department, it is understood the President decided to make no move during the night.

There is a disposition among some Administration officials to believe that even if begun tomorrow, the progressive plan for the strike never will be carried to conclusion. Before next Wednesday, the day by which it is proposed to make the walkout effective throughout the country, they believe a compromise will have been reached.

Precedents under which the Government might take a hand in the situation were being searched for last night.

Had the Sixty-fourth Congress, which adjourned early this month,

(Continued on page eight, column two)

OFFICIAL NEWS OF THE WAR FROM CAPITALS

The British have made further gains on the western front. London reports that the area of the German withdrawal has extended toward the south and that the British have occupied German trenches on a front of 2½ miles, from south of St. Pierre-Vaast Wood to the north of the village Saillisel. The French have also made gains east of Canny-sur-Matz, where they have penetrated the German positions to a depth of 800 meters. Steadily increasing activity is reported from the Macedonian theater. The British have advanced their line southwest of Doiran, 1000 yards over a front of 3500 yards; whilst the Italian troops are advancing on Bulgarian and German positions between Lake Presba and Lake Malik.

BERLIN, Germany (Friday, by wireless to Sayville)—The official statement issued yesterday from army headquarters reads:

Western front: During the rainy weather the artillery fire in most sectors was limited.

In the Champagne French attacks on the northwest slope of Hill 185, south of Ripont, were not developed, under our annihilating fire.

Reconnoitering advances took place in the Somme sector and on the west bank of the Meuse (Verdun front), where a post held by the French south of Cumieres was captured by

(Continued on page six, column seven)

GERMANS TO TAKE ACTION AGAINST SPANISH JOURNAL

El Liberal Claimed That Chilean and German Officials Were Implicated in Cartagena Plot

Special Cable to The Christian Science Monitor from its European Bureau

MADRID, Spain (Friday)—A new sensation is produced almost daily in connection with the discovery of explosives, etc., left at Cartagena by a German submarine. In connection with the matter, the Spanish Government is bringing four Germans and numerous Spaniards to trial.

It is now announced that finding the position difficult as a result of the piling up of new charges against German officials, proceedings are about to be taken against the newspaper El Liberal, at the instance of the German Ambassador who complains of articles published recently on German espionage in Spain. El Liberal, commenting on the threatened proceedings, states that part of the information in the article complained of appeared in the Conservative journal, La Epoca, the previous day, and asks if the German Ambassador will dare take proceedings against the Conservative organ.

The new turn of events has created enormous interest and startling revelations are expected. For some two or three weeks El Liberal, which has just discovered that cases deposited by the submarine contained 1800 kilos of trinitrolol, has been carrying on a vigorous campaign against German espionage in Spain, and admittedly its revelations have forced the Government to action against the Germans in the country. As a result, German diplomacy in Spain is in a difficult position, and it was evident Prince de Ratibor would be compelled to take some action.

In the issue, of which the German Ambassador complains, El Liberal indicated that in some degree Chilean and German officials were implicated in the Cartagena plot and that one of the chief Germans implicated, Herr Kallen, endeavored to escape in an automobile that had belonged to the Chilean Minister in Madrid. The latter immediately published a statement to the effect that he had sold the automobile the previous day. Herr Kallen was subsequently arrested and brought back to Madrid.

NOMINATIONS TO TARIFF BOARD ARE OPPOSED

Makeup of Commission Displeasing to Republican Senators — Ratification of Colombia Treaty Under Consideration

Special to The Christian Science Monitor from its Washington Bureau

WASHINGTON, D. C.—There is a question as to whether or not the Tariff Commission just named by the President will be confirmed at the present session. Strong Republican opposition will have to be faced, especially from the high protectionists, who view with displeasure the make-up of the commission as just nominated. It is intimated that committee opposition may keep the nominations from being reported at this session.

The Senate this afternoon appointed a committee to notify the President that unless he had further business for them, they were ready to adjourn until April 16, the date of the extra session.

Administration senators have given up hope of having the Colombian treaty ratified during the special session of the Senate and have consented to put it over until the extra session on April 16. In the meantime efforts will be made to have the State Department agree to "slight modifications" expected to make the treaty acceptable to the Republican opposition.

MR. BONAR LAW TALKS ON THE IRISH QUESTION

Informs House of Commons Attitude of Nationalists May Cause Appeal to Country — Government Declaration Asked

Special Cable to The Christian Science Monitor from its European Bureau

LONDON, England (Friday)— Mr. Bonar Law, Chancellor of the Exchequer, in a statement on the Irish question in the House of Commons today said the attitude of the Nationalists in opposition might have the effect of compelling an appeal to the country. If the good will of the country could settle the question it would be done tomorrow.

John Dillon had asked whether there would be any one present to answer for Ireland. A rumor had reached him that orders had been issued to Dublin people to keep indoors tomorrow, St. Patrick's Day. Mr. Bonar Law said he knew nothing of the circumstances mentioned.

The Chief Secretary for Ireland had proceeded to Ireland so that there was no one to answer with authority for the department.

On the report stage of the vote of credit, Sir Henry Dalziel asked for an announcement of the Government's intentions regarding Ireland, and proposed the establishment of a powerful commission to deal with the matter. It was important in view of the grave state of affairs in Ireland and at a time when revolutions were in the air that they should have a frank declaration from the Government. His own information was not reassuring.

Friday—Mr. Bonar Law, in moving the new vote of credit in the House of Commons yesterday, explained it was a very disagreeable surprise to him that he had to ask for an additional vote. In spite of every precaution that might have been taken it would have been impossible when estimating for £200,000,000 on Feb. 12 to anticipate the circumstances which now necessitated his occupying the House for two days with the question of further new money.

When examining the figures presented to him early in February he thought the margin rather fine and mentioned the matter to his advisers, and it occurred to him then that an additional £10,000,000 might wisely be added, but it was small satisfaction to feel even if he had taken the precaution that it would still not have avoided the present supplementary estimate.

The additional £60,000,000 asked for is made up as follows: Wheat from Australia £18,000,000, advances to the allies and dominions £23,000,000, additional expenditure on munitions and expenditure by the Shipping Controller for increasing the supply of merchant ships £19,000,000.

In connection with figures covering the extra munitions and ships expenditure, the Chancellor said it should be a distinct satisfaction to the House, as it certainly is to the Government, to find they are getting these merchant ships more rapidly than they had reason to anticipate when the last vote was introduced. The total amount of the credit voted during the present year would now be £201,000,000; excluding £350,000,000 voted for next year the aggregate vote of credit since the beginning of the war reaches the enormous total of £3,792,000,000.

ENEMY STEAMER CAPTURED

LONDON, England (Friday) — A small enemy steamer, attempting to cross the Tigris River, was set afire and ultimately captured, practically undamaged, today's official report from the Mesopotamian expeditionary force asserted. The capture occurred on Tuesday. The vessel carried 250 rifles and a quantity of ammunition.

CHANCELLOR TO VISIT VIENNA

Special Cable to The Christian Science Monitor from its European Bureau

AMSTERDAM, Holland (Friday)—It is announced that the German Chancellor is to visit Vienna at the end of the week to return Count Czernin's recent visit.

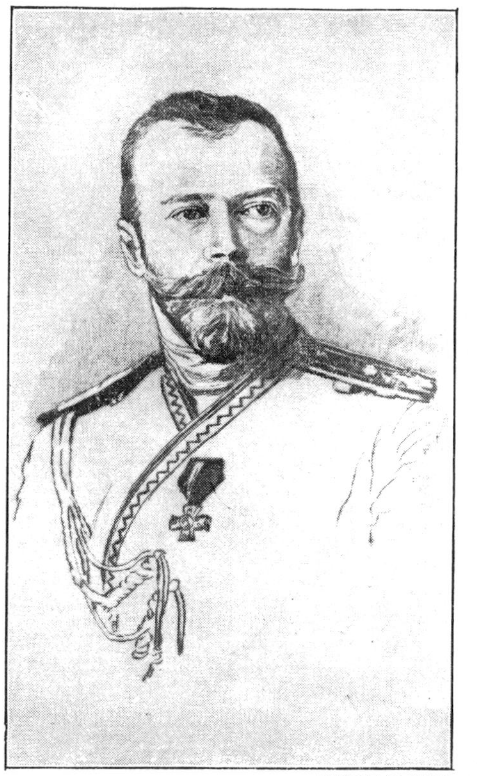

Etching by W. Renison

Nicholas II of Russia

BILL TO PERMIT CHALLENGING OF JUDGES FAVORED

Legislative Committee Makes a Report on Important Judiciary Measure, and House Passes It to Its First Reading

Legislation to permit either party in a suit in the Massachusetts Superior Court to challenge a judge on the ground of "personal bias or prejudice," is provided for in a bill favorably reported in the Massachusetts House today by the joint Committee on the Judiciary. Six of the 16 members of the committee dissented to the report, and it understood that a sharp contest will be made when the measure comes up for its second reading early next week. It took its first reading today as a matter of course, as do most measures receiving a favorable committee report.

This bill is one of the most radical relating to the judiciary that has come out of committee with a favorable report in many years. If enacted, it would permit either party at a civil or criminal session of the Superior Court, who had reason to believe that the judge sitting on the case had personal bias or prejudice against him or in favor of any opposite party to the suit, to file with the clerk of the court an affidavit to that effect, in which event the judge would be automatically removed and another judge satisfactory to both parties would be appointed to the case by the Chief Justice.

The dissenting members of the committee are Senators Hobson of Palmer and Sanford of Boston and Representatives Kennard of Somerville, Abbott of Haverhill, Burr of Boston and Wolcott. The bill is a redraft of a bill introduced on petition of Representative Simon Swig of Boston.

A unanimous report of leave to withdraw was made by the Committee on Public Lighting, on Representative Sullivan's bill for repeal of the sliding scale gas act regulating the price of gas in Boston.

The same report was made unanimously by the same committee on the report of the Gas and Electric Light Commission, under a resolve of 1915, relative to the continuance, terms and extension of the sliding scale for the price of gas.

The Social Welfare Committee reported a bill that the Board of Parole may grant a special permit to be at liberty from the State prison to a prisoner who has served half his minimum term, if it appears that he is likely to lead an orderly life and not depend on charity.

The Committee on Public Institutions reported an appropriation of $11,450 for improvements at the Lyman school for boys, of which $5700 is for the purchase of the Bailey place adjoining the school.

Leave to withdraw was reported by the Committee on Federal Relations on the petition of the Massachusetts Real Estate Exchange that a resolution be adopted asking Congress to investigate the subject of age pensions.

Ought not to be adopted was re-

(Continued on page five, column six)

BRIEF SKETCH OF THE CAREER OF FORMER TSAR

Nicholas II Since 1894 Has Been One of Enigmas of Europe — How Duma Arose

Nicholas II, the Tsar of all the Russias, has, ever since he succeeded his father in the November of 1894, been one of the enigmas of Europe, at any rate to all except those few who had some grasp of the true facts. As is recalled by Mr. Gardiner in his able sketch of the Russian Emperor, written nearly 10 years ago, Mr. Heath, the Tsar's English tutor, relates how that one day he and his pupil were reading together "The Lady of the Lake," and when they came to the stirring passage which tells how the gates of Stirling Castle were flung wide open, and King James rode out amidst the shouts of the populace, "Long live the Commons' King, King James!" the boy exclaimed eagerly, "The Commons' King, that is what I should like to be."

Mr. Gardiner goes on to make the cogent comment, that Nicholas II is one of those unhappy figures in whom "emotion is divorced from conduct, an idealist faithless to his ideals, a visionary doomed to violate his visions." This is, perhaps, as just a summary of the matter as could be made.

From his earliest childhood, Nicholas II has been the same. He received the ordinary education of all Russian

(Continued on page seven, column two)

BY-ELECTION FOR LIEBKNECHT'S SEAT

Special Cable to The Christian Science Monitor from its European Bureau

AMSTERDAM, Holland (Friday)—A Berlin telegram states that the by-election for Dr. Liebknecht's vacant Reichstag seat for the Spandau, Potsdam and Ostsavelland constituency resulted in a victory for the Majority Socialists, whose candidate, Herr Emil Stahl, obtained 12,886 votes against 3930 secured by Dr. Franz Mehring, Socialist Minority candidate, who carried Dr. Liebknecht's Prussian Diet constituency by a large majority. Results have still to arrive from some districts, but Herr Stahl's election is certain.

Berlin papers state that Herr Stahl organized a great house-to-house canvass, while Conservatives gave him their support and workmen in the large factories in Spandau were given special leave to go to poll and civil servants took an active part in the election.

AIR RAID ON WESTGATE

LONDON, England (Friday)—A hostile aeroplane bombarded Westgate, a suburb of Margate in Kent, without casualties early today. A statement issued by Lord French, commander in chief of the home forces, declared the material damage was slight.

BRITISH DESTROYER SUNK

LONDON, England (Friday) — A British destroyer of an old type struck a mine in the English Channel yesterday and sank, the Admiralty announced today. One man was killed and 28 are missing.

LIBERAL PARTY SECURES SIGNAL VICTORY IN SPAIN

Special Cable to The Christian Science Monitor from its European Bureau

MADRID, Spain (Friday)—The elections of provincial assemblies have passed without incident resulting in an overwhelming victory for the Liberal Party, supported by the Conservatives, in the form of a monarchist coalition.

The returns show 150 members of this coalition have been returned, 20 Regionalists, 17 Carlists, 17 Republicans and 25 Maurists. The Socialists gave their entire support to the Republicans, but the latter were divided into several groups.

RUSSIAN ARMY TO HAVE FINAL SAY IN POLICY

New York Russoye Slavo Says if Army Stands With People Future of Country Is Settled—Food Situation Brought Crisis

NEW YORK, N. Y.—Michel Pasvolsky, Russoye Slavo, Russian daily paper of New York, said today:

"We expected a conflict between the pro-German and the anti-German parties," he said, "but hadn't looked forward to the tremendous success which seems to have attended the move of the Duma. Only a few days ago the pro-German party, of which Stürmer, Protopopoff and Rasputin were sturdy pillars, displayed its strength by exiling Amfiteatrov, editor of the Petrograd Russkaya Volya.

"He had recently returned to Petrograd from exile under the promise that he would not be disturbed. Evidently those who made the promise were not strong enough to protect him. It was interpreted here as a sign of weakness on the part of the Liberals. The direct attempt of the Tsar to prorogue the Duma, too, made many believe that the pro-German influence was almost too strong. The success, then, of the anti-Germans came as a most welcome surprise.

"If the Army stands with the people, Russia's problem is settled. The people are overwhelmingly with the Duma. The need for change has been brought strikingly home to almost every one because of the apparent food shortage. The personal element in the problem assures the interest of all. They, too, have in mind that the Council of Empire at the opening of the Duma passed a resolution declaring that the food situation resulted from the failure of the administration to cooperate with the people.

"The army will have final say and hopes are high. The old units of soldiers such as defended the Czar and reactionaries in 1905 are gone—wiped out in the first big smashes of the war. Russia now has a citizen army. The rank and file is overwhelmingly anti-German and strong for a decision in the war. If the Petrograd garrison stands by the Government until the idea permeates the empire it won't be long until Russia will have solved her problem."

The Russian newspaper Novy Mir says: "The people will not be satisfied. We may expect any day to see the temporary Government give way to a more radical one. If the radicals succeed, it is not likely to effect peace."

EXCLUSION OF CHINESE ONLY BY COURT ORDER

Federal Tribunal Holds Immigration Officials Can Act Only Under General Law

Special to The Christian Science Monitor from its Southern Bureau

NEW ORLEANS, La.—What is considered one of the most significant victories won by Chinese in their dealings with immigration officials, is a decision rendered by the United States Circuit Court of Appeals in New Orleans. The court ruled that immigration officials can deport only Chinese charged with violating the Immigration Act, which applies to all aliens alike.

Where the charge is a violation of the Chinese Exclusion Act of 1893, the court holds that the facts in the case must be determined by the judicial department of the Government, and not by the immigration branch.

The case decided was that of Lee Wong Him versus John P. Mayo, Commissioner of Immigration at New Orleans. The Court of Appeals made a distinction between the immigration act and the Chinese Exclusion Law, ruling that the immigration authorities are empowered to act only under the former. The immigration act gives the immigration officials power to exclude undesirable aliens, regardless of their nationality.

RUMANIA TO OBTAIN LOAN FROM BRITAIN

Special Cable to The Christian Science Monitor from its European Bureau

JASSY, Rumania (Friday)—At the Cabinet Council held on March 8 an announcement was made that England had agreed to advance 1,000,000,000 francs at par to Rumania. The interest is to be at the rate of 5 per cent.

REVOLUTION IN RUSSIA BRINGS MANY CHANGES

Executive of Duma in Charge of Affairs in Capital—Reactionaries Arrested — Efficiency Aim of New Movement

Russia's popular assembly, the Duma, is undoubtedly in control of the situation in that country. As the details of the revolution of the past few days continue to come in, it is clear that the effect of the overturn is the virtual elimination of the reactionary and pro-German influences, and that the country has taken a long stride in the direction of popular liberty. While it is now stated that the abdication of the Tsar has not been actually effected, the revolution is regarded as indicating the end of autocracy in Russia and a more united and more effective action in the prosecution of the war.

All the leading members of the reactionary bureaucracy have been deposed from power, and are either imprisoned or in flight. These men were regarded as friendly to Germany in the present war situation, and the revolution which throws them out of power is regarded as a distinct triumph for the Allied cause.

Present reports indicate that the revolution was remarkable for the openness with which it was discussed in advance, and for the completeness with which it was carried out. It was also notable for the far-reaching results achieved with practically no bloodshed and comparatively little disturbance.

Special Cable to The Christian Science Monitor from its European Bureau

PETROGRAD, Russia (Friday)—The inevitable has happened. The people of Petrograd have risen against influences which they believe have sought after a separate peace; influences that for this purpose they believe have deliberately thrown out of gear the machinery of distribution, so that while grain rots in one part of the country there may be starvation only 100 miles distant; influences that for this purpose also have suspended the Duma.

The revolution has been carried through so far with ease and success exceeding any one's most sanguine hopes, although looking back it seems that one could scarcely have anticipated any other result. For it is the case that for months past in Petrograd, where, at one time to breathe the word revolution was to take instant departure for Siberia, revolution has been on every one's lips. It has been freely talked of in streets, on tramcars and wherever two or three persons are gathered together. It has been on the lips of soldiers, wounded or on leave, in Petrograd, and a common expression has been "when all is ready we will return and clear this matter up." This in strict faith they have done, and today Nicholas II is no longer Tsar of Russia.

His brother, the Grand Duke Michael, has been appointed regent. Nearly every Minister of State is in prison and the Duma is supreme.

The executive committee of the Duma, which is maintaining order, has published the following list of members of the new national Cabinet:

Prince Lvoff, president of the alliance of Zemstvos, is President of the Council, Premier and Minister of Interior.

M. Miliukoff is Foreign Minister.

M. Kerenski is Minister of Justice.

M. Nekrassoff, vice-president of the Duma, is Minister of Ways and Communications.

M. Konovaloff is Minister of Commerce and Industry.

Professor Maniuloff of Moscow University is Minister of Public Instruction.

M. Gutchkoff, who is a member of the Council of Empire and was formerly President of third Duma and President of United Committees of Mobilized Industry becomes Minister of War and Marine ad interim.

M. Schingareff becomes Minister of Agriculture.

M. Terestchanko is Minister of Finance.

M. Godneff is Controller of State.

It was, of course, the food question which finally precipitated the revolution. The shortage of food and the lack of organization in a land of plenty had been generally attributed to the methods of M. Protopopoff, Minister of Interior, who was generally known shortly as the "Madman." On Friday the streets of Petrograd were full of slowly-moving crowds, including strikers from factories and the general public. Tramcars were stopped and bridges were closed by the authorities to prevent this movement as far as possible.

Through the crowds moved cavalry, Cossacks and infantry with fixed bayonets. Here and there cheering was to be heard, the people cheering the sol-

(Continued on page six, column one)

MONITOR INDEX FOR TODAY

THE CHRISTIAN SCIENCE MONITOR

INTERNATIONAL EDITION | Copyright 1917 By The Christian Science Publishing Society | BOSTON, MASS., THURSDAY, APRIL 12, 1917—VOL. IX, NO. 115 | PRICE TWO CENTS

SUPPORT URGED FOR THE NEW RUSSIAN REGIME

Army Representatives Spurn Idea of Peace Without Consent of Allies—Workmen Reminded of Duty to the State

Special Cable to The Christian Science Monitor from its European Bureau

PETROGRAD, Russia (Thursday)—The meeting arranged by the party of the country and national Army representatives of the Petrograd garrison decided to submit to the Committee of Workmen's and Soldiers' Delegates and to the Provisional Government resolutions in favor, on the one hand, of continuing the war until the new liberties of Russia are guaranteed and, on the other hand, of continuing the war to a complete victory, restoring the ancient frontiers of the State.

The Army considers that a peace without the consent of the Allies would be a shameful peace, threatening Russian liberty, branding Russia as a traitor and separating her from free England, republican France, Belgium, Serbia, Montenegro and Rumania, which had suffered devastation for their friends, and would make the Russians perjurers in view of their solemn oath to restore free Poland, including the German and Russian sections of Poland. To achieve these objects the resolution submitted various demands to the Committee of Workmen's and Soldiers' Delegates.

First, a demand was made upon the committee to use all its authority in support of the Provisional Government so long as it safeguarded the interests of the people and could maintain order.

Second, the resolution called upon them in effect to act exclusively through the Provisional Government, as the Government to which the country and Army had taken the oath of fidelity.

Third, a demand was made for a termination of all dissensions among the workmen and administration and technical staffs of factories and workshops, since disorganization of industry threatened the Army with innumerable calamities.

Fourth, a demand was made upon the committee to submit its economic demands to a committee of experts for examination, without ceasing indispensable work and, finally, it was asked to increase the productivity of works of defense and to postpone initiation of the eight hours' day, in view of the fact that the Army was always working in the trenches.

The resolution also made certain requests to all soldiers and officers in the direction of concentration of work preparatory to battles. As to discipline the resolution pointed out that freed from gross submission the soldiers should establish a more vigorous discipline on the basis of the new order of democracy in the Army

(Continued on page seven, column two)

OFFICIAL NEWS OF THE WAR FROM CAPITALS

A heavy snow storm, an unusual thing for this time of the year in Northern France, has for the moment held up the British advance. It is difficult to direct gun fire and impossible for aeroplanes to scout effectively in such conditions, and without this it is scarcely safe for infantry to advance. Sir Douglas Haig has utilized the time in securing his position on the ridge at Vimy and on the heights at Monchy le Preux. From the ridge and from the top of the heights the surrounding country is commanded, and therefore the possession of them is essential to the holding of this country.

For this reason the German staff has poured out attack upon attack in a constant endeavor to recapture the lost terrain, but instead of this being successful Sir Douglas has slowly pushed forward down the slopes and along the flat ground both to the north and south of the ridge. Monchy itself lies some six or seven miles to the south, and commands the country between la Scarpe and la Sensée rivers, through which the great high road from Arras to Cambrai runs. Early this morning the breach in the enemy's front was farther widened by an advance from the northern end of the ridge, which enabled General Haig to get astride of la Souchez River near the town of the same name.

Key Position Taken

Monchy le Preux Falls Into Hands of British Forces

Special Cable to The Christian Science Monitor from its European Bureau

LONDON, England (Thursday)—The battle of Arras has quieted somewhat, but yesterday morning an important success was achieved in the Arras neighborhood itself by the capture of Monchy le Preux, near the Arras-Cambrai road and about six miles east of Arras. Monchy constituted a key position by reason of the fact that it is situated on a plateau

(Continued on page seven, column one)

AUTHORITATIVE VIEW ON THE SPANISH CRISIS

Senor Prieto May Take Over Premiership — Public Opinion Said to Favor Neutrality

Special Cable to The Christian Science Monitor from its European Bureau

MADRID, Spain (Thursday)—Although the Cabinet difficulties continue serious it is not believed the Government is in real danger. The opinion held in the best-informed circles is that the utmost that may occur is that Senor Garcia Prieto may take over the premiership. He has a strong following and a reputation for tactfulness.

Difficulties, it is believed, exist between Senor Alba, the Finance Minister, and Senor Gasset, Public Works Minister. The opinion of a high political authority is it should not be assumed that the crisis is upon the question of Spain's continued neutrality, although the entry of the United States into the war may increase the difficulties of her situation commercially and in regard to supplies of necessities.

Spain, this authority states, must inevitably persist with her neutrality, because public opinion in the country is hard against any further participation in wars of any kind, of which she has had more than enough in recent years, and all unprofitable. The same authority believes Spain's absence from the conflict will not prejudice her prospects after the war, since the Allies understand her position and sympathies.

Despite such statements, however, it is clear important movements are in progress, and long interviews of French and other ambassadors with the Premier have been commented upon.

CLUB WOMEN ARE UNITED FOR CONSERVATION

One Thousand, in New Orleans Meeting, Promote Ways and Means for Producing and Saving—Loyalty Pledged

Special to The Christian Science Monitor from its Southern Bureau

NEW ORLEANS, La.—One thousand club women here devoted practically all of Wednesday to discussion of plans for conserving the present food supply of the country and increasing the planting of gardens and other methods of adding to production all over the country. Mrs. John D. Sherman, chairman of the conservation department, took charge of the meeting, which was impromptu, and not included in the general program of meetings.

The teaching of conservation and the increase of food production by practical methods in all the schools of the United States was urged by Miss Mary E. Parker, chairman of the educational department. She proposed that the club women of every port make it their business to teach immigrant women how to raise at least part of the food for their own families This, she said, would assist materially also in the Americanization of aliens newly come to the United States.

Special attention also was paid to rural schools, which now have more than 12,000,000 pupils, and the club women were urged to cooperate with the teachers in these schools in preparing the pupils to become self-supporting immediately on leaving the schools.

That education is the only remedy for war, was advocated by several speakers. Prohibition of the sale of all bird feathers also was urged, and the extermination of all cats was demanded to protect feathered life.

Plans for pleasure trips about the

(Continued on page seven, column four)

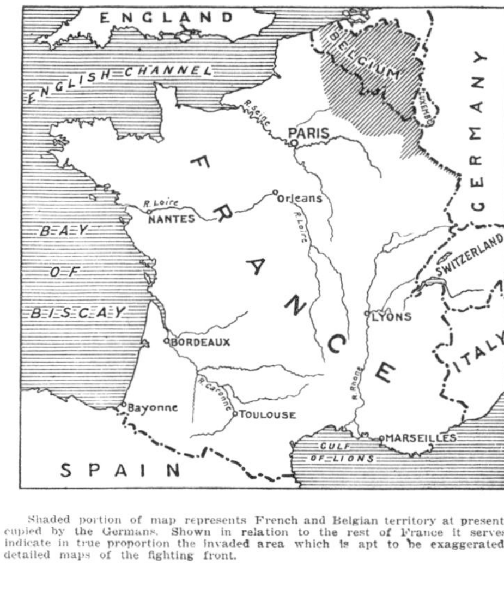

Shaded portion of map represents French and Belgian territory at present occupied by the Germans. Shown in relation to the rest of France it serves to indicate in true proportion the invaded area which is apt to be exaggerated by detailed maps of the fighting front.

BRITISH LOSSES BY SUBMARINES ARE LESSENED

Of 4773 Large Ships Arriving or Departing 17 Sank Week Ending April 8, Smallest Percentage in Seven Weeks

Special Cable to The Christian Science Monitor from its European Bureau

LONDON, England (Thursday)—An Admiralty statement of British shipping losses by gun and submarine for the week ended at 3 p. m., April 8, gives the following particulars:

Merchant vessels of all nationalities and local craft, arrivals, 2406; departures, 2367. British merchant vessels of 1600 tons gross or over sunk by mine or submarine, 17; under 1600 tons gross, 2; British merchant vessels unsuccessfully attacked by submarine, 14; British fishing vessels sunk, 6.

The 17 vessels of 1600 tons or over included one sunk during the week ended March 25, and one during the week ended April 1.

The two vessels under 1600 tons lost include one sunk during the week ended March 25, and three during the week ended April 1. The six fishing vessels sunk include one during the week ended April 1.

The following table, compiled from figures given out by the British Admiralty, shows results of seven weeks of the campaign the German submarines are conducting against British shipping. The number includes ships sunk by mines and those sent down by U-boats, the Admiralty states:

Week ending	Arrivals and departures	Vessels sunk	% sunk	Beat off attacks
Feb 25	4,541	21	0.46	12
March 4	5,005	23	.45	12
March 11	3,944	17	.43	16
March 18	5,082	24	.47	19
March 25	4,747	25	.52	13
April 1	4,680	31	.66	18
April 8	4,773	19	.40	14

WIRE STOCKADE FOR ALIENS

NEW YORK, N. Y.—Construction of a wire stockade for the internment of alien enemies has been begun on Ellis Island, and it was announced that a heavy guard of United States regulars would be quartered on the island.

M. NABOKEFF MAY BE NAMED AS AMBASSADOR

Russian Liberal Reported to Succeed George Bakhmeteff as Representative to United States

NEW YORK, N. Y.—That George Bakhmeteff, Ambassador from Russia to the United States, has been recalled by the new Russian Government, reported in despatches received here by the Russian newspaper Russko Slav. It was stated Russia would send M. Nabokeff, a widely known Liberal, to succeed M. Bakhmeteff. M. Nabokeff was a member of the first Russian Duma and later editor of the newspaper Retch.

M. Bakhmeteff was strongly allied with the most conservative group of the old autocratic Government. His wife is an American, sister of the late John R. McLean, multi-millionaire of Cincinnati and Washington. M. Bakhmeteff spends much of his time at Newport, R. I., and it is seriously doubted whether he will return to Russia under existing conditions.

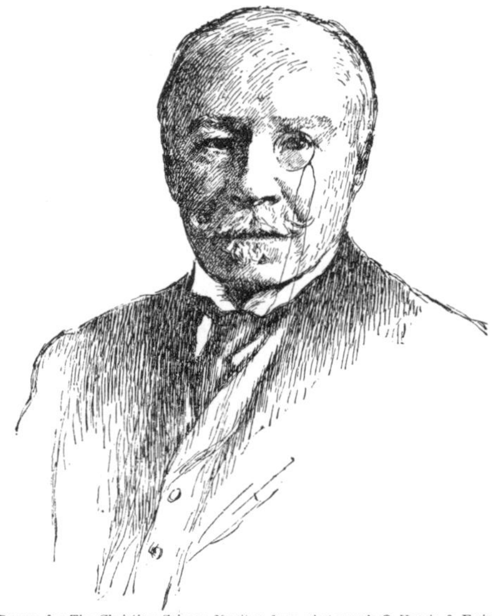

Drawn for The Christian Science Monitor from photograph © Harris & Ewing

George Bakhmeteff

Present Russian Ambassador to the United States

Knowledge of Recall Denied

Special to The Christian Science Monitor from its Washington Bureau

WASHINGTON, D. C.—Both the State Department and Russian Embassy deny knowledge of the reported recall of Ambassador Bakhmeteff. The first secretary of the Russian Embassy said that no official information whatever had been received indicating that there was any change contemplated in the Russian diplomatic corps here.

In the office of Assistant Secretary of State Phillips, it was stated that no such information had been received.

RHODE ISLAND SENATE PASSES SUFFRAGE BILL

PROVIDENCE, R. I.—The State Senate has passed, 32 to 3, an act giving women of Rhode Island the right to vote for presidential electors. Senator Guy Norman of Newport cited in opposition Miss Rankin's recent vote in Congress on the war resolution.

"Miss Rankin," he said, "was not equal to the occasion recently when the war resolution came up. The statement she made on the floor of Congress is equal to saying, 'I know what my duty is, but, being a woman, I can't do it.'"

ITALIAN SHIPPING LOSSES

Special Cable to The Christian Science Monitor from its European Bureau

ROME, Italy (Thursday)—The Ministry of Marine issues the following statement of the Italian shipping losses for the week ended April 8. Arrival of merchant ships of all nationalities at Italian ports, 494, with tonnage of 470,560 tons; departures, 477, with tonnage of 496,692 tons; Italian steamers under 3000 tons sunk, 5; sailing ships under 300 tons sunk, 10. One steamship was unsuccessfully attacked by submarine.

COURTESIES EXCHANGED

Special Cable to The Christian Science Monitor from its European Bureau

LONDON, England (Thursday)—King George has received from President Poincaré a telegram of congratulations on the splendid British success. King George has replied conveying the heartfelt gratitude shared by the British people and himself for the friendly congratulations so kindly expressed.

CONGRESSIONAL ELECTION

Special to The Christian Science Monitor from its Eastern Bureau

NEW YORK, N. Y.—Thomas F. Smith, secretary of Tammany Hall, is expected to be elected to Congress today in the special election to fill the vacancy of the Fifteenth New York Congressional District. His opponents are John Neville Boyle, Republican, and J. D. Cannon, Socialist.

UNITED STATES FLAG CHEERED BY JAPANESE

War Declaration Against Germany Deemed an Automatic Establishment of a Japanese-American Alliance

Special to The Christian Science Monitor from its Pacific Coast Bureau

SAN FRANCISCO, Cal.—The Japanese-American News, published here, has received the following cable message regarding the Japanese attitude toward the United States' entrance into the war.

"America's declaration of war to chastise German arrogance has been deemed by the Japanese people as an automatic establishment of a Japanese-American alliance. Americans are welcomed wherever they go and are greeted with cheers. The American flag is displayed everywhere. The war message of President Wilson and the war debates in Congress were minutely reported and printed in all the leading papers of the Empire and were read with great enthusiasm.

"Especially the passage of President Wilson's message challenging German bureaucracy, not the German people, for the defense of the rights of humanity and civilization and for the peace of the world was welcomed with great enthusiasm."

A cable message to the New World, a Japanese newspaper, said: "When extras announced America's participation in the war a flood of Japanese officials and leaders went to the American Embassy to express congratulations, while the populace surrounded the Embassy and cheered the American flag. Charge Post Wheeler, head of the American Embassy, had a long conference with Foreign Minister Viscount Motono."

John R. Noggle of the firm of Lanman & Kemp, New York chemical manufacturers, said recently that 2000 Chinese soldiers en route to France arrived at Vancouver a few days ago on the steamer Empress of Russia, on which he was a passenger. While he says the Chinese were all in blue field uniforms with khaki overcoats and officered by Chinese and 10 British officers, it was reported they were not to be used in the line but for agricultural and other work.

DAYLIGHT SAVING BILL IS AGAIN BEFORE CONGRESS

Provides for Advance of One Hour in Standard Time on the Last Sunday of April

Special to The Christian Science Monitor from its Washington Bureau

WASHINGTON, D. C.—Representative Borland of Missouri has introduced into the National Congress a bill to save daylight and to provide standard time for the United States, in which he asks that, between the last Sunday in April and the last Sunday in September, clocks everywhere in the United States be advanced one hour.

The bill, which has been presented in similar forms to former congresses, comes this year with the indorsement of many associations of commerce and industrial organizations in the United States. It provides that the territory of the United States shall be divided into five zones, clearly defined, and that at 2 o'clock a. m. of the last Sunday in April of each year, the standard time of each zone shall be advanced one hour. At 2 o'clock a. m., on the last Sunday in September, the time shall be returned to the normal.

SUNDRY CIVIL BILL PASSED BY SENATE

Special to The Christian Science Monitor from its Washington Bureau

WASHINGTON, D. C.—The Senate has passed the Sundry Civil Bill of $154,000,000 which included an amendment providing $10,000,000 for control of the lower Mississippi and the Sacramento rivers, which was supported by Senator Johnson of California in his first speech in Congress.

BRAZIL SEVERS RELATIONS WITH GERMAN EMPIRE

Official Word of Break Has Reached Washington — No Verification of Uruguay Action

Special to The Christian Science Monitor from its Washington Bureau

WASHINGTON, D. C.—Official word has reached Washington of the severing of relations with Germany by Brazil.

Brazil's official explanation of the break with Germany is as follows:

"Considering that the inquiry and the conclusions cabled by the legation at Paris on the subject of the torpedoing of the steamer Parana established the fact that the Parana was proceeding under reduced speed, was illuminated outside and inside, including the shield with the name 'Brazil,' and considering that the steamer received no warning to stop, according to the unanimous deposition of the crew, and further that the steamer was torpedoed and was shelled five times, and that the submarine made no attempt to save life, then, in the presence of such aggravating circumstances and in accordance with the note of Feb. 9 and the telegram of Feb. 13, sent by the Brazilian Government to the legation at Berlin, the Brazilian Government severs relations with Germany."

General public rejoicing greeted the announcement of Brazil's formal severance of diplomatic relations with Germany. In many circles, however, the view was expressed that the republic should go further and actually enter the war. Several newspapers began a

(Continued on page seven, column six)

PERU BEGINS CRUSADE FOR PROHIBITION

Process Is to Be Gradual at First, and Will Include Compulsory Teaching of Evils of Intemperance in the Schools

Special to The Christian Science Monitor from its Southern Bureau

NEW ORLEANS, La.—The Peruvian Government is planning to establish Nation-wide prohibition, by first eliminating the stronger alcoholic liquors and then reducing the percentage of alcohol in other beverages until it reaches the vanishing point, according to Porfirio Adan, a business man of Lima, and member of the ayuntamiento, or council, of that city, who is here buying merchandise and studying American business methods.

"Intemperance has become a serious problem in Peru," said Mr. Adan, "especially in the mining sections, and the Government has asked the State and city and town officials to assist the Federal authorities in stamping it out. The National Government has offered a prize of $500 gold, for the best textbook teaching temperance, to be used in the public schools. The author of this book also will receive a royalty on each copy published, and the study of it will be made compulsory in all educational institutions, whether public or private, so that there is considerable financial incentive to the successful writer.

"The copy for the textbook, which must be written in Spanish, but can be submitted by a person of any nationality, will be passed upon by a committee composed of the Director of Public Instruction, the Director of the Public School for Men, a member of the National Temperance Society of Peru, and a teacher to be chosen by vote of all the teachers of the public schools of Lima.

"Meanwhile, for the benefit of the present generation, strict laws are to be passed forbidding the making or the importation of drinks containing more than one and one-half of 1 per cent of alcohol. Eventually these also will be eliminated, and the Government is even now experimenting with the production of non-alcoholic drinks which gradually can be substituted for the harmful drinks. It is estimated that nearly 75 per cent of the adult

(Continued on page six, column four)

ALLIED LEADERS TO UNITE IN WAR CONFERENCE

Administration at Washington Preparing to Receive Representatives From Great Britain and France

Special to The Christian Science Monitor from its Washington Bureau

WASHINGTON, D. C.—That the proposals put forward in the President's address to Congress on April 2 for close cooperation with the nations at war with Germany are to be given heed, is indicated clearly in the developments Wednesday in the war situation. Reports from London that Arthur J. Balfour, Secretary of Foreign Affairs of the United Kingdom, and other British officials, together with a commission from France, are coming to Washington, are confirmed here.

The announcement is taken to mean the most momentous conference of the war, and in potentiality it will involve the consideration of steps, the most important in the history of nations, for it will involve a program of measures and procedure that will be generally accepted as shaping the future of the family of nations. It will be the initial act in the development of the federation of the world and the concert of nations the President so often has presented in his public utterances, a purpose which lies behind all the vast preparations now in progress for the participation of the United States in the war.

The date of the arrival of the representatives of the Allies is not announced, and even if it were, the day or even the approximate date, could not be published. But Administration officials have no hesitancy in saying that the conference is to take place, for it is the logical sequence of the President's address.

In addition to the Foreign Secretary of the United Kingdom, the Governor of the Bank of England, the Rt. Hon. Lord Cunliffe, will be included in the party from London. Others mentioned are Rear Admiral Sir Dudley De Chair and Brig.-Gen. George Bridges.

Unofficial information is that the French commission will be composed of Rene Viviani, formerly Premier, now vice-president of the Council of Ministers, and Minister of Justice; Marshal Joffre, formerly Commander-in-Chief of the Allied armies, the defender of France; General Foch, formerly commander of the northern armies of France, and considered one of the greatest strategists of the Entente armies; an Admiral of the General Staff of the French Navy; Octave Homberg, who served on the Anglo-French loan commission to the United States as the chief aid of Mr. Ribot, then Minister of Finance, and Franklin Bouillon, president of the Inter-Parliamentary Union, and a member of the Chamber of Deputies.

On the part both of the Allies and this Government it is felt that a better understanding may be reached and quicker results attained by personal conferences, than by negotiations carried on in the ordinary diplomatic channels. Mr. Balfour has always been a close friend of the United States, and his selection for the duty he is to assume on behalf of the United Kingdom is considered here a most happy one. He was First Lord of the Admiralty in the preceding Cabinet. His last public manifesto on the subject of the relations with Germany, addressed to this Government in January, while the peace proposals of Germany were under discussion, are still fresh in memory. On that occasion he gave expression to sentiments, also entertained by his predecessor, Sir Edward Grey, favoring a concert of nations that would assure lasting peace after the present war is concluded. It is regarded as certain that this subject, which is close to the heart of both men, will be discussed by the British Foreign Secretary and the President, when they meet in the United States capital.

As to the general character of the conferences that are to follow the arrival of the commissioners of the Allies, abundant light is furnished by the President's address to the joint session. His references to cooperation with the nations at war with Germany were contained in the following words:

"It will involve the utmost practicable cooperation in counsel and action with the governments now at war with Germany, and, as incident to that, the extension to those governments of the most liberal financial credits, in order that our resources may so far as possible be added to theirs."

"In carrying out the measures by which these things are to be accomplished we should keep constantly in mind the wisdom of interfering as little as possible in our own preparation and in the equipment of our own military forces with the duty, for it will be a very practical duty, of supplying the nations already at war with Germany with the materials which they can obtain only from us or by our assistance. They are in the field, and we should help them in every way to be effective there."

The Government is already in possession of information in a general way as to the needs of the Allies. For present activities the Allies are understood to be well supplied with munitions, and to have as many men

(Continued on page seven, column four)

MONITOR INDEX FOR TODAY

THE CHRISTIAN SCIENCE MONITOR

AN INTERNATIONAL DAILY NEWSPAPER

THREE CENTS | Copyright 1918 by The Christian Science Publishing Society | BOSTON, U. S. A., TUESDAY, NOVEMBER 12, 1918 | Sixteen Pages | VOL. X, NO. 298

THANKSGIVING AND REJOICING IN ALL ALLIED CAPITALS

Popular Enthusiasm Breaks Out as British and French Premiers Announce the Signing of Armistice to the Crowds

Special to The Christian Science Monitor

LONDON, England (Monday)—Universal rejoicing broke out in Europe today as the news was given out during the morning that the German delegates at Allied Headquarters had appended their signatures to the armistice terms, which the Entente governments had granted them, at 5 o'clock p. m., and that the great war would come to an end six hours later. Amidst the ringing of church bells, the sounding of familiar air-raid signals and the flying of flags, Mr. Lloyd George from the door of his residence told the London crowds of the great event, after which, at his wish, the houses of Parliament adjourned their sessions to attend a thanksgiving service at St. Margaret's, Westminster, while at the same time in St. Paul's Cathedral the announcement of the armistice was made, followed by the singing of the Old Hundredth, and the national anthem, and the sound of gun-firing without.

In Paris, M. Clemenceau read the armistice terms to the Chamber of Deputies in a memorable session, with cannon-salvos, illumination of buildings and general rejoicing proceeding throughout the capital.

Similar rejoicings are reported from Rome and from every capital of the nations who have now accomplished their victory over military despotism.

London Stops Work to Rejoice

Special cable to The Christian Science Monitor from its European Bureau

LONDON, England (Monday)—London has stopped work to rejoice. By 11 o'clock Whitehall was thronged with cheering crowds, the War Office and Admiralty are beflagged, soldiers of the Allies and the people are thronging all vehicles. Promptly at 11 o'clock, the Premier from No. 10 Downing Street announced to the crowd in the street that the war was over. A dense crowd before Buckingham Palace cheered the King's and Queen's appearance on the balcony.

LONDON, England (Monday)—Waving flags and cheering, a large crowd pressed into Downing Street before noon today shouting "Lloyd George! Lloyd George!" Finally the cheers and shouts brought the Premier and Andrew Bonar Law, Chancellor of the Exchequer, to a second floor window of the Premier's residence.

When order and silence had been secured, he spoke as follows:

"You are entitled to rejoice. The people of this country and of their allies and the people of our overseas dominions and of India have won a glorious victory. It was the sons and daughters of the people who have won it. It was the most wonderful victory for liberty in the history of the world. Let us thank God for it."

Evacuation Period Prolonged

Special cable to The Christian Science Monitor from its European Bureau

LONDON, England (Monday)—The French Government's wireless service transmits the German plenipotentiaries' communication to the German High Command concerning the signing of the armistice and the prolongation of the delay for evacuation.

The period given for the evacuation of the left bank of the Rhine by the German forces has been extended by 24 hours, according to a French wireless dispatch received here.

PARIS, France (Monday)—(Havas)—Before the signing of the armistice, L'Echo de Paris says it understands telegrams were exchanged by the Entente governments and the United States to decide whether the new situation in Germany was of a nature to cause prolongation of the 72 hours' time given the enemy armistice delegates.

Paris en Fête

PARIS, France (Monday)—Official announcement of the signing of the armistice and the termination of hostilities was given to the Paris press at 11.30 o'clock.

A Havas dispatch says that as soon as the official announcement was made, all official buildings, embassies and legations in Paris were bedecked with flags, and church bells were rung. Workers flocked from offices and shops and formed processions which paraded through the principal streets. The marchers sang allied national hymns and carried allied flags.

Further reports state that Jules Pams, the Minister of the Interior, has notified the prefects throughout France to decorate public buildings and have public illumination tonight. He also ordered them to have the military authorities fire salvos to inform the populace that the armistice had been signed and to cause all bells to be rung.

London Press Cautious

LONDON, England (Monday) — In view of the irregular and uncertain position of the new German Govern-

(Continued on page five, column one)

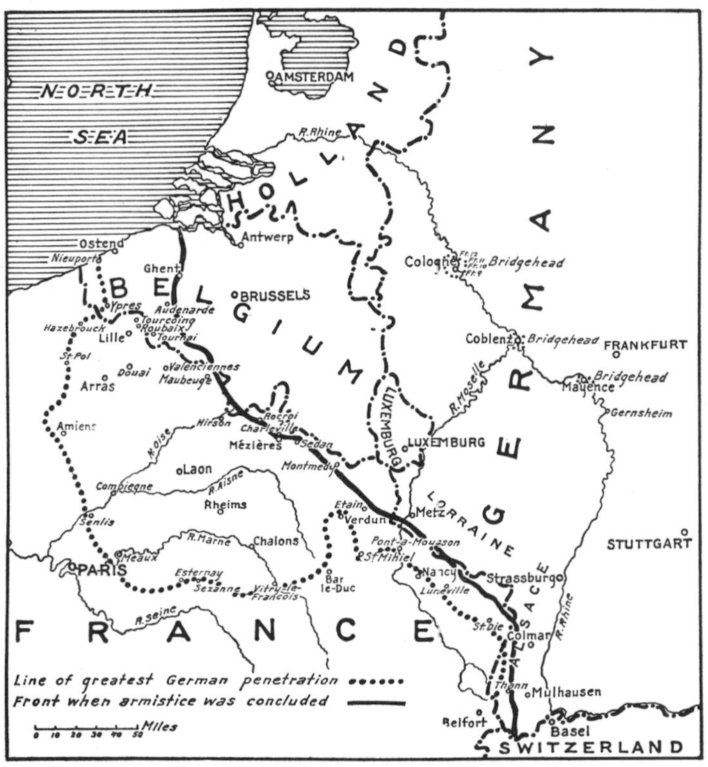

Drawn for The Christian Science Monitor

Military terms of the armistice granted to Germany

1. Evacuation of invaded countries: Belgium, France, Alsace-Lorraine and Luxemburg.
2. Evacuation of the countries on the left bank of the Rhine, in other words the territory between the river and France, Luxemburg and Belgium.
3. Occupation by allied and United States garrisons of the principal crossings of the Rhine, Mayence, Coblenz and Cologne, together with the bridgeheads at these points in a 30-kilometer radius on the right bank.
4. A neutral zone shall be reserved on the right of the Rhine between the stream and a line drawn parallel to it 40 kilometers to the east from the frontier of Holland to the parallel of Gernsheim, and as far as practicable a distance of 30 kilometers from the east of the stream from this parallel upon the Swiss frontier.

DR. MASARYK ENDS HIS LONG EXILE

Leader of Tzecho-Slovaks to Return to Europe to Shape Policies of the Recently Formed Independent European State

Special to The Christian Science Monitor from its Washington Bureau

WASHINGTON, D. C.—While Prof. Thomas G. Masaryk has been promoting the interests of the Tzecho-Slovak nation during his four years and more of exile with such success that he has won for it the recognition of the Allies and the United States as an independent nation, events have been shaping themselves for the complete fruition of all the work that has been done by him and his associates. A committee has had charge of affairs in Bohemia, and has maintained the integrity of the sturdy little nation against the assaults of the Austro-Hungarians.

The time has now come when Professor Masaryk is asked to return to his country and personally help the new republic to work out its destiny. A constitution must be adopted, boundaries settled, and other important matters worked out, in order that Bohemia may take her place among the nations which she enjoyed in former days and establish her prosperity along modern progressive lines. Two telegrams have been transmitted to Professor Masaryk by the Department of State in Washington. One from the United States legation in Berne, reads:

"We are on the soil of Switzerland after four years of indescribable suffering, and we send to you a salute most sincere, and thanks more fervent of a grateful nation.

(Signed)

"KRAMARZ, STANEK, KLOFAC, HABERMAN, KALINO, SVOBODA PREISS."

The men whose names are signed to this telegram represent all the political parties and factions in Bohemia, and their united action indicates that Professor Masaryk will have no opposition when he returns.

A second telegram from Paris, also transmitted through the American Department of State, contains the following message from Mr. Benes to Professor Masaryk:

"After interview with Kramer and his friends at Geneva, following decisions were taken: Government to be republican, our Cabinet to be immediately completed upon its return to Bohemia. You, as president of the Republic, should return at once, and in the meantime give to Kramer right to sign in your name as president of the council. General political and social situation in Bohemia is such that your presence is necessary. Your authority is unlimited, and you are awaited. All our activities approved with general enthusiasm. I retain portfolio of Foreign Affairs and remain in Paris for the present. Milan keeps the Ministry of War. I am sending you detailed information."

Professor Masaryk will heed this summons and very shortly will start for Prague. Bohemia is likely to be established with less friction, with more security, and more speedily, than any of the new states that are expected to be carved out of the old countries which have fallen to pieces in the test to which they have been submitted since the war began.

CONTROL OF THE NEW POLAND

American Jewish Committee Asks for Effectual Guarantees of Equality in Charter

Special to The Christian Science Monitor from its Eastern Bureau

NEW YORK, N. Y.—Merely to make stipulations for the equality of all inhabitants in a treaty or protocol will not be sufficient; effectual guarantees must be added to the articles of the Polish charter, according to the report of the American Jewish Committee which was established "to prevent the infraction of the civil and religious rights of the Jews throughout the world."

The report continues: "Will the new Poland be controlled by enlightened and broad-minded men who will administer it as a great civilized state on the basis now recognized to be the foundation of all modern civilized nations, or will the new state be the victim of those extreme chauvinists whose motto has been publicly proclaimed as 'Poland for the Poles' and who propose to arrive at this ideal by sending half of the Jews of Poland to America and half to Palestine?"

The report also draws attention to the analogous case of the Jew in Rumania, where they say that the "oligarchy found no difficulty in circumventing the provision of the treaty of Berlin guaranteeing civil and political equality to all inhabitants irrespective of creed." It is claimed also that a new naturalization law granted in the treaty of Bucharest, providing for the citizenship of Jews born in Rumania, was really valueless except in the cases of children then under the age of fifteen.

SAILORS ARE URGED TO BREAK THE TRUCE

Special cable to The Christian Science Monitor from its European Bureau

LONDON, England (Monday)—The British Admiralty announces that a wireless message which was sent from the command and Soldiers' Council of the German cruiser Strassburg to all warships, torpedo-boat destroyers and submarines in the North Sea and Baltic, quotes an extract from the armistice terms.

The message concludes: "This would be the destruction of us all. German comrades defend your country against such an unheard-of presumption. Strong English forces are reported in the region of the Skaw. All submarines in the Baltic except those on outpost duty are to assemble at once at Safnitz harbor."

PLAN FORMED TO RESTORE LOUVAIN

Nicholas Murray Butler of Columbia University Heads Commission in the United States to Undo Work of the Enemy

Special to The Christian Science Monitor from its Eastern Bureau

NEW YORK, N. Y.—A national commission in the United States for the restoration of the University of Louvain has just been established, with Nicholas Murray Butler, president of Columbia University, as chairman, and with a secretary's office to which those eager to aid in the undertaking may send books, in the J. P. Morgan library, according to the announcement sent out by the committee.

"The wanton destruction of the ancient and celebrated university halls of Louvain, including the treasures of its splendid library, has evoked the unanimous indignation of the entire civilized world," the announcement states. "This application, after the sacrilegious invasion of Belgium, of the policy of monstrous terrorization by which it was planned that kultur should be substituted for European culture, developed through the ages, is to receive universal condemnation by the restoration of the university. Founded in 1425, the University of Louvain has for five centuries been an international center of science and learning, attended by students from all nations."

National committees are being organized in all the leading nations to cooperate with the international committee for the restoration of the University of Louvain.

Two former presidents of the United States, William Howard Taft and Theodore Roosevelt, are members of this committee, the personnel of which includes several heads of American universities, other educators, publicists, financiers and diplomatists.

H. M. S. BRITANNIA SUNK AT GIBRALTAR

Special cable to The Christian Science Monitor from its European Bureau

LONDON, England (Monday) — A statement issued by the British Admiralty tonight says that the battleship Britannia was torpedoed at the western entrance of the Straits of Gibraltar on Saturday and sank three and one-half hours later. It was stated that 39 officers and 673 men were saved.

The Britannia was a battleship of the King Edward VII type and was completed in 1906. The vessel had a displacement of 16,350 tons, a speed of 18 knots and carried a complement of 820 men. Its armament consisted of four 12-inch guns, four 9.2-inch, 10 6-inch guns, and 12 12-pounders, 17 three-pounders and machine guns, and it had four torpedo tubes.

DR. SOLF APPEALS FOR EASIER TERMS

German Foreign Secretary Asks for Mitigation of Truce Conditions — Revolution Reported Secure in Fourteen States

Special cable to The Christian Science Monitor from its European Bureau

LONDON, England (Monday)—A wireless message from Berlin says Dr. Solf, the Foreign Secretary, in addressing an appeal to President Wilson, pleads for a mitigation of the armistice terms, while a further dispatch says that negotiations are in progress for the establishment of a common government to include representations from the Socialists, Independent Socialists and Middle class parties from the late majority group.

Rumania's Liberation

Special cable to The Christian Science Monitor from its European Bureau

AMSTERDAM, Holland (Sunday)—A Vienna message reports that General von Mackensen's army is marching through Hungary, while the Rumanians have occupied Lugos and Groskanisza.

Demonstrations in Alsace

Special cable to The Christian Science Monitor from its European Bureau

PARIS, France (Sunday)—Alsatian soldiers on leave are participating in demonstrations in Strassburg in favor of the return of the province to France, according to a Zurich dispatch to Le Journal.

Crowds, including soldiers, paraded bearing banners inscribed, "We want to be re-tied to France, our motherland."

The police did not actively interfere with the demonstrations, merely begging the populace to remain calm.

Anti-Bolshevist Campaign

Special cable to The Christian Science Monitor from its European Bureau

AMSTERDAM, Holland (Sunday)—The Frankfürter Zeitung reports that a Munich meeting discussed means for uniting the two German Socialist Reichstag groups, and appointed a committee for considering the matter. Meanwhile, the Vorwärts joins the entire German press in urging an anti-Bolshevist campaign.

Berlin Prison Stormed

AMSTERDAM, Holland (Monday)—Armed workers and soldiers stormed the prison in the Alt-Moabit Street in Berlin, but at the request of Herr Baechener, a deputy, they released only those incarcerated as "war victims," including former Captain von Beerfeld, who was concerned in the distribution of the memorandum of Prince Lichnowsky, which accused Germany of starting the war.

Utilities Uninterrupted

LONDON, England (Monday) — The Soldiers' and Workmen's Council, according to a German wireless message picked up here, has decreed that public utilities employees, physicians and domestic servants are exempted from the general strike.

The German Independent Socialists have proposed Dr. Karl Liebknecht, Hugo Haase and Herr Barth as members of the government, a German wireless message announces.

Regarding the negotiations between both groups of Socialists, the leader of the Social-Democrats announces, the message adds, that both parties are seeking a Socialist republic, but will ask the people and a constituent assembly to decide.

Revolutionary Progress

COPENHAGEN, Denmark (Monday)—(By The Associated Press)—Fourteen of the 26 German states, including all the four kingdoms and all other important states, are reported in the hands of the revolutionists.

The kingdom of Württemberg has been declared a republic and the King has announced he will not stand in the

(Continued on page four, column three)

BOSTON SALOONS ARE ALL CLOSED

Specially for The Christian Science Monitor

BOSTON, Mass.—Saloons, hotel and club bars, and, in fact, places holding any class of liquor license, without distinction, were closed today by order of the Boston Licensing Board, in cooperation with Mayor Peters and Police Commissioner O'Meara. This action was taken to diminish the abuse of the sentiment to celebrate the end of hostilities, and to aid the observance of the higher meaning of the day in a more wholesome way, while saving from themselves those who might use intoxicants to excess in the guise of enthusiasm. This order remains in force until further notice from the board, Mayor and police commissioner.

CAUSE OF FOOD COST RISE TRACED

United States Food Administrator Says Larger Production Expense and Inflation Are the Chief Causes of Advances

Special to The Christian Science Monitor from its Washington Bureau

WASHINGTON, D. C.—"With the war effectually over, we enter a new economic era, and its immediate effect on prices is difficult to anticipate," said Herbert Hoover, United States Food Administrator, who is soon to leave for Europe to take up the work there of feeding the people who have suffered most severely from the war. He warns speculators that an embargo will prevent depletion of supplies below necessities by hungry Europe. It is admitted that the price of some foods will increase in price because of the great demand for them, but that of others will decrease, because new supplies can be released.

"For the first 12 months of the Food Administration the prices to the farmer increased, but decreased to the consumer by elimination of profiteering and speculation. During the last four months, prices have increased, due to transportation and wage increases. The currents affecting food are less controlled in the Unitad States than in the other countries at war," said Mr. Hoover. He continued: "The powers of the Food Administration extend:

"First—To the control of profit by manufacturers, wholesalers and dealers, and the control of speculation in foodstuffs, but not to the great majority of retailers, to public eating places, or the farmer, except so far as on a voluntary basis.

"Second—The controlled buying for the allied civil populations and armies, the neutrals and the American Army and Navy, dominates the market in certain commodities at all times, and in other commodities part of the time. In these cases it is possible to effect, in cooperation with producers and manufacturers, a certain amount of stability in price. I have never favored attempts to fix maximum prices by law. The universal history of these devices in Europe has been that they worked against the true interests of both producer and consumer.

"All indexes show an increase in farmers' prices and a decrease in wholesale prices of food during the year ending July 1, 1918. In other words, a great reduction took place in the middlemen's charges.

"The course of retail prices corroborate these results also. Since October, 1917, the Food Administration has had the services of 2500 voluntary, weekly retail price reporters throughout the United States. These combined reports show that the combined prices per unit of 24 most important foodstuffs were $6.62 in October, 1917. The same quantities and commodities could be bought for $6.55 average for the spring quarter, 1918—that is, a small drop had taken place. During this same period the prices of clothing rose from 74 per cent to 136 per cent over 1913, or a rise of about 62 per cent, according to the Department of Labor indexes.

"Since the spring quarter, ending

(Continued on page eight, column three)

PRESIDENT TELLS CONGRESS THAT THE WAR IS OVER

Mr. Wilson Reads Armistice Terms to Enthusiastic Audience and Counsels Friendly Helpfulness to the Conquered

Special to The Christian Science Monitor from its Washington Bureau

WASHINGTON, D. C. — President Wilson addressed a joint session of Congress on Monday in the House chamber and read to the two branches the terms of the armistice with Germany which went into effect at 6 o'clock on Monday morning, when hostilities in the war for peace ceased. His remarks evoked much enthusiasm in the audience which filled the Representatives' Hall.

Following the reading of the terms, which in their entirety leave Germany powerless to renew the conflict, the President said: "It is not now possible to assess the consequences of this great consummation." He meant that it was not possible to comprehend in a moment the fullness of meaning of an event which frees all mankind of the curse of a war that has disturbed in one way or another most of the individuals dwelling on the earth. So, realizing the hopelessness and impossibility of setting forth an inventory of what the end of hostilities comprehends, he pointed out some of the tremendous problems into which the shattered and war-torn nations have suddenly been plunged in the midst of whom the United States stands, still fresh from her late coming into the conflict, in a position now to help to their feet all those peoples who sincerely and honestly seek to establish themselves on a permanent basis.

Armistice Terms

Resumption of War Made Practically Impossible

WASHINGTON, D. C.—Before a joint session of the Senate and House on Monday President Wilson read the armistice terms, as follows:

1—Military clauses on western front:

One—Cessation of operations by land and in the air six hours after the signature of the armistice.

Two—Immediate evacuation of invaded countries: Belgium, France, Alsace-Lorraine, Luxemburg, so ordered as to be completed within 14 days from the signature of the armistice. German troops which have not left the above-mentioned territories within the period fixed, will become prisoners of war. Occupation by the allied and United States forces jointly will keep pace with evacuation in these areas. All movements of evacuation and occupation will be regulated in accordance with a note annexed to the stated terms.

Three—Repatriation beginning at once and to be completed within 14 days, of all inhabitants of the countries above mentioned, including hostages and persons under trial or convicted.

Four—Surrender in good condition by the German Armies of the following equipment: 5000 guns (2500 heavy, 2500 field), 30,000 machine guns; 3000 minenwerfer, 2000 aeroplanes (fighters, bombers — firstly, D. 73s and night-bombing machines)—the above to be delivered in situ to the Allies and the United States troops in accordance with the detailed conditions laid down in the annexed note.

Five—Evacuation by the German armies of the countries on the left bank of the Rhine. These countries on the left bank of the Rhine shall be administered by the local authorities under the control of the allied and United States armies of occupation. The occupation of these territories will be determined by allied and United States garrisons holding the principal crossings of the Rhine, Mayence, Coblenz, Cologne, together with bridgeheads at these points in a 30 kilometer radius on the right bank and by garrisons similarly holding the strategic points of the regions. A neutral zone shall be reserved on the right of the Rhine between the stream and a line drawn parallel to it 40 kilometers to the east from the frontier of Holland to the parallel of Gernsheim and as far as practicable a distance of 30 kilometers from the east of the stream from this parallel upon the Swiss frontier. Evacuation by the enemy of the Rhine lands shall be so ordered as to be completed within a further period of 11 days, in all 19 days after the signature of the armistice. All movements of evacuation and occupation will be regulated according to the note annexed.

Six—In all territory evacuated by the enemy there shall be no evacuation of inhabitants, no damage or harm shall be done to the persons or property of the inhabitants. No destruction of any kind to be committed. Military establishments of all kinds shall be delivered intact, as well as military stores of food, munitions, equipment not removed during the periods fixed for evacuation. Stores of food of all kinds for the civil population, cattle, etc., shall be left in situ. Industrial establishments shall not be impaired in any way and their personnel shall not be moved. Roads and means of communication of every kind, railroads, waterways, main roads, bridges,

DAILY INDEX FOR NOVEMBER 12, 1918

THE CHRISTIAN SCIENCE MONITOR

AN INTERNATIONAL DAILY NEWSPAPER

THREE CENTS | BOSTON, U.S.A., THURSDAY, JANUARY 30, 1919 | Sixteen Pages | VOL. XI, NO. 58

Copyright 1919 by The Christian Science Publishing Society

DRY AMENDMENT IS DECLARED PART OF UNITED STATES LAW

Acting Secretary of State Issues a Proclamation Completing Work of Executive Department of Federal Government

Special to The Christian Science Monitor from its Washington News Office

WASHINGTON, District of Columbia—Frank L. Polk, Acting Secretary of State in the United States, issued a proclamation on Wednesday declaring the Federal Prohibition Amendment a part of the Constitution of the United States and, therefore, a part of the fundamental and organic law of the land. The amendment becomes operative on Jan. 16, 1920, one year after the day when the thirty-sixth state ratified it. As the amendment itself states, its provisions will become effective either by Act of Congress or by state legislation. The states named by the Acting Secretary of State in his proclamation are the first 36 whose official notifications were received in Washington, and are not the first 36 which took ratification action.

The official act which completed the executive department work of the federal government in making national prohibition a fact was performed in the office of the Secretary in the presence of the men who have been leaders in the contest. The ceremony took place late in the forenoon, Morris Sheppard, Senator from Texas, author of the resolution; William J. Bryan, former Secretary of State; Charles H. Randall of California, the prohibitionist member of the House of Representatives, being present together with the following:

Members of the W. C. T. U.—Miss Anna Gordon of Evanston, Illinois, national president; Mrs. L. L. Yost, legislative representative; Mrs. Frances E. Beauchamp of Lexington, Kentucky, one of the national officers, and Mrs. Stephen J. Berben of New Jersey;

Members of the Anti-Saloon League of America—Dr. H. H. Russell, founder of the league; E. C. Dinwiddie, legislative superintendent; Laura R. Church, his secretary; Ernest H. Cherrington, Westerville, Ohio, general manager of the publishing interests of the league, Ed. J. Richardson, assistant manager of the publishing plant, and Wayne B. Wheeler, counsel;

The Rev. Dr. Charles H. Scanlon and Mrs. Scanlon, of Pittsburgh, Pennsylvania, the former being general secretary of the Presbyterian Board of Temperance; Frank M. Waring, Board of Temperance, Methodist Episcopal church and Wilbur F. Crafts, of the International Reform Bureau; Ben. G. Davis, chief clerk of the State Department and other State Department afficials.

When Frank L. Polk, the Acting Secretary of State, penned his name on what some call a new Declaration of Independence, or the Magna Charta of American manhood, he by the stroke of a pen liberated a nation from the domination of the saloon power. There were those in the room who recalled the days of the early '80's when Maine and Kansas and Iowa were the only States where prohibition laws had been enacted, who remembered the early contests of the prohibition orators like Dickie and others who went about pleading for the abolition of the thing that was the enemy of the home, and before whose eyes passed the review of the struggles of the years to this day.

"The announcement by the Secretary of State of the United States that three-fourths of the states had ratified the amendment, is the official proclamation under section 205 of the revised statutes that the amendment is a part of the organic law of the nation," said Wayne B. Wheeler, general

(Continued on page five, column one)

LANGUAGE TEACHING LIMITED BY BILL

Special to The Christian Science Monitor from its Western News Office

LINCOLN, Nebraška—The State Senate, on Wednesday, passed a bill making it unlawful to teach in any private church, denominational, parochial or public school, any language other than English, until the child has passed the eighth grade. No foreign language shall be taught as a language in any such schools below the ninth or above the eighth grade, unless such teaching has been prescribed in the curriculum designated by the state superintendent of instruction. This places the teaching of foreign languages in colleges, universities and normal schools under the state superintendent.

NEW MOVEMENT IN THE BRITISH UNIONS

Large Number of Strikes Shows Need for Revision of Structure of Trade Unions Based on Shop-Steward Movement

Special cable to The Christian Science Monitor from its labor correspondent

LONDON, England (Wednesday)—The industrial situation, although still strained, is somewhat easier this week. Each morning, however, brings its crop of strike surprises, the only redeeming feature of which is that, with the news of each fresh outburst, comes the announcement of the settlement of another. In spite of the strenuous efforts of strike promoters, the numbers affected on the Clyde fall far short of the hope of its supporters. Contrary to general expectations, none of the municipal services are affected. Cars, electricity, gas, and water undertakings proceed as usual. The workers principally in the dispute are the shipwrights, boilermakers, and engineers, who, as can always be confidently expected, have gone one better than their colleagues in other centers by demanding a 40-hour week.

Not a single shipyard, however, on the whole length of the river has been completely stopped as a result of the strike. The conclusion arrived at by the present writer, during a personal tour of the Clyde a few weeks ago, is that the discontent fomented by the irreconcilables is more political than industrial in character, and if the present demands were conceded, there is no justification for the hope that peace would be restored. Rather would the movement thrive and grow impudent with the success attained, and steps be almost immediately taken to formulate further proposals. The leaders of the movement declare quite openly and candidly at their own party conferences that they are hostile to the present government, that their ultimate object is the control of industry, first having reduced industry to a condition that it no longer pays the employer to carry on.

It is not to be supposed for a moment that the rank and file are cognizant of the true position of the policy behind the demands. The shop-stewards' movement has sufficient insight and tactical knowledge to formulate only such demands as are acceptable and common to all trades, insuring thereby the cooperation of every craft and grade of workmen. Questions of demarcation which formerly divided the various crafts, and prevented joint action, have been relegated to the limbo of forgotten things. The outstanding feature of the present strikes is the remarkable degree of unity attained by all sections of workers in a given industry.

Another feature in common is that they are unofficial in character, and have been declared in opposition to the national executives, whose posi-

(Continued on page four, column three)

DAILY INDEX FOR JANUARY 30, 1919

BOLSHEVIST RULE BANE OF RUSSIA

Mme. Breshkovsky, in New York, Appeals to People of United States to Understand Desires of People in Crisis

Special to The Christian Science Monitor from its Eastern News Office

NEW YORK, New York—Russians in this city, evidently of all shades of political opinion, some carrying armfuls of red flowers, congregated in the Grand Central Station on Wednesday morning and startled various porters by kissing and kissing again a venerable woman, whose kindly face shone ruddy under her white hair. Mme. Catherine Breshkovsky, "the Grandmother of the Russian Revolution," for more than a score of years in exile in Siberia, more recently hidden away for months in Russia, as a protection against the Bolsheviki, had finally reached New York, after traveling from Omsk since last November.

Later, seated at a long table in the Henry Street Settlement, surrounded by representatives of the press, Mme. Breshkovsky explained the difference between a Socialist and a Bolshevik, the hopelessness of believing that any good can come to Russia through the latter, predicted a more glorious day for her nation in the future, and in answer to the question, "What can America do for Russia now?" said, with a characteristic smile, "Strive to understand her."

It is to help America understand Russia that Mme. Breshkovsky has come to this country. In all her public speeches, in all her conversations with her own and the American people, she is striving to drive home what she hopes is the truth about Russia. And this truth, as stated by her around the table on Wednesday, is that Bolshevism is anarchy, and true socialism, founded upon honesty of purpose, and honorable execution of that purpose, will spell salvation for her people.

Mme. Breshkovsky said she could not relate the details about the excesses to which the Bolsheviki had stretched their doctrines. Chaos was the word one thought of while she was describing the upheaval brought about by the forcible impression upon the people of Bolshevist theories and Bolshevist rule. New decrees came from Lenine and Trotzky every day. The people did not know what to expect next. There was no more law, no more order. The soviets had been corrupted by the Bolsheviki, there were no elections any more, the Constituent Assembly, the hope of the people, had been disorganized by the Bolsheviki, the only semblance of control now was exercised by revolutionary committees with power to enforce that control in a military manner.

"Oh," appealed Mme. Breshkovsky, "don't mix socialism with Bolshevism. I don't profess to know what the theory of Bolshevism is. But I do know what true socialism is. Yes, I am, and always have been, and always will be, a true Socialist. But a Bolshevik—never."

Mme. Breshkovsky's eyes grew more tender when she said there were 4,000,000 orphans in Russia, children robbed of their parents, either by the war or by the excesses of the Bolsheviki. Her expression became radiantly hopeful when she mentioned the need of education among the people.

"Send us books," she pleaded, "send us education."

Such aid, she added, could be sent to the cooperative societies, to the Zemstvos. As for the destruction of any such efforts to help Russia, by the Bolsheviki wherever they are in power, Mme. Breshkovsky smiled warily.

"Ah," she said, tapping her finger on the table, "we have ways of communicating information and help—underground ways."

She expresses the need for education in rather a quaint manner. "Alphabets," she says, nodding her head emphatically, "alphabets for our children. Give us alphabets."

But always she returned to the subject of Bolshevism. The Bolshevist propaganda, she said, began in Petrograd before the revolution, and it spread under the rosy promises of an overturn of affairs so that the people always would be on top. When the Constituent Assembly was in process of organization, the Bolshevist antidote for true representative government was:

"You will never get your rights if you wait for the Constituent Assembly. You must act now. You must take those rights now or never."

Peace was also a Bolshevist bait, and money at the front, German money, and the cry of no more war, no more separation of families, nothing but happiness for the people, all for the people always.

But the pendulum swung too far. Now there was no order where the Bolsheviki tried to rule. There was only suffering for the people; the railroad from Omsk to Vladivostok, every station along the way, was crowded with refugees, women and children fleeing from the Bolsheviki. The Bolshevist soldiers had the arms and ammunition, practically martial law held sway; there was not hope for Russia in Bolshevism.

But in true socialism, yes, that was Russia's hope. And in a correct understanding of Russia by the great powers, by the United States especially. As for armed intervention by the Allies, Mme. Breshkovsky said whether that was good or bad depended entirely upon whether it was unselfish or selfish.

"If you come in to help us, and only to help us, and not for your own purposes," she explained, "very well. But if not——" and she shrugged her shoulders.

BRITISH MINISTRY'S AGRARIAN SCHEME

Parliament on Assembling Next Tuesday to Consider Plans for Establishing Soldiers on Cooperative Farms

Special cable to The Christian Science Monitor from its European News Office

LONDON, England (Wednesday)—When Parliament assembles next Tuesday in accordance with the whip already dispatched to the members, Lieut.-Col. F. B. Mildmay will propose, and Sir Henry Dalziel will second, the reelection of Mr. J. W. Lowther as Speaker of the House of Commons. Mr. Lloyd George is expected back from Paris, and Mr. Bonar Law will also be present.

Urgent questions, such as industrial unrest, await their attention, and problems connected with demobilization will be placed well in the front of the new parliamentary program. The position of the depleted non-Coalition Liberals, with regard to the official opposition is not yet clear, nor is their strength a certain quantity. Sinn Feiners are the most numerous non-Coalition Party. But the Labor Party will occupy that position among the parties actually in attendance.

While the Labor members, according to a recent arrangement, are to sit on the opposition benches, Liberal Privy Councilors and former ministers also propose to sit there, with their small following.

The task before the new Parliament involves sweeping social changes, the effect of which upon the structure of the Coalition will be keenly watched.

The land question will be amongst the first to be discussed.

The Christian Science Monitor learns that agricultural laborers are to be given priority for army release, owing to shortage of farm labor. The situation with regard to the 1919 harvest makes more interesting and important the coming bill embodying a scheme for settling the demobilized soldiers on the land. Three classes of farming are contemplated. Men with experience, and who either possess capital or can obtain it from the state, will be settled in small holdings. The larger numbers, who live mainly by seasonal work in neighboring towns, or as workers on the land, will have a cottage and an acre of land for fruit growing, or poultry keeping. Co-partnership farms will be established on intensive lines under a skilled manager, all workers in the concern to benefit by the progress and profits.

The land will be acquired either by cash purchase, by rent for 35 years with renewal, by compulsion, or by annuities charged on the county rates. The security of tenure is insisted on, and the county councils are given freedom of action through the proposal to meet their deficiencies nationally.

PASTOR FINED FOR HOLDING SERVICES

Special to The Christian Science Monitor from its Western News Office

LOUISVILLE, Kentucky—The Rev. H. Boyce Taylor, pastor of the Baptist Church at Murray, Kentucky, was fined $100 on Wednesday in the County Court for his refusal to observe the orders of the Health Board in connection with the ban instituted as an alleged preventive of the so-called influenza epidemic. He insisted on holding services at the Murray Baptist Church despite the closing order and he was arrested.

The Rev. Mr. Taylor declared that in spite of the fine and the order of the court he would continue to hold services. He was warned by the county attorney that he would be arrested again if he continued to defy the law and that warrants would be sworn out for every person who attended the services while the ban is on.

The Baptist minister's fine follows his forcible removal from his pulpit and taking to jail by the sheriff of Calloway County on the charge of violating a court order secured by the State Board of Health prohibiting public meetings. The order of the court was read at his Sunday morning service, but no effort was made to stop the services. However, when the evening services began the sheriff entered the church and asked the minister if he proposed to disregard the court order. When answered in the affirmative the sheriff placed the minister under arrest and took him to jail. He was released on his own recognizance.

ARMENIAN DEMAND FOR RECOGNITION

Special cable to The Christian Science Monitor from its European News Office

PARIS, France (Wednesday)—At a meeting of Armenians, a resolution was passed demanding recognition of the Armenians' right to independence, and that representatives should be admitted at the Peace Conference.

GOVERNOR REMOVES CUSTOMS MINISTER

Australian Statesman Deprived of Office After Inquiry Into Purchase of Wireless From Roman Catholic Priest

Special to The Christian Science Monitor from its Australasian News Office

MELBOURNE, Victoria—Following the report of a Royal Commission on the sale to the Commonwealth, by a Roman Catholic priest, of wireless works at Randwick, N. S. W., a Federal Minister has been removed from office by the Governor-General and a Senator has resigned.

The Royal Commission on Navy and Defense Administration reported to the Federal Government on the purchase of the Shaw Wireless works, called after Father Shaw, the Roman Catholic priest who sold the works to the government, and on the purchase by the Navy Department of certain vessels. Prior to the report, Mr. J. Jensen, Minister for Customs, who was Minister for the Navy when the wireless works and the two vessels were bought had not taken his seat as a Minister for some little time, awaiting the finding of the commission. When the report was made, he considered himself exonerated of wrongdoing, refused the request for his resignation made by the Prime Minister and colleagues of the Cabinet, and resumed his seat in Parliament as Minister for Customs.

Mr. W. A. Watt, the acting Prime Minister, communicated the facts by cable to Mr. W. M. Hughes, the Prime Minister, who was in London. Not receiving a reply, Mr. Watt took the next step, an appeal to the Governor-General who removed Mr. Jensen from office.

The commission stated in its report that it found that the Rev. Father Archibald John Shaw had obtained an option of purchase of the works of the Shaw Wireless Company for £25,000, and on the same day, May 15, 1916, had offered to the Minister for the Navy, Mr. Jensen, the works and patents for £57,000. On July 15, 1916, Mr. Jensen offered Father Shaw £55,000 and this offer was accepted on July 18, 1916. Father Shaw withdrew from the purchase money sums amounting to £5300, of which sum the commission believed that Senator Long, a Tasmanian representative in the Federal Parliament, who had drafted Father Shaw's offer, had received £2400 as consideration for political influence used in connection with the purchase, or believed by Father Shaw to have been used, or represented by Senator Long to have been used. As to the disposition of the remainder of the money drawn out by Father Shaw the commission reports:

"The commission has not been able to secure any positive evidence as to the disposition of the balance of the sum of £5300 drawn on the Saturday morning, but as Father Shaw withdrew a further sum of £50 from his account on Monday morning, Aug. 21, 1916, and at the time of his death (on Aug. 26), had only a very small sum in his possession, it is evident that the money in question had been disposed of by him in some undisclosed way between Saturday, Aug. 19, and Monday, Aug. 21."

Dealing with the purchase of the works, as a business question, the commission refrains from undue criticism as the plant was bought at a period of intense war activity. It finds, however, that the works were undoubtedly too large for the Navy Department, and perhaps were unnecessary for the Commonwealth. They are situated in an unsuitable district and contain a quantity of obsolete and useless machinery and stock. Being burdened with such a high capital charge, much in excess of what might have been the price if business methods had been followed, the works are unable, it says, to compete effectively with other workshops, and as they have been conducted at a loss even in war time they cannot be expected to do nearly as well under peace conditions.

Referring to Mr. Jensen, the commission found that "the evidence does not disclose that the Minister or any person other than Senator Long received any portion of the £5300 withdrawn by Father Shaw on Aug. 19, 1916."

Dealing with the purchase of two vessels for the navy, the responsibility of the purchase being taken by Mr. Jensen, as Minister, who had considered purchase better than the cost of continuous hire.

When presenting the report of the Royal Commission to the federal Parliament, Mr. Watt, the Acting Prime Minister, said that the Ministry had adopted the conclusion of the commission that there was no evidence to connect Mr. Jensen with the receipt of money in connection with the acquisition of the Shaw Wireless Works, but had decided that the findings of the commission and the matters disclosed in the report rendered it undesirable that he should remain a member of the government.

As to the finding of the commission with respect to Senator Long, the Acting Prime Minister said that the Cabinet had further determined that eminent counsel be asked to consider and advise whether the evidence taken disclosed any facts which would justify or demand action in a court of law, and further to advise as to the powers, precedents, and procedure of Parliament in cases of this character.

Meanwhile the silence of Mr. Hughes, in response to the cable message or messages, has left the government in some doubt as to his approval or disapproval of the removal of Mr. Jensen from office, especially as Mr. Jensen is a Hughes man and not a Liberal—the other wing of the Nationalist Party.

PACKERS FORCING THEIR PROPAGANDA

Testimony Submitted in Congressional Hearing Designed to Supplement Campaign Waged Against Trade Commission

Special to The Christian Science Monitor from its Western News Office

CHICAGO, Illinois—In following the reports of the meat-packer hearings at Washington, the public may well bear in thought, remarks a local student of the meat-packing industry, that the packers went to Washington to influence American public opinion to their point of view. They are trying, commented this observer, to do in another way what they have been endeavoring to accomplish for months at great expense through nation-wide advertising in the newspapers and farm papers. They enjoy, at the present moment, the tremendous advantage over their advertising campaigns, that they are voicing their propaganda from here the sounding board of the national capital.

A large part of the ground covered is technical, continued the packing-house observer, and therefore it may behoove the public, in the face of this sustained packing-house argument and criticism of the Federal Trade Commission, to hold its ground against being carried away into conviction by repeated declarations, and wait for the weighing of the facts. The comment of this observer was further set forth as follows:

It is to be remembered, despite the attacks of the packers and of the federal trade committee of the Chamber of Commerce of the United States, and by various other persons prominent in business or manufacturing, that the Federal Trade Commission is a regularly constituted government body, and that its investigation of the packers was made in such capacity, and furthermore, that the public, as represented by the government, was represented by the trade commission. Without undertaking any comment on the commission in its investigation, it certainly stands as fact that until the commission did undertake its work the public knew practically nothing about the packing industry. The old phrase "closed book" applied to its workings, and today, despite inquiry and hearings, there is a large part of the business which is still regarded as "closed book" to outsiders. The public is only at the threshold of the packing industry.

The right of the packers to declare their point of view is unquestionable. But in following this point of view, as reported at length in the press, the foregoing in regard to the trade commission may well be remembered; also that other point, that the packers had a distinct motive in going to Washington en masse with their lawyers and publicity men; further, that that motive was evidently to keep things as they are in their business, or as much so as is possible, to protect their profits and to discredit the trade commission; and finally, that the subject is largely technical, and much of the knowledge of it, thanks to the packers' policy of secrecy in the past, is new, and in some fields incomplete; certainly, so far as the public goes, very incomplete.

Furthermore, the public may well remember, continued the observer, that back of all these questions raised is the problem of packers' profits, which cannot finally be hidden by side issues raised, by the argument of efficiency, or by being overshadowed in the press reports, as it sometimes seems to have been, by the personalities of these leaders of the industry on the stand, by lack of understanding of significance of replies in cross-questioning, or otherwise.

"As a matter of fact," concluded the speaker, "there are those who have followed this packing-house situation who regard what is going on at Washington as being bigger than the packers. They view, whether rightly or wrongly, the issue as American industry brought to the bar of regulation. The government, through the Federal Trade Commission, made an investigation of the meat packers. The packers have turned on the commission and are seeking to destroy it in the public confidence. The government, through the Food Administration, sought to regulate the packers. The packers reversed the regulation, and are now using it to protect themselves. The most effective weapon of the times has been utilized by the packers. It is publicity. They are getting today, incidentally, in the way of publicity, what they could not have bought in the advertising columns of the press for millions. If they win the fight, there are those who regard the struggle as meaning that big business generally wins with them; while if they are put under some measure of actual control, then the people have made some start toward the government of business. It is, of course, a great new field, and in the case of the packers, as of other business, a great need is knowledge of the wisest means of control, if control there is to be."

GERMAN COLONIES DISCUSSED AT THE PEACE CONFERENCE

Two Different Doctrines in Discussion on Territory—Australian Objections to Internationalizing Pacific Islands

Special cable to The Christian Science Monitor from its European News Office

PARIS, France (Wednesday)—Territorial adjustments are engaging the attention of the Peace Conference, and consequently the papers are full of irresponsible talk about the claims of one power or the demands of another. It is said that the Quai d'Orsay debates have revealed two different doctrines in the matter of territorial adjustments. According to the first, which finds expression in General Smuts' pamphlet on the League of Nations, territorial questions should be handled by different methods, according to whether they concern the colonies of the enemy, or whether they treat of territory forming part of Austria-Hungary, the Ottoman Empire, or Russia.

The other thesis, which would seem to be that of the United States, demands that the major part of the territorial question method should be uniform and consist essentially of allowing the League of Nations to regulate the disposition of territories in Europe, no less than in the case of the German colonies.

On Tuesday night, following on the meetings at the Quai d'Orsay, when the questions of German colonies in the Far East, the Pacific and Africa were considered, there was a rumor of disagreement between China and Japan over Kiaochow. With regard to the Pacific islands, Mr. William M. Hughes, Prime Minister of Australia, has received a cable from the Commonwealth Government emphatically protesting against the proposal to internationalize the Pacific islands or to place them in possession of any other power than Great Britain or Australia.

Mr. Hughes on Monday night, in an address to the Australian Y. M. C. A., said that Australia had fought for the national safety, for the islands in the vicinity of the Australian coasts in which the German eagle had fastened its claws. What Australia had won, she was entitled to hold, and no nation would be threatened by her possession of the Pacific islands.

The same could not be said in case some other nation became possessed of them, for such possession would constitute a menace to Australia.

On Tuesday evening, the French League of Nations Society entertained the allied representatives of the League of Nations associations. M. Louis Klotz, Finance Minister, represented the French Government. Lord Robert Cecil, Signor Orlando, Mr. Venizelos and representatives of America, Belgium, Serbia, Rumania, and China, were present.

M. Léon Bourgeois said that the allied League of Nations associations had already had several meetings, and an agreement was almost complete. In a few days, they would be able to communicate to the allied governments the ideas on which they were in unanimous agreement. All had the same cause at heart, and wished to make it triumph. They desired to see the Society of Nations established on a basis of world-wide friendship, but to insure true, durable, sincere, and reciprocal friendship involved mutual concession and sacrifice. It was essential in the Society of Nations that each should consider the interests of universal peace and right superior to the interests of their own country. In accepting the decisions of the league, each nation would at the same time defend his own liberty and full rights.

It was necessary that the nations should consent to put all their resources, intellectual, moral, economic, financial, and, in case of need, their military force also in the service of the common cause. They were unanimous in a confident belief that the dream of yesterday and the hope of today would become the living reality of tomorrow.

Lord Robert Cecil has granted an interview to Señor Mitre, editor of La Nacion, Buenos Aires, regarding the neutral countries in the League of Nations. Señor Mitre pointed out that the disproportion in the representations between the neutral and belligerent countries was too big to allow the former to discuss the plan of a League of Nations, when once it had been accepted by the great powers. While fully appreciating the high spirit and justice embodied in the idea of a League of Nations, the neutral countries must see in their disproportion the shadow of a danger for their sovereignty. Lord Robert replied that the neutral countries could not, of course, take part in the deliberations directly concerning war problems, but, so far as the League of Nations was concerned, if the neutral countries prepared a practical plan for submission to the conference, the representatives of the great powers would be glad to consider it, although it must be a plan containing concrete issues, not theoretical solutions drawn upon paper.

Señor Mitre called Lord Robert's attention to what has been described as "Universalization of the Monroe doctrine," saying that the league was supposed to protect the territorial integrity of its components, which would appear redundant when applied to the American nations.

Lord Robert said that the Monroe

THE CHRISTIAN SCIENCE MONITOR

AN INTERNATIONAL DAILY NEWSPAPER

THREE CENTS | Copyright 1920 by The Christian Science Publishing Society | BOSTON, U.S.A., THURSDAY, FEBRUARY 12, 1920 | Fourteen Pages | VOL. XII, NO. 69

DEMOCRATS REJECT PROPOSED CHANGE IN ARTICLE TEN

Senator Hitchcock Says Treaty Modification by Republicans Is Not a Compromise but a Demand for Surrender

Special to The Christian Science Monitor from its Washington News Office

WASHINGTON, District of Columbia—First overtures from Republican leaders yesterday for a compromise on the reservation to Article X of the covenant of the League of Nations were summarily rejected by Gilbert M. Hitchcock (D.), Senator from Nebraska and acting minority leader. The battle for ratification of the Treaty has centered down to the probability of an agreement on Article X, "the heart of the covenant," and the compromise offered was framed as an opening wedge to break the deadlock between Mr. Hitchcock and Henry Cabot Lodge (R.), Senator from Massachusetts and majority leader.

Senator Hitchcock declared that the proposed modification which was informally submitted to him was not a compromise but a demand for "surrender." He insisted that, to all intents and purposes, it carried all the odium attached to the Lodge reservation in inner administration circles. The aim of those senators who framed the compromise was to secure a rapprochement on this vital point before the fight was taken to the floor.

Senator Lodge, who is determined that the substance of the pivotal reservation shall not be changed, accepted the new draft tentatively and agreed to use his influence to get it accepted by the rank and file of his "middle-ground" followers within the Republican ranks. Irvine L. Lenroot (R.), Senator from Wisconsin, drafted the proposal submitted to Senator Hitchcock and to which the latter refused to agree.

While preparations were under way for a finish fight on the Article X reservation, Mr. Hitchcock sought the advice of the President as to how far he should go in compromising with the Republican opposition. The policy of the minority leader apparently precludes an agreement on reservations unless the consent of the President has first been secured.

Text of Proposed Reservation

Following is the text of the proposal which the Nebraska senator declared was in effect a demand for surrender:

"The United States assumes no obligation to preserve, by the use of its military or naval forces, or by the economic boycott, or by any other means, the territorial integrity or political independence of any other country, or to interfere in controversies between nations, whether members of the League or not, under the provisions of Article X, or to employ the military or naval forces of the United States under any article of the Treaty for any purpose, unless in any particular case the Congress, which, under the Constitution, has the sole power to declare war, shall, by act or joint resolution, so provide."

"Not a Compromise, but a Surrender"

"The reservation is not a compromise, but a surrender," said Senator Hitchcock. "It is put in a much more obnoxious form than the reservation considered by the bipartisan conference, which the President said was not acceptable to him. It is simply the Lodge reservation under another wording. Its acceptance would eliminate every weapon the United States has to give its moral support to the decisions of the League."

Rumors that President Wilson was in a more yielding mood and had changed his attitude to a considerable extent since his Jackson Day ultimatum were heavily discounted by Senator Hitchcock. He did not believe, he asserted, that the President has reached the point where he is prepared to accept whatever compromise the Democratic senators are able to secure in the coming fight on the floor of the Senate.

President's Policy to Clarify

The minority leader refused to anticipate what would be the result of failure on the part of the Administration senators to accept the best possible terms that they can secure in the coming showdown. His policy now is to work for "interpretative" reservations, which, as he and President Wilson interpret that phrase, would merely clarify and not modify the obligations which the United States undertakes in entering the League of Nations.

Speaking of the modification of the Lodge Article X reservation, Senator Lenroot, its author, said:

"I did not understand from the President's letter that the President surrendered to the extent that he would accept any reservation on Article X. I understand that the President for the first time said that he would accept certain reservations. The reservation was drafted at a meeting of the mild reservationists, and Senator Lodge has agreed to it. It will receive the support of practically all the Republicans except the irreconcilables."

He said that he did not know the extent of the Democratic support the compromise reservation would receive, but that he expected many Democrats would vote for it, judging from their talks with him.

BOSTON MAYOR AND EAMONN DE VALERA

Specially for The Christian Science Monitor

BOSTON, Massachusetts—Andrew J. Peters, Mayor of Boston, yesterday issued the following statement in reply to many inquiries following reports that he would not receive Eamonn de Valera should Mr. de Valera again visit this city:

"I have not been asked to receive Mr. de Valera, nor have I been asked to accord him recognition in any capacity which would conflict with the international amenities and established diplomatic custom that give the Government of the United States exclusive control of international affairs between citizens of the United States and other nationalities. Mr. de Valera did not raise the question of nationality during his visit last year, and I do not contemplate that he will now.

"However deeply the American people may sympathize with the struggle for liberty in other lands, they cannot permit their citizenship and their obligations to the United States to be forgotten.

"If de Valera does come here and calls on me, I shall be glad to renew the acquaintance I made with him last year. . . . I will, as I have done to other Irishmen who have been here recently, give him my cordial personal greeting."

When Mr. de Valera visited Boston last summer, Mayor Peters was away and he was received by the acting Mayor, Francis J. W. Ford.

LEAGUE OF NATIONS MEETS IN LONDON

First Business Session Is Held in St. James Palace—Public Attendance Small — Chairman Deplores America's Absence

Special cable to The Christian Science Monitor from its European News Office

LONDON, England (Wednesday)—The League of Nations held its first business session in St. James Palace today, in the palace picture gallery, a long, spacious apartment hung with portraits of a score or more of the kings of England. The democratic nature of the proceedings was in marked contrast to the autocratic environment, and the event seemed typical of the passing of the old dispensation.

The chamber is admirably suited to such gatherings and provided space for the delegates, who were placed round the baize table, with, directly under Henry VIII's portrait, the press seated at a table running the whole length of the room, and about 150 invited guests. The public attendance was markedly small, little of the accommodation reserved for the public being occupied.

A. J. Balfour, the British representative on the League council, welcomed the delegates, expressing with obvious sincerity regret that there were only eight delegates when there should have been nine and fervently hoping that the difficulties preventing the United States from collaborating would shortly be removed. Leon Bourgeois, the French representative, associated himself with this and Mr. Balfour was then elected to the chair.

The chairman's speech stated that the delegates, while favoring publicity, felt it would handicap the necessary frankness of discussion and had, therefore, decided to split into committees, which would deliberate privately and communicate the results to the public in plenary session. The committees would sit this afternoon and tomorrow, and he anticipated that the next plenary meeting would be on Friday. The proceedings then terminated, having lasted under half an hour.

The council gave the impression of a businesslike intentness, and it is noteworthy that it is moving along parliamentary lines. Today may, therefore, have witnessed the establishment of a real world-parliament, and if the rest of the nations are speedily brought in and certain sections take the League seriously, much may be done through this organization to free the world from the curse of war, the hope of which motived millions of the fighting men. The League has serious flaws, but to many seems the only alternative to a repetition of the tragedy of the recent war on a vastly larger scale.

SIR LYNDEN MACASSEY AT DOCKERS' INQUIRY

Special cable to The Christian Science Monitor from its European News Office

LONDON, England (Wednesday)—The court of inquiry into the dockers' case, under the chairmanship of Lord Shaw, reassembled today when Sir Lynden Macassey continued his speech for the employers, giving reasons in support of the district rate rather than the national wage minimum. He showed how differential rates had arisen and contended that the result of introducing the 16s. a day minimum would be simply to lift up the whole differential system of wages.

Sir Lynden maintained that there was no case for a uniform national minimum, or for attempting to lay down a minimum for each portion on the basis of the cost of living. He submitted that what the court had to do was to examine the rates as they existed today in different districts and see whether they were adequate.

WOMEN EXPECT TO VOTE IN PRIMARIES

Ratification by the Last Six States Needed Is Looked for This Month — Suffrage Association Plans Last Convention

Special to The Christian Science Monitor from its Eastern News Office

NEW YORK, New York—The Federal Woman Suffrage Amendment has a good chance of being ratified before the beginning of the spring primaries in March, in the belief of the National American Woman Suffrage Association. Arizona and New Mexico are expected to ratify the Anthony Amendment this week. Oklahoma's Governor has promised to call a special session within 30 days from February 6. These three would bring the number of ratifying states up to 33, and Washington and two eastern states are expected to complete the necessary 36. Oklahoma and Washington are expected to be the last of the equal suffrage states to ratify the amendment. Suffragists have been hoping that Sunday, February 15, when they celebrate the centenary of their pioneer leader, Susan B. Anthony, might also see the celebration of their final victory.

At the fifty-first annual convention of the association, which opens in Chicago today, and which is expected to be the last suffrage convention held in the United States, distinguished service certificates are to be presented to active workers in the fight for woman suffrage, and a "receiver" appointed for winding up the association affairs preparatory to its going out of business.

The chief business of the convention will be the determination of the part to be taken by women voters in the coming presidential election, the working out of a legislative program, and the election of a national president for the League of Women Voters, Mrs. Carrie Chapman Catt, president of the association, having refused to be a candidate for that office. Mrs. Catt's call to the convention reads:

"Arise, women voters of east and west, and North and South, in this your union together, strong of heart, fearless of spirit; let the nation hear you pledge all that you have and all that you are to a new crusade—a crusade that shall not end until the electorate of the Republic is intelligent, clean, and loyal."

Interview With Mrs. Catt

Special to The Christian Science Monitor from its Western News Office

CHICAGO, Illinois—Ratification of the suffrage amendment within a very short time is assured, declared Mrs. Carrie Chapman Catt, president of the National American Woman Suffrage Association, in commenting on the fact that the convention of the association, which opens here today, has been announced as the last convention of the organization.

Those who do not know what is being done toward ratification of the federal amendment may think there is some doubt about early ratification, but Mrs. Catt declared that the suffrage leaders had confidential information which made them positive that ratification would be completed soon.

The first presidential primary will be held on March 9 in New Hampshire, which has ratified, and an effort is being put forth, said Mrs. Catt, to secure ratification in time to permit the women of New Hampshire to take part in the primaries.

Mrs. Catt declared it probable that the present association would merge into the League of Women Voters. This organization was planned to stimulate political education among women and to secure legislation, which suffragists believe necessary for the betterment of political conditions.

Schools will be conducted to instruct teachers in political matters, the first to be held at the close of the convention. Each state is expected to take up the task and carry on political instruction.

Suffrage Session Expected

Special to The Christian Science Monitor

HARTFORD, Connecticut — "We hope to be able to announce to the National Suffrage Convention that Connecticut will call a special session to consider ratification of the suffrage amendment," said Miss Katharine Ludington, president of the Connecticut association, before she left Hartford on her way to the Victory Convention in Chicago. She pointed out that the men's Republican ratification committee was very active in behalf of a special session. In suffrage quarters, Idaho, New Mexico, Arizona, and Oklahoma are expected to give favorable action this week. Others regarded as possibilities are Washington, Vermont, Tennessee, and Maryland.

Arizona Plans Action

Special to The Christian Science Monitor from its Western News Office

PHOENIX, Arizona—The Arizona Legislature meets in a special session today for the sole purpose of ratifying the federal suffrage amendment.

The measure will be introduced by one of the four women members of the House of Representatives. The Senate has no women members. Women also are to fill all clerical positions, the Governor having offered the services of 20 attachés already on the state pay roll. The sessions will last three days.

BOLSHEVIST PLANS FOR TRANSPORTATION

Special cable to The Christian Science Monitor from its European News Office

LONDON, England (Tuesday)—A Moscow wireless message states that the Supreme Soviet of National Economics has decided to organize a special Chief Department of State Transport with executive powers. Its first task will be the creation of transport and forwarding agencies with frontier posts in Esthonia and Petrograd, and it has begun the registration of all nationalized transport undertakings in Siberia and Turkestan, which will play an important part in the trade exchange with other countries.

MINERAL LEASING MEASURE PASSED

Action of Conference Puts Development Plan Affecting Public Coal, Oil, and Phosphate Lands Up to the President

Special to The Christian Science Monitor from its Washington News Office

WASHINGTON, District of Columbia—After years of dispute, a comprehensive, definite bill has finally been passed by both houses of Congress providing for the mining of coal, phosphate, oil, gas, and sodium on the public domain. The conference report on the measure was agreed to by the House last Friday, and by the Senate yesterday, and it now goes to the President for his signature.

This was pronounced by Frank W. Mondell (R.), majority floor leader, a few days ago, "the greatest triumph of the cause of proper conservation of public resources up to the present time." By the terms of the bill, coal under 50,000,000 acres of land, gas and oil in the remaining 700,000,000 acres, and the phosphate and sodium in the public domain, will be reserved to public ownership.

The rights to develop the minerals will be given to individuals under leases, the proceeds of rentals and royalties being divided between the states in which the minerals are found and the federal government. The government's share is to be applied mainly to the reclamation fund for the benefit of future irrigation projects, a certain proportion being used for roads and schools.

Coal lands are to be divided into 40-acre tracts or multiples of that amount, as the Secretary of the Interior finds most convenient for efficient mining purposes, no tract, however, to exceed 2560 acres. He is to offer these lands from time to time for leasing as seems best in his judgment, and shall dispose of the leases by competitive bidding or such other methods as may be deemed advisable under certain regulations.

Claimants Protected

The Secretary of the Interior is required to recognize the rights of occupants or claimants; prospecting permits may be issued where exploratory work is necessary, for two years for tracts of land not to exceed 2560 acres, and if at the end of that time the permittee shows that the land contains coal in commercially paying quantities, he will be entitled to a lease of a part or all the land.

No lease of coal land shall be approved or issued until after 30 days' notice has been given by advertising in a newspaper of general circulation of the country in which the deposits are situated; no company or corporation operating a railroad shall have a lease except for its own use for railroad purposes with certain guarded exceptions.

The royalties to be paid to the United States are to be not less than 5 cents per ton, and an annual rental to be fixed by the Secretary of the Interior at not less than 25 cents an acre for the first year, not less than 50 cents up to the fifth year, and not less than $1 a year after that.

Prospecting Encouraged

In regard to oil and gas, the Secretary of the Interior is authorized to issue a prospecting permit which will give the exclusive right for not longer than two years to prospect for oil or gas upon not to exceed 2560 acres of land, upon conditions that the permittee begin drilling operations within six months, and shall within a year drill one or more wells for oil or gas to a depth of not less than 500 feet, unless deposits are discovered sooner, and must within two years drill to a depth of 2000 feet. Upon the discovery of oil or gas, the permittee is to be entitled to a lease of one-fourth of the land embraced in his prospecting permit for a period of 20 years.

All unappropriated deposits of oil or gas within the known geologic structure of a producing oil or gas field, and the unentered lands not subject to the preferential lease, may be leased to the highest bidder under certain regulations for 20 years.

No individual or corporation is allowed to hold more than one coal, phosphate or sodium lease, nor more than three oil or gas leases in any one state. If any lands or deposits leased under this act are subleased, possessed or controlled so that they in any wise form an unlawful trust or are the subject of any contract or conspiracy in restraint of trade in the mining or selling of coal, oil, gas, sodium or phosphate, the lease is to be forfeited.

PRESIDENT TO ACT ON WAGE DEMANDS

Director-General of Railroads Refers Controversy With Employees to Mr. Wilson at Request of Union Representatives

Special to The Christian Science Monitor from its Washington News Office

WASHINGTON, District of Columbia—Final decision on the demands of 14 unions of railroad employees for increased wages will be given by President Wilson, to whom the whole controversy between the employees and the United States Railroad Administration was referred last night. The conferences, according to spokesmen of both sides, have been friendly, but Walker D. Hines, Director-General of Railroads, said he was unable, just prior to relinquishment of federal control, to agree to their demands.

How long President Wilson will take to consider the representations of the employees and of Mr. Hines was not conjectured officially last night. In a general way he has been kept informed of the progress of negotiations, and so it is expected that he will make an early decision, possibly by the end of this week. He will then either summon representatives of the unions to the White House to receive his award, or deliver it through Mr. Hines.

Maintenance of Way Demands

In the meantime, the special demand of the Brotherhood of Maintenance of Way Employees for an increase in pay, failing to obtain which they will strike on Tuesday next, will be considered by Mr. Hines today in conference with a committee of 10 representatives of the union who came to Washington from Detroit, Michigan, to notify him of the intention to strike and the terms on which such action could be avoided.

A. Mitchell Palmer, Attorney-General of the United States, conferred with Mr. Hines yesterday on the legal phase of the proposed strike. After this conference, Mr. Palmer would not say whether the government would resort to the use of the injunction, as in the bituminous coal strike, but both the Lever Act and the act creating the United States Railroad Administration were said to be applicable.

"I am hopeful," said Mr. Palmer, "that the difficulty between the Railroad Administration and the maintenance of way employees will be straightened out before the date on which the strike is announced to begin."

Further than this, neither Mr. Palmer nor Mr. Hines would go, but there was manifest in official circles a degree of optimism. Among the leaders of the railroad employees other than of the maintenance of way employees, and, to a lesser degree, the Brotherhood of Railway Trainmen, a disposition to reach an amicable agreement was evident.

Mr. Hines' Statement

The request to place the issues before President Wilson for final adjudication was made by the representatives of the employees. Mr. Hines last night issued the following announcement of the move:

"Since February 3, the Director-General has had frequent conferences with the chief executives of the railroad labor organizations for the purpose of devising means for disposing of the pending claims for wage increases. During these conferences the executives of the labor organizations have expressed their views with great ability and frankness. The Director-General has not been able to agree with them as to how the problem should be disposed of, in view of the early termination of federal control, and is now laying before the President the representations of the executives of the organizations, and also his own report, for the purpose of obtaining the President's decision in the premises.

"In any event, the conferences have been decidedly helpful in bringing out a clearer development as to the real issues involved, and as to the character of evidence pertinent to those issues, and the discussion throughout has been characterized by courtesy as well as candor, and with a sincere purpose on the part of all to try to find a solution."

There has been marked reticence on both sides with regard to the specific demands of the employees and the counter propositions of Mr. Hines. When the wage increases were first asked last July Mr. Hines estimated that they would add a total of $800,000,000 a year to the pay roll of the railroads for 2,000,000 employees.

CONFIDENCE VOTED IN H. H. ASQUITH

Action Taken Following Address to Night-Shift Workers' Meeting by the Liberal Candidate in the Paisley By-Election

Special cable to The Christian Science Monitor from its European News Office

GLASGOW, Scotland (Tuesday) — Following Lord Robert Cecil, Lord Lambourne, better known as Colonel Lockwood, a former Unionist M. P., has written to H. H. Asquith, the former British Premier and Liberal candidate in the borough of Paisley by-election, wishing him all success, and "indorsing every word" of Lord Robert's. Mr. Asquith also received, last week, a cordial letter of support from Mr. Gladstone's three sons. The common opinion in Paisley is, however, that these letters and external expressions of opinion will not turn half a dozen votes.

Early yesterday Mr. Asquith addressed a nightshift workers' meeting and, at the close, a vote of confidence was carried by a narrow majority, although the audience had listened courteously and appreciatively. Apart from this one, however, the meetings have been notoriously unsatisfactory from the standpoint of political feeling. To judge by the meetings, indeed, Mr. Asquith's victory would be certain. At the same time, there is apparent in Paisley a widespread conviction that Mr. Asquith will not be returned.

Mr. Asquith's agents were not only pleased but amazed at the result of a canvass taken recently, and speak of a 1500 majority. As against this, Labor expressed itself as being equally satisfied with the canvass and hopes for a 2000 majority. The Coalition candidate, it is commonly thought, will be at the bottom of the poll, but several good judges declare he has gained much ground lately, thereby endangering Mr. Asquith's prospects.

To the night-shift workers yesterday, Mr. Asquith developed his thesis of no essential antagonism between Liberalism and Labor as distinct from the Labor Party. He enumerated the Liberal achievements for Labor and deprecated "Alpine climbing" in politics as a waste of energy. The former Premier is very little heckled now, although occasionally taken to task for his daughter's aggressive criticisms of trade unions' autocracy.

J. M. Biggar, the Labor candidate, yesterday had a women electors' meeting and at night had Philip Snowden assisting him.

MR. HOOVER'S NAME ON GEORGIA BALLOT

Special to The Christian Science Monitor from its Southern News Office

ATLANTA, Georgia — Herbert C. Hoover's name will appear on the Democratic ticket for the presidential nomination at the preferential primary to be held in Georgia on April 20. The required number of signatures requesting that Mr. Hoover's name shall appear was forwarded to the Democratic State Executive Committee chairman yesterday by voters of Hall County.

TRIAL OF JOSEPH CAILLAUX

PARIS, France (Tuesday)—The trial of the former Premier, Joseph Caillaux, for conspiring to bring about a premature and dishonorable peace with Germany will open before the Senate, sitting as a high court, on February 17.

THE CHRISTIAN SCIENCE MONITOR

AN INTERNATIONAL DAILY NEWSPAPER

Published daily, except Sundays, by The Christian Science Publishing Society, 107 Falmouth Street, Boston, Mass. Subscription price, payable in advance, postpaid to all countries: One year, $9.00; six months, $4.50; three months, $2.25; one month, 75 cents.

Entered at second-class rates at the Post Office at Boston, Mass., U. S. A. Acceptance for mailing at a special rate of postage provided for in section 1103, Act of October 3, 1917, authorized on July 11, 1918.

INDEX FOR FEBRUARY 12, 1920

BRITISH PREMIER STATES POSITION ON RUSSIAN ISSUE

Mr. Lloyd George, in Speech Before House of Commons, Says Russia Must Be Put "Into Circulation" to Restore Europe

Special cable to The Christian Science Monitor from its European News Office

WESTMINSTER, England (Wednesday)—The essential part of the Prime Minister's vigorous speech in the House of Commons yesterday was its Russian section. As to the by-elections, Mr. Lloyd George attributes the government's troubles to the after-war reaction.

He indicated that the government, which had been hitherto preoccupied with peace problems, would soon come into the open and fight. The Coalition was crowding its bills into the first two years, so as to have time to administer, construct and develop, and when the time came it would have achieved, not bills, but something which the bills had achieved.

On the question of Russia, he insisted that they must begin by recognizing the facts. They could not restore Europe without putting Russia "into circulation." He declared he had never believed they could crush Bolshevism by force and they could not pay others to do it. His remedy was to save Russia by trade, although he would not make peace with the Bolshevist Government.

Military Power Exaggerated

As to the danger that Bolshevist Russia might attack Poland or make trouble in central Europe, he reasoned that the military power of Bolshevism was exaggerated. It could not make war outside its own territory, he declared, but more especially had no motive to do so, seeing that the outside territories were worse off than Russia.

He concluded by warning the House of the dangers of high prices. "These dangers are not in Russia, they are here at home," he said. "I speak with knowledge, apprehension, and responsibility, and I warn the House, in fact, of a thing that may happen. We must take every legitimate weapon to contend against these things and we must fight anarchy with abundance."

LONDON, England (Wednesday) — William Bruce, president of the South Wales Miners Federation, speaking in the House of Commons in behalf of Labor today, moved an amendment to the reply to the speech from the throne delivered yesterday by King George, expressing regret for "the absence of any proposal to nationalize the coal mines of the country along lines recommended by the majority of the members of the Royal Commission on the Coal Industry, which was appointed to advise the government as to the best methods of reorganizing the industry."

Mr. Bruce, who was the first speaker when the debate on the speech from the throne was resumed today, contended that the miners had been led to suppose that the government would accept the recommendations of the majority of the Coal Commission. He declared that nationalization would not mean bureaucratic control. The government might delay nationalization, but, he predicted, it could not prevent nationalization coming.

Drink Question Discussed

The drink question was alluded to by Sir Donald Maclean. "The fact that America has gone dry is an economic fact of the gravest importance to Great Britain," he said. He declared the British expenditure for drink absolutely staggered him. The country spent more than £164,000,000 for drink in 1914, he said, and this expenditure increased steadily until it was £259,000,000 in 1918, while it was estimated that the expenditure for the year ending March 31 next would be nearly £400,000,000. He was unaware what the duty on the consumption for the last named period would produce for the public revenue, but the duty of 1918 was £48,500,000. It was a form of revenue that all chancellors of the exchequer would be pleased to be able to dispense with, he said. He hoped the measures proposed by the government would prove to be a serious attempt to grapple with the evil.

Reply to Address From Throne

The reply to the address from the throne was made yesterday by Col. Sydney Peel, coalition Unionist, who said in part:

"It will be a grievous disappointment to us if the United States finds itself unable to take part in the work of reconstruction. But she must be master in her own house, as we are in ours."

Sir Donald Maclean, urging revision of the Peace Treaty, said: "One of the essentials of the guarantee to us, is the fact when Opposition agreed to it, that the signature of the President of the United States was appended. It does not now look as though this is going to be honored. I only hope I am wrong," he added, as Mr. Lloyd George indicated his dissent.

Replying to Sir Donald Maclean's inquiry, the Premier also said he was glad to be able to say that the coming budget would balance, and more than balance.

Dealing at length with the situation in Russia, Mr. Lloyd George said he agreed with the view that Europe

THE CHRISTIAN SCIENCE MONITOR

AN INTERNATIONAL DAILY NEWSPAPER

THREE CENTS
FIVE CENTS AT NEWS STANDS

Copyright 1920 by The Christian Science Publishing Society

BOSTON, U.S.A., FRIDAY, AUGUST 27, 1920

Sixteen Pages

VOL. XII, NO. 238

BOLSHEVIKI AGREE TO ALLIED DEMAND ON POLISH TERMS

Foreign Minister Declares Willingness to Accede to Request to Exclude Proletariat Army From the Peace Conditions

Special cable to The Christian Science Monitor from its European News Office

LONDON, England (Thursday) — The Russian Soviet Government, replying to Arthur J. Balfour's note, sent to Leo Kameneff, the Bolshevist representative in London, on Tuesday, states that, subordinating everything else to its paramount desire to secure the establishment of peace throughout the world, it agrees to withdraw its conditions that the Poles should provide arms for a workmen's militia of 200,000 men. This decision, it is claimed, meets the wishes of the British and Italian governments.

LONDON, England (Thursday)—The following is a portion of the long note of George Tchitcherin, the Russian Soviet Foreign Minister, to Arthur J. Balfour, in which, alluding to the proposed Polish civic militia, he says:

"Although our interpretation of this point in our peace terms is thoroughly justified, we nevertheless are willing to remove this, the only point of divergency, in order to establish a full understanding between us and the above governments.

"As to the terms of peace with Poland, we first of all declare we never considered our terms as an ultimatum, and are still, as we have been all the time, willing to discuss them with the Polish Government, with whom alone we are treating for peace. Any undertakings we may give thereanent will, therefore, be given to Poland alone.

"In view, nevertheless, of our earnest desire to obtain important results for the world's welfare and a peace arising from peace with Great Britain, we are willing to inform the British Government that the Russian Government is resolved to make a concession on this point. It will not insist upon the clause referring to the arming in Poland of a workers' civic militia, thus securing full agreement with Great Britain as to all the terms of peace with Poland."

Poland Cautioned

French Government Advises Poles to Avoid Further Risks

Special cable to The Christian Science Monitor from its correspondent in Paris

PARIS, France (Thursday) — Some significance lies in the renewed representations of France to Poland that moderation must be shown. Alexander Millerand, the Premier, has shown too often his desire to see the Bolsheviki crushed for any doubt to be entertained that, if it were thought possible to pursue the present victory without risk of fresh disaster, it would be pursued. French representatives have, however, insisted once more on the necessity for stopping at the frontiers of Poland.

If France was opposed to peace on the Bolshevist conditions, she is desirous that the Poles at Minsk, or elsewhere, should present counter-propositions which will be accepted. This does not indicate a changed view on the part of the French Government on the general question of Bolshevism. General Wrangel is being aided, and his forces are growing, while Hungary is filled to the bursting point with munitions, largely supplied with consent of the western countries.

But Poland is too important a factor in Europe to be put in peril. France joins heartily in the exhortations of England to take advantage of the actual situation, which, it is always possible, may be reversed.

The remarkable demonstration of the Poles on the departure of General Weygand confirms the impression that the French general saved Poland. It is claimed that the victory is due entirely to French intervention. General Weygand is both a French and Polish hero.

British Policy

Premier's Firm Attitude Toward Soviets Shows Unexpected Trend

Special cable to The Christian Science Monitor from its correspondent in Paris

PARIS, France (Wednesday)—The ultimatum sent by Arthur J. Balfour, on behalf of the British Prime Minister, to Leo Kameneff, the Bolshevist representative in England, appears to contradict the belief of those in France who considered that Mr. Lloyd George and John Giolitti, the Italian Premier, were in reality pursuing the same policy of an understanding with Russia, while offering a sop to French opinion by further menaces in form. It is now generally claimed that the three allies are in accord on the Millerand policy, which is to break with the Bolsheviki. Should this interpretation prove true it will be in contradiction with certain definite expressions which have been given out from the Lloyd George entourage. It can perhaps be explained by the resentment of the British Premier at the idea that he has been deceived regarding the proposed Russian terms. The Bolsheviki claim that there has been no breach of faith; that the condition of a proletariat army was included in the original terms.

The general impression here is that the double defeat, diplomatic and military, will seriously shatter the Moscow Government, and that, unless there is an unexpected change in the situation, the Bolsheviki must finally succumb, after being so near victory. All reports speak of the crushing defeat in Poland, and, in some of them, put the figure of prisoners as high as 100,000.

Not only the Poles, but the forces of General Wrangel, are making progress. General Wrangel has called on the Cossacks of Kuban to revolt, and if he is able to launch an offensive, the occasion is exceedingly favorable. General Weygand is returning to Paris, which indicates that he considers his work accomplished. Mr. Millerand, in sending a telegram to Sir Reginald Tower, the High Commissioner at Danzig, tactfully made it clear that the French Government appreciated his difficulties. The message reminds the High Commissioner of Article 104 of the Treaty, and calls on him to guarantee to Poland free transport of goods and munitions. Should Danzig dockers refuse to work, other labor must be immediately found. Allied ships will protect the unloading and allied troops will be sent to Danzig, if necessary. The approval of the United States of America and Japan is sought.

The Premiers' Meeting

Special cable to The Christian Science Monitor from its correspondent in Paris

PARIS, France (Wednesday)—Although nothing is definitely settled regarding the proposed meeting of Alexander Millerand, the Premier, and John Giolitti, Premier of Italy, at Aix-les-Bains, the representative of The Christian Science Monitor is informed that it will take place about September 10. Officially Mr. Lloyd George has not signified his desire to take part; but if arrangements permit, there is little doubt that he will do so. The situation in England, where a coal strike is threatened, may, it is declared, compel the return of the British Premier.

Bolshevist Methods Rejected

Special cable to The Christian Science Monitor from its correspondent in Paris

PARIS, France (Wednesday)—The Confédération Générale du Travail, now holding its national counsel, has pronounced against union with the Third International. Leon Jouhaux was loudly acclaimed when he said they could accept no instructions from anyone, and invited Nicholas Lenine to attend to his own affairs. He added that they had every sympathy with Russia, but intended to pursue their own path. The extremists were routed. The federation is turning definitely from the revolutionary counsels, which have recently been heard.

Possible Counter-Offensive

Special cable to The Christian Science Monitor from its European News Office

LONDON, England (Thursday)—The Russian northern army has made several desperate attempts to break through near Mlava, but these were all repulsed by the Poles excepting that a portion of the Red army succeeded in escaping eastwards. The Bolsheviki are retreating on the whole front in Eastern Galicia to avoid a flank attack, which is threatening them from the north.

The French General Lanezan is taking command of the Polish Southern front.

A Berlin message states that 24,000 Russians have now crossed the German frontier.

The Russians are preparing for a new great counter-offensive behind the River Niemen, and a message states that enormous masses of troops have been observed.

Moscow wireless transmits appeals to the Russian people, recalling General Denikin's and General Judenitch's defeats, and, although the Poles are beating them, their answer will be a blow by overwhelming mass attack, such that no trace shall remain of the enemy. "If they fling us back from Warsaw beyond Brest-Litovsk, we are not only able to return, but we shall advance further until we finally crush the enemy."

NATIONAL MEDICAL SERVICE PROPOSED

Special to The Christian Science Monitor from its Australasian News office

WELLINGTON, New Zealand — A report has been submitted to the New Zealand Minister for Public Health by the New Zealand branch of the British Medical Association favoring the establishment of a national medical service.

Included in the Medical Association proposal is the formation of district health areas, the extension of the Department of Public Health, and a national service for remote and sparsely populated areas and mining districts. It is interesting to note that the association's scheme proposes that the members of the Board of Health should be elected by the medical profession which will thus have complete control. A national service is also favored for the poor in the cities and larger towns, a system of part-time medical officers being recommended.

The report proposes that there should be no honorary staffs of hospitals, the work carried out being adequately paid for on a part-time basis. As a corollary the report advocates a considerable increase in the state control of hospitals.

It is proposed by the association that the control of the national medical service should be in the hands of a board, the majority of members being elected by the medical profession and the Department of Public Health having representation.

The fate of the recommendations is not yet known.

DEALERS ADVANCE THE PRICE OF COAL

Increase Is Declared to Exceed Rates Which Would Be in Proper Proportion to the Higher Cost of Transportation

Special to The Christian Science Monitor from its Washington News Office

WASHINGTON, District of Columbia—Advances in the prices of anthracite coal for household use have been the first result, so far as indications have appeared here, of the increased freight rates which have just gone into effect.

Since anthracite and bituminous coal comprise about one-third of the freight hauled on the railroads of the United States, coal prices would naturally show the effect of the new rates as quickly as anything, and, owing to the bulk of coal in comparison to its value, the increased rates would naturally be more noticeable than in other commodities.

So far as information has been received here, the forecasts made by opponents of the freight rate advances that dealers would make their own profit on the increases in transportation costs, appear to be borne out.

Advance in Retail Rates

In Boston, Massachusetts, for example, a city at a considerable distance from the producing fields, anthracite prices are now given as $16 a ton, as against $14.50 for June, 1920. These rates are for a ton of 2000 pounds. Freight rates from the principal anthracite regions to Boston, per ton of 2240 pounds were, before the advance, $3.20 a ton, for the grade of coal carrying the highest rate.

A 40 per cent advance on $3.20 would be $1.28 and the retailer in Boston would be justified in adding $1.20 to the June cost, making allowance for the sale of the short ton instead of a long ton. Unless other factors enter into the situation, however, it would appear that an increase of $1.50 a ton in coal rates in Boston is adding 30 cents to the cost of the freight increases and passing it on to the consumer. On steam coal the advance in freight rates would be about $1.10 a ton, and the profit 40 cents.

It cannot be contended that there has been any advance in labor costs since June, for the Anthracite Coal Commission's reports now lie before the President, awaiting his signature, and have not been made public. In all probability an advance in wages will be permitted, and that will be the basis for a further advance in the cost to the consumer.

Previous Increases

Shippers and others who protested against the recent freight advances contended that by the time the amount awarded to the railroads had reached the consumer it would be increased from two to five times. In reply to these contentions figures were introduced to show that no large increases were necessary, and the figures were not questioned.

The probable necessity of a rise in the cost of commodities to cover freight rates was not considered by representatives of the shippers, railroad employees and the public, an index of the probable course of prices. Nevertheless, figures made public by the anthracite coal miners when they presented their case for increased pay indicated that there had already been increases in the price of anthracite coal to the consumer, ranging from $1.50 to $2.63 for the period from January, 1919, to June, 1920, according to the distance from the mines. It was also shown that, although labor cost of coal from 1914 to December, 1918, was $1.41, the advance in retail prices of coal at Scranton, Pennsylvania, in the anthracite district, averaged $3.33, and in Boston $4.48.

Officials Expect a Reduction

Department of Justice officials say they expect a drop in coal prices. It is known that business advisers in many instances have cautioned their clients against taking advantage of the freight increases to raise prices; the reaction against exorbitant clothing and shoe costs was cited to show that the public would not stand further profiteering. Production of coal is increasing, according to government reports, and the government officials base their forecast of reduced prices in part on this. However, cold weather is not far ahead and that, in all probability, will mean increased demand and lowered production. If the break in prices comes for the reason that production is advancing, it may be only temporary.

Agents of the department are said to be active at Baltimore, Maryland, and at Hampton Roads, Virginia, where they are seeking evidence of profiteering. "Flagrant violations" of the Lever Act are said to be mainly confined to the Atlantic coast. Where investigations are under way, coal prices were said to be showing a downward tendency before the rate increase effects were given a chance to come into play. Those, however, may check the downward trend.

Existence of Emergency Declared

In an effort to stimulate production of coal, the Interstate Commerce Commission yesterday issued a service order declaring the existence of an emergency, due to the shortage of equipment and congestion of traffic, which justifies discrimination against "wagon mines" where quick-loading facilities are not available for placing coal in open top cars. From August 26, 1920, until April 1, 1921, therefore, the coal-carrying roads are directed to observe the following regulation: "Upon any day when a common carrier by railroad is unable to supply any mine upon its line with the required open top cars, open top cars shall not be furnished or supplied by it to wagon mines which are not in a position to load such cars upon private tracks and from a tipple or other arrangement which permits the coal to be dumped from an elevation into the car, until all other mines have been fully supplied with open top cars. Open top cars supplied and furnished wagon mines on private track and so equipped with a tipple or other arrangement for dumping coal from an elevation into a car must be counted against such wagon mines under uniform mine ratings and car distribution rules, the same as are applied to established tipple mines."

Coal Price Increased

Boston Dealers Blame Railroad Rates for Added Cost

BOSTON, Massachusetts—The Metropolitan Coal Company announced yesterday an increase of $1.50 per ton for anthracite coal, making the price for egg, stove, nut and broken coal $16 per ton, and for pea coal $14.25. Householders are especially affected. The new freight rates are given as an excuse for the raise. Reference is also made to the increase in the prices at the mines since May 1.

Local dealers say that anthracite coal at the mines has increased about 40 cents per ton since May 1, and that with an additional increase of 40 per cent in freight rates the jump of $1.50 per ton will hardly cover the cost increase. They claim that stove coal is being sold at from $8 to $14 per ton at the mines, while some of the premium coal sells at a minimum of from $8.75 to $9.25.

Boston dealers had already increased the price of coal to its former price of $14.50 per ton on the basis of a 27 per cent increase in miners' wages as sought in a minority report of the Anthracite Coal Commission, appointed by President Wilson to adjust wages in the anthracite coal industry. The majority report, however, grants the miners less than 27 per cent increase demanded.

TROOPS DISPERSE BELFAST CROWDS

Serious Rioting Breaks Out as Rival Factions Clash—Further Outrages Committed Against Soldiers and the Police

Special cable to The Christian Science Monitor from its European News Office

BELFAST, Ireland (Thursday)—Rioting broke out on Wednesday evening in the Newtownards district of Belfast, when Sinn Feiners and loyalists came into collision. The outlook was becoming serious, when an armored car arrived, and, upon its opening the machine-gun ports, the crowds quickly dispersed. Several trams were damaged and, after darkness had set in, there was further looting and setting on fire of public houses and groceries in various parts of Ballymacarett, where one person was killed and 20 injured during the rioting.

The crowds were dispersed by the police and military, who on one occasion had to fire over the heads of the mob to disperse it. A number of persons were also injured in baton charges by the police.

The fire brigade was called out 26 times in seven hours, the total number of incendiary fires in Belfast being 40. The police have arrested 30 persons. Troops are still on duty in the streets today.

Special cable to The Christian Science Monitor from its European News Office

DUBLIN, Ireland (Thursday) — The assassination of police and soldiers still continues without abatement. Constable McNamara was fatally shot by four armed and masked men at Glengariff on Tuesday night, and Constable Patrick Cleary was seriously wounded. Constable Hough was fatally shot in Bantry on Wednesday afternoon, three constables who were with him making good their escape. The attacking party was hidden in a grove in the chapel grounds.

A party of Cameron Highlanders, who were engaged in removing a wooden hut near Queenstown were attacked on Wednesday afternoon by a large number of armed civilians. Three of the soldiers on guard were wounded, one of them fatally. After shooting them, the raiders beat the soldiers with batons and took possession of their arms. The police were quickly on the spot, but the raiders made good their escape.

BELA KUN IN RUSSIA

Special cable to The Christian Science Monitor from its European News Office

COPENHAGEN, Denmark (Thursday)—The special correspondent of the "Berlingske Tidende" at Helingsfors, states that Bela Kun has arrived in Petrograd, where he was received with great honors. In an interview, he declared that the Bolsheviki need have no fear regarding Hungary, as it was impossible to send troops from there to Poland.

WHY MINERS MAY STRIKE IN BRITAIN

Labor Leader Ascribes Threatened Deadlock to Capitalistic Viewpoint of Parliament and Miners' Bad Living Conditions

Special cable to The Christian Science Monitor from its European News Office

LONDON, England (Thursday)—The case for the miners, giving their reasons for the threatened coal strike, has received little or no attention in the newspapers here, the onus of responsibility generally being put on the shoulders of their leaders. In an interview with a well-known Labor leader on Wednesday night, the representative of The Christian Science Monitor was informed that during the hearings before the coal commission last year the newspapers were uniformly fair in the presentation of the miners' viewpoint, and most of them went so far as to say that the miners had made out a good case.

Since that time, however, the ownership of many newspapers has changed hands, and at the last general election many members were elected to the House of Commons whose main interest is in upholding the position of the capitalists. The influence of these members is evident in the recent determination of the government to take a firm stand against a further rise in workmen's wages, independent of whether the cost of living goes up or not.

There has been a steady stream of propaganda against further increase of wages, more particularly in relation to coal miners, and an attempt has been made to throw full responsibility for the reduced output of the mines on the miners. This, the representative of The Christian Science Monitor was informed, cannot be considered fair. For one thing, during the war, operations in the sinking of some 40 new shafts were suspended, which, by this time, would have been each giving an output of some 1000 tons per day, or nearly 15,000,000 tons per year, to take the place of seams which have run out in the interim.

Bad Equipment Discussed

The coal owners have themselves stated that the uncertainty as to whether the mines are to be decontrolled, or to become nationalized, has caused them to hold up the investment of about £50,000,000 of capital obtained from earnings which, in the ordinary course, would have been turned to the extension of operations, additional plant, improvement, in mechanical haulage and other investments, all of which would have tended to increase the output.

In many mines, at the present time, there is a shortage of equipment. Mechanical haulage has not been extended, so that miners in some cases have to push tubs half a mile from the haulage gear to the operating face and back again by manual labor.

As compared with the mines in America, the miners there load about eight tons per day, as against one ton per day in England. This, the representative of The Christian Science Monitor was informed, casts no reflection on the skill or activity of the British miners, for, whereas in English mines the total seams vary from 15 inches to 30 inches in depth, and to reach an operating face entails a walk of some three miles for the workmen after they reach the pit bottom, in America the seams go straight in from the hillside, following veins six to 20 feet deep, with the consequent ease in getting and loading, combined with larger cars, shorter hauls and easier access.

Coal Owners' Profits

The government's move in increasing the price of domestic coal by 14s. 2d., while bringing the sale price of coal up to the cost of production, increases the mine owners' profits to such an extent, under the government allowance, that they now receive £30,000,000 annual profit as against £14,000,000 before the war, and the excess profits on high-priced export coal, falling to the British Exchequer amount to some £66,000,000. This, the miners' leaders consider, is a distinct tax on coal users toward the relief of taxation of those well able to bear it, and the increased price is advanced as a reason why miners cannot receive increased wages.

It is obvious that the government increased the domestic price of coal with decontrol in view, so that mines could be handed back to the owners on a profitable basis. The miners, on the other hand, consider that, if the mines are nationalized on the lines of the Sankey report, and the workmen are given a share in the management, much needed capital investment will be made in improving the mechanical haulage and equipment, resulting in a greatly increased output, as the miners will not then be working under the present disadvantageous conditions.

As to the increased wage of 2s. per day, demanded, this sum is necessary to keep step with the increased cost of living since the last rise was granted. Much propaganda has appeared, stating that the miners are earning fabulous amounts, but the informant assured the representative of The Christian Science Monitor that the general average did not exceed 18s. per day. If the miners were now paid on the sliding scale, obtaining before the war, much higher wages would prevail. Under this system, the wages rose and fell with the price of coal, but the present high world price of coal is so exceptional, that it is given as a reason for not reverting to the sliding scale.

In the steel trades, the sliding scale is still in force and the present high price of steel has resulted in steel workers receiving very much higher rates than the miners at the present time. Miners therefore feel that they are not getting a square deal.

Bad Housing Conditions

The representative of The Christian Science Monitor was informed that the deplorable conditions of the housing of the miners revealed before the coal commission has not been improved in the slightest since the report was made, as there are now more workmen, and practically no additional houses have been erected on account of the war. Despite a bill being passed through Parliament providing for bathing and drying room facilities at the pithead, a restrictive clause was inserted enabling the mine owner to escape providing the facilities if he could prove that their maintenance involved expenditure greater than quite a normal number of pence per week per man.

This was not difficult to prove, and consequently few mines have installed these necessaries, which are so common in Germany and America. The consequence is that miners with two sons, on reaching home, have to spread their pit clothes, reeking with perspiration and moisture, before the fire in a small one-tenement house, to be dried for the next day, resulting in deplorable conditions, seeing that, in some 25 per cent of the homes, more than one family is living in one tenement.

Mine owners who have adopted wash-houses and drying rooms at the pithead have been rewarded one hundred fold by the increased loyalty of the workmen and the additional output. These conditions, the miners and their leaders feel, must be remedied, and their only way of calling attention, they consider, is by the strike method. While there is a prospect of a last hour compromise, the miners' leaders feel that there is every likelihood that there will be an overwhelming majority in favor of a strike, and if the government maintains its present obdurate attitude, the strike is inevitable.

THE CHRISTIAN SCIENCE MONITOR

AN INTERNATIONAL DAILY NEWSPAPER

Published daily, except Sundays, by The Christian Science Publishing Society, 107 Falmouth Street, Boston, Mass. Subscription price, payable in advance, postpaid to all countries: One year, $9.00; six months, $4.50; three months, $2.25; one month, 75 cents.

Entered at second-class rates at the Post Office at Boston, Mass., U. S. A. Acceptance for mailing at a special rate of postage provided for in section 1103, Act of October 3, 1917, authorized on July 11, 1918.

INDEX FOR AUGUST 27, 1920

RATIFICATION OF EQUAL SUFFRAGE LAW PROCLAIMED

Notice of Certification of Vote by Tennessee Legislature Is Received and Formally Announced by Secretary Colby

Special to The Christian Science Monitor from its Washington News Office

WASHINGTON, District of Columbia—Ratification of the Susan B. Anthony Federal Suffrage Amendment to the Constitution of the United States was proclaimed by Bainbridge Colby, Secretary of State, early yesterday morning.

Mr. Colby, in describing the conditions under which this significant document was signed, touched lightly upon his evasion of the motion picture melodrama which had been planned, and seriously declared his deep interest in the extension of suffrage and his profound and modest pride that it had fallen to his good fortune to enact a rôle in the great drama.

The package, for the coming of which both representatives of the State Department and of the suffrage organizations kept anxious vigil, arrived in Washington a little before four o'clock in the morning and Charles L. Cook of the State Department at once notified Mr. Colby. The Secretary explained that he did not sign the proclamation at that time both because he regarded the hour as unseemly for so important an event, and because there was a point of law on which he wanted the opinion of his legal advisors before doing so. At eight o'clock, however, he signed it at his own home.

Messages Received

Mr. Colby said that he had received a great many messages urging him to sign at the moment that he received the certification, there being an apprehension that the anti-suffragists would effect some judicial action that would interfere with the issuing of the proclamation.

"While it was not becoming that I should exhibit undue eagerness to sign," explained Mr. Colby, "I saw no reason why I should conspicuously loiter in the matter."

Eight o'clock seemed to him the earliest hour at which the matter could be taken up with seemliness. A number of women belonging to the National Woman's Party had planned to be present when the document was signed and to have the scene photographed for moving pictures. The action of the Secretary in signing at his home prevented this. He was asked to have the scene reproduced so that it might still be photographed, but he replied that after the act had been done it was difficult to know of what the ceremony should consist; and that he had been more concerned with prompt ratification of the amendment that with feeding the cameras.

Process Completed

Mr. Colby said he believed the process was complete when the action was done; women deserved the greatest credit for it. His preference for simplicity in solemn moments was not due to an aversion to stage setting, but it was impossible to sign at the earliest moment and at the same time arrange for the "movie" scene. This great act of enfranchising women was too great to be made a plaything. He had had a very definite duty to perform and had thought that nothing would lose through simplicity. The temper and spirit of the amendment have launched women upon a new sea of action, he declared.

The journals of both branches of the Tennessee Legislature accompanied the certification of the Governor.

Mr. Colby said it was not for him to go behind the Governor's certification. If there were difficulties to be met they were not within his province. His act was only a ministerial one.

Secretary Colby's Statement

Secretary Colby's statement follows:

"The certified record of the action of the Legislature of the State of Tennessee on the suffrage amendment was received by mail this morning. On its receipt the record was brought to my house. This was in compliance with my directions and in accordance with numerous requests for prompt action. I therefore signed the certificate required of the Secretary of State this morning at 8 o'clock in the presence of Mr. F. K. Neilson, the solicitor of the State Department, and Mr. Charles Cook, also of the State Department. The seal of the United States has been duly affixed to the certificate and the suffrage amendment is now the Nineteenth Amendment of the Constitution.

"It was decided not to accompany the simple ministerial action on my part with any ceremony or setting. This secondary aspect of the subject has, regretfully been the source of considerable contention as to who shall participate in it and who shall not. Inasmuch as I am not interested in the aftermath of any of the frictions or collisions which may have been developed in the long struggle for the ratification of the amendment, I contented myself with the performance in the simplest manner of the duties devolved upon me under the law.

"I congratulate the women of the country upon the successful culmination of their efforts which have been sustained in the face of many dis-

THE CHRISTIAN SCIENCE MONITOR

AN INTERNATIONAL DAILY NEWSPAPER

THREE CENTS
FIVE CENTS AT NEWS STANDS | BOSTON, U.S.A., WEDNESDAY, NOVEMBER 3, 1920 | Sixteen Pages | VOL. XII, NO. 296

Copyright 1920 by The Christian Science Publishing Society

OVERWHELMING HARDING VICTORY SEEMS CERTAIN

Early Returns Leave Little Doubt That Republicans Will Retain Their Control of Both Houses of the Congress of the United States

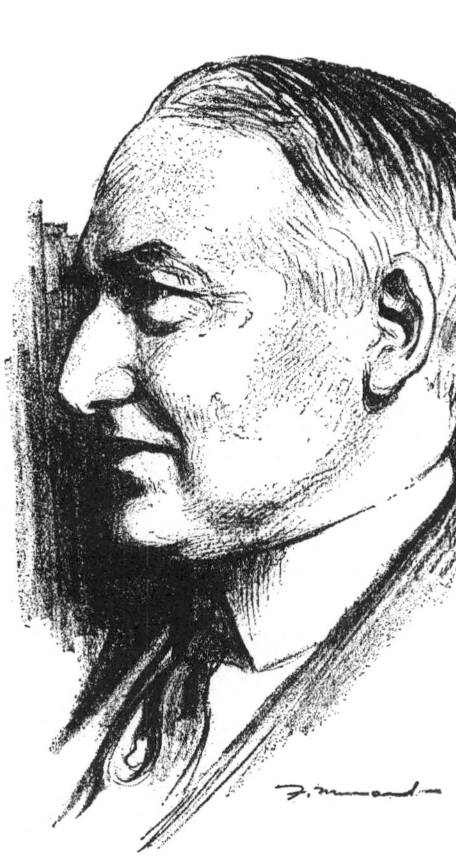

Drawn for The Christian Science Monitor

Warren G. Harding

United States Senator from Ohio, successful candidate for President. Early returns from the election of yesterday indicate this result

Special to The Christian Science Monitor from its Eastern News Office

NEW YORK, New York—Senator Warren G. Harding (R.), of Ohio, was elected President of the United States yesterday over Gov. James M. Cox (D.), of Ohio.

At 11 o'clock last night George White, chairman of the Democratic National Committee, conceded the election to Senator Harding and Gov. Calvin Coolidge of Massachusetts, Republican candidate for Vice-President, and a Republican Congress.

At midnight the Republicans had gained one seat in the United States Senate, with results in several contested states still unsettled. The Republican claims of a Harding landslide were supported by early returns from western states. The first returns from Nebraska showed Mr. Harding leading, 2 to 1; in Wyoming 3 to 1, and in Montana almost 2 to 1.

The first state outside the Democratic "Solid South" that gave Mr. Cox an early lead was Kentucky, where, with more than one-third of the precincts reported, Mr. Cox was leading by 16,000. Scattered returns throughout Delaware indicated a decisive Harding victory.

The Republicans claimed the election of Nathan L. Miller over Gov. Alfred E. Smith of New York by 100,000, but Tammany Hall held that New York City would reelect Governor Smith by overcoming Judge Miller's up-state majority. Judge Miller's majority was conceded to be 305,000 on returns from 1444 precincts out of 2575 in the State, but Governor Smith, it was claimed, then showed an indicated lead of 336,000 in the city.

Outside the city, 2240 districts gave Senator Harding 599,085 and Governor Cox 265,111; and 440 of the city's 2753 precincts gave Mr. Harding a lead of 62,597.

Senator James W. Wadsworth Jr., won his race for the United States Senate over Harry C. Walker (D.), Mrs. Ella A. Boole (Pro.), and Miss Rose Schneidermann (Farmer-Labor).

Although definite figures were not available, the Socialist and Farmer-Labor vote, apparently, was not so large as was expected.

Figures showing whether the new Legislature will be disposed to repeal the 2.75 beer law will not come in until later, but New Jersey elected at least five of her eight dry Republican legislative candidates.

With 266 electoral votes needed to insure his success, Senator Harding at midnight had won 199 without doubt, and for him 132 others were claimed. The certain Democratic electoral vote at midnight was 116, representing the "Solid South."

The Republicans claimed that Colorado, New Hampshire, Kansas, California, Arizona, Washington, Idaho and Oklahoma, which President Wilson carried in 1916, had swung to Mr. Harding. George White, Democratic national chairman, called the Oklahoma claim absurd, insisting that the state had gone for Mr. Cox and that eight of its 11 congressional districts were Democratic.

The states were lined up as follows:

Certain for Mr. Harding: Pennsylvania, New York, Massachusetts, Vermont, Ohio, Illinois, Maine, Kansas, Connecticut, New Jersey and Delaware.

Claimed for Mr. Harding: Indiana, Colorado, New Hampshire, Iowa, Michigan, Minnesota, California, Wisconsin, Oklahoma, Kentucky, Arizona, Oregon, Washington and Idaho.

Certain for Mr. Cox: West Virginia, North and South Carolina, Virginia, Alabama, Florida, Georgia, Louisiana, Mississippi and Texas.

The New York Times, which supported Mr. Cox, conceded Senator Harding's election with 276 electoral votes.

The vote in Indiana and Missouri was believed to be close.

Concession of the election of Senator Harding by the Dayton Daily News, Governor Cox's newspaper, was generally accepted in political quarters here as final evidence of a sweeping victory for Mr. Harding.

Governor Cox Concedes Defeat

Mr. Cox later announced that he authorized The Dayton News extra conceding Mr. Harding's election.

Mr. White's statement follows:

"The abandonment by some of the most prominent Republican leaders of the League of Nations which they helped to construct has been successful. The people have succumbed to the confusion wrought by these distinguished men and to the misrepresentation of those who would not and did not understand the League of Nations. I hope it may yet be rescued from the political morass and be saved to mankind.

Returns from California

A late dispatch from Los Angeles said that incomplete returns from 100 precincts in California gave: Harding, 13,097; Cox, 3904.

At midnight Republicans had gained one seat in the United States Senate. Samuel D. Nicholson (R.), defeated Senator C. S. Thomas (D.), running as an Independent, and Tully Scott, regular Democratic nominee, in Colorado.

Returns indicated the reelection of Senators Frank B. Brandegee, Connecticut; Charles Curtis, Kansas; George H. Moses, New Hampshire; James W. Wadsworth Jr., New York; Boies Penrose, Pennsylvania, and W. P. Dillingham, Vermont, all Republicans.

William B. McKinley (R.), was elected to the Senate from Illinois, succeeding Lawrence Y. Sherman (R.).

Close senatorial fights were being waged in Indiana, Oklahoma, and Wisconsin. James E. Watson (R.), was leading Thomas Taggart (D.), in Indiana.

In New Jersey, the Republicans apparently gained two seats in Congress.

Late reports gave Eugene V. Debs, Socialist candidate for President,

(Continued on Page Four Column One)

SUDDEN FALL OF PERSIAN MINISTRY CAUSES SURPRISE

Approaching Debates Regarding Ratification of Anglo-Persian Agreement May Have Helped to Cause the Resignations

Special cable to The Christian Science Monitor from its European News Office

LONDON, England (Tuesday)—The Persian Cabinet has suddenly and inexplicably resigned, this event taking place a week ago on the eve of the meeting of the Majlios, the Persian Parliament, which, after so many delays, was to consider the Anglo-Persian agreement with a view to its ratification. No details are as yet available to explain the fall of Mushir Ed Dowleh's government, but in the British official view, it may be due to the influence of General Starosselsky, commander of the Russian Cossack division which, under Persian pay, has been fighting the Bolsheviki.

The position of this force, which numbers from 7000 to 8000 rifles, would no doubt be affected by confirmation of the Anglo-Persian agreement, as would that of many other servants of the Persian state, the representative of The Christian Science Monitor is informed by an authority well versed in the affairs of that nation, and undercurrents of Persian politics are always determined by considerations comparatively unknown to western civilizations. Corruption and self-interest are so rampant in the administration of Persia, as in other oriental countries, it is stated, that expert opinion outside Persia is unable to forecast what is likely to happen in regard to the Anglo-Persian agreement, except to be certain that opposition to it will come from those who see a threat to illicit perquisites in the establishment of a less corrupt administration.

The British aim, the informant declared, is to support any government in Persia that will keep the country immune from outside aggression, and the British representative in Teheran has therefore supported both the last Persian Cabinet and its predecessors. Already, even before the Anglo-Persian agreement is confirmed by the Majlios, the financial benefits which it brings have accrued to Persia, for the Financial Commission has begun its operations and has succeeded in augmenting to a considerable extent the Persian state revenues, while bigger royalties have been paid by the Anglo-Persian Oil Company through extensions inaugurated under the agreement.

Sepahdar Azam is mentioned as a possible new Prime Minister. Little is known of him outside Persia, but in Persian circles in London his assumption of office is looked upon as likely to be favored by British opinion. The identity of the new Cabinet is, however, utterly unknown, for the last Cabinet fairly well exhausted the number of prominent Persians qualified by European experience to fill such responsible positions.

RUMANIA NEEDS AMERICAN SUPPLIES

Special to The Christian Science Monitor from its Eastern News Office

NEW YORK, New York—Rumania needs foodstuffs, farm machinery, clothing, shoes, automobiles and other supplies from America, according to Dr. Mircea St. Angelescu, who has arrived here to serve as Rumanian consul-general in Washington. Rumania could export petroleum in return, he said. There was plenty of work in Rumania. Workmen were coming to industrial centers from all parts of the kingdom. They had resisted Bolshevist propaganda and Rumania was on a sound industrial and commercial basis. Industrial relations with merchants of other nations were being established.

LABOR DEFEATED IN MUNICIPAL ELECTIONS

Special cable to The Christian Science Monitor from its European News Office

LONDON, England (Tuesday)—The municipal elections, which took place yesterday throughout England, have resulted in the crushing defeat of the Labor candidates. Labor made a special effort in these elections. The results have been returned, so far, of 202 Labor candidates, who went to the polls in 18 districts, of whom only 20 were successful. There were in all about 300 municipalities contested in England and Wales for the election of one-third of the councilors, who retired this year.

In Liverpool, none of the 23 Labor candidates was returned.

SOCIALISTS TO DEMONSTRATE

Special cable to The Christian Science Monitor from its European News Office

GENEVA, Switzerland (Tuesday)—The Left Socialist Party in Switzerland and the young Communists invite the Swiss proletariat to demonstrate on November 7 in favor of the Russian revolution and the international Communists.

MR. GIOLITTI'S PLANS

Special cable to The Christian Science Monitor from its European News Office

ROME, Italy (Tuesday)—The "Giornale d'Italia" states that John Giolitti, the Premier, will proceed to London at the end of November, or the beginning of December, the object of his journey being to conclude a commercial and economic agreement.

MUNICIPAL ELECTIONS TAKE PLACE IN ITALY

London Times News Service

MILAN, Italy (Monday)—In the municipal elections which are taking place in 8400 communes in Italy, 5771 had voted up to October 24. Of these, 2935 communes were won by the Constitutional Party, 1733 by the Socialist, and 1031 by the Clericals.

Yesterday the elections resulted in victories for the Constitutional Party, both in Rome and Venice, where a coalition of all parties had been formed against the Socialists. The latter, however, were victorious in Bologna, Novara, Modena, Ferrara, Pavia, and other small centers.

In Milan, the elections take place on Sunday next. The Socialists have formed a group of extremists, all moderate elements being excluded. Unfortunately the group is assured of victory as the Liberals and Clericals could not agree to form a coalition group as at Rome and Venice.

The figures of the present elections confirm the fact that Bolshevism and Clericalism are both weak south of Rome, while their forces constantly increase in the north.

GREEKS TO VOTE ON WHO SHALL REIGN

Should Mr. Veniselos Win Elections, the Constantine Party Will Then, It Is Thought, Furnish the Written Guarantees

Special cable to The Christian Science Monitor from its European News Office

ATHENS, Greece (Tuesday)—Eleutherios Veniselos, the Premier, replying to the protest of Mr. Gounaris and Mr. Stratos, leaders of the opposition, that he refused to allow the people to decide the dynastic question, declared that he accepted the opinion of Mr. Gounaris and Mr. Stratos that the people should be left to decide the question. He admitted that the question would be put at the elections, but he asked for the cooperation of the opposition in order to avoid disorders that might occur during the electoral struggle.

At the meeting of the Chamber of Deputies, at which Admiral Coundouriotis was elected regent, the only opposition deputy present at the sitting proposed the return of former King Constantine in order to calm the nation. Mr. Veniselos protested and stated that the return of Constantine, who endeavored to smash the constitution, was impossible. On the contrary, his complete abdication was necessary for the peace of the country.

Special cable to The Christian Science Monitor from its European News Office

LONDON, England (Tuesday)—The reply of Prince Paul of Greece to the government's conditional offer of the throne, as cabled to The Christian Science Monitor, the Greek authorities in London characterize as a bald attempt on the part of the Constantine party to confuse the issue at the forthcoming Greek elections, now postponed until November 14. Prince Paul's written reply, the representative of The Christian Science Monitor was informed, has been drafted with the object of creating the impression in Greece that he has refused the throne of Greece, whereas careful perusal shows that a loophole of ample dimensions for his acceptance of the throne has been left by the Constantine party, should the elections go against them. The loophole is obvious in Prince Paul's statement: "I would only consent to ascend the throne in the event of the Hellenic people not desiring the return of my august father and excluding Prince George from the right of succession."

The aim of the Constantine party, the informant said, is to upset the minds of the populace and cause great numbers to vote against the Veniselos Government purely out of fear that Prince Paul's refusal of the crown would force a republic on the country and completely upset the Greek national policy.

Very little doubt is felt by the Greek authorities that the Veniselist party will be returned with a handsome majority. The Constantine party, it is thought, will then accept the inevitable and furnish a written guarantee, as already demanded by Mr. Veniselos, that both Constantine and Prince George forever renounce all claims to the Greek throne.

Special cable to The Christian Science Monitor from its European News Office

LUCERNE, Switzerland (Tuesday)—Mr. Streit, formerly Greek Minister of Foreign Affairs, declared that the elections would not be a certain criterion to discover whether the people did or did not ratify the fall of the former King Constantine. A plebiscite would be necessary during the temporary absence of Eleutherios Veniselos, the Premier, in order that Greece, having recovered her full national independence, might make known her will; and if she considered as definite the removal of Constantine and the elder branch of the family, Mr. Veniselos would not be able to postpone decision by the people.

Mr. Streit said that Constantine has regained confidence since the loss of King Alexander, and the Greek people, again masters of their fate, would declare that their uncompromising attitude was dictated to them.

FRENCH INTEREST IN AMERICAN ELECTIONS

Special cable to The Christian Science Monitor from its correspondent in Paris

PARIS, France (Tuesday)—Probably never has such interest been taken in the American presidential election in France as is now taken in the great issue being decided today. The result, in consequence of the difference of the hour, will not be known here tonight, but preparations for publication of special editions of the morning papers tomorrow are being made. Photographs of the candidates and particulars of their careers and of their policies are extensively published.

The reason of this interest is easy to understand, for, in reality, what is being decided, in the opinion of France, is the whole relations of America to Europe, and the fate of the League of Nations. Newspapers describe today as one of the most solemn days in history. Not only is the great American democracy deciding its own destinies, but it is determining in a large measure the policy of the old, as well as the new world.

Some appeals are made in the press that America should not desert Europe, whatever is the result of the election. France, says the "Gaulois," is necessary to the United States, to the prosperity and security of America. That expresses the general sentiment of France and indicates from what standpoint the election is regarded.

MANY ATTACKS ON POLICE IN IRELAND

Irish Chief Secretary Announces That Fifteen Serious Incidents Followed the Obsequies of Lord Mayor of Cork

Special cable to The Christian Science Monitor from its European News Office

WESTMINSTER, England (Tuesday)—Following the Lord Mayor of Cork's obsequies, according to an account given by Sir Hamar Greenwood, the Irish Chief Secretary, in the House of Commons last night, there were 15 cases in which policemen had been killed or attacked during the last week-end. These cases were as follows:

A patrol of a sergeant and three constables was ambushed at Killybegs, County Donegal, one constable being wounded. District Inspector Killegher was fatally shot in Kiegan's Hotel, Granard, County Longford. Sergt. Henry Cronin of Tullamore, Kings County, was fatally shot. A police patrol was fired upon at Dungannon, County Tyrone, one constable being wounded. Constables Casely and Evans of Killorglin, County Kerry, were fatally shot. An attempt was made to assassinate a military officer at Killenaule, County Tipperary, a military sergeant being wounded. A police patrol was fired on at Ballyduff, County Tipperary, one man being killed and one wounded.

A police patrol at Abbeydorney, County Kerry, was attacked, Constable Madden being fatally shot and another being seriously wounded. A police patrol in Listowel, County Kerry, was fired upon, there being no casualties. Two constables were wounded at Causeway, County Kerry. A naval wireless operator was wounded in Tralee. Constable Doyle of Clonark was seriously wounded at Kielty. Two constables were fired upon at Thomastown, County Kilkenny, there being no casualties. Policemen were ambushed at Castledale, County Galway, one constable being killed and two wounded.

REMOVAL URGED OF JAPAN'S INFLUENCE IN CHINESE AFFAIRS

China's Friends Think Republic, Left to Itself, Could Settle Problems — Say Its Integrity Is Threatened by Meddling

Special to The Christian Science Monitor from its Eastern News Office

NEW YORK, New York—Among China's friends here, the opinion is expressed that the powers ought to support the international consortium by enforcing a moratorium, so to speak, for the next few months, on meddling with Chinese affairs. It is believed that the results would be surprisingly gratifying to those who desire to see the Chinese on the way to the realization of their Republican ambitions. It is said that China would settle her affairs in short order if Japanese influence could be removed for six months.

One of the straws indicating the direction of the political wind in China is held to be the split in the south, between what may be called the southern military oligarchy at Canton and the liberal element, led by Wu Ting-fang, Sun Yat-sen and other leaders now at Shanghai.

Cleavage Emphasized

The cleavage between these two elements was emphasized only yesterday when the report that the Peking Government had issued a proclamation declaring a reunion between the north and the south was accompanied by information of a manifesto from the Constitutional leaders, Sun Yat-sen and Tang Shao-yi, refusing to recognize this proclamation as having force and declaring that the persons in the south who had made the alleged peace agreement with the north were irresponsible, both Peking and Canton merely aiming to create the impression, among the powers, that unity had really been brought about.

The Constitutional leaders say they are working in the interests of the people of China, and that their People's Party insists upon a constitutional government which shall be genuinely representative of the whole people and which shall work not merely in the interests of an official or militaristic class. Ma Soo, representative of that party in the United States, is now in China. He went there soon after the People's Party convention in Philadelphia, Pennsylvania, a few months ago.

In this connection it is of great interest to note that Dr. Paul S. Reinsch, before he left China to campaign for the United States Senate, issued a statement reviewing China's condition and urging a constitutional convention for the adoption of a really representative form of government for the whole country. A significant feature of Dr. Reinsch's opinion is that representation should be based on some group arrangement rather than upon geographical lines.

Interests Outside Consortium

Those who apprehend continued Japanese meddling in China's political affairs find significance in the fact that there are in China private Japanese activities on a large scale arranged with private or unofficial Chinese interests, which are no more affected by the operation of the consortium than similar American, British or French activities. These include the development of projects in Japan's Manchurian sphere, such as those entered into between Chang Tso-lin and Japanese capital-

THE CHRISTIAN SCIENCE MONITOR

AN INTERNATIONAL DAILY NEWSPAPER

Published daily, except Sundays, by The Christian Science Publishing Society, 107 Falmouth Street, Boston, Mass. Subscription price, payable in advance, postpaid to all countries: One year, $9.00; six months, $4.50; three months, $2.25; one month, 75 cents.

Entered at second-class rates at the Post Office at Boston, Mass., U. S. A. Acceptance for mailing at a special rate of postage provided for in section 1103, Act of October 3, 1917, authorized on July 11, 1918.

INDEX FOR NOVEMBER 3, 1920

THE CHRISTIAN SCIENCE MONITOR

AN INTERNATIONAL DAILY NEWSPAPER

FIVE CENTS   Copyright 1921 by The Christian Science Publishing Society   BOSTON, U.S.A., THURSDAY, NOVEMBER 3, 1921   { Fourteen Pages }   VOL. XIII, NO. 295

FRANCO-TURKISH AGREEMENT HAS SURPRISED BRITAIN

Treaty With the Kemalist Turks Gives France Valuable Concessions and Is Thought to Infringe Rights of Allied Powers

Special cable to The Christian Science Monitor from its European News Office

LONDON, England (Wednesday) — Profound surprise has been aroused in British official circles at the terms of the Franco-Turkish treaty, the text of which was delivered to the British Foreign Office last night. Although it was well known that the French Government was negotiating with the Kemalist Government at Angora, it had been understood that the discussions were proceeding along lines of nothing more than a local agreement.

The surprise may be judged by the fact that it is now discovered that far from a mere local agreement a full fledged peace treaty has been signed by one of the Allies without consultation with the others and apparently with total disregard to the terms of the Pact of London.

In official circles it is considered that the terms not only go far beyond anything that had been expected but the net result will be that some very searching questions will undoubtedly be asked by the British Government. These questions will, of course, be based on the assumption that a reasonable explanation will be readily forthcoming, and every effort will be made to keep the discussions on frank and friendly lines.

Territory Renounced

At the same time it cannot be disguised that the utmost tact will be needed on both sides. For notwithstanding the French declaration that the document in question is purely an agreement with Kemal Pasha, the only meaning that the British official mind has so far been able to read into the pact is that it is a definite treaty of peace.

Furthermore, according to Article VIII of the Franco-Turkish agreement or treaty, a large stretch of the Cilician territory assigned to France under the Treaty of Sèvres is renounced in favor of Turkey. The new frontier runs from north of Alexandretta between Killis and Aleppo, leaving in Syrian territory part of the Baghdad railway up to the Euphrates. The control of the railway between the Euphrates and Nisibin will be in Turkish hands. From Nisibin the frontier goes along the Tigris to Jezireh Ibn Omar, following the caravan route.

In Article III, it definitely lays down: "In a period of two months at the most, dating from the signature of the present agreement, the Turkish troops will withdraw to the north and the French troops to the south of the line described in Article VIII." On the other hand, and apparently in return, she is granted some remarkably valuable concessions in way of iron, chrome and silver mining rights over a period of 99 years.

Value of Concessions Obtained

Another point in the treaty that is considered to have significant value is the right for French teachers to be appointed to Turkish schools with the object of teaching the French language. It is fully expected that the French authorities will use the argument that by the cessation of hostilities they are released from the necessity of maintaining troops in Syria and Cilicia. This fact is frankly acknowledged by the British authorities, but at the same time it cannot be

disguised that in the matter of concessions—whether intentional or not—French interests have undoubtedly got in ahead of their allies.

Another point which it is considered will be the subject for serious consideration is that France by signing this treaty has by virtue of this act given de facto recognition to the Kemalist Government at Angora. This alone may lead to serious complications.

Another matter that vitally affects British interests in the East is contained in the latter part of the terms of treaty whereby either French or Turkish troops have the right to be transported over that portion of the Baghdad railway which is returned to Turkey. As to what action France would take in the event of Turkey interpreting this clause to her advantage as regards an attack on the newly formed kingdom of Irak (Mesopotamia), British authorities find it difficult to express any opinion.

Particular attention is drawn to Article 6, which is considered to be quite unsatisfactory. The article reads: "The government of the Turkish Grand National Assembly declares that the rights of minorities solemnly recognized in the national pact will be confirmed by it on the same basis as that established by conventions concluded on the subject between the powers of the Entente, their adversaries and certain of their allies."

Much value and many precautions,

it is stated, have been devoted to the protection of minorities in Asia Minor by western powers. According to this wholly unsatisfactory clause it is considered that these much-suffering peoples have every reason to express anxiety as regards their future safety if this treaty is to stand.

Taken in its entirety, this act on the part of France in effect would render null and void the solemn Pact of London, entered into in 1915, whereby each ally undertook not to sign any treaty of peace with an enemy power without the full agreement of her partners, taking into consideration the fact that the Sèvres Treaty with Turkey has not been ratified.

ARMISTICE DAY A NATIONAL HOLIDAY

WASHINGTON, District of Columbia—Armistice Day, November 11, 1921, will be declared a national holiday. Congressional action on a resolution requesting the President and all state governors to proclaim the day a holiday was completed yesterday through adoption by the Senate. Issuance of the proclamation by Mr. Harding is expected within a few days.

THE CHRISTIAN SCIENCE MONITOR
AN INTERNATIONAL DAILY NEWSPAPER

Published daily, except Sundays, by The Christian Science Publishing Society, 107 Falmouth Street, Boston, Mass. Subscription price, payable in advance, postpaid to all countries: One year, $9.00; six months, $5.00; three months, $3.00; one month, $1.10 Entered at second-class rates at the Post Office at Boston, Mass., U.S.A. Acceptance for mailing at a special rate of postage provided for in section 1103, Act of October 3, 1917, authorized on July 11, 1918

IRISH CONFERENCE AT TURNING POINT

Two Lines of Compromise, Both Dependent Upon Attitude of Ulster, Mentioned as Having Been Examined by Delegates

Special cable to The Christian Science Monitor from its European News Office

LONDON, England (Wednesday) — From passages in Mr. Lloyd George's speech in the House of Commons on Monday, and from feeling in both Sinn Fein and government circles, the Irish negotiations bear every appearance of being near some definite solution or else a complete breakdown. The conference has been proceeding since early last month and has now reached a critical point, it seems, where the consultation of Ulster has become necessary.

Since Eamon de Valera's message to the Pope, which started the discussions at Downing Street, somewhat prematurely on the question of the allegiance of Southern Ireland to the King, the delegates of each side have been taking soundings. The Sinn Fein representatives have, there is reason

to believe, endeavored to find how they could secure the unity of Ireland as a whole if they consented to waive their objection to allegiance, and the government has been trying to discover how far Sinn Fein would persist in its declared aim, namely, the establishment of a republic, and whether there was not a quid pro quo which might be exchanged for the surrender of the republican demand.

Although the Indian leader has recently been trailing his coat and issuing challenges to the government,

County Option Proposed

Two lines of compromise, both dependent upon the attitude of Ulster, are mentioned as having been examined with a view to finding a way out of the deadlock. One is to give the Ulster counties by the method of county option an opportunity to declare whether they will join the Southern Irish state or not. This plan would result in Tyrone and Fermanagh voting themselves out of the Northern Parliament, if the statistics compiled in the 1911 census are accurate at this period 10 years later, thus leaving Ulster a four-county area.

This plan would hardly be approved by the Ulster people, it is held, and there is more hope in the second plan which visualizes a federated Ireland in which the jurisdiction of the Northern Parliament instead of being curtailed would actually be extended to include the three Roman Catholic counties of Donegal, Cavan and Monaghan. Ulster, under those circumstances, would be a unity, and, by the infusion of a stronger Roman Catholic element into the Northern Parliament, the parties would be more evenly balanced than they are at present. The Southern Parliament would then function for the rest of Ireland, and there would be a supreme All-Ireland Parliament over both.

In addition to these two lines of settlement, it is also proposed that there shall be an alteration in the powers and status of the Irish Council, which is intended by the Government in the Ireland Act to link the Northern and Southern Parliaments, but the attitude of prominent Ulstermen on this point is so well known that the proposal only needs to be stated to be seen as improbable of fulfillment.

Optimism Prevails

Whatever the merits of these schemes, it is acknowledged that no agreement can be effective without Ulster's spokesmen being consulted. It now remains for Mr. de Valera to sink his objections to Sir James Craig being admitted to the conference as an equal instead of as the representative of a minority in Ireland, and until the invitation has been sent to Sir James, and either accepted or rejected, Mr. Lloyd George cannot go to the House of Commons and inform that that all has been done that can be done.

Optimism prevails in both Sinn Fein and government circles as the result of Tuesday's conversations. The work of discussion is being carried on by the sub-committee of the conference,

and it may be that when the next full meeting of the conference is summoned it will either be to approve the terms of settlement or to be informed that it is impossible for the negotiations to proceed.

Peace still hangs in the balance, and although optimism prevails the veil of secrecy surrounding the conference is not lifted, so that judgment may be brought to bear upon the grounds for optimism.

INDIAN AGITATORS GUILTY OF SEDITION

Ali Brothers and Another Noncooperator Sentenced to Imprisonment—No Action Meanwhile Against Mr. Gandhi

Special cable to The Christian Science Monitor from its European News Office

LONDON, England (Wednesday) — The Ali brothers and Dr. Kitchlaw have received a sentence of two years imprisonment for sedition, as a result of their trial at Karachi, which concluded on Tuesday. It is yet early to estimate the results of the conviction.

have recently been trailing his coat and issuing challenges to the government, the question of his prosecution has been for the moment shelved, if it was ever seriously considered, and the tedious byways of Indian procedure will keep the problem out of sight from the responsible authorities until after the visit of the Prince of Wales to India.

Situation in Malabar Area

The situation in Malabar is by far the most serious task to be tackled at the moment, and the neighboring districts are becoming restless at the failure to deal finally with the Moplahs. The measures taken against them have been much improved recently by the use of non-British troops in combination with white troops, and there have been several successful actions in which large bands of Moplah tribesmen have been rounded up.

One battalion of Gurkhas from Nepal and one battalion of Burmese troops from the Chin Hills, both accustomed to country which favors guerrilla tactics, have been drafted to Malabar and are being utilized with success in driving the Moplahs into the arms of the Dorset and Leinster regiments, who, armed with artillery and armored cars, patrol the roads and villages. Two more battalions of native troops are being sent into the district in the hope of hastening the fall of the rebels.

Difficulties of Troops

The difficulties in connection with intelligence work are proving formidable to the government troops. Although the Moplah police are proving most loyal, according to reports, the inhabitants, who might otherwise be favorably inclined toward the British forces, are terrorized by the rebels so that they refuse to give information to the punitive expeditions. The Hindu elements are being persecuted to an extent that cannot be exactly estimated and, owing to the protection afforded by the bush to the aggressors, it has been found impossible to protect them universally.

Sir Thomas Holland, whose career in India was recently brought to an end by his action over the Calcutta munitions case, is now on his way home to England. It is probable that he will be succeeded as Minister of Commerce of the Government of India by Sir Louis Kershaw, head of the Labor department of the India Office.

KRUPP CONCESSION IN CHILE IS HALTED

Land Title Flaws Now Expected to End Lease Negotiations for Great Tract of Virgin Territory Rich in Minerals

By special correspondent of The Christian Science Monitor

SANTIAGO, Chile — It is now generally believed in Chile that the Krupp concession in southern Chile which was so much talked of early this year will never materialize. The Germans have discovered serious flaws in the land titles and are unwilling to take over the territory until the government is able to guarantee a clear title.

The Chilean Government's title to the enormous territory which it granted to the Germans in exchange for establishing a branch of the Krupp iron and steel industry dates back to the crown grants, but almost every tract is disputed by settlers claiming squatters' rights and the Germans would be required to maintain a separate legal action for each parcel of land, the suits continuing over probably 15 years.

The Krupp representatives have also learned that the water rights in the Petrohue River, which they considered one of the most valuable features of the concession, were granted several years ago to other parties who, although they are not exercising these rights, could remove all the water from the river at their pleasure any time after the Krupp people were ready to use it.

These and other legal knots which have been discovered since the government granted the concession present difficulties which the Germans are not willing to assume and the indications are that they will allow the time limit to expire without filing their acceptance of the terms of the concession, whereupon it automatically becomes canceled.

The concession was granted to two Germans, Otto Lenz and Paul Guerich, on behalf of the Krupp Company, and gave them rights to 346,000 acres of forest lands for a term of 30 years, renewable on the expiration of that operation. This land extends southward from the shore of Lake Todos los Santos almost to the outlet of Reloncavi Sound, westward to the base of Calbuco Volcano, and eastward to the foot of the Andes range, the Petrohue River flowing through the entire length of the territory.

The contract provided that the concessionnaires should, within two years of the date of the decree, commence the installation of a siderurgical industry in the country and within five years of the same date, the installation was to be in working order.

The industrial enterprise thus established was to be under obligation to manufacture iron, steel, and the complementary products of the same industry which Chile needs.

In the event of noncompliance with the terms of this convention, which was signed by the Inspector-General of Colonization on behalf of the executive, Messrs. Lenz and Guerich on the other, this will constitute sufficient authority for the annulling of the contract and eviction from the lands in question.

The site of this valuable concession is the coast of Reloncavi Sound, in the northeast part of the Gulf of Ancud, near Puerto Montt, and is in the heart of Chile's primitive forests and virgin soil. There is a wealth of many millions of dollars in saleable lumber and paper pulp material, apart from the material for charcoal necessary for the smelting, to say nothing of the undoubted existence of petroleum springs waiting to be tapped; while the cleared land would produce beets for conversion into sugar by the factory.

RESIGNATION OF PRUSSIAN CABINET

Special cable to The Christian Science Monitor from its correspondent in Berlin

BERLIN, Germany (Wednesday) — The sudden resignation of the Prussian Cabinet, which is due to party intrigues and possesses little political significance, has occasioned very little interest among the general public. It is evident that a reaction, after the Upper Silesian excitement, set in and that tax and food price problems alone possess engrossing interest. It is not yet settled when Dr. Wirth's Cabinet will introduce its tax proposals, but it is expected that a preliminary skirmish will take place on the subject in the Reichstag on Friday night. The German People's Party, which represents the big industrial interests, announced its determination to oppose the tax plans which Dr. Wirth is understood to be preparing on the ground that they will complete the crushing of the much-burdened middle class. The Social Democratic Party is also restless on the taxation question. The leading democratic organ, however, the "Vossische Zeitung," tonight declares that the hopeless taxation situation in Germany is mainly due to the "cowardice displayed by all parties, the Social Democrats included, during the past year, which prevented them, for fear of offending a large body of electors, from attempting to reduce the enormous bureaucratic machine in Germany, through which billions of marks are being wasted in the payment of unnecessary salaries."

AUSTRALIAN LAND SETTLEMENT
Special cable to The Christian Science Monitor from its European News Office

MELBOURNE, Victoria (Wednesday) — W. M. Hughes outlined to a premiers' conference held here a comprehensive scheme of land settlement which he calculates will absorb all the Australian unemployed together with the British soldiers. He stated that he believed he would be able to borrow £50,000,000 for the purpose of the scheme.

COST OF ALLIED TROOPS IN GERMANY HEAVY

Special cable to The Christian Science Monitor from its correspondent in Paris

PARIS, France (Wednesday) — The report is expected from the special commission which is studying the question of the cost of the armies of occupation. So far the occupation of Germany has cost 4,000,000,000 gold marks, and if such charges, which must be paid by Germany, are regarded as part of the sums due for reparations, it is obvious that the prospects of real reparations are extremely small. This priority will absorb all the early payments of Germany.

There is a growing feeling of the necessity of reducing the expenditure of a military character to the minimum. There have been some abuses signaled in shape of too luxurious lodgement of officers and excessive expenditure, which it is hoped to cut down radically. The delegates are leaving for Coblenz to study this problem on the spot.

LITTLE ENTENTE DEMANDS REMOVAL

Dr. Benès's Note to the Council of Ambassadors Calls for Dethronement of Hapsburgs in Perpetuity and Disarmament

Special cable to The Christian Science Monitor from its correspondent in Paris

PARIS, France (Wednesday) — The Council of Ambassadors considered today the note of Dr. Benès which was moderate in tone. The Czecho-Slovakian Premier intimates that a proclamation of the ineligibility of the Hapsburg dynasty for the Hungarian throne will be regarded as sufficiently appeasing the fears of the little entente.

The Council thereupon decided to demand from the Horthy Government the dethronement in perpetuity of the Hapsburgs. This proclamation must be made not later than November 7. It is hoped that the little entente will disarm. The alarm that was felt in Paris at the attitude of the little entente, which made demands directly upon Budapest including demands for the reimbursement of sums spent on military preparations, is dissipated by the declarations of Dr. Benès.

Czecho-Slovakia, he says, follows and intends to follow a policy of peace and is doing all in her power to prevent an armed conflict. But this attempt of former Emperor Charles in the second made in six months to trouble the peace of central Europe. In April only half measures were taken, and thus the insurrection of Burgenland and the dash of former Emperor Charles were rendered possible. Czecho-Slovakia, therefore, intends to finish loyally with these provocations, but is nevertheless resolved to act in accord with the great powers. The great powers should understand that the danger was greater than was supposed at Paris, London, and Rome. The departure of the former Emperor is not adequate. The Hapsburgs must abdicate and Hungary must disarm.

Dr. Benès denies having sent any ultimatum to Hungary, nor has the little entente fixed a date for the invasion of Hungary. It has merely taken the indispensable measures of precaution and energy.

It is obvious from the tone of Dr. Benès's note that no steps of a hostile character are contemplated without the consent of the Allies on this occasion, but at the same time it is clear that any further disturbances in central Europe will compel the neighbors of Hungary to act without delay. Realizing this fact, the Allies appear equally determined to put an end to the peril. The Council of Ambassadors further examined in what conditions the internment of former Emperor Charles could be effected and what measures of surveillance were necessary.

Special cable to The Christian Science Monitor from its European News Office

BUDAPEST, Hungary (Wednesday) — Former Emperor Charles and his wife, former Empress Zita, were taken from their sanctuary at Tihany Abbey early on Tuesday morning and by half-past 8 they were safely aboard the British river gunboat Glowworm, which shortly afterward left for Galatz, where it is expected the royal exiles will be kept pending further decision of the allied powers. The removal was effected without incident.

The special train left Tihany at 5 o'clock in the morning, an early hour being decided upon to avoid the possibility of a public demonstration, and was preceded and followed by special trains carrying armed troops. The trains stopped at Baja, whence the former emperor and empress were conveyed in a carriage to the gunboat. Their removal was carried out under the personal supervision of British, French and Italian military attachés.

CHINA DESIRES TO WIN POLITICAL AND FISCAL FREEDOM

Basic Policy at the Washington Conference Will Be Demand That She Be Party in All the Agreements Affecting Her

SAYINGS OF THE CONFERENCE

"I am, therefore, in favor of every question being discussed openly with as much publicity as possible, and after all the difficulties have been thoroughly ventilated and discussed, an equitable solution is not unlikely to be found."—Viscount Haldane.

"Competitive armaments are based on the mad theory that mankind is a beast only to be ruled by fear."—Henry van Dyke, former United States Minister to the Netherlands.

"I hope the Conference may find it possible to outlaw war."—Bishop William F. Anderson of Cincinnati.

"So far as I am concerned, and here I speak not only as the responsible head of the British Admiralty, but as one of the official delegates, I come in a spirit of quiet confidence that the results of this Conference will be such as amply to justify President Harding's far-seeing initiative, and, personally, I am not prepared to contemplate the possibility of failure."—Lord Lee of Fareham, First Lord of British Admiralty.

Special cable to The Christian Science Monitor from its Washington News Office

WASHINGTON, District of Columbia—That China is the important factor in the Far Eastern question will be accepted as an underlying and fundamental premise, when the powers that are about to gather in the Washington Conference turn to the problems of peace and progress in the Pacific. Whatever differences may exist as to various phases of the items in the Conference agenda, the fact that China is the storm center in the Far East is regarded as axiomatic.

For this reason the attitude of China, and what she proposes to say to the world powers through her delegations, is of supreme importance. The aim of the delegation is to present a categorical statement of policies and aspirations which is, in effect, a demand for a complete break with the paternalism and internationalism of the past, and a new deal for the future.

Without going into details as to the attitude of the Chinese delegation concerning specific questions which may be brought up in connection with the Far Eastern discussion, it is possible to state here on undisputed authority that the aims of the delegation will center around two leading propositions, one the maintenance of the political independence of China, and the other to secure complete financial autonomy.

All Control Opposed

It is recognized that the trend of events during the last few years among some of the world powers has been in direction of the belief that some form of international control of these is inevitable. It is flatly stated that the policy of the delegation will be to take direct issue with this viewpoint.

China, in effect, will tell the powers that the time has come when there must be an end of the traditional policy whereby one strong power signed treaties with another strong power, in which Chinese political independence and sovereignty were mere pawns. She will also say that, the financial consortium notwithstanding, what China needs is not more international control of finances, but the scrapping of the policy whereby the powers control her revenues and make it impossible for her to exercise fiscal freedom.

The paternalism which found expression in such agreements as the Anglo-Japanese alliance, the Root-Takahira agreement, the Lansing-Ishii compact, in all of which certain declarations regarding China have been made, is frowned on by the Chinese delegation, which is authorized to declare to the powers that any agreements touching on China in the future must be with China herself.

The paternal attitude toward China has been and is, considered by the Chinese delegation to be detrimental to her complete political independence. It is humiliating to them to think of themselves as dependent upon the good will and benevolent intentions of other powers. They believe the policy of other nations toward China should not be expressed in agreements among themselves in which China has had no part, but that the only vehicle in which policies toward China should be promulgated is direct agreements with China. The delegation is authorized to make this clear to the powers.

Treaty Right Claimed

For the reason stated, China looks with disfavor upon the Anglo-Japanese alliance, the Root-Takahira agreement, the agreement between France and Japan concerning China, and all similar arrangements. China can see no reason why it is not as advantageous to other nations to declare their policies in direct agreement with China as in agreements between themselves in which China has not been consulted. China does not wish at this time to call in question the good intentions of the powers in making declarations with China. It only objects to having them made without her. She calculates will absorb all policy in China that is disadvantageous to her policy in China. It does claim the right of regulating its own policy by treaty or agreement with all nations with which she has diplomatic relations. She also maintains that the

Map illustrating Franco-Turkish agreement

Under the new pact signed by representatives of Paris and Angora, the Turkish frontier, as shown by the heavy dotted line, runs from a point just north of Alexandretta, crosses and recrosses the Baghdad railway as far as Nisibin, at which point it turns slightly northeast until it reaches the Mesopotamian frontier at Jezireh Ibn Omar

THE CHRISTIAN SCIENCE MONITOR

AN INTERNATIONAL DAILY NEWSPAPER

FIVE CENTS | BOSTON, U.S.A., WEDNESDAY, DECEMBER 7, 1921 | Fourteen Pages | VOL. XIV, NO. 11

Copyright 1921 by The Christian Science Publishing Society

IRISH FREE STATE IS NEW MEMBER OF BRITISH EMPIRE

British Cabinet Has Unanimously Approved the Settlement and Parliament Is Being Summoned at Once to Ratify the Treaty

Special cable to The Christian Science Monitor from its European News Office

LONDON, England (Tuesday)—At a full meeting of the British Cabinet today, the terms of the Irish settlement were unanimously approved and a new session of Parliament will, it is stated, be summoned for Wednesday next which, it is believed the King will open in person. The business of the new session will be confined exclusively to the Irish settlement and after ratification and the passing of certain resolutions, the House of Commons will probably be either prorogued or adjourned to a later date.

Mr. Lloyd George, Winston Churchill, Lord Birkenhead, Austen Chamberlain on the one side and Michael Collins, Arthur Griffith, and R. C. Barton on the other side were the signatories to the formal document, a copy of which was dispatched without delay by the hand of one of the Prime Minister's secretaries, who traveled by special train and fast destroyer to Sir James Craig, Premier of the Northern Government in Ireland.

In government circles there is every hope that Ulster will find the agreement acceptable, but, if this hope is not well founded, it is within her power to refuse it so far as she is concerned without torpedoing the settlement.

As for Southern Ireland the agreement still remains to be ratified by Dail Eireann, but as the Sinn Fein signatories to it enjoy, without doubt, the status of plenipotentiaries there is every confidence that at any rate the majority of the Dail will approve of what has been done at Downing Street. There is thus the prospect of a considerable reduction of the numbers in the British forces in Ireland being effected.

Monday's conferences between the Sinn Fein and the British representatives lasted nearly 12 hours in all, broken intermittently by private party conferences, and when the last meeting broke up only the newspaper men outside No. 10 Downing Street and the policemen in Whitehall were about to hear that at least there were prospects of the age long quarrel between the two parts of the United Kingdom being satisfactorily settled.

The King sent the following telegram to the Prime Minister today from Sandringham:

"Am overjoyed to hear the splendid news you have just sent me. I congratulate you with all my heart on the successful termination of these difficult and protracted negotiations, which is due to the patience and conciliatory spirit which you have shown throughout. And I am indeed happy in some small way to have contributed by my speech in Belfast to this great achievement. GEORGE R. I."

Congratulations are showering on Mr. Lloyd George from all quarters.

Details of Agreement

Ireland to Have Similar Status to Dominion of Canada

Special cable to The Christian Science Monitor from its European News Office

LONDON, England (Tuesday)—The full text of the treaty terms between Britain and Ireland which were drawn up and signed at the peace conference, which ended so dramatically in the early hours this morning, were issued tonight. The document is styled: "Treaty between Great Britain and Ireland." Articles of agreement. Signed Dec. 6th, 1921."

The articles number 18 and the Irish delegates' signatures thereto are subscribed in Gaelic.

The first article lays it down that: "Ireland shall have the same constitutional status in the community of nations known as the British Empire as the Dominion of Canada, the Commonwealth of Australia, the Dominion of New Zealand and the Union of South Africa, with a parliament having powers to make laws for the peace, order and good government of Ireland, and an executive responsible to that parliament, and shall be styled and known as The Irish Free State."

Subject to certain provisions set out in the agreement, the position of the Irish Free State in relation to the Imperial Parliament and the government shall be that of the Dominion of Canada and the law, practice and constitutional usage governing the relationship of the Crown and the Imperial Parliament to the Dominion of Canada shall govern their relationship to the Irish Free State.

The representative of the Crown in Ireland to be appointed in like manner as the Governor-General of Canada and according to the practice observed in making such appointments.

Article IV deals with the oath to be taken by the members of Parliament of the Irish Free State; said oath being in the following form:

"I . . . do solemnly swear true faith and allegiance to the Constitution of the Irish Free State as by law established, and that I will be faithful to His Majesty, King George V, his heirs and successors by law, in virtue of the common citizenship of Ireland with Great Britain, and her adherence to, and membership of, the group of nations forming the British Commonwealth of nations."

The Irish Free State is to assume liability for the service of the public debt of the United Kingdom as existing at the date of the agreement, and toward the payment of war pensions as existing at the same date in such proportion as is fair and equitable.

Naval Defense

Articles VI, VII and VIII refer to coastal and other defense, it being agreed that until an arrangement has been made between the British and Irish Governments, whereby the Irish Free State undertakes her own coastal defense, the defense by sea of Great Britain and Ireland shall be undertaken by the Imperial forces, this, however, not preventing the construction or maintenance by the Irish Free State Government of such vessels necessary for the protection of revenue or fisheries.

The foregoing provisions shall be reviewed at a conference of the representatives of the British and Irish Governments to be held at the expiration of five years from the date of the agreement with a view to Ireland undertaking a share in her own coastal defense.

The Government of the Irish Free State is to afford His Majesty's Imperial forces in time of peace such harbor and other facilities as indicated in an annex to the agreement, and, in time of war or of strained relations with a foreign power, such harbor and other facilities as Britain may require for purpose of such defense.

Limitation of Armaments

With a view to securing "the observance of the principle of international limitation of armaments," if the government of the Irish Free State establishes and maintains a military defense force, it is agreed that the establishments thereof shall not exceed in size such proportion of the military establishments maintained in Great Britain as that which the population of Ireland bears to the population of Great Britain.

The ports of Britain and the Irish Free State shall be freely open to ships of the other country on payment of the customary port dues.

Provision is made for the Ulster Parliament to decide, within one month of the passing of the Act of Parliament ratifying the agreement, whether Ulster will come into the Irish Free State or maintain her present powers under the Government of Ireland Act, 1920.

If Ulster decides on the latter course, a commission, consisting of one representative of the Irish Free State, one of the Northern Ireland Government, and a chairman appointed by the British Government, shall be appointed to determine the boundaries between Northern Ireland and the rest of Ireland.

Ulster to Decide

If the Ulster Parliament passes no resolution either way within the stipulated month, then the Irish Free State Government shall have the same powers in the North as in the rest of Ireland in relation to matters in respect of which the Northern Parliament has no powers to make laws under the 1920 Act.

In such a case, however, the Northern Ireland Government and the provisional Southern Ireland Government may meet for the purpose of the discussing of safeguards in Northern Ireland, the settlement of financial relations between Northern Ireland and the Irish Free State and the establishment and powers of a local militia in Northern Ireland and the relations of the defense forces of the Irish Free State and Northern Ireland respectively.

Neither the Irish Free State nor the Northern Ireland Parliament shall make any law to endow any religion or make any religious discrimination. Steps are to be taken forthwith for the summoning of a meeting of the Southern Parliament elected since the passing of the 1920 Act and for constituting a provisional government, every member of which shall signify in writing his acceptance of the agreement.

Naval Reservations

Article XVIII concludes the agreement in the following terms: "This instrument shall be submitted forthwith by His Majesty's Government for the approval of Parliament, and by the Irish signatories to a meeting summoned for the purpose of the members elected to sit in the House of Commons of Southern Ireland, and, if approved, shall be ratified by the necessary legislation."

An annex to the agreement reserves to Britain the maintenance of harbor defenses at Berehaven, Queenstown, Belfast Lough and Lough Swilly, with certain Admiralty property rights; also aviation facilities.

A convention is to be concluded between Britain and the Irish Free State with a view to preserving British submarine cable and wireless rights. It is also provided that a convention shall be made between the same governments for the regulation of civil communication by air.

Ulster Considers Terms

Special cable to The Christian Science Monitor from its European News Office

BELFAST, Ireland (Tuesday)—After considering the Irish peace terms for over two hours tonight, the Ulster Cabinet adjourned further consideration till tomorrow.

HOW GERMANY IS SUBSIDIZING TRADE

State Subsidy on Bread and Coal, Aid to Railways and Rent Restrictions Help Her to Undersell Allied Manufacturers

Special cable to The Christian Science Monitor from its European News Office

LONDON, England (Tuesday)—The logic of events in the shape of growing unemployment and trade stagnation is compelling the business men and statesmen of Britain to give the German reparations question close consideration. Britain is between Scylla and Charybdis. On the other hand, if she with her allies brings pressure to bear on Germany to meet her reparations payments, there will be added to the already impoverished Central Europe a broken, bankrupt Germany. This would be a catastrophe of the first magnitude.

As Sir Robert Horne, Chancellor of the Exchequer, said last night at Manchester: "It would be a disaster not only from an economic point of view, but no man can foretell what its reverberations would be in the political sphere."

But if Germany is able to meet her obligations under the London reparations agreement, payments can be made only in the form of an excess of exports over imports. These exports can find entry into foreign markets only if they are cheaper than British and American manufactures. So that even if German goods are not sold in England, British manufacturers are excluded from foreign markets by this artificial competition.

Dr. Walter Rathenau is still in London endeavoring to reach an agreement, first with financiers to float a loan on German industries, and second with the British Government to arrange for delay in the reparations payments, and if possible to reduce the amounts demanded by the Allies. He has not been too successful in either of his quests, The Christian Science Monitor is informed.

The finance committee of the Cabinet is meeting today to consider proposals with regard to the next German reparation payment. But there seems little disposition on the part of the British Government to advocate a moratorium, and French uneasiness as to Britain reaching an agreement with Germany behind her back is needless, as the Cabinet is determined to maintian the solidarity of the Allies despite the Wiesbaden agreement which lays France open to criticism on this very point.

In her endeavor to meet the reparations payment, Germany has in effect been subsidizing her exports. This has not been done directly but in a roundabout way. In the first place manufacturers are able to employ German workmen at lower wages on account of the bread subsidy. This is done at the expense of German taxpayers and results in a deficit in the state revenue.

State railways are operated on loans amounting to about £1,250,000 monthly. The low freight charges resulting therefrom enable the German manufacturer to carry his goods to the seaboard below cost of transportation.

Rent restrictions, while robbing the landlords, have resulted in this item being almost negligible in the weekly budget of the German workman, whose rate of pay has increased many times while his rent remains practically stationary.

The state subsidy on coal is such that fuel is being sold in Germany at about half the price being paid elsewhere in the world today.

It is certain that if the Allies give Germany any easement in reparation payments, they will call for guarantees that she shall make her taxation sufficient to yield a revenue to meet her expenditure, and cease to use the printing press to manufacture paper marks to meet her deficit. This is the chief reason for the depreciation of the mark which, in fact, is another subsidy added to those enumerated above which enables the German manufacturer to underbid British goods.

All this brings the question back to the need for revising the schedule of reparations payments. The present scheme forces Germany to export greatly in excess of her imports, and these articles are necessary to enable her to do so. If no revision is granted by the Allies, they will have a bankrupt Germany on their hands, and if, by a gigantic effort, Germany meets their demands there will be trade stagnation in every exporting country.

PROTECTION FOR IRISH MINORITIES

Special cable to The Christian Science Monitor from its European News Office

BIRMINGHAM, England (Tuesday)—Speaking at a Birmingham Conservative Club luncheon this afternoon, Lord Birkenhead said it was proposed within the area of Southern Ireland to make those entitled to speak for the overwhelming majority of the population masters of their own household. The experiment would be tried upon the most generous lines, upon the lines tried in South Africa. The state to be created would be known as the Irish Free State.

No difficulty had been experienced in inducing Sinn Fein representatives to contemplate reasonable arrangements for the protection of the minority in the South of Ireland.

If Ulster determined that it would rather retain her existing powers, she would so retain them. If she also indicated her intention to retain her membership of the British House of Commons, her wish would be respected in the paramount interest of peace itself. If Ulster exercised the option to remain thus closely associated with England there must be a rectification of frontiers.

The Sinn Fein representatives were prepared to recommend to Dail Eireann that the newly-constituted Irish Free State should not be merely a matter of treaty but of association with the British Commonwealth for all purposes.

At an early date in the new year, Parliament would be summoned and the proposals would be submitted. Lord Birkenhead hoped they would meet with the assent of Parliament, but if they did not, an early opportunity would be taken of ascertaining the views of the people. With all the difficulties, he hoped they were about to carry this great and priceless vessel into harbor.

MR. HARDING MAY GET TARIFF POWER

Bill to Grant Wide Discretionary Authority to the Executive Is Offered by Senator Smoot Following Annual Message

Special to The Christian Science Monitor from its Washington News Office

WASHINGTON, District of Columbia — Reed Smoot (R.), Senator from Utah, introduced in the Senate yesterday amendments to the tariff bill designed to carry out the President's proposal with reference to the American valuation plan and his recommendation that he be given discretionary power to proclaim elastic rates quickly responsive to changing conditions in competition and foreign exchange.

They were introduced on behalf of the Senate Finance Committee and will be considered by it in connection with its hearings on the tariff which are to be resumed today.

In the case of dutiable merchandise from a country whose currency has depreciated more than 5 per cent, Senator Smoot proposes that the President shall by proclamation levy equalizing duties not to exceed 50 per cent of the value of the respective imported articles, provided he shall modify them or take them off when the occasion arises.

Another amendment authorizes the President to change duties so as to equalize any difference he may find to exist in favor of foreign producers in marketing products in the United States, within 30 days, by an increase or a decrease not exceeding 50 per cent of the rates provided in the tariff act.

The President also would be authorized, through the United States Tariff Commission, to investigate all phases and conditions affecting competition.

As regards American valuation, the amendment reads:

"That in case of merchandise which is subject to an ad valorem duty or to a duty based upon or regulated in any manner by the value thereof, if the President shall find by reason of the depreciation of the currency or other unstable conditions in the country of origin of such merchandise that the value as defined in section 402, title 4, of this act, is not a certain basis for the assessment of duties he may direct and proclaim that any ad valorem rate of duty or any rate based upon or regulated in any manner by the value of such merchandise shall be levied, collected and paid upon the wholesale selling price of such or similar products in the principal market or markets of the United States at the time of exportation of the imported merchandise: provided, however, that in such cases said duties may be increased or decreased in accordance with section 1 and 30 days after the date of such proclamation such imported merchandise shall be thus valued for the purpose of the assessment of duties."

LIBERALS CARRY CANADIAN ELECTION

Returns Show Sweeping Victory Against the Meighen Government, Premier Being Defeated in His Own Constituency

United Press via The Christian Science Monitor Leased Wires

MONTREAL, Quebec — Incomplete returns in yesterday's general election in Canada showed a large majority against the Meighen Government. In the Prime Minister's own district in Manitoba, the voting gave a majority of about 800 to Henry Lauder, the Farmer candidate. The Cabinet was crumbling as returns came in from districts where the Premier's advisers were running, nine of them having fallen in the east and, with the Farmers taking a considerable number of seats in western provinces, it looked as if the Cabinet would be almost entirely wiped out.

W. Mackenzie King, leader of the Liberals, was elected in his district, North York, in Ontario. T. A. Crerar, leader of the new farmers' party, was elected in Manitoba, and the returns showed that eight of the 16 seats in that Province had gone to the agrarian party.

Sir Lomer Gouin, formerly Premier of Quebec, won his contest in Montreal. Every one of the 65 seats in Quebec were won by Liberals, Hon. C. C. Ballantyne, Minister of Marine and Fisheries in the Meighen Cabinet and sponsor of the Canadian merchant marine, being defeated by H. C. Marler, a Montreal notary.

Miss A. MacPhail of Ontario is the first woman elected, according to returns so far. She ran on the farmers' ticket. Prince Edward Island went solidly Liberal, all four seats going to candidates of that party.

Of 235 seats in the House, the Liberals have won 103, according to returns at the time of writing, the Farmers 17, government 42, Labor 2, Independent 1.

In the 1917 election the government won 153 seats while the opposition took 82.

United Press via The Christian Science Monitor Leased Wires

OTTAWA, Ontario—Early returns of the federal election give the Liberal Party the majority of seats, swamping out the government party with its solid Quebec Liberal vote. The Progressive Farmers are sweeping the Prairie Provinces and will likely be the second party in the House.

ALLIED EFFORTS FOR PEACE IN NEAR EAST

Special cable to The Christian Science Monitor from its correspondent in Paris

PARIS, France (Tuesday)—The date and place of the proposed conference on the Greco-Turkish conflict expected this week was not known late this afternoon. But Aristide Briand has discussed the matter with Lord Harding, the British Ambassador. There is in Paris, Ferid Bey, representative of the Angora Government.

Mr. Briand, Lord Curzon and the Italian delegate will be the principal figures in the conferences which will discuss the whole problem of the Near East, the Sèvres Treaty, the Angora pact and the prospect of general peace through the mediation of the Allies. It is the French wish to confine the conversations to these matters, but nevertheless an opportunity may be taken to discuss other urgent questions such as Germany's capacity to pay her debts.

PHILIPPINE REPORT ACCEPTED

WASHINGTON, District of Columbia—President Harding is understood to have accepted the conclusions and recommendation of the Wood-Forbes mission, which studied conditions in the Philippine Islands and recently submitted a report.

THE CHRISTIAN SCIENCE MONITOR

AN INTERNATIONAL DAILY NEWSPAPER

Published daily, except Sundays, by The Christian Science Publishing Society, 107 Falmouth Street, Boston, Mass. Subscription price, payable in advance, postpaid to all countries: One year, $9.00; six months, $5.00; three months, $3.00; one month, $1.10.

Entered at second-class rates at the Post Office at Boston, Mass., U. S. A. Acceptance for mailing at a special rate of postage provided for in section 1103, Act of October 3, 1917, authorized on July 11, 1918.

INDEX FOR DECEMBER 7, 1921

SHANTUNG DISCUSSIONS REVEAL WIDE SEPARATION BETWEEN VIEWPOINTS OF CHINESE AND JAPANESE DELEGATIONS

Failure to Make Marked Progress Toward a Settlement Causes Suspicion in Representatives of China as to Power of the Conference Formulas to Turn Into Concrete Benefits Promises Carried on the Surface

SAYINGS OF THE CONFERENCE

"When what the Prime Minister is pleased to call the President's clarion call to humanity went out, the first to respond were the English-speaking peoples on our northern border and across the sea."—John W. Davis, president of the American branch of the English-Speaking Union.

"I hope and believe that the international cooperation toward which all these powers are honestly working with the United States for a common end is going to be a prelude to other international actions directed with equal genius and equal unselfishness." —Arthur James Balfour.

"We should stress our belief in the vital necessity for the Christians of the world, at this time, to unite their efforts in rendering every possible service toward making the Conference successful."—From a statement by the Congregational Churches of Japan.

The Christian Science Monitor News Service. Copyright, 1921.

WASHINGTON, Tuesday Night — There is an unpleasant suspicion of truth in Dr. Tyau's charge that so far the Conference has produced nothing but negative results so far as China is concerned. Some excellent principles, he declares, have been submitted to the sub-committees, where they have been most successfully tied up. As a result, the sovereign rights of China are persistently ignored. What China ought to claim, he insists, is not merely restoration of her rights in the present, but an indemnity for the past. Dr. Tyau puts into words what a good many people no doubt are thinking, and backs his words with his resignation as secretary-general to the Chinese delegation. But Dr. Sze and Dr. Koo have greater responsibilities, and cannot rid themselves of them so easily. Still it would be interesting to hear candidly just what they think about it.

Take, for instance, the statement issued by Mr. Hanihara on the subject of Shantung. Mr. Hanihara is of the opinion that Japan has been remarkably generous in the matter. He thinks, indeed, that the Japanese have gone further than the Americans or British would have gone. Now, incidentally, what Great Britain or the United States would have done in the matter is nothing whatever to the point, the point is, What has Japan done? Japan coming into the war proceeded, by a very simple, and not in the least costly, military operation, to oust Germany from the Kiaochow enclave, an operation she would never have dreamed of attempting if Germany had not been fighting for her life in Europe. Having expelled Germany, owing to these circumstances, Japan demands compensation. But from whom? Why, from one of her own allies in the war, China. No doubt Japan would argue that what she is claiming are rights which she acquired by conquest from Germany. But, first, the Kiaochow concession was a non-transferable concession: it was to Germany, and to nobody else. And, in the second place, the prospect opened up by the claim of conquest leads to immense possibilities.

In the conquest of Kiaochow, a British force was associated with the Japanese, therefore Great Britain could equally claim rights in Shantung. Then imagine what would happen if each of the allies had claimed their particular conquests in the war as their peculiar property. There would have been no need to have issued a mandate for German Southeast Africa, and Palestine would have become a British province. Of course, the Treaty of Versailles passed over Kiaochow to Japan, but this was done with China protesting and declining to sign. On the whole, perhaps, the less attention Japan draws to her sacrifices and rewards in Kiaochow the better. They are far too like most of the methods by which China has been deprived of territorial and economic rights in the past.

As for Mr. Hanihara's argument that Japan could not possibly be holding the forty millions of Chinese in Shantung in subjection by means of the 2700 troops engaged in policing the railway, nobody can know better than he does that this is absurd. What Japan is protecting with these 2700 men is all the claims she has made in Shantung, and she is manifestly protecting these claims against the 40,000,000 who, if they safely could, would certainly throw the 2700 into the sea tomorrow. What does Mr. Hanihara suppose Rome held her empire with? The number of legionaires under arms, or the knowledge of what would follow an attempt at revolt? How does Great Britain keep peace amongst the warring elements of the Indian Empire today? By the employment of a few thousand bayonets, or by the knowledge of the power behind them? Mr. Hanihara has only got to tell the Chinese in Shantung that they have nothing to fear but the presence of 2700 Japanese troops on the railway, and the Shantung question will be solved for him in an afternoon.

Shantung Sessions Continue

Chinese and Japanese Seem Far Apart in Viewpoint

Special to The Christian Science Monitor from its Washington News Office

WASHINGTON, District of Columbia —Shantung and the shadow of Versailles hung over the Conference on Limitation of Armament yesterday. Several sessions of Japanese and Chinese delegates appointed to settle the vexed controversy outside the Conference have come and gone, and so far as can be ascertained the two sets of conferees are as far apart as ever on the fundamental issues at stake.

The failure of the two delegations to make any material progress toward a settlement has materially increased the suspicion and apprehension which has invaded the Chinese delegation as to the futility of the efforts of the powers toward solving the problem of China and the extent to which the formulas adopted by the Conference carry concrete benefits proportionate to their surface promises.

Japan Concedes Little

The dissatisfied element is not confined to the Chinese officials who have left the Conference. Others who must see it out agree that much that is conceded by the powers is merely a shell while the kernel is being retained by the powers that possess it now.

Not much more, it is contended, can be said for the maximum of concession that the Japanese delegation is willing to make on the question of Shantung. That it should be left to be decided outside the Conference with American and British representatives in the rôle of advisers was the only way that the Conference leaders could see, in view of the fact that seven of the powers participating in the Conference are signatories to the Treaty of Versailles.

Up to the present time the Japanese delegation has not gone beyond the proposals made to China on several occasions heretofore and which were invariably regarded as an inacceptable basis of settlement. Japan is willing to concede to China everything in the leased territory except the material resources on which the economic life of the region in great part depends, that is the railroad and the mining projects.

The retaining of a half interest in these and possibly also in other public property in the leased zones, such as telephones and water works, will in all probability be insisted upon. The restoration of the latter class of property to China was discussed at yesterday's session of the two delegations, but the brevity and baldness of the communiqué indicated that no real progress has been made.

Half Interest to Be Kept

Masanao Hanihara, one of the Japanese delegates, at the conference with the press yesterday took the position again that Japan, in only retaining a half interest in the railroads and the mining developments, is giving to China one-half of what actually belongs to Japan by right of conquest and under the terms of the Versailles Treaty. Mr. Hanihara did not state this in so many words, but there is no doubt that Japan is proceeding on the assumption that she is giving something to China for nothing, rather than on the assumption that she is withholding from China something that belongs to the latter.

Whatever changes may come in Japan's attitude as the conference between the two delegations proceeds, there is no doubt whatever that Japan's delegates went into the conference with the determination to stand pat on the question of retaining a half interest in the railroads and the mines of the leased territory. It was on this very proposition that negotiations between Peking and Tokyo broke down before, and the showdown in the present instance is expected when this question is broached. The effort now is to postpone it while the two delegations are discussing other matters which are less vital to a solution.

No Time Limit Set

In their claim for a half interest in the railroad and the mining properties the Tokyo Government has specified no time limit during which the right demanded should extend. Failure to specify such a limit, the Chinese contend, is in direct conflict with one of the demands made by China at the opening of the Conference, namely, that a definite duration should be fixed for claims and concessions which otherwise bid well to extend into perpetuity.

Mr. Hanihara said yesterday that the matter of duration of Japanese claims had not been discussed and that he could not say at this stage whether or not they would be in perpetuity. This same official indicated that although Japan is mainly inter-

THE CHRISTIAN SCIENCE MONITOR

AN INTERNATIONAL DAILY NEWSPAPER

FIVE CENTS | Copyright 1921 by The Christian Science Publishing Society | BOSTON, U.S.A., TUESDAY, DECEMBER 13, 1921 | Fourteen Pages | VOL. XIV, NO. 16

INDIAN GOVERNMENT TAKES FIRM ACTION AGAINST SEDITION

As a Result of Determination That Peaceful Citizens Shall Be Protected Many Agitators Have Recently Been Arrested

Special cable to The Christian Science Monitor from its European News Office

LONDON, England (Monday)—As a direct result of the firm attitude now adopted by the Government of India many arrests have recently taken place of Extremist leaders, owners and editors of Indian newspapers advocating sedition. Among these the noted Extremist leader, Pundit Moti Lal Nehru, has been arrested at Allahabad, also his son and nephew, the latter being manager of The Independent.

For some time The Independent has been carrying on violent propaganda against the Government of India and, despite numerous cautions, refused to moderate its tone. C. R. Das, president-elect of the Indian National Congress and a prominent attorney who gave up his practice in compliance with Mahatma Gandhi's program, was arrested on Saturday morning. The Government of India some days ago proclaimed various non-cooperative associations.

In its determination that peaceful citizens shall be protected, the government has caused arrests during the last few days numbering, according to various estimates, from 260 to 600. Within the last two weeks the government has brought into force "The Prevention of Seditious Meetings Act, 1911"; also the "Criminal Law, Part II, Amendment Act, 1908." These laws have been put into effect in various districts where it was deemed necessary with the result that disturbing factors have been quickly brought to book.

Editors Arrested

The editor of "India" has also come under the notice of the government and has been arrested. This vigorous policy has had the effect of rousing the more moderate inhabitants to organize themselves into bodies with the object of combating the efforts of the Extremists to incite people to violence. Another editor named Lalla Lajpat Rai, who was chiefly notorious for his endeavor to stir up feeling in America during the war against British rule in India, has also been arrested.

It is significant that disturbances in the majority of cases have taken place in British India. Very little scope has been given for that kind of work in Indian provinces which are ruled by native princes. The bare facts are that Indian princes will allow the Extremists no latitude within the sphere of their influence, and any action on the part of non-cooperators or other disturbers of the peace is quickly and not infrequently summarily dealt with.

Considerable criticism has been leveled at the Government of India for not adopting similar action. It is pointed out that it is traditional of British rule that the natives of India should be given every opportunity to express themselves by speech and action, provided the latter remained within reasonable bounds.

Owing to the violent action of the few which culminated in riots in Bombay, the Government of India has determined that coercive acts on the part of non-cooperators and Caliphate agitators must be stopped. Little has been heard of late regarding Mr. Gandhi, leader of the non-cooperators' movement, and the Prince of Wales' visit to Lucknow where he arrived on Friday has passed off successfully. Prearranged protest meetings and a strike planned by the non-cooperatives to show Indian feeling against Great Britain came to nothing.

Caliphate Movement

It remains to be seen whether Mr. Gandhi has learnt his lesson from the fatal acts of his followers in Bombay. These violent measures on the occasion of the Prince's visit it is considered did more harm to Mr. Gandhi's cause than all his previous attempts to embarrass the government of the country.

The main cause of the disturbance in India today is the question of the Caliphate. Though the Ali brothers' arrest has to a great extent quietened the more violent sections, there still remains an impression that Great Britain is not friendly toward the Muhammadan population. The reason for this feeling arises from the subtle propaganda regarding the Greco-Turkish conflict, and not until peace in Asia Minor is concluded will it be possible to arrest the discontent of the Muhammadan people in India.

The Afghan treaty has done much toward easing the situation, but anxiety will continue until this disturbing factor in the Near East has been removed. Over 70,000,000 people in India are concerned in what is called the Caliphate question, and the Government of India sees little hope for a real settlement of the country before their confidence in the British attitude can be restored.

Of course Kemalist agitators and Kemalist funds are greatly responsible for creating the feeling that Great Britain as a great Muhammadan power in refusing support to the Turks, is not true to her trust. It is of little account to the native mind that such support is also refused to the Greek forces.

Meantime the Prince's visit will do much to create good feeling among more moderate Indians; the enthusiasm with which he is being everywhere received will go far toward dispelling many disturbing factors in India.

BRITISH COAL WINS AMERICAN MARKET

Commerce Officials Point Out Competition Has Extended From a Fight to Hold Foreign Customers to Those at Home

Special to The Christian Science Monitor from its Washington News Office

WASHINGTON, District of Columbia—Six months ago concern was being expressed by coal experts and government officials because American coal was being pushed out of certain European and South American markets by the competition of cheaper British fuel. High officials of the Department of Commerce pointed out yesterday that this competition has grown to such an extent that the coal interests of the United States are having to fight not only to keep a grip on the foreign markets, but actually to maintain their control of the markets on the Atlantic seaboard.

Indications of the weakened position of this country in the coal trade of the world, it was pointed out, have become increasingly frequent since the rapid recovery of British coal production following the strike in the English mines last summer. As early as August, 1921, it was noted that American coal was being underbid in price in the northwestern European market and in the Mediterranean, Scandinavian and Baltic markets. The British, due to shipping conditions, being able to secure return cargo, were also placed in a position of advantage in one of the most promising American markets for export trade, South America.

It appears now, in the opinion of Commerce Department officials, that American dealers may lose a considerable part of trade along the Atlantic seaboard unless they are enabled to lower their prices to meet British competition, having lost a great number of their foreign markets, chiefly in the Boston and New York markets. Ships which formerly sought American coal are now doing their bunkering elsewhere. It has recently been noted that British interests are outbidding American dealers in the West Indies. In short they are faced by a serious prospect, that of being pushed out of domestic as well as foreign markets.

The reason, according to officials, is that American coal production is still on a war basis as to costs of mining and transportation, while English mines are practically back to a 1913 basis.

LARGE TRACTS OF OIL LANDS SOLD IN MEXICO

Special to The Christian Science Monitor from its Pacific Coast News Office

SAN FRANCISCO, California—Large purchases of oil lands and leases on other extensive tracts are reported by the Department of Commerce and Industry of the Mexican national government in the last issue of the "Diario Oficial." Three states are involved in these purchases and leases, Hidalgo, Tamaulipas and Nuevo Leon, and much of the territory is in unproven sections of the oil belt, which is commonly supposed to extend from an inland point on the Rio Grande, in the north of Mexico, to the peninsula of Yucatan, in the extreme southeastern portion of that Republic.

According to this report, the Corona Company has bought 198,000 acres just east of Monterey, in the State of Nuevo Leon. This is the farthest inland of all the land on which drilling for oil is now proceeding in Mexico. The International, Huasteca, and Transcontinental companies jointly have purchased 128,000 acres in the State of Tamaulipas, 9000 in the State of Hidalgo, and 4000 in Nuevo Leon.

The Texas Oil Company has purchased 228,000 acres in unproven territory in the State of Nuevo Leon. The International and the Oriental companies have taken leases on 205,000 acres in the Chintepec, Zacallanguia, and Jojutla districts in the State of Hidalgo. Permission to drill 54 wells was asked and obtained by 32 companies during November.

RAILROAD OFFICIALS OPPOSE PENDING BILLS

WASHINGTON, District of Columbia—Daniel Willard, president of the Baltimore & Ohia Railroad, and Alfred E. Thom, counsel for the National Association of Railway Executives, appeared yesterday before the Senate Interstate Commerce Committee, in opposition to pending legislation designed to repeal provisions of the Transportation Act, which are said to curtail rate-making authority of state commissions.

The proposed legislation, Mr. Willard said, would lead to absolute failure of the Transportation Act, which he commended as important constructive legislation which has not yet been given a fair trial.

Mr. Willard said the only alternative to the Transportation Act was government ownership. The pending bills, he added, would prevent the railroads from securing sufficient funds to provide facilities of transportation demanded by the public.

EXTENSION WORK FREEDOM PLANNED

Assistant Secretary of the United States Department of Agriculture Tells of Federal Efforts in Aid of the Farmers

Special to The Christian Science Monitor

AMHERST, Massachusetts—Greater administrative freedom for extension work in each state is expected to result from the reorganization now taking place in the United States Department of Agriculture, said C. W. Pugsley, Assistant Secretary of Agriculture, in an address before the annual conferences of county agents and extension workers at the Massachusetts Agricultural College.

The reorganization is a step for a unified community program in extension work, he said. It will do away with the division along the line of age and sex and make it possible for a development of extension work in each state according to the method most needed there. The old organization of the Department of Agriculture so far as it concerns state and national extension work has hindered this united program for agricultural improvement, he continued. The reorganization does not mean that any change will be necessary in the state systems of extension teaching but merely means that each state may have greater freedom in assisting communities for better farm life.

Extension Idea Traced

Mr. Pugsley traced the history of the extension idea in agricultural teaching from the early instruction at fair meetings through the era of agricultural trains and institutes when, as he put it, "the agricultural speakers got into town on one train, gave a blunderbuss talk and got out of town on the next train, before anyone could ask them any questions." Then came the movable school which brought specialized instruction to the community. "But the specialists only stayed a week and then left never to return. The United States Department of Agriculture finally developed a system of permanent county agents, and it was the original intent of the department to place a specialist in each county who could take care of every possible problem in agriculture.

"It soon became apparent that the county agent could not be a specialist on all subjects and the need for a central force of specialists at the agricultural college to be on call in the counties has been filled.

"The new office of extension work will have three divisions, first a project division where economists will gather the facts of the international situation in agriculture and illuminate these facts to provide intelligent guidance in the formation of extension programs. Such an office is needed so that the stimulus inevitably given to agricultural production by extension work may be based on the economic needs of the world. For instance, we need some office to tell extension directors that next year's corn crop can be 20 per cent perhaps less than this year's and meet all world needs. Both the corn growers and the rest of us will profit by the use of the land and labor so saved for other production. This office, too, will advise as to the proper division of funds between work for farmers, for home makers and for boys and girls in each community. The department believes that all members of the family must be working for a better farm life in order to bring it about.

Results of Research Work

"The second division is concerned with the $30,000,000 to $40,000,000 a year the department spends on research work. It will be the duty of this office to make the results of that research of the greatest use in extension work.

"The third division is one of organization, composed of specialists to assist state extension workers in organizing their field work."

Among the important projects accepted to guide the extension teaching of the year were farm management surveys; soil fertility demonstrations; an orchard development program to include better orchard management and improvement of nursery stock; the development of fruit manufactures; and the construction of more fruit storage facilities.

To promote better farm management, farm tours to successful farms will be held, and good farmers will be urged to keep production records of both crops and dairying which will be summarized and placed at the disposal of the county agents for study to determine the factors influencing farm profits. Each county agent agreed to accept a project to devote one week to a survey of the typical farming area in this county, the records gathered to be summarized by the Agricultural College.

NEW GREEK PATRIARCH OPPOSED

LONDON, England (Sunday)—The Greek Government announces its intention not to recognize the Most Reverend Meletois Metaxakis, the newly-elected Patriarch of the Greek Orthodox Church in Constantinople, says a Reuter dispatch from Athens. It also announces the breaking off of relations with the patriarchcate in the belief that the patriarchs of Jerusalem, Alexandria and Antioch and the metropolitans in the newly annexed territory will do likewise.

FRANCO-TURKISH TREATY PUBLISHED

Special cable to The Christian Science Monitor from its European News Office

LONDON, England (Monday)—A copy of the Franco-Turkish agreement on Cilicia was published here tonight. The usual formalities as to the state of war ceasing, release of prisoners of war, withdrawal of troops and the granting of complete amnesty are set forth in the preliminary articles of the agreement, also a special administrative régime for the district of Alexandretta and fixing of the frontier line.

By article 10 the government of the Grand National Assembly of Turkey agrees to the transfer of the concession of the section of the Baghdad railway between Bozanti and Nisibin, as well as of the several branches constructed in the vilayet of Adana, to a French group nominated by the French Government. A mixed commission, according to another article, was to be constituted with a view to concluding a customs convention between Turkey and Syria; while Aleppo was authorized to obtain a water supply from the Euphrates in Turkish territory.

FRANCE SOUNDING BELGIAN OPINION

Mr. Loucheur Consults With Belgium's Minister of Finance—Views Expected to Agree on the January Payments

Special cable to The Christian Science Monitor from its correspondent in Paris

PARIS, France (Monday)—While René Viviani in a telegram to Aristide Briand confirms the statement that he will leave Washington on Wednesday next, there is much kite-flying respecting the new conference at Washington. The suggestion is received in France with considerable reserve. If the proposal really comes from the American Government there is little doubt that France will accept once more to participate in an international meeting so far off, but it is nevertheless pointed out that Mr. Briand has only just returned after a prolonged absence and has duties at home which he should now perform. There is skepticism about the reality of such a gathering. It is represented that this hint of a conference is inspired by Mr. Lloyd George who now has his hands free of Irish affairs, and is ambitious of settling even greater problems in obtaining the influence of America for the forwarding of his views.

The Washington Conference on the Pacific question has been so successful that it is felt in some quarters that the great economic problems of the world, reparations, fluctuations of the rate of exchange, excessive fiduciary circulation, inter-allied debts, unemployment and even the enigma of Russia might well be considered in a world congress.

When Mr. Briand goes to London for conversations with Mr. Lloyd George, it is not improbable that something will be said concerning the possibility of convening, either in Europe or in America, such a congress, to which, it is believed, the Washington Government would not be unfavorable. But it is not thought possible that Mr. Briand will accept the suggestion of leaving at once.

British diplomacy, rightly or wrongly, is extremely anxious to settle once for all the problems which are of vital importance, and their settlement is becoming increasingly difficult without the cooperation of America. At least it is held to be desirable that they should take place under the auspices of America, who assuredly has direct interest in whatever may be decided.

But France, as already asserted by the correspondent of The Christian Science Monitor, could not allow her claims to be reduced under some sort of moral coercion, and it is inevitable that this proposal should either not be taken seriously or should be regarded with suspicion. In fact caution will be shown by Mr. Briand in the London conversations.

There is a wish to preserve the entente and to find some common policy, but a common policy cannot be found if France is asked to forgo her rightful cred'ts on Germany. This feeling dominates all others. Fresh concessions would have serious consequences, and if England chooses to forgo her own demands on Germany, France asks that her share of the indemnity shall be respected as a special and prior payment which has become necessary.

Belgium in these negotiations is largely on the side of France. Louis Loucheur is today engaged in conversations with Mr. Theunis, the Belgian Minister of France at Brussels, and Belgian support will almost certainly be accorded France since an immediate moratorium would suppress the January payments, which by virtue of the recognized priority should go to Belgium.

Where the attitude of Belgium is more doubtful is or the Wiesbaden accord, which, unless precautions are taken, might divert to France payments due to the rest of the Allies. The need of an exchange of views is therefore clear, and the Loucheur-Theunis conversations will partly determine the issue of the Briand-Lloyd George conversations next week.

ULSTER OPPOSES IRISH AGREEMENT

Sir James Craig Declares the People Feel Chiefly About the Question of Finance and Proposed Boundary Commission

Special cable to The Christian Science Monitor from its European News Office

BELFAST, Ireland (Monday)—Speaking in the Northern Parliament this afternoon, Sir James Craig, the Ulster Premier, accused Mr. Lloyd George of breach of faith in connection with the Irish treaty. He stated that Ulster was not included in the treaty. They were not invited to sign. In conformity with Ulster's attitude throughout they refused to interfere with any attempt to determine a settlement between Sinn Fein and the British Government, but they reserved to themselves the right to go into the conference with the British Prime Minister where Ulster's rights and privileges became affected.

Mr. Lloyd George had given him a statement which he had read a short while ago that Ulster's rights and privileges would be neither sacrificed nor prejudiced. He accused Mr. Lloyd George of a breach of the pledge.

Sir James advised his hearers, however strongly they might feel on the subject, to take no action which would not be constitutional, and recommended them to leave their interests at present in the hands of their representatives in the Imperial Parliament. Ulster, he said, felt principally on two points—finance and the proposed boundary commission. He did not want to anticipate the arguments that would be used in the Imperial House of Commons upon these heads.

Sir James recommended the Ulster people to maintain their dignified attitude of calm and courage and hopeful optimism, because they had triumphed in the past over many great difficulties. He asked them to trust their leaders.

On Sir James' arrival this morning he met the members of the North Ireland Cabinet at his Belfast residence. Afterward he presided at an adjourned party meeting of the Ulster Unionists held at the old Town Hall. The meeting lasted two hours, and the official statement issued at the close merely announced that Sir James Craig made a detailed statement on the situation.

It is understood, however, that Mr. Lloyd George has made no concessions to Ulster on finance or boundary questions. The general impression is that his attitude amounts to this: "There are the terms. You can take them or leave them."

Ireland's Honor Not Involved

Special cable to The Christian Science Monitor from its European News Office

DUBLIN, Ireland (Monday)—Eamon de Valera issued the following statement here today. "I have been asked whether the honor of Ireland is not involved in the ratification of the agreement arrived at. The honor of Ireland is not involved. The plenipotentiaries were sent on the distinct understanding that any agreement they made was subject to ratification by Dail Eireann and by the country, and could be rejected by Dail Eireann if it did not commend itself to the Dail, or by the country if it did not commend itself to the country.

"The Parliament of Britain and the people of Britain will on their side similarly consider the agreement solely on its merits. If the British Parliament desires, it can reject it; so can the British people. Ratification is then no mere empty formality. The United States refused to ratify a treaty signed even by the President. The honor of the nation is not involved, unless and until the treaty is ratified."

Special cable to The Christian Science Monitor from its European News Office

DUBLIN, Ireland (Monday)—Eamon de Valera had conversations with Arthur Griffith, Erskine Childers, E. J. Duggan, Alderman Cosgrave and R. C. Barton at the Mansion House here today.

YAP AGREEMENT REACHED BETWEEN UNITED STATES AND JAPANESE—EVE OF AN ANNOUNCEMENT ON NAVAL RATIO

Pacific Isle to Be Governed From Tokyo With Two Countries Guaranteed Equal Cable Privileges and Americans' Right to a Radio Station Suspended While Japanese Give Satisfactory Service—Senate in Lively Debate

SAYINGS OF THE CONFERENCE

"We make the experiment here in this treaty of trying to assure peace in that immense region by trusting the preservation of its tranquillity to the good faith of the nations responsible for it."—Henry Cabot Lodge, Senator from Massachusetts.

"In the name of the Government of the French Republic, whose authority I am borrowing now, and who speaks through my voice, I am glad to bring here, in its full amplitude, without any reticence or any reservations, our full adhesion to the pact that has just been read."—René Viviani.

"I want to seize this opportunity to state that I feel that in my country, Holland, this treaty will be received with great sympathy."—H. A. van Karnebeek delegate from Holland.

"Any measure aiming to the creation of guaranties for the safeguarding of peace in the world cannot but meet with our fullest consent."—Senator Schanzer, delegate from Italy.

The Christian Science Monitor News Service. Copyright, 1921.

WASHINGTON, Monday Night—After the field day of Saturday the delegates have retired to their committee rooms, and the next phase of the proceedings is there being hammered out. The points of immediate interest are the naval ratio and Shantung, and after these the question of fortifications in the Pacific. It is in such circumstances that the Japanese passion for keeping half a dozen different issues going at the same time is seen most clearly. The Westerner could settle the question of the naval ratio on its merits. Not so the Japanese. He sees the reaction of the settlement in a thousand microscopic ways, and finds an entanglement with another decision where to the Western mind none exists. Take, as an example, the naval ratio. To the Western mind if the ratio of limitation is maintained on the present averages no power can be any worse off than it is today. Therefore it is difficult to see what this has to do with the question of the Pacific defenses, which question will have eventually to be settled on a basis of equality for all. None the less, the Japanese mind can find a point of entanglement.

As a matter of fact the point at which an argument could be raised on the subject would be of the ability of the nations, in the immediate future, to undertake building programs in competition. But this competition is purely a question of finance. It has no limitation whatever save the power of the purse. Reduced to this Japan has no hope whatever of outstripping either Great Britain or the United States and there are no other powers in the competition. Therefore, from the Western point of view, it matters not one atom in fixing the naval ratio what may be decided with regard to fortifications in the Pacific. If, as just at the moment is conceived probable, the determination is taken to extend the naval holiday to the building of fortifications, the status quo will be preserved as in the building of capital ships. But even if the nations agreed to go on building fortifications, each at their good pleasure, what reaction could that possibly have on the building of fleets, if the naval holiday is to take place; whilst, on the other hand, if the fortifications are to remain stationary why should that affect the naval holiday or the naval ratio?

Even more distinct is the question of Shantung. The question of Shantung has now resolved itself, as was pointed out in this service a few days ago, into a matter of compensation. The Japanese are steadily becoming more amenable to the Chinese view of this subject. They realize that the claim to perpetual rights in the railways and mines of the German concessions is a discredited one and that the Chinese offer of liberal compensation for expenditures actually made in the development of the concession is all they are morally entitled to. To claim more than this would be approaching too dangerously close to the methods of the mailed fist to be good diplomacy, and there appears, therefore to be every chance of the matter being worked out on the basis of the Chinese proposal. If Japan should evacuate Shantung through such an agreement, and France and Great Britain should evacuate the concessions made to them as a consequence of the Shantung concession, something would really have been done toward freeing China. There will remain, of course, the much older concession of Hong Kong and the much more dangerous concessions in Manchuria. But if a beginning is made within the Great Wall, an extension may be made outside later on. As a matter of fact, the original Manchurian concession expires in 1925, and the validity of the ninety-nine years extension is seriously in dispute, and presents a question which will have to be faced separately.

Yap Agreement Reached

Negotiations Began Last June Result in Complete Understanding

Special to The Christian Science Monitor from its Washington News Office

WASHINGTON, District of Columbia—Negotiations which have been under way between the United States and Japan since last June have finally resulted in a mutual agreement regarding Yap and other mandated islands of the Pacific Ocean lying north of the Equator. The terms of this agreement were made public by the Secretary of State yesterday, with the explanation that the rights of the United States in regard to these islands were now fully protected.

In this case, as in others now being dealt with, the rights of the powers signatory to the Versailles Treaty were specifically defined, but the protection thus secured to them did not run to the United States and it was therefore necessary to enter upon a special treaty in order that the United States might have her full share of cable privileges and that no discrimination might lie against the United States.

It was further explained that the islands to the north of the Equator were in a different category from those lying to the south, most of which belong to the British Empire.

Japan Granted Mandate

By the agreement reached yesterday the controversy between the United States and Japan, which at one time threatened to reach dimensions out of all proportion to the size of the island, becomes extinct. The trouble arose over the action of the Supreme Council in May, 1919, giving Japan a mandate over Yap. Mr. Wilson claimed to have made specific reservations concerning Yap, but aside from that, Mr. Hughes contended that the United States had never vested the Supreme Council or the League of Nations with authority to bind the United States and that the right accruing to the United States through its participation in the war could not be ceded to Japan or to any other power except by treaty, and that no such treaty had been made.

There was considerable talk in the Senate, some of it behind closed doors, to the effect that the Yap incident pointed the way to the necessity for a stronger navy in the Pacific.

With a peaceful settlement of the Yap question, the approaching agreement on the naval situation and the gradual working together of the influences that tend to remove causes of irritation in the Far East, the spokesman for the American delegation yesterday again indicated that real progress is being made at the Conference on Limitation of Armament.

Mr. Hughes' Announcement

The announcement made by the Secretary of State, Mr. Hughes, yesterday, was as follows:

"The United States and Japan have reached an agreement with respect to the Island of Yap and the other mandated islands in the Pacific Ocean, north of the Equator. The negotiations have been in progress since last June and the terms of settlement were almost entirely agreed upon before the meeting of the Conference on Limitation of Armament. The last steps in the negotiations now have been taken. The points of the agreement are as follows:

"1. It is agreed that the United States shall have free access to the Island of Yap on the footing of entire equality with Japan or any other na-

THE CHRISTIAN SCIENCE MONITOR

AN INTERNATIONAL DAILY NEWSPAPER

Published daily, except Sundays, by The Christian Science Publishing Society, 107 Falmouth Street, Boston, Mass. Subscription price, payable in advance, postpaid to all countries: One year, $9.00; six months, $5.00; three months, $3.00; one month, $1.10.

Entered at second-class rates at the Post Office at Boston, Mass., U. S. A. Acceptance for mailing at a special rate of postage provided for in section 1103, Act of October 3, 1917, authorized on July 11, 1918.

INDEX FOR DECEMBER 13, 1921

THE CHRISTIAN SCIENCE MONITOR

AN INTERNATIONAL DAILY NEWSPAPER

THREE CENTS IN GREATER BOSTON
FIVE CENTS ELSEWHERE

Eighteen Pages

BOSTON, FRIDAY, MARCH 10, 1922—VOL. XIV, NO. 90

COPYRIGHT 1922 BY THE CHRISTIAN SCIENCE PUBLISHING SOCIETY

AMERICA DEMANDS $241,000,000 FOR TROOPS' EXPENSES

Rhineland Costs Come Before Reparations, Allies Are Informed

PARIS, March 10 (By the Associated Press)—A demand from the United States that $241,000,000 for its expenses in connection with the occupation of the Rhineland be paid before any reparations were paid was presented to the Allied Finance Ministers at their meeting this morning.

The distribution of this year's German payments, it was learned on good authority, already had been practically decided before the American note was received. The total was not to exceed 800,000,000 gold marks, and the ratio of sharing this amount was practically the same as was decided upon at the recent meeting of the Supreme Council at Cannes, which was a slight modification of the percentages worked out at the Spa conference.

According to this schedule France would receive 52 per cent of the payment and Great Britain 22 per cent. The appraised value of the Saar Valley coal mines, estimated at 300,000,000 gold marks, being charged against France's receipts, this schedule would leave France about 35,000,000 gold marks.

WASHINGTON, March 10 (By the Associated Press) — Charles Evans Hughes, Secretary of State, refused today to comment on the news from Paris that representatives of the United States had presented a demand to the Allied Finance Ministers that expenditures aggregating $241,000,000 sustained by the United States in the occupation of the Rhineland be paid before any reparations.

There was nothing that could be said on the subject at this time, Mr. Hughes declared.

Wiesbaden Agreement Being Reviewed at Paris

PARIS, March 10 (By the Associated Press)—The question of extending the scope of the Wiesbaden reparations agreement between France and Germany, to make Germany's payments in kind applicable to all the Allies, ocupied today's session of the meeting of Allied Finance Ministers who are here discussing the general subject of German reparations. Some such alteration of the Wiesbaden Accord, signed last year by Louis Loucheur and Dr. Walter Rathenau, was originally proposed at the recent meeting of the Supreme Council at Cannes.

The point at issue is the amount of deliveries Germany should make to France for the devastated regions, some of the Allies desiring to limit the amount to 900,000,000 gold marks' worth of material, so as to leave part of Germany's capacity for payments in kind available for the other Allies, Belgium, Italy and Great Britain.

SWEEPING REDUCTION OF WAGES IN BELGIUM

BRUSSELS, March 10—(By The Associated Press)—The Central Industrial Committee has decreed decreases in the salaries of workmen of all categories. The decree will immediately affect the miners, whose wages will be reduced 10 per cent, and the steel and iron workers, whose pay will be reduced 20 per cent. The present wage scale will be maintained provisionally in the textile industry, but decreases in pay will later be aplied to gas and electrical workers and other branches of industry and commerce.

The reduction in pay for the miners is equivalent to 6 francs per ton. The miners' union met today and decided not to accept the decree. It was considered probable that they would call a strike in protest.

CERTIFICATE BONUS PROPOSAL WORST YET, SAYS MR. BORAH

Senator From Idaho Declares Enactment of Such Bill Would Show Republican Party Had Suffered Moral Breakdown

WASHINGTON, March 10 (Special) Enactment of a soldier bonus bill on the basis of the latest proposal of a certificate issue, discountable at national banks, would be a signal to the nation that the Republican Party, placed in power by enormous majorities a little over a year ago, had suffered a "complete and ignominious moral breakdown," William E. Borah (R.), Senator from Idaho, declared in a statement to The Christian Science Monitor today.

Senator Borah is only one leader out of many in both Houses who believes that effort to put this scheme up to President Harding, compelling him to assume the responsibility of either signing or vetoing the legislation is an "iniquitous procedure" on the part of representatives of the people. He believes, however, that it is a "first step"—not really a sincere effort on the part of Congress to give the one-time service men a bonus.

"I sincerely think," said the Idaho senator, "that the latest plan proposed is much worse from a financial, and certainly from a moral, standpoint than anything that has hitherto been proposed. Certainly if we owe these boys a bonus there is a high and honorable way to meet it, but to turn them loose with a certificate which they may pawn and pledge and barter like, mendicants in the street is a shameless procedure which no self-respecting nation should brook for a moment. The very proposal is unbelievable. Of course, the truth is that it is not intended that the proposal should get further. It is merely a maneuver—a first step.

A Complete Breakdown

"If I thought Congress would pass such a measure, I would unhesitatingly conclude that the Republican Party had suffered a complete and ignominious moral breakdown which would shock the conscience of the country."

Condemnation by D. R. Crissinger, Comptroller of the Currency, of the insurance certificate scheme for financing the bonus as the "worst kind of frozen credit," aroused a great deal of criticism here, where Republican House leaders, on the eve of the Ways and Means Committee meeting, are making desperate efforts to check the rising tide of opposition to the new scheme for defraying bonus.

Aroused by what they term "uncalled-for interference" with the bonus arrangements by the Comptroller of the Currency, Republican leaders of the Ways and Means Committee are making ready to demand on the floor of the House the reasons for the Treasury official in giving out such a statement to the country. James A. Frear (R.), Representative from Wisconsin, for one, served notice that he

(Continued on Page 2, Column 1)

TREATY ADVOCATES REFUSE ARMISTICE

Administration Leaders Block Attempt to Delay Debate

WASHINGTON, March 10—A request to lay aside, temporarily, the Four-Power Pacific Treaty in the Senate today was blocked for the time being by Administration leaders, who insisted that the ratification debate continue.

Several senators had prepared addresses on a bill to reorganize the Federal Judiciary, but Senator Henry Cabot Lodge of Massachuetts, the Republican leader, declined to let that bill have the right of way.

The "Irreconcilables" indicated that they were not anxious to keep up the active offensive they began yesterday, several of them saying they preferred to postpone further discussion until they had heard the speech in support of the treaty to be made tomorrow by Senator Oscar W. Underwood, of Alabama, the Democratic leader. Senator H. W. Johnson (R.), of California, is expected to reply to him Monday.

Although the treaty remained as the actual business before the Senate, discusison at the beginning of today's session took little cognizance of it, ranging over a variety of subjects from Muscle Shoals to nominations of postmasters.

Renewing his charge that the four-power Pacific treaty was negotiated "secretly," Senator J. T. Robinson (D.) of Arkansas, declared on the Senate floor today that while the negotiations were in progress Charles E. Hughes, Secretary of State, as head of the American delegation, had misled newspaper correspondents and through them the press of the country by denying that he knew of any such scheme.

Correspondents who were assigned to the Conference, the Arkansas Senator asserted, not only were unable to obtain any authoritative information as to what was going on, but many of them suffered professionally

(Continued on Page 2, Column 4)

STRIKE ON RAND IN ACUTE STAGE

Circumstances Aggravated by Attack on Natives

JOHANNESBURG, Transvaal, Mar. 10 (By The Associated Press)—Martial law was proclaimed here today. Fighting between bands of strikers and the police has broken out in the entire extreme eastern section of the Rand.

LONDON, March 10 (Special Cable)—The increasingly serious situation on the Rand has resulted, The Christian Monitor learns from South African authorities here, in the calling up of six units of the civil defence force. Apart from defiance of the police authorities and intimidation of the whites the gravity of the circumstances are much aggravated by the wanton attack on the natives.

South African officials here view this new phase of the situation as a deliberate attempt to induce the natives to revolt. As the average ratio of colored labor, apart from that used in the mines, is three to one in the cities and seven to one outside, the danger of the new move is obvious. Europeans urgently demand martial law, but as this would be reckoned a Nationalist victory, General Smuts, the Premier, will not accede. Artillery, cavalry and infantry have been sent to assist in keeping order in Johannesburg and drastic steps are being taken to prevent further wanton shooting of natives by strikers.

The general strike called by the Industrial Federation has not been brought off, though drivers, stokers and guards have been intimidated into striking through threats of strikers to burn their homes. In Johannesburg, business is at a standstill, there being no light, trams or trains and public buildings are closed.

All efforts at reconciliation between the Industrial Federation and the Chamber of Mines have failed.

INDEX OF THE NEWS

FRANCE DEPLORES AMERICAN DECISION CONCERNING GENOA

Responsible Personage Voices Regret at America's Action but Maintains Confidence

PARIS, March 10 (Special Cable)—Extreme regret was expressed by a responsible personage at the decision of the United States to refrain from participation in the Genoa conference. "We are genuinely sorry for we realize the importance of American cooperation. But we are convinced that in her own time and in her own way, America will again draw closer to Europe. Our interests are one. Without speaking of common sentiments, it is imperative that the interdependence of two continents be clearly appreciated. But of course there is no desire to influence America or ask her to alter her judgment which in her wisdom she now adopts.

The French Government was doubtful about the advisability of the Genoa conference and it should be remarked that before the Poincaré cabinet gave its consent to a policy to which it was largely committed before its advent, it insisted upon precaution. It demanded that if France is to sit down with Russia, definite conditions must be imposed. The necessity for reconstruction, whether of Russia or elsewhere, cannot be questioned but guarantees are essential. France has certainly no intention of improperly exploiting the situation in which Russia finds herself in consequence of economic disorder produced by misgovernment.

With regard to the political character of the gathering, while there may be inevitable political questions, the efforts of France have been directed to getting the conference on economic terrain. There is no question of abandonment of the Genoa conference, which should be useful in clearing the ground and, deeply as the abstention of America will be regretted, we shall endeavor to obtain from the conference all the beneficial results legitimately possible while proceeding cautiously."

Newspapers now comment with more freedom. L'Eclair remarks on the contradiction in American policy. "If the States refuse to be drawn into the current European affairs, they demand to be told where the current is flowing. Too occupied with their own concerns to intervene in ours they nevertheless request that nothing definite be done without them. Is this just, cordial or even logical?"

Among reasons which Liberal papers urge is the recent frank statement of Louis Loucheur which, if understood by financiers, is found incomprehensible by the masses. The American attitude is also interpreted as disapproval of present relations of France and Germany and the menaces of war which still darken the European sky. Not until there is a real pacification and disappearance of complications, hostilities, and diplomatic intrigues will America believe it is possible to rebuild with hope of success. "Le Temps" remarks that the method of disarming first to balance budgets and restore confidence is putting the cart before the horse.

European Unity Essential

First there must be confidence and credit and then general disarmament. It pleads that the basis of settlement is cancellation of inter-allied debts and debts toward America which will permit reduction of the German debt in corresponding proportion. Indeed these manifestations of American opinion have at least the effect of making many Frenchmen understand that at all costs there must be cessation of the policies which divide Europe into opposing camps. European unity must be substituted for European schism.

Le Journal Des Debats points out another cause of the American attitude, namely, the incredibly bad management of the French case at the Washington Conference. La Liberty puts its finger on the part of the American note dealing with Russia, declaring that if America is still opposed to the Soviets it is rather because she is against the allies, Great Britain or Japan obtaining hegemony over Russia. What she has most in mind is the possibility that the powers should obtain concessions of mines and petrol wells at the expense of other countries. Without mingling in European affairs, America wants to exercise control over them.

Generally opinion is pessimistic. There are fears of a fiasco and, although reserve is shown, sometimes commentators break out into sharp criticisms.

Germans Little Concerned By American Genoa Decision

BERLIN, March 9 (Delayed in Transmission) (Special Cable)—Conflicting telegrams from Washington and Paris referring to the United States Government's decision on the general question of the Genoa conference published this morning caused great confusion among the general public. The German Government itself this forenoon was unacquainted with the nature of America's decision and the brief telegram from Paris to the effect that the United States had definitely decided not to attend the Conference was first described as a French maneuver by the mid-day newspapers Later telegrams from Washington on the subject were construed here as meaning that America will not attend the conference, but that the terms of its refusal suggest that, if Europe consents to certain stipulations of the United States and

(Continued on Page 9, Column 5)

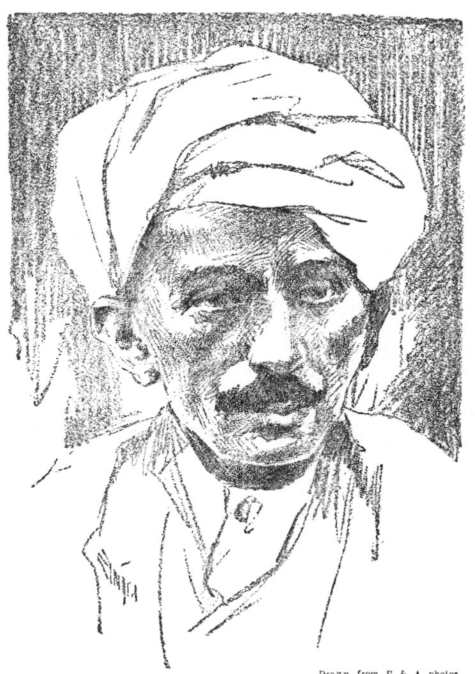

Drawn from P & A photos

Mahatma Gandhi

The Government of India has decided to arrest the leader of the Non-Cooperation movement because of disorders which followed his preaching of civil disobedience in various parts of the country.

DISOBEDIENCE POLICY IN INDIA GETS OUT OF GANDHI'S CONTROL

Leader of Non-Cooperation Movement Finds Himself Helpless to Direct Course of Anti-Government Struggle, for Which He Is Responsible

DELHI, India, March 10 (By The Associated Press)—The Government has definitely decided to arrest Mahatma Gandhi, the non-cooperation leader. He is now in the Ajmere district, about 220 miles southwest of this city.

(By an Anglo-Indian)

LONDON, Feb. 16 (Special Correspondence)—Mahatma Gandhi, mystic, ascetic, and revolutionary, whose preaching of civil disobedience in India has been followed by serious disorder in that far-off land, is a small, lean, brown-skinned man to whom one would hardly give a second glance if one met him in an Indian street.

When I last saw him he was addressing a densely crowded meeting of the Indian National Congress in Calcutta. At that time Mr. Gandhi was chiefly known for work he had done in ameliorating the social condition of emigrant coolies from India in the Transvaal and Natal. In politics he was a moderate, and he was an energetic advocate of temperance. Only gradually has he since grown into a visionary fanatic, unable to realize in his mental exaltation that he has been creating among a people singularly susceptible to emotional appeals, conditions of excitement and race hatred he is quite unable to control.

After the visit of the Prince of Wales to Bombay, when his preaching was followed by riots, in which some 50 people were killed and 200 injured, he retired in disgust and declared he was going to fast until his followers had purged themselves of violence—a threat he was subsequently prevailed upon by his friends to withdraw.

Preferred to Leave Him at Large

His bona fides had been so obvious, however, that the British authorities long thought that to leave him at large was preferable to making a martyr of him as would be the case if they deprived him of freedom. In consequence of growing disturbances following upon his preaching they have now reversed this decision, and E. S. Montagu, British Secretary of State for India, who at one time publicly claimed Mr. Gandhi for his friend, has been driven to admit that it may become necessary to arrest him. Speaking from his place in the House of Commons on behalf of the British Government so lately as Feb. 14, Mr. Montagu said:

"Mr. Gandhi began with certain activities, which nobody will stigmatize, for the promotion of temperance and for social reform, and has gradually started into one of the maddest political campaigns, step after step, and stage after stage, in each one of which he has failed, and been repudiated by the good sense of India. It is not a sin to think you are going to get Home Rule by spinning a cobweb, and it is not a sin to think you are going to get Home Rule by stopping your practice as a barrister. What happened was that at each stage Mr. Gandhi failed in his promises, and became discredited by thinking people. Now that he has embarked on things which are dangerous in his anarchical mood, the Government of India is entitled to call upon the support of every well-thinking and loyal Indian in the measures that it may be necessary to take."

Mr. Gandhi's influence rests largely upon the Indians' admiration for self-denial and personal saintliness. Unfortunately, when these attributes are combined in the person of an active political propagandist, they lead to sanction for deeds which would not otherwise be tolerated. Mr. Gandhi's intentions are of the best. He has challenged the forces of law and order, however, to combat, and after the struggle has commenced he has found himself helpless to direct its course. He is being carried forward by forces of popular excitement, stronger than himself, and has no definite idea as to where he will stop.

Mahomed Ali, another prominent Indian extremist, has been among Muhammadans very much what Mr. Gandhi has been among Hindus. His position has differed from that of Mr.

(Continued on Page 2, Column 5)

UNIONIST OFFERED VACANT INDIAN POST

Lord Derby Likely to Succeed E. S. Montagu, Thus Straining Coalition Feelings

LONDON, March 10 (Special Cable)—Lord Derby will be offered the post of Secretary of State for India in succession to E. S. Montagu today, The Christian Science Monitor learns. He will probably accept. Thus a Unionist is likely to succeed a Liberal, involving a further strain on the feelings of the divided coalition.

The Christian Science Monitor is also informed that Mr. Montagu will address his constituents tomorrow, violently attacking Mr. Lloyd George, the premier, and will "prove" that Lord Curzon could have prevented publication of Lord Reading's memorial had he wished to do so, and alleging that his dismissal is the Premier's sop to the "die-hards."

There was considerable movement and excitement behind the political scenes last night and the lobby was deeply stirred over the Montagu incident. The Christian Science Monitor is informed that an important ministerial meeting was held last night when the political situation, as affected by this incident, was discussed. Lord Reading's resignation, of course, is widely expected and The Christian Science Monitor is reliably informed that it will very probably follow. But this is not so much the cause of excitement as the possibility of the Premier's resignation.

The ties binding the Premier to office are wearing very thin. He is accustomed to handle lots of troubles all at one time, but this quality is nullified by the fact that he is in no mood to remain, but rather go, if this would not damage the interests he has at heart. Into his political calculations have entered simultaneously America's refusal to participate in the Genoa Conference and the Montagu blunder. In any case his resignation is only suspended and should he feel no successful results are now expected from Genoa he would almost certainly quit office.

On the other hand, The Christian Science Monitor was assured, yester-

(Continued on Page 2, Column 1)

BRITAIN TO RAISE GARRISON IN INDIA TO FULL STRENGTH

Seriousness of Situation Prompts Stern Measures—Boycott to Be Suppressed

LONDON, March 10 (Special Cable)—Owing to the seriousness of the Indian political situation, the British Government has issued orders that the British garrison in India be immediately raised to full strength. To save time, 6000 soldiers of Irish battalions in India, who are under disbandment orders under the Irish treaty will be given an opportunity of transferring to units that are to remain in India.

So acute has the situation become in its various phases that other measures are to be taken by the Government. The attempted boycott of the Prince of Wales at certain stages of his Indian tour has moved the Government of India, with the sanction of E. S. Montagu, who has just resigned as Secretary of State for India, to decide upon legislation to suppress the political boycott, a start being made with Burma, where the political agitation is worst.

An Anti-Boycott Bill is being introduced immediately, which will make unlawful the use of the boycott "for the furtherance of political purposes." The measure provides the severest penalty, not for the individual boycotter, who too often is merely a dupe in the hands of political agitators, but for the instigators or instigator of the movement. This is expected to have a salutary effect as hitherto the tendency has been to punish merely the pawns in the revolutionary agitation, while the leaders and "wirepullers" enjoyed immunity.

Similar measures are shortly to be enacted for the whole of India.

Montagu Incident Compromises British Position in Near East

LONDON, March 10 (Special Cable)—Mr. Lloyd George's Government had no alternative to acceptance of the resignation of E. S. Montagu, yesterday, when it became known that his responsible Minister, without consulting his colleagues, had gravely compromised the Cabinet's freedom of action in delicate negotiations of the greatest international importance now pending with Turkey. All further unity of action would have been impossible had so deplorable an example of the lack of coordination been overlooked.

Why a statesman of Mr. Montagu's experience committed such a blunder is not completely explained by publication of the correspondence between himself and the Premier. He has certainly been an earnest propagandist of Indian Moslem ideas, his activities in this respect even during the Paris conference being noteworthy, and it is possible he allowed his enthusiasm for his adopted cause to outrun his discretion. In any case, he is no loss to the Government, for he is certainly unpopular and his policy in India consistently encountered considerable opposition. His disappearance from the cabinet, however, scarcely affects the grave international results precipitated by the publication of the Viceroy's telegram.

On the other hand, Austen Chamberlain's significant statement in the House of Commons that the terms exceed those demanded by the warmest friends of the Turks clearly suggests that they are regarded as unacceptable in official circles, and the fact that there is little difference of opinion in this matter either within or without the House does not affect the gravity of the difficulties Mr. Montagu's action has produced.

Lord Curzon, the British Foreign Secretary, now goes to the allied meeting in Paris to discuss affairs in the Near East with the whole case for Turkish policy hitherto adopted by the British Government compromised by the fact that Great Britain's own representatives in India not only hold strongly, but have been allowed to express publicly views entirely inconsistent with that policy.

The anomaly is so great that The Christian Science Monitor understands it is exceedingly doubtful whether it is possible for Lord Reading, the publication of whose dispatch was the immediate cause of the split, to continue as Viceroy of India, though no direct blame attaches to him since, as long ago laid down by Lord Morley, the position of British Viceroy is only that of agent to the British Secretary of State above him.

Whether Lord Reading goes or stays does not affect the seriousness of the result upon Great Britain's growing difficulties in India, as the excitement there is such that it would be difficult to convince the Muhammadan population that the discarding of their champion in the British Cabinet does not represent failure of the British Government to recognize the weight of their case. This case has already been strongly pressed by Lord Northcliffe and most carefully considered. So far as it has not been adopted, The Christian Science Monitor learns, this was not because of any failure to recognize the strength of India's Moslem sentiments behind it, but because of the inherent difficulties of carrying it into effect without violation of British commitments during the war, especially those with an independent Moslem power, which now controls the principal holy places of Islam.

British Prestige at Stake

While the tendency in some quarters here, particularly in the Northcliffe press, favors capitulation, the

(Continued on Page 2, Column 3)

Greatest Title, 'American Citizen;' Desires No Other, Says Earldom Heir

Chicago Lawyer, Heir to British Estate, Satisfied to Remain What He Is

CHICAGO, March 10 (By The Associated Press)—Cyril Woodward Clubley Armstrong, self-made Chicago lawyer, today learned that he was heir to an English earldom. The news had little effect on him, however, for he calmly informed newspaper reporters that he already possessed the greatest title in the world, that of an American citizen, and desired no other.

Mr. Armstrong received a communication which had been sent to friends by the Consular Department in Washington in response to queries from relatives in India asking that he be located. He produced many letters and documents to prove that he was the man sought, but said he knew nothing of the title he is supposed to have inherited, for he became separated from his family when a child and had worked his way up to membership in the bar through night schools. Previously he sold newspaper subscriptions for a living, worked on Canadian farms, and finally became a reporter.

The letter asking that Mr. Armstrong be traced was written by the British Vice-Consul in charge at Nairobi, East Africa, to the State Department at Washington. It stated that the Armstrongs recently had fallen heir to an earldom, that Cyril was the immediate heir, and that his younger brother, Capt. St. John Shelverton, was seeking Cyril. The letter was forwarded from Washington to Mayor P. J. O'Brien of Quincy, who located Mr. Armstrong in Chicago.

"I know nothing of the title," said Mr. Armstrong today, "but I do know that I am the Armstrong sought. If the reports of a title prove correct—well, I'll cross that bridge when I come to it. I came to this country, became an American citizen, fought my way up to a position of respect in this community and it will always be foremost in my mind that I hold the greatest title in the world—that of American citizen. This is a bad day for any other title and I have no desire to change. I am satisfied to be an American. If they really have a title and a big estate for me as it is reported—I don't know what I'll do. I claim no title now."

THE CHRISTIAN SCIENCE MONITOR

AN INTERNATIONAL DAILY NEWSPAPER

THREE CENTS IN GREATER BOSTON
FIVE CENTS ELSEWHERE

Sixteen Pages

BOSTON, SATURDAY, FEBRUARY 17, 1923—VOL. XV, NO. 70

COPYRIGHT 1923 BY
THE CHRISTIAN SCIENCE PUBLISHING SOCIETY

EDUCATION NEEDS UNFETTERED POST, SAY CLUBWOMEN

Presidents, Meeting in Chicago, Decide to Open Drive to Save Department

Special from Monitor Bureau

CHICAGO, Feb. 17—Women's club presidents from 100 organizations, mostly from Chicago, but including several in near-by states, in conference here took up as part of their program the proposal for a health-educational-welfare combination cabinet department and decided vigorously to oppose anything short of the Department of Education as outlined in the Towner-Sterling bill. Mrs. Charles S. Clark, president of the conference of club presidents, which includes in this move for an education Cabinet officer, gave to The Christian Science Monitor today the following statement in connection with their action:

The success of a democracy—especially our democracy—rests primarily upon the public schools. Theories of government, political parties, may change, or utterly fail, and we would persist as a great Nation. If our public school system fails, the democracy fails with it. The mothers deeply sense this fundamental need and I believe will stand firmly for an unfettered educational bill.

The astounding record of illiteracy in our army is convincing proof that education should be given the importance—the dignity—of being represented in the Cabinet. Later there will have to be a shifting of some of the present ill-sorted interests to the educational department. The conference of club presidents considered the Towner-Sterling bill yesterday, and more than 100 of the larger clubs will throw their influence for the present Towner-Sterling bill unpampered and unhampered.

N. E. A. to Fight Plan

Dr. William B. Owen, president of the National Education Association, said yesterday to a representative of The Christian Science Monitor:

The National Education Association is on record to support the Towner-Sterling bill and we shall not accept any lesser measure or modification which in any way subordinates education to a health department or a war veterans' bureau.

The National Education Association cannot afford to accept any compromise that gives away anything less than an educational department headed by a secretary on education.

That is the fundamental object of the Towner-Sterling bill, and although there may be changes in details, we will oppose vigorously any measure that will give us less than our department. We would object to a welfare department in which education had a minor place—especially would we object to being a division of a general department which might be headed by a physician.

It seems incredible that the oft-defeated scheme of political doctors can succeed now. Congressmen will do well to canvass their constituencies before voting for it. Never were there so many medical heretics as now, and never since its inauguration was "state medicine" so wabbly—even various regular doctors now denouncing it.

There are two ironies of fate bound up in the possibilities of this proposed department. One is that it would come into existence at the moment when the medical influence is at its lowest point and so would be a source of Administration weakness. The other is that the chief instrumentality, in securing this long coveted elevation for allopathy, should be a homeopathic physician, Dr. Sawyer, is heaping coals of fire on the American Medical Association or can it be that he is an innocent tool of clever politicians?

Allopathic Recognition

Homeopathy, osteopathy and other pathological schools of healing, with the exception of allopathy, will oppose the measure bitterly, it is declared among homeopaths here. "The aim of the American Medical Association is to get a man in the Cabinet so as to give them more power and give allopathy wider national recognition," Dr. J. B. S. King told a representative of The Christian Science Monitor. Continuing, he said:

The allopaths would saddle a lot of bureaux and boards on the public and spend great sums of the people's money. In a national way as they are doing now in a state and local way through the state and local health departments. They would continue their propaganda on diseases intended to make fear and start epidemics. Such a cabinet division would just make the health situation more critical.

I oppose this kind of paternal government. People get along about as well without this patriotic attitude on the part of the American Medical Association as they would without it meddling with their health. There is altogether too much of the paternal attitude for the public's well being.

Medical Liberty Threatened

The move to set up a federal department in which public health would dominate, which has been launched by state health officials, physicians and Brig.-Gen. Charles W. Sawyer, a close friend to President Harding, will meet with vigorous opposition by American citizens who stand for medical liberty," declared Mrs. Lora C. W. Little, secretary of the American Medical Liberty League, to the representative. She added:

Such a measure would go one more step toward establishing a medical autocracy. It would increase the power of the allopathic fraternity and would serve them as a great propaganda medium.

It seems incredible that the oft-defeated scheme of political doctors can succeed now. Congressmen will do well to canvass their constituencies before voting for it. Never were there so many medical heretics as now, and never since its inauguration was "state medicine" so wabbly—even various regular doctors now denouncing it.

There are two ironies of fate bound up in the possibilities of this proposed department. One is that it would come into existence at the moment when the medical influence is at its lowest point and so would be a source of Administration weakness. The other is that the chief instrumentality, in securing this long coveted elevation for allopathy, should be a homeopathic physician, Dr. Sawyer, is heaping coals of fire on the American Medical Association or can it be that he is an innocent tool of clever politicians?

High Wage Demands Threaten Building

Special from Monitor Bureau

NEW YORK, Feb. 17

WALTER KRASLOW, who is conducting building operations in the Ocean Avenue section of Flatbush, part of Brooklyn, involving more than $3,000,000, says he intends stopping work immediately if plasterers insist upon their demand for $20 a day, lathers for $18 a thousand to nail up lath, and plumbers for the placing of a foreman over every two men on a job.

PRIORITY FOR COAL DENIED BY FEDERAL COMMERCE BOARD

President Against Any Embargo on Fuel for Canada—Calls Other Methods Better

WASHINGTON, Feb. 17—(By The Associated Press)—Over the protest of F. R. Wadleigh, Federal Fuel Distributor, the Interstate Commerce Commission today refused to issue general priority orders to expedite the movement of anthracite to northeastern New York and New England.

Special from Monitor Bureau

WASHINGTON, Feb. 17—President Harding is opposed to an embargo on coal exportations to Canada, despite the demands now being made in Congress by New England, New York and other northern delegations for immediate relief of the shortage in anthracite prevailing in those sections.

Mr. Harding let it be known that he "does not look with favor" on the proposed embargo on anthracite and expressed the opinion that coal could be supplied to New England through the adoption of other methods. In this position the President has the backing of Herbert Hoover, Secretary of Commerce.

Although no definite assurances of action on an embargo can be obtained, Henry Cabot Lodge (R.), Senator from Massachusetts, is hopeful of getting relief legislation through in the final shuffling of bills during the closing days of the session.

Just returned from a trip to New England and New York, John Jacob Rogers (R.) Representative from Massachusetts issued a statement today, in which he decided the Interstate Commerce Commission hearing in the metropolis as a "love feast" in which representatives of railroads, officials of Pennsylvania, officers of the anthracite mines and Charles A. Magrath joined in urging that no restrictions be placed upon the exportation of anthracite to Canada.

"All, to use the words of Mr. Magrath, want to continue to have Canada treated as a forty-ninth state of the Union," said Mr. Rogers. He then added:

We do not wish to punish Canada, but we do wish to take some action for our own essential well-being, so that which Canada has herself taken in declaring in the past embargoes against the United States.

The Interstate Commerce Commission has power to declare the embargo. I hope it will exercise that power. I hope that even if it does not, Congress will by act will enforce it. In the last analysis, the adjournment on March 4 makes it too late.

LITHUANIA RAISES JUDICIAL ISSUE

Appeal Made to World Court to Define Power of League

By Special Cable

GENEVA, Feb. 17—No official information has been received here regarding the Lithuanian resistance to the establishment of Polish administration over the portion of the neutral zone allotted to Poland by recommendation of the Council of the League of Nations on Feb. 3. At Paris last month the Council adopted a report by the neutral zone replaced by a provisional frontier line, Poland accepting the plan and Lithuania rejecting it. Lithuania now asks the World's Court to decide whether the Council has a right to modify the neutral zone, and if so whether the modification is enforceable if one party does not accept it.

A telegram has been received from the Lithuanian Government by the League Secretariat requesting the submission of the following questions to the Permanent Court of International Justice:

Firstly, Has the League Council under the circumstances, the right under the convention to make the recommendation, and are the terms of the declaration of Feb. 10, in conformity with the convention?

Secondly, Does the convention confer on one party the right to act according to the recommendation of the Council, despite the opposition of the other party?

The request will come before the Council at its next meeting.

JOHN H. BARTLETT MAY GO TO HEAD OF POSTAL DEPARTMENT

WASHINGTON, Feb. 17—John H. Bartlett, former Governor of New Hampshire, now First Assistant Postmaster-General, is being considered for promotion to Postmaster-General in case President Harding should decide not to appoint Senator New of Indiana.

Photograph © Underwood & Underwood, New York

America's Trio of Women in Congress

Left to Right: Miss Alice Robertson (R.), Representative From Oklahoma; Mrs. Winifred Mason Huck (R.), Representative From Illinois, and Mrs. Mae Ella Nolan (R.), Representative From California. Mrs. Huck Succeeded Her Father, William E. Mason, and Mrs Nolan Took the Post Left Vacant by Her Husband. This Photograph Was Taken a Few Days Ago When the Three Statesmen Met at the Capital for the First Time

---

SENATE APPROVES DEBT BILL CUTTING "FAVORED" CLAUSE

Vote of 70 to 13—House to Concur in Two Amendments and Send on to President

Special from Monitor Bureau

WASHINGTON, Feb. 17—Passed by an overwhelming majority in Congress that places the American public squarely behind its terms, the British debt settlement bill is expected to be sent to President Harding early next week.

Concurrence by the House in two important amendments added in the Senate will follow quickly, so that the final stamp of approval can be placed upon the settlement terms within a few days. In the last analysis, the settlement of the British debt of $4,600,000,000 would tend to bring about that stabilization of international credit so essential to make economic readjustment possible. As passed by the Senate, with only 13 opposing votes, the bill contains two important amendments.

Two Amendments

The first strikes out the provision in the House bill that the debts of other countries should not be settled on more favorable terms than those accorded Great Britain. Substituted for this is a provision authorizing settlements with other debtor nations on such terms as the "commission may deem just, subject to the approval of the Congress by act or resolution." This was sponsored by Joseph T. Robinson (D.), Senator from Arkansas, and was accepted not only by Reed Smoot, member of the Debt Commission, but also by Andrew W. Mellon, Secretary of the Treasury, and chairman of the commission.

The other amendment proposed by William J. Harris (D.), Senator from Georgia, also accepted, increases the membership of the Debt Commission to eight, the three new members to be appointed from the Democratic side, heretofore unrepresented on the commission.

All other efforts to amend the bill were defeated by decisive votes.

Mr. Borah Opposes Bill

The vote by which the measure passed the Senate late yesterday, under a unanimous consent agreement curtailing debate, was 70 to 13. Forty-six Republicans and 24 Democrats comprised the majority. The opposing votes were cast by nine Democrats and four Republicans. These Republicans—William E. Borah of Idaho, Robert M. La Follette of Wisconsin, Joseph I. France of Maryland, and George W. Norris of Nebraska. Democrats—Henry F. Ashurst of Arizona, Peter G. Gerry of Rhode Island, J. Thomas Heflin of Alabama, Gilbert M. Hitchcock of Nebraska, Kenneth McKellar of Tennessee, James A. Reed

---

City-Wide Liquor Raids Fill Capital Stations

By The Associated Press

Washington, Feb. 17

POLICE and prohibition enforcement officers today launched their second city-wide liquor clean-up since the beginning of February. With 50 warrants, they began before noon a series of raids which reached into every section of the capital and which filled up rapidly all available detention space at several station houses.

of Missouri, Park Trammell of Florida, David I. Walsh of Massachusetts, Thomas J. Walsh of Montana.

After the first test vote to require Great Britain to pay a higher rate of interest, which was defeated, 16 to 21, the opposition, such as it was, made no further attempts to record the votes of senators on various amendments.

As finally approved, the bill provides for payment by Great Britain of interest at the rate of 3 per cent for the first 10 years and 3½ per cent thereafter, the whole period for settlement of the $4,600,000,000 extending 62 years.

MR. FORD RAISES WAGES

PITTSBURGH, Pa., Feb. 17—A wage increase of approximately 30 per cent for the employees of the Allegheny Plate Glass Company of Glassmere, near here, was announced late yesterday by D. K. Albright, general manager of the plant, which was purchased several days ago by Henry Ford. The Ford wage scale, he said, would be applied as well as the Ford plan for investing in the company.

INDEX OF THE NEWS

Nomad Tribes in Revolt on West Coast of Africa

By The Associated Press

Cadiz, Spain, Feb. 17

THE Spanish cruiser Reina Regente was ordered today to Cape Juhi, on the west coast of the Sahara, opposite the Canary Islands, where a number of nomad tribes are reported to be in revolt.

LUXOR EXCAVATORS FIND MORE RELICS OF ANCIENT EGYPT

Splendors of Bygone Age Revealed in Inner Chamber of Tomb of Tut-ankh-amen

LUXOR, Egypt, Feb. 17 (By The Associated Press)—Examination of the inner chamber of the tomb of King Tut-ankh-amen yesterday showed the sarcophagus of the Pharaoh to be still in the same position in which it was placed more than 3000 years ago.

When the explorers, after removing the delicate seals, broke their way through the masonry of the inner chamber door, they were confronted with splendors which, upon the first cursory examination, appeared to surpass even those of the ante-chamber which have held the interest of the entire world.

The exploring party, headed by Howard Carter, was amazed to find the center chamber, which is about 14 feet square, occupied by an immense gilded canopy, richly inscribed.

An Immense Gilded Canopy

One feature of the discovery in the inner chamber was a magnificent statue of a cat, richly painted, which has stood sentry over the Pharaoh through the centuries he has lain there. The chamber is filled with splendid furniture, in orderly array. It also holds several superb gold chariots, an exquisite ivory and ebony box and many beautiful alabaster vases.

"Marvelous, I congratulate you," exclaimed Professor Breasted to the Earl of Carnarvon, when the Earl and Mr. Carter and the other members of their party emerged from the tomb.

LONDON, Feb. 17—A dispatch to the Exchange Telegraph from Luxor explains that there are two chambers in the Pharaoh's tomb, the first containing the canopy sarcophagus and a chamber beyond, filled with treasures, including a number of gilded chariots, standing on their wheels. The dispatch adds that the tomb has been closed for the official opening, which will take place tomorrow.

Interest may be found in a brief outline of the salient historical and geographical features of ancient Thebes, and of Luxor, the name that

(Continued on Page 3, Column 1)

TURKISH FOREIGN TRADE THREATENED BY NEW DECISIONS

Dismissal of Christians Spells Chaos at Ports—Curb Placed on Use of Languages

By CRAWFURD PRICE

By Cable from Monitor Bureau

LONDON, Feb. 17—The developments in the Near East are inevitably overshadowed by the events in the Ruhr, but with the arrival of Ismet Pasha at Constantinople there is a revival of interest in the fate of the Treaty of Lausanne. Most competent observers retain an open mind. The decision, of course, rests with the Angora Assembly and that is a "packed house" largely made up of individuals chosen at the time of the Nationalist revival for their power to

(Continued on Page 3, Column 1)

ISMET PASHA NOT SATISFIED WITH LAUSANNE PARLEY

By Special Cable

CONSTANTINOPLE, Feb. 17—Ismet Pasha, Turkish Foreign Minister, arrived yesterday from Rumania.

In diplomatic circles and in part of the Constantinople press it is hoped he will influence the Angora Assembly to sign the peace project on the ground of alleged last-minute concessions communicated to him at Bucharest. However, the Bucharest conversations do not appear to be substantial, to judge from the last declarations of Ismet Pasha to representatives of the Rumanian press.

In his interview, he expresses discontent with the Lausanne Conference for trying to force him to set aside the National Pact.

Dr. Breitscheid Consults British Labor Leaders

By Cable from Monitor Bureau

LONDON, Feb. 17—Dr. Rudolph Breitscheid, one of the leaders of the Social Democratic Party in the German Reichstag, interviewed by a correspondent of the Christian Science Monitor, said he arrived here last Friday and had since been in close touch with the leaders of the British Labor Party, with a view to pressing the adoption by Britain of a "policy whereby Germany, and not only Germany but the whole of Europe, might be freed from the great dangers threatened by French occupation of the Ruhr."

Dr. Breitscheid said the Social Democrats welcomed the movement of British Liberals to refer this matter to the League of Nations, their great anxiety being lest the indignation against the French, which now fired all classes in Germany should pass from its present passive resistance stage into that of violence. German industry, he thought, could not hold out for more than eight or nine months against the Ruhr coal blockade, but the saw no prospect of a peaceful surrender upon the part either of the German people or of the Cuno Government.

Should the German coal magnates come to any arrangement of their own with the French Government, he held this would not make for peace, since it could not be acquiesced in by his country generally.

Dr. Breitscheid returns to Germany on Monday.

PARIS TOURISTS GET NEW MOTOR SERVICE

Special from Monitor Bureau

NEW YORK, Feb. 17—Passengers on International Mercantile Marine steamships calling at Cherbourg, France, on their voyages from New York, are to be provided, beginning March 1, with automobile service between Cherbourg and Paris by road, about 230 miles, will be covered, according to plans, in 10 hours by touring cars. Stops will be made for rest and meals. Choice of two routes, both of which pass through Normandy, the many picturesque villages and several large towns on the way, will be given.

GERMANS TO SHUT ELECTRIC CURRENT OFF FROM ESSEN

Workers to Cut Off Supply as Result of Fine Imposed on Director of Plant

ESSEN, Feb. 17 (By The Associated Press)—The employees of the municipal electric works have decided to cut off Essen's supply of electricity as a result of the imposition of the fine of 5,000,000 marks on Herr Buszmann, director of the local plant.

The French imposed this fine yesterday as punishment for interference with the supply of electricity to the Kaiserhof Hotel, the French headquarters, and at the same time sentenced Herr Haverstein of Oberhausen to three years' imprisonment and Vice-Lord Mayor Schaefer of Essen to two years in jail and a fine of 10,000,000 marks for similar measures in opposition to the French.

An appeal has been lodged for the revision of all the sentences.

Britain Ready to Surrender Sector of Railway to France

By Cable from Monitor Bureau

LONDON, Feb. 17—Yves le Trocquer, French Minister of Public Works, left last night for Paris to consult the other members of the Poincaré government on the subject of the concessions Great Britain is prepared to make regarding the French use of the railways which traverse the British zone in the Cologne area. The exact nature of these concessions has not been made public here, but it is understood that while they include the surrender to France of a short sector of the railway just inside the British territory they exclude the use of lines in the zone generally as incompatible with a continuation of the British occupation.

The question now is: Will France prefer unrestricted use of the lines of communication through Cologne, which they might find costly to safeguard if the British withdrew, or the restrictions coupled with the continued British presence in this region? How far Germany is prepared to go to keep the British where they are is shown by the fact that so lately as last Thursday the Cuno Government intimated to Great Britain that it would continue to guarantee this short sector of its line of communication with the Ruhr.

Light upon the German attitude is also thrown by today's Breitscheid interview, cabled separately, which strongly urges international intervention. The British Labor Party's resolution, which made intervention one of its points, was defeated by a large majority in the House of Commons here last night, but this was only because the Government speakers took the line that the time for anything of the kind was not yet "opportune."

Stanley Baldwin's contribution was upon a note heard but seldom in the House of Commons. "No gospel of hate," he said, "will ever seize the hearts of the people of Great Britain." Instead, he pinned his faith on four inspiring monosyllables: "Faith, hope, love, and work."

GREEKS AND TURKS READY FOR EXCHANGE OF PRISONERS

Rival Generals Will Be Returned at Island Before Smyrna—Reconstruction Proceeding in Armenia

By Special Cable

MYTILENE, Feb. 17—The exchange of prisoners of war between the Greeks and the Turks starts on Monday on the Island of Clasaiteman, in front of the port of Smyrna. The first men to be exchanged will be rival generals, Jafar Tayar, former Turkish commander of the Adrianople forces, taken prisoner by the Greeks, will be traded for General Tricoupis, former Commander-in-Chief during the Turkish offensive, after the resignation of General Hadjianestis.

Turkey Must Be Used

Measures have already been taken to evacuate Adrianople at its civil population to give ample opportunity for the movement of military forces. Strict use should be made of the railway in all writing undertaken for business purposes by foreign companies in that city. This is aimed directly at the foreign companies established there, and is declared to be an infringement of the rights enjoyed by foreigners, among whom the French suffer most.

News of reconstruction efforts in Armenia is encouraging. The ministers there are devoted to the uplift and betterment of the small nation, whose land is barren, and whose territory is so small as to make it incapable at present of supporting all its inhabitants. The Government is engaged in trying to transform the sterile ground into fertile and thorough artificial irrigation. A textile factory is being established at Alexandrianople, where 2000 orphans are being cared for by Americans.

Patriarch Attacked

The Turkish press is engaged in bitter attacks upon Meletios Metaxakis, Patriarch of Greek Orthodox Church at Constantinople, raking up ancient slanders against him from the past and demanding his expulsion. The Patriarch's action in promoting and leading his people to freedom from Turkish oppression and despotism in 1896 in Avnie, by revolting against the despots, is now loudly denounced by the Turkish press as a movement that caused the destruction of many Turks. The Government does nothing to suppress the attacks.

The Kemalist independence tribunals are at work, and many have fallen victims. Refugee Armenians assembled at Constantinople are the cause of immense anxiety to the Armenian authorities, who are deprived of adequate means to support and to shelter these unfortunates. Negotiations are being carried on by Mr. Maguinizdah, diplomatic representative of the Armenian Republic at Constantinople, to transport part of the refugees to Armenia. The Government will distribute the land and agricultural implements, which it is hoped will be provided for them by foreign philanthropic organizations.

COPYRIGHT 1923 BY
THE CHRISTIAN SCIENCE PUBLISHING SOCIETY

Fourteen
Pages

BOSTON, FRIDAY, AUGUST 3, 1923—VOL. XV, NO. 210

FIVE CENTS } A COPY
TWOPENCE

HARDING PASSES ON—COOLIDGE IS PRESIDENT

MR. COOLIDGE TAKES OATH BY THE LIGHT OF OIL LAMP AS THIRTIETH PRESIDENT

Pledge Administered by His Father in Vermont Farmhouse While Neighbors Look On—New Executive Starts at Once for Capital

Calvin Coolidge—Public Servant

Reared in Plymouth, Vt.; worked on father's farm and attended school in village of Black River, later in St. Johnsbury Academy.

Entered Amherst College in 1891, graduating in 1895.

Began study of law in Northampton, Mass., and was admitted to the bar on July 2, 1897.

City councilor, Northampton, 1899 and 1900; city solicitor, 1900, 1901.

Member of Massachusetts House of Representatives, 1907 and 1908.

Mayor of Northampton, 1910 and 1911.

Member of Massachusetts Senate, 1912 to 1915; president of Senate, 1914 and 1915.

Lieutenant-Governor, 1916, 1917, 1918; Governor, 1919, 1920.

Nominated as Republican candidate for Vice-President in Chicago, June, 1920; elected on Nov. 2, 1920.

PLYMOUTH, Vt., Aug. 3 (AP)—Calvin Coolidge became President of the United States at 2:47 a. m. today, eastern standard time, when he took the oath of office in the living room of his father's farmhouse in this little mountain village where he was born.

Three hours earlier he had been notified of the passing of President Harding and had expressed briefly his estimate of his "chief and friend" and his purpose of carrying out the "policies which he has begun for the service of the American people." President Coolidge made immediate preparations to start for Washington. It was arranged that he should motor to Rutland, where a special train was ready to take him for New York.

A messenger who had hastened here from Bridgewater, the nearest telegraph office, brought the news from San Francisco to Mr. Coolidge in the form of a telegram from George B. Christian Jr., Mr. Harding's secretary.

Mr. Coolidge's Statements

Mr. Coolidge's father, John C. Coolidge, received the message shortly before midnight and took it upstairs, where he made it to the Vice-President, who was in bed. Mr. Coolidge quickly dressed in a suit of black and came downstairs, followed a moment later by Mrs. Coolidge. Shocked by the news but outwardly showing his accustomed calm, he dictated two brief statements to his secretary and then distributed copies to the newspaper men who had gathered in the living room of the farmhouse. His first statement was as follows:

"Reports have reached me which I fear are correct that President Harding is gone. The world has lost a great and good man. I mourn his loss. He was my chief and my friend. It will be my purpose to carry out the policies which he has begun for the service of the American people, and for meeting their responsibilities wherever they may arise. For this purpose I shall seek the co-operation of all those who have been associated with the President during his term of office. Those who have given their efforts to assist him I wish to remain in office that they may assist me. I have faith that God will direct the destinies of our Nation."

A little later Mr. Coolidge made this statement:

"It is my intention to remain here until I can secure the correct form for the oath of office, which will be administered to me by my father, who

is a notary public, if that will meet the necessary requirements. I expect to leave for Washington during the day."

Message to Mrs. Harding

To Mrs. Harding, Mr. and Mrs. Coolidge joined in sending the following telegram:

"We offer you our deepest sympathy. May God bless you and keep you."

Mr. Coolidge, who had come here for a complete rest, had welcomed the absence of a telephone from his father's home and had walked several times a day to the village store to receive over the telephone there the latest word from San Francisco. But with the news of the President's passing, telephone company officials immediately set to work to give Mr. Coolidge every possible facility for communicating with Washington and elsewhere, and within an hour a telephone had been installed in the farmhouse.

It was through a telephone communication with Washington that the Vice-President obtained the exact form of oath which the Constitution requires the President to take upon assuming office. Then in the presence of Mrs. Coolidge, Representative Porter H. Dale (R.), Representative from Vermont, and a little party of friends and acquaintances, Mr. Coolidge quietly went through the simple ceremony that made him President. His father read by the light of an oil lamp on the table the impressive words of the oath of office:

"I do solemnly swear that I will faithfully execute the office of President of the United States and I will to the best of my ability preserve, protect and defend the Constitution of the United States."

Mr. Coolidge calmly and clearly repeated the words and added: "So help me God."

The ceremony ended, the President turned at once to preparations for his journey to Washington.

President Coolidge Has Devoted Career to Public Service; Police Strike Gave Him National Fame

Calvin Coolidge has made his career the public service, a career starting with membership in the City Council of Northampton, Mass., and now culminating in the office of President of the United States.

Descended from Puritan ancestry, Mr. Coolidge is a native of Plymouth, Vt., where his people now live. He grew up to farm life, but in 1891 left to attend Amherst College, graduating with honors in 1895, and entering on the study of law in Northampton. He still maintains an office there, although his practice is carried on by associates.

It was not long, however, before Mr. Coolidge's bent for the public service asserted itself, and he won election to the City Council. He progressed to the office of City Solicitor, and later Mayor, then represented his district first in the House of Representatives of the Commonwealth and then the Senate.

Twice Governor

Senator Winthrop Murray Crane recognized the abilities of Mr. Coolidge as he rose to the presidency of the state Senate and then to higher state offices. For three successive years, 1916, 1917 and 1918, he served as Lieutenant-Governor, giving distinguished service in an office that permits of slight distinction. In November, 1918, he ran successfully for Governor and was re-elected in 1919.

As a legislator Calvin Coolidge was identified with the conservative group.

He has consistently regarded the public service as a public trust. In his official utterances he has avoided the sensational and the demagogic, at the same time avoiding the appearance of commonplaceness by discriminating silence at times when others in similar position would choose to rush into print.

The Police Strike

It was the Boston police strike of September, 1919, however, that lifted Calvin Coolidge from the realm of state politics and state office to a position in the national political firmament. The issues involved in this strike attracted the eyes of the entire nation. The manner in which Mr. Coolidge met them attracted the attention of the nation, swept him overwhelmingly into office again as Governor, and brought him the nomination for the Vice-Presidency when the Republican Party convened in national convention in Chicago in 1920.

The formation of a union of Boston policemen affiliated with the American Federation of Labor was understood. Edwin U. Curtis, the Police Commissioner, forbade this unionization and enforced his decree by the suspension of 19 policemen. On Sept. 9, about three-fourths of the police force went on strike. Lawlessness and rioting followed, and the next day Governor Coolidge called the state guard to police the city while a new force was being recruited.

For several days the strike con-

(Continued on Page 2, Column 1)

Warren Gamaliel Harding

WARREN G. HARDING'S LAST PLEA WAS FOR MORE OF CHRIST SPIRIT

Tolerant Executive's Final Official Words Invoked the Wayshower's Humility—Speech Read in Los Angeles

LOS ANGELES, Cal., Aug. 3 (Staff Correspondence)—The last official words of President Harding, urging "more of the Christ spirit, more of the Christ practice, and a new and abiding consecration to reverence for God," were delivered here yesterday by George B. Christian Jr., Mr Harding's secretary, at a presentation of the Knights Templars' international traveling beauséant to California Knights. President Harding, a member of the Marion, O., Commandery, was to have presented the beauséant in person in behalf of his fellow Masons, and between 15,000 and 20,000 people gathered here to hear the message brought by Mr. Christian. The address follows:

Sir Knights and Brothers:

I am deeply sensible of the honor implied in my selection as the medium for the transfer of this sacred banner from the custody of the grand jurisdiction of the commanderies of Ohio to the temporary keeping of the Knights of California. I am especially gratified that this designation has been made by my own home Commandery, composed of brother Knights, with whom I have lived in more or less intimate, neighborly association throughout the greater part of my life.

It was a beautiful idea which brought about the reproduction of the banner under which the Knights of the Holy Grail went forth to battle to the death with the Saracens for the restoration of the Holy Land and its shrines to Christian hands, and to send it on a pilgrimage to the temples of the latter-day Christian Knights to reawaken or reanimate their faith and devotion. The reproduced beauséant will not encounter the storms, the fanaticism, and the romances of knighthood which attended the original banner, but I trust its journeys will encounter no less of conscience and no less of noble purpose.

"Not Mere Symbolism"

I am sure the mission of the beauséant will be a failure if its travels are made simply a matter of symbolism and pageantry. It bears emblazoned upon it the supplication, "Not unto us, O Lord, not unto us, but unto Thy name be the glory." We should glorify the Holy name, not by words, not by praise, not by displays at arms, but by deeds and service in behalf of human brotherhood.

Christ, the great Exemplar of our order, repeatedly urged this truth upon his hearers. There was nothing mystical or mystical in the code of living preached by Jesus Christ. The lessons he taught were so simple and plain, so fashioned to be understood by the humblest among men, that they appealed to the reason and emotions of all. His words to the fishermen bore conviction to the learned men of the Roman bench. All of his teachings were based upon the broad ground of fraternalism, and justice, and understanding, from which flows always peace.

"A new commandment I give unto you—that ye love one another." Surely in this was "all the law and the prophets."

I make bold to say, in reflective de-

liberation, there is nothing in Templar Knighthood, nothing in obligation, lecture or exemplification, nothing in practice where obligation is kept, which could not be openly, and in equal simplicity, proclaimed to the world.

"Need More Christianity"

Someone has said, in speaking of our present-day civilization, that "we need less of religion and more of Christianity." This may be couched expressed, but it contains a great truth. With the universal observance of Christ's commandment we would have the essentials of all religions. Perhaps I will best express my thought if I say we need less of sectarianism, less of denominationalism, less of fanatical zeal and its exactions, and more of the Christ spirit, more of the Christ practice, and a new and abiding consecration to reverence for God.

I am a confirmed optimist as to the growth of the spirit of brotherhood. Science and genius are lending their aid to the removal of the obstacles to intercourse and attending understanding among the peoples of the world. We do rise to heights at times, when we look for the good rather than the evil in others, and give condemnation to the viewof all. The inherent love of fellowship is banding men together, and when envy and suspicion are vanquished, fraternity records a triumph, and brotherhood brings new blessings to men and to peoples in the larger sense.

"All for Brotherly Love"

Because I am holding, temporarily, a position of official prominence, I have been privileged in being invited into association with many of our so-called secret fraternal societies. I find that each of them has as its foundation and the reason for its existence the further-

(Continued on Page 2, Column 3)

INDEX OF THE NEWS

AUGUST 3, 1923

COOLIDGES FORCED TO DROP SIMPLICITY

Assumption of White House Duties Means Sharp Change From Favorite Way of Living

Special from Monitor Bureau

WASHINGTON, Aug. 3—The transition from the Willard Hotel, where Mr. and Mrs. Calvin Coolidge maintained a suite of rooms since he became Vice-President, to the White House will be almost as marked as that from Northampton to Washington.

The Coolidges have lived simply, their position considered. They have entertained little; at no time in a large way. They have, however, participated in the social and official life of the capital, making the guest list of functions of widely varying character.

Their two sons are at school at Mercersburg (Pa.) Academy, but, in their short vacations, join their parents at the hotel and get sidelights on the Government at Washington and honored guest when the wheels go 'round." Mr. Coolidge's father, too, is a frequent and honored guest at his son's affairs that his son plays in them. Both Mr. Coolidge, the father, and the young Coolidges were always to be found in the galleries watching the Senate proceedings when they were in Washington.

Mr. and Mrs. Frank Stearns of Boston, close personal friends of Mr. and Mrs. Coolidge, have been their guests in Washington more frequently than anyone outside the family.

Of Modest Means

It is well understood why the Coolidges have lived as they have in Washington. The Vice-President did not have the private fortune necessary to have maintained a large establishment and to have entertained on a commensurate scale. He could easily have been financed by friendly or political patrons but he desired above all things to maintain his independence. The Coolidges were not ashamed to admit that they could not afford to do things but they would have been greatly humiliated to have accepted the wherewithal from anyone else.

The frugality and independence which went so far toward making New England pre-eminent in the early days persist strongly in this son of Vermont.

Just as he does not desire to accept personal favors, Calvin Coolidge regards the Government not as the source of benefits but as the object of service. "We cannot look to Government," he says in his speech On the Nature of Politics. "We must look to ourselves. We must stand not in the expectation of a reward but with a desire to serve." In the White House, the Coolidges will have an enlarged sphere of social responsibility and the expectation based on observation of their conduct in Washington the last two and a

(Continued on Page 2, Column 6)

ATTENDANTS HAD ISSUED OPTIMISTIC STATEMENTS FOLLOWING HOPEFUL DAY

Mrs. Harding Was Reading To Husband When Change Came—Body To Be Taken To Washington for Ceremonies

President Harding's Achievements

Washington Conference on Limitation of Armament. United States took bold position and important treaties were evolved.

Peace re-established with Germany and Austria. Army of occupation withdrawn.

Declaration in favor of American participation in World Court.

Treaty with the Republic of Colombia ratified, settling long-standing dispute.

Budget system established and the Government enabled to carry on its business with greater efficiency and economy.

Extension of credit to farmers.

Firm stand on enforcement of prohibition laws.

Regulation of immigration by modified restriction.

Settlement of British war debt; also that of Finland, with Czechoslovakia and Jugoslavia in prospect.

Influence extended in Central and South America.

SAN FRANCISCO, Aug. 3 (AP)—Warren G. Harding, twenty-ninth President of the United States, passed away at the Palace Hotel here last night. The late President's body will be sent to Washington tonight. Mr. Harding had been confined to his room less than a week. He passed on after having served his country as President for nearly two and one-half years.

With the passing on of President Harding, Calvin Coolidge, Vice-President of the United States, becomes actual head of the Government. He has already been sworn into office by his father, John Coolidge, a notary public, of Plymouth, Vt., where he was visiting when the news reached him from San Francisco.

Mrs. Harding, with her characteristic devotion and solicitude, was reading to the President when the end came. She summoned aid, but it was too late. The President, by virtue of his office and his personality, one of the world's outstanding figures, passed away at a time when his physicians had predicted recovery. Government officials and members of the President's party had been encouraged by the improvements of the last few days, and a feeling of confidence that the Chief Executive would soon recover was universal.

Three hours before the President passed away the most optimistic bulletin issued since the President had been confined was issued. It said that he had spent the "most comfortable day since his illness began." This bulletin resulted in a letting down of the watchfulness and members of the Cabinet and attendants started to speculate as to when the trip back to Washington would start.

Warren G. Harding Became President in Midst of After-War Problems; Worked His Way on Weekly Newspaper as Boy

Special from Monitor Bureau

WASHINGTON, Aug. 3.—Warren G. Harding came to the Presidency at a time when the aftermath of the World War was clogging ordinary channels of international intercourse and commerce and when domestic issues, in part incident upon the war and the shaking of all the countries of the earth were seething and seeking new forms and outlets.

The Coolidges have lived simply, their position considered. He did not bring to this stupendous task no proportionate equipment of tried and proved statesmanship. He did face it with a touching humility, an expressed desire to learn, and a yearning to do the right thing for all the people. Those who saw him from time to time at close range, watched his mental processes and his political and official acts, observed Mr. Harding groping for the right move, listening to the counsel of trusted friends and of those whose position entitled them to be heard, and then striking out for what he believed to be the best thing for the American people, sometimes at the cost of opposing those whom he preferred to please.

President Harding continued to be a politician, but he was less so than Senator Harding; that is, his sense of proportion had accommodated itself to his larger responsibilities. That was not invariably true, for Mr. Harding was swayed by personal influences to a large degree in many instances, but that he was able to adopt a comparatively independent line at times is what many persons who knew him well had not expected.

Duty Always First

Perhaps there was no better way of understanding the purposes, the changes, and the character of Mr. Harding than by following him week by week at his conferences with the press. These occasions not only gave the President an opportunity to let the country know through the newspapers the facts before him in which they have so great a stake, but his attitude as a representative of the press, like the correspondents before him, occupying for the time a position which called for a different line of action but never interrupting his sympathies with the aims and obligations of journalism.

Frequently when asked a question which went so far toward making he looked about, half humorously, half appealingly and said: "I love you—that ye love one another. Understand that it is your duty, but I have a duty that prevents my doing it. I wish I could."

The scene of the President's activities, the figures that appeared upon it, and the complications that ensued

were for the most part not such as he anticipated. Although no one will deny that his grasp of public affairs became larger and firmer as he advanced in his administration, at the same time found ever new perplexities to cope with. The political field with which he was most familiar took on an adverse aspect. The schism within his own party, the attacks by men who wore nominally the same party as himself gave him increasing concern.

Mr. Harding was comparatively happy in his political family. There were divergences within the Cabinet. It could not be otherwise with men of such varying caliber and experiences, but so far as the country knew they were all loyal to their chief. The President leaned on Mr. Hughes for his international policy and Mr. Hoover's advice was listened to in regard to matters at home and abroad. Mr. Mellon's financial views were never challenged. The changes that took place in the Cabinet were not such as to affect its equilibrium.

Introduction of League

The League of Nations as an issue entered very largely into the campaign which resulted in the election of Mr. Harding. In his inaugural address he assured the country that the cardinal maxim of his foreign policy would be to keep the country free from any "permanent military alliance." At the same time he declared that the United States would be willing to associate itself with the nations of the world, great and small, for the promotion of peace through friendly counsel, sympathy and understanding and through the reduction of military armament.

"Our eyes will never be blind to a developing menace and our ears never deaf to the call of civilization," he asserted, and intermittently for some time after he became President he asserted his desire for an association of nations. It was characteristic of Mr. Harding, however, that in the antagonisms developed he did not find it feasible to enunciate a clear-cut definition of how this was to be brought about or what the substitution of the party-banned League of Nations was to be.

He did, however, co-operate with his Secretary of State in the plan for reducing armament by means of an international conference held in Washington, and this gave a prestige to the early part of his Administration that persisted to the end. At the Washington Conference was settled a part of vexed mandate questions, especially that exemplified by the Island of Yap, and the State Department, with the approval of the Presi-

---

COPYRIGHT 1924 BY
THE CHRISTIAN SCIENCE PUBLISHING SOCIETY

Eighteen Pages

BOSTON, WEDNESDAY, NOVEMBER 5, 1924—VOL. XVI, NO. 290

FIVE CENTS A COPY

British Prime Minister Busy Forming New Government; Awaits Reply to Invitations

Several Members of Lloyd George's Cabinet Mentioned for Office

LORD CURZON SLATED FOR HIGH POSITION

Winston Spencer Churchill, It Is Reported, May Be Given Portfolio

By Cable from Monitor Bureau

LONDON, Nov. 5—Invitations have gone out to those selected by Stanley Baldwin for membership in the new Cabinet, and he is today considering the acceptances and refusals. While the situation as regards the new national executive is still fluid therefore, and likely to remain so until tomorrow night, when an authoritative statement is promised, it has become possible to give semiofficial indications of the general trend of expectations in this matter.

The most reliable forecast on Government circles is that so far as changes from the last Conservative Government are contemplated, they are in two directions. Firstly, those leading ministers are to be included who stood 'aside when Mr. Lloyd George gave place to Mr. Bonar Law. This affects especially Austen Chamberlain, who is mentioned for the Foreign Office, the Earl of Birkenhead who may go to the India Office and Sir Robert Horne who is named for the Chancellorship of the Exchequer, if his business commitments allow. The Earl of Balfour, it is rumored, may be Lord President of the Council. An office is also now expected for Winston Spencer Churchill.

In the second place, the number of peers in the Cabinet is likely to be reduced, though a high office is certain to be offered to Marquess Curzon. Parliament's reopening will be postponed, probably until Nov. 25, the King's Speech being delivered a week later, followed by formal business, which may relegate contentious measures to January.

BRITISH EXULT OVER VICTORY OF REPUBLICANS

Conservatives Especially Enthusiastic—Look for Co-operation

By Cable from Monitor Bureau

LONDON, Nov. 5—The reported victory in the United States of Calvin Coolidge and Brig.-Gen. Charles G. Dawes has evoked the friendliest British reaction, which is especially marked in the new Government circles here. The Conservatives, themselves fresh from the polls, are especially enthusiastic. They recall with pride the association of their own last administration with the Dawes committee which, as they see it, has done so much for Europe at this critical time.

They look forward hopefully to continued co-operation upon similar lines, since they recognize that a settlement of the European imbroglio must precede any real industrial recovery in Great Britain. They also welcome the return to power in the United States of a party which they regard as of a somewhat similar political completion to themselves.

French See Popular Reaction

PARIS, Nov. 5 (P)—The Republican victory in the American election is seen by Le Temps today as a popular reaction against "tendencies regarded as dangerous to the constitutional régime." The newspaper says the election of Calvin Coolidge as President and Charles G. Dawes as Vice-President assures continuance of the recent American policy "in the direction of more active co-operation with Europe, and that it is only by private means for the solution of the problems of peace."

The Intransigeant, commenting upon the election of Brig.-Gen. Dawes, says: "America owed this homage to the author of the Dawes plan."

"BOY EMPEROR" LEAVES PALACE

PEKING, Nov. 5 (P)—In consequence of the decision of Feng Yu-hsiang, head of the new Chinese military régime, to take over the Imperial City in accordance with the Manchu abdication agreement, the "Boy Emperor," Hsuan Tung, and his entire family this afternoon left the imperial palace and took up their residence at the palace of Prince Chun, the former regent.

The Manchu dynasty was overthrown as a result of a revolution which broke out in 1911. The Emperor abdicated on Feb. 12, 1912, being guaranteed favorable treatment and a pension of $4,000,000 a year by the new Republic.

Hsuan Tung, the former Emperor, has been living in the Imperial Palace in the "forbidden city" since his abdication, but his pension has long been in arrears. On several occasions it has been reported that Hsuan had been forced to sell valuable heirlooms of his family in order to meet expenses.

World News in Brief

Mexico City—Foreign or nonunion laborers will not be permitted to work as strike breakers in the Corona Company's oil fields, the Federation of Labor is assured by President Obregon. The federation had protested to the President against an alleged plan by the company to import workers from Holland.

Mooseheart, Ill.—James J. Davis, Secretary of Labor, has been elected Mayor of Mooseheart, more than 1200 children of all ages participating in the voting. Mr. Davis, founder of the Moose children's city, is the first to be honored with election to this office.

Walla Walla, Wash.—The Walla Walla Times, a daily newspaper published by union printers and supported financially by the International Typographical Union and by union printers of the northwest, has ceased publication. Oct. 2, 1922.

Cape Girardeau, Mo. (P)—Persons of every religious faith have united in a movement to make the church dominant in Cape Girardeau. A fund subscribed by business and professional citizens maintains three illuminated signboards and systematic newspaper advertising during the year. Part in church also observes separately. All churches reported unprecedented increases in attendance and budgets.

Berlin (P)—Amazing changes have come about in Berlin. High-priced hotels are crowded; there are theater and opera openings almost nightly; various German commercial organizations are holding conventions and conferences; directors of various shipping companies are planning for an extension of their activities.

Warsaw—Poland is the most expensive country in the world in which to live, says the Journal of Polonne. The reason given is that nearly 50 per cent of the state expenditures are invested in unproductive armaments.

Zurich (P)—Zurich, the past summer, like most other Swiss cities, has had more American visitors than at any other period in history. At the height of the season when all the hotels and pensions were filled every night, the city authorities turned a schoolhouse over to be used temporarily for those who were unable to find quarters for the travelers.

London (P)—Negotiations are expected to be completed shortly whereby the garret in Heathfield Hall, Handsworth, in which James Watt conducted the experiments which led to the development of the steam engine, will be removed bodily to London to be perpetuated in the South Kensington Museum. All first went to Heathfield Hall in 1768.

STATE DRY LAW VOTE LOOKS TO BE VERY CLOSE

Referenda Tabulation Not Complete — Child Toil Ban Meets Defeat

The vote on seven state-wide referenda had not been tabulated in full this afternoon but the disposition which the voters made of four of them was fairly accurately indicated by the returns from 1081 out of 1155 precincts outside of Boston.

It was previously decided that the vote on the most conspicuous of these questions—liquor law, gasoline tax, child labor and daylight saving—would be counted before any other referenda.

The vote of the 1353 precincts, including all but two Boston precincts, gave on the referendum questions:

No. 3, Liquor law, Yes, 412,099; No, 414,001; No. 4, Gasoline tax, Yes, 251,015; No, 504,908; No. 6, Daylight saving, Yes, 453,295; No, 393,794; No. 7, Child Labor, Yes, 222,988; No, 639,411.

On the question of approving a law which provides that no person shall manufacture or transport liquor without a Government permit, thus virtually setting up a state law instead act and giving full effect to the Eighteenth Amendment, prohibition leaders were hoping for victory this afternoon, although the vote would be close.

The citizens of the Commonwealth strongly voiced their disapproval of the proposed amendment giving Congress the power to limit, regulate or prohibit the labor of persons under 18 years of age. This was one of the big issues of the campaign and received special attention by the Democrats who inserted a plank favoring this amendment in their platform.

On the basis of 1353 precincts, the gasoline tax, providing that an excise levy of 2 cents a gallon be placed on gasoline and other fuel used for motor vehicles, appears to have been "snowed under" by a 2-to-1 vote.

Daylight saving appears to have been retained in so far as the voice of the people can make itself felt on Beacon Hill.—The fact that the "yeses" had it in cities and towns outside Boston, which include the farming communities where daylight saving is supposed to be in great disfavor, leads to the opinion that it will win. It is generally accepted as a fact that the industrial centers favor the change in the hands of their clock and the proponents of this practice feel confident that the final tabulation will show an even greater margin in favor.

AUSTRALIA REPORTS REGARDING MANDATES

By Special Cable

GENEVA, Nov. 5—The Mandates Commission yesterday discussed the Australian Government's reports on New Guinea and Nauru, Sir Joseph Cook supplying supplementary information on a number of points. The first named report, as illustrated by numerous photographs, contained the report of the canning inquiry into the alleged forced labor and the flogging of natives, but no questions were asked on this point, the commission being apparently satisfied.

Sir Joseph stated that the forced labor existing under German rule had been abolished, and all the work was now paid for under contract. The chairman expressed the commission's satisfaction with both reports.

GANDHI IN CALCUTTA

By Special Cable

CALCUTTA, Nov. 5 — Mahatma Gandhi arrived secretly in Calcutta some time within the last 48 hours. He alighted from the Punjab mail at Bandel, 30 miles from Calcutta, and motored to C. R. Das's house. The utmost secrecy was maintained regarding his arrival, but large crowds went out in the early morning in the hopes of seeing him.

GILLETT SEEMS TO BE ELECTED BY SMALL MARGIN

In Other State Contests Massachusetts Polls Big Republican Majorities

STATE TICKET

GOVERNOR
Alvan T. Fuller of Malden, R.

LIEUTENANT-GOVERNOR
Frank G. Allen of Norwood, R.

SECRETARY
Frederic W. Cook of Somerville, R.

TREASURER
William S. Youngman of Boston, R.

AUDITOR
Alonzo B. Cook of Boston, R.

ATTORNEY-GENERAL
Jay R. Benton of Belmont, R.

Unofficial and nearly complete returns today indicated the election of Speaker Frederick H. Gillett for the United States Senate over Senator David I. Walsh by a margin estimated at about 6000 votes. Victory in this important contest will make the Republican landslide that carried Calvin Coolidge in for President complete in this State, so far as the state ticket is concerned.

With all but two of Boston's 274 precincts, and 1082 of the 1158 precincts outside of this city completed, the totals gave Speaker Gillett 511,446, Senator Walsh 505,427. This plurality, estimated at 6019, if official figures later verify it, seems small when compared with the plurality of more than 300,000 for President Coolidge over John W. Davis, Democratic candidate for President and about 110,000 for Lt. Gov. Alvan T. Fuller of Malden, candidate of the Republicans for Governor over Mayor James M. Curley of Boston, but weeks ago the closeness of the contest between the Speaker of the national House of Representatives and the Junior Senator from Massachusetts was conceded and the last efforts of the leaders of both parties were directed to this contest.

Same Political Proportions

The same political proportions are maintained in the delegation of 16 Representatives sent from Massachusetts to the lower house of Congress—13 Republicans and 3 Democrats.

The counting of the legislative returns was delayed as the election boards, generally, made their first counts on President, United States Senator, and Governor. After those official counters, the election officials counted the returns of national Representatives and, frequently, because of the great interest taken in them, the seven referenda of state-wide import.

The legislative count, unofficial and (Continued on Page 4, Column 1)

COOLIDGE-DAWES TICKET SWEEPS NATION WITH 10,000,000 PLURALITY

Calvin Coolidge   *Charles G. Dawes*

Brennan Hold on Illinois Is But a Memory

Democratic Strife Stirred at N. Y. Convention Proves Boomerang

Special from Monitor Bureau

CHICAGO, Nov. 5—Democratic discord which George E. Brennan, Illinois' political boss, invoked in the New York Democratic convention, reacted on him yesterday. Brennan's candidates for Governor of Illinois and United States Senator were blotted out, and what is more vital to a boss, his entire county ticket was crushed.

Despite all the factionalism which has broken up Republican unity here, the Republican local candidates received majorities numbered by the hundreds of thousands. Surviving in the Harding landslide of four years ago, one Democratic county officeholder ran again yesterday. He was retired.

Brennan's Illinois lieutenant at Madison Square Garden, Michael Igoe, popular and able, for whom every effort had been expended, lost the highly important state's attorneyship by 250,000 votes. Brennan's arts had been exhausted on Igoe, but his opponent ran 40,000 ahead of the other Republican candidates.

Playing to both wets and drys, the Illinois boss' strategy had led him to pick a dry for Governor, but by 490,000 to a Republican Governor laboring under singularly heavy disadvantages. Brennan's wet candidate for Senator simultaneously was rejected by upward of 300,000 and failed to carry much wet territory in his own city of Chicago, losing Chicago by more than 100,000.

Assuming a commanding position in national Democratic councils on the passing of Charles F. Murphy, the Tammany leader, the Illinoisan led the fight against William G. McAdoo at the New York Democratic convention, and was credited with an important rôle in the conduct of the campaign. However, he was judged by close political observers to make his moves on the national stage in response to cues given by the local situation in Chicago and Illinois.

This campaign, however, moved on broader lines. It recalls that once before Mr. Brennan played a part in dictating the nomination of a Democratic Presidential candidate, whose nomination was followed in 1920 by a Republican landslide, comparable only to that of 1924.

Thanksgiving Proclamation
By the President of the United States of America

WE APPROACH that season of the year when it has been the custom for the American people to give thanks for the good fortune which the bounty of Providence, through the generosity of nature, has visited upon them. It is altogether a good custom. It has the sanction of antiquity and the appropriation of our religious convictions. In acknowledging the receipt of divine favor in contemplating the blessings which have been bestowed upon us, we shall reveal the spiritual strength of the Nation.

The year has been marked by a continuation of peace whereby our country has entered into a relationship of better understanding with all the other nations of the earth. This is owing in no small way to which we could perform very great service through the giving of friendly counsel, through the extension of financial assistance, and through the exercise of a spirit of neighborly kindliness to less favored peoples. We should give thanks for the power which has been given into our keeping, with which we have been able to render these services to the rest of mankind.

At home we have continually had an improving state of the public health. The production of our industries has been large and our harvests have been bountiful. We have been remarkably free from disorder and remarkably successful in all those pursuits which flourish during a state of domestic peace. An abundant prosperity has overspread the land. We shall do well to accept all these favors and bounties with a becoming humility, and dedicate them to the service of the righteous cause of the Giver of all good and perfect gifts. As the Nation has prospered, let all the people show that they are worthy to prosper, by rededicating America to the service of God and man.

THEREFORE, I, Calvin Coolidge, President of the United States of America, hereby proclaim and fix Thursday, the twenty-seventh day of November, as a day for national thanksgiving. I recommend that the people gather in their places of worship, and at family altars, and offer up their thanks for the goodness which has been shown to them in such a multitude of ways. Especially I urge them to supplicate the Throne of Grace that they may gather strength from their tribulations, that they may gain humility from their victories, that they may bear without complaining the burdens that shall be placed upon them, and that they may be increasingly worthy in all ways of the blessings that shall come to them.

IN WITNESS WHEREOF, I have hereunto set my hand and caused to be affixed the great seal of the United States.

DONE at the City of Washington, this fifth day of November, in the year of our Lord one thousand nine hundred and twenty-four, and of the independence of the United States the one hundred and forty-ninth.

(Signed) CALVIN COOLIDGE.

RHODE ISLAND OVERTURN PUTS REPUBLICANS IN POWER

PROVIDENCE, R. I., Nov. 5—Giving its five electoral votes to Calvin Coolidge and Charles G. Dawes, Rhode Island at the same time swept its Republican state ticket into office yesterday, elected Jesse H. Metcalf to the United States Senate on that ticket and returned Clark Burdick and Richard S. Aldrich to Congress. Jeremiah E. O'Connell, Democratic nominee from the Third Congressional District, was the only opposition candidate to survive the débacle. Aram J. Pothier, named by the Republicans to combat the candidacy of Lieut.-Gov. Felix A. Toupin, stormy petrel of Rhode Island politics, who aspired to the gubernatorial chair, defeated his opponent by more than 32,000 votes, and Nathaniel W. Smith swamped Robert E. Quinn, who sought to carry on as Mr. Toupin's successor in the president's chair of the Rhode Island Senate.

The strong Democratic minority in the Senate is wiped out by yesterday's election and their high numbers, inasmuch as the plurality for Coolidge and Dawes, in the largest outpouring of votes ever known in the State yesterday, was nearly equal to the poll for all presidential candidates in 1912.

Pluralities for the five Republican Congressmen elected ranged from 6912 for James P. Glynn, Fifth District, over P. B. O'Sullivan of the present incumbent to 34,907 for Schuyler Merritt (R.) Fourth District, over William English Walling (D.) of Greenwich, well-known writer. In each of these districts one of the missing cities is still to be heard

regarded by party leaders as the most remarkable vote ever rolled up for a Republican candidate in the State, exceeding the plurality for President Harding four years ago by about 37,000 votes. The total vote for President was Coolidge 255,993, Davis 109,788, La Follette 37,539.

With pluralities for the state ticket ranging from 125,394 for Lieut.-Gov. Hiram Bingham, Republican nominee for Governor over Charles G. Morris, Democrat, up to 131,086 for the Republican nominee for state Treasurer, it was indicated that the 37,171 votes cast for the La Follette-Wheeler electors in the State, with two cities missing, were drawn quite largely from the Democratic electorate. It compared rather closely with the vote collected for former President Roosevelt in the Progressive campaign of 1912, when La Follette added Government ownership of railroads as

Great Republican Plurality Rolled Up in Connecticut

NEW HAVEN, Conn., Nov. 5—With the vote of the State all in, a tabulation shows a total plurality for Coolidge and Dawes in Connecticut of 146,205 over Davis and Bryan,

Victory Called Confidence Vote in Mr. Coolidge

Not Due to G. O. P., But Is "Personal Triumph," Says Observer

By FREDERIC WILLIAM WILE

WASHINGTON, Nov. 4—No presidential election was ever so easy to diagnose as the landslide which has swept Calvin Coolidge to victory. It is a personal triumph, pure and simple, almost unparalleled in our modern political history. The result is immeasurably less a vindication of the Republican Party, or even of Republican fundamentals, than it is a stupendous vote of confidence in Calvin Coolidge. That is the long and short of the presidential election of 1924.

There will be arguments in plenty to prove why the victors conquered, and why the conquered were vanquished. There will be talk of the wave of prosperity on the farms, which sent the rural west to the polls in an avalanche for Mr. Coolidge. There will be explanations that Davis was hopelessly handicapped from the start by Democratic strife and by the Bryan millstone. But when all is said and done, all the credits and debits have been balanced, it will be discovered that it was overwhelmingly the country's deep-seated, impregnable confidence in the President that elected him.

What They Voted For

Nothing else seriously counted. Hardly anything else was in the voters' minds. Their thoughts were concentrated on what Senator Moses of New Hampshire called "the calm and cautious Christian character of Calvin Coolidge." That is what the country voted for overwhelmingly—east and west, north and southwest. That is why, with the exception of the invincible Democratic south and a couple of southwestern border states and La Follette's Wisconsin, the Nation almost made the election of Mr. Coolidge unanimous.

There are, of course, correlated reasons for the President's smashing victory. Prosperity is the foremost of them, but over and above it is directly associated with the paramount cause of "confidence in Coolidge." Prosperity having arrived, the people determined to risk no loss of it by a mid-stream change of Administration in Washington. They convinced themselves that there would be an incalculably stronger prospect of keeping the times good by perpetuating Mr. Coolidge in the White House than by displacing him. The Nation directly links up the President's "calm" and "caution" with prosperity. Indeed the Coolidge landslide plainly indicates that without those qualities in the leadership of the United States at this juncture, the people felt their welfare might be in jeopardy. They decided not to make a change. They voted to "let well enough alone."

Rout for Radicalism

Against that stone wall of reasoning, the attacks of the Democratic and Progressive parties were launched in vain. It was almost as if the country had shut its collective ear to the pleadings, the arguments, and the invectives of the opposition. As for Mr. La Follette, his introduction of the Supreme Court issue, with its frontal attack on the fundamentals of the Constitution, presented to the Republicans defensive material that probably would if not itself might have been sufficient to win in the country.

When Mr. La Follette added Government ownership of railroads as

Latest Returns Swell Republican Totals in Nation's Record Vote

PRESIDENT LEADING IN WESTERN POLLS

Texas and Wyoming Elect Women Governors—Smith Re-Elected in New York

WALSH IS DEFEATED IN MASSACHUSETTS

Coolidge Polled 18,000,000 Vote, Davis, 8,000,000, and La Follette, About 4,000,000

NEW YORK, Nov. 5 (P)—As returns from the states continued to roll in today, they served only to swell the tide upon which Calvin Coolidge is riding to an apparent overwhelming victory over his two opponents in the 1924 presidential contest.

In eight states, all of them in the west, the result still was in doubt at midday, but the President had a lead in seven of them, including Minnesota, North Dakota, and South Dakota, which followers of Senator Robert M. La Follette had expected to win the Independent candidate their electoral votes.

Returns in the congressional contests were slow and at noon they still were insufficient to show whether Mr. Coolidge will have a real working majority of his party in either the House or Senate. The Republicans had made a net gain of 12 in the House, and apparently, of three or four in the Senate. Nicholas Longworth of Ohio, the Republican leader in the House, has been re-elected as has Finis J. Garrett (D.) Representative from Tennessee, the Democratic House leader.

Davis and La Follette

John W. Davis succeeded in capturing certainly only states generally reckoned as irrevocably Democratic. Even at that he lost Kentucky, on the face of the incomplete returns, although Mr. Cox had carried it against Mr. Harding in 1920. The same returns indicated that he had brought back into the Democratic fold two of the states taken away by Mr. Harding—Oklahoma and Tennessee.

Senator La Follette, with a popular vote of about 4,000,000, which approximates Mr. Roosevelt's in the memorable year 1912, was assured the electoral vote of only one State—his own, Wisconsin—Roosevelt captured 90 electoral votes in 1912—enough to defeat his Republican opponent, Taft, and elect his Democratic adversary, Wilson.

It was estimated that President Coolidge polled 18,000,000 popular votes—2,000,000 more than were given to Mr. Harding. Mr. Davis, it was estimated, had 8,000,000 as against 9,000,000 for Mr. Cox. More voters trooped to the polling places and dropped their ballots yesterday than ever before in the history of the Nation.

Overwhelming Majorities

In many of the states carried by Mr. Coolidge his majority over both of his adversaries was overwhelming. In New York State where the Republican national ticket made a clean sweep both in the metropolis and upstate, the plurality over Mr. Davis was more than 800,000. In New England states, Mr. Coolidge's one time neighbors piled up a lead for him which in some cases ran up to 10 to 1. In Ohio and Illinois the majorities likewise were tremendous, and out on the Pacific coast the tale of the ballots was almost the same. California California indicated the Republican margin there will be more than 100,000.

There was underflow of this roaring tide of Coolidge strength pulled down to defeat a number of Democratic state tickets and Democratic members of Congress who had been confident of election, but in New York, Governor Alfred E. Smith withstood the handicap of a sweep for the Republican national ticket, and bested his Republican opponent for re-election, Theodore Roosevelt, by an estimated 100,000 plurality. Mr. Roosevelt came down from the upstate districts with a lead that seemed for a time to make his election certain, but the metropolis rose to the occasion and repelled the invasion at its borders.

Women Elected Governors

In Ohio another Democratic Governor, Vic Donahey, battling with a similar handicap, was about holding his own today in a nip and tuck race for re-election against the Republican nominee, former Governor Harry L. Davis. The sweep of the Coolidge slide appeared, on the other hand, to have reversed the expectations of the wiseacres and to have landed Ed Jackson, the Republican candidate for Governor in Indiana, in the Governor's chair at Indianapolis.

In Texas, Mrs. Miriam A. Ferguson, wife of an impeached Governor, who won her nomination on the Democratic ticket in Texas after a fight against Klan sympathizers, and obtained a place on the ballot, only after a further fight in the courts, apparently had been rewarded with the distinction of being the first woman ever elected to preside over the destinies of a state. Very fragmentary and inconclusive returns from Wyoming gave the lead for Governor in that State, too, to a woman, Mrs. Nellie Ross, the Demo-

THE CHRISTIAN SCIENCE MONITOR

AN INTERNATIONAL DAILY NEWSPAPER

COPYRIGHT 1925 BY THE CHRISTIAN SCIENCE PUBLISHING SOCIETY | Fourteen Pages | BOSTON, MONDAY, APRIL 27, 1925—VOL. XVII, NO. 128 | ATLANTIC EDITION | FIVE CENTS A COPY

HIGH CHARGES ON MORTGAGES CHECK BUILDING

National Real Estate Organization Seeks to Convince Investors of Their Safety

COMMISSION UP TO 15 P. C. IN CHICAGO

Basis of Facts Sought as Solution of Problem Embarrassing Construction Men

Special from Monitor Bureau

CHICAGO, April 27—"There is no question but that the risks in second mortgages are generally overemphasized, and that in many communities unduly high charges have tended to restrict home building," said Arthur E. Curtis, secretary of the mortgage finance division of the National Association of Real Estate Boards. "It is an unstandardized business, but more money is going into it every year, and we hope at the coming convention of the association, when we shall take up this question in our mortgage section, to make a start toward improving the situation.

"We are making an investigation to determine the risks, and we believe that the facts will show that they do not justify the high charges, but will show comparatively few losses.

Survey by School Dean

"Here in Chicago an illuminating inquiry into the second mortgage situation has just been completed by Harry A. Atkinson, dean of the School of Commerce at the Central Y. M. C. A.

"Mr. Atkinson's investigation shows that the average commission charged here is about 10 per cent, with interest of 6 or 7 per cent in addition. On a second mortgage of $2000 made for one year this would mean a commission of $200 with interest of $140, a total of $340, which is deducted at the time the loan is made, so that the borrower receives $1660.

"If the mortgage ran for two years the commission probably would be 15 per cent and the interest 7 per cent; for three years, 18 per cent, same interest. I have known of instances where as much as 25 per cent was charged."

In such an excessive charge as the last, the commission on a $2000 second mortgage would amount to $500, and if it ran three years with interest at 7 per cent would total $420, or a combined payment of $920 for the use of $1360 in actual money for three years.

Has One Good Factor

"This, however, should be said of second mortgage rates," added Mr. Curtis. "It is true that they sometimes discourage the individual of small means who wants to build a home but just falls short of the means to finance it. At the same time they often shut out the weak builder and others who, if financing were too easy, would try to operate on a shoe-string and get into difficulties they could not overcome. In other words the good side of these high charges is they have served to restrict speculative building.

"What we need is a basis of fact. Charges have grown up in different cities along different lines, until today they are levied indiscriminately. The mortgage and finance division of the National Association of Real Estate Boards has taken this question up in earnest and we hope to make a substantial beginning toward its solution this year."

15 to 18 Per Cent Rates Shown in Louisville Survey

LOUISVILLE, Ky., April 25 (Special) — Second mortgage interest rates in Louisville run around 6 per cent, plus discount fees, which brings the total up to as high as 15 or 18 per cent, depending on the time the second mortgage runs, according to authorities here. The discount is subtracted from the amount of money lent. The average total rate amounts to 11 or 12 per cent.

C. C. Hieatt, chairman of the taxation committee of the National Association of Real Estate Boards, remarks that a second or third mortgage is usually only for a small part of the cost of a house, and then the high interest on it adds only a very small percentage to the cost of the principal loan. The system here, Mr. Hieatt observes, is not so much of a hardship as it appears.

Second Mortgage Problem National, Kansas City Reports

KANSAS CITY, Mo., April 25 (Special)—Interest amounting to 6 and 7 per cent is charged on Kansas City second mortgages. These, if they are marketed, must be discounted anywhere from 10 to 20 per cent. The discount, which often is figured in at the time the mortgage is made, varies with the estimated value of the property.

The second mortgage is regarded here as a problem by both building and real estate interests. These explain that the problem is in no sense local, but national. Home building operations in Kansas City are well up to market demands, and several times in the last four years have been ahead of demand.

ALLIED AMBASSADORS TO DEBATE VIOLATIONS

PARIS, April 27—A meeting of the Allied Council of Ambassadors has been called for next Wednesday to take up the supplementary report of Marshal Foch, as head of the Allied Military Committee, on the German violations of the Versailles Treaty.

Japanese From California Are to Farm Lands in Ohio

Colony of 500 Will Locate in Richland County and Take Individual Leases

MANSFIELD, O., April 25 (Special Correspondence) — Five hundred Japanese will be brought from Imperial Valley, Calif., to lease and farm the mucklands between Plymouth and Willard, Richland County, according to an announcement by J. O. Parsons of Plymouth, this county's president of the Ohio Farms Company, which owns the land. The Japanese will take over 1500 acres.

Work on the construction of 50 houses to shelter the first 50 families of the colony will begin at once, Mr. Parsons said. The land, he added, is being reclaimed and prepared for the tenants, many of whom are citizens of the United States through birth in Hawaii. The orinetal tenants are expected to pay a good rental price. Most of the land, Mr. Parsons said, already has been reclaimed.

It had been the intention of the company to bring in the better class of southern Europeans for colonization purposes, but it is stated that a sufficient number of these could not be induced to come here to properly farm 4000 acres of land owned by the company. For this reason it became necessary to change the original policy. This led to the investigation of the Japanese.

Fifty families are expected here by July. Some of them will come at once, the remainder after they complete the harvest of their California crops. It is expected that at least 100 families totaling 500 persons will be on the mucklands eventually. The crops will be put in the land this spring. Lettuce, celery, onions and other vegetables, the most suitable products of the soil, will be raised.

Commenting on the character of these Japanese as citizens, Mr. Parsons said that the pastor of the Japanese church they attended in California had been educated at Oberlin College, Oberlin, O., and that the members of the committee which came here to investigate the proposition are graduates of American colleges and universities. The families that will be brought here are Christions and Americanized, he declared, and added that they are taking up the leases individually.

The coming of these Japanese to Ohio brings the first colony of farmers of that nationality into this State and will place Ohio third in the number of Japanese in the United States, it is estimated here.

SAFE DRIVING LAW ASSURED

Jail Terms to Be Mandatory for Drunken Driving Second Offenders

Final touches have been added to the so-called drunken driver bill, which provides jail sentences for a person found guilty a second time of driving an automobile under the influence of liquor, and Governor Fuller has said that he will sign the measure which is to be enacted today by both branches of the Legislature.

Engrossing the bill is the mechanical process alone that may prevent the bill's becoming law today.

Clarence S. Luitweiler of Newton, state Representative, who introduced this bill which has been fought and fought hard by many men opposed to this legislation which will make it mandatory for the judges to send to jail drivers of motor vehicles who have been convicted of driving while intoxicated within six years of their arrest for that offense.

Jail Term Mandatory

The "Drunken Driver" bill was ready for enactment today when the Legislature came in at 11. The amendments put on the measure last week were but perfecting expressions and stipulations in the bill, House 1284, as it finally passed to the enactment stage. Several amendments were offered which would have vitiated the purpose of Mr. Luitweiler.

Several judges have disregarded the present law providing for giving jail sentences to second offenders for intoxication while operating motor vehicles on the ground that the wording of the statute really left their course optional with themselves when dealing with this specific offense.

Governor Fuller, in his address yesterday before the Tremont Temple Brotherhood on the annual "Governor's Day" meeting, said that this measure shows the power of public opinion when it is determined to have its way in matters of government.

Public Opinion's Power

The "drunken driver" bill, the Governor added, was made possible by the growing indignation on the part of the great body of the people at the danger to which innocent persons are put when operating cars on the road or even walking near the highways.

"I am satisfied with the 'Drunken Driver' bill as it now has been framed," said Mr. Luitweiler today to a representative of The Christian Science Monitor. "It now positively makes it impossible for judges in municipal courts to suspend sentences or to place on probation motorists guilty of second offense intoxication within six years. It makes the measure really safe, because persons under suspended sentences cannot appeal to the Superior Court; so the bill, when finally law, will be sound."

LITTLE ENTENTE NOT TO DISCUSS GREECE AND POLAND

By Special Cable

BUCHAREST, April 27—The Rumanian Foreign Minister, I. G. Duca, has informed the correspondent of The Christian Science Monitor that the Little Entente Conference has been definitely set for May 9, 10 and 11, at Bucharest. The Foreign Minister says the admission of Greece and Poland is not under consideration.

The tentative program of the conference comprises a discussion of Hungary's military expenditure, the Bulgarian situation and minor questions involving Russia.

The Foreign Minister categorically denied current rumors of Bolshevist disturbances in Bessarabia, and that Rumania is considering military intervention in Bulgaria. He expressed the belief that the Zankoff Government is competent to control the situation without outside intervention.

NEPAL SLAVES BEING SET FREE

Emancipation Work Encouraged by Another Grant of 3,900,000 Rupees

By Special Cable

CALCUTTA, April 27—Khatmandu messages report that a prompt and willing response has been made to the antislavery appeal issued by the Maharajah of Nepal.

The work of emancipation, already well advanced, has been further encouraged by the grant of another 3,900,000 rupees for this purpose, making the total grant 5,300,000.

The plea for the abolition of slavery has been so successful that it has been found possible to do away with the period of seven years during which emancipated slaves originally bound were to continue their labors with former masters.

Slaves are brought daily from various parts of the kingdom to gather at Khatmandu durbars — councils — at which the Maharajah declares them free men.

FEDERAL CLUBS SEEK TO AROUSE LAGGARD VOTER

New Organization Also Would Establish College of Political Science

Special from Monitor Bureau

WASHINGTON, April 27—Arousing every citizen of the country to cast his ballot at the polls at every election, impressing voters with the value of good citizenship, and ultimately the establishment of a college of political science in the National Capital, are among the purposes of the National Association of Federal Clubs, with headquarters in Washington.

The association is really a nucleus for a large number of local clubs to be formed in the cities of the country, one to each city. Four have already been organized, and are now on a working basis, in Baltimore, Boston, Philadelphia and New York, it was announced at association headquarters today, with another in the process of formation and about to have its organization completed, located in Indiana.

Apathetic Voter Objective

Steadily decreasing interest in voting has been manifested since the presidential election of 1896, when 78 per cent of the citizens eligible to vote cast their ballots, according to figures compiled by the association. This ratio went down to 61 per cent in 1912, with a slight uptrend to 70 per cent in 1916, after which there was a sharp decline, in 1920 the percentage being 49 and in 1924 slightly below 50, or, to be exact, 49.7. It is pointed out by the department of research of the association, headed by Alfred Anthony, that in the latter year President Coolidge received 26.8 per cent of the eligible vote.

It is to overcome this apathy on the part of voters that the Association has been formed. To this end, the application form of the Association calls attention to the fact that there is a growing tendency among the citizens of the country "to neglect the responsibilities of citizenship" and "that such negligence constitutes a meanace to our Nation and hinders its progress as a true Republic."

To bring about the training of qualified leaders in the science of government is another one of the objectives of the association. This is found necessary, in the belief of those sponsoring the association, because the administration of government, federal, state, and municipal, is daily becoming more complicated, "and has now reached a point where efficient operation of all government is impaired through the lack of qualified leaders." This training of leaders can best be brought about, they

(Continued on Page 3, Column 8)

CHILD WELFARE CASES SHOW ADVANTAGES OF PROHIBITION

Eighteenth Amendment Has Brought Large Decrease of Intemperance as Reflected in the Records of S. P. C. C.—Secretary Submits Report

Prohibition has cut intemperance more than half as a factor in child welfare cases handled by the Massachusetts Society for the Prevention of Cruelty to Children, it is shown in the annual report issued today by Theodore A. Lathrop, general secretary.

Enactment of the Eighteenth Amendment brought at once a decrease of fully 60 per cent in intemperance, and this factor, although observed to vary through fluctuating enforcement of the law in this State, has always been at least 50 per cent less than in the days of license.

"Intemperance in Massachusetts," the report states, "as reflected by the work of the society, discloses that in 1916 a prosperous pre-war year, it appeared in 47.7 per cent of our cases. In 1921, the first year of national prohibition, it dropped to 16.8, nearly two-thirds. In 1922, it increased to 20.2 per cent, and in 1923, to 23.2 per cent. It was thought that these increases were due to the superiority of the illegal liquor traffic over law enforcement, which in this State was without state law concurrent with the federal. This year, 1924, intemperance has decreased to 21.9 per cent. The peak seems to have been passed.

Improvement in Children

"Whatever other statistics may show as to the value and effectiveness of national prohibition to suppress the evils of intemperance, our records show that, since national prohibition, intemperance has at all times been less than half that prevailing before. The family man is noticeably less in evidence because of intemperance. The condition of women and children has correspondingly improved.

"While the decrease of intemperance noted in 1924 is encouraging, now that Massachusetts law is concurrent with the federal law it is reasonable to expect better law enforcement and further decrease of this menace to home life."

Other statistics contained in the report show that the society was called upon to render aid to 13,351, which comprised 5342 individual families. In four out of every five families reform was possible without court action, and out of 2000 children protected by court action only 347 were permanently removed from their homes.

"The more we analyze our work," Mr. Lathrop explains, "the more evident it becomes that ignorance and incompetency of parents as to the fundamentals of their job account for a large part of our work, and that prevention of child abuse and neglect will come, for the most part, only through education of parents. The building of an ideal home and the proper rearing of children, is life's most important task. Parents should have as complete training for this as they would have for any other human undertaking."

See Need for Expansion

John H. Sturgis, general treasurer, reports that total expenses for the year were over $178,000, while income from contributions and from investments were only $132,000 leaving a deficit of $45,000 which was met out of unrestricted bequests, and that the work last year increased 9 per cent over the year before.

As to the financial condition of the society, Mr. Sturgis says, "there is a need of an increase of 50 per cent in current contributions to keep up with present demands upon us, but for any assurance of permanence we must depend on bequests, many small ones, a few large ones, and some day a monumental gift that will forever identify the giver's name with the work of setting children free from oppression."

GOVERNORS TO MEET JUNE 28 TO JULY 4

PORTLAND, Me., April 27—The governors' conference will be held at Poland Spring from June 28 to July 4, it has been definitely decided. President Coolidge is expected to attend the conference and it is considered probable tht he will come to Portland in the presidential yacht, the Mayflower, and from here go to Poland Spring by automobile.

Governor Brewster is arranging to have the Army and the Navy send a squadron of hydroplanes and airplanes to Poland Spring or to Portland.

ITALIAN AIRMAN LEAVES BAGDAD

ROME, April 27 — Commander Francesco de Pinedo, chief of the Italian Air Staff, has arrived at Bagdad on his attempted flight from Rome to Tokyo, according to dispatches reaching here today. De Pinedo, using a hydro-airplane, started his flight last Tuesday.

BAGDAD, April 27—Commander de Pinedo left here today for Bushire, Persia.

AUSTIN HOST TO TEACHERS AND PARENTS

Enforcement, Clean Press, Censorship, Are Topics at Convention

AUSTIN, Tex., April 27 (Special)—Delegates to the 29th annual convention of the National Congress of Parents and Teachers, representing a membership of about 700,000 mothers and educators, have met here to advance their program of work for children.

The discussions are to cover a wide range of subjects, including law enforcement in the United States and its relation to the home, the educational influence of the daily newspaper, motion picture censorship, child labor, and other social questions of current importance.

Men are having a prominent place in the proceedings this year for the first year in the history of the organization which, until last year, had been known as the National Congress of Mothers and Parent-Teachers Associations. The idea of training men to deal with children is expected to have an important part in the six days' sessions.

Inception in 1855

Dr. Walter M. W. Splawn, new president of the University of Texas, was chosen to deliver the chief address at the first evening session. He was to discuss modern factors in child education. May Day exercises by Austin school children in the university stadium and tree planting exercises are among the novel features of the program.

The organization had its beginning in thought and ideals as long ago as 1855 when mothers' meetings were held in connection with the inauguration of the kindergarten movement in the United States. It was, however, in 1897—February 17—that the present organization, under the name of National Congress of Mothers, was founded in Washington. It was Mrs. Theodore W. Birney of that city, heading a large group of men and women drawn together by a common appeal—the highest welfare of children and the manifold interests of the home—who realized her dream of an intelligent and sympathetic motherhood in the founding of the congress.

Mrs. Phoebe A. Hearst, at that time widely known for her interest in the welfare of children, financed the movement. The annual celebration of Founders' Day (or Child Welfare Day) on Feb. 17 has become an international observance when appreciative tributes are paid to these two women in hundreds of parent-teacher associations throughout all parts of the land.

Name Is Changed

With increasing realization of the essential importance of active cooperation between the home and the school, the name was changed in 1908 to National Congress of Mothers and Parent-Teacher Associations. In 1924, the marked participation of fathers in the work brought about a request for the more inclusive name now designating the organization.

Aims and purposes adopted by the founders have guided the activities of the congress throughout its 29 years of service for the childhood of America. It was foreseen by the early leaders that the home side of a child's education was a dominant force in his life and their stated aims pointed toward that side, making parental intelligence and guidance the great purpose of the organization's activity.

To raise the standard of the home, to develop wiser, better trained parenthood, to interest men and women to work together for truer, purer homes, to surround the child with that wise care in the impressionable years that will make good citizens, to bring into closer relation the home and the school, that parents and teachers may co-operate intelligently and constructively in the education of the child, and to rouse the whole community to its responsibility for the moral, civic and educational environment of its children — these

(Continued on Page 3, Column 4)

INDEX OF THE NEWS

MONDAY, APRIL 27, 1925

Germans Outline Attack on Everest

Berlin, April 27

THE German Alpine Club is preparing an attempt this summer to reach the summit of Mt. Everest, highest mountain in the world, making the ascent from the Nepal side of the Himalayas.

The expedition plans to leave Venice, Italy, on July 2, seemingly being confident that the British Government will grant the necessary permit.

CHOICE OF GERMANS FOR PRESIDENT FALLS ON VON HINDENBURG

Ex-Commander-in-Chief of Reich Forces is Elected Over His Two Opponents By Majority of Over 800,000

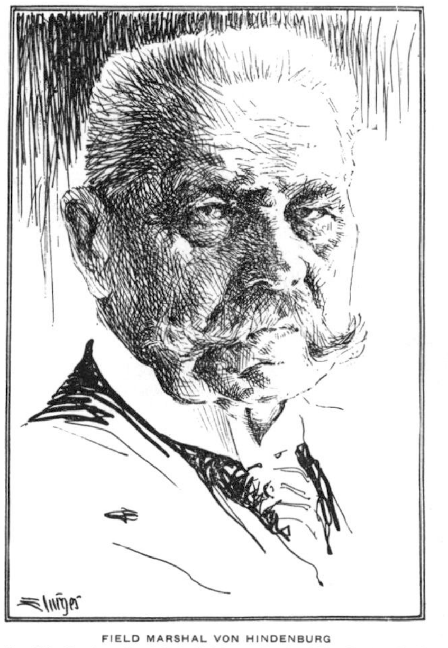

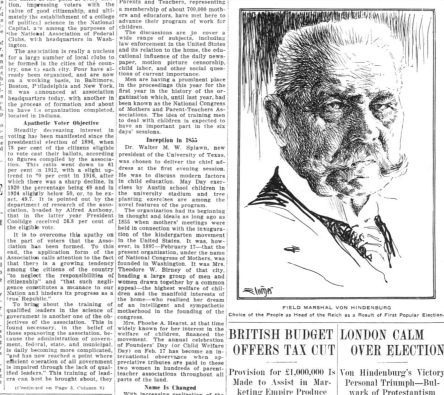

FIELD MARSHAL VON HINDENBURG

Choice of the People as Head of the Reich as a Result of First Popular Election.

RACE CLOSE UP TO MOMENT OF COUNT

Supporters of the Two Other Candidates Are Not Discouraged by Their Defeat

By Special Cable

BERLIN, April 27—Field Marshal von Hindenburg has been elected President of the Reich with 14,639,399 votes, against 13,752,640 for Dr. Wilhelm Marx and 1,931,591 for Ernst Thaelmann, according to figures published this morning at 10 o'clock, that is, with a majority of some 880,000 over Dr. Marx.

Die Welt am Montag heads its report of the election results this morning with the words "Poor Germany," while Germania speaks of the "Victory of Unreasonableness." Another reason for General von Hindenburg's victory is the fact that many did not vote at all or voted against Dr. Marx out of antipathy to Roman Catholicism.

BERLIN, April 27 (AP)—Field Marshal von Hindenburg's "front porch" campaign, conducted from his home in Hanover, has been successful, and next week he will be inducted into office as the first popularly elected President of Germany. The first President, the late Friedrich Ebert, was named by the National Assembly immediately after the revolution which established the Republic, but General von Hindenburg was chosen by direct vote of the people. Running as the choice of the Nationalist-Conservative bloc, consisting of the parties of the united Right, he received 14,639,399 votes, or 48.3 per cent of the total valid ballots cast in yesterday's polling. He obtained a pulrality of 886,659 over his principal opponent, the former Chancellor, Dr. Wilhelm Marx, candidate of the Republican bloc, who received 13,752,640 votes. Ernest Thaelmann, the Communist, trailed with 1,931,591.

The race was close from the start, the two chief candidates running neck and neck almost until the official count. Dr. Marx, backed by the Centrists, Democrats and Socialists, conducted a whirlwind campaign on the American plan, delivering several scheduled addresses daily as well as speaking from the rear platform of his train when occasion offered.

General Did Not Vote

General von Hindenburg took little active personal part in the fight, and did not even vote himself, but his supporters were busy everywhere waging a strenuous campaign. His most important speech was delivered before a great gathering of Nationalists at Hanover, when he denied that he represented reaction or that his candidacy was inimical to the republic.

His only other public utterance of significance was a final appeal, radiocast last Friday night. On that occasion the grizzled war veteran, who has spent his life in the military service of the fatherland, made this statement:

"I affirm before the whole world that it has always been my holiest endeavor to prevent new horrors of war and to help to the utmost the victims of past wars. This aim can best be attained by unity, and to serve our people as leader in this sense will be my holiest task."

Opinion on Dawes Plan

When questioned by the Associated Press during the progress of the campaign as to his attitude on the Dawes reparation plan, the field marshal stated that only the future could show whether the scheme was capable of fulfillment.

"Germany," he asserted, "will not be able to fulfill the conditions unless the foreign powers participating in the pact evince political and economic loyalty."

The women's votes and the heavy turnout of former stay-at-homes are believed to have been responsible for his victory over such a seasoned political campaigner as Dr. Marx.

The latter, however, failed to arouse enthusiasm in the ranks of the Democratic Party, which was but an unwilling partner in the so-called Weimar coalition. Dr. Marx's supporters also freely admit that anti-Catholic feeling militated strongly against their candidate's prospect.

The Reichstag will reconvene next Tuesday, and Gen. von Hinderburg, if he follows established custom, will have the Republican oath administered to him some time during the next fortnight by the Socialist Reichstag president, Paul Loebe, in the presence of a parliament in which he probably has more opponents than supporters, as the Centrists, Democrats, Socialists, and Communists command 277 seats against only 216 for the Rightists.

Early Voting Prevailed

Early voting was the rule in Berlin and the crush at many of the polling places was so great that violent encounters at times broke out and the police were busily occupied in separating the fighters. More serious trouble occured at Karlsruhe, where two persons were killed and a number wounded in a clash between Republicans and Nationalists.

Disturbances also took place at Ratibor, in Silesia, when an erroneous announcement was published to the effect that Dr. Marx was leading General von Hindenburg by nearly 2,000,000 votes. The Nationalists, roused by this, gathered and began marching through the streets.

BRITISH BUDGET OFFERS TAX CUT

Provision for £1,000,000 Is Made to Assist in Marketing Empire Produce

By Cable from Monitor Bureau

LONDON, April 27—The main features of tomorrow's budget are now confidently forecast in informed circles, though Winston Churchill's proposals have yet to be revised by the Cabinet, which is sitting here today for this purpose. The only taxation reduction expected is 6d. in £1 off the income tax, though the question of increasing this by an additional 6d. either later this year or in 1926 is understood to have not yet been finally settled.

In this connection, caution is preached in Government circles, where it is argued that it will be especially dangerous to depart from Great Britain's traditional policy of paying its way from revenue at a moment like the present when financiers are making their plans upon the expectation that at least a partial restoration of the gold standard is to take place almost immediately.

Several other announcements are also anticipated. These are, first, for a comprehensive social insurance scheme to cover contributory pensions for widowed mothers, also old-age allowances and insurance against unemployment and other loss of earnings; second, for a remission of British import duties upon such empire-grown produce as dry fruits and sugar and the provision of £1,000,000 to assist in marketing empire produce; third, for the reimposition of duties upon imported automobiles, musical instruments, films and time pieces, with new provisions for tightening up the collection of arrears of existing taxation and an inquiry with a view to a reduction of the heavy civil service expenditure.

AIR MAIL TO CUT DAY FROM LOS ANGELES CROSS-NATION TIME

WASHINGTON, April 27—Speeding up the transcontinental air-mail service has been ordered by Harry S. New, Postmaster-General, in order to cut down transit time between San Francisco and New York from 31 hours and 35 minutes, to 28 hours and 50 minutes, and at the same time to advance Southern California air mail practically one full day.

Departures from San Francisco will be made at 8:45 a. m., effective May 1 instead of 6:30 a. m., as at present. This will enable mail leaving Los Angeles at 6 p. m. to be placed on the transcontinental airplane leaving San Francisco the next morning, instead of being held there 24 hours. The change will not affect time of arrival at New York.

COLOMBIAN CABINET RESIGNS

BOGOTA, Colombia, April 27—The Colombian Cabinet resigned today, the ministerial situation having been brought to a crisis by the resignation of Foreign Minister Velez, who surrendered his portfolio because, despite his protest, the Congress adjourned without acting on the Peruvian-Colombian treaty.

LONDON CALM OVER ELECTION

Von Hindenburg's Victory Personal Triumph—Bulwark of Protestantism

By Cable from Monitor Bureau

LONDON, April 27—News of Field-Marshal von Hindenburg's election to the German presidency is on the whole taken calmly here. Though one observer described it as "putting the clock back a couple of years," the general attitude is to regard it more as a storm signal than as an actual storm. It is recognized that presidential powers in Germany are very circumscribed, approximating more to the French than the American model. Moreover, Gen. von Hindenburg's success is looked on by many as a purely personal triumph, for one who has the reputation of being transparently honest, above intrigue and who is also a strong bulwark of Protestantism.

Although the election clearly clearly shows that Germany has not forgotten the days of Frederick the Great and Bismarck, it is not expected here to lead to any immediate change in Germany's foreign policy, such as breaking off the pourparlers for peace pacts with France and other neighbors of Germany. Nevertheless, it is admitted on all sides that it will make these pourparlers more difficult, and will strengthen Aristide Briand's hands in his demand for Germany's unconditional entry to the League of Nations before taking up the serious negotiations for a security pact. In fact, the most serious apprehensions that are felt here about General von Hindenburg's election are concerned with the reaction it will inevitably provoke in France.

The Christian Science Monitor representative finds little echo in responsible circles of the fears expressed in some quarters that the process of German—and with it European—reconshtruction will be seriously affected because the much-needed credits will be withheld owing to fears that Germany is backsliding into militarism. It is thought that at the worst, these credits will be somewhat delayed, and that as soon as capital sees there still are profitable investment avenues in Germany, it will begin to flow again in that direction—perhaps even faster than before to make up for lost time.

GOVERNMENT PLANS TO LINK UP BUREAUS

Special from Monitor Bureau

WASHINGTON, April 27—Transfer of the bureau of mines from the Interior Department to the Department of Commerce will probably be the next move in carrying out the recommendations of the Joint Congressional Committee for regrouping of Government bureaus, it is indicated by Herbert Hoover, Secretary of Commerce.

Transfer of the bureau of mines has the approval of Hubert Work, Secretary of the Interior, of Mr. Hoover, and of the President. Before it can be carried into effect, however, the Attorney-General will have to determine the legality of the transfer.

THE CHRISTIAN SCIENCE MONITOR

AN INTERNATIONAL DAILY NEWSPAPER

COPYRIGHT 1925 BY THE CHRISTIAN SCIENCE PUBLISHING SOCIETY

Fourteen Pages | BOSTON, WEDNESDAY, JULY 22, 1925—VOL. XVII, NO. 200 | PACIFIC EDITION | FIVE CENTS A COPY

AIRSHIP TYPES CONTEST FOR LEADERSHIP

Rigids Have More Speed, Semirigids Have Bigger Disposable Lifts

DESCRIPTION "RIGID" CALLED MISLEADING

Even Primitive Mooring Methods Prove Worth in Winds Up to 25 Miles an Hour

Special from Monitor Bureau

LONDON, July 8—Regarding all divisions of aircraft, whether heavier or lighter than air, it is advisable at the present early stage of development to avoid fixity of opinion. There has not been enough investigation, nor of operational research, in any branch to lead to absolutely definite selection; but from time to time the ulterior needs of the moment have led to a temporary supremacy of this or that type. Thus, throughout the history of flying there have been periods when either the biplane or the monoplane was most in vogue.

The periods to which airship development conforms being longer than those for the comparatively cheap and quickly built airplane, it may be easier to become committed to a wrong policy. It is, therefore, necessary from time to time to survey the situation. It may not be probable, but it is not impossible that the circumstance that Germany was the principal airship country in pre-war days, and was heavily committed to the type developed by Count Zeppelin, may have diverted attention from the possibilities of nonrigid and semirigid types. It is true, Great Britain used nonrigids before the war and extensively during the war, but for obvious reasons the types were hastily chosen or chosen under pressure of circumstances for one purpose, that of war.

Commercial Development

The new era of airship history now entered upon is essentially development for commercial purposes. It is true that airships may yet be employed in war, but the indications are that heavier-than-air aircraft will be able to do all that the airship can do, for the big sea-going flying boat appears more and more likely to serve for long-range naval reconnaissance. The airship should, then, rather be considered for transport.

Belief in the rigid airship, to the exclusion of the semirigid and nonrigid, is by no means universal, and there are authorities on the subject who claim that for commercial purposes the claims of advanced types of nonrigids and semirigids now proposed ought to be carefully weighed. In Germany the Parseval Company is designing both nonrigids and semirigids, and the company represents a line of consistent development almost as long as that of the Zeppelin type. They are supported by some British experts, and a British aeronautical firm recently established, and which includes Commander F. L. Boothby, are their representatives, being also holders of Zeppelin rights in Britain. Commander Boothby advocates the semirigid for the smaller sizes of airships; but it must be remembered that "smaller" is a relative term, and may mean anything up to a cubic capacity of about 2,000,000 cubic feet.

Formerly the Parseval airships were of the nonrigid type, but the company have now developed a big semirigid which consists of a keel extending the whole length of the ship supported by a gas container which is divided not only transversely but also longitudinally. The gas bags are under steel nets, and the outer cover inclosing them leaves a six-inch space between it and the bags, a space which can be filled with a noninflammable gas.

Advantage of Semirigid Type

Important advantages of this system, as compared with the rigid, are its comparatively small initial cost and the simplicity and cheapness

(Continued on Page 2, Column 2)

INDEX OF THE NEWS

WEDNESDAY, JULY 22, 1925

Veterans Beat Stills Into Kitchen Utensils

Special Correspondence

Phoenix, Ariz., July 18

THE Scriptural admonition of beating swords into plowshares has found an application here in the turning of illegal whisky-making apparatus into utensils of lawful and domestic value.

Following the active enforcement of the Eighteenth Amendment by civil officers here, a large number of copper and brass stills were accumulated, but for a long time they have been stored awaiting orders. Now they are being turned over to a shop in Prescott run by disabled veterans from Whipple Barracks, who use the metal in the production of works of art—book ends, trays, etc.—and utensils for the kitchen.

NEW MONTANA LINE WILL OPEN 1,500,000 ACRES

Winter Wheat Empire Next to Canadian Boundary Will Be Available

SCOBEY, Mont., July 22 (Special) —Eight hundred farmers have invested $325,000 with the Great Northern Railway to build 50 miles of railway extension and a new empire about twice the size of the State of Rhode Island is being opened in Montana. This line which will be extended west from Scobey, Mont., paralleling the Canadian boundary, is to cost about $1,250,000. The farmers and a few business men purchased $325,000 of Great Northern treasury stock at par and the Hill line will furnish the balance of the money needed to build the line.

This is the first time in the history of the northwest that farmers have assisted in financing an extension line. These farmers have been hauling their grain to market in wagons and motor trucks, some of them being obliged to travel 65 miles to sell their products. Five new towns will be established in this new domain, and each of these towns will draw grain, live stock and other farm products from about 15 townships.

Twenty miles of this new railway will be completed this fall, and the rest will be built next year. Considerable area in Canada also will be served by this railway extension. By next year, when the road is completed, it is estimated an additional 1,500,000 bushels of wheat will be marketed from this section. Most of the wheat raised in this upper region of Montana is sought by eastern millers because of its high protein content.

Modern Towns Planned

The new empire which the extension of this line will open is a dependable wheat region under the summer fallow system of agriculture. About 1,500,000 virgin acres will be cultivated. The townsites are to be put on sale in September and plans are under way to build the most modern towns architects can design. The new stockholders consist of about 95 per cent farmers and 5 per cent small town business men.

For years the farmers of Daniels and Valley counties lying next to the Canadian boundary have sought a branch line of the Great Northern Railway, but the war came on and the building of extensions was, of course, out of the question. When the railways finally were turned back to private control, the Great Northern Railway found itself with the rest of the lines of the United States, occupied entirely with rehabilitating its main line system. So these Montana farmers had to go on hauling their products to market by wagon and motor truck.

Stock Was Oversubscribed

Finally the Great Northern announced that if the farmers of the two commodious Montana counties

(Continued on Page 2, Column 3)

To Open State Filling Stations

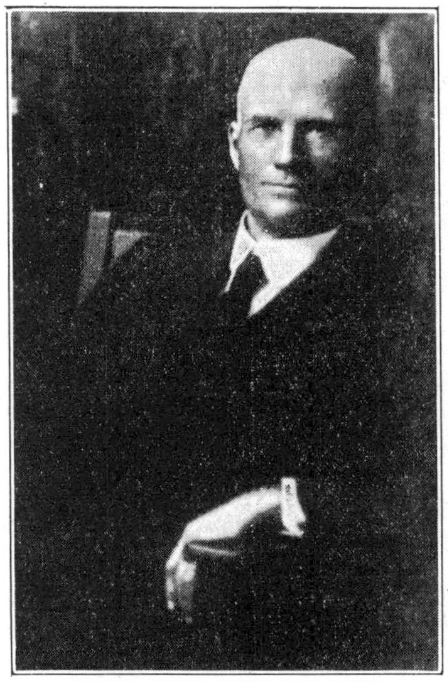

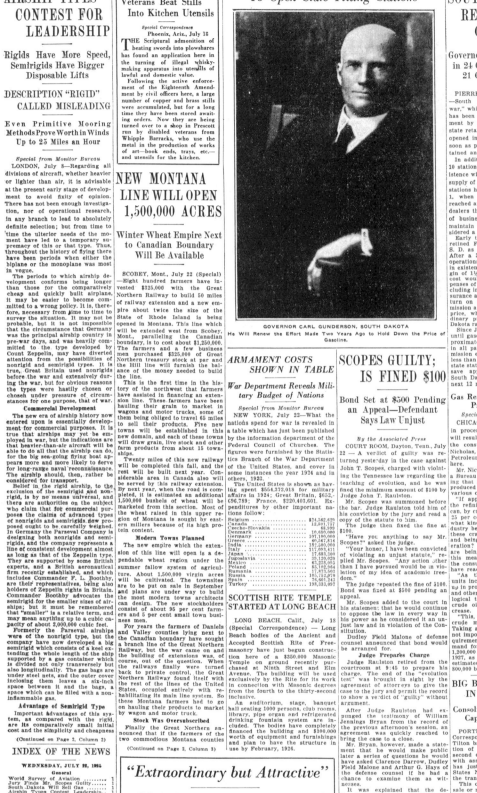

GOVERNOR CARL GUNDERSON, SOUTH DAKOTA

He Will Renew the Effort Made Two Years Ago to Hold Down the Price of Gasoline.

ARMAMENT COSTS SHOWN IN TABLE

War Department Reveals Military Budget of Nations

Special from Monitor Bureau

NEW YORK, July 22—What the nations spend for war is revealed in a table which has just been published by the information department of the Federal Council of Churches. The figures were furnished by the Statistics Branch of the War Department of the United States, and cover in some instances the year 1924 and in others, 1923.

The United States is shown as having spent $554,372,018 for military affairs in 1924; Great Britain, $652,-696,789; France, $220,403,601. Expenditures by other important nations follow:

Belgium	$24,562,629
Canada	12,801,737
Czecho-Slovakia	68,999
Denmark	10,680,000
Germany	107,100,000
Greece	40,567,814
India	182,500,000
Italy	117,093,411
Japan	17,683,300
Jugoslavia	39,120,020
Mexico	63,238,095
Poland	85,102,964
Rumania	17,873,503
Russia	105,752,070
Spain	76,601,243
Turkey	198,333,097

SCOTTISH RITE TEMPLE STARTED AT LONG BEACH

LONG BEACH. Calif., July 18 (Special Correspondence) — Long Beach bodies of the Ancient and Accepted Scottish Rite of Freemasonry have just begun construction here of a $350,000 Masonic Temple on ground recently purchased at Ninth Street and Elm Avenue. The building will be used exclusively by the Rite for its work in connection with Masonic degrees from the fourth to the thirty-second inclusive.

An auditorium, stage, banquet hall seating 1000 persons, club rooms, library, pipe organ and refrigerated drinking fountain system are included. The bodies have completely financed the building and $100,000 worth of equipment and furnishings and plan to have the structure in use by February, 1926.

SCOPES GUILTY; IS FINED $100

Bond Set at $500 Pending an Appeal—Defendant Says Law Unjust

By the Associated Press

COURT ROOM, Dayton, Tenn., July 22 — A verdict of guilty was returned yesterday in the case against John T. Scopes, charged with violating the Tennessee law regarding the teaching of evolution, and he was fined the minimum amount of $100 by Judge John T. Raulston.

Mr. Scopes was summoned before the bar. Judge Raulston told him of his conviction by the jury and read a copy of the statute to him.

The judge then fixed the fine at $100.

"Have you anything to say Mr. Scopes?" asked the judge.

"Your honor, I have been convicted of violating an unjust statute," replied Mr. Scopes. "Any action other than I have pursued would be in violation of my idea of academic freedom."

The judge repeated the fine of $100. Bond was fixed at $500 pending an appeal.

Mr. Scopes added to the court in his statement that he would continue to oppose the law in every way in his power as he considered it an unjust law and in violation of the Constitution.

Dudley Field Malone of defense counsel announced that bond would be arranged for.

Judge Prepares Charge

Judge Raulston retired from the courtroom at 9:45 to prepare his charge. The end of the "evolution test" was brought in sight by the agreement of attorneys to give the case to the jury and permit the record to show a verdict of "guilty" without argument.

After Judge Raulston had expunged the testimony of William Jennings Bryan from the record of the previous afternoon's session, an agreement was quickly reached to bring the case to a close.

Mr. Bryan, however, made a statement that he would make public later a series of questions he would have asked Clarence Darrow, Dudley Field Malone and Arthur G. Hays of the defense counsel if he had a chance to examine them as witnesses.

It was explained that the defense's testimony on which it relied to acquit Mr. Scopes having been excluded, the defense would state to the jury that it could not ask a verdict of "not guilty," and was satisfied to have a conviction in this court that an appeal might be made to the Supreme Court of Tennessee and possibly eventually to the United States Supreme Court.

At the opening of court Monday afternoon Clarence Darrow, of counsel for the defense, extended an apology for his remarks at Friday's session, and Judge Raulston accepted this, thus disposing of the citing of the attorney for contempt of court.

"Great Issue Involved"

Among the comments in the court room at the conclusion of the case was the following expression by William Jennings Bryan:

"This case has stirred the world, because it goes deep and wide.

"Here has been fought out a little case, of little consequence as a case, but one in which a great issue is involved.

"Some day it will be settled, but there can be no settlement without discussion.

"Human beings are mighty small, your honor, and we are sometimes apt to magnify the individual. But causes go on forever. We who have been associated in this case have attached ourselves to a mighty issue."

"Extraordinary but Attractive"

Under the above caption the Rochester Democrat and Chronicle, one of the leading newspapers of New York State, recently published the following editorial:—

The Christian Science Monitor has projected a series of seven articles about motion pictures; it has some experts at work gathering information and formulating opinions; on July 27th the first of these articles is to find its way into the Monitor. Apparently this is a research project much like many other newspaper enterprises—even enterprises that have to do with motion pictures.

But in one important particular these Monitor articles promise to be quite other than most of those undertaken. The title of this series of articles is to be "What's Right with the Movies" and the task given the writer, or writers, is to find the constructive and educational work that has been accomplished, and is being accomplished, by motion pictures.

This is quite topsy-turvy procedure. To be sure, it can be defended as sensible. A tremendous majority would agree that there is much more good than evil in motion pictures and this majority would like to see the good increase and the evils diminish. But it is the usual mode of procedure to make a target of the evils with such vehemence and with such an ignoring of the good that the whole business is often made to look like a doubtful asset to good living.

Yet it seems logical to find out just how much of an asset we already have in motion pictures; to show how much good is done and how much more can be done. If the same amount of sensible statement—aloof from propaganda—were devoted to the good that is in things, that is devoted to the evil, there might be more public excitement about increasing the good, which would automatically get rid of much that is bad. Once in a while this way of accomplishing uplift is adopted. When it is, it deserves the attention of intelligent people.

SOUTH DAKOTA RENEWS SALE OF GASOLINE

Governor to Open Stations in 24 County Seats—Says 21 Cents Is Enough

PIERRE, S. D., July 22 (Special) —South Dakota's "gasoline price war," which started in August, 1923, has been renewed in the announcement by Gov. Carl Gunderson that state retail gasoline stations will be opened in 24 county seat towns as soon as pump equipment can be obtained and gasoline distributed.

In addition to these new stations, 10 stations which are already in existence will be reopened as soon as a supply of gasoline is received. These stations have been closed since June 1, when the gasoline commission reached an agreement with the large dealers that the State would go out of business if the dealers would maintain what the commission considered a fair price.

Early this spring the commission retined F. H. Harmon of Redfield, S. D. as director of gasoline sales. After a 30-day examination of the operations of the State stations then in existence, he reported that a margin of 1½ cents over the laid-down cost would cover all operating expenses of a $10,000 filling station, including interest, depreciation and insurance and allowing a per cent return on the investment. The commission adopted this margin as a fair price, which would make the ordinary price of gasoline in South Dakota range around 21 cents.

Since June 1 prices have advanced until gasoline is now selling for approximately 25 cents on the average, in all parts of the State. The commission expects the price to drop to less than 22 cents a gallon when the state stations are opened, which will save approximately $3,000,000 on South Dakota's gasoline bill for the next 12 months, it is estimated.

Gas Refining Costs Cut; Price Drop Is Predicted

Special from Monitor Bureau

CHICAGO, July 22—Improvements in processes of cracking crude oil will result in lower gasoline prices to the consumer, according to L. V. Nicholas, president of the National Petroleum Marketers Association, here.

Mr. Nicholas referred to a report of a Bureau of Mines economist asserting that 26 per cent of the gasoline produced during May resulted from various crcking processes. He said:

"If approximatly 15 per cent of the refining capacity of the country can, by cracking, produce better than 25 per cent of the gasoline supply, what kind of a situation will the industry be facing in May, 1926, when these cracking plants now building and being contracted for are in operation? Gasoline production costs are being lowered every day and this means, too, that the price to the consumer will be decreased. We have reached the peak, I believe.

"As the percentage of cracking units increases and fuel oil, gas oil, up in production of gasoline, it seems and other cheap by-products are used logical to assume that demand for crude oil will correspondingly decrease.

"This, in our opinion, means easy crude markets and lower prices. Taking a two-year look ahead, it is not impossible that our crude oil requirements to supply the entire demand for gasoline will not be over 1,200,000 barrels per day for the year 1927, as compared with our present estimated daily requirements of 1,-800,000 barrels per day."

BIG BANK MERGER IN PORTLAND, ORE.

Consolidated Institution Has Capital of $58,000,000

PORTLAND, Ore., July 18 (Special Correspondence) — The Ladd and Tilton bank, oldest financial institution of the Pacific northwest, and second oldest on the Pacific coast, with assets aggregating $25,927,112, has just been sold to the United States National Bank of Portland, the transfer being effective at once.

This constituted the biggest bank sale or merger ever consummated in the northwest. Announcement that the sale had been effected came as a surprise event to those best informed in financial circles of the city.

The United States National Bank, as a result of the deal, has become the largest financial institution north of San Francisco and west of Minneapolis. Its combined deposits, since the merger amount to approximately $58,000,000.

Charles Pratt & Company of New York, chief owners of the Ladd and Tilton bank felt they were too far away to continue active direction of the bank here.

PRESIDENT UNMOVED BY COAL SITUATION

SWAMPSCOTT, Mass., July 22 (AP) — President Coolidge believes that anthracite operators and miners will reach an agreement on a new wage scale and that there will be no deadlock resulting in a suspension of mining operations on Sept. 1.

The President's opinion is based largely on the report as to the situation given him late last week by James J. Davis, Secretary of Labor, and on press dispatches regarding the wage negotiations at Atlantic City. He is receiving no report, official or otherwise, and apparently is not in any way disturbed over the outlook.

Dry Law Enforcement Gaining, Pennsylvania Police Head Proves

By the Associated Press

Harrisburg, Pa., July 21

SENTIMENT in support of the prohibition laws is growing with the result that enforcement is improving, in the opinion of Maj. Lynn G. Adams, head of the Pennsylvania State Police. Arrests for violations of the prohibition laws by his force totaled 4074 in 1924, compared with 4191 the year previcus.

Major Adams' estimates showed less than one-third the amount of alcoholic beverages is being consumed in the United States as compred with ante-Volstead days, and he asserted that the Federal blockade of rumrunners has reduced the amount of smuggled intoxicants about 75 per cent on the Atlantic coast. As to beverages now sold, he said they largely were manufactured from alcohol diverted from commercial channels and "camouflaged by counterfeit bottles, labels and revenue stamps."

"It is my opinion that enforcement is gradually gaining strength," he said. "I think people are beginning to see the question is not peculiarly a police problem; that the police are helpless without the support of the courts; and the courts are nearly helpless without the support of the people as represented by the jurors. People are beginning to realize more and more that the tremendous sums paid out in the form of bribes are not only getting exemption from the liquor-law violators, but are gradually beginning to undermine the very foundations of law enforcement. I believe it is gradually coming into the consciousness of the people that it is the 'otherwise eminently respectable' citizen who patronizes the bootlegger who is furnishing the bribe money which is causing most of our troubles."

WORK PLENTIFUL IN THE NORTHWEST

Farms and Building Activity Absorb Idle Labor

PORTLAND, Ore., July 18 (Special Correpondence —Little or no unemployment exists in the northwest. Midsummer farming, construction activities and the harvest have increased the demand for men, despite the shutdown in the lumber camps of Washington.

In Portland the situation is reported to be especially favorable, reports say. More than 400 men have been sent from here to the harvest fields to fill orders from Pendleton and other wheat districts where early operations are already under way. Building construction, road work and highway work, together with the demands for seasonal workers have absorbed all the surplus labor. Some scarcity of berry pickers exists.

About 90 per cent of the fir sawmills along the west coast have resumed cutting after the briefest shutdown in three years. There are no unemployed sawmill workers here and common labor in general is well employed.

In Washington 40 per cent of the lumber camps will remain closed indefinitely for repairs, while others are running on the one-shift plan. Even so, there is little unemployment, as the men are being absorbed in other lines of seasonal work.

Eugene reports a strong demand for labor of all kinds, particularly for farm work and railroad construction.

ATHENS CRITICIZES ACCORD WITH TURKEY

By Special Cable

ATHENS, July 22—The Greco-Turkish accord, which was approved by the Cabinet Council last Saturday night in its entirety, except a few points concerning the unexchangeable Greeks in Constantinople and Western Thrace respectively, requiring clarifications through further conversations with Angora, has provoked discontent in opposition and refugee circles. Certain quarters comment bitterly and reproach the Government in that, before approval, it refused to consult the parliamentary commission on foreign affairs, despite the urgent pleading of Alexander Papanastasiou, thus, it is alleged, affording ample proofs of its despotic dispoistion.

Compulsory arbitration as a means of improving Greek relations with Balkan friendly states was advocated by K. Rendis, Foreign Minister, who added that the Greco-Serbian alliance would today be a reality had both parties agreed to submit to arbitration.

DA SILVA MINISTRY RESIGNS IN PORTUGAL

LISBON, Portugal, July 22 (AP)— The Premier, Antonio da Silva, presented his resignation again yesterday and President Gomes accepted it.

Senhor da Silva resigned Friday, after a nonconfidence vote by the Portuguese Chamber of Deputies, but reconsidered the resignation Saturday, when the Senate gave his Cabinet a vote of confidence.

WORLD SURVEY OF AVIATION IS HOOVER PLAN

Movement Expected to Develop Information to Stabilize Industry

Special from Monitor Bureau

WASHINGTON, July 22—A world survey of commercial aviation, undertaken jointly by the Department of Commerce and the American Engineering Council, is the latest step taken by the Government in its endeavor to promote commercial aviation to a point where it will be an important factor in the economic life of the country.

It was announced by Herbert Hoover, Secretary of Commerce and one of the most ardent advocates of commercial flying, that this survey of air transportation in the leading nations of the world is the first of its kind in this or any other country. It will consume about six months, and is expected to develop information which will put the industry upon a stable basis by encouraging the private financial support upon which it must depend, at least for the present.

Has Important Bearing

That this is one of the most extensive and significant surveys to which the Government has put its hand in recent years, is the belief of aviation experts here. The survey is described as "an economic study of civil aviation in the leading nations and a constructive analysis of the economic possibilities of civil aviation in the United States."

The work will be directed by a committee of six, headed by J. Walter Drake, Assistant Secretary of Commerce. The field staff will be headed by Prof. Joseph W. Roe, head of the Department of Industrial Engineering in New York University.

Extensive preliminary studies have been made, both by the Department of Commerce and the aircraft committee of the American Engineering Council, according to Mr. Hoover's announcement.

As stated by Prof. Roe, vice-chairman of the committee, the purpose is "to provide a fact-finding review of civil aviation and other conditions necessary for successful civil air routes in this country."

In a statement outlining the scope of the survey, Professor Roe said:

"At the outset a comprehensive survey will be made of commercial air lines in other countries, including services offered, volume of traffic, safety regularity, financial status and equipment, cost of operation, government aid, and maps showing routes, landing fields, distances and density of traffic.

"This will be followed by a similar study of what has been done in the United States, where most of the experience is confined to the air mail. There will be a study of the geographic, economic and operating conditions in the United States, the volume of business possible for mail, express and passengers, the possible routes and their relation to existing forms of transportation."

President Asks Naval Survey With View to Cut in Expenses

Mr. Coolidge Believes Many Activities Should Be Discontinued and Money Used for Construction

SWAMPSCOTT, Mass., July 22 (AP) —Frederick Hale (R.), Senator from Maine and chairman of the Senate Naval Committee, has been asked by President Coolidge to make an intensive study to determine whether there are useless naval activities that could be abandoned with a view to reducing appropriations.

Mr. Hale, during a conference Monday with the President, reported on an inspection he had just completed of naval bases on the Pacific coast and in Hawaii. He expressed the opinion that a strong naval base should be established on the west coast, preferably at Alameda, Calif.; that improvement of the Pearl Harbor, Hawaii, base should be expedited, and that increased attention should be paid to aviation without unduly weakening other branches of the naval service.

After his conference with the President, Mr. Hale declared himself in favor of reducing appropriations wherever possible, but said that care should be taken not to destroy efficiency for the sake of too rigid economy.

In proposing a survey of naval activities with the view to making retrenchments, President Coolidge had in view the necessity of making appropriations during the next few years to carry out the comprehensive building program authorized at the last session of Congress. President Coolidge believes that a number of activities should be discontinued, and that the money now expended for them should be applied toward absorbing at least part of the cost of the new construction program.

EDUCATORS HAIL PLAN FOR FINER WORLD CITIZENS

Conference at Edinburgh Would Make Learning "the Servant of All"

DELEGATES SEE DAWN OF ERA OF GOOD WILL

Universal Geography and International Exchange of Teachers Proposed

By Special Cable

EDINBURGH, July 22—The conference of the World Federation of Education Associations launched into the third day of its program with the determined purpose of making education "the servant of common humanity." The enthusiasm of the delegates for intelligent, co-operative effort in behalf of world citizenship is proving truly remarkable. Group discussions of yesterday and today bear out that fact indisputably. The preschool, elementary, secondary, university, and adult groups are moving rapidly forward to an understanding of their common aim and purpose.

Prof. Patrick Geddes of the University of Jerusalem, discussing the subject of higher education, paid a tribute to the educational freedom of American universities nothwithstanding the apparent denial of freedom in the Tennessee situation.

"Our thought," he said, "is now environed by the afterwar situation and despite all perplexities, overcloudings and discouragements, reconstructive endeavors are exceedingly manifest. Especially hopeful in this world fermentation is the increase of sympathetic aspirations and endeavors which are now becoming more influential and evident Witness movements like those of international associations and of international bibliography and also the League of Nations committee for international Intellectual Relations which is now preparing to take up its center in Paris.

Great Progress in Education

"At this time, when the American attitude toward educational freedom and progress is being so popularly misrepresented by the world's press as centering in Tennessee, it is but fair to recall that actual progress in higher education today is, in some ways, unparalleled since the thirteenth century.

"Evidence of this is afforded in the recent admirable advances of Columbia and Dartmouth toward supplying the much needed introduction to higher education in all its faculties and departments in terms of general courses in which each and every special subject of higher studies, humanistic and scientific alike, is indicated in its historic origin and development, its appropriate place and its significance toward the understanding of nature and of civilization, not only in its separate but its coadaptive evolution."

Revision of textbooks on geography occupied the attention of the group on elementary education during today's session. Methods for an exchange of materials instructive of geographical environment of other peoples were advised. Discussions of this group were led by Miss Thedera George of Paris.

Standardization of Geography

Every speaker urged an arrangement of the subject matter in geographical textbooks so that the teachers of one country might be mutually helpful to the teachers of other countries.

The secondary education group discussion on Tuesday resulted in the appointment of a committee under Prof. N. G. Welinkar of India to bring in a report on the introduction of international themes in high school curricula.

The committee under T. C. Thors of Denmark is also to report on the international exchange of teachers in secondary schools. Speakers before this group included Dr. Roman of Poland, Miss E. H. Pagan of Greece, Alexander Szorenyi of Hungary, Paul Otlet of Belgium and S. B. Lucas of London.

Mr. Okamote of Japan recommended that high schools introduce courses in international economics, as well as studies in the international aspects of history, music, literature and biography. He asked for a more liberal consideration of Oriental peoples, their history and customs, in the curricula of Western education. Only in that way, he maintained, was it possible to modify conditions for the better.

Acute relations between the East and West, the present situation between Asiatics and Europeans, the speaker said, had come to the place where the politician must be supplanted by the educator.

An International Forum

The Tuesday noon luncheon to the delegates proved to be an international forum of great educational significance. Speakers represented every shade of world opinion. There was a welcome unanimity of opinion on the nature and purpose of education. Speakers included Dr. Chu, Chinese Minister to the Court of St. James's; Prof. Sarolea of Belgium; Dr. Kundt of Budapest University; Dr. Vocadlo of Czechoslovakia; Miss Ruth Conway of Liverpool; Lord Aberdeen, former Governor-General of Canada and Gilbert K. Chesterton.

Each speaker forged an additional link in the chain of education, intended to bind the world closer and closer together. The youth movement was officially brought before the delegates yesterday by the address of Thomas Harrison, national secretary of the American Fellowship of

THE CHRISTIAN SCIENCE MONITOR

AN INTERNATIONAL DAILY NEWSPAPER

COPYRIGHT 1926 BY THE CHRISTIAN SCIENCE PUBLISHING SOCIETY — Fourteen Pages — BOSTON, WEDNESDAY, MAY 12, 1926—VOL. XVIII, NO. 141 — PACIFIC EDITION — FIVE CENTS

NORGE FLIES OVER POLE ON WAY TO NOME

Dirigible Under Amundsen and Ellsworth Duplicates Byrd Party's Feat

TRIP FROM KINGS BAY MADE IN 15 HOURS

Italian-Built Craft Under Norwegian Flag Making 50 Miles an Hour

NEW YORK, May 12 (AP)—Capt. Roald Amundsen's dirigible Norge has crossed the North Pole, in its flight from Kings Bay, Spitzbergen, to Nome, Alaska, the New York Times and the St. Louis Globe-Democrat announce.

The great balloon duplicated within three days the feat of the three-engined airplane Miss Josephine Ford, piloted by Lieut. Commander Richard E. Byrd, with the difference that Commander Byrd returned to Kings Bay, Spitzbergen, in a 1600-mile nonstop flight, while the Norge continued a 2750-mile journey toward Nome.

Captain Amundsen, commander of the third expedition to reach the North Pole and first explorer to reach the South Pole, wired to Ralph Lomen, Norwegian Consul at Nome, to have 100 men ready to lower the dirigible. He said he would keep Mr. Lomen advised of progress by radio, and the Consul had four anchors placed in readiness to hold the ship down.

Seventeen Members in Crew

The Norge left Spitzbergen at 10 a. m. Norwegian time or 5 a. m. New York daylight saving time yesterday and sailed over the pole with the 17 members of its crew at 1 a. m. today Norwegian time, or 7 o'clock last night, eastern standard time. The news reached the New York Times and St. Louis Globe-Democrat and the first message ever received direct from the pole announced the news at 3:05 a. m. eastern standard time.

Commander Byrd saw the Norge off but remained at Kings Bay to prepare, in the words of Lieut. Alton N. Parker of his party, to "investigate every foot of real estate near the pole for Uncle Sam."

The Norge is 343 feet long, was inflated with 19,000 cubic meters of hydrogen at Kings Bay, and loaded with 6000 kilograms of benzine for fuel. Its best speed is 62 miles an hour. It was built in 1923 by the State Airship Factory at Rome as the N-1 for the Italian Air Service, and originally bore a luxurious special cabin for the King of Italy. It carried the Italian flag at its stern beside that of Norway on its trip from Rome to Pulham, Eng.; Oslo, Norw.; Leningrad, Rus.; Spitzbergen, and thence to the pole.

Uses Three Motors

The Norge is described as a "blimp with a deck nose." The metal keel runs from stem to stern, and on it is an 18-inch runway. The vessel has three motors, and is steered by a wheel, like any other ship. Sun compasses in the control cabin were used to check against the magnetic compasses, which are apt to be misleading so near the magnetic pole. The ship was equipped with a sled, tents, and other essentials for a possible forced landing.

The American Amundsen was beaten to the North Pole by Robert E. Peary. He set out for the South Pole by dog sled, reaching it Dec. 14, 1911, beating four rival expeditions from as many countries. His nephew, Lieut. Gustav Amundsen of the Norwegian Navy, is a helmsman of the Norge. Captain Amundsen last year made the first attempt to reach the North Pole by airplane, but failed. Mr. Ellsworth and Captain Amundsen in 1924, when he paid for three airplanes Captain Amundsen had ordered in Italy. He accompanied the Norwegian on his polar dash last year and was made secretary of the Norge expedition.

Vilhjalmur Stefansson, Canadian explorer now in New York, expressed delight that the Byrd and the Ellsworth-Amundsen expeditions could

(Continued on Page 6, Column 3)

46

Norge Seeks First Dirigible Honors in North Pole Race

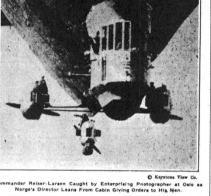

© Photograph by Central News From Underwood & Underwood, N. Y.

© Keystone View Co.
Commander Reiser-Larsen Caught by Enterprising Photographer at Oslo as Norge's Director Leans From Cabin Giving Orders to His Men.

ARBITRAL GUIDE TO BE PUBLISHED

American Association Plans Code for Guidance of Disputants

Special from Monitor Bureau
NEW YORK, May 11—Publication of an official guide to civil and commercial arbitration as it is being practiced and developed by American business and professional men will be undertaken by the American Arbitration Association, according to Lucius R. Eastman, chairman of the association. This has been made possible, he announced, by a special grant received through "the generous interest and co-operation" of Col. Michael Friedsam of B. Altman & Co.

"The development of arbitration," he continued, "has been largely through the individual and uncoordinated efforts of some 200 trade associations and chambers of commerce, with the result that an official handbook is badly needed to bring before business as a whole information about arbitration and a codification of the standard procedure under the federal law, the various state laws, and the sanction of trade and professional associations which have formally adopted arbitration as the procedure for settling disputes within their own memberships."

The first part of the guide will be general in character, dealing with the function of arbitration, its legal status in 1926, and its status as a trade practice, together with a general description of arbitral tribunals and procedure.

The second part, which, according to Mr. Eastman, will be most valuable, will contain a directory of every commercial organization which is practicing or has indorsed arbitration and with which the association can get in touch.

The American Arbitration Association plans to devote the summer to the editing of this official guide, for publication in the fall. So far as is known, this will be the first directory of its kind to be published either here or in Europe.

TO OPEN FOREST TRAILS

ASHLAND, Ore., May 8 (Special Correspondence)—Improvement work to the extent of $54,000 will be begun in the Crater National Forest on June 1. Approximately 80 miles of trails will be established. Other improvements will include the building of lookout houses, and establishment of new telephone lines and roads.

World Fraternity Stressed in Nations' Economic Plans

Sir Josiah Stamp Tells Chamber of Commerce Reconstruction Depends on Unselfishness

Special from Monitor Bureau.
WASHINGTON, May 12—"Economic interest has come to defy national boundaries and the barriers of oceans," said John W. O'Leary, president of the United States Chamber of Commerce, stressing the worldwide responsibility for prosperity and well-being at the opening of the fourteenth annual meeting.

Although tradition has led American agriculture to avoid political entanglements, this policy should not interfere with the development of a broad international nature, he asserted. "It is desirable that we know our neighbors in the world better.

"We are accomplishing this desire by our participation in the International Chamber of Commerce, by our support of adherence of the United States to the Permanent Court of International Justice, and by the spirit of understanding and sympathy in our support of the settlements negotiated by the American Debt Funding Commission.

"At the present time agriculture

holds the forefront in the political arena. Claims to the contrary notwithstanding, the destiny of American agriculture will be achieved through the policy of self-government and not, as some would have us believe, through paternal control by the Federal Government."

Dr. Julius Klein, director of the Bureau of Foreign and Domestic Commerce, spoke as one of the group luncheons on American dependence upon foreign controlled raw materials. "More than 50 per cent of our total imports, valued at more than $840,000,000, are jeopardized through the arbitrary dictates of foreign political control—materials which are the very foundation stones of industry in this country," said Dr. Klein. "Great sections of our agriculture could not exist without certain foreign fertilizers and sisal binder twine. Rubber is absolutely indispensable for those two fundamental elements in our economic mechanism — automotive transport and the electrical industry.

"The professed purpose of these controls is stabilization at a reasonable level, but the actual result of each control has all too frequently been to raise prices periodically to exorbitant levels. The high standard of living and prosperity of our people based on their efficiency and high wages, makes these products more essential to us than to foreign nations. These facts are better recognized among producers abroad than among consumers in this country."

Self-Denial Called For

"The making of a better permanent structure—out of the battered remains of the old economic conditions calls for self-denial and a sound sense of life's purposes," Sir Josiah Stamp, British member of the Chamber Committee, said in a speech before the American Committee of the International Chamber of Commerce.

"We are engaged not merely in snatching or securing the best possible immediate advantage for ourselves," he explained, "but we have put our hands to something which may run right across dictates of today's opportunism or the short period desires of a single country—reconstruction.

"It is better to endure hardship in the process than live from day to day feasting and idling. For only the fit structures, wisely made, and the best life of world commerce in the future will live. Life is too long if spent in idleness; it is too short if spent in business; but we cannot measure its value in terms of time at all if it is spent in service.

"We have gone far enough along the road of reconstruction now to see that it is no picnic of a day. It calls

(Continued on Page 1, Column 2)

Middlesex Stream Yields Pearl of Unusual Beauty and Value

Gem of Deep Pink and Uncommon Luster Found by Wellesley Man in Fresh Water Clam

What is believed to be the record fresh water pearl found in New England has been offered for inspection at the museum of the Boston Society of Natural History by its owner and finder, R. W. Denton of Wellesley, and has been found to weigh 16.2 grains and to have a commercial value of $1312.

The pearl is an exceptionally deep pink in color, a perfect sphere in shape and has an uncommon luster. It was found by Mr. Denton in a fresh water clam taken from one of the streams of Middlesex County in Massachusetts.

Acquisition by the society of numerous small items for its variety of collections is noted in the quarterly bulletin just issued and officials take occasion to point out the public benefit and educational service represented in gifts which, if they sometimes seem relatively inconsequential in themselves, may very possibly contribute missing links in important natural history records.

A new mineral for New England has been added to the mineralogy materials of the greatest service is noted by officials. It is a report of Glover M. Allen, librarian, newly bound volumes of Thoreau, Stefansson, John Muir, Bradford Torrey, Dallas Lore Sharp and Hornaday; also the Walden edition of Thoreau complete in 20 volumes, Bade's Life and Letters of John Muir, Barrus' Life and Letters of John Burroughs and three books by Lacy on historical and philosophical phases of zoology have been catalogued.

versity, who has presented a group of thulite specimens, of the rose-red variety of zoisite (a calcium aluminum silicate) discovered recently at Haddam, Conn. Two smoky quartzes of unusually fine quality have been added to the New England gem collection through the gift of F. Wesley Fuller. These were cut from material found by Mr. Fuller in the Quincy granite quarries. Mr. Fuller also has cut and polished a ball of rhodonite from material at the museum originally obtained from Cummington, Mass.

In the insect section a catalogue of the holotypes, allotypes, paratypes and cotypes of insects in the New England collection, including the "type" collection, which comprises approximately 612 species.

In the library, according to report of Glover M. Allen, librarian, newly bound volumes of Thoreau, Stefansson, John Muir, Bradford Torrey, Dallas Lore Sharp and Hornaday; also the Walden edition of Thoreau complete in 20 volumes, Bade's Life and Letters of John Muir, Barrus' Life and Letters of John Burroughs and three books by Lacy on historical and philosophical phases of zoology have been catalogued.

Two Spanish Airmen Land in Philippines

By the Associated Press
Manila, May 12
CAPTAIN LORIGA and Captain Gallarza, the Spanish aviators, flying from Madrid to Manila, have landed safely at Aparri, on the Island of Luzon, from Macao, China, with but one more hop ahead to reach their destination.

The aviators came down at 2:20 p. m., thus completing their flight across the China Sea in 6h. 55m. Later they will hop off for Manila, on the last stretch of their flight.

SCOUTS PLEDGE WORLD UNITY AT CAMPFIRE

Girl Leaders of 31 Nations Dedicate Camp to Fellowship Advancement

By a Staff Correspondent
CAMP EDITH MACY, Briarcliff Manor, N. Y., May 12—One of the most impressive and significant ceremonies in the annals of world fellowship was held here, when 450 delegates to the International Council of Girl Guides and Girl Scouts, representing 31 countries, dedicated this camp as the principal training ground for Girl Scout leaders in America.

Following a brief ceremony in the great lodge house, the delegates moved out to the terrace where, on a promontory overlooking the large estate, there was kindled America's first world council fire, to be held in the United States. In the widening circle stood girls from many lands, united for one purpose. Dean Sarah Louise Arnold, president of the Girl Scouts, made a brief address signalizing the purpose of the fire.

One by one the delegates from the foreign lands came up, dressed in the Scout uniform of her country, each bearing a small bundle of twigs, symbolic of participation in the council and as a contribution to the union of world womanhood.

Their Offerings

Australia brought her wool. Belgium gave her lace, unfolding a pattern of service and sisterhood. Austria, the music of her great composers.

Canada brought the exemplified in her unarmed common border.

And so on down the list the nations came—Chile, China, Czechoslovakia, Denmark, Egypt, France, Germany, England, Ireland, Scotland, Hungary, Italy, Jugoslavia, Latvia, Luxembourg, the Netherlands, Norway, Palestine, Poland, Portugal, South Africa, Suomi (Finland), Sweden, Switzerland, Turkey, the United States and Uruguay—each making a gift of its national hope for

(Continued on Page 4, Column 4)

MEXICAN TROOPS ENTER GUERRERO

Federal Forces Are Sent to Garrison Towns and Protect Ranchers

MEXICO CITY, Mex., May 12 (Special)—Steady movement of federal troops into the state of Guerrero from adjoining states indicates that revolutionist activity in that state is more serious than at first reported. Joaquin Amaro, Minister of War, has reached the capital of Guerrero to take charge of the campaign against the revolutionists, should development so require.

As military trains and automobiles bearing troops have been moving toward Guerrero for several days, the number of troops in the state is now estimated at more than 15,000. The object of the heavy movement of troops is said to be to hamper the movement of revolutionists, to afford protection for ranches and rural property, and to garrison towns should further revolutionist activity develop.

Airplanes of the government forces, scouting in Guerrero, report that the revolutionists are divided into several parties along the coast and foothills of the state which is one of the most mountainous in Mexico. Mexican gunboats continue guarding the coast to prevent communication by sea between revolutionists and outside help should any present itself, though none has developed so far, as the department reports the Guerrero situation under control.

LOS ANGELES WORKS ACTIVELY FOR GOOD-WILL DAY EXERCISES

Broad Interest Taken in Observance Planned by Council on International Relations of Southern California

LOS ANGELES, May 3 (Staff Correspondence)—Extensive plans for the observance of International Good Will Day, May 18, are being made in the schools and elsewhere, largely under the leadership of the Council on International Relations of Southern California.

Acting upon the recommendation of Mrs. Susan M. Dorsey, superintendent of city schools, 38 public schools in Los Angeles already have applied to the council for speakers to participate in exercises, while many other schools are preparing to hold observances without the assistance of outside speakers.

A number of student speakers which the council has drawn from cosmopolitan clubs of local colleges and high schools will deliver addresses at these gatherings. These students represent several countries, among them the Philippines, Japan, China, and Syria. Adult speakers from the speakers' bureau of the council will complete the lists.

Facilities Rapidly Extended

The fact that the Council on International Relations can undertake to furnish speakers to so many meetings occurring on the same day is the result of vigorous growth of that body's facilities during the past few months. In its efforts to promote permanent peace through better international understanding, the council has established a speakers' bureau as a principal means of spreading authentic information about foreign peoples generally throughout this vicinity. Affiliated councils already spreading to other cities in this vicinity. Affiliated councils already exist at Long Beach and Pasadena. There is a similar organization at Fullerton, and one is at present being formed at Riverside. A number of other cities throughout the State, but how far the idea has been carried is not known here.

The council maintains a headquarters in the Chamber of Commerce building here.

BRITISH STRIKE CALLED OFF SUBSIDY WILL BE RESUMED

Lockout Against Miners to Be Withdrawn and Special Board Established to Revise Wages

TRADE UNION CONGRESS ACTION FOLLOWS VISIT TO THE PREMIER

News Flashed to Anxious Public Throughout Country by Radio—Walkout Termination Based on Negotiations Conducted Unofficially

By Cable from Monitor Bureau
LONDON, May 12—The general strike was officially declared off today.

LONDON, May 12 (AP)—The conditions on which the general strike was called off are as follows:

The governmental subsidy to the coal industry will be resumed temporarily.

The lockout against the miners will be withdrawn.

A wages board will be established to revise the miners' wages, with the understanding that there shall be no revision without sufficient assurances that the measures recommended for reorganization of the mining industry by the Royal Coal Commission shall be put into effect.

The Trade Union Congress, which initiated the movement in sympathy with the striking miners, visited the Premier, Stanley Baldwin, and his Cabinet Ministers at No. 10 Downing Street at noon and announced that the strike was over.

This action was taken, the chairman, Arthur Pugh, said, in order to enable resumption of the negotiations or settlement of the miners' grievances, which negotiations the Government had declared could not be resumed while the general strike lasted.

Premier Receives Leaders

The Trade Union Congress forthwith dispatched telegrams to the affiliated unions throughout the country.

The individual unions, before acting, must await definite instructions from their own executive councils. However, it is expected the Trade Union Congress instructions will have quick effect and that the wheels of industry, stilled since last Monday midnight, will begin to turn again almost immediately.

The official statement of the settlement, issued from the Premier's residence in Downing Street, reads:

"The Prime Minister, who was accompanied by the Minister of Labor, the Secretary for India, the Secretary for War, the First Lord of the Admiralty, the Minister of Health and the Secretary for Mines, received the members of the general council of the Trade Union Congress at 12:20 o'clock this afternoon at No. 10 Downing Street.

"Mr. Pugh announced, on behalf of the General Council of the Trade Union Congress, that the general strike is being terminated today." Mr. Citrine, secretary of the Trade Union Congress, afterward made the following statement:

"In order to resume negotiations, the general council of the Trade Union Congress has decided to terminate the general strike today. The telegrams of instructions are being sent to the secretaries of all the affiliated unions.

News Conveyed by Radio

"The members before acting must await definite instructions from their executive councils.

(Signed) Arthur Pugh, John Bromley, W. Citrine."

Almost as soon as the decision was made known to the Cabinet, it was flashed throughout the country by radio to the anxious public, who had been informed earlier that persistent peace rumors were in the air.

In the London hotels and restaurants, announcement of the news was received with cheers and handclapping, and a moment later when an orchestra on the radio struck up "God Save the King," thousands sprang to their feet and stood at attention.

The general strike began last Monday at midnight, being called to support the miners in their stand

(Continued on Page 4, Column 1)

RAIL LABOR BILL UP TO PRESIDENT

Voluntary Arbitration Plan Passes Senate 69 to 13, Without Amendment

WASHINGTON, May 12 (AP)—The "Treaty of Peace" agreed upon by executives of a number of large railroads and union leaders awaits only the approval of President Coolidge to become law.

Embodied in the Watson-Parker bill, the plan has been approved by the Senate, 69 to 13, exactly as it came from the House, despite vigorous efforts to change some of its provisions.

Abolition of the Railroad Labor Board and substitution of new machinery for handling disputes between employers and workers in the industry is provided for in the measure. It will be signed by President Coolidge if he is convinced the public interest is adequately safeguarded in its provisions.

Main Point of Debate

This proved the main point of contention during the debate on the measure in Congress. Although advocated by representatives of large carriers and the railroad brotherhoods, opposition was registered by executives of some of the smaller lines and the National Manufacturers' Association, which held shippers and the public generally were not given sufficient voice in labor disputes involving transportation costs.

Numerous amendments, most of them based on this objection, were offered, but all were rejected, proponents of the bill insisting upon its passage "without the dotting of an 'i' or the crossing of a 't'." In one and 39 Republicans, 29 Democrats and one Farmer-Labor Senator voted in the affirmative with nine Republicans and four Democrats casting the negative ballots.

Voluntary Boards Provided

The bill provides for establishment of voluntary boards of adjustment to conduct negotiations in labor disputes within the industry. If these fail to bring about agreement, it authorizes the President to appoint a Federal board of mediation of the members to seek a solution. Should no settlement be reached in this way a strike be threatened, the President would set up an emergency board to study and publish the facts involved in the dispute, which would be held in status quo for 30 days after the board's report.

Passage of the measure cleared the way in the Senate for consideration of the McFadden Branch Banking Bill, which failed at the last session. It has been rewritten this year by the banking committee.

Virginia Provides Muskrat Detours

Eight-Inch Tiles Built as Runway to Save the Country's Roads

RICHMOND, Va., May 10 (Special Correspondence)—Detours for muskrats as well as for automobilists have to be built by the Virginia highway commission. Department officials gravely put their heads together and planned muskrat detours for 3.89 miles of the Richmond County approach to the Tappahannock Bridge.

This is no laughing matter to those engaged in road construction. In some sections of the state, near the swamps, muskrats have been known to wreck a fill by tunneling through. The little animals move along in definite paths and when they find obstructions they do not turn aside, but bore in. To meet this determined characteristic in the little fur bearers, the road men place eight-inch tiles through the fill at the point where the "rats" usually are found. The muskrats accept the changed conditions in good part and use the tiles instead of disturbing the road.

In order to further mollify the rats the department builds nests for them, or rather places for them near the nests; pipes placed at an angle that will accommodate the average sized muskrat family.

Horse Sense

SPUNK was a pony, and he had to be shipped from his home in Scotland to be sold. Although he had to jump overboard, he did so in order to get back. Read about this SCOTTISH GRIT.

in

Tomorrow's
MONITOR
Editorial Page

THE CHRISTIAN SCIENCE MONITOR
AN INTERNATIONAL DAILY NEWSPAPER

COPYRIGHT 1927 BY
THE CHRISTIAN SCIENCE PUBLISHING SOCIETY

Eighteen Pages

BOSTON, MONDAY, MAY 23, 1927—VOL. XIX, NO. 150

ATLANTIC EDITION

FIVE CENTS A COPY

ECONOMISTS AT GENEVA FAVOR LOWER TARIFFS

Export Taxes on Raw Material Opposed, Also Subsidies to Bolster Up Industries

SOVIET DELEGATES TO ABSTAIN FROM VOTING

Conference of Ministers of Commerce Likely to Act Soon on Resolutions Presented

By Wireless via Postal Telegraph from Halifax

GENEVA, May 23 — The main points of the resolutions presented by the commerce committee at the plenary session of the Economic Conference, on the eve of adjournment, are as follows:

1. High tariffs are an obstruction to trade and ought to be lowered, beginning immediately with the exaggerated post-war protection by the conclusion of commercial treaties.

2. The instability of tariffs should be corrected and the most favored nation treatment generally adopted as one of the primary conditions of free normal development of trade.

3. Import and export prohibitions hamper the normal play of competition and are not counterbalanced by any advantages in improvement of exchanges.

Subsidies Should Be Avoided

4. Export taxes on raw materials, especially of a discriminating character, should be condemned.

5. Indirect protection to industry, in the form of state subsidies should be avoided.

6. Nomenclature of tariffs should be simplified.

The committee on industry approved the tenets of rationalization as calculated to secure to the community the greatest stability, a higher standard of living and lower prices to the consumer with goods better adapted to his needs, but, it is added, the process must be applied with care for the legitimate interests of the workers.

In a resolution on cartels the general advantages and the necessity for big industrial undertakings are admitted.

"There is, however, considerable divergence of views as to the working of international trusts, which will find expression in the final proposals laid before the conference, the workers' representatives insisting on expression of opinion for safeguarding the consumer by some measure of control.

The Soviet delegation caused a mild surprise on Saturday by voting against the resolutions on the grounds that they are inconsistent with their economic system of state monopoly in trading, but today when the resolutions will be presented en bloc it is understood they will abstain from voting, so that the resolutions will go to the council as the unanimous expression of opinion.

Conference of Ministers

Surprise has been caused by the Soviet delegates' action on Saturday, because, according to the agreement reached behind the scenes, they were not to vote against the resolutions on condition that a decision was made recognizing the co-existence of the Communist and capitalist systems. It is true the Russians have not obtained the specific declaration they desired, but they were apparently contented with an acknowledgment of the essential equality of all the delegations, which comes to much the same thing. But abstention is not regarded as an infringement of the unanimity principle.

The conference will close early this week and when the Council of the League has adopted the resolutions they will be transmitted to the governments concerned. It is opined that such a strong body of opinion for lowering the present high tariffs and for the abolition of postwar restrictions in trade can hardly be ignored. It is, therefore, expected that a conference of ministers of commerce will meet in the near future for the purpose of reaching an agreement between their governments regarding the disposal to be taken by means of international conventions.

Additional importance is now attached to the diplomatic convention for simplification of tariff regulations, which is to be held in November.

CLEVELAND WELCOMES SAFETY DEPOSIT MEN

CLEVELAND, O., May 23 (Special)—Bankers in charge of safety deposits are custodians of the Nation's sentiments, delegates to the convention of the Safety Deposit Associations of the United States were told by H. C. Robinson, Cleveland banker.

Lloyd L. Jones, chief of the Federal Bureau of Investigation and Statistics in Cleveland, said people write more boldly when writing a check, reflecting the unusual feeling of importance that comes over them during the process. Newton D. Baker, Cleveland, urged the bankers to co-operate in world peace. New York was selected as the association's 1928 convention city.

UTAH GIRL IS WINNER OF ORATORICAL PRIZE

LOS ANGELES (Staff Correspondence)—Miss Dorothy Carlson of Salt Lake City won first place in an oratorical contest in which the winners of similar events in eight districts of the Southwest competed for the right to represent this section at the fourth national oratorical contest in Washington May 27.

Whisky Manufacture Authority Decided On

By the Associated Press

WASHINGTON, May 23

MANUFACTURE of whisky for medicinal purposes will be begun under Treasury supervision in time to utilize the fall corn crop, Assistant Secretary Andrews announced today. The Treasury, he said, would authorize such manufacture by possibly five corporations.

It was the original intention to authorize two companies to engage in making the spirits, but when the question of violation of the antitrust laws was brought up, it was decided to allow enough corporations to enter the industry to provide competition.

CORPORATE TAX LEADS IN CALLS FOR REVISIONS

Decrease in 13½ Per Cent Rate Will Be Proposed Again to Congress

Special from Monitor Bureau

WASHINGTON, May 23—Leaders of tax legislation in Congress are of the view that tax revision at the coming session of Congress will revolve about a plan for cutting the present 13½ per cent corporation tax.

During the last session all serious deliberations about tax revision centered on this item. Since the closing of Congress there have been indications that Administration tax experts were concentrating their attention on reducing the corporation tax. A press statement by Ogden L. Mills, advocating the desirability of examining the corporation tax field, was accepted in Congressional quarters as confirming the strong impression held there that the corporation tax would be the chief point of attack in the tax revision program of the Administration.

Senate and House Divided

The present rate of 13½ per cent on corporation returns was a last-minute arrangement in the 1926 tax bill differences between the two houses of Congress. The Senate revised drastically the tax measure as it came from the House. Among these changes were provisions repealing the estate taxes, reducing the corporation tax, and considerably increased reductions of the so-called nuisance taxes. The House balked on the repeal of the estate taxes, insisting that its schedule of reduced rates be retained. In the give and take that ensued between the conferees of the two houses it was decided to raise the corporation tax to 13½ per cent in order to provide the amount of additional income that the House insisted must be assured.

There was some dissent from Administration leaders in the Senate but the demand for prompt action was urgent and the item was allowed to stand. During the last session when tax reduction was strenuously advocated by the Democrats, repeated proposals were made to reduce the corporation tax. One on occasion, Mr. Mills, then a member of the House and the Republican leader in tax matters there, was challenged by the Democrats to permit the introduction of a tax reduction measure which would be confined solely to the corporation tax. He countered with the proposal of receiving guarantees from the Democrats that the Senate would not tamper with their bill.

Combination Proposal

At one time this year there was a possibility that action in combination would be sought in the Legislature. This would have called for naming of party nominees by conventions, with those candidates not named still having a chance to be named in a subsequent primary. If convention nominees were unsatisfactory to various groups of voters, there would still be a chance for the people to select a nominee in the primary, it was said by sponsors of the plan.

This proposal was opposed on the ground that it had a self-evident weakness. The nominee of the party convention, it is believed, would gain such an advantage that any candidate not indorsed by the convention would seldom win. The combination of primary and convention systems was also regarded as extra expensive to the State.

Interest in Campaign

The campaign this summer, which will be entirely nonpartisan, is anticipated to be one of intense interest, for the groups seeking to repeal the primary law have made plans for a thorough canvass of the State by means of the radio, newspapers and otherwise. Among those to be invited here to speak against the primary are Col. Theodore Roosevelt and Charles G. Dawes, Vice-President of the United States.

The issue is drawn sharply. There is no legislation asked to modify, strengthen or change in any way the direct primary law. The referendum seeks a vote on whether or not the entire primary law shall be wiped off the statute books, thus making possible a return to the old convention system.

In the opinion of some political observers, those drawing up the referendum petitions have chosen for themselves the more difficult of two possible courses. The alternative was to ask for a combination of the primary and a modified convention plan, a combination known to be favored by many who do not care for either the primary or the old type of convention system.

GAINS REPORTED BY BOYS CLUBS OF TWO NATIONS

Syracuse Session Speaks for 220,000 Youths—Great Britain, Canada There

SYRACUSE, N. Y., May 23 (Special)—Representatives of 220,000 boys, including delegates from Great Britain and Canada, met in convention here today to observe the twenty-first anniversary of the Boys' Club Federation. The federation has clubs in six foreign countries. Thirty states were represented, it is reported, as the convention opened. The convention will last three days. Registrations for the convention exceed those of any other year in the history of the federation.

For the first time in the history of the federation, the National Association of Boys' Clubs of Great Britain will be represented at the convention, there being 19 English boys' clubs now enrolled in the federation. The Canadian delegation this year will be three times as large as any other group of representatives from the Dominion.

Growth of Federation

Organized in Boston in 1906, the federation has grown from a small group of New England boys interested in the underprivileged boy to a large international organization which now numbers 275 boys' clubs in the United States and six foreign countries, with a total membership of 220,000 boys. Figures recently compiled by William E. Hall, president of the federation, shows that since 1921 the number of clubs has increased from 163 to 275, the number of boy members from 115,414 to more than 220,000, the number of clubs having camps from 83 to 158, the number of clubs with vocational classes from 87 to 142, and the number of classes from 340 to 638. The number of club newspapers in the same period has increased from 38 to 91.

$11,500,000 Investment

More than $11,500,000 is now invested in Boys' Clubs in the United States, according to the most recent returns received at federation headquarters, indicating a marked upward trend in the growth of Boys' Club building values. Since 1921 the number of buildings having increased in the same length of time from $4,668,650 to $11,675,000. This does not include Settlement buildings and Community.

Fight to Save Direct Primary Starts With Call for Election

Maine to Vote on Question of Repeal on Oct. 18, and Opponents of Return to Convention Are Invited to Mass Meeting at the State Capitol

AUGUSTA, Me., May 23 (Special)—Following the issue of a proclamation by Gov. Ralph O. Brewster, calling for a special election on Oct. 18 on the issue of whether or not the direct primary shall be retained, a call was issued this afternoon for a public meeting in the State House on Thursday to consider a campaign of education regarding "the gross abuses" of the old convention system.

This call was signed by Frank H. Holley of North Anson, president of the Maine Senate; Mrs. Althea G. Quimby of Portland, president of the Maine W. C. T. U.; Merle J. Harriman of Readfield, State lecturer of the Maine Grange; John Wilson, Mayor of Bangor and chairman of the Penobscot County Republican Committee; and Mrs. William R. Pattangall of Augusta, National Democratic Committee member.

Two years ago the Governor declined to issue a call for a special election on the ground of alleged illegalities in the signature, but the combination of primary and convention systems was also regarded as extra expensive to the State.

Royal Australian Tour Is Completed

By the A. P.

PERTH, W. Aus., May 23

THE Duke and Duchess of York have completed their Australian tour. They departed on the cruiser Renown this morning. In a farewell message, the Duke expressed gratitude for the wonderful welcome and countless kindnesses accorded them, saying the demonstrations of loyalty and wholehearted affection and devotion to the throne far surpassed anything they imagined, and they were deeply moved by them. A special message to the children contained, "Love and Best Wishes," from the Duchess and the Duke.

The Renown will call at Suez, Malta, and Gibraltar, and is due at Portsmouth, Eng., June 27.

New Brigadier-General Welcomed

Front Row, Left to Right—Col. Charles D. Roberts, Maj.-Gen. Preston Brown, Commanding First Corps Area; Brig.-Gen. James C. Rhea, Lieut. R. J. Burgess and Maj. Rapp Brush. Back Row—Private Mario Kopecx, Sergt. Charles Scott and Private Alexander Pelletier.

QUARRY WASTES IN INDIANA NOW YIELDING PROFIT

Odd Sizes and Colors Used to Advantage Under Efficiency Methods

Special from Monitor Bureau

CHICAGO, May 23—Mountains of rock waste, accumulating for years around the quarries and mills of the Indiana Limestone Company, in the famous Bedford stone district in Indiana, have yielded nearly $1,000,000 in usable material the last year. Formerly this had been considered "rubbish."

Lawrence H. Whiting, Chicago financier and chairman of the board of the Indiana Limestone Company, made this announcement in reviewing the year's work of the concern.

In the "rubbish" heaps was an odd assortment of stone, rejected as not suitable for originally intended purposes, or fragments chipped off during the operations and discarded as of apparently no use.

Efficiency engineers, studying the properties after Mr. Whiting effected the consolidation of 24 formerly independent quarrying and milling concerns into his one big company, discovered the potential fortune in the huge piles of waste around each quarry.

Now these mountains of broken rocks are being reduced by working the odd pieces into usable shapes when the mills are not otherwise busy. A specialty is being made of ashlars suitable for residence ledges. Another element in the rock piles was stone rejected because of the color variations. It "didn't match" with the bulk of an order and was thrown out. But now these peculiarly shaded pieces are being sought by architects intent on balancing the light and dark shades in various situations to obtain suggestions of height and mass and other effects in new structures, according to recent theories of color.

METHODISTS TO HAVE SKYSCRAPER CHURCH

SAN FRANCISCO (Staff Correspondence)—Construction of a 23-story church and hotel in San Francisco has been announced by a committee headed by Charles Wesley Burns, bishop of the Methodist Episcopal Church here. The structure will cost approximately $3,000,000. Plans have been prepared and ground will be broken within four months, it is said. The building will in many ways follow the plans of combination church-and-hotel and church-and-office building structures in New York and Chicago.

COMMITTEE TO STUDY PLAYGROUND METHODS

SAN ANTONIO, Tex. (Special Correspondence)—A permanent organization for continuous exchange of information about play methods and projects is being formed as the result of decision made here during the recent round-table meetings of the Southwestern District, Playground and Recreation Association of America.

Truth About China Sent With Laundry

Boston Chinese Inclose Folder in English About Nationalistic Aims

Laundry checks are still written in the curious hieroglyphic chirography of Chinese characters, but Boston customers are receiving with their bundles of clean shirts and collars a four-page leaflet, written in the best "King's English," and printed in the most approved modern fashion, setting forth an "Appeal to the American People by the National Government of China."

The folder, signed the Kuomintang, Boston Branch, 17 Hudson Street, Boston, Mass., outlines the aims and ambitions of the new Nationalist Government in China, and appeals against armed intervention.

TAX CASE BEING CLOSED

WASHINGTON (AP)—Oral argument in the $30,000,000 Ford tax case is being conducted before the board of tax appeals. Counsel for the petitioners, opposing the assessment of that amount of back taxes in connection with their sale of minority holdings in the Ford Motor Company, A. W. Gregg, general counsel for the Internal Revenue Bureau, presents the Government's case, assisted by W. H. Trigg, special attorney.

INDEX OF THE NEWS

Army Base Gives Greeting to Citizens' Camp Leader

Brigadier-General Rhea, Newly Promoted After Interesting Career, Is Received With Military Ceremonies—Is Veteran of Second Division in France

Received with full military honors including a salute of 11 guns, Brig.-Gen. James C. Rhea, leader of the Citizens Military Training Camps in the First Corps Area, in the New England States, who was promoted to that rank last Saturday, arrived at the Army Base, South Boston, today to assume his new duties. He was officially welcomed by Brig.-Gen. Preston Brown, First Corps Area commander, and a group of army officers.

Accompanied by his aide, Lieut. Ralph J. Burgess, General Rhea inspected the first battalion of the Thirteenth Infantry which was drawn up in full military dress to receive him as a guard of honor. The new brigadier-general took the oath of office in Washington and came here to take charge of his work from offices in the headquarters building of the Army Base. The ceremony at the base today was no less colorful than the biography of the new general, a native of Iowa, who was appointed from Texas to the United States Military Academy at West Point, N. Y. Upon graduating in 1899 he was assigned to the Seventh Cavalry in Cuba for duty until 1902. He served with the same regiment in the Philippines from 1905 until 1907.

After attending the Army School of the Line and the Army Staff College

(Continued on Page 2, Column 5)

LINDBERGH'S OWN VERSION OF HIS FLIGHT

"There Wasn't Anything to Do but Just Keep Going," He Tells Press

PARIS, May 23 (AP)—Capt. Charles Lindbergh told the story of his flight from New York to Paris to a group of newspapermen in the Embassy, and when he had finished, everyone was firm in the belief that he was a real flier.

"Being newspapermen," he began, "I suppose you gentlemen are interested first in knowing what was the most dangerous thing about our flight. The most dangerous thing of all was that landing at Le Bourget, bringing that ship down on a field with all that crowd running. I had more concern at that moment for the welfare of our plane than at any other time in the whole flight.

"The first part of the flight was better and easier than any of us expected. The field in New York was muddy, which made the takeoff a little long; but we got away all right.

"All the way up the American coast to Newfoundland we had uncommonly good weather. Lots better than we expected. But for the next 1000 miles it couldn't have been much worse for us."

At this juncture the Ambassador remarked: "When Lindbergh says 'we,' he means the ship and himself."

All the way through, except when asked for a personal opinion of something the flier used the first person plural in describing the voyage.

Fog, Rain and Hail

"After we got away from land," continued the aviator, "we ran into fog, then into rain, then hail. Sometimes we flew not more than 10 feet above the water, and the highest was 10,000 feet. We went up that high to try to get above the storm, but the average altitude for the whole second 1000 miles of the flight was less than 100 feet.

"Gales compare favorably with 1926, generally considered a record year," said Mr. Cox. "New England firms that are now showing good profits are facing squarely the new competition and are reducing costs, adapting modern merchandising methods, eliminating wastes and are going after business with policies which incorporate the most advanced methods.

Mr. Dennett outlined the part played by the Chamber in the development of this new attitude. He said, "The Chamber is making, saving, or causing to be more widely spent millions of dollars for the benefit of Boston and New England. The Chamber expresses the opinion of thousands of business and professional men in the community, many of whom have wide spheres of influence."

Mr. Johnson outlined the plans of the chamber for spreading this movement for co-operation throughout this section. He said: "This is a very logical part of the chamber's efforts. It requires the support of every progressive business and professional man in this territory."

RECREATION BOARD SEEKS FINANCE PLAN

Special from Monitor Bureau

CHICAGO, May 23—Some new plan of financing the work of the Chicago Recreation Commission will be sought next month in deliberations which will begin upon the return of A. R. Brunker, chairman of the commission, from Europe, according to C. P. Axelson, secretary of the commission, consisting of 250 members, was appointed by former Mayor William E. Dever, to stimulate more wholesome recreation and provide wider interest in music, opera and other arts, but its progress now is said to be handicapped by the lack of any city council appropriation or other funds to carry on its program.

MR. GOODWIN TO BE SPEAKER

HOLYOKE, Mass., May 23 (Special)—Frank A. Goodwin, State Registrar of Motor Vehicles, will address the Western Massachusetts Association of Chambers of Commerce at its next meeting in Westfield, June 15. Reports on the plan to extend the Mount Tom Reservation and also from the insurance rates committee are on the program.

FRENCH NATION OPENS ARMS TO CAPT. LINDBERGH

President Receives Him at Palace and Awards Legion of Honor Cross

FLIER RECOUNTS EVENTS OF TRIP

Flight Is Called Better Than Treaty as Aid to Franco-American Amity

BY SISLEY HUDDLESTON
By Special Cable

PARIS, May 23—France's welcome to Capt. Charles A. Lindbergh was unprecedented in its warmth, sincerity, tenderness, and pride. Yes, it is pride that Paris feels at Lindbergh's landing, for the question of nationality disappears. It is a triumph for humanity. From the long wait on Saturday to the thrilling moment of his arrival, throughout the night, during the whole of Sunday, and again today, the enthusiasm for his exploit has manifested itself in an extraordinary manner. The immense acclamation has surpassed anything ever seen for monarch, minister, or movie actor.

The foolish stories that France would display jealousy have been utterly refuted. There is nothing but fraternal pleasure in the American success. The failure of Nungesser and Coli is regretted, but certainly does not provoke the unpleasant sentiments of spite or envy. At Le Bourget, 100,000 people, at the lowest estimate, assembled and went wild when the plane dipped from the light. Their undisciplined ardor may be deprecated, but its generosity cannot be doubted. The boulevards were thick with excited throngs.

American Flag Flown

"Vive l'Amerique" was the cry which went up everywhere when the marvelous feat of Lindbergh became known. Raymond Poincaré, the Prime Minister, who is not a demonstrative man, ordered the American flag flown on the Louvre which all crowned the French government. Aristide Briand, Foreign Minister, followed suit and the American flag flies above the Quai d'Orsay. Captain Lindbergh will be received officially by the Municipal Council. Fêtes are being prepared and it is hoped to induce him to fly over Paris. Honors are showered upon him and thousands of messages from the highest personages to the humblest citizens have been received. It is not likely that Lindbergh will be spoilt by this tremendous ovation. Myron T. Herrick, United States Ambassador, has behaved with fatherly affection, housing and protecting the boy from important visitors, even lending him his pajamas and borrowing a suit for him.

It is the juvenility of Lindbergh which is the most striking thing. His simplicity and modesty captures the imagination. He seemed unaware that he had done anything particular, and he searched for a letter of introduction to Mr. Herrick, remarking naively that he knew nobody in Paris. He was astonished at the reception.

Saluted Unknown Soldier

His first thought after his amazing journey was to salute the unknown soldier before sleeping. His next thought was to telephone his mother in Detroit and a connection between Europe and America was established. Another thought was to call on Captain Nungesser's mother. He seems instinctively to do the right thing. The verdict of the newspapers is unanimous. The flight is perhaps the greatest achievement in the records of mankind, though at the time M. Blériot's crossing the Channel seemed more impossible. It was less than 20 years ago. Now Blériot is a regular Channel service, then Garros traversed the Mediterranean. Today Africa is joined to Europe by a regular service.

It is generally prophesied that 10 years hence perhaps five transatlantic air services will function. Lindbergh has renewed confidence. In a practical sense he has given points to those who prefer an air-cooled engine to a water-cooled motor. But above all it is asserted that Lindbergh has affected a rapprochement between the peoples that the diplomats could not. He has physically brought nearer two countries and morally made them realize their common humanity.

PARIS, May 23 (AP)—Capt. Charles Lindbergh came, was seen and has conquered the hearts of all Frenchmen. From stately homes to humble cottage, his feat in flying alone from New York to Paris is still the sole topic of conversation, while his name is heard in every bar and city café his name is heard repeatedly.

When President Doumergue pinned on Captain Lindbergh's breast the Cross of the Legion of Honor, the President on a real sense acted in the name of the whole Nation. It is felt everywhere that this fine young American has done more in a few hours to promote genuine sympathy between the two peoples than volumes of speeches and reams of literature.

Received at Elysée Palace

President Doumergue received Captain Lindbergh in the Elysée Palace and congratulated the young American warmly on his achievement.

"It's just one joy after another," said Captain Lindbergh, after thanking the President, "and this is one of the greatest."

The French Chamber of Deputies will pay the flier a signal honor on Wednesday, when he will be the

(Continued on Page 4, Column 1)

TRADE ADVANCE IN NEW ENGLAND SEEN BY MR. COX

Chamber of Commerce Is Commended for Part in Winning Co-operation

Marked improvement in New England business during the last quarter were outlined by Channing H. Cox, vice-president of the First National Bank and formerly Governor of Massachusetts, at a special luncheon of the Chamber of Commerce to more than 200 of its members today. Speakers praised the efforts of the Chamber in developing New England into a stronger co-operative force. Carl P. Dennett and E. C. Johnson, vice-presidents of the Chamber were also speakers.

Sir Alan Greets Him

All heads turned. The voice was that of Sir Alan Cobham, the greatest of British long-distance aviators, the pioneer of routes to South Africa, India, and Australia.

"It is Sir Alan Cobham," several said, and made a path for him to approach Lindbergh, who grasped the Briton's hand and said: "I am mighty glad to meet you, sir. I have heard a great deal about you. We—[did it all by dead reckoning. My name is Cobham, and I believe that did you do the whole flight by dead reckoning? I am a flier myself; my name is Cobham, and I believe that from London a few minutes ago to see you and tell you, you have done the greatest thing I have ever heard of."

"What points did you fly over in crossing from Ireland to France?" Lindbergh replied.

"Hand me the map; I'll tell you."

In answer to another question he said he did not feel either hungry or sleepy during the flight, and as to his meals—"I had a sandwich and a half and drank about a half a glass of water. I kept the windows open all the way. But, you see, our ship, the way she is built, we are protected from straight winds, and so we didn't have that discomfort."

"How did you fly from Cherbourg on to Paris?"

"Oh, just came in on a straight

(Continued on Page 4, Column 7)

Prohibition: Its Economic and Industrial Effects

Has Prohibition Reduced Discharges for Drunkenness?

This question will be answered by Professor Feldman's fourth article

in

The Christian Science Monitor

TOMORROW

(Continued on Page 2, Column 4)

THE CHRISTIAN SCIENCE MONITOR

AN INTERNATIONAL DAILY NEWSPAPER

COPYRIGHT 1927 BY THE CHRISTIAN SCIENCE PUBLISHING SOCIETY

Sixteen Pages — BOSTON, THURSDAY, AUGUST 4, 1927—VOL. XIX, NO. 211 — **ATLANTIC EDITION — FIVE CENTS / TWOPENCE } A COPY

POWERS ADJOURN NAVAL CONFERENCE AT GENEVA; NO AGREEMENT REACHED

Last-Hour Discussions Fail to Break Deadlock on Auxiliary War Vessels

MOTION TO SUSPEND PARLEY IS ADOPTED

Obstacles Are Not Accepted as Terminating Efforts at Future Naval Limitation

By Special Cable

GENEVA, Aug. 4—Last-hour discussions failed to provide a solution for the cruiser problem which has been engaging the attention of the tripartite naval conference here. The conference ended this afternoon

GENEVA, Aug. 4 (AP)—The Tripartite Naval Conference came to an unsuccessful end today. After nearly seven weeks of discussion the delegates of the United States, Great Britain and Japan found themselves unable to reach an agreement on the limitation of cruisers, destroyers and submarines which was the object of the conference.

The last act of the conference was the adoption of the joint motion of adjournment with the declaration that the governments of the three powers represented be invited to give new consideration to the problems involved in the hope that the governments would be able to reach an early solution.

In this joint declaration, the conference also registered its conviction that the obstacles encountered at Geneva should not be accepted as terminating efforts to bring about future limitation of naval armaments.

Hugh Gibson's Address

The declaration says: "On the contrary the delegates trust that the measure of agreement which has been reached here will make it possible for consultations between the governments to find a basis reconciling the divergent views and lead to early conclusion of an agreement for limitation of auxiliary naval vessels which will permit of substantial economy, and, while safeguarding national security, promote a feeling of mutual confidence and good understanding."

In his final address to the conference restating the American position, Hugh Gibson, head of the American delegation, pointed out that the invitation to the conference by President Coolidge left no room for doubt as to the nature of the proposals the American delegation would make. Those proposals, he said, had conformed strictly to the spirit of the invitation and he recalled that the Japanese had indicated willingness to negotiate on the basis of minimum figures suggested by the American delegation.

"From the first, however, we encountered a serious difficulty in the claim of the British Government that it needed a considerably larger number of cruisers than it now possesses," Mr. Gibson said.

He added that while the British claim had been defended on the ground of absolute naval needs of the Empire, the American delegation never had been able to reconcile "the conception of absolute naval needs with the negotiations of a treaty to fix limitations on the basis of mutual concession."

"Further," he said, "we have not yet been able to understand why, in a time of profound peace and at the moment that we are seeking to reduce the burdens of naval expenditures the British Government considers a considerable program of naval expansion as an absolute and even a vital necessity."

Calling attention to the British suggestion for strict limitation of the larger type of cruiser armed with 8-inch guns and for limiting all smaller craft to 6-inch guns, Mr. Gibson said the smaller ships would

(Continued on Page 2, Column 3)

INDEX OF THE NEWS

Junker Plane Breaks Reich Endurance Record

By the Associated Press

Dessau, Germany, Aug. 4

THE German endurance record for airplanes was broken this morning by the Junker plane, piloted alternately by Cornelius Edzard and Johann Risticz, which went aloft shortly before 6 o'clock yesterday morning.

At 9 o'clock this morning the plane had been in the air 27 hours, completed 3300 kilometers and was still going. It was flying normally in its shuttle circuit between Dessau and Leipzig.

FARM-TO-CITY MOVE IS URGED AS BEST RELIEF

Politics Institute Debate Also Turns on Costs of Dictatorships

By a Staff Correspondent

WILLIAMSTOWN, Mass., Aug. 4—Whether American farmers, representing a quarter of the Nation, are being discriminated against, or whether the farm problem is due simply to there being too many farmers, was keenly debated from the different viewpoints of banker, economist, sociolologist, farm editor and farmer, at a round-table conference under Henry A. Wallace of Des Moines, Ia., at the Williamstown Institute of Politics.

At another round table the similarity in the evolving makeup of the British Commonwealth, to a "smaller league of nations" was brought out by Prof. Herbert Heaton, Queens University, Canada.

Dr. D. S. Tucker, economist at Massachusetts Institute of Technology, analyzing the American farm problem, concluded that the question is simply one of the relatively larger increase in production on the part of the farm element extending back for years, as compared with the smaller ratio of productive increase on the part of manufacturers.

This, he said, has brought agriculture to overproduction. In other words, farmers are producing "too

(Continued on Page 4, Column 3)

SACCO-VANZETTI LOSE; GOVERNOR UPHOLDS COURTS

Special Board in Unanimous Accord That Men Had Fair Trial

"I find no sufficient justification for executive intervention."

So said Alvan T. Fuller, Governor of Massachusetts, in his decision, just before midnight Wednesday, on the appeal of Nicola Sacco and Bartolomeo Vanzetti for commutation of the extreme penalty imposed for a crime committed more than seven years ago.

His decision was in full accord with the unanimous findings of a board of three appointed by him at the beginning of his review of the case May 3, and reached by them by an entirely different and separate route.

There have been charges of unfairness in the conduct of the trial of these men and that they were convicted more because they were radicals than because they were proved guilty of the crimes charged, but the Governor states in the conclusion of his report:

"I believe with the jury, that these men, Sacco and Vanzetti, were guilty and that they had a fair trial. I furthermore believe that there was no justifiable reason for giving them a new trial."

This case, which was echoed throughout the world, began when Frederick A. Parmenter, paymaster of the Slater & Morril Company in South Braintree, Mass., and his guard, Alexander Berardelli, were shot on April 15, 1920. Bandits who had driven to the factory in an automobile seized the factory pay roll and escaped.

The Governor's decision follows in substance:

Substance of Decision

The first verdict was followed by seven motions for a new trial and two appeals to the Supreme Court for the Commonwealth, all of which were heard and later denied. Prior to the trial of the two men in this case, Vanzetti had been arrested, tried and convicted of an attempted hold-up on Dec. 2, 1919, at Bridgewater, Mass., and sentenced to 15 years imprisonment.

This appeal, presented to me in accordance with the provision in the Constitution of our Commonwealth, has been considered without intent on my part to sustain the courts if I became convinced that an error had been committed or that the trial had been unfair to the accused.

I realize at the outset that there were many sober-minded and conscientious men and women who were genuinely troubled about the guilt or innocence of the accused and the fairness of their trial

I believed that I could best reassure these honest doubters by having a committee conduct an investigation

(Continued on Page 4, Column 1)

'Teacher's Pet' Becomes Chum of Pupils in Chicago School

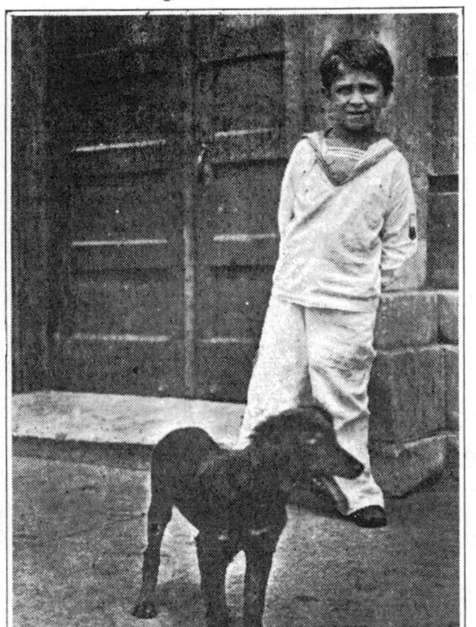

"Honey" Being Watched Over by Tony Paniko of the Dore School, Chicago.

Silky-Haired Black Pup, Picked Up From Doorstep, Is Principal's Assistant and Sets Example of Classroom Decorum Quite Unlike Mary's Lamb

Special from Monitor Bureau

CHICAGO—Few dogs can boast of having attended public school, but Honey, once a nameless, homeless puppy, has a proud record of three months' regular attendance at the Dore School here as the faithful companion of Miss Nora Dolan, the principal.

From early April, when Miss Dolan found the little black dog shivering on a doorstep in a belated snowstorm, to the end of June, when school was out, Honey trotted at the heels of the principal on her rounds, to the delight of 900 or more boys and girls.

In this school, set down in the midst of a quarter crowded with many nationalities, a happy atmosphere is regarded as a first requisite for education, and the old jingle about Mary's little lamb is reversed. Here it runs something like this:

Teacher had a little dog,
It's hair was very black:
And everywhere that teacher went
The pup was on her track.

It followed her to school each day
And never broke a rule,
But trotted closely at her side
And supervised the school.

Unlike the classical lamb, too, Honey causes no disturbance among

(Continued on Page 6, Column 7)

Chicago Schools Add Course in Aviation

By the Associated Press

Chicago

HIGH SCHOOL students of Chicago are to learn in the classroom the fundamentals of flying.

The subject will be incorporated in a general mathematics course, and J. Lewis Coath, president of the board of education, has invited aviation and radio experts to assist in a preliminary study which will enable adaptation of such training to public school use.

The study will be the first of its sort in the United States, Mr. Coath believes, and will be eagerly sought because of the renewed interest in aviation.

BRITISH EMPIRE MERGER SOUGHT IN TRADE WORLD

Sir Alfred Mond Favors United Front in Dealing With Other Countries

By Wireless from Monitor Bureau via Postal Telegraph from Halifax

LONDON, Aug. 4—A new commercial policy for the British Empire, involving the formation of a world-wide merger of the British Dominions to bargain with other coun-

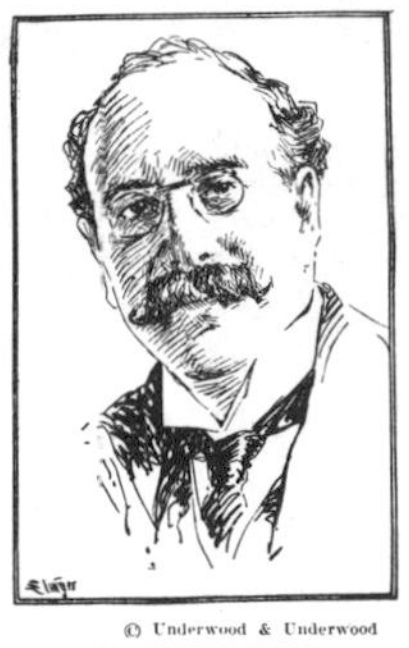

© Underwood & Underwood

SIR ALFRED MOND

tries, including the United States, is proposed by Sir Alfred Mond in a statement published here today.

Sir Alfred's scheme is unofficial, but is taken seriously as from one who has himself effected big British combines in chemicals, nickel and anthracite. Whether it will be fathered by the British Government may depend upon the report the Colonial Secretary, L. C. M. S. Amery, brings back from the British commonwealth tour on which he started on July 22.

Would Organize Empire

Sir Alfred advocates organizing the Empire as a self-contained fiscal unit with one general tariff against non-Empire goods and a central organization to arrange amalgamations and fix quotas of production. He says there is now no united front either in theory or in practice and that each Empire unit is consequently liable to get only the minimum benefit from its resources and efforts.

"I have seen that," Sir Alfred continues, "in the negotiations, for example, between Canada and the United States. Bartering and bargaining go on about the resources of Canada which, for instance in pulp and lumber, are by no means negligible. What would be the bargaining power of a united front? It would be a very different atmosphere, a very different reception when knocking was heard on the doors of Washington. It would not be so much a question of asking a favor as of stating what would be acceptable."

Sir Alfred goes on to claim that his scheme would give the British Empire "such trade as no other unit in the world could hope to achieve."

Mixed Reception

His proposals, while generally favored by the Conservatives, do not find support in Opposition circles. This is shown at the Liberal summer school conference now proceeding at Cambridge. Walter T. Layton, editor of the Economist, for example, there yesterday welcomed the Geneva economic conference declaration against high and constantly changing tariffs and saw no future for the creation of fresh customs duties. On the contrary, Mr. Layton claimed Britain's "hundred years of free trade" to be "the first chapter in the tendency to comparative world free trade."

Sir George Paish, ex-Governor of the London School of Economics, takes a different line from either. At this week's League of Nations Union meeting at Oxford, Sir George said that America was "creating credit" on a scale which could not last. A great smash must come unless America changed its financial policy. Germany had borrowed vast amounts in order to buy what it required, and Italy, another debtor, was unable to sell enough to buy what it needed. How were they going to repay America? Yet the nations of the world were imposing restrictions on trade which were literally driving the world into bankruptcy.

PREMIER SHOWS BRITAIN'S NEW TRADE OUTLOOK

New Industrial Balance Is Aimed At, Says Mr. Baldwin in Ottawa Speech

OTTAWA, Ont., Aug. 4 (Special)—For over half an hour yesterday Stanley Baldwin, the British Prime Minister, spoke frankly and freely to the members of the Ottawa Canadian Club and a number of distinguished guests, including W. L. Mackenzie King, Canadian Premier; Sir Robert Borden, William Phillips, United States Minister, and dominion cabinet ministers, on present commercial and industrial conditions and the future possibilities of his home land.

Referring to the utterance of gloomy forebodings, more especially from Englishmen themselves, "which often misleads a stranger, not always to his advantage," Mr. Baldwin said "it is wrong to state that England is in a state of industrial decline. We are feeling our way toward a new industrial balance, just as commercially we are moving toward a new orientation in our markets," following the setback due to the war.

Britain's Main Difficulties

The main difficulties of Great Britain, he pointed out, arose from her geographical situation as a predominantly manufacturing nation. Before the war the country had lived by a system which had been inherited—a constant exchange of goods, primary goods coming in and manufactured goods going out and a perfect system of banking and credit.

"How happy we were that the whole world, as it seemed, obediently brought us what we needed and took away what we made—in the halcyon days before the war, life for the ordinary man in England, indeed in Europe, was probably more comfortable than at any time in man's history and more comfortable than it will be again for many years.

Rebuilding of Trade

"When the shock came, our geographical position turned us into a shock absorber. We had broken contact with outer markets, but so sensitive had we become to the reaction of markets that each local convulsion within them was reflected in our own system. The vastness of the area over which we had previously operated was in itself a handicap to us. Wherever a market for our goods had been disturbed by the war, there for us and from our standpoint was devastated territory. We had to build up again the organization of the world's commercial system. Our policies abroad and our troubles at home are the story of that rebuilding."

Mr. Baldwin referred extensively to industrial troubles in England, and said that there was a tendency abroad to say that the working classes were revolutionary and out for trouble.

"That is a very gross exaggeration and a gross calumny on a very fine lot of men," he stated emphatically. There was, he said, material for trouble in the industrial disruption that followed the war, and there were numbers of men intent on fomenting trouble, but they were a minority and a very small minority.

In closing, the Premier told his hearers that he had spoken as he could in no other country but England, adding that he regarded Canada as England.

Prince's Busy Day

If yesterday in the Dominion's capital is typical of the Prince of Wales's daily round, then he is indeed a busy man. During the morning he received a group of invalid soldiers at Government House, then he drove out to the Hunt and Golf Club for a game of golf and a luncheon. In the afternoon he dedicated an altar within the sanctuary of the Peace Tower, wherein lies the Book of Remembrance to the 60,000 Canadians who fell in the war, unveiled the statue of Sir Wilfrid Laurier on Parliament Hill, visited the World's Poultry Congress, taking a keen interest in the numerous exhibits, and in the evening dined in state at Government House.

The unveiling of the statue was the occasion for an eloquent tribute from W. L. Mackenzie King, the Premier, Sir Robert Borden and Rodolphe Lemieux, to the memory of one of Canada's greatest men. His great natural endowments were enriched by a nobility of character that made his personality one of rare dignity and serenity, said the Canadian Premier. "Wherever he went, he seemed to shed a constant influence, a peculiar grace, he was singularly devoid of jealousies and prejudice, singularly charitable in his estimates of others and singularly forgiving. In all things he was a great gentleman."

Laurier Statue Unveiled

Sir Robert Borden, who divided with Sir Wilfrid the government of the country for many years, said "that like Sir John MacDonald, he inspired his party with the deepest emotion of love and devoted loyalty, even his strong political opponents cherished for him a feeling of warm affection.

"For more than 10 years I led the Opposition, while he was in power, and in all that concerned the maintenance of the wholesome traditions of Parliament and the principles of parliamentary government I am glad to acknowledge that I was a disciple of Sir Wilfrid Laurier."

Rodolphe Lemieux, Speaker of the House of Commons, referred to the difficulties of governing a country with such problems as Canada. To find a happy mean and determine the proper equation between two races, and two creeds, to reconcile the East and West, constituted an almost superhuman task. To those who have followed Laurier's career closely, it was evident that he had been destined for this great rôle.

REPUBLICANS AWAIT CLEARING OF COOLIDGE ANNOUNCEMENT; PRIMARY STATUS IS NEW PHASE

President Definitely Out of Race, Is Opinion at the Summer Capital

STATEMENT IS TERMED UNEQUIVOCAL STAND

Observers at Rapid City Say Mr. Coolidge Acts Like Man Relieved of Burden

RAPID CITY, S. D., Aug. 4 (AP)—A marked change in the general attitude of President Coolidge—like one who had a burden lifted—has been noticed since he made the announcement that "I do not choose to run for President in 1928."

Mr. Coolidge is described by those who are brought into closest contact with him as a much happier man. He is more talkative, although still far from loquacious, freer in his greetings, and he seems to get more enjoyment out of the little incidents of daily life.

This change has been noticed for several days before the statement was issued and it is believed by many to show that he reached his decision some time before it was announced.

Opinion Near Agreement

The opinion that President Coolidge's statement that he does "not choose to run for President in 1928" might have more than one meaning dwindled further in the summer capital and the belief has become almost positive that he has unequivocally eliminated himself from occupancy of the White House after March 4, 1929.

Several reasons for this belief come most prominently to the fore in Rapid City. First, it is pointed out, Mr. Coolidge could scarcely have used any other than the word "choose" in making his pronouncement and still keep the country from thinking him to be presumptive to the extent of believing the nomination next year actually was his. Had he said: "I will not run for President in 1928," he would have presumed, it is held, that the Republican convention would nominate him.

It is argued further at the summer capital that if Mr. Coolidge said: "I

(Continued on Page 2, Column 2)

Mr. Hoover Indorsed By Henry Ford

By the Associated Press

Detroit, Mich, Aug. 4

HERBERT HOOVER was indorsed as the logical candidate for the Republican presidential nomination to succeed Calvin Coolidge, in a statement issued here today by Henry Ford. Mr. Ford said the President is sincere in his decision not to become a candidate.

French Opinion Regrets Action of Mr. Coolidge

Press Comment Shows Appreciation of Dawes Plan Co-operation

By Wireless via Postal Telegraph from Halifax

PARIS, Aug. 4—Though the opinions of foreign countries cannot affect the course of domestic politics in the United States, there is a gratifying unanimity in the French press regarding the Coolidge Administration, and regret is widely expressed at the President's choosing not to run in 1928.

Without pretending to examine Mr. Coolidge's internal policy beyond the general statement that he has been a President who encouraged prosperity and tranquillity, the French consider that in foreign affairs his influence has been good, especially in regard to Europe. It is to the Coolidge régime and active American co-operation that arrangements for the payment of reasonable reparations by Germany are due, it is felt here.

This was the beginning of a new pacific period. From it flowed Locarno and the reconciliation of western European nations. On many occasions, it is said, judicious help

(Continued on Page 2, Column 1)

Overwhelming Call That Mr. Coolidge Run Again Seen by Mr. Burton

THIRD-TERM ISSUE MAY HAVE DECIDED

Declaration Bars President From Party Primaries, Appeals Judge Thinks

Special from Monitor Bureau

WASHINGTON, Aug. 4—Whether the third-term issue entered into President Coolidge's decision not to be a candidate for re-election to a determining degree, he has not made clear. It was one of several reasons, it is thought by his friends. At any rate, he has given himself a place in the history of the country by turning aside from the possibility of infringing upon this tradition.

Mr. Coolidge will have served considerably less time as President than Theodore Roosevelt did and the latter was converted to the idea that to be elected again would not be a third term, certainly not in the technical sense. President Grant wanted an out-and-out third term when he had served two full terms. The men who spoke definitely against a third term for the Presidency were those who were at the head of the nation in its formative days, when the country was not so solidly established nor so far from the monarchistic idea as today.

At any rate Calvin Coolidge has, with the simplest of gestures, declined to be a candidate at the end of his first elected term and a part of a term in succession to President Harding. Even those who regret that he felt impelled to make it admire him for it.

"The third term has been put to sleep for a long time," said an official here. "It will be a long time I think, before it awakens."

Door Opened to Candidates

As the finality and significance of the President's statement sinks in, conjecture as to candidates grows apace covering a wide field. It is seldom that favorite sons have appeared so early in a pre-campaign. It is accepted that Mr. Coolidge is not the man to designate a successor or to throw the influence of his office or his person in favor of any man. This gives the greater opportunity to increase the number of candidates. Charles E. Hughes, Vice-President Dawes and Herbert Hoover are still most frequently mentioned, but "dark horses" are crowding the paddock.

Potential candidates and their friends intend, whatever the feeling may be in other quarters, to take President Coolidge's declaration as a sincere and definite determination not to run for the office. Those who would "draft" the President, in spite of his statement, assert that it would be no reflection upon Mr. Coolidge's sincerity to nominate him, that it would be merely an indication of the wish of the people, before which the President would bow, sacrificing personal inclination.

Sees Demand for Mr. Coolidge

Theodore E. Burton (R.), Representative from Ohio, and temporary chairman of the Cleveland Republican convention, believes it will be Mr. Coolidge again. He said:

"President Coolidge's statement has put him in a position where neither he, his political advisers, nor his closest friends can work for his nomination. If he gets the nomination now it must come to him by an overwhelming demand. Whether such a demand will be made the future will tell.

"Undoubtedly his announcement has made his nomination less assured than it was before he spoke. I believe President Coolidge meant what he said. I believe he personally does not wish the nomination. And he probably went even further than that when he issued his statement.

"When a man has been in the White House as long as President Coolidge it is inevitable that he should make some enemies. Look at his vetoes, for instance. He has shown his courage. Possibly he made more friends than enemies. But consider his feelings when he pictures a great bloc of farmers arrayed against him. These things are to be considered.

Considering Other Candidates

"On the other hand, when a man says he does not wish an office, the public is more likely to wish him to have it anyhow. This probably will make people want to look at his record as President. The public may feel that the records of the other candidates in public office cannot equal his and may send him the overwhelming demand that will force him to run again.

"This, I believe, is certain. If the fight in the Republican Convention reaches a point where it is likely to be any man's race, the party will turn in overwhelming force to demand that Mr. Coolidge save it. Unless an outstanding leader is found, it will certainly be Coolidge again."

In analyzing the strength of the three foremost candidates for the moment, it is pointed out that both Mr. Dawes and Mr. Hoover would be acceptable to the business interests of the country. There would be opposition to Mr. Hoover wherever wheat is grown, as one man put it. To offset that is the prestige among the people at large, enhanced by his latest work in the flood district. "It is Mr. Hoover's greatest opportunity," said a friend of his, "but I am inclined to believe that he will not make it. Certainly the politicians would not take him if they could help it."

Mr. Dawes has prestige of another sort. He would be a better cam-

Nation's View on Prohibition to Be Objective of Conference

Workers in All Parts of Country to Be Called on for Aggressive Stand to Offset Wet Campaign in Political Campaigns

Special from Monitor Bureau

NEW YORK, Aug. 4—A conference that has as its goal the adoption of a nation-wide program by dry law supporters and which will probably have far-reaching effects in the political campaigns to be waged next year will be held in Atlantic City, Oct. 5 and 6, it has just become known here.

The names of the group of prominent prohibition workers who have united in calling the meeting were not made public, but The Christian Science Monitor correspondent is authoritatively informed that the conference is being called by outstanding supporters of the dry law who are convinced that the rank and file of drys throughout the country are depending upon organized workers to wage an aggressive and intelligent campaign to offset the strong offensive the wets are expected to stage during the next 12 months.

The conference will be attended by about 75 men and women, among whom will be those who have figured most prominently in prohibition work for many years. They will attend the meeting as individuals and not as official representatives of their organizations.

National Outlook Sought

In informed quarters it was learned that the discussions would center around the prospects for prohibition progress for the country as a whole and would not be confined to the activities of particular organizations. In this way it is expected that a broader consideration of the prohibition question in the United States will be possible than would be the case if attention were given merely to group interests. The findings of the conference, however, are expected to influence the attitude and activities of the various prohibition and law enforcement organizations during the coming year.

The conference will also consider the results of a survey now being made by Charles Stelzle at the request of prohibition leaders. The investigation, which is designed to determine "what America actually thinks of prohibition," will be nation-wide, and will also include the results of prohibition investigations recently completed by several professional groups, which will be used for comparison. A number of leading economists, sociologists and statisticians will assist in the preparation of the material when full returns have been received.

"This study will not be undertaken for the purpose of proving that prohibition is a good thing," Mr. Stelzle said. "Nor will the persons to be enlisted in making this study in various parts of the United States be selected because they favor prohibition.

To Be Chosen for Knowledge

"They will be chosen mainly because of their official positions in local communities or because they have had the opportunity to obtain accurate knowledge of the facts to be sought."

Among those who will be consulted during the investigation will be secretaries of chambers of commerce, high school superintendents, chiefs of police and other municipal officers, newspaper editors, labor officials, officers of employers' associations, librarians, clergymen, social workers, officers of fraternal organizations and such others as have actual contacts with typical Americans of various classes or groups, Mr. Stelzle said.

The prohibition leaders "wish to get accurate data regarding the people's attitude, as a whole, with respect to the dry law," he added, "so that their own efforts, looking toward enforcement, may be more intelligently directed."

The letter of invitation to the Atlantic City conference declares that "the conference is being convened in recognition of a large amount of correspondence from friends of the cause of prohibition concerning the importance of the months leading up to the next presidential election.

"These inquiries reveal anxiety as to whether the temperance forces are doing all that should be done for this great cause," it continues. "It is apparent that the organized liquor traffic is preparing to make a titanic effort to nullify and defeat that which has been accomplished by the Constitutional Amendment and Volstead Act."

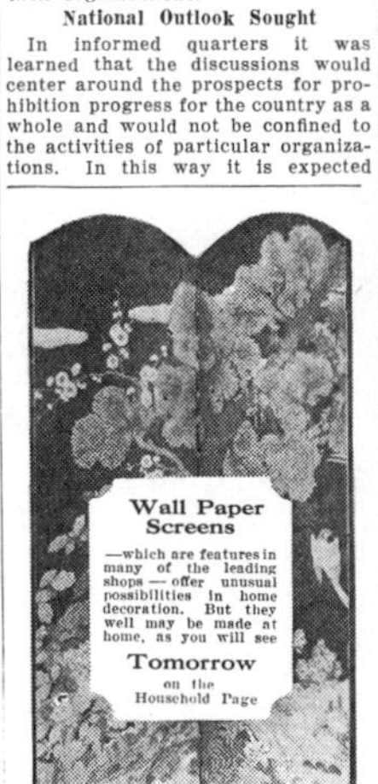

Wall Paper Screens
—which are features in many of the leading shops — offer unusual possibilities in home decoration. But they well may be made at home, as you will see
Tomorrow
on the Household Page

THE CHRISTIAN SCIENCE MONITOR

AN INTERNATIONAL DAILY NEWSPAPER

COPYRIGHT 1928 BY THE CHRISTIAN SCIENCE PUBLISHING SOCIETY

Fourteen Pages | BOSTON, MONDAY, JUNE 18, 1928—VOL. XX, NO. 173 | PACIFIC EDITION | FIVE CENTS A COPY

FRANCE BACKS OCEAN FLIGHT FOR FIRST TIME

Official Support Is Being Given to Attempt to Fly to United States

HYDROAIRPLANE NOW BEING GOT READY

Flight Under Government Auspices May Be Precursor of Air-Mail Service

By Cable from Monitor Bureau

PARIS—The French Government is, for the first time, officially backing a transatlantic flight, The Christian Science Monitor representative is informed by the Foreign Affairs ministry. Two Gnome-Rhone motors on a large hydroplane now settled on an inland sea called Étang de Berre, near Marseilles, are receiving a final tuning up. The machine will be flown by Lieutenant Paris of the French Navy and it is expected to reach the United States, via the Azores. It has, with an eight-ton load, a cruising radius of nearly 3000 miles.

While this ocean-crossing under government auspices may be the precursor of a regular transatlantic air-mail service, it will in no sense inaugurate such a service. The report from North America saying that a postal air route from France would soon be opened is not confirmed here, the postal authorities at least knowing nothing about it.

Many Airplanes Preparing

The French Government refuses to recognize or help any ocean-crossing attempted with machines incapable of landing on water. This attitude, however, has not deterred preparations now in full swing of six airplanes for transatlantic flight. There are rumors of others being got ready secretly.

Sergeant Détroyat, a war ace flying a Bernard plane, is given by experts an excellent chance of being the first Frenchman with private backing to reach the other continent. Then there is Capt. Louis Coudouret waiting also with a Bernard airplane called the Oiseau Tango, being the same one which made a start but had to return last year. A new Breguet is having motors fitted for the famous world fliers Dieudonné Costés and Joseph Lebrix.

Other Pilots Preparing

René Couzinet has built a trimotored graceful monoplane specially for the transatlantic hop and this is now being tested by its pilot of fine flying record, Maurice Drouhin. Two young commercial pilots, Nirmier and Wackenheim, are putting the finishing touches on a Potez airplane of a type used for several years by a French company between Paris and Constantinople. Finally, of those attempts of which there is definite information, the Polish aviators, Maj. Louis Idzikowski and Maj. Casimer Kubala, are standing by for a westward flight.

It is unwise to predict when any plane will actually start, nevertheless it would surprise no one to hear

(Continued on Page 3, Column 2)

WESTERN CANADIAN AIRPLANE SERVICE

Special to The Christian Science Monitor

VICTORIA, B. C.—Western Canada's first airplane passenger and mail service will be inaugurated between Victoria, Vancouver and Seattle on July 1 by the Western Canada Airways, Limited. Two eight-passenger Fokker cabin seaplanes will be used in the service, which will provide two arrivals and two departures a day from each of the three cities on the triangular route.

The service will connect at Seattle with the Pacific Air Transport and the West Coast Air Transport, passenger and mail lines operating to Portland and San Francisco. Thus it will be possible to reach San Francisco the day after leaving Victoria or Vancouver with a night's stopover at Seattle. The Western Canada Airways also are planning a service to Prince Rupert and Ketchikan.

INDEX OF THE NEWS

MONDAY, JUNE 18, 1928

Federal Power Investigation Confirms Monitor Story of City Plant's Profit

Special from Monitor Bureau

Washington

EVIDENCE that The Christian Science Monitor published a true and unbiased report of the success of municipally owned public utilities in Ponca City, Okla., has been introduced into files of the Federal Trade Commission, which is conducting an investigation of public utilities.

Edward F. McKay, manager of the Oklahoma Utilities Association, during his testimony before the commission, exhibited a letter written to him by Sam T. McQuarrie, director of the New England Bureau of Public Service Information, Boston, calling attention to an article published in the Monitor of Jan. 19, 1927.

The article pointed out that a municipally owned public utility can be made profitable, recounting that in Ponca City, for the five years ending June 30, 1926, the municipal electric plant had cleared approximately $550,000, with the citizens paying no larger rates than are paid elsewhere in the State and in some instances less.

"The Christian Science Monitor is published in Boston," Mr. McQuarrie wrote, "but evidently it has an active correspondent in Ponca City, Okla. If you have the time and the inclination, I should be very glad to have an authoritative statement from you as to why you permit a municipal light plant to make so much money."

"The sad part of it is," Mr. McKay said in his reply to Mr. McQuarrie, "that this story is true, and another sad part is that the secretary of the Ponca City Chamber of Commerce is a very capable and energetic newspaper man, who has an irresistible impulse to market his wares."

"The real explanation demanded in the last paragraph of your letter," Mr. McKay continued, "is found in the inclosed sheet, paying tribute to Arthur Brisbane's reference of a year or more ago to this same situation. The difference is that Mr. Brisbane was too sweeping in his reference to the Ponca City tax situation, while Mr. Corb Sarchet, the Ponca City correspondent of The Christian Science Monitor, has kept within the facts."

The "inclosed sheet" declared that Mr. Brisbane had given a false impression as to the desirability of municipal ownership of public utilities by saying in his syndicated editorial comment that profits on Ponca City's light, water, and power plants were sufficient to make the city free from taxes.

Investigation into the facts, Mr. McKay replied, showed that instead of being free from taxes, the citizens of Ponca City pay sums comparable with those paid in other cities of similar size in Oklahoma and elsewhere.

Mayor Callahan explained that the "citizens are relieved from city taxes only so far as they are required for the operation of the city government. State, county, and school taxes are levied as usual."

North Carolina to Take Stock of Resources

Entire State Is Enlisted in Move to Pave Way to Development Program

Special to The Christian Science Monitor

RALEIGH, N. C.—With a program designed to enlist the entire State of North Carolina in a new era of progress, the State Department of Conservation and Development has taken the first steps in a survey of natural and industrial resources whereby information necessary to promoters and investors may be made immediately available.

One unit of the survey, a study of the forest resources of the State, is already under way, and others are about to be launched. The work of tabulating and issuing the survey is under the direction of Park Mathewson, statistician and assistant director of the department.

Broadly speaking, the survey will be an inventory of the natural resources of the State, including raw materials, such as agricultural products, forests, minerals, fisheries, climate and population. This will mark the first attempt toward indexing the resources of the State in a comprehensive and systematic fashion. It is an effort to show the materials which the State is able to furnish for use either in their natural condition or in the processes of industry.

The survey seeks to determine to what extent the possibilities for development have been exploited and what opportunities exist for increased exploitation. More than a mere effort to seek indiscriminate utilization of natural resources, it is said, rather to be a move to guide the State in channels that promise to be of greatest benefit to the individual and the community.

The department characterizes it as an effort to collect fundamental information and to make it available to those whom it may serve in building a bigger and better State along sound and economic lines.

Gov. A. W. McLean, Director Wade H. Phillips of the Department of Conservation and Development; H. L. McLaren, former chairman of the Division of Commerce and Industry, and his successor, Benjamin B. Gossett, are all said to have been instrumental in developing the idea of a state-wide survey as well as in planning its details.

Mr. Phillips has announced that the survey will be carried out entirely with the department's force and with the co-operation of other state agencies. The divisions of the department will assist. In the field of mineral resources, co-operation of Dr. Jasper L. Stuckey, head of the Department of Geology, North Carolina State College; Dr. A. L. Greaves-Walker, professor of ceramics, State College, and Harry T. Davis, curator of geology, State Museum, has been promised.

SWEDEN EVINCES ITS LOYALTY TO THE KING

By Wireless to The Christian Science Monitor

STOCKHOLM—Unusually splendid scenes marked the celebration of King Gustav's birthday owing to the fact that the date almost coincides with the twentieth anniversary of his ascending the throne. Sweden's loyalty to the monarch is taking the form of a public subscription which the King has specially requested shall be for the benefit of the Swedish people as a whole.

On Sunday he will attend a religious service in the open air on the Ladugardsgarde parade ground when the troops march past at the conclusion of the ceremony. The Austrian-Sweden Bank committee has arranged a special Te Deum at the Lutheran church in Vienna on the same day as a mark of gratitude for the help given by Sweden to Austrian children during the war.

ALIENS TO FACE IDENTIFICATION TEST BY CARDS

On and After July 1 Immigrants Will Have to Show Proof of Legal Entry

Special from Monitor Bureau

WASHINGTON—Identification cards will be issued to all immigrant aliens, except students, who enter the United States on and after July 1. George J. Harris, acting commissioner of immigration, describes the innovation as "a milestone in immigration practice." It is expected to provide a practical means of differentiating between those who enter the United States legally and the many supposed to be smuggled in.

Identification cards will be issued by American consuls at points of departure and will contain the name and description of the immigrant, with his photograph attached. They are expected to prove popular with all legally admitted aliens who have hitherto lacked a convenient means of proving their status.

On the other hand, the alien who has entered in violation of the American Quota Act will find his stay much complicated by the absence of such a card, immigration officials say. It has been estimated that more than 1,000,000 immigrants are now in the United States illegally.

The certificate system will not be made retroactive, but lack of a card in aliens claiming to have entered after July 1, 1928, will be prima facie evidence of illegal entry.

The new system is an outgrowth of past experiences. About 15 years ago the service issued certificates for the use of Chinese immigrants. Later, identification cards were issued to aliens living contiguous to cities on the border to facilitate crossing to and fro. Last year indorsements were given for the first time to passports of those admitted as non-immigrants. This left the largest class of all still uncared for, the quota and non-quota immigrants.

"The card," Mr. Harris said, "not only will be a ready means of identification, but it will also prove a valuable record and afford the government an unfailing index to the official files which contain all the data respecting the status of aliens."

E. F. Albee

An interview that offers a clue to the professional ideals and practice of the leading figure of a dominant vaudeville circuit in the United States, will appear

Tomorrow

ROTARY SEEKING TO LINK WORLD IN CLOSER TIES

Interchange of Hospitality for Members' Sons to Be Proposed to Clubs

Special to The Christian Science Monitor

MINNEAPOLIS, Minn.—A plan designed to forge closer friendships among business and professional men of the world by sending their sons to live in each other's homes and study each other's businesses has been drafted for presentation to the nineteenth convention of Rotary International meeting here this week.

About 2000 foreign delegates, including a chartered boatload of 300 British, Irish and continental Rotarians, came here to meet with thousands of Americans from every state in the interest of a better business order throughout the world. The European delegation is reported to be the largest that has ever come to the United States for a Rotary convention.

The plan of exchanging "employee-students," an idea of European origin, received the approval of Rotary's board of directors in its general outlines at a conference held in Chicago last week. The board recommended it as an activity for individual clubs, however, not as a program to be guided from headquarters.

Plan Drafted at Zurich

It agreed with its subcommittee consisting of an American, a Mexican, and a Canadian, who investigated proposals brought by European delegates for this new activity, that the individual clubs or groups of clubs should be encouraged to go ahead on lines which already have had a tryout in Europe.

European Rotarians brought to the convention a definite working plan for the exchange of vocational residence which they drafted this spring at a meeting held for the purpose at Zurich. It represents the views of Rotary Clubs of Holland, Italy, Germany, Austria, France, Belgium, and Switzerland.

Their idea, which is expected to be carried out after it receives the approval of the convention, provides for a central agency to act as a clearing house for the clubs exchanging young men. Vocational students would be transferred like

(Continued on Page 2, Column 4)

Labor Conference Ends at Geneva

Another Milestone Seen as Being Passed on Road to Industrial Welfare

By Wireless to The Christian Science Monitor

GENEVA—The minimum wage draft convention was finally approved by a vote of 76 to 21 at the International Labor Conference. The delegates after unanimously deciding to frame a convention or recommendations for the consideration of governments on the question of the prevention of accidents next year, listened to an eloquent speech by President Saavedra Lamas, Argentine, reviewing the work of the conference which he pronounced to be another milestone on the road to social justice, and the progress of good understanding to all concerned in industry.

Tom Moore, Canada, who returned thanks to the chair on behalf of workers' delegates declared that a meeting representative of so many countries and interests could not fail to strengthen the bond between all those who were striving for the peace and prosperity of the world.

Thus ended the eleventh session. Just before the close of the conference, an incident occurred which evoked a loud burst of applause, for Mitsusuke Yonkubo, the Japanese workers' delegate asked for the president's official hammer, in order that the debates on the Japanese workers' movement might be directed with the same harmonious rhythm that ruled the running of the International Labor Conference.

SHIPPING PARLEY CLOSES IN LONDON

By Wireless from Monitor Bureau

LONDON—The international shipping conference has closed. It was agreed to accept the American recommendation regarding a reduction in f. o. b. oil tankers. There was also noted with satisfaction the recommendation of last year's economic conference for increased co-operation between the League of Nations and the organizations which permanently study transport questions.

McNARY, FARM BILL CO-AUTHOR, BACKS HOOVER

Solution Plan for Agricultural Problem Expected Soon

Special from Monitor Bureau

WASHINGTON—Hoover supporters believe that before the Presidential election occurs in November they will have gone a long distance toward modifying the farm resentment manifested in the stand of Frank O. Lowden and his sympathizers.

The first action came almost simultaneously with the return to the capital of delegates to Kansas City, when Charles L. McNary, Senator from Oregon, coauthor of the McNary-Haugen bill, following a visit to Mr. Hoover, issued a statement sympathetic to Mr. Hoover's candidacy and to the Republican farm plank at the convention, and sidetracking the equalization fee. Later in the day Mr. McNary was closeted again with Mr. Hoover in another conference.

The second action, looking to swift formulation of a farm program, is likely to follow shortly, with a statement from Mr. Hoover or from his assistants, offering a farm solution in the direction of federal aid in marketing surplus crops. It is hoped that the plan will be acceptable both to the "McNary-Haugenites" of the West, and to those who oppose the equalization plan.

Dry Law As Big Issue

Incidentally, if the proposal achieves its object and partially removes the farm controversy from the center of the stage, then by that much it will center the wet-dry dispute in the spotlight, as the major issue in the coming election.

On all sides it is agreed that the McNary statement is of major assistance to Mr. Hoover, coming as it does from one of the men who has lent his name to the farm bloc's battle from the beginning. It serves notice to that bloc that Mr. McNary will have nothing to do with efforts at a bolt in the western rural communities.

Mr. McNary states his belief that Mr. Hoover will carry every state in the "Corn Belt." Furthermore he puts the equalization fee proposal aside, and virtually promises to the farmers that a compromise measure will be evolved with Mr. Hoover's sympathetic assistance, which can be passed in the December session, or in the Congress that will assemble in 1929, following the inauguration of the new President.

Farm Relief Promised

"The agricultural plank in the Republican platform commits the party to enactment of legislation that will place agriculture on a basis of economic equality with industry," Mr. McNary said in his statement. He added that Mr. Hoover was "sympathetic and anxious to relieve the distress of our farm population."

On coming from his first conference with the Secretary of Commerce, Mr. McNary expressed the belief that if the farm bill which passed the last session of Congress had been stripped of its equalization fee feature, it would still have improved the condition of agriculture. He said:

"In a word, the plan contemplates the creation of a Federal Farm Board, abundantly financed to make loans to co-operative associations and farmer control stabilization corporations for the purpose of preventing violent price fluctuations and of controlling agricultural surpluses through the process of orderly marketing."

Opposes Equalization Fee

Mr. Hoover, it is well known, feels as does President Coolidge on the equalization fee. He does not consider it a practical solution of the problem, nor does he agree with Representative Haugen and the others of that school that the equalization fee idea offers the only way out of the mire into which the farmer is sinking.

The Hoover supporters believe that the farm resentment against the administration on account of the twice-vetoed bill is not so great as has been pictured. They believe that if they can prove that Mr. Hoover is the friend of the farmer, there will be little talk of bolting the ticket in the West. They believe that nothing could be more effective to this end than a statement from Mr. Hoover elaborating in general terms the Party's platform plank.

Friends of Mr. Hoover say he has rather definite views on the farm situation, but that he has never been called upon to express them. As Secretary of Commerce, the farm field was not his province, and it is only now as nominee of his party that he could set them forth.

Nations Compete to Capture "Luxury" Shipping Trade With South America

Special from Monitor Bureau

LONDON—International competition for the capture of the "luxury" shipping trade between Europe and South America was referred to by Lord Kylsant, in his address at the recent annual meeting of the Royal Mail Steam Packet Company.

"On the company's main service to Brazil and the River Plate," Lord Kylsant said, "we have been confronted with intense competition, particularly as regards first-class passengers. Ships of increasing size and speed are being placed on this route by lines of many nationalities, with the result that there is a superabundance of high-class passenger tonnage.

"The total volume of traffic has not increased to such an extent as to insure satisfactory complements of passengers for all the passenger vessels engaged in the trade. This competition has been intensified by the fact that in many cases our foreign competitors receive substantial aid from their governments."

The French Government subsidized the Compagnie-de-Navigation Sud Atlantique with an annual payment of £384,000 for 25 years.

The Brazilian Government had made provision for a subsidy amounting to about £434,300 per annum in respect of the transatlantic and coastwise service of the Lloyd Brazileiro.

"I venture to reiterate," said Lord Kylsant, "that Great Britain could find in the Argentine a still larger market for her maunfactured goods."

"Lady Lindy" Triumphs Over Atlantic

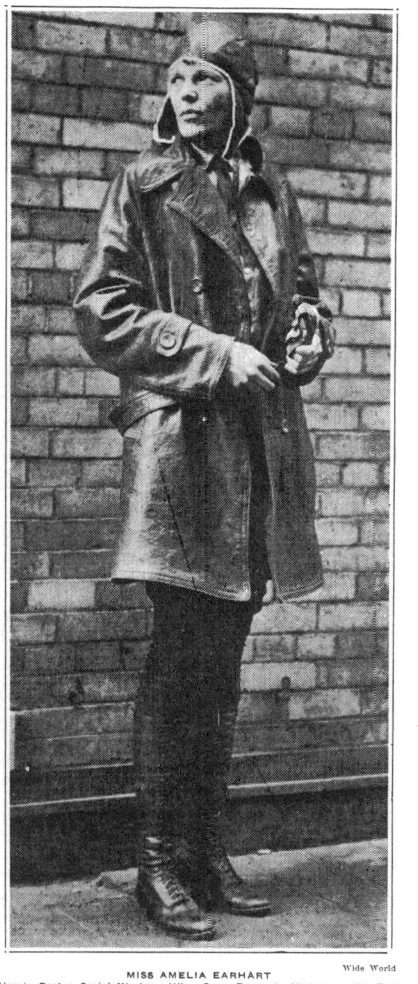

Wide World

MISS AMELIA EARHART

Heroic Boston Social Worker, Who Goes Down to History as the First Woman to Have Crossed the Ocean by Air.

BREWSTER FIRM IN HIS SUPPORT OF PROHIBITION

Favors Stricter Law and Larger Funds to Stop Illicit Traffic

Special to The Christian Science Monitor

AUGUSTA, Me.—A strong stand in favor of the national prohibition law and its vigorous enforcement was taken by Gov. Ralph O. Brewster in reply to a questionnaire by the Maine Civic League which constitutes one of the last-day events of the campaign between him and Senator Frederick Hale for Republican nomination to the United States Senate.

Declarations that if the Volstead Act is to be amended it should be in the direction of strengthening rather than weakening and that the Nation must soon mark the patron of the bootlegger as an accessory are outstanding features of his statement. The text of the questionnaire and Governor Brewster's answers follow:

"First. Do you believe the prohibition enforcement law, the so-called 'Volstead Act' as it now stands needs changing in any way, if so how?"

Heavier Penalties Advised

"Answer. I believe that the Volstead Act may be materially strengthened from time to time as the forces that are opposed to prohibition shall indicate the need. I believe it is already apparent that very much more substantial penalties might wisely be imposed for certain offenses.

"I also believe that the Nation must soon recognize that the patron of a bootlegger is an accessory to the crime.

"If it is wrong and criminal to sell liquor, it must be recognized that it is wrong and criminal to buy liquor. Without the patrons the stream of bootleg liquor would soon dry up and disappear.

"Meanwhile those elements in society that instigate this crime by their patronage will give more serious thought to the consequences when they realize that the outcast with whom they deal may at any time turn state's evidence and send their otherwise respectable customer to the nearest county jail."

Favors Larger Fund

"Second. Would you give your support to granting a larger appropriation to the prohibition bureau in order that they may carry on a stricter program of federal enforcement than is now possible?"

"Answer. I believe that the more quickly the Federal Government shall demonstrate its determination to crush out illegal traffic in liquor

(Continued on Page 2, Column 8)

Museum's Fund Gets Two Gifts of $200,000 Each

New York Institution's New Building Assured by Last Minute Donations

Special from Monitor Bureau

NEW YORK—Gifts of $200,000 each from John D. Rockefeller Jr. and James Speyer have just been announced by the Museum of the City of New York, completing its $2,000,000 building fund.

The gifts were made only a few hours before the time limit for raising the money expired. Under an agreement with the city, donation of site for the proposed museum was contingent upon the raising of the required funds. A total of $1,607,000 was raised by public subscription during a six weeks' campaign.

According to Robert LeRoy, secretary of the board of trustees of the museum, construction of the building will begin without delay. The plans were drawn by Joseph H. Freedlander, president of the Fine Arts Federation. The site is in Fifth Avenue, between 103rd and 104th Streets.

The Museum will house a complete record of the historical and commercial development of New York City. It will cover the 300 years from the period when Peter Minuit bought the lower end of Manhattan Island—now the most valuable real estate property in the world—by giving the Indians trinkets valued at $24, to the present time.

The Museum plans call for a U-type building of colonial design, with a formal garden between the wings. On the north and south sides of the garden will be arcades suitable for outdoor exhibits of colonial doorways and other works, and in the west ends of the structure there will be niches for the statues of Dewitt Clinton and Peter Stuyvesant.

UNIVERSITY GETS $1,000,000

By a Staff Correspondent

LOS ANGELES—Dr. Rufus B. von KleinSmid, president of the university of Southern California, has announced subscriptions totaling $1,000,000 received by the university's semicentennial fund. Approximately $10,000,000 is expected by 1930, when the university will celebrate its fiftieth anniversary. The fund will be used in construction of new buildings, and to endow teaching departments.

FIRST WOMAN TO FLY ATLANTIC LANDS IN WALES

Miss Earhart Makes Welsh Coast 20 Hrs. 49 Min. From Newfoundland

TAKEOFF MADE IN PERFECT WEATHER

Friendship's Radio Keeps the World in Touch With Crew of Plane During Flight

LONDON (AP)—The first air crossing of the Atlantic Ocean by a woman has been accomplished. The American hydroairplane Friendship, carrying Miss Amelia Earhart, Wilmer Stultz and Louis Gordon, was reported in a Press Association dispatch to have landed in Burry Estuary, off Burryport, Wales, at 12:40 p. m. (6:40 a. m. eastern standard time), just 20 hours and 49 minutes after hopping off from Trepassey, Newfoundland.

About 11 a. m. (5 a. m. eastern standard time) the plane had been sighted 75 miles southeast of Cobh, Ireland, by the American steamship America. The Llanelly dispatch said that a motorboat put off immeditaely to ascertain the crew's intentions. The Friendship was stated to have come down in the sea about two miles from Burryport coastguard station. The tide was out and the plane came to a standstill close in shore. Coastguards immediately went out in a boat. Burryport is on the south Carmarthenshire coast, four miles west of Llanelly. It is in approximately the same latitude as the southern coast of Ireland.

TREPASSEY, N. F. (AP)—Miss Earhart and her two companions hopped off on Sunday morning at 9:51 eastern standard time with the intention of reaching Valentia, Ire., in 18 hours. From this sleepy little harbor on the southern end of the Avalon peninsula the big pontoon-equipped Fokker monoplane rose into the air to circle over the village and then headed east into a cloudless sky.

Dumping of Gasoline

The takeoff was made only after five unsuccessful attempts, and the dumping of 80 gallons of gasoline, which reduced the fuel supply to about 700 gallons—less than 20 hours consumption for the three 220-horsepower Wright Whirlwind motors.

The same confidence which Miss Earhart had shown during the 13 days she and her companions awaited favorable weather prevailed as she took her place in the cockpit with Stultz, the pilot, and Gordon, the mechanic. "We are going today in spite of everything," she said as she rose early in the morning and scanned the weather reports, which promised favorable conditions with following winds for all but 700 miles of the almost 2000-mile journey, "and we'll make it."

Then with her companions, she entered a dory and was rowed out to where the big Fokker rose and fell to the harbor swell. Half an hour later the fliers were started on their great adventure.

They were reported by a steamer as they cleared the tip of Newfoundland and started out along the steamer track toward their destination. Through the day and early hours of the night other steamers reported them, either by sight or through the medium of the Friendship's radiocasts. Stultz was acting as both pilot and radioman. When he was sending, Miss Earhart was at the controls. The plane had two sending sets, one working on 600 meters, the other an emergency set for use if the plane should be forced down on the water and the engines stilled.

Plane Bought From Byrd

Mrs. Frederick Guest, wife of the former British Secretary of State for Air, is the backer of the flight. Mrs. Guest, the former Amy Phipps of Pittsburgh, when she finally identified herself as sponsor for the flight, said it was being made in the hope that it would be another link in the friendship chain between England and the United States and "truly helpful to aviation."

To that end she commissioned George Palmer Putnam, New York publisher, her American representative, to take all possible safeguards for the flight.

The plane was purchased from Commander Richard E. Byrd, who had bought it for his South Polar expedition. It was equipped with pontoons and given rigid tests for over a month at Boston, where the start was made two weeks ago.

It is tri-motored, equipped with all up-to-date air navigation instruments and, with the pontoons, is probably as well equipped as any plane used in ocean flying to date. It is almost a duplicate of the Southern Cross which Captain Kingsford-Smith and his three companions flew from the United States to Australia.

Miss Earhart, a Boston social service worker, is a qualified pilot with a record of over 500 hours in the air. She learned flying on the Pacific coast. She is slim, blonde and has a striking resemblance to Colonel Lindbergh. She repeatedly denied that she was making the flight as a commercial adventure. Stultz, chief pilot, and ex-army flier, is an aviator of long experience. He was a pilot for Mrs. Francis Wilson Grayson on her unsuccessful attempts to make a European flight from Old Orchard, Me., last summer. On one of the attempts Stultz piloted the Grayson plane several hundred miles to sea, when motor trouble developed and he turned back. Last winter he made a non-stop flight to Havana with Charles A. Levine and Miss Mabel Boll.

Gordon is an experienced flier and mechanic, formerly in the army air service. His home is in San Antonio.

THE CHRISTIAN SCIENCE MONITOR

AN INTERNATIONAL DAILY NEWSPAPER

COPYRIGHT 1928 BY THE CHRISTIAN SCIENCE PUBLISHING SOCIETY | Twenty Pages | BOSTON, WEDNESDAY, NOVEMBER 7, 1928—VOL. XX, NO. 293 | ATLANTIC EDITION | FIVE CENTS A COPY

HOOVER AND CURTIS WIN IN LANDSLIDE

HOOVER QUIETLY HEARS RETURNS WITH FAMILY

Accepts Victory as He Lived—Simply and With Profound Humility

FRIENDS 'LISTEN IN' AND WATCH HIS CHARTS

Sousa's Band and Stanford Students "Serenade" Nation's New Leader

By a Staff Correspondent

PALO ALTO, Calif.—The Presidency came to Herbert Hoover as he has lived—simply, quietly and with profound humility.

It was 8:30 p. m., Pacific coast time, Nov. 6, when it became certain that his election was assured by a poll that set new political forces and alignments into action. The President-elect was in the drawing-room of the unostentatiously charming home he and Mrs. Hoover built on the Stanford University campus that they both knew as students together and love so deeply and to which they have always returned after great service and to prepare for new labors.

With them were their two sons, Herbert Jr. and Allan, and the former's wife, and a group of friends and neighbors, mostly members of the university faculty. It was like a home gathering in spirit and person. There was no clamor, no tumult, no ceremony, no pose.

Hoover Prepared Chart

The little group, joined from time to time by another close friend, gave its attention to a chart that Mr. Hoover had prepared which gave a comprehensive tabulation of the trend of the count.

The chart was chalked on three classroom blackboards. Two carried the list of states, with the number of precincts in each, and spaces for the report as it came over the wire. The third board listed the states and their electoral vote as they were recorded for the two major candidates.

Mr. Hoover and Mrs. Hoover greeted their friends simply and graciously. They mingled with the group, chatting in friendly undertones. For the newspaper men Mrs. Hoover thoughtfully provided a tasty luncheon in the large room that had been fitted up for them.

Hears Smith's Message

In the simple dignity and humility with which he had accepted the nomination and made his campaign, Mr. Hoover received the recognition from his opponent that he was the victor. There was no change in his manner, nor in that of his family and friends.

The group was seated in the room before an improvised screen, on which the news reel cameramen,

(Continued on Page 5, Column 4)

Curtis Beams 'That's Great!'

Told of Republican Landslide as His Train Stops in Chicago

CHICAGO, Ill. (AP)—Informed of the Republican landslide, while still clad in pajamas aboard the train which is carrying him to Washington, Vice-President-elect Charles Curtis exclaimed, "That's great!" as a smile beamed over his face.

"I am gratified with the returns," the Senator said. "Mr. Hoover made a wonderful campaign. Personally, I am grateful to the American people for the splendid indorsement given the Republican ticket."

COLLEGE PRAISES BOOK ON MINING BY HOOVER

Special to The Christian Science Monitor

EUGENE, Ore.—"Principles of Mining," a volume by Herbert Hoover, has been in use as a text for the past 10 years at the Oregon Agricultural College school of mines, and is still considered the best authority in its field, it is declared by Dr. James H. Hance, dean. The text is used by mines seniors in their last term in college.

The book deals with fundamentals and is a condensation of lectures delivered by the author at Columbia and Stanford Universities. It is used by many other mine schools and colleges.

RAILWAY COMBINE TO RUN TRAMWAYS

By Wireless from Monitor Bureau

LONDON—The County Council, after an all-night sitting, has agreed by 63 to 44 votes to the proposals for the taking over of the tramways by the Underground Railway combine.

The proposal is designed to reduce the heavy loss now incurred in tramway operation by reducing the duplication of services, but has been strongly opposed on the ground that it makes for private as against public ownership of essential city utilities.

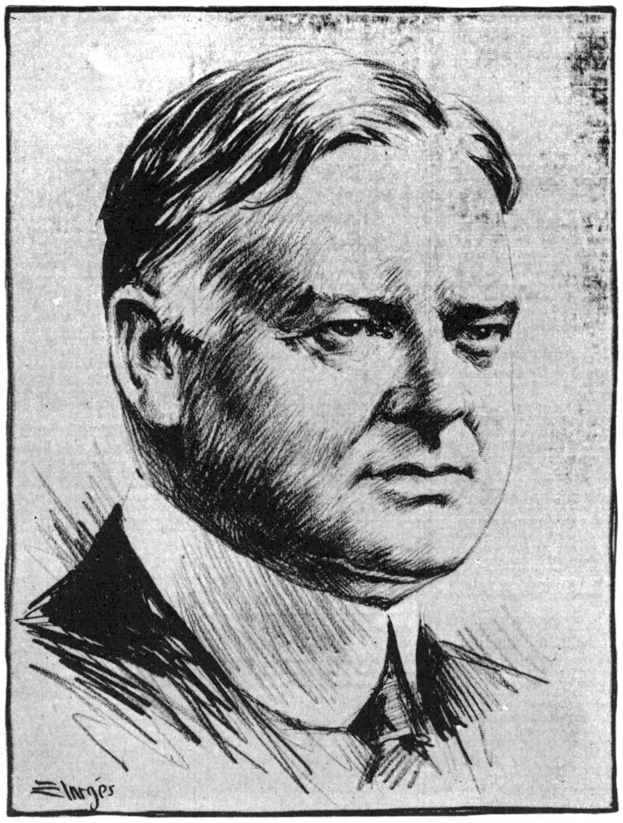

HERBERT HOOVER

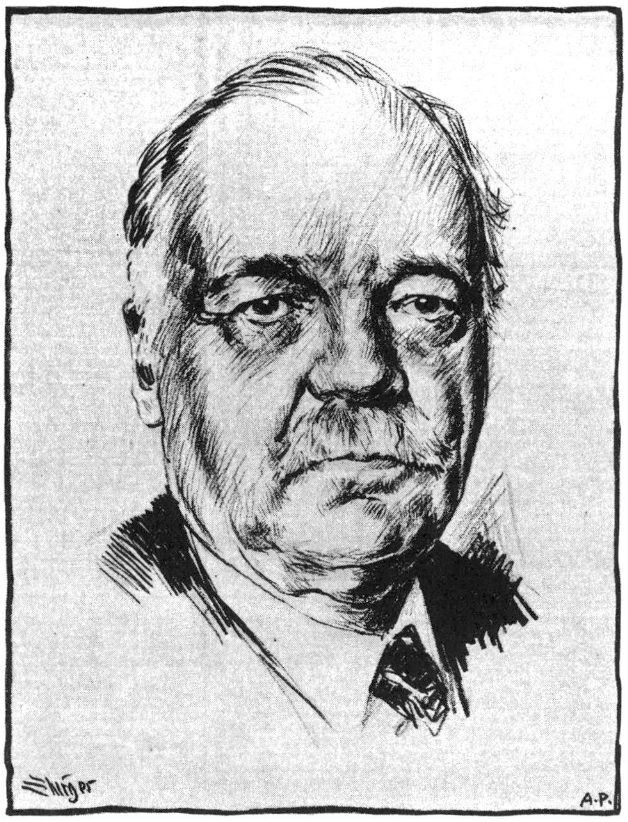

CHARLES CURTIS

Socialists' Chief Sees Break-Up of Democratic Party

Norman Thomas Says Own Group Will Take Its Place as Center of Opposition

NEW YORK (AP)—Norman Thomas, Socialist candidate for President, viewed the overwhelming Republican victory as a "long step" toward the disintegration of the Democratic Party and the rise of the Socialists as the principal party of opposition.

Mr. Thomas said the Socialist vote here exceeded expectations and indicated increasing strength. He received 48,179 votes in the city, after predicting that he would get 45,000. The party's national headquarters had no figures on the voting elsewhere.

"I don't think Governor Smith was defeated by the religious or any other one issue," the Socialist candidate said. "It was a complex of forces. Regardless of his religion or Tammany Hall, he would have lost.

"From my observations on my stumping of the country, the Democrats were badly organized and split internally. That, in my opinion, was a bigger factor in the defeat than religion, although this issue did play a part.

"I predicted Democratic defeat because it seemed to me the Republicans were better organized. I look upon this as preceding the disintegration of the Democratic Party and political realignment upon clear-cut issues. I expect the Socialist Party to rise as the new party of opposition."

Imported Fishballs Must Pay Customs

Potato Flour in Them Does Not Put Product in Vegetable Class

Special from Monitor Bureau

WASHINGTON—Fishballs and fishcakes must pay duty when imported into the United States, the Bureau of Customs has ruled. Strange that that commodity, generally accepted as of native origin, should be imported.

Whether or not this delectable New England food is dutiable hung on whether it was a vegetable. There are fishcakes which run largely to flour, but they are not the kind most highly approved by New England. Potato flour, it is now stated, does not fall within the term "vegetables" as used in the customs regulations.

"There has been some confusion resulting from the various decisions in regard to the classification of articles produced from vegetables where the articles have lost their identity as vegetables," the customs ruling says. "The department is of the opinion that fishballs containing a small amount of potato flour are dutiable at the rate of 25 per cent ad valorem."

NAVAL ACCORD DROPPED, SAYS LORD SALISBURY

Conservative Leader, in Upper House, Declares Response Not Encouraging

By Wireless from Monitor Bureau

LONDON—The Marquess of Salisbury, leader of the Conservatives, speaking for the Government in the House of Lords at the opening of Parliament, made it clear that the much-criticized Anglo-French naval agreement is now entirely dropped.

Asked by Lord Beauchamp for the Liberals whether the position was now like a "clean slate" he said: "Undoubtedly the naval agreement is at an end. We were confronted by a response to our effort, which was not at all encouraging. I very much regret it. I do not really know how this disarmament problem—and it is a great problem—is to be solved, unless there are preliminary understandings which are at once communicated to the other interested parties. I do not see upon what other principle you could proceed."

Lloyd George Amendment

The House of Commons will discuss the situation next Tuesday upon the address of the amendment which Mr. Lloyd George is to move attacking the Government's handling of the naval agreement. The Cabinet, a representative of The Christian Science Monitor understands, is much concerned at the widespread international misunderstandings which this compromise, however harmless its intentions, admittedly caused, and is anxiously looking to redressing the situation. Its uneasiness is reflected in the prominence given in the King's speech to Great Britain's desire to assist in "formulating plans for a general reduction of armaments."

How far-reaching the issues involved are is shown by the fact that even the resignation of the Poincaré Cabinet is associated with it here. The Daily News, for example, says: "The Pact has helped to bring down Poincaré's Government. At the Angers congress the French Radicals showed that they, at any rate, were under no illusions as to what unlimited multiplication of trained reservists means. They attacked severely the increasing military expenditure of France and the new long service army. The revolt which has proved fatal to the Government was, that is to say, a direct result of the outcome of the pact negotiations, and was largely inspired by animosity to them."

New Angle on Disarmament

An opportune proposal on the now approaching disarmament question from a new angle is made in a letter in The Times by Dr. Abraham Flexner, noted American educator and this year's Rhodes memorial lecturer at Oxford.

Dr. Flexner in a special non-official inquiry, says: "I have read with

(Continued on Page 7, Column 2)

Intimate Glimpses of Hoover Career Give Keys to Success

"Action Pictures" Illustrate How He Grows to Meet Each Job, Wins Loyalty of Helpers—Failed in College Test but Gained Teacher's Respect

By ROBERT S. ALLEN

Every now and then some enthusiastic journalist or other writer who has come under the sway of the genius of Herbert Hoover rushes into print with an exclamatory article about the "new Hoover." The author of such an exposition is always right. The "new Hoover" is there, but that fact is neither new nor unusual, for the most outstanding characteristic of the President-elect is his constant and limitless capacity for growth.

He comes by that rare talent naturally. He is the son of a long line of American pioneers among whom each generation marched to a new frontier, building in its turn new homes and communities, new churches and schools. His father's people pioneered from Maryland to North Carolina before the days of the Revolution. The War of 1812 was not yet history when they reached Ohio, and as the years leading up to the Civil War unfolded they were to be found always on the advancing frontier. By the time the sectional conflict took place they were in Iowa and afterward pushed on to the shores of the Pacific.

Constant Advance

This constant advance with the vanguard of American civilization was not merely removal from one region to another. In every instance it was the beginning of a new center of American activity, a new community where men and women worked and worshiped God and built homes and farmed broad acres.

From such sturdy, valiant, profoundly American stock the next President of the United States sprang. Herbert Hoover is racially and instinctively wholly American, and despite more than a quarter of a century during which his profession called him to every quarter of the globe, he has remained completely so.

It was said of him by an old comrade of many years' standing that although Mr. Hoover had lived for many years in England he never showed the slightest trace of that residence in his speech. Mr. Hoover is a man indissolubly linked with his origins.

Dealt With Unusual

Nothing shows more strikingly the President-elect's genius for growth and coping with great problems than the manner in which he took up and so successfully dealt with the unusual, and to him peculiarly trying, demands of a presidential campaign. To understand fully just what an unwelcome task it was for Mr. Hoover it must be kept in mind that political campaigning was not merely a new experience for him, but one that was contrary to all his past experience and to his most fundamental instincts.

For although he is a man of worldwide activities and friendships, and no man seeks the comradeship of people more than he, or has performed greater humanitarian service for whole nations, yet few men are more utterly modest, shy and reserved.

A noted observer of men, who has known Mr. Hoover for many years both in mutual labors and comradeship, described him as a "man who seeks society, and yet no man is more charged with an essential unassuaged loneliness." This same intimate friend expressed the opinion

(Continued on Page 3, Column 1)

Wall Paper Comes to Life!

THE artist and printer may think they lay their designs flat on the paper, but, what child does not daily revel in the antics and capers on his wall? Sisley Huddleston gives us a page cut of childhood's book

Tomorrow on the EDITORIAL PAGE

INDEX OF THE MONITOR

TAMMANY'S VOTE FELL FAR SHORT OF EXPECTATION

Broadway Crowds Thrilled and Chilled by Rapid Changes in Returns

Special from Monitor Bureau

NEW YORK—The greatest vote that New York ever cast has resulted in the State going for Herbert Hoover for President. The five boroughs of New York City did not return the vote for Gov. Alfred E. Smith that the Democrats hoped for, and Mr. Hoover and Charles Curtis came down to the New York County line with such an avalanche of votes that the big Tammany vote in the city was submerged.

It was not a Hoover landslide in so far as the entire State vote was concerned, but within a few hours after the polls closed, the Hoover victory was apparent. Indeed, a little after midnight, Governor Smith sent a dispatch to Mr. Hoover in Palo Alto, congratulating him on his victory and wishing him well.

At the time this is written, Franklin D. Roosevelt, Democratic candidate for Governor, is leading Albert Ottinger, Republican, by about 60,000 votes. Three hundred and fifty precincts are yet to be heard from. At Republican state headquarters it was said that Mr. Ottinger's strength was considerable in these precincts.

Copeland's Election Indicated

Incomplete returns indicate the reelection of Dr. Royal S. Copeland, Democrat over Alanson B. Houghton, former Ambassador to the Court of St. James's. The election of Mrs. Ruth Pratt, Republican candidate for the House of Representatives from the

(Continued on Page 6, Column 7)

Germans See Vote as Dry Law Gain

Hoover Victory Welcomed as Aid in Settling Question of Reparations

By Wireless to The Christian Science Monitor

BERLIN—Herbert Hoover's election is described here as "a victory for prohibition." Under his Presidency it is said furthermore, the reparations question—in which Germany is naturally most interested—will be solved in a reasonable and practical manner.

Mr. Hoover's popularity in Germany is best proved by the heading which one noonday paper gives to its report which runs as follows: "Herbert Hoover, the man who supplied Germany with foodstuffs after the war, has been elected.

Interest in the United States elections was weakened temporarily by the sudden resignation of Raymond Poincaré as French Premier since this affects Germany more immediately.

Leader Against Alcohol Affirms Belief in Hoover

Friends of Prohibition, Says E. H. Cherrington, Know He Will Aid Enforcement

Special from Monitor Bureau

WASHINGTON—"Friends of prohibition are convinced that the character of President-elect Hoover as well as his statements made during the campaign assure the Nation of his honest intent to do everything possible in fulfillment of the oath to 'preserve, protect and defend the Constitution,'" said Ernest H. Cherrington general secretary of the World League Against Alcoholism.

"There is a positive obligation upon the supporters of this law to do all within their power to make easier and more successful the task of enforcement of national prohibition.

"Especially important is the educational program upon which ultimately this great social policy must depend. The advocates of liquor, although repeatedly beaten in the polls and in legislative bills have not yet abandoned the fight to regain a traffic that would today probably be worth $5,000,000,000 if it could obtain legal sanction once more.

"The continuance of prosperity, the steady decrease in our death rate, the drop in our criminal ratio, the disappearance of poverty and the slum, the new moral idealism which is replacing the disrespect for law fomented by the liquor group and the progress made in developing our swift, closely integrated civilization, are all unanswerable arguments in favor of prohibition, evidencing its title to the fullest adhesion on the part of the American people.

"President-elect Hoover should be assured of the fullest and most active co-operation that can be given to him by the countless millions who believe in, obey and support the Eighteenth Amendment."

KONIGSBERG PARLEY FAILS OF AGREEMENT

By Wireless to The Christian Science Monitor

BERLIN—The report that no agreement has been reached by Lithuania and Poland at the Königsberg conference is received here with regret and disappointment. The deadlock is due to the fact, it is said, that it is practically impossible to solve minor questions without tackling the Vilna problem.

It is now up to Geneva to take the situation in hand at the next meeting of the League of Nations in December, it is declared here.

UNEMPLOYMENT FIGURES

By Wireless

LONDON—The weekly returns gives the total number of unemployed as 1,347,700 which is 30,513 more than a week ago, and 268,643 more than a year ago.

WOMEN'S VOTE BIG FACTOR IN RECORD POLL

G. O. P. Nominees Break 'Solid South' and Carry New York

ALL BORDER STATES GO TO REPUBLICANS

New President Stressed His Philosophy of Economic-Political Liberalism

By a Staff Correspondent

WASHINGTON—Herbert Hoover has been elected thirty-first President of the United States by a popular and Electoral College majority that swept aside sectional and party lines. He "broke" the "Solid South" by apparently winning Virginia, Florida, North Carolina and possibly Texas, and took all the border states listed as "doubtful," Maryland, West Virginia, Kentucky, Tennessee, Oklahoma and Missouri. He started his landslide sweep by carrying New York and Wisconsin, the two states the Democrats had considered "certain." He ran unexpectedly strong throughout the entire East.

Of the 43,000,000 registered voters it is believed more than 35,000,000 went to the polls, a new record for all time. The unusually keen interest taken by the women all over the country in the campaign was a big factor in the unprecedented popular vote.

For the first time since the formation during the reconstruction days that followed the Civil War of the so-called solid South, a Republican presidential candidate carried some of these states.

Campaign Characteristic of the Man

The campaign as a whole was characteristic of the simplicity and straightforward dignity of the man. He addressed himself strictly to placing before the electorate in a series of learned deliberations his philosophy of an economic-political liberalism in dealing with the moral and economic problems that confront the Nation.

It was primarily the moral element, it is declared, which was responsible for the breaking of the solid South, as it was in the winning by Mr. Hoover of such states as New York, Wisconsin, Tennessee, Kentucky, Nebraska, New Jersey and Connecticut. This controlling moral factor as viewed by these leaders, was involved in every issue of the campaign, prohibition, agriculture, water power, foreign affairs and tariff.

No force except such a profound conviction, it was held, could have produced the victory that Mr. Hoover scored. Mere political and economic matters could not have moved the Nation to such an unprecedented ballot and to give to a candidate of Mr. Hoover's reserve and restraint such a tremendous majority.

Presages New Order

The election to the presidency of Herbert Hoover, political leaders declare, presages not only a new order in federal government administration and policies but of equal importance the emergence of a new leadership and alignment in party lines. Such a development is inevitable, it is said, because the type of administration that Mr. Hoover, with his rare capacity and experience, is certain to give the Nation in response to the demands of a new era in national affairs.

Every device was used in southern states to compel allegiance to the party candidate. In Virginia state Democratic leaders frankly declared they were "whipping" support into line, adding, "and when we say 'whip' we mean just that." This was also so in other southern states where every pressure and influence was resorted to to maintain Democratic Party lines in the national contest.

Expanding Industrialism

A factor that political leaders say also entered to a considerable extent in the winning by Mr. Hoover of "solid south" states was the expanding industrialism of the section. This fact has done much to break down the long-standing sectional barriers of the region and coalesce it with the rest of the Nation in a sense that it has not known since the Civil War.

The leadership of both major parties is certain to undergo great changes in the next few years. Political leaders declare that the Smith candidacy will result in the eventual disappearance from power and authority of many Democratic chiefs who supported him. It is known on the highest authority that Mr. Hoover is determined to reorganize the Republican Party and to remove from influence elements which have gained ascendancy in recent years.

Washington Calm

Washington took the election of Hoover and Curtis calmly. The crowds in front of the newspaper offices were expectant and interested but not noisy. It was not until late in the evening when the size of the Republican victory became so overwhelming that a few horns began to toot and men hugged their neighbors in a spasm of delight. Toward

THE CHRISTIAN SCIENCE MONITOR

AN INTERNATIONAL DAILY NEWSPAPER

COPYRIGHT 1929 BY THE CHRISTIAN SCIENCE PUBLISHING SOCIETY | Sixteen Pages | BOSTON, MONDAY, OCTOBER 28, 1929—VOL. XXI, NO. 282 | — ATLANTIC EDITION • | FIVE CENTS A COPY

PACIFIC NATIONS BEGIN 12-DAY PARLEY IN KYOTO

Japan Greets 200 Delegates to Third Biennial Conference of Institute

WOMEN TAKE PART FOR THE FIRST TIME

Settlement of Disputes on Borders of Pacific to Be Theme of Discussion

BY CABLE TO THE CHRISTIAN SCIENCE MONITOR

KYOTO, Japan—The third biennial conference of the Institute of Pacific Relations opened Oct. 28. Delegates, their families and friends, filled the large hall at the opening sessions. Further meetings, however, will be smaller and held in local hotels.

Lord Hailsham, heading the British delegation, stressed the purpose of the Institute, which was to study, not to decide.

Messages of welcome were read from Premier Hamaguchi, President Hoover, the Prime Minister of Australia and the Premiers of New Zealand and Canada.

Following the meeting, Dr. Jnazo Nitobe was host at a large luncheon attended by more than 400, when the Japanese council of the institute welcomed the delegates of the other countries.

The most interesting part of the program begins next week with round table discussions on Manchuria, these being held behind closed doors in order that publicity may not prevent those present talking freely.

Beginning Oct. 29, the machine age and its effects on industry, food population and land utilization will be discussed for three days.

On Nov. 1 and 2, discussion on Chinese foreign relations is expected to prove highly significant. The large number of world-famous experts on various subjects here makes, the gathering an exceptional opportunity to bring together varying points of view.

Women Included

This is the first time women have been included in a conference held in the Orient to discuss questions of international import.

Russia, Mexico, France, the League of Nations and the International Labor Office will have observers present, with the main body of the conference members coming from China, Japan, the United States, Great Britain, Hawaii, Australia, Canada, Korea, New Zealand, and the Philippines.

Many of the 200 conferees present will have gone round the world by the time they reach home after the Kyoto

(Continued on Page 3, Column 2)

Edge, as French Ambassador, to Widen His Field

SPECIAL FROM MONITOR BUREAU

WASHINGTON—A new policy in diplomatic representation is contemplated by Walter E. Edge (R.), Senator from New Jersey, when he assumes his post as Ambassador to France in the near future.

It is Mr. Edge's intention not only to be his country's diplomatic and political representative, but also to place himself before the French people as his Nation's official business and industrial ambassador.

To this end he proposes to visit other cities and sections of France, particularly the great industrial centers. In this way Mr. Edge believes that he can do an extremely valuable service to both countries.

Mr. Edge's idea is understood to have the hearty approval of President Hoover and Henry L. Stimson, Secretary of State. With the new Ambassador they consider such a conception of his diplomatic mission as in keeping with the present-day leadership that the United States has in world affairs in industry, commerce and finance.

Among the great French cities that Mr. Edge contemplates visiting and spending some time in studying are Marseilles with a population of 647,705; Lyons, 564,566; Bordeaux, 254,386; Lille, 200,000; Nice, 191,304; Le Havre, 156,000; Nancy, 113,572; Toulouse, 178,457.

France today is one of the most prosperous industrial countries of Europe. It has no unemployment and its factories are expanding and working to capacity. The output of coal, iron ore, pig iron and steel has enormously increased in the past few years. Its textile industry has been very prosperous. Its silk industry, which escaped the havoc of the war, has enjoyed unprecedented prosperity.

The United States for the past five years has been France's chief source of supply and her fourth best customer. The industrial, commercial and financial ties between the two countries are continually expanding, and it is Mr. Edge's view that this fact should be vividly brought to the attention of the people of the nations, and that if this is effectively done the traditional bonds of friendship between them will be strengthened.

INDEX OF THE MONITOR

MONDAY, OCTOBER 28, 1929

Planning Ways to Settle Disputes Around Pacific

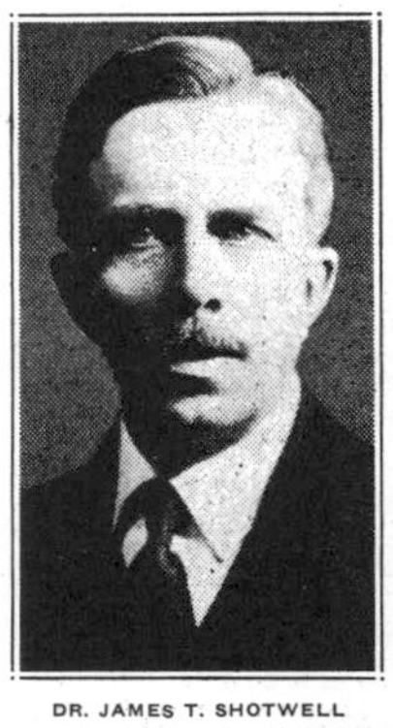

DR. JAMES T. SHOTWELL

Who Has Been Re-elected Chairman of the International Research Committee of the Institute of Pacific Relations.

Italy Honors Eighth Year of Fascismo

Throngs Cheer Mussolini as He Calls Citizens to Continued Service

BY RADIO TO THE CHRISTIAN SCIENCE MONITOR

ROME—Impressive celebrations in every town and village of Italy ushered in the eighth year of Fascist rule. In Rome Premier Mussolini reviewed the Fascist contingents of the army, navy and air forces and after the parade the Black Shirts assembled in the Piazza Venezia to hear the address of their leader.

After briefly referring to the progress of the last seven years, the Duce affirmed that it was useless, and might be dangerous to disturb the magnificent harmony which existed today in Italy from the Sovereign and the Crown Prince to the peasant in the humblest village.

Difficult times might come, not only for Italy but for Europe and the whole world, but Italy today is as he wishes it to be—an army of citizens and soldiers ready for the tasks of peace, hardworking, silent and disciplined.

"If tomorrow," concluded the Duce, "anyone sought to disturb this harmony will you answer my call, would you follow me every instant?" The Duce's words were welcomed with tremendous cheers.

All the monuments of classical antiquity, including the newly opened markets in the Trajan Colosseum were illuminated by powerful reflectors.

ROME (AP)—Premier Mussolini inaugurated the Academy of Italy in a solemn session at the capital Oct. 28. In a speech he stressed the universality of its composition, with representatives of music, mechanical progress, philosophy, achitecture, archeology, and futurism.

"Therein are all traditions of Italy's past," he said, "the certainties of her present, and the anticipations of her future."

Prince Boncompagni Ludovisi, Governor of Rome, welcomed the Duce and the academicians.

Soviet Uses Force Against Opponents

BY RADIO TO THE CHRISTIAN SCIENCE MONITOR

MOSCOW—Determination of the Soviet Government to crush any resistance to its decrees is evidenced by sentences of capital punishment meted out to groups of persons charged with anti-governmental activity in the provincial towns of Kirmi and Ivanovo-Vognesensk.

Intense opposition has been aroused by the attempt of the authorities to gather grain from the peasantry and convert small land holdings into co-operative farms.

In Kirmi a priest, two members of the church council, and two rich peasants were sentenced to execution, nine others received sentences of imprisonment and exile varying from three to ten years because last May they are alleged to have headed a popular demonstration against closing the church.

At Ivanovo-Voznesensk a priest, choir singer and two rich peasants of the village of Ari were shot on the charge of inciting a mob of peasants to attack local Soviet supporters who escaped by flight.

PARLIAMENT TO HEAR 'COLOR LINE' PROTEST

LONDON (AP)—The question of the color bar against Negroes in England will be raised in Parliament by James Marley, Laborite, at the earliest opportunity, he has just announced. Protests by two widely-known American Negroes against alleged discrimination because of their race have raised the question in England in an acute form for the first time.

Mr. Marley has assured Robert S. Abbott of Chicago of his intention of pushing the matter in Parliament. Mr. Abbott, who was a member of Gov. Frank O. Lowden's Race Relations Commission in 1919 and president of the Hampton (Institute) Alumni Association, complained of discrimination against him on the British steamship Aquitania.

STOCKS CRASH AGAIN, SOME TO NEW LOW LEVEL

Promised Banking Support Caused Losses 5 to 45 Points —Flood of Sales

NEW YORK (AP)—Deprived of the banking support which many traders understood had been arranged for last week, the stock market plunged downward in spectacular fashion again Oct. 28 as "bears" renewed their assaults on the market, and thousands of weakened speculative accounts were thrown overboard. Prices of scores of issues broke 5 to 45 points, with most of the leaders selling below the low levels reached in last Thursday's record-breaking session.

Trading was again in enormous volume, with the ticker falling an hour behind the market by early afternoon. Total sales crossed the 3,000,000-share mark before mid-day, with indications that the day's total would exceed 8,000,000 shares.

Indications that bankers might again be called upon to stem the tide of selling were seen in the visit early this afternoon of Charles E. Mitchell, chairman of the National City Bank, the country's largest banking institution, to the offices of J. P. Morgan & Co. Unless the tide of selling is stemmed, other bankers probably will be called into conference.

With the market undergoing another drastic "cleaning out" process little attention was paid to the day's news. Nothing happened over the week-end to alter the views of President Hoover and leading bankers that fundamental business conditions were sound, and that there was no sign of a general recession in industrial activity.

Directors of the General Refractories Company have declared an extra dividend of 25 cents and raised the annual rate from $3 to $4. Wall Street is fervently hoping that good news will be forthcoming from the quarterly meeting of the United States Steel Corporation after the close of the market tomorrow. Several weeks ago, there were rumors of a possible stock split-up or extra dividend on Steel, but these gradually disappeared as the date of the meeting approached.

General Electric was the hardest hit in today's selling, breaking 43½ points to 254, as contrasted with a low of 283 last Thursday. Westinghouse Electric broke 29¼ points to 150, Western Union fell 27½ points, Johns Manville 26¼, and Case Threshing 25. American Can, Standard Gas & Electric, Underwood Elliott Fisher, Eastman Kodak, Allied Chemical, Peoples Gas, American Telephone, International Business Machines, Air Reduction and A. M. Byers were among the many issues to sell 15 to 20 points lower.

U. S. Steel common broke 10½ points to 193, carrying it fractionally below the low level established last Thursday.

Stock	Thurs. Low	Today's Low	Low
U. S. Steel	$193.50	$193.50	$10.00
General Elec.	283.00	255.50	42.00
Westinghouse Elec.	160.00	152.50	26.75
Western Union	220.00	203.00	27.50
Stand. Gas & Elec.	134.25	129.00	17.00
J. I. Case	210.00	200.00	25.00
Underwood Elliott	133.00	130.00	15.00
Eastman Kodak	211.00	202.87	20.12
Allied Chemical	265.00	261.00	20.00
American Telephone	245.00	247.50	18.50
American For Pow.	88.00	83.50	15.50
Johns Manville	140.00	134.50	26.00
Peoples Gas	308.00	292.00	16.50
Stand Oil N J	61.62	68.00	5.75
Amer Water Works	93.00	90.00	14.00

Hungary Opposes Reparations Changes

BY RADIO TO THE CHRISTIAN SCIENCE MONITOR

BUDAPEST—Hungary could never agree to increased reparations burdens, as now demanded at the Paris eastern reparations conference, Dr. Louis Waldo declared at the last meeting of the Foreign Affairs Committee.

Hungary also desired the settlement of many matters still outstanding so as to be able to meet the liabilities she has agreed to shoulder after 1943. In the same committee the Premier, Count Stephen Bethlen, stated that just as the great powers have seen the problem of German reparations solvable only by a roundtable conference, so must due consideration be given to Hungary.

The Hungarian Government cannot accept new unauthorized demands and an attempt is now being made to bring the reparations question into relation with the optants question (the claim of the Hungarian land owners for their estates expropriated in Translyvania by the Rumanian Government) contrary to the peace treaties.

BRITISH SEEK TO GIVE WELCOME TO PREMIER

LONDON (AP)—There is a growing demand in England for a great public welcome to the Prime Minister, Ramsay MacDonald upon his return from the United States and Canada. It is felt in political circles that this can surely be arranged, the only doubt being over Mr. MacDonald's own personal attitude toward the proposal. Steps are being taken to ascertain what the Prime Minister thinks about it.

If the tentative program is finally approved, it is certain to include the conferring of the freedom of London upon both Mr. MacDonald and Philip Snowden as one of its items.

AIR-RAIL TIME REDUCED

SPECIAL FROM MONITOR BUREAU

NEW YORK—The air-mail schedules between New York and Los Angeles on the "Great Circle Line" will be reduced from an elasped time of approximately 67 to 52 hours by a supplementary service to be inaugurated about Dec. 10 by Western Air Express, it has just been announced here.

Deployed Around Lakes and Lagoons, Sweden's Fair Has Ideal Site

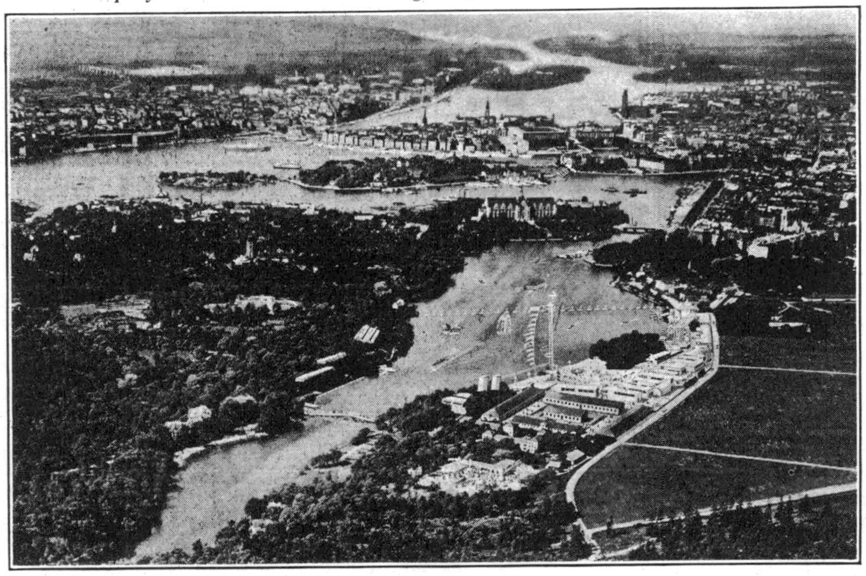

Location of Stockholm Exhibition as Seen From Air. Foto Aero Material A B.

REBELS REPEL CHIANG'S ARMY IN HONAN AREA

Reports Indicate End of Political Maneuvering as Clashes Are Renewed

BY RADIO TO THE CHRISTIAN SCIENCE MONITOR

SHANGHAI—Although there has been only minor clashes in China's latest revolt, which at one stage was believed to be more political than military, thereby engendering hope of a peaceful solution, renewed activity is reported from Honan where northwestern rebels are reported gradually gaining ground, and forcing back government troops in the vicinity of the Peiping-Hankow Railway, where additional reinforcements were rushed.

As many political factors and questionable loyalties as usual are obscuring the situation and hampering the effectiveness of the Government's plans against the revolters, it is difficult to estimate the strength of the rebel position, but its seriousness is fully realized at Nanking, when President Chiang Kai-shek, after much dallying, has decided to leave for Hankow, which is the rebel objective, in order to direct operations.

In a manifesto issued to the country General Chiang calls the people to assist him in suppressing the northwestern military combination which is the biggest obstacle to the reconstruction program of the central Government. The most amazing feature of the situation is the personal activity of Gen. Feng Yu-hsiang, who recently was reported "arrested" by Gen. Yen Hsi-shan but as the latter is adopting a noncommittal attitude toward Nanking, preferring to remain neutral, it is believed this neutrality may be benevolent. General Chiang's departure toward Hankow will be the signal for ending political maneuvering and beginning military action.

Three Receive Roosevelt Medal for Rendering Notable Service

Award Goes to Owen D. Young, Henry Putnam and Owen Wister—Sister of Former President Tells of Beauty of Early Home Life

SPECIAL FROM MONITOR BUREAU

NEW YORK—Owen D. Young, well known for his work on the reparations problem; Owen Wister, noted author, and Herbert Putnam, librarian of Congress, received the Roosevelt Medal for Distinguished Service at an anniversary dinner just held in honor of Theodore Roosevelt at his birthplace on East Twentieth Street.

Characterizing Mr. Young as "envoy extraordinary of a new age," the citation accompanying his award declared "that his name belongs not to this country alone, but to mankind as a symbol of intelligent and effective statesmanship."

Mr. Putnam's achievement as director for 30 years of "the destinies of the Nation's treasure house of knowledge, wisdom, and imagination," the citation said, was that of a "creative dreamer, before whose expanding vision the functions, as well as the facilities, of his institution have expanded," into a "university where none shall affirm or propound, but scholar and student shall lead each other out toward the sun and all the other stars."

Mr. Wister was eulogized for having caught an era in its flight," and held it "for all time for all to see."

Charles E. Hughes, who was introduced by Mrs. Douglas Robinson, younger sister of the former President, paid a notable tribute to Theodore Roosevelt.

Mrs. Robinson recalled the happy atmosphere in the Roosevelt home.

"I think the reason Theodore Roosevelt always laid such stress on what home should mean," she said, "was because in his early childhood he saw demonstrated in his own home that most beautiful thing in the world—perfect love and understanding."

SPECIAL TO THE CHRISTIAN SCIENCE MONITOR

OYSTER BAY, L. I.—More than 1000 persons, including a representative of the President of the United States, famous aviators, neighbors and friends of Theodore Roosevelt joined in annual memorial exercises in honor of the former President here.

Brig.-Gen. Hugh A. Drum, representing President Hoover, and members of his staff, took part in unveiling a bronze tablet at Christ Church, of which Mr. Roosevelt was for 30 years a member.

Nine airplanes swooped over the Roosevelt plot to drop flowers, then gathered into a V formation and dipped together in salute. Col. Clarence D. Chamberlin, transatlantic flier, formed apex for the V. Col. James Fitzmaurice, copilot of the transatlantic airplane Bremen, was one of the pilots.

After the hilltop ceremonies, Col. Chamberlin flew toward Sagamore Hill, residence of the former President, and soared a few hundred feet over the lawn where members of the Roosevelt family were gathered, and dropped a wreath.

Before their visit to Oyster Bay, the aviators flew over the old Roosevelt neighborhood in East Twentieth Street, New York City, and the Natural History Museum, where a new Roosevelt wing is being built.

Brazil Settling Frontier Disputes With Neighbors

RIO DE JANEIRO (By U. P.)—Work on demarcation of Brazil's many frontiers, long indefinitely outlined because of the inaccessible character of the country, is getting under way at all points, the Foreign Ministry announces. Settlement of the outstanding boundary disputes between Brazil and several of its neighbors was one of President Washington Luis' campaign promises.

The Anglo-Brazilian commission will assemble April 16 on the British-Guiana frontier to begin demarcation of that boundary. The Brazilian-Venezuelan commission is scheduled to assemble Dec. 1 at San Carlos to carry out the boundary definition in accordance with the treaty of July 24, 1928. The Brazilian commission is now at San Carlos.

Demarcation of the Brazil-Bolivian frontier, in accordance with the treaty of December, 1928, will begin in April, 1930. The boundaries between French Guiana and Brazil and between Brazil and Uruguay are included in negotiations and the final act in the boundary dispute with Paraguay was written last Saturday when the Chamber of Deputies at Asuncion approved the Ibarra-Mangabeira treaty between the two countries, whereby Brazil recognizes Paraguay's title to territory on the west bank of the Paraguay River between Bahia Negra and the mouth of the Apa River.

CABINET OF UDRZAL RESIGNS AT PRAGUE

PRAGUE Czechoslovakia (AP)—Defeated in the Czechoslovak general elections Oct. 27, Prime Minister Frantisek Udrzal has handed the resignation of his Cabinet to President Masaryk. The President asked him to remain at his post until a new Government could be formed.

Parliament was dissolved Sept. 25 and the general elections were set for Oct. 27, after defeat of the coalition Government. The voting was for parties and not for individual candidates. Formation of another Coalition Government is expected. There was little excitement over the election among the people.

Army Officers See Bushel of Wood Make Truck Move 38½-Ton Weight

SPECIAL FROM MONITOR BUREAU

SAN FRANCISCO, Calif.—An invention which, in the opinion of officers of the United States General Staff, is destined to revolutionize motor transport throughout the world, but particularly in countries where wood is plentiful, has been subjected to an exhaustive test at the ninth corps area headquarters here.

It was brought to this country from France at the instance of Lloyd M. Robbins, San Francisco attorney, who discovered it and the inventor during a recent trip abroad. The inventor of the machine, which produces a gas which runs motor engines from nothing more than scrap and waste wood, was present to watch the tests by the United States officers. He is Col. Jean Imbert of Sarre-Union, France. He served in the French Army during the World War, and developed his new gas-producer because of the high price of motor petrol in France.

The machine consumes nothing but wood. About two bushels of wood scraps are dumped into a hopper. This is sufficient to run a motor truck for six hours. The wood is ignited from the bottom. A crank is then turned for three minutes. This works a blower which serves to start the gases generated from the burning wood following into a series of condensers beneath the motor truck.

When sufficient gas is generated to start the engine, the blower is run by the motor itself. The gases are mixed with coal tar products in the wood, which are broken up by the heat, and all are mixed with air in the condensers, just as vaporized gasoline is mixed with air by a carburetor in a gasoline motor. The blended gases, air and coal tar products are forced directly to the intake manifold of the motor, and in the combustion chambers of the cylinders they are ignited.

Colonel Imbert calls his invention a "gasogen." In the tests it ran an old army motortruck perfectly. The truck equipped with the invention at one time pulled and carried 38½ tons dead weight. It did everything that a gasoline-driven truck can do, and did it quite as efficiently.

Col. Robert B. McBride of the United States General Staff, who watched the tests closely, declared: "I am satisfied that this invention will revolutionize motor transport in countries where wood is available. Its possibilities are limitless."

At Standard, Calif., where two of the inventions have been in daily use for two weeks at a lumber mill, it is stated a saving of $4 a day per truck is realized from the use of this invention. The fuel costs nothing, and the invention generates gas from any kind of wood. Its inventor claims that it saves from 65 to 95 per cent of the cost of operating motor trucks.

Mr. Robbins has bought the rights to the invention in this country, and he said they will be manufactured in San Francisco. They cost only $400 installed.

LAND OF THE SOVIETS FLIES TO DETROIT

DETROIT (AP)—The plane. Land of the Soviets, flying from Chicago, arrived at the Ford airport in Dearborn, Mich. The crowd which turned out to greet the Russian fliers was so large that airport guards and police experienced difficulty in keeping order.

HALLS OF GLASS NOVEL PLAN FOR STOCKHOLM FAIR

Contents of Palaces to Be Visible From Without at Coming Exposition

SPECIAL TO THE CHRISTIAN SCIENCE MONITOR

STOCKHOLM—Large numbers of comparatively small halls with walls made almost entirely of glass is to be one of the striking features of the Stockholm Exposition, preparations for the opening of which on May 15 next, are already being pushed ahead. The effect of this plan is that in the evenings, when the halls are closed, the articles exhibited may be seen from the outside through the glass walls, as the halls will be brilliantly lighted from within, showing up their entire contents. These groups of small halls are separated by flowered gardens with benches, where the visitor may sit.

In a tour through the grounds with the general director, Dr. Gregor Paulssen, and the head architect, E. G. Asplund, the representative of The Christian Science Monitor found the buildings already roofed in, so that in the spring there will remain only the placing of the objects on exhibit in their halls.

The exposition is unique because it lies practically in the center of Stockholm, often called "the Venice of the North." One of the most beautiful parks of the city, Diplomats Park, containing many fashionable residences, has been chosen as the site. This park surrounds a body of water called Djurgardsbrunn Bay, a part of Stockholm's Strom, and for exposition purposes the two banks of the river are connected by a new bridge.

Sailing boats such as one finds in Hamburg on the Alster will be seen on this expanse of water, and aquatic sports, rowing, sailing and swimming races will take place here, ending up with a display of fireworks every evening. A large illuminated fountain will be installed by the French firm, Lumi-Or. This fountain rises 25 meters above the water, and when it plays full force uses 18,000 liters of water a minute.

A big open space, holding 50,000 people, in the center of the exposition, on the banks of the stream, will be devoted to orchestral performances and even to festival plays, performed by Sweden's best artistic and dramatic talent. Dominating this open space will be a tower 80 meters high, with an elevator to the top from which the environs of Stockholm may be viewed. Here will be a radio station and megaphone announcer as well as a room for the press.

English Art Exposition Opened at Stockholm

BY RADIO TO THE CHRISTIAN SCIENCE MONITOR

STOCKHOLM—An English art exposition was opened at Stockholm by the new English Minister, Sir Howard Kennard, in the presence of the Crown Prince, the Crown Princess, Princess Ingrid, Prince Carl and Princess Ingeborg.

Sir Howard presented a telegram of greeting from the Prime Minister, Ramsay MacDonald, hoping that the good feeling between the two countries would be forwarded by the exposition and that the British pictures would be as much esteemed as the Swedish sculpture exhibited at the Tate Gallery.

DORNIER MAY REDUCE FACTORY OPERATIONS

FRIEDRICHSHAFEN, Ger. (AP) — The Dornier airplane works is reported to be contemplating laying off 60 per cent of its employees Jan. 1, because of lack of orders.

A huge seaplane manufactured by the Dornier company recently set a world record for all aircraft by taking up 169 persons on a single flight.

BRIAND AGREES TO RETURN TO FOREIGN OFFICE

Socialist Group in Chamber Agrees to Join French Cabinet

PARTY'S INDORSATION NEXT STEP NECESSARY

Daladier Reported as Favoring Vigorous Action Looking Toward Disarmament

BY CABLE FROM MONITOR BUREAU

PARIS—The parliamentary group of the Socialist Party has pronounced in favor of the participation in the Radical-Socialist Government so that Edouard Daladier, Radical leader, has crossed the first river toward the promised land.

It still remains to be seen whether the National Council of the Socialist Party will indorse this decision. The permanent administrative commission of the party is to meet earlier to give the Council its advice and, as Pierre Renaudel and J. Paul-Boncour are not on this commission, it may reverse the decision of the parliamentary group. The majority of the Socialist deputies, however, appear to be so strongly in favor of forming a Coalition Government that whatever the administrative committee may say, the national council is likely to approve the vote.

Edouard Daladier has, in the meantime, secured a promise from Aristide Briand that he will resume the office of foreign secretary in the Radical and Socialist government. This is a great feather in Daladiers cap and he is making the most of it in his visits to the leaders of the various groups whom he also wants to draw into his coalition. To have an absolute majority, M. Daladier must gain the support of the Radicals of the Left and the Left Union who number in all 72 including the Independents of the left.

If these be added to the Socialists and Republican Socialists, Mr. Daladier will have done the trick. He is said to be also making overtures to the Republican Left who number 53, for M. Briand has advised M. Daladier to make the foundations of his government as wide as possible. To satisfy all these groups, M. Daladier will have to offer them some of the spoils of office, and in this matter the Socialists are likely to drive a hard bargain.

The danger is that they may split into rival groups in spite of the majority decision to collaborate with the Radicals. Léon Blum, Socialist leader, is not at all pleased with the decision, and if he refuses to take office he may end by becoming a critic of the new Government, thus forming an extreme Left, like the group led by James Maxton in the English Parliament.

Paul Faure will also be a dangerous man to leave outside the Government and if these two Socialists appeal to the Socialist congress there may be wigs on the green in the near future. M. Daladier is, however, very hopeful that he will be able to include half a dozen leading Socialists in his Cabinet and thus gain the support of a great majority of the Socialist Party.

What is he to offer to the other groups? They will certainly expect some portfolios and M. Daladier is too clever a politician not to know that it is an excellent thing to take hostages in this way. But hostages cannot be taken without concessions to the opinions of the parties which permit their members to take office in a coalition government, and at the same time M. Daladier has to think of his own party who will certainly demand the chief prizes of office.

It will be seen that it is not all plain sailing for M. Daladier and that he will be a busy man as he tacks his course through the shoals of parliamentary intrigue. It is indeed not an easy task to form a government in France, and the choosing of ministers is a difficult job, for so many men must be left disappointed. M. Daladier may do a great deal with the blessing of M. Briand.

The news that M. Briand has consented to become Foreign Minister again is of the utmost importance for foreign governments, for it means that if this new government is formed it will carry out the Hague agreement and fulfill M. Briand's pledge of the early evacuation of the Rhineland. Moreover, M. Daladier talks of making a vigorous push for disarmament. Thus his appointment as president of the Council might facilitate the work of the five-power naval conference.

BULGARIA WATCHING PACT NEGOTIATIONS

SOFIA, Bulgaria (AP)—All Bulgaria is anxiously watching the progress of the negotiations at Pirot to bring about an agreement between Bulgaria and Jugoslaivia on their frontier.

While the two nations are negotiating, a provisional agreement has been put into effect. It establishes police measures for the security of frontier districts, permission for people living in the disputed zone to cross the frontier to look after property divided in two portions by the delimitation, and a mixed commission to regulate disputes.

SWEDE HEAD OF PRESS UNION

BY RADIO TO THE CHRISTIAN SCIENCE MONITOR

STOCKHOLM — Fritz Henrikson, Councilor of Legation and director of the press department of the Swedish Foreign Office at Stockholm, was elected president of the International Union of Press Associations at the eighteenth congress at Barcelona, where 20 countries were represented.

THE CHRISTIAN SCIENCE MONITOR

AN INTERNATIONAL DAILY NEWSPAPER

COPYRIGHT 1929 BY THE CHRISTIAN SCIENCE PUBLISHING SOCIETY | Twenty-Two Pages | BOSTON, SATURDAY, NOVEMBER 30, 1929—VOL. XXII, NO. 5 | ATLANTIC EDITION | FIVE CENTS A COPY

MOSCOW PUSHES PEACE WITH MUKDEN—REJECTS PROPOSALS OF NANKING

Manchuria May Meet Russians at Dairen Conference

WASHINGTON AWAITS REPLY FROM NATIONS

Peace Pact Signatories Not to Act If Independent Peace Is Likely

Definite word that Nanking had expressed a desire to enter into negotiations with the Soviet has reached Washington, though the Chinese Foreign Minister denies that arrangements for such a discussion have yet been made. Tentative proposals from Nanking have been rejected by Moscow.

Meanwhile Moscow states unequivocably that parleying between Manchuria and Moscow is on the way, and dispatches from Tokyo declare that a conference at Dairen is anticipated, at which Nanking, which appears to have been left out in the cold, may attempt to intervene.

Washington is awaiting replies from the five governments to which proposals have been made for taking action among signatories of the Kellogg pact. Such action, it is declared, would not be pushed if the disputants show signs of settling their quarrel between them.

SPECIAL FROM MONITOR BUREAU

WASHINGTON—The State Department is interested in seeing the Manchurian crisis settled peacefully and is not concerned with the agencies by which the agreement is reached. This was the comment from the State Department when word reached Washington that the Chinese had expressed the desire to enter into negotiations with Russia to settle the Chinese Eastern Railway dispute.

At the same time, authoritative information reached the Capitol confirming previous reports that at no time have large masses of Russian troops been operating against the Chinese, and that most of the looting and killing in the retreat of the Chinese troops was committed by Chinese soldiers, who had been left leaderless after a preliminary sanguinary encounter with Red forces.

The diplomatic representatives of Italy and Japan were at the State Department during the day, but pending the return to the city of the Secretary of State no announcement was made of the reply of the five great powers to America's latest proposal for discussions of appropriate steps in Manchuria.

Relaxation of tension through the apparent capitulation of the Chinese and the restoration of the status quo of the railway were believed likely to forestall action under the State Department's proposal to Great

(Continued on Page 6, Column 5)

Mexican Issues to Be Debated at Washington

SPECIAL TO THE CHRISTIAN SCIENCE MONITOR

MEXICO CITY—The almost simultaneous arrival in Washington from Europe of Elias Plutarco Calles, former President, still seen as a guiding hand in Mexican politics, of President-elect Ortiz Rubio, and of Dwight W. Morrow, American Ambassador, indicates in the opinion of conservative observers of United States and Mexico relations that it will be during these three men's stay in the United States that a program will be mapped out on disputed questions.

These include the block settlement of American claims, the resumption of interest payment by Mexico on its international obligations and an agreement on payment to be made to Americans whose lands have been expropriated under provisions of the Mexican agrarian laws.

Mr. Morrow is departing for Washington Dec. 6. General Calles is reported due in New York about the same time, and the latest information available on the departure of Ortiz Rubio is that he will arrive shortly before the others.

The solution of these three problems hinges entirely on the future stability of Mexico and improved economic situation that will be the natural result if the Ortiz Rubio Administration prospers.

Until this stage is reached there will be ample time for the London naval conference, which Mr. Morrow will attend as a member of the American delegation, to conclude its work with the presence of the Ambassador in Mexico not essentially needed during this transient stage when it will be possible for a clearer vision to be gained on the prospects of an undisturbed future for Mexico.

INDEX OF THE MONITOR

SATURDAY, NOVEMBER 30, 1929

Labor Introduces Road Traffic Bill

BY THE ASSOCIATED PRESS

London

ABOLITION of the speed limit for light motorcars and heavier penalties for dangerous driving are features of the Government's new road traffic bill.

Thirty miles an hour is the limit fixed for motorcoaches and other heavy passenger-carrying motor vehicles.

It was understood the Government hope the bill will be regarded as a nonparty measure.

Reichstag Vote Defeats Attack on Young Plan

Bill Against 'Enslavement of German People' Now Goes to Referendum

BERLIN (AP)—The Nationalist bill for rejection of the Young plan was defeated in the Reichstag Nov. 30 and the measure will now be referred to a referendum by the German people on Dec. 22.

The first of the four sections of the proposed law "against enslavement of the German people" was defeated 318 to 82 with four abstentions.

This clearly indicated that the whole law would be defeated and the second section was voted down by acclamation.

The terms of the bill, about which much controversy has centered, were as follows:

1. The German Government shall notify all foreign powers immediately and solemnly that the enforced acknowledgment of war guilt in the Treaty of Versailles is contrary to historical truth, is based on false premises and is not binding in international law.

2. The German Government shall use all endeavors to secure the annulment of the war guilt acknowledgment contained in Article 231 and Articles 429 and 430 of the Treaty of Versailles. It shall also undertake to secure the immediate and unconditional evacuation of the occupied German territories without any remaining control commissions, independently of the acceptance or the rejection of the Hague convention.

3. No further financial burdens or obligations based on the war guilt acknowledgment shall be assumed, inclusive of those arising from the recommendations of the Paris reparations experts.

4. Chancellor and ministers or representatives of the Reich who lend their signatures to agreements contrary to the provisions of Paragraph 3 shall render themselves liable to prosecution for high treason.

A fifth paragraph simply said the law entered into force at the moment of its proclamation.

In order to present this bill to the Reichstag it was necessary for the Nationalists to obtain 4,000,000 signatures, representing one-tenth of the electorate at the last presidential election. As it was only with great difficulty that the Nationalists succeeded in getting the necessary 4,000,000 signatures, it is generally believed that it will be impossible for the bill to obtain a majority in a plebiscite throughout the country.

Curtius Declared Worthy Successor to Stresemann

BY RADIO TO THE CHRISTIAN SCIENCE MONITOR

BERLIN—Dr. Julius Curtius's great initial speech Nov. 29 in the Reichstag is regarded as having proved his mettle as a worthy successor of Dr. Gustav Stresemann. The address was characterized by lucidity of expression, directness of purpose, and subtle irony, and won him hearty applause.

He said the Reich Government begged the Reichstag to decide as quickly as possible concerning the referendum bill for which the Government demanded and expected rejection. He said rejection of the referendum was not significant to agreement on the Young plan, regarding which he remained reserved. The German Hague delegates and the Government are aware of the heaviness of the Young plan burden, but compared with the Dawes plan the Young plan would bring considerable alleviation which would benefit German economics and German peoples and no arithmetical arts could dispute this. Dr. Curtius declared the Government would confidently pursue its course and continue to strive for sensible co-operation with the nations. Dr. Alfred Hugenberg did not respond to loud cries for him to defend the bill, and Herr Oberfohren, who spoke for him, made a poor impression.

AUSTRALIAN LABOR DISPUTE SETTLED

SYDNEY, N. S. W. (AP)—A conference between mine owners and miners has settled the labor dispute in the Newcastle coal fields on a basis of a reduction of 12½ per cent in hewing rate of 12 cents a day in wages. The mines will probably reopen on Dec. 12.

The settlement followed an announcement by the Government of New South Wales that if an agreement was not reached the Government would go ahead with state operation of the mines and have them working during the Christmas season.

Course to Pole and Man Who Followed It

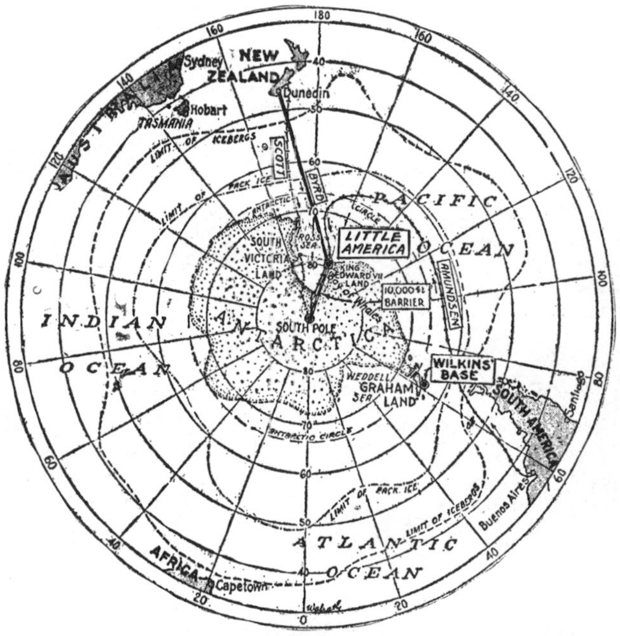

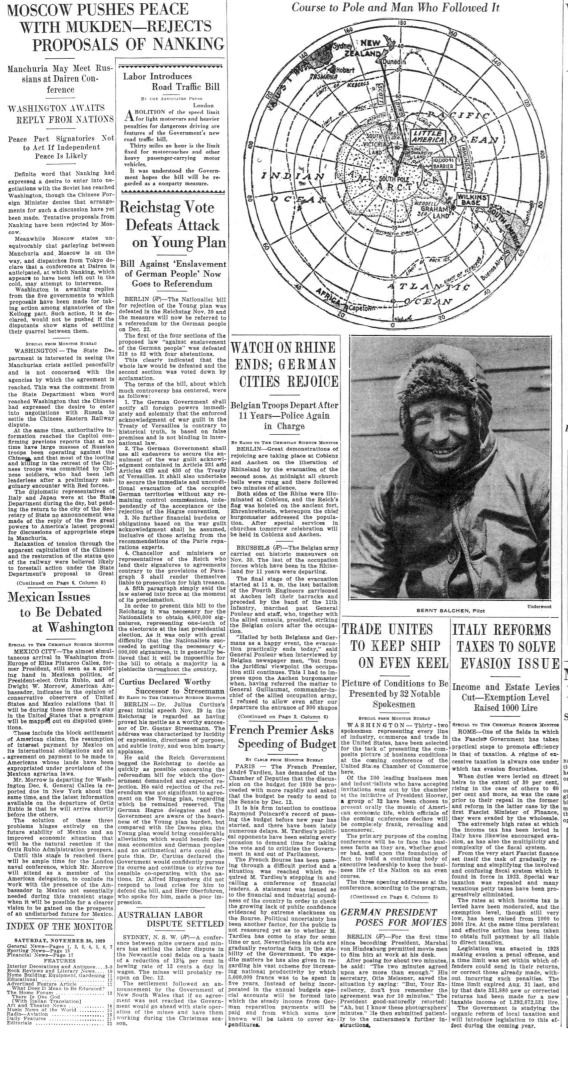

WATCH ON RHINE ENDS; GERMAN CITIES REJOICE

Belgian Troops Depart After 11 Years—Police Again in Charge

BY RADIO TO THE CHRISTIAN SCIENCE MONITOR

BERLIN—Great demonstrations of rejoicing are taking place at Coblenz and Aachen on the liberation of Rhineland by the evacuation of the second zone. At midnight all church bells were rung and there followed two minutes of silence.

Both sides of the Rhine were illuminated at Coblenz, and the Reich's flag was hoisted on the ancient fort, Ehrenbreitstein, whereupon the chief burgomaster addressed the population. After special services in churches tomorrow celebration will be held in Coblenz and Aachen.

BRUSSELS (AP)—The Belgian army carried out historic maneuvers on Nov. 30. The last of the occupation forces which have been in the Rhineland for 11 years were departing.

The final stage of the evacuation started at 11 a. m. the last battalion of the Fourth Engineers garrisoned at Aachen left their barracks and preceded by the band of the 11th Infantry, marched past General Pouleur and staff, who, together with the allied consuls, presided, striking the Belgian colors after the occupation.

"Hailed by both Belgians and Germans as a happy event, the evacuation practically ends today," said General Pouleur when interviewed by Belgian newspaper men, "but from the juridical viewpoint the occupation still continues. This I had to impress upon the Aachen burgomaster when, having referred the matter to General Guillaumat, commander-in-chief of the allied occupation army, I refused to allow even after our departure the entrance of 300 shupos

(Continued on Page 2, Column 6)

French Premier Asks Speeding of Budget

BY CABLE FROM MONITOR BUREAU

PARIS — The French Premier, André Tardieu, has demanded of the Chamber of Deputies that the discussion on the budget for 1930 be proceeded with more rapidly and asked that the budget be ready to send to the Senate by Dec. 12.

It is his firm intention to continue Raymond Poincaré's record of passing the budget before new year has started, and there have been lately numerous delays. M. Tardieu's political opponents have been seizing every occasion to demand time for taking the vote and to criticize the Government in and out of Parliament.

The French Bourse has been passing through a difficult period and a situation was reached which required M. Tardieu's stepping in and calling a conference of financial leaders. A statement was issued as to the financial and industrial soundness of the country in order to check the growing lack of public confidence evidenced by extreme slackness on the Bourse. Political uncertainty has been another factor, for the public is not reassured yet as to whether M. Tardieu has come to stay for some time or not. Nevertheless his acts are gradually restoring faith in the stability of the Government. To expedite matters he has also given in regarding his vast scheme for increasing national productivity by which 5,000,000 francs was to be spent in five years. Instead of being incorporated in the annual budgets special accounts will be formed into which the steady income from German reparation payments will be paid and from which sums now known will be taken to cover expenditures.

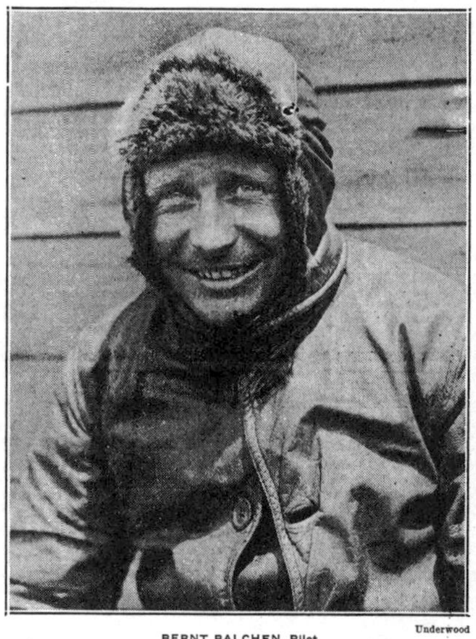

BERNT BALCHEN, Pilot — Underwood

TRADE UNITES TO KEEP SHIP ON EVEN KEEL

Picture of Conditions to Be Presented by 32 Notable Spokesmen

SPECIAL FROM MONITOR BUREAU

WASHINGTON—Thirty-two spokesmen representing every line of industry, commerce and trade in the United States, have been selected for the task of presenting the composite picture of business conditions at the coming conference of the United States Chamber of Commerce here.

Of the 200 leading business men and industrialists who have accepted invitations sent out by the chamber at the initiative of President Hoover, a group of 32 have been chosen to present orally the mosaic of American economic life, which officials of the coming conference declare will be completely frank, revealing and uncensored.

The primary purpose of the coming conference will be to face the business facts as they are, whether good or bad, and upon the foundation of fact to build a continuing body of executive leadership to keep the business life of the Nation on an even course.

The three opening addresses at the conference, according to the program,

(Continued on Page 6, Column 3)

GERMAN PRESIDENT POSES FOR MOVIES

BERLIN (AP)—For the first time since becoming President, Marshal von Hindenburg permitted movie men to film him at work at his desk.

After posing for about two minutes, he said: "The two minutes agreed upon are more than enough." His secretary, Otto Meissner, saved the situation by saying: "But, Your Excellency, don't you remember the agreement was for 10 minutes." The President good-naturedly retorted: "Ah, but I know these photographers' minutes." He then submitted patiently to the cameramen's further instructions.

ITALY REFORMS TAXES TO SOLVE EVASION ISSUE

Income and Estate Levies Cut—Exemption Level Raised 1000 Lire

SPECIAL TO THE CHRISTIAN SCIENCE MONITOR

ROME—One of the fields in which the Fascist Government has taken practical steps to promote efficiency is that of taxation. A régime of excessive taxation is always one under which tax evasion flourishes.

When duties were levied on direct heirs to the extent of 30 per cent, rising in the case of others to 60 per cent and more, as was the case prior to their repeal in the former and reform in the latter case by the first Fascist Minister of Finance, they were evaded by the wholesale.

The extremely high rates at which the income tax has been levied in Italy have likewise encouraged evasion, as has also the multiplicity and complexity of the fiscal system.

From the very start Fascist finance set itself the task of gradually reforming and simplifying the involved and confusing fiscal system which it found in force in 1922. Special war taxation was repealed and many vexatious petty taxes have been progressively eliminated.

The rates at which income tax is levied have been moderated, and the exemption level, though still very low, has been raised from 1000 to 2000 lire. At the same time persistent and effective action has been taken to obtain full payment by all liable to direct taxation.

Legislation was enacted in 1928 making evasion a penal offense, and a time limit was set within which offenders could send in their returns, or correct those already made, without incurring such penalties. The time limit expired Aug. 31 last, and by that date 331,980 new or corrected returns had been made for a new taxable income of 1,392,672,531 lire. The Government is studying the organic reform of local taxation and will introduce legislation to this effect during the coming year.

WORLD ACCLAIMS BYRD FLIGHT TO SOUTH POLE AND RETURN, 1600 MILES ACROSS ICY WASTE

Tops Both Ends of Earth

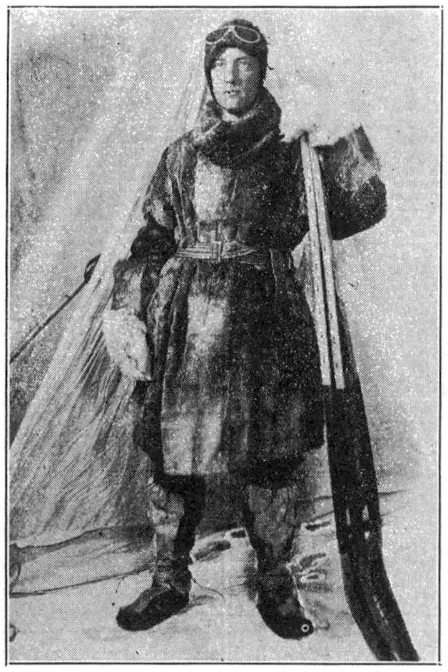

COMMANDER RICHARD E. BYRD — Wide World

Photographer and Radio Operator of the Flight Who Did Much to Help Conquer the Antarctic Waste

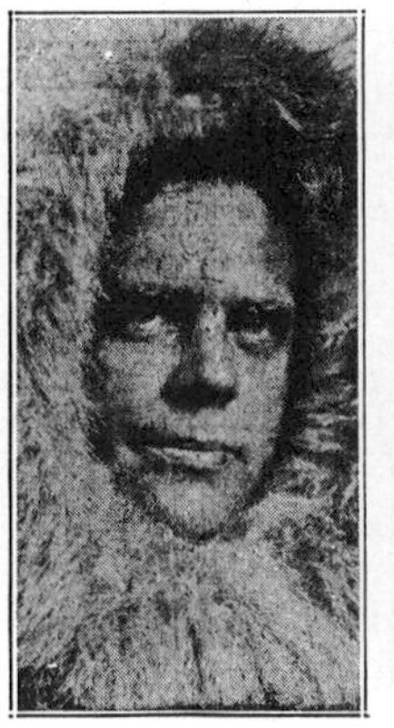

CAPT. ASHLEY C. McKINLEY

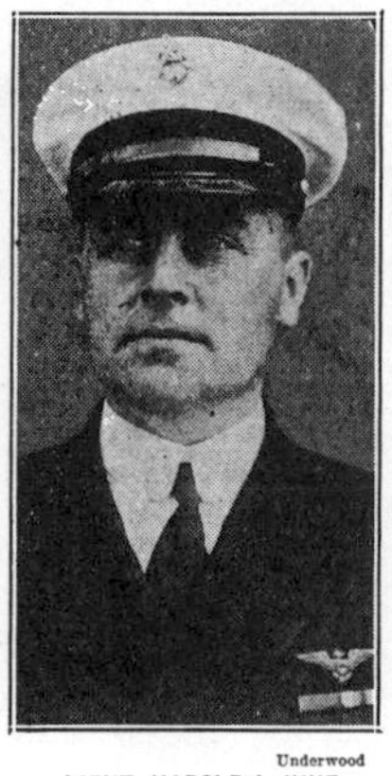

LIEUT. HAROLD I. JUNE — Underwood

Three Companions on Trip Share Glory—Top Peaks 15,000 Feet High

VOYAGE TAKES PLACE WITHOUT ANY MISHAP

Soar Over Jagged Mountain Range and Frozen Plains, Bare and Desolate

NEW YORK (AP)—The New York Times, the St. Louis Post Dispatch and newspapers affiliated with them in publishing reports from Commander Richard E. Byrd's expedition, announce that Commander Byrd safely returned to his base, Little America, Nov. 29, after a successful flight across the south pole, during which he surveyed much adjacent territory. The flight was without mishap and everything worked well.

The Times announced it had been directed by President Hoover to forward through its wireless station the following message to Commander Byrd:

"Commander Richard E. Byrd,
"Little America:

"I know that I speak for the American people when I express their universal pleasure at your successful flight over the south pole. We are proud of your courage and your leadership. We are glad of proof that the spirit of great adventure still lives. Our thoughts of appreciation include also your companions in the flight and your colleagues whose careful and devoted preparation have contributed to your great success.

"Herbert Hoover."

BY THE ASSOCIATED PRESS

Commander Richard E. Byrd, safely back at his base, Little America, from a flight to the south pole, holds the unique distinction of being the only man to fly over both poles of the earth.

By bending to the use of his courage and skill the tools supplied by modern mechanical and natural scientific progress, he achieved within 3½ years what no other polar explorer has accomplished in a lifetime—visits to the top and bottom of the globe by air.

Flying to the south pole, he did in less than a day what it had previously taken more than three months to accomplish.

The antarctic flight was beset with difficulties far greater than those encountered in Byrd's trip to the north pole, which was made May 9, 1926. The distance of each flight was about the same, 1600 miles.

On the flight to the north pole and back, made in 15 hours, 30 minutes, there was no stop.

Commander Byrd navigated his plane to and from the south pole over a jagged mountain chain with sentinel-like peaks that rise anywhere from 10,000 to 15,000 feet. The antarctic is mostly barren of plant life and without human inhabitants and even animals, due to its severe climate. Even in summer, which is at hand there now, there are no inhabitants. In the arctic there are Eskimos and summer vegetation.

Byrd Flew Over South Pole

Commander Byrd flew from Spitzbergen to the north pole over floating ice fields, arising only a few feet above sea level, with here and there open leads of water. From the edge of the southern ice barrier he flew 400 miles over an accumulation of ice rising 150 feet or more above the sea and solid as land and then soared over mountains to the polar plateau and back again.

Commander Byrd's flight to the south pole is a striking demonstration of the conquest of modern methods of travel and communication of distance and other physical obstacles encountered in polar exploration when compared with similar feats accomplished by older methods. Commander Byrd flew from his base on the Bay of Whales to the pole and back in less than a day.

Capt. Roald Amundsen, the first explorer to reach the south pole, using dog sledges and starting from a base which was near Little America, required 97 days to reach the pole. The trip there and back, a total of 1545 miles, was made in 148 days. He left his base Oct. 20, 1911, reached the pole Dec. 14, averaging about 15 miles a day.

World Gets News by Radio

Just as the airplane enabled Commander Byrd to travel as far in an hour as Captain Amundsen did in six days, the radio, sending its waves at the speed of 186,000 miles a second gave the instantaneous news of his feat, a radio message was sent from his plane at the pole to New York via a relay.

It was 153 days after Capt. Robert E. Peary reached the north pole on April 6, 1909, before he was able to reach the northernmost telegraph office at Indian Harbor, Labrador, to send a message announcing the fact.

Commander Byrd with a company of 77 and using three ships to transport his planes and supplies arrived at the edge of the great antarctic ice barriers last December. In addition to a crew of pilots and mechanics for the planes, the party included radio operators and natural scientists with equipment for making and recording observations of conditions prevailing in the region.

After establishing a base which was named Little America and a series of emergency supply stations in the direction of the pole, the party made several exploration flights over the barrier. The existence of Scott

Mysteries of Antarctic Regions May Unfold Through Byrd Flight

Students Surmise That Observations May, Among Other Things, Show Whether Antarctica Is One or Two Continents

NEW YORK (AP)—The greatest natural scientific mystery of antarctica which the Byrd expedition may help to clarify, is whether it is one or two continents.

Commander Byrd's camp is on the outer tip of the world's largest glacier, called the Barrier, which bites far southward into the land masses of the continent. Around on the other side of antarctica, nearly opposite his camp, is another huge bay that extends southward far toward the interior. It is the Weddell Sea. Explorers long have claimed that fragmentary evidence indicated there might be a connection between the water beneath the Barrier, where Little America lies, and the Weddell Sea. One of the Darwins pointed out that tides indicated this possibility.

The elevation of the country where this break in the continent might exist would go far toward answering the riddle. If the elevations are thousands of feet, natural scientists believe the heights would indicate dry land buried in the ice beneath. Should there prove to be a low, comparatively flat plain between the Weddell Sea and the Barrier, it would be taken as indicating the possibility of a thick coating of ice overlying either shallow water or a series of low islands, about which water might flow beneath the ice.

Mountains Stick Through Ice

Commander Byrd already has made some short flights in the general direction of the Weddell Sea. In those flights he has found granite mountains sticking up through the ice.

One of the reasons for interest in this possible division of the great polar continent is to learn more about the origins of the earth itself. It is thought that if two continents are found, one may prove to be a continuation of the old world southward, while the other will mark the southernmost extension of the new world. Geologists have learned that there is much sameness in the forms, texture and time of building millions of years ago of the mountains that reach from Alaska to the tip of South

(Continued on Page 2, Column 8)

Jack and Jill Go Scouting

THIS LITTLE PAIR, ALREADY WELL KNOWN TO READERS OF THE CHILDREN'S PAGE, TRY OUT A NEW SLED, AND YOU WILL ENJOY READING ABOUT THE RESULTS

Monday

1930-1949

COPYRIGHT 1930 BY THE CHRISTIAN SCIENCE PUBLISHING SOCIETY   Eighteen Pages   BOSTON, WEDNESDAY, MARCH 12, 1930—VOL. XXII, NO. 89   ATLANTIC EDITION ***   FIVE CENTS TWOPENCE } A COPY

CLUB WOMEN MASS FORCES FOR DRY LAW

12,000,000 of Them, Say Leaders, Mean to See It Maintained

INDUSTRIAL HEADS PROVE DRY STAND

Bankers, Merchants, Manufacturers Rally to Deny Charge of Drinking

Special from Monitor Bureau

WASHINGTON — Led by Mrs. Henry W. Peabody of Beverly, Mass., general chairman of the Woman's National Committee for Law Enforcement, more than a score of representatives of the largest and most influential state and national women's organizations appeared before the House Judiciary Committee on March 12 and demanded complete retention and preservation of the Eighteenth Amendment.

They said 12,000,000 club women indorsed the dry laws and meant to see that there was no repeal.

Immediately upon the heels of the impressive presentation of the women, Carlton M. Sherwood, executive secretary of the Citizens' Committee of One Thousand for Law Enforcement, filed with the Judiciary Committee a large sheaf of telegraphic messages from business leaders from all sections of the United States emphatically denouncing testimony by wet witnesses that most big business men violate the Eighteenth Amendment.

Among the scores of outstanding industrial leaders who repudiated the committee decisive refutations of law violation among their class were T. J. Gillespie, president Lockhart Iron & Steel Co. of Pittsburgh; Capt. Robert Dollar of San Francisco; J. H. Marshall of Minneapolis, president of Federal Wholesale Druggists' Association; Clarence H. Kelsey, chairman of the Title Guarantee & Trust Co. of New York; Clarence H. Howard of St. Louis, Mo., of General Steel Castings Corporation; J. C. Penney of the Penney chain stores; Ralph H. Burnlage, Portland, Ore., president of Wilapa Lumber Company; John W. Sherwood, president of Sherwood Brothers of Baltimore, Md.; E. L. Smith, president of National Association of Clothiers and Furnishers; S. C. Gilmore of the Hires-Turner Glass Company of Philadelphia; E. E. Linthicum, president, National Cast-Iron Pipe Company, Birmingham, Ala.; Orrin R. Judd, vice-president of the Irving Trust Company, New York; William H. Crosby, president of Crosby Company, Buffalo, N. Y.

Says Business Men Libeled

In submitting to the committee this array of dry sentiment among business leaders, Mr. Sherwood declared that the wets in the testimony of Grayson M. P. Murphy of the Guaranty Trust Company of New York, had "libeled the average American business man with the statement that 'he did not know a single leading business man who does not drink.'"

Mr. Sherwood declared that such statements were "harmful to the

(Continued on Page 2, Column 1)

Belfast Education Bill Backs Simple Teaching of Bible

By Cable from Monitor Bureau

LONDON—The King's speech read at the opening of the Northern Ireland Parliament at Belfast March 11 announces the impending introduction of an education bill which promises to be contentious.

The measure, as described in the speech, proposes "certain amendments and additions to education acts for the purpose of making secure the position of simple Bible teaching in public elementary schools, making further provision for representation on regional and board education committees, the better regulating of school management committees, and for other purposes calculated to increase the usefulness of measures taken by Parliament since 1922 to improve the educational system."

The question at issue concerns the church influence upon schools. An act passed seven years ago when Lord Londonderry was Minister of Education sought to abolish the old system of denominational education and to transfer control of the schools from the churches to elected authorities with the schools financed by local and state taxation.

The Roman Catholics, however, have stood out and in part only partially. The Protestants complain that there is no guarantee as to the religious attitude of the controlling authorities. They have also pointed out that while the Roman Catholic Church retains full advantage of keeping its schools without any firm foundation for the tenets of their religion. This has militated against the success of the existing system and the bill now to be introduced is to endeavor to meet this situation.

British Labor Government Defeated, but Remains in Office

MacDonald Refuses to Accept Incident as Vote of Confidence, but Daily Herald Sees It as Pointing to General Election

By Radio from The Christian Science Monitor Bureau

LONDON—The Labor Government suffered its first defeat in the House of Commons on March 11 by the narrow margin of eight votes on its Coal Miners Bill, and it is regarded in Conservative circles as the beginning of the end of Ramsay MacDonald's present term of office.

The real explanation is that the Government is tied by its election promises to secure for miners shorter working hours without lowered wages, and that the mine owners have only agreed to this upon condition of being helped to prevent uneconomic pricecutting in the home market. To what extent the amendment now passed may affect this bargain, to which both branches of the Opposition object, is still to be seen.

Ramsay MacDonald, the Prime Minister, made it clear that the Government does not regard the vote as one of confidence. Excited Opposition shouts of "resign" when the results of the vote were announced were, however, more than a theatrical gesture, since it was a trial of strength in which all the parties had made the utmost efforts. Only three members of the Conservative Party were unaccounted for in the division, and Labor voted equally solidly. Indeed, it would have reduced its unaccounted-for absentees to two but for the unusual incident of the warning bell in the Education Minister's quar-

(Continued on Page 15 Column 3)

WHEAT GROWERS WARNED TO CUT ACREAGE 10 P. C.

Chairman of Farm Board Tells Western Governor Action Is Imperative

Special from Monitor Bureau

WASHINGTON—Demand that the wheat growers of the country reduce their acreage by at least 10 per cent or the Federal Farm Board will not be able to safeguard the grain market was promulgated by Alexander H. Legge, chairman of the board, in a letter sent by him on March 11 to George F. Shafer, Governor of North Dakota, in response to a telegram of inquiry from the State executive.

Mr. Legge states the wheat case bluntly and asks the growers for their full co-operation. A 10 per cent reduction in acreage, he advises, would put the grain trade "on a fairly healthy basis"; a 20 per cent cut would make the "tariff fairly effective." He favors the 20 per cent drop, but would be satisfied with the smaller cut.

No solution of the wheat problem is possible unless the growers co-operate by acreage reduction, Mr. Legge asserts. He sharply criticizes the wheat industry, declaring that no other group "in the world blindly produces without any attention to potential market possibilities."

"In endeavoring to stabilize prices of agriculture," he says, "it is essential that agriculture adopt some of the basic principles of other industries."

Coming as it does in the midst of sharp questioning in congressional and agricultural quarters of the board's wheat marketing activities the statement is viewed in the nature of a retort by Mr. Legge and his colleagues. A demand is now under consideration by the Senate Agricultural Committee for an inquiry of the board's operations and policies. Mr. Legge and several other members of the board have been before the committee in executive session and are to return for further discussion.

ANTI-PEASANT MOVE DECRIED IN MOSCOW

MOSCOW (AP)—Echoing the recent warning of Joseph Stalin, chairman of the central committee of the Communist Party, to Soviet village officials not to use force in recruiting peasants for collective farms, the Pravda of March 11 cautions all Communist Party workers and village officials that neither administrative measures nor open coercion must be resorted to.

In all cases, the Pravda says, membership in these farms must be based upon the voluntary consent of the peasant himself.

The paper also hints that administrative measures must not be used in converting peasants from their religious beliefs. At the same time, it says, these warnings must not be interpreted as a weakening of the party's struggle to exterminate the kulaks, or rich peasants, as a class.

"There have been many cases where poor and middle class peasants have who have joined collective farms under duress are free to leave such farms.

BIG EXPANSION PLANS ON FOOT FOR STOCKHOLM

Architects Vie in Effort to Beautify City in Coming Time of Growth

Special to The Christian Science Monitor

STOCKHOLM — "Greater Stockholm" is the subject of an exhibit called "Svea Rike" or the "Kingdom of Sweden" at the Stockholm Exposition, which opens in May and runs until September. The general development plan will be set forth in picture and model.

In Sweden each municipality has its department of city planning, to which all architects' plans are submitted before any building may be erected. City development, therefore, does not destroy the harmonious contours of a town through freedom for personal eccentricity, as happens in countries where this control does not obtain.

Since the Swedes remained an agricultural people longer than the peoples of most European countries, the country's municipal authorities had time to establish building control on a sound basis. After 1870 Swedish industrial progress was rapid. The population increased to about four times what it was before that period.

Stockholm proper, not including the suburbs, has about 500,000 inhabitants. Many other Swedish cities are small in comparison with those of the Continent.

Although the municipal governments, in general, have taken no responsibility for building, but have rather encouraged individual undertaking along these lines, they have assumed definite control over conditions for building and for city planning, for which laws apply to the entire country. These laws are just now being revised. According to previous laws, the government of each commune lays down regulations for its city plan according to the desires of the local authorities. This concerns such matters as height of buildings, sub-division of plots allowing for sufficient garden room, according to the demands of hygiene and beauty.

Control of Buildings

Style of houses put up in a given neighborhood is also under city control. Each town has its own architect, who provides plans for buildings of different types at reasonable rates, or who supervises plans turned in by the individual builder. This control has had a most favorable effect on the general appearance of a town and has proved to be of service to the individual rather than a handicap. In general it assures the maintenance of property values.

Another active policy directed toward forwarding the building question, from a social point of view, is that of city-owned property in the heart of, and on the outskirts of, a city. This policy has been carried on by the communes since the beginning of the nineteenth century and has been found a great protection to property, whether used for residence or for industrial purpose. Sweden's

(Continued on Page 7, Column 2)

Locomotive Without Boiler Fire Runs Under Own Steam Pressure

Special from The Christian Science Monitor

CHICAGO—Can a locomotive run under its own steam, yet have no fire in its boiler?

The answer, according to engineers attending the thirty-first annual meeting of the American Railroad Engineering Association here, is emphatically "Yes." And by doing so, they added, it can reduce smoke and increase economy of operation.

The practice is known as "direct steaming." Shortly before a locomotive is needed for service, a high-pressure steam line is connected to its boiler, and steam and hot water are furnished from a stationary power plant, until working pressure is built up. The locomotive then moves from the engine house under its own pressure but without any fire, to a specially assigned firing-up track, where its fire is lighted.

Of course, such fireless trips are exceedingly short, but they represent a distinct advance in railroading, a report submitted to the convention declared. An analysis of one direct steaming installation showed a saving of 20 per cent in the cost of bringing a locomotive up to working pressure, and a saving of 35 per cent in the time required.

News of great interest to amateur gardeners who struggle each year to uproot a large crop of weeds came to light in a report on roadbed maintenance. The railroads, it seems, are now able to eliminate weeds growing in railway ballast and along the edges of the track, at the rate of 30 miles an hour. A work train merely sweeps by at slow speed, spraying chemicals from nozzles close to the ground, and the weeds are doomed.

BRITAIN TO SAVE £605,000 IN 1930 ON COST OF ARMY

Number of Men Reduced by 16,000—Work Curtailed on Singapore Base

By Radio from Monitor Bureau

LONDON—The British Army estimates for 1930, published March 12, show that the Government has succeeded in making a further cut of £605,000 (about $3,025,000) in its annual military expenditure, although the force it has hitherto maintained at German expense on the Rhine has come home and contributions for the cost of maintenance of British troops in Cairo has stopped.

The number of men on establishment has been diminished by 16,000. But this is not the full extent to which the British Army has been reduced as the attractiveness of the unemployment insurance system has proved to be such that, despite the prolonged trade depression, recruiting has fallen off and the strength of the British Army is 10,000 below the authorized establishment, to which result anti-war propaganda has also contributed.

In all Britain is to spend during the coming year upon the army £40,000,000 ($200,000,000), or roughly two-thirds of the corresponding outlay of the United States.

The estimates include the defense works at Singapore, regarding which the official statement says: "Provision for 1930 is only sufficient to meet outstanding liabilities and complete work which if left unfinished would involve loss to the public through deterioration; all other work has been suspended."

In connection with the introduction of mechanical transport, the statement says: "There is ample evidence that the types of vehicles rendered by the army are making transport possible in places hitherto inaccessible, thus contributing to the commercial development of the resources of the Empire."

King of Albania Backs Education on Modern Lines

By Radio to The Christian Science Monitor

TIRANA, Albania—King Zog has sent a letter to the new Prime Minister of Albania, Pandeli Vangeli, outlining the main features of the Government's policy.

If possible, he says, taxes and administrative fees must be lowered, agrarian reform put through, a new commercial law passed, measures taken for improving the economic situation, and special attention must be given to the education of youth in the ideals of modern culture and progress.

The head of the new Cabinet has taken an active part in politics here during the last decade. He was called from post of president of Parliament to accept that of Premier, and is expected to serve as a faithful executor of the King's wishes.

The Foreign Minister in the new Cabinet remains the same, Rauf Fitso, former Minister Plenipotentiary in Turkey and Jugoslavia. Other new ministers are: Justice, Vassil Avrami; Education, and at interim Public Works, Hil Mosi; Finance, Koi Thatchi; Public Economics, Mehdi Frasheri. The Portfolio of the Interior is held by Mr. Fitso ad interim.

PARADING STUDENTS ARRESTED IN SPAIN

By Radio to The Christian Science Monitor

MADRID—Arrest at Valencia of seven noisy students parading the streets, marks the beginning of application of severe methods recently announced for repression of disturbances.

Possible reaction on universities, where it is thought may take the opportunity of displaying solidarity with their comrades, is being watched with interest at a time when quiet reigns throughout Spain.

Rotarians have issued an appeal that owners of securities alarmed over depreciation of the peseta should refrain from giving practical expression of their uneasiness, thus fulfilling a patriotic duty. The manifesto assures them that all is well with Spain. It has been circulated to Rotary Clubs throughout the country, explaining the situation, which in general opinion, is that the Spanish business world is so solid economically that Spain could if necessary withstand greatest adversity without flinching.

Holland Takes 50,000-Acre Bite Out of Zuider Zee

Flat Reaches of Holland's Famous Inland Sea Are Pierced by a 12-Mile Dike, or Dam, Here Seen in Perspective as It Strikes Across the Entrance to the Wieringermeer, or Northwest Polder. The Water on the Left of the Dike Is to Be Pumped Out Into the Main Portion of the Sea to the Right, Partly by the Pumping Station of Medemblik, the White Building Seen on the Dike. The Main Barrage That Will Cut Off the Larger Waters of the Zuider Zee Runs Northeasterly From the Far End of the Dike Shown Above.

N. V. Vereenigde Fotobureaux, Amsterdam

Plan to Cut Draining Cost of Zuider Zee

Huge Estimate Modified as Work on Dike Shows Ways to Effect Economy

Special to The Christian Science Monitor

AMSTERDAM—Although the cost of draining the northwest polder of the Zuider Zee, as a preliminary part of the work which will add another 535,000 acres to the present Dutch territory of 33,000 miles, has vastly exceeded the original estimate, the Minister of Waterways, Dr. P. J. Reymer, declares that the experience gained in work on this polder will enable reductions to be made in the cost of work as a whole.

The main dike, he points out, will cost 120,000,000 florins, instead of the estimated 128,000,000 florins. Moreover the difficulties to be contended with in the northwest polder, or Wieringermeer, are largely eliminated in the diking-in of the other polders since this work will take place within the closed-in Zuider Zee, and thus will not be exposed to tidal movement.

Difficulties over the polder have raised the cost of drainage from the original estimate of 16,000,000 to 128,000,000 florins and the considerably increased cost of the whole project has aroused some concern among certain sections of the population. As it is, the total cost of draining the Zuider Zee, estimated at 230,000,000 florins in 1914, is now put at 948,000,000 florins, and has been diminished.

Singer to Get $4000 a Minute in Talkies

Special to The Christian Science Monitor

CULVER CITY, Calif.—Unique in the history of business agreements, a term contract between Mary Lewis, Metropolitan Opera Company star, and the Pathe Studios was consummated by recording the obligations of both parties on a sound film. No other contracts or written agreements were recorded.

With E. B. Derr, executive vice-president of the Pathe Studios, and Laura Hope Crews, studio director, as representatives of the film company, and Miss Lewis and her business manager seated in front of the microphone, the terms of the contract were repeated verbally, every word and movement of the principals being recorded.

After appearing for a number of performances in the East next month, Miss Lewis, who is still under contract to the Metropolitan, will return to Los Angeles to start her first Pathe picture. By the terms of the studio contract, Miss Lewis will receive approximately $4000 for every minute in which her voice will be heard in her first picture.

Arab Delegation Plans London Visit

By Radio to The Christian Science Monitor

JERUSALEM—Representatives of the three middle and east territories are about to visit London for direct negotiations with the Government in regard to the unsatisfied national claims and conversations on unsettled points in the agreements pending with Great Britain. The Arab delegation from Palestine expects to leave the middle of the month and to arrive in London about the time of the publication of the report of the commission which inquired into the August disturbances.

Mousa Kazin Pasha, chairman of the Arab executive, heads the delegation, comprising Hajj Muhammad Amin El Husseini, Grand Mufti, and Rah Geb Nashashibi, the Mayor of Jerusalem, and others. Advance reports from London foreshadowing the commission's recommendations as favorable to the Arab claims to limit Jewish immigration and restrict land sales greatly encouraged the delegation.

The impatience over the protracted Anglo-Irak conversations regarding the future relations of mandatory and ward decided the Arab National-ists to send a delegation to London to accelerate the agreement. It is also sending a delegation headed by Nahas Pasha, the Premier, to complete the Anglo-Egyptian conversations for finally securing Egypt's independence, which were begun under the predecessor, Mohammed Mahmud Pasha, last year.

Spanish Women Await Vote for the Cortes

By Radio to The Christian Science Monitor

Madrid

THE question of parliamentary vote for women must stand over until the Cortes can decide, it is stated in regulations for the new census which the Government has just issued.

Women have the municipal vote, and it was believed that the right to vote at the election of the Cortes would be extended for the purpose of carrying the support of women for the monarchy under the influence of the church party.

GANDHI VOICES 'SALT MESSAGE' ON PILGRIMAGE

Dares Indian Government to Arrest Him for Delivering Speech

ASLALI, India (AP)—Mahatma Gandhi, in a speech here March 12, called the "message of salt," defied the Government to arrest him.

Aslali was the first halt of the volunteer civil disobedience marchers who set out with Gandhi from Ahmedabad early in the morning beginning their campaign for Indian independence.

Gandhi said that the Government had arrested his lieutenant, Vallabhai Patel, for his intention of addressing a public meeting. "Let the Government arrest me for actually doing so," said Gandhi.

His 79 volunteers come from all parts of India. Two of them are Moslems, and one is a Christian; the remainder are Hindus. Nine teachers, 25 are students, and 12 are graduates. Thirty-three belonged to the various departments of the Ashram.

Disorders in Bombay Mark Campaign's Start

BOMBAY, India (AP)—Disorders occurred in Bombay March 12 as a consequence of demonstrations in celebration of Mahatma Gandhi's inauguration of the civil disobedience campaign at Ahmedabad.

Show cases were smashed in two provision stores when a crowd paraded through the streets saw European customers inside. Windows of the offices of the Times of India were also smashed.

Two thousand schoolboys demonstrating in the afternoon clashed with police. Several boys were injured.

The Indian Government is keeping close contact with the Bombay Government with regard to the situation caused by inauguration of Mahatma Gandhi's civil disobedience campaign. The movement is regarded more or less in the light of an all-India matter.

RECEIVED IN MEXICO

MEXICO CITY (By U. P.)—The Spanish Minister, Viscount Grana Real, presented his credentials to President Ortiz Rubio March 11. He was the first diplomat to be received by the President since the inaugura-tion.

THREE-POWER NAVAL PACT VISUALIZED

Britain, United States and, Japan May Draw Up Separate Treaty

OFFICIAL LONDON STILL OPTIMISTIC

American Change of Face Reported Ordered From the White House

By ERWIN D. CANHAM

LONDON—With both the United States and Great Britain apparently firmly decided against entering any political arrangement with the French, the most authoritative opinion in London is now inclined to feel that the likeliest outcome of the conference will be a three-power pact limiting navies, with France and Italy adhering only to the technical provisions which have been so laboriously hammered out in London.

It is now generally concluded, as it was speculated before, that Mr. MacDonald's rejection of entangling alliances on his radicast speech on March 9, together with the American delegation's unofficial statement on March 11, have rendered any form of political settlement, even a consultative pact, highly improbable.

At the same time the French have inspired a statement that they regard as extremely valuable technical settlements on the model category tables of exempt and special ships and other drafted provisions. This French claim will materially facilitate the work of the general disarmament conference when it meets and they are eager to adopt them now.

Maxima of Tonnage

If tonnage figures are mentioned at all in the five-power agreement, the French would prefer they would be purely on a provisional basis, covering the technical points on which a unanimous agreement can be reached and including the larger British, American and Japanese agreement.

An opposition motion to refrain for two months from promulgating the Young plan legislation found the support of 173 members of the Reichstag, which are sufficient, but the government parties immediately countered by introducing a motion declaring the Young plan and the connected legislation "urgent." This means that if the National Council (Reichsrat) also agrees, as seems certain, President von Hindenburg may promulgate it despite the opposition's motion.

The Reichstag adopted the urgency motion by a vote of 283 to 174. The Reichsrat will be convened March 13 and is certain to approve it.

The German Nation's decision on the settlement of the reparation plan entered its final and decisive stage.

The Chancellor declared several times in his speech that the burden Germany was forced to shoulder under the Young plan is heavier than ever and again he emphasized that Germany is sincerely willing to fulfill its obligations under this plan.

Germany's economic development needs order and peace, and the settlement of the reparation question in the form of the Young plan meets this need, he declared.

But the creditor nations, too, must loyally fulfill the plan, he continued. They must realize that solution of the reparations problem lies in interest of all and is not solely a task to be performed by Germany. All, therefore, must co-operate.

"Its coming into force," he continued, "means the liberation of the Rhinelands," and he expressed the hope that liberation of the Saar would follow.

The Chancellor then turned against the machinations of the Fascisti and Communists to overthrow the present regime and declared the Government sufficiently strong to master both enemies.

Germans Give Final Sanction to Young Plan

Chancellor Declares Nation Will Loyally Strive to Fulfill Obligations

BERLIN (AP)—The Reichstag on Mar. 12 finally approved the Young plan. The vote was 270 in favor of the plan and 192 against it, with three abstentions.

The measure now only requires President von Hindenburg's signature and publication of the ratification in the Official Gazette for the plan, by which the financial aftermath of the World War has been liquidated, will become law as far as Germany is concerned.

By Radio to The Christian Science Monitor

BERLIN—After the Young plan was passed by the Reichstag on second reading by a vote of 263 to 174, with 25 abstentions, the Chancellor, Dr. Hermann Mueller, opened the third reading with a speech in which he explained the Government's reasons for supporting the Young plan, and asked the Reichstag to co-operate with the Government to obtain a spare Germany grave difficulties.

Several film companies, including one German, accompanied the party taking films.

The secretary of the Gujarat provincial Congress committee, in a message to Pandit Jawaharlal Nehru, president of the All-India Congress, said that Gandhi began his civil disobedience march amid unforgettable scenes unprecedented in the history of Gandhi's seminary.

Millionaires and laborers, he said, vied in wishing God-speed to the marching column. Thousands of men, women and children followed the procession for miles in orderly array, while thousands lined the route and showered coins, currency notes, flowers and saffron on the Mahatma. One woman gave a horse to Gandhi.

Swiss Watch Fascist Activities in Ticino

By Cable to The Christian Science Monitor

GENEVA—The Swiss authorities of the canton Ticino have been keeping a sharp eye on the activities of the Fascist organizations in view of the kidnapping incident which recently occurred, when an anti-Fascist was carried over the frontier. As a result, several Italians have been arrested on the suspicion of being connected with the Fascist organization, carrying on irredentist propaganda in Ticino, or endeavoring to interfere with the welfare of anti-Fascist residents in Switzerland.

The Swiss Government is considering such steps as it deems necessary, such as whether they can be dealt with under the federal penal code or not, or whether there is sufficient justification for expelling them from the country. It is obviously a difficult and delicate matter for the Swiss Cabinet to decide what steps they should take to deal with such activi-ties.

Middle Ground Proposed

A middle ground in which the British accord a fairly high French figure in lieu of a naval pact, and the French concede favorably, for the future dangers of surrender are held to be infinitely more undesirable than

(Continued on Page 3, Column 4)

COPYRIGHT 1931 BY
THE CHRISTIAN SCIENCE PUBLISHING SOCIETY

Sixteen Pages

BOSTON, THURSDAY, JULY 2, 1931—VOL. XXIII, NO. 184

ATLANTIC EDITION **

FIVE CENTS A COPY

MORAL FORCE PUT FIRST IN ENFORCEMENT

Education, Colonel Woodcock Says, Is Better Than Courts

SEES NO LIMITS TO POSSIBILITIES

Upholds Effectiveness of Injunctions to Control Liquor Nuisances

By A Staff Correspondent of
The Christian Science Monitor

CHARLOTTESVILLE, Va., July 2—Moral forces are far more important to prohibition enforcement than courts and investigators, Col. Amos W. W. Woodcock, director of prohibition, told the Institute of Public Affairs here today.

While the hands of the latter are tied by the constitutional fundamental of "private immunity," there are, he declared, "no limits to what may be done by education."

Colonel Woodcock's address was delivered at the third session at which prohibition has been a feature during the first week of the institute. These sessions have attracted larger audiences than any of the numerous discussions of social and economic questions, held on the historic campus of the state university founded by Thomas Jefferson.

The proposed revision of all American business and farmers was enlarged upon today by its sponsor, Carl Vrooman, former Assistant Secretary of Agriculture. Problems of adult education and local taxation also assumed important places on the program.

No sweeping changes in federal procedure against violators is necessary, Colonel Woodcock told the law enforcement round table investigators, and courts ought to be more efficient, but that efficiency will come "not from sweeping changes, but from better men, more earnest and better trained," he added. The law and practice in removal cases in his opinion is the only phase of procedure which needs clarification.

Colonel Woodcock mentioned the following improvements in enforcement that have marked his first year of administration ended yesterday: Decrease in the percentage of cases where conviction failed reduction of cases awaiting trial by approximately 3000, and the introduction of a policy of hiring young, intelligent and honest men as investigators. He defended the grand jury system, characterizing it as "a most valuable check-up on possible oppressive zeal by the professional prosecutor."

He likewise declared himself a "firm believer in the system of trial by jury," adding that the defendant should have the right to waive such trial if he desires.

"I do not believe the somewhat frequent assertion that juries will not convict in prohibition cases," Colonel Woodcock declared.

"I have observed a tendency in some places, in the trial of prohibition cases, in a wave of enthusiasm by those who

(Continued on Page 4 Column 4)

Chinese Block Andrews And Haardt Trips

By Radio to The Christian Science Monitor

PEIPING, China, July 2—Both the Rev. Dr. Roy Chapman Andrews archaeological expedition to Mongolia and the National Geographic-Haardt expedition across the Gobi Desert are seriously threatened by the new attitude of the Nanking Government.

Dr. Andrews has been definitely refused permission to resume his expedition and the Haardt expedition has been forbidden to enter Chinese Turkestan, it is learned here that correspondence of the Chinese Commission for the Preservation of Antiquities.

The Commission, in its letters, has declared a substitute Chinese expedition is already planned and Dr. Andrews's "arrogance" has made further coöperation difficult.

Dr. Andrews, when interviewed, declared the Commission had informed him last November that he might complete his Mongolian researches.

The published letters show that Dr. Andrews informed the Chinese in April the museum trustees had unanimously decided it would be disastrous to the final results of the expedition to leave the work uncompleted and asked the Commission to name the conditions and requested a personal interview. The Chinese reply to this first letter has not been published, but Dr. Andrews declared they refused to grant an interview or name any conditions, declaring that the Chinese have already sent an expedition to Sinkiang wherefore it is not necessary for Dr. Andrews to continue.

Dr. Andrews replied that Mongolia is 1000 miles from the Chinese operations and again requested an interview, warning that the Chinese attitude could not fail to bring discredit. The final Chinese reply, as published, declared, "Your arrogant attitude alone is responsible for coöperation being so difficult."

The Commission's decision regarding Dr. Andrews immediately follows its action yesterday in demanding that the Sino-French Haardt expedition be recalled.

PEIPING, China, July 2 (AP)—The Haardt Asiatic expedition, collaborating with the National Geographic Society in a 13,000-mile trek over the legendary trail of Marco Polo, has been forbidden by the Nationalist Government to enter Chinese Turkestan.

INDIAN PRINCES APPROVE IDEA FOR FEDERATION

Groups Disagree, However, on Form the Union Should Take

By ALEXANDER INGLIS
By Radio to The Christian Science Monitor

BOMBAY, July 2—Acceptance of the general idea of federation for India has been substantially confirmed by the princes of Indian states in a series of meetings held here during the last three days. There are, however, two camps whose followers hold opposing views as to the form this federation should take.

The first group, headed by the Nawab of Bhopal, Chancellor of the Chamber of Princes, and supported by a majority of the most important states, stands by the scheme of federation proposed by the Round Table last year. The other group, led by the Maharaja of Patiala, supported by minor states, seeks first some form of federation among the states themselves as a preliminary to a federal

(Continued on Page 3, Column 6)

Plans for New Spanish Constitution Held Model of Clarity and Foresight

By SISLEY HUDDLESTON
By Cable to The Christian Science Monitor

MADRID, July 2—At last official publication of the projected constitution, as passed by the plenary commission, and made ready for presentation by the Government of the constituent Cortes, has enabled us to judge what manner of men are these so-called revolutionaries who are constructing the Spanish Republic.

If the draft goes through without serious modification, Spain will have a constitution which is in many respects a model of clarity and foresight. It takes from France and the United States some of the best features. Considerable autonomy will be allowed to the provinces which desire it, but the central government must remain master of relations between the church and state, international policy, diplomatic representation, the army and navy, fortification of frontiers, maintenance of public order, public debt, treaties of commerce, railroads, canals and air routes, judicial organization, monetary systems, post, telegraph, telephone and radio, and other matters which properly belong to the Spanish nation as a whole. Nor must regional laws run counter to the general laws of the state.

A good deal has been said about the presumed clash between Catalonia and Castile, but it would certainly seem agreement can be realized on the lines of the constitution. It is affirmed that all Spaniards are equal before the law, and birth, titles, political ideals and religious beliefs cannot confer any privileges.

Titles are not recognized. Each citizen is free to practice whatever religion he pleases, for there is no state religion. Provisions are made for the inviolability of the domicile and of correspondence. The rights and duties of citizens are set out at length in a special chapter.

The President of the Republic, like the French Presidents, will be elected by Congress and the Senate united in a national assembly. There are barred from the Presidency, naturalized persons, military men, ecclesiastics, and members of former reigning families. The President shall sit for six years, he shall choose the Prime Minister and authorize ministerial decrees. He cannot declare war without a law, which must become effective after international obligations have been solemnly fulfilled. His powers are indeed limited in the sense that his acts must always be countersigned by the Government. He will be criminally responsible for deliberate infraction of the constitution, or gross negligence.

However, how farm prices may force relief of some kind. What form it will take, if any, is what political leaders are anxiously concerned about.

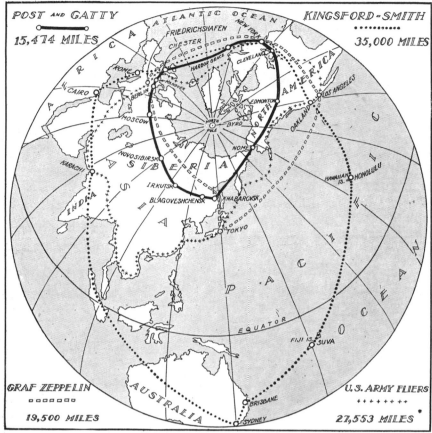

Fliers Ring Globe in 4 Days 10h. 8m. Flying Time

POST AND GATTY — 15,474 MILES

KINGSFORD-SMITH — 35,000 MILES

GRAF ZEPPELIN — 19,500 MILES

U.S. ARMY FLIERS — 27,553 MILES

HOW DIFFERENT FLIERS HAVE GONE ROUND THE WORLD

The Map Is Self-Explanatory as to Routes Followed, but It Must Be Borne in Mind That Post and Gatty Were Actually the Only Ones Who Deliberately Set Out to Cut the Time to a Minimum. The Army Flight Was Leisurely. So Was Wing Commander Kingsford-Smith's. It Is the Australian Flier Who Thus Far Has Made the Closest Actual Bisecting of the World. The Graf Zeppelin, While Not Out for a Time Record, Was, Nevertheless, Eager to Clip the Time.

World Opens Wide Its Heart In Praise of Post and Gatty

New York Gives Fliers Who Circled Globe in 4 Days, 10h., 8m., Flying Time, Tumultuous Welcome—Wife Meets Winnie Mae's Pilot

Special from The Christian Science Monitor Bureau

NEW YORK, July 2—A welcome in keeping with the best traditions of Father Knickerbocker's hospitality was accorded Wiley Post and Harold Gatty here today following the completion last night of an air flight which took them around the world in 4 days, 10h., 8m., of actual flying time.

Exactly 8 days, 15h., 51m. after leaving Roosevelt Field on the start of their world-circling flight, which was aimed at lowering the record of globe circumnavigation, they returned there, completing their record-breaking accomplishment with a perfect three-point landing.

The difference between this time and their actual flying time was accounted for by their refueling stops, a halt of nearly 11 hours in Berlin and a stop of nearly 12 hours in Moscow.

When the fliers brought their plane to a stop at Roosevelt Flying Field, New York took from the portals of the general post office here, the inscrip-

tion thereon and pinned it to its crowns it placed upon their heads:

"Neither snow nor rain nor heat nor gloom of night stays these couriers from the swift completion of their appointed rounds."

Everywhere the achievement of Wiley Post as a pilot and of Harold Gatty as a navigator was acclaimed as a "relentless subjugation of time and space."

Mrs. May Post, wife of the aviator, and Mrs. Vera Gatty, wife of the navi-

(Continued on Page 5, Column 1)

Federal Farm Board Facing Finances Issue

Special from Monitor Bureau

WASHINGTON, July 2—Of the many complex problems facing the Federal Farm Board none is more disturbing than the question of its future finances.

Yesterday, the beginning of the new fiscal year, the board received the $100,000,000 final allotment of the $500,000,000 appropriated as a revolving fund for its operations a little over two years ago.

With this $100,000,000 the board has on hand a total cash balance of $160,-000,000, it was stated at the board offices today. This means that some $340,000,000 of the board's money is tied up in grain holdings, cotton holdings, coöperatives and a number of other marketing activities.

How much will be lost and how much recovered only time will show. The board is carefully keeping the details of its holdings and operations secret, on the ground that to make these facts known would be to give valuable aid to its opponents.

There is much conjecture here as to the likelihood of a demand at the next Congress, by either the board or from agricultural quarters, for additional funds. With a $1,000,000,000 Treasury deficit such a proposal faces serious obstacles.

FRANCE'S CHALLENGE TO DEBT HOLIDAY PUT BEFORE WORLD

American Note to Paris Warns of Consequences of Reich's Collapse

DOOR STILL OPEN FOR CONCESSIONS

Agreement on French Plea for Relief From Guarantee Fund Is Possibility

While Washington has sent a firmly worded note to the Paris Government, warning it of the grave consequences which will result if the debt-holiday plan fails and the Berlin Government is compelled to declare a moratorium, opinion on both sides of the Atlantic is that the success of the plan is now so essential that means will be devised to overcome the Franco-American differences. Then, it is expected, the issues between France and Germany can be adjusted.

The American note is under discussion in France, and a Paris dispatch indicates that it is regarded as conciliatory, although not offering concessions on the main points in dispute.

The day's news does, however, intimate that there is a possibility of meeting the French demand for relief from the guarantee fund in case of a German moratorium on conditional reparations. This would come by agreement of the signatories of the Young plan, and in this the United States is not involved.

Today the British Government offered its services in calling a conference of the interested powers if the Franco-American negotiations fail. This is taken by Washington as referring to the French demand regarding the reparations fund.

Rumania has joined with other governments which have accepted the Hoover plan without conditions.

By ROBERT S. ALLEN
Staff Correspondent
Special from Monitor Bureau

WASHINGTON, July 2—The United States Government has taken to the world's public opinion on the French Ministry's challenge of President Hoover's debt suspension proposal.

Confronted with a gravely disturbing French viewpoint that presented the serious possibility of jeopardizing the whole success of the President's plan, the American Government has taken its case to the people of the world—including those of France.

This it did in the form of a friendly but firmly frank memorandum delivered to the French Ministry yesterday by Walter E. Edge, American Ambassador in Paris. The note warns the Paris Government of the danger of economic collapse in Germany and indicates that if the American plan fails and Germany declares a moratorium, France will stand to lose more than $100,000,000.

Thus for the first time there is available to the great mass of people everywhere, including France, the full import of the French Government's demands. Just what these conditions are, what they imply, and the grave consequences that face the world, including France, if the American plan fails is unsuccessful, are candidly discussed in the American note.

The note makes a distinct departure in recent international negotiations. The American Government, supported by the approval of the President's plan by all the interested governments, except France, made public to them in its unusual diplomatic communication the case for the debt holiday in its original form.

Way Open for Negotiations

Washington has summarized the case against France's demands without in any way closing the door to an accord or further negotiations. In fact these are actively under way. Mr. Edge and Andrew W. Mellon, Secretary of the Treasury, now in Paris, are holding conversations with Paul Claudel, French Ambassador.

President Hoover and his advisers are still hopeful and confident that reason the military heroes and heroines of the Old Testament," he said, "and has, spoken, condescendingly of the pagans to whom missionaries must be sent. The school has taught that man is a fighting animal and always would fight. The battles of great military heroes have been fought over again in the classrooms."

Dr. Van Kirk named, as the direct cause of the World War competitive armaments, faulty diplomacy, and

(Continued on Page 4, Column 2)

Debt Plan Hinges on Guarantees

THE crux of the Franco-American debt discussion centers upon guarantees. A guarantee fund was devised by the Young plan to operate in case Germany declared a moratorium.

Into this fund France, being recipient of the largest share of non-postponable annuities, is to pay $120,000,000 in the event of declaration of the moratorium. The fund would be used by the Bank for International Settlements to make good the proportion of annuities to creditor nations getting smaller sums, which would. otherwise suffer through the moratorium.

Germany's right to call a moratorium is allowed by the Young plan, which divided the 59 payments into non-postponable annuities of $165,-000,000 a year, and others, varying in amount, to be subject to two years' moratorium after due notice from Germany. The Hoover plan calls for postponement of both types of annuity.

France holds that its $120,000,000 payment into the guarantee fund should not be made in the event of Germany declaring a moratorium during the period of debt postponement, but that this amount should be made up by France from annuity money which the Hoover plan would reloan to the Germans.

Washington opposes this view on the ground that it would impose a double burden on Germany.

Reports that Britain will call a conference on the debt question are interesting in view of the hope expressed by President Hoover that other governments concerned would be willing to free France from any prospect of actually having to produce the $120,000,000.

CANADIAN HOUSE URGED TO EXTEND DROUGHT RELIEF

Bennett Outlines Situation and Announces Plans for Aid

Special to The Christian Science Monitor

OTTAWA, July 2—"Tremendously serious" and perhaps constituting "the greatest national calamity that has ever overtaken this country," was the way in which the Prime Minister, R. B. Bennett, referred to the drought conditions in the prairie provinces when Parliament assembled yesterday.

Recalling that it was Dominion Day, the sixty-fourth anniversary of confederation, he said one might well "contemplate the past with some degree of satisfaction and pride" and the future with "great courage and hope and confident faith."

With respect to the present he said the fact must be faced from information received by the Government "that in consequence of lack of moisture and of great heat a very considerable portion of Saskatchewan and smaller portions of Alberta and Manitoba will not this year produce a crop.

"In some areas," Mr. Bennett continued, "this is the third successive year in which no crop has been produced, in others it is the second, while in the smaller areas it is the first year that such a calamity has overtaken them."

Mr. Bennett said that the Government of Saskatchewan was carrying on a survey the results of which in part had already been received and which made clear that the heat not only had gravely affected livestock over a substantial area, but at least 5,000,000 acres so far as crop is concerned.

Under such circumstances, Mr. Bennett said, Parliament and never been hesitant in coming to the assistance of other countries when such a disaster had overtaken them. "Before the House rises," he continued, "it is the purpose of the Government to submit a measure that will, we believe, at least in part, show the desire and purpose of the Canadian people to assist those who are less fortunate than the inhabitants of other parts of Canada in this particular crisis."

While he hoped that his worst "fears were groundless," in regard to what happened to the "greatest national calamity that has ever overtaken this country," there was unfortunately evidence to show that "at least 100,000 people are directly affected and their herds as well," and there was no doubt but that the situation was "tremendously serious."

In replying W. L. Mackenzie King, Liberal leader, assured Mr. Bennett that "coöperation will be given in the fullest measure and with the most hearty accord by all members on this side of the house." He suggested that, as apparently very large sums of money would have to be spent to take care of this calamity as well as for unemployment relief this coming winter, the administration consider the establishment of a National Relief Board, "which will face this situation as a national emergency and a national obligation and become responsible through the minister to this Parliament for the expenditure of public money from this source."

Federal Aid Promised To Northwest Farmers

KANSAS CITY, Mo., July 2 (AP)—Promise of Federal drought relief went out to stricken areas of North Dakota and Montana today.

Arthur M. Hyde, Secretary of Agriculture, who was here for a conference with Gov. George E. Shafer of North Dakota and a group of state officials and farmers from the two states, agreed to extend all the aid possible under the law.

Mr. Hyde said agricultural credit loans would be extended and he believed the department had authority to make seed and feed loans. He said he would seek a ruling from the Comptroller-General.

He based his decision on the plea of Governor Shafer and upon the report made by John G. Brown, special representative of the department.

Brown reported that a desperate situation exists in 31 counties of northwestern North Dakota and northeastern Montana, a region impoverished by crop failure last year, in which farmers borrowed $4,000,000 to finance this year's crop.

Canada Wheat Rate Drops

WINNIPEG, Man., July 2 (AP)—The condition of western Canada's wheat crop on June 30 was 59 per cent of normal, the bi-weekly report of the Canadian wheat pool said yesterday. This condition rating compares with an estimate of 70 per cent two weeks previously and 82 per cent at the end of June in 1930.

She Is Only Candidate For N. E. A. Presidency

MISS FLORENCE M. HALE

Teacher Jobs Problem Put Up to States

Standards Held Too Low by Education Association Speakers

By MARJORIE SHULER
Staff Correspondent of
The Christian Science Monitor

LOS ANGELES, Calif., July 2—An appeal to state departments of education to take action on teacher unemployment has gone forth from the sixty-ninth convention of the National Education Association in session here.

While conditions differ greatly between the states, there are some states with a tremendous oversupply of certificated teachers but as indefinite a supply of adequately trained teachers, it was pointed out. This is the crux of the problem, the association was told. If two years beyond high school education is to be the minimum standard for a teacher, it was said, then it can be said with assurance that the country lacks adequately trained teachers.

At present, teaching is one of the easiest professions to enter, a special report on the economic status of the teaching profession sets forth. This report, prepared by Frank W. Hubbard, assistant director of research for the association, under the direction of a committee, headed by Dr. B. R. Buckingham of Harvard University, indicates that the answer to the problem is the raising of standards for entry into the profession. Such action on the part of state departments of education together with intelligent planning, to train only such numbers of teachers as will be demanded, will answer the problem of unemployment for teachers, Dr. Buckingham said, in presenting his report to the convention today.

Educators must keep their attention centered on simple, thrifty living, said Joseph Rosier, of Fairmont, W. Va., to whom was assigned the task from the association's objectives. He urged that the first grade through the university remain open and that the association develop leadership to preserve American ideals.

Both the church and the school have contributed toward the prejudices in human thinking which cause dissension, Dr. Walter Van Kirk, secretary of the Federal Council of Churches of Christ in America, said at a general session of the convention devoted to education and its auxiliary agencies.

"The church has exalted beyond

TREASURY SETS 1931 DEFICIT AT $900,000,000

Mills' Report Says Total National Debt Has Reached $16,801,000,000

Special from Monitor Bureau

WASHINGTON, July 2—The Treasury has set up its accounts for the fiscal year 1931 just over and recorded the end of an 11-year era of heavy surpluses with a deficit of $903,000,000. The year closed with the total gross public debt at $16,801,000,000, compared to $16,185,000,000 on June 30, 1930.

The following table shows that government revenues in the depression year fell off while expenses increased, due chiefly to relief measures.

The most essential figures in the report issued by Ogden L. Mills, acting Secretary of the Treasury, are, in millions of dollars, as follows:

	1930	Budget estimate '31	Actual figures '31
Receipts	4178	3835	3311
Expenditures	3994	4015	4222
	$184 surplus	$180 deficit	$903 deficit

Mr. Mills points out that the total ordinary receipts declined $861,000,000 from 1930, while expenditures were $226,000,000 larger than a year ago.

The Treasury, according to Mr. Mills' admission, underestimated the impending deficit by $723,000,000.

Under "receipts" the following table, compiled from Mr. Mills' figures, shows the 1931 figures, and the falling off from 1930, again in millions:

	1931 Receipts	Drop from 1930
Income tax	$1860	$561
Customs	378	209
International revenue	510	42
Miscellaneous	569	49

The drop in income tax collections was the most notable feature among these decreases. Estimated income tax receipts had been placed by the Treasury at $2,190,000,000.

On the "expenditure" side, preliminary figures, Mr. Mills says, show the following principal items of increase and decrease (millions again omitted):

Increased Expenditures—1931	
War Dept., increased construction	$25
Agricultural Dept., highway and drought relief	119
Farm Board, farm loans	31
Commerce Dept.	12
Post Office, increased deficiency	44
Veterans' loans, adjusted service certificate fund	112

Reduced Expenditures—1931	
Navy Dept., unmanned construction	$20
Public debt interest, lower interest rates	48
Tax refunds	66

Mr. Mills points out that money market conditions during the year permitted the issue of new debt securities at "unusually low rates with consequent reduction in annual interest charges on the public debt."

The annual rate of interest on the interest-bearing debt on June 30 was 3.56 per cent compared with 3.80 per cent a year ago.

THE CHRISTIAN SCIENCE MONITOR

AN INTERNATIONAL DAILY NEWSPAPER

COPYRIGHT 1932 BY THE CHRISTIAN SCIENCE PUBLISHING SOCIETY

BOSTON, WEDNESDAY, NOVEMBER 9, 1932—VOL. XXIV, NO. 294

*** ATLANTIC EDITION — FIVE CENTS / TWOPENCE A COPY

The MARCH of the NATIONS

By RUFUS STEELE

America Changes Presidents

Roosevelt Gets a Free Hand

Britain Welcomes New Head

France Sees War Debts Fall

Japan Hails Stimson's Recall

Hoover Grows Great in Defeat

THE United States changes horses in the middle of the stream. It elects a new President to replace the old, and does it with a determination that annihilates the force of the old order in the Senate, the House and wherever else it seemed to be a factor in the times. The result is regarded as not, primarily, Mr. Hoover's defeat, and still less as Mr. Roosevelt's victory; it is the voting mass venting an almost heedless passion for change. The result is an emotional protest against economic conditions as they are, an irresistible, if emotional, demand for a new order in the hope that, somehow and with some speed, it may bring in a new condition. The personalities of the two presidential candidates seem hardly to have counted; the economic arguments seem to have fallen on ears in no mood to listen. The President made a great plea for protection of vast recovery machinery in operation, but no plea could have been effective—No policies and no pleas could throw back that upheaving ocean's tide.

¶ The Administration of Franklin D. Roosevelt will have an exceptional opportunity. Besides having an abundance of substantial men from whom Cabinet selections may be made, the new President will have a Senate and a House wholly sympathetic to him politically. It is something that in planning and proposing the all-important measures that must come on economic recovery, tariffs, finances, the veterans' bonus, liquor, and foreign relations, the new President will not have to face bitter fights on Capitol Hill—No menace awaits the "new deal," whatever that may be.

¶ Britain shows the keenest interest in the election of Franklin D. Roosevelt. The London Times says the American people have chosen as their leader "a man who by birth and training is an aristocrat, by sympathy and principle is a democrat, and whose character and courage no enemy dare impugn." The Evening News sees new vigor and new liberalism brought to national policies. London admires President Hoover—It sees him a good sportsman in taking his defeat.

¶ France is pleased with the outcome of the American election. The French newspapers regard President-elect Roosevelt as more favorable to reduction of war debts than President Hoover. They see as a probability lower tariff on manufactured goods and the possibility of an American market for French wines. France remembers that President Wilson, who proposed the League of Nations, was a Democrat and that Roosevelt was a member of his Administration—It thus hopes the United States will take active part in European affairs.

¶ Italy believes it will benefit greatly by a change of régime in the United States. It sees its war debts reduced and a lowering of the tariff barriers that are keeping out Italian goods. The Fascists, under a rigid system of dictation, are fond of expressing contempt for popular elections, but they followed this one with the deepest interest, realizing its importance in world affairs. The present Italian-American relations are extremely cordial—Italy does not believe these will be destroyed by foreign policy changes.

¶ Japan is delighted with the election, one Tokyo journal announcing the result three hours before it was actually known. Tokyo sees a weakening of the American policy in the Far East. It sees a partial repudiation of the Stimson doctrine, which has given Japan most of its apprehension over the outcome in Manchuria. It anticipates a favorable lowering of tariffs, and silk and securities go up in response. One newspaper expresses the general feeling—"In foreign policy Roosevelt is certain to be more liberal."

¶ Already the figure of President Herbert Hoover begins to loom large in defeat. Bitter as repudiation must be to him, in the midst of a gigantic task well on its way, the able, courageous, hard-working man in the White House must see from the very hurricane vote itself that any man in his position would almost certainly have shared his fate. Financial hardships bred a passion that demanded a change—a change to almost anything—a change. When passion has spent itself, its immediate victim will undoubtedly find himself high in the public esteem. His works are his monument; they will not be scrapped; they will be carried on. A shift having been effected, the country will see more clearly now—Mr. Hoover is a great President, a great and beloved man.

Croats Demand Federal State Under Rule of One Monarch

Desire for Separation From Serbs Makes Big Problem for Yugoslav Kingdom—Memories of Old Autonomy Strong in Croatia

YUGOSLAV SERIES—*Fourth of Five Articles*

Special to The Christian Science Monitor

BELGRADE, Yugoslavia — The antipathy of the Croatians toward the Serbs of Belgrade constitutes a supreme Yugoslav problem. There are somewhat less than 4,000,000 Croatians, and somewhat more than 4,000,000 Serbs. No distinct ethnological boundary separates them, so that it would be very difficult to divide them.

What Croatians say is that they seek merely a "free Croatia." Just how this "free Croatia" would be organized, and what its relation would be with Serbia and other states, the masses are willing to leave to their leaders. But, as Dr. Machek, their leader, has often said, the Croatians require effective and guaranteed freedom. They would accept nothing less than complete autonomy or self-government.

In Croatia the common people are much more extreme than their leaders, who serve not to stir them up, but to hold them back. There is no patriotic Croatian press, no popular meetings, and not the slightest possibility of any public agitation, yet local patriotism demands Croatian liberty.

If one should ask the peasants if they didn't consider some kind of an agreement with the Serbs of Belgrade still possible, they would answer: "We have made a hundred agreements, and they have all been broken." That is their attitude.

So unanimous and extreme is public opinion in this respect that Dr. Machek, the most popular person in the recent history of Croatia, never visits Belgrade, lest his people think he is trying to conclude some deal and lose faith in him. The Croatians wish no negotiations with any Serbian politician, be he with or against the dictatorship. They are not trying to overthrow any government, or to put an end to a political régime. What they want is the reorganization of the state on a completely new basis. According to Dr. Machek the least they will accept is a confederation of an independent Croatia and Serbia, and perhaps other provinces, with a common monarch, Alexander.

The Croatians for decades enjoyed a form of autonomy under Austria. And before that they had a kingdom of their own. They say the Serbs have robbed them of the freedom they once enjoyed, and feel that they are being dominated by a foreign usurper.

Croatians consider their former situation as part of the Austro-Hungarian Empire better than their present state. Their "slavery" under Hungary was far lighter than their "freedom" under Belgrade.

The majority of the Slovenes also demand a federative constitution. The relatives of the very Bosnian Serbs who started the World War to gain freedom from Austria are opposing the present Serbian dictatorship, while many Serbs are opposing the present régime.

Yugoslavia was one of the good fruits of the war. With its great resources, natural beauty, vital location, and extremely vigorous inhabitants, it should be one of the most prosperous and enviable states in the world. It is not too late for King Alexander to give his country the future it deserves. And if he establishes a régime of freedom, equality and justice, Bulgaria might also join it, thus guaranteeing a long period of Balkan peace.

LONDON PRESS CITES RECORD OF ROOSEVELT

Note of Sympathy Voiced for Hoover in Taking Defeat Gallantly

By Press Wireless from Monitor Bureau

LONDON, Nov. 9—Quotations on American securities were marked up on the London Stock Exchange today upon the results of the presidential election. Keenest interest in Gov. Franklin D. Roosevelt's triumph is displayed upon every newspaper poster. A note of sympathy is also struck for President Hoover who, in British parlance, has taken his defeat like a sportsman.

All of the evening journals here give prominence to what the Standard refers to as Mr. Roosevelt's "good record" as Governor of New York. The President-elect's welcome here is also the more friendly for the early association of "the new lady of the White House" with England where her girlhood is still appreciatively remembered.

The Evening News says: "If new vigor and new liberalism to national politics can restore the American people's vanished prosperity then Franklin D. Roosevelt has it in him to supply them."

The Times of London in a contributed article says: "The American people have chosen for their leader a man who by birth and training is an aristocrat, by sympathy and principle a democrat, and a man whose character and courage no enemy has dared to impugn."

French Press Sees Trade Gain in Election Result

By Cable from Monitor Bureau

PARIS, Nov. 9—France is greatly pleased at the outcome of the elections in the United States, judging by the practically unanimous comments in the press today.

Lower tariffs on its manufactured goods and the possibility of selling its wines soon to America are the principal benefits the French press as a whole finds in the Democratic victory. Most papers also express opinion that Gov. Franklin D. Roosevelt will be more favorable to the reduction of war debts, and some journals voice the hope that the Democratic régime will tend to take a much more active part in European affairs generally.

Newspapers today also expressed pleasure at the news from Berlin that the Chancellor, Herr Franz von Papen, finds the French disarmament proposals a "great step forward" and "a satisfactory basis for discussion."

Italy Expects Change In American Debt Policy

By Press Wireless from Monitor Bureau

ROME, Nov. 9—Never before has an American presidential election been followed with such close attention in Italy. Fascists have hitherto looked upon political elections abroad with open contempt, considering them to be of little value as an indication of the nation's will.

But in contrast with their political doctrines they seem to have made an exception for this year's American election since they realize the tremendous influence its result would have on world affairs.

It is felt, however, that Italy will greatly benefit from a change in régime in the United States on at least two fundamental issues, namely, reduction of war debts and tariffs. At the same time it is felt whether Republicans or Democrats are in power, the United States will follow one foreign policy, namely, a distinctly American policy.

Roosevelt Wins by Record Plurality; Democratic Congress Also Sweeps In Under Evident Control of Wet Forces

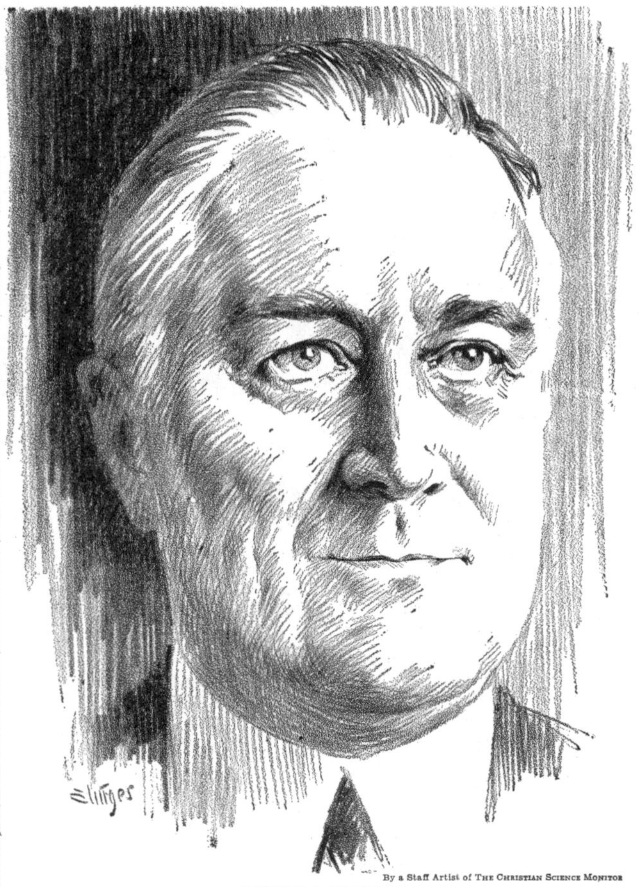

By a Staff Artist of The Christian Science Monitor

FRANKLIN D. ROOSEVELT

Governor Evidently Wins 42 States, Piling Up Unprecedented Vote

PROTEST IS AGAINST ECONOMIC TURMOIL

Dry Senators Go Down in G. O. P. Debacle; Returns Still Incomplete

Special from Monitor Bureau

WASHINGTON, Nov. 9—The Roosevelt-Garner ticket has won the 1932 election by the largest vote and the largest plurality in American history.

With about 72,000 of the nation's 119,723 election districts reported, Gov. Franklin D. Roosevelt appears to have secured a total of 472 electoral votes from 42 states, the 59 votes of the six remaining states going to President Hoover. In 1928 Hoover received 444 and Smith 87.

Four years of business decline has transmuted the great Hoover victory of 1928 into the even bigger defeat of today.

The Roosevelt tornado was still blowing today, and as additional tabulations were received, the states previously recorded in his column were for the most part holding their position by greater majorities.

From the East, the West, the North and the South, the big popular Roosevelt vote piled up. Only in a few rock-ribbed Republican strongholds in the East was President Hoover successful. Late returns indicate that these successes probably will be confined to six states, with 59 electoral votes.

Governor Roosevelt appears to have won California, his rival's own State, and on the eastern extreme, the great Empire State has gone Democratic by the huge plurality of more than 800,000.

Congratulates Successor

President Hoover, winding up a gallant struggle, in which he battled on despite all obstacles, and almost alone in behalf of his party, sent a cordial message to Governor Roosevelt last night, to which Governor—now President-Elect—Roosevelt responded with a statement recognizing his new responsibility. Friends and foes of Mr. Hoover alike join in expressing their admiration for his plucky election effort and acknowledge that the Chief Executive went down—fighting to the last—overwhelmed by economic forces over which he had slight control.

In the general Republican debacle some of the best-known senators were carried into defeat. The tentative list of the more important Republican defeats includes those of Senator James E. Watson of Indiana, Senator Reed Smoot of Utah, Senator Wesley L. Jones of Washington, Senator George H. Moses of New Hampshire, Senator Hiram Bingham of Connecticut, and Senator Otis F. Glenn of Illinois. This list will have additions and may have subtractions in later returns, but the net verdict of a Republican debacle will stand.

The Democrats have won not only the Presidency, but the new Senate and the House of Representatives. The gift of the nation to Governor Roosevelt is a working majority in both branches of the Legislature. This means that the Chief Executive will have a free hand when he comes into office. It means, too, that the responsibility for subsequent developments will rest squarely on the Democratic Party.

Drys Suffer Reverses

The drys suffered heavy reverses in the election. Already plans are under way among dry leaders for a defensive contest to rally their forces. Some nine states voted on a state referendum, or for repeal of a state enforcement law, and in six of these the wets appear to have won, while reports from the other three are not yet complete.

Wet victories, according to early reports, have been recorded in California, Washington, Oregon, Arizona, Colorado and Wyoming. The states yet to be heard from are New Jersey, Louisiana and North Dakota.

In addition to this, the Democratic Party which now comes to power is officially pledged to outright repeal; while at the same time a number of the defeated Republican Senators, like Mr. Jones of Washington, were leaders in the dry ranks.

The United States Senate will have another former Cabinet officer in its ranks in Mr. William Gibbs McAdoo (D.), from California, whose election was conceded late last night by his Republican opponent, although the vote was to be close. Mr. McAdoo will find his old Cabinet associate, Senator Carter Glass (D.) of Virginia in the upper house.

Woman Mentioned for Cabinet

With the Roosevelt landslide, speculation in Washington at once turned to the question of the new Democratic Cabinet. This speculation is of an entirely tentative character, and concerns itself more with possibilities than with actual forecasts. The speculation is bound to continue, however, and will be a regular feature of newspapers for months to come, until Governor Roosevelt finally announces the names of the men who will help him.

A list of prominent men are available for the Cabinet posts, and rarely has the Democratic Party had such a wealth of material. Mr. Norman H. Davis and Mr. John W. Davis have been discussed as possibilities as Secretary of State; Mr. Owen D. Young and Mr. Bernard M.

(Continued on Page 3, Column 3)

CANADA TO EASE FLOW OF CREDIT AND CURRENCY

Prime Minister Pledges Rigid Restrictions to Keep Money Sound

Special to The Christian Science Monitor

OTTAWA, Nov. 9—Canada intends to follow the lead of Great Britain and the United States in easing money and credit. This significant announcement was made by the Prime Minister, Mr. R. B. Bennett, in Parliament yesterday.

"So far as I am aware," said Mr. Bennett, "the best and most conservative opinion throughout the world is committed to the idea that an easing of money and credit is highly desirable in the interests of business recovery. The credit situation in Great Britain has been materially improved.

"In the United States a recent enactment gives power to the national banks to create new note issues aggregating nearly $1,000,000,000 against the security of certain classes of Government bonds, and this measure supplemented a central bank policy of easing money which resulted in bringing the Government bond holding of the Federal Reserve System to a figure in excess of $1,800,000,000."

Mr. Bennett explained the recent "borrowing" of $35,000,000 from the banks. The banks had purchased two-year notes of the Dominion of Canada, bearing interest at the rate of 4 per cent. The banks will use these notes as security in obtaining an advance of an equivalent amount under the Finance Act, thereby swelling their cash reserves and substantially increasing their loaning capacity.

It was because of Canada's sound banking situation that transactions of this type must be carefully restricted, Mr. Bennett said. Advances under the Finance Act are now at a very low level, he pointed out, having dropped from $112,900,000 in 1929 to only $38,700,000 in 1931, and even when full advantage is taken of the recent arrangement, the total this year will only exceed $40,000,000. Not only are such advances at a low level, but today Canada's gold holdings are larger than they were a year ago, indicating the soundness of its financial position. The Prime Minister said that once this present loan operation is completed the Dominion is finished with the market for some time to come.

"After having proved our ability to ride out the storm, I feel that we were justified—to the very limited degree necessary in our case—in joining other countries in the adoption of monetary measures designed to encourage recovery," continued Mr. Bennett. "However, any broad action along this line is unnecessary and, as I have stated frequently on previous occasions, this country will not depart from the established principles of sound money."

VIRGIN ISLANDS BILL DRAWN

ST. THOMAS, Virgin Islands, Nov. 9 (By U. P.)—The American Congress will be asked to pass a new and permanent organic act for the Virgin Islands when it convenes in December. The proposed act is now being drafted by Mr. Lawrence W. Cramer, Lieutenant-Governor of St. Croix. Gov. Paul M. Pearson is expected to go to Washington next month to urge passage of legislation on behalf of the Virgin Islands.

JAPAN PLEASED OVER VICTORY OF DEMOCRATS

Partial Repudiation of Stimson Policies in Orient Expected

By Radio to The Christian Science Monitor

TOKYO, Nov. 9—The prices of securities and commodities advanced sharply here at the morning session of the stock exchanges, largely due to the Democratic victory in the United States which traders interpreted bullishly, believing it means a weaker American policy in the Orient and partial repudiation of the doctrines of the Republican Secretary of State, Mr. Henry L. Stimson.

The silk market at Yokohama also advanced, gaining six yen a bale. All prices eased in the late afternoon under profit taking.

Officials of the stock exchange said a Democratic victory was most likely to improve Japanese-American commercial as well as diplomatic and general relations, because the Democrats were pledged to lower tariffs and greater and more general international cooperation.

The Nichi Nichi editorially says: "Viewed from the standpoints of foreign policy, also of international economic policy, the Roosevelt Administration is certain to be more liberal and realistic than that of President Hoover. . . . We firmly believe the Roosevelt victory will improve Japanese-American relations on all fronts. Relations have been needlessly strained under President Hoover. The cause of the strain has now been removed."

It is understood here that the American Ambassador, Mr. Joseph C. Grew, may tender his resignation as a matter of form, but it is expected that he will continue his ambassadorship since Gov. Franklin D. Roosevelt is reported to favor the continuation of career diplomats in their present posts. It is understood that Mr. Nelson T. Johnson will also continue as Minister to China.

The press issued frequent election extras. The Asahi announced that Mr. Roosevelt had been elected at 10 a. m., Tokyo time, obviously a case of intelligent anticipation, since President Hoover's admission that he had been defeated only reached Tokyo at 3 p. m.

THE MONITOR INDEX

THINGS PRESENT

Should college players be paid? Many persons profess to see little difference between paying athletes a salary and the dodge of providing a hundred and one little ways for them to make money on the side. An editorial sums up the arguments.

Note to the thrifty housewife: Have you looked into the possibilities of turning that knitted jacket or skirt? See the Women's Enterprises and Fashions page.

The Spaniard who is studying English, or the Englishman who is studying Spanish, will find parallel translations on the Home Forum page which will help him in his studies.

If you have time for only one thing on the Daily Features page, let that one thing be "Courage" in For the Scrapbook.

AND THINGS TO COME

Reports of the International Goodwill Congress start tomorrow.

Thursday, of course, is a big day with the youngsters. Look for the Young Folks' page.

Friday brings "The World Court Month by Month." This summary appears monthly (usually on the eleventh day).

Bulgarian Joke Proves Identity And Court Acquits

Special to The Christian Science Monitor

SOFIA, Bulgaria—Humor has been put on trial before the Sofia district court and acquitted. A former Bulgarian Minister of Justice, Dr. Kuncho Milanoff, brought suit against Mr. Raeko Alexieff, one of the most distinguished and popular Bulgarian caricaturists and humorists, because of many jokes which Alexieff made at the minister's expense.

The court, however, accepted the point of view of the humorist who declared that he put no malice into his caricatures and that his jokes were free from evil intentions. So the case was dismissed.

Although a rather stringent press law exists in Bulgaria, caricaturists here are allowed almost unbounded freedom and fill the daily press with ludicrous pictures of prominent persons without causing any offense. Mr. Alexieff, in fact, is an intimate and highly esteemed friend of most of the persons whom he most frequently caricatures.

The most talented caricaturists in the Balkans are found in Bucharest, whose 15 daily papers carry many of the most brilliant articles appearing in southeast Europe. A great majority of the leading Bulgarian caricaturists are "left wingers," a number of them being Communists.

WESTERN AUSTRALIA'S CROPS

Special to The Christian Science Monitor

PERTH, W. Aust.—Official statistical estimates disclosed that 3,548,000 acres of land have been sown with wheat this year, being an increase of 160,000 on last season. The yield of 1931-32 was 41,360,000 bushels, giving an average of a little over 13 bushels of wheat to the acre.

HOOVER OFFERS HIS SUPPORT TO GOV. ROOSEVELT

Receives News of Defeat Surrounded by Neighbors and Friends

By ERWIN D. CANHAM

Staff Correspondent of The Christian Science Monitor

PALO ALTO, Calif., Nov. 9—Herbert Clark Hoover, defeated for reelection to the Presidency of the United States, early today congratulated his victorious opponent, Gov. Franklin D. Roosevelt, for his "opportunity for service," dedicated himself to "every possible helpful effort," and prepared to take up the serious task that awaits him at Washington before his job ends officially March 4, next.

Today he made his plans to return to Washington at the end of this week by the Santa Fe route. He is taking four days of rest at his home, in preparation for a strenuous period with Congress before March 4.

The President is taking his defeat with complete philosophic calm, indeed his whole attitude when correspondents chatted with him today seemed to be one of relief. He plans to leave Washington as soon as President-elect Roosevelt is inaugurated, and will retire to California.

(Continued on Page 3, Column 1)

Career of Present Roosevelt Similar to That of Theodore

Both Harvard Men, Each of Them Entered Field of New York Politics, Was Governor of State and Assistant Secretary of Navy

Special from The Christian Science Monitor Bureau

NEW YORK, Nov. 9—The election of Franklin Delano Roosevelt as the thirty-first President brings the third Democrat to that high office since James Buchanan made way for Abraham Lincoln. Mr. Roosevelt's party predecessors — Grover Cleveland and Woodrow Wilson—are both written big in the nation's history, and, were these Roman times, today's circumstance no doubt would see a turning to the oracle for a prophecy.

Like Cleveland and Wilson, Mr. Roosevelt's Presidency is coincident with a great national emergency, and no sign is lacking that he, too, will make history, for, besides a world in turmoil, reasons for this spring from the man himself. He is ambitious, and the mark of his fifth cousin, Theodore Roosevelt, who went to the White House at the turn of the century, has been on every one of the 22 political years of this Roosevelt of "the other branch of the family."

He, too, like Theodore Roosevelt, entered politics through the New York Legislature, became Assistant Secretary of the Navy and was nominated for the Vice-Presidency when he was 38—four years younger than Theodore when the latter was nominated on the McKinley ticket in 1900.

Again as did Theodore, he attains the Presidency, a graduate in the fullest sense of one of the hardest schools of politics in a country of political complexities—the New York Governorship.

If the casual eye sees a phenomenon in his political rise, marveling

Continued on Page 2, Column 3)

New York Breaks State Record Of The Republicans

Special from Monitor Bureau

NEW YORK, Nov. 9—New York State, its traditional Republicanism in presidential politics cast aside like an outworn garment, today heads the list of smashed precedents in the national political shake-up, its 47 electoral votes swept into the Democratic column by a more than 500,000 plurality—the first time in 40 years that the Empire State has gone to the Democratic presidential candidate.

Gov. Franklin D. Roosevelt and Speaker John N. Garner, the Democratic candidates for President and Vice-President, have piled up a 622,000 lead over the Republican national ticket and swept into office the other Democratic candidates, on the state-wide ticket, returns indicate.

Lieut.-Gov. Herbert H. Lehman won the New York governorship over Col. William J. Donovan, Republican, by a plurality estimated at 904,832, with 392 up-state election districts unreported. Senator Robert F. Wagner overwhelmed United States Attorney George Z. Medalie, Republican, for reëlection with a plurality estimated at 875,000.

In New York City Tammany Hall felt the strong wave of protest when its mayoralty candidate, Surrogate John P. O'Brien trailed the Democratic ticket with Acting Mayor Joseph V. McKee, whom the Wigwam had turned down, the "write in" choice of thousands. While the down-state machine helped roll up a lead of more than 800,000 for Governor Roosevelt in the city, however, far better than it did four years ago for its own brave, Alfred E. Smith, who lost the State to President Hoover by more than 100,000

War Debts and Manchurian Situation Lead in Issues to Face Democrats

WASHINGTON, Nov. 9 (AP)—War debts, disarmament and the new-born state of Manchukuo are three international subjects of pressing importance with which the new Administration will have to deal after March 4.

Other international questions upon which the policy of the incoming Administration must be decided are:

Shall Soviet Russia be recognized?

Shall the United States join the World Court?

Shall the present policy of Haitienization be pursued in Haiti?

Shall the United States continue its coöperation with the League of Nations in rehabilitating Liberia?

Shall El Salvador be recognized?

Shall the United States continue in its joint efforts with neutral Latin-American countries to settle the Chaco dispute?

Shall the United States take any steps in Cuba under the Platt amendment to prevent anarchy?

Shall the St. Lawrence seaway treaty be ratified?

Shall independence be granted to the Philippines?

War debts and disarmament agreements involve tariff policy and the various plans suggested for restoring economic and financial conditions the world around through international coöperation.

European debtors of the United States say they can meet their obligations only in manufactured goods and they complain that tariff barriers prevent this.

The Democratic platform declares against cancellation of foreign war debts and Congress is strongly on record against cancellataion.

The Manchukuo policy is in a stalemate, pending action of the League of Nations on the Lytton report on the Manchurian situation.

Efforts during the campaign to get Governor Roosevelt to announce his attitude toward Soviet Russia were unsuccessful.

THE CHRISTIAN SCIENCE MONITOR

AN INTERNATIONAL DAILY NEWSPAPER

BOSTON, MONDAY, OCTOBER 16, 1933—VOL. XXV, NO. 273

• ATLANTIC EDITION—FIVE CENTS A COPY

COPYRIGHT 1933 BY THE CHRISTIAN SCIENCE PUBLISHING SOCIETY

The March of the Nations

By Rufus Steele

Arms Parley Goes on in Week

Surprised Nations Keep Cool

Germany's Act Revises Means

Shut U. S. Banks Pay Billion

Mexico's Army Is Gold Braid

Palestine Arabs Protest Jews

THE nations, recovering from surprise at Germany's withdrawal from the Disarmament Conference and the League, look cautiously to the future. They find the situation serious, but containing no hint of any immediate conflict. The Disarmament Conference is postponed for one week, after two long Sunday sessions by delegates of four powers. Arthur Henderson, president, declares the struggle for disarmament must go on and that the Covenant of the League shall not be treated as a scrap of paper The weakened condition of the League, with only three of the six great powers left in it, is recognized, but it is regarded as still effective. "Nail your flag to the mast of the League," Henderson cries amid applause—"The reign of law must triumph over international anarchy that breeds war."

¶ France maintains Germany must not be allowed to rearm and holds the Versailles Treaty unimpaired. France is not unfavorably impressed by Chancellor Hitler's implied bid for direct negotiations on arms. Britain insists the demand for disarmament and no rearmament has been strengthened by Germany's walkout; the other powers could reach an agreement and offer it as the last word to Berlin. Norman H. Davis, voicing President Roosevelt and Secretary of State Hull, declares every effort must go on to solve the vital armament problem. Czechoslovakia says the League and the conference can and must function without Germany. Japan, gratified, feels the Russo-Japanese tension may be lessened. Austria gives a mixed expression—It opposes Hitler, but it is pleased to see a defeated nation strike back.

¶ World observers begin to construe Germany's sudden act. They see the Reich's recent huge mass demonstrations as succeeding fully in their purpose of inflating the national spirit. In such an hour Chancellor Hitler could consolidate public sentiment by playing upon the obvious fact that the allied powers have not kept faith under the Versailles Treaty and reduced their own armaments as agreed. The Berlin press declares France or Britain has had no intention of disarming; the same papers praise Hitler for having blown away the fog of refined hostile diplomacy that was deep over Germany. The German act throws into the melting pot many plans and perhaps the whole machinery for solving disputes—Will new and clarified methods for settling world questions which must be settled now emerge?

¶ America's closed banks prepare to yield $1,000,000,000 to needy depositors in the next few weeks under beneficent thawing by the R. F. C. President Roosevelt announces the setting up of the Deposit Liquidation Board, headed by Carroll Burnham Merriam of Topeka, Kas., for the purpose of advancing cash up to 50 per cent of sound but frozen deposits. This applies to banks which have closed during the current year. The scheme supersedes slower methods which had been planned—Holiday spending will be rosier by a billion than it had expected to be.

¶ Mexico City is set to wondering by a report from the War Department on the army. The official figures show a total of 49,731 enlisted men and 21,750 lieutenants. This is almost one lieutenant for every two high privates. The number of generals is given as 398. If, as seems, disarmament is beginning, it is in the ranks, and that is not a bad sign—No army that is wholly gold braid will greatly disturb the peace of the world.

¶ Virginia bids formal good-by to its favorite son, Admiral Richard E. Byrd as his two ships prepare to sail for the antarctic. Coming into the Norfolk hall by radio, American officials and Admiral Sir William Goodenough of London, president of the British Geographical Society, voice their good wishes. A European as well as an American audience listens in to impressive speeches and music. Soon the frozen South will swallow up Byrd and his brave band for two years—But every day this same wonderful radio will keep them and the world in close touch with each other.

¶ Jerusalem and other cities in Palestine are torn with Arab outbursts against the influx of Jewish refugees from Germany. The police charge a crowd of 2000 at the New Gate of the ancient capital and both rioters and policemen are injured. A similar parade and protest is planned for Jaffa on Oct. 27. The Arabs, who greatly outnumber the Jewish population, naïvely refer to the Jewish people as newcomers and interlopers. The Children of Israel have been in Palestine several thousand years, but the Arabs brush aside that impressive fact—Arabs have been there much longer, airily they claim.

Himalayan Clouds and Snow-Clad Peaks From an Aviator's Window

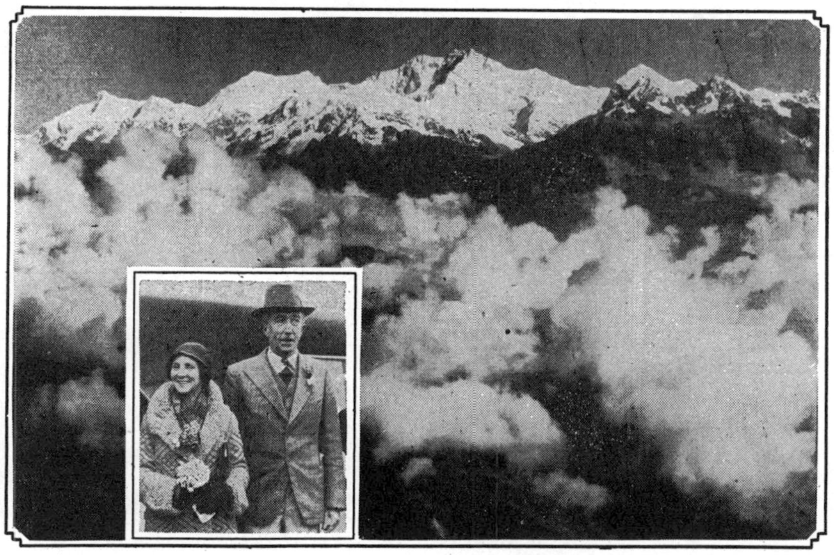

THE CHRISTIAN SCIENCE MONITOR—Publishers' Photo Service. Inset—© Keystone

Inset—Leader of the Houston-Mt. Everest Flying Expedition, Air Commodore P. F. M. Fellowes, and Mrs. Fellowes

Librarians Expect More Book Call In Increased Leisure

American Association Opens Fifty-Fifth Annual Convention

Special from Monitor Bureau

CHICAGO, Oct. 16 — Convinced that the library is becoming more and more an educational center for communities and less a "cemetery of books," and preparing for still greater demands which increased leisure is expected to make up on it, the American Library Association opened its fifty-fifth annual meeting here today.

Concurrently, librarians from some 15 lands, composing the Committee of the International Federation of Library Associations, are holding their first meeting on American soil here. The presence of this distinguished international group is of great value to American librarians, said Mr. Harry Miller Lydenberg, of New York, president of the American Library Association.

"It fills us with humility and gratitude to see what these men are doing," Mr. Lydenberg said. The emphasis in Europe and the Orient is upon the library as a handmaiden of productive scholarship and research, but some countries like Denmark, Holland, Russia and England have also done much in developing libraries as an instrument for the diffusion of popular education."

That the people's library is growing in many parts of the earth is indicated in a volume published for this conference by the American Library Association, called "Popular Libraries of the World." Reports contributed by librarians in nearly 50 countries, from Argentina to the Virgin Islands, show democratic trends in library development or at least democratic aspirations.

Poland, for example, has had libraries since the eleventh century, five of its existing libraries dating

(Continued on Page 7, Column 3)

Everest Leader Tells Story Of Splendid 'Insubordination'

His Pilots Made Second Flight Over the Top Against British Orders, Interpreting Clouds as Flat Spaces Allowed to Be Rephotographed

Special from The Christian Science Monitor Bureau

NEW YORK, Oct. 16—The "inside story" of the second flight made by the Houston Expedition which conquered Mt. Everest, the world's highest peak, was told by Air Commodore P. F. M. Fellowes, leader of the expedition, in an exclusive interview with a correspondent of The Christian Science Monitor here. This flight not only has astonished the world, but was made in complete disregard of orders from England. It has been described as "a piece of magnificent insubordination."

"The photographs taken on the first flight over Everest were disappointing because the dust haze went up much higher than we had expected and interfered with visibility," Commodore Fellowes said. "This dust haze went up to 19,000 feet, while we had not expected to find it higher than a few thousand feet.

Photographs Are Object

"Since photographs were one of the chief objects of the expedition, it was important we should try again. The Nepalese, who had refused to give us permission to make more than one flight, satisfied that the first one had been well organized and carried out, agreed to let us make a second. But we had hardly won their consent when orders came from England that no more flights over Everest were to be attempted.

"When the weather cleared after 10 days of thunder and gales, the pilots were eager to try the conquest of Everest again. I said, 'I cannot give directions contrary to orders from home. But I will give you permission to fly into the mountains as long as you remain within flying distance of flat spots which would make possible landing places.'

"I gave them to understand that they might consider any place as a landing spot that looked anyways like one. They took the tops of the clouds as flat spaces and flew the entire way over the summit."

On the flight over Mt. Kunchinjunga, a neighbor of Mt. Everest and one of the last Himalayan heights to be conquered, Commodore Fellowes said he found the wind disturbances near the summit much greater than he had expected. Kunchinjunga, which is a vast field of sharp-toothed peaks, is a much more stupendous sight from the air than Mt. Everest, he said.

On the Nepal-Tibet Border

Mt. Everest, whose summit men saw for the first time in the history of the world when two of the expedition's airplanes, with the Marquis of Clydesdale as chief pilot, flew over it on April 3, 1933, clearing its ice-bound heights by a mere 100 feet, is on the borders of Nepal and Tibet.

The explorers could not get permission to fly over Tibet, and were allowed to fly over Nepal only on one definitely charted course which they were obliged to follow closely both going and returning, Commodore Fellowes said.

The reason for that was that the Nepalese do not want any encroachments of western civilization into their territory, he explained, and they were unwilling to run the risk of having to admit a rescue expedition from outside should the Houston expedition's airplanes crash in Nepal.

India Affords Contrasts

Commodore Fellowes, who arrived here recently on a lecture tour, accompanied by Mrs. Fellowes, expects that his next undertaking will be to develop aviation among native Indian princes. He is enthusiastic about the future of aviation in India, where excellent visibility, vast distances to be traversed and magnificent scenery encourage travel by air.

A dramatic contrast of modern and ancient methods of transportation in India occurred while the Houston expedition, which Commodore Fellowes headed, was there last spring. The Maharajah of Nepal, with a procession of richly caparisoned elephants, came to welcome the British air men, who had flown all the way from England, and to whom he had granted permission to fly over his territory on condition that their work would serve a definitely scientific purpose.

Mrs. Fellowes is also an aviation enthusiast and flew with Commodore Fellowes on the trip from England to India, about 1000 miles of which was through dust storms in Egypt and Arabia.

Tufts Houses New School Of World Affairs

Roscoe Pound, Denys P. Myers and Others Direct Advanced Study

By a Staff Correspondent of The Christian Science Monitor

MEDFORD, Mass., Oct. 16—An antiquated gymnasium at Tufts College has been transformed into what promises to be a training ground for future world-famous diplomats.

"Goddard Gym" the students for years have called the little brick building half-way up College Hill. Now it is "Goddard Hall." Within its walls has been started a unique educational venture of world-wide significance. Its interior is much changed. The old basketball court now is an imposing auditorium. Book shelves and tables fill the rooms that once held showers and lockers. Rooms for physical exercising now contain facilities for mental gymnastics.

These changes in Tufts' traditional landmark are the result of a unique agreement between two colleges and a world peace organization sending the "Fletcher School of International Law and Diplomacy" down the ways on Oct. 2 with a representative list of 21 students from a dozen states and 19 institutions.

Includes Superb Library

Tufts College provides the location and the funds, Harvard University offers a large part of the faculty, and the World Peace Foundation contributes its superb Beacon Hill library of international knowledge, said to be the finish collection of its kind in the United States.

Along with the library goes the services of the Foundation's research director, Mr. Denys P. Myers, who will be Research Librarian.

Thanks to the foresight of two men—one an educator, the other a philanthropist—Tufts will become a focal point for the study of international relations. When the late Austin B. Fletcher, Tufts alumnus, gave $1,000,000 to the college just 10 years ago, he specified it should go toward a new school of law. As early as 1924 Prof. Halford L. Hoskins broached the idea of an international school of law and drew up a prospective curriculum. President John A. Cousens of Tufts agreed with him that a law school of the orthodox type was not needed in Massachusetts, that the great demand was for something more far-reaching.

Students Carefully Selected

The Fletcher trust fund having grown to nearly $1,500,000 this year, the time was deemed opportune for starting the school. Professor Hoskins was appointed dean.

Only proved talent is acceptable. From 100 applicants for admission, only 22 were accepted on their past records. It is the dean's wish that the enrollment at no time shall exceed 50 students.

"The success of the institution," he declared, "depends to a large extent upon individual instruction. To invite an unlimited number of students would defeat this purpose."

Several students already have their masters' degrees. With the prospective expansion of the curriculum next year, the dean said, the school would offer the degree of Doctor of Philosophy. Tuition is $300. The school will be administered by Harvard and Tufts jointly, and the Fletcher fund by the Tufts College trustees. Dean Roscoe Pound of Harvard Law School is one of a group of 10 charter faculty members.

The three-cornered agreement also solves the problem of how to expand the usefulness of a library that has more information to distribute than the public can consume. In its new location, it will have three outlets. First, it will be the center of Fletcher School information. Second, its services will still be available to the public. And finally, by some agreement, it is hoped to make it useful for the regular students of both Tufts and Harvard.

Young Readers Turn Skeptics In Scanning Daily Newspapers

Special from The Christian Science Monitor Bureau

CHICAGO, Oct. 16—A new type of newspaper reader is being developed in the United States.

It is a discriminating reader, one who knows the good from the bad, who can detect misleading propaganda and discount it; one who may not be fooled simply because he "saw it in the papers."

Once a year the nation has a chance to see its new reading public in action, as it did here last week, but usually it doesn't pay much attention. It is composed of such a lot of youngsters—many boys who look as if they were still new to long trousers, many girls whose pigtails are not long forgotten.

Nevertheless the conventions of the National Scholastic Press Association advertise a great new trend in newspaperdom. They signify that probably 40,000 high school students are studying the press as part of their regular school work. Each year a new crop comes on.

Some 1500 high schools, it is estimated, are teaching journalism. It is a new movement. It didn't begin its national expansion until 1920. Today there are so many journalism teachers in the high schools that they have their own national organization. Its membership now runs between 500 and 600, and normally should be twice or thrice that.

Now for the results, as reported by one of the teacher leaders here Saturday:

"A bit of movie propaganda was spotted by one of my students recently. The class stopped to consider it. We decided that movie stars should not be put upon pedestals and everything they do copied by the young folks. That was exactly what movie managers wanted to have happen, it was agreed. Why do it?

"When boys and girls come into my classes in their third year in high school, usually all they have regularly read in the newspapers is the comics. Some occasional boys have read sports, and a few have read murders.

"Then we start to study what a newspaper is, its history, its aims, what it is made of, and how it is made. The children go home and often nearly break up the family routine. They want to read the newspaper first."

"A speaker from the world's fair told us the other evening that the exposition had been built for adults. But it had been found, he said, that the children many times knew more about the exhibits and explained them to their parents. I think it is working out the same way with the newspapers.

"Thousands of children are being trained every year into the intelligent reading of the daily paper. Many of them are passing on their newspaper knowledge to their parents."

This working convention of youthful editors and writers from high school papers acted in the judgment of observers as if journalism was no frill. The general sessions brought nearly a thousand together and round tables were crowded to the door.

The Monitor Index

Monday, Oct. 16, 1933

Things Present

There is a timely and important protest in the editorial "No Devil's Island."

Today marks the last Monday appearance of the Casual Day. But take heart from the announcement you will find about halfway down. Editorial page.

Waddles is back on the Children's page.

You need read no more than the first two lines of "Over-Night Camp" to agree that words have power. Home Forum page.

The inside back page offers more Hymnal Notes, another article in the State Flower series, and another interesting typewriter drawing.

And Things to Come

Tuesday brings the Progress in Education page, Home Building and Gardening page, more Vocations, and another Junior Cross-Word. Are these latter too easy?

Arms Conference Postponed, Due to Break by Reich; Hitler Rejects Inferiority

German People Believed United in Support of Chancellor's Appeal

Seeks Equal Status

Plebiscite of Nov. 12 Held Likely to Find Solid Vote for Hitler

By Press Wireless from Monitor Bureau

BERLIN, Oct. 16—Germany's decision to retire from the Disarmament Conference and the League of Nations is presented to the world both as an appeal to the moral forces which support disarmament and a justification of the Reich's own attiude.

Refusal to yield any more to conditions laid down by the "spirit of Versailles" finds strongest support among all sections of the population, whatever their views about National Socialism. Herr Hitler, by basing his radio broadcast appeal on Germany's humiliation and refusal to now continue as an inferior nation has united all Germans on the régime's foreign policy. Thus there appears but one answer to the question prescribed for the Nov. 12 plebiscite, namely, do the German people agree with its Government's foreign policy, and is it ready of its own free will to declare and acknowledge this as an expression of its own position.

Humiliation and degradation are used as the main basis of appeal, and they pervade the whole speech of Herr Hitler. In replying to the question of M. Edouard Daladier, French Premier, at Vichy, why Germany demands arms which must later be abandoned, Herr Hitler declares that the German people always demanded "not arms, but equal status."

The German Government entered the League of Nations hoping to find therein a forum for just compromise in the interests of all nations, for genuine conciliation with its former opponents. But the primary condition for this, it is declared, must be recognition of Germany's reinstatement as a nation of equal status. It was under this condition that Germany entered the Disarmament Conference. "Degradation to the position of an inferior member in such an institution of conference is for an honor-loving nation of 65,000,000 people, and a no less honor-loving government, an unendurable humiliation," the declaration said.

Germany feels itself fighting with moral righteousness against the world on a problem which cannot be settled in any other way than by recognition of its claim to fair play. The German middle class, who comprise the main portion of the National Socialist movement, are absolutely behind Herr Hitler in this matter.

In this country, with its government-controlled press, public opinion can know largely only what the Government wants it to know, and regarding foreign recognition, it feels, is likely to serve to weld moderate opinion to National Socialism as its defender.

Germany's conviction that it alone of all powers has fulfilled its duties in disarmament, together with the Reich's present military unpreparedness, are facts underlying every reference to this subject. For not only does Herr Hitler repudiate any responsibility for the last war on Germany's part, but contends that "never has a defeated nation so honorably endeavored to coöperate with its enemies in the healing of wounds as have the German people in the long years of dictatorship imposed upon it."

Misgivings Abroad

Herr Hitler appealed to France declaring that Germany desires peace and understanding with its neighbors. Acting on the assumption that the Saar territory will be returned to Germany, he then adds: "Only a madman could think of war between both states, for which we see no moral or reasonable grounds."

Comment cannot be omitted here that it is unfortunate for Germany that just when Anglo-Saxons are reading these words, they will also

(Continued on Page 4, Column 2)

Adamant

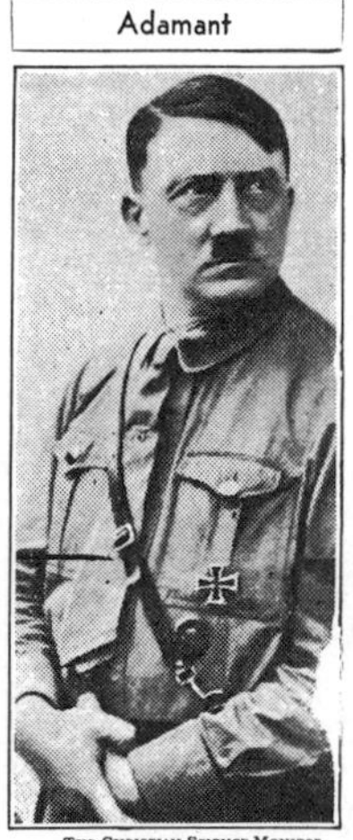

THE CHRISTIAN SCIENCE MONITOR

Chancellor Hitler

Washington Holds Air of Precaution In European Upset

Ready to Talk Disarmament, but Not Old World Politics

Special from Monitor Bureau

WASHINGTON, Oct. 16—Outwardly, and with some slight show of ostentation, the American Government today withdrew from the warm support of Britain and France it had evinced when the European crisis exploded on Oct. 14, and took up a position of extreme caution. The general Administration attitude is:

"We went to Geneva purely for disarmament reasons. We are not there for European political discussions. When the disarmament talks poach too extensively on the political field, we shall withdraw."

Mr. William Phillips, Undersecretary of State, acted as spokesman for the Government today instead of Mr. Cordell Hull, Secretary of State, who on Saturday frankly lined the nation up solidly behind France and Germany. From today's statements, hints, and impressions at the State Department, a definite withdrawal from the continental turmoil is to be seen.

Attitude Is Strategic

This new attitude of reserve matches the "keep calm," and "wait and see" postures adopted in chief European capitals. It is strategic. The United States is, of course, deeply concerned in European peace or war, and the State Department is following the proceedings at Geneva, Berlin, Paris, and London with utmost concern. But it does not wish to alarm the American public, which to a man is anxious to avoid involvements in future hostilities.

Hence Mr. Phillips told the nation, at the State Department press conference, that the United States Government is interested in disarmament alone. He did not deny, on direct questioning, that disarmament and continental politics are now inextricably intertwined. But he carefully disassociated the United States from purely political complications.

The State Department spokesman, however, did remind his questioners that European governments are keeping very quiet about the crisis, and in effect disclosed that the great powers are imposing a compact of silence upon official comment so

(Continued on Page 4, Column 5)

More Time Needed to Examine Situation After Walkout

League Feels Brunt

Geneva Questions Merit of Berlin's Assertions of Pacific Intentions

By Press Wireless from Monitor Bureau

GENEVA, Oct. 16—The Disarmament Conference which was to resume work today after a four months' interval has adjourned to Oct. 26 as the result of Germany's leaving both conference and the League of Nations.

The adjournment decision was reached after two long private meetings of representatives of the four major powers was held yesterday under the chairmanship of Mr. Arthur Henderson.

Germany's action establishes an entirely new situation which renders imperative changes in disarmament procedure from that which had already been agreed upon. There has not been any question of adjourning the Disarmament Conference indefinitely or even for a long period.

Determination of the United States, Great Britain and France to go ahead on lines traced by Sir John Simon, British Foreign Secretary, in his report to the bureau last Saturday has not been diminished in any way by Germany's blunt walkout. At the same time, however, it is recognized that the governments concerned need time to examine the new situation. It is believed that an adjournment of one to two weeks will be sufficient.

Convention to be Framed

For the moment the idea seems to be to intensify disarmament efforts so as to reach agreement on a convention to be signed by the largest possible number of states and leave it open for eventual acceptance or rejection by Germany. Certainly no attempt will be made to induce the German Government to resume its place at Geneva, but the conference will go ahead just as it did last year when Germany also abandoned it.

The League of Nations is still under the shock of the heavy blow. That Germany would abandon the Disarmament Conference is not altogether surprising in view of the stubborn, insistence for acknowledgement of its claims of equality. But that it would also withdraw from the League is indeed incomprehensible, and its breaking from the only international peace machinery in existence forecasts, indeed, the most grave case against its declared pacific intentions.

One of the first results of Germany's cessation said here is that it has virtually killed the four-power pact which was to operate strictly within the framework of the League. It is extremely doubtful whether the French Government in view of the changed circumstances will care to ratify the pact which was to insure 10 years of peace in Europe. How Germany can collaborate with other powers in the maintenance of general peace after it has turned its back upon Geneva is most difficult to say and for this reason that part of Chancellor Adolf Hitler's speech broadcast Saturday night in which he laid stress on Germany's pacific intention is considered to be in open contradiction to his actions.

Views by Henderson and Cecil

No nation, however just its cause, can be considered loyal to the cause of peace if it refuses to participate in the world's peace machinery.

This verdict of Mr. Henderson directly applying to the German situation was given this morning when he received the resolution adopted at a mass meeting of international peace organizations held here yesterday.

The resolution urged adoption of a convention providing for the equality and security of all nations. It specifically urged the abolition within a specific period of aggressive weapons, including air weapons, substantial reduction of armaments and limitation of expenditure, permanent organization to exercise strict supervision and preparation for further disarmament.

It was not true that the conference has been destroyed by Germany's action, Viscount Cecil told the gathering. The conference must continue in spite of Germany's effort to prevent international disarmament. He suggested that the obstacles to disarmament are chauvinism and fear. Chauvinism makes demands which from disarmament point of view are completely inadmissable. It glorifies armaments and war and adds direct negative to all proposals for international disarmament.

Recklessness Increases Anxiety

"The flaming propaganda and reckless policy of which we have just had such a striking example has increased anxiety in Europe," he said. The policy which Lord Cecil recommends is, first, the absolute necessity of conclusion of a disarmament treaty. Second, proper international machinery through permanent disarmament commission to control and supervise execution of the treaty. If clearly proved that any country has failed to perform its duties under the Covenant, then economic sanctions similar, for example, to those adopted by Great Britain in the recent dispute with Soviet Russia after the arrest of British

(Continued on Page 4, Column 4)

Reich Rests Case on Treaty

GERMANY'S declaration of withdrawal from the arms conference and the League is a reply to Geneva's latest compromise on arms proposed by Britain.

The plan, following closely the French plan of Oct. 9, provides for a four-year trial period, during which European armies would be put on a militia basis under control of a special commission.

After that, another four-year period would gradually reduce armaments of the former allied powers, finally allowing Germany complete equality.

This proposal was intended to accord with the preamble to the Versailles arms clauses, which said: "In order to render possible the initiation of a general limitation of armaments of all nations, Germany undertakes strictly to observe the military, naval and air clauses. . . ."

Germany strongly objected to Geneva's offer, because, despite the technical equality allowed it by the powers last fall, the proposal now left Germany unable to rearm or to have "prototypes" of all armaments possessed by the other powers, including the tanks, airplanes and submarines forbidden to Germany. Berlin further objected to the four-year trial, and demanded equality of naval rights with the other great powers.

Although Germany announces withdrawal from the great peace efforts, it is still bound by provisions of the Locarno pacts and the Kellogg pact, while its association with the League Covenant cannot be severed till the two-year period of notice has elapsed.

THE CHRISTIAN SCIENCE MONITOR

AN INTERNATIONAL DAILY NEWSPAPER

BOSTON, WEDNESDAY, DECEMBER 6, 1933—VOL. XXVI, NO. 9

**ATLANTIC EDITION—FIVE CENTS A COPY

COPYRIGHT 1933 BY THE CHRISTIAN SCIENCE PUBLISHING SOCIETY

The March of the Nations

By Rufus Steele

RFC Enters New York Banks

Italy Makes League Demands

President Appeals on Liquor

Lindberghs Fly the Atlantic

U. S. Wheat Acres Do Not Fall

Americans Meet Odd Delusion

THE Washington Administration makes another effort to loosen money in the banks and pour it over the wheels of industry and business. To this end the RFC arranges with 12 big New York banks to buy more than $90,000,000 in preferred stock or notes from them, thus filling up their reservoirs of ready capital. Previously about $400,000,000 of RFC funds had been sent to banks all over the country to stimulate purchasing of goods and granting of credit. Before the operation is complete, the RFC expects to put out $1,000,000,000 in this effort at credit inflation—The Government takes a step toward the biggest banks in the seeming socialization of banking.

¶ Italy lets it be known that its continuance in the League of Nations hinges upon the League's drastic reform of itself. Premier Mussolini wants the League separated from the Versailles Treaty, not enforcing the will of the conquerors on the conquered. Power must be given mainly to those nations which will carry the responsibility, little nations having less to say. Mussolini wants all the great powers as members—Doubling the Four-Power Pact would about fit the plan he is going to push.

¶ Utah's enforcing ratification of the prohibition repeal amendment is followed by a presidential proclamation and warning. President Roosevelt repeals four special taxes yielding $212,000,000 a year, and appeals to the people to exercise temperance with license. He wants respect for law, protection of dry states, banishment of bootleggers. He strikes at the old liquor conditions—A return to them would be "a living reproach to us all."

¶ Natal, Brazil, welcomes Col. and Mrs. Charles A. Lindbergh as they land after an 1870-mile hop from Bathurst in British West Africa. Their powerful seaplane crosses the south Atlantic at from 110 to 125 miles an hour. Mrs. Lindbergh, proving herself an expert wireless operator, keeps in touch with South American stations. Many other modern instruments besides radio are on Lindbergh's plane and were unheard-of when he first startled the world in 1927—And with these new aids he simply goes on startling the willing world.

¶ Will the United States' spending of $100,000,000 to curtail its wheat crop prove all in vain? Nat C. Murray, noted Chicago crop statistician, finds practically the same acreage sown to wheat as a year ago. The thousands of farmers now receiving bonus checks are faithfully withholding the plow, but the money offer has stimulated farmers in hitherto wheatless sections to turn to wheat. One hope of securing the 15 per cent reduction remains. Wheat crop variation is said to depend 70 per cent on yield and only 30 per cent on acreage—So a generous Government may now have to hope for a poor yield.

¶ Montevideo and 200 dignified statesmen suffer a terrific shock to their dignity. Secretary of State Hull, nine Foreign Ministers and all the delegates to the Pan-American Conference wait in a marble corridor an hour and a half for Carlos Yereguy, Chief of Protocal, to arrive with the place cards for the banquet given by President Terra of Uruguay. Without the cards the all-important matter of proper precedence cannot be settled. Señor Yereguy bursts in at last; he had been kidnaped by laughing Communists—But there is little laughter among warm delegates who sit down to a cold dinner.

¶ Austria is amazed to see the Roman Catholic bishops require their clergy to withdraw from all political activity. In a country where priests hold many offices this order upheaves the entire political system. Premier Engelbert Dollfuss is not believed to be losing the church support, but the church is apparently thinking of its own future. In Italy and Germany it mixed deep in politics and in the changes has suffered in both countries—Change looms in Austria, the church of Rome uses wisdom.

¶ In countless American cities and towns certain citizens wake up in an unhappy state of remembrance. They embraced prohibition repeal fervently for the boundless new joy it was to pour into human existence, but on the morning after they hold only a heavy and heated head. Something seems wrong. Somewhere all the joy has jarred out. But of course there must be some big compensation for a fellow in the cold gray of the subsequent morning. And by and by, if the bright fellow be a philosopher and persistent, he will realize what his cordial compensation is—He has a legal alcoholic headache to reward his years of yearning.

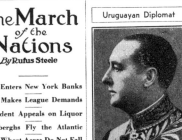

Uruguayan Diplomat

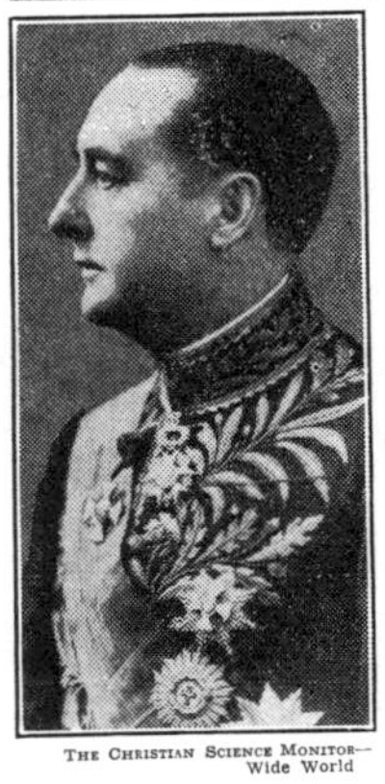

THE CHRISTIAN SCIENCE MONITOR—Wide World

Enrique E. Bucero

Temporary Secretary-General of Pan-American Conference.

Chaco Dispute Kept on Agenda At Montevideo

Friendly Peace Note to Bolivia and Paraguay Under Consideration

MONTEVIDEO, Dec. 6 (AP)—The Chaco war was kept on the agenda of the Pan-American Conference today, despite an effort in the peace committee to suppress a discussion of the struggle.

Chile, with the support of Salvador, Uruguay, Nicaragua and the Dominican Republic, kept the matter before the 21 nations in face of the opposition of Peru and Argentina.

A subcommittee was named to study the advisability of sending a joint friendly peace plea to the belligerents, Bolivia and Paraguay.

Consideration of war in general was given by the conference in naming a subcommittee to study prevention of war and conciliation and the Pan-American declaration of 1932 against recognition of conquered territory.

A study of the Argentine antiwar treaty was turned over to another subcommittee.

Peruvian delegates desired to suppress virtually the whole peace agenda, to clear the way for economic discussions, but Dr. Miguel Cruchaga of Chile, chairman of the committee on peace, who desires the conference to act in some manner on the Chaco strugle, appointed the subcommittees.

He did so only after sympathizers with his objective suggested that the subcommittee not be empowered to act of the Chaco question without consent of the steering committee.

Dr. Cruchaga proposed that any peace message should be couched in the most amicable terms, assuring the warring sides that the conference action merely enabled them to indicate if they wanted to stop the war.

South American Ties With Old World Kept In View by Delegates

Special to The Christian Science Monitor

SANTIAGO, Chile—The necessary contacts having been established between the various delegations at Montevideo, the seventh Pan-American Conference is ready for a diligent study of the economic aspects of international collaboration.

All the Central and Southern American countries depend for their very existence on the supply of raw materials, and have been stricken to a greater degree than their sister nation in the north and the rest of the world by the crisis in commodity prices.

No matter how the agenda may be framed, there will be an irresistible drift in the conference endeavors to tackle their economic problems.

At the same time the southern delegates recognize the difficulties inherent in the numerous schemes

(Continued on Page 9, Column 3)

The Monitor Index

Wednesday, Dec. 6, 1933

Things Present

What the American press thinks of lynching, and of officials who seem to feel that there are times when it is to be tolerated, may be judged from some editorial statements collected under the heading "Mirror of World Opinion" on the Editorial page.

Our "Etiquette in Daily Living" article today gives a few helpful hints on manners over the telephone. Women's Activities—Fashions—Foods page.

Next to strolling with a poet in the autumn is the reading about such an adventure. See "Autumn with W. H. Davies" on the Home Forum page.

A recent note from the retail collection department of one of the world's largest lumber companies reported remarkable success with a letter to delinquent accounts. It had been based on some collection letters which had been submitted in a contest conducted by the Word a Day. Following our publishing of the expression of appreciation, there have come numerous requests for the republication of the original letters. You will find them on the Daily Features page.

And Things to Come

Thursday brings the Young Folks' page and a collection of the best cartoons of the week.

Repeal Adds New Problems To Old Ones

Liquor Flows Freely in 19 States With Six More Expected

Difficulties Appear

Dry Territory Is Wide Open to Wet Advertising as Old Law Fails to Work

Special from Monitor Bureau

WASHINGTON, Dec. 6—With prohibition repealed, the nation today was assessing the probable results of its action; awake to the realization that legal liquor is no longer glamorous but a stark actuality which will require just as much attention as illegal liquor did during pre-prohibition days.

According to latest reports the sale of liquor is now legal in 19 states. The other states remain dry, at least for the moment. In a half dozen or so, however, legislatures or legislative groups are considering changes in local laws and it is possible that by the end of the week the number of states classified as unconditionally wet will total more than 24.

The anti-climactic change from prohibition to repeal came at 5:32 p. m. (E. S. T.) yesterday, just 13 years, 10 months and 19 days after the United States embarked on its great national experiment in liquor control through absolute prohibition. The change was attended by remarkably little excitement. Judging by the apathy of crowds in the major cities of the country popular enthusiasm for repeal has been greatly exaggerated.

President Offers Plea

Utah delivered the final blow when it became the thirty-sixth state to ratify the Twenty-first Amendment to the Federal Constitution. Seventeen and a half minutes later Mr. William Phillips, acting Secretary of State, officially proclaimed that, having received official notice from the lawfully required number of states, prohibition was no longer part of the basic law of the United States.

President Roosevelt, on his part, then issued a proclamation to the same effect as a prelude to announcing removal of special nuisance taxes levied by the last Congress. The Recovery Act specified that they should remain in effect only until the Eighteenth Amendment should

(Continued on Page 6, Column 2)

Civil War Strikes At Rule of Soviets In Outer Mongolia

TOKYO, Dec. 6 (AP)—Civil war has flared in Outer Mongolia, with Nationalists rising against the Soviet's nine-year domination of the régime which has Urga as its capital, according to Japanese military reports to the War Office today.

Moscow's recent efforts to tighten control over the area, said the reports, resulted in Nationalist outbreaks in the Urga and Kerulen districts.

The Soviet Embassy and military and commercial representatives at Urga are pretending neutrality, added the reports, but it was understood that Moscow has ordered their return home.

Outer Mongolia proclaimed its independence of China in 1911 after the fall of the Manchu dynasty. A revolution in 1924, allegedly fostered by Soviets, resulted in establishment of the Mongolian Peoples Republic, modeled along lines of the Soviet Government. China has never abandoned a technical claim to the country.

Striking Instances of Fraud And Deception Are Revealed In Revised Drug Control Act

Supporters of Measure Show Where Dishonesty and Subtlety Appear in Every Form of Publicity Employed by Many Drug Makers

Special from The Christian Science Monitor Bureau

WASHINGTON, Dec. 6—Unquestionably the most striking passage in the new Food and Drug Act, on which hearings open tomorrow, and which has earned it much of the opposition with which it is faced, is the flat statement that no drug has any effect in the treatment of a long list of diseases.

Prepared by physicians of highest standing, to refute the claims of manufacturers that drugs are beneficial in the treatment of these diseases, the act speaks frankly and specifically. It declares:

". . . any advertisement of a drug representing it directly or by ambiguity or inference to have any effect in the treatment of any of the following diseases shall be deemed to be false." There follows a list of 36 diseases, many of them including in one general term a far larger subordinate number.

Another section of the law makes it obligatory for a drug product to bear on its label a statement that the product "is not a cure for" a specified disease, even though it may be accepted as a palliative. This regulation is strongly opposed. It is also stipulated that drug buyers have a fundamental right to know what they are buying, and each label must bear an accurate and full statement of the contents. In opposition to this proviso, some critics plead that it would "give away every manufacturer's formula." Others say that a prospective user of drugs should not know what he is taking: that some physicians find that by informing a user exactly what drug is being administered they often nullify the effect of the drug!

An editorial comment in a trade magazine defends this point by saying: "A patient often reacts to medicines in an entirely different way if the ingredients are known. This fact will be testified to by the leading physicians of the country who, many times, demand that the patient shall not know the ingredients of prescriptions."

Mr. Walter G. Campbell, chief of the Food and Drug Administration, who has been an official in this field since the original Act in 1906, says that labeling of drugs "is simply a

(Continued on Page 9, Column 1)

U. S. Funds Start Pouring Into Banks Of New York City

Credit Inflation Sector Releases $93,700,000 to 12 Institutions

Special from Monitor Bureau

WASHINGTON, Dec. 6 — The credit inflation sector of the Administration's far-flung financial battle line blazed into prominence today as an additional $93,700,000 of federal cash was released by an agreement with half of New York's big banks.

Thus far, some $400,000,000 of Reconstruction Finance Corporation funds have been sent out to banks all over the country to stimulate the purchase of goods, grant credit to the small merchant and manufacturer, and in general, aid in business recovery. Before the operation is complete, Mr. Jesse H. Jones, RFC chairman, believes the figure may reach $1,000,000,000.

Almost forgotten by the public in the greater interest in the spectacular Administration dealings on the gold market, the process of credit inflation is nevertheless an integral part in the vast financial operation which the Government is now pushing. Another wing has been the open market operations of the Federal Reserve Board, also designed to inflate credit, but these operations recently were suspended.

At the same time RFC credit inflation is being speeded. By every means in his power, President Roosevelt is carrying through the program announced in his radio speech of Oct. 22 of restoring commodity price levels, to be followed by dollar stabilization. At that time he declared that if the result were not achieved by one means, another would be used.

It is as part of this program that the RFC casually announced last night that 12 of the biggest New York banks had agreed to sell more than $90,000,000 in preferred stock, or notes, to the RFC, with the National City Bank leading the list with a huge amount of $50,000,000. So far has the "socialization of credit" and the extension of state capitalism gone that the an-

(Continued on Page 9, Column 7)

Massachusetts As Road Safety Model Proposed

Survey Plan Under M.I.T. Direction Considered by State CWA

Plans to make Massachusetts a model highway safety state through the channels of a project coming under the Massachusetts Civil Works Administration have been submitted to Maj. Joseph W. Bartlett chairman of the board, by Maj. Paul Hines, Boston safety authority.

A comprehensive survey of the causes of accidents to be conducted by the Massachusetts Institute of Technology as a basis for remedies for reducing the increasing toll of auto fatalities and injuries, is proposed.

The project was outlined to Major Bartlett at a conference yesterday in the State House. Present were Dr. Vannevar Busch, vice-president of M. I. T.; Col. R. C. Eddy; Prof. Irwin Shell, members of the Institute faculty and Major Hines. Dr. Busch expressed his belief in the necessity of such a survey and offered the services of the Institute to direct the entire study.

Dr. Busch said that he would go into the scheme only because it was felt it would be a public benefit and that Technology in such cases feels it a public obligation to undertake such work when requested.

It was suggested that Technology be asked formally by Gov. Joseph B. Ely to undertake the direction of the survey from a purely technical standpoint. Supporters of the project point out that the highway safety campaign would provide immediate work of upwards of 1000 men and women.

Major Bartlett agreed to see Governor Ely on the project after he had learned that Prof. Miller McClintock of Harvard University, an internationally famous traffic safety expert, had indorsed the plan.

Investigational phases suggested for study by Technology included a statistical survey of the record of accidents in the State; the actual investigation and testing of motor equipment to determine replacement periods of vehicle parts; formulating a standard code of instruction and examination of driving license applicants: a study of educational work among pedestrians, motorists and particularly children, a study of traffic control equipment; a survey of localities where accidents occur more than once; a study of legal aspects involved and recommendations for legislation; the effect of road improvements as it effects increase in accidents; the study of lighting effects such as headlights, glare, etc., and finally liquor and its effects on drivers.

Such a complete survey would be, it is said, the first of its kind to be carried out systematically in the country. Its findings, indorsers of the project say, undoubtedly would have a national influence upon the needs for greater highway safety.

Sixty-Eight Men in Wellesley Unite in Big Boy Scout Troop

By a Staff Correspondent of The Christian Science Monitor

WELLESLEY, Mass., Dec. 6—Down to the "ole swimmin'" hole and a plunge into its soothing waters. Long, vigorous hikes over mountain and wooded trails. Congenial chats around a blazing camp fire. No longer are these boyhood haunts just pleasant memories to a group of 68 men in Wellesley. Instead they are again realizing these unforgettable pastimes of former days.

They call themselves the Back to Boyhood Training Troop. Each Monday night they gather at the Alice Phillips Junior High School where they do everything from playing games to the more serious things of tying knots and learning all the practical phases of Scouting.

The Norumbega Council of Boy Scouts of America is their host, under the direction of Mr. Liscom A. Bruce, Scout executive of the Norumbega Council. Here they are put through their paces in Scout work; they learn the importance of it in helping the boy of today in his development and preparation for the morrow.

After completion of this course these men will be the more competent to become leaders among the boys in their community, better fit to impart to them the comradeship which should exist between man and boy, father and son.

Many activities are planned for this grown-up troop, one of which will be an all-night hiking trip, possibly up in the wooded areas of New Hampshire. Here the men will be put on their own resources and be required to put into practice the things taught while partaking of the course.

The council's main objective, however, is to bring a boy in understanding contact with a man. In fact it is the objective of the whole Boy Scout movement.

"It's too bad," Mr. Bruce told the Monitor correspondent, "that the world in general feels that we Scouts are a bunch of 'sissies.' They have got to be convinced differently. It takes courage, grit, determination and ability to be a Scout. And that is what these men of the Back to Boyhood Training Group are trying to instill into the boys in their community."

Chile Voids Decrees of 'de Facto' Rulers

SANTIAGO, Chile, Dec. 6 (By U. P.)—A special judicial commission headed by Señor Juan Esteban Montero, former President, has presented a report declaring unconstitutional all "laws by decree," totaling 687, signed by de facto governments between June 6 and Sept. 30, 1932.

The report declared that all such legislation by de facto governments during the country's disturbed period must be considered a legislation imposed by army occupation.

Chignecto Canal Report Now in Its Final Stage

Special to The Christian Science Monitor

TRURO, N. S.—Expectation that the Royal Commission report on the proposed Chignecto Canal project will be tabled during the pending session of the Parliament was expressed recently by Mr. R. K. Smith, member from Amherst, N. S.

"Of course I cannot say definitely," Mr. Smith explained, "but my understanding is that the report is now in the final stages of completion and that in allprobability it will be in the hands of the Government before the session opens."

Airmada Reaches Fort Lamy

FORT LAMY, French Congo, Dec. 6 (AP)—The French Black Squadron of 28 planes, flying back to France from Bangui, French Congo, arrived here today from Fort Archambault.

Italy to Quit Unless League Revises Scope

Would Unite Big Powers in Pact to Control World for Peace

Details Not Yet Ready

Fascist Grand Council Moves to Include Germany, Russia and United States

By Press Wireless from Monitor Bureau

ROME, Dec. 6—Italy's continued coöperation with the League of Nations has been made conditional on drastic reform of the League itself.

Failure to speedily revise the League constitution, procedure and objectives along lines acceptable to Premier Mussolini will result in Italy's withdrawal from the League.

This is the final decision on Italy's future relations with Geneva, taken by the Fascist Grand Council, Italy's supreme executive body, in a long night session which ended early this morning.

The Grand Council's motion must be interpreted as a step to open discussion on the vital problem of the League's future. It is contended here that the League as at present organized cannot fulfill the mission for which it was created, and that reform has become necessary to permit entry or reëntry of those states which are now outside.

Italy plans fully to study the whole question, and will make definite proposals at the opportune moment. Italy, however, will listen with open mind to any suggestion from other countries. The difficulty of the task is by no means minimized, since reforms need to be voted unanimously by the Assembly, but it is confidently anticipated that they will be carried through in a spirit of good will and international coöperation.

Experience Dictates Reforms

It would be premature to enumerate at present the particular proposals that will be advocated by the Fascist Government. Articles of obvious official inspiration published

(Continued on Page 14, Column 1)

Truck Owners Face Federal Summons In Motor Strike Case

Individual truck owners involved in the extended western Massachusetts trucking strike, are expected to be summoned to Washington by the National Labor Board to explain their reasons for noncompliance with the findings and recommendations of the New England Regional Labor Board, it was announced today.

The strike has tied up motortruck transportation to and from many points in New England for several weeks.

The New England Board, in a decision rendered by Judge John J. Burns, chairman, following a study and a hearing, recommended that the workers return to their jobs immediately without discrimination, pending the sending to Springfield of a mediator to discuss wages and hours with the employers. The trucking officials, however, evidently have disregarded the board's findings and consequently Washington is stepping into the dispute.

Much controversy has arisen in the strike in regard to a temporary injunction granted the trucking interests by a state court. As a result, employees involved have filed a petition in United States District Court in Boston seeking removal of the injunction on the grounds that it is a matter for the federal courts to decide. Judge Elisha H. Brewster will hear the petition of the workers tomorrow.

Lindberghs Greeted By Gala Throngs On Arrival in Brazil

'We' Again

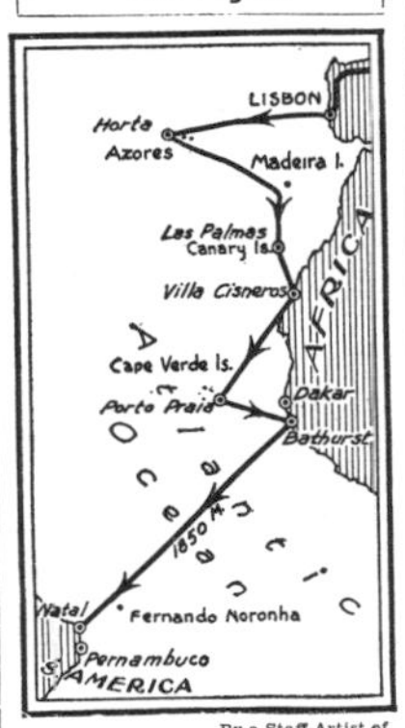

By a Staff Artist of The Christian Science Monitor.

Lindberghs' Course

Flying Colonel and Wife 15 Hours 55 Minutes in Air From Africa

Atlantic Spanned Second Time on Trip

Business Houses Close So Natal Can Don Its Festive Attire

NATAL, Brazil, Dec. 6 (AP)—Col. and Mrs. Charles A. Lindbergh arrived here today, after a 1875-mile flight across the south Atlantic Ocean from Bathurst, Gambia, Africa.

The great monoplane landed on the harbor here at 2:55 p. m., Brazilian time (12:55 p. m., E. S. T.).

The streets and docks were thronged with huge crowds of Brazilians who had waited throughout the day for the arrival of the famous American couple.

By general agreement, all business houses and stores in the city were closed for nearly an hour before the Lindberghs arrival in celebration of the great event.

Streets Gayly Decorated

The streets were gayly decorated for the "fiesta." For more than a week past the populace had been excited by the reports that Colonel Lindbergh and his wife, the former Miss Anne Morrow, would return to the American continent through their city.

For Colonel Lindbergh, it was the third aerial spanning of the Atlantic. His first flight, in 1927, skyrocketed him to the attention of the whole world. On that occasion, flying the famous old ship Spirit of St. Louis, he stayed in the air 33½ hours before the lights of Le Bourget appeared before him. The distance on that occasion was 3610 miles, almost double what he did today with his wife at the wireless set.

He flew the Atlantic again this summer, but it was by easy stages that time, as he surveyed a proposed north Atlantic air route for the Pan American Airways, of which he is technical adviser.

On the flight today the Lindbergh monoplane averaged 118 miles an hour. It was in the air 15 hours 55 minutes from the time of the takeoff at Bathurst, Gambia.

Flies Atlantic Again

NEW YORK, Dec. 6 (AP)—Lindbergh flying the Atlantic again—and no one getting very excited about it!

That shows how far aviation has come since the day in 1927 when the Flying Colonel arrived in Paris with his uneaten sandwiches in his pocket and his letters of introduction in his hand.

The gulf between the first horseless carriage and the modern motorcar is hardly greater than the difference between ocean aviation of 1927 and of 1933. Flying the Atlantic six years ago was high adventure, fraught with peril every mile of the lonely way. Lindbergh's present jaunt, besides being much shorter, lacks daredevil thrills—thanks to natural science.

World Waited Anxiously

Winging from New York to Paris, Lindbergh was lost to the world for more than 36 hours. He had no wireless, and the anxious millions could only wait. Flying from Gambia, W. Af., to Natal, Brazil, he communicated frequently with Pan American Airway's wireless stations strung along the South American coast.

The earth inductor compass, marvelous gadget in 1927, is obsolete in 1933. Now Colonel Lindbergh uses a Gatty navigation sight, a device which enables Mrs. Lindbergh to peer down through a glass and through a revolving belt with holes in it to the waves below, thereby determining drift and speed. This apparatus makes dead reckoning, the simplest form of navigation, a very sure thing.

Have All Modern Devices

Colonel Lindbergh now has a radio direction finder which, should he lose his way, would enable a wireless station to draw him to his destination as surely as a child retrieves a ball at the end of a string. He has a gyroscopic compass which holds a course despite buffetings; a plane that develops 700 horsepower against the "Spirit's" 220 and streamlines that can send it zipping through the air at 160 miles an hour.

He has an adjustable pitch propeller, which does for an airplane what the gear shift does for a car. The 1927 plane had a fixed pitch blade—imagine driving a car with no gear shift!

Above all, the Colonel is not alone this time. He has a navigator, copilot and a wireless operator who—as the professionals say—has "a good fist" at the sending key. The name of this three-in-one crew is Mrs. Anne Morrow Lindbergh.

Pennsylvania to Pay Bonus

HARRISBURG, Penna., Dec. 6 (AP)—The Senate today passed finally two bills to permit the payment of a bonus to the State's veterans. The State is authorized to issue bonds up to $50,000,000. Payments would be computed at the rate of $10 for each month of service, no veteran to receive more than $200.

Austrian Priests To Quit Politics On Bishops' Edict

Action of Roman Catholics Expected to Revolutionize Republic's Affairs

By Press Wireless from Monitor Bureau

VIENNA, Dec. 6—The surprise decision of Austrian Roman Catholic Bishops to require the clergy to refrain from political activity, which has just been announced, is expected to have incalculable results in the whole Austrian political situation.

In accordance with this decision after Dec. 15 no priest will remain in the Parliament, city and district councils or other active posts, and participation of any clergyman in politics will not be permitted without special permission from the Bishops.

This will give a completely new aspect to political life here because for a full half-century, through the Christian Socialist Party, Roman Catholic priests have played a leading rôle in both houses of Parliament, the governments of Austrian provinces and municipal councils of countless towns and villages.

Roman Catholic churches in this predominantly Roman Catholic country have been accused of becoming centers of political agitations, and priests have been accused of using their pulpits as stumps for campaign speeches. The clergy have taken a leading part in the long and bitter struggle against Marxism here.

Furthermore the clergy, the Roman Catholic Church and the Christian Socialist Party have been the chief support of Chancellor Engelbert Dollfuss in his fight for preservation of Austrian independence and preventing Austro-German union.

This support was manifested in an especially demonstrative manner last summer during "Catholic Day" here, when the church impressively gave Chancellor Dollfuss its blessing.

The action of the Bishops is a serious blow to the Christian Socialist Party and the Dollfuss Government, but is hailed with delight by the Opposition.

Rivalry Over Entertaining Lindberghs Starts Storm in Teacup Among Iberians

Special to The Christian Science Monitor

MADRID—Col. Charles A. Lindbergh, who has spanned the great Atlantic in one stride, made several unsuccessful attempts to cross from Tuy, Spain, to Valença, Portugal, separated only by the Minho River—300 yards wide.

After being forced to land at Santoña near Santander, he set off again and was once more obliged to come down on account of fog in the Minho, the boundary line between Spain and Portugal.

Inhabitants in both Tuy and Valença became excited when Colonel Lindbergh seemed to hesitate as to whether and where he and Mrs. Lindbergh would come ashore and stay until the fog lifted. The difficulty was that nobody spoke a word of English and the Colonel not a word of any other language.

So "Hurrah, Portugal!" was all he could say when he discovered that the Portuguese on their side had taken offense.

The two sides were pacified by mutual concessions, however, the Mayor of Tuy contenting himself with an invitation from the Portuguese authorities to row across the Minho and inspect their illustrious guests who were being regaled to one of the best banquets the town could put on.

Young ladies flocked in from the neighboring farms, picturesquely dressed, and offered to Mrs. Lindbergh a bouquet of flowers. They had arranged for an exhibition of the Fade, the national dance, but the flyers retired to the hydroplane at 9 o'clock.

A gang was improvised from the carabineers to clear the river bottom, and when the fog lifted, he was able to take off for Lisbon.

Unfortunately domestic complications seem to have arisen out of the visit as the Mayor of Tuy, in his eagerness to reach the hydro from the Spanish side, even at the risk of transgressing regulations, fell foul of the officer in charge of the carabineers. As a result, he announced that as soon as Colonel and Mrs. Lindbergh left, he would resign his post.

Many columns in the Madrid press are devoted to Colonel Lindbergh, in spite of his complete silence regarding himself or his trip. Experts as well as the peasant folk say they are amazed at the skill with which he came down on the river, since he had chosen a spot where there are only three feet of water and a rocky bottom.

El Sol, which considers Colonel Lindbergh the most interesting figure in aviation today, says he has proved that he never merited the nickname, the "mad flyer," given him in his early days, not only because of his tremendous and steadfast energy, but because of the equanimity with which he bears his popularity.

THE CHRISTIAN SCIENCE MONITOR

AN INTERNATIONAL DAILY NEWSPAPER

BOSTON, MONDAY, JULY 2, 1934—VOL. XXVI, NO. 183

** ATLANTIC EDITION | THREE CENTS IN GREATER BOSTON | FIVE CENTS ELSEWHERE

COPYRIGHT 1934 BY THE CHRISTIAN SCIENCE PUBLISHING SOCIETY

The March of the Nations

By **Rufus Steele**

Hitler Holds Germany in Hand

His Power Increases in Crisis

Roosevelt Signs Bills, Sails

World's Women Make Pleas

U. S. Railroaders Get Pensions

She Holds Canada's Parliament

GERMANY sees Chancellor Adolf Hitler in seemingly more complete control than ever after defeating the so-called "second National Socialist revolution." The number of high officials and others executed or slain in the clean-up process is placed as high as 200. These include Capt. Ernst Roehm, deposed commander of the Storm Troopers, Karl Ernst, Berlin commander, Gen. Kurt von Schleicher, Edmund Heines, Munich Trooper commander, Hubert von Bose of the Vice-Chancellor's staff. Under arrest are Vice-Chancellor von Papen and Prince August Wilhelm, son of the former Kaiser. Propaganda Minister Goebbels intimates more punishments to follow, while Chancellor Hitler issues stern warning regarding loyalty and conduct of the Storm Troopers—The view is that a necessary housecleaning in the Nazi forces has been well done.

¶ Berlin's official statement declares a Putsch to be carried through on Saturday for the overthrow of Hitler was defeated by his swift action. Its leaders are named as Capt. Roehm and former Chancellor Gen. von Schleicher. Public condemnation of Roehm is encouraged by official exposure of alleged gross immorality in his private life. Europe watches with mixed feelings the great stir in Germany. Italy approves Hitler's despotic suppression of the uprising, his continuance in power promoting Mussolini's plans. Chancellor Dollfuss takes a bolder stand against National Socialists in Austria. France has not been displeased by evidence of lack of German stability —How nations do measure one another's troubles in the light of their own profit or loss.

¶ President Roosevelt, after swift action on momentous bills passed by Congress, sails on the cruiser Houston for his long trip to the Caribbean and Hawaii. Mrs. Roosevelt waves good-by to her husband and two younger sons at Annapolis and goes for her own "off the record" vacation. The President signs the Frazier-Lemke bill. This gives farmers a five-year moratorium on their debts and is called the Administration's most radical measure. He also signs the railroad pension bill, names commissions—A perspiring nation tries to figure out all that these new laws may mean.

¶ France welcomes to Paris the triennial session of the International Council of Women, representing 40,000,000 women in 42 countries. Through the ICW civilized womanhood lifts its voice in definite and emphatic pleas. On the basis of the fundamental equality of nations, both international and sex barriers must break. Male and female must be equal in education, moral standards, right to earn, right to choose national status, and in legislative and administrative bodies. The world's youth must be educated in understanding as between races, nations, classes—And this is striking straight at the roots of war and of the world's major problems.

¶ The American Brotherhood of Railway Trainmen figures that 100,000 trainmen will retire this year on pay under new pension laws. Congress passed these after four years of lobbying. The railroaders also get an increase in wages of $4,000,000 under the April 26 agreement between labor and management. The 10 per cent wage cut of two years ago will be fully restored by April 1, 1935. The railroad men have very generally fared better than other workers—Again and again they have shown the fruits of powerful organization.

¶ Paris sees a military tribunal restore, under strange circumstances, the good name of five soldiers shot for mutiny in 1915. After 10 years of continuous effort the widows of Sergeant Morange and Private Prevost win clearance of the soldiers' records and seven cents damage for the widow of each. Fifth Company of the Sixty-third Regiment was slashed to pieces in St. Mihiel, refilled with raw recruits and did not leap over the top in a terrific barrage when ordered to do so. The five shot were chosen by lot—Simple raw recruits will balk at the sheer folly of being slaughtered.

¶ Canada's Parliament finds itself held in session by its sole woman member. With the Governor-General on his way for scheduled adjournment ceremonies, Miss Agnes McPhail protests too much military control in prisons and stands on her rights for investigation and debate and Premier Bennett holds the members in Ottawa. Parliament had already made something of a record, establishing a central bank, requiring a permit for possession of arms, and forfeiting lottery prizes to the state —Ireland's profitable sweepstakes must now worry along without Canada's help.

Richberg Rises To Pilot's Seat At the Capital

General Counsel of NRA Put in Power During President's Vacation

Farm Bill a Bugaboo?

Debt Moratorium to Benefit Holders of Mortgages, Too, Administration Argues

The Washington Day** with **The Monitor Bureau

WASHINGTON, July 2—President Roosevelt, in his last official act before leaving on his vacation, reached down below the top crust of his executives and picked Mr. Donald Richberg, general counsel for NRA, to head a new temporary committee which will exercise a large degree of executive authority during his absence.

In the order made public today he at one and the same time settled the question as to who would control the Government while the President is out of immediate touch with affairs and established a new super authority to supervise the activities of all the relief agencies of the Government during the renewed drive for recovery which the summer is to witness.

Mr. Richberg's vastly expanded authority will rest on three new positions. First, he becomes director of the Industrial Emergency Committee, the new agency to consist of the Secretary of the Interior, the Secretary of Labor, Brig-Gen. Hugh S. Johnson as Industrial Recovery Administrator, and Mr. Harry L. Hopkins as Emergency Relief Administrator.

Concentration of Power

Second, he will temporarily take Mr. Frank Walker's place as executive director of the National Emergency Council—the coördinating agency for all federal relief activities. Third, he will be executive secretary of the Executive Council—the super-Cabinet of the Roosevelt Administration.

The acts combine in Mr. Richberg a greater concentration of power and authority than have been in the hands of any single individual other than the President not only under the Roosevelt Administration, but in recent American history. It makes him the center and the clearing point for all administrative activity while the President is out of town.

Mr Roosevelt, however, was careful in his order to make it clear that the duties of the new industrial emergency committee are "to make recommendations to the President, through its director, with respect to problems of relief, public works, labor disputes and industrial recovery and to study and coördinate the handling of joint problems affecting these activities."

Thus all major problems affecting the Government will be coördinated in Mr. Richberg's hands and he will

(Continued on Page 2, Column 4)

Mexico's 45th President

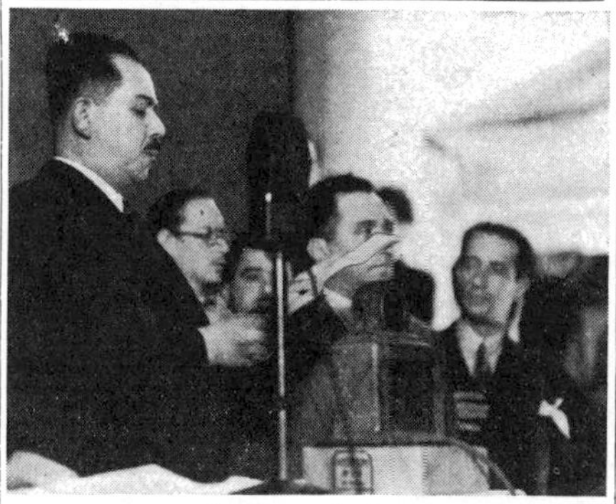

Gen. Lazaro Cardenas

Successful Candidate, Shown Reading His Speech Accepting Administration Party's Nomination.

Mountain 'Hikers' Protest Invasion Of Peaks by Auto

Appalachians Point Out That Sky-Line Drives Will Ruin Trails

By a Staff Correspondent of The Christian Science Monitor

RUTLAND, Vt., July 2—Mountain peak invasion by horn-blowing, gas-fuming automobiles today threatens to wipe out major portions of the famous Appalachian Trail, a 2050-mile "hikers' empire" from Maine to Georgia.

Opposition to this invasion turned out to be the main theme of the three-day Appalachian Trail Conference which closes today at the Long Trail Lodge. Nearly 100 representatives of the trail building organization are waxing indignant over "skyline" road projects being forwarded in New Hampshire, Pennsylvania, Virginia, North Carolina and Tennessee. Each of these would wipe out lengthy sections of the trail which now stands only 112 miles short of completion.

Each delegate is leaving the conference today vowing to oppose strenuously these skyline roads, which not only will displace the trail, but will defeat forest conservation efforts and mar wilderness scenery. They are not opposed to motor roads which follow the valleys and occasionally ascend to the gaps. It is skyline roads passing over mountain peaks and cutting wide treeless swarths on mountainsides which meet their disfavor.

Best Views From Valleys

In fact the delegates actually approve wilderness penetration by a reasonable number of valley-line, gap-line roads, for these highways would take motorists to the natural beauties to which they are entitled. But, they pointed out, skyline highways become monotonous. Scenery

(Continued on Page 6, Column 4)

Cardenas Elected Mexican President By 96 P. C. of Votes

Two Defeated Candidates Charge Irregularities in Counting Ballots

MEXICO, D. F., July 2 (AP)—A revolutionary veteran of mixed Spanish and Indian descent, Gen. Lazaro Cardenas, was assured election today as the forty-fifth constitutional President of Mexico.

The election yesterday was the most orderly and one-sided in the history of the nation. One person, an election judge in Ocotzintla, Vera Cruz, was shot in a scuffle, but there were only minor clashes elsewhere.

Both defeated candidates asserted today, however, that the National Revolutionary (administration) Party supporters of General Cardenas violated election laws in rolling up an estimated 96 per cent of the total vote.

Gen. Antonio Villarreal and Col. Adalberto Tejeda both charged numerous irregularities and said they would not recognize the results of the election.

Headquarters for General Villarreal, nominee of the Confederation of Independent Democratic Parties, issued a statement:

"Villarreal is the President-Elect. The day of justice is approaching."

Colonel Tejeda, nominee of the Left-Socialist Party, said he would await the decision of Congress as to the legality of the election, "and after that, the people can judge."

Official returns were not available, but those gathered by the Administration Party gave 96 per cent to Cardenas, 2 per cent to Villarreal and 1 per cent to Tejeda. The rest went to Señor Hernan Laborde, a Communist, although his candidacy was not recognized officialy as legal.

The Administration Party also claimed a clean sweep in the election of 170 deputies and 49 senators.

General Cardenas, former Minister of War and revolutionary campaigner, is scheduled to be sworn in Dec. 1, to succeed President Rodriguez.

General Cardenas will bring to the Presidency experience gained during 18 years of military campaigning interspersed with brief periods of office holding.

The General—who is 39 years old —will be the youngest of all the nation's 45 chief executives, with the exception of Gen. Francisco I. Madero. General Madero was 38 when he assumed office in 1911 after heading the uprising which ousted Gen. Porfirio Diaz.

In 1928 he was elected Governor of Michoacan. His record as Governor shows that he dealt severely with the Roman Catholic Church, aided the Indians by large grants of land, encouraged industrial development and built roads and schools.

He left the Governor's post for various intervals to combat the Escobar revolution and to serve as Minister of the Interior, president of the National Revolutionary Party and Minister of War, from which position he resigned to become presidential candidate.

Call Issued for Safe Fourth

Massachusetts Serves Nation

Woolen Workers Defer Strike

Motor Registrar Cites Last Year's Highway Toll and Marshal Asks Care With Fireworks—Landis, Smith and Kennedy Promoted

The Boston Day

Muzzle-loaders swelled casualty lists in 1776. Today, as America prepares to celebrate its 159-year-old independence, automobiles and fireworks provide the same lethal force.

With the Fourth approaching attention turns more than ever to the need for safety on the highway, on the picnic ground, in the back yard.

Registrar Morgan T. Ryan recalls the 11 automobile deaths last year on this day, pleads with drivers to follow these rules:

1. Don't speed.
2. Don't race railroad trains to grade crossings.
3. Dont' throw lighted firecrackers from moving automobiles.

State Fire Marshal Stephen C. Garrity warns against improper use of fireworks, reminds celebrators that carelessness in handling even the most simple pieces causes fatal accidents, costly fires.

Registrar Ryan offers food for thought in announcing last week's highway fatality figure—17. Eight were pedestrians, five occupants of a car struck by a train. Going on, Mr. Ryan notes 185 operators were convicted of drunken driving during the week, 99 more than in the previous week. But 15 of these went to jail.

Totaling up the highway fatalities of the year so far to 440, Mr. Ryan looks ahead to clogged roads over the holiday this week, says he doesn't intend to tolerate speeding. As proof he has suspended the licenses of 100 drivers convicted of speeding on the Worcester Turnpike.

The entire division of inspectors of the registrar's office, 150 men, will patrol the roads before, on, and after the holiday.

Government

Landis, Smith and Kennedy

Massachusetts gives three more of its sons to the nation. And looks about for someone to take their places.

Dr. James M. Landis was a professor of legislation at the Harvard Law School. Last October he became Federal Trade Commissioner and moved his desk to a weather-beaten, war-time office in Washington. Now he becomes a member of the important Federal Securities and Exchange Commission. Dean Roscoe Pound at Harvard says when Dr. Landis gets through helping America back on its feet, Harvard wants him back on its teaching staff.

Mr. Edwin S. Smith was appointed Massachusetts Commissioner of Labor and Industries in December, 1931, and friends of labor saw a new era. The new era came, with a policy of honesty and realism in dealing with labor conditions. Mr. Smith now goes to Washington as a member of the new Federal National Labor Relations Board. Labor approves the appointment, but looks wonderingly in the direction of the Governor's office, from which the name of a new appointee soon will come. The names of Mr. James T. Moriarty, president of the Massachusetts branch of the American Federation of Labor, and Mr. Robert J. Watt, secretary of the local federation, have been mentioned. The Massachusetts Con-

(Continued on Page 6, Column 1)

The Monitor Index

Monday, July 2, 1934

Things Present

Keep abreast of the news behind the news in the nation's capital, by reading "An Intimate Message From Washington," every Monday on the Editorial Page.

Your friend who is studying French will welcome the opportunity of comparing the article and its translation, on the Home Forum Page.

Another Parable of Safed the Sage graces the inside back page.

And Things to Come

Inasmuch as Henry A. Wallace, U. S. Secretary of Agriculture, is an important ace in the New Deal, readers of the Monitor will await with interest his article "The World at the Crossroads," appearing in the Weekly Magazine Section tomorrow. Another thought-provoking article is "Let's Celebrate Interdependence," by Robert and Dorothy Desmond.

Tuesday brings the Progress in Education Page, Home Building and Gardening Page.

Public Schools Of U. S. Stand At Crossroads

Wide Range of Opinions on Changes Shown at N. E. A. Convention

Is a Tsar Needed?

Commission on Emergency to Call State Meetings of Educators and Citizens

By Marjorie Shuler

Special from Monitor Bureau

WASHINGTON, July 2—Public school education in the United States ought to be changed. Ten thousand teachers attending the seventy-second annual convention of the National Education Association here this week agree to that. But as to what those changes should be there are about as many different opinions as there are blueberries growing on Vermont hillsides. In fact the diversity of opinion is such as to cause the average citizen to throw up his hands and inquire whether education needs a "tsar," such as Mr. Will H. Hays is to the movies or Judge Kenesaw M. Landis to baseball.

It may not take an umpire to adjudicate between those who think that the communities which have dropped kindergartens are wise and those who urgently seek to reëstablish such instruction for very young children at public expense. It may not require the voice of single authority to reconcile the classical school-teachers who want more Latin and the modernists who are all for substituting industrial preparation for instruction in a dead language.

Series of State Conferences

But so far the Joint Commission on the Emergency in Education whose report was given this morning by Dr. John K. Norton, professor of education, Teachers College, Columbia University, is not prepared to arbitrate.

However, Mr. Norton told his audience today that the commission is preparing to call a series of state conferences enlisting the aid of prominent citizens as well as educators in writing a new program for education.

"To a far greater extent than in the past professional organizations should seek the active coöperation of larger numbers of laymen," Mr. Norton warned, adding: "The platform must be as defensible as careful research and mature experience will permit."

The commission, which up to now has occupied itself mainly with attempts to protect adequate financing of schools, will continue that activity, and in addition is offering materials to state education associations to help them in developing long-term programs, and is preparing to encourage coöperation between the teaching profession and outside citizens to determine the rôle which education should play in solving economic and social problems.

Many Committees at Work

This year the commission has discovered 400 educational committees and commissions which have either prepared reports or are now conducting investigations tending toward educational recovery and reconstruction.

A number of these, together with descriptions of their work, have been

(Continued on Page 5, Column 1)

Brain Trust Wins Vote of Approval By College Group

Special to The Christian Science Monitor

CLEVELAND, Ohio, July 2—Criticism directed toward the "Brain Trust" employed by President Franklin D. Roosevelt was repudiated by the American College Publicity Association in annual convention here June 28-30. The President was commended for calling on college specialists to aid him in solving the problems confronting the nation.

Directors of public relations from 54 colleges in 25 states joined in indorsing this and other resolutions directed toward furthering higher education.

"It is you who direct publicity who have the duty and high honor to beat back the tide of senseless slaughter of our colleges and schools and lay the broad foundation in the hearts and minds of our citizens for the development through higher education of a truly educated leadership and citizenry in our country," declared Dr. A. Caswell Ellis, dean of the downtown branch of Western Reserve University, host institution.

"We are in the midst of a race not merely between education and disaster, but between disaster and the development of adequate publicity departments and methods for our institutions of higher learning," Dr. Ellis further pointed out. "The staggering blows that higher education has received in the last few years are part of our punishment for the niggardly support and casual attention that our institutions of higher learning have given to their Departments of Public Relations.

"The colleges and universities must wake up and develop personnel, materials and technique equal to the present need and opportunity or they will continue to pay a frightful price for their neglect."

The delegates indorsed the proposal to set aside one week each year as National Higher Education Week.

Hitler Faces Cabinet Crisis As Storm Trooper Revolution Is Smothered by Swift Action

Hitler's Iron Fists

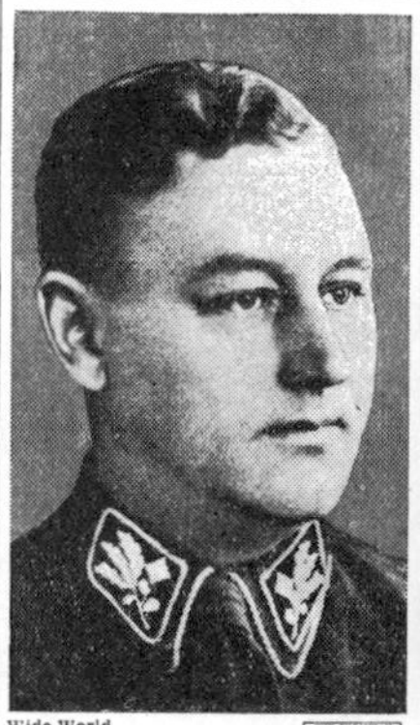

Wide World

Viktor Lutze

Newly Appointed National Commander of Storm Troops

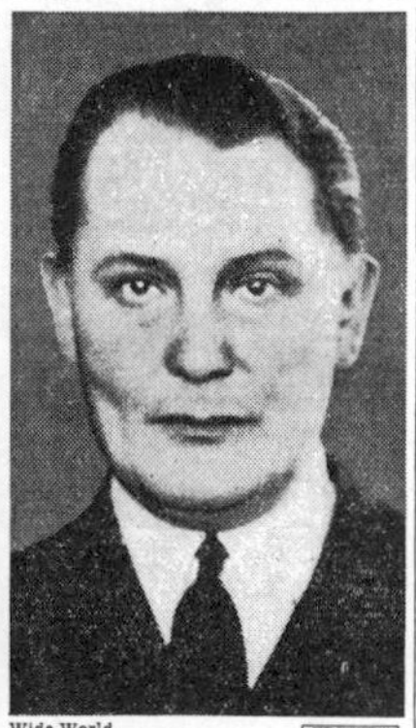

Wide World

Hermann Wilhelm Goering

Prussian Premier Who Moved Swiftly to Quell Uprising

Old Line-Ups Bother Dictator

* * *

Political, Economic, Social Differences Also Thwarted Bismarck in 'First Reich'

* * *

Herr Adolf Hitler, after a year and a half as Chancellor, has been confronted with one of the primary facts that faces every dictator.

"Dictatorship," says an Italian diplomatist, "is a blanket of political uniformity, but it cannot at once alter fundamental divisions that have previously expressed themselves in political, economic and social differences."

Such divisions, which Bismarck dared not crush when he forged the "First Reich," form the background for the "Second Revolution" in the "Third Reich," which Hitler has so drastically suppressed.

The First Reich

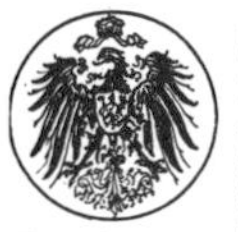

When Bismarck in 1871 welded the Germans into a single unit, he recognized the cultural, religious and economic differences then existing in the various separate kingdoms and principalities. Even under Kaiser Wilhelm II states had their own armies, postal systems and railroads. Protestants in Prussia, Roman Catholics in Bavaria, landed proprietors in the North, small farmers in the South, traders in the Hansa cities, industrialists in the Ruhr—these formed a highly varied realm. These elements Herr Hitler has compressed into a single political party, now virtually identical with the state itself.

The Second Reich

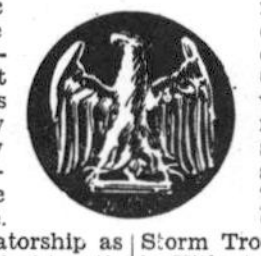

With the Republic which followed the World War, the Socialists held the largest share of power, but as many as thirty to forty political parties not only complicated the elections, but weakened the parliamentary machine. Herr Hitler offered dictatorship as an escape from this political ineptitude. The country, smarting under injustices of the peace treaties, riven by economic difficulty, fell into hostile camps: the "Red Front" Communist army, which was banned; "Steel Helmet," war veterans' association of monarchist and aristocratic leaning; "Reichsbanner," the Socialist private army; Storm Troops, originally organized by Hitler to protect the party speakers at political meetings, which grew into the Brown Shirt force.

The Third Reich

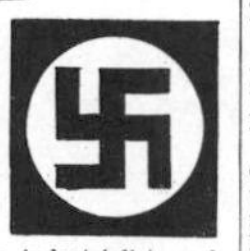

The theory of the totalitarian state has room for but one party and one instrument of enforcing its will. During Hitler's first year in power, political unification — "gleichschaltung" — became a major preoccupation, sweeping aside state governments, banning all other parties, ousting or imprisoning political opponents and attempting a measure of control of religion. The opposition crystallized slowly in these major divisions:

1. **The Conservatives**—Aristocrats of the old régime, industrialists and landed proprietors, sought to save a crumbling political house by placing Hitler in a chancellery which they intended to control. But the Chancellor, despite his coalition partners, embarked upon an unexpectedly extreme path. Many of them, like General Kurt von Schleicher, were believed ready to seek a restoration of the monarchy. Others, like Vice-Chancellor Franz von Papen, have sought to work with Hitler to force him to modify his course.

2. **The Roman Catholics**—The National Socialists' differences with the Roman Catholics began in party campaigns where the Hitlerites criticized the part which the priests played in politics. A concordat negotiated with the Holy See, which implies removal of priests from political activity, has not yet been ratified by the German Government. A major issue is the desire of both the Roman Catholic Church and the National Socialist Party to control education of the youth. The Roman Catholics also take vigorous issue with what they call the Nordic paganism of the new Germany.

3. **The Evangelical Church**—A section of National Socialist opinion organized in church affairs as the "German Christians" would not only incorporate doctrines of the Nordic race in religious teaching but would make the church subservient to the state. An important section of Evangelical pastors have organized against this move and are resisting as well the Government's effort to "unify" the admittedly cumbersome divisions of the old Protestant church through decrees issued by a Reichs Bishop who was given virtually commissarial powers by Herr Hitler.

4. **The Left Wing**—Radical elements within the National Socialist Party became discontented because Herr Hitler did not allow rein for many of the more extreme measures discussed in the heat of political campaigning. Such men as Capt. Ernst Roehm, creator of the Storm Troops, became focal points of this element, which demanded not only socialistic schemes where Herr Hitler was proceeding slowly in the face of grave economic problems, but also demanded a clean sweep of remaining opposition.

The 'Second Revolution'

Talk of a "Second Revolution" had for months been heard on the part of radical elements within the National Socialist Party. Repeated warnings had been issued by Chancellor Hitler in an effort to maintain discipline. The problem was complicated by the fact that, with their own organizations suppressed, Communists and Socialists "changed faith," entered the Brown Army and attempted to foment reaction from within.

Following his traditional "ruthless offensive," Herr Hitler has apparently halted the Left Wing extremism and moved against other opposition as well. Conservatives, however, who are "with the National Socialists but not of them" appear to have won a victory of some proportions, for Herr Hitler has prevented the radical Brown Shirts from completely liquidating the once-Nationalist Steel Helmet organization, which thus retains something of its old identity, although under strict Government control.

Storm Troop Rising Had Been Planned Saturday Noon

Von Papen Expected To Resign His Post

Roehm and Other Leaders of Nazi Revolt Lined Up and Executed

By J. E. Williams

By Cable from Monitor Bureau

BERLIN, July 2—That Saturday's "putsch" plans had already been thoroughly worked out by the higher leaders (Oberfuehrer) of the Storm Trooper organizations is declared established by detailed information now made available here.

In fact, certain circles have even gone so far as to say that 13 of the Oberfuehrer, that is a majority, were for a "putsch" and that Government authorities only came to hear of it through one of these men betraying the plot.

The time planned for the "putsch," according to present information, seems to have been uncertain—either, Saturday last or in September. That it was not to have been immediate appears evident to some from the fact that the Berlin Oberfuehrer, Karl Ernst—stated by friends to have been by no means a coward—one of those shot, was arrested at Bremen when he and his wife were about to embark for a vacation trip to Madeira.

Concerning the number of those shot or killed by their own hand, official statistics are not yet available, but a reliable estimate puts them at least 50 to 60. Among these may be mentioned Herr Gregor Strasser who earlier played an important rôle on the Socialist side of National Socialism.

Von Papen's Status

The position of Vice-Chancellor von Papen is at the moment not clear but it is considered likely that he will resign the vice-chancellorship, and General Goering will be named as his probable successor. That Herr von Papen cannot continue to hold office seems beyond doubt in view of events of the past week-end. His Marburg speech increased his unpopularity in National Socialist circles, arousing a great wave of resentment which is by no means abated, and which, together with suspicion which certain circles have felt that among his coöperators there was a connection with a foreign power—that is France—whereof official mention is made in official communiqués made him persona non grata in official circles. At the same time it is generally believed he personally had no connection with General von Schleicher.

For the past two days Herr von Papen has been prisoner in his own home, and not permitted to leave. Within his own house two of his coöperators, Herr von Bose and Herr Klausner were shot. A copyrighted Associated Press dispatch from here states that President von Hindenburg has made the Reichswehr personally responsible for the safety of the Vice-Chancellor.

It is significant that the German press, has as yet reported nothing that happened at Herr von Papen's home.

Both in Germany and abroad the question is being asked why such peremptory treatment has been meted out to these Storm Trooper leaders? Why weren't they arrested and brought before a military or other court, and then sentenced? Some foreign journals go so far as to describe this action as murder and illegal.

Technically Legal

Whatever may be the individual feelings in the matter, there is no question but that what has happened was legal. For both Storm Troops and the Schutz Staffel (Hitler's personal bodyguard) stand under special jurisdiction and there is no necessity to bring them before an ordinary court. They have all sworn a special oath to Chancallor Hitler as members of these organizations and the consequences of betraying that oath were known to them personally ever since the decree of special jurisdiction was sanctioned on April 28, 1933.

There is no doubt in the mind of Germans that if this "Putsch" had succeeded then Germany would have soon been in the throes of civil war wherein the struggle would have been primarily between Storm Troopers and the Reichswehr, with the possibility of foreign intervention.

If the radical "Putschists" had won, it is regarded as certain that an unimaginable rule of terror for this country would have followed.

Bodyguard Loyal

Throughout all these events, Herr Hitler's personal bodyguard has been absolutely true and it was upon them and the Goering police that reliance was placed and has been shown justified.

The action of Saturday is regarded here as a cleaning-up process—as the beginning of the introduction of a stronger order. Purging of the undesirable elements has been considered long overdue in moderate circles. It is generally regarded as further evidence that Herr Hitler and his prin-

(Continued on Page 4, Column 4)

THE CHRISTIAN SCIENCE MONITOR

AN INTERNATIONAL DAILY NEWSPAPER

COPYRIGHT 1934 BY
THE CHRISTIAN SCIENCE PUBLISHING SOCIETY

BOSTON, MONDAY, AUGUST 20, 1934—VOL. XXVI, NO. 224

PACIFIC EDITION—FIVE CENTS A COPY

The March of the Nations

By Rufus Steele

Chinese Eastern Sale Looms

A. F. of L. Predicts Good Trade

London Wheat Parley Fails

Louisiana Gives All to Long

Virginia Clings to Its Dances

California Does Gobble Cement

INCREASING friction between Japan and Russia over the Chinese Eastern Railway, with serious clashes in Manchuria, may be ended by an extraordinary circumstance, the railroad's sale. Moscow learns that negotiations have come much nearer to satisfactory results than has been supposed. Russia, which is said at first to have demanded 625,000,000 yen for its half interest, is understood to have dropped to 160,000,000, with two-thirds payment acceptable in Japanese goods. Japan, which bid 50,000,000 yen, has raised to 120,000,000. Observers see the breach closing and losing its grave threat of trouble—Manchukuo may become nominal owner of the Chinese Eastern, but Japanese steam will make the wheels go round. ✦ ✦ ✦

❡ The American Federation of Labor predicts a substantial upturn in the nation's business, beginning in September. Seasonal decline will end a steady rise set in, says the announcement. Normal improvement and stimulation by the NRA are given the credit at the Atlantic City conference of the Federation's Council. The sincerity of Labor's prediction is assured by the many important strikes it is planning—Labor's strategy is to strike when there is appear to be substantial prizes to fight for. ✦ ✦ ✦

❡ London hears the "big four" wheat exporting nations admit collapse of their efforts to agree on a 1934-35 schedule for export quotas. Argentina demands a quota of 150,000,000 bushels, but Australia, Canada and the United States refuse to agree unless Argentina will guarantee acreage reduction commensurate with their own. Argentinian and Russian delegates profess to lack instructions and the conference goes to pieces. America, owing to drought, may have little to send abroad—And somehow plans to limit production while some men go hungry do not succeed. ✦ ✦ ✦

❡ Louisiana's Legislature completes its transferring to Senator Huey P. Long dictatorial powers about equal to those of Adolf Hitler. In Long's effort to defeat his chief enemy, Mayor T. Semmes Walmsley of New Orleans, and forcibly gain control of that stronghold of his opposition, new laws nullify restraining powers of the courts, give him an investigating court of his own, and a large constabulary to operate all over the State. Senator Long has taken over the law—It remains to be seen what the popular sentiment of an American state will do about it. ✦ ✦ ✦

❡ Germany and former Chancellor Hitler's two-hour pre-plebiscite speech interesting as climax of an extraordinary campaign. Even Germany, where the Government controls all channels of public information and propaganda has been developed to the farthest degree, never saw anything like it. Paris interprets the speech as an attempt to gain confidence of the world through protestations of peace. Propaganda Minister Goebbels says propaganda becomes the German's daily bread—A people that assents to this will certainly reflect their leaders' will. ✦ ✦ ✦

❡ Virginia watches White Top Mountain vibrate in rhythm as the Folk Music Festival draws absorbed crowds. The tuneful ballads and spirited dancing steps that have characterized the life of these mountaineers for 150 years have more exponents than ever. Many of the 300 performers have wavy hair and long beards. The old dances hold their power, for 40 per cent of the dancers are under 30 years. The 24 fiddlers from Pennsylvania come to join in the "speed the plow" competition—"Cacklin' hen" and "flop-eared mule" express the life of a wholesome, rugged people. ✦ ✦ ✦

❡ Austria understands that Britain and France have asked Chancellor Kurt Schuschnigg to enlarge the basis of his Government. This move, advised to prevent dictatorial government, would involve persuading Social Democrats or National Socialists to assume Cabinet portfolios. The latter would be unacceptable; the former, remembering stability of their comrades, might refuse. Again, the Franco-British request may not please Italy. Working out of the Austrian situation still requires clearest thought—The right solution is of the utmost importance to the whole of Europe. ✦ ✦ ✦

❡ Southern California finds enough concrete going into aqueducts to lead Colorado River water to 14 cities to build a highway from Los Angeles to New York. This $220,000,000 water distribution project requires 5,670,000 barrels of cement, or 160,000 more than needed to build the sister project of Boulder Dam 150 miles upstream from the intake. In 29 separate bores 91 miles of 16-foot tunnel are being put through. The whole history of engineering holds nothing comparable to this—Southern California does one more thing in its grave, matchless manner.

'Paradise' in Manchukuo Fails To Meet Japanese Predictions, Analysis of Resources Shows

Manchuria Hasn't Produced Cotton, Iron and Beans as Needed by Japan, While Demand for Japanese Manufactures in Manchuria Is Disappointing

Special to The Christian Science Monitor

HARBIN, Manchuria—At the moment when the Japanese first entered Manchuria the subsidized press was full of articles leading the public to believe that Manchuria was now on the road to a sort of earthly paradise, generally spoken of as "Wang Tao."

Two years have already passed and this earthly paradise does not seem to be closer than on the day when it was first written about, and it is generally recognized that difficult and enormous obstacles lie in the path of Japan.

The most extraordinary point in the situation is that apparently the Japanese invaded Manchuria without having any real plan as to what they would do with the conquered country.

There is an institution in Japan which is called "The Overseas Office," and as it really represents civilian interests it has been consistently against the military proposals regarding economic penetration into Manchuria. Present reports from Japanese sources rather lead to the assumption that some kind of an agreement has been arrived at between the military and the civil parties regarding the exploitation of Manchurian resources, but notwithstanding the importance of the question, the bloc does not seem to be advancing in any way, this being contrary to the defined plan which was entered into by Soviet Russia.

The idea of the Japan-Manchukuo bloc is the attainment of such conditions in economic relation between the two countries as will make them

one body in a certain number of years, entirely independent of all foreign countries.

It might be said that there is a certain likeness between the objects of the bloc and the Soviet Five-Year Plan by which the latter country is putting itself on a self-supporting basis.

The idea of the bloc are quite clear but there are many obstacles which will probably entirely hinder the attainment of the scheme that all raw materials should be supplied by Manchuria and manufactured goods by Japan. An investigation of the figures published annually regarding Japan's foreign trade clearly indicate that raw cotton and wool, iron and steel, wheat, beans and their by-products—cakes, sugar and rubber—represent the greater part of her imports. If Manchuria were actually able to supply all the above raw materials the scheme would be a very excellent one and would solve the economic problems of Japan, but it is extremely doubtful as to how much Manchuria can supply in the above lines, even though the cultivation of some of them may be increased.

Although it 'is emphasized that the finished products are for the use of the unemployed and will not be sold on the general market, many protests against what is called "government competition" are being received at federal emergency relief headquarters. A recent announcement that the unemployed would be put to work making rough furniture for their homes brought 700 letters of protest from furniture manufacturers.

Wide Range of Articles

The list of articles which state relief officials are now manufacturing with the use of federal funds includes, besides mattresses and furniture, sheets, pillow cases, towels, shirts, underwear, pajamas, nightgowns, children's play suits, coats and dresses and slips for women and young girls—in fact, all kinds of clothing for men, women and children. Relief officials defend their program on the grounds that the people who receive the clothing would not be buying it, but would be wearing rags.

The estimated quantity of cotton required for the mills of Japan is 600,000 tons of which fully 90 per cent is imported from the United States and India, and only 10 per cent from China and Korea. So far Manchuria has not produced more than 13,000 tons, while Korea has given about 7000 tons per annum. As the cotton plant cannot be cultivated in all parts of Manchuria, there seems

(Continued on Page 2, Column 6)

Cry Against U.S. In Business Grows Louder

Sixty Thousand Jobless Women Put to Work Making Mattresses

Many Articles Made

Protests Continue in Face of Plea of 'No Sales' in General Market

Special from Monitor Bureau

WASHINGTON, Aug. 20 — With announcement that 60,000 unemployed women are being put to work making mattresses in 650 sewing rooms throughout the country, the Government takes another step into the manufacturing business.

Investigation reveals that relief workers paid out of federal funds are already making a wide range of clothing and canned goods for use of the unemployed. Many of the plants have been set up in factory buildings that private industry has had to abandon in the last three or four years.

The sewing and canning programs are giving work to some 300,000 persons in the states, a large part of which are women. Relief officials like the projects because they give really productive work to the unemployed and at the same time train them; along these lines may enable them to find work later. Unable to see the end of the new applicants for relief, officials hope that the self-help scheme will aid the Government to get out from under the tremendous burden it is shouldering. With factories lying idle as well as men and women, they believe the natural thing is to bring the two together.

In the fall the Government's manufacturing program will be extended to use the thousands of hides of cattle bought in the drought regions. Federal authorities have promised the tanning industry that they will keep these hides off the market. Instead, they will be used for shoes, jackets and gloves for the unemployed.

Located in Every State

Mattress factories will be located in almost every state, Mrs. Ellen H. Woodward, director of the women's work division of the FERA, announced. The 250,000 bales of cotton used is of low grade, purchased by the surplus relief corporation out of surplus stocks. Each mattress will be stamped with a warning that it must not be sold.

Pointing out that in one southern state 60 per cent of the people on relief rolls had no mattresses, Mrs. Woodward predicted that the Government manufacture would help private manufacturers by accustoming people to mattresses.

(Continued on Page 8, Column 3)

Schuschnigg Advised to Give Wider Base to Austrian Rule In New Franco-British Move

Monitor's Review of Week in Europe Finds Reich Reaching Far Afield for Voters in Hitler Plebiscite—Danes Drop 'No Arms' Policy

By Press Wireless from The Christian Science Monitor's European Bureau

LONDON, Aug. 20 — The British and French Governments, the Monitor understands, have privately advised Dr. Kurt Schuschnigg, Austrian Chancellor, to enlarge the basis of his Government. It is understood he has already been approached by the Social Democrats in this connection.

While the Anglo-French démarche is regarded as an important evidence of the attitude of these Governments toward the present dictatorial régime in Austria, it is not expected to have startling results. In the first place, the Social Democrats are unlikely to have forgotten what happened to their comrades during the February shootings.

Moreover, a broadening of the base of the Austrian Government, whether in the direction of the Social Democrats or the National Socialist would scarcely be palatable to Signor Mussolini, who, as the financial backer of the existing Heimwehr-clerical coalition expects to be allowed to call the turn in Austria.

At the same time, Downing Street, the Quai d'Orsay and other chancelleries are receiving pessimistic reports about the prospects of the present Austrian Government. Competent observers feel it must either persuade the Social Democrats or the National Socialists to support it or go under—with incalculable effects on the European situation.

Plebiscite, War Guilt in Reich

The campaign for yesterday's plebiscite in Germany was by no means confined to the Fatherland. Four base, chartered by the German Consulate at Geneva carried voters from that swiss city. A number of German residents in Istanbul, Turkey, were taken by a German steamer out into the Black Sea where they recorded their votes beyond the limit of Turkish territorial waters. In addition, the vote was carried out to German nationals far beyond the frontiers of the Reich.

Stauning Reverses Arms Policy

Mr. Thorwald Stauning, Prime Minister and leader of the Danish Socialist Party, which long has been advocating total disarmament, is un-

(Continued on Page 8, Column 1)

Sticks to Guns

By Eugene Hutchinson

Miss Viola Ilma
President of Central Bureau for Young America

Youth Congress Is Still Divided When It Closes

Each Side Elects Heads and Adopts Program for Achievement

Special from Monitor Bureau

NEW YORK, Aug. 20—Miss Viola Ilma of New York City was elected chairman of the board of governors of the First American Youth Congress at the closing session of the congress Friday night at New York University.

Taking its first step to organize on a permanent, nation-wide basis, eight months ago by Miss Ilma, as president of the Central Bureau for Young America, concluded its three-day program by electing a board aiming to be as widely representative of the United States as a whole as possible.

The opposing faction, having Mr. Waldo McNutt of Topeka, Kan., as chairman, passed a resolution protesting discrimination against Negroes, particularly in the South, when this discrimination deprives them of public school facilities. Negro teachers in the public schools should receive pay equal to that paid white teachers, provided their work is equal, it was advocated in another resolution. Politically and economically controlled institutions that prevent academic freedom were condemned.

This same group, which objected to being termed "radical," voted for the abolition of all forms of military training in high schools and colleges, and for the diversion of the millions now so spent for increased educational and relief facilities; the abolition of the Citizens Military Training Corps; freedom of all imprisoned in Fascist countries for their opposition to Fascism; the defense of the Democratic rights gained by the masses of people; against all forms of exploitation and hatred against national and racial minorities, Jews, Negros, Mexicans, Japanese; for the immediate withdrawal of all American armed forces from colonial countries, China, the Philippines; for the support of the peace proposals of the Soviet Union; for complete disarmament. It was stressed that the "only constructive proposals toward peace at international conferences have been offered by the Soviet Union."

Johnson to Stay NRA Head Until It Is Reorganized

General Intimated He Was to Remain Indefinitely but Reports Say 'No'

Special from Monitor Bureau

WASHINGTON, Aug. 20—President Roosevelt and Brig.-Gen. Hugh S. Johnson on Saturday consulted over NRA's future for the first time since the latter's return a week ago and segmented with the announcement that the General was staying on with the NRA.

But while the General's own version of the conference with the President implied that the NRA chief was staying on indefinitely at the request of the President it was explained that the President had asked him to stay only "until" the re-organization of the NRA is complete and the new system is running smoothly.

General Johnson, on emerging from the conference said, "The President told me I could not get away from the NRA or the Administration. He wants me right here with my feet nailed right down on the floor. And, of course, I'm staying."

Almost simultaneously it was learned that the President was not thinking in terms of keeping the General on indefinitely, but only of keeping him during the transition stage. Thus rumors of his early dismissal are officially scotched but indications that the turbulent Blue Eagle chief would be dispensed with ultimately are confirmed.

There is as yet no positive indication when the reorganization of the NRA will be complete, except that this stage is not likely to be reached before the elections. It is considered most likely that the reorganization will be started as soon as possible to head off official campaign attacks on the actual form of the NRA, but that completion of the process will not arrive until sometime after the elections, probably in the early spring.

Thus the Administration will make every possible effort to turn aside the blows of industrial opposition without at the same time admitting dissatisfaction with General Johnson.

The Monitor Index

Monday, Aug. 20, 1934

General News—Pages 1, 2, 3, 8
News of Sports—Page 4
Financial News—Page 6

Features

The Children's Page 9
The Home Forum 7
  Constructive Thinking
  [With Hungarian Translation]
Daily Features 9
Editorials 10

Things Present

What does the farmer think about the New Deal for agriculture? Professor Parker summarizes some Kansas views, in the Wide Horizon, on the Editorial Page.

The Lacey's planning for a vacation trip reminds us of a balloonist's meticulous preparation for a stratosphere flight. See "One More Canvas Bag," on the Home Forum Page.

An article on the Children's Page discusses the insect orchestra piece by piece, and tells how and when each is played.
Another Parable of Safed the Sage appears on the inside page.

And Things to Come

Tuesday brings the Home Building and Gardening Page, with its Hobbies Column; the Progress in Education Page; and a layout of seascapes sent in by members of the Monitor Camera Club.

Textile Situation Kept Close Under Government's Eye

Feeling in Washington Is That Labor Is Being a Little Unreasonable

Special from Monitor Bureau

WASHINGTON, Aug. 20 — The Federal Government, from President Roosevelt down, has been keeping a sharp eye on developments in the textile industry where strike warnings threaten to take somewhere up to 500,000 men out of work and tie up the first major industry to come under NRA supervision.

While there is no disposition to minimize the potential dangers of the situation here, it is felt that as yet there is no reason for direct federal intervention. It is pointed out that the authority to order a general textile strike, which is vested in the executive committee of the United Textile Workers of America, is an optional, not a mandatory, authority.

The White House remains extremely cool to the suggestion of direct presidential intervention from the union headquarters in New York. It strongly deprecates the tendency in each recurring strike situation to seek Mr. Roosevelt's personal mediation. It is certain that the Chief Executive has not the slightest in-

(Continued on Page 8, Column 6)

Hitler Polls Huge 'Ja' Vote In Plebiscite

More Than 38,000,000 Give Approval to Assumption of Presidency

'No' Vote Increased

But Absolute Power Is Won by Der Führer in Appeal to German Electorate

BERLIN, Aug. 20 (P)—Germany has given former Adolf Hitler a 38,000,000 vote "Ja."

In Sunday's one-man election, called to let the people say by ballot if they approved Chancellor Hitler's action in naming himself, upon the death of President von Hindenburg, as President, too, the vote was:

"Yes"—38,362,760.
"No"—4,294,654.
"Invalid"—872,296.

Waning Enthusiasm

Some see in these preliminary official figures a waning in enthusiasm for Herr Hitler, pointing out that yesterday's "No" votes were more than twice the number that were cast in last November's plebiscite. Attention is also called to the sharp decline in the volume of National-Socialist Party votes as compared with the November voting.

In the November plebiscite there were 43,453,000 "Ja" votes, and in the November Reichstag election the Nazi vote was 39,655,224.

With but few exceptions, the 35 major voting districts produced in yesterday's election fewer "Ja" votes than were cast in November. Some observers see this as a failure of the German voters to respond to the appeals of Nazi orators during the past few days that a larger affirmative vote be cast so that the world might know the nation is solidly behind "Mein Hitler."—President-Chancellor Hitler.

"Yes" votes placed 89.9 per cent of the total, as against 95 per cent in the plebiscite of nine months ago. The public cast a total of 43,529,710 votes, according to preliminary final figures, or approximately 96 per cent of the whole 45,202,667 registered, qualified voters.

Nazis Exultant

Regardless of how the balloting may be interpreted abroad, the results have been accepted by Nazis as full evidence of their strength.

Today has been set aside as a "Day of Victory" with National Socialist flags unfurled throughout the Third Reich in celebration of the new conquest. The victory came after a day of quiet, orderly voting, unmarred by disturbance. There were scenes of wild enthusiasm when the polls closed.

In Berlin thousands stood for hours in the rain in front of the Chancellery hoping for a glance of Herr Hitler. Women in summer dresses were drenched but still cheered for "Der Führer" long after midnight.

Marching columns of men added to the formalities of the victory celebration, but the rain stopped a scheduled torchlight procession.

Herr Hitler himself did not vote.

Some Losses; Some Gains

The results of the voting showed a distinct loss of his support in certain provinces and major voting districts. Hamburg voting district, where Herr Hitler, ironically enough, made his personal campaign appeal, showed a sharp drop, compared to the November balloting. Instead of 736,404 "Yes" votes turned out then, there were only 650,872 votes of approval, or 71.5 per cent for the district, a former Communist stronghold.

East Prussia, which is dominated by the large land-holding interests, rolled up a 97.1 per cent affirmative vote but cast less approval ballots than it did in 1933.

The Oppeln voting district which is strongly Roman Catholic, provided 723,216 affirmative votes, as against 835,459 in the November balloting, the percentage dropping from 95.5 to 90.8.

The province of Pomerania, home of small farmers, polled 1,185,259 votes of approval, compared to 1,178,403 "for" last November.

In the Berlin district 224,558 persons voted against Hitler, while 986,334 voted for him. Ballots of 32,235 persons were declared void.

The failure of Hitlerism to exceed past election results is expected in political circles to influence the Nazi program.

Stratosphere Flight Ends in Yugoslavia

MARIBOR, Yugoslavia, Aug. 20 (P)—The Belgian stratosphere balloonists, Prof. Max Cosyns and M. Nérée Vanderlist, settled gently to the earth in a corn field near Zinovlje Saturday night after almost all hope for their safety had been abandoned.

At the delicate scientific instruments with which the balloonists went aloft at Hour-Havenne in Belgium were intact, but the instruments not attained. The scientists, exhausted but uninjured, believed they had gone up nearly 16 miles far short of their goal.

As the great gas bag descended in the gathering dusk farmers fled in terror. The strange sight was believed by the simple peasants to be of infernal origin.

The village gendarmes came to the scene quickly and informed the bewildered scientists that they were in Yugoslavia.

Stronger Laws Advocated For Drunken Driving

A. A. A. Urges More Uniform, Adequate and Rigidly Enforced Penalties

Special from Monitor Bureau

WASHINGTON, Aug. 20—Revealing that in many states it is legally possible for a motorist convicted of driving while drunk to escape with a fine of as little as 1 cent or one day in jail, Mr. Thomas P. Henry, president of the American Automobile Association, declares that more control can be acquired over drunken driving by providing "more uniform, adequate, reasonable and rigidly enforced penalties."

The A. A. A. survey, among other things, shows:

Penalties that may be legally imposed for first offense convictions range from 1 cent to $5000.

Jail sentences provided by law range from one day to five years.

Seven states, namely, Florida, Illinois, Indiana, Minnesota, Nebraska, Oregon and West Virginia, make jail sentences mandatory for first convictions, while two states, Kentucky and Mississippi, have no provisions either for an optional or a mandatory jail sentence for first offenses.

Three states, New Hampshire, Virginia and Rhode Island, have definitely provided by law that sentences for second convictions cannot be suspended.

Suspension or revocation of driving permits is mandatory for first offenses in 31 states.

Mr. Henry recommended as reasonable the standard furnished in the Uniform Motor Vehicle Code as recently amended by the Fourth National Conference on Street and Highway Safety. For first convictions the code prescribes a fine of not less than $100 and not more than $1000, or a jail sentence of not less than 10 days and not more than one year, or both. For second offenses it prescribes a minimum mandatory jail sentence of 90 days, with an additional fine in the discretion of the court.

Japan Denies Intent To Interfere With Philippine Affairs

TOKYO, Aug. 20 (P)—A Foreign Office spokesman declares: "The Japanese Government has no intention of interfering in the domestic affairs of the Philippines or the relations between the United States and the Philippines."

His statement was to comment on an address by Count Atsushi Kimura, Japanese consul-general at Manilla, who told Filipino students that there might be "serious effects" from tariff increases by the Islands.

Commenting upon another phase of Japanese foreign relations, the spokesman said, "No negotiations are in progress looking to an Anglo-Japanese political agreement. It is probable that the impending British mission evoked rumors to this effect, but the mission is purely economic and non-political, and I think is not concerned with the possibility of British recognition of Manchukuo."

The mission is to be headed by Lord Barnby, director of Lloyds Bank, will cross America in September on its way to the Orient. The spokesman said Japan will seek to promote an accord on views of naval issues with Great Britain in conversations in October in London but that no larger agreement was

Accord Looming On Railway Issue, Moscow Reports

Soviet Newspapers Carry Contrary Predictions of Forcible Seizure

Special to The Christian Science Monitor via Press Wireless

MOSCOW, Aug. 20 — Disclosure that Russo-Japanese negotiations concerning the sale of the Chinese Eastern Railway have come much nearer agreement than was generally suspected revives hope here that a settlement may be possible in the early fall, despite present friction in Manchuria.

The official Soviet statement reveals that the most recent Japanese offer fixed the price at 120,000,000 yen, or about $36,000,000, whereas the Soviets have agreed to accept 160,000,000 yen, about $48,000,000.

As evidence of its willingness to settle the matter reasonably, Moscow reveals full details of the negotiations, showing that the Soviets originally asked 250,000,000 gold rubles for the railway, which equaled 625,000,000 yen. The Japanese offer fixed the price at 120,000,000 yen the Soviets have disclosed a decided spirit of compromise, and that the Japanese have also indicated a disposition to increase the price sufficiently to make settlement possible.

With the offers so nearly equal, it is reasonable to suppose that a settlement—

(Continued on Page 8, Column 3)

Little California City Seeks To Take World Into the Home

Special to The Christian Science Monitor

CULVER CITY, Calif.—An impressive exhibition of what a small city can do toward interesting its residents in world affairs was provided here recently when Culver City young people produced the first Community International Night.

Culver City, which had the stated purpose of promoting "world friendship and international and interracial understanding among the various peoples of the earth," was held in the city hall after six weeks of effort in securing an attractive and informative schedule of speakers and entertainment.

But Community International Night really had its genesis at a much earlier date. It was discussed a year ago by young men and women who had attended Pacific coast universities where world affairs were emphasized, and this group began to plan a program that would awaken the home city to a wider appreciation of the world.

The result was that a young people's inter-church committee took concrete action operation as a nucleus about which definite plans could grow. Care was taken, however, to make the event a community, and not a church, enterprise. This was accomplished partly by securing the indorsement of 100 professional and business people. Still greater care was taken to consolidate the community interest by securing cash subscriptions from 75 persons and organizations.

With the generation of a large measure of interest, the enterprise

went forward with vigor. The young sponsors found ready support, and soon learned that it could be self-financed, for many persons were willing to loan and donate needed things. Thus when the assigned evening approached, Community International Night was found with a full program and a ready audience. Culver City is in the 5000 population class, but the city hall was packed, literally, with an eager group of citizens who had come to see the consular delegation from Los Angeles and to hear a group of speakers.

Mayor Frank H. Dobson opened the serious discussion by telling how important he thought a study of world affairs could be to a community like Culver City, and he was followed by Mr. Geoffrey Morgan, Chautauqua lecturer, who described what could be called an international point of view.

As a part of the program, the consular representatives in the Los Angeles from Czechoslovakia, Argentina, Dominican Republic and China, Costa Rica were introduced to the audience, and then a program of musical entertainment representing 14 countries was presented.

Mr. Malcolm Alexander, general chairman, said following the celebration that the committee had sought to present world affairs not as a person to person basis, and not from the standpoint of politics and economics. The possibility of holding another Community International Night is being discussed.

'On Ships of State, Prue'

Mussolini, My Dear Sister, Would Make His Vessel Into a Gunboat, and on a Communist Ship We'd All Take Turns at the Boilers!

Meanwhile, British Treacly Puddings

Richard L. Strout of the Monitor's Washington staff, breaks away from his old friends in "Claverly Street" to revisit England, mellowed by memories of his former sojourns there. His letters will appear at irregular intervals. This is the second.

S. S. Aquitania, At Sea, Thursday

Dear Prue:

The difficulty about all this voyage, my dear sister, is to believe that it is real. In all my preparations I neglected the essential one, I find, of sitting down and convincing myself that all this was happening to me. Here I am, a sedentary and bookish man, piled loose from my rut, and actually in mid-Atlantic. "And a very good thing, too!" I hear you say. Well, mind Waldo, the cat, then, and see he gets his fish on Friday, and I shall do what I can.

I think the menu was what really convinced me we were sailing for England. The Cunard Company has done well by us. But the British prejudices peep through. There is an honest effort to Americanize this bill of fare; there is friendly rivalry to irritate us with a stratosphere flight. See "One More Canvas Bag," meticulous breakfast, and there is ice cream for dinner. But there is also a selective choice of British beef, British veal, British lamb; something called "Oxford brawn" (connected perhaps with the athletic attainments of the university); all served with standard British sauces and mustard, and followed when desired by hearty, British treacly puddings.

Good, solid, substantial stuff, if you go British on the menu; the kind of food that made tight little England great.

Young Jones, the newspaper man from Washington who shares my cabin, says the ship resembles the aristocratic state. First class, he says, looks down on second class; second class on third class, and third —well, it looks down on the fish!

This condition of affairs appears to irritate young Jones. Let me say to irritate young Jones. But there is also in second class to irritate young Jones. Let me say journalistic cockiness there is a certain bump of astuteness. I tell him I enjoy such definite class divisions; I am a conservative.

"You know where you are in such a social scheme," I say. "A pure democracy would be a cabin ship. I suppose—all one class; Mr. Musso-

(Continued on Page 8, Column 1)

THE CHRISTIAN SCIENCE MONITOR

AN INTERNATIONAL DAILY NEWSPAPER

COPYRIGHT 1935 BY
THE CHRISTIAN SCIENCE PUBLISHING SOCIETY

BOSTON, THURSDAY, FEBRUARY 14, 1935—VOL. XXVII, NO. 67

••—ATLANTIC EDITION—FIVE CENTS A COPY

The March of the Nations

By Rufus Steele

Germany Accepts London Plan

Macon's Crew Wins High Praise

Japan's House Votes War Sums

Hauptmann Gets Chair Decree

Britain Bids for Irish State

Hitler Seeks Trade With Motor

GERMANY replies to France and Britain on the London proposals, specifying questions yet to be cleared up, but accepting the basis for negotiating a European settlement. A report that Berlin would demand a plebiscite in Austria on Anschluss is not borne out. Germany appears willing to sign an Austrian noninterference pact to counterbalance Italy. Germany is not willing to assume a mutual assistance pact, holding its army too small, but it is in favor of the air convention. Germany wants it understood that Part V of the Versailles Treaty limiting its arms is definitely at an end—But Chancellor Hitler does appear to make the unity of five big powers complete by joining in.

¶ Washington moves to get at the reason for the collapse of the navy dirigible Macon. Statements of officers and crew in San Francisco show a coolness and bravery displayed all through the emergency that could hardly have been surpassed. President Roosevelt halts all airship building plans. Its Akron (Ohio) builders stoutly defend the Macon—From Germany Dr. Hugo Eckener points to his long record of safety with the Zeppelins and says his faith is unimpaired.

¶ Japan's House of Representatives overwhelmingly passes the military expenditures budget of $297,000,000 and sends it to the House of Peers. The sum, largest in Japanese history, represents 46 per cent of the entire year's expenditures. The militarists have won their long, hard fight on the score of "an international crisis" and the opposition is nearly silenced. A dreadful dictum an admiral has demanded that the people accept—He has said Japan must maintain an equal navy even if its citizens are reduced to a diet of rice gruel.

¶ Bruno Richard Hauptmann is found guilty of first degree murder of the Lindbergh child and is sentenced to electrocution in the week of March 18. The jury of eight men and four women is unanimous on the degree of guilt on the first ballot, but four more ballots are taken and much discussion ensues during 11 hours before the two women and one man who favored life imprisonment vote with the others. Circumstantial evidence, which many sought to discredit during the trial, receives the full approval of the jury—In fact, the verdict shows that circumstantial evidence, when convincing, is the strongest kind.

¶ British and Australian newspapers rush out editions carrying the Hauptmann verdict in enormous headlines. Popular opinion in those countries, where the papers carried full cable reports, appears to approve the verdict. London papers comment that gowns and wigs were omitted and cigarettes allowed in recesses in the Flemington court. In line with American sentiment, they regret the theatricalism press and radio gave the trial, but commend the dignity and fairness maintained by Justice Trenchard. The conviction does not bring back the Lindbergh child—But the world is quietly gratified to know that the parents could not be made to suffer such an outrage with impunity.

¶ Britain sees J. H. Thomas, Secretary of Dominions, hold out the olive branch to the Irish Free State. He tells the Constitutional Club in London that should the Free State say it wishes to remain an integral part of the Empire in this year of the King's Silver Jubilee, the event would be celebrated by the United British Commonwealth of Nations. This step follows logically the recent trade understanding. Mr. Thomas says there is no hostility toward the Irish in the thoughts of the British—"Only a single-minded desire to see the Empire united."

¶ Cuba hunts for miscreants who bomb the Bank of Nova Scotia at Santiago, perhaps to injure the U. S. Consulate above it. A panic and slight injuries follow the explosion. Havana calls out the armed forces to commemorate the 37th anniversary of the blowing up of the U. S. battleship Maine in Havana harbor. The mysterious explosion that cost 261 officers and men their lives has never been cleared up. The date has more than sympathetic interest for the Cubans—War followed and Cuba escaped from 400 years of Spanish rule.

¶ Reichsführer Adolf Hitler announces that Germany will win its way back into the world markets with a new automobile that requires little fuel. He opens the auto show, saying Germany solves the problem of the cheap car because it must. He cites one costing no more than a middle-priced motorcycle and having "the least imaginable fuel consumption." The motor makers enthuse—They feel the new car becomes the object of first importance for export.

Italy's Grand Council Meets To Decide Action on Ethiopia; Prospect of Hostilities Fades

Reinforcements Prepare to Leave for Eritrea and Somaliland

Copyright 1935 by the Associated Press

ROME, Feb. 14—The first detachment of Italy's African expeditionary force will leave Sicily for Eritrea and Italian Somaliland Saturday, a Government spokesman announced today.

This information was divulged as Premier Benito Mussolini prepared to confer with the Fascist Grand Council to determine his policy in view of the communication sent him by Emperor Haile Selassie of Ethiopia.

The official spokesman said other expeditionary contingents would follow the first unit on Sunday and succeeding days. He emphasized this move does not necessarily presage war, but the troops are being dispatched to reinforce colonial garrisons and obviate the danger of further Ethiopian attacks.

The number of troops scheduled to leave was not disclosed, but it was learned 15,000 will be on their way before the end of next week.

"This shows definitely our mobilization was not merely a bluff, the spokesman said.

More than 1000 troops with full equipment arrived in Rome this morning from northern cities. They were to spend the day here in barracks, undergoing inspection of their equipment, and then were to move on to Sicily.

There appeared to be less concern in government circles over the prospect of hostilities in Africa, although an authoritative source said Italy was prepared to spend $850,000,000 in a two-year African campaign if war breaks out.

Whether or not the expeditionary force is sent apparently depends on Il Duce's reaction to Emperor Haile Selassie's vigorous note de-

(Continued on Page 4, Column 3)

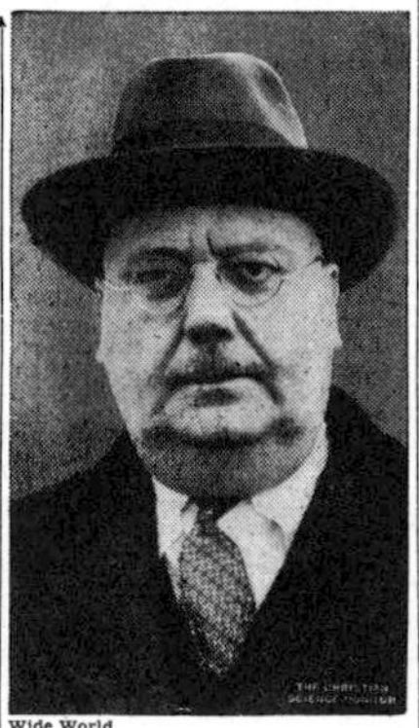

Wide World

George C. Hanson

Who Has Been Named United States Chargé d'Affaires at Addis Abeba

Huge Profit On Cruisers Is Admitted

Newport News Company Made $5,601,851 on Two Ships

Say It Was Surprise

Special from Monitor Bureau

WASHINGTON, Feb. 14—Senate munitions investigators today disclosed that the Newport News Shipbuilding Company made 35 per cent profit on two naval cruisers in 1927, but officials of the company described the gain as entirely unanticipated.

Homer L. Ferguson, president of the company, contended that the Government received extra advantages in later bids to offset the large profit on the Houston and Augusta. He produced a letter which F. P. Palen, vice-president of the company, wrote to H. E. Huntingdon, owner, predicting that there would be a "moderate" profit on the two ships.

"Nobody on this committee was more surprised than I was when I heard about the 35 per cent profit," Mr. Ferguson declared. "We don't charge 35 per cent on any ship. I think it's rotten business in addition to not being right. It is just as bad from my point of view to over-estimate costs as to under-estimate."

Admits Huge Profit

The shipbuilders admitted that they made a $5,601,851 profit on the two vessels. They explained that after the bids were made, design costs were cut down by the establishment of a joint marine engineering corporation which served all the large companies and by reductions in overhead brought about by an increase in volume of production and an improvement in plant efficiency.

Mr. Ferguson described the so-called "protective" as a bid to protect the customer. Asked if it did not protect the company's competitors in the field, he replied, "I have nothing to do with other companies. They mean nothing to me."

He explained that if his own yard does not want a certain ship, then it bids high on it; if it is anxious to get the contract it bids low. Bids, he said, run all the way from cost to 10 and 12 per cent profit.

"We bid solely in accordance with what we consider the necessities of our own business," Mr. Ferguson told the committee.

Appeals Sometimes Prevail

"Company estimators," he said, "are sometimes moved by appeals from workers in the vicinity of the plant to cut their estimates to the bone in order to assure business for the plant."

Mr. Ferguson described to a "natural process" the fact that there was almost an even split of contracts in the merchant marine program over a period of three years between his company, New York Shipbuilding Corporation and Bethlehem Newport News, it was revealed received $33,000,000 worth of business; Bethlehem $33,000,000 and New York, $31,700,000.

He said he was "surprised" when he found his company had bid the same on the Manhattan and Washington as Bethlehem. Both bids were $9,750,000. The New York company bid $9,515,000 and received the contract. It had been charged before the committee that the larger bids were put into "protect" the New York company's bid.

The committee deviated from its munitions topic long enough to question Mr. Ferguson about the Morro Castle which his company built. The shipbuilder said the ill-fated ship was equipped with all modern fireproof appliances and met specifications laid down in the convention for safety of life at sea which this country has not yet ratified.

Europe's Traders Decry Air Barriers

Balkan Situation Worst With Secret Zones Closing Vast Areas

Special from Monitor Bureau

LONDON — British and French business men are now joined in protest against international air travel restrictions imposed on account of military and naval interests, in certain localities.

Chief among these obstacles are the "prohibited areas" across which flying is forbidden and the narrow corridors through which entrance to a state is allowed. In many cases both entail long detours. They are almost entirely for the purpose of guarding military or naval secrets connected with fortifications and defenses.

The London Chamber of Commerce has now approached the Air Council on the matter, and the Air Transport Committee of the International Chamber of Commerce has compiled a list of air traffic barriers in force in 30 different countries and asks for a simplification of formalities.

A map of Roumania shows how that country has frontiers to six others as well as a stretch of the Black Sea, and for those six countries it provides only narrow corridors on its closed frontiers. Even where the frontier is open it may be a prohibited area in the adjoining country.

There are many other cases which have come to the notice of the aviation section of the Automobile Association. The big area round the fortified harbor of Cherbourg is one. This is practically on the direct route between London and the Channel Islands between which there is a daily service. The prohibition necessitates a longer sea route at a greater distance from the land than would otherwise be necessary. Taxi aircraft, too, meeting ships arriving at, or departing from Cherbourg have to enter by a narrow corridor from the south.

A prohibited area on the Czechoslovak-Hungarian frontier necessitates an extra 65 miles flying between Cracow and Budapest. A prohibited area in Switzerland, coupled with those in Italy, causes pilots to take a narrow, winding route, instead of the direct one over the St. Gotthard Pass. It is hoped that the protests from business men will result, at least, in relaxing some of the prohibitions and a diminution in the size of some of the prohibited areas.

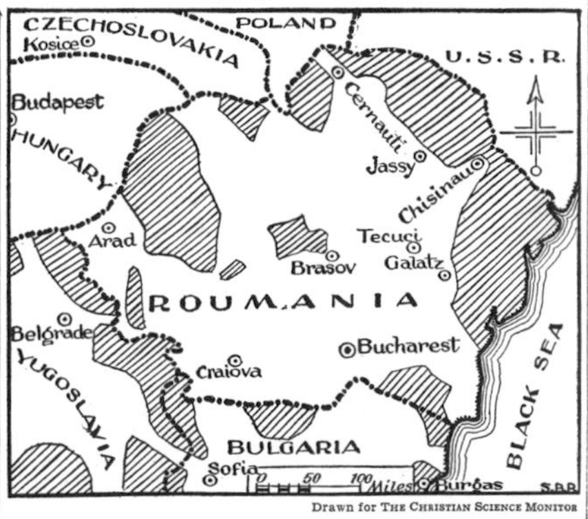

Drawn for THE CHRISTIAN SCIENCE MONITOR

Air Lanes Sharply Restricted

Shaded Portions of This Map Show Prohibited Areas for Fliers. The Map Sets Forth Roumania's Territory as Typical of Conditions All Over the Balkans and Central Europe.

Reich Replies It's Ready To Discuss Pact

Franco-British Proposal Approved in Principle, According to Report

Air Locarno Pleases

Germany Expected to Hesitate on Lending Armed Support to Other States

By Press Wireless from Monitor Bureau

BERLIN, Feb. 14—Germany's reply to the London proposals was handed to Sir Eric Phipps, British Ambassador, and Ambassador André François-Poncet of France this afternoon.

The reply of the German Government is understood to indicate the Reich's willingness to accept the proposals of Britain and France as a suitable starting point for negotiations. The reply also emphasizes a number of important questions which Germany considers require further clearing up.

In Gen. Hermann Wilhelm Göring's words at Dresden last week end, Germany's "complete equality of rights in all directions" must be the basis for future discussions.

Right to Rearm

Thus the new armaments agreement, which is to replace the discriminatory armaments policy laid down in Article V of the Versailles Treaty must admit from the first Germany's right to such armaments as it considers necessary in view of the military strength of other states. Germany considers the proposed air convention as a definite step toward this equality. Consequently Berlin is understood to be giving the strongest support to this proposal.

Regarding the East European pact, Baron Constantin von Neurath's reply is expected to indicate that in no case is Germany willing to sign a treaty of mutual assistance in case the frontiers of any one of the signatory states is attacked. It maintains that its army is too small for sanctions purposes.

Austrian Plebiscite

Germany also is understood to desire fuller information regarding Franco-Russian relations at the present time.

On the question of the Austrian noninterference pact in connection with which some press reports have asserted that Germany would demand a plebiscite in Austria as a condition of agreement, informed circles here doubt whether Germany will wish to raise such a controversial problem as that of an Austrian plebiscite just now.

Germany's immediate aim in Austria appears to be rather to become a signatory of a noninterference pact provided it would enable Berlin to counter-balance Italian influence in Vienna, at the same time allowing "natural" forces to work for that close co-operation between Austria and Germany—whether in a direct "anschluss" or other looser connections is immaterial—which most Germans believe is only a matter of time.

Germany strenuously denies ever having engaged in any violent interference in Austrian affairs and maintains that it stands for Austrian independence.

Meanwhile the practical question asked is what is to happen to 40,000 Austrian National Socialist refugees now in Germany.

Mitchell Advises Against Dropping Airship Program

Unwise, He Tells House, in View of Situation in Far East

WASHINGTON, Feb. 14 (AP)—Congress was warned today by Brig. Gen. William Mitchell, retired, that "it would be very foolish to give up our airship development, particularly in view of conditions in the Far East at this time."

Testifying before the House Patents Committee in what Representative William Sirovich (D) of New York, chairman, announced as an investigation into the loss of the airship Macon in the Pacific, the commander of the United States air force during the World War abroad, championed the lighter than aircraft in the midst of criticism on Capitol Hill and elsewhere following the Macon disaster.

"If we continue to disarm," he said, "we will be an easy target for any Asiatic country that comes along. If we had 50 Zeppelins properly manned and equipped, in the future, we could go straight to any Asiatic country and Destroy it."

Germans Are Mystified By Disaster to Macon

By Press Wireless from Monitor Bureau

BERLIN, Feb. 14—The Macon mishap cannot be construed as evidence of the failure of the airship as a future means of transport, it is declared in official airship circles here.

Dr. Hugo Eckener, famous commander of the Graf Zeppelin, interviewed today declared himself unable to pass judgment on the mishap with the scanty information available, but considers it likely that Commander Wiley's references to some fractures in the rear of the airship and the report that two gas cells had been damaged, is the only apparent explanation, especially as similar things were reported concerning the Akron.

Dr. Eckener refuses to accept the opinion that the airship could have been tossed onto the surface of the water by storm, and therefore rejects categorically any inference from mishap regarding future airship development.

Captain Hans von Schiller of the Zeppelin Company at Friedrichshafen declared the mishap to be incomprehensible, since the airship had been built by the American Zeppelin Corporation similar to the Graf Zeppelin, which has weathered many severe storms.

"Our belief in airship transport

(Continued on Page 2, Column 4)

Lowell Interviewed: 'Good Morning, Sir'

For a decade a State House reporter on numerous occasions has tried—unsuccessfully—to interview Dr. A. Lawrence Lowell, Harvard University's press-dodging president emeritus.

And not once did the reporter even come face to face with the educator, nor cross the Lowell threshold.

Today, Dr. Lowell came to the reporter for assistance. He approached the "news hawk" in the State House and asked to be directed to the hearing room. The reporter "made" the educator talk. He said, "Good morning, Dr. Lowell." The educator replied, "Good morning, sir."

It wasn't much of an interview after waiting 10 years, but it was a beginning. The reporter is now wondering whether Dr. Lowell would even have asked directions, had he known he was talking to the "press."

Mail Order Head To Help President Spend Relief Fund

General Wood Will Advise on $4,880,000,000 If Senate Passes It

Special from Monitor Bureau

WASHINGTON, Feb. 14—Brig. Gen. Robert E. Wood, West Point graduate, Acting Quartermaster General in the World War, head of Sears Roebuck & Co., was announced today as the man who will head a special advisory committee to aid President Roosevelt in the allocation of his prospective $4,880,000,000 relief fund.

Even as this announcement was being made by Daniel C. Roper, Secretary of Commerce, after a White House conference, a slashing attack on the huge bill was opening in the Senate, where Frederick Steiwer (R), of Oregon, declared the lump sum proposal to be "the most radical perversion of the American concept of government yet seen."

Appointment Timed

Word of General Wood's appointment was carefully timed by the Administration to coincide with the introduction of the relief bill from the Appropriations Committee in the Senate. While Senator Steiwer was declaring that the bill vested limitless discretion in the President, and that there was nothing to deter him from "setting the Government up in direct competition with industry, even to the extent of building factories," Mr. Roosevelt was giving out the name of the Chicago business leader as the "dollar-a-year" man who will aid in guiding the vast relief expenditures.

Opponents of the measure were quick to point out that General Wood's position is purely advisory and that there is nothing in the bill which requires the President to take his advice if he does not like it.

General Wood will head a special advisory committee, Mr. Roper said, of which the other members have not yet been chosen. The committee will be selected from the business advisory council of the Commerce Department. It will act, said Mr. Roper, "in an advisory capacity to President Roosevelt's board or whatever method, agency or instrumentality he may adopt for allocation of this money."

West Point, '00

General Wood is 56 years old, graduated from West Point in 1900, immediately saw two years active service in the Philippine insurrection, had service in the quartermaster's corps in Panama, and by the time of the World War was acting quartermaster general. He entered business life in 1915.

Senator Steiwer opened the attack by conservatives, who believe the blanket appropriation goes too far; Senator Pat McCarran (D.) of Nevada prepared to open a second attack, in behalf of the A. F. of L., on the ground that the bill does not go far enough.

"Congress is asked to spend $4 for relief where $1 is now being spent," Senator Steiwer said, "which means that the public debt for relief purposes will grow four times as fast as it has grown under the present system and that the deficit will be four times as large as it would be under a direct relief system."

He advocated direct relief as sounder and cheaper.

The Monitor Index

Thursday, Feb. 14, 1935

Lehman's Fiscal Bills Passed By Senate Despite Republican Attack on Unbalanced Budget

Stiff Opposition to Program Expected in Assembly, With Rise in Gasoline Tax Main Point of Difference—Governor Urges Town Economy

Special to The Christian Science Monitor

ALBANY, N. Y., Feb. 14—Eleven major fiscal measures of Gov. Herbert H. Lehman's $294,000,000 budget for 1935 await Assembly ratification today, following their passage in the Senate late yesterday.

Republicans in the upper house opposed the legislation, and although Senator George R. Fearon of Syracuse, leader of this bloc, voted affirmatively on the main bill he prefaced his vote with a denunciation of it as failing to comply with the constitutional provision for a balanced budget, and charged that the Governor had juggled the figures.

A battle over this main fiscal business of the session is expected in the lower House, where strong opposition has mobilized against the rise from 3 to 4 cents in the emergency tax on gasoline to bring in an estimated $16,250,000.

Controversial Item

This is the most controversial item in the proposed $55,750,000 tax increase program, but the Governor has served notice that the only alternative to the petrol tax is a sales levy.

In his attack on the budget program, Mr. Fearon asserted that the record showed the Governor constantly blundered in estimating revenues and forecast that, instead of the $3,000,000 surplus hoped for at the end of the next fiscal year, there will be a $100,000,000 deficit.

None of this unduly delayed the passage of the budget bills, however, and meanwhile the Governor went before the annual dinner meeting of the State Association of Towns to urge support of his program for governmental simplification and reform of overlapping local government structures in the State.

Too Many Units

"It must be conceded there are too many units of government in the State of New York," he said, "and that the resulting complexity of local government cannot produce efficiency or economy."

The Governor urged town officials to sponsor actively the Fearon constitutional amendment to pave the way for such reforms, outlining a four-point program for changes as follows:

A budget system of fiscal affairs for all towns and counties; greater restrictions of debt limits of local units, consolidation of special district bodies and reduction in the number of justices of the peace.

Ban Put on Politics In Michigan Contest For Judicial Posts

Special to The Christian Science Monitor

GRAND RAPIDS, Mich.—Reams have been written about "taking the judiciary out of politics," but it has remained for three Kent County circuit judges, all residents of this city, to act upon the proposal.

It all came about when Prosecutor Bartel J. Jonkman, who is seeking one of the judgeships, suggested that the candidates refrain from campaigning in the drive preceding the Republican primary to be held next month. Other candidates agreed to the plan, which said:

"It is hereby agreed by and between the undersigned, candidates for circuit judge of Kent County, that we will refrain from conducting, directly or indirectly, any campaign for the nomination, and we agree not to attempt to influence the voters directly or indirectly, by ourselves or through others, but leave them to their free choice, uninfluenced by political propaganda."

The three judges, Willis B. Perkins, William B. Brown and Leonard D. Verdier, not only signed the pact but added an amendment to make it ironclad.

This addition, written "so there may be no uncertainty as to what is intended by the term political campaigns," reads:

"It is our understanding that in addition to the general terms used, this agreement prohibits candidates from printing or circulating campaign cards, printing, circulating or publishing any campaign advertising, attending or addressing either public or private meetings, or assemblies of any kind, campaign meetings, or making any use of radio broadcasting, personal solicitation of votes by any method, hiring or employing workers, either before or at the polls."

So instead of spending their time seeking the votes the three will be attending to their court calendars.

Hauptmann Guilty Sentenced to Die; Appeal Next Move

Counsel for Defense to Fight Conviction to U. S. Supreme Court

FLEMINGTON, N. J., Feb. 14 (AP)—A request for a stay of the death sentence imposed upon Bruno Richard Hauptmann will be the next move of his attorneys if they go forward with their announced intention of appealing his conviction.

Edward J. Reilly, chief counsel for Hauptmann, said the defense would fight the conviction all the way to the Supreme Court of the United States if necessary. That court, however, has consistently declined to review any case in which no constitutional question is involved.

The bulk of the defense exceptions were based upon the final charge given to the jury by Justice Thomas W. Trenchard, and the attorneys indicated their arguments for reversal would be aimed at that charge.

General Exception

The defense took a general exception to the whole charge and then recited numerous assertions of the court for which they begged and were allowed specific exceptions.

Prison precedent combined with judge and jury to fix the night of March 22 as the tentative date for Hauptmann's electrocution. He was sentenced to "suffer death" the week of March 18, and Friday is the day on which executions generally take place.

Edward J. Reilly, chief of defense staff, said an appeal would be carried to the United States Supreme Court if necessary.

The first tribunal expected to hear the plea, the State Court of Errors and Appeals, meets for its next term late in May. The Court of Pardons will not hear it before October.

The jurors who sentenced him showed more emotion than did Hauptmann as he stood before them at 10:45 p. m., yesterday. The jurors required more than 11 hours to reach their verdict.

The 12 jurors were unanimous on

(Continued on Page 6, Column 5)

North Carolina Club Plans to See Own State

Special to The Christian Science Monitor

ASHEVILLE, N. C., Feb. 14—There are said to be New Yorkers who have never glimpsed the Statue of Liberty, and there are North Carolinians who have never seen the Blue Ridge of the Southern Appalachians, but an organization has been formed here, known as the Carolina Mountain Club, whose members are determined to visit regions in this section never before seen by them.

The club has mapped out a schedule of 31 visits, which will begin Feb. 17 and continue through next Dec. 8. Picnics, overnight trips, luncheon parties in the mountains and other events are planned. The itinerary will lead through remote areas of the Great Smoky Mountains National Park and into sections less known from a national standpoint and little visited by native urbanites of this section.

Arrival of Cape Verde Sail Packets Reported

PROVIDENCE, R. I., Feb. 14 (AP)—The schooners Trenton and Winnipesaukee, which sailed from New Bedford in November, bound for Brava, have arrived there safely, Frank J. Silva of this city said he had been assured today.

Mr. Silva, long associated with the Cape Verde Islands packet trade, said he had learned that relatives of passengers on the two schooners have received letters reporting their safe arrival. The schooner John R. Manta, which left Providence on Nov. 9, is still unreported.

Irish Free State Invited to Return To British Family

LONDON, Feb. 14 (AP)—Mr. J. H. Thomas, Secretary of the Dominions, held out the olive branch to the Irish Free State today in a speech which political quarters interpreted as a move by the Secretary toward effecting peace between England and Ireland in King George's Silver Jubilee year.

Mr. Thomas told the Constitutional Club that should the Irish Free State answer affirmatively as to whether it desires to remain an integral part of the empire, "then how happy we would all be in this year above all others in saying we are celebrating the great event—the event that is celebrated by the United British Commonwealth of Nations."

The Dominions Secretary said there was no bitterness or hostility toward the Free State in the minds of the British and instead there was "only a single-minded desire to see the empire united."

Unique Stamp of 1856 Tagged for London Sale

NEW YORK, Feb. 14 (AP)—A small scrap of dull-red paper had a price on it today probably in excess of $50,000.

The treasured bit is said to be the world's most valued postage stamp, a one-cent Magenta issued by British Guiana in 1856, and the only one of its kind.

The tiny etching of a sailing vessel will be put up for sale next month by Mrs. P. Costa Scala, of Utica, N. Y., widow of Arthur Hind, philatelist, most of whose $1,000,000 collection she has already disposed of.

The stamp was purchased by Hind in Paris in 1922 for $32,500. It will be sold in London.

America Backs General Pact On Arms, Wilson Tells Geneva

GENEVA, Feb. 14 (AP)—Hugh Wilson, United States Minister to Switzerland, told a special committee of the Disarmament Conference today that the dearest hope of the United States is a general convention for the limitation of armaments.

The committee, which will attempt to hit at the evils of arms manufacture and traffic, was just opening its session when Mr. Wilson spoke.

Alluding to negotiations with Germany for a European air securities pact and to other antiwar projects, the American representative called them "important" and said he believed success in handling a specific subject such as the arms traffic "would materially aid the success, which we all ardently desire, of general negotiations."

"The American Government," continued Mr. Wilson, "attaches peculiar importance to the success of the threefold project now before us: For the regulation of arms traffic and manufacture, for the establishment of a supervisory body, and for the publicity of expenditures.

"It is conceived as something which will not only be a definite contribution itself but will facilitate the preparation of a general convention on the limitation of arms. It has never been our (the United States's) intention to divert the work of this conference from a general convention of the limitation of arms."

He then moved the adoption of this plan as a basis for the future discussions of the committee meetings. The committee accepted this American plan as a basis.

[A summary of events during the Disarmament Conference's adjournment is given on Page 4.]

Attack on Nucleus of Atom Designed In 'Doughnut' Electric Generator

COLUMBUS, Ohio, Feb. 14 (AP)—A contrivance that generates 1,000,000 volts of electricity a second was announced yesterday by Ohio State University's department of physics.

It is something new in high energy, different from any other mechanism in America and Europe that produces electrical currents equaling the power of lightning. As set up in the laboratory, it is a wooden shell in the form of a doughnut, its outer surface a smooth copper skin. The interior is entirely hollow. Through the hole in the middle runs a silk belt. The belt does not touch the doughnut, which hangs from the ceiling by cables.

The belt carries electricity. As it whizzes through the hole, the "juice" brushes off and spreads over the outside surface of the copper covering. A million volts will store up on this surface in a second or two.

Electrodes inside draw off this electricity as needed. The apparatus was developed by Dr. Willard H. Bennett. As in the case of other high power machines, its purpose is investigation of the nucleus of the atom.

The thrill in this investigation lies in the fact that 99 per cent of everything that exists, living or inert, on earth or elsewhere, lies in the still unknown nucleus of atoms. When physicists succeed in solving the nature of the atomic nucleus, they expect to produce new sources of power and new forms of chemistry.

62

THE CHRISTIAN SCIENCE MONITOR

AN INTERNATIONAL DAILY NEWSPAPER

COPYRIGHT 1935 BY THE CHRISTIAN SCIENCE PUBLISHING SOCIETY

BOSTON, SATURDAY, SEPTEMBER 21, 1935—VOL. XXVII, NO. 251

CENTRAL EDITION—FIVE CENTS A COPY

The March of the Nations

By Rufus Steele

PWA Yields to A. F. of L.

Relief Goes on Union Wage

Private Industry Regrets

Hot Potato Can Grow Cold

Canada Wants Short Hours

Borah Tells About Peace

THE American government in business compromises a former stand in a way that does not endear it to the hearts of private employers with whom it is in competition. All through the long hard fights in Congress when huge emergency measures were setting up jobs for the unemployed the American Federation of Labor officials contended for wages at the going scale, while the Administration pleaded that only relief wages could be paid out of its funds and that equal wages would defeat the whole spirit of its undertaking. Now Harry L. Hopkins, WPA Administrator, yields to pressure and rules that State PWA Administrators may reduce hours below the alloted 40 at their discretion. This raises the hourly rate—It puts the relief worker on pay parity with the thrifty artisan who has managed to hold onto his job.

¶ Mr. Hopkins issues the compromise order after a conference with A. F. of L. leaders of the building trades in Washington. Gen. Hugh S. Johnson, WPA Administrator for New York City, meets the labor men with a bid of $1.50 an hour for workers in the skilled trades in the metropolis, where union strikers and passive resistance by loafers on jobs have threatened relief projects with failure. The Hopkins order does not allow for extension of the weekly time of relief workers, but only for lifting of the hourly rate. The Administration is regarded as deserting the stand on which it fought organized labor for so long before Congress. Presently the advantages of this may appear—But the first reaction of private enterprise is of one more fault to find with Government for unfair competition.

¶ The American Government has now had perhaps more experience than any other government in history in autocratic or co-operative participation in private industry. Yet experience does not appear to have made its administration more skilled or its commercial ways more appealing to businessmen. Mistrust has sometimes extended to its motives, and often to its ability to get anything done as economically and satisfactorily as private management could do. Even now there is the unhappy hint that with a Presidential election ahead concessions by the Administration to organized labor are in order. Somehow the basic concepts are too low—When government dips into business it should do it according to the rightest rules.

¶ The PWA makes its disturbing announcement just as Comptroller General McCarl withdraws what was getting to be a very hot potato from the public scene. In the closing days of the congressional session someone conceived the idea that the potato men had the same right to be protected from overproduction as the cotton men, corn men, hog men, tobacco men, sugarcane men and others. So in the full spirit of AAA crop restriction the humble spud was sent through for a system of proper regimentation. With the time for enforcement of the act at hand, vast complications loomed. The potato had the law on its side but few friends. Comptroller McCarl adroitly discovered there were no funds to enforce the potato tax. The spud steps out of politics—And the country is probably saved one more example of the fallacy of prosperity through restriction.

¶ Canadian workers lift their voices on the subject of hours and machines. The Trade and Labor Congress at Halifax, representing 100,000 workmen, repeats its demand for a six-hour day and a five-day week. Seeing the purchasing power of the masses decreasing, the delegates declare that hours of labor must be shortened to permit of more persons being brought into industry. The old bugaboo of the machine plays its frightening part. The machine is seen as swallowing more and more jobs. But some day the scene will shift—That same old machine will actually and happily be made to lift all major burdens off the muscles of men.

¶ Senator William E. Borah of Idaho tells the nation by radio that the strongholds of war are in those countries where the people have been silenced. Where constitutional government has gone and arbitrary power has usurped the place of the public will war finds its chief advocacy. Wherever the people are free, where the voice of the people is heard, where speech is untrammeled and liberty of action unchained, the cause of peace leaps ahead. The Senator carries his analysis to an interesting conclusion. If we look alone to the attitude and action of governments, the friends of peace may well despair —It is in the wishes and desires of the people for peace that the hope of it lies.

Ancient Reich Town Has Novel Fetes

Special to The Christian Science Monitor

Berlin

THE ancient town of Münder in the Deister Hills, Hanover, chose an exceptional method of celebrating its 600th anniversary recently.

Four days before the anniversary a pageant of the town's history was given, and then on the day the whole population marched round the boundaries of the municipal forest. At each boundary post, the youths formed a ring and danced. Every dancer was boxed on the ear and exhorted not to forget the boundaries—as has been done for centuries past!

Soviets Create New Brand Of State Nobility

Elaborate System of Orders With Titles and Special Privileges Set Up

By a Staff Correspondent of The Christian Science Monitor

MOSCOW—The Soviet state is creating a well-defined aristocracy by an elaborate system of orders, honors and distinctive designations which take the place of titles, ranks and honorary degrees in other European countries. To an increasing degree these distinctions, conferred only by the state—and approved by the ruling Communist Party—set off favored individuals from the undistinguished mass. They confer not only prestige, but a whole series of material advantages.

All of these orders and ranks are granted on sufferance. They may be withdrawn at any time by the same government organs which are empowered to grant them. Because of the prestige and material benefits which they confer, few holders are likely to risk losing them by antagonizing the responsible authorities. They help to assure the loyalty of the most ambitious and energetic individuals in Russia.

Many Privileges

There are four official orders—the Orders of Lenin, of the Red Star, of the Red Banner and of the Red Banner of Labor. The intrinsic value of these orders is impressive. Holders receive from the state 30 rubles in cash monthly for their first order and 25 additional rubles monthly for each subsequent order. They are freed from income tax up to 500 rubles a month, and get a reduction in rent of from 10 to 50 per cent, depending upon their salary.

Their children are admitted free to any school, they are entitled to pensions in one third less time than ordinary citizens, they ride free on tram cars and may take two free

(Continued on Page 3, Column 4)

Dictatorship Breaks Down In Louisiana

Heads of Long Machine Start Free-for-All Hunt for Jobs

Milder Laws Due

By a Staff Correspondent of The Christian Science Monitor

NEW ORLEANS, La., Sept. 21—Dictatorship in Louisiana is crumbling.

Break-up of the machine put together by Senator Huey P. Long, the strongest political organization in any state, is forecast by the scramble for jobs following his passing. Likewise abandonment of the Senator's autocratic legislation appears destined.

The free-for-all hunt for the big offices breaking out this week, in which every man has gone for himself, emphasizes the disappearance of the dominant central control.

Possibly the strangest part of the struggle is the paradox furnished by Gov. O. K. Allen. Senator Long invested him with more authority than any other Governor.

Worked Through Others

The Senator could not vote to himself directly the domination he sought, but had to lodge it in the state administration and very largely in the Governor. Mr. Long worked through the Governor and other state officials to exercise his abnormal powers.

Today Governor Allen, so far as the laws go, is dictator. But he has been unable to keep his own people in line enough to agree among themselves on a ticket for the Democratic state primary four months off. Various of the principal Long leaders have determined to run for the choice offices, such as Senator and Governor, without asking agreement of the rest of the faction. Those who entertained similar ambitions themselves but held back for common action, as Governor Allen had urged, do not relish being elbowed aside.

The character of the Long machine has been illumined to the general eye during the last fortnight. Previously the public concentrated on the Senator. Now that his leaders have stepped into the spotlight, it is realized what a curious set of elements had been welded by the hand of the master politician of this State, and how unlikely it is that they will continue to co-operate without his commanding direction.

A Divergent Team

Senator Long drove a strong team of powerful men dissimilar and divergent. Some were conservatives and leaders of excellent standing whose sole departure from the routine was their adherence to Mr. Long. Meanwhile with them labored radicals like the Rev. Gerald L. K. Smith, chief of the Senator's

(Continued on Page 4, Column 7)

The World's Day

Its News in Focus

Saturday, Sept. 21

SEC—Kennedy Resigns Chairmanship

Special to The Christian Science Monitor

HYDE PARK, N. Y.—The resignation of Joseph P. Kennedy as chairman of the Securities and Exchanges Commission was announced yesterday by President Roosevelt. The news was greatly regretted in financial circles, since Mr. Kennedy was a Wall Street man, and regarded as one of the ablest administrators in Washington. Mr. Kennedy will return to private business after a vacation in Europe.

Thus the crucial chairmanship of the commission which is to carry out the law that levels utility holding company superstructures becomes open. Rumors of Mr. Kennedy's resignation got current when the "death sentence" provision for utility holding companies was being urged on Congress by the President, and was reported opposed by Mr. Kennedy. That clause was not included in the final bill, and the reports subsided.

In view of the President's "breathing spell" policy toward business and finance, and of the forthcoming holding company dissolutions, the selection of a new chairman will be regarded as an important indication of Roosevelt policy.

Spain—Lerroux Cabinet Resigns

MADRID—No important upset in the present reactionary Government appeared likely, as the Lerroux Cabinet resigned yesterday. The immediate cause was a dispute between the Agrarian Party and the Catalonian regional group, the Associated Press reports. The Cabinet had transferred certain public works appropriations to Catalonia, and the Agrarians objected.

Premier Alejandro Lerroux is expected to form another Cabinet with increased Agrarian and Catalonian representation. The remainder of the Cabinet will come from the present Conservative and Roman Catholic groups, as before.

Philippines—May Ask to Join League

MANILA, P. I.—The new Philippine Commonwealth may seek American permission to join the League of Nations, it was suggested yesterday by the newly elected President, Manuel Quezon, as reported by the Associated Press. Or it may, "if," said Mr. Quezon, "the League doesn't crack up now." He doesn't expect to push the issue yet, however.

In an interview, Mr. Quezon said he would work for less politics and more government . . . declined to discuss military defense plans . . . favored establishing a Philippine base for the Pan American Airways' projected transpacific airline . . . said tariff matters would be put off until a reciprocal conference with the United States, early next year, takes place.

Labor—Miners and Longshoremen Aggressive

On the labor front yesterday via reports of the Associated Press:

Washington: Edward F. McGrady, Assistant Secretary of Labor, informed deadlocked soft coal operators and labor leaders that the Government wanted an agreement within 48 hours, in order to avert the strike threatened for Sunday midnight. Otherwise, Mr. McGrady said, he would insist that both miners and operators lay their case before the public.

Valley View, Penna.: An anthracite mine railroad of the Susquehanna Company was dynamited by independent miners today, and state troopers went on guard.

New York City: Longshoremen today opened negotiations with ship owners for higher wage scales. They want $1 an hour for a 40 hour week, as compared with the existing 95 cents an hour for a 44 hour week. They want $1.50 an hour for overtime as against $1.35 now.

Vera Cruz, Mexico: Approximately 1200 railroad workers went out on

(Continued on Page 4, Column 7)

Dark Corner of Africa Is Full of Riches

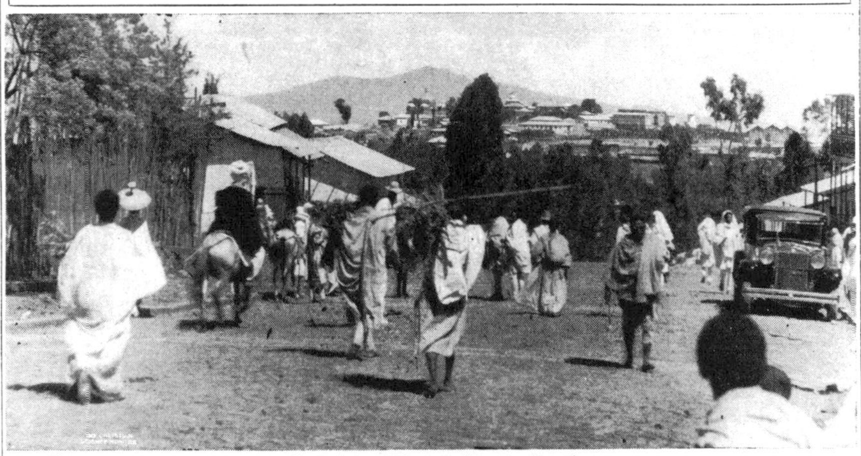

Newman Photo

The Capital of Ethiopia Is "The New Flower"

Above Is a General View of Addis Ababa in the Near Distance, With the Emperor's Palace Clearly Seen to the Right and the Cathedral to the Left

Duce Seeks to Avoid Blame for African Rift; U. S. Hopes for Peace But Speeds Neutrality Act

State Department Talks Over Situation With Italy's Ambassador

Stock Market Reacts

By a Staff Correspondent of The Christian Science Monitor

WASHINGTON, Sept. 21 — The State Department is asking itself if there is no way out of the "war which nobody wants," and is still looking for an avenue to peace.

At the same time, it is putting into effective shape the machinery for preserving American neutrality, passed by the recent session of Congress, and at the same time, speeding up decision on the crucial matter, left undecided by Congress when it adjourned, of what constitutes "implements" of war.

Augusto Rosso, Italian Ambassador made an unexpected call at the State Department yesterday where he discussed the Ethiopian situation with William Phillips, Under-Secretary of State.

Mr. Rosso said that the call was merely to keep the department informed of up-to-the-minute developments in Europe and carried no major significance. No comment on the visit was forthcoming from the State Department.

U. S. to Keep Informed

Meanwhile, President Roosevelt has turned his attention to the Ethiopian crisis with a series of conversations at Hyde Park with well-informed authorities, including Jesse I. Straus, American Ambassador to France, who will return shortly to the center of European turmoil, fully conversant with the viewpoint of the Administration in the matter.

The American Government moved also yesterday to insure a source of free, uncensored and direct communication with one of the prospective belligerents, when the Navy Department announced dispatch of four expert radio men to Addis Ababa with equipment for erecting an emergency transmitting station at the American Legation. It was announced that these radio men sailed aboard the S. S. President Harding from New York, two days ago.

The purpose of the mission, according to navy announcement, is to facilitate maintenance of com-

(Continued on Page 3, Column 3)

League Plans New Ethiopia

The Committee of Five set up by the League Council at Geneva has proposed the following solutions to the Italo-Ethiopian dispute as a basis for negotiations:

A Central Organization is to be set up by the League, probably composed of the heads of executive departments, also chosen by the League.

There is no bar of nationality on the international governing body under the porposal. Either Italian, British or French could serve if nominated by the League and approved by the Emperor. Nor is there anything in the plan as presented both at Rome and at Addis Ababa to prevent an Italian from presiding over the League's governing body, directing procedure in Ethiopia.

Territorial concessions to Italy are not so definitely established although it is understood that Danakil and Ogaden are suggested to be made Italian territory. A free port for Ethiopia at Djibouti with a corridor to Zeila are part of the compensation for Ethiopia.

Public services are to be modernized. Economic and financial reforms are to be made.

The system of justice is to be overhauled, as well as the systems of public instruction and hygiene.

Foreign capital is to be attracted to invest in agriculture, mines, commerce and industry.

Technical advisers from abroad are to work out comprehensive reorganization of public works, facilities of transportation, postal service, telephone and telegraph systems.

Organization of a police force and gendarmerie to suppress slavery, prohibit private carrying of arms and to insure safety of town and country alike, also patrolling frontiers and suppressing banditry.

Foreign trade and commerce would be encouraged.

State monopolies are envisaged for revenue purposes.

A budget would be established and taxes would be authorized and collected regularly.

Loans, based on national securities, would be floated to take care of the development and to execute the reforms.

The Fertile Land of Ethiopia

Its Bounties Remind of France, Its Beauties of Bavaria—Tropical and Temperate Life Both Flourish—Three Crops a Year

This is the fourth of a group of descriptive articles by THE CHRISTIAN SCIENCE MONITOR'S *staff correspondent, recently sent to Addis Ababa to cover developments there. Previous articles appeared on Sept. 10, 12 and 18.*

By R. H. Markham

Staff Correspondent of The Christian Science Monitor

ADDIS ABABA — Africa is a continent of extremes. Those areas that are good are "very very good" and those that are bad are "horrid." Most of Ethiopia is among the parts that are very very good. It is one of the most healthful, attractive and richly endowed lands in the world.

Practically all of its entrances are back doors. It has no fine front yard. From most parts of the fertile plateau one descends into hot and barren deserts; from others one goes down into hot and swampy jungles. There are almost no grand approaches. Yet when one reaches central Ethiopia, he finds it is a magnificent, friendly land, vying in bounty with France, Hungary or Ohio.

Climbing Rails

I found it takes a minimum of two days by rail to reach the capital from the French port of Djibouti. During almost the whole of the first day one traverses a desert. The beginning of the second day, also, is spent in rather unproductive land. One sees little more than grass there and seldom comes across fields or signs of agriculture. Large flocks abound, tended by people living in clusters of tiny thatched huts, scattered over the prairies. The cattle are small, with long, graceful horns and large humps above their shoulders, making them resemble buffalo. The sheep and goats are also small, and their meat, skins and milk are of a rather poor quality.

By noon of the second day the train has mounted well up onto the plateau and verdure abounds on every side. The barren wastes have completely disappeared and the land is filled with surging, throbbing life. The soil with but little cultivation and no enrichment yields three crops yearly. The weather is delightfully cool. The landscape rivals the best in Europe and there are no especially disagreeable seasons or pests.

Yet Ethiopia loses none of its mysterious African glamour as it mounts from torrid deserts to a broad, temperate plateau. One still

(Continued on Page 3, Column 2).

Knox Urges Tariff And Export Bounty To Protect Farmer

SHENANDOAH, Iowa, Sept. 21 (AP) —Col. Frank Knox, Chicago newspaper publisher, in a speech last night, proposed restricted imports of staple agricultural products and the establishment of an export bounty for American farmers as substitutes for the New Deal's policy of restricting production to increase farm prices.

Colonel Knox, regarded as a possible Republican presidential nominee, addressed the Seventh Congressional District Republican rally here. Asserting that the future prosperity of American business depends upon "an intelligent, sound, successful farm policy," Colonel Knox said that in his opinion such a policy must include:

"A tariff high enough to insure the full domestic market to the American farmer.

"Some form of export bounty which would insure to the individual farmer, whether his particular product was sold in the domestic market or sold abroad, the benefit of the domestic price.

"An intelligent, persistent expansion of world markets for American farm products.

"Utilization of farm-grown commodities in industry," by applying "the tremendous strides which organic chemistry has made in the last few years."

Firm British and French Attitude Disquieting to Rome Officials

Solo Mandate Sought

By a Staff Correspondent of The Christian Science Monitor

ROME, Sept. 21—Disquiet in high Italian quarters over the firm attitude taken by both the British and French Governments in relation to the Italo-Ethiopian dispute was expected to find practical expression in Italian counter-proposals to the latest 'League of Nations plan for settlement,' it was learned here yesterday.

It was expected, however, that the plan of the Council Committee of Five will be rejected—like the British and French Paris proposals—because they do not give to Italy that military security she is so anxious to obtain for her East African colonies, and is not granted the much-needed opportunity to expand.

At the same time, it was realized in Rome that the moment had arrived for Italy to make specific demands, if only to throw upon the shoulders of other governments or the League responsibility for breakdown of pacific negotiations.

Exclusive Mandate

Il Duce, it is believed, would make capital out of the most important admission made by the Committee of Five—namely, that Ethiopia needs outside assistance for its own good government and economic development.

He is therefore expected to ask the League either to re-examine the Ethiopian situation thoroughly, taking into consideration how the present Ethiopian Empire was formed; and to restore it to the area inhabited by the Amharic race. Alternatively, Italy would ask a full, exclusive mandate over the whole of Ethiopia.

Il Duce would pledge himself to respect interests of Britain and France in Ethiopia, as defined by existing treaties. The idea of a "collective" mandate over Ethiopia is entirely disagreeable to Italy.

Are Britain and France sharing between themselves, or with other countries, territories placed under their mandate? It is asked. And why should an exception be made

(Continued on Page 4, Column 6)

Emperor Sees League's Plan As Aid to Empire Development

By a Staff Correspondent of The Christian Science Monitor

ADDIS ABABA, Sept. 21 — Although no communication has been issued, it is certain that the League committee's proposals are in the main acceptable to the Ethiopian Government.

The League plan is interpreted as meaning that Ethiopia will engage a larger number of competent foreign assistants in vital posts. The Emperor is completely in accord with such a plan. However, it is emphatically pointed out in governmental circles that this does not mean foreign control, which would be categorically rejected. Nor is international supervision of any sort acceptable.

If the League recommends five able foreign assistants, the Emperor is not opposed to appointing such as his helpers, and with their co-operation will engage other competent foreigners for important administrative positions. The League itself would not carry out the reforms but would merely aid the Emperor to realize long-desired improvements.

Ethiopia is not opposed to reorganization of its police with the aid of foreign experts, but it is emphasized that life and property are already safer here than in many lands. All reasonable aid to hasten the ending of slavery is welcome. Although the budget here is always balanced and no state debt exists, any method of improving finances would be gladly accepted.

The Emperor informs The Christian Science Monitor also that all foreign aid in developing the country's resources will be welcome, but that there must be free political conditions and no special privileges shall be given to Italy or any other power. In inviting foreign aid now the Government is unwilling to recognize the sphere of influence of any foreign state and refuses to promise any special predominance of Rome in the development of Ethiopia.

In fact, if world peace depends on Ethiopian co-operation with the League on the basis of the committee's report, it is certain there will be no war.

The Monitor Index

Saturday, Sept. 21, 1935

Italy Gains By Change In League Plan

No Nationality Ban Put on Officials to Rule Over Ethiopia

Emperor's Approval Necessary to Choice

Proposals of Committee of Five Must Yet Pass Council to Be Effective

Extraordinary tension pervaded all nations as they await Signor Mussolini's reply to proposals of the Council's Committee of Five, made to Rome and Addis Ababa for a last-minute way out of the African deadlock.

Il Duce was understood to be working on counter-proposals to the League plan, the result of which might be to delay action by further discussion. The Emperor of Ethiopia, the Monitor correspondent in Addis Ababa understands, in the main approves of the League proposals.

The seriousness with which Britain views the situation is seen in the proposal to broaden the basis of the present national Government by the addition of members of the Labor Party.

Meanwhile, as Britain rushes its preparations to meet all contingencies in the Mediterranean, London was anxiously awaiting news from Paris, whose co-operation is considered vital to collective action, and which has so far refrained from giving any indication of the line it proposes to take.

By a Staff Correspondent of The Christian Science Monitor

GENEVA, Sept. 21 — It is now possible to give a more or less complete picture of the present contents of the document drawn up by the Council's Committee of Five, which have become known bit by bit during the past few days. It must be emphasized, however, that they are subject to alterations and additions.

It is recalled in the preamble that the League's duty is to respect the territorial integrity and political independence of its members, and, among other things, to lend assistance to such states as desire it. Since Ethiopia has asked for aid it is obviously proper to collaborate with it on a collective basis with a view to constructive action. But to carry out a settled plan it will be necessary that Ethiopia sign a protocol admitting of the co-operation and officials as delegated by the League.

Welcomed by Hawariate

In this connection it is recalled that on September 11 Tecle Hawariate, Ethiopia's delegate, declared from the tribune of the Assembly that Ethiopia would welcome suggestions designed to raise the economic, financial or political level of his country, provided it emanated from the League and would be applied according to the intentions of the covenant.

In these conditions and within the framework of international law, the report passes in review the public services which should be brought up-to-date by European experts. There must be complete reorganization of these public services and development of the economic resources of the country together with financial reforms.

Sweeping Reforms

The system of justice should be overhauled; public instruction and hygiene are to be taken in hand. A regime for agriculture, mines, commerce and industry should be instituted in such way as to make the investment of foreign capital feasible. Public works, transport, posts, telegrams and telephone, all are to be reorganized by means of a comprehensive scheme worked out by technical advisers to the Emperor.

Perhaps the most important part of the plan is the constitution of a police force and gendarmerie officered by specially appointed foreigners. They would have large tasks confided to them, namely, to see that laws are strictly applied to suppress slavery, to prohibit the carrying of arms by unauthorized persons, and to insure safety to foreign residents in towns and countryside. They would also patrol the frontier, pursue slave-merchants, bandits and marauding tribes.

To Invite Commerce

In the domain of commerce the keynote of the report is the provision of extended possibilities of trade with foreign countries on the basis of equality and reciprocity.

Foreigners must be allowed to participate in the exploitation of the natural riches of the country, now neglected.

As for finances, a budget must be established with adequate control of expenditures. Taxation must be collected by regularly authorized officials.

State monopolies are envisaged for purposes of revenue.

Loans may be raised against national securities in order to develop

(Continued on Page 3, Column 6)

[Financial repercussions of the tension at Geneva: Financial Page.]

THE CHRISTIAN SCIENCE MONITOR

AN INTERNATIONAL DAILY NEWSPAPER

COPYRIGHT 1935 BY THE CHRISTIAN SCIENCE PUBLISHING SOCIETY

BOSTON, THURSDAY, OCTOBER 3, 1935—VOL. XXVII, NO. 261

CENTRAL EDITION—FIVE CENTS A COPY

The March of the Nations

By Rufus Steele

Italians Have Wild Hopes

After Ethiopia Is Britain

England Is Held Decadent

Vast Black Army Is Plan

Rift Has Bred the Dream

Powers Grimly Back League

DOES Dictator Mussolini of Italy, about to crash his war machine over the Ethiopian border, regard Great Britain as his real foe and one from which he can take much booty? The very question is so new that it startles. Yet its framing in all seriousness is forced by a résumé of facts coming from what the Monitor regards as unimpeachable sources. These facts may seem more significant to Italian eyes than they will when considered by world observers. Again, they are subject to change. But at the moment the shrewd appraisal is that Il Duce may be motivated by the belief that he can make sure, quick conquest of Ethiopia and that that conquest will give him prestige to play for the mightier stake—As master of the Red Sea area, would he seek to take prizes from Britain and break the prestige of the British Empire?

¶ Informed Italians are earnestly talking of war with Britain and as earnestly believing in the possibility of success against what they call an overrated power. The cordial feeling which began between Italy and Britain some 13 years ago has, during two years, drifted steadily toward iciness. Italy was greatly comforted when through the years Britain almost invariably backed Italian foreign policies. England did this even when France was in doubt or opposed. Then came the Franco-Italian accord. Britain strongly approved this settling of difficult questions. But Italy used it to stage a changed attitude toward its former best friend—Rome astonished Downing Street with a sudden showing of arrogance where only confidence had been.

¶ The Monitor's intimate information is to the effect that Il Duce now seeks to form an Italian Empire that will revive the glories of ancient Rome. Along his new highway through the ruins of the old Forum Il Duce is believed to see visions of new Roman legions moving homeward victoriously with the spoils of far conquest brimming their gasoline-driven chariots. Specifically, his campaign plan is said to be conquest of Ethiopia at the earliest moment that so large a task may be completed, and then the formation of an Italian colonial army embracing more than 1,000,000 black troops. With such a conquest and such an army Il Duce's prestige would be enormous, not to be gainsaid—He would then strike, if he had not already initiated the striking, as befitted the master of the Red Sea.

¶ The blow would hope to be a crumpling blow at Britain. With a horde of swart soldiers at a base close to the Suez Canal, it seems to the Italian thought that the route to India could be readily threatened and the prestige of the British Empire set to shriveling by steps that were logical and not to be gainsaid. This Italian vision is based upon something besides the dream of imminent Italian power; that is, upon the firm belief that British prestige is today overestimated. England, Italy suddenly assumes, is a decadent nation. After Ethiopia, Il Duce believes, Italian Fascism would be so strong that the world couldn't stop it for at least two generations—In its new strength it would strike and Britain would yield things to make the new Rome outshine the old.

¶ Under circumstances that smite the eye Italy seems guilty of daydreaming. The great British fleet patrols the Mediterranean, definitely held there against a day of harmonious settlements. Britain has come out unequivocally for the League Covenant. It has taken what might seem the strongest stand possible to a strong nation. It is ready to push sanctions on an aggressor. But Italy whispers that Britain and all the others have been wrong about Fascism failing in recent years; it believes Fascism is about to mount the platform from which it can utter a world challenge for its acceptance. Mussolini first wanted economic concessions; now he sees territory and power—Power tempts to the further emulation of his model and mentor, conquering Julius Caesar himself.

¶ World observers will probably be more interested than alarmed by this reflection of what is going on in the excited heart of Italy. The world recognizes Benito Mussolini as an able, ambitious master of his country who sees far, dreams deep. But knowledge of this farthest dream will serve as a forceful warning in a time of warnings. The powers have their own plans, which embrace even Italy's legitimate future. The powers are acting through the League. Geneva is the legislative branch of world power, the World Court at The Hague articulates international justice. Out of the present crisis the powers may achieve that other arm they feel they so much need—They may gain that international police force to halt squabbles and to bring offenders to their common bar.

President Says U.S. Must Keep Free From War

Pledges Himself to Act Against Any Entanglements in Europe

Starts Long Cruise

By **Erwin D. Canham**

Chief of the Washington Bureau of The Christian Science Monitor

SAN DIEGO, Calif., Oct. 3—With a determined anti-war pledge rounding out the account of his stewardship which President Roosevelt has presented during his trip across the continent, the Chief Executive is today cruising off the shores of Lower California, far from every direct preoccupation of government.

This significant succession of speeches and declarations is obviously intended to mark a milestone in the present Administration, and by promoting the current business recovery, to open a period of normal activity which would be expected to end in Mr. Roosevelt's re-election.

Pledge Stands Out

In the tense world situation, the President's peace pledge takes on much greater importance than its actual content would otherwise warrant. Yet, if any proof were needed that the American people want to be told the obvious truth that they are determined to remain out of war, it was furnished when upward of 60,000 people in magnificent San Diego Stadium cheered long and discriminatingly at this passage in Mr. Roosevelt's speech.

The President frankly expressed a "deep sense of apprehension" at the world situation, and received the ovation of his intent audience at the simple words:

"Despite what happens in continents overseas, the United States shall and must remain 'unentangled and free.'"

No Hint as to Means

Yet Mr. Roosevelt gave no hint of the policy he intends to follow as the best way to remain unentangled and free: his only possible reference to the means of waging neutrality came when he said:

"We not only earnestly desire peace, but we are moved by a stern determination to avoid those perils that will endanger our peace with the world."

Presumably the way to "avoid those perils" would be by rigorously denying the sponsorship of the American flag to exports not alone of munitions, as now provided, but for borderline contraband of war-like cotton, steel, oil and copper. But on these points the President was silent.

Touches Religious Issue

Besides ignoring the precise mechanics of nonentanglement, Mr. Roosevelt immediately proceeded to outline a moralizing foreign policy which, while impeccable of itself, bears strong interventionist implications. He said, to the extent of two long paragraphs, that freedom of religious worship was endangered abroad, that the United States could do nothing direct about it, yet that "in our inner individual lives we can never be indifferent."

He was considered by close observers to have referred in the first instance to Mexico, and in the second to Germany, in these strictures on free religion. Large groups in the United States have been pressing for diplomatic protest to both powers; Roman Catholics for action regarding Mexican policy, and Jews in respect to Germany.

Verbal Consolation

In his speech, the President gives them considerable verbal consolation, without, however, pledging the United States to any diplomatic action.

To that extent, his remarks about religious freedom steered away from the Scylla of intervention. Whether the "unentangled" declaration is interpreted abroad as a new burst of nationalistic isolationism will determine if the policy encounters the

(Continued on Page 2, Column 1)

Now Chicago Claims Another Superlative With 'Longest' Street

By a Staff Correspondent of The Christian Science Monitor

CHICAGO—Finding superlatives is a favorite game in Chicago. Now it's "the longest urban street in the world" that is claimed.

The street is Western Avenue. It runs like a straight ruled line from north to south, including in its length 23 miles of Chicago and an almost equal amount of suburbs, making a total of 40 miles.

The Chicago Association of Commerce, which made the claim for Western Avenue, fortified its position by comparing the lengths of other long American streets. It places Figueroa Street and Vermont Avenue of Los Angeles in second and third places respectively, the former credited with a length of 27.5 miles, the latter with 22.8. Halsted and Ashland Avenues in Chicago are ranked third and fourth. Other cities with long streets are Detroit, New York City, Philadelphia and Cleveland.

Broadway appears twelfth on the list with a length of 14.5 miles. European claimants are not given, nor South American. Knowing the propensity of European streets to make turns and change their names as they go, the Association of Commerce may feel safe in omitting them. But to claim the title for the world is a little risky in these days of bigger and bigger telescopes.

Why Italy Is Prepared to Challenge British Power Shown in Confidential Survey of Mussolini's Policy

United Nation Carefully Prepared by Propaganda Has Risen to Mussolini's Imperialistic Plans; Difficult to Turn Back Now

Rome Still Counts on Paris' Backing; London May Yet Avoid Actual Conflict

Italian Posters Attack Britain

By the Associated Press

ROME, Oct. 3—As soon as the nation-wide mobilization was called yesterday, a special guard of 300 police and infrantrymen was thrown around the British Embassy.

Throughout the city were pasted posters declaring: "We find it simply monstrous that this nation (Great Britain) which dominates the world refuses us a strip in the poor land of Africa."

Copyright 1935 by The Christian Science Publishing Society

What is behind Mussolini's effort at conquest of Ethiopia?

Why is Italy willing to risk opposition of Great Britain?

What do Italians feel about the "African Adventure"?

These three questions—holding the most important keys to the Italo-Ethiopian crisis—are illuminated in a confidential memorandum published with permission today by The Christian Science Monitor.

The memorandum, obtained from an American authority recently returned from Italy, was originally drafted for private use and speaks with unusual frankness. It draws its information from what the Monitor believes to be unimpeachable sources. It explains the Italian thought against a background of accurate and close knowledge of Fascist policy.

It reveals Mussolini's concept of empire. It infers Britain was once willing to give Italy a free hand in Albania, provided Italy would refrain from conflict with British interests in Africa. It reveals personal difficulties between diplomatists. It shows basic differences between French and British policy over Italian expansion.

But, beyond these details, the document is of importance because of the clear picture it presents of the official and popular Italian views which bear on the present crisis.

Despite the diplomatic conflict that the memorandum reveals, it does not picture an Anglo-Italian war as inevitable. But it delineates with unrestrained clarity a situation of major importance in today's efforts to keep the peace.

Text of the Memorandum

The views expressed in this memorandum are the result of a very thorough examination of the present Italian situation. Its conclusions are based on extensive observation of events under the Fascist regime, and upon conversations with high officials, foreign diplomatists and a number of military authorities.

The most delicate and serious problem at the present time is the crisis which has unexpectedly broken out between Italy and Britain.

I do not refer to the differences which have arisen between Rome and London over the method of settling the Ethiopian conflict, but to the radical change which has taken place in the political relations between Italy and England, between two countries, that is, which up to only a few months ago were believed by all to be the best of friends without conflicting interests.

The crisis between Rome and London is much more serious and deep than appears on the surface, and whether it will end in an armed conflict between the two nations—a conflict unfortunately anticipated by many in Italy—must depend upon the adjustment of basic Anglo-Italian differences.

Fundamental Friendship

All observers of Italian events, without any exception, including also the diplomats with whom I have discussed the Italian problem in recent years, were entirely of the opinion, which I also shared, that Italy might have followed a policy contrary to France, or contrary to Germany, or contrary to any other European power, but never, for any reason, opposed to England.

Anglo-Italian friendship, in fact, had always been reckoned as the fundamental and immutable basis of Fascist foreign policy. This was the opinion in the epoch preceding Fascism's arrival. Benito Mussolini himself, in his most important speech on foreign policy (June, 1928) had declared that friendship with England was the cardinal point of Italian policy. During the whole of the 13 years of the Fascist regime Italian relations with the more important countries of Europe (France, Germany, the Little Entente) have passed through periods of acute tension, but with Britain everything had proceeded smoothly.

Sudden Change?

There was absolutely nothing to lead one to expect the brusque change which has now occurred. The only serious incident between the two countries worth mentioning was the Corfu affair in 1923. Except for this crisis, which was of brief duration but which, evidently, must have left deep traces in the mind of Signor Mussolini, Britain had always supported Fascist foreign policy, even when certain other great European powers, notably France, opposed some of its tendencies.

When two years ago Sir Eric Drummond was appointed Ambassador to Italy, his predecessor, Sir Ronald Graham, before leaving Rome, said to him:

"I leave in your hands a situation which is excellent in all respects. Except for the question of the Italian language at Malta, there is no question in suspense and no disagreement between us and Italy."

New Diplomacy

As the situation has worked out, Sir Eric has necessarily represented a political school wholly opposed to the ideas of Signor Mussolini. This is said to have rendered the personal relations between them very difficult. I do not believe I am mistaken in saying that Signor Mussolini has anything but personal liking for Sir Eric. These factors, and the international situation, have prevented the frank relations which existed between Il Duce and Sir Ronald Graham.

No Common Ground

A short time ago it was said that, in spite of all the efforts he had made, Sir Eric had never succeeded in making Mussolini understand the reasons why the British Government was so attached to the League and wanted League intervention in order to solve the Ethiopian difficulty. They had always approached the same problem—Ethiopia—from entirely different angles and with a different frame of mind, and were both unable to find common ground on which to meet.

In this way, the Anglo-Italian differences, instead of being narrowed, seemed, at each interview between Il Duce and Sir Eric, to become wider and wider.

Miscalculations

It is curious how both Britain and Italy have made the same error in judging each other's attitude toward the Ethiopian affair. From the outset Britain considered that Mussolini was bluffing and that he would not resort to war against Ethiopia if generous concessions were offered to him. On his part, Mussolini has based his whole policy in East Africa on the assumption that there would be trouble with England, but that the latter would in no circumstances go to war either to defend her own vital interests, threatened by an Italian occupation of Ethiopia, or to uphold the Covenant of the League.

Both England and Italy are now realizing that neither of them was bluffing. This, in the face of a publicly declared attitude, makes it the more difficult for either side gracefully to withdraw.

Smooth Surface

Until the Ethiopian crisis broke out, relations between Rome and London were excellent. This, however, was only on the surface. The facts of today provide an explanation of many things which up to now were incomprehensible and which, strangely enough, had escaped the attention of all, diplomats included.

I have just re-examined the whole attitude of Signor Mussolini toward the major international problems; I have reread most of his speeches, keeping in mind the present tension between Italy and England; I have reached the conclusion that there also is a basic division between Signor

(Continued on Page 4, Column 3)

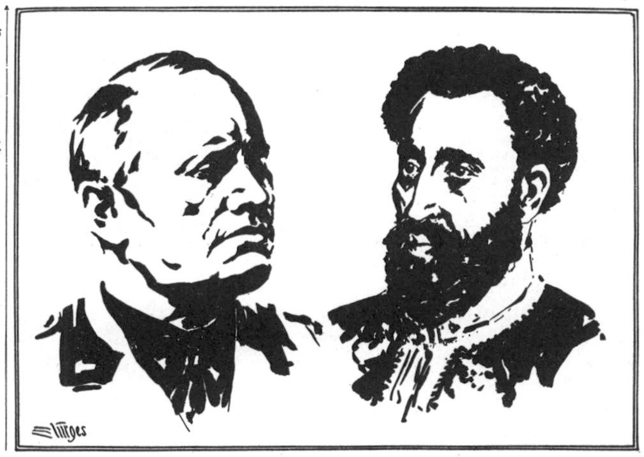

By a Staff Artist — Benito Mussolini — Haile Selassie

U. S. Backs Plans For World Action To Prevent Wars

Thought to Indicate Full Co-operation in Move to Remove Basic Causes

NEW YORK, Oct. 3 (AP)—Selling on the stock exchange yesterday, on reports of a start of hostilities between Italy and Ethiopia, caused many leading issues to lose $1 to $3 a share, and in Chicago world wheat prices jumped sharply to the highest levels of the season.

By a Staff Correspondent of The Christian Science Monitor

WASHINGTON, Oct. 3 — The American Government yesterday met the reported outbreak of hostilities between Italy and Ethiopia with a strong stand for readjustment of the basic world conditions which have caused the present situation.

Cordell Hull, Secretary of State, in a hastily prepared statement, indorsed recent European proposals for world co-operation which would look toward a "more equitable distribution" of the world's store of raw materials.

After declaring that the first requisite for peace and stability is "a firm, cool determination on the part of governments to preserve peace and to abstain from all aggression," Mr. Hull said:

"Then, under conditions of peace, steps must be taken to assure the process of lessening trade restrictions, to build up again a freely operating international monetary system, and effective plans must be formulated to assure an adequate

(Continued on Page 4, Column 1)

Citizens Organize In Northwest To Make Roads Safer

Special to The Christian Science Monitor

WENATCHEE, Wash. — Aroused by the appalling number of recent traffic accidents caused by reckless and drunken driving, a group of 100 "vigilantes," calling themselves the Citizens' Highway Safety Committee, is co-operating with sheriffs and state highway patrol offices in three north-central Washington counties in a drive against traffic violators.

The "vigilantes' have been supplied with special card forms upon which they enter any road violations, noting the automobile or truck license number, and mail these to authorities, who then check up on the violations. Letters are mailed to offenders on first report. If the same number is received twice, its owner must appear before officers, and drastic measures will be taken upon further violations.

Failure to stop at arterial highways, driving on the wrong side of the road and reckless passing of other cars were the most frequent offenses reported as the vigilante campaign got under way. This offensive, sponsored by a committee of Legionnaires, was followed up by the sheriff's office here which stopped more than 500 cars in four hours after midnight one recent Saturday.

"We're going to make the highways safe for sober drivers," Sheriff Tom Cannon announced. "From now on it will go hard with anyone involved in a traffic accident if he has the smell of liquor on his breath, or if there is an unsealed liquor bottle in his car."

The Monitor Index

Thursday, Oct. 3, 1935

'My Peace I Give Unto You'

An Editorial

AMID the wars or rumors of wars reported today we have need more than ever of the peace Jesus spoke of, the inner assurance of spiritual harmony. With the material manifestations of warring human thought thrown at us in aggravated and more evident form by the news from Ethiopia, mankind in this hour must turn all the more firmly to the active understanding that true peace is indestructible and eternal.

We would not cry, "Peace, peace, when there is no peace." But we would remember that the hate and greed and other passions that make war are no more real, but only more ripe for destruction when they spring into visible expression.

At a time like this we realize that suspicion will not remove suspicion, hate will not heal hate, greed will not cure greed, injustice will not remedy injustice, war will not end war. Only by applying the opposites of these evils shall we achieve any permanent peace. And only as we begin to understand, as Jesus understood, when he said, "My peace I give unto you," the actual spiritual unity and harmony of men as the sons of one Father shall we be able to practice the trust, the love, the generosity, the justice and the harmony which represent the underlying reality.

In reporting, as a newspaper, the story of warlike measures, the Monitor as a Christian Science publication also bespeaks its readers' attention to the fact of peace.

The World's Day

Its News in Focus

Thursday, Oct. 3

President—Off to Sea to Think

By a Staff Correspondent of The Christian Science Monitor

SAN DIEGO, Calif.—The President's program: an extremely important speech, the review of a major portion of America's battle fleet, and off to sea for a long, quiet think.

The President speaks peace, watches mock war, and puts to sea to think it over: Page 1.

Bulgaria—Plot Brings State of Siege

By a Staff Correspondent of The Christian Science Monitor

SOFIA, Bulg.—This country was in a stage of seige yesterday. The Government claims to have upturned a revolt, aimed not merely at the Cabinet but at overthrowing the King and establishing an agrarian republic. A number of alleged plotters were under arrest. Chief among them was Colonel Veltcheff, who, it is said, had set out to end oppression and Macedonian terrorism, and to bring Bulgaria within the community of Balkan nations and the Balkan Entente.

Colonel Veltcheff returned secretly from Yugoslavia, and was seized by the Government, it is reported. Should his liberal faction be thoroughly dispersed by the armed dictatorship, a belligerent policy and more difficult relations with Yugoslavia and Turkey are thought likely.

Mussolini—Rallies Fascists for Action

By a Staff Correspondent of The Christian Science Monitor

ROME—Premier Mussolini yesterday informed his mobilized Fascist legions that "A solemn hour is about to strike."

At the same time he opened the way for League economic sanctions, without their precipitating a war with the League powers.

The real French people, he said, will not support sanctions, in his opinion. The real British people, he believed, will not spill blood.

But to economic sanctions Italy will answer with "our discipline, our spirit of sacrifice and our obedience." To military sanctions, Italy will answer "with acts of war."

". . . I shall do everything in my power to prevent a colonial conflict from taking on the aspect and weight of a European war."

Text of Mussolini's speech: Page 1.

Hull—Indorses British Plan

By a Staff Correspondent of The Christian Science Monitor

WASHINGTON—Secretary Hull yesterday indorsed Britain's plan for a world conference to discuss the more equitable world distribution of raw materials

America ready to discuss how the "have" nations will help the "have nots": Page 1.

Ethiopia—Emperor Charges Italian Invasion

From Associated Press Dispatches

ADDIS ABABA—An Italian military invasion of a 15-mile area of Ethiopian territory was charged yesterday by Emperor Haile Selassie, in a protest note to the League of Nations. The Emperor asked the League Council to send observers to see for themselves.

The report, from French sources, said that Italy had established advance fortifications at the juncture of Eritrea, Ethiopia and French

(Continued on Page 8, Column 4)

The Bible: Beacon Light of the World

The fourth installment in this series of 54 daily articles, written for The Christian Science Monitor by Albert F. Gilmore, will be found on

Page Three

Duce's Force Over Border, Negus Wires

Invasion Alleged to Have Occurred at Somaliland-Eritrea Junction

20,000,000 Hear Mussolini Speak

Fascist Mobilization Begins With Radiocast of Warlike Talk

By a Staff Correspondent of The Christian Science Monitor

GENEVA, Oct. 3 — The Emperor of Ethiopia notified the League of Nations yesterday that Italian troops have crossed the Ethiopian frontier south of Mount Moussa Ali, Province of Aussa, and are preparing an extensive attack from that base. As the region is near the sea and French Somaliland, confirmation is easily obtained by the Council. It is believed here that the actual outbreak of hostilities is imminent.

The cabled protest of Haile Selassie read as follows:

"We inform you for communication to the Council and the states members that Italian troops have violated the Ethiopian frontier in the region south of Mount Moussa Ali, in the Province of Aussa, between that mountain and the frontier of Ethiopia and French Somaliland and have established themselves in Ethiopian territory preparing a base for extensive attack.

"The proximity to the sea of this region and its easy access through the territory of French Somaliland make it possible with the Council either to send observers or to obtain confirmation of this violation of Ethiopian territory through the Government of French Somaliland."

The text was signed "Selassie."

Rome Abandons Hope Of League Settlement; Prepares to Strike

By a Staff Correspondent of The Christian Science Monitor

ROME, Oct. 3—Mobilization of the whole Fascist forces in the Italian Kingdom and the colonies was held yesterday, according to orders broadcast by Achille Starace, secretary general of the Fascist Party.

The salient event of this imposing manifestation of Fascist strength was the speech by Il Duce, broadcast all over Italy, in which he virtually gave the signal to begin Italian operations in East Africa.

The "Great Day"

Reports from foreign sources that the Italian advance in Ethiopia has already begun find no confirmation here but the holding today of the Fascist rally suddenly brought vividly before all Italians in every town and village from the Alps down to the most remote corner of Sicily the fact that the "Great Day" has at last come.

Already by mid-afternoon the Fascists of Rome had begun to concentrate in their respective headquarters to await orders broadcast to them by the Secretary of the Fascist Party. The people in the streets were in the wildest state of excitement.

Loyalty to Duce

The international implications of the Italo-Ethiopian dispute are for the moment forgotten and the Italian people were called together to prove their loyalty to Premier Mussolini in his African adventure.

Everybody feels that all hopes for an eleventh hour settlement have now definitely vanished. The die, it seems to them, has been cast. Italy, having completed her military preparations, is now ready to settle old and new accounts with Ethiopia and seek by her own forces expansion in East Africa, which the world claims to deny her.

Text of Speech

The following English translation of Premier Benito Mussolini's speech in Rome was received here yesterday by the National Broadcasting Company:

Black Shirts of the Revolution; men and women of all Italy; Italians all over the world, beyond the seas—listen.

A solemn hour is about to strike in the history of the country. Twenty million Italians are at this moment gathered in the squares of all Italy. It is the greatest demonstration that human history records: 20,000,000, one heart alone, one will alone, one decision.

This manifestation signifies that the tie between Italy and Fascism is perfect, absolute, unalterable. Only brains softened by puerile illusions, by sheer ignorance can think differently because they do not know what exactly is the Fascist Italy of 1935.

Marching in Unity

For many months the wheel of destiny and of the impulse of our calm determination moves towards the goal. In these last hours the rhythm has increased and nothing can stop it now.

It is not only an army marching towards its goal, but it is 44,000,000 Italians marching in unity be-

(Continued on Page 4, Column 7)

THE CHRISTIAN SCIENCE MONITOR

AN INTERNATIONAL DAILY NEWSPAPER

COPYRIGHT 1936 BY THE CHRISTIAN SCIENCE PUBLISHING SOCIETY

BOSTON, WEDNESDAY, NOVEMBER 4, 1936—VOL. XXVIII, NO. 290

C * * * ATLANTIC EDITION—FIVE CENTS A COPY

The Franc: Devaluation Aids Trade

Paris Reports a Modest but Clear Rise in Business Lines

Exports Expanded

Success of World's Fair in 1937 Is Seen, With 50 Countries Participating

By a Staff Correspondent of The Christian Science Monitor

PARIS—Signs of a slight but unmistakable improvement in business have become visible in France since the devaluation of the franc.

There has been nothing like the rush to buy goods of all kinds which followed the fall of the franc in 1926. But most French merchants and manufacturers report a modest but evident increase in sales.

The exporting industries especially seem to have felt the effects of devaluation very quickly. Although official figures are not yet available, it is widely stated that a satisfactory increase in orders from abroad has been registered by many exporting firms. Furthermore, high hopes are entertained in France that the Anglo-Franco-American monetary accord will lead before long to general economic disarmament, and thus to a general revival of world trade.

Success of Fair Foreseen

Another cause of optimism here is that devaluation of the franc is felt to have assured success of the Paris 1937 Exposition. Already more than 50 countries have announced their intention of participating. With the franc "aligned" there is every reason to believe that the French "World's Fair" will bring a record number of visitors who will give a great impetus to economic recovery in France.

At the same time, it cannot be claimed that French recovery is already an accomplished fact by any means. Apprehension is still expressed in many quarters. In particular, the criticism is heard that the franc was not sufficiently devalued—that the rate of reduction should have been 40 or 45 rather than 25 or 30 per cent.

Balanced Budget Demanded

This agitation is naturally regretted and denounced in official circles as prejudicial to French economic recovery, since it implies the possibility of a new devaluation later on. For instance, Paul Raynaud, a former Minister of Finance, stated in a recent speech in Paris: "Let us cease this light talk, which one so often hears, of a fresh devaluation. I declare that if the Government of the country does its duty there will be no necessity for renewed devaluation."

The "duty" referred to by M. Reynaud means, as he has often made clear, primarily two things. First, the present rise in prices must be checked or at least slowed down; and secondly, the budget must be balanced, at least in so far as ordinary expenditures are concerned.

Already there are predictions that nearly all the profit reaped by the State Treasury from devaluation—about 17,000,000,000 francs—will be absorbed by this year's deficit while for next year a new deficit of at least 20,000,000,000 francs is envisaged if the program of expenditures for various social schemes is adhered to by the Popular Front Government.

Money Still Hoarded

These pessimistic previsions, however, need not necessarily be realized. Even a partial improvement in business activity in France and a revival of world commerce would mean increased revenue, higher tax returns and a rapid return toward a balanced budget. Once confidence is restored, hoarded money—which so far still seems slow about coming out of its woolen stockings and linen closets despite the devaluation of the franc—would return to circulation, and a conversion loan would enable the State to reduce the heavy burden of interest charges on the public debt, now carried at 4, 5 or even 6 per cent.

Thus, although the "alignment" of the franc has not precipitated the rapid return to business prosperity for which the Government had hoped, nor removed all obstacles to economic recovery, it has nevertheless put France in a position to share in the improvement visible elsewhere in the world, and given an undoubted if slight impulse to French industry and commerce.

The Monitor Index

Wednesday, Nov. 4, 1936

The Holy Land
Thirtieth of 51 Articles, Page 4

Weekly Magazine Section

U. S. Envoy Ignores Claim to Ethiopia

By the Associated Press

Rome, Nov. 4

UNITED STATES AMBASSADOR WILLIAM PHILLIPS presented his credentials today to King Victor Emmanuel of Italy.

The official documents addressed the Italian ruler only as the "King of Italy" and did not refer to him as "Emperor of Ethiopia."

Mr. Phillips read his address of presentation to the King in the Quirinal palace. The monarch replied in English, assuring the Ambassador of co-operation between his Government and the United States.

Austria Ousts Heimwehrmen From Cabinet

By a Staff Correspondent of The Christian Science Monitor

VIENNA, Nov. 4—Elimination of the pro-Starhemberg Heimwehr influence from the Austrian Cabinet has been finally effected by the reconstruction of the Austrian Government, which was announced last night.

Despite the fact that the official communiqué represents the changes as merely a matter of personnel, not policies, it is generally regarded as strengthening the pro-German elements in the Government.

Duties Divided

The main feature is the division of the Ministry of the Interior, which was previously occupied by Vice-Chancellor Eduard Baar-Baarenfels, one-time friend of Prince Ernst Rüdiger von Starhemberg, between the National Socialist exponent in the Cabinet, Dr. Edmund Glaise-Horstenau, who takes over the general affairs of this ministry, and the present Minister to Hungary, Udo Neustädter-Stürmer, a friend of Major Emil Fey and known to have pro-German leanings, who is entrusted with public security.

Starhemberg Men Dropped

The former Starhemberg-Heimwehr ministers who have now been evicted are Ludwig Draxler, former Minister of Finance, and Fritz Stockinger, ex-Minister of Trade and Communications. The other cabinet minister dropped is Hans Hammerstein-Equord, Minister of Justice.

The position of Vice Chancellor is given to Field Marshal Ludwig Hülgerth, new commander of militia.

New Cabinet Members

Rudolf Neumaier becomes Minister of Finance; Dr. Wilhelm Taucher is the new Minister of Trade, and Communications (Commerce); Herr Neustädter-Stürmer heads the new Ministry of Security, and Dr. Atolz Pilz is the new Minister of Justice.

Dr. Glaise-Horstenau who became Minister of the Interior, was Minister-without-Portfolio in the former Cabinet.

Eduard Baar-Barrenfels, Dr. Draxler and Dr. Hans Pertner were announced as resigning Oct. 10 last, when Chancellor Schuschnigg announced the dissolution of all private armed forces and their merger in the State militia.

Federal Accord Sought to End Shipping Strike

Labor Officials Resent Roper Viewpoint on Hiring Halls

Union to Aid Lines

By a Staff Correspondent of The Christian Science Monitor

WASHINGTON, Nov. 4—Federal efforts to settle the seamen's strike now paralyzing American shipping were complicated today by a conflict of attitude toward the situation by two government departments here.

Pressure was being brought to bear on Daniel C. Roper, Secretary of Commerce, to authorize the establishment under federal control of hiring halls on the Pacific coast through which non-union labor could obtain work on the strike-tied ships.

Mr. Roper insisted at a press conference that he is giving the Department of Labor his full co-operation, but added that he had not definitely vetoed the hiring-hall proposal which is anathema to the Department of Labor.

Suspicions Aroused

Department of Labor officials said they had heard nothing whatever about co-operation from Mr. Roper and added privately that if he wanted to co-operate he would stop talking about hiring halls under federal control. Such a proposal, they explained, inflames the suspicions and anger of the strikers, who would look upon such a development as a deliberate attempt by the Government to break their strike.

The Department of Labor is bending every effort to extract a promise from strikers to put maintenance crews on ships and to get representatives of both sides around a table together. These efforts, they feel, are made more difficult by the kind of talk which is current in the Department of Commerce, which, quite properly, is the branch of the Government where the interests of the employers are heard.

Intervention Held Justified

The hiring halls constitute a proposal of Joseph B. Weaver, director of the Bureau of Marine Inspection and Navigation, who believes that there is a similarity between mutiny and strikes against shipping which justifies federal intervention.

That any such proposal will be put into operation is doubted here, although it is pointed out that what President Roosevelt may do when he returns from election congratulations to the business of government is an unknown quantity. It is conceivable he might accept the recommendations of Mr. Roper on the subject, as well as of other individuals who favor putting navy crews on the idle ships to protect them against damage incident to the strike.

The most probable course is federal intervention solely in the form of efforts to bring the hostile groups around an arbitration table together. But pressure on shipowners through the subsidy control of the

(Continued on Page 2, Column 6)

The World's Day

Its News in Focus

Wednesday, Nov. 4

Power—Ruling for Projects Put Before Court

Weather vanes, pointing toward a show-down between the New Deal and public utilities, were fixed on election day, when Attorney General Cummings filed a brief in the Supreme Court in which he asserted that the crux of the issue over government loans for public power projects involved the validity of "co-operation between the central government and the states." The brief will come in handy next week, when administration attorneys argue the case brought by the Duke Power Company and the Southern Utilities Company, attacking a PWA loan for construction of a power plant on the Saluda river.

Peru—Office Denied to Chosen President

Dr. Luis Antonio Eguigureu, apparently elected to the Presidency of Peru yesterday, today may be imagined as looking wistfully toward America, whose re-elected President will certainly not be denied entrance to the White House. Señor Eguigureu and his colleagues of the Social Democratic party are less fortunate. Although they amassed enough votes to elect, they have been informed that the Constituent Assembly has rendered a "thumbs down" verdict on their ascendency to power, contending that the Social Democrats were supported by an outlawed party.

Election—Calls Startled Comment From Europe

The world applauds America's decision to retain the New Deal while showing less enthusiasm for American securities. From far-off Moscow and Shanghai, across Europe to South American capitals, come words of congratulation. "Roosevelt, we think you're grand!" was the phrase used by Lord Beaverbrook's London Daily Express, and that seems to be the general sentiment abroad. Paris finds the Rightists and Leftists momentarily united in expressions of satisfaction; Fascist Rome applauded the New Deal victory; Soviet Moscow approved America's choice, because it indicated no change in Russo-American relations. Nazi Germany welcomes the return of President Roosevelt "because of his fearlessness"; inscrutable Tokyo declares the continuance of New Deal policies will favorably affect Japanese-American relations. But on the London market American securitiies took a drop. Brokers described the decline as "a sharp technical reaction," however, and said the long term trend is likely to be higher, a prediction born out by a subsequent stock recovery.

Dublin—Question of British Relations Postponed

Eamon de Valera won't be pushed; and so the fears of those who predicted a breach wider than St. George's Channel, between Ireland and Great Britain, are somewhat allayed.

Said the head of the Irish Free State Government before the general congress of Fianna Fail:

"I won't be forced by anyone to take up a position which I cannot hold. Unilateral action on our part isn't going to end partition or get the British out of our ports, and we might as well recognize that."

However, his words indicate that the Free State will be demanding

(Continued on Page 6, Column 3)

The President of the United States

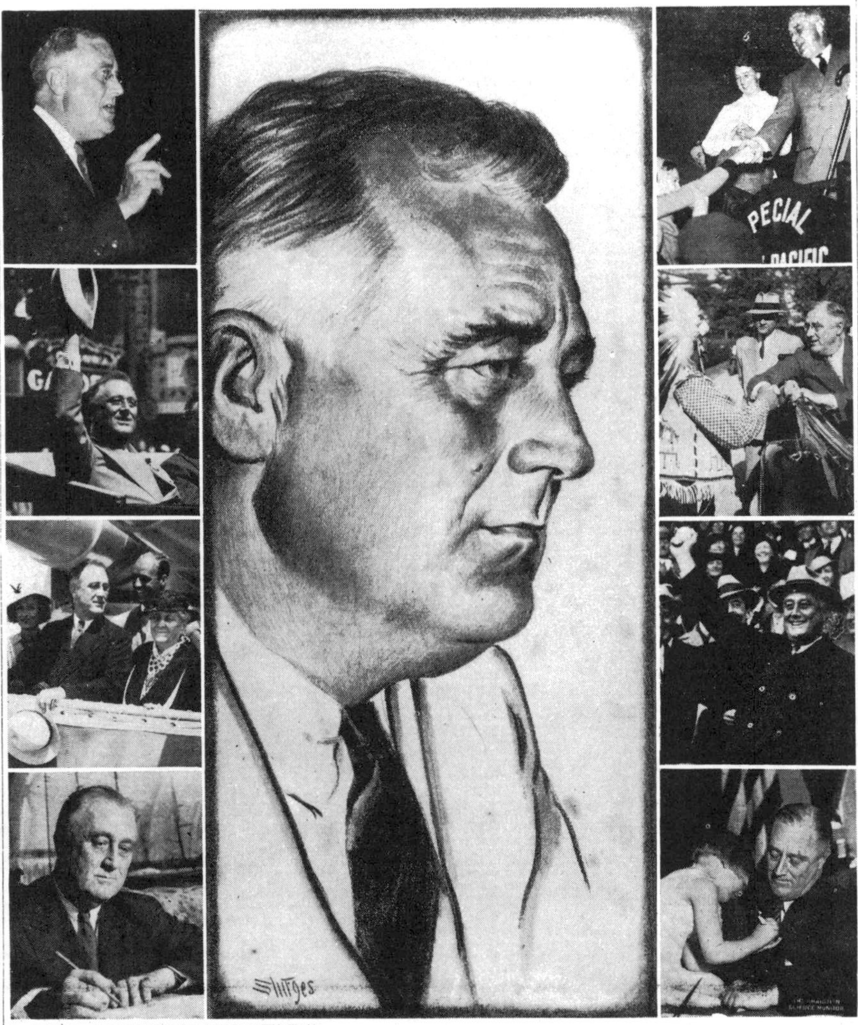

By a Staff Artist; © Harris & Ewing; Associated Press; Wide World

Australia Defers Defense Pending Empire Parleys

Special to The Christian Science Monitor

MELBOURNE, Vic.—So rapidly has the international situation been changed by rearmament that Australia has decided to abandon its second three-year defense program until after the Imperial Conference in London next year. By then it is expected that a completely new policy for the co-ordination of Empire defense will have been evolved.

The Commonwealth Council of Defense, supreme military, naval and air authority for Australia, which met here recently, decided that it would be unwise and unsafe to push ahead with rigidly planned development while there was a distinct possibility that the requirements of national defense would alter completely within a short period.

New Air Forces Pushed

Air force expansion will be pushed ahead with all speed, and made a feature of future defense programs. The Minister for Defense, Sir Archdale Parkhill, announced after the meeting that the Salmond plan for air defense would be amended to provide for a considerable increase in the number of machines originally contemplated.

Every effort will be made to increase the number of qualified pilots for an emergency by developing a citizens' air force and the encouragement of fliers' clubs and civil aviation.

Main Arm of Defense

It is rapidly becoming accepted by defense authorities that Australia will largely have to rely upon its air force to resist possible invasion. Its problem in this respect is entirely different from that of Great Britain,

(Continued on Page 7, Column 1)

Spain's President Moves Into Catalan Monastery

BARCELONA, Spain., Nov. 4 (AP)—President Manuel Azaña of Spain today took up residence at a monastery at Montserrat, a short distance outside of Barcelona.

When he came to Barcelona from Madrid several weeks ago, the President lived at the Parliament building, normal headquarters for the nation's Chief Executive. It was reported reliably his change of residence was made out of respect for the political sentiments of the Catalan people, who prize their autonomy and regard Luis Companys, President of the Catalan Generalitat, as their national leader.

More New Deal at Decreased Tempo Expected of President

By Richard L. Strout

Staff Correspondent of The Christian Science Monitor

WASHINGTON, Nov. 4—Returned to the White House with a fresh mandate from the American electorate, there is every indication that President Roosevelt's next four years in office will represent a continuance and consolidation of the activities of the first.

Due to economic and political factors there is not likely to be the same adventuresome efflorescence of new agencies which marked 1933-1936 apart from any similar period in American history; but, on the other hand, it is unlikely that he will veer appreciably to the conservative side.

With Emphasis

Mr. Roosevelt's record-shattering electoral majority obviously recorded the confidence of the great majority of voters in his leadership and this confidence may well affect the next four years. The victory was the more remarkable and emphatic, in view of the type of campaign waged against him.

Outside of the South, probably 70 per cent of all the newspapers were hostile to the President, often bitterly so. In spots like Chicago and New England only a few newspapers favored him, despite which Mr. Roosevelt won Illinois and most of the New England states, including even New Hampshire.

Abuse Fails

A campaign of abuse carried in one large newspaper chain and picked up by some high Republican leaders, charged that he was allied with the Communists. Despite all this he won handily.

These factors can hardly be disregarded by the New Deal in charting the course of the next four years. Though the period of rapid experimenting is probably over, the solid foundation which Mr. Roosevelt obviously has with the masses, as contrasted with the propertied classes, is likely to be a guiding factor in the unfolding story.

Calming Words

The representative of the cities, the slums, the workingman and the underprivileged is obviously in control. Though the shock of Mr. Roosevelt's overwhelming victory will be hard for many partisan minority opponents, the calming words of the impartial English correspondent of the Times of London may be of profit:

"He (the conservative) should see that slowly, but surely, the forces of democracy in America have broken away from the form of government originally contrived to limit their power, and that the end is not yet."

In this English view, Mr. Roosevelt's victory is more expressive of a deep mass movement in the United States than of a personal victory for any one candidate.

It can hardly be denied that in the four years to come the New Deal will not be greatly affected by the cry of "Communist," if the same cry has had so little effect in the past.

How Not to Do It

The election just concluded, in fact, apparently illustrates how NOT to defeat Mr. Roosevelt. The masses who approved Mr. Roosevelt were not affected by charges of radicalism against him. The very heat of the conservative newspapers appears to have reacted in his favor, as witness Chicago; exaggerated last-minute canards against the Social Security Act countenanced by high Republican officials appear to have been a boomerang, which strengthened labor's support. Obviously, with such a victory, Mr. Roosevelt is likely less than ever to fear the "radical" label.

Easier Ride Expected

Three immediate brakes are apparent on the giddy rush of New Deal legislation which featured Mr. Roosevelt's first term of office, and the national caravan is likely to see a calmer and more comfortable ride. This will be due in part to easier springs in the Roosevelt car itself and secondly to an easier economic road. Also any need for drastic changes, economic improvisations and emergency measures has passed. Many of the experiments of the New Deal—at least of those left by the Supreme Court—have been accepted now even by Mr. Roosevelt's opponents.

The New Deal is becoming the "Old Deal." Already some of the measures which seemed startling and revolutionary in 1933 and '34 and '35 are being looked upon as the normal scheme of things—control of stock markets, banks, regulation of utilities.

Looking Forward

Accepting at the outset the promise that Mr. Roosevelt is a moderate liberal, whose economic views are a little left of center, and who is quite prepared to improvise, compromise, or play the opportunist for the time being in order that his program as a whole should be furthered, certain aspects of the next four years stand fairly revealed.

Good and Bad Criticism

To begin with there may be certain general factors that will moderate the pace of the New Deal.

Even though the Republicans fail

(Continued on Page 6, Column 1)

New Constitution In Dublin Avoids Rift With Britain

Special to The Christian Science Monitor

DUBLIN, Nov. 4—The statement of Eamon de Valera, president of the Free State Executive Council, before the general congress of the Fianna Fail party yesterday, is generally regarded as reassuring, in so far that it shows there is to be at least some postponement of any possible open breach with Britain.

This view places emphasis upon Mr. de Valera's declaration that "unilateral action on our part is not going to end partition or get the British out of our ports and we must recognize that position. We will do everything in our power to solve these problems as time goes on, but they cannot be solved by unilateral action only. I won't be forced by anyone to take up a position which I cannot hold."

British Issue Reserved

On the other hand it is recognized that the bill, of which he announced immediate introduction to "give us a constitution which the Irish people would themselves freely choose if Britain were a million miles away," involves very grave potentialities. It is noticed, however, with satisfaction, that it is to be concerned mainly with internal affairs, while the question of relations with Britain and the Commonwealth are to be reserved for some subsequent occasion.

Popular Vote Planned

There is every reason to believe that Mr. De Valera has planned to have the constitution passed in the Dail by Christmas so that it may be submitted to the people toward the end of January or early in February, 1937.

The constitution will be the big item of the Dail session which opened today and if, as anticipated, it is introduced during the first week, the second reading should take place shortly after the middle of November, and the first of December should see things reaching the committee stage which is really the most important period of progress and, in view of the big issues involved, likely to be the most protracted as well as the hardest fought.

Wide Field of Debate

These issues embrace the position of the Saorstat in relation to the British Commonwealth; the place of the Crown; the office of the Governor-General; the proposal to set up a new office of Supreme Head of the

(Continued on Page 6, Column 5)

Roosevelt Sweeps 46 Of 48 States In U. S. Vote

New Deal Adds to Its Power in Congress and in States

Landon Pledges His Full Support

President Says Nation Will Pull Together in Implementing His Policies

By Erwin D. Canham

Chief of the Washington Bureau of The Christian Science Monitor

Closer to electoral unanimity than since the "era of good feeling" in 1820, the American nation, by a decision inadequately called a landslide, has returned President Roosevelt to office with 523 electoral votes, leaving only Maine and Vermont's eight votes to Governor Landon.

This tremendous mandate stands as a personal endorsement of the buoyant Chief Executive, a vote of confidence for the New Deal as contrasted with the Republican alternative. The great strength shown by the President surprised most observers by carrying along with it the rest of the Democratic ticket in most states, producing both a Senate and House probably more heavily Democratic than in the 1932 and 1934 landslides. President Roosevelt is assured of a supporting Senate—as far as party lines are certain—for the whole of his term, and a towering majority in the House.

Some Republican Victories

Isolated Republican victories cropped up here and there, the most notable being Henry Cabot Lodge Jr.'s sound defeat administered to Governor James M. Curley in Massachusetts. This success was in spite of President Roosevelt's heavy sweep in the State, and the close victory of Charles F. Hurley, State Treasurer, the Democratic candidate for Governor, over John W. Haigis, Republican.

Other leaders who stood for re-election in their own right were also successful: Senator William E. Borah won in Idaho as handily as President Roosevelt did in the same State, while Senator George W. Norris, running as an independent with President's warm support, was managing to keep ahead of both Republican and Democratic rivals.

Never in modern American two-party history has such an overwhelming electoral vote been piled up. In 1932, President Roosevelt swept into office with 472 votes to 59 for Mr. Hoover. Today the six states that went Republican then are whittled down to three and possibly two.

All Will Pull Together

"The nation has spoken," telegraphed Governor Landon to President Roosevelt from Topeka as soon as the electoral results were manifest. "Every American will accept the verdict, and work for the common cause of the good of our country. That is the spirit of democracy. You have my sincere congratulations."

To which President Roosevelt immediately replied: "All of us Americans will pull together for the common good."

Facing the astounding returns, which grew more tremendous with every passing hour of the night and early morning, observers came to one major conclusion: that the victory could not be explained as a triumph along class lines, but was an overwhelming expression of public opinion so emphatic as to be unchallengeable; that the very nature of the victory should dissipate much of the bitterness produced in the campaign.

Farley Regrets Bitterness

Speaking for the Democratic higher command on this point, James A. Farley said today:

"I have an idea that the people who so viciously assailed the President during the campaign, who called him a Communist, a would-be dictator, and an enemy of business, are now rather ashamed of the bitterness they brought into the campaign. For myself, I hope these attacks will be forgotten.

"I am sure that the President entertains no bitterness even to those who in the fury of political struggle so grossly assailed him. He realizes, I feel justified in saying, that he is more than ever the President of all the people, for all of the people contributed to the splendid endorsement he has received."

Records Crash

Record after record fell with the avalanche. The popular vote seemed likely to exceed 43,000,000 and perhaps would go above 44,000,000, as against the previous high of 39,500,000 in 1932.

As election night wore on, state after state rolled in with totally unexpected Roosevelt leads. Connecticut was one of the early surprises, with Delaware and Kansas at its heels, but the results were entirely conclusive when Pennsylvania consistently held a 2-to-1 lead for Roosevelt and Illinois began to return the same totals. One of the major surprises was that President Roosevelt carried downstate Illinois, a typical Mid West farming region with scattered industrial and mining towns, as well as running to 500,000 plurality in Cook county.

Outstanding in the senatorial re-

(Continued on Page 4, Column 1)

THE CHRISTIAN SCIENCE MONITOR

AN INTERNATIONAL DAILY NEWSPAPER

COPYRIGHT 1937 BY
THE CHRISTIAN SCIENCE PUBLISHING SOCIETY

BOSTON, SATURDAY, JULY 3, 1937—VOL. XXIX, NO. 185

••• ATLANTIC EDITION—{ FIVE CENTS / TWOPENCE } A COPY

Tower reViews

by Clearwy

The Week in Focus

**Ben's Timely Prayer;
Franc Finds Support**

On June 28, 1787, just 150 years ago last Monday, Benjamin Franklin turned the United States Constitutional Convention toward success by an appeal for divine guidance.

His words echo forward with timely conviction this week to a world of confused events, groping amid labor strife, wars and rumors of war.

"In this situation of this assembly," Franklin said, "groping as it were in the dark to find political truth, and scarce able to distinguish it when presented to us, how has it happened, sir, that we have not hitherto thought of humbly applying to the Father of Lights to illuminate our understandings."

He concluded by moving that each day's deliberations be opened with prayer. History records that moment as the beginning of fruition. The Constitution moved forward to completion as a charter of human liberties.

✦ ✦ ✦

Franc Unpegged

As ambassador to France, Franklin once spoke up against the waste of candles due to late rising and late working. He surely would join with Britain this week in counseling Paris to set its budgetary house in order. London sees the crisis of the franc as primarily budgetary, and only secondarily monetary.

In June, nearly 8,000,000,000 francs' worth of gold left the country. When the Chautemps Government assumed office a week and a half ago, the Treasury had only 20,-000,000 francs, or less than $1,000,-000. To meet current expenses, 400,-000,000 francs had to be borrowed.

Onto the dock at Havre Monday morning stepped the man charged with finding a way out for France. Georges Bonnet, on his way home from the United States, had received a record batch of radiograms as Paris kept him advised of each new turn.

The Cabinet asked full powers of Parliament to deal with the financial and economic crisis. The Blum Government had fallen on a similar request, but Parliament voted the powers to the Chautemps Cabinet until Aug. 31.

The Bourse was closed to stop speculation in the franc. A temporary moratorium was declared on all payments in gold and foreign currencies.

Behind these moves lay the intent of further devaluing the franc. It is to be left free to find a new level, possibly near 4 cents, its ratio to the dollar from 1928 to 1933.

✦ ✦ ✦

Partners Stand By

France, like Britain and the United States, has maintained a fund to prevent inroads on the linked values of three currencies. On Tuesday Paris advised Washington that France might be forced to withdraw from the three-power pact of last Sept. 25.

The French gold reserve equalization fund, originally 10,000,00,-000 francs, was founded firmly behind the three-power pact. Even with the franc dropping well below the 4.35 figure at which the original agreement pegged it, Secretary Morgenthau indicated that America would stand by during France's "temporary difficulties."

Britain had announced nearly a week earlier the increase of its exchange equalization fund from £350,000,000 to £500,000,000. With the United States, Britain is standing by while France recovers.

✦ ✦ ✦

Fire Over Asia

From financial tension in France, the week's attention turns to diplomatic tension in Asia.

There, as in Europe, the nations endure severe provocation without resorting to general war. On Monday the Versailles Treaty was 18 years old, and for France the world learned of war threats in Asia while Europe uneasily waited for the next move of the Fascist powers in Spain.

Japan and Russia came to blows over two islands in the Amur River. This river divides eastern Siberia from the Japanese-controlled Manchoukuo. Tokyo charged that Russian troops had "invaded" the islands of Bolshoi and Sennukha, near Blagoveschensk. Ownership of the islands has been in dispute between Manchoukuo and Russia.

Not that the islands are worth much. They are little more than sandbanks, mostly submerged when the Amur reaches high water. But border incidents have long troubled relations in East Asia.

Moscow had acceded to Tokyo's protest by agreeing to withdraw the troops, when on Wednesday a new incident occurred. Japanese-Manchoukuan land troops reported sinking one Russian gunboat, inflicting heavy damage on another, and driving off a third near Blagovestchensk.

For some years Russia has avoided trouble with Japan, and has again chosen this course. Moscow ordered withdrawal of her troops and gunboats from the scene of conflict.

Internal difficulties, shown this

(Continued on Page 2, Column 7)

By the Canadian Press

Tweedsmuir Starts North Canadian Tour

Quebec, July 3

A vice-regal party leaves here today on a 10,000-mile tour that will make Lord Tweedsmuir the first governor general in Canada's history to cross the Arctic Circle.

The tour, believed the longest continuous journey ever made by a governor general in Canada, will take Lord Tweedsmuir and members of his staff down the Mackenzie River to Aklavik on that great river's delta, across a narrow strip of water by air to Herschel Island in the Beaufort Sea, and back to civilization by air. The tour will end in Ottawa Sept. 5.

The journey will mark the first time a governor general has flown on a long trip with sanction of the Government.

Farm Tenant Aid Bills Pass Both House and Senate

WASHINGTON, July 3 — Both Houses of Congress have now given their approval to a program of aid to tenants in acquiring farms of their own.

Differences in the House and Senate bills are being ironed out in conference.

The Senate yesterday passed the Administration's bill, introduced by Senator John H. Bankhead (D), of Alabama, as a substitute for another bill approved earlier in the week by the House.

Following in general the recommendations made by President Roosevelt's committee on farm tenancy, the Senate bill provides for the purchase of land by the Government and resale to tenant farmers and farm laborers on long-term contracts.

A new Government agency, to be known as the Farmers' Home Corporation, is authorized to retain an option to repurchase the farm in case the purchaser wishes to sell. This procedure is designed to provide protection against speculative excesses.

The President's committee emphasized the importance of preventing any farm tenant aid from contributing to a speculative rise in land values, and a repetition of what happened to a large part of the homestead land provided farmers by the Government years ago.

Because of the Administration's economy drive, the tenant-aid program will be tried out first on a modest scale. For the first year an appropriation of $10,000,000 is authorized; for the second year, $25,-000,000 and thereafter, $50,000,000 annually.

The Jones bill, passed by the House, follows the ordinary banking procedure of making loans to individual tenants, though is de-

(Continued on Page 2, Column 8)

De Valera Gets Lead in Vote; Aide to Cosgrave Defeated

DUBLIN, July 3 (AP)—Trickling returns from the Irish Free State's general election today gave Eamon de Valera's Government Party a lead over the opposition headed by William T. Cosgrave.

Incomplete returns assured de Valera supporters of 17 seats in the Dail (Parliament), Cosgrave eight, the Labor Party two, Independent Labor one and Independents four.

Both Mr. de Valera and Mr. Cosgrave were returned to their Dail Seats, but full election results were not expected to be known until next week, including the fate of the proposed new constitution.

In County Clare, Mr. de Valera polled 14,012 votes, almost double the number of his nearest opponent. Mr. Cosgrave received 9508 votes in County Cork, about 1000 over the nearest government candidate.

The greatest political sensation thus far was the defeat of Mr. Cosgrave's second-in-command, Gen. Richard Mulcahy, former chief of the Free State Army. He was beaten in the Dublin northeast district by James Larkin, Independent Labor candidate.

The new Dail will have 138 members in comparison with the 153 who formerly sat in the Parliament. On the constitutional question, a majority of 11,026 votes was rolled up

in South Dublin favoring the document.

County Sligo, in far western Ireland, was the first constituency thus far to reject the constitution, by a margin of 1136 votes.

Civil Flying Force For Relief Service Started in Holland

Special to The Christian Science Monitor

THE HAGUE—New and useful tasks are looming up for amateur airmen in the Netherlands who recently united in a volunteer organization of "sporting fliers." Only the best and well-trained licensed amateur pilots are admitted to membership.

The activities will include taking supplies to areas isolated by ice or floods in winter time. In case of shipwrecks on the coast, when the lifeboats fail to effect a connection between the stranded ship and the coast, the amateur pilots will endeavor to drop cable lines on ships in distress.

In times of emergency the Netherlands can call on its amateur pilots. In case of war they would act as reserve military pilots.

(Continued on Page 6, Column 8)

Youth Festival Witnessed By British Royalty

Every Sports Organization in Britain Represented in Wembley March

Massed Bands Play

Special to The Christian Science Monitor

WEMBLEY, Eng., July 3 — King George VI and Queen Elizabeth and the two little princesses were present at the Empire Stadium here today when 11,000 young men and women from all parts of Britain took part in a great Festival of Youth, the first to be organized in this country.

Members of the Cabinet, the diplomatic corps and foreign ambassadors in London were also present. The festival was organized by the British Sports and Games Association, the proceeds to be devoted to King George V's Jubilee Trust Fund.

Horse Guards Participate

A fanfare by the State Trumpeters of the Royal Horse Guards, the trumpeters who performed in Westminster Abbey at the Coronation, heralded the entry of the King and Queen into the Royal Box. A second fanfare was the signal for the National Anthem to be played by the massed bands of the Brigade of Guards, at which all flags were lowered in salute.

To the music of these massed bands 1400 boys and girls marched past the King and Queen. In this great parade was a contingent, headed by standard-bearers, from every sporting organization in the country. Each section was attired in the dress or uniform of the organization it represented. Among those represented were: The Boys' Brigade, The Girl Guides Association, the League of Health and Beauty; The Church Lads' Brigade, Dr. Barnardo's Homes; The Y. M. C. A., the Women's Amateur Games Association and the English Folk Dance Society.

Display of Gymnastics

Two thousand factory girls, domestic servants, shop assistants and typists in the London area and from most of the big towns in the home counties represented the National Council of Girls' Clubs which has a total membership of 250,000. For 12 minutes they gave a display of gymnastics and skipping to the music of the massed bands. These girls had paid their own expenses, many of them having saved up for weeks to be present on this occasion.

Picked teams from 40 organizations representing thousands of sports clubs then gave a display of outdoor games and athletics. The area of the Empire Stadium was specially marked out by 1000 small wooden disks so that each performer knew exactly where to stand for the mass displays.

It is hoped to make this Festival of Youth an annual event.

Old and New World Start New Permament Link

By a Staff Artist; Wide World

Capt. Harold E. Gray
Commanding the Pan American Plane

Survey Flight Prepares Way for Regular Service Between Europe and America

Top—Pan American Clipper, Which Will Make the Eastward Flight
Center—The Route Which the Two Planes Will Follow
Below—The Caledonia, Which Will Fly Westward

Capt. A. S. Wilcockson
Commanding the Imperial Airways Plane

American Plane Starts First Leg Of Atlantic Flight

PORT WASHINGTON, N. Y., July 3 (AP) — Well on its way toward bridging the north Atlantic by commercial airline, the Pan American Clipper III, 45,-500-pound flying boat, coasted to a landing on Shediac Bay, N. B., at 10:52 a. m. (E. S. T.) today.

By a Staff Correspondent of The Christian Science Monitor

NEW YORK, July 3—The Pan American Clipper, huge flying boat of the Pan American Airways, took off from Port Washington, L. I., at 7:20 o'clock (Daylight Saving Time) this morning on the first leg of an exploratory flight over the Atlantic Ocean preliminary to the establishment of a regular passenger and mail service between the United States and Europe.

The Clipper's first stop will be at Shediac, N. B., 601 miles from New York, where Pan American Airways has established an intermediate base and set up one of its long-range direction-finders to assist the Clipper on her trans-Atlantic flight. This constituted a change from the announcement by Pan American Airways yesterday, when it said the Clipper would fly directly to Botwood, N. F.

The Clipper, a 45,500-pound Sikorsky flying boat, is under command of Capt. Harold E. Gray, and carries a crew of six. Simultaneous with the taking off of the Clipper from Port Washington, the Imperial Air-

(Continued on Page 6, Column 8)

Laws Urged to Stop Beer's New Threat to Temperance

Tighter Liquor Control Declared Necessary to Meet Situation

By a Staff Writer of The Christian Science Monitor

NEW YORK, July 3—The nation-wide program of tighter liquor control through vastly strengthened laws and enforcement machinery represents the only way to meet the challenge of the United Brewers', Industrial Foundation's new drive to propagandize America into drinking more beer and lining the pockets of the brewers, according to many authorities on the liquor problem.

The Foundation's potential $1,000,-000-a-year propaganda campaign to try to make beer respectable is seen as an adroit effort to wrest control of the traffic in beer from state and federal authorities and repose it with the brewing industry, where the tender uses of self-interest can make what capital they will with this power. Temperance leaders insist that the foundation's ambitious pressure-for-beer, drive calls for a showdown between the public and the brewers that can be met only by a vigorous counter-offensive to achieve an effective liquor control program.

Grounds Reviewed

Such a program is viewed as imperative on the following grounds:

1. Abuses are many and increasing under the present status of liquor control.
2. Existing regulatory laws and enforcement are inadequate.
3. The Brewers' Foundation could not, if it would, meet the abuses of the liquor industry through self-regulation.
4. The foundation will actually increase existing abuses, for its purpose is to divert the nation from practical means of regulation by specious claims about the brewery industry's ability to regulate itself.

That enforcement is lax and laws inadequate is admitted by the brewers themselves. Speaking of the present status of the liquor problem, Herbert F. Leisy, Cleveland brewer, writing in the Brewers' Journal, said:

"There has been practically no enforcement."

Brewers' Own Lobby

Despite the fact that the brewers during repeal promised to promote temperance, bar the saloon and protect the dry States from importations of liquor, the effect of their activities since repeal has been to tie the hands of the Federal Alcohol Administration.

It was the brewers' own lobby that persuaded Congress that there should be no excessive federal regu-

The Facts on Beer

A propaganda campaign using all the devices of modern publicity subtly to influence the American public in favor of beer has been initiated by brewers in the United States. This campaign, operating through the newly formed United Brewers' Industrial Foundation, is a major effort to capture the thinking of the people and mold social policy in the interest of a special group—this time the brewers. This is the last of 12 articles disclosing the methods, objectives, and ultimate consequences of this campaign.

lation of the beer industry. The brewers told Congress that less than 20 per cent of the beer traffic moved in interstate commerce. Subsequently, the Federal Alcohol Administration, through question-naires, ascertained that 73.5 per cent of the brewers of the United States whose total production amounted to 92.9 per cent of all the beer produced were doing a portion of their business in interstate commerce.

The result has been the existence of a great void, a no-man's land in the nation's liquor enforcement ma-

Jurisdiction Lacking

The extent to which the Government's hands so far have been tied is illustrated by the fact that some 60 or 70 cases have been investigated by federal enforcement agents, but in only two did the FAA have enough jurisdiction to turn them over to the

(Continued on Page 7, Column 7)

Propaganda Seen Adroit Effort to Wrest Control From U. S. and States

chinery. The liquor laws, as they now stand, give the Federal Government no power to move against the abuses of the "tied-house," commercial bribery and false and misleading advertising, in so far as these abuses relate to the brewery industry, except in such cases as state laws of a similar nature are violated by an interstate brewer.

If a brewer in Milwaukee sells beer in Texas and Texas has a fair trade law which the Milwaukee brewer violates, the Federal Government can act, but if it is a Texas brewer who is breaking the law, or if Texas does not have a law similar to that of the other, Washington cannot act.

Now for Inflated Week-Ends

By a Staff Correspondent of The Christian Science Monitor

WASHINGTON, July 3 —Should holidays always fall on Monday?

By the Fourth of July coming on Sunday this year, most of the United States gets a long week end holiday, starting Saturday and ending Tuesday morning.

Now a Monday-holiday group has been formed in Congress. It believes that American holidays should be reallocated, rearranged and readjusted, to the end that the last full measure of week end pleasure should be squeezed from the event. What good does a week-day holiday do, anyway?

Senator Edwin C. Johnson (D) of Colorado is leading the proposal. He has introduced a bill providing for the observance on Mondays of certain legal public holidays, just as Labor Day now invariably is. England regularly follows this scheme on its great "bank holidays."

His proposal is that whenever New Year's, Washington's Birthday, Memorial Day, July 4 or Thanks-

giving occurs on any day other than Monday, public observance shall be held on the nearest Monday to the date in question.

Sounds silly, doesn't it—observing "July 4th" on July 5!

But that is exactly what the United States is doing this week end.

Dorothy Round Wins Wimbledon Net Title

WIMBLEDON, Eng., July 3 (AP)—Dorothy E. Round, 27-year-old daughter of an English clergyman, defeated Jadwiga Jedrzejowska, buxom Polish sweater, 6—2, 2—6, 7—5, today and won the women's singles title of the All-England's tennis championship for the second time in four years.

Details of Wimbledon final matches: Sports Page.

Moscow-Tokyo Accord Ends Threat of War

Concessions on Both Sides Made in Amur Island Boundary Dispute

Joint Inquiry Due

Tokyo Pleased by Action Which Led to Withdrawal of Soviet Troops

By a Staff Correspondent of The Christian Science Monitor

MOSCOW, July 3—As dispatches in The Christian Science Monitor anticipated, the Amur River dispute has been settled by mutual concessions.

Japanese and Soviet authorities have withdrawn their patrols from the disputed islands, thus restoring the status quo ante until a fundamental settlement of the entire boundary dispute can be arranged. Immediate prospect of more serious friction is thus removed.

Joint Inquiry Likely

Meanwhile both Governments have agreed to set in motion machinery to determine exactly where the boundary lies between Manchuria and Siberia. They have tentatively agreed to appoint a joint commission for study and negotiations which, it is hoped, can reach an agreement upon a demarcation boundary.

Without a settlement of this fundamental question, it is probable that incidents similar to those of the past week would recur as they have in the past.

If either government sought a pretext for war, such incidents obviously might serve. The fact that recent incidents were settled so promptly is interpreted by independent observers here as evidence that neither side desires war at present.

Soviet Troops Evacuate Disputed Amur Islands; Tokyo Welcomes Accord

By a Staff Correspondent of The Christian Science Monitor

TOKYO, July 3—The conflict over the occupation of the Amur islets ended today with an apparent clear-cut victory for Japan, since the evacuation which Foreign Commissar Maxim Litvinoff promised Japanese Ambassador at Moscow, Mamoru Shigemitsu, began this afternoon.

There was no indication whether the Japanese claim that the islets belong to Manchoukuo will find expression through the dispatch of Japanese-Manchoukuan forces there.

The Kwantung army fired a last verbal shot in the incident in endorsing the settlement in a public statement this afternoon, but adding a warning that no future illegal acts of the Soviet army will be tolerated.

The Japanese Foreign Office had emphasized the necessity of the restoration of the status quo under which neither side maintained military units on the islets and the Soviet Government agreed to satisfy this demand.

The Soviet consent to evacuate the islands and its failure to press a demand for compensation for the presumptive fatalities in the sinking of the gunboat were interpreted in some quarters here as signs of weakness after the recent purge and as an indication that the Soviet Union will not fight unless no alternative remains.

Basque Government Legitimate Wherever It Is, Says Leader

BAYONNE, France, July 3 (AP)—Basque Government officials here announced that President de Aguirre and the remnant of his army had abandoned their last stand in Basque territory of northern Spain.

The President, fleeing with his forces, made a protest to the world against what he termed "plundering of which we, the Basques, have been made victims in the twentieth century."

Señor de Aguirre's statement, given out by a spokesman here, said "our territory has been conquered," but that "the Basque Government, wherever it is, remains the legitimate Government of the Basques, interpreting the feelings of a race which has not been conquered."

The President expressed, "indignation" that he and his men were forced to give up their fatherland, and said that feeling was "still greater because in order to take the fatherland from us, the Spanish Fascists were forced to call in mercenary forces — Germans and Italians."

SECRET HEADQUARTERS OF THE BASQUE GOVERNMENT, SOMEWHERE IN NORTHERN SPAIN, July 3 (AP)—Jose Antonio de Aguirre, President of the conquered Basque republic, accused the Valencia-Madrid regime today of leaving his insurgents without means to "own resources" to resist insurgent attackers.

Señor de Aguirre's statement set the number of casualties in the Basque defense of Bilbao during the three-month insurgent offensive that brought the capital's fall June 19, at 45,000 dead and wounded.

"We have been without help either from within or without (Spain)," he said. "We have had all kinds of promises but none of them has been fulfilled."

C. I. O. Steel Rallies Set; Paris Hotels Avert Lockout

PARIS, July 3 (AP)—Threat of a nation-wide shutdown of hotels, restaurants and cafes was averted today as employers and workers signed an agreement on working conditions.

Details of the accord were not immediately disclosed.

Its signature followed an announcement last night during which came as the Premier Camille Chautemps' office that a "compromise in principle" had been reached.

Owners had scheduled a shutdown to begin today as a protest against a five-day, 40-hour week decreed for their employees by the Chautemps' Government just after it took office.

Announcement of the compromise came as the French Government, battered by labor disputes, prepared to go into action on eleventh-hour negotiations.

There was considerable confusion, both on the part of hotel owners and their guests. Several Paris hotels posted notices that they would close. Others, still foreseeing an agreement, declared they were undecided what they would do if the lockout were called.

Some newspapers suggested Parisians open their homes to tourists and furniture dealers lend the necessary beds and mattresses.

Swift settlement of a truck-drivers' holiday that halted truck deliveries in Philadelphia left the labor crisis centered around the steel-producing area. Calm generally prevailed throughout the Mahoning Valley and Calumet areas, although Youngstown, Ohio, and Johnstown, Penna., waited tensely for the outcome of huge strikers' rallies scheduled for their cities tomorrow.

The C. I. O. has taken definite steps to remove troublesome elements which are being blamed for unauthorized strikes and other acts of insubordination.

The National Labor Relations Board remained the chief hope of labor as troops provided protection for back-to-work movements throughout the steel-producing mid-west.

The steel strike resulted in Washington, D. C., as the Senate Civil Liberties Committee wound up its hearings on the Memorial Day riot in Chicago and as the C. I. O. built a fire under a heated debate in the House.

Other labor
developments:
Page 4.

Independence Day

As legal observance of the Fourth of July is on Monday, July 5, all editions of The Christian Science Monitor will be omitted.

The Monitor Index

Making the Constitution

A day-by-day account of the concert session of the Federal Convention of 1787 that drew up the United States Constitution is "reported" by a Monitor staff correspondent:
Page 2

THE CHRISTIAN SCIENCE MONITOR

AN INTERNATIONAL DAILY NEWSPAPER

BOSTON, SATURDAY, MARCH 12, 1938—VOL. XXX, NO. 89

CENTRAL EDITION—FIVE CENTS A COPY

COPYRIGHT 1938 BY THE CHRISTIAN SCIENCE PUBLISHING SOCIETY

Hitler's New Austrian Coup Brings Union in All but Name; German Troops Take Control

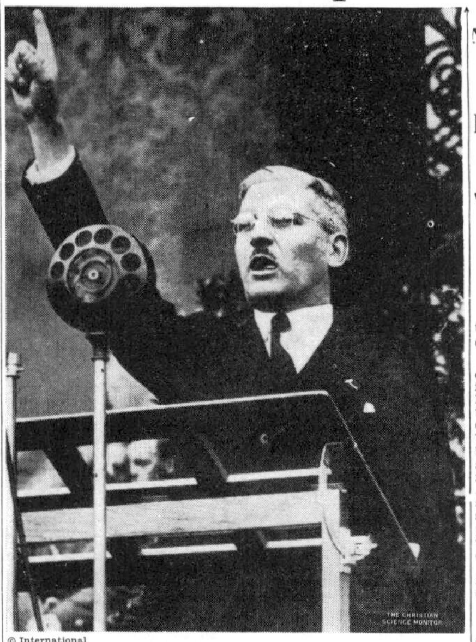

© International

Ousted Chancellor Kurt Schuschnigg

National Socialist Leader Succeeds Schuschnigg as Chancellor

Rome-Berlin Axis Seen as Shaken

Violence Is Not Expected as Reich Acts at Opportune Moment

By a Staff Correspondent of The Christian Science Monitor

VIENNA, March 12—Austria has taken a long step toward union with Germany.

It has passed under the domination of the National Socialist Party and its chief, Reichsführer Adolf Hitler. Hubert Klausner, leader of the Austrian branch of the party, speaking early this morning to multitudes in Vienna who were exultantly celebrating what they call "freedom," said "we Germans now have one fold, one Reich, and one Führer."

This is essentially true. Austria still retains its independence in form and has its own government, composed exclusively of Austrians, but it will be completely under the influence of Germany.

Economically, culturally and in military matters Austria will be part of German Union.

New Austrian Chapter

Thus the sudden ultimatum from Germany, the marching of German troops into Austrian territory, the cancelling of the "independence" plebiscite which had been set for this Sunday, and the resignation of Chancellor Kurt Schuschnigg, has opened an entirely new chapter in Austria.

Dr. Arthur Seyss-Inquart, who was previously named Minister of Interior at Reichsführer Adolf Hitler's express request, has become temporary Chancellor of Austria. Dr. Seyss-Inquart also has taken over the portfolios of War Minister and Minister of Police, making him the virtual master of Austria under Herr Hitler. And a new Cabinet has been appointed, made up largely of untried, but moderate, men. None of the old radical "illegal" National Socialist agitators are in it.

This "revolution" is expected to bring about the complete reorganization of the administrative apparatus. Practically all of the district governors, mayors, and high police officials will be changed immediately. The Mayor of Vienna, Richard Schmidt, has already been removed. His place has been taken provisionally by present vice-mayor, who is a moderate pro-German.

Little Violence Expected

This week end is to be given up to exuberant jubilation all over Austria, but violence is not expected.

There may be a few cases of personal violence, but Austrians by nature are remarkably tolerant. All relics of Marxism, of course, will be suppressed, but the workers are inclined to rejoice at least that they may now get work.

The great tragedy may be the Jewish persecution and there are about 200,000 Jews in Vienna who will now be subject to the same anti-Semitic influences that are current in Germany.

Arrangements are to be made very soon for a larger degree of trade and industrial co-operation with Germany and from this program economic improvement is expected.

In foreign politics there must be changes. The Hapsburg restoration movement is regarded as completely crushed and chances for the Danubian Federation are believed to have disappeared.

Rome-Berlin Axis

The position of the Rome-Berlin axis—co-operation between Herr Hitler and Signor Mussolini—is something that only time can clarify. On the one hand, it appears clear that the relationship is gravely shaken by the sudden action of Germany. For the axis was committed to the independence of Austria—just as Germany guaranteed this independence in its agreement with Austria in 1936.

Yet it is also true that, as the price of Herr Hitler's co-operation, Mussolini is believed to have looked forward to a period of German expansion in Austria. It is recalled here that it was first Signor Mussolini and not Herr Hitler who tried to Coerce Chancellor Schuschnigg into taking pro-Germans into his Cabinet and he has just informed the Yugoslav Government that he would not partake in any protest against the changed regime here.

Dr. Schuschnigg in his fight against Herr Hitler found little substantial support from Rome. Of course, Herr Hitler knew this. The international situation was therefore extremely favorable for his coup.

Russia and France

Russia is thought greatly weakened and France is without a Government.

Italy had been Herr Hitler's partner and the German Foreign Minister yesterday was the guest of the British King. So Herr Hitler thought he had free hand here and used it.

The new masters of Austria now constantly refer to this conutry only as "German Austria." The distribution of most foreign papers is forbidden here today. The Fatherland Front has been completely abolished and all of its buildings

(Continued on Page 4, Column 1)

Tower Views

by Clearway

An Appeal to Benevolence
Youth Sizes Up Warfare
Vienna at the Zero Hour

¶ **Mobilization for Human Needs**—The ideal of the good neighbor, exemplified in every community, is invoked by President Roosevelt as the twenty-fifth anniversary of the establishment of community chests and councils is signalized by the launching of this year's Mobilization for Human Needs. Says the President: "Only in jobs and more jobs at good pay shall we find national stability and individual security." The Government, he asserts, aims to provide jobs for "normal people who can give useful work to the country," but private benevolence is called upon to assist the "unemployables." • 'Tis opportunity. Warm hearts seldom shiver from want.

¶ **Youth and War**—Washington learns what American youth thinks of war. On the basis of a survey made in Maryland, the American Youth Commission estimates that one lad out of nine would definitely refuse to fight; 60 per cent of some 13,000 youths of both sexes think war is "needless and preventable"; another 27 per cent consider it a "necessary evil"; while a weak minority feels that it's justifiable. However, one-third of the boys interviewed would volunteer, another third would not evade the draft, a tenth would fight if America were invaded. The general comment seems to be: "We don't care to risk our lives in other people's quarrels, but if they bring the quarrel to us, we'll fight." • Ah, but they'll bring the quarrel to us if we don't help to bring peace to them.

¶ **Austrian Caldron**—Approaching its "surprise" plebiscite, Austria seethes with political cross-purposes and escaping steam bubbles from 'neath its loosely-set lid of independence, throwing strange shadows on the face of Europe. In southern Germany troops maneuver ostentatiously. In Berlin word goes forth that the Reich won't use force, but simultaneously it is declared there that only Dr. Schuschnigg can determine whether Austria shall be National Socialized peacefully or with bloodshed. Then comes notification that the referendum is called off. Whispers have it that something like an ultimatum changed Herr Schuschnigg's mind. • Chancellor Schuschnigg, trying his strength, kicks fuel under the caldron of central Europe and finds the fire too hot.

¶ **French Foreign Policy**—With Austro-German relations heated to combustive temperature, Paris feels the need of an asbestos foreign policy, but Premier-designate Léon Blum refuses to disclose the cut or fabric of the garment until assured of Radical-Socialist support. Yvon Delbos, Foreign Minister in the last Cabinet, confers with the German Ambassador, however, freely admitting concern over the German troop movements, and later there's talk with the Austrian Minister, and an exchange of confidences between Paris and London. • M. Blum, seeing a possible need for a united front outside France's borders, first demands unity within.

¶ **Ribbentrop Conversations** — Joachim von Ribbentrop, Reich envoy to London, ends his first round of conversations, as retiring Ambassador to London but remains for further considerations. With his decision likelihood of a better Anglo-German understanding seems less uncertain. Germany's demand for straight restitution of the colonies as a right, and Premier Chamberlain's refusal to consider their return except as part of a general European appeasement, remain obstacles. Disappointment, therefore, is tempered with hope, for while Anglo-German relations are cool, Anglo-Italian understanding seems improving. • As strain is put on the Rome-Berlin axis, Mussolini finds gravitation toward Britain attractive.

¶ **New England Wants Barriers**—Secretary of State Hull's ideal of a world's pacification induced by reciprocal trade finds few echoes of applause in highly competitive industrial New England. Responses to New England Council inquiries, voiced at mass protest meetings, reveal that more than 30 New England industries oppose trade treaties to nine which favor them. Explaining their position, James W. Hook, president of the New England Council, holds up a cautioning hand. We mustn't give up foreign trade, he points out. But it's well to think beyond the confines of one's own business and consider fundamentals. A nation capable of producing surpluses in almost every line should be careful to keep in line with world prices, lest it find its economy disrupted. • The most successful world traders are the most persistent world thinkers, we take it.

¶ **Where's Your Chivalry, Men?**—"We need the money!" cry Representatives in the House in extenuation of their denial to head the "powder puff bloc" and repeal the 10 per cent cosmetics tax. The women even pleaded: "Be sporting!" But the men shout "No!" vehemently, crassly. Cosmetics are a $17,000,000 tax item and with the budget in its present condition, they prefer the shekels to powdered noses. • Boors! Morons!

President Says Job Program Is Vital to Nation

Tells Welfare Workers U. S. Progress Depends on Masses Spending

Must First Earn

By a Staff Correspondent of The Christian Science Monitor

WASHINGTON, March 12—Representatives of 36 national welfare organizations meeting here yesterday heard President Roosevelt defend the Federal Works Program as necessary to the American Economic System and Charles P. Taft, son of another President, propose a revision in the present set-up to give states and local communities more responsibility.

Making his annual address to the gathering, held in behalf of local charity drives, the President declared that industrial production in the United States cannot progress unless "our masses have income with which to buy its products." The Federal Works Program, he held, "not only serves the unemployed, it saved the jobs of those who have jobs."

After their initial meeting in the East Room of the White House where the President spoke, the Mobilization for Human Needs Conference moved to a hotel for the remainder of their two-day sessions.

The Small Gift Tells

Although people of means give a substantial part of the $80,000,000 raised annually in community chest drives, yet it is the small giver on whom success of these money-raising campaigns depends, Mr. Taft declared.

"In our own community," he said, "nearly 20 per cent of the population are on our rolls as contributors. We are really a people's movement, standing for all the highest social aims of the community."

Later, at a luncheon meeting, Mr. Taft outlined the proposal he presented to the Senate Committee on Unemployment and Relief last month, giving states and local communities a larger share in relief responsibilities.

Would Match States

The amount appropriated by the Federal Government, under Mr. Taft's proposal, would be a definite sum available only upon condition that it be matched by the states in prescribed proportions. Each State would apportion to local communities upon any basis it may decide compatible with relief needs.

Other features of Mr. Taft's plan include: Local and state administration by non-political citizens' boards; co-ordination within each State of all welfare agencies receiving federal funds; creation of a federal commission to study and recommend a long-range program on relief and public welfare; special federal grants for care of transients.

Text of President's speech to welfare conference: Page 2.

Aid for Schools Asked In Prairie Drought Area

Dominion Parliament Called On by Teachers to Send Funds West—Books and Materials Needed in Saskatchewan

Special to The Christian Science Monitor

TORONTO—The Canadian Teachers' Federation has urged the Dominion Government to make emergency grants to those prairie schools of Western Canada which are most desperately in need of help. The "adoption" plan, by which 300 needy schools were to be assisted by teachers and students in Eastern Canada, has been declared inadequate, in the face of the drought problem.

In the past six months, 432 teachers have left the profession in Saskatchewan, because of the stricken condition of the areas in which they were situated, it has been reported. The provincial government provides an annual grant of $300 to needy school districts; but certain of the grants were long overdue, and local efforts to raise funds for education were hampered because so many residents, in some cases 95 per cent of the municipality, were on relief.

There is no lack of experienced teachers in the province, but there is danger that many children will grow up without proper schooling because the municipalities in which they live lack money to buy books and materials for the classrooms. Foster-schools in Eastern Canada have been of assistance, sending supplies west; and individual schools in Ontario, Manitoba and other parts of the prairies have made themselves responsible for keeping their needy, adopted friends equipped, that the work of education may go on.

In one Toronto school the students pay voluntary fines for minor infractions of rules. This money is collected and sent by four teachers who have undertaken the task of keeping in touch with the western school and supplying its needs. Bazaars and fairs have been held, with the object of collecting funds for needy Westerners; and in the past 15 months, 57 boxes of clothing have been distributed, and over $12,000 has been shared by 1,000 teachers in the drought areas.

A teacher writing from Trossachs, Saskatchewan, tells a typical story of the daily struggle in the dust bowl, where crops have been destroyed for the past seven years.

"Our attendance is much below normal, because of the lack of funds to pay the students' expenses. Many of them come over long distances, walking, riding bicycles or horses, while others are prevented from coming by hard times.

"We do not wish to stand with our hands out. I think we will manage to get by and conditions will become better, as we have more soil moisture than we have had in any recent year at this time."

Another teacher related that neither he nor his wife had been able to buy underclothing for three years. In that time he had been able to buy only one suit at a cost of $12. He made the clothes last by taking them off as soon as he came home from school and donning his rags. This teacher received $80 for five months' work.

The support of 50 Members of Parliament has been pledged in answer to the Teachers Federation's appeal for additional funds, it was announced by A. C. Lewis, President of the organization, which includes teachers from the Atlantic to the Pacific.

President Begins Work On Four New Messages

By a Staff Correspondent of The Christian Science Monitor

WASHINGTON, March 12—President Roosevelt said yesterday that he is working on three or four new messages to send to Congress, and that he contemplates making clear his views on the pending tax revision bill. This was an intimation that he may fight for passage of the essential parts of the Treasury's tax revision program.

Whether the President will send a message or letter on taxes to Congress, or address the nation in a fireside talk, was unclarified. Incidentally, however, the President refused to be drawn into an unfavorable comment on the proposed tax on distilled liquors, which has been substituted for the levy on closely held corporations. Whether you pay a whisky tax or not, said the President, is a voluntary proceeding anyway. Citizens who don't want to pay a whisky tax, he implied, only have to refrain from buying whisky.

As to the three or four pending messages, observers already have a pretty good idea of their subjects. An anti-monopoly message, but without recommendation of legislation, is in preparation. A message on world distribution of phosphates, and their vital usefulness to civilization, is also being drafted.

A third message on the railroad problem is contemplated, after the President concludes the railroad conferences which he will begin next week. And a possible fourth message concerns the shipping problem, which is still acute.

However it is unlikely that any of these presidential papers will require legislation in Congress this year, and they are unlikely to prevent adjournment when the legislators get through their pending work.

Of most application to Congress, however, were the President's remarks on taxation. The objective of present tax revision, he said, is the ending of special privilege where it exists under present revenue laws.

Thus, he said, if Mr. A and Mr. B, both in the higher income brackets, make the same profits ought they not pay the same amount in income taxes? If you find they are not paying the same amount, continued the President, and when you try to rectify the situation by tax revision, should your proposals be called punitive in headlines and newspaper leads? "Punitive" is the very last word that should be applied to this equalizing effort, said Mr. Roosevelt. The objective was a restoration of equality of taxation upon people making the same profits.

These inequalities, he said, arise from the different methods of taxation—corporation, partnership, individual." And the Presdient concluded by saying that he might go into the specific matter of inequalities further a little later, and cite some concrete cases.

From this final touch, it was inferred that the President may make an effort—at least, before the forum of public opinion—to justify the tax program drawn up so carefully by the Treasury experts. But there was no clear indication whether he would make an aggressive campaign, or

(Continued on Page 2, Column 2)

Fly 'Acquitted' of Speeding

By the Natural Science Correspondent of The Christian Science Monitor

LANCASTER, Pa., March 12—Back to things mechanical goes the world's speed record as Dr. Irving Langmuir, Associate Director of General Electric's Research Laboratory and Nobel prize winner publishes investigations exploding—with proofs—the fantastic yarn about a fly that travels 818 miles an hour.

Sound travels 740 miles an hour, so that according to the speed record credited to Cephenomyia, or the deer botfly by Entomologist Charles T. Townsend, if someone were to shout across the street to a friend "Watch out, here comes a speed demon" the fly would be there before the sound of the speaker's voice.

Dr. Langmuir is no bugologist, but as a researcher whose physicochemical investigations netted him the $50,000 Nobel award 1933, he found the story so hard to swallow he made a leaden fly the size of Cephenomyia (sef-en-omi-ah), tied it on a string and figured out mathematically just what would happen to such a speedster. He found, according to his report in Science, official organ of the American Association for the Advancement of Science:

1. The flat-headed fly at such a speed would encounter a wind pressure against its head of about eight pounds per square inch, enough to crush it.
2. Power consumption at 800 m.p.h. would be about a half a horsepower—too much to expect of any living creature.
3. Crediting the fly with as high a thermodynamic efficiency as mankind, the fly must consume almost twice his weight in food every second of flight.
4. The solder fly (made to imitate ones Dr. Townsend reported seeing in flight at the top of the Andes Mountains) were visible only as a blur in a brightly-lighted white-ceilinged room when the fly was swung at a speed of 13 miles per hour. At 26 miles per hour it was barely visible and at 43 m.p.h. it appeared only as a faint line, disappearing entirely at 64 m.p.h.

"Aviators," Dr. Langmuir concludes, "need no longer hang their heads in shame because they can hardly surpass 400 m.p.h. with today's planes. Twenty-five miles per hour is a reasonable estimate for the deer fly, while 800 m.p.h. is utterly impossible." Dr. Langmuir himself holds an airplane pilot's license.

Entomologists back Dr. Langmuir's estimate of deer-fly speed: Page 5.

The Monitor Index

Saturday, March 12, 1938

Stockholm Dines Again

STOCKHOLM, March 12 (AP)—Stockholm's hotel and restaurant lockout ended yesterday. Meals were served for the first time since Jan. 17.

An average wage increase of 15 crowns (about $3.75) a week was included in the settlement. Every available table was booked for a carnival tonight.

For two months the lockout has disorganized not only hotels and restaurants, but in some measure the social life of Sweden itself. Its effect on trade in general has been serious. The sight of Cabinet Ministers and high officials carrying their sandwiches and thermos flasks became an every-day occurrence, as restaurants were unable to supply them with mid-day lunches.

Something like 20,000 workers were involved in the dispute, to which had to be added 500 restaurant musicians, porters, and drivers.

The trouble started when the question arose of a new agreement to replace the one expiring Dec. 31. The employers were willing to accord an average increase of 10 per cent in salaries and to shorten hours of work. But the employees demanded an increase of between 20 and 40 per cent, and increased guarantees for tips.

The Government appointed a commission to mediate between the parties, without, however, curtailing the expected two-month duration of the strike. The fact that the trade unions had very large funds made it virtually certain that the workers would hold out for that length of time.

Air Route Approved: Alaska-Puget Sound

Special to The Christian Science Monitor

TACOMA, Wash.—Pacific Alaska Airways, said to be a Pan American subsidiary, has been issued a permit to operate a Puget Sound-Alaska route and will start passenger and express service this spring. Approval of the Post Office Department and an appropriation are necessary before it can become an airmail line.

The situation is further complicated by the need of an agreement with Canada to operate planes up the Canadian Coast with commercial stops. For the present it is planned to route the planes around Vancouver Island, but Canadian authorities, according to a bulletin issued by the Tacoma Chamber of Commerce, are in favor of eliminating the coastal regulations in the interest of direct plane service from Puget Sound, through Vancouver, to Alaska.

World Labor Group to Study Farm Problems

Permanent Committee Is Set Up by Geneva Organization

Opens New Field

By a Staff Correspondent of The Christian Science Monitor

GENEVA—A vast new field for international research and collaboration has been taken up by the International Labor Organization of the League of Nations with the formation of a permanent agricultural committee.

The Labor Office, which hitherto has largely confined its attention to industrial problems, now proposes to tackle the allied problems of agriculture, and has set up the new committee to serve as a permanent contact between the I. L. O. and the agricultural world.

The first meeting of the new committee brought 30 experts from 22 countries to Geneva, together with officials of many important agricultural organizations in four continents. Among those present was the President of the International Institute of Agriculture at Rome, who accepted appointment as Vice-Chairman of the committee, thus making it clear that the Rome Institute will continue to co-operate with the I. L. O., even though all other Rome-Geneva connections have been broken.

Agriculture Lags

Preliminary discussions, in which most of those present participated, may be briefly summarized as follows:

Agricultural workers, constituting a majority of all workers, have lagged behind industrial workers in attaining a suitable standard of living. The world-wide economic depression has fallen with especial severity upon agriculture, not only upon workers but upon owners of land, both large and small.

At the same time, technological advances and discoveries have immensely widened the possibilities for agriculture, and have so altered agricultural methods in many countries that a complete readjustment is necessary to assure satisfactory relationships among those engaged in agriculture and between agriculture and governments, and among the various governments. Many of the problems posed by these new conditions can be settled only by international collaboration, and the International Labor Organization is one of many instruments designed for this purpose.

Harold Butler, director of the I. L. O., pointed out that agriculture, formerly a national industry, has now become the most international of all industries, as evidenced by the international regulations adopted for rubber, tea and sugar. He said that most agricultural problems, whether social or economic, have acquired international significance.

Questions Classified

One set of agricultural questions, Mr. Butler explained, falls entirely within the competence of the I. L. O. These are the questions dealing with protection of workers, and include hours of work, holidays with pay, children's work and wage-fixing machinery. Another set of questions, Mr. Butler pointed out, require collaboration among the I. L. O., the

(Continued on Page 11, Column 7)

British-German Rivalries Seen as Rearmament Factor

By Argus

Written for The Christian Science Monitor

The fresh crop of rearmament figures coming in this month carries the world outpourings of wealth on preparation for war to new staggering heights. They present, superficially at any rate, a picture without coherence, designed according to no rational laws.

What is the connection between the United States Congress debating an arms authorization measure of a billion dollars, in addition to the $900,000,000 budgeted for defense, and the British and French forcing through extra-budgetary arms programs, the former for a billion and a half, the latter for $500,000,000, or the Japanese adding $1,392,000,000 to the ordinary defense budget, or the Russians, with the largest army in the world, spending nearly 20 times as much on arms as they did six years ago, or Czechoslovakia and Hungary spending, the one $150,000,000 and the other (sweeping aside all treaty restrictions) nearly $200,000,000 on new defense needs?

Nations of utterly different needs, circumstances and geographical positions all seem motivated by the same impulse to arm to the teeth, with apparently only one thing clear—that the race began at three points as Germany, Italy, and Japan refused to adhere to arms limitation treaties that failed to accord them equality. Germany had shown herself willing, providing the allied powers consented to reduce their own armaments, which they failed to do. Delving deeper into fundamental motives there is again confusion, for who can tell precisely which nations consider themselves to be arming on a defensive basis, and which are preparing to extend their own national interests?

These strange contradictions remained with scarcely a break until Feb. 20 last, when the resignation of Foreign Secretary Anthony Eden suddenly delineated, in sharp relief, the alternatives which Britain's foreign policy had been facing. Premier Chamberlain made it clear that the issues between democracy and fascism were not under consideration by his Government at this juncture and that his main concern was a settlement with Italy and Germany. His explanations left no doubt but that he was swayed by one of the governing ideas of the past half century—the sense of unavoidable struggle between the two empires of Britain and Germany.

With the dramatically sudden rise of National Socialism and Fascism, throwing new values into the world's political make-up, there is a

(Continued on Page 5, Column 2)

Economics in the News

Shortage of Capital—Complaints Lead to House Rejection of 'Third Basket' in Tax Bill—Repairing the Pump

By H. B. E.

The reference which I made some time ago to business complaints that both credit and capital are "tight" has been amply reinforced in subsequent discussion.

First the distinction between credit and capital should be kept in sight. It was often blurred in the speech-making at the Small Businessmen's conference on Feb. 2. Credit is accommodation extended by a commercial bank to finance waiting. A manufacturer, say, wishes to be reimbursed for the raw materials which he has bought and which he is using in the fabrication of some article or other. The bank accommodates him. Its loan is repaid when the manufacturer sells his finished product to the jobber or retailer. Meantime, however, the manufacturer has bought some more raw materials. This is one type of credit loan which the banks extend. In the nature of things credit does a short-term service; then it returns to itself, and is destroyed.

In a credit economy it is essential that the credit service should be maintained. In American practice, unfortunately, credit gets alternately loose and tight. It is loose in booms and tight in slumps. According to Walter Bagehot, the great authority on banking, this is the reverse of what should happen. Bankers should behave in just the opposite way from the rest of the community. That is, when there is a boom, bankers should be cautious, and when there is a slump, they should be generous. Alas, American banking is still highly competitive and hydra-headed—the penalty of continued addiction to unit banking and 49 systems. So the bankers behave much as businessmen behave. The result is that slumps are exacerbated by banking caution.

For the Great Depression, Col. Leonard P. Ayres, well-known Cleveland banker-economist, placed "the over-cautious policies of banks with regard to the issuance of business credits" among the great responsible factors. Another banker voice has just been raised warningly in respect of the present exigency. It is that of Dr. W. Randolph Burgess, economist of the Federal Reserve Bank of New York. At the last meeting of the American Statistical Association Dr. Burgess pointed out wherein the present "cheap money" was not synonymous with "easy money." "Because of uncertainty as to the future," he said, "the position of the borrower is scrutinized with the utmost care, and money is not easy to obtain by any but prime borrowers." "Little Business" no doubt thinks that "prime" means "big"; most probably, with reason.

Capital, properly speaking, has nothing to do with the commercial banks. It comes out of savings—both the savings of business and the savings of private persons.

As to the former, the undivided profits tax doubtless impeded its accumulation, especially by small business. The new tax bill would ameliorate this state of things. I would say, in parenthesis, that, though the new bill partly cleans out one channel of capital, nevertheless it is still a criticizable measure, inasmuch as "the third basket" is both discriminatory against family-held corporations and not discriminating enough as between operating companies and holding companies. The House, however, rejected "the third basket" as much because it was a vestigial obstruction in business capital generation as because of the other arguments.

Other tax reforms are likewise necessary. The capital gains tax is a levy on capital. Moreover, the impost upon incomes in the higher brackets has blocked a good deal of capital from going into local industries. In the old days a lot of neighborhood capital energized local industries; nowadays it flows into the Security markets, latterly into tax-exempts.

Last Nov. 10 Secretary of the Treasury Morgenthau said "the basic need today is to foster the full application of the driving force of private capital." That is even more the basic need today. The machinery, of course, is of no avail without the confidence to use it. But in an exigency which has been marked, as the present exigency has been marked, by the failure of the priming of the pump of capitalist enterprise, the obvious next course is to examine the pump to see whether it needs repair. Equally obviously the pump is the source of private capital. There is here a series of obstructions between the investor and the user which requires investigation.

The lack of availability of capital to business enterprise is now engaging the attention of a Senate committee. It deserves such notice. As a Securities and Exchange Commission witness told the Committee, "a shortage of capital in small business enterprises is a matter of serious concern to the entire nation." The remark comes with particular force from the agency which was set up to restrain investment. It seems to show that nowadays recovery should take precedence over reform, if only to preserve past reforms.

THE CHRISTIAN SCIENCE MONITOR

AN INTERNATIONAL DAILY NEWSPAPER

COPYRIGHT 1938 BY THE CHRISTIAN SCIENCE PUBLISHING SOCIETY

BOSTON, MONDAY, MARCH 14, 1938—VOL. XXX, NO. 90

• ATLANTIC EDITION { THREE CENTS IN GREATER BOSTON / FIVE CENTS ELSEWHERE

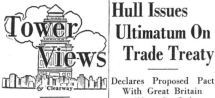

Tower Views

by Clearway

Europe Faces "Realism"
They That Live by Sword
Leon Blum Leads France

¶ **Anschluss Arrives**—Friendly, poised, waltz-loving Austria loses its identity, disappears into the maw of National Socialism, and Reichsführer Hitler's ambitions, as set forth in his book "Mein Kampf," gain another great stride toward fulfillment. The news at the week's beginning reveals an Austria surrendered, to become a part of the German Reich; Czechoslovakia, defiant and armed, awaiting the unfoldment in action of Acting Chancellor Göring's hints at ambitions thitherward, protesting vigorously against German Army fliers passing over its territory; France all set to expand its treaty to protect Czechoslovakia, and significantly rushing troops into the Maginot Line; England veering its too, too "realistic" diplomacy toward France's support and Italy's self-interest; and Italy, outwardly acquiescent to Austrian absorption, eyeing the Brenner Pass with cold eyes, and turning toward Britain with warmer approval. • Austria is gone. German ambitions remain. Europe studies an elastic map.

¶ **Britain on the March**—Lord Lothian addresses a letter to the London Times. He says: "Democracy will only recover its health and confidence when democratic peoples are ready to place universal national service alongside universal individual liberty as a basis of society." The majority of English people find the suggestion displeasing and Prime Minister Chamberlain recently pledged that the present Parliament would not consider it. But the seizure of Austria arouses a general feeling that since no moral consideration is likely to bind the Reich ambitions, it is imperative for Britain to present a front of munitions and men which will discourage attacks on British interests. The attitude seems to be that, after Austria, Herr Hitler's assurances to Czechoslovakia, Italy, and Poland are but empty words. When the Reich drew the sword in Austria, it drew the sword throughout Europe. • There's a Scriptural text applicable to the situation too obvious to need quoting.

¶ **France Gets a Government**—Again headed by Leon Blum, the Popular Front comes into authority. After four historic days of European readjustments, during which France remained rudderless, agreement is reached on a Cabinet. The new Premier himself acknowledges that it's not the Government the public wants or that present circumstances demand but it is the best available. It faces two immediate problems, namely, money for self-defense and a foreign policy potent enough to meet Pan-Germanism. • Few doubt that the problems will be solved (whether by the present government or the next) for France is always her best in an emergency.

¶ **Britain in Wordy Battle**—Entering the competition of vernacular radiocasts in South America, Great Britain goes "on the air" with programs designed to offset the Fascist propaganda already carried on by radio and designed to capture not only more Latin-American trade but likewise Latin-American loyalty. Transmitted through the British Broadcasting System in Spanish and Portuguese, the programs deal with British aims and policies. It is believed the United States will likewise add official to unofficial appearances before the microphone in the ethereal debate. • If the followers of Mars can be induced to become followers of Marconi, future wars may be auditory rather than predatory.

¶ **Anglo-American Trade**—Some 400 witnesses and 25 Congressmen participate in public hearings on the current negotiations for a British Trade Agreement. On the outcome of the hearings depends the course of America's future tariff policy. If a mean of agreement is reached, permanent adoption of the reciprocal trade principle probably will follow; if it is muffed, we may look for a return to the old scratch-and-grab system of tariff acts. • In matters of trade the short view is distorted by selfishness, while the long view reveals the pitfalls, clarifies the advantages.

¶ **Advice From Tokyo**—The newspaper Nichi Nichi prints an advertisement addressed to America and sponsored by "The Purple Cloud," a patriotic organization. "The United States," it says, "will instantly realize its desire for peace in the Orient when it acknowledges . . . Japan's position as the greatest power of the Orient." • Without engaging in any debate about it, America's concept is of an even greater power which must be recognized before stability can be brought to any section of the world —the power of right principles rigorously observed.

¶ **Spring Vigor**—Dr. Robert Oleson, Assist. U. S. Surgeon-General, laughs at the theory that Spring weather either stimulates or slows one down. At the Public Health Service in Washington he declares: "It's the mental outlook that counts!" • Spring in the heart makes spring in the step, so to speak.

Hull Issues Ultimatum On Trade Treaty

Declares Proposed Pact With Great Britain 'Must Go On'

Hearings Open

By a Staff Correspondent of The Christian Science Monitor

WASHINGTON, March 14—Pleas for protection made today by spokesmen for a variety of American industries at first public hearings on the proposed Anglo-American Trade Agreement were partly drowned by an ultimatum from Cordell Hull, Secretary of State, that the reciprocal trade program must go on.

The Secretary's defense of this key Administration policy and his insistence on its continuance on a "non-partisan" basis were set forth in a letter to 12 Republican members of Congress from New England who recommended delay in negotiation of further agreements.

Most of these same members were in the vanguard of 400 witnesses who have asked to testify in regard to the most ambitious trade treaty yet undertaken by the State Department—that with the United Kingdom. Of 26 members of Congress scheduled to enter pleas in behalf of industries in their districts at the first public session, 13 were from New England and nine from Massachusetts.

Disaster Forecasts

While the Congressmen were predicting disaster in their districts from increased foreign competition, Secretary Hull was maintaining that "abandonment of our liberal policy would signal a revival of economic warfare which would inevitably result in an increase in political tension throughout the world."

Mr. Hull charged that the New England Congressmen's proposal that trade agreement negotiations be suspended "until the cost of production is ascertained in the countries with which negotiations are contemplated" was a disguised attempt to force abandonment of the entire trade agreement program, that any such action would vitally damage New England's industrial interests, and that conclusion of the British agreement would be of inestimable benefit not only to American farmers, but also to New England manufacturers.

The Secretary, writing jointly to the group, emphasized that Britain takes over a third of all American agricultural exports and about half of all agricultural exports other than cotton. He pointed out that this market amounted in 1929 to $445,000,000, but in 1937 had recovered from depression lows only to $259,000,000. He said that conclusion of the British trade agreement "would obviously constitute an important contribution toward the solution of the problem of expanding market outlets for our farm products.

Large Crops Expected

Emphasizing the prospects of large surplus crops this year, it held it would be a disservice to American industry or labor, as well as to the former, "to become suddenly indifferent toward the preservation and expansion of foreign markets."

Turning to New England specifically he said:

"Let there be no illusion concerning New England's state in this whole situation. Because New Eng-

(Continued on Page 14, Column 2)

In the Boston Section:

Rhode Island forces organize for horse racing referendum hearing tomorrow.

El trustees in surprise move come out for State ownership.

Farnum calls for return to before-the-war civic type of leadership.

Many cities backward in collecting excise tax, Lœffler says.

And News From All New England
In the Second Section, Beginning on Page 11

'Off-the-Record' Talks Released by President

By a Staff Correspondent of The Christian Science Monitor

WASHINGTON, March 14—An intimate and informal picture of the four years in history known as the first presidential term of Franklin D. Roosevelt is afforded for the first time today in the transcripts of many of the President's press conferences, made available from hitherto secret stenographic transcripts, with the "off-the-record" material also revealed.

From 30,000 to 35,000 words of press conference discussions are made public. But they are culled from only 15 selected press conferences, between March 8, 1933, and Dec. 29, 1936. During that period, no less than 350 press conferences were held in all, although those quoted were the longest and most important. So it is a safe calculation that well over 700,000 words were uttered by the President at these bi-weekly meetings with the Washington correspondents, and might have been published.

Even the 35,000-word selection published is an astonishing record of democratic publicity. From the very outset, the President is seen making his effort to shape the public thought through the press, permitting—as he explained at his first conference—the venturesome method of verbal questioning, and giving out information in three carefully chosen categories. First category was straight information, in which the President may be quoted indirectly, as: "Mr. Roosevelt said that . . ." Second category was "background," in which reporters could publish information the President told them on their own responsibility, or by saying something like "It is learned that . . ." Third category was "off-the-record," and reporters were supposed not to print this information or use it in any way—not even to communicate it to their editors.

Whether the President ever thought he could tell 100-150 men

(Continued on Page 2, Column 6)

Britain Enters Radio Race To Influence South America

LONDON, March 14 (AP)—Britain begins shortwave radiocasts tonight to South America, in Spanish and Portuguese, in an effort to offset radio propaganda from other foreign countries.

Special to The Christian Science Monitor

SANTIAGO, Chile, March 14—The official inauguration of British competition in vernacular radiocasts to South America is scheduled for today. The Latins, sensitive of the honors conferred upon them through the ether, believe that the United States will also officially join in soon. Unofficial private broadcasts have been going on for some months. They are following the moves in Washington, where many high officials are concerned about the success attending European propaganda and hear with interest the suggestions in Congressional circles that a Government transmitting station be prepared for South America.

Great Britain, to transmit through the British Broadcasting Corporation in Spanish and Portuguese, was forced into the South American sphere by a parliamentary and commercial outcry against anti-British propaganda. The chief objection appears to be against the cumulative effect of news presented according to authoritarian viewpoints, resulting in a misrepresentation of ultimate British aims and policies. As Great Britain leads all powers, including the United States, in South American investments, the radio challenge had to be accepted.

The Fascist states do not disguise the fact that they are using the radio for political purposes. The achievements of their regimes are lauded, obviously to impress South Americans and make them sympathetic to that system of rule. Great Britain emphasizes the cultural side of its mission and makes clear that the British viewpoint will be expounded in its radio news and talks. All offer plenty of music for the entertainment of the South Americans and appeal to their artistic tastes. But, no matter how much all the competitors—German, Italian, British and Americans, if the United States participates—emphasize that they intend to explain and simultaneously entertain, the South Americans see themselves rapidly being drawn against their desire, into the great radio contest between Fascism and Democracy.

On the one hand, Latin Americans are proud to think they are getting so much world attention, but on the other hand, they resent not being able to control incoming propaganda—news, viewpoints, or whatever it is called—through the ether. With one notable exception—for the tendency in Brazil has yet to be accurately determined—South American states are, at least in their official tendencies, bent on getting into the middle of the doctrinal road, away from the side paths of fascism and communism. Their internal and external policies, even where the governing authority is dictatorial, are shaped towards this end.

Importers and distributors of radio apparatus report increased sales of short wave sets due to stimulated South American interest since the British program inauguration date was announced. Interest is especially keen in Chile, Peru and Bolivia, where large numbers of Spanish-speaking residents of British ancestry look forward to a permanent cultural connection with the land of their fathers. Many of these are exiled in distant mining camps

(Continued on Page 15, Column 1)

Economics in the News

The 'Third Basket'—Retaining Undistributed Profits Tax in Respect of Closely Held Corporations—Argument Over Discrimination

By H. B. E.

Discrimination is a word which both sides have flung into the tax debate on the "third basket." Advocates of this section say it would end discrimination. Opponents argue it introduces discrimination. The seizure of the same word by both sides has no doubt confused the layman. Which side is really entitled to it? I must reply "both." The senses are different—that is all.

The "third basket" is Title 1—b in the new tax bill and imposes a penalty tax upon closely-held corporations keeping over a certain amount of their income. It is only against this class of corporation that the undistributed tax penalty is retained. Thus, to take a brace of examples, the Ford Company, a private corporation, would be "penalized," but the General Motors Corporation, a public corporation, would escape. Representative Lamneck last week put the difference in treatment in terms of percentages. He said that if a widely-held corporation and a family-owned corporation of equal income both retained all their earnings, the family-held corporation would have to pay a tax 56 per cent greater than the widely-held corporation. Obviously there is discrimination here. And this is the burden of the complaints of the closely-held corporations.

With equal force, however, the President retorts that the purpose of the "third basket" is to end discrimination. And this is how. Mr. Ford, say, could escape taxation in the highest personal income tax brackets by letting his share of the Ford profits remain in the enterprise. General Motors, however, is under obligation to its owners or stockholders to disburse dividends or profits upon which those owners have to pay a personal income tax. Thus General Motors stockholders are "penalized" and Mr. Ford escapes.

Now we can put the word discrimination in its proper perspective. As among corporations the "third basket" is discriminatory; as among individual taxpayers it removes discrimination.

I think the House of Representatives at this time chose the wiser course in dwelling upon the former argument and rejecting 1—b.

I say "at this time" because the country is in the throes of what Secretary Morgenthau calls an "acute" setback. That setback is without parallel in the business annals of America. First, it is peculiar to America, despite the fact that recovery in the other major industrial countries was two years ahead of American recovery. And, secondly, it has overcome America before there has been any evidence of over-expansion. In other words, this is a synthetic depression with its proximate cause clearly outlined as an impediment in the flow of private capital into business enterprise. Accordingly, the first duty of a "managing" government is clear. Statesmanship—or, in its original form, steersmanship—requires the liberation of private capital.

This, I take it, is the reason the House set its face against "discriminatory" treatment of family corporations. The steep fall in the business indexes is throwing the economy back to the subsistence levels of several years ago. Unemployment has increased rapidly. Recovery, in consequence, has become the No. 1 Reform. To quote the President, at the annual meeting of the Mobilization for Human Needs: "Only in jobs, and more jobs, at good pay, shall we find national stability and individual security." Job-providers would be discouraged by 1—b. In my own calling, for instance, that great family corporation, the New York Times, acted as Santa Claus for unemployed newspapermen in the great depression. At one time it was said to be double-staffed with the throwouts of "impersonal" corporations. I doubt whether that same sense of social responsibility would have been forthcoming if there had been any "third basket" statute.

The "third basket," of course, deals with a situation that requires rectification—present and possibly future. As such there should be no complete balking at a remedy from fear of disturbing business. The nucleus of the remedy, however, it at hand in the section of the Revenue Act of 1924 directed against corporations "formed or availed of" for income tax avoidance. Originally, the undistributed profits tax was intended to plug this "leak" of income into so-called incorporated pocketbooks. Is it beyond the wit of legislators and administrators to spot these companies from the closely-held corporations which plow back earnings for honest-to-goodness, job-creating expansion? At this time a rifle is preferable to the shotgun.

Blum Forms Another Paris Popular Front

Minority Parties Obstruct Premier's Proposal for National Regime

11 Are Socialists

By a Staff Correspondent of The Christian Science Monitor

PARIS, March 14—After being stranded without a Government for four historic days during the gravest European crisis since the World War, France today finally has a Popular Front Cabinet headed once again by Léon Blum.

But in M. Blum's own words, "It isn't the government of public opinion I wanted nor the kind of government the present circumstances demanded." Despite really heroic efforts France's first—and now its second—Socialist Premier, M. Blum was obliged by the resistance of minority parties of the right to abandon his attempt to form what he himself described as a "truly National Government, by which I mean a Government grouping a Popular Front of the Democratic and Republican forces of the nation."

Few French observers today deny that his failure through no fault of his own to constitute such a Cabinet by uniting all French parties from Communists to Conservatives is more important than his success in setting up a second Popular Front Cabinet.

This Cabinet is essentially a revised version of his first Ministry formed in June, 1936. It contains 23 Ministers of whom 11 are Socialists, 9 radicals and 3 members of Joseph Paul-Boncour's Social Union group.

Problem of Finance

Besides the premiership, M. Blum has taken charge of the treasury and intends to devote his chief energies to solving the serious financial problems.

Simplified and summarized, the situation in France today is this: two men, M. Blum and M. Daladier, are facing two immediate problems; one, financial and other, international. Can Premier Blum get M. Daladier the money he must have for the building up of defense forces as Minister of National Defense? Shorn of its detailed complications this is the question.

Unconfirmed reports today credit Premier Blum with the intention of

(Continued on Page 4, Column 6)

Champion Swapper Starts With Knife And Gets an Auto

MAYFIELD, Ky., March 14 (AP)—County Patrolman Fayette Cherry started trading when he had a 10-cent pocket knife, and 10 weeks later had an automobile he value at $200.

Net profit claimed: $199.90.

There were at least 100 trades between the pocket knife and the car, Mr. Cherry said.

He doesn't remember them all, but among things for which he swapped were other knives, cash, radios and watches.

Mr. Cherry has been trading seriously for 40 years. "I've never seen the time I couldn't get a trade out of something," he said, adding:

"When I was six years old, going to school at Antioch (southeast of Mayfield), I exchanged a pencil for an apple."

Mr. Cherry for many years operated a second-hand furniture store and trading post at Kentwood, La., returning here five years ago—still in a swapping mood.

There's nothing unusual about the trade he has just completed, Mr. Cherry said.

Take, for example, that time 25 years ago, when he started with a horse and buggy. Three months later, he said, he owned a house and lot.

Another time, on a "trade day," Mr. Cherry swapped all day and found himself the possessor of a horse.

He had started out with—a halter.

Ssh! Roosevelt's At His Income Tax

By a Staff Correspondent of The Christian Science Monitor

Washington, March 14

A suspicious blank appeared on President Roosevelt's engagement pad for this afternoon. No callers, no consultations, no plans were announced.

Nobody would say so officially, but the real fact is that Mr. Roosevelt, like many a John Doe, has put off preparing his income tax statement until the day before the deadline. And so, far into the White House night. . . .

The Monitor Index

Monday, March 14, 1938

Germany Annexes Austria; Process of Nazification Is Speeded on All Fronts

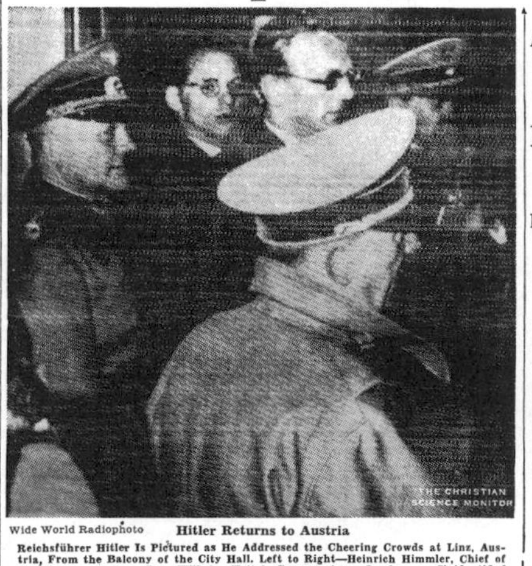

Wide World Radiophoto **Hitler Returns to Austria**

Reichsführer Hitler Is Pictured as He Addressed the Cheering Crowds at Linz, Austria, From the Balcony of the City Hall. Left to Right—Heinrich Himmler, Chief of the German Police; Gen. Wilhelm Keitel, German Army Leader; an Unidentified Person; Dr. Arthur Seyss-Inquart, Austrian Chancellor, and Herr Hitler

Army, Press, Radio and Youth Movements Are Absorbed by Reich

Plebiscite Set; Little Violence

Indifference, Sadness and Jubilation Split New Hitler Province

VIENNA, March 14 (AP)—Adolf Hitler today triumphantly entered Vienna, capital of the German state he has absorbed in his greater German Reich.

Herr Hitler, who had changed to an open motor car during his 100-mile journey from Linz, entered Vienna standing up, bowing, smiling to hundreds of thousands lining the route.

Behind his slow moving automobile was another car carrying Heinrich Himmler, chief of all German police, and other high officials of the Reich.

By a Staff Correspondent of The Christian Science Monitor

VIENNA, March 14—One of Europe's 25 states has disappeared. Austria has ended its career as an independent nation and has become the eighteenth province in the Third Reich.

Six and one half million people were incorporated into the foreign state without a man, woman, or child raising his hand in forcible resistance. The entire Austrian Army was swallowed up by the German Army and placed under the command of Gen. Fedor von Bock, commander of the Munich eighth army corps, without a single sword leaving its scabbard. Soldiers of the neighboring state assumed control of all Austrian cities. So complete was the German domination that the outward expression was only one of flowers, cheers, and waving of German flags.

The Patriotic Front, which boasted 2,000,000 members, failed to produce one patriot who was willing to do anything bolder than to make speeches.

Hitler Reaches Goal

Reichsführer Adolf Hitler sat in a modest hotel in the little Danubian City of Linz, his own home town, and dictated two paragraphs. One was telephoned to Vienna and became law: the other was telephoned to Berlin and also became law. They were announced over the radio and the Austrian State disappeared from the world.

Thus Herr Hitler's dream of uniting all Germans in one Reich came true. His law, proclaimed from Vienna, says Austria is a province of the German Reich. His law, proclaimed from Berlin, says the German Reich takes cognizance of this new fact.

Austria is being integrated into the Reich with dizzying rapidity. The National Socialist machine is working here with the precision speed of an airplane. Friday night the Austrian regime collapsed. Saturday Herr Hitler appeared in Austria, where he was received with frenzied enthusiasm.

Radio System Absorbed

Sunday President Miklas was forced to resign and Austria took its place in the one Reich with the other Germans. As these formalities of "Gleichschaltung"—unification—of the Austrian State were being coercively carried out, every single phase of Austrian life was being transformed in no less expeditious manner, so that in the course of a single week end Austria, both in appearance and in essence, became a province of the Third Reich, hardly distinguishable from Bavaria, Saxony or Baden.

The Austrian radio system became part of the Reich radio system and was placed under the control of Dr. Joseph Göbbels Sunday afternoon. Already by Sunday morning the whole Austrian press was "co-ordinated."

Youth, sport, and gymnastic organizations were integrated into the German system at a single stroke. German Youth Leader Baldur von Shirach flew to Vienna from Germany and on Sunday reviewed a parade of Austrian Hitler youth and maidens that lasted until midnight.

Other Sweeping Change

The Roman Catholic gymnastic associations were dissolved. The youth organization of the Fatherland Front were incorporated into the Hitler system. Its "patriotic" leader, who for years has taught these youths to work for Dr. Kurt Schuschnigg, the former Chancellor, and a free Austria, spoke over the radio and urged them now to join the Hitler youth movement in the new Reich.

The Austrian National Socialist party of course became part of the German party and as was expected, it took over buildings of the Fatherland Front as their headquarters as most of the members of the Fatherland Front will soon be its members. Labor organization has been incorporated into Germany's labor front. "SS" and "SA"—Blackshirt and Brown Shirt Guards—are very prominent. They have taken charge of all public buildings and as commissioners in all public institutions see that National Socalist measures are carried out.

The Austrian Army was almost completely co-ordinated in a sud-

(Continued on Page 5, Column 7)

London: New Arms Warning; Berlin: Bars All Hindrances

LONDON, March 14 (AP)—Prime Minister Neville Chamberlain today plainly warned Germany that Britain would expand her vast rearmament program to match force with force in answer to Reichsführer Hitler's absorption of Austria.

However, the Prime Minister, in a vital statement of policy before a House of Commons packed and tense, did not promise British backing to France if she should go to war to save Czechoslovakia from Pan-Germanism.

Mr. Chamberlain said Czechoslovakia had been in consultation with Britain but he refused to discuss what Britain would do to guard the Central European Republic for whose 3,500,000 Sudeten Germans Herr Hitler had proclaimed himself protector.

Mr. Chamberlain bluntly rejected a German statement that Britain had no right to interest herself in Austrian independence, the German answer to British protests over the annexation.

Reaffirms British Rights

Mr. Chamberlain insisted that Britain "must be interested in developments in Central Europe."

"These events cannot be regarded by His Majesty's Government with indifference: They are bound to have effects which cannot yet be measured.

"The methods adopted throughout these tense events call for the severest condemnation and have administered a profound shock to all who are interested in the preservation of European peace.

"It is untrue to suggest that we ever gave Germany our assent or encouragement to enforce the absorption of Austria into the German Reich.

"The hard fact is that nothing could have arrested this action by Germany unless we and others with us had been prepared to use force to prevent it.

"Accordingly we have decided to make fresh reviews and in due course we shall announce what further steps we may think it necessary to take."

Baron Constantin von Neurath, head of Germany's new Secret

(Continued on Page 4, Column 2)

By J. Emlyn Williams

Staff Correspondent of The Christian Science Monitor

BERLIN, March 14—Achievement of Austro-German Anchluss, due in no small measure to Italy's benevolent neutrality and in defiance of a strongly worded Anglo-French protest, is regarded here as indicating once more that where German racialism is concerned, "necessity knows no law."

Continued official assertions that the Third Reich's intervention in Austria was essentially an aid to weaker brothers and Germany's appreciation of Italy's attitude ran through week-end speeches and press comments.

Description of the German troops' invasion as an essential guarantee for a free plebiscite in Austria has, however, changed in the press today. It now is being celebrated as the "dawn of a great German Reich." Inquiries as to how quickly Austrian co-ordination in the Third Reich will be achieved, are the only note of speculation.

To Strengthen Armed Forces

Germany also announced through Field Marshal Hermann Göring yesterday that despite, or rather because, of what has happened Germany has decided further to strengthen the armed forces in the interests of peace—presumably for Pan-Germanica.

Field Marshal Göring was named by the Reichsführer as acting Chancellor just before Herr Hitler left for his journey into Austria. Today, at the German war memorial, the Field Marshal clearly indicated Germany's determination to go its own way unhindered, driven to this policy in the present instance, he affirmed, by the "treachery" of ex-Chancellor Schuschnigg.

Herr Hitler's personal letter to Premier Mussolini, delivered Friday last by Philip of Hesse, husband of the Italian Princess Mafalde, has not been published here. In this letter the Führer explained the reason for his action—maltreatment of Germans of Austria by a régime having no legal basis—and gave definite

(Continued on Page 4, Column 4)

The European Situation

Written for The Christian Science Monitor

Austria became a province of Germany over the week end. All that remains is to formally enact the statutes which will give effect to "Anschluss"—union of Austria and Germany—reducing the former remnant of the Hapsburg empire to the status of a German state.

In Austria

Behind his troops, which effected a bloodless occupation of Austria, Reichsführer Adolf Hitler rode toward Vienna in triumph.

President Miklas was forced to resign. Dr. Arthur Seyss-Inquart took over the President's duties—in addition to the post of Chancellor, Minister of War, and Minister of Police. A purge of former foes of the National Socialists in Austria was immediately begun. City and Provincial Governments passed into National Socialist hands.

Having obtained postponement of Austria's "independence" plebiscite, the National Socialists announced themselves that they would hold a referendum April 10 to give popular "approval" to the unification of Austria and Germany.

In Europe

Great Britain, key to whatever action appears imminent by the Great Powers, heard Prime Minister Neville Chamberlain declare that the German absorption of Austria remained a "matter of British concern." Although declining to state that Britai would come to the armed defense of Czechoslovakia, the Prime Minister warned that rearmament would be speeded against such dictatorial encroachment.

France meanwhile formed a Cabinet, although Premier Leon Blum's success fell short of the anticipated inclusion of all of the major political parties.

Rome—officially agreeing to "Anschluss" and whistling to keep up the Rome-Berlin axis—nevertheless was gravely concerned over a move which made Il Duce diplomatically subservient to Reichsführer Hitler.

Germany—its populace somewhat mystified by the suddenness of the Austrian coup—welcomed the new expansion of the Fartherland.

European currencies tumbled. The French franc fell to the lowest level in 11 years and the pound sterling decreased to a new low for the year. Swiss, Belgian and Netherlands currencies also declined.

THE CHRISTIAN SCIENCE MONITOR

AN INTERNATIONAL DAILY NEWSPAPER

BOSTON, TUESDAY, MAY 2, 1939—VOL. XXXI, NO. 133 R CENTRAL EDITION—FIVE CENTS A COPY

COPYRIGHT 1939 BY THE CHRISTIAN SCIENCE PUBLISHING SOCIETY

Provinces Act To Force Job Plan in Canada

Enabling acts passed in Ontario and Quebec—Legislators increase taxes—8 cents on gas.

Special to The Christian Science Monitor

OTTAWA, May 2—In a joint attempt to force the Federal Government to take some action toward establishment of an unemployment insurance scheme before the Parliament session ends, the Governments of Ontario and Quebec adopted measures which empower the provinces to enter into any such plan.

This acquiescence smooths the way for the King Government, which has pleaded lack of cooperation on the part of the provinces as well as constitutional difficulties in explaining why some legislative action has not been taken in the past.

An imposing body of legal opinion now supports the view that the British North America Act—the equivalent of a Constitution in Canada—will, as it now stands, permit such a move. Thus the Federal Government may introduce a pre-election measure to establish a social service which has been one of the planks in the Liberal platform since 1919.

The Legislatures of both provinces prorogued on notes of reaffirmed loyalty to the crown and keen anticipation of the royal visit.

Gasoline Tax Raised

The legislators approved two-cent increases in the gasoline tax which brought the levy to eight cents in each province and in Quebec was closely linked with a proposed $50,000,000 road program to occupy the Department of Highways for the next four years.

Taxation took the spotlight in the closing hours of the Quebec Legislature when approval and royal consent were given to a sweeping measure which will increase corporation taxes by $2,000,000 a year, according to Provincial experts. The revision is aimed at 1,500 "big companies," Premier Duplessis told the House. Some 7,000 "ordinary" firms will bear no added burden, but trust and insurance companies, tobacco firms, public utilities and banks are facing greater imposts on paid-up capital and a higher levy on their business places. Since there are several national head offices in Montreal, this provision will have a wide effect. The tax on insurance premiums was raised from 1½ per cent to 2 per cent.

Cities Get More Funds

In Ontario a revision was made in the Corporation Tax Act, less sweeping than the Quebec legislation, whereby the levy on paid up capital was reduced and the tax on income was increased. By a change in the Assessment Act, northern municipalities, many of them in financial difficulties, were given the power to collect added revenue from the mines. All municipalities will share in the gasoline tax increase through subsidies amounting to one-half mill on their assessments.

A further move towards centralized authority in the Quebec Government was seen by opposition critics in the Government's action in extending the powers of the four-member Treasury Board.

A proposal to abolish liquor advertising in Quebec was given swift and harsh treatment in the Treasury benches. Because Ontario does not permit the advertising of liquor a considerable amount of printing goes to the neighboring province each year where there is no such restriction. The suggestion was "inappropriate, unwarranted, and inopportune," said Mr. Duplessis as it perished.

Rebuke to Meddlers

Reaffirmation of the theory that Quebec needed the Padlock Law to fight the Communists and a stern rebuke to the United States and Britain to attend to their own affairs were heard in the House from Mr. Duplessis who spoke with resentment of a movement abroad which he blamed for giving the Province a bad reputation as a nest of Fascists. Mr. Duplessis was also heard in an attack on the Federal Government's record defense estimates. Quebec wanted bread not guns for its people, he said.

In Ontario the Legislature agreed to ask the Federal Government for the repeal of the Canada Temperance Act as it applied to Ontario. This would leave the Ontario Liquor Control Act as the sole authority in the few localities where the seniority of the Provincial legislation is now challenged.

The Monitor Index

Tuesday, May 2, 1939

Why Doctors Oppose Sickness Insurance

Bureau of American Medical Association declares compulsory system would lead to deterioration in quality of medical service; physicians would become 'routine' workers.

Objections to compulsory sickness insurance—a major issue in the California legislature, a subject before Congress, and a question just revived in Canada—are reviewed in part in the following article, second of a series of six.

By a Staff Correspondent of The Christian Science Monitor

CHICAGO — Introduction of compulsory sickness insurance in the United States would lead to a deterioration in the quality of medical service available to a great portion of the population and so would be hurtful to many seeking medical care, reports the Bureau of Medical Economics of the American Medical Association.

The Bureau bases this judgment on study of systems of compulsory sickness insurance in many foreign countries where long established, particularly Germany and Great Britain.

"The compulsory insurance system drops the doctor in it to a routine," commented an official of the Bureau, pointing out a single objection. "It doesn't make much difference to him whether or not he gives the best he's got, he can get away with it.

"We don't think the average American going to a physician would get as good treatment from an insurance doctor as he can receive under the present system of private practice."

Main Objections Cited

Analyzing in detail the compulsory feature of the National Health Program recently laid before Congress, the American Medical Association, largest body of physicians in the country, finds the depressing effects of compulsory insurance on medical practice to include the following:

1. Many doctors in the typical insurance system are overworked, because of being required to look after too many patients.

2. The trend of compulsory insurance is toward the mechanization of medicine, which because of the great human element involved in treatment of the sick, would suffer from mass mechanical methods.

3. Treatment of patients becomes in many cases superficial.

4. Too many minor and frequently unnecessary cases are thrust upon the physician, encouraged in part by the opportunity or temptation to claim insurance money. In an overemphasis on mild cases, the serious cases may during times of pressure be slighted or overlooked.

5. Independence of thought and self-help on the part of the medical profession is not encouraged by the imposition of a great machinery of governmental regimentation.

6. Physicians would not be kept alert as many are today by the requirement of making

(Continued on Page 4, Column 7)

P.-T. A. Told How to Lead Child to Self-Realization

Special to The Christian Science Monitor

CINCINNATI, Ohio, May 2—Home and school should maintain a closer relationship in assisting children to develop their best individualities, it was emphasized at the National Congress of Parents and Teachers here, where the roads to fuller self-realization were carefully explored.

Through reading, conversing, and having interests with the child in the home, parents may work hand in hand with schools in directing the child toward the finer things, making them part of his life. It was brought out by Dr. Bess Goodykoontz, Assistant Commissioner of Education, United States Office of Education, that the home and the school should strive to establish similar codes of conduct in order to give the child a definite standard for building character.

Responsibility Pointed Out

"Our responsibility as parents and teachers is to plan together, to avoid conflict in standards for children, to be as uncritical of each other as possible, to be ready to explain or to modify our own standards," declared Dr. Goodykoontz. "To realize one's best self a person needs to know how to use the tools (reading, writing, etc.) to keep on learning, to know how to keep well, to have long-time interests and standards by which to steer his course."

Dr. William G. Carr, Director of Research, National Educational Association, also emphasized the important place the home plays in developing the self-realization of the child. There, he declared, is the starting point for democracy and as the home becomes a democracy instead of a dictatorship the child begins his right growth toward freedom.

Religious Problems

Turning to the need for education to teach the child economic effectiveness, Dr. Carr stated that education today is one sided, teaching pupils how to be producers rather than cosumers as well. An educated person, he said, should be an educated consumer, knowing how to buy and invest wisely, and not swayed easily by appearances and promises.

"Education, too, should not

(Continued on Page 4, Column 5)

Chicago Opens 'New Frontier' For Business

Forums and campaign to raise $250,000 advertising fund mark move to reawaken city.

By a Staff Correspondent of The Christian Science Monitor

CHICAGO—Out to get "a new frontier for Chicago business," the Chicago Association of Commerce is launching a series of 100 business men's forums which it hopes will ultimately set the city's cash registers ringing.

An immediate objective is the raising of a $250,000 fund to advertise Chicago as a vacation center. But the Association aims to go farther and recommend basic improvements in the city which will make it more attractive to permanent residents as well as visitors, improvements which will bring new industries here and keep old ones from leaving.

The program launched in recent days is the outcome of a year of planning, according to Oscar G. Mayer, President of the Association. Changing economic conditions, an altered relationship between government and business, and new conditions surrounding business enterprise in Chicago are given as the factors which prompted the Association to take steps for what it calls "the reawakening of Chicago."

Non-Members Called

The plan is to call in not only members of the Association but non-members as well to get the widest range of recommendations for the betterment of the city. Well known business men have been chosen to preside at each of the so-called "business clinics." Fred D. Fagg, former assistant secretary of the United States Department of Commerce is in general charge of the meetings.

Four specific questions are to be put before the clinic groups, as follows:

1. What three or four major problems are now most deserving and in need of aggressive, united action by the business men of Chicago?

2. What can the Association of Commerce do that it is not now doing to help my business?

3. What new enterprises can be undertaken by the Association to bring about an immediate improvement in the several major lines of business endeavor?

4. What can Chicago business men, banded together, do to bring about a "Greater Chicago," and a revival of the old Chicago "I will" spirit?

To Bring Visitors

Answers made by individuals are to be tabulated and used as a guide for a new program of the Association.

A specific project now being urged by the Association is the raising of funds to finance a campaign to bring summer visitors to Chicago as they were brought during the two years of the Chicago Century of Progress Exposition.

This Changing World

Hitler's Speech—A Condition and Not a Theory Still Facing the World After The Reichstag Oration—Germany's Living Room

By H. B. Elliston

Bismarck said that history is made where things happen. On this dictum no history was written when Chancellor Hitler addressed the Reichstag on Friday. History will be fashioned in Poland, perhaps in Rumania, any place that Nazi Germany chooses to absorb. Nevertheless Herr Hitler's speeches always are interesting, if only for the rationale he provides for his history-making. He knows that in this slogan-drugged world only a veneer of plausibility is needed in order to justify Nazi imperialism.

Always Herr Hitler's speeches are tuned to the harshness of the Treaty of Versailles. Such a denunciation used to be a surefire hit with this writer, a veteran of the World War. I was fighting in France soon after my nineteenth birthday, and with millions of others found secular solace only in the prospect that after the war, we could all, Germans as well, remold the world nearer to the heart's desire.

Ah, disillusion! Peace "broke out" with a new set of warriors in the saddle, so-called statesmen. Their idea of a peace was to squeeze the Germans till the pips squeaked. This was their very language, and it reminded this demobilized soldier of his bayonet practice. He accepted the first opportunity to be a war correspondent in this post-war world.

* * *

Somewhere in Schiller you will find the saying that a wrong once committed increases in geometrical ratio until it is rectified. This is what happened under the Treaty of Versailles and the League of Nations which was embalmed in the Treaty. Except that on top of the old wrong were piled heaps of new wrongs. It would be idle to enumerate them, for the fact now is that the ex-allies have made amends. Reparations are gone. The Rhineland is back in German hands. The encirclement of Germany, or what the French used to call the cordon sanitaire, is a thing of the past.

Nazi Germany, in sum, stands forth today far greater in area and population than the Kaiser's Germany. True there are no colonies. But, as I showed some time ago, the former German colonies were unimportant in feeding the Germans and their industry. Still the British have many times offered to consider a colonial adjustment as part of a general settlement. They are even now guided by a willingness to go more than halfway to rectify past injustices.

Encirclement, however, is a useful word in the mouths of demagogues. It keeps stirred up a sense of the old wrongs. On Friday Herr Hitler emitted another slogan which has lately been tickling the ears of the groundlings. This far greater Germany still has no Lebensraum. Encirclement and living room! Add them to the old "have-not" slogan, and you have the wordy dynamite to blow up "my" people.

The other day, at a conference of university professors, a German banker got off a variant of this plea that poverty excuses everything. A similar justification had already come to me from readers of my examination of the colonial argument. It was that Germany had to indulge in barter because it had no liquid resources.

Of course Nazi Germany has no liquid resources, and for a very simple reason. It is not interested either in gold or foreign exchange, but in raw gold and foreign exchange will buy. So that every dollar of money or ounce of gold earned in trade or obtained by conquest is turned right away into real goods. Alas! that so many of them are for armament purposes. As much as 28 per cent of the national income is now spent on armament.

* * *

Germany is a poor country in extent of natural resources. But many other countries are poorer. Yet they don't think that any "right" is conferred upon them to apply pressure-barter in eking out supplies. Every nation has something to contribute to the common economic good. The Swiss made their Alps extremely valuable even though there is nothing of much value under them. The Chinese found the hair on their women's heads a great economic asset. Denmark was a poor country which became individually wealthy by the ingenuity it applied to farming. Without adding a square foot to its territory a nation can make living room by developing the skills of the people, and then by exchanging the surplus products of those skills.

Here in the blocked exchange or trade of the world is what makes for international trouble. The "have-not" problem is merely a symptom of that disease. Clear out the channels uniting our several skills, and strife would be healed. It is a psychological more than an economic problem nowadays. We simply shrink from recognizing subjectively in our human relations the world neighborhood which we have already wrought objectively. However, both Britain and America have tendered economic olive branches to Germany. So that a sign is still required from Germany that it will join in a quest for new economic co-operation. Until this is shown, the Hitler speeches merely underline Cleveland's warning that a condition and not a theory confronts the world in the Nazi phenomenon.

Television Moves Forward Another Step

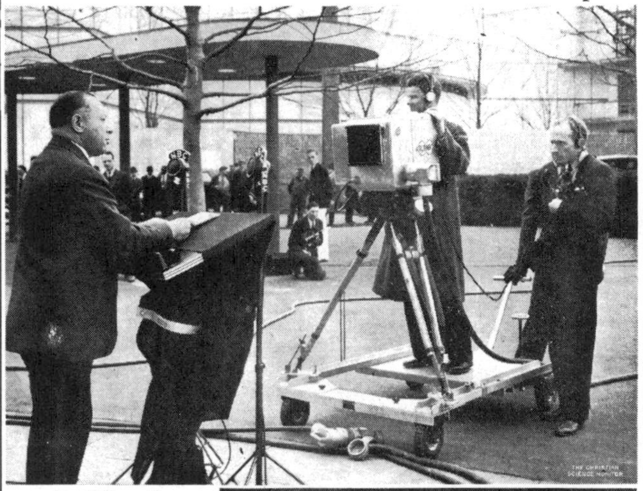

David Sarnoff

President of the Radio Corporation of America, televised as he delivered speech April 20 dedicating RCA Exhibit Building at the New York World's Fair.

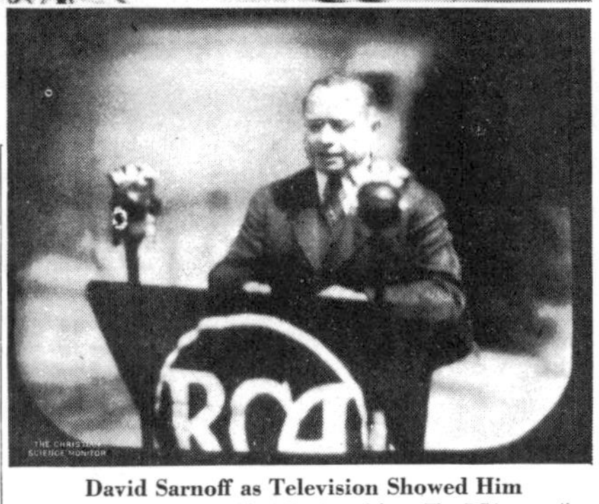

David Sarnoff as Television Showed Him

This shows the "other end" of the top picture. The RCA executive as he appeared in the receiving set in New York City eight miles away.

Television Test At Fair Reveals Marked Advance

By Volney D. Hurd

Staff Correspondent of The Christian Science Monitor

NEW YORK, May 2—Fascinated groups of men and women, jamming sidewalks at several store windows April 30, indicated an interest that presages the success of television which was inaugurated at the Fair. Two hours of events at the World's Fair grounds, climaxed by the televising of President Roosevelt as he spoke, opening the Fair, made up the first spot news program in official American television, received by probably 200 sets in Greater New York.

Newspaper technical workers were as delighted as the crowds seeing television for the first time—for the transmission was better than anything seen before. Whatever doubts may have existed in their minds before today were wiped out. Television had advanced to the point where it was a feasible art.

The first scene showed the Court of Peace, with the trylon and perisphere in the background. Bright sunlight and lovely clouds gave these symbols a perfect setting. That clouds, nebulous as they are, should have come through so clearly was one of the first intimations that excellent television was being seen.

Cascading Fountains

Next was the playing of the cascading fountains, their white streams spraying out, moving gently up and down as fountains will. The fact these fountains showed up so well was a pleasant surprise.

Then came the camera swinging around, taking in various foreign buildings and their flags. A gentle breeze swung the banners out in undulating folds and television cameras picked them up with marked fidelity.

Finally came the parade. Soldiers, men and girls in native costumes, military bands, a bagpipe band, all swung by with easy identification. After the parade came the speeches, climaxed by the President's address. That spot news pickup of television can be exciting was proved by the period preceeding the arrival of the President. The police came and cleared the way. The camera swung from the speakers stand, down along a ramp up which the Presidential car would come. The build-up was as eager and intense as though one were present. Finally came cries of "He's coming!" the band struck up and in rolled the presidential car. It was all very stimulating—and an experience to remember as one sat in New York City in an easy chair, seeing things as they happened at that split second, and from the choice viewpoint cameramen always seem to get.

Proves Its Value

Of course, the novelty helped to hold interest. But to be able to watch happenings at the Fair for nearly three hours showed possibilities of television in giving lengthy pickups of news events.

One complaint against television has been that continual looking was tiring. But not a single one of some dozen spectators in the NBC office where we viewed the affair reported any fatigue.

The display marked an event which is expected to carry long beyond the World's Fair, as great a success as that may be. It gave sight-at-a-distance as a public service which, if it improves in the next 10 years as much as radio did in its first 10, may become one of the greatest influences the world has ever seen.

World unity stressed at New York Fair: Page 2.

Chamber Asks Fight on Trend Toward Central Government

By a Staff Correspondent of The Christian Science Monitor

WASHINGTON, May 2—A call to businessmen to unite against a "dangerous trend" toward central Government "and away from our American system of representative Government" was issued yesterday by John W. O'Leary, in conjunction with the annual meeting of the United States Chamber of Commerce.

Mr. O'Leary spoke as the Chairman of the Executive Committee of the Chamber before the National Council and did not mince matters in his appeal to American businessmen. His speech is believed to reflect a new and more militant drive against the Roosevelt Administration, reflected at other points in the Chamber's advance four-day program. There has been a partial truce between the New Deal and the Chamber for a number of years. Now with the possibility of a turn in the political tide, sharper hostilities appear to be breaking out.

Mr. O'Leary called for "a greater unity in determination to hold the line—against the 'dangerous trend'" which he envisaged. It is the business of the national Councilors of the Chamber of Commerce, he declared in the first formal address of the convention, to supply the leadership in this drive. The year, he declared, has brought "a new courage and hope."

Mr. O'Leary referred to the year's business advertising program featuring slogans of "What Helps Business Helps You—Less Taxes More Jobs." The most fundamental and imperative task before the country at the moment, he declared, is the revival of private enterprise. Past days of American prosperity were associated with reduced taxation and balanced budgets, he said. He called for present removal of "uncertainties," revision of laws and taxes, reduction of Government spending, and modification of restrictive legislation to restore prosperity today. Winding up, he likened the condition under the New Deal with that in Britain under the Labor Government. The Labor Government was finally ousted, he recalled. "In 1927 it became possible for England to bring order to its monetary siauation and from that time forward the Nation prospered," he said.

Mr. O'Leary spoke at a preliminary session as 2,000 business spokesmen were arriving at the annual meeting, theme of which this year is—"What Is Holding Business Back?"

Harvard Romps to Victory In Hoop Race at Wellesley

By a Staff Writer of The Christian Science Monitor

WELLESLEY, Mass., May 1—"Peggy" Read of Villanova, Pa., won the traditional May Day hoop race at Wellesley College before breakfast this morning and for this spurt was awarded the "bride's bouquet." That means first of the senior class to marry—perhaps.

Following the shrilling, shrieking pursuit of elusive hoops down the slope from Tower Court to Chapel, everything was at sixes and sevens—as it is every year. But, possibly, everything would have gone as merry as a wedding bell if "Peggy" hadn't puffed, "Thank you, very much."

The thank-you was vibrant, Robert-Taylor-at-his-best, but it certainly was not feminine. Up went a Greek chorus of exasperated "Oh's" and "Ah's" and "Peggy," whose brown wig had gone a bit askew—proving that it was a disguise—was stripped of cap and gown and hustled to Lake Waban and dumped in. Prowess in hoop rolling thereupon was enhanced by proof that a Harvard junior can swim.

How Edward Cameron Kirk Read, of Eliot House, Harvard '40, President of the Lampoon, and "Peggy" in the race, really got in is still undisclosed—although certain events point to inside aid. The hoop race is inexcusably early, in student eyes; in fact, the sophomores or "little sisters" of the seniors, have to rise around six to baste seniors' black gowns for greater facility in running, and to stand by to adjust bandanas or scarves over mortar-board caps.

Yet just at the moment the signal was given, "Peggy" dashed into the line and before any explanation could be demanded was taking the lead down Tower Hill.

Harvard's champion could not be reached to comment on his victory. Two impending classes in Cambridge rather than any innate modesty, plus the need of a dry suit of clothes, drove him from the campus in a hurry.

Tabulation of results disclosed that Miss Margaret Cahill of Park Avenue, N. Y. C., and Miss Phyllis Sweetser of Lincoln Street, Newton Highlands, were runners-up. Both girls are engaged: Miss Cahill, according to the Wellesley News office, since last October to Thomas McGrath, Dartmouth '38, and Miss Sweetser to Paul B. Hooper, Harvard '37, dating from yesterday.

"Can he cook?" one of the girls asked.

Parents in School Drive

Special to The Christian Science Monitor

PHILADELPHIA—A campaign for legislative relief and increased taxes to keep the City's schools open has been launched by thousands of parents of public school children in South Philadelphia.

New Air Link To China Is French Plan

Proposed plane route to connect French Indo-China with Yunnan Province.

The News

PARIS (AP)—The Government-subsidized Air France Company has announced plans to operate a line between French Indo-China and Yunnan Province, China.

The new air line is expected to give Generalissimo Chiang Kai-shek a route paralleling the Hanoi-Yunnan Railroad. The Japanese Government has complained that the French were shipping munitions to the Chinese Government along this line.

The new link will provide an all-air service between Chinese Government territory and western Europe.

Behind the News

By a Staff Correspondent of The Christian Science Monitor

CHUNGKING, China — The price of an airplane trip from Hong Kong to Chungking, China's new National Capital, is, among other things, a night's sleep. For there is now a pronounced aversion on the part both of the two commercial airline operators and the traveling public to daytime flights over territory in which Japanese airplanes are likely to be on patrol.

That caution dates back to the forcing down and machine-gunning of one big American-built transport last September with a dozen fatalities and minor incidents — happenings which first caused complete suspension of service, and which later allowed gradual resumption only under extraordinary conditions.

There are no "sleeper planes" in China nor have the airlines any facilities for night flights aside from excellent German radio direction-finding apparatus and the usual blind-flying equipment. The planes are multi-motored—China National Aviation Corporation, partly American-owned, has twin-engined craft, and Eurasia, partly German-owned, uses tri-motors—but while this decreases the prospect of forced landings there are no such emergency landing fields with light equipment as safeguard night flights elsewhere.

The answer is to take off sometime in the general neighborhood of 2 to 3 a. m. and make the necessary midway refuel landing after daylight has broken. Passengers are not told the precise take-off time, so they usually get out sometime after midnight and get what sleep they can in the plane.

Routes Carefully Chosen

The present writer started from Hong Kong at 3:22 a. m., the plane starting on a course by no means directly for the objective—a theoretical 750 miles into China's hinterland. The companies do not object to burning a little extra gasoline in the interest of taking what is regarded as a safe route. Originally the ticket had been printed to include provision of a free $10,000 (Chinese currency) life insurance policy, but one of the stamps read:

"In case of being unable to reach the destination due to air attack on the plane, this corporation is not responsible for any loss to the passengers or for taking them back to the starting station."

Coming near the landing the Chinese steward drew all the window blinds, evidently to prevent passenger observation of the landing field. But once the plane had landed and busy coolies had begun to pour gasoline into the tanks from five-gallon tins, there was no objection to the passengers' getting out for a look at things.

History of 4,200 Years

"Beautiful, aren't they?" I remarked to the German pilot as I looked at the still-misted volcanic hills, projecting up from the plain.

"To me they are not beautiful!" said the pilot, and one recalled how little margin there had been between the point of visibility and the actual hilltops as the plane coasted down.

Up again and riding the clouds at 3,500 meters with the sun shining, until after 10 a. m., when the plane began to coast down through the cloud layers again. Suddenly rocky hills, paddy fields, red soil of western China, and glimpses of broad rivers. The plane circled about over the Yangtze, slipping past the fantastic rock-clambering houses and endless stone steps of Chungking, stretching out on its peninsula to the intersection of the Yangtze and the Kialing. And an instant later the plane bumped on the stone runway on an island landing field.

Taxi Monopoly Clause Eliminated in Atlanta

Special to The Christian Science Monitor

ATLANTA, Ga.—The Atlanta City Council has revised the taxicab ordinance, eliminating the monopoly clause, and allowing a slight increase in taxi rates.

THE CHRISTIAN SCIENCE MONITOR

AN INTERNATIONAL DAILY NEWSPAPER

COPYRIGHT 1939 BY
THE CHRISTIAN SCIENCE PUBLISHING SOCIETY

BOSTON, FRIDAY, SEPTEMBER 1, 1939—VOL. XXXI, NO. 236

ATLANTIC EDITION—FIVE CENTS A COPY

British in Last Warning to Hitler; Warsaw Bombed, Poland Is Invaded; Duce Neutral; U. S. Hopes to Keep Out

Roosevelt Puts Army Needs At $1,000,000,000

President expected to ask Congress to appropriate sum for defense if extra session is called.

By a Staff Correspondent of The Christian Science Monitor

WASHINGTON, Sept. 1—President Roosevelt will ask Congress in special session, if and when it is called, to appropriate $1,000,000,000 for immediate strengthening and expansion of the American Army, it is reported by authoritative sources today.

Enlargements will not be in any sense for the purpose of paving the way for an American expeditionary force, it is emphasized in War Department circles here—such a denial already appears in preparatory recommendations which have been drawn up—but will be designed to put the American Army in the strongest possible defensive position.

While War Department plans for these enlargements, and the specific recommendations, actually antedated the recent war maneuvers and are not to be considered as a result of disappointment with those exercises, the general sense of dissatisfaction with the Army is expected to stimulate Congress's willingness to vote the increases.

Artillery Needed

Of the rough total of $1,000,000,000 which it is contemplated will be asked at once from Congress, some $317,000,000 is earmarked for guns and other artillery equipment, noitably for development of anti-tank guns and other such facilities in which the American Army is deficient. Another $300,000,000 is intended for supplies. Another objective is to provide for an increase in the Army Air Corps to 6,000 planes as speedily as American aviation plants, working three shifts a day, can produce them.

But in the main, the projected recommendations are to build up a more effective mobile defense force. With the 300,000-man American Army no wscattered over wide areas, a mobile force of only about 15,000 men is available for use in any single emergency spot, it is estimated in expert quarters. A far larger mobile force, with the best equipment, is desired.

Primarily, therefore, the proposed enlargements are a direct reply to European war threats, intended to prevent any possible aggressive acts in the Western Hemisphere.

Equipment Out of Date

Recommendations were worked out by the highest officials here, with the Navy Department taking a sympathetic interest, but not seeking any enlargements of its own because shipyards already are working to capacity. The Army, also, received generous appropriations from the first session of the Seventy-sixth Congress, but so far behind had its equipment and personnel slipped that it is expertly contended that a new appropriation of $1,000,000,000 will be no more than enough to meet new needs.

Already this year the Army receved totals of $803,788,614 from Congress — substantially all it asked for in regular session—divided between $508,789,824 in the regular Army supply bill for 1940, $223,398,047 in the supplementary Military Appropriations Act, $69,738,287 in the second deficiency bill for military appropriations, and an extra $1,862,456 for War Department military activities.

These funds were intended to raise the Army Air Corps to a strength of 5,500 planes by July 1, 1941; to spend almost as much in the Ordnance Department, strengthen seaboard defenses, and purchase other Army equipment. Flying fields and facilities, educational orders for manufacturing plants, and strengthening of the Panama garrison were included in the expansion program.

Rapid Progress Planned

Now, with this program barely started, the Army plans to march ahead more rapidly. Its new mobile defense force, the major purpose of the recommendations, would be able and expected to co-operate with the Navy in preventing the landing of any aggressive force in the Americas. It is aimed, therefore, at a potential long-range threat of fascist powers in Latin America.

Congress showed no reluctance at the last session in voting military expenditures, and a reasonable expectation would be that the special session, to be calied only in the event of war, would be equally generous.

This Changing World

Appears Today On Page 7

The Monitor Index

Friday, Sept. 1, 1939

Hitler 'Positive' In Answering U. S.

By the Associated Press

Washington, Sept. 1

Adolf Hitler sent President Roosevelt today his reply to the President's appeal for peace last week.

The Germany Embassy forwarded it to the State Department this morning and the Department was expected to make it public shortly.

A well-informed person described the reply as being "very positive."

V. F. W. Approves Neutrality Plan; Demands Congress

By a Staff Writer of The Christian Science Monitor

BOSTON, Sept. 1—Dual steps "to keep America out of war" were taken today by the National Convention of the Veterans of Foreign Wars. First the veterans passed an 18-point neutrality program. Then the convention unanimously called upon President Roosevelt to summon Congress immediately, lest "a diplomatic blunder" involve the United States in the present European turmoil.

The resolve calling upon the President to summon Congress came after Past Commander James E. Van Zandt, himself a United States Representative, warned that unless Congress has a voice in American relations at this time "a diplomatic blunder" might drag the United States into war against the wishes of the people.

Blames 1917 'Blunder'

Congressman Van Zandt, (R) of Pennsylvania, told the 40th Encampment of the V. F. W. in its closing session this morning that it was a diplomatic blunder by the Executive Branch of the Government which brought the United States into war in 1917. That mistake might now be repeated, he warned, unless Congress meets at once to direct America's policy for the people.

When the question was put to the convention the 2,000 veterans present, representing every State in the Union, thundered their approval.

A telegram asking the President to summon Congress was sent to the White House immediately by Eugene I. Van Antwerp, retiring National Commander of the V. F. W. from the First Corps' Armory in Boston where business sessions of the veterans' organization have been held.

On the 18-point neutrality program the veterans took the position that since the World War "did not advance the ideals of democracy" but rather brought about the totalitarian form of Government, it would be "infinitely better for the cause of civilization" as well as for the United States itself, for this Nation to keep out of today's or future war.

Briefly summarized, this program called for absolute neutrality on the part of the United States from wars in Europe, even to the extent of refusing protection to civilians and property. However, if such wars penetrated the zone of American influence prescribed by the Monroe Doctrine, that zone should be defended by arms if necessary. Finally, if the United States should become involved in a war to prevent European nations from getting a foothold in the Americas, then the profits should be taken out of any such war.

Pension Action

A resolution demanding outright pensions for all World War veterans 65 or over and more liberal pensions to the disabled stood approved by the Veterans of Foreign Wars today as the Fortieth Encampment, held in Boston throughout the week, came to a close.

The following officers were elected and installed before the encampment finally adjourned late this afternoon: Otis N. Brown of Greensboro, N. C., Commander-in-Chief, without opposition; Dr. Joseph C. Menendez of New Orleans, Senior Vice-Commander in Chief, also unopposed; Max Singer of Boston, Mass., Junior Vice-Commander in Chief; Robert B. Handy, Jr., of Washington, D. C., Quartermaster General; Robert Merrill of Shelby, Mont., Judge Advocate General; Dr. Samuel C. Bostic of New York City, Surgeon General; and the Rev. Daniel Monaghan of Milan, Ill., National Chaplain.

Roosevelt appeals to nations to refrain from bombing cities.

By a Staff Correspondent of The Christian Science Monitor

WASHINGTON, Sept. 1—President Roosevelt sincerely hopes and believes that the United States can stay out of war, he earnestly told his press conference today.

At the same time, he asked the co-operation of press and radio in sticking to fact and avoiding exaggerated or distorted news, to the end that public calm may prevail and what the President called the common sense of the American people should dominate.

After an almost sleepless night, interrupted early by news of the outbreak, the President outlined his activities with utmost calmness to his press conference.

Asked by a correspondent what his estimate was of the possibilities of the United States staying out of war, the President immediately authorized for quotation the following considered and solemnly pronounced statement:

> Only this: That I not only sincerely hope so, but I believe we can, and that every effort will be made by the Administration so to do.

Appeal to Nations

With the avoidance of American participation his first objective, the President already had sent an urgent appeal to five nations to refrain from air bombardment of civilian populations. The two facts are interconnected, for it has been asserted by many authorities that widespread bombing of open cities would inflame American public opinion and lead to involvement as nothing else would.

Within a few hours, the British and French Governments replied favorably to the President's note. The British Government declared that it would refrain from bombing civilians and unifortified cities as long as Britain's military adversaries likewise refrained. Handed to Cordell Hull, Secretary of State, by Lord Lothian, new British Ambassador, the note said:

> His Majesty's Government welcomes the weighty and moving appeal of the President of the United States against the bombardment from the air of civilian populations or of unfortified cities.
>
> Deeply impressed by the humanitarian consideration to which the President's message refers, it was already the settled policy of His Majesty's Government, should they become involved in hostilities, to refrain from such action and to confine bombardments to strictly military objectives upon the understanding that those same rules will be scrupulously observed by all their opponents.
>
> They had already concerted in detail with certain other governments the rules that in such an event they would impose upon themselves and make publicly known."

Awaits Developments

The President made plain he would not summon a special session of Congress or invoke the Neutrality Law until further events develop in Europe. Thus, the present position, as interpreted here, is that while German forces have invaded Poland—the President used this phrase—war has not yet been declared, and it is not entirely clear whether general war will result Events in Europe today and tomorrow, said Mr. Roosevelt, will have an important bearing on American policy.

The assumption here is that if a general war broke out, the President would call Congress into extra session, and would also apply the Neutrality Law pending its revision or repeal by Congress. But he is cautiously waiting for a declaration or its imminence be-

(Continued on Page 2, Column 7)

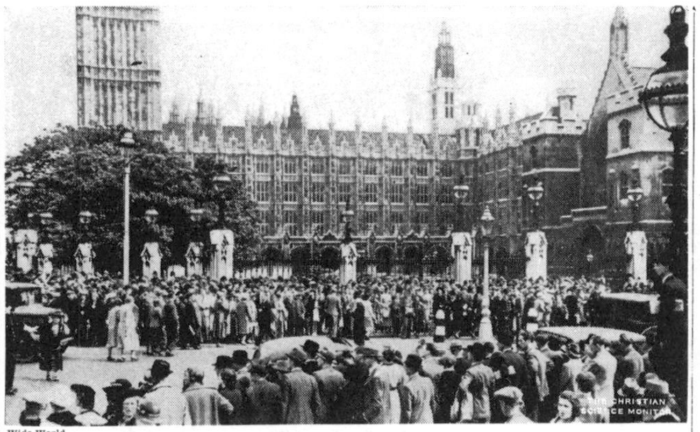

THE CHRISTIAN SCIENCE MONITOR

Wide World

Crowd Outside British Parliament Buildings Watches Members Arrive

This was the scene Aug. 31 as Prime Minister Neville Chamberlain reviewed the international crisis and secured passage of the bill giving the Government virtually complete dictatorial powers.

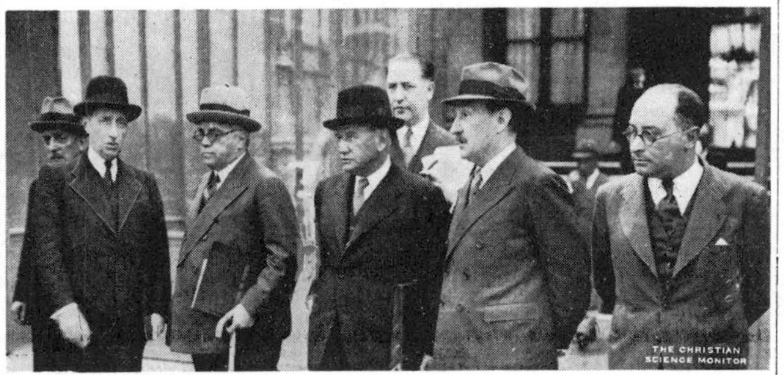

THE CHRISTIAN SCIENCE MONITOR

Wide World

Premier Edouard Daladier and Part of French Cabinet Leaving Palais de l'Élysée

Left to right: Dr. Henri Queuille, Minister of Agriculture, partly hidden; Paul Marchandeau, Minister of Justice; Albert Sarraut, Minister of the Interior; Premier Daladier; Raymond Patenôtre, Minister of National Economy and Production, partly hidden; Camille Chautemps, Vice-Premier in Charge of Co-ordination, and Jean Zay, Minister of Education.

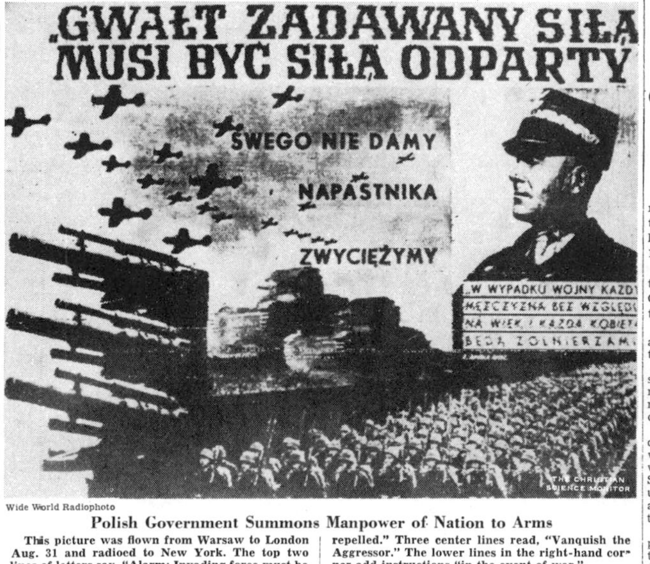

„GWAŁT ZADAWANY SIŁĄ
MUSI BYĆ SIŁĄ ODPARTY"
SWEGO NIE DAMY
NAPASTNIKA
ZWYCIĘŻYMY
„W WYPADKU WOJNY KAŻDY
MĘŻCZYZNA BEZ WZGLĘDU
NA WIEK I KAŻDA KOBIETA
BĘDĄ ŻOŁNIERZAMI
THE CHRISTIAN SCIENCE MONITOR

Wide World Radiophoto

Polish Government Summons Manpower of Nation to Arms

This picture was flown from Warsaw to London Aug. 31 and radioed to New York. The top two lines of letters say, "Alarm: Invading force must be repelled." Three center lines read, "Vanquish the Aggressor." The lower lines in the right-hand corner add instructions "in the event of war."

Hitler decrees Danzig a part of Reich and in 16 points demands vote on Corridor 'ownership'—Appoints line of succession; Göring and Hess next.

Britain today issued a last warning to Germany and France was reported preparing an ultimatum—both demanding an immediate halt in German military action against Poland.

This in response to Poland's plea for aid, brought the great powers to the verge of final action as Reich troops thrust across the Polish borders and Warsaw and other Polish cities felt the impact of German bombing.

The British Parliament appropriated £500,000,000 to carry on a war as yet undeclared. The Government took control of British railways.

Prime Minister Chamberlain placed the responsibility on the shoulders of Adolf Hitler in a vigorous address to Parliament.

But Italy—momentarily at least—remained neutral. A Cabinet meeting in Rome announced the Italians would refrain from starting military operations.

Hitler Praises Soviet Russia

Italy's action was interpreted as a sequel to Reichsführer Hitler's Reichstag address in which he complimented Italy but said Germany needed no outside aid. Hitler paid high tribute to Soviet Russia, where the Russo-German nonaggression pact was formally ratified by the Soviet parliament.

Danzig was decreed a part of the German Reich. The action was taken almost simultaneously with a 16-point demand by Hitler including immediate cession of the Free City and a "plebiscite" in the Polish Corridor.

Blockade of Gdynia Reported

Reports from the various agencies in Warsaw agree that German troops have advanced on to Polish soil at each side of the Corridor, also at a point between the Vistula and Deutsch Eylau in East Prussia southeast of the Corridor and northward through Zakopane, in Slovakia.

Apart from troop movements, the German Navy is stated to be blockading Poland's great port of Gdynia, while bombing raids from the air are reported to have been carried out by the Germans at Warsaw, Katowitz, Grodno, Cracow, and other points.

President Roosevelt, at press conference today, expressed the belief that the United States could stay out of the European conflict and he added "every effort will be made by the Administration so to do."

Awaiting the next turn of events in Europe, President Roosevelt today reserved his decision on whether to invoke the Neutrality Act or call Congress in session.

Germany Invades Polish Borders; Allies Mobilize

By the Associated Press

Reuters, British News Agency, reported from Berlin today that the German Supreme Command had issued this announcement at 11:40 A. M. (5:40 A. M., E. S. T.):

"In the fulfillment of their task to offer resistance to Polish force, German troops have crossed all the frontiers to counterattack.

"The air arm has also come into action. The Navy has taken over the protection of the Baltic."

The announcement, Reuters said, was broadcast by the German radio soon after it was announced that bombs had been dropped on Warsaw.

Subsequenaly the German High command issued a communiqué which said that the German troops which started from Pomerania Silesia and East Prussia were well under way toward their objectives, and that the Air Force is "controlling Polish air."

At the same time London dispatches stated that King George today signed an order in council for complete British Army, Navy, and Aviation mobilization and a similar order was made in France to take effect tomorrow.

The attitude of Britain's dominions was indicated, as far as Canada was concerned, when the Ottawa Government placed all militia and naval and air forces of the Dominion on an active basis under proclamation of the war measures act of 1914.

Swastika Flies

Prime Minister W. L. Mackenzie King announced that, as soon as Parliament assembles Sept. 7 in emergency session, it would be asked to authorize the Government to give the most effective co-operation to Great Britain in the present crisis.

The German radio announced that the League of Nations Commissioner for Danzig, Prof. Carl Burckhardt, and his staff left Danzig this morning.

The German swastika immediately was raised over the red brick house which had been head-

(Continued on Page 2, Column 3)

British Forces Called to Colors By King George

LONDON, Sept. 1 (AP)—(Passed by the British Censorship)—Great Britain and France have sent their last warning to Germany, Prime Minister Neville Chamberlain told the British Parliament tonight.

"If the reply to this last warning is unfavorable, and I do not suggest that it is likely to be otherwise," Mr. Chamberlain said, "his Majesty's Ambassador is instructed to ask for his passport."

His declaration was in answer to a plea from Poland that Britain take action in support to its pledge to give military assistance to the Poles.

Earlier King George VI signed an order for complete British Army, Navy: and Air Force mobilization.

The House of Commons approved a bill providing £500,000,000 to prosecute war, for defense, and for maintenance of public order.

The British Ministry of Transport took over the British railroads.

To Parliament Prime Minister Chamberlain said that Reichsführer Hitler "has not hesitated to plunge the world into misery in order to serve his own senseless ambitions." He added:

"We will stand at the bar of history, knowing that the responsibility for this terrible catastrophe rests on one man.

"Had there been the least desire, on the part of the German Government," he went on, "the crisis could have been averted.

"Last night the Polish Ambassador saw Her von Ribbentrop and expressed to him that they were willing to negotiate with Germany about their dispute on an equal basis.

"The German Government without any further warning crossed the Polish frontier at dawn."

Text of Prime Minister Chamberlain's declaration, Page 7.

Poles Ask Anglo-French Aid

LONDON, Sept. 1 (AP)—(Passed through the British Censorship)—The Polish Ambassador to London today notified Foreign Secretary Viscount Halifax that Poland invoked the British-Polish mutual assistance treaty on the grounds of German aggression.

The Polish Ambassador took the momentous step in a personal call on Lord Halifax.

[The mutual assistance pact, signed Aug. 25 by Great Britain and Poland, provides: "Should one of the contracting parties become engaged in hostilities with a European power in consequence of aggression by the latter against that contracting party, the other contracting party will at once give the contracting party engaged in hostilities all the support and assistance in its power."]

WASHINGTON, Sept. 1 (AP)—The Polish embassy today confirmed the report that Poland had invoked the aid of Great Britain and France.

A spokesman said:

"The Polish ambasadors to Great Britain and France have notified the respective governments that Germany has invaded Poland.

"In the consequences, the treaties of alliance between Poland and Great Britain and between Poland and France apply."

Exporters to Get Ample U. S. Credit

By a Staff Correspondent of The Christian Science Monitor

WASHINGTON, Sept. 1 — The first important announcement of what will be America's economic role in the event of a general European war has been made here. There will be no lack of credit for American exports to Europe in the event of a war, Jesse Jones, Federal Loan Administrator, declared at the White House, following a full canvass of the situation with President Roosevelt.

In effect Mr. Jones' statement was an advance intimation on the all-important part which the United States will play in supporting Great Britain and France if a war occurs. Although it was couched in general terms, and carefully avoided stressing the fact that in the event of war the markets open to American exporters will be confined to the democracies because of the British sea-control, Mr. Jones' statement revealed the direction in which the Administration is thinking. He explained that the RFC has vast unused credit which could be extended to business and industry. He added significantly that neither the RFC nor the Export-Import Bank are subject to the Johnson Act, which forbids purchase or sale of bonds of nations which are in default on their obligations to the American Government.

Thus, in brief informal words in the foyer of the White House, Mr. Jones outlined a course which may very well make the United States the economic ally of France and Great Britain, to all intents and purposes, from the moment war breaks out.

Always using the general term "Europe" Mr. Jones explained that the export of goods there could be financed through Export-Import Bank credits to individual exporters. He added quickly, however, that he did not think there would be severe pressure on government agencies for such service, but that nevertheless the RFC is ready to aid business and industry if the need arises.

Mr. Jones indicated that he thought the immediate requirement of credit, if any were forthcoming, would be to finance farm surplus exports. However, the credit was available, he said, for industrial products also although in no circumstances would it assist or underwrite export of war materials.

The Federal Administrator explained that public corporations established by Congress are specifically exempt from the Johnson Act provisions.

COPYRIGHT 1940 BY
THE CHRISTIAN SCIENCE PUBLISHING SOCIETY

BOSTON, MONDAY, JUNE 24, 1940—VOL. XXXII, NO. 177

* ATLANTIC EDITION | THREE CENTS Greater Boston Newsstands | FIVE CENTS Elsewhere

Mexico Plans Arms Curb During Election Period; Benefit Helps Red Cross

The World's Day—At a Glance
June 24, 1940

Mexico to Curb Sale of Arms

MEXICO, D. F. (AP)—Sale of arms and the carrying of weapons will be prohibited during the two weeks preceding and following the national elections July 7 under an order issued by the Ministry of National Defense.

Hollywood Benefit Raises $79,000 for Red Cross

HOLLYWOOD, Calif. (AP)—Red Cross officials reported they had received $79,000 from the movie and radio star benefit radiocast on June 22. Howard Hughes, flier, was one of the largest contributors, giving $25,000. Seven thousand persons were crowded on two film studio sound stages where the show was held.

War Summary: Italo-French Armistice Awaited

France's negotiations with Italy proceeded apace today with expectations of prompt conclusion of the Italo-French armistice. [Details: Page 5.]

Terms dictated by the Reich virtually transform France into a passive German ally, permit the Nazis to occupy more than half the country, and would demobilize both the French army and fleet. [Details: Pages 1 and 4.]

Remnants of French resistance were being organized to aid Britain as the London Government formally dealt with the General-in-Exile Charles de Gaulle. [Details: Pages 1 and 4.]

Britain struck from the air against Germany's Krupp plants at Essen, claiming explosions. On land, French resistance faced Italian and German onslaughts in the hours preceding armistice. Warfare spread rapidly to the Mediterranean and Africa with land raids against Ethiopia, and widespread air raids. [Details: Page 4.]

Turkey's concern over possible Italian occupation of French-mandated Syria and seizure of rich Mosul oil fields in northern Iraq was reflected in reports that Iraq Government officials would confer with Turkish officials in Ankara.

King Farouk and party leaders discussed plans for a new Cabinet following acceptance of the resignation of Premier Ali Maher Pasha's Cabinet.

Soviet denial was attached to rumors that Turkey's Foreign Minister, Sukru Saracoglu, was going to Moscow for talks.

United States Ambassador Joseph P. Kennedy appealed to Americans to contribute to their Red Cross, stating that "everything indicates England will be called upon to meet the greatest siege in the history of man."

American refugees from France were aided by Spanish waiving of visa formalities for from 500 to 1,000 persons en route to the United States through Spain.

Estonia's New Government announced its intention to dismiss dishonest state employees, dissolve Parliament, guarantee rights of minorities. The Government was re-formed under Soviet guidance.

The Duke and Duchess of Windsor dined with Sir Samuel Hoare, British Ambassador to Spain, in Madrid.

Belgium's Refugee Government has no intentions, as rumored, of abandoning the fight against Germany, Henri Jaspar, Belgian Cabinet Minister, declared.

At sea Britain announced the torpedoing and sinking of its 11,000-ton freighter Wellington Star, while Britons acclaimed British naval and air attacks which damaged the 26,000-ton German battleship Scharnhorst. [Details: Page 5.]

Appeals Court Affirms Browder Conviction

NEW YORK (AP)—The United States Circuit Court of Appeals today affirmed the conviction of Earl Russel Browder, General Secretary of the Communist Party in the United States, of willfully using a passport obtained by false statements. Browder was sentenced to four years imprisonment and fined $2,500 upon conviction by a Federal jury last Jan. 22.

Mexican Pledges Aid If U. S. Attacked

NEW YORK (AP)—The full support of Mexico should the United States be invaded was pledged by Dr. Francisco Najera, Mexican Ambassador to this country.

"Any attack on America by a non-American nation concerns the entire continent," he told reporters. "If the United States is invaded, we will stand by it."

In Washington: CCC Enrollment Eased

The Civilian Conservation Corps hereafter will enroll sons of parents not on relief, if the boys are unemployed and actually need jobs.

Better employment conditions have reduced applications for CCC work, a spokesman said, and therefore it was decided to drop the previous requirement that some come from relief families.

Army Role for Noncombatants

By a Staff Correspondent of The Christian Science Monitor

LONDON—Formation of a Noncombatant Corps so that conscientious objectors may join the Army in a nonfighting capacity, is announced by the War Office here. Entry into the Corps is limited to those who have been registered by military tribunals as liable to be called up for service, but for reasons of conscience to be employed only in noncombatant duties. No arms will be issued to the members of the Corps.

The nature of the training and duties, as indicated in Army Council instructions, is that they will receive foot drill without arms, physical training, passive air defense, and antigas instruction, lessons in decontamination and special duties, including cooking and clerical work. Training is to be supervised by officers and noncommissioned officers of the recently formed Pioneer Corps.

Work of the corps is to be on the construction and maintenance of hospitals, barracks, camps, railways, roads, and recreation grounds; the care of baths and laundries; passive air defense; quarrying, timber cutting, filling of trenches; and duties not involving the handling of "military material of an aggressive nature."

The formation of such a noncombatant Corps is seen here as a necessary complement of the tribunal system for dealing with conscientious objectors, which becomes more necessary now that wider measures of general conscription—of persons and of wealth—are being introduced.

Experience of the tribunals has been that there are many men, especially since the intensification of the war effort, who are anxious to do service that will directly help the nation, but which is genuinely noncombatant.

Return Is Sought Of Wright Airplane

MIAMI, Fla., June 24 (AP)—Dr. Ralph Greene, Eastern Air Lines medical director, disclosed June 22 he had suggested the removal of the Wright brothers' first successful airplane from England.

Dr. Greene requested Senator Claude Pepper (D) of Florida to enlist President Roosevelt in an effort to persuade Orville Wright to give his permission for the return of "this priceless treasure."

Mr. Wright, incensed because the Smithsonian Institution listed the Langley steam-driven airplane as the first heavier-than-air machine capable of flight, rejected all previous proposals for bringing the plane back from a British museum. The Langley plane crashed into the Potomac when launched.

Workers and the Workshop

International; © Harris & Ewing

Drafters of the New Republican Platform

Upper: The drafting Subcommittee of the Resolutions Committee of the Republican Party (left to right in the rear), Judge Thomas J. Guthrie of Des Moines, Iowa; Henry P. Fletcher of Rhode Island; O. G. Saxon of Connecticut; Herbert Hyde of Oklahoma City, Okla.; (seated, left to right), Robert Williamson of Augusta, Maine; Alf M. Landon of Kansas, the 1936 Republican standard-bearer; George Wharton Pepper of Pennsylvania, Chairman of the Subcommittee, and C. B. Smith of Michigan. Inset: Gov. Harold E. Stassen of Minnesota, keynoter and Temporary Chairman of the Convention. Lower: Front and east side view of the new Philadelphia Municipal Auditorium, which is Convention Hall for this convention.

Elephant Turns Sphinx: Philadelphia Asks 'Who?'

By J. Roscoe Drummond
Staff Correspondent of The Christian Science Monitor

CONVENTION HALL, Philadelphia, June 24—In an atmosphere made anxious and tense by the gravity of the war, the twenty-second National Convention of the Republican Party was called to order at 11 o'clock this morning in this City which gave birth to American Constitutional Government.

At a time when democracy is being challenged and crushed in many parts of the world, 1,000 delegates from every American State and possession are gathered here in this massive Convention Hall to perform a vital function of free government; to make a free choice of the Party's nominee for President of the United States.

There is every evidence here that it will be a free choice, for as John Hamilton, Chairman of the Republican National Committee, formally opened the organizing session of the Convention, it was evident that the most certain thing about this assembly is that the nomination is uncertain, that no candidate is yet assured of the necessary majority, that the balance of power clearly rests with a large and decisive bloc of unpledged and uncommitted delegates.

Indeed the most significant and obvious fact about this 1940 convention is that it is the most completely open, tremendously uncertain, and wholly unbossed convention in Republican history. It is not an exaggeration to say that the national party leaders and the most influential party bosses are waiting to find out where the delegates are going to jump in the hope that they can step in at the last minute and lead them.

This plus the fact that at least 11 names will be put in nomination with appropriate oratory, second-ing-speeches, demonstrations, and hurrahs, means that Philadelphia is likely to witness and the nation is likely to be following one of the longest of Republican conventions.

Philadelphia Enthusiastic

But Philadelphia is ready and enthusiastic. Even before the important business of the week is really under way, this vast, flag-bedecked, elephant-dotted auditorium is filled to overflowing by more than 15,000 persons, of whom nearly 2,000 are delegates and alternates, another 1,000 are newspaper and radio correspondents, and the remainder a part of the 100,000 visitors who have poured into this City either to watch this great spectacle of democracy at work or to play some small part in it.

It is an audience which is excited and expressive, which is plainly looking forward to all the band-playing, aisle-parading exhibitions which decorate the surface of national political gatherings. But beneath all this is a mood of tenseness which quiets and chastens the delegates, a mood which recognizes that flag-waving, name-calling, carnival politics has little place in a world torn by strife and will have little popularity with a Nation which today feels the ominous peril of war itself.

Although the Convention will have headline matters before it for the next three days—Gov. Harold E. Stassen's keynote speech tonight, former President Herbert Hoover's address Tuesday night, and action on the national platform Wednesday—virtually all interest continues to be focused upon the prospective nominee.

For the first time since 1923, when Frank O. Lowden and

Continued on Page 2, Column 7

Intimate Message From Philadelphia

Convention Is Uncertain and Hence Interesting—Strange Stories Are Appearing—Hopeful Looks on Familiar Faces of Faithful

By the Convention Bureau of The Christian Science Monitor

Philadelphia

This is in many ways the most uncertain and by that token the most interesting national convention for 20 years. In only one of the conclaves held since 1920 was the outcome so problematical, and that was the tedious Democratic convention of 1924.

Today it is not merely uncertain. Large issues are at stake: The orientation of the Party on world affairs, the task of choosing a nominee strong enough to defeat the prospective candidacy of President Roosevelt, the very survival of the Republican Party, which could ill support in its present form four more years in the wilderness.

This convention marks the revolt of the little man, but a state leader can be certain of his delegation. Though Pennsylvania's mighty phalanx of 72 votes, supposedly controlled by Joseph E. Pew, is held nominally for Gov. Arthur H. James, it may split off at any time a sizeable bloc for Wendell L. Willkie. Though Alf M. Landon of Kansas has been frankly critical of Mr. Willkie, his own delegation is in open and democratic revolt and may give a good share of its votes to the utilities man.

Though Representative Joseph E. Martin, Jr., has supposedly great influence over the Massachusetts delegation, and is not yet friendly to Mr. Willkie, the Bay State group will certainly give much of its total to him.

Prior Pledges Undergo Some Hammering

These three cases merely illustrate the problems of party leaders in every State. Mr. Willkie said last night that he has promises of votes from all but three of the 48 States. He expects to start small and build up. A barrage of letters and telegrams from his supporters is hammering at individual delegates. These individuals are much impressed in many cases, and are breaking away from the old-line leaders trying to hold them for their prior pledges. In other instances, delegates resent the pressure and assert it reminds them of the holding-company fight in Congress—a bad memory for Mr. Willkie.

Seldom was there a convention of more conflicting reports. You expect delegate-zealots to tell different and inconsistent stories. But newspapermen and impartial watchers have caught the contagion. One man thinks that "Dewey can't be stopped." Another says: "Dewey is all washed up." A third insists: "I can't see big Willkie thing at all. Wall Street runs straight down the Mississippi River, and he will get hardly a single vote west of it." A fourth says: "Willkie has strength everywhere." Old-line politicians insist that the Taft organization is the best here, but it delegate strength it is hampered by inclusion of many Southern delegations which are artificially assembled. Nevertheless the Taft group operates very smoothly and professionally. They know how to do these things well in Ohio.

Any convention is bound to have one sensational newspaper story; this is likely to have many, but it began well Sunday night with a copyrighted piece in the Philadelphia Inquirer asserting that Governor Landon had been in conference with Senator Burton K. Wheeler, Democrat of Montana, who was to become either presidential or vice-presidential nominee, with either John L. Lewis or Governor Landon as a running mate. Governor Landon categorically denied the story as "absurd and ridiculous."

Nevertheless, a good deal of mystery hovered around the Kansan's movements. He was believed by many of his friends to have left town during most of Sunday, and when he returned and dined with a group of them—including this writer—he said little of his activities. However, Governor Landon had helped bring to a successful conclusion the drafting of an agreed plank on foreign policy in the face of resolute extremism on both the isolationist and the to-the-Allies ends.

Events of Future Will Shape Policies

What most middle-of-the-roaders worked for was a platform that would leave it up to the nominee to shape his policy in coming weeks and months according to events which will have taken place. It is grimly speculated that the issue of aid to the Allies—or Ally—may be academic by October, or that on the other hand an antiwar pledge may then run afoul of the Monroe Doctrine. The draft, it was hoped, would leave the way open for future decisions.

This is the convention of the individual delegate. Never has he been so much wooed. Parties and perquisites are flung in his and his wife's way. Philadelphia is being immensely hospitable, but so are many of the prospective 11 men whose names will be presented. The hotel lobbies are hives of high-pressure political salesmanship. Campaign buttons have swollen until some of them are six or eight inches across. There is free food and drink in one candidate's headquarters, but despite that he won't get many votes. Lobbyists and old political ghosts are everywhere. "Big Bill" Shearer of Geneva fame is striding about the hotel lobbies, and so are the representatives of almost every interest, making contacts on behalf of their employers. Faces once familiar in Washington but unseen here for these eight or ten years gone have turned up here, looking just the same as ever.

There are hopeful looks on the familiar faces. For these Republican faithful haven't given up the fight yet, even if they are uncertain about their nominee. They know for sure that he will be a vigorous man, a two-fisted political warrior, and they are almost sure—as they sniff the hope-scented atmosphere of the smoke-filled rooms—that maybe life begins, again, in forty.

French and Italians Negotiating; Europe Enters Upon New Epoch; Roosevelt Speeds Defense Bills

Naval situation caused by French Armistice is carefully studied by Washington.

Richard L. Strout
Staff Correspondent of The Christian Science Monitor

WASHINGTON, June 24—President Roosevelt returned to the White House today to sign bills appropriating billions of dollars for the emergency preparedness program and to discuss with State Department advisers the New World situation created by the drastic armistice terms imposed by victorious Germany on prostrate France.

There was no immediate comment here on the peace terms but the Administration was concerned in the possibility that the French warships might be added to the German and Italian fleets and that the British armada might also later call on fall into the hands of the axis powers.

President Roosevelt frankly contemplated such a possibility in comments before leaving Hyde Park and declared that the United States may have to shift its whole Navy to the Atlantic, leaving the Pacific dominated by Japan.

Comparison of Navies

President Roosevelt quoted naval advisers to the effect that a victory by the Axis powers which gave them the French and British fleets would leave the United States greatly outnumbered in vessels. He showed this by a simple arithmetical formula presenting the world's relative naval strength in weighted index numbers. The fleets are rated:

United States	100
Great Britain	100
Japan	100
France	50
Italy	50
Germany	33

Navy Chief Interest

A German–Italian fleet of 83, plus the French fleet would give the Axis powers a total of 133 under this calculation. If the worst came to the worst and the British Navy was added to this total, the American fleet would be faced with desperate odds in the case of eventualities. Officials here, accordingly, watched with anxious inter-

Continued on Page 6, Column 2

[map]

By a Staff Artist

France Under Terms of Hitler Armistice

More than half of France is to be occupied by Germany under terms of the armistice. The occupied section is shown shaded on the map. Terms include full demobilization of the French armed forces, including a demand for disarmament of the fleet. Germany, according to terms as reported from London, reserves the right to cancel the armistice if France does not fulfill all its obligations. Nazis impose severe terms upon France: Page 4.

Why Did France Fall? Some Reasons Listed

By Mallory Browne
European Editorial Manager of The Christian Science Monitor
and former head of its Paris Bureau

LONDON, June 24—Why did France collapse?

Why has the French Government at Bordeaux, headed by Marshal Henri Pétain, hero of Verdun and author of the immortal "They shall not pass," signed the armistice dictated by Reichsführer Hitler?

What happened to the French Republic and its great army?

Although the full answer to these questions must await the verdict of history, it is important for Britain—and perhaps also for America—to know the answer now.

Unless democracy can learn from the hard lessons of experience and

Some Conclusions

From a careful inquiry into recent events in France, from close questioning of many who recently have come to Britain from France, as well as from a background of seven years' experience there, it is possible to draw the following tentative conclusions:

1. The failure of France is due primarily to the failure of its democratic political institutions. It is not the failure of democracy. It is not the failure of the French people.

But it is the failure of a political system to prove its power at a great moment in human history to rise to the occasion and meet the merciless onslaught of dictatorial militarism.

It is the leadership, or rather lack of great leadership, which let France down—political leadership primarily, military leadership secondarily.

When the records are examined, it will be seen that there were many younger generals both in France and in Britain who foresaw exactly the form which the German attack would take and who tried in vain to get their Governments to organize proper measures to meet it. But the inertia and short-sightedness of the politicians in both countries stifled these warnings.

Initiative Sapped

2. The passive acceptance of the theory that France was secure behind the Maginot Line, and excessive devotion to the doctrine of defensive strategy—these sapped the initiative and vigor of many members of the French High Command.

Undoubtedly there were some who were either "fifth columnists"—traitors—or else were guilty of an incompetence scarcely less criminal.

3. The French poilu—and even officers in the lower ranks

Continued on Page 6, Column 4

One France has gone and another is in the making after yielding to Hitler's terms.

ROME, June 24 (AP)—France's armistice delegates, carrying new instructions from the Bordeaux Government, met the Italians today for the second time to negotiate terms to restore peace to the beaten French.

Fascist leaders believed an agreement would be reached today.

Fighting between the Germans and the French is not to stop until six hours after notification has been received by the German command of the French-Italian armistice.

By a Staff Correspondent of The Christian Science Monitor

LONDON, June 24—A new epoch in the history of France—and therefore of Europe—has begun with signature of the armistice by the Bordeaux Government, and the simultaneous setting up of a French National Committee in London.

The importance of these two events, considered together, can hardly be overestimated. Whatever the immediate future may hold, they mean that one France has died and another France is born.

That France, which is of the past, has agreed to give over more than half of its territory to German occupation. A summary of the Reich's terms, issued by the British Ministry of Information, also discloses that complete demobilization of France would be required, including the surrender of its Fleet, the actual disposition of which is not yet clear.

Right of Denouncement Kept

But perhaps the most striking provision in the terms is that paragraph which would permit Germany to denounce the Armistice and do as the leaders of the Reich wish in the event that France does not fulfill its obligations. And patently it is Germany which intends to remain the judge of that fulfillment.

As to the new France, it is too soon and the war outlook is too clouded, to say what form it will take or just when it will emerge. But no one who knows France can doubt for an instant this essential fact: The signing of the armistice can only mean the prelude to a fresh start for France.

It is France's darkest hour before the dawn. Will this dawn come from the French National Committee formed here by Gen. Charles de Gaulle with the agreement and support of the British Government?

In any case it is already clear that General de Gaulle's provisional committee has rallied to its support military commanders, and in some cases civil authorities, as well as overseas France.

Pledges of Resistance Given

Syria, where a French force of several hundred thousand is still under arms, has proclaimed its determination to fight on.

In Tunis, the Resident General has announced that he intends to continue the struggle.

In Morocco, Senegal and the Cameroons assurances of continued resistance have been received.

Algeria, unlike Morocco and Tunisia, is a French Department and politically is almost an integral part of France. Its strategic, economic and agricultural importance is immense. Unless it joins France's other North African possessions in continuing the fight, their will to resist is likely to prove vain.

The other vital question is the fate of the French fleet. The Nazis have demanded as one of the terms of the armistice that it be collected in specified ports, demobilized and

Continued on Page 6, Column 7

French Colonies to Carry On

LONDON, June 24 (AP)—The Evening Star, liberal newspaper, said today that it was being strongly urged in "influential quarters" that full British nationality be offered at once to all units of the French army, navy, air force, and merchant marine.

LONDON, June 24 (AP)—The British Government has announced it has received pledges of support from the French colonial empire, determined to carry on the war against Germany despite the armistice signed at Compiègne Forest.

The following statement was issued yesterday on the French-German armistice:

"The signature of the armistice by the French Government brings to an end the organized resistance of the French forces at home. In the French colonial empire, however, there are encouraging signs that a more robust spirit prevails.

"In Syria, General Mittelhauser, the French Commander-in-Chief, has proclaimed the determination of the French forces to fight on.

In Indo-China, the Governor-General has declared that he will not lower his flag. In Tunis, the Resident General is firm in his intention to continue the struggle.

"In Morocco, Senegal, the Cameroons and Jibuti, assurances of loyal support have been received from the military or civil authorities.

"His Majesty's Government are prepared to make financial arrangements to enable the French colonial empire to play its part. As stated by the Prime Minister, the British aim is the complete restoration of the metropolitan and overseas territory of France."

THE CHRISTIAN SCIENCE MONITOR

AN INTERNATIONAL DAILY NEWSPAPER

COPYRIGHT 1940 BY THE CHRISTIAN SCIENCE PUBLISHING SOCIETY

BOSTON, WEDNESDAY, NOVEMBER 6, 1940—VOL. XXXII, NO. 291

**ATLANTIC EDITION | THREE CENTS Greater Boston Newsstands | FIVE CENTS Elsewhere

Roosevelt Elected for Third Term; Willkie Urges End to Antagonisms; Saltonstall Leads in Close Contest

Massachusetts Returns In U. S.-State Contests; Nazis Claim Heavy Sinkings

The World's Day—At a Glance

Nov. 6, 1940

Returns in Massachusetts

President
(1,698 out of 1,810 precincts)

Willkie (R)	869,248
Roosevelt (D)*	981,571

Senator
(1,577 precincts)

Parkman (R)	727,569
Walsh (D)*	914,394

Governor
(1,782 precincts)

Saltonstall (R)*	975,894
Dever (D)	969,007

Lieutenant Governor
(1,639 precincts)

Cahill (R)*	879,826
Gallagher (D)	807,196

Secretary of State
(1,639 precincts)

Cook (R)*	941,448
Foley (D)	737,733

State Treasurer
(1,639 precincts)

Hurley (R)*	855,996
Donahue (D)	768,462

State Auditor
(1,639 precincts)

Wood (R)*	806,232
Buckley (D)	819,571

Attorney General
(1,639 precincts)

Bushnell (R)	859,766
Brennan (D)	802,550

*Incumbent

War Summary: Nazis Estimate Allied Sea Losses

At sea Germany claimed that Allied merchant shipping losses had reached a total of 7,162,200 tons since the war's outbreak. [Details: Page 6.]

British bombers started 30 fires among petroleum tanks at Germany's naval base at Emden, and damaged shipyards at Bremerhaven and Bremen, according to the British Air Ministry.

Lone German bombers gave London its longest night raid, but did not attack on a large scale. The industrial Midlands and Eastern Scotland shared the brunt of these attacks.

Swiss protest over alleged violation of its territory by British bombers during the night, was directed to London. The Swiss High Command announced that, beginning tomorrow, Switzerland would be blacked out every night after 10 o'clock in an effort to hinder the movement of foreign aircraft.

Hull Hails Indorsement of Foreign Policy

Washington (AP)—Secretary of State Hull said today the nation now could go forward in the "firm continuance of those foreign policies" which he said were given "nationwide approval" in yesterday's election. [Details: Page 2.]

Workmen Build Bleachers for Inauguration

Washington (AP)—All the votes weren't counted yet, but workmen hammered and sawed away today, building wooden bleachers for the Jan. 20 inauguration on the east steps of the Capitol. With 11,000 spectator seats to put up, the contractor declined to take a chance on the weather, got an early start.

Popular Democrats Lead in Puerto Rico

San Juan, Puerto Rico (AP)—The Popular Democratic Party, a new force in Puerto Rican politics, was leading this morning in five of the island's seven Senatorial districts, but the Republican-Socialist coalition which heretofore has held a big majority in the Legslature refused to admit defeat. The Popular Democrats claimed they had elected 12 of the 19 Senators, 20 of 37 Representatives and a new Resident Commissioner to Washington. Coalition leaders, however, insisted they would retain power by a small margin.

In Africa: Italians Claim Advance

Egyptian campaign showed signs of renewed activity today when Italians claimed they had driven more than 30 miles to the southeast of Sidi Barrani, their outpost along the coast, in pursuit of British units.

British airmen carried out reconnaissances over Libya. Bombing expeditions, partly undertaken by South African airmen, raided Eritrea, Italian Somaliland, and other points.

In the Balkans: Greeks Reported in Koritza

Greek Advance in Albania was reported to have virtually encircled Koritza, important Italian base. One report said that the Greeks had actually entered the city. [Details: Page 1.]

Defending armies of the Greeks appeared to be holding the Italians elsewhere all along the line.

British raiders were said to have bombed Naples for the third time.

College Mates Meet in Senate

By a Staff Correspondent of The Christian Science Monitor

WASHINGTON, Nov. 6—Two men who were college roommates have apparently won their election to the United States Senate the same year. They are Ralph O. Brewster (R), elected ot the Senate in the Maine September election, and Harold Burton (R), leading in the Senate race in Ohio.

The two were roommates at Bowdoin College, Maine, during most of their college career. Mr. Brewster was elevated this fall from Congressman ot Senator and Mr. Burton has been serving as Mayor of Cleveland.

In this case both men ran on the Republican ticket, unlike Wendell L. Willkie and Paul V. McNutt, who were fraternity brothers at Indiana University, but who have been on opposite sides of the fence politically.

The Monitor Index

Wednesday, Nov. 6, 1940

Greeks Enter Italian Base In Albania?

Capture of thousands of Italians is reported by mountaineer troops in area of Koritza.

SALONIKA, Greece, Nov. 6 (AP)—The Greeks were reported in frontier advances today to have entered the Albanian city of Koritza, Italian military base for the Greek offensive, and to have captured thousands of Italians.

LONDON, Nov. 6 (AP)—Britain has advanced £5,000,000 in credits to Greece for war supplies, the Foreign Office announced today.

ATHENS, Nov. 6 (AP)—Fortifications on a range of hills guarding Koritza, Albanian base for the Italian drive into Macedonia, were reported today to have been captured by Greek mountain troops after fierce hand-to-hand fighting.

Retreating Italian forces were shelled by their own tanks, the Greek High Command declared.

A communiqué said many Italian prisoners were taken in the battle, and artillery pieces, howitzers, and machine guns were seized in the abandoned fortifications.

Meanwhile, the City of Koritza itself was shelled almost continuously by Greek Alpine gunners on heights previously taken in bayonet charges.

The Greek Air Force, aided by British planes, attacked Italian troop and supply positions in Albania, while in Greece the civilian casualties from Italian air raids the first nine days of the war were counted at almost 1,000.

Greek planes were said to have bombed airdromes at Koritza and Argyrocastron, Albania, destroying some Italian planes which were on the ground.

The Greek communiqué blamed Italian planes for the bombing yesterday of the Yugoslav town of Bitolj, pust across the frontier from the Greek-Albanian battlefront.

The Greeks declared their lines were holding firm in western Macedonia, where the Italians are driving at Florina, and in Epirus, along the north bank of the Kalamas River, barring the Italian push toward Ioannina.

Naples Raided

ROME, Nov. 6 (AP)—The Italian High Command reported today that British warplanes had bombed the area around Naples during the night, killing 14 persons and injuring 10.

The raid was the third in less than a week on Naples, center of many important Italian war industries.

On the northern flank of the Greek war front, the High Command said, "Italian forces yesterday repelled Greek attacks between Lake Presba and Kapestica Pass after violent fighting.

The Italians asserted that their air force had heavily bombed the station at Florina cutting a railway

Continued on Page 7, Column 6

Saltonstall Leads in Close Contest

Democrats also defeat G. O. P. governors in Rhode Island and Connecticut.

The Associated Press at 3 p. m. claimed that Gov. Leverett Saltonstall led by 10,000 votes with on. five precincts yet to be heard from.

A recount was indicated.

Gov. Leverett Saltonstall leads for re-election—but just barely.

In a sizzling last-minute fight that developed unexpectedly early this afternoon, hours after his victory had been generally acknowledged, Governor Saltonstall, Republican, found his lead over Attorney General Paul A. Dever, Democratic aspirant for the gubernatorial chair, nibbled down to, at one time, a scant 4,400 votes.

The latest returns, with 28 precincts yet to be heard from, gives Saltonstall 975,894 votes; Dever 969,007, a scant 6,887 lead for the Governor.

Just as the Governor was receiving congratulations at the State House this morning—his lead having reached 30,000—the wires began to bring in reports that took first 1,000, then 200, then another 2,000 from his majority.

The Governor and his aides awaited the news which was hours in coming. Impatiently, demands were sent for news as to what districts were yet to be heard from. Were they normally Republican or Democratic?

No one knew. Some were in Quincy, others in Fall River. They might mean anything since these industrial cities have districts that run both ways, and strongly.

Shortly before one this afternoon, the lead was cut to the 4,400 figure. Then, gradually it began to climb. Close political observers were of the opinion he would win; but a recount seemed likely regardless of the outcome.

Two other Republican Governors, William H. Vanderbilt of Rhode Island and Raymond E. Baldwin of Connecticut, had already been swept under by the Democratic trend which duplicated 1936 in leaving only Maine and Vermont true to the region's once traditional Republicanism. J. Howard McGrath, former U. S. District Attorney, was elected Governor of Rhode Island, and Robert A. Hurley, Commissioner of Public Works, was chosen Governor of Connecticut.

The President's plurality in New England was cut 100,000 below his record of fours years ago.

Democrats Gain Seats

Democrats gained six seats in the lower House of Congress, picking them up in Rhode Island and Connecticut.

Details of New England elections: Pages 13, 14, 15 and 16.

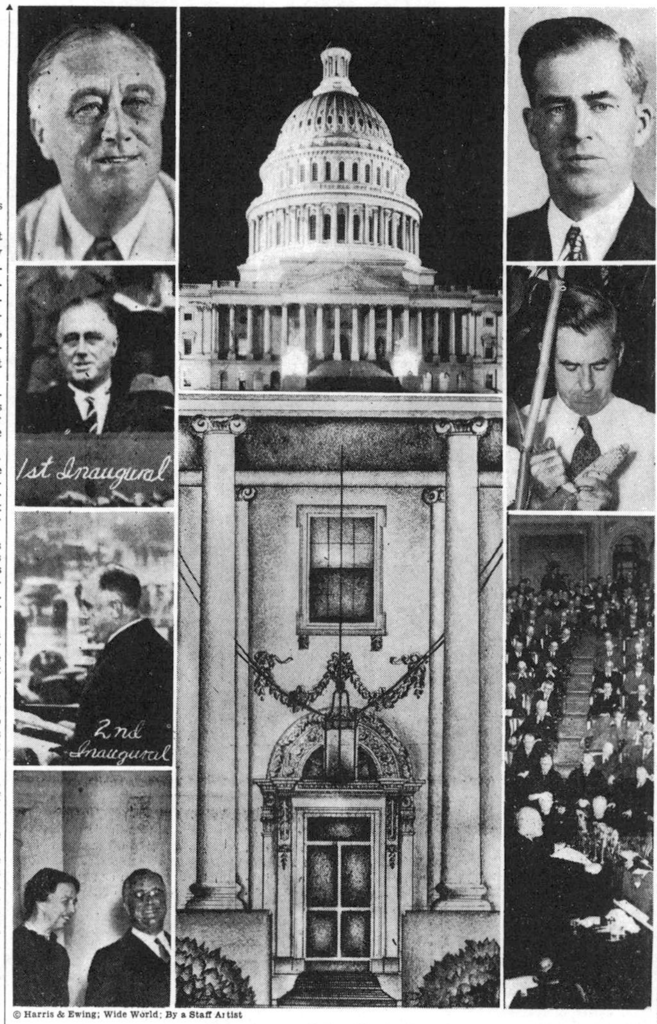

© Harris & Ewing; Wide World; By a Staff Artist

Government Is by All the People

President Roosevelt again heads the Government but the Capitol still looms large.

Upper left and right: The President today and Vice-President-Elect Henry A. Wallace, former Secretary of Agriculture.

Left row shows President Roosevelt in different inaugurals and at bottom with Mrs. Roosevelt receiving as hosts at the White House.

Middle of right row shows Mr. Wallace inspecting an ear of corn. He is a noted specialist in corn culture.

Lower right: President Roosevelt addresses a joint session of the Senate and House and the Supreme Court in the Senate Chamber on the occasion of the 150th anniversary of the Constitution.

The door to the White House and the Capitol Dome hold the center of the picture, symbolizing the co-ordinate branches of the Government.

Roosevelt Elected for Third Term

Roosevelt sweep also increases Democratic control in the House; War big issue.

By J. Roscoe Drummond
Staff Writer of The Christian Science Monitor

Franklin Delano Roosevelt stands elected today as the first President in American history to be chosen to serve three terms in the White House.

With returns still coming in, it is indicated that Mr. Roosevelt will amass an electoral vote of 468 to 63 for Wendell L. Willkie, the Republican nominee whose dynamic campaign helped to produce a record-breaking national ballot. Mr. Roosevelt has either won or is leading in 39 States, Mr. Willkie in 9.

There is every evidence that the leadership of the President has brought unexpected strength to the Democratic Party throughout the country, has in large part reversed the Republican trend which showed itself significantly in 1938 and has guaranteed his Administration effective control of Congress during the next two years.

Democrats Gain in House

The Democrats are actually making a net gain in their numerical strength in Congress. In the face of Republican predictions that, irrespective of the Presidency, they would add at least 50 seats in the House and perhaps acquire control, the Democrats increased their already large House majority by nine members. The net turn-over in the Senate, according to present results, adds only two to the Republican minority.

Since the campaign turned largely on foreign policy, this result does not assure the President a guaranteed go-ahead signal on New Deal domestic policy. A Republican and conservative Democratic coalition, as has come into being during the past two years, will likely continue to stand as a Congressional balance-wheel to Executive dominance. The President's positive Congressional majority will, however, assist him to proceed along his established course in foreign affairs.

The Popular Vote

Latest returns give President Roosevelt a total popular vote of 23,175,051, as against 19,388,426 for Mr. Willkie.

America is today practicing its precious democracy and in one of few nations of the whole world where the ballot is still supreme. millions of free-voting Americans who honestly disagreed over politics and policy yesterday are today dedicating themselves to the substance of national unity at home in the face of the perils of war and totalitarianism abroad.

As a Democratic newspaper which this year supported the Republican candidate, the New York Times struck the note of national unity in its election editorial when it declared: "The choice is made. We must close our ranks. . . . We glory in the fact that ours is still a system of government in which the will of the majority prevails, and the minority gives ungrudging support to the majority in the achievement of every truly national purpose."

Willkie's Strength

President Roosevelt's popular vote does not extend to the landslide proportions of 1936, but it is a decisive majority, national in scope and unquestioned. Mr. Willkie has proved himself a stirring campaigner, a strong exponent of political and economic ideas which he is confident will ultimately prevail and a national leader who has earned such a devoted and popular following as to provide the New Deal with a counter-balance during the four years to come.

There is general agreement that the President's second re-election is a mandate in the field of foreign affairs which issue he himself put foremost as his reason for asking the American people to give him a third term, that it is not a mandate in the field of New Deal social reform. A significant feature of the campaign was that toward its close Mr. Roosevelt and Mr. Willkie were both advocating policies and objectives in many ways parallel with each other and it is therefore evident that the electorate has chosen a President to become the instrument of a unity which is urgently desired and which is already in the making.

Third Term Issue

It is not apparent that the third term issue exerted, under the impact of the war and its related issues, any very considerable influence in the final decision.

It is apparent that the Presi-

Continued on Page 6, Column 4

Willkie Congratulates; Calls on America for Unity

By a Staff Correspondent of The Christian Science Monitor

NEW YORK, Nov. 6—Calling on the American people to unite for national unity, completion of the defense program, greater aid to Britain, and "removal of antagonisms in America," Wendell L. Willkie today in a radio talk to the Nation accepted his defeat in the presidential race "with complete good will." Shortly before, he had sent a congratulatory message to President Roosevelt on his re-election.

"Congratulations on your re-election as President of the United States," the Republican nominee telegraphed his Democratic opponent in yesterday's election.

"I know that we are both gratified that so many American citizens participated in the election. I wish you all personal health and happiness."

The President accepted with "sincere thanks" Mr. Willkie's message. In a talk today, Mr. Willkie still the man on "crusade" bent said:

"I accept the result of the election with complete good will.

"The popular vote shows the vitality of our Democratic principles and the adherence of our people to the two-party system.

"I extend my thanks to the thousands who so zealously and wholeheartedly worked for my election in various organizations, and supported me individually. I know that they will continue as I shall to work for the unity of our people, in the completion of our defense effort, in sending aid to Britain and in insistence upon removal of antagonisms in America—all to the end that government of free men may continue and may spread again upon the earth.

"I have received too many kind and encouraging messages to permit of individual answer to all. To the senders of them I express my gratitude and thanks."

Proud to Lead

Mr. Willkie was photographed during and after his appearance before the microphones and then came into the press room of his Commodore Hotel headquarters for a chat in the easy and companionable way that has characterized his attitude toward reporters throughout his publicized and far-flung undertaking to win the Nation's highest office. There were easily 75 newsmen on hand for the statement of the 1940 titular head of the Republican Party.

"I am proud to have led the crusade I did," he told them in the informal interview. "I believe completely, and if anything, more deeply, in it than I did before.

"I believe the ultimate adoption of the principles I set forth in my Madison Square Garden speech are indispensable to the free way of life.

"I entered the campaign without bitterness, and I leave it with no ill-will or bitterness toward anyone."

Last night Mr. Willkie kept vigil over election charts in his Commodore Hotel campaign headquarters. The lobby and ballroom floors fourteen stories below were a scene of tension and high drama as the immense bulletin board told the story of the historic vote that rejected his crusading bid for the Presidency.

With the Republican challenger throughout the evening were Mrs. Willkie and their son, Philip, and his suite as midnight neared was a reception place for many promi-

Continued on Page 6, Column 3

Foreign Policy to Dominate Third Term

By Richard L. Strout
Staff Correspondent of The Christian Science Monitor

WASHINGTON, Nov. 6—President Roosevelt's unprecedented third term is likely to be dominated by foreign issues and a possible postwar economic readjustment rather than by new domestic social legislation.

So far as Roosevelt foreign policies go they have been fairly well indicated. They will be an extension of what has gone before. There will be aid to England "short of war," if the program is followed and a continuing "good-neighbor" policy towards Latin America.

There will be an effort to keep the balance of power in the Pacific, while, if peace returns to the harassed world in the next four years, and if he accepts reappointment, Cordell Hull will once again push his great tariff-reducing drive which was a feature of his efforts before the outbreak of hostilities.

More Aid for Britain

Where aid can be given abroad to the revival of democracies it obviously will be given in the next four years. Whether the United States can keep out of direct participation in the conflagrations in Europe and Asia remains to be seen; Mr. Roosevelt in his election speeches repeatedly emphasized that he is striving for peace, and even in the most warlike acts of sending munitions and ships and airplanes to Great Britain supported a policy which he hopes will protect the United States from war.

President Roosevelt gave certain indications of his further policies in the five major political speeches before election. In answer to Republican attacks he repeatedly stressed that he was not leading the country into war but was "arming for peace."

In an extemporaneous talk on Nov. 2 in upstate New York when he attacked Representative Joseph W. Martin (R) of Massachusetts, Republican National Chairman, for an alleged "whisper campaign" charge that he would send the fleet against Japan the day after election, Mr. Roosevelt made an important statement on fleet maneuvers. He declared he would not send the fleet westward from Hawaii. "That would lead us into war," he said. "Such a step would be regarded properly as a hostile act."

On the domestic side, Mr. Roosevelt interpolated a comment in his Nov. 1, Brooklyn speech, regarding old age and unemployment insurance. After saying these should operate "on an increasingly wider base" he interpolated, "so that it will eventually include every man and woman in the country."

For the most part the campaign speeches added little to earlier Roosevelt programs.

With the 1940 election now over it is important to recall that at no point were the cardinal issues of America's foreign policy turned into a political football. The methods of carrying out the program, as between President Roosevelt and Mr. Willkie were stressed, but the essential goods were the same.

Burden of Defense

The burden of defense is certain to remain heavy throughout the third term. The four years will see a "two-ocean navy" become a reality, under present defense plans, and the Nation armed more heavily in peacetime than ever before in history.

This vast program, already started, will have economic and social consequences of an incalculable sort in the years ahead. With industrial output breaking all records and men going back to work in defense industries, the problem of unemployment will be considerably mitigated and a business boom is anticipated by all economists.

This boom is based, of course, on deficit spending and on an armaments industry attributable to the Government rather than private business. In a sense it is an example of state-capitalism in action. Just what will happen if and when the need for the vast defense

Continued on Page 6, Column 6

'Same Franklin,' Roosevelt Says

By the Associated Press

Hyde Park, N. Y., Nov. 6

President Roosevelt filled chart after chart in today's early hours with figures telling a story of an overwhelming electoral vote lead in his historic race for a third term, and then, after describing the election trends as "fine," went to bed at 2:35 a. m., E. S. T.

To a group of his neighbors, the Chief Executive remarked:

"We, of course, face difficult days in this country. But I think you will find me in the future just the same Franklin Roosevelt you have known a great many years."

THE CHRISTIAN SCIENCE MONITOR

AN INTERNATIONAL DAILY NEWSPAPER

COPYRIGHT 1941 BY THE CHRISTIAN SCIENCE PUBLISHING SOCIETY

BOSTON, MONDAY, JUNE 23, 1941—VOL. XXXIII, NO. 176

• • — ATLANTIC EDITION—FIVE CENTS A COPY

British Pledge Aid to Soviet; U.S. Condemns Hitler Attack; Nazis Push Ahead in Russia

Allies Push War in Syria; RAF Bags 64 Nazi Planes; Neutrality Repeal Urged

The World's Day—June 23, 1941

Middle East: British Reach Palmyra Outskirts

Allied forces driving across the Syrian desert have reached the outskirts of Palmyra, important French post, the French admitted. Mopping up operations proceeded around the Syrian capital at Damascus, captured by the British June 21. [Page 7.]

Air and Sea: RAF Claims 64 Nazi Planes Downed

An offensive sweep by the RAF over France for the seventh successive day shot down seven German bombers, making a total of 64 in three days, the British reported. During the night the RAF carried out their 12th successive assault, causing heavy damage at Wilhelmshaven, Nazi naval base.

A second American squadron is being formed as a part of the RAF for Americans who have volunteered to serve with the British.

British patrols intercepted the 4,422-ton German supply ship Babitonga, disguised as a Dutch merchant ship, headed for Brest from Brazil.

Germany claimed sinking of nine British merchantmen totaling 37,500 tons. Italy asserted it had sunk 50 British ships since war began.

An Irish merchant marine consisting of two former United States ships and a former Yugoslav freighter will carry foodstuffs from the United States to Ireland.

In Washington: Repeal of Neutrality Act Urged

Senator Claude Pepper (D) of Florida, proposed that Congress implement President Roosevelt's demand for maintenance of the freedom of the seas by repealing the Neutrality Act which prevents American shipping from entering war zones.

The Senate Judiciary Committee approved unanimously President Roosevelt's nomination of Associate Justice Harlan F. Stone to be Chief Justice of the United States. Action was delayed on the nomination of Attorney General Robert H. Jackson to succeed Justice Stone as an Associate Justice because Senator Tydings (D), of Maryland, asked to be heard regarding Mr. Jackson's qualifications.

The War Department recommended to President Roosevelt that the National Guard be kept on active duty beyond the current single year of service which ends Sept. 16; legislation is required.

The President gave speedy approval to a bill under which he has virtually unlimited authority to regulate entry into and departure from the United States of both aliens and citizens.

William H. Davis, Vice-Chairman of the National Defense Labor Mediation Board, was designated by President Roosevelt to be the new Chairman, succeeding Dr. Clarence A. Dykstra, who is to retire July 1.

The Office of Production Management announced a plan for curtailing civilian use of rubber, and Price Administrator Leon Henderson said a ceiling on tires would be established as of June 16 prices. [Financial Page.]

Nathan Straus, Administrator of the U. S. H. A., ordered that substitutes for steel, copper, bronze, and other metals be used in constructing U. S. H. A. homes.

Government acted today to halt the departure of Italian nationals from the United States. The action duplicated steps taken against the Germans in this country June 18. The step was taken, the Justice Department said, to insure compliance with the executive order of the President of last June 14, regulating transactions in foreign exchange and foreign-owned property.

A Senate Appropriations subcommittee was reported to have decided that $500,000,000 for 15 new munitions plants should be provided in a pending $10,000,000,000 military supply bill.

The Army made public orders consolidating its mobile general air headquarters air force and the service branches of the air corps into a "single unified organization" to be called the "Army Air Force" to provide unity of command under an officer responsible only to the Chief of Staff.

In Africa: British Take Jimma in Ethiopia

Capture of Jimma, in southwestern Ethiopia, resulted in taking of 8,000 prisoners, including 11 generals, the British announced in Cairo.

German bombers attacked the British naval base at Alexandria, Egypt, according to German reports, while Italian dispatches told of RAF raids on the Libyan port of Bengasi.

In Orient: Japan Watches Russo-German Action

Far Eastern repercussions of the Nazi attack against Russia sent Japanese officials into urgent conference. Strict neutrality was the order in Tokyo. [Page 4.]

China saw supplies from Russia dwindle. The Chinese must now look almost exclusively to the United States for war materials to use against the Japanese invader.

Fingerprinting and registration of all aliens in the Philippine Islands are required under a bill signed by President Manuel Quezon. An estimated 100,000 aliens will be affected.

Diplomatic: Germans and Russians Come to Grips

German and Russian armies came to grips along a 2,000-mile front extending from the Arctic to the Black Sea, climaxing a war of nerves between the two countries whose treaty of friendship and mutual nonaggression in August, 1939, laid the groundwork for the original German attack on Poland. [Pages 1, 4, and 5.]

Prime Minister Winston Churchill in a special radiocast offered the Soviet all possible assistance in defense. [Text: Page 7.]

Italy joined Germany in its declaration of war on Russia, and Finnish and Rumanian troops advanced with the Nazi legions across the Soviet frontiers.

Germany charged Russia with treachery in the Baltic and Balkans, with plotting with the British and the United States, and with violating Germany's frontiers.

A Lithuanian "independence" coup and declaration of Latvian "Government-in-Exile"—both pledging alliance with Germany against Russia—threatened U. S. S. R.'s Baltic defenses. [Page 7.]

National: U. S. O. Drive Passes Half-Way Mark

New York—Thomas E. Dewey, national campaign manager, announced that the United Service Organizations' campaign to raise $10,765,000 to furnish recreation facilities for the Nation's armed forces had passed the half-way mark with $5,411,083 donated.

New York (AP)—Prices rose $1 to more than $3 a share in leading stocks today, and blocks of several thousand shares changed hands frequently as traders interpreted bullishly the involvement of Germany with Russia, with a consequent lessening of the pressure on Britain.

New England: Saltonstall for State-Owned 'L'

Complete public ownership of the Boston Elevated Railway System was recommended today by Governor Saltonstall in a special message to the Legislature.

The Massachusetts League of Women Voters launched a campaign for an all-out citizen effort to assist the "Battle of Production."

Radio Station WRUL at Boston announced plans for a 100,000-watt transmitter, thereby doubling its present power and giving the City the largest shortwave station in the world.

The Christian Science Monitor Index

Monday, June 23, 1941

Higher Estate, Gift Taxes Are Voted

By the Associated Press

Washington, June 23

The House Ways and Means Committee voted tentatively today in favor of higher estate and gift taxes designed to produce about $113,700,000 additional revenue.

Chairman Robert L. Doughton (D) of North Carolina announced that the present exemption of $40,000 for both estate and gift tax purposes would be unchanged.

The Committee's decision on the estate and gift levies was interpreted to mean that between $900,000,000 and $1,000,000,000 of additional revenue would have to be raised through more and higher excise taxes in order to reach the goal of $3,500,000,000 of new revenue.

Communists Call for U. S. Aid to Soviet

By Wyona Dashwood

Staff Correspondent of The Christian Science Monitor

NEW YORK, June 23—With the Daily Worker, chief Communist organ in the United States, denouncing the Nazi war against the Soviet Union, in banner headlines as "a wanton act," its front page today features a statement by the Communist Party in the United States calling for full American support and co-operation in the Russian defense.

The statement signed by William Z. Foster, Chairman, and Robert Minor, Acting Secretary of the party, calls the new Axis blitzkrieg "an unprovoked criminal attack upon the greatest champion of peace, freedom and national independence." It focusses solely, however, on the "armed assault by German Fascism and its satellites" in explicit exclusion of endorsement of the war aims of the British War Cabinet or of American foreign policy, continuing to refer to the European conflict as the "second imperialist world war," in which the rulers of Fascist Germany were engaged in a "desperate struggle with their imperialist rivals in England and the United States."

Of the Russian role in the remapping of the continent, it declares that the Soviet Union had liberated the peoples of the Western Ukraine, White Russia, Bessarabia and the Baltic States," while the "reactionaries and imperialists of both sides" had conspired against its peace and neutrality.

New 'Party Line'

The new "party line," ending a period since the signing of the Nazi-Soviet non-aggression pact just before the war started in September, 1939, in which American Communists have soft-pedaled the subject of Nazi aggression for concentration on United States domestic problems and strong criticism of the Roosevelt all-out British aid policy as a war-making program, was drawn at a meeting of the party's "political committee."

Acting for Earl Browder, party secretary, now a prisoner in Federal penitentiary for passport fraud, Mr. Minor with Mr. Foster cleared the statement to all New York newspapers by wire last night, three hours later than it had been promised, with the assertion that the latest German aggression was "an attack upon the people of the United States and of the entire world."

Couched in fervid terms of Communist ideology, the preamble acclaims a Soviet policy based, it declares, "upon rendering aid to those nations that were waging a just struggle for national independence and liberty," instancing Russia's aid to the Chinese people and the Spanish republic.

"With the fullest support of all its people," the statement reads, "the Soviet Government is now waging a struggle not only in defense of the most vital interests of the peoples in all countries. It is waging a just struggle for the cause of the freedom of all nations and peoples . . .

"Hitler is calling upon his friends and supporters in all the capitalist countries to join hands in war against the Soviet Union, in war against the working people and oppressed masses throughout the world.

A New Munich

"The rulers of Fascist Germany are dangling before the imperialists of all countries, especially in England and the United States, the vision of a new Munich, a new conspiracy to redivide the world at the expense of the peoples of all nations, to crush the Soviet Union, to exterminate democracy in Europe and to strengthen reaction throughout the world. This was the message Hess brought to England. The friends of fascism in the United States and England are reaching out for this reactionary vision.

"The Scripps-Howard Press, just before the attack of Hitler began, cynically declared, 'that's one war we could really favor. . . .' This is likewise the position of the Social-Democratic lickspittles of big capital who have long been demanding war against the Soviet Union.

Civil Service Field Widened By New Laws

Merit system is making gains as States act on many measures affecting the average citizen.

By a Staff Correspondent of The Christian Science Monitor

CHICAGO—If you live in Kansas, political pull will no longer land you a job with the State. For Kansas was one of several States this year to create or extend a civil service system. If you live in New York you may soon find your neighborhood undergoing a transformation under the terms of a new low-rent housing law just passed by the Legislature. And if you own property in Oregon you'll find your next property tax bill charging you on the basis of an assessment made on Jan. 1.

That's just a sample of some of the miscellaneous laws passed by our State Legislatures this year, and how they affect Mr. Average Citizen. They are laws by the people, for the people, and with thousands of others, most of them dealing with vitally important subjects, they form the real foundation of the American governmental system. The lawmakers of the 48 sovereign States after all do more of the kind of legislating that is felt in terms of one's everyday homelife, than those in Washington.

Kansas System

The Kansas merit system law covers some 4,500 State employees, and incidentally was put into effect by the Legislature only after the voters of the State last fall ratified the idea by a big majority.

A really major advance in this civil service field, though, was the passage by the New York Legislature of a bill extending the merit system to every jurisdiction within the State. Vermont and North Carolina legislators also established new merit systems.

All wasn't clear sailing for the merit system idea, however, for New Mexico, after but a year under a civil service system for seven State agencies, decided to abandon it. The records of the Commission have all been carefully packed and carted over to the University of New Mexico "for future use if needed," says Ralph Trigg, commission chairman.

Measures Pending

Meanwhile at the time of writing Florida, Nebraska, New Hampshire, Oklahoma, Pennsylvania, South Carolina, and Texas legislators had pending before them some sort of merit law proposals.

The low-cost housing bill in New York is the first of its kind in the country. It is of special interest because it permits municipalities to offer private corporations special inducements to build large-scale, low rent housing projects. The idea is to give private enterprise a legitimate place in the low-cost housing field, so far monopolized by public agencies under Federal auspices. The New York law restricts the activities of these private groups by various controls to assure the work being always in the public interest. Similar legislation is pending in Illinois, and was introduced also this year in Utah.

The matter of the assessment date change in Oregon may not seem important on the face. It's part of a move, though, to establish uniformity in State property tax assessment dates.

Soviet war with Nazis considered helpful to America — Aid for Moscow hinted.

By Joseph G. Harrison

Staff Correspondent of The Christian Science Monitor

WASHINGTON, June 23—The one great issue before the American people today is to stop Nazi Germany, and all help in this aid, no matter from what source, is welcome, the United States Government declared today.

Although calling the principles and doctrines of Communism as intolerable as those of Naziism, Sumner Welles, Acting Secretary of State, said that Russian resistance to Germany will hasten the end of Adolf Hitler and consequently will contribute to America's own defense and security.

While warning that President Roosevelt himself did not yet know if Russia would be eligible for aid under the lend-lease program, Secretary Welles strongly hinted that this would be so, saying that the measure clearly empowers the President to assist those powers whose defense is deemed necessary to that of the United States.

It is believed that the United States is waiting for the Soviet Union to make formal application for such aid and that, in granting it, this Government would make clear its dislike of Russia's internal and external policies. So far, no communication has been received from Moscow, the Acting Secretary said.

Warning of Nazi Intent

Describing the German attack as proof that Berlin negotiates nonaggression pacts only as subterfuge and in a different light than do "civilized" nations, Secretary Welles declared that such pacts "constitute a dire warning on the part of Germany of hostile and murderous intent.

"To the present German Government, the very meaning of the word 'honor' is unknown."

The statement was issued after Mr. Welles had conferred with the President twice in the course of the morning. It is seen as preparing the American people for a measure of wartime collaboration with Russia, which most Americans would find distasteful except in the most critical times.

This preparation is believed to have dictated inclusion of that part of the statement excoriating the principles of both Communism and National Socialism. Strong stress was made of the point that "neither kind of imposed overlordship can have or will have any support or any sway in the mode of life, or in the system of government, of the American people."

The immediate issue, however, as seen by this Government, is whether Herr Hitler's plan for universal conquest and enslavement of all peoples and the destruction of democracy can be stopped. Since this is so, the Government holds that any opposition to Hitlerism can only "redound to the benefit of our own defense and security."

The statement ends with the un-

Continued on Page 21, Column 6

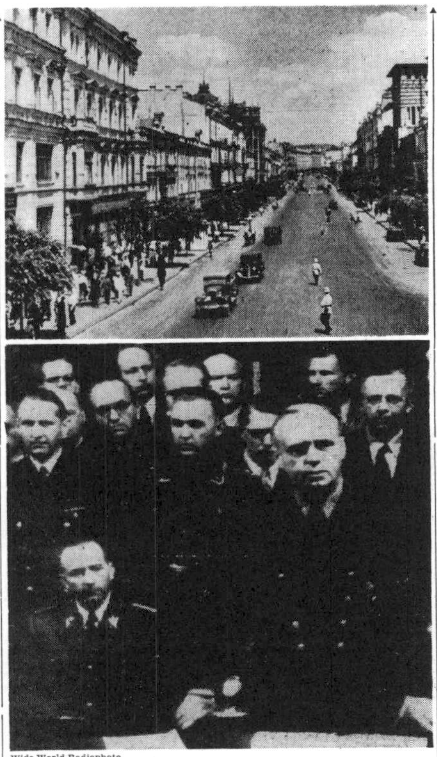

Wide World Radiophoto

As War Widens in Russia

Above: A view of Kreshchatik, the central street in Kiev, Russia, which was one of the main targets of the German air attacks as the Nazi forces advanced against Russia. Below: Joachim von Ribbentrop, German Foreign Minister, pictured as he read the anti-Russian declaration.

Newest Hitler campaign is seen as cementing British unity in war still further.

BERLIN, June 23 (AP)—Adolf Hitler's legions have driven ahead "on schedule and successfully" in their first lunges against Soviet Russia along the 2,000-mile-long battle line of Germany's new eastern front, the High Command declared today.

Specific details of German progress in the conflict pitting two of the world's largest military machines in one of the most meaningful struggles of history were omitted from the communiqué, however.

A Russian submarine base on the Black Sea was especially hard hit in an attack by German bombers yesterday, DNB, official German news agency, said, adding that oil stores were set afire.

By Mallory Browne

European Editorial Manager of The Christian Science Monitor

LONDON, June 23—Prime Minister Winston Churchill's promise of all possible aid to Russia and his pledge never to parley nor negotiate with Reichsführer Hitler has behind it the full support of the British people, more united now than ever in the new awareness of the need for redoubled efforts to meet the increased peril implied by the Nazi attack on the Soviets.

If Herr Hitler hoped to weaken British resistance by stirring up dissension through class appeal on the grounds of an anti-Bolshevist crusade he has failed completely.

On the contrary the German attack on Soviet Russia has had the opposite effect. It has rallied to the Government's support the only group in the country where some signs of defection had become visible recently. The extreme left wing of labor, which is under Communist influence, which has been more and more vocal in favoring a compromise peace movement, now appears to have been brought over into camp among the Government's strongest supporters.

Communists' Stand

Thus the Communist Party of Great Britain in an official statement declares "Hitler's attack against the Socialist Soviet Union is Fascism's supreme aggression against the people of the world" and Mr. D. N. Pritt, Labor Member of Parliament, and Treasurer of the People's Convention declared "If Britain and the United States will fight the Nazis with all their power this new move will be the end of Fascism."

Mr. J. Tanner, President of the Amalgamated Engineering Union, which only last week sprang a surprise by voting for a peace program based on the people's Convention, now states "every effort must be made to remove any differences we have with Russia and to trace the steps to bring about an active alliance with her, both economic and military."

By promising full British aid for the Soviets, Mr. Churchill has thus rallied the extreme left-wing elements here who have been causing some concern lately to the move for stronger support of the Nation's war effort.

Compromise Barred

And simultaneously he reaffirmed "we are resolved to destroy Hitler and every vestige of the Nazi regime. From this nothing will turn us—nothing. We will never parley, we will never negotiate with Hitler or any of his gang."

Thereby he has abolished in advance any notion that the British Government might be tempted to temporize or compromise with the Nazis now they have returned to their old anti-Bolshevist position.

Furthermore, if Herr Hitler hoped to lull the British into a false sense of security by turning eastward he has miscalculated. Mr. Churchill's trenchant warning that "the invasion of Russia is no more than a prelude to the attempted invasion of the British Isles" is echoed prominently and unanimously in editorial comments of the British press.

Feeling of Relief

It is true there was certain feeling of relief at first on the part of the man-in-the-street here at the news that Germany had attacked Russia. One heard some comments along the line that Herr Hitler would now lose himself in the vastness of Russia like Napoleon did.

Mr. Churchill's speech, however, soon made clear the vanity of any such expectations. Today there is general agreement with the Prime Minister's prediction that Herr

Continued on Page 21, Column 1

Churchill pledges aid to Russia: Page 7.

Hitler's declaration of War on Russia: Page 7.

Soviet's Baltic Bulwark Is Pounded by Germans

By the Associated Press

Monday, June 23

The Baltic bulwark which Soviet Russia erected by threats and persuasion against the possibility of just such an attack by Germany as is now raging along its great western frontier appeared today to be crumbling.

Combined military and political blows within and without the three little States—Lithuania, Latvia, and Estonia—which the Russians took into camp and started fortifying a year ago, threatened to link them with Adolf Hitler.

According to Berlin advices, based in turn on radiocasts from the Kaunas radio, Lithuanians have risen up, forming a new Government pledged to help Germany fight Russia.

An effort to cut Latvia also out of the Russian camp was indicated when the Germans radiocast a declaration by a Latvian "Government-in-Exile" that Latvia, too, would fight alongside Germany presumably when and if Russian rule could be cast off.

Revolts Expected

Helsingfors reports said that Estonia, farthest removed of the three from the German-Russian battle line, was expected to follow suit. Baltic political refugees, themselves anti-Russian, said Russia had expected revolts in the three States.

Finland, who lost territory to Russia by war, declared, at the same time, that it would maintain neutrality as long as possible—this despite Reichsführer Hitler's classification of it as his ally.

Meanwhile, Germany launched its attack on Russia on June 22 upon a front stretching from the Arctic Ocean to the Black Sea—a front lined with 5,000,000 men.

It was, in scope and in its meaning for the world, a major development of perhaps the greatest war in history.

It meant that Adolf Hitler had given up hope of a quick conquest of Britain.

Breaking his treaty with Russia—signed in August, 1939, to secure the Eastern Front while Germany launched its attacks in the West—Herr Hitler charged the Soviets with sabotage and double dealing.

In return, the Russians accused the Germans of a cynical repudiation of the Nazi-Soviet nonaggression pact, immediately put the Red air fleet aloft and early reports told of heavy air battles over Germany's East Prussia.

Advance Under Way

As to ground forces, the Nazis offered only the general statement that their advance was everywhere under way.

The Italians joined the Germans in a declaration of war upon the Soviet.

The initial maneuvers in Tokyo indicated that Japan, although a member of the Axis alliance would stay out of the fighting.

Spain made it clear that it sympathized with Germany.

Two-Edged Nazi Strategy in Russia; Stalin Policy Seen Dictated by Fear

—Berlin—

By Joseph C. Harsch

Berlin Correspondent of The Christian Science Monitor who is now in the United States.

Adolf Hitler's long predicted attack on Soviet Russia is a shrewd double play intended to give German high strategy the advantage of two alternative courses of action either one of which the Führer can develop or abandon as events unfold in this new phase of world war.

It is first and primarily a hedge against a protracted war involving the stupendous power of the United States. It is an attempt to protect himself against this by gaining absolute control of the resources of European Russia which he had found himself unable to obtain by means short of war.

It is, secondly, an effort to consolidate the basis for a peace offensive which Herr Hitler's strategists have always wanted to keep in reserve as a means of bringing the war to a quick end if the going became too difficult.

Disunity Is Sought

Incidental to both of these two purposes behind the move, and involved in both of them, is the idea that by suddenly turning on Russia, Germany will be able to promote disunity and indecision both in Britain and the United States.

In fact the first result Herr Hitler and his diplomatic strategists hope to achieve by the Russian move is a reduced tempo of intervention by the United States and with it a revival of the appeasement movement in Britain.

But Berlin took far more than this possibility into its considerations in pressing Russia to the point where Joseph Stalin made the one decision he probably never expected to make during the course of this war—namely to fight or surrender. The move proves that Britain has actually won a great military victory during the dark months of defeat in Greece, Crete,

Continued on Page 21, Column 5

Monitor Writers Tell Background of War

Reasons behind the war between Russia and Germany cannot—because of censorship—be freely analyzed from the capitals of those countries. But two correspondents of The Christian Science Monitor, writing from intimate knowledge of these countries where they have recently served, today tell the meaning of the new moves.

Joseph Harsch, recently returned to the United States, served in Germany from the beginning of the war.

Edmund Stevens, back in America after coverage which has included the Finnish, Norwegian, and Greek campaigns, writes from long experience in Moscow.

—Moscow—

By Edmund Stevens

Special Correspondent of The Christian Science Monitor who spent 5½ years in Russia.

"No matter how much you may feed a wolf, he still gazes longingly at the fields and forests."

Joseph Stalin has proved to himself and the world that this old Russian proverb applies to the Nazi wolf and the fields and forests of the Ukraine.

It often is easier to quote proverbs or give advice to a neighbor than to act on it oneself. For more than five years the Soviets, through their Geneva mouthpiece, Foreign Commissar Maxim Litvinoff, warned the world against appeasing the aggressors. When Neville Chamberlain stepped off the plane at Croydon after his memorable Munich flight, declaring he had brought back "peace in our time" in his leather briefcase, the Soviets were the most outspoken in predicting that war had been postponed only slightly. A few months later, just as the warnings against appeasement proved their correctness, the Soviets themselves embraced appeasement.

The Russians were threatened by the same danger as the rest of Europe—Adolf Hitler. They were offered the hand of friendship and alliance against the common foe by Britain. But Mr. Stalin saw, or thought he saw, a dagger up the sleeve and preferred an under-

Continued on Page 21, Column 3

THE CHRISTIAN SCIENCE MONITOR

AN INTERNATIONAL DAILY NEWSPAPER

COPYRIGHT 1941 BY THE CHRISTIAN SCIENCE PUBLISHING SOCIETY

BOSTON, MONDAY, DECEMBER 8, 1941—VOL. XXXIV, NO. 12

• •— ATLANTIC EDITION—FIVE CENTS A COPY

Congress Declares War on Japan; 3,000 Casualties in Hawaii Air Raid

Senate votes 82 to 0, House 388 to 1 within 33 minutes after President's address—Two U. S. warships sunk, others damaged—Nation mobilizes resources to battle Axis on all fronts.

By Roscoe Drummond
Staff Correspondent of The Christian Science Monitor

WASHINGTON, Dec. 8—With Congress unhesitatingly and overwhelmingly voting a declaration of war against the Japanese Empire, President Roosevelt began immediately today to mobilize to the limit the military and industrial power of the Nation to fight the Axis in two oceans.

As the Senate, by a vote of 82 to 0, and the House, by a vote of 388 to 1, accepted the verdict of the Japanese attack—accepted it with a unity greater than when the United States entered the World War in 1917—it was evident in Washington that America's support of all the anti-Axis nations was not to be weakened, but that the war would be prosecuted on all fronts with greater vigor.

America's war operations against the attacking Japanese force in the Pacific, now in the first stages of the second day, have destroyed "a number of Japanese planes and submarines," the White House announced today.

But the damage wrought by Japan's sudden blow at United States defenses in Hawaii, the Philippines, Guam and Wake Islands is more serious than at first known and casualties at the Hawaiian air and naval base of Oahu alone have mounted to 3,000, including 1,500 fatalities.

Large-scale retaliatory attacks against Japanese air and sea power in the neighborhood of the Hawaiian Islands are continuing, the White House disclosed, and the outcome of the first battle of the Pacific awaits clarification.

Losses in Pearl Harbor

The Government confirmed the loss in Pearl Harbor of "one old battleship" and a destroyer, which was blown up.

Several other small ships were seriously damaged, several hangars were destroyed and a large number of Army and Navy planes were put out of commission.

Numerous bombers arrived safely from San Francisco while the Hawaiian air attack was in progress and more reinforcements of aircraft are being rushed today. Repair work on ships, planes and ground facilities is under way.

Striking out in all directions, invading Thailand, assaulting British Malaya, thrusting at Singapore and bombing American defenses, Japanese air and sea power is being immediately confronted by a powerful coalition of Pacific nations.

As the American and the Japanese fleets were reported to be battling near Honolulu, Britain declared war, Canada declared war, the Netherlands declared war, Australia declared war.

World War in Fact

Thus the struggle for world conquest which Adolf Hitler started on Sept. 1, 1939, became today a World War in fact as well as in name. The pattern of conquest of the Axis partners has now met in the Pacific and as the United States of America stood in its way, the Axis attacked.

It was a severe and surprise attack. It was an attack which Cordell Hull, Secretary of State, branded as "treacherous and utterly unprovoked."

But it is an attack which finds the United States prepared and united as never before. Congress is ready to support President Roosevelt, who promptly ordered the Navy and Army into action,

Continued on Page 10, Column 6

Defense officials, far from diluting aid to Britain and the Near East, are acting to bring a total mobilization of industrial and financial resources—as pledged by Congress in its war resolution.

A speed-up of all munitions production and a rigorous new curtailment of civilian manufacture were promptly undertaken by the Supply Priorities and Allocations Board at the direction of Vice President Henry A. Wallace.

Today less than 20 per cent of the nation's industrial facilities are devoted to defense. SPAB's new program calls for commandeering two thirds to three quarters of America's productive capacity in order that aid to the democracies may be continued unabated.

Aimed at Japan

Today's declaration of war was specifically directed against Japan in the Pacific because of its "dastardly and unprovoked" attack, but the war which the United States is now beginning to conduct will be against the Axis everywhere in the world.

Donald M. Nelson, Executive Director of SPAB, indicated no less when as the first high official to go on the air since the bombing of American fortifications he declared that the Japanese attacks were inspired by Berlin and that the prime task of America is to defeat Hitler.

Only 33 minutes after President Roosevelt stood before a joint session of both houses this afternoon to announce that hostilities exist and to proclaim that "America . . . will win through to absolute victory, so help us God," Congress voted to proclaim the existence of a state of war.

The Senate vote of 82 to 0 and the House vote of 388 to 1 bespoke more powerfully than words the support, the unity, and the determination with which the country and the Congress took the inevitable decision.

Describing the Japanese attack on American defenses throughout the Far East as "deliberate and dastardly," the President spoke accurately when he said that "the people of the United States have already formed their opinions and well understand the implications to the very life and safety of our nation."

In the face of the rain of Japanese bombs on Hawaii, Guam, Wake and the Philippines, Congress had already formed its opinions, and Mr. Roosevelt's request for a declaration of war was but to request what was ready to be

Continued on Page 10, Column 3

Roosevelt message to Congress stresses Japanese duplicity: Page 10.

Japanese Bomb Manila; Malayan Invasion Foiled; 'Moscow Capture' Delayed

The World's Day—December 8, 1941

War: British Thwart Malayan Invasion

Malayan invasion was thwarted by British troops who threw back Japanese landing parties.

The Philippines were again blasted by Japanese, particular targets being United States military establishments, bases and harbors. Manila was bombed late today, the raiders smashing at Fort William McKinley and Nicholas Airfield.

Canal Zone police began rounding up Germans and Italians in a drive co-ordinated with the roundup at Colon where Panama police have taken 11 Germans into custody and are combing the city for more Axis nationals.

Thailand ceased resistance following Japanese invasion at four points.

Nauru and Ocean Islands were attacked in new Japanese air thrusts.

Hong Kong was surrounded by Japanese troops reported about to stage an invasion after delivering heavy air attacks.

Singapore casualties resulting from Japanese air raid were estimated at between 50 and 100.

Shanghai's International Settlement was seized by Japanese troops.

At Tientsin, 200 United States Marines, all that remained of the American Marine detachment in China, were interned.

In Hawaii, United States forces were putting up active resistance to continued Japanese air attacks.

Guam was attacked by Japanese forces.

Wake Island was said to have been captured by a Japanese landing party.

Midway Island was attacked by Japanese forces.

American losses at Pearl Harbor, Hawaii, from the Japanese surprise attack Sunday, total two warships and 3,000 dead and wounded, according to the White House, although Tokyo claimed two battleships, two destroyers and damage to four battleships and four heavy cruisers.

Japanese losses in the Pearl Harbor attack were said to have been several planes and submarines. There were reports that a Japanese airplane carrier had been sunk.

A naval battle is reported in progress somewhere between Hawaii and the Philippines following the United States Fleet's departure from Pearl Harbor.

Japanese aliens numbering 736 were arrested during the night in the United States and Hawaii.

Fiorello La Guardia and Mrs. Eleanor Roosevelt, Director and Assistant Director of Civilian Defense, respectively, flew to California from New York to aid in organization of civilian defense.

Panama began interning Japanese aliens, ignoring demands by the Japanese Minister that they be released.

The General Hugh Scott, United States Army transport, was reported sunk 1,600 miles from Manila.

A lumber-laden transport was said to have been torpedoed 1,300 miles west of San Francisco.

Diplomatic: U. S. Congress Declares War

The United States declared war on Japan following President Roosevelt's war message to Congress, the Senate voting 82-0, the House 388-1.

War declarations against Japan were also made by Great Britain, Canada, the Netherlands East Indies, Australia, Costa Rica, Haiti, Honduras, the Dominican Republic, and Polish and Free French authorities in London.

Thailand was reported negotiating with Japan and was said to have granted Japanese troops passage to British Malaya, where the Japanese claimed the British had opened an attack on Thailand.

Russia: Nazis 'Hold Off' on Moscow

German plans do not envisage the capture of Moscow this year in view of the coming of winter, a military spokesman in Berlin declared today.

Washington: Contempt Convictions Reversed

The Supreme Court reversed contempt of court convictions against the Los Angeles Times and Harry Bridges, West Coast C. I. O. labor leader.

William Green, President of the American Federation of Labor, called for an end to strikes in defense industries, stating that Japanese "treachery and aggression had aroused in American workers an unconquerable determination to see this fight through to a victorious finish at any cost."

All private airplanes in the United States and its possessions except commercial airliners, were ordered grounded by the Civil Aeronautics Authority.

Maxim Litvinoff, the new Soviet Ambassador, arrived in Washington via San Francisco and the Pacific after a month's journey by air from the Russian capital at Kuibyshev.

Strikes: 'Captive' Mines to Have Union Shop

A union shop for "captive" coal mines owned and operated by steel companies was voted by the President's three-man arbitration board, assuring full production of coal for national defense until April 1, 1943. The two to one decision requires all miners in the "captive" mines to join the United Mine Workers of America.

Philip Murray and Thomas Kennedy, President and Secretary-Treasurer, respectfully, of the C. I. O., refused to withdraw their resignations from the National Defense Labor Mediation Board as requested by President Roosevelt.

Naval officials at San Francisco said they had been advised that a nation-wide strike of welders, scheduled for Dec. 9, had been cancelled because of the Japanese attack on the United States.

National: Four Naval Vessels Launched

Four small naval vessels and two merchant ships were launched Dec. 7 at shipyards in Maine, Rhode Island, New York, New Jersey and North Carolina.

Clipper Off for Lisbon; U. S. Officers Are Aboard

NEW YORK, Dec. 8 (AP)—The Atlantic Clipper left for Lisbon today with all of its scheduled 48 passengers on board including eight representatives of United States armed forces. Expected cancellations as a result of the war in the Pacific failed to materialize.

Among the military and naval men were Col. John Reynolds, going to Dublin to serve as military attache; Lieut. Col. Aaron Bradshaw, Lieut. Harold Broudy, Sergeant William Finney and Private Harold McIntire, on an observation mission; Naval Lieuts. Jonus D. Hardy and Charles Frazer, couriers for the State Department, and John Wehle, an attaché of the Marine Corps.

The Christian Science Monitor Index
Monday, Dec. 8, 1941

Navy Takes Over Hotel

Special to The Christian Science Monitor

RICHMOND, Va.—The Navy Department has disclosed completion of contract negotiations to take over the Chamberlin Hotel at Old Point Comfort, Va., for housing transient officers and families of officers of the Army and Navy.

Rush to Enlist Hits New York As City Arms

By a Staff Correspondent of The Christian Science Monitor

NEW YORK, Dec. 8—War reaction flared in the Metropolitan District today as the man-in-the-street digested the sensational sequel of bulletins that blazed over the radio networks yesterday on the Japanese attack in the Pacific, and Army, Navy and Marine Corps recruiting stations were open at 7:30 a. m., instead of the usual hour of 9 a. m. Applicants even sought immediate enlistment yesterday, with the Federal Building in Newark, N. J., reporting the arrival there of a truckload of young men from the Oranges with this objective. They were told to return today.

Meanwhile, with the New York area regarded by military authorities as "a possible, but not a probable, danger zone," full military and civil defense precaution was in process here to protect it from such an attack as surprised Pearl Harbor. The Federal Bureau of Investigation moved instantly into the picture with a detail of 100 detectives assigned to round up Japanese nationals, 85 of whom were in custody on Ellis Island by morning and hundreds of others on the list for detention pending action in Washington.

Coincidentally, at Albany Gov. Herbert H. Lehman directed the Mayors of the State "to take all steps necessary to prevent sabotage in defense plants, public utilities, waterworks, bridges and all other places of strategic importance in your jurisdiction and to protect all Japanese nationals residing in your city."

Defense Measures Implemented

Rear Admiral Adolphus Andrews, Commander of the North Atlantic Squadron; Mayor Fiorello H. La Guardia, in his dual capacity as Federal Director of Civilian defense, and Police Commissioner Lewis J. Valentine moved instantly to put into practical effect, their blueprints on war conditions. As a result, today guards had been strengthened against sabotage, with special patrols for all bridges, piers,

Continued on Page 4, Column 7

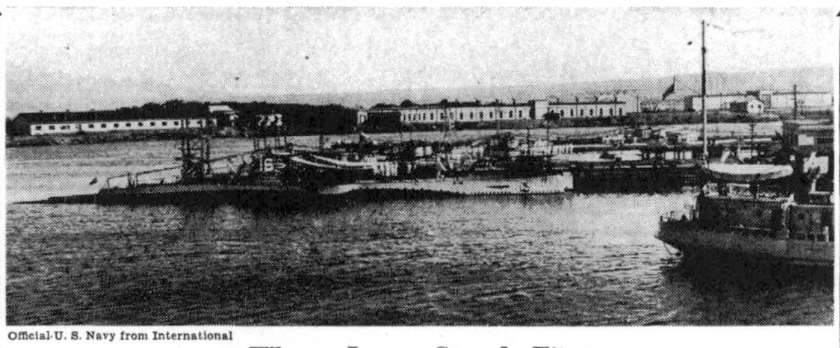

Official U. S. Navy from International

Where Japan Struck First
View of Pearl Harbor Naval Base in Hawaii

U. S. Navy Suffers a 'Scapa Flow'; Britain Hails U. S. as Ally in Pacific

By a Naval Expert
Written for The Christian Science Monitor

The United States has suffered its Scapa Flow.

Why the American Navy permitted itself to be surprised in the Pacific will take some major explaining from a command which almost at the same moment was declaring its marine forces "second to none" in the world.

But at the same time it is vital to understand that Japan's tactical success—its sudden air-and-water blitz—will be a Pyrrhic victory, in the face of the superior force which Britain and the United States and their Allies can mass against Nippon.

But the United States, which was highly critical of Britain when a German submarine in a surprise attack sank the Royal Oak at Scapa Flow on Oct. 13, 1939, has given evidence of its own lack of vigilance.

Unpreparedness Cited

How were Japanese aircraft carriers and other surface vessels permitted to approach within so short a striking distance of strategic Pearl Harbor? Where was the continuous reconnaissance over these strategic waters which was presumed to have been in constant operation in the air?

Where were Army dawn fighter patrols which should have been aloft to protect the Hawaiian Islands from surprise bombing attack?

How were Japanese naval concentrations permitted to arrive without observation within striking distance of Wake Island and Guam—the immobilizing of which not only interferes with passenger service in the Far East, but will seriously hamper air re-enforcements.

The answer to these questions can only lie in psychological unpre-

Continued on Page 11, Column 1

Peace and War
By Mary Baker Eddy
In The First Church of Christ, Scientist, and Miscellany, page 277, lines 18-23

Whatever weighs in the eternal scale of equity and mercy tips the beam on the right side, where the immortal words and deeds of men alone can settle all questions amicably and satisfactorily. But if our nation's rights or honor were seized, every citizen would be a soldier and woman would be armed with power girt for the hour.

LONDON, Dec. 8 (AP)—Britain declared war today on the Tokyo Government without waiting for Washington first to formulate an American declaration.

Said Prime Minister Winston Churchill: "It only remains now for the two great democracies to face their tasks with whatever strength God may give them"

At the same time Britain made allies of Thailand and Free China.

Mr. Churchill told the House of Commons that instructions had been forwarded to the British Embassy at Tokyo, and that at 1 p. m. (7 a. m., E. S. T.) a note was handed to the Japanese Charge d'Affaires here "stating that in view of Japan's wanton acts of unprovoked aggression the British Government informed them that a state of war existed between the two countries."

Mr. Churchill recalled that "with the full approval of the nation and of the Empire I pledged the word of Great Britain about a month ago that should the United States be involved in war with Japan, a British declaration would follow within the hour."

He declared that Britain had assured Thailand "that an attack on her will be regarded as an attack on us," and that he had informed Gen. Chiang Kai-shek of

Continued on Page 11, Column 6

The Pacific—Ocean of War by Choice of Japan

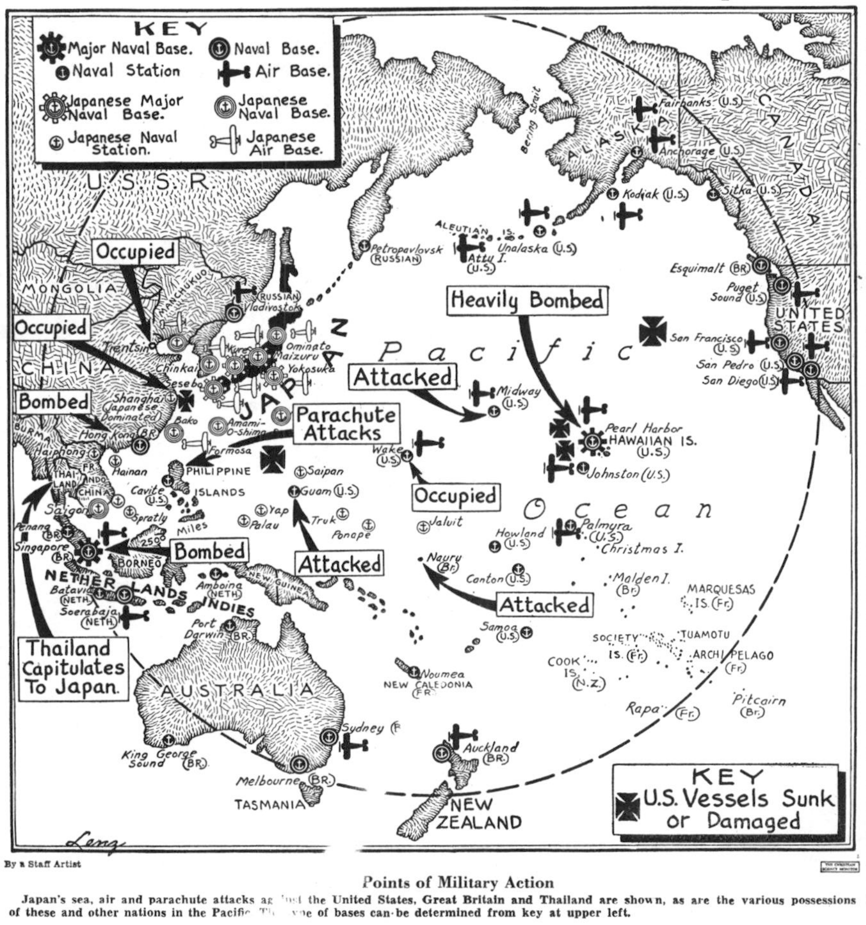

By a Staff Artist

Points of Military Action

Japan's sea, air and parachute attacks ag[illegible] the United States, Great Britain and Thailand are shown, as are the various possessions of these and other nations in the Pacific. [illegible] of bases can be determined from key at upper left.

Dramatic Scenes in Congress Attend Declaration of War

By a Staff Correspondent of The Christian Science Monitor

WASHINGTON, Dec. 8 — A grim-faced Congress forgot oratory and declared the existence of a "state of war" with Japan in record-breaking time today amid scenes that revealed a new atmosphere of unity and determination.

The historic scene, including a short, rugged speech by President Roosevelt to a joint session, attended by the Cabinet and the Supreme Court, was over less than 24 hours after raiding Japanese warplanes delivered their treacherous attack in the Pacific.

The vote on the war resolution in the House was one of the fastest in history. The Clerk read through the House list at breakneck speed, and member after member cried "Aye!" save for one exception.

"Rankin of Montana," cried the clerk.

"Nay!" said a woman's voice—the same Jeanette Rankin, who voted against the World War declaration. Miss Rankin had previously tried to get the floor but had been unsuccessful.

That was the only negative vote. At 1:27 the total was announced 388 to 1.

The Senate had previously voted 82 to 0.

Crowds Line Approaches

Scenes leading up to the vote were crisp and grim, in keeping with the mood of the day. There was an outburst of cheering of an unusually fervent sort as President Roosevelt's big limousine, flanked by outriders, swept up Pennsylvania Avenue just after noon. Packed crowds cheered his arrival outside the Capitol.

It was a dull midwinter day, with the sky overcast as the President arrived, and swept almost free of clouds in the brief interval before his departure. The last brown leaves still clung to a few of the big trees on the Capitol Plaza. Crowds lined the approaches. They cheered as the President's procession arrived. Inside the Capitol a big display of police kept order, and at the House side were Marines with fixed bayonets.

At 12:20 the Senate trouped into the House Chamber. Galleries were packed to the last degree. Eyes turned to Mrs. Roosevelt in the distinguished visitors gallery.

Then came in the black-robed

Continued on Page 4, Column 1

THE CHRISTIAN SCIENCE MONITOR

AN INTERNATIONAL DAILY NEWSPAPER

COPYRIGHT 1941 BY THE CHRISTIAN SCIENCE PUBLISHING SOCIETY

BOSTON, TUESDAY, DECEMBER 9, 1941—VOL. XXXIV, NO. 13

ATLANTIC EDITION—FIVE CENTS A COPY

Tokyo Reported Bombed; West Coast Hunts Carrier; Hemisphere Aid for U. S.

The World's Day—December 9, 1941

War in the Pacific:

Latin America

President Vargas issued a decree placing the financial operations of citizens of all non-American warring countries under the control of the Bank of Brazil.

All police reserves in the Brazilian State of Sao Paulo—which contains the greater part of Brazil's 170,000 Japanese residents—were ordered to duty immediately.

Outright declarations of war against Japan were made by eight Latin-American countries as expressions of solidarity with the United States poured into Washington.

Mexico and Colombia severed diplomatic relations with Japan.

Argentina, Brazil, and Chile refrained from war declarations but co-operated with hemisphere defense. Argentina proposed to let United States warships use its ports. Brazil's Foreign Minister, Oswaldo Aranha, said his country would "do its part."

Chile sponsored a conference of American Foreign Ministers on the Pacific war. The United States, Brazil, and Argentina supported the idea. Plans are under way.

Asia

Bombing of Tokyo and Kobe and the Japanese island of Formosa was reported in an unconfirmed CBS radiocast from Manila.

The Burma Road was the objective of a reported Japanese land thrust across northern Thailand. [Page 4.]

Attack on Singapore area was announced by Japan. British reports said reinforcements were rushed to area north of the port to thwart fresh Japanese troop landings.

Bangkok was occupied by Japanese troops who reached the Thailand Capital after Thai troops ceased resistance.

Invasion of Hong Kong was begun by Japanese troops, who had surrounded the recently-reinforced British crown colony.

West Coast

A Japanese aircraft carrier off the California coast was being sought by the United States Army and Navy following reports of reconnaisance flights by squadrons of Japanese planes over the San Francisco Bay area last night.

First official casualty list naming 37 officers and men killed in action in Japanese attack on Hawaii was released by the War Department. At the same time House Naval Committee members requested high officials to appear and explain how Japanese reached Hawaii.

British Columbia, observing total black outs during the night, expected a Japanese attack on the Pacific Northwest.

Oceania

Japanese off the Aleutian Islands, in the narrow Bering Strait between Alaska and Siberia, stirred new alarms in the Pacific.

The Island of Guam was attacked by 18 light and medium Japanese bombers at 8:45 a. m. yesterday. About half a dozen planes made a second attack at 2:45 p. m., United States Naval Headquarters announced at Manila.

The Philippines continued to receive heavy assaults. Manila was bombed heavily; Japanese soldiers attempted a landing on an island in Manila Bay; air raids were carried out on Fort William McKinley and Nicholas Airfield.

Hawaii was quiet following the heavy attacks Dec. 7 in which Japan sank a battleship, a destroyer and caused 3,000 casualties, half of them fatalities, according to the White House.

Midway Island was attacked by Japanese forces.

Russia: Germans Reported Driven Back

In Russia, Moscow press claimed that the Germans in the south were being pushed back west of Taganrog. Severe cold was bringing operations to a standstill in most other sectors.

Africa: Rommel Regroups Army in Libya

Gen. Erwin Rommel was reported in Cairo to be regrouping his Libyan army for a resumption of fighting in Libya after withdrawing westward to a line from Tobruk to Bir el Gobi.

Washington: All Axis Nationals 'Enemy Aliens'

President Roosevelt placed Japanese, Italians and Germans in this country in the category of "enemy aliens" and prescribed by proclamations the conduct they must follow.

All Japanese banks and business were seized by the Treasury and from 700 to 1,000 Japanese nationals taken into custody by the F. B. I.

Leon Henderson, Federal Price Administrator, told the Senate Banking Committee that he has a new draft of a drastic price control bill which he will urge as a substitution for the bill passed by the House. [Financial Page.]

The White House declared that Germany "obviously" did all it could "to push Japan into the war" in the hope it would end the lend-lease program but this program, the statement said, "is and will continue in full operation."

The House completed Congressional action on legislation to hold all Navy enlisted men in service for the duration of the war.

A Red Cross drive to raise $50,000,000 to be used for armed forces of the United States was announced by Chairman Norman H. Davis.

The State Department asked an unidentified neutral nation to negotiate an exchange of nationals between the United States and Japan.

Maxim Litvinoff presented his credentials as Russian Ambassador to the United States to President Roosevelt, after which the two conferred on the war situation.

National: Railroads to Ask Fare Increase

The Association of American Railroads decided to ask for a 10 per cent increase in basic passenger fares to help compensate for an estimated $300,000 annual pay roll boost incurred in the compromise settlement of their employees' wage demands.

The Christian Science Monitor Index

Tuesday, December 9, 1941

Costa Rica Ignored

NEW YORK, Dec. 9 (AP)—A German radio dispatch from Tokyo today said a Government spokesman told foreign correspondents Japan would ignore Costa Rica's declaration of war, and presumably those of other Central American nations.

The spokesman was quoted as saying the only real state of war existed with the United States and the British Empire, and as expressing doubt that the South American nations would declare war on Japan without having "the least interest in the Far East."

Eastern Seaboard Has Air-Raid Tests; U. S. Planes Hunt 'Raider' in Atlantic

'Safety Valve' Role Assumed By Congress

By Richard L. Strout

Staff Correspondent of The Christian Science Monitor

WASHINGTON, Dec. 9—Congress has buckled down to its new role in the Japanese war.

A flood of new legislation and legislation that has gained new importance awaits action.

Congress also has its traditional role of safety value and watchful observer of military matters. Already Representative John D. Dingell (D) of Michigan has demanded courtmartial proceedings against five top Army and Navy commanders, including Admiral Husband E. Kimmel, Commander in Chief of the United States Fleet for the "Naval debacle" at Pearl Harbor.

No war has even been fought by America yet in which scattered Congressmen did not demand somebody's courtmartial nearly every week. In the Civil War Congress at one point almost took operations out of Lincoln's hands but fortunately refrained. On the whole, the role of Congress is invaluable, when kept within proper bounds, in spurring on the Executive, in watching jealously the course of operations, in giving popular sentiment a vehicle of expression, and exposing inefficiency, bungling and selfishness.

Price Bill Hearings Start

Immediate problems before Congress are specific. The Senate Banking and Currency Committee started hearings today on the admittedly inadequate House price control bill. With war declared there is more danger of inflation than ever. Long, hard, dull, constructive toil is needed by legislative committees to frame proper controls. The work of this character in Congress may be as important in the long run as that of the ships at sea. Selfish interests and political blocs have been reduced in the common patriotism of the start of this war, but all sorts of sectional considerations must still be taken into account.

That isn't all. The Treasury wants money more than ever. Sec-

Continued on Page 6, Column 3

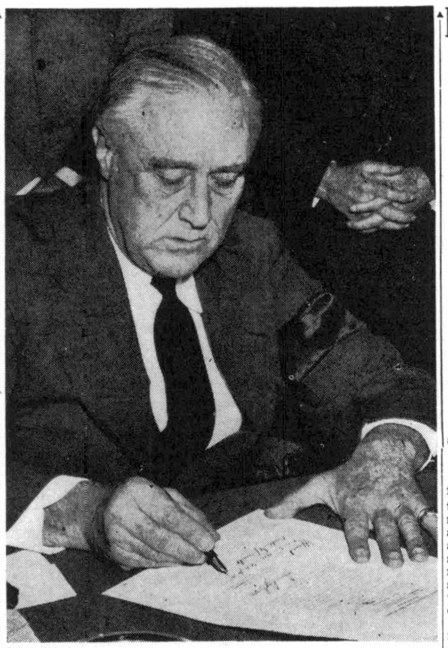

International

President Signs Declaration of War

An historic moment at the White House. President Roosevelt affixes his signature to the resolution passed with only one dissenting vote by Congress proclaiming the existence of a state of war between the United States and Japan.

Hitler Seen Guiding Hand Behind Japanese 'Blitz'

By Randall Gould

Former Chief Far Eastern Correspondent of The Christian Science Monitor

WASHINGTON, Dec. 9—Berlin is today the military Capital of Japan.

Adolf Hitler's role has suddenly become enlarged to make him arch-plotter not merely of Europe but of the world.

Forecasts of Japanese political and military action have consistently, and naturally, been made on a basis of Japanese psychology coupled with estimates of the Japa-

Continued on Page 7, Column 1

Russia Faces Decision On Pacific War

KUIBYSHEV, Russia, Dec. 9 (AP)—Official Russia kept its silence today on receipt of the news of the Japanese-American conflict.

Expiration of the Russian-Japanese fishing pact at the end of this month may bring the first clarification of relations between Japan and the Soviets.

The Far Eastern fisheries Pact, which gave the Japanese the right to fish in Russian waters, expires Dec. 31. Diplomats are watching to see whether the deadline will bring a renewal prolonging anomalous relations between the two countries or a break.

By Edmund Stevens

Special Correspondent of The Christian Science Monitor and an authority on Soviet Russia.

With no direct news in as yet from the Soviet Far East, the question how Russia is affected in the new Pacific war is best clarified by asking what will be America's new attitude to the war in Europe. Russia would lose as much by a Japanese victory or even temporary success in the Orient as America would by a Nazi victory in Europe or North Africa.

Just as Japan is utterly committed to a victory of its Nazi partner, America's future is tied up with the Allied cause. It is all one war.

The Russians, who have long insisted on the indivisibility of war and have shown considerable realism in their strategy, are fairly certain to appreciate where their interests lie in the Far East.

Tactical Considerations

Within the last few days Great Britain, in response to Russian pressure, declared war on Finland, Hungary, and Rumania, on the grounds that those countries were fighting Britain's ally. On a reciprocal basis, Russia is therefore committed to declare war on Japan whenever Britain requests her to.

But apart from these general

Continued on Page 7, Column 4

Russians press back freezing Germans: Page 6.

Boston and New York school pupils dismissed—Fore River ship plant closes as warning is sounded—Mitchel Field civilians are evacuated from danger zone.

The United States—whose Pacific possessions since Sunday have felt the impact of total war—experienced on its two seaboards within 24 hours the grim prospect of enemy air raids.

New England and New York, experiencing sudden test warnings with reports of enemy planes off the coast, quickly took thorough air-raid precautions.

Passenger automobiles were ordered off Boston streets. Civilian employees were evacuated from the Boston Navy Yard. Schools emptied their children. The Bethlehem Shipbuilding Company's largest plant at Fore River, near Boston, was evacuated completely. The Navy's huge air base at Quonset, R. I., sounded an air alarm. Boston sounded the "all clear" signal at 2:19 p. m.

New York meanwhile was experiencing two air-raid alarms. Planes at Mitchel Field took to the air. Families were evacuated from the military reservation. The city's million school children were dismissed. The first alarm sounded at 1:25 p. m., E. S. T., lasted 20 minutes. The second came as the result of a mistaken fire alarm.

The Army in Washington would not confirm the report that hostile planes had been sighted off the Atlantic Coast, but Cordell Hull, Secretary of State, did warn his press conference that the country should be on guard against a sudden German move supporting Japan in fulfillment of the Axis Tripartite Pact.

As the Atlantic Coast experienced its first air-raid warnings, Pacific Coast defense forces combed the California coast to see if there were any Japanese aircraft carriers harboring the enemy planes that last night were reported making reconnaissance flights over the San Francisco Bay area. Black-outs were experienced by numerous Coast cities, and radio stations were put off the air.

Tokyo, Kobe, and the Japanese Island of Formosa were bombed, according to a radiocast by CBS from Manila, though such bombings remained unverified.

The United States' speedy declaration of war against Japan, signed by the President shortly after passage by Congress, was accompanied by a growing list of such declarations by anti-Axis nations. Seventeen nations to date have ranged themselves with the United States in the Pacific war.

American possessions in the Pacific continued to suffer heavily from Japanese blows from the air. Manila, severely bombed yesterday, was attacked again today as were other strategic points in the Philippine Islands. Japanese troops were said to have landed on the Island of Lubang, near Manila Bay, aided by "fifth columnists" posing as fishermen. Tokyo claimed the capture of Guam and Wake Islands. The status of Midway Island was in doubt.

American Army and Navy officials are giving no reports on enemy losses in air and naval action, but they do deny that the seaplane tender Langley had been bombed during a Japanese attack on Davao.

Japanese land armies simultaneously began an invasion of Hong Kong in the north, and attempted fresh troop landings in British Malaya, just north of Singapore, Straits Settlement.

Japanese fleet units were reported off the Aleutian Islands between Alaska and Siberia, resulting in predictions in blacked-out British Columbia that the Pacific Northwest coast would be attacked.

Japanese Moves on the War Front in the Pacific

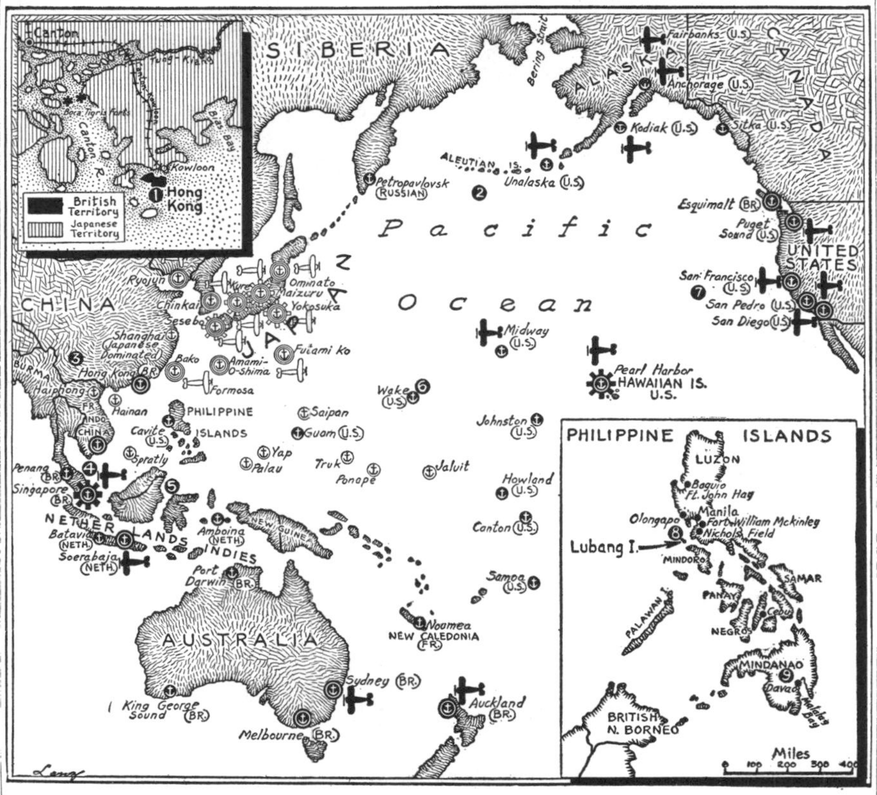

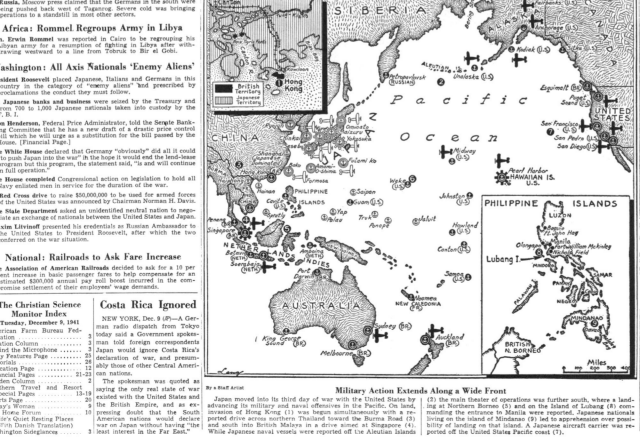

By a Staff Artist

Military Action Extends Along a Wide Front

Japan moved into its third day of war with the United States by advancing its military and naval offensives in the Pacific. On land, invasion of Hong Kong (1) was begun simultaneously with a reported drive across northern Thailand toward the Burma Road (3) and south into British Malaya in a drive aimed at Singapore (4). While Japanese naval vessels were reported off the Aleutian Islands (2) the main theater of operations was further south, where a landing at Northern Borneo (5) and on the Island of Lubang (8) commanding the entrance to Manila were reported. Japanese nationals living on the island of Mindanao (9) led to apprehension over possibility of landing on that island. A Japanese aircraft carrier was reported off the United States Pacific coast (7).

New York Tests Its Defenses In Air-Raid Alarm

NEW YORK Dec. 9 (AP)—Public safety officials disclosed today that a series of air-raid alerts and alarms which electrified the Eastern Seaboard this afternoon were merely a dress rehearsal and that reports of approaching enemy planes were false.

By a Staff Correspondent of The Christian Science Monitor

NEW YORK, Dec. 9—A wartime New York awoke today to regular air patrol and daily drill for its 115,287 air raid wardens and 25,000 auxiliary firemen, as the First Interceptor Command called to active duty 40,000 volunteer civilian aircraft spotters at 1,300 posts scattered through 13 Eastern coastal States and the District of Columbia.

It is an East on guard on land, in the air, and on the sea, and New York City is on the alert, transformed over night from an easy-going metropolis into a community ready to go on complete war-footing at the first alarm.

Task Taken in Stride

In hundreds of ways the fact was being driven home to citizens today that the United States had entered hostilities as City, State, and Federal Government authorities buckled on the preparedness armor. Corollary to the whole was the lineup outside every Army, Navy and Marine Corps recruiting office in the City now on a 24-hour schedule and reporting three times as many applicants for enrollment as on April 6, 1917. Navy and Marine offices listed 1,200 applicants by yesterday mid-afternoon, with 1,000 more turned away for return at a later date.

As the war plans of the Army and Navy for protection of the city and seaboard took form, citizens took the big new moment of his-

Continued on Page 8, Column 1

New U. S. Policy: To Fight Axis On World-wide Front

By a Staff Correspondent of The Christian Science Monitor

WASHINGTON, Dec. 9—The most significant evidence developed today to show that the United States is undertaking total war against the Axis.

Congress is ready formally to declare war on Germany and Italy at the least sign of Nazi aid to Japan.

Proof that such aid already is being given by Berlin, both instigating and strengthening Japanese attacks on the United States, is already in the possession of the White House, it was authoritatively learned.

In consequence, new steps against the Axis in Europe—as well as against the Axis in Asia—which cannot yet be announced, have been taken.

The purpose of President Roosevelt's radiocast to the nation tonight is to prepare the way for acceptance of war on the widest possible front and it is in light of this fact that the announcement that Mr. Roosevelt will deal with "the Nazi pattern" behind Tokyo's multi-thrusts in the Pacific takes on its largest meaning.

Evidence that the war will be fought against the Axis on every front where America can make its force felt came from extraordinarily reliable sources and was illustrated in numerous develop-

Continued on Page 24, Column 1

Congress war "safety valve": important legislation awaits it: Page 1.

Canada's new western front calm: Page 5.

Far West's businessmen map economic war against Japan: Page 6.

Relief tempers amazement as Oregon readies for war: Page 4.

Los Angeles' festive color hides concern over war: Page 2.

THE CHRISTIAN SCIENCE MONITOR

AN INTERNATIONAL DAILY NEWSPAPER

COPYRIGHT 1941 BY THE CHRISTIAN SCIENCE PUBLISHING SOCIETY

BOSTON, THURSDAY, DECEMBER 11, 1941—VOL. XXXIV, NO. 15

* * — ATLANTIC EDITION—FIVE CENTS A COPY

U. S. Formally at War With All Axis; Bomber Sinks Japanese Battleship

U. S. Regains Aparri Area; Senate Opens A.E.F. Way; African Command Shifts

The World's Day—December 11, 1941

War in the Pacific: Aparri Area Recovered

At Sea

The Philippine Army was reported unofficially but reliably to have recaptured the region around Aparri, on the north coast of Luzon, and to be driving the Japanese back to the seacoast.

Sinking of the 29,000-ton Japanese battleship Haruna by a United States Army bomber off the northern coast of Luzon in the Philippines was announced by Secretary of War Stimson.

Tokyo claimed Japanese forces occupied Agana, the capital of Guam, and captured 350 Americans including Capt. George G. McMillin and other officers.

No attacks have been made against the Hawaiian Islands since Dec. 7, the Army Command announced. The islands, blacked out last night, are under martial law.

The Americas

The Panama Canal was closed until further notice from 6 p. m. to 6 a. m. by the United States Army while precautionary blackouts were ordered for the Canal zone and the city of Panama.

More than 1,000 Germans, Italians and Japanese were detained by Panama police for transfer to the Canal Zone quarantine station.

Lazaro Cardenas, former President of Mexico, was appointed commander of Mexico's Pacific forces by President Avila Camacho.

Colombia, after severing relations with Japan, let it be known that a declaration of war against the United States by Germany or Italy would bring similar action.

El Salvador ordered universal military training for all male citizens from 15 to 50 years.

The Bolivian Government expressed solidarity with the American nations which have declared war against Japan and offered its collaboration without actually declaring war.

Asiatic Continent

In Malaya the British admitted that Japanese air attacks had knocked out several airdromes. No new reports of fighting on the Malay-Thailand border were published.

Australian bombers based in the Netherlands East Indies raided a Japanese air base on the island of Pobra between the Celebes and Japanese-mandated Palau Islands southeast of Manila.

Hong Kong fighting continued although British reports said Japanese attacks had been repelled. Japan claimed sinking of two British gunboats off Hong Kong.

Tokyo black-out has been ordered by the Japanese Government, according to German radio dispatches.

President Roosevelt sent a message to Generalissimo Chiang Kai-shek of China, confident of success in the mutual struggle. [Page 8.]

Washington: Senate Lifts Ban on A. E. F.

The Senate, by a vote of 86 to 0, approved legislation lifting present restrictions against use of selectees and National Guardsmen outside the Western Hemisphere.

Sale of rubber tires and tubes was prohibited by the Office of Production Management Priorities Division, effective until Dec. 22, pending the formulation of "a more permanent" plan for controlling rubber distribution. [Page 3.]

American "Benedict Arnolds"—citizens suspected of being "fifth columnists," of propagandizing in behalf of the Axis, and whose loyalty was questioned—were being listed for F. B. I. study.

The nation's radio facilities were placed at the disposal of the Army and Navy by President Roosevelt, but no "general taking over or operation of private radio by the Government is contemplated," an official spokesman said.

Enough food for all in the United States and some for Allies abroad is on hand for winter, the Department of Agriculture said.

Production of giant four-motored bombers will be increased from the present number of 500 a month to 1,000 under a plan announced by William S. Knudsen, Director of the OPM.

The State Department said funds for the personal needs of employees of the Japanese Embassy and consultants here had been released on a reciprocal basis; it also announced German newspaper correspondents were being held for investigation.

Miss Harriet Elliott's resignation as consumer adviser in the OPM was accepted by President Roosevelt, effective at once.

Africa: Britain Changes Army Commander

A shift in command in Britain's African army replaced Gen. Sir Alan Gordon Cunningham with Maj. Gen. Neil Methuen Ritchie as commander of the British Eighth Army.

National: Tobacco Firms, Officials Fined

Reynolds, Liggett and Myers, and American—three big tobacco companies—and 13 officials, were denied a new trial on price-fixing and monopoly convictions and fined $15,000 each by the United States District Court in Lexington, Ky.

Australia: Government Firms Its Policy

Australian Government, according to Prime Minister Curtin, is recasting its entire war strategy following Allied naval losses. Appeals to public, he said, are at an end. The public must now accept whatever decrees the Government finds necessary to issue. [Page 5.]

In Europe: New Axis Pact Against Allies

War declarations against the United States were made by Reichsführer Hitler and Premier Mussolini. [Pages 1 and 18.]

Executions in France were renewed with the shooting of 11 residents of Brest for possession of arms and explosives.

Prime Minister Churchill warned of heavy losses already sustained by the Allies in the Far East, but added that combined naval might of the Allied democracies was "still largely superior to the combined forces of the three Axis powers." [Page 7.]

German forces both in the Moscow and the Rostov sectors were stated to be continuing their withdrawal in Russia, harried by guerrillas.

New England: Freighter Sinks in Collision

At least eight bodies and several survivors from the freighter Oregon were brought into New Bedford, Mass., today, approximately 24 hours after the vessel went to the bottom following a collision with a U. S. Navy ship.

The Christian Science Monitor Index

Thursday, December 11, 1941

Substantial Gains Made by Ohio Drys

Special to The Christian Science Monitor

CLEVELAND, Ohio—Substantial gains made by Ohio dry forces in local option elections held this fall, according to Secretary of State John E. Sweeney. Official returns show that 28 communities which were wet voted dry. Through other votes on various phases of liquor retailing, the drys registered gains in a total of 31 counties. In only one instance did a community that had been dry vote wet.

Joint War Plan Urged as Need Of U. S.-Allies

By Mallory Browne
Staff Correspondent of The Christian Science Monitor

LONDON, Dec. 11—As Germany and Italy declare war on the United States, they make mandatory a single world-wide grand strategy plan on the part of the democratic powers—a world conception of strategy which has too long been lacking in this war.

President Roosevelt's reference in his Tuesday night talk to the importance of the working out of such a common strategy has been welcomed here as one of the most important portions of his speech.

The President's reiteration that Germany and Japan were conducting their military and naval operations in accordance with a joint plan has been swiftly documented by the joint Axis declaration of war on America.

But so far Britain and the United States have not even established their mutual status as allies, in striking contrast to Germany, Italy and Japan who today signed full alliance. Britain, the United States, and China are merely associated against common enemies and there has been no American statement so far even of association with Soviet Russia.

Combatting "Total Treachery"

Military experts here—speaking now as Allies and not only as observers of United States strategy—emphasize that America and Britain, with the Dominions, China, and Russia must at once adopt and carry out a "grand design" for war if they are to match successfully the "total treachery" of Hitler, Mussolini, and Tojo.

For the present situation is the result of certain facts which clearly imply that the war has entered a drastically different phase.

For one thing, Germany has been stopped in Russia. Hitler's hopes of seizing Moscow and Rostov and of destroying the Soviet armies before the winter sufficiently to turn westward with freer hands for a blow at Britain have been frustrated.

American Moves Help

Another important factor was the American move in modifying the Neutrality Act, in speeding up production, and in generally coming more and more openly into the war even before the Japanese attack.

These two developments, combined with increased British production, especially of tanks and planes, undoubtedly influenced the Nazi leaders to try a new tack by impelling Japan to strike now.

Japan's entrance into the war has overnight presented Hitler with a powerful ally who is strongest where Germany is weakest, namely, on the sea.

Hitler undoubtedly calculated that this fact will force Britain and America to draw upon their naval resources in the Atlantic in order to meet the grave menace in the Pacific—or at least he counts on America and Britain being unable to strengthen their Atlantic fleets.

Attack on Africa Seen

There is reason to believe that Hitler intends to capitalize on this ituation by pushing southward into Spain and Portugal and from there into northwest Africa, thereby gaining many new bases from which to intensify the Battle of the Atlantic and even to threaten South America iself.

There is a clear realization here on the part of the general public, the Government, and naval and military authorities that the conflagration has now spread to every continent.

But careful inquiries here disclose no signs that anything is being done either to work out one all-embracing battle plan or even to set up some sort of joint General Staff capable of co-ordinating and unifying the separate strategic schemes of the anti-Axis nations.

Co-operation in Pacific

The only thing approaching such united action, so far as can be ascertained here, is a certain amount of apparent co-operation between the British, American, and Dutch fleets in the Pacific, as well as the inevitable co-ordination of convoy activity on the Atlantic arising out of the virtual repeal of the Neutrality Act.

Apart from this, there is no evidence that either in London, Moscow, Washington, or Chungking is anything being done by the Governments about this urgent need for such a world-wide grand strategy.

Well-informed observers here agree that Germany is staking everything on a sudden shift of strategic emphasis from the Rus-

Continued on Page 9, Column 2

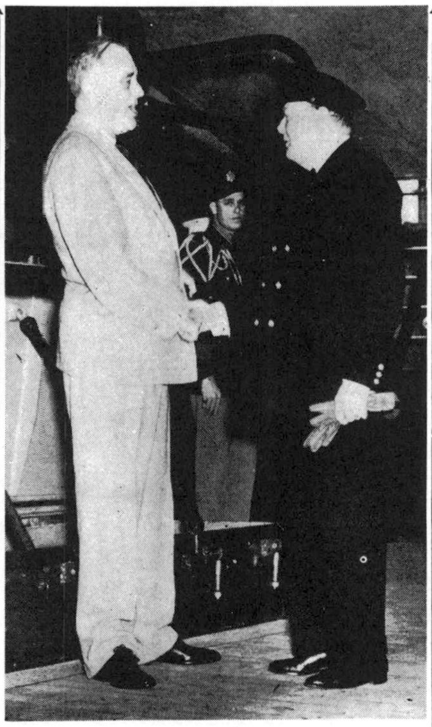

'In Freedom's Crowning Hour'

Today the two great democracies are linked in the indivisible task of establishing the world order foreseen by President Roosevelt and Prime Minister Churchill in the Atlantic Charter.

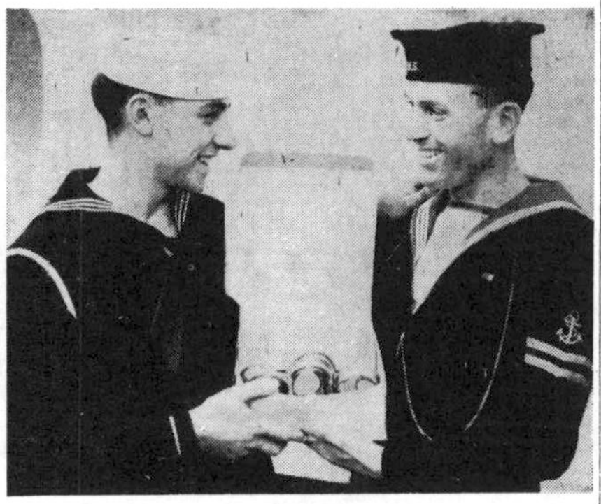

'To mightier issues than we planned'

Joint patrol of seven seas, with new meaning, links British and American seamen. Two are pictured at the Atlantic Charter meeting.

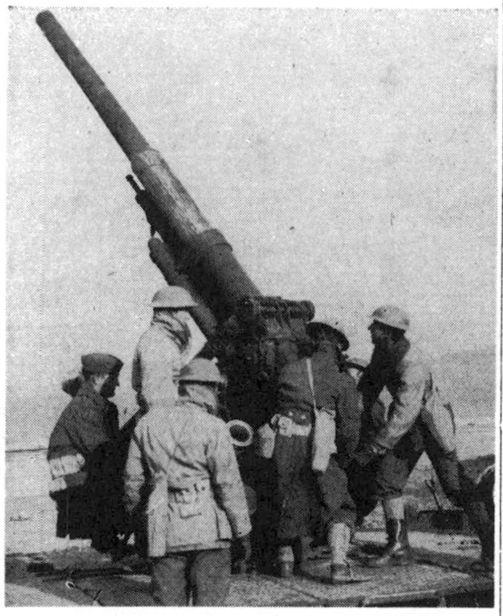

'Oh fearless men . . . I call'

These alert antiaircraft gunners manning one of the Army's powerful weapons are guarding a vital shore position in the vicinity of Boston. Other crews have been stationed at strategic spots along the New England coast.

Photographs: Wide World and by a Staff Photographer

Pacific War Balance Less Uneven Now

By Joseph G. Harrison
Staff Correspondent of The Christian Science Monitor

WASHINGTON, Dec. 11—The balance of war in the Pacific, which tilted strongly against the United States and its allies during the first four days of conflict, swung back somewhat today as American forces sank a 29,000-ton Japanese battleship and confined Japanese attacks upon the Philippine Islands to a small area in northern Luzon.

Simultaneously, Secretary of War Henry L. Stimson announced that while American plane losses in Hawaii were heavy, "this loss can be and immediately is being made good."

Speaking calmly and confidently, the Secretary said that the chief concern today was not to place blame for past mistakes, but to push forward with present efforts to strengthen American offensive and defensive power in all parts of the world.

Partial Compensation

The Air Corps' success in sinking the Japanese battleship, which is believed to be the 29,330-ton Haruna or one of its class, has offset to a degree the heavy initial loss in capital ships suffered by the Allied powers.

The United States Government has already conceded the loss of one old battleship in Pearl Harbor, while the British have lost the new Prince of Wales and the older Repulse.

The sinking of the Haruna reduces to 10, or possibly 11, the number of Japanese battleships available for service. Estimates differ as to how many of America's 17 battleships were in the Pacific when the war broke out, although it is known that some were in the North Atlantic.

The Haruna was one of the least powerful of the Japanese battleships, carrying but eight 14-inch guns and having been built in 1913.

Democracy's Momentum

Bespeaking a full realization of the long and immensely hard road before the American people, Secretary Stimson said that "when we survey the situation in cold blood we must expect initial reverses. They are almost always to be expected in fighting an autocratic nation which has been at war for several years.

"All students of history know, however," the Secretary said, "that a war falls into three periods. First is the period of the war's onset. Second is the period of drag, and finally there is the finish.

"In the first period the free governments inevitably are at a distinct disadvantage. In the later period, however, when it becomes a contest of endurance the democracies win the war. The last shots are the ones that count and not the first. The democratic nations have a momentum which cannot be possessed by a nation ruled by one man."

The Secretary then recounted an

Continued on Page 6, Column 7

Churchill grave at Allied losses at sea: Page 5.

Germany and Italy declare war first, with action by Congress and President following quickly —New Berlin-Rome-Tokyo alliance—Japanese 'chutists reported at Luzon airport.

The United States today is officially at war with Germany and Italy. Acting swiftly after Rome and Berlin declared war on the United States this morning, the United States Congress listened to a request for a war declaration from President Roosevelt and responded in record time with action that put the nation at war with Italy and Germany. President Roosevelt immediately signed the declarations.

Meanwhile Hitler, addressing the Reichstag, announced a new military alliance with Italy and Japan. Members of the tripartite pact from today on are locked in a finish fight with Britain and the United States.

United States air forces were credited with sinking an enemy cruiser and destroyer at Wake Island.

In the battle over the island of Luzon in the Philippines, reliable but unofficial reports claimed that Philippine troops had recaptured the region around Aparri, on the north coast of Luzon and were driving the Japanese back to the coast. Japanese 'chutists, however, seized the airport near Iligan in Eastern Luzon and Washington confirmed the sinking of the Haruna, a 29,000-ton Japanese battleship by a United States bomber off the northern coast of the island.

Hawaii, which bore the brunt of the Japanese initial attack on Sunday, reported no new raids. Martial law was proclaimed in the territory.

Throughout the Western Hemisphere, the imminence of Axis action or the realization of its danger was driven home. The Panama Canal was closed from 6 p. m. to 6 a. m. as a war precaution. Mexico's President Avila Camacho named his predecessor, Lazaro Cardenas, Commander-in-Chief of all the country's Pacific forces.

The outbreak of war in the Pacific and American reverses forced the United States to revise upward its already mounting war-production program. Basic arms industries henceforth will be pouring out tanks, planes, and arms 24 hours a day, seven days a week, OPM Director Knudsen announced. A billion dollars a week is America's war bill now envisioned.

Berlin-Rome-Tokyo Axis Pact Pledges 'No Separate Peace'

By the Associated Press

Thursday, Dec. 11

Germany and Italy simultaneously declared war on the United States, fulfilling the Rome-Berlin-Tokyo alliance of totalitarianism against democracy.

To cheering throngs in Berlin and Rome, Hitler and Mussolini made the declarations at approximately 8 a. m., E. S. T.

Premier Mussolini spoke from his balcony post at the Palazzo Venezia in Rome, Führer Hitler before the German Reichstag.

Both had been foreshadowed, a Japanese spokesman having declared yesterday that "Japan expected Germany and Italy to declare war on the United States" in fulfillment of the Rome-Berlin-Tokyo alliance of totalitarianism against democracy.

Soon after word reached Tokyo that Germany and Italy had joined Japan in war on the United States, the Nippon Government announced that all three Axis powers had

Continued on Page 6, Column 1

How Hitler declared war on U. S.: Page 8.

Mussolini hails 'privilege' of fighting at Japan's side: Page 8.

Congress Quickly Moves for United War Against Axis

By Roscoe Drummond
Staff Correspondent of The Christian Science Monitor

WASHINGTON, Dec. 11—The United States today accepted war with Germany and Italy and pledged a rapid and united effort to insure a world victory over the Axis.

President Roosevelt, without troubling to go to Congress in person so inevitable was the verdict, informed the House and Senate that Germany and Italy, pursuing their course of world conquest, had declared war against the United States.

Without hesitancy, without debate, Congress replied in kind and this verdict strengthens and clarifies the nation's whole plan of war strategy.

How Congress Voted

The Senate vote for war against Germany was 88 to 0, for war against Italy 90 to 0. Two Senators reached the chamber for the second vote but missed the first. The House vote for war against Germany was 393 to 0, for war against Italy 399 to 0. But in each instance Representative Jeanette Rankin (R) of Montana, who voted against war with Japan Monday and against war with Germany in 1917, voted "present" rather than for or against a war declaration.

Since Germany's action, joining Japan formally in attacking the United States, was regarded as certain, the verdict today is welcomed.

Its immediate effect is to enable the President to conduct a united Allied war against the united Axis, to pool, wherever strategy requires, the naval, air, and land forces of the United States and Britain.

The great value of the declaration is that it gives clear-cut Congressional and national support to the plan of battle which recognizes Nazi Germany as the main and major enemy; it permits the greatest possible flexibility in conducting the war on a world scale and presents a common allied front to the Axis on every front.

"Never before has there been a greater challenge to life, liberty and civilization," the President told Congress in a briefly, tersely worded message.

Mr. Roosevelt said that Hitler's declaration of open war on America was long expected and its certainty long known.

Congress could not be more united. There were no isolationists against the war which Germany declared. There were no Republicans opposing the Administration. There were only American Con-

Continued on Page 6, Column 7

[A detailed study of resources of United States, Great Britain and their allies and those of the Axis powers is given in a tabulation compiled by the U. S. Department of Commerce: Financial Page.]

Plea for Spiritual Guidance Opens Congress War Session

By a Staff Correspondent of The Christian Science Monitor

WASHINGTON, Dec. 11—Prayer for the spiritual guidance of the American people and the American Government through the deep trials which must be faced fearlessly preceded the first war sessions of the United States Congress.

Before the Senate unanimously passed its resolution authorizing the President to defend the country against Japanese attack it heard its Chaplain urge reliance on God to "keep us fine and true in our individual and corporate lives," and appeal to Congress to be receptive to the "intuition and courage" which comes from divine reliance.

The Chaplain of the House, prior to the joint session addressed by President Roosevelt, asked the legislators to turn to divine leading whereby the nation will be kept free "from passion and hate" and be blessed "with the enduring prizes of national unity, honor, and integrity."

Thus the prayers which opened this historic meeting of Congress are really the prayers of the whole country today and deserve special contemplation at this time.

Prayer in Senate

The Rev. Zebarney T. Phillips' prayer in the Senate follows:

O thou blessed Christ, companion of our days, mediator of the infinite God, and the creator of a new world of being which men may know if they follow thee and in which thy tender love is ever available to lonely and despairing souls: help us to find in thee a sustaining sense of justice which shall become a passion for the amelioration of the wrongs of men, as honor calls us to the defense of every sacred ideal of our beloved country.

Keep us fine and true in our individual and corporate lives, steadfast in purpose that we may endure with patience and calm determination every trial, discipline, and sacrifice through which we may be called upon to pass, as we meet the exactions of these days out of which must emerge the future destiny of mankind.

Bless thou the Congress with intuition and courage; strengthen our President with the strength of thine own indwelling, and comfort him with the knowlege that today the loyalty of every citizen is pledged under his leadership to the service of the nation as it undertakes its solemn task.

Do thou have in thy holy keeping those who have given their lives in the service of our country, and grant that in the new life they may serve thee with clearer vision and greater

Continued on Page 6, Column 2

THE CHRISTIAN SCIENCE MONITOR

AN INTERNATIONAL DAILY NEWSPAPER

COPYRIGHT 1942 BY THE CHRISTIAN SCIENCE PUBLISHING SOCIETY | BOSTON, WEDNESDAY, MAY 6, 1942—VOL. XXXIV, NO. 137 | **ATLANTIC EDITION | THREE CENTS Greater Boston Newsstands | FIVE CENTS Elsewhere

Stuttgart Again Bombed; Time Payments Curbed; Church War Duty Cited

The World's Day—May 6, 1942

The War: RAF Raids Stuttgart Second Night

In the air: Industrial plants around Stuttgart, southeast Germany, were bombed by the RAF for the second successive night; RAF admitted loss of four bombers. London asserted that British warplanes made 175 attacks on 62 targets in Europe, the Mediterranean and Pacific war theaters during April. At Malta 247 civilians were admitted killed during April.

At sea: RAF airmen were said belatedly to have scored a hit on the Nazi battleship Tirpitz when it was in Kiel harbor prior to the transfer to Trondheim, Norway.

Russia: Germans announced communications had been re-established with long encircled Nazi force, apparently in the Staraya Russa sector.

Burma: RAF bombers attacked a convoy of Japanese barges laden with troops up the Chindwin River, Burma, while United States bombers destroyed 40 Japanese grounded planes and damaged 25 others near Rangoon.

Australia: Allied airmen renewed attacks on Lae in New Guinea and Rabaul in New Britain, damaging troopship in those waters.

Atlantic: The United States Navy announced that a medium-sized Norwegian merchant vessel had been torpedoed and sunk off the Atlantic Coast. Survivors have been landed at an East Coast port.

Washington: New Installment Buying Curb

The Federal Reserve Board, carrying out President Roosevelt's anti-inflation program, tightened restrictions on installment buying and broadened them to include all charge-account purchases. [Financial Page.]

C. E. Wilson, President of General Motors Corporation, refused to comply with a National War Labor Board order to extend for three weeks the double time provision of the corporation's expired contract with the United Automobile Workers union as hearings opened before a NWLB panel. [Page 3.]

Gasoline consumption in the East will be slashed 50 per cent below normal starting May 16, the War Production Board announced, with many motorists limited to five or six gallons a week. [Page 1.]

Reversing its previous stand, the House Military Affairs Committee voted to knock out a rider in the service pay increase bill that would have limited issuance of Army commissions to officer-trained men, except in the cases of doctors, dentists, veterinarians, and chaplains.

New England: Sewall Stresses Church's Duty

"Tremendous responsibility" of the church in helping those in armed forces to gain a foundation for better citizenship in peacetime was emphasized by Gov. Sumner Sewall of Maine. [War Activities in New England: Page 2.]

Senate confirmation of the promotion of Rear Admiral Adolphus Andrews to Vice-Admiral was held up when Senator Ralph O. Brewster (R) of Maine asked if he was in any way responsible for the liner Normandie fire. [Page 2.]

Head of National War Labor Board and of United States Conciliation Service are coming to Boston to give the City's new Industrial Relations Council an auspicious send-off. [Page 2.]

The 40-hour week was assailed as one cause of higher prices for civilian goods before the Boston Rotary Club by James R. Bancroft, investment counsellor. [Page 5.]

John L. Lewis' plan of organizing dairy farmers was disapproved by an American Federation of Labor leader, who said the A. F. of L. rejected it, probably before Mr. Lewis picked it up. [Page 2.]

Railroads serving Boston agreed to forego dockage and wharfage charges on ships discharging ballast. [Page 2.]

National: Grand Jury Exonerates Flynn

Edward J. Flynn, National Democratic Chairman, was exonerated of charges that New York City materials and city labor were used in paving a courtyard on his Lake Mahopac estate by a Bronx County Grand Jury after five weeks of investigation.

Far East: India Plans Mission to Moscow

An Indian delegation will leave India shortly for Moscow on a good-will mission the British Radio announced, according to CBS.

In Europe: Prisoners' Food Shipments Ready

Food shipments for British war prisoners in Hong Kong and Singapore are ready to be sailed to the Far East as soon as the Japanese Government agrees to grant them a safe passage, Foreign Secretary Anthony Eden announced.

Cruiser 'Sunk' by Japanese Arrives at East Coast Port

WASHINGTON, May 6 (AP)—The United States light cruiser Marblehead, which the Japanese have several times claimed to have sunk, has arrived at an East Coast port, the Navy announced today, badly damaged and torn by bombs but "very much afloat."

The 7,050-ton cruiser has steamed half way around the world, making a portion of the trip with its steering gear disabled and sometimes barely managing to keep afloat, to "bring her wounds of war home for healing and testify," the Navy said, "to the struggles of captain and crew to keep their badly damaged ship going, even though war at times poured like a torrent through her sides."

The epic journey of about 13,000 miles was made after the cruiser was bombed, twice hit directly and once damaged under water by a near miss, during the preliminary phases of the battle for the utch East Indies when the Japanese were advancing southward through Macassar Strait.

"Her's is the story of a ship that was doomed to hell," a Navy account of the voyage and fighting said, "and was brought right out of it again by a crew that doesn't know the meaning of the word 'abandon.'"

Tokyo on Madagascar: 'We Are Prophets'

By the Associated Press

New York, May 6

The Tokyo Radio, as heard by CBS, had this to say last night on the British landing at Madagascar:

"Radio Tokyo predicted it. We are great prophets."

15,000 Pounds of Sugar Reported by a N. J. Man

NORTH BERGEN, N. J., May 6 (AP)—A North Bergen man reported as he signed up for sugar rationing that he had 15,000 pounds of the sweetener.

Ralph Mazzei, local rationing administrator, said the man, whose name was withheld, declared he bought the sugar two years ago in anticipation of the present shortage.

Mr. Mazzei said he would ask state officials what should be done.

The Christian Science Monitor Index

Wednesday, May 6, 1942

Weather Predictions

FAIR | WARMER | RAIN | COLDER

TONIGHT

Complete Weather Predictions for New England on Page 2

New England Reassured On Fuel Oil Cut

50 per cent reduction in deliveries called temporary measure to build up reserves.

The War Production Board's order to cut delivery of light fuel oil to New England dealers 50 per cent beginning May 15 is only a "stop gap" until reserves can be built up for this winter, Clyde G. Morrill, Executive Secretary of the Independent Oil Men's Association of New England, said today.

"New Englanders needn't get panicky over this announcement," Mr. Morrill said, "for when the cold weather sets in we hope to have built up enough fuel oil reserves to give people who heat their homes with oil 80 or 90 per cent of what they used last year. Certainly this should cause no hardship on anyone."

Mr. Morrill admitted that the light fuel oil situation is serious in New England and in order to protect the surplus on hand for use in industrial plants working on war orders the WPB deemed it necessary to cut deliveries 50 per cent.

No cut, however, has been ordered in deliveries of kerosene, known as number one oil, because so many people use this to cook with throughout the year, Mr. Morrill added.

Transportation Problem

"At the present time," he pointed out, "the railroads are hauling heavy loads of coal attempting to stock up New England with reserves enough for this winter. When this is done then more tank cars of oil will be hauled helping to build up a surplus of this fuel for those customers."

New England's oil and gasoline requirements by way of tank cars are about 1,500 tank cars a day. So far the best the railroads have done is 865 tank cars in one day.

Speaking of the gasoline situation in New England Mr. Morrill felt that from five to seven gallons a week would be about what the average motorist would get when the real rationing program gets under way May 15.

He felt, however, that allowances would be made for those entirely dependent upon automobiles to get to their work, whether it be in war industries or otherwise.

5 to 7 Gallons Seen

Officials in Washington, on the other hand, would not venture to say what the individual quota for nonessential drivers would be, but unofficial mathematicians figured there would not be more than five or six gallons a week available to

Continued on Page 2, Column 1

Corregidor and Manila Bay Forts Fall, Philippines Still Battling Japanese; Epic of U.S. Industry in War to Unfold

Nation-wide tour of all war production plants to reveal tremendous strides made.

"Production for Victory" in the United States has stepped up from the phase of tooling to mass output. Rolling back the curtain of secrecy which has guarded this unprecedented industrial effort, the National Association of Manufacturers has arranged a tour by 20 news correspondents. In collaboration with Army and Navy officers, the party will check up on progress made since the similar N. A. M. survey of June, 1941. The Christian Science Monitor's representative today outlines the trip's scope and purpose.

By Joseph G. Harrison

Staff Correspondent of The Christian Science Monitor

WASHINGTON, May 6—The forges of America are today ringing with the most stupendous industrial effort the world has ever seen—or imagined.

And now this torrent of production, carefully concealed behind barbed-wire, military guards and official secrecy, is to be uncovered with the special permission of the country's war agencies.

Sponsored by the National Association of Manufacturers, official body of most of American industry, 20 newspapermen are starting today on a 24-day tour of the main production centers in the eastern half of the country. We shall cover every major phase of the United States' war effort with what amounts to a virtual blow-by-blow description of the industrial war against the Axis.

Warplane plants, shipyards, gun factories, tanks, arsenals, smokeless powder plants, machine tool companies—all these and many others are being thrown open so that we may give a report to the nation on just how production stands today and how it will stand tomorrow.

Plenty to See

There'll be certain things we cannot see. There'll be more which we can see but cannot describe. But there'll be enough that we can both see and describe to permit America to judge for itself as to the basis for the new-found optimism with which President

Continued on Page 21, Column 4

Madagascar defense stiffens against British invasion — Allies report air victories.

By the War Editor of The Christian Science Monitor

Drawn from dispatches of the Associated Press and other sources

Surrender of the four Manila Bay forts to the Japanese four months after the capture of Manila and following close on the heels of the collapse of Mandalay is another heavy blow to the prestige of the United Nations. The continuous run of failures has been relieved by increasing evidence of Allied aerial ascendancy at certain points, although the British Madagascar expedition, which otherwise showed vigor and initiative, appears to have run into initial difficulties.

The destruction of 40 Japanese planes and serious damaging of 25 others by an American bombing squad at Mingaladon, near Rangoon, though too late to save defeat in Burma, at least shows sufficient Allied domination of the air to impede the Japanese in turning their victory to account. British bombers also appear to have damaged considerably troop-laden barges heading up the Chindwin River far in the interior of Burma.

Pending more detailed information from Madagascar, it would appear that the British landing party is taking some time to cut through the jungle from Courrier Bay to the naval base of Diego Suarez a few miles away, although there were reported to be only some 5,000 French and Colonial troops to oppose them.

Assuming that the three cruisers originally reported at the island, in default of any news from them, are not actually at Madagascar, the sinking of two French light naval units in the initial fighting in the bay may be regarded as a serious loss.

The main question appears to be whether the British can take the main bases of the large island before Japanese or German expeditions have time to put in an appearance.

Meanwhile in the Australian theater Allied airmen are maintaining their ascendancy with renewed attacks on Lae in New Guinea and Rabaul on New Britain. It is significant, however, that the latest raids have been attacking troopships rather than airfields, which may indicate that Japanese troops are being assembled for a new offensive.

Madagascar

London reports the British are meeting determined resistance in Madagascar and that casualties have been "heavier."

A joint Admiralty-War Office communiqué said:

"The advance of our forces in northern Madagascar is being resisted with determination and casualties today have been heavier. Operations continue with the support of our naval aircraft."

A British Government military commentator in London said Diego Suarez and the neighboring community of Antsirana were the chief objectives of the invaders, who, he said, were making satisfactory progress although French resist-

Continued on Page 9, Column 1

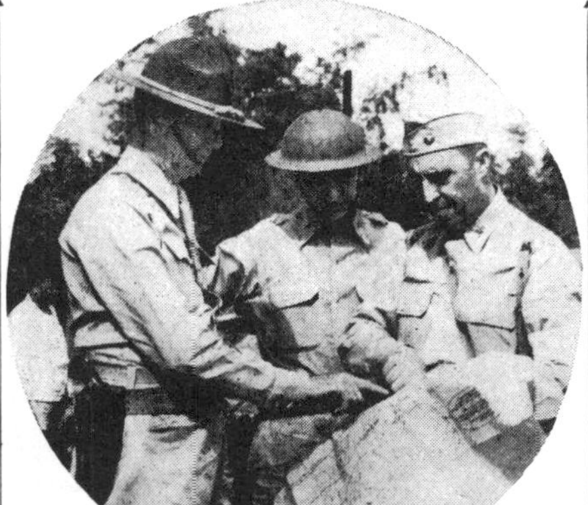

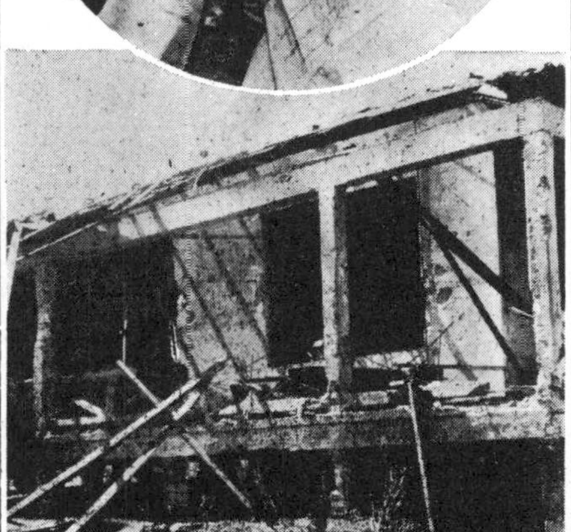

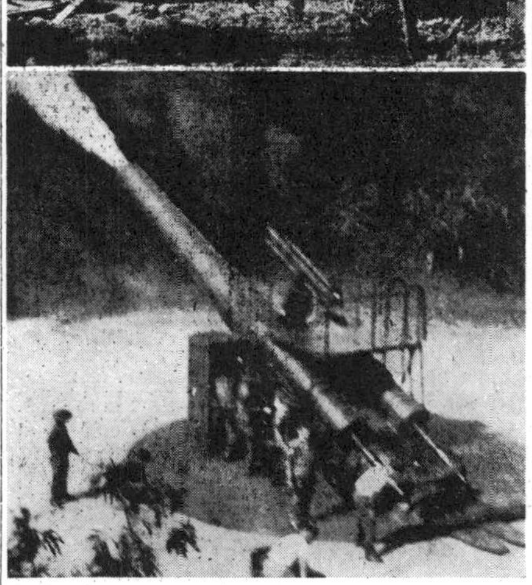

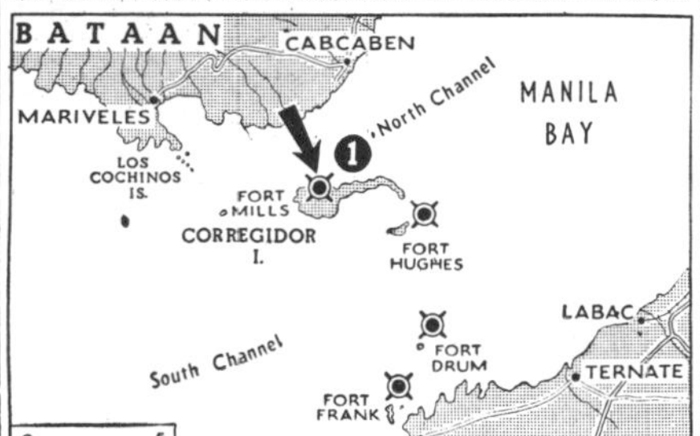

Associated Press; International

Remember Corregidor!

Corregidor has fallen after an epic defense against the might of Japan. Its gallant fight against overwhelming odds illumines one of the brightest pages of American military history. Top: Lieut. Gen. Jonathan M. Wainwright, left, who took over the command of the Philippines after Gen. Douglas MacArthur was ordered to Australia to command the forces of the United Nations in the Southwest Pacific, studies a map with his staff. Upper center: This shrapnel-marked building was the home of General and Mrs. MacArthur during their stay on Corregidor. Lower center: It was big guns like this that enabled the forts in Manila Bay to stave off the Japanese so long. This is a 12-inch disappearing rifle in action on Fort Mills. Below: The arrow shows where Japanese shock troops landed on Corregidor in the attack that preceded the final surrender of the fort. The Japanese used steel barges to ferry their troops across the narrow stretch of water separating Corregidor from the Bataan Peninsula. Even though Corregidor and the other forts in the Bay have been forced to surrender, the battle of Philippines is not over. From various sections of the islands comes word that small forces of American troops are still carrying on the fight.

Wainwright surrenders after Japanese land on isle—6,500 U. S. troops taken.

By Roscoe Drummond

Staff Correspondent of The Christian Science Monitor

WASHINGTON, May 6—Though Corregidor has fallen, the Philippine fight goes on.

Corregidor's fortress and three other islands dominating Manila Bay are today, after an unceasing 27-day assault by overwhelming man power and materiel, in the hands of the invading Japanese.

Five months after the attack on Pearl Harbor and Manila, the last garrison of American and Filipino troops—some 6,500 with an undetermined number of civilians—surrendered to the temporary conqueror, the War Department in Washington and Gen. Douglas MacArthur's headquarters in Australia, have announced.

Resistance is not ended. Persistent and harassing guerrilla warfare continues.

Terms are being negotiated covering the capitulation of the men of Corregidor whom President Roosevelt described as "the living symbols of our war aims and the guarantee of victory—brave and dogged defenders vastly outnumbered, admittedly weary and at the end of their available resources."

Time Most Important

But of even greater importance, it is pointed out, is the time gained for preparation and production of the vast volume of war material in the United States during the months that these brave defenders fought their glorious battle to delay the Japanese.

The crushing of Bataan and now the final and successful blow at Corregidor constitute a significant strategic victory for the enemy, but it would have been vastly more valuable two months ago, three months ago—the deadline when military judgment said the Philippines would be expected to fall.

They didn't fall three months ago. They didn't fall two months ago. And it is for this reason that it can be said that the garrisons on Corregidor and her sister forts have carried out their assignment—unyielding, last-ditch resistance and infliction of the greatest possible toll upon the enemy.

"The defenders did their job and did it well," one military official declared. "The Japanese have paid a high price to control Manila Bay."

But they still do not have unmolested control of the Philippines.

Both American and Filipino officers are directing guerrilla warfare and both American and Filipino soldiers are fighting it.

Weapon of Starvation

The weapon of starvation which the Japanese have employed in their seige of Bataan and Corregidor will not be an effective weapon against the guerrillas. They can live on the country; they will be fed and sheltered by Filipino sympathizers.

To hunt them down, surround, and defeat them is not an easy or inviting task. To end such resistance the Japanese will have to invade some 7,000 islands, most of which are not even named, and to control the coasts the Japanese

Continued on Page 21, Column 7

Text of communiqué on Philippines: Page 8.

Corregidor's one weakness: Lack of air defense: Page 8.

Australia Waits and Watches For Next Thrust by Japanese

By Joseph C. Harsch

Staff Correspondent of The Christian Science Monitor

SOMEWHERE IN AUSTRALIA, May 6—For Australia and for the American forces here these days are a period of suspense, like those that England and France endured after the fall of Poland in September, 1939, when an enemy attack is fully expected somewhere, but there is no clear public knowledge of what may happen.

It is a feeling of expectancy which Canberra fosters as an antidote to the complacent tendency which developed when the Japanese turned toward Burma after the fall of Java instead of coming this way.

The Government spokesmen and press are daily warning the people that an attack is possible any moment at almost any point around the huge periphery of Australia, or against its vital supply lines.

The fact is that so far as is known the enemy still has both the military initiative and sufficient war facilities to exercise it along several different lines. But even that much is not too sure. It is possible that the enemy is exhausted and needs a recuperative period.

Japan's Next Move

After wiping up the Philippines and Malaya, the Japanese turned immediately to the Burma Road, as it looks now, primarily to bottle up China and cut its main supply line to the outside world.

That job is finished now and troops presumably can be released both from that front and the Philippine front or, at least, Japan itself needs no longer send heavy supply streams to those areas, but instead can move further supplies to other fronts.

Unless one can assume—which certainly is unsafe—that Japan needs a breathing spell, this would appear to mean a new offensive on a new front. The latest news from India might make that country appear in Tokyo's eyes like a ripe plum. American reinforcements in Australia are certain to have given this continent the character of a major threat to Japan.

Last Saturday and Sunday, Allied attacks were reported on enemy transports in Rabaul Harbor, whereas previously most of the Allied air attacks have been reported as directed against airdromes.

The enemy still has several cleaning-up jobs on his hands which may be bothering him slightly. Reports of further enemy landings on Mindanao in the Philippines shows even with the fall of Corregidor, he is still some distance from the complete conquest of the islands, while there is reported to be still some guerilla opposition in Java, Sumatra, and other Netherlands islands.

Indian Ocean Front

Details of these Dutch activities cannot be obtained. If communication still exists, details are being carefully guarded as a protection for the forces still holding out. All that we are sure of is that some Dutch units still are carrying on but where and how effectively is unknown here.

Another front blanketed with

Continued on Page 21, Column 3

Capture of Gallant Soldiers Big U. S. Loss at Corregidor

By Walter Robb

Former Philippine Correspondent of The Christian Science Monitor

PASADENA, Calif., May 6—The loss of Corregidor stems directly from the loss of the Bataan Peninsula on April 9. Having Bataan Peninsula, Gen. Tomoyuki Yamashita could set up nine-inch guns behind the crown of Mariveles Mountain and lob shells over on Corregidor with impunity. Maj. Gen. George I. Moore was not able to blast out these fatal emplacements and the emplacements, therefore, served in lieu of a victorious Japanese fleet to hammer to uselessness our larger batteries on Corregidor and enabled troop convoys to approach the island in force.

General Moores responsibility was the command of the coast artillery. Lieut. Gen. Jonathan Wainright was over him with mixed forces. More accurate than a roll call is the fact we surrendered at Corregidor 2,000 or 3,000 of our best Marines, all our Coast Artil- units practiced under fire, and our star Coast Artillery commander, in addition to General Wainwright and his herioc remnant of troops from the peninsula.

The steep shores of Corregilor were not easily pregnable to infiltrators. Japanese landings there involved men in force. Parachutists would be cut down to a man. It was a job for landing parties who could expect to lose 6 to 8 men out of 10, getting ashore, and it probably was in this action that General Wainwright's troops, marines and sailors included, took the brunt

Continued on Page 21, Column 5

Patriot Day Observance Held On Corregidor

WASHINGTON, May 6 (AP)—Fighting men from Massachusetts on Corregidor recently observed Patriots' Day, the anniversary of the Battle of Lexington, the War Department stated today in a delayed report from the fortress.

The Massachusetts men held an informal meeting, with Brig. Gen. Charles C. Drake of Brockton presiding.

Among those attending were Col. Frederick A. Ward, Quincy; Col. Thomas W. Doyle, Lowell; Col. Chester H. Elmes, Concord; Col. Francis S. Conaty, Taunton; Maj. Joseph J. Hughes, Mattapan; Capt. Harry W. Schenck, West Roxbury; Capt. Albert C. Darcy, Jr., Somerville; Capt. Walter A. White, Everett; Chief Warrant Officer Raymond Morgan, South Weymouth, Master Sergeant Harry E. Morrison, Forge Village; Technical Sergeant Maurice J. Bracken, Marlboro, and Technical Sergeant Robert Doyle, Dorchester.

The Army Nurse Corps was represented by Lieutenants Florence MacDonald, Brockton; Catherine M. Acorn, Belmont; Rita George Palmer, Brookline; Letha McHale, Haverhill, and Helen Mary Cassiani, Bridgewater.

THE CHRISTIAN SCIENCE MONITOR

AN INTERNATIONAL DAILY NEWSPAPER

COPYRIGHT 1942 BY THE CHRISTIAN SCIENCE PUBLISHING SOCIETY | BOSTON, MONDAY, NOVEMBER 9, 1942—VOL. XXXIV, NO. 294 | C * * * ATLANTIC EDITION—FIVE CENTS A COPY

Landing in Africa Key to Allies' Plan; F. D. R. Says: 'On Through Tunisia'

Job of Rebuilding World Put Up to United Nations

Plan envisages making capital available to all nations as well as equipment and technological assistance needed to rehabilitate world trade on a free and equal basis without any taint of imperialism.

By a Staff Correspondent of The Christian Science Monitor

WASHINGTON, Nov. 9—A co-operative venture by all the United Nations designed to spread the benefits of modern industry throughout the world free from the taint of imperialism was proposed today by the National Planning Association.

The project envisages the formation of an International Development Authority on which investing and borrowing nations would be represented and, the report affirms, holds out distinct hopes for establishing the basis for an expanding trade in the postwar world.

The Association, a private research institute, whose members are drawn from varied fields of government, business, labor, the sciences and the professions, holds that in this manner capital can be made available on an international basis and the advantages of modern technology widely distributed without imperialistic exploitation.

Showing how war-born developments have made it clear that industrially backward areas will undertake national self-development with or without co-operation of the industrially mature nations, the Association's report asserted that enlightened self-interest would necessitate such a venture because:

Why It Is Necessary

1. If industrially advanced nations attempt to interfere with and hinder developments elsewhere in the world, it is likely that the Second World War will be followed by renewed conflicts in which not only ideologies but even continents or races may be ranged against one another.

2. If the backward areas embark on their programs of national development without the benefit of loans or technical assistance of other nations, either because such aid if not offered or is offered on unacceptable conditions, the future will be one of great uncertainty.

On the other hand, the report said, "national developments in every country in the world, undertaken simultaneously and co-operatively, will provide the expansionary environment in which world trade can be reorganized on a multilateral, non-discriminatory basis." Private capital responding to profit incentives as well as public capital will be required for the development of international trade and investment.

Citing a need for international investment in the postwar period, when the task in many countries will change from one of finding the resources to fill demands to one of finding demands to use resources, the report said:

"Most of the countries of the world are undertaking national development or will undertake it after the war on the basis of imported capital equipment — locomotives, steel, tractors, steam shovels, cement mixers, turbines.

"In some instances, they have foreign assets which can be used to purchase this equipment. In the majority of cases, however, they will be able to acquire it only by cutting down imports of consumer goods and pushing exports, to develop an export surplus, or by borrowing.

"Private investors in London, New York, Paris, Amsterdam, and Zurich, after the experience of the last 20 years, will probably not be willing to lend monies in sufficiently large amounts or low rates of interest to enable national development in debtor areas to get off to a good start. The alternative is for governments in creditor countries to guarantee the loans, or to lend the funds themselves.

"The governments of the countries to be developed will want so far as practical to finance the developments themselves; the principal emphasis in any scheme of development should be domestically recruited capital, materials and labor.

Key to Productive Expansion

"The availability of foreign funds, foreign technicial assistance and foreign machinery, however, will transform the process of national development from one which would threaten to disrupt international economic relations and trade into one which can make a key contribution to the expansion of world income and the reorganization of world trade."

The report concludes that a co-operative venture by United Nations to spread the benefits of modern technology and modern capital equipment throughout the world holds out distinct hopes for establishing the basis in the postwar world of expanding trade, in which maladjustments can be overcome through adaptation to the world markets and economic advancement for all the world.

"If the backward areas of the world embark on their program of national development without the benefit of loans and technical assistance from industrial nations," it says, "either because such aid is not offered or offered on unacceptable conditions, the future is uncertain.

"If the industrially advanced nations attempted to interfere with and hinder development elsewhere in the world, there seems a considerable likelihood that the second world war will be succeeded in the not too distant future by renewed conflicts in which not only ideologies but even continents or races may be ranged against one another."

French Canadians Aid Allies By Plea to Homeland Kinsmen

By a Staff Correspondent of The Christian Science Monitor

OTTAWA, Nov. 9—French Canada is using the weight of its blood relationship with France to impress upon the French people the real meaning of the American landings in North Africa.

The crusade was begun Nov. 8 when the Quebec Premier Adelard Godbout, Gen. George Vanier, former Canadian Minister, to France, Louis St. Laurent, Federal Minister of Justice, and others broadcast to their kinsmen in France that "the day of deliverance is approaching." They spoke as brothers from across the sea emphasizing that the American troops "drive the enemy out of your colonies to give them back to you."

Meanwhile the Vichy Minister still remains at Ottawa, although at any hour the word may be received from his Government severing the last slender diplomatic thread joining France with the United Nations.

Prime Minister W. L. Mackenzie King has explained that the British without diplomatic relations with Vichy attached no less importance than Canada to the maintenance of Canada's relations with Vichy "which have proved of value to the Allied cause in many ways."

The ties of kinship, the Prime Minister said, bind France more closely to Canada than to any other of the United Nations. "It is our mission to remove from the minds of the French people that we are no less eager to help them and to help them soon to win back the liberty which has never seemed so precious as since it was lost."

Canada Weighing Break With Vichy

OTTAWA, Nov 9 (AP)—Canada's diplomatic relations with the Vichy Government of France appeared to be nearing the breaking point as the French resisted the American Expeditionary Force in North Africa.

Prime Minister Mackenzie King said in a statement that the policy, up to now, of maintaining relations with Vichy had been "misunderstood in Canada just as it was in the United States." He did not, however, give a definite indication of future policy.

The statement said that even if United Nations forces met resistance in Africa it could not mean that "we are at war against the Real France."

The Prime Minister said that "In spirit, France has always been of the company of the United Nations," and he asked Canadians not to be deceived by a deluge of propaganda which he expects from the Vichy radio.

Most Helpful Blow

OTTAWA, Nov. 9 (AP)—Lieut. Gen. A. G. L. McNaughton, commander of Canada's overseas army, said in a message intended for the Soviet Union on the twenty-fifth anniversary of the Russian revolution that "we watch our time to strike so that our contribution may have its maximum effect against the despoilers of other peoples' rights and liberties."

The Christian Science Monitor Index

Monday, November 9, 1942

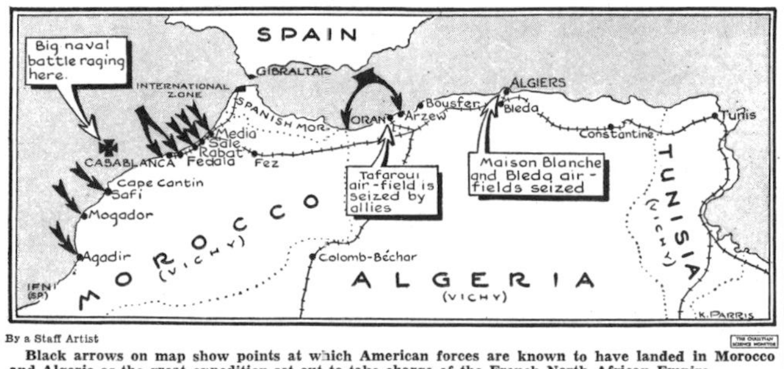

By a Staff Artist

Black arrows on map show points at which American forces are known to have landed in Morocco and Algeria as the great expedition set out to take charge of the French North African Empire.

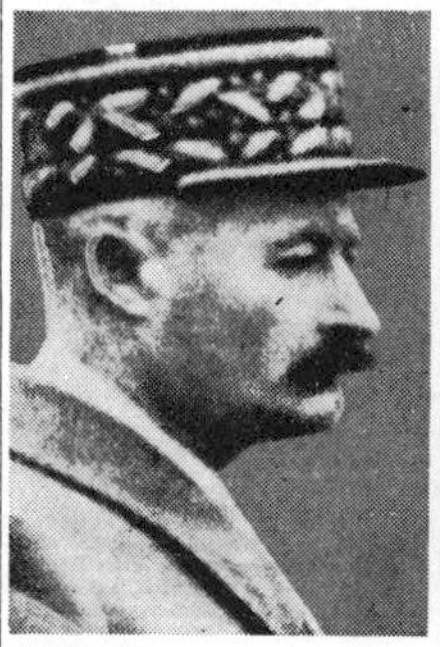

Associated Press

Gen. Henri Giraud

French collaborator with Allies in battle for French Africa.

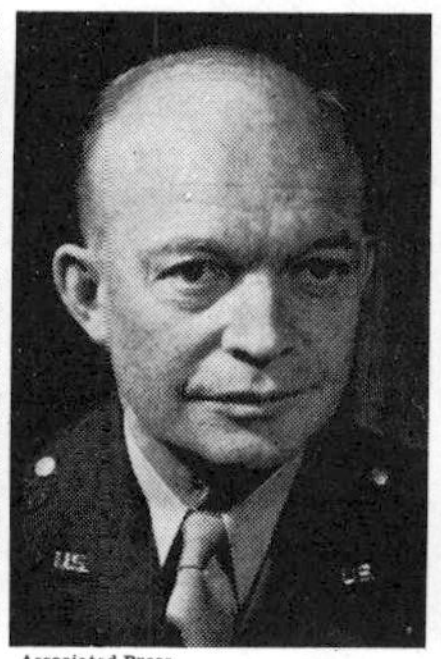

Associated Press

Lieut. Gen. Dwight D. Eisenhower

Commander in Chief of Anglo-American operations.

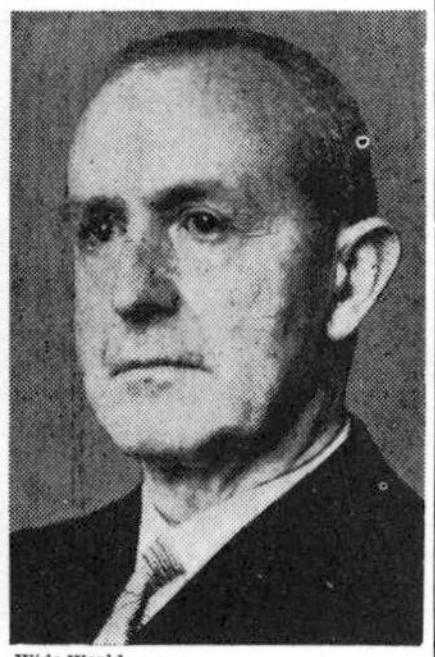

Wide World

Admiral Sir Andrew Cunningham

In command of naval operations in American invasion.

Vichy-U. S. Break: All Trade Banned

By Joseph G. Harrison

Staff Correspondent of The Christian Science Monitor

WASHINGTON, Nov. 9 — The United States formally and completely broke relations with Vichy today as the following train of events unfolded:

Gaston Henry-Haye, the Vichy French Ambassador, was handed his passport.

Secretary of State Hull told his press conference that the U. S. was taking into protective custody all Vichy French ships in the country's ports.

Secretary of the Treasury Henry Morgenthau, Jr., announced that all France within continental Europe would be considered "enemy territory under restrictions against trade and communications with the enemy."

Simultaneously with the start of the North African conquest and the quick succession of the above events here, Washington had obviously launched a powerful diplomatic drive among the nations and peoples of the Mediterranean.

Occupation Temporary

By far the most important aspect of this diplomatic campaign is the American attempt to convince the French people that the occupation of France's rich and strategic North African empire is only temporary and is a major step toward the restoration of French liberty.

At the same time, Washington has assured the Governments of Spain and Portugal that the sensational Allied move does not menace in any way their countries or territories. Although neither Madrid nor Lisbon had any immediate statement to make on the move, it is felt certain that both Governments were strongly impressed by the strength, speed and efficiency of this country's first major offensive of the war.

The smooth manner in which the opening phases of the conquest were carried out is also expected to produce strong and favorable reaction among Moslem populations all the way from the Vichy French port of Dakar in French West Africa to Turkey. This should also have effects, it is said, in such far-distant places as India, to say nothing of Latin America.

Washington is acutely aware that a friendly acceptance of the latest Allied move by Frenchmen in France and by both Frenchmen and Moors in North Africa will greatly facilitate the long-range plan to use North Africa as a starting point for at least one of the great United Nations drives against the European heart of the Axis.

Why America Struck

This is believed to be one of the reasons why American troops, wrapped in the cloak of traditional Franco-American friendship, were chosen to open the drive in Northwestern Africa, although British engrossment in Egypt and Libya was also a determining factor.

Preliminary reports indicate that neither the French nor the native troops in North Africa had much desire to oppose the invasion. It is believed that this fact will greatly simplify the task of establishing harmonious relations between the newcomers and those on the spot.

> **. . . More . . .**
>
> *There is, in the newspaperman's phrase, "more to come."*
>
> *Opening of the North African front has placed a heavy strain on communications. Dispatches from correspondents of individual newspapers will be cleared as soon as cable and radio facilities permit.*
>
> *Stories by The Christian Science Monitor staff writers are presumably among those delayed.*

In his note to French Chief of State Marshal Philippe Pétain, President Roosevelt stressed the fact that the move was designed particularly to achieve "the liberation of France and its Empire from the Axis yoke."

While a break with Vichy had been expected here and has been viewed almost with indifference, there is sharp speculation as to whether Premier Laval will seek a declaration of war against the United States and Great Britain. It is thought probable that Berlin will seek such a move. Particularly it now seems likely that the German Army will feel itself forced to occupy all of France as a protection against a possible Allied invasion of Europe along the French Mediterranean coast.

It is pointed out, however, that Vichy has fought the British in Syria, in Madagascar and at Mers-el-Kebir without declaring war against its former Ally.

In a special press conference, Secretary of State Cordell Hull revealed that America's continued, and much-criticized, maintenance of diplomatic relations with Vichy prepared the way for the present successful invasion of North Africa.

Hull Explains Policy

The Secretary explained that American observers in France and French North Africa had provided invaluable service to the Allied cause by keeping tabs on French military strength, Axis maneuvers and official trends. American policy in regard to Vichy was aimed at:

1. Encouraging French resistance to German demands and keeping before the French people the ideals of liberty, equality and fraternity.

2. Keeping in closest touch with the development of Franco-German relations in order to be able the better to counter Berlin's influence.

3. Staying as close to Germany as possible, thereby being in a position to gather news as to German military plans and diplomatic maneuvers.

4. Preparing the way for the North African move.

Although it is doubtful that the Secretary's explanation will serve to quiet all criticism of this country's past policy toward Vichy, it would seem that the present successes in North Africa will go far toward bringing this policy into a new light.

Allied Move Against French Africa Planned Months Ahead

By Roscoe Drummond

Staff Correspondent of The Christian Science Monitor

WASHINGTON, Nov. 9—The rapidly advancing American invasion of French North Africa is the visible outcome of 11 months of preparation—preparation not for this operation alone but for major offensive action against Germany.

The long and thorough training of American troops, the accumulating production of American arms are just beginning to make themselves powerfully felt against the Axis.

This is the start of the nation's massive war effort in execution and it is the prevailing military judgment in Washington that the pressure of offensive will not now be let up until the end.

American troops in both the United States and Britain have long been schooling themselves for this three-pronged attack in Africa and it represents one of the most ambitious water-borne operations in military history.

Many of the American forces were carried thousands of miles from the shores of the United States across submarine-infested waters and others were gathered from their training bases in Britain.

Uncer the protective convoy of a huge Anglo-American armada embracing battleships, aircraft carriers, and a screen of destroyers and lighter vessels all advanced against the Africa coast. After having split into three separate spearheads somewhere at sea, each struck at almost precisely the same hour, 3 a. m. Sunday morning, in a perfectly timed maneuver.

That French resistance has appeared to be slight from the very beginning is accepted here as evidence not only of their lack of desire to oppose the entry of American troops, but also as some indication of the decisive magnitude of the invasion force soon to be augmented still further by British units.

Acted Ahead of Axis

But the occupation of this whole strategic area is not a "second front." But it is a prelude to a second front. The United States is now in process of taking possession of bases from which a full-fledged invasion of the European continent is practicable. Such a step is believed to be imminent. It is considered the immediate next step to follow the early consolidation of the Allies in their present position and the complete elimination of the Rommel army—an elimination now proceeding nicely.

The decision to place Lieut. Gen. Dwight D. Eisenhower in charge of the Africa invasion is revealing, General Eisenhower is the American commander in the European theater of operations and it seems reasonable to conclude that the present operation is not an extension of General Eisenhower's command but closely related to it.

Thus the occupation of the key French African air and naval bases along the Mediterranean sea discloses itself as a flanking movement preparatory to direct attack against the Axis forces in Europe and the possible joining with Russian forces through Iraq and Iran.

In his statement from the White House coincidental with the American landings, President Roosevelt described the move as "designed to prevent an occupation by the Axis armies on any part of Northern or Western Africa."

In addition, the President said that "it provides an effective second front assitance to our heroic allies in Russia."

The invasion of Africa is only secondarily assistance to Russia because it is only a preliminary action itself.

But it is a forerunner of the real thing—a land invasion of Axis territory where the Axis is weakest and where Germany will be forced to divert all the troops it can spare.

The President frankly said as much in the opening communiqué. There is no longer need nor opportunity to conceal the strategy.

"This expedition," it was stated, "will develop into a major effort by the allied nations."

In the forthcoming battle it will be the United Nations which will be in a position to decide where the initiative will be taken and to determine the terrain on which it will be fought. That is the purpose of acting first to eliminate Axis power and influence entirely from Africa.

The Allies have struck when Germany is in the worst position to respond. Not a single German plane was free to attack the easily detectable concentration of British and American naval forces at Gibraltar. The Nazis are still deeply and unsuccessfully engaged at Stalingrad and the Caucasus and apparently are in no position to withdraw with impunity in order to resist the accumulating pressure of the forthcoming invasion of the Continent at points yet to be revealed.

Italy Next, Duce Thinks

At the same time Berlin cannot divert its strong holding forces in Northern Europe at which points it really expected attack and through which it can never be

Continued on Page 2, Column 5

Allied forces continue to land on 1,000-mile coastline as grip is tightened.

By the War Editor of The Christian Science Monitor

Drawn from dispatches of the Associated Press and other sources

United Nations forces continued to pour into French North Africa after 70 transports had yesterday unloaded 140,000 ground troops, Marines and Rangers at various points along a 1,000-mile length of the Moroccan-Algerian coastline in the greatest naval landing undertaking of the war.

Within 24 hours, Algiers, Capital of Algeria, surrendered —thanks, it is said, to the efforts of Gen. Henry Giraud, who co-operated with the Allies. Fighting, however, was still in progress around Oran and Casablanca, in Morocco and elsewhere.

President Roosevelt notified the Bey of Tunis that he desired passage for his troops through Tunisia—thereby indicating that the United Nations might find themselves close upon General Field Marshal Erwin Rommel's headquarters of Tripoli.

By expert timing between air and ground troops, the united forces, under Lieut. Gen. Dwight D. Eisen-hower, quickly captured two airfields at Algiers, one near Oran, and possibly the main Moroccan base of Rabat.

Axis dive-bombers reported to be joining in the battle.

The British fleet, commanded by Admiral Sir Andrew Cunningham, was reported in action off Casablanca. Whether this was with the French Fleet, moved from Toulon, as Berlin reported, was not clear. London denied the French Fleet had moved.

Landings made at more than 10 places, extended to Agadir, 245 miles below Casablance on the West Coast of Africa.

Fighting French were reported, without confirmation, ready to close in from Equatorial Africa in the South.

Gen. Charles de Gaulle, head of the Fighting French, sent word to the North African French: "Forward! The great moment has arrived."

Marshal Philippe Petain ordered the French to fight. Resistance was organized by Gen. Auguste Nogues, commander of the Vichy troops at Morocco, and presumably by Admiral Jean Darlan, commander of all Vichy's forces. It was visible at various points, notably at Oran in Alberia and at certain other coastal points where naval and coastal guns opened firfe on the Allied forces.

Thus two master strokes, dealt by the United Nations with remarkable speed and precision have not only proved Allied generalship equal to the Axis, but have completely changed the strategic outlook in the Mediterranean.

Continued on Page 4, Column 1

Sweep into French territories discloses master United Nations program for assault on Hitler; Nazis to be fought on all sides with control of North Africa opening Mediterranean.

By Joseph C. Harsch

Staff Writer of The Christian Science Monitor

Now at last after the long months of uncertainty and doubt we know what the Allied master plan for victory is to be.

With American troops landing along the north and northwestern coasts of French Africa, the die is cast—we are going to lay siege to Hitler's fortress of Europe from all sides and draw in those siege lines where they are most remote from the enemy's citadel.

This is the plan, instead of attempting the costly and dangerous alternative of trying to carry the main gate by storm while his back doors are still open for supplies and for forays against our own lines.

The whole picture fits together now—the reason for Gen. Bernard L. Montgomery's powerful attack on General Field Marshal Erwin Rommel at this time, the reason for the great supply and repair bases in the Middle East, the reason for fleet and shipping concentrations at the western end of the Mediterranean, the reason for our diplomatic dallyings with Vichy, the reason for the recent bombings of Northern Italian ports, even the reason for the heavy American troop concentrations in Great Britain, and the reason for the methodic development of a great chain of air bases across Central Africa.

Civil War Precedent

It is to be peripheral warfare instead of the frontal attack.

In many ways it is a readaptation of the grand strategy which finally proved successful in the American Civil War. The attack in Africa bears the same relationship to the grand strategy of this war that the drive to control the Mississippi bore to the ultimate strangulation of the Confederacy.

We are going to try now to gain control of the entire coast of North Africa.

When we do the Mediterranean is open to our shipping.

Our siege lines will be shortened by thousands of miles and our strain on shipping relieved by millions of tons.

We will be within easy reach of Persia and the Caucasus and able to increase our supplies to Russia several fold.

More than that, if we succeed in gaining all of North Africa and opening the Mediterranean we will be in a position to attack Hitler where he is weakest, "from underneath," instead of being forced to attack him where he is strongest, from in front.

Most Logical Course

It is the course of wisdom and logic. No other strategy for the European theater would so directly bear on the protection of America. At the same time no other strategy could bring us to grips with the enemy at anything like the same advantage of our forces, nor could any other course give such equal aid to all other countries which have borne the brunt of war to this date.

The greatest danger which has existed to our military cause has been that Hitler would burst out of Europe through the Middle East, join hands with Japan in the Indian Ocean on one side and gain a jumping off point on the bulge of Africa on the other for the hop across the South Atlantic to South America.

His plan to that end was a giant pincers, one arm being the drive into the Caucasus and the other Marshal Rommel's drive toward Suez.

Had this succeeded, Hitler would have been the besieger and we the besieged.

But now the picture changes.

We have placed our own pincer on Marshal Rommel's position in Libya. We have restored the plan which existed when France was still in the war. With the Army of the Nile driving westward into Libya and Marshal Rommel trying to extract enough of his forces to make a stand in his rear, we have taken the offensive to squeeze that rear and wipe out Hitler's great salient in the Mediterranean.

Enormous Possibilities

The possibilities for success are enormous. The move comes at a moment when Italian morale is at its lowest ebb. One can scarcely resist the temptation to count one's chickens before they are hatched.

One can foresee the Italian fleet out of action and Mussolini's bombastic Fascism crumbling under air attack from a great fringe of United Nations air bases along the southern coast of the Mediterranean.

One can foresee from that United Nations troops landing in Italy with the welcome of a disillusioned Italian people and establishing a position on the Brenner Pass from which to aid revolts flaming in the Balkans and to pound at Germany's southern industrial areas from the air.

Hitler's Middle Eastern pincers can be turned on himself. The great highways which he strode southeastward can open for us in reverse. With the long haul around South Africa no longer necessary our shipping can supply attacks through the Balkans and up the

Continued on Page 2, Column 4

Rommel Rout Laid to Axis Air Weakness

By Mallory Browne

Staff Correspondent of The Christian Science Monitor

LONDON, Nov. 9—While United States troops were landing at the western end of the North African coast line, the British Eighth Army today continued its pursuit of remnants of Nazi Marshal Erwin Rommel's decimated army.

The Axis retreat from Egypt has now clearly become a rout. Only weak units are now straggling across the frontier into Libya closely followed by the vanguard of the Allied forces and harassed by British and American fighters and bombers.

Enemy air activity has become negligible, according to today's mideast communiqué, and columns of retreating transports, it says, are "left without protection from our continuous fighter attacks."

Continuous Air Attacks

The reference to the continuous activity of Allied fighters illustrates the speed with which British, American, South African, and Australian fighter squadrons are being moved up to new airfields from which they can operate against Marshal Rommel's fleeing columns.

Bombers, too, have been busy and it is reported that they have partially destroyed the road leading through the narrow Halfaya Pass.

At the same time, enemy rearguard elements which have been holding out near Mersa Matruh finally capitulated yesterday.

The result is that Axis efforts to cover the rear of their retreating forces has now been practically abandoned.

The reasons for this are, first, effective and unrelenting bombing and strafing from the air; second, Marshal Rommel's shortage of petrol, and, third, the fact that the vast bulk of Axis armor has now been destroyed or captured.

In fact, it is estimated that more than 500 Axis tanks have now been destroyed or captured by the Eighth Army and messages from the front assert that Marshal Rommel's cracked Afrika Korps now contains only a couple of dozen tanks in all.

The explanation of these enor-

Continued on Page 2, Column 4

THE CHRISTIAN SCIENCE MONITOR

AN INTERNATIONAL DAILY NEWSPAPER

BOSTON, THURSDAY, SEPTEMBER 9, 1943—VOL. XXXV, NO. 241

CENTRAL EDITION—FIVE CENTS A COPY

COPYRIGHT 1943 BY THE CHRISTIAN SCIENCE PUBLISHING SOCIETY

Allies Land at More Points in Italy; Germans Offer Resistance at Naples

Hull's 'No' to Argentina Lists Aid to Axis Powers

Request for Lend-Lease benefits in airplanes and other supplies flatly turned down—Hull reports Argentine financial transactions with enemies of United Nations—Rio agreements violated.

By Mary Hornaday
Staff Correspondent of The Christian Science Monitor

WASHINGTON, Sept. 9—The time has passed for gestures of friendship toward Argentina, only one of the American republics which has not broken relations with the Axis, Secretary of State Cordell Hull has sternly informed that nation's new government.

The Secretary, with the advice of President Roosevelt, flatly turned down an Argentine request for Lend-Lease airplanes, spare parts, armaments and machinery, made through Vice-Admiral Segundo Storni, Foreign Minister.

"Since Argentina, both by its words and its actions, has indicated clearly that the Argentine armed forces will not under present conditions be used in a manner designed to forward the cause of the security of the New World, and thereby, the vital war interests of the United States, it would be impossible for the President of the United States to enter into an agreement to furnish arms and munitions to Argentina under the Lend-Lease Act," Mr. Hull wrote in reply.

A "neutral" request for Lend-Lease arms is also reported to have been made by Generalissimo Francisco Franco of Spain, but if there has been a reply to him, it has not been published.

"Volunteers" From Spain

The Office of War Information reported a German broadcast this week in which it was said that 1,000 Spanish "volunteers" were on their way to join the German armies on the Eastern Front. The "volunteers," the broadcast said, included "numerous soldiers who have been fighting in the East repeatedly and have particularly distinguished themselves at Leningrad and Volkhov."

The Argentine entreaties to the United States might almost be described as groveling, but Secretary Hull was stern, and a little sarcastic, in his reply. Admiral Storni denied that Argentina's new regime looks upon the Axis with great sympathy, but hinted it might be unchivalrous to join the United Nations "when defeat is inexorably drawing closer to the countries of the Axis."

Secretary Hull detailed Pan American commitments which Argentina has failed to live up to.

Financial transactions of direct benefit to the enemies of the United Nations have been authorized by agencies of the Argentine Government, Secretary Hull said, in direct violation of resolution V, adopted by the consultative meeting of Foreign Ministers at Rio de Janeiro.

Axis Agents Busy

Axis agents have operated in Argentina in violation of resolution XVII adopted at Rio, Mr. Hull added. "It is notorious," he said, "that Axis agents in Argentina have been and are engaging in systematic espionage which has cost the United Nations ships and lives. Vicious propaganda aimed at the United Nations appears in publications which are supported by subsidies from Axis sources. These publications have benefited by a Government decree which enables them to receive supplies of newsprint at favorable prices through the intervention of the Argentine Ministry of Agriculture."

In maintaining radiotelephone

Continued on Page 4, Column 6

It's Hard World Question If This Library Is Stumped

By Dorothea Kahn
Staff Correspondent of The Christian Science Monitor

CHICAGO—A Chicago businessman can call State 1760 and get answers to such questions as these:

What magazine published in Latin America would be suitable for advertising American fur coats?

What is the electric current and voltage in Trinidad, and can I use my radio when I go there? Did Great Britain find a way to curb black markets?

The staff of Chicago's unique Library of International Relations is waiting for such calls. The library has been building up a collection of current material about foreign lands ever since it was founded by Miss Eloise Requa in 1932. Now it possesses books and equipment valued at about $46,000, and has a staff skilled in digging out facts these publications contain. As a result, it is being used more and more by Chicago business and professional people.

The staff are pleased at the variety of organizations that come to them for help. A labor union, for example, recently called up to ask if the United States had ratified certain conventions of the International Labor Office. A magazine editor, checking the facts in a short story, inquired if there was a Rue Michelet in Algiers. (There is.) An educational film company asked the number of secondary schools in five Latin American countries, hoping to learn whether there was a reasonable market for his product there.

A biographical service inquired the names of members of the new Argentine Cabinet. A lawyer sought the answer to the question, "Who holds the salvage rights for the Admiral Graf Spee?" The research staff of "Quiz Kids" checked on the answer to a question about the government of a South American country so that the person who put the question would be sure of his facts before asking the kids.

Nearly always the staff can give the answer, but sometimes there are difficulties. For instance, this question about the Admiral Graf Spee. When it was asked in 1939 the ship had just been scuttled and salvage rights had not been granted. When a Uruguay junk dealer bought the wreck a year later from the German Government the library staff informed the lawyer, but this still didn't settle the matter of salvage rights. It wasn't until about two years after that they were granted by the Uruguay Government to the purchaser. When that happened the Library staff made another phone call to the lawyer, believing the matter concluded. But it wasn't. In the course of their research, the librarians learned later that the junk dealer who bought the wreck and got the right to salvage it couldn't do anything because of the dynamite shortage. Their latest call to the lawyer was to relay that information.

Another poser was a question put by a Chicago food packer. He wanted the original French of Napoleon's saying "An Army marches on its stomach." He didn't want a translation made to order; he wanted the original words. The staff of the library looked long and hard, exhausing 18 books of quotations including a number of French ones. It found the saying only once, and then it was listed as anonymous. So they sought out a University of Chicago historian who specializes in Napoleana. He undertook a search and came out with the conclusion that Napoleon never said just those words, but that he expressed the sentiment in his dictated memoires from St. Helena, under date of November, 1816. The Windsor Magazine in one of its 1904 issues used the epigram and attributed it to Napoleon. Ever since the Corsican has had the credit, the librarians found. They hope the packer's next question will be an easier one, like "What is the extent of use of retail credit in Brazil as compared with the United States?" which they answered for a publisher here without batting an eye.

The Christian Science Monitor Index

Thursday, September 9, 1943

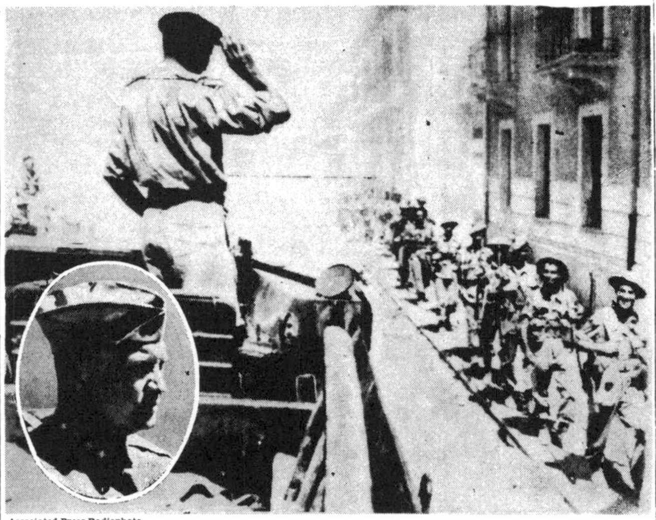

Associated Press Radiophoto

Victors in the Capitulation of Italy

Gen. Sir Bernard L. Montgomery, Commander of the British Eighth Army, salutes his men as they file through a street in Reggio Calabria, Italy. This is an official British picture received by the Office of War Information from Algiers. Inset—Gen. Dwight D. Eisenhower, Commander in Chief of Allied Forces in the Mediterranean theater.

The Fall of Italy

Monitor Correspondents Analyze the News

The Front

By R. Maillard Stead
Staff Correspondent of The Christian Science Monitor with The United Nations Forces in the Mediterranean Theater

ALLIED HEADQUARTERS IN NORTH AFRICA, Sept. 9—Unconditional surrender of the Italian armed forces, as the rising tide of Allied military might surges up to the shores of their Nazi-garrisoned country, swings the full weight of Gen. Dwight D. Eisenhower's immense military machine in this theater of war against the Germans alone and confronts them with a prodigious new problem in the South while the Russians roll back their armies in the East and the menace of invasion from Britain rises in fresh starkness in the West.

It is a problem the Germans doubtless have foreseen and one they are expected to attempt to solve by holding a line as far south of the German-Italian border as possible.

But this isn't going to prevent Italian airfields from being used against them at the same time as soon as the Allies have turned Italy into the first bridgehead and vast assembly ground on the European continent for the coming land offensives against the Nazis.

Bases for Heavy Bombers

There are well over 100 airfields in Central and Southern Italy. From those areas heavy bombers can reach Berlin or Warsaw and strike northeast nearly to Odessa. There isn't a spot in Germany that couldn't be reached from Northern Italian bases in the Plains of Lombardy from which bombers could reach Copenhagen, Brest, and the whole of France.

Here's a setup for an aerial pincers movement, a two-way bombing campaign, far transcending anything yet seen. If the Germans envisaged this, no wonder they conserved their aircraft in operations over what now emerges as their extreme perimeter defenses in Africa, Sicily, and Southern Italy.

Implementation of Marshal Pietro Badoglio's undertaking of unconditional surrender of the Italian armed forces—an implementation which hadn't occurred at the time of this writing—promised valuable accession of ships to Allied naval resources in this theater of war and equivalent to another accession by release from surveillance duty of Allied ships hitherto contained by the mere existence of the Italian Navy in Mediterranean waters.

Estimate on Ships

Excluding Italian warships damaged but since repaired and in commission again, the Allies destroyed during the war 5 heavy Italian cruisers, 7 light cruisers, 35 destroyers and large torpedo boats, a considerable number of submarines and light craft.

But this leaves 7 battleships, 2 heavy cruisers [both damaged], 9

Continued on Page 2, Column 7

The Strategy

By Joseph C. Harsch
Staff Writer of The Christian Science Monitor

Having served the interests of Berlin up to the last moment of any value, Rome yesterday recognized a long-existing fact, surrendering Italian armies and whatever Italian territory its German allies have not chosen to occupy.

The Italian capitulation serves some purpose in clarifying the war in Europe. The Anglo-American advance is moving now against Germans without any of the distractions or uncertainties which persisted so long as Italy remained technically at war. Italian capitulation will undoubtedly carry the defection of other lesser satellites in its wake, whenever they can succeed in tearing themselves away.

But before capitulating, the Badoglio Government in Rome gave Germany the maximum amount of time possible to consolidate a German defense line in northern Italy. Germany has taken the strategic frontier of its own choosing in Northern Italy. The Italian Army acted since Mussolini's downfall only as a screen for this operation. It is reasonably complete now and the screen was falling apart anyway.

Uncertainty Removed

So today what we witness primarily is the final removal of a tattered screen which still partly obscured the real position of the real enemy.

Its removal does not, and could not possibly, give us all of Italy. Germany has taken what it wants of Italy. It was never in the power of Rome to surrender its entire country. It surrenders only what the Germans have chosen to aban-

Continued on Page 7, Column 6

The People

By Saville R. Davis
Former Rome Correspondent of The Christian Science Monitor

Unconditional surrender of the Italian Government is the logical end, so far as the Italian people are concerned, of fighting a war which they never wanted, for a Fascist Government which they abhorred.

The agony of the Italian people is not at an end. Presumably the German Army will continue fighting somewhere on the Italian peninsula, at a point yet undeter-

Continued on Page 7, Column 4

British Stage Full Rehearsal Of Channel Invasion of Europe

LONDON, Sept. 9 (AP)—In a full-dress rehearsal of invasion plans for the future, all arms of the British services have completed a giant amphibious exercise in the English Channel, it was announced officially today.

Announcement of the completion of the maneuvers came within a day of the surrender of Italy, and coincided with what appeared to be the mightiest blows yet delivered by the Allied Air Forces against French Channel ports.

A brief communiqué issued jointly by the Admiralty, the War Office and the Air Ministry said:

"A full scale amphibious exercise has recently taken place in the English Channel. It has been most successful and valuable lessons have been learned by the service and civil authorities concerned."

WASHINGTON, Sept. 9 (AP)—What made today the "favorable moment" for announcing and thereby putting into effect the surrender of Italy?

This question intrigued the capital and produced considerable speculation that new Allied moves are in immediate prospect.

The phrase "favorable moment" was used by Gen. Dwight D. Eisenhower to describe the time for making the armistice with Italy effective and disclosing it to the world, but he offered no explanation as to why the time chosen was favorable.

Although military men do not say so, one of the purposes of the maneuver might well have been to contribute to Germany's indecision at a time when the Allies were walking into Italy. Even the threat of a cross-channel invasion might have proved a confusing factor to the Nazis in arranging their dispositions of troops.

U. S. Fifth Army engages Germans as troops from North Africa are put ashore—Capture of Stalino gives Russians two thirds of grain lands in Ukraine; rail line to Mariupol cut.

By the War Editor of The Christian Science Monitor
From Associated Press and other direct news dispatches

Unconditional surrender of Italy's armies is being followed today by landings of American and British forces near Naples and at other points on Italian soil.

American forces, already engaged with strong German forces in the Naples sector, are commanded by Lieut. Gen. Mark W. Clark, indicating that the Fifth Army, long held in reserve in North Africa, has come into action.

Other landings on Italian soil include one at Vilo Valenzia in the Gulf of Eufemia about 30 miles north of Palmi, which had been occupied by British and Canadians.

Historic events of the previous day were as follows:

While Premier Joseph Stalin was announcing the recapture of the city of Stalino and the clearing of Germans from all the Donets Valley, General Eisenhower, Allied Commander in Chief, radiocast at 12:30 p. m. eastern war time that a military armistice with Italy became effective "this instant."

Hostilities then ceased, although the truce was actually reached Sept. 3 at Allied advanced headquarters in Sicily. It was agreed that the armistice should come into effect at a time most favorable to the Allies. "That moment has arrived," said the official Allied statement.

Terms of the armistice were approved by the Governments of the United States, Britain and Soviet Russia.

Hitler has lost the help of some 38 Italian divisions in the Balkans, putting his 15 divisions there in peril. The situation of about 15 German divisions in Italy now becomes uncertain.

The truce obliges Italy to "comply with the political, economic and financial conditions" which the Allies will impose later.

General Eisenhower promised that "all Italians who assist in the fight against the Germans will have the support of the United Nations."

Marshal Badoglio, in a proclamation, disclosed that the Italian Government asked for a truce "some weeks ago" and a meeting thereupon took place in neutral territory.

The Italian Prime Minister ordered Italian troops to drop the fight against the Allied forces, but to "oppose attacks from any other quarter."

The recapture of Stalino, which the Germans had held since October, 1941, restores little of the former great industrial center to the Russians—for the city is largely in ruins—but it signalizes the return to the Russians of two thirds of the Ukraine's valuable grain lands. From the strategic standpoint it cuts the Stalino-Mariupol railroad feeding the south end of the German line, which rests on Budennovka, 30 miles east of Mariupol. The Russians are also across the trunk railroad running west to Dnepropetrovsk on the Dnieper some 140 miles away.

Between the present battle line and the Dnieper is little territory of a defensive nature. If the Russians can keep up their present pressure, a considerable German withdrawal from the coasts of the Sea of Azov may be expected, forced on by successive blows north of Konotop, west of Kharkov and north of Stalino.

In New Guinea, General MacArthur's men were losing no time in following up the week-end moves which landed some battalions of paratroops on the Markham River west of Lae and other sea-borne troops on the Huon Gulf 10 miles east of that base. Once the paratroops had located their field artillery, which had been dropped in sections by parachute in the tall grass of Nadzab airport, they formed up and pushed along the Gulf toward the base. Already the two airfields at Lae and Salamaua's one air base have been rendered useless for the Japanese by Allied airmen.

Surrender Proclamations By U. S.-Italian Chiefs

Eisenhower

From the Associated Press

Text of General Eisenhower's broadcast on the unconditional surrender of Italian armed forces:

"This is General Dwight D. Eisenhower, Commander in Chief of the Allied Forces. The Italian Government has surrendered its armed forces unconditionally. As Allied Commander in Chief, I have granted a military armistice, the terms of which have been approved by the Governments of the United Kingdom, the United States, and the Union of Soviet Socialist Republics. Thus, I am acting in the interests of the United Nations.

"The Italian Government has bound itself to abide by these terms without reservation. The armistice was signed by my representative and the representative of Marshal Badoglio, and it becomes effective this instant.

"Hostilities between the armed forces of the United Nations and those of Italy terminate at once. All Italians who now act to help eject the German aggressors from Italian soil will have the assistance and support of the United Nations."

Badoglio

From the Associated Press

Text of Marshal Pietro Badoglio's proclamation on the unconditional surrender of the Italian armed forces:

"The Italian Government, recognizing the impossibility of continuing the unequal struggle against the overwhelming power of the enemy, with the object of avoiding further and more grievous harm to the nation, requested an armistice from General Eisenhower, Commander in Chief of the Anglo-American Allied forces.

"This request has been granted.

"The Italian forces will, therefore, cease all acts of hostility against the Anglo-American forces wherever they may be met. They will, however, oppose attacks from any other quarter."

Roosevelt-Churchill Mapped Surrender

By Richard L. Strout
Staff Correspondent of The Christian Science Monitor

WASHINGTON, Sept. 9—The great news for which Winston Churchill has been waiting in Washington came yesterday—Italy surrendered.

From authoritative sources it is known that Messrs. Churchill and Roosevelt are also hourly expecting developments in regard to closer relations with Russia.

Messrs. Churchill and Roosevelt were familiar with and directed all developments regarding Italy's surrender to General Dwight D. Eisenhower.

The leaders of the two democracies had dinner together Sept. 7, according to Stephen T. Early, the President's Secretary, and were closeted from dinner on.

They met again yesterday morning, and Mr. Roosevelt had eliminated all but one minor appointment on his schedule.

The sense of great impending developments had hung over the capital for days, as Mr. Churchill prolonged his stay here.

Italy's surrender, spectacular though it is, does not close the door to other momentous matters which the two leaders are considering.

What to Do Now

There are four major subjects:

1. Winding up Italy's affairs, now that it has surrendered.
2. Working out closer relations with Russia, regarding which major developments are occurring.
3. Preparing new battle thrusts.
4. Considering postwar relations, particularly those between Britain and the United States.

For obvious reasons, it is concerning the last that most of the information has been divulged. Mr. Churchill has spoken openly on the subject in his Harvard address. In addition to this, with the obvious desire of both sides, authoritative supplementary information has been made available.

As to war plans, nothing will of course be given out here. And the first information will come when the thrust occurs.

To a lesser degree, developments on Italy's surrender are apparently so imminent that the public is getting information.

In a third field, closer relations with Russia, a little information is trickling out. The state of the hourly developments can be appreciated however from the Roosevelt press conference indication Sept. 7 that progress in the current negotiations with Russia may be expected soon.

From a non-American, authoritative, source it has been learned that a Soviet-U. S.-British parley "on the Foreign Ministers' level" has actually been agreed upon and is being carried out. Apparently it is in connection with this conference that Mr. Roosevelt expects news shortly.

Simultaneously, in connection with the problem of closer contact with Russia, has come a further bit of information. A Mediterranean commission is being considered, including Russia as well as the United States and Britain.

Outlet for Russia

The particular significance of this has not been emphasized by Anglo-American sources. But its creation would mark diplomatic recognition of Russian interest in the Mediterranean, a status which Britain has been loath to recognize in the past. It would release Russia from the Black Sea.

Oddly enough, at his press conference Sept. 7, Cordell Hull, Secretary of State, said he was in the dark on the subject. But Mr. Roosevelt at his press conference a few hours later confirmed the report.

That leaves the big question of postwar Anglo-American relations.

The same authoritative, non-American, source from which other information has been gathered discussed the subject in the course of the conferences here.

Now the American equivalent of such interpretation has been made available to correspondents.

Both dealt with the subject of the Churchill proposal for continued Anglo-American collaboration after the war.

The Churchill proposal, according to this second authoritative source, is less startling than it momentarily appears on the surface.

Only the innocent any longer believe, this authority holds, that when the final shot is fired there

Continued on Page 4, Column 3

'Military Instrument' Only, London States

By the Associated Press

London, Sept. 9

Downing Street, official residence of Prime Minister Churchill, said the unconditional surrender by the Italian Government was "strictly a military instrument." It does not include the political, financial and economic terms which will be imposed later.

Furthermore, it is evident that the present position does not permit public announcement of the contents of a military document signed in these circumstances.

Surrender:

Italy Gives Up Unconditionally

Gen. Dwight D. Eisenhower announced unconditional surrender of Italy in the greatest ernment ordered its troops to drop the fight against Allied forces, but victory for Allied arms in four years of war.

Russia, as well as the United States and Great Britain, approved

Continued on Page 2, Column 1

INVASION EDITION

THE CHRISTIAN SCIENCE MONITOR

INVASION EDITION

AN INTERNATIONAL DAILY NEWSPAPER

VOL. XXXVI NO. 161 | COPYRIGHT 1944 BY THE CHRISTIAN SCIENCE PUBLISHING SOCIETY | BOSTON, TUESDAY, JUNE 6, 1944 | FIVE CENTS A COPY

Allied Armies Smash Across Channel; Invasion Beachheads on French Coast

Roosevelt Warns U. S. Hard Road Still Ahead

President, on invasion eve, says that war will be won, but not until after tough and costly fight—Marshall calls invasion battle to Allied victory—Pershing says unconquered people will rise again.

By Roscoe Drummond
Staff Correspondent of The Christian Science Monitor

WASHINGTON, June 6—President Roosevelt's counsel to the nation today, as the Allied liberation of Europe now is actually under way, is that final victory over Germany "still lies some distance ahead."

In a White House radiocast—his first since last Christmas—delivered on the eve of the invasion he knew was about to begin, he gave the assurance that the road to victory will be covered in due time, but said that it will be tough and costly.

Mr. Roosevelt's 15-minute address at 8:30 last night hailed the capture of Rome as "one up and two to go," but he emphasized that it would be unwise to inflate its military importance.

Conscious of the news which soon would be breaking, the President kept his speech signally free from heroics and oratorical effects, and devoted himself largely to a tribute to the United Nations forces and leadership which drove the Nazis from Rome.

Government Offices Active

Many government departments were ablaze with activity from the earliest morning hours when the words of the offensive reached the Capital. Elmer Davis, Director of the Office of War Information, was at his office shortly after midnight. The public-relations staffs of the Army and Navy were on duty all night long.

Only a few high-ranking civilian and military officials of the War Department were at the Pentagon Building when the invasion started.

Gen. George C. Marshall, Chief of Staff, stayed at his desk most of the night, leaving his office shortly before dawn.

Secretary of War Henry L. Stimson remained at home during the early hours of the battle.

One of the very few persons in Washington to know in advance exactly when operations would begin, President Roosevelt retired early in the evening after his radiocast, but was reported up early this morning to study the latest official dispatches.

OWI "Blankets" World

In less than five minutes after the first communiqué from Gen. Dwight D. Eisenhower's headquarters, the Office of War Information, through its short-wave transmitters in New York and San Francisco, was blanketing the world in 39 languages and dialects with the news that the liberation of Europe was under way.

Gen. John J. Pershing, who commanded the American armies in France in World War I, issued the following statement:

"American troops have landed in western Europe.

"As the overvastering military might of the Allies advances, it will be joined by the men of the occupied countries, whose land has been overrun by the enemy but whose spirit remains unconquered.

"Twenty-six years ago, American soldiers, in co-operation with their Allies, were locked in mortal combat with the German enemy. Their march of victory was never halted until the enemy laid down his arms in defeat. The American soldier of 1917-1918, fighting in a war of liberation, wrote, by his deeds, one of the most glorious pages of military history.

Sons Fight War Now

"Today, the sons of American soldiers of 1917-1918 are engaged in a like ware of liberation. It is their task to bring freedom to people who have been enslaved. I have every confidence that they together with their gallant brothers-in-arms, will win through to victory."

When General Marshall was given the Order of Suvorov, First Degree, the highest honor of the Soviet Union, at the Russian Embassy here last night he said: "The final action in this terrible European war is now focused on a single battle in which every Allied force will be represented. It is to be a battle to the death for the Nazis and a battle to victory for the Allies."

Roosevelt Speaks

President Roosevelt said, in his speech:

Yesterday, June 4, 1944, Rome fell to American and Allied troops. The first of the Axis capitols is now in our hands. One up and two to go!

It is perhaps significant that the first of these capitals to fall should have the longest history of all of them. . . . The United Nations are determined that in the future no one city and no one race will be able to control the whole of the world. . . . It will be a source of deep satisfaction that the freedom of the Pope and of the Vatican City is assured by the armies of the United Nations.

It is also significant that Rome has been liberated by the armed forces of many nations. The American and British armies—who bore the chief burdens of battle—found at their sides our own North American neighbors, the Gallant Canadians. The fighting New Zealanders from the far South Pacific, the courageous French and the French Moroccans, the South Africans, the Poles, and the East Indians. . . .

The prospect of the liberation of Rome meant enough to Hitler and his generals to induce them to

Continued on Page 5, Column 2

Boston Greets Invasion Day With Subdued Excitement

Subdued excitement was the first reaction of Boston's population today to the official news of Allied invasion thrusts across the English Channel to France.

Although news from Allied Headquarters was announced at 3:32 a. m., for many the first knowledge of the long-awaited, dramatic news came with announcement of the Allied land, sea and air blows over Boston's public address system by Mayor Tobin at 7:38 a. m.

Windows were opened in homes as the stirring tones of the national anthem was played over the address system. An impromptu news desk had been set up at the fire-alarm telegraph headquarters in the Fenway, and Mayor Tobin arrived there shortly after 7:30 to radiocast over the air-raid-alarm system.

In his brief announcement over the loudspeakers, Mayor Tobin said that churches of the entire city are open for those who wish to enter and pray, and that schools would be open as usual.

"I strongly urge every man, woman, and child to go to the churches sometime during the day and pray," the Mayor declared, adding that "the future of the entire world depends on the success of the invasion."

Deeply moved by the news from across the water, Governor Saltonstall said from his Chestnut Hill home, "President Roosevelt said last night that it was one down and two to go when Rome was captured. Let us pray that it will be two down and one to go as soon as possible."

Soldiers in army camps in the New England area took the invasion announcement "in stride," public-relations offices announced.

Regular training program for the soldiers at Fort Devens continued on this D-Day—but the sole topic discussed between drills, exercises, and formations was the progress of Allied arms on the Continent. Sleepy-eyed K. P.'s were electrified when in the early morning hours they were dragged out of bed for a day's kitchen detail—the radio announced the invasion.

The Christian Science Monitor Index

Tuesday, June 6, 1944

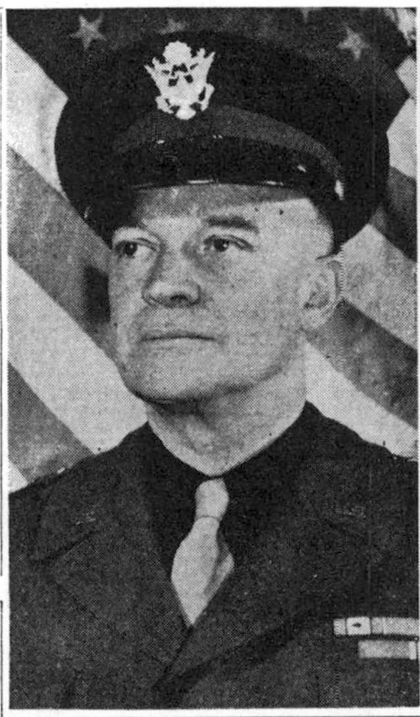

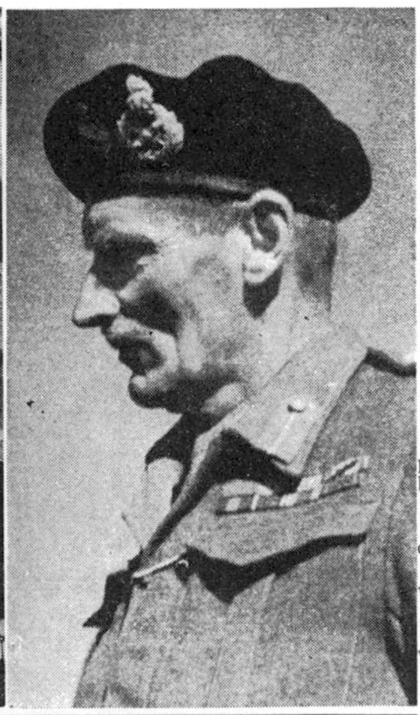

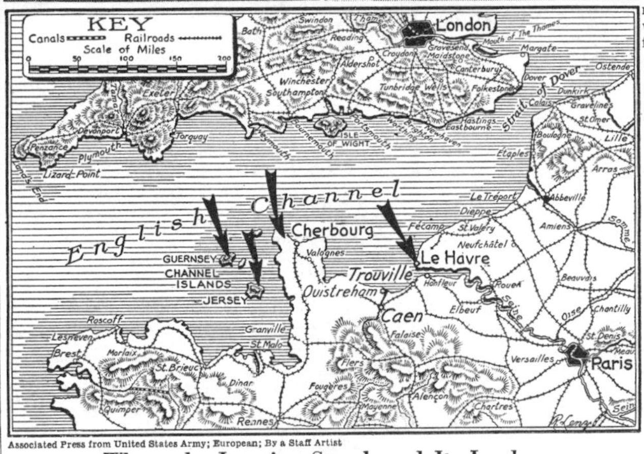

Associated Press from United States Army; European; By a Staff Artist

Where the Invasion Struck and Its Leaders

Upper left: This new picture of Gen. Dwight D. Eisenhower, Supreme Allied Commander, was made at headquarters of the Allied Expeditionary Force in Britain shortly before the invasion started. Upper right: Striking picture of Gen. Sir B. L. Montgomery, who is in direct field command of the invading Allied armies. Lower: Arrows indicate points between which Allied landings have been effected on the Normandy coast, and also upon German-held Channel islands.

'It's Come': Analysis of Armies

Allies Have Plenty Of Men and Arms

By Joseph C. Harsch
Staff Writer of The Christian Science Monitor

The Allied armies which stormed Europe's western walls today are the tempered, polished, sharpened spearhead of the gigantic armed force which British and American arms have forged—but only the spearhead.

Behind that spearhead is an enormously greater force of men, most of whom never will cross the Channel. Those who have crossed today and who will follow them as the beachheads widen and deepen must fight through to the final decision against German forces probably their equal and perhaps even their superior in numbers on the immediate battlefields.

But what will give these men their advantage on the evenly contested fields is the weight which propels them and sustains them from behind. Germany mans its fortress walls with every last recruit who could be ferreted from the crannies of an empty manpower barrel. The walls are strongly held, but there is no last reserve inside those walls. The fortress is being assailed from all sides.

Quality Has Been Goal

The German plan was always to fight first on one side and then the other—first Poland, then France, then Russia, then the Anglo-Saxon Powers in the final victory blow. Today the one thing German strategy planned above all else to avoid has become a reality. The Russian front bears down on the reserves which, according to German plans, should be available to back up defenders

Continued on Page 10, Column 7

Where Are Troops Of Nazis Deployed?

By Lieut. Gen. Sir Douglas Brownrigg
Former Adjutant General to the British Field Forces
Written for The Christian Science Monitor

SUPREME HEADQUARTERS, ALLIED EXPEDITIONARY FORCE, June 6—The Duke of Wellington said that the best general was the one who most accurately could guess what lay on the other side of the hill. Despite the advent of air power, this saying remains fundamentally true today.

Air photographs can tell a great deal, but every new weapon or military device invites an anti-

Continued on Page 11, Column 4

Battle-Wise Soviet Poised to Strike

By Edmund Stevens
Staff Correspondent of The Christian Science Monitor

MOSCOW, June 6—The landing of the liberation armies on the beaches of Western Europe finds the Red Army fully poised to carry out its share of the Allied master plan, awaiting only the signal to synchronize its operations with the second front.

Soon not only the German Army but the entire "greater Reich" will find themselves embraced in a mighty constricting bear-hug. Bismark's old nightmare of a simultaneous attack from the East and West will come to pass on a scale

Continued on Page 10, Column 7

This Is It!

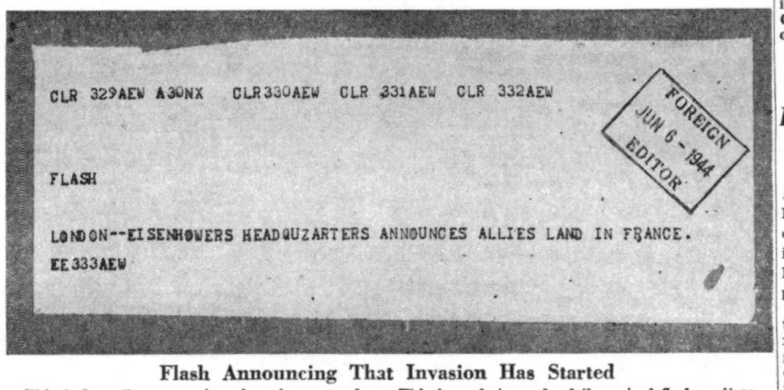
CLR 329AEW A30NX CLR330AEW CLR 331AEW CLR 332AEW

FLASH

LONDON--EISENHOWERS HEADQUZARTERS ANNOUNCES ALLIES LAND IN FRANCE.

EE333AEW

Flash Announcing That Invasion Has Started

This is how the momentous invasion news for which the world has waited so long wash flashed to newspapers and radio stations throughout the United States early today b the Associated Press. This is a photograph of the actual flash as it appeared on the teletype machines in the News Room of The Christian Science Monitor shortly after 3:30 o'clock this morning.

Four Divisions of Paratroops Hop West Wall in Normandy

Other forces land on Channel Islands while air-borne divisions cascade down on Germans as far inland as Caen, France—Battleships shell enemy defenses—11,000 planes give Allies air control.

By the War Editor of The Christian Science Monitor
From Associated Press and other direct news dispatches

The hour of invasion has arrived.

The signal that all the world awaited boomed out around 6 a. m. G. M. T. this morning.

"The eyes of the world are on you," said General Eisenhower. "The hope and prayers of all liberty-loving people go with you."

Some 4,000 vessels, said Prime Minister Churchill, with several thousand smaller crafts, appeared off the Normandy coast. They effected landings between 6 and 8:30 a. m. between Cherbourg and the Seine, and secured several beachheads.

Other forces landed at Jersey and Guernsey in the Channel Islands.

Paratroop divisions—four British accompanied by Americans and Canadians—simultaneously dropped at points on the coast and inland as far as Caen, 30 miles west of LeHavre.

Battleships of British and American navies shelled invasion points at long range. Some were reported entering the Seine River.

They did their work so well that German resistance was surprisingly small.

Radiocasters accompanying the expedition declared there was no resistance at all until within a mile or two of the shore.

Some small German E-boats and a few destroyers offered the only naval resistance reported.

On land, this mighty expedition, commanded by General Montgomery, met no initial strong resistance. German aircraft reacted slowly to the paratrooper attack. It appeared to be overwhelmed by the 11,000 first-line aircraft which, according to Mr. Churchill, are available for the invasion.

Rapidity with which the great flotilla of minesweepers cleared the way for the invading armada and the help of artificial fog, produced by naval units, enabled the infantry to make quick landings.

The success of the paratroopers at the airfields had yet to be announced.

Announcement that heavy guns opened fire across the Straits of Dover at midday indicated that the invasion might be spreading eastward.

Channel waters were choppy and cloudy weather prevailed, but apparently not sufficiently to impede the invading forces.

Since French patriots had been warned to keep out of an area within 22 miles of the coast, their activities did not begin immediately.

Details of the landings show these occurred west of the Orne River on the Cherbourg Peninsula, near Ouistreham, Arromanches, Carentan, Harfleur, and St. Vaast—all dotted along the Normandy coast.

The attack was preceded by a raid by 1,300 great bombers which roared over the Channel during the night in the heaviest aerial attack on the French coast.

Ten attacks were executed between 11:30 p. m. and sunrise.

The German Radio flashed news of the invasion three hours before Allied Headquarters came through with the report. General Eisenhoweer, it is said, waited to be sure of the initial success of the landings before releasing the intelligence.

Invasion:

First Blow Reported In Cherbourg Area

Although the German Radio said the landings were made from Le Havre to Cherbourg, along the north coast of Normandy and the south side of the Bay of the Seine, Allied headquarters did not specify the locations. They left no doubt, however, that the landings were on a gigantic scale. One correspondent wired that as far as he could see there was no oppostiion to the landings.

The German Radio filled the air with invasion flashes for three hours before the formal Allied announcement came at 7:32 a. m. Greenwich mean time (3:32 a. m., eastern war time).

It acknowledged deep penetrations of the Cherbourg Peninsula by Allied parachute and glider troops in great strength.

The assault was supported by gigantic bombardments from Allied warships and planes, which the Germans admitted set the coastal areas ablaze.

A senior officer at Supreme Allied Headquarters said rough water caused "awful anxiety" for the sea-borne troops but that the landings were made successfully, although some soldiers undoubtedly were seasick.

The sun broke through heavy

Continued on Page 6, Column 1

First Attack Succeeds, Churchill Tells Commons

LONDON, June 6 (AP)—Prime Minister Winston Churchill told the House of Commons today that an immense Allied armada of 4,000 ships, with several thousand smaller craft, had carried Allied forces across the English Channel for the invasion of Europe.

Mr. Churchill also said that massed air-borne landings had been successfully effected behind the Germans' lines.

"The landings on the beaches are proceeding at various points at the present time," Mr. Churchill said.

"The fire of shore batteries has been largely quelled."

He said that "obstacles which were constructed in the sea have not proved so difficult as was apprehended."

The Prime Minister said the American-British Allies are sustained by about 11,000 first-line aircraft, which can be drawn upon as needed.

"So far," he said, "the commanders who are engaged report that everything is proceeding according to plan."

"And what a plan!" he declared.

Mr. Churchill said the vast operation was "undoubtedly the most complicated and difficult which ever has occurred."

To cheers by Parliament members, Mr. Churchill took "formal cognizance of the liberation of Rome," and added:

"American and other forces of the Fifth Army broke through the enemy's last lines and entered Rome, where

Continued on Page 7, Column 4

Tough Paratroopers Cascade Behind Hitler's Atlantic Wall

WITH UNITED STATES PARACHUTE TROOPS, June 6 (AP)—The toughest fighting men on the Allied side landed behind Hitler's Atlantic Wall today. American paratroopers — studded with battle-hardened veterans of the Sicilian and Italian campaigns—cascaded from faintly-lit skies in an awesome operation. Twin-engined C-47's—sisters of America's standard airline flagships—bore them across the skies, simultaneously towing troop-laden CG4A gliders—to merge in a single sledge-hammer blow paving the way for frontal assault troops.

By Daedalus
Military Aviation Correspondent of The Christian Science Monitor

Current operations against Europe comprise not only a cross-Channel invasion, but an invasion from the skies. The theory of "vertical envelopment" is receiving its first really complete test.

In many respects the Allied attempts at "vertical envelopment" are likely to encounter conditions similar to those which the Germans met at Crete. That is to say that, barring a surprise move, the Allied troops will come across fierce ground resistance by seasoned opponents. They will also, as did the Germans, enjoy air superiority, if not supremacy, and, in contrast to the Germans on Crete, an at least initial superiority in numbers.

A factor of major importance in

Continued on Page 4, Column 5

Eisenhower Stands Lonely Battle Watch

SUPREME HEADQUARTERS, ALLIED EXPEDITIONARY FORCE, June 6 (AP)—As the battle opening the Western Front raged in Northern France, Gen. Dwight D. Eisenhower occupied a lonely post on this side of the Channel.

After inspecting parachute troops before they went into the fray, the director of history's greatest amphibious strike stood on the roof of a house watching the huge air armadas roar across the Channel.

Eisenhower's order of the day: Page 6.

THE CHRISTIAN SCIENCE MONITOR

AN INTERNATIONAL DAILY NEWSPAPER

VOL. XXXVI NO. 229 | BOSTON, FRIDAY, AUGUST 25, 1944 | c •••ATLANTIC EDITION | FIVE CENTS A COPY

COPYRIGHT 1944 BY THE CHRISTIAN SCIENCE PUBLISHING SOCIETY

French Armored Troops Enter Paris; Nazi Forces Put Up Stiff Resistance; Red Army Speeds Ahead in Romania

Hull and Dulles in Accord On World 'League' Points

Report 'agreement of views on numerous aspects of this subject'—Dulles places organization for security outside partisan politics—Other phases of foreign policy open for discussion.

By Robert R. Mullen

Staff Correspondent of The Christian Science Monitor

WASHINGTON, Aug. 25—At least a tentative agreement answering the specific question that there shall be a new world peace organization, or "league" and that it shall have teeth, appeared to have been reached between Secretary of State Cordell Hull and John Foster Dulles here today.

In a joint statement, the two men, after three days of conferences between themselves and with high-ranking Senators, and after telephone consultations between Mr. Dulles and Gov. Thomas E. Dewey, announced that there is "agreement of views on numerous aspects of this subject."

Political Innovation

In a long talk with the press just after he emerged from Secretary Hull's office this afternoon, Mr. Dulles made it clear that while one specific area of the peace problem had been explored, meaning the security organization, and that an effort is to be made to lift this phase above partisan politics, all other phases of foreign affairs are open for partisan discussion. He referred with emphasis to "past conduct of foreign affairs."

"However," Mr. Dulles added, "we feel we have made a great achievement and have done something perhaps unique in American politics. We have found a practical way to implement the purpose of bipartisan peace discussions."

It was reported here, although not directly confirmed, that the area of agreement between Mr. Hull and Mr. Dulles was aimed at two points:

1. There shall be a world security organization or "league."
2. The delegate, or delegation, from each nation on the executive council of this organization shall have power to call out armed forces of his nation to put down aggression without waiting for approval of his government. This means, for example, that the American delegate could order out the troops without asking Congress.

Allies' Doubts Raised

The Hull-Dulles statement was not phrased in enthusiastic enough language, nor was it sufficiently specific to greatly bolster Russian and British interest in the present Dumbarton Oaks conference on co-operative peace enforcement.

This not to say that there is any evidence of waning interest on the part of these two nations. It is simply to point out the obvious doubts that must have arisen in British and Russian thoughts as they saw Governor Dewey's representative, Mr. Dulles, suddenly projected into the headlines even as the Dumbarton Oaks conferees assembled. Here was history, they might have said, repeating itself.

That the shadow of Woodrow Wilson's experience was cast over hopes for winning the peace just as the war with Germany was reaching a resounding crescendo was at first a sharp disappointment to Mr. Hull, it can be reported.

Mutual Interests

There was absolutely no prearrangement in his talks with Mr. Dulles. These talks resulted spontaneously and directly from a question asked Mr. Hull by a newspaperman. In answering, Mr. Hull without visible enthusiasm said he would be glad to talk with Mr. Dewey or his representative.

But when Mr. Dulles was actually seated in Mr. Hull's office, it can be reported that the mutuality of long years of rather parallel interests in foreign affairs took effect. The discussion inevitably rose above narrow partisanship and as two Americans—though with admitted reservations between them as to nuances in policies—they pondered how their country can do its part in preserving future world order. This is an objective near to the desire of all Americans, though there may be differences of opinion as to how best achieve that objective.

Mr. Dulles is authority for the information that Mr. Hull laid before him the full story of the American proposals at Dumbarton Oaks. These include the idea of a "league" and for enforcement implementation, and appear to have won the general approval of Britain and Russia.

Whether Mr. Hull asked directly for Mr. Dulles' support is not known, but Mr. Dulles unquestionably recognizes the full implications of the Republican position, and how acutely a domestic fight over international issues might affect the delicate fabric of world peace.

Apparently he already favored, or was won, to the central necessity for (A) a "league" with (B) teeth in it.

He then consulted with some of his party's leaders in the Senate, where the league ran onto the rocks two decades ago. What he learned after talking with those of both isolationist and internationalist coloration was at least suf-

Continued on Page 5, Column 5

Roosevelt Contacts Willkie, Who Seeks to Delay Parley

By Richard L. Strout

Staff Correspondent of The Christian Science Monitor

WASHINGTON, Aug. 25—President Roosevelt told his press conference today that he has been in touch with Wendell L. Willkie, his opponent in 1940, who has to date maintained an aloof position between Republican and Democratic candidates since his own campaign ran aground in Wisconsin last spring.

Earlier reports of communications on the part of the White House to Mr. Willkie brought a "technical" denial from President Roosevelt. However, the reports were based on evidence which appeared conclusive to correspondents familiar with the state of affairs, and information of a new Roosevelt approach to Mr. Willkie has also now become available.

In answer to a direct question Mr. Roosevelt explained that he sees lots of people privately and that he had been in private contact with Mr. Willkie.

Mr. Roosevelt, to further questions, said that he knew of no plans for a "private" meeting with his 1940 opponent but he added that this did not mean he would not meet him. In any event no date had been set.

Initiative by President

It is assumed that Mr. Roosevelt has taken the initiative in getting into touch with Mr. Willkie, and that whatever political motive may be behind the move, the subject of politics has been omitted and the approach has

Continued on Page 5, Column 6

By Wyona Dashwood

Staff Correspondent of The Christian Science Monitor

NEW YORK, Aug. 25—Continuing to avoid taking sides in the presidential campaign, Wendell L. Willkie again reiterated today his wish to postpone any discussion of foreign or domestic policies with either President Roosevelt or Gov. Thomas E. Dewey, Republican nominee, until after the election.

Following close upon the heels of President Roosevelt's remarks at his press conference in Washington this morning that he wanted to talk over the situation with Mr. Willkie, the 1940 Republican standard bearer, who piled up the biggest popular vote any Republican or any defeated candidate for President ever received, issued a brief formal statement in which he said:

"It is true that Mr. Roosevelt has written to me asking that I confer with him. Naturally, I would much prefer that no such conference occur until after the election, but if the President of the United States wishes to see me sooner, I shall, of course, comply."

Willkie Stand Unchanged

Mr. Willkie's statement hews close to the policy line he has followed since the Democratic and Republican conventions in Chicago.

It will be recalled that Governor Dewey tried to reach Mr. Willkie at midnight Aug. 19 to ask him to come to Albany to confer with him and John Foster Dulles, chief Dewey adviser on foreign affairs, prior to Mr. Dulles' conferences with Secretary of State Cordell Hull and Republican congressional leaders in Washington. Mr. Willkie had retired when his telephone call from Albany was put through and could not be reached by the Governor, who, on the following day, sent him a telegram asking him to join in the Dewey-Dulles talk. Mr. Willkie declined, but agreed to see Mr. Dulles in New York for a nonpartisan, man-to-man talk, which was held at the Dulles' home late on the afternoon of Aug. 21.

Mr. Willkie's attitude regarding the campaign, indicating his determination to come out in sup-

Continued on Page 5, Column 7

The Christian Science Monitor Index

Friday, August 25, 1944

Changes in Allied Shipping Situation

Big changes in the shipping situation are coming about as more and more ports fall into Allied hands and as the Allied navies gain more complete ascendancy in the Atlantic and Mediterranean.

One great gain to the Allies will be the releasing of important naval units from western waters for concentration of overwhelming naval force against Japan in the Far East.

This situation is examined in detail by The Christian Science Monitor's naval expert, Capt. Frederick L. Oliver, U. S. N. (retired) on the first page of the second section.

U.S. and Britain Scan Bulgarian Plea for Peace

By J. Emlyn Williams

Staff Correspondent of The Christian Science Monitor

LONDON, Aug. 25—Bulgaria's direct, formal plea for an armistice, transmitted through the British ambassador at Ankara, is now receiving official consideration in London and Washington, according to information here today, thus hastening the collapse of Germany's Balkan front and the end of the war.

Such a development is to be expected, especially after Romania's surrender. If, also the Ankara report that all German forces have been withdrawn from Bulgaria is correct, then that State should have little difficulty in "working its passage home," provided there is a real realization in Sofia that the victorious Allies will not tolerate a continuance of the unsavory intrigues which have hitherto marked the rather scandalous scramble for safety of Germany's satellites in the Balkans.

Peace Terms

Britain and the United States, from their past official declarations and from their loyalty to Allies, Yugoslavia, and Greece, who suffered at the hands of the Bulgars, will certainly insist upon, first, unconditional surrender of Bulgaria and, secondly, of its acceptance of the principle that no enemy state shall be allowed to continue to hold territorial gains resulting from aggression.

Hitherto there has been little indication that Bulgaria was willing to accept this standpoint as regards to Thrace and Macedonia, rather hoping, apparently, that continued diplomatic relations with Russia would benefit them.

This is hardly conceivable and now there seems, from London's standpoint, little to be done except for Bulgaria to accept. Presumably, final decisions concerning the details of frontiers will be made, not now but later under more normal conditions.

Close Allies of Axis

Hungary, also, is obviously making attempts to appease the Allies, but equally with Bulgaria, is largely responsible for the instability of the Balkan's relations.

Both were close allies of totali-

Continued on Page 5, Column 4

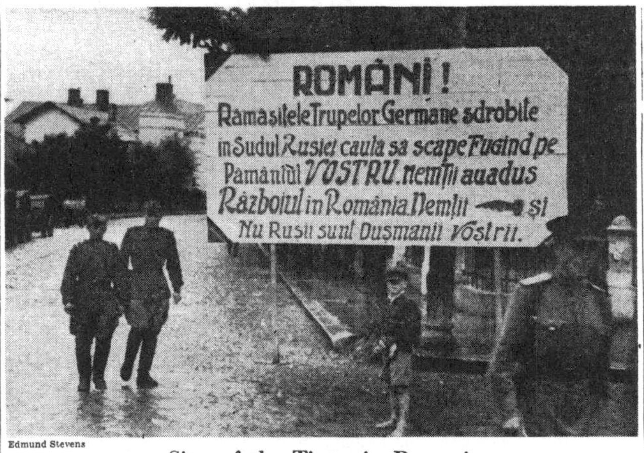

Edmund Stevens

Sign of the Times in Romania

This sign, photographed by a staff correspondent of The Christian Science Monitor while in Romania in July, was erected in a frontier city. It reads: "Romanians! The remnants of the German troops smashed in the south of Russia seek to escape by fleeing across your soil. Germans brought war to Romania. The Germans and not the Russians are your enemies."

Paris Slip-Up Fails to Dim Enthusiasm; Allies in Rush to Trap Nazis at Seine

By Peter Lyne

Staff Correspondent of The Christian Science Monitor

LONDON, Aug. 25—Two developments today are in large measure helping to counter the disappointment and puzzlement here over the confusion in Paris following the premature announcement of the Capital's liberation by French Forces of the Interior.

One is the news that Gen. Leclerc's Second French Armored Division has reached the center of Paris.

The second is a formal Anglo-French agreement assuring France its full share in armistice and peace plans, and providing for the earliest handing over of the civil administration of France to the French themselves.

Today Supreme Headquarters made its first positive contribution to solving the mystery of Paris by announcing that elements of the Second French Armored Division had entered the outskirts of the French Capital.

Further headquarters information, which appears since to have

Continued on Page 2, Column 5

What Went Wrong in Paris? Page 5.

Rule Set in Motion In Liberated France

By the Associated Press

Washington, Aug. 25

Arrangements to administer liberated France until the French people choose a permanent form of government went into effect today, the State Department announced.

These arrangements were set in motion through an exchange of letters between General Eisenhower, as Commanding General of Allied Forces, and General Koenig, Commander of the French Forces of the Interior.

They deal with administration of civil affairs and related matters.

Nazi Supplies To Italy Hit By Riviera Grip

By Ronald Stead

Staff Correspondent of The Christian Science Monitor With the United Nations Forces in the Mediterranean Theater

ALLIED HEADQUARTERS, Italy, Aug. 25—One of the effects of the Riviera invasion has been to deprive the Germans of any means of getting supplies or reinforcements from France to their hard-pressed armies in Italy.

In Northern Italy itself, communications have been so blasted that the Germans now have to rush their supplies into the Gothic Line at night across rivers over pontoon bridges which they dismantle before dawn to avoid their being bombed.

In the Rhône Valley toward which the Allied southern forces

Continued on Page 2, Column 6

By William H. Stringer

Staff Correspondent of The Christian Science Monitor Accredited to the Allied Invasion Forces

LONDON, Aug. 25 — Allied armies are employing the swiftest techniques of modern warfare, from air-borne bulldozers to quarterback split-second decisions, in their drives east of Paris and in the race to close a new and bigger trap in Northwest France on the battered German troops retreating toward the Seine.

The speed of the Allied advance has required the development of a whole new lightning technique of engineering, bridge-building, airfield laying, supply hustling.

This is true for Lieut. Gen. George S. Patton's eastward-racing spearheads, for American armored columns rumbling down the lower bank of the Seine, and equally requisite with advancing British and Canadian troops pushing northeastward up the coast toward Le Havre.

Swift Daily Advances

While the Battle of France as a whole is unfolding directly according to the excellent over-all strategy conceived months ago by the Allied high commanders, yet the swift daily advances are requiring quick judgment to exploit enemy weaknesses and push through lines of least resistance—tactics similar to those of a victorious football quarterback in a crucial game. Local strategy is subject to change without notice, but pays vast dividends.

Thus even the slower-moving

Continued on Page 2, Column 8

Hard Fight in Senate Is Seen For Anglo-American Oil Pact

By a Staff Correspondent of The Christian Science Monitor

WASHINGTON, Aug. 25 — The new Anglo-American Oil Agreement must run the gantlet of the Senate two-thirds treaty rule which has wrecked many treaties in the past and which defeated the League of Nations.

Mr. Roosevelt cut through controversy over whether the new oil pact is an "agreement" — which generally requires only majority approval of both houses—or a "treaty"—which requires approval by a two-thirds vote of the Senate alone, under the Constitution—by suddenly sending the controversial arrangement to the Senate in the form of a treaty.

He thereby precluded a controversy arising out of the charge that he was ignoring the Senate, but at the same time, it is believed here, probably engendered a new controversy over the Anglo-American Oil Agreement. He also set the stage for the procedure likely to be followed in the series of postwar international understandings following World War II. It appears that agitation to alter two-thirds treaty procedure will have little effect, and that the traditional two-thirds Senate majority will be the required hurdle for important postwar understandings.

Dates From Early Days

The two-thirds treaty provision, adopted by something of a fluke in the early days of the Republic by

Continued on Page 5, Column 6

N. H. Folks Turn Out For Good Roads Day

TEMPLE, N. H., Aug. 25 (AP)—Tomorrow is Good Roads Day for this hilltop village town.

Annually, men from all sections of this community turn out with tools, teams, and trucks and improve some piece of road for the benefit of everyone. Townswomen prepare and serve dinners and the event is a community reunion in which everyone participates.

Good Roads Day, officials point out, is a survival of early times when "everyone got together and worked for the common good."

Roosevelt Address Political? Socialists Granted Radio Time

WASHINGTON, Aug. 25 (AP)—Responding to a contention that President Roosevelt's Aug. 12 address at Bremerton, Wash., was "political," the War Department today acceded to a Socialist Party request for equal radio time to radiocast to soldiers overseas.

Further, the War Department said, correspondence embracing the Socialist Party's request and its reply has been furnished to the other major political parties.

Mr. Roosevelt spoke at Bremerton from the deck of a destroyer upon his return from a visit to Hawaii, where he conferred with Gen. Douglas MacArthur and Admiral Chester Nimitz, and to bases in the Aleutian Islands.

The War Department announcement was made in reply to a press inquiry. It said:

"The Socialist Party has written the War Department that it definitely considers the President's speech of Aug. 12 at Bremerton a political address and has requested the War Department, in accordance with Title V, Public Law 277, to give equal radio time for a Socialist Party political address.

"The War Department has indicated to the Socialist Party that, under the statute, it will accede to this request. The other major political parties have asked for and been furnished copies of the correspondence between the War Department and the Socialist Party in this connection."

The text of the correspondence was not made public by the War Department.

Public Law 277 is the soldier-vote law, and Title V, recently amended, is the section which governs the dissemination of political news and propaganda to troops under official sponsorship.

Car Tagged Daily: Police? No, Buyer!

WILLIAMSPORT, Pa. (AP)—A local motorist has a market for his automobile any time he decides to sell. Daily for the past few weeks a prospective buyer has left his name, address and this note tied to the auto: "I need a car like yours."

Hitler Wants More Credit For Robot-Bomb 'Success'

LONDON, Aug. 25 (AP)—Nazi robot bombs sent against England at the rate of 100 a day have caused "heavy casualties" and "shocking damage to property," the Government asserted today in a fresh appeal to Londoners to keep their children away from the Capital.

The British Information Service declared that flying-bomb salvos had reached such a pitch that 17,000 homes were being destroyed or damaged by them every 24 hours.

By a Staff Correspondent of The Christian Science Monitor

LONDON, Aug. 25 — Amid the present flood of Allied victories, the voice of Nazi propagandists is raised in indignant protest that the Germans are not getting enough credit for what they call the greatest and most prolonged bombardment ever achieved in the history of warfare—the 10-week nonstop bombardment of London by flying bombs.

From southern England's viewpoint, there is no noticeable improvement in the flying-bomb situation. In some areas it is worse.

When every other radio station in the world seemed to be talking about the liberation of Paris, "Quisling" commentator William Joyce, speaking in English from Berlin, was trying to get in his say about "the greatest bombardment of all time." For 10 weeks he and Propaganda Minister Dr. Joseph Goebbels' other satellites have been stoking up a fiery picture of doomed London.

Dr. Goebbels' difficulty is in having to describe for 10 weeks the allegedly ever-worsening conditions of London which the Germans had already pictured as a smoke-shrouded ruin.

The fact that today London is still functioning fully and calmly, that Allied troops are sweeping the Germans from France and that everywhere signs are increasing of a Nazi crack-up is all very embarrassing for Dr. Goebbels' propaganda about Germany's remarkable new weapons and the destruction of London.

The Nazi propagandist tried to be more specific. He claimed that small-arms factories are being evacuated from London away from flying bombs. Even supposing his claim is true, it represents a big comedown from earlier reports of the complete destruction of London. Any reasonable listener would ask what appreciable effect there would be from removal of such small-arms factories at the present stage of the war, when Allied arms and supplies are pouring onto the Continent along countless Allied avenues.

Mr. Joyce only confirmed what was obvious already, that the Nazi robot bombardment is nothing but a terror weapon of revenge as it is being used at the present stage of the war. Its future aspects remain to be seen, but in the meantime the accumulative effect of the bombardment is causing acute suffering—all to no purpose in its bearing on the war's outcome.

Radiocast by Partisan-controlled station says commander of Germans in Capital has surrendered to Leclerc, leader of French unit sent in by Bradley.

By the War Editor of The Christian Science Monitor

From Associated Press and other direct news dispatches

French armored troops have entered Paris and now are operating there, General Eisenhower's aides have announced.

One report radiocast by a Partisan-controlled station said the commander of the German forces in the city had surrendered to General Leclerc, leader of the French troops. This report is unconfirmed from other sources.

Earlier, it was indicated that General Leclerc had led armored units into the center of Paris against strong German opposition.

Heavy fighting was said to be still going on in some areas. Nazi SS units were described as resisting desperately. They set fire to the Navy Ministry and the Hotel Crillon and early today the sky was red in the direction of Neuilly and Vincennes.

According to one dispatch, the Germans were entrenched in a triangular area covering the Champs-de-Mars, the Place de la Concorde, and the Champs Elysées.

General Leclerc's troops were believed to be the vanguard of a substantial Allied force headed by General de Gaulle, which was dispatched to the aid of patriot fighters inside the city. The bulk of this force which includes some American units, is believed to be in the Pont de Sèvres suburbs, six miles to the southwest. General de Gaulle is said to be waiting to make a triumphal entry. Churchbells can be heard ringing in the city over the sound of bombs and shells.

Northwest of Paris, converging American and British Empire forces have reduced the pocket in which disorganized enemy forces are fleeing across the Seine to an area less than 15 miles in depth.

RAF pilots said it appeared that Marshal von Kluge was preparing his next stand along the Somme-Marne line.

There has been no further word of General Patton's spearhead which swung around Paris beyond Sens.

In southern France, troops of General Patch's Seventh Army have opened a heavy attack on four remaining enemy strong points in Marseille after capturing two German generals and 5,000 prisoners.

Other troops have captured the famous resort city of Cannes and near-by Grasse in a push eastward from the center of the beachhead. It remains to be seen whether this is the opening of a drive to the Italian border, to which thousands of Nazis are said to be fleeing.

Somewhat balancing the continued swift progress in France is the news that the Nazis have greatly intensified their robot-bomb assaults on London, perhaps with heavier missiles than used heretofore. A British Government statement says the bombs are causing "heavy casualties" and "shocking damage to property."

Meanwhile, the Nazis have announced a shakeup in the Hungarian Cabinet because of "political tensions" arising from events in Romania. Details are lacking.

Soviet armies are pushing deeper into Romania and Bessarabia with something approximating blitz speed in an effort to capitalize on Romania's defection before the Nazis can reorganize their Balkan defenses.

In 24 hours, the Russians have taken 25,000 prisoners and more than 550 towns and villages, including Chisinau, the Bessarabian Capital.

In Estonia, Soviet forces have captured Tartu, Marshal Stalin has announced.

To add further to Germany's woes, General Eisenhower's Headquarters has just announced that production of finished oil products for the Reich was reduced an estimated 49 per cent by Allied air bombardments during May, June, and July.

Paris:

In spite of the fact that the French 2d Armored Division is operating inside the city, fighting

Continued on Page 2, Column 1

Moscow Says Romania Must Earn Armistice

LONDON, Aug. 25 (AP)—Russia officially informed Romania today that it must earn an armistice with the Allies by ordering its troops to fight "hand in hand with the Red Army" during the remaining days of the war.

Such assistance "is the only means for speedy cessation of military operations on Romanian territory and for the signing of an armistice," said a statement issued by the Soviet Commissariat for Foreign Affairs.

The radiocast Moscow statement, first official reply from an Allied government to Romania's announced decision to accept Allied peace terms, came simultaneously with reports that Washington and London were considering a Bulgarian armistice move.

From various quarters came reports that Romanians already were beginning to fight the Germans. Moscow said Romanian soldiers were surrendering in droves as the two-pronged Russian offensive drove more deeply into northeastern Romania and Bessarabia.

The Soviet Foreign Commissariat made it clear that Romanian troops would be welcome allies either in helping drive the Germans from Romania or in attacking the Hungarians through Transylvania, half of which was stripped from Romania in the 1940 Vienna Dictate and given to Hungary.

Russia thus gave backing to Romania's announced intention of regaining this lost territory.

The Soviet Government has disavowed entirely any desire to acquire Romanian lands, to infringe upon the Kingdom's independence, or interfere with its internal affairs.

THE CHRISTIAN SCIENCE MONITOR

AN INTERNATIONAL DAILY NEWSPAPER

VOL. XXXVI NO. 280 | COPYRIGHT 1944 BY THE CHRISTIAN SCIENCE PUBLISHING SOCIETY | BOSTON, WEDNESDAY, OCTOBER 25, 1944 | **—ATLANTIC EDITION | FIVE CENTS A COPY

MacArthur: Jap Fleet Routed; U. S. Planes Spearhead Attack; Soviets Drive Deep Into Reich

Dewey Reiterates Support For U. S. League Delegate With Power to Act Swiftly

Republican nominee for President says he long has favored that American representative be granted authority to vote action against aggressor without asking Congress—Flays New Deal 'isolationism.'

By Roscoe Drummond
Chief of the Washington Bureau of The Christian Science Monitor

MILWAUKEE, Wis., Oct. 25—Gov. Thomas E. Dewey of New York has acted today to bring about the total elimination of all foreign-policy disagreements between President Roosevelt and himself in the 1944 campaign.

The purpose of the Republican nominee is to make the voting on Nov. 7 turn as completely as possible on domestic issues.

His endeavor is to persuade the country that it can safely vote against a domestic Administration he believes it does not want without risking a peace program he is convinced it does want.

Dewey Purposes

In reputedly isolationist territory journalistically dominated by the Chicago Tribune, which is now tearfully criticizing him, Governor Dewey is acting to accomplish his purpose:

By publicly advocating the proposal which the President presented last Saturday night, and which Governor Dewey says he has long favored, that the American delegate be empowered to vote to bring the world-security council into action against aggressors without, as he says, "having to return to Congress for authority every time he has to make a decision."

By expressly classifying the withholding of such authority from the American representative as a "nullifying amendment" which he would oppose.

Support of G. O. P. Leaders

By bringing to his support the Republican leaders of the next Congress whose indorsement of his foreign-policy views he now announces, in making public a series of telegrams from them.

By seeking to demonstrate that Republican internationalist Senator Joseph H. Ball of Minnesota, in whose State he delivered his speech last night, acted prematurely, unnecessarily, and unwisely in jumping the ranks of the G. O. P. in giving his allegiance to President Roosevelt on the foreign-policy issue.

By pledging that on Jan. 20 next year work on the future peace "will become a bipartisan effort, bringing to it the ablest men in our country from both political parties."

By bringing up the President's past record to show that Mr. Roosevelt at times has been an isolationist, and by emphasizing that what are important are not the "past mistakes of any individual in either party" but "what the next Congress will do."

Centers on Congress

It is on this point—on the point of what the next Congress will do—that Governor Dewey centers his major criticism on Mr. Roosevelt and contends that the prospects of a secure peace are better under a Republican President desirous and qualified to work harmoniously and co-operatively with Congress.

He accuses Mr. Roosevelt of attempting "to ride roughshod over Congress" and of trying "to dictate the course it should follow before it has even been acquainted with the facts."

He asserts that such an attitude represents "trifling with the hope of the world."

He charges Mr. Roosevelt with 'deliberately seeking to precipitate a hardening of minds" on the issues of the peace and declares that "if this stubborn course is pursued, it can only result once again as in 1919, in a disastrous conflict between the President and the Congress."

Partnership With Congress

The Republican candidate says he does not have "the slightest doubt that a Congress which is working in partnership with the President will achieve the result we all consider essential and grant adequate power for swift action to the American representative" on the proposed security council.

But, he adds, "we must not find ourselves after next Jan. 20 stalled on dead center as a result of this series of recriminations between my opponent and the Congress."

Governor Dewey's own support of the proposal to endow in advance the American delegate with authority to vote the use of force against aggressors, which the President advocated last week and which won him Senator Ball's indorsement, came when, in his Minneapolis reply to Mr. Roosevelt's latest speech, he put the withholding of such authority by Congress in the class of "nullifying amendments" which he opposed.

Not Subject to Reservation

Governor Dewey cited this sentence from his own address before the New York Herald Tribune forum: "We must make certain that our participation in this world organization is not subjected to reservations that would nullify the power of that organization to maintain peace and to halt future aggression."

He then added:

"That means, of course, that it must not be subject to a reservation that would require our representative to return to Congress for authority every time he had to make a decision. Obviously, Congress, and only Congress, has the constitutional power to determine what quota of force it will make available and what discretion it will give our representative to use that force."

"Appeasement" Criticized

Governor Dewey's latest speech manifestly aligns him still more firmly on the international side of foreign policy. His main criticisms of his opponent were in the field of his "isolationist" acts of the past. He cited the cool words the

Continued on Page 6, Column 5

Governor Dewey's address in Minneapolis: Page 6.

President Continues Campaign But Not 'in Ordinary Sense'

By Richard L. Strout
Staff Correspondent of The Christian Science Monitor

WASHINGTON, Oct. 25—President Roosevelt worked today on week-end speeches which he will deliver in two of the three largest cities in America, Philadelphia and Chicago. Last Saturday he toured New York, America's biggest city. He is expected to continue to feature foreign affairs in his addresses and to hammer home charges of alleged past and present Republican isolationism. At a press conference here yesterday he denied that he was campaigning "in the ordinary sense" and smilingly insisted that he was following out the second part of his July 20 acceptance speech:

"I shall, however, feel free to report to the people the facts about matters of concern to them and especially to correct any misrepresentations."

The three cities where Mr. Roosevelt is directing campaign efforts have all had unexpectedly high registration of civilian voters. The Congress of Industrial Organizations Political Action Committee claims some of the credit for this, and Democrats have found considerable comfort in the figures.

In addition the President will make a platform talk en route between Philadelphia (Friday night) and Chicago (Saturday night) at Fort Wayne, Ind. Another platform talk is scheduled Friday at Wilmington, Del., afterwards driving to Camden, N. J.

Trip in Pivotal Section

Significance of the trip is that it carries the President through a pivotal section of Electoral College states. Pennsylvania has 35 votes; Illinois, 28.

With his initial bonus of electoral votes from the Solid South, President Roosevelt will probably win a fourth term if he can break even in this tier of big, industrial and uncertain eastern states, Democrats believe.

The President will do more than speak in the two cities, it is understood; he will tour Philadelphia by car, repeating in effect his four-hour trip through New York last Saturday. Another big campaign procession is expected through downtown Chicago.

From the Democratic viewpoint the campaign moves into new ground with the Dewey speech last night, declaring that the American delegate to the proposed security organization must have power to act, without referring each case to Congress. Democrats profess pleasure that Governor Dewey has "followed" the President, and that appears to be shaping as the new party line, mingled with genuine satisfaction that this great issue has been moved out of the political campaign.

Test of Rival Fervor

Democrats, who have taken Senator Joseph H. Ball (R) of Minnesota to their bosoms since he bolted the Republican presidential ticket, were asked today how his argument stood, now that Governor Dewey had approved giving the security delegate power to act. The reply was to quote Senator Ball's press conference statement here that after Mr. Dewey's first two speeches on foreign affairs, in which he did not take up the security delegate issue directly, any statement following Mr. Roosevelt's New York speech would seem to be forced from him, for political purposes.

Vice-Presidential candidate Harry S. Truman also seems to be indicating the new Democratic point of attack in his demand that Governor Dewey "repudiate" eight alleged Republican "isolationists" now seeking re-election to the Senate.

Once more the situation seems to be professed agreement on major goals and objectives by the two big parties, but sharp difference over the rival ability to carry them into effect, and the fervor with which they will be pushed.

Monitor Newscast Series to Change

The present series of daily newscasts by The Christian Science Monitor, entitled "The World's Front Page," will end Friday, Oct. 27. Future radiocasting plans for this paper will be announced later.

Dewey Places Faith In Strong Congress

Special to The Christian Science Monitor

Minneapolis, Minn., Oct. 25

Calling for Congressional co-operation behind United States participation on a world security council, Gov. Thomas E. Dewey of New York in his major campaign speech here last night as the Republican Presidential nominee said:

"I have not the slightest doubt that a Congress which is working in partnership with the President will achieve the result we all consider essential and grant adequate power for swift action to the American representative. But those who would attempt to ride roughshod over Congress, and to dictate the course it should follow before it has even been acquainted with the facts, are trifling with the hope of the world."

Voting Time To Be Settled In N. Y. Soon

By Wyona Dashwood
Staff Correspondent of The Christian Science Monitor

NEW YORK, Oct. 25—All facets of the 1944 national presidential contest glistened for the voter eye here today as the quadrennial race accelerated to finale speed.

Gov. Thomas E. Dewey's return to Albany from his midwestern reply in the controversy on America's position in the postwar world is expected to bring decision on the plea of New York City spokesmen, civic and official alike, for extension of the State voting time to accommodate the big metropolitan registration.

Minnesota's Republican insurgent, United States Senator Joseph H. Ball, further projected his defection from the Dewey standard on the issue of adequate foreign policy for a lasting peace, declaring that, in his pronouncement in Minneapolis last night, Governor Dewey "again declined to state clearly his own position on the vital question of whether the proposed security council should be empowered to use force against an aggressor without reference back to Congress in each action."

"These controversial issues are not new or strange," Mr. Ball said. "They are the same ones on which the League of Nations was wrecked, and the people can decide the issues only if candidates state their positions on them clearly and unequivocally."

Political Commotion

Here as featured spokesman at a vote-for-freedom rally of the Americans United for World Organization, Inc., Senator Ball has made political commotion in his announced preference for Mr. Roosevelt as definitive voice on the question of granting authority for the use of force against aggressors.

"Governor Dewey's speech," he said of the Republican candidate's response to President Roosevelt's major address before the Foreign Policy Association here Saturday night, "if we did not know the record on Selective Service, Lend-Lease, repeal of the Neutrality Act and other measures, would almost convince us that it was President Roosevelt and the Democrats who were isolationists and opposed these preparedness measures before Pearl Harbor. Fortunately we do know the record.

"Governor Dewey took the strange attitude that efforts to get congressional candidates to be honest with the voters on these issues are an attempt to dictate to Congress. Apparently he does not want a mandate from the people

Continued on Page 8, Column 7

Red Armies sweep by signpost with single word in bold Russian: 'Germania'

By Alexander Werth
Special Correspondent of The Christian Science Monitor

MOSCOW, Oct. 25—A Russian Army is in Germany. Outside Eydtruhnen, long a frontier station between the Russian and German empires. The Red Army has put up a large signpost with one word written in Russian "Germania."

How much this signpost symbolizes can be seen from the deep emotion that has seized every Russian soldier crossing into Germany.

They all think of the thousands of Russian towns and villages destroyed by the Germans. They remember those 40 months of war, when the German boot was arrogantly stepping on Russian soil. One Russian soldier, who had just crossed into Germany, was saying with emotion that his truck had travelled all the way from Stalingrad.

Stalin Order

In the last few days the Red Army has conquered much more than was announced Oct. 23 by the Stalin order to Gen. Ivan D. Cherniakhovsky, commander of the Third White Russian Front.

In a wide sector, north of General Cherniakhovsky's Army, troops of the First Baltic Front have overrun that whole strip of the country called Memelland with the exception of the town of Memel itself.

All this strip on the right bank of Niemen is now in Russian hands. A Russian communiqué refers to it as the Klaipeda area.

The fighting has been extremely heavy in East Prussia. Not only inside the German borders but also at the approaches to East Prussia, the Germans have built a formidable network of fortifications. These included masses of field fort fortifications in addition to the whole chains of concrete forts, some with roofs and walls two yards thick. There was a network of barbed wire entanglements and more mines per square mile than perhaps anywhere in the world.

Reich Forts Strong

An example of the thoroughness of German fortifications can be seen from one of the command posts captured by the Russians. They call it "The Palace." It consists of five underground rooms with powerful concrete walls and roof, comfortable living quarters and an artesian well.

All this had to be smashed up by an intensive artillery barrage, combined with air blows. One of the peculiarities of this Russian offensive is the exceptionally important part played by the air force.

There is probably a larger Russian air concentration here than in any fighting on the Russian front. Seldom if ever have the Russians enjoyed such overwhelming air superiority.

An important factor in the East Prussian battle is the system of continuous "psychological attacks"

Continued on Page 5, Column 1

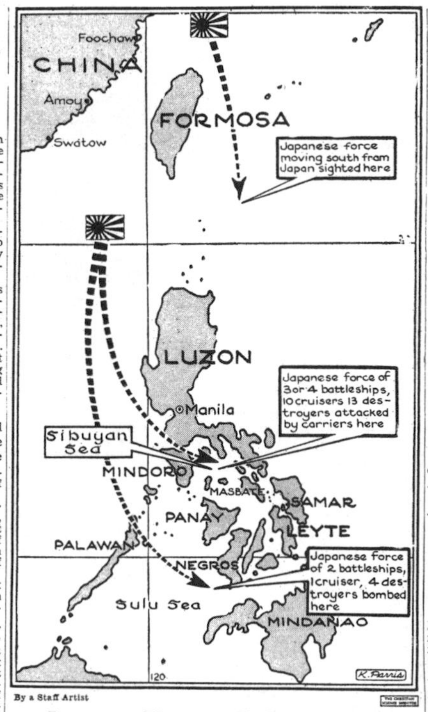

By a Staff Artist

Japanese Fleet on Fighting Prowl

Details so far announced of the great naval battle of the Philippines show the position of two Japanese naval forces close in to the archipelago and a third coming southward at a point southeast of Formosa.

U. S. Forces on Leyte Win Supply Docks at Tacloban

By Gordon Walker
Staff Correspondent of The Christian Science Monitor

WITH AMERICAN FORCES INVADING THE PHILIPPINES, Oct. 23. Delayed—At Tacloban, Leyte's capital, American forces have won sizeable docking facilities which will speed up the unloading of supplies. In a small way, therefore, Tacloban has the same relative importance to the Philippines invasion as Cherbourg had to the landing in Normandy.

Unloading of supplies has been one of the biggest problems here on the Leyte beachheads. I made a quick trip to each of the beachheads yesterday and watched men slaving in fierce heat to perform the almost superhuman task of unloading and moving inland mountains of food, ammunition, and mechanized equipment.

Here on these two tiny strips of sand in the central Philippines there were probably as many, if not more, troops put ashore on the first day as on Europe's D-Day at Normandy.

Need Supplies Quickly

After four divisions of troops had been landed ashore here they had to be supplied and quickly. Cargo-landing craft were able to drop their ramps on a dry beach at several points. On others, however, beaches were too gradual and the big landing ships for tanks were forced to pull back out into the bay until pontoon ramps could be assembled to serve as improvised docks.

Even then the problem of transporting supplies inland from the beach was made difficult by the presence of unexpected swamps discovered a few hundred yards in from some beaches.

Most of this problem has been cleared up now and the invasion is now taking on the aspect of a major shift of forces rather than merely the transporting of an assault force. Not only are combat troops and equipment pouring ashore in gigantic numbers and weight but engineers and engineering equipment are being thrown ashore to begin the big job of converting Leyte into a first American base.

Meanwhile, men were loading trucks and hauling supplies on beaches while over their heads warships still lobbed shells, and dive-bombers still screamed down to soften up enemy positions further inland.

Walking along the beaches was like trying to push through a political convention hall on the last night. Men worked all day in tropical heat—oblivious of the war around them. And when night came they continued to work under artificial light occasionally intensified by bursting of star shells to spot night artillery and naval bombardment.

Troops lounged on the beaches in myriads of foxholes, where the assault troops dug in on the first night. Bulldozers cut roads out of an overgrown palm grove just ahead of long lines of trucks and amphibious jeeps.

And in the midst of this maelstrom of a four-day-old beachhead, a few Filipino mothers with

Continued on Page 2, Column 5

Flash! Philippine Guerrillas Strike on Long-Planned Signal

WITH AMERICAN FORCES INVADING THE PHILIPPINES, Oct. 25 (AP)—A weak signal from a radio set on the island of Panay heard in the late fall of 1942 set in motion machinery to aid the guerrillas—aid which culminated in a full-scale invasion of the Philippines, Gen. Douglas MacArthur disclosed today.

In a special communiqué issued from his headquarters and radiocast in English to the Philippines, the General paid tribute to the guerrillas.

For two years, he said, the inadequately armed patriots, some of them Americans who never surrendered, others who escaped from prison camps, and men sent in to carry out specific missions have fought the Japanese.

"Following the disaster which, in the face of overwhelming superior enemy power, overtook our gallant forces, a deep and impenetrable silence engulfed the Philippines," the General said. "Through that silence, no news concerning the fate of the Filipino people reached the outside world until broken by a weak signal from a radio set in the island of Panay, which was picked up in the late fall of the same fateful year by a listening post of the War Department and flashed to my headquarters.

Curtain of Silence Lifted

"The signal, weak and spotty as it was, lifted the curtain of silence and uncertainty and disclosed the start of a human drama with few parallels in military history. In it I recognized the spontaneous movement of the Filipino people to resist the shackles with which

Continued on Page 2, Column 7

Candidates' Stand on Swift U. S. Peace Power

By the Associated Press

Here is what President Roosevelt and Gov. Thomas E. Dewey have to say on the controversial issue of the powers to be vested in the American representative on an international peace agency:

Governor Dewey

Speaking at Minneapolis, last night:

"I have emphasized . . . that 'we must make certain that our participation in this world organization is not subjected to reservation that would nullify the power of that organization to maintain peace and to halt future aggression.' That means, of course, that it must not be subject to a reservation that would require our representative to return to Congress for authority every time he had to make a decision. Obviously Congress, and only Congress, has the constitutional power to determine what quota of force it will make available, and what discretion it will give our representative to use that force."

President Roosevelt

In his Foreign-Policy address, Oct. 21:

"The council of the United Nations must have the power to act quickly and decisively to keep the peace by force, if necessary. A policeman would not be a very effective policeman if, when he saw a felon break into a house, he had to go to the town hall and call a town meeting to issue a warrant before the felon could be arrested.

"It is clear that, if the world organization is to have any reality at all, our representative must be endowed in advance by the people themselves, by constitutional means through their representatives in the Congress, with authority to act."

American light carrier Princeton sunk—MacArthur reports general advance on Leyte—11,000 Nazi troops sealed off by Canadians—Russians in Norway.

By the War Editor of The Christian Science Monitor
From Associated Press and other direct news dispatches

The Japanese fleet has suffered the "most crushing defeat of the war," said Gen. Douglas MacArthur in a broadcast statement.

Japan's Navy, forced out of its seclusion by the landings on Leyte, has come out to challenge American naval power in the Pacific.

All indications are that a mighty trial of strength between the two navies is in progress.

So far, three Japanese naval forces have been sighted and attacked by carrier-borne planes—two of them close to the Philippines, the third southeast of Formosa, going southward.

Japanese losses, reported by Admiral Nimitz, include one large carrier sunk, two others damaged, five or six battleships damaged and at least one torpedoed, and 150 planes destroyed.

American losses so far include the sinking of the light carrier Princeton, which exploded following damage from shore guns on Oct. 23, when the three Japanese forces were sighted. Practically all the crew was reported saved.

The Japanese say they sank four American carriers, two large cruisers, one destroyer, and four transports.

The great fight appeared to be still in its initial stages and details so far are meager.

The first Japanese force sighted apparently consisted of three or four battleships, 10 cruisers, and 13 destroyers. It was moving eastward into the Sibuyan Sea, south of Mindoro, in the west center of the Philippines. It was heavily attacked by carrier planes.

The second was sighted farther south in the Sulu Sea—on the west side of the islands. It was a smaller force, consisting of two battleships, one cruiser, and four destroyers. This, too, was attacked by carrier planes.

The third, sighted late in the afternoon of Oct. 23, was driving southward from Japanese home waters at a point southeast of Formosa.

No reports came from Pearl Harbor regarding any Japanese warcraft on the east of the Philippines, where the advance on Leyte Island is continuing.

The Japanese Domei agency, however, radiocast a report that the American fleet east of the islands was "surrounded."

On Leyte, General MacArthur's forces recorded a general advance the whole length of their bridgehead, reaching Taboutabon, eight miles northwest of Dulag, and the San Pablo airfield, seven miles west of Dulag.

Tacloban, the island's Capital, is being used as a port for shipping large quantities of supplies to the invading forces.

Events on the Eastern Front showed little major change beyond a Russian advance, so far reported only by the Germans, from bridgeheads on the Narew River, about 14 miles north of Warsaw.

The Russian Army has crossed the frontier into Norway, Marshal Stalin announced tonight.

Berlin announced German evacuation of the important arctic port of Kirkenes, 30 miles west of Petsamo.

In the West British were fighting in the streets of 's-Hertogenbosch, an important road center, causing the Germans to retreat on a 15-mile front.

A Canadian advance into South Beveland in the Schelde estuary has sealed off 11,000 German troops.

Pacific:

Jap Warships Hit; U.S.S. Princeton Lost

The text of Admiral Chester W. Nimitz's communiqué is as follows:

"On Oct. 23 (west longitude date), searchers from carriers of the Third Fleet located two enemy

Continued on Page 2, Column 1

Japanese Risk Navy in Defense Of Philippines

By Joseph C. Harsch
Staff Writer of The Christian Science Monitor

A substantial portion of the Japanese fleet has now been committed to possible decisive action for the third time since the Pacific war began.

This conclusion, which is all that information up to this moment justifies, gives the measure of importance of the Philippine Islands in the scheme of Japanese war plans.

For this is the first time that Japan has risked its fleet in substantial strength in what is for Japan the defensive phase of the war.

Its two previous commitments in comparable scale were the related battles of the Coral Sea and Midway where Japan was attempting to complete its plan of conquest. Not since the effort to paralyze American sea power, which those engagements represented, has Japan risked a major fleet action.

Yet now, after allowing the approaches to its inner seas to be torn away one by one without accepting the challenge it finally does commit major strength to the defense of the Philippines.

Both the scale of this commitment—a minimum of five battleships, 11 cruisers and 17 destroyers—and the pattern of action of the three forces involved, expresses an effort to make one last use of the advantages of holding the Philippines and controlling the passages through them.

Two of the forces located are placed in the waters of the central Philippines. The third was found steaming south from the area of Formosa. This is enough to define the Japanese plan of action which is obviously based on possession of the inner passages through the islands. It represents a squeeze maneuver which is still theoretically possible, but will cease to be possible once the passages are in American hands.

The enemy undoubtedly hopes to catch Admiral William F. Halsey's forces between its force moving south from the Formosa area and the two others debouching through the inner passages. It has the advantage up to this time of passages between the island which must be assumed to be still under enemy control either from artil-

Continued on Page 5, Column 1

Unconditional Surrender Still Goes, Says Churchill

LONDON, Oct. 25 (AP)—Prime Minister Churchill reiterated in the House of Commons today that "unconditional surrender in the sense of no bargaining with the enemy is still the policy of the Government."

He suggested the House should bear in mind also the three-power declaration of May 12 to Axis satellites, in which they were warned to quit Germany.

The Prime Minister declined to engage in a foreign affairs debate, declaring it would be unwise to go into details on delicate international matters "on the spur of the moment." There will be an opportunity for debate after his report Friday on his Moscow mission, he said, but added he hoped it would be short.

He left unanswered questions as to how unconditional surrender was reconciled with former enemies becoming "apparent allies" and as to whether Nazis who surrendered unconditionally would be given government posts in Germany.

Earlier, Richard Law, Minister of State, told the House Britain and Russia had made no decision during the recent Moscow talks on respect zones of influence in the Balkans.

Although Bulgaria has declared war on Germany, he said, the country is still technically at war with the Allies and could not yet be recognized as a cobelligerent.

Mr. Churchill turned aside a question as to whether Germany would be made to pay for the "worthless marks" with which she flooded occupied countries.

Woman Made Model Of Portable Ports

LONDON, Oct. 25 (AP)—Mrs. Masika Lancaster told members of Parliament yesterday all about the prefabricated ports which made the Normandy landings possible—a secret she had kept until the British and United States Governments announced it.

Mrs. Lancaster, wife of an officer, made the original cardboard models from which the two ports were constructed at a cost of $100,000,000. An artist, she has no technical or engineering training.

THE CHRISTIAN SCIENCE MONITOR

AN INTERNATIONAL DAILY NEWSPAPER

VOL. XXXVI NO. 292 | COPYRIGHT 1944 BY THE CHRISTIAN SCIENCE PUBLISHING SOCIETY | BOSTON, WEDNESDAY, NOVEMBER 8, 1944 | **—ATLANTIC EDITION | FIVE CENTS A COPY

Roosevelt Gets War-Peace Mandate; Democrats Increase Lead in Congress

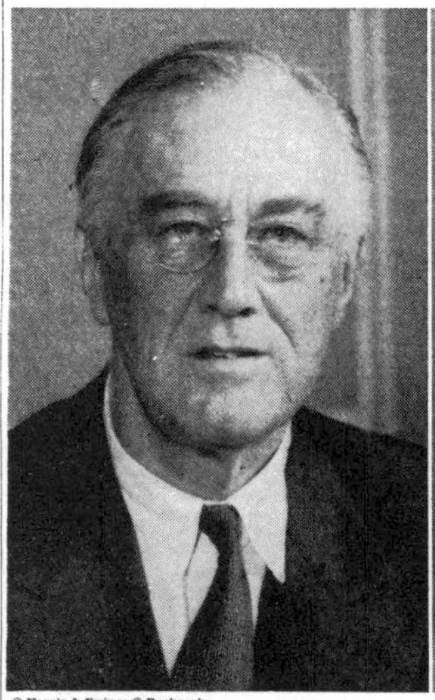

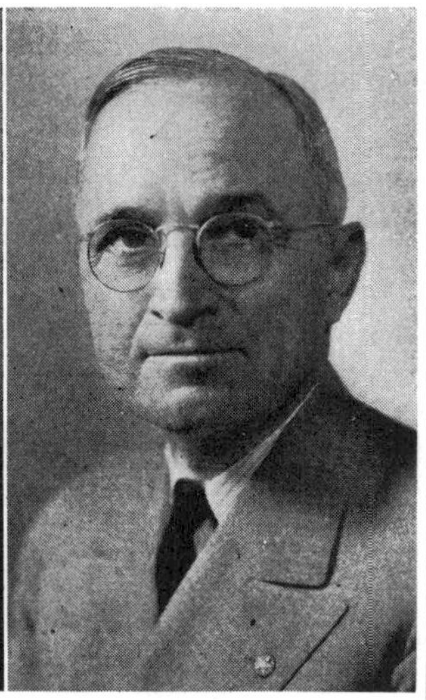

© Harris & Ewing; © Bachrach

Franklin D. Roosevelt
Re-elected to fourth term in White House

Harry S. Truman
Elected to the Vice-Presidency

President re-elected for fourth term with possibility late returns from doubtful states will give him greater Electoral College majority than he had in 1940.

Associated Press tabulations this afternoon reported President Roosevelt's fourth-term victory was looming larger hourly, and Mr. Roosevelt now held the prospect of defeating Gov. Thomas E. Dewey by a popular-vote margin and an Electoral College vote greater than he piled up against Wendell L. Willkie in 1940. It shows signs of engulfing Michigan, which was one of the 10 Republican States four years ago. Ohio, after hours in the Dewey-Bricker column, is shown by the Associated Press to be changing over. Oregon went into the Roosevelt-Truman column at an advanced hour.

The incomplete popular vote reached 20,865,595 for Mr. Roosevelt and 18,343,397 for Mr. Dewey.

By Roscoe Drummond
Chief of the Washington Bureau of The Christian Science Monitor

In the wake of a national vote for both candidates still mounting toward a new high, President Franklin D. Roosevelt's re-election to a fourth term today stood as an indorsement of his leadership both in prosecuting the war and in carrying America into full participation in the peace.

There was every evidence that the issues of the war and the peace dominated the campaign and determined the verdict.

In re-electing the Commander in Chief—and it was primarily as Commander in Chief that Mr. Roosevelt submitted his Administration to the fourth-term test—it is clear that the American people have acted to give the President an effective working majority in the Senate and in the House of Representatives with which to carry forward the objectives on which the nation is so fully united.

As the full proportions of the Democratic victory emerge today, these significant features of the voting stand out:

1. The full scale of the President's indorsement is still in the making. With New Jersey and Oregon swinging to Mr. Roosevelt, the electoral vote stands at 413 to 116 for Mr. Dewey; with Michigan and Ohio, both of which the Republican nominee is holding with the narrowest margin, the President's winning total would go to 457 to 74 for Mr. Dewey. Mr. Willkie in 1940 won 82 electoral votes and amassed the largest popular vote ever given to a Republican Presidential candidate, defeated or elected.

2. But Mr. Roosevelt's victory remains clear-cut and emphatic and with it the voters have assured the President of a strengthened Democratic majority in the House of Representatives and in the Senate. There will not be a divided Congress.

3. Moreover, there are major evidences of a notable anti-isolationist trend which cannot fail to result in helping the President win the approval of Congress for the postwar security program he advocated in his campaign speeches. The most significant manifestation of this trend is the defeat of a whole group of the most implacable isolationist leaders of the Republican Party, including Senator Gerald P. Nye of North Dakota, Richard J. Lyons, Chicago Tribune senatorial candidate in Illinois, Senator John Danaher in Connecticut, and Representative Hamilton Fish, whom Mr. Dewey himself opposed, in New York. The strength of the internationalist vote and its apparently decisive alignment on the side of the President was also illustrated in the Democratic capture of Minnesota, home state of Senator Joseph Ball, who broke ranks with his own Party to support the fourth term on the issue of foreign policy.

G. O. P. Trend Reversed

4. As in other national election years, the President's manifest vote-getting ability has reversed the Republican trend throughout the country. Thus, while the Republicans showed remarkable strength in 1938, picking up some 80 seats in the House, they were stopped in 1940, and while the G. O. P. trend was resumed again in 1942, when Mr. Roosevelt was not himself a candidate, it was turned back yesterday at nearly every political level—in the House, in the Senate and in the Governorships.

5. Finally—and on this both Parties were united in their ap-

Continued on Page 4, Column 6

Isolation Wall Battered In Senate Race

By Richard L. Strout
Staff Correspondent of The Christian Science Monitor

WASHINGTON, Nov. 8—Democrats will control the United States Senate in the historic forthcoming debate on League of Nations No. 2, with a ratio of about 3 to 2, according to latest election returns.

Voters showed a tendency in close senatorial contests yesterday either to knock off, or to threaten, candidates of known isolationist views, but despite this a number of so-called "nationalists" were returned.

Republicans had lost one Senate seat, in Connecticut, where Democrat Brien McMahon had defeated Incumbent John A. Danaher.

Danaher Record

Senator Danaher had voted against both Neutrality Act revision bills, against both draft-act bills and against Lend-Lease, prior to Pearl Harbor.

Republicans were being threatened with the loss of two other seats, those of James J. Davis of Pennsylvania, running behind Francis J. Myers (D), and Gerald P. Nye of North Dakota, running behind John Moses (D).

Senators Davis and Nye also voted against all five bills which Senator Danaher opposed.

On the other side of the picture, Republican Bourke B. Hickenlooper won the seat from Iowa held by Senator Guy M. Gillette (D). In New Jersey, H. Alexander Smith (R) was running ahead of Elmer H. Wene, Democratic incumbent.

On the other side of the picture, Republicans were threatening two seats now held by Democrats.

In Iowa, Bourke B. Hickenlooper (R) was running ahead of

Continued on Page 4, Column 2

1,000 Planes Destroyed, 71 Nippon Warships Hit; Patton Advances 3 Miles

Bitter fight rages at Leyte against reinforced foe—U. S. warned attack by robots is possible.

By the War Editor of The Christian Science Monitor
From Associated Press And other direct news dispatches

Complete figures of last week end's carrier-plane attack at Manila raise to 1,000 the total Japanese aircraft destroyed, and to 71 the total Japanese warships sunk or damaged since the landing on Leyte.

Saturday-Sunday blows by Hellcats, Helldivers, and Avengers destroyed 440 Japanese planes and sank a subchaser, a destroyer, three cargo ships, and an oil tanker.

On Leyte Island, however, the situation is not so favorable as was first reported. Organized Japanese resistance has not ended, as was declared. Indeed, the American 24th Division has run into some of the heaviest fighting of the Pacific war as it pushed southward from Pinamopoan toward the port of Ormoc. Elements of the Japanese 1st, 13th, and 102d Divisions, pushing north, have brought up heavy artillery into the hills and now are shelling the American lines far behind the front.

Where the Japanese came from has not been stated. Apparently General MacArthur's men have been taken by surprise and possibly new dispositions of the troops will have to be made.

However, American artillery also appeared to be shelling the enemy behind the lines toward Ormoc, and American planes are flying freely into newly built airfields on the Island.

On the Western Front, General Patton's Third Army launched a new attack at the south end of the 500-mile line between Metz and Nancy, gaining three miles.

Farther to the north, General Hodges' First Army had run into heavy resistance. Late front dispatches said the assault had run down with the loss of most

Continued on Page 2, Column 3

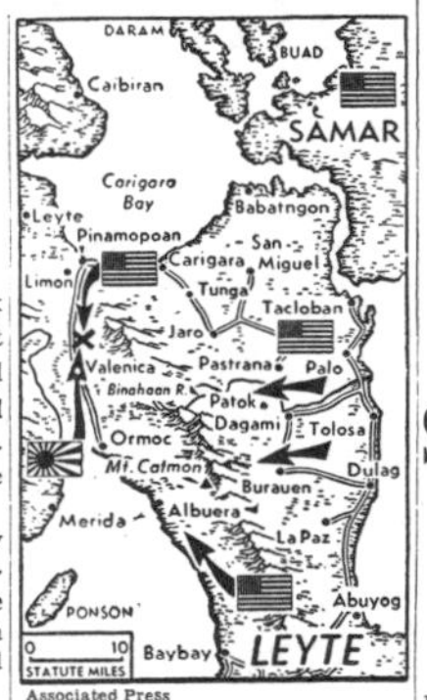

Associated Press

Climactic Fight on Leyte

Cross indicates approximately where Japanese risistance is holding up American advance on Leyte Island.

Japanese Use Strong Force West of Leyte

By Gordon Walker
Staff Correspondent of The Christian Science Monitor

ALLIED HEADQUARTERS IN THE PHILIPPINES, Nov. 8—Elements of the American 24th Infantry Division meeting Japanese reinforcements thrust on the west side of Leyte Island have run into the stiffest enemy resistance and sharpest fighting of the entire campaign.

Within the next week, this fighting is likely to become even more intense.

However, no serious threat has yet appeared to contest American gains on the island.

Japanese forces pushing northward from Ormoc have been identified as elements of the Japanese 1st, 30th, and 102d divisions.

The 1st division, which has been modernized from the old Japanese square-type 1st Division, is believed to be one of the enemy's topmost fighting units. The other two divisions are of mediocre quality, employing some tanks of a type slightly better than has previously been encountered in Southwest Pacific fighting—but still not the enemy's best mechanized equipment.

These units may still complicate the job of cleaning up on Leyte.

The fighting north of Ormoc

Continued on Page 2, Column 7

F. D. R. Exercises Wire 'Prerogative'

By the Associated Press

New York, Nov. 8.

President Roosevelt, who a Western Union spokesman said has the authority to modify, alter, or rescind" the Board of War Communications ban on congratulatory telegrams, today wire messages to political associates and opponents on the election outcome. The President sent messages to Gov. Thomas E. Dewey and Senator Harry S. Truman.

J. L. Egan, Vice-President of Western Union, upheld his Company's acceptance on the ground that "if the President had the authority to authorize issuance of the ban, he has the authority to modify, alter, or rescind it."

Second Session Of 'Big Three' Expected Soon

WASHINGTON, Nov. 8 (AP)—President Roosevelt's re-election makes it virtually certain that he will hold an early meeting with Premier Joseph Stalin and Prime Minister Winston Churchill.

Turning on key questions of postwar co-operation, the conference will largely shape the course of Mr. Roosevelt's fourth-term foreign policy.

The proposed second session of the "Big Three," a year after their first gathering at Teheran, becomes possible now because the outcome of Tuesday's voting has restored to diplomacy the stability lost during hectic campaign weeks. Then foreign governments did not know whether they would have to reckon with Mr. Roosevelt or Gov. Thomas E. Dewey in the weeks ahead.

May Come Soon

Consequently, diplomatic authorities here now expect an acceleration in international affairs beginning with the projected "Big Three" session, which some officials hope may even be held this month.

It appears certain that attempts will come soon to speed organization of the proposed world security organization and to get agreement with Britain, Russia and other Allies on control of a defeated Germany.

The great political issue to be settled in the "Big Three" meeting is basic to American foreign policy: How far are Russia, Britain, and the United States willing to go in harmonizing their interests? Since the United States and Britain have had long experience and share much confidence in their bilateral solution of this problem, the question really boils down to Anglo-American vs. Russian interests.

Mr. Stalin is believed to be looking to Mr. Roosevelt and Mr. Churchill for answers to these two fundamental questions: (1) Will the United States take part, this time, in a world security organization? and (2) can Britain be depended upon to work with Russia rather than against it in Europe?

These questions also pose for the President one of his greatest domestic problems—holding popular support for the proposed new world organization against the attacks that are certain to develop. These are due to come to an issue in Congress over Senate approval

Continued on Page 2, Column 1

P. A. C. Viewed as Key To Party Realignment

By a Staff Correspondent of The Christian Science Monitor

WASHINGTON, Nov. 8—Most controversial and in some ways most spectacular new feature of the 1944 presidential election is the emergence of the Congress of Industrial Organizations Political Action Committee, now agreed to have been responsible for much of the increased worker registration in the big cities. Its post-election fate is looked to as an index of possible realignment of America's political parties.

In yesterday's elections, it was the big labor majority piled up in the cities which often swung the state results, frequently in areas where the P. A. C. had been active. Labor played a large role in the Roosevelt victory and supplied the most militant element in his organization, in contrast to the often apathetic, or actually hostile, southern Democrat old-guard leaders.

Future of P. A. C.

On the labor front the victory aids C. I. O. prestige and is a blow at John L. Lewis, President of the United Mine Workers, who was again unable to throw support of his miners to the Republicans, according to results in Pennsylvania.

The future of the P. A. C. will be decided at the annual convention of the C. I. O., starting Nov. 20 in Chicago. Prospect is, according to information here, that the P. A. C. will be laid on the shelf in stand-by condition, and that later efforts will be made to establish a broader-based organization—or "citizens group"—which was the original plan a year ago, with some permanent organization worked out with the American Federation of Labor and the railway brotherhoods.

The big vote yesterday is causing renewed national interest in the P. A. C. activities, criticism, condemnation, and some praise, depending on the success or failure of the candidates indorsed or attacked by P. A. C. The organization was denounced by the Dies subcommittee as "Communist" in the campaign and the charge was taken up by the G. O. P., although strongly denied by Sidney Hillman. The "clear it with Sidney" phrase will pass into history as the most frequently repeated slogan in the bitter campaign.

Huge Financial Goal

Although the P. A. C. started out with a financial goal of $3,000,000, it never reached even a third of that, according to latest figures on its report of contributions submitted to Congress.

However, the P. A. C. and affiliated groups in their publicity department did an extraordinary large job of publication, the national office putting out some 110,000,000 pieces of literature, it is estimated, including 25,000,000 pieces in one eight-day campaign spurt alone.

Far-reaching implications surround the emergence of the P. A. C. which will be discussed factually by friends and foes for months to come to see where the new trend is carrying the American labor movement.

Samuel Gompers, father of the modern American labor movement opposed political action centered in a distinctively labor party. He argued that labor should reward its friends and punish its enemies, not as members of an independent party, but as individual Democrats or Republicans. This view is adhered to by the powerful A. F. of L. and rail brotherhoods, whose leaders have attacked P. A. C. as endangering

Continued on Page 4, Column 4

Democrats Get Firmer Grip Over House

By Neal Stanford
Staff Correspondent of The Christian Science Monitor

WASHINGTON, Nov. 8—The Democrats have not only retained their control of the House of Representatives, they have substantially increased it.

Reversing a trend that had carried the Republican Party to within six seats of control, yesterday's balloting saw the President's Party picking up seats here and there that assured it a comfortable majority in the 79th Congress. Although several of these were vacancies that had occurred in the 78th Congress (all of them previously held by Democrats), most of the increase was at the expense of incumbent Republicans.

In the House, Democrats elected 219 (218 is majority). They captured 23 seats now held by Republicans. Republicans elected 127 including five seats now held by Democrats and one held by a Progressive. Undecided seats, 89.

Thus President Roosevelt is assured of substantial Party control of the House, which should aid him considerably in carrying out his war and postwar policies.

Perhaps the most surprising defeat in the House was that of Representative Hamilton Fish (R) of New York, by Augustus W. Bennet, the Republican Democrats and others nominated to beat him. Representative Fish, a pre-Pearl Harbor isolationist whose candi-

Continued on Page 6, Column 4

Roosevelt Tops 1940 Margin In N. Y. Incomplete Returns

By Wyona Dashwood
Staff Correspondent of The Christian Science Monitor

NEW YORK, Nov. 8—New York's electorate has thrown its crucial 47 Electoral College bloc into the fourth-term column in a Roosevelt sweep that goes for the entire Democratic state-wide ticket.

With state-wide returns still lacking in 290 of 9,121 districts, President Roosevelt had exceeded his 1940 home State plurality of 224,400 over Wendell L. Willkie in a lead of 325,000 out of a 6,241,685 popular-vote total that is taking steep toll of normally Republican upstate territory.

Complete returns give Mr. Roosevelt a 769,849 plurality in heavily Democratic New York City, with 2,039,932 votes of a 3,310,015 total, which compares with the 3,225,000 vote cast here in 1940. It includes a better than the estimated Roosevelt vote lead in the most populous of the city's five boroughs—Manhattan, the Bronx and Kings. A combined American Labor Party and Liberal Party tally of 694,466 greatly bolstered Mr. Roosevelt's party margin of 1,347,446 to the 1,270,083 Republican votes for Governor Dewey.

Also inclusive were 241,082 war ballots that tallied 175,648 for

Continued on Page 6, Column 6

Norwegians in Moscow Talk Future Relations With Soviet

NEW YORK, Nov. 8 (AP)—Norwegian army regulars now are fighting alongside the Red army against the Germans in Norway, Foreign Minister Trygve Lie of the Royal Norwegian Government said today in a radiocast from Moscow reported by the Norwegian Information Service.

By a Staff Correspondent of The Christian Science Monitor

LONDON, Nov. 8—The arrival of a Norwegian delegation in Moscow indicates the necessity of the closest co-operation between Norway and the Soviet Union now that Russian troops are on Norwegian soil and new military developments may demand a greater clarification of future relationship between both countries.

Norwegian Foreign Minister Trygve Lie, Minister of Justice, and Ambassador to the Soviet Union, flew from Stockholm to Moscow on the first direct flight from the Swedish capital which has occurred since Dr. Juhn K. Paasikivi followed the same route for Finnish-Russian peace talks.

The first questions for discussion will be of a practical nature concerning problems arising from Russian entry into, and German withdrawal from, northern Norway. It is also felt that other issues of a more permanent nature are under consideration.

Following its agreement with Finland, the Soviet Union naturally is showing greater interest in the extreme north of Europe where Norway adjoins Finland.

The liberation of Norway in the north naturally involves Norwegian sovereignty for the time being and the delegation in Moscow will work out the details of future plans as affecting sovereignty. This is a more-or-less routine matter since agreement in principle between both countries was reached some time ago.

In some circles here there is reference also to the present conversations marking a move toward a closer co-ordinated Scandinavian policy as part of a greater European agreement.

By Scandinavia in this connection is meant Norway, Denmark, and Sweden, since Finland is considered much more within the Russian orbit. Whatever the discussion, it is generally accepted nowadays that success depends upon incorporation within the greater framework of international order, such as the Soviet Union and Britain have long been working out.

Reports from Finland and northern Norway indicate that the Germans are already making preparations for evacuation. The Norwegian war of liberation, according to Swedish reports, has already begun in earnest though no attempt is made to disguise the fact that liberation by land will be a slow process and that geographical conditions call for action from the sea. And it is confidently hoped that Allied navies will soon actively participate and speed up the fighting in that region.

Tromso is said to be full of Germans awaiting transport further south, while from Narvik the Germans are reported to have removed much war material including antiaircraft guns and armored weapons and to have mined bridges, quays, and other essential war installations. Morale among the German wounded is said to be extremely low mainly due to the terrible strain under the abnormal conditions in northern European lands.

Among the Norwegians, however, feeling was described by a Swedish journalist recently there as solemn but neither panicky nor fearful and full of hope that liberation will soon come. The Germans are in preparation for a new and feared Allied campaign in Norway and already are taking many hostages.

Swedish official actions and press comments indicate the country is following closely all Russian and German activities in Norway. At the same time Sweden continues to comment fully upon developments inside Finland where a number of problems left over from the Russo-Finnish peace pact still are not fully worked out. To Norway, Sweden has granted a credit of 100,000,000 kroner and plans for more aid in foodstuffs.

Prices Rise 122 Per Cent On 69 Items in Norway

Special to The Christian Science Monitor

WASHINGTON—Prices in Norway for 69 essential items of consumers' goods average 122 per cent above the price level of 1939, despite the Nazi price freeze in April, 1940, reports the United States Department of Commerce.

Meats, which are practically unobtainable, did not increase as sharply in price as some other commodities, such as various garments which range from an increase of 75 per cent for men's trousers to 246 per cent for dress shirts.

Saltonstall Wins Senate Seat Against N. E. Roosevelt Tide

By a Staff Writer of The Christian Science Monitor

BOSTON, Nov. 8 — Mayor Tobin, of Boston, Democratic candidate for Governor, and most of the Democratic state ticket were swept into office on a heavy wave of votes which carried President Roosevelt to his fourth successive Bay State victory and gained for him 32 of New England's 40 electoral votes.

Running counter to the tide, Governor Saltonstall scored a smashing victory in his contest for the United States Senate against Mayor John H. Corcoran of Cambridge, amassing a plurality of more than 300,000 votes. District Attorney Robert F. Bradford, Republican candidate for Lieutenant-Governor, and Frederic W. Cook, G. O. P. Secretary of State seeking re-election, were the othe Republican winnes.

Incompleted returns indicated that the new Democratic Governor would have an Executive Council evenly divided in political tinge. The present Council is seven-to-one Republican.

President Roosevelt won Massachusetts' 16 electoral votes handily, captured Connecticut's eight electoral votes by a slightly lower margin than in 1940, increased his Rhode Island plurality to take that State's four votes and won New Hampshire's four votes by a comfortable margin.

Maine and Vermont gave their electoral votes to Gov. Thomas E. Dewey.

Gov. Raymond E. Baldwin (R) of Connecticut withstood a Roosevelt sweep of Connecticut to poll a 25,000 vote margin over former Democratic Gov. Robert A. Hurley in their third successive gubernatorial match.

Representative Clare Boothe Luce (R) of Connecticut won re-election in the Fourth Congressional District in an extremely close contest with Miss Margaret E. Connors. The only other Republican Representative to win re-election in Connecticut was John E. Talbot in the Fifth Congressional District.

Lieut. Gov. Mortimer R. Proctor (R) of Vermont scored a heavy victory in the Green Mountain State's contest for Governor, as did Senator George D. Aiken (R) and Representative Charles A. Plumley (R) for re-election.

In New Hampshire Mayor Charles M. Dale (R) of Portsmouth won a commanding lead for Governor over Col. James E. Powers, Democratic nominee, while Senator Charles W. Tobey (R) of New Hampshire won re-election in an unexpectedly close contest with Joseph J. Betley, Manchester City Solicitor. Senator Tobey has been under attack as a pre-Pearl Harbor isolationist.

New Hampshire's two seats in the U. S. House of Representatives remained in Republican hands, although Representative Chester E. Merrow in the First Congressional District held only a very narrow lead, as the count neared completion, while Sherman Adams (R), Speaker of the New Hampshire House of Representatives, won easily in the Second District.

Gov. J. Howard McGrath won a third term in Rhode Island by a heavy plurality.

Brien McMahon, of Norwalk, Conn., former United States Assistant Attorney General, and a protégé of Homer Cummings, former U. S. Attorney General, defeated Senator John A. Danaher (R), who was seeking a second term, but who found his pre-Pearl Harbor record too great a handicap.

The Democrats retain the two Congressional seats in Rhode Island, re-electing Representatives John E. Fogarty and Aime J. Forand.

In Connecticut the Democrats recaptured four of the State's six Congressional seats.

Returns in Massachusetts indicated that Massachusetts Republicans have retained their hold on 10 Representative in Congress seats, while the four Democrats seeking re-election were victorious.

Nazis Reduce Size of 'Space'

Special to The Christian Science Monitor

NEW YORK, Nov. 8—Germany is now talking in terms of "Small Space" instead of the "Grossraum" and "Lebensraum" (enlarged living space) which marked the original Nazi propaganda.

Deputy Reich Press Chief Helmuth Sündermann in a talk to what remains of the foreign press in Berlin, declared that Germany was fighting for the preservation of the National Socialist "Kleinraum."

The term appeared twice in Herr Sündermann's speech. In the very first sentence he stated that preparations for the "successful defense of the European 'small-space'" had been carried out "with German thoroughness."

Expert in Propaganda

And again in his closing remarks he said that the "National Socialist 'small-space' of Europe" would neither be shaken nor conquered by any Allied offensive to come.

Herr Sündermann is one of the important current figures in German propaganda. His words carry considerable weight despite the fact that only nine days earlier Dr. Joseph Goebbels, Reich Propaganda Minister had proclaimed that the safeguarding of the Reich's national existence within "enlarged boundaries" was one of the basic prerequisites of peace.

Difference in Direction

The day before Herr Sündermann's disclosure, Gestapo Chief Heinrich Himmler told German refugees from the eastern territories that "sooner or later" the German Army would "reconquer the territorial forefield needed by the Greater Germanic Empire."

This obvious contradiction can, however, be explained by the fact that Dr. Goebbels' and Herr Himmler's words were intended for home consumption, while Herr Sündermann talked to a small group of foreigners who are not allowed to divulge their knowledge to German citizens. It is clearly in the interest of the Hitler Government to make its own people believe that a relatively favorable peace is still within reach, and only an interim solution. On the other hand Germany can only benefit from spreading rumors abroad about its willingness to make peace under condition that the National Socialist structure of Germany proper will be left intact.

Mrs. Luce Wins in Connecticut

By Mary Hornaday
Staff Correspondent of The Christian Science Monitor

WASHINGTON, Nov. 8 — Representative Clare Boothe Luce, blonde playwright and wife of the publisher of Time, Life and Fortune was the nation's political queen today.

Overcoming charges of "carpetbagger" and "absentee," Mrs. Luce won re-election in Connecticut's Fourth District over Congress of Industrial Organizations-supported Margaret E. Connors, Bridgeport woman lawyer, for whom President Roosevelt and Vice-President Wallace had campaigned.

Intense national interest in the Luce-Connors battle was evidenced in President Roosevelt's reference to it during his speech to his Hyde Park neighbors last night when he noted with satisfaction that Margaret Connors was running ahead at the moment.

Mrs. Luce devoted every waking moment of the last two weeks to her own re-election campaign after stumping the country as the Republican's No. 1 woman speaker for Presidential Nominee Thomas E. Dewey.

The overseas G. I. in whose behalf Mrs. Luce addressed the Republican National Convention last summer appears to have been a major factor in her success at the polls yesterday.

In Congress, after January, Mrs. Luce may have to share glamor interest with Mrs. Helen Gahagan

Continued on Page 12, Column 1

THE CHRISTIAN SCIENCE MONITOR

AN INTERNATIONAL DAILY NEWSPAPER

VOLUME 37 NO. 118 | COPYRIGHT 1945 BY THE CHRISTIAN SCIENCE PUBLISHING SOCIETY | BOSTON, SATURDAY, APRIL 14, 1945 | ••—ATLANTIC EDITION | FIVE CENTS A COPY

World Honors Roosevelt in Prayer and Praise; U.S. Armies Close In on Dresden and Leipzig

B-29's Blast Tokyo In Biggest Assault

By the War Editor of The Christian Science Monitor
From Associated Press, Reuters, and other direct news dispatches

The amazing march of Allied troops through an apparently defenseless Germany continued as General Patton's United States Third Army drove on toward Dresden, cutting Berlin's main highway and railroad links with south Germany.

General Simpson's Ninth Army won a second crossing of the Elbe and pushed on against stiffening resistance toward Berlin.

In a 32-mile dash, General Bradley's 12th Army Group forces went 25 miles past the northwest tip of Czechoslovakia.

Farther south, the Third Army entered Bayreuth, home of the Wagnerian opera, which is deep in the mountain redoubt supposed to be reserved by Hitler as the site for his final desperate stand.

To the north, General Hodges' First Army drove to Leipzig, great Saxony city of 1,000,000 inhabitants, encircled it, and pushed four miles beyond.

At the most northerly end of the line, the British Second Army had captured Ülsen, 49 miles southeast of Hamburg.

Altogether, Germany has already lost more than half its 58 cities of more than 100,000 inhabitants.

Where the Germans would make their last determined stand, if any, had not yet appeared. Already three armies of the western Allies are less than 100 miles from the Russian lines on the Oder. The nearest to the Red Army is the United States Third Army, which, beyond Dresden, is only 88 miles away.

Meanwhile, German remnants were being attended to. The remnants of the German fleet gathered around Kiel Harbor were attacked during the night by upward of 750 heavily loaded RAF Halifax and Lancaster bombers. The harbor was reported to be filled with all kinds of shipping which had escaped from the captured Baltic

Continued on Page 6, Column 1

Nippon Suicide Air Attacks On U.S. Navy Told

By Gordon Walker
Staff Correspondent of The Christian Science Monitor just returned from 28 months of war coverage in the Pacific

The hitherto unpublished story of Japan's desperate bid to break up and block the American invasion of the Philippines can be told now with Fleet Admiral Chester W. Nimitz officially lifting what has been a tight censorship ban on Japanese suicide air tactics.

When American forces made their first invasion of the Philippines on the island of Leyte, the first weapon the Japanese used against them was the so-called Kamikaze Corps.

The Kamikaze Corps, which was made up of young warrior-type airmen who had volunteered to fly on suicide crash missions, was organized originally as an instrument to combat America's growing aircraft-carrier strength.

It provided a hazard, but failed as a decisive weapon.

Japanese Program

The Kamikaze Corps pilot was supposed to dive his light bomber into the target, remaining in the cockpit of his plane until it exploded on contact with the target. Thus his wing load of bombs were sure to find their target, while his gasoline tank, bursting in the crash, would throw flaming petrol over the target.

The Japanese High Command, with its often noticed flare for wild schemes, reasoned that it would take two Kamikaze crash

Continued on Page 2, Column 5

Danish Pastor Flees Gestapo, Directs Blows Against Invader

By Melita Spraggs
Staff Correspondent of The Christian Science Monitor

LONDON, April 14—With the Allied armies pushing through Holland toward the North Sea, which washes the west coast of Denmark, and with the Russian armies advancing along the Baltic Sea which sweeps its eastern shores, the little Danish peninsula, though outwardly calm, is tensing Underground.

"The finest people in Denmark are in the Underground," said Pastor Harald Sandbaek, one of its leaders who is on a visit to London to take part in the services commemorating the fifth anniversary of the invasion of his country by the Nazis.

Outwardly the scene may have changed a little since the German armies swept through the defenseless sea-girt land which leads from Holland to the Scandinavian Peninsula. Though the Wehrmacht is established in Jutland, most Danes go about their work during the day as though nothing unusual were happening.

Civil Service administers the country with the least possible contract with the Germans. But Underground there is an unending struggle between the German Gestapo chief and the resistance movement under secret leaders.

Resistance Powerful

The power of the Danish resistance movement was made clear to the Gestapo chief last year, when thousands of people went on strike because of German restrictions, including curfews and conscription of Danish workers for German labor camps.

"The Danes listen eagerly to the news over BBC," Pastor Sandbaek said. "They follow step by step the course of the Allied armies as they get nearer their own frontier."

Sabotage continues and it is coordinated with Allied strategy. British contribution is the raiding of Gestapo headquarters. For Pastor Sandbaek, one of these Mosquito raids on Oct. 31, 1944, came just in the nick of time.

In broken English he told a thrilling story of his release from a German inquisition by the British bombing of German headquar-

Continued on Page 6, Column 6

Inviting You

to follow the

San Francisco Conference

Beginning April 25

with a Distinguished Group of

THE CHRISTIAN SCIENCE MONITOR'S

Editors, Correspondents and Reporters

Who will REPRESENT YOU at this historic conference through daily eye-witness stories

Erwin D Canham • Roscoe Drummond
Richard L. Strout • Rodney L. Brink • Carlyle W. Morgan
Kimmis Hendrick • Doris Peel

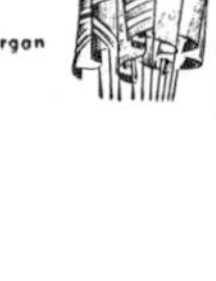

Pan-America: Foreign-Policy Ties Face Test

Written for The Christian Science Monitor

Pan-American Day, 1945, is an April 14 when candid stocktaking discloses one great unbridged gap between the American peoples and their most cherished democratic hopes. That gap is the distance between many governments and the peoples they are supposed to represent.

Argentina's fascist military clique is a glaring example, not only because the Farrell-Perón regime continues to oppress the Argentine people, but because the other American Governments have just recognized President Farrell.

From the standpoint of Pan-American unity it is easily understandable that the prolonged semi-absence of Argentina aroused misgivings. Return of Argentina to the family shortly before Pan-American Day is being made the subject of relieved oratory. The question is: Who has returned in the name of Argentina?

The democratic Argentine people never went away from their allegiance to the cause of embattled freemen. The men who gave Argentina the reputation of being fascist and pro-Nazi are precisely the military politicians who now have been rewarded with recognition. In this paradoxical situation burns the central flame of challenge to the Americas during their next phase of living together.

Aid for Oppressed

For one brief period of months when former Secretary of State Cordell Hull was nearing the end of his long tenure in the mellow gray pile on Pennsylvania Avenue, it seemed that Washington had launched a new diplomatic offensive on behalf of Latin-America's oppressed peoples.

The Argentine military dictatorship—the very one just recognized—was publicly accused by Mr. Hull of being fascist, pro-Nazi anti-democratic, and a menace to the friendship and security of the Western Hemisphere.

President Roosevelt, in an extremely bold and unusual move for a Chief of State, went out of his way to second Mr. Hull's indictments—and did this in a public statement.

Liberals, in exile or hiding from the Farrell regime as well as the Vargas regime in Brazil and several similar dictatorships, lifted their heads and dared to hope again. A strong voice in Washington had been raised in their defense. At least so it appeared.

State Department Policy

Actually, State Department policy never departed from a line laid down early during the war by Mr. Hull. That line makes a sharp division between the foreign policies of governments and their domestic policies. When a regime of unmistakable fascism, such as the Vargas dictatorship in Brazil, slanted its foreign policy toward the Allies, its fascism at home was overlooked.

The same pattern has now resulted in recognition of the fascist Farrell-Perón clique.

It is a pattern that can be explained not only against the immediate background of this war, but in the deeper setting of Pan-American relations during the 120 years since Simón Bolívar invited the first Congress of American powers at Panama in 1826.

Yet it is a pattern that does not yet come to grips with the central political dilemma of the hemisphere. Until some way is found whereby governments representative of their peoples can be enabled to speak for them, Pan-American relations will continue largely sterile in human values.

Argentina's case drives this point home forcefully.

Brazil is a close parallel.

Central America, where two encrusted tyrannies were over-

Continued on Page 9, Column 1

The Christian Science Monitor Index

Saturday, April 14, 1945

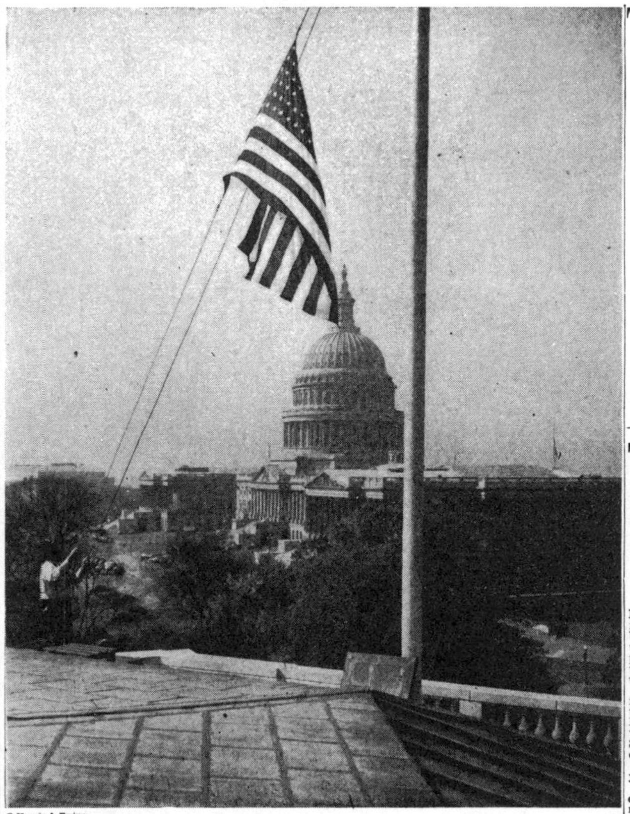

© Harris & Ewing

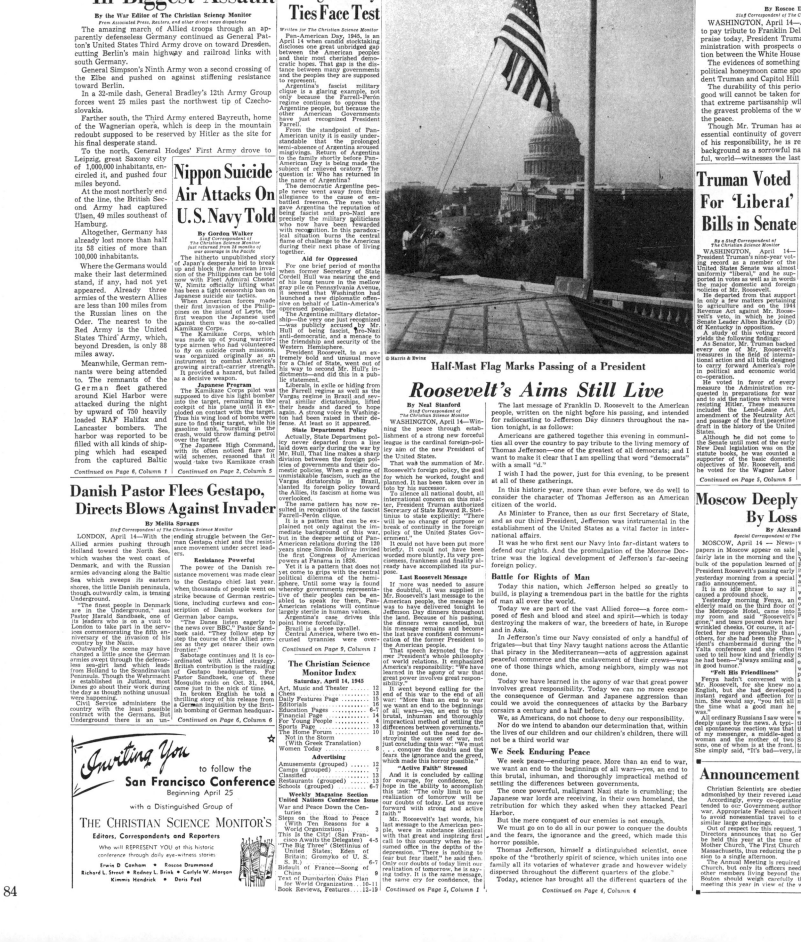

Half-Mast Flag Marks Passing of a President

Roosevelt's Aims Still Live

By Neal Stanford
Staff Correspondent of The Christian Science Monitor

WASHINGTON, April 14—Winning the peace through establishment of a strong new forceful league is the cardinal foreign-policy aim of the new President of the United States.

That was the summation of Mr. Roosevelt's foreign policy, the goal for which he worked, fought and planned. It has been taken over in toto by his successor.

To silence all national doubt, all international concern on this matter, President Truman authorized Secretary of State Edward R. Stettinius to state explicitly: "There will be no change of purpose or break of continuity in the foreign policy of the United States Government."

It could not have been put more briefly. It could not have been worded more bluntly. Its very preciseness, frankness and finality already have accomplished its purpose.

Last Roosevelt Message

If more was needed to assure the doubtful, it was supplied in Mr. Roosevelt's last message to the American people, the message he was to have delivered tonight to Jefferson Day dinners throughout the land. Because of his passing, the dinners were canceled, but his message remains and become the last brave confident communication of the former President to the American people.

That speech keynoted the former President's whole philosophy of world relations. It emphasized America's responsibility: "We have learned in the agony of war that great power involves great responsibility."

It went beyond calling for the end of this war to the end of all war: "More than an end to war we want an end to the beginnings of all wars—yes, an end to this brutal, inhuman and thoroughly impractical method of settling the differences between governments."

It pointed out the need for destroying the causes of war, not just concluding this war: "We must . . . conquer the doubts and the fears the ignorance and the greed, which made this horror possible."

"Active Faith" Stressed

And it is concluded by calling for courage, for confidence, for hope in the ability to accomplish this task: "The only limit to our realization of tomorrow will be our doubts of today. Let us move forward with strong and active faith."

Mr. Roosevelt's last words, his last message to the American people, were in substance identical with that great and inspiring first call to this country when he assumed office in the depths of the depression. "There is nothing to fear but fear itself," he said then. Only our doubts of today limit our realization of tomorrow, he is saying today. It is the same message, the same cry for confidence, the

Continued on Page 5, Column 1

The last message of Franklin D. Roosevelt to the American people, written on the night before his passing, and intended for radiocasting to Jefferson Day dinners throughout the nation tonight, is as follows:

Americans are gathered together this evening in communities all over the country to pay tribute to the living memory of Thomas Jefferson—one of the greatest of all democrats; and I want to make it clear that I am spelling that word "democrats" with a small "d."

I wish I had the power, just for this evening, to be present at all of these gatherings.

In this historic year, more than ever before, we do well to consider the character of Thomas Jefferson as an American citizen of the world.

As Minister to France, then as our first Secretary of State, and as our third President, Jefferson was instrumental in the establishment of the United States as a vital factor in international affairs.

It was he who first sent our Navy into far-distant waters to defend our rights. And the promulgation of the Monroe Doctrine was the logical development of Jefferson's far-seeing foreign policy.

Battle for Rights of Man

Today this nation, which Jefferson helped so greatly to build, is playing a tremendous part in the battle for the rights of man all over the world.

Today we are part of the vast Allied force—a force composed of flesh and blood and steel and spirit—which is today destroying the makers of war, the breeders of hate, in Europe and in Asia.

In Jefferson's time our Navy consisted of only a handful of frigates—but that tiny Navy taught nations across the Atlantic that piracy in the Mediterranean—acts of aggression against peaceful commerce and the enslavement of their crews—was one of those things which, among neighbors, simply was not done.

Today we have learned in the agony of war that great power involves great responsibility. Today we can no more escape the consequence of German and Japanese aggression than could we avoid the consequences of attacks by the Barbary corsairs a century and a half before.

We, as Americans, do not choose to deny our responsibility.

Nor do we intend to abandon our determination that, within the lives of our children and our children's children, there will not be a third world war

We Seek Enduring Peace

We seek peace—enduring peace. More than an end to war, we want an end to the beginnings of all wars—yes, an end to this brutal, inhuman, and thoroughly impractical method of settling the differences between governments.

The once powerful, malignant Nazi state is crumbling; the Japanese war lords are receiving, in their own homeland, the retribution for which they asked when they attacked Pearl Harbor.

But the mere conquest of our enemies is not enough.

We must go on to do all in our power to conquer the doubts and the fears, the ignorance and the greed, which made this horror possible.

Thomas Jefferson, himself a distinguished scientist, once spoke of the "brotherly spirit of science, which unites into one family all its votaries of whatever grade and however widely dispersed throughout the different quarters of the globe."

Today, science has brought all the different quarters of the

Continued on Page 4, Column 4

Ties With Congress Welded by Truman

By Roscoe Drummond
Staff Correspondent of The Christian Science Monitor

WASHINGTON, April 14—As nation and world paused to pay tribute to Franklin Delano Roosevelt in prayer and praise today, President Truman is beginning his new administration with prospects of unusually close co-operation between the White House and Congress.

The evidences of something more than the conventional political honeymoon came spontaneously from both President Truman and Capitol Hill itself.

The durability of this period of executive-congressional good will cannot be taken for granted, but it seems likely that extreme partisanship will be muted in dealing with the gravest problems of the war and the greatest issues of the peace.

Though Mr. Truman has acted alertly to maintain the essential continuity of government during the first days of his responsibility, he is remaining deliberately in the background as a sorrowful nation—and, indeed, a sorrowful, world—witnesses the last rites for the first President to succumb in office since Warren G. Harding in 1923.

While President Truman, in taking up the reins of government, is at the moment keeping his activities to the minimum, several developments already are shedding light on the likely direction and personnel, the tone and character, of his Administration. These deserve to be noted:

Decisive Action Planned

1. There is every indication that Mr. Truman's will not be a "do nothing" Administration. He is showing himself aware of the urgency of the times and the need for decisive action. While personally he is unassuming and quiet, Mr. Truman intends, there is reason to believe, to exercise the responsibilities of his office. This is partly evident in his decision to address a joint session of Congress at once—on April 16—and to deliver a radiocast to the armed services on April 17.

2. It is premature to attempt to forecast what changes will take place in the immediate entourage of the White House. There will

Continued on Page 4, Column 4

Truman Voted For 'Liberal' Bills in Senate

By a Staff Correspondent of The Christian Science Monitor

WASHINGTON, April 14—President Truman's nine-year voting record as a member of the United States Senate was almost uniformly "liberal," and he supported in votes as well as in words the major domestic and foreign policies of Mr. Roosevelt.

He departed from that support in only a few matters pertaining to agriculture and on the 1944 Revenue Act against Mr. Roosevelt's veto, in which he joined Senate Leader Alben Barkley (D) of Kentucky in opposition.

A study of this voting record yields the following findings:

As Senator, Mr. Truman backed every one of Mr. Roosevelt's measures in the field of international action and all bills designed to carry forward America's role in political and economic world co-operation.

He voted in favor of every measure the Administration requested in preparations for war and to aid the nations which were resisting Hitler. These measures included the Lend-Lease Act, amendment of the Neutrality Act and passage of the first peacetime draft in the history of the United States.

Although he did not come to the Senate until most of the early New Deal legislation was on the statute books, he was counted a supporter of the basic domestic objectives of Mr. Roosevelt, and he voted for the Wagner Labor

Continued on Page 5, Column 5

Moscow Deeply Moved By Loss of U. S. Friend

By Alexander Werth
Special Correspondent of The Christian Science Monitor

MOSCOW, April 14 — Newspapers in Moscow appear on sale fairly late in the morning and the bulk of the population learned of President Roosevelt's passing early yesterday morning from a special radio announcement.

It is no idle phrase to say it caused a profound shock.

Yesterday morning Fenya, an elderly maid on the third floor of the Metropole Hotel, came into my room and said "Roosevelt's gone," and tears poured down her wrinkled cheeks. Of course, it affected her more personally than others, for she had been the President's chambermaid during the Yalta conference and she often used to tell how kind and friendly he had been—"always smiling and in good humor."

"Felt His Friendliness"

Fenya hadn't conversed with Mr. Roosevelt, for she knew no English, but she had developed instant regard and affection for him. She would say, "you felt all the time what a good man he was."

All ordinary Russians I saw were deeply upset by the news. A typical spontaneous reaction was that of my messenger, a middle-aged woman and the mother of two sons, one of whom is at the front. She simply said, "It's bad—very, very, very bad."

I asked why. She replied, "He's been doing right things for years. You knew where you were with Roosevelt. He knew how important it was to help us in this war. We wanted to build up a real peace after the war." And she added, "It's very, very bad he went now when he's needed more than ever." To the Russian people, no other foreign statesman was considered as much a friend whom Russia could rely upon.

Front-Page News

Large portraits of Mr. Roosevelt with a black border round his name and warm appreciating notices as well as the texts of the Stalin-Molotov-Kalinin telegrams of condolence occupied nearly the whole front page of every newspaper. There is the feeling that a great personage who worked for a better world is gone and the future as far as the United States is concerned becomes a question mark.

The great question is to what extent Mr. Roosevelt's great work will be continued. It is realized that but for his great personality that imposed itself on the world and his own country, the United States might not have been able to play the great role it is playing in this war.

Announcement by Directors

Christian Scientists are obedient to the laws of the land as admonished by their revered Leader, Mary Baker Eddy.

Accordingly, every co-operation has been, and will be, extended to our Government authorities in the prosecution of the war. Appropriate Federal authorities have requested the public to avoid nonessential travel to conventions, trade shows, and similar large gatherings.

Out of respect for this request, The Christian Science Board of Directors announces that no General Activities Meetings will be held this year at the time of the Annual Meeting of The Mother Church, The First Church of Christ, Scientist, in Boston, Massachusetts, thus reducing the program from a three-days session to a single afternoon.

The Annual Meeting is required by the Manual of The Mother Church, but only its officers need be in attendance. Therefore, other members living beyond the metropolitan area of Greater Boston should weigh carefully the question of attending the meeting this year in view of the war emergency.

THE CHRISTIAN SCIENCE MONITOR

AN INTERNATIONAL DAILY NEWSPAPER

VOLUME 37 NO. 137 | BOSTON, MONDAY, MAY 7, 1945 | ** — ATLANTIC EDITION | FIVE CENTS A COPY

COPYRIGHT 1945 BY THE CHRISTIAN SCIENCE PUBLISHING SOCIETY

Germans Surrender

Tuesday Set as VE-Day, Great Britain Announces

By the War Editor of The Christian Science Monitor

Germany has signed a preliminary instrument of surrender to the Allies. Tomorrow will be observed as V-Day in Europe, the British Ministry of Information has announced.

Reuters carried word from London of the signing of the preliminary document—a monumental instrument of 15 pages.

Radiocast announcements are scheduled to be made tomorrow by Prime Minister Churchill at 3 p. m. and by King George at 9 p. m. The day will be observed as a public holiday in Britain.

On Sunday at 8:41 p. m. (E.W.T.), according to the Associated Press, unconditional surrender of the German High Command took place at General Eisenhower's headquarters in a schoolhouse at Rhéims.

The Associated Press—after carrying a dispatch from Paris saying that filing privileges of the Associated Press Paris Bureau had been suspended—declared that today was not VE-Day, but that "Surrender Day" was correct.

A radiocast by Edward R. Murrow from London said Prime Minister Churchill and President Truman were ready to give official announcement of the end of the war today, but that Marshal Stalin was not ready.

Delay in the final announcement also appeared due to fighting in Czechoslovakia, where General Patton had captured the great arms center of Pilsen and was pushing on to Prague.

In a brief ceremony, the greatest and most destructive war in history virtually came to an end.

According to Associated Press reports, the capitulation, which ended 5 years, 8 months, and 6 days of bloodshed and misery, was signed by four generals.

It was signed for Germany by Col. Gen. Gustav Jodl, new Chief of Staff of the German Army; for the Supreme Allied Command in the West by Lieut. Gen. Walter Bedell Smith, Chief of Staff for General Eisehhower; for Russia by Gen. Ivan Susloparoff; and for France, by Gen. François Sevez.

General Eisenhower was not at the signing, but immediately afterward General Jodl and his fellow delegate, Admiral Hans Georg Friedeburg, were received by the Supreme Commander.

They were sternly asked if they understood the surrender terms imposed upon Germany, and if they would be carried out by Germany.

They answered yes.

Heralding the news of the final capitulation over the air, the voice of German Foreign Minister, Count Lutz Schwerin von Krosigk, said that Admiral Dönitz had ordered the unconditional surrender of all fighting German troops.

The Dönitz order came 40 minutes after Britain's BBC reported the complete capitulation of German forces in Norway.

German troops in Norway will march into Sweden for internment within a few hours, according to the Stockholm newspaper "Expressen."

A few hours previously Admiral Dönitz had ordered commanders of all German U-boats to cease hostilities, since German forces in Norway, where most of Germany's submarine bases were located, were about to surrender.

The German commander in Prague broadcast his refusal to recognize an announcement radiocast from Flensburg that Admiral Dönitz had ordered all German force fighting to surrender.

"In our area," said the Prague radiocast, "the struggle will be continued until the Germans on the East are saved and until our way back into the homeland is secure."

Col. Gen. Gustav Jodl, who signed the uncon-

Continued on Page 2, Column 2

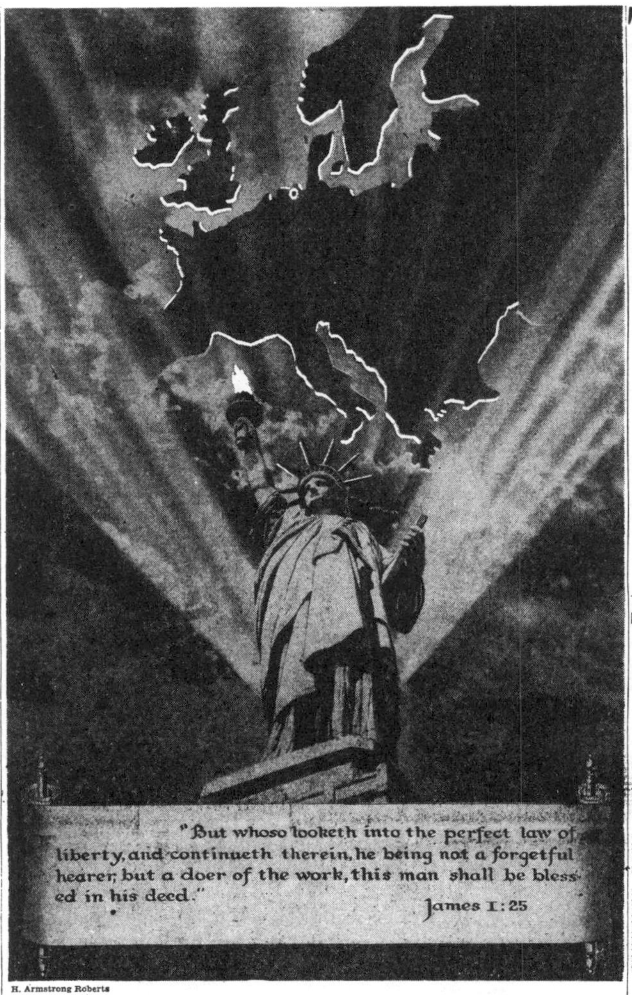

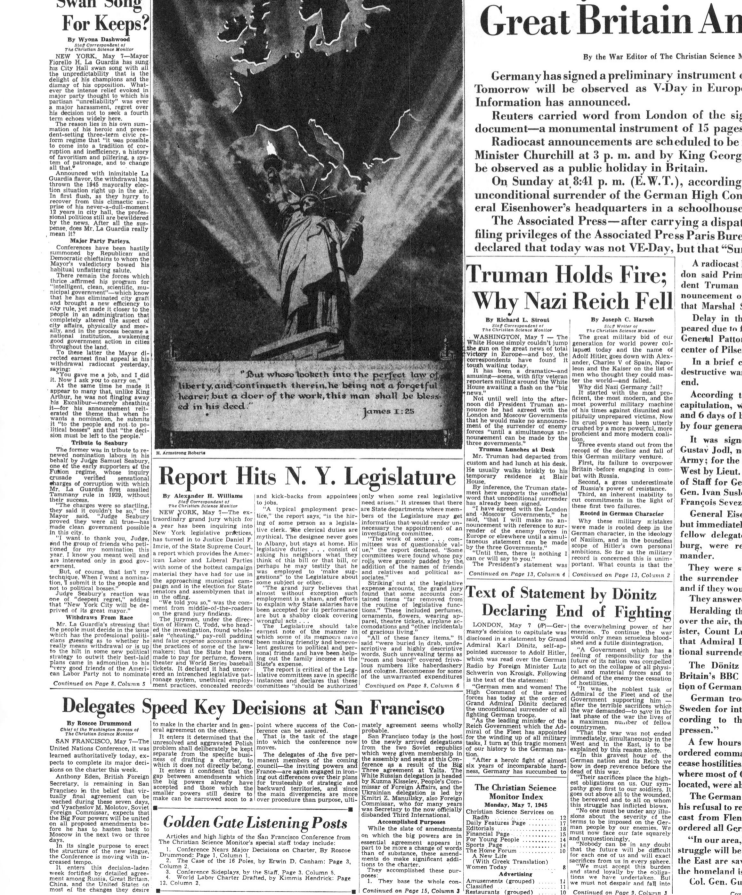

"But whoso looketh into the perfect law of liberty, and continueth therein, he being not a forgetful hearer, but a doer of the work, this man shall be blessed in his deed."
James 1:25

H. Armstrong Roberts

La Guardia: Swan Song For Keeps?

By Wyona Dashwood
Staff Correspondent of The Christian Science Monitor

NEW YORK, May 7—Mayor Fiorello H. La Guardia has sung his City Hall swan song with all the unpredictability that is the delight of his champions and the dismay of his opposition. Whatever the intense relief evoked in major party thought to which his partisan "unreliability" was ever a major harassment, regret over his decision not to seek a fourth term echoes widely here.

The reason lies in his own summation of his heroic and precedent-setting three-term civic reform regime that "it was possible to come into a tradition of corruption and inefficiency, a history of favoritism and pilfering, a system of patronage, and to change all that."

Announced with inimitable La Guardia flavor, the withdrawal has thrown the 1945 mayoralty election situation right up in the air. In first flush, as they hurry to recover from this climactic surprise of his never-a-dull-moment 12 years in city hall, the professional politicos still are bewildered by the news. After all the suspense, does Mr. La Guardia really mean it?

Major Party Parleys

Conferences have been hastily summoned by Republican and Democratic chieftains to whom the Mayor's valedictory bowed his habitual unflattering salute.

There remain the forces which thrice affirmed his program for "intelligent, clean, scientific, municipal government"—which know that he has eliminated city graft and brought a new efficiency to city rule, yet made it closer to the people in an administration that completely altered the aspect of city affairs, physically and morally, and in the process became a national institution, awakening good government action in cities throughout the land.

To these latter the Mayor directed earnest final appeal in his withdrawal radiocast yesterday, saying:

"You gave me a job, and I did it. Now I ask you to carry on."

At the same time he made it appear to many that, unlike King Arthur, he was not flinging away his Excalibur—merely sheathing it—for his announcement reiterated the theme that when he wants a nomination, he submits it "to the people and not to political bosses" and that "the decision must be left to the people."

Tribute to Seabury

The former was in tribute to renewed nomination labors in his behalf by Judge Samuel Seabury, one of the early supporters of the Fusion regime, whose inquiry crusade verified sensational charges of corruption with which Mr. La Guardia first assailed Tammany rule in 1929, without their success.

"The charges were so startling, they said it couldn't be so," the Mayor said. "Judge Seabury proved they were all true—has made clean government possible in this city.

"I want to thank you, Judge, and the group of friends who petitioned for my nomination this year. I know you meant well and are interested only in good government.

But, of course, that isn't my technique. When I want a nomination, I submit it to the people and not to political bosses."

Judge Seabury's reaction was one of "deepest regret," adding that "New York City will be deprived of its great mayor."

Withdraws From Race

Mr. La Guardia's stressing that the people must decide in the issue which has the professional politicians guessing as to whether he really means withdrawal or is up to the hilt in some new political strategy to outwit their best-laid plans came in admonition to his "very good friends of the American Labor Party not to nominate

Continued on Page 8, Column 5

Report Hits N. Y. Legislature

By Alexander H. Williams
Staff Correspondent of The Christian Science Monitor

NEW YORK, May 7—The extraordinary grand jury which for a year has been inquiring into New York legislative practices, has turned in to Justice Daniel F. Imrie, of the State Supreme Court, a report which provides the American Labor and Liberal Parties with some of the hottest campaign material they have had for use in the approaching municipal campaign and in the election for State senators and assemblymen that is in the offing.

"We told you so," was the comment from middle-of-the-roaders on the grand jury findings.

The jurymen, under the direction of Hiram C. Todd, who headed the investigation, found wholesale "cheating," pay-roll padding and false expense accounts among the practices of some of the lawmakers; that the State had been made to pay for perfume, flowers, theater and World Series baseball tickets. It declared it had uncovered an intrenched legislative patronage system, unethical employment practices, concealed records and kick-backs from appointees to jobs.

"A typical employment practice," the report says, "is the hiring of some person as a legislative clerk. The clerical duties are mythical. The designee never goes to Albany, but stays at home. His legislative duties . . . consist of asking his neighbors what they think of this bill or that bill, or perhaps he may testify that he was employed to 'make suggestions" to the Legislature about some subject or other.

"The grand jury believes that almost without exception such employment is a sham, and efforts to explain why State salaries have been accepted for its performance are but a shabby cloak covering wrongful acts . . .

The Legislature should take earnest note of the manner in which some of its members have been making friendly and benevolent gestures to political and personal friends and have been helping out the family income at the State's expense.

The report is critical of the Legislative committees save in specific instances and declares that these committees "should be authorized only when some real legislative need arises.' It stresses that there are State departments where members of the Legislature may get information that would render unnecessary the appointment of an investigating committee.

"The work of some . . . committees was of questionable value," the report declared. "Some committees were found whose pay rolls were grossly padded by the addition of the names of friends and relatives and political associates."

Striking out at the legislative expense accounts, the grand jury found that some accounts contained items "far removed from the routine of legislative functions." These included perfumes, ornaments, flowers, wearing apparel, theatre tickets, airplane accomodations and "other incidentals of gracious living."

"All of these fancy items," it said "were buried in drab, undescriptive and highly descriptive words. Such unrevealing terms as "room and board" covered frivolous numbers like haberdashery and cologne. Recompense for some of the unwarranted expenditures

Continued on Page 8, Column 6

Truman Holds Fire; Why Nazi Reich Fell

By Richard L. Strout
Staff Correspondent of The Christian Science Monitor

WASHINGTON, May 7 — The White House simply couldn't jump the gun on the great news of total victory in Europe—and boy, the correspondents have found it tough waiting today.

It has been a dramatic—and amusing—scene, with fifty veteran reporters milling around the White House awaiting a flash on the "big news."

Not until well into the afternoon did President Truman announce he had agreed with the London and Moscow Governments that he would make no announcement of the surrender of enemy forces "until a simultaneous announcement can be made by the three governments."

Truman Lunches at Desk

Mr. Truman had departed from custom and had lunch at his desk. He usually walks briskly to his temporary residence at Blair House.

By inference, the Truman statement here supports the unofficial word that unconditional surrender has already been signed.

"I have agreed with the London and Moscow Governments," he said, "that I will make no announcement with reference to surrender of the enemy forces in Europe or elsewhere until a simultaneous statement can be made by the three Governments."

"Until then, there is nothing I can or will say to you."

The President's statement was

Continued on Page 13, Column 4

By Joseph C. Harsch
Staff Writer of The Christian Science Monitor

The great military bid of our generation for world power collapsed today and the name of Adolf Hitler goes down with Alexander, Charles V of Spain, Napoleon and the Kaiser on the list of men who thought they could master the world—and failed.

Why did Nazi Germany fail?

It started with the most proficient, the most modern, and the most powerful military machine of his times against disunited and pitifully unprepared victims. Now its cruel power has been utterly crushed by a more powerful, more proficient and more modern coalition.

Three events stand out from the record of the decline and fall of this German military venture.

First, its failure to overpower Britain before engaging in combat with Russia.

Second, a gross underestimate of Russia's power of resistance.

Third, an inherent inability to cut commitments in the light of these first two failures.

Rooted in German Character

Why these military mistakes were made is rooted deep in the German character, in the ideology of Naziism, and in the boundless scope of Hitler's own personal ambitions. So far as the military record is concerned this is unimportant. What counts is that the

Continued on Page 13, Column 2

Text of Statement by Dönitz Declaring End of Fighting

LONDON, May 7 (AP)—Germany's decision to capitulate was disclosed in a statement by Grand Admiral Karl Dönitz, self-appointed successor to Adolf Hitler, which was read over the German Radio by Foreign Minister Lutz Schwerin von Krosigk. Following is the text of the statement:

"German men and women! The High Command of the armed forces has today at the order of Grand Admiral Dönitz declared the unconditional surrender of all fighting German troops.

"As the leading minister of the Reich Government which the Admiral of the Fleet has appointed for the winding up of all military tasks, I turn at this tragic moment of our history to the German nation.

"After a heroic fight of almost six years of incomparable hardness, Germany has succumbed to the overwhelming power of her enemies. To continue the war would only mean senseless bloodshed and a futile disintegration.

"A Government which has a feeling of responsibility for the future of its nation was compelled to act on the collapse of all physical and material forces and to demand of the enemy the cessation of hostilities.

"It was the noblest task of Admiral of the Fleet and of the Government supporting him — after the terrible sacrifices which the war demanded—to save in the last phase of the war the lives of a maximum number of fellow countrymen.

"That the war was not ended immediately, simultaneously in the West and in the East, is to be explained by this reason alone.

"In this gravest hour of the German nation and its Reich we bow in deep reverence before the dead of this war.

"Their sacrifices place the highest obligations on us. Our sympathy goes first to our soldiers. It goes out above all to the wounded, the bereaved and to all on whom this struggle has inflicted blows.

"No one must be under any illusions about the severity of the terms to be imposed on the German people by our enemies. We must now face our fate squarely and unquestioningly.

"Nobody can be in any doubt that the future will be difficult for each one of us and will exact sacrifices from us in every sphere.

"We must accept this burden and stand loyally by the obligations we have undertaken. But we must not despair and fall into

Continued on Page 9, Column 3

The Christian Science Monitor Index

Monday, May 7, 1945

Delegates Speed Key Decisions at San Francisco

By Roscoe Drummond
Chief of the Washington Bureau of The Christian Science Monitor

SAN FRANCISCO, May 7—The United Nations Conference, it was learned authoritatively today, expects to complete its major decisions on the charter this week.

Anthony Eden, British Foreign Secretary, is remaining in San Francisco in the belief that virtually final agreement can be reached during these seven days, and Vyacheslov M. Molotov, Soviet Foreign Commissar, expects that the Big Four powers will be united on all proposed amendments before he has to hasten back to Moscow in the next two or three days.

In its single purpose to erect the structure of the new league, the Conference is moving with increased tempo.

It enters this decision-laden week fortified by detailed agreement among Russia, Great Britain, China, and the United States on most of the changes they desire to make in the charter and in general agreement on the others.

It enters it determined that the unresolved and aggravated Polish problem shall deliberately be kept separate from the specific business of drafting a charter, to which it does not directly belong.

It enters it confident that the gap between amendments which the big powers already have accepted and those which the smaller powers still desire to make can be narrowed soon to a point where success of the Conference can be assured.

That is the task of the stage into which the conference now moves.

The delegates of the five permanent members of the coming council—the inviting powers and France—are again engaged in ironing out differences over their plans for trusteeship of strategic and backward territories, and since the main divergencies are more over procedure than purpose, ultimately agreement seems wholly probable.

San Francisco today is the host to the newly arrived delegations from the two Soviet republics which were given membership in the assembly and seats at this Conference as a result of the Big Three agreement at Yalta. The White Russian delegation is headed by Kuzma Kisselev, People's Commissar of Foreign Affairs, and the Ukrainian delegation is led by Kmitri Z. Manuilsky, also Foreign Commissar, who for many years was Secretary to the now officially disbanded Third International.

Accomplished Purposes

While the slate of amendments on which the big powers are in essential agreement appears in part to be more a change of words than of substance, these amendments do make significant additions to the charter.

They accomplished these purposes:

1. They base the whole con-

Continued on Page 15, Column 3

Golden Gate Listening Posts

Articles and high lights of the San Francisco Conference from The Christian Science Monitor's special staff today include:

1. Conference Nears Major Decisions on Charter, By Roscoe Drummond: Page 1, Column 1.
2. The Case of the 16 Poles, by Erwin D. Canham: Page 3, Column 2.
3. Conference Sideplays, by the Staff. Page 3. Column 5.
4. World Labor Charter Drafted, by Kimmis Hendrick: Page 12, Column 2.

THE CHRISTIAN SCIENCE MONITOR

AN INTERNATIONAL DAILY NEWSPAPER

VOLUME 37 NO. 138 | COPYRIGHT 1945 BY THE CHRISTIAN SCIENCE PUBLISHING SOCIETY | BOSTON, TUESDAY, MAY 8, 1945 | **—ATLANTIC EDITION | FIVE CENTS A COPY

Allies Proclaim Complete Victory in Europe; President Designates May 13 as Day of Prayer; 'V' News Speeds Forging of Peace Machinery

Haste Urged On Issues At Golden Gate

By Roscoe Drummond
Chief of the Washington Bureau of The Christian Science Monitor

SAN FRANCISCO, May 8—The end of the war in Europe is speeding the successful beginning of the United Nations peace machinery.

It is hastening vital decisions on the charter which otherwise would have been delayed. It is enhancing the spirit of agreement.

Vyacheslav M. Molotov, Anthony Eden, Edward R. Stettinius, and T. V. Soong, the "Big Four" Foreign Secretaries, today are urging all the delegations to seize the urgency of events as the final impetus to bring the Conference to a united conclusion in the shortest possible time.

Major Developments

The effect of this appeal already is evident, although there are hurdles which the deliberations still must mount before differences are reconciled.

On the broad canvas of the larger issues before the Conference, these developments stood out:

1. On the authority of Mr. Molotov — who certainly likes unanimity when it's on his side—Russia, Britain, the United States, and China now have reached complete unanimity on all important and controversial amendments. This agreement, he said, reaches to the wording of the two changes the United States submitted independently on review of unhealthy world situations and on regional defense pacts.

Assurance by Vandenberg

2. Senator Arthur H. Vandenberg (R) of Michigan emphatically discounts reports that the effect of Mr. Molotov's press conference yesterday was to give a narrower and different interpretation than that which has come from the American delegation on its amendment to empower the assembly to investigate and recommend changes in any situation it believes will improve world peace.

Specifically, Mr. Molotov held that the agreed authority of the assembly to examine "any situations, regardless of origin, which it deems likely to impair the general welfare" does not—to use his own words—embrace "treaties signed by defeated aggressors" or "treaties concluded by some of the United Nations with a view to averting renewal of aggression in this postwar period by defeated Axis countries."

Vandenberg Explains

Senator Vandenberg agrees with Mr. Molotov, but obviously they both give a different emphasis to the agreed wording and the agreed meaning of the same amendment. Mr. Molotov says what it can't do. Senator Vandenberg says what it can do. He says that while it is true that the assembly cannot recommend treaty revision for its own sake, it can deal with "any situation" which, resulting from a treaty, tends to impair the general welfare or endanger the peace.

In a statement he issued late last night, Senator Vandenberg puts it this way:

"I do not read into our proposal any latitude in respect to treaties or agreements of this nature—I agree with Mr. Molotov in this regard. Our proposed amendment deals with other subjects. It recognizes that other situations may arise, as the result of a vast area of war decisions, which may not have been answered, under the pressures of expediency, in the best manner to serve justice and peace. It proposes that these situations, regardless of origin, shall be legitimate subjects of inquiry and recommendation by the assembly, so that we are not called upon to freeze injustice in a static postwar world."

Senator Vandenberg, who fought for the amendment on this point, is satisfied with the phrasing which the Russians have accepted. Evidently the American delegation is prepared to leave it to the assembly itself to interpret the scope of its investigatory powers. Since Mr. Molotov has accepted the amendment, the United States is not quibbling over Russia's press-conference interpretation, particularly since in the assembly, where this authority is to be used, the big powers have only one vote.

Regional Problem

3. One serious and significant problem continues to plague the Conference leaders. It concerns the danger of whittling away the effectiveness of the security council by the renewed efforts to take regional defense decisions from its jurisdiction. Already it is agreed that the member nations may act independently against future aggression by the present enemy countries.

Now, the 20 Latin-American countries are asserting en bloc their dissatisfaction with the United States proposal that collective action in the Western Hemisphere against a non-Axis aggressor first must come under the jurisdiction of the council. They want the Western Hemisphere to

Continued on Page 11, Column 3

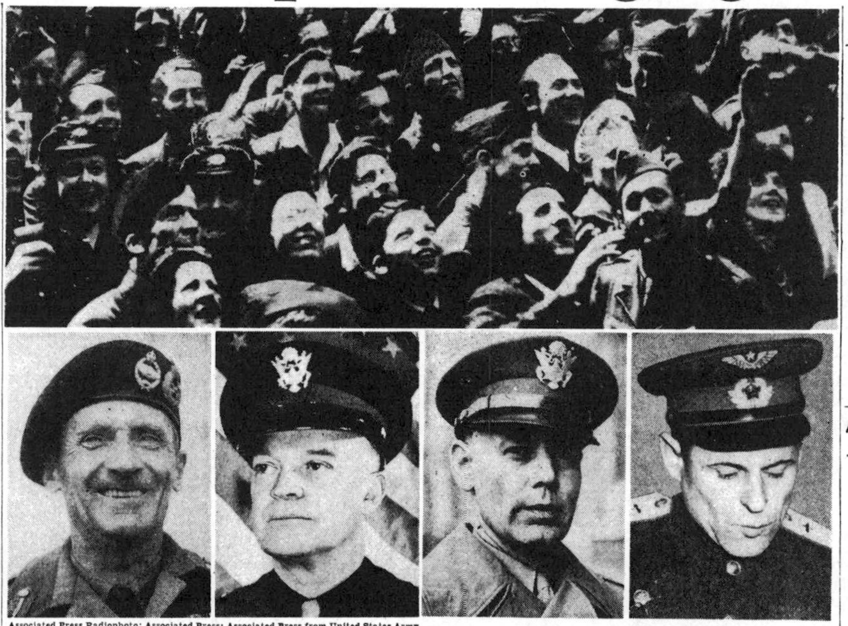

Associated Press Radiophoto; Associated Press; Associated Press from United States Army

Victory Celebration in London—and Some of the Men Behind It

Upper: Service men and women of the Allied forces celebrate the news of Germany's surrender in Piccadilly Circus, London. Lower, left to right: Field Marshal Sir Bernard L. Montgomery, Gen. Dwight D. Eisenhower, Lieut. Gen. Walter Bedell Smith, and Gen. Ivan Susloparov. Generals Smith and Susloparov signed the capitulation document.

'VE Is Won—On to Tokyo!'

Churchill

By Mallory Browne
Staff Correspondent of The Christian Science Monitor

LONDON, May 8—Prime Minister Winston Churchill told the people of Britain today that hostilities will end officially at one minute after midnight tonight, May 8, British time, and that "the German war is therefore at an end."

Radiocasting from the Cabinet room at 10 Downing Street, the Prime Minister broke the news that the unconditional surrender is being ratified and confirmed in Berlin today, where Marshal Gregory Zhukov is to sign the surrender agreement on behalf of the Soviet High Command, while Field Marshal Gen. Wilhelm Keitel and the Commanders in Chief of the German Army, Navy, and Air Force sign for the Germans.

All over London, all over Britain, all over the Dominions and colonies, the people who have fought this European war from the beginning and now have seen it through to a victorious end listened to their leader with mingled seriousness and rejoicing.

Watching thousands of Londoners massed in front of Buckingham Palace, I was struck by the thought that these people received the formal announcement

Continued on Page 4, Column 5

Grim Finale in Europe

By Ronald Stead
Staff Correspondent of The Christian Science Monitor

TANGERMÜNDE, Germany, May 7. Delayed.—The end of the European war was marked here today with a scene of intense and spectacular drama. It was a picture that might have been "in glorious Technicolor," it was so vividly and theatrically produced—by the events themselves in the last phase of fighting on this front.

It was the battle of Tangermünde Bridge. Its title could have been "the abject end."

It showed the flight of the last German troops and civilians across the Elbe into American lines and the Russians' victory over the rear guard that covered it. I watched it from a tent on the western bank of the Elbe, with the Red Army's mortars bursting a few yards away in the water and shell fragments periodically whizzing overhead. I saw it blow by blow as one might witness a match from the ringside.

Never in my experience as war correspondent since hostilities started have I seen such a composite presentation of both the fighting and the suffering it entails for civilians.

Visually it was the great climax following all that has gone before. I saw Germans blown to pieces by Russian mortars. I saw German artillerymen firing upon advancing Russians and German infantrymen digging in for a last futile stand with machine guns and small arms.

I saw panic-stricken German soldiers and civilians swim-

Continued on Page 4, Column 1

Truman Call

By Richard L. Strout
Staff Correspondent of The Christian Science Monitor

WASHINGTON, May 8—President Truman called upon every American today "to stick to his post until the last battle is won."

He gave solemn and reverential thanks to God for victory in Europe, warned Japan of terrible retribution unless its submits to "unconditional surrender," declared that the great Allies must stick together in peace as they have in war, and added that what the world is striving to, and will, get at San Francisco is a framework of peace "based on justice and law."

Mr. Truman made these declarations at an unprecedented and historic 8:30 a. m. White House press conference just prior to going on the air with his radio address of victory. The conference was attended by his Cabinet, his military advisers, and by legislative leaders of both parties in Congress. A great number of newspapermen crowded the oval study.

Mr. Truman had four formal statements ready from which he read excerpts aloud, interlarding observations, emphasizing and stressing certain points, and telling correspondents the matters on which he laid particular importance.

Save for a brief touch of humor at the outset, as he observed this was his anniversary, and many people would be celebrating it over the world, he struck a solemn and subdued note. However, when he turned to the military prospect that now faces Japan, his customarily even voice noticeably changed. It was rather in the tone than in the informal words themselves, as he slowly explained matters that he seemed to be sounding a note of doom.

He was informed by this Chiefs of Staff and by the Secretaries of War and Navy, he declared, that with the end of the war in Europe, Japan is going to face a terrible time—from now on.

The four prepared releases, upon which Mr. Truman made verbal variations to the press, were as follows:

A formal radio address to the nation, calling upon it to "work, work, work," and declaring that

Continued on Page 8, Column 5

Party Chiefs Quiz La Guardia 'Bow Out'

By Wyona Dashwood
Staff Correspondent of The Christian Science Monitor

NEW YORK, May 8—The axiom that it is well to beware of gifts from enemies dates from the Trojan war. That is the way Democratic and Republican organization leaders in New York State and this city's five counties react to Mayor Fiorello H. La Guardia's declaration of intention to take a rest from office holding and bask in the sun awhile after Jan. 1 next.

They are a little more than dubious that he will turn his back on the classical outlines of City Hall. Even if it turns out to be fact, they are gloomily aware that he can make plenty of campaign trouble meanwhile. Whether or not he is a candidate for re-election to a fourth term, he will be a key figure against maneuverings to break with the system of nonpartisan, nonpolitical government he has so fiercely fought to perpetuate.

Fusionists under the leadership of Judge Samuel Seabury are hastily recanvassing the situation, but are hopeful they need not take the La Guardia announcement as final. Mr. Seabury has an appointment for a talk with the Mayor in a few days.

Suitable Successor

It is certain he again will try to prevail upon Mr. La Guardia to reverse his decision, especially in view of the very great difficulty of finding a candidate of suitable coalition caliber. The Mayor has said he knows several who would fit into the picture, but gave no names.

In the process, however, he managed to pay unflattering respects to fusion City Comptroller Joseph D. McGoldrick, leading as a coalition prospect with Republican-Liberal forces which are inimical to renewed La Guardia support, and to fan his feud with the Republicans by implicating this leadership in the charge of an attempted "dirty deal" concerning support of Gov. Thomas E. Dewey for a second term next year in return for Republican mayoralty support.

If Judge Seabury fails to persuade Mr. La Guardia it is his duty to again enter the mayoralty lists, he will call upon the Mayor to name his preferences for a vigorous new fusion drive.

The dilemma of these nonpartisan independents can be seen in primary enrollment figures which list 1,978,111 Democrats, 821,013 Republicans, and 194,602 American Labor Party members.

Skepticism Not General

Skepticism in major party circles and among Liberal Party spokesmen regarding the temporary La Guardia retirement is not general. There are persons close to the Mayor who do not doubt the irrevocableness of his decision.

They base their certainty on belief that Mr. La Guardia has canvassed the situation with care and has concluded that the forces lined up in opposition might result in his defeat—something he would be the last to risk.

Moreover, it would serve to strengthen the Republican organization in the city and State for next year's governorship and United States Senate races and extend into the 1948 national scene. All parties concerned here see in the oncoming city election the key to their fortunes in the larger picture.

This does not mean the Republicans would win the municipal election even though the Democratic-American Labor Party coalition now looming in the new turn of events fails to eventuate and a three-corner race develops. It would, however, improve Dewey organization stance in the 1946 vote for Senator from the Empire State.

Bid for Senate Seen

By absenting himself from city politics at the end of his third term, Mr. La Guardia would be in a position to make a formidable bid for the senatorial toga due to slip next year from the shoulders of the New York junior incumbent, James M. Mead. The latter is increasingly to the fore as Democratic-American Labor Party nominee for Governor against the expected Dewey bid for return, with the A. L. P. at dedicatory pitch to frustrate this Dewey ambition.

Viewed from this angle, the La Guardia renouncement of the

Continued on Page 10, Column 3

The Christian Science Monitor Index

Tuesday, May 8, 1945

Moscow Fails to Share In Peace Announcement

By the War Editor of The Christian Science Monitor
From Associated Press, Reuters, and other direct news dispatches

Victory celebrations spread over Europe and America today as President Truman and Prime Minister Churchill, at 9 a. m. (E. W. T.), proclaimed the complete victory in Europe and the end of a war involving 27,000,000 men.

The day, however, was very generally observed as one of thanksgiving rather than of extreme exultation, for, as both statesmen reminded their hearers, the war in the East still continues and many trials lie ahead.

There was no immediate proclamation from Premier Stalin. At 10 a. m. (E. W. T.) the Moscow Radio broadcast to Germany warning isolated units of the German Army still fighting against the Red Army to "cease hostilities immediately."

During the day Marshal Stalin announced continuing events in the field—the capture of Olmutz in Moravia and Dresden.

Marshal Tito's Yugoslav Partisans had liberated Zagreb, Croatian Capital, the last major Yugoslav city in German hands, the Belgrade Radio said.

Mr. Churchill said that hostilities would cease one minute after midnight, British time, tonight (6:01 p. m. E. W. T. today).

Admiral Dönitz, Hitler's successor, in a Flensburg broadcast to the German people this morning announced that all German arms would be silent at the same hour.

Mr. Churchill said that the surrender will be ratified and confirmed in Berlin today where Air Chief Marshal Tedder and General De Tassigny will sign on behalf of General Eisenhower, and Marshal Zhukov on behalf of the Soviet High Command. German representatives will be Marshal Keitel and commanders of the Army, Navy, and Air Forces.

Offering of Thanks

President Truman, going on a radio hook-up at 9 a. m., called upon persons of all faiths to "unite in offering joyful thanks to God for the victory we have won."

He set Sunday, May 13, as a day of prayer.

"General Eisenhower informs me," he said, "that the forces of Germany have surrendered to the United

Continued on Page 2, Column 2

Truman Forges Fourfold Aims

By a Staff Correspondent of The Christian Science Monitor

WASHINGTON, May 8—Four historic documents were issued by President Truman today in connection with his announcement of the end of war in Europe.

They included a statement calling upon Japan to surrender unconditionally, the President's radiocast statement announcing final victory in Europe, a proclamation which the President also radiocast declaring Sunday, May 13, to be a national day of prayer, and a series of congratulatory messages to United Nations leaders.

The President's statement on Japan came as Prime Minister Winston Churchill in London was radiocasting a special message to British subjects in the Far East, who are yet under Japanese control, announcing the war's end in Europe, and saying: "The time of your liberation is also at hand. . . . Lift up your hearts, for we are coming." At the same time, in faraway Chungking, Generalissimo Chiang Kai-shek appealed to the Allies to employ all their forces to smash Japan.

The texts of the four Truman documents follow:

The President's statement on Japan:

Nazi Germany has been defeated.

The Japanese people have felt the weight of our land, air, and naval attacks. So long as their leaders and the armed forces continue the war, the striking power and intensity of our blows will steadily increase and will bring utter destruction to Japan's industrial war production, to its shipping, and to everything that supports its military activity.

The longer the war lasts, the greater will be the suffering and hardships which the people of Japan will undergo—all in vain. Our blows will not cease until the Japanese military and naval forces lay down their arms in unconditional surrender.

Just what does the unconditional surrender of the armed forces mean for the Japanese people?

It means the end of the war.

It means the termination of the influence of the military leaders who have brought Japan to the present brink of disaster.

It means provision for the return of soldiers and sailors

Continued on Page 9, Column 4

UNRRA Rushes Relief to Nazi 'Slaves'

By Josephine Ripley
Staff Correspondent of The Christian Science Monitor

WASHINGTON, May 8—VE-Day finds help already on its way to Germany's surviving slave laborers.

More than 100 teams of United Nations Relief and Rehabilitation Administration workers are on the job today on German soil.

Others are being rushed to the scene at the rate of 12 a week. The Army has called for a total of 450 to handle the tremendous tasks ahead.

Meanwhile, Gen. Dwight D. Eisenhower has appealed to the millions of liberated peoples from all over Europe still in German territory to remain there until help arrives and their repatriation can be arranged.

Thousands of French laborers have already hitchhiked their way home, by air, rail, or over the road in any conveyance they could find to give them passage.

Problem Difficult

Army authorities see great danger in this uncontrolled human flood toward the Rhine, and the Eisenhower order has been radiocast to Europe in 10 different languages so that there will be no doubt as to its meaning and importance.

UNRRA relief teams are hastening to the aid of displaced peoples wherever they are. They are working in camps, hospitals, hotels, public buildings, or wherever the refugees may be billeted.

They are providing food, clothing, medical care, housing and other services which may be required while the liberated slave laborers await transportation to their homelands.

It has been estimated that there were 15,000,000 foreign workers in Germany. The exact figure was never known, and it may never be possible to gauge it accurately. The Nazis have destroyed many of the documents which would have revealed the number, and thousands of these people have been done away with during the war in extermination camps.

Workers Recruited

Recruiting of UNRRA relief workers for this task which VE-Day brings into sudden focus is going forward at a rapid pace. Personnel officers at UNRRA headquarters in Washington are interviewing 200 applicants a day. In France, more than 1,000 workers have already been recruited.

In fact, 60 per cent of the total recruitment is being done on the Continent.

The training period for workers who are being groomed in the United States for a European assignment has been telescoped from a six-weeks course into two weeks. Nearly 200 graduates a month are leaving the UNRRA training center at the University of Maryland for destinations overseas.

Trained Men Needed

There they report immediately to the European regional office in London where they are organized into teams and sent over to the Continent.

UNRRA recruiting officers have been scouring the United States, Canada, and South America, for qualified candidates for relief and rehabilitation work.

Greatest need is for men who can

Continued on Page 10, Column 3

'Monty' Springs Surprise

WISMAR, Germany, May 7. Delayed. (AP)—On the steps of a three-story brown stucco house which once belonged to the gauleiter of this little Baltic port, Field Marshal Sir Bernard L. Montgomery sprang the news on Soviet Marshal K. K. Rokossovsky today that the war had ended.

The two army commanders were going through the formalities of making welcome speeches to each other and posing for photographers when Marshal Montgomery, through an interpreter, surprised Marshal Rokossovsky with the information.

The Commander of the Second White Russian Army broke into smiles and grabbed Marshal Montgomery's hand vigorously while Russian generals lined up behind the two leaders chatted and laughed excitedly.

Up to that point the meeting had been stiff with military pomp.

THE CHRISTIAN SCIENCE MONITOR

Registered in U. S. Patent Office
AN INTERNATIONAL DAILY NEWSPAPER

VOLUME 37 NO. 214 | COPYRIGHT 1945 BY THE CHRISTIAN SCIENCE PUBLISHING SOCIETY | BOSTON, TUESDAY, AUGUST 7, 1945 | **—ATLANTIC EDITION | TWO SECTIONS | FIVE CENTS A COPY

Japs Say Atomic Bomb Halted Trains

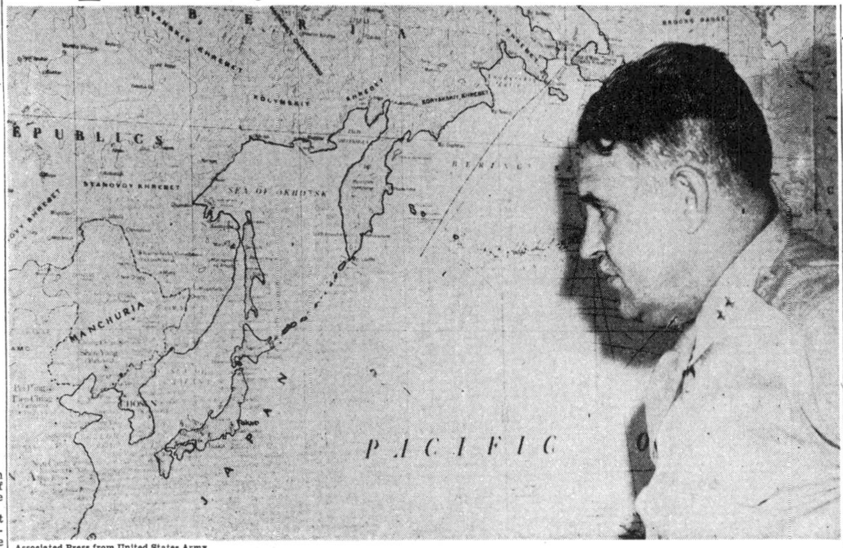

Associated Press from United States Army

Builder of Atomic Bomb Picks a Target

Maj. Gen. Leslie Richard Groves directed the development of the atomic bomb. He supervised the building of the three atomic-bomb production plants. He is shown looking at a map of the Western Pacific.

Potsdam Agencies And New Charter: Will Aims Dovetail?

By Neal Stanford
Staff Correspondent of The Christian Science Monitor

WASHINGTON, Aug. 7 — In three specific fields the Potsdam communiqué deals with matters that may strengthen or weaken the new world organization. In different ways it might do both.

1. It sets up a permanent Council of Foreign Ministers—or Big Five—that will work outside the world organization.

The only specific reference to the Council's permanency in the Potsdam communiqué was in reference to its "permanent secretariat" to be set up in London. But it is learned authoritatively here that the Council now takes its place alongside the new world organization as a separate, stable institution—in so far as anything can be called permanent in these times.

2. It specifically recommends for membership in the United Nations organization ex-enemy European states—except Germany—and neutrals, except fascist Spain.

3. It confirms Russian interest in territorial trusteeships, particularly former Italian territories.

The newly established Council of Foreign Ministers, or Big Five, becomes the third exclusive international group concerned with resolving the problems of the world.

There is the Security Council of the United Nations Organization, composed of the Big Five, but also six other nonpermanent nations. Because the Council's primary responsibility is to "keep peace and maintain security," it may not be possible or appropriate for that body to involve itself in many matters that actually require big-power consideration.

Council of Ministers

There is also the Crimea-established Council of Foreign Ministers—a Big Three body and therefore more exclusive—that will probably hold "periodic consultations" presumably on matters that require quick and unanimous decisions by the Big Three.

This Potsdam-approved Council of Foreign Ministers, though assigned the immediate task of drawing up peace treaties for submission to the United Nations, is to have a permanent secretariat in London — similar, though on a much smaller scale, to the secretariat that will be established at the site chosen for the new United Nations organization.

By establishing this permanent Big Five Council, in addition to the more nebulous Big Three Council of Ministers, the Big Three at Potsdam established an organ for big-power control of world issues that can either aid and complement, or undermine and supplant, the activities and duties of the United Nations Organization's Security Council.

There is no reason to believe this Big Five Council of Foreign Ministers was established with any deliberate design to weaken the authority and activity of U. N. O.'s Security Council. It may even strengthen it by pre-assurance of Big Five on matters before the Council.

The very fact, however, that there are restrictions in the Charter on the responsibilities of the 11-member Security Council appears to justify if not require some such authority as is provided for by this Council of Foreign Ministers.

That each of the Big Five powers retains a veto on matters that should get Council attention is seen in the short paragraph of the communique reading: "Other matters (than the peace treaties) may from time to time be referred to the Council by agreement between the member governments."

Obviously should one big-power disagree, there would be no agreement. Thus the key of the Security Council's success—big power unanimity — becomes the touchstone for results to flow from the Council of Foreign Ministers.

The Potsdam communiqué clarified another problem growing out of the United Nations Conference at San Francisco, namely what nations other than the original 50 could be sure of getting Big Three approval for mempership in the new world organization. A secondary issue revolved around how soon they could seek membership.

Place for Italy

Ot Potsdam the Big Three clearly stated they were hopeful of making the new world organization a truly world-wide organization. They stated it was "their desire (once a peace treaty with a recognized and democratic Italy had been concluded) to support an application from Italy for membership of the United Nations."

They added that once peace treaties had been concluded with other ex-enemy states (Bulgaria, Finland, Hungary, Romania) they

Continued on Page 8, Column 6

Göring's Own Car On Board Transport

By a Staff Writer of The Christian Science Monitor

Boston, Aug. 7

Hermann Göring's personal car, a Mercedes-Benz, with bullet holes in its silver-plated sides, and crated for transport, was the center of interest today on board the transport George Shiras, after a ship's officer reported its presence.

While not officially admitted, the report was current that the car would be taken to Castle Island, where it would be uncrated.

The automobile is consigned to the Commanding General of the 20th Armored Division, Camp Cooke, Calif., and is believed to have been captured when the 20th took several high-ranking Nazis into custody in Salzburg, Germany, in June.

Question of Ideals Rises As Exporters View Markets

By Theodore N. Cook
Staff Correspondent of The Christian Science Monitor

NEW YORK, Aug. 7—International trade circles here are currently the scene of much deep pondering and rather self-conscious soul-searching. For evidently the resumption of foreign trade from this port, the busiest in the world, is not going to be as simple as it might sound offhand.

The bottleneck—at least as things stand at present—will not, of course, be lack of markets or hulls to move the goods in. It is more complicated than that. It boils down to a question of ideals. And consequently, many leading businessmen who deal heavily in exports are currently tripping all over themselves in an effort to decide whether they are going to be idealists or whether they are going to be "practical."

Things are reaching the point where three or more exporters cannot assemble for more than 10 minutes without turning to the troublesome subject. This, as a matter of fact, is encouraging, because the question should have been settled long before now.

Here is a sample of how the question enters discussions, and how vital and at the same time explosive it can become.

Indian Speaks

They had a forum at the New York Board of Trade on postwar trade with India a day or so ago. Principal speaker was A. D. Schroff, director of the Tata Industries of Bombay, which roughly corresponds to United States Steel in this country. In the audience was a group of export members of the Board's international section.

Well, Mr. Schroff was welcomed by the Chairman as a man who spoke their own language—"quite unlike those government bureaucrats we've been listening to recently," he added. Mr. Schroff bowed, and commenced to tell the gathering of the "tremendous possibilities" of postwar trade between India and the United States.

He told of India's vast road construction program for after the war, calling for building of 300,000 roads in 15 years, and pointed out that there would be a big market in India for road construction. The audience liked that. Then he told of a projected system of hydroelectric plants near Bombay. There would be a big market for generators and electrical equipment, he said. His listeners enjoyed that, too.

Plans for Textiles

But then he turned to India's plans for boosting textile production 50 per cent. And it was here that the faces in the audience presented an interesting study from the press table. Some looked quite eager to help. Others, it must be recorded, looked as if the monsoon had just landed. And it was at this point that the subject of idealism came to the foreground.

Mr. Schroff emphasized that India urgently needs more textile machinery, and that Great Britain cannot meet its requirements. At the same time, manufacturers of such equipment in the United States do not appear interested in adapting their machines to India's needs.

With the textile industry as its mainstay, all this puts India on the spot, Mr. Schroff said, asking, meanwhile, would America help India out of its predicament.

Slowly a gentleman in the audience rose from his chair. "Do you think it would be wise," he asked Mr. Schroff, "for the United States to ship machinery to India when, with your low wages and low prices, you could eventually cut into our textile business?"

Issue Clear-Cut

Here was the issue—"to be or not to be" an idealist.

Mr. Schroff evidently anticipated the question, and had a ready reply. Shipment of such equipment to India, he asserted, would make possible a great expansion of the textile industry in that country, going a long way toward boosting the miserable living standards of India's 300,000,000.

Continued on Page 8, Column 3

The Christian Science Monitor Index

Tuesday, August 7, 1945

How Many, How Soon Is Query on Missile

By Joseph C. Harsch
Staff Writer of The Christian Science Monitor

There is not the slightest doubt about what one atomic bomb can do. But the skeptics are asking just how many such bombs can be produced how soon.

The same skeptics have been fooled before. In this case the secrecy surrounding the atomic bomb plants is so deep and tight that the answer is anyone's guess.

But here are the points being made by those who are inclined to say, "Don't go off any deep ends":

1. The atomic bomb has come out sooner than those who were on the fringes of knowledge about it expected. The assumption in their opinion is that one was rushed out and dumped on Japan in a hurry to underline the 12-day-old ultimatum to the Japanese to surrender.

2. It is noted, in this connection, that propaganda broadcasts to Japan have been based immediately on the dropping of the single atomic bomb. In other words, its first employment is without doubt a careful part of the whole Allied offensive in psychological warfare.

3. The official statements are extremely careful to minimize the postwar availability of atomic energy for industrial and commercial purposes. By implication, the process of packing atomic energy into a bomb casing is very expensive. Energy has to be used to harness energy. Coal and water power are the existing sources of energy, and there is a limit to the amount which can be used for impounding atomic energy, either for war purposes now or for commercial purposes later.

Production Big Factor

From all of this the skeptical point of view is that Allied war power is capable of dropping atomic bombs on Japan from time to time. They have had one, and now we sit back and, in effect, say: How do you like that?

And then there will be another. And then another. Perhaps there can be one a week or even one a day. But it remains to be seen whether production is up to the point where such bombs can be employed with a frequency in any way comparable to conventional bombs.

One theory current here is that this dropping of a single atomic bomb on Japan is best compared to the original bombing of Tokyo by Lieut. Gen. James Doolittle's fliers coming from the deck of an aircraft carrier. That was a warning of what would come later. But it was also a military "tour de force." The launching of medium bombers from an aircraft carrier never was employed a second time. It took over two years after the initial bombing of Tokyo before the real aerial offensive against Japan could begin.

Destruction Underestimated

No one is quite as skeptical as to believe that it will be years or even months before a second atomic bomb can be dropped on Japan. The planes exist which can carry them and they have the bases from which to do it. All that is necessary is for the plants to produce the bombs. And if they have produced one they certainly can produce more. But there will be much and pleasant surprise, among these same cynics, if such bombs can be dropped on Japan oftener than once a week, if that often.

The biggest factor behind all this thinking is that atomic energy is not something like electricity

Continued on Page 2, Column 4

By the War Editor of The Christian Science Monitor
From Associated Press, Reuters, and other direct news dispatches

The new atomic bomb is attached to a parachute and explodes in midair, according to the Tokyo Radio. While the details of yesterday's earth-shaking atomic attack on the city and military depot of Hiroshima remained—so far as American sources were concerned—cloaked in a cloud of debris eight miles high and reinforced by an iron-clad censorship, the first dazed enemy reaction came over the ether waves.

The first intimation of what had happened was an announcement that train service in the Hiroshima area had been halted. Several hours later the Japanese were still at a loss to explain the destructiveness of the explosion and unable to realize that it was the work of a single missile.

Thus the Japanese version of the attack said that shortly after eight o'clock yesterday morning a small number of enemy planes appeared over the city of Hiroshima and dropped a number of new type bombs. As a result of this attack, it added, a considerable number of houses in the city were demolished while fires were started at several points.

This description of the damage appeared like an understatement which ill-accorded with the hysterical tone in which other radiocasters denounced the "diabolical" new weapon. Seeking to derive some consolation from this new disaster, the enemy attributed employment of the new weapon to Allied "impatience at the slow progress of the projected invasion of Japan's mainland."

Later enemy radiocasts declared that, while the new bomb's destructive power "cannot be slighted," it should cause no undue alarm as effective countermeasures were being worked out. Added the announcer: "The history of war shows that a new weapon, however effective, will eventually lose its power as the opponent is bound to find methods to nullify its effect."

Air Operations

News and speculation over the atomic bomb obscured the routine air operations against the home islands—the conventional bombing and strafing seemed tame and old-fashioned by comparsion. Nevertheless, the boys of the B-29's carried on as usual and from Gen. Carl Spaatz's air head-

Continued on Page 2, Column 1

Air Power Can Win, Rickenbacker Says

By the Associated Press

New York, Aug. 7

Capt. Edward V. Rickenbacker expressed the opinion today that Japan can be defeated by air power alone.

The World War 1 Ace and Eastern Airlines President said in a statement:

"I believe that in a very short time the Japanese people and industry will be so demoralized and battered by the daily ration of atomic, demolition, and incendiary bombs that they will cry quits.

It is my firm belief that this is the first war which will be won exclusively by air power, notwithstanding all experts' feelings that we will have to land troops on the home islands themselves."

Atom Bomb: Second Ultimatum

Reich Exiles Aided Project

By William H. Stringer
Staff Correspondent of The Christian Science Monitor

WASHINGTON, Aug. 7—Nazi Germany, with its discriminatory racial laws, its persecution and exile of Jewish natural scientists and intellectuals, contributed to Hitler's failure to win the race in the development of the atomic bomb.

A number of the top physicists in the British-American teams that developed the atom bomb were exiles from the Third Reich.

Many more of the thousands of researchers and technicians in the university and industrial laboratories which were utilized in the fantastically involved exploitation of this new power were refugees from Hitler's purged Reich.

A few of the original explorers into the mysteries of atomic energy were Germans who later quit their homeland because of its political fanaticism and intellectual intolerance.

Three of the top natural scientists in the British-American team that are engaged in developing the atom bomb are fugitives from Nazi injustice: Prof. Rudolph Peierls and Dr. Otto Robert Frisch, who are now in the United States, and Dr. Franz Eugene Simon, now in London.

All three quit Germany in 1933 because of discrimination and persecution. All three went to London and continued their studies that put them among those working on the atomic bomb. All three took out British citizenship.

Dr. Simon, born in Berlin, fled Germany because of Hitler's racial laws. He became reader in thermodynamics at Oxford.

Professor Peierls, Professor of Applied Mathematics in Birmingham University, was born in Berlin in 1907. A product of German schools, he won a Rockefeller Fellowship in 1932 that enabled him to travel, visiting Rome and Cambridge, England.

But Hitler's rise to power and the persecution of the Nazis forced him to quit Germany. He went to live in England in 1933. He became a Research Fellow in Manchester University, then worked in the Royal Society Laboratories in Cambridge. In

Continued on Page 11, Column 2

New Bomb Shades Potsdam

By Jon Kimche
Reuter's Military Correspondent

LONDON, Aug. 7—The strategic decisions taken at Potsdam, Teheran, and Yalta are already outdated by the atomic bomb.

Security no longer will be definable by the control of the Dardanelles and of the Suez Canal. Possession of the port of Königsberg by the Soviet Union would be of practically no strategic advantage in the event of a further conflict.

Possession of the Rhine and of Cologne with its radiating roads might be economically an advantage to France, but it can no longer be claimed as a measure of strategic necessity. The same is evident of many other claims to strategic frontiers in eastern and southeastern Europe. Nothing less than international peace will give security.

Atom-Smashing History Traced

By Robert K. Shellaby
Staff Writer of The Christian Science Monitor

As the age of atomic energy dawns, military security veils much of the detail of splitting the uranium atom. Yet enough information is available to piece together the story of this most prodigious achievement of modern physics.

The final lap in the race for releasing atomic energy began in 1939. Just before the war began in Europe, a German mathematician, Dr. Lise Meitner, was bombarding uranium atoms with neutrons and then submitting the uranium to chemical analysis.

Uranium, probably the most essential element in the new bomb, occurs in 100 different metals, though its principal sources are from uraninite, pitchblende, and carnotite. Pitchblende, for instance, is the source of radium. Like radium, uranium is radioactive, that is, it gives off rays or electron showers.

Vast Energy Stored

Because of the nature of atomic structure, it had been suspected long before Dr. Meitner's experiments that if a way could be found to split an atom, vast stores of energy could be obtained. An atom is made up of negatively charged electrons, positively charged protons, and other electrical and non-electrical particles. The atom keeps its shape because of the attraction of negative and positive

Continued on Page 4, Column 5

Control of Atom Physicists' Goal

By Mallory Browne
Staff Correspondent of The Christian Science Monitor

LONDON, Aug. 7—Britain is justly proud of the important part which British natural scientists played in the development of the atomic bomb, and now the whole nation's interest is centered on the question whether the new discovery is to mean the destruction or liberation of mankind.

The achievement of the atomic bomb is compared here in importance with the invention of gunpowder. It is stated unhesitatingly that the potentialities of the new discovery far transcend anything yet attained by such physical forces as those derived from coal, oil, steam, or electricity.

Sir John Anderson, who was Minister of Home Security prior to Winston Churchill's accession to the Premiership, was officially responsible for supervision of work on the atomic bomb in Brit-

Continued on Page 2, Column 6

Potsdam Made Bomb Decision

By Roscoe Drummond
Staff Correspondent of The Christian Science Monitor

WASHINGTON, Aug. 7 — The decision to unleash the atomic bomb on the foundering Japanese home islands represented a last-minute reversal of high-command policy, it was learned today.

As the full military possibilities of the greatest secret weapon in the history of warfare still were being assayed, these facts developed from a variety of sources:

1. Two months ago President Truman and the American joint chiefs of staff had reached an agreement that, at least in that stage of the Pacific war, the atomic bomb was not to be used, and the contrary decision was made during the course of the Potsdam Conference. Henry L. Stimson, Secretary of War, to whom President Truman yesterday gave great credit for the development of the new weapon, went to Potsdam to share in this decision. While no official explanation of the conclusion to use the bomb at once has been forthcoming, it seems evident that it was felt justified to end the fighting in the Pacific in the shortest possible time.

Things to Come

2. The best information here is that large-scale use of the atomic bomb is not imminent, and that, therefore, the smashing to Hiroshima is more in the nature of showing the Japanese the shape of things to come—unless there is unconditional surrender—than it is a launching of mass destruction. On this basis, the Hiroshima atomic bombing is seen as somewhat in

Continued on Page 11, Column 1

Trial of Pétain Expected To Wind Up by Next Week

PARIS, Aug. 7 (AP)—The trial of Marshal Philippe Pétain, now in its 14th day, is expected to go to the jury by the end of next week. Twenty-three defense witnesses remain to be heard, and attorneys for Marshal Pétain expect to call them at the rate of five daily.

Prosecutor André Mornet and chief defense attorney Fernand Payen said they then hoped to complete their respective summations in two days apiece.

Marcel Peyrouton, former Vichy Minister and Governor of Algeria, today told the court that Britain maintained contact with the Marshal's regime throughout 1940 through Spain and Switzerland.

He said Marshal Pétain and Laval were at loggerheads within six months after the Vichy Government was set up and that Laval was arrested on the night of Dec. 13, 1940, after Marshal Pétain had consulted the Cabinet of which he was Interior Minister.

Minister of the Interior is 1940 and 1941, M. Peyrouton organized the "Groupes de Protection," special independent police force which surrounded the Vichy Government building and arrested Laval in December, 1940.

After serving as Ambassador to Argentina, M. Peyrouton's appointment as Governor General of Algeria in January, 1943, by the faction of Gen. Henri Giraud unleashed a storm of controversy. He was placed under arrest at the end of the year as the resistance faction gained the upper hand.

Prosecutor Mornet charged yesterday that Marshal Pétain and Hitler exchanged letters three weeks after Allied landings in North Africa relative to German help for France "to assist her in reconquering her colonial domains."

In a surprise move, M. Mornet interrupted defense testimony in Marshal Pétain's treason trial to introduce the fragment of a letter he said was dated Dec. 6, 1942, and written by Marshal Pétain in reply to a communication from Hitler.

The portion M. Mornet read to the court said "you consider, and correctly that it is inconceivable for a nation to exist in the long run without a disciplined, obedient army. I have made it my first duty to reconstruct an army capable of assuring the safety of France and her empire.

"Von Rundstedt, (the Field Marshal then German commander

Continued on Page 8, Column 5

Aftermath of Conflict: Europe Struggles to Rise

Vienna Plans

By Joseph G. Harrison
Staff Correspondent of The Christian Science Monitor

VIENNA, Aug. 7—Although war-pummeled Vienna is going to need a major face-lifting job, its architects will be able to preserve the character and charm of this lovely city.

As in London the town fathers of Vienna are now drawing plans which will use the present disaster as a means for beautifying the city and enhancing its efficiency, without destroying its attraction.

Preliminary surveys show that 40 per cent of the City's buildings were hit to some extent during the street-fighting and bombing.

Of these, 19 per cent are still inhabitable, although they may be uncomfortable, due to shattered windows, and unhinged doors. The remaining 21 per cent, however, are considered uninhabitable and must be either replaced or extensively overhauled.

It is perhaps interesting to note how this destruction took place. Thus, of the 21 per cent unusable buildings, 8½ per cent were destroyed during street fighting between Russians and Nazi Elite Guards, another 8½ per cent were partially damaged through Allied bombing, while the remaining 4 per cent were wholly destroyed through bombing.

Although Vienna came off far more fortunately than many of the great cities in Germany, it still gives the impression of being a badly battered town. Anywhere you stand in the city you can see more or less damaged structures around you.

What is more, many streets are still clogged with towering piles of rubble, upon the top of which the Viennese have thrown their

Continued on Page 5, Column 4

Berlin to Get News Unvarnished

BERLIN, Aug. 7—Berlin residents, who got their news spoon-fed under Hitler, will begin getting it straight and undiluted tomorrow from the American-published Allgemeine Zeitung.

The first issue of the four-page, thrice-weekly paper will carry such factual news as accounts of the new United States atomic bomb, chitchat about persons down the Strasse, and statements from Berlin's four leading political parties.

News of Germany will be obtained by interchange with nine other newspapers published in the American zone under Military Government supervision, and local news will be gathered by a bicycling staff of eight German reporters.

UNRRA Spurred

By Mary Hornaday
Staff Correspondent of The Christian Science Monitor

LONDON, Aug. 7—The shadow of the atomic bomb hung over London's county hall today when representatives of 44 nations who are members of the United Nations Relief and Rehabilitation Administration council met in Europe for the first time to plan a wider international effect against the degredation in which another world war could spawn this coming winter.

Resounding in the ears of the delegates as they were welcomed by Britain's new Foreign Secretary Ernest Bevin were the worldwide warnings in the wake of the atomic-bomb disclosure that another world war would mean destruction of all regulated life.

A sense of urgency resulting from the bomb disclosure was felt deeply as the delegates tackled the enormous problems of finance, supplies, transport, and traditional European political squabbles that threaten to keep UNRRA from meeting its goal of rehabilitating those nations unable to help

Continued on Page 5, Column 4

Nazis Displaced

By a Staff Correspondent of The Christian Science Monitor

LONDON, Aug. 7—The decision by the Big Three at Potsdam on the removal of Germans from Poland, Czechoslovakia, and Hungary did not come soon enough to avert considerable chaos and suffering under the "eye-for-eye" expulsion policy that has been troubling American civil affairs officers in their occupation zone.

In accord with the Berlin declaration, Czechoslovakia, Poland, and Hungary are being asked to suspend further expulsions of Germans from their areas until orderly and humane plans for their removal can be arranged.

Germans Herded Out

Stories about the fury with which the Czechs and others tried to drive the Germans from their country when the Germans capitulated are just now reaching London. Some instances have been reported where the treatment the Germans received is said to have been not unlike that which they themselves meted out to "slave" peoples.

Describing their actions as "purification," the Czech National Guard, made up of young Leftists,

Continued on Page 5, Column 5

Reich Warned

By J. Emlyn Williams
Staff Correspondent of The Christian Science Monitor

BERLIN, Aug. 7—Gen. Dwight D. Eisenhower told Germans in the United States zone of occupation that they may form local unions and engage in local political activities with the aim of helping prepare for the coming winter, which he predicted will be hard.

The speech was in the nature of an account of the General's stewardship in the past three months since the final defeat of German arms. In the main, it followed the lines which the Potsdam communiqué laid down for the treatment of Germany, declaring: "German power to make war will be destroyed."

But it stressed a note of hope that if the Germans help one another to overcome the difficulties and hardships of the coming months, and in fact until the "time comes for you to select your own government," they would find the Americans ready to do their part.

Willing to Work

In appealing to the Germans to reduce their hardships "by steady work," General Eisenhower will find a ready response—not only because these persons realize their own interests but also because there are few people in Europe—or in the world, for that matter—who are less idle or more disciples of the theory that man has to work. They will gather wood from the forest all right — they have done it for years, especially in the country districts.

What the Germans look for from the Americans is an opportunity either to rebuild some of their peacetime industries or, in keeping with the Potsdam declaration help in intensifying German agriculture.

Following is the text of Gen-

Continued on Page 5, Column 1

THE CHRISTIAN SCIENCE MONITOR

Registered in U. S. Patent Office

AN INTERNATIONAL DAILY NEWSPAPER

VOLUME 37 NO. 221 | COPYRIGHT 1945 BY THE CHRISTIAN SCIENCE PUBLISHING SOCIETY | BOSTON, WEDNESDAY, AUGUST 15, 1945 | ★★—ATLANTIC EDITION | TWO SECTIONS | FIVE CENTS A COPY

The World at Peace

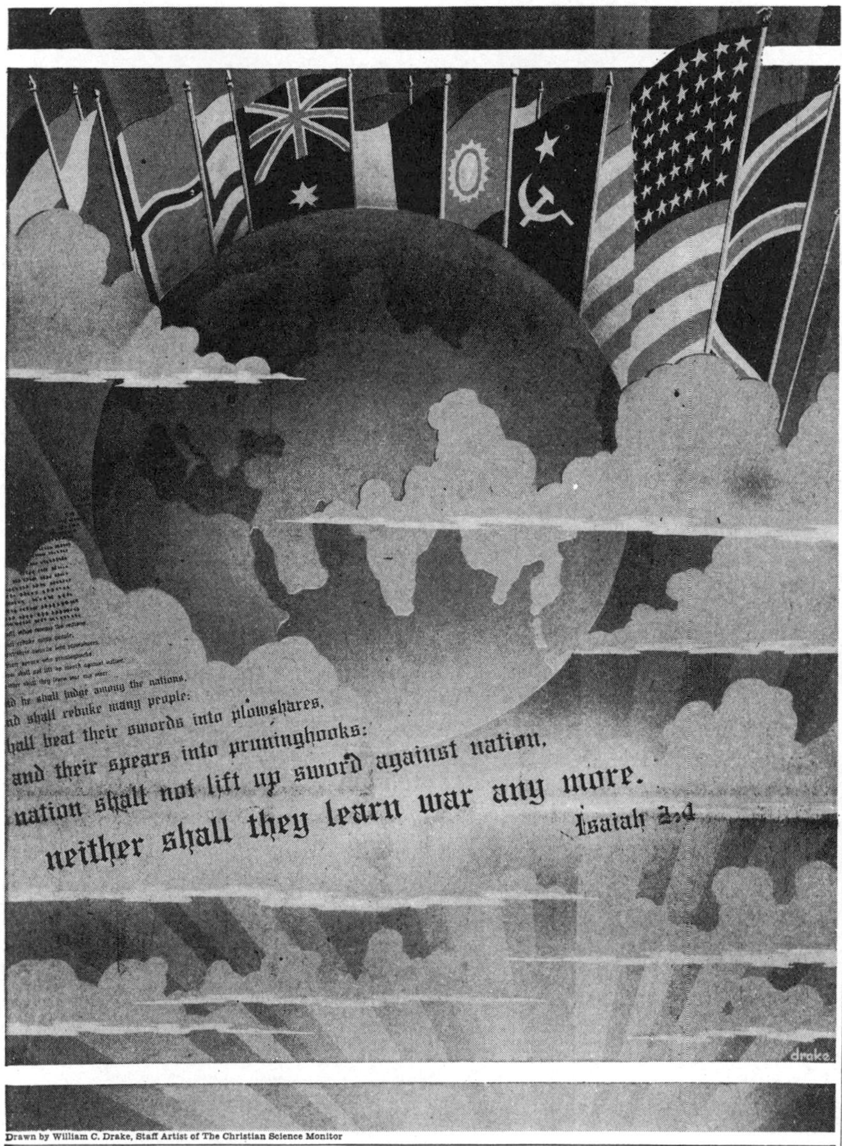

nd he shall judge among the nations,
nd shall rebuke many people:
hall beat their swords into plowshares,
and their spears into pruninghooks:
nation shall not lift up sword against nation,
neither shall they learn war any more.
Isaiah 2:4
drake.

Drawn by William C. Drake, Staff Artist of The Christian Science Monitor

Gasoline and Fuel Oil Ration Ends; U.S. Industry Geared to Peacetime

Allies Prepare To Occupy Japan

By a Staff Writer of The Christian Science Monitor

As peace broke out today—in all its glory, complexity, promise, and responsibility—the United Nations moved swiftly to formalize the Japanese surrender and to occupy the enemy homeland.

At the present moment, relations between the Allied powers and Japan are in a state of truce. This will continue for several days until Gen. Douglas MacArthur, who has been named Supreme Commander for all Allied forces in the Far East, can accept a written Japanese surrender on the basis of the Potsdam declaration.

Immediately after the news of the surrender decision was flashed to the world last night, General MacArthur sent word to the Japanese authorities instructing them to send a representative to Manila to arrange for the formal act of capitulation.

Today he dispatched a second note ordering the Nipponese envoy to fly in an all-white plane decorated with green crosses. With a sense of poetic justice, General MacArthur told the Japanese to use the code word "Bataan" for all communications between the envoy and American forces.

Program for Envoy

The surrender plane will leave Kyushu Island on Friday morning and will fly to an American airport on Ie Shima, a short distance from Okinawa. Six hours' advance notice of exact departure time and route must be given. From Ie Shima, an American plane will carry the surrender party to Manila.

General MacArthur warned the Japanese that the envoy must bring competent Army, Navy, and Air Force advisers with him and to bear credentials enabling him to represent Emperor Hirohito.

In Manila, it is assumed that the Japanese delegation will receive instructions regarding the technical details of the Allied occupation and similar problems. The surrender party is expected to return at once to Tokyo after conferring with General Mac-

Continued on Page 2, Column 5

'Cease Fire' Ends War in Pacific

By the War Editor of The Christian Science Monitor
From Associated Press, Reuters, and other direct news dispatches

The "cease-fire" order reverberated through the far-flung war areas of the Pacific today as Allied commands acted to halt operations in midair.

The crews of a vast armada of Superforts heard the good tidings as they were winging back to their bases from a heavy strike at the Japanese homeland.

Hundreds of other warplanes, including carrier-based craft of the Third Fleet and medium bombers of the Far Eastern Air Force based on Okinawa, jettisoned their bombs in the sea off Honshu as orders to halt offensive operations flashed to their radio operators.

Twelve hours after the announcement of Japan's surrender a pair of bomb carrying Japanese Kamikaze suicide planes crashed into Ihya Island, 30 miles north of Okinawa tonight, injuring at least two American garrison troops in a futile raid which left Okinawa fuming with fury. It caused a two-hour blackout alert over Okinawa and nearby islands.

The Kamikaze planes, something rare at Okinawa since the large-scale raids during the campaign for the island, flew in under a bright moonlight about 8 p. m. to strike the astounding blow.

Raids on Okinawa in the last two months have been chiefly high altitude reconnaissance and bombing missions aimed at shipping and airfields. They have caused almost nightly alerts. No Kamikaze attacks, however, had been launched for many weeks.

Japanese Order

A radio dispatch from Domei, the Japanese news agency, stated that Japanese Imperial Headquarters was endeavoring to transmit the Imperial order to end hostilities to every branch of the forces but that before this order took full effect a part of the Japanese Air Force was reported to have made an attack on an Allied base and on Allied naval units.

The Domei dispatch concluded, "While the Imperial Head-

Continued on Page 2, Column 1

Master Reconversion Plan Unveiled by Government

By a Staff Correspondent of The Christian Science Monitor

WASHINGTON, Aug. 15—The rationing of gasoline, canned fruits and vegetables, fuel oil, and oil stoves was ended today by the Office of Price Administration. Dealers may now sell these freely without further notice.

Rationing continues for meats, fats, oils, butter, sugar, shoes, and tires "until military cutbacks and increased production bring civilian supplies more nearly in balance with civilian demand."

"Right now," said Price Administrator Chester Bowles, "it's impossible to estimate" when other items will be released, but "it certainly cannot come too soon."

By William H. Stringer
Staff Correspondent of The Christian Science Monitor

WASHINGTON, Aug. 15—As the gigantic American war economy shuddered with the command "Reverse engines," the Administration unveiled today its master reconversion program bull's-eyed straight toward a peacetime production surpassing anything in history.

A fact-jammed 31-page cover-all report from John W. Snyder, Director of Reconversion, became the cover-all charter by which the Government hopes to map the way, bridge the war-to-peace transition, and avoid permanent dislocation.

War-contract cancellations reaching $35,000,000,000 within a few weeks, and temporary unemployment rising to 8,000,000 jobless before next spring, are the fundamental shocks which require expert handling by Government in collaboration with industry, the Snyder report warned.

Even as the War Department was announcing contract cancellations which would total $23,500,000,000 in a year, the reconversion charter was propounding that "only a peacetime production, vastly expanded over anything this or any other nation has ever seen," will provide jobs for all and a rising standard of living.

Immediate Steps Planned

Mr. Snyder announced these immediate steps in the nation's task of shaping weapons into the plowshares and production of peace:

1. The Army's vast munitions procurement program is being cut immediately "by 94 to 100 per cent." The tremendous food procurement for the Army will be cut "as fast as demobilization will permit." Navy reductions will be smaller and more gradual.

2. At least 7,000,000 men will be demobilized from the armed forces within the next year. The Army's demobilization rate will climb in several months from its current 170,000 a month to 500,000. The Navy will demobilize some personnel now, but must await determination of its future role and police duties before taking drastic action.

3. Many wartime production and distribution controls will be removed at once. Some must remain in force to expedite production, break bottlenecks, thwart inventory hoarding, and maintain economic stabilization. The Director of Reconversion and the War Production Board agree heartily on this.

4. Rationing of scarce commodities must continue, but restrictions on others will be lifted immediately. Transportation controls must continue—rail travel may become

Continued on Page 2, Column 8

A. F. of L. Sees Washington Bar to Labor Adjustments

By Ralph Cessna
Staff Correspondent of The Christian Science Monitor

CHICAGO, Aug. 15—The American Federation of Labor seems to be looking toward Washington, rather than the employer, as the worker's worst enemy. It sees also that the reconversion unemployment period just ahead offers opportunity, through following a conciliatory policy toward management, to recoup ground lost to its unruly but dominant stepchild, the Congress of Industrial Organizations.

The Federation's Executive Council, meeting here in place of the regular convention, closed its sessions yesterday, almost simultaneously with the final peace announcements, on a rising note of conservatism.

The Council is headed by William Green, President of the A. F. of L., and representing some 7,000,000 workers at its meeting here re-emphasized its conservative character in several specific ways.

Anti-Communistic

To recapitulate: It continues to refuse to join the recently formed World Federation of Trade Unions, because the C. I. O. and the Soviet Union are represented. The Federation has been and is today more than ever bitterly anti-Communistic. Here it has something in common with American industry, and here it differs with the C. I. O. which has, throughout its leadership and membership a leftish tinge.

Unlike its rival, the Federation, Mr. Green says, will try to avoid strikes now that peace has come, whether or not the no-strike pledge is still in force.

Mr. Green pointedly urges Washington to see to it that industry is helped over the reconversion hump.

As a matter of fact, the Federation's attacks in the field of labor relations are invariably aimed at Congress or some Federal agency, rather than at employers.

Mr. Green at a press conference here, with dignified sarcasm referred to one case in which a poor innocent stove maker has been prevented by the War Production Board from reconverting to peace production because, it was claimed, to do so would give it an advantage over its competitors.

Views on Production

"Employers," Mr. Green said, with a smile that took in what many classes or organized workers would consider "'that capitalism crowd,' should have been given a chance to prepare for postwar manufacture."

The Council was almost merciless in its criticism of the proposal of Senators Ball, Burton, and Hatch, that the Labor Relations Act be amended to provide for permanent Federal arbitration machinery.

Such legislation, Mr. Green announced, would freeze management-labor negotiations under bureaucratic government agencies. Industry and Labor he plainly implied, can get along much better without such machinery. The C. I. O. objection to the same legislation is on the ground of the unworkability of the machinery, rather than on the assumption that labor and management can get by on their own.

A proposal, howtver, which has the hearty approval of the Federation, is amendment of labor legislation to provide for election of minority unions within plants holding representation elections. This would, of course, give the A. F. of L. craft unions a new foothold in industries where C. I. O. industrial units have held control through majority voting.

Again, in its attitude toward the

Continued on Page 14, Column 4

See for Yourself

The incredible story of radar, almost rivaling the atomic bomb in drama, is released from censorship for the first time today. The entire First Page of the Second Section is devoted to this subject.

It includes actual pictures looking through a late type of radar screen from high above the earth, showing how aviators can actually see what they are bombing, either through clouds or darkness.

The Christian Science Monitor Index

Wednesday, August 15, 1945

Exit Thor: Now the Tasks of Peace

U. S. Molds Dynamic Pattern Based on Global Co-operation

By Roscoe Drummond
Staff Correspondent of The Christian Science Monitor

WASHINGTON, Aug. 15—Once more the world is at peace and once more we have an opportunity to keep it.

This time the end of the war finds the United States putting its total influence—its political, economic and military as well as moral influence—behind the peace.

This may well be the difference which can spell success for World Peace II: That after this "one world" has suffered the travail of two vast wars and a total of at least 37,000,000 military casualties in one generation, the United States is joining the peace, not seceding from it; is placing its maximum power behind creating a good peace and securing it.

This time the timetable of peace-making has outsped the timetable of war-making, and now the abrupt climax to the fighting in the Pacific finds the beginnings of the peace already well advanced.

Peace Must Be Dynamic

The new league of United Nations has been framed and its 50-nation interim commission is already at work in London.

The pattern of the war settlements in Europe, laid down at the Potsdam Conference, is being slowly but steadily realized.

The essential outlines of the war settlements in the Pacific, partly established by the Cairo declarations, are already visible.

The cessation of destructive hostilities does not guarantee the beginning of constructive peace, and World Peace II shows signs of being neither Utopian nor easy nor automatic.

For peace is dynamic, not static, and whether we keep World Peace II or throw it away depends on how the United Nations use it.

For its part the United States has, there is reason to

Continued on Page 4, Column 1

World Faces New Challenge To Reshape Mental Concepts

By Henry Sowerby
Staff Writer of The Christian Science Monitor

The war is ended. The victory is ours. The heroic work of our young men who fought has been accomplished. The greatest evil that has ever menaced the entire human race has been beaten down. An orgy of destruction such as has never before stained the annals of the nations is a thing of the past.

World War I was called Armageddon. There is no name in the vocabulary vast enough to embrace these six years of conflict—infinitely more ravaging in their drain on men and resources, in their destructiveness and in their shattering effect upon the faith and hopes of humanity.

After World War I we looked for the voice to thunder: "It is done!" It never came.

Road to Freedom

Today as the "tumult and the shouting dies," and the "captains and the kings depart," we know it is not yet done. The Four Freedoms have yet to be established and protected. The prayer of all hearts is:

"Lord God of Hosts, be with us yet
Lest we forget, lest we forget!"

Today we know, as we did not in 1919, that victory has brought us, not an end to the struggle, but only the right and the responsibility to resolve the chaos that remains in our own way—the opportunity to set humanity on a better road to faith and harmony.

We have learned since 1918 that victory does not of itself leave democracy strong. In this war we carried no glittering emblems of a war "to end war," or a war "to make the world safe for democracy." Millions of young men who went out to fight in Europe and the Far East understood the call without slogans. They knew that the evil menacing all our concepts of freedom and justice must be destroyed, or democracy must go under.

We are in no mood to boast of our military victory. We

Continued on Page 2, Column 1

Supreme Allied Commander

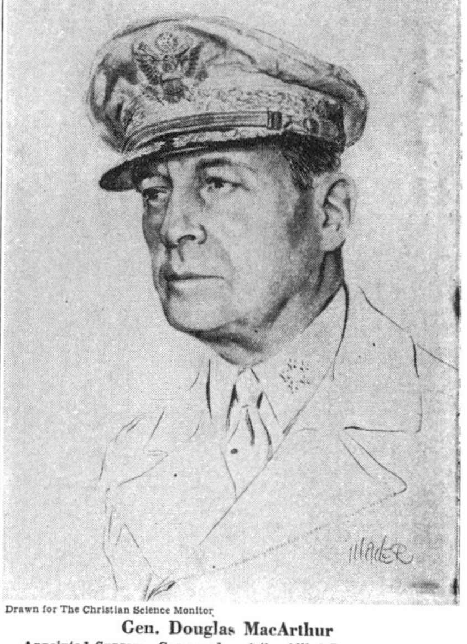

Drawn for The Christian Science Monitor

Gen. Douglas MacArthur

Appointed Supreme Commander of the Allied Powers and given authority to accept the surrender of Japan and to fix terms for the occupation and control of the island empire.

THE CHRISTIAN SCIENCE MONITOR

Registered in U. S. Patent Office
AN INTERNATIONAL DAILY NEWSPAPER

VOLUME 38 NO. 38 | COPYRIGHT 1946 BY THE CHRISTIAN SCIENCE PUBLISHING SOCIETY | BOSTON, THURSDAY, JANUARY 10, 1946 | * * * ATLANTIC EDITION | TWO SECTIONS | FIVE CENTS A COPY

Truman Ready to Increase Price Level to Get U. S. Over Hump of Vital Wage Disputes

Steel and Labor Hold Conference

By Richard L. Strout
Staff Correspondent of The Christian Science Monitor

WASHINGTON, Jan. 10—With the Truman Administration prepared to allow price increases in basic industries, the heads of the United States Steel Corporation and the Congress of Industrial Organizations met in New York today to avert the threatened steel strike.

Benjamin F. Fairless, President of United States Steel, and Philip Murray, President of the C. I. O., conferred at the Corporation's offices, the result of which may not only settle the steel dispute but open the way for a solution to the wage-price controversies which have blocked the nation's reconversion efforts.

The meeting in person of Mr. Fairless and Mr. Murray as the negotiations approach a climax follows closely the Administration's plan to allow price increases in steel, meat, and other commodities as the cost of getting America's production over the hump of wage disputes.

The steel negotiations already have made history.

The administration has retreated on the price line, although officials argue that this does not set a precedent.

The steel corporations have won their big point, not to negotiate with the union until assured that they might count on some price increases.

Mr. Murray—unlike Walter Reuther, C. I. O. leader in the General Motors strike—has not barred out price increases in demanding wage increases. On the contrary, he wants wage increases regardless of where the money comes from.

Reflecting an inflationary trend and hope of a steel settlement, stocks averages reached 15-year highs yesterday.

Legislative Hopes Fade

While hope of industrial peace grew, prospect of congressional labor legislation similarly declined.

The C. I. O. steel union indicated willingness to compromise its $2-a-day wage increase demand.

Not only did the Government make known that it was prepared to allow steel prices to go up, but at Chicago, Edgar L. Warren, chief of the United States Conciliation Service, told the two big packing houses, Swift and Armour, that the Government would permit higher

Continued on Page 3, Column 5

Wire Strike Stalls Wire Strike Orders

By the Associated Press

Omaha, Neb., Jan. 10

Members of the Northwestern Union of Telephone Workers in Iowa, Nebraska, Minnesota, and North and South Dakota do not know if the current communications workers' strike will bring a sympathy walkout.

The reason—strike-slowed communications.

E. G. Albrecht, union President, of Minneapolis, explained here yesterday his group is waiting for directions from the National Federation of Telephone Workers in New York.

The Western Union strike has cut their normal route of communications, and long-distance phone communications in the metropolitan area are jammed.

Democrats Offer Target In N. Y. Roles

By a Staff Correspondent of The Christian Science Monitor

NEW YORK, Jan. 10 — Although the Democrats are the "ins" at New York City Hall, they are the "outs" at the Albany State Capitol, and this situation is providing independent New York voters with an opportunity to observe a political party playing two different roles at the same time.

Any party in control at one key point, but a decided minority at another, invariably faces the difficulty of maintaining consistent party policy. There is evidence that the challenges as will as the opportunities of such a position are fully grasped by both the Democratic and G. O. P. leaders.

Big Guns Open Fire

For a long time, the State Democratic Party has criticized G. O. P. legislators in Washington for condemning without offering constructive solutions. Having gone on the record against such practices, the Democratic Party in Albany is currently faced with a tidy problem along this very line.

Governor Dewey has just made his Legislative address, and the

Continued on Page 5, Column 3

Phone Workers To Quit in N. Y.

By the Associated Press

Some 7,000 long distance telephone workers including operators will start leaving their jobs at 7 a. m. (EST) tomorrow in New York City, John J. Moran, a union spokesman announced, marking the start of a threatened nationwide shutdown of telephone service in sympathy with an installation workers walkout.

The New York walkout would be simultaneous with establishment of picket lines, which installation workers said they would set up across the nation tomorrow.

Installation workers — 8,000 of whom went on strike in 44 states yesterday — said they expected telephone operators generally would refuse to cross their picket lines.

Status of Service

The American Telephone & Telegraph Co. said, however, that although a prolonged strike of equipment workers and of Western Electric Company employees would handicap installation of new sets, dial service could be maintained "many months—barring accidents" such as major breakdowns.

Telephone service in Washington was curtailed for the second time in six days when switchboard operators of the Chesapeake & Potomac Telephone Co. started leaving their posts today to attend a union protest meeting.

The walkout, which the union contended was in protest against "overworking" supervisors and operators, interrupted White House communications. Incoming calls were blocked and outgoing calls were routed through Army and Navy tie lines.

In Washington, meanwhile, a report by the Government's fact-finding board in the General Motors wage dispute was ready for President Truman's consideration. Chairman Lloyd K. Garrison declined to disclose the recommendations.

Special Conference

Walter P. Reuther, U. A. W.-C. I. O. Vice-President and director of the union's General Motors Department, notified all G. M. locals by telegraph of a special U. A. W.-G. M. conference for Sunday, Jan. 13, at 1 p. m., in Detroit.

He advised the locals that the G. M. Fact-Finding Board had submitted its report to the President on the long strike which has made more than 175,000 workers idle.

The Washington telephone tie-up, the Washington Telephone Traffic Union said, bears no relation to a sympathy walkout planned by other affiliates of the National Federation of Telephone Workers in a strike of 17,000 Western Electric Company employees in New York and New Jersey.

In Hollywood, Calif., the controversy over whether studio office workers must pay dues to the A.

Continued on Page 11, Column 1

Congress Prepares Probe Of Demobilization Policy

By William H. Stringer
Staff Correspondent of The Christian Science Monitor

WASHINGTON, Jan. 10—G. I. discharge demonstrations at Manila, Frankfurt and other points are building high steam pressure for a congressional investigation of Army demobilization policies as first order of business when Congress reconvenes Monday.

Meanwhile, support is growing for still more adequate on-the-spot information to America's citizen-servicemen, to tell them just why they are detailed to ship demobilized Jap troops back to Japan, dismantle German factories, or just plain "sit it out" on dull Pacific islands.

When soldiers and sailors are kept informed by their commanders, not merely concerning the broader occupation policies, but why this or that perplexing task is necessary; when they are given up-to-the-minute demobilization facts not subject to reversal from Washington—then, the feeling is, demonstrations will end.

Hoped to Head It Off

The War Department hoped to head off a congressional investigation by releasing the statement of Gen. Dwight D. Eisenhower, Chief-of-Staff, assuring that the entire demobilization pace is being reviewed and that a detailed new program shortly will be forthcoming.

General Eisenhower directed that all troops no longer needed in overseas posts be returned to the United States "without delay."

Notwithstanding these steps by the War Department, Senator Edwin C. Johnson (D) of Colorado demanded that General Eisenhower be summoned before the Senate Military Affairs Committee to present a clear picture of the Army's demobilization policies. He said overseas demonstrations constituted "near mutiny" which Congress could not ignore, adding that "the causes for this deplorable situation must be brought into the open."

Senator Johnson was named chairman of a special Senate military subcommittee today to explore the whole demobilization situation.

Actually, a fundamental cause behind the whole furore appeared to be the 60,000-and-more "men who aren't there." This is the figure by which new enlistments are falling behind demobilizations due to insufficient selective service inductions and inability to make immediate use of the 400,000 new volunteers recruited up to Jan. 1.

In addition it is the belief of War Department officials that the pool from which volunteers are being drawn will gradually dry up and the critical manpower situation may worsen in the coming months.

Nevertheless, individual members of Congress continue to hammer for faster demobilization schedules, while Representative Charles R. Savage (D) of Washington has urged that the recruiting drive be sparked anew with increased pay and other incentives.

Senator Elbert Thomas (D) of Utah, Chairman of the Military Affairs Committee, denied that an investigation of the Army's discharge system was necessary, arguing that discharges were being carried out even faster than the Army had predicted.

The bulk of European theater veterans possessing discharge points will have been rewarded by demobilization during January, during which month one of the largest flow of homebound men will take place with about 800,000 then reaching the United States. The War Department is making a big effort to fulfill Gen. George C. Marshall's expressed hope that all two-year veterans would be out of service by late March, but this is not guaranteed.

As one small contribution to the problem, a stepped-up information and education program was begun at Andrews Field near Washington—where a protest demonstration occurred Jan. 7—to keep personnel better posted on new demobilization developments.

Declaring that Monday's demonstration resulted from lack of information among his men, Col. Curtis D. Sluman, Base Commander, asked all squadron commanders to call regular meetings of their men for open discussions, adding that complete bulletins on all incoming demobilization rules would be posted in barracks immediately on arrival. He also suggested a weekly "question and answer" section in the biweekly post newspaper.

It is similarly suggested that if overseas commanders, utilizing whatever information they can obtain as well as the facilities available through the Army's Information and Education Divi-

Continued on Page 10, Column 4

The Christian Science Monitor Index

Thursday, January 10, 1946

UNO Assembly of 51 Nations Meets With Grim Faith to Make Peace Work

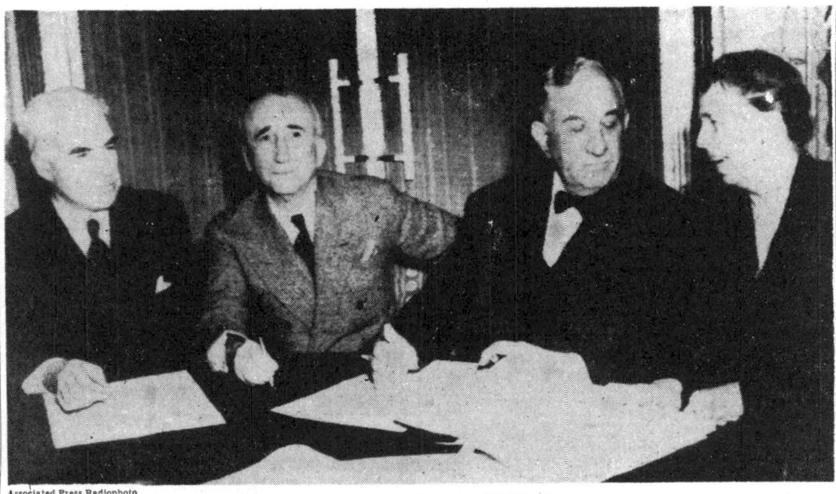

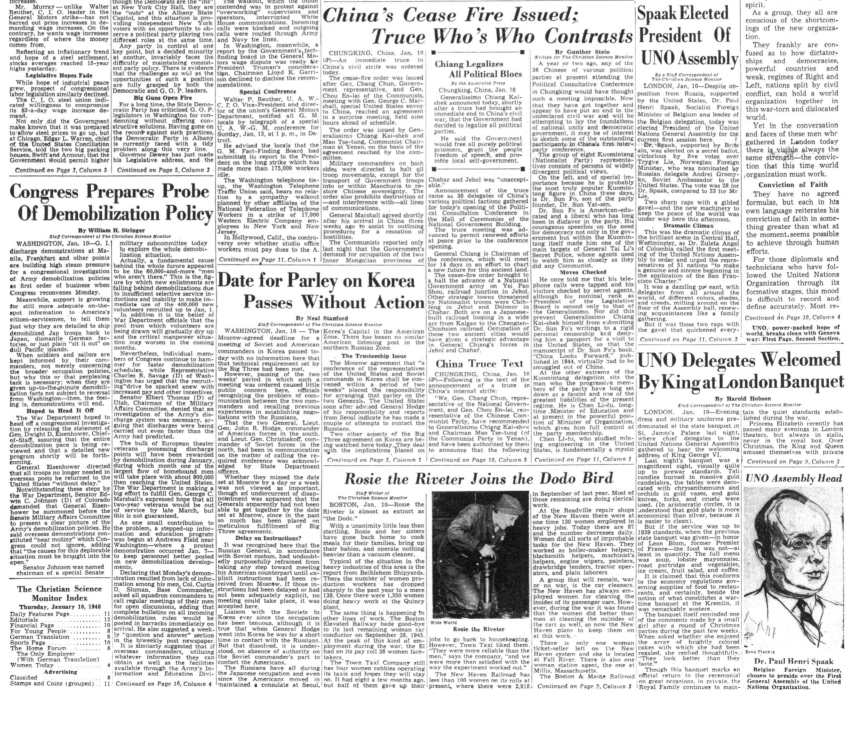

Associated Press Radiophoto

American Delegates Unify UNO Strategy

Seated at a table in a London hotel, members of the United States delegation to the United Nations Organization General Assembly confer as they prepare for the opening of the Assembly. Left to right: Edward R. Stettinius; Secretary of State James F. Byrnes; Senator Tom Connally, and Mrs. Eleanor Roosevelt, who represent the United States at today's functions.

New 'League' Accents Action, Not Eloquence

By Saville R. Davis
Chief of the London News Bureau of The Christian Science Monitor

LONDON, Jan. 10—Never did the hopes of the world rest on so few illusions—or on so profound a conviction that the forces of atomic warfare must be overcome by mankind.

The new world peace organization began its work here today after a welcoming speech to the chief delegates by King George VI last night at a state dinner.

The leading statesmen of 51 United Nations took their places on the floor of the General Assembly in a mood which was in sharp contrast to the bright bustle around tables and the proud draperies of Central Hall.

Grimly Determined

They came heavy in spirit.

As a group, they all are conscious of the shortcomings of the new organization.

They frankly are confused as to how dictatorships and democracies, powerful countries and weak, regimes of Right and Left, nations split by civil conflict, can hold a world organization together in this war-torn and dislocated world.

Yet in the conversation and faces of these men who gathered in London today there is visible always the same strength—the conviction that this time world organization must work.

Conviction of Faith

They have no agreed formulas, but each in his own language reiterates his conviction of faith in something greater than what at the moment seems possible to achieve through human efforts.

For those diplomats and technicians who have followed the United Nations Organization through its formative stages, this mood is difficult to record and define accurately. Most re-

Continued on Page 10, Column 4

UNO, power-packed hope of world, breaks clean with Geneva way: First Page, Second Section.

China's Cease Fire Issued; Truce Who's Who Contrasts

CHUNGKING, China, Jan. 10 (AP)—An immediate truce in China's civil strife was ordered today.

The cease-fire order was issued after Gen. Chang Chun, Government representative, and Gen. Chou En-lai of the Communists, meeting with Gen. George C. Marshall, special United States envoy to China, reached an agreement in a surprise meeting, held nine hours ahead of schedule.

The order was issued by Generalissimo Chiang Kai-shek and Mao Tse-tung, Communist Chairman at Yenan, on the basis of the agreement reached by the committee.

Military commanders on both sides were directed to halt all troop movements, except for the transport of Government troops into or within Manchuria to restore Chinese sovereignty. The order also prohibits destruction of—and interference with—all lines of communications.

General Marshall agreed shortly after his arrival in China three weeks ago to assist in outlining procedures for a cessation of hostilities.

The Communists reported only last night that the Government's demand for occupation of the two Inner Mongolian provinces of Chahar and Jehol was "unacceptable."

Announcement of the truce came as 38 delegates of China's various political factions gathered for today's opening of the Political Consultation Conference in the Hall of Ceremonies of the National Government Building.

The truce meeting was advanced to permit renewed efforts at peace prior to the conference opening.

General Chiang is Chairman of the conference, which will meet for 14 days in an effort to chart a new future for this ancient land.

The cease-fire order brought to a halt the advance of a National Government army on Yei Pao Shou, railroad junction in Jehol. Other strategic towns threatened by Nationalist troops were Chihfeng in Jehol and Dolonor in Chahar. Both are on a Japanese-built railroad looping in a wide arc from Kalgan to the Chengten-Chinhsien railroad. Occupation of these two ancient cities would have given a strategic advantage to General Chiang's forces in Jehol and Chahar.

Chiang Legalizes All Political Blocs

By the Associated Press

Chungking, China, Jan. 10

Generalissimo Chiang Kai-shek announced today, shortly after a truce had brought an immediate end to China's civil war, that the Government had decided to legalize all political parties.

He said the Government would free all purely political prisoners, grant the people freedom of speech, and promote local self-government.

China Truce Text

CHUNGKING, China, Jan. 10 (AP)—Following is the text of the announcement of a truce in China's internal strife:

"We, Gen. Chang Chun, representative of the National Government, and Gen. Chou En-lai, representative of the Chinese Communist Party, have recommended to Generalissimo Chiang Kai-shek and Chairman Mao Tse-tung (of the Communist Party in Yenan), and have been authorized by them to announce that the following

Continued on Page 10, Column 5

By Gunther Stein
Written for The Christian Science Monitor

A year or two ago, any of the 38 Chinese of various political parties at present attending the Political Consultative Conference in Chungking would have thought such a meeting impossible. Now that they have got together and appear to have put an end to the undeclared civil war and will be attempting to lay the foundations of national unity and democratic government, it may be of interest to sketch some of the outstanding participants in China's first inter-party conference.

The group of eight Kuomintang (Nationalist Party) representatives consists of persons of widely divergent political views.

On the left, and of special importance because he is probably the most truly popular Kuomintang figure in China these days, is Dr. Sun Fo, son of the party founder, Dr. Sun Yat-sen.

Dr. Sun Fo is American-educated and a liberal who has long been in disfavor in the party. His courageous speeches on the need for democracy not only in the government but within the Kuomintang itself made him one of the main targets of General Tai Li's Secret Police, whose agents used to watch him as closely as they did any Communist.

Moves Checked

He once told me that his telephone calls were tapped and his visitors checked by secret agents, although his nominal rank as President of the Legislative Board is second only to that of the Generalissimo. Nor did this prevent Generalissimo Chiang Kai-shek himself from submitting Dr. Sun Fo's writings to a rigid personal censorship and denying him a passport for a visit to the United States, so that the manuscript of Dr. Sun Fo's book, "China Looks Forward," published in 1944, virtually had to be smuggled out of China.

At the other extreme of the Kuomintang delegation sits the man who the progressive members of the party have long set down as a fascist and one of the greatest liabilities of the present regime. He is Chen Li-fu, longtime Minister of Education and at present in the powerful position of Minister of Organization, which gives him full control of the party membership.

Chen Li-fu, who studied mining engineering in the United States, is fundamentally a mystic

Continued on Page 11, Column 1

Spaak Elected President Of UNO Assembly

By a Staff Correspondent of The Christian Science Monitor

LONDON, Jan. 10—Despite opposition from Russia, supported by the United States, Dr. Paul Henri Spaak, Socialist Foreign Minister of Belgium and leader of the Belgian delegation, today was elected President of the United Nations General Assembly for the current first session here.

Dr. Spaak, supported by Britain, was elected on a secret ballot, victorious by five votes over Trygve Lie, Norwegian Foreign Minister, who was nominated by Russian delegate Andrei Gromyko, Soviet Ambassador to the United States. The vote was 28 for Dr. Spaak, compared to 23 for Mr Lie.

Two sharp raps with a gilded gavel—and the new machinery to keep the peace of the world was under way here this afternoon.

Dramatic Climax

This was the dramatic climax of the brilliant scene in Central Hall, Westminster, as Dr. Zuleta Angel of Colombia called the first meeting of the United Nations Assembly to order and urged the represenatives of 51 nations "to make a genuine and sincere beginning in the application of the San Francisco Charter."

It was a dazzling pageant, with delegates from all around the world, of different colors, shades, and creeds, milling around on the floor of the Assembly hall, renewing acquaintances like a family gathering.

But it was those two raps with the gavel that quickened every-

Continued on Page 11, Column 3

Date for Parley on Korea Passes Without Action

By Neal Stanford
Staff Correspondent of The Christian Science Monitor

WASHINGTON, Jan. 10 — The Moscow-agreed deadline for a meeting of Soviet and American commanders in Korea passed today with no information here that that technical requirement set by the Big Three had been met.

However, passing of the two weeks' period in which such a meeting was ordered caused little public concern here, officials recognizing the problem of communication between the two commanders and recalling previous experiences in establishing negotiations with the Russians.

That the two General, Lieut. Gen. John R. Hodge, commander of American forces in the south, and Lieut. Gen. Christiakoff, commander of Soviet forces in the north, had been in communication on the matter of calling the required conference was acknowledged by State Department officers.

Whether they missed the date set at Moscow by a day or a week was not viewed as important, though an undercurrent of disappointment was apparent that the Generals apparently had not been able to get together by the date set at Moscow, since in the past so much has been placed on meticulous fulfillment of Big Three agreements.

Delay on Instructions?

It was recognized here that the Russian General, in accordance with Soviet custom, had undoubtedly purposefully refrained from taking any step toward meeting his American counterpart until explicit instructions had been received from Moscow. If those instructions had been delayed or had not been adequately explicit, no meeting could take place, it was accepted here.

Liaison with the Soviets in Korea ever since the occupation has been tenuous, although it is true that when General Hodge went into Korea he was for a short time in contact with the Russians. But that dissolved, it is understood, on absence of authority on the Soviet commander's part to contact the Americans.

The Russians have all during the Japanese occupation and even since the Americans moved in maintained a consulate at Seoul, Korea's Capital in the American Zone. There has beeen no similar American listening post in the northern Russian Zone.

The Trusteeship Issue

The Moscow agreement that "a conference of the representatives of the United States and Soviet commands in Korea shall be convened within a period of two weeks" placed the responsibility for arranging that parley on the two Generals. The United States soon after advised General Hodge of his responsibility and reports from Seoul indicate he has made a couple of attempts to contact the Russians.

Two other aspects of the Big Three agreement on Korea are being watched here today. They deal with the implications placed on

Continued on Page 5, Column 1

Rosie the Riveter Joins the Dodo Bird

Staff Writer of The Christian Science Monitor

BOSTON, Jan. 10—Rosie the Riveter is almost as extinct as "the Dodo."

With a unanimity little less than startling, Rosie and her sisters have gone back home to cook meals for their families, bring up their babies, and operate nothing heavier than a vacuum cleaner.

Typical of the situation in the heavy industries of this area is the report from Bethlehem Shipyards. There the number of women production workers has dropped sharply in the past year to a mere 138. Once there were 1,350 women doing heavy work at the Quincy plant.

The same thing is happening in other lines of work. The Boston Elevated Railway bade good-bye to its last remaining woman car conductor on September 28, 1945. At the peak of this kind of employment during the war, the El had on its pay roll 38 women faretakers.

The Town Taxi Company still has four women cabbies operating its taxis and hopes they will stay on. It had eight a few months ago, but half of them gave up their

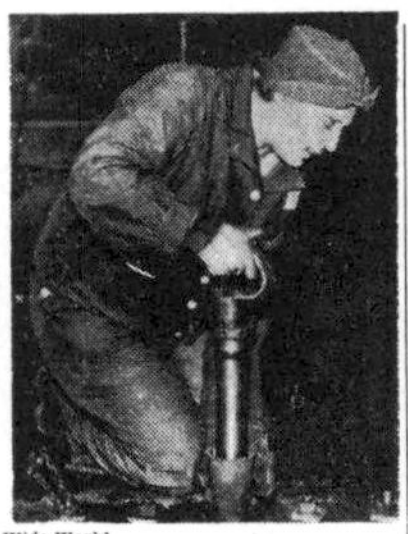

Wide World

Rosie the Riveter

jobs to go back to housekeeping. However, Town Taxi liked them. "They were more reliable than the men," says the company, "and we were more than satisfied with the way the experiment worked out."

The New Haven Railroad has less than 100 women on its rolls at present, where there were 2,918 in September of last year. Most of those remaining are doing clerical work.

At the Readville repair shops of the New Haven there were at one time 130 women employed in heavy jobs. Today there are 87 and the number decreases daily. Women did all sorts of improbable tasks for the New Haven. They worked as boiler-maker helpers, blacksmith helpers, machinist's helpers, engine wipers, painters, drawbridge tenders, tractor operators, and plain laborers

A group that will remain, war or no war, is the car cleaners. The New Haven has always employed women for cleaning the insides of its passenger cars. However, during the war it was found that the women did better than men at cleaning the outsides of the cars as well, so now the New Haven plans to keep them on at this work.

There is only one woman ticket-seller left on the New Haven system and she is located at Fall River. There is also one woman station agent, the one at Millis, Massachusetts.

The Boston & Maine Railroad

Continued on Page 9, Column 3

UNO Delegates Welcomed By King at London Banquet

By Harold Hobson
Staff Correspondent of The Christian Science Monitor

LONDON, Jan. 10—Evening dress and military uniforms predominated at the state banquet in St. James's Palace last night, where chief delegates to the United Nations General Assembly gathered to hear the welcoming address of King George VI.

Last night's banquet was a magnificent sight, visually quite up to prewar standards. Tall candles burned in massive gold candelabra, the tables were decorated with chrysanthemums and orchids in gold vases, and gold knives, forks, and cruets were used. (In aristocratic circles, it is understood that gold plate is more economical than silver, because it is easier to clean).

But if the service was up to 1939 standards, when the previous state banquet was given—in honor of Leon Blum, former Premier of France—the food was not—at least in quantity. The full menu was soup, lobster mayonnaise, roast partridge and vegetables, ice cream, fruit salad, and coffee.

It is claimed that this conforms to the economy regulations governing supplies of food to restaurants, and certainly, beside the notion of what constitutes a wartime banquet at the Kremlin, it was remarkably austere.

The banquet itself reminded one of the comments made by a small girl after a round of Christmas parties during the past few weeks. When asked whether she enjoyed the array of brightly colored cakes with which she had been regaled, she replied thoughtfully, "They look better than they taste."

Though this banquet marks an official return to the ceremonial on great occasions, in private, the Royal Family continues to maintain the quiet standards established during the war.

Princess Elizabeth recently has passed many evenings in London theaters, but always in stalls, never in the royal box. Over Christmas, the King and Queen amused themselves with private

Continued on Page 9, Column 3

UNO Assembly Head

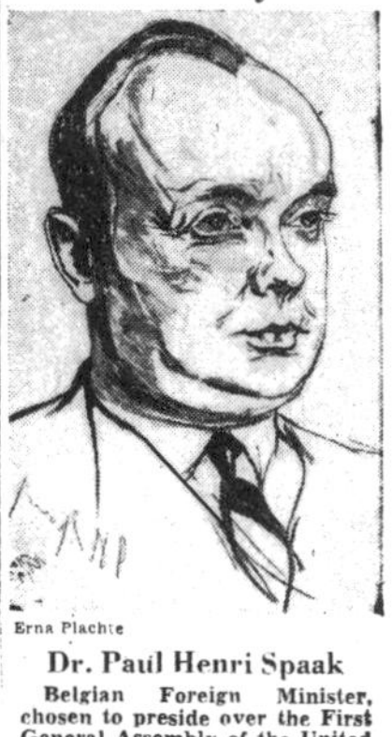

Erna Plachte

Dr. Paul Henri Spaak

Belgian Foreign Minister, chosen to preside over the First General Assembly of the United Nations Organization.

THE CHRISTIAN SCIENCE MONITOR

Registered in U. S. Patent Office

AN INTERNATIONAL DAILY NEWSPAPER

VOLUME 38 NO. 84 | COPYRIGHT 1946 BY THE CHRISTIAN SCIENCE PUBLISHING SOCIETY | BOSTON, WEDNESDAY, MARCH 6, 1946 | • ATLANTIC EDITION | TWO SECTIONS | THREE CENTS Greater Boston Newsstands | FIVE CENTS Elsewhere

President Calls for Spiritual Uplift; Churchill Speech Stirs British Fears

Strike Front Focuses On Rails, Phones

By the Associated Press

Two of the nation's vital industries—railroads and communications—were threatened with strikes today, but there were hopes of settlement or delay of both scheduled walkouts.

As the deadline for the country-wide work stoppage of 250,000 telephone workers—6 a. m. Thursday—drew near, Federal conciliators reported "some progress" as they sought to effect a settlement of a wage dispute between the American Telephone & Telegraph Company and the Federation of Long Lines Telephone Workers.

A walkout of about 300,000 locomotive engineers and trainmen reportedly was set to start March 11 on most major railroads, but there were indications that Railway Labor Act procedure would delay the strike for at least 30 days.

Although officials of the two big railroad brotherhoods in several cities disclosed receipt of calls for the walkout of engineers and trainmen, presidents of the unions at headquarters in Cleveland, Ohio, did not confirm or deny that a strike date had been set. In Chicago, a railroad spokesman said no railroad had been notified officially of the reported walkout.

Statement Expected

A statement by presidents of the two brotherhoods, A. F. Whitney of the trainmen and Alvanley Johnston of the engineers, was expected today.

Belief was expressed by observers that the mediation procedure would be followed after the strike call, with President Truman naming an emergency fact-finding commission which would have 30 days in which to study the strike threat and report recommenda-

Continued on Page 14, Column 5

Talks Deadlocked In Fishing Tie-Up

Complete breakdown of negotiations in the Boston fishing fleet tie-up which began Dec. 27 was announced by Thomas D. Rice, Executive Secretary of the Federated Fishing Boats of New England and New York, Inc. Thirty-five of the major trawlers with crews totaling 600 fishermen are held idle.

Mr. Rice said that the boat owners had negotiated with the union almost continuously for the past three weeks, and that discussions had reached the point where the union demands were too stiff and they would not yield. He declared the union insistence on a 60-40 share, instead of 50-50, of the net returns of the catch too extreme, and said the employers had asked the union to come out with something a little better and it had refused.

Some Editors Turn English Into—English

By Herbert B. Nichols
Natural Science Editor of The Christian Science Monitor

The language of research and engineering is exceedingly precise and sufficient unto itself, so that when one specialist talks to another there can be no doubt about what is meant.

But this same preciseness accounts for the fact that when men of research gather in large conventions and divide up into their small groups of specialties, one natural scientist can hardly understand another should he happen to wander into a session on subject

Continued on Page 2, Column 3

Republicans In Spain Hit Note's Calm

LONDON, March 6 (AP)—The Admiralty states that units of the British Home Fleet would sail from Portland, England, tomorrow for six weeks of maneuvers which will include battle exercises off Gibraltar.

A Foreign Office spokesman, in answer to a question, said the maneuvers were not in any way related to the three-power declaration of the United States, Great Britain, and France calling for the removal of the Franco regime in Spain.

By Arno Dosch-Fleurot
Special Correspondent of The Christian Science Monitor

MADRID, March 6—Republican sentiment inside Spain, so far as it can be sounded out in the disrupted state of the country's opposition parties, found the American-British-French note, published here yesterday, disappointing. It expected something stronger.

The Monarchists saw in it delay, accompanied by constant pressure on Generalissimo Francisco Franco which fits their book. As to General Franco he has heard stronger language directly from both the United States and British Ambassadors.

Due to a curious circumstance, the form in which the note was given to the Spanish press for publication made it stronger than the original. Portions of the note summarized in order to avoid mention of General Franco's name had the effect of eliminating several qualifying phrases which weakened the original.

The Spanish public consequently had a version which indicated more likelihood of action on the part of the three powers than the original note would justify believing.

One of the chief effects as seen from here is to diminish the importance of French unilateral action in closing frontiers to Spain. The possibility of breaking relations was hedged by qualifications which to those who saw the original text puts the possibility of action off to an undefined future.

Violence Ruled Out

The tone of the note indicated the three expected opposition to General Franco to manifest itself within Spain but also washed their hands of any violent form of opposition. In point of action many Spaniards see this as a contradiction, as there is no practical way to upset a government which established itself by revolution except by another revolution.

The Franco regime remains physically strong. It has upward of a million men under arms who are well dressed, trained, armed, fed and lodged. The Civil Guard which with the Security Police keeps a finger on the pulse of the biggest cities to the smallest villages is also under leadership which stemmed from the Civil War. This correspondent never at

Continued on Page 18, Column 3

U. S. Food Leaders Confer

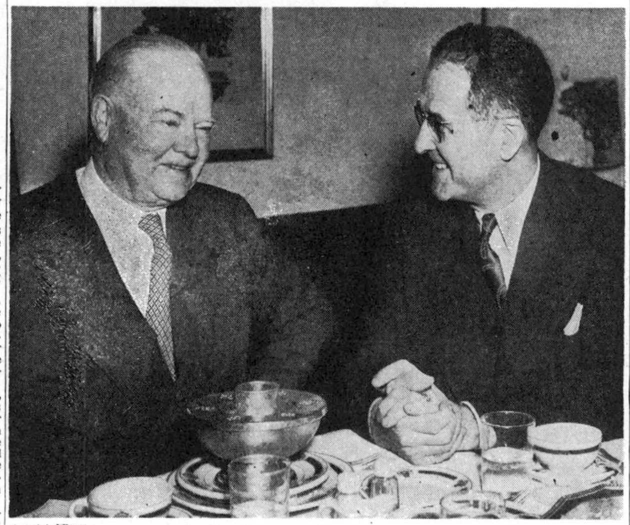

Associated Press

Herbert Hoover, former President (left), discusses over breakfast at his hotel in Washington with Clinton P. Anderson, Secretary of Agriculture, plans for his trip to Europe to survey food needs of that Continent. The former Chief Executive is to leave on the tour next week.

Soviet Problem Now Out in Open

By Saville R. Davis
Chief of the London News Bureau of The Christian Science Monitor

LONDON, March 6—Mr. Winston Churchill's relentless charge that the Russians want "the indefinite expansion of their power and doctrines" is visibly increasing the distress of the British people who already were greatly worried over the Russian problem.

It is not that everyone agrees with the former Prime Minister in detail. First reactions disclose a number of specific criticisms, and Labor leaders in particular feel that his brand of implacable anti-Communism is not a happy spokesman for the Labor Government's more flexible approach to the Soviet problem.

But Mr. Churchill pointed up and sharpened the fears that have been sinking deeper into most everyone's feelings here for the past few months. The effectiveness of what he said lay in the fact that those who would like to contradict him sternly, now feel less able to do so.

Serious Doubts Aroused

The sequence of events leading from Security Council clashes, through Premier Stalin's speech of Feb. 9 to the continuing of Soviet troops in Iran, and the steady procession of anti-Russian headlines and commentary by the press and radio here, have shaken most of the middle grounders and have prepared the way for the most formidable doubts which Mr. Churchill's speech is serving to crystallize.

The result, sooner or later, will be to force a clarification of Foreign Secretary Ernest Bevin's own policy. The difference between the two is that Mr. Churchill has crystallized his thought on the point that Russia's aim is unlimited evil and that nothing but combined Anglo-American force exerted to the utmost will stop Communist totalitarianism.

Mr. Bevin, whatever his apprehensions may be, is keeping his thoughts partly open. For all of Mr. Bevin's plain speaking, he has been refraining more and more from saying those irrevocable things that Mr. Churchill said, which might cause the Russians to abandon any hope of collaborating with the West.

Labor Unions Protest

Labor unions and Left Wing organizations here already are beginning to make a vigorous protest against Mr. Churchill's fatalism. But unless Mr. Bevin should revive the hope of the average

Continued on Page 15, Column 7

Truman Cites Housing Needs

By William H. Stringer
Staff Correspondent of The Christian Science Monitor

COLUMBUS, Ohio, March 6—President Truman in an address prepared for delivery here today called for a spiritual awakening throughout the nation, and simultaneously summoned Americans individually and in their churches to a practical Christianity which should be manifest in:

1. Full support of the Government's housing program, with its goal of 2,700,000 low-cost homes within the next two years, plus the sharing of existing homes with veterans.

2. Sharing food and eating less so that millions of hungry humans overseas shall have "a crust of bread."

3. Rooting out juvenile delinquency by ending war-caused abnormalities in home and community living and by bringing "moral uplift" to the nation's youth.

Leading Speaker

President Truman was the leading speaker on the program of the three-day meeting of the Federal Council of the Churches of Christ here, where approximately 500 Protestant ecclesiastical leaders are gathered to discuss issues regarded as of greater importance than those confronting the Federal Council's meeting immediately following World War I.

Under the chairmanship of Bishop G. Bromley Oxnam, world needs are being reviewed under five headings: World order and reconstruction, community tensions, returning service

Continued on Page 12, Column 4

Truman links religious aims to freedoms of democracy: Page 12.

Light N. E. Effect Seen As Phone Walkout Nears

By Frederick W. Carr
Staff Writer of The Christian Science Monitor

Telephone service within New England appeared today likely to suffer less from the national telephone strike set for tomorrow than any other section of the country. This is due to comparatively few of the telephone employees here going on strike, most of them belonging to other unions which are staying aloof from the walkout.

The effects of New England are expected to be due mostly to what happens to service outside of this region. Local community telephone service will not be interrupted.

Another national strike meantime cast its shadow on New England when the Brotherhood of Railroad Engineers set strike schedules for March 11 on the Boston & Albany and for March 12 on the Boston & Maine, New Haven, and Maine Central Railroads. Between 4,000 and 5,000 engineers and trainmen are involved. Strike orders call for the handling of all milk and troop movements but nothing else.

However, there seemed to be much more possibility of the railroad strike being averted than the telephone tieup. Both company and union officials said today they felt the telephone strike very likely.

The one cheerful spot in the local labor situation was found in the return to work today of 700 marine warehouse employees and 60 lumber handlers. Their three-week stoppage was ended by mutual agreement to arbitrate.

Beside the movement of merchandise and food in and out of 21

Continued on Page 2, Column 4

Wheat Saving Plans Rushed To Aid Europe

By Josephine Ripley
Staff Correspondent of The Christian Science Monitor

WASHINGTON, March 6 — America's food-saving program is off to a flying start in the 120-day race against famine abroad.

Within the next four or five weeks, it is expected that foods actually saved here will be arriving in Europe.

By that time Herbert Hoover, former President, Chairman of President Truman's Famine Emergency Committee, will be overseas supervising the distribution of these supplies and speeding their delivery to the neediest areas.

But for some, even this will not be enough. There just isn't sufficient to go all the way around. Starvation is forecast to take place in some countries.

That is the sad admission of Clinton P. Anderson, Secretary of Agriculture. To prevent this, the United States should send abroad 20,000,000 tons of wheat before June.

There are only 12,000,000 tons

Continued on Page 9, Column 5

Army Drills Germans In U. S. Democracy

By the Associated Press

Washington, March 6

The Army disclosed today that hand-picked prisoners of war are given a six-day course in the principles of democracy and sent back to Germany or Austria as free men.

Some 16,000 prisoners have received the instruction. They will be discharged as civilians when they reach their homeland.

Ceylon Elbows British Trade In New Power

By Ronald Stead
Staff Correspondent of The Christian Science Monitor

COLOMBO, Ceylon, Delayed.—British trading interests are diminishing numerically on this island off the southern extremity of India, as the native administration gains increased governmental power.

I came through on the way to

Continued on Page 15, Column 4

Churchill And Truman Swap Yarns

By a Staff Correspondent of The Christian Science Monitor

ABOARD TRUMAN-CHURCHILL SPECIAL TRAIN, March 6—What do a former Prime Minister and a President talk about at dinner?

Well, on good authority, conversation within the Truman-Churchill dinner party in the President's private car hasn't risen above the anecdotal levels during some meals. But even the anecdotes are famous.

For instance: Winston Churchill was deploring the Irish neutrality during the war and remarking how useful south Irish ports would have been in the submarine warfare. He was reminded, he told President Truman, of the story of two Irishmen who managed to enlist in Great Britain and fly for the RAF.

Clinches His Argument

It seems the Irishmen were having an intense argument over Eamon de Valera, Eire Premier, as their bomber began to encounter heavy flak in its flight over Berlin. As they separated, each to his machine gun or bombardier post, the defender of Mr. de Valera hurled a parting shot at his comrade: "At least ye must admit, Patrick," he shouted, "that de Valera has kept us Irishmen out of the miserable war."

With some relish Mr. Churchill also told Mr. Truman how the other day the Sons of the American Revolution had invited him to become a member. His mother, being an American of early and fighting stock, he was eminently qualified. However, he concluded, since his father was a Britisher and he had forbears on both sides, he felt he should adopt a strictly "unbiased attitude" and did not join.

It is the correspondents' consen-

Continued on Page 14, Column 6

Anglo-U. S. Military Link Advocated by Churchill

By William H. Stringer
Staff Correspondent of The Christian Science Monitor

FULTON, Mo., March 6—Winston Churchill, British wartime Prime Minister, struck while the iron was hot in vigorously espousing March 5 a virtual military federation between the United States and the British Commonwealth of Nations.

At a moment when demands are increasing for a vigorous stand against limitless Soviet expansion, Mr. Churchill referring directly to Russia from the platform at Westminster College here, made the kind of forthright speech that some Americans have wished to hear from their own officials.

By urging, further, that the United States, Great Britain, and Canada retain the secret of the atomic bomb in the present lack of world harmony, Mr. Churchill left his remarks open to the interpretation that he was espousing the Anglo-Canadian-American-Commonwealth amalgamations as a kind of superguardian of the peace.

Britain's wartime chief cried out with all his eloquence against appeasement of Russia. He had been preparing his speech in days when sentiment against further concessions was crystallizing in speeches by Secretary of State James F. Byrnes, Senator Arthur H. Vandenberg, and Britain's Foreign Minister Ernest Bevin. But Mr. Churchill, who always had spoken his mind vigorously to Generalissimo Stalin, went further than the rest in one of the strongest protests against unilateral Russian action to date.

His remedy, virtual Anglo-American alliance, would, in a major degree, end the sometimes-

Continued on Page 14, Column 7

Text of Churchill speech: First page, second section.

STATE OF THE NATION

By ROSCOE DRUMMOND
Chief of the Washington Bureau of The Christian Science Monitor

WASHINGTON

The proposed $3,750,000,000 loan to Great Britain, public hearings on which began this week, will have a rough time in Congress. There is division in both parties on this issue. Senator Robert A. Taft (R) of Ohio, chairman of the minority steering committee, has indicated that the Republicans will put off a decision for some weeks, and an Administration spokesman frankly has said that the Democratic congressmen facing election this fall are the most uncertain in their support of the loan.

All of this suggests that the Administration's task is to demonstrate not only to Congress but to the country that a line of credit of this size is conceived in the common interest of both the United States and Britain, and that both countries will suffer if it is defeated and both countries will gain if it is approved. Here are some of the facts:

Its Size— The loan will add approximately 1 per cent to the public debt of the United States. It will be an amount equal to what we spent in less than 16 days of war.

Its Purposes—The essential economic purposes of the credit are: (1) to facilitate British purchases of goods and services in the United States; (2) to help restore the economy of our best customer, whose finances were more shattered by the common war than those of any nation in the world; (3) to enable Britain to join with the United States and other countries in reopening the channels of world trade.

Its Consequences - The American negotiators of the loan are convinced that, far from imperiling the admittedly large national debt of the United States, it will help create conditions by which it can be cut down more rapidly. Senator Warren R. Austin (R) of Vermont, for example, who is far from being a deficit spender, takes the position that the proposed credit will promote employment and production, so that the Federal debt can be retired more steadily, and will help restore the world to a sound peacetime economy, which will be a maximum boon to the United States. He sees the loan as an investment in economic stability.

Its Long-Range Significance—The simple question which needs to be asked and answered wisely is: Will America's interests and America's ideals be served by a weak and depleted or by a virile and dynamic Britain? Twice in one generation Britain has held the outposts against aggression while the United States and the Western Hemisphere have been able to prepare their defenses. Neither has fought each other's war. Each has fought side by side against the common threat to their common freedom.

Each has stood because they have stood together; each has stood because in these two terrible perils they have united their battle plan. The struggle for peace and freedom has not been won; it is a perpetual struggle, and the economic collaboration which the proposed loan would bring into being is part of that united battle plan which will help each to survive the buffets which still are ahead.

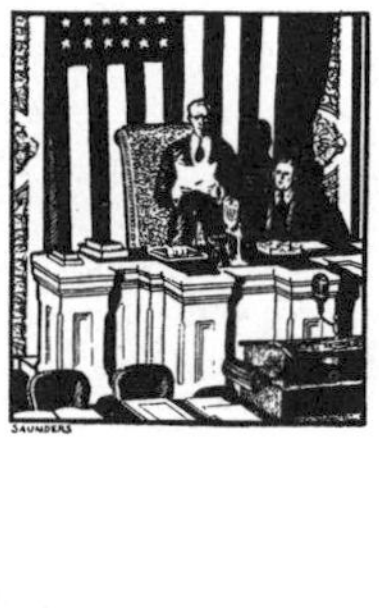

The United States and Britain over the years have been the world's major forces for political freedom and human rights — witness the Philippines; witness the evolution of the British colonies into independent, self-governing dominions, with India soon to follow. The cause of political freedom and human rights the world over is going to need a strong Britain and a strong America as it never has before, not to coerce any nation but to preserve the freedoms for which they stand. In this cause, Britain's strength is America's strength, and America's strength is Britain's strength.

Its Alternatives — Britain needs this assistance to help finance its transition from war to peace, and if it is not available, then Britain will be forced to resort to trade and financial practices—barter and a closed Commonwealth economy—which will be contrary to the best interests of the United States. It is these circumstances which set the British loan apart and which enabled President Truman to assure Congress last week that it would not be a precedent for other loans.

There is good reason to believe that the United States can afford this loan much better than it can afford the danger of an economic world divided against itself.

The decision which Congress shortly will be called upon to make goes to the very heart of whether America is to give lip service to world co-operation or intends to practice it; for economic collaboration and political collaboration must go hand in hand or neither will succeed.

New Japanese Constitution Bars War and Armed Forces

TOKYO, March 6 (AP)—A new Japanese Constitution renouncing war for all time and prohibiting the maintenance of armed forces was announced today.

Gen. Douglas MacArthur, reporting that it was drafted with his full approval, emphasized that "the foremost of its provisions . . . that abolishing war as a sovereign right of the nation . . . renders (Japan's) future security and very survival subject to the good faith and justice of the peace-loving peoples of the world."

Emperor Hirohito, who will be reduced from "a sacred and inviolable" monarch to a symbol of state with very limited formal functions, issued a special rescript stating:

"It is my desire that the Constitution of our Empire be revised drastically upon the basis of the general will of the people and the principle of respect for the fundamental human rights.

"I command hereby the competent authorities of my Government to put forth in conformity with my wish their best efforts

Continued on Page 18, Column 1

The Christian Science Monitor Index

Wednesday, March 6, 1946

Weather Predictions

Fair

Complete Weather Predictions For New England on Page 2.

King Urges National 40-Mile Speed Limit for a Year

The World's Day
Reg. U.S. Pat. Off.

Boston: Speed Curb Asked Till Tires Are Safe

A national 40-mile speed limit plan for one year "until four good tires are on all our cars," is proposed by Rudolph F. King, Massachusetts Registrar of Motor Vehicles. [Page 2.]

Four pairs of shoes this year for every man, woman, and child in the country is the prediction by Maxwell Field, Executive Vice-President of the New England Shoe and Leather Association, who estimates 1946 output at 550,000,000 pairs. [Page 2.]

Thousands of New Englanders are getting butter these days—by churning their own. Local stores report rapidly mounting sales of heavy cream, and housewives tell how it's done. [Page 4.]

Three hundredth anniversary of application to the General Court of Massachusetts for the first American patent, by a Lynn ironworker for "engins to go by water," was noted by the National Patent Council. [Page 2.]

Far East: Censorship Ended Throughout China

Abolition of censorship throughout China was announced today by K. C. Wu, Chungking Minister of Information.

Shipment of 100,000 copies of the Bible, printed in Japanese, first consignment of 300,000 donated by the American Bible Society, has arrived in Tokyo by plane.

Washington: Ickes Reports Notes in Bank Vault

Harold L. Ickes told the Senate Naval Affairs Committee his memoranda on conversations with Edwin W. Pauley are locked in a bank vault and that because he did not receive word until 6:45 p. m. yesterday he was to testify, he was unable today to produce his notes for examination.

The Hyde Park home of Franklin D. Roosevelt will be formally dedicated as a national historic site April 12. Acting Secretary of the Interior Oscar L. Chapman said President Truman will attend the ceremonies and deliver the principal address. Mrs. Eleanor Roosevelt also will speak.

A request for $2,051,000,000 to continue Government subsidies on food and other materials during the fiscal year beginning July 1 was asked of the House Banking Committee by James F. Brownlee, deputy to Economic Stabilization Director Chester Bowles.

In Europe: Swiss-Norwegian Treaty Concluded

A Swiss-Norwegian commercial treaty has been concluded under which Switzerland would grant Norway a credit of about $1,160,000 to import vital goods needed for Norwegian reconstruction, a Bern report said.

Middle East: More Palestine Terrorists Caught

An additional 19 suspected terrorists have been rounded up by Jerusalem police, bringing the total of arrests during the past two days to 47, a dispatch from Palestine said.

IT'S BACK . . . ★

Your complete **Movie Guide** . . . this **Thursday** and every **Thursday** in **The Christian Science Monitor.** It lists some 200 current films . . . describes them briefly . . . classifies them for mature people . . . young people . . . children.

★

THE CHRISTIAN SCIENCE MONITOR

Registered in U. S. Patent Office

AN INTERNATIONAL DAILY NEWSPAPER

VOLUME 38 NO. 260 | COPYRIGHT 1946 BY THE CHRISTIAN SCIENCE PUBLISHING SOCIETY | BOSTON, TUESDAY, OCTOBER 1, 1946 | **—ATLANTIC EDITION | TWO SECTIONS | FIVE CENTS A COPY

Göring, Ribbentrop Sentenced to Hang; Hess Gets Life Term, Dönitz 10 Years

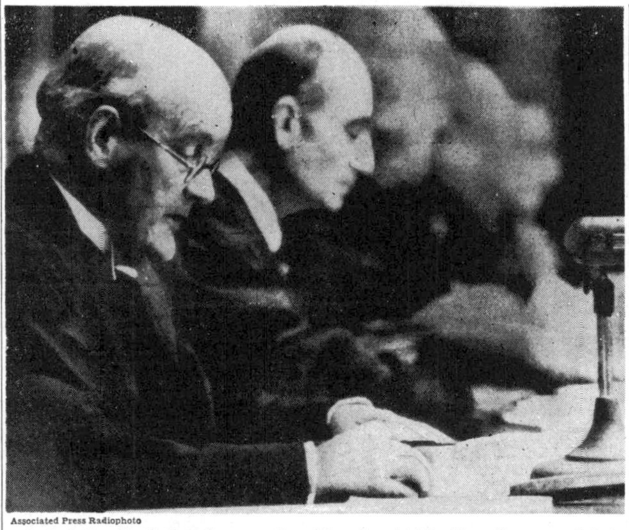

Associated Press Radiophoto

Lord Justice Sir Geoffrey Lawrence (foreground) reads verdict of four-power International Military Tribunal at trial of 21 Nazi leaders who have been tried for 10 months as war criminals. Justice Francis Biddle, United States judge at the trial, sits at right.

Russians Dissent On 3 Acquittals

By J. Emlyn Williams
Staff Correspondent of The Christian Science Monitor

NUREMBERG, Germany, Oct. 1 — Capital sentences were today decreed for 12 Nazi leaders here. Seven others received prison terms. Three—Hjalmar Schacht, Franz von Papen, and Hans Fritzche—were acquitted.

Of the military and naval leaders, Field Marshal Wilhelm Keitel and Col. Gen. Alfred Jodl were sentenced to be hanged. Grand Admiral Karl Dönitz, who surrendered Germany to the Allies, was sentenced to 10 years' imprisonment; Grand Admiral Erich Raeder to a life term.

The verdicts were not unanimous. After sentencing Hermann Göring, Joachim von Ribbentrop, Alfred Rosenberg, and nine others to be hanged, the International War Crimes Tribunal stated that Russia had dissented from the three acquittals.

The Soviet Judge, Maj. Gen. I. T. Nikitchenko, declared that Rudolf Hess should have been sentenced to hanging instead of being awarded a life sentence. He also disagreed with the decision exonerating the German General Staff and High Command.

Jackson Regrets Acquittal

United States Justice Robert H. Jackson expressed regret at the acquittals and the freeing of the General Staff from culpability.

The Tribunal broke up at 2:46 this afternoon on the 219th day of the 10-month trial—longest in judicial history.

Execution of those under sentence to the extreme penalty is to take place in the jail of the Nuremberg Palace of Justice. Those who have received prison terms will be confined in a four-power jail in Berlin.

Lord Justice Lawrence read the sentences in a calm, impassive voice, using the same formula to announce each of the sentences as each of the defendants filed into court at two- or three-minute intervals to hear his sentence.

There was complete silence in the court during the delivery of the judgments.

The Case for Schacht

Though almost from the beginning it was considered improbable that Dr. Schacht, former Reichsbank President, would be condemned to capital punishment, it also was not imagined that he would be immediately discharged.

The Tribunal also found that though Dr. Schacht was a central figure in Germany's rearmament and that steps he took were responsible for Nazi Germany's rapid rise as a military power, nevertheless "rearmament of itself is not criminal under the Charter," for to be a crime against peace under Article 6 of the Charter, "it must be shown that Schacht carried out this rearmament as part of the Nazi plans to wage aggressive war."

Not in 'Inner Circle'

Dr. Schacht's "participation in the occupation of Austria and the Sudetenland [neither of which is charged as an aggressive war] was on such a limited basis that it does not amount to participation in the common plan charged in Count 1. [Dr. Schacht actually was charged on only two counts.] He was clearly not one of the inner circle around Hitler which was most closely involved with this common plan," the verdict stated.

The Austrian Ministry of Justice announced that it would ask for extradition of Franz von Papen and Baldur von Schirach, Hitler's former Youth leader and Governor of Austria, for trial in Austria. The latter has been sentenced to 20 years' imprisonment at Nuremberg.

'Little Man' Acquitted

As for Hans Fritzche, it has been felt that he was too small a man to be indicted at this trial and his acquittal had been expected.

Some surprise was expressed in circles here concerning the pronouncement of guilt on all counts against Consantin von Neurath, but the Tribunal's statement of mitigation because of certain leniency while Protector in Bohemia and Moravia allows him to escape the supreme penalty.

Hermann Göring, declared guilty on all counts, the Tribunal maintained, never opposed Hitler on ideological or legal grounds.

"Nothing is to be said in mitigation. . . . His own admissions are more than sufficiently wide to be conclusive of his guilt. His guilt is unique in its enormity. The record disclosed no excuses for this man," declared the Tribunal.

'Von Ribbentrop Served'

Nor does von Ribbentrop fare much better in the Tribunal's judgment. "It was because Hitler's policy and plans coincided with his own ideas that von Ribbentrop served him so willingly to the end."

As for Rudolf Hess, the Tribunal rejected any extenuation on health ground. "That Hess acts in an abnormal manner, suffers from loss of memory, and has mentally deteriorated during this trial may be true. But there is nothing to show that he does not realize the nature of the charges against him or is incapable of defending himself," the court said.

Nuremberg verdict analyzes top Nazis' crimes: First Page, Second Section.

The Sentences

Special to The Christian Science Monitor

Nuremberg, Germany
Oct. 1

These International Military Tribunal sentences:

Hermann Göring, Reichsmarshal and Hitler's designated successor: Sentenced to be hanged. Convicted of conspiracy, crimes against the peace, namely: Planning, preparing, initiating, or waging aggressive war; war crimes, namely: Violations of the laws or customs of war; and crimes against humanity, namely: Murder, extermination, enslavement, deportation of civilians, before or during the war; or persecutions, political, racial, or religious.

Rudolf Hess, Deputy Führer: Life imprisonment for conspiracy and crimes against the peace. Acquitted of crimes of war and against humanity.

Martin Bormann, Hitler's Deputy: Execution in absentia for war crimes and crimes against humanity. Acquitted of conspiracy.

Joachim von Ribbentrop, Nazi Foreign Minister: To be hanged for conspiracy, crimes against the peace, war crimes, and crimes against humanity.

Wilhelm Keitel, Chief of Reichswehr: To be hanged for conspiracy, crimes against the peace, war crimes, and crimes against humanity.

Ernst Kaltenbrunner, Chief of the Gestapo: To be hanged for war crimes and crimes against humanity. Acquitted of conspiracy.

Hans Frank, Governor of Poland: To be hanged for war crimes and crimes against humanity. Freed of conspiracy.

Alfred Rosenberg, Editor of Hitler's Völkische Beobachter, and Nazi Commissioner in the East; To be hanged for conspiracy, crimes against the peace, war crimes, and crimes against humanity.

Julius Streicher, anti-Jewish propagandist and editor of Der Stürmer: To be hanged for crimes against humanity. Acquitted of conspiracy.

Wilhelm Frick, Interior Minister: To hang for crimes against the peace, war crimes, and crimes against humanity. Acquitted of conspiracy.

Walther Funk, Nazi Minister of Economics: Life imprisonment for crimes against the peace, war crimes, and crimes against humanity. Acquitted of conspiracy.

Karl Dönitz, Grand Admiral: Ten years' imprisonment for crimes against the peace and war crimes. Acquitted of conspiracy.

Baldur von Schirach, Hitler Youth Leader: Twenty years for crimes against humanity. Acquitted of conspiracy.

Hjalmar Schacht, Chief of the Reichsbank: Acquitted as not guilty of conspiracy or of crimes against the peace.

Erich Raeder, Navy Commander in Chief: Life imprisonment for conspiracy and crimes against the peace and war crimes.

Fritz Sauckel, Slave Labor Commissioner: To be hanged for war crimes and crimes against humanity. Acquitted of conspiracy.

Franz von Papen, onetime Chancellor of Germany: Acquitted as not guilty of conspiracy or of crimes against the peace.

Alfred Jodl, Reichswehr Chief: To be hanged for conspiracy, crimes against the peace, war crimes, and crimes against humanity.

Arthur Seyss-Inquart, Nazi Governor in Holland: To be hanged for crimes against the peace, war crimes, and crimes against humanity.

Albert Speer, Nazi Munitions Minister: Twenty years' imprisonment for war crimes and crimes against humanity. Acquitted of conspiracy and crimes against the peace.

Hans Fritszche, Deputy Propaganda Minister and Radio Director: Acquitted of conspiracy or of war crimes and crimes against humanity.

Constantin von Neurath, "Protector" of Bohemia-Moravia: Fifteen years' imprisonment for conspiracy, crimes against the peace, war crimes, and crimes against humanity.

Turtle Hop Accents Atom Peril

By Richard L. Strout
Staff Correspondent of The Christian Science Monitor

WASHINGTON, Oct. 1—Carrying a crew of four, a baby kangaroo, and the possibility of extending atomic bombing half way round the earth, the big United States Navy patrol bomber Truculent Turtle set a new long-distance flight mark today with a nonstop 11,237-mile flight.

Never had man flown so far in one trip: 55 hours of continuous flying, from Australia to two thirds across America, to Columbus, Ohio.

Washington military and commercial officials watched the flight with intense interest. Either for peace or war man's conquest of distance is speeding up.

The two-motored plane took off from Pearce, near Perth in western Australia, at 5:10 a. m. eastern standard time on Sept. 29. Its speed averaged well over 200 miles an hour in the initial part of its journey.

Three Stories High

Dimensions of the huge bomber can be gauged from the fact that it rises to the height of a three-story building.

The circumference of the earth at the equator is just under 25,000 miles.

Thus, a year after ending World War II, man has learned to make nonstop flights approximately halfway around the world.

The trip was also a test of the ability of human beings to stand pilot fatigue. A crew of only four men to pilot the massive craft meant almost continuous duty, and a maximum of individual responsibility.

Wives of the crew had assembled here in Washington on the possibility that the bomber would reach the capital. There was even some talk of its proceeding on to Bermuda, the theoretical range of the plane being 13,000 miles. For 14 hours over the Pacific, as the craft approached North America, there was radio silence. This was broken as contact was first established at the Alameda naval air station in California.

Heavy Weather

Later, the Turtle radioed from Cheyenne, Wyo., that it was encountering heavy weather. It was this that limited continuance of the flight from an even more spectacular distance.

Aside from the romantic adventure of the great flight which kept its haggard crew between stars and the Pacific, and then over the North American land mass for nearly two days, the flight symbolized the shrinking of the earth, and the awful potentialities for good or ill that lie in the bringing together of the far corners of the globe.

In five or 10 years, it is being forecast here, a plane will be built that will girdle the earth.

The extension of the flying radius cannot be separated from man's thoughts of the atomic bomb.

The flying Turtle was stripped of all nonessential equipment even of long-distance radio equipment to make room for its enormous load of gasoline—25 tons. Its calculated range, 13,000 miles, is a primary consideration in patrol planes.

Shift in Strategy

It was so heavy at take-off that it required jet-propulsion devices to get it into the air.

Measured from a starting point at New York, the following distances give an approximation of the scope of the new plane—3,500 miles to London; 5,000 to Honolulu; 7,800 to Bombay; 8,500 to Tokyo.

Carrying such a load of gasoline, the Turtle could not have carried bombs. But bigger and faster planes mean that in a short time, no area on earth theoretically will be free from such assault.

This is the situation which confronts military strategists. Here in Washington it was announced that work on all unimportant naval bases had been reduced to a minimum and work concentrated on a few bases of major importance; Pearl Harbor, Guam-Saipan and Kodiak, particularly.

In mankind's groping for peace, the flight of the Truculent Turtle, with the human element always underlined by the carrying of the pet baby kangaroo as mascot, will be studied carefully.

Picture showing route of Truculent Turtle: Page 3.

Navy Plane Completes 11,237-Mile Flight

By the Associated Press

Columbus, Ohio, Oct. 1

The Truculent Turtle, Navy patrol bomber, landed at Port Columbus at 12:28 p. m. (E. S. T.) today, completing a record-breaking nonstop flight of 11,237 miles from Perth, Australia. The unofficial elapsed time was 55 hours and 18 minutes.

The twin-engined Lockheed Neptune P-2V, carrying a crew of four men and a baby kangaroo, thereby exceeded by 3,321 miles the nonstop mark of 7,916 miles set last November by the Army's B-29 Dream Boat.

Allied Council to Execute Doomed Nazis

By a Staff Correspondent of The Christian Science Monitor

NUREMBERG, Germany, Oct. 1—The International Military Tribunal having completed its work with sentences on 22 Nazi leaders here, it will devolve upon the Allied Control Council, representing the United States, Britain, Russia and France, to impose the sentences.

There was a general impression among American observers that any of the three acquitted Nazi leaders returning to the United States zone of occupation probably would be tried by the Germans under the denazification law in the zone.

Since Hjalmar Schacht and Franz von Papen have property in more than one zone, it was uncertain to which they might return. The general belief was that Hans Fritzche, the third one to be acquitted, might be returned to the Russians, since they had arrested him in Berlin and turned him over to Nuremberg for trial.

Appeals Planned

The defendants have four days in which to appeal to the Allied Control Council, which is their last court of appeal. The executions are expected to take place Oct. 16 unless the Council grants an appeal for clemency. All defense attorneys had announced they would appeal in the event of capital sentence against their clients.

One by one the Nazi leaders were marshed into court to hear their fate. Göring, minus uniform and medals, strode in between two stalwart military policemen in a shabby gray suit, and heard Justice Lawrence's cold legal voice announce the sentence in the glare of kleig lights.

Von Ribbentrop was helped out of the room by police after hearing the sentence. The military and naval officers, Keitel, Jodl, Rader, and Dönitz, all remained completely impassive. The lightness of the sentence on the last-named (10 years) surprised many spectators.

Von Ribbentrop was described by the court as the willing tool of Hitler, adding "it was because Hitler's policies and plans coincided with his own ideas that Ribbentrop served him so willingly to the end."

Pleas Rejected

The Court described as "untrue" von Ribbentrop's statement that Hitler made all the important decisions.

The Tribunal convicted Keitel in a 1,000-word document. It brushed aside the Marshal's defense of "superior orders" saying "there is nothing in mitigation where crimes as shocking and extensive have been committed consciously, ruthlessly, and circumstances were listed in connection with charges against Admiral Dönitz, the court saying that in view of all the circumstances of naval warfare, he could not be held guilty for his conduct of submarine warfare.

The Tribunal maintained that "any signifiicant participation in the affairs of the Nazi Party or Government is evidence of a participiation in a conspiracy that is in itself criminal." It is further apparent that the Nazis had planned to wage wars as early as Nov. 5, 1937 (date of conference in the Reich Chancellery when Hitler described to the Party's leading representatives his warlike ideas). At the same time, however, "evidence establishes with certainty the existence of many separate plans rather than a single conspiracy embracing them all."

Inside Reading:

Tuesday, October 1, 1946

Anderson Shuts Lid On Price Decontrol Of Meat in October

By Josephine Ripley
Staff Correspondent of The Christian Science Monitor

WASHINGTON, Oct. 1—Meat continues to be in the news rather than on the table.

Cattle, hogs, and sheep took a headline bow today—on the Secretary of Agriculture's short supply list. This constitutes a virtual "no" on price decontrol of meat for another month, at least.

Under the present price control law, Secretary of Agriculture Clinton P. Anderson is required to designate each month all agricultural commodities in short supply. Any commodities dropped from that list are decontrolled automatically.

In New Mexico, where he is vacationing, the Secretary explained that while the supply of cattle on the range may be adequate and "on many ranges more than adequate," he must consider as "supply" only meat itself—pork and mutton and beef.

Indignation Mounting

These, according to receipts at Chicago and Kansas City, are "in short supply," he said.

Speaking to a group of cattle growers in his home State, the Secretary appealed directly for "co-operation in trying to bring meat back to the American public in lawful trade at legitimate prices."

In other sections of the country, there is evidence that tempers and patience are growing short. Official "posses" are already on the meat hunt to uncover any hidden stores that may be deliberately withheld from the market in a "conspiracy against the public."

Those are the words of New York's Mayor William O'Dwyer, who has followed the lead of Massachusetts' Governor Maurice J. Tobin in launching an official inventory of local meat supplies.

Governor Tobin's discovery of 6,000,000 pounds of meat in a Boston plant brings up the possibility of legal action against those found to be withholding meat depriving hospitals, public institutions, and private individuals of available supplies.

Moves Closely Watched

All this indicates a rapidly mounting public resentment against what is suspected as an unnecessarily acute shortage of meat. It is believed that it may have a salutary effect on the situation. At any rate, it is a development which authorities here are watching with close interest.

It is hoped that this pressure of public indignation, plus the firm stand of the President against decontrol, together with Mr. Anderson's firm shake of the head, will convince the meat industry that agitation for decontrol is useless at this time.

This, it is argued, should convince cattle growers that nothing is to be gained by any withholding of livestock and encourage any holding stocks of meats in storage to dispose of these at current ceiling prices.

Such a movement already is in evidence, according to Roy L. Thompson, Chairman of the Price Decontrol Board. He told a group of newsupaperwomen yesterday that there is an upward trend in livestock receipts and that he believes that trend will continue.

He anticipates "a little better situation before too many weeks," but warns that meat is going to be short, in relation to demand, for the next 12 months.

The Decontrol Board head disclosed that Congress has been appealing to the Board to disregard the laws which Congress itself has laid down with respect to price control on meat.

Mr. Thompson said that the Board has been receiving wires from congressmen calling the Board "bullheaded" for not taking controls off of meat, and insisting that that be done.

Congressional Protest

"You would expect these people to know," he commented, "what they had placed in our lap." According to the laws which Congress made, and under which it decreed that the Decontrol Board should operate, price control may not be removed from meat except under certain conditions — and one of those conditions is an adequate supply.

These letters and telegrams protesting action by the Board have come from Democratic and Republican congressmen alike, Mr. Thompson stated.

When asked what he considered the causes of the meat shortages were, Mr. Thompson replied that, as far as he had been able to determine it stemmed from three main causes:

1. The rush of meat into deep freeze lockers during the "price holiday."

2. Quantity storage in the private lockers of public eating houses.

3. The flooding of cattle to market during the "price holiday," some of which were ready for market and some not.

Truman Step Hinted

WASHINGTON, Oct. 1 (AP)—Representative Brent Spence (D) of Kentucky said he "gathered the impression" at a conference with President Truman today that the Government may "take remedial action" to ease the meat shortage.

Mr. Spence, Chairman of the House Banking Committee, told reporters after the White House conference that he was "not at liberty to discuss" what the action may be.

Mr. Spence said he had talked to Mr. Truman aboue the Office of Price Administration and the "dissatisfaction of the people" about it.

U. S. Efforts Fail to Halt Ship Strike

By a Staff Correspondent of The Christian Science Monitor

WASHINGTON, Oct. 1—Failure of Labor Department conferences here to bring about a contract agreement today brought on the second great maritime strike within a month.

Thus the Government's strenuous efforts to confine the strike to the West Coast fell apart, even as Labor Department conciliators frantically tried to avert the new walkout right to the last.

The talks between East Coast and Gulf ship operators and the unions broke up with no contract agreement in sight. The contracts of the two unions involved expired last midnight and today's efforts were devoted to saving a situation that already deteriorated badly.

Shipping Setback

The two unions involved are the C. I. O. Marine Engineers Beneficial Association and the A. F. of L. Masters, Mates and Pilots.

This second major shipping tie-up came so quickly on the heels of the 17-day strike of seamen and other unlicensed merchant marine personnel early in September that shipping, that had begun to get back into swing, was thrown for a disastrous loss.

Meanwhile, the Associated Press reported, several men were injured in Hollywood, Calif., in a clash between police and sheriff's deputies and parading pickets at Metro-Goldwyn-Mayer studio, where two unions are involved in a jurisdictional dispute. A call was issued for police reserves and ambulances after officers used night sticks to force back a parade of strike sympathizers, who, the police said, ignored a court injunction against mass picketing.

Pittsburgh Parley

Meanwhile, Federal conciliators planned to resume negotiations with union-management officials in an attempt to end the eight-day power strike in Pittsburgh.

The first joint session of negotiators in the strike ended after two hours of talks early today with no apparent break in the deadlock which developed Sept. 28. At that time, the company withdrew an offer of a 5 per cent wage raise after it had been flatly rejected by the union membership. The union seeks a 20 per cent boost, which would increase average base pay from $1.18 to $1.41.

The strike has closed most of Pittsburgh's downtown businesses and offices, slowed down industrial production and, indirectly, halted all streetcar and bus traffic because operators refuse to cross picket lines.

In addition, about 2,000 A. F. of L. employees of Pittsburgh's eight major hotels walked out at midnight, when their two-year contract expired.

Chief matter of dispute in discussions of a new contract was the union's demand for a 20 per cent wage raise.

State of the Nation

By ROSCOE DRUMMOND
Chief of the Washington Bureau of The Christian Science Monitor

WASHINGTON

The issue of placing the Pacific islands wrested from Japan under American-United Nations trusteeship will not be settled for some little time.

The factors which are working for delay are greater than those which are working for an early decision. Although the United States is working on its trusteeship proposals, there is little evidence that they will be ready for the next meeting of the U. N. General Assembly. There are several reasons.

One is that there is no solid agreement yet between the State Department and the Navy on what, if any, jurisdiction should be offered to the United Nations over the Pacific islands which the Navy expects to administer. Or whether the former Japanese mandates—the Marshalls, Carolines, and Marianas—and the other Japanese islands, like Okinawa and Iwo Jima, should be brought under the same kind of trusteeship system or treated differently.

The fact is that while the Navy agreed to the theoretical terms of abstract trusteeship in the United Nations Charter, it never has really gone along with the State Department on any degree of actual U. N. trusteeship which would give it less than exclusive, unquestioned strategic control. This issue within the Administration has not been resolved.

The second reason the Pacific trusteeships are not likely to be settled quickly is that the former Japanese islands which the United States expects to control have not been legally placed in American hands. Therefore, the United States Government is not in a position to propose a trusteeship agreement with the United Nations over former enemy territory which has not been ceded to it.

While President Truman has said that the United States will obtain the Japanese Pacific islands by agreement, that is easier and more quickly said than done. What islands? All of the ex-enemy islands, including Okinawa? By agreement with whom? By agreement, of course, with the nations which will write the Japanese peace settlement: in the first instance, the Big Five—the United States, France, Britain, China, and Russia.

Remember the veto? It applies to the decisions of the Big Five Foreign Ministers on the peace treaties as well as to the decisions of the Security Council. Obviously, the United States is not going to toss the Pacific islands to another power. Obviously, the United States will continue to sit in these islands if agreement cannot be reached on their disposition. But the legal basis for an American-United Nations trusteeship for them can be laid only within the terms of the future Japanese peace settlement. Looking at Paris, one can believe a Japanese peace treaty won't be ready very soon.

Finally, there is reason to believe that President Truman would like to see at least the beginning of a stronger, less veto-ridden United Nations before putting the Pacific islands very largely into its cumbersome machinery. Collective security still is a hope, not a reality, and to entrust a large degree of the nation's security to the U. N. will be the fruitage of a stronger U. N. The United States is proposing to strengthen the United Nations, not on its fringes but at its center, and when the United Nations is ready to control atomic energy, it will show that it is ready to control such things as the common defense of the Pacific.

The United States already has before it the proposals of three of the Allies—New Zealand, Australia, and Great Britain—for converting some of their mandated territories into United Nations trusteeships, and none of them contemplates permitting U. N. jurisdiction over the military defense of the trust territories.

Furthermore, Russia, in addition to its vast land acquisitions in eastern Europe and Asia, has obtained by outright acquisition a cluster of Pacific islands—the Kuriles—without any reference to trusteeship responsibilities or intentions. There can be no United Nations trusteeship jurisdiction over any part of the Kuriles, strategic or otherwise, because these islands already have been incorporated into Soviet territory as one of the quid pro quos given at Yalta as a condition of Russia's joining the war against Japan.

There undoubtedly will be value in establishing a thoroughgoing United Nations trusteeship for the common defense in the Pacific, but it will have to be a standard accepted by all the Big Five, not just one or two.

EDITOR'S NOTE—*Mr. Drummond has started on a cross-country trip to take some political soundings. His first dispatch in a series on the congressional elections will appear Thursday.*

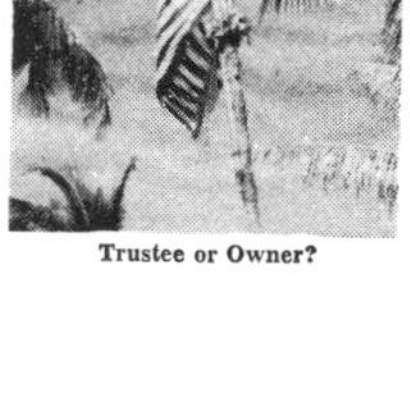

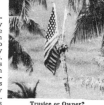

Trustee or Owner?

THE CHRISTIAN SCIENCE MONITOR

Registered in U. S. Patent Office

AN INTERNATIONAL DAILY NEWSPAPER

VOLUME 39 NO. 174 | COPYRIGHT 1947 BY THE CHRISTIAN SCIENCE PUBLISHING SOCIETY | BOSTON, FRIDAY, JUNE 20, 1947 | PACIFIC EDITION | TWO SECTIONS | FIVE CENTS A COPY

Roving Farm Labor Poses New Problem For Western States

By Robert R. Brunn
Staff Correspondent of The Christian Science Monitor

San Francisco

The Hope bill, providing a permanent farm-labor program for migrants, has brought a sharp divergence of opinion in the West, as almost 250,000 itinerants swing into the annual crop cycle.

Receiving support from growers' associations, the American Farm Bureau Federation, and the California State Chamber of Commerce, the bill has been attacked by labor unions and the Farm Research and Legislative Committee.

The Legislative Committee, a state-wide organization dormant during the war, is reviving its activity in the face of what it believes to be "a possible cycle of distress."

The Hope bill would turn Federal migrant-labor camps throughout the West over to specially designed State agencies, to other State agencies at the direction of governors, or sell them to growers' associations. The Legislative Committee terms it "a growers' bill."

Influx Eyed

Eyeing an unprecedented postwar influx of former war-plant workers, out-of-state migrants, and big-city unemployables, the Committee asks three things:

1. That hearings on the Hope bill be adjourned to California, the State with the biggest stake in migrant labor. They say that the people of this state should have time to study the recent report made by the Federal Interagency Committee On Migrant Labor.

Explaining that the Hope Bill provides no minimum wage, permanent housing, or community integration for migrants, and that it is "full of loopholes," they ask that the people of California become thoroughly familiar with the Interagency report before action on the Hope bill is taken.

The Federal migrant-labor survey recommended legislation to protect children of migrants, extension of worker compensation laws to migrants, and broadening of the Interstate Commerce Act to cover their private transportation.

Changes Asked

Also asked were removal of state-residence requirements for health, education, welfare, and recreation services, grants-in-aid to assist states in meeting such needs, extension of the minimum wage to migrants, and camp and employer licensing.

2. Concurrent resolutions by both houses providing for continuation of present Federal supervision under Public Law 40 insuring housing and health services for migrants.

3. That the United States Public Health Service be called in to survey California's migrant areas to avert what the Committee believes to be a coming crisis due to the postwar floodtide of migrants.

The existing law provides for Dec. 31, 1947 liquidation of the housing and camp activity of the Labor Branch of the Production and Marketing Administration of the Department of Agriculture. This office now administers 30 packed camps caring for 18,000 migrant workers and their families in California and Arizona.

Action Urged

The California State Chamber of Commerce says action in Washington is necessary to prevent the closing of these camps during the present harvest season. The Hope bill and continuation of provisions under Public Law 40 are alternative measures.

The Department of Agriculture's Labor Branch now is tapering its activity following budget restrictions. The Hope bill is designed to fill the vacuum and is the result of compromise between the American Farm Bureau Federation, the National Grange, and various growers' committees from the three major migrant states—California, Oregon, and Florida.

Should the Hope bill be voted out of the House Agricultural Committee, now terminating hearings, it is expected that it will be passed by Congress with little opposition—the legislative calendar permitting.

In California, there is some question as to the ultimate administration of the 28 Federal camps in the state. Although preserving loose Federal supervision, the Hope bill asks the state to step forward with a special administrative agency.

Alternatives

Gov. Earl Warren could designate another state agency to handle the camps or they could be sold to growers' associations under the Hope bill's provisions.

Most logical successor to the Labor Branch would be California's Agricultural Extension Service. Today the service and its partners maintain farm labor information stations in California, Arizona, Idaho, Nevada, Oregon, Utah, and Washington.

Although primarily educational agencies, the extension services have done a remarkable job of spreading the thin supply of itinerant labor over the West during the past five years.

Wool Vote Step to Isolation?

Tariff Threat Alarms Europe

By Richard L. Strout
Staff Correspondent of The Christian Science Monitor

WASHINGTON, June 20—Resurgent American isolationism is seen by some observers in two current Washington developments: Congressional approval of the wool tariff bill and the protracted legislative attack on the "Voice of America" foreign radio programs.

By their timing—coincident with European efforts to implement the great new "Marshall doctrine" of global aid—the two domestic legislative developments take on deep significance.

The Senate June 19 approved the wool price support bill 48 to 38. The bill authorizes higher trade barriers on foreign wool. The vote disregards threats of a veto but is less than the two-thirds majority needed to override a veto.

Strong Pleas Made

The State Department hitherto has used its strongest arguments against the wool bill, and in favor of the overseas foreign radiocast.

Both issues are precipitated by the impending end of war powers, July 1. At that date wartime support of the wool price and the 460,000,000 pounds of accumulated government-owned wool come to an end, unless extended.

Simultaneously, the present State Department program of radiocasts to foreign nations and allied educational efforts must be discontinued July 1, unless some substitute is provided.

The State Department pleaded against passage of the wool bill in its present form. The State Department also urged passage of funds for the "Voice of America" program. The latter program is blocked in the House at least temporarily with only a few days left for enactment.

Clayton Flies Back

The State Department did not object to the wool price support measure as originally passed by the Senate. This amounted to a potential subsidy that would come out of the taxpayer's pocket. But when the House proposed to insert a provision for the possible imposition of import fees or quotas, Will Clayton, Assistant Secretary of State, hurriedly flew back from the International Trade Conference at Geneva to fight the measure. The State Department charged that passage might wreck the Geneva Conference.

It was the Conference report containing a modified quota provision on which the Senate acted today. The House passed the same measure after bitter debate. The House nearly beat the wool measure on a motion to recommit, which failed, 191 to 166.

Friends and foes of the revised wool bill do not agree in their interpretation of the House provision under which the President could apply fees or quotas on wool imports.

Sponsors of the bill like Senator George D. Aiken (R) of Vermont, deny that this section is mandatory upon the President. Senator Aiken is frank to say that he would have preferred to have had the provision left out. He proposes that the President sign it and issue a statement reassuring foreign nations that he does not wish to use the proposed power.

Attack Resumed

Foes of the measure, who resumed their attack before the June 19 vote, reiterated the grave view of the State Department. Senator Leverett Saltonstall (R) of Massachusetts opposed the House amendment. In a previous speech Senator A. Willis Robertson (D) of Virginia told the Senate he had just talked to Mr. Clayton. "He said that the nations with whom he is dealing at Geneva regard this proposed step as a high-tariff, isolationist move," Senator Robertson reported.

According to a carefully researched article in January Fortune Magazine, the wool tariff added $136,000,000 to America's clothing bill in 1946; or about $10,000,000 more than the value of all the wool produced in the United States that year.

America ordinarily imports twice as much wool as it produces. In normal times the tariff is equivalent to 100 per cent protection, Senator Robertson said. On the basis of abnormally high wool prices last year, the tariff was equivalent to 63 per cent protection.

"I am satisfied the State Department will ask the President to veto the bill," Senator Robertson added, "and if he does, there will be no likelihood that the Congress will pass the bill over the President's veto. That will mean that no measure on this subject will be enacted into law."

Government sets up wool-testing laboratory in Denver: Page 3.

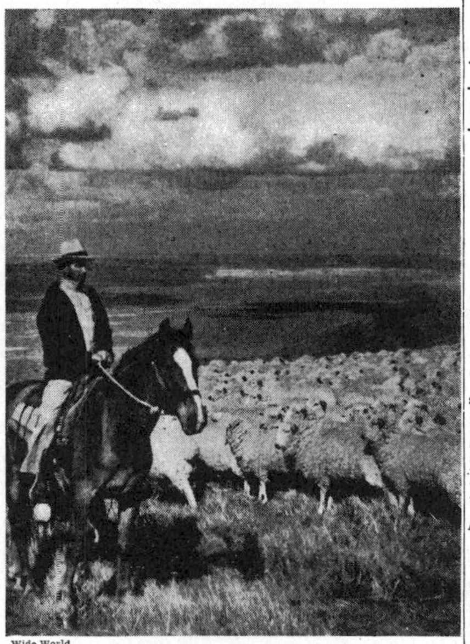

Wide World

A herder in the western United States rides with his flock, guiding them to pastures, guarding them from predatory animals, and bringing them to the pens for shearing. Here begins the wool tariff question now agitating Congress, the Administration, and the Geneva Conference.

Marshall Program of Aid Advances in U. S., Europe; Impact on Soviet Bared

Exclusive Report on Russia: Contradictions Burn No Bridges

Special to The Christian Science Monitor
Copyright, 1947, by The Christian Science Publishing Society

Stockholm

The impact of the Truman Doctrine on the Soviet mentality and on Soviet policy cannot be gauged yet in its full extent.

As processed through the Soviet press, the implications of the United States' outspoken intention of opposing Soviet infiltration and expansion wherever they manifest themselves have been disclosed only gradually to the Russian reader.

The purpose of this delayed reaction has been to avoid too much of a sudden shock at a time when the people and country are having to face tremendous internal hardships.

For more than a year, at least, ever since Winston Churchill's speech in Fulton, Mo., the Soviet Government had been warning its people of the perils of new capitalist encirclement. It had been forecasting that the United States, having emerged as the most powerful capitalist state of the postwar world, would head up the forces of world "reaction" in opposition to the Soviet Union.

Alarms Overdone

Not that the Soviet leaders necessarily regarded a new war as imminent, but such propaganda was calculated to stimulate the people to greater reconstruction effort to counteract the natural tendency toward postwar relaxation, and also take their thoughts off certain shortcomings.

From the standpoint of this internal propaganda line, the Truman Doctrine was a windfall. It seemed to confirm just what the Communist Party spokesmen had been saying all along. At the same time, however, it also came at a time when the cry of "Wolf! Wolf!" had been rather overdone.

Alarmist propaganda had reached the stage where it had passed its peak of usefulness, and instead of stimulating the people to greater effort, it had an unsettling and demoralizing effect. Russia's people were beginning to say: "What's the point of building up things if they're all going to be blasted away by atom bombs?"

Propaganda Softened

Such comments and the mood they reflect became so widespread that the Russian Communist Party ever sensitive to the popular mood through its feelers, reacted accordingly. Statements were made in high places like the Stalin quizzes—which, without exactly altering the general line, injected notes of reassurance to the effect that perhaps war wasn't just around the corner after all.

This countercampaign was at its height on the eve of the Moscow Conference, which was exploited to the full, incidentally, as evidence that the Soviet Union was not isolated, that the problems of big-power unity were not, after all, insoluble.

At the same time, the attacks on American policy continued.

Contradictory Logic

This apparent inconsistency is in full accord with the Marxist ideas of the unity of opposites, a peculiar form of logic whereby contradictory, and, to the non-Marxian way of thinking, mutually exclusive proposition, can be simultaneously affirmed.

Back in wartime, a party army propagandist explained in a moment of rare frankness:

"We have two lines about America, one praising, one attacking. We can turn either on according to instructions."

The desired balance is maintained or shifted according to requirements by first one and then the other line. It is all rather like Alice in Wonderland regulating her size by nibbling first on a bit from the left side of the mushroom and then from the right side.

And now, the Soviets have discovered that during the past year, they had rather overdone the capitalist danger angle to the extent of undermining the individual's sense of security and confidence in the future. And the Truman Doctrine appeared to confirm the first proposition with such emphasis that it made the task of reassuring public opinion still harder.

'Two Americas' Pictured

But Soviet propagandists, nothing if not resourceful, have devised new arguments and angles to cope with their task.

The main device has been to intensify the anti-American campaign, but at the same time to shift its content. The present line, while condemning the Washington Government and its policy, is to play up and magnify the importance and strength of left-wing opposition to the Truman Doctrine inside the United States.

Hardly a day now elapses without lengthy quotations from Henry A. Wallace or Senator Claude Pepper being printed in Pravda. The activities of various left-wing organizations in the United States also are made prominent and an over-all impression thus fostered that the majority of the American people are against the Government.

There is much talk of the "two Americas," the America of Lincoln and Roosevelt as opposed to the America of Truman and the "imperialists." At the same time there is a tendency to minimize the American economic and military potential.

Sell U. S. Short

As regards policy there is an attempt to redefine, from the standpoint of the party line, not only the United States' role in the postwar world, but also the American war contribution. The object is to picture the Soviet Union as winning the war virtually single-handed, to minimize America's part, and thus reduce the reserve of good will which the United States banked with the Russian people in wartime.

This is no easy task, in view of the instinctive admiration and sympathy for the United States among the average citizenry, especially as American aid, through the United Nations Relief and Rehabilitation Administration has continued in important areas down to the present time.

The entire propaganda machine has been mobilized for the task of selling America short.

The foremost publicists, journalists, economists, historians, and fiction writers have been put to work. Sometimes overlapping, each group carries out its assignment in its given field. The publicists and journalists "expose" the imperialist, militarist trend of American policy.

Out of the mass of reports filed by Tass from the United States, those items which fit in with the official thesis are culled for publication. Articles on conditions in the United States emphasize the seamy sides of race relations (lynchings seldom are overlooked), or corruption in politics, or labor strife (wage agreements like the steel settlement are not reported).

The picture of life in general is blackened sufficiently to make the Soviet reader consider himself well off by comparison (assuming he believes what he reads).

Depression Forecast

The economists paint a somber picture of the United States as tottering on the brink of economic chaos and depression. On this the Soviets bank especially. The assumption that depression in the United States is inevitable is basic to their entire foreign policy.

It is hard to gauge how successful this propaganda is convincing the public. The people naturally get most of their information from official Soviet sources.

At the same time barriers to outside information have been widely breached, breached beyond repair, by the foreign newscasts in Russian, particularly the British and American, and by such publications as British Ally and Amerika, which exert an influence far beyond actual circulation.

Contrary to the general impression abroad, the number of persons in Russia who like to think for themselves is increasing, especially among the war veterans and younger intellectuals.

Clayton Favors Vandenberg Plan

By Harlan Trott
Staff Correspondent of The Christian Science Monitor

WASHINGTON, June 20—Substantial progress in the Administration's program for giving American aid to Europe is manifested in a number of new diplomatic developments. Among the more encouraging developments now unfolding are:

1. Undersecretary of State William L. Clayton's indorsement of the proposal advanced by Senator Arthur H. Vandenberg (R) of Michigan to set up a bipartisan council which would survey the nation's resources to determine how far the United States could go in extending economic aid abroad.

2. The exchange of notes between the United States and Greece in which the latter outlines its specific aims for effecting a far-reaching rehabilitation program and sweeping governmental reforms to insure the efficient administration of such a program.

3. The joint decision of the British and French Foreign Offices to invite Vyacheslav M. Molotov, Soviet Foreign Minister, to confer with them soon on the European reconstruction program recently proposed by Secretary of State George C. Marshall.

Study Under Way

Mr. Clayton's reference to Senator Vandenberg's proposed bipartisan council as a very wise suggestion is regarded as encouraging evidence of the American teamwork which is helping to advance the Administration's aid-to-Europe program. It is presumed that the names of outstanding men who will constitute such a council already are under consideration.

The Undersecretary of State for Economic Affairs told a press conference that a study of the relation of American exports to the price structure is being undertaken by the State Department's planning staff. Mr. Clayton also agreed that Herbert Hoover's proposal for surveying the relation of United States' exports to imports was essential.

Mr. Clayton explained that the program for aiding Europe still is far from complete. He suggested that the emergency economic commission for Europe might be called upon to assist in developing the views of European nations with regard to an American economic program abroad.

Logical Start Seen

The Undersecretary described the meeting of the British and French Foreign Ministers as a logical start in the unfoldment of a concerted understanding of specific goals. He said that official communications from the Governments of the Low Countries have been received in Washington voicing support for the project and citing the advantages of their customs unions as a practical indication of the feasibility of European co-operation.

Speaking at a State Department press conference in the absence of Secretary Marshall, Mr. Clayton said that while no time limit has been set within which the undertaking should be launched, economic conditions abroad are getting progressively worse. He declined to say whether he thought Congress should be called into special session to expedite the program.

Washington naturally is interested in reports from Moscow regarding Russia's reaction to Secretary Marshall's plan for extending economic aid to Europe. No official Russian reaction to Secretary Marshall's Harvard address has been received here, but Mr. Clayton indicated that he hoped Russia would side with the plan.

Greek Aid Spurred

In view of the favorable reply of the Greek Government regarding the steps it purposes to insure the best possible use of the $400,000,000 American loan, the State Department has directed Lincoln MacVeagh, United States Ambassador in Athens, to begin negotiations on a formal agreement.

President Truman's nomination of Edwin C. Wilson, United States Ambassador to Turkey, to be chief of the American Mission for aid to Turkey means that Mr. Wilson's assignment in Turkey will parallel that of former Gov. Dwight Griswold of Nebraska in Greece. Mr. Wilson will remain as Ambassador to Turkey.

Appointment of George C. McGhee as co-ordinator of the Greek-Turkish aid program is intended to expedite the preliminary phases of the planning.

He will supervise the administration of the Greek program at the Washington end.

The President also nominated Brig. Gen. Charles E. Salzman, Vice-President of the New York Stock Exchange, to be Assistant Secretary of State. General Salzman, a graduate of the United States Military Academy and a former Rhodes scholar, will fill the post now held by Assistant Secretary of State John H. Hilldring, who is in charge of occupied areas.

Picture of two Greek aid chiefs: Page 11.

State of the Nation

By ROSCOE DRUMMOND
Chief of the Washington Bureau of The Christian Science Monitor

WASHINGTON

Serious split in party ranks is not something which plagues only the Democrats. Whatever they say publicly, the Republicans are gleefully eying the widening breach between President Truman and Henry Wallace. They will be saving themselves future trouble if they begin eying the widening breach within their own congressional ranks.

Bolder and more outspoken isolationism is revealing itself in Congress today, and it is using the Republican Party as its main instrument of political power.

Republicans have long been handicapped—sometimes fatally handicapped—in national elections by the extent to which the isolationists have controlled the party machinery and party policy. It is the isolationists who have gained from such an alliance, not the GOP.

As a result of the 1944 elections, the isolationist forces suffered an overwhelming setback, and what remained went underground. For three years their role has been small and their influence slight in Congress.

But now the voices of isolationism, particularly economic isolationism, are beginning to be raised in stronger tones. They are still in the great minority, but it is evident the time is at hand to attempt openly to check a foreign policy which rests on the premise that the United States must live with the world as well as in the world.

As before, most of the congressional isolationists are in the Republican ranks, and they are seeking mostly to use the Republican Party to further their ends. In this fact lies the greatest danger to the Republican cause in 1948, because it holds the prospect of splitting the GOP just as seriously as Henry Wallace holds the prospect of splitting the Democrats.

Emergent isolationism is right now manifesting itself in three actions on Capitol Hill:

1. The extent and character of the opposition to the State Department's international information program, including the "Voice of America" radiocasts, offer the clearest evidence that the isolationists have chosen this issue on which to make an open stand.

The Mundt bill authorizing the information program was recommended unanimously by the Republican-controlled House Foreign Affairs Committee, but the GOP isolationists, aided only by representative John E. Rankin (D) of Mississippi, have been purposefully and skillfully delaying and diluting it. They attack it obliquely; they attack it misleadingly. They don't admit they are opposing America raising its voice around the world because they want America to try to withdraw from the world. But that is the premise, and that is the effect of their position.

2. At a time when the Government is acting internationally to reopen the channels of freer world trade, the Republican majority in both houses of Congress has acted to raise the barriers against trade with the United States in passage of the new wool tariff bill.

In the judgment of conservative spokesman Mark Sullivan, this action combines the worst features of the most contradictory domestic and foreign policy. He says this because it uses Government funds to increase prices when the need is to decrease prices, and because it serves to shut off foreign trade when American exports are outrunning imports by billions of dollars a year.

3. Finally, important Republican members of Congress are engaged in a hit-and-run attack on the whole Reciprocal Trade Act which has been approved by the American people for a decade and which was indorsed by the Republican platform and by the Republican presidential candidate in 1944. Thus Republicans present themselves as acting simultaneously to co-operate with the world politically and to shun the world economically—a policy and a party divided against itself.

The split in Republican ranks on foreign economic policy can be as harmful to the 1948 GOP presidential nominee as the split in Democratic ranks on foreign political policy to President Truman. None of the three leading Republican presidential prospects—Governor Dewey, Senator Vandenberg, Harold Stassen—could run effectively on any platform which would be satisfactory to the Republican opponents of the "Voice of America" and the reciprocal trade treaties or to the Republican adherents of the wool tariff bill, which President Truman will successfully veto.

The prospect in 1948 is not that the GOP isolationists will split away from the party—as Henry Wallace probably will from the Democratic Party. The danger is that they will nestle under the tent and thereby cause voters to split away from the Republican Party.

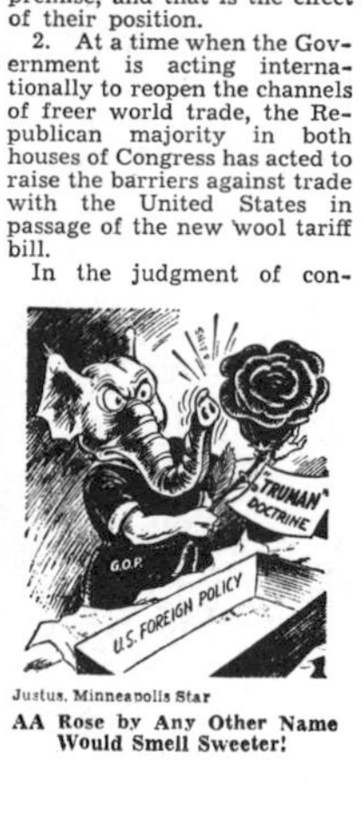

Justus, Minneapolis Star

AA Rose by Any Other Name Would Smell Sweeter!

Of All Things . . .

Buckfast and Tithe

PLYMOUTH, England (Reuters)—Home of Sir Francis Drake—Buckfast Abbey—and its tithe barn, one of the largest and best in England, has become national property, it was announced here.

It is understood that the abbey and tithe barn will be used as a Drake naval and folk museum on lines which are still subject to discussion and negotiation.

Mountain Chain Mapped

LONDON (Reuters)—Soviet natural scientists have mapped a huge mountain chain in the Tian-Shan Mountains between Turkestan and China, one of the world's most inaccessible regions, Radio Moscow said.

The Tian-Shan Mountains, called "Nameless Range" by the Russians, penetrate deep into Sinkiang area of China, scene of the Mongolian incursion.

They form a huge chain about 1,600 miles long and between 100 and 300 miles broad, and rise to heights up to 23,000 feet.

Soviet Meteor

MOSCOW (Reuters)—A meteor which collided with the earth last February in a mountainous area about 300 miles northeast of Vladivostok, weighed about 100 tons, according to evidence brought back by an expedition from the Soviet Academy of Science sent out to investigate the phenomenon.

The expedition brought back five tons of splinters—remnants of the shattered meteorite.

One hundred and sixty craters made by the impact—the largest over 30 yards in diameter—also were discovered.

Soviets Use Food Rations to Win Poles

By Joseph C. Harsch
Special Correspondent of The Christian Science Monitor

Warsaw

The familiar remark that Communism thrives on misery and shortages takes on a new meaning here in Poland. Communism thrives not so much because shortages produce unrest but because shortages provide a wonderful opportunity for patronage and favoritism.

In theory, rationing equalizes the shortage of goods for all. But here rationing is not for everybody but only for the favored. The masses are served by the free market at extremely high prices. Rations are granted only to workers, Government employees, and schoolteachers.

Communists Explain

A justification is offered for this which, in the abstract, sounds reasonable enough.

It is pointed out that the Polish economy is so badly depleted by the war, and Government organization so disrupted, that a total rationing system would be impossible to establish.

It is argued further than reconstruction of the country is a priority undertaking for which workers, Government employees, and schoolteachers must be unhampered by the daily hunt for food.

That is all very well and would be fair enough, were the ranks of these classes recruited nonpolitically. But practice suggests strongly that this is not the case.

The security of employment appears to improve visibly when membership is registered with one of the Government parties, particularly with the Communist-led Workers Party.

Housing Involved

It's not only a question of food. Every Government department in Warsaw is "required" to provide living quarters for its officials. The result is that the first apartment houses repaired go to Government officials. Thus proper political "orientation" proves in practice the way to get the better not only of the food speculator but also of the tailor and the landlord.

Under this treatment it is not surprising that Workers Party membership has grown from 200,000 a year ago to 850,000 at the latest report. The Socialists still claim they are the strongest single party, but they count only 700,000 registered members.

Of course, this raises a question regarding the depth of such political conversions. It is reported here, perhaps apocryphally, that a prominent Pole recently asked Prime Minister Joseph Stalin his opinion of the Polish Communists. It is said Stalin compared them to radishes: Beautifully red on the outside, but . . .

Communism Modified

After long talks with Poland's highest Government Communists, I personally am inclined to question Stalin's lack of faith in his Polish followers—at least, so far as it applies to high officialdom. These men make a strong point that Communism has adjusted itself to special conditions in Poland. Such an adjustment is perfectly orthodox Communist strategy and already has paid big dividends.

The only possible western answer obviously lies in destroying the patronage system on which the Communists thrive through use of consumer goods.

One fact supremely apparent here in eastern Europe is that the revised, economic-aid version of the Truman Doctrine is immensely more effective than the original military-dress version.

Communist sources attempt to counter it by charging the United States with attempting to buy support. Yet no matter how politically tainted American gold may be, no Government would dare to decline it if proferred.

New Truman Approach

The original version of the Doctrine may have provided some boost in spirits among the friends of the West, but it played superbly into Communist hands for an excellent reason. Even the Poles, for all their inherited distaste for the Russians, descending from Cossack days, have no taste any more for a battleground life. That first version was easily represented as an invitation to the Poles for race suicide.

But the revised version is quite a different matter, for instead of threatening it invites, and the invitation is most tempting. At first the Truman Doctrine repelled—but now it attracts. America in civilian clothes is proving a more successful propagandist than Uncle Sam in a soldier suit.

N. Y. City Educators Assail Dewey Fund As Crumb of Relief

By John Beaufort
Chief of the New York News Bureau of The Christian Science Monitor

New York

The crisis in education continues.

Problems facing the nearly 800 schools here in the nation's financial capital once more acutely illustrate this crisis in its political and economic aspects.

Gov. Thomas E. Dewey's Committee on a State Educational Program has just recommended that the State spend $182,000,000 a year to help New York's cities and towns pay their educational way. This represents $56,000,000 more than has been provided by the "Friedsam Formula," which was revised in 1945 and under which state assistance has been distributed in former years.

Governor Dewey has made the new recommendation official by endorsing it in his budget message to the New York Legislature.

New York City would receive an increase of $16,000,000 for permanent school aid under the new system. Of this amount, $6,600,000 represents the latest recommendation of the Dewey education committee, the remaining $9,400,000 is an emergency assistance which would be made permanent.

City Disappointed

On the face of it, this looks like a substantial increase. But New York City educators are keenly disappointed. They would have liked to see the city receive at least a $100,000,000 increase "to wipe out school slums."

The Public Education Association felt that a minimum increase of $40,000,000 would be required.

Mayor William O'Dwyer asked for $30,000,000.

In terms of such figures, the $6,600,000 of new aid looks rather small to them. In effect, educators here feel they have asked the Dewey administration for bread and have been offered a crumb.

New York City spent $230,671,-000 on its schools in 1947. Of this amount, the State contributed upward of $52,000,000. (New Yorkers are quick to point out that most of this amount came from their own taxes.) The New York City schools have an enrollment of some 800,-000—about equal to the population of Cleveland or Baltimore.

High Taxes Cited

According to the Public Education Association, New York City's grammar and high-school students total about half the secondary-school population in the entire State. Furthermore, this City pays half the State's income taxes, but receives only one fifth of the State's education assistance.

Without oversimplifying the enormously complex aspects of the problem, the foregoing suggests the essence of the crisis now facing New York City—and other large communities in the State.

The Public Education Association points out that Dr. Francis T. Spaulding, Governor Dewey's own Education Commissioner and the only educator on the Dewey education committee, dissented from the majority report. Dr. Spaulding wanted $60,000,000 in new state aid to schools, in addition to the emergency funds that now have been made permanent. Of such an increase, New York City would have received $20,600,000 of new funds.

Politics Charged

In a testily worded comment on the Dewey program, the PEA remarked, "This could hardly be called an educational report—it's a political document." The Association intends to fight the report and strengthen its efforts on behalf of the Republican-sponsored Young-Milmoe bill, which would give an increase of $40,000,000 for New York City.

Dr. Paul R. Mort of Columbia University, whose 1947 study of the New York City situation received widespread attention, described the Dewey committee's statement as "woefully inadequate." Dr. Mort declared that the new, Dewey-approved formula contains "many fine features" and that it would help the poorer communities and "centralized" (country community) schools of the State. Most of these are in strongly Republican upstate New York. However, he added, "it all but ignores the problems of cities over 100,000."

The new formula would allocate $200 for each elementary pupil and $240 for each secondary pupil. The community would contribute an amount represented in a $7 per $1,000 real estate tax, compared to $2.65 per $1,000 as at present. The rest would come from the State. The present formula allocates $100 and $130, respectively, for each grammar and high school student.

The majority report of the Governor's committee stressed the priority which education should receive and declared that "no individual child should be deprived of educational opportunities because he lives in an area which is lacking in resources sufficient to supply a minimum educational program."

Inside Reading:

Friday, January 30, 1948

State of the Nation
The GOP, . . . the ERP, . . . the Election

By ROSCOE DRUMMOND, Chief, Washington Bureau, The Christian Science Monitor

Washington

The Marshall Plan is presenting the Republican Party with its most difficult and critical political test at a time when the highest reward is at stake—the winning of the Presidency in 1948.

The oncoming vote on the European Recovery Program is bringing to the surface a Party disagreement on foreign policy which, unless averted, would have these consequences:

It would reveal GOP disunity at a moment when disunity hardly can fail to imperil its chances in the presidential election.

It would deepen the already substantial differences between Senator Arthur H. Vandenberg and Senator Robert A. Taft, the two most influential Republican spokesmen in Congress.

It could make it impossible for the Party to nominate either Gov. Thomas E. Dewey or Senator Vandenberg or Harold E. Stassen, strong Marshall Plan supporters, and, if one of them were nominated, would put him in the weak position of asking the support of the country in behalf of a foreign policy on which his own Party was seriously divided.

It would topple the whole bipartisan foundation of foreign policy, inject foreign policy into the heat and scuffle of a divisive national campaign, and thereby weaken the effectiveness of the nation when it most needs it.

It would imperil a Repub-lican 1948 victory as almost nothing else could, since on the two central foreign-policy decisions before the 80th Congress—the Marshall Plan and renewal of the reciprocal trade treaties—the voters have shown themselves substantially in favor of both.

All this is why a group of 20 Senate Republicans who met in private 10 days ago to devise ways of defeating ERP ended up looking for ways to pass ERP with only sufficient alterations to salve the isolationists but without alterations which would endanger the program itself. They went into a huddle as opponents of the Marshall Plan, and after several hours of candid talk decided that to defeat it might well defeat the Republican Party. Their objective now is to bridge the differences between the isolationist and internationalist wings of the Party in order that they will not have to go into the 1948 campaign with their differences too greatly exposed.

An informal committee of five GOP senators now is seeking sufficient compromises to, avoid an open split when it comes to vote. They include Senators Joseph H. Ball of Minnesota, C. Wayland Brooks of Illinois, William F. Knowland of California, Homer E. Capehart of Indiana, and Edward V. Robertson of Wyoming.

The high lights of the Republican voting record which gave the senators pause and caused them to think again before widening the breach still further were these:

A breakdown of these Party votes shows a conspicuous geographical division within the GOP and the opposition to the bipartisan foreign policy to be where the GOP is politically strongest—the Middle West and Rocky Mountain states. The vote in the special session authorizing the $504,000,000 for interim aid is illustrative. In the Senate on the test vote to cut it to $400,000,000, of the 20 Republicans for slashing it, 17 came from the middle and central plains states. The vote in the House followed the same geographical pattern.

The paramount foreign-policy issues on which the 1948 election may turn in large part if bipartisan collaboration is seriously broken in the present session would be the Marshall Plan and renewal of the Reciprocal Trade Act. Fortunately for the country, both parties will have to face these issues squarely and openly before the campaign begins. Most observers agree that the Republicans face the prospect of losing the election if they impose upon their presidential nominee, whoever he may be, the burden of a grievously divided Party. To avoid such a divided Party is the Republicans' biggest political problem in this session of Congress.

Cabinet Wins In Bid to Void Franc Notes

By Joan Thiriet
Special Correspondent of The Christian Science Monitor

Paris

Premier Robert Schuman's delicately balanced coalition Government has won an important victory in approval by Parliament of its decision to withdraw all 5,000-franc notes from circulation. The National Assembly vote was 307 to 286; in the Council of the Republic, 167 to 126.

More important than this vote itself, perhaps, is the fact that it paves the way for favorable Assembly action on the Cabinet's highly controversial bill for free trade in gold and certain hard currencies. The franc invalidation measure was what persuaded the Socialists to support the gold bill.

Withdrawal of the 5,000-franc banknotes has caused a sensation not only in financial circles but among the little people of France, who long have had the squirrel-like habit of storing banknotes away in household hiding places instead of putting their savings in bank accounts or bonds.

Vast Amounts Involved

The Government's idea was to tap this huge source of hidden savings before free markets for gold and certain hard currencies were established. Some idea of the amounts involved can be gained from the fact that with 330,000,000,000 francs' worth of these notes in circulation, the nationalized banks are said to have only about 10,000,000,000 worth in vaults.

The question for the average French citizen, and for his deputy in the Assembly during the debate, was how soon and how much the Government would repay on the notes now to be turned in.

One result of the Government's action in calling in the notes will be the possibility of estimating hidden wealth of certain categories of citizens.

Thus, small farmers, liable under Finance Minister René Mayer's new plan for a supertax, have been trying to organize resistance and avoid payment on the plea they simply have not got the money.

This plea will fall flat if, as Government officials estimate, a large proportion of the 5,000-franc notes are held by these same farmers.

Socialists Placated

Behind the timing of the decision was the Government's undoubted desire to placate the Socialists and to hold the Government majority together.

The proposed law to authorize a free market in gold and some national currencies runs contrary to the basic principles of Socialist doctrine. It threatened to upset the delicate balance of Premier Robert Schuman's "third force" Government.

M. Mayer's decision to call in the bank notes is not a new idea, but such an abrupt announcement—and indeed the very surprise which greeted the news even in Finance Ministry circles—suggests it may have been a decision finally taken purely on the spur of the moment.

As to the real effect of the note recall, opinion is sharply divided. Opposition in the Assembly itself came from both the far Left and the far Right.

Anderson Reverses Stand

© Harris & Ewing

Secretary of Agriculture Clinton P. Anderson reversed his stand that United States-owned privately leased distilleries in Omaha, Neb., and Muscatine, Iowa, would get no grain and now will allow the plants limited quantities. Mr. Anderson is shown conferring with Senator Theodore Francis Green (D) of Rhode Island at a recent hearing.

Federal Distilleries Get Grain

By Harlan Trott
Staff Correspondent of The Christian Science Monitor

Washington

Right when President Truman is asking Congress to extend Federal controls on grain for distillers to help feed Europe, the Administration is an active "partner" with private interest in the whisky business.

Two large distilleries acquired by the Government during the war to produce industrial alcohol are now making whisky for private corporations under Federal leases from grain supplies through the help of the Administration.

On Dec. 17, Secretary of Agriculture Clinton P. Anderson declared at a conference with leaders in the liquor industry that the United States-owned, privately leased distilleries at Omaha, Neb., and Muscatine, Iowa, would not be permitted to have any grain.

Quota System

The Secretary of Agriculture subsequently has reversed himself.

Under the quota system, which expires Jan. 31 and which the President has asked Congress to extend until Oct. 31 of this year, the Farm Crops Processing Corporation has received a monthly allocation of 60,000 bushels of corn and other grains and the Grain Processing Corporation of Muscatine gets 50,000 bushels.

The Department of Agriculture's order allocating grain to distillers provides that "no distilling plant owned or operated by the United States Government or by any agency or instrumentality thereof shall, during the effective period of this order, use grain or grain products in the manufacture of distilled spirits or neutral spirits for beverage purposes."

However, Department regulations provide that "any person affected by this order who considers that compliance herewith would work an exceptional or unreasonable hardship on him may file a petition for relief."

Appeals Filed

"Hardship" appeals were filed by both plants. As a result Mr. Anderson waived the ban on grain and granted grain quotas.

A Department of Agriculture spokesman admitted that considerable pressure, both industrial and political, has been exerted on the Administration since the failure of the industry to cooperate in maintaining voluntary controls on grain used for whisky.

Considerable conjecture is going on in Government quarters here as to the political channels, if any, through which the whisky lobby may be exerting pressure. It is pointed out, for example, that one of the leading officers of the Farm Crops Processing Corporation, the lessee of the Government's Omaha Distillery, is J. L. Walsh, a former partner of Senator Hugh L. Butler (R) of Nebraska in the Butler-Welsh Grain Company.

Interest Held Sold

Senator Butler's office explained today that the Senator had sold out his interest in the Butler-Welsh partnership when he came to the Senate seven years ago. And one of Mr. Anderson's aides said that they had been out of contact with Senator Butler for "several months."

Asked about the "hardship" aspects of the appeals lodged by the Omaha and Muscatine distilleries, an Agriculture Department spokesman said such considerations as the likelihood of throwing distillery employees out of work, "of course," entered into the decision. President Truman recently belittled this argument when he was fighting the grain holiday.

The Agriculture Department official stressed that the private op-erators of the Government whisky plants are getting what amounted to "token" allotments.

He said that on the basis of the volume of production in these two plants, the Omaha distillery normally was entitled to 92,000 bushels of grain a month and the Muscatine plant 82,000, but that Mr. Anderson had decided to cut grain-for-whisky quotas of the Government plants to 60,000 and 50,000 bushels, respectively. The Agriculture Department official laughingly suggested this could be considered "a compromise with our conscience."

Officials concede, however, that there is no suggestion of compromise with the whisky industry in anything that President Truman stated in his special message to Congress Jan. 29 asking for extension of grain controls for liquor.

On the contrary, the President put "the national interest" above that of the whisky interests. And he called the grain situation of most European countries "extremely grave."

Plant Sought

Meanwhile the Farm Crops Processing Corporation is trying to buy the Government plant in Omaha, but the sale is being held in abeyance by the WAA pending some action by the House and Senate Agriculture Committees.

Both congressional groups are debating whether to sell the plants or keep them as a means of processing farm commodity surpluses once farm production returns to normal and the United States no longer has to help feed Europe.

There is a strong inclination in Congress to keep the plants, based somewhat on the lingering impression of pictures which appear in the newspapers ever so often showing mountains of potatoes and other farm crops rotting for lack of markets.

Whenever there is a surplus of grain or potatoes, it is suggested, the Government plants could be put to work making distilled spirits out of these unmarketable commodities.

Large Plant

The Omaha plant is one of the largest single distilleries in the United States. At one time, the Schenley Whiskey Company was reported interested in buying it.

The plant was thrown together out of odds and ends of machinery when wartime priorities impeded the manufacture of new distillery equipment.

Some of the vats were shipped in from a Texas oil tank farm, it is reported, and some of the boilers are said to have beer. resurrected from an obsolete street railway power house. Despite its low book value and high depreciation factor, the Government's Omaha distillery is believed to be one of the most profitable single beverage alcohol plants.

Congress Asked To Banish 'Billion'

By the Associated Press

Washington

Banishing the word "billion" from the English language has been proposed by Representative Robert J. Twyman (R) of Illinois. He suggested that a thousand million be substituted.

"The trouble with billion, he said in a statement, is that it is "a very confusing word." People frequently use million when they mean billion, and vice versa, he said.

"A billion dollars is a thousand million dollars," Mr. Twyman added, "Why slur over this tremendous amount?"

Moscow Rebuke Balks Unification Plan of Satellites

By William H. Stringer
Chief of the London News Bureau of The Christian Science Monitor

London

Russia apparently has decided to call a halt to, and rechannel, the unification and federalization which its trusted lieutenants have been busily promoting in the Balkans and Eastern Europe.

Rather surprisingly, Russia appears to have admitted openly that the only kind of unification it is willing to permit in eastern Europe is unity of the central command from Moscow.

This is unity through the mechanism of tightly reined local Communist parties—not the broad economic-political unification of a common customs union and confederation.

This is the most likely interpretation being placed by diplomatic spokesmen and independent European observers here on the unexpected rebuke administered by Pravda, official organ of the Russian Communist Party, to George Dimitrov, Bulgarian Prime Minister, "hero of the Reichstag fire," and General Secretary of the old Comintern.

This Russian rebuke, veritably in the man-bites-dog category, is regarded here as the diplomatic sensation of the week.

Considering the deviousness of Russian policy, and considering the fact that many of the Kremlin's decisions often have complex motivation, with several horses being ridden at once, no one can be sure of the precise meaning of Pravda's statement contradicting Mr. Dimitrov and declaring that the Balkans require neither federation nor a customs union.

The most favored and indeed the most obvious interpretation is that Russia has no intention of permitting a broad and strong east European federation to be built up for the simple reason that such a federation might grow into a powerful state—which some day conceivably would have a mind of its own and resist Moscow's dictation.

That Moscow may fear the harmonizing and unifying effect of a customs union and a common economic policy, such as the Benelux countries have been developing and such as is included in the British proposals for western Europe, seems implicit in Pravda's seemingly "inspired" decision that such instruments are not suitable for eastern Europe's development.

Kremlin Misgivings

The kind of unity Russia really wants in the Balkans, it is believed here, was evidenced in the kind of unity it was promoting for Germany during the London sessions of the Big Four Council of Foreign Ministers. This was unity to be accomplished almost entirely under the banners of the Communist - dominated political parties of Germany—a unified Germany which could be advanced, checked, altered, or revised virtually by phone call from Moscow.

Formation of an east European federation, such as Mr. Dimitrov said Bulgaria, Yugoslavia, Albania, Romania, Hungary, Czechoslovakia, Poland, "and perhaps Greece" were preparing for the future, might well have been more acceptable to Moscow in the easier days when the western powers were not so insistently challenging Soviet expansionism.

Now the Kremlin appears to have apprehensions lest such a federation eventually should get out of hand, feel its own strength, and most especially, be inclined to make its own economic terms and trade pacts with the West.

There may be other long-term implications in l'Affaire Dimitrov. It is conceivable that Russia is looking to the day when the Slav

Pravda's Statement

Pravda's statement said:

"The editors believe these countries do not need a problematic and artificial federation or confederation or customs union; what they do need is consolidation and protection of their independence and sovereignty through mobilization and organization of domestic popular democratic forces, as has been correctly stated in the declaration of the non-Communist parties."

Here are some other explanations being offered here:

1. It is suggested that Russia is re-emphasizing its oft-professed interest in maintaining the sovereignty of small nations—an emphasis of which will be distinctly usable in Communist propaganda that the Marshall Plan is undermining the independence of western European nations.

2. It is suggested that the rebuff is chiefly a personal rebuke to Mr. Dimitrov with the intention of definitely second-rating him as regards the Balkan rivalry between Yugoslavia's Marshall Tito and himself. Marshal Tito is the man with more recent Communist training in line with the new Cominform strategy. It is further suggested that Mr. Dimitrov may have overstepped the mark in warning Bulgarian oppositionists to remember the fate of Nikola Petkov, recently executed.

Realistic View

3. It is suggested that Russia is being very realistic as regards the economics of east Europe—and well realizes that a customs union between backward Bulgaria and industrially forward Czechoslovakia, for instance, would have exceedingly hard sledding. In short, the Soviet line may be opposing the customs union and federation idea as impracticable, some persons feel.

The central point, as seen by diplomatic spokesmen here, is that the rebuff to Pravda, which usually reflects official policy, seems an answer to the question frequently raised lately, namely, whether the Soviet Government really wishes a powerful new federated state on its flank, even though such a state would be closely allied to Moscow—and be subject to the internal weaknesses incident to all new federations. The indicated Soviet answer seems to be "No!"

Gandhi, Shot by Hindu, Led Indian Climb to Freedom

By the Associated Press

New Delhi

Mohandas K. Gandhi, who was shot and killed, by one of the Hindus he led to independence, stands as one of the monumental figures in the history of troubled Asia.

The 78-year-old Indian leader, whose voice long was the political and religious articulation of millions of Indians, was killed by three bullets fired at close range at his prayer meeting on the lawn of the sumptuous Bir a Mansion—the estate of an Indian industrialist who had long supported him.

Police arrested the assassin immediately. They said only that he was a Hindu from Poona. He was held incommunicado at police headquarters.

Mr. Gandhi's passing came less than a year after he achieved his life's main goal of independence from Great Britain for the teeming subcontinent of India. Paradoxically, however, he considered his triumph a failure because India and its 400,000,000 people were divided into separate dominions of India (Hindu) and Pakistan (Moslem). The partition resulted in destructive communal warfare between Moslems on one side and Hindus and Sikhs on the other.

It was in an effort to end the bloodshed that Gandhi undertook this month the last of his many fasts. After five days in which he threatened to starve himself to death, the Hindus and Moslems of New Delhi adopted the Gandhi program and set up a committee of 130 of all religions to meet nightly and review the progress toward his aims.

[Reuters reported that the fraternize with Moslems on the next Mohammedan festival, as in the old days. He asked that mosques which had been converted into Hindu temples or dwelling places be returned to their original uses.

The communal leaders in New Delhi adopted the Gandhi program and set up a committee of 130 of all religions to meet nightly and review the progress toward his aims.

[Reuters reported that the assassin was named Nathuran Vinayak Gode—a young man between 30 and 35 years of age.]

Mr. Gandhi, born to the upper Hindu caste, espoused the cause of the Untouchables in later years. Educated as a lawyer in London, he organized his first civil disobedience campaigns among Indians in South Africa early in the century. He returned to India in 1915 and became recognized leader of the nationalists in 1925.

He attracted world attention in 1930 by leading 70 volunteers on a march from Ahmadabad to Dandi on the Gulf of Cambay to make salt illegally, in a protest against the British salt tax.

A victim of violence, Mr. Gandhi throughout urged his followers to campaigns of nonviolence, even when the Japanese threatened and actually invaded India. His brushes with the British caused him to spend a total of 12 years in prisons.

High lights of Gandhi's career:
Page 6.

Associated Press

A Recent Photograph of Mohandas K. Gandhi

93

THE CHRISTIAN SCIENCE MONITOR

Registered in U. S. Patent Office

AN INTERNATIONAL DAILY NEWSPAPER

VOLUME 40 NO. 145 | BOSTON, SATURDAY, MAY 15, 1948 | * ATLANTIC EDITION | THREE SECTIONS | FIVE CENTS A COPY

COPYRIGHT 1948 BY THE CHRISTIAN SCIENCE PUBLISHING SOCIETY

Buildings Sought For Boston Use

By Courtney R. Sheldon
Staff Writer of The Christian Science Monitor

In almost the same predicament as house-hunting newlyweds, Boston's governmental units are seeking modern accommodations—shelters which will be fire and collapse proof.

Among the projects now taking shape is a proposed $500,000 garage, repair shop and office building for the Boston Traffic Commission.

The Boston Finance Commission requested last night that this and other projects be delayed pending further investigation of the need. However, Mayor Curley immediately rejected this proposal, commenting that qualified municipal officials were agreed on the necessity of the program.

Leo F. Curley, Traffic Commissioner, and his aides believe they have several compelling reasons for a change of scenery.

Old Wooden Stable

First, the Commission's trucks are now garaged in an old wooden stable which has been condemned by the Fire Department.

Also, the activities of the Commission are now located in three separate places — offices in the Sumner Tunnel Terminal building, parking meters in the basement of the City Printing Department, and garage on Atkinson Street.

"We don't care where we go as long as it is centrally located," Commissioner Curley informed City Councilors who must pass on the project.

However, he indicated that the Boston Real Estate Commission had at least two satisfactory sites available on Albany Street. The land is already owned by the city, it was pointed out.

Called 'Fire Trap'

The present garage—where 60 men work—was described as a "fire trap." Fire Department officials inspected the building, Commissioner Curley said, and found that the "building violated every law on the books."

Traffic Commission officials estimate they will need a one and one-half story garage building. In the basement would be the garage storage space.

On the first floor would be room for a repair shop, paint shop and the parking meter division. The offices of the Commission could be fitted into the one-story above the first floor.

According to the Commission's proposals, $50,000 would be spent for foundations, $50,000 for architects, engineers and other contingencies, $20,000 for equipment, and $380,000 for building construction.

For 16 Trucks

The building would be 80 feet by 150 feet and be large endugh to house the 16 trucks of the Commission, plus equipment and supplies.

Merely requesting money for the structure, however, does not assure its construction. The Commission's request is only part of a $4,315,000 loan order being considered by the Finance Committee of the City Council.

Nation Hears Call For New Action In Citizenship Tasks

By Josephine Ripley
Staff Correspondent of The Christian Science Monitor

Washington

The clash of ideologies which resounds throughout the world today gives the job of intelligent, active citizenship a new meaning and urgency.

For that reason the Third National Conference on Citizenship, in session here May 16-19, is attracting nationwide interest, to be thrown into dramatic focus with "America's Town Meeting of the Air" on "How should democracy deal with groups that aim to destroy democracy?" as a feature of the evening session of May 18.

Senator Robert A. Taft (R) of Ohio, Thurman W. Arnold, former Assistant Attorney General, Representative Richard M. Nixon (R) of California, and Ralph E. McGill, Editor of the Atlanta Constitution, will be the participants.

1,000 Delegates

This year's conference is drawing together 1,000 delegates from all over the country, and for the first time finds the United States Department of Justice stepping forward as a direct cosponsor with the National Education Association.

Speakers will include some of the nation's most impressive authorities on what makes a good citizen "tick." One of these speakers is Judge Carl B. Hyatt of the United States Department of Justice.

Judge Hyatt was the man responsible for transforming citizenship induction from a drab mumbling of words into an impressive, dramatic event through his book, "Gateway to Citizenship," which established a new manual of principles and procedures for the naturalization ceremony.

Another featured speaker, Dr. William G. Carr, Associate Secretary of the NEA, was one of the moving spirits behind the formation of the United Nations Educational, Scientific and Cultural Organization.

The conference will open with greetings from the President of the United States, from Charles Evans Hughes, Honorary Chairman of the Conference, and with a personal message of welcome from Attorney General Tom Clark.

Ferretting out the program director, Richard B. Kennan in the throes of conference preparation behind a paper-strewn desk at the NEA, we learned how the idea of dramatizing citizenship in a national conference first started.

Mr. Kennan proved the right source for this information, for it was he who originated the idea, although he modestly passes over that as "unimportant."

It was in 1945 during the war when Mr. Kennan, a well-known educator and former University of Vermont professor, first came to the NEA, that he saw the need for anticipating and heading off, if possible, the inevitable letdown in patriotic enthusiasm which comes after a war has been won.

He queried all national organizations with citizenship programs, such as the American Legion and the Girl Scouts, for their material on citizenship.

What he received was disappointingly meager and filled with vague generalization. What he envisioned was something definite and workable in the way of a program, something which would not only fan the impulses of patriotism but carry them into action in citizenship practices.

Idea Caught Fire

Mr. Kennan felt very strongly that citizenship training was not something to be learned in school and then dropped. He felt that training was even more important later, as the student, oftentimes disillusioned in the let-down from theory to practice, becomes of voting age.

The idea caught fire, and as a first step the NEA joined with the American Legion to sponsor a National Citizenship Day proclamation, introduced in Congress as a joint resolution.

Just about that time from out of the West came the "I Am An American Panegyric Society of California" promoting "I Am An American Day."

For some reason Congress seemed to feel that it would be easier to get approval of an "I Am An American Day." NEA and Legion officials quickly agreed to the compromise, and "I Am An American Day" ceremonies have become a preliminary to the citizenship conference.

Elephants Come to Town And Boston Gets a Parade

By Everett M. Smith
Staff Writer of The Christian Science Monitor

Oompah! OOMpah! OOMPAH!

Welcome strains of Merle Evans' circus band, toot-tootles from the calliope, and chimes from the bell wagon awakened Boston today to its first real old-fashioned circus parade in 28 years.

Young Bostonians were out in mass crowding every inch of the long parade route, and doubly keyed up for the fun by yesterday's postponement on account of rain. Being Saturday and a holiday for many workers, Dads and Mothers joined in the fun, too.

As early as 8:30 a. m. they were on hand to renew one of their childhood pleasures.

Memories of circus parades of years gone by are perhaps more precious than fine gold. Nostalgic associations stirred as the circus band blared a Sousa march or the stepped-up tempo of a Viennese waltz.

The role played in today's Childrens' Crusade parade by the Ringling Brothers and Barnum and Bailey Circus was a small one compared with the circus parades of more than a quarter of a century ago, but it was no less impressive.

Fifteen trumpeting elephants including Tiny, Big Minny, Eva, Jewel, and other ponderous pachyderms were looking for peanuts all along the route and they were not disappointed.

Familiar strains on the calliope were played by the Bay State's own Mike Doyle. Chimes on the bell wagon were rung out by a veteran clown, Johnny Tripp, more than a half-century in the business.

For real old-fashioned memories, however, it remained for the Barnum and Bailey's original circus wagon of 1884 to awaken memories.

Other circus equipment in the big parade included the Do-see-do carriage driven by tramp clown Emmett Kelley, the jack-in-the-box spectacle with little Prince Paul, another Boston boy, and Lulu, the circus lady clown, in attendance.

Throughout the parade circus clowns in their gay make-up and costumes were augmented by beautiful riding horses with even more beautiful girls smiling their best to the assembled throngs.

There was also another gay wagon from the circus spectacle in the Noah's Ark float with the tiny members of the Doll [illegible]mily in charge. Bystanders didn't know it but they had Pat Valdo of B&B to thank. He had rounded up much of the circus personnel who volunteered for the parade.

All in all it was a huge spectacle—when viewed through the rose colored glasses of yesteryear and it satisfied many a nostalgic longing.

Vermont Republicans Open State Convention

The World's Day
Reg. U.S. Pat. Off.

New England: Vermont GOP Opens Convention

Vermont Republicans opened their State convention in Montpelier with Representative Charles A. Halleck (R) of Indiana charging noncooperation by President Truman with the Republican-dominated Congress. [Page 18.]

Albert Gray, Jr., of Staten Island, N. Y., was appointed Town Manager for Meredith, N. H. He will be graduated from the University of Maine's public management course in June.

Bostonians had a view of the noted Brookhaven National Laboratory's Atomic Energy display as Mechanics Building was the stage for the interesting exhibits. [Page 2.]

Washington: Truman Urges Surpluses for Poor

President Truman proposed that future farm surpluses be fed to the poor to assure farmers prosperity and improve the national health. [Page 19.]

Disagreements between Congress leaders clouded the prospect for any early action on the draft.

The House plunged into a hot debate on a bill to put tight hobbles on American Communists.

Europe: British to Get More Milk in Derationing

More milk for Britons and more bread for Germans are in the offing. Beginning tomorrow, Britain will end restrictions on the sale of milk for three weeks after nearly 10 years of rationing. In western Germany, British and American officials said the bread ration would be boosted by over two pounds a person a month.

1,320 persons have been executed in Greece since June, 1946, Press Minister Michael Alianos announced in Athens. They were convicted for "high treason," not for "political or civil crimes." London, Paris, and Moscow have commented on the severity and frequency of the sentences.

National: Krug Accents Private Oil Development

Secretary of the Interior J. A. Krug, in Tulsa, Okla., told the world's top oil men that private industry—not the Government—should develop synthetic fuels.

Far East: Americans Granted Visas to Dairen

Visas to enter Dairen, northeast China port held by Russia, have been granted to American consular personnel in a surprise move. All but a few foreigners have been denied entry since the war's end.

Electric power for South Korea remained shut off for a second night by North Korean power plants under Soviet control. The move is regarded as retaliatory for the strong anti-Communist trend in the recent South Korean elections.

Weather Predictions: Clearing (Details, Page 2.)

Inside Reading:

Saturday, May 15, 1948

Soviet Press Assails U. S. Balk on Talks

By Edmund Stevens
Staff Correspondent of The Christian Science Monitor

Moscow

Disappointment over the American attitude toward Soviet Foreign Minister Vyacheslav M. Molotov's proposal for bilateral Soviet-American negotiations is written large in the latest editions of the Soviet press.

The Soviet press has been vigorous in its attack on the American position.

But there are some diplomatic observers here who believe that this episode is only the opening gambit in a much larger play. And they await the next moves.

What has happened is clearly regarded here as sort of diplomatic reconnaissance, with both sides trying to sound out the other's position and ascertain whether the other was prepared to yield at any point.

U. S. Blunder Inferred

Some observers here feel that by taking the initiative the United States unavoidably placed itself at a bargaining disadvantage, opening itself to inferences it was prepared to concede. The manner in which the Soviet press presented Ambassador Walter Bedell Smith's declaration and Mr. Molotov's reply tended to give this impression.

The restatement of the American position embodied in Mr. Smith's note does not get great emphasis in this reasoning—nor was it given top emphasis by the Soviet press.

Instead, President Truman and Secretary of State George C. Marshall are pictured as seeking to scuttle the whole issue and of going back on the previous American declaration.

In this connection the well-known Pravda commentator Victorov cites statements by the President and the Secretary of State that United States policy remains unchanged, and Secretary Marshall's further remarks that the United States has no intention of discussing bilaterally with the Soviet Union questions involving other states.

Subterfuge Alleged

He attempts to contrast these subsequent utterances with what he describes as the initial widespread favorable reaction in the United States to Soviet-American diplomatic exchange, which seemed to augur well for early realization of good intentions voiced by both governments.

But now, he asserts, American leaders have disclosed their true intentions. "As though at the wave of a magic wand," claims Victorov, "the tone of the American press cooled off, as did public utterances of politicians."

The American State Department, Victorov asserts, never really intended to negotiate with the Soviet Union. It was simply looking for ways of reducing war hysteria in the United States, "which has reached proportions that of late have placed United States ruling circles in an embarrassing position."

American Critics Cited

Victorov declares that the State Department's handling of the whole affair has been sharply criticized in America, and that even leading conservative papers like the Washington Post and the New York Herald-Tribune have deplored its apparent failure to make the best of the opportunity for settling differences with the Soviet Union.

Tass, like Pravda, expresses the immediate reaction, rather than indicating any long-range aspects of the interchange. A Tass dispatch from Washington singles out those portions of a dispatch from the correspondent of The Times of London, to the effect that President Truman's statement is generally regarded as unsatisfactory.

Foreign Press Quoted

As for Secretary Marshall's declaration, The Times correspondent is quoted as saying that a majority of the people eager for peace would not inquire into American motives and would prefer that Americans took the risk that accompanies this hope rather than affirming a cautious position which for the remainder of the world can only mean a perpetuation of fear.

The subject of American motives is dealt with in other press comment quoted by Tass from other capitals.

Thus, Pierre Courtade of Paris' L'Humanité (Communist daily) is cited as writing that in making its initial approach to Moscow, Washington had been forced to backwater "under pressure of democratic and peace loving forces throughout the world."

Israel Recognized by U. S.; Nation Launched Minus Pomp

Few Foreigners At Tel Aviv Ritual

By Francis Ofner
Special Correspondent of The Christian Science Monitor

Tel Aviv, Israel

It was a simple, almost informal, ceremony of 40 minutes which established the Jewish state of "Israel."

Thus was born the first Jewish state in the Holy Land since 135 A. D. when the Bar Kohba state in the Holy Land rebellion was suppressed by the Roman legions.

David Ben-Gurion, first Premier of the newly proclaimed Israel, announced the official rebirth of the Jewish nation in Tel Aviv Museum. Scarcely 400 people listened inside the small building, protected by a Haganah guard of honor.

Jews attended the ceremony with almost religious fervor, and many of them did not even notice that no official representatives of the outside world were present.

Study in Contrasts

Two years ago when I witnessed the birth of another state, the coronation of King Abdullah of Transjordan, not only high dignitaries of the Arab world but also diplomatic and consular representatives of a number of western powers were there.

Lt. Gen. Sir Alan Cunningham, High Commissioner of Palestine, as well as a number of other British civil and military personalities were among the guests then and watched the colorful parade of Bedouin tribes, of Abdullah's picturesque camel-mounted forces, and of the Arab Legion on the airfield of Amman.

At Tel Aviv's historic act, only newspapermen represented the foreign world.

Among some 400 persons assembled, I saw the man who witnessed the whole history of Zionism from its inception to its fulfillment He is the venerable Viennese Dr. Isidor Schalit, who was secretary to Dr. Theodor Herzl, the founder of world Zionist organization.

Topped Fondest Hopes

Dr. Schalit was organizer of the first Zionist Congress at Basel, Switzerland, in 1897, and at this proclamation of the state of Israel was guest of honor.

"When 51 years ago we decided at Basel to make Hatikvah the Zionist anthem and blue and white the colors to the Zionist flag, even a young optimist like myself did not dare to hope I should see with my own eyes how this flag and this anthem would become the national insignia of our state," Dr. Schalit told me with tears in his eyes.

While the streets of Tel Aviv, provisional Jewish capital, and other parts of Israel still were echoing from joy which had been increased by the unexpected and speedy United States recognition, the Jewish provisional government commenced, in spite of the Sabbath, its deliberations on fateful problems which the new state is facing.

The first act of the new 13-man Jewish cabinet was to revoke the British White Paper of 1939, restricting Jewish immigration and land purchase rights.

All other Palestine laws remain in force.

Questions of threatened Arab invasion, application for membership at the United Nations, and the problem of immigration are the first items on the agenda.

Immigration Speeded

Deliberations on the first two items are veiled with complete secrecy. Concerning immigration, the provisional Jewish government is deciding to transfer to Israel 24,000 Jews interned at Cyprus in the course of the next two months. A few thousand others aree xpected from Europe in the same period. The first day of existence of the new state, May 15, two ships are scheduled to arrive here with immigrants from Cyprus.

Preparations are being made to open passport offices and visa sections throughout the world. Palestine offices of the Jewish Agency, which hitherto existed in various parts of the world, are to act as visa sections of the state of Israel.

Official circles hope that absorption of the new flow of immigrants will not be too difficult as existing industry needs urgently some 20,000 more workers.

Seven hours before the state of Isreal was proclaimed in Tel Aviv, some 60 miles northward in Haifa the final ceremony of winding up the British mandate took place.

Exactly 30 years ago British General Allenby marched into Haifa and was greeted by both Arabs and Jews with flowers and cheers. This latest ceremony was not the case when another British General, Sir Alan Cunningham, last British High Commissioner for Palestine, was leaving the same town. The British, who showed much administrative and political ability in various parts of the world, did not win support for their Palestine administration.

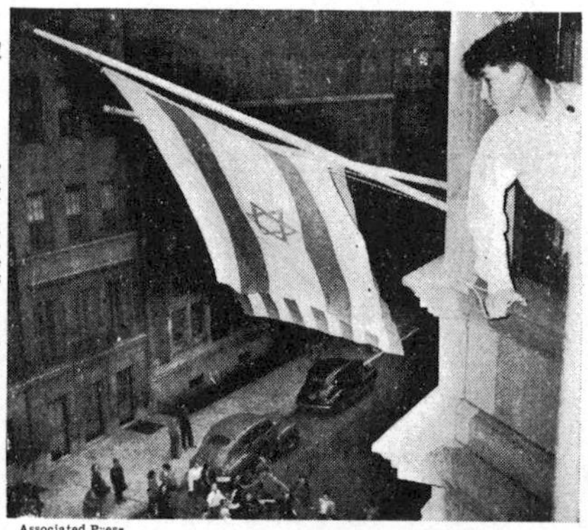

Associated Press

Haim Shertok, teen-age son of Moshe Shertok, Foreign Minister designate of the newly proclaimed Jewish state of Israel, looks out the window of the Jewish Agency at New York City as young Jews dance in the street to celebrate the raising of the Zionist flag next to the American flag in the window of the Agency.

Zionists Elated; Arabs Stunned

By Neal Stanford
Staff Correspondent of The Christian Science Monitor

Washington

President Truman recognized the new Jewish state of "Israel" in Palestine with lightning speed.

His action, taken only 20 minutes after the British ended their mandate and the Jewish state came into being, caught Washington by complete surprise. It immediately touched off a wave of elation among Zionists. It left the Arab world stunned and angry. It confounded and confused the United Nations, which even as the Truman statement was issued, was futilely debating the Palestine crisis.

It was unquestionably one of the best kept secrets in recent Washington history. State Department officials, except for Secretary of State George C. Marshall and one or two others, knew nothing of it. The United States representatives at Lake Success had not been told.

Decided About May 1?

The President is understood to have made up his mind on this step about May 1, contingent on failure of the UN to settle the situation before the British pulled out.

One of the few who is said to have had foreknowledge of this action was Judge Samuel I. Rosenman of New York, a close friend and adviser of the White House. Whether he played any part in helping the President reach his decision is not known.

Mr. Truman's announcement received the immediate approval of Senator Arthur H. Vandenberg (R) of Michigan, President of the Senate, whose support will be enormously helpful in solidifying congressional support for any future aid-to-Palestine measures.

Said the Chairman of the Senate Foreign Relations Committee: "It is the logical and proper step.... It takes account of the reality that no other authority can fill what would otherwise be a cruel and dangerous vacuum....

Boost for UN

"It responds to a basic decision of the United Nations taken at our instance. It is positive action after many months of critical and unhappy indecision.

"If the present course of the United States is followed by other governments, I am unable to believe that the parties in controversy cannot be successfuly summoned to the bar of the United Nations in behalf of an urgent truce.

"The restoration of law and order and an environment of peace is indispensable to the best evolution for all concerned."

Recognition immediately raised the issue of what next. Following the White House statement, Presidential Secretary Charles G. Ross shed some light on next moves by stating that the United States intended to continue working for a truce between Jews and Arabs in Palestine.

Arms Embargo Unsettled

As to whether the United States will lift its arms embargo, which has kept American weapons from legally reaching the Jewish forces in Palestine, it appeared Washington had not yet made up its mind. Informed quarters said that recognition did not carry with it the lifting of the embargo, and suggested, though not saying so flatly, that for the mement there would be no change There will be what one might call a wait-and-see policy.

Mr. Truman's formal words recognizing the new Jewish state follow:

"This Government has been informed that a Jewish state has been proclaimed in Palestine and recognition has been requested by the provisional government thereof. The United States recognizes the provisional government as the de facto authority of the new state of Israel."

De facto recognition, it is pointed out here, is the normal procedure for governments in the process of creation. The assumption is that in time de jure recognition is extended almost automatically.

Transjordan Case Stalls

Informed quarters here say that for a time, the White House had also seriously considered recognizing Palestine's neighboring Arab state of Transjordan, whose King Abdullah is expected to occupy the Arab portions of Palestine with his British-trained army. But the suspicions and rivalries between the Transjordan King and the other Arab chiefs discouraged the project. Its consequences might have caused more trouble than it was worth.

Despite the fact that Arab forces are today reported b[illegible]ing Tel Aviv and invading [illegible]tine, Washington of late has less alarmed over the possib[illegible] of an all-out fight in the Holy Land than a month or so ago. One reason appears to be the military strength and skill exhibited by the Palestinian Jews. Another, the military weakness and disunity of the Arab League countries.

Now with American recognition behind them, the Palestinian Jews also can be counted on to press diplomatically for a lifting of the arms embargo. Already the White House and State Department are feeling the pressure to that end—a pressure that is sure to mount with the days.

UN Delegates Rap U.S. Shift on Palestine

By Homer Metz
Staff Correspondent of The Christian Science Monitor

Lake Success

It was in an incredible atmosphere of consternation and confusion caused by the swift recognition accorded to the new Jewish state of Isreal by the United States that the General Assembly of the United Nations wound up its special session by adopting—37 to 7—a resolution to send a UN mediator to Palestine.

The American recognition of Isreal announced in Washington by President Truman—without the knowledge of the American delegation here, incidentally—overshadows everything else for the moment in the tense Palestine drama, including the dramatic birth of a new nation and the likelihood of large-scale warfare in the Holy Land.

New About-Face

It is seen here as another astonishing shift in American policy as regards Palestine.

It puts the seal of legality on the partition of the Holy Land into independent Jewish and Arab states—the very thing the United States fought so viciously to avoid, first in the Security Council and later in the social session of the Assembly, where it sought to have a UN trusteeship imposed upon the Holy Land.

It left the assembly shocked and breathless.

U. S. Policy Scored

As the meeting drew to a close, delegate after delegate arose to criticize the United States' course. American prestige in the UN has been severely compromised.

The general view here is that the American action will have two immediate results:

1. It will virtually nullify the chances of a UN mediator to achieve a military truce or a political compromise between the Jews and Arabs, at least for some time to come.

2. It will drive at least one part of the Arab world into the open arms of Russia.

Seen as Peace Move

On the other side, the American action may in the long run convince the Arabs that it is futile to continue major military operations against the Jews and thus remove a threat to world peace in Palestine.

At the same time, it must be recognized that there may be more than meets the eye in the President's astonishing move.

A hint of this conceivably may be read into the immediate reaction of British delegates here.

According to an authoritative British spokesman, the British had planned to recognize Israel, but only after they receive assurances from the Jerusalem provisional government that Britain will be compensated financially for the maintenance of 32,000 "illegal" Jewish refugees on Cyprus.

This suggests that a three-way deal may be in the making by the British, the Jewish Agency, and King Abdullah of Transjordan, whereby the Transjordan monarch would leave the Jewish part of Palestine more or less alone in exchange for a free hand elsewhere in the Holy Land.

It remains to be seen, of course, whether this supposition is correct.

The effects of the American action are likely to be far reaching. The Arabs, for example, are voicing veiled threats to withdraw American oil concessions in the Middle East and to take other summary action.

The French are displeased because they had no prior knowledge of the action.

Gromyko Blasts Move

Soviet delegate Andrei A. Gromyko accused the United States of having got the UN into "a ludicrous situation" and of wrecking whatever chance there might have been of effecting a compromise between the Jews and Arabs.

The majority of the smaller and intermediate powers and the Latin-American states assert that the UN "has been dealt a grave blow."

A French-American resolution calling for the establishment of a UN trusteeship in Jerusalem to protect that city's holy places was rejected by the Assembly by a vote of 20 to 15, with 19 abstentions.

Council Still Seeks Truce in Holy Land

By the Associated Press

Lake Success

The United Nation's Security Council's American-French - Belgian consular truce commission remains operative in Palestine. The Jerusalem Mayor and the Palestine mediator are expected to go into the Holy Land soon.

Any steps to stop the fighting still rest with the Council, which so far has done nothing beyond naming the truce commission.

The Council now has an appeal before it from the Jewish Agency to halt the reported invasion of Palestine by armies of Arab nations. No meeting has been set.

Of All Things . . .

Kansas Gets Rain Test

By the Associated Press

Hollywood

Mrs. J. E. Morris won some rain, but she hopes to move it to Kansas.

Mrs. Morris, who lives in Santa Ana, Calif., and has only 30 feet of front lawn, was named winner of a farm contest on radio station KMPC. It entitles her to "an opportunity to have the clouds above her ranch seeded with dry ice."

Her front lawn does not need any rain, so Mrs. Morris asked KMPC if she could transfer the test to land she owns near Winfield, Kan. The station agreed, and promised to contact the Physics Department of the University of Wichita, Kan., for advice.

Concrete 'Bust'

By the Associated Press

Champaign, Ill.

Attorney John L. Franklin's asparagus crop is sprouting, but he's not happy.

Mr. Franklin planted the asparagus in his yard three years ago. It didn't come up so Mr. Franklin built a driveway over the barren patch. For surfacing he used four inches of gravel and two inches of asphalt.

Now the driveway is splitting and the asparagus is peeking through the cracks. Mr. Franklin thought he had something for natural science. But Lee Somers of the University of Illinois College of Agriculture shrugged him off with this story:

An ivy vine less than an inch in diameter once threw old University Hall completely out of plumb.

'Solar Suit' Shown

By the Associated Press

Chicago

A department store let out its imagination today and came up with an "atomic-sola suit" for the 21st-century male.

The suit does away with collars, neckties, buttons, shoelaces, lapels and pockets. It is made of wrinkle-proof, water-repellent plastic, and can be cleaned with a damp cloth.

In lieu of pockets, the wearer sports a wristband containing a watch, and—the store predicts—an electronic communications set that can put the owner in touch with any point in the world.

The suit was designed by Goldblatt Bros., Ltd., and the clothiers who supply it.

The store explained the name by saying the coming age is an atomic one and sola, short for solar, means the suit would let the sun's rays in.

THE CHRISTIAN SCIENCE MONITOR

Registered in U. S. Patent Office

AN INTERNATIONAL DAILY NEWSPAPER

VOLUME 40 NO. 289   COPYRIGHT 1948 BY THE CHRISTIAN SCIENCE PUBLISHING SOCIETY   BOSTON, WEDNESDAY, NOVEMBER 3, 1948   ** ATLANTIC EDITION   TWO SECTIONS   FIVE CENTS A COPY

Truman Elected; Dewey Concedes After Close Race; Dever Nets Record Plurality, Saltonstall Survives

Democrats Rule Congress

By Richard L. Strout
Staff Correspondent of The Christian Science Monitor

Washington

Democrats took control of the 81st Congress in the most spectacular election overturn in modern times.

Democratic National Chairman J. Howard McGrath issued a statement asserting that control of the House had passed to the Democratic Party.

"This ensures that the liberal, progressive program of legislation proposed by President Truman will now be carried out with both houses of the Congress safely in Democratic control," Senator McGrath said.

"The jury of the people has returned its verdict upon the donothing Congress, thanks to a frank and effective presentation of the case by President Truman. One needs only to recall the voting record of most of those who are returning to the hall of Congress to recognize that a mandate for progressive liberalism has been returned by those who gave the final word."

Capture of Congress by the Democrats represents one of the most significant upsets of advance newspaper and "scientific" poll forecasts since the Literary Digest magazine erroneously predicted the election of Gov. Alf Landon over Franklin D. Roosevelt.

An element in the situation which apparently received too little attention was the upsurge of the vote of organized labor, spurred by the Taft-Hartley Act. A pattern appeared to be forming as returns came in as to the Republican congressmen replaced by Democrats. In many cases advocates of the recent labor legislation were being knocked off.

New Chairmen

Capture of Congress means that every committee of the legislature will have a new chairman. Most notable of the senators involved is Arthur H. Vandenberg (R) of Michigan, whose Democratic counterpart on the Foreign Relations Committee is Senator Tom Connally (D) of Texas. Actually the switch of these two men would not greatly affect foreign policy. They have seen eye to eye on international cooperation.

Another big factor in the congressional upset appears to have been President Truman's relentless, unremitting attack on the "do-nothing 80th Congress" which he called the "second worst in history."

Never was the record of Congress so figured in a national election. In many states the incomplete returns showed that voters had "split" their tickets, with many supporters of Governor Dewey voting against Republican congressional incumbents.

Congress Statistics

Statistically, the situation in Congress was as follows.

In the Senate, the Republicans have held a 51-to-45 vote majority. This meant that the Democrats needed to make a net gain of four seats to take over the upper chamber where 32 senators out of 96 were up for election.

If Democrats hold their own in the races where they now lead they will have 263 seats in the House to 171 Republicans and 1 American labor.

According to press association counts the Democrats had won a certain 239 house seats, or 21 more than a majority. They were leading Republican opponents in 24 other congressional districts.

At the same time 139 Republicans were elected and 32 were leading.

In the Senate the Democrats were in control.

The indicated line-up was 54 Democrats to 42 Republicans. Democrats had elected 19 candidates in contests for the 32 seats. Republicans had elected eight and were leading in another.

In the Senate, the Democrats seemed to be within easy control with results not all in.

In the House membership of 435 a total of 432 remained to be chosen, three Maine Republicans already having been selected at the earlier Maine election. In the 80th Congress the relative party position was 246 Republicans, 187 Democrats and 2 American Labor. This meant the Democrats needed to pick up 34 seats to give them control.

Control Claimed

Even while the returns still were incomplete, Democratic leaders were claiming, and advance results then supported the contention, that the Democratic Party had captured control in the two houses.

Prof. Paul Douglas, a Democratic liberal, defeated Senator C. Wayland Brooks (R) of Illinois, one of the most far reaching and politically extraordinary incidents of the election. Senator Brooks is an crypto-isolationist of the Chicago Tribune school; Professor Douglas a strong New Deal internationalist. At the same time in Illinois another so-called reform candidate, Adlai Stevenson defeated the incumbent Gov. Dwight H. Green. Democrats already have a mayor in Chicago.

Victory for Bowles

Another former New Dealer elected in the Democratic upsurge appears to be Chester Bowles (D) as governor of Connecticut.

Under Democratic control, Representative Sam Rayburn (D) of Texas will replace Representative Joseph W. Martin (R) of Massachusetts as speaker. In an interview, Mr. Rayburn declared Democrats would challenge the seating of Representative J. Parnell Thomas (D) of New Jersey, chairman of the Un-American Activities Committee, now under investigation on charges of irregularities in connection with his office pay roll, Representative John McDowell (R) of Pennsylvania, another prominent member of the committee, was defeated by a Democrat who had strong tradeunion support.

Knutson's Status

One prominent Republican having election difficulties was Representative Harold Knutson (R) of Minnesota, chairman of the Ways and Means Committee.

The position of Senator Alben W. Barkley (D) of Kentucky is peculiar. If Mr. Truman is elected, Senator Barkley becomes presiding officer pro tem. That means the new governor of Kentucky will name Senator Barkley's successor in the Senate seat. If Mr. Dewey is elected, Senator Barkley still remains in the Senate in his own right and will be majority leader in case of expected Democratic control.

The apparent overturn in Congress leaves a temporary non-plussed feeling of confusion in Washington. To say that it is a stunning surprise hardly describes the mood.

The political difficulties in the situation are apparent.

Chief of the problems is the fact that the Democrats in the 80th Congress actually opposed President Truman almost as much as the Republicans did. In case after case a majority of the Democrats, like the bulk of the Republicans, voted to override Mr. Truman's veto.

Labor Bill Stand

Thus, on the Taft-Hartley veto, a majority of the Democrats of both the Senate and House voted against their own President in favor of the Taft-Hartley Act.

The same was true on the Presidential third veto of the tax-reduction measure.

Thus, whoever is the next President of the United States, he will almost certainly have trouble with Congress.

Even with the accession of new Democratic members in the Senate and in the House, the combined conservative group in the legislature would appear to be more than a majority in regard to the New Deal position Mr. Truman has taken.

Weather Predictions: Cloudy, Cool (Details Page 2)

President Truman
Associated Press

Hoover Urges U.S. to Rally Behind Truman for Peace

By the Associated Press

Comments on the Democratic victory:

Herbert Hoover, former Republican President: "All Americans will now rally unitedly to the President's support that we may have peace on earth and prosperity for our country."

Senator J. Howard McGrath, Democratic national chairman: "It marks a tremendous victory for American labor, for to the organized political effort of the American labor movement much of the credit must be given."

Brien McMahon, United States Senator from Connecticut (D): "President Truman has scored the most remarkable personal victory in American history. He didn't have anyone with him but the people, and that is enough in a democracy."

Gov. Thomas E. Dewey, after conceding defeat, sent this telegram to President Truman: "My heartiest congratulations to you on your election and every good wish for a successful administration. I urge all Americans to unite behind you in support of every effort to keep our nation strong and free and establish peace in the world."

Jack Kroll, director of the CIO's Political Action Committee:

"The people of America have given their mandate. They look to the Democratic Party to carry out its platform, the people of the United States have demonstrated their genuine unity in defense of the cherished principles of the New Deal."

George Meany, treasurer of the AFL's Labor League for Political Education, speaking about the Taft-Hartley repeal pledge:

"That's our fight and we mean to continue it. If we don't get repeal now, we're going to look forward to 1950. We concentrated our fire where we were strongest. We feel that we were responsible for getting out the big vote.

"We worked hard and we feel we were instrumental in changing about eight senators and at least 50 representatives in Congress—all on the basis of the Taft-Hartley Act."

Sen. Alben W. Barkley, who retired at his home here last night after listening to early vote returns on his radio, didn't sleep too well.

The running mate of Truman, who wound up a two-fisted campaign here the day before election, got up during the wee small hours of the morning, checked latest returns and declared:

Cook Leads

By Courtney R. Sheldon
The Christian Science Monitor

Republican domination of Beacon Hill crumbled today as Paul A. Dever's record-shattering Massachusetts gubernatorial triumph approached a plurality of 300,000.

Senator Leverett Saltonstall and Secretary of State Frederic W. Cook apparently were the only statewide Republican candidates to weather the hailstorm of Democratic votes.

Returns from 1,635 of 1,879 precincts netted Dever 1,041,003 and Bradford 747,204.

Mr. Dever's achievement set a new record for pluralities in a Massachusetts gubernatorial race.

'Silent Vote' Speaks

Meanwhile, the Bay State's "silent vote"—apparently unheard in public-opinion polls—awarded the state's 16 electoral votes to President Truman.

With 1,685 of 1,879 precincts counted, the presidential vote was Truman 1,005,778, Dewey 825,485, and Wallace 32,060.

The New York governor lost to President Roosevelt in 1944 by a 114,946 margin.

In the majority of cities and towns, Dever was stronger than Truman, while Bradford lagged behind Dewey.

Well-organized opposition to the birth-control referendums and to the three labor referendums resulted in their rejection.

Referendums Key Factor

These issues were potent drawing cards in drawing an all-time high of voters—much to the advantage of the Democrats.

As the Democratic victories reached landslide proportions, the Democrats gained working control of the Executive Council by a 5-to-4 margin. Three seats now held by Republicans are unresolved.

Meanwhile, the Associated Press tabulation showed the Democrats close to control of the Massachusetts Senate. At least 20 of the 40 seats have already been captured by Democrats and several contests are undecided.

The Republicans controlled the Governor's Council by a 8-to-1 margin before elections and the Senate by a 22-to-18 edge.

In statewide contests, Senator Saltonstall is securely ahead of John I. Fitzgerald (D). However, the senator's current lead of about 150,000 is about 300,000 below the anticipated plurality.

Secretary of State Frederic W. Cook is maintaining a slim lead over Edward J. Cronin (D) in his bid for a 15th term. With 1,601 of 1,879 precincts counted, Mr. Cook leads by 27,417 votes.

A tight battle for state treasurer was apparently resolved in favor of John E. Hurley (D). In 1,601 precincts, Mr. Hurley earned a 151,867 margin over the State Treasurer Laurence Curtis.

Barnes Trails

The only Democrat now holding statewide office, State Auditor Thomas J. Buckley, again was too strong for Russell A. Wood (R). Mr. Buckley is ahead in 1,601 precincts by 369,786.

In the Attorney General contest, the Democratic challenger, Francis E. Kelly, leads Attorney General Clarence A. Barnes by a vote margin of 81,207.

Congressional contests in Massachusetts, influenced by the Democratic trend in the pluralities recorded, resulted in on Democratic victory in the Second District, making the score Republicans 8 and Democrats 6.

Mr. Dever's overpowering victory margin parallels a nationwide Democratic upsurge.

The most plausible explanation offered for this unexpected development is that the electorate was rebuking the Republicans for their congressional record on prices, housing, and labor legislation.

At the same time, it is likely that many persons admired the President for taking a definite stand on many issues and also maintaining a man-in-the-street approach.

Local Factors Play

However, local factors—such as the apparent united support of the groups turning out to defeat the birth control and labor referendums—were important ingredients.

Also, unity within the local Democratic Party surpassed the teamwork efforts of the Republicans.

Boston accounted for about 168,000 of Mr. Dever's plurality, but other industrial cities joined in amassing pluralities for the Democratic candidate.

Thus, Governor Bradford never began to pile up the anticipated margins outside Boston. He gained over his 1946 totals in many towns, but higher percentage gains were made by his Democratic opponent.

Early in the evening, as the Boston voting trend was learned, Mr. Dever claimed victory. Shortly after midnight, Governor Bradford conceded the election.

Part of Governor Bradford's failure in the vote department is being ascribed to lack of dramatization of the two-year record of his administration. Also, the attacks on Governor Bradford, including the 15-cent MTA fare issue, were found difficult to combat.

Bay State Returns

GOVERNOR		
(1,635 of 1,879 precincts)		
Dever (D)		1,041,003
*Bradford (R)		747,204
LIEUTENANT GOVERNOR		
(1,601 of 1,879 precincts)		
Sullivan (D)		945,752
*Coolidge (R)		752,685
SECRETARY		
(1,601 of 1,879 precincts)		
*Cook (R)		855,472
Cronin (D)		828,055
TREASURER		
(1,601 of 1,879 precincts)		
Hurley (D)		915,043
*Curtis (R)		763,176
AUDITOR		
(1,601 of 1,879 precincts)		
*Buckley (D)		1,016,677
Wood (R)		646,891
ATTORNEY GENERAL		
(1,601 of 1,879 precincts)		
Kelly (D)		879,131
*Barnes (R)		797,924
UNITED STATES SENATOR		
(1,601 of 1,879 precincts)		
*Saltonstall (R)		932,715
Fitzgerald (D)		781,374

* Incumbent.

State of the Nation

By Roscoe Drummond
Chief, Washington News Bureau, The Christian Science Monitor

The American people have rewarded Harry S. Truman's dauntless, dogged, outspoken campaign by voting the President a full four-year term in the White House and by giving the Democratic Party a conclusive national victory.

Though the victory is not overwhelming numerically—far from it—it is decisive at every point.

Republican nominee Thomas E. Dewey conceded defeat in a congratulatory statement to the President shortly before noon.

"My heartiest congratulations to you on your election," the governor wired to Independence, Mo., "and every good wish for a successful administration, and I urge all Americans to unite behind you in support of every effort to keep our nation strong and free and establish peace in the world."

This word from Independence, New York came as the final returns were ensuring Mr. Truman's victory. His lead was holding up in Ohio, and that's all he needed. His advantage appeared secure in Illinois. He was forging visibly ahead in California.

Best Pollster of All

The President replied, commending Governor Dewey for his "fine sportsmanship," and said all his efforts would be devoted to "the cause of peace in the world" and to prosperity and happiness at home.

Almost singlehandedly, with his party grievously split to the right in the South and to the left by the Wallace Progressives, the President reversed the onrushing Republican trend of 1946 and turned a general forecast of defeat into a sensational upset.

He proved to be the best pollster of them all.

To the President go the full fruits of his gallant and successful efforts. They add up to an impressive, meaningful political triumph. They are these:

An assured Electoral College majority over Gov. Thomas E. Dewey.

Full control of the House of Representatives, clinched by 238 assured votes, which is 20 more than needed to control. The Republicans had 145 at the last count, with 51 in doubt and one going to American Labor.

Control in Senate

Working control of the Senate, with 50 seats assured to the Republicans' 40. Six remained in doubt.

A popular plurality of more than 1,500,000, or 3 per cent of the total vote, over Governor Dewey, which is kept smaller by the Thurmond and Wallace minority votes.

The election of liberal candidates to Congress in both parties, thus giving to a new Truman administration the prospect of wider backing for his policies in both House and Senate.

The election of a majority of Democratic governors, which means that now in more than half of the 48 states the Democratic Party is reinvigorated and ascendant.

When Governor Dewey conceded the Truman victory, the President had forged ahead for the first time in California, was leading in Illinois by approximately 72,000 votes with only 6 per cent of the electorate to be reported, and was leading by 14,422 votes in Ohio with only 164 precincts to be heard from. These were the key states around which the contest revolved in its final hours.

The popular vote, at latest count, stood as follows:

Truman	20,308,873
Dewey	18,770,581
Wallace	953,674
Thurmond	783,846

President Truman in the end was leading in 28 states, with a total of 304 electoral votes, 38 more than needed to win. Governor Dewey was leading in 16 states, with a total electoral vote of 189. Governor Thurmond led in four states, with 38 votes.

Salient Facts

Three salient political facts stand out today in the wake of the fullest returns:

1. The President defeated the Republican 80th Congress more than he defeated the Republican presidential nominee, Governor Dewey. Mr. Truman made the 80th Congress and its record his principal antagonist—and he defeated that Congress conclusively. He defeated it overwhelmingly in the House. He defeated it significantly in the Senate. He defeated it even more than the Democratic numerical majority indicates because his campaign helped to bring into office liberal Republicans as well as Democrats.

2. Mr. Truman's definite Electoral College victory would have been greatly enhanced had it not been for the Wallace and Dixiecrat defections within the Democratic Party. It is significant that the President won despite these defections. They drew almost entirely from Truman strength, and without this handicap the President would have a minimum of 85 additional electoral votes. These would be made up of the 38 electoral votes Mr. Thurmond carried in Louisiana, Mississippi, Alabama, and South Carolina, plus the 47 electoral votes of Governor Dewey's home state of New York, which would have gone to Mr. Truman easily if Mr. Wallace had not been in the race.

Small Wallace Vote

3. The total Wallace vote throughout the nation proved smaller than his most earnest critics dared hope. It was a massive repudiation of what the former vice-president stood for, which was principally allout opposition to the nation's bipartisan foreign policy and appeasement of the Soviet Union.

Though Democrats were winning all over the nation—senators, representatives, governors —the real victory was Harry S. Truman's very own. It was a victory which was given to him by the voters, who believed to what he said and believed what he said. It was an uphill, hard-fought, and at times a lonely campaign which the President waged.

He owes little to the big-city machines, which tried to keep him from being nominated.

He owes little to other figures in his party, many of whom supported him only halfheartedly and without any real expectation of winning.

Today Harry S. Truman is President-elect because of Harry S. Truman—and the big outpouring of voters who decided on balance that the President was nearer right than his opponent and that his specific policies and programs were more to their liking than the considerable generalities of Mr. Dewey.

Never Cried 'Uncle'

It is likely that if he were to be completely candid, Mr. Truman would admit that he was surprised by his own election. He conducted a chin-up, nevercry-uncle campaign, but when we asked him once if he were confident of the outcome, he didn't say yes. He said quickly and frankly, as is his manner: "A pessimistic candidate isn't any good."

Though his political intimates admitted in the middle of the campaign that the President was, in gridiron parlance, on his own 10-yard line with the game nearly over, Mr. Truman was not a pessimistic candidate—and he proved to be good.

Mr. Truman is not the kind of politician who ducks a battle or runs from the field when the going gets tough.

He is literally the man from Missouri. He had to be shown. They told him he couldn't be nominated. He said: "Show me!" He was nominated, and he put new fight into the Democratic crusade.

'Show Me' Demand

They told him, after he was nominated, that he couldn't win. He said: "Show me!" He won, and he carried Democratic senators, democratic congressmen, Democratic governors— and some liberal Republican congressional candidates—to victory on his shoulders.

From the very moment of his near-dawn nomination in Philadelphia at the depth of Democratic despair—a despair which if he felt it he never showed—President Truman made the issues in this astounding election and carried the fight incessantly to his opposition.

Traveling by rail and plane 25,000 miles from Sept. 6 in Detroit to preelection eve in Independence, Mo., and delivering some 280 speeches, Mr. Truman put his case to the jury of the American voters as few candidates have in the past.

President Polled, Says . . . 'I'm Just Happy'

By the Associated Press

Kansas City, Mo.

President Truman promised today to dedicate himself "to the cause of peace in the world" and "prosperity and happiness at home" as he won one of history's greatest upset victories.

He promised to "serve the American people to the best of my ability" in the four years ahead.

And he acknowledged the congratulations of his defeated opponent, Gov. Thomas E. Dewey, and commended him for his "fine sportsmanship."

"I feel very deeply the responsibility which has fallen to my lot as the result of the election," said his simple statement. "I shall continue to serve the American people to the best of my ability. All my efforts will be devoted to the cause of peace in the world and the prosperity and happiness of our people here at home.

Thanks Dewey

And he wired Governor Dewey, "I thank you sincerely for your congratulations and good wishes. Your fine sportsmanship is deeply appreciated. We jointly owe consolations to the American people who have once again shown the world the vitality of our free institutions."

As he left the hotel, the President was asked, "Can you tell us how that Truman Poll works."

"No, I can't," he said. "When you win you can't say anything about it, I'm just happy."

Then he said, "Talk to Charlie, he'll tell all about it." He referred to press secretary Charles Ross.

Mr. Truman not only had forecast his own victory in campaign talks but Democratic control of both houses of Congress.

His voice cracked with emotion and his face beamed with happiness as he received the best wishes of scores of friends and Missouri neighbors who crowded into his penthouse quarters in the Hotel Muehlebach.

Too Happy to Gloat

He spoke almost humbly to those who showered him with praise and congratulations and refused to talk of his own predictions of a victory for himself and of a Democratic Congress in the face of contrary pollsters' opinions.

The pollsters were red-faced, but the President did not gloat.

He was too happy for that.

Cheers went up from his headquarters in the Hotel Muehlebach penthouse as word of Governor Dewey's concession of defeat was conveyed to him.

A long line of old friends, including newspapermen who have covered his campaign, swarmed into the living room of the suite to shake the President's hand and to congratulate him on the fiery campaign which upset the dopesters.

The impromptu celebration also included secret service men, who dropped their nonpolitical role to shower their congratulations upon

"the boss," to whom the whole White House detail is devoted.

Single-Handed Victory

The President was smiling as the full import of his victory became apparent.

Almost single-handedly, in a series of strenuous cross-country stopping tours, the President had saved victory from apparent defeat and swept a Democratic Congress into office with him.

Charles E. Ross, the President's secretary and an old high-school mate of Mr. and Mrs. Truman in Independence, beamed at everyone he saw.

"The President was certain some hours ago of his election," Mr. Ross said.

Nevertheless, when the press association bulletins on Governor Dewey's concession were brought in Mr. Truman smiled broadly.

The President was expected to issue an official statement later in the day.

Ex-Partner on Hand

A fat, little man came out of an adjoining room where he was closeted briefly with the President. He was Eddie Jacobson, former haberdashery store partner of the President. Almost overcome with joy, he told a reporter:

"I cried and I prayed for this."

Barney Allis, the short, rotund and genial operator of the Hotel Muehlebach, was all over the place.

When the President comes to town, the 11th floor suite becomes the temporary White House.

The President arrived at his hotel hide-away early in the day. In the Hotel Muehlebach at dawn, to tell how he slipped away to Excelsior Springs Nov. 2 to spend election night in a hotel hide-away.

Sitting in his shirt sleeves, with sleepy-eyed reporters huddled on the floor around him, the President looked happy and confident, but he awaited a certification as others on his hard-fought struggle with Gov. Thomas E. Dewey, the GOP nominee.

He indicated there was a possibility of a statement after he had gone over some correspondence, eaten breakfast, and taken a nap.

While newspaperman wondered as to his whereabouts he left his hide-away residence at 3 p. m. on Nov. 2 to drive to Excelsior Springs, 32 miles away to spend the night in the Elms Hotel.

"I got there about four, took one of their hot spring baths and rubdowns," he said. "Then I ate and went to bed.

President Sleps

"I woke up around midnight, heard a news broadcast and went back to sleep. I woke up again about 4:30 a.m., heard another broadcast, and decided I'd better drive back to town and have breakfast in the penthouse."

Charles Ross, the President's press secretary who had retired at 4:30 a.m., joined other members of the presidential party who were clustered around the chief executive talking excitedly of the returns still coming on the press association printers in an adjoining room.

The President would not talk about the election returns, other than to say that he had made the fight of his career because he believed in the campaign he made.

A grin on his face, he showed little of the strain of a preconvention and preelection stumping tour which carried him 31,500 miles to make 351 speeches in every corner of the country.

Heads for Washington

One of the President's first acts upon reaching the penthouse was to telephone Mrs. Truman and his daughter, Margaret.

Mr. Truman was to leave later for Washington by train.

Whatever the outcome, he had upset the calculations of the public-opinion samplers, to bear out his prediction that they would be among the most "red-faced" people in the country.

He felt that his 351 speeches in cross-country campaigns from June to Nov. 1 had aroused the people to change the complexion of Congress by replacing Republicans with "liberal" Democrats.

THE CHRISTIAN SCIENCE MONITOR

Registered in U. S. Patent Office

AN INTERNATIONAL DAILY NEWSPAPER

VOLUME 41 NO. 142 | COPYRIGHT 1949 BY THE CHRISTIAN SCIENCE PUBLISHING SOCIETY | BOSTON, FRIDAY, MAY 13, 1949 | • • ATLANTIC EDITION | TWO SECTIONS | FIVE CENTS A COPY

State Road Builders Face $100,000,000 Job Minus 'Strings'

By Courtney Sheldon
Staff Writer of The Christian Science Monitor

Massachusetts' Department of Public Works is standing by to undertake a $100,000,000 highway program—restricted as to area, but not as to projects.

The Legislature—except for a few minor formalities — has sanctioned the most extensive and expensive highway plan in Bay State history.

A Department of Public Works official today interpreted the Legislature's action as "setting up the areas," but "not tying the hands of the department."

No Promises Made

Philip H. Kitfield, chief engineer of the department, said "no promises have been made to anyone as to what projects will be constructed."

According to Mr. Kitfield, the department may, if it wishes, vary from the priority listings of the "Master Highway Plan for the Boston Metropolitan Area" and "The Report on Massachusetts State Highway Needs, exclusive of Metropolitan Boston"—both mentioned in the highway legislation.

Legislators indicated during debate that this also was their interpretation of the highway measure.

The Senate vote for the program—backed by Governor Dever and almost identical with the plan endorsed by Governor Bradford last year—has been unanimous on every test of the over-all bill.

Bipartisan Vote

Earlier this week, the House approved the same bill by a voice vote with the cooperation of Democratic and Republican leaders.

Passage of the bond issue by the Senate ended the legislative fight against the Embankment parkway. An $8,000,000 bond issue for the parkway was incorporated in the over-all bill.

It was apparent to foes of the parkway in the Senate that they lacked strength to hold up the highway bill and force deletion of Embankment parkway provisions.

Just for the record, Senator Charles Innes (R) of Boston, attempted at today's Senate session to amend the bill to remove sections concerning the Embankment parkway

No Roll-Call Vote

This move failed on a voice vote. No attempt was made to force a roll-call vote.

Final legislative action on the highway measure is expected May 16, when there will be a larger attendance in both branches of the Legislature than today.

It is unlikely that any further attempts will be made to amend the bill before it is enacted and sent to Governor Dever for signature.

Despite the unanimity on the final vote, Republicans and Democrats disagreed as to the history of the $100,000,000 bond issue.

Senator Harris S. Richardson (R) of Winchester, Republican floor leader in the Senate, recalled that the highway program was blocked by 16 Democratic senators last year.

The Republican floor leader pointed out the change in Democratic positions by quoting from Governor Dever's campaign speeches.

According to Senator Richardson, Governor Dever described the highway program as a plan that "might have enriched certain bankers but would not necessarily build roads."

Governor Dever charged then, Senator Richardson said, the Public Works Department would be able to "approve of any project without restriction and without having furnished a program nor prepared a systematic plan.

"This might have provided well for certain contractors, but not necessarily for integrated highway system. Finally, it gave unlimited power to the maladministered Public Works Department to take public and private property without limitation, even to the taking of parks and cemeteries."

In rebuttal, Senator John E. Powers of Boston, Democratic floor leader, said the situation is different this year:

"We now have a public works commissioner who, we believe, is competent. The bill contains an allocation plan. There are many things different. It is in no sense a blank check. No party can claim a monopoly on the desire to improve highways."

The bill provides for 10-year bonds to be paid for from the proceeds of the highway fund.

Area Stipulations

It stipulates that $37,000,000 be spent in the metropolitan area; $8,000,000 for the embankment parkway; $2,000,000 for highway signs and signals; and $53,000,000 in the remainder of the state.

This year, the bill was amended to insure that four areas outside of Metropolitan Boston receive a minimum of $5,000,000 each out of the total allotment of $53,000,000.

Senator Edward W. Staves (R) of Southbridge—chairman of the Legislative Committee on Highways and a consistent champion of an immediate road-building program—asked his fellow party members not to ask for restrictive amendments as the Democrats did last year.

The Senate turned down an amendment designed to allow court stays of eviction up to six months for occupants of property taken by eminent domain. The vote was 15 to 12.

Also rejected was an amendment to require that all contracts be given to the lowest qualified bidder and that no payments beyond 10 per cent above the contract could be paid for extra costs.

Freedom Rings on Every Page

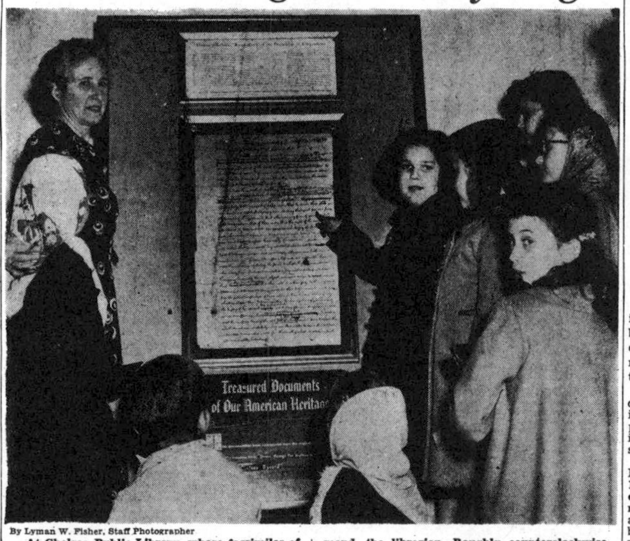

By Lyman W. Fisher, Staff Photographer

At Chelsea Public Library, where facsimiles of 26 of the Freedom Train documents are now on display, scores, even hundreds of children come daily to look and wonder. Here the Declaration of Independence is the center of interest for children gathered around Miss Sylvia B. Richmond, the librarian. Roughly counterclockwise, the children are: Eileen Bishop, Edmund Hovasse, Cynthia Sokolowska, Carol Ann von Handorf, Sandra Cooper, Roberta Frank, Pauline Pedi, Freda Aronas, Annette Picarello. A variety of national origins is represented here. (Story page 2.)

CIO Cries 'No Injunctions'!

By Harlan Trott
Staff Correspondent of The Christian Science Monitor

Washington

That dreaded word "injunction" still is keeping labor leaders from throwing their full strength behind the administration's efforts to repeal the Taft-Hartley Act at this session of Congress.

Again this week, the CIO has made its official position plain to the Senate and House Labor Committees:

"The CIO definitely and unequivocally labels—as it has done throughout this campaign—any amendment providing for injunctions in national emergency or other labor disputes as completely unacceptable."

Despite last week's setback in the House brought about by the Dixie-Republican coalition, and the closeness of the vote which sent the Wood bill—the bill labor called the Taft-Hartley Act by another name—the CIO is holding out.

Why Labor Is Adamant

Many observers now are saying that unless labor gives way on this issue, Congress may recess with the Taft-Hartley Act still on the statute books.

Why is labor so stubborn about inserting a provision in the administration's labor bill spelling out the President's power to seek a court injunction whenever a strike or lockout in an industry endangers the national health or safety?

The answer is interwoven through labor's struggle to organize workers into unions for the purpose of bargaining over hours and wages and other working conditions. Some of it is written in blood.

Sapped Bargaining Power

For years, the wide use of court injunctions restricted the development of unions and sapped organized labor's bargaining strength by circumscribing its right to strike.

Without freedom from unrestricted use of court injunctions, however, labor leaders admit even the Wagner Act, which was designed to safeguard the right of workers to organize and bargain collectively through representatives of their own choice, would not have been very effective.

In 1932, Congress passed the Norris-La Guardia Act providing that no federal court should have any jurisdiction to issue any restraining order or injunction in any case involving or growing out of a labor dispute.

Issuance of injunctions in labor disputes was to be permitted only if there was a threat of unlawful acts which would inflict irreparable damage on the employer and his property greater than that which the workers would suffer from the granting of an injunction.

The Norris-La Guardia Act also provided that an injunction could be granted only if the complainant had no adequate remedy at law and the local police were unable or unwilling to furnish adequate protection for his property. The law applied only to federal court injunctions, but a number of states promptly enacted similar legislation.

The Taft-Hartley Act imposed exceptions to the Norris-La Guardia antiinjunction law by empowering the President to ask for a court injunction in labor disputes that threatened the national health or safety.

Unwritten Right Cited

Organized labor devoutly cherishes the Norris-La Guardia Act as a bulwark in upholding constitutional safeguards against "involuntary servitude"; but strikes in the coal mines and on the railroads since World War II created such grave national emergencies that the public became alarmed.

Congress included in the Taft-Hartley Act a provision for dealing with "national emergency" strikes by empowering the President to seek injunction against the strike in the federal courts.

During the hearings on the administration's labor measure, the Thomas-Lesinski bill, William Davis, former head of the National War Labor Board, argued that the fewer restraints congress set up around labor-management relations the better, but that it didn't matter much one way or the other whether it kept the "national emergency strike" provisions of the Taft-Hartley Act, because the President had unwritten powers to put down such a strike anyway.

Clause Held Unnecessary

Labor spokesmen agreed with this point of view, but went on to insist that since the President had sufficient powers, it was unnecessary and unwise to insert any injunction provision in the bill to repeal the Taft-Hartley Act.

Dr. William H. Leiserson, who served on the NWLB with Mr. Davis, told the Senate Labor Committee there was no need to retain the 80-day injunction clause set out in the Tart-Hartley Act to deal with national emergency strikes.

Only a police state can abolish strikes, Mr. Leiserson declared. Later, he asserted that "no country which values free labor can abolish strikes in any industry, however affected with public interest, so long as the employers are private persons or corporations. A free government does better not to expose its own impotence."

Ford Refuses Contract Talks

By the Associated Press

Detroit

An authoritative source here says the Ford Motor Company "flatly refuses" to open 1949 labor contract talks until its workers end their present strike.

The source, who declined use of his name, said Ford has informed the CIO United Auto Workers of its stand.

The union previously had asked Ford to open the 1949 talks not later than May 16, 60 days prior to expiration of the present pact.

The report came as top-level negotiators once again went to the bargaining table in an effort to solve the stubborn "speed-up" dispute which resulted in the strike of 65,000 workers here.

[Other details on the Ford strike: Page 17.]

Berlin Big 4 Meet to Cut Export Knot

By Reuters

Berlin

Four-power talks have been held in Berlin for the first time for many months, a British spokesman has disclosed.

Details of the talks are being kept secret for technical reasons but it can be assumed on good authority that their main subject is that of exports from Berlin to the West.

By J. Emlyn Williams
Central European Correspondent of The Christian Science Monitor

Berlin

Trains and trucks are rolling into Berlin from the west and barges are slowly moving on the canals and other waterways carrying much-needed supplies to this former beleaguered city.

The airlift also is continuing its deliveries—over 6,700 tons during the last 24 hours—so that improvements in variety food and in increased employment soon should be evident.

Along the superhighway from Helmstedt to Berlin, an estimated 1,500 trucks and passenger cars entered the city May 12, and it now is hoped that the restrictions and inconveniences due to soviet bureaucratic methods at the check points along the route will be reduced to a minimum.

[Soviet-controlled Berlin papers charge that the West ban on exports to the Soviet zone has not been lifted, the Associated Press said. According to the same source, Lawrence Wilkinson, economic adviser to General Clay, has promised an immediate investigation.]

More Trains Asked

German rail experts plead for an increase in the number of daily freight trains and free use of other and more convenient gateways into Berlin. This, they claim, would save much time and personnel.

It is believed, however, that such a development is a long way off unless the Soviets are willing to transfer decisions of this kind to conferences between the east and west German sections of the Reichsbahn.

The May 12 celebration of the end of the blockade passed quietly here in Berlin. Outstanding were the two large public meetings, one in the United States sector and the other in the East sector.

These meetings typified better than any long explanations, the fundamental difference between West and East, between democracy and totalitarianism. The former was a voluntary, happy gathering, the latter bore all the marks of compulsory attendance under apprehension of reprisals of some kind or another.

200,000 Gather

The crowd of more than 200,000 which assembled before the Schöneberg Rathaus came of its own accord to hear members of the west Berlin city council and representatives from the Parliamentary Council at Bonn pay tribute to the Berliners for their great stand, and to the airlift instituted by the western allies.

The other meeting, held in the Soviet sector, was in marked contrast.

Most of them had been compelled to march directly from their work places. As happened in Nazi demonstrations of this sort and in the Communist-organized processions of May 1, at the first opportunity large numbers slunk off soon after reaching the parade ground.

The Bonn delegates who had attended the Schöneberg meeting flew to Frankfort immediately after the meeting to witness the signing of the new constitution by the three western military governors.

Gen. Lucius D. Clay for the United States, Gen. Sir Brian Robertson for Britain, and Lt. Gen. Pierre Koenig for France signed the document.

They stipulated reservations designed to make sure no "jokers" in the document's wording would allow the Germans to violate the occupation statute, establish an armed force, change state borders, grant western Berlin a vote in the new government, or concentrate too much authority in the central government.

Ratification of the constitution by the 11 Länder is expected before the end of May.

Soviets Hail CFM As Peace Omen; British Vote Pact

Hope Seen For Accord

By Edmund Stevens
Moscow Correspondent of The Christian Science Monitor

Moscow

Optimism over prospects for a four-power German settlement at the forthcoming Council of Foreign Ministers meeting is voiced by the current issue of New Times.

In the first Soviet editorial opinion since the Berlin agreement and the scheduling of a CFM meeting, the authoritative foreign affairs weekly sees a reconciliation of differences on Germany as a possible turning point toward a postwar settlement.

The four-power communiqué announcing an accord on Berlin and restoring the CFM, the editorial notes, revived hopes of people throughout the world that the fifth anniversary of victory over Hitler, a year from this month, may see completion of a European peace settlement.

It is a logical assumption that a responsible publication such as New Times has good reason for its optimism.

The editorial blamed past difficulties in Germany on the western powers, reiterating charges they had violated the Yalta and Potsdam decisions, and credited the Soviet Union with repeated attempts to find a solution.

New Times traced the origin of "the so-called Berlin question" to western attempts "to dismember Germany," beginning with the London conference of last year.

It cited documents on the Berlin question published by the Soviet Foreign Ministry as evidence of Soviet good will during the Moscow talks last summer.

Who Backed Down?

In this connection it also cited conversations in Paris last fall with Juan D. Bramuglia, then President of the United Nations Security Council, as well as Premier Joseph Stalin's answers to a Pravda correspondent last October and to the American correspondent Kingsbury Smith last January.

The recent change in the situation and swiftness of tangible agreement on Berlin is ascribed by New Times to abandonment by the western powers of their previous position.

They were influenced in this, New Times suggests, by "a broad movement of protest against the North Atlantic Pact and the aggressive policy it embodies."

The impression thus is given that the Berlin settlement and the reconvening of the CFM represents a major success and vindication of Soviet policy in Germany, which forced the western powers to back down.

New Times does not indicate the Soviet position at the impending CFM session. It gives as grounds for its optimism the fact that the machinery set up by the Potsdam agreement in the shape of the Council of Foreign Ministers has been set in motion again after a long interruption.

Bevin View: War Skirted

By Peter Lyne
Parliamentary Correspondent of The Christian Science Monitor

London

In Westminster, the British House of Commons has endorsed the North Atlantic Treaty.

The vote was 333 to 6. It came after Foreign Secretary Ernest Bevin had described heightened hopes of peace and the Russian lifting of the Berlin blockade as first fruits of the pact.

Mr. Bevin threw a clear light on reasons for American military aid to Europe and the organization of Western Union. He indicated how near the world approached last year to another war.

Mr. Bevin said the Atlantic Pact had led the Russians to give second thought to their tactics of preaching peace and promoting disturbance, a policy which if allowed to continue unchecked would, in Mr. Bevin's view, have led inevitably to war.

Shift in Tactics

But now the unity of the western world, as shown in the Atlantic Pact, has caused the Russians to change their tactics, he said, adding that the new situation might well lead to a settlement

This was the optimistic side of Mr. Bevin's speech. On the other hand, he emphasized the great difficulties which must be faced in the four-power conference and in combating Soviet policies elsewhere; in the Far East, for example.

Endorsement of the Atlantic Pact by the House of Commons does not mean Britain has ratified it. The House of Lords will debate the pact next week and overwhelming endorsement is expected.

But the British constitution does not really require parliamentary endorsement for a treaty to be ratified. The King has power to ratify a treaty entered into by his government. In practice, however, his ministers prefer to have Parliament's endorsement first.

Canada already has ratified the pact and the Canadian Parliament has endorsed it.

There were high tributes in the Commons debate, from a number of speakers, to the United States for its economic aid and part in the Atlantic Pact.

Winston Churchill declared, "The hope of mankind is that the present valiant and self-sacrificing policy will be the means of preventing a third World War."

Scores Leftists

Giving the extreme left-wing section of the socialist back benches a merciless stare, Mr. Churchill reminded those inclined to scoff at United States motives that not all Americans were millionaires

In fact, Mr. Churchill rubbed it in, this vast help to Europe was being paid for by just ordinary folk paying their taxes in the United States.

Mr. Churchill could not refrain from reminding the Commons that the Atlantic Pact did, in fact, give practical form to his Fulton, Mo., speech of March, 1946, for which speech he had been severely censured. More than 100 members of Parliament supported a vote of censure on him at that time.

Defense Steps Urged

And what had Churchill on this occasion to say about the future of relations with Russia? He described the future as shrouded in obscurity resulting from having to deal with the incalculable Russian leaders. No one knows what they will do, so it is imprudent to prophesy, he said.

But he urged the western powers to press forward with making their defenses more than mere paper plans. He said he was concerned at the lack of coordination of military plans and forces in Europe and at the shortcomings in British defenses.

He called the absence of Spain a weakness in strategic plans for western defense, but he did not advocate going further than restoring diplomatic relations for the present.

Hidden Opposition

The Commons vote of 333 to 6 was not a very heavy one considering that there are some 650 MPs.

Open opposition to the pact came mainly from a handful of Communists and fellow travelers, who charged that the pact was a warmongering act and would poison the new relationship with the Soviet Union.

But there was a higher proportion of socialist absentees from the voting lobbies than was expected. About one in four of all Socialist MPs is reported to have been missing, despite the fact a strong whip had been sent out.

There was an excuse of activity in another local election. But this cannot hide the fact that an appreciable section of the Labor Party is not happy about the policy toward Russia.

Their case is stated this way: This "ganging up" against Russia and the threat of force is only building up still greater Russian arms and resentment, and failing to build a really secure peace. What will happen, it is asked, when the United States monopoly of the atomic bomb ends?

Burke's Peerage Peers Into Mine For Missing Peer

By the Associated Press

London

One of Britain's 13 missing baronets has been traced to his hole—a coal hole.

Some days ago the editors of Burke's Peerage, which keeps the aristocracy neatly classified, expressed concern because a baker's dozen of the baronets had vanished into thin blue air.

Now they have found Sir John Henry Dunn, son of a former lord mayor of London. He is contentedly doing his job, which is checking coal trucks as they come from an open-pit mine near Barnsley.

"I certainly am not missing, because here I am," said Sir John.

"I don't use the title because the popular notion is that baronets are supposed to live in a mansion and not work.

"I have no mansion and don't mind working."

State of the Nation

Senator Douglas Is a Man to Watch

By ROSCOE DRUMMOND, Chief, Washington Bureau, The Christian Science Monitor

Washington

You are going to hear the name of Paul H. Douglas of Illinois more often before this 81st Congress completes its work—or at least completes its term.

The fact is that, with little more than four months of the 1949 political season behind us, freshman Senator Douglas is already on the varsity team. None of the first-year senators has made a more favorable and friendly impression or exerted more influence than this refugee from the classroom at the University of Chicago.

True, he never would make the grade in a Hollywood version of the college professor turned politician. He doesn't flaunt his scholarship either in his manner or in his language. Perhaps he lost just enough of it when he served in combat as a marine during the last war. He is not ivory-towerish, he is not doctrinaire, he knows how to shake the hand of a voter as well as did Al Smith or Boss Ed Kelly.

What seems evident by now is that Senator Douglas is coming to the top of his party during the first months of his first term the way Senator Robert A. Taft did when he broke into the Republican ranks back in 1938. Two years later Senator Taft was a serious contender for the GOP presidential nomination.

It is premature to put Mr. Douglas into the presidential race, but on the basis of the prestige and respect he is winning, anything could happen if there is a wide-open contest for the 1952 Democratic nomination.

Senator Douglas came to Washington in the wake of his defeat of Senator Wayland Brooks ticketed by his opponents as a starry-eyed radical and political theorist. His supporters always have hailed him a full-scale New Dealer. Mr. Douglas counts himself a Democratic "liberal" and a genuine supporter of President Truman.

But what stands out from the record thus far is that the senator is proving himself to be a political independent, is a discriminating, not a just-tell-me-what-you-want ally of the White House, and seems to be in the process of coming right in about the center, rather than on the left, of the Fair Deal.

In his campaign last fall Senator Douglas began by establishing himself at once as a clean-cut, clear-headed opponent of the Communists and the Communist Party-line pseudoliberalism. His principal opponent was isolationist "Curly" Brooks, who stood at the extreme right of Republican policy. But this didn't prevent the Wallace third party people in Illinois from centering their fire on Mr. Douglas because he strongly endorsed the Marshall Plan and the nation's bipartisan foreign policy.

Senator Douglas earnestly supports having the federal government do something to protect the civil rights of minority groups in the United States against which there are still grave discriminations. To this end he opposed the recent Senate compromise on the filibuster which really was calculated to kill any prospect of civil rights legislation at this session.

But only last month Senator Douglas pitched into the middle of the battle to protect the long-range, public housing bill from an amendment which its chief opponent, Senator John Bricker (R) of Ohio was trying to slip into the measure before it came to a final vote. Senator Bricker was blandly asking the Senate to rule that no state could get any federal housing funds for any project where there would be racial segregation. That was nice poison bait to throw at the civil rights liberals and Senator Douglas helped the housing bill advocates not to bite.

He replied that it was not that he preferred civil rights less but a public housing bill more, that a housing bill which was defeated because of a civil rights rider would promote neither housing nor civil rights. He did some of the best work on the floor in turning the Bricker stiletto aside.

The signs that Senator Douglas is to the right of the President, and perhaps at about mid-center of his own party, are these:

He favors considerable strengthening of the administration's Taft-Hartley substitute—if it ever can pass a substitute.

He voted to send the administration's $2,400,000,000 Labor-Social Security appropriations bill back to committee to be trimmed. His position is that Congress must do its part of the job of balancing the federal budget.

He wants to take the water out of the budget before considering an increase in taxes. He is opposed to deficit financing "except when the country is in desperate straits."

He is an opponent of a spawning officialdom.

"It is," he says, "a case of the people vs. officialdom. Many of the officials are trying to build up empires—they have become a sort of third party. They are not the perfect judges of their own importance or how much money they should have to spend."

Professor Douglas is doing well as a first-year man in the senatorial classroom and with his calm, quiet-voiced, Old World courtesy is making telling points without making any terrible enemies.

End of 'Biggest Sellers' Market in History' Seen

The World's Day

Reg. U.S. Pat. Off.

Boston: Business Loans Show Sharp Decline

Business loans by Boston banks have dropped off about $63,000,000 during the past four months, indicating the end of "the biggest sellers' market in history," informal discussions at the annual convention of the Massachusetts Bankers Association in Swampscott disclosed. [Page 2.]

The United States will be placed under a completely controlled economy in the event of another war, Edward V. Hickey, production director of the National Security Resources Board, told a Portland, Maine, Rotary Club meeting.

Europe: British Conservatives See 'Handwriting'

Britain's Conservative Party claims to see "the handwriting on the wall" as the Labor government continues to receive heavy setbacks in returns from municipal elections. [Page 6.]

Dr. Philip C. Jessup, American ambassador at large, arrived in Paris for talks with French and British officials preparatory to the Big Four foreign ministers meeting. [Page 10.]

Washington: Matthews Named to Succeed Sullivan

Francis Patrick Matthews, Omaha lawyer, was named Secretary of the Navy. The White House announced that Mr. Matthews has been picked to succeed John L. Sullivan.

Mrs. Gearhart Eisler was rearrested for deportation while the Justice Department laid plans to bring her husband back from his flight across the seas. [Page 17.]

Kirill Alexeeve, former commercial attache of the Soviet Embassy in Mexico City, testified that all Soviet diplomatic officials have a "spy responsibility." He was heard by the Senate Judiciary Committee.

The House Armed Services Committee unanimously approved a bill to boost the pay of members of the armed services. The wage increase will cost $406,000,000 a year.

National: Explosion Damages Holland Tunnel

The Holland Tunnel under the Hudson River may be stopped up for a month as the result of the explosion of drums of chemicals aboard a burning truck. Walls and ceilings of the tunnel were badly damaged and 30 persons were overcome with fumes of carbon disulphide.

Los Angeles was shaken by an earthquake which startled residents out of their beds, but apparently did no damage. This was the second shock felt this month in southern California.

Americas: Argentina Agrees to Trade With Japan

Argentina has agreed in principle to a trade pact with Japan, the Ministry of Economy announced in Buenos Aires. The chief of the Japanese mission there is awaiting instructions from occupation authorities before completing details.

Weather Predictions: Fair (Details Page 2)

THE CHRISTIAN SCIENCE MONITOR

Registered in U. S. Patent Office

AN INTERNATIONAL DAILY NEWSPAPER

VOLUME 41 NO. 253 | BOSTON, FRIDAY, SEPTEMBER 23, 1949 | • ATLANTIC EDITION | TWO SECTIONS | FIVE CENTS A COPY

COPYRIGHT 1949 BY THE CHRISTIAN SCIENCE PUBLISHING SOCIETY

Coop Bank League Told High Taxes Jar Financial Structure

By W. Clifford Harvey

Staff Writer of The Christian Science Monitor

Swampscott, Mass.

A sharp warning that it is high time that government began to economize rather than to think in terms of taxing bank dividends to spend more money and create new tax demands was issued today by Harry R. Andrews, President of the Massachusetts Cooperative Bank League, meeting here.

Addressing the 61st Annual Convention of the 175 cooperative banks of Massachusetts, Mr. Andrews declared that if government does not begin to economize soon "it may be too late for all of us."

Even at the present rate of taxation, he said, the structure of the state's banking system has been seriously weakened. He hesitated to say what might happen if government further reduces the incomes of banks or be further penalized by reductions in dividends.

Sober Reflection

In the corridors, as well as on the platform of the league's convention at the New Ocean House, there was developed an atmosphere of sober reflection on the disintegrating effects of heavy taxes.

This atmosphere permeated the full day's sessions of the bankers addressed by national, state, and city officials, bank representatives, and business executives. Further taxation was said to be a threat to the cash reserves of every bank in the Commonwealth of Massachusetts.

On the other hand, William K. Divers, Chairman of the Home Loan Bank Board, sounded a more pleasant note in referring to the $2,800,000,000 in government insurance dividends to veterans, "much of which should find the way into cooperative banks and other savings institutions."

"Millions of veterans have learned the value of thrift over the last few years," Mr. Divers stated. "While many of the veterans will use their insurance dividends to pay current expenses, many will take advantage of the opportunity to set up sizable savings accounts."

Other speakers pointed out that nearly $27,000,000 in GI loans had been written by Massachusetts cooperative banks since the war. This represented about one-fourth of all the mortgage loans held by these banks, totaling $107,531,000.

Warner K. Allen, secretary-treasurer of the league, declared that very few defaults had been registered on GI loans

The ratio of defaults, he said, would be less than 1 per cent.

Most of the cooperative banks are still writing GI loans, Mr. Allen added. But they are more selective than they were, and the loans have dropped off radically in the last six months. Some of the banks' portfolios are completely filled, he said.

Family Affair

Aside from the benefits of veterans' insurance funds flowing into savings banks, Mr. Divers saw them as a sharp stimulus to business. The veterans' funds are counted upon in Washington as part of the administration's overall inflationary effort.

Yet Franklin Hardinge, vice-president of the United States Savings and Loan League, told the bankers that if every family would look upon the prospects of a deficit in the federal finances in the same light as their own family "going into the red" some of the broad steps taken toward a welfare state would be arrested.

What this nation needs, Mr. Hardinge insisted, is "a council of war around every family hearthstone to repel the efforts of government to spend billions of the taxpayers money. When the family starts going into the red, it starts to economize. But no such effort is evident in Washington."

Other speakers stressing the advantage of free enterprise were H. Phelps Gates, circulation manager of The Christian Science Monitor; Col. Robert B. Brooks, Jr., of the Roy Wenzlick Forecasts; M. H. K. Murphy, president of the Federal Savings and Loan League, Herbert N. McGill, representing a commodity service organization, and Timothy J. Donovan, Massachusetts Commissioner of Banks.

Adenauer Heckler Gets 'Attention'

By Reuters

Bonn, Germany

As Dr. Konrad Adenauer, new German Chancellor, was making his declaration on the future of the Deutsche Mark Sept. 20, a left-wing member of the House interrupted, "I can see you already in the uniform of an American general."

Dr. Adenauer replied, "Then you'll have to stand at attention in front of me."

Inside Reading:

Friday, September 23, 1949

State of the Nation

Soviet Armed Might—Steel or Paper?

By JOSEPH C. HARSCH, Chief, Washington News Bureau, The Christian Science Monitor

Washington

No man ever could accuse Senators George of Georgia and Byrd of Virginia of being soft on either communism or Soviet Russia. Their conservatism is impeccable and their anti-Communist record irreproachable.

Yet Senators George and Byrd have gone off the administration reservation on arming western Europe against the possibility of Russian aggression or Communist insurrection.

Senator George favored trimming the appropriation to a figure lower than administration spokesmen long have contended is a minimum necessity to protect western Europe. And Senator Byrd voted against any appropriation.

This straying from the reservation by two conservative senators provides a classic example of what can happen when figures are used incautiously.

In many an argument over many a foreign policy issue, and over budgets for the armed services, it has been customary to use a certain set of figures about Russia's armed strength. One figure is that Russia can put 300 divisions in the field today and probably could increase the figure to 500 divisions by the end of the first year of a war. Another figure is that Russia possesses somewhere between 12,000 and 18,000 military airplanes; which is of course several times the number of operational front-line planes in the American plus the British air forces.

Figures like that have been useful to impress Congress in several legislative pinches over the past three years. But they have one implication which Senators George and Byrd have now seized upon. If Soviet Russia can put 300 first-class divisions into the field now, and even 10,000 first-line military planes into the air, then it is quite silly to talk about defending the Rhine with the kind of military force which can be bought with the $1,500,000,000 involved in the present military aid bill.

All the bill which the Senate has just passed can do is to modernize the equipment of nine French divisions and perhaps three more from the Benelux countries and improve communications and warning systems for the western European countries. And obviously 15 divisions cannot hold the Rhine for a week against the type of Soviet forces so frequently alleged to exist.

The purpose of the bill, of course, goes beyond 15 divisions on the Rhine. The long-range plan calls for a western European defense force totaling somewhere in the vicinity of 40 to 50 divisions which it is estimated might have a good chance to hold the Rhine until British and American reinforcements could be brought up.

But even 50 western divisions look like a fairly futile goal if one assumes that the Soviet Army already numbers 300 divisions just as good as any of the western divisions to be constituted. The question raised by Senators George and Byrd is, really, why spend more money on what would seem to be a hopeless task?

The answer is that there is a second side to the Russian figures. On paper, Russia may have 300 divisions. But there is reason to doubt that they compare with American divisions. In fire power, a good average Russian division is now said to equal an average American brigade. On paper, Russia may have 15,000 operational military aircraft. But its best bomber is a copy of the now obsolete American B-29. Also it is extremely doubtful that Russia can put into the air anything like what it shows on paper.

The two Russian fliers who deserted in Vienna early this year came from a unit which supposedly possessed about 50 operational aircraft. Yet the fliers said that on the day they left Russia there were only five planes in their unit capable of taking the air.

If Russian military strength is to be measured by such qualifications as the above, then arming western Europe is by no means a hopeless task. And 30 good divisions in western Europe would be a powerful guaranty against Communist insurrection, and a powerful boost to the confidence of western Europe.

The moral of the story is that, if you overstate your case one day, you may find yourself trying to explain it downward the next.

Speakers at Bank Parley

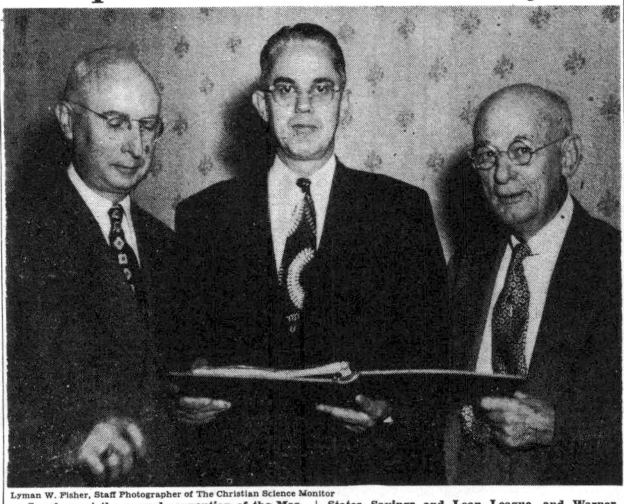

Lyman W. Fisher, Staff Photographer of The Christian Science Monitor

Speakers at the annual convention of the Massachusetts Cooperative Bank League were, left to right: Harry R. Andrews, league president; Franklin Hardinge, Jr., vice-president of the United States Savings and Loan League, and Warner Allen, secretary-treasurer of the Cooperative Bank League. The conference was held in Swampscott, Mass.

Chinese Puzzle Challenges UN

By Ronald Stead

Staff Writer of The Christian Science Monitor

Communist China emerges today as a new political entity with impact on the current session of the United Nations General Assembly.

For years this has been a menacing probability. Now it is an accomplished fact.

An immense new ally, more than 200,000,000 strong, has lined up beside Soviet Russia and the other Communist states. This vastly outweighs Yugoslavia's defection.

Problems caused by the formal establishment of the "People's Republic of China" are expected to illustrate rather clearly just how much unity the United Nations lacks. For sharp divisions of opinion will be made sharper by considerations relative to the new rulers of half of China.

An appeal for concerted international action against these rulers was made Sept. 22 in the UN by the Nationalist spokesman for China's other half.

Warned by Tsiang

This delegate, Dr. T. F. Tsiang, warned: "The strident voice of Mao Tze-tung [China's Communist leader] tells the world that Chinese Communists are a new and mighty contingent in the armies of world revolution, which is to spread to southeast Asia and finally to cover the whole world. In case of a third war, Communist China, according to Mao, will fight on the side of the Soviet Union."

This warning came in one introductory speech as the Assembly opened, but the distinct impression at Flushing Meadow Park was that formal action would be initiated by the Chinese delegate next week. Reaction among the other delegates was cautious, inasmuch as the issue could prove highly explosive.

Nationalist China claims administration over just about as much Chinese territory as the Communists do. But this parity is not likely to continue long.

Communist forces are poised for a renewed military offensive in southern China which threatens immediately both the Nationalists' temporary capital, Canton, and the strategic easterly seaport of Amoy. Meanwhile the remaining ranks of the Nationalists are riven by defections, corruption, and inefficiency.

Key Port Attacked

Amoy, the best port remaining to the Nationalists, is under heavy attack. Late dispatches said the island had been invaded by Communist forces, and some Communist sources claimed its capture. Nationalists, however, spoke of heavy Communist losses. The port is 140 miles west of the Nationalist bastion of Taiwan (Formosa).

While Nationalist China is disintegrating in the south, a new Communist-dominated "coalition" government is being put together in the north, for formal inauguration Oct. 10.

This date, the 10th day of the 10th month, is known in China as "the double 10th" and is nationally celebrated each year to commemorate the institution of the Chinese Republic in 1912.

That was the year when the last of the imperial dynasties, the Manchus, was supplanted by the regime which is now tottering. Even so, this regime still is the legal government of China and rates among the United Nations as one of the Big Five permanent members of the Security Council, vested with a veto power it never yet has exercised. The other four are Soviet Russia, which has used the veto 38 times, the United States, Britain, and France.

Global Dispute Brews

It is not doubted that before long, Communist China will seek United Nations membership. Or, to use the words of China's Communist chieftain, Mao Tze-tung, it will move to "join the big family of peace- and freedom-loving nations of the world."

As this latter phrase refers to Soviet Russia in particular, the support of that "freedom-loving nation" is assured. And so are the makings of a far-reaching international dispute.

China's Communists already have gratified Soviet Russia by opening up to it exploitation possibilities in Manchuria which once furnished Japan's chief economic strength.

It now looks as though the United States, as the main occupying agent, will have Japan on its hands, economically, a great deal longer than the satisfied converter of Japanese militarists into Japanese democrats—Gen. Douglas MacArthur—has supposed.

It is clear that Soviet Russia and the "People's Republic of China" together can become—indeed, already are—a very harassing antiwestern combination.

The Russians are expected to give full diplomatic recognition as soon as possible to the government.

In ceremonies at Peiping this week, the new republic was approved by more than 600 Chinese delegates purporting to represent all grades of national life. They called themselves the "People's Consultative Conference."

The United States and Great Britain are not likely to extend the glad hand enthusiastically as Russia, even though economic urgencies make the British more willing than the Americans to regularize diplomatic relationships with Communist China.

Recognition scarcely can be withheld, however, unless China's Communists do something outrageous in the matter of mistreating western foreigners or repudiating existing Chinese international obligations. The most spectacular of the latter is the Chinese lease agreement with the British over Hong Kong.

The recognition issue scarcely can have eluded the discussions pursued in Washington by the Secretary of State Dean Acheson, British Foreign Secretary Ernest Bevin, and French Foreign Minister Robert Schuman.

Indeed, their acceptance of the impending decision can be inferred from what is understood to be their agreement on the impracticability of aiding Nationalist China in its current extremity.

At this point the Chinese Nationalist Government has turned to the United Nations and is expected to accuse Soviet Russia formally of aiding China's Communists in violation of a friendship agreement with the Nationalist government.

Communists Rushed

The Nationalist move to explode this monumental Chinese firecracker in the face of the United Nations is seen to have inspired China's Communists to announce their new government ahead of the historic "double 10th" in order to be in a better position to counterattack.

Further fireworks will be touched off if Russia, in due course, leads a campaign to have Communist delegates replace the Nationalists at Lake Success.

It is noteworthy in this connection that the Nationalists, with whom Russia now exchanges recognition, already have paid $1,000,000 of their current United Nations membership fee — reportedly the earliest payment they ever made.

Knowing how anticlimactic Chinese climaxes are apt to be, and having seen at first hand the amount of devious dealings entailed in China's civil war, I can well imagine that China's two governments are likely to perform concurrently for far longer than generally expected. In fact, an imaginable outcome is partition, which would make the Chinese puzzle even more puzzling.

Belgian Ponders 49th State Status

By the Associated Press

Ghent, Belgium

Gaston Eyskens, Prime Minister of Belgium, said here his country wouldn't mind becoming the 49th state of the United States.

He jokingly told guests at a Belgian-American luncheon, "provided our national integrity is preserved, I think it would be a good way of solving the pending problems of American customs tariffs."

Steel Talks Start Again; Coal Knotted

By the Associated Press

Contract talks that may settle the threatened steel strike were resumed today.

But the coal strike, entering its fifth day, seemed likely to continue some time—possibly a long time.

The United States Steel Corporation and the CIO United Steelworkers of America, resuming negotiations, have one week before an Oct. 1 strike deadline.

They are at odds over pension and insurance demands by the union. The million-member steel union complied Sept. 22 with President Truman's request for extension of the steel strike truce —previously set to end Sept. 25 at midnight.

The steel industry agreed Sept. 21 to the extension, and also agreed to resume bargaining. The union, arranging the United States Steel talks, told 52 other steel companies that it is ready to negotiate.

A fact-finding board named by Mr. Truman has vetoed a fourth-round wage increase for steelworkers. But it recommended a company-paid pension and insurance program equal to 10 cents hourly a worker. The union accepted the report, but United States Steel balked at accepting without further bargaining.

Coal Deadlock

Prospects for settling the coal strike seemed more bleak in the wake of John L. Lewis's statement that his 480,000 United Mine Workers, who had been on a three-day week, now are on a "no-day week."

Mr. Lewis bluntly rejected a proposed two-year extension of the old UMW contract, which expired in July. He said the steel dispute is blocking a wage settlement for the miners. He reverted to his old policy of "No contract, no work."

His talks with mine operators in the North and West were recessed to Sept. 29. Both sides reported a deadlock.

The miners walked out Sept. 19 in protest against suspension of pension and disability payments from the miners' three-year-old welfare fund.

The steelworkers reported Sept. 22 that the Standard Steel Works of Lewistown, Pa., a subsidiary of Baldwin Locomotive Company, had accepted the fact-finding board's recommendations in full. Standard Steel officials could not be reached for comment. The company has about 2,500 employees.

The steelworkers also have conferences scheduled with Northwestern Steel & Wire at Waukegan, Ill. Talks with Rustless Steel, a subsidiary of American Rolling Mills, began Sept. 22.

Long Negotiation List

The union said bargaining sessions with steel firms will be held in all the major steel centers in the country.

On the negotiation itinerary are United States Steel in Pittsburgh, Bethlehem Steel in New York, Republic Steel in, Cleveland, Youngstown Sheet and Tube in Youngstown, Ohio, Inland Steel in Chicago, Great Lakes Steel in Detroit, Jones & Laughlin in Pittsburgh, and Continental Steel in Indianapolis.

Other labor developments:

In Washington, one Pennsylvania miner has filed a federal court suit charging illegal use of the UMW health and welfare fund. He asked for court appointment of new trustees for the fund.

In Altoona, Pa., state police were sought to help prevent recurrence of violence in Blair County coal fields. Mine operators used shotguns Sept. 22 to hold 300 roving pickets at bay until police arrived. The pickets had threatened to dump truckloads of coal.

In Detroit, Ford and the CIO United Automobile Workers planned to resume bargaining Sept 24 on pensions. Tension seemed eased by postponement of the steel strike threat.

UE rightists hint secession if union cuts ties with CIO: Page 17.

Atom Explosion Set Off in Russia, Truman Reports

By the Associated Press

Washington

President Truman announces "we have evidence that within recent weeks an atomic explosion occurred in the U.S.S.R. [Russia]."

The White House said the President gave the information to the cabinet this morning.

In a statement sent to reporters, Mr. Truman said the development emphasizes the necessity "for that truly effective enforcible international control of atomic energy which the government and the large majority of the members of the United Nations support."

His statement made it clear that top American officials regard the development as meaning the Russians have learned to make the atomic bomb.

Mr. Truman said the probability that some other nation might develop an atomic bomb "has always been taken into account by us."

Text of Truman Statement

The text of Mr. Truman's statement:

"I believe the American people, to the fullest extent consistent with national security, are entitled to be informed of all developments in the field of atomic energy. That is my reason for making public the following information:

"We have evidence that within recent weeks an atomic explosion occurred in the U.S.S.R.

"Ever since atomic energy was first released by man, the eventual development of this new force by other nations was to be expected. This probability has always been taken into account by us.

"Nearly four years ago I pointed out that 'scientific opinion appears to be practically unanimous that the essential theoretical knowledge upon which the discovery is based is already widely known. There is also substantial agreement that foreign research can come abreast of our present theoretical knowledge in time' and, in the three-nation declaration of the President of the United States and the Prime Ministers of the United Kingdom and of Canada, dated Nov. 15, 1945, it was emphasized that no single nation could in fact have a monopoly of atomic weapons.

"This recent development emphasizes once again, if indeed such emphasis were needed, the necessity for that truly effective enforcible international control of atomic energy which this government and the large majority of the members of the United Nations support."

By Richard L. Strout

Staff Correspondent of The Christian Science Monitor

Washington

Short-range joy, long-range anxiety—that's the administration's reaction to the Senate's 55 to 24 passage of the $1,314,010,000 European military aid bill.

As for the Senate itself, it figures the vote brings it a whole lot closer to the recess which venerable senators yearn for so eagerly.

The Senate passed the big Military Aid Program bill in just four days' debate, which is par for the course so far as anybody around Washington can remember.

Simultaneously administration leaders are figuring out the last list of additional "must" bills which the first session of the 81st Congress should act on before it is allowed to go home.

Shifting the air of home, Congress now may well quicken its pace in the weeks ahead.

The State Department's mingled feelings over Senate passage of the big military aid bill boil down to the question, "So far good, but what next?"

It is agreed that Senate action marks some sort of a landmark. It will reassure America's Atlantic Pact allies that the United States is willing to sign its name to checks as well as to high-sounding treaties. But there are a lot of "ifs" and "buts" involved, too.

Proposed Allocations

Here is how the money would be allocated, as the Senate wrote the big program:

For western Europe, $1,000,000,000.

For Greece and Turkey, $211,370,000.

For Korea, Iran, and the Philippines, $27,640,000.

For China, the President may use $75,000,000 for that area in his discretion.

And surplus arms valued at $450,000,000 may be distributed.

This looks like a resounding victory on paper. There are tangibles and intangibles involved, however, which write something of a question mark after it.

First of all, the House passed a different bill allocating only half as much money for the western Europe area. The two bills now must be reconciled somehow in conference.

Secondly, this is an authorization, not an appropriation. The whole thing has to be done a second time later on for specific appropriations. If the economy drive increases in Congress, cash payment may be hard.

Third, the Senate tied two restrictive amendments to its approval Sept 22, neither of which the State Department likes. First, half of all military aid sent abroad must go in United States ships. Second, all but $100,000,000 of Europe's funds must be held up till a formal "integrated" European defense plan is achieved; the administration wants the funds made available right away and wants this very much. It hopes this "Ferguson amendment" will be dropped in conference.

Those are the tangible difficulties. The intangibles are long-range affairs; in a way they could cloud the sky at a moment when it should look sunniest.

Basic question is, is the bipartisan coalition on foreign affairs breaking apart?

Like the final vote on passage of the Reciprocal Trade Agreement Law last week, the net result seems to belie this fear. Senate passage of the MAP bill Sept. 22 (55 to 24) was by a bigger majority than leaders hoped. Democrats voted for passage, 36 to 10; Republicans, 19 for and 14 against. That seems conclusive.

Focus on Amendments

But as in the fight over the Reciprocal Trade Agreement Act last week, the real battle was not over the theory of the law (which nearly everyone nominally approved) but over certain specific amendments which advocates of internationalism declared would disable the measure. On some of these amendments the party line-up and the line-up of leadership within the parties was disconcerting to say the least.

Morgan Memorial Retires From Community Fund

The World's Day

Reg. U.S. Pat. Off.

Boston: Morgan Membrial Withdrawal Date Set

Morgan Memorial has withdrawn from the Community Fund because Red Feather campaigns have not raised enough money to keep it going. The withdrawal takes effect Dec. 31, 1949. [Page 2.]

New England department store sales for the week ending Sept. 17 declined 3.5 per cent below the sales for the equivalent week last year, the Federal Reserve Bank of Boston announced. Downtown Boston store sales declined only 1.3 per cent, and Cambridge sales were up 7.2 per cent for the week as measured against last year.

Quincy voters, heading for their first Plan E-City manager election on Nov. 8, are priming themselves on how to vote under the proportional representation method of voting. [Page 5.]

Europe: U.S. Plans North Pole Air Training

Air training at the North Pole may begin for United States Air Force, Col. Bernt Balchen announced in Oslo. Colonel Balchen, a noted Arctic flier, recently made a nonstop flight from Alaska to Norway in a C-54.

Linking of the Marshall Aid countries' electric power systems was recommended by a western European technical aid mission. Lower costs, less duplication of generating plants, and better coordination of power were cited as the advantages.

France, Belgium, and Holland are joining Britain and the United States for the first time in week-end aerial war games over England. Daylight and night bombers, as well as fighters, will test Britain's defenses.

Italy's 16-day-old shipping strike gave a wide berth to the Italian liner Vulcania, which sailed for New York without hindrance. Several crews have been returning to their ships, but the strike has not been settled.

Washington: Civil Rights Issue May Be Put Off

The big civil rights issue in Congress is likely to be postponed until next year in the House as well as the Senate. Chairman Lesinski (D) of Michigan said an understanding has been reached by the Labor Committee not to press for action until the second session of the 81st Congress, which begins in January.

About 30 senators lined up behind a move to cut the pay increases being proposed for cabinet members and civilian workers who get $5,000 or more yearly from the government. But Senator Lucas (D) of Illinois brought before the Senate a companion measure to raise the pay of the armed forces about $348,000,000 yearly with signs of only scattered opposition.

National: GOP Group Attacks Brannan Farm Plan

Republican leaders, seeking recommendations for a farm program from farmers themselves—a group which has been credited with swinging the 1948 election to the Democrats—opened a conference in Sioux City, Iowa, with attacks on the Brannan farm plan by Representative Hope (R) of Kansas and Guy C. Gabrielson, Republican national chairman.

Federal Judge George Harris in San Francisco set Nov. 14 as trial date for Harry Bridges' citizenship case despite protests of "persecution" from the CIO Longshoremen's leader's attorney. The government charges Bridges fraudulently concealed his membership in the Communist Party when he obtained citizenship papers.

Far East: ILO Adopts 29-Point Asiatic Plan

A 29-point program for the development of technical and vocational training in Asiatic countries was adopted by the International Labor Organization conference in Singapore.

The Chinese Communist dollar has been fixed at 4,000 to one United States dollar. The former rate was 3,700 to one.

Weather Predictions: Showers (Details Page 2)

THE CHRISTIAN SCIENCE MONITOR

Registered in U. S. Patent Office

AN INTERNATIONAL DAILY NEWSPAPER

VOLUME 41 NO. 255 | COPYRIGHT 1949 BY THE CHRISTIAN SCIENCE PUBLISHING SOCIETY | BOSTON, MONDAY, SEPTEMBER 26, 1949 | • ATLANTIC EDITION | TWO SECTIONS | FIVE CENTS A COPY

Traffic Drive Brings Lower Insurance To Bay State Motorists

By W. Clifford Harvey
Staff Writer of The Christian Science Monitor

Massachusetts highway-safety efforts, which have made this state the safest in the country for motorists and pedestrians, today "paid off" again in terms of a $600,000 reduction in the over-all rates for automobile liability insurance.

Thus for the second straight year the 10-year-old campaign of Rudolph F. King, Registrar of Motor Vehicles, to get speeders, drinking drivers, and other accident-prone motorists off the roads has settled the issue of who benefits most from safe driving.

"The individual driver is always the chief beneficiary," declared Mr. King today.

Some Protests Made

Not all the communities, however, were satisfied with the reductions released in the tentative schedule for 1950 by Charles F. J. Harrington, State Insurance Commissioner.

Protests from Revere, which displaced Chelsea from top place in the list of high-rate communities, today took the form of a drive to set up a new state system of uniform rates.

At least 18 communities which did not share in the rate reduction displayed more than passing interest in Revere's intention to get the insurance issue on the state ballot as an initiative referendum.

The 18 communities paying higher rates for 1950 are Ashland, Ayer, Easton, Fairhaven, Foxboro, Groveland, Haverhill, Mansfield, Marion, Mattapoisett, Milford, Milbury, North Brookfield, Northboro, Norwell, Raynham, and Swampscott. The increases ranged from $2.20 to $3.20.

Chelsea Drops

Revere rose to the highest rated community in the state by virtue of its $56,30 rate, as compared with a 1949 figure of $57.50. Chelsea, for the first time in many years, dropped out of first place by a reduction of $6.70 in its rate from $60.40 to $53.70.

Other large reductions were recorded in Billerica, Randolph, Saugus, Franklin, Scituate, Medway, Sudbury, Chicopee, Middletown, Bridgewater, Cohasset, and Hingham. Boston continued with the third highest rates of $50.10, which represented a drop of $1.10.

These rates, based on the safety records of the individual communities over the previous five-year period, are released tentatively for consideration at a public hearing to be held on Oct. 10.

They represent the continuing campaign for safety launched by Mr. King four years ago and culminating this year in a system of close cooperation between most of the communities and the Registry of Motor Vehicles.

The increasing success of these safety drives virtually assure motorists of additional insurance cuts in 1951. It is due largely to the fact that 229 communities now have driving training as part of their school curriculums. When Mr. King came to office in 1944 only 48 communities had such courses.

In addition, the registrar has studied highways upon which the accidents occur most frequently and blanketed the road with inspectors or remedied conditions that help to cause the trouble. All of the 78 cities of 10,000 persons and over are now holding regular safety conferences with the registrar.

Beyond that, 53 towns with less than 10,000 population are cooperating with the registrar in conference. Gradually this effort is being extended to the smaller communities.

Greater Gains Seen

"So, you see, safety is a continuing development," Mr. King pointed out, "and promises even greater dividends to Massachusetts motorists commensurate with their cooperation."

The action in Revere aimed to establish a system of uniform rates throughout the state also is a continuing one. Opponents of the present system of basing insurance rates upon the number of accidents and fatalities in each community declare that it represents flagrant discrimination.

How? Because it charges accidents occurring in Boston, for instance, against the communities from which the drivers come, they say. In other words, hundreds of accidents occur in Boston that are not charged against Boston in the rate-fixing.

Actually, the accident records of Newton drivers, operating in Boston, for instance, are leveled against the city of Newton, even though it was Boston's congestion that could be held to blame.

At any rate, the opponents of the present system insist that a uniform rate throughout the state would discriminate against no one, save a tremendous amount of bookkeeping, and distribute the insurance costs to permit a reasonably low rate.

Table: Page 15

South Africa Due To Ration Gasoline

By the Associated Press

Capetown

Gasoline rationing will go into effect in South Africa as soon as administrative machinery can be set up, Eric H. Louw, Minister of Economic Affairs, has announced. It is expected to come into operation in about two months.

Mr. Louw said the curtailment of gasoline consumption would help the union conserve its foreign exchange. Last year gasoline cost the union more than £10,000,000.

This Is Not an Atom Bomb

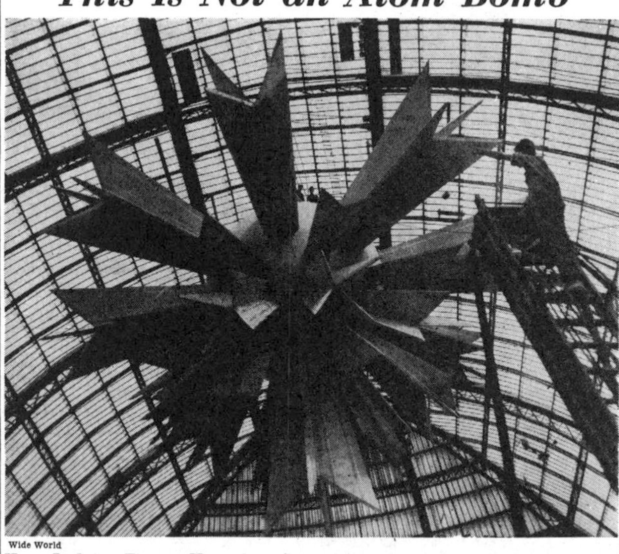

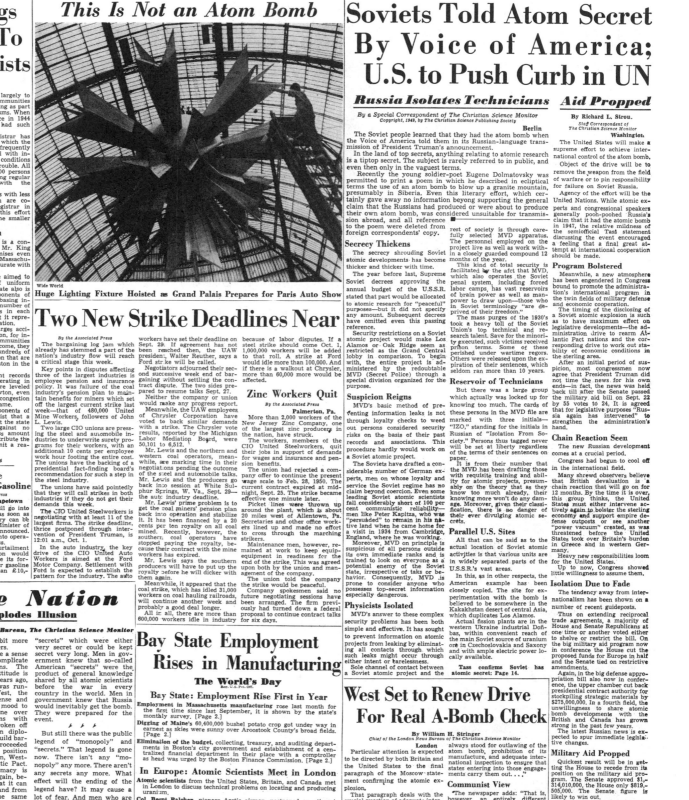

Wide World

Huge Lighting Fixture Hoisted as Grand Palais Prepares for Paris Auto Show

Two New Strike Deadlines Near

By the Associated Press

The bargaining log jam which already has stemmed a part of the nation's industry flow will reach a critical stage this week.

Key points in disputes affecting three of the largest industries is employee pension and insurance policy. It was failure of the coal industry's pension plan to maintain benefits for miners which set off the largest current strike last week—that of 480,000 United Mine Workers, followers of John L. Lewis.

Two large CIO unions are pressing the steel and automobile industries to underwrite surety programs for their workers, with an additional 10 cents per employee work hour footing the entire cost. The unions have the backing of a presidential fact-finding board's recommendation for such a step in the steel industry.

The unions have said pointedly that they will call strikes in both industries if they do not get their demands this week.

The CIO United Steelworkers is negotiating with at least 11 of the largest firms. The strike deadline, thrice postponed through intervention of President Truman, is 12:01 a.m., Oct. 1.

In the auto industry, the key drive of the CIO United Auto Workers is aimed at the Ford Motor Company. Settlement with Ford is expected to establish the pattern for the industry. The auto workers have set their deadline on Sept. 29. If agreement has not been reached then, the UAW president, Walter Reuther, says a Ford strike will be called.

Negotiators adjourned their second successive week end of bargaining without settling the contract dispute. The two sides prepared to resume talks Sept. 27.

Neither the company or union would make any progress report.

Meanwhile, the UAW employees of Chrysler Corporation have voted to back similar demands with a strike. The Chrysler vote results, reported by the Michigan Labor Mediation Board, were 50,101 to 6,512.

Mr. Lewis and the northern and western coal operators, meanwhile, are marking time in their negotiations pending the outcome of the steel and automobile talks. Mr. Lewis and the producers go back into session at White Sulphur Springs, W. Va., Sept. 29—the auto industry deadline.

Mr. Lewis' prime problem is to get the coal miners' pension plan back into operation and stabilize it. It has been financed by a 20 cents per ton royalty on all coal mined. Recently, however, the southern coal operators have stopped paying the royalty, because their contract with the mine workers has expired.

Mr. Lewis says the southern producers will have to put up the royalty before he will dicker with them again.

Meanwhile, it appeared that the coal strike, which has idled 31,000 workers on coal hauling railroads, will continue another week and probably a good deal longer.

All in all, there are more than 600,000 workers idle in industry because of labor disputes. If a steel strike should come Oct. 1, 1,000,000 workers will be added to that roll. A strike at Ford would idle more than 100,000. And if there is a walkout at Chrysler, more than 60,000 more would be affected.

Zinc Workers Quit

By the Associated Press

Palmerton, Pa.

More than 2,000 workers of the New Jersey Zinc Company, one of the largest zinc producers in the nation, have struck.

The workers, members of the CIO United Steelworkers, quit their jobs in support of demands for wages and insurance and pension benefits.

The union had rejected a company offer to continue the present wage scale to Feb. 28, 1950. The current contract expired at midnight, Sept. 25. The strike became effective one minute later.

Picket lines were thrown up around the plant, which is about 20 miles west of Allentown, Pa. Secretaries and other office workers lined up and made no effort to cross through the marching strikers.

Maintenance men, however, remained at work to keep equipment in readiness for the end of the strike. This was agreed upon both by the union and management of the company.

The union told the company the strike would be peaceful.

Company spokesmen said no future negotiating sessions have been arranged. The firm previously had turned down a federal proposal to continue contract talks for six days.

Soviets Told Atom Secret By Voice of America; U.S. to Push Curb in UN

Russia Isolates Technicians

By a Special Correspondent of The Christian Science Monitor
Copyright, 1949, by The Christian Science Publishing Society

Berlin

The Soviet people learned that they had the atom bomb when the Voice of America told them in its Russian-language transmission of President Truman's announcement.

In the land of top secrets, anything relating to atomic research is a tiptop secret. The subject is rarely referred to in public, and even then only in the vaguest terms.

Recently the young soldier-poet Eugene Dolmatovsky was permitted to print a poem in which he described in ecliptical terms the use of an atom bomb to blow up a granite mountain, presumably in Siberia. Even this literary effort, which certainly gave away no information beyong supporting the general claim that the Russians had produced or were about to produce their own atom bomb, was considered unsuitable for transmission abroad, and all reference to the poem were deleted from foreign correspondents' copy.

Secrecy Thickens

The secrecy shrouding Soviet atomic developments has become thicker and thicker with time.

The year before last, Supreme Soviet decrees approving the annual budget of the U.S.S.R. stated that part would be allocated to atomic research for "peaceful" purposes—but it did not specify any amount. Subsequent decrees have omitted even this passing reference.

Security restrictions on a Soviet atomic project would make Los Alamos or Oak Ridge seem as restricted as the Grand Central lobby in comparison. To begin with, the entire project is administered by the redoubtable MVD (Secret Police) through a special division organized for the purpose.

Suspicion Reigns

MVD's basic method of preventing information leaks is not through loyalty checks to weed out persons considered security risks on the basis of their past records and associations. This procedure hardly would work on a Soviet atomic project.

The Soviets have drafted a considerable number of German experts, men on whose loyalty and service the Soviet regime has no claim beyond coercion. Even some leading Soviet atomic scientists fall considerably short of 100 per cent communistic reliability—men like Peter Kapitza, who was "persuaded" to remain in his native land when he came home for a visit in 1934 from Cambridge, England, where he was working.

Moreover, MVD on principle is suspicious of all persons outside its own immediate ranks and is trained to look on everyone as a potential enemy of the Soviet state, irrespective of taks or behavior. Consequently, MVD is prone to consider anyone who possesses top-secret information especially dangerous.

Physicists Isolated

MVD's answer to these complex security problems has been both simple and effective. It has sought to prevent information on atomic projects from leaking by eliminating all contacts through which such leaks might occur through either intent or carelessness.

Sole channel of contact between a Soviet atomic project and the rest of society is through carefully selected MVD apparatus. The personnel employed on the project live as well as work within a closely guarded compound 12 months of the year.

This kind of total security is facilitated by the afct that MVD, which also operates the Soviet penal system, including forced labor camps, has vast reservoirs of brain power as well as manpower to draw upon—those who in Soviet terminology "are deprived of their freedom."

The mass purges of the 1930's took a heavy toll of the Soviet Union's top technical and research talent. Save for the minority executed, such victims received prison terms. Some of these perished under wartime regors. Others were released upon the expiration of their sentences, which seldom ran more than 10 years.

Reservoir of Technicians

But there was a large group which actually was locked up for knowing too much. The cards of these persons in the MVD file are marked with three initials—"IZO," standing for the initials in Russian of "Isolation From Society." Persons thus tagged never will be set at liberty regardless of the terms of their sentences on paper.

It is from their number that the MVD has been drafting those with requisite training and ability for atomic projects, presumably on the theory that as they know too much already, their knowing more won't do any damage. Moreover, given their classification, there is no danger of their ever divulging atomic secrets.

Parallel U.S. Sites

All that can be said as to the actual location of Soviet atomic activities is that various units are in widely separated parts of the U.S.S.R.'s vast areas.

In this, as in other respects, the American example has been closely copied. The site for experimentation with the bomb is believed to be somewhere in the Kakakhstan desert of central Asia, which duplicates Los Alamos.

Actual fission plants are in the western Ukraine industrial Donbas, within convenient reach of the main Soviet source of uranium ore in Czechoslovakia and Saxony and with ample electric power locally available.

Tass confirms Soviet has atomic secret: Page 14.

Aid Propped

By Richard L. Strou.
Staff Correspondent of The Christian Science Monitor

Washington

The United States will make a supreme effort to achieve international control of the atom bomb.

Object of the drive will be to remove the weapon from the field of warfare or to pin responsibility for failure on Soviet Russia.

Agency of the effort will be the United Nations. While atomic experts and congressional speakers generally pooh-poohed Russia's claim that it had the atomic bomb in 1947, the relative mildness of the semiofficial Tass statement discussing the event encouraged a feeling that a final great attempt at international cooperation should be made.

Program Bolstered

Meanwhile, a new atmosphere has been engendered in Congress bound to promote the administration's international program in the twin fields of military defense and economic cooperation.

The timing of the disclosing of a Soviet atomic explosion is such as to have maximum effect on legislative developments—the administration drive to rearm Atlantic Pact nations and the corresponding drive to work out stability of economic conditions in the sterling area.

After an initial period of suspicion, most congressmen now agree that President Truman did not time the news for his own ends—in fact, the news was held back till after the Senate passed the military aid bill on Sept. 22 by 55 votes to 24. It is agreed that for legislative purposes "Russia again has intervened" to strengthen the administration's hand.

Chain Reaction Seen

The new Russian development comes at a crucial period.

Congress had begun to cool off in the international field.

Many shrewd observers believe that British devaluation is a chain reaction that will go on for 12 months. By the time it is over, this group thinks, the United States must either intervene actively again to bolster the sterling economy and support empire defense outposts or see another "power vacuum" created, as was threatened before the United States took over Britain's burden in Greece and in western Germany.

Heavy new responsibilities loom for the United States.

Up to now, Congress showed little willingness to assume them.

Isolation Due to Fade

The tendency away from internationalism has been shown on a number of recent guideposts.

Thus on extending reciprocal trade agreements, a majority of House and Senate Republicans at one time or another voted either to shelve or restrict the bill. On the big military aid program now in conference the House cut the proposed funds for Europe in half and the Senate tied on restrictive amendments.

Again, in the big defense appropriation bill also now in conference, the upper chamber cut back presidential contract authority for stockpiling strategic materials by $275,000,000. In a fourth field, the unwillingness to share atomic bomb developments with the British and Canada has grown strong in the past few years.

The latest Russian news is expected to spur immediate legislative changes.

Military Aid Propped

Quickest result will be in getting the House to recede from its position on the military aid program. The Senate approved $1,314,010,000, the House only $819,505,000. The Senate figure is likely to win out.

Again, a willingness to cooperate with Britain and Canada on atomic information is reviving fast.

The changed mood embarrasses the administration in one respect. The Senate dropped $800,000,000 from air force funds because Mr. Truman thinks 48 groups are sufficient rather than the 58 approved in the House bill. Now the drive to restore the House figure will be revived in conference in the big defense appropriation bill.

Economic Burden

Less spectacular, but just as important, is the field of economic cooperation, particularly in the sterling area. British devaluation has set off a chain reaction. Some 25 countries have now devalued.

Devaluation puts an indirect economic burden on American manufacturers already: It means cheaper competitive textiles, suits, coats, shoes, leather goods, chinaware, small cars, wool from Australia, and luxury goods from France. On top of this are tariff concessions just made at the big conference at Annecy, France. This is a double blow for some American producers.

And the great creditor country, the United States, has other problems to face in its uncomfortable world role. They won't stop with tariffs.

State of the Nation

Russian Explosion Explodes Illusion

By JOSEPH C. HARSCH, Chief, Washington News Bureau, The Christian Science Monitor

Washington

President Truman's announcement that the Russians had an atomic explosion made a lot of long, black headlines. It also caused an almost record crop of statements by just anyone and everyone. So it was big news.

But there are two kinds of news. There is one kind that leaves you saying, "So what?" And there is the other kind that means that the world never will be the same again. Which kind of news is it—this news that Russia undoubtedly already has built one atom bomb and therefore, presumably, will go on now building more?

Obviously, this is something more than just a dramatic incident, with no meaning in history. But it probably is not so much more than that as our group thinking would have assumed in advance of the event. It was something which many men feared. Now it is here. And it isn't really so awesome after all.

It doesn't bring the danger of war any closer. The United States did not launch a preventive war against Russia when Russia had no bomb. The United States isn't likely to launch such a war because Russia has a bomb or perhaps bombs. That issue presumably has been settled long ago. Russia didn't risk a war when the United States had a monopoly on bombs. It hardly seems likely it would risk a war now when the United States still is several years in engineering and quite a number of bombs ahead.

Does it make the danger of war any less? You can argue that the Russian mind will become more belligerent now that the Russians have a bomb, too. But you can argue more plausibly that the Russians now are free from any reason for an inferiority complex about atom bombs, and therefore likely to be a bit more calm about such matters.

There is nothing like a sense of inferiority to complicate international relations. The United States' own attitude is evidence itself. Two years ago, when the cold war was running against the West, the United States was tense and frightened and in no mood to negotiate with anyone over anything. Negotiations with the Russians were broken off deliberately. American diplomacy wanted time to build bargaining position. It proceeded to build bargaining position with the Marshall Plan, Western Union, and Atlantic Pact. Now American diplomacy is willing to negotiate again, because it is satisfied that it can speak with authority and from strength. Perhaps the same applies to the Russians. Perhaps now that they have a bomb they will feel that they can bargain from a position of equality.

That's all speculative, but it is difficult to see how the Russian mastery of the bomb really makes any serious difference to prospects of war or peace.

It does explode one thing—the mental sense of monopoly. The American Government never has operated on the assumption that the United States possessed a permanent monopoly on atom bombs. Nor has the American Government believed that it possessed "secrets" which were either very secret or could be kept secret very long. Men in government knew that so-called American "secrets" were the product of general knowledge shared by all atomic scientists before the war in every country in the world. Men in government knew that Russia would inevitably get the bomb. They were prepared for the event.

But still there was the public legend of "monopoly" and "secrets." That legend is gone now. There isn't any "monopoly" any more. There aren't any secrets any more. What effect will the ending of the legend have? It may cause a lot of fear. And men who are afraid tend to run off to extremes. We already have such extremes in the suggestion that the United States now abandon Europe, and the companion suggestion that Mr. Truman immediately go and meet Mr. Stalin. One is obviously as silly as the other.

But if the public does not panic, and does not rush to extremes out of fear, then the single probable result of the end of the legend is that opposition will diminish to the United States reviving its old atomic partnership with Britain and Canada.

Of course politics will be made of the news. It already is. The Republicans have the edge and might be able to persuade some voters that Russia got the bomb because of Washington security leaks. The Democrats would have to defend, which is the politically weaker position.

All in all, the principal thing the news does is to end an illusion which has existed in public consciousness, but not in government operations or planning. Perhaps that will shake the world, but there is an excellent chance that it won't.

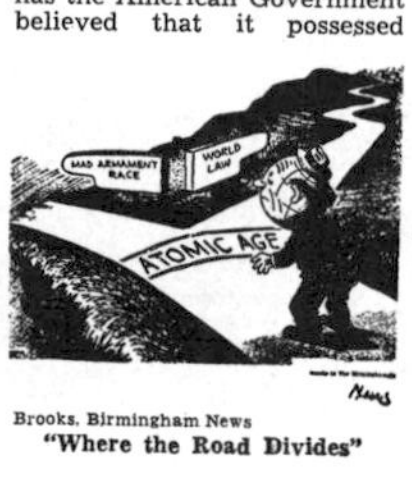

Brooks, Birmingham News

"Where the Road Divides"

Bay State Employment Rises in Manufacturing

The World's Day

Reg. U.S. Pat. Off.

Bay State: Employment Rise First in Year

Employment in Massachusetts manufacturing rose last month for the first time since last September, it is shown by the state's monthly survey. [Page 2.]

Digging of Maine's 60,400,000 bushel potato crop got under way in earnest as skies were sunny over Aroostook County's broad fields. [Page 2.]

Elimination of the budget, collecting, treasury, and auditing departments in Boston's city government and establishment of a centralized financial department in their place with a comptroller as head was urged by the Boston Finance Commission. [Page 2.]

In Europe: Atomic Scientists Meet in London

Atomic scientists from the United States, Britain, and Canada met in London to discuss technical problems on locating and producing uranium.

Col. Bernt Balchen, pioneer Arctic airman, postponed an attempt at a nonstop flight from Norway to Washington because of strong north Atlantic winds.

Washington: Reciprocal Trade Extension Signed

President Truman signed an extension of the Reciprocal Trade Agreements Act until 1951, proclaiming it will aid "expanded world trade at a time when it is most urgently needed."

A speedy return to friendly relations with Franco Spain as a step toward strengthening North Atlantic defenses was urged by Senator Taft (R) of Ohio, who told a reporter he isn't proposing military aid, but said "there is no reason why we shouldn't recognize her fully in a diplomatic way and send an ambassador to Madrid." [Page 3.]

First general pay boost for the armed forces in 40 years comes up for Senate vote late this afternoon with approval generally regarded as certain. Increases are bigger for the higher ranks because top levels have had no pay adjustment for many years while enlisted men have had recent increases.

National: Glidden Tour Rolls Into Virginia

The Glidden caravan's 89 ancient automobiles and one motorcycle left Luray, Va., for Richmond on the second leg of their 650-mile tour of five states. The "faster" ones made the initial 125 miles from Gettysburg, Pa., to Luray yesterday in five hours, but some of the "oldsters" took up to 11 hours.

Far East: Australian Elections Set for Dec. 12

Australia's general elections will be held Dec. 12, Prime Minister Joseph Chifley announced. The Labor Party, which was reelected in 1946, has been in power since 1941.

A Far East expenditure committee of United States congressmen arrived in Batavia, Java, to confer with Dutch officials. Next stop: the Indonesian Republican capital of Jogjakarta.

Prices have been frozen in Hong Kong at predevaluation rates as an antiinflation measure.

Weather Predictions: Sunny (Details Page 2)

West Set to Renew Drive For Real A-Bomb Check

By William H. Stringer
Chief of the London News Bureau of The Christian Science Monitor

London

Particular attention is expected to be directed by both Britain and the United States to the final paragraph of the Moscow statement confirming the atomic explosion.

That paragraph deals with the crucial question of adequate international inspection of atomic energy plants, which Russia hitherto has rejected in spite of semantically handsome words.

The final Russian paragraph states: "Concerning control over the atomic weapon, it has to be said that this control will be essential in order to check up on the fulfillment of the decision on the prohibition of production of the atomic weapon."

Soviet Foreign Minister Andrei Y. Vishinsky in his opening address to the United Nations General Assembly also urged "establishment of an adequate and rigid international control."

What Does Russia Mean?

But heretofore, although the Russians used the phrase "international control," they meant inspection by the Russians' own officials and not by an international agency, as urged in the Baruch plan adopted by the United Nations Atomic Energy Commission.

On this point, the whole effort to formulate international control of atomic energy has foundered in the past. The crucial question is: Do the Russians mean anything different this time, now that they, too, have at least a prototype bomb?

Purporting to elucidate Soviet policy, the London Daily Worker declares: "The Soviet Union has always stood for outlawing of the atom bomb, prohibition of its manufacture, and adequate international inspection to ensure that states entering into those engagements carry them out. . . ."

Communist View

The newspaper adds: "That is, however, an entirely different thing from giving the ownership and control of all atomic enterprises in the world to a so-called international body dominated by the United States and the Marshall countries which are dependent upon it. Such a piece of imperialits megalomania has nothing in common with genuine international cooperation."

Skipping the abuse, is there anything new here? Britain and the United States will wish to know, and undoubtedly will seek through the United Nations or the Council of Foreign Ministers, to discover whether Russia now is prepared to submit its own atomic enterprises as well as those of the United States and other nations to some degree of international inspection.

Great Britain's earlier request for a full share in the United States' atomic information is expected to be reemphasized as result of disclosure of Russia's atomic developments.

Britain as well as Canada may ask for information on the Eniwetok tests, and Britain may even conceivably ask for a stockpile of American atomic bombs.

But strong pressure from public opinion also will be exerted to induce the British Government, in concert with the United States, to make another major try at reaching an agreement for control of atomic energy with Russia.

1950-1969

THE CHRISTIAN SCIENCE MONITOR

Registered in U. S. Patent Office

AN INTERNATIONAL DAILY NEWSPAPER

VOLUME 42 NO. 183 | COPYRIGHT 1950 BY THE CHRISTIAN SCIENCE PUBLISHING SOCIETY | BOSTON, FRIDAY, JUNE 30, 1950 | • ATLANTIC EDITION | TWO SECTIONS | FIVE CENTS A COPY

President Orders Ground Troops To Stem Korean Break-Through

Five Towns Vote School Pooling Plan

By Theodore N. Cook
Staff Writer of The Christian Science Monitor

Citizens of five Massachusetts towns have put aside petty rivalries and false pride to provide, together, the modern high school facilities they could not offer their children on their own.

The five towns—Holden, Paxton, Princeton, Rutland and Sterling—have voted to form Massachusetts' first regional school district, and one of the first in New England.

Establishment of the regional high school is assured with Holden's vote of 771 to 373 in favor of the plan yesterday. The other towns voted overwhelmingly in favor of the proposal on June 17.

Aid From State

Under the terms of present state aid for school construction—which was specifically designed to encourage establishment of regional schools—the state will pay 65 per cent of the cost of the building.

What the new school will mean to the individual communities may be seen in terms of present high school conditions in the towns.

Figures in the latest report of the Massachusetts Department of Education reported an enrollment of only 26 in Princeton's high school, 60 in Rutland, and 250 in Holden. Paxton and Sterling, lacking their own high schools, sent their pupils to other communities on a tuition basis.

By pooling their resources, the five towns expect to have a building capable of accommodating an enrollment of from 800 to 900. This size school will be necessary to provide for rapidly-growing school populations in each of the towns in coming years.

Better Facilities Seen

A larger building and a broader financial base for the school are also expected to make available to the children in the region the kind of facilities that are taken for granted in today's large, modern high schools, but which are virtually impossible to finance in single communities with low enrollments.

Facilities for teaching agricultural courses, along with laboratories, arts and crafts, gymnasium, driver training, mechanical drawing and blueprinting equipment, auditorium, home economics rooms, and music now are well within the range of possibility for children in the five towns.

Details of the curriculum for the new school will be worked out by a regional district committee made up of representatives from each town.

For the purposes of discussion, a $1,500,000 building has been under consideration and preliminary sketches drawn. The proposed site, which is to be in Holden, would cover between 25 and 30 acres.

Significant Development

The remaining cost of the building after deducting state aid will be distributed in proportion among the five towns on the basis of net average membership and equalized valuation.

This action by the five towns is regarded by some educators as perhaps the most significant development in Massachusetts education in 100 years.

A special legislative commission on education found in 1949, that there were 176 one-teacher schools in the state where one teacher tries to teach eight grades, and 60 small towns with high schools—representing one-fourth of all high schools in the state—with a student membership under 100.

John E. Marshall, administrator of the School Building Assistance Commission, who has the responsibility of encouraging regional schools as well as approving all buildings proposed for state aid, was heartened by the vote in the five towns showing 75 ptr cent in favor.

"I hope," Mr. Marshall said, "it will show the educational and financial advantages of the regional school and lead Massachusetts away from the weak, small high school."

State Population Goes Up 395,032

Massachusetts' population gained 395,032 in the past decade with a new high of 4,711,753 reached in the 1950 census, it was announced today by Paul G. Carney, area supervisor for New England of the United States Bureau of the Census, with headquarters in the Boston Federal Building.

The figures are preliminary, pending final checking in Washington. The 1940 census gave Massachusetts 4,316,721.

Middlesex County with a new peak of 1,082,036 accounted for 110,646 of the state's gain over the 1940 figures of 971,390.

Lie Queries Nations On South Korea Aid

By a Staff Correspondent of The Christian Science Monitor

Lake Success

Secretary-General Trygve Lie has asked the 59 members of the United Nations—including Russia—to notify him as to what type of assistance, if any, they plan to supply South Korea.

Calling the members' attention to the June 27 resolution of the Security Council recommending military sanctions, Mr. Lie said, "In the event that your government is in position to provide assistance, it would facilitate the implementation of the resolution if you were to be so good as to provide me with an early reply as to the type of assistance."

Pledges of aid already have been received from Great Britain, Australia, New Zealand, and Belgium. The Netherlands and India have expressed support for the resolution.

Plans for Australian TV Accepted by Cabinet

By Reuters

Canberra, Australia

The cabinet has approved plans for television in Australia, Postmaster-General H. L. Anthony announced here.

The first experimental station would be finished in about two years. Private enterprise would be allowed to participate.

Tax Relief Seen Tucked Into Budget

By Edgar M. Mills
New England Political Correspondent of The Christian Science Monitor

Hard-pressed Massachusetts taxpayers may reap some financial relief through a little-discussed, but highly important, spending curb tucked into the recently passed $218,875,739 state budget.

That curb is contained in provisions barring the governor and state departments from spending more than one-half of their full year's appropriations in the first six months of the fiscal year opening tomorrow.

This stop sign against accelerated spending is considered by Republican leaders as one of the most important concessions won through their long battle to cut the budget.

Brake on Overspending

Both Senator Harris S. Richardson (R) of Winchester, Senate president, and Representative Charles Gibbons of Stoneham, House GOP floor leader, consider it an important means of trimming down or eliminating completely department overspending. This overspending, in the past, has resulted in substantial deficiency appropriations in the last half of most recent fiscal years. For the fiscal year closing tonight, the deficiency budget totaled $3,392,292.

Senator Richardson is convinced $5,000,000 can be saved through this Republican-sponsored provision.

"With the state faced with the necessity of raising $40,000,000 to $45,000,000 more in new revenue next year to continue the present level of state government, it is imperative that every possible saving be effected in the new budget," he added.

Mr. Gibbons is like-minded. He considers it an extremely important concession capable of producing substantial intangible savings.

Balks Preelection Spree

They and other GOP leaders point out the spending curb will prevent the Dever administration from possibly speeding up spending during the four months just prior to election day, for the political advantages involved.

There are several parts to the spending curb. They include:

1. The major provision limiting departments to no more than one-half of their appropriations during the first six months of the fiscal year.

2. Exemptions from this main provision include seasonal activities in the state department of conservation, summer recreation work, and the like, as well as supplies delivered on long-term contracts.

3. The state comptroller is required to report to the Legislature as soon as possible after Jan. 1, 1951, the balance in each department account.

4. Allotments for the last three months of the year cannot be made until the 1951 Legislature specifically permits.

Senator Richardson and Mr. Gibbons asserted that one reason Senate Republicans finally backed down on their $3,000,000 budget cut proposal was that they feared if the second budget were killed, the third budget would not include the spending curb provisions.

Eyewitness Bares Plight

By Gordon Walker
Chief Far Eastern Correspondent of The Christian Science Monitor

Gen. Douglas MacArthur's Advance Headquarters, South Korea

As a result of Gen. Douglas MacArthur's visit here June 29, the South Korean war, including the South Korean Army, has passed directly under supervision and direction of the Supreme Commander, Allied Powers.

The South Korean Army still is an individual fighting organization.

But it is receiving both tactical and strategic orders from General MacArthur through his field commander, Brig. Gen. John H. Church.

General MacArthur has ordered United States planes to bomb air installations in North Korea. Targets in Pyongyang, capital of North Korea, already have been struck, according to Clarence Ryee, South Korean Information Director.

Island Attack Reported

In addition, Mr. Ryee said South Korean troops had reentered the suburbs of Seoul.

[The North Korean radio in Seoul announced Communist troops had occupied Kanghwa Island, 20 miles northwest of Inchon, Seoul's port, the Associated Press said.]

The South Korean war, therefore, has changed its complexion entirely.

Legal aspects notwithstanding, it now is war between the United States and North Korea, with the American Far East command furnishing air, sea, and logistic support, and the South Korean Government furnishing ground forces.

On June 27 this American advance headquarters consisted of 17 men, with equivalent rations.

Now the number of men has multiplied many times, although rations have not been increased commensurately.

Ammunition Priority

The method by which I arrived here early June 30 gives an adequate answer.

We left a southern Japanese airfield before dawn aboard a four-engine transport plane carrying 7,500 pounds of rocket shells.

There was no equipment for advance headquarters, such as food and blankets, simply because first priority was given to the South Korean ground troops who must stop the North Korean tanks massed on the north bank of the Han River, south of Seoul.

Weaving through valleys at 150 feet, our plane managed to get through Yak fighters to land on an isolated cement strip in the middle of rice fields near the fighting front.

At one end of the strip was the wreckage of a previous transport plane which had been strafed by Yaks and whose rockets had exploded.

Shooting War

Nearby was a grounded F-82 fighter which had been strafed and wrecked before it could get off again.

Literally diving into a landing, our ammo transport was unloaded by Korean troops and was off again before 30 minutes had elapsed.

Driving along in a truck loaded with rockets, we witnessed the final seconds of an American jet fighter which had been hit while strafing North Korean positions just south of Seoul.

The pilot parachuted to the ground on one side of us, while his plane crashed into some paddy fields 200 yards to our right. This and other eyewitness scenes here emphasize only too strongly that this is a shooting war.

The pressing problem is to give the South Korean Army sufficient equipment and sufficient stiffening to prevent another major break-through such as occurred north of Seoul earlier in the week.

Morale Strong

Right now the South Korean Army has plenty of carbines but only a handful of bazookas and a single 105 mm. artillery piece—the remainder of its artillery was lost when the army was evacuated from Seoul.

The South Korean Army has tended to disintegrate badly. But this is understandable in view of the fact they have little or nothing with which to block the advance of the North Korean mechanized columns.

But there is nothing wrong with their fighting spirit once they are given proper equipment.

The feeling among many observers here, however, is that unless the United States brings in its own ground troops, air and logistical support will not be enough.

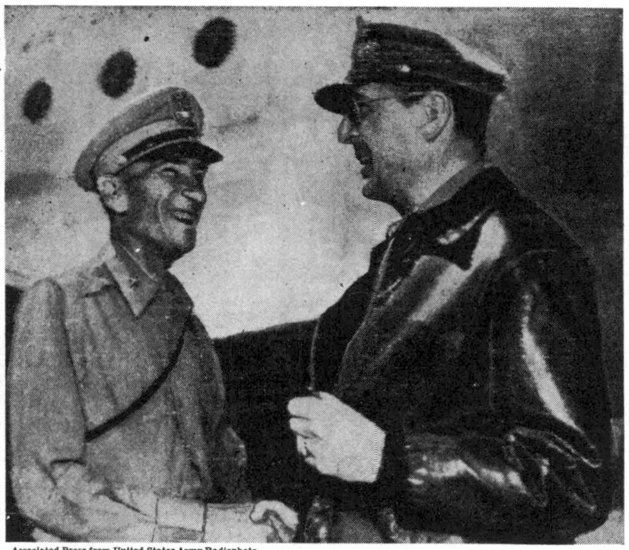

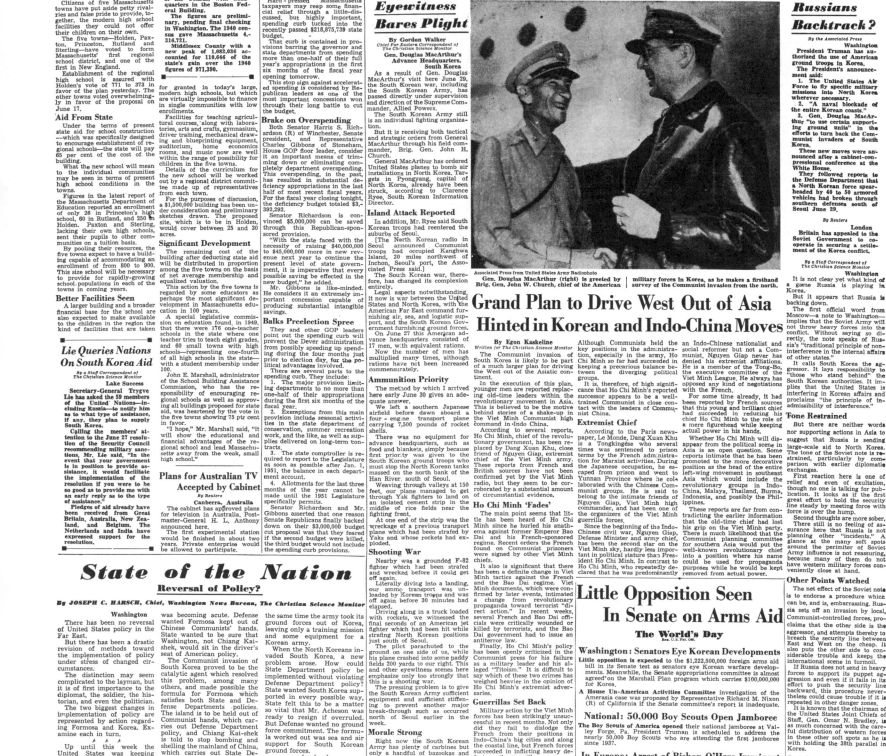

Associated Press from United States Army Radiophoto

Gen. Douglas MacArthur (right) is greeted by Brig. Gen. John W. Church, chief of the American military forces in Korea, as he makes a firsthand survey of the Communist invasion from the north.

Russians Backtrack?

By the Associated Press

Washington

President Truman has authorized the use of American ground troops in Korea.

The President's announcement said:

1. The United States Air Force to fly specific military missions into North Korea wherever necessary.

2. "A naval blockade of the entire Korean coasts."

3. Gen. Douglas MacArthur "to use certain supporting ground units" in the efforts to turn back the Communist invaders of South Korea.

These new moves were announced after a cabinet-congressional conference at the White House.

They followed reports to the Defense Department that a North Korean force spearheaded by 40 to 50 armored vehicles had broken through southern defenses south of Seoul June 29.

By Reuters

London

Britain has appealed to the Soviet Government to cooperate in securing a settlement of the Korea conflict.

By a Staff Correspondent of The Christian Science Monitor

Washington

It is not clear yet what kind of a game Russia is playing in Korea.

But it appears that Russia is backing down.

The first official word from Moscow—a note to Washington—implies that the Soviet Army will not throw heavy forces into the conflict. Without saying so directly, the note speaks of Russia's "traditional principle of noninterference in the internal affairs of other states."

It calls South Korea the aggressor. It lays responsibility to "those who stand behind" the South Korean authorities. It implies that the United States is interfering in Korean affairs and proclaims "the principle of inadmissibility of interference."

Tone Restrained

But there are neither words nor supporting actions in Asia to suggest that Russia is sending large-scale aid to North Korea. The tone of the Soviet note is restrained, particularly by comparison with earlier diplomatic exchanges.

First reaction here is one of relief and even of exultation, though no one is talking for publication. It looks as if the first great effort to hold the security line steady by meeting force with force is over the hump.

Second thoughts are more sober.

There still is no feeling of assurance here that Russia is not planning other "incidents." A glance at the many soft spots around the perimiter of Soviet Army influence is not reassuring, because many of them do not have western military forces conveniently close at hand.

Other Points Watched

The net effect of the Soviet note is to endorse a procedure which can be, and is, embarrassing. Russia sets off an invasion by local, Communist-controlled forces, proclaims that the other side is the aggressor, and attempts thereby to breach the security line between East and West on the cheap. It also puts the other side to considerable trouble and keeps the international scene in turmoil.

If Russia does not send in heavy forces to support its puppet aggression and even if it fails in its effort to push the security line backward, this procedure nevertheless could cause trouble if it is repeated in other danger zones.

It is known that the chairman of the United States Joint Chiefs of Staff, Gen. Omar N. Bradley, is as much concerned with the careful distribution of western forces in these other soft spots as he is with holding the 38th parallel in Korea.

Satisfaction Noted

With this much said, it is undeniable that the Soviet note has caused some very solid satisfaction here. Those responsible for the nation's over-all security planning have not expected Russia to go all out in any such local adventure—certainly not at this time. Since this is known to be their best judgement, it can be presumed that they regard this affair as an effort by Russia to score a big diplomatic success by shock, without committing the Soviet Army directly.

This effort is being rebuffed. To that extent, the Russians have lost.

The really serious problem is caused by the fact that they might have won. Had President Truman and his advisers of both parties not reacted as they did, the Russians might have succeeded. The line between success and failure is that thin.

The problem ahead, therefore, is how to avert similar adventures elsewhere, in which western forces might be less close to the scene and less able to act decisively.

Grand Plan to Drive West Out of Asia Hinted in Korean and Indo-China Moves

By Egon Kaskeline
Written for The Christian Science Monitor

The Communist invasion of South Korea is likely to be part of a much larger plan for driving the West out of the Asiatic continent.

In the execution of this plan, younger men are reported replacing old-time leaders within the revolutionary movement in Asia. This is believed to be the motive behind stories of a shake-up in the Viet Minh Communist high command in Indo China.

According to several reports, Ho Chi Minh, chief of the revolutionary government, has been replaced by Dang Xuan Khu, close friend of Nguyen Giap, extremist chief of the Viet Minh army. These reports from French and British sources have not been confirmed yet by the Viet Minh radio, but they seem to be corroborated by a substantial amount of circumstantial evidence.

Ho Chi Minh 'Fades'

The main point seems that little has been heard of Ho Chi Minh since he hurled his anathema against former Emperor Bao Dai and his French-sponsored regime. Recent orders the French found on Communist prisoners were signed by other Viet Minh chiefs.

It also is significant that there has been a definite change in Viet Minh tactics against the French and the Bao Dai regime. Viet Minh documents, which were confirmed by later events, intimated a change from revolutionary propaganda toward terrorist "direct action." In recent weeks, several French and Bao Dai officials were critically wounded or killed by terrorists, and the Bao Dai government had to issue an antiterror law.

Finally, Ho Chi Minh's policy has been openly criticized in the Communist press for his failure as a military leader and his alleged "Titoism." It is difficult to say which of these two crimes has weighed heavier in the opinion of Ho Chi Minh's extremist adversaries.

Guerrillas Set Back

Military action by the Viet Minh forces has been strikingly unsuccessful in recent months. Not only did they fail to dislodge the French from their positions in Indo-China's big cities and along the coastal line, but French forces succeeded in inflicting heavy defeats on the guerrillas.

Viet Minh guerrillas had to abandon their strongholds in the northern Indo-China "rice bowl." Their troops which infiltrated into Cambodia, a French controlled kingdom in southern Indo-China, last May were repulsed by a French counteroffensive.

On the other hand, Viet Minh has continued to entertain relations with Marshal Tito's Yugoslavia despite apparent Moscow pressure to sever this diplomatic link. Nguyen Duc Quy, Viet Minh representative in Thailand, told an American newspaperman recently that these contacts would be maintained in the future. He also pointed out that Ho Chi Minh's government was not Communist-dominated but that it represented all groups and classes of the Indo-Chinese people.

Precarious Balance

A number of unbiased observers in Indo-China have affirmed that the Viet Minh was a "national front" movement which included democratic nationalists, as well as socialists and Communists. Yet the Communist minority always dominated the other factions. Although Communists held the key positions in the administration, especially in the army, Ho Chi Minh so far had succeeded in keeping a precarious balance between the diverging political groups.

It is, therefore, of high significance that Ho Chi Minh's reported successor appears to be a well-trained Communist in close contact with the leaders of Communist China.

Extremist Chief

According to the Paris newspaper, Le Monde, Dang Xuan Khu is a Tongkingese who several times was sentenced to prison terms by the French administration for Marxist activities. During the Japanese occupation, he escaped from prison and went to Yunnan Province where he collaborated with the Chinese Communist groups. He is said to belong to the intimate friends of Nguyen Giap, Viet Minh high commander, and has been one of the organizers of the Viet Minh guerrilla forces.

Since the beginning of the Indo-Chinese civil war, Nguyen Giap, Defense Minister and army chief, has been the second star on the Viet Minh sky, hardly less important in political stature than President Ho Chi Minh. In contrast to Ho Chi Minh, who repeatedly declared that he was predominantly an Indo-Chinese nationalist and social reformer but not a Communist, Nguyen Giap never has denied his extremist affiliations. He is a member of the Tong-Bo, the executive committee of the Viet Minh League. He always has opposed any kind of negotiations with the French.

For some time already, it had been reported by French sources that this young and brilliant chief had succeeded in reducing his chief Ho Chi Minh to the role of a mere figurehead while keeping actual power in his hands.

Whether Ho Chi Minh will disappear from the political scene in Asia is an open question. Some reports intimate that he has been promoted to the more decorative position as the head of the entire left-wing movement in southeast Asia which would include the revolutionary groups in Indo-China, Malaya, Thailand, Burma, Indonesia, and possibly the Philippines.

These reports are far from contradicting the earlier information that the old-time chief had lost his grip on the Viet Minh party. There is much likelihood that the Communist planning committee for southern Asia would put the well-known revolutionary chief into a position where his name could be used for propaganda purposes while he would be kept removed from actual power.

Little Opposition Seen In Senate on Arms Aid

The World's Day
Reg. U.S. Pat. Off.

Washington: Senators Eye Korean Developments

Little opposition is expected to the $1,222,500,000 foreign arms aid bill in its Senate test as senators eye Korean warfare developments. Meanwhile, the Senate appropriations committee is almost agreed on the Marshall Plan program which carries $100,000,000 for Korea.

A House Un-American Activities Committee investigation of the Amerasia case was proposed by Representative Richard M. Nixon (R) of California if the Senate committee's report is inadequate.

National: 50,000 Boy Scouts Open Jamboree

The Boy Scouts of America opened their national jamboree at Valley Forge, Pa. President Truman is scheduled to address the nearly 50,000 Boy Scouts who are attending the first jamboree since 1937.

In Europe: Arrest of Bishop O'Hara Imminent

Arrest of Roman Catholic Bishop Gerald P. O'Hara, Papal Nuncio to Romania, may be imminent, according to a Vatican spokesman, following the charge at a Communist-staged trial in Bucharest that the American Bishop had hired a spy in the guise of a chauffeur.

New England: May Employment Totals 3,130,200

Employment in New England totaled 3,130,200 persons in May, 1950, amounting to an increase of 28,400 jobs more than the previous month's total, and 16,900 more than in May, 1949, according to the United States Department of Labor. [Page 2.]

Different attitudes toward Boston's $63 tax rate have been expressed by tax experts, real estate operators, homeowners and former mayoralty candidates. [Page 2.]

Far East: Gas Rationing Ending in Pakistan

Gasoline rationing ends in Pakistan July 1, the government announced in Karachi.

Canada: Parliament Votes Millions for Defense

Canada's Parliament recessed after a noncontroversial session which voted $425,000,000 for defense and the last of some $2,400,000,000 for government expenditures.

Anti-Communist Russian displaced persons living in Canada have been trying to enlist in Canada's army, officials in Ottawa said. The Canadian Army accepts only citizens and resident British subjects.

Weather Predictions: Cloudy, Cool (Details Page 2)

State of the Nation

Reversal of Policy?

By JOSEPH C. HARSCH, Chief, Washington News Bureau, The Christian Science Monitor

Washington

There has been no reversal of United States policy in the Far East.

But there has been a drastic revision of methods toward the implementation of policy under stress of changed circumstances.

The distinction may seem complicated to the layman, but it is of first importance to the diplomat, the soldier, the historian, and even the politician.

The two biggest changes in implementation of policy are represented by action regarding Formosa and Korea. Examine each in turn.

Up until this week the United States was keeping hands off Formosa. Now the United States Seventh Fleet is protecting Formosa. This is a contrast in action, but does not represent change in policy. Formosa is not of itself a matter of major policy. Formosa is a problem which has to be resolved in carrying out both state and defense policies.

The State Department policy most actively touched by Formosa is the policy of avoiding American involvement in the Chinese civil war. The Defense Department policy involved in Formosa is of avoiding the loss of any further sea and air bases to hands which, in case of war, might put them at Russian disposal.

Up until this week no formula had been developed for handling Formosa in a way which would satisfy both of these policies. It was a problem which had not been acute because the Chinese Communists were not ready yet to move against Formosa. But it was becoming acute. Defense wanted Formosa kept out of Chinese Communists' hands. State wanted to be sure that Washington, not Chiang Kai-shek, would sit in the driver's seat of American policy.

The Communist invasion of South Korea proved to be the catalytic agent which resolved this problem, among many others, and made possible the formula for Formosa which satisfies both State and Defense Departments policies. The island is to be held out of Communist hands, which carries out Defense Department policy, and Chiang Kai-shek is told to stop bombing and shelling the mainland of China, which carries out State Department policy. Both departments and both policies are satisfied. It is an excellent solution, recognized as such by both. But there is no reversal of policy involved for either.

Then take Korea. It has been all along, and still is, State Department policy to support the independence of the Republic of Korea, which was set up in South Korea under United Nations auspices and is the only government in Korea recognized by the western world and the UN.

It also has been all along, and still is, Defense Department policy to avoid commitment of American ground forces in Korea. These policies involved no conflict so long as the North Koreans kept north of the 38th parallel. Under State Department policy, the Korean Government was given all American aid available toward building up Korean strength and independence. At the same time the army took its ground forces out of Korea, leaving only a training mission and some equipment for a Korean army.

When the North Koreans invaded South Korea, a new problem arose. How could State Department policy be implemented without violating Defense Department policy? State wanted South Korea supported in every possible way, State felt this to be a matter so vital that Mr. Acheson was ready to resign if overruled. But Defense wanted no ground force commitment. The formula worked out was sea and air support for South Korean ground forces.

Defense hopes that circumstances will not lead to demands for ground troops in Korea as well. Perhaps that step will be taken as a last resort. But that will not represent a reversal of Defense Department policy. It will be a temporary departure from that policy forced by unusual circumstances. You may be sure that if United States ground forces go to Korea they will be taken out again at the very earliest possible moment.

So it is not accurate to say that policy reversals have taken place. Mr. Acheson has not been reversed over Formosa. Mr. Johnson has not been reversed over Korea. But formulas have become possible in a situation of emergency which satisfy the immediate needs of both Formosan and Korean problems within the framework of the basic policies of both State and Defense Departments.

Houston Places Port Under 24-Hour Alert

By the Associated Press

Houston

The port of Houston has been placed on a 24-hour alert, with orders that port police are to approach suspicious persons with their guns drawn. Gen. W. F. Heavey, port director, issued the order.

THE CHRISTIAN SCIENCE MONITOR

Registered in U. S. Patent Office

AN INTERNATIONAL DAILY NEWSPAPER

VOLUME 43 NO. 115 | BOSTON, WEDNESDAY, APRIL 11, 1951 | ** — ATLANTIC EDITION | TWO SECTIONS | FIVE CENTS A COPY

COPYRIGHT 1951 BY THE CHRISTIAN SCIENCE PUBLISHING SOCIETY

MacArthur Ouster Laid to Pentagon; Truman's Action Confuses Japanese

U.S. Prestige Wanes In Iran as Aid Lags; Moscow Makes Hay

MEN AGAINST THE JUNGLE—CRISIS IN IRAN

This is the eighth article in a group of exclusive features under the general title "Men Against the Jungle."

Rapidly moving events have focused the spotlight of world attention on the crucial, oil-rich area of southwest Asia. Thus the first phase is entitled "Crisis in Iran." These articles present a clear picture of what is happening in that country and why it is important for the whole free world. Later articles will deal with southeast Asia.

The next article will appear Friday.

By Edmund Stevens

Chief of the Mediterranean News Bureau of The Christian Science Monitor

Teheran, Iran

American prestige in Iran has waned considerably during the past 10 months and the downhill process is continuing. Basic reason for this is failure of expected large-scale American economic financial aid to materialize.

Few persons in Teheran nowadays have a good word for the late Premier, Gen. Ali Razmara, except his immediate kin. Indeed there is a widespread campaign to blacken General Razmara's character posthumously.

Yet few premiers ever assumed office under better auspices and with brighter hopes or greater popular support. He announced at the outset a program of sweeping reforms of large-scale economic undertakings embodied in a seven-year plan.

U. S. Support Expected

According to bazaar gossip, General Razmara attained office with American support. But at the time, this was not said as criticism.

To the average Iranian citizen, it meant that General Razmara could count on the backing of the great American republic in implementing his plans. General Razmara himself seemed to share this view.

These expectations were enhanced by the appointment to Teheran of Ambassador Henry F. Grady, fresh from a big spending program in Greece.

Altogether, American popularity in Iran reached a peak as did the Iranians' own enthusiasm and eagerness to work for their country's future. That was last June.

But the United States, which elsewhere distributed billions with a lavish hand, showed no inclination to even modest generosity toward Iran. Applications for loans encountered endless red-tape technicalities.

The Iranians, unfamiliar with complex loan procedure, received requests for detailed economic financial data unavailable in a country where few statistics are kept—where even the size of the population is a matter of rough estimate.

Aid Whittled Down

Requests for direct aid netted a total grant of half a million dollars under President Truman's Point Four. Request for a seven-million dollar loan from the International Bank to improve port facilities was whittled down to three million dollars, which the Iranians rejected. Last October, after lengthy negotiation, the Export-Import Bank granted a 25-million dollar loan to Iran, which had asked 500 million dollars. General Razmara felt so humiliated at this reduction that he hesitated to submit loan to the Iranian Parliament, which has not accepted it yet.

Apologists for the American attitude cite Iran's governmental instability, corruption, faulty tax-collecting system and vagueness of many requests for aid. While admitting that these arguments contain an element of truth, pro-Iranians point out that they apply equally to Greece, Italy, and others receiving lavish American aid which those cases justified because those countries were essential to defense of the free world.

Turn Against West

But surely oil-rich Iran, open gateway to the entire Mideast, is no less vital, it was felt here. As for political instability, American aid would have strengthened the government. As for vagueness of requests, it is pointed out that it was up to the Americans to assist Iranians in formulation of their requests.

Many American officials here feel the Iranians got so little attention in Washington largely because they had nobody to lobby for them or press their case before Congress.

In any event, the American attitude caused keenest disappointment, which swiftly ripened into resentment.

Premier Razmara, who saw his brave program dissolve like a dream, in bitter disillusionment turned against the West. Iranian foreign policy shifted from its previous consistent all-out support of the West in the United Nations and elsewhere toward a position of neutrality.

Russia Cultivated

Parallel to this estrangement from the West, General Razmara began cultivating better relations with the Soviet Union. Most important step was the announcement on Nov. 3, 1950, of a barter agreement with Russia. Soviet-Iranian trade, which had been at a virtual standstill since 1946, was partially resumed under terms of the trade and naval treaty of March, 1940.

This reinvoking of a prewar accord still formally operative avoided the necessity of submitting the matter to Parilament for approval.

In agreeing to this resumption of trade, General Razmara left to subsequent negotiations the settlement of Iran's claims for $12,000,000 in gold and $8,000,000 in currency removed from the country by the Soviets during the wartime occupation. A boundary dispute was left to a joint commission.

No Reciprocity

The agreement provided that Soviet-Iranian trade be channeled through Iranian state corporations organized specially for the purpose, with one in each area where the Soviets wished to trade. Since then, there has been difficulty in raising capital for this purpose, and consequently the Soviets are permitted in most areas to send commercial representatives who deal directly with private business.

Needless to say, there is no reciprocity in this, and whereas Iranians are no more free to travel in the Soviet Union than any other foreigners and no longer have consulates in Baku and Batum, Soviet agents in the guise of trade representatives now can roam Iran.

General Razmara shifted toward a soft policy toward the Soviet Union in other respects, although the pro-Communist Soviet-sponsored Tudeh Party has been illegal ever since an assassination attempt on the Shah in 1949.

Curb Eased

General Razmara gradually relaxed police measures against the Tudeh Party. Most sensational event was the escape from prison of 10 Tudeh top leaders last December.

In sum total, these developments have greatly enhanced Soviet influence and prestige to the further detriment of American prestige. Moreover, they have resulted in intensification of Soviet underground activities, which, here as everywhere, aim eventually at bringing the Communists to power and reducing the country to the status of a Soviet satellite.

In this connection, the Soviets' strongest allies are extreme poverty, the masses which having lost faith in America are turning toward the Soviet Union, not because they are Communists but because they feel that in their case any change is preferable; upper-class resentment against the West, which they feel let them down, and finally the continued mistakes committed by the West in Iran.

Tokyo Sees Asia 'Lost'

By Gordon Walker

Chief Far Eastern Correspondent of The Christian Science Monitor

Tokyo

Segments of United Nations headquarters here and the Japanese Government and people have been stunned into confused silence following President Truman's action in relieving Gen. Douglas MacArthur of his UN command and position as Supreme Commander, Allied Powers, in Japan.

An atomic bomb dropped along the avenue which separates the Imperial Palace and General MacArthur's Dai Ichi building office could have had hardly more profound an effect.

Tokyo Stunned

Aside from the immediate aspects of relieving General MacArthur of one of the biggest military positions in American history, there already is a rumble of running rumors—not only in Tokyo but throughout Asia—that tremendous changes in American Far East policy are imminent, that America now may decide to abandon Asia completely to communism and turn its entire attention to Europe.

News of General MacArthur's dismissal reached Tokyo while the general was lunching with Senator Warren Magnuson (D) of Washington and other friends.

There was no inkling of the momentous news when the battle-jacketed general strode down the steps of the Dai Ichi building and into his new black Chrysler at 2:30 p.m. on April 11 here.

The usual crowds of curious occupationaires and Japanese thronged about the front steps of the office as they have done for the past six years.

Rift Periled Morale

An hour later the presidential decision was announced here publicly.

Two hours later Japanese newspapers, reflecting the extreme shock of the average man in the street, came out with extras and editorials rimmed in black.

Mr. Truman's spectacular announcement climaxed a fortnight of tension here as local newspapers chronicled what was obviously a growing policy rift between General MacArthur and Washington.

The feeling here, among both Japanese and military circles, however, had been that the general was such a powerful political figure in the United States and has such a brilliant record that the most Mr. Truman could do would be to give him a stern reprimand.

Unfaltering Stand

The fact remains, nevertheless, that the open debate which has been taking place between General MacArthur and Washington over such vital questions as Formosa, utilization of Chinese Nationalists, and extension of the Korean war into Manchuria, was eating into the morale of all concerned here with the United Nations military venture.

It was also, in the opinion of most observers here, providing the enemy with the most decisive sort of propaganda aid and comfort.

As far as local SCAP headquarters was concerned, there never has been any middle ground as far as General MacArthur and his definitive views on Asia problems are concerned. One was either for General MacArthur or against him.

And among those who supported the general—particularly his close lieutenants of past military campaigns—feeling is so strong on elements of America's Asiatic policy that little short of General MacArthur's removal could change the situation to any extent.

Undoubtedly under Lieut. Gen. Matthew B. Ridgway the UN command will take on an entirely different complexion.

And on this point alone, the average Japanese here is fearful to the extreme.

Held in Highest Esteem

For six years the Japanese have come to regard General MacArthur as something of a savior rather than a conqueror.

To them he spelled a soft occupation and material gain.

They felt, moreover, that the MacArthur influence was largely responsible for the fact that America was solidly entrenched in Asia: that without General MacArthur America might abandon Japan as some persons feel it abandoned Nationalist China.

Likewise, Chinese Nationalists, who also looked upon General MacArthur as their strongest supporter, already have shown signs of extreme dismay.

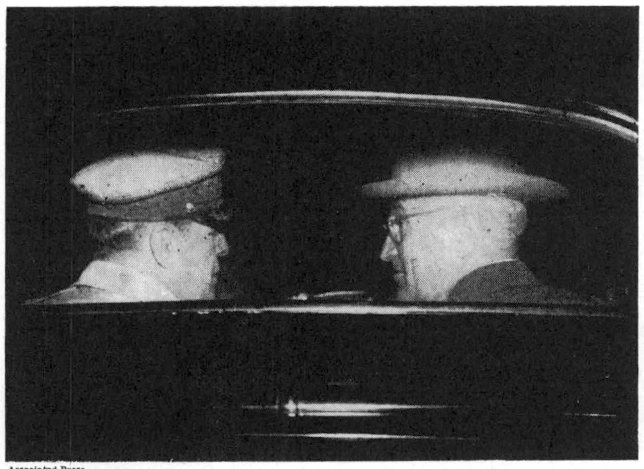

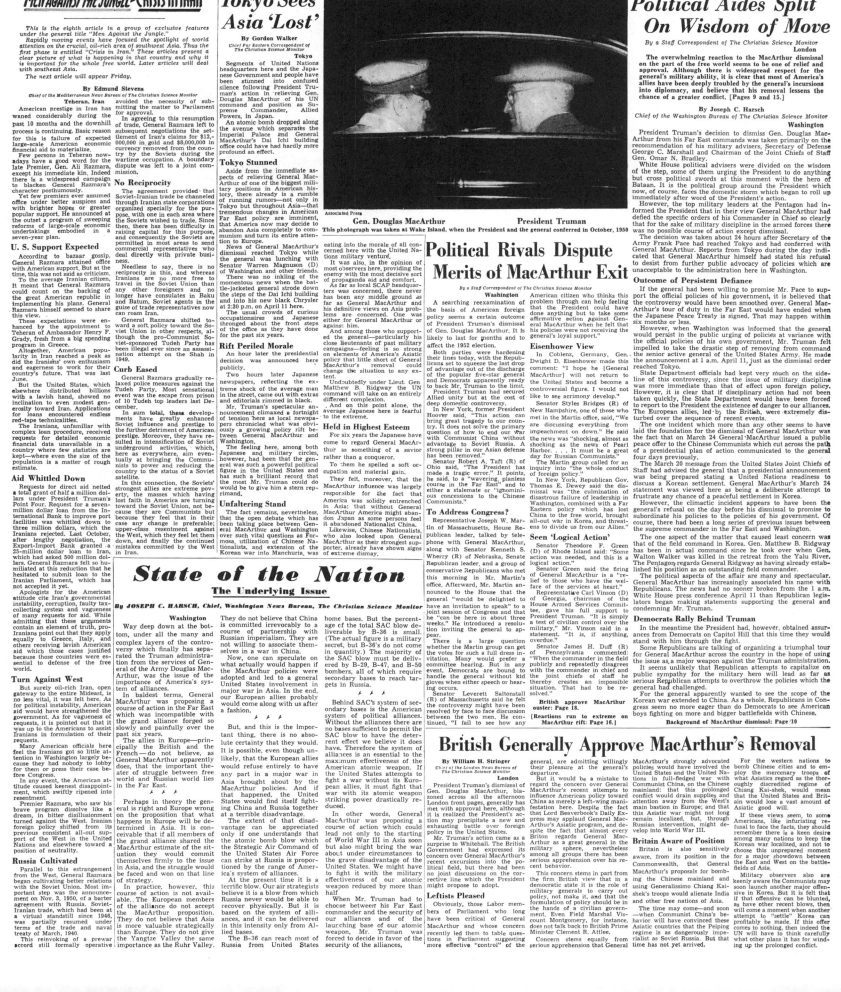

Associated Press

Gen. Douglas MacArthur — **President Truman**

This photograph was taken at Wake Island, when the President and the general conferred in October, 1950

Political Aides Split On Wisdom of Move

By a Staff Correspondent of The Christian Science Monitor

London

The overwhelming reaction to the MacArthur dismissal on the part of the free world seems to be one of relief and approval. Although there is widespread respect for the general's military ability, it is clear that most of America's allies have been deeply troubled by the general's incursions into diplomacy, and believe that his removal lessens the chance of a greater conflict. [Pages 9 and 15.]

By Joseph C. Harsch

Chief of the Washington Bureau of The Christian Science Monitor

Washington

President Truman's decision to dismiss Gen. Douglas MacArthur from his Far East commands was taken primarily on the recommendation of his military advisers, Secretary of Defense George C. Marshall and Chairman of the Joint Chiefs of Staff Gen. Omar N. Bradley.

White House political advisers were divided on the wisdom of the step, some of them urging the President to do anything but cross political swords at this moment with the hero of Bataan. It is the political group around the President which now, of course, faces the domestic storm which began to roll up immediately after word of the President's action.

However, the top military leaders at the Pentagon had informed the President that in their view General MacArthur had defied the specific orders of his Commander in Chief so clearly that for the sake of military discipline in the armed forces there was no possible course of action except dismissal.

The decision was taken about 24 hours after Secretary of the Army Frank Pace had reached Tokyo and had conferred with General MacArthur. Reports from Tokyo during the day indicated that General MacArthur himself had stated his refusal to desist from further public advocacy of policies which are unacceptable to the administration here in Washington.

Outcome of Persistent Defiance

If the general had been willing to promise Mr. Pace to support the official policies of his government, it is believed that the controversy would have been smoothed over. General MacArthur's tour of duty in the Far East would have ended when the Japanese Peace Treaty is signed. That may happen within six months or less.

However, when Washington was informed that the general would persist in the public urging of policies at variance with the official policies of his own government, Mr. Truman felt impelled to take the drastic step of removing from command the senior active general of the United States Army. He made the announcement at 1 a.m. April 11, just as the dismissal order reached Tokyo.

State Department officials had kept very much on the sideline of this controversy, since the issue of military discipline was more immediate than that of effect upon foreign policy. However, it is clear that if disciplinary action had not been taken quickly, the State Department would have been forced to report to the President the existence of danger to our alliances. The European allies, led by the British, were extremely disturbed over the sequence of recent events.

The one incident which more than any other seems to have laid the foundation for the dismissal of General MacArthur was the fact that on March 24 General MacArthur issued a public peace offer to the Chinese Communists which cut across the path of a presidential plan of action communicated to the general four days previously.

The March 20 message from the United States Joint Chiefs of Staff had advised the general that a presidential announcement was being prepared stating a United Nations readiness to discuss a Korean settlement. General MacArthur's March 24 statement was viewed here as being a deliberate attempt to frustrate any chance of a peaceful settlement in Korea.

However, the climactic incident appears to have been the general's refusal on the day before his dismissal to promise to subordinate his policies to the policies of his government. Of course, there had been a long series of previous issues between the supreme commander in the Far East and Washington.

The one aspect of the matter that caused least concern was that of the field command in Korea. Gen. Matthew B. Ridgway has been in actual command since he took over when Gen. Walton Walker was killed in the retreat from the Yalu River. The Pentagon regards General Ridgway as having already established his position as an outstanding field commander.

The political aspects of the affair are many and spectacular. General MacArthur has increasingly associated his name with Republicans. The news had no sooner broken from the 1 a.m. White House press conference April 11 than Republican legislators began making statements supporting the general and condemning Mr. Truman.

Democrats Rally Behind Truman

In the meantime the President had, however, obtained assurances from Democrats on Capitol Hill that this time they would stand with him through the fight.

Some Republicans are talking of organizing a triumphal tour for General MacArthur across the country in the hope of using the issue as a major weapon against the Truman administration.

It seems unlikely that Republican attempts to capitalize on public sympathy for the military hero will lead as far as serious Republican attempts to overthrow the policies which the general had challenged.

For the general apparently wanted to see the scope of the Korean war extended to China. As a whole, Republicans in Congress seem no more eager than do Democrats to see American boys fighting on more and bigger battlefields with Chinese.

Background of MacArthur dismissal: Page 10

Political Rivals Dispute Merits of MacArthur Exit

By a Staff Correspondent of The Christian Science Monitor

Washington

A searching reexamination of the basis of American foreign policy seems a certain outcome of President Truman's dismissal of Gen. Douglas MacArthur. It is likely to last for months and to affect the 1952 election.

Both parties were hardening their lines today, with the Republicans set to squeeze the last drop of advantage out of the discharge of the popular five-star general and Democrats apparently ready to back Mr. Truman to the limit.

President Truman had secured Allied unity but at the cost of deep domestic controversy.

In New York, former President Hoover said, "This action can bring great tragedy to our country. It does not solve the primary question of how to end our war with Communist China without advantage to Soviet Russia. A strong pillar in our Asian defense has been removed."

Senator Robert A. Taft (R) of Ohio said, "The President has made a tragic error." It points, he said, to a "wavering, planless course in the Far East" and to either a stalemate or "ignominious concessions to the Chinese Communists."

To Address Congress?

Representative Joseph W. Martin of Massachusetts, House Republican leader, talked by telephone with General MacArthur, along with Senator Kenneth S. Wherry (R) of Nebraska, Senate Republican leader, and a group of conservative Republicans who met this morning in Mr. Martin's office. Afterward, Mr. Martin announced to the House that the general "would be delighted to have an invitation to speak" to a joint session of Congress and that he "can be here in about three weeks." He introduced a resolution inviting the general to appear.

There is a large question whether the Martin group can get the votes for such a full dress invitation. Many would prefer a committee hearing. But in any event, Democrats are bound to handle the general without kid gloves when either speech or hearing occurs.

Senator Leverett Saltonstall (R) of Massachusetts said he felt the controversy might have been resolved by face to face discussion between the two men. He continued, "I fail to see how any American citizen who thinks this problem through can help feeling that the President could have done anything but to take some affirmative action against General MacArthur when he felt that his policies were not receiving the general's loyal support."

Eisenhower View

In Coblenz, Germany, Gen. Dwight D. Eisenhower made this comment: "I hope he [General MacArthur] will not return to the United States and become a controversial figure. I would not like to see acrimony develop."

Senator Styles Bridges (R) of New Hampshire, one of those who met in the Martin office, said, "We are discussing everything from impeachment on down." He said the news was "shocking, almost as shocking as the news of Pearl Harbor. . . . It must be a great day for Russian Communists."

The Martin group called for an inquiry into "the whole conduct of foreign policy."

In New York, Republican Gov. Thomas E. Dewey said the dismissal was "the culmination of disastrous failure of leadership in Washington, combined with a Far Eastern policy which has lost China to the free world, brought all-out war in Korea, and threatens to divide us from our Allies."

Seen 'Logical Action'

Senator Theodore F. Green (D) of Rhode Island said: "Some action was needed, and this is a logical action."

Senator Green said the firing of General MacArthur is a "relief to those who have the welfare of the services at heart."

Representative Carl Vinson (D) of Georgia, chairman of the House Armed Services Committee, gave his full support to President Truman. "It is simply a test of civilian control over the military," Mr. Vinson said in a statement. "It is, if anything, overdue."

Senator James H. Duff (R) of Pennsylvania commented: "When the commander in the field publicly and repeatedly disagrees with the commander in chief and the joint chiefs of staff he thereby creates an impossible situation. That had to be resolved."

British approve MacArthur ouster: Page 18.

[Reactions run to extreme on MacArthur rift: Page 16.]

State of the Nation

The Underlying Issue

By JOSEPH C. HARSCH, Chief, Washington News Bureau, The Christian Science Monitor

Washington

Way deep down at the bottom, under all the many and complex layers of the controversy which finally has separated the Truman administration from the services of General of the Army Douglas MacArthur, was the issue of the importance of America's system of alliances.

In baldest terms, General MacArthur was proposing a course of action in the Far East which was incompatible with the grand alliance forged so slowly and painfully over the past six years.

The allies in Europe—principally the British and the French—do not believe, as General MacArthur apparently does, that the important theater of struggle between free world and Russian world lies in the Far East.

Perhaps in theory the general is right and Europe wrong on the proposition that what happens in Europe will be determined in Asia. It is conceivable that if all members of the grand alliance shared the MacArthur estimate of the situation they would commit themselves firmly to the issue in Asia, and the struggle would be faced and won on that line of strategy.

In practice, however, this course of action is not available. The European members of the alliance do not accept the MacArthur proposition. They do not believe that Asia is more valuable strategically than Europe. They do not give the Yangtze Valley the same importance as the Ruhr Valley. They do not believe that China is committed irrevocably to a course of partnership with Russian imperialism. They are not willing to associate themselves in a war in China.

Now, one can speculate on what actually would happen if the MacArthur policies were adopted and led to a general United States involvement in major war in Asia. In the end, our European allies probably would come along with us after a fashion.

But, and this is the important thing, there is no absolute certainty that they would. It is possible, even though unlikely, that the European allies would refuse entirely to have any part in a major war in Asia brought about by the MacArthur policies. And if that happened, the United States would find itself fighting China and Russia together at a terrible disadvantage.

The extent of that disadvantage can be appreciated only if one understands that the atomic bomb blow which the Strategic Air Command of the United States Air Force can strike at Russia is proportioned by the range of America's system of alliances.

At the present time it is a terrific blow. Our air strategists believe it is a blow from which Russia never would be able to recover physically. But it is based on the system of alliances, and it can be delivered in this intensity only from Allied bases.

The B-36 can reach most of Russia from United States home bases. But the percentage of the total SAC blow deliverable by B-36 is small. (The actual figure is a military secret, but B-36's do not come in quantity.) The majority of the SAC blow must be delivered by B-29, B-47, and B-50 bombers, all of which require secondary bases to reach targets in Russia.

Behind SAC's system of secondary bases is the American system of political alliances. Without the alliances there are no bases sufficient to permit the SAC blow to have the deterrent effect we believe it does have. Therefore the system of alliances is an essential to the maximum effectiveness of the American atomic weapon. If the United States attempts to fight a war without its European allies, it must fight that war with its atomic weapon striking power drastically reduced.

In other words, General MacArthur was proposing a course of action which could lead not only to the starting of World War III in Asia soon but also might bring the war about under circumstances to the grave disadvantage of the United States. We might have to fight it with the military effectiveness of our atomic weapon reduced by more than half.

When Mr. Truman had to choose between his Far East commander and the security of our alliances and of the launching base of our atomic weapon, Mr. Truman was forced to decide in favor of the security of the alliances.

British Generally Approve MacArthur's Removal

By William H. Stringer

Chief of the London News Bureau of The Christian Science Monitor

London

President Truman's dismissal of Gen. Douglas MacArthur, blazoned across all the afternoon London front pages, generally has met with approval here, although it is realized the President's action may precipitate a new and exhausting battle over foreign policy in the United States.

Mr. Truman's action came as a surprise to Whitehall. The British Government had expressed its concern over General MacArthur's recent excursions into the political field, but there had been no joint discussions on the corrective line which the President might propose to adopt.

Leftists Pleased

Obviously, those Labor members of Parliament who long have been critical of General MacArthur and whose concern recently led them to table questions in Parliament suggesting more effective "control" of the general, are admitting willingly their pleasure at the general's departure.

But it would be a mistake to regard the concern over General MacArthur's recent attempts to influence American policy toward China as merely a left-wing manifestation here. Despite the fact that Lord Beaverbook's Daily Express may applaud General MacArthur's Asiatic program, and despite the fact that almost every Briton regards General MacArthur as a great general in the military sphere, nevertheless among all groups there has been serious apprehension over his recent behavior.

This concern stems in part from the firm British view that in a democratic state it is the role of military generals to carry out policy, not make it, and that the formulation of policy should be in the hands of a civilian government. Even Field Marshal Viscount Montgomery, for instance, does not talk back to British Prime Minister Clement R. Attlee.

Concern stems equally from serious apprehension that General MacArthur's strongly advocated policies would have involved the United States and the United Nations in full-fledged war with Communist China, on the Chinese mainland: that this prolonged conflict would drain supplies and attention away from the West's main bastion in Europe; and that this Asiatic war might not long remain localized, but, through Russian intervention, might develop into World War III.

Britain Aware of Position

Britain is also sensitively aware, from its position in the Commonwealth, that General MacArthur's proposals for bombing the Chinese mainland and using Generalissimo Chiang Kai-shek's troops would alienate India and other free nations of Asia.

The time may come—and soon—when Communist China's behavior will have convinced these Asiatic countries that the Peiping regime is as dangerously imperialist as Soviet Russia. But that time has not yet arrived.

For the western nations to bomb Chinese cities and to employ the mercenary troops of what Asiatics regard as the thoroughly discredited regime of Chiang Kai-shek, would mean that the United States and Britain would lose a vast amount of Asiatic good will.

If these views seem, to some Americans, like infuriating refusal to face the facts, they should remember there is a keen desire among many nations to keep the Korean war localized, and not to choose this unprepared moment for a major showdown between the East and West on the battlefields of Asia.

Military observers also are keenly aware the Communists may soon launch another major offensive in Korea. But it is felt that if that offensive can be blunted, as have other recent blows, then will come a moment when another attempt to "settle" Korea can profitably be made. If this offer comes to nothing, then indeed the UN will have to think carefully what other plans it has for winding up the prolonged conflict.

THE CHRISTIAN SCIENCE MONITOR

Registered in U. S. Patent Office

AN INTERNATIONAL DAILY NEWSPAPER

VOLUME 43 NO. 282 | BOSTON, FRIDAY, OCTOBER 26, 1951 | • ATLANTIC EDITION | TWO SECTIONS | FIVE CENTS A COPY

COPYRIGHT 1951 BY THE CHRISTIAN SCIENCE PUBLISHING SOCIETY

Churchill Wins Clear Majority; U. S. Weighs Impact of Swing

Communists Retreat From 38th Stand In Korean Truce Talks

By Henry S. Hayward

Chief Far Eastern Correspondent of The Christian Science Monitor

Tokyo

For the first time Communist representatives at the Korean armistice conference have proposed dividing the line between the belligerents not based on the 38th parallel.

While the proposal made at a subcommittee session in Panmunjom on Oct. 26 has almost no chance of acceptance by the United Nations, it nevertheless represents a major retreat by the enemy from the former relentless insistence on the old political boundary between North and South Korea as the line of demarcation.

It grants the Allies roughly 1,000 square miles of North Korean territory while the Communists retain only a little South Korean territory.

Face-Saving Aspect

The official Allied release from the advanced base camp at Munsan complains that the Communist plan would require "withdrawal by the United Nations command forces from militarily important positions along practically all present ground of the battle line."

This release fails to mention the larger implications of the new Communist stand. Having relinquished their flat demand for the parallel, the Communists doubtless have set the "asking price" as high as possible—for face-saving purposes. But the fact remains that fruitful ground for a compromise exists between the line slightly north of the parallel the Communists propose and a line slightly south of the present battle front.

Proposed Line Traced

The Communist proposal was pinpointed by small towns largely unfamiliar and included on only detailed maps of Korea. Generally, however, it follows the parallel in the west across Ongjin Peninsula, clipping south of Kaesong and then continuing along the parallel to a point near Korangpori—at which point the line leaves the parallel and slants gradually northeastward into North Korea.

It passes well south of such places as Chorwon and Kumhwa, two towns forming the base of the Iron Triangle area the Allies captured with difficulty early last summer. These would be returned to the Communists.

The line likewise runs south of the Punch-Bowl area and Heartbreak Ridge—captured at heavy cost by United Nations soldiers—and passes not far north of Yanggu and the Hwachon Reservoir.

Criticism From UN

Viewed militarily, the enemy plan would, as the United Nations points out, force the Allies to move back as much as 15 miles along a front 100 miles long. It bears, as the United Nations also emphasizes, little relationship to the present battle front—which is the basis for the Allied proposal of Oct. 25.

"In exchange for bitterly won military positions in the east," the United Nations declares "the Communists offer to withdraw their troops from sections in the Ongjin Peninsula in the west which have never been of military importance but over which the Communists retained administrative control."

The Allied command, including Gen. Matthew B. Ridgway, himself, has frequently pointed out the uselessness of Ongjin Peninsula as a bargaining point since it is militarily indefensible as far as forces in South Korea are concerned. Such disadvantages inherent in the Communist plan are obvious, however. So, too, is the fact that such a line will not be the line finally agreed to.

Enemy Admission

What seems vastly more important to observers here is the fact that the Communists — in their own proposal — finally are willing to give the Allies a sizable chunk of North Korean territory while demanding a small portion of South Korean territory.

In effect the enemy is admitting publicly that the war has not resulted in even a stalemate at the old parallel line — and that a slice of North Korea has been lost at the bargaining table. This must hurt the Communists just as much as the suggestion that the Allies lose hard-earned ridgetops on the east front hurts them.

The initial United Nations reaction naturally is strongly opposed to the surrender of positions in the Iron Triangle, on Heartbreak Ridge, and in the Punch Bowl — all names now synonymous with heavy Allied losses of men and materiel.

Rejection Seen

All indications are that the United Nations intends to reject the Communist proposal as a result. Brig. Gen. William P. Nuckols' briefing officer stated that the withdrawal in the east is "completely unacceptable." He added that the line proposed by the enemy is not regarded as defendable militarily by the Allies.

But the rejection of the proposal does not mean that negotiations are not proceeding well. Actually they are moving at a more rapid pace than at any time since the early days of the Kaesong talks.

In two days both sides have stated their positions, both have made some concessions, both have indulged in give and take. And the way ahead now seems clear for the serious horse trading to narrow down the area of disagreement between the belligerents.

When studied on a large map of all Korea, the disputed area is now quite small. Although the differences are crucial with both parties fresh from a long recess, there seems justification for cautious optimism that difficult Item 2 of the agenda can be solved in the near future.

Italy to Build Jets In Mass Numbers

By the Associated Press

Rome

Italy expects to be mass producing British - designed Vampire jet fighter planes by the end of the year.

Defense Minister Randolfo Pacciardi disclosed this Oct. 24 and said another jet fighter, all-Italian in design and manufacture, will be ready for testing by the end of this month.

Mass production here is the result of more than a year's retooling of Italian aircraft plants.

Clubwomen Told to Fight For Schools

By Betty Driscoll Mayo

Staff Writer of The Christian Science Monitor

Education is the determining factor today in the battle between the free world and the slave.

This is the firm conviction of the General Federation of Women's Clubs which is holding its first regional workshop on education in New England in an effort to alert the citizens in the area to the importance of working together with educators for better education.

Mrs. Edwin Troland of Malden, Mass., chairman of the General Federation's Public Education Division who arranged the workshop, hopes that from the information disseminated at the meeting, clubwomen will be encouraged to do something about their public-school situations if they have problems in their local areas.

Safeguards Urged

Miss Chloe Gifford, chairman of the General Federation's Education Department, who was introduced by Mrs. Troland, stressed that education must shoulder the major responsibility today.

Emphasizing the necessity for interest in and support of education at all levels, elementary, secondary, and higher, Miss Gifford said, "We cannot isolate our children from the uncertainty of the world in which we live. We can and we must equip them to meet and cope with the problems that face them.

"Individual self-reliance and independence is essential. They must not be enslaved mentally, morally, or spiritually. We must safeguard the education, health, and welfare of our most precious possession, our children."

Vital Questions Asked

Pointing out the importance of being better informed about the situations in our public schools, Miss Gifford asked:

Is there a woman on your school board?

Is membership considered a post of high honor and great responsibility?

Is your superintendent selected on the basis of experience, training, and administrative ability?

Are your teachers well qualified?

Is the physical plant adequate?

What is your school doing to guide the students in their daily life through clubs, sports, and social activity?

What does a good school cost?

What steps are being taken in your state to secure and hold good elementary teachers?

What new school laws have been passed by your state legislature?

What further improvements are needed?

Others to Speak

What new problems in education of children are raised by comics, radio, television, and how can the schools and homes help to meet them?

How does your school promote moral and spiritual values?

Also scheduled to speak were Dr. Earl C. McGrath, United States Commissioner of Education, and the commissioners or deputy commissioners of education in the six New England States John J. Desmond, Jr., Massachusetts; Hilton C. Buley, New Hampshire; A. John Holden, Jr., Vermont; Michael F. Walsh, Rhode Island; Ermo Scott, Maine; and William H. Flaherty, Connecticut.

Republicans Encouraged

By Richard L. Strout

Staff Correspondent of The Christian Science Monitor

Washington

The world has shrunk so that elections no longer are domestic. The British election is the biggest piece of news in America, and it is acknowledged that the British swing to the right may vitally affect the United States.

On domestic politics, the swing away from the Labor government in Britain is bound to give encouragement to Republicans here. To an extent this is deceptive, because the British so-called "Conservatives" are well to the left of the Republicans in social legislation and in willingness to run nationalized industries. Nevertheless, the development in Britain marks a political trend that may jump the Atlantic.

It is in foreign affairs that the biggest interest centers, however. It presumably means the return to Downing Street of Winston Churchill, one of the three titans of World War II, to talk again with the other remaining titan, Soviet Prime Minister Joseph Stalin.

Truman-Attlee Paired

Here again there is an inevitable transference in the United States that finds reflection in comments in Washington. This is the common habit of Americans to link Mr. Attlee with Mr. Truman, rightly or wrongly, as more common-place figures after the great war characters. The return of Mr. Churchill to the stage strikes a dramatic chord in Washington because he is a glamorous figure.

American sympathy for Mr. Churchill is somewhat like British sympathy for President Roosevelt—it is disassociated with problems which the two figures had at home and involved primarily their role as international characters.

Return of a Conservative government may make it a little easier for American free-enterprise businessmen to work with Britain. For example, recently Hugh Gaitskell, President of the Board of Trade, was in Washington urging Britain's need for an additional 800,000 tons of steel. If the Steel Nationalization Act is halted under the Conservative Party in Britain, it may make the road somewhat smoother for sending American steel abroad. However, this aspect may be exaggerated, for there have been close working relations between the heads of the American and British economies in the past.

Bevanite Vote Watched

The State Department naturally is leaning over backward in expressing its neutrality in the British election, and that correct position also is followed by the entire administration.

On the other hand, the neutralist views of Aneurin Bevan, who resigned from the British Labor Government in protest over the speed of rearmament, have caused some concern.

Mr. Bevan now is out of office, and his wing of the Labor Party will have slight influence on the prospective new government. But even out of office, the Bevan forces have rather dramatically expressed the apprehensions of many Englishmen, and the size of the vote which Mr. Bevan and his lieutenants are getting is a matter of continuing interest, since it involves a variety of anti-Americanism, neutralism, and an emphasis on putting social gains ahead of rearmament.

Industrially, the chief equation here is whether the withdrawal of the Labor Party and trade unions from political control will mean more strikes and work stoppages in Britain. It has been argued that British workers were restrained from striking in some cases because it would be against "their own Labor Party." American observers count on the high social intelligence of the British nation, as represented by the extraordinarily high turnout in the election itself, to meet this problem.

Taft Urges Study

By the Associated Press

Pittsburgh

In the wake of a Conservative victory in the British election, Senator Robert A. Taft (R) of Ohio continued here to press the vigorous conservative domestic line which he hopes will bring a similar result in the United States.

Calling for a recheck of military expenditures, he said "we've just about reached the limit on taxes."

"We have to be as selective with our military projects as anything else," Senator Taft declared. "We can't run the entire world. There's an economic limitation on the United States."

Senator Taft called for establishment of a joint civilian-military commission to reappraise military expenditures. This commission, he suggested, would:

"Determine exactly how large an expenditure is necessary to assure the peace and security of the United States and at least eliminate the waste and extravagance which is likely to permeate a military establishment."

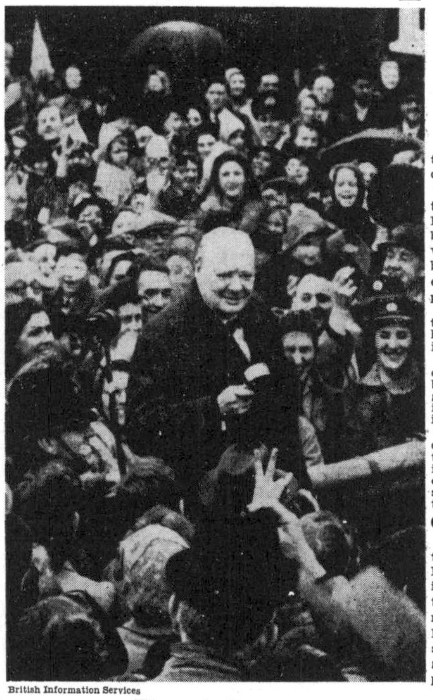

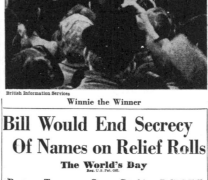

British Information Services

Winnie the Winner

Bill Would End Secrecy Of Names on Relief Rolls

The World's Day

Reg. U.S. Pat. Off.

Boston: Taxpayers Group Drafting Relief Bill

Secrecy of the names of recipients of government relief would be withdrawn and inspection of the public welfare rolls given to properly authorized investigators by a bill being drafted by the Massachusetts Federation of Taxpayers Associations. [Page 2.]

Target date for prorogation of the record-length 1951 Bay State legislative session has now shifted to next week end. [Page 2.]

Washington: Mossadegh Resumes Talks in Capital

Iranian Premier Mossadegh began the fourth day of his visit to the nation's capital apparently not committed as yet, despite official United States blandishments, to a new start at settling the Anglo-Iranian oil dispute.

A Senate Rules subcommittee has five investigators checking into charges on which Senator William Benton (D) of Connecticut bases his demand that Senator Joseph R. McCarthy (R) of Wisconsin be ousted from Congress, said Senator Thomas C. Hennings, Jr. (D), of Missouri, acting chairman of the subcommittee.

Mrs. Flo Bratten, long-time secretary to Vice-President Barkley, has turned over her 1949 and 1950 income tax returns to a Senate subcommittee conducting a new inquiry into government loans.

National: Scheduled A-Bomb Drop Postponed

A scheduled atomic bomb drop was called off at Las Vegas, although planes were in the air, presumably ready to loose their nuclear weapons. Storm conditions were said to be the explanation for the postponement.

The federal government placed a new perjury charge against economist William Remington in New York after failing in a previous attempt to jail him.

Gambler Frank Erickson is due for release from Rikers Island penitentiary in New York, but will face further court action in New Jersey and New York.

Federal mediators have abandoned efforts to end New York's crippling wildcat dock strike amid claims by insurgent union leaders that the walkout will spread to still more East Coast ports. [Page 3.]

Asia: 2 Soviet-Made MIGs Shot Down Over Korea

Allied air pilots shot down two Russian-made MIGs and damaged three others in the sixth straight day of aerial dogfights over Korea.

Gen. J. Lawton Collins, United States Army Chief of Staff, arrived in Formosa from Manila on his Asiatic tour.

Six members of a congressional subcommittee on expenditures arrived in Tokyo for a tour of the Far East Command supply installations.

Russia's mission in Tokyo invited Japanese officials to an official function for the first time since the end of the Pacific war.

In Europe: Soviet Names New Envoy to Prague

Russia appointed Deputy Foreign Minister Anatole I. Lavrentiev as Soviet Ambassador to Czechoslovakia, replacing Mikhail A. Silin.

UN: Korea to Be Major Item on Assembly Agenda

Korea will be a major item on the agenda at the Paris meeting of the UN General Assembly, Secretary of State Dean Acheson said as he sailed from New York.

Weather Predictions: Sunny (Details Page 2)

Atom Arms Still in Blueprint?

By the Associated Press

Chicago

It probably will be two to three years before we have tactical atomic weapons—bombs for use in battle.

This was the interpretation some natural scientists placed on the talk of Senator Brien McMahon (D) of Connecticut recently before about 2,000 physicists.

The dating of the new weapons was attributed to Senator McMahon's remarks: "Our men cannot fight in 1951 with new atomic weapons, which will not exist until 1953 or 1954."

The context for this statement was an explanation of Senator McMahon's proposal in September calling for $6,000,000,000 annually for the next several years to expand atomic weapon production.

The senator's proposal was, at the time, widely interpreted to mean that the atomic weapons program had gone ahead faster than anticipated and that revolutionary atomic weapons were at hand.

Piccadilly Panorama

By John Allan May

Staff Correspondent of The Christian Science Monitor

London

In Piccadilly Circus at 1:30 a.m. there was a silence in which you could hear a government drop.

The Circus was packed. Under the steel-blue glare of television lights, the great boisterous crowd bobbed and swayed, looking always upward at an election scoreboard where colored lights flashed each change in the state of the polls.

At 1:30 this notice flashed on the signboard: "Labor majority has been wiped out—Labor now in minority of one."

The crowd roared. Then suddenly the roaring wave of sound broke and was shattered in a gasping silence. This, one felt, was it. This was the moment of meaning.

It was also, I think, a moment of bewildered silence. For while that notice said that Labor was in the minority, the actual figures on the scoreboard at the time showed labor holding 73 seats then to the Conservatives' 60.

Cheers—and Boos

Then quickly the solution to the puzzle ran through the crowd. Labor already had lost 12 seats it previously had held. Even if the night and the following morning brought no further losses, the figures on the Tory side of the scoreboard were bound gradually to overtake the apparant Labor lead.

A new wave of cheering broke—wild, jubilant cheering from Tory supporters countered by loud groans and boos from Laborites.

Next to me, one Conservative young woman turned round on a vociferous socialist who was bellowing in her ear and struck him playfully on the head with a blue balloon. That was the most violent action I saw throughout the night.

The crowds were superbly good humored. There was shown here among the people not one ounce of that great weight of bitterness the politicians have dragged about the country for the past three weeks. In fact, Piccadilly at midnight was in favor of coalition.

Piccadilly Jammed

From 10 o'clock at night until 3 a.m. Piccadilly Circus was jammed. Busses and cars were diverted to other streets and the traffic lights of the circus flashed on and on—red, yellow, green, red, yellow, green, in mechanically disinterested fashion.

Lights on the scoreboard—set above a theatrical billboard which read "And This Was Odd"—twinkled red, yellow, and blue to more purpose. When the electric stars twinkled red, the crowd knew a Labor win was about to be added to the total; when blue, a Conservative victory; when yellow, a liberal score, and folks prepared to cheer or boo accordingly.

Like Football Crowd

In fact, they took it as they would take a football match, only it happens that the British take their football seriously.

It was a night of festivity and color. It was a night of balloons, of hot-chestnut men on street corners with red coals glowing through their braziers, of street orchestras and escapologists "busking" in the side streets, of motor horns and rattles, of students marching in gay processions singing irrelevant songs and carrying satiric banners, of squibs and Chinese cracker fireworks, of jokes and laughter.

On my way to Piccadilly, I was stopped several times by little cockney urchins with entreating eyes and cheeky faces. Each would be dragging a soap-box cart on which was seated an effigy of Guy Fawkes, the man of November five, and each would call "Penny for the Guy, mister. Give us a penny for the Guy."

'Cube Law' Explained

A penny seemed cheap for the service of being reminded that Britain's only violent political traitor was an amateur who got caught red handed and that now he is remembered only by a happy children's festival.

But in case you should think all this excessively light headed, let me hasten to add that in Piccadilly Circus between the bouts of cheering I heard serious discussion of "the cube law."

This is a statisticians' "law"—supposedly applicable to British elections—stating that the ratio of seats in Parliament won by the two parties is the cube of the ratio of votes cast for them.

I listened while a Tory London bobby gravely explained the cube law to a socialist London housewife as figures of voting were flashed on a screen. "Really," she said, "really. It's amazing, isn't it."

It is. That's exactly what it is. It is amazing.

Middle-Road Policy Due

By Peter Lyne

Parliamentary Correspondent of The Christian Science Monitor

London

The hand of Winston Churchill is grasping the doorknob of No. 10 Downing Street.

Britain is preparing for a new government as Labor's slim majority of the last Parliament shapes into a small majority for the Conservatives in the new Parliament.

But the final signal for Mr. Churchill to enter Downing Street at the head of a Conservative government will be no clear-cut, decisive bugle call, but rather a victory calculated in decimal points.

Net Gain of 20

With 21 of the 625 seats in the House of Commons still remaining to be counted, the latest result stands as follows:

Conservatives—310.

Labor—288.

Liberals and others—6.

This means a net gain of 20 for the Conservatives, and a net loss of 18 for Labor and of two for the Liberals.

The closeness of the voting is shown by the fact that both Conservatives and Labor received almost exactly the same percentage of votes, just under 49 per cent, with the Liberals obtaining just over 2 per cent and the Communists receiving but 0.5 per cent.

[The Associated Press reported Winston Churchill as saying: "Now, perhaps, there may be a lull in our party strife which will enable us to understand more what is good in our opponents and not be so very clever finding all their shortcomings."]

All through the counting of votes, both experts and nonexperts here have marveled at what has turned out to be a most remarkable election. There is no parallel in British politics for the doggedness with which voters have clung to their existing political convictions despite tremendous events both at home and abroad.

Almost Equally Divided

The British political mold is shown to have set into two almost equal halves with even greater fixedness than appeared in the near stalemate election of 1950. The vast majority of the 625 contests have this time reported "no change." The same party and the same candidate are returned to Westminster.

What are the deductions from the election results?

They are, first, that Mr. Churchill appears certain to become Prime Minister again, bringing a fresh team to grapple with Britain's grave problems, which have just about worn out the Attlee team.

But second, this election result is no major defeat for the Labor Party or for the welfare state. In the course of the past 6½ years, the British people have been in the throes of a tremendous social experiment and at the end of it there is a turnover in votes in most constituencies of perhaps 1 per cent. Indeed, it must be ranked, in this moment of victory for Mr. Churchill, as a notable achievement for Clement R. Attlee.

Third, as result of this remarkably small change in political opinion, there is no mandate for Mr. Churchill to make any drastic changes. In fact, he never promised to in his preelection campaign. His manifesto was just right of Center, while Mr. Attlee's was just left of Center.

Center Course Looms

Mr. Churchill's mandate will be to try to do better what Mr. Attlee already was doing, and in particular to restore confidence in Britain both at home and abroad.

Britain's future course, therefore, would seem to be about dead center. But it must be remembered that the center of today would seem markedly left of grandad's day or even mother's earlier political days.

A French observer watching the election results come through put his characteristic Gallic pith: "Your Conservatives are a part of the Right but are determined to keep Left."

UN to Send Query On Forced Labor

By the Associated Press

Geneva

The United Nations Committee on Forced Labor has decided to ask each country to provide full information on forced labor practices in its territory. Private organizations and individuals also were asked to help the committee's investigation.

The three-member committee unanimously approved a questionnaire to governments requesting detailed information on the laws under which persons "convicted of offenses against the established constitutional or political order may be forced to perform certain labor."

The Soviet bloc vigorously opposed the establishment of the committee by the UN General Assembly. The Soviet Union, where most of the forced labor camps under investigation are located, is regarded as certain to ignore the questionnaire.

State of the Nation

The Need of a Solid Bipartisan Policy

By ROSCOE DRUMMOND, Chief, Washington News Bureau of The Christian Science Monitor

Seattle

Any wide-scale contact with public opinion across the country, which it has been my useful experience to have during the past two weeks, shows it is imperative to keep defense and foreign policy resting on a solid bipartisan basis.

It is clear there is an evident willingness to support, regardless of party, the sacrifices and actions necessary to win the cold war.

However, what is equally clear—and what needs to be recognized in Washington—is that this support is not likely to stand up against any bitter, partisan effort on the part of the leaders of either party to claim overriding credit for the measures which now are beginning really to pay off.

The fact is that credit for the sacrifices and actions which are beginning to win the cold war belongs not to either party, not to the leaders of the administration, nor to the leaders of the sometimes united, sometimes disunited, factions in Congress. In an overriding sense, the credit belongs to the whole American people, who have accepted these sacrifices and actions—from the loan to Greece and Turkey to the defense of Korea, to the Japanese Peace Treaty—not as Democrats or Republicans, but as Americans intent upon safeguarding the nation.

Often I have been asked the sharp question: "Do you believe that credit for the measures which now are making headway toward winning the cold war belong to Secretary Acheson and President Truman?" My answer is: "The principal credit belongs to neither of them. It belongs to you."

Questions like this one come from every audience I meet—audiences often predominantly Republican. And I have found this answer lifts the issue above partisan division.

The reason is that it is true. It is the fact of the matter, not just a nice set of words. Fancy phrases would make no impression whatsoever. The facts to which I find opinion eager to respond are these:

The measures which are producing the beginning of victory in the cold war are: (1) The loan to Greece and Turkey, (2) the Marshall Plan, (3) the North Atlantic Alliance, (4) the defense of Korea, (5) the rearmament program, and (6) America's constructive relations with Japan.

The initiative and responsibility for these measures are divided as follows:

The Greek-Turkish loan was initiated by President Truman and was made possible by the Republican Congress elected in 1946.

The Marshall Plan was initiated by Secretary Marshall and Undersecretary Acheson and was valuably remodeled by the Republican Congress with its appointment of Paul G. Hoffman as administrator was made possible by the wise influence of Republican Senator Arthur H. Vandenberg.

The North Atlantic Alliance was initiated singlehandedly by Republican Senator Vandenberg and approved overwhelmingly by both parties in Congress.

The defense of Korea and the mobilization program belong to no party; they belong to the nation.

America's constructive relations with Japan were significantly shaped by General MacArthur, and the successful negotiation of the Japanese Peace treaty was the nearly exclusive work of Republican John Foster Dulles, with the helpful backing of President Truman.

This is the record.

The evidence is that the nation will continue to support whatever measures are still requisite if these measures are kept on a bipartisan basis.

But if the politicians start to tamper with the facts and paw the truth in the coming presidential year, they are going to stir up a bitter, divisive controversy which will risk the gains we have made and imperil the nation.

THE CHRISTIAN SCIENCE MONITOR

Registered in U. S. Patent Office

AN INTERNATIONAL DAILY NEWSPAPER

VOLUME 44 NO. 61 | COPYRIGHT 1952 BY THE CHRISTIAN SCIENCE PUBLISHING SOCIETY | BOSTON, WEDNESDAY, FEBRUARY 6, 1952 | • ATLANTIC EDITION | TWO SECTIONS | FIVE CENTS A COPY

Communists Seek Asia Peace Parley Tied to Korea Truce

By Henry S. Hayward

Chief Far Eastern Correspondent of The Christian Science Monitor

Tokyo

The Chinese Communists have now made clear they are seeking not only a truce in the Korean fighting, but an over-all peace settlement for all Asia.

And they also have made clear that their basic terms include recognition by the United Nations Allies in Korea of both Communist China and the People's Republic of North Korea.

This is the interpretation placed here upon a surprise Communist move in the Korean Truce talks, Feb. 6, in which the enemy proposed that 90 days after an armistice is achieved, a political peace conference be called.

Communist Proposals

The Communists recommended:

1. A political conference at a higher level to commence work on peaceful settlement of the Korean question.

The Chinese proposed specifically that such a conference be composed of five delegates from the United Nations represented in Korea, on the one hand, and Communist China and North Korea on the other.

2. Withdrawal of all foreign forces in Korea to be the first item for consideration by the proposed political conference.

3. Coupling the Korean settlement with a general Asiatic settlement.

Bares Hand on Key Aims

After listening to the statement, the UN requested a recess to study the proposals. Several things are clear immediately, however:

1. The Communists intend to shift the difficult problem of early troop withdrawal from Korea to a later political conference—and give it priority for consideration. Thus, the only connection of the troop issue with the present armistice conference would be to decide if and when it would be discussed later.

2. The Communists now are formally admitting the government of the People's Republic of China is concerned in the Korean affair and should be represented and recognized at the peace conference. Hitherto their contentions have been that Chinese troops were in Korea only as volunteers.

3. The UN would be faced with recognition of both the Peking Chinese and Pyongyang North Korean regimes in the sense it would be dealing with them in the political realm whereas the present negotiations have been only on a military level.

Some Issues Not Clear

Not clear were these points:

1. What the Communists mean by the proposal of a peace conference to deal with "other questions related to peace in Korea."

This could include such broad issues as the Chinese Communist claim to Nationalist-held Formosa, neutralization of waters between Formosa and the Chinese mainland by United States naval forces, termination of the Allied-imposed economic blockade of China, Communist threat to Burma and Indo-China, and formal recognition of Communist China and North Korea.

2. The Communist plan also leaves unclear the status of South Korea.

The Communists repeatedly have refused to recognize the South Korean Government as a legitimate regime.

Garbage Pickups Resumed

Garbage and refuse collections in Boston resumed today after a 129 to 112 vote by the collectors who were out on strike for two days.

They settled for a 10-cent-an-hour pay boost, giving them $1.60 an hour for a 44-hour week and for two more paid holidays, bringing the total to 10.

Contractors will absorb the entire cost of the wage increase, which will amount to a total of approximately $100,000 for a full year.

The new salary rates will be retroactive to Jan. 1, 1952. Immediately following today's vote collections started in all sections of the city.

Curtis Bids For Top Spot In Bay State

By Edgar M. Mills

New England Political Correspondent of The Christian Science Monitor

Laurence Curtis, 1950 GOP nominee for lieutenant governor, is the first announced Republican candidate for Governor.

His announcement to a group of friends and campaign workers at the Parker House came only a few hours after disclosure that Republican leaders, headed by Sinclair Weeks, Republican National Committeeman, were pressuring Representative Christian A. Herter (R) of Massachusetts to make the gubernatorial run.

Sources close to Mr. Herter have confirmed the move to influence him to stand for the GOP nomination for Governor but state no decision has yet been made.

Meanwhile, Mr. Curtis, former state treasurer, former state senator, and former city councilor, has made his anticipated move.

Strong in Primaries

While Mr. Curtis is regarded as particularly strong in Republican primaries, many GOP leaders are of the belief he cannot win the election. Thus, the present move to get Mr. Herter to make the run.

But Mr. Curtis was quick to counter this contention by pointing out that although he lost the lieutenant governor contest in the November, 1950, election he polled the highest vote of any GOP statewide office candidate in that election. His 870,542 votes were 46,473 more than Arthur W. Coolidge polled for governor.

For several months Mr. Curtis has been working diligently building up his statewide organization.

Whether or not he would step down for Mr. Herter, should the latter decide to run, is considered unlikely by some of his supporters.

Top-Level Support

Meanwhile, it is reported that Senator Sumner G. Whittier (R) of Everett is cooling off his ardor for the GOP gubernatorial nomination. It is understood he may not now run and will not run if the Weeks' forces are successful in getting a "yes" answer from Mr. Herter.

Senator Whittier would be eager to tackle Mr. Curtis in a two-man contest, but undoubtedly would back away from a battle in which the political cards are stacked against him.

And they would be stacked against him if Mr. Herter enters the field, inasmuch as the latter has been promised top-level support. That includes Senator Leverett Saltonstall and other top GOP leaders.

Two Sovereigns of Britain

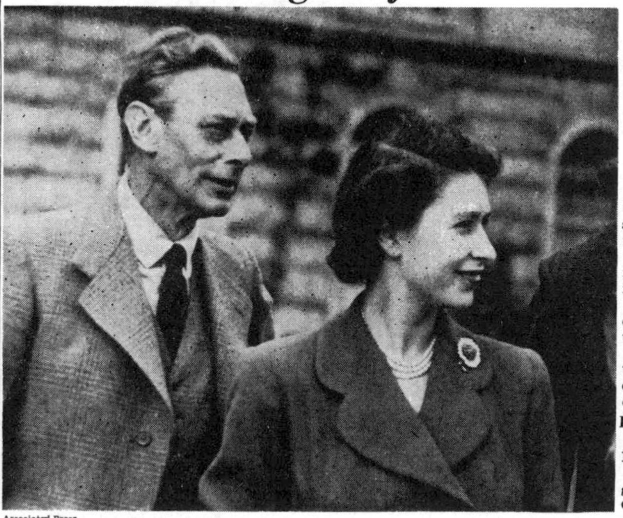

Associated Press

King George VI — Queen Elizabeth II

Foreign Policy Battle in Commons Temporarily Eased as Nation Unites

By Peter Lyne

Parliamentary Correspondent of The Christian Science Monitor

London

A new Queen has come to the throne—and the biggest foreign-policy battle for 12 years has been postponed.

Former Prime Minister Clement Attlee took a dramatic and unusual course in the current foreign-affairs debate in the House of Commons by moving a censure motion not against the Conservative government but against Prime Minister Winston Churchill personally for his speech to Congress.

Mr. Attlee echoed sections of the American press which have suggested that Mr. Churchill spoke with two voices on policy in China—one voice to please the Americans by suggesting that Britain is ready for all-out war with Communist China and another to placate the British who are against commitments in China.

Mr. Attlee called that "good salesmanship but bad statesmanship."

Tension Eased

But political tension in Parliament as a result of this censure motion has been lessened — at least for the moment — by the sudden passing of King George VI.

The Commons, which was about to meet to renew the biggest foreign-policy battle this country has known since the beginning of World War II, abandoned its second day of debate and met instead to mourn the loss of a sovereign who was loved and respected on the Laborite as well as on the Conservative benches.

But current foreign-policy issues are far too fundamental to be shelved for more than a short respite. The political battle therefore, will be resumed. At the same time, an event such as the King's passing and the succession to the throne of the much-loved new Queen inevitably will have a twofold restraining effect. There will be a tendency to greater national unity and the foreign-affairs clash will be temporarily overshadowed.

Compromise Move

Mr. Attlee's course in the clash with Mr. Churchill was a novel one. It was also a compromise with his own left-wing Bevan followers.

Mr. Attlee and a majority of his followers were not keen on the idea of breaking with bipartisanship in foreign policy. They remembered the times when Mr. Churchill and the Conservatives had supported them when they were in power.

But they were genuinely concerned at Mr. Churchill's Far Eastern foreign policy as they considered it was reflected in his speech to Congress. The Bevanites and other Labor back benchers were threatening to split the Labor Party unless it censured Mr. Churchill.

Then Mr. Churchill put up Foreign Secretary Anthony Eden instead of himself to open the debate. This was a further complication because the Labor Party as a whole likes Mr. Eden and likes to support him. So Mr. Attlee and the Labor shadow cabinet—which has no Bevanite representative on it — made a compromise decision.

They introduced this motion: "That this house takes note of the Foreign Secretary's statement, welcomes his adherence to the policy followed by His Majesty's previous administration [the Attlee government] with regard to the Korean conflict and the relations between Great Britain and China, but regrets the Prime Minister's failure to give adequate expression to this policy in the course of his recent visit to the United States.

This looked not merely like a compromise solution of the Labor Party's differences, but also a Laborite attempt to split Mr. Churchill from his government and party. Indications in Commons were that Mr. Attlee had no chance whatsoever of achieving any such split.

Mr. Attlee's main emphasis in his attack on Mr. Churchill was on Mr. Churchill's so-called "two voices" — one for the United States and one for Britain. He accused Mr. Churchill of trying to "please his audience in the United States." "I cannot but think," Mr. Attlee declared. "that he tended to represent us (Britain) as an ally, even a comparative minor ally, in an American war.

Significance Seen

It is significant that he only mentioned the United Nations once in the whole of that speech to Congress and that was only very much in passing."

Mr. Attlee was here confirming the view held in certain high Conservative circles that the issue in the Churchill-China commitments controversy is not that he made any new commitments but that he came down heavily on the side of the Anglo-American alliance rather than on the United Nations as the best means of keeping the peace.

But Mr. Eden's speech showed that British foreign policy is still based on the United Nations, the western defense organization, and the North Atlantic Treaty Organization.

Is this compatible with Mr. Churchill's primary reliance on the Anglo-American alliance? Mr. Churchill, Mr. Eden, and the Conservatives think yes. Mr. Attlee and his party think no.

Moran Convicted in N.Y. On Shakedown Charges

The World's Day

Reg. U.S. Pat. Off.

National: Friend of O'Dwyer Faces Sentence

James J. Moran, friend and political protege of former Mayor William O'Dwyer, was convicted as the mastermind of a $500,000-a-year shakedown racket run by New York City firemen. [Page 15.]

Africa: Queen Elizabeth to Fly Back to England

Queen Elizabeth, no longer a princess but a sovereign, will fly home from Africa to take her place at the head of the British Commonwealth and empire.

New England: Bid to Save R.I. Textile Industry

Proposals to save the textile industry for Rhode Island were made by Kenneth B. Cook, president of the Rhode Island Textile Association. [Page 4.]

Just how well was the city of Boston treated by the 1951 Massachusetts Legislature? The Boston Municipal Research Bureau has outlined most of the important bills enacted, especially those affecting the pocketbooks of Boston taxpayers. [Page 2.]

Europe: Red Cross Rebuffed Again in Korea

The International Red Cross said another effort to aid allied prisoners of war in Korea has been rebuffed by Communist authorities.

Washington: Hearings Opened on Vet Housing

New houses bought by veterans under government-guaranteed loans began to crack and come apart within a year, Representative Lyle (D) of Texas told a House banking subcommittee which opened hearings on widespread charges of faulty construction by builders and lax inspection by government agents.

The Senate Banking Committee decided to ask democratic leaders for a floor test as soon as possible to see whether the lawmakers want to keep or abolish the Reconstruction Finance Corporation.

American, British, and French experts will meet soon to discuss new ways to bolster Yugoslavia's economy against the danger of Soviet aggression.

Burnet R. Maybank, chairman of the Senate Banking Committee, started a bill through Congress to continue for one year the government's power to control wages, prices, rents, credit, and raw materials.

The House Armed Services Committee agreed on the main points of a bill under which all qualified 18-year-old youths would be called up for six months of universal military training.

Mideast: Czech Consul Fails to Return to Prague

The Czechoslovak Consul General in Jerusalem, Frantisek Necas, has not returned to Prague, although called home Feb. 1. The Israeli Foreign Ministry reports no request for asylum.

Far East: UN Tank Force Blasts Supply Lines

A United Nations tank-infantry force rammed six miles into Communist territory on the Western Korean front and blasted enemy supply lines and installations with direct fire for three hours.

Weather Predictions: Clear, Colder (Details Page 2)

Deposits of Uranium Reported in Sweden

By the Associated Press

Stockholm

Rich uranium deposits have been discovered in Sweden's rocky soil, a high atomic energy official disclosed here.

Harry Brynielsson, director of the part government-controlled atomic energy company, told interviewers that at Kvarntorp, near Stockholm, heavy shale deposits were found to contain about 175 grams to the ton. In some samples, he said, the uranium content ran as high as 3,000 grams a ton. (There are 29 grams to one ounce.)

Other big finds have been made in Oestergotland, southwest of the capital, Mr. Brynielsson added.

Russian Acclaims Atomic Research

By Reuters

London

The president of the Soviet Academy of Sciences, Alexander Nesmeyanov, claimed in Moscow that Russia has made great strides in atomic research in the past year.

A Tass agency message picked up in London said he reported artificially produced radioactive atoms were being used successfully in plant nutrition, physiology, and industry.

George VI Passes; Elizabeth to Fly Back to London

By a Staff Correspondent of The Christian Science Monitor

London

A new Queen Elizabeth of England today prepares to fly back to her homeland with all possible speed as this island kingdom and the worldwide British Commonwealth of Nations mourn the passing of King George VI, "the commoners' King."

Until the return of Queen Elizabeth II to London the commonwealth is without a constitutional head, an event unique in recent British history.

The young monarch has been vacationing in the African colony of Kenya prior to undertaking a state tour of Australasia. She is expected back in London Feb. 7.

Meanwhile, a meeting of the Privy Council has been called to proclaim Elizabeth Queen. This Council is a group of advisers drawn from the ranks of the nation's leading political figures of all major parties.

Proclamation Awaits Return

The actual proclamation is expected to be made after Queen Elizabeth's return in an ancient ceremony at St. James's Palace.

The young Queen reigns as the first ruling Queen since the great Queen Victoria, and the fifth in English history since Queen Mary in the 16th century.

It is inevitable, however, that her accession should bring to the thoughts of the British people the historic memories of a former Queen Elizabeth, in whose reign the English nation flourished and the English character grew great—the Elizabethan Age when William Shakespeare wrote, when Sir Francis Drake with the aid of a "great wind from heaven" drove off the invading Spanish Armada, and when Francis Bacon laid the foundations of modern natural scientific method.

Now, grouping its loyalties under the new Queen Elizabeth, is the British nation challenged to meet dangers as great as the dangers of that age and to produce men and women as great as the giants that swaggered through that era.

Empire Uncertain of Future

Britain, the mother country, gasps with the exertion of climbing the final slopes of its economic Everest. The empire and the commonwealth, home of one-quarter of the population of the world, feel uncertain of their future. It is a time for giants.

Elizabeth and her husband, Prince Philip, had set out on a 30,000-mile voyage to the farthermost ends of the commonwealth to represent the well-loved King George VI on this significant good-will mission.

They were to rest first in Africa. On Feb. 6 they had just come back from an exciting night in a treetop "hotel" in the Kenya jungle when the solemn news came through from England.

The new Queen wept. Then quickly, it is reported, standing straight to her queenliness, she regained her poise. Immediately she ordered a plane to be made ready at Nairobi so that she might return to her capital and to her duty.

Here at home in view of the noted improvement in the King's health the announcement from Sandringham carried an extra voltage of surprise. Immediately the course of the day's affairs, not only at Buckingham Palace and the government offices, but in the courts, business houses, shops, private homes, and even on the streets came to an astonished stop.

British United Like Big Family

And in that moment the underlying national unity of the British people—which, where their sovereign is concerned, becomes more like family unity—began to assert itself.

At Westminster the parliamentary debate on foreign affairs, which a few hours before was the focal point of national interest and involved delicate questions of Anglo-American relations and the visit of Prime Minister Winston Churchill to Washington was dropped for the time being.

The parliamentary Labor Party was holding a council of war on the debate when word of the King's passing came. Labor leader Clement Attlee was called from the room and returned to announce the news. The meeting ended immediately and members left the Parliament Building.

In Downing Street sober and silent crowds gathered to watch members of the Cabinet arrive for a meeting at "Number Ten."

A thousand or more persons watched outside Buckingham Palace while an attendant lowered the window shades.

In "the City," London financial district, markets closed. The British Broadcasting Corporation canceled all programs except scheduled news bulletins, signals to ships, and weather reports. Television officials said there probably would be no television programs for the next few days.

Tributes From All Over World

From all over the world came tributes and condolences for the Royal Family, the British people, and peoples of the commonwealth. Commonwealth members sent tributes to the sovereign who, as Sir Thomas White, Australian High Commissioner in London, said, "showed all those qualities of a King and of a man which will leave imperishable memories in the minds of the people of the empire and commonwealth."

From all over the British Isles messages and reports reached London expressing the affection which warmed and deepened British esteem for him.

The simplest tribute was the commonest and the one most deeply felt: "He was a good man."

Meanwhile protocol and procedure, the pomp and practical circumstances which usually accompany momentous events in the British scene, already had begun their march.

Plans to adjourn Parliament were announced immediately after the Cabinet meeting in Downing Street. A Privy Council meeting was scheduled to announce the new Queen's accession to the throne.

Later an assembly of members of Parliament to take an oath of allegiance to the new Queen was scheduled at Westminster.

After Queen Elizabeth returns to London on Feb. 7 the Prime Minister and his ministers will go to the palace, surrender their seals of office, receive them back again, and, having kissed her hand, resume their functions at the helm of the British nation.

Elizabeth Trained for Task

Elizabeth is the first Queen of England to reach the throne in direct accession to her father. Britain's other Queens followed relatives to the throne, not parents. And Elizabeth, unlike these former Queens, has been trained specially for the work she has to do.

The Queen's work is never done. She is "the Crown"—the historic symbol that links nearly 100 lands, colonies, protectorates, trusteeships, dominions. She has but little political power, but she can wield tremendous influence. The crown is what the sovereign makes it.

Beside the new Queen there stands the figure of Prince Philip, Duke of Edinburgh. The duke is expected to take the title Prince Consort, the rank granted to Prince Albert of Saxe-Coburg-Gotha when he married Queen Victoria almost exactly 112 years ago.

The British people have more than loyalty for the handsome couple who are the Queen and her Consort. For King George VI, called unexpectedly to the throne, raised kingship to a new majesty. Because he was human, simple, and good, he was popular.

Now must the British people show that they are kingly.

Other stories and pictures: Page 6

State of the Nation

Newbold Morris: The Case for Waiting and Seeing

By ROSCOE DRUMMOND, Chief, Washington News Bureau of The Christian Science Monitor

Washington

Most citizens—if not most politicians—will consider Newbold Morris innocent until proved guilty.

Most citizens—if not most politicians — will rightly assume that Mr. Morris, an independent Republican brought up in the La Guardia school of clean government, is intent upon doing a constructive, fearless, heads-up job of bringing federal wrongdoing into the open until it is proved that he isn't.

Mr. Morris is beginning his assignment under the most difficult circumstances. He deserves the opportunity to show that he has the courage and the stamina and the skill to carry through before he is condemned with political epithets —or buried with political epitaphs.

This is a campaign year. While most politicians cannot restrain themselves from reaching for invective instead of fact, most citizens can refrain from being overimpressed by invective until the facts have been established; that is, until Mr. Morris has had a chance to prove by performance whether he has the qualifications and the will to do his part of the much-needed cleanup job.

It needs to be borne in mind that there are some Republican politicians who want to discredit Mr. Morris before he has even begun, who do not want the probing and the purging of the federal government to be really successful for fear it will rob them of a winning campaign issue.

It needs to be borne in mind that there are some Democratic politicians who want to thwart Mr. Morris before he gets very far, who do not want the investigation to be honest and uninhibited for fear it will enmesh the administration in so much scandal it will give the opposition a winning campaign issue.

This is why Harold Ickes, whose personal integrity was unsmirched and whose knowledge of the operations of government was vast and never cynical, warned the public, in the last column he wrote before he passed on, to be on the alert against the political tendencies of both political parties when it comes to the corruption issue.

Most persons, whether they voted Democratic or Republican in the past, want Mr. Morris to expose and prosecute every instance of corruption and bad ethics and impropriety in government even if it buries the administration in an avalanche of disgust.

Most persons, regardless of party affiliation, would like to see the promised cleanup so scorching and so complete and evil officials so routed from the federal service that the issue of corruption could be reduced to its proper proportions in the 1952 election.

This is the assignment which Mr. Morris will need to take, if it hasn't been given to him.

He is going to have a hard enough time fulfilling it without the politicians breaking out of their glass houses to attack him before he has started. At the very least, he merits a reservation of judgment until he has had time to show by action whether he is going to match promise with performance. He deserves nothing less.

President Truman said he was going to create a nonpartisan commission of experienced and distinguished private citizens to investigate and prosecute federal wrongdoers and confirmed the appointment of Judge Thomas F. Murphy to head it. The project fell through.

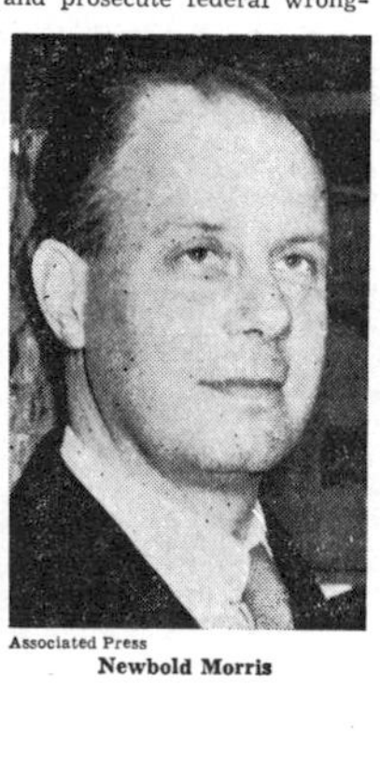

Associated Press

Newbold Morris

The President, firing Attorney General Howard McGrath's assistant in charge of tax prosecutions without consulting Mr. McGrath, later canvassed the field for another Attorney General.

He failed to find what he wanted or, for one reason or from Mr. McGrath himself, decided he didn't want to appoint whom he found—and the project for getting a new Attorney General fell through.

Mr. Truman then determined that, as chief enforcement officer of the government, Mr. McGrath was the man to take "continued drastic action" against federal corruption — wherever necessary, as he said.

Now Mr. Morris is Mr. McGrath's special cleanup assistant and has been in office a matter of hours.

In the wake of these developments and as a subordinate to Mr. McGrath, Mr. Morris may find some locked doors or some locked records or some would-be intimidations and no-trespassing signs along his path.

But Mr. Morris' record in dealing with matters of this kind does not suggest that he is intimidated easily or that no-trespassing hints necessarily will deter him.

As The Christian Science Monitor's New York bureau has reported, Mr. Morris was publishing information about New York gangsters long before the Senate Crime Investigating Committee appeared on the scene. And in his 1949 campaign for Mayor, he named Frank Costello as the real boss of the city and said that because of his power "every mobster, every extortioner, every bookmaker feels safe as long as O'Dwyer is in City Hall."

Mr. O'Dwyer was given the balm of an ambassadorial appointment to Mexico by President Truman, but he was given no balm by Mr. Morris.

Those who know him best believe Mr. Morris will insist upon the necessary freedom of action to do his job fully and fearlessly—or he will throw it back in the President's lap.

THE CHRISTIAN SCIENCE MONITOR

Registered in U. S. Patent Office

AN INTERNATIONAL DAILY NEWSPAPER

VOLUME 44 NO. 170 | BOSTON, SATURDAY, JUNE 14, 1952 | • • —ATLANTIC EDITION | TWO SECTIONS | FIVE CENTS A COPY

COPYRIGHT 1952 BY THE CHRISTIAN SCIENCE PUBLISHING SOCIETY

Taft and Eisenhower Battle for Delegates In Key State Blocs

By Richard L. Strout
Staff Correspondent of The Christian Science Monitor

Washington

With three weeks before the Republican convention Gen. Dwight D. Eisenhower is concentrating on an effort to mobilize popular pressure upon delegates, while Senator Robert A. Taft of Ohio is concentrating on taking control of the convention machinery.

These distinctive approaches reflect the different advantages possessed by the two neck-and-neck rivals: In the case of General Eisenhower, public-opinion polls indicate that he has greater popular support than the senator; on the other hand, the rank and file of professional Republican politicians are believed to favor Senator Taft.

In the harsh controversy that has developed, some observers see the possibility that the Republicans will water down the election issue upon which they had counted most heavily, the so-called "morals issue."

'Ruthless' Tactics Charged

High-handed methods of excluding Eisenhower delegates from certain southern states are bringing cries of "fraud" and "corruption" from that faction of the party, while Senator Taft replies that the Eisenhower forces, when in control, have been just as "ruthless." It will be harder to make telling attacks on the Truman administration for corruption if the GOP Chicago convention itself features charges of corruption among its own leading candidates.

There are some signs now that the Republican state leaders are looking about for some way out of the fratricidal Taft-Eisenhower battle. The situation has not apparently jelled yet, but the expectation of many would be that well before the convention a tacit understanding may have been achieved as to who will get the nomination. The situation seems politically ripe.

A likely prospect is that Messrs. Taft and Eisenhower may enter the convention with only 50 or 75 votes separating them and with neither having enough for a first-ballot nomination. Taft leaders believe they are within striking distance of a first ballot nomination but this is yet to be proved.

Three Key States

The situation is so close that certain relatively obscure leaders who have handy little bags of unpledged delegates in their pockets might well be able to get together and write their own ticket. These are the kingmakers who so often in the past have picked American candidates and American Presidents.

The decisive factor might well turn out to be batches of delegates from contested southern states which rarely if ever have voted Republican.

Or it might be the leaders of big industrial states, who, irrespective of the direction of preference primaries, will decide how their puppet-delegates will vote.

Attention now centers on leaders of three states, Pennsylvania, Michigan, and Maryland. Like a chemical reaction in which different components dance about together briefly in a test-tube before crystallizing into a firm pattern the Republican leaders of these states are now in communication, and a "deal" may be shaping that will have decided who will be the candidate well before the convention meets. In normal circumstances, the deal will not be disclosed till the convention starts balloting.

The three men involved are Gov. John S. Fine of Pennsylvania, Arthur Summerfield, Michigan GOP national chairman, and Gov. Theodore McKeldin of Maryland. Between them, they control about 85 delegates. If politics is to be regarded simply as business without consideration to personal aspirations or policies, it obviously would be reasonable procedure for them at this point to pool resources, unite their strength, accept competitive bids from either camp, drive the hardest bargain in patronage and prestige, and name the next candidate — and possibly the next American President.

Whether or not this process is going on, it is significant that General Eisenhower has taken his campaign first into Pennsylvania and now into Michigan, while Senator Taft in turn will soon meet with the Pennsylvania delegation and his lieutenants are also active in Michigan.

Personal Row Rises

Meanwhile, the decisions in the Taft-dominated Republican convention machinery are going consistently against General Eisenhower. There are 70 to 80 delegates in contested southern states who represent still another uncertain bloc that might, conceivably, decide the outcome.

A violent personal row has broken out between Eisenhower lieutenant Senator Henry Cabot Lodge, Jr., of Massachusetts, and Walter S. Hallanan, West Virginia national committeeman, the Taft supporter who has been named as temporary chairman of the convention in which post he can make vital decisions over the contested southern delegates.

Mr. Hallanan is the obscure type of man who emerges briefly every four years to help pick a President.

Senator Lodge calls upon him to resign, another Eisenhower supporter, Senator James Duff of Pennsylvania, calls his selection as preposterous as picking one of the players to be umpire. Mr. Hallanan retorts in kind, that he is quite neutral and that Senator Lodge is a "completely spoiled political child."

Technical Decisions

One of the technical decisions going against Candidate Eisenhower is that the convention will decide contests only of delegates elected at large (namely by the whole state) while contests over the bulk of delegates from individual districts will be referred back to the states.

Most state organizations in the South are well in control of the Taft machinery, so this is a big advantage for the latter. Eisenhower forces want the contests decided by impartial committees at the convention or, if necessary, on the convention floor under the blaze of television.

From the present view here, General Eisenhower is going to be disappointed on both grounds.

Clouds Seeded With Conflict As Rain Makers Duel Stoppers

By the Associated Press

Yakima, Wash.

Cloud formations moving toward central Washington's Yakima and Wenatchee Valleys are being bombarded daily by opposing experiments financed by wheat growers who want rain and fruit farmers who don't.

One set of attacks is designed to punch holes in the clouds to bring rain. The other seeks to disperse the clouds without rain.

Both sides are secretive about the operations, but Yakima and Wenatchee newspapers reported the "wet" and "dry" campaigns were under way, with the dry forces claiming a preliminary victory.

It's a critical time for both, with rain needed in the wheat fields at the time the cherry harvest is starting. Rain causes ripening cherries to split and damages other "soft fruits" at harvest time.

Farmers in central Washington's big wheat-producing district has hired the Water Resources Corporation of Denver as a rain maker the past two years.

The firm uses ground generators principally to bombard clouds with silver iodide, but cherry growers here said they heard that rain makers also were operating from planes this week.

Soft-fruit growers, blaming rain makers for damage to their crops last year, hired an anti-rain maker this year for the first time. Growers voted to assess themselves $1 a ton of cherries, and Jack M. Hubbard, Olympia, Wash., meteorologist, was hired to ward off the rain.

Mr. Hubbard has been elusive and mysterious about his operations, methods, and equipment, but the Yakima Republic reported he was "dashing from point to point in the valley to aid his ground forces as black clouds threaten."

Dr. Phil E. Church, University of Washington meteorologist, said the anti-rain makers probably would use the same method as the rain makers—only more. He said the likely method would be to overseed.

Overseeding, he said, would result in wider distribution of the limited moisture particles on the silver iodide, preventing it from forming large and heavy enough drops to fall.

The rain stoppers claimed success as the cherry harvest got under way with only occasional showers this week that caused little or no damage in the Wenatchee and Yakima fruit-producing areas.

Jungle to Singapore Is Story of No Tails

By Reuters

London

A party of British show people, after a 6,000-mile tour entertaining troops in the Malayan jungle, were refused dinner in the mess at Army headquarters in Singapore because they were not in evening dress.

George Jeger, Labor member of Parliament, has declared he will take the matter up in Parliament, asking War Minister Anthony Head for a statement.

He says he wants the minister to insure proper treatment of performers who go out to Malaya to entertain British troops fighting Communists in the jungle.

Gen. Sir Gerald Templer, British High Commissioner for Malaya, last April said there were "too many parties and too much golf" in the federation. "The Communists work," he said. "They seldom go to races, give dinner parties, cocktail parties, or play golf."

15 Stars for 'Old Ironsides'

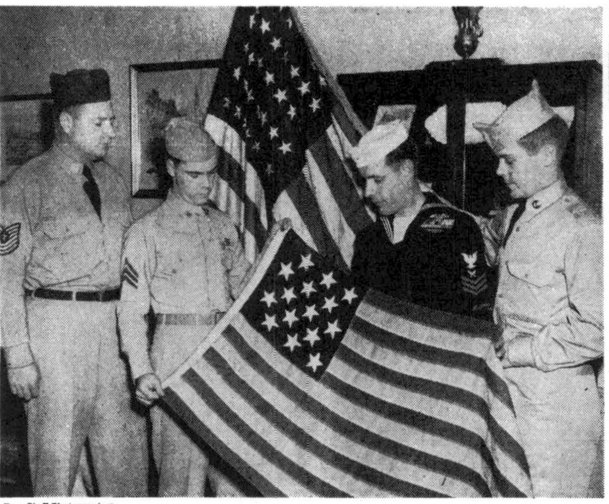

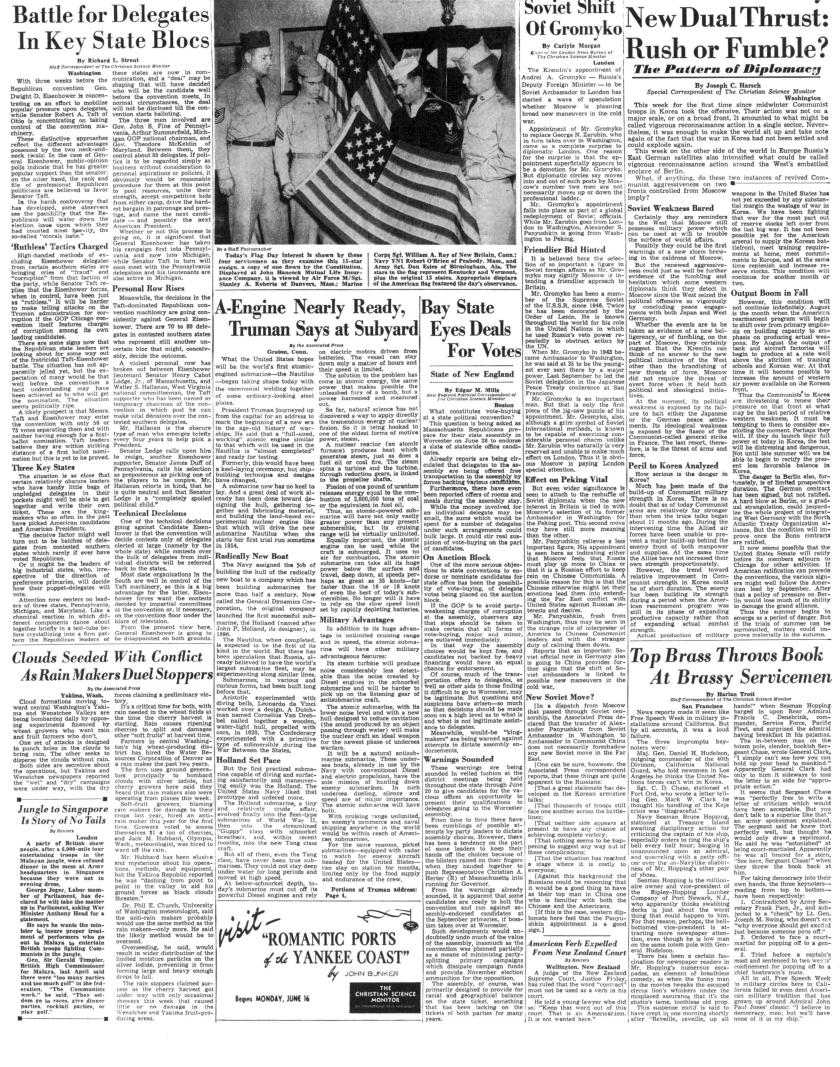

By a Staff Photographer

Today's Flag Day interest is shown by these four servicemen as they examine this 15-star ensign, a copy of one flown by the Constitution. Displayed at John Hancock Mutual Life Insurance Company, it is viewed by Air Force M/Sgt. Stanley A. Roberts of Danvers, Mass.; Marine Corps Sgt. William A. Roy of New Britain, Conn.; Navy YN1 Robert O'Brien of Peabody, Mass., and Army Sgt. Don Estes of Birmingham, Ala. The stars in the flag represent Kentucky and Vermont, plus the original 13 states. Appropriate displays of the American flag featured the day's observance.

A-Engine Nearly Ready, Truman Says at Subyard

By the Associated Press

Groton, Conn.

What the United States hopes will be the world's first atomic-engined submarine—the Nautilus—began taking shape today with the ceremonial welding together of some ordinary-looking steel plates.

President Truman journeyed up from the capital for an address to mark the beginning of a new era in the age-old history of warships. He said that a "full-sized, working" atomic engine similar to that which will be used in the Nautilus is "almost completed" and ready for testing.

Formerly, this would have been a keel-laying ceremony, but shipbuilding technique and designs have changed.

A submarine now has no keel to lay. And a great deal of work already has been done toward designing the hull, gathering together and fabricating material, and building the land-based experimental nuclear engine like that which will drive the new submarine Nautilus when she starts her first trial run sometime in 1954.

Radically New Boat

The Navy assigned the job of building the hull of the radically new boat to a company which has been building submarines for more than half a century. Now called the General Dynamics Corporation, the original company launched the first successful submarine, the Holland (named after John P. Holland, its designer), in 1896.

The Nautilus, when completed, is expected to be the first of its kind in the world. But there has been speculation that Russia, already believed to have the world's largest submarine fleet, may be experimenting along similar lines.

Submarines, in various and curious forms, had been built long before that.

Aristotle experimented with diving bells, Leonardo da Vinci worked over a design. A Dutchman named Cornelius Van Drebbel nailed together a wooden, water-tight hull, propelled with oars, in 1620. The Confederacy experimented with a primitive type of submersible during the War Between the States.

Holland Set Pace

But the first practical submarine capable of diving and surfacing satisfactorily and maneuvering easily was the Holland. The United States Navy liked that prototype and ordered more.

The Holland submarine, a tiny and relatively crude affair, evolved finally into the fleet-type submarines of World War II, then into the streamlined "Guppy" class with schnorkel breathers, and, within recent months, into the new Tang class craft.

But all of them, even the Tang class, have never been true submarines. They could not stay deep under water for long periods and moved at high speed.

At below-schnorkel depth, today's submarine must cut off its powerful Diesel engines and rely on electric motors driven from batteries. The vessel can stay down only a matter of hours and their speed is limited.

The solution to the problem has come in atomic energy, the same power that makes possible the unleashed fury of a bomb, but a power harnessed and measured out.

So far, natural science has not discovered a way to apply directly the tremendous energy of nuclear fission. So it is being hooked to one of the oldest forms of motive power, steam.

A nuclear reactor (an atomic furnace) produces heat which generates steam, just as does a fuel oil or coal fire. The steam spins a turbine and the turbine, through reduction gears, is linked to the propeller shafts.

Fission of one pound of uranium releases energy equal to the combustion of 2,600,000 tons of coal or the equivalent in fuel oil.

Thus, an atomic-powered submarine will have not only vastly greater power than any present submersible, but its cruising range will be virtually unlimited.

Equally important, the atomic engine can be used while the craft is submerged. It uses no air for combustion. The atomic submarine can take all its huge power below the surface and travel, deep down, at speeds perhaps as great as 35 knots—far faster than the 16 or 18 knots of even the best of today's submersibles. No longer will it have to rely on the slow speed limit set by rapidly depleting batteries.

Military Advantages

In addition to its huge advantage in unlimited cruising range and in speed, the atomic submarine will have other military advantageous features:

Its steam turbine will produce noise considerably less detectable than the noise created by Diesel engines in the schnorkel submarine and will be harder to pick up on the listening gear of antisubmarine craft.

The atomic submarine, with its lower noise level and with a new hull designed to reduce cavitation (the sound produced by an object passing through water) will make the nuclear craft an ideal weapon for the newest phase of undersea warfare.

It will be a natural antisubmarine submarine. These undersea boats, already in use by the Navy with conventional Diesel and electric propulsion, have the sole mission of hunting down enemy submarines. In such undersea dueling, silence and speed are of major importance. The atomic submarine will have both.

With cruising range unlimited, an enemy's commerce and naval shipping anywhere in the world would be within reach of American submarines.

For the same reasons, picket submarines—equipped with radar to watch for enemy aircraft headed for the United States—can stay on station for months, limited only by the food supply and endurance of the crew.

Portions of Truman address: Page 4.

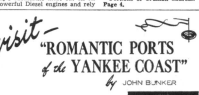

visit—
"ROMANTIC PORTS of the YANKEE COAST"
by JOHN BUNKER
Begins MONDAY, JUNE 16
THE CHRISTIAN SCIENCE MONITOR
an international daily newspaper

Bay State Eyes Deals For Votes

State of New England

By Edgar M. Mills
New England Political Correspondent of The Christian Science Monitor

Boston

What constitutes vote-buying at a state political convention?

This question is being asked as Massachusetts Republicans prepare for their state assembly in Worcester on June 28 to endorse a slate of statewide office candidates.

Already reports are being circulated that delegates to the assembly are being offered free transportation to the assembly by forces backing various candidates.

Furthermore, there have even been reported offers of rooms and meals during the assembly stay.

While the money involved for an individual delegate may be small, the sums which would be spent for a number of delegates under such arrangements could bulk large. It could stir real suspicion of vote-buying on the part of candidates.

On Auction Block

One of the more serious objections to state conventions to endorse or nominate candidates for state office has been the possibility of vote-buying, of delegate votes being placed on the auction block.

If the GOP is to avoid party-weakening charges of corruption at the assembly, observers say that steps should be taken to make certain that all forms of vote-buying, major and minor, are outlawed immediately.

In that way the assembly choices would be kept free, and candidates not backed by heavy financing would have an equal chance for endorsement.

Of course, much of the transportation offers to delegates, as well as other aids to those finding it difficult to go to Worcester, may be legitimate. But questions and suspicions have arisen—so much so that decisions should be made soon on a high level as to what is and what is not legitimate assistance to delegates.

Meanwhile, would-be "kingmakers" are being warned against attempts to dictate assembly endorsements.

Warnings Sounded

These warnings are being sounded in veiled fashion at the district meetings being held throughout the state through June 20 to give candidates for the various offices an opportunity to present their qualifications to delegates going to the Worcester assembly.

From time to time there have been rumblings of possible attempts by party leaders to dictate assembly choices. However, there has been a tendency on the part of some leaders to keep their hands off the choices because of the blisters raised on their fingers when they banded together to push Representative Christian A. Herter (R) of Massachusetts into running for Governor.

From the warnings already sounded, it is apparent that some candidates are ready to bolt the convention and run against assembly-endorsed candidates at the September primaries, if bossism takes over at Worcester.

Such developments would undoubtedly undo much of the value of the assembly, inasmuch as the convention was planned partially as a means of minimizing party-splitting primary campaigns which dissipate campaign funds and provide November election ammunition for the opposition.

The assembly, of course, was primarily designed to provide for racial and geographical balance on the state ticket, something that has been lacking on the tickets of both parties for many years.

British Eye Soviet Shift Of Gromyko

By Carlyle Morgan
Chief of the London News Bureau of The Christian Science Monitor

London

The Kremlin's appointment of Andrei A. Gromyko — Russia's Deputy Foreign Minister — to be Soviet Ambassador to London has started a wave of speculation whether Moscow is planning broad new maneuvers in the cold war.

Appointment of Mr. Gromyko to replace George N. Zarubin, who in turn takes over in Washington, came as a complete surprise to diplomatic London. One reason for the surprise is that the appointment superficially appears to be a demotion for Mr. Gromyko. But diplomatic circles say moves into and out of such posts by Moscow's number two men are not necessarily moves up or down the professional ladder.

Mr. Gromyko's appointment falls into place as part of a global redeployment of Soviet officials. While Mr. Zarubin goes from London to Washington, Alexander S. Panyushkin is going from Washington to Peking.

Friendlier Bid Hinted

It is believed here the selection of so important a figure in Soviet foreign affairs as Mr. Gromyko may signify Moscow is intending a friendlier approach to Britain.

Mr. Gromyko has been a member of the Supreme Soviet of the U.S.S.R. since 1946. Twice he has been decorated by the Order of Lenin. He is known throughout the world for his role in the United Nations in which he used Russia's veto power repeatedly to obstruct action by the UN.

When Mr. Gromyko in 1943 became Ambassador to Washington, he was said at 35 to be the youngest ever sent there by a major power. Last September he led the Soviet delegation in the Japanese Peace Treaty conference at San Francisco.

Mr. Gromyko is an important man. But that is only the first piece of the jig-saw puzzle of his appointment. Mr. Gromyko, also, although a grim symbol of Soviet international methods, is known to be capable of exercising considerable personal charm unlike Mr. Zarubin who naturally is very reserved and unable to make much effect on London. Thus it is obvious Moscow is paying London special attention.

Effect on Peking Vital

But even wider significance is seen to attach to the reshuffle of Soviet diplomats when the new interest in Britain is tied in with Moscow's selection of its former Ambassador in Washington for the Peking post. This second move may have still more meaning than the other.

Mr. Panyushkin relieves a less important figure. His appointment is seen here as indicating either that Moscow feels that Russia must play up more to China or that it is a Russian effort to keep rein on Chinese Communists. A possible reason for this is that the Chinese otherwise might let their emotions lead them into extending the Far East conflict with United States against Russian interests and desires.

Mr. Panyushkin, fresh from Washington, thus may be seen in the strange role of interpreter of America to Chinese Communist leaders and with the stranger duty of calming them down.

Reports that an important Soviet official now in Germany also is going to China provides further signs that the shift of Soviet ambassadors is linked to possible new maneuvers in the cold war.

New Soviet Move?

[In a dispatch from Moscow that passed through Soviet censorship, the Associated Press declared that the transfer of Alexander Panyushkin from Soviet Ambassador in Washington to Ambassador in Communist China does not necessarily foreshadow any new Soviet move in the Far East.

[One can be sure, however, the Associated Press correspondent reports, that these things are quite apparent to the Russians:

[That a great stalemate has developed in the Korean armistice talks;

[That thousands of troops still face one another across the battlelines;

[That neither side appears at present to have any chance of achieving complete victory;

[That nothing seems to be happening to suggest any way out of these complications;

[That the situation has reached a stage where it is costly to everyone;

[Against this background the Russians could be reasoning that it would be a good thing to have as their top man in China one who is familiar with both the Chinese and the Americans.

[If this is the case, western diplomats here feel that the Panyushkin appointment is a good sign.]

American Verb Expelled From New Zealand Court

By Reuters

Wellington, New Zealand

A judge of the New Zealand Supreme Court, Justice Finlay, has ruled that the word "contract" must not be used as a verb in his court.

He told a young lawyer who did so: "Keep that word out of this court. That is an Americanism. It is not wanted here."

Communists Try New Dual Thrust: Rush or Fumble?

The Pattern of Diplomacy

By Joseph C. Harsch
Special Correspondent of The Christian Science Monitor

Washington

This week for the first time since midwinter Communist troops in Korea took the offensive. Their action was not on a major scale, or on a broad front. It amounted to what might be called vigorous reconnaissance action in a single sector. Nevertheless, it was enough to make the world sit up and take note again of the fact that the war in Korea had not been settled and could explode again.

This week on the other side of the world in Europe Russia's East German satellites also intensified what could be called vigorous reconnaissance action around the West's embattled enclave of Berlin.

What, if anything, do these two instances of revived Communist aggressiveness on two fronts controlled from Moscow imply?

Soviet Weakness Bared

Certainly they are reminders to the West that Moscow still possesses military power which can be used at will to trouble the surface of world affairs.

Possibly they could be the first warnings of a new storm brewing in the caldrons of Moscow.

But the renewed aggressiveness could just as well be further evidence of the fumbling and hesitation which some western diplomats think they detect in Moscow since the West seized the political offensive so vigorously by concluding peace engagements with both Japan and West Germany.

Whether the events are to be taken as evidence of a new belligerency, or of fumbling, on the part of Moscow, they certainly suggest that the Kremlin can think of no answer to the new political initiative of the West other than the brandishing of new threats of force. Moscow did not require the threat of overt force when it held both political and ideological initiatives.

At the moment, its political weakness is exposed by its failure to halt either the Japanese or the German peace settlements. Its ideological weakness is exposed by the fiasco of the Communist-called general strike in France. The last resort, therefore, is to the threat of arms and force.

Peril to Korea Analyzed

How serious is the danger in Korea?

Much has been made of the build-up of Communist military strength in Korea. There is no doubt that as of today Communist arms are relatively far stronger than when the truce talks began about 11 months ago. During the intervening time the Allied air forces have been unable to prevent a major build-up behind the enemy front of both manpower and supplies. At the same time the Allies have not increased their own strength proportionately.

However, the trend toward relative improvement in Communist strength in Korea could be of short duration. The enemy has been building its strength during a period when the American rearmament program was still in its phase of expanding productive capacity rather than of expanding actual combat strength.

Actual production of military weapons in the United States has not yet exceeded by any substantial margin the wastage of war in Korea. We have been fighting that war for the most part out of reserve stocks left over from the last big war. It has not been possible yet for the American arsenal to supply the Korean battlefront, meet training requirements at home, meet commitments to Europe, and at the same time replenish and increase reserve stocks. This condition will continue for another month or two.

Output Boom in Fall

However, this condition will not continue indefinitely. August is the month when the American rearmament program will begin to shift over from primary emphasis on building capacity to emphasis on producing actual weapons. By August the output of tank and aircraft factories will begin to produce at a rate well above the attrition of training schools and Korean war. At that time it will become possible to increase the amount of western air power available on the Korean front.

Thus the Communists in Korea are threatening to renew their pressure on that front at what may be the last period of relative western weakness. It must be tempting to them to consider exploiting the moment. Perhaps they will. If they do launch their full power of today in Korea, the test will be distressing and dangerous. Not until late summer will we be able to begin to rectify the present less favorable balance in Korea.

The danger to Berlin also, fortunately, is of limited prospective duration. The German contract has been signed, but not ratified. A hard blow at Berlin, or a gradual strangulation, could jeopardize the whole project of integrating West Germany with the North Atlantic Treaty Organization alliance. But the condition will improve once the Bonn contracts are ratified.

It now seems possible that the United States Senate will ratify before its members adjourn to Chicago for other activities. If American ratification can precede the conventions, the various signers might well follow the American lead by September. After that a policy of pressure on Berlin would lose much of its ability to damage the grand alliance.

Thus the summer begins to emerge as a period of danger. But if the trials of summer can be surmounted, matters could improve materially in the autumn.

Top Brass Throws Book At Brassy Servicemen

By Harlan Trott
Staff Correspondent of The Christian Science Monitor

San Francisco

News reports made it seem like Free Speech Week in military installations around California. But by all accounts, it was a loud failure.

The three impromptu keynoters were:

Maj. Gen. Daniel H. Hudelson, outgoing commander of the 40th Division, California National Guard, who told newsmen in Los Angeles he thinks the United Nations forces can't win in Korea.

Sgt. C. D. Chase, stationed at Fort Ord, who wrote a letter telling Gen. Mark W. Clark he thought his handling of the Koje crisis was "disgraceful."

Navy Seaman Bruce Hopping, stationed at Treasure Island awaiting disciplinary action for criticizing the captain of his ship, especially orders to ring the ship's bell every half hour; barging in unannounced upon an admiral, and quarreling with a petty officer over the un-Navylike shabbiness of Mr. Hopping's other pair of shoes.

Seaman Hopping is the millionaire owner and vice-president of the Ripley-Hopping Lumber Company of Port Newark, N.J., who apparently thinks swabbing decks is just about the worst thing that could happen to him. For that reason, perhaps, the bell-bottomed vice-president is attracting more newspaper attention, even though he is low man on the same totem pole with General Hudelson.

There has been a certain fascination for newspaper readers in Mr. Hopping's numerous escapades, an element of breathless comedy, as when the funny man in the movies tweaks the escaped circus lion's whiskers under the misplaced assurance that it's the studio's tame, toothless old prop.

This suspense motif is said to have crept in one morning shortly after "Reveille, reveille, up all hands!" when Seaman Hopping barged in upon Rear Admiral Francis C. Denebrink, commander, Service Force, Pacific Fleet, and surprised the admiral having breakfast in his pajamas.

The in-between man on the totem pole, slender, bookish Sergeant Chase, wrote General Clark, "I simply can't see how you can hold up your head to mankind." Apparently General Clark had only to turn it sideways to toss the letter to an aide for "appropriate action."

It seems that Sergeant Chase was "perfectly free to write a letter of criticism which would have been acceptable. But you don't talk to a superior like that." an army spokesman explained. The sergeant said he knew that perfectly well, but thought he would only draw a reprimand. He said he was "astonished" at being court-martialed. Apparently he was all braced for a stern, "See here, Sergeant Chase!" when they threw the book back at him.

For taking democracy into their own hands, the three keynoters—reading from top to bottom—have been respectively:

1. Contradicted by Army Secretary Frank Pace, Jr., and subjected to a "check" by Lt. Gen. Joseph M. Swing, who doesn't see "why everyone should get excited just because someone pops off."

2. Ordered to face a court-martial for popping off to a general.

3. Tried before a captain's mast and sentenced to two weeks' confinement for popping off to a chief boatswain's mate.

All in all, Free Speech Week in military circles here in California failed to even dent American military tradition that has grown up around Admiral John Paul Jones' classic: "I believe in democracy, men; but we'll have none of it in my ship."

THE CHRISTIAN SCIENCE MONITOR

Registered in U. S. Patent Office

AN INTERNATIONAL DAILY NEWSPAPER

VOLUME 44 NO. 291 | COPYRIGHT 1952 BY THE CHRISTIAN SCIENCE PUBLISHING SOCIETY | BOSTON, WEDNESDAY, NOVEMBER 5, 1952 | R | • ATLANTIC EDITION | TWO SECTIONS | FIVE CENTS A COPY

Eisenhower Tide Engulfs East-West, Cracks South; Herter, Kennedy, Fingold, Whittier, Buckley Win

Emil Weiss

'Ike' Faces Congress Difficulties

By Richard L. Strout

Staff Correspondent of The Christian Science Monitor

Washington

President-Elect Dwight D. Eisenhower must lean heavily on Democratic support on a bipartisan basis to carry through the terms of his announced foreign policy in a legislative line-up that almost certainly bodes stormy weather ahead for continuation of the present Truman-Acheson program of international cooperation.

Almost certainly the result of the election upon which America's free allies in Europe have waited breathlessly will depend on the degree to which General Eisenhower can translate his immense prestige and internationalism into action through a Congress that gives signs by its make-up of being cautious, if not suspicious, about present policies.

An irony is that the Eisenhower sweep has returned to Congress and particularly the Senate a group of Republicans known as the "class of 1946," whose voting records are almost diametrically opposed to the general's proposed foreign policy.

House Control Looms

Basic question is whether responsibility placed on Republicans after 20 years will alter a position on foreign policy which has caused grave concern abroad. General Eisenhower obviously believes it will.

With incomplete returns, it appears that Republicans will take control of the House and organize the committees. The chairmanships of the key committees will be largely what they were in the controversial 80th Congress, with Illinois holding four and New York and Michigan three each, and the other 16 scattered. It appeared that GOP control of the House would be by a slim margin. A House majority is 218. In the outgoing House there are 232 Democrats, 202 Republicans.

The big question is the Senate. The size of the Eisenhower vote makes possible Republican control, which was previously thought unlikely. The present Senate shows 49 Democrats, 46 Republicans and 1 independent, Wayne Morse of Oregon. There has not been a split Congress in presidential election since 1916. Voting control in the Senate requires 49 seats. Thirty-four Senate seats were at stake.

Possibilities Surveyed

Three possibilities appeared, as control wavered in the balance:

1. If the result turned out to be 48 Democrats and 47 Republicans with 1 independent (Morse), Senator Morse might vote with the Republicans, giving a tie vote. But Vice-President Alben W. Barkley will be in office till Jan. 20 and could break a tie vote till then on the Democrats' side.

2. Vice-President-elect Richard M. Nixon takes over Jan. 20, when the GOP could break a tie and organize the Senate.

3. Republicans may take control if they can squeeze through in Senate contests still pending.

'Class of 1946'

Particular attention fell on 10 freshmen senators of the "Class of 1946" up for reelection whose views differed from General Eisenhower's. These were:

Bricker, John W., Ohio, reelected.

Cain, Harry P., Washington, defeated by Henry Jackson, an internationalist.

Ecton, Zales N., Montana, trailing Mike Mansfield, an internationalist.

Jenner, William E., Indiana, reelected.

Kem, James P., Missouri, defeated by W. Stuart Symington, internationalist.

Langer, William, North Dakota, reelected.

McCarthy, Joseph R., Wisconsin, reelected.

Malone, George W., Nevada, reelected.

Martin, Edward, Pennsylvania, reelected.

Watkins, Arthur V., Utah, reelected.

The above senators would be unimportant in themselves in a total of 96, but with the majority of them reelected on Eisenhower coat tails, they presumably will cooperate with a similar group already in the Senate, or make common cause with Democrats like Pat McCarran of Nevada, whose views are similar. The foregoing senators have been more extreme in their Republicanism than Senator Robert A. Taft of Ohio, but they have been among his most ardent supporters.

Storm Warnings Up

Almost without question Senator Taft will be the most powerful man in the new Senate under either party. It appears likewise that there will be a continuation of coalition government with the majority consisting of internationalist Republicans and Democrats, but held in close check by Senator Taft.

General Eisenhower and Senator Taft cooperated in the election and should do so for a honeymoon period after it.

But storm warnings are up. There were differences with Senator Taft on world affairs even in the campaign agreement. The Eisenhower election speeches obscured rather than recognized these differences.

General Eisenhower is committed to large and difficult goals—an effort to settle the Korean war, to slash the budget, cut military expenditures, review foreign aid, and ultimately reduce taxes. Where these goals leave the Truman-Acheson foreign policy is anyone's guess.

A big victor in the election is GOP Senator Joseph R. McCarthy. He won in Wisconsin, though by a smaller majority than either General Eisenhower or Gov. Kohler. Senator William Benton (D) of Connecticut, who introduced a resolution for Mr. McCarthy's Senate expulsion a year ago, was defeated. Undoubtedly Senator McCarthy will argue that his two big campaign speeches helped the defection of Democrats, particularly Irish Roman Catholic votes.

Massachusetts Vote

President
(1933 of 1967 precincts)

Eisenhower	1,262,678
Stevenson	1,064,642

United States Senator
(1879 precincts)

Kennedy (D)	1,145,109
Lodge (R)	1,078,850

Governor
(1934 precincts)

Herter (R)	1,154,480
Dever (D)	1,145,141

Lieutenant Governor
(1913 precincts)

Whittier (R)	1,163,119
Sullivan (D)	1,057,204

Secretary of State
(1913 precincts)

Cronin (D)	1,111,071
Mullaney (R)	1,057,664

State Treasurer
(1913 precincts)

Furcolo (D)	1,119,804
Papalia (R)	1,048,915

State Auditor
(1913 precincts)

Buckley (D)	1,173,607
Mintz (R)	1,008,014

Attorney General
(1913 precincts)

Fingold (R)	1,254,604
Kelly (D)	924,911

Inside Stories on Election

Triumph Slated to Unite Nation; General Runs Far Ahead of Party

By Roscoe Drummond

Chief of the Washington News Bureau of The Christian Science Monitor

Washington

Gen. Dwight D. Eisenhower becomes the 34th President of the United States in a towering, national, personal triumph which dramatically ends the 20-year Democratic rule and restores the American two-party system to vigor and vitality.

There is a Homeric quality to the general's five-star victory.

Its sweep, its magnitude, and its healthy conclusiveness are its significance. It is a presidential election which helps to unite, rather than divide, the nation.

General Eisenhower, who will shortly be making his plans to go to Korea, is President-elect:

By the largest popular vote in American political history.

By the largest popular majority the Republican Party ever has won.

By the largest electoral vote since President Roosevelt defeated Wendell L. Willkie 12 years ago.

By breaking the now-unsolid South for the first time since Alfred E. Smith lost to Herbert Hoover in 1928 with about the same electoral vote as Gov. Adlai E. Stevenson has lost to his soldier opponent—the first general chosen for the presidency since Gen. Ulysses S. Grant—in 1952.

Carries All Big States

By carrying every large state in every section of the country, from Massachusetts to California and including the Governor's home state of Illinois.

By winning decisively the farm vote of the Midwest and a substantial portion of the labor vote in the populous industrial areas of the country.

There is one restraining factor in this nationwide verdict: The Republican presidential nominee—himself a figure new to politics and considered by many of his supporters to be above politics—ran ahead of the Republican Party everywhere.

This means that while the voters chose General Eisenhower overwhelmingly, they chose the Republican Party narrowly, and this is demonstrated in the thin, uncertain control the Republicans have in the Senate.

Democrats Remain Strong

In 1948, many Democratic senatorial and congressional candidates far outdistanced President Truman and helped him to office. This year General Eisenhower has far outdistanced the Republican senatorial and congressional candidates and in close contests has helped just enough of them into office to give the GOP little more than organizing control of the Senate.

But in such states as Massachusetts, where his earliest supporter, Senator Henry Cabot Lodge, Jr., lost out, and Washington, where Republican Senator Harry P. Cain was defeated, the general's personal popularity was not sufficient to carry his party with him.

This is why General Eisenhower's victory is a personal victory, even though of landslide proportions.

The very least that can be said from this fact is that the Democratic Party remains strong in opposition and will be a constant challenge and check upon an Eisenhower administration.

For many years and throughout this latest presidential campaign, all the polls showed the Democratic Party trusted by the voters more than the Republican Party. Something of this attitude is reflected in the fact that while the Democratic Party was literally submerged in the presidential contest, it lost Congress only narrowly and remains a potent force on Capitol Hill.

For the first time in 22 years, since the Senate went to the Democrats in the middle of the Hoover administration, the Republicans control the national government.

The dissolution of the coalition which kept the presidency in Roosevelt and Truman hands is shattering. That coalition was made up of the farmers and organized labor and the minority groups in the large cities which, until General Eisenhower became the party's standard bearer, the Republicans have hardly been able to dent.

The general more than dented the coalition this time. It literally fell apart under the impact of his fame, his force, and his earnest appeal to apply fresh ideas and fresh vision to seeking a way to peace in a dangerous world.

America's war-famed President-elect is in an ideal position to lift his leadership beyond the boundaries of partisan politics and solidify his hold upon the country.

He has drawn his support from every area of the nation and from every segment of the electorate. He is not captive of any voting group, but he is the beneficiary of nearly every voting group—farmer, worker, urbanite, Easterner, Westerner — and Southerner.

What is most important about General Eisenhower's break into the Solid South is not just the fact that he already had carried four southern states and might well take two more but rather the fact that he has piled up significant popularity votes in virtually every southern state.

This can be the foundation of the development of a two-party system in the South.

Three Major Issues

Korea, communism, and corruption—plus the general's own force and fame—combined to make the winning issues for the Republican nominee. Governor Stevenson, relatively unknown until his nomination, made a strong and appealing personal candidate, but it now is clear that he had little chance of offsetting the accumulated resentments against the Truman administration.

The result was that Governor Stevenson was able to retain only the shattered façade of the once-solid South along with one or two border states to put together a defeat which, in its bid for the presidency, the Democratic Party has not experienced for 24 years.

National Election Scoreboard

By the Associated Press

This was the national election picture at 10 a.m.:

Eisenhower elected President by largest popular vote ever given GOP candidate, possibly any presidential candidate.

Eisenhower's popular vote, 27,027,230; Stevenson's, 22,039,899 in 113,599 of 146,361 precincts.

Eisenhower led in 39 states with 442 electoral votes; Stevenson in 9 with 89.

Eisenhower swept key states in North, Midwest farm area (voted Democratic five past elections), several southern states including Florida, Virginia, Texas, possibly Tennessee, Louisiana, and won border states like Maryland and Oklahoma.

Senate: 35 races—Democrats elected 10, holdovers 35, total 45; Republicans elected 19, holdovers 26 (counting Morse, now independent), total 45. Needed to control, 49. GOP picked up 2 seats from Democrats (Connecticut, Maryland); Democrats picked up 3 seats (Missouri, Massachusetts, Washington). Democrats leading 2, Republicans 4 in undecided races.

House: 435 races—Democrats elected 189, Republicans 199, independent 1, undecided 46. Needed to control, 218.

Governors: 30 races—Democrats elected 8; Republicans 16 (gain of 3). Republicans leading in 5, Democrats 1 (total GOP gains if present leads hold—6).

State of the Nation

By a Staff Photographer

John F. Kennedy (D)
United States Senator-Elect from Massachusetts

By a Staff Photographer

Christian A. Herter (R)
Massachusetts Governor-Elect

Surprises Dot Vote

Representative Christian A. Herter has won the gubernatorial election against Governor Dever. With all precincts counted, Mr. Herter had an 18,495-vote margin.

By Edgar M. Mills

New England Political Correspondent of The Christian Science Monitor

Representative Christian A. Herter appears to be a winner over Governor Dever today in the closest Bay State gubernatorial election in more than a decade and possibly in the state history. The margin was at 5,000 votes with only 40 precincts to be counted.

Furthermore, a recount appears to be a certainty.

The Herter-Dever contest, which narrowed dramatically and suddenly as the Democratic Governor made a late rush, took the day-after-election spotlight in Massachusetts away from Gen. Dwight D. Eisenhower's spectacular 210,000-vote margin victory to capture the state's 16 electoral votes.

Overshadowed, too, was Representative John F. Kennedy's unseating of three-term Senator Henry Cabot Lodge, Jr., by approximately 70,000 votes.

Governor Dever was involved in the previous close battle for Governor back in 1940 when he was defeated by Leverett Saltonstall by 5,588 votes.

Dever Overtaken

At one time Governor Dever was far ahead, only to be overtaken by Mr. Herter. Then as the final returns slowly trickled in, the Governor made a dramatic comeback.

So the Herter bid to unseat the two-term Governor attracted almost complete voter attention away from the other contests.

But the Republicans had plenty to cheer about, even with the Herter-Dever outcome indecisive and Senator Lodge going down to defeat.

Young hard-hitting Senator Sumner G. Whittier (R) of Everett unseated two-term Democratic Lt. Gov. Charles F. Jeff Sullivan, and crusading George F. Fingold, former Assistant Attorney General, defeated Democratic Attorney General Francis E. Kelly.

But even the tremendous Eisenhower victory could not provide a sweep of the state offices for the GOP. Split-ticket voting saved Democrats Edward J. Cronin, Secretary of State; Foster Furcolo, State Treasurer, and Thomas J. Buckley, State Auditor.

The fact that Mr. Herter ran such a close race with Governor Dever while Senator Lodge was losing was a major surprise in many quarters. Many had felt the tall, handsome congressman did not have the campaign fire necessary to ignite a political bonfire under the Governor.

But Governor Dever ran well behind his 1950 strength in many areas, particularly Democratic cities. He held up well in Boston, yet even here his 144,000-vote margin of 1950 was whittled to 123,000.

But in industrial areas hit by unemployment, the Herter claim that the Dever regime had meant loss of jobs in Massachusetts proved effective.

Lawrence, one of the hardest-hit areas, gave Governor Dever a 26,527-to-13,632 margin, but two years ago the Dever spread was 29,574 to 7,470.

New Bedford, carried by Dever two years ago 27,957 to 17,105, was carried this time by Dever by a wafer-thin 26,376 to 26,048.

'Ike' Leads Ticket

General Eisenhower ran well ahead of his ticket throughout the state. By carrying the state, he became the first Republican presidential nominee to win Massachusetts electoral votes since Calvin Coolidge turned the trick in 1924.

But it had been anticipated that if he carried the state by 200,000 votes or more he would be able to carry Lodge and Herter with him.

Several factors worked in young Mr. Kennedy's favor and against Senator Lodge. And his victory was more a victory for him than a defeat for Senator Lodge.

As far as the state as a whole is concerned, the young congressman is a new, fresh figure. His campaign was costly but highly effective. He drove an effective wedge into Senator Lodge's usual ability to corral heavy portions of the Democratic vote.

Unlike Governor Dever, he did not have a much-criticized administrative record.

In the tremendous GOP surge in Massachusetts, incomplete returns indicate the Republicans have recaptured the Massachusetts House of Representatives and strengthened their hold on the State Senate.

Attorney General-Elect Fingold made one of the most amazing runs of the entire election, to become the first Jewish-American ever to be elected to Massachusets statewide office.

Nov. 5, 1952

THE CHRISTIAN SCIENCE MONITOR

Registered in U. S. Patent Office

AN INTERNATIONAL DAILY NEWSPAPER

VOLUME 45 NO. 84   COPYRIGHT 1953 BY THE CHRISTIAN SCIENCE PUBLISHING SOCIETY   BOSTON, FRIDAY, MARCH 6, 1953   K   • ATLANTIC EDITION   TWO SECTIONS   FIVE CENTS A COPY

For and Against?

Dulles Treaty Position Waited

By Neal Stanford
Staff Correspondent of The Christian Science Monitor

Informed official and private sources in the Capital hint that Secretary of State John Foster Dulles may approve the much-debated "Bricker resolution" in theory but oppose it in practice.

The resolution would tighten up the treaty-making provisions of the Constitution to protect national sovereignty.

Reasons for feeling this way are varied, but collectively impressive:

1. As a private citizen before his appointment, Mr. Dulles agreed that treaty law could override the Constitution and cut across the Bill of Rights. But he questioned the need for remedying the Constitution to remedy this situation, suggesting rather that a little more "vigilance" by both President and Senate in writing treaties might do the trick.

2. Now that Mr. Dulles is and not out of the government, when the responsibility for making treaties is his, it is natural to expect he would be more cautious than before to see his treaty-making powers restricted. He would probably prefer the present latitude, however confined, to any added obstacles to treaty-writing.

No Added Restrictions

3. While President Eisenhower has not publicly expressed himself on this matter, there are reports that he has privately made it clear he wants no added restrictions put in the way of writing treaties and could not go along with the present Bricker Amendment.

4. If Secretary Dulles should now openly advocate the Bricker restrictions on treaty writing, he would not only be reversing the position of the previous administration, which felt such a change was both unnecessary and unwise, but be going counter to his

'Slavery' Blast Lands on Shelf

By the United Press

Washington

Soviet Prime Minister Joseph Stalin's passing appears to make in doubt certain President Eisenhower's amended "anti-enslavement" resolution will be shelved indefinitely in Congress.

The resolution, designed to put this country on record against Soviet violation of the Yalta and Potsdam Agreements, previously had become the subject of a Republican-Democratic Senate clash that jeopardized its prospects.

With the passing of Stalin, all hands agreed the resolution should be held up at least until the situation in Russia becomes clearer.

Details Page 14

legal advisers in the department. Some of them are his own appointees, not holdovers from the Democratic regime.

A fifth consideration may enter into the attitude that the Secretary of State finally adopts on this issue.

While the American Bar Association has worked with Senator John W. Bricker (R) of Ohio in drafting a treaty-procedure amendment to the Constitution, its one recalcitrant branch, the New York Bar Association, has constantly and determinedly opposed such action.

That branch, significantly, is the Secretary of State could hardly do less than back the Bricker Amendment, or a reasonable substitute, when he or his legal counsel appears on Capitol Hill to testify on Senate Joint Resolution 1.

'Difference of Opinion'

But further on in the same speech, Mr. Dulles, who was then a private citizen, said: "Senator Bricker has made important proposals for a constitutional amendment which would prevent treaties from impinging on present constitutional rights of the Congress, the states, and the peoples."

"There is room for honest difference of opinion as to whether our Constitution needs to be amended as proposed, or whether the President and the Senate should retain their present powers for possible emergency use, at the same time insuring vigilance to the end that treaties will not undesirably and unnecessarily encroach on constitutional distribution of power."

If the first quote suggests that Mr. Dulles would favor the Bricker Amendment, the second expresses his doubt about the wisdom of thus tying the hands of future Presidents and members of the Senate.

amendment such as Senator Bricker has proposed.

The general presumption in the capital has been that Mr. Dulles, when his turn comes to testify on this measure, will throw the administration's support behind the Bricker Amendment. But there would seem to be equal if not greater reason to expect that, while he will agree to the senator's analysis of the trouble, he will end up by questioning the remedy proposed.

Dulles Position

Supporters of the Bricker Amendment have generally assumed that Secretary of State Dulles would support the measure.

They quote a speech he made last April in which he said: "The treaty-making power is an extraordinary power, liable to abuse. Treaties make international law and also they make domestic law. Under our Constitution, treaties become the supreme law of the land. They are, indeed, more supreme than ordinary laws, for congressional laws are invalid if they do not conform to the Constitution, whereas treaty law can override the Constitution.

"Treaties, for example, can take powers away from the Congress and give them to the President; they can take powers from the states and give them to the federal government or to some international body, and they can cut across the rights given the people by the Constitutional Bill of Rights."

Taken by itself, this sounds as if the Secretary of State could hardly do less than back the

---

Herter Firings Rock 'Hill'

Long-run political effect of the firing of 44 Dever supporters from the State Department of Corporations and Taxation and their replacement by 19 Herter backers is being assessed on Beacon Hill today.

Friends of Governor Herter's administration are disturbed that the swap may be interpreted by the public that patronage will be a big feature in the Herter regime and that it will undermine plans for increasing the efficiency and economy of the state government.

Governor Herter himself has stated that the other 25 vacancies, which resulted from the discharges, will not be filled. The firings affected several Democratic legislators tucked into the tax department by Governor Dever in the last days of his administration.

Generally impartial observers hail the firings as in the interest of good, efficient government, but their enthusiasm is tempered by the appointment of the 19 to succeed them.

This is particularly true in view of the fact that the Governor's patronage chief, Elmer C. Nelson, chairman of the Republican State Committee, had a hand in selecting the appointees, as disclosed by the Governor himself.

Further Details: Page 2

State of the Nation

Purpose Behind Taft's Teamwork With Eisenhower

By ROSCOE DRUMMOND, Chief, Washington News Bureau, The Christian Science Monitor

Washington

By now you probably have read a spate of articles about the cooperative teamwork which is marking the relations between President Eisenhower and Senator Robert A. Taft.

What is surprising is that so many persons should consider it surprising.

It is not unexpected to find General Eisenhower a teamplay leader. That is his forte.

It is not surprising to find Senator Taft devoting his energies to making the first Republican administration in 20 years a success. That is his principal dedication.

President Eisenhower knows that his administration cannot succeed without the genuine cooperation of Senator Taft.

Senator Taft knows that the Republican Party cannot hold any long tenure of office unless he and his followers in Congress give President Eisenhower substantial support.

Each is acting on that premise. It is a solid premise, and it is producing teamwork between the two which is noteworthy but not surprising given the political facts as they are.

There are four political facts which give Senator Taft the maximum incentive to be a team player, though not a rubber stamp, in the Eisenhower administration. They are these:

1. He has a greatly increased confidence in the President's basic conservatism, and on most domestic policies there is much more that unites them than separates them.

2. Mr. Eisenhower has amply demonstrated that he desires and intends to work with the senator and to consult and regard his views on policy—as long as there is a spirit of give and take on Mr. Taft's part. Thus far there has been that spirit.

3. Senator Taft realizes full well that the Republican Party won only half a victory last fall, that the voters refused to give the Republicans the nor-

mal presidential election year congressional majorities. He is aware that unless the Republican Congress and the President achieve a substantially united front this year and next the party will face the greatest difficulties of holding the House of Representatives after only two years in office.

4. Senator Taft's great desire is for the Republican Party to remain sufficiently long in office—and he would see two full terms as the minimum—in order to effect a permanent change in the tone, temper, and direction of federal policy. He has said he does not intend again to seek a presidential nomination, and there is no evidence that his current actions, in Congress and in his relations to the White House, are influenced by presidential ambition.

At nearly every point in recent weeks Senator Taft has been putting his huge influence in Congress to the support of the Eisenhower program.

He advocated renewal of the Reorganization Act without change while some Republican leaders in his recognizing that there is a difference between being spokesman for the opposition and spokesman for a party in power. His record has been a record of responsibility and cooperation with the President.

To continue this record will require Senator Taft to resist the pressure of some of his own most ardent congressional admirers who already are beginning to berate the senator for not standing out against Mr. Eisenhower. But Mr. Taft is aware that it was Mr. Eisenhower's brand of Republicanism which won the massive support of the voters last November, and it is evident he is going to do his best to support it in the interests of the party.

Certain underlying differences between the two could sometime explode, but the restraint against them doing so is the knowledge that at any such explosion it would be the Republican Party which would get hurt.

pressure within his party, Senator Taft has strongly favored, in line with White House leadership, deferring any tax reduction until the President and Congress have proved that they can balance the budget.

He has supported the position of the President against rushing into any blockade of China without the support of our principal Allies and, actually reversing the position he took when he was seeking the nomination, Mr. Taft has been counseling against any go-it-alone policy in Asia.

Finally, he has been more willing than many of his colleagues to back the administration in favor of the temperate resolution which Mr. Eisenhower and Secretary of State John Foster Dulles sent to Congress condemning, not the Yalta and Potsdam agreements per se, but their perversions and violation by the Soviet Union.

Senator Taft has been foremost among the Republican congressional leaders in recognizing that there is a difference between being spokesman for the opposition and spokesman for a party in power. His record has been a record of responsibility and cooperation with the President.

Practice Swings

Scott Long, Minneapolis Tribune

Unity Asked

By Eddy Gilmore and Thomas P. Whitney
Staff Correspondents of the Associated Press

Moscow

The body of Prime Minister Joseph Stalin awaits a state funeral befitting world communism's second great leader and one of the most powerful men in history.

The Soviet man of steel, whose power and influence reached a third of the world's people, passed on in the Kremlin at 9:50 p.m. (1:50 p.m., e.s.t.), March 5. For 29 years he had led the 200 million people of the Soviet Union and called the turn for Communists throughout the world.

Giving no hint of who might succeed him, a joint statement by the Soviet Communist Party and the government called for continuation of such Stalin policies as strengthening the nation's armed forces, increased vigilance at home, and tighter bonds with Communists throughout the world.

The statement said Stalin's body would lie in state in the beautiful Hall of Columns in Moscow's House of Trade Unions—only a few hundred yards from the large Lenin mausoleum in Red Square, where the body of the founder of Russian communism lies embalmed in a glass coffin.

Committee Appointed

A committee of top Soviet leaders was appointed to arrange the funeral, but its date was not announced immediately. Nor was there any word of Stalin's final resting place.

The passing of the man who sparked the development of Russia from a near-feudal farmland to a great industrial power exceeded only by the United States was announced first by Moscow Radio at 4:07 a.m., March 6 local time (8:07 p.m., March 5 e.s.t.) in a broadcast beamed to Soviet provincial newspapers.

Two hours later, Moscow Radio's star announcer, Yuri Levitan, told the saddened nation that its chief had succumbed. Mr. Levitan twice read both the official announcement and the final bulletin from the 10 Kremlin doctors who had been in constant attendance on Stalin since his stroke March 1. The radio then played the solemn last movement of Tchaikovsky's "Pathétique" symphony.

The official announcement said: "There has ceased to beat the heart of a comrade-in-arms and genius-continuer of the cause of Lenin, the wise leader and teacher of the Communist Party and the Soviet people—Joseph Vissarionovich Stalin. The death of Stalin, who gave all his life to dedicated service to the great cause of communism, is the heaviest loss for the party and workers of the Soviet nation and for all humanity."

It was issued in the name of Communist Party's Central Committee, the Council of Ministers (government cabinet), and the Presidium of the Supreme Soviet.

The Russian people appeared

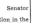

Joseph Stalin

stunned and grief-stricken by the news. To many, Stalin had seemed like a father. "Excuse me," said one Muscovite chauffeur of his own tears, "he was a real person."

All over Moscow, black-bordered red flags snapped in the cold wind that whipped the snow-blanketed city. Thousands of yards of black crepe were being hung on buildings and homes.

The House of Unions—where the bier of virtually every Soviet leader has been placed to be viewed by the people—was made ready to receive Stalin's body. A huge portrait of the leader hung above the main doors.

25,000-Word Blueprint

The last months had been a period of intense activity for the Soviet chief. He wrote his latest book, "Economic Problems of Socialism in the U.S.S.R.," a 25,000-word partial blueprint for Russia's economic future, and took a leading role in last fall's big Soviet Communist Party congress.

Last Nov. 7 he spent long hours reviewing the huge parade marking the anniversary of the 1917 revolution that brought the Communists to power in Russia. He made several public appearances at the Bolshoi Theater and recently received the Argentine and Indian Ambassadors to Moscow.

Black-bordered editions of Pravda, the Communist Party newspaper, and all other journals in the Soviet Union published the news of Stalin's death today, along with a large portrait of the Prime Minister in military uniform, the last medical bulletins, and the announcement that the body would lie in state.

Along with these, they published the proclamation of the party and the government appeal-

ing for unity and increasing power against capitalism and calling for a spirit of "implacability and firmness in the struggle with internal and foreign enemies of the U.S.S.R."

Policy Due to Continue

Most of the statement reiterated policy lines that have been long emphasized in Soviet declarations, indicating that the government plans to continue the essentials of Stalin's foreign and domestic policies.

It declared that both the party and the government stood for strengthening the Soviet armed forces to "constantly heighten our readiness for a crushing response to any aggressor." But it also called for the development of international cooperation and ties with all nations.

It asserted the Soviet Union would tighten bonds with Communist China, the people's democracies, and workers in capitalist countries, and would continue policies of strengthening peace and fighting against progressions for a third world war.

The newspapers announced the official commission appointed to arrange Stalin's funeral is headed by Nikita Khrushchev, secretary of the Central Committee of the Communist Party.

Other members include: Lazar Kaganovich, deputy president of the Council of Ministers; Nikolai Shvernik, president of the Presidium of the Supreme Soviet (Parliament); Marshal Alexander M. Vasilevsky, Minister of the Armed Forces; M. A. Yasnov, chairman of the City of Moscow; N. M. Pegov, a member of the Communist Party secretariat and an alternate member of the Presidium, and P. A. Artemyev, commander of the Moscow Military District.

Historic Changes Noted

By Ernest S. Pisko
Staff Writer of The Christian Science Monitor

With the passing of Joseph Vissarionovich Djugashvili, better known under the name of Stalin, an individual who may well have wrought greater changes in the world than any historic figure since Napoleon has left the scene.

But, unlike Napoleon, he was spared a Waterloo and could send his opponents to St. Helena. He could carry on at the place which for the past 25 years had been the center and the symbol of his power—the Kremlin. There, where in ornate halls, in carpeted corridors, on winding stairways, and in secret underground passages the memories of Ivan the Terrible, Peter the Great, of Catherine, and the last Romanovs linger, was his home.

There he worked, ate, and slept, and from there, under the ringing of church bells, the beat of muffled drums, he will be carried to the Red Square, probably to be placed temporarily next to Lenin's sarcophagus until a final resting place, bigger than Lenin's, will have been erected for him.

With these last ceremonies an epoch will have come to an end not only in the history of the Soviet empire but in the history of the world. And regardless of whether Stalin's beliefs are condemned by free men as aberrations and his deeds as evil or whether they are praised by fanatics, the epoch that has closed was to no small extent dominated by Stalin.

35-Year Era Belonged to Stalin

The 35 years from October, 1917, when the Bolsheviks seized power, until October, 1952, when Stalin addressed the 19th Congress of the Soviet Communist Party and put his seal of approval on the new blueprint for distribution of power in the Soviet state—these years were his era despite the fact that the first seven of them stood under Lenin's sign.

Though Lenin was by far the greater intellect of the two and the father of the Soviet system, his time was too short to finish the task he mapped. He had to spend the first three years of his rule clearing the ground for the Communist society he wished to set up, and during his last two years he was incapacitated and rarely able to exercise a more than nominal authority.

It is tempting but idle to speculate over the course history would have taken had Lenin been allowed to finish his work. The Soviet Union might have developed in a strikingly different manner; but, on the other hand, it might not, for the one thing Lenin and Stalin had in common—apart from their belief in the ultimate validity of Marxian dialectic—was their willingness to switch signals, reverse directions, and change tactics without ever changing their strategic concept.

Compromised on Means but Not on Goal

They both were willing to compromise about means without ever compromising about their ends. The ultimate goal for both was the same—the conquest of the world by and for the dictatorial communism under the slogan of a proletarian revolution.

The difference between Lenin and Stalin was one of character rather than of intentions. Lenin was more of an architect, Stalin more of a contractor. But what Stalin built was all taken from the vast collection of blueprints Lenin had drawn.

The four great tasks before Stalin were:

Securing the economic basis of the Soviet Union; making the "party" superior to all other institutions; regaining Russia's former position among the big powers; preparing the ground for a perpetuation of the Soviet system.

When Stalin began to gather the reins of government in his hands after Lenin's passing in 1924, the Soviet Union was in the middle of the so-called NEP period. NEP, which stands for New Economic Program, was essentially a return to private enterprise and the profit system.

After the end of the revolution and the civil war, Russia was nearly bankrupt. Its industry, underdeveloped, short of skilled labor, and starved for raw materials, could not produce even a fraction of the necessary goods. As a result the peasantry, who are counted as more than half of the Russian population, refused to supply food unless they would be paid for in kind instead of in rubles, for which there was nothing to buy in the stores.

Collectivization Ousts NEP Program

Introduction of NEP changed the situation almost overnight. And the years from 1922 until about 1927 may look in retrospect to the older Soviet generation as the best years of their lives.

It was clear to Stalin that NEP could be only a temporary experiment. To allow it to take root in the Russian soil plowed up by the Bolshevist upheaval would have meant to forgo any plans for spreading communism. If Stalin wanted to carry out the program of Marx and Lenin, he had to abolish NEP. The vital problem was how to continue and expand the country's industry, without which no stable economy could be developed, and at the same time secure adequate output from the agricultural sector.

Stalin solved this problem by the compulsory collectivization of Russia's independent farmers. This process, which started in 1929 and extended until about 1932, brought ruin and misery to millions of Russian farmers and was the first step in Stalin's grand plan of turning the peasantry into a wing of the industrial army.

By 1933 the majority of independent farmers had been merged into collectives and Stalin called a halt to the brutal methods that had been used in transforming the agricultural sector. There was no doubt, however, that further steps had to be taken to safeguard the prerogatives of Soviet communism. For even collectivization could not destroy the seeds of independence in the individual farmers.

Spectacular Successes in Foreign Policy

Stalin's greatest achievement—from the standpoint of the Marxist-Lenin program—was the streamlining of the Soviet Communist Party which he developed into a second administration and trusted with the task of supervising every sector of public life and even considerable portion of the private lives of Soviet citizens.

Most spectacular were Stalin's successes in the field of foreign policy. It is probably no exaggeration to say that in the diplomatic game he had no match among his opposite numbers from abroad, though neither was there anyone among those who was so unhampered by moral scruples, and so ready to deceive as Stalin. A considerable part of Stalin's diplomatic successes has to be credited to the creation and skillful use of Communist fifth column with branches all over the world.

The Soviet empire which Stalin has left to his heirs is, in fact, bigger than the Russia of pre-World War I days. Although some parts of Poland and Finland are outside the Soviet Union, this loss has been compensated for by acquisitions in Romania, Czechoslovakia, central Asia, and the Far East, and far more than compensated by what amounts to undisputed domination of all the Balkan countries except Yugoslavia, and of parts of central Europe.

Ever since the middle 1930's Stalin has paid special attention to building a one-way street at the end of which was devotion to the "new Soviet man." Natural and social sciences, arts and education—they all were pressed in the service of transforming the Soviet people in their thinking and in their emotions. This work, which was interrupted during the war years, was taken up with great vigor after 1946, but it was here, according to all indications, that Stalin ran into powers with which he was unable to cope.

The measure of Stalin's importance does not lie only in what he has achieved in the Soviet Union. It also lies in the effort which this and future generations will have to make to undo much of what he built without in this process transforming East and West into one vast expanse of smoking ruins.

Stalin's career from cobbler to dictator: First page, second section

---

British Sight Big Red Changes

By Carlyle Morgan
Chief of the Christian Science News Bureau of The Christian Science Monitor

London

The passing of Joseph Stalin, Soviet dictator, marks the beginning of a new era in Russian relations with the rest of the world, it is generally agreed in informed London circles.

Although Stalin has left ex-

plicit instructions as to how a successor should carry on, many here expect that once the power struggle in the Kremlin is settled, radical changes in Soviet policy are likely to emerge.

The argument back of this expectation is that a strong man will not be content merely to follow in Stalin's footsteps, and a weak man will be unable to. Pressures for change which

Stalin was able to resist will probably increase and the possibility is that a weaker man than Stalin may be unable to resist them.

Whether consequent shifts of the Soviet's policy toward its satellites and allies and the free world will clash more forcibly with world policies of the Eisenhower administration, or whether an internal struggle will oblige Moscow to seek compromise in its foreign policy is one question being asked here.

Its answer could mean the difference between peace and war.

It seems accepted here that the United States is firmly set on a "tougher policy" toward international communism. For this reason, Stalin's passing has raised almost as many questions about what the United States may do, in view of it, as about what the Soviet Union may do.

Moderate and Conservative opinion here feels that to try to take advantage of Russia's present difficulties would be, in the words of the weekly Spectator, the "worst of all policies." British officials feel that an attempt to do so would be premature anyhow, because no one knows yet what form a power struggle in Russia might take or when it might offer. Even the fact of a power struggle might show itself only very gradually, they point out.

Cracks in the Soviet empire Stalin has built may come sooner, it is believed. Already reports have reached London from Belgrade of anti-Communist underground action in Albania. These say Marshal Tito has moved tanks to the Yugoslav-Albanian border.

American efforts to encourage immediate anti-Communist uprisings in Soviet satellite states, however, would cause most anxiety here. On the other hand, there would be strong support for a program of western economic aid to those nations, and there is little doubt here that they would welcome it.

They have been forced to make excessive shipments of manufactured goods to Russia and consequently face serious shortages themselves.

MTA Reorganization Bid Wins Legislative Approval

The World's Day

E.S. U.S. Pat. Off.

Boston: MTA Plan One of Many Major Projects

Governor Herter's plan for reorganizing the Metropolitan Transit Authority became the first of the Governor's many major reorganization proposals to win final legislative approval. [Page 2.]

Dollar value of sales in New England department stores for the week ended Feb. 28, 1953, showed an increase of 8.8 per cent over the corresponding period in 1953, according to the Federal Reserve Bank of Boston.

Washington: Ammunition Report Stirs Senators

Senate military leaders expressed grave concern over secret testimony of Gen. James A. Van Fleet on ammunition shortages in Korea. Senator Russell (D) of Georgia said General Van Fleet presented a "very disturbing" picture to the Senate Armed Services Committee.

A British move to tighten controls on strategic shipments to Communist China was reported shaping up at the Anglo-American Conference on cold war policy.

National: Minnesota Not to Rehire Weinberg

James L. Morrill, president of University of Minnesota, said that Dr. Joseph W. Weinberg, so-called "Scientist X," would not be rehired by the university. Dr. Weinberg was acquitted of federal perjury charges in denying he was a Communist Party member.

Far East: Nationalist Air Force to Be Expanded

The Chinese Nationalist Air Force will be expanded, United States Air Secretary Harold E. Talbott said after a one-day tour of the island.

Europe: Three Czechs Jailed as Slansky 'Aides'

A Prague military court has jailed three Czechs for allegedly working with American intelligence to release "traitor" Rudolph Slansky from his Communist jailers.

Weather Predictions: Fair Tonight (Details Page 2)

March 6, 1953

THE CHRISTIAN SCIENCE MONITOR

Registered in U. S. Patent Office

AN INTERNATIONAL DAILY NEWSPAPER

VOLUME 45 NO. 190 | COPYRIGHT 1953 BY THE CHRISTIAN SCIENCE PUBLISHING SOCIETY | BOSTON, FRIDAY, JULY 10, 1953 | * * ATLANTIC EDITION | TWO SECTIONS | FIVE CENTS A COPY

Malenkov Scores in Kremlin Coup, Jails Beria as Agent of Capitalism

U.S.-Rhee Pact Near

By the United Press

Seoul, Korea

South Korea and the United States have reached virtual agreement on a compromise armistice plan, reliable sources have said.

They said the agreement may not satisfy the Communists, who were reported demanding that the United Nations use military force to hold South Korean President Rhee in line.

But the reports were the most optimistic since three weeks ago when Mr. Rhee upset the all but signed truce agreement by ordering the release of 27,000 anti-Communist North Korean prisoners.

It appeared that the compromise agreement worked out by Mr. Rhee and United States presidential envoy Walter Robertson might give UN commander Gen. Mark W. Clark sufficient ground on which to assure the Communists South Korea would go along with a truce.

Gap slowly narrowed on U.S.-Rhee terms: Page 5.

Stand on McCarthy Taken by President

By Roland Sawyer

Staff Correspondent of The Christian Science Monitor

Washington

More and more President Eisenhower is being forced by events to take a public position on the methods and practices of Senator Joseph R. McCarthy (R) of Wisconsin—something Mr. Eisenhower has sought to avoid ever since he went into politics.

Every indication is that the President, in a showdown, would take and hold a stand in opposition to the activities of the senator.

The President's telegram to the three clergymen who appealed to him against the sweeping "attack" by J. B. Matthews, Senator McCarthy's staff specialist, on Protestant ministers, bares Mr. Eisenhower's position.

The President began by stating he wanted the Protestant, Roman Catholic, and Jewish clergymen to know "at once" that he shared their convictions.

Then he said the issues "here" are clear.

These opening sentences suggest what the President's aides have been saying, that while Mr. Eisenhower would refrain from attacking the senator personally, he would pick some suitable occasion to speak out against McCarthy methods.

Refers to 'Attacks'

The clergymen wired the President about a specific "attack." But Mr. Eisenhower's reply twice refers to "attacks."

This suggests that the President has had in mind several episodes involving Senator McCarthy.

The clergymen's telegram says the Matthews article indicting the loyalty of the Protestant ministry on the Communist issue weakens the position of the church, "the greatest American bulwark against . . . communism."

Mr. Eisenhower's reply, while in full agreement, makes no mention of communism by name, but refers, rather, to the struggle against the forces of "godless tyranny."

On another issue involving Senator McCarthy, the State Department's policy on books in its overseas libraries, the President likewise is being forced into an increasingly public position.

The latest directive by the department, the 12th, announced by Dr. Robert L. Johnson, is one specifically approved by Secretary of State John Foster Dulles and broadly endorsed by the President.

Johnson Is Called

Senator McCarthy has called this new policy "ridiculous," and he has summoned Dr. Johnson to appear before the senator's committee and answer questions about it.

Thus, Dr. Johnson will be speaking, in effect, for the President when he testifies.

It is assumed that Dr. Johnson will defend the new policy, which stipulates that it is the content of books, and not the authors, which will determine whether certain books are placed on shelves of United States Information Service Libraries overseas.

Dr. Johnson's resignation takes effect at the end of the month, and his statement explaining and supporting the new policy is such a strong one as to make it inconceivable that he could back down before the senator's questions.

Should Dr. Johnson do so, President Eisenhower's present position would dissolve, and Senator McCarthy would emerge stronger than ever.

'Time Runs Out'

Such an outcome is not indicated by the President's statements to date, including his remarks at Dartmouth College on "book burners," nor by reports by White House aides on the President's private views about Senator McCarthy, which are said to be very strong.

For instance, an aide was asked whether President Eisenhower's immediate reply to the clergymen had any significance.

He replied: "Time runs out on these things, you know."

On the day that the President and the clergymen exchanged telegrams, Mr. Matthews' resignation as executive director was accepted by Senator McCarthy.

On this same day the senator challenged Dr. Johnson's statement of future policy of United States libraries, saying that he did not see how any book by a Communist author could serve democratic ends.

Senator McCarthy directed Dr. Johnson to "have present the individual or individuals responsible" for the new policy directive.

Leadership Felt

If Dr. Johnson were to carry out this order to the letter, it probably would mean that the Secretary of State and perhaps the President himself would be called upon to appear.

Dr. Johnson at once defended his new policy in his reply to the senator indicating he would testify. Thus, in this case as well as in the Matthews episode, President Eisenhower has now been placed in a position where his influence and prestige will be affected.

The Matthews case suggests that, for the present at least, the President's leadership is being felt.

Mr. Matthews is out, with Senator McCarthy's written expression of "deep regret." And Mr. Matthews' attack on the Protestant clergy is called by the President of the United States "irresponsible" and "contempt for the principles of freedom and decency."

Four letters: Page 12

Purge Looms

By the Associated Press

Washington

Secretary of State John Foster Dulles has ordered the United States Ambassador to Moscow, Charles E. Bohlen, home for consultation on the dismissal of Lavrenti P. Beria from the Soviet Government and Communist Party.

The State Department said Mr. Dulles wants to get Mr. Bohlen's views while the Big Three foreign ministers' meeting is under way here.

By the United Press

Moscow

Secret police chief and First Deputy Prime Minister Lavrenti P. Beria, arrested on treason charges presented by Prime Minister Georgi M. Malenkov, faces trial for plotting to seize leadership of the government and overthrow communism in Russia.

He was stripped of all his power and expelled from the Communist Party as an enemy of the state, July 10.

In his place as Interior Minister was named Sergei N. Kruglov, unknown outside Russia but a man who had held the interior ministry prior to Mr. Beria.

[Western statesmen gravely were pondering whether the reference to Mr. Beria's "capitulatory policy" might be the remarkable peace offensive which Russia has staged in recent months and whether it now is due for a reversal.]

Scrutiny Demanded

Pravda, organ of the Soviet Communist Party, called for a careful and systematic scrutiny into the operation of the internal affairs ministry.

"It is necessary to check systematically and unremittingly the activity of the U.S.S.R. Ministry of Internal Affairs," Pravda said. "This is not only the right but the direct duty of party organizations."

Pravda accused Mr. Beria of selecting men in his ministry on the basis of their loyalty to him while he "wormed himself into confidence and threaded his way to leadership."

Pravda said Mr. Beria was guilty of:

1. Sabotaging the enforcement of the Soviet laws.
2. Becoming a "bourgeois degenerate" and "actual agent" of international imperialism.
3. Attempting to undermine the collective farm system and cause difficulties with the food supply.
4. Trying to cause national animosities among the people of the Soviet Union.
5. Attempting to turn the Ministry of the Interior into a privately dominated force.
6. Advocating a policy of capitulation which might have led to a restoration of capitalism.

Communiqué Issued

The Beria case was disclosed in a communiqué of the Central Committee of the Soviet Communist Party. It said:

"A plenary meeting of the Soviet Communist Party was recently held. After listening to and discussing a report of the presidium of the central committee by G. M. Malenkov as regards criminal antiparty, antistate actions of L. P. Beria intended to undermine the Soviet state in the interests of foreign capital, and manifested in perfidious attempts to place the U.S.S.R Ministry of Internal Affairs above the government and the Communist Party of the Soviet Union, the plenum of the Soviet Communist Party Central Committee decided to remove L. P. Beria from the Central Committee of the Soviet Communist Party and to expel him from the ranks of the party as an enemy of the Communist Party and the Soviet people."

United Press

Georgi M. Malenkov

Associated Press

Lavrenti P. Beria

Sovfoto from Associated Press

Sergei N. Kruglov

West Expects Tougher Russia

By Joseph G. Harrison

Overseas News Editor of The Christian Science Monitor

One great question overshadows all others on the international scene today.

It is whether and to what extent the victory of Soviet Prime Minister Georgi M. Malenkov over his rival for power, former Deputy Premier and secret police head Lavrenti P. Beria, will change the current Soviet policies toward the West, toward international understanding, toward conditions within the Soviet Union itself, and toward the treatment of the satellite nations.

Does the triumph of Mr. Malenkov, generally held to be a rigid follower of Stalin's policy of pushing communization as fast and as far as it could go, weaken the opportunity for an end to the cold war? Does it lessen the chance, so devoutly hoped for by the West, that a period of lesser tension was in the offing?

The first indications would seem to imply that, so far as a lessening of Soviet Bolshevization is concerned, this is a turn for the worse. The fact that the arrested Beria is charged with favoring capitalism, of fostering internal nationalism, of seeking to weaken the collectivization of agriculture, in other words of doing the very things which the West has applauded, are taken as strong indications that left-wing Marxism again is triumphing in the Soviet Union.

In other words, there apparently has been, at least for the moment, a reversal in the trend which the world has noted during the past three or four months—a trend which some had hoped might even result in a less aggressive and more cooperative Russia.

Important Factors

Whether this trend actually has been reversed would seem to depend upon several factors. One of these is whether the struggle between Messrs. Malenkov and Beria was one over power or over principles.

A second is the extent to which Mr. Beria's successor, Sergei N. Kruglov, believes the Soviet people should be held down by repressive measures.

Another is whether Mr. Malenkov, even if he wished to return to the sterner programs followed under Stalin, can do so now that everywhere in the world, inclusive of Russia itself, men have been hoping for less communism and more peace.

For there are those who hold that to attempt to reimpose the more rigid lines of Stalinist Marxism today would create stresses and strains within the Soviet Union and its satellites which would hasten the breakup of that huge empire. Thus latest reports from the Ukraine, the single richest Russian province, tell of a drop in both industrial and agricultural production, a dislocation of urban and rural life, and a general atmosphere of deep dissatisfaction with postwar life in the Soviet Union. With such conditions prevailing, will Moscow, under any ruler, dare to push the people too far in the name of Marxist theory?

Those who have followed the course of world communism most closely during the past few months believe that the following signs should be watched for if one is to anticipate the course which Moscow will follow under Mr. Malenkov:

1. Will there be a reversal of the recent more lenient policies in the satellites? Will the concessions granted to workers in Hungary, Czechoslovakia, East Germany, and so on, be withdrawn and will harsh repressive measures be reintroduced?

2. Will there be an increase in antiwestern, but particularly anti-American propaganda? This would indicate a lessened Russian desire to end the cold war and reach an international understanding.

Was Washington Right?

3. Will such areas of international tension as Korea, Berlin, Indo-China, Malaya, and Austria show a heightened sensitivity?

If any or all of the above-mentioned conditions arise, will this prove that the United States has been correct during the past few months in viewing the new policy of Russian "softness" with a wait-and-see attitude?

This American stand has contrasted with that adopted in Europe, where there has been much hope that a fundamental change had come over the official Russian outlook. Up to now Europe has been inclined to accuse the United States of not being sufficiently receptive to Soviet overtures. Will the rise of Mr. Malenkov show that Washington correctly assessed the situation?

If this is so, many observers believe it will result in a restoration of American diplomatic prestige in Europe, that it will aid in the completion of those Western European military alliances which have languished of late, and that it will greatly strengthen the position of such pro-American European statesmen as West German Chancellor Konrad Adenauer and Italian Premier Alcide de Gasperi.

How Did It Occur?

Among questions most frequently asked regarding the victory of Mr. Malenkov over Mr. Beria is, how did the former manage to pull it off?

Most observers had felt that it was Mr. Beria's star, not Mr. Malenkov's, which had been rising steadily in the Soviet sky. They attributed this to Mr. Beria's control of the MVD (secret police), which, it was felt, gave him a distinct tactical advantage over his rival.

How, it is being asked, did Mr. Malenkov manage to neutralize, or absorb, the power of the MVD? Did he do so through the help of the Army, or did Mr. Beria make some false step which cost him the loyalty of the police commanders upon whom his security rested?

The fact that Mr. Beria has been arrested for "criminal" and "antistate activities," as an agent of "foreign capital," and as "an enemy of the party (Communist) and the Soviet people" clearly indicates, if past Russian performance is any guide, that only one fate awaits him—capital punishment. And his downfall may also bring in its train the downfall of many others as well, for there has been abundant evidence during the past months that Mr. Beria was putting his own men in positions of importance in many areas of the Soviet Union. Thus another drastic Soviet purge may well be in the making.

Possible Strategy

This triumph of Mr. Malenkov has gone far toward restoring the reputation he enjoyed under Stalin as a shrewd, long-range thinker and as an able and ruthless maneuverer. It is now suggested that Mr. Malenkov may well have permitted Mr. Beria to appear to be in a stronger position than he actually was, so that, in the end, Mr. Malenkov could use this as an argument against him.

Thus, Mr. Malenkov may have been able to point to the anti-Communist riots in East Germany, the drop in production in Czechoslovakia, the unrest in Hungary as an example of what happens under "Beriaism."

Related Stories: Page 3

Beria Fall Deals Blow To Revolutionary Myth

By Paul Wohl

Written for The Christian Science Monitor

Exactly four months after Stalin's passing, the Soviet volcano has erupted.

It has claimed its first major victim.

The fall of Lavrenti P. Beria, who for three months was believed to have held the Kremlin in tutelage, is at once a shattering blow to the Soviet legend of legitimacy and to the revolutionary myth of the Communist world movement.

It was Mr. Beria who endorsed George M. Malenkov as Prime Minister before the Supreme Soviet, Mr. Beria who introduced him as the new chief at Stalin's bier. This is the central fact in Mr. Beria's expulsion from the party and in his arrest and impeachment as a traitor. Yesterday it was Mr. Beria. Tomorrow it may be Mr. Malenkov—or Vyacheslav M. Molotov.

Seen in this perspective, the dramatic emergence of the party's 236-men central committee under Messrs. Malenkov and Nikita S. Khrushchev, reinforced by a Muscovite workers' chorus in revolutionary trappings, is of secondary importance. It will take Mr. Malenkov and his associates a long time to repair the authority of party and state, if repaired it can be.

False Front Collapses

From now on personalities once again must come to the fore. The false front of government by a committee has collapsed. Few people inside Russia can have doubted that behind the façade of Communist solidarity Stalin's successors were remorselessly struggling for power. But no one knew when the decision would fall or who would come out on top.

Mr. Beria won the first rounds. He was identified with the multinational principle as opposed to Great-Russian preponderance, with a balanced, conciliatory economic policy as opposed to Stalin's attempt to stamp out the last vestiges of capitalism in the countryside. Both, a multinational line and economic retrenchment have characterized Kremlin policy in recent months.

Nothing indicates that Mr. Malenkov, who in the eyes of real Great-Russians is a Bashkir, a man from the part-Russian periphery, will aggressively raise the banner of Great-Russianism. In the economic field the new Prime Minister has come out strongly for "maximum satisfaction of economic and cultural requirements of the workers."

Far more than Mr. Beria, who for 15 years headed the dreaded secret police, Mr. Malenkov is a spokesman of the large new middle class of managers and technicians. He also has become identified with the younger generation. Only in his agricultural policies, which hitherto have followed those of Party Secretary Khrushchev, has he taken a "tough" and doctrinaire attitude. But that was at the 19th congress last October, with Stalin looking on. Among Stalin's successors such questions are matters of expediency rather than of principle.

According to one source, Mr. Beria lost out when he went to Berlin after the June 17 riots on behalf of the party and the government.

If the report is correct, Mr. Beria may have gone to Berlin with the secret intention of taking over the East German agenda, which hitherto had been Mr. Malenkov's domain, and thereby add to his own power. If he went, he also must have thought that the situation in Moscow was under control.

Mr. Kruglov was Mr. Beria's first assistant even before the war. When the People's Commissariat of the Interior was split for the first time into a People's Commissariat of the Interior and of State Security, Mr. Kruglov was entrusted with the Interior, both commissariats being under Mr. Beria as Commissar General of National Security.

Malenkov Tactics

There have been a few indications in their power race that Mr. Malenkov was drawing ahead of Mr. Beria. Mr. Malenkov's publicized appearance at the Bolshoi theater on June 26, accompanied by the entire presidium of the party was a demonstration which highlighted Mr. Beria's absence from the capital.

The following day, Pravda came out with an attack on the official news agency Tass which is known to operate under the control of the foreign division of the secret police.

On July 7, the government organ, Izvestia, quoting Mr. Malenkov's speech of 1946, came out with a mighty appeal for party unity and a threat that all dissenters would be "crushed." This, it appears now, was the flourish of trumpets with which the central committee was opened where Mr. Beria suddenly found himself under attack.

His fall brings crashing down with him the legend of party unity and orderly succession. The feet of clay of the Soviet Colossus have been heard.

State of the Nation

New Library Directive Restores Esteem

By ROSCOE DRUMMOND, Chief of the Washington News Bureau of The Christian Science Monitor

Washington

The State Department's book-burning mishmash has been resolved constructively, courageously, brilliantly — and past criticism should be turned into esteem.

There is verve, vigor, candor, and bigness in every thought and in every sentence in the new directive governing the government's overseas libraries which Dr. Robert A. Johnson, the Information Director, and Secretary of State John Foster Dulles have drafted and released.

This new directive, written by men with heads up and proudly published, doesn't look or sound anything like that petty, frightened, pusillanimous thing which created the ignominious mess.

This directive makes Mr. Dulles look and sound like a Secretary of State and Dr. Johnson a Director of the International Information Administration—which is natural to them.

* * *

But the catalyst, the foremost influence, the principal corrector of policy who finally rescued the overseas libraries from the hands of fear and timidity and brought them into the democratic sunlight is President Eisenhower.

"Don't join the book burners!" General Eisenhower told the graduating class at Dartmouth College.

And when he returned to Washington and held his next meeting with the correspondents, they disclosed to the President that the State Department already had joined the book burners.

General Eisenhower was frank to say that he wasn't referring at all in his Dartmouth speech to the cleaver-like removal of books from the USIS libraries. He said he hadn't known about it, but enough newspapers were crying out against this shame so that before long everybody knew about it, including the President.

And he did something about it. He did everything that was needed about it. The forecast of what was to come was imbedded in the brief, low-voiced announcement the President made that he was asking Mr. Dulles to come to his office to talk over the matter with him. That's quite a big carpet the President has in his office.

* * *

In spirit and in letter the new directive faithfully follows the views which General Eisenhower expounded at his press conferences.

Vital changes are made.

Neither books nor authors are banned because they are "controversial."

The content of the book will be the principal factor in determining whether a book goes over the line from "controversy" into "conspiracy."

The libraries shall provide "a representative cross section of contemporary American writing," and Dr. Johnson adds with vision that "controversy is as American as the varied sounds in the bleachers of a ball park."

They, of course, will not circulate books propagandizing for communism or calculated to further the forceful overthrow of free government.

And on top of all this it is pleasant to report that the State Department has receded now from its previous untenable and expedient position that the policies governing the overseas libraries and the lists of books either removed from or restored to the shelves were part of "cold war strategy" and couldn't be made known to the American people. Even temporary reliance upon this shabby theory shows what a government official gets himself into when he tries to be disingenuous rather than straightforward. The simple fact was that the new directive wasn't ready, and rather than admit the fact honestly — which was certainly no crime — its spokesman contrived the theory that such information was just too, too hush-hush. The President pulled the rug from under that one, too, when he said he did not hold with any such secrecy.

* * *

But why did this all have to take place in the first place? Why did it take 11 fumbling, faltering directives before this present directive came into being and into force?

Every Washington correspondent knows that Secretary Dulles and Dr. Johnson were trying to please and to appease Senator Joseph R. McCarthy and that to do so they put their names to a directive they didn't believe in. It brought them only trouble. They didn't buy a half hour's breathing space from Senator McCarthy who was quick to characterize the new directive as "completely ridiculous."

It must be encouraging to President Eisenhower, in reading the able Dulles-Johnson declaration, to see how two of his top officials rise to heights when he provides for them the atmosphere of freedom and support which brings out their best.

Defense Opens in Fort Devens Court-Martial

The World's Day

Reg. U.S. Pat. Off.

Bay State: Attempt to Dismiss Charges Fails

After several unsuccessful attempts to dismiss charges and obtain a directed verdict of acquital defense counsel Emanuel H. Bloch opened the defense's case in the unprecedented court-martial trial of Lt. Sheppard Carl Thierman, accused of concealing Communist ties at Fort Devens, Mass. [Page 2.]

New England department store sales for the week ending July 4 were up 5 per cent in dollar volume over the same period in 1952, the Federal Reserve Bank reported. Sales were higher by the same percentage over the June 6 level. In downtown Boston the increase was 9 per cent, while suburban sales slumped 14 per cent in comparison to the July 4, 1952, level.

In Europe: Hogan Wins British Open Golf Title

Ben Hogan, U.S. Open Golf Champion, won the British Open with a final record 68 for 72-hole aggregate of 282. [Page 14.]

East Berlin Communist police shot a West Berliner on the newly reopened East-West border for allegedly trying to talk them into deserting to the West.

A three-member inquiry mission from the International Confederation of Free Trade Unions arrived in Berlin from Stockholm for an on-the-spot study of the East German labor situation.

Washington: Dulles Evaluates Beria Incident

Secretary of State Dulles told a Big Three foreign ministers meeting today that the Soviet purge of L. P. Beria means that "a new convulsion is under way" in Russia. He spoke shortly after the State Department had announced he has summoned Ambassador Charles E. Bohlen home for personal consultation on the ouster of the boss of the Soviet secret police.

Senate-House conferees agreed on a $5,157,232,500 program for foreign aid in the fiscal year which began July 1.

Three members of the Senate Investigations subcommittee, including Chairman Joseph R. McCarthy (R) of Wisconsin, today told Allen Dulles, director of the Central Intelligence Agency, his supersecret organization is neither "sacrosanct" nor immune from investigation.

President Eisenhower signed a bill to ban display of international or foreign flags "in equal or superior prominence" to the American flag, but said he hoped Congress would clarify its language later to avoid international misunderstanding.

The House Ways and Means Committee approved a bill to take the 20 per cent federal tax off tickets to movie theaters. It does not remove the tax from admissions to sports events, legitimate theaters, and other places of amusement.

National: Dewey Denies Published Report

Gov. Thomas E. Dewey of New York denied as "sheer fiction" a published report that President Eisenhower has "let it be known" to him that he would like him to run for governor next year, and that Mr. Dewey acceded.

Far East: Bombers Rush Aid to UN Infantrymen

Waves of bomb-laden American warplanes swarmed to the aid of Allied infantry and artillerymen in the struggle for Pork Chop Hill and Arrowhead Ridge in western Korea.

The American expedition trying to scale Mt. Godwin Austen (K-2) in the Himalayas has begun preparations for the final assault, news reaching Karachi said.

South China's Yunnan Province, hard hit by floods and then droughts early this year, has now been struck by swarms of insects.

Mideast: Israeli-Jordan Border Clash Reported

An armed clash on the Israeli-Hashemite Jordan frontier in the Judean Hills killed two Israeli soldiers and wounded one.

Weather Predictions: Sunny (Details Page 2)

THE CHRISTIAN SCIENCE MONITOR

Registered in U. S. Patent Office

AN INTERNATIONAL DAILY NEWSPAPER

VOLUME 45 NO 204 | BOSTON, MONDAY, JULY 27, 1953 | • • ATLANTIC EDITION | TWO SECTIONS | FIVE CENTS A COPY

COPYRIGHT 1953 BY THE CHRISTIAN SCIENCE PUBLISHING SOCIETY

Calm Reigns on Korean Battle Front As Diplomats Take Over Peace Quest

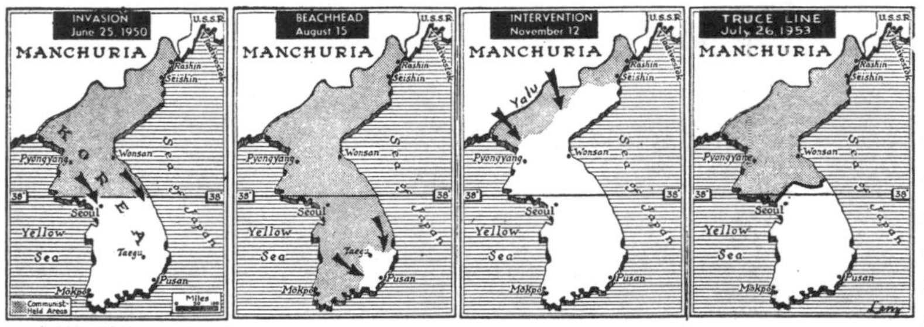

Russell H. Lenz, Chief Cartographer

No Celebrations Greet Armistice

By Henry S. Hayward

Chief Far Eastern Correspondent of The Christian Science Monitor

Seoul, Korea

Quiet hangs over the battlefields of Korea, where for three years, one month, and two days one of history's least decisive wars has been fought.

Fighting flared briefly just before the zero hour—10 p.m. Korean time, 9 a.m. e.d.t. July 27—then ceased abruptly as front-line commanders executed the final order.

And as the dust from Communist artillery barrages began to settle, new activity marked the front-line positions of United Nations soldiers.

Bunkers and fortifications were coming down. Trucks began rumbling up to the front to carry men and equipment back to rear areas.

As the Korean night settled down over the front there was a new feeling of peace—not solid peace, but at least the kind which gave front-line troops a long-sought chance to sleep.

There were no handsprings. For in the words of their top commanders: "It is not the moment for exultation, but for prayer."

Pens held by Lt. Gen. William K. Harrison, Allied chief delegate, and Lt. Gen. Nam Il, Communist chief delegate, at the united signing, scratched across 36 copies of the armistice document in the garish, barn-like structure that had been erected in Panmunjom at 10 a.m. July 27—2 years and 17 days after cease-fire negotiations commenced.

Three hours later, at the base camp at Munsan, Gen. Mark Clark signed 18 copies of the armistice and completed the signing so far as the Allies are concerned. Presumably at Kaesong Communist leaders Peng Teh Huai of China and Kim Il Sung of North Korea likewise have signed their 18 copies.

They refused to come to Panmunjom because the Allies insisted that the free world press be present.

Conspicuously absent at the Panmunjom ceremony were any South Korean representatives. Their absence bespoke their profound opposition to terms of the settlement agreed upon—terms that leave Korea temporarily divided and the northern portion still occupied by one million Communist enemy troops.

At the Munsan ceremony, however, Maj. Gen. Duk Shin Choi of South Korea was present. He declared he came as an observer on unexpected sudden instructions from Syngman Rhee, President of the Republic of Korea. For roughly 400,000 South Korean troops the occasion was not one to celebrate, although, like any soldier exposed to heavy combat, they welcomed the termination of hard fighting.

Grim and Drab

The occasion at Panmunjom was notably lacking in glitter and color. It was grim, businesslike, and drab. Only by remembering that this action affected nearly two million fighting men who have surged up and down this country in bitter battle—and countless millions of others in over a score of nations large and small—could one summon a sense of history.

United Nations military officials representing those countries with fighting or service forces in Korea were present for the ceremony. They sat quietly at one end of the pagoda.

At the other end sat Chinese and North Korean representatives neatly divided into two groups.

Promptly on schedule General Harrison and Nam Il entered the vast unpainted auditorium from opposite doors and marched to tables in the center. General Harrison wore no decorations. General Il was in full regalia with rows of medals.

No Word Spoken

Without a word the two men sat down and commenced signing armistice copies laid before them by aides. As each copy was signed it was carried to a smaller table between the two at which General Harrison and Nam Il sat.

General Harrison's face was grim as he signed. General Nam Il wore his usual bland expression. The two men did not appear to look at each other although occasionally they glanced out of the corner of their eyes.

The Munsan ceremony followed a similar pattern—but without any Communists present. General Clark was accompanied by the Eighth Army commander, Lt. Gen. Maxwell D. Taylor, the naval commander, Vice-Admiral Robert P. Briscoe, and the Air Force commander, Lt. Gen. Otto P. Weyland.

Signing Ceremony

Without a word General Clark signed the documents while General Choi, directly behind him, sat ramrod stiff and staring straight ahead. Within five minutes General Clark finished signing and read a brief statement.

"I cannot find it in me to exult in this hour," he said soberly.

"Rather it is a time for prayer that we may succeed in our patently difficult endeavor to turn this armistice to the advantage of mankind.

"If we extract hope from this occasion it must be diluted with the recognition that our salvation requires unrelaxing vigilance and effort," he warned.

General Clark added, however, that he was thankful "we have stopped shooting" and said this "means much to fighting men and their families and it will allow some of the grievous wounds of Korea to heal."

He emphasized that the armistice was "only a step toward what must yet be done."

The task, he said, "is to put the cease-fire agreement into full effect as quickly as we can and get down to working out an enduring settlement of the Korean problem."

On this note, within eight minutes after the actual ceremony started, the Korean truce was as complete from a documentary standpoint as the UN can make it.

Now it depends on the ability of the statesmen of all the nations concerned to discover answers for the tremendous issues that lie ahead.

Their work will determine whether or not Korea can be unified—and lasting peace finally descend upon this battered peninsula.

Further Details: Pages 4, 5, 11, 12

Bulletin

By the United Press

Panmunjom, Korea

Communist prisoners of war will begin moving out of their camps at once toward the demilitarized zone where they will be handed over to Communist authorities.

A report from Pusan said some of the prisoners held on Koje Island, off the south coast of Korea which was the scene of riots a year ago, will be the first to be moved.

United Press

Waving Flags Greet Korean Armistice

Collective Security in Action

UN Faces Korea Tasks Soberly

By William R. Frye

United Nations Correspondent of The Christian Science Monitor

United Nations, N.Y.

Achievement of an armistice in Korea represents for the United Nations the climax of the world's first experiment with collective security in action.

As Lester B. Pearson, Assembly president, summoned the 60-nation "parliament of the world" into session for Aug. 17 to write an official "finis" on the fighting and to set up a peace conference, diplomats and observers are asking:

Did the United Nations achieve what it set out to achieve on that tense Tuesday in June, 1950, when it voted to repel aggression by military force?

Has collective security—the theory of all for one and one for all—been proven practical in the 20th century?

What problems lie ahead for the UN?

Diplomats and public figures in virtually every corner of the globe—outside the Iron Curtain—are making formal public statements pointing with pride to the UN's "victory" and the "defeat of aggression." UN headquarters is fairly ringing with them.

Express Restraint

In more candid moments, however, and in private, many of these same public figures are much more restrained. The consensus is that the UN was not defeated; aggression did not succeed; but the practical value of collective security has been far from proved—in fact, may have been cast in some doubt. And many serious problems remain unsolved.

The UN's basic objective, as defined on June 27, 1950, was to "repel the armed attack and to restore international peace and security in the area." The "area" was not defined.

Now that an armistice has been signed, with the aggressor roughly where he started—a little further north—the armed attack has been "repelled" and peace has been "restored." But it would take an optimistic person indeed to contend seriously that "security" has been established "in the area."

On Oct. 7, 1950, the Assembly amplified its earlier definition of objectives by recommending that "all appropriate steps be taken to insure conditions of stability throughout Korea." It is clear that this objective has yet to be achieved.

Goal Achieved 'in Part'

Thus diplomats here answer the question, "Did the UN achieve its goal?" with the candid answer: "In part."

To the second—and more far-reaching—question, "Has collective security been proved practical?" the answer given is, "No. The UN still has a long way to go."

Partly because Gen. Douglas MacArthur was never enthusiastically receptive to the dispatch of heterogeneous forces, partly because many nations had other commitments, partly because of inertia and timidity, only 16 countries contributed to the UN police force which went to South Korea's rescue, and the United States' contribution was overwhelmingly the largest. There are 55 non-Communist UN members.

On the credit side of the ledger is the fact that, as a result of the Korean experience, the UN General Assembly now is in a position to circumvent the veto power which the Big Five possess in the Security Council.

Thus if, at some future time, there is universal desire to establish a true international police force, it no longer will be possible for an aggressor to block, or even to seriously delay, such action.

The UN also once again has proved its worth as a peacemaking organ. It was the UN General Assembly which broke the deadlock into which the truce negotiations had fallen on the question of prisoner repatriation. A formula put forward by India and voted by the Assembly was substantially the formula ultimately accepted by the Communist enemy.

Most informed persons also would list, as an important item on the credit side, establishment of voluntary repatriation of prisoners as a new principle of international law. The UN's firm stand that no prisoner of war should be forced home against his will has led now to its acceptance in practice, albeit grudgingly and qualifiedly, by the Communist world. And this instance can be cited as a precedent.

Curbs Terror for PWs

If ever there is again a line-up of Communist and non-Communist soldiers across a battle line, this precedent is expected to be a powerful impulse to Communist desertions.

It closes the books on the picture of World War II prisoners being whipped and driven back across the Iron Curtain from which they had fled to assist or collaborate with Russia's enemies.

Many serious problems lie ahead, however, before the UN can be said to have succeeded in its Korean venture.

South Korean President Rhee's defiance provides one of the major challenges. Another is the possibility of new Chinese Communist aggressions in Asia—notably in Indo-China, or elsewhere in southeast Asia.

United Korea Issue

The whole knotty problem of China lies ahead. The western alliance is deeply split on how best to break up the Chinese-Russian axis. It is clear that the Korean war placed severe strains on this Moscow-Peking alignment. But now this source of strain has been removed.

So far as Mr. Rhee is concerned, the UN is expected to tackle in earnest a question it previously dodged: What are the obligations of the victim state to the world community?

What can be done if the Communists refuse—as they presumably will refuse—to permit a united free Korea?

There is no simple answer. But such questions must be answered before the UN can be said to have restored "peace and security" in the area.

Looking at Asia as a whole, the UN and the free world have before them the immense challenge of restoring "peace and security" to Indo-China, Formosa, Hong Kong, Malaya, and Burma, to mention only the most obvious trouble spots.

The key to the puzzle is Communist China. Great progress in its solution would be made, it is believed here, if the government controlling the hundreds of millions who make up China were disassociated from Moscow's influence and support.

Louisiana Purchase—1953

Louisiana Purchase! Just 150 years ago that great slab of land from Louisiana north to Montana was acquired from the French by the United States. As the sesquicentennial is celebrated, three staff correspondents of The Christian Science Monitor are touring that spreading region to report on the state of the purchase—1953. A series of articles begins today on the first page of the second section.

State of the Nation

The Truce and What Lies Behind It

By ROSCOE DRUMMOND, Chief of the Washington News Bureau of The Christian Science Monitor

Washington

The truce is here.

Is it the "honorable end" to the Korean war which President Eisenhower said he would try to find and which he hopes it is?

Is it the tragic mistake, serving the ends of the Communists and fastening forever a divided nation upon the Korean people, which President Rhee fears it is and hopes it isn't?

Is it a pathway to peace in Asia, or is it a dead-end alley concealing more dangers than it resolves?

* * *

At the moment it is easier to ask than to answer. But here is an attempt to provide part of the answers to some of the questions which cannot fail to be uppermost in the minds of all as the news of the signing of the truce, after 25 months of hard and often interrupted negotiation, comes from Panmunjom.

Q. Why are the Chinese Communists accepting the truce?

A. The reasons usually attributed are that Russia is reluctant to keep up the flow of military supplies (which the Chinese are forced to pay for), that Communist China wants to get on with its economic reconstruction, that the Chinese Communists are convinced they can impose more divisive peace problems upon the free world than the Korean fighting imposes divisive war problems.

Numerous Washington officials have been convinced that the Chinese have eagerly wanted the truce for some time. They figure that China by now has got all it could out of the war; that since there is no chance of conquering South Korea, it is better to pull out and expend its energies elsewhere—either to strengthen itself internally or to push out in another direction.

Q. When all incidental arguments are put aside, what are the central differences between President Rhee and the United Nations?

A. Both agree that there is little prospect of uniting Korea by force of arms. Both agree that there is no guarantee and only a moderate hope that the Communists will accept a united Korea by negotiation.

* * *

The differences between us, then, are these:

In this bleak situation President Rhee considers continuing the fighting—for a united Korea—the least hopeless of all alternatives.

We don't.

President Rhee is willing to take the casualties which continuing or extending the war would mean.

We aren't.

Q. Balancing all factors, is the truce wise?

A. Candidly, nobody is sure. The fact is that nobody in American public life is honestly advocating the measures—almost unlimited military spending, total mobilization, higher taxes or vastly increased debt, new inflation controls, etc.—which we would have to be ready to take if we set out to get a military decision in Korea, extending the war to whatever extent it might be necessary and risking World War III.

* * *

Under these circumstances, the truce seems the only practicable alternative. It is possible that the timing is better than could be humanly contrived. It comes when, inside Russia and inside its satellites, the Kremlin is suffering the most acute dissension and strife. It is possible that its internal strains are imposing upon Soviet policy a wish for peace which is not its normal state. The truce in Korea and the stresses and fissures within the Soviet world may well combine to make a negotiated settlement in Asia attainable. The dominant view here is that it is worth trying, and that, on balance, the truce is desirable.

Q. Do President Rhee's attacks on the truce and his refusal to sign mean that the United States is tied to any wild initiative which he might undertake by himself?

A. No, it's not that bad. We will not support Mr. Rhee in any violation of the truce terms or any aggression on North Korea. He has promised not to obstruct the truce for at least six months. We believe the danger of South Korean violation of the truce in six months will not be great.

Q. Will the United States lose interest in Korea once the fighting is stopped?

A. There is no evidence that we will. We won't unless we lose sight of our own best interests. This week end President Eisenhower asked Congress to earmark $200,000,000 as a first installment toward the economic reconstruction of Korea. It is virtually certain that Congress will approve this week. Obviously some of the savings in military outlay which the truce makes possible should be instantly channeled into rehabilitation, and the sooner the better. The devastation to Korea exceeds our capacity to imagine it—not only the vast and horrible physical destruction, but millions of Koreans have been uprooted and hundreds of thousands of children have been orphaned.

* * *

The quick action to deal with these economic problems, even before the ink is dry on the truce, is the best assurance that America is Korea's ally in peace as well as in war.

Few things could serve the free world more than to have in Korea a healed and reconstructed nation, a strong, peace-serving, dynamic democracy—to which Mr. Rhee will have to contribute some reforms—on the doorstep of Communist tyranny in Asia.

Related Washington Stories: Pages 3 and 10

The World's Day

Reg. U.S. Pat. Off.

Washington: $200 Million for Korea Asked

President Eisenhower formally requested Congress to provide an initial $200 million for Korean relief, as United Nations Commander Gen. Mark Clark announced that the President has authorized him to begin the immediate delivery of 10,000 tons of food to Korea.

The Defense Department anticipates that monthly draft calls will drop 4,000 in about three months if reasonably stable conditions are achieved in Korea within that time.

National: Atomic Energy Plant Workers Strike

For the first time in Oak Ridge, Tenn. labor history, production workers in two atomic energy plants struck to back up wage increase demands.

Europe: Air Cargo of Food En Route to Berlin

The first air cargo of American food for hungry East Germans left Hamburg for West Berlin aboard two DC-4 planes.

New England: Tobey Successor Choice Awaited

Choice of a successor to the late Senator Charles W. Tobey (R) of New Hampshire is awaited in the Granite State as names of five possible candidates for the post received consideration. [Page 2.]

Weather Predictions: Clearing Tonight (Page 2)

New England Takes Truce News Quietly

By a Staff Writer of The Christian Science Monitor

New England's calm reception of the truce news was quite different from the explosive celebration of Allied victories in Europe and Japan—the VE and VJ-Days that had brought wildly cheering crowds into the streets.

Soberness of reaction generally was a measure of the difference between the clearcut victories of World War II and the prolonged deadlock of the Korean police action.

Coming as it did—in the midst of a summer Sunday evening—the armistice news found many families clustered around radio or television sets. Many others were hearing the news on their way home from the mountains or beaches, where they had spent a day not noticeably different from a hundred other Sundays.

Few Crowds

Earlier in the day, many persons had gone to church in an expression of gratitude for the prospective cessation of hostilities and with a prayer for guidance in the days still ahead.

By 9 p.m., the streets of Boston were relatively empty, save for small crowds at Boylston and Tremont Streets and at Scollay Square. Most Bostonians were near radio or television sets to hear the President and other notables speak about the historic occasion, its significance, and its meaning for the future.

Pealing church bells then mingled with wailing air raid sirens, clanging fire bells, and honking automobile horns.

Some people telephoned the newspapers to find out what all the noise was about.

Others, knowing, said they saw little to cheer about. "We didn't win the war," they said.

Others, with sons or brothers in Korea, were jubilant. They talked of how soon their kin would be home, and how grateful they were that the shooting would stop.

Servicemen, for the most part, moved through the streets quietly. At military installations in New England the news was received matter-of-factly.

Governor Herter expressed, on behalf of Massachusetts, "tremendous happiness we feel at this wonderful news, and also a profound humility and thanks to the young men from our state in Korea who have laid down their arms, we trust, for good."

He added: "To those who will never return, we bow our heads and promise to remember, treasure, and profit by their supreme sacrifice on our behalf."

'Not a Guarantee'

In Connecticut, Gov. John D. Lodge spoke of the armistice as "only an opportunity—not a guarantee." He called upon citizens of his state to "show the same responsible vigilance, understanding, and patience which have been demonstrated by our sons who wear the uniform on our behalf."

Mayor Hynes said he was "glad for the GIs in Korea that the hostilities have come to an end, for the time being at least." The Boston Mayor said he is "hopeful that the armistice agreement will be observed."

"Although to me the agreement has ominous undertones," Mayor Hynes said, "it may well be that it will turn out to be a truce that will lead to real understanding in the world."

The Rt. Rev. Henry Knox Sherrill, Presiding Bishop of the Protestant Episcopal Church, said, "While the future is still greatly clouded, we can all thank God that an armistice has been signed. At least—and it is a great deal—the daily loss of life is at an end."

Rabbi Samuel I. Korff, secretary of the Council of Orthodox Rabbis of Greater Boston, said, "Our thoughts turn to those who have made the supreme sacrifices for the glory of God, the love of the United Nations and the service of humanity. We pray that their sacrifices be not in vain."

THE CHRISTIAN SCIENCE MONITOR

Registered in U. S. Patent Office

AN INTERNATIONAL DAILY NEWSPAPER

VOLUME 46 NO. 146 | COPYRIGHT 1954 BY THE CHRISTIAN SCIENCE PUBLISHING SOCIETY | BOSTON, TUESDAY, MAY 18, 1954 | K | **—ATLANTIC EDITION | TWO SECTIONS | FIVE CENTS A COPY

Reds March Against Hanoi As Molotov Muffles 'Nyet'

By Edmund Stevens
Staff Correspondent of The Christian Science Monitor

Geneva

An atmosphere of guarded expectation prevails here as the Geneva conference goes into restricted session on Indochina for the second consecutive day.

[The French High Command has announced the first official news that a Vietminh Communist army of 30,000 men is marching on the Red River delta, last French bastion in northern Indochina.]

The man of the hour is Soviet Foreign Minister Vyacheslav M. Molotov, whose amiability May 17 led western delegates to believe he might seriously mean to find a solution. The second meeting is expected to show whether this reading was warranted.

When French Foreign Minister Georges Bidault, fully backed by his western colleagues, pressed his previous plea that Cambodia and Laos get separate, special treatment and that withdrawal of the Vietminh invading forces from these two kingdoms be the starting point of a gradual cease fire throughout Indochina, Mr. Molotov's reaction, though somewhat vague, was far from his usual curt "nyet" manner and indicated a willingness to bargain and to jettison the Communist phantoms of Khmer and Pathet Lao in return perhaps for something more substantial elsewhere.

Maps Unrolled

Likewise, when M. Bidault again, with support of western representatives, insisted again that a cease fire and political settlement should be treated separately, Mr. Molotov, without actually renouncing his previous stand that at least some political issues be settled in connection with a cease fire, agreed to discuss such details as zones of concentration of contending forces.

At this point, maps were unrolled and the delegations summoned their respective military experts with a view to setting up a subcommittee to work on details.

Allied observers believe that the issue of whether the cease-fire and political-settlement aspects of the Indochina question should be dealt with separately is a subject of debate in the Communist camp, with Mr. Molotov inclined to make concessions, whereas the Chinese and especially the Vietminh, after recent victories in the field, are in no mood for compromise.

Thus, in trying to meet any western demand on this point, Mr. Molotov must make a special effort to bring his eastern allies along with him. Significantly, at the May 17 meeting he acted as spokesman for both Communist China and the Vietminh.

Prior to discussing the substance of the cease-fire question, the meeting spent its first two hours in a rather heated discussion of snags in the evacuation of Dien Bien Phu wounded.

The western allies repeated their charges that the Vietminh command was discriminating against Vietnamese wounded, refusing to let them be evacuated along with the French, that they had failed to make the air strip serviceable, and that, by demanding suspension of air activity over Highway 41, main road from Dien Bien Phu toward Hanoi, had sought to exploit the prisoner issue to facilitate movement of heavy equipment for an attack on the Red River delta. The Communist side replied.

But instead of prolonging the argument it was agreed that simultaneous negotiations on the subject would be conducted between the respective commands on the spot and between French and Vietminh delegates here at Geneva.

This last was a concession on the part of the French, who hitherto had steadfastly refused to deal directly with the Vietminh, which they do not recognize. Ever since the French raised the issue of evacuating the wounded early in the conference, before the fortress fell, Mr. Molotov had been trying to use it to force the French into negotiations with the Vietminh.

On May 17, M. Bidault, with his western colleagues concurring, decided to give in on this for the sake of the Dien Bien Phu wounded, who at last count included more than 2,000 stretcher cases, only 11 of which have so far reached Hanoi.

Eyewitness sources confirm that the May 17 restricted meeting was completely informal and the speeches brief and to the point, although the absence of simultaneous interpretation and consequent consecutive interpretation of everything into three languages slowed down the proceedings.

Two Allies Stiffen

While the start of the French-American talks in Paris on the subject of Indochina has somewhat miffed the British—first because they were not informed thereof in advance and, second, because they fear such talks may prejudice the chances for agreement here—other observers believe that signs of renewed determination in both Paris and Washington not to write off Indochina, but to prevent its engulfment by the Communists, may be having a sobering and salutary effect on the Communist delegates here.

Proceeding from the presumably valid premise that the Soviet Union is anxious to avoid a spread of fighting which could lead to a general conflagration, it is believed Mr. Molotov's present mood of seeking a settlement is genuine.

Soviet delegates and reporters in private conversations have also been most emphatic on this point, thus indicating that the desire to prevent a third world war, which all parties share, is the most powerful incentive toward agreement.

Policy Rift Grows In Bonn Coalition

By the Associated Press

Bonn, Germany

A rift in Chancellor Konrad Adenauer's four-party coalition government has been widened by growing belief in West Germany that the European Army project is finished and that some quick alternative must be found to win back German sovereignty.

The break in the pro-West Chancellor's governmental ranks came from a revolt by the rightist Free Democrat Party.

The Free Democrats announced May 17 after a stormy conference with Mr. Adenauer that "the future resumption of German diplomatic relations with the Soviet Union is necessary."

Stalled Army Hearings Put Spotlight on Major Conflict

The Washington Scene

By William H. Stringer
Chief of the Washington News Bureau of The Christian Science Monitor

Washington

It is well to see just what is at stake in the perplexing move and countermove which have, temporarily at least, halted the Army-McCarthy hearings in Washington.

President Eisenhower had every constitutional right to wrap the same cloak of inviolability around executive conferences, documents, and meetings that has been extensively employed by other Presidents from George Washington down to Harry S. Truman. The real problem and confusion derives from the reaction of the subcommittee senators, Democrats and Republicans alike, to this action, and the behavior of Senator Joseph R. McCarthy (R) of Wisconsin.

The Democrats threw down the first challenge to the presidential order—strange conduct for members of a party which for 20 years throve on the zealous employment of presidential prerogatives. The Republicans, of course, welcomed the opportunity suddenly offered by Senator McCarthy to get the damaging hearings off the television screen.

Senator McCarthy says he cannot adequately pursue his case—cannot adequately question and cross-examine—if the presidential order stands. But it is important to note that the presidential order does not in any way prohibit the disclosure of conversations, sessions, or communications between members of the legislative department and members of the executive branch. All that it prohibits is disclosure of conversations and sessions within — purely within—the executive branch.

Room to Continue

The present Army-McCarthy dispute chiefly concerns relations between an Executive Department, the Army, and a legislative organ, the McCarthy subcommittee. There is no ban on testimony about these relations. Questioning could go right ahead regarding what Army counsellor John G. Adams said to subcommittee counsel Roy M. Cohn, and vice versa. Or regarding those so-far-suppressed monitored phone calls between Mr. Cohn and Army Secretary Robert T. Stevens' office. All of the immediate principals and subordinates can testify all about the alleged McCarthy-Cohn request for preferential treatment for Pvt. G. David Schine, and all about the alleged Army attempt to blackmail Senator McCarthy and Mr. Cohn.

As for the possibility that Mr. Stevens was not acting on his own in developing his case against Senator McCarthy, it would be surprising indeed if he did not seek, and receive, advice and perhaps a directive or two from the administration in which he is an official. It might be useful if the President could see his way to modify his order to the extent of permitting Mr. Adams to admit just that.

But what Senator McCarthy would like to get on the record is that there is a great "plot" to be exposed here, larger than a mere Army "blackmail" concerning Messrs. Cohn and Schine, and master-minded from high levels.

He is apprehensive that six months ago a high-level decision was made within the administration to allow Senator McCarthy's investigating techniques to weave a web of circumstances around him that would gradually checkmate, immobilize, and discredit him.

Something is happening to him, he knows: opinion polls indicate a dwindling popularity. The hearings are hurting him. And now comes the President's order to checkmate his penetration—past and planned—into the executive area. Belatedly restoring the executive prestige, Mr. Eisenhower is behaving like a strong President.

To break out of this web, Senator McCarthy perhaps still hopes to silence the hearings before he or Roy Cohn ever have to face a major grilling on the subcommittee's witness stand. But that failing, he would like to use his cross-examination time at the hearings to explore and prove the existence of a high administration strategy against him, perhaps under the direction of Attorney General Herbert Brownell. And he would "expose" such a strategy, not as a mere effort to cut down his investigative excesses, but as an administration "plot" to halt his investigation into Communists within the government.

'McCarthy for President'

The White House is aware of what is at stake in all this. This is an inflammable issue, and Senator McCarthy presents the major national challenge to President Eisenhower's leadership. A "McCarthy for President in 1956" organization is setting up shop in Washington, although Mr. McCarthy has written to its organizer that he prefers to concentrate on being a senator "at this time."

By a remarkably slow process, Mr. Eisenhower has moved to checkmate the Wisconsin senator.

It is being argued that the President would have avoided the present confusion and controversy if he had acted to halt the erosion six months and more ago. But he now, at last, has acted—vigorously.

It will be interesting to see whether the subcommittee senators now support Senator McCarthy in his desperate effort to turn the tables on the administration strategists, for that is what is being attempted. Or whether, when the chips are down, they support the President.

United Press

INDOCHINA WAR HEROINES: Brigitte Friange (left), French war correspondent, who parachuted into Indo china fighting zones with French Union forces on several occasions, and Capt. Valerie Andrée, of the French Army, honored for piloting a helicopter in front-line areas to evacuate wounded French and Indochinese soldiers. Miss Friange is in the United States for a TV appearance.

Political Meddling Charged

India Curbs Missionaries

By Gordon Graham
Special Correspondent of The Christian Science Monitor

Calcutta

The whole pattern of Christian mission work in India, built by generations of missionaries from overseas, is today in danger of severe curtailment.

This has been brought about in the short period of one year by the political activities of a minority of European and American missionaries who have allowed their zeal for the progress of their flocks to make them not only pastors but political advocates.

In the remote hills of Assam, for example, a group of American Baptists who have been working among the Naga hillmen for 80 years, have become identified with the Nagas' unacceptable demand for independence from New Delhi.

Similarly, in Madhya Pradesh, central India, the state government has formed a committee to inquire into the allegedly unfair methods of conversion employed by missionaries in aboriginal areas.

The result is that missionaries wishing to come to India are very often refused visas, while missionaries returning to the West may not be permitted reentry. This trend is the reverse of events from 1947 to 1952 when the number of non-Indian Christian missionaries in India increased from 2,271 to 4,683. The Government of India has not revealed the current figure, but the presumption is that it is either on the decline or static.

[Prime Minister Jawaharlal Nehru said May 18 his government's objections to foreign missionaries are based solely on political grounds, not religious, according to the Associated Press.

[During a foreign affairs debate in Parliament, he said Christianity is one of the oldest religions in India and foreign missionaries had done excellent work here, especially in education and social welfare.]

Money Lure Seen

Behind the opposition to foreign mission work is the hard core of Hindu conservative thought, which notes with alarm that thousands of Indians, mainly Harijans (formerly untouchables) and remote, underprivileged tribes are adopting the Christian faith. This proselytization, the Hindus challenge, is not genuine. In the words of B. D. Khaitan of Calcutta, "our people are poor and they fall a victim to the allurements of money and this is how hundreds of thousands of our brethren have been compelled to accept Christianity."

In Parliament, recently, Miss Maniben Patel, daughter of the late Sardar Vallabhai Patel, made similar accusations claiming that missionaries concentrate on "poor illiterate people and small children."

In the hands of Prime Minister Jawaharlal Nehru and Home Minister Kailas Nath Katju, who are responsible for the Government of India's official policy, the extreme Hindu attitude is tempered. India is a secular state and there is no opposition to Christianity, the government makes clear, but it would prefer, it implies, that Christianity should be propagated by Indians.

Numerical Stress

The 100 mission organizations in India, many of which are administered by Indians although they include missionaries from overseas, rest their case squarely on the Indian Constitution which states: "All persons are equally entitled to freedom of conscience and the right to profess, practise, and propagate religion."

They draw particular attention to the use of the word "persons," which shows that these rights are not confined to Indian citizens.

The pity of the situation is that those missionaries who concentrate on numerical proselytization and may use questionable means to achieve this are a very small minority. But this minority is undermining the acknowledged achievements of the others who give education, medical aid, and social service without aiming at conversion beyond the voluntary response of those who may admire the Christian example.

The emergent trend is that Christianity in India, like most other things, is becoming subject to a policy of national self-sufficiency, and those Christian organizations which are most deeply Indianized have the best chance of growth. This gives a head start to the Roman Catholic Church, which appointed the first Indian Cardinal last year.

Decision on Schools Finds South Poised

By Bicknell Eubanks
Staff Correspondent of The Christian Science Monitor

Dallas, Texas

What to do about the Negro and public schools in the South now rests with state and community.

A judicial revolution which has been sweeping the South since 1930 has been all but completed. There still will be a lot of litigation on both sides. But any future suits will be aimed at postponing or adjusting to the foregone conclusion that segregation will be completely abolished in good time.

First reaction to the Supreme Court decision on the part of southern leaders has been one of caution and temperateness over the large area affected, with serious defiance centered in Georgia and South Carolina. Governors of nearly every state involved said they would call special legislative and administrative groups into session at once. Gov. Herman E. Talmadge of Georgia was the only one to say flatly that his state would refuse to accept the decision, but Gov. James F. Byrnes of South Carolina had said as much earlier, and now said he was "shocked" by the decision.

'Years to Comply'

The task now is to get the Constitution, as interpreted, into everyday practice.

As many of the South's leaders point out, the answer will depend on the amount of community action and responsibility which the South imposes on itself.

This holds for Negroes as well as whites, it is pointed out.

All sides agree that it will "take years to comply" with the Supreme Court decision. The high court itself appears to recognize the need for ample time to survey the full import of its decision, described by Dr. Charles Johnson, president of Fisk University in Nashville, Tenn., as the greatest advance in, racial relations since the Emancipation Proclamation.

Gov. Allan Shivers of Texas reflects the generally temperate view taken by most southern chief executives. Mr. Shivers, chairman of the Southern Governors Conference and former chairman of the National Governors Conference, points out that the ruling on time and method of enforcement, still to be announced, are "all important."

"I hope that it can be worked out so as not to cause damage to the schoolchildren and that the children themselves will not be placed at a disadvantage," the Governor explains.

In the Deep South, where a heavy preponderance of the southern Negro population makes the problem more acute, one state legislator feels that the delay on the part of the Supreme Court in completing its decision will "be helpful in allowing a period for emotions to subside."

He is Representative George W. Howell of Aberdeen, Miss., who has played a major role in legislative debate on state public school problems. Mr. Howell is a member of the 25-man advisory committee set up by Gov. Hugh White to study the legal and educational problems of bringing Mississippi's public school system up to a more efficient level. It was originally designed to set up a program for making public school facilities for Negroes equal to those for white children. The program is scheduled to go into effect July 1.

Similar Plans

Governor White indicates he will go ahead with the program as scheduled. He calls for coolness and careful thought.

Still pending for action by a possible special session of the Mississippi Legislature — which some members expect the Governor to call in light of the court decision — is a proposal by Walter Sillers, Speaker of the House, for an amendment to the state Constitution which would permit the Legislature to turn the public schools over to private corporations. Appropriations would be made to individual pupils by the state to pay for their tuition. The Sillers plan has drawn heavy fire, however.

Similar plans exist in Georgia and South Carolina.

"It would be a terrible folly if southern politicians make good their threats to turn the public schools over to private interests," Hodding Carter, editor of the Greenville, Miss., Delta Democrat-Times, declares in an editorial on the court decision.

Mr. Carter considers it "significant" that all sections of the country and shades of economic and political beliefs are represented in the unanimous opinion of the Supreme Court. He observes that the decision comes as no surprise to those who have followed the trend of high court opinions on southern racial problems. He considers it a major American victory in the ideological war with world communism and writes that from a practical point of view, it should be a great help in establishing solid and friendly relations with the yellow and brown races of Asia.

The South must keep calm and not get excited, he cautions, and he points out that southern states have brought the decision on themselves by "violating" the terms of their own Constitutions which call for separate but equal facilities. Instead, he points out, Negro children have been put in schools much inferior to those for white pupils.

Slow Process Seen

Another liberal southern editor, Harry Ashmore of the Little Rock, Ark., Arkansas Gazette, expects integration to be a slow process. In his book, "The Negro and the Schools," based on a study by the Fund for the Advancement of Education, financed by the Ford Foundation, and published just a few days ago, Mr. Ashmore predicts a "rather lengthy" transition period, which might require thousands of separate law suits in districts not covered by the five test casts before the high court.

In addition, he writes, a pattern of voluntary segregation, enforced by "public pressure," might keep separate Negro and white schools going in many areas for many years. On the other hand, he suggests that where small Negro populations, such as in mountain areas, make separate schools a financial burden, segregated schools probably will be dropped without much fuss.

South studies ruling: Page 10.

State of the Nations

The Constitutional Issue

By JOSEPH C. HARSCH, Special Correspondent of The Christian Science Monitor

Washington

In assessing President Eisenhower's order closing to senatorial eyes the books on the meeting of Jan. 21, at which members of his staff discussed the relationship between the executive establishment and Senator McCarthy of Wisconsin, it is first necessary to dismiss as trivial and intended only for the political record the protests made by Democrats.

These Democrats cannot, and do not, intend to have themselves taken very seriously when they question the propriety and even the duty of the executive establishment to protect the confidence of its own internal deliberations. The same Democrats were on the other side of the fence within recent years when the President in the White House was a Democrat. Without implying any unusual political behavior to these Democrats, it must be taken for granted that their role in this affair is only to emphasize the existence of a division within the rival Republican Party between the President and some of its members in the Congress.

The issue is joined in this case not between the major political parties but between the President and Senator McCarthy.

The next step in clearing away the debris to get at the heart of the matter is to be clear about what happened on Jan. 21. It was a meeting of high officials of the executive establishment—Sherman Adams of the White House staff, Herbert Brownell, Jr., the Attorney General, Henry Cabot Lodge, Jr., a close personal political adviser to the President in addition to being an ambassador at the United Nations, and John G. Adams, a counsel to the Department of the Army.

The subject of discussion at that meeting was the relationship of the executive establishment of the government toward the McCarthy hearings. It was a White House political strategy conference. It considered how the executive establishment should conduct itself toward the pressures which at that time were bearing upon the Department of the Army from Senator McCarthy.

The President now has declared that deliberations of this sort are the private and exclusive property of the executive establishment. The Attorney General has backed this declaration with precedents from George Washington to Harry S. Truman. The heart of the President's argument is continued in the statement that:

". . . It is essential to efficient and effective administration that employees of the executive branch be in a position to be completely candid in advising each other on official matters. . . ."

The fact that Senator McCarthy is assertedly hunting Communists is as irrelevant to the real issue as the mock protests of the Democrats. It doesn't matter whether the senator is hunting Communists, butterflies, or troglodytes. The thing that matters is whether the members of the President's personal staff can discuss problems of internal administration privately, and therefore candidly, or must always be subject to the possibility of congressional review of everything they have said and done.

The senator now contends that the current Senate hearings cannot be brought to a proper conclusion if the discussions of Jan. 21 are to be kept secret from the senators conducting the hearings. This

Justus, Minneapolis Star

Difficult Enough Without a Handicap

may or may not be the case. However, it is clear that the executive branch of the government cannot maintain the independence entrusted to it by the Constitution if its internal deliberations are to be opened at the will of Congress to congressional scrutiny.

If the President were to open the Jan. 21 records to Senator McCarthy, and to the Cheshire Cat Democrats (who do not really want them opened), he would be throwing away not only his presidential heritage but also abandoning an essential feature of the Constitution which he is under oath to protect. That too-little-read document states that "the executive power shall be vested in a President of the United States." If the President were to open the private deliberations of the executive branch to congressional scrutiny at congressional direction, then the executive establishment would cease to be executive; instead, it would become an instrument of the Congress.

If that happened, the United States would cease to be governed under a system of coordinate and coequal branches of government; it would be governed by an all-powerful parliament of which the presidential office was an appendage.

The end result of such a development in the United States might be strong government by the parliament, as in Britain, or weak government by the parliament, as in France, or something in between, but it would not be government as provided in the Constitution and as intended by the founding fathers.

The issue is the independence of the executive establishment from the Congress. Is the President master in his own household, or is the Congress the master not only of the legislative, but also of the executive establishment? That is the issue on which President Eisenhower has decided he must stand as his predecessors, including Herbert Hoover and George Washington as well as Harry S. Truman, also decided that they had to stand.

Stockbrokers of Italy Stage Protest Walkout

By a Staff Correspondent of The Christian Science Monitor

Rome

Strikes are so popular in Italy in the sunny springtime one never knows who or what will strike next.

Latest to follow suit was the highly conservative and affluent profession of stockbrokers. Instead of staging one-day protest strikes like Rome's municipal transport workers who left the citizens stranded on April Fool's Day, for several days the stockbrokers forced exchanges throughout Italy to close down and brought all trading in securities to a virtual standstill.

So as not to be confused with working-class agitation, the brokers did not call their action a strike. They simply explained they had decided to suspend operations indefinitely for fear of the probable adverse impact on security values of the latest government proposals for putting teeth into income tax enforcement.

The provision to which the brokers most strenuously object is one that would require them to prepare and produce daily statements of their market operations listing clients' names and the amounts involved. The government's purpose in presenting this measure is to plug one of the present major loopholes for legal tax evasion.

Hitherto Italian investors have managed to avoid reporting their profits from securities transactions simply by instructing their brokers to hold the shares for them without effecting any formal transfer of title—in Italy, stock certificates are made out in the owner's name. The brokers insist that the requirement of statement greatly would curtail the volume of trading besides causing a general market slump.

They have further charged that as long ago as last October the gist of the government proposals with reference to stock transactions had been leaked to certain persons and that this advance knowledge had enabled such persons to reap handsome profits. The implication of this charge is one of carelessness if not deliberate dishonesty on the part of certain Finance Ministry officials.

As a further complaint the brokers declared that the additional bookkeeping involved in the preparation of daily statements would unduly complicate their operations and add to their overhead.

Such is the excitement stirred up by the mere publication of the government's tax enforcement proposals to Parliament. It looks like the kickoff for an intensive campaign to defeat the measure; the effort doubtless will reach its maximum some weeks hence when Parliament begins debating the controversial proposals. It is not hard to imagine the amount of pressure that will be exerted both on single deputies and on whole party groups by opponents who even at this early stage are prepared to tie up the country's stock exchanges indefinitely.

Reds Close Ranks

By the Associated Press

Moscow

The eight Communist nations represented in the Soviet-sponsored European Security Conference have called for integration of their armed forces and establishment of a joint command if the West ratifies the Paris accords to rearm West Germany.

The conference, snubbed by the western powers, ended its work Dec. 2 by adoption of a declaration to this effect.

Communist China's observer, Chang Wen-tien, said his country threw its full support behind the eight-nation declaration.

A Soviet Union marshal is expected to be named supreme commander.

Solid Pledge, but . . .

U.S.-Formosa Pact Lets Peking Guess

By Gordon Walker

Chief Far Eastern Correspondent of The Christian Science Monitor

Tokyo

Asian defense experts here are waiting further word on just how far the United States is prepared to go to defend Formosa from Chinese Communist attack.

They point out that Secretary of State John Foster Dulles' statement announcing a new American - Formosan defense pact still leaves several questions unanswered.

Washington, it would appear from the Dulles announcement, is prepared to accede to President Chiang's recent demands for some sort of solid commitment.

It even is willing to go as far as to serve notice on Peking that in event of attack United States military forces will retaliate.

What appears to be noticeably lacking in the defense pact, however, is any firm commitment on the extent of retaliation—notably where, when, and in what force.

Quemoy Position Veiled

It also is left to the Communists to guess whether or not the United States would take any significant commitment if Communist amphibious forces were to try to seize Quemoy, the Tachen Islands, or any of the other coastal islands aside from the Pescadores, which comprise Formosa's secondary line of defense.

What appears to be happening there roughly is this:

Peking, through its recent tentative attacks on Quemoy and the Tachens, has indicated it is engaged in a preliminary testing operation to see how far the United States will go to underwrite defense of Formosa.

The United States, rather than submit to the charge of being merely a paper tiger, now is prepared to buttress its hitherto verbal military commitment with a slightly more solid formal type of military backing, but not of the type which forewarns the Communists that "if

you cross this line you risk World War III."

Just how much the embryonic theory of coexistence has played in Washington's new formal agreement with Formosa is difficult to assess.

Coexistence Set Back

It seems fairly clear here that while coexistence may be considered a feasible possibility vis-a-vis the Soviet Union, here in the Far East it still is a distant prospect which has been recently set even further back by Peking's insupportable conviction of 13 Americans for alleged espionage plus the Chinese Communist Government's continued series of provocative military acts in building up North Korean airfields against armistice terms, attacks on Nationalist-held islands off the Chinese mainland, and continued military support for the Vietminh.

It seems more likely from this observation point that Washington's thinking is conditioned far more by military practicalities.

It would be a relatively simple matter on paper for the United States to pledge all-out support for General Chiang's Nationalist armies in event of attack.

But it would be an entirely different matter if in carrying out that pledge the United States fleet should engage Communist forces in the Formosan Straits and one or more capital warships of the Seventh Fleet should be sunk in the process.

Such a possibility is viewed in Far Eastern capitals, including probably Peking, in the light of the following frequently asked question: "Would American public opinion figure Formosa was worth it, and would the Eisenhower administration be willing to risk another Korea?

U.S. closes gap in Pacific chain of treaties: Page 3.

British scan U.S.-Nationalist China pact: Page 10.

State of the Nations

The Churchill Touch

By JOSEPH C. HARSCH, *Special Correspondent of The Christian Science Monitor*

Washington

Sir Winston Churchill has not chosen to explain precisely why he picked this period of history, when the world is full of talk of coexistence and he himself favors a spring meeting with the Soviets, to disclose the details of his precautionary measures taken in 1945 against the Soviet military advance westward in Europe.

The statement of what he then did has shocked some of his compatriots and brought him editorial reprimands from most of the responsible newspapers of his own country. But, be it noted, he was reprimanded not so much for what he had done in 1945 as for disclosing it in 1954. The charge against him is that it was unwise to disturb the atmosphere of today by recalling his deep distrust of the Soviets in Europe on the eve of victory in Europe and the measures he then took to halt their military advance as far westward as lay within his power.

It may sound slightly unorthodox, but I submit that the Churchill remarks of this period are just as prudent as were the actions which he took in 1945, and that this controversial disclosure exhibits the extraordinary instinct Sir Winston Churchill possesses for dealing with the great currents of power which ebb and flow through this world of ours.

It was prudent because nothing in modern history has ever challenged an old and basic assumption about Soviet behaviorism: That Soviet power is a commodity which flows like water wherever there are no barriers either natural or man-made to check the flow.

In 1945 this was certainly true. The collapse of the German armies removed ancient barriers to the westward flow of Moscow's power and it was pouring into all the empty lowlands lying before it. Sir Winston almost alone in those days urged the

farthest possible eastward advance of western armies. He drove Field Marshal Montgomery's armies as fast and far as they could go along the Baltic coast. He was prepared, we know now, to rearm the Germans themselves, if such a step had proved necessary to erect barriers against the Soviet flow.

One of the arguments used against Churchill policies at that time was that such action would exhibit lack of confidence in an ally and might cause resentment in Moscow. Yet there was no evidence at

tional disturbance and resentment in Moscow is to assume that the men who run Soviet foreign policy make their decisions on a basis of human, emotional reactions. Such assumptions were not supported by events in 1945. They will not, I think, be supported by events in this year, or next.

What has happened is that Sir Winston has given all of us a practical example of how to combine "coexistence" with prudence and, to use his own word, vigilance.

It was both prudent and vigilant on his part in 1945 to be prepared even to rearm Germans, if necessary, in order to fix a limit to the westward flow of Soviet power. To disclose this story now is to exhibit to Moscow an example of a prudent attitude.

It certainly would not be prudent for the West to base its policies toward Moscow on the assumption of an emotional affection between eastern and western worlds. Moscow does not respond to such human qualities as affection, trust, confidence, gratitude any more than does a river. Soviet power is impersonal. It knows neither gratitude nor resentment.

What Sir Winston has done by his so-called "indiscretion" is to remind the men of Moscow that the West can also be impersonal, prudent, and practical. It can shun atomic war. It can be willing to experiment with coexistence. But at the same time it can remember the necessity of 1945 to erect barriers against the westward flow of Soviet power.

The reminder tends, I think, to put the trend of western policy into balance, like Teddy Roosevelt's favorite combination of soft words and a big stick. Sir Winston probably made his remarks more out of instinct than out of intent. Time will, I think, confirm the soundness of his instinct.

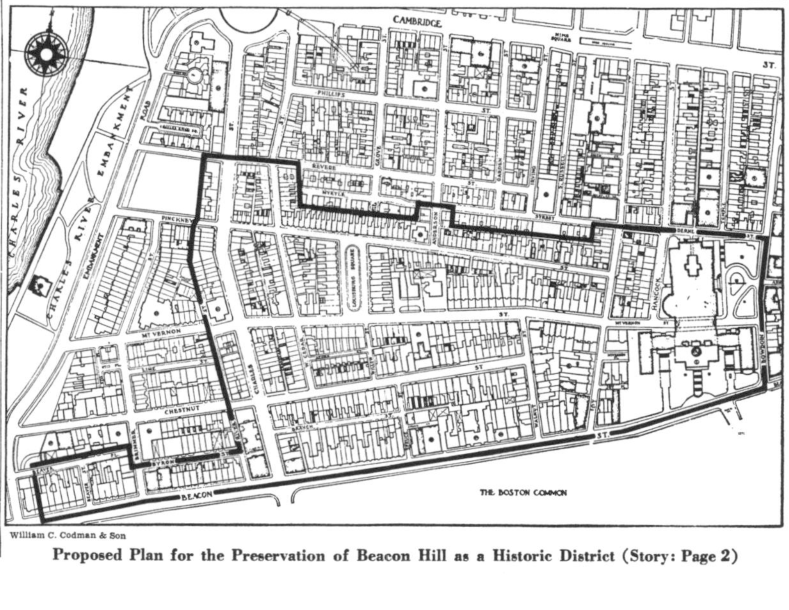

Ceylon's Prime Minister Greeted in New York

Sir John Kotelawala, Prime Minister of Ceylon, is welcomed to New York's Idlewild Airport by James O'Brien, representing Mayor Robert F. Wagner. The Ceylon leader will visit the White House and tour America as Mr. Eisenhower's guest. Story: Page 5.

Associated Press

Missionary Trend: International Units

By Betty Driscoll Mayo

Staff Writer of The Christian Science Monitor

The era of American missionaries dominating foreign missions and institutions is over.

In drawing this frank conclusion, foreign missionary officials of the National Council of the Churches of Christ in the U.S.A. point out that the American missionaries' job is not finished. But, they add, the new pattern will be sharing the work with nationals of other countries.

The Rev. E. Bruce Copland, associate secretary of the National Council's Division of Foreign Missions, commenting on this situation, states that there is resistance to any one national group to missionaries in a country.

In India, for example, if a team of all Americans—or all of any other country—were to come in, it would be resisted. National pride is touched off when foreigners play too prominent a role, he indicated.

New Trend Cited

The old concept in America, the Rev. Mr. Copland said, is that of a missionary taking Christianity and Christian civilization to the rest of the world. He contrasted this idea with the new trend of exchange of

missionaries, which is a pattern catching hold within the younger churches in Asia.

Invitation of a young Indian student to come to that country is typical, he said.

C. I. Itty, a student at the Union Theological Seminary in New York, belongs to the Syrian Orthodox Church. He told a division session Dec. 1 of his call by the Indonesian National Council of Churches to work among university students.

'World Level'

This is truly the beginning of an ecumenical era and the end of the old missionary era, he said, when the Indonesian church, of Dutch Reform background, asks one who is not even a member of a Protestant church to come and work in its field.

Working with Mr. Itty as an international team were missionaries from the United States, Australia, the Philippines, Holland, Switzerland, Germany and India. "Christianity was on a world level, with no one country or color predominating," he said.

Of equal importance, along with the exchange of missionaries, are the lay missionary efforts by many different countries —an example of new emphasis in the Christian missionary field.

At one of the sessions, a representative of the Canadian Council of Churches said the council is interested in the question of the nonofficial missionary—the representative of business or industry who goes into a country with the consciousness that he can be a Christian missionary in an unofficial way by his Christian dealings with the nationals and others of the country.

'Christian Witnesses'

Indonesia, it was pointed out, needs engineers. Australian engineers have been willing to go to that country and be paid the prevailing wage of Indonesian engineers, with the viewpoint of going "as Christian witnesses through their work," the council was told.

England, too, it is reported, is trying to send abroad Christian conviction to work abroad — often to countries where they would not be accepted as regular missionaries.

Although America is reported to be slow in developing this phase of the nonofficial missionary, there are some evidences of this activity.

For example, in Nepal, a Foreign Missions Division report states:

"Where large-scale Christian worship is forbidden, the members of the American Technical Cooperation Mission meet regularly on Sunday, and a letter says, 'The high government officials . . . seem to respect us for such worship.' In another capital city, the ambassador said, 'I have always noticed a difference in the morale and general spirit of the American colony when there is a strong Union Church there.'"

'Prestige Suffers'

These "profound impressions" are attributed to "the quiet testimony of the religiously motivated lives of such congregations, and the sense of the importance of worship. . . ."

At the same time, however, the division reports:

"It is a tragic truth that the prestige of this country has suffered a serious slump in recent years. Part of this is due to the mere fact of our economic and political power, which is viewed with fear or jealousy or both. Part of it is due to Communistic propaganda. But too much of it results from the attitudes and actions of many individual American citizens — business and professional people and tourists."

Related stories: Page 8.

Censure Vote Sets Precedent, Raises U.S. Prestige Abroad

By Richard L. Strout

Staff Correspondent of The Christian Science Monitor

Washington

Profound consequences to American politics will flow from the Senate censure vote of Senator Joseph R. McCarthy (R) of Wisconsin.

The McCarthy issue split the Republican Party down the middle while leaving the Democrats a solid unit in the 67-20 vote.

The methods and attitude of Senator McCarthy are simultaneously condemned by his colleagues and peers in the Senate.

Only three times in Senate history has the easy-going body censured a member. Though the Wisconsin senator professes to carry the result jauntily, the shadow of having been condemned by his own colleagues in the Senate "club" will be difficult to efface.

The last senator censured, Hiram Bingham, a Republican from Connecticut, did not seek reelection. Senator McCarthy's term expires in 1958.

The Senate action will have profound consequences abroad. Americans who have visited foreign countries are aware of the impression Mr. McCarthy has made on Europeans. Foreigners not conversant with American affairs or aware of the steadiness of constitutional processes, have viewed so-called "McCarthyism" with deep and exaggerated misgivings.

U.S. Critics Stirred

Critics of the United States, and even its friends, have been stirred by the apparent freedom of Senator McCarthy to make his own rules unchecked. It is no exaggeration to say that reports of "McCarthyism" have been one of the most unfavorable factors to the United States abroad. Foreigners will interpret the overwhelming vote in the Senate against him as indicating that Senator McCarthy's influence is less than they had supposed and American institutions stronger than they realized.

The effect of the censure vote on the investigation of communism in the United States

should be to alter the procedures but not the basic determination to expose Communist infiltration. Senator McCarthy will lose his chairmanship of the Senate Government Operations committee, in any case, to the Democrats. Aside from campaign oratory, few responsible observers believe that Democrats are not as hostile to Communist infiltration as Republicans. The work will go on.

The consequences of the Senate action upon Senator McCarthy himself are problematical. He announces that he will push his continuing investigation after the Senate recesses and until the Democrats take over in January. Whether he can get a quorum under the new circumstances remains to be seen. A large majority of his colleagues condemn him for having done violence to the repute and dignity of the Senate and for having brought the chamber into disrepute. It is a grave offense in the eyes of fellow senators who jealously guard

their prerogatives and dignity. Whatever Senator McCarthy does in the remaining years of his Senate service, this condemnation will remain.

Finally, the Senate action sets a precedent of disciplining a member. Both advocates and opponents of the action agree that this is a new field. Opponents of the action have said, and with justice, that in many respects the proposal is unprecedented. Now there is a precedent. Only time and the Senate can tell whether this marks the beginning of a closer watch on the actions of individuals and committees by the chamber — the only upper house of a democratic legislature in the world that has increased its power in the generations. Most upper houses have shrunk in power or disappeared.

Republicans Split

The most striking immediate development is the split in the Republican Party.

The first tentative vote to censure was 67 to 20. On it Democrats were solidly for censure (as they were on every anti-McCarthy vote taken in the first series). The Republicans, however, split 23 for the motion and 20 against.

Even more significant—the top GOP leadership, led by Senator William F. Knowland (R) of California, took Senator McCarthy's side. This seemed to be the final burning of the bridges by Senator Knowland in his new relation to the White House. He has split emphatically with President Eisenhower and Secretary of State John Foster Dulles on foreign affairs. Now he has come down on the side of Senator McCarthy in domestic affairs, while the pro-Eisenhower Republicans almost universally voted against Senator McCarthy.

A congressional leader who takes an independent line from the President of his own party is a new thing in American politics. Normally the majority leader would resign. Senator Knowland shows every indication of staying. When he voted against the Bricker amendment last year Senator Knowland symbolically left the majority leader's chair to indicate that he was adopting an independent course. In his vote against censure, however, he was in his chair. The Eisenhower wing of the party will not try to oust Mr. Knowland, which illustrates how weak the support for the President i. on certain controversial issues.

Midwest Supporters

Analyzing the 20 "pro-McCarthy" Republicans, only three came from states east of the Appalachians. The others were primarily the Midwest isolationists with a sprinkling of other senators.

Senator Knowland's action left the chairman of the committee, Senator Arthur V. Watkins (R) of Utah, in a grim mood. The committee senators were dragooned to take the unwanted assignment and reluctantly assented to Senator Knowland's appeal. He said after their appointment that he would trust

Senator Watkins

Senator McCarthy

Senator Knowland

his life to their fairness. Now, however, Senator Knowland has voted against the Watkins committee report, on the side of the man whom they had condemned.

Explaining his vote, Mr. Knowland said that he had reached it "prayerfully." He based it on the argument that an unwritten statute of limitations covered Senator McCarthy.

The Knowland speech changed the strategy of the minority leader, Senator Lyndon B. Johnson (D) of Texas. He rose to the defense of the Watkins committee. The "real issue," he declared, was whether other senators "will permit abuse of a duly appointed committee seeking to carry out the will of the Senate."

Senate Is Tense

The scene of the final voting was as tense as that for the first ballot in a presidential nominating convention.

Galleries were jammed.

Senator McCarthy fought to the last and brought in "forgery" charges at the last minute, which did not interrupt the voting though they caused the appointment of a two-man committee—Senators Homer Ferguson (R) of Michigan and Walter F. George (D) of Georgia—to investigate.

A whitewash substitute resolution by Senator Everett McKinley Dirksen (R) of Illinois was defeated 66 to 21. It set the tone for what followed. Democrats stood solid and Republicans were about evenly split.

How Senate voted: Page 19.

McCarthy says public isn't fooled: Page 19.

India May Seize U.S. Military Cargo

The World's Day

Reg. U.S. Pat. Off.

Asia: Two U.S. Ships Detained in Bombay

Military cargoes carried by two United States ships now in Bombay port may be confiscated by the Indian Government on grounds that the Indian Sea Customs Act of 1878 prohibits bringing in or taking out of India any military stores. The United States consulate in Bombay declared the cargoes were merely in transit from one United States Government agency to another in United States lines. [Page 20.]

Washington: Senate May Weigh Nominations

President Eisenhower's nominations of a new atomic energy commissioner and two high defense officials were lined up for possible Senate action today at the windup of the session called to consider censure charges against Senator McCarthy (R) of Wisconsin. Also awaiting Senate consideration were promotions for more than 10,000 military officers.

Boston: Council of Churches Elects Blake

The Rev. Eugene Carson Blake, Stated Clerk of the Presbyterian Church in the U.S.A., Philadelphia, was unanimously elected president of the National Council of the Churches of Christ in the U.S.A. [Page 9.]

Middle East: Soviets Sign Pact With Iran

The Soviet Union signed a pact with Iran agreeing to settle Iranian war debt claims (11 tons of gold and $8,000,000) and iron out frontier differences dating back to Czarist times.

National: Assembly of the States Opens

Officials of the states got together in Chicago to talk over their common problems. The occasion was the start of the biennial Assembly of the States. The meeting is sponsored by the Council of State Governments, an organization that serves as a clearinghouse of information on governmental subjects.

Europe: West Defense Pact Debate Delayed

Foreign Affairs Commission of the French National Assembly turned down Premier Pierre Mendès-France's plea that debate on ratification of the Paris agreements on western defense begin Dec. 14. The commission decided instead to propose beginning debate Dec. 20.

Americas: Economic Parley Near Adjournment

The first Inter-American Economic Conference in Quitandinha, Brazil, headed for adjournment today on a friendly note. The United States pledged financial help to Latin America but kept a firm hold on its purse strings.

Weather Predictions: Cold Tonight (Page 2)

Cambridge map —

Proposed Plan for the Preservation of Beacon Hill as a Historic District (Story: Page 2)

William C. Codman & Son

THE CHRISTIAN SCIENCE MONITOR

Registered in U. S. Patent Office

AN INTERNATIONAL DAILY NEWSPAPER

VOLUME 47 NO. 63 | COPYRIGHT 1955 BY THE CHRISTIAN SCIENCE PUBLISHING SOCIETY | BOSTON, WEDNESDAY, FEBRUARY 9, 1955 | CENTRAL EDITION | TWO SECTIONS | FIVE CENTS A COPY

State of the Nations

Weakness in Moscow

By JOSEPH C. HARSCH, Special Correspondent of The Christian Science Monitor

Washington

It is not a happy or encouraging thing that on the heels of a further reduction in the United States arms budget we learn that Moscow has raised the Soviet arms budget by 12 per cent and has decreed a new "Iron Age" of emphasis upon heavy industry at the expense of consumer goods.

It is as though an olive branch extended from Washington had been answered by more tanks from Moscow.

Inevitably under such circumstances there is an immediate and perhaps entirely justified assumption that Moscow's brief indulgence in a "breathing spell" had been brought to an abrupt end in a new burst of arms production. There is an ominous overtone in such a development, and one can only regret that the Muscovites have withdrawn what appeared to be an investment in less danger in the world.

This Is the Greatest All-Steel Breadbasket in Existence!

However, just as the happy interpretations placed upon the period of emphasis on consumer goods in Moscow may well have been overdrawn, it is also possible that the meaning behind the 12 per cent raise in the Soviet arms budget is not quite as alarming to the outside world as it may sound on its face.

It is never easy for westerners to know what is going on inside the Soviet state and never possible to know the real reasons behind the major policy decisions of the Kremlin. At best, the West can only grope and guess. But the speeches and announcements made during the current meeting of the Supreme Soviet in Moscow suggest internal as well as external reasons for what is happening and that this renewed emphasis on heavy industry may be a reflection of weakness rather than a reflection of new menace.

For example, Nikita S. Khrushchev, first secretary of the Communist Party and a man who appears to have become the most powerful figure in the Soviet hierarchy, made a speech to the central committee of the party on Jan. 25 which contained some extremely interesting assertions. One was that the Soviet Union has less livestock today than it had in 1928. Another statement was that sometimes as much as a fourth of the Soviet grain crop is lost through delayed harvesting, due in turn to insufficient machinery. The proposed Khrushchev remedy for all this was that his country should imitate the United States and go in for a corn-hog program designed to double livestock production over the next six years.

Add to the above that the new Soviet budget calls for a major increase in government bond purchases by the public, and also a campaign to raise savings accounts.

Note finally that under the now discredited Malenkov "relaxation" policy, Soviet wages were raised and prices reduced.

What happens when a government raises wages, cuts prices, and fails to increase food production? The only possible answer is that under such circumstances the public tries to buy more food than is available.

But does an assertedly all-wise government admit that it has offered its people an improvement in the standard of living which it is incapable of providing? The answer, of course, is no. Instead, it revives the old bogey of foreign menace and thus shoves off the blame for its own shortcomings on the imaginary enemy. Then, of course, it must try to take back some of the extra purchasing power granted in a moment of over-optimism and seek once more to raise productivity to the point where more food and consumer goods can, in fact, be provided.

If a fourth of the grain crop is sometimes lost due to insufficient machinery the answer is more machinery before there can be more food.

Obviously, this is not the whole explanation of the new Soviet budget. This would explain only a renewed emphasis on machinery production, not the 12 per cent boost in the arms budget; unless the arms budget is only a cover for the deficiencies in the agriculture and consumer goods programs. But there may be reasons for the arms budget boost less immediately alarming than would appear on the surface.

For example, the Soviet Union undoubtedly has the largest conventional army in the world. It has vast numbers of divisions of infantry equipped with beep guns and the most numerous artillery of any country in the world. But western armed forces are well along toward reorganization on a new basis. Has the Soviet Army become obsolete? It never was demobilized after World War II. Is Moscow under the necessity of reequipping its vast armies at the same time that its economy is struggling under the impact of higher purchasing power on lagging production of food and consumer goods?

One can only ask the questions. We do not know the answers. But just as we may have been unduly cheerful about the consumer goods phase of Soviet development, we may be unduly alarmed about the change of direction in Moscow. It is not happy news. It may be dangerous news. But it is not necessarily dangerous. It could mean that the new regime in Moscow is in serious difficulty on its home front.

Tougher Kremlin Policy Forecast As Bulganin Replaces Malenkov

Associated Press

Marshal Nikolai A. Bulganin

Associated Press

Nikita S. Khrushchev

Associated Press

Vyacheslav M. Molotov

Associated Press

Georgi M. Malenkov

By Ernest S. Pisko
Staff Writer of The Christian Science Monitor

Less than two years after Georgi M. Malenkov became Soviet Prime Minister he has relinquished this post to Defense Minister Nikolai A. Bulganin under circumstances which strongly suggest a toughening of domestic as well as foreign policy.

The announcement of Mr. Malenkov's resignation was read to the Supreme Soviet Feb. 8.

Mr. Malenkov himself was present at the session. An Associated Press report from Moscow said that when the announcement was made "a gasp of surprise swept through the diplomatic and press galleries."

The statement said:

"I ask you to release me from my post as First Chairman of the Council of Ministers in order to strengthen the Council of Ministers with people who are of more experience, because my lack of experience has had a negative influence on work in the economic sphere."

Downfall Foreseen

What is the meaning of this event? First of all it should be said that Mr. Malenkov's downfall was expected. It had been forecast for some time by most students of Soviet affairs.

Right from the beginning, it had been obvious that Mr. Malenkov's position in the Council of Ministers could not be compared with the position Stalin had held.

At the time of Stalin's passing, March 5, 1953, Mr. Malenkov was First Secretary of the Communist Party. A few days after he had become Prime Minister he relinquished the leadership of the party to Nikita S. Khrushchev.

This was not simply following the Stalin pattern, because Stalin was the supreme authority in all sectors of Soviet life and the persons in charge of the various top offices always remained strictly subordinate to him.

Watched Carefully

In contrast, when Mr. Malenkov gave up the party leadership to Mr. Khrushchev, this evidently meant that his colleagues in the Politburo were careful not to allow any of their members to accumulate too high a degree of power.

It also appeared evident that the new Prime Minister's performance would be carefully watched by four of the deputy Prime Ministers—Mr. Khrushchev, Marshal Bulganin, Vyacheslav M. Molotov, who assumed the post of Foreign Minister, and Lavrenti P. Beria, Interior Minister and chief of the secret police.

The Soviet leaders at that time gave the impression they were attempting a "government by committee," something that never in history has worked for any length of time.

It didn't work in Moscow, either.

Although the reports about the so-called Beria case are full of contradictions, and many of the details are obscure, it seems reasonably safe to assume that the former police chief, who had proposed Mr. Malenkov for Prime Minister, tried to take the top place.

How far Mr. Beria's scheme had grown out of personal ambition and how far it was the result of strong differences of opinion regarding the domestic and foreign political course of the Soviet Union, no outsider can say. Whatever the motive, part of Mr. Beria's plan leaked out, and all other members of the Politburo joined in a common front against the dangerous rival.

Laid to Malenkov

After Beria's elimination, the committee of strong men was reduced to four.

Soon indications multiplied that the next round would be fought between Mr. Malenkov and Mr. Khrushchev. Judging from all accounts, these two men seem not only very different in temperament and character but also in their views regarding the economic program of their country and the tactics to be used in dealing with the non-Communist world.

Mr. Malenkov is considered the chief advocate of a "soft course."

Difficult as it is to pinpoint the responsibility for any decision on a single person, it seems that the temporary thaw in the cold war after Stalin's passing was due to Mr. Malenkov's initiative. Without abandoning the ultimate aims of Soviet communism, he may indeed have thought it was necessary to relax East-West tension and to increase the production of consumer goods in order to fulfill a fraction of the promises which Stalin made to the Soviet people in a succession of back-breaking and austere five-year plans.

Mr. Khrushchev is considered chief advocate of a "hard course," or perhaps, it might be better to say, of unrelenting dynamism.

He is more a man of direct action than Mr. Malenkov and he proved this efficiency in the merciless manner in which he enforced farm collectivization in the Ukraine in the 1930's and mobilized partisan resistance against the German Army in the same area during the war.

Farm Policies Differ

Probably the fundamental difference between Mr. Khrushchev and Mr. Malenkov concerned Soviet farm policy. Food production in the Soviet Union still is insufficient to meet the demands of a population growing by roughly 3,000,000 every year. In some respects it has not been able to rise beyond the level of 1928 and in some it is at about the level of 1913.

In part these conditions are due to unwillingness of the Soviet peasants to produce under the terms imposed upon them by the government. In part they are due to lack of mechanized farm implements, lack of fertilizer, and backwardness in agricultural methods.

Mr. Khrushchev a few years ago tried to tackle the farm problem by establishment of "agrogorods"—that is, by merging of a number of collective farms into giant supercollectives where the farmers would be under the constant close supervision of party functionaries and where their position would correspond exactly to that of a factory worker.

This program ran into so much opposition from the farmers as well as from some members of the Politburo that it had to be shelved.

It is unlikely, however, that Mr. Krushchev has dropped it for good, though for the time being he has embarked on a new program to raise food production by granting the farmers higher prices for their crops and by plowing up millions of acres of virgin land.

The latest plan foresees cultivation of a total of 70,000,000 acres in parts of the country that heretofore have lain barren.

Powers Relocated

This farm program put a heavy drain on Soviet manpower at a time when East-West relations in Asia have come close to the breaking point and when the prospect of West German rearmament threatens to upset any Soviet plans for further expansion in Western Europe.

Under these circumstances, it seems plausible that Mr. Khrushchev had a legitimate interest in cutting down the stature and influence of Mr. Malenkov, who as Prime Minister was tied up with "normalization" in the diplomatic field and higher living standards for the Soviet people.

The exact relocation of power in the Council of Ministers is a matter of conjecture. It seems certain that Mr. Malenkov's share has been drastically curtailed and that most of what he has lost will be Mr. Khrushchev's gain.

The relocation of industrial power can be sketched with greater assurance. There will be more tanks, more tractors, and fewer television sets. The crucial question is, whether there also will be more food.

Malenkov statement: Page 6.

Britain ponders Moscow outcome: Page 12.

Bonn, Brussels Weigh Bulganin

By the Associated Press

"Election of Nikolai Bulganin (as new Soviet Prime Minister) can be very bad for us," a high West German official declared. Federal Chancellor Konrad Adenauer and his foreign-policy advisers were studying the Moscow events closely.

Members of the Belgian Parliament generally considered the news as a "hardening" of the Soviet regime in the Stalin pattern.

U.S. Reacts Gingerly To Soviet Big News

By Neal Stanford
Staff Correspondent of The Christian Science Monitor

Washington

Washington could not help reacting to the big news from Moscow. But most of the quotable reaction was something less than profound—such as "Developments have to be watched carefully," and, "This could be serious."

Most of those in a position to say something significant were not talking. President Eisenhower and Secretary of State John Foster Dulles held their fire, presumably until whatever they said could have some real meaning.

Usually well-informed sources in the capital, it can be said, showed surprise at the timing and method of Georgi M. Malenkov's demotion, but not at the result. They had never accepted his elevation to Prime Minister as final, and they do not now accept Marshal Nikolai A. Bulganin's promotion as more than a stopgap. They tend to feel that the man to watch is the First Secretary of the Communist party, Nikita S. Khrushchev—the man who nominated Marshal Bulganin for Prime Minister.

Malenkov Blamed

There have been signs for months that Mr. Malenkov was slipping and Mr. Khrushchev's star was rising. Somebody had to take the blame for the disastrous agricultural situation in the U.S.S.R.; someone had to be the scapegoat for the new "guns for butter" policy; somebody had to be the "fall guy" for the loss of Soviet prestige in the world struggle between the United States and Communist China.

When Mr. Khrushchev and Foreign Minister Vyacheslav M. Molotov, so the argument goes, pointed their fingers at Mr. Malenkov in a Politburo showdown, the Prime Minister found he had nothing to point back at them. Mr. Khrushchev, as Communist Party leader, had the secret police at his call. Mr. Molotov, who is trusted by the Army, had the Soviet divisions. So Mr. Malenkov had no choice but to go gracefully to his disgrace or suffer the fate of Beria.

There seems little doubt here that Mr. Khrushchev has consolidated his power by this move. Marshal Bulganin is a political general—a party man. How long he will last as Prime Minister is anyone's guess. But the best guessers here give him only a year or two before Mr. Khrushchev repeats the tactics of his mentor Stalin and eases himself into the top job in the Kremlin.

Reactions to this political shift in Moscow came from all over the United States. Former President Truman, out in Kansas City, Mo., was quoted as saying it could be an improvement, for "things can't get any worse in Russia."

George Kennan, former policy planning chief in the State Department and ex-Ambassador to Moscow, would only comment at Princeton, N.J., that "I'm not surprised." Friends of his say he has always been a little amused at efforts to cast Mr. Malenkov in the top role and rather considered Mr. Khrushchev the real Soviet leader since Stalin.

Senators Wary

At the Capitol, senators began limbering up for comment not long after the announcement. Typical were the following:

Minority Leader William F. Knowland (R) of California: "I believe developments have to be watched carefully. Prudence would dictate that we not forget the lessons of history."

Senator Mike Mansfield (D) of Montana: "Khrushchev is undoubtedly the man behind the whole setup."

Senator Alexander Wiley (R) of Wisconsin: "This indicates a ferment is working. No man is wise enough to say what will happen tomorrow."

Senator John J. Sparkman (D) of Alabama: "This could bode trouble for us if Bulganin and Khrushchev are more insistent on closer cooperation with Communist China as reported."

Defense Secretary Charles E. Wilson fell back on his old definition of the Formosa crisis in describing the Bulganin flash: "Just another ripple" as far as United States long-range defense planning is concerned.

It is not entirely correct to say that Secretary Dulles had no quotable views for the day. Trapped by correspondents in a corridor of the State Department, he was allowed to escape only after giving the following: "We have been expecting something like this. There have been signs of internal trouble. I have nothing further to say. Sorry. I have nothing further to say."

One angle of this bloodless palace revolution that intrigued Washington was the fact it was—so far—bloodless. Whether it would remain so was the absorbing question. But the most immediate and interesting reaction to this upheaval was that the headlines went to the wrong characters. Whereas Malenkov and Bulganin hit the headlines, it was Party Leader Khrushchev who hit the jackpot.

Arms Headlined

Moscow Budget Blares Warning

By Paul Wohl
Written for The Christian Science Monitor

The outstanding feature of the vast new Soviet budget just submitted is armaments and more armaments.

This fact, coupled with the choice of a military man as new Prime Minister of the Soviet Union, is one hardly likely to decrease world tension or to further the chance for lasting peace, in the opinion of those whose daily task it is to follow internal Soviet developments.

By stressing their country's war potential and announcing their determination to increase its military might, Soviet leaders have sounded a double warning: a warning to the United States and its Atlantic allies and a warning to the officialdom and other articulate elements of the population.

The former is related to Moscow's campaign against the Paris agreements and to the Chinese conflict; the latter quashes hopes of those "woebegone theoreticians," as First Party Secretary Nikita S. Khrushchev recently called the unrepentant advocates of abundance for the Soviet consumer, whom the new budget is to convince that the course definitely has been set in the direction of bigger and better arsenals.

For the first time since 1952, the Soviet Union has increased its military budget. It is to be 112,100,000,000 rubles, 1,700,000,000 rubles less than in the peak year of 1952.

Tenuous Relation

Its share is now 19.9 per cent of the total, compared to 17.8 per cent last year, 20.8 per cent in 1953, and 23.9 per cent in 1952. It is true that the increase is not very great, that ever since 1947 the military outlay has gone up and that its share in the total has risen steadily.

But after the somewhat lower military outlay of the first two post-Stalin budgets, a return to the upward trend was not expected. Nor is there any explanation for the exceptionally high allocation of 34,000,000,000 rubles for "scientific research" — about one-third more than last year's budget provisions for transportation.

According to Finance Minister Arseni Zverev's report, developments on the international scene have made it necessary to strengthen the "defense capacity" of the country.

Yet the relationship between the military budget and the defensive capacity is a tenuous one. United States and European experts have mustered evidence from official sources which shows that the military budget covers only a very small part of the U.S.S.R.'s defense spending. Recent disclosures of Maj. Ivan Miroshnikov, a former Soviet ordnance officer, indicate that these calculations actually were below the mark.

This means that the Kremlin did not have to ask the Supreme Soviet to vote a military budget 12 per cent larger than that of 1954 because Marshal Bulganin's Defense Department needed an additional 12,000,000,000 rubles.

False Comparisons

The larger defense appropriations were demanded because the Kremlin wanted to bring home to those concerned that the political climate has changed. For propaganda purposes Moscow still likes to compare the much lower share of defense allocations in its own budget with the share of defense spending in the American budget.

This has been a steady theme in the Finance Minister's reports since 1948. This year Soviet propaganda suggested facetiously that American military spending now accounted for 65 per cent of the budget, while in the Soviet Union the share of defense expenditures was still less than one-fifth.

In fact, the two budgets do not compare. Pensions and compensations for veterans, which represent a large share of the American military budget, come in the Soviet Union under the heading of "social-cultural appropriations." Soldiers' families are taken care of out of local budgets. The building of arsenals, barracks, airfields, etc., figures under "general construction." Expenses on military schools are paid out of the amount allocated for general education.

Percentages Analyzed

Prices of military equipment and ammunition are fictitious. In 1943, the even then low prices for arms and munitions were cut in half. In the same year, armament, shipbuilding, and aviation enterprises were freed from the turnover tax which under Soviet conditions sometimes more than doubles the price. These facilities have not been withdrawn; they remain in force.

The extent to which other industries contribute to defense expenditures was shown in a study by Prof. Gardner Clark of Cornell University, which assembles evidence to the effect that in 1937, 23.2 per cent of the total iron and steel output of the Soviet Union was used for munitions and 24.7 per cent for construction of a military nature. In the following year, close to 60 per cent of the country's total iron and steel output went to the military establishment, while appearing in the budget mainly as "capital investment."

Soldiers' Pay

Another difference between the American and Soviet military budgets is the low pay to Soviet soldiers. Whereas the American private receives around \$80 a month, the Soviet private, in accordance with the old continental system, receives only pocket money amounting to 17.5 rubles, or \$4.35 at the official rate of exchange.

On this basis, the pay of the Soviet Union's more than 4,000,000 soldiers would represent approximately 0.7 per cent of the total defense budget. The corresponding figure for the United States would be close to 10 per cent. The actual figures are different because Soviet officers, always in accordance with the old continental system, are fairly well paid. A captain, for instance, receives 800 rubles a month, 47 times as much as a private, whereas in the United States this relationship would be approximately five to one.

The low cost of maintenance also is an important factor. Whereas the United States Defense Department pays market prices for food, Soviet ordnance receives food out of state reserves at the nominal price which the government pays the collective farms for compulsory deliveries.

During maneuvers, the upkeep of the armed forces is at the charge of local authorities. A substantial part of the Soviet Army is stationed abroad at the expense of the satellites. Financially, the additional 12,000,000,000 rubles voted by the Supreme Soviet for the military budget is a mere drop in the bucket. Its political significance, however, is considerable.

News Background In Three Series

Vital questions of international interest are currently discussed in three 10-article series in The Christian Science Monitor.

Today on Page 2: "Red Chinese Giant."

Friday: "New Germany: Will Democracy Win?"

Monday: "Social Democracy and Western Defense: Is Marx in Moth Balls?"

Molotov Flays U.S.

By the Associated Press

Moscow

Foreign Minister Vyacheslav M. Molotov has bitterly arraigned the United States, declaring it guilty in China of aggression "which must be condemned by the United Nations if the UN wants to retain its respect."

He added that the Soviet Union regards Formosa as "undoubtedly the territory of the Chinese People's Republic."

Mr. Molotov delivered a major statement of Soviet policy before the joint session of the Supreme Soviet Feb. 8. He accused the United States of capturing Formosa and the Pescadores, the stronghold of Nationalist China's Generalissimo Chiang Kai-shek now being threatened by the Chinese Communists.

The Soviet Foreign Minister, in effect, repeated previous Soviet pronouncements on the tense Far East issue, but he repeated them with marked emphasis.

"We believe," he said, "that troops should be withdrawn from the Far East, and then peace will be established."

Apparently he meant American and Chinese Nationalist troops.

"While the attitude and position of the United States in the Far East leads to the increasing of tension, the attitude of the Soviet Union is for reducing tension there," he said.

In words reminiscent of the days of Stalin, Mr. Molotov accused the United States of seeking world domination—"They want to spread the capitalistic system over the whole world, and this means preparation for war."

He said the western capitalist countries, under United States leadership, want to "turn back the people's democratic countries to capitalism" and to restore capitalism in the Soviet Union.

But he said such attempts would fail, that communism moreover was making great strides in "the people's liberation movement against colonialism" in Asia. He forecast that such movements would also come to pass in Africa and that the "colonial imperialist powers will not be able to stop these movements."

"Along with India, Indonesia and Burma now have established republics and thrown out colonialism," Mr. Molotov said. "We now hope that Pakistan as well as Ceylon will find its path to real national freedom and economic survival.

"In the Near East we can say that the Arab countries have not progressed as much in development as the countries of the Far East. But it is obvious that soon it will be impossible to strangle the national liberation movement in the Near East as freely as they (the western powers) are doing it now with the peoples of Africa.

"The continents of North and South America are now standing aside from that road on which the people of Europe and Asia are moving forward. But the iron curtain with which they want to isolate the American people from other people is not so strong as it seems to be."

THE CHRISTIAN SCIENCE MONITOR

Registered in U. S. Patent Office

AN INTERNATIONAL DAILY NEWSPAPER

VOLUME 47 NO. 110 COPYRIGHT 1955 BY THE CHRISTIAN SCIENCE PUBLISHING SOCIETY BOSTON, WEDNESDAY, APRIL 6, 1955 CENTRAL EDITION TWO SECTIONS FIVE CENTS A COPY

First High-Level Purge Bared by Peking Chiefs

By Frank Robertson
Special Correspondent of The Christian Science Monitor

Hong Kong

The Chinese Communist Party has undergone its first major purge since coming to power, and official Peking Radio has indicated that others may follow.

An official communiqué also disclosed that the Peking regime for more than 12 months has kept secret the fact that the party's central authority was openly challenged during 1953 for the first time.

The principal purge victims were Kao Kang, who until his sudden disappearance over a year ago was counted among the top three or four Chinese Communist leaders, and Jao Shushih, until his downfall a powerful figure in high party councils.

They were charged with having conspired to seize power of the party and state.

The communiqué announcing expulsion of the two leaders stated that Mr. Kao refused to admit his guilt and took his own life "as a complete expression of his betrayal of the party."

The fact that Mr. Kao was not made to confess is most unusual, and if indeed he did take his own life on a question of policy or principle it would suggest that the rift within the party leadership was quite a serious matter.

Purge Kept Secret

Messrs. Kao and Jao, the communiqué stated, planned to "seize the supreme power of the party." Mr. Kao refused to admit his guilt, the official announcement said, and took his own life, though when this occurred is not stated. Mr. Jao's downfall, it seems, came several months later.

Peking kept the facts of the purge secret for so long, it is believed, in order to allow time for stringent measures to be taken to prevent the spread of disaffection. The time lapse certainly suggests strongly that the leadership was seriously concerned.

A rigorous campaign aimed at tightening discipline, combating disunity, and exacting unquestioning obedience at all levels was set in motion by party theoretician Liu Shao-chi in February of last year, and the reason for this now is apparent. This campaign lasted through most of 1954 and it is interesting that during this time all party members were required to study Chapters 10 and 11 of a Short History of the Soviet Communist Party (Bolsheviks) which deal with events in the Soviet Union that led to great purges of 1937 and later.

The report on the Chinese-Communist purge was delivered to the fifth plenary session of the party on April 4. The report stated that Kao Kang, who was both political and military administrator of Manchuria, regarded his region as his own independent kingdom. Mr. Kao was transferred to Peking in 1953 following his appointment as chairman of the state planning commission and at this time the report stated his "anti-party activities became even more rampant," adding that he attempted to enlist Army leaders on his side.

Charges Outlined

He also advocated that the party should be divided with one section controlling the center and the other the Army and regional areas. Mr. Kao sought authority over the second section the report charged.

Charges against Jao Shu-shih went back to 1943 in spite of the high position he had maintained since then. His indictment stated he had "resorted to ignominious frauds within the party on numerous occasions in order to seize power and followed a rightist policy of capitulating to capitalists, landlords and rich peasants."

Mr. Jao is said to have formed an alliance with Kao Kang after he was transferred to Peking from Shanghai in 1953. The purge was cited as a "decisive victory" for the party.

Discipline Tightened

Similar cases may occur in the future, however, it was stated, and it was announced that a central disciplinary inspection committee has been formed to guard against "corrupt degeneracy and violations of discipline."

Mr. Kao at one time was regarded as a contender for eventual leadership of the party. In addition to his important post as Communist regional boss in Manchuria, he was a member of the Politburo and Vice-Chairman of the Central People's Government.

Mr. Jao has recently been chairman of the East China Administrative Area and political council head of the powerful Organization Bureau of the party and a member of its Central Committee.

The report on Messrs. Kao and Jao was passed on to the fifth plenum by a national conference of the party which was held in Peking from March 21 to 31, presided over by Chairman Mao Tse-tung.

The plenary session also approved changes in Communist China's first five-year plan—details of which were not given—and measures to ensure tighter party discipline.

Peking radio also disclosed that two new members have been admitted to the Politburo.

They are Teng Hsiao-ping, Secretary General of the Central Committee—who delivered the report on Messrs. Kao and Jao; and Gen. Lin Piao who has been inactive for the past five years—presumably because of illness.

Churchill Steps Down as Premier As Palace Ceremony Ends Tension

By Peter Lyne
Parliamentary Correspondent of The Christian Science Monitor

London

An amazing end to a phenomenal political career was enacted here in London April 5 as Sir Winston Churchill stepped down from the British Prime Ministership.

Into his place stepped his long-time deputy, Sir Anthony Eden, whose appointment as First Minister was announced on the morning of April 6. The shift heralded few changes in the Cabinet or in the government's policy, but was expected to mean that the Conservatives would get down to serious preparations for a national election, possibly on May 26.

Despite this business-as-usual prospect for the British political scene, the attention of most Londoners was focused on the events which had taken place under the gradually strengthening sunlight of April 5.

The 80-year-old statesman flashed his famous "V" sign as he drove past crowds on his way from No. 10 Downing Street to Buckingham Palace, where he informed Queen Elizabeth II of his wish to resign.

Late in the afternoon, after a 43-minute audience with the Queen, the message was flashed that "Her Majesty was graciously pleased to accept."

Many of the things that have happened in his life have been extraordinary. But nothing has been more extraordinary than his retirement.

Officially there was no preknowledge of his decision to hand over to Sir Anthony Eden. All the same, there was no denying that the political world of London had reached an all-time high of agogness. It just happened that the House of Commons had one of the biggest attendances in its history April 5 in expectation that "the old man" would take his final curtain as Prime Minister.

Londoners Gather

And then, at the very last moment, it was announced that Sir Winston would not take his place in the Commons at question time after all. If ever there were a performance of Hamlet without the Prince of Denmark it was here in Westminster April 5.

No official reason was given for Sir Winston's decision not to attend the Commons for this last appearance as Prime Minister. Unofficially it was suggested that the occasion might prove too emotional for a man who is prone to be emotional.

But whatever drama the packed House of Commons missed, Londoners in general gained. In spite of the dearth of news occasioned by the city's 12-day-old newspaper strike, crowds gathered wherever the scenes of this dramatic last act of the Prime Minister's career were staged.

They assembled in curiosity the night of April 4 outside No. 10 Downing Street as Sir Winston played host to the Queen and to his old wartime military and political companions. They collected there again in mounting excitement as members of the Churchill Cabinet gathered for the last time the morning of April 5.

And they thronged outside that traditional home of Prime Ministers later in the day as Sir Winston, jaunty in an old-fashioned frock coat, left for Buckingham Palace to make his resignation official.

Final Scene

London

Reuters reports the details of that last historic drive as follows:

At 23 minutes past 4 the black door at No. 10 Downing Street opened and Sir Winston appeared.

He doffed his topper, waved, and for several seconds posed in the doorway of his official town home, in response to shouts from photographers, "This way, Winston."

Mounted police jogged in front of the Prime Minister's black limousine as he drove to the palace. He drove through the wrought-iron gates of Buckingham Palace at 4:29 p.m.

Once inside he was escorted immediately by officials of the royal household to a room where the young monarch awaited him.

With portraits of past kings and queens staring down from the walls the old statesman bowed low and kissed Queen Elizabeth's hand. He then formally requested her to relieve him of the burdens of his office.

Eden Tapped

The Queen, under whose great-great grandmother, Queen Victoria, Churchill served as a cavalry officer, then asked him to recommend a successor. He named Sir Anthony Eden, his dapper Foreign Secretary, who has been his right-hand man and political "heir" for many years.

As the historic meeting went on, crowds waited outside the palace forecourt as they always do on state occasions. A warm spring sun shone down on the scene, banishing the grayness in which earlier events of the resignation had taken place.

Soon after Sir Winston had left the palace—again flashing his "V" sign—and returned to Downing Street, the formal announcement of his resignation was issued:

"The Right Honorable Sir Winston Churchill had an audience of the Queen this evening and tendered his resignation as Prime Minister and First Lord of the Treasury, which Her Majesty was graciously pleased to accept."

Political Limelight

With that, the venerable statesman-politician was Prime Minister no longer. He had been Britain's first minister for a total of eight years, seven months, and 25 days—including five years that alone would place him in the first ranks of history, his years as the nation's indomitable leader in World War II.

While Britons showered tributes on their great leader, politicians in both the Conservative and Labor Parties began to prepare for the aftermath of the Churchill resignation, a snap general election.

Foreign capitals, under no compunction to worry about Britain's impending tight political race, continued to lavish eloquent praise on the man who in the past had dominated so many such campaigns.

Premier Edgar Faure of France commented, "No political career has been so full, so fruitful, so prodigious.

"He has been the champion of liberty and democracy. For this we give him our grateful thanks."

In Washington, leaders of both parties in Congress paid tribute to Sir Winston.

Achille Van Acker, Premier of Belgium, said in Brussels, "Never perhaps in humanity's history has a man so deeply embodied the spirit of his people as Sir Winston Churchill during the Second World War. . . . The Belgian people takes this opportunity of renewing its profound gratitude to Sir Winston Churchill."

Churchill engraves name in history: First Page. Second Section.

Emil Weiss

Churchill and Eden

Chicago's Election of Daley Sends Democratic Stock Spiraling

By Godfrey Sperling, Jr.
Staff Correspondent of The Christian Science Monitor

Chicago

Democrat Richard J. Daley is the next Mayor of Chicago. His victory was a relatively easy one, despite a coalition opposition that was energetically led by a Democrat maverick, Robert E. Merriam.

The Merriam defeat cannot be cast off lightly. His name carried more than ordinary voter magic since his father had been a reform mayoral candidate before him. Many independents and liberal Democrats did him honor as they did to no man except Adlai E. Stevenson. Eisenhower Republicans accepted him, liked him, and worked hard for him. Yet he lost.

'Regulars' Stay Home

The defeat must, therefore, be measured as a bigger blow to the Republicans here than even the loss of Chicago by General Eisenhower to Mr. Stevenson in 1952. "Ike" had so much going for him then, but he got only 45 per cent of Chicago's votes. But "Young Bob" Merriam seemed to have the Eisenhower following plus a good segment of the opposition. Yet he lost.

The reason emerges clearly in an examination of the precinct returns. One Republican precinct captain told this reporter that there were 258 of his Republicans who did not vote in this election. This was in a precinct with 700 registrants. "They are 'regular' Republicans" he said, "who didn't care for 'Ike' and they like Merriam even less."

This serves to indicate why the liberal-moderate GOP formula, so successful generally, does not work out here in a Chicagoland where many Republicans are inclined to distrust "internationalists."

Right-Wing Apathy

This right-wing apathy also showed up in the over-all total of about 1,290,000 votes cast for the office of mayor, some 110,000 ballots fewer than were forecast for the sunny, 70-degree day. A Merriam victory was predicated on this 100,000-plus vote. But much of his potential victory margin apparently sat at home, uninspired at the thought of voting for a man who had been a Democrat until just a few months ago.

Apparently, some 48,500 citizens who voted for other candidates in the election did not vote for either candidate for mayor.

It is recalled that a "regular" Republican, Robert L. Hunter, in a 1,200,000-vote mayoral election four years ago—a race that held none of the dramatic elements of the current contest—came within 154,000 votes of Mayor Martin H. Kennelly.

Nationally, the returns here must be recorded as a further indication of a Democratic resurgence, a trend that has persisted since the presidential election.

National implications are present in this mayoral race more than usually. The Democratic organization normally has held this city by plugging local issues and its candidate, and by merely "getting out the vote." This time the Merriam threat prompted Mr. Daley and his Democratic colleagues to lean on national issues—and on Mr. Stevenson, Senator Douglas, and Stephen A. Mitchell, former national party chairman.

This urgent request for help from above helped put the local Democrats in a position to exult in victory. But, for the first time in 24 years at City Hall, they must give important credit to a power outside their efficient precinct captains.

'—Some Strings'

In Mr. Daley, Chicagoans are getting a product of 22 years' training in the local Democratic organization. The mayoralty has been described by the long-time Democratic political leader of Cook County, Jacob N. "Jake" Arvey, as Mr. Daley's "diploma."

Mr. Daley brings to his new job a long experience in public life, as state legislator, as state auditor under Governor Stevenson, as county clerk and as chairman of the Cook County Democratic Committee.

The new Mayor has, during the campaign, matched Mr. Merriam's promises for a streamlined city council, for a cleanup in the police force, for improved public schools, for better transportation, and for increased civil service.

Besides Mr. Daley's impressive record and an integrity which has not even been questioned by an extremely questioning opposition, a new factor for city betterment has emerged in this hard-fought campaign.

It has been more than hinted—in fact, a man high up in the Democratic Party has privately disclosed—that Mr. Stevenson's support of the local organization had some strings attached to it.

Mr. Stevenson, it appears, now has a special interest in seeing that the local Democratic Party clean house, and, most of all, that election promises be fulfilled. And, for the first time, the titular head of the Democratic Party has a special friend in the Mayor's chair who will be happy to listen to him—and a local organization that is now obligated to heed his advice.

Thus the exclamation of a Democratic alderman, uttered in the flush of victory, may not hold true. Said the alderman, dancing a jig: "Chicago ain't ready for reform."

It is too early to say, but it is very possible that some measure of reform now may come from within the local Democratic Party.

Close Election

By the Associated Press

Chicago

Although decisive, the Chicago mayoral result was one of the closest since Anton J. Cermak wrested the mayoralty from William Hale Thompson in 1931.

The only narrower margin in the six Democratic Mayor victories preceding that of Richard J. Daley was that of 114,020, by which the late Edward J. Kelly won his third term in 1943.

The victory and Democratic gains in Michigan were hailed by Democratic National Chairman Paul M. Butler as evidence of the party's "resurgence" of strength. To Illinois Republican leaders, it meant that the city's traditional Democratic leaning had not been altered, and with the Chicago Democratic organization intact, there might be trouble ahead in the 1956 presidential and state contests.

Results in aldermanic races indicate that Mr. Daley will have 38 Democrats among the 50 aldermen in the City Council.

The total vote in the election was 1,338,554—more than 68 per cent of the 1,946,477 registration. But 48,423 voters apparently did not vote for either Mayor candidate.

Mr. Daley, a native of the southwest "back of the yards" area and veteran of more than 25 years in party service, is the father of seven children.

Larger Pluralities

In a news conference, he said an effort to get aid of the Legislature to boost Chicago's police force by 2,000 will have top priority in his agenda.

He said he will resign both his party chairmanship and his job as County Clerk before he takes the Mayor's chair for a four-year term April 20 from Martin H. Kennelly, who retires after two terms.

Mr. Kennelly lost his bid for a third term in the Feb. 22 primary.

"As Mayor of Chicago I shall have only one goal," he said in a statement, "to make this city a better and more beautiful place in which to live."

An unusual aspect of the election was that three running mates of Mr. Daley won by larger pluralities than the mayoral victor.

The ticket leader was Morris B. Sachs, owner of two clothing stores, who received 735,747 votes for City Treasurer, defeating Republican John L. Waner by 217,452 votes.

The Democratic City Clerk candidate, John C. Marcin, polled 708,228 to defeat Charles R. Barrett by 170,645. In a contest to fill a Municipal Court vacancy, Democrat Edward M. Koza received 508,211 to Republican Saul A. Epton's 391,174.

Four bond issues totaling $95,750,000 for new school buildings, sewers, street lighting, and a traffic sign shop were overwhelmingly approved.

Results of 14 aldermanic run-off elections indicated the 50-member City Council will be composed of 38 Democrats, 11 Republicans, and 1 Independent. But unofficial results were very close in two run-off races, and the official canvass could change the line-up.

Chicago's Mayor-Elect Daley Flashes Victory Smile

State of the Nations: President, Secretary, and Admiral

By JOSEPH C. HARSCH, Special Correspondent of The Christian Science Monitor

Washington

Eight days after the famous "Carney dinner" at which the Chief of Naval Operations indicated his opinion of the imminence of war with China, and four weeks after Secretary of State Dulles had returned from the Far East sounding like an oracle of doomsday, the State Department quietly announced that 76 Chinese students who have been kept in the United States against their wishes might return to Communist China.

The first two of these events are not easily reconciled with the third. If it is as urgent as Mr. Dulles was saying through March that the United States prove it is not a "paper tiger," and if war with Communist China may start any hour after the dawn of April 15, as Admiral Carney indicated, then it would make very poor sense indeed to choose April 2 as the date for sending 76 Chinese students, many of them highly skilled technicians well versed in American industrial and natural scientific techniques, back to Communist China.

The truth of the matter is, I think, that the obvious irreconcilability of the release of the students and the things the admiral and the secretary were saying through the month of March is symptomatic of a condition in Washington in which many men propose, but only the President disposes; and that we make a mistake every time we deduce a decision of the President from remarks of the secretary, the admiral, or Senator Knowland.

Certainly the time has not come yet when every act of government in the great area of war or peace is tailored to Dulles or Carney approaches, for were it so tailored the Chinese students never would have been released.

This release belongs in a different context from the Dulles pessimism of March and the Carney theory that the only proper response to the expected Chinese attack on the Matsus would be a general United States military attack upon all sources of Chinese military strength throughout China and Manchuria.

It belongs to the stream of events which opened with the Geneva conference of last summer. At that time the allies of the United States pointed out the incongruity of the United States demanding the release of prisoners held in China while Chinese students were being held in the United States. It progressed from that through the Dag Hammerskjold visit to Peking of early January, and through a period since then when the Western Allies have maintained a continuing interest in what they regard as a desirable "rectification" of the United States position. It culminates now in the release of the students, which will be followed, it is hoped, by release of the prisoners.

Thus the thread of long-range negotiation with Peking never has been totally broken, the channels of communication never totally closed, the opportunity for the President to return to the path of negotiation never allowed entirely to lapse.

Running alongside this stream of events has been the other stream of a rising sense of tension which can be dated from the late February visit of Secretary Dulles to the Far East. Beginning on March 2 and continuing through March 21 Mr. Dulles produced a series of statements, speeches, and inspired news stories which built up a cumulative impression of mounting crisis.

It is easy in retrospect to see where Admiral Carney made his tactical mistake of assuming that the time for willingness to fight China was at hand. His "dinner" on March 25 must have seemed to him a logical sequel to the Dulles forebodings of preceding weeks. He, like some Washington reporters, must have assumed that the Dulles words reflected a matured change of high policy rather than only a Dulles view of what should be done.

The admiral must have been both startled and surprised when the White House roof virtually fell in on him, for if the situation were as bad as Mr. Dulles had been saying, then what more logical than that the military should expect to fight?

But the President did repudiate the admiral; and the secretary, whose position never had become quite so radical in public, then saved his own position by narrowing down his emphasis to the technical fact that the United States is not committed to defend anything but Formosa and the Pescadores.

The end conclusion is justified, it seems to me, that the President himself is the only real source of high foreign policy decision; that he still clings to the hope of a peaceful resolution of the Formosa crisis; that he sometimes is deflected by Dulles anxiety or by Carney-Radford eagerness or by Knowland activism; but that in the main his course remains fixed on the goal of a peaceful resolution of the Formosa issue; and that Mr. Dulles, by releasing the students and by adjusting his views on the Formosa situation, has completed his March detour and is back now in step with the President.

I still want to know what the President says.

THE CHRISTIAN SCIENCE MONITOR

Registered in U. S. Patent Office

AN INTERNATIONAL DAILY NEWSPAPER

VOLUME 48 NO. 291 | BOSTON, MONDAY, NOVEMBER 5, 1956 | • ATLANTIC EDITION | TWO SECTIONS | FIVE CENTS A COPY

COPYRIGHT 1956 BY THE CHRISTIAN SCIENCE PUBLISHING SOCIETY

Egypt Invaded—Israel Rejects Police Force; UN Demands Moscow Lift Heel From Hungary

Campaign Hits Peak

President Eisenhower has busied himself with what is generally assumed to be the best politics for an incumbent at such a time: conducting his nonpolitical business of being President. He made a personal appeal to Soviet Premier Nikolai A. Bulganin to refrain from reimposing a regime of terror on Hungary, and conferred with officials on the Middle East crisis. He will make his election-eve talk in an hour-long Republican program statring at 11 p.m. e.s.t.

Both President Eisenhower and Adlai E. Stevenson are beaming final vote bids into Massachusetts. At 8:55 p.m. over WBZ-TV, Channel 4, the President will cap a Republican Bay State team effort with a five-minute address.

Mr. Stevenson, flying to Massachusett sto see his new grandson, born to Mrs. Adlai E. Stevenson, Jr., will make a windup speech over WNAC-TV, Channel 7, at 10 p.m.

Before leaving for Boston, Mr. Stevenson fired another round at the administration's conduct of foreign policy during a campaign breakfast in Minneapolis. He said President Eisenhower's "negligence on questions of peace and war may plunge the whole world into the horror of hydrogen war. And negligence," Mr. Stevenson said, "is precisely what we are getting."

Vice-President Richard N. Nixon will join President Eisenhower on the 11 p.m. broadcast program.

Senator Estes Kefauver is campaigning in Ohio, and will go to Washington tonight. From there he will take part in the Democratic windup broadcast at 10 p.m.

Related Stories: Pages 2, 3, 5, 6

Washington Scene

Foreign Affairs Win Spotlight

By WILLIAM H. STRINGER
Chief, Washington Bureau, The Christian Science Monitor

Washington

Suddenly, at the very finish of the presidential campaign, foreign policy became a very big issue. And the question of which candidate would be better equipped to lead the nation through the intermittent international storms visible ahead became a matter of importance to every voter.

Traditionally, foreign affairs sway few votes. Indeed, it was one of the frustrations of Adlai E. Stevenson's campaign that, though he wanted to make foreign policy a major issue, it didn't catch on very well. He made his pitch on banning H-bomb tests, but that speedily became a problem of great complexity and he didn't get much mileage out of it.

Then, suddenly, there came the uprisings in Poland and Hungary, the Soviet reentry into Hungary and the surprising Anglo-French march against Egypt. And all this has so illumined the churnings and changes at work in the world that a high diplomatic official, at a very recent Washington gathering, tossed out the suggestion that if events in Europe continued their course we might even glimpse, some distance down the road, the prospect of German unification.

⁂

To the Democrats, these dramatic events gave new last-minute life and point to the Stevenson attack. The Democratic contender, in the closing hours of the political battle, charged that developments belie the Eisenhower assurances of "good news" in the Middle East and peace in general. The only Democratic lament was that the Hungarian uprising and the British - French - Israeli advance on Egypt came at the last moment of the campaign. Had they come two weeks earlier, Mr. Stevenson would have had more time to make an issue of them.

The signs and polls suggest, at this writing, that the Democrats have not been able to exploit sufficiently their domestic issues: The plight of the "little man," the troubles on the farm, the "give-away" and "big business" issues. There was a shift to Mr. Stevenson of some voters who in 1952 were for President Eisenhower, but it was minor, not major. Then came the sudden urgency on the foreign front, but its belated impact on the campaign is difficult to gauge.

All politics aisde, however, it is at last obvious that the next few years are probably going to see surprising shifts and changes abroad. Four years ago when President Eisenhower took office, there was need in the main for conciliation and accommodation, for patience and good will, standing firm and yet in de-fusing the most dangerous phases of the cold war.

There has since been a major easing of global tensions—an easing indeed which allowed some nations like Hungary to believe they could strike out for freedom. At Trieste, in Iran, in Austria, at the Formosa Strait, the perilous tension subsided. It was a significant change in the atmosphere.

There still will be need for patience and good will in American foreign policy. And there still will be times when the best American policy will be to sit tight and let other nations work out their destiny. But the next four years also is going to be a period when American statecraft will need to deal with empires in transition like the Soviet Union, with alliances like NATO which demand new forms and functions, with rising, impatient nationalisms and perhaps with other men like President Nasser who will seek to ride these risky tides beating against the status quo.

And this will be a time when there will be need for a planning staff at the State Department which can develop new policies, and for gifted individuals who can sense the new trends and the paths around the pitfalls. And when America's voice will need to speak out boldly and with imagination—to speak from the heart and from an understanding of the rights of the individual.

⁂

In short, the next four years will not make the same kind of demands on United States policy as have the last four years. It will not be enough merely to develop a "cease-fire" in Egypt. Some kind of more permanent, guaranteed, enforced Middle East settlement will be requisite. And if in Europe there does loom, down the long road, the prospect of German unification, it will not come to pass until all the risks and possibilities of a general European agreement (tacit or formal) have been considered, and these include rectification of the Polish frontiers, European demilitarization on each side of Germany, and guarantees against a resurgence of German militarism.

Which candidate, which party could most ably mobilize and energize American statecraft and talent to meet these new challenges and opportunities? Historians surely will say this was one of the most fundamental questions facing the voter in 1956.

Brutality Hit

By William R. Frye
United Nations Correspondent of The Christian Science Monitor

United Nations, N.Y.

What next for Hungary and the Soviet empire?

This is the great question mark hanging over Central Europe in the wake of a ringing United Nations denunciation of what has been called one of the most wanton massacres in human history.

Is the Kremlin headed back into the blackness of all-out Stalinism? Or does it merely intend to guarantee that its empire does not slip beyond Titoism to liberal democracy?

On the answers to these questions depends the immediate fate of Poland and the future fate of other satellite countries. If Soviet Communist Party Secretary Nikita S. Khrushchev has lost his dominance within the Politburo and the Kremlin is turning back the clock to the Stalin era, Poland may soon be the scene of another tragedy on the Hungarian model.

If, on the other hand, the crushing of the Hungarian revolt by Soviet tanks and planes is to be explained by the fact that the regime of Imre Nagy tried to go too fast and too far toward genuine freedom, the process of Titoization of the Soviet empire—a process very much in the West's interest—may not have been halted.

Diplomats and observers listened carefully to Soviet delegate Arkady A. Sobolev Nov. 4 as he tried to defend his government's action before a special emergency General Assembly of the United Nations—the second to be convened in three days.

Kremlin Warned

Between the lines, Mr. Sobolev appeared to suggest that it was liberal democracy, not Titoism, to which the Kremlin objected—in other words, that the basic Khrushchev policy had not been changed, but merely executed with the all-out brutality of a Stalin.

Western diplomats, taking the UN podium in a series of eloquent, emotion-packed speeches, did what they could to warn the Kremlin away from a return to Stalinism and to indict it for the crimes committed in Hungary.

They passed 50 to 8 with 15 abstentions and 3 absentees, a United States resolution which did these things:

¶Condemned the use of Soviet armed might "to suppress the efforts of the Hungarian people to reassert their rights" and "noted" the "grave loss of life and widespread bloodshed" which it said had resulted;

¶Called upon the Soviet Union "to desist forthwith from all armed attack on the peoples of Hungary" and to "withdraw all of its forces without delay from Hungarian territory";

¶Directed Secretary - General Dag Hammarskjold to establish an investigating committee and try to send it into Hungary—a step which, however, few expect the new Hungarian regime will permit;

¶Asked Mr. Hammarskjold and the UN specialized agencies, along with governments and private humanitarian organizations, to go to Hungary's aid with "food, medicine, and other similar supplies."

Soviet Action Scathed

Sir Leslie Knox Munro of New Zealand acknowledged bitterly that the action may have come too late to save Hungary "for the time being." But he added that it was useful for the world to voice its "anger" at the "ruthless exercise of Soviet power," lest silence lead to the question: "Who tomorrow? And who the day after that?"

Selim Sarper of Turkey, in a voice so thick with emotion he scarcely could speak, said, "Tanks and guns can open gates of cities, but they are powerless to conquer the hearts and minds of human beings." He warned the Kremlin in effect that it was sowing the wind and would reap a whirlwind.

Henry Cabot Lodge, Jr., of the United States denounced what he called the "unutterable cynicism" with which the Soviet delegate was "raising his hands in horror" over bloodshed in Egypt while the Soviets were committing "wholesale brutality" in Hungary.

Mr. Lodge pointedly recited the so-called "Bandung principles"—including nonintervention in the affairs of other states and peaceful coexistence. He recalled how Soviet Premier Nikolai A. Bulganin and Mr. Khrushchev had paid lip service to these principles on a tour of Asia and on other occasions.

13 Hold Aloof

If this was a bid to Asia and Africa to join in the protest, it did not succeed. Of the 29 countries which signed the Bandung declaration on April 24, 1955, 23 are members of the UN. Of these 23, only 8 voted for the condemnation of Soviet action in Hungary.

Thirteen refused to take a stand. They were Afghanistan, Burma, Ceylon, Egypt, India, Indonesia, Iraq, Jordan, Libya, Nepal, Saudi Arabia, Syria, and Yemen. Two were absent when the vote was taken.

A number of these Bandung countries are sullen over what they regard as an effort to distract attention from the Egyptian crisis. They also resent United States resistance to sanctions against Britain, France, and Israel, and Washington's effort to promote a lasting peace settlement with Israel. Some wish to destroy Israel, not negotiate with it.

Ground Lost

The aloofness of many Bandung countries was also ascribed by numerous observers to a lack of moral courage often noted among this group when issues involving the Soviet Union are at stake.

There was little doubt that the action in Egypt had had a tragic impact on Hungary, splitting the Western alliance as it did, giving the UN a major preoccupation, and relieving the Soviet Union in large measure from the intense pressure of world opinion which the West had managed to build up.

Many believed the Kremlin never would have sent its troops back into Hungary, after first withdrawing them, if world attention had been focused exclusively on Budapest.

UN diplomacy Nov. 4 was an effort to restore the lost pressure, but few diplomats felt it had been successful. The studied indifference of the 13 Bandung powers was one measure of the ground that had been lost.

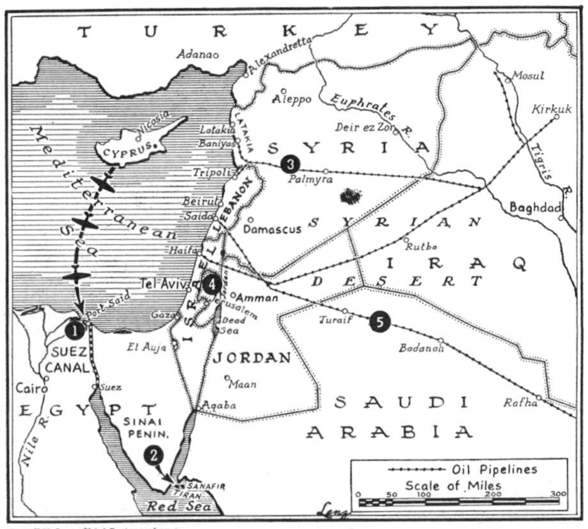

Russell H. Lenz, Chief Cartographer

British and French paratroopers from Cyprus have invaded Port Said area of Egypt (1). Israel is believed to have occupied islands of Tiran and Sanafir (2) in Gulf of Aqaba. London confirms that Iraq Petroleum Company oil pipeline has been sabotaged in Syria (3). Iraqi and Syrian troops continue to pour into Jordan (4). American-owned Trans-Arabian Pipeline (5) is believed to be still intact. Latest news hints Port Said is about to surrender.

Freedom Torn From Hungary

By Ernest S. Pisko
Staff Correspondent of The Christian Science Monitor

Vienna

Hungary's battle for freedom from Soviet Communist domination has clearly been lost—at least temporarily.

The revolt which started some two weeks ago was ruthlessly crushed Nov. 4 by four Soviet tank armies, Soviet treachery, and the sudden side-switching by Janos Kadar, recently appointed First Secretary of the Hungarian Communist Party.

Only a day or so previous, it looked as if Hungarians had succeeded in an attempt to break away from Moscow.

Premier Imre Nagy had accepted all demands of anti-Communist groups, representing some 90 per cent of the Hungarian people, and had formed a coalition government in which the Smallholders and Social Democrats had three members each, the Petöfi Party, formerly the Liberal Peasant Party, and the Communist Party, two each. The Cabinet also contained Maj. Gen. Pal Maleter, "hero of Hungary," in the post of Defense Minister.

Stage Set by Ruse

On the evening of Nov. 3 Mr. Mr. Nagy dispatched General Maleter and the Chief of Staff, Maj. Gen. Istvan Kovacs, to the Soviet high command to negotiate the terms of withdrawal of Soviet troops. Who actually was in command on the Soviet side is still unclear. There are strong indications, however, that Marshal Georgi K. Zhukov, Soviet Defense Minister, was in Hungary.

First reports on the military talks suggested that the Soviets asked for two or three weeks to take out their troops. This seemingly reasonable demand evidently was a ruse to win time for the tank armies to approach their respective goals.

In the early morning of Nov. 4, a thousand Soviet tanks which had surrounded Budapest began to attack. Three more tank armies moved on other key cities such as Pécs, Györ, Székes Fehérvár, and Szombathly.

Envoys Seized

When the Budapest attack started, Mr. Nagy immediately recalled General Maleter and Kovacs; he did not know that in the meantime they already had been arrested by their Soviet opposite numbers.

Then he broadcast a dramatic appeal, telling that Hungarian troops were fighting Soviet troops whose aim was to overthrow the government and completely subdue the country.

The Hungarian news agency MTI in a telephone talk to the Vienna office of the Associated Press said all of Budapest was under fire and asked help in Premier Nagy's name.

When the phone connection broke down, MTI over tele-type gave an incredibly graphic step-by-step description of the fighting, again and again interrupting the account of the Budapest battle to ask urgently whether there was any news of approaching help.

"The government waits for your answer," the MTI editor said. "We have no time to lose. Nagy personally asks for help and diplomatic moves by the western powers."

Later the editor reported that the Soviets were using incendiary ammunition and that the agency's main office was under fire. "I don't know how long I shall be able to keep the line to Vienna open," he said. And he ended, "Long live Hungary and Europe. We shall die for Hungary and Europe."

By 8 a.m. on Nov. 4 the battle was over. Radio Budapest was silent, and all other communications with the capital had broken down.

Earlier, Pécs, where the Hungarian uranium mines are located, had fallen. Gyö and other cities followed.

The Soviets arrested the entire government with the exception of Social Democratic leader Anna Kethly, who managed to escape from Sopron and now is reported on the way to the United Nations, and Mr. Kadar, who had secretly worked with the Soviets, had asked their intervention, and now has been appointed head of the new government.

Soviet tanks have sealed the main roads to the Austro-Hungarian frontier. Nobody is allowed in or out, and a number of Western correspondents are believed to be stranded in Hungary. Refugees have been arriving in Austria in increasing numbers by side roads.

Casualty figures are not available yet. Whether any will be made public is doubtful. The British estimate three days ago spoke of some 30,000 killed and wounded in the first stage of the revolt.

Casualties Estimated

Hungarian circles here have given the total casualties and fatalities as 15,000. This figure, which is held to be correct, now is certain to be surpassed many times by the number of victims of the end battle in which Hungarians literally fought Soviet tanks with bare hands.

Radio Szombathely, which has been in Soviet hands since mid-morning Nov. 4, ordered the rebels to surrender their arms. "Unmasking of the counterrevolutionaries is under way," it announced, and added, "Long live the friendship with the Soviet Union."

[The Associated Press announced that Premier Kadar had vowed to restore "order and calmness . . . in the whole country in the next few days" and then bring freedom and democracy to the country. He repudiated Mr. Nagy's appeal to the UN to guarantee a free and neutral Hungary.

[Hungarian refugees denounced Mr. Kadar as a traitor whose name would live in infamy akin to that of Norway's World War II Quisling.

[Josef Cardinal Mindszenty, Roman Catholic prelate freed from house arrest only a week ago, took refuge in the United States legation in Budapest.

[A red sky glowed over Budapest, indicating that many buildings were afiire.]

British Enter Port Said

By Harry B. Ellis
Assistant Overseas News Editor of The Christian Science Monitor

Even as the first British and French paratroopers hit Egyptian soil the awesome consequences of the invasion of Egypt began to reverberate around the world.

First consequence was the fact that the United Nations General Assembly's unanimous call for an international police force to end Mideast fighting had run into snags.

Israeli Ambassador Abba Eban told the Assembly that "the stationing of a force on the territory of Israel is not possible without the consent of the Government of Israel."

Earlier, in Jerusalem, Walter Eytan, director general of the Israeli Foreign Office, was quoted in a copyrighted article in the New York Herald Tribune as saying that the 1949 Palestine armistice was dead, that there was no possibility of reviving it, and that Israel wanted neither a UN police force nor mediation, but direct negotiation with Egypt.

New Borders Sought

Israel appeared to feel that for the first time since the Palestine war of 1948 possibility existed of a new general agreement between Arabs and Israelis which would create and stabilize new borders and guarantee Israel's position in the Middle East.

The Assembly resolution setting up a UN command, however, called for withdrawal of Israeli and Egyptian forces behind their original armistice lines, with the imposition of a strong UN force to guarantee these lines.

There was no immediate response from embattled Cairo, intent at the moment on repelling the Anglo-French invasion of Egypt which began in the dawn hours of Nov. 5 following round-the-clock aerial bombardment of Egyptian military bases and road convoys since Oct. 31.

At this writing, a reported 3,000 British and French paratroopers have been dropped in the Port Said area at the northern entrance to the Suez Canal in an operation which returning pilots said went off like clockwork. Port Said airport was believed to be under the invaders' control.

Egypt Contradicted

Egyptian claims that the paratroop force was "annihilated" were contradicted by Anglo-French headquarters on Cyprus, which said the operation was going well. At a press conference on Cyprus, Gen. Sir Charles Keightley, commanding the Anglo-French offensive against Egypt, said that both British and French paratroopers "have had some very tough fighting" in Egypt.

An Anglo-French invasion armada left Cyprus Nov. 4, but there was no indication when or where it would land. Headquarters on Cyprus announced that Egypt had sunk three ships at Suez to block the Suez Canal.

Thus the canal is blocked at its southern terminus of Suez and also midway in its course at Lake Timsah, where British planes on Nov. 1 sank a vessel which the British later claimed the Egyptians were towing with the purpose of sinking in the channel.

Resolution Passed 57-0

In the Sinai Peninsula, meanwhile, Israel was in complete control. It appeared almost certain that Israeli forces had captured the two islands of Tiran and Sanafir at the mouth of the Gulf of Aqaba, from which Egyptian guns had barred the gulf to Israeli shipping since 1949.

Back at the UN, the General Assembly police-force resolution, passed 57-0 with 19 abstentions, appointed Maj. Gen. E. L. M. Burns, now chief of the UN truce machinery in Palestine, as commander of the force still to be raised.

UN Secretary-General Dag Hammarskjold reported that Colombia, New Zealand, and Norway had agreed to take part in the force. Canada also was expected to do so. Mr. Hammarskjold will seek the necessary troops from among 71 of the UN's 76 members, barring only the big powers—Britain, France, the United States, the Soviet Union, and Nationalist China.

Employment of the UN force, observers believed, would raise grave problems. Should Israel refuse to accept the force and should the UN persist in sending it, it was possible that Israel would attack Jordan to stabilize its eastern frontier before a UN force blocked any move.

Thus the UN resolution designed to end Mideast fighting might indirectly cause its extension if Israel should decide that the experience of the past eight years had made its present boundaries intolerable.

This was an immediate danger. Even should both sides accept the presence of UN forces and agree to pull back to the original armistice lines, the problem would merely have reverted to the old status quo, which bred the present fighting.

Tension Builds Up

Thus tension might be expected to grow in the future, ready to explode when UN screening forces eventually were withdrawn.

Meanwhile, the first evidence of expected Arab sabotage of Western oil installations was announced. The British Foreign Office acknowledged that two pumping stations of the Iraq Petroleum Company had been sabotaged over the week end, halting the flow of pipeline oil from Iraq.

Blaming the Syrian Army for the sabotage, the Foreign Office called on the Syrian Government to repair the damage and restore the line to use. The Syrian Government was not expected to comply.

Indeed, the sabotage was merely the first of many incidents which might be expected to take place in the Arab world as Arab anger mounted over the Israeli-British-French invasion of Egypt. So far, the American - owned Trans - Arabian Pipeline Company, running from Saudi Arabia to Lebanon on the Mediterranean Sea, appeared to be intact.

This type of sabotage would not be expected to end in the event of Anglo-French conquest of Egypt. Some observers foresaw the eventual need of Anglo-French occupation of much of the Arab world if widespread sabotage were not to disrupt or halt the flow of oil to Western Europe. The consequences throughout Asia and Africa of such occupation would be incalculable.

Port Said Talks Surrender Terms

By Reuters

London

British Prime Minister Sir Anthony Eden told the House of Commons he had received a signal from the commander in chief of Britain's Midde East forces saying the Governor and military commander of Port Said was now discussing surrender during a cease-fire.

Demands Increase For Eden's Ouster

By Peter Lyne
Parliamentary Correspondent of The Christian Science Monitor

London

Demands for the resignation of Sir Anthony Eden as Prime Minister have become more and more insistent as Britain passed through one of the tensest and most eventful political weekends in modern history.

Wild scenes took place in Whitehall on Nov. 4 when some 10,000 Londoners staged an anti-Eden demonstration which led to some angry clashes with horse-mounted police.

Meanwhile, the outcome of Sir Anthony's venture in Egypt remains as big a question mark as ever.

Militarily, it is assumed in Britain that the venture will be successful—at least initially. But what happens after?

Sir Anthony had broadcast and televised in defense of his policy on Nov. 3. Opposition Leader Hugh Gaitskell's counterappeal to the nation was unprecedented in its uncompromissing and bitter denunciation of the Prime Minister and its plea that if the Conservative Party would force Sir Anthony's resignation then the Laborite opposition would support a new Conservative Prime Minister in bringing the fighting in Egypt to an end.

Events of political significance crowded on each other thick and fast at the weekend. Sir Winston Churchill broke his silence with a wholehearted endorsement of Sir Anthony's policy and a warning that in his view "recent months have shown that it is not possible to hope in this area [the Middle East] for American cooperation on the scale, and with the promptness, necessary to control events."

That was a highly significant pronouncement from perhaps the greatest advocate of all time of the Anglo-American alliance.

It became known at the weekend that one of Sir Anthony's closest Cabinet colleagues had resigned in protest against the Eden policy in the Middle East. He is Anthony Nutting, youthful Minister of State and protégé of Eden.

Parking Overhaul In Boston Urged

The World's Day

Reg. U.S. Pat. Off.

New England: Hub Unit Urges Complete Study

A complete overhaul of Boston's off-street parking program after a reappraisal of major policy decisions now in force, was urged by the Boston Finance Commission, in line with earlier recommendations made by the Boston City Council. (Page 5.)

Striking draftsmen at the Bethlehem Steel Company's Fore River Shipyard in Quincy, Mass., reduced their picket line to a token force, allowing production workers who were respecting their lines to go back to work. Union officials said they had proved that the production force respected their strike for a wage increase.

Mideast: India to Represent Egypt's Interests

India has agreed to take charge of Egyptian interests in Britain and France following Egypt's rupture of diplomatic relations with those two countries, the Egyptian Middle East News Agency said.

National: Steady Rain Welcomed in Texas

Steady rains ranging up to nearly 6 inches yesterday have brought many areas of Texas their best rainfall of the year. The slow, soaking rains that extended over most of the eastern half of the state and into West Texas assured green pasturage for winter and poured water into shriveled ponds and lakes.

United States Weather Bureau forecast for election day, Nov. 6: Showers through the Western Plains from the Dakotas into portions of the Mississippi Valley with considerable cloudiness and fog over the Great Lakes Region; some cloudiness for the Southeast and Northwest with snow flurries in the Rockies; fair dry weather for the Ohio Valley, mid and North Atlantic states.

Asia: Prime Ministers to Discuss Mideast

The Prime Ministers of India, Pakistan, Burma, Ceylon, and Indonesia will meet Nov. 12 in New Delhi to discuss the Middle East crisis, an official Indian spokesman said. Indonesia asked for the meeting.

Earl Attlee has canceled a week's tour of Pakistant and is leaving Nov. 5 for London. It was reliably reported that the Pakistan Government suggested he cancel an up-country tour in view of possible embarrassment by anti-British demonstrators.

Weather Predictions: Cool Tonight (Page 2)

Art, Music, Theater, Radio, TV: Page 7. FM: Page 11

Inside Reading:

THE CHRISTIAN SCIENCE MONITOR

Registered in U. S. Patent Office

AN INTERNATIONAL DAILY NEWSPAPER

VOLUME 48 NO. 293   COPYRIGHT 1956 BY THE CHRISTIAN SCIENCE PUBLISHING SOCIETY   BOSTON, WEDNESDAY, NOVEMBER 7, 1956   R   • ATLANTIC EDITION   TWO SECTIONS   FIVE CENTS A COPY

Eisenhower Scores Great Personal Victory;
Democrats Forge Ahead in Massachusetts

Events Spin World

Events are moving with great rapidity in many parts of the world. Although military action has ceased in the Middle East, guns are still speaking in Hungary. And in New York, the United Nations is girding itself to deal with both situations.

The UN General Assembly is meeting today to take up both the details following the cease-fire in Egypt and to try to find means of sending an observer team into Hungary.

In Egypt itself, Britain, France, Egypt, and Israel have all accepted the cease-fire. However, the full consequences of the recent military action there are still to be assessed.

In Hungary, the courageous resistance of freedom-minded Hungarians to Soviet and Communist attempts to reimpose a totalitarian dictatorship continues.

In Washington, the United States Government, having played a leading role in inducing a Middle East cease-fire, is assessing the important international repercussions of the Eisenhower electoral victory. This victory has been widely hailed in almost all parts of the world.

Fuller details may be found on The Christian Science Monitor's special and additional page one (First Page, Second Section).

Senate to GOP

Furcolo Victor In Bay State Test

By Edgar M. Mills
New England Political Correspondent of The Christian Science Monitor

Massachusetts Democrats have won a series of smashing state victories, restoring the governorship to Democratic control, solidifying their hold on the Massachusetts House, but failed to engulf the state Senate as well.

In the face of President Eisenhower's amazing plurality of more than 400,000, nearly double his 1952 margin, Foster Furcolo, Longmeadow Democrat, soared into the governorship by a margin of close to 140,000 votes over Lt. Gov. Sumner G. Whittier.

As the balloting neared an end, Democrats just missed capturing the Senate. This would have given them complete control of the redistricting machinery in the 1957-58 Legislature.

It now appears that the GOP has maintained its 21-19 margin in the upper branch as a means of maintaining a strong bridgehead in the Governor's office for the 1958 campaign.

GOP Holds Veto

By blocking Democratic Senate control, the GOP can at least force an acceptable compromise on reapportionment or can block any reapportionment at the next session. Such a development might well throw the whole issue into the courts, inasmuch as the state Constitution requires a redistricting of legislative districts after every decennial state census. (The census was taken in 1955, but the figures were not complete in time for 1956 action.)

Only Republican Attorney General George F. Fingold, up for a third term, survived an otherwise complete Democratic office sweep.

The Democratic successes were particularly stunning in view of President Eisenhower's tremendous plurality, one of the highest in state history.

It was an unprecedented display of split-ticket voting. Despite this crossing of party lines up and down the ballot, or perhaps because of it, the ballot casters retained all 14 Massachusetts representatives in Congress, seven Republican and seven Democrats.

Of particular national interest was the reelection of Representative Thomas J. Lane (D) of Massachusetts in the heavily Democratic 7th District, only two months after he completed serving a four-months federal penitentiary sentence for income-tax evasion. Thus he became the first member of Congress to win reelection after

Gordon N. Converse, Staff Photographer

Foster Furcolo (D)

serving a prison sentence while in office.

In addition to victories generally on the state level, the Democrats also captured for the first time Middlesex County's district attorney's office, to make almost a clean sweep of offices in that county previously a GOP stronghold. Representative James L. O'Dea, Jr. (D) of Lowell defeated Republican District Attorney Ephraim Martin by about 18,000 votes.

On the statewide level, former Representative Robert F. Murphy (D) of Malden, former House Democratic floor leader, won the Lieutenant Governor contest from Representative Charles Gibbons (R) of Stoneham, House minority leader. His margin was about 70,000 votes.

Republican leaders had hoped to win the lieutenant governorship even in the face of a Whittier defeat for Governor as a means of maintaining a strong bridgehead in the Governor's office for the 1958 campaign.

Whittier Trails

Throughout the state, Mr. Whittier ran substantially behind President Eisenhower and behind the totals piled up by Governor Herter in his winning fight against former Governor Dever in 1952. Mr. Whittier even trailed Mr. Furcolo in his home community of Everett, by a margin of 11,883 to 10,111.

Political observers are busy determining the reasons why Mr. Whittier was defeated in the face of the tremendous Eisenhower victory in Massachusetts.

There are several factors involved in the Whittier defeat. They include:

1. The long-held belief that Massachusetts is basically a Democratic state which elects a Republican for Governor only when the GOP comes up with an outstanding candidate such as Governor Herter or in a period of Democratic unpopularity.

2. The almost solid Italo-American voter support of Mr. Furcolo, whose father is an Italo-American and whose mother is an Irish-American.

Democrats United

3. A Democratic Party more united than at any time since the 1948 victory of Governor Dever. Mr. Furcolo apparently suffered little or no cutting among Irish-Americans because of his Italo-American name.

4. Failure of Mr. Whittier to make a strong favorable impression on television. Many observers feel Mr. Whittier's frequent TV appearances tended to hurt rather than help him.

5. Undermining of Mr. Whittier's legislative record on such issues as old-age assistance and labor in a manner which the lieutenant governor labeled as distortion.

The Democratic majorities if they hold up, are so thin, however, that the party will be unable to force through legislation without Republican help.

Thus a kind of coalition seems inevitable.

It would appear likely that the coalition will continue about as it has—a conservative-center coalition with the Democratic

'. . . To Work for 168,000,000 Americans . . . and for Peace in the World'

Drawn by Emil Weiss for The Christian Science Monitor

Democrats Hold Lead

Coalition Congress Seen

By Richard L. Strout
Staff Correspondent of The Christian Science Monitor

Washington

It appeared that in a contest between a popular Republican President and a popular Democratic Party the GOP had won the White House and the Democrats had recaptured one and possibly both houses of Congress.

If the Democrats do retain control of the legislature in spite of the Eisenhower landslide, it will be the first time it has happened since 1848. Then Gen. Zachary Taylor came in as a popular hero of the Mexican War, but failed to bring his party along with him.

It was a ding-dong battle for the Senate with the prospect that the result might linger some time in doubt.

As the situation stood, with results still coming in, Democrats had won 16 Senate seats and led in two others, Oregon and South Dakota. Republicans had won 15. Two, Kentucky (Morton-Clements) and Nevada are nip and tuck.

Tie Would Aid GOP

If there were a tie, 48 to 48, Vice-President Richard M. Nixon would have the deciding vote and Republicans would organize the upper chamber. Chief value of this for the party would be that the GOP would take over the important committee chairmanships. If Democrats keep control, the chairmanships will stay as they are.

The Democrats have elected 211 members to the House, only seven short of a numerical majority, and were ahead in 22 of the undecided 39 contests. Republicans had won 185 seats and were ahead in 17 others. To attain the 218 needed for a majority, Republicans would have to win 33 of the outstanding 39 contests, many of them in normally Democratic areas.

Whichever party wins control of the Senate, the indications are for continuing coalition rule in Congress.

President Eisenhower had a Republican Congress only in his first two years of office. Democrats took control in 1954 at midterm.

The unfolding situation is unprecedented in modern times. Now Mr. Eisenhower becomes a second-term President, barred by the 22d Amendment from succeeding himself.

Tradition Broken

In Washington it has been a political rule of thumb that if the opposing party took control of Congress at midterm it would sweep on to victory at the next presidential election. But what happens if the two parties split the executive and legislative functions right at the start?

There is no parallel for the situation, just as there seems to be no parallel for the personal popularity of Mr. Eisenhower that primarily brings such a situation into being.

Mr. Eisenhower's coattails have not been broad enough to bring his party back to power in Congress, it would appear.

Greatest Party Asset

Even in Mr. Eisenhower's moment of triumph over Mr. Stevenson, he hinted that he now felt he had cut himself free from the fetters of the GOP Old Guard. This is not the kind of approach likely to endear him to congressional conservatives.

Mr. Eisenhower is still the party's greatest asset, even if he

southerners going along in many matters with the middle-road Republicans.

At either end will be minority groups — the Republican "Old Guard" on the right, and the remnant of the Fair Deal-New Deal members on the left.

There are various estimates about how this coalition will work.

Historically there have often been times of legislation stagnation and actual stalemate in this divided government, which could not occur under a parliamentary system.

Gloomy forecasts were made of such a stalemate after the midterm election of 1954. But it did not develop. Congress managed to turn out a respectable batch of new legislation.

Various reasons for this past cooperation have been given. The country is immensely prosperous and there is little demand for radical new legislation. President Eisenhower did not try to push Congress as some chief executives have done and friction with the White House generally was kept out. Mr. Eisenhower has been immensely popular both with voters and with most congressmen; this helped maintain peace. Foreign affairs, furthermore, seemed to be going well. There was a minimum of difficulty here. Finally, the center position of the administration accorded pretty well with the center position of the Democratic Party.

Observers wonder if these generally harmonious conditions can be continued for another two or four years.

Two Conservatives Lose

One or two conservative senators have been defeated and their absence may play a part in Mr. Eisenhower's announced intention to remake the GOP as a "modern Republican" Party.

One of these defeats is that of Senator Herman Welker (R) of Idaho, an erratic figure who generally backed Senator Joseph R. McCarthy (R) of Wisconsin (not up at this election). Senator Welker was defeated by a young Democrat, Frank Church.

From Kentucky, the President gets the support of a new liberal Republican senator, John Sherman Cooper. He is of the pattern Mr. Eisenhower seeks to encourage.

Again, Senator-elect Jacob K. Javits (R) of New York is liberal enough to be classified in many respects almost as a New Dealer.

But the calibration of the GOP in Congress is generally to the right both of the White House and of the Republican state governors. Men like Bricker, Bridges, Butler, Capehart, Goldwater, McCarthy, Jenner, and others remain in the Senate. They have gloomily noted President Eisenhower's reference to "New Republicanism."

does not seem able to rub his popularity off on all followers.

The President will be helpful in the next midterm election—1958—and even though he cannot run himself he will be important in 1960 with the voters.

Nevertheless, as a President in his final term who has given up the weapon of his availability will have to exercise exceptional leadership to preserve his influence.

If past precedents hold, even the unique Mr. Eisenhower will face a test when he tries to push any very controversial legislation through Congress.

President's Vote Tops 1952 Mark

By William H. Stringer
Chief of the Washington News Bureau of The Christian Science Monitor

Washington

The landslide victory of giant proportions won by President Eisenhower has given him a resounding personal vote of confidence and the support of a united nation as he confronts the urgent Middle Eastern and Eastern European crises.

Mr. Eisenhower's triumph, exceeding most advance forecasts in its prodigal size, is a towering tribute to the genial general's personal popularity with the American people.

In his bid for reelection, President Eisenhower has won over Democratic contender Adlai E. Stevenson with an avalanche of ballots which almost approximates Franklin D. Roosevelt's one-sided wins of 1932 and 1936. Near-final results gave the President 41 states and 457 electoral votes as against Mr. Stevenson's 7 states and 74 electoral votes.

This tops the 1952 proportions, when Mr. Eisenhower won 39 states and 442 electoral votes and Mr. Stevenson won 9 states and 89 electoral votes.

But powerful as was the Eisenhower appeal, the Eisenhower coattails, on which many a candidate sought to ride, produced no Republican sweep of House or Senate or state governorships. With the Democrats winning control of the House of Representatives and possibly able to capture the Senate by a workable margin, it was apparent that the Republican Party, without the Eisenhower dynamism, was still numerically the weaker party in the nation.

Mandate From People

The "time of peril" abroad apparently served to enhance the Eisenhower triumph, making it even more desirable to voters to decide not to "swap horses."

Mr. Eisenhower thus has powerful approval for a "vigorous" second-term presidency, with undiminished influence over Congress and over legislation.

He has a mandate to act energetically to shore up the Western coalition and oppose the new Soviet efforts to incite disaster in the Middle East. He has a mandate to proceed with liberal legislation in Congress, including his four-year school-construction campaign promise.

Following are the latest results as compiled by the Associated Press:

President Eisenhower has built up a margin of more than eight million votes. The count of popular votes has reached: Eisenhower 29,503,903, Stevenson 21,376,316.

Five Races Undecided

Despite Mr. Eisenhower's landslide defeat of his Democratic opponent—a victory that might reach a nine-million-man margin in popular votes — Democrats appeared to be pulling into a commanding lead in the battle for the House. The Democrats also attained a favorable position in their efforts to retain control of the Senate.

The Democrats have already elected 210 of the 218 members needed to hold onto the House. Republicans have elected only 178, despite Mr. Eisenhower's sweep.

In 47 undecided races, Demo-

crats led in 26 and Republicans in 21.

The political complexion of the Senate—which also appeared likely to remain Democratic—hung on the results of five undecided races.

Democrats edged nearer control of the Senate by winning 15 seats in the Nov. 6 voting for a total of 46, including holdovers. They needed to win at least three of the five undecided races, in all of which they were leading. These were in Colorado, Kentucky, Nevada, Oregon, and South Dakota.

Republicans also had won 15 Senate seats, which with 30 holdovers gave them 45 Senate votes. They would have to come from behind in the undecided races even to hold their own.

Mr. Eisenhower's vote, pointing toward a possible nine-million edge, compared with the 6,612,449 by which he won in 1952. The Eisenhower count only six states in the Deep South — Alabama, Arkansas, Georgia, Mississippi, North Carolina, and South Carolina—together with Missouri, for 74 electoral votes.

Here is a brief summary:

Senate: (35 races) Republicans elected 15. Holdovers 30, total 45. Democrats elected 15. Holdovers 31, total 46. Needed to control 49.

Undecided: (5) Colorado, Carroll (D) ahead of Thornton (R); Kentucky, Clements (D) ahead of Morton (R); Nevada, Bible (D) ahead of Young (R); Oregon, Morse (D) ahead of McKay (R); South Dakota, Holum (D) ahead of Case (R).

House: (435 races) Republicans elected 176; Democrats

elected 210. Needed to control 218.

Undecided: 49, with Democrats leading in 24, Republicans in 25.

Governor: (30 races) Republicans elected 12 in Delaware, Indiana, Nebraska, New Mexico, New Hampshire, North Dakota, Ohio, South Dakota, Utah, Vermont, West Virginia, Wisconsin. Democrats elected 13 in Arizona, Arkansas, Colorado, Florida, Iowa, Kansas, Maine, Massachusetts, Michigan, Missouri, North Carolina, Texas, Washington.

Two late developments: Gov. William G. Stratton (R) of Illinois put on a last-minute spurt and defeated Democrat Richard B. Austin and won a second term. In Pennsylvania, Senator James H. Duff, Republican candidate for reelection, conceded victory to his Democratic opponent, Joseph S. Clark.

Vigorous Program

The presence of running-mate Richard M. Nixon on the ballot did not detract from the triumph. Indeed Mr. Nixon, now reendorsed by the same popular mandate, is projected powerfully forward as the most likely Republican presidential candidate for 1960.

It was said, however, that the heavy campaigning of the Vice-President in 36 states across the nation, while it served to galvanize and energize the Republican Party, did not rescue any significant number of beleaguered senatorial and congressional candidates from defeat.

The immediate victory statement of President Eisenhower, emphasizing youth and the future and declaring "I think that modern Republicanism has proved itself," strongly suggested that the victorious Chief Executive would carry forward vigorously that reshaping and rejuvenating of the GOP on which he has labored in the past four years.

The President's task of party-building was made somewhat easier, but not really easy, by the election. The voters retired a few Old Guardists like Senator Herman Welker of Idaho, but they also sent a once-defeated Old Guardist back to the Senate in the person of Chapman Revercomb of West Virginia.

And they failed to elect to the Senate the President's handpicked candidate in Washington state, Gov. Arthur Langlie. Nor did Mr. Eisenhower's election excursions to Pennsylvania and Ohio save Senators James H. Duff or George F. Bender from defeat at the hands of powerful opponents, as it now looks.

As forecast, the gallant contender Adlai E. Stevenson ran behind his party. Somehow he "failed to communicate," in competition with the President, in 1956 as well as he did in 1952.

Stevenson congratulates President: Page 4.

'Inside Stories' Of U.S. Election

Key contests in the election are reported by members of the staff of The Christian Science Monitor as follows:

The Eisenhower sweep again fragmented the Solid South, with the President retaining his hold on Florida, Texas, Virginia, Oklahoma, and Tennessee and also sweeping Kentucky and, suprisingly, Louisiana, a state which has not voted Republican in 80 years. [Page 7.]

Mr. Eisenhower captured every electoral college vote in the Far West from Colorado to California, from Washington to New Mexico, but Democrats captured some vital senatorial seats. [Pages 11 and 13.]

In the Midwest, President Eisenhower brought victory out of what looked like near defeat for GOP Senator Everett McKinley Dirksen of Illinois and Bourke B. Hickenlooper of Iowa. Elsewhere in the area farm discontent and traditional Democratic strength won statewide posts for that party's standard-bearers. [Page 13.]

A tidal wave swept President Eisenhower to victory in New Jersey and Pennsylvania. [Page 6.]

The Eisenhower victory in New York State carried with it a win for Attorney General Jacob K. Javits in his bid for a Senate seat. [Page 5.]

Bush Triumphs

President Wins 40 N.E. Votes

By a Staff Writer of The Christian Science Monitor

President Eisenhower's personal popularity has not only repeated a sweep of New England's 40 electoral votes, but pushed a Connecticut United States senator to an unexpected by huge plurality, and was a big factor in the near election of Rhode Island's first Republican Governor in 18 years.

So huge were the Eisenhower pluralities in all the New England states, record-high in most of them, that he aided numerous GOP candidates, even though he failed to save the Massachusetts governorship for Lt. Gov. Sumner G. Whittier.

Probably the most stunning GOP feat in New England's party 40 history was scored by Christopher Del Sesto, Providence attorney, who still has a chance to unseat Democratic Gov. Dennis J. Roberts. Although Mr. Roberts only holds a 190-vote lead, 11,000 absentee ballots remain to be counted on Dec. 5.

The Del Sesto feat was a combination of President Eisenhower's significant run and Mr. Del Sesto's Italo-American background. Italo - Americans constitute the fourth largest ethnic group in Rhode Island. Even before the election it was obvious that a major part of this group was swinging to Mr. Del Sesto after voting Democratic for a number of years.

The results, even though not yet conclusive, move Rhode Island out of the one-party state category, in which it had been placed until the 1952 election when President Eisenhower captured it for the GOP for the first time since 1924.

May Defeats Ward

The Eisenhower repeat victory in Little Rhody had been anticipated because of widespread Democratic dissatisfaction over Mr. Stevenson's position on banning further H-bomb tests and

an early end to the military draft, as well as his divorce. The Roman Catholic vote is heavy in Rhode Island.

But Mr. Del Sesto has been given only a fighting chance of tipping over Governor Roberts. Rhode Island's two representative in Congress seats remained in Democratic hands.

GOP leaders were highly encouraged by the big plurality run up by Connecticut's Senator Prescott Bush in winning a

full six-year term by defeating Representative Thomas J. Dodd (D) by a vote of 609,367 to 404,209. His 1952 plurality, when he was elected to fill out the four years remaining in the term of the late Senator Brien McMahon (D), was only 30,000 votes. Election forecasts had labeled this contest as close this year.

Other important result in New England was the victory of Edwin H. May, Jr., young Hartford insurance company executive, in Connecticut's 1st Congressional District. Democratic-held since the 1948 election, this seat went to Mr. May by a margin of 160,632 to 133,805 votes over State Senator Patrick J. Ward (D) of Hartford, president pro tem of the Connecticut Senate and a CIO labor leader.

The May victory completed a GOP sweep of Connecticut's six representative in Congress seats. The five GOP incumbents were reelected easily. Mr. May's triumph was due to his own resourceful campaign and the Eisenhower sweep.

Bush Is Elected

There is no doubt that in Connecticut the Eisenhower coattails were particularly strong and long. His plurality of more than 300,000 votes was nearly 2½ times his 1952 margin and was the largest ever scored in Connecticut history.

The largest previous Connecticut plurality for the presidency was that scored by Christopher Del Sesto ... in the 1924 when President Coolidge, former Massachusetts Governor, carried the state by 136,138.

In the rest of New England, the line-up remained unchanged. In Maine, the President piled up a record plurality of 137,000

votes, about 25,000 higher than the previous record he established in 1952. With only three small precincts missing, the President's vote, Nov. 6 was 249,024 to 101,797 for Mr. Stevenson.

Although New Hampshire's Gov. Lane Dwinell (R) had been expected to be closely pressed by the Democratic nominee, John Shaw, because of GOP party splits, he won a second term handily by a 24,000 plurality, about 4,000 more than he defeated Mr. Shaw in 1954.

Branon Loses Again

In addition, Representative Chester E. Merrow (R) of New Hampshire won an eighth term in Congress, piling up a margin of more than 11,000 votes over James B. Sullivan (D), Manchester attorney. Two years ago Mr. Merrow was reelected by only 400 votes.

Representative Perkins Bass (R) of New Hampshire had no trouble winning a second term in the 2d District, while Senator Norris Cotton (R) of New Hampshire won a second Senate term by a wide margin.

Thus the GOP won all four major spots in traditionally Republican New Hampshire while President Eisenhower was carrying the state by about 85,000 votes, well over his 1952 plurality of 60,000.

In Vermont, Democrats had hoped to end the 100-year GOP hold on the governorship; but Republican Gov. Joseph B. Johnson won by 27,000 votes over Democratic nominee E. Frank Branon.

Two years ago, Mr. Branon came within 5,200 votes of tipping over Mr. Johnson. But even though he increased his vote total by about 5,000 this year, he still lost ground to the Governor.

Macdonald Wins

President Eisenhower increased his Vermont victory margin to 74,000, compared to 66,000 in 1952. Both Senator George D. Aiken (R) and Representative Winston L. Prouty (R) won reelection by margins of about 2 to 1.

Massachusetts congressional results continued the present 7 to 7 division of the 14 seats between the two major parties. The only really close contests were in the 8th and 10th Districts.

Governor Roberts (R.I.)

November 7, 1956

THE CHRISTIAN SCIENCE MONITOR

Registered in U. S. Patent Office

AN INTERNATIONAL DAILY NEWSPAPER

VOLUME 48 NO. 306 | COPYRIGHT 1956 BY THE CHRISTIAN SCIENCE PUBLISHING SOCIETY | BOSTON, FRIDAY, NOVEMBER 23, 1956 | * ATLANTIC EDITION | TWO SECTIONS | FIVE CENTS A COPY

Ruling Cuts Hub Prices On Gasoline

By Everett M. Smith
Staff Writer of The Christian Science Monitor

Motorists were able to buy gasoline at cut prices today in many Greater Boston filling stations which had dropped prices one and two cents a gallon.

The action followed a ruling on Wednesday by Federal Court Judge Charles E. Wyzanski, Jr., dismissing a suit which the Esso Standard Oil Company had brought against Secatore's, Inc., of East Boston, which operates several filling stations in that area.

In dismissing the Esso petition, Judge Wyzanski vacated a temporary injunction he had issued against Secatore's on Oct. 5.

Appeal Promised

Attorney Charles W. Bartlett, counsel for the Esso company, indicated today that the decision by Judge Wyzanski would be appealed.

Most of the major oil companies, with the exception of Shell and Sun, have adopted the fair price agreement. They have contended that such fixing of prices will benefit dealers and tend to straighten out what were termed "chaotic price wars in Massachusetts, Rhode Island, and Connecticut."

In his ruling, Judge Wyzanski said that the Esso company, by selling its gasoline directly to trucking firms and other large-scale commercial users in quantity lots, was engaging in competition with many of its dealer-operated filling stations for this type of trade.

His decision was hailed by numerous North Shore gasoline dealers, who previously had cut their prices in that area below those established under the Massachusetts Fair Trade agreement, not only as a victory for themselves, but for the motoring public.

Everett Prices Cut

"It has given us back our liberty to run our business as we see fit," said Franklin Secatore, who added that his stations have returned to "competitive prices.

"I have no intention of cutting prices," he added, "but I just want the right to sell at prices I think are right, and to meet competition. I felt that it was my duty as a citizen to find out why the gasoline companies had a right to control not only the prices at which they sold gasoline to us dealers, but also the prices which we charged our customers."

Clifton F. Lord, operator of an Esso station on Broadway, Everett, who long has opposed fair trade price fixing, immediately dropped his prices—regular gasoline from 26.9 to 24.9, and high test from 29.9 to 28.9 cents a gallon.

"I think we have been shown justice by this decision," he said. "The gasoline companies have been in competition with us for the trucking business, and that is one point on which the decision was made.

'Victory for Public'

"Prior to this decision, the gasoline companies were able to sell gasoline to the trucking firms in bulk lots at the prices we pay, or even less.

"Free enterprise should be allowed. This is a victory for those gasoline dealers who have been trying to give the public a break for 25 years, and it also is a victory for the motoring public.

"Gasoline is a necessity, and not a luxury. I feel that it should be sold on a competitive basis."

On this score, only on Tuesday, Special Assistant Attorney General John J. Galgay, referring to another gasoline case, told Federal Judge George C. Sweeney that in his opinion gasoline is not a commodity which should be included in any fair trade agreement.

Judge Wyzanski ruled that the Esso Company was in competition with Secatore's, Inc., and therefore did not fall within the exemptions of the Miller-Tydings Act and the McGuire Act.

United Press

Refugees Look at America

A trio of Hungarian refugee children look out the window of an Army bus at Camp Kilmer, N.J., following their arrival from abroad at McGuire Air Force Base. They were among a group of 60 Hungarians, the vanguard of 5,000 refugees from Soviet oppression who will be settled in the United States. Another planeload of 70 already has arrived in this country.

Austria Appeals For Refugee Aid

By Frederick Brook
Special Correspondent of The Christian Science Monitor

Vienna

Austria has appealed to the free world to think afresh about the growing problem of refugees still pouring out of martyred Hungary.

Austrians have reaffirmed that they will never fail to fulfill their duty as good neighbors by granting asylum to every refugee who arrives on their frontiers. And they have praised the generous help offered from all parts of the Western world in sharing this human burden.

But they have warned that such generosity may be pinched, if not strangled, by the red tape of bureaucracy. They hold that the emergency on their eastern borders has now become too great for normal processes of examination and selection to be carried out there.

Some countries, such as the United States, have already tried to anticipate this crisis by amending the normal procedure to issue immediate regular visas to Hungarians. But what Austrians have now asked is that all receiving countries take away their agreed quotas of refugees direct by plane or train from Austria's frontiers—leav- all formalities of immigration until the refugees arrive at their future homes.

8,000 Set Record

This Austrian plea was made in vibrant words, unusual in the cool tones of diplomacy. The difficulties in responding to it are obvious enough. But what must be understood is the background.

The appeal was sent out after the Austro-Hungarian border had lived through the most agitated and tragic night since the Hungarian uprising started a month ago.

In one 12-hour period, between dusk and dawn, no fewer than 8,000 Hungarians crossed into the Austrian province of Burgenland. Many arrived soaked and nearly frozen, having waded through the icy waters of canals which run close to the frontier. Others had been shot at by Soviet or Hungarian patrols.

Some had lost their wives and children in the confusion. Most were so exhausted that once asleep on Austrian soil, it was impossible to rouse them.

This batch of 8,000 was a record. But there was no sign that the flow would drop far below that rate in the near future. For though the fighting has ceased in Hungary, it is now the threat of deportation to the Soviet Union which is stalking the land. And this is striking fear into thousands of Hungarian patriots who could stare unflinchingly into the barrels of Soviet tank guns.

Meaning for Austria?

What does all this mean for Austria?

First, the significance of the figures themselves must be borne in mind. Over the last fortnight between 60,000 and 70,000 refugees have entered Burgenland Province from Hungary. They have included a traveling circus complete with its performing animals, a prima ballerina disguised as an old woman, infants without their parents, pushed across the border in baby carriages, whole families fleeing on carts, tractors, and even a diesel locomotive.

And, to complete the picture, dogs and other pets have crossed into freedom in search of their missing masters.

Faster Evacuation

Burgenland, which now resembles a great open-air camp, is strained to its limits in providing even the transit accommodations which the flood of refugees requires. Its own population is only 300,000, and it is in some ways the poorest.

The whole country is, of course, helping with the transport of refugees as swiftly as possible to other reception centers in the interior. But what is really needed is a faster rate of evacuation from Austria itself. So far, little more than 10,000 refugees have started out for the eight principal countries which have offered them a near home.

Only a few hundred have gone to the United States, though this rate will soon quicken as the long-distance "refugee airlift" develops.

But the fact that alarms Austrians is that the grand total of a fortnight's evacuation action is little more than the influx of one night.

Series of UN votes supports Hungary: Page 4.

Hungarian refugee in U.S. depicts Soviet brutality: Page 5.

Eisenhower Move Eases Dock Crisis

By Harry C. Kenney
Staff Correspondent of The Christian Science Monitor

New York

President Eisenhower's decision to put into operation the emergency provisions of the Taft-Hartley Law to halt the Atlantic and Gulf Coast dock strike has eased pressurized anxieties among workers and business firms alike.

The President acted, he said, to protect "the health and safety of the nation" at a very critical time in national and world affairs.

Plainly for days the International Longshoremen's Association and the New York Shipping Association had maneuvered the strike issues into a hard and knotted deadlock. Ports from Maine to Texas were idled, and the cost to the nation was about 20 million dollars a day.

As a result of the President's move to provide an 80-day "cooling-off" period, it is expected that the 60,000 longshoremen along the whole affected area will be back on the job the first of next week.

Court Takes Action

Actually, fast-moving events were precipitated when it became evident that the deadlock centered around the ILA's insistence upon "some kind of national bargaining," and the shippers' refusal on the grounds that such a contract would be stretching their rights and powers.

Consequently, on Nov. 22, District Judge Frederick Van-Pelt Bryan ruled, enjoined, and restrained the ILA from demanding that the shippers negotiate any contract affecting longshoremen beyond the limits of New York. This ruling was a hard blow to the NLA "national bargaining" procedure, but as Capt. William V. Bradley, president of the union, indicated, "there are many other issues yet to be settled."

The new result was that even though the National Labor Relations Board secured the federal court restraining order, evidence continued to pile up that the ILA and the shippers were still far apart and that the strike would go on indefinitely.

It was at this point that President Eisenhower decided the seven-day strike had gone on long enough and that the issues were so involved that federal intervention was necessary. The reluctance of the President to do this is evidenced by the fact that only twice before has he invoked the emergency provisions of the Taft-Hartley Law.

Board Begins Hearings

The President has appointed a three-member fact-finding board, as required by law, to start an investigation into the issues of the strike. The board is headed by Thomas W. Holland, professor of labor economics at George Washington University; Arthur Stark, labor arbitrator of New York, and Jacob J. Blair, professor of industry at the University of Pittsburgh. The board already has been sworn in and hearings have started with representatives from both the ILA and the shipping association.

This will be a fast-moving inquiry. the Board is expected to give the President its views within hours. From the board's report the President could instruct the Attorney General to process a court injunction halting the strike for 80 days.

Here in New York, an official of the independent ILA expressed his opinion that the union would honor an anti-strike injunction if one were issued. While there is no guarantee that an 80-day cooling-off period would result in a settlement it is assumed that such would be the case.

Hope for Settlement

In announcing the President's action, James C. Hagerty, presidential secretary, said 'Mr. Eisenhower had expressed the hope that the strike would be settled quickly without resorting to the Taft-Hartley Act. He noted that the strike "was serious and has repercussions which spread far beyond the maritime industry." He added that he hoped "that both labor and management will resolve their private differences across the bargaining table."

There were several times when evidence indicated that the ILA and the shippers were very close to signing. In fact, it is the contention of ILA officials that a settlement had been virtually reached on the troublesome "national bargaining" issue but that the shippers had reneged at the last moment.

The ILA claims that the shippers were ready to relax and compromise on port bargaining from Portland, Maine, to Hampton Roads, Va. The union, in turn, indicated it was ready to ease up on several of its demands. However, now there are denials all around on all points of this issue.

It is possible that the federal court procedure and the President's decision to act may result in a quick settlement of the strike. If not, a settlement is expected soon by all concerned since it is believed that the wage issue is all but solved, leaving to final discussion the issues of sling loads, "call-in" pay, and length of time for work contract.

New U.S. Policy Seen For Asia and Mideast

UNEF Positions Mapped

By Mario Rossi
Special to The Christian Science Monitor

United Nations, N.Y.

The stationing of United Nations Emergency Force units on both sides of the armistice line between Israel and Egypt has reportedly been agreed on by UN Secretary-General Dag Hammarskjold during his recent conversations in Cairo with Egyptian President Nasser.

This information is believed to have been included in the first and second draft of the Secretary-General's report on "basic points for the presence and functioning in Egypt of the United Nations Emergency Force," the fourth and final draft of which was submitted to the General Assembly Nov. 21.

Mr. Hammarskjold is said to believe that the international force should police the Suez Canal area until the withdrawal of British, French, and Israeli forces has been completed and then be moved to both sides of the demarcation line between Egypt and Israel.

Army Contact Avoided

The Secretary-General is reported to feel that the Israeli and Egyptian armed forces should not be allowed again to come into contact until the explosive Palestine situation has been clarified.

In their conversations with Mr. Hammarskjold prior to the issuing of the report, the French, British, and Israeli representatives are said to have opposed any reference to a decision which reportedly was taken without prior consultation with the Israeli Government.

The General Assembly, in its Nov. 7 resolution, approved the principle that it could not request the international force "to be stationed or operate on the territory of a given country without the consent of the government of that country."

On Nov. 22, meanwhile, Asian-African nations including India decided to introduce a resolution under which Britain, France, and Israel would be called upon to withdraw their forces from Egypt "forthwith."

Though the UN resolutions of Nov. 2 and Nov. 7 had called for "immediate" withdrawal of invading forces, the three powers concerned have indicated their withdrawals will be staged to coincide with the arrival of the United Nations Emergency Force along the cease-fire lines.

Withdrawals Claimed

France claims already to have withdrawn one-third of its forces involved in the invasion of Egypt. Britain plans the withdrawal of one battalion of its forces soon. Israel declares it has achieved a partial withdrawal by pulling back in Sinai an average of 25 miles along the entire front.

The intention of Asian-African nations to introduce a new resolution indicated their belief that withdrawal was not proceeding swiftly enough to comply with the standing UN resolutions.

In his report Nov. 6 to the first emergency session of the General Assembly, the Secretary-General specified that the function of the international force can "be assumed to cover an area extending roughly from the Suez Canal to the armistice demarcation lines established in the armistice agreement between Egypt and Israel."

The following day the Secretary-General clarified that "the United Nations force will have to come in at what is at present the dividing line between the Egyptian and Israeli forces. It is at whatever may come to be the dividing line that they will have to function. As the situation is, that means that the United Nations activities will have to start close to the Suez Canal, but that, after the expected compliance with the recommendations of the General Assembly, they would end up at the armistice demarcation line."

This clarification would indicate, therefore, that the international force would eventually be stationed along the demarcation line but on the Egyptian side only.

Fairness Sought

The Secretary-General now is reported to feel, however, that in fairness to the Egyptians and to ensure a fuller implementation of the armistice agreement, the international force should be deployed on both sides of the demarcation line, including the Israeli side.

In UN circles it is felt that a solution of this problem requires as a first step a clarification of Israel's intentions. So far the position of the Israeli Government has been that "Israel will willingly withdraw its forces from Egypt immediately upon the conclusion of satisfactory arrangements with the United Nations in connection with the emergency international force."

Premier David Ben-Gurion's government has specified that the "satisfactory arrangements" which Israel seeks "are such as will ensure Israel's security against the recurrence of the threat or danger of attack, and against acts of belligerency by land and sea."

Sinai Pondered

This statement is interpreted to mean that Israel is unwilling to withdraw its military forces from the Sinai until it receives assurances that the Egyptian Army will not reoccupy the peninsula.

In this connection it has been reliably reported that policy planners at the Pentagon in Washington have urged President Eisenhower to support any measures that would effectively separate the Israeli and the Egyptian Armies. The Pentagon is further said to favor the demilitarization of the Sinai Peninsula.

The military are said to consider that the Soviet Union's penetration of the Middle East is far deeper than currently known and that unless some radical measure is being taken the West might be confronted soon with a situation threatening its security.

Oil Weighed

By William H. Stringer
Chief of the Washington News Bureau of The Christian Science Monitor

Washington

The pulling and hauling over how urgently the United States should act to alleviate Europe's Suez-caused oil shortage can be better understood if Washington's new policy toward the Arab-Asian world is clearly perceived.

So far, in planning emergency oil aid, the United States is preferring to deal with "Europe" rather than individual countries, even when requested for special consideration by some nations.

Washington does not want to alienate the Arab world and risk its revived reputation by rushing openly to the rescue of Britain and France. Behind this is the wish to take advantage of the situation developed when Washington opposed the British-French hostilities in Egypt.

New Diplomatic Era

In the succinct words of one official, the United States has "emancipated itself from all associations with colonialism in the Middle East." It may be able, now, to revise and vastly improve its relations with India and other Asian and African countries—develop virtually a new era of American-Asian-Middle Eastern relations.

Indian Prime Minister Jawaharlal Nehru is due to visit President Eisenhower in mid-December. The time is ripe, Washington officials believe, to bring to pass an era of larger mutual trust between the United States and the underdeveloped and Asian-African nations.

This does not mean that Washington is ready to forget its British alliance, or its North Atlantic Treaty Organization connections. But the President and his advisers believe that, in the Middle East and in Asia, the United States can better serve that alliance and those connections if it "goes it alone" for the present, labors to revive mutual trust all around, and works primarily through the United Nations.

'European' Problem

Officials here well understand the British-French reluctance to withdraw their troops from Suez until firm guarantees for free and secure navigation of the canal are obtained. They sympathize when R. A. Butler, deputizing for Prime Minister Sir Anthony Eden, tells the House of Commons that Britain and France must be left free to judge just when the UN force at Suez is "competent" to insure action to restore "freedom of navigation" through the canal.

But Washington feels that, in the interests of all concerned and in the hope of furthering an ultimate settlement, it must press now for the withdrawal of British-French troops from Suez and handle the oil crisis as a problem confronting "Europe," not individual nations.

There are Pentagon officials who would have preferred to see Britain and France press forward unimpeded with their conquest of the canal, eventually toppling Egypt's President Nasser and ridding the Middle East of a dangerous center of Soviet penetration. But this military advice was not followed. Such a sourse might have risked Soviet intervention; certainly it would have provoked further Arab sabotage against the pipelines and the Western position in the Middle East.

So now the United States sometimes finds itself on the side of India and the East at the UN. It is working to help Europe with its emergency oil needs, but acting primarily through the Organization for European Economic Cooperation, as it did in the old Marshall Plan days.

Nations Prod U.S.

European nations — affected countries besides Britain and France—think the United States could act more effectively if it called together the Middle East Emergency Committee, composed of oil industry experts under government chairmanship, which was set up after Egypt nationalized the Suez Canal Company last July and which developed an emergency oil plan involving tanker pools and shifts in oil shipments.

The State Department has had representatives of Austria, Greece, Italy, Norway, Spain, Switzerland, and West Germany call on it this week, asking about American oil plans. They have stressed that Europe faces serious oil shortage, and that it is not their fault.

They have further urged the United States to lend its official aid to formation of a tanker pool and to the rearrangement of routes so to get available oil to Europe faster. It is recognized that the main problem is transportation rather than oil. The United States, with increased oil flow from Texas, Louisiana, and other fields, plus the big output of Venezuela, could probably make up a good part of the actual oil shortage caused by Syrian pipeline sabotage.

State of the Nations

Suez—the Task Ahead

By JOSEPH C. HARSCH, Special Correspondent of The Christian Science Monitor

Washington

An important advance in United States Government thinking about the problem of Suez is marked by the statement John Foster Dulles made on emerging from the hospital to begin his convalescence in Florida.

"It would, however, be a great mistake," he said, "to believe that stability and tranquillity can be permanently established merely by emergency measures to stop the fighting. It is necessary to attack the basic problems of the area."

It would not be fair to say that no attempts have been made in the past to attack the "basic problems of the area."

There have been efforts made to provide for the permanent resettlement of the Arab refugees from Israel.

There has been the persistent effort led by Eric Johnston to use a Jordan River development program as a solvent for the differences between Israel and Jordan and Syria.

And the Aswan Dam proposal was intended in part to reduce Egyptian resentment against Israel by giving it an opportunity for its own economic development at home.

These three programs did constitute an effort to get at basic problems and reduce them and enlist the countries in the area in programs for economic development which might, in time, have persuaded all concerned that they could coexist economically in the Middle East without seeking the annihilation of either Israel or the military power of the Arab League.

Yet it is also true that the major effort of the would-be peacemakers from the time of the establishment of the State of Israel to recent resort to military action by the Israelis was marked primarily by an effort to "stop the fighting" and prevent new outbreaks of fighting.

The hope always was that if border warfare could be kept to a minimum, Israelis and Arabs would settle down, accept the status quo, and acquire a habit of allowing each other to live.

Perhaps this might in the end have worked out if the United Nations had been able to establish a buffer strip along the frontiers of Israel. The British and French proposed this in January of this year—a strip to be policed by UN forces. Had that project been achieved, it is probable we would not have seen the resort to arms of this period.

'Is It Real or a Mirage?'

But there were basic problems which no peacemaker wanted to touch. One was the Egyptian ban on use of the Suez Canal by Israeli shipping which worked a serious hardship on the economy of Israel, and was also a violation of the doctrine of unrestricted passage through the canal.

Another was Egyptian pressure to prevent the development of Elath as an Israeli seaport on the Red Sea.

Another was the Gaza strip which, by its very existence, was a source of friction between Egypt and Israel.

These were "basic problems" which everyone knew had to be settled some day before there could be stability and tranquillity.

Another basic problem then, and now, is whether the Arab countries will accept the permanence of the State of Israel. So long as they challenge that existence, and assert a policy of destroying Israel, there can be neither stability nor tranquillity.

All of these unsolved basic problems contributed to the problem which caused Britain and France to send troops into Suez. The unsettled state of Israel-Arab relations jeopardized Western Europe's access to Middle Eastern oil. It was this which finally, and more than any one other thing, launched British and French troops into Suez.

A solution to be permanent must secure Western European access to oil. But to do that there must be assurance that Egypt will not arbitrarily interfere with that access, or act as an agent of Moscow to the disadvantage of Western Europe. Europe cannot tolerate either the Nasser or the Moscow hand around its economic throat.

But before this assurance can be gained, there must be a permanent settlement of the status of Israel. That can only come when the Arab countries make their peace with Israel and recognize its existence, and its permanence.

There is a great deal of peacemaking to be done. The task is difficult and will be long protracted. But the beginning is the recognition by Mr. Dulles that merely maintaining a truce is not good enough. A truce can be used to protect the task of peacemaking. But the task must be taken in hand, and progress, or the warring factions almost will inevitably violate the truce again, as they already have so many times.

Shipping Officials Probe Ship Damage

The World's Day
Reg. U.S. Pat. Off.

New England: Etrusco Freed From Grounding

Shipping officials in Boston prepared to investigate the extent of the damage done to the freighter Etrusco before it was freed at Scituate yesterday. [Page 2.]

National: Three-State Area Hit by Snow

A biting wind off Lake Erie blew a tumult of up to 26 inches of heavy wet snow over adjacent sections of Ohio, Pennsylvania and New York State and socked in highway and air travel with drifts up to seven feet deep.

Nearly 11 months of negotiations climaxed by a marathon 72-hour session in Chicago, attended by government mediators, has resulted in an agreement calling for pay increases for some 50,000 operating employees on the nation's railroads. The new pact between the Brotherhood of Locomotive Firemen and Enginemen and the railroads was announced Wednesday by the National (Railway) Mediation Board.

Europe: Disarmament Study Is Concluded

Consultations between Britain, France, and the United States on the latest Soviet disarmament proposals have been concluded, and a statement may be made shortly in the United Nations, a British Foreign Office spokesman says.

Asia: Peking Premier Arrives in Cambodia

Chinese Communist Premier Chou En-lai has arrived in Cambodia by air from Hanoi, North Vietnam.

Weather Predictions: Cold Tonight (Page 2)

Art, Music, Theater: Page 15. Radio-TV, FM: Page 14

THE CHRISTIAN SCIENCE MONITOR

Registered in U. S. Patent Office

AN INTERNATIONAL DAILY NEWSPAPER

VOLUME 49 NO. 4 | BOSTON, THURSDAY, NOVEMBER 29, 1956 | • ATLANTIC EDITION | TWO SECTIONS | FIVE CENTS A COPY

COPYRIGHT 1956 BY THE CHRISTIAN SCIENCE PUBLISHING SOCIETY

Furcolo Faces Test

Pressure Exerted To Repeal Port Act

By Edgar M. Mills

New England Political Correspondent of The Christian Science Monitor

Governor-elect Foster Furcolo of Massachusetts faces the first major test of his political judgment as a result of pressure from top Democratic leaders seeking his support in a move to repeal the new Massachusetts Port Authority in the 1957 Legislature.

The pressure is being exerted, reliable sources report, by former Governor Dever and Joseph J. Mulhern, Boston attorney and director of the highly successful 1956 Democratic voter registration drive which was a big factor in the size of the Furcolo election victory.

Civic and business interests which strongly backed the successful authority-establishing act in the 1956 legislative session hope the Governor-elect will resist the Dever-Mulhern pressure.

Mr. Dever and Mr. Mulhern were chief architects of prolonged Democratic opposition to the Massachusetts Port Authority at the 1956 session. Now, with a Democratic Governor due to take office in January and the Democratic margin in the House substantially increased, it is understood they are hopeful that the port-authority measure will be repealed.

Political Ties Noted

Mr. Dever and Mr. Mulhern have been particularly close politically to Mr. Furcolo. Former Governor Dever persuaded Mr. Furcolo in 1952 to resign from his United States House seat to accept appointment to fill a State Treasurer vacancy, a move which first projected Mr. Furcolo into the statewide political picture. For some time he had been considered Mr. Dever's choice to succeed him as Governor in the 1952 election until Mr. Dever decided to seek a third term himself.

The Democratic registration drive conducted by Mr. Mulhern, the design of which attracted nationwide Democratic attention, moved Mr. Mulhern to high rank in the Furcolo political entourage.

Thus both men are in a position close to the Furcolo ear.

As yet, it is understood, Mr. Furcolo has made no commitment on the port authority issue. The organization was set up by a 1956 act to take over the Logan International and Bedford Airports, state-owned Boston port facilities, the Sumner Tunnel, and Mystic River Bridge and to build a second harbor crossing to East Boston.

Civic Groups Watch

Boston civic and business interests which view the port authority as a vehicle for major economic development of the Greater Boston area are watching the developments very carefully.

While spokesmen for these groups now are maintaining public silence, it is anticipated they will fight hard to block repeal, if Mr. Furcolo decides to favor such a course.

At present the port authority is awaiting final reports on which to base decisions on whether to undertake floating of a big bond issue soon to finance taking over of state-owned airport, port and tunnel facilities, as well as the Mystic River Bridge from the existing bridge authority.

Ephraim A. Brest, chairman of the Massachusetts Port Authority, said he expects the final reports to be available at the end of next week. Preliminary reports, he said, have been very encouraging.

Despite the present tight money market, Mr. Brest expressed confidence that the authority can float in the first quarter of 1957 the necessary bonds within the 4 per cent interest limit set by the legislation. Originally plans called for issuance of the bonds before the end of this year.

Confidence Voiced

If repeal is to be undertaken, it must be done before the bonds are sold. Otherwise, the state would have to satisfy financial claims of the bondholders.

Mr. Brest has voiced confidence that the port-authority program can be undertaken successfully, if allowed to proceed. He has long advocated the authority approach as the key to Greater Boston's economic expansion in the transportation field.

He and other authority supporters strongly believe the authority should be given a real chance to operate.

Opponents of the port authority have argued that development of transportation facilities planned by the authority can be undertaken cheaper through state tax-supported bonds than through authority bonds. They claim the state can float bonds at a more favorable interest rate.

Repeal Bid Filed

However, authority backers insist the authority will proceed faster with development and that freedom from state red tape will lead to better over-all results.

Already repeal legislation has been filed by Representative Rico Matera (D) of East Boston, long a vociferous foe of the authority plan.

Although the authority legislation was adopted with strong bipartisan support at the 1956 session, the situation might change in 1957 if Governor-elect Furcolo were to throw the full weight of his administration behind repeal. The vast powers of the Herter administration constituted a major factor in the 1956 passage of the bill.

Democratic leaders in both branches of the Legislature were and are opposed to the authority. If repeal should be the Furcolo course, they can be expected to go all out along that line.

But civic groups interested in Boston's development are hopeful the Governor-elect will successfully resist attempts to enlist his aid in crushing the authority even before it can prove itself.

Associated Press

United States Starfighter—World's Fastest Fighter Plane?

Test Pilot Tony LeVier is set to take aloft the XF-104 Starfighter, whose small frontal area is designed for fastest speeds yet attained by fighters. Its wingspread is only 21 feet, 11 inches; its length, 55 feet. The jet speedster is tested at Edwards Air Force Base, Calif.

Business Scans Oil Crisis

Free World A-Union Urged

By Nate White

Business and Financial Editor of The Christian Science Monitor

New York

An anxious, but hopeful, group of 250 business leaders of 38 Nations of the free world are debating here at their third international meeting since 1951 what steps they, as businessmen, can take to set the world's course for peace and thwart the growing industrial might of Soviet Russia.

Many of these men came to New York with anxious hearts. Western Europe, the industrial and native home of more than a hundred of them, lies stalemated by the Middle Eastern crisis and the drought in oil. The ferment and torture of Hungary pounds at their own countries' windows and doors.

Even so, hope prevails here at the Hotel Plaza as the International Conference of Manufacturers, sponsored by the United States' National Association of Manufacturers, gets under way.

Atomic Union Proposed

John Jay Hopkins, president and chairman of General Dynamics Corporation, proposed that the free world nations of Asia, the British Commonwealth, the Americas, Western Europe, and Africa join in a united atomic treaty organization for the pooling of atomic energy resources to counteract the nuclear power of the Soviet Union and its satellite system. His is the firm which built the Nautilus, the first atomic-powered submarine.

He said, "I have certain knowledge that the good and the true must prevail—for only the good and the true are real."

"I am enough of an optimist to know that we cannot fail," Mr. Hopkins told the meeting, "enough of a pessimist to state that we dare not fail, enough of a realist to believe in the triumph of moral principle, of individual courage, of the cooperation of free men under God."

Mr. Hopkins' "geological time limit" for free world dependence on oil as an energy fuel is a scant 20 years. His "politico-economic time limit" has expired. By pressure diplomacy, a five-year delay may be obtained. Mr. Hopkins believes, before the Soviet Union finally dominates the nations of the Middle East and controls their oil "by seizure, sabotage, or inflamed nationalism."

NATO Sets Pattern

Against these deadlines, Mr. Hopkins calls on the citizens of the non-Soviet world, the political leaders, "the men of science and religion," the military men, and the industrialists to form now "a new economic alliance, an atomic alliance, a united atomic treaty organization—Unatom."

Specifically, the Hopkins proposal would be directed toward making the free world totally independent of Middle East oil resources. He would pattern the new economic alliance in formative stages after the North Atlantic Treaty Organization, because NATO has taught member nations how to cooperate and because it preserves national sovereignty but enlists and programs the resources of all.

The current "energy crisis" in the blocking of Middle Eastern oil is so serious, in Mr. Hopkins' view, that the Berlin blockade which brought NATO into existence pales by comparison.

"What I visualize generally," he urged, "is a flexible alliance of the free nations aimed as much at eradicating poverty through the wide-scale application of nuclear power as it is at providing rapidly a worldwide equalization of energy resources. Specifically, Unatom would expedite not only nuclear power development, but advance nuclear science and technology so that all member nations might, in the shortest space of time, achieve energy self-sufficiency—and hence the political independence that economic independence provides."

The United States industrialist called for "a massive cooperative effort on the part of free world industrialists" to clear away the roadblocks to international nuclear development by providing credit and know-how.

Soviet Goal Stressed

Fritz Berg, president of the Federation of German Industries, while hailing the "mutual and growing feeling of neighborliness" among the peoples of the free world, solemnly warned that the "recent tragic events in Hungary unfortunately are conclusive proof" that Eastern communism's principal goal is "universal penetration and world domination."

"We should not underestimate the economic possibilities of the East," Mr. Berg cautioned the industrialists. He contrasted steel and energy production in the United States, in the free countries of Europe, and in the Soviet Union. "In 1955," he said, "raw steel production amounted to 106 million tons in the United States, 78 million tons in Europe, and 45 million tons in the Soviet Union.

"In relation to 1950, this represented an increase by 20.5 per cent in the United States, by 2 per cent in Europe, and by 67 per cent in the Soviet Union. During the same period, the relative increase in electricity production amounted to 61.1 per cent in the United States, 35.1 per cent in Europe, and 86.9 per cent in the Soviet Union."

Unless the free world intensifies its efforts, the German leader said, "we shall not only lose our lead, but the East will overcome us." He set the tasks of the businessmen and nations of the free world as follows: Providing the "new" nations of Africa and Asia with technological advice, training facilities for their own workers, schooling for their juveniles, goods, credits, and investments.

Protective Code

As a foundation of this growth and development, Mr. Berg proposed a world Magna Charta for the protection of investments abroad, an international code, based on the rule of law.

The "new" nations hope to make their jump from an underdeveloped economic status to fully developed industrial systems without spending the 200 years which the West required for the same progress, Mr. Berg said, and told the industrialists that they and their countries must find ways to aid in the development. He also urged that if the satellites of the Soviet Union were to request economic aid, as Yugoslavia has done, the free nations should provide it.

Leaders of the industrialists' working groups on how to bring about free world cooperation in the industrial application of atomic energy are under Dr. Franz Josef Mayer-Gunthof, vice-president of the Federation of Austrian Industries; Quinto Quintierie, vice-president of the General Federation of Italian Industries; Wilhelmus Hendrik van Leeuwen, president of the Netherlands Productivity Center; and Christian von Sydow, chairman of the Federation of Swedish Industries.

Nations with industrialists participating at this conference are besides the United States and Canada: Austria, Belgium, Denmark, Finland, France, West Germany, the Irish Republic, Italy, the Netherlands, Norway, Portugal, Spain, Sweden, Switzerland, the United Kingdom, Argentina, Bolivia, Brazil, Chile, the Dominican Republic, Ecuador, El Salvador, Honduras, Mexico, Panama, Paraguay, Uruguay, and Venezuela.

Pro-West Iraq Under Fire

By Harry B. Ellis

Assistant Overseas News Editor of The Christian Science Monitor

As change and rumors of change continue to sweep the Middle East, the strongest pro-Western voice in the Arab world is under increasing pressure from elements which are basically anti-Western.

This voice is the Iraqi Government of Premier Nuri es-Said, which consistently has opposed the pro-Soviet counsels of Egypt, Syria, and, to a lesser extent, of Jordan. The Iraqi Government now finds itself threatened by anti-Western sentiment within its own country.

How widespread Iraqi feeling against the West is, and how immediate a threat it poses to Es Said, is unclear.

Iraq denies the Syrian claims that dozens of Iraqis have been killed in anti-government riots in Iraq's main cities in the past few days. Damascus Radio declared 104 Iraqis were killed in four days of rioting in the Moslem holy city of Najaf, in southwest Iraq.

In denying these claims, Es Said's government asserted only two civilians were killed and several police and civilians were wounded in a clash at Najaf. At the same time the Iraqi Government urged its people to be calm and not to yield to "subversive elements" who were inciting trouble.

These "subversive elements" Iraq claims, are Syrian and Egyptian agents who are seeking to turn Iraqi masses against the leadership of Es Said.

Anti-West Drift

Independent observers report that a number of Iraqi Army officers and Iraqi politicians are becoming disaffected with the pro-Western stand of Es Said, and are leaning toward the anti-Western views of President Nasser of Egypt and a pro-Soviet Syrian clique led by Lt. Col. Abdel Hamid Serraj, Syrian Army intelligence chief.

In the face of these reports, the military governor of Baghdad has broadcast an appeal to the people to be calm. In an interview with the Associated Press, Khalil Ibrahim, Iraqi director of information, declared:

"One of the biggest dangers in the Arab world today is that 'the streets' are tending to lead the governments. Our response to such attempts is to try to calm the streets." Mr. Ibrahim referred to the historic tendency of Arab opposition leaders to arouse street mobs against their governments.

These developments occurred as tension between Syria and Iraq rose apparently near the breaking point. The Iraqi Government deplores Syria's current gravitation toward Soviet control, and sees in this trend a threat to Iraq's northern oil fields.

Invasion Plan Charged

Syria claims that Iraq, and possibly Turkey, intend to invade Syria, Thus Damascus has launched a full-fledged radio and newspaper campaign against the government of Es Said. In this campaign Syria is echoed by the Soviet Union and Egypt.

In other developments, the Jordanian Parliament gave the Jordanian Government a 39-1 vote of confidence Nov. 29 on its decision to abrogate its 1948 defense treaty with Britain. Jordanian Premier Suleiman Nabulsi announced Nov. 27 that the treaty would be scrapped as soon as Syria, Saudi Arabia, and Egypt implemented their pledge to furnish Jordan the $33,000,000 yearly which Britain now provides.

The Soviet Government newspaper Izvestia accused Israel of threatening its Arab neighbors since the day the Israeli state was established, and warned that "Israeli rulers are pushing the country on the road to suicide."

Reflecting all-out Soviet support for the Arabs, Izvestia asserted that the "very existence of Israel as a state is now at stake."

Israeli Premier David Ben-Gurion called upon the United Nations and the big powers "to halt the persecution of Jews in Egypt." Mr. Ben-Gurion charged Nov. 28 that thousands of stateless Jews had been expelled from Egypt, that many other Jews had been deprived of Egyptian nationality, and that others had been placed in concentration camps.

Israeli Charge Denied

Egypt has denied that any Jews except "enemies of the country" have been deported or imprisoned.

In Damascus, the Syrian Foreign Ministry proclaimed Syria's "positive neutrality" between East and West, and denied United States charges that Syria was receiving "substantial shipments" of Soviet arms.

Most of these factors touched in one way or another on Iraq's basic problem, namely that its government's stanch adherence to the West was not widely supported among the Iraqi populace.

Until recently this populace did not take sides on the question, partly, no doubt, because the Iraqi Government has launched a gigantic seven-year economic development program which already is beginning to benefit wide segments of the Iraqi population.

This program is financed by income from oil. This income now is sharply reduced by the Syrian sabotage of Iraqi pipelines crossing Syria to the Mediterranean. Syria and Egypt now are appealing directly to the Iraqi people to join their Arab brethren in opposing the West.

The situation is made difficult for Es Said by the fact that Iraqis, differing little from Syrians or Jordanians in background and outlook, are susceptible to the kind of Arab nationalism now being voiced by Cairo and Damascus radios and newspapers. It is this fact which constitutes the present threat to his position.

Chapin Sentence Commuted to Life

The World's Day

Reg. U.S. Pat. Off.

Boston: Council Votes 6 to 3 on Chapin

The capital sentence for Kenneth Chapin was commuted to life imprisonment today on a six-to-three vote of the Governor's Council, after Governor Herter had recommended this step to them.

Australia: U.S. Lead Over Soviets Increased

Charley Jenkins of Cambridge, Mass., provided an upset in the Olympic Games, winning the 400-meter gold medal as Americans increased their unofficial point lead over the Soviets, 318-219½. [Page 10.]

National: Refugee Aid Coordinator Named

President Eisenhower today named Tracy S. Voorhees, former Undersecretary of the Army, to coordinate the Hungarian refugee program and study whether more than 5,000 should be admitted to the United States. White House press secretary James C. Hagerty said at Augusta, Ga., Mr. Voorhees, now a New York attorney and a consultant to the Defense Department, is taking over the new assignment immediately and will serve without pay.

Weather Predictions: Cold Tonight (Page 2)

Art, Music, Theater, Radio, TV: Page 10. FM: Page 22

November 29, 1956

Suez Troop Decision Hangs Over Britain

By Henry S. Hayward

Chief of the London News Bureau of The Christian Science Monitor

London

How long British troops are to remain in Egypt and under what conditions they are to be withdrawn—if a withdrawal is ordered—these are questions all Britain is waiting to hear.

As this is written, the hope was that Foreign Secretary Selwyn Lloyd could clarify the situation for the House of Commons on Nov. 29.

The prospect for an immediate clarification dimmed, however, with an announcement French Foreign Minister Christian Pineau is consulting with London Nov. 30—a move expected to delay any government statement on troop withdrawal.

Since Prime Minister Sir Anthony Eden's departure for Jamaica on Nov. 23, the British Government, Parliament, and people have been marking time awaiting the outcome of Mr. Lloyd's labors at the United Nations in New York.

Now that the Foreign Secretary has returned and consulted with Acting Prime Minister R. A. Butler and the Cabinet, an important policy statement seems urgent.

The situation is described as unparalleled since World War II in tenseness.

Not only is troop withdrawal—and the threat of a major revolt in the Conservative Party if it is permitted—up for consideration.

Members of Parliament likewise are eager for Mr. Lloyd's report on the status of the Anglo-American alliance—plus, if possible, an explanation of what the government's attitude toward American policy is likely to be.

Overshadowing the situation is growing speculation in unofficial Whitehall circles that trouble in Syria may inject a new element into the Mideast crisis. Some Conservatives appear anxious for what might be termed a "second-front diversion" that would have the effect of "taking the heat off Britain."

U.S. Stand Decried

As far as relations with the United States are concerned, criticism of President Eisenhower's stand against talks before withdrawals continues here. "United States policy at the moment can be summed up in one word—golf," was one comment on a television show.

About one hundred and thirty conservative MPs, meanwhile, have endorsed the motion accusing the United States of "gravely endangering the Atlantic Alliance." This is a sizable proportion of the government's backbench supporters.

A countermotion, on the other hand, has been drafted stating that the Anglo-American tie is "the main safeguard of peace in the world." Support so far is 25 Tory MPs. Included are some of the most prominent Conservative backbenchers.

Some would say the ratio of backers for the two opposing motions accurately reflects the current tide of opinion in Parliament.

Commons Storm Brews

There nevertheless is awareness—at least at high government levels—that a formal rebuke to the United States in the form of a House of Commons motion would present the Soviet Union with a fantastic triumph in the Communist campaign to drive the two foremost Western allies apart.

In the present mood of the Commons it is difficult to see how the Foreign Secretary could advocate or announce an unconditional British withdrawal from Suez. If he refuses to so advocate, however, the animosity of the Labor opposition is believed certain to burst forth once more in an unruly Westminster scene.

Mr. Lloyd is regarded as having indicated his position Nov. 28 upon his return from the UN. He admitted the "acute difference of opinion" with the United States about the Mideast, but insisted that the two governments were trying to bridge the gap.

Stern Task Looms

The Foreign Secretary also refused to accept the suggestion that Britain has been "let down" by its trans-Atlantic ally, replying, "No, I would not put it that way. They (the Americans) do not think the way we do."

He pointed out that "the atmosphere at the UN has undoubtedly improved as far as Britain is concerned," stressing the change in voting alignments. He said Britain is slowly persuading people that this is an opportunity to get a permanent Mideast settlement.

He warned, however, that "if people think it is the right thing to go back to the state of things as they were before, they are wasting an opportunity and making a great mistake."

Mr. Lloyd's difficult task in the Commons is to present developments at the UN and in the United States in perspective without either promising anything he cannot deliver—or making it seem that his mission was fruitless.

The debate obviously will continue for more than one session, with government officials attempting to hold the line and find a formula to close what now seems to be an open rift in the Conservative ranks.

State of the Nations

Road to Suez Settlement

By JOSEPH C. HARSCH

Special Correspondent of The Christian Science Monitor

Washington

There have been two theories in high government quarters in Washington about how to begin the task of getting a Suez settlement.

One theory is that it could only begin with a complete and unconditional withdrawal of British and French troops.

The other theory is that the presence of the British and French troops is a fact which is in many ways regrettable but a fact which has changed the old situation in the Middle East and which, if properly managed, can be converted into one means of aiding a long-term permanent settlement.

The first theory was the dominant theory from the day of the Anglo-French ultimatum until Nov. 27 and the theory on which operating policy was based.

It led to the reported alignment of the United States with the Afro-Asian or Bandung powers bloc in United Nations voting down through Nov. 24. It caused a rupture in effective diplomatic conversations with the British and French and the growing belief throughout Western Europe that the United States had decided to abandon the NATO alliance.

The operating policy based on this first theory included a refusal to discuss any serious matter with Britain and France until after they had first withdrawn their troops. This meant that they were given no assurance that the United States would attempt after the withdrawal to work for a satisfactory long-term solution of Middle East problems or in the meantime cooperate with them to devise ways and means to protect their economies from a dangerous oil shortage.

This amounted, in its effect, to the imposition of economic sanctions. Washington was using the threat of an oil shortage as a weapon to induce the troop withdrawal. In British and French eyes the Suez crisis was precipitated by a United States refusal to apply sanctions on Egypt. Matters had reached the point where Washington was threatening to use a more dangerous weapon against its own principal allies than it ever had been willing to use against Egypt for seizure of the canal or against the Soviet Union for what it had done in Hungary.

This policy was not achieving its purpose. The French refused to budge. The British took out a token battalion, but then dug in their heels. Great nations do not lightly give way to pressure of this kind. An old rule in diplomacy is that an ultimatum should be used only when the user is willing to go to war to enforce its demands. An ultimatum is never used against an ally, not if there is any intention of retaining the alliance.

The second theory permits a much more flexible operating policy toward Britain and France. It starts with the proposition that the purpose is to achieve a settlement in Suez. It recognizes that British and French troop withdrawal is necessary to a settlement, but it puts settlement ahead of troop withdrawal. Therefore, it seeks to fit the troop withdrawal into the pattern — rather than making it the prime purpose.

Washington's operating policies went over from the first to the second theory basis this week. The British and French were assured both publicly and privately that President Eisenhower regards the NATO alliance as an "essential" feature of United States foreign policy. He authorized an immediate revival of an oil committee which will organize world oil deliveries to guarantee British and French economic survival. It was made clear to the British and French that the United States is interested in, and will help to achieve, a real settlement in the Middle East.

Essential to the Game

Thus, although not all the steps are yet public at this writing, the road is cleared in fact for a withdrawal of British and French troops from Suez. It is cleared because the hard policy which had alarmed London and Paris, and induced obstinacy arising out of that alarm, has been repudiated by President Eisenhower.

The next question is how to manage the transition from British and French to UN forces in the Suez area in a manner which will not result in merely restoring the condition which existed in advance of the Anglo-French intervention. That old situation was impossible and intolerable. It led to the explosion. Washington, no more than London and Paris, desires merely to see President Nasser reconfirmed in his ability to disturb the peace.

Nasser policy is seeking a restoration of the status quo. But the status quo will not, in fact, be restored so long as the UN police force remains in the area. The probable development will be a staged replacement of British and French troops by UN troops. This will remove the obstacle of British-French troops to a settlement without depriving the rest of the world of the bargaining power of the UN forces in negotiations with Egypt and Israel.

At least one can see some light ahead—for the first time in weeks.

Seaway Advances

By the Associated Press

Washington

Eisenhower Lock, one of two being constructed by the United States in its portion of the St. Lawrence Seaway, now is better than one-third completed.

This was reported by Lewis G. Castle, administrator of the St. Lawrence Seaway Development Corporation. He said about 50 per cent of the total concrete in the huge lock will have been placed before winter weather forces a construction shutdown.

More than 200,000 cubic yards of cement have been placed in the lock as of Oct. 31, Mr. Castle said in his latest progress report of seaway construction.

He said work on the Eisenhower Lock and also on the Grasse River Lock is ahead of schedule. Work on the latter was 24 per cent complete as of the end of October.

Also under construction by New York State and Ontario is a huge power development in the International Rapids section of the St. Lawrence.

U.S. Hits Arms Aid By Soviets to Syria

By the Associated Press

Washington

The United States State Department says the Soviet Union is "adding to tensions" in the Middle East by shipping arms to Syria.

It disclosed that the American Ambassador has expressed to Syria the United States Government's concern over continuing Soviet weapons deliveries.

A department spokesman said: "We know of substantial shipments of Soviet arms of various types and weights to Syria in recent months. We understand that since the Middle East crisis, further shipments have been made."

He did not say what specific types and quantities of Soviet weapons had gone to Syria. But officials said more than $30,000,000 worth of such Communist military equipment has been delivered.

THE CHRISTIAN SCIENCE MONITOR

Registered in U. S. Patent Office

AN INTERNATIONAL DAILY NEWSPAPER

VOLUME 49 NO. 186   COPYRIGHT 1957 BY THE CHRISTIAN SCIENCE PUBLISHING SOCIETY   BOSTON, FRIDAY, JULY 5, 1957   ★ ATLANTIC EDITION   TWO SECTIONS   TEN CENTS A COPY Five Cents in Greater Boston

GOP Caucus Bends

Jobless Benefits: Compromise Due

By Edgar M. Mills

New England Political Correspondent of The Christian Science Monitor

The Massachusetts Senate stage is being set for organized labor's last-ditch struggle to win a major advance in unemployment compensation benefits from the 1957 Legislature.

Already defeated in the Senate on three big employment security issues, labor forces are expected to gain an increase in dependency benefits from $3 a week to $4.

Both the Massachusetts Federation of Labor and the Massachusetts State CIO have been driving for a $5-a-week level on benefits allotted for each dependent minor in addition to the basic benefit the unemployed worker receives. The maximum basic benefit is $35 a week for 26 weeks.

GOP Caucus Divides

Labor is ready to accept a compromise figure of $4 on dependency benefits. The Senate Committee on Ways and Means has brought out such a compromise, after a GOP caucus failed to agree to establish a solid party front against any advance.

Business groups such as the Greater Boston Chamber of Commerce and the Associated Industries of Massachusetts have campaigned for retention of the present benefit level.

They are opposed to the compromise plan but some of their spokesmen anticipate its passage.

On every other measure involving increased benefits for unemployed workers, the organized business groups have been victorious in the Republican-controlled Senate this year.

Only last week the Senate threw out three major labor bills for benefits liberalization. They were:

Rumblings of 1958

1. A bill to grant unemployment compensation benefits to strikers after a strike had lasted six weeks.

2. A measure to make eligible for benefits a worker who voluntarily quits his job for causes not attributable to his employer, after he serves a four to 10-weeks penalty period. The present law requires such a worker to return to the labor market and work at least four weeks before becoming eligible for benefits.

3. Legislation to permit an unemployed woman worker to refuse employment between 10 p.m. and 6 a.m. without losing benefits rights.

These measures were rejected as a result of GOP caucus action binding members to a vote against them.

Largest Check $74

When a similar stand was sought on the dependency benefit measure, it failed. Some GOP senators, in districts where the political division is narrow, desire to vote for some labor-backed legislation to sweeten up their labor record. They have the 1958 state election firmly in mind.

When some Republican sena-

tors showed a desire to vote for the $5 dependency benefit, a move was immediately started for a $4 compromise. The pending bill from the Senate Committee on Ways and Means is the result.

Senator Ralph C. Mahar (R) of Orange, chairman of the committee, today said the $4 dependency limit would cost about $500,000 to $750,000 a year.

He added that it would solidify Massachusetts' position as the most liberal state in its overall unemployment compensation benefits.

Sentaor Mahar said that 10 states, the District of Columbia and Alaska now pay dependency benefits, but all these government units, except Massachusetts, limit the number of dependents for which benefits will be paid. The only limit in Massachusetts, he said, is that the total benefits must not exceed the average salary of the worker. He said that in 1956 the largest weekly benefit check in Massachusetts was for $74.

Other Rates Cited

Disclosing the dependency benefits in the other government units, Senator Mahar said North Dakota and the District of Columbia pay $1 a week per dependent up to three dependents, Maryland $2 a week for up to four dependents, and Ohio and Wyoming $3 weekly on up to two dependents.

Illinois, he said, pays $3 weekly on up to four dependents, but only if the unemployed worker earned $573 or more in his highest quarter year. Connecticut's dependency benefits, he added, are $3 weekly up to a maximum of $17 a week.

Michigan pays varying benefits up to a maximum of $24 for dependents, while the Nevada allowance is $5 a week for up to four dependents, and Alaska pays $5 weekly for up to five dependents.

Demoted in Soviet Shake-Up

Associated Press

These four top-ranking Soviet officials have been demoted from Communist Party leadership. Deputy Premier Georgi M. Malenkov, upper left; First Vice-Premier Vyacheslav M. Molotov, upper right; and industrial expert Lazar M. Kaganovich, lower right, were ousted from the party presidium. Dmitri T. Shepilov, lower left, lost his post as secretary of the Soviet Communist Party's powerful central committee, it was reported.

Cairo Change Scented

Nasser Bids for Arab Unity

By Geoffrey Godsell

Mediterranean Correspondent of The Christian Science Monitor

Cairo

As the results of the Egyptian elections of July 3 are beginning to come in, the most interesting news item is one which gets much less play in Egyptian newspapers than the names of those chosen to sit in the new National Assembly.

This is the unheralded departure for Saudi Arabia of one of President Nasser's closest and most trusted associates, his Minister of War and Commander in Chief, Maj. Gen. Abdel Hakim Amer.

It has not been officially disclosed why President Nasser has sent General Amer to Saudi Arabia at this particular time. The general assumption, however, is that he is to have talks with King Saud as part of attempts which are apparently being made to sweeten—outwardly at

any rate—relations between Egypt and Syria on the one hand and Saudi Arabia on the other, which have become increasingly embittered since King Saud threw his support behind King Hussein of Jordan in the latter's firm repression of pro-Egyptian and pro-Syrian factions in Jordan.

Developments since the Jordanian crisis have seen an increasing isolation of Egypt and Syria from the other Arab governments. Behind this, Egyptian and Syrian propagandists see a process to see the cunning machinations of the United States State Department.

There is a parallel belief that Egypt and Syria would not have suffered their recent diplomatic defeats in Jordan if King Saud had not backed King Hussein in the latter's risky but resolute action. The atmosphere was subsequently acerbated by charges of plots and counterplots exchanged between the Governments of Jordan on the one hand and of Syria and Egypt on the other.

Egyptian officials have refrained from direct criticism of King Saud, but there has been more outspokenness in Syria. Last month the Syrian Minister made this remark in the knowledge that steps were being taken seen whether General Amer's visit to Saudi Arabia is part of the same pattern.

The Secretary General of the Arab League, Abdel Khalek Hassouna, has just returned to his Cairo headquarters after a visit to King Saud. He said he had firm hope that the Arabs were about to turn a new page in the history of their unity and solidarity. Only events will show whether Mr. Hassouna made this remark in the knowledge that steps were being taken to try to close the widening gap in this unity and solidarity.

As for the Egyptian election results, it is difficult to interpret them at this stage. Voters placed at Mecca and Medina gives him both a peculiar awareness of the urge for Arab unity and a uniquely influential role throughout the Arab world.

In results so far announced, it there will have to be a second ballot in runoff elections on July 14 in a surprisingly large number of electoral districts because no candidate on the list managed to get the necessary over-all majority in the first ballot.

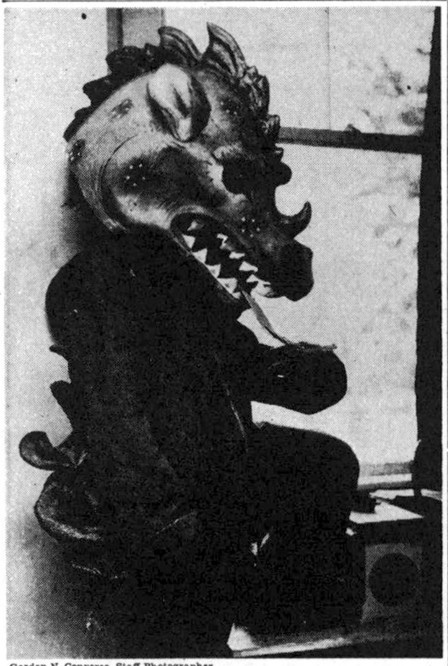

Craving for Unity

It is one of the paradoxes of the Arabs that although they find it so hard to agree among themselves, they have in their hearts a deep craving for Arab unity. One of the factors contributing to this yearning is the overwhelming majority of Arabs. King Saud's position as protector of the Moslem holy

ser, many observers noted that he was refraining—notably during his visits to his erstwhile dynastic foes in Baghdad and Amman—from public pronouncements or denunciations likely to widen the breach that was developing with Egypt.

Exchange Reported

In an interview on the independent British television network earlier this week, the following exchange took place between Colonel Nasser and a reporter—according to a text released in Egypt:

Question: What about your relations with the Saudi Arabian Kingdom?

Nasser: My personal relations with King Saud are good. But the things that we want to create trouble from trying to create doubts.

Question: Does it bother you to see King Saud have American leanings?

Nasser: The leanings of King Saud must be Arab.

Reports from Damascus say King Saud and President Kuwatly of Syria have this week exchanged messages about improving relations between their two countries. It remains to be seen whether General Amer's visit to Saudi Arabia is part of the same pattern.

Gordon N. Converse, Staff Photographer

Fierce but Friendly

This beastly looking beast is actually somebody's loving pet. Good and gentle, she never shows her fangs except when helping her master, handsome hero of "The Land of the Dragon," rescue the beautiful princess from prison. Madge Miller's play is the first of three productions to be put on this summer by the Magic Circle, Tufts children's theater. In private life, when she isn't frightening away subversive Oriental courtiers, the dragon is nine-year-old Jane L. Shapiro of Somerville, Mass. Here she waits for a curtain call and feels her dragon tongue. Performed this morning, the play will be put on again at 10 a.m. July 11 and 12. [Other pictures: Page 2.]

Big A-Test Success

By the Associated Press

Atomic Test Site, Nev.

What may have been the most powerful atomic test weapon ever exploded in the United States has burst with earth-shaking fury over a brigade of entrenched marines.

The 1,090 marines were safely dug in 5,700 yards from the detonation site.

The weapon, rated unofficially at between three and four times as big as the World War II atomic bombs which devastated the Japanese cities of Hiroshima and Nagasaki, was singled from a balloon 1,500 feet in the air. It went off at 4:40 a.m. July 5.

As the tremendous blast went off a wave of heat enveloped News Nob, 13 miles away, where reporters and photographers were assembled.

KhrushchevClinchesControl, ShovesStalinistsDownLadder

Army Star Rises

By Paul Wohl

Written for The Christian Science Monitor

Soviet Party Chief Nikita S. Khrushchev has set up a new and larger party Presidium in which he is virtually unopposed.

Its members, with the exception of Marshal Georgi K. Zhukov, Soviet Defense Minister, and President Voroshilov, are servants of the apparatus who gained their experience in organizational, propagandistic, and coercive party work.

At the same time the political weight of the Army has risen.

Marshal Zhukov, who has become a full member of the Presidium, must have supported Mr. Khrushchev.

The Army, moreover, now that the high ministerial bureaucracy has been dispersed and politically chastised in the person of its foremost representatives, has emerged as the only other all-union (federal) hierarchy besides the party apparatus. Six of the remaining eight industrial ministries have become part of the defense establishment.

Foreign Relations Aided

Not since the days of the slave-labor trusts of Lavrenti P. Beria's MVD has any single government department exercised control over a similarly large sector of the economy.

On the international scene the political significance of the shake-up is believed to be the following:

1. By dropping Stalin's most prominent associates, Mr. Khrushchev makes it appear that the Soviet Union has entered a new era of experimentation and flexibility, described as "living Marxism in action." The eclipse of Vyacheslav M. Molotov, especially, is likely to gain good will for Moscow in western Europe.

2. Now that the so-called Stalinist faction is out of the picture, the Kremlin in its dealings with the satellites can afford to steer what appears to be a middle course while concentrating its fire on the "revisionists" or "liberals." This was the line of both Czechoslovakian party secretary Jiri Heidrych and of Hungarian Premier Janos Kadar, whose speeches were extensively summarized in Pravda June 21 and 29—the date of the central committee's decision. Premier Nikolai A. Bulganin's and Mr. Khrushchev's imminent departure for Prague gives these statements programmatic significance.

Domestic Issues Aired

3. On the eve of Chinese Communist chairman Mao Tse-tung's arrival, the disappearance from the political scene of the three full presidium members who always had remained aloof from a close pro-Chinese orientation may ease the situation of the Soviet negotiators.

Domestically the reasons for the shake-up may well have been those given by the central committee. The decentralization of industrial management has led to many complaints from onetime ministerial executives who naturally turned for support to the men who were considered to be their spokesmen in the party presidium. It also is possible that Mr. Khrushchev's agricultural policies have reached an impasse which he expects to open in his own way without the "I told you so" of his old associates.

Whatever the reasons, the few specific accusations listed in the central committee's communiqué appear to consist of distortions and outright lies which informed Soviet readers are unlikely to take any more seriously than Mr. Malenkov's confessions of guilt and inexperience of February, 1955.

Serious Charge

Deputy Premier Georgi M. Malenkov was listed first among the members of the alleged anti-party group. Yet the indictment was directed mainly against Mr. Molotov.

Although organized antiparty activity is the most serious accusation which can be leveled against a Communist, no proof of collusion was offered or claimed.

At first sight the ouster of the four men seemed to confirm

State of the Nations

By William H. Stringer

Chief, Washington News Bureau, The Christian Science Monitor

Washington

It's useful that a large number of Americans saw Soviet Party Boss Nikita S. Khrushchev on the CBS television interview recently. For the shrewd, dynamic Khrushchev now has had his position greatly strengthened—as the most powerful man in the Soviet Union.

He is no Stalin, and never will be. He starts under differing conditions, and he is too old ever to hope to amass the absolute power which Stalin wielded. But by the dismissals of Molotov, Kaganovich, and Malenkov, by the installation of more Khrushchev protégés in the Soviet Presidium, and by the circumstances of the whole dramatic shift the short, burly First Secretary of the Communist Party emerges as much more than a mild "chairman of the board" of the Kremlin's collective leadership.

The aptest title for him now would be simply "the driving force." For it is in the name of this ebullient man of the people, with his intense energy and will, that the three great innovations in Soviet policy since the 20th party congress were initiated and are being carried out.

He has been the central figure behind the daring debasement of Stalin, the bold push to open virgin lands for agriculture, the mammoth move to decentralize Soviet industry.

Each of these stupendous shifts from past rigidities still requires tremendous applications of skill and drive. That precarious balance of forces and politics which elevates and demotes men in Moscow has found in Khrushchev the strong man of the hour for the job: for carrying forward the recoupment of Soviet prestige in matters of Communist ideology—made necessary by the shattering of the Stalin image—for boosting Soviet agricultural production, and for regionalizing Soviet industry.

We can place the sudden Moscow dismissals in clear perspective if we compare them with the purging of Lavrenti P. Beria, MVD chief back in 1954. When the "collective rulership" was set up after Stalin's passing, Beria refused to surrender his control over the Soviet secret police. This meant that every top Soviet official who looked straight down the gun barrel of the dreaded police. It was an intolerable situation, and, with the Army's help, Beria was seized and executed.

The misdeeds of Molotov, Kaganovich, and Malenkov are of a different caliber. They argued, interminably, against Khrushchev's policies. The old Bolsheviks, Molotov and Kaganovich, feared the relaxations following the demolition job on Stalin, said "we told you so" to satellite unrest, criticized the foreign tours of "B and K," sought to insert their own followers in important posts. Eventually Khrushchev, with the Army's approval, lowered the boom on them.

Soviet experts in Washing-

New Members Listed

They believe that the basic conflicts probably had been decided immediately before and during the 20th congress of February, 1956. The disciplined momentum and were unable to put up effective resistance. Under these circumstances it was easy for Mr. Khrushchev to have them ousted by a cooperative central committee.

Six of the new men, full members of the Presidium Averky B. Aristov, Leonid I. Brezhnov, Nikolai G. Ignatov, Otto V. Kuusinen, and alternate members Demyan S. Korochenko and Alexei N. Kosygin, belonged to Stalin's Presidium of October, 1952. Pyotr N. Pospelov, a new alternate member, was Stalin's chief party theoretician. The other newcomers have risen in the party ranks under Mr. Khrushchev.

Marshal Bulganin and oldtimer First Deputy Premier Anastas I. Mikoyan are the only remaining full members with nonmilitary government experience. Of the technocrats of yore only atom chief Mikhail G. Pervukhin remains, demoted to alternate member of the Presidium. Maxim Z. Saburov, who directed the recent session of Comecon (Mutual Economic Assistance Organization) lost his seat in the Presidium but remained a member of the central committee.

Seen from this angle, the shake-up appears to be an outright victory for Mr. Khrushchev and his party professionals over high state officials and technocrats.

ton were surprised to find former Premier Georgi M. Malenkov in this group. He favors no return to Stalinism. He has argued strenuously, however, for a deemphasis of heavy industry in favor of more consumer goods.

Khrushchev probably included him among the dismissed to get a potentially dangerous rival out of the way. Malenkov has been regarded by many Western diplomats in Moscow as the most intelligent member of the Presidium, the man most likely to talk sense to them and not spout ideological dogma. He is 10 years younger than Khrushchev. If any of Khrushchev's hazardous programs had faltered attention would have shifted to Malenkov. But now he probably will be banished, like a defeated Roman politician of old, to the provinces—and some minor provincial post.

We are not likely to see any blood bath, any treason trials, any executions. Although the planned campaign of vilification against the trio is mounting, it is a measure of Mos-

KHRUSHCHEV

The Man at the Wheel

cow's strength and maturity that the dismissal of onetime key figures can be accomplished with no earthquake shock. But under Leninist ground rules, an "opposition party" led by Molotov could not be permitted.

Are the changes helpful, as far as the United States is concerned? We have only to consider what Washington's dismay would have been had unyielding, stony - visaged Molotov triumphed.

Khrushchev will need a few weeks, and further dismissals, to consolidate his triumph. He has won new prestige just in time to greet Communist China's Mao Tse-tung on the latter's European tour. It will be interesting to see whether he attempts to show Mao that Muscovite communism, too, has an ideological "new look."

Before long we shall probably see Khrushchev proposing another "summit" conference, Washington believes. He will speak highly of peaceful coexistence and urge a settlement of outstanding differences in politics and disarmament. And it will be well to examine what he has in mind. But the old, hard knots of German unification, Soviet Middle East meddling, and foolproof disarmament inspection will not be solved merely by Khrushchev's friendly talk and boosted prestige.

Inside Reading:

New Kremlin Faces
Names and Pictures
      Page 4

Tito Vindicated
Yugoslavs Pleased
      Page 4

Hungary's Skies Clear
Blow to Stalinists
      Page 13

Washington Reacts
No Official Alarm
      Page 15

Eisenhower Vacation Plans Uncertain

The World's Day

Reg. U.S. Pat. Off.

New England: Holiday Plans Tied to Congress

President Eisenhower's summer vacation plans cannot be made at this time for "family reasons" and "because so much depends upon how long Congress will be in session," the President wrote in a letter to Governor Roberts of Rhode Island.

Mideast: American Faces Charges in Cairo

American archaeologist Charles Arthur Muses will be charged with the theft and smuggling of precious antiquities from a newly discovered pyramid, the local prosecutor announced in Cairo.

National: Verbal Storm Brews Over Warning

A verbal storm brewed today in devastated southwest Louisiana after Senator Russell Long (D) of Louisiana charged what he called a 12-hour error by the Weather Bureau "led the people to stay here" the night before Hurricane Audrey ripped inland.

Africa: Bomb Explodes at U.S. Consul Office

No one was injured and damage was slight when a home-made bomb exploded outside the United States Consul General's office in Algiers July 4.

Americas: Venezuela Asked to Expel Perón

The Argentine Ambassador has asked the Venezuelan Government to expel Juan D. Perón immediately, reliable sources said in Caracas.

Washington: International Agency Proposed

Formation of an international agency within the United Nations

to undertake and manage development projects in the Middle East, to lend money either to public or private agencies there, and to carry on research in soil fertility and basic engineering surveys, has been proposed by Senator Humphrey (D) of Minnesota.

Agriculture Department officials said losses to this year's wheat crop caused by adverse weather in the western Great Plains might make a small dent in present wheat surpluses.

Weather Predictions: Cooler Tonight (Page 2)

Art, Music, Theater: Page 5. Radio, FM, TV: Page 6

Demoted Reds Accused

By the Associated Press

Moscow

The Soviet Army has accused the four deposed Kremlin leaders of treachery and of threatening to undermine the Soviet Union's defenses.

These grave charges appeared in the July 5 edition of Red Star, official newspaper of the Soviet Defense Ministry headed by Marshal Georgi K. Zhukov.

The campaign of denunciation gathered up momentum at meetings and rallies throughout the Soviet Union. Lazar M. Kaganovich, one of the four leaders, was singled out for new and stronger accusations which could foreshadow legal action against him.

The Army and Navy publicly announced their endorsement of Nikita S. Khrushchev in his ousting of Mr. Kaganovich, Vyacheslav M. Molotov, Georgi M. Malenkov and Dmitri T. Shepilov from their high posts.

THE CHRISTIAN SCIENCE MONITOR

Registered in U. S. Patent Office

AN INTERNATIONAL DAILY NEWSPAPER

VOLUME 49 NO. 255 | COPYRIGHT 1957 BY THE CHRISTIAN SCIENCE PUBLISHING SOCIETY | BOSTON, WEDNESDAY, SEPTEMBER 25, 1957 | ATLANTIC EDITION | TWO SECTIONS | TEN CENTS A COPY

Sloth, Confusion Reported

Soviets Falter on Grain

By Paul Wohl

Written for The Christian Science Monitor

This year's Soviet grain crop will not be as good as that of 1956.

Kazakhstan, where most of the new lands lie, had unfavorable weather. In the rest of the country the weather seems to have been rather good, and if the weather alone counted, the over-all grain crop should have been fair. But there were other factors which have darkened the prospects—poor leadership, poor teamwork, and insufficient preparation.

Despite dry weather, huge harvest losses have been piling up. In the new lands of Asia the situation is especially tense.

What happened there is believed to be significant for what is going on in the Soviet Union at large. The old discipline based on strict regimentation and fear seems to have disappeared and the interplay of self-interest, patriotism, and decentralized flexible management, advocated by Soviet Party Chief Nikita S. Khruschev, has not yet been translated into practice.

Drop Admitted

According to extensive spot reports, harvesting does not proceed normally. Sloth, confusion, and incompetence prevail. Administrative duplication slows down the pace. Moscow's insistence upon a new harvesting technique also may have something to do with the harvest difficulty.

As early as Aug. 13 Pravda admitted that Kazakhstan, which last year had delivered more than one billion pood of grain (16,400,000 metric tons), this year was expected to deliver only several hundred million pood. On Sept. 10, grain deliveries to the state had reached 203,000,000 pood. Last year on Sept. 15 more than four times as much was reported.

This year's grain is of much poorer quality than last year's. On Sept. 15 Izvestia complained that at one large reception point in western Siberia, half of the grain contained 27 per cent water.

An example of poor harvesting was given in Izvestia's report on the Kazakh province of Akmolinsk which last year was the second-largest grain producer in Kazakhstan. The state, wrote Izvestia, has supplied the province with grain driers and cleaners. "At reception points there are 320 powerful driers and 20 elevators. Unfortunately every day 140 driers are out of commission; 102 driers have not yet been set up because the 20 specialists and 300 skilled workers required for the job, are not available." For the same reason some of the new elevators do not function.

Harvest Method

The new harvesting method prescribed by Mr. Khrushchev seems to have confused many officials. The idea is to harvest in two stages: first, to mow the grain and to bundle it and later to thresh it. This was the way it used to be done before the giant combines took care of both operations together.

Last year the Soviets reversed themselves, and two-stage, or progressive-stage" harvesting was declared to be the only efficient method. By allowing bundled grain to ripen in the field, harvesting operations allegedly were sped up.

As a result of Moscow's prodding, the two-stage harvesting method now has been generally introduced. The results were described in a report from Novosibirsk in Pravda of Sept. 12. "Last year less than 18 per cent of the grain was harvested in accordance with the progressive-stage method. This year it was applied to the whole grain crop." But work did not proceed "in an organized manner." On nearly 900,000 hectares (2,250,000 acres) "the grain still stands in bundles in the field; more than half of it was mowed more than 10 days ago."

New Facilities Planned

On Sept. 14 Izvestia complained that in the Altai region, vast quantities of grain were waiting bundled in the field, because the equipment for taking delivery and processing the grain is not ready. . . . Out of many thousand driers only 150 functioned at the beginning of September. In several districts the authorities . . . continue to place damp and pressed down grain into elevators because the driers are not ready for use.

'For the beginning of the harvest it was intended to have new storage facilities and powerful elevators, asphalted storage platforms and mechanical equipment at delivery points were planned. Graphs had been designed showing for each operation when the work was supposed to be completed."

But in practice hardly anything had been done.

According to other reports, some delivery points lack scales, large quantities of threshed grain lie around in the open and much is stolen.

The main responsibility is said to rest with the Ministry of Grain Procurement and with the trucking agencies, now under the regional economic soviets.

Reports from the Ukraine are much more positive. There and in Byelorussia large increases over 1956 are reported, but this does not mean too much, because the grain crop was a failure in both republics last year. More encouraging sound reports that in some provinces this year's targets have been substantially exceded.

Despite the poor showing in the Asian newlands, Mr. Khrushchev has not given up his idea of farming further millions of acres.

Yugoslavs set harvest record: Page 2.

Hoffa Is Indicted On Perjury Counts

By the Associated Press

New York

James R. Hoffa, vice-president of the International Brotherhood of Teamsters, was indicted Sept. 25 on five counts of perjury by a federal rackets grand jury.

The indictment charged that the union leader, a candidate for the presidency of the Teamsters to succeed Dave Beck, lied to the grand jury, during its probe into alleged wiretapping of Teamster Union headquarters in Detroit.

The grand jury also indicted Benjamin Franklin Collins, secretary-treasurer of Local 299, which is headed by Mr. Hoffa. It accused him of 12 counts of perjury in connection with the same investigation.

Negro Students Get Protection; Eisenhower Lashes at 'Mob Rule'

'Anarchy'

By William H. Stringer

Chief of the Washington News Bureau of The Christian Science Monitor

Washington

President Eisenhower's history-making move in sending federal troops to remove the mob-raised barriers to integration at Little Rock is being watched throughout the nation for its impact and effect on the embattled school desegregation issue.

In Arkansas, in the White House view, the President was faced with a constitutional crisis. Federal court rulings upholding the Supreme Court's desegregation decision were being flouted by mob violence. "The President had no choice," declared his Democratic campaign rival, Adlai E. Stevenson.

'At Bayonet Point'

Thus in an earnest radio-television address to the nation President Eisenhower called on the people of Arkansas—and the South—to "preserve and respect the law even when they disagree with it." He explained that federal troops had been dispatched to Little Rock to prevent "mob rule" and "anarchy."

Some southern opinion reacted bitterly to the presidential decision to move federal troops—paratroopers of the elite 101st Airborne Division — into Little Rock. It was argued that this action was very nearly the kind of enforcement of desegregation "at bayonet point" against which Senator Richard B. Russell (D) of Georgia had warned in denouncing the original version of the civil rights bill in Congress.

Supremacy Asserted

Southern governors noted that the President had moved to assert the federal supremacy over Gov. Orval Faubus and his obstructionist tactics. The National Guard on which he relied had been ordered into the Army and he had no longer had it under his command.

In high Washington quarters it was obvious, however, that the Eisenhower administration had no intention of proceeding generally against the Deep South and its antiintegration attitudes by use of federal troops. In Arkansas, a graduated program, to which the city authorities of Little Rock were agreed, had been wrecked when Governor Faubus ordered out the National Guard. A federal district court's order had been disregarded. Mob violence, instigated by racial agitators, many from outside Little Rock, had flouted the President's proclamation calling on citizens to "cease and desist" from blocking the court's ruling.

Little Rock, in short, was an individual case. Circumstances were not at all the same in the Deep South states.

In Little Rock there was a substantial segment of opinion which, however much it disliked desegregation, intended to obey the law. The Arkansas Gazette at Little Rock, for instance, declared:

"The reckless course the Governor embarked upon three weeks ago has raised old ghosts and tested the very fiber of the Constitution. . . . He has by his acts and words dealt a major and perhaps lethal blow to the cause of segregation which he purported to uphold."

Democrats Split

Immediate attention was focused, of course, on whether the nine Negro children would return successfully to Little Rock Central High School, and whether agitators and troubled parents would allow the white children to attend peacefully, or would seek to stage a scholastic strike of nonattendance in an effort to defeat the federal troops indirectly.

At Sea Island, Ga., southern governors in their annual conference had proposed that a committee of governors be set up to meet with President Eisenhower in a 10th-inning effort to avert use of federal troops. But the White House had determined — after a shrieking, powerful mob on Sept. 23 had induced city authorities to call out the Negro students at Central High—that the situation was sufficiently grave to require quick action.

Obviously Mr. Eisenhower's action in using federal troops will have strong political repercussions. Democrats are divided in their comment, northerners approving the action but castigating the President for allowing the racial situation to deteriorate. Southern Democrats have denounced the action, and it will take some earnest wallpapering by Senator Lyndon B. Johnson (D) of Texas, the national Democratic harmonizer, to cover over the newly felt party rift.

On the Republican side, gone for the moment, at least, is the impression of presidential vacillation and indecision.

Despite the "nevermore" croakings of a few columnists, it appeared that the President possessed ample authority to use federal troops. Woodrow Wilson when he was President sent federal troops into the same state of Arkansas in his first term, to end disorders among coal miners. In the present case the President is using troops to uphold, not a law of Congress, but a decision of the Supreme Court, which has equal validity under the Constitution.

Text of President's talk: Page 7

United Press

GUARD COMMANDER: The Army has placed Maj. Gen. Edwin A. Walker in command of federalized Arkansas guardsmen for action in quelling school integration disorders in Little Rock, Ark. General Walker, a Texan, is commander of the Arkansas Military District, a paratrooper, and an Army ranger.

No Trouble At Scene

By a Staff Correspondent of The Christian Science Monitor

Little Rock, Ark.

Faculty members here at Central High School are reported determined to use their influence with the student body to receive quietly the Negro children that have entered, and to help avert any possible violence inside the school itself.

Presence of the regular Army soldiers of the 101st Airborne Division on the school grounds assured peaceful entry of the Negroes. What concerns school officials now is the reception the Negroes will get in the early days inside the school.

Faculty members, especially coaches and athletic assistants, have been assigned special duty in the corridors to break up any movement toward harming the Negroes. Several student leaders, who have absented themselves from school, are known to have agreed to be on hand in the classrooms to use their influence with other students to preserve peace and assure the right atmosphere if possible.

Students Hear General

As part of this movement, the commanding officer, Maj. Gen. Edwin A. Walker, spoke to the students assembled this morning. He tried to explain why the troops are here in simple terms, referring to law in the same way that the President did last night —that "the United States is a nation under law and not under men."

The general also tried to reassure the children, saying, "I believe that you are well-intentioned, law-abiding citizens, who understand the necessity of obeying the law, and are determined to do so."

In strong contrast to the screaming and fury of Sept. 23, there was quiet outside Central High Sept. 25. There were no catcalls and no real incidents as the six Negro girls and three boys walked calmly into the previously all - white school. They were escorted by the federal troops.

In a great arc at least two blocks from the school soldiers kept breaking up clusters of people and moving them back. In this process two civilians were hurt. One tried to grab a paratrooper's rifle and was struck by the soldier. Another, apparently slow in obeying an order, was slightly cut.

There seemed to be no mass exodus of students after the entry. A school official said there were more than 1,200 students in the school, meaning that about 750 are absent. This is only a small increase over the number absent Sept. 24.

South Jolted

The presence of federal troops in a southern capital to enforce court-decreed integration of races in public schools has jolted southern leaders into a search for a more basic solution to the Little Rock crisis, lest it spread across the South.

While paratroopers of the United States Army's 101st Airborne Division from Fort Campbell, Ky., bivouacked in the Arkansas capital, governors of southern states, meeting in the Atlantic coast resort at Sea Island, Ga., have taken under consideration a proposal by Gov. Frank Clement of Tennessee for an emergency committee to study the situation.

"This crisis is no longer one of whether certain students should go to a certain school," Governor Clement has emphasized. "This crisis has reached the proportions of whether federal troops should be used against citizens of a sovereign state."

Precedent Scented

"Governors of good will have been described by the President as his partners in government. If a crisis arises in business, the partners are going to sit down and discuss it. A crisis has arisen in our partnership. Why shouldn't the partners sit down and discuss it instead of fighting it out in the newspapers, with lawyers in between?"

Governor Clement is apprehensive that the President may be setting a precedent which could be applied to other internal troubles in a state. He explains that "the next problem involving the use of federal troops may not involve the schools at all. It might be labor trouble or anything else. If we can possibly avoid setting such a precedent, we should do it."

The rapid pace of the Little Rock crisis, and its impact on the constitutional framework on which state and federal relations rest, is putting southern leaders to the test. The Tennessee chief executive himself met a similar test forthrightly last year when he sent National Guard troops into Clinton, Tenn., to restore order after violence erupted when Negro students were integrated in the town's public schools. The Tennessee militia protected the young Negroes and brought the town back to order. This year, the Clinton schools resumed without any disturbance.

Here in Little Rock the Army has made one effort to avoid trouble by saying that Negro members of the airborne division will not be used as guards or as patrols. They will be engaged only in support work in reserve.

Faculty Prepares

There are signs that even the most ardent prosegregationists are a bit alarmed over the whirlpool of events which is drawing the nation into its most serious constitutional crisis since Reconstruction.

In Little Rock itself, a meeting Sept. 24 of the local White Citizens Council heard a warning that every effort must be made to "avoid violence." Recognized newsmen were barred from the meeting in Little Rock's Hotel Lafayette, attended by an overflow crowd of about 800 men and women. While leaders insisted that the council "deplores violence," some statements were made which were interpreted as suggestions to Negroes to think of the future.

Amis Guthridge, Little Rock attorney, a strong segregationist, commented that "we will be here long after the troops have gone home."

Further coverage of Little Rock crisis: Pages 7, 10, and 14.

South Governors To Ask Troop Exit

By the Associated Press

Sea Island, Ga.

Southern governors, worried over states' rights because of federal troop intervention at Little Rock, Ark., voted Sept. 25 to send a committee to Washington seeking withdrawal of the soldiers "at the earliest possible moment."

The resolution, adopted at the Southern Governors Conference, grew out of a suggestion by Gov. Frank Clement of Tennessee.

A five-man committee headed by Gov. Luther Hodges of North Carolina was named to seek a conference or conferences with President Eisenhower and Gov. Orval Faubus of Arkansas as soon as they can be arranged.

United Press

TROOPS ARRIVE: Citizens of Little Rock, Ark., watched from behind barricades as members of the 101st Airborne Division arrived to take up positions around Central High School. Their arrival brought out a crowd of 200 to 300 persons.

State of the Nations

Gomulka's Balance Sheet

By JOSEPH C. HARSCH, Special Correspondent of The Christian Science Monitor

Lodz, Poland

Wladyslaw Gomulka became Poland's strong man almost a year ago. He was tossed up to the supreme position of power in his country by an imperative wave of national revulsion and hope. The Poles had stood all they could stand of the Soviets at their table and of Communist incompetence in their government. They looked, in what they call their national rebirth, to a man who himself had been a personal victim of Stalinism.

Now, a year later, they are asking themselves, as are many others: How much of the great hopes of a year ago have been realized?

Since Poland's "rebirth" was launched by Mr. Gomulka there has been one serious disturbance in Poland — a streetcar strike in the textile center of Lodz. To this reporter Lodz seemed the logical place to come to in search of an answer.

Lodz is a city that looks unloved. If there is a new postwar building or an old one repainted I have not found it. Relatively undamaged by the war, it has been consistently neglected ever since. Vestiges of ancient paint flake from cracked plaster. Were it not full of people, one would think it an abandoned city.

Off on one side stands a brick textile mill built about a hundred years ago, behind a fortress wall. Across the street stands the brick-barracks tenement built for workers in the mill at the same time as the mill, and still mostly inhabited by them. An apartment in this barracks is one room about 12 by 15 feet partitioned at one end into a tiny kitchen where a coal stove is the only "appliance." The rest is bed and sitting room.

On our arrival we were regarded with apprehension and suspicion. The first door we knocked on opened slowly and gave us admittance reluctantly. When we left we were surrounded by many scores of eager children and smiling adults. We drove hurriedly away lest the fast-growing crowd attract unfriendly police attention on these people who have so little and who expected much more—a year ago.

At the last apartment the parting words of our host were: "Thank you for coming. It is like a father. You are the first person who has come to ask us how we are getting along."

The story that poured from mouth after mouth, first haltingly and then in a torrent, was always the same.

Yes, there has been great "moral improvement." They can talk freely. The secret police have disappeared. The regular police do not bother them any more. The factory manager is less unfair and less arbitrary. They are no longer forced to work two days for free for every day they stay away sick. They are not afraid to talk to an American when he visits them. Some abuses have ended. The streetcar company manager who took his workers' annual customary "13th - month" bonus to build himself a villa is in jail.

'Mama, is communism something we can eat?'

But physically and materially, they are no better off. The textile workers have had a raise. Their pay has gone up from 900 zlotys a month to 1,200 zlotys. But it takes 3,000 zlotys to buy a suit of clothes. A worker feeds his family of five by working eight hours a day at the mill and another eight hours pushing a fruit cart. He makes more from the cart than from the mill.

But food prices have gone up as much as the raise. And streetcar workers have not had their promised raise yet, although it is supposed to come on Oct. 1.

Why didn't the textile workers strike with the streetcar workers? The frank and immediate answer was, "We were afraid."

It costs 1,000 zlotys a month to feed one person, one worker asserted. Yet there were families of four and five and six living on 900 zlotys a month. They managed, just, somehow. They cannot explain how they do it. They know that materially they are no better off than before. The wants most frequently expressed were for cheaper lard and a better grade of ham.

Mr. Gomulka has changed many things. The Soviets have gone away. Poland is run by Poles. There is no doubt about a new sense of freedom in the air—freedom to talk, if not freedom to strike, although they said that since the streetcar strike the directors have been more assertive and threatening.

Mr. Gomulka never promised to raise the standard of living in a year. He told them honestly at the beginning that the country was almost bankrupt and that higher wages would only mean inflation. He told them they must be patient, and go on working just as hard for no more money. The record is not out of line with the promise.

Somewhere down Mr. Gomulka's road lies a deadline—none can say just where. These Polish workers are infinitely patient. They have endured much and can endure much more. But life in an ancient textile mill in Lodz is about as drab and hard as it can well be. It would be more endurable if some of their own government people would only come and do what we did—show just a simple interest in them as human beings, and in their problems.

Who is to go among the people for Mr. Gomulka? His party is the Communist Party. But individual Communists are better, for Mr. Gomulka deprived them of their power and their privileges.

Mr. Gomulka alone cannot visit all the people to make them understand the need for patience. Nor can he alone break through the economic chaos left by the Stalin years and start Poland toward economic rebirth. He needs a party of devoted followers who believe in the people and sincerely seek their welfare. In Lodz can be seen all around the evidence that the Communists never did and never can.

The real question for Mr. Gomulka is whether he can disentangle himself in time from the bankruptcy of communism.

A-Ban Bid Tests U.S. in UN

By William R. Frye

United Nations Correspondent of The Christian Science Monitor

United Nations, N.Y.

Formal proposals by Japan, India, and the Soviet Union, that the testing of nuclear weapons be halted, have highlighted one of the principal diplomatic problems facing the United States at the United Nations.

How can the United States explain—and successfully "sell" —its viewpoint that tests must continue until the whole nuclear arms race is brought under control?

The Soviet Union is riding high on the test-ban issue. Moscow has managed to portray itself as on the side of the angels.

The Soviets have proposed that tests be halted for two to three years, under UN control. Japan has suggested a suspension for approximately one year, beginning as soon as there is agreement "in principle" on inspection. India asks an immediate and wholly unconditional suspension, without any provision for control. The ban would continue indefinitely.

The United States, on the other hand, is in the position of insisting on "all or nothing." Washington has made the suspension of tests part of a "package" disarmament plan. No one part, Washington says, may be separated from the whole. Britain, France, and Canada agree.

Western Plan Outlined

Other parts of the Western plan include:

¶Air and ground inspection to guard against surprise attack.

¶Diversion of all future production of atomic fuel to peaceful uses, under strict control.

¶Reduction of manpower, conventional armaments, and arms budgets.

¶Steps (as yet unspecified) to curb the development of space missiles.

Must the United States and its allies hold out for the whole program? Diplomats are asking. A growing number of countries favors beginning with the test suspension. So many countries, in fact, feel this way that the United States may not be able to muster the necessary majority for a UN endorsement of its package.

In other years, the United States has escaped from a similar dilemma by one of two devices: either by combining all outstanding ideas into a single omnibus UN resolution which, when passed, can be hailed as a "victory" because it includes the "right" subjects; or else by referring all proposals to the disarmament subcommittee "for further study," thus avoiding a showdown.

Difficult Task

This year, however, it will be difficult if not impossible to take either tack. UN draftsmen are skilled with language. But even they would find it hard to write a resolution which endorsed both a "package" and a single step at one and the same time.

Referral to the subcommittee is a device which can be used to save face when both sides are willing to have their faces saved, or when one side is the Soviet Union and therefore a majority of the UN is willing to disregard its wishes.

But when one side includes Japan and India, which want action, the diplomatic problem is far greater. The United States wants to retain their friendship. This is why their proposals—and especially that of Japan—are causing United States diplomats serious concern.

Secretary of State John Foster Dulles attempted to explain to the Assembly in his major "state of the world" speech Sept. 19 why the United States feels it must go on testing its bombs. British Foreign Minister Selwyn Lloyd added further reasons Sept. 24.

Cool to Dulles Plea

The Dulles case was that it is important to make atomic and hydrogen weapons "cleaner"—that is, less productive of fall-out—and better adapted to defense.

"The Soviet Union seems not to want the character of nuclear weapons thus to be refined and changed," he said. "It seems to like it that nuclear weapons can be stigmatized as 'horror' weapons. Does it calculate that, under these conditions, governments subject to moral and religious influences will not be apt to use them?"

This argument was not particularly effective in the UN, where it is hard for many to think of atomic bombs as anything but "horror" weapons, whatever their size and cleanliness. Nor did Mr. Dulles meet the concern of many over the effects of radioactive fall-out test explosions.

Mr. Lloyd took a new tack, contending that a test ban would not be a disarmament step. "It does nothing to reduce armaments," he said. "It does not prevent further countries emerging as possessors of nuclear weapons."

Lloyd View Disputed

This argument was not much more successful. Advocates of a test ban, while agreeing that the step would not be "disarmament" in the strictest sense, vigorously disputed Mr. Lloyd on the second point. Few countries, they said, would invest the huge sums necessary to build nuclear weapons which they could not legally test.

The West's problem, therefore, remains unsolved. It might be easier, observers feel, for the case to be presented simply and persuasively, if the government in Washington were wholly agreed within itself that its test program is essential. There is, however, no such agreement.

And even if the United States were to decide to bow to popular pressures, Britain and France —especially France—might well hold out.

Some diplomats and observers here, recalling earlier suggestions that the United States offer to stop testing its largest weapons, wish some such initiative as this had been taken before Washington was pushed into its present uncomfortable position.

THE CHRISTIAN SCIENCE MONITOR

Registered in U. S. Patent Office

AN INTERNATIONAL DAILY NEWSPAPER

VOLUME 49 NO. 264 | BOSTON, SATURDAY, OCTOBER 5, 1957 | K | ***ATLANTIC EDITION | TWO SECTIONS | TEN CENTS A COPY

COPYRIGHT 1957 BY THE CHRISTIAN SCIENCE PUBLISHING SOCIETY

Made-in-U.S.S.R. 'Moon' Circles Earth; Space Era Advent Jolts Washington

By William H. Stringer

Chief, Washington News Bureau, The Christian Science Monitor

Washington

The first earth satellite, hurtling around the earth in its manmade orbit, evoked several Washington reactions:

¶Congratulations to the Soviet Union for its feat in hoisting the first mechanical moon above earth.

¶Chagrin that Moscow had beaten the United States, which is not scheduled to launch its earth satellite until next spring, although the date conceivably could be advanced.

¶Surprise at the size of the Soviet satellite, which is more than eight times heavier than the contemplated American vehicle.

¶Sharp awareness that the Soviet accomplishment indicated a very high degree of skill and development in the field of far-flying missiles.

¶And finally, a startled look ahead to the not-so-distant future when still heavier satellites, capable of carrying instruments for "inspecting" other countries' territory and eventually capable of carrying weapons, would be circling this earthly sphere.

Comment Sparse

There was no Congress in session in Washington to comment on the outstanding Soviet achievement, there were few available American diplomats, and President Eisenhower had flown off for a quiet weekend at Gettysburg. So capital comment came largely from the physicists and specialists engaged in preparing the American earth satellite, some attending an International Geophysical Year conference here.

In the international fraternity of natural science there was a sporting amount of congratulations to the Soviets.

Lloyd Berkner, nuclear physicist and American IGY official attending a party at the Soviet Embassy celebrating the IGY rockets and satellites conference here, offered plaudits to A. A. Blagonravov, a top Soviet satellite expert.

"It would have been nice if the United States had been first, but let's be glad that it's been achieved," Dr. Berkner declared.

'Moonwatch' Gains?

Joseph Kaplan, chairman of the United States National Committee for the IGY, said:

"I am amazed that in the short time in which the Soviets had to plan—obviously not any longer than we had — they made this remarkable achievement.

"From the point of view of international cooperation the important thing is that a satellite has been launched. They did it and did it first.

"I hope they give us enough information so that our 'moonwatch' teams can help learn the scientific benefits."

Experts pointed out that if the Soviets could launch a satellite 23 inches across and weighing 185 pounds, they soon could launch still heavier ones. It was also obvious to experts that the launching rocket must have been close to the intercontinental-missile class.

Soviet expert Blagonravov termed the Soviet launching merely the first of mankind's steps into space. He reported that he had sent his own dog 90 miles skyward in a rocket in 1951, without ill effects. The next step would be to send an animal up in a satellite, and then "men will penetrate space."

'Second Round' Moscow's

The Soviet natural scientist said there was no danger to any of the earth's peoples from this man-made moon, for it would disintegrate from friction when it began to fall back into the earth's heavier atmosphere.

However, American officials were not unaware of the intense meaning of the Soviet accomplishment in terms of rockets and missiles.

"The Soviet satellite gives the Russians no military advantage as such," declared Dr. Fred L. Whipple, director of the Smithsonian Observatory, "but it indicates the Russian potential in the area of missiles. We won the first round with the H-bomb, but they took the second with the satellite."

Admission that the Soviets have scored a considerable propaganda victory and are likely to use the circling satellite as proof that the U.S.S.R can outdistance the United States in military prowess—a propaganda note likely to be influential with some undecided nations.

There was a very penetrating realization in Washington—and at the Pentagon—that the Soviets again had demonstrated the excellence of their basic research, and the speed with which they are able to translate research into actual, usable hardware.

'Pressure Off' Now

Undoubtedly, had Congress been in town, there would be questions as to why the Soviets had been allowed to outdistance the Americans. As if in reply to this unstated query, William M. Holaday, Special Assistant to the Secretary of Defense for Guided Missiles, said the achievement would not be evidence of Soviet technological superiority in missile and rocket developments.

The Soviets may have placed great emphasis, time, and money in getting the satellite into orbit first in order to embarrass the United States, Mr. Holaday suggested. Quite conceivably, they had given the project higher priority than has the United States, which is not scheduled to launch its first full-scale satellite until next spring. This autumn, four small test spheres will be fired as part of the advance testing program and some of these may go into a globe-circling orbit.

Rear Admiral Rawson Bennett, whose Office of Naval Research has charge of launching the American satellites, said the United States never regarded the program as a "race with the Russians." A very opposite impression was given by American experts at the Soviet Embassy reception when they commented, "Now the pressure to win is off, and we can concentrate on doing a good job."

Simultaneously no American official was belittling the prospect that before many years larger satellites would be available, carrying instrumentation for observing more than celestial secrets, and able to position nuclear weapons over enemy territory.

At present, it is believed, the Soviets have sent up a simply-instrumented satellite. Later, more elaborate satellites with more scientific instrumentation will be attempted. So far, the Soviets have indicated a willingness to share discovered data of nonmilitary value, although they did shift the vehicle's transmitting frequency.

The Soviet launching secrecy was assumed to stem from the likelihood that components of Soviet military missiles were used to hoist the satellite into its orbit.

By Robert C. Cowen

Natural Science Editor of The Christian Science Monitor

There's a brand new "moon" circling the earth and it carries the label "made in the U.S.S.R."

Until Soviet rocket scientists put this first artificial satellite into the sky, unmanned flight beyond the atmosphere for any length of time has been only a hope and a dream. But today there is a manmade object circling round and round the earth out there which, to one way of thinking, is the first crude "space ship."

The old familiar world of vast continents and trackless seas will never be the same again. It has become in practical fact what we have known it is in theory—a planet, to be girdled by the machines of men.

Not even the swift around-the-world flights of jet aircraft have brought this fact home with the impact of that little sphere of metal that every 95 minutes is sweeping over the United States.

Dr. Richard Porter, chairman of the International Geophysical Year Technical Panel on the Earth Satellite, called it "a magnificent step forward in science."

According to a Moscow announcement, the satellite is traveling in a southwest-northeast direction along an orbit that cuts a 65 degree angle with the equator and is about 560 miles high. Weighing 185 pounds, the 23-inch Soviet vehicle is more than eight times heavier than the 20-inch spheres scheduled to be launched by the American earth satellite project, Project Vanguard.

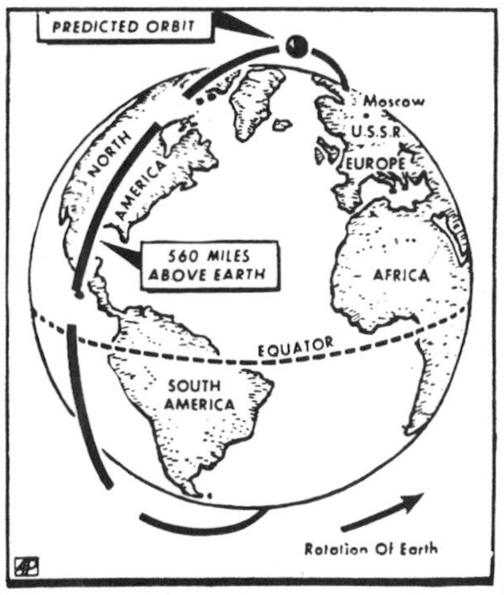
PREDICTED ORBIT
Moscow
U.S.S.R
EUROPE
NORTH AMERICA
560 MILES ABOVE EARTH
AFRICA
EQUATOR
SOUTH AMERICA
Rotation Of Earth

Orbit of Soviet 'Moon'

'Really Fantastic'

Moscow added that later satellites will be bigger and heavier than the first.

Commenting on this, Dr. Joseph Kaplan, chairman of the United States National Committee for the IGY was quoted by the Associated Press as exclaiming that the 185 pound weight and 23-inch span "is really fantastic. If they can launch that they can launch much heavier ones."

The United States Project Vanguard, which has postponed the schedule for its satellite launchings from last September to sometime next spring, has never contemplated such heavy satellites. In terms of the rocket power with which Vanguard engineers are working, such weights are out of the picture.

Dr. Kaplan said he is "amazed that [the Soviets did it] in the short time which they had to plan—obviously not any longer than we had—I think it was a remarkable achievement on their part."

A more somber note was added by Dr. Fred Whipple, director of the Smithsonian Astrophysical Observatory which is handling visual tracking of the IGY satellites. In response to a question about possible military implications of the Soviet "moon," he observed, "It is not a military advantage as such, but it indicates the Russian potential in the area of missiles."

Claims Buttressed

Dr. Whipple was referring to an axiom widely held among rocket experts that any country which has the capability to successfully launch a satellite such as that of the Soviets also has the rocket capability of launching successful intercontinental ballistic missiles.

Thus the successful satellite that now is circling the planet will lend substantial weight to Soviet claims of having developed at least a working prototype of the most awesome weapon envisioned by military planners today.

Indeed, this latter Soviet claim had led many observers to speculate that it might soon be followed by a satellite launching. Thus the sudden appearance of an artificial "moon" on Oct. 4 was not completely unexpected even if it did catch the rest of the world offguard.

Rocket experts from many nations including the Soviet Union were nearing the end of a week-long IGY conference on satellites at Washington when the Soviet announcement broke without previous warning. But any chagrin the others may have felt at not being told in advance—both the Soviet and American satellite programs are part of scheduled IGY activities — melted in overwhelming realization that a new age has dawned upon mankind.

Observers Keep Vigil

It was this same realization that maintained an air of subdued excitement throughout the long night vigil held by a small group of us at the only center outside the Soviet Union that was prepared to compute the orbit of the new satellite—the Computation Center of the Massachusetts Institute of Technology, which is handling orbit calculations for the Smithsonian Astrophysical Observatory.

There is another such center at Washington, but it will handle only radio observations of satellites. These were unavailable because the Soviet sphere broadcasts on a frequency well below that to be used by the Vanguard satellites.

Data Fed Computer

The first report came in from Terre Haute, Ind., followed by sightings from Columbus, Ohio, and Whittier, Calif. Only three good sightings were needed. But so far none of the reports had been accurate enough.

G. Rossoni of International Business Machines Corporation stood by at IBM's big 704 Computer in the MIT center, checking out his computing program. The reports, he said, were too uncertain. He couldn't trust them for computation.

Then, as the dawn of the new space-flight age brightened over Cambridge, the answer came. The orbit of the satellite had passed through the plane of the sun. No part of it touched the twilight zone and thus it was not observable from the ground.

Dr. Whipple said that the earlier sightings had been erroneous, just misidentified meteors or high flying aircraft. Disappointing, perhaps, but in their hearts no one cared. The first man made satellite was in the sky.

Soviet "moon" announcement: Page 2.

California Aroused

GOP Duel Buoys Democrats

By Harlan Trott

Staff Correspondent of The Christian Science Monitor

Sacramento, Calif.

California politics has burst out of the long doldrums with Republican Senator William F. Knowland's formal announcement he is a candidate for Governor next year.

While this news surprised no one, any sign of anticlimax has been dispelled by Gov Goodwin J. Knight's defiant response to Senator Knowland's challenge.

If California Democrats cannot cook up any excitement commensurate with their 3-to-2 edge over the state's Republican voter registrations, no matter. The Republicans are going to take care of that themselves.

United Press Telephoto

Senator William Knowland

The prospect of an all-out, gloves-off Knowland-Knight contest in next June's primary is the very thing Democrats have been counting on. Since we cannot stop the Republicans, then hurrah, let the Republicans beat themselves.

Democrats See 'Walk In'

If the Knowland-Knight rivalry keeps up this sizzling pace, Democrats like to think their top officeholder, Attorney General Edmund G. "Pat" Brown, will walk into the governorship over the Republican pieces.

It seems probable Mr. Brown will run for Governor. A cautious, in-and-out politician, vocal one day, silent the next, the leading Democrat never has ventured very far from his foxhole in the California Department of Justice.

In a state where personalities outweigh partisan issues because voting procedure permits candidates to run on both tickets, Mr. Brown never felt like risking his popularity against Earl Warren, now Chief Justice of the United States, nor more recently like testing Governor Knight's grip on President Eisenhower's coattails.

Now, for only the second time in this century, California Democrats are enthusing out loud about their chances of electing a Governor. And their enthusiasm soars with every verbal salvo between Governor Knight and Senator Knowland. Governor Knight's strategy at the moment is to cast Senator "Bill" Knowland in the role of a party wrecker, a Bill in a china shop, a brash disturber of the Republican peace.

The Governor implies, too, that Senator Knowland is an out-of-step right-winger, and that Governor Knight alone is the true torch bearer of modern Republicanism here in the second pivotal state.

Moving with the precision of a politician who had seen this shaft coming, Senator Knowland fished a letter out of his blue serge pocket, an embossed letter on crinkled White House stationery, in which the President warmly commended him for his fine service in the hard role of minority leader in the last session of Congress.

GOP Duel Intense

Announcement day at Sacramento was a day of heavy shelling on the Republican redoubts. Shortly after Senator Knowland broke the news that wasn't news, Governor Knight held a press conference calling the Knowland statement something all "reasonable people" view as a "hydraheaded bid for the presidency of the United States."

This was intended to de-fuse Senator Knowland's lofty disclaimer: "I have made my decision . . . with no purpose other than if nominated and elected governor to devote myself faithfully to the duties of the office for the term or terms to which I might be elected."

At the same time the senator seemed to be leaving the night latch off in explaining that "no one has a crystal ball," and as for 1960 or 1964, "I expect to serve out my term. I hope I shall be permitted to do so."

Senator Knowland showed he has been studying the historical techniques of reluctant candidates by declaring his was not a "Sherman-like statement" but one "in keeping with my whole record in public life." It was Civil War Gen. William T. Sherman who once said when presidential drafts were blowing: "If nominated I would not run. If elected I would not serve."

Rapid Cross Fire

And so the shelling went on across the State House lawn, between the Governor's office and the Knowland parlor in the dreamy old Senator Hotel. Reporters panted, and pencils shriveled as Senator Knowland countered Governor Knight's press conference with another statement clarifying his position on topics such as the right-to-work issue.

He said his program for labor democracy included a "labor's bill of rights." And he proposed to give rank-and-file members control over union affairs, "including election of officers, welfare funds, and union dues." If elected, Senator Knowland said he would propose legislation embodying a right-to-work plan and would sign such a bill if "fair and equitable."

Governor Knight takes an opposite view on this hot labor issue of whether a man should be barred from a job unless he joins a labor union.

Senator Knowland's ponderous sincerity makes it easy for his backers to believe his unquestioned integrity will enable him to surmount Governor Knight's formidable "me too" assets in next year's primary fight.

Case for Knowland

Their faith is fortified by recent polls among Democrats showing a distinct preference for Senator Knowland over Governor Kinght. A follow-up to the national poll here in California likewise favored Senator Knowland. Some observers see in this some Democrats' yearning for a Knowland build-up that will help to counteract gathering Nixon strength.

All this is a jolt to Knight supporters who realize he has done very well in enlisting union support in California much in the Warren manner. At the same time, he has posed arm in arm with California bankers who promised to help finance his campaign for reelection—active leaders at one time in public campaigns on behalf of ballot measures sponsored by monopoly powers such as oil and electric power industries.

Governor Knight's opponents call this carrying water on both shoulders. But the balancing act, if such it is, has paid off. And this powerful, aggressive, tireless, ambitious candidate for reelection warns that "this will be no pantywaist campaign."

Thus the Republican slugfest rings in the straight-up ears of the cautious Attorney General, Mr. Brown, like McNamara's band. This was one of Mr. Brown's braver days, and he hailed the "fine choice" the Republican titans are offering "between an incumbent dead duck and a foolish modern McKinley."

Such confidence has not blown its top in Democratic Party circles in California since Culbert Olsen blew into the governship on Franklin Roosevelt's coattails, and blew right out again the next time around.

Trend of Economy

Pivotal Issues Test U.S.

By NATE WHITE, Business and Financial Editor of The Christian Science Monitor

Boston

Two pivotal decisions charge the atmosphere in the United States at the present time. Each is a fundamental test of the basic principle of America, whether individuals can enjoy life, liberty, and the pursuit of happiness without harm from their fellow man.

In the Little Rock crisis, symbolizing as it does the basic failure of education to lead the way to a better understanding of man's relation to man, democracy as practiced in the United States faces stringent testing.

On the second front—the economic — the pivotal decision is just as important. Here again the educational system has not prepared the way for a better understanding of the problem. Again the United States system of economic democracy faces stringent testing.

The two tests are not as far apart as they seem.

In Little Rock the test is whether race can live beside race in full enjoyment—not partially—of the privileges of democracy.

On the economic front the test is whether all segments of the economy can live together in full enjoyment of the privileges of democracy.

If the United States proceeds to build an economy in which its businesses and people are in overwhelming debt —a bankers' economy—then the general purposes of economic democracy are defeated. Debt has its function, but a creditors' monopoly would destroy democracy.

If the United States builds an economy in which labor unions monopolize economic power, then a people's economy is defeated.

If the United States puts itself in the straitjacket of oligopolistic business, where "administered" prices do not reflect the market or the ability of the consumer to pay, then a people's democracy has been defeated.

The test today is whether all of these segments can be brought into and kept in balance, so that no special segment dominates or can dominate another.

We are in a fight for the balanced control of our economy. It is a fundamental struggle between the economic theories of specialists.

On the one side stands the specialist who says: Let us curb high prices by making it hard to borrow money even if we squeeze the small man out of business. Let us also tax so heavily that the government will have the spending power which it has withheld from the consumer.

On another side stands the specialist who says: Let us take the straitjackets of control off the economy. Let us increase the money supply. Let us lower taxes. Let us lower interest rates. Let us have freedom, even if prices soar and even if the dollar loses in value.

The socialist would end the debate. He would nationalize industry, nationalize the professions, and organize the system under rigid controls, a truly managed economy. In this kind of economy he could administer prices, wages, profits, and fees, and he could impose heavy taxation.

These basic questions are never far away in a democracy. It is all too easy to drift into attitudes which clear the way for a change.

The United States is as strong economically as its people's understanding of the economy. It is weak when the understanding of the economy is weak.

The key to a successful economic democracy is productivity. This means the amount of wealth which can be created by the combination of men's ingenuity and labor with the use of machines and mechanical aids. It is the measure of this total combination according to each worker hour. But the product must also be sold. There must also be consumption.

If productivity lags, the economy will lag and one sector can get dominance over another.

If the pricing system kills off consumption this in turn kills off productivity.

If the wage system costs so much that the pricing system becomes unrealistic this in turn kills off productivity and consumption.

If the borrowing system costs so much and gets so out of hand that it destroys incentive to save and the will to work, this in turn kills off productivity and consumption.

What is being said is that there is no substitute for working and saving, for ingenuity and careful management, for restraint on greed, for astute marketing, and that there comes a time when the public welfare must be placed above the special welfare or the selfish interest.

When we believe that the stock market is a key to the economy we are not understanding the economy. The stock market is not an entity with either intelligence or power. It as much a marketplace as the fruit stands at Faneuil Hall, in the Manhattan Market, or the Farmers Market. And people behave in this marketplace just the same way they behave in any of these markets, when they are following good judgment. They search for good investments. But if they try to build a meal out of bananas when a better balance would include potatoes, corn, peas, and roast beef, they may slide on the skin of the banana they drop.

The country is strong. It is not in trouble. Individual businesses must make adjustments, but when was this not true? Individuals must reassess their own situation but when could an individual sit back and sleep and assume that his own work would be done for him?

To let the economy grow in every sector so that all can prosper without the distortion of inflation which favors some group and hurts others, without governmental control which stifles all is the goal ahead.

This is a pleasant goal. Its achievement is possible with intelligent cooperation by leaders in all sectors, with avoidance of frozen positions which may be economically untenable, and with an abeyance of the selfish motive which would put one class above another in the economic scale.

Dr. Sumner H. Slichter states his views on inflation: Page 12

Polish Students Stage New Riot

By the Associated Press

Warsaw

Angry students and other Poles battled police, security troops, and militia in Warsaw's streets the night of Oct. 4 in the second violent antigovernment demonstration in two days.

The street battling even rolled up to the doors of Communist Party headquarters, where the central committee was reported in emergency session, before the demonstration was smashed.

Unlike the fighting of the previous night, which was confined to an area around the polytechnic school, the violence this time spread to three sections of Warsaw. And for the first time, other Poles joined the 2,000 students in their defiance of government force.

State of the Nations

Little Rock and Politics

By WILLIAM H. STRINGER, Chief, Washington Bureau, The Christian Science Monitor

Washington

It is too early to plot precisely the shifts in American voting patterns and party allegiances which the Little Rock crisis is likely to bring about. Conceivably they will be of some magnitude.

National and regional opinion has suddenly been jolted by a southern Governor's defiance of the federal courts, by a President's dispatch of federal troops, and by a revived mental churning over the racial issue which has been with us since pre-Civil War years. It would be surprising if new political patterns did not emerge. So far, political experts add up the picture something like this:

1. On the Republican side the party has found a greater unity, which may improve its effectiveness. At last the persistent Old Guard-modern party rift has been mitigated by the discovery of a new major issue—an issue which is not basically economic—on which both party wings can unite. The GOP politicians are heartened to have something "positive" rather than "divisive" to talk about.

Again, President Eisenhower has been firm and decisive—"at his best" in the Arkansas crisis, and this is a boost to party morale. It doesn't mean that "modern Republicanism" is again in the ascendant; business organizations will continue their drumfire assault against presidential policies which involve strong spending and big budgets. But the party as a whole — White House, Old Guard, and liberals—is in a revived mood with discovery of an issue which benefits the GOP and divides the Democrats.

2. The Republican Party stands to gain among the Negroes in the North. The gains are likely to be concentrated among the more prosperous and the younger people, who have less allegiance to or less memory of the Rooseveltian New Deal days and the great depression-born Negro shift to the Democrats. A very gradual "shift back" to the Republicans has been under way for several years; now this has been accelerated somewhat.

However, this new allegiance attaches itself more to President Eisenhower than to the Republican Party or to the general run of GOP candidates. Whether it would benefit Vice-President Richard M. Nixon as a candidate who has exerted himself vigorously in the civil rights battle awaits further Negro assessment of Mr. Nixon. Whether the Republican gains are maintained or soon lost will depend in great measure on how the Republicans handle those potent "pocketbook" issues of inflation and the high cost of living.

LITTLE ROCK

Hold Onto Your Hats, Boys

3. The Republicans, of course, have lost ground seriously in the South. "Operation Dixie"—that hopeful project for building GOP strength south of the Mason and Dixon's line — is a forlorn prospect now. This doesn't mean that, in the long-term sense, there isn't the possibility of establishing a two-party system in the South. Northerners and new industry continue to move southward. But Republican hopes of adding congressional seats from Texas, Florida, North Carolina, or elsewhere have gone glimmering. It's a sharp setback.

4. On the Democratic side, a party which believed it had eased past the divisive civil-rights issue successfully in Congress now finds itself again suffering from rifts and recriminations. Southern Democrats are castigating their northern brethren for "urging 'Ike' on." Northern liberals are intimating that perhaps the party would be better off without its southern wing.

Some southern moderates in Congress are feeling they now must talk in extremist tones or risk losing out to extremist opponents in the next primary elections. Northern Democrats believe they must take a powerful stance for desegregation or lose the Negro vote in the big cities.

5. There is talk of setting up a third party in the South. Whether this truculence is translated into political action depends on how long the Little Rock crisis survives and whether new bitterness is generated. It also depends on finding an acceptable leader. The "obvious choice," Senator Richard Russell of Georgia, does not believe in third-party movements.

6. Democratic division and recrimination could hamper congressional election campaigning, could induce voters to sit on their hands and stay home, and could prevent the orderly development of persuasive issues. Fortunately for the Democrats the party possesses one very potent peacemaker, Senator Lyndon Johnson of Texas, the Senate majority leader. He has been saying nothing publicly but doing a lot of conferring behind scenes.

When tempers have cooled, his persuasive arguments will be heard in campaign committees and party councils, warning his colleagues that the party could be wrecked on the shoals of racial fury. But he has a tough job ahead of him. So far, the Republicans have come out ahead politically at Little Rock.

THE CHRISTIAN SCIENCE MONITOR

Registered in U. S. Patent Office

AN INTERNATIONAL DAILY NEWSPAPER

VOLUME 50 NO. 158 | BOSTON, MONDAY, JUNE 2, 1958 | ***ATLANTIC EDITION | TWO SECTIONS | TEN CENTS A COPY

© 1958, THE CHRISTIAN SCIENCE PUBLISHING SOCIETY All Rights Reserved

De Gaulle Spurs Reform Program; Relief and Doubt Mix in Washington

By Neal Stanford

Staff Correspondent of The Christian Science Monitor

Washington

There are two distinct and official Washington reactions to Gen. Charles de Gaulle's elevation to the premiership of France.

One is gratification and relief that France passed through this immediate "hour of peril" without civil war and anarchy.

This was the public White House comment welcoming General de Gaulle's assumption of power and anticipating "continuation of the intimate and friendly relations which have always characterized our long association with France."

It was anticipated in President Eisenhower's press conference comment last week: I like de Gaulle.

It was reaffirmed, after General de Gaulle's election to the premiership, by Secretary of Defense, Neil H. McElroy who told a TV audience that General de Gaulle's rise to power would be "beneficial" to United States efforts to build up Western European defenses.

The other reaction is quite different. It is one of concern and uncertainty of both General de Gaulle's intentions and his ability to accomplish the goals for which he was elected—sweeping revision of the Constitution, settlement of the Algerian war, and the overseas territories problem.

Numerous Causes

This reaction is just as official as the first, but not attributable to any office or authority. It has numerous causes.

One is the fact that General de Gaulle is still largely an unknown quantity.

Another stems from the fact that the investiture vote the general received, a margin of little more than 100, was hardly the mandate he had expected and may need.

A third is the mounting disappointment in Algiers over the membership of the new Cabinet, particularly selection of General de Gaulle's predecessor, Pierre Pflimlin, as Minister of State. Only last week the Algerian crowds were demanding: "Pflimlin to the gallows."

In other words, while Washington breathed a sigh of relief that General de Gaulle had moved into the premiership without civil war or violence, it was not entirely confident that he could accomplish the purposes for which he was elected. The opposition at home and the disillusionment expressed by his followers abroad suggested the task would not be as simple or easy as the general may have expected.

And then there was a third definable line or reaction discernable in Washington. This centered entirely on speculation as to what the general's impact on a possible summit meeting between East and West would be.

Summit Considered

While the prospect of a summit meeting has receded of late, it is still a possibility, and General de Gaulle's presence at such a conference could raise all kinds of complications and embarrassments.

For while current reports on the general's mellowed character and less arbitrary attitudes continue to flow across the Atlantic, United States officials have little experience with the general to go on except what the wartime leaders have noted—and that was generally far from complimentary.

In fact, President Eisenhower's "I like de Gaulle" is a highly oversimplified statement of his wartime feelings toward the French general, for he actually more or less agreed, as his memoires show, with President Roosevelt that General de Gaulle was too much "a prima donna."

Washington, therefore, has already put out feelers looking to a visit here of the new French Premier, prior to any summit meeting—a visit that would give President Eisenhower and Premier de Gaulle an opportunity to find what common ground there was in any approach to the Soviets.

The United States is aware that the new Premier has his hands full at home and that a trip to the United States is therefore not an immediate possibility. But the prospect of General de Gaulle occupying a summit seat is one that has Washington concerned. It is not that Washington officials distrust him so much, as that they do not know him—and they want to get to know him fully and well.

De Murville Hailed

One thing that does seem to please all Washingtonians, officials, diplomats, and what is left of the capital's populace, is that France's former Ambassador to the United States, Maurice Couve de Murville, has been named Foreign Minister.

Mr. de Murville is highly esteemed and liked by American officials and in diplomatic circles. He was more recently French Ambassador to West Germany, and officials here consider his selection a sign of General de Gaulle's desire to work closely and harmoniously with West Germany.

Associated Press Radiophoto

General de Gaulle Enters Elysée Palace for Meeting With New Cabinet

By Joan Thiriet

Special Correspondent of The Christian Science Monitor

Paris

The National Assembly has voted Gen. Charles de Gaulle the six-month emergency powers he demanded, but with even fewer votes than it confirmed him as the 26th Premier of the Fourth Republic.

While the investiture vote of June 1 was 329 to 224, the June 2 vote for the emergency powers was 322 to 232. There is no need to read too much into the switch of seven votes from the pro-de Gaulle bloc to the opposition; but it is an indication of the wavering sentiments of the deputies.

The emergency bill has already been sent to the Council of the Republic (senate) where it is expected to be passed in short order.

Thus, General de Gaulle has cleared the main hurdle—in Paris. There still remain some formidable obstacles to be cleared in Algeria.

Insurgents Contacted

[The Associated Press reported that General de Gaulle's contacts with the insurgents in Algeria took on something of a cloak-and-dagger aspect. Gen. Raoul Salan, French Commander in Algeria, announced June 2 that he had received a telephone call from General de Gaulle saying the general would arrive there June 4. General de Gaulle's office confirmed the phone call, but only after several hours.

[It was learned, too, that Leon Delbecque, a fiery political leader in the Algerian Junta, had come to Paris for secret talks with General de Gaulle.]

It was evident as the general spoke June 1 that the 11-year-old regime of the Fourth Republic was about to vanish, with its government by Assembly and consequent kaleidoscope of governments alternately supported and opposed by party maneuvers, personal ruses, and the powerful lobbies that have succeeded in toppling the weak coalitions which have never had the time or the unity to carry out broad and energetic policies.

Brief Statement

General de Gaulle's declaration was given with a military shortness that contrasted strongly with the length and detail of his predecessors' in the task of winning the Assembly's investiture.

He asked for Parliament to hand over full powers to the government for a six-month period, "hoping that, at the end of that period, with order restored in the state, hope rediscovered in Algeria, and unity reestablished in the nation, the public powers will be able to resume the normal course of their functioning."

He then mentioned his plan for constitutional reform, to be based on three principles: universal suffrage, a proper division of powers, and the responsibility of government to Parliament.

Work on Bills Begun

Such a reform involves, if it is to go directly to the people for the referendum General de Gaulle desires, prior change in Article 90 of the present Constitution. This states that only Parliament can carry out constitutional reform, and provides for a referendum only in cases where a stipulated two-thirds or three-fifths majority is not attained in either Assembly or Senate.

Before retiring for a long vacation, at least until October, deputies will therefore be called on to vote General de Gaulle the powers he demands, as well as the alteration in Article 90. They have already begun work on these bills, to be rushed through Parliament so that General de Gaulle can go to Algiers within the next few days.

Apart from the emphasis on the present state of France with which the general opened his short speech, there was virtually no program indicated. General de Gaulle in fact offered little but leadership, asked for the needed powers, and left all details of his policies still to come.

His opening words made it clear that in his view this was no time to go through the habitual procedure of minutely considering every brand of trouble and the remedies it called for.

Situation Appraised

"The state still rushing headlong into degradation, French untiy directly threatened, Algeria plunged into affliction and agitation, Corsica suffering from a feverish contagion, opposing factions in France itself whose passions and activities are increasing hourly, the Army long tried by bloody and meritorious tasks but scandalized by the bankruptcy of authority, our international position breached to the very heart of our alliances—such is the situation of our country today," said General de Gaulle in a grave but noticeably undramatic voice.

The 15 names of his Cabinet members (most previous governments have had at least 30 and once 44) are an adroit mixture of old and new, of political background from the now discredited "system," and technical ability drawn from outside political circles.

Pinay Joins Team

The four ministers of state, a sort of political advisers' group, are Felix Houphouet-Boigny, from the Ivory Coast, an enlightened product of Negro Africa who has already sat in several Cabinets, and three Fourth Republic political leaders: outgoing Premier of the Roman Catholic Popular Republican Movement, Pierre Pflimlin; Conservative Louis Jacquinot (known for moderately liberal views on Algeria), and former Premier Guy Mollet, secretary-general of the Socialist Party, but now in a weak position since the bulk of his colleagues did not follow his plea for support of General de Gaulle.

At the Finance Ministry will be another former Premier, conservative Antoine Pinay, who has for some time been saying privately that a liberal solution for Algeria must be found.

Related Stories: Page 14

God's Power Cited At Annual Meeting Of Mother Church

Scientific reliance on God's power is needed to meet the challenges of the space age, The Christian Science Board of Directors said today.

"Although some people may view this new age with trepidation, Christian Scientists welcome it and the opportunities that accompany it," they declared.

More than 7,000 church members from many parts of the world heard the Directors' message at the Annual Meeting of The Mother Church, The First Church of Christ, Scientist, in Boston, Massachusetts.

Warning against reliance on materialism, the Directors pointed out that modern inventions "are not really solving the basic problems confronting humanity, but seem, in fact, to be increasing them."

Thoughtful people, they said, "are beginning to realize that only by availing themselves of a higher power, a force far more powerful than that obtained through nuclear fission or fusion, can men hope to hold in check and nullify the evil elements of the human mind which would threaten to misuse the inventions of the space age."

New President Named

Leonard T. Carney of Boston, Massachusetts, a member of the Board of Trustees of The Christian Science Publishing Society, was named President of The Mother Church for the coming year. He succeeds Miss Mabel Ellen Lucas, a Christian Science practitioner of Brookline, Mass. Roy Garrett Watson and Gordon V. Comer were reelected Treasurer and Clerk, respectively.

Seven new members were appointed to The Christian Science Board of Lectureship:

Neil H. Bowles of Atlanta, Georgia; Francis William Cousins of Manchester, England; Richard L. Glendon of Los Angeles, California; Mrs. Lona Koch-Meisen of Boston, Massachusetts; Herbert E. Rieke of Indianapolis, Indiana; Mrs. Gertrude E. Velguth of Flint, Michigan; and Paul K. Wavro of Jacksonville, Florida.

In his keynote address Mr. Carney, the new President, stressed the need for spiritual maturity. "It is yielding to materiality," he said, "that blocks our progress. The shackles of materiality fall away as we advance spiritually."

He added that the "dominance of the spiritual over the material has been proved through the ages as God's law of progress has been acknowledged in the thoughts of men."

Healings Reported

Reports of complete and permanent healings in Christian Science of alcoholism, tuberculosis, cancer, blindness, hay fever, arthritis, epilepsy, multiple sclerosis, and many other difficulties were mentioned at the meeting.

The audience filled the Extension of The Mother Church as well as the adjoining original edifice and a nearby theater. The members traveled from every state in the union and from Europe, Africa, Asia, South America, Australia, and other distant points to attend.

Many arrived in time for Sunday services yesterday. In addition to today's comprehensive session, they will attend a series of meetings on various special subjects tomorrow and Wednesday.

New Projects Announced

New projects were announced at the main session by key officials:

1. Reporting for the Trustees of The Christian Science Publishing Society, John H. Hoagland, Manager, announced the release of a motion picture in color showing the publishing operations of The Christian Science Monitor in Boston and activities of national and overseas correspondents. Mr. Hoagland invited the gathering to attend special previews of this 30-minute documentary entitled "Assignment: Mankind" in the Uptown Theater on June 3 and 4.

2. In the Clerk's report, Mr. Comer announced that air conditioning of the original edifice of The Mother Church, the Extension, and the Publishing House will be completed in a year's time.

3. The Trustees under the Will of Mary Baker Eddy announced that a Danish translation of "Science and Health with Key to the Scriptures" by Mary Baker Eddy, Discoverer and Founder of Christian Science, is in the hands of the printer now.

4. Will B. Davis, Manager of Committees on Publication, announced that a new hour-long motion picture in color entitled "The Mother Church in Action" would be released in the early spring of 1959.

Milestones Marked

Four anniversaries — the founding of The Christian Science Journal 75 years ago, the Christian Science Sentinel and the Publishing Society 60 years ago, and the Monitor 50 years ago—were celebrated by the Publishing Society during the year, it was reported.

A long-sought victory was reported by Richard H. Chase, Manager of Christian Science Activities for the Armed Services. "In 1957 the British armed forces," he said, "exempted Christian Scientists from compulsory medication and surgery."

Many new branches of The Mother Church were established during the year, it was reported, including those in: Letchworth and in Whitby, England; Lindau, Ludwigsburg, and Uelzen, Germany; Zwolle, the Netherlands; Roturua, New Zealand; Sudbury, Ontario, Canada; and Porto Alegre, Brazil.

Other stories on Annual Meeting: Pages 6 and 7.

Report Deepens Galíndez Mystery

By Frederick W. Roevekamp

Staff Correspondent of The Christian Science Monitor

New York

The report by Morris L. Ernst, noted American lawyer, on the disappearance of Dr. Jesús de Galíndez may deepen rather than dispel that two-year-old mystery.

While it rejects one batch of theories that have sprung up around the case, it encourages speculation in still another direction.

Mr. Ernst, in effect, clears the Dominican Republic's strongman Generalissimo Rafael L. Trujillo of any part in the case. Prevalent theories had linked him to the disappearance of Dr. Galíndez, an outspoken foe of General Trujillo. Mr. Ernst was retained by the Dominican Government to make the investigation.

By implication, the New York attorney relates the disappearance of the Basque exile and Columbia University lecturer to his role as a million-dollar fund raiser for the Basque government-in-exile.

Rebuttal Published

In its efforts to repair the damage to its reputation within public opinion in the United States and elsewhere, the Dominican dictator could hardly have picked anyone more effective. Mr. Ernst is widely known as a lawyer and an opponent of authoritarian regimes.

Mr. Ernst was paid a $50,000 retainer and $50,000 in expenses to start the probe last July after a heavy accumulation of rumors regarding Generalisimo Trujillo's role in the Galíndez case.

In the 94 pages and 53 exhibits published June 1, Mr. Ernst concluded that:

"No accusation concerning the Dominican Republic or any of its officials with the disappearance of Galíndez is supported by any evidence: And this covers all theories. . . ."

Mr. Ernst presented some evidence which conflicts with the reports in the most prevalent of all theories about Dr. Galíndez.

That theory contends that the Basque scholar was kidnaped in New York on the night of March 12, 1956, taken by ambulance to Zahn's Airport, Amityville, Long Island, New York, and flown via Florida to Monte Christi Airport in the Dominican Republic.

The pilot who allegedly flew the plane was Lester Gerald Murphy, an American who has been tied to Dr. Galíndez's disappearance by several sources. The United States State Department sent a note on May 2, 1957, saying that "sufficient evidence has now been uncovered to indicate that Mr. Murphy may have been connected with the Galíndez disappearance, acting on behalf of or in association with certain Dominican and American nationals."

Widespread Publicity

There has been massive newspaper and magazine publicity attempting to tie Mr. Murphy to Dr. Galíndez's disappearance.

The American pilot, according to a Dominican Government report, was killed in a personal conflict by Octavio de la Maza, a fellow pilot in the Dominican airlines for which Mr. Murphy worked later.

To buttress his implications that Dr. Galíndez's disappearance may have been connected with questionable practices in his fund-raising activity, Mr. Ernst points to a $62,852 claim by the United States Internal Revenue Service against the Galíndez estate filed last July 10.

The public administrator representing the Galíndez estate here has fought the federal tax claim with the contention that there was no evidence to prove that Dr. Galíndez had kept any "allegedly undeposited collections."

The Ernst report itself quotes José Antonio de Aguirre, president of the Basque exile organization as saying in Paris that "every last penny had been accounted for, and there was no question of Galindez's financial integrity."

State of the Nations

Modern Elizabethans

By HENRY S. HAYWARD, Chief, London News Bureau, The Christian Science Monitor

London

Britons and Americans recently have had an opportunity to see Prime Minister Harold Macmillan interviewed on television.

Something he said in the course of the Columbia Broadcasting System "See It Now" interview is of basic importance in understanding the British national philosophy of today.

His American interviewers, Edward R. Murrow and Charles Collingwood, at one point asked Mr. Macmillan the forthright question: Is Britain in decline?

Quite true, the Prime Minister replied, compared with the nineteenth century, the material power of England is much reduced.

Then Mr. Macmillan went into one of his favorite themes. While Britain's dominant position is gone, he said, it never held a dominant position—except for about 100 years of its history.

He was, of course, referring to the century between the defeat of Napoleon and World War I, when the British Empire reached its greatest expanse, influence, resources — when Britain became, virtually beyond challenge, the greatest power on the face of the globe.

⁂

Everyone knows of that century. Some Britons still have a tendency to hark back to it. Not Mr. Macmillan.

"English people had better forget about the nineteenth century and think a little more about the sixteenth, seventeenth, and eighteenth centuries, which were far the most glorious in their tradition," the British leader asserted.

What did he mean?

Those who have heard him personally discourse upon this theme aver he meant that Britain was a massive world power only for a relatively brief span of one century. It drew to a close in 1914 or 1918. But for at least three centuries prior to the big century, Britain was a small, but important, island power that administered many a naval and economic defeat to the larger powers of the day.

Mr. Macmillan sees Britain today not as declining, but as paralleling its older historic role and pattern—as a smaller power, yet as a power none can afford to ignore.

'I'd Love to See Sir Francis Drake Run This Thing!'

Britain's real power, he points out, always has rested in its ability to make coalitions to defeat vaster forces.

That ability is as available today as in the time of Hitler, the Kaiser, Napoleon, or Philip II of the mighty Spanish Empire, whose ships were scattered by those from a tiny island state.

As a student of history, Mr. Macmillan is aware of the England of Elizabeth I—of its physical smallness, compensated by naval prowess, and particularly of its emerging mercantile power, the trade that built an empire. It was the first Elizabeth who encouraged the expansion of trade with Asia and the New World, who backed seaborne adventurers — the Drakes, Raleighs, Hawkinses, and Frobishers. Her captains learned to trade as well as fight. Yet her country, for all its growing power, remained what could be termed "Little England" with scarcely five million people.

Under the second Elizabeth today, a Britain of 52 millions still is finding difficulty in adjusting to a more moderate position in world affairs. It clearly is to be a position somewhere between the first Elizabeth's Little England and the gargantuan domain of Victoria, Edward VII, and George V.

The retrenchment is not an easy task. But the Prime Minister in effect has told both Britons and Americans it is under way — and moreover that the smaller Britain yet can have a great future.

His inference is that it need no more be second-rate than were the ships and men who defeated the Spanish Armada in 1588 — or the sea rovers and traders who have continued under the second Elizabeth as under the first.

⁂

History, it is pointed out, is seldom made by those who look backward. And it would be wrong to give the impression that either the Prime Minister or his countrymen spend much time so occupied.

They are not specifically concerned with breeding a new Elizabethan race of Armada-smashers, East India traders, and New World colonizers emanating from a tiny island-bound Britain.

But men such as Mr. Macmillan are giving voice to the conviction that Britain can remain great—indeed become greater than ever in trade inventiveness, leadership, and the democratic practices — even without vast possessions.

Mr. Macmillan, in effect, is calling for new Elizabethans. Some already are visible in action. Others are striving to find their new role and fulfill it. The old Elizabethans would recognize them.

Emil Weiss

Charles Malik

The Lebanese Foreign Minister, who is to present Lebanon's complaint against United Arab Republic at UN Security Council.

Beirut delays UN airing: Page 2

THE CHRISTIAN SCIENCE MONITOR

Registered in U. S. Patent Office
AN INTERNATIONAL DAILY NEWSPAPER

VOLUME 50 NO. 183 | © 1958, THE CHRISTIAN SCIENCE PUBLISHING SOCIETY All Rights Reserved | BOSTON, TUESDAY, JULY 1, 1958 | ••—ATLANTIC EDITION | TWO SECTIONS | TEN CENTS A COPY

Alaska Statehood Slated to Bring New Evolution for United States

Senate Approves 64 to 20

By Richard L. Strout
Staff Correspondent of The Christian Science Monitor

Washington

The vote giving statehood to Alaska marks a new stage in the evolution of the United States.

As for Alaskans, they have no doubt of their future. They do not talk about the present but of the expected expansion ahead. They believe the new forms of transportation and communication will bring commerce and population to their immense, mineral-rich area.

The Senate vote opens the way for later admission of Hawaii, already asking statehood, and perhaps for other distant territories.

Thus the meaning of "United States of America" may have to be stretched a bit. Hawaii, for example, is well offshore in the Pacific.

Alaska's admission means a readjustment of thinking—political, economic, social.

64-to-20 Vote

The vote for Alaska's admission in the Senate, June 30, was 64 to 20. Presidential approval is required, following which a statehood referendum will be submitted to Alaska's citizens.

Alaska probably will have an election this summer to pick a new governor, two senators, and single member of the lower house.

In domestic politics the immediate effect is in the Senate. Alaska's present population is estimated at around 210,000, dispersed over an area twice as large as Texas, in a frontier civilization. The capital Juneau, for example, has only 7,100 people, without any rail or highway connections with the United States or Canada.

Alaska, whose population is about the size of Worcester, Mass., will get two United States senators. These two votes in the upper chamber are a powerful lever in the hands of a small population state. Like Nevada, Alaska will be able to use its Senate votes to win federal aid and subsidies.

Out of 350 million acres only about 1 per cent are estimated to be potential farm land, with 20,000 acres now under cultivation.

The Alaskan economy is at present sustained by federal spending, largely defense. Out of an Alaskan income of about 500 million dollars a year, 70 per cent comes from the United States Government.

Higher Costs Likely

Of the total population about 45,000—or over a fifth—are members of the armed forces and their dependents; another 34,000, or 16 per cent, are Aleuts, Eskimos, and Indians.

The cost of the territorial government of Alaska is around 28 million dollars annually. The United States Treasury has been putting back into Alaska well over the 100 million dollars it collects from that territory in income and excise taxes. The total of United States expenditures there is estimated at 300 million dollars or over.

With statehood, Alaskan citizens must assume the cost of court administration, schools (now operated by the Alaska Native Service), borough government, roads, and the like. One estimate is that this will cost Alaskans 14 millions more annually.

The shift from a territorial to an independent economy is not easy and grave doubts have been raised of Alaska's fiscal viability by opponents on the Senate floor. There also has been some opposition in Alaska itself. However, an emotional wave of sentiment for the "49th state" has swept all material obstacles aside.

For years both of the American political parties have publicly favored statehood, though there is no evidence that they have considered the matter very carefully.

Statehood Irrevocable

Once statehood is granted it is irrevocable.

Representative Leo W. O'Brien (D) of New York, declared here that the House Insular Affairs Committee, of which he is a member, will approve Hawaiian statehood next week. Congressional action on making Hawaii the "50th state" is hardly likely at this session however.

The United States, in admitting Alaska and possibly Hawaii, is following the French pattern of centralizing government in Washington, rather than the British pattern of dispersing government in outlying commonwealths. However Alaska was acquired in a straightforward purchase.

Puerto Rico is the exception in the United States. Puerto Rico has been happy with its self-governing and self-taxing "commonwealth" status.

Each new senator added dilutes the power of the compact bloc of southern senators which has thus far been used effectively on segregation issues.

Indeed, with the addition of two senators from Alaska, it would seem more likely than in a hundred years, that the old Senate rules under which southern filibusters occur, could be revised.

In Alaska, enthusiastic statehood supporters hardly could believe the news that their 42-year fight was nearly over. They had noted the House vote, May 28, which favored statehood 208 to 166.

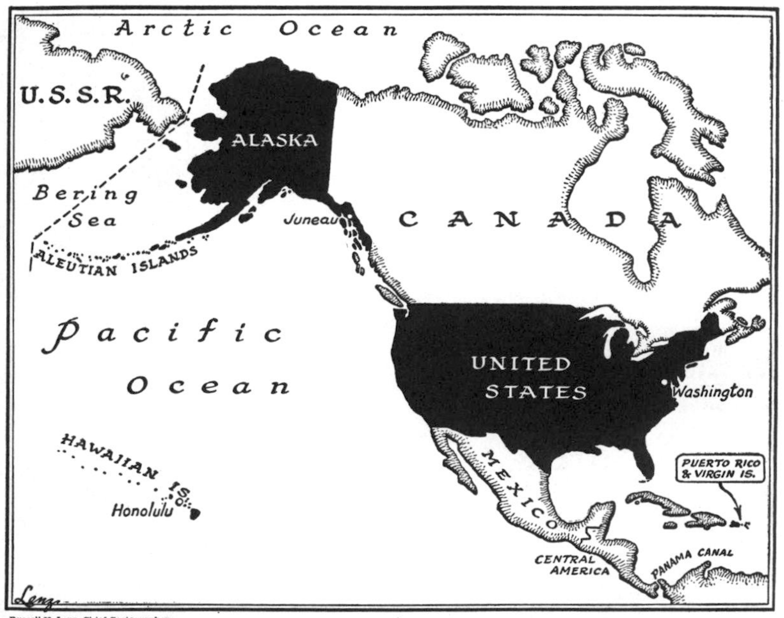

Russell H. Lenz, Chief Cartographer

ALASKA MADE IT! On this map it is shown in its position in the Western Hemisphere and its relationship to the United States and its possessions. This is a Van der Grinton projection, the whole world placed on a flat circle, in this case with the United States at the center. The projection slightly distorts so that the northern regions, including Alaska and Canada, are larger than is actual with respect to the United States. The question now is "Will Hawaii be next?" Puerto Rico has already decided not to ask for statehood, but stands as a commonwealth within the union.

Nasser Contact Cited

Infiltration Ebb Set in Lebanon?

By William R. Frye
United Nations Correspondent of The Christian Science Monitor

United Nations, N.Y.

United Nations Secretary-General Dag Hammarskjold has told key UN diplomats he believes infiltration from Syria into Lebanon will taper off and stop, it has been learned here.

It is generally assumed that Mr. Hammarskjold bases his confidence on the conversation he had with President Nasser of the United Arab Republic June 22.

Whether President Nasser's assumed promise to "ease up" on Lebanon was permanent or temporary, whether it was conditional or unconditional, and whether the Cairo leader has sufficient authority over the Syrians to make his word "stick," are all unanswered questions.

Lebanese diplomats here indicate they are willing to wait a reasonable time to see whether Mr. Hammarskjold's optimism is justified before demanding further UN action. Infiltration, they say, has not yet shown any signs of stopping.

One correlative aspect of the revolt, however, to which Lebanon has objected — attacks on President Chamoun in the Cairo press—has eased up. News of the fighting is still being given major prominence, but according to Arab sources, denunciations of Mr. Chamoun have become less virulent.

Report Delayed?

If Mr. Hammarskjold has been able to persuade Colonel Nasser to abandon or substantially modify his support of the Lebanese rebels, it will have been a major stroke of peacemaking, all agree. Until he went to Beirut and Cairo, there was a possibility the West and the Soviet Union were headed for a collision.

The UN Observer Group in Lebanon (UNOGIL) has not yet submitted a report on the charge of intervention by Colonel Nasser. The first such report now is said to be due July 2, but few here would be surprised if it were further delayed.

Until a report is submitted, Mr. Hammarskjold, through the UNOGIL, has valuable leverage on President Nasser. A verdict unfavorable to the President would damage him greatly in the eyes of the world, and might well open up the floodgates for counterintervention by the UN, the West, or the West on behalf of the UN. Colonel Nasser has considerable incentive to act in such a way as to avoid that kind of verdict.

Bargaining Leverage

There was just the slightest hint of a warning to President Nasser in a preliminary report made public by the Secretary-General June 30. The observer group, the report said, "has received information concerning prisoners, said to be Syrians, taken by Lebanese authorities. Such prisoners, when made available to the group, are being interrogated by the executive member of the group. . . ."

Translating this passage from the diplomatic idiom, UN observers said it meant: "We are on the trail of some hard evidence against you. If you don't follow through with your promises to ease up, we will spread the evidence on the public record."

It would be in character for Mr. Hammarskjold to withhold publication of the report as long as possible, diplomats say, in order to prolong the life of this bargaining leverage. Once a verdict is passed in either direction, the asset is largely consumed.

Observers here point to the fact that on July 24, the Lebanese Parliament is due to elect a new President. Mr. Hammarskjold is said to want to delay a showdown, if possible, until that time, feeling that the outcome of the voting may be sufficiently acceptable to all factions so that the rebellion would come to a natural end.

One major objective of the rebels—to prevent a new term of office for President Chamoun—would be achieved as of that date if, as now seems certain, someone else were elected.

Election Date Waited

If violence and infiltration were to continue beyond July 24, or resume after that date once they had stopped, there would then be much less basis for the contention that the whole affair was simply a domestic struggle for political power.

The contention that President Chamoun shared blame in that he sought to perpetuate himself in office would lose persuasive power, and the moral lines would be much clearer, it is said.

Meanwhile, efforts are being made to give the UNOGIL access to all the facts. The group now numbers 109 officers from 11 countries. Two helicopters have been put into operation, and four light observation planes have been requested.

There is a "regular patrolling system" of areas accessible to the group, Mr. Hammarskjold reported June 30. Five such areas are under almost constant surveillance, he said. Seven permanent "out stations" have been set up as branches of the Beirut headquarters, and patrols regularly go out from these stations in radio-equipped jeeps.

The observers also have contacted rebel leaders to seek freedom of movement in rebel-held areas. The chief military observer, Lt. Col. Maurice Brown, had lunch with one rebel leader, Tawfik Haidar, at Labweh June 30.

Attempted Revolt In Jordan Reported

By Reuters

Beirut, Lebanon

The Beirut independent newspaper Al-Jarida said July 1 that 12 Jordanian Army officers have been arrested for an attempted coup d'état in Jordan.

The newspaper said Jordan had asked Iraq for urgent military help and that Iraq promised to send 5,000 troops immediately.

The officers arrested ranged in rank from a second lieutenant to a lieutenant colonel.

Independent observers in Beirut said their information suggested that the Al-Jarida report was "as least partially true."

But when Jordanian authorities in Amman were telephoned for comment on the report, they refused to say anything but "Wait for the result of our investigation."

Jordan and Iraq proclaimed a federation of their two governments last February.

Inside Reading:

Other stories on Alaska will be found on page 4:

What Is Alaska?

Reaction to the News

Senate Roll Call on Vote

When States Admitted

Alaskans Celebrate Good News

By Hal Painter
Special to The Christian Science Monitor

Anchorage, Alaska

Alaska's reaction to the Senate's passage of the Alaska statehood bill, to put it mildly, is hysteria.

Some grand, unnamed feeling swept across this 586,000-square-mile land like a skyrocket. Statehood proponents, opponents, the indifferent alike, are celebrating.

As word came shortly after 2 p.m., June 30 in Anchorage, the Anchorage District Court—a murder trial in session—was immediately dismissed. Judge, jury, and all but the defendants rushed to the street as the city air-raid and fire sirens blew—at last, the sweet sound of Alaska statehood.

Bonfire Lights City

A 49th star was added to a giant United States flag that all but shrouded the Anchorage Federal Building. This building has long been a symbol of the federal control exerted over the former Territory of Alaska.

On the night of statehood, the sky barely darkened as the long summer sun still hovered, the leaders of Operation Statehood, a hard-driving, deliriously victorious citizens' group, lit a 50-ton bonfire in the center of the city—49 tons for Alaska, an extra ton for Hawaii's statehood ambitions.

The roar of its flame was lost in the din and uproar, honking horns, firecrackers, a sizable citizens' arsenal, loud speakers, and cheering.

People Dance in Streets

The bonfire was the scene of organized dances and much disorganized pushing and shoving, and the burning of the Jones Act which has been held to be a stranglehold on Alaska's economy, supporting high shipping rates.

North, in Fairbanks, Alaska's second largest city, the Chena River ran through town dyed a brilliant gold. A bonfire was lit and a balloon bearing a high 49th star soared into the sky. Here, too, was wild celebration.

In Juneau in the south, Alaska's third largest city, bonfires were lit, sirens sounded, the bells of all its churches rang and there were prayers for the future of Alaska. People danced and sang in the streets.

As one reporter put it in answer to a national wire service query:

"It's pandemonium. Second Avenue (Juneau's main street) is an unending traffic jam."

In the widespread villages and towns of the north, word was spread by Eskimo. Only the Eskimos know what the words were, but the results were spectacular: more singing, more dancing, more bonfires.

The whole of the new state was virtually afire, north to its Arctic, south to the panhandle, west to the Aleutians.

What is ahead no one knows. At the moment, no one cares. Alaska is too happy to worry.

Big Issue Remains

"Stunned," "great," "fine," "can't find words to describe it" were some of the phrases used by Alaska's statehood leaders. They had few words for the future, only an occasional cliché they managed to retain in the throes of an ecstatic reaction.

John Manders, Anchorage attorney and outspoken critic of Alaska statehood, summed up perhaps what is left of the feeling of statehood opponents as elation sweeps this new state:

"What are you going to do with a million-dollar yacht if you can't run it?"

This is the question Alaska will now have to answer: What to do with this rich land, how do we make it produce?

But as the current reaction might indicate, Alaskans have been waiting a long time to roll up their sleeves and dig for the answer.

The most immediate prospect is oil. Already it has produced over $2,000,000 since its discovery in July, 1957. Then comes fishing, vital metals, lumber, and in this age of promotion and travel—tourists.

There is no doubt Alaska is rich. Only the means are needed: more people, more capital.

These granted, there is little doubt here Alaska will find a prosperous place in the union.

Hawaii Statehood Pushed

By the Associated Press

Washington

President Eisenhower has prodded Congress to act on legislation to grant statehood to Hawaii, now that the Alaska bill has been approved.

The President's call was reported to newsmen by Senate Republican leader William F. Knowland of California after he and other GOP leaders from Congress concluded their regular weekly meeting with the President. Senator Knowland said the general feeling at the conference was that the Democratic leaders of both the House and Senate are practicing rank discrimination against Hawaii.

The senator added that from an economic standpoint Hawaii has perhaps an even greater claim on statehood than Alaska does.

The Hawaiian statehood bill is on the Senate calendar and could be called up for action at any time. Similar legislation is pending before the House Interior Committee with no prospects for action.

Leaders in Hawaii hailed the Senate vote to make Alaska the 49th state and they too expressed hope that Hawaii would follow soon as the 50th.

Gov. William F. Quinn, a Republican, sent a telegram to the Governor of Alaska, Mike Stepovich, stating:

"Overjoyed to learn of Senate action. All praise, honor, and glory to 49th state. All Hawaii rejoicing."

Hawaii's Democrats immediately arranged a "victory celebration."

William S. Richardson, territorial Democratic chairman, said, "This is the best news we've had in a long time. This is the closest Hawaii has ever got. We ought to pull all the stops now."

Mayor Neal S. Blaisdell of Honolulu, a Republican, said:

"Now that Alaska statehood has been granted Hawaii can't be far behind."

United Press International

President Confers With Shah of Iran

Shah Mohammed Reza Pahlevi of Iran, the American Chief Executive, and other top officials have discussed the problems of the Shah's homeland and the broader issues affecting the whole Middle East during the visitor's three-day informal stay in the United States. The Shah has spoken publicly of the farm ties between the two countries. He said Iran had demonstrated its friendship by standing firmly with the West during the Middle East crises.

State of the Nations

The Next Congress—?

By WILLIAM H. STRINGER, Chief, Washington Bureau, The Christian Science Monitor

Washington

If the portents of a Democratic victory in the congressional elections this fall continue to show up as they are doing now, the United States is going to have a Congress with a pronounced liberal conviction next year.

But there are political experts in Washington who forecast—and they have been right before—that such a large-scale Democratic victory would neither overturn the mid-road congressional leadership by Texas Democrats nor mean a spate of rip-roaring New Deal legislation pouring out of the mills on Capitol Hill.

Much would depend, of course, on the size of the Democratic triumph — how many additional senators and representatives were elected on the Democratic ticket in the West, the Midwest, the East, and New England. If the election were held tomorrow, it would indeed be a Democratic landslide. But, as an astute observer remarks, "Elections are never held tomorrow."

Right now the field reports coming in—to both parties—suggest that the impact of the recession, sputnik, troubles abroad, farm discontent—and now the Adams - Goldfine furor—means a formidable Democratic triumph in November.

But there could still be shifts in the political weather: That brisk economic recovery which a minority of economists is already forecasting; something of value achieved somewhere on the foreign-policy front (or a deeper crisis which would rally the country behind President Eisenhower); a felicitous "era of good feeling" among the farmers.

Senator Lyndon B. Johnson

Present indications are that any upturn in Republican fortunes would come too late. But Democratic strategists, remembering the great upset of 1948, are not counting their chickens yet.

Given anything but a great landslide of votes bringing additional Democrats in droves to the halls of Congress, the mid-road Democratic leadership on Capitol Hill insists it can maintain its hold on the legislative reins, and believes also that the legislative flow from Congress will not be extremist.

Perhaps the Lyndon Johnson leadership is misjudging future tempers. But the able, adroit Senate leader from Texas has been right before—he dissented when liberal columnists were forecasting that a civil-rights battle would perilously split the Democratic Party, and when they opined that Democratic support of Eisenhower legislation would redound only to the benefit of the Republicans. The Democratic Party was not wrecked by the civil-rights fight, and the Democrats today have a campaign slogan: "If you like what's being legislated by Congress, send us more Democrats."

One thing is certain: The roster of prospective Democratic candidates discloses few of the "wild man" type. Muskie of Maine, Leader of Pennsylvania, Engle of California, to select a few, are certainly not extremists.

The Democratic leadership suggests that if the nation wants to see the kind of legislation the next Congress will produce with a reinforced Democratic majority, it has only to note some of the measures which this Congress failed to pass. In the Senate, for instance, seven or eight more votes could have passed a school bill; one additional vote would have rescued the Kennedy amendment to the foreign-aid bill, permitting more assistance to Soviet satellite countries.

Seven or eight more votes would have passed the Democratic farm bill (maintaining high price supports) over the President's veto. Five or six more would have approved a public power development of Hells Canyon.

Most certainly, a big Democratic victory in the North and West would send to Congress enough "liberals" so that the old coalition of conservative Republicans and southern Democrats could be overridden. But the Texas leadership would say that this alliance is already obsolete. The effective coalition, it is argued, is that of North-South Democrats working together.

So the present Democratic leadership insists that Congress, next session, will continue its mid-road course, while other Democrats are forecasting that a Democratic landslide would spawn "extremist" measures. The Republicans could help Congress hold the mid-road course by reversing the present evidences of discouragement within the GOP and winning more seats for the Republicans than now forecast.

'Political Blackmail' Rejected by Dulles

Compiled from Associated Press and Reuters Dispatches

Americans held captive in foreign lands were in the forefront of the news July 1.

French diplomatic sources reported that the crew of a United States Air Force plane forced down in the Soviet Union June 28 will be handed back to United States authorities shortly.

At his press conference in Washington, Secretary of State John Foster Dulles declared that the United States refuses to pay political blackmail for the release of Americans held captive in East Germany and Cuban rebel territory.

At the same time the Soviet Embassy in Washington told the State Department again that United States efforts to free nine United States soldiers and their helicopter must be taken up through East Germany, not the Soviet Union.

Mr. Dulles told newsmen that East Germany is trying to force United States recognition of the Communist government in negotiating the release of the men.

Four United States citizens are still held in Communist China, and Mr. Dulles reported that the United States is planning to propose that negotiations over this and other Washington-Peking issues be switched from Geneva to Warsaw.

Further details: Page 4

THE CHRISTIAN SCIENCE MONITOR

Registered in U. S. Patent Office

AN INTERNATIONAL DAILY NEWSPAPER

VOLUME 51 NO. 31 | BOSTON, FRIDAY, JANUARY 2, 1959 | ***ATLANTIC EDITION | TWO SECTIONS | TEN CENTS A COPY

© 1959, THE CHRISTIAN SCIENCE PUBLISHING SOCIETY All Rights Reserved

Germany in Crisis: 9

Wartime Rancor Left Far Behind

By Erwin D. Canham
Editor of The Christian Science Monitor

Two weeks in today's Germany left this editor, who cannot often stray from his home base, with the desire to see in equal detail what has been happening in Britain, in France, in Italy, in Japan, and of course in the Soviet Union and in Communist China. These hopes must be presently unfulfilled.

But one set of broad conclusions emerges: that the settlement of World War II as regards Germany and Japan has been a mighty triumph over hate and revenge. If it were not for the tragic confrontation that exists with Moscow and Peking, it could be said that the aftermath of World War II has been more healing than that of any great war of modern times. The "if," alas, is mountainous.

Yet there is basis for great satisfaction that Japan and Germany have come back into the family of like-minded nations. I do not ignore the elements of misunderstanding and delusion which led these nations into the morass of World War II. Moreover, we on the other side should not forget our own errors of omission and commission. But the fact remains that after extensive occupation by military forces—and 13 years later alien military forces are still on German and Japanese soil, though not as occupiers—relations of friendship and respect exist between the great nations which so recently were battering one another.

No small part of this healing results from American policy. Marshall Plan aid, and other assistance rendered to Japan and Germany, made a tremendous contribution to the recovery of those now powerful industrial nations. Italy, even sooner, was put on its feet economically, and revived in terms of national morale and self-respect.

Freed of False Systems

Thus the peoples who were so recently in the grip of false systems have become free. Moreover, the Germans and the Japanese, like the Italians, have been preserved, largely from the infection of communism. If, as a result of hate and resentment, the powerful economic potentials of Germany and Japan had been drawn into the Communist orbit, this would be a very different world. As it is, the balance of the free world is increased, perhaps decisively, by the vigorous dynamics of these two nations.

Their peoples, many lessons learned, are applying their abundant energies to the growth of their economies and the restoration of their substance. Their young people entering higher education have little memory of actual war. And these young people, it is generally agreed, are thinking in universal, idealistic terms to a degree not matched in earlier generations. The space age is upon them.

Germany's role in Western Europe is very important. The European movement itself is hopeful, though fraught with problems. It is vital that no one nation should dominate. Thus the revival of France under Premier Charles de Gaulle is of greatest significance. A weak France and a powerful Germany could lead to disaster. The sturdy, reliant strengths of Belgium and the Netherlands are helpful. Italy, especially its industrial complex in the north, plays a counterbalancing role. And if Britain comes more and more to participate in the European movement, it will help, perhaps decisively, to prevent excessive German dominance, which would be as bad for the Germans as for anybody else.

Progress Clear

A strong, interrelated Europe from Scandinavia to Italy, with hopes for Greece and Turkey, is a barrier to Communist penetration which is fully as important as the military power of NATO. When we remember how many Europeans were barely subsisting on the 1,000 calorie daily diets of the grim winter of 1945-46, when we recall the huts and holes in which many of them lived and half froze, when we remember their appalling cities and factories and roads, their big-eyed children, their hollow-eyed wives, one can feel that incalculable progress has been made.

Had they not been helped to recovery by American aid, had they not been able to work hard and effectively for themselves, had they not produced a new generation of statesmanlike political and economic leaders, the world indeed would have been a different place and communism would have reigned.

So Germany is only part of the picture. And one's conclusions have to be tentative. The German "miracle" has all taken place in boom times. The stress of depression has not been felt. There has been a kind of protective barrier against communism—American deterrent military power. During this period of rebuilding, both capital and labor have tended to be on their best behavior. When both get their strength back, will they be as reasonable? Under what circumstances could the delusions of the 1930's return? Questions must remain.

Full Credit Deserved

But questions need not taint confidence and respect. And certainly the West German Federal Republic and its government and people deserve all credit for their remarkable achievement. Nobody could have foreseen quite such a marvel, after the years of racial hate, after the death and torture camps, after the devastation, after the dismantling, after the hunger, after the military occupation.

I cannot forget the other Germans—all 17,000,000 of them—living under Communist rule. I remember those who deliberately choose to remain there, though they detest the regime, because they want to serve Germany and to prove something about the dignity and inviolability of man. They have lived under great difficulty and strain for many years: since 1939, at least; since 1933 for some; since 1914 for others. For those of us who have lived these years under governments and in societies in which we had confidence and pride, unsullied and undisgraced, and have felt free at all times to hold up our heads and speak or write our minds, there can be no concept of life in chains, mental or physical.

But one can also remember that many of these people are turning to inner lives, and finding spiritual outlets and rewards which are sometimes of transcendent value. I am sure that many of them are achieving heroism and nobility. And of course there are many others like them, farther east, in all the domains of communism. Boris Pasternak has written their story.

Helpfulness Acknowledged

I cannot end these articles without recording the great courtesy and friendliness with which my visit was arranged by the West German Government. The officials in the Foreign Office who helped organize the itinerary and schedule the interviews were eager to obtain anybody for whom I asked, including some harsh critics of the government. No questions were asked: anybody I wanted to see was unhesitatingly sought. Much of the respect with which I was received is due to the Monitor's long-time German correspondent, J. Emlyn Williams. He has been covering Central Europe since the mid-1920's, and Germany since the early 1930's. His knowledge and judgment about German problems are second to no man's. His regular dispatches tell much more than I can hope to summarize.

Germany in crisis: a crisis precipitated by Nikita S. Khrushchev. Berlin under ultimatum. Soviet arms a few minutes' drive from Hamburg. A nation divided.

And yet a nation partially reborn. A nation enormously restored. A nation capable of playing a strong and useful role in the holding of the West, and in the ultimate adjustment of livable arrangements with the East. Germany's destiny was never more signally a part of man's universal hope for peace than it is today.

Last of nine articles

Soviets Announce Lunar Resolution

By the Associated Press

London

The Soviet Union says its natural scientists will be in position to send a rocket around the moon in 1959 and declare the new year will see the first trials of nuclear-powered civil aircraft.

Moscow radio said Jan. 1 that the problem of nuclear reactions is high on the priority list of Soviet scientists for 1959 and beyond.

"The prospects of conquering these sources of concentrated power are closely linked with the problem of penetrating into cosmic space," the broadcast declared.

The year 1959 "will see still greater development in the field of interplanetary rockets and sputniks," the French-language broadcast continued. "Here progress of technology and automation will without doubt make it possible to send an interplanetary rocket around the moon in 1959.

"Soviet scientists have been working a long time on the problem of efficient use of atomic engines for civil aviation, and the results already obtained make it possible to state that 1959 will see the first trials in this field."

The American magazine Aviation Week said Nov. 30 that the Soviet Union had completed a nuclear-powered bomber six months before and that it had been flying in the Moscow area for at least two months.

The magazine said a number of foreign observers from countries on both sides of the Iron Curtain had witnessed the test flights.

Toppling of Dictatorship in Cuba Puts Isle at Political Crossroads

Associated Press Wirephoto

Cuban Government Reins Fall to Fidel Castro, Center

This photo was taken at the rebel leader's mountain hideout in May, 1957

By Bertram B. Johansson
Staff Writer, Latin-American Affairs, The Christian Science Monitor

Democracy-conscious Latin America is minus one more ruling dictator today.

After a slow-motion guerrilla war of two years' duration between Cuban Government and Castro rebel forces, Cuba suddenly has become the scene of swiftly moving events.

President Batista's government in Cuba has collapsed and fled.

Advance spearheads of Fidel Castro's bearded guerrilla fighters rolled into Havana by the truckloads over the central highway from the eastern provinces of Matanzas and Las Villas.

A provisional Cuban government headed by Dr. Manuel Urrutia is scheduled to be established in Havana this afternoon.

Cuba's overthrow of dictator Batista falls in the pattern of Latin America's more recent history of banishing dictators except that the independence movement worked more in the open and over a period of several years before it deposed Cuba's dictator.

There are only two left—President Trujillo of the Dominican Republic, and Gen. Alfredo Stroessner of Paraguay. But President Duvalier's government in Haiti is regarded as a virtual dictatorship now.

Base at Santiago

In January of last year, dictator Pérez Jiménez was toppled in Venezuela where absolute government had been exerted for nearly 100 years. Free elections have since been held.

In September, 1955, dictator Juan Perón was turned out by the military in Argentina. Peru ousted Gen. Manuel Odria in July, 1956, and Colombia followed suit in May, 1957, by ordering out Gen. Gustavo Rojas Pinella.

In each instance, the primary problem following has been how to nurture the fragile plant of democracy in the first months and years of new governments where one-crop economies are beset with financial problems, underdevelopment, the highest population increase rates in the world, and general poverty. There is a recently stepped-up exploitation of these conditions by a fringe of Communists.

[Armed Cuban rebels fired Jan. 2 on the Havana Post building and arrested three Associated Press staffers covering the city's postrevolt convulsion, according to the AP.

[Those herded out of the building at gunpoint were George Kaufman, chief of the Havana AP bureau, a Cuban national; Larry Allen, roving AP correspondent who has been covering the Cuban revolution, and Harold Valentine, AP photographer from Miami.]

To install Señor Urrutia, the Castro contingent must travel across half of Cuba to Havana. Señor Castro has ordered a mass public demonstration in Havana for 4 p.m. Jan. 2 for the installation.

Just what Fidel Castro's role will be in the government is an open question.

Embassy Reins Shift

A political idealist, law school graduate, son of a millionaire sugar plantation owner — rebel Señor Castro chose Señor Urrutia for the presidential post several months ago, declaring he himself had no presidential ambitions. Señor Castro is three years too young to become President under the constitutional age requirement of 35 years.

Señor Urrutia, a quiet-spoken lawyer, was smuggled into eastern Cuba about three weeks ago in preparation for setting up a provisional government.

His appearance in the Sierra Maestra rebel-held territory of eastern Cuba was a tipoff to Cuban exiles and to Castro supporters in Cuba that the expected Christmas - New Year offensive would really be launched.

Washington, though it has followed Cuban events closely, has remained noncommittal on the question of whether it would readily recognize a Castro-dominated government.

The White House said United States naval vessels are ready to evacuate Americans from Cuba if they are in danger, but the United States Embassy in Havana is not advising United States citizens to leave. It is only informing them how they can depart, if they wish.

The Cuban Embassy in Washington shifted gears smoothly. Cuban Ambassador Nicholas Arroyo resigned and designated Dr. Emilio Pando, the embassy's economic counselor, as chargé d'affaires.

Officials Take Flight

Ernesto Betancourt, Castro forces representative in Washington, asked that Señor Pando be placed in charge "until an ambassador can be chosen by the rebel government which will take over in Havana in a day or so."

In Cuban embassies and consulates around the world, particularly in Latin America, the changeover of personnel was rapid, and in most cases without violence.

Though Havana was relatively quiet by early Jan. 2, an undercurrent of tension was building up.

A black-book file has been kept of all Batista police and officers who persecuted and tortured their fellow Cubans. There have been many victims. Many of these officers face the ultimate penalty for the cruelties they have inflicted.

Cuban consular records throughout the world were ordered seized by the Castro government as part of a move decided on months ago to prevent loss or destruction of records that might be of use to the new government as evidence in trials of war criminals.

As a consequence, dozens of Batista Cabinet members and government officers have fled to Miami, New Orleans, Jacksonville, and New York by plane and boat.

Erstwhile dictator Batista has removed himself to that other haven of dictators, the Dominican Republic, ruled by President Trujillo.

Argentina's former dictator, Juan Perón, has been accorded sanctuary and restless ease on the Dominican island for some months in a palatial hotel suite.

At this writing, Cuba technically had no government.

Junta Left Behind

Fleeing President Batista assigned what crumbling authority he had to a three-man military junta. They appointed Carlos Piedra, a lawyer, as provisional president.

The Cuban Supreme Court re-

Associated Press Wirephoto

Manuel Urrutia Lleo

Cuba provisional President?

fused to swear him in, however, until Fidel Castro's approval, which he withheld.

The military junta gave up trying to form a government, leaving the field wide open for the Castro forces.

Basic problem facing the Castro forces will be the maintenance of order after years of repressive dictatorship, and the setting up of a functioning governmental administration.

There is bound to be confusion in the first weeks and months. Sugar cane harvesting is about to begin. The crop supplies about 40 per cent of United States sugar consumption. There may be some difficulty in transporting the harvested cane to sugar mills and to Cuba's seaports, especially in eastern Cuba where rebels have blown up hundreds of roads, bridges, and railroad tracks in preparation for the year-end offensive.

There is the question also of what the new government's attitude will be toward foreign firms operating in Cuba.

In 1955, Fidel Castro spoke often of needed nationalization of United States financed and operated utilities in Cuba. Associates say he has retreated drastically from this position. He favors a program of public housing and rural electrification and participation of all Cubans in industrial and utility enterprises.

Sugar futures in New York dropped sharply in heavy trading as a result of developments in Cuba, which produces about one-eighth of the world's sugar.

Dealers reported general selling, predominantly by commission houses, in the belief the end of the war will increase Cuba's exports and hike global supplies, but they doubted the decline in futures would affect the price of sugar to consumers.

Uneasy quiet falls over Havana: Page 6.

49-Star U.S. Digs In '59 Policy Heels

By Richard L. Strout
Staff Correspondent of The Christian Science Monitor

Washington

The United States is getting a new state, a new flag, and a new Congress all at once, but there are few signs that it is getting a new approach to the problem of expanding production or to world peace.

Alaska will be proclaimed the 49th state Jan. 3.

This means a new star will be added to the flag for the first time since 1912, when Arizona became the 48th state. The new flag will become official July 4, but millions will be issued before that.

As for the new Congress — the 86th — it starts work here Wednesday, Jan. 7.

The more things change in Washington, however, the more they remain the same.

Conservatives Hold On

After one of the biggest midterm election explosions in history, established conservative leaders of both parties in Congress are clamping on the lid to block the new liberal forces from taking over.

Simultaneously, the White House, instead of proposing drastic new policies on domestic or international fronts, appears rather to be digging in its heels on the old.

On foreign affairs the latest New Year's Eisenhower-Khrushchev exchange of notes shows the deadlock much as before, while on the home front President Eisenhower is placing increasing emphasis on economic retrenchment and fiscal orthodoxy with a balanced budget.

This is the background for the assembling of the new Congress following an overwhelming Democratic election victory last November. The November result was generally interpreted not as a vote of confidence in the Democrats but of dissatisfaction with the Republicans.

On the economic side the recession has cut down revenues on which federal taxes are based to produce an indicated 12 billion-dollar budget deficit. While the Soviet Union seeks an economic growth rate of more than 8 per cent annually, the American growth rate in recent years has been less than 2 per cent.

On the foreign field the Soviets have been stimulated by their sputnik military strength to push a series of offensive maneuvers, first in one part of the world then in another, and the United States and its allies have been left largely on the defensive.

What Congress is apt to produce in its first days, at least, is a series of sharp skirmishes representing efforts by the established leaders of both parties to hold the line against the thrust of the incoming new members against conservative institutions.

Filibuster Fought

Four of these skirmishes are immediately significant.

1. **Senate filibuster:** For generations a southern Senate minority has been able to stop civil-rights legislation by blocking cloture (i.e., refusing to shut off debate). A determined bipartisan group of liberals now wants to amend Senate rules to allow a majority to impose cloture after a period of debate that might run as long as two months.

Resisting change is Senate Majority Leader Lyndon B. Johnson (D) of Texas, who proposes a "compromise" which would allow two-thirds of senators present and voting to apply cloture. In practical effect, the liberals insist, this would hardly alter the present veto power of the South.

Minor Reforms Seen

Prospect: The Johnson compromise will prevail; simultaneously Vice-President Richard M. Nixon will identify himself with the "liberals" at least in part.

2. **House Rules Committee:** House Speaker Sam Rayburn (like his fellow Texan Mr. Johnson in the Senate) now appears to be mobilizing strength against parallel drive of House liberals. This is directed against the autocratic House Rules Committee, which has power to bottle up legislation. GOP House leader Joseph W. Martin, Jr., of Massachusetts, told newsmen here he has an agreement with Mr. Rayburn to leave the Rules Committee line-up unchanged. Prospect: Chances of liberal success are extremely doubtful, but minor reforms are likely.

3. **GOP Senate revolt:** Ten or a dozen Senate Republican liberals, alarmed by the 1960 party prospects, want a stronger voice in party affairs and in the ear of the White House. They have boldly entered their own ticket for Senate minority leader — John Sherman Cooper of Kentucky—and Thomas H. Kuchel of California for "whip" (second in command). Prospect: Mr. Cooper will lose, Mr. Kuchel will win, and the liberals will remain a thorn for the conservatives for two years.

4. **Status of Representative Dale Alford:** Northern Democrats do not want to let Representative-elect Alford of Arkansas, anti-integrationist "independent" who defeated a regular Democrat by a write-in campaign, join their party. Southern leaders support Dr. Alford as a "Democrat." This may precipitate a North-South battle. Prospect: Uncertain.

State of the Nations

Where We Stand: 2

By JOSEPH C. HARSCH, Special Correspondent of The Christian Science Monitor

There was an uncomfortable contrast (for Westerners) during the year 1958 in the appearances of leadership on opposite sides of the so-called Iron Curtain.

What news there was of positive action initiated by great governments came largely from Peking and Moscow. Peking initiated radical social change, and the bombardment of Quemoy. Moscow initiated pressure on West Berlin, trouble in the Middle East, and a new seven-year plan for bringing the Soviet Union abreast of the United States in industrial production.

⁂

Washington responded to the bombardment of Quemoy defensively, and to trouble in the Middle East by landing troops in Lebanon. But 1958 was not a year during which the West generated either excitingly successful responses to challenges or any long-range projects for either strengthening its own side or thwarting the presumed purposes of its opponents.

The West was, in fact, heavily preoccupied during 1958 with its own individual national problems. The United States was concerned primarily with its own second postwar economic recession and with its unsolved racial problems. France spent the year primarily in saying a wistful farewell to the Fourth Republic and getting the first real taste of the Fifth Republic designed for it by Charles de Gaulle. In Britain, the main effort was to rebuild the pound sterling and defend the economy against the expected secondary effects of the American recession.

The biggest foreign-relations problem of the year for France and Britain was not anything Moscow did, but their own differences over Britain's trade relationship with the continent. France, having agreed to a customs union with West Germany, Italy, and the Low Countries, refused to twin this project with a free trade area involving Britain. In effect, Paris was denying to Britain its traditional trading beachhead in Europe. In London, the Battle of Waterloo—fought a century and a half earlier to defend that beachhead — seemed closer and more vitally related to the present than Moscow's deeds or misdeeds.

And Field Marshal Viscount Montgomery of Alamein provided for Britons a rationale for turning away from the Soviet problem, by laying it all at the door of Dwight D. Eisenhower. According to the Montgomery thesis it was General Eisenhower's failure to adopt a proper strategy over the Normandy landings in 1944 which had opened the way for Soviet armies, and Soviet influence, into the heart of Europe. By implication, although not by specification, what General Eisenhower had done, President Eisenhower should cope with. In fact, if not consciously, most West Europeans were, in 1958, treating the Soviet problem as one which Washington should handle.

Washington spent the year trying to handle it by building bigger and better Space Age weapons. But while Washington kept up with the Ivanovitches in weaponry — so far as a layman could tell — the Ivanovitches hung on to all the real estate they had at the start of the year and ended it with an excellent prospect of getting into the Middle East — at Iraq — on their own, not vicariously through President Nasser of Egypt.

On the surface, it was a poor year, power politics-wise, for the West—an excellent one for Muscovites.

But was it really such a good year for the men of Moscow? Of all the men who joined Nikita S. Khrushchev in a collective sigh of relief when Stalin had disappeared, actively, from the scene six years before, and had pledged each other to the doctrine of live and let live (among themselves), there was only one really important survivor with Mr. Khrushchev still in the Politburo — Anastas I. Mikoyan.

Mr. Khrushchev had found himself forced (according to his own standards) to dispense with all the others. In 1958 he became more powerful, in fact nearly all-powerful in Moscow. But he must also have become more lonely and more concerned about how his problems were going to be surmounted by his own imagination alone.

⁂

Mr. Khrushchev had become master in the Communist household, but he could not run it in the arbitrary manner of his predecessor, Joseph Stalin. He had to negotiate with the Chinese, almost on terms of equality. He did in fact, in midsummer, negotiate on remarkably fair terms even with Wladyslaw Gomulka of Poland. The time was past when the lesser satellite leaders were merely executors of orders from Moscow.

As in the case of the Roman Empire, the proconsuls and provincial governors of the Soviet empire were beginning to think and act for themselves, were perceptibly exercising local autonomy. They could no longer even be replaced on Moscow's arbitrary whims.

Summit Series

THIS IS a photograph of Japanese Premier Nobusuke Kishi taken in Tokyo by Gordon N. Converse, chief photographer of The Christian Science Monitor. On the first page, second section, of this edition there is an interview with the Japanese Premier by William H. Stringer, chief of the Washington News Bureau of the Monitor, second in a series of interviews with the world's leaders.

THE CHRISTIAN SCIENCE MONITOR

Registered in U. S. Patent Office

AN INTERNATIONAL DAILY NEWSPAPER

VOLUME 51 NO. 90 | BOSTON, FRIDAY, MARCH 13, 1959 | ••—ATLANTIC EDITION | TWO SECTIONS | TEN CENTS A COPY

© 1959, THE CHRISTIAN SCIENCE PUBLISHING SOCIETY All Rights Reserved

'Unifier' vs. 'Divider'

Mideast Struggle Falls Into Focus

By Harry B. Ellis
Mediterranean Correspondent of The Christian Science Monitor

Beirut, Lebanon

Of great interest and significance are the names now being attached to Premier Abdel Karim Kassem of Iraq and President Nasser of the United Arab Republic by the pro-Nasser press throughout the Arab world. General Kassem is being called a "divider" of the Arabs, the word "divider" being a literal translation of the Iraqi Premier's last name.

President Nasser, on the other hand — whose name is derived from the Arabic for "victory"—is labeled "unifier" of the Arabs. In this choice of names, Mr. Nasser has an enormous advantage over the man who has emerged as the U.A.R. President's chief rival for Arab leadership, since a dominant theme of Arab thinking generally is the unity of the Arab lands and peoples.

The pro-Nasser press in Cairo, Beirut, and Damascus is merely reflecting the conviction of most Arabs when it describes Mr. Nasser as champion of Arab unity and General Kassem as an opponent of that unity. Indeed, it has become clear that the apparent showdown battle now looming between the rival regimes in Baghdad and Cairo will be fought out on that theme—unity of the Arabs versus communism in the Arab homeland.

Neutrals Watch

Arab reaction to developments in Iraq show that in this battle General Kassem can count in the main only on the Communists and pro-Communists for support, while Mr. Nasser will have on his side Arab nationalists throughout the Middle East.

Striving to remain neutral in this great struggle will be certain Arab minorities such as some Christians of Lebanon and supporters of King Hussein of Jordan.

[The battle lines were drawn more sharply March 13 when President Nasser charged publicly in Damascus, Syria—according to the Associated Press—that Iraqi Communists tried to create a Syrian-Iraqi union dominated by "an Iraqi brand of communism."

[Mr. Nasser spoke to crowds who transformed the funeral of a slain Iraqi rebel into one of the biggest anti-Communist demonstrations ever staged in the Arab world.

[It also was—the Associated Press said—the biggest anti-Kassem rally since the conflict of the two powerful Arab leaders broke into the open following the revolt at Mosul in northern Iraq.

[Mr. Nasser told the cheering crowds he offered four times to meet General Kassem "to close the Arab ranks" but that General Kassem always refused.

[The crowds chanted "There is no God but God" and "Death to Kassem" as they accompanied the body of Col. Mohammed Said Shehab, Iraqi rebel wounded in the fighting at Mosul. He escaped to Syria despite his wounds and passed on in Damascus.

[Marchers carried hundreds of banners bearing such slogans as "Death to Kassem," "Death to the traitorous Communist Party," and "There is no place in the Arab motherland for Communist agents."]

Speaking of Arab Communists earlier, Mr. Nasser declared they were agents of the foreigner and wished to "drag their country into foreign spheres of influence." This clear implication of the Soviet Union in Iraqi affairs was strong language for Mr. Nasser and showed his deep concern at the tightening Communist control of public opinion in Iraq.

Mr. Nasser also accused the Iraqi Air Force of attacking the Syrian village of Hammoudiya during the Mosul revolt, and declared the U.A.R. Air Force had been capable of returning a doubly strong blow, but that he refrained "because the villages we would have hit are purely Arab villages with whom we have close Arab ties."

The U.A.R. President was quite right in saying his Air Force could have returned the blow doubly strong since Egypt alone possesses an estimated 50 to 60 Soviet Ilyushin twin-jet bombers, while the Iraqi Air Force has virtually no bomber strength.

Processions Held

Despite the provocation of the alleged Iraqi attack on Hammoudiya, Mr. Nasser clearly had no desire to alienate public opinion in northern Iraq by bombing Iraqi centers in return.

The atmosphere in Baghdad reportedly has returned to something approaching normal March 13 following three days of wild demonstrations in favor of Premier Kassem, and against Mr. Nasser. The Syrian crowds in Damascus, by contrast, continued to throng the streets shouting against General Kassem and the Iraqi Communists.

The slain Iraqi's funeral in Damascus recalled the giant funeral procession mounted in Baghdad March 11 for the Iraqi Communist leader Kamel Zazanchi, killed by Iraqi nationalists at Mosul March 8. Western observers estimated that two-thirds of Baghdad's population either marched in or watched Mr. Kazanchi's funeral procession.

The Syrian Ministry of the Interior announced in Damascus March 12 that large numbers of Iraqi refugees from the Mosul area were entering Syria. These refugees reportedly included Capt. Mohammed Afrir, described as adjutant to Col. Abdel Wahab el-Shawaf, leader of the Mosul revolt.

Newspapers Wrecked

Captain Afrir is quoted as saying he left Mosul "in a state of chaos, with corpses filling the streets." The heavy loss of civilian lives in Mosul was confirmed in Baghdad March 12 by the Communist newspaper Ittihad el-Shaab, which wrote of "scores and hundreds" of soldiers and civilians having been killed.

[Reuters reported from Baghdad that the offices of three right-wing nationalist newspapers were wrecked there March 11. No editions of the newspapers appeared on the streets the next morning.

[A fourth newspaper was officially suspended and officials said they had seized a clandestine press allegedly owned by the "Arab Liberation Party." The press had been printing pro-Nasser leaflets.]

Jubilation Rolls Into Waikiki

By Jack Teehan
Special to The Christian Science Monitor

Honolulu

Hawaii celebrated statehood March 12 with a reservation recalling its early missionary forebears.

Statehood—long on the threshold—had walked in the front door. But it met a stunned populace. Everything had happened just a little too fast for the islanders. But within a few hours after the announcement, Waikiki—the Miami Beach of Oahu—was transformed into a giant midway and vehicular traffic piled up for blocks.

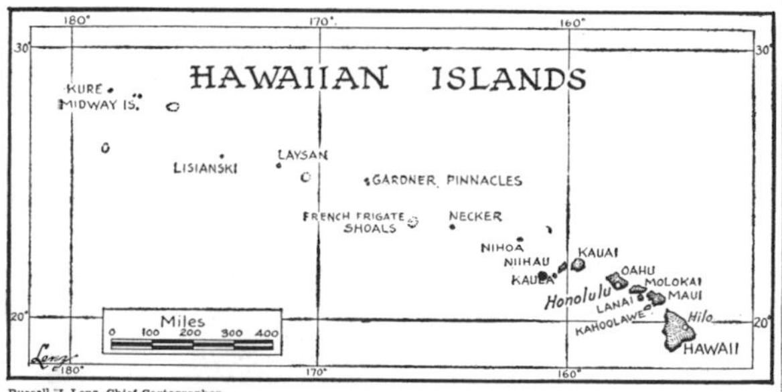

Russell H. Lenz, Chief Cartographer

Cheers and Tears

Navy destroyers offshore fired barrage after barrage of pyrotechnics and overhead military planes strung necklace after necklace of Very flares.

Thousands of Oahuans strolled along Kalakaua Avenue—Waikiki's tourist strip—almost as though they sought reassurance that all the glitter and gold was still theirs.

Earlier in the day the news of the favorable House action was transmitted to the territorial Legislature by a special telephone hookup with Delegate John A. Burns. At the time word of victory also came from Gov. William I. Quinn, who made a last-minute trip to the capital.

Mr. Burns' voice, fed into a public address system, was drowned out by cheers and a barrage of firecrackers set off just outside the chamber.

Tears coursed down the cheeks of Robert F. Ellis, administrative assistant to the Governor. Said he, to no one in particular: "I'm a grown man — why am I crying?"

Texan Chimes In

As sirens shrieked the long-awaited news, the Honolulu Advertiser, only morning paper in the islands, was already on the street with a "Congress Says Yes" extra.

Motorists took up the cry with their horns and business offices throughout the downtown area unleashed a storm of confetti.

Intermittent showers, an old Hawaiian good omen, sprinkled the city.

In Waikiki, a Texan, clad in the traditional 10-gallon hat, roamed the streets shouting "Welcome — welcome."

At the Palolo Elementary School as in schools throughout the city, youngsters raced outdoors with hastily fashioned statehood signs when the news came.

Meaning Explained

At Palolo, Mrs. Miyo Y. Tanaka, the principal, explained the meaning of statehood. "Now maybe one of you," she said to 1,500 upturned faces, "may some day be President of our great country."

Veterans of the Nisei 442d infantry battalion, which carved out a heroic record in Italy in World War II, were taking active roles in the celebrations.

A 12-foot statehood torch—erected by the local gas company—flickered out the night before statehood was assured, but was back in operation within a few hours.

More than 30,000 were expected to attend a statehood celebration show March 13 climaxing the two-day statehood holiday.

The front page of the Honolulu Star-Bulletin, largest daily in the islands, carried a strip of eight photos, representing the major racial groups in the islands. It was captioned simply "First-Class Citizens Now."

Associated Press Wirephoto

Honolulu Headline Tells the Story

Newsboy Chester Kahapea's grin underlines exultation

UN Scans Hawaii

By the Associated Press

United Nations, N.Y.

United Nations delegates got a formal report — probably their last—on how Hawaii is doing as a dependent territory of the United States.

Under the UN Charter, member nations are required to keep the world organization informed each year on economic and social progress in non-self-governing areas. The current report, dated March 6, tells about the fight for statehood during the past few years. It was already being processed when the March 12 vote came in Washington.

The report indicates everything is rosy in Hawaii. It says the territory has been enjoying economic prosperity and that its standard of living is comparable to that of the mainland. It states that Hawaii enjoys the same personal freedoms and human rights as those enjoyed on the mainland.

"No serious racial problems are reported," the document declares.

Related stories: Page 6

Bowles Suggests Economic Steps

By a Staff Correspondent of The Christian Science Monitor

Washington

The United States can avert serious economic dips if it is willing to take steps which might now appear unorthodox, according to Representative Chester Bowles.

The Connecticut Democrat, a former head of the Office of Price Administration and onetime Ambassador to India, suggests that the President set up a commission to find out precisely the relationships between wages, prices, profits, productivity, and output per man-hour.

The public should have some way of finding out economic truths among many conflicting voices, Mr. Bowles said in an interview with Courtney Sheldon, a Washington correspondent of The Christian Science Monitor.

Details: Editorial Page

Foreign Aid Plea Echoed in Crises

By Neal Stanford
Staff Correspondent of The Christian Science Monitor

Washington

The President's budget request for $3,930,000,000 for his mutual-security program this coming fiscal year may have to be increased.

World events, Moscow's unremitting drive to subvert neutrals and the free world, the Berlin and other crises are what would force the President's hand.

This was the high light of the President's sober, and at places impassioned, message to Congress March 13 for approval of his "minimal" request.

The bipartisan committee he appointed last November to study the military-assistance program is about ready to turn in its interim report, the President announced. It is already clear from what is known of its findings that it will, to quote the President, "recommend an increase in the level of commitments for vital elements of the military-assistance program, primarily for the provision of weapons to the NATO area."

Earnest Plea Made

The message once again made an earnest and eloquent plea for congressional approval of the mutual-security request—a program that is better known as "foreign aid," though the administration does not like the term. For, as the President stressed in his concluding paragraphs: mutual security is not a "giveaway" program, an "aid to foreigners at the expense of domestic programs."

It is rather, he insisted, just as vital and necessary for the security of the United States as the $41,000,000,000 he is asking for the country's own military forces; and, dollar for dollar, he asserted, it buys "more security than far greater additional expenditures for our own forces" would.

Is the United States to be "the richest nation in the graveyard of history?" the President asked in his concluding plea for congressional support for this mutual security program.

Vulnerable Item

He is fully aware that mutual security, or foreign aid, is possibly the one budget figure that Congress views with the greatest suspicion. And the practice is for Congress to cut a billion or more each year from presidential requests. Yet this time, the President insisted he is asking for a minimum—and may well have to ask for more after his special committee has reported.

Thus the Congress this time is warned that rather than accept a foreign-aid cut this year the President may be stepping up his demands on Congress. All of which makes this perhaps the most crucial foreign-aid struggle the Eisenhower administration has faced.

In defending his mutual-security requests the President spotlighted certain world developments and factors in the East-West cold war that have so far been obscure or hazy.

For example, through its allies the United States has the use of some 250 free-world bases in highly strategic locations; has the cooperation of some 5,000,000 men stationed where the danger of local aggressions is acute; has the support of 30,000 aircraft of which some 14,000 are jets; has behind it some 2,500 combat vessels belonging to Allied naval forces.

For example, the Soviets, who five years ago opened their great diplomatic and economic campaign of wooing the new nations of Asia and Africa, have extended more than a billion dollars in credits to 17 nations in 1958 alone—or a total of $2,400,000,000 in the 5 years. It also has supplied 2,800 technicians to these 17 countries this last year.

Peril Sighted

For example, the $3,929,995,000 President Eisenhower is asking is slightly less than asked last year; it is well under 1 per cent of the gross national product of the country, it is only 5 per cent of the national budget.

At one point in his message, the President asserted that if the Soviets' demands on Berlin remained "unmodified" they could have "perilous consequences." Here again he was saying, but in different form what he told his news conference this week, that a nuclear war over the West's rights in Berlin and West Germany was "not impossible."

Talk of cuts greets aid bill: Page 4.

President to Speak To Nation on Crisis

By the Associated Press

Washington

President Eisenhower will make a nationwide television-radio address March 16 on the Berlin crisis and the general security position of the United States and its allies.

Announcing this, the White House said President Eisenhower will speak over all networks from his office for 30 minutes starting at 9:30 p.m., e.s.t.

"The President will make a report to the American people on the evolving Berlin situation and the general security position of the United States and its allies," James C. Hagerty, press secretary, said.

U.S. Oil-Curb Order Protested Abroad

By Bertram B. Johansson
Staff Writer on Latin-American Affairs for The Christian Science Monitor

President Eisenhower's announcement of curbs on foreign oil imports is causing reverberations in hemisphere relations, especially in Venezuela and Canada.

The curbs are being greeted in these two nations with expressions of concern, with moderated diplomatic language, and, in some cases, with anger.

Venezuelans, who find oil import quotas an additional problem for their new democracy which exports some 390,000,000 barrels annually of petroleum to the United States, have reacted with restraint, at least on official levels.

There is little doubt but that anti-American, nationalist, and extremist groups in Venezuela will treat the oil quotas as evidence of a new "imperialism."

It is difficult for Venezuelans to understand why United States firms will invest huge amounts in petroleum extraction in Latin America only to have quotas imposed on their output by their home country. The Venezuelan Government derives a huge revenue of more than $815,000,000 annually from oil production.

Canada Voices Concern

Canada has expressed mounting concern about the imposition of the United States oil import quotas, which will affect its burgeoning petroleum industry.

Prime Minister John G. Diefenbaker said that continuing representations would be made to the United States against the import restrictions.

Lester B. Pearson, opposition leader in Parliament, said the United States was "adding insult to injury" in seeking to justify the new curbs on grounds of national security.

Mr. Pearson termed the quota announcement as "inadmissible" action at a time when Canada's defense policy is being more closely integrated with that of the United States.

President Eisenhower said in his March 10 announcement that the basis of the new quota program "is the certified requirements of our national security which make it necessary that we preserve to the greatest extent possible a vigorous, healthy petroleum industry in the United States."

Industry Need Cited

The President added that "in addition to serving our own direct security interests, the new program will also help prevent severe dislocations in our own country as well as in oil industries elsewhere which also have an important bearing on our own security."

It is the contention of much of the United States petroleum industry that if it is not making sufficient profits the industry cannot explore and prepare for exploitation of the nation's petroleum reserves in a manner sufficient for mobilization of the nation's resources in the event of a war.

There is another view that United States petroleum reserves are being depleted too rapidly and that it would be wiser, in the long run, to import as much petroleum as possible and conserve United States resources. This view apparently is rejected by the President's quota announcement.

The new quotas, which will restrict competition from foreign fuel oils, seem almost certain to increase consumer costs. The President's announcement said it would watch prices and implied the government might police price increases.

Advance Notice Noted

The Venezuelan Embassy in Washington disclosed that it had advance notice of the substance of the oil import curb order from the State Department.

The embassy said, nevertheless, in restrained diplomatic language that "it notes with concern that residual fuel oil has been included among the products under import controls."

The Embassy pointed out that the "burden of the limitations would fall almost entirely on Venezuela which directly or indirectly supplies the largest of the United States imports of residual fuel oil."

In Caracas, Juan Pablo Pérez Alfonso, Minister of Mines and Hydrocarbons, said he was not pessimistic about the import curb announcements.

He told reporters Venezuela would have to wait to see what effect the mandatory restrictions would have, but he did not expect a drop in Venezuela's oil production — which is over 3,000,000 barrels daily.

Nearly Half to U.S.

Of a total of 940,300,000 barrels of petroleum exported from Venezuela, the largest percentage, 41.88 per cent (about 390,600,000 barrels) goes to the United States.

Canada, though now a petroleum exporting nation, imports about 10.4 of Venezuela's export. Europe, mainly the Netherlands and Great Britain, receives 22.5 per cent, while the remainder of about 25 per cent is exported to Latin America and the rest of the world.

Venezuela exports petroleum products in South America to Argentina, Brazil and Uruguay. However, recent oil negotiations between Venezuela and Uruguay have broken down, and Uruguay has felt obliged to turn more and more to the Soviet Union for supplies.

Paris Hand in News Shakes Public Faith

By Volney D. Hurd
Chief of the Paris News Bureau of The Christian Science Monitor

Paris

Two factors here have shaken the faith of those who had hoped that French officials were today more fully prepared to face hard facts than has been the case in the past.

These factors are (1) official wishful thinking in regard to the recent election and (2) the seizure by the government of the weekly L'Express because it ran a factual interview with an Algerian underground officer.

On March 8 it became apparent that French Communists had regained practically all of their former electoral strength in the first round of the municipal elections held that day. However, the government delayed giving the final, official figures and only incomplete returns were issued.

Total Vote Rose

After three days had passed, Interior Minister Jean Berthoin called a press conference in which he sought to prove statistically that the average Communist vote throughout the country was 16.3 per cent against 16.0 per cent at the last municipal elections in 1953.

French newspapermen were quick to point out, however, that M. Berthoin had omitted to mention that this was because the Communists had deliberately refrained from putting up candidates in many rural areas.

In fact, the total Communist vote actually rose by 300,000. In the main cities, where the comparison between 1953 and 1959 is felt to be most valid, the percentage rose from 26.1 in 1953 to 27.2 this time. This is held to show that not only did the Communists recover from recent setbacks but added new strength.

Le Monde's comment on this is as follows:

"After three days of reflection, the Interior Minister discovers that the comeback of the extreme Left is, after all, a setback. He cites figures which, we have to regret, we believe to be false."

The seizure of L'Express was, in the government's own words, "because by giving prominence to a scandalous interview it indecently praised the rebel forces against which the nation and army are fighting."

The interview was with the rebel leader Si Azzedine, who described how the French Army tried, unsuccessfully, to negotiate a local cease-fire with him last winter under the de Gaulle directive to seek such agreements in order to bring about peace. There was nothing sensational in the account and critics of the government charge that French chagrin over the fact the effort failed lies behind this seizure.

L'Express answered by having the reporter who wrote the interview, Jean Daniel, do a new special article actually much more forceful than the original, in which the main elements are still given, and the paper then using the government seizure for a snew springboard, L'Express efficiency turned the affair to its own profit journalistically.

Communiqué Issued

The weekly issued a communiqué in which it said that the text of the government seizure order itself "shows a disquieting lack of sang-froid."

It continued in part, "What is it about? the report of Jean Daniel on his meeting at Tunis with Si Azzedine. The record of this conversation is obviously of political interest. It is one report which confers an understanding of why the 'peace of brave men' [offered by Premier Charles de Gaulle to the underground] has not been taken up on the Algerian battlefields.

"The French public has the right to know these things. What journalist would be so cowardly as to let himself be intimidated by official pressure to the point of not trying to carry out his profession of informing the public about an issue which affects the very life of the nation? . . ."

Today everyone here is familiar with the newspaper story because of the government publicity given it. And people avidly seek to read this news which the government thinks should be denied them.

State of the Nations

Between Scylla and Charybdis

By JOSEPH C. HARSCH, Special Correspondent of The Christian Science Monitor

When British Prime Minister Harold Macmillan was in Moscow, the Soviets said they regarded him as dangerously inflexible.

By the time he reached Bonn via Paris, he was being called from Washington an appeaser and charged with being too flexible.

The way of the would-be peacemaker is always open to misunderstanding. As a reporter watches Mr. Macmillan wend his way among the pitfalls attending anyone who tries to find a compromise solution to positions long regarded as irreconcilable, he is reminded of the Greek legend of Ulysses and his precarious and less than totally successful passage between the twin dangers of Scylla and Charybdis.

✓ ✓ ✓

He is trying to be flexible without committing appeasement—firm without overlooking any possibility for reconciliation which may conceivably produce an acceptable compromise solution to the Berlin crisis.

On the one hand he runs the risk of closing off further negotiation. On the other, he runs the risk of encouraging the Soviets to think that by a strategy of intractability they can get more than otherwise they might.

The essence of what he is trying to do is contained in the one word, negotiation. He preached this to the Soviets in Moscow, he preaches it now to the French and Germans, and he will preach it again in Washington.

It is a very long time since there has been any real negotiation between East and West. There are only two examples of really serious negotiation since World War II. One serious negotiation produced the lifting of the Berlin blockade, and the other produced the mutual withdrawal of occupation forces from Austria.

Betwixt and Between

These incidents established certain simple facts. In both cases there was mutual advantage in finding a solution. In both cases a solution was possible without major strategic loss to the position of either side. In both cases the negotiators were dealing with geographically small and uncomplicated situations.

If they proved that negotiation is possible, they did not prove that it is possible when the issue has such broad implications as the future shape of Germany. One cannot say that because Austria was neutralized and the blockade of Berlin lifted it will necessarily be possible to submit a far broader problem to successful negotiation.

If Mr. Macmillan can induce both sides to approach the meetings of coming months in the spirit of true negotiators, then a better settlement is conceivable than has yet been reached. But he must persuade both to accept the concept of negotiation—and that is where the trouble lies.

The West is deeply committed to the proposition that West Berlin must remain free and attached to the West. It can negotiate over recognition of the East German regime because the difference between the de facto situation which now exists and de jure recognition is not in itself wide or too serious.

The idea of two Germanys has existed for a long time, and the West is not so strongly opposed to a formalization of this condition as its official policies say. To put it simply, no Western government would go to nuclear war rather than accept the two-Germanys theory. But it cannot negotiate over the integrity of Berlin without thereby committing an act of withdrawal which could undermine the Western position the world around.

As far as one can tell, the Soviets are equally committed to the proposition that the Western enclave in Berlin must be wiped out, not necessarily tomorrow but in the foreseeable future.

For the West to give up Berlin would be to advertise to all the world that it is not willing to accept the risk of war for one place it has repeatedly labeled as vital. For Moscow to give up its demand for Berlin would be to give up its best chance of consolidating its entire western power frontier. It is difficult to doubt that Moscow wants Berlin quite as much as the West wants to hold it.

✓ ✓ ✓

Mr. Macmillan has no easy task trying to find room for maneuver and negotiation between these positions. He himself stanchly refuses to consider giving up Western access to Berlin. There is no evidence that the Soviets have considered giving up their declared intention to choke off that right of access.

One way out may exist. Some of the more optimistic diplomats think that a compromise might lie down the road of trading Western recognition of East Germany, plus measures to seal West Berlin off from East Germany, in return for continuation of Berlin's connections with the West. This is where Mr. Macmillan's explorations are currently directed. It is far too early to estimate his chances for success.

THE CHRISTIAN SCIENCE MONITOR

Registered in U. S. Patent Office

AN INTERNATIONAL DAILY NEWSPAPER

VOLUME 51 NO. 218 | BOSTON, WEDNESDAY, AUGUST 12, 1959 | R | • ATLANTIC EDITION | TWO SECTIONS | BEYOND 30 MILES TEN CENTS | FIVE CENTS

© 1959, THE CHRISTIAN SCIENCE PUBLISHING SOCIETY All Rights Reserved

Soviets Hint Basic Veering

Associated Press Wirephoto by Radio from Moscow

Moscow Crowd Greets a Distinguished Visitor

United States Chief Justice Earl Warren leans for a handshake

Rapprochement?

By Paul Wohl

Written for The Christian Science Monitor

The Soviet picture of the world is evolving toward a more peaceful conception.

An evolutionary and more realistic view of world affairs is, according to published evidence, winning out over communism's traditional mythology of a continuous war between capitalism and socialism—a political, social, and economic war, which ultimately must lead to Armageddon.

According to the published statement of a group of leading Soviet scholars, capitalism is now viewed as being both a vigorous and resourceful opponent of communism in the seemingly endless tug-of-war in which both sides simultaneously operate with economic power and political ideas. Somewhere beyond the horizon socialism is expected, in Communist eyes, to prevail thanks to the claim that it has greater efficiency and reasonableness.

The statements given above are the gist of a forum on "current problems of world politics" held by the Soviet Academy's Institute of World Economy and International Relations, of which the Kremlin's veteran international prognosticator Prof. Eugene Varga is a director.

The conclusions of this forum were published as the leading article in the July issue of the institute's magazine, which went to press shortly before First Deputy Premier Frol R. Kozlov left for the United States. First Deputy Premier Anastas I. Mikoyan's son Sergei, who in January accompanied his father to this country, is listed among the authors.

Reduction of Tension Foreseen

Their 40-page report reviews the entire world situation, including the foreign policy of the Soviet Union and its bloc, the "basic political and strategic tendencies of the imperialist powers," the "national liberation movement and its impact in international relations," and then analyzes, one by one, "key points" of world affairs. The concluding chapter is entitled "Prospects of reduced international tension."

At the very beginning it is stated that "the world situation has radically changed. . . . A new era has started. . . . A capitalist encirclement of the Soviet Union does not exist." This represents a sharp departure from former views.

Another important new development is that now "the danger of a restoration of capitalism in the U.S.S.R. is excluded." In other words there no longer is any basis for a continuous struggle against so-called internal class enemies.

The over-all comparison of the socialist and capitalist camp follows the usual pattern: The capitalist world is becoming weaker, the socialist world is becoming stronger. In the capitalist world uneven economic development deepen inner contradictions and makes for sharper competition. In the socialist world continually growing economic and political collaboration makes for greater unity.

After having paid lip service to this official formula just mentioned, the authors make considerable qualifications. Capitalism's "economic crisis of 1957-1958" is described as a thing of the past and the detailed analysis of the five key points of world affairs—Western Europe, the Near East, Africa, Southeast Asia and the Far East, and Latin America—represents the contest between the two systems as a long, drawn-out affair in which there are no simple solutions in the old style.

Everywhere the report points to complex factors, new developments which do not fit into the black-and-white pattern of the Stalinist catechism.

'New Initiatives' Set as Goal

The foreign policy of the Soviet Union and its bloc is said to have two basic features. On the one hand it must constantly display new initiatives in order to force the ruling circles of the allegedly imperialist powers to seek peaceful solutions. On the other hand it must strengthen the unity of the members of the socialist commonwealth.

[In this connection the report points to the continually growing economic cooperation among socialist countries which is supposed to have received new impetus through the Moscow conference of the CEMA countries in May, 1958. The political unity of the bloc is to be consolidated through regular mutual visits of the kind Premier Nikita S. Khrushchev made to Albania in May.]

Other important features of Soviet foreign policy are "further rapprochement" with the noncommittee countries of the so-called peace zone, which includes the former colonial and underdeveloped countries, and improved relations with neighboring countries also are given a big play. Ultimately a "mutually beneficial" modus vivendi with the "imperialist powers," especially with the United States must be established. "These two countries have the responsibility for (assuring) peaceful coexistence."

'Imperialist' Strategy Viewed

So far as policy and strategy of the "imperialist powers" go, the report claims that there are two trends: (1) the adventurous policy of the great American monopolies which are out to dominate the world and to stop (Marxism's) pre-ordained course of history. This "reactionary" force seeks to establish a new kind of "fascism camouflaged as democratic and patriotic." (2) The other trend is represented by the forces of reason which understand that the balance of power has changed decisively in favor of the socialist bloc and that under present conditions war would be a catastrophy. This second force, like the Soviets today, seeks empirical solutions through mutual concessions and compromise.

The kernel of the ideological contest between the two systems will be their efforts to win over and to influence the "movement of national liberation" in colonial and underdeveloped countries.

The analysis of the West European problem centers on the German question. West Germany, according to the Soviet forum, now has emerged as the second imperialist world power after the United States.

In the Middle East it is admitted that there exists a genuine trend among the Arabs, which opposes their joining the "socialist camp." Africa is seen as a permanent trouble spot for the capitalist world. Communist "selfless aid" is to guaranty the neutrality of Southeast Asia and the Far East.

In South America the Soviet bloc is to counter American influence through trade and improved "technical and financial relations."

Another "more realistic Geneva conference" is expected for 1959.

State of the Nations

Satellite Empire, New Diplomacy

By JOSEPH C. HARSCH

Special Correspondent of The Christian Science Monitor

The new personal diplomacy relationship between East and West—inaugurated early in the year by British Prime Minister Harold Macmillan and taken up now by Washington with arrangements for the Eisenhower-Khrushchev meetings—would make poor sense if we were to assume an inevitable continuation of Soviet behavior on the pattern of the past.

It can make sense if we are to assume that for several fundamental reasons there is a viable chance of a change in Soviet behavior.

There is a theory which has become increasingly respectable in Western foreign offices over recent months that chances for such a change exist. One of the reasons derives from an assessment of change within the Soviet power empire in the relationship between the Soviet Union and the other Communist countries.

It is the history of power empires that they expand to a certain point and then find themselves restrained for either external or internal reasons or sometimes by a combination of the two.

One of the crucial questions for those who live under the shadow of such empires is whether they must take up arms to prevent further expansion. Most, but not all power empires have been restrained by external resort to arms. This was necessary in cases both of the Napoleonic and the German empires. Neither Napoleon nor Hitler was stopped by internal reasons before they were brought to bay by external force.

But while external arms were used to restrain Roman expansion, it did make its own internal decision for internal reasons to consolidate its frontiers and rest on them under Hadrian, and in modern times the British Empire came to rest and began contracting largely for internal reasons.

There are reasons internal to the new Soviet empire which give some prospect of exerting a restraining influence. One is that communism has lost its early momentum. There is still some crusading ardor among the faithful ideologists in the Soviet Union, but the hierarchy seems to be increasingly concerned with individual position rather than with external victory for the symbol of hammer and sickle.

Furthermore, ideological differences have opened up between Moscow and other Communist countries. Yugoslav deviationism has infected Communist doctrine elsewhere, particularly in Poland. Communist China is in a clearly different state of doctrinal evolution from that of the Soviet Union.

The fact that Vice-President Richard M. Nixon could be received in Poland, and that the regime could tolerate a massive demonstration of popular affection for the United States in connection with the Nixon visit, testifies not only to a weakness of pure communism in Poland but also to Moscow's recognition of the fact that pure ideological conformity cannot be imposed wisely or safely upon the Polish people or its government.

In medieval times provinces of empire tended to evolve varying degrees of autonomy. This process operated in the Turkish Empire in more recent time and even appeared in Napoleon's empire although not in time to spare the allies the necessity of taking to arms.

Men may differ over the extent to which regional autonomy plus ideological deviation plus public inertia have become significant factors in the Soviet power empire. But there can be no reasonable room for doubt that these factors are all present and distinguishable now and that they exert some restraining influence on the external policies of the Soviet state.

The time has passed when Moscow speaks in either ideological or in foreign policy matters for the whole Communist world without having first to consider the views of the other Communist capitals. One no longer may assume automatically that every Communist aggression originates in Moscow.

By itself the growth of internal ideological and foreign policy differences within the Soviet orbit could hardly be considered sufficient reason to trust in the theory of change. Coupled with other reasons it could provide a reasonable basis for thinking that the Soviet empire has reached the normal limits of its expansiveness and for its own welfare had best relax and attempt to hold what it now has.

It has become a reasonable if not necessarily and proven proposition, however, that the Kremlin is increasingly aware of the fact that further attempted expansion not only could induce such external resistance as might threaten disastrous nuclear war but also could put an intolerable strain on the fabric of the power empire itself. Other reasons will be explored in subsequent articles in this column.

Inside Reading

Criticisms rise against MTA; new nominees sought for general manager. **Page 2**

Greater Boston milk dealers get price-war ultimatum. **Page 2**

American guides steal show in Moscow. **Page 3**

Foreign ministers of American states open conference. **Page 3**

Queen honors Ghana's Kwame Nkrumah. **Page 4**

London prepares for Eisenhower visit. **Page 6**

Texas confronted by financial crisis and tax impasse. **Page 7**

Franco faces uphill climb in strengthening Spain's economy. **Page 10**

Japanese security company highlighted. **Page 12**

Stengel evaluates Chicago White Sox. **Page 13**

Talbert sees U.S. retaining Davis Cup. **Page 13**

Mr. K Accepts UN Bid

By the Associated Press

United Nations, N.Y.

A United Nations official has said Soviet Premier Nikita S. Khrushchev probably will address the 82-nation General Assembly in the week of Sept. 20.

The official said Mr. Khrushchev had accepted an invitation from Secretary-General Dag Hammarskjold to visit the United Nations on his stay in the United States, but that the exact date for his speech to the General Assembly had not been set.

Mr. Khrushchev is due in the United States Sept. 15—the day the General Assembly opens. He plans to stay in Washington two days, then come to New York.

The United Nations official said the invitation was extended by Mr. Hammarskjold soon after it was announced that the Soviet Premier had accepted President Eisenhower's invitation to come to the United States.

Diplomats said at that time that they expected Mr. Khrushchev would address the Assembly.

After opening preliminaries including the election of a new president, the General Assembly hears foreign policy statements by heads of the various delegations. The United Nations official said it is during this period—probably the week of Sept. 20—that Mr. Khrushchev will speak for the Soviet Union.

Sparkman Revives Housing Bill Fight

By the Associated Press

Washington

Leading a move to revive a vetoed housing bill, Senator John J. Sparkman (D) of Alabama said Aug. 12 the measure would provide for necessary programs at minimum levels of expense.

Senator Sparkman's remarks urged the Senate to reverse President Eisenhower's veto of the $1,375,000,000 measure. The prospects appeared to favor an Eisenhower victory.

Senator Sparkman, chairman of the housing subcommittee, criticized Mr. Eisenhower's veto message as "intemperate, misleading, and incorrect." He specifically denied that the bill was extravagant, as Mr. Eisenhower had said.

Despite its large over-all total, Senator Sparkman said, the bill's spending impact on the President's budget in the current fiscal year would be only a few million dollars, and so would not cause any deficit.

Even if the Senate votes to override, the House appeared unlikely to do so.

Little Rock Attempts Peaceful Integration

By the Associated Press

Little Rock, Ark.

Three Negro girls walked into Hall High School today, opening Little Rock public schools to integration. There was no demonstration from some 20 spectators, watching from residential lawns across the street.

The girls arrived in a private automobile. They got out of the car in the street in front of the school. They walked calmly together into the building.

By Bicknell Eubanks

Staff Correspondent of The Christian Science Monitor

Little Rock, Ark.

This Arkansas capital may at last be returning to normal after two years of strife. Tight security regulations have been worked out by a Little Rock city government determined to keep peace in its reopened high schools.

It is a recognition of facts. Little Rock's leaders recognize they have only two choices now—either public schools with integration, or no schools at all.

[Police threw up barricades in front of Hall High School shortly before integrated classes were scheduled to start, according to the Associated Press.

[Fifty patrolmen blocked off streets of the upper-income residential area with sawhorses. An hour before the school was to open, there was no sign of the three Negro girls or the 736 white students assigned to Hall.

[Hall was the first of two once-white public high schools scheduled to open on an integrated basis.

[Pickets showed up early at the Capitol to protest integration. Six pickets walked back and forth in front of the building with signs. "Race mixing is communism," one sign read. Business went on at the Capitol as usual.]

They have tried a whole year without public high schools. They had been assured by Gov. Orval Faubus that he had a way out. They had tried private schools. Every plan thus far put forth by Governor Faubus has been struck down when he tried to use it to block desegregation.

And the Governor's trump card, the operation of a high school for white students on a private basis, has failed. He could not get state funds diverted to help finance it. And public support has not been strong enough to keep it going. So it has had to close its doors.

Some of the most ardent segregationists are ready to accept integration, at least on a token basis, with only grudging acquiescence. Their attitude is the same as it was when I talked with them last spring. They have tried every kind of legal tactic available. None of them has worked.

Segregationists have looked hopefully to Governor Faubus for "something new." But in a statewide television broadcast, the Governor told them Aug. 11 that they would have to accept the fact of integration, at least temporarily.

In a talk which did not put the Governor definitely on record for or against a public demonstration at the schools, he accused the city administration and Chief of Police Eugene Smith of being "puppets" controlled by elements that want complete integration. He compared Little Rock with Hungary and said outside elements, especially federal authorities, were imposing conditions on the Arkansas capital contrary to the will of the local citizens.

In his television talk, Governor Faubus said it would be "futile" to try to prevent the immediate token integration by force. But he urged that those opposing integration continue to fight by other methods. He suggested that they fight in the political arena and held himself ready to lead them in any way he could.

Recall Election Hit

There was a note of disappointment if not desperation in the Governor's voice as he sought to explain to Little Rock that despite its successful recall of segregationist Little Rock school board members, they actually had not known what they were doing. He continued his adamant refusal to accept the recall election, which rebuked him so strongly, as being conclusive. He insisted that the successful candidates had falsely portrayed their stands.

They don't like it, but they have to admit privately that federal fiats are supreme in this situation.

Meanwhile, Mrs. L. C. Bates, state president of the National Association for the Advancement of Colored People, reported three shots had been fired at her house from a speeding car. The shots struck a nearby house occupied by a white family, Mrs. Bates said.

Actually, the integration in Little Rock's two all-white high schools is the barest possible minimum. Under a pupil placement procedure, the Little Rock school administration has been able to return all but six Negro pupils to Horace Mann High School, an all-Negro school. Of the six, three have been assigned to Hall High School and three to Central High School. Hall High has had no integration before.

Newsmen Briefed

Police Chief Smith is determined that Hall High and Central High will reopen peacefully. He has checked every newsman carefully and will allow no one but faculty members and pupils with proper credentials to enter the high-school grounds.

Newsmen have had to sign an agreement to abide by the emergency regulations. Each has been given special credentials. Newsmen have been promised briefings twice a day. The police are under firm control of the police chief himself.

Although Governor Faubus is in a strong political position—stronger perhaps than any other Arkansas chief executive since the Reconstruction period—he has been countered at every turn by the federal government and has not been able to produce the promised solution to keep the schools from being integrated.

Negros are not satisfied with the meager amount of integration. They are seeking a reassessment of the pupil placements and are attacking the plan in court.

The school board has been reconsidering some of the assignment, but the feeling is that while the city may be ready to resume full school operation with token integration, it would be a mistake to push too hard right now.

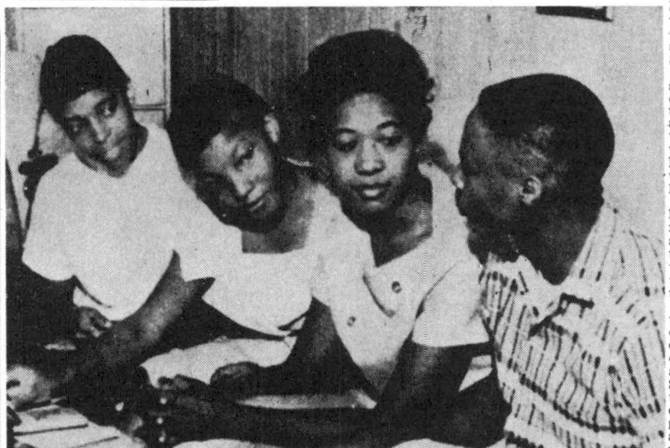

Associated Press Wirephoto

Little Rock Foursome Awaits New School Year

Four Negro pupils who will enter formerly all-white high schools in Little Rock, Ark., Aug. 12 chat prior to the schools' reopening. They are (left to right): Elsie Robinson, Estella Thompson, Effie Jones, and Jefferson Thomas. The girls will attend Hall High School, while young Thomas will enter Central High School. The schools are opening earlier than usual.

Visit Details Unfold

By the Associated Press

Gettysburg, Pa.

President Eisenhower has disclosed that Soviet Premier Nikita S. Khrushchev is being invited to see some military installations during his visit to the United States if he wishes.

The Soviet leader will be given a wide range of choice on the kind of installations open to him, the President told a news conference. If he does not want to see any establishments, that's suitable with Mr. Eisenhower too.

Discussing the unprecedented Khrushchev visit beginning in mid-September, Mr. Eisenhower said he intends to tell the Soviet leader that United States bases abroad are purely defensive and threaten no one.

He also plans, Mr. Eisenhower said, to ask why Mr. Khrushchev does not permit the progress in improvement of East-West relations which Mr. Eisenhower considers necessary for a summit conference.

Mr. Eisenhower said he is most anxious for Mr. Khrushchev to see the fine, small, modest homes in which Americans live, including those in such specific places as the Levittown development and the community around the Fairless steel plant in Pennsylvania.

Presumbably Mr. Eisenhower had in mind the Levittown development on Long Island.

Mr. Eisenhower said in fact he would like to take Mr. Khrushchev on a flying trip around Washington, D.C., in his "chopper" — (helicopter) so Mr. Khrushchev could see the fine homes which have developed in the areas around Washington.

Switch Jars DPW Patronage

By Edgar M. Mills

New England Political Editor of The Christian Science Monitor

Most political observers on Beacon Hill today remained unconvinced that Massachusetts legislators would carry through to final passage an initially approved measure to take State Department of Public Works patronage from the Legislature and the Governor's office.

The issue has become a growing problem to legislators plagued with constituent requests for temporary jobs in the Public Works Department during the summer months.

While the House, on Aug. 11, voted 108 to 93 for legislation to require the Public Works Department to hire summer temporary help from lists in the State Division of Employment Security, the crucial test will come later.

The initial vote was too close to be conclusive. Furthermore, nearly a score and a half of the House members did not vote.

It is no secret, however, that the patronage issue has been disturbing to many serious legislators, even to many legislators who have been the greatest users of the present system.

But there is some question among some members as to the legality of using the employment security system for filling the public works summer jobs. The state is not a covered employer under the employment security system. State employees are not eligible for unemployment compensation benefits. Thus, some legislators aver that the state cannot use the employment security division in the hiring of state workers.

Furthermore, many legislators are unwilling to give up patronage, although this year patronage in the Public Works Department has been scarce because of budget cutting and the schism between the Legislature and Governor Furcolo.

Most observers believe, however, that some workable controls are needed to cut down patronage for the sake of economy and efficiency.

One of the strong advocates of the employment security approach to the patronage issue is Representative Frank S. Giles (R) of Methuen, House minority leader. He served as the House patronage chief while Governor Herter was in office.

Mr. Giles told the House that more than $2,000,000 is squandered annually because of inefficient temporary employment methods.

He teamed up with Representative Cornelius Desmond, Jr., (D) of Lowell in pushing for the pending measure, which the House Committee on Ways and Means had proposed be sidetracked into a recess study. Mr. Desmond had filed the original bill.

The latter said he filed the bill because "public works patronage has become an unwholesome part of government."

Representative Cornelius F. Kiernan (D) of Lowell, House majority leader, charged that Mr. Giles, his Republican counterpart, had the least right to favor such legislation because he was the Herter patronage chief in the House for four years. Mr. Kiernan favored the study as the proper approach.

Mr. Giles replied that he had not made any accusations, adding that there had been patronage abuses under both Republican and Democratic administrations.

The World's Day

Reg. U.S. Pat. Off.

National: U.S. Air Force Reports Successes

The Air Force has made additional successful test flights of both the super Bomarc-B antiaircraft missile and the Atlas missile at Cape Canaveral, Fla. The Atlas flights have buoyed United States hopes for an operational intercontinental ballistic missile by Sept. 1.

Nearly 20 forest and brush fires are still burning in California, but most are now under control.

Boston: Car Owners to Use '59 Plates in '60

Massachusetts car owners will continue to use 1959 registration plates through 1960, with windshield stickers validating continued registration, Clement A. Riley, State Registrar of Motor Vehicles, announced.

Europe: De Gaulle Presides at Meeting

French President de Gaulle broke his vacation to preside over a cabinet meeting called as a preliminary to his meeting with President Eisenhower next month.

Asia: Kishi Would Meet With Rhee on Dispute

Japanese Prime Minister Nobusuke Kishi said today he would meet with President Rhee if it would settle the Japan-South Korea dispute. Such a meeting would depend on the Republic of Korea-Japan talks resuming tomorrow.

Weather Predictions: Fair, Mild Tonight (P. 2)

Arts, Music, Theater: Page 11. Radio, TV, FM: Page 14

THE CHRISTIAN SCIENCE MONITOR

Registered in U. S. Patent Office

AN INTERNATIONAL DAILY NEWSPAPER

VOLUME 52 NO. 137 | BOSTON, FRIDAY, MAY 6, 1960 | * ATLANTIC EDITION | TWO SECTIONS | BEYOND 30 MILES TEN CENTS | SEVEN CENTS

© 1960, THE CHRISTIAN SCIENCE PUBLISHING SOCIETY
All Rights Reserved

Majesty, Tradition, Trace of Fantasy

Princess Margaret Weds

By Henry S. Hayward
Chief of the London News Bureau of The Christian Science Monitor

London

The lovely princess has wed the handsome commoner who once came to the palace to take her picture.

She thereby became: Her Royal Highness the Princess Margaret, Mrs. Antony Armstrong-Jones, and they drove off together in a glass coach.

To celebrate the event, London put on an impressive display of official pageantry and personal warmheartedness unmatched since her sister's Coronation nearly seven years ago.

It was a tableau rich with color, majesty, tradition, and a trace of fantasy.

Princess Margaret, with her dark hair piled high on her head and circled by a sparkling diadem, was a stunning bride.

Happy Procession

At her side as they rode through streets lined with cheering crowds, some of whom had camped on the pavements overnight to be sure of witnessing the spectacle, was the youthful-looking former photographer who now has become a member of the Royal Family.

This happy procession—from the abbey where monarchs have been crowned and buried; past Parliament Square, the seat of one of the oldest and most active legislatures in the world; down Whitehall, the heart of the British Government; through Horse Guards Parade, the symbol of Britain's military tradition in ages past; and down the Mall to Buckingham Palace, residence of Queen Elizabeth II—fulfilled for many of the watching millions there and at home the full fairy-tale aspect of this romance.

Westminster was wholly given over to the occasion, and much of London and the country at large came to a standstill to watch the wedding on television.

Caribbean Honeymoon

At Buckingham Palace, after a short delay, the bride and groom, with the Queen, Prince Philip, the Queen Mother, Prince Charles, Princess Anne, and other high-ranking members of the Royal Family, appeared on the balcony to acknowledge the cheers of crowds massed in the Mall and around the Victoria Memorial.

Following the wedding reception at the palace, Princess Margaret and Mr. Armstrong-Jones were scheduled to drive through crowded London streets once more to Tower Pier, where they were to board the royal yacht Britannia to set sail for their Caribbean honeymoon.

Princess Margaret was escorted to Westminster Abbey by Prince Philip. As they paused at the head of the long aisle, lined with the highest of the nation's civilian and royal dignitaries and the 11 visiting Commonwealth prime ministers, she was a picture of radiant expectancy.

Dazzling White Gown

Philip appeared to whisper a few reassurances, and once the bride seemed almost on the verge of a giggle. Then, full of grace and composure, she moved forward to meet the waiting bridegroom, a petite figure in her dazzling white gown with its long train, her high hair-do lending weight and dignity, a gentle joy on her face.

The abbey ceremony was marked by the firm, quiet answers of the wedding couple—Antony Charles Robert and Margaret Rose, they were called—and the magnificent voice and presence of the Archbishop of Canterbury, who performed the rites.

Everything went without a hitch. It was a tribute to the mountain of preparations, the miracle of timing, the triumph of organization by the British royal institution itself.

Uniforms, personalities, buildings, and settings combined in a burst of color that was described as like an artist's palette that can hold no more.

"We want Margaret!" and "We want Tony!" the crowds chanted outside the palace.

It was Margaret's day, and her fresh loveliness held every eye. The other notables present—the Queen and Royal Family, Sir Winston and Lady Churchill, Sir Anthony and Lady Eden, Prime Minister and Lady Macmillan, Lord Mountbatten, and all the rest—seemed almost deliberately to do nothing that might for an instant divert attention from the Princess.

But for Tony Armstrong-Jones, the day's transformation must have seemed even more unbelievable.

He left for the abbey in a limousine with his best man, Dr. Roger Gilliatt, one of many in a great procession. An hour later, he returned at the head of the parade, riding behind plate glass in a famous coach, with his Princess-bride at his side—and two Queens, Queen Elizabeth II and the Queen Mother—following in the carriage behind.

As a man with an eye for details of a scene, he must have marveled that all this display and reception was at least partly for him.

Whatever the future may hold, life truly can never again be quite the same for this young man.

Earlier, the teeming crowd outside the abbey, to whom the service was relayed, came to utter silence when the Princess said her clear: "I will."

Superb Backdrop

Following are some of the other high lights people are likely to remember:

Prince Charles, the Prince of Wales, at 11 very interested but a model of boyish good behavior in his Scottish kilt and white ruffle.

Princess Anne, an excellent bridesmaid at the age of nine, standing alone behind the couple as they plighted their troth.

The Queen, solemn and obviously touched by her younger sister's great occasion. During the ride home, however, she brightened and waved in her usual gay spirits.

And finally, the Queen Mother, as ever her cheerful, attractive self, giving no outward indication of the deep emotion and affection the scene must have conveyed to her.

All this against the superb backdrop of London itself, of the perky, talkative London crowds who abandon their reserve on such occasions—and the proud panoply of jingling breastplates, the clatter of horses hooves on asphalt, and the waving of long plumes on burnished helmets.

At the wedding breakfast in in the palace, it was Prince Philip who proposed the toast of the bride and bridegroom. Princes Margaret, helped by her husband, cut the three-tiered cake.

With such a beginning, and as their yacht steamed toward the horizon, who could doubt the bridal pair would indeed live happily ever after.

Multitudes observe wedding: Page 20.

Associated Press Wirephoto

Newlyweds Wave From Buckingham Palace Balcony

Associated Press Wirephoto

Floral Cascade for Royal Wedding

Physicists Back A-Test Ban

By Robert C. Cowen
Natural Science Editor of The Christian Science Monitor

American scientists who favor a ban on nuclear tests are speaking out strongly again to put their case in what they regard as its proper perspective.

It is a political perspective rather than a technical one.

The burden of their argument is that objections to a test ban have been improperly raised on technical grounds when what is needed is a political decision as to how much risk of Soviet cheating would be acceptable.

Since one can never be absolutely guaranteed of no cheating, they maintain this fact must be faced maturely. It should not in itself be allowed to scuttle a test ban.

Voices Raised

The voices are being raised in strong scientific quarters.

One is the American Federation of Scientists, a group which has long supported a test ban with inspection and which includes many highly respected scientists.

The other is the lone voice of Dr. Hans Bethe, one of the great men of American physics. Normally he shuns publicity, preferring to work quietly in the background. However, during the past two weeks he has given several public speeches on the test-ban issue.

To put the argument of these scientists into other words, they point out that the objections are based on the acknowledged fact that, below a certain explosive strength and given techniques of muffling, underground nuclear blasts would be quite difficult to detect with present methods. This, they say, is specious ground on which to base objections for the following reasons.

Possibility Ignored

First, they say it ignores the very good possibility that detection methods can be substantially improved under a determined and well-supported research program.

Second, and more important, they say it glosses over the fact that, technically, detection can never be made 100 per cent certain any more than a tire manufacturer can guarantee you will never have a flat.

When you go for a drive, you accept a certain small risk of tire failure and prepare as best you can to cope with it. In like manner, it is argued, the United States will have to accept some risk of test ban cheating or never have a test ban, with the much greater risk of uncontrolled arms racing this may imply.

The Federation of American Scientists made these points in a statement released May 2. Although it is not particularly surprising for this group to speak out once again in this vein, its statements are not issued lightly.

Responsible View

They are carefully prepared by knowledgeable scientists and thus represent an important segment of responsible opinion.

Here are a few relevant paragraphs from the FAS statement:

"In considering the risk and advantages of the proposed (test ban) agreement, one must look not only at the technical problems of detecting evasion but also at the political and human factors involved.

"As scientists we are aware of the risks necessarily involved in any test limitation. Nonetheless, the proposed monitoring system . . . has great value as a first practical step in controlled disarmament. Furthermore . . . virtually no effort has yet been directed toward improving surveillance techniques. . . . Scientists know that ingenious techniques for test detection are as likely to be developed as are ingenious techniques for evasion.

"As scientists, we further recognize that 100 per cent certainty of detecting and identifying underground explosions is not likely to be achieved. But we also recognized that the benefits . . . outweigh by far the risks involved in allowing, for a limited time, undetected small tests."

Dr. Bethe has been taking substantially the same position. He further maintains that there is more military risks in unlimited testing in which the Soviets would continue to improve really powerful bombs, than in a ban in which they might sneak in a few tests of small-scale weapons.

Dr. Bethe's arguments are impressive, considering his background. Dr. Edward Teller, the principal scientific opponent of a test ban and one who has raised many technical objections, is generally regarded as the chief architect of the hydrogen bomb. Although he is publicly less well-known, Dr. Bethe has an equal if not superior claim to the title.

But Dr. Bethe has never been interested in pressing that particular claim, nor has he had a taste for public debate on the technology of test ban inspection. The fact that he is speaking out so strongly now indicates he believes something very valuable is at stake, namely the future of civilization as we know it.

Called First Step

As with many other scientists, Dr. Bethe sees a test ban with reasonable, if not absolutely foolproof, inspection as the first step toward effective arms limitation. Similarly he sees a failure in the test ban talks as a step toward nuclear disaster.

The strength of his feelings is also indicated by his remarks concerning Dr. Teller.

Dr. Bethe is a kindly man and has long refrained from personal attack. But Earl Ubel, science editor of the New York Herald Tribune, reported that, during a speech in Washington, "the anger crackled when Dr. Bethe accused Dr. Edward Teller . . . of obstructing the [test ban] negotiations by throwing in 'silly' technical objections, objections based on the premise that if testing is to stop the United States must be 100 per cent sure the Russians won't cheat."

There are many facets to the test-ban issue. They include such sticky questions as how effective any inspection system for the U.S.S.R. will be if neighboring China is not included; as how to get France, China, and other potential nuclear countries to respect a ban themselves, etc.

All of these questions are political. The point that the scientists reported here want to make is that the "technical" question of the adequacy of inspection to detect underground tests is essentially a political question, too.

UN Chief Deplores Arms-Bypass Talk

By the Associated Press

United Nations, N.Y.

Dag Hammarskjold, United Nations Secretary-General, has spoken out vigorously against recent discussion of an international police force at the 10-nation Geneva disarmament talks.

Mr. Hammarskjold said this issue is closely linked with the UN structure and any attempt to deal with it outside the UN would be unsound and a bypassing.

Story: Page 4

President Signs Civil-Rights Bill

The World's Day

Reg. U.S. Pat. Off.

Washington: Act Called 'Historic Step'

President Eisenhower has signed the 1960 civil-rights bill keyed to new protection for the voting rights of Negroes. The President called the act "an historic step forward in the field of civil rights," although Congress failed to include some of his recommendations.

Boston: Civil Liberties Union Protests

The Civil Liberties Union of Massachusetts protested to Mayor John F. Collins of Boston the action of Richard Sinnott of the Boston Licensing Division, in censoring portions of the musical play "Lock Up Your Daughters." The CLU said the action "violates the constitutional guarantees of freedom of expression and is repugnant to a free society." Mr. Sinnott said he will stand firm on his ruling.

Africa: Khrushchev Accepts Ghana Invitation

Soviet Premier Nikita S. Khrushchev has accepted an invitation to visit Ghana at "a convenient time," the Soviet news agency Tass reported.

Europe: Prosecution Extension Bill Opposed

A bill to extend the time limit for the prosecution of certain crimes committed during the Nazi era has been passed to committee by the Bonn lower house. The bill is opposed by the Justice Ministry is not expected to be approved.

Weather: Fair Tonight and Saturday (Page 2)

Art, Music, Theater: Page 11. Radio, TV: Page 22. FM: Page 20

State of the Nations

On the Eve of the Summit

By JOSEPH C. HARSCH
Special Correspondent of The Christian Science Monitor

This is being written 10 days before the second summit conference opens in Paris and at the apparent peak of Premier Nikita S. Khrushchev's power in the Soviet Union and in the world.

He has chosen this occasion to demonstrate his unusual influence in his own country by reshuffling his hierarchy. He has jettisoned the last holdover from the old Bulganin clique, Nikolai A. Mikhailov. He has taken the No. 2 label off Alexei Kirichenko by sending him to the provinces and pinned it, instead, on Nikolai Kosygin. Only a man in solid authority over his own household could do these things so easily.

He also has used the presummit period to polish up his world bargaining power and in the process make it very clear to us of the West that easier relations with him and his country can be had only at an uncomfortably high price. His price is very clearly a new status for Berlin which would reduce the ties between the Western half of that city and both West Germany and the Western countries. He has no intention of allowing West Berlin to continue indefinitely as a Western outpost and show window behind his front lines.

'Put Me Down As "Nikita the Bold"'

He is equally tough and confident in his handling of the nuclear testing question. A bargain on this matter is obtainable but again only at a high price to be paid by us. He would admit our inspectors to the Soviet Union, but in return he requires what would amount to a permanent restraint on our desire to test our new nuclear warheads.

The summit itself, Mr. Khrushchev would like to make us believe, could be meaningless and a failure impossible to disguise unless we will pay the required price on these two points. Presumably we will pay the nuclear-test price, since the alternative would mean the unleashing of still another round in the arms race and the most expensive one yet. It also would mean abandoning the first and only real chance yet seen of breaking through the isolationism of the Soviet Union with Western inspectors.

It is on West Berlin that the price will be most distressing. The established Western position has very little flexibility in it. Washington, in particular, cannot pay the required price without an obvious retreat from positions long held by John Foster Dulles when he was Secretary of State, and it would be extremely embarrassing for the Republican Party in an election year to be caught in such a retreat.

The most curious fact of all is that Mr. Khrushchev has chosen this moment to make it even harder, not easier, for us to pay the price he is asking and which conceivably Washington and certainly London would be willing to pay provided he would do his utmost to smooth our path rather than his surprising utmost to make the path harder.

His speech to the Supreme Soviet was a very tough speech, tougher than Baku, tougher than necessary to polish up his presummit bargaining position, tougher than would be necessary for domestic home consumption. True, he did not revive the Berlin ultimatum to the point which would make it impossible for President Eisenhower to go to the summit conference, but he did break a tacit rule by gloating over the shooting down of our jet. Planes have been shot down before in the cold war, but the rule is to do it and keep quiet. This is the first overt case of gloating afterward.

All of this means one very disturbing thing. Mr. Khrushchev is playing his hand for every ounce it is worth. And it is a very strong hand. "Relaxation" already is well established as an attitude in the West. Mr. Eisenhower desires to go down in history with a great peacemaking achievement crowning his career. British Prime Minister Harold Macmillan's whole body of policy and doctrine is built around relaxation. Western parliaments are thirsting for a chance to cut taxes—not for the hard task of reverting to larger arms budgets.

To refuse to pay the Moscow price would mean reversing gears when men's collective minds are well established along the thought patterns of relaxation and its prospective benefits. This is a situation which strengthens the Khrushchev bargaining position.

The worst of it all is that the one way out is even more intolerable for Western political leaders than the type of summit ordeal which has been projected by Mr. Khrushchev's speech. Under different circumstances Mr. Eisenhower, Mr. Macmillan, and French President de Gaulle could agree to call off the summit. To do so now would be to play into the Moscow propaganda hand.

The side which would call off this summit inevitably would appear to be the side least interested in peace. It is merely a political fact of today that neither Mr. Eisenhower nor Mr. Macmillan would dare to do so. Perhaps General de Gaulle could get away with it but not the English-speaking pair.

Summit forecasts must be downgraded. What was billed even a few weeks ago as a harmless exercise in conversation has become a prospective exercise in power maneuvering which will test the stamina of the Western participants. It begins to look rather unpleasant.

Washington Hit By Shock Wave Of Plane Issue

By Neal Stanford
Staff Correspondent of The Christian Science Monitor

Washington

Soviet Premier Nikita S. Khrushchev's announcement in Moscow that an American plane had been shot down over Soviet territory and that if there is any more air trespassing the U.S.S.R. will reply with rockets has Washington concerned as at no time since the Berlin crisis of 1948.

Official reaction is careful and studied.

The White House is making a thorough investigation. The United States Ambassador in Moscow, Llewellyn E. Thompson, has been asked to get all the details.

State Department officials are weighing the effect of this incident on the United States' allies and what effect a soft or hard reply would have on their loyalties and emotions. Defense Department officials are trying to see what the shooting down of an American plane by a Soviet antiaircraft rocket on the first shot means to the West's reliance on retaliatory bombers in global military strategy.

Kremlin Brandishes Rockets at West: P. 4

Shock Registered

Congressmen—not unanimously and vocally—are registering shock and anger over the incident, some even demanding that President Eisenhower call off the summit meeting in Paris May 16 and cancel his visit to the U.S.S.R. as a result of Mr. Khrushchev's belligerency.

In considering the incident, provocative and explosive as it may be, these things are being weighed here by responsible government officials:

1. This is not the first, and can hardly be expected to be the last, of a series of plane incidents that have touched off intermittent crises with the U.S.S.R. since the end of World War II. With the United States almost alone responsible for patrolling the West's air frontier with the Communist bloc, the surprise may be not that these incidents occur but that they do not occur more frequently.

[Actually, this is the 12th American aircraft lost in encounters with Soviet or satellite forces during the past 10 years of the cold war, points out the Associated Press.]

Issue Provided

2. The plane incident provides Premier Khrushchev with a perfect and ready-made issue with which to whip up Soviet emotions at the meeting of the Supreme Soviet and lay the basis for blaming the West if the Big Four summit conference fails to ease tensions.

Whatever else the speech may mean, Washington officials are persuaded it is, in part, a presummit tactical move to put the West on the defensive and try and bring pressure on the West for concessions.

The West had more or less expected a presummit tough, even belligerent, stand by Mr. Khrushchev—but it had not counted on its providing the basis for it.

The Soviet Premier, of course, took just the opposite view—that the plane incident was a deliberate, aggressive, and provocative act by the United States "aimed at wrecking the summit conference." He did not charge President Eisenhower with ordering the air violation but rather with being the victim of "imperialists and militarists" around him.

3. The plane incident and blistering denunciations by Premier Khrushchev, dangerous as they may be, was but part of the Premier's address to the Supreme Soviet, in which he renewed his demand for an end to Western occupation of West Berlin, spoke disparagingly of Vice-President Richard M. Nixon, and warned the United State's allies that in letting the United States use bases on their territories they were playing with fire — missile and rocket fire.

Economic Changes

The speech also, it is kept in mind, discussed economic changes in the Soviet Union — a 10-fold boost in the norminal value of the ruble, renewed promises to abolish the individual income tax by 1965 — suggesting to many here that the Premier was also concerned over domestic discontent and that he needed some good issues with which to whip up up popular support and anti-American sentiment.

4. Then, too, the speech, and the plane incident, and the Premier's emotional denunciations of the United States have to be taken in context with Moscow's relations to its satellites, to Communist China, all of them have been pressing the Kremlin to be stiffer and tougher with the West.

[According to the Associated Press, the United States is expected to deny vigorously and quickly in the United Nations the Soviet charge that a United States military plane deliberately committed aggression by flying over Soviet territory.

[Premier Khrushchev told his Parliament that such a complaint would be made to the UN Security Council. A Soviet delegation source said May 5 no instructions along that line had been received yet from Moscow.]

Related story: Page 4.

Congress Speeds Legislative Mill

By Richard L. Strout
Staff Correspondent of The Christian Science Monitor

Washington

This has been one of the most eventful weeks in recent legislative history.

President Eisenhower sent a message to Congress asking it not to play politics. Since this is an election year, Congress continued, as expected, to play politics.

The administration sent up its hastily assembled care-for-the-aged bill, which many think was composed with politics in mind. If any important organization has so far endorsed it Washington isn't giving it much play.

Device Taken Off Shelf

It has found no favor with the American Medical Association, with the AFL-CIO, with Senator Barry Galdwater (R) of Arizona, on the right, and with New York Republican Gov. Nelson A. Rockefeller on the left, who argues the subject should be included under social security.

Mr. Eisenhower attacked the pending Democratic distressed area bill is his May 3 speech as tending to "perpetuate insecurity." The House promptly passed the $251,000,000 bill, 201-184, by using the spectacular "calendar Wednesday" device that hasn't been taken off the shelf before for 10 years.

The Democratic Senate showed every sign of approving the House measure before the week-end.

Defense Bill Speeded

Nor was this all.

In a nationwide TV speech Monday night Mr. Eisenhower asked the public to protect his $4,175,000,000 foreign-aid bill against threatened congressional slashes of a billion dollars.

As though anticipating the speech, the Senate—a few hours before he made it—passed an authorization, 60-25, giving the President substantially all he asked for. The real struggle, however, will come when Congress considers actual appropriations. The initial authorization merely provides a ceiling.

Another big action came in an extraordinarily busy week.

The House passed and sent to the Senate, 377 to 3, a defense bill for the year costing $39,337,000,000. While this totaled close to Mr. Eisenhower's original request there was the most widespread reshuffling of funds within the bill.

Any week that produces a presidential TV speech about Congress to the nation (May 2), and a second direct message to Congress by the President (May 3), is memorable. On top of this the White House tossed Congress its controversial care-for-the-aged bill (May 4).

The energetic Eisenhower action—and the spasmodic congressional response — were breath-taking but at few places did they seem to meet; they were like violently revolving gears that did not mesh.

President Appeals

Mr. Eisenhower's forceful appeal to Congress for full amounts for foreign aid seem unlikely to be accepted.

The White House aid-for-the-aged bill, or "medicare," probably encouraged the leaders of the Democrats, rather than the reverse, to make a new drive for a voluntary system of their own.

The House defense bill is a drastic revision of administration proposals.

Mr. Eisenhower's sharp attack on the pending distressed areas bill, as representing "dispiriting misplaced benevolence on the part of the distant central government" (Washington), helped goad House Democrats into a convulsive reaction.

They passed the bill and told Mr. Eisenhower to veto it—if he cared—in an election year.

THE CHRISTIAN SCIENCE MONITOR

Registered in U. S. Patent Office

AN INTERNATIONAL DAILY NEWSPAPER

VOLUME 52 NO. 138 | BOSTON, SATURDAY, MAY 7, 1960 | * * ATLANTIC EDITION | TWO SECTIONS | BEYOND 30 MILES TEN CENTS | SEVEN CENTS

© 1960, THE CHRISTIAN SCIENCE PUBLISHING SOCIETY All Rights Reserved

Moscow Says Pilot Caught Spying; U.S. Doubt Voiced on 'Confession'

By Reuters

Moscow

The pilot of an American plane shot down over the Soviet Union May 1 is alive and in Soviet hands, Premier Nikita S. Khrushchev said May 7.

The Soviet Premier said the pilot, Francis G. Powers, was on an espionage flight and may stand trial here. Mr. Khrushchev told a tumultuous session of the Supreme Soviet (Parliament) that he thought "it would be right to put the pilot on trial."

He said Mr. Powers, a former captain in the United States Air Force before transferring to the Central Intelligence Agency in 1956, was shot down by a rocket near Sverdlovsk in the Ural Mountains.

The pilot was under orders to kill himself to avoid capture but was now "alive and kicking" in Moscow, Mr. Khrushchev said. Mr. Khrushchev said he did not disclose that the pilot was in Soviet hands in his original announcement of the incident three days earlier because he wanted to wait for the State Department version.

Militarists Blamed

(The State Department has suggested the pilot might have lost consciousness through lack of oxygen and the plane strayed over Russian territory.)

Mr. Khrushchev said he wanted to believe President Eisenhower's word that he knew nothing about the mission.

But if that were the case, Mr. Khrushchev said, it showed the militarists and generals were in actual power in the United States. Mr. Khrushchev told the supreme Soviet the purpose of the American's flight was to get information on Soviet guided missiles and radar defenses.

He said the plane photographed defense installations.

There was an uproar in the hall when Mr. Khrushchev showed photographs purporting to be taken by the planes of airfields and industrial buildings.

Mr. Khrushchev said Mr. Powers escaped from the plane by parachute without using the ejector mechanism. The plane had self-destroying equipment and would have exploded if he had used the ejector seat, the Premier added.

He said Mr. Powers had been told to kill himself rather than fall into Soviet hands. The pilot, he said, had been given a special pin, one prick from which would kill him instantly.

Mr. Khrushchev said the aircraft took off from Inkirklik, near Adana in Turkey.

U.S. Suggestion Hit

The pilot said the purpose of his flight was officially to carry out the study of cosmic radiation, but in reality to carry out spying activities, Mr. Khrushchev said.

He trained for a long time for his mission, the Premier said, by flying along the Soviet frontier to study Soviet radar defense.

He flew from Turkey to Peshawar in Pakistan and from there over Kazakhstan to Sverdlovsk, where he was shot down, according to the Khrushchev version.

He was slated to land in Bude, Norway, after flying over Murmansk and Archangel, Mr. Khrushchev said. He said secret equipment from the plane, which he described as a "most genuine" military reconnaissance aircraft, was in Soviet hands and would be shown to the delegates later.

The Soviet Premier said that the Americans had used an aircraft capable of very high speeds and heights and that they counted on Soviet aircraft and antiaircraft artillery's being unable to shoot it down.

But the Soviet antiaircraft forces got it "and should American aircraft fly higher, we would also get it," he said amid wild applause.

Mr. Khrushchev dismissed an American suggestion that the plane might have strayed over Soviet territory when the pilot lost consciousness at high altitudes.

Flight Detailed

He said the American version was a "complete lie" and said the men who advanced it had counted on the pilot being killed.

But he said the pilot was alive and well in Moscow. Wreckage of the plane had also been brought to the capital.

Mr. Khrushchev said he did not disclose the pilot was alive in his original announcement of the incident May 5 because the State Department would have issued another version.

"Now they have already told us a lot of foolish things," he said. "I am sure they will give more of these things."

Detailing the flight—which he said was scheduled to last for three hours and forty minutes—Mr. Khrushchev said the plane took off from Inkirklin near Adana, Turkey.

He said it flew from Turkey to Peshawar in Pakistan and from there over Soviet Kazakhstan to Sverdlovsk, where it was shot down.

Mr. Khrushchev quoted the pilot as saying the official reason for the flight was to carry out studies of cosmic radiation, but in reality it was to carry out spying activities.

Mr. Khrushchev said the Soviet authorities would show all the pilot's "suicide equipment" to foreign diplomats.

He said the Americans called themselves Christians and the Communists atheists. But the Communists had never committed such crimes against a human being and never would, he added.

Associated Press Wirephoto

Francis G. Powers

Pilot of missing plane

The pilot was given a large sum of Soviet rubles, he said, but the men who gave him the money did not think of the difficulties he would run into because of the new "heavy" ruble (announced earlier in the session).

He was also given a large sum of French gold francs, West German marks, and Italian lira, as well as two gold watches and gold bracelets, according to the Soviet Premier.

Referring to the gold francs, Mr. Khrushchev asked, "For what purposes had he French gold francs—for taking samples of air?

"Perhaps his mission was to fly even higher to Mars and supply these things to them," he said amid loud laughter.

Noiseless Pistol Reported

Mr. Khrushchev said the pilot carried a noiseless pistol.

The French gold francs were carefully wrapped in cellophane. "What were these for, to gain altitude?" he asked.

The pilot also had seven women's rings—"Was he going to fly to Mars and seduce Martian women?" Mr. Khrushchev asked amid laughter.

It is possible, Mr. Khrushchev said, that the countries where American aircraft are based did not know what was being done by the Americans.

But they ought to know for their own good, he warned, because they might suffer from the Americans playing with fire. He mentioned Pakistan, Turkey, and Norway in his warning.

He said he had dwelt at such length about what happened because many people in the United States believed in the version put out by the Americans—that the flight was an innocent weather reconnaissance aircraft.

Referring to the Eisenhower "open skies" proposal, he said: "The Americans decided themselves to open the Soviet sky."

By Richard L. Strout

Staff Correspondent of The Christian Science Monitor

Washington

"Fantastic" was the comment applied by administration officials here to the charge of Soviet Premier Nikita S. Khrushchev that a downed American pilot, Francis G. Powers, had confessed to flying a spying mission over Soviet territory.

The charge, made dramatically in a second attack before the Supreme Soviet (Parliament), heightened speculation here that President Eisenhower might call off his June visit to the Soviet Union. State Department officials still discounted the likelihood of such a cancellation.

Premier Khrushchev declared that Mr. Powers was alive and well, that he had confessed to spying, was on a high-altitude photographic mission, that some of his pictures were captured, and that he carried a suicide kit. The charges fell into this capital like a brick into a beehive.

Broad Hint Dropped

In a casual conversation with George Meany, AFL-CIO president, May 6 Mr. Eisenhower dropped a broad but seemingly calculated hint in the presence of reporters that his trip to the Soviet Union after the summit conference is on a hypothetical "if" basis.

The President's assistants had opportunity to clear up the ambiguity if they cared to but pointedly abstained.

The official American attitude, as disclosed by high officials prior to the latest Khrushchev attack, was that Mr. Eisenhower probably would make the trip unless Mr. Khrushchev by further actions created an atmosphere that made it undesirable.

Mr. Khrushchev's renewed assault raises speculation about the trip and the summit conference, scheduled in just over a week.

The Soviet leader on his second appearance told his Parliament that he had purposely held back part of the alleged espionage story in order to trap the United States Government into lies.

There were hints that the Soviet Union planned to try the downed United States aviator as a spy.

In a guarded first comment, State Department officials said merely that they were glad Mr. Powers was alive and that they were, to say the least, "skeptical" of the Khrushchev story.

Presummit Impact

Off the record other officials pointed to alleged inconsistencies in the charges; they aruged that a rocket hit (as claimed by the Soviets) would demolish a small, relatively light plane, and that the alleged route of the plane in the Soviet version would have required a fuel capacity out of the question.

It is the American version of the affair that Mr. Powers, an hour after leaving his home base on a routine weather research flight, complained over the radio that something was the matter with his oxygen system and that he was turning back.

Here in Washington, a State Department spokesman, Lincoln White, speculated that the civilian pilot had lost consciousness in the oxygen failure and that the automatic pilot had continued the plane's course with a blacked-out pilot into Soviet territory.

Whatever the results of this particular incident, it is acknowledged here that it can have imponderable effects on presummit relations and upon American prestige in cold-war propaganda.

There is no secret that both the Soviet Union and the Western powers are engaged in tireless efforts to keep abreast of internal developments across their adversaries' borders.

Most of the burden of patrolling the far-flung Soviet frontier falls on the United States, and over the years a series of trespass incidents has occurred. Officials here say they will be surprised if they do not intermittently occur in the future.

Officials here speculated after the initial Khrushchev charges of a downed American plane that it might be motivated by two factors: a desire by the Soviet leader to place the blame for failure of the summit conference on the West in advance, and an almost pathological sensitivity over the integrity of Soviet borders caused by a history of invasions.

As American public opinion seemed to be forming on the incident there was a wait-and-see attitude. If the American plane were actually over Soviet territory it ran the risk of being destroyed, the man in the street seemed to think, just as would a Soviet plane over this country (though it would probably be signaled here first).

But Mr. Khrushchev's triumphal propaganda use of the incident and what seemed to be distortions of most of the probabilities of the affair cast a gloom over the presummit atmosphere.

Red Defense Shift?

By Reuters

London

Soviet Premier Nikita S. Khrushchev told the Supreme Soviet May 7 that the Soviet Union is switching completely to guided missiles. A command of strategic intercontinental missiles has been established, the Soviet Premier announced.

His speech was broadcast by Radio Moscow and monitored in Britain.

Mr. Khrushchev said the ballistic missile command has been established under Marshal Mitrofan Ivanovich Nedelin, Commander in Chief of Soviet Army Artillery.

Speaking directly to the newly appointed commander of intercontinental guided weapons, Mr. Khrushchev said: "So I would say, Comrade Nedelin, do not trust in God, but rather devote your attention to the armed forces and technical means, with which . . . you would be ready at any moment to deliver a return devastating blow to the enemy."

Gordon N. Converse, Staff Photographer

Preparing for Greek Tragedy at Wellesley College

Securing the drapery on Menelaus's costume, Miss Barbara McCarthy, professor of Greek, readies the cast for tomorrow's outdoor production of Euripides's "The Trojan Women." Hidden by masks, but watching the production, are Mrs. Alan Lefkowitz (left), who portrays Cassandra, and Miss Lynda Gregorian, Talthybius. [Story and pictures: Page 2.]

Revise Bay State Charter?

Citizen Bid

By Edgar M. Mills

New England Political Editor of The Christian Science Monitor

Amherst, Mass.

Formation of a top-level citizens commission to make an exhaustive study of the Massachusetts Constitution and recommend changes to the Massachusetts Legislature was advocated by Representative Thomas C. Wjotkowski (D) of Pittsfield at an all-day session on the methods of revising the Constitution here May 6.

The session was staged by the Amherst League of Women Voters on whether or not a popular constitutional convention, with elected delegates, should be called to consider broad revision of the state's basic law; or whether the Constitution should be revised by the slower and piecemeal method of legislative amendment, considered at joint sessions of the Massachusetts House and Senate.

Mr. Wjotkowski pointed out that a citizens committee could be appointed by the Governor or the Legislature.

He said its proposals for legislative amendments could be presented with a program of mass education of the voting public. If the Legislature gave the proposed amendments the required approval at two successive Legislatures, they would be submitted to the people for ratification.

Set Up in Other States

The Pittsfield legislator pointed out that such citizens commissions have been set up in a number of states, including New York, California, Pennsylvania, Georgia, Louisiana, Tennessee, and Vermont, among others, with the Georgia Constitution having been redrafted completely through such means.

Secretary of State Joseph D. Ward strongly advocated calling a popular constitutional convention. He said that only through such a method can needed changes in the Constitution be obtained.

Mr. Ward pointed out that proposals for a graduated state income tax amendment have been before the Legislature for many years, and still no such constitutional amendment has final approval. Similarly, an amendment for a four-year term for Governor and other statewide constitutional offices have failed to gain legislative approval.

Limit on Debt Urged

Supporting Mr. Ward's position on a constitutional convention, Kermit C. Morrissey, state budget commissioner, insisted that a constitutional convention is the only way to bring about changes in the Constitution necessary for the efficient management of government.

Among Mr. Morrissey's suggested constitutional changes was a limit on the state debt. The budget commissioner favored a debt limit of the total amount spent for state government operations in any one year, only to be exceeded if the legislature makes adequate provisions for amortization of the bonds.

Mr. Morrissey was sharply critical of the present debt, pointing out that of the existing $780,000,000 debt, at least $50,000,000 was avoidable debt for items which should have been financed out of current revenue, such as purchase of typewriters and repairs.

Revision Item Noted

He said a constitutional convention is necessary to provide a flexible and adequate tax structure and to write into the Constitution mandatory provisions for equalized valuations among cities and towns on which to base distribution of state aid.

Elwyn E. Mariner, research director of the Massachusetts Federation of Taxpayers Federations, favored legislative amendment of the Constitution rather than a popular constitutional convention.

He argued against placing in the Constitution mandatory equalized-valuation provisions, saying there would be no way to force the Legislature to make such frequent valuation revisions.

He added that the Legislature has not complied with many existing constitutional provisions, such as requirements for decennial reapportionment of legislative districts. In answer to arguments that a convention is necessary to bring about reorganization of the state government, Mr. Mariner said that reorganization of the executive branch can be made by statute without constitutional revision. He further argued that the present Constitution gives the Legislature wide latitude to revise the tax structure.

He insisted that the present problems of state governments "are the product of human frailties, not of alleged deficiency of the Constitution.

Others who participated in the all-day panel sessions were Gerald J. Grady, assistant director of the Bureau of Government Research, University of Massachusetts; Representative James DeNormandie (R) of Lincoln, John L. Saltonstall, Jr., of Boston attorney, and Russell M. Keith, state house correspondent of the Springfield Union. Moderating the panels were John S. Harris, chairman of the Department of Government, University of Massachusetts, and this correspondent.

State of the Nations

Humphrey-Kennedy Debate

By WILLIAM H. STRINGER, Chief, Washington Bureau, The Christian Science Monitor

Charleston, W.Va.

Senators Humphrey and Kennedy both thought the televised joint debate in which they participated the other evening in West Virginia was just fine—as a campaign format for the autumn, between the two chosen presidential candidates.

But as a debate between two primary contestants who think pretty much alike on most issues, and who are equally fervent Democrats, the West Virginia debate left much to be desired.

The main criticism heard afterwards was that it wasn't a debate. It was mainly two nice guys answering questions mailed in, beforehand. Each had his turn at responding, and somehow each managed to work in an occasional rebuttal and even a surrebuttal. But the technique was faulty.

* * *

Both senators, questioned later, laid some of the blame on the questions. They just weren't challenging enough to test the mental acumen of Messrs. Kennedy and Humphrey.

It was just too easy, being asked about admission of Communist China into the United Nations, or the purchase of Cuban sugar at the presently boosted price, or the record of the Democratic Congress versus the Eisenhower administration. The senators were in happy agreement on most answers, and for an adept senator this kind of questionnairing is "duck soup."

Questions could have been put asking Senator Kennedy just how much he is spending in West Virginia, and whether this doesn't give him an unfair advantage over his less well-heeled rival.

Or to Senator Humphrey concerning the charge made by his followers that he was offered the vice-presidential nomination if he would "quit the race." Or to both candidates asking them specifically about their bold programs for assistance to West Virginia—how soon could these be enacted, how much money could they require from the federal till?

* * *

Even then, this would have been no Lincoln-Douglas debate, or even the sort of Dewey-Stassen debate which was arranged in Oregon before the primary in May of 1948. In that debate the rival candidates, Harold E. Stassen and Thomas E. Dewey, argued the question whether the Communist Party should be outlawed in the United States. Interest was keen on the problem of internal subversion in those days. Stassen was for outlawing the party; Dewey was not, believing outlawry would simply drive the Communists underground.

The contest was carried over 900 radio stations. Governor Dewey showed the greater debating skill, won the debate, won the Oregon vote, and this became one of those primary contests which killed off a candidate. Former front-runner Stassen was eliminated.

The West Virginia talkfest was more like the Stevenson-Kefauver debate in Miami during the 1956 campaign. There again the contestants were polite and complimentary. They hurled cream puffs at 50 paces, no sparks flew, and the debate decided nothing.

It is good campaign tactics to challenge your opponent to public debate, as Senator Kefauver had done in Florida and as Senator Humphrey repeatedly had done during the Wisconsin primary campaign. The difficult moment arrives when your opponent accepts the challenge, as Senator Kennedy finally did in West Virginia. This ends the psychological advantage which a challenger possesses, but it puts both men on their mettle to make the contest meaningful.

* * *

In West Virginia, thousands of citizens applauded the televised close harmony. They finally had the opportunity of seeing the two candidates together in quiet focus, thoughtfully discussing important issues of the day. Many didn't mind at all that no one resorted to histrionics or fisticuffs. As an intelligent hour of able exposition of the Democratic position, it was a success—indeed, such a success that the Republican national chairman has since demanded "equal time."

But if this debate technique is to be used more frequently, the rules should be improved. Questions from the audience—yes.

But let them be tough questions which challenge and measure the ability of the candidate. And let there be questions and challenges from one candidate to the other, and full opportunity for rebuttal and surrebuttal.

And of course—as would be the case next autumn—the rivals must be further apart ideologically than Tweedledum and Tweedledee.

Associated Press

Checking Itinerary for a Summer in Europe

Five students from the Lincoln-Sudbury Regional High School smilingly point out where they expect to be this summer. They are going abroad as part of the school's annual foreign students' exchange program, funds for which are being raised at a "fair of friendship" at the school today. The students participating in the European trip are (left to right) Doris Grason, Betty Ellis, Penny Child, Dick Dinosky, and David Garrison.

Eisenhower Urges Export Expansion

By the Associated Press

Washington

President Eisenhower has called for a nationwide observance of World Trade Week starting May 15.

The White House proclamation called attention to the government's export expansion program to boost the sale of United States goods abroad and improve the capacity of American industry to compete in world markets.

Increased exports, Mr. Eisenhower said, "are essential to our healthy economic growth, add substantially to the millions of jobs already generated for our people by export trade, and contribute significantly to our capacity to sustain our international investment, travel and trade."

Inside Reading

Voroshilov Resigns as Soviet President

The World's Day

Reg. U.S. Pat. Off.

Europe: Brezhnev Succeeds Marshal in Post

Marshal Klementi Y. Voroshilov has resigned his post as president of the Soviet Union because of poor health, the Soviet news agency Tass announced today. He will be replaced by Leonid Ilyich Brezhnev.

Soviet Premier Nikita S. Khrushchev will arrive in Vienna June 30 for a week-long state visit, it was officially announced today.

Boston: Half of Drawbridge to Close for Repairs

One-half of the drawbridge over the Charles River Dam will be closed to traffic starting Monday morning, the Metropolitan District Commission has announced. Emergency repairs will be conducted on a 24-hour basis and are expected to be completed in about 10 days. Motorists are requested to use the expressway if possible.

National: Nebraska Democrats Climax Drive

Senators Stuart Symington and John F. Kennedy join Nebraska Democrats whooping it up at a big fund-raising meeting today in Omaha climaxing the primary election campaign. The primary is Tuesday, May 10. Senator Kennedy is the only entrant in the primary.

Texas Democrats are holding precinct conventions with presidential significance today. The conventions climax a day of voting in which the party will nominate thousands of candidates.

Weather Outlook: Showers, Cool Sunday (Page 2)

Art, Music, Theater: Page 7; Radio, TV, FM: Page 17

THE CHRISTIAN SCIENCE MONITOR

Registered in U. S. Patent Office

AN INTERNATIONAL DAILY NEWSPAPER

VOLUME 52 NO. 294 | BOSTON, WEDNESDAY, NOVEMBER 9, 1960 | EASTERN EDITION | TWO SECTIONS | TEN CENTS A COPY

© 1960, THE CHRISTIAN SCIENCE PUBLISHING SOCIETY All Rights Reserved

U.S. Gains Vigorous President With Kennedy's Close Victory

Associated Press Wirephoto

Richard M. Nixon

John F. Kennedy

A long, grueling campaign over, the two candidates awaited the public's decision

By Richard L. Strout

Staff Correspondent of The Christian Science Monitor

Washington

In one of the crucial elections of the century Americans picked for the presidency a man committed to strong government and social change.

President-elect John F. Kennedy of Massachusetts is the 34th man chosen President. He is the youngest man ever elected and succeeds the oldest. And he is the first Roman Catholic.

Senator Kennedy's election restores to Washington a united party government for the first time in six years with executive and both chambers of Congress controlled by Democrats.

In world affairs Mr. Kennedy's selection means that an American of 43 will deal with a generation of European leaders—Soviet Premier Nikita S. Khrushchev; Dr. Konrad Adenauer, West German Chancellor; President de Gaulle of France; and British Premier Harold Macmillan—who are 30 years his senior. It brings to the presidency the first man born in this century.

Aims Outlined

In domestic affairs it elevates a vigorous, self-confident and articulate legislator committed to be a "strong" President who has stated that he intends to use unique powers of the American presidency to the utmost.

As he outlined his conception of these powers in his speech to the National Press Club here Jan. 14 he said it was "imperative" that the new President take leadership into his own hands, guide foreign policy himself, and be willing to serve the public "at the risk of incurring their momentary displeasure."

"He must be prepared to exercise the fullest powers of his office," he declared.

Mr. Kennedy's election was one of the most dramatic of the century, recalling 1948 when Harry S. Truman made a spectacularly unexpected victory, and 1916, when Charles Evans Hughes went to bed mistakenly thinking himself victor.

Count Seesawed

It was a race. The nation waited with bated breath for the election results from Illinois, California, New Mexico, Minnesota, and Alaska.

This was one of the closest presidential elections in American history. The margins between Vice-President Richard M. Nixon and Senator Kennedy in three small states kept swinging back and forth.

There was some doubt also about both Illinois and California for hours.

Most advance polls showed Senator Kennedy the probable but close victor and he started off on election eve with a burst of popular votes from populous Eastern cities. This seemed to confirm the forecast.

Then, however, as later results came in from Western states and as rural votes swelled from the big battleground areas, majorities began to decline. The final victory will be the closest since 1948.

Dramatic Moment

A complicating factor was a batch of 11 electoral votes in Mississippi won by a group opposing Senator Kennedy but not supporting Republican Mr. Nixon.

As Mr. Kennedy's electoral count hung beneath the needed 269, there was a remote possibility in the early hours of Nov. 9 that they might prevent either candidate from getting an outright majority, in which case the election would go into Congress. Under such circumstances each of the 50 states would have one vote.

At 3:15 a.m., e.s.t., Nov. 9, Vice-President Nixon made what some interpreted as a qualified concession of defeat to a moved and cheering group of supporters in California.

But he made it plain that he would be negative only if the trend continued. Now Illinois, California, New Mexico, Minnesota, and Alaska are still undecided.

At his home at Hyannis Port, Mass., Mr. Kennedy went to bed without claiming victory. It was one of the most dramatic scenes in the political history of the century.

Thanks From Nixon

The big audience which sat up to see the final act of the drama watched uncomfortable TV announcers point out that the Kennedy lead, which at one point stood at almost 2,000,000 in popular votes, slowly dwindled to less than 1,000,000. There seemed no reason to most to doubt the ultimate outcome, but Mr. Kennedy needed one more state to clinch the result.

Finally TV cameras switched to Mr. Nixon and his wife "Pat," moving from their hotel room down to the crowd of Republicans in the big auditorium below.

The crowd seemed to sense Mr. Nixon's state of mind and by applause sought to prevent his speaking.

Mr. Nixon had full control of himself and spoke cheerfully and good-humoredly. Mrs. Nixon, fighting back emotion, stood at his side. The Vice-President thanked supporters, said that if the then current trend continued without significant change "Senator Kennedy will be the next President of the United States," and thereupon made an appeal for national unity. He offered his own "wholehearted support" to his rival if elected. Then he added that he was going to bed.

Promptly television attention was switched to the exterior of the illuminated Kennedy house at Hyannis Port. Mr. Kennedy's press secretary, Pierre Salinger, told the press that the senator, too, was calling it a day, or a night, and would go to bed without further comment before 10 a.m.

For spectators it all made a spectacular photofinish.

In the words of Leonard W. Hall, Mr. Nixon's campaign manager, "This one is a squeaker."

Mr. Kennedy's associates seemed to consider that the Massachusetts senator was elected.

Patterns Examined

As this phase of the battle closed, Mr. Kennedy was leading in two big states, California and Illinois, though by diminishing majorities. Either state could put him over and indeed; the vote was so close that even the delayed 3 electoral votes of Alaska would have served.

Meanwhile, in Washington, President Eisenhower called a Cabinet meeting, Nov. 9, to smooth transition to the new administration.

Analysis indicated Mr. Kennedy had lost in some areas by being a Roman Catholic but had gained a great deal more elsewhere. One spot check by the Columbia Broadcasting Corporation showed that Mr. Kennedy got about 62 per cent of the vote in designated "Catholic" areas, or a little less than the expected 70 per cent, and 19 per cent more than Adlai E. Stevenson got in 1956, in the same areas.

On the other hand, according to this study, Mr. Kennedy got 46 per cent of the total in selected areas chosen as "Protestant," or 6 per cent more than Mr. Stevenson did in the same precincts.

Kasavubu Bid Put Before UN

By Geoffrey Godsell

Assistant Overseas News Editor of The Christian Science Monitor

Congo President Kasavubu's appearance before the United Nations General Assembly seems to be bringing closer a moment of decision in his country's troubled story. But whether that means bringing closer the restoration of law and order in the Congo is quite a different question.

Mr. Kasavubu's 15-minute speech before the Assembly Tuesday has:

¶ Made imminent a decision by the United Nations on who should occupy the Congo's seat, vacant since that country was admitted to membership Sept. 20. It seems likely to go to Mr. Kasavubu or his representatives.

¶ Strengthened the image in the eyes of the more radical African nationalists—represented by Ghana and Guinea—of Mr. Kasavubu as a client of the West. To them the true voice of the Congo is Mr. Kasavubu's arch-foe, Patrice Lumumba.

Unity Cited

¶ Resharpened the irritation which from time to time hinders understanding between the West and the young nationalist-neutralist nations of Africa and Asia.

¶ Given the Soviet Union a renewed opportunity to pose as the understanding friend of nationalism in areas which have recently emerged or are still emerging from colonial rule.

In his address to the Assembly less than 24 hours after flying into New York from Léopoldville, Mr. Kasavubu appealed for the seating of a delegation headed by himself as the rightful occupants of the empty chairs behind his country's nameplate.

The Credentials Committee of the UN General Assembly was expected to act on Mr. Kasavubu's request for recognition of his delegation later Wednesday. There are nine members of the committee—Costa Rica, Haiti, Morocco, New Zealand, the Philippines, Spain, the Soviet Union, the United Arab Republic, and the United States.

Three Committed

Of these, only three—Morocco, the Soviet Union, and the United Arab Republic — have openly committed themselves against Mr. Kasavubu by supporting Mr. Lumumba.

Mr. Kasavubu will almost certainly argue that the legality of his position has been accepted by Secretary-General Dag Hammarskjold's special representative in the Congo, Rajeshwar Dayal.

Mr. Dayal, in his progress report published last week, wrote: "In the confused political situation which prevails [in the Congo] the only two institutions whose foundations still stand are the office of the Chief of State and the Parliament."

But cables from the presidents of both chambers of the Congolese Parliament, relayed to Mr. Hammarskjold through Ghanaian diplomatic channels, challenge Mr. Kasavubu's current mission to the United Nations.

The cable from the president of the Chamber of Representatives, Joseph Kasongo, said Mr. Kasavubu's journey was not official and "he does not speak for the Congolese nation."

Mr. Kasavubu, Mr. Kasongo alleged, had left the Congo "without informing Parliament, accompanied by his Belgian and French advisers."

Colonialism Cited

This theme was repeated by Guinea's spokesman, Ismael Touré, who went to the rostrum in the UN General Assembly immediately after Mr. Kasavubu had spoken. Mr. Kasavubu's speech, Mr. Touré said, "was drafted in Paris and Brussels. We know who was behind this trip and that the aim was not honorable. This hoodwinks no one."

Hastening to exploit African suspicions about Western and particularly Belgian and French intentions in Africa, Soviet delegate Valerian A. Zorin said that Mr. Kasavubu was being used by colonialists, and that Mr. Lumumba was the only legally elected representative of the Congolese people.

The afternoon session of the Assembly adjourned without any formal Western statement from the rostrum.

The expected debate on Mr. Kasavubu's claim officially to represent his country could lead to a split among the newly independent African countries now members of the United Nations.

A large group of these countries were former French territories, and their present leaders seem to hew more closely to French policy than to the radical African nationalism of Ghana or Guinea.

Dahomey Speaks Up

It did not escape notice that on Monday a parliamentary move in the Assembly favoring Mr. Kasavubu was initiated by the spokesman of Dahomey, a member of the French Community.

To African nationalists such moves are at least equivocal, and many observers wonder whether African opinion at home may not eventually force such governments as that of Dahomey to take a less pro-French and more radically African stand.

In the Congo itself, relations between the United Nations and Colonel Mobutu—strongly censured in Mr. Dayal's progress report—deteriorated further. Colonel Mobutu accused the UN Tuesday of being involved in a plot to deprive him of authority and restore Mr. Lumumba to power.

To this, UN officials in Léopoldville replied: "Sheer nonsense."

Slight Gains for Republicans

Congress Shifts Degree to Right

By Courtney Sheldon

Staff Correspondent of The Christian Science Monitor

Washington

The membership of the next Congress—a product of countrywide crosscurrents — appears a trifle more conservative, in the net.

What this means in terms of legislation largely depends on how the new President exercises his power, especially in the early honeymoon period of the next administration.

The Republicans have gained two seats in the Senate. Democratic seats were picked off by Gov. J. Caleb Boggs of Delaware and Representative Keith Thomson of Wyoming.

Democrats retain overwhelming control of the Senate, however. The present Democratic margin is 66 to 34. If the present returns hold up, the edge will be 64 to 36.

In the House, where the results of many races were tied to the late count on the presidential race, the indications were that Republicans would make moderate gains, perhaps upwards of 18 seats.

As in the Senate, this would not lift the Republicans to a majority. The present House line-up is 280 Democrats and 151 Republicans.

The Republican gains strengthened the coalition of Republicans and Southern Democrats which operates openly on social welfare and fiscal legislation.

Some of the Democrats knocked out of Congress were younger liberals who had been swept in with the heavily Democratic elections of 1958.

Most of the Republican gains were made in traditionally Republican states. Five were in the New England states of Vermont (1), Connecticut (2), and Maine (2).

The Republicans also increased their delegations from several Midwestern states, according to uncompleted returns.

States which added to their Democratic representation in Congress included New York, Massachusetts, New Jersey, and Idaho

Senator J. Allen Frear, Jr. (D) of Delaware, a conservative, was the only incumbent running for reelection who lost favor with the voters. His replacement, Governor Boggs, is generally regarded as a moderate conservative.

Four Republican liberals who retained their seats, although in two instances—New Jersey and Massachusetts—their states were won by Senator Kennedy, were:

Senator Leverett Saltonstall of Massachusetts, Senator Clifford P. Case of New Jersey, Senator John Sherman Cooper of Kentucky, and Senator Margaret Chase Smith of Maine.

Mrs. Smith will no longer be the lone woman in the Senate. She will be joined by Mrs. Maurine B Neuberger who captured the Oregon Senate seat for the Democrats.

Eleven Southern Democrats were returned to the Senate without much difficulty. One Southern Republican, Senator Cooper of Kentucky, more than held his own in running ahead of Mr. Nixon in his state.

Northern Democratic fixtures in the Senate, Paul H. Douglas of Illinois and Hubert H. Humprey of Minnesota, won handily.

Also victorious on the Democratic side were Senators E. L. Bartlett of Alaska, Pat McNamara of Michigan, Clinton P. Anderson of New Mexico, and Robert S. Kerr of Oklahoma.

These will be the new faces in the Senate:

Claiborne Pell (D) of Rhode Island, a liberal whose primary interest has been in international affairs. He replaces Senator Theodore Green, a liberal, who is retiring.

Edgar V. Long (D) of Missouri, who was appointed Sept. 21 to fill the unexpired term of the late Senator Thomas C. Hennings, a businessman pledged to follow Mr. Henning's liberal record "insofar as possible."

Mrs. Neuberger (D) of Oregon, a liberal who now takes the seat held by her husband, the late Senator Richard L. Neuberger.

Gov. J. Caleb Boggs (R) of Delaware, who followed a fairly conservative line while a member of the House from 1947 to 1953.

Jack Miller (R) of Iowa, state senator since 1956, a tax lawyer who specializes in farm tax problems and appears conservative on fiscal matters

Keith Thompson (R) of Wyoming, a three-term member of the House who is regarded as a conservative.

Representative Lee Metcalf (D) of Montana, a liberal who succeeds Senator James E. Murray, a liberal who has retired.

State of the Nations

On Using the Interregnum

By Joseph C. Harsch

Special Correspondent of The Christian Science Monitor

The new President of the United States faces the usual problem at such times of using to best advantage the weeks which intervene before he becomes President of the United States in fact.

It is an interregnum, unavoidable under the United States system of government in which one man continues to hold the de jure power while another the de facto power which he cannot use formally but which exists and which can be used in certain ways which pave the road to his assumption of office and the earliest possible commencement of useful business thereafter.

The most useful thing which the new President can do right now is to remove such uncertainties as are inevitable in the aftermath of the election campaign about future foreign policy. They would not be resolved by indulgence in public pronouncements about matters which happily can be treated now with more circumspection than is employed on the hustings. They could be abated by two possible steps.

The first would be earliest possible announcement of the name of his new Secretary of State. The second would be personal meetings between that person and the foreign ministers of allied governments. It would be improper for the next Secretary of State to open negotiations with foreign governments, but it would be perfectly proper for him to meet individuals in those governments and begin personal relationships which would save time when actual negotiation can begin.

It of course should not be a "good-will" mission either among allies or satellite countries. It is an important business, that of getting acquainted with the new men who will hold both power and responsibility in Washington after Jan. 20.

The foreign ministers of the Western alliance will be gathering shortly in Paris for the annual NATO meeting. It would be an occasion at which the next Secretary of State could make the acquaintance of his future colleagues. His presence there would have the further advantage of letting Moscow know by indirection that the priority concern of the new government will be with the allies and the alliance. This in itself would be the first new "situation of strength" which can be built.

There almost certainly will be an East-West confrontation of some form during the coming year. The strength of alliance bargaining power at that time will depend heavily on whether there has been previous reappraisal of alliance policies and agreement among the allies on new ones.

The present situation makes such an early reappraisal both urgent and promising.

It is urgent because over Berlin, over the Congo, and over Asia communism is pressing with increasing boldness against the outposts of the alliance and also against the uncommitted nations. Considerable and dangerous Communist breakthroughs are possible at a number of points and can be prevented only by a degree of coordination among the allies and between allies and uncommitted nations which does not exist now.

Opportunities for a reappraisal are promising because the allies are as aware of the dangers as is anyone in Washington — perhaps even more aware. The time when the allies complained of Washington leadership and were tempted by the road of neutralism has passed and has given way to a new receptiveness. Not in a long time have the allies been as keen to get on with the job of finding new ways for better coordinating their relations with Washington.

The isolation of neutralist sentiment in Britain in the schismatically inclined left wing of the British Labor Party is a case in point. With Labor chieftain Hugh Gaitskell backing an alliance policy, Prime Minister Harold Macmillan is freer today to give full support to the alliance than at any previous time since he became Prime Minister, as he is doing.

But the basis of the relationship among allies must be recast. The United States is still the strongest single power in the alliance but no longer by a wide enough margin to be able to command. The power and influence of Western Europe would instantly and automatically equal that of the United States should it become an economic and political federation. This development is a possibility. The alliance structure will have to be based more on partnership and less on Washington leadership than in the past.

Moscow will recognize growing strength in the alliance if the President-elect's first step expresses interest in the alliance and an intent to modernize its structure.

Adenauer Greets U.S. Victor

By J. Emlyn Williams

Central European Correspondent of The Christian Science Monitor

Bonn, Germany

Chancellor Konrad Adenauer, who had already sent a congratulatory telegram to John F. Kennedy, as President-elect, before the outcome of the election was certain, also has made a statement.

In it he noted that because of the special position of the United States, the President of that country more than any other government chief carries the responsibility not only for his own nation but also for the well-being of the whole world.

The personality and principles of John F. Kennedy are a guarantee that he "will represent with prudence and strength the cause of peace in freedom," the statement declared.

Dr. Adenauer particularly expressed hopes that Mr. Kennedy, during his period in office, can ensure security of all, can lead the way to controlled disarmament, and give the world genuine and permanent peace. And in these efforts for world peace, the new President and the American people will always find the German people on their side, the statement ended.

'Glad It's Over'

West Germany's most sincere reaction to the American presidential election is thankfulness that it is all over and the Western world can now return to face the fundamental foreign policy tasks set by Communist aggressive tactics against freedom and democracy.

From the beginning of the campaign it has been regarded as primarily an internal American affair, especially as both Mr. Kennedy and Vice-President Richard M. Nixon by their statements had shown that "Germans could have the same unrestricted confidence in the new President as they have in Dwight D. Eisenhower," and that United States foreign policy would not change fundamentally.

Hermann Höcherl, chairman of the Christian Social Union (the Bavarian branch of Dr. Adenauer's coalition), satisfactorily noted American unconditional support for Berlin. And since this issue might be the main theme at a summit conference expected next spring, Herr Höcherl assumed that Dr. Adenauer would shortly visit the new American President.

Social Democratic spokesman Fritz Erler said that Mr. Kennedy's apparent election marks a change in style of American politics. He indicated a belief that though basic principles will remain, there probably will be changes in methods and details which might be important for Germany.

Split Avoided?

But to him the greater importance of the election was that it might speed what he defined as the "modernizing of the United States' military, economic, and cultural power." In one word, according to Herr Erler, the election would mean a move to "more mobility."

Seeking explanations for the Kennedy votes, many persons attribute it to Americans wanting a change after eight years of Republican rule, to the Democratic candidate's ability as campaign organizer, to his personal appeal to some sections of the population, especially over television, and to the fact that President Eisenhower's popularity could not be transferred to Mr. Nixon.

One important consequence of the election underlined here is that for the next four years, at least, the President and majority in Congress apparently will belong to the same party, thus avoiding the conflict between the White House and the Capitol existing since 1954.

Democrats are seen here as more prepared to experiment than Republicans, leading to expectation of greater activity than at present in Washington, though there is caution about its application in foreign policy.

On two things Germans of different political opinions agree, namely that, to cite the rightest independent Deutsche Zeitung Dusseldorf, a new generation has come to power through new methods in use of power.

No New Dulles

"Paradoxical thought it may seem, older statesmen act as though they have heaps of time, while the younger believe they must achieve final results immediately and everywhere possible," the comment added.

Also there is general agreement that whoever will be the next Secretary of State, he will not play as independent a role as did John Foster Dulles under Mr. Eisenhower.

Commons Told Queen's Comet In No Danger From German Jets

By the Parliamentary Correspondent of The Christian Science Monitor

London

Official investigators have reported there was no danger of a collision between the Comet airliner in which Queen Elizabeth II was returning from Copenhagen to Britain on Oct. 25 and two F-86 fighters of the West German Air Force.

This was announced by Air Minister Julian Amery in the House of Commons Nov. 9. The finding is contrary to the original impression given by the Comet pilot on landing safely at London Airport.

Britons were given the impression that the Queen's Comet was buzzed by German fighters. Mr. Amery now has stated that the German fighters broke off "short of buzzing range."

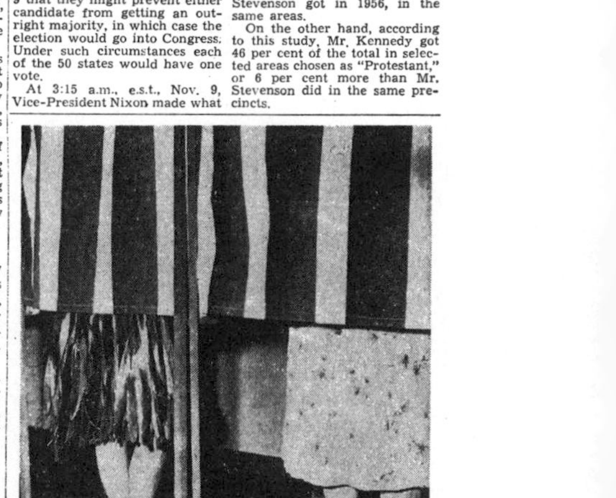

Associated Press Wirephoto

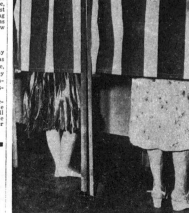

Casting the Grass-Skirt Vote

Hawaii voted Tuesday in a United States presidential election for the first time, and this barefoot, grass-skirted hula dancer took time out from her job as a welcomer for the Hawaii Visitor's Bureau to vote. Voter at right wears more conventional garb.

THE CHRISTIAN SCIENCE MONITOR

Registered in U. S. Patent Office
AN INTERNATIONAL DAILY NEWSPAPER

VOLUME 53 NO. 116 | © 1961, THE CHRISTIAN SCIENCE PUBLISHING SOCIETY All Rights Reserved | BOSTON, WEDNESDAY, APRIL 12, 1961 | EASTERN EDITION | TWO SECTIONS | TEN CENTS A COPY

West Retools Alliance

By William H. Stringer
Chief, Washington News Bureau, The Christian Science Monitor

Washington

As West Germany's Chancellor Konrad Adenauer confers with President Kennedy, it can be said that the United States and its key allies are on the threshhold of fashioning an Atlantic partnership more meaningful and much broader-ranged than the original alliance of the North Atlantic Treaty Organization.

This is only the inception, and much remains to be accomplished, including a successful dialogue between President Kennedy and France's imposing President de Gaulle.

Yet from early steps, hints, and indicia it is possible to envisage—provided all goes well—an Atlantic community in which:

- Britain will have become a fairly full-fledged member of the Common Market, though retaining special ties with the Commonwealth.
- West Germany will be honoring its wide obligations as a prosperous member of the Atlantic community by extensive participation in joint programs to bring the underdeveloped world to self-sustaining economic maturity.

Historic Forces

- The Senate-ratified Organization for Economic Cooperation and Development will be serving as a major adjunct to NATO in knitting together Atlantic community nations and initiating common policies concerning economic growth, corporate activity, balance-of-payments, general finance, trade and aid.

The United States is not clutching to itself the credit for the early trends visible. Its spokesmen are suggesting rather that historic forces and economic winds are pushing the Atlantic community closer together. But the very presence in Washington of a new administration, as well as the policies initiated by the Kennedy team, have helped very considerably.

British Prime Minister Harold Macmillan during his recent Washington consultations asked his United States counterparts directly what the Washington reaction would be if Britain joined up with the Common Market. The Kennedy reply was that the United States would be delighted.

Opinion Veers

This was not a new United States position, as some members of the London press have been making out. Washington has long favored having Britain join the Common Market; it objected only to previous British proposals which contained so many reservations and exceptions as to threaten to weaken the Common Market itself if Britain were accepted under such terms.

Now opinion is veering in Britain toward fuller association with the six-nation grouping, as London becomes concerned at the faster growth rate attained by several continental countries and at the prospective raising of tariff walls against British manufactures—which threaten, for instance, seriously to handicap sales of British automobiles in the traditional Netherlands market.

Bonn Role

The Washington reply assured Mr. Macmillan that the United States intends to give strong support to the Organization for Economic Cooperation and Development. This means the visible presence of the United States and Canada in the Atlantic economic family; Britain would not be alone and by itself, breaking historic tradition by moving, 400 years after it quit Calais, into closer association with the continent.

London still may not take the plunge. President de Gaulle conceivably could rule that Britain was not welcome. But West Germany is in favor, since the British adherence would assist that great objective of Chancellor Adenauer: to anchor West Germany solidly into the family of the West. The general opinion is that Britain would be accepted.

Meanwhile, Washington believes that West Germany and Chancellor Adenauer are increasingly responsive to the role which Bonn's economic power and balance-of-payments strength entitle it to play in helping the free world avoid payments crises and in rendering assistance to the emergent nations.

First Step Seen

In its talks with German Foreign Minister Heinrich von Brentano and since, the Kennedy administration has avoided seeming to demand help from Bonn so as to balance the United States budget.

President Kennedy has said in effect: "We can get along all right by ourselves"; what is wanted from the Germans is that they assume their responsibilities as a member of the Western club. Both Chancellor Adenauer and his possible successor, Professor Ludwig Erhard, have manifested a willingness to allocate German resources realistically to foreign aid.

Indeed at the development assistance group sessions recently concluded in London (embracing the chief Western industrial powers plus Japan) it was agreed to establish a permanent organization for the pooling of data on development requirements, plus data on what respective nations already are doing in various lands.

The State Department regards this as an essential first step in formulating an effective assistance program in any recipient country.

Man Leaps Free of Earth Shackles

By Neal Stanford
Staff Correspondent of The Christian Science Monitor

Washington

Shortly after the Soviet Government officially announced it had orbited a man in space, returning him safely to earth, President Kennedy sent off a congratulatory statement to the Kremlin.

But the President's congratulations were accompanied by considerable official and congressional disappointment that the United States had again been beaten by the U.S.S.R. in one of the greatest scientific adventures in man's history.

Actually the Soviet success did not come as much of a surprise to Washington, for the Soviet spacecraft launchings this past year left no doubt the time for a man orbiting the earth was not far off.

The best that the United States was prepared to do was shoot an astronaut down the Atlantic Missile Range in a shot that would take some 16 minutes in an up-and-down flight, giving him possibly six minutes of space weightlessness. The earliest possible date for this shot was April 28, with orbiting of an astronaut not possible before December.

Redstone on Pad

Your correspondent, who was down at Cape Canaveral this week, saw, sitting on its pad, the Redstone rocket that would boost a man into space—with the whole staff down there hoping that the United States would get a man down the Atlantic range before the Soviets put one in orbit. For the Atlantic run, however spectacular, could only be a poor show to a man in orbit.

But now the Soviets have put a man in space, to the disappointment of a lot of Washington officials who had recognized that the psychological and propaganda impact of such a victory could far transcend its immediate scientific value.

Since the Soviets opened the space age on Oct. 4, 1957, with the launching of Sputnik I, they have orbited 16 satellites to 40 for the United States. What the Soviets have, that the United States hasn't, is a clear immediate superiority in rocket engine thrust which permits them to put a five-ton satellite into orbit. Such an engine is way beyond America's present potentialities.

Weights Compared

America's Mercury capsule weighs about one ton, as compared to Moscow's five-ton payload. This is pictured by many as a space race between quantity and quality, between size and precision, with the Kremlin ahead in the first two heats.

The rocket that the Soviet "cosmonaut" rode probably developed more than 800,000 pounds of thrust. The Redstone which the United States will use to shoot an astronaut down the Atlantic range has a rating of only 78,000 pounds; and even the Atlas, the modified ICBM, that is slated for use in orbital shots, generates only 360,000 pounds of thrust.

America's Project Mercury sustained a series of launch mishaps this past fall that required additional tests to qualify the system.

On Nov. 8 a space capsule failed to separate from a "Little Joe" rocket fired from Wallops Island, Va., in a test of the capsule escape system.

Two weeks later, a Redstone, topped by a capsule, fizzled because of a faulty connection which caused the escape tower to fire, leaving the rocket and capsule on the pad. This test had to be repeated before Ham, the space chimpanzee, was sent up on a short trip Jan. 31.

An engine thrust regulator stuck on the chimp shot, creating excessive thrust which lofted Ham higher and farther than intended. Another Redstone was fired to prove out corrections made in the regulator, again delaying the manned trip.

Another setback occurred March 18 when a repeat of the "Little Joe" escape tower test fizzled. Another try is set for about April 20 and must succeed before the Redstone now on the pad hurls an astronaut aloft.

Soviet Tests Cited

In contrast, as far as Washington can ascertain, the Soviets have been quite successful in their tests. Last year they launched three giant spacecrafts, each capable of carrying a man.

The first, launched in May, carried a man-sized dummy.

The second, the most spectacular of the three, was launched in August. It was a five-ton spacecraft that brought back safely to earth two dogs and other living creatures for the first time from an orbiting satellite, after circling the earth 18 times at an altitude of more than 200 miles.

The third spacecraft, also a five-ton job and carrying living things, was successfully launched into orbit Dec. 1. But something went wrong with the recovery mechanism, and the craft went out of control and burned out as it plunged into the earth's atmosphere, after a signal was given for it to return to earth.

Comments Sparse

Dr. Hugh S. Dryden, Deputy Administrator of NASA, the United States space agency, would only comment on the Soviet success: "This is the day we have been expecting." And congressmen echoed his words. James Webb, NASA administrator, had this to say: "A splendid achievement, a significant event in terms of the Soviet timetable."

Both Mr. Webb and Dr. Dryden expressed the hope the U.S.S.R. would "make available to the scientific community the information gained from this experiment."

Dr. Wernher von Braun, operations director of the Army's Missile Center, Huntsville, Ala., said he thought "the Russians did this to impress the African nations." He said the United States still was ahead of the Soviet Union in several fields of space science.

Dr. Ralph Lapp, who worked on the A-bomb at the 1946 Bikini tests, said the Soviets had the capability of launching two men into space instead of one.

'Not Unexpected'

Said Representative Overton Brooks (D) of Lousiana, chairman of the House Space Committee, this was "not unexpected. We knew the Soviets had that capability. At the same time it is an amazing feat. We have to move on with a stepped-up plan."

There is also the mystery that needs clearing up as to why the original stories apparently leaked out of Moscow had a man in orbit three days earlier, and had him returned but suffering from aftereffects. Did the Soviets have two spaceships on pads—the first one a fizzle, but the second a success?

Such questions and mysteries, though, do not detract from the fact of the astonishing success of putting a man in orbit and bringing him back alive. Shooting an astronaut down the Atlantic range can only be anticlimatic, however successful.

Wrong Number!

By Reuters

Moscow

There are eight households listed in Moscow's new telephone directory under the name Gagarin, but none of them say they are related to the Soviet spaceman. Their telephones have been ringing constantly.

When a Reuters reporter rang the numbers, six of the Gagarins said "Nyet" (No).

One man said: "I am fed up with this. My phone has been ringing all day."

Another man hung up without answering.

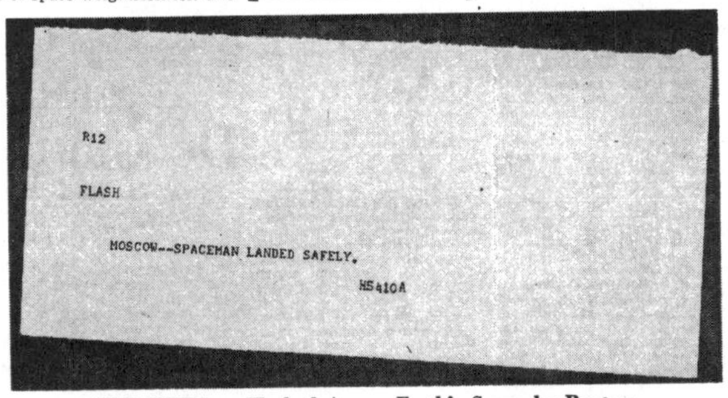

R12

FLASH

MOSCOW--SPACEMAN LANDED SAFELY.

H5410A

THE NEWS as Flashed Across Earth's Space by Reuters

By Robert C. Cowen
Natural Science Editor of The Christian Science Monitor

Considered apart from national rivalries, the successful orbiting and return of the Soviet cosmonaut, the first man in space, is a magnificent achievement on behalf of all mankind.

Maj. Yuri Alekseyevich Gagarin's satellite flight is a culmination of the development begun when men dropped superstition and magic and turned to reason and objective study to understand and deal with their environment.

Considered in the context of the cold war, his flight is another pointed reminder of how determined the Soviet space effort really is, both for military and scientific research purposes.

It was completely predictable on the basis of previous Soviet performances and announced intentions. It likewise was to be expected that the United States would most likely place second in the race to put a man into orbit.

This is the hard fact of the matter that must be faced by those in Western nations, especially in the United States, who wonder why the Soviets are walking away with this and other spectacular first prizes for space achievement.

On this first trip through space, April 12, the cosmonaut rode in a satellite ship named Vostok. Including the passenger, but excluding the final stage of the launching rocket, it reportedly weighed 10,640 pounds.

Low Orbit

The orbit was a relatively low one, ranging between 189 miles and 109 miles at its farthest and nearest points. It took 89½ minutes to make a complete circuit of the earth.

During the flight, Major Gagarin was strapped into a specially designed couch within the sealed cabin. According to the Associated Press, he reported over the radio that he was "withstanding the state of weightlessness well."

Later, after being brought safely to the ground at a predetermined location, he said, "I feel well. I have no injuries or bruises."

The Soviets have been pushing their space program hard for a number of years. The United States began to take such a program seriously only after the first sputnik was launched in the fall of 1957.

Before that time, space flight was generally considered a wild idea in the United States, not worth the expense of a substantial national effort.

A Determined Runner

It is hard to catch up with a determined runner when one starts the race so late. As Dr. H. Guyford Stever of the Massachusetts Institute of Technology, a leading government consultant on space research, has been quoted as saying, the United States manned satellite program is "running a fraction of a year to one year behind the Russians. We did not have a chance of beating them."

Moreover, the Soviet success is due entirely to Soviet engineers and scientists.

Questions are frequently raised, particularly in the United States, as to whether the Soviets may not be using German experts to bolster their own technical manpower in the rocket field. This does not appear to be the case, although there may be some East Germans associated with the Soviet work.

Prof. Eugen Sänger, renowned German rocket and space flight authority, has said he believes the Soviets are more or less going it alone.

Germans Drafted

During a visit to the United States last month, Professor Sänger explained in conversation that in the earlier years of the Soviet space program shortly after World War II, many German specialists were pressed into service. They worked along with Soviet engineers in special camps.

Later, Professor Sänger said, the Soviet engineers went off on their own, and the Germans were generally free to return home. This took place before any of the sputnik work. He said he believes the visible space successes of the Soviets are more or less the work of their own engineers.

Thus the breakthrough in human adventure and scientific exploration which the Soviets have announced would seem to be a fully expectable result of a hard-driving, well-supported, and ably manned domestic program.

In any event, and considered in the perspective of human history, this is one of the great moments for all mankind.

Purists may object that it was a "technological" rather than a "scientific" achievement. They may note that Major Gagarin is more of a pilot than a scientist.

Spark to Success

This certainly is true as far as the immediate developments leading to the flight are concerned.

But in the larger context of the full history of space research, this is the fulfillment of the vision and the researches of many pure scientists.

It is the questing drive for new knowledge, the urge to explore ever further into the unknown that characterizes scientific research that has supplied the long-term drive toward space flight over the decades of the past.

Major Gagarin's flight is also a beginning as well as a fulfillment. It dramatically symbolizes the opening to human experience of a bit more of the grand universe of which the planet Earth is such a tiny and circumscribed part.

What effect this broader horizon will have on human thinking is virtually impossible to foresee. Its long-term impact should be as revolutionary as the rise of scientific research itself.

'You Know—I Thought I Heard Balalaika Music the Other Night!'

Adenauer Seeks Defense Backing

By the Associated Press

Washington

German Chancellor Konrad Adenauer visited President Kennedy April 12 seeking personal assurance of full United States support for West Berlin and the defense of Western Europe.

Flanked by advisers, the Chancellor arrived at the White House at 9:55 a.m. and was quickly led into the President's office.

Administration officials forecast that the President would give the Chancellor the reassurance he wants as to the future course of United States foreign policy.

State of the Nations

Deterrents Should Deter

By Joseph C. Harsch
Special Correspondent of The Christian Science Monitor

London

Speaking before the NATO military committee in Washington, President Kennedy said that NATO's nuclear deterrent should "do what we wish, neither more nor less."

Speaking at the Massachusetts Institute of Technology, Prime Minister Macmillan said that "the first essential is that the deterrent should deter."

These and other recent similar statements sound as though some sensible and practical rethinking is going on about deterrents. As a matter of fact, there has been a good deal of rethinking in this area.

* * *

What is happening is that governments are reaching a new stage of maturity in their ability to think and talk about nuclear weapons. It was not easy to apply objective thinking about them in earlier days. They were too new, exciting, and emotion arousing.

The West went through a Phase 1 in which their original possessors, in Washington, operated on a blithe assumption that a monopoly existed which could be perpetuated for a long time. President Truman clutched the Washington bomb possessively to his bosom and attempted to deny the technical knowledge about it even to those—the British—who had participated through the original development stages.

In this Phase 1, Washington proposed to renounce possession and use in return for a complete international inspection system. It may have sounded both high-minded and generous at the time, but it was also self-defeating.

In effect, it offered the Soviets a choice between submitting to inspection by outsiders and setting to work themselves to obtain the secrets by their own devices. A combination of curiosity, pride, and reluctance to be inspected caused them to seek their own. They got it.

The British, deprived of the end result of the process but possessing all the original knowledge, also went their own way. They had to spend considerable money in solving the production problem which they would have preferred to use for other things, but had no serious difficulty in producing their bombs.

The French lagged a bit behind the others but eventually came up with their own bombs.

So the experience in Phase 1 showed that the original Washington approach to nuclear weapons had the reverse effect from what was intended. The intent was to prevent the generalization of nuclear weapons in the hands of others. But the effect was to produce four nuclear-possessing countries where originally there had been one.

In Phase 2, when the Washington stockpile was plentiful and others had fewer, Washington indulged in the doctrine of massive retaliation. The intent of this was to deter the Soviets from allowing Communists to cross any more frontiers. Had it worked, the power frontiers of the world would have been frozen and the Soviets would have been perforce satisfied with what they had.

But the effect was to turn the Soviets to means of crossing frontiers which would not engage nuclear weapons. They have been busily crossing frontiers ever since. Again the deterrent did not do what was wanted. It may have deterred the Soviets from using nuclear weapons, but it did not deter them from thinking and acting aggressively.

Now the West enters Phase 3 and the new thinking. The Kennedy - Macmillan phrases show that the lessons of Phases 1 and 2 have been noted and recognized. The capabilities of the nuclear weapon are being bounded. We of the West have learned that it is not an all-purpose weapon sufficient to all our purposes or needs.

It can deter others from using similar weapons—provided bombs in sufficient numbers and quality and the vehicles for conveying them to target are maintained. But they do not prevent others from getting them and do not prevent the waging of the power struggle by other means. Nor are they convincing when overused. Massive retaliation has ceased to be convincing—if it ever was.

* * *

The new thinking involves deciding what the West wants from them within the framework of what it can get. We want them to deter the use of similar weapons by others. That we can have. But we also want if possible to prevent the further proliferation of ownership. To get that we must reach agreement with the Soviets and Chinese Communists. That road is being studied.

The West also wants security for free-world frontiers. The nuclear deterrent is probably useless for this purpose. Hence we now are reviving reliance on conventional weapons. And we want our deterrent to be convincing. To be convincing we must never threaten to use it where under test we might not use it.

The biggest single step taken is the recognition that it is a limited-purpose, not a general-purpose weapon. We have certainly not yet "harnessed the bomb," but we have begun to harness our own thinking about it with some practical, even rational, conclusions. It sounds hopefully like the first toddling footsteps toward sanity on the subject.

Reform Rift Jostles Wagner

By Frederick W. Roevekamp
Staff Correspondent of The Christian Science Monitor

New York

A top city hall official privately warned Mayor Robert F. Wagner more than a year ago that by advocating charter reform in this election year he was inviting disunity within his own party and unity among his opponents.

The first part of this warning has already proved accurate.

Increasingly bitter opposition among Democrats, especially county leaders, to the proposed charter reform found dramatic expression in the 22-3 vote of the Democratic City Council against the Mayor April 11. The council passed a bill that would set up a charter commission in open competition with the one appointed by the Mayor, a Democrat himself, less than two weeks ago.

This overwhelming vote, in which one of the three dissenters was a Liberal Republican, also was seen to indicate the disapproval among Democratic leaders of the way in which the Mayor has courted the Democratic insurgent group led by former Senator Herbert H. Lehman.

Fusion Movement?

The soundness of the second part of the warning, namely that the Mayor might encourage a fusion movement against him among other parties and groups, so far has been neither proved nor disproved.

However, the primaries are still five months away and, while there is as yet no sign of any alliance between the Republican and the Liberal parties, such a development is not completely ruled out by observers.

Whatever may be said about Mayor Wagner's political judgment in insisting on charter reform, observers do not overlook that he had no easy choice.

Had he backed away from what he advocated for several years, Republicans, Liberals, and insurgents could have attacked him for expediency.

There is little doubt among observers that the Mayor made a conscious strategic decision in this respect. He apparently hoped that his posture of consistency would win him more votes than the hostility within his own party would cost him.

Broke With DeSapio

The chief threat to his reelection is seen to lie in the possibility that a growing number of anti-Wagner Democrats may team up with the forces of Carmine G. DeSapio in backing a candidate against him in the primaries in early September.

Mayor Wagner broke openly with Mr. DeSapio some time ago, an act which, politically, was interpreted as part of his effort to appeal to Liberals and insurgents.

A hard primary fight might create a climate for a fusion movement, which is the only way for parties other than the Democrats to win the mayoralty in this city.

While the city council's dislike of charter reform had been well known, the overwhelming vote to take the reform away from the Mayor surprised even some insiders.

Backed by Governor

Majority leader Joseph T. Sharkey, leader of the party in Brooklyn and politically the strongest figure in the council, repeated his charge that Mayor Wagner had been "playing together" with Republican Gov. Nelson A. Rockefeller on charter reform. The Governor had backed the bill passed by the GOP-controlled State Assembly which gave the Mayor full powers to set up his own charter commission.

United Press International

Mayor Robert F. Wagner
Trouble in New York Democrats' camp

Associated Press Wirephoto via Radio From Moscow

Back From Space, Just as the Soviets Planned It
The first man in space, Maj. Yuri Gagarin

2nd Cl Post Pd at Boston, Mass., and add'l offices

THE CHRISTIAN SCIENCE MONITOR

Registered in U. S. Patent Office
AN INTERNATIONAL DAILY NEWSPAPER

VOLUME 53 NO. 123 © 1961, THE CHRISTIAN SCIENCE PUBLISHING SOCIETY All Rights Reserved BOSTON, THURSDAY, APRIL 20, 1961 **EASTERN EDITION** TWO SECTIONS TEN CENTS A COPY

Cuba and Laos: U.S. Faces Up to Two-Front Crisis

Facing Facts on Prestige

By William H. Stringer
Chief, Washington News Bureau, The Christian Science Monitor

Washington

The first round in the struggle for Cuba may have been won by Castro, and Moscow and Castro now will have a propaganda heyday over the "defeat" of what they alleged is "Yankee imperialism."

Though Washington did not mount the landings, the Kennedy administration prestige is hurt all around the globe. Castro has made remarkably quick use of the formidable armaments furnished him by the Soviet bloc, and he has mobilized a potentially powerful militia. This could be a tough combination to beat.

The Cuban Revolutionary Council has had mainly the middle class on its side. Castro has the "dispossessed" on his side, and Khrushchev's communism is shrewdly and coolly exploiting the unrest of the impoverished classes all around the globe. To the great credit of the Kennedy administration, its new-development partnership with Latin America is aimed to reach the "shirtless ones" and to build therefrom a middle class eventually.

This takes long years. What will Washington do in the meantime? One step will be a careful reassessment of what Khrushchev is up to.

For a few weeks after President Kennedy took office, the Soviet Premier obligingly refrained from heating up the atmosphere. Then Moscow exploited the deterioration in Laos—no doubt egged on by Peking—and expressed a surprising unconcern at the nuclear-test-ban negotiations at Geneva. And now in Cuba Moscow has shown none of the restraint concerning a flame-up close to United States territory that Washington showed, rightly or

State of the Nations

wrongly, during the Hungarian revolt in the Soviet sphere of influence.

Yet Cuba is not even Khrushchev's first concern, by any means. He has told Walter Lippmann that his priority worry is Berlin, and Germany—the prospect that Bonn will acquire nuclear arms and drag NATO into a major war for the recovery of Germany's lost territories.

But side by side goes this unrestrained effort to exploit every situation in the undecided (and weak) countries of the world—even as Khrushchev proclaimed he would do in his review of Soviet grand strategy late in 1960. This should be no surprise.

Moving into this arena with development programs and a newly sensitized approach to the emergent nations, President Kennedy has reminded Premier Khrushchev that free peoples do not accept his claim of the "historic inevitability" of the Communist revolution. And the United States, along with Britain, has forcefully demanded that Moscow quit stalling on the Laos cease-fire.

Still the basic question here is whether there now is going to be any kind of Soviet-American détente or Kennedy-Khrushchev understanding at all—any progress in areas which seemed so recently promising, such as arms control.

If Moscow presses military advantage in Laos and if it adds to the Soviet "base" in Cuba, this is going to cancel any prospect of constructive talks, through normal channels or at the summit. The cold war will be on again in full force.

Perhaps this is the only definition of "peaceful coexistence" that Khrushchev can muster today, pressed as he is by his Chinese colleagues and emboldened by his own propaganda.

In that case President Kennedy will have to step up his mild start toward beefing up United States conventional forces, augmenting the Army's airlift, training the new guerrilla teams. They may be needed, alongside a revamped NATO, a more perceptive foreign-aid program, and effective representation at the United Nations.

Perhaps only when Moscow is stopped in its tracks at various points around the globe (as it has been stopped to a surprising degree in the Congo through the UN "presence" there) will the Soviets be ready for any kind of détente, even an amelioration of the arms race.

If Moscow's behavior of the past few weeks is normal operating procedure now, the United States will face the hard facts. If Khrushchev wants a better atmosphere, he will have to reverse course pretty quickly.

Red China Links Up Crises

By Takashi Oka
East Asia Correspondent of The Christian Science Monitor

Hong Kong

Communist China has linked the Cuban crisis with the Lao civil war in a new propaganda onslaught against the United States.

The virulence of this campaign exceeds that of Moscow. There is almost an "I told you so" quality about Peking's renewed insistence that the Kennedy-Rusk administration represents only a continuation of the Eisenhower-Dulles policies—since this has been Peking's consistent contention from the day President Kennedy was elected.

The massive nature of Peking's offensive, its obvious effort to inflame opinion throughout the Asian-African world, casts a shadow over the West's peace-making efforts in Laos.

The campaign appears to be bearing out Indian Prime Minister Jawaharlal Nehru's concern that the Cuban development may have snarled the solution of other problems such as disarmament and Laos.

"United States aggression against Cuba has taken place at a time when the socialist countries and all other peace-loving countries are striving for a solution to the Laotian question," Peking self-righteously declared in an official statement broadcast by the state radio April 20.

'Peace Hoax'

"The United States Government has declared that it is willing to settle the Laotian question peacefully," the broadcast said, "but it is inconceivable that one can stand for peace in one region while deliberately creating war in another. The United States act of war against Cuba has exposed its peace hoax concerning Laos."

Whereas Moscow's official statement on the same subject said "the present United States Government, which declared itself an heir of the Roosevelt policy, is in essence pursuing the reactionary imperialist policy of Dulles and Eisenhower," Peking stated succinctly that "the armed United States aggression against Cuba has removed the Kennedy administration's mask of peace and proved that Kennedy and Eisenhower are jackals of the same lair."

Report From India

The official New China News Agency's ticker is crammed with items purporting to come from all over the world expressing indignation about alleged United States interference in Cuba.

One of the few non-Cuban items is from India and noncommittally reports that Prime Minister Nehru praised the Kennedy administration's helpful attitude toward underdeveloped countries.

This fits in with Peking policy since the clash with India over Tibet, which without attacking Mr. Nehru by name has frequently linked him with the Western camp and has emphasized India's pro-United Nations policy in the Congo at a time when the Communist bloc and some African states were attacking the UN as a United States tool.

Reassessment?

One reason for Peking's emphasis on Cuba at this time may be the paucity of favorable domestic developments. Communist Chinese newspapers have been most uniformative recently about the food situation, about steel targets, railway construction, and other economic affairs.

Some observers here are speculating that the Communist leaders maybe in the process of reassessing the entire domestic situation in the light of the disasters of last year and that until a new official line is set, the Communist papers have little to report.

Cuba, Laos, the Congo, Angola, and the Soviet man in space help newspaper cadres to tide over this unproductive season.

Rebels Infiltrate Hills?

By Bertram B. Johansson
Latin America Writer of The Christian Science Monitor

The propagandists have taken over the fighting of the Cuban civil war which, one can be virtually certain, is far from ended, even if it should not be resumed immediately.

The Castro government has announced all anti-Castro rebel action has been crushed. (This proclaims the efficiency of the Cuban Government.)

The anti-Castro Revolutionary Council has announced anti-Castro rebels have infiltrated the Escambray Mountains and that this "completed the first phase" of operations against Premier Fidel Castro. (This downplays the rebel effort, whereas most communication media have overplayed it.)

Another Revolutionary Council spokesman in Puerto Rico has said other landings in Cuba by rebels will come shortly. (This says the rebel efforts have only begun, and could continue indefinitely until Premier Castro has fallen.)

If one were to take these statements at their face value, without examination, one would be led to believe that a huge anti-Castro effort had fallen flat and ingloriously on its face.

The result is that the United States has been made to look as if it had committed the sin of intervention in Cuba; as if that intervention were a failure; as if Communist support has helped perpetuate a glorious Castro government.

Soviet Myth Cited

The intent of Communist propaganda around the world, as evidenced in Soviet statements and in student riots on both sides of the Iron Curtain, is to blacken the name of the United States, as in the U-2 "spy" episode, and to defame President Kennedy by associating his policy with that of President Eisenhower, and by charging it is a continuation of the "same old" imperialist policy the United States always has pursued.

The inevitable result of this will be an attempt at a new stridency of Castro supporters in Latin America, a quickening of Communist organization.

In all of these propaganda implications, the United States must struggle against the myth which the Soviet Union has managed to perpetuate in world thinking today that it is acceptable practice for the Communist world to send in supplies to Laos (now at the rate of 200 airlift planes a day), or to train Pathet Lao troops (which has been going on in Viet Nam at least since 1955), but that it is not acceptable for the United States to counter such Communist action in either Laos or Cuba.

What actually has been happening to the "pea" under the three walnut shells which information manipulators have been swiftly shifting?

There is no doubt there have been rebel setbacks.

But it is doubtful that they were on as grand a scale as is purported.

"The revolution," says the Castro communiqué, "has emerged victorious though paying a high toll in courageous lives of revolutionary fighters who faced the invaders and attacked them incessantly without a moment of respite, thus destroying in less than 72 hours the army which was organized over many months by the imperialist government of the United States."

A few hours before this announcement, the anti-Castro Revolutionary Council expressed "astonishment" at a report that thousands of "invading" insurgents had been killed by Castro forces.

The council said only a few hundred men had been employed in the operation, though the newsplay of some of the communications media would have indicated far, far more.

Losses Admitted

The anti-Castro council said, further:

"Regretfully, we admit tragic losses in Wednesday's action among a small holding force . . . which courageously fought Soviet tanks and artillery while being attacked by Soviet MIG aircraft—a gallantry which allowed the major portion of our landing party to reach the Escambray Mountains."

The communiqué attempted also to put the insurgent action more into context. It said:

"We did not expect to topple Castro immediately or without setbacks. And it is certainly true that we did not expect to face, unscathed, Soviet armaments directed by Communist 'advisers.' We did and survived!

"The struggle for freedom of 6,000,000 Cubans continues."

Then the council delivers its most telling sentences, which say:

"The recent landings in Cuba have been constantly, though inaccurately, described as an invasion.

"It was, in fact, a landing mainly of supplies and support for our patriots who have been fighting in Cuba for months and was numbered in the hundreds, not the thousands. . . ."

The grave questions facing the United States, thus, are:

How does the Kennedy administration begin to make its Latin America "Alliance for Progress" proposals concrete and credible, in the face of Communist propaganda diversions?

Where does its policy on Cuba go from here? Will it have to intervene militarily for the sake of United States national security? How can it not only counter organized Communist propaganda, but anticipate it so fully that it outwits it?

Criticism Hits Washington

By William R. Frye
United Nations Correspondent of The Christian Science Monitor

United Nations, N.Y.

The Cuban case is beginning to look more and more like a diplomatic and military fiasco.

The United States has taken, and is still taking, a severe chastising in the United Nations. Country after country has stated or strongly implied criticism of the United States' presumed role, while friends of the United States—with the single exception of Britain—have remained silent or given very qualified support.

Meanwhile, there are increasing indications that all this diplomatic punishment has been absorbed without achieving the main goal sought: the ouster of Premier Fidel Castro. While it is too early to say for certain, the revolution appears to have failed, or to be on the verge of failure—and Señor Castro may emerge even stronger than ever.

UN diplomats are likening the Cuban incident to the Suez war of 1956, in which Britain, France, and Israel unsuccessfully attempted to overthrow President Nasser of Egypt.

Only all-out United States intervention now could save the Cardona revolution, it is believed here. The United States must decide within the next 24 hours whether to take such action or to let the revolt fail, informants say.

Reconciliation Sought

It is not an easy dilemma. On the one hand, outright intervention would increase manyfold the diplomatic damage—and might be too late to save the military situation.

On the other hand, to stand by and let the revolt fail would be to give Dr. Castro and his Sino-Soviet allies a firm foothold from which to subvert the Western Hemisphere. Later efforts to oust him would be much harder to mount.

Some delegates here hope that there can still be a reconciliation between Havana and Washington, but few believe the prospects are bright. It was more than four years after Suez before President Nasser would resume full diplomatic relations with Britain, and he still has no relations with France. Of course, the United States repeatedly has denied direct involvement in the Cuban affair.

Dr. Raul Roa, the Cuban Foreign Minister, sought to implicate United States personnel Wednesday, charging that a United States pilot had been shot down and identified.

Criticism Cited

This charge is not, however, regarded as proved. If the United States had intervened directly with its own manpower, it is not thought likely that the revolt now would be on the verge of failure.

What the United States is accused of doing is financing, training, and helping supply the rebels. It is generally taken for granted that the rebels would not have been in a position to mount an attack, even on the relatively limited scale involved, without such help.

Among the non-Communist countries directly or indirectly criticizing the United States for its action have been Mexico, Ecuador, India, Burma, Nepal, and Iraq. India's criticism was particularly telling.

What these countries have said, in substance, is this:

- That the United States has complained when the Soviet Union sought to overthrow governments by organizing and supplying revolutions — and should practice what it preaches.
- That the United States even sponsored an "essentials of peace" resolution in 1950 which condemned the practice of "fomenting civil strife."
- That although cleansing the Western Hemisphere of Communist influence is an understandable motive, the end does not justify the means.

Britain Defends U.S.

Sir Patrick Dean of Britain, defending the United States, said his government had found from long experience that its word could be trusted, and that he therefore believed there had been no direct American involvement. Canada also went a certain distance in the United States' direction.

Several Latin - American friends of Washington are seeking to shunt aside the worst of the criticism by offering an inconclusive resolution to replace Communist-sponsored condemnations and a Mexican-sponsored rebuke. Their generalized document is believed to have the best chance of passage in the Assembly.

Meanwhile, however, the United States has been having a difficult time in several other spheres of UN activity as well. An approach it offered to the Palestine refugee problem has been defeated to the tune of severe Arab tongue lashings. Washington's stand on the admission of Outer Mongolia proved unpopular.

Tibet and Hungary, which the United States wanted debated, apparently will be shelved until the fall. American efforts to establish the principle of collective responsibility for Congo expenses are having very limited success.

The Assembly is due to adjourn April 21. It will not be any too soon for Washington.

On-Stage Echoes: Cuba, Algeria

By Harold Hobson
London Drama Critic of The Christian Science Monitor

London

With the orientation of British drama which is considerably more left-wing than the country as a whole, between the discussion of political problems on the stage, events in Algeria and Cuba strongly affected the atmosphere of Wednesday's first night of Jean-Paul Sartre's "Altona" at the Royal Court Theater.

Theater people in England today, often to the resentment of some sections of the community, intervene in matters of public policy ranging from campaigns to abolish capital punishment to marches in protest against the British hydrogen bomb on a scale which would have been incredible a few years ago.

In spite of disagreement with them, it would be a mistake to underrate the importance of these interventions, for the contemporary London theater is as strong a political influence as is political journalism.

Probably more prominent theatrical figures came to Wednesday's first night after signing political manifestos than to any previous performance event at the Royal Court, always the most politically minded of London theaters.

M. Sartre, the play's author, is one of 121 writers and actors of French nationality who have signed a declaration asserting that they would sympathize with French soldiers who refused to fight in Algeria.

This has brought on them the disapproval of the French authorities and for some time M. Sartre anticipated arrest. The danger has passed, although the signatories are not allowed to appear on the French radio.

Amongst those signatories, another member of the Royal Court was in the first night audience, Roger Blin. M. Blin is now rehearsing for the Royal Court

Associated Press Wirephoto

Adlai E. Stevenson
U.S. envoy to UN listens

Jean Genet's play "The Blacks." This piece is a fierce and scathing attack on white imperialism and is expected to wring the withers of the British and French Governments.

But America, too, is under attack from professional members of the first night audience. Kenneth Tynan, drama critic of a London paper, was fresh from printing in The Times, of London, of that morning a letter on Cuba which called on the United Nations "to condemn America's part in this invasion in the strongest possible terms."

Amongst the signatories of this letter were the actress Constance Cummings, the film critic Penelope Gilliatt, wife of Dr. Roger Gilliatt who was best man at the marriage of Princess Margaret; John Osborne, the author of "Look Back in Anger" which in 1956 at the Royal Court began a series of socially conscious dramas which have rejuvenated the British theater.

It would be a mistake to suppose that these views have much popular support in Britain. But the adhesion to them by a significant part of the theater is an influential factor.

During the performance one or two doors were noisily banged. Occasional murmurs could be heard. Now and again there was an inexplicable trampling of feet at the back of the theater. But political feelings were speedily stunned by the thumping weight of M. Sartre's interminable rhetoric which went on for three and a half hours.

School Named For Jane Addams

By the Associated Press

Chicago

The social service school at the University of Illinois has been renamed to honor Jane Addams, founder of Chicago's Hull House.

The U of I trustees, meeting in Chicago Wednesday named it the Jane Addams Graduate School of Social Work in recognition of the Nobel Prize winning social worker. She passed on in 1935.

Tougher Policy Pondered

By Courtney Sheldon
Staff Correspondent of The Christian Science Monitor

Washington

The United States has hastily sanctioned more military aid for Laos. It indignantly condemns the Castro government's actions against individual Americans.

These steps are regarded by American officials as minimal among the possible tough policies to counter Communist designs in Laos and Cuba.

To not be prepared to take further steps, it is conceded, would display a weakness that the Communists would be sure to capitalize on.

The United States goal in Laos is still to freeze the military situation so diplomatic wrestling at the conference table can begin.

What the United States can hope to salvage in the Cuban situation is much less apparent.

It is not yet clear here whether the Cuban revolutionists are going to be able to carry the day with open and material support from the United States.

Associated Press Wirephoto

Raul Roa
Cuban charges U.S. at fault

Red Infiltration

The hour of testing for United States policy could come eventually if enough of a beachhead is established in Cuba by the anti-Castro forces to proclaim that they are the "legitimate government."

Should the revolutionists then fail, while pleading unavailingly for help from the United States, American officials admit that communism will have dealt the free world one of the severest blows of the cold war.

The Communist infiltration of other Latin-American countries would be stepped up tremendously.

If the Kennedy administration means what it said in its recent white paper that "because the Castro regime has become the spearhead of attack on the inter-American system, that regime represents a fateful challenge to the inter-American system," it is far too early to rule out military moves beyond that of the past indirect aid and sympathy.

Events such as the summary execution of two American citizens, coupled with further evidence that—as in Laos—Communist arms aid is entrenching Castro could provoke the Kennedy administration to action beyond its present intentions.

Mr. Kennedy, meanwhile, has canceled a scheduled weekend cruise aboard the aircraft carrier Independence and scheduled the third full-cabinet session of his administration — actions which appear related to the administration's concern over Cuba.

Laos Cease-Fire?

American officials acknowledge that the decision "to help redress the military balance in Laos" by converting the United State civilian advisory group there into a military advisory group is to put pressure on the Soviets for a quick cease-fire.

As one American source put it, no one here wants to go to the conference table and see another Dien Bien Phu occur.

This is a reference to the fact that the Geneva conference on Indochina in 1954 started before there was a cease-fire and the Communists took advantage of the situation to conquer Dien Bien Phu.

As much as the United States would like to see a cease-fire Thursday, April 20, as proposed to Moscow by the British, it feels that if the Communists are at all receptive they will pick a day of their own choosing.

Lincoln White, State Department spokesman, branded the Castro government's execution of two Americans as "a violation of the elementary standards of justice practiced by civilized nations of the world."

Executions Scored

Inquiries are being made, through Switzerland, which represents United States interests in Cuba, about reported arrests of other Americans, including news correspondents.

Mr. White said that the executions of Howard F. Anderson of Yakima, Wash., and Angus McNair, Jr., of Miami "as far as we know . . . have taken place, perhaps without a trial, but in any case without a fair trial."

It was also Mr. White who announced that the additional assistance the United States is sending to Laos "should help redress the military imbalance in the country which has resulted from the continuing flow of materiel and personnel to the rebel forces over an extended period."

He acknowledged that the new United States military advisory group would go into the field with combat units to give tactical advice.

Soviet Airlift Noted

Under the 1954 Geneva agreement ending the Indochina war, only the French were allowed to have military forces in Laos. But the American position is that the United States never signed the Geneva agreement and it would be farcical to permit Communists to aid the Communist Pathet Lao and not permit help from the outside to the royal government Army.

Unofficial estimates are that the Soviet airlift is now at the rate of 200 planes a day.

It has only been in the last month that the Kennedy administration emphasized the intensified Soviet arms supply, though it has been going on steadily over recent months.

Only when several correspondents visited the headquarters of the Pathet Lao and reported a huge arms build-up did the State Department call their reports a real service to the United States and start to talk consistently about the arms build-up threat.

A similar approach has been taken on the Communist arms build-up in Cuba.

The administration was working mostly behind the scenes and plainly entertained hopes that the Soviets would become more concilatory and help reduce tension by holding back on arms supplies.

Arms Pour In

But this did not happen. And early in April the United States spread the Communist military assistance program in Cuba on the record.

In a white paper it declared that "since the middle of 1960, more than 30,000 tons of arms with an estimate value of $50,000,000 have poured from beyond the Iron Curtain into Cuba in an ever-rising flood.'

Associated Press Wirephoto

José Miró Cardona
Heads Revolutionary Council

Lyman W. Fisher, Staff Photographer

Marking the 'Shot Heard Round the World'

Ambassador and Mrs. W. M. Q. Halm of Ghana link arms with Lt. Martin Bashain of the Lexington, Mass., Minutemen, before the first war memorial erected in the United States. Delegates from 15 African nations and G. Mennen Williams, Assistant Secretary of State for African Affairs, were invited to Lexington to join in Patriots' Day festivities celebrating the Battles of Lexington and Concord, where the first shots of the American Revolution were fired. In the spirit of the occasion Ambassador Halm tried on Lieutenant Bashain's hat.

Africa looks to Lexington: Page 9.

2nd Cl Post Pd at Boston, Mass., and add'l offices

THE CHRISTIAN SCIENCE MONITOR

Registered in U. S. Patent Office
AN INTERNATIONAL DAILY NEWSPAPER

VOLUME 53 NO. 136 | BOSTON, FRIDAY, MAY 5, 1961 | NEW ENGLAND EDITION | TWO SECTIONS | BEYOND 30 MILES TEN CENTS | EIGHT CENTS

© 1961, THE CHRISTIAN SCIENCE PUBLISHING SOCIETY
All Rights Reserved

U.S. Enters Man-in-Space Era

Rocket Lifts Capsule Safely After Two-Hour Delay

By Neal Stanford
Staff Correspondent of The Christian Science Monitor

Cape Canaveral, Fla.

The United States has put a man in space, and brought him back.

Astronaut Alan B. Shepard, Jr., Commander, United States Navy, took 15 minutes to ride into and out of space—and into history.

He now joins Soviet cosmonaut Yuri A. Gagarin as the only humans to have entered space, fulfilling the dream of centuries.

His accomplishment May 5 closes Chapter I in United States space exploration, begun 2½ years ago—an adventure in faith that has cost $400,000,000 to date—and will cost untold billions in the future.

And it opens another chapter that will include not only a manned orbit of the earth, but trips to the moon, planets, and beyond.

Astronaut Shepard took off here from Missile Pad 5 at 9:35 a.m. e.s.t., in his Mercury-Redstone spacecraft. Range control announced, "OK—go, go!" The missile angled over at about 40 degrees down range. Fifteen minutes later he had gone 115 miles up and 290 miles down the Atlantic missile range, hurtling through space at 5,100 miles per hour.

Trip Smooth

Commander Shepard's first words were, "What a beautiful view!"

Col. John Powers reports that "pilot is in good voice." Astronaut Shepard said all is "go, go."

Over the Cape Canaveral loudspeakers, the trip was announced as "smooth."

It was a beautiful shot, and a roar went up from the huge crowd of newsmen and other observers as the missile took off.

Shouting, "Go, go, go," the crowd listened to the loudspeaker words that "excellent voice communication" was continuing for the first minutes of the flight.

At the peak of reentry stress, undergoing a stress of 20 G's, Commander Shepard kept saying, "OK, OK." He then weighed more than 3,000 pounds. All systems in cockpit were operating correctly. Drogue parachute was properly deployed. Mercury control center reported pilot fine all the way.

When sighted from Carrier Lake Champlain at 9:45 a.m., e.s.t., a round of applause broke out from assembled newsmen.

Official sighting reported at 9:48 a.m., e.s.t., coming down in perfect view of the waiting carrier, four miles away from the spacecraft. Helicopters were on the way to the point of impact before Commander Shepard had impacted the water.

Astronaut Shepard touched the water and the parachute flattened out at 9:50 a.m., e.s.t. Within four minutes helicopters were lowering the sling to Astronaut Shepard, who was apparently out of the capsule.

In a matter of minutes, the United States's first astronaut was being hurried to the carrier by helicopter inside the capsule. No questions were permitted by newsmen when he first reached the carrier.

Satisfaction General

After being picked up by helicopter in the expected landing area, Astronaut Shepard was rushed to the Grand Bahamas Tracking Station as planned. There he will spend several days telling officials his story of space travel—later being flown to Washington to meet President Kennedy—and the American Press.

The sigh of relief, satisfaction, and pride that went up from the assembled thousands of officials, newsmen, engineers and technicians as the spacecraft rose majestically from its pad could almost have shot the astronaut into space itself, if it could have been harnessed. Such was the determination that this attempt at space penetration should not fail.

Astronaut Shepard had gone to bed at 10:30 p.m., May 4, after watching some TV.

At 1:05 a.m. he was awakened by Dr. William Douglas. Breakfast at 1:50 consisted of a fillet wrapped in bacon, two poached eggs, toast, and orange juice.

After a physical examination at 2:25, Commander Shepard was pronounced by the doctor as in superb health, relaxed, and optimistic.

The astronaut was helped into his space suit at 3 a.m., and by 3:30 had checked the suit's pressure and found everything working properly.

At 4 a.m., with the visor of his helmet open, Commander Shepard climbed into a van to leave Hangar S, where he has stayed during the days of waiting. He was heard to say to an accompanying nurse, "Here I go."

Arriving at Pad 5 at 4:23, Commander Shepard left the van at 5:10 and climbed on the elevator to ascend to level 3 of the rocket.

At 5:20, under a clear, windless sky Commander Shepard climbed feet first into the Mercury capsule to begin the final two hours of countdown.

In spite of holds for weather uncertainties and a fairly long hold to correct an undisclosed technical difficulty with the rocket, the launching went off reasonably smoothly. The weather turned satisfactory and the technical snag was resolved. In all, the launching was fairly "routine."

James Webb, National Aeronautics and Space Administration Director, had earlier issued this warning of the dangers involved as well as a picture of what success would mean: "Our nation's space program will soon enter a new era—man's participation in the exploration of space by our first astronaut.

"The Mercury-Redstone flight is a most important step in the United States program—a step that will lead on to man's ultimate conquest of this new and hostile environment.

"It is also a most serious step; for it cannot be taken without risk to human life. It is the kind of risk that Lindbergh took when he crossed the Atlantic, that Chuck Yeager took in the X-1's first supersonic flight. . . ."

Although Commander Shepard's brief penetration beyond the atmosphere cannot be considered a match for Major Gagarin's full orbit, it is a significant step in the American manned space flight program.

It has tested an astronaut's performance under many of the stresses of true space flight. Both on take-off and reentry into the atmosphere, severe acceleration pressures were experienced.

There also was a full five minutes of weightlessness, far longer than any American has experienced. Special flights in aircraft have produced weightless moments lasting a few tens of seconds. Now at least one astronaut has had an "extended" period of weightless with which to experiment.

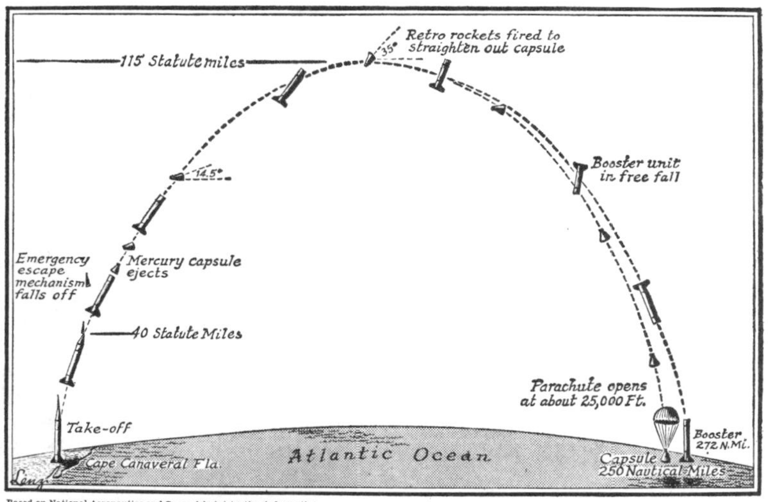
115 Statute miles
Retro rockets fired to straighten out capsule
14.5°
Booster unit in free fall
Emergency escape mechanism falls off
Mercury capsule ejects
40 Statute Miles
Parachute opens at about 25,000 Ft.
Take-off
Cape Canaveral Fla.
Atlantic Ocean
Booster 272 N.Mi.
Capsule 250 Nautical Miles

Based on National Aeronautics and Space Administration information

Stages in Astronaut Shepard's Suborbital Space Flight

Gordon N. Converse, Staff Photographer

Parents of Alan Shepard at Home

Mr. and Mrs. Alan B. Shepard shown at the organ in their East Derry, N.H., home recently. Today they received news that their son had become the first United States space man.

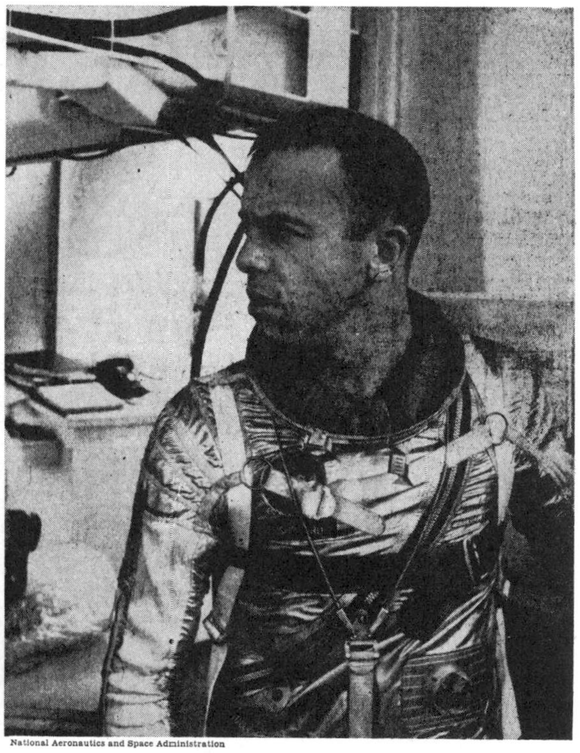

National Aeronautics and Space Administration

Alan B. Shepard, First United States Astronaut

Wearing flight pressure suit, Commander Shepard waits out final countdown

City's Transit: No Bridge?

By Michael Liuzzi
Staff Writer of The Christian Science Monitor

A transportation tug of war between city planners and state political leaders is beginning to stir in Massachusetts.

The gulf between planners and politicians has never been wider.

This is Boston's biggest "space" obstacle.

There are two immediate issues:

1. The turnpike extension versus the inner belt.
2. Limited diesel-car railroad service versus rapid transit.

Political momentum today is still moving in favor of the turnpike extension in Boston and diesel-car railroad service on the Old Colony line to the South Shore.

Bond Effort Set

Behind this momentum are two of the state's most powerful political figures — William F. Callahan, chairman of the Massachusetts Turnpike Authority, and John E. Powers (D) of Boston.

Both made major moves on Thursday.

A spokesman for Mr. Callahan announced that a second attempt to sell the turnpike extension bonds will be made before July 1.

Senator Powers blocked any further consideration of the Governor's rapid transit bill, and substituted instead a "package plan" involving a subsidy to the New York, New Haven & Hartford Railroad for limited commuter service, using diesel cars leased from some other source.

Yet, professional transportation planners agree almost unanimously that what the Boston area needs most is an "inner belt" and rapid transit extensions.

No 'Voice on Hill'

Their problem is that they have not yet found an effective political voice on Beacon Hill.

Backers of the turnpike and limited railroad service have no such problem.

Senator Powers consistently has supported the railroad service as opposed to rapid transit—to the point of personally persuading one legislator to switch his vote after a 19-to-17 roll call had apparently passed the Governor's rapid transit bill earlier this week.

As for Mr. Callahan—former state Public Works Commissioner under four governors — both his critics and supporters like to say: "He has never lost a vote in the Legislature yet."

There is much conjecture as to whether Mr. Callahan has played a role in delaying construction of the inner belt.

'By 1970' Tag

Even though the turnpike's consultants have twice averred that the inner belt will be a "help" to the turnpike, rather than a competitor, they have carefully added two words—"by 1970."

They have established a definite priority: first the crosstown turnpike; then, "by 1970," an inner belt.

This is the reverse of what all city transportation planners have recommended.

They have consistently given the inner belt "No. 1" priority in all their plans — and urged immediate construction.

And some have specifically stated that a turnpike extending within the inner belt is not desirable.

At the very least, the planners don't want to see the inner belt delayed because of the turnpike.

But they are still searching for a voice on Beacon Hill.

Up to Volpe?

There have been signs during the past few months that some of the old centers of political power and decision-making are crumbling, withdrawing, or becoming ineffective.

Many observers were waiting for Gov. John A. Volpe to step into what appeared to be a growing vacuum.

But the Republican Governor apparently has not yet found the key for dealing with strongly Democratic and sometimes hostile Legislature.

Setting up of a metropolitan planning agency may be the only step that can give professional planners an effective political voice.

Shepard Home Abuzz but Confident

By Jewel Spangler Smaus
Special to The Christian Science Monitor

East Derry, N.H.

Even the constant jangling of the telephone did not disturb the quiet sense of expectancy at the home of Bart and Renza Shepard in the village of Derry, N.H., Thursday night.

Alan Shepard, Sr., had attended a meeting earlier in the evening. Renza, his wife, and mother of the astronaut, had been about her usual affairs including a committee meeting of the Colonial Dames (of which she is vice-president for her area), chatting with neighbors, and keeping her home in its usual spotless order.

"You know," one of the members of the committee commented, "we knew she would be there even with all the excitement."

There were the usual lovely flower arrangements in profusion in her home. On a desk tucked in among piles of letters was a glass filled with the modest arbutus—better known as the mayflower—first harbinger of spring in New Hampshire. A neighbor had brought them from the woods and they filled the room with their fragrance.

Letters Piled High

Letters and clippings were piled on the dining-room table. The mail has been very heavy.

About 9 o'clock sister Polly (Mrs. Gordon L. Sherman) arrived from North Attleboro, Mass., with David, age 10, in a Cub Scout uniform. David was as excited about the circus his den had seen that afternoon, the fact that he had been let out of school early to see the circus and would have a holiday the next day, too, for the space shot, as he was about the forthcoming space trip of his famous uncle.

David's sister Betsy had not come on the visit because she is still a bit young (eight years) to be up so late, and also she had a piano lesson.

"You know," David commented excitedly, "I can't pick up a paper without seeing a picture of Uncle Alan."

Excitement, Yes

At 9:30, Mr. Shepard put in a telephone call to Alan, Jr., at Cape Canaveral. Polly and Renza each got on an extension phone and they had a bit of the togetherness that has made them a close-knit family. They chatted about the events of the last day, what Alan had for dinner, and the all-important weather.

Everything was fine, Alan, Jr., assured them, and Alan, Sr., reported the same for New Hampshire.

There was excitement, of course. Reporters kept calling. The local TV repairman arrived with a new set. He was not pleased with the one he had fixed that afternoon and wanted to be sure the reception was perfect.

The woman who helps with the cleaning called to see if she could be of assistance.

As the phone rang shrilly for the umpteenth time, Mrs. Shepard laughed, "You know," she said, "after having only one phone all these years it is hard to get used to three."

From green fields surrounding the colonial home came the high chorus of spring peepers, mixed with the occasional bass of a frog. A cold wind swept the meadows, and the slender spire of the Congregational Church across the way, built even before Revolutionary days, shone pale in the evening light.

"The stars are out," Mrs. Shepard exclaimed. "How lovely they are." And so they were—shining calm and steady in the clearness of the New England night.

Again, the telephone rang, and again Mr. Shepard answered it in his calm, firm voice. Yes, there was underlying excitement in the now well-known home in East Derry, N.H. And there was expectancy. But above all there was still an air of quietness and confidence.

The World's Day

Reg. U.S. Pat. Off.

Washington: Kennedy Sets News Conference

President Kennedy scheduled a news conference for 2:30 p.m., e.s.t., today. The session will not be carried "live" on radio or television.

President Kennedy signed with "great satisfaction" the bill putting 3,624,000 additional workers under the minimum-wage law and increasing the minimum for those already covered.

Europe: Attitude of France's Allies Praised

Foreign Minister Maurice Couve de Murville, today praised the attitude of France's allies—particularly the United States—during the recent Algerian crisis. Speaking in the Foreign Affairs Commission of the National Assembly, he referred to rumors that the United States Central Intelligence Agency was involved in the Algiers revolt.

More than 3,000 persons were homeless today in Evreux, France in the wake of a tornado Thursday night which killed 4 and injured more than 100.

Boston: Maasdam Sails on Initial Voyage

The SS Maasdam of the Holland American Line sailed from the Port of Boston at noon today, marking the initial voyage between the Hub and Galway, Ireland.

Weather: Clear Tonight, Fair Saturday [Page 2]

Arts and Entertainment: Page 7. TV: Page 10. Radio, FM: Page 18

State of the Nations: Season of Discontent

By Joseph C. Harsch
Special Correspondent of The Christian Science Monitor

London

Britain's sad discovery that its former "man in Berlin" actually was working for the Soviets all the time adds one more item to the growing list of misfortunes experienced of late by the major Western governments.

Washington has had its Cuba, Paris its Algeria, London its George Blake, and Bonn the Eichmann trial. Each is embarrassed, and there is little reason to believe that we are yet at the end of a season in which the West will find it difficult to chalk up successes outweighing its misfortunes.

Ahead lies the uncertain question of whether agreement can be reached in Geneva which will end in anything less than the substance of a Communist take-over in Laos. South Viet Nam is being more deeply infiltrated by Communists than even is Laos. It remains extremely doubtful that Communist China will be kept out of the United Nations beyond this year.

To add to the list of difficulties, Washington invoked for its Cuban venture a doctrine which in essence is based on the concept of great power spheres of influence. This already has boomeranged by raising again the Matsu-Quemoy issue which had been dormant for several years.

The West is not visibly gaining ground at this stage against its competitors in the marketing of influence.

The question is, What is wrong, and what does the West do about it?

What is wrong basically is that Moscow and Peking have brought their strategies up to date, whereas Western strategy has not been overhauled and revised significantly since early cold-war years. In essence it still is official Washington doctrine that communism should be contained at all points around the circle which was forged in Truman-Acheson and early Eisenhower-Dulles years.

At that time a ring of military bases was built around the Soviet Union and its satellite system and a fabric of treaties built to support the bases. The treaties, in turn, depended on the ability of the government involved to command the loyalty of its people. In the pyramid of containment the people were at the bottom and the military base on top. But the base was only as effective as the inclination of the people underneath.

Soviet strategy has long since gone over from attacking the Western bases to infiltrating the population on which they rest. And, in the meantime, evolution of new weapons has in many cases made the bases obsolete.

Western strategy has changed gradually but not fast enough to compete effectively where the Soviet operation is most effective. Too much the West still is clinging to bases around the rim of the circle even when the popular ground under the bases has gone soft and when the bases themselves have ceased to be of important military value.

The old strategy of the circle of containment was valid until roughly the time of the Geneva summit conference of 1955. It was weakened there by recognition that the nuclear weapon would not be used in contests along the circle. It was undermined decisively by Soviet achievement of long-range missiles in 1957.

Surely President Kennedy must find a way to change Western thinking from the assumption that it can and must defend lines to an understanding that a military line cannot be held in the days of weapons which can reach from continent to continent. The issue in the areas between the great centers of military power will be determined by the inclination of the masses of people inhabiting the twilight zone.

Under the Truman Doctrine there was no twilight zone but only opposite sides of a line. The lines are being eaten away both by Communist infiltration and by considerable disinterest among the peoples. Many would prefer to be uncommitted in the twilight than committed in daylight. People in Laos continue to show a considerable reluctance to fight one another.

The effective new strategy for the West is not yet clear. Adjustment from the old and familiar strategy will be distressing. But the landscape shows that the former strategy is old and out of date. It failed to save the 1954 settlement for Southeast Asia. Iraq still survives in the twilight zone, but because it was left alone not because the Truman Doctrine was applied.

Probably the key to the new strategy lies in learning to leave situations like that alone as was done in Iraq.

White House Gets Drawing

By the Associated Press

Washington

Mrs. John F. Kennedy has informally accepted the first major acquisition of the White House Fine Arts Committee—a $30,000 pencil and sepia drawing by Jean Honoré Fragonard.

The White House said the drawing, "Apotheosis of Franklin," was donated by Georges Wildenstein, New York art historian and dealer.

It was hung on the west wall of the Blue Room.

The drawing will be formally accepted by the Fine Arts Committee and become the property of the government when the committee is legally established. The group was formed, with Mrs. Kennedy's cooperation, to supply the White House with worthy pieces of art.

Fragonard's 18th century drawing is an allegory which shows Benjamin Franklin, crowned with laurel and clad in classic drapery, seated on clouds. As the White House described it, Franklin's "right hand evokes Athena to protect with her shield the seated figure of America; his left hand encourages Mars to chastise the two foreground figures, Avarice and Tyranny."

The drawing measures 18⅞ inches by 14¾ inches.

THE CHRISTIAN SCIENCE MONITOR

Registered in U. S. Patent Office

AN INTERNATIONAL DAILY NEWSPAPER

VOLUME 53 NO. 220 | © 1961, THE CHRISTIAN SCIENCE PUBLISHING SOCIETY All Rights Reserved | BOSTON, MONDAY, AUGUST 14, 1961 | EASTERN EDITION | TWO SECTIONS | TEN CENTS A COPY

Latin America Forges Plans

By Bertram B. Johansson

Latin America News Editor of The Christian Science Monitor

The inter-American economic conference at Punta del Este, Uruguay, moved a giant step toward concord of views this weekend with the help of United States Senate support of long-term foreign aid provisions in President Kennedy's legislation.

Within hours of the time that Maj. Ernesto "Che" Guevara, Cuba's economic chieftan, had, with calculation, asserted that the Latin countries could not depend on continued aid from the United States, the Senate defeated, 56 to 39, an amendment to cut long-term borrowing provision from the bill.

Cuba Shifts Stance

The Senate action was like a tonic at Punta del Este to the United States delegation, according to news reports. The hope is that by Tuesday, an agreement of principles supporting land, tax, education, housing, and other reforms will have been produced by the conference, attended by some 1,500 persons from Latin America and the United States.

Cuba's gambit this week in both Havana and Punta del Este has been to soothe Latin-American countries to the point where they do not see any particularly urgent reason for the Organization of American States to oust Cuba from the Latin community because of its announced predeliction for Communist aid.

In Havana Fidel Castro quickly returned the Pan American World Airways DC-8 hijacked last week by a French artist. He has offered to exchange Eastern's $3,000,000 Electra for a $40,000 Cuban patrol boat sequestered in the United States.

Advice Proffered

At Punta del Este, Major Guevara has allowed that the $20,000,000,000 United States suggested aid for the next decade could help the hemisphere. His appearance there likewise indicates Cuba's apparent desire to stay in the OAS framework, if only for propaganda purposes.

Major Guevara's position notwithstanding Cuba abstained Sunday from going along with the major committee of the conference which approved a United States pledge to pump more than $1,000,000,000 in lightning aid into the continent's most threatened nations.

The committee by a unanimous hand vote accepted President Kennedy's promise of emergency aid. The committee is drafting the "declaration of Punta del Este" to put Mr. Kennedy's Alliance for Progress program into operation.

Even as the delegates deliberated on the draft of resolutions they hope to issue by Tuesday, the United States received some blunt advice from a Latin-American writer for the Fund for the Republic who advocated a less obsessive approach to Premier Castro and a more positive approach to the hemisphere as a whole.

"Brazil's President Quadros was right," said Jaime Benitez, Chancellor of the University of Puerto Rico writing for the Center for the Study of Democratic Institutions of the Fund for the Republic, "when he described Fidel Castro as a 'nuisance,' as someone who was preventing him, as he is preventing all other Latin-American leaders, from getting down to the real business at hand. This is equally true of Castro in relation to the United States."

Change at Stake

The central issue in Latin America, Señor Benítez writes is not Cuba "but how shall the relations between the United States and Latin America be so governed that the whole hemisphere will benefit."

He said the problem of Latin America is not so much Marxism as an ideology of social change. "It is the dangerous possibility that other movements and tendencies — especially those passed in protest against legitimate grievances and those thriving upon and reflecting long-standing weaknesses in Latin-American societies and elites—will be taken over and subverted for the cynical aims of communism."

Señor Benítez said, "Unfortunately, the obsession of the United States with Fidel Castro and Fidelismo has maneuvered it into a clear and dangerous expression of negative thinking, of which the events of the week of April 17 were the logical climax. . . ."

Principles Espoused

Among those principles he listed the following:

First: the United States must state its acceptance of the "right of all governments in the hemisphere to amend their laws so as to do over their systems of land tenure, to overcome injustice, and to give a fair chance to the destitute."

Any limitations on this right, even those represented by the vested interests of the United States, he said "need to be firmly condemned and repudiated."

Second: the United States should offer its help in developing a reservoir of trained Latin American personnel who could give badly needed economic, technical and administrative leadership in their countries.

"Capital and machinery are of minor importance," compared to the need for skilled manpower, Señor Benitez said.

Third: The United States "must be willing to state just how much it is willing to put up with. It must recognize that it cannot do the job for Latin America. Even if it wanted to, it could not do it, for people are not saved, they save themselves."

Berlin Seal Builds Up Pressure

Associated Press Wirephoto via Radio from Berlin

West Berliners Watch East German Soldiers Erect Barbed-Wire Barrier

By J. Emlyn Williams

Central European Correspondent of The Christian Science Monitor

Bonn

The East German Communist regime finally has halted the flow of refugees to West Berlin, but only by a flagrant violation of agreements on the four-power status of the divided city.

That some drastic steps soon would be taken to prevent catastrophic consequences for East Germany's economy and prestige were to be expected after the Volkskammer [People's Chamber] meeting August 11. But it generally was assumed that even the tempestuous and doctrinaire Walter Ulbricht, chairman of the State Council, would have been checked by the Soviet Union before the present step was taken since it meant complete disregard for the agreements which the Soviets themselves had solemnly accepted.

Actually this move was not taken by East Germany alone but on "instructions" of the Warsaw Pact states. They say that the East German Government should post reliable guards around the whole area of West Berlin and close its borders with "democratic" [East] Berlin and exercise effective control.

Pledges Broken

By being a partner to this action the Soviet Union has broken its solemn promises given in agreements in 1945 and again in 1949 after the end of the Berlin blockade. These agreements, made with the United States, Britain, and France as the occupational powers, guaranteed free movement within the four sectors of the city, free choice of working places for all, and free travel between Berlin and East Germany.

Until two hours after midnight Aug. 13, East Germans and East Berliners had moved with few restrictions into and throughout the divided city.

Afterward the border with West Berlin was manned by large contingents of East German troops and Volkspolizei, barriers were erected, and most persons desiring to cross over into the free sectors of the city were turned back.

Public Informed

Later a special announcement over the East German radio informed the public what was happening.

After stating that measures had been taken in agreement with the political council of the Warsaw Pact states, an announcement was added that East Germany for its own interests and "security of the socialist camp" would:

First, introduce along West Berlin's borders controls which were "customary along the frontier of any sovereign state."

Second, require from all East Berliners entering the western sector a special pass to be issued in East Berlin—until West Berlin became a "demilitarized and free city."

Third, "peaceful" West Berliners entering the eastern sector must submit identification papers. What were called "politicians of revenge and agents of West German militarism," however, were forbidden to enter.

Fourth, West Germans still were to be allowed to enter East Berlin according to the procedure introduced Sept. 1, 1960. They will be granted a one-day pass on submitting their personal identification papers.

West Berliners Jeer

In practice the new action already has meant that direct trains on the overhead railroad running between all parts of the city are being interrupted at sector borders.

Some 49,000 border crossers living in East Berlin but working in the western sector have been ordered to report for work at East Berlin labor exchanges.

Only 13 of 80 border crossings between East and West Berlin now are open and these are barricaded and with stronger military and police controls.

The result as far as fleeing refugees is concerned is that whereas on Aug. 12, the day before the border closing, a record number of 4,900 reported at the Marienfelde refugee center in West Berlin, on Sunday the number was only a few hundred.

How fantastic is the situation on the sector borders within Berlin can only be realized when one has seen for oneself. In some places, the border is at a road crossing, or between the two sides of a street, or even, in some cases, the front part of a house or street is in West Berlin and the back is in East Berlin.

Troops at Key Points

It is even more fantastic in some places, than at the Brandenburg Gate and the Potsdamerplatz where Berlin has been hermetically sealed off and where West Berliners generally gather for protest meetings against Communist activities. Sunday night thousands of West Berliners assembled at such border points jeering at the heavily armed and strongly reinforced border police across barbed-wire fences.

In East Berlin, tension certainly is rising and West Berliners expect that strong attempts will be made by some living near the border line to cross over despite strong military and police guards.

That the East German government reckons with the possibilities of dramatic developments is indicated by the announcement a few days ago that Marshal Ivan S. Konev soon will take over command of Soviet forces in East Germany. This obviously is intended as a warning to the East Germans. Strong concentrations of East German troops with tanks are evident at strategic points—not only at the borders but also where there are likely to be protests from East Germans such as the Hennigsdorf Works where the revolt started on June 17, 1953.

Adenauer Confers

What the Western powers now do is the question on everybody's lips, both in West Berlin and in Bonn.

Willy Brandt, Lord Mayor of West Berlin, at a press conference stated that the Berlin Senate, the West German Government, and the Western Allies are all united in the necessity for energetic actions against Soviet measures but he abstained from stating what such measures would be.

In Bonn, Chancellor Konrad Adenauer conferred with the American, British, and French ambassadors here. Chancellor Adenauer, who has interrupted his election campaign, appealed to all Germans to remain firm but calm in the face of the Communist challenge but also to undertake nothing which would make the situation worse.

Hot Chestnut Thrust at West

Red Action Hit

By William H. Stringer

Chief of the Washington News Bureau of The Christian Science Monitor

Washington

East Germany's blockade of the escape hatches to West Berlin has thrust a new, sharp challenge on President Kennedy and his foreign policy advisers.

On the one hand there are humanitarian, legal—and propaganda — motives for vigorously protesting the blockade. Secretary of State Dean Rusk immediately denounced it as a flagrant violation of the four-power German occupation agreement.

On the other hand there is apprehension here lest the angry agitation of East Berliners against the blockade erupt into an open uprising akin to that of June 1953, when German workers braved Soviet tanks barehanded.

Administration officials did not feel, initially at least, that the tensions in Berlin had reached the peak of those of June 16, 1953, the day before the workers' uprising in East Germany.

U.S. Maps Protest

Yet if a serious uprising occurred, Washington's dilemma would be whether to stand by and watch as Soviet troops suppressed the rebellion—as in Hungary—or to intervene and risk open war with the Soviet Union.

President Kennedy, briefed at Hyannis Port over the weekend on Berlin developments, conferred Monday in Washington with the United States Ambassador to the Soviet Union, Llewellyn E. Thompson, Jr., on the meaning of Soviet Premier Nikita Khrushchev's latest speeches and the Soviet decision to blockade the Berlin escape hatches.

A vigorous United States protest was to be lodged with Moscow on the travel blockade. The ambassadors of the United States, Britain, and France held urgent talks on the crisis in an emergency meeting with the West German Government in Bonn, and the three Western commandants conferred in Berlin to assess the seriousness of the public mood there.

The Washington protest by Secretary Rusk took the form of a statement approved by President Kennedy. The Secretary of State said the East German authorities were trying to remedy Communist failures "by the dangerous course of threats against the freedom and safety of West Berlin."

Mr. Rusk made clear there was no indication so far that the travel blockade between the Berlin sectors would be accompanied by a blockade of the West's access routes into the Communist-ringed city. But he declared:

"The refugees are not responding to persuasion or propaganda from the West, but to the failures of communism in East Germany. These failures have created great pressures upon Communist leaders who, in turn, are trying to solve their own problems by the dangerous course of threats against the freedom and safety of West Berlin.

Crowds Kept Back

"Having denied the collective right of self-determination to the peoples of East Germany, Communist authorities are now denying the rights of individuals to elect a world of free choice rather than a world of coercion.

"The pretense that communism desires only peaceful competition is exposed; the refugees, more than half of whom are less than 25 years of age, have 'voted with their feet' on whether communism is the wave of the future."

Actually Washington has been expecting some such clampdown as this, as the tide of refugees from the puppet state reached record proportions. The refugee total for the last "open" day, Aug. 12, was 4,900, surpassing by more than 1,000 the previous one-day peak just before the 1953 revolt.

Washington would doubtless prefer to extract the greatest amount of worldwide notice from this Berlin blockade, without seeing the situation become a formidable "crisis" through open revolt of the East German population. An open revolt, with shooting near or at the former escape gates, could conceivably involve West Berlin police or West German forces—and then the North Atlantic Treaty Organization.

Complex Situation

It was noted initially that both West German police and East German military forces were keeping the milling crowds — on both sides — a hundred yards or so away from the border itself, to minimize incidents.

This border furor has built up, just as indications were multiplying in Washington that the United States was preparing to step up its campaign to tell world opinion that it is the Soviet Union which is threatening world peace by its behavior in Berlin and by its attitudes toward the nuclear test ban, disarmament, and the United Nations. Even so, the Kennedy diplomatic team faces a very complex situation here.

Momentarily, it would seem that the West has been given a big propaganda advantage in the border clampdown by the East Germans. But it is a touchy situation requiring the greatest delicacy in handling.

State of the Nations

Britain and Berlin

By Henry S. Hayward

Chief of the London News Bureau of The Christian Science Monitor

London

Holiday season or not, people here are deeply concerned about the Berlin crisis. It has been easy to make the mistake, as some already have done, of accepting as valid the charges of indifference or softness on the part of the British people.

But the fact is that today the British are asking themselves serious and fundamental questions about the causes of a future Berlin crisis—and what it will mean to all Western alliance members.

"What is this particular crisis all about?" They ask one another. And if you know the British temperament, you may regard this as a pretty clear sign. The British like to talk about their problems before they make up their collective mind and take a stand. As with the recent European Common Market debate, before all the talking subsides, one usually has a good idea what the British intend to do.

✈ ✈ ✈

Evidence that the British now are pondering the Berlin problem is everywhere. The subject creeps into social conversation. It burgeons in newspaper letters, columns, and editorials. In one day's selection in one London paper, a man airs suspicion that Allied policy is too much under the influence of the West Germans, and a mother inveighs against complacency in exposing children and future generations to nuclear war for the sake of West Berlin.

In the same columns, another Briton decries what is termed the "emotional" American attitude toward communism and the British Foreign Secretary's firm declarations. A fourth writer reviews past Communist proposals for reunifying Germany with internationally controlled free elections.

By this process of public discussion, considerable clarification of British thinking is taking place now. Half-forgotten moves that make the picture look different are recalled. Familiar arguments pro or con are knocked down by fresh submissions.

✈ ✈ ✈

Such is the general atmosphere here. But there are plenty of specific queries as well. For instance, many Britons want to know more definitely what the American and British Governments mean by taking "a firm stand." The phrase strikes them as meaningless if the access routes to Berlin are not actually interfered with. For then there seems nothing to stand firm on. And few indeed are ready to risk war only for the nonrecognition of East Germany.

Another point that furrows British brows is whether or not the Western powers really would contemplate taking offensive military action along the access routes with patently inadequate and numerically inferior ground forces. People here believe such spearheads would be stalled by superior Communist formations.

Then the unpleasant choice for the West presumably would be between initiating a nuclear holocaust—or accepting a far more humiliating climbdown from its bluff than recognition of the East German regime would have entailed in the first place. Now at least, Britons say, we can still bargain and negotiate.

✈ ✈ ✈

Yet even this British position needs to be understood clearly. If the United States decided to take the initial offensive against the Communists over, say, East German regulation of the access route, Britons probably would prefer to stand aside—if circumstances gave them any option. But if the first real aggression were on the Communist side, the British probably would be ready to fight. The distinction between these two British attitudes is important.

With so much at stake, people here therefore are striving to get the crisis in perspective. Despite the notorious unreliability of Communist promises, the Soviet leader, it is evident, has made an impact on British intellectuals with his statement that the lawful interests of the Western powers in Berlin would not be infringed upon by him, and that there is no question of a Berlin blockade. There is some tendency on the part of these intellectuals to overlook the fact that Stalin would probably have said exactly the same thing up to an hour before he imposed the Berlin blockade.

But, others challenge, do East German leaders see things the same way? Herr Ulbricht is suspect. Only two months ago, he asserted that after a peace treaty with Moscow, his regime would stem the refugee tide and close the Templehof Airport escape hatch. So few trust him not to interfere on the autobahn, canals, railways, and air corridors, too. Which leaves Britons staring at another piece in the puzzle: Who will speak for the Communists on Berlin—Khrushchev in the Kremlin or Ulbricht in Pankow—after a treaty is signed? That, too, makes a difference.

✈ ✈ ✈

But make no mistake: Britain's instincts are intact today. So are its basic principles. It will be firm and reliable in the fight against wrong—whenever wrong is seen actually to be done.

This crisis, in the opinion of many here, has not yet reached that stage, however. The dim outlines of bargains and concessions are still discernible. So although the Communist negotiators are know to be tricksters, Britons still vastly prefer a Churchillian jaw-jaw to war-war. But Churchill, it is worth remembering, was not the man who went to Munich.

Rockefeller Roused

By R. Stafford Derby

Chief, New York News Bureau, The Christian Science Monitor

New York

Gov. Nelson A. Rockefeller is on the move:

- As Governor he has called an "extraordinary session" of the State Legislature to meet in Albany on Aug. 21 and consider the school situation in New York City.
- As state GOP leader he has journeyed to Gettysburg and talked with former President Eisenhower about politics in general and specifically the New York City mayoralty campaign.

The Rockefeller move on the controversial school mess in this city was strictly in accord with his established reputation for action to meet specific problems by seeking out root troubles and removing them.

Part of Design

The Eisenhower meeting was held as part of the Rockefeller design to enlist every source of strength to bolster the GOP campaign to put Attorney General Louis J. Lefkowitz into City Hall this November. And, from the smiles of those who emerged from the meeting with General Eisenhower, the former President's two visits to this city during the final weeks of the campaign will not be wasted. No dates or plans for an Eisenhower participation were announced, however.

The school situation, which has been confronting New York City for a long time, is a mammoth operation. In 1961, for example, the school budget is $650,000,000 of which the state contributes (through a tax return formula) $225,000,000.

School properties are spotted all over the city. They range from antiquated, unsanitary, over-crowded buildings to the latest in modern school architecture with many of the frills.

In addition to the mountain of problems which arises from the physical operation of the schools, there are the many which are inherent in any system which covers such a variety of educational needs.

These basic situations have been heated to the boiling point by charges and countercharges of maladministration by the New York City Board of Education and the Superintendent of Schools, John J. Theobald. Corruption has been charged in the letting of contracts.

The state and Governor Rockefeller enter into the picture officially as the state has the basic responsibility to provide for the "maintenance and support of a system of free common schools, wherein all the children of this state may be educated."

Action Demanded

This responsibility is delegated to the municipalities, however, and all comes under the scrutiny of the State Commissioner of Education. At present this is Dr. James E. Allen, Jr. He has watched the gyrations in New York, called for prompt action in making the current board clean house or get out, and on Aug. 12 requested the Governor to call a special legislative session.

The Rockefeller role, while it may be interpreted as politically inspired—especially by Mayor Robert F. Wagner (running for re-nomination on a reform ticket)—is expected to produce a long overdue and effective overhaul of the school operation in this city.

African Scholarshippers

By Mary Hornaday

Staff Correspondent of The Christian Science Monitor

New York

Diogo Adel Hippolyte Innocent has arrived here to become one of French-speaking Africa's first students to study in the United States.

Along with four fellow students from his native Dahomey and 188 other American students sponsored by the African scholarship program of American universities, Diogo touched down here Aug. 11 and was immediately whisked away for college orientation.

Largest Numbers

Waiting to greet Diogo, who wore flowing robes and a big cowboy-type hat, were representatives of the Council on Student Travel, the Experiment in International Living, and the African-American Institute—all of which are having a hand in the greatly expanded program.

Last year the scholarship program, with headquarters in Cambridge, Mass., brought 24 Nigerians to the United States on a pilot project. This year the Africans have been awarded full four-year scholarships to nearly 100 universities in 31 states.

Colleges which have accepted the largest number of Africans are Oregon state, 8; Purdue, 7; New York University and the University of California at Berkeley, 6 each; Harvard and Princeton, 5 each, and Howard and UCLA, 4 each.

This year's students, including 11 women, are from 18 countries: Nigeria, South Rhodesia, Tanganyika, Kenya, North Rhodesia, Uganda, Cameroun, Zanzibar, Dahomey, Ivory Coast, Nyasaland, Liberia, Mali, the former French Congo, the former Belgian Congo, Togo, Gabon, and Sierra Leone.

The students were selected in Africa by committees of African and American educators, including Prof. Edward J. Geary of Harvard, Prof. Morton Briggs of Wesleyan, Rixford Snyder, Director of Admissions at Stanford, Helen McCann, Director of Admissions at Barnard, Archibald Macintosh, vice-president of Haverford, and David Henry, Director of the International Students Office at Harvard.

Each participating university provides full tuition scholarships for the African students. The International Co-operation Administration provides room, board, and living expenses. The students' home governments pay for the round-trip travel between Africa and the United States.

Expenses Split Up

The students reported that it is becoming easier for American-trained young folks to get important jobs in the newly independent countries of Africa without taking refresher courses in either Britain or France.

According to an Institute of International Education survey, there were 2,831 African students in the United States in 1960-61, 44.5 per cent more than in the previous year. The largest group is studying social sciences, followed by the natural and physical sciences, humanities, and engineering.

2nd Cl Post Pd at Boston, Mass., and add'l offices

THE CHRISTIAN SCIENCE MONITOR

Registered in U. S. Patent Office

AN INTERNATIONAL DAILY NEWSPAPER

VOLUME 54 NO. 73 | © 1962, THE CHRISTIAN SCIENCE PUBLISHING SOCIETY All Rights Reserved | BOSTON, TUESDAY, FEBRUARY 20, 1962 | NEW ENGLAND EDITION | TWO SECTIONS | BEYOND 30 MILES TEN CENTS | EIGHT CENTS

Sullivan Returns Fire

By Edgar M. Mills
New England Political Editor of The Christian Science Monitor

All-out assaults on the authenticity of the CBS-TV "Biography of a Bookie Joint" and relevancy of vital prosecution evidence concerning alleged contract splitting and conflict of interest appear to constitute the basic strategy of Boston Police Commissioner Leo J. Sullivan in battling against ouster.

Gov. John A. Volpe's ouster proceedings against the commissioner entered the second day today, with John V. Bonner, Mr. Sullivan's counsel, poised for a continued attack against the reliability of the CBS television film showing alleged bookie operations at Swartz's key shop in Boston's Back Bay.

Governor Volpe has charged Commissioner Sullivan with "neglect of duty" on the ground that he failed to investigate the bookie situation portrayed and to take appropriate action, if warranted, against any Boston police officer found to be involved.

Letter From Network

James D. St. Clair, special counsel to the Governor, already has read into the record a letter from Richard S. Salant, president of CBS News, stating flatly that "no paid actors or trick photography" were used in the "Biography of a Bookie Joint." Mr. Salant insisted the program shown nationally, with Boston blacked out, was an accurate portrayal of conditions at the Back Bay key shop.

Under close cross-examination today by Mr. Bonner is Harold Hestnes, legal assistant to Governor Volpe. Mr. Hestnes has testified that he and Mr. St. Clair went to New York in January to confer with Joseph DeFranco, CBS counsel, and Jay McMullen, CBS News producer, concerning authenticity of the "Biography of a Bookie Joint." He testified that the CBS officials assured them of the film's reliability.

Already Mr. Bonner has attacked the testimony as violating the rule concerning hearsay evidence and has attacked the admissibility of letters of CBS officials on the same ground.

Program Attacked

What other methods Mr. Bonner will employ in his attempts to show the CBS film as unworthy and unreliable is not yet known. He has attacked the program as a "falsehood and deliberate fabrication."

As the case progresses it appears likely that once Governor Volpe makes his anticipated ouster recommendation to the Executive Council, the latter will hold its own hearing into the case.

Furthermore, Mr. Bonner obviously has been laying the legal foundation for an appeal to the Supreme Judicial Court on a number of grounds, in the event the council votes Mr. Sullivan's removal. At almost every point Mr. Bonner has reserved his rights when repeatedly overruled by Governor Volpe on his challenges against the relevancy or admissibility of evidence being put in by Mr. St. Clair and his witnesses.

Legality Challenged

In addition, Mr. Bonner has challenged the legality of the hearing before the Governor. He contends that by demanding Mr. Sullivan's resignation in a letter he already had made his decision to oust the commissioner and therefore should convene the Executive Council to act on the ouster. This challenge may serve as the basis of a future court test.

In addition to the "neglect of duty" charge, the Governor is seeking to remove the commissioner on the grounds that he split contracts to avoid public bidding requirement and that he engaged in the insurance business while commissioner.

During the opening day testimony, Mr. St. Clair produced:

- Testimony that Commissioner Sullivan was partner with his brother Charles in an insurance firm which did business with the Police Department during his term as commissioner.
- A series of contracts to show that the commissioner had split projects for flooring and lighting into a series of small contracts to avoid the public bidding requirement on contracts of $2,000 or more.

Evidence Presented

Mr. St. Clair has emphasized that if evidence proves that Mr. Sullivan is guilty of even one of the four charges against him, he can be removed from office.

The afternoon session was devoted partly to presentation of evidence concerning Commissioner Sullivan's partnership in the 18 Tremont Street insurance concern with his brother.

Mr. St. Clair placed Mrs. Marguerite M. Ryan, clerk in the State Department of Banking and Insurance, on the stand to offer records showing that Commissioner Sullivan did not sever conditions with the insurance firm until March 6, 1961. A letter from Commissioner Sullivan was read into the record stating that he was "no longer connected with the firm" as of that date.

Later Sgt. Arthur W. O'Leary of the State Police Bureau of Photography and Fingerprinting, testified that he had photographed the office of Charles G. Sullivan & Co. on Jan. 2, 1962. The photograph showed the names of Charles G. Sullivan and Leo J. Sullivan on the office door.

Payments Approved

Earlier Joseph P. Lally, former City Auditor, testified he had approved payments to the Sullivan company for bonding police officers. He said that when he approved the payments he did not know the commissioner was a partner in the firm.

During the morning session, Joseph T. Leonard, Boston City Auditor, presented 49 contracts for $975 each for the Dorgan Electric Company, for electrical work at police headquarters. Later 43 of the contracts were canceled.

Former City Auditor Lally said he refused to approve payment on the contracts as well as eight to the John J. Curtin Flooring Company, because they violated the law requiring public bidding on similar work costing $2,000 or more.

Fraud Recital On Roads Grows

By a Staff Writer of The Christian Science Monitor

Among major points that emerged in the testimony of witnesses Monday before the House special subcommittee investigating Massachusetts land takings in the federal-aid highway program are:

- **As early at the fall of 1957—only a year after passage of the Interstate Highway Act—Bay State land appraisals were found to be well above the maximum set by a five-man Real Estate Review Board.**
- **Although there was clear indication in Massachusetts that things were very wrong, nothing was done about the problem of the appraisers.**
- **A meeting of Bay State Department of Public Works and United States Bureau of Public Roads officials late in 1957 concluded that land-damage claims reached in court without trial were binding on the bureau, even though the BPR had no control over the land settlements.**

Related Story: Page 2

Big Step to Moon

Atlas Hurls Glenn Into Orbit

Associated Press Wirephoto

Astronaut Glenn Atop Atlas—Accelerating Smoothly to 17,500 M.P.H.

By Robert C. Cowen
Natural Science Editor of The Christian Science Monitor

The breathtaking space ride of Astronaut John H. Glenn Jr. is further evidence that men, however haltingly, are breaking the bonds that have tied them to one planet.

Travel to other stars may be considered out of the question by even the most imaginative space scientists.

But the orbital flight of Colonel Glenn and the earlier orbits of the Soviet cosmonauts have given the scientists more reason to believe the world that men can explore and, to some extent inhabit, can be expanded to include the planets of our own solar system.

Difficulties Clear

On the other hand, the delays and postponements that preceded the Glenn flight have again emphasized how hard is the job of opening this new frontier for mankind.

Men have taken up a daring challenge. But they have also tackled one of the toughest engineering problems humanity has ever faced.

They have undertaken to learn to survive, travel, and work in the alien environment of interplanetary space.

At this writing, Colonel Glenn's flight is off to a successful start. It looks as though it will become one of the many intermediate achievements that, together with many failures and setbacks, will mark the long development path to the know-how and hardware needed to explore the moon and planets.

To succeed in such an effort, the United States must make an expensive effort for many years to come. There will be no guarantee that specific goals, such as manned landing on the moon, will be attained on schedule.

Yet the costly effort has to be sustained consistently through periods of discouragement, as well as in achievement, if it is to succeed at all.

Prestige Committed

The United States has committed its prestige to this kind of effort, at least up to the point of manned exploration of the moon. The public has come to regard this as a race with the Soviets, although the government has avoided committing itself officially to any such competition. The year 1967 is widely discussed as a rough target date.

It is worthwhile reviewing a few basic facts relating to the United States ability to meet this goal in the light of the Glenn flight.

In the first place, the launch is convincing proof, if this is still needed, that American technology has not sagged in the space field.

Project Mercury like the Vanguard satellite project before it, is a marginal program in that technology is being pushed to the utmost.

Many aspects of the project would have been easier technologically if more powerful rockets had been available. As it was, every item in the payload had to more than pay its way in terms of performance.

It is a tribute to the engineers and designers that, in spite of stringent weight limitations, they have produced a rocket-capsule combination in which a man can safely ride into space and return.

At the same time, the Mercury vehicle is no match for the Soviet Vostoks.

No amount of wishful skepticism of Soviet abilities will obviate the fact that the Soviets are also excellent in space technology and superb in manned space flight. Moreover, they started earlier with the development of big rockets.

Given engineering excellence on both sides, it was inevitable that the Soviets should have the present edge in space.

Among other things, their rockets have enabled them to give their cosmonauts a vehicle that can sustain a man in orbit for over a week and can come down on sea or land as desired.

To put it in other terms, the Soviet manned space flight program has not been a technological marginal effort. This has enabled them to be first with big satellites and first with manned orbital flight. There is a good possibility it will also enable them to be first to the moon.

If one thinks in terms of the 1967 target date, the United States moon program is again a marginal effort.

The rockets that will be available by that time will just barely have enough power to land a moon expedition if technology is pushed to the utmost. The really adequate rockets planned for the program won't be available until several years later, perhaps not before the early 1970's.

All of this means that, if the United States is racing the Soviets to the moon, it will take a very determined effort to win. Even if one thinks of space exploration with no sense of competition, the United States still faces a very difficult engineering problem if it is to put men on the moon within this decade.

Thus, as a spectacular and, for Americans, the unprecedented adventure, Colonel Glenn's flight is the culmination of a difficult and ingenious engineering program. But it is also the prologue to a longer and much more demanding national effort if the great promise of that flight is to be realized.

By Neal Stanford
Staff Correspondent of The Christian Science Monitor

Cape Canaveral, Fla.

Astronaut Glenn took the 9:47 a.m. daring, nonstop flight into space today, intensifying the space race and becoming the first American to orbit the earth.

This was a day for the history books. Everything combined to make this a perfect orbital shot—the weather and the Cape.

Before sunrise the sky was overcast, but it cleared up shortly thereafter. Recovery forces in the Atlantic reported good weather and calm seas; and the Atlas booster, the Mercury space vehicle, and the pilot John H. Glenn Jr., were "go" from about 6 this morning.

There were a number of minor mechanical troubles that developed with the Atlas. These were quickly rectified. Shortly after 9 a.m. there was no doubt here but that Colonel Glenn would be on his way.

Tension Stepped Up

As the countdown proceded one could clearly notice the increased tension and excitement on the Cape among newsmen and space officials. They had waited out 10 postponements of this shot before watching the 93-foot rocket and spaceship blast off.

The first words relayed from Colonel Glenn were "Zero G and I feel fine and the view is tremendous."

Then he reported seeing a large cloud pattern. "It's a beautiful sight," he commented.

Colonel Glenn subsequently reported that, after more than an hour of weightless flight, he had experienced no ill effects.

Within minutes after the Atlas blasted off Pad 14, in a cloud of smoke and flame, Colonel Glenn was reporting everything "go" within the capsule. All of the telemetry equipment was functioning perfectly.

The booster engine dropped off on schedule. The 16-foot escape tower was jettisoned after the rocket had risen 40 miles.

When it reached about 100 miles, out of the earth's atmosphere, the Atlas dropped off, and Colonel Glenn was on his way. He traveled at a speed of 17,500 miles an hour, encircling the globe at between 100 and 150 miles altitude.

He reported no particular stress during his thrust out of the atmosphere where he was subjected to more than 7½ G's (7½ times the force of gravity).

This was a triumphant moment for Colonel Glenn, for the nation, and also for the thousands of space scientists and engineers and others who had planned and worked and lived for this moment.

Three Orbits Possible

At the speed at which Colonel Glenn is encircling the earth, he is going to record a full day and night within 90 minutes, which means the shortest day and the shortest night ever chalked up by an American.

Astronaut Glenn took off early enough in the morning so that it is still possible for him to make three orbits of the earth, if officials find everything going well.

Had the shot been delayed beyond 12:30, they could not have done more than one orbit as they want to keep three hours of daylight in the recovery areas to pick him up and carry him to Bermuda for a well-deserved rest.

The two most critical moments in an orbital flight are those of liftoff and of re-entry into the earth's atmosphere. At both there are numerous factors that make it dangerous for a pilot.

Extra Measures Taken

There is the gravity pull of 7 to 12 Gs. There is the heat generated as the craft hurtles toward the earth, reaching 3,000 degrees Farhenheit. And there is the matter of recovering the spacecraft and pilot after he has landed in the ocean.

Pilot Glenn's voice is being clearly heard and picked up as he reports on his own condition, the various instruments in his cabin, and what he is seeing through his telescope.

He is now entirely on his own—alone—although in constant touch with the ground and the tracking centers below. Either he himself, or those in the control center, can bring him down after one, two, or three orbits, as desired.

Another Atlas and another Mercury spacecraft are already here on the Cape. They will be assembled in short order. This means that even before they learn the full results and lessons of the Glenn flight, they will start preparing and assembling the next one.

Related stories: Page 22

Glenn Sees Lights Of Perth, Australia

By a Staff Writer of The Christian Science Monitor

Astronaut John H. Glenn Jr. reported that he could see the lights in Perth, Australia, on his first orbit.

The citizens of the town had earlier announced that they would turn on all their lights in the hope that Colonel Glenn would see them.

The astronaut responded with an official "thank you" from more than 100 miles overhead.

State of the Nations

At the Plimsoll Line

By Joseph C. Harsch
Special Correspondent of The Christian Science Monitor

London

Prof. Walt W. Rostow of the State Department planning staff is in Paris trying to persuade NATO that the Washington cause against Cuban Premier Fidel Castro is a common cause of the Western Alliance.

It will be fascinating to see how he makes out.

This is one of the toughest assignments President Kennedy has yet handed one of his traveling salesmen headed for friendly countries.

Regrettable or otherwise, the plain fact is that United States's European allies feel themselves massively unengaged in the issue against Señor Castro.

In Washington eyes he may be the beachhead of communism in the Americas, but in European eyes he looks more like a rather entertaining Robin Hood stealing from the rich to give to his own poor. They simply do not take him seriously as a beachhead.

Dr. Rostow's highest hurdle in trying to bring around the Allies is the disparity in size and power of Cuba and the United States. It frequently was said in Washington at the time of Sir Anthony Eden's Suez venture that he made the mistake of equating President Nasser of Egypt with Adolf Hitler. It is said in Western European capitals these days that one cannot seriously equate Fidel Castro with Joseph Stalin.

Another hurdle is that to Europeans there is an unavoidable appearance of similarity between United States's Cuban problem and, let us say, various European colonial problems. Cuba is regarded as something like a former American colony and the United States's Cuban problem to be precisely the same decolonialization issue which has so troubled France in Algeria, Belgium in the Congo, Portugal in Goa and Angola, and Britain in most of Africa.

Had Washington sided resolutely with its military allies against their rebelling colonies, then the Allies would feel obligated, in turn, to help Washington against Señor Castro. But Washington has taken a less than totally sympathetic attitude toward the occasional vestiges of colonial inclination in Britain, France, Belgium, and the more than vestiges in Portugal. The inevitable sequel is an inclination in the allied countries to feel some sympathy toward what they see as a rebelling American colony.

Dr. Rostow has taken his mission to Paris. It was prudent of him not to plan to come to London. In London he would find the Labor Party strongly in favor of anticolonialism but regarding Cuba as being quite as entitled to freedom from Washington influence as any other colony. British Tories, moreover, are half-inclined to say "Had you been willing to help us we might be willing to help you get back Cuba." Feeling in London is particularly sensitive on any colonial issue at the moment because of Washington pressure to speed the pace of independence for such colonies as Kenya. The British Government believes that given 25 years it could prepare any colony for self-government. It would take a chance, if necessary, on 10 years. But it regards anything less than 10 years for an orderly transition as extremely hazardous.

Washington, however, strikes some Britons as pressing for the fastest possible release of all important remaining British colonies.

This is simply not a time when Dr. Rostow could expect much sympathy in London or Paris for his case against Señor Castro—particularly when he is asking the allies to join in a trade boycott of Cuba.

For a good 12 months now a new high has been achieved in smooth meshing of Washington and London policies. On Berlin, disarmament, and summitry, London has ceased to make news simply because its official line is identical with Washington's. There hasn't been room for a razor blade between the two capitals.

Foreign Secretary Lord Home has done this at a price. He has had trouble with right-wing Tories while Labor Party leader Hugh Gaitskell has had equal trouble holding the Labor Party left.

The Home-Gaitskell combination can hold the rebels in line on Berlin disarmament and summitry. But it would be quite beyond their capacity to hold them on boycotting Cuba.

To load that project on the ship of Anglo-American harmony would be loading it beyond the Plimsoll line.

Dr. Rostow is a most persuasive person. But his chances of selling a Cuban boycott in London are precisely as good as would be London's chance of selling an abandonment of Formosa in Washington.

Kennedy Asks Federal Pay Reform

By the Associated Press

Washington

President Kennedy has urged Congress to provide a $1,000,000,000 pay raise over three years for the government's white-collar workers. The aim, he said, to put federal pay on a par with that outside so that competent people can afford to work for Uncle Sam.

The President said in a special message Tuesday that he was proposing "federal pay reform, not simply a federal pay raise."

For the whole field of white-collar workers, the increase would amount to 10 per cent of the present $10,000,000,000 annual payroll. But for individuals, the raises would range from 3.7 per cent to about 33 per cent for the three-year period. The first increase would come Jan. 1.

New Approach

Mr. Kennedy said he is proposing a wholly new, "common sense" approach to the problem of putting federal salaries on a basis comparable to those in non-federal service.

This would be done for all but the highest-level officials. And for them, Mr. Kennedy said, "the most vital single element" in the proposal is pay adjustments for top executive and professional positions. Many of these top-rank employees, he said, are being drawn away by higher pay outside. Low government wages endanger national security, said Mr. Kennedy.

Everyone to Benefit

The pay reform would apply to 1,640,000 employees spread throughout the world. It would not affect approximately 660,000 blue-collar workers in skilled trades and crafts who work at such places as navy yards and arsenals.

Everybody in the white-collar category would get some sort of raise. For the lowest grade, GS-1, the entrance salary of $3,185 would go up to $3,225 next Jan. 1, to $3,265 a year later, and to $3,305 in the third step.

The biggest group in any one class is the 168,000 workers in GS-4. These are mainly clerical workers—file clerks, stenographers, or clerk typists. The top salary in this grade would reach $5,475 at the end of the three-year salary reform program compared with a present peak of $4,985.

A recent college graduate without experience would start in at grade 5 at $4,345 under present schedules. Under the new plan he would enter federal service at $4,565 as of next year. The figure would build to $4,690 by Jan. 1, 1965. At this point the top salary for his grade would be $6,130.

Take a man with a doctor's degree as a physicist with a year or two working experience. Under the present pay scale he would start in at $9,380 a year. His top pay could reach $12,215 in his grade, GS-12. Under the Kennedy proposal, this grade would be in for a raise of about 16 per cent over the three-year period. By Jan. 1, 1965, the starting pay would be $10,270 and the maximum in the grade would be $13,375.

The administration proposal calls for about a 33 per cent salary increase for the present top grade, GS-18, from $18,500 to $24,500.

The way things would work out, some top career officials would get more pay than their bosses—the members of the Cabinet and the sub-Cabinet. But Mr. Kennedy said the executive branch is ready to co-operate with Congress "in determining what executive and congressional pay scales would be appropriate following the terms of the present incumbent."

Cabinet salaries customarily are at the level of congressional salaries—now $25,000 a year.

Comparisons Given

Mr. Kennedy said that the federal employee's top salary, if he stays to reach it, will be less than half that of his counterpart in private enterprise.

Even some state and local governments, the chief executive said, do better by their top employees than Uncle Sam does. A Cabinet member, he said, now draws a smaller pay check than a head of a department in the New York State government and "less than the average salary paid to the superintendents of schools in cities over 500,000 population."

He said the highest paid federal employees under the civil-service classification act—they get $20,315 a year—would receive more pay if they worked in the state career service in Georgia, Ohio, New York, Pennsylvania, Illinois, Michigan, or California—or for the cities of St. Louis, Denver, Detroit, San Francisco, Los Angeles, or Philadelphia.

Kennedy Seeks Debt-Ceiling Hike

The World's Day

Reg. U.S. Pat. Off.

Washington: House Expected to Approve Bid

The House of Representatives in Washington was expected Tuesday to approve by a wide margin President Kennedy's request for a $2,000,000 000 increase in the temporary national debt ceiling—raising it to $300,000,000,000.

Boston: Huge Income Tax Evasion Charged

Several hundred million dollars in taxes are evaded annually on the profits organized crime makes on its illicit enterprises: gambling, prostitution, narcotics peddling, and high-jacking, Elliot L. Richardson, former United States Attorney from Massachusetts told the Kiwanis Club.

Europe: West German Export Surplus Drops

A sharp drop in foreign sales last month caused West Germany's export surplus to nose dive, the Federal Bureau of Statistics reported Tuesday in Wiesbaden, West Germany.

National: N.Y. Trio Vie for Vacant House Seat

Two Democrats and a Republican contested Tuesday in New York for a vacant seat in the House of Representatives. Benjamin S. Rosenthal, one of the Democrats, has the backing of President Kennedy, Mayor Robert F. Wagner, and the Liberal Party in his bid for the Sixth District seat.

Weather: Fair Tonight and Wednesday [Page 2]

Arts, Entertainment: Page 7. Radio, FM: Page 21. TV: Page 10

THE CHRISTIAN SCIENCE MONITOR

Registered in U. S. Patent Office

AN INTERNATIONAL DAILY NEWSPAPER

VOLUME 54 NO. 281 | BOSTON, THURSDAY, OCTOBER 25, 1962 | R | NEW ENGLAND EDITION | TWO SECTIONS | BEYOND 30 MILES TEN CENTS | EIGHT CENTS

© 1962, THE CHRISTIAN SCIENCE PUBLISHING SOCIETY All Rights Reserved

Cuba Quarantine Holds; Some Ships Shift Course

By the Associated Press

New York

A congressman said today a regional briefing session by the State Department was told that a Russian tanker bound for Cuba had been intercepted but allowed to proceed earlier today.

The congressman told newsmen the briefing session was told the tanker's captain had furnished information to the Navy that he had petroleum aboard and was allowed to proceed.

By Robert R. Brunn

Staff Correspondent of The Christian Science Monitor

Washington

The stealthy, knifelike pre-Pearl Harbor-type tactic of the Soviet thrust in Cuba is being blocked so far by an unyielding limited United States action.

In a somber Washington the United States moves with extreme caution. At this writing six Soviet ships have changed course while a Polish ship farther out leads others toward quarantined waters.

Having chosen its own time and place in which to check Soviet aggression, the United States may well have upset a Communist timetable tied to Berlin.

More Talk Seen

Now, informed sources believe Premier Nikita S. Khrushchev is trying to fog up the atmosphere with a screen of words, and interesting talk about a summit talk while, it is speculated, he and the Presidium ponder further steps.

[The United States Navy maintained an apparently air-tight arms blockade of Cuba today amid indications the Russians could be giving ground, at least temporarily, by diverting some of their Cuba-bound 25 cargo ships, the Associated Press reported.

[Word that some of the oncoming Russian ships had changed course prompted a feeling that perhaps munitions-laden vessels were turning away while others bearing food or other nonprohibited cargo might be steaming on toward Cuba.

Submarines Warned

[Meanwhile, the United States took formal steps to flush any unidentified submarines that might be detected in the quarantine area.

[Through the State Department, it notified other governments that American forces contacting an unidentified submarine will drop four or five "harmless explosive sound signals."

[Along with these signals, the Navy craft may send out an international code signal meaning "rise to the surface."

[If a submarine did not rise as ordered, it probably would be depth charged. But if it did surface it would be boarded and searched.]

What follows is a summation from informed sources of the principal factors and possible repercussions flowing out from the United States decision to react massively to the Soviet power drive:

● **United Nations moratorium.** Secretary-General U Thant's proposal for a two- or three-week moratorium with a suspension of the quarantine is considered unacceptable by the United States in its present form.

No Guarantee Yet

No guarantee against further delivery of arms to Cuba is provided in the plan to stop the Soviet military build-up. On-the-spot UN inspection would be necessary to be sure the missile sites are being dismantled or, at a minimum, work is stopped.

● **Summit talks.** To move rapidly on the apparent Khrushchev proposal for talks made in a telegram to Bertrand Russell would be unwise.

First the question of the approaching ships must be eliminated.

'Peace Pose' Resumed

Next, the United States is not exactly in a mood for a Khrushchev - Kennedy meeting with 1,000- and 2,500-mile range missiles pointed at the United States, possibly with nuclear warheads available.

The Soviet words are taking the familiar Soviet "peace pose." Premier Khrushchev spoke of a summit talk when the United States landed troops in Lebanon in 1958 but it never took place.

Mr. Khrushchev said "take no rash decisions. . . . Avert a war"—the Soviet Union will "not let itself be provoked." This message may have taken some of the edge off the tension but it has not changed the basic problem of missiles in Cuba.

A Khrushchev note to President Kennedy handed to Ambassador Foy Kohler, it is understood, did not contain any direct proposal for a summit meeting.

Riposte Awaited

● **Soviet tactics.** Apart from the Communist-bloc ships approach, any action by the Soviets in the form of a riposte to counter the quarantine effect may come rather slowly.

Premier Khrushchev is capable of a good deal of caution if brought up short. But to protect his political position is a tough response inescapable?

A Soviet response around its power periphery is considered likely, but the timing of any move is, of course, uncertain. Berlin still is given priority as a major possibility.

Washington knows that the Soviet Union completely understands there is little "give" in the Western response plan.

By Russell H. Lenz, Chief Cartographer

Cuba Shipping Routes and Missile Sites

Eight to 10 missile bases—each with about four rocket launchers—are located near four Cuban cities, Assistant Secretary of Defense Arthur Sylvester has disclosed. The cities are: (1) San Cristobal, (2) Guanajay, (3) Sagua La Grande, and (4) Remedios. Dotted lines show shipping lanes.

Ifs Answered

Why Crisis Flared Up

By Richard L. Strout

Staff Correspondent of The Christian Science Monitor

Washington

Reporters are asking these questions and receiving these replies from officials in the Cuban crisis:

● **Did President Kennedy want a crisis?**

No. Again and again he told press conferences he did not believe that Soviet arms build-up in Cuba constituted "significant offensive capability" (Sept. 4) or "a serious threat" (Sept. 13). Republicans repeatedly attacked lack of action, Richard M. Nixon calling for "a quarantine" (Sept. 18) and Sen. Kenneth B. Keating (R) of New York charging (Oct. 14) he had evidence of offensive missiles. Mr. Kennedy (Indianapolis, Oct. 13) condemned "self-appointed generals and admirals."

● **Why did Mr. Kennedy suddenly alter his position?**

Aerial photos reached him, Oct. 16, indicating that in addition to surface-to-air missile sites (range around 30 miles, termed "defensive") bigger "offensive" installations were being set up. Corroborative pictures came quickly, interrupting his political trip Saturday, Oct. 20. A conclusive briefing came next day.

● **Can this evidence really be trusted?**

Blown-up photographs of extraordinary detail leave no doubt with military technicians. They are supported by espionage and refugee information. The Soviets do not deny the presence of big missiles; merely argue they are "defensive."

● **What is the definition of "offensive"?**

This is a vague term. Washington defines it substantially as something beyond that needed to protect a coast against invasion and big enough in this case to hit the United States or Latin-American mainland. Long-range missiles being set up in Cuba could shoot more than 2,000 miles.

● **Are the missile bases alone the cause of the United States "quarantine"?**

No. There is a deeper issue. Officials argue Moscow knew United States aerial photography would disclose the big missile sites, built despite protestations by Soviet Foreign Minister Andrei A. Gromyko to Mr. Kennedy Oct. 18 and others that only "defensive" arms were involved. Moscow, it is argued, tested and challenged American determination, in conjunction with Soviet Premier Nikita S. Khrushchev's repeated assertion to visitors that the United States was "soft" and would not react in Cuba or Berlin.

● **Suppose the United States had not reacted?**

If Washington had remained passive, the United States's "credibility," in the language of the "balance of terror" cold war, would have been long in doubt.

● **Isn't this just another passage in the continuing struggle?**

No, this appears to go deeper; it is about the first naked Kennedy-Khrushchev confrontation of wills in what looks like a showdown.

● **In diplomacy it is good policy to leave a way out for an adversary to save face; has the United States done that?**

Officials say planning has covered this point, but they are close-lipped about possibilities of negotiation. It won't include a Berlin swap in any event, they maintain.

● **Is the United States alone?**

No. There is the unprecedented, 19-0 approval (Uruguay abstained) of an American-sponsored resolution by the Organization of American States calling for use of force if necessary to prevent a Cuban arms build-up. In addition, NATO allies of the United States, though not consulted before Washington's unilateral action, appear to be going along.

● **If it is wrong for the Soviet Union to mount long-range missiles in Cuba, why isn't it wrong for the United States to have them in Turkey and Italy?**

Washington's answer is that (A) American bases were not mounted surreptitiously; (B) American bases were set up only after Moscow threatened Western Europe with nuclear attack. At no time has the United States threatened Cuba with nuclear attack.

● **Why doesn't the United States invade Cuba?**

Because its goals are limited ones, directed at nuclear offensive weapons, so a limited quarantine has been established.

● **Isn't "quarantine" another name for war?**

International law is ambiguous. The United States wants to avoid a shooting war if it can, but it leaves no doubt it will shoot if necessary to stop vessels carrying a prescribed list of offensive weapons.

● **Can't airplanes bring in such weapons?**

Some heavy parts need vessel transportation.

● **Is a United States troop invasion being planned?**

Troops are being deployed. It might be an invasion if other action—by the UN, by the OAS, or by neutrals—does not achieve removal of long-range missile capabilities.

● **How is Moscow's initial reaction appraised?**

Reaction is "relatively mild—for Moscow," comments one official. However, this was before any actual contact between Soviet supply ships and the United States Navy.

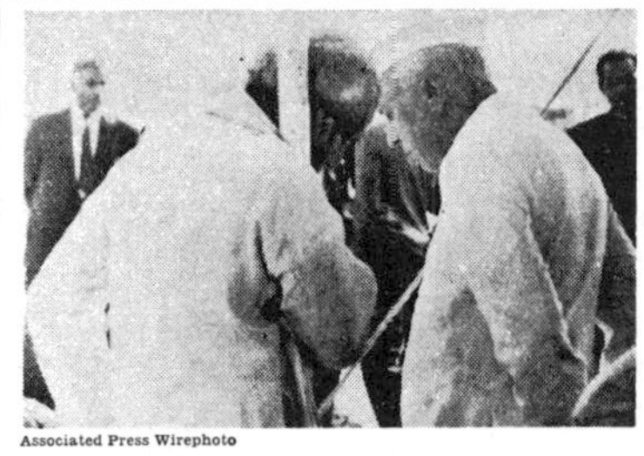

Associated Press Wirephoto

Tent-Pole Conference in India

Indian Defense Minister V. K. Krishna Menon drapes arm around tent pole as he and Prime Minister Jawaharlal Nehru presumably discuss India's border conflict with Communist China. They were bidding good-by to a Romanian delegation.

Cuban Missile Control Seen Peril

By Bertram B. Johansson

Latin America Editor of The Christian Science Monitor

Nongovernmental submarine sources have stated the Soviet Union has had an estimated 45 submarines off the Atlantic coastline in past weeks.

Some of them are capable at least of delivering 300-to-400-mile and longer range missiles.

If this is so, why has so much attention suddenly been riveted on missile bases in Cuba?

And, if the stated United States objective in Cuba is to dismantle Soviet missiles there, how is this to be accomplished?

These and a number of other strategic questions are concerning analysts of the Soviet military build-up in Cuba as the protagonists spar for time and advantage.

Major Risk

It is possible that the answer to the first question is:

Not just that land bases are more stable.

Not just that mobile launching pads can be set up in only a few days.

Not just that a demarcation line simply had to be drawn by the United States against further Soviet "salami slicing," upsetting of the balance of power, and potential political blackmail in future negotiations.

But also that the Kennedy administration, quite aware of Soviet submarine activity, could not possibly risk accidental touch-off of panic buttons by an anger-possessed Castro government which might not be as responsible about missiles as the Soviet Union which understands their capability.

The answer to the second question: How are Soviet missiles in Cuba to be dismantled? is acknowledgedly more complicated.

The answers would seem to lie in the direction of diplomacy, increased blockade pressures, or invasion.

Thus far, the United States has invoked an air- and sea-going quarantine on transport of strategic "offensive" weapons into Cuba.

'Petroleum Attrition'

But Cuba already has refused any possible inspection of missile sites, let alone dismantling of them. The Soviet Union has not in any of its statements at the United Nations and from Moscow even acknowledged its missiles are in Cuba, which is the main focus of Mr. Kennedy's attention, insisting they are defensive only.

Though blockade of petroleum imports has been mentioned, and then taken out of current consideration by Washington officials, it still exists as a possibility that "petroleum attrition" could be the next step.

Cuba depends completely on imported petroleum, all of which it now receives from the Soviet bloc.

Dependent on Oil

Cuba depends almost entirely on petroleum for generation of electricity, since it has no coal resources. Cut-off of petroleum imports probably could bring Cuba to a complete standstill within a month, in order to force compliance with the Kennedy missile dismantling request.

What next, if compliance were still refused?

There could be internal rebellions, which are not thought very possible at this stage.

Then? United States forces might be ordered to penetrate Cuba, militarily, to enforce the dismantling. The Soviet Union may, in fact, want to force such an eventuality, for propaganda and face-saving purposes.

Armored Cars Extended

By Emilie Tavel

Staff Writer of The Christian Science Monitor

The Federal Reserve Bank of Boston, hit by the $1,551,277 Aug. 14 United States mail truck robbery, is extending as fast as possible its own armored car service from a 65-mile radius of Boston to include "greater parts" of Massachusetts, Connecticut, Rhode Island, as far north as Bangor, Maine, and ultimately all of New England.

George H. Ellis, president, made the announcement in Boston today at the annual meeting of the Federal Reserve Bank's 254 commercial bank members in New England.

Mr. Ellis said this action is in direct response to the Aug. 31 request of Postmaster General J. Edward Day for assistance in reducing the volume of currency shipped by banks via registered mail.

Service Widened

His announcement came as spectacular developments are occurring in the Cape Cod robbery climaxing nine weeks of intensive investigation by postal inspectors and other agents.

Mr. Ellis told bankers that at the time of the highway stickup, biggest cash robbery in United States history, the Federal Reserve Bank provided currency and coin service by armored car to 259 banking offices within about a 65-mile radius of Boston.

"On Oct. 16," he said, "an additional run was inaugurated to service 20 additional banking offices." As fast as arrangements can be made, he said, the service will be extended. "When completed," he said, it "will include virtually all of the New England points having banks which are large shippers of currency."

Mr. Ellis's comments were a follow-up to his Oct. 16 letter to all member banks. In it he pointed out that the Post Office Department has set a limit on the maximum amount of currency it will accept for registered mail at one time.

Banks Prodded

He said, however, that "very few banks" will be affected by this limitation, although it may mean splitting cash shipments and their arrival at different times of day or different days of the week.

He urged all banks reached by the Federal Reserve System's armored-car service to limit their shipments to this mode of transportation.

Studies, he said, reveal that shipments of cash from banks are often offset shortly afterward by orders for cash. To reduce such duplicating shipments, Mr. Ellis asked member banks to plan ahead and increase their holdings to meet immediate needs.

Text of affidavit leading to search of North Weymouth, Mass., home: Page 10.

U Thant Calls for Cooling Off

By William R. Frye

United Nations Correspondent of The Christian Science Monitor

United Nations, N.Y.

United Nations Acting Secretary-General U Thant has attempted to point a way out of the perilous Cuba crisis.

His effort met with some skepticism in American circles but with considerable praise elsewhere in the free world. The Communist reaction was not known at this writing.

It was possible, however, that U Thant's proposals would run into a rejection from the United States, the Soviet Union, and Cuba, the three powers primarily concerned.

The United States already had indicated it would not halt the arms blockade on the basis of a neutral-nation appeal. And both the Soviet Union and Cuba have made it plain they intend to maintain the arms build-up in Premier Castro's island.

Urgent Appeal Made

The Secretary-General suggested in the 11-nation UN Security Council Wednesday that a two- to three-week cooling-off period be agreed upon during which:

1. The American blockade would be suspended.
2. Arms shipments to Cuba would be halted.
3. Further construction of missile bases in Cuba would be barred.
4. The United States, the Soviet Union, and Cuba would sit down with him and attempt to hammer out a solution.

U Thant earlier appealed "urgently" to President Kennedy and Premier Nikita S. Khrushchev to "refrain from any action which may aggravate the situation and bring with it the risk of war."

Some 50 nonaligned countries had asked him to make this appeal. They followed through by proposing formally that the Security Council direct U Thant to confer with "the parties."

The phrase "the parties" is used to mean Washington, Moscow, and Havana. The United States is reluctant to negotiate with Cuba, though it has offered to talk with the Soviet Union.

Associated Press Wirephoto

U Thant

Before UN Security Council

Scrutinizing the "Thant plan," Western diplomats said it would not provide adequate assurance against the introduction of further weapons into Cuba. How, it was asked, would Soviet assurances on this point be verified?

The same question was asked about Cuban missile-site construction. Intelligence surveillance could help, it was acknowledged; but the United States nevertheless fears secret activity. Once built, there would be little short of bombing or invasion that could be done about new sites.

Criticism Voiced

Critics of American policy ask, however, how a "quarantine" of Cuba applying only to the import of further offensive weapons could affect installations already in place. There is doubt that a partial blockade can achieve the stated purpose of forcing their withdrawal.

Britain, France, Nationalist China, Venezuela, and Chile all supported the United States in the council Wednesday.

Ghana and the United Arab Republic were critical of the blockade.

U Thant also implied criticism of Washington. He said "some of the measures" which had been taken and the UN had been asked to approve were "very unusual, and I might say even extraordinary except in wartime."

Boston Considers Low-Rent Housing

By George B. Merry

Staff Writer of The Christian Science Monitor

What could be an important partial solution to one of the Boston urban renewal program's most perplexing problems—the provision of new low-rent relocation housing—is now under consideration.

The Boston Redevelopment Authority is expected to take action at its next meeting, Nov. 14, on a proposal for expansion of the Washington Park renewal project area to provide sites for up to 980 new dwellings.

If approved, the present 796,781-acre project boundary would be extended across Washington Street in two places near the Egleston Square and Dudley Street Metropolitan Transit Authority stations.

Reasonable Rates

And if carefully timed and carried out successfully enough, new homes at reasonable rentals within the project area would be available when the first families are displaced by demolition in other sections of the huge Washington Park tract.

This would do much to stem the tide of criticism directed at Boston Redevelopment Administrator Edward J. Logue, Mayor John F. Collins, and the redevelopment authority, for the lack of new relocation housing for persons in low-income brackets within the city.

Other Sites Weighed

Negotiations are already under way for the acquisition of the 16.4-acre property of the Academy of Notre Dame on Washington Street between Townsend Street and Codman Hill. The academy is relocating in Hingham, Mass.

Mr. Logue told the authority that two other sites—the 8.4-acre New England Hospital property, on Dimmock Street in this same area, and eight acres used by the MTA for housing buses at Washington and Bartlett Streets—may later become available.

With some 575 families scheduled to be displaced by the early phases of the Washington Park project, it is hoped that some, if not all, of the additional land can be obtained and used for relocation housing. The clearance of existing buildings on the proposed expansion area would not involve the moving of any families.

State of the Nations

Cuba, the Root of the Issue

By Joseph C. Harsch

Special Correspondent of The Christian Science Monitor

London

There will for some time to come be a massive output of involved argumentation over the rights and wrongs of who has done what over Cuba. It would be well for all of us to be very clear about what lies at the root of the matter.

The root of the matter is that the Soviet Union made a move on the chessboard of power which, if unchecked, would have produced a sudden and important change in the balance of military power in the world. It would have upset the status quo.

Nothing in the relations of great-power states is so disturbing to general tranquillity and so dangerous to the peace as a sudden change in the balance of military power.

⁂

It is never power in familiar, accepted and contained relationship which causes the great moments of danger to the peace. It's the sudden change in the power status of one or another which tempts one to strike for consolidation of a new advantage or another to prevent the loss of position.

Foreign Secretary Lord Home expressed this point in the most relevant passage in the British Government's comment on the affair which reads:

". . . Guilty of deliberately opening up a new area of instability."

In the game of power the most dangerous possible deed is precisely to "open up a new area of instability."

From the Castro revolution in Cuba through Sept. 16 the relationship between Cuba and the Soviet Union was galling to American pride, unsettling to American concepts of the Monroe Doctrine, and potentially a Communist base in the Western Hemisphere. It did not involve any major change in the world balance of military power.

On or about Oct. 13, both medium and intermediate-range ballistic missile sites were discovered in advance stages of completion. For two reasons this triggered Washington reaction.

First, it exposed an extraordinary Soviet capacity for quick deployment of nuclear striking capacity.

Second, the number of launching pads and missiles added up to a startling fact. Within a matter of weeks, unless something were done by Washington, Moscow would very nearly double its capacity to hit targets in the United States with nuclear weapons.

It is irrelevant and a waste of time to discuss such matters either in ethical or legal terms. Ethics and law have no more to do with the growth or decline of national power than with the growth or decline of the wealth or property holdings of an individual. It's a fact that when one power reaches for a doubling of its capacity to injure another, that other power either takes defensive action or submits to a drastic reduction in its power position in the world.

Washington faced precisely that choice. Within a matter of days—since several of the bases already were operational — either Washington would move to choke off this increase of Soviet nuclear capacity against the United States or have to face the consequences. These would have been a loss of capacity to influence world events or counterbalancing action which would have increased massively the size and cost of the American military establishment. It is uncertain whether anything could have fully balanced off the increment in Soviet striking capacity against the United States.

⁂

To recapitulate, we have witnessed a suddenly discovered attempt by the Soviet Union to seize a substantial increase in its military capacity against the United States. We have seen Washington take sudden emergency action to avert the change in the balance of power.

The immediate question is how Moscow will react to the thwarting of a power move which was well advanced and almost within completion. The Moscow communiqué on the second day seemed to threaten nothing more specific than argument and noise in the United Nations Security Council.

China Reds Capture Town in India

The World's Day

Reg. U.S. Pat. Off.

Asia: Towang Taken by Advancing Troops

Communist Chinese troops have taken Towang, a monastery and administrative center in northeast India near Bhutan. It is the first capture of an Indian civilian town by the Chinese Communists. [Story: Page 12.]

Washington: Report on Military Censorship

Senate investigators reported today that they found ineptness and capriciousness in censorship of military speeches but no evidence of appeasement. The special Armed Services Subcommittee added that while the troop information program can be improved, they did not find any evidence that "it is approached with a 'softness on communism' attitude or policy."

Bay State: Peabody Campaigns Atop 'Wagon'

Endicott "Chub" Peabody continues to campaign throughout the state for the governorship, using a station wagon topped by a sound-equipped platform which his aides have dubbed a "chariot." [Story: Page 2.]

Weather: Cloudy Tonight and Friday [Page 2]

Arts and Entertainment: Page 11. TV, FM: Page 10

THE CHRISTIAN SCIENCE MONITOR
Registered in U. S. Patent Office
AN INTERNATIONAL DAILY NEWSPAPER

VOLUME 55 NO. 233   © 1963, THE CHRISTIAN SCIENCE PUBLISHING SOCIETY / All Rights Reserved   BOSTON, THURSDAY, AUGUST 29, 1963   WESTERN EDITION   TWO SECTIONS   TEN CENTS A COPY

U.S. Blows Rail Whistle

By a Staff Correspondent of The Christian Science Monitor

Washington

An impending rail strike is being avoided by the first compulsory arbitration ever voted by Congress.

An overwhelming Senate vote set the pace, and the House approved as was expected well before the midnight strike deadline on Wednesday.

At the crux of the union-management dispute is the long-delayed effort by the railroads to eliminate century-old work procedures now anachronisms because of improved technology.

Arbitration would be run by a seven-man board to reach binding settlement on the two major issues — the fireman jobs and the make-up of train crews. Arbitration must start within 30 days with a decision filed with the court in another 60 days and to be effective in another 60 days.

Order Canceled

With the strike deadline only hours away the Senate Tuesday evening voted 90 to 2 for the arbitration legislation. Only Sens. Wayne Morse (D) of Oregon and John G. Tower (R) of Texas voted against the bill.

The House Rules Committee cleared the bill for two hours of debate. Then passage followed by a 286-to-66 vote.

Railway management then canceled the new work rule order and the threat of the strike was over. Management says that about $600,000,000 can be saved annually with the changes by removing firemen from diesel locomotives in freight and yard service, and by removing some conductors and brakemen from regular service.

The final bill provides for a 180-day arbitration and action period, although the House bill originally was for 150 days. This was the only important difference between the two measures.

The bills bar strikes and lockouts for either 150 or 180 days and require the status quo to be kept intact.

The bill sets up, a special board. Two members would be appointed by the carriers, two members by the unions. Then the four appointed would themselves appoint three more. If the management-union panel members cannot agree on the three other panel members within 10 days President Kennedy will appoint them.

Looking ahead to the arbitration, leaders of the rail unions have agreed for a long time that some work rules are overdue. But whenever the issue comes up management asks for more than the unions will agree with.

Four-Year Debate

This is at least what most observers say has been the upshot of the argument. A presidential panel studied the complex dispute earlier this summer.

Almost four years have been taken trying for a meeting of minds over the so-called featherbedding issue. So far it defies solution; but congressmen hope that this enforced arbitration will bring a final settlement that will have a historic impact on union-management relations.

Apart from the two major issues the two parties under the House-Senate bill would resume collective bargaining on other issues, such as pay structure, interdivisional runs, and combinations of yard and road work.

Africans Press UN Racial Protest

By Earl W. Foell
United Nations Correspondent of The Christian Science Monitor

United Nations, N.Y.

The drive for African equality continues to parallel the American Negro drive for domestic equality.

Diplomacy and distance do not permit mass marches on the United Nations. But the African bloc here has been mounting a series of ambassadorial and foreign ministers protests at the Security Council against the remaining bastions of racial discrimination and colonialism in southern Africa.

The latest of these arises from a unanimous African request for a Security Council session on or about Sept. 5 on the subject of Southern Rhodesia.

Geographically this is a logical addition to the diplomatic campaign the African nations are waging against the Republic of South Africa and the Portuguese territories of Angola and Mozambique. This bloc of white-controlled lands constitutes a geographical unit.

Timing Questioned

But diplomatically, the timing of the Africans' push on Southern Rhodesia is rated as questionable by disinterested political tacticians here.

In this analysis, the Africans' action may tend to upset the delicate negotiations by which Britain is seeking to avoid granting independence to Southern Rhodesia until some system of future racial equality is guaranteed.

This, of course, is not the Africans' intention. Nor do they wish to risk driving the white-controlled Southern Rhodesian government of Prime Minister Winston Field in Salisbury into the arms of South Africa.

Apparently the African bloc's strategy is to nail down, through Security Council action, London's informal promises to the Africans. These promises have been essentially not to let go of Southern Rhodesian military power until a program of increased voting power for Africans is instituted.

Air Threat Seen

The African bloc here will base its case in the Security Council on the threat to peace the African spokesmen say would follow the transfer of the British-controlled Southern Rhodesian Air Force to Salisbury's control.

Under Ghanaian leadership, the bloc plans to introduce evidence to the effect that a force of 15 Canberra jet bombers would put Mozambique, Angola, Bechuanaland, and Southwest Africa within easy striking distance of Southern Rhodesian bases.

This may be technically correct. It may foreshadow the future. But Western diplomats and some UN officials feel that the African arms are stretching the UN charter when they assert that a transfer of power not yet in sight to a government not yet committed to aid its white neighbors threatens the peace through bombing raids.

A high neutral official with intimate knowledge of Rhodesian affairs recently reported that Prime Minister Field, having staged to pressure London into quick independence for Salisbury, now sees political realities differently and is searching for a means of either moderating his government's racial stand or adhering to the status quo until the end of his term.

Pressure Reacts

In this situation, severe African pressure at the Security Council could work against Britain's efforts at persuasion instead of reinforcing it.

The Ghanaians, who have led the African bloc into calling for next week's council meeting, feel this argument is just another of a series of stalls by European leaders.

The persistence of Ghana's President Nkrumah is generally credited with having brought the Rhodesian question before the Security Council—on which Ghana is the only African member. A majority of African diplomats had previously felt that the timing was bad.

But the momentum of the Africans' post-Addis Ababa unity drive is such that no one leader can appear publicly to lag far behind any other in his enthusiasm for projects such as this. In this again, the Africans' racial equality drive parallels the American Negro campaign, in which no leader can afford to appear less militant than any other.

■ **Diem Regime Says U.S. Unjust**

By the Associated Press

Saigon, Vietnam

President Ngo Dinh Diem's regime has charged that the United States State Department declaration of Aug. 21 which deplored methods used by Vietnamese security forces against Buddhists early on the morning of Aug. 21. Pagodas throughout the nation were sacked and thousands of Buddhist monks and nuns were beaten, shot, or arrested.

"The government of Vietnam reaffirms its intention to continue its policy of conciliation toward the Buddhists," the latest note said, "but it is also resolved to unmask all political saboteurs hiding under various disguises."

Behind the crisis in Vietnam: Page 2.

Negroes Call for Equal Rights

World Responds To March

By Reuters

London

Sympathizers in Western, neutralist, and Communist countries alike expressed support for American Negroes in their big freedom march on Washington Wednesday.

Delegates of Afro-Asian, Caribbean, and other groups went to the United States embassy in London to present a message backing the United States civil-rights movement.

In Tel Aviv, Israel, some 50 Americans marched to the American embassy carrying banners with such slogans as "The Civil War Is Over" and "Black and White Together."

The All-China Federation of Trade Unions and nine other Chinese Communist organizations announced they had sent a message to the Washington march organizer; Cleveland Robinson, expressing support for "all the oppressed peoples in their struggles for freedom, equality, and liberation."

Equality Bid Seen

The Soviet news agency Tass said Wednesday the civil-rights march in Washington "rivets attention to the most acute domestic problem of the biggest capitalist power."

"The present march on Washington, the biggest and most impressive in the history of the country, aims at securing not only political, but also economic equality for Negroes in the United States," Tass said.

A front-page editorial in the progovernment Ghanaian Times said "the voice of the Afro-American cries out loud for freedom in America."

American Negroes and Ghanaians also planned to picket the United States embassy in Accra in support of the Washington march.

Dr. Anne Vondeling, floor leader of the Dutch Labor Party, wrote United States Ambassador John Rice to say the treatment of American Negroes was a "shameful affair for your country."

The letter said, however, that the Labor Party was "delighted" about President Kennedy's recent proposals for ending racial discrimination and expressed the hope Congress would approve them.

Algerian Reaction

In Cairo the Middle East News Agency said representatives of African movements arranged to march from the headquarters of the African Association in Zamalek suburb to the American embassy to present a petition to Ambassador John Badeau and hold a two-hour demonstration.

The Cairo march was organized by representatives of Zanzibar, Northern and Southern Rhodesia, Southwest Africa, South Africa, Kenya, Swaziland, Basutoland, and Mozambique.

In Munich, Al Hoosman, an American Negro ex-boxer who lives in Germany, prepared to lead a group of Germans and Americans in a march to the American consulate.

Associated Press Wirephoto
Air View of Marchers Gathered at Washington Monument

Then ... Tramp, Tramp

By Josephine Ripley
Staff Correspondent of The Christian Science Monitor

Washington

Washington had never seen anything like it.

The great 'freedom march' began so quietly, at the Constitution Avenue starting point, all you could hear was the shuffling of feet and the shrill song of the locusts in the green elms that arched above.

There was no fanfare. There seemed to be no signal.

It was as if this tremendous crowd, fed by the constant streams of newcomers from arriving buses, had suddenly filled the Washington Monument grounds to capacity — as it had — and spilled over into the street. And the march was on as simply as that.

Voices Ring Out

Placards blossomed out, like square white flowers. Placards calling for "An FEPC Law," for "Jobs and Freedom," "No U. S. Dough To Help Jim Crow," placards identifying church groups, labor groups, the Negro organization.

All come down, however,

No Fanfare

at a certain specified point in the march and singing began, with the "Freedom Song" rolling out from tens of thousands of throats like a mighty revival hymn.

From the beginning, it was an orderly crowd. It was a neatly dressed, dignified crowd.

There was no feeling of tension, no sense of militance—just a kind of joy reflected in happy, confident faces.

The crowds were slow in arriving. At 9 o'clock, there were less than a hundred persons on the scene.

Negro ushers from local NAACP headquarters were apprehensive lest the turnout be less than impressive.

Cool and Sunny

They need not have feared. Soon bus after chartered bus came roaring up Constitution Avenue with marchers from New York, New Jersey, Pennsylvania, and many other states.

They swarmed back down the sidewalk to the monument grounds in a throng which became so heavy it

was almost impossible to pass through.

Although many had ridden most of the night, they did not seem weary.

After all, the sun was shining, it was cool, and they were obviously people with a mission.

There was a flourishing business in march buttons and freedom banners.

At the march headquarters there was a sign: "Have Brush, Will Paint." That was the counter where placards were being painted on the spot—at cost.

Soon the familiar songs began. A small group of CORE members from Jackson, Miss., began singing and clapping: "Everybody Wants Freedom, Freedom, Freedom."

Queue Up for Phone

There was the soft undertone of spirituals at other points, all blending in a kind of harmony from which one word emerged loud and clear —"Freedom!"

Oddly, one of the most popular stopping places for new arrivals was the telephone booth. There were long waiting lines.

"Are you telephoning friends?"

New Peking Troop Move Reported

Hong Kong

Two Communist Chinese armies with a total of about 100,000 men reportedly have been moved from the northeastern province of Kwangtung to the sparsely settled northwestern province of Sinkiang where Communist China meets the Soviet Union along a 1,500-mile stretch of border.

The movement took place during the past few weeks, according to accounts by refugees, who also report that it was facilitated by the recent completion of a 60-mile railroad link from Canton to Samshui.

Previous Moves

Canton is the largest city and port on the southeastern coast of Communist China. Samshui, due west, is a terminus of a rail network to western and northwestern China. The linking up of the two cities by rail is of considerable economic as well as military importance.

These reports of troop movements to the northwest are strikingly similar to reports several weeks ago about troop movements to the northeastern cities of Dairen, Port Arthur, and Harbin.

The Soviet Union had a major interest in both regions until relatively recent years.

Until 1954, the Soviet Union was in control of Dairen and the naval base at Port Arthur. It had built a variety of factories in the northeast including an electrical machinery plant, a ball-bearing plant, and an electric-meter factory in Harbin; a crane factory and locomotive works in Dairen; and a large electric plant in northern Manchuria.

In the northwestern province of Sinkiang, joint stock com-

By Edward Gamarekian
Special to The Christian Science Monitor

panies had been set up from which the Soviet Union withdrew in 1955.

The Soviet Union had also set up some atomic test reactors in Sinkiang and had obtained uranium from the province.

However, in the opinion of observers here the movement of Communist Chinese troops to the border appears to be more a sign of nervousness in Peking

than aggressiveness in Moscow. A Soviet excursion across the border at this point is thought to be highly unlikely.

Revolt Reported

There is speculation here about one other possible reason for sending troops to the northwest.

Back in 1961, according to reports here, the commander and political commissar of the

Sinkiang Military Region, Wang En-Mao, defected and took to the hills with 8,000 of his men to form a guerrilla band whose objective was to make the province independent. He reportedly has been receiving some aid from the Soviet Union.

A report earlier this year described an organized revolt in Sinkiang that "caused heavy casualties to Chinese troops virtually paralyzing the military administration."

"Strong reinforcements" were rushed to the area to quash the revolt, the report said.

Soviet Influence

Peking may now be afraid, say some observers here, that the Soviet Union will give the rebels there enough support to make a revolt successful.

Sinkiang is the largest province of Communist China, accounting for one-sixth of its area but only 1 percent of its population.

Letters from people in Communist China to relatives in Hong Kong disclose considerable anxiety and tension on the Chinese Communist side of the Sino-Soviet border.

Entire factories are being shifted to the interior in what may be the beginning of a large-scale movement of industry to safer places. People with the wrong kind of family background also are being moved away from the border area or are being kept under surveillance.

Students of the Chinese Communist scene feel that the present trouble with the Soviet Union could trigger off revolts among groups who are still hostile to the Peking regime and the domination of the country by the Han race.

[map of Soviet Union / China border region labeled: SOVIET UNION, Lake Baikal, Alma Ata, Ulan Bator, MONGOLIA, Urumchi, SINKIANG, MANCHURIA, Pekingo, TIBET, CHINA, NEPAL, INDIA, BURMA, FORMOSA, HAINAN]

By Russell H. Lenz, Chi.f Cartographer

Critical Area Watched

Map shows Province of Sinkiang, where Chinese Communist troops reportedly have moved from Kwangtung Province. Also shown is the railroad link between Canton and Samshui.

Washington Witnesses 'Declaration of Conscience'

By William H. Stringer
Chief of the Washington Bureau of The Christian Science Monitor

Washington

The early consensus—as the tens of thousands of weary participants in the "Washington march for jobs and freedom" headed homeward —was that the giant demonstration would have a modest impact on the nation as a whole, and the largest impact on the marchers themselves.

These marchers—clergymen, unionists, businessmen, college students, women, young organizers from rural Southern counties in overall garb, and thousands of just plain people —will return to New York, Philadelphia, Cleveland, Pittsburgh, Mississippi, Florida— encouraged to struggle for civil rights.

They would. they said. continue writing to their congressmen, demonstrating for equal hiring on construction projects, organizing support in Southern counties (and facing intimidation for it) and seeking to speed school desegregation.

Sea of Faces

The march on Washington— a sea of determined faces, a parade swelling down historic avenues from Washington's spire to Lincoln's memorial— rolled across the nation's capital under a blue summer sky.

Americans watching on television — and other lands via Telstar and Eurovision — were given a glimpse of the coordinated new Negro leadership in the United States and what it can accomplish.

When the first buses and trains full of Negroes and whites began discharging their cargoes, from Mississippi and Florida, Chicago and New York, Philadelphia and the West Coast, it was uncertain whether the total eventually would swell as predicted to 150,000. But one hour before the march it reached 100,000.

The intense resolve of the Negro leadership and of the police forces along the route that this would be a totally nonviolent, completely orderly demonstration was evident.

As its originator, A. Philip Randolph, had said in his deep oratorical voice, the march is intended as a "solemn declaration of conscience" and simultaneously as an effort to reach the conscience of the American people.

The marchers were both white and Negro, but heavily Negro. The parade began unexpectedly early and swept along Constitution Avenue toward the Washington Monument to the Lincoln Memorial.

Leaders of the parade barely managed to catch up and get themselves in front of the parade.

A Bit of Lobbying

Signs had been prepared in advance with such slogans as "We March for Freedom." But some placards were introduced at the last moment by individuals. One read "The Justice Department Is A White Man." It is estimated that about half of the government workers in Washington did not report for work. Commuters buses were relatively empty and car-traffic lanes were not crowded as usual. Washingtonians had been warned of possible traffic jams.

Negroes went to the Capitol and met with Senate and House leaders of both parties.

Senate Majority Leader Mike Mansfield (D) of Montana told newsmen later that it was a cordial and courteous meeting at which no commitments were asked and none given.

The Rev. Dr. Martin Luther King Jr., president of the Southern Christian Leadership Conference, said, "We had a very good discussion, and I think it will lead to fruitful results."

A few of the top 10 leaders, in statements prepared for delivery to the vast assemblage from the podium of the Lincoln Memorial with the statue of the Great Emancipator looking or, were more militant. John Lewis of the Student Nonviolent Coordinating Committee called the administration's civil-rights bill "too little and too late," and inveighed against both Republicans and Democrats for "immoral compromises."

Moderate Tone

Another leader, James Farmer of the Congress of Racial Equality sent his message from the jail in Louisiana where he is behind bars for carrying on a demonstration. He declared:

"Our direct-action method, bringing down barriers all over America — in jobs, in housing, in schools, in public places—is giving hope to the world."

In more moderate tone Roy Wilkins, executive secretary of the National Association for the Advancement of Colored People, declared:

"We have come asking the enactment of legislation that will affirm the right to life, liberty, and the pursuit of happiness, legislation that will place the resources and the honor of the government of all the people behind the pledge of equality in the 'Declaration of Independence.'"

President Sees Negroes Gain

By the Associated Press

Washington

President Kennedy says "the cause of 20 million Negroes has been advanced" by the civil-rights march on Washington.

The President pledged that the executive branch of the government will continue its efforts "to obtain increased employment and to eliminate discrimination in employment practices, two of the prime goals of the march."

In addition, he said, the push to civil-rights legislation "will be maintained," as will administration attempts to win congressional passage of proposals "to strengthen the educational system and expand the opportunities of young people."

While declaring that the summer of 1963 has seen remarkable progress in translating civil rights from principles into practices," Mr. Kennedy said:

"We have a very long way yet to travel."

"One cannot help but be impressed," he said, "with the deep fervor and the quiet dignity that characterizes the thousands who have gathered in the nation's capital from across the country to demonstrate their faith and confidence in our democratic form of government."

Mississippi Runoff A Slap at Kennedy

By the Associated Press

Jackson, Miss.

Lt. Gov. Paul Johnson Jr., militant anti-Kennedy segregationist, has ended 16 years of political frustration, winning the Democratic nomination for Governor of Mississippi by a record vote.

Mr. Johnson overwhelmed former Gov. J. P. Coleman after a bitter runoff campaign which centered on white voters' deep-rooted opposition to President Kennedy and his civil-rights program.

Mr. Johnson reminded voters he still faces federal contempt of court charges for his part in temporarily blocking James H. Meredith from enrolling in the University of Mississippi last September.

He also called Mr. Coleman the "Kennedy satellite candidate." Mr. Coleman supported the President in the 1960 presidential race.

Mr. Coleman argued that he was anti-Kennedy, too, saying he erred in 1960.

With 1,861 of the state's 1,877 precincts reporting, Mr. Johnson had 258,427 votes, highest ever given a gubernatorial candidate, to 193,021 for Mr. Coleman.

The previous high for a winning candidate was 233,237 votes for Mr. Coleman in his 1955 runoff victory over Mr. Johnson.

Mr. Johnson faces Republican Rubel Phillips in the Nov. 5 general election. A newly expanded Republican state headquarters had promised Mr. Phillips would be more than the usual token GOP candidate in this overwhelmingly Democratic state and there were indications many anti-Johnson democrats might vote for Phillips.

An independent has also announced for the general election.

Mr. Johnson, son of a former Governor, lost three previous races for the nomination, including one to Coleman in the 1955 runoff. He also was defeated in a race for the United States Senate before being elected lieutenant governor four years ago.

Gov. Ross R. Barnett, barred by law from succeeding himself, joined the crowd of cheering Lieutenant Governor Johnson fans at an election party. He said he voted for Mr. Johnson.

THE CHRISTIAN SCIENCE MONITOR

Registered in U. S. Patent Office
AN INTERNATIONAL DAILY NEWSPAPER

VOLUME 56 NO. 1 | BOSTON, MONDAY, NOVEMBER 25, 1963 | EASTERN EDITION | TWO SECTIONS | TEN CENTS A COPY

© 1963, THE CHRISTIAN SCIENCE PUBLISHING SOCIETY All Rights Reserved

U.S. Rallies in Crisis

By Bachrach

John F. Kennedy
'Ask not what your country can do for you . . .'

Associated Press Wirephoto

Lyndon B. Johnson Sworn In as 36th President of the United States
Former Vice-President takes oath of office from Judge Sarah T. Hughes in presidential plane at Dallas

Continuity Of Presidency

By Richard L. Strout
Staff Correspondent of The Christian Science Monitor

Washington

"And so my fellow Americans: ask not what your country can do for you—ask what you can do for your country."

The American presidency is a continuing office. These words were uttered by a President slain by a sniper's bullet in Dallas, Texas, but it was a President still—though another man—who returned to Washington, and with heavy heart urged the nation to give him its help, and picked up the awesome responsibility of Chief Executive.

As Lyndon Baines Johnson succeeded John Fitzgerald Kennedy as 36th President of the United States a stunned nation asked how such things could be, but at the same time rallied behind the figure in the White House, as it always has rallied at every great crisis.

Over the Pacific a lonely military transport plane suddenly turned in its course and made a great circle back to Washington. It bore Secretary of State Dean Rusk and other Cabinet members who had been heading to a meeting in Tokyo.

'Monstrous Act' Denounced

A special train pulled out of a town in the Ukraine and, according to reports, sped back to Moscow, carrying Premier Nikita S. Khrushchev who had just learned of the assassination. Eulogies of the murdered President were heard over all Soviet news media.

In Washington, away from public view, a stoic widow of 34, who had held her wounded husband in her arms in a vain dash to the hospital, and still maintained her composure as she sat beside the coffin on the return trip to the capital, told her two children that they were fatherless.

Caroline Kennedy will be six on Wednesday, and John three on Monday. Mrs. Kennedy lost her third-born child last August.

In London a grizzled statesman, who had seen generations come and go, Sir Winston Churchill denounced "this monstrous act" that had taken the life of his friend of only 46, the youngest man ever elected President and the first Roman Catholic.

And in Dallas a suspect in the crime, Lee Harvey Oswald, 24, chairman of a "fair play for Cuba committee," who spent three years in the Soviet Union seeking to renounce his American citizenship, after hours of examination sullenly denied having anything to do with the crime.

Many Precedents Broken

But in this turmoil, which affected the chancelleries of the world, and caused a $10 billion loss of paper profits in a dazed Wall Street before the stock market was arbitrarily closed, chief attention centered, as always, on the living President. White House officials accustomed themselves to the name, President Johnson.

Almost every precedent was broken as the tall, spare, quietly tense Texan took the oath of office under circumstances as incongruous in their way as those of Calvin Coolidge, sworn in by his justice-of-the-peace father, on the family Bible, by kerosene lamp in Vermont.

President Johnson was the first to receive the oath from a woman, Federal Judge Sarah T. Hughes. She used a small Bible as he took the solemn oath, to defend the Constitution, which most Presidents take on the portals of the Capitol before admiring crowds.

For the first time in history the oath was administered in an airplane. And for the first time it was administered in the tragic presence of the slain predecessor's wife and before the coffin of the slain President.

After the stark rite, President Johnson embraced Mrs. Kennedy and then his wife, Lady Bird Johnson, and the President's secretary, Mrs. Evalyn Lincoln. Only then, according to some observers, in the forward compartment of the plane, did tears come to Mrs. Kennedy.

Reporters Wait Awed and Silent

Meanwhile, in Washington, reporters waited at the White House for President Johnson's arrival. The party came from Texas by jet plane, and then the new President left by helicopter from Andrews Air Force Base at 6:26 p.m.

Two hundred reporters and broadcasters left the floodlit, noisy foyer of the executive wing of the White House where news bulletins in all languages had been jabbered into phones for the wondering world, and moved bareheaded out into the cool, mild November night on the fenced grounds of the executive mansion.

It was historic ground, where Lincoln paced, where the smiling Franklin D. Roosevelt was bodily lifted up on his fourth and wartime inaugural to take the oath.

In the haze a crescent moon made an intermittent spot of light. At hand rose tall magnolia trees. To the right the windows of the old State Department building were aglow as charwomen cleansed, and directly ahead rose the tall floodlit Washington Monument with a single red window at the top.

Continued on Page 10, Col. 5

Directors' Message

The tragedy which has deprived the American nation of its President, and a family of its husband and father, should awaken all to the shocking price of political or ideological fanaticism and hate-filled thinking. The depraved state of thought that motivated the assassination of President Kennedy needs to be faced squarely and overcome by every individual.

Never before has the United States faced a more compelling need than it does today to lift itself out of the fruitless, self-defeating mesmerism of hate that turns brother against brother, nation against nation, and race against race, and has culminated in this tragic event. The Christian ideals of government by law and of brotherly love, upon which the United States was founded, must be so rekindled, so revitalized, that this event will become a turning point toward a more rational approach to the solution of today's crucial issues.

We unite with members of all faiths in our heartfelt sympathy to the President's wife and family.

THE CHRISTIAN SCIENCE BOARD OF DIRECTORS

Historical Imprint Of a Brief Term

By a Staff Correspondent of The Christian Science Monitor

Washington

Only two years and ten months in the White House; but President Kennedy has left his undoubted mark on history.

He had charm and wit; warmth and decency; he also had drive and an Irish determination. All this made the White House exciting, and gave a special verve to Kennedy-era Washington.

Sure the press corps liked the President; its members sympathize with all presidents perhaps, because they see, close up, the harassments and burdens borne.

Mrs. Kennedy of course added a special high style to Washington.

Who will forget the candlelight supper given for Pakistan President Ayub Khan at Mount Vernon; the painstaking, authentic redoing of the White House by the First Lady; the deft sallies at a presidential press conference; the speeches which made soaring use of the English language.

Matters of show rather than substance, these? Not really. Critics also said Mr. Kennedy was more interested in playing politics than in standing for solid programs—that he compromised too often.

But the late President had studied the careers of Woodrow Wilson, and Theodore Roosevelt, and Franklin D. Roosevelt, and he wanted to go down in history as one of the "strong" presidents of this century. He had a program to enact, to "get America moving." It included urban renewal, stronger federal aid to education, rapid transit, medicare, a bold tax cut, revised foreign aid, a new trade act.

Continued on Page 3, Col. 1

Johnson Pledges 'My Best'

Basic Policies Expected to Stay

By William H. Stringer
Chief of the Washington Bureau of The Christian Science Monitor

Washington

A tall restless Texan with a homespun accent and a driving energy has succeeded John Fitzgerald Kennedy as President of the United States.

In his first hushed statement, before the microphones at Andrews Air Force Base, Lyndon Baines Johnson declared with complete simplicity:

"I will do my best. That is all I can do. I ask for your help, and God's."

President Johnson has come a long way, from his boyhood in Stonewall, Texas, to that solemn moment of swearing-in, in the forward suite of the presidential jetliner waiting to speed back to Washington. He has, through sorrowful circumstance, broken the ban which decreed that no Southerner had a chance to become President.

Strong 'Rights' Stand

He will undoubtedly maintain unchanged the basic foreign policy of his predecessor, though his method of operation will differ from that of the late President Kennedy. He is likely to retain Secretary of State Dean Rusk, whom he greatly admires, though as time goes on other Cabinet members may be replaced by his own appointees.

Having little over a year to go before he must stand for reelection, President Johnson probably will launch few new policies, domestic or foreign, but devote his energies to tidying up programs for presentation to the electorate in 1964.

Though a Southerner—or Southwesterner — President Johnson has taken a civil-rights position about as strong as was Mr. Kennedy's. He has worked long hours to carry out fair - employment practices through the presidential Fair-Employment Commission he has headed.

Some Southerners call him a "renegade" for this, and for presiding as Senate majority leader over the passage, in 1957, of the first civil-rights legislation since Reconstruction days. He doesn't seem to mind; his position has given him national stature.

Busy Traveler

As Senate majority leader he found a formula for enacting much "Eisenhower" legislation, by giving a Democratic twist to needed bills proposed by the Republican administration.

Associates sometimes wondered whether this vibrant six-foot-three individual would not rust away in the obscurity of the vice-presidency, but by means of trips as presidential emissary — to Southeast Asia, the Berlin wall, Scandinavia, and the NATO countries—Mr. Johnson managed to keep the vice-presidency alive.

Most observers believe that, having been defeated by Mr. Kennedy in the 1960 presidential contest, he was looking ahead to 1968 for another try at the White House, when Mr. Kennedy would not have been eligible for a third term.

Probably the biggest omission in the Johnson travel itinerary has been the Soviet Union. Now he must establish relations with the redoubtable Premier Nikita S. Khrushchev.

Mr. Johnson inherits a foreign policy stance—bolstered by this acknowledged nuclear superiority of the United States and with a more acceptable regime consolidating power in South Vietnam. But he still will have the problems of negotiating on European unity with French President de Gaulle and a new government in West Germany.

Career Began in '31

Mr. Johnson entered political life in December, 1931, as secretary to Rep. Richard Kleberg of Texas. Six years later he was elected to the 75th Congress over 10 opponents.

He became a political protégé of Franklin D. Roosevelt and Sam Rayburn—Mr. Roosevelt personally encouraging him to run for the Senate when incumbent Morris Sheppard passed on in 1941. He lost by a slim vote but in 1948 was elected to the Senate by an 87-vote margin.

Four years later the Senate Democrats chose him as their minority leader, the youngest in history. When the Senate political alignment changed, he became majority leader, and earned a strong reputation for skilled maneuver.

Kept Informed

When 1960 rolled around, Senator Johnson, aided by his friend, House Speaker Rayburn, sought to contest the presidential nomination with Senator Kennedy, but the Kennedy band wagon was too superbly organized.

When the Massachusetts senator won the nomination he picked Mr. Johnson to be his running mate—and thereby held Texas and several other sorely needed Southern states in the Democratic column.

Besides serving as the Fair-Employment Commission chairman and directing the administration's space program, Mr. Johnson had been kept closely informed by the late President on all policy affairs, so he faces no long apprenticeship during which he must learn policies and programs afresh. Continuity has been good here.

President Johnson is a compelling personality. Deeply concentrating on the business at hand, he usually accomplishes what he has set out to do. As President he is likely to demand untiring zeal and hearty loyalty from subordinates. He had a serious heart attack nearly a decade ago, but is reported to have completely recovered.

President Johnson does not have the command of rhetoric that Mr. Kennedy had, but no one will have any trouble in understanding what President Johnson wants and intends; he comes through loud and clear.

World Reaction

In London, Britons in sympathy reached out for American neighbors **(Page 16)**. In West Germany, for some time people could not believe what they heard in the news and telephoned British and American friends **(Page 2)**.

In East Asia, President Kennedy is likely to be remembered as the man who tried to defuse the cold war **(Page 6)**. In New Delhi, India felt the loss of a "true friend" and the world a man who strove for international understanding **(Page 6.)**

Tribute Expressed By Khrushchev

By Reuters

Moscow

Premier Nikita S. Khrushchev has led the Soviet people in a tribute to President Kennedy.

Mr. Khrushchev and Foreign Minister Andrei A. Gromyko went to the American Embassy on Saturday afternoon where American Ambassador Foy D. Kohler escorted them to a small table in the reception room.

A loose-leaf album had been laid out to receive the signatures of foreign diplomats and top Soviet officials.

Mr. Khrushchev described the President's passing as "a heavy blow to all people who hold dear the cause of peace and Soviet-American cooperation," the Soviet news agency Tass reported.

In a cable addressed to President Johnson, Mr. Khrushchev noted that the "heinous assassination" of Mr. Kennedy at a time when there appeared signs of relaxation of international tension and a prospect for improving relations between the Soviet Union and the United States evoked the "indignation of Soviet people against the culprits of this base crime."

Soviet newspapers reporting the assassination of Mr. Kennedy were sold out quickly here as the United States Embassy began 30 days of mourning.

Soviet citizens on snowswept Red Square in the heart of Moscow early Saturday openly expressed deep regret at the assassination.

One of the guards on Lenin's red-and-black granite mausoleum, a Soviet Army captain, told a correspondent:

"We very much regret this. As we say, each country has its villains. . . ."

One of a group of young male students standing near Saint Basil's Cathedral at the end of the square, summed it up: "It is bad for the American people and for our people. . . . What might have happened if there had been another President at the time of Cuba?"

Dallas Tries to Regain Equilibrium

By Bicknell Eubanks
Staff Correspondent of The Christian Science Monitor

Dallas

Even as a shocked Dallas struggled to regain its equilibrium after seeing the President of the United States murdered and the Governor of Texas seriously wounded, the staff of District Attorney Henry Wade began preparations to prosecute Lee Harvey Oswald, a self-styled pro-Communist who was arrested only hours after President Kennedy was assassinated.

A second man, alleged to be a friend of Oswald, was arrested the day after the slaying.

The city itself reeled under the impact of the events which left a mark that it will be a long time erasing.

Room Rented

President Kennedy was killed as his motorcade was leaving downtown Dallas to go to the Trade Mart, where he was to deliver a speech at a colorful luncheon which was to have climaxed his trip across north-central Texas. Gov. John Connally of Texas was wounded. [Speculation on whether the Governor was the prime target of the assassin has been roused by the disclosure of an Oswald letter to Mr. Connally, who was Secretary of the Navy until December, 1961, appealing Oswald's "undesirable" discharge from the Marines.]

Mayor Earl Cabell of Dallas joined with the Dallas City Council in emphasizing that the action in no way could be connected with the people of the city itself. Mr. Cabell pointed out that Oswald was not a permanent resident of Dallas, although he had rented a room in the city itself about a month ago.

"There are maniacs all over the world and in every city of the world," Mayor Cabell said. "This was a maniac. It could have happened in Podunk as well as in Dallas."

Movements Traced

Councilmen Carie Welch, who is Mayor pro tem, said:

"This still should not reflect on the image or character of Dallas. There were too many sincere people extending Mr. Kennedy a warm greeting, filling the streets, standing along the roadways, cheering from office windows. I challenge anybody who says that this act reflects the character of the people of Dallas. This was the horrible action of a mentally deranged person.

"I just can't conceive that it happened here."

State Jurisdiction

Others pointed to the warmth with which the President had been received when his plane landed at Love Field. He had walked along the fence, shaking hands with and speaking to the thousands who had gathered at the airport to greet him.

As the civic leaders struggled to redeem the city in world opinion, investigators sought to trace Oswald's movements prior to the shooting. They found that he had worked in the building from which the shot was fired and had rented a room in a section of the city not far from the building.

He moved into the roominghouse on Oct. 14 and gave his name as O. H. Lee. His landlord, A. C. Johnson, described him as polite and a gentleman. Mr. Oswald came and went quietly and never seemed to have any friends or any words for anybody or any interests.

The prosecutor's staff began to prepare the case which it will present in one of the county criminal district courts.

The case will be tried in the state courts because even though a federal law makes it a violation to threaten the life of a president, there is no federal law covering the assassination of one.

Mr. Wade pointed out that neither is there a specific state law applying to murder of a president other than the general laws of murder.

To counter any insanity plea Mr. Wade said he would arrange for psychiatrists to examine the accused man.

The test of legal sanity under Texas criminal laws is whether the defendant can distinguish between right and wrong and is aware of the nature of the consequences of his acts.

Mr. Wade said he would argue that, since Oswald fled from the scene it is obvious that he knew the nature of his acts.

World Business Suspended in UN

By Earl W. Foell
United Nations Correspondent of The Christian Science Monitor

United Nations, N.Y.

The world's business literally stood still here in grief and dismay this weekend. And none among the hundreds of UN diplomats showed more shock and perplexity than members of the Communist bloc.

But if there was perplexity about the future there was also abnormal clarity about the present. Seldom is the real course of diplomacy so stripped of all its serpentine intricacies and seen in such simple outline as it was after the assassination news spread here Friday afternoon.

Delegate after delegate interviewed — African, Communist, Latin American—came, by whatever private route of grief or shock, to essentially the same point. It was that President Kennedy had, in the seven months since his American University speech, deflated suspicion and turned the curve of the cold war dramatically downward. The question uppermost in the minds of most of these diplomats was whether the Kennedy approach would go on.

Recollections, hearsay, and news reports on Lyndon B. Johnson are being eagerly cannibalized. The return of Ambassador Adlai E. Stevenson from the first meetings of Johnson advisers is anxiously awaited.

In all this snatching for straws the question of continuity of policy is paramount.

One high UN official, eying clusters of sober diplomats in the delegates' lounge, said thoughtfully: "If they want to honor him, Kennedy's successors could find no better way than to continue his two great programs. I mean civil rights at home and patient negotiating with the Russians abroad."

Continued on Page 2, Col. 3

2nd Cl Post Pd at Boston, Mass., and add'l offices

THE CHRISTIAN SCIENCE MONITOR

Registered in U. S. Patent Office

AN INTERNATIONAL DAILY NEWSPAPER

VOLUME 56 NO. 187 | BOSTON, MONDAY, JULY 6, 1964 | EASTERN EDITION | TWO SECTIONS | TEN CENTS A COPY

© 1964, THE CHRISTIAN SCIENCE PUBLISHING SOCIETY All Rights Reserved

Convention Guide

The Christian Science Monitor today presents a compact-size supplement Convention Guide to the nominating conventions of the Republican and Democratic Parties.

It is offered as a reader service to help make the convention process more understandable and interesting. Candidates' views on issues, stories on their careers, discussions of platforms and dark horses of other years, and charts which capsule key current and historical facts are included.

An election guide highlighting information on the campaign and the political parties before voters make a final choice in November will be published on Oct. 26.

U.A.R. Test

Yemeni War Sputters On

By John N. Rigos

Special Correspondent of The Christian Science Monitor

Beirut, Lebanon

For the last 20 months the Yemen has been in a state of war.

On the mountaintops, controlled by the followers of Imam al-Badr, one can see men training in modern weapons, bands of soldiers moving toward contested points singing marching songs in their high-pitched voices.

Barefooted fighters, dancing war dances, wave their "jambiyas" (curved swords) over their heads before they leave for the front.

Evidences of the war are not hard to find as one comes across bombed villages or destroyed castles in royalist-held areas.

Along the main roads and around major cities the large Egyptian camps and motorized columns remind one that this country is the test case of the U.A.R.'s efforts to reassure itself of its ability to overthrow reactionary regimes and to promote its socialist revolution throughout the Arab world.

Money From Both Sides

Three significant internal reasons prompted the coup that took place in September, 1962, against Imam al-Badr:

- First, the natural tendency of Yemenis to resist a strong central authority.
- Second, the excessively oppressive regime of Imam Ahmed, the father of Imam al-Badr.
- Third, the desire of a few educated Yemenis to open up their country to the world and, through such contact, to begin its long-overdue modernization.

One may also add a fourth outside reason: the need of the U.A.R to advance socialism and revolution into the Arabian Peninsula from the south.

"The revolution and ensuing fighting seemed like the best thing that could have happened to most of the mountain tribes," a well-placed foreign observer in Sanaa told this correspondent. "They saw central authority falling to pieces. They were needed by the new government and by the Imam, and both were ready to pay to win their favor. Many tribes profited by receiving money from both sides."

The truth, according to this observer, is that most of this money was spent to rebuild destroyed homes or to buy food which was becoming more expensive.

The really great gain for the Yemenis themselves was the free distribution of arms and ammunition by both the Imam and the republicans. Previously a life's savings went for the purchase of a good rifle. Now there is hardly a man or a boy in Yemen without a rifle.

German Rifles Prized

German World War II rifles are the prize possessions. American M-1's are next; British and Canadian-made Enfields follow. Egyptian semiautomatic rifles are not considered very desirable because they are too heavy, and Soviet rifles are too small. I remember how for a whole evening an old sheik pestered a young prince, commanding an area in northwest Yemen, to give him a new German rifle in return for an M-1.

The oppressive and tyrannical measures of Imam Ahmed, who ruled from 1948 until 1962, were unprecedented in the history of Yemen and, if it had not been for the interference of Crown Prince al-Badr, many of today's revolutionary leaders would not have lived to see the revolution.

Continued on Page 2, Column 5

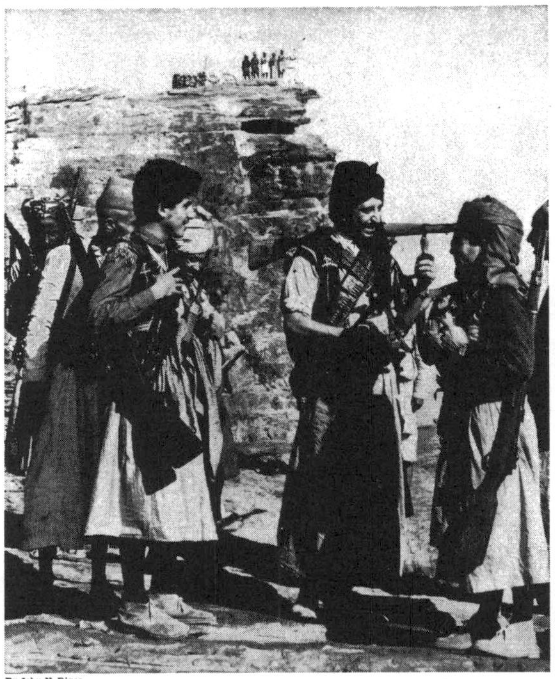

By John N. Rigos

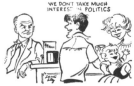

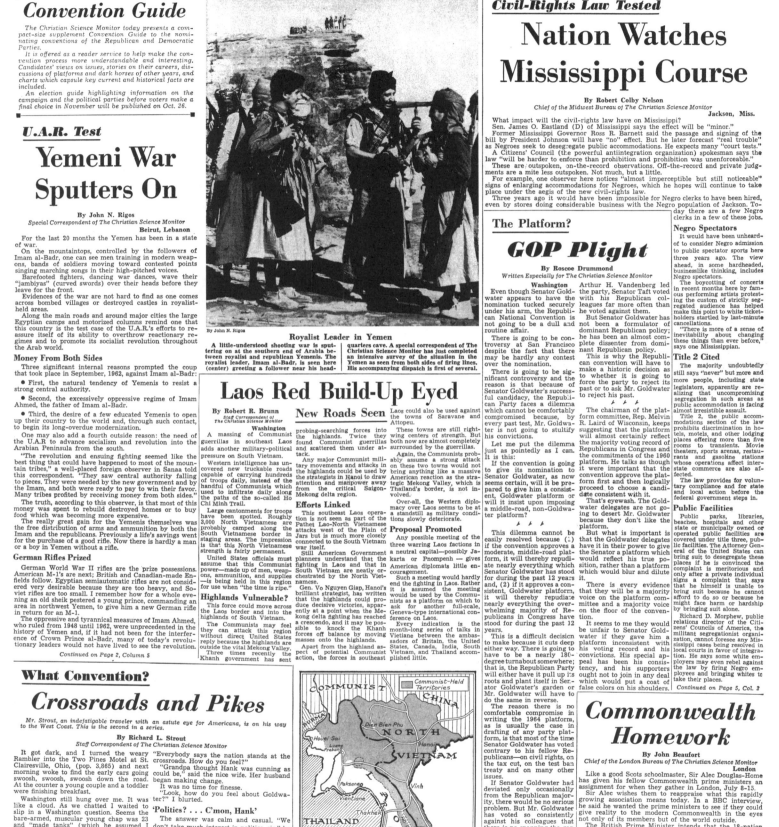

Royalist Leader in Yemen

A little-understood shooting war is sputtering on at the southern end of Arabia between royalist and republican Yemenis. The royalist leader, Imam al-Badr, is seen here (center) greeting a follower near his headquarters cave. A special correspondent of The Christian Science Monitor has just completed an intensive survey of the situation in the Yemen as seen from both sides of firing lines. His accompanying dispatch is first of several.

Laos Red Build-Up Eyed

By Robert R. Brunn

Staff Correspondent of The Christian Science Monitor

Washington

A massing of Communist guerrillas in southeast Laos adds another military-political pressure on South Vietnam.

Western intelligence has uncovered new truckable roads capable of carrying hundreds of troops daily, instead of the handful of Communists which used to infiltrate daily along the paths of the so-called Ho Chi Minh Trail.

Large cantonments for troops have been spotted. Roughly 3,000 North Vietnamese are probably camped along the South Vietnamese border in staging areas. The impression is that this North Vietnamese strength is fairly permanent.

United States officials must assume that this Communist power—made up of men, weapons, ammunition, and supplies—is being held in this region for use when "the time is ripe."

Highlands Vulnerable?

This force could move across the Laos border and into the highlands of South Vietnam.

The Communists may feel they can attack this region without direct United States reply because the highlands are outside the vital Mekong Valley.

Three times recently the Khanh government has sent

New Roads Seen

probing-searching forces into the highlands. Twice they found Communist guerrillas and scattered them under attack.

Any major Communist military movements and attacks in the highlands could be used by the strategists in Hanoi to draw attention and manpower away from the critical Saigon-Mekong delta region.

Efforts Linked

This southeast Laos operation is not seen as part of the Pathet Lao-North Vietnamese attacks west of the Plain of Jars but is much more closely connected to the South Vietnam war itself.

Still American Government planners understand that the fighting in Laos and that in South Vietnam are neatly orchestrated by the North Vietnamese.

Gen. Vo Nguyen Giap, Hanoi's brilliant strategist, has written that the highlands could produce decisive victories, apparently at a point when the Mekong delta fighting has reached a crescendo, and it may be possible to knock the Khanh forces off balance by moving masses onto the highlands.

Apart from the highland aspect of potential Communist action, the forces in southeast Laos could also be used against the towns of Saravane and Attopeu.

These towns are still right-wing centers of strength. But both now are almost completely surrounded by the guerrillas.

Again, the Communists probably assume a strong attack on these two towns would not bring anything like a massive American reaction as the strategic Mekong Valley, which is Thailand's border, is not involved.

Over-all, the Western diplomacy over Laos seems to be at a standstill as military conditions slowly deteriorate.

Proposal Promoted

Any possible meeting of the three warring Laos factions in a neutral capital—possibly Jakarta or Pnompenh — gives American diplomats little encouragement.

Such a meeting would hardly end the fighting in Laos. Rather it is assumed the meeting would be used by the Communists as a platform on which to ask for another full-scale, Geneva-type international conference on Laos.

Every indication is the month-long series of talks in Vietiane between the ambassadors of Britain, the United States, Canada, India, South Vietnam, and Thailand accomplished little.

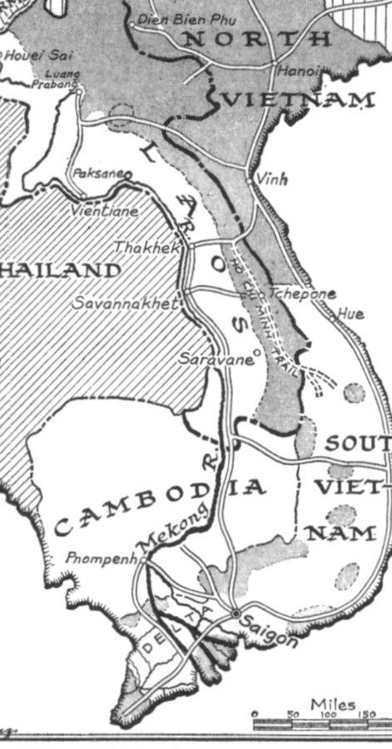

By Russell H. Lenz, Chief Cartographer

Communist Supply Trails Spotted

What Convention?

Crossroads and Pikes

Mr. Strout, an indefatigable traveler with an astute eye for Americana, is on his way to the West Coast. This is the second in a series.

By Richard L. Strout

Staff Correspondent of The Christian Science Monitor

It got dark, and I turned the weary Rambler into the Two Pines Motel at St. Clairesville, Ohio, (pop. 3,865) and next morning woke to find the early cars going swoosh, swoosh, swoosh down the road. At the counter a young couple and a toddler were finishing breakfast.

Washington still hung over me. It was like a cloud. As we chatted I waited to slip in a Washington question. Seems the bare-armed, muscular young chap was 23 and "made tanks" (which he assumed I would understand), and his wife is 19. The toddler was Hank, and there would be another one in August.

Question Put Artfully

"About the time of the Democratic convention?" I said artfully.

They had been visiting Grandpa, he replied, without taking the bait.

Every summer they visited him. They would be leaving now, soon's they got the bill.

"I am a Washington correspondent," I said impressively, "driving to the San Francisco convention." I paused to let it sink in.

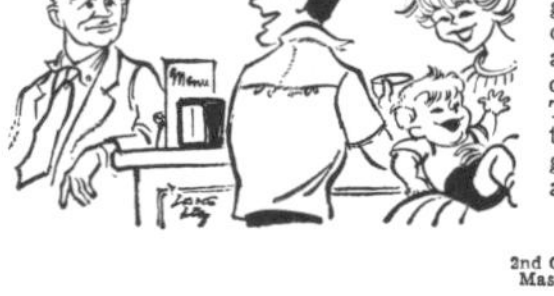

"Everybody says the nation stands at the crossroads. How do you feel?"

"Grandpa thought Hank was cunning as could be," said the nice wife. Her husband began making change.

It was no time for finesse.

"Look, how do you feel about Goldwater?" I blurted.

'Politics? . . . C'mon, Hank'

The answer was calm and casual. "We don't take much interest in politics, sir," he said politely. He might have been saying thanks, he didn't follow the hockey scores. "C'mon, Hank." They left.

I suppose nobody else can understand it. I braced myself and my jaw sagged. I don't get out of Washington often enough. I thought of the interminable, 24-hour debate in Washington. "What is the country thinking?" I took a big, wonderful breath. The country was doing a lot less thinking about Washington, I suddenly realized, than Washington supposed. Inside me I could feel the crunch of values shifting.

The speed limit on the Ohio Turnpike is 70. Even my car, the "Rabler," as we have dubbed our M-less, seemed a little surprised at first. Mostly on turnpikes further east the limit is 55 or 60. Everybody goes 5 or 10 miles above it. But here, I noticed, as we gradually climbed the scale and settled down to a tranquil, even pace a bit above a mile a minute, the traffic stream on the divided highway seemed visibly to relax. The distance between cars lengthened out; there was not the competitive pressure to get ahead, when everybody was traveling at an easy 70.

Continued on Page 5, Col. 5

2nd Cl Post Pd at Boston, Mass., and add'l offices

Civil-Rights Law Tested

Nation Watches Mississippi Course

By Robert Colby Nelson

Chief of the Midwest Bureau of The Christian Science Monitor

Jackson, Miss.

What impact will the civil-rights law have on Mississippi?

Sen. James O. Eastland (D) of Mississippi says the effect will be "minor."

Former Mississippi Governor Ross R. Barnett said the passage and signing of the bill by President Johnson will have "no" effect. But he later forecast "real trouble" as Negroes seek to desegregate public accommodations. He expects many "court tests."

A Citizens' Council (the powerful antiintegration organization) spokesman says the law "will be harder to enforce than prohibition and prohibition was unenforceable."

These are outspoken, on-the-record observations. Off-the-record and private judgments are a mite less outspoken. Not much, but a little.

For example, one observer here notices "almost imperceptible but still noticeable" signs of enlarging accommodations for Negroes, which he hopes will continue to take place under the aegis of the new civil-rights law.

Three years ago it would have been impossible for Negro clerks to have been hired, even by stores doing considerable business with the Negro population of Jackson. Today there are a few Negro clerks in a few of these jobs.

Negro Spectators

It would have been unheard-of to consider Negro admission to public spectator sports here three years ago. The view ahead, in some hardheaded, businesslike thinking, includes Negro spectators.

The boycotting of concerts in recent months here by famous performing artists protesting the custom of strictly segregated audience has helped make this point to white ticket-holders startled by last-minute cancellations.

"There is more of a sense of inevitability about changing these things than ever before," says one Mississippian.

Title 2 Cited

The majority undoubtedly still says "never" but more and more people, including state legislators, apparently are realizing that uncompromising segregation in such areas as public accommodation is facing almost irresistible assault.

Title 2, the public accommodations section of the law prohibits discrimination in hotels, motels, and other lodging places offering more than five rooms to transients. Movie theaters, sports arenas, restaurants and gasoline stations whose operations affect interstate commerce are also affected.

The law provides for voluntary compliance and for state and local action before the federal government steps in.

Public Facilities

Public parks, libraries, beaches, hospitals and other state or municipally owned or operated public facilities are covered under title three, public facilities. The Attorney General of the United States can bring suit to desegregate these places if he is convinced the complaint is meritorious and only after a private individual signs a complaint that says that he himself is unable to bring suit because he cannot afford to do so or because he might face harm or hardship by bringing suit alone.

Richard D. Morphew, public relations director of the Citizens' Councils of America, the militant segregationist organization, cannot foresee any Mississippi cases being resolved in local courts in favor of integration. He says some white employers may even rebel against the law by firing Negro employees and bringing whites to take their places.

Continued on Page 5, Col. 2

The Platform?

GOP Plight

By Roscoe Drummond

Written Especially for The Christian Science Monitor

Washington

Even though Senator Goldwater appears to have the nomination tucked securely under his arm, the Republican National Convention is not going to be a dull and routine affair.

There is going to be controversy at San Francisco despite the fact that there may be hardly any contest over the nomination.

There is going to be significant controversy and the reason is that because of Senator Goldwater's successful candidacy, the Republican Party faces a dilemma which cannot be comfortably compromised because, by every past test, Mr. Goldwater is not going to stultify his convictions.

Let me put the dilemma just as pointedly as I can. It is this:

If the convention is going to give its nomination to Senator Goldwater, as now seems certain, will it be prepared to give him a consistent, Goldwater platform or will it insist upon imposing a middle-road, non-Goldwater platform?

This dilemma cannot be easily resolved because (1) if the convention approves a moderate, middle-road platform, it will thereby repudiate nearly everything which Senator Goldwater has stood for during the past 12 years and, (2) if it approves a consistent, Goldwater platform, it will thereby repudiate nearly everything the overwhelming majority of Republicans in Congress have stood for during the past 12 years.

This is a difficult decision to make because it cuts deep either way. There is going to have to be a nearly 180-degree turnabout somewhere; that is, the Republican Party will either have it pull up its roots and plant itself in Senator Goldwater's garden or Mr. Goldwater will have to do the same in reverse.

The reason there is no comfortable compromise in writing the 1964 platform, as is usually the case in drafting of any party platform, is that most of the time Senator Goldwater has voted contrary to his fellow Republicans—on civil rights, on the tax cut, on the test ban treaty and on many other issues.

If Senator Goldwater had deviated only occasionally from the Republican majority, there would be no serious problem. But Mr. Goldwater has voted so consistently against his colleagues that there is no spanning the gap between them.

One of the arguments often used by the Goldwater supporters is that the party never has given a representative of its right wing an opportunity to demonstrate how effective such a candidate would be in a national campaign and that, after denying the nomination three times to the late Sen. Robert A. Taft, the time has come to give the Republican conservatives their chance.

There is some validity to this thesis, but it needs to be understood that Senator Goldwater confronts the platform-makers with a more difficult problem than did Senator Taft.

During his years in the Senate, Mr. Taft was a prime formulator of Republican policy and, except for some aspects of foreign affairs where the late Sen. Arthur H. Vandenberg led the party, Senator Taft voted with his Republican colleagues far more often than he voted against them.

But Senator Goldwater has not been a formulator of dominant Republican policy; he has been an almost complete dissenter from dominant Republican policy.

This is why the Republican convention will have to make a historic decision as to whether it is going to force the party to reject its past or to ask Mr. Goldwater to reject his past.

The chairman of the platform committee, Rep. Melvin R. Laird of Wisconsin, keeps suggesting that the platform will almost certainly reflect the majority voting record of Republicans in Congress and the commitments of the 1960 platform. He talks as though it were important that the convention approve the platform first and then logically proceed to choose a candidate consistent with it.

That's eyewash. The Goldwater delegates are not going to desert Mr. Goldwater because they don't like the platform.

But what is important is that the Goldwater delegates have it in their power to give the Senator a platform which would reflect his true position, rather than a platform which would blur and dilute it.

There is every evidence that they will be a majority voice on the platform committee and a majority voice on the floor of the convention.

It seems to me they would be unfair to Senator Goldwater if they gave him a platform inconsistent with his voting record and his convictions. His special appeal has been his consistency, and his supporters ought not to join in any deal which would put a coat of false colors on his shoulders.

Commonwealth Homework

By John Beaufort

Chief of the London Bureau of The Christian Science Monitor

London

Like a good Scots schoolmaster, Sir Alec Douglas-Home has given his fellow Commonwealth prime ministers an assignment for when they gather in London, July 8-15.

Sir Alec wishes them to reappraise what this rapidly growing association means today. In a BBC interview, he said he wanted the prime ministers to see if they could give reality to the modern Commonwealth in the eyes not only of its members but of the world outside.

The British Prime Minister intends that the 18-nation "talking shop" should discuss ways and means of marshaling Commonwealth resources for the development of schemes of technical assistance and cooperation. He believes that older and more prosperous Commonwealth countries can strengthen the foundations of newly independent members.

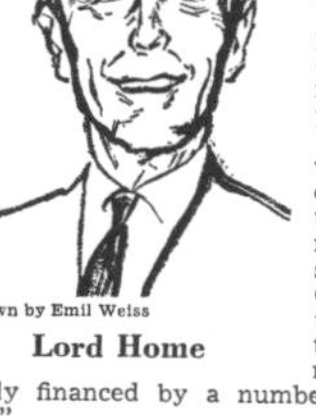

Drawn by Emil Weiss

Lord Home

"I think we want, as far as we can, to make this a cooperative effort," Sir Alec told his BBC listeners. "It may be, therefore, that we should explore the field of Commonwealth projects so that certain projects, in particular in the field of technical assistance, should be jointly financed by a number of Commonwealth countries."

Sir Alec should give his ministerial colleagues some kind of prize if they come up with a new, generally satisfying definition of "this great mixture of nations." Not long ago, an anonymous Conservative contributor to the Times challenged many a cherished notion by writing that "the Commonwealth has really become a gigantic farce."

Continued on Page 2, Column 6

THE CHRISTIAN SCIENCE MONITOR

Registered in U. S. Patent Office
AN INTERNATIONAL DAILY NEWSPAPER

VOLUME 56 NO. 274 | BOSTON, FRIDAY, OCTOBER 16, 1964 | R NEW ENGLAND EDITION | TWO SECTIONS | TEN CENTS A COPY

© 1964 THE CHRISTIAN SCIENCE PUBLISHING SOCIETY All Rights Reserved

Top Bureaucrats Oust Khrushchev; Wilson Poised to Take British Reins

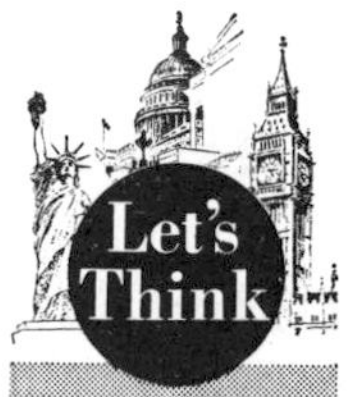

By Erwin D. Canham

As The Christian Science Monitor makes clear in its editorial comment on the subject, nothing is more important than basic integrity in the choice of a president. And as was pointed out in this space two days ago, the issue of personal character is already biting deep in the campaign.

What will be the tangible effect of the Jenkins case? Will there be still more sensations? And on which side?

Unless new and clearly mitigating facts come to light, it seems to me that the Jenkins case will hurt President Johnson seriously. The Republican Party officials may be right who regard the issue of personal integrity as the biggest issue of the campaign.

⁂

On the narrow question of whether Walter Jenkins should have been permitted to stay on a high-security job, having a blackmailable police record, there can be little doubt.

President Johnson tells us he knew nothing of the situation. Normal security investigation evidently antedated the first arrest. The probe by the Federal Bureau of Investigation which President Johnson has ordered may bring new information to light as to how such a risk could have continued for 5½ years.

⁂

On the broader question of President Johnson's total record, there is more argument. Personally, I think he is vulnerable on a number of points. It seems to me improper for an official in his position to make a fortune out of a governmentally regulated enterprise, television and radio, even though others have. His first Senate election, in 1948, is very difficult to explain. The Bobby Baker case has not been fully explored. There are other unanswered questions.

There is now no avoiding these questions. In 1952, public opinion—and Dwight D. Eisenhower—demanded that Richard M. Nixon should give a full explanation of his campaign funds. He did so, although not without continuing controversy. In 1920, late one night, a group of Republican Party leaders turned to Warren Gamaliel Harding and demanded if there were anything in his private life which should prevent him from being the party's nominee. His negative answer remains a blot on American history. The sad consequences may well have had some relationship to the cover-up.

⁂

If President Johnson is called upon to clarify elements relative to the integrity issue, so is Senator Goldwater. Published reports concerning Las Vegas and Phoenix underworld characters deserve full and frank disclosure in order to dispel them. The Lockport Felt Company's relationship to Rep. William E. Miller should also be clearly explored.

Let us hope the American air can grow sweeter rather than fouler in the 2½ weeks to election. Neither candidate is by nature a mud slinger. The American people do not want a mud slinger as president. They want a man of integrity.

⁂

Bland ignoring never healed any problem. The facts, even if they seem to hurt, will ultimately heal. The American people respect candor. The air is already filled with innuendo, and some fact.

The moment of truth is approaching. It is a time when we all need the whole truth. We need to be able to recognize it. We need to dismiss in our own thoughts any condemnation not based on knowledge and fact. The 1964 campaign, even now, can lend luster to American statecraft if it is marked by honest speaking, responsible restraint, and careful, unemotional weighing of fact by troubled voters.

Close Margin

By Peter Lyne
Parliamentary Correspondent of The Christian Science Monitor

London

Harold Wilson has emerged as Britain's next Prime Minister in a dramatic, closely fought election.

The Conservative and Labor Parties engaged in a ding-dong battle right down to the finish Friday. The Labor Party emerged victorious but with a majority so slender that political uncertainty threatens.

All night Thursday and Friday morning, Britons had been glued to TV sets and radios as the fortunes of the two main parties swayed back and forth.

'A Bare Majority'

By early Friday afternoon however, Mr. Wilson was able to announce: "We have just a bare majority" in the House of Commons.

At that point, Labor had won 315 votes, one short of a majority in the 630-member Commons. However, it held a plurality of one over the other two parties, with 11 more constituencies to be heard from.

The Tories at the same time had some 300 seats to their credit.

Thus ended 13 years in the political wilderness for the Labor Party.

Earlier, analysts and the computers had been forecasting a final Labor lead over the Conservatives of perhaps 17 seats in a 630-seat House of Commons.

This was smaller than the majority Labor supporters had hoped for as the results were coming in.

The Liberal Party was expected to win perhaps 7 or 8 seats, thus reducing Labor's over-all majority in the Commons to 10.

Test for Government

The close outcome will test how small a majority a British government can effectively work with.

Some of the newly elected Labor MPs were saying that a keen new Socialist administration could manage with a House of Commons majority of a dozen or less.

Tory MPs, on the other hand, were contending that parliamentary government in Britain is apt to become "degraded" by very small majorities. They cited the parliaments of 1950 and 1951, when majorities ranged between 8 and 16 seats.

The news that Nikita S. Khrushchev had been replaced as Soviet leader started Britain's election night off in a mood of high drama.

A Wilson victory in Britain would mean two new world political figures within 24 hours.

There was speculation, too, about whether Sir Alec Douglas-Home's Conservative administration would have benefited if the news from Moscow had come a little earlier. Would Sir Alec's tougher line on defense have won his party more votes in light of new uncertainties in world affairs?

British Tories were cautious about commenting on Mr. Khrushchev's deposition. Mr. Wilson indicated he would like to know more about the circumstances of the changeover in Moscow.

Kosygin Described

He added that he was well acquainted with Alexei N. Kosygin, new Soviet Premier. Mr. Wilson had found him "tough, able, efficient, and a notable specialist in industrial matters."

Mr. Wilson was asked whether if he became British Prime Minister in the next 24 hours he would seek a visit to Moscow. He replied in effect that the Western alliance would have top priority with him. He would like to visit the American president first.

Meanwhile, as Britons went to work Friday, they still did not know for certain who their prime minister was to be. The 1964 election has proved once again how closely divided the British people are into two main political camps.

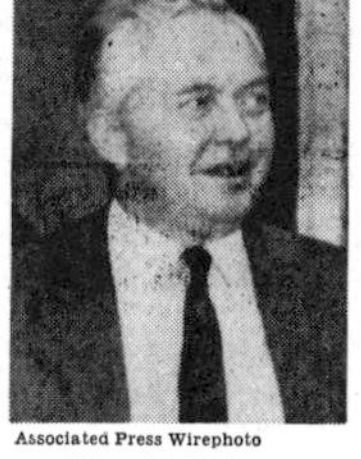

Associated Press Wirephoto
Harold Wilson

Red China Fires A-Device

By Reuters

Peking

Communist China Friday exploded a nuclear device.

A press communiqué stated:

"China exploded an atom bomb in the western region of China at 1500 hours (Peking time) on Oct. 16, 1964, and thereby conducted successfully its first nuclear test."

The announcement was made by the official New China News Agency.

The blas made Communist China the fifth nuclear power after the United States, the Soviet Union, Britain, and France.

Raido Peking announced the test was a success.

It was the explosive result of a long drive by Mao Tze-tung's regime to join the world's nuclear club.

The blast ended speculation started by United States Secretary of State Dean Rusk several weeks ago that Communist China would set off a nuclear device "in the near future."

The New China News Agency had been warning subscribers to stand by for an important announcement. At 11 p.m. Peking time. The news flash on the explosion of the bomb came right on schedule.

'Morality Issue' Gets New Impetus

By Richard L. Strout
Staff Correspondent of The Christian Science Monitor

Washington

Washington believes that the so-called "morality issue" will be the dominating feature of Sen. Barry Goldwater's drive for the presidency in the final two weeks of the campaign. It has been given an extraordinary, if disagreeable, boost by the case of Walter W. Jenkins, just resigned as President Johnson's confidential assistant.

There have been some signs that Senator Goldwater's political rating was rising on the opinion polls and many believed that this trend would continue in any event in the final days. Under the present circumstances, the Jenkins episode is bound to be held responsible for any Goldwater upturn, though whether it is actually responsible will be hard to determine till after the election.

Many conservatives over the country, it is believed, who have hitherto taken a critical attitude toward Senator Goldwater may use the Jenkins incident as a bridge for returning to their former home, the Republican Party.

Wide Poll Gap

Washington has pretty well written off Senator Goldwater's presidential chances, though the surprising victory of President Truman in 1948 is recalled. Senator Goldwater is much further behind than Mr. Truman was; in fact, the present gap is wider than at any previous time since Dr. Gallup began taking measurements.

An antiadministration reaction in the last minute might have sweeping political consequences in marginal election districts. It could make the difference in a variety of close legislative races, particularly in the House.

President Johnson's own feelings are not forgotten. He is a proud and sensitive man, and this scandal in his official family, following the Bobby Baker case, must have the most poignant meaning. The two men who were close to him in his career as majority leader have both resigned under a cloud.

Formula of Attack

It is not thought that Senator Goldwater will refer to the Jenkins case immediately in his campaign, but his previous formula of attack fits the new situation. He declared recently at Kansas City, for example, that a sterner morality is needed at the apex of American political life:

"As it is, the White House remains silent in the face of scandal, grave suspicion and a sense of national doubt unequalled in our time," he said. He referred to the Baker case.

Continued on Page 3, Col. 3

Khrushchevism: UN View

By Earl W. Foell
United Nations Correspondent of The Christian Science Monitor

United Nations, N.Y.

Which parts of Khrushchevism will survive—which be repudiated?

Eastern Europeans and Westerners here who have served in or specialized in the affairs of Moscow are waiting to see signs of what basic Soviet forces lie behind the new duo of Leonid I. Brezhnev and Alexei N. Kosygin before hardening their answers.

But among a wide range of diplomatic Sovietologists here, there was informed speculation viewing the fall of Nikita S. Khrushchev as:

- A propaganda triumph for Peking in the new Bolshevik-Menshevik struggle among world Communists.
- A possible retrenchment to warier and tougher competition with Washington.
- A change not likely, however, to alter Moscow's need to gain infusions of Western European capital — particularly German—on long-term credit.
- The forerunner of a period of uneasy caution and less freedom of diplomatic action for Eastern European leaders.
- A difficult problem for the UN, currently set on a Soviet-American collision course over financing, which neither Moscow's new leaders nor the American President may now have much latitude to resolve.
- The start of a period of manipulating Soviet farm policy, which may serve as a litmus test as to whether Khrushchevian incentives or old-style pressures will be used on the economy.

Cause of Downfall?

All these preliminary assessments were of course conjectural in the early hours of this latest great change in Soviet leadership. Analysts were still digesting the opening policy declaration of the new leaders, waiting to see how performance matches words, and hedging until their longevity in office becomes more clear.

A view shared by many Eastern and Western Europeans here was that Mr. Khrushchev had lost out basically because he was having difficulty with Russia's ancient problem of trying to avoid a two-front struggle.

He had destroyed relations with Communist China to the east without successfully ending competition to the west.

This in itself was felt to be excusable as long as the split and thaw bore fruit. But the schism in almost every part of the Communist world, accompanied by the failure of Mr. Khrushchev's bold agricultural policies apparently gave the opponents too much ammunition.

One astute neutral delegate with long service in Moscow pointed to another superficial but psychologically important factor: Khrushchev's earthy behavior.

"His shrewd buffoonery irritated many of the old stalwarts in the leadership. When Khrushchev almost fell from power once before, it will be remembered, it was recorded that Vyacheslav M. Molotov had said, 'We're not going to send that clown Nikita Sergeivitch to that meeting, are we?'

"The traditionalists have been offended, but they just had to bide their time until the party splits throughout the length and breadth of communism and economic difficulties at home became decisive."

News Hits Hard

The scene here at the United Nations as the news filtered in was one of consternation. The shock wave was of a lesser magnitude than that caused by last year's assassination news. But it was accompanied by the same deep concern over change at the helm of one of the two world super powers.

Secretary-General U Thant was reportedly left momentarily speechless with pen in midair while he digested the news that the man he had visited in Moscow this summer no longer ruled.

For the Secretary-General it meant new soundings, new attempts to get the big powers to find limited areas of agreement under which the UN could resume the slow easing of tensions that has prevailed since the test-ban treaty was signed.

Eastern Europeans were probably hardest hit by the news. Some expressed concern that Washington had not been able to make more gestures in recent months to back Mr. Khrushchev's Westward efforts.

Other Special Reports

Washington
British Labor Party's views are well known to United States officials. **Page 2**

London
Britons look to the tasks ahead as the Labor Party for the first time in 13 years musters a majority in the House of Commons. **Page 4**

New Delhi
India is deeply concerned about its economic ties with Moscow following the Khrushchev replacement. It wonders if the new regime will be as 'pro-Indian.' **Page 7**

Bonn
West Germans wait to see if the new Soviet leaders will carry out the scheduled Khrushchev visit to Bonn. **Page 7**

Moscow
Profiles of the two new chiefs in the Kremlin. **Page 7**

Change Made in Secrecy

By Paul Wohl
Written for The Christian Science Monitor

The Soviet Communist Party's upper echelons have won out over the rank and file and the people at large.

Premier Nikita S. Khrushchev's fall from power represents a victory of the bureaucratic traditionalists.

It also was a victory for Peking. The Soviet Union's "internal Chinese" were joined by many of their political opposites who stand for more leeway in world communism.

The suddenness of the move shows that the Soviet Union continues to be ruled by cabal rather than by constitutional processes, and that the people themselves have little say.

The "Khrushchevchina" or the Khrushchev circus, as critical Soviets called the former Premier's regime, ended almost as dramatically—and for the outsider unexpectedly—as the "antiparty group" of Messrs. Molotov, Malenkov, and others in 1957.

Not so long ago Mr. Khrushchev had spoken of his intention of being around in 1980. His robust alertness impressed recent visitors. Yet Tass reported that he resigned because of his "advanced age and deterioration of his health."

His son-in-law and personal foreign envoy, Izvestia editor Alexei Adzhubei, a Central Committee member, was reportedly ousted on Thursday. For the first time in history, his newspaper failed to appear. The printing or distribution of the issue must have been stopped by order of the party. This seems to indicate that the popular Premier, through his son-in-law had tried a last-minute appeal to the people.

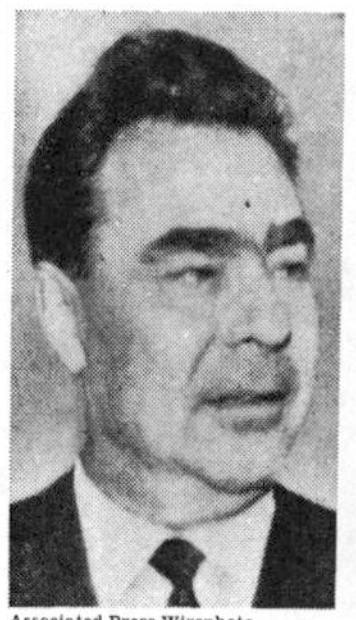

Associated Press Wirephoto
Leonid I. Brezhnev
Party First Secretary

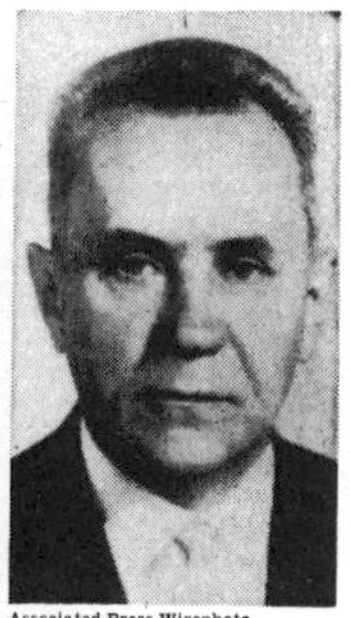

Associated Press Wirephoto
Alexei N. Kosygin
New Premier

Decided in Plenum

The crucial decision to oust Mr. Khrushchev was taken at an unscheduled plenum of the party's Central Committee. According to one report, the plenum convened on Monday, Oct. 12, while the Premier was vacationing on the Black Sea coast.

Because of the committee's surprise meeting, Mr. Khrushchev on Tuesday rushed to Moscow and granted only a few minutes to French Atomic Minister Gaston Palewski, who had come especially to confer with him.

The new setup in which Leonid I. Brezhnev succeeded Mr. Khrushchev as First Party Secretary and former First Deputy Premier Alexei N. Kosygin became Premier is an interim regime.

Mr. Brezhnev last December was described to this writer as "a reed painted the color of steel." Mr. Kosygin is a politically faceless technician who, since Stalin's day, has been identified with consumer goods and light industry.

No Change Suggested

Messrs. Brezhnev and Kosygin present a façade which outwardly looks like a continuation of the popular policies of Mr. Khrushchev.

Actually Mr. Brezhnev, shorn of Mr. Khrushchev's support, will have to lean upon the military high command. His political career was made in political administration of the armed forces.

Mr. Kosygin, once a favorite of Stalin, who at a critical moment entrusted him with the reorganization of Soviet finances—and took him along on a Black Sea cruise as his only companion from among the members of his Cabinet—stands for tradition rather than reform. His personal dignity and know-how are respected but he completely lacks popular appeal.

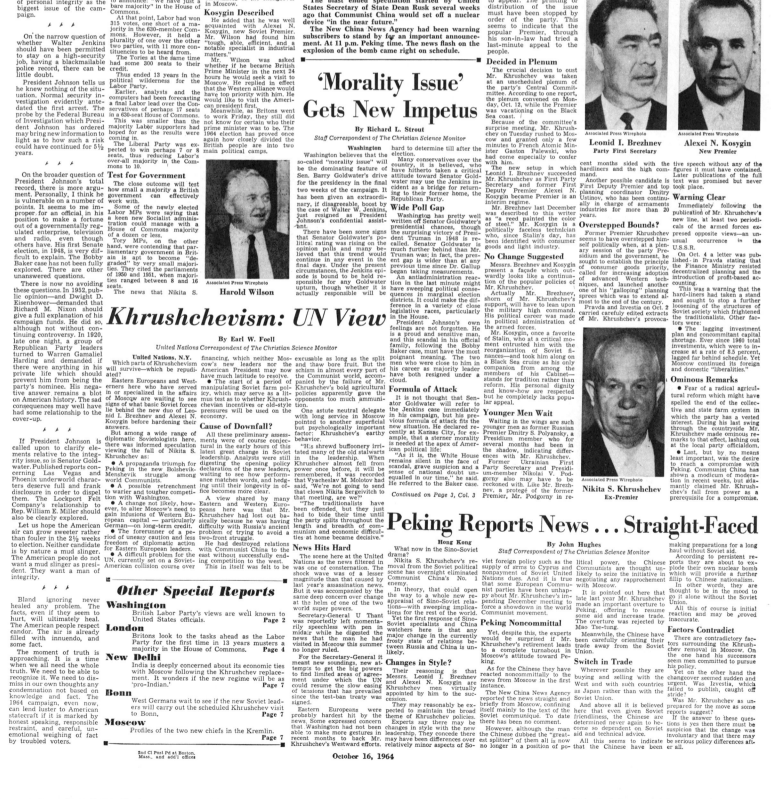

Younger Men Wait

Waiting in the wings are such younger men as former Russian Premier Dmitry S. Polyansky, a Presidium member who for several months had been in the shadow, indicating differences with Mr. Khrushchev.

Former Ukrainian First Party Secretary and Presidium-member Nikolai V. Podgorny also may have to be reckoned with. Like Mr. Brezhnev, a protegé of the former Premier, Mr. Podgorny in recent months sided with the hardliners and the high command.

Another possible candidate is First Deputy Premier and top planning coordinator Dmitry Ustinov, who has been continually in charge of armaments industries for more than 20 years.

Overstepped Bounds?

Former Premier Khrushchev seems to have overstepped himself politically when, at a plenary session of the party Presidium and the government, he sought to establish the principle of consumer goods priority, called for increasing adoption of advanced Western techniques, and launched another one of his "galloping" planning sprees which was to extend almost to the end of the century.

Pravda and Izvestia on Oct. 2 carried carefuly edited extracts of Mr. Khrushchev's provocative speech without any of the figures it must have contained. Later publications of the full text was promised but never took place.

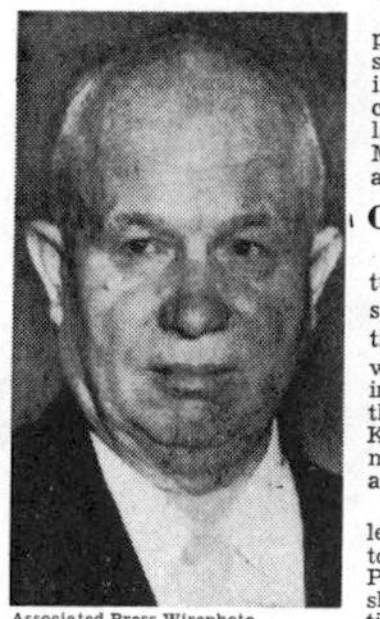

Associated Press Wirephoto
Nikita S. Khrushchev
Ex-Premier

Warning Clear

Immediately following the publication of Mr. Khrushchev's new line, at least two periodicals of the armed forces expresed opposite views—an unusual occurrence in the U.S.S.R.

On Oct. 4 a letter was published in Pravda stating that the Finance Ministry resisted decentralized planning and the introduction of profit-based accounting.

This was a warning that the hard-liners had taken a stand and sought to stop a further loosening of the structures of Soviet society which frightened the traditionalists. Other factors were:

- The lagging investment plan and concommitant capital shortage. Ever since 1960 total investments, which were to increase at a rate of 8.5 percent, lagged far behind schedule. Yet Moscow continued its foreign and domestic "liberalities."

Ominous Remarks

- Fear of a radical agricultural reform which might have spelled the end of the collective and state farm system in which the party has a vested interest. During his last swing through the countryside Mr. Khrushchev made ominous remarks to that effect, lashing out at the local party officialdom.
- Last, but by no means least important, was the desire to reach a compromise with Peking. Communist China has shown a modicum of moderation in recent weeks, but adamantly claimed Mr. Khrushchev's fall from power as a prerequisite for a compromise.

Peking Reports News ... Straight-Faced

By John Hughes
Staff Correspondent of The Christian Science Monitor

Hong Kong

What now in the Sino-Soviet drama?

Nikita S. Khrushchev's removal from the Soviet political scene has overnight eliminated Communist China's No. 1 enemy.

In theory, that could open the way to a whole new reappraisal of Sino-Soviet relations—with sweeping implications for the rest of the world.

Yet the first response of Sino-Soviet specialists and China watchers here is that any major change in the currently frosty state of relations between Russia and China is unlikely.

Changes in Style?

Their reasoning is that Messrs. Leonid I. Brezhnev and Alexei N. Kosygin are Khrushchev men virtually appointed by him to the succession.

They may reasonably be expected to maintain the broad theme of Khrushchev policies.

Experts say there may be changes in style with the new leadership. They concede there may have been differences over relatively minor aspects of Soviet foreign policy such as the supply of arms to Cyprus and nonpayment of Soviet United Nations dues. And it is true that some European Communist parties have been unhappy about Mr. Khrushchev's impending December meeting to force a showdown in the world Communist movement.

Peking Noncommittal

Yet, despite this, the experts would be surprised if Mr. Khrushchev's retirement leads to a complete turnabout in Moscow's attitude toward Peking.

As for the Chinese they have reacted noncommittally to the news from Moscow in the first instance.

The New China News Agency reported the news straight and briefly from Moscow, confining itself mainly to the text of the Soviet communiqué. To date there has been no comment.

However, although the man the Chinese dubbed the "greatest splitter" of them all is now no longer in a position of political power, the Chinese Communists are thought unlikely to seize the initiative in negotiating any rapprochement with Moscow.

It is pointed out here that late last year Mr. Khrushchev made an important overture to Peking, offering to resume some aid and increase trade. The overture was rejected by Mao Tse-tung.

Meanwhile, the Chinese have been carefully orienting their trade away from the Soviet Union.

Switch in Trade

Wherever possible they are buying and selling with the West and with such countries as Japan rather than with the Soviet Union.

And above all it is believed here that even given Soviet friendliness, the Chinese are determined never again to become so dependent on Soviet aid and technical advice.

All this seems to indicate that the Chinese have been making preparations for a long haul without Soviet aid.

According to persistent reports they are about to explode their own nuclear bomb which will provide a further fillip to Chinese nationalism.

In other words, they are thought to be in the mood to go it alone without the Soviet Union.

All this of course is initial reaction and may be proved inaccurate.

Factors Contradict

There are contradictory factors surrounding the Khrushchev removal in Moscow. On the one hand his successors seem men committed to pursue his policy.

Yet on the other hand the changeover seemed sudden and urgent. Was Izvestia, which failed to publish, caught off stride?

Was Mr. Khrushchev as unprepared for the move as some reports suggest?

If the answer to these questions is yes then there must be suspicion that the change was involuntary and that there may be serious policy differences after all.

THE CHRISTIAN SCIENCE MONITOR

Registered in U. S. Patent Office
AN INTERNATIONAL DAILY NEWSPAPER

VOLUME 56 NO. 290 | BOSTON, WEDNESDAY, NOVEMBER 4, 1964 | NEW ENGLAND EDITION | TWO SECTIONS | TEN CENTS A COPY

© 1964 THE CHRISTIAN SCIENCE PUBLISHING SOCIETY All Rights Reserved

Johnson-Humphrey Landslide Sharpens U.S. Image Before the World

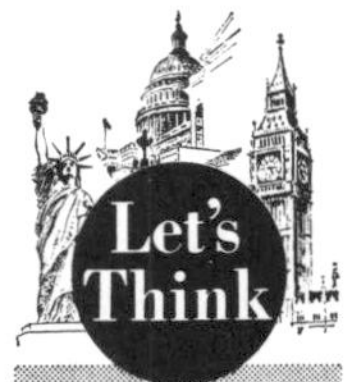
Let's Think

By Erwin D. Canham

What can the American nation learn from this election? What can the rest of the world conclude?

For Americans, one of the great lessons may be that to depart from the traditional, deeply rooted path of political moderation bears great dangers. The Johnson landslide, resulting from the Goldwater nomination, has grievously damaged two-party government in much of the nation. Only restraint on the part of the victors will preserve balanced power. But, as in 1936, balance could soon be restored.

For the world, the steadiness of Americans in pursuit of the goals they have followed for a quarter of a century is reaffirmed. A great wave of relief now arises from many nations.

The ardent minority which supported Senator Goldwater has most to ponder today. Many of them upheld him and voted for him for the best of reasons. Only a few—but they were very vocal—really partook of actual extremism. The rest were sincere, thoughtful, dedicated people who believed in curbing the trend toward ever bigger federal government, who wished to "win" over communism, who were distrustful of President Johnson's political maneuverings.

These people should not blame the eloquent outcome on press reporting, on manipulation, or on skulduggery of any kind. Their candidate lost because the overwhelming majority of Americans flatly rejected an extremist position, and were unpersuaded of the presidential qualifications of Senator Goldwater.

The test which the right-wing elements in American partisanship have long desired has taken place. Its results prove that most citizens of the republic are in the vast middle ground of political thought, where the Republican and Democratic parties have shared presidential office almost equally during this entire century.

Many of the people who voted for President Johnson split their tickets and supported local Republicans. Never before has a Republican or Democratic nominee run so far behind the rest of his ticket as did the Arizona Senator. But the magnitude of the sweep removed temporarily from public life many useful Republicans, most of them moderates. The consequences will be felt in both houses of Congress and in many state houses from coast to coast.

President Franklin Roosevelt's sweep in 1936 — the most comparable election result in this century — was soon followed by his effort to alter the membership of the Supreme Court. Congress refused to follow him. But the complexion of the court soon changed through its own internal processes.

By 1938, the power of New Deal majorities was greatly curbed. In the years just ahead, President Johnson may also find a Congress impressed by his tremendous sweep and responsive to his political prowess but nevertheless determined to be near the middle of the road.

President Johnson has himself shown many signs of political moderation and restraint. He owes the magnitude of his victory (alongside the limitations of his opponent) to his appeal to the vast middle ground. He will lead the nation effectively as he continues to be the President of all the people.

The United States is instinctively a two-party nation. Its parties, indeed, always have been coalitions balanced from within. The first effort to "realign" them into monolithic conservative and liberal groups has led to an adverse landslide.

Over all, Americans have spoken with unmistakable urgency. They want moderate government; not left-wing or right-wing government but steady, balanced progress toward solution of pressing problems.

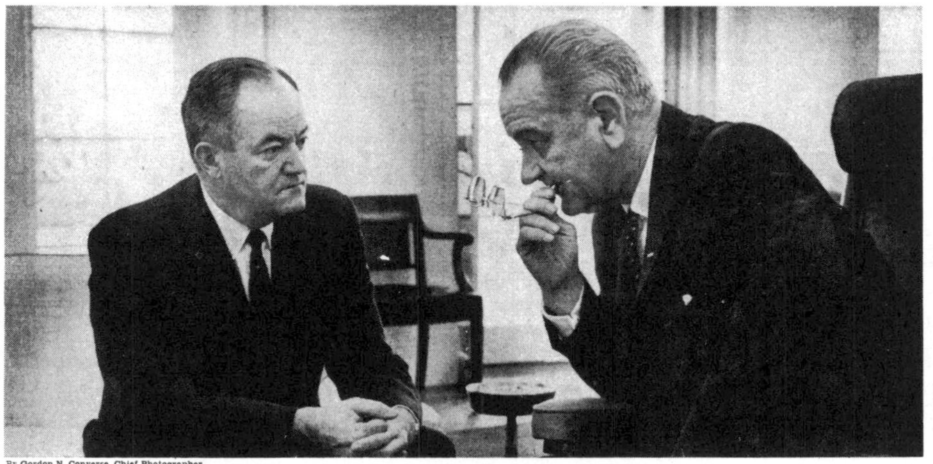

By Gordon N. Converse, Chief Photographer

The Johnson-Humphrey Team Face to Face

Brooke and Richardson on Team

Split-Ticket Vote Carries Volpe In

By Edgar M. Mills
New England Political Editor of The Christian Science Monitor

Split-ticket-voting Massachusetts has done it again.

It has elected former Governor, John A. Volpe, to the governorship in a cliff-hanger finish.

It has reelected Republican Attorney General Edward W. Brooke by a plurality of close to 400,000 votes.

It has elected Elliot L. Richardson of Brookline, former United States Attorney, as Lieutenant Governor, over Executive Councilor John W. Costello (D) of Boston, by a close margin.

But at the same time it gave President Johnson the state's 14 electoral votes with the greatest plurality in the state's history.

And Sen. Edward M. Kennedy (D) almost matched the Johnson plurality in winning a full six-year term in the Senate his brother, the late President Kennedy, left to assume the presidency in 1961.

The situation is similar to that in 1960 when Mr. Volpe was elected Governor despite President Kennedy's 511,000 plurality in his home state.

Strong GOP Team

In Tuesday's election President Johnson's margin far outstripped the Kennedy 1960 plurality. His lead over Sen. Barry Goldwater was approximately 900,000, or about 3 to 1.

The Volpe, Brooke, and Richardson victories in the face of the Johnson Kennedy runaway triumphs saved the Bay State Republican Party from political disaster.

As Governor, Mr. Volpe will face a strongly Democratic Legislature in which Republican minorities have slipped below effective levels. But as Governor in 1961 and 1962 he had to work with a Democratic-controlled Legislature.

The Volpe-Brooke-Richardson wins give Massachusetts a team of corruption fighters in the top three statewide offices. All three men have records of action against corruption in high places. They had been regarded as the strongest Republican team in the statewide field in many years.

Mr. Volpe, Mr. Brooke, and Mr. Richardson will hold the three most powerful statewide offices in Massachusetts. But the Democrats maintained control of the other statewide posts.

Secretary of State Kevin H. White (D) won his third-term bid by a wide margin over State Rep. Wallace B. Crawford (R) of Pittsfield.

Similarly State Treasurer Robert Q. Crane (D) also won election to a full term, defeating State Rep. Robert C. Hahn (R) of Stoughton handily.

State Auditor Thaddeus Buczko (D) easily triumphed over Republican Elwynn J. Miller of Medford, a CPA.

Attorney General Brooke's big victory had been widely anticipated. But all observers rated the Volpe-Bellotti and Richardson-Costello contests as extremely close. The results proved them to be correct.

The gubernatorial triumph was welcome vindication for former Governor Volpe. Two years ago he lost his reelection bid to the present Gov. Endicott Peabody by 5,431 votes. At that time he was charged with failure to campaign sufficiently hard and with overconfidence.

This year Mr. Volpe hit the campaign trail early and hard.

Candor Praised

He and Mr. Richardson made political capital of their support of referendum question No. 5 under which the voters backed restriction of the powers of the Executive Council.

Governor-elect Volpe won wide praise for his candor in advocating a program of new taxes to solve state and municipal fiscal problems. His advocacy of a limited sales tax as one means of meeting financial needs projected that into the campaign as a major issue. But he weathered the possible adverse effects of such boldness, while Lieutenant Governor Bellotti suffered from charges that he failed to meet the problem head on.

A factor in the Volpe victory was the projection of a better public image than Mr. Bellotti. The latter was hurt by rumors concerning the source of his voluminous campaign funds.

In addition the vote for Lieutenant Governor Bellotti was cut heavily in Democratic Boston. He had a Boston plurality of 46,000 votes, far below the normal Democratic margin.

Continued on Page 2, Col. 4

Related stories: Pages 2, 4, and 5

'Extreme Center'

By Richard L. Strout
Staff Correspondent of The Christian Science Monitor

Washington

No election ever concludes with the words, "The end"; it is always, "To be continued."

President Johnson has won a landslide of the century; now comes the task of interpretation . . . and conciliation.

Americans "voted as many but . . . must face the world as one," President Johnson declared.

Sen. Barry Goldwater delayed the normal statement conceding the election. One of his aides indicated that the conservative fight would be continued.

Huge Majority in Congress

In foreign affairs, Mr. Johnson's overwhelming victory makes the United States Government the most stable element in a quivering world.

It crushingly rejects a tougher American line to the Communists and accepts, instead, the policy of continuing search for agreements with the Kremlin.

In domestic affairs, it accepts a policy of gradual federal expansion rather than curtailment, carried through by a President who is described as not of the extreme "Right," nor of the extreme "Left," but of the "extreme Center."

President Johnson not only won a personal victory, but carried into office a bigger majority than ever in Congress. It gives him great momentum when Congress meets to carry into effect his economic and social proposals.

In foreign affairs, it gives him opportunity to reappraise American policies toward the Communist world, and Vietnam, if desired.

Few GOP 'Moderates' Emerge

Only a few major figures among the Republican "moderates" emerged through the storm.

With 91 percent of the voting units reporting, Mr. Johnson had 39,505,022 votes and Mr. Goldwater 24,889,651.

In Michigan, Republican Gov. George Romney survived the double stress of a Johnson landslide and disaffection of some Goldwater supporters. The state went 2 to 1 for Mr. Johnson.

In Illinois, attractive Republican gubernatorial candidate Charles H. Percy was defeated by Democratic incumbent Gov. Otto J. Kerner.

The New York Senate race attracted almost as much attention as the presidential race. Young Robert F. Kennedy, former United States Attorney General and brother of the late President, defeated anti-Goldwater incumbent Kenneth B. Keating. He will join his younger brother, Edward M. Kennedy (D) of Massachusetts, in the Senate.

Continued on Page 16, Column 6

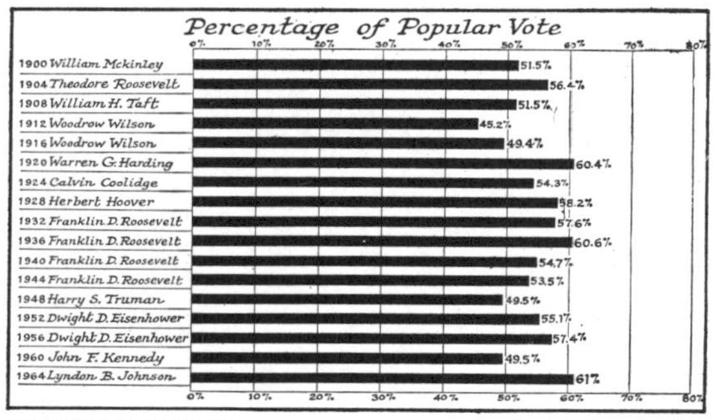
Percentage of Popular Vote
0% 10% 20% 30% 40% 50% 60% 70% 80%
1900 William Mckinley 51.5%
1904 Theodore Roosevelt 56.4%
1908 William H. Taft 51.5%
1912 Woodrow Wilson 45.2%
1916 Woodrow Wilson 49.4%
1920 Warren G. Harding 60.4%
1924 Calvin Coolidge 54.3%
1928 Herbert Hoover 58.2%
1932 Franklin D. Roosevelt 57.6%
1936 Franklin D. Roosevelt 60.6%
1940 Franklin D. Roosevelt 54.7%
1944 Franklin D. Roosevelt 53.5%
1948 Harry S. Truman 49.5%
1952 Dwight D. Eisenhower 55.1%
1956 Dwight D. Eisenhower 57.4%
1960 John F. Kennedy 49.5%
1964 Lyndon B. Johnson 61%

By Russell H. Lenz, Chief Cartographer

Based on nearly complete returns

Top GOP Survivors?

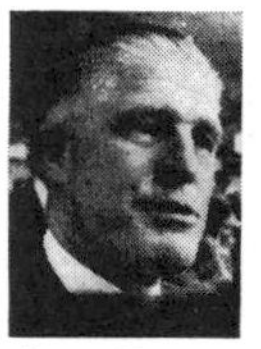

George Romney

Gov. George Romney has become a man of the hour of the Republican Party. He won reelection to a second term in Michigan despite the two-to-one margin by which President Johnson carried the state. Governor Romney's edge over Rep. Neil Staebler was approximately 6 percent. A moderate Republican, Governor Romney declined to endorse Sen. Barry Goldwater. He now is in the front row of contenders for the GOP nomination for the presidency in 1968. [Story: Page 6.]

The name of Taft may once more rise high on the national Republican horizon. Robert Taft Jr., son of the longtime "Mr. Republican," is in a seesaw battle with Sen. Stephen M. Young. Mr. Taft held an early lead and had been thought the winner. A moderate Republican with conservative leanings, Mr. Taft for the past two years has been the Ohio representative at large. He would be a possible presidential candidate for 1968 if he won.

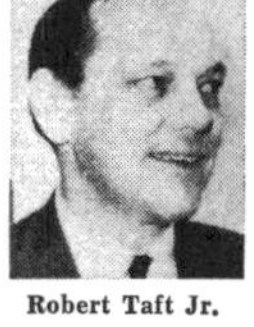

Robert Taft Jr.

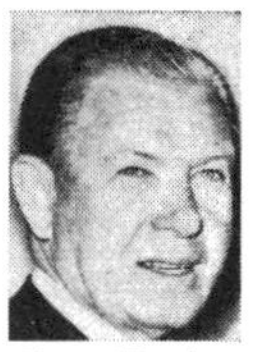

George Murphy

George Murphy has surprisingly bounded to the fore among Republicans in the West. This actor-turned-businessman appears to have unseated Sen. Pierre Salinger, former press secretary to President Kennedy. As a Senator from populous California, he could play a major role in forming national Republican policy. He is considered conservative to moderate in political philosophy. President Johnson captured California's 40 electoral votes by a plurality of well over one million popular votes. [Story: Page 3.]

Sen. Hugh Scott is the most prominent leader of the GOP Eastern liberal wing likely to survive the Johnson landslide. Although the Democratic presidential ticket carried Pennsylvania almost two to one, Senator Scott edged out his Democratic senatorial opponent, Miss Genevieve Blatt. He likely will be increasingly influential in party councils, especially if the GOP liberals and moderates succeed in taking over leadership of the party. [Story: Page 6.]

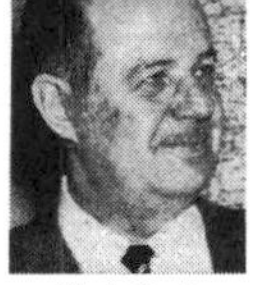

Hugh Scott

Republicans: Which Way?

By William H. Stringer
Chief of the Washington Bureau of The Christian Science Monitor

Washington

Though retired to private life, Sen. Barry Goldwater remains the "titular" head of the Republican Party and its chief conservative spokesman. The party plainly faces a tough rebuilding job following the Johnson landslide.

The question immediately posed is how tightly—and for how long—will the deeply conservative GOP faction symbolized by such Goldwaterites as Dean Burch, chairman of the national committee, and Denison Kitchell, Senator Goldwater's campaign director, be able to maintain their hold on the party's machinery and destiny?

Question for '68

Mr. Kitchell seemed to be looking far to the future when he declared, as the Johnson victory was piling up, "It doesn't look like we're going to win this first round. Four years from now, we're going to get the government back to where it belongs."

Defeated candidates Thomas E. Dewey and Richard M. Nixon were unable to maintain a tight enough hold on their party to give their own candidacies a second round. Very few observers now believe that Senator Goldwater will again be a candidate in 1968—if indeed he would run again.

Will the Goldwaterites be able to maintain such a position of influence within the party that they can dictate the choice of candidate and the party platform in 1968? This depends on evolving sentiment within the Republican Party, and on the stature and outlook of those Republicans in Congress and the governorships who survived the Johnson triumph.

Gov. Robert Smylie of Idaho argues that Nov. 3 did not produce a "Democratic Party" landslide—that many highly eligible Republicans survived, even though such men as Charles H. Percy, the promising GOP candidate for the Illinois governorship, and Sen. Kenneth Keating of New York went down to defeat.

Besides Republican congressmen elected in the Deep South for the first time, the party can point to such vote-getters as Sen.-Elect Robert Taft Jr. of Ohio, congressman John Lindsay of New York City, and the reelected Governor of Michigan, George Romney. Any Northern Republican who survived the Johnson landslide obviously had to be a potent vote-getter.

Will these individuals, plus such incumbent governors as Nelson A. Rockefeller of New York, Mark O. Hatfield of Oregon, and William W. Scranton of Pennsylvania, move gradually to counter the Goldwaterites' hold on the Republican Party, arguing that the Goldwater philosophy stands discredited by the Senator's resounding defeat?

If past history is any guide, long before the 1968 convention, Republicans who are not of the Goldwater "establishment" will begin major efforts to oust the Goldwaterites from their positions as state chairmen and potential delegates. This happened to the Dewey faction after the former New York Governor was defeated in the 1948 upset.

Leadership Attacked

Power in a party which does not control the White House tends to drift to the congressional leadership, with the state governors exercising additional influence. The conservative Dirksen-Halleck leadership of the GOP in Congress is coming under attack from liberals on the grounds of relative ineffectiveness.

To rebuild strength and influence in the face of what is likely to be a resourceful, strongly led Democratic Party, the Republicans will need the help of every effective individual, GOP leaders acknowledge. Here the role of Senator Goldwater will be thoughtfully discussed in the weeks ahead.

Before undertaking his campaign, the Arizona Senator said in interviews that he would not wish to contest the presidency if there were the prospect of going down to such serious defeat as to discredit his brand of conservatism for years to come. Experts now are seeking to assess how serious was the Goldwater defeat.

Formula Misses

The election returns show that, despite the earnest and dedicated efforts of Senator Goldwater, his brand of sharp conservatism captured a majority almost nowhere outside the Deep South, where the civil-rights issue played a strong role. He did not win the Northern suburbs, where receptivity to the Goldwater philosophy might have been expected to be stronger.

The Goldwater victory formula, which counted on the capture of Midwestern and Western states, failed completely.

This would suggest that the rebuilding of the GOP will lie more in the hands of the Romneys, Tafts, Hatfields, Scrantons, and Lindsays, than in the Goldwater camp. Still, the Goldwaterites are strongly entrenched in the party machinery and the zeal of this militant minority—looking about for another candidate as attractive as Barry Goldwater—will not be easily turned aside.

Bonn Admiral Resigns Post

By Reuters

Bonn

Vice-Admiral Helmut Heye, parliamentary defense commissioner (ombudsman) for West Germany's armed forces, has resigned, the speaker of the Bundestag (lower house) said.

Admiral Heye was sharply criticized for his recent demand for a professional West German army of 250,000 volunteers.

The resignation was accepted, the speaker's office said.

TV: Page 4
FM, Arts: Page 7

2nd Cl Post Pd at Boston, Mass., and add'l offices

THE CHRISTIAN SCIENCE MONITOR

Registered in U. S. Patent Office

AN INTERNATIONAL DAILY NEWSPAPER

VOLUME 57 NO. 20 | BOSTON, FRIDAY, DECEMBER 18, 1964 | WESTERN EDITION | TWO SECTIONS | TEN CENTS A COPY

© 1964 THE CHRISTIAN SCIENCE PUBLISHING SOCIETY All Rights Reserved

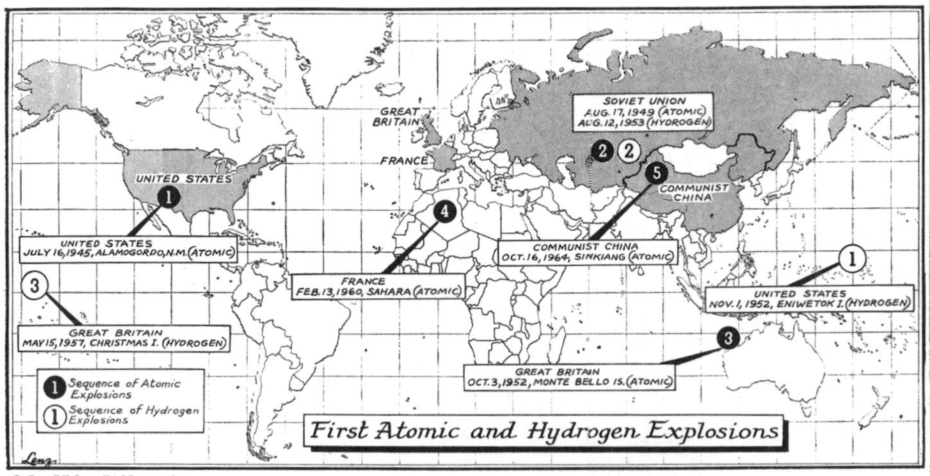

By Russell H. Lenz, Chief Cartographer

The World's Five Nuclear Powers

Johnson Prods

Task Force Reports Pour In for 'Great Society'

By William H. Stringer
Chief of the Washington Bureau of The Christian Science Monitor

Washington

As President Johnson surveys the prospects of his first full term in office, he is highly enthusiastic over the prospects for building what he calls the "Great Society" in the United States.

In particular the President is encouraged at the reports flowing in from the task forces he has appointed, and from Cabinet and sub-Cabinet members—reports which touch on virtually every phase and challenge of modern society.

As a matter of fact, Mr. Johnson would undoubtedly say that the "Great Society" is already here—represented by the gigantic material productivity and idea fertility of the democratic system. The job of government, as he sees it, is to assist this American society to realize its full potential.

President Johnson does not intend to high-pressure Congress to remake America overnight. And he is relaxed about such foreign issues as the multilateral force.

But his enthusiasm for the nation of tomorrow can be seen in the fact that among his nightly "reading papers"—and he frequently reads in bed until 1 a.m.—are the documents and memoranda which educators, businessmen, the foundations, the authorities in health, transport, and even nuclear proliferation have prepared on request.

Fifteen or 16 task forces have reported their suggestions and counsel to the President. In addition, the 10 Cabinet officers, plus 40 sub-Cabinet officials, have been commissioned by the President to say what "bold new steps" they should be taking—in the areas, for instance, of trade, tariffs, mass transport, urban renewal, communications, economic growth, and antipoverty.

Joint Enterprise

For instance, a study group on foreign aid and trade, embracing Aid Chief David E. Bell, Bill D. Moyers, Douglas Cater, and other White House aides met Wednesday, with President Johnson walking into the conference from time to time.

The President frequently asks his officials, "How are we going to keep up with the times?" He may seek answers on the economy from Dr. Paul A. Samuelson of Massachusetts Institute of Technology, on aid to education from Dr. Clark Kerr of the University of California, on automation from George Meany, president of the AFL-CIO.

Having nominated a new Secretary of Commerce, John T. Connor, he immediately asked Mr. Connor to meet with Secretary of Labor W. Willard Wirtz so they might learn to operate in tandem, not as competitors but as cooperators in a joint enterprise.

President Johnson realizes the pitfalls of talking too big about the "Great Society." He does not want to give the impression that he is a Rexford Tugwell, arrived in Washington with the intention of revamping the nation in a few weeks.

Task for Humphrey

But the President does believe that powerful forces are at work which could reshape the United States in harmful ways, unless they are realistically tackled. He notes, for example, that population is exploding—there are 2.5 million more persons living in the United States today than when he first became President, and 10 million more than when John F. Kennedy took his oath of office.

Some 2.3 million youngsters will turn 18 this year, and many may find that they have neither colleges to go to, nor jobs to fill.

The nation is fast becoming urbanized, which means more and more citizens condemned to spend two and more hours daily commuting to work.

The Negro rights revolution is continuing.

There are more white-collar than blue-collar workers, and more service employees than production employees.

The President has asked Vice-President-designate Hubert H. Humphrey to work with poverty-czar Sargent Shriver to provide leadership and direction for Cabinet members as they tackle the challenges incident to their own departments.

Pressure Builds To Oust Burch

By Godfrey Sperling Jr.
Chief of the New York Bureau of The Christian Science Monitor

©1964 The Christian Science Publishing Society
All Rights Reserved

New York

Sentiment for a change of leadership is continuing to build among members of the Republican National Committee.

The Christian Science Monitor has learned of a group of national committeemen, at least half of whom were early Goldwater supporters, who have made recent soundings among all 132 members.

- Their findings indicate that from 67 to 72 members would vote for the removal of Dean Burch as national chairman if the vote were taken today. Their preference for a replacement: Ray Bliss, Ohio state chairman. Some expectations even point to an imminent resignation by Mr. Burch.

Repudiation of Burch Shunned

In addition to those openly advocating new leadership, there appear to be another 29 members who could best be termed "fluid." They feel that a change in leadership would be advisable. But in no way would they want to do anything that would look like a repudiation of either Mr. Burch or Senator Goldwater. Thus, if a showdown comes in the meeting of the Republican National Committee in Chicago, Jan. 22, there could be no certainty of how many of these 29 would be against Mr. Burch.

Actually, this private poll indicates there are only about 10 "hard-core Burch supporters" on the committee who would not consider a change under any circumstances. Another 20 want no change, but are described as "at least being willing to listen" to a discussion of the subject.

Will the growing pressure on Mr. Burch cause him to step aside?

On this question the response from the members is much less certain.

There is wide hope expressed that this will come about, thus avoiding a head-on collision in Chicago—a collision that could be harmful to the party.

But there is considerable anxiety being expressed over what is seen as a strong possibility that a bitter showdown may be inevitable.

Bitter-End Theory Traced

Said one committee member: "Did you notice what Dean Burch said right after the 'summit' meeting of Eisenhower, Nixon, and Goldwater? He didn't retreat. Instead he said, 'Let's face it. The headlines, if I were deposed in Chicago, would not be "Dean Burch Deposed." It would be "Goldwater Rejected by the Republican Party," and it's as simple as that.' "

Thus, some committee members express the hope that the growing pressure will bring about a graceful bowing out by Mr. Burch any day now.

But there are many others who see this as a bitter-end possibility. The thinking behind the bitter-end theory goes like this:

The real objective of Senator Goldwater, Mr. Burch, and the conservatives is to bring about a new realignment within the party. They would prefer to force out the moderates and liberals and seek to become the party of the Right.

They are not really concerned about 1966 or even 1968. They are willing to give up a few elections if they can put together a party that, they think, could become a majority in time.

Thus, they may prefer to stand their ground on this national leadership issue.

Bliss says, 'I will not discuss it': Page 11

U.S. Tests 'Nuclear Winds' in Asia

Peking Capabilities Upgraded

By Robert R. Brunn
Staff Correspondent of The Christian Science Monitor

Washington

Peking's planes continue to drop weekly onto an airstrip in the Takla Makan Desert in Sinkiang where the Chinese Communists are readying another nuclear explosion.

But the next nuclear shot may not go off before March. Chinese technicians and scientists are deep in theoretical work and are only beginning a series of tests that will last for months.

Some American analysts have upgraded Chinese technical development as a result of tests of chemical debris drifting eastward from the first Chinese explosion.

Thus Washington strategists face the following uncertainties:

- Will the next detonation be a product of Uranium 235, as was the first? Or will it be a plutonium explosion?

If the next cloud that rises above Lop Nor is the product of another rather sophisticated U-235 device, the Chinese capabilities will be seen as fairly advanced. But experts do not want to credit the Chinese with too much ability, yet.

- A hydrogen bomb is what would lie directly down the U-235 path after a long series of experiments.

Five Years Away

Even then it is assumed that the construction of a hydrogen bomb is five or even more years away.

- Peking's development of short-range missiles began in about 1958 and could lead to missile production around 1970 or before. Such 750-to-1,000-mile-range rockets could reach India and all of Southern and Southeast Asia.

Beyond this it is speculated here that it would take between 10 and 15 years for Peking to develop an intercontinental missile with a nuclear warhead.

At the moment what interests analysts is the question of a Chinese gaseous-diffusion plant.

If the Soviets did not give the Chinese some U-235, and it is certainly unlikely that they did, the easiest path for the Chinese would have been the building of a gaseous-diffusion plant.

This is a complex plant, much more complicated than the comparative simplicities of a nuclear reactor which could have produced plutonium for a plutonium detonation.

French Effort

The only other way of developing U-235 would have been an electromagnetic process. This is regarded as theoretically possible, but not likely.

If a Chinese gaseous-diffusion plant is in operation, it would have leapfrogged the French Atomic program in the field. A French effort to build a gaseous-diffusion plant at Pierrelatte has been going on for four years and is still incomplete.

If a gaseous-diffusion factory is working, experts say it may not be functioning at full blast, that is in continuous production.

Rather it could be producing U-235 on what scientists call the batch process, turning out small sporadic clumps of U-235.

For the Chinese to build a single, true atomic bomb, to be followed by a factory assembly line, calls for extremely sophisticated techniques. This is considered unlikely.

Even to set off the first Chinese "bang" in Sinkiang's Tarim Basin two months ago took hundreds of highly trained personnel.

Continued on Page 2, Col. 5

Indonesia Faces Hurdles in Road to A-Club

By John Hughes
Staff Correspondent of The Christian Science Monitor

Jakarta, Indonesia

Although it has impressive conventional forces and weaponry, Indonesia is far from ready to join the ranks of nuclear nations.

This is the consensus of Western intelligence and diplomatic reports here despite the recent assertion that Indonesia might produce an atomic device next year.

The assertion was made by Brig. Gen. Hartono, director of the Indonesian Army's Logistic Service.

Reliable sources say that assertion was pure political "gimmickry." It was designed to startle the Indonesian government itself into adopting a serious nuclear program.

According to these sources, it was a shock tactic by a top-ranking member of the military, intended to put pressure on the government for funds for rocket and atomic development.

If this reading of General Hartono's statement is correct, he was simply using tactics also employed in other countries, including the United States, where the generals lobby and politick for increased military spending.

Still a Long Road

Indonesia has a small atomic reactor at Bandung, provided by the United States. There have been rumors in Jakarta that the Soviets might be planning to build one in this area. But since the Soviets have been more circumspect toward Indonesia of late, this seems unlikely. Communist China might be a likelier prospect.

But this is a long way from production of an atomic bomb, according to the experts. They believe Indonesia has neither the skilled scientists nor the immediate resources to complete such a project for at least five years. Even that is the minimum estimate, and the likelihood is that it would take far longer.

There is the possibility that Indonesia might acquire ready-made atomic weapons from one of the existing nuclear powers. But this possibility is a slim one.

There is no question of either the United States's or Britain's supplying Indonesia with atomic weapons. France is a similarly unlikely prospect.

Unlikely Sources

There remain the two Communist powers. Communist China's nuclear program, despite the successful detonation of an atomic device, is still in its early stages. With priority on its own program, it is thought unlikely that Communist China would divert its effort toward Indonesia.

As for the Soviet Union, it is seeking stability in Southeast Asia. For all its public announcements, it does not want enlargement of existing conflicts. It is therefore seen as extremely unlikely that the Soviets would provide Indonesia with nuclear weapons.

In diplomatic circles it is speculated that President Sukarno asked the Soviets for modern missiles during his visit to Moscow earlier this year. If he did, all the evidence indicates that he was turned down.

Indonesia has tested simple rockets, designed and manufactured in Indonesia itself. These are believed to have been ground-to-air rockets with a range of about 11 miles.

In addition, Indonesia is known to have been supplied with ground-to-air rockets by the Soviet Union. These are purely defensive and of limited range. They rouse no serious anxieties among Western military experts.

Soviet technicians are helping to install these, and it is not known whether they are yet operational.

President Sukarno did, on his Moscow visit earlier this year, win a Soviet commitment for more military aid. But it is not certain how much of this is covered by earlier Soviet credits.

In other words, Western experts are not sure how much of the Soviet military shipments still due in Indonesia is really new and how much is covered by earlier contracts.

In their delegation to Moscow, the Indonesians included parachute experts. It is believed they asked the Soviets for parachute equipment for two Indonesian divisions. This would be used to drop Indonesian paratroopers from Soviet transport planes already in Indonesia. But the Soviet response to the request is unknown.

Soviets Unhappy?

Hints dropped in Jakarta by Soviet diplomats indicate the Soviets are less than happy with the return they have got for their substantial military assistance to Indonesia.

The official Communist Party of Indonesia, the Partai Komunis Indonesia, seems well aligned with Peking. Outside the party, the government, whenever it agrees with the Communist line, seems to agree more with Peking than Moscow.

The Soviets were particularly incensed by the recent visit to Indonesia of Chinese Communist Foreign Minister Chen Yi. The Chinese official had long talks with Indonesian leaders, including President Sukarno himself, and is thought to have wielded some influence upon Indonesian foreign-policy plans.

All this has produced a much more withdrawn attitude toward Indonesia on the part of the Soviets.

State of the Nations: Mr. Wilson's Deftness

By Joseph C. Harsch
Special Correspondent of The Christian Science Monitor

London

Harold Wilson's deftness as a politician and the stroke of the statesman was manifested in his speech in the defense debate in the House of Commons.

His task in the speech was to lead his party toward, if not fully into, the NATO nuclear force without mortally offending his restless left wing.

The solution to the problem had about it that element of simplicity which is of course the essence of effective politics.

In the opening part of his speech he mentioned that he had invited the new Premier of the Soviet Union to visit London and that Alexei N. Kosygin had accepted and would be coming early in the new year.

⁂

Then he proceeded to report on what had happened in Washington. The essence of what happened in Washington was that Mr. Wilson had not definitely refused to take Britain in to a mixed-manned fleet. He had not even slammed the door irrevocably on a mixed-manned surface fleet—the variety which Washington prefers and London likes least.

Yet it is precisely British membership in a new nuclear force, or for that matter any kind of nuclear force, which is most distasteful to Mr. Wilson's political left wing.

The true believers in that area regard force of any kind as bad and American nuclear force as worst. They would be happy only with complete renunciation of all British association with nuclear weapons.

⁂

But they are pleased every time anyone from London goes to Moscow or vice versa.

Mr. Kosygin is hardly likely to conduct major diplomacy while in London. He is Premier in Moscow, but Moscow is a city where it counts more to be head of the party than head of the government. The head of the party has not accepted the invitation.

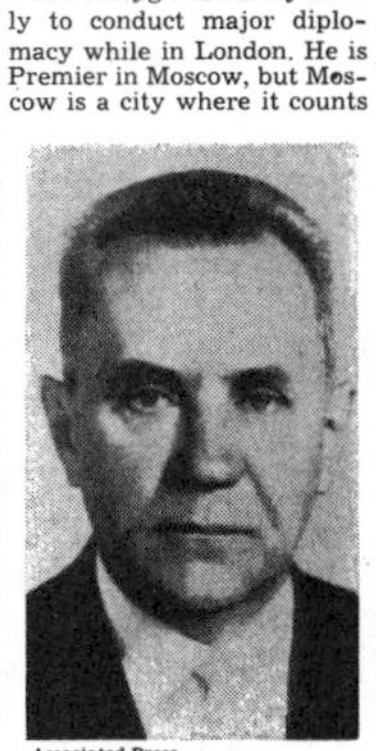

Associated Press

Alexei N. Kosygin

Also, it seems fairly clear to most Western experts that the present Soviet leadership is interim rather than permanent. Messrs. Brezhnev and Kosygin are regarded as good quiet people who can preside with dignity over minimum action until the new Kremlin ruler emerges. Since he has not yet become apparent, no Western government would at this time initiate important negotiations with Moscow.

Thus this is to be a sort of ceremonial or "state" visit, marked by maximum expressions of goodwill and supported by a minimum of serious business. Concealing might be a more accurate word.

⁂

There will be no serious harm in such a visit. There is no evidence that Washington regards the affair as anything more than an inevitable and probably harmless political exercise. Mr. Kosygin might obtain some valuable impressions of life in the Western world.

But it has the immediate virtue in London of satisfying the longing on the Labor Party's left for chummy relations with anyone from Moscow. It should do that, and give them one thing to be happy about when there is so much else to be unhappy about.

It was kind of Mr. Wilson to do this because in truth the left can scarcely desert him. There is no place to the farther left for them to go. Their only way of deserting Mr. Wilson would be to leave the party, which would only reduce their influence in it.

Meanwhile, the Labor government has in fact moved toward an ultimate accommodation with Washington and the West Germans on an Atlantic nuclear force. Mr. Wilson is doing what loyalty to the alliance requires of him.

Congress Closes Door on Bracero Labor

By James Nelson Goodsell
Latin America Correspondent of The Christian Science Monitor

Washington

The era of the bracero is fast coming to an end.

For years, Mexican farm workers have swarmed across the border into the United States to help harvest crops in a dozen southwestern states.

Not only have they taken back to Mexico more than $35 million annually, they also have served to keep costs down in the United States on tomatoes and lettuce, strawberries and melon.

Now this is ending.

With the start of 1965, the bracero program closes because Congress refused to extend the 1951 act under which Mexican migratory labor could legally enter the United States.

Debate Focused

Debate in Congress and elsewhere on the program has centered on the unemployment problem in the United States—and the need to get some of these unemployed into the harvesting field.

With the ending of the program, concern is being expressed by farmers in the Southwest, packers in California, and farm officials in Mexico.

Solutions to the need for inexpensive labor are hard to come by. Most observers agree with the farmers that it is difficult to obtain United States domestic labor to do harvesting. The work is difficult and, unless the pay is high, thus forcing consumer prices up, few domestic harvesters want the work.

Mechanization is a possible answer. But so far, development of mechanized harvesters is lagging.

Aerojet-General Company last month announced that it may soon work on development of harvesting machines. Such machines, the firm said, were "not only economically feasible but necessary to the continuing health of this segment of our market economy."

In Mexico City, the great concerns deals with the economic problems facing Mexico when the program goes out of existence:

- The $35 million earned by braceros presently account for roughly one-third of Mexico's favorable balance-of-payments situation.
- More important, perhaps, is the fact that Mexico has a bulging labor market, and those who will not go to the United States now will add to this labor surplus—one of Mexico's most acute problems.

Problem Spotlighted

Mexico's new government is committed to a major attack on the unemployment problem. Estimates of the number of unemployed reach seven million in Mexico's 40 million population—a significant political and economic factor for Gustavo Díaz Ordaz, the new chief executive who took office Dec. 1.

The bracero program (so called from its derivative of the Spanish word "brazo" meaning arm) was begun shortly after World War II when a severe labor shortage on United States farms compelled growers, especially in the Southwest, to seek help from abroad to harvest their crops.

Over the years, thousands of heads of family crossed the border to work. Relatively high wages helped them to feed close to a million dependents — through the $35 million or more they annually took home.

Work quotas of the United States have been reduced sharply during the past several years. But during the peak of the program in 1956, about a half-a-million Mexican farm workers received employment yearly.

In 1962, the number dropped to 300,000. Last year, it was only 200,000 — and work permits for this number were again issued in 1964.

For President Díaz Ordaz, the cutoff clearly represents a challenge. He hailed the United States Congress's decision as an opportunity for his nation. Mexico can, he said, "face up once and for all to our rural problems."

Farmers Concerned

While Mexico grapples with its aspect of the problem, many farmers and packers in the Southwest — particularly in Texas and California — are worried.

They have used the braceros to keep costs down. Paying braceros $1 to $1.25 an hour, the farmers have been able to harvest their fields quickly and relatively inexpensively. If domestic harvesters were employed, the cost of harvest would be increased by at least 50 percent, the farmers say.

Social-welfare and labor groups in the United States, however, argue that use of the Mexican labor is wrong on two points:

- Mexicans are employed at low wages and provided with living conditions which one social agency in California termed "near feudal." The social agencies in particular attack the program on humanitarian grounds saying Mexicans are forced to live in squalor for wages hardly equal to United States wage scales.
- United States unemployment is such, say labor groups, that domestic harvesters ought to be used in the field. The bracero program, these groups argue, has tended to keep United States unemployment running at a fast pace.

To these arguments, supporters of the bracero program point to the difficulty of obtaining United States domestic labor to handle the so called "stoop" labor — the back-wrenching job of harvesting the fruit and vegetable crops of the Southwest.

2nd Cl Post Pd at Boston, Mass., and add'l offices

THE CHRISTIAN SCIENCE MONITOR

Registered in U. S. Patent Office
AN INTERNATIONAL DAILY NEWSPAPER

VOLUME 57 NO. 56 | © 1965 THE CHRISTIAN SCIENCE PUBLISHING SOCIETY All Rights Reserved | BOSTON, MONDAY, FEBRUARY 1, 1965 | EASTERN EDITION | TWO SECTIONS | TEN CENTS A COPY

U.S. Economy

'E' Stands For Expansion

By Richard L. Strout
Staff Correspondent of The Christian Science Monitor

Washington

President Johnson is putting the fourth birthday candle on an extraordinary economic expansion, Feb. 1.

The expansion began in the United States in February, 1961. It now enters its fifth year.

It is the longest expansion since the war.

Short of two months, it is the longest peacetime period of uninterrupted economic growth in modern times and economists say that its rival, the 1933-37 expansion (50 months) really doesn't count because it started from an abyss and spent most of its time just scrambling out.

This new expansion is the pride and joy of the administration.

"Never one like it!" they coo fondly, like new parents.

It isn't too fat; it isn't too thin, they say. It's just what it ought to be — moderate.

No End in Sight

Most remarkable of all, at the beginning of its 49th month, it seems to have no end in sight.

Most of economic Washington is holding its breath. The expansion just keeps rolling along.

In the eight prior years of President Eisenhower there were three recessions (1953-54; 1957-58; 1960-61). In the past four years there has been no recession.

The trough of the last recession was February, 1961. Then little expansion was born.

Economic growth has been extaordinary. In February, 1961, gross national product was $622 billions.

President Johnson expects that of 1965 to be $660 billions.

Other economic indices show similar phenomenal four-year advances.

In the past, economic gains have exploded still faster but they were generally wartime bursts accompanied by inflation.

Clues Researched

In the civil war an expansion lasted from June, 1861 to April 1865; 46 months. But then came a contraction.

In World War I expansion lasted 44 months. Before and during World War II there was the granddaddy of all United States expansions, lasting 80 months. It ended with the cost of living just about doubled!

Compared to those incandescent flames this cozy expansion is like a well-behaved living-room fire: The wholesale price index is virtually unchanged; it stood at 100.4 in 1958; averaged 100.5 for 1964 (1957-59 — 100).

Here are reasons given by experts for the prolonged expansion:

- Built-in stabilizers (unemployment and similar insurance; the countercyclical income tax; spread of private pensions.)
- Stable wholesale prices.
- Steady fiscal - monetary programs (the deficit, the budget, interest rates, and the money supply).
- Countercyclical government policy that headed off a threatened recession in 1962.
- Business and labor "statesmanship" (prices and wages).
- Government policy in boosting expansion by tax cuts.

Clouds on Horizon

Are recessions things of the past? "No," say experts. But there is strong hope that they will be shorter from now on, due to remarkable advances in economic expertise.

Under this theory, the "retardation" of 1962 was a recession that never occurred. The big news was that nothing happened. It was a combination principally of good timing, and good management.

Clouds on the horizon — yes! The unemployment rate is too high, and the balance of payments gap is too wide.

"All things considered, however," says Julius Shiskin, chief economic statistician of the Census Bureau, "it is difficult to point to a previous expansion which represents a better performance."

And so — light that fourth candle.

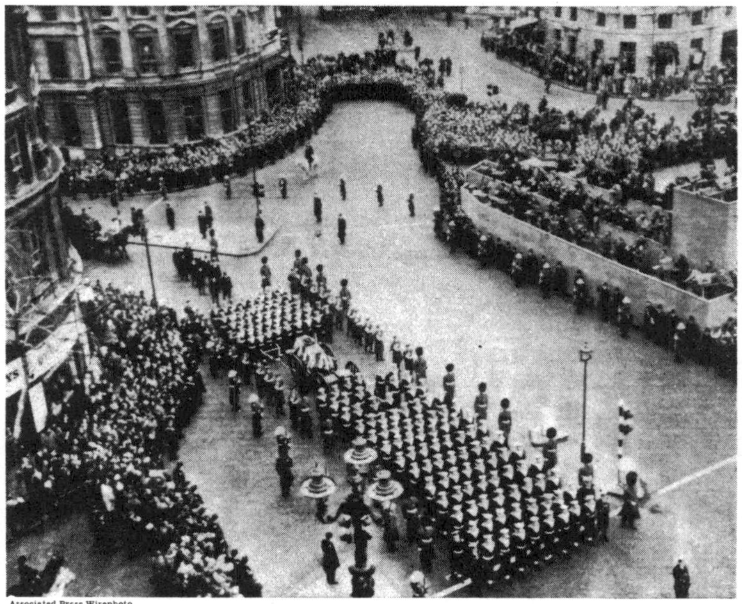

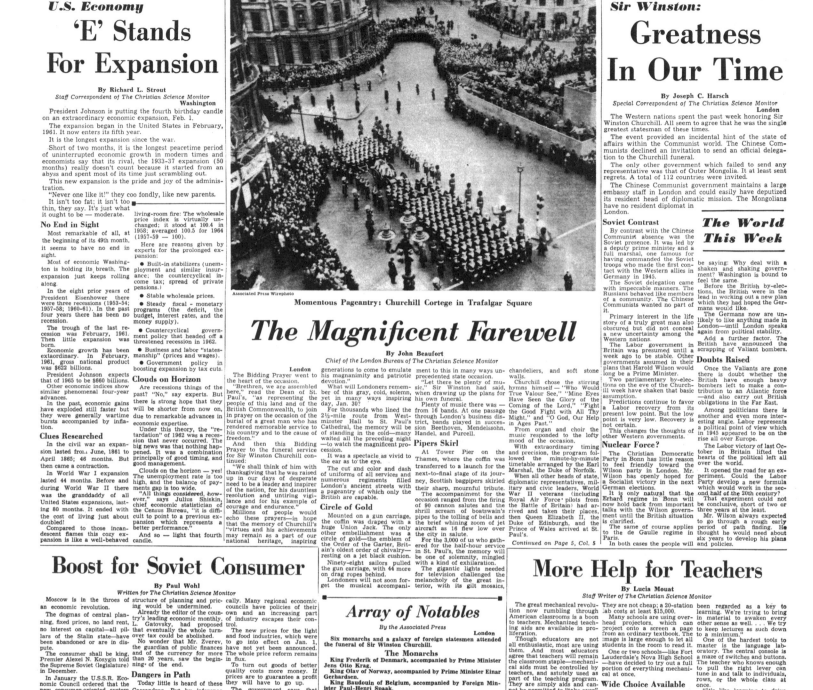

Associated Press Wirephoto

Momentous Pageantry: Churchill Cortege in Trafalgar Square

The Magnificent Farewell

By John Beaufort
Chief of the London Bureau of The Christian Science Monitor

London

The Bidding Prayer went to the heart of the occasion.

"Brethren, we are assembled here," read the Dean of St. Paul's, "as representing the people of this land and of the British Commonwealth, to join in prayer on the occasion of the burial of a great man who has rendered memorable service to his country and to the cause of freedom."

And then this Bidding Prayer to the funeral service for Sir Winston Churchill continued:

"We shall think of him with thanksgiving that he was raised up in our days of desperate need to be a leader and inspirer of the nation, for his dauntless resolution and untiring vigilance and for his example of courage and endurance."

Millions of people would echo these prayers—in hope that the memory of Churchill's "virtues and his achievements may remain as a part of our national heritage, inspiring generations to come to emulate his magnanimity and patriotic devotion."

What will Londoners remember of this gray, cold, solemn, yet in many ways inspiring day, Jan. 30?

For thousands who lined the 2½-mile route from Westminster Hall to St. Paul's Cathedral, the memory will be of standing in the cold—many waited all the preceding night—to watch the magnificent procession.

It was a spectacle as vivid to the ear as to the eye.

The cut and color and dash of uniforms of all services and numerous regiments filled London's ancient streets with a pageantry of which only the British are capable.

Circle of Gold

Mounted on a gun carriage, the coffin was draped with a huge Union Jack. The only other embellishment was a circle of gold—the emblem of the Order of the Garter, Britain's oldest order of chivalry—resting on a jet black cushion.

Ninety-eight sailors pulled the gun carriage, with 44 more on drag ropes behind.

Londoners will not soon forget the musical accompaniment to this in many ways unprecedented state occasion.

"Let there be plenty of music," Sir Winston had said, when drawing up the plans for his own funeral.

Plenty of music there was — from 16 bands. At one passage through London's business district, bands played in succession Beethoven, Mendelssohn, Handel, and Purcell.

Pipers Skirl

At Tower Pier on the Thames, where the coffin was transferred to a launch for the next-to-final stage of its journey, Scottish bagpipers skirled their sharp, mournful tribute.

The accompaniment for the occasion ranged from the firing of 90 cannon salutes and the shrill scream of boatswain's pipes to the tolling of bells and the brief whining zoom of jet aircraft as 16 flew low over the city in salute.

For the 3,000 of us who gathered for the half-hour service in St. Paul's, the memory will be one of solemnity, mingled with a kind of exhilaration.

The gigantic lights needed for television challenged the melancholy of the great interior, with its gilt mosaics, chandeliers, and soft stone walls.

Churchill chose the stirring hymns himself — "Who Would True Valour See," "Mine Eyes Have Seen the Glory of the Coming of the Lord," "Fight the Good Fight with All Thy Might," and "O God, Our Help in Ages Past."

From organ and choir the music responded to the lofty mood of the occasion.

With extraordinary timing and precision, the program followed the minute-by-minute timetable arranged by the Earl Marshal, the Duke of Norfolk.

When all other heads of state, diplomatic representatives, military and civic leaders, World War II veterans (including Royal Air Force pilots from the Battle of Britain) had arrived and taken their places, then Queen Elizabeth II, the Duke of Edinburgh, and the Prince of Wales arrived at St. Paul's.

Continued on Page 5, Col. 5

Sir Winston:

Greatness In Our Time

By Joseph C. Harsch
Special Correspondent of The Christian Science Monitor

London

The Western nations spent the past week honoring Sir Winston Churchill. All seem to agree that he was the single greatest statesman of these times.

The event provided an incidental hint of the state of affairs within the Communist world. The Chinese Communists declined an invitation to send an official delegation to the Churchill funeral.

The only other government which failed to send any representative was that of Outer Mongolia. It at least sent regrets. A total of 112 countries were invited.

The Chinese Communist government maintains a large embassy staff in London and could easily have deputized its resident head of diplomatic mission. The Mongolians have no resident diplomat in London.

Soviet Contrast

By contrast with the Chinese Communist absence was the Soviet presence. It was led by a deputy prime minister and a full marshal, one famous for having commanded the Soviet troops who made the first contact with the Western allies in Germany in 1945.

The Soviet delegation came with impeccable manners. The Russians behaved like members of a community. The Chinese Communists wanted no part of it.

Primary interest in the life story of a truly great man also obscured but did not conceal a new uncertainty among the Western nations.

The Labor government in Britain was presumed until a week ago to be stable. Other governments assumed in their plans that Harold Wilson would long be a Prime Minister.

Two parliamentary by-elections on the eve of the Churchill week have shaken that basic assumption.

Predictions continue to favor a Labor recovery from its present low point. But the low point is very low. Recovery is not certain.

This changes the thoughts of other Western governments.

Nuclear Force?

The Christian Democratic Party in Bonn has little reason to feel friendly toward the Wilson party in London. Mr. Wilson has openly hoped for a Socialist victory in the next German elections.

It is only natural that the Erhard regime in Bonn will now hold back from important talks with the Wilson government until the British situation is clarified.

The same of course applies to the de Gaulle regime in Paris.

In both cases the people will be saying: Why deal with a shaken and shaking government? Washington is bound to feel the same.

Before the British by-elections, the British were in the lead in working out a new plan which they had hoped the Germans would like.

The Germans now are unlikely to like anything made in London—until London speaks again from political stability.

Add a further factor. The British have announced the scrapping of Valiant bombers.

Doubts Raised

Once the Valiants are gone there is doubt whether the British have enough heavy bombers left to make a contribution to an Atlantic force—and also carry out British obligations in the Far East.

Among politicians there is another and even more interesting angle. Labor represents a political point of view which in 1945 appeared to be on the rise all over Europe.

The Labor victory of last October in Britain lifted the hearts of the political left all over the world.

It opened the road for an experiment. Could the Labor Party develop a new formula which would work in the second half of the 20th century?

That experiment could not be conclusive, short of two or three years at the least.

Mr. Wilson always expected to go through a rough early period of path finding. He thought he would need about six years to develop his plans and policies.

The World This Week

Boost for Soviet Consumer

By Paul Wohl
Written for The Christian Science Monitor

Moscow is in the throes of an economic revolution.

The dogmas of central planning, fixed prices, no land rent, no interest on capital—all pillars of the Stalin state—have been abandoned or are in dispute.

The consumer shall be king, Premier Alexei N. Kosygin told the Supreme Soviet (legislature) in December.

In January the U.S.S.R. Economic Council ordered that the new consumer-oriented system be applied for 400 of the best shoe and clothing factories as of April 1.

This is only a beginning.

"We shall plan on the basis of consumer orders not only in the consumers industries, but in all branches of production," Mr. Kosygin has promised.

Slowness Charged

The new businesslike approach to economics is sweeping the country like a tidal wave.

At the recent Supreme Soviet session, Konstantin N. Belyak, chairman of the economic council of the Voronezh region, lambasted the government for having gone too slow.

"Attempts have been made to plan from below, but this had a declarative character: Whatever the factories proposed was swept away mercilessly by the central planning organs," said Mr. Belyak. He also attacked former Premier Nikita S. Khrushchev by name.

There is likely to be more backbiting of this kind.

Formidable Opposition

In 1962 Mr. Khrushchev denounced the old system of quantitative planning without regard for profit and quality. He actually approved economist Yevsei Liberman's ideas of "freedom of economic maneuver," profitability, and "direct links between producers and consumers."

At the time this speech was interpreted as an attempt to kill Libermanism by paying it only lipservice.

It is known today that Mr. Khrushchev was up against formidable opposition, spearheaded by such an authoritative figure as long-time Minister of Finance Arseny G. Zverev.

Mr. Zverev feared that as a result of the reform the whole structure of planning and pricing would be undermined.

Already the editor of the country's leading economic monthly, L. Gatovsky, had proposed that eventually the whole turnover tax could be abolished.

No wonder that Mr. Zverev, the guardian of public finances and of the currency for more than 20 years, saw the beginning of the end.

Dangers in Path

Today little is heard of these Cassandras. But by inference we know that in the inner councils of the regime their voices have not been silenced.

However sensible the tenets of profitability and consumerism, the reform is fraught with dangers.

Mr. Kosygin gives the impression of knowing what he wants. He has the reputation of being an excellent economist. But he ranks second behind First Party Secretary Leonid I. Brezhnev. The latter, significantly, was the leader of the Soviet delegation at the recent Warsaw Pact conference.

Much of the reform, moreover, is being carried out locally. Many regional economic councils have policies of their own and an increasing part of industry escapes their control.

The new prices for the light and food industries, which were to go into effect on Jan. 1, have not yet been announced. The whole price reform remains in flux.

To turn out goods of better quality costs more money. If prices are to guarantee a profit they will have to go up.

The government says that this may not be necessary because costs must come down, and the Soviet economy has indeed been working at incredibly high costs.

But to cut costs is a slow process. The fast and easy way out is to shift the burden to the consumer. In practice this means inflation. This is one danger.

The Soviet Union is undergoing a change as significant and far reaching as was Lenin's New Economic Policy of 1921, and, six years later, Stalin's entry into the era of five-year plans. This time the change goes into new and still uncharted directions.

Array of Notables

By the Associated Press

London

Six monarchs and a galaxy of foreign statesmen attended the funeral of Sir Winston Churchill.

The Monarchs

King Frederik of Denmark, accompanied by Prime Minister Jens Otto Krag.

King Olav of Norway, accompanied by Prime Minister Einar Gerhardsen.

King Baudouin of Belgium, accompanied by Foreign Minister Paul-Henri Spaak.

Queen Juliana of the Netherlands, accompanied by her husband Prince Bernhard and Foreign Minister Joseph Luns.

King Constantine of Greece.

The Grand Duke Jean of Luxembourg.

Among the Statesmen

President de Gaulle of France.
President Asgeirsson of Iceland.
President Shazar of Israel.
President Giannattasio of Uruguay.
Former President Eisenhower of the United States.
Prime Minister Lester Pearson of Canada.
Chancellor Ludwig Erhard of West Germany.
Former Prime Minister Nobusuke Kishi of Japan.
Prime Minister Sir Robert Menzies of Australia.
Prime Minister Keith Holyoake of New Zealand.
Prime Minister Ian Smith of Rhodesia.
Chancellor Joseph Klaus of Austria.
Prime Minister Moise Tshombe of the Congo.
Deputy Premier K. N. Rudnev and Marshal Ivan S. Konev of the Soviet Union.

More Help for Teachers

By Lucia Mouat
Staff Writer of The Christian Science Monitor

The great mechanical revolution now rumbling through American classrooms is a boon to teachers. Mechanized teaching aids are available in proliferation.

Though educators are not all enthusiastic, most are using them. And most educators agree that teachers will remain the classroom staple—mechanical aids must be controlled by teachers, and astutely used as part of the teaching program. They are simply aids and cannot be permitted to "take over" a classroom.

One of the best-known aids is instructional television. It reaches an estimated three million youngsters during their daily lessons. (It is so common that some schools are caught in disputes about whether "star" teachers should belong to a labor union of video performers or get extra pay for programs syndicated out of state.)

'Language Labs' Boom

Almost equally well-known are electronic language laboratories. Their number has jumped from fewer than 100 in 1958 to close to 5,000 in 1965. They are not cheap; a 20-station lab costs at least $15,000.

Many schools are using overhead projectors, which can project onto a screen a page from an ordinary textbook. The image is large enough to let all students in the room to read it.

One or two schools—like Fort Lauderdale's Nova High School—have decided to try out a full portion of everything mechanical at once.

Wide Choice Available

Nova is a frankly experimental school. Three resource centers, located in the science, math, and language buildings, replace the traditional library.

Here, close to pertinent materials, a student in his individual booth can dial any of 67 languages or lecture tapes. He can telephone to a TV center on campus for a video tape, study microfilm cards selected quickly by an IBM file system, or, of course, read a conventional book.

"Every bit of our instructional process revolves around the latest in mechanized teaching," says principal David Fitzpatrick.

"The visual sense has long been regarded as a key to learning. We're trying to bring in material to awaken every other sense as well. . . . We try to keep lectures as such down to a minimum."

One of the hardest tools to master is the language laboratory. The central console is a maze of switches and buttons. The teacher who knows enough to pull the right lever can tune in and talk to individuals, rows, or the whole class at once.

"It's like learning to drive a car—you have to keep doing it or you forget how," says Dr. C. Burleigh Wellington, professor of education at Tufts University. He is one of the instigators of a demonstration classroom on campus to train teachers to use mechanical aids.

Main value of the language lab is for pronunciation and grammar practice. Although this device is now becoming the norm rather than the exception, some teachers question its effectiveness.

'The Machine'

"It's designed to produce language illiterates who are lost as far as self-expression goes," bristles one Maryland teacher. "The pupil has to listen to a specialized conversation which is tolerable at best when heard once—impossible to bear day after day."

Far more controversial than the lab is programed instruction—otherwise known as the teaching machine. Based on Socrates' favorite method of asking easy questions leading to a logical conclusion, it was revived just a few years ago after a fadeout in the 1920's. Already more than 100 firms are putting out programed instruction materials.

Subject matter and form are limitless. A student may learn the same program through a 50-cent paperback or an expensive machine-complete with electronic buttons.

"The great hope of programed learning is to take the bulk of elementary and intermediate courses off the back of the elementary teacher," says Donald A. Murray, professor of modern languages at Beloit College.

"Many teachers would like to spend more time on more challenging things."

Related story: Page 4.

Point of View

Presidential Disability Law Now?

By Roscoe Drummond
Written Especially for The Christian Science Monitor

Washington

It was not, of course, planned that way.

But Lyndon Johnson's nighttime ride to the hospital came at a moment when it can do some good.

It showed the deep concern that comes when the nation is not quite sure whether it has a functioning president.

Mr. Johnson's slight illness again brought into sharp focus a vital question: Can we afford to be without a president for any time at all?

⁂

In this case we weren't. But the scene of the ambulance drawing up at the White House should provide the extra spark toward getting Congress to take the needed action.

I believe Congress will approve at this session an amendment to remove the vagueness on presidential disability. It was lost in the hectic days of last year's election-eve adjournment. Any further delay would be downright reckless.

⁂

The Constitution leaves three vital issues up in the air as to what happens when a president is incapacitated. It does not define "disability." It does not state who shall decide when disability exists. It does not say whether the "powers and duties" or the "office" itself shall be taken over by the vice-president.

Time was when a president could take a three-hour afternoon nap or go on summer vacations and hardly be missed. But these times went out when we split the atom, sent spaceships to the moon, and began $100 billion budgets.

The vagueness of the law on how to deal with the problem of a president when he cannot perform his duties isn't just theory. It is very concrete and can bring the White House to a standstill.

⁂

Take the case of Woodrow Wilson. He was ill for months, but he was so fearful that if his "powers and duties" were taken over by the Vice-President, he could never get them back. He even fired his Secretary of State because he dared call a Cabinet meeting on his own when needed decisions were not being made.

Four times in the past 10 years the prospect of a president being unable to perform his duties has come up. President Eisenhower was sidelined three times and President Johnson was hospitalized the first week of his own administration.

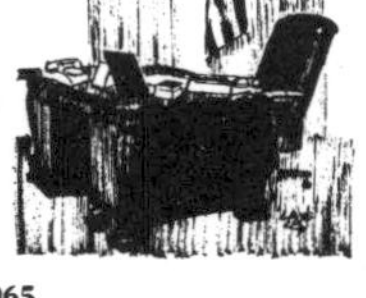

How often must this happen before we learn the lesson? We must be prayerfully concerned with the health of the president and we must take steps to see that there is no confusion about what will happen if there is a void in the White House. It is not safe in today's nuclear world to have the president unable to perform his duties even for a few minutes.

⁂

There is mounting support for the amendment which Sen. Birch Bayh of Indiana, with 33 other sponsors, is again putting forward.

It would remove all danger of a vice-president usurping the office. It would do it in this way:

He would become only acting president. If a president refused or was unable to affirm his disability, the Cabinet would have to approve before the vice-president would take over. If the president sought to resume before he was ready, the vice-president could not stop him—only Congress. (My own view is that it would be better to have the Cabinet make this decision instead of Congress, thus keeping the separation of powers.)

Also, we would not again be without a vice-president—which has occurred 16 times already. If the office became vacant, the president would fill it—with the consent of Congress. This would virtually insure a vice-president of the same party and partake of the elective process.

2nd Cl Post Pd at Boston, Mass., and add'l offices

THE CHRISTIAN SCIENCE MONITOR

BOSTON, THURSDAY, MAY 6, 1965 — *An International Daily Newspaper* — VOL. 57, NO. 136 TWO SECTIONS — WESTERN EDITION ✦ 10¢

FOCUS on U.S.

What's ahead . . .

Plans to dam up both ends of the Grand Canyon may yet detonate a major storm in the American West.

The federal government wants to build two electric power dams on the Colorado River, which snakes through the canyon. They would belong to the Central Arizona Project, a $1.3 billion scheme to water Arizona's dry heartland.

The lower dam would form a new lake, backing up deep into the Grand Canyon itself.

The storm will break first in Congress, when hearings open. Public-power groups strongly champion it. But wilderness and park groups bitterly oppose it. Everybody wonders what will happen when these two powerful pressure blocs collide over the issue.

⊕

A bill in New York may be breaking ground for a nationwide movement to make rear windshield wipers mandatory on cars.

The New York Senate has just passed a bill that would require most new autos to come equipped with them by June, 1967.

It still must pass the Assembly and win the Governor's signature.

Its prime mover was a state Senator's wife, Esther Greenberg. Two years ago she went driving with Senator Greenberg in heavy snow.

"So I said to Sam," she says, "why shouldn't there be a law making them put windshield wipers on the back window? There are laws for other safety features in cars."

She may have started something.

⊕

Civic leaders from all over, faced with waves of new problems even before the old are solved, will consult each other often this summer.

Mayors from some 400 American cities meet in St. Louis May 29-June 2. Two weeks later (June 14-20) some of these same American civic chief executives will go to Belgrade to discuss mutual problems with overseas counterparts.

And in September, city managers of the United States and Canada will gather in Montreal for more talk.

New dimensions in local government triggered by the war on poverty and by mounting civil-rights drives will key many of these agendas.

And an old theme—more cash needed—will pervade almost all.

⊕

A showdown over drunk driving is building in California.

A bill now in the Legislature would let the state take away a driver's license if he gets in a smashup and then refuses to submit to an alcohol test.

The California Council on Alcohol Problems insists it would cut the accident toll in half, reduce personal injuries one-fourth, lower auto insurance rates, and protect the guilty as well as the innocent.

California liquor interests are ranged against it. Though willing to see it pass in the Assembly, they are counting on the Senate to kill it. Chance of passage is slim.

Trends . . .

Perhaps the fastest-growing aspect of roughing it, climbing it, walking it, and viewing it, is bicycling it.

The Bicycle Institute of America says a million more bicycles were sold in the United States last year than the year before. This is viewed as a phenomenal jump.

It has in part triggered a stepup in the American youth hostel business too.

Youth hostel membership has doubled in the last five years. And hostels expect to be inundated by a record 53,000 this summer. Some 116 of these cut-rate overnight havens for youth now dot 20 states.

Youth hostels have traditionally been better known in Europe, where they enjoy government support.

The next step for youth hostels in the United States as a trend continues to move their way may be to ask government aid too. They are accustomed to operating on a shoestring—or is it a bicycle chain?

How and why . . .

Florida is caught up in a modern gold rush, perhaps better described as a doubloon rush.

Florida-owned ocean bottoms abound in sunken Spanish galleons. Many were wrecked off the Florida coast in the 16th century.

Some sites are known, others are unmapped. But with the growth of skin and scuba diving, new finds constantly crop up. The latest was in water so shallow that silver coins were retrieved by waders.

Florida has so far limited treasure hunting permits to 17 individuals or firms. But pirating and poaching is rampant. And now the state is preparing to crack down harder. A new law will make it a felony to take treasure without a license.

Where to look

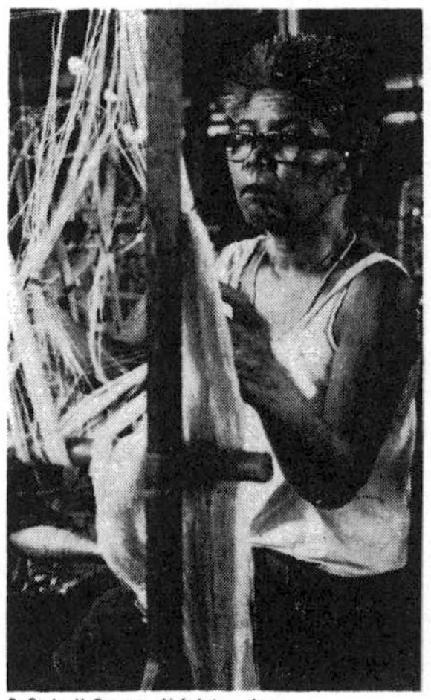

By Gordon N. Converse, chief photographer

Silk spinner

Much silk is spun in Thailand's impoverished northeast. Mulberry trees grow well there, and women such as this one can make extra money for their grandchildren's schooling.

Reds aim at Thai 'soft spot'

By John Hughes
Staff correspondent of The Christian Science Monitor

Nong Khai, Thailand

As always, the Communists have selected with care and cunning the battleground for their new assault on Thailand.

They have chosen the backward northeast, most vulnerable to Communist propaganda and subversion.

Six provinces are considered the most critical ones. These are the ones snuggled under the shoulder of Laos and strung along the Mekong River. And this river serves more as a pathway between Laos and Thailand than a barrier.

Land here in the northeast is the poorest in all Thailand. Rainfall is the lowest. It falls for the shortest period. Thus the northeast is beset more by droughts and floods than any other part of the country.

Incomes compared

This is an area not suited to rice growing—the main and most important crop in a primarily agricultural country. The yield here per acre is about half the yield elsewhere in Thailand.

Thus per capita income in the northeast is about $45 a year compared with $98 in the rest of the country.

Superimpose on these harsh economic factors the years of long neglect of the area by the central government in Bangkok.

Then add the problem of significant minority groups in the northeast. Several million Laotians, for example, who speak Lao rather than Thai. People of Cambodian origin who speak Khmer. A potential fifth column of some 30,000 to 40,000 Vietnamese refugees heavily indoctrinated by their Communist cadres.

Communists watched

Total all this up, and one has a situation highly inviting to communism's dabbling fingers.

There is little doubt but that the invitation has been accepted. There is overwhelming evidence of a campaign of Communist subversion in the area. The Thai Government is apprehensive lest such a campaign soon flare into open insurrection.

However, there is one important positive factor. The anti-Communist forces know the Communists have begun their campaign. They know where the Communists are working. They have a good idea of how they are

★ Please turn to Page 4

Phantom bases . . .

With the bombings of North Vietnam the aircraft carrier has come into its own again.

The Vietnamese Army and United States marines and Army personnel tangle with Viet Cong guerrillas on the ground. High priority targets of those guerrillas are the air bases that serve as home to air force bombers.

At sea, however, the airfields are constantly on the move. And the United States Navy takes its toll as carrier-based Phantoms, Skyhawks, Skyraiders, and Crusaders streak over the South China Sea toward North Vietnamese targets.

For an eyewitness account from a giant United States aircraft carrier, please turn to Page 8.

2nd Cl Post Pd at Boston, Mass., and add'l offices

Dominican revolution as seen from rebel side

By James Nelson Goodsell
Latin America correspondent of The Christian Science Monitor

With the rebels in Santo Domingo

A tour of the rebel section of this embattled city shows the extent to which antigovernment forces have dug in.

I spent five hours wandering through the 10-square-mile section of the city which includes the National Palace, Fort Ozama, and the commercial and business heart of the city.

My conclusions are these:

- Virtually to a man the rebel elements feel they have a cause which is important to preserve, that of fighting for constitutionalism and returning the deposed President Juan Domingo Bosch to office.
- While there are Communists in their midst, the top rebel command is in the hands of non-Communist elements who fiercely proclaim their opposition to communism.
- There remains a significant balance of good will toward the United States despite the marine and airborne occupation of other parts of the city—even the understanding that the Marines had to come to rescue American lives.
- But the rebels are questioning the continued presence of United States forces and seem determined to resist any further encroachments on rebel territory by United States forces.
- It may be possible to dislodge the rebel force with superior arms, but the rebels would probably put up a real struggle, for they possess large stores of weapons and ammunition stores.

Friendliness shown

Friendliness greeted me as I walked alone through the rebel territory. People seemed pleased to talk with a newsman, if nothing more than to get their points of view across.

"Tell the world we are not Communists," was a repeated refrain. Spoken in a variety of ways, this view was virtually unanimous.

Col. Francisco Caamaño Deno, military leader of the rebel forces and apparently the top man in the whole effort, said, "We just do not have a Communist problem."

But the colonel, who is looked to with respect by thousands of Dominicans in the rebel area, admitted there are Communists in the midst of the rebel movement.

Another rebel chieftan added, After all, we will take any support we can get."

Still another said, "But do not forget that we have control of the situation, and this is not a communist revolution. It is a constitutional movement to restore constitutionalism."

Looking for Reds

This seems the driving force of the rebel movement. A number of Mr. Bosch's longtime associates and members of his political party are in key command positions in the rebel hierarchy.

However, some American spokesmen here cite the names of 53 known Communists who occupy positions of authority in the rebel command. On the other hand, not all United States officials in Santo Domingo agree with this assessment.

I tried to locate several of those whose names are on the list. I was not successful. But in the rebel headquarters in downtown Santo Domingo, as I went from office to office, I could find no evidence that they were anywhere in these key command positions. (This is not to suggest they do not operate with rebel forces, but merely to indicate they are not visibly in evidence as the United States spokesmen had affirmed they would be.)

A large supply of weapons and ammunitions — including some tanks and some large weapons — are in rebel hands. They are stored at a variety of spots throughout the rebel territory.

United States presence in the Dominican Republic, to the extent of 15,000 troops, is viewed with growing alarm by the rebels. There is clear good will and even an understanding of President Johnson's decision to safeguard American lives.

U.S. involvement

"But we understand you've removed these Americans," said a rebel major who added: "Isn't it time for you to get out and allow us the opportunity to win the struggle against the forces of those opposed to constitutionalism?"

The major was speaking of the military under the command of last week's hastily formed military junta, headquartered at San Isidro Air Force Base east of Santo Domingo.

The United States forces began landing in the Dominican Republic at a time when the heart appeared to have been going out of junta cause — and rebels were on the point of gaining the advantage — despite some reports inspired by the junta to the contrary.

There are many questions in the rebel territory about the next United States action in Santo Domingo.

"We will fight against Americans as we have fought against fellow Dominicans. We believe our cause is just, and we are willing to die for it," said one rebel.

His view is general, although of course expressed differently by others.

While I spent only five hours in the rebel area, my observations are in general corroborated by neutral observers who have been in the same territory in the past several days.

U.S. Dominican stand: Page 9

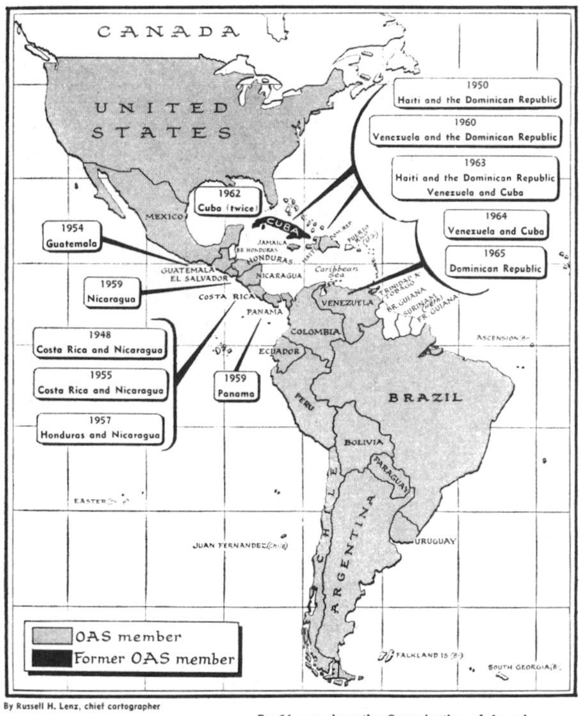

By Russell H. Lenz, chief cartographer

OAS record

On 14 occasions the Organization of American States has applied the 1947 treaty providing for inter-American defense and peace keeping. Shown here are the times and places that OAS has intervened. Sometimes this has been with sanctions, other times with observer missions or mediation teams. If an OAS peace-keeping force is created in the current Dominican Republic crisis, it would be the first such force in OAS history.

South Africa

Race policy holds

By Robert M. Hallett
Staff correspondent of The Christian Science Monitor

Cape Town

Will time allow South Africa to carry through its bitterly condemned experiment in race relations—apartheid?

There is considerable confidence, in fact determination, among Nationalists that it will.

Politically the current within the country is clearly running in the government's direction. Internationally the world is deeply enmeshed in Vietnam and other problems that have a higher priority than South Africa.

A professor at Stellenbosch University, an Afrikaaner institution, said in an interview that he believes the country will have its chance to try apartheid.

Opposition restrained

His explanation: social, cultural, and economic advancement is progressing at such a rate, thanks to the South African boom, that by and large the overwhelming masses are daily having it better than they ever had it before.

There are also antigovernment analysts who feel that economic progress is a restraint on political agitation and opposition to apartheid.

"There is some question, however," said the Stellenbosch professor, "whether the outside world will, either out of malice, as in the case of the socialist or Communist nations, or out of overhasty moral indignation in the case of the Western powers, upset this delicate situation."

Historically, he pointed out, South Africa, as most societies, has had broad class distinctions. Unfortunately in South Africa these have coincided with color and cultural distinctions.

Africans form the bottom social layer, coloreds and Indians a buffer above them, with a narrow white end of the pyramid on top.

'Escape from prejudice'

In most Western countries, he said, this stratification has been solved through evolution of democratic processes and broadening of political and civil rights.

"However a man of color in South Africa, even though he has merit, still carries his skin color with him," he continued. "It is difficult not to identify him with the broad class from which he has emerged.

"But once we establish a separate hierarchy for the Bantu we can accept a man as an equal because he will be identified with the hierarchy. One can appreciate him as a medical man, politician, or leader.

"This is what Dr. [H. F.] Verwoerd [Prime Minister] means when he sees apartheid as a way of escaping from prejudice."

The professor granted that some present apartheid laws and regulations were "cruel and uncalled for." Much criticism has been heard recently of "petty apartheid," such as banning mixed audiences in Cape Town, which has a long tradition of racial tolerance.

A cohesive society

He attributed such tactics to "bungling bureaucrats."

Critics, realizing that Cape Nationalists have a reputation for being less fanatic on the apartheid issue than their upcountry cousins, have wondered why moderates stay silent in the face of such government actions.

"A situation is created where a front has to be maintained in support of the government in spite of unpopular measures," was how the professor explained it.

"This government after all is elected," the professor continued. "It has to pander to the prejudices of the broad masses of its electorate, as happens in every country. And we still have quite a large number of whites, like southerners in the United States, who are prejudiced.

"They believe Africans are inferior and should be kept in their place. Others fear economic competition from nonwhites."

The Coloreds (who number about 1,700,000) have been "caught between the grinding surfaces of the white and black mill stones," he said.

Pressure resisted

"But once the Bantustan idea has been developed to a stage where it has absorbed a significant proportion of the numerically preponderant masses of Africans, the chances of these remaining elements [Coloreds, Malays, and Indians] merging into a cohesive society would be improved," he declared.

But the government hope is to relieve the pressure of nonwhites on the white economy and society.

In 1948 and for some time thereafter the term used by Nationalist leaders to describe their racial policies was "wit baaskaap" ("white boss-ship" or domination). The pressure of world events altered that approach. The terminology of freedom was introduced and apartheid became "separate development" and then "freedom based on separation."

First of three articles. The next will discuss the Black Sash, a society of white women who aid Africans in their apartheid problems.

© 1965 THE CHRISTIAN SCIENCE PUBLISHING SOCIETY
All Rights Reserved

THE CHRISTIAN SCIENCE MONITOR

BOSTON, SATURDAY, MAY 22, 1965 — An International Daily Newspaper — VOL. 57, NO. 150 TWO SECTIONS — WESTERN EDITION 10c

FOCUS on business

What's ahead . . .

France's new friendship with Communist China is about to sprout wings.

The French airline, Air France, will be the first Western airline to fly into Peking.

Only two other foreign lines, Indonesia's Garuda Airways and the Pakistan International Airways, now fly there. Air France would be the third.

Its officials have been negotiating in Peking. No documents have yet been signed. But it is understood that general agreement prevails. Only outstanding technical points are left to clear up.

It is one of the first signs that the cultivated new Paris-Peking amity is paying off in tangible form.

⊕

The new excise tax-cut proposals are out of the bag. Now both the White House and Congress are girding for an uprising of trucking, shipping, and airline lobbies.

None of them like the new user taxes the President hooked on to his proposed $4 billion excise tax cut.

The Johnson tax-cut message this week proposed an increased duty on trucks, on highway diesel fuels, and on tread rubber for heavy trucks. That is certain to trigger a trucking industry tempest.

His message also proposed a tax on fuel used in inland waterways—sure to stir up the shipping interests.

And commercial airlines are expected to fight the proposed tax hike in aviation gasoline and jet fuels.

⊕

More and more the walls in houses, the roofs, the floors, the insulation, and the plumbing fixtures are coming up plastic.

Last year builders used two billion pounds of plastics for construction in the United States. By 1970 they will likely be using twice — even three times — as much. That is not a lot when the total amount of building materials used in the country last year was 250 billion pounds.

But it is a fast-growing slice of all construction and bound to grow even faster in the years ahead.

Plastic plumbing fixtures, walls, insulation, roofs, and floors will account for most of the growth.

Trends . . .

One of Britain's biggest rail passengers today is the family car.

More and more cars are taking the train. It is becoming a booming business.

Ferry trains now connect London with Scotland, Wales, Ireland, and Devon and Cornwall.

The next development in this movement will be the building of a single central car-by-rail terminal in London—at Olympia in Kensington.

Some nine platforms will service car-laden trains in and out of Olympia terminal. And any motorist wanting to take himself and his car by train in the future will go there first.

It may not be long before Britons can catch a car-train to France, via, it is hoped, the Channel Tunnel.

To turn around an old advertising adage: "Next time tell your car to try the train."

⊕

Germany's Frankfurt is blossoming as a key international financial center.

This is a new, almost overnight development. It comes partly because of the United States equalization tax and the drastic curtailment of American foreign borrowing.

From 1957 to 1963, foreign fixed interest issues in Germany amounted to 760 million Deutschmarks. This was 135 million less than in 1964 alone.

Frankfurt last year floated 2½ times the volume of foreign issues floated in Switzerland. Until then Switzerland usually raised six times as much as Frankfurt.

The trend is expected to pick up steam as Germany's exchange situation continues strong and Switzerland's continues quiet.

How and why . . .

Communist bloc banks may do business Communist style, but they prefer to carry out their clearing operations in a capitalist country.

Clearing is the way banks settle their mutual payments.

Moscow's International Bank for Economic Cooperation boasts that last year it handled 126,000 clearing operations for the Comecon, the Soviet bloc's Council for Mutual Economic Aid.

But many, if not most, of these were actually cleared through two banks in Vienna and merely recorded in Moscow.

The Chinese Communists never clear through the Comecon bank. And both Poland and Romania prefer the services of two private Austrian banks, where they settle up in very un-Communist dollars.

Where to look

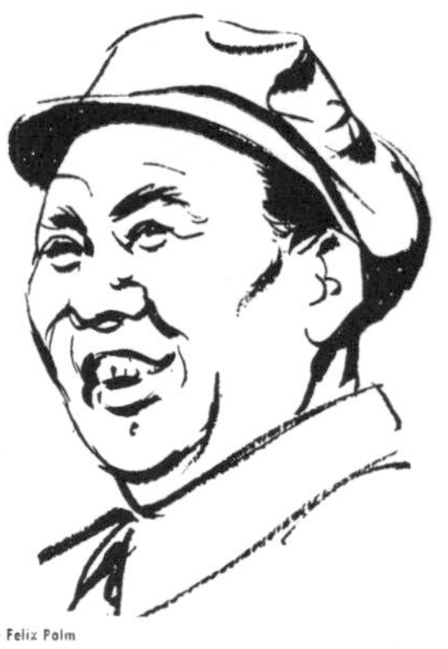

By Felix Palm

Mao Tse-tung
. . . in Lenin's footsteps

Chinese Comintern scented

By Paul Wohl
Written for The Christian Science Monitor

A new Communist International, embracing Europe and oriented toward Peking, soon may come into being.

European pro-Chinese Communists are to hold a conference in Switzerland in August. The outcome may be the nucleus of a Chinese Comintern.

Such an organization of "white Chinese" would represent a determined effort by Peking to wrest control of the international Communist movement from Moscow.

"White Chinese" is the name pro-Moscow or noncommitted Chinese have given the European pro-Peking Communists.

In Europe these two brands of Communists are openly at loggerheads.

While the Chinese and Soviet Communist Parties still address each other officially as "dear comrades," European dissident and "orthodox" Communists have stopped "comrading" each other.

The term "mister," deeply insulting among Communists, is not yet used. Instead, the contestants refer to each other by their family names.

Only the independents, grouped around the Italian Communist Party, still go on "comrading" right and left.

At the August conference of pro-Peking European Communists, the Italians are slated to play a peculiar role.

Decisive role seen

Theoretically they seem to be on the right wing of what Peking disdainfully calls "revisionism." Actually they have thrown their weight into the balance in favor of a modus vivendi between Moscow and Peking.

Although the Italians are unlikely to participate in the conference officially, the position of the Italian party is expected to be the decisive factor.

If Peking refrains from attacking the Italians, as it has done so far, the Italian party and its independent European comrades may take a noncommittal, albeit sympathetic attitude toward the new Peking-oriented European Communist organization which the Chinese apparently seek to set up.

In trying to set up a new international Communist organization — first for Europe, later for other continents and ultimately for the world—Chinese Chairman Mao Tse-tung follows in the footsteps of Lenin.

When Lenin established the Communist International or Comintern in 1919, only

★ Please turn to Page 4

Kennedy supports gun curb

By Josephine Ripley
Staff correspondent of The Christian Science Monitor

Washington

It obviously was not easy for Sen. Robert F. Kennedy (D) of New York to speak on a subject so closely related to the assassination of his brother, the President—the subject of mail-order guns.

It was a gun obtained by mail order, under a false name, in the hands of a mentally disturbed man that killed President Kennedy.

Senator Kennedy is one of the sponsors of the bill to ban the mail-order delivery of guns to individuals.

His appearance before the Senate subcommittee on juvenile delinquency, now holding hearings on the legislation, was brief and moving.

He called S. 1592 "a necessary bill."

"It would," he said, "save hundreds of lives in this country and spare thousands of families all across this land the grief and heartbreak that must come from the loss of a husband, a son, a brother, or a friend."

This was the closest he came to any reference to the assassination of his brother.

Questioning avoided

Out of deference to his personal feelings, he was not questioned by Sen. Thomas J. Dodd (D) of Connecticut, subcommittee chairman, author of the legislation.

He posed briefly for photographers as he entered the hearing room—but not in front of the mail-order gun display including a model of the rifle used in the assassination.

And he departed abruptly, brushing aside photographers and reporters who followed him.

In Senator Kennedy's opinion, the bill "would meet the firearms problem in a moderate and careful fashion."

He said it "would only subject deadly weapons to the same controls we have always imposed on automobiles, liquor, or prescription drugs. The use and sale of these things are carefully regulated by federal, state, and local government. The same should be true of firearms."

All this can be done, he contended, "without unduly curtailing the use of firearms for legitimate sport shooting or hunting, and without curtailing the lawful activity of sport gun clubs."

Campaign criticized

He said there has been a "massive publicity campaign against the bill . . . which has distorted the facts of the bill and misled thousands of our citizens. . . . The campaign is doing the nation a great disservice."

He departed from his text to say that he, personally, had received far more mail against this bill than on any other issue since he had become a senator.

"We have a responsibility to the victims of crime and violence," he said, chiding opponents of the legislation.

The first opposition witness was Harry R. Woodward, director of the Colorado Game, Fish, and Parks Department.

He opposed the bill largely on grounds that it would "restrict a nonresident hunter's ability to bring firearms into Colorado with which to hunt. . . ."

Senator Dodd quickly challenged Mr. Woodward on this point. "You point out to me anything in this bill that says a man can't carry a shotgun or a rifle into Colorado and I'll eat it," he snapped.

Asked if he had actually read the bill, the Colorado official conceded he had not but said his staff had prepared a report on it.

Senator Dodd expressed shock that the witness "could be so misinformed about the bill."

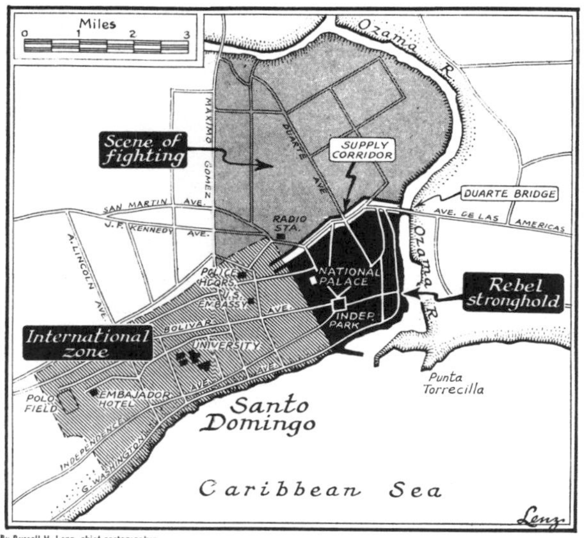

By Russell H. Lenz, chief cartographer

Divided city: zones of three forces

Details of Dominican cease-fire: Page 2

Dominican pledges of U.S. put to test

By Saville R. Davis
Staff correspondent of The Christian Science Monitor

Washington

The pledge of the United States in Vietnam and the Dominican Republic—to establish free government and then withdraw—is being sorely tested in Santo Domingo.

The Johnson administration continues to insist it is not taking sides between the two contending parties there. It says it is not supporting the forces of political reaction; it is not aiding the military junta to crush the rebels.

Meanwhile the President and his soldiers and diplomats on the spot continue to be drawn into actions—against his will or with it—that seem to do just those things.

This is the leading topic in Washington today. It is being hotly debated. But much of the argument is private. The situation is considered so serious that most responsible officials and news correspondents are trying to be constructive and to avoid reckless charges.

The President's critics say he proclaims impartiality while his agents still consider the Caamaño military forces to be Communist led at key points, and seek to have them quickly defeated. This dichotomy, it is argued, brings the credibility of the United States into question.

Fully committeed

The President's defenders say that the actions of the American military are being misunderstood and distorted. When the full story is told, they argue, it will appear that the President's instructions were honorably carried out in the main and that the United States consistently sought to halt the fighting.

One thing appears certain in the midst of this quietly desperate debate where neither side appears entirely sure of its ground:

President Johnson by now stands fully committed to letting the Dominican people choose their own government. If the people elect a coalition government or one controlled by the so-called constitutional rebels, it will be seen whether they are Communist controlled or not.

If the forces behind the military junta win in a fair ballot, it will soon be proved whether they are reactionaries and indulge in political repression or not.

Meanwhile the forces of popular democracy in the Americas are critical of the Johnson "impartiality" even when it is taken at face value. A typical Latin-American observer here explained this attitude in these words:

"First the United States rescued the militarists from possible defeat (after they admitted they no longer could keep control), supplied and financed them, fought with them in 'keeping order,' confined the Caamaño forces to a narrow area, and gave the military leaders time to prepare an assault on the so-called rebels.

Given equal basis

"It now seeks to be 'impartial' between its own sorry creation and the forces of democratic revolt.

"We cannot permit this. It would be like asking the forces of resistance in Europe during World War II to form a coalition with the Nazis."

To Mr. Bunker this meant impartiality. To most of his listeners it meant that he did not regard the leaders of one side as more deserving than those of the other. It also suggested that he considered the Dominican "population" to be divided.

Most correspondents on the scene have reported that the junta was as widely unpopular as the so-called constitutional forces were popular.

The degree to which the United States now seeks to place the military junta and the Caamaño forces on an euqal footing was shown by the speech of United States Ambassador Ellsworth Bunker to the Organization of American States.

He recommended that the armed forces of the Dominican Republic should "be accessible to both factions, so as to avoid friction. . . ." He spoke of "the depth of the bitterness and hostility engendered by the war," not only between "the opposing military leaders" but also "in the population generally."

OAS finds road hard: Page 3

Soviet soldiers tucked away

Hungary profits from Communist thaw

By Eric Bourne
Special correspondent of The Christian Science Monitor

Budapest

Candid stories about the Soviet Union have recently been told in Yugoslavia as well as here.

But here in Budapest their authors do not get sent to prison.

Recently a Hungarian writer published a frank piece about aspects of Soviet behavior when the Red Army came in pursuit of the Germans.

Publication during the recent anniversary of the allied victory over Hitlerism was considered in bad taste, but there was no Soviet protest—as in Belgrade when Professor Mihajlov's Moscow diary appeared in a local weekly—if only presumably because the Soviets keep their military presence here an exceedingly unobtrusive affair.

Unfortunate time

Nor will the Hungarian writer have to go to prison for nine months as Mr. Mihajlov will if his appeal against the recent sentence fails.

Instead, he was reprimanded, and his stipend from the Writers Fund suspended. But this done, a publishing house came up with an offer of advances for a book which in effect assure the Hungarian author of no loss of income.

An intellectual who himself has been a victim of the ups and downs of the past two decades told us: "Nothing at all would have happened if he had not written harsh things about the Soviets at a time when the victory over Germany was being celebrated."

The milder, more sophisticated approach seems typical of Hungary. Just now Communist officials concede that the withdrawal of the 60,000 Soviet troops would be good psychologically. But they make it clear that this is not going to happen until there is a general East-West agreement on the reduction of foreign bases.

And they seem right enough when they assert that the Soviets tuck themselves away in their rural encampments so well that most Hungarians have almost forgotten they are here.

On two visits within the past month this writer has seen not a solitary Soviet uniform on the streets of Budapest.

Soviet presence apart, the Kadar regime's policy of cautious liberalization proceeds and is certainly bearing fruit. From conversations one gets both an impression that the regime considers making further concessions and that the man-in-the-street is becoming more willing to accept.

But one also gets the impression that the government is not quite sure how far it can afford to go.

Trade with West

His regime—like others in Eastern Europe—begins to show a marked urge toward greater openings to the West. The old complaining hostility toward the Common Market and the petulant talk of "discrimination" has been dropped.

Instead, talk is of expanded trade and business with the West, including factory-building partnerships, even with West Germany despite the Hallstein doctrine and political uneasiness.

Communists here make the stock show of anger about American policy in Southeast Asia. But it often sounds more in sorrow than in anger that the deadlock over Vietnam should prevent not only a mending of fences in relations with the United States but should also hold up growth of better relations between East and West from which the Hungarians obviously expect to become more "masters in their own house."

Free speech and pay-TV

California's much-publicized experiment with pay-television, which began to roll last July, screeched to an abrupt halt in November when voters outlawed pay-TV after a bitter campaign.

Now a justice of the Sacramento Superior Court has ruled that the voters' action was unconstitutional because in effect it was a ban on free speech.

While Californians wonder whether pay-TV opponents will appeal, it is probable that proponents of pay-TV will put their experiment back on the air.

Further details: Page 3

2nd Cl Post Pd at Boston, Mass., and add'l offices

© 1965 THE CHRISTIAN SCIENCE PUBLISHING SOCIETY
All Rights Reserved

THE CHRISTIAN SCIENCE MONITOR

BOSTON, WEDNESDAY, JUNE 9, 1965 — *An International Daily Newspaper* — VOL. 57, NO. 164 TWO SECTIONS — WESTERN EDITION — 10c

FOCUS on world affairs

What's ahead . . .

A quiet peace effort is smiling wanly through in the Middle East.

Despite grating Arab-Israeli border abrasions that often erupt into violence, a few leaders on both sides are circumspectly seeking new approaches to possible peace talks.

Some of the impetus springs from Tunisian President Bourguiba. He wants to treat the Palestine problem as diplomatic rather than military.

To those Arabs yearning to drive Israel into the sea, his idea is heresy.

But Israeli diplomats are under orders to pinpoint Arab leaders who might be willing to talk in private to third parties—to scholars and diplomats in netural nations perhaps.

Some Israelis feel the big Jewish and Arab communities in the United States and Latin America might make good points of initial contact.

Nobody knows if it will work, but the idea is in the wind.

⊕

Poland's perennial Premier, Jozef Cyrankiewicz, may be on the skids.

When the Polish Sejm (Parliament) held elections recently, he ranked ragtag last among candidates in his home town, Cracow.

Most of Mr. Cyrankiewicz's trouble stems from within the Communist-led United Worker Party. The so-called hard-liners are in ascendency there. And whenever in the past they have been, the Premier has come under attack.

His political decline coincides with a rash of recent Polish defections to the West. These have triggered a tightening of police pressures.

The basic hard-liner rise in Warsaw is laid to uneasiness over West Germany's recent political and economic inroads in Eastern Europe. The hard-liners are also pressuring party chief Wladyslaw Gomulka to cultivate political relations with Peking. And Peking has little use for Mr. Cyrankiewicz.

⊕

Latin America could become the world's pioneer region in birth control.

Some 75 cooperative studies are plowing ahead simultaneously under the general wing of the Alliance for Progress. The United States is pouring about a million dollars a year into them.

President Johnson mentioned this assistance in his state of the Union message last January. And the program has been quickly and quietly mounting ever since.

Even Roman Catholic church groups are getting some study help. The impression is growing that the church in the hemisphere concedes the need to brake the birth rate.

What may happen is tacit church acceptance of population-control policies without actually publicly endorsing them.

Trends . . .

A bevy of Soviet party chiefs is roaming Europe talking up "an opening to the right."

They would have Europe's Communist parties, big and small, warm up to the Social Democrats—those in the political spectrum to the right of the Communist left.

When the Austrian Communist Party held its recent 19th congress, a Soviet team turned up urging new approaches to the Social Democrats. A Soviet party delegation has taken a like tack in France.

The Kremlin insists it does not aim this time at repeating prewar popular-front tactics. These are still rejected as a Stalinist deviation.

But the new drive does mean that Soviet policy inside world communism now has drawn close to what the late Italian party leader, Palmiro Togliatti, urged—autonomy of national parties, Communist unity in diversity, and mending of fences with China.

How and why . . .

The West has the jitters over the prospects of a possible East-West clash in Africa.

Here is how the reasoning runs:

Moscow and Peking are both quick to identify closely with militant African movements to "liberate" southern Africa—Rhodesia, South Africa, and Portuguese territories—from white minority domination.

Western powers favor a gradual trend to majority rule there too. But not by resort to violence.

Other African states intent on rooting out these white regimes, lack the muscle to do it. Nor does it seem likely that southern Africans can overthrow their well-armed white governments.

Will the Africans then, tap Communist power to help them? What would the West do? To side with the white minority would call down the ire of black Africa. But not to would be to give communism a foothold.

The situation is still iffy. But there is enough to it to stir Western qualms.

Where to look

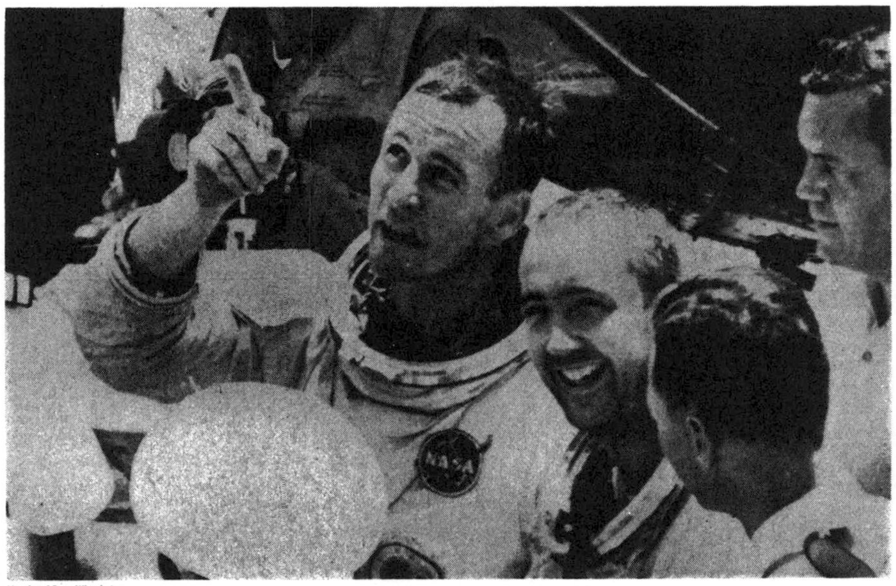

Associated Press Wirephoto

Earthmen again

Astronauts Edward H. White II, pointing, and James A. McDivitt enjoy a hearty welcome aboard the carrier Wasp. The pair are wearing 62-orbit beards.

Vietnam escalator tests U.S.

By David K. Willis
Staff correspondent of The Christian Science Monitor

Washington

Louder and more insistent grow the questions:

Where is the United States headed in Vietnam?

Is congressional and public debate keeping pace with change in Southeast Asia?

Over the weekend, the State Department again defined the role of United States ground troops, indicating they have attacked the enemy while defending American installations.

A department spokesman also says United States units can go to the help of hard-pressed Vietnamese units if asked.

Does all this add up to a gradual escalation into a full-scale ground war between the Viet Cong, reinforced by North Vietnamese forces, and American units?

The State Department says there is no shift in basic United States policy—to let the South Vietnamese do the fighting, but to give them every support.

So far, the support has taken the form of military advisers to help with strategy on the ground, massive air cover, and various kinds of assistance from the Navy.

Character changes

But the character of the support has been slowly changing.

United States planes now seek out targets in the north and bomb them. United States Navy guns shell enemy targets.

The State Department still insists the primary task of United States forces recently flown in is to protect American installations—such as the big air base at Da Nang.

Earlier in the war, government troops guarded the bases. But since March, they have been needed at the front, and marines have taken over.

The redefinition by the State Department was interpreted by some newsmen as the first time the United States had publicly announced that American ground troops were attacking the Communist guerrillas to defend installations.

The statement, issued by department spokesman Robert J. McCloskey, said that troops recently sent to Vietnam to guard installations "naturally" return fire if fired upon.

Debate sought

"It should come as no surprise therefore that our troops engage in combat in these and similar circumstances," Mr. McCloskey said. But South Vietnamese government troops were still "carrying the brunt of combat operations."

Asked to explain the words "similar circumstances," Mr. McCloskey said he was referring to "clear-and-hold" operations.

Critics among university faculties and members of Congress feel that basic United States policy now needs a full public airing.

The recent all-day "teach-in," beamed to campuses across the nation from Washington's Sheraton-Park Hotel, was welcomed, but has resulted in demands for more debate.

It is realized, of course, that the President is in a difficult situation. Critical debate could always be construed abroad as a weakening of the United States position.

Yet there is some feeling in Congress for a fuller debate. Twenty-eight House Democrats—seven of them from the House Foreign Affairs Committee—have urged the committee to hold public hearings on Vietnam.

Dominican intervention

Bosch assails U.S.

By James Nelson Goodsell
Latin America correspondent of The Christian Science Monitor

San Juan, Puerto Rico

To Juan Domingo Bosch, the deposed President of the Dominican Republic in whose name the current revolt was started, that revolt is "a true revolution and not merely a disorder."

He says he regards United States policy in his nation as "a very sad mistake . . . and an irreversible one."

As a result of the United States intervention, Dr. Bosch believes that "anti-Americanism in Latin America, as in my country, has jumped."

Dr. Bosch outlined his views during a two-hour talk in the home he is using here in his San Juan exile.

Revolutionary current

Although he foresees a long United States stay in his country, he holds that Washington "is ignorant of the problems facing us."

Washington's view that Communists were a threat to the revolt which began April 24 is simply wrong, Dr. Bosch said.

"You equate revolution with communism and by so doing you show no understanding of the Latin-American situation today."

A revolutionary process is under way in Latin America and the Dominican revolt is part and parcel of this process, he argues.

"The great tragedy of our hemisphere is that Washington does not understand that Latin America is in a revolutionary stage," he says.

During our talk, Mrs. Bosch came into the room and spoke in her gentle way of her

★ Please turn to Page 6

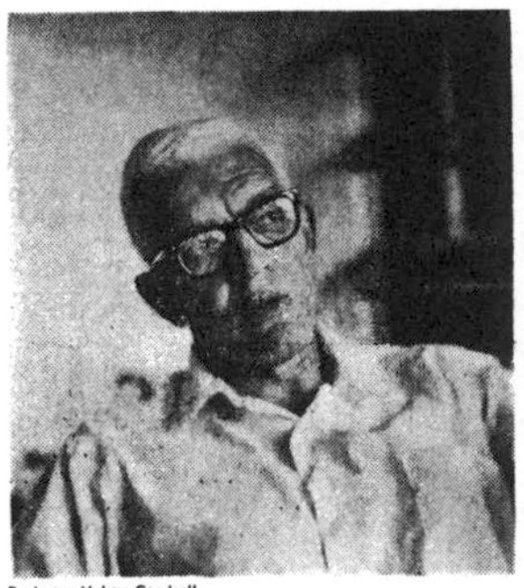

By James Nelson Goodsell

Juan Domingo Bosch

U.S. policy: a sad mistake

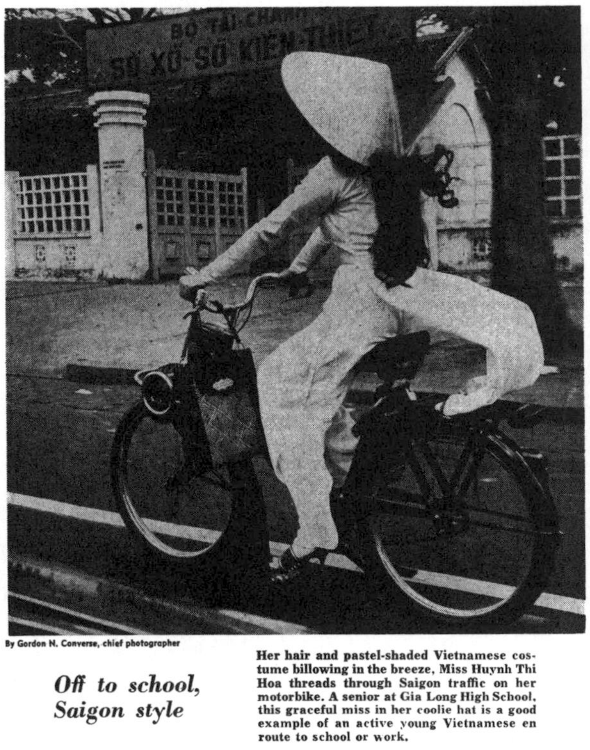

By Gordon N. Converse, chief photographer

Off to school, Saigon style

Her hair and pastel-shaded Vietnamese costume billowing in the breeze, Miss Huynh Thi Hoa threads through Saigon traffic on her motorbike. A senior at Gia Long High School, this graceful miss in her coolie hat is a good example of an active young Vietnamese en route to school or work.

Space trails blazed

By a staff writer of The Christian Science Monitor

Astronaut Edward H. White's 20-minute walk in space was a harbinger of the future.

It previewed one of the most important kinds of activity in many of tomorrow's space flights.

This is why it is the event that stands out for the flight of Gemini 4 that ended so successfully Monday.

As space flight develops, there will be more and more need for astronauts to leave their craft to carry out what the National Aeronautics and Space Administration insists on calling "extravehicular activity" (EVA).

To maneuver and work in space means the ability to repair one's own spacecraft. Major White literally walked all over Gemini 4 in a preview of this.

Detection task

It means being able to assemble structures such as manned laboratories from smaller pieces that individually are easy to send into orbit.

It means being able to move from one vehicle to another easily and important for the military, to inspect at firsthand suspicious unmanned satellites.

To do all or any of these things is not straightforward. Besides having to have a protective suit with life-support equipment, the astronaut has to use new tools and develop new ways of moving and working.

Outside his ship, he is himself a tiny satellite. He is weightless. He cannot move by pushing his feet against the ground or swimming through water or even air. Like his spacecraft, he has to use small jet thrusters.

Or, if he does push against an object like the spacecraft, he may float off from the reaction to his push in a way he does not intend.

Traction difficult

Major White illustrated this in walking on Gemini 4.

When his feet pushed on the craft, it bounced and he tended to move away from it. He had a hard time maintaining traction. He had to hold himself down with his golden tether to walk at all. A space mechanic working on a craft will need magnetic or suction-gripping shoes.

Had he tried to use ordinary tools, say a wrench to tighten or loosen a nut, Major White would have had even more trouble. He likely would have only turned himself around and around—not the nut.

Special tools are being developed to cope with this aspect of weightless working. They undoubtedly will be tried out on some future flight.

The hand-held jet propulsion unit Major White used typifies the individual's means of moving around in space. Some sort of hand-held or strapped-on jet device will always be needed.

For short moves, such as between two nearby vehicles, one might push off from the first and drift over to the second. But for anything more complex, a small motor will be needed.

Tethered to craft

Major White's device jetted oxygen from bottles of the compressed gas. It was jetted from two nozzles that extended out on thin arms. They were arranged so the jets shot to either side of Major White's body. He held the device so that their combined force passed through his center of gravity.

In this way he could slowly drift about. His 25-foot tether removed any danger that he would drift beyond his range for returning to the spacecraft.

Someday, the maneuvering units will enable one to move about over sizable areas of space. Bigger units may be like scooters. They may be large enough to hold considerable fuel and shaped so a man can ride them or hang on and be pulled along by them.

The seven-day mission of Gemini 5, to take place probably in August, does not now include any outside activity. But it is certain that the feat of Major White will be extensively developed on many later American space flights.

Likewise, the Soviets can be expected to move well beyond Lt. Col. Alexei Leonov's space walk of last March.

Spacemen have important date: Page 5

Storm center

The 1964-65 term of the Supreme Court of the United States has alarmed some, pleased others. Dissenting opinions pointed up disagreements among the justices. Majority judgments reflected certain patterns of decision in line with past rulings.

This week, the court ruled that televising a criminal trial over objection of the defendant deprives him of constitutional rights.

It also struck down Connecticut's 1879 Anti-Birth Control Law.

For a report on this week and this year in the Supreme Court please turn to Page 3.

2nd Cl Post Pd at Boston, Mass., and add'l offices

June 9, 1965

© 1965 THE CHRISTIAN SCIENCE PUBLISHING SOCIETY
All Rights Reserved

THE CHRISTIAN SCIENCE MONITOR

BOSTON, WEDNESDAY, DECEMBER 29, 1965 — *An International Daily Newspaper* — VOL. 58, NO. 28 TWO SECTIONS — EASTERN EDITION ★ 10¢

FOCUS on Europe

What's ahead . . .

Who's to succeed Franco? It's a question that will roll more and more off the Spanish tongue in the year ahead.

Spain's caudillo is planning to step down someday soon as Chief of State. What happens then?

The problem boils down to picking a king to take over. General Franco declared Spain a kingdom as long ago as 1947. But the throne still stands vacant. The big dilemma is deciding which descendant of the Spanish Bourbon line will mount it.

Pretender Don Juan is next in line, ready and eager to be king. General Franco deposed Alfonso XIII, Don Juan's father, in 1931. The late monarch fled, but never abdicated.

General Franco would prefer to have Don Juan's son, young Juan Carlos, wear the crown. And official talk in Madrid tends more and more that way.

However, Don Juan doesn't intend to be cut out. In early January he is expected to reassert, by declaration, his place next in line of succession.

⊕

Europe's Common Market may try to avoid being derailed by simply resetting its timetable.

A "third stage" in the development of the European Economic Community (EEC) is coming on fast. And it is the major reason that the Common Market is gripped in crisis.

The idea is now afoot to postpone this "third stage." That would also mean putting off a fully completed Common Market until 1973 (instead of 1970).

The "third stage" is more political than economic anyway. It rests on the concept of majority voting and "supranationalism," which France bridles against. Putting it off would not hold up a European customs union. Industrial tariffs could still be shorn away by mid-1967. The common farm market could be fully planted by 1970.

Dangers of a direct clash between France and the EEC Commission would be eased. And the pressure of an immediate deadline would be gone.

France and its five Common Market partners will meet in mid-January to try to heal their breach. They may reset the timetable.

Trends . . .

Europe's department stores are beginning to befriend in a big way the exports of underdeveloped nations.

It's a new idea in foreign aid. Several major department and chain stores not only buy an emerging nation's exports, but they vigorously promote the country.

The Italian chain, "La Rinascente" is the pioneer in all this. Its buyers not only rove nations staked out for special promotion, but they take along historians, artists, writers, and educators, too. This team portrays the nation and its economy and gives the portrayal full coverage.

"La Rinascente" insists that organized export operations in some developing nations are often rudimentary, sometimes nonexistent. The department store has come along and organized them for the first time.

How and why . . .

The dust kicked up by the French elections has settled. But the European air hasn't cleared yet.

All the allied nations wait now to learn how a reelected President de Gaulle will interpret his new mandate.

Bonn especially is bracing itself. During his election campaign, President de Gaulle said no one could know how the future Germany would turn out, hence it should be denied nuclear arms.

But a hand on the nuclear helm, including eventual "copossession" of warheads, is just what West German Chancellor Ludwig Erhard seeks.

This basic Paris-Bonn chasm is a gaping one. Europeans see little hope of bridging it.

⊕

Concern is mounting in Europe over what might follow Chancellor Erhard in Bonn.

Nationalism is on the rise in West Germany. And President de Gaulle isn't the only European who envisages the possibility someday of an extremist government coming to power there. Some fear such a regime might engineer a drive to take over East Germany, which even liberal West German periodicals call "Middle Germany."

The Bonn bid for a voice in nuclear planning abets this uneasy feeling. So does the fact that a West German is about to become assistant secretary-general of NATO — in charge of political affairs. So does Bonn's recent suggestion that NATO's northern army group, hitherto British-led, should come under German command.

All these signs may mean nothing. But they make many Europeans edgy.

Where to look

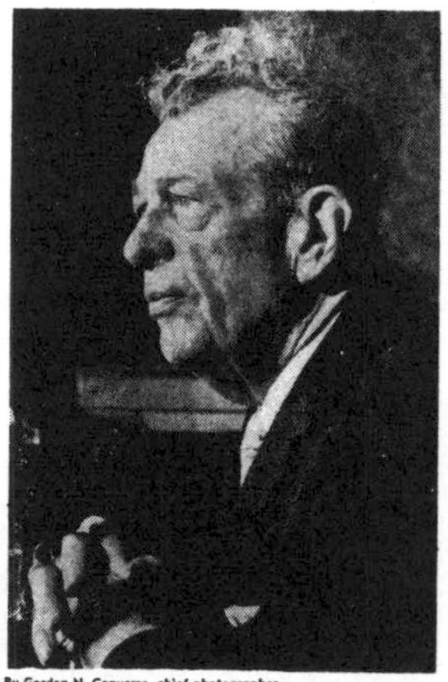

By Gordon N. Converse, chief photographer

Minority Leader Dirksen

'It is the people involved who are making Vietnam an issue today.'

Dirksen primes Viet debate

By Godfrey Sperling Jr.
Staff correspondent of The Christian Science Monitor

Washington

In the forefront of Senator Dirksen's approach to the next session of Congress is his concern with the increasingly difficult role he must play.

The questions confronting him:

- What does the continuing escalation in Vietnam mean to the loyal opposition?
- How does the leader of the loyal opposition continue to express this loyalty and, at the same time, raise questions about the war?

In an interview with The Christian Science Monitor, Everett McKinley Dirksen, who sets the tone of the GOP challenge in the upper chamber, said that Vietnam would have to be an issue in 1966—"not because a political party is raising the issue but because the people are making it an issue."

'All shades of politics'

"There are all shades of politics among those fighting in Vietnam," said the Senate minority leader "There are young Republicans and young Democrats, fighting side by side. These are the people who are making Vietnam an issue today. Together with the parents of those who are in battle. And also those who know they could be called to the defense of their country.

"All these," he said, "are the ones who make Vietnam an issue. Not a political party."

Within this rationale is the Dirksen explanation for a hardening Republican position on Vietnam. It can be measured in this way: Until a few days ago, Senator Dirksen was expressing support for the administration. Now he says he still backs the administration "for being in Vietnam," but faults United States leadership for what he views as an unnecessarily protracted conflict.

Resolution stressed

Senator Dirksen now assumes the Republican congressional leadership is trying to bring about an early resolution of the Vietnam war. He thinks a quarantine would be good. He'd like more use of naval and air power.

Further, as he was saying in the phone interview, he has determined that the pushing of such a policy will be within the spirit of bipartisanship. "The people," he repeated, they were the ones who were insistent that answers be found.

A major aspect of this issue, the Senator said, would be the question of financing Vietnam. "Will there be cutbacks in spending on social, welfare, and other domestic programs? Or will there be tax increases? This has not yet been indicated. I suspect that at this very moment the President is wrestling with this at the ranch."

Measures hinted

The Illinois Senator did some speculation on the kind of tax increase that could come. He wondered whether the President would revise the tax tables so as to put a heavier load on those in the higher-income brackets. Or whether there might be a sales tax. Or something else.

"I really can't tell you," he said. "Everyone is so close-mouthed about it."

The Senator said that much of the session would be devoted to repairing legislation passed in 1965. "The poverty legislation," he said, "is so full of loopholes and abuses and enormous extravagances."

"Besides this," he said "14(b) will be an issue [the right-to-work dispute]. We are going to bring it up and we are going to fight. There has been some speculation that I might be willing to compromise on 14(b) or on reapportionment [the Dirksen amendment]. But I won't compromise."

2nd Cl Post Pd at Boston, Mass., and add'l offices

Parley or escalation

Pause pressures Hanoi

By Saville R. Davis
Staff correspondent of The Christian Science Monitor

Washington

The silent gesture of the United States toward peace—suspending the bomb raids on North Vietnam with no public explanation—contains both an opportunity and a warning.

If both sides could be persuaded to transfer the conflict to the conference table, the rapidly intensifying war could be ended now.

If not, a full-scale ground war could soon develop in South Vietnam. And destruction by bombing of North Vietnam's highly prized industrial complex could well come at once.

World diplomacy is once again being given an opportunity to move in, during this suddenly fluid holiday and year-end period. Many different channels are known to be trying to mediate. But which, if any, sparked President Johnson's second pause in the bombing is a tightly held secret.

[The Associated Press reported from Saigon early Tuesday that the Viet Cong announced it would observe a four-day New Year's holiday cease-fire against Vietnamese government forces from 12:01 a.m. Jan. 20 to midnight Jan. 23.]

Washington divided

At this writing, as the hours continue to pass and no bombs are dropped in the north, Washington is divided. Some officials are quietly hopeful that both sides have had enough, despite skepticism in Washington and a recent hard line in Hanoi.

Others continue to be pessimistic. They doubt whether anything short of defeat would cause the determined and resourceful men of Hanoi to negotiate on anything short of their own terms.

The official line is that Hanoi has to choose. It can talk or face a great deal more war. But these stark alternatives, aimed at the other side, are only part of the picture.

It is well known here that leading officials have grave doubts about the value of talks at this time. Hanoi has not really been hurt, they say, by the bombing of the north.

In the south, the expanding American armies have kept the Viet Cong from total victory. But they have not yet made much progress against the guerrilla forces or the regular North Vietnamese Army units sent down from the north.

Both sides, it is argued, still think they can win.

The peacemaker element in the United States Government is a minority. But it is reinforced by important segments of opinion in Congress and the country and of world opinion.

Positions changed

It wants active peacemaking, which will reach out to the other side and seek to attract and persuade it to the conference table.

President Johnson appears to have decided to give the latter group its chance. If the pause continues beyond the brief five days of last May's sudden suspension of bombing, this will be confirmed.

One virtue is seen in this new development by both the militant and the peacemaker factions here.

During the past year, suspicion has grown in neutral and hostile countries that it was the United States that was chiefly obsessed by military victory and was blocking any peace talks. This criticism was fed by reports, both accurate and false, of peace feelers that were turned down by President Johnson.

They had some basis in an honest concern of the President. He felt that any negotiations before the United States turned the tide this past year would have amounted to surrender. This the President was not prepared to do.

Meanwhile Hanoi was represented by some as eager to stop the war.

In more recent months, Mr. Johnson has seemed genuinely anxious to hold at least beginning talks without conditions — provided the other side would do likewise. And Hanoi has emerged as the side that refused. Its line has steadily hardened.

Quiet diplomacy

No official source will say openly, now, that President Johnson wants to prove that he is willing to talk, and to let Hanoi — if it rejects the mediation that is undoubtedly going behind the scenes — stand self-convicted as the barrier to settlement.

But this is widely thought to be one of the President's motives. If an agreed truce should come, everyone benefits. If not, he is released from blame. So the argument goes.

There is intense speculation in Washington as to what secret diplomacy may be accomplishing now. Fingers are pointed to Vice-President Hubert H. Humphrey's trip to the East, to Pope Paul's continued efforts to bring about a truce, to the presence of the North Vietnamese Deputy Premier in Hungary, to the recent world trip of Senator Mike Mansfield and several congressional colleagues, to Prime Minister Harold Wilson's comment here that "we have many lines open to Hanoi," and to the statements of Soviet leaders that no mediation could succeed without a halt to the bombing.

It is assumed there are other leads. There is no hint as to which might be producing results.

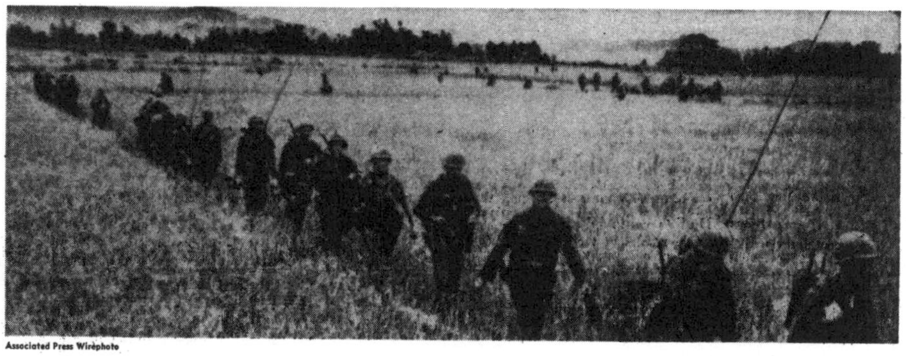

Associated Press Wirephoto

GIs press Viet struggle with long, risky treks

Truce experiment behind them, troops of the 2d Battalion of the 7th Cavalry of the United States 1st Air Cavalry Division walk through paddies in central Vietnam on another thrust against the Communist Viet Cong.

U.S. foreign-policy balance sheet

The Christian Science Monitor has gathered widely divergent opinions from government officials on American foreign-policy ventures of 1965. Most readers will have reached their own conclusions. This report gives some of the informed thinking in Washington.

By David K. Willis
Staff correspondent of The Christian Science Monitor

Washington

Sizing up '65

Opinion among government officials is sharply divided on whether the United States comes out with a profit or a loss on its foreign balance sheet for 1965.

Some officials see a bright side to the year. American goals were brought closer, they say.

Others are much more gloomy. They point to the escalation in Vietnam, intervention in the Dominican Republic, troubles in Europe, in Africa, and in the Indian subcontinent.

These pessimistic officials make deep, subtle criticisms of American policy.

They are concerned that the men at the top of the Johnson administration are spending too many hours of the day worrying about the Vietnam war—about "nuts and bolts questions," as one source put it to this newspaper.

They complain that Vietnam looms too large on the American foreign policy horizon—that too many other policy issues are clouded because of it.

Vietnam has chilled relations with Moscow and Eastern Europe, has made disarmament and a nuclear nonproliferation treaty harder to get, and has stirred misgivings in Asia and elsewhere.

They question whether, in 10 years, the war will look so important in retrospect. Some even believe that Mr. Johnson should offer to negotiate openly with the National Liberation Front in South Vietnam, as well as with Hanoi.

American policy during 1965 was unbalanced, they say. Along with greater military pressure on Vietnam perhaps could have gone—they believe—a dramatic disarmament move; along with support for the strong military government of Castelo Branco in Brazil, perhaps some greater help to Chile; and along with the Dominican intervention, even greater efforts to bolster the Alliance for Progress.

These officials say the United States is floundering in Vietnam; certainly, the war is far from won.

They freely admit that Peking had its setbacks, too: that Washington-London ties are closer now than might have been expected during the sterling crisis early in the life of the Wilson government; that the Middle East was quiet; that events in Indonesia look better than before the Nov. 30 attempted coup.

More optimistic officials make much of these last points.

Without wanting to minimize the seriousness of Vietnam, Santo Domingo and Rhodesia they look at the past year in another light.

Americans would do well to remember, they say, that 1965 was a bad year for "extremists" — for dogmatic world leaders

★ Please turn to Page 4

Cairo spy trial points at U.S.

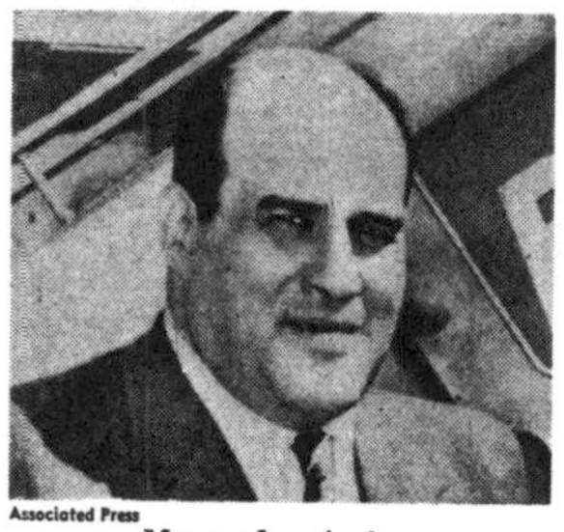

Associated Press

Mustapha Amine

Spy—or diplomatic pawn?

By John K. Cooley
Staff correspondent of The Christian Science Monitor

Cairo

The espionage trial of Cairo publisher Mustapha Amine may disclose as much about some of Egypt's internal problems as it does about United States-United Arab Republic relations.

Mr. Amine went on trial here Dec. 28 on charges of selling state secrets of President Nasser's regime to the United States Central Intelligence Agency.

When arrested, Mr. Amine was in the company of Bruce Taylor Odell, United States Embassy attaché afterward recalled and reassigned by the State Department.

The prosecution says Mr. Odell was a CIA agent first spotted as such by United Arab Republic intelligence in Iraq. It says it will prove its case by playing tape recordings of Amine-Odell meetings.

Mr. Amine was seized in Alexandria on July 23. This was the thirteenth anniversary of the nearly bloodless military coup which made Lt. Col. Gamal Abdel Nasser Egypt's ruler and the most prominent person in the Arab world.

Mustapha Amine, and his twin brother Ali Amine, pioneered in the Egyptian press coverage of this revolution and its aftermath.

Mustapha Amine studied at the American University in Cairo, then at Georgetown University, Washington. He returned to Egypt as a crusading popular journalist.

In 1947, as Zionists and Arabs prepared for the armed showdown over independence of the state of Israel, a young reporter named Mohammed Hasseinine Kaykal worked for

★ Please turn to Page 6

December 29, 1965

© 1965 THE CHRISTIAN SCIENCE PUBLISHING SOCIETY All Rights Reserved

THE CHRISTIAN SCIENCE MONITOR

BOSTON, FRIDAY, JUNE 3, 1966 — *An International Daily Newspaper* — VOL. 58, NO. 159 TWO SECTIONS — EASTERN EDITION ★ 10¢

FOCUS on Washington

What's ahead . . .

Washington's NATO oracles are climbing out on two limbs.

They are predicting French President de Gaulle will pull all his divisions out of West Germany this year.

And they forecast that he won't sign a nonaggression pact when he goes to Moscow in mid-June. He will do some other headline-snatching thing instead. Just what, the oracles can't yet make out.

Not all Washington experts agree French troops will leave Germany. Indeed, until recently most thought they wouldn't.

But now well-placed Washington sources see signs that President de Gaulle wants to bring his men home and will. It would save Paris money and still leave plenty of other German-based NATO forces to shield France from any Communist attack.

As for the June journey to Moscow, nobody knows what the general has in mind. Everybody knows, however, that the Soviets will try to capitalize any way they can on the French-triggered rift in NATO's ranks.

⊕

If President Johnson has a tax hike in mind—to check inflation—he won't spring it until late in the congressional year.

The President has decided to postpone the issue until then.

It was a political decision. If more money became available in this election year, Congress would spend it. However, the need is not to spend more but less—to ease inflationary pressures.

Not until that last, traditional, pell-mell congressional dash for adjournment, when an administration can often whisk through an emergency act, will it be politically safe to enlarge the government's tax income without spending it.

As of now the President is much more likely to ask for a tax hike than not. But not until nearer session's end.

⊕

Tax or no tax, Vietnam needs more money

The President won't be able to avoid much longer asking Congress for it.

Many high Washington officials expect to see Vietnam war costs approach $2 billion a month. At that rate, they will more than double what was written into the 1967 budget last January—$10.3 billion.

When tapped for more Vietnam money, Congress is likely, at the same time, to press additional defense funds on the President that he doesn't now want—for the advanced manned bomber and the antimissile missile. Even if such extra money is voted, the White House probably won't spend it.

Trends . . .

Labor chiefs backed the new American immigration law because they thought it would protect American jobs.

And it does—so well that now, after six months' trial, the pressure is on to relax restrictions and let more workers in.

Only aliens with close relatives in the United States or with exceptional skills or talents can readily get in. Others can enter only if they seek jobs no American worker wants.

The law is so well enforced that so far, for the most part, it has only reunited divided families.

Advocates who originally hailed it as "more liberal" now want it made more liberal still. Sen. Edward M. Kennedy (D) of Massachusetts and Rep. Emmanuel Celler (D) of New York are both pressing for a more relaxed law.

Labor's response to the Kennedy-Celler push is awaited with interest in Washington.

⊕

When the financially well-developed Western Big 10 meet to reform the world gold standard they must decide whether to let in the Eastern underdeveloped.

The decision will sting either way. Without the developing nations the new order may just make the rich richer and the poor poorer.

But with the underdeveloped lands present, the Big 10 must make concessions that are hard to make. It's like including the poor in a program to help the poor.

Washington is predicting that the Big 10 finance ministers, meeting in July, will swallow hard and let the underdeveloped in. Most of the ministers know that the present restrictive system of world currency is by and for the West — in a world which demands to include the needy East.

Where to look

Photos stream back

Surveyor—touchdown and talking

By Curtis J. Sitomer
Staff correspondent of The Christian Science Monitor

Pasadena, Calif.

Surveyor A was a winner all the way. Some 63 hours and 36 minutes after leaving Cape Kennedy, Fla., it landed on the moon softly enough to have deposited astronauts safely on the lunar surface.

It took the Soviets five tries to make a successful soft landing on the moon.

Surveyor engineers made it on their first attempt. With this one stunning success, they wiped out the sting of being three years behind on their original schedule and of running into costs 10 times the original estimate for the Surveyor program.

In every respect, the Surveyor spacecraft and its Atlas-Centaur launch vehicle have performed faultlessly. The fact that one of two low-gain antennas did not fully deploy was considered of no significance.

Robert Seamans, Deputy Administrator of

★ Please turn to Page 4

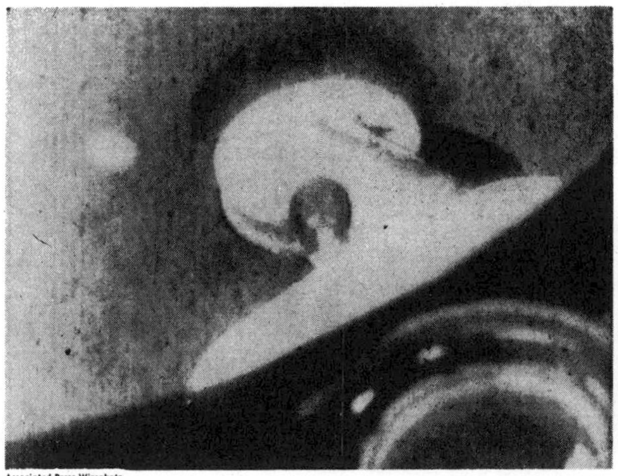

Associated Press Wirephoto

Footprint on the moon

Surveyor's 'foot' caused a slight, shadowy depression in the moon's surface. Picture was made by 200-line-per-picture transmission. Camera was six feet from area photographed. Bright spots at left are sun reflections. Dark rings in lower right are reflections of television tube as seen in the camera's mirror.

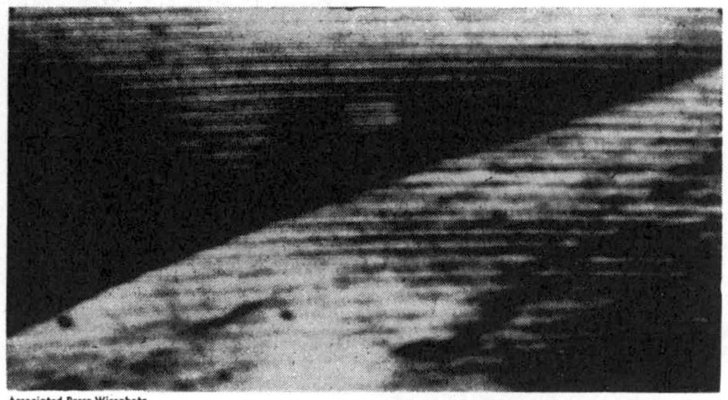

Associated Press Wirephoto

Edge of triumph

Surveyor's camera saw this horizon of the moon this week. The photo was taken and relayed back to earth by the Surveyor transmitters.

Indonesia and Malaysia step nearer peace

By John Hughes
Staff correspondent of The Christian Science Monitor

Hong Kong

Though there is no sign of peace in Vietnam, wars in Asia can end and can be forgiven.

Evidence of this has just come from Bangkok, Thailand, where leading spokesmen of Indonesia and Malaysia have gone a long way toward ending the sputtering war between their two countries.

The peace talks did not end in quite the same rosy glow as they began. The participants refused to be drawn into an admission that confrontation had actually ended.

But they are taking back various peace proposals to their respective governments. And if these are ratified, there seems little doubt that confrontation will eventually fade quickly away.

Certainly the proposal to restore normal relations between the two countries is in striking contrast to the tensions of the past three years during which Indonesian troops have harassed Malaysia's Borneo borders and Indonesian terrorists have been dropped by air and put ashore by boats on the Malaysian mainland.

After a roaring start, the peace talks apparently slowed down over the issue of Malaysia's continued control of its Borneo territories of Sabah and Sarawak. President Sukarno has consistently demanded a new referendum in those regions to determine whether the populace really wanted to be under Malaysian administration. Indonesia's new leadership, represented in Bangkok by Foreign Minister Adam Malik, is understood to be willing to waive Mr. Sukarno's demand.

Economic pressure involved

But discussion between the Indonesian and Malaysian negotiating teams apparently lengthened over some suitable alternative.

Some observers speculate that the failure to reach complete and final conclusion to the war at Bangkok may be part of that important Asian requirement for face-saving on Indonesia's part. The decision by Indonesia's new leaders to seek an end to confrontation is one they took at considerable political risk. For in so doing they had to cut across the nationalistic fervor whipped up in Indonesia by President Sukarno's violent and inflammatory anti-Malaysian course.

Hard economic facts have compelled the new Indonesian leadership to this pride-swallowing course. The country is in such economic crisis that it cannot continue the extravagance of confrontation.

Nevertheless, the Indonesians may well have been looking for some face-saving device. Complete agreement at Bangkok would have underlined the completeness of Indonesia's surrender.

But a holdup on the question of the Borneo territories, with perhaps a little more maneuver and discussion, may enable the Indonesians to assert that they extracted concessions from the Malaysians—and saved some face.

[Meanwhile Reuters reported that as Mr. Malik prepared to leave Bangkok, he told reporters that Malaysia, Indonesia, the Philippines and Thailand have agreed to join a proposed union of cooperation among Southeast Asian countries.]

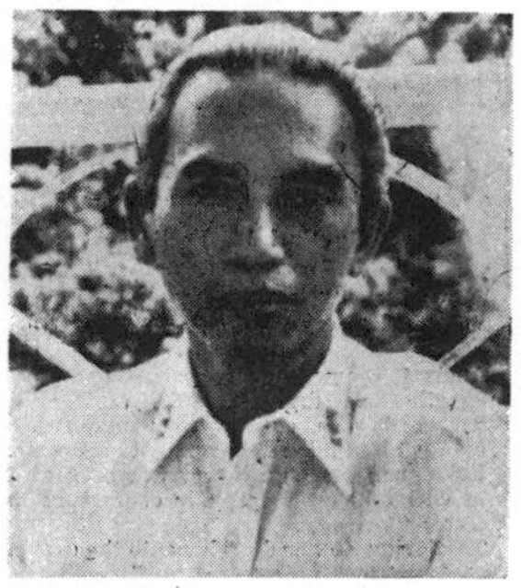

Associated Press Wirephoto

Foreign Minister Adam Malik

A face-saver for Indonesia

'Rights' crosswinds

The lid blew off at the White House Conference on Civil Rights — apparently with President Johnson's blessing.

It had been thought the President might seek to mute criticism of the lagging civil-rights drive. Not so. Conference rules were changed, the agenda opened up, and critics had their say.

President Johnson himself, in an unannounced appearance, admitted mistakes had been made, that more are likely, but that "we are moving . . . and that we shall not turn back."

The mood of the conference was one of emergency. **Story: Page 4**

Paris, Moscow hold keys

Summit prospect brightens

By William H. Stringer
Staff correspondent of The Christian Science Monitor

London

The enticing prospect of an East-West summit conference on European security, proposed by the Soviet Union, depends not on London or Washington but on the Soviets themselves, and on France's President de Gaulle.

This is the frank Anglo-American appraisal of the prospect of a high-level East-West confrontation—a proposal to be discussed at the NATO ministerial meeting in Brussels starting June 6.

But since Moscow first launched the idea, significantly omitting to say that the United States would be present at such a conference, several developments have altered the picture:

1. It can be reported on reliable authority that an eastern European country, seeking clarification of the summit proposal from Moscow, was told that, after all, the Americans would evidently have to be present if the conference were to be meaningful at all.

2. American officials have had to knock down stories appearing in the British press that the United States is definitely preparing to pare its European garrison from five to one division by 1970. Such forecasts are long range and uncertain, United States officials insist. But by the same token, if a European summit conference could establish a larger element of East-West security, then the American contribution to the NATO forces could indeed be reduced.

3. The official British reaction to the Soviet proposal is that, if the conference were carefully prepared beforehand, and if it dealt realistically with the German reunification issue, and if the Americans were present, then it might "accomplish something." Neither London nor Washington ruled out such a conference.

Increased emphasis adheres to the Soviet proposal from the fact that France's Presi-

★ Please turn to Page 14

Dominican voters seek stability in Balaguer

By James Nelson Goodsell
Latin America correspondent of The Christian Science Monitor

Santo Domingo, Dominican Republic

The clear victory of Joaquín Balaguer in the Dominican presidential election is much more a defeat for his opponent, Juan Domingo Bosch, than a personal triumph for Mr. Balaguer.

Moreover, the Balaguer victory is a defeat for the moderate left in the Dominican Republic. It could push this political element, represented by Dr. Bosch's Dominican Revolutionary Party, further leftward.

While the vote count was still incomplete at this writing, it was obvious that Mr. Balaguer would win. Dr. Bosch led the voting here in Santo Domingo, the capital city, but not by margins sufficient to offset a big countryside ballot in favor of Mr. Balaguer.

With about half the vote counted, Mr. Balaguer had 319,474 votes and Dr. Bosch 225,776. A third candidate, Rafael F. Bonnelley, was out of the race.

In early analyses of the vote, there was some feeling that Dominican voters feared the consequences of a Bosch victory and hoped that a Balaguer win would promise a return to stability in this troubled land.

Such may not be the case. But observers agreed that Dr. Bosch, by staying in his house and campaigning only by radio, had harmed his campaign.

Many Dominicans, even those who voted for Dr. Bosch so overwhelmingly in 1962, were not pleased with his campaigning performance.

The Dominican electorate is frankly tired of the titanic civil struggle which has wracked the nation in the past 13 months.

Goals remain

Mr. Balaguer is considered a rather colorless figure who, in contrast to the more colorful Dr. Bosch, campaigned vigorously around the nation.

Most observers here are quick to emphasize that Mr. Balaguer's victory should not necessarily be taken as a repudiation of the goals of the April, 1965, revolution which sought to restore Dr. Bosch to the presidency. He had been ejected in a coup d'état by the Dominican military in September, 1963.

There is wide support here for the sort of reform which Dr. Bosch has long sought—and this desire for basic changes in the nation's social structure will continue to be felt in the months ahead.

Potential for trouble

Indeed, if Mr. Balaguer fails to take these desires into account, he could well face serious attempts to overthrow his government.

Such a prospect exists because the extreme left will be just as unhappy with Mr. Balaguer as the extreme right would have been if Dr. Bosch had won.

This extreme left has the potential to cause trouble—and while it does not have widespread popular appeal, its strength has grown since the start of the April, 1965, revolution.

Interestingly, some observers here think the extreme left will profit more from a Balaguer victory than it would from a Bosch triumph.

Dr. Bosch, in the eyes of many extreme leftists here, has frequently undercut their position because he speaks the same reform language and often steals their thunder.

With Mr. Balaguer in office, the left will be freer to carry out its calls for reform than it would be under Dr. Bosch. Such calls often lead to demonstrations and public protests which in turn sometimes, in the charged Dominican atmosphere, lead to violence.

A Balaguer administration will not face an easy future. Stanch opposition from Dr. Bosch and his party, which until now has been the leading political force in the nation in recent years, can be expected.

Observers here are watching closely for signs of what Dr. Bosch will do now. Even in defeat he will remain a force with which to reckon in Dominican politics.

And the elements which began the April, 1965, revolution in his name are equally, if not more so, a force to be considered.

The Dominican civil war is not terminated. The present lull in the struggle is in the view of many here merely a hiatus which could end at any time with a resumption of fighting.

2nd Cl Post Pd at Boston, Mass., and add'l offices

© 1966 THE CHRISTIAN SCIENCE PUBLISHING SOCIETY
All Rights Reserved

THE CHRISTIAN SCIENCE MONITOR

BOSTON, SATURDAY, AUGUST 20, 1966 — *An International Daily Newspaper* — VOL. 58, NO. 225 TWO SECTIONS — EASTERN EDITION ★ 10¢

FOCUS
on business

What's ahead . . .

Space contractors are about to be asked some pointed questions about how they manage big government contracts.

Both Congress and the National Aeronautics and Space Administration want answers. There's a feeling in Washington that some space failures aren't really necessary.

Rep. Joseph E. Karth (D) of Minnesota is heading up a congressional probe. It's only an informal look at present. But if his group turns up evidence of mismanagement the entire space program may be opened up for formal hearings.

NASA hopes to head that off with a probe of its own. With its budget already in peril of being trimmed, the agency doesn't want any unnecessary publicity.

The current Karth investigations are aimed at Gruman Aircraft Corporation, General Electric, TRW Systems, and Ball Brothers. All manage major satellite contracts.

NASA's Goddard Space Center may also come in for a hard look—by NASA itself. But the Karth group may not be far behind.

A new helmsman has grabbed the American Stock Exchange tiller. And he probably will steer with a reformer's zeal, but without rocking the boat too much.

When Amex named Ralph S. Saul as its new president, nobody was too surprised. As director of the Securities and Exchange Commission's trading and markets division, he had policed all the nation's exchanges. Some time back he headed a committee that issued a basically critical report on the operation he now will direct.

Mr. Saul has a reputation as a trading reformist. He was the force behind many of the guidelines SEC laid down for all exchanges. He was a strong government regulator, but he also was noted for reaching compromises with the industry.

SEC officials expect him now to follow closely the reform pattern mapped out for Amex by his predecessor, Edwin D. Etherington, who has quit to be president of Wesleyan University.

Trends . . .

More top executives are paying more attention now to their credit managers.

With bank loans becoming costlier and harder to get, cash-hungry firms are pressing their suppliers for more credit on easier terms.

All size companies are getting top heavy with trade receivables—the money another company owes them for goods and services. For small manufacturers receivables make up about 28 percent of their assets—more than any other single thing.

The average manufacturer now has the equivalent of 39 days of sales tied up in receivables. That's 3.8 percent more than last year.

So executives are turning to their credit managers who in turn are watching their customer payment records—with an eye to weeding out marginal risks before they turn into uncollectible accounts.

Inland waterways in the Midwest are cargo-clogged and booming.

In tonnage moved and in new plants being built along their banks, they lead the nation.

Seventy-five percent of river-steaming barge loads are still bulk cargo—petroleum, wood, stone, coal, grains, sugar, and dry chemicals. But barges also are taking on other cargoes, too—cattle, liquid oxygen, and liquid sulphur.

Traffic on the upper Mississippi for one, is up 25 percent this year.

One indicator of this waterway boom is the number of new industries springing up along the river banks. Roughly half of all such new building in the second quarter this year was along Midwest waterways.

Twenty-six new plants started rising on the Mississippi this year, 13 on the banks of the Ohio, 12 at the edge of Lake Michigan, and 11 along the Gulf Intracoastal Waterway.

International business gets more international every day.

Konam of the Netherlands, which is half owned already by Celanese of America, is hooking up now with Courrieres-Kuhlmann of France.

Deutsche Entwicklunges of West Germany now owns 30 percent of Brazil's Traubomatic, not to mention 20 percent of Afghanistan's Wollindustrie.

Fiat of Italy is linking up automotively with Villares of Brazil, Westinghouse of the United States, and Afne-Astilleros of Argentina. Besides, it is selling a car plant to the Soviet Union.

Brown, the American paper group, is opening an Italian branch of its Brussels sales company. Goodyear Rubber is building a new tire plant in West Germany. French food suppliers are buying interests in Spanish supermarkets.

Anybody for a subsidiary in Timbuktu?

Where to look

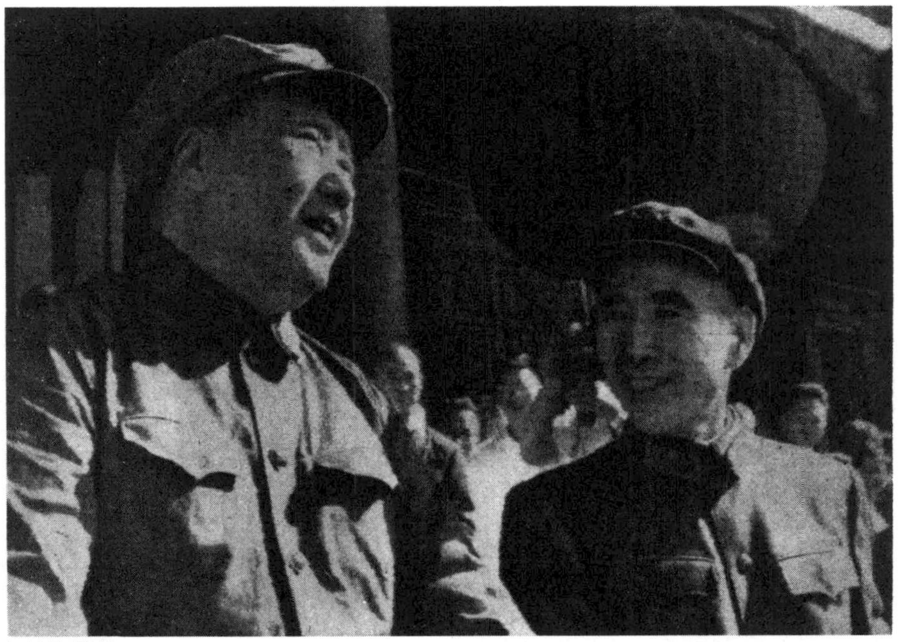

Associated Press Wirephoto

Red China's heir?

Chinese Communist Defense Minister Lin Piao, right, is shown standing side by side with party leader Mao Tse-tung at a rally in Peking, in this Chinese radiophoto monitored in Tokyo. Marshal Lin has emerged as No. 2 man in the party hierarchy and may already be succeeding Chairman Mao as Communist China's leader.

Hall organizes Romney backers

By Godfrey Sperling Jr.
Staff correspondent of The Christian Science Monitor

Washington

The group that will form the nucleus of any Romney-for-president effort now is taking shape.

The veteran political professional, and nationally known, figure involved in this early phase is Leonard W. Hall, chairman of the Republican National Committee under former President Eisenhower, and a man who is strongly identified with the moderate wing of the party.

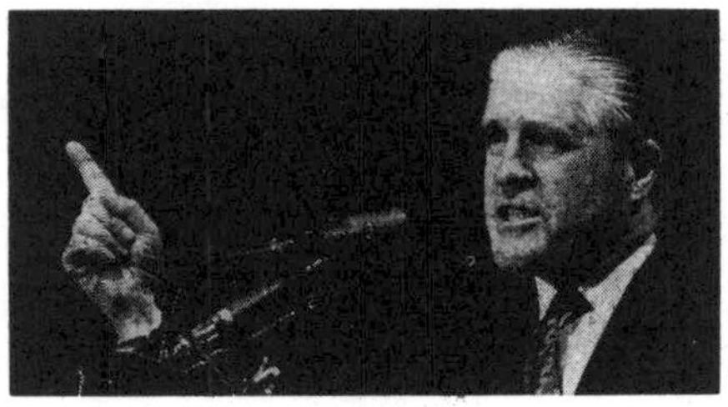

Michigan Governor Romney
The long road to '68

Mr. Hall already has been instrumental in setting up some speeches for the Michigan Governor. It was Mr. Hall who put together the Nassau County (New York State) dinner where New York Gov. Nelson Rockefeller came out so strongly for Governor Romney as a possible presidential candidate.

Frequent phone calls

Others in the small group come under the heading of old friends and long-time supporters. One is J. Willard Marriott, president, Hot Shoppes, Inc. (restaurant chain) and owner of Marriott Motor Motels, whose friendship with Governor Romney dates back to the '30's. He is a financial backer. Mrs. Marriott is also heavily committed to Governor Romney and active in his behalf. She is a vice-chairman of the Republican National Committee, moving into that post after Ray C. Bliss became national chairman last spring. The Marriotts, like Governor Romney, are Mormons.

Finally, there is John Clifford Folger, ambassador to Belgium under President Eisenhower and now a member of the investment firm here of Folger, Nolan, Fleming & Co., Inc.

Governor Romney is aware of the group's existence and of its hopes for him. These are people who call him, fairly frequently, on his private phone in the Michigan Capitol.

The Governor, himself, is right in the midst of a state campaign — seeking his third term. At no point is he openly expressing any aspirations that go beyond the governorship.

But he does know that his name is receiving prominent mention these days as a possible presidential nominee. And he cannot be unmindful that his friends are in the tentative, but beginning stages of preparing the groundwork for a national campaign in his behalf.

Nixon counterpart

It is understood that Mr. Hall, who has strong political contacts throughout the United States, is "getting the lay of the land." Both on the phone and in his travels about the country Mr. Hall is seeking to make an assessment of Governor Romney's prospects — as well as being quite persuasive in Mr. Romney's behalf.

The Romney group has a Richard M. Nixon counterpart, led by men who worked closely with Mr. Nixon when he was Vice-President. Leaders in this group include former Secretary of the Interior Fred A. Seaton and former Budget Director Maurice H. Stans. The Nixon people have a much broader base, however, with some 50 prominent Republicans around the nation meeting from time to time in behalf of the former Vice-President.

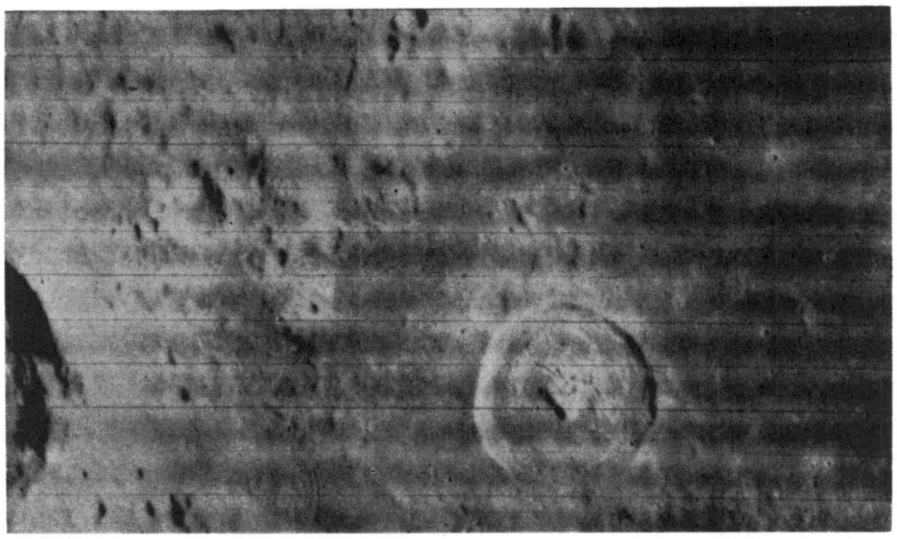

Associated Press Wirephoto

A new look at the moon's surface

Lunar Orbiter's first photograph of the moon's surface shows a 59-by-92-mile area. Crater in lower center is about 18 miles in diameter. Despite the clarity of this photograph, there were early indications that Orbiter's picture-taking system was not functioning properly. **[Story: Page 13.]**

Lin's rise lifts Army in Peking

By John Hughes
Staff correspondent of The Christian Science Monitor

Hong Kong

China's 700 million people have awakened to discover that they apparently have a new Communist emperor.

Climaxing months of foreign speculation, Defense Minister Lin Piao has emerged either as Mao Tse-tung's designated successor, or the man who already has quietly succeeded him as China's new ruler.

For China's own people, however, all this has been accomplished without their being canvassed, without their concurrence, and all the product of internal palace maneuver among an elite group of party influentials.

Equality of position

Marshal Lin, the man thus arbitrarily presented to them as their new ruler, is a battle-seasoned soldier of many wars. He is probably China's greatest expert on guerrilla warfare. For a while he commanded the Communist armies in the Korean war.

For China, his elevation means strict adherence to the hard and unyielding ideological line of Mr. Mao. His mission is to preserve and guard China's Communist revolution as it passes to a younger generation of whose political fervor the old guard is doubtful.

Few experts doubt that Thursday's mass rally in Peking was designed to stress the ascendancy of the Army and the fact that Marshal Lin now is at least equal to Chairman Mao, if he is not quietly in charge.

Chairman Mao himself wore the olive-green uniform of the People's Liberation Army with red collar insignia. Marshal Lin was constantly at his side. The two were always a little apart from others in the leadership lineup.

Comrades in arms

Meanwhile, Premier Chou En-lai, in his speech, pointedly called on the people to "respond to the call of comrade Lin Piao." And Liu Shao-chi, the head of state who has long been tipped as an interim successor to Mr. Mao until the real power struggle for the succession took place, was relegated to seventh place in the official New China News Agency's list of leaders present.

The import of all this in a land where such details are highly significant seems clear. Indeed the question now occupying many observers is whether Marshal Lin is merely the successor designate or whether he in fact has taken power, and Chairman Mao is merely a figurehead.

Whatever the real situation, Marshal Lin can be counted on to follow Mr. Mao's policies. Fifty-eight years old, he is one of Mr. Mao's oldest comrades in arms.

He was an early student at the famed Wampoa Military Academy under Chiang Kai-shek. There he also got political instruction from a man called Chou En-lai. A colonel in the Kuomintang Army at 20, he switched to the Communists and fought brilliantly throughout the legendary Long March.

Army in ascendancy

With Marshal Lin either close to or in the seat of power, China can expect endorsement of the current purge of antiparty elements called the "cultural revolution." However, there are some signs the party leadership is applying the brakes to the purge, and that it might end this fall. Marshal Lin, however, approves of the new "great leap forward" which now is getting under way.

For the pragmatists in the party, and the intellectuals who favor modifications of Mr. Mao's policies, Marshal Lin's elevation is a grim affair. The Army now is riding high. Whether it will continue to be kept subservient to the party, as under Chairman Mao, now depends on Marshal Lin.

However, he has consistently backed Chairman Mao on this point.

Just what kind of power struggle may have gone on among party leaders must for the moment remain a mystery to foreign observers. It seems clear that Chairman Mao's lengthy absence for part of last year and this was not routine. He may well have been ill.

News-agency reports of Thursday's rally said that although he looked fit a nurse helped him from time to time.

Whatever the cause of Chairman Mao's absence, it seems probable that Marshal Lin was either ordered by Mr. Mao into the vacuum, or himself seized the initiative.

Johnson on the go

Beset by inflationary pressures at home and a hard-to-win war in Vietnam, President Johnson is out strengthening his image among the electorate.

He has a big stake in the outcome of November's congressional elections: Votes from the 48 freshman Democratic congressmen have been invaluable to his legislative programs these past two years. He wants to see as many as possible reelected.

Story: Page 6

© 1966 THE CHRISTIAN SCIENCE PUBLISHING SOCIETY All Rights Reserved

THE CHRISTIAN SCIENCE MONITOR

BOSTON, MONDAY, JUNE 12, 1967 — An International Daily Newspaper — VOL. 59, NO. 167 TWO SECTIONS — EASTERN EDITION ★ 10¢

FOCUS on business

What's ahead . . .

Starting July 1 public attention will be focused on industrial smokestacks that billow pollutants into the air.

On this date the United States Environmental Science Services Administration (ESSA) will begin issuing air-pollution forecasts.

Advisories will be fed to major metropolitan and industrial areas from Weather Bureau computers in suburban Washington.

It's the first step in a broad ESSA program to forecast and pinpoint air-pollution problems. The agency now is working on an on-the-spot forecasting method, using balloons and instruments installed on towers.

The program is to begin in Philadelphia and eventually expand to 25 metropolitan areas.

Government officials admit this new service probably puts the squeeze on industry to install abatement equipment as soon as possible.

But there's a possibility the government may increase subsidies to industry to speed such installations.

A British firm has introduced a bricklaying machine whose zany speed would put Bugs Bunny to shame.

It can lay 20 bricks a minute.

Even allowing for the time it takes to set up the machine so that it will leave space for doors and windows, the machine increases output over conventional methods by at least five times.

Europe's three "communities" are due to join hands July 1.

It should facilitate a common "energy policy" for the six-nation Common Market. Jean Rey, president-elect of the merged community, says he expects some solution in "a short time."

At present, the European Coal and Steel Community controls coal policy; Euratom governs atomic power; and the European Economic Community looks after oil.

This split in responsibility has made it difficult for the community to devise a common policy coordinating every area of energy.

Any agreement on policy would be of vital concern to industry, the international oil companies, and even the European householder, figuring out the most economical way to heat his home.

The Common Market is about to discriminate in favor of oil companies based inside the European Economic Community, and against those outside — mainly American and British firms.

European companies will get favored treatment, including tax concessions, exploration loans, and aid for research.

These companies include the Compagnie Française des Petroles, Italy's ENI, and Royal Dutch Shell.

Trends . . .

Computers, it is believed, can do wonders for Britain's wool industry.

A new research team has been formed jointly by International Computers and Tabulators and Britain's Wool and Allied Textile Employers Council.

Its objective is the almost total computerization of British wool buying, stock control and manufacturing.

At the outset the team is estimating that computers can cut costs by 5 percent on ordering and storing wool. And by 10 percent over-all, if production processes are included.

Here are other advantages claimed for computerization:

Exporters of cloth will be able to give firmer delivery dates. Growers will be able to gauge demand more closely. Violent price fluctuations will be avoided. And greater stability will be given to the trade as a whole.

There's a mountain of wool involved. Last year the British industry bought 139 million pounds of wool from Australia, 136 million pounds from New Zealand, 62 million from Argentina, 39 million from Uruguay, and 40 million from South Africa.

How and why . . .

Few items come closer to the pocketbook than the price of gasoline.

It could be directly affected by a long-range plan of the Federal Trade Commission now reaching culmination.

Major American oil companies, whose pricing and marketing practices are held suspect by the FTC, may soon face government suits. The action will end several years of quiet on the FTC oil front.

For five years the commission has filed no suits against oil companies on charges of illegal marketing practices. And since 1964 it has suspended the processing of pricing complaints brought against oil companies.

During this period the commission has been making an intensive study of oil marketing practices across the country — checking local gasoline prices. Now the study is nearly done and due to be released in the next few weeks.

Where to look

Arts	4	Sports	7
Business	12	The Home Forum	8
Family Features	15	Women Today	10

Middle East at crossroad

By Joseph C. Harsch
Special correspondent of The Christian Science Monitor

Washington

"It" did not happen the way any government in the world (except possibly the one in Israel itself) expected. The large elements of surprise complicate calculations for the future.

Western governments, including Washington, had long calculated that Israel still had a military edge over the neighboring Arab states. But the edge was supposed to have declined since 1956.

The expectation was for Israeli caution. If war came it was expected to be a much longer one than in 1956.

Pattern of diplomacy

One can only guess at Moscow's calculations. The extent to which Moscow gave verbal support to the Arab cause after the fighting started would seem to indicate that the Kremlin rated the Egyptian Army higher than did the Western governments.

Cairo itself must have assumed that it could at least get a draw. Otherwise it hardly would have pushed the issue over the brink of war.

The result is that this is a moment of readjustment, by every foreign office, except the one in Israel. There, the new problem is how to cope with the consequences of one of the most decisive victories in military history.

Washington is suddenly full of high hopes. At the White House it is happily assumed that the magnitude of the disaster to Soviet policy provides an opportunity to enlist Moscow's cooperation in a big drive to get a permanent solution to the problems of the Middle East.

The State Department is not so optimistic. This is why the new special committee to handle the post-crisis problems of the Middle East has been set up at the White House; not at the State Department.

In planning the cleanup problem and charting the effort to reach a long-term solu-

★ Please turn to Page 6

Inside . . .

Was White House unaware? Page 3

Soviet aid to Nasser called key: Page 3

Moscow breaks Israel ties: Page 2

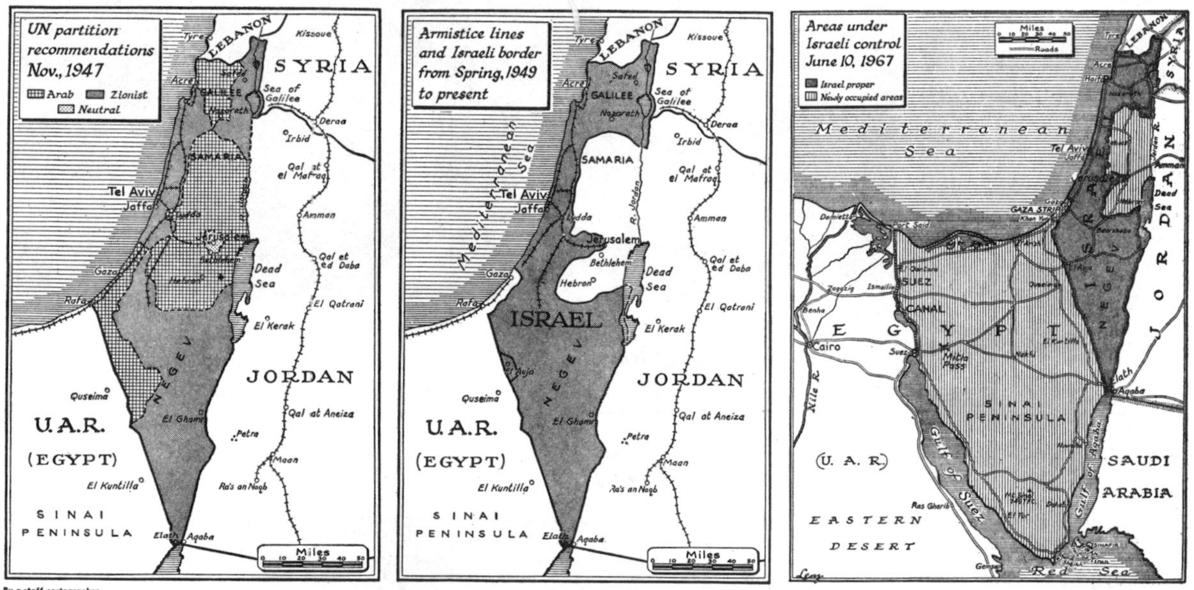

By a staff cartographer

From partition to hot war

Not the least of problems before the United Nations involving Israel and the Arab nations will be the settling of boundaries. Shown here are the fluctuations of borders from the days of UN partition recommendations in November, 1947, left, to the vast expansion of Israeli control over territory today, accomplished since June 5. Center map shows Israel's borders from the armistice of early 1949 to the present. Map on right indicates extent of territory currently under Israeli military control, including the Jordanian bulge up to the River Jordan, and the entire Sinai Peninsula up to the east bank of the Suez Canal as claimed by the Israelis.

UN digging into seeds of conflict

By Earl W. Foell
Staff correspondent of The Christian Science Monitor

United Nations, N.Y.

As soon as firing halted on the Sinai front, Mideast specialists here said privately that they expected the Israeli armed forces to turn its attention to Syria, which Israel blames as the original goad to the war.

Through long hours Friday and Saturday, the UN Security Council wrestled with the Syrian-Israeli problem.

Three factors develop

The Council was hard put to determine: whether Israel had invaded Syria; if so how far; the relatively obscure point of who fired first; and above all how to enforce its cease-fire order that both sides had accepted.

It gradually became clear that the cease-fire could eventually be made to stick. Israeli Defense Minister Moshe Dayan met Saturday with the UN truce supervisor, Gen. Odd Bull, and worked out details for halting the fighting.

But three other factors also became clear during the course of the marathon Security Council sessions:

1. That the UN truce observer teams — the Security Council's eyes and ears on the spot — would need to be strengthened if the Council was to receive fast, impartial information in coming days.

2. That the battles fought on the Syrian front while the UN tried to enforce its cease-fire there would probably further complicate an already tremendously difficult peace settlement problem.

3. That, as Britain's Lord Caradon said with eloquent feeling, a step-up of existing UN aid to Arab refugees fleeing into Jordan would be needed.

Exodus reported

Lord Caradon, who once worked in the area of those Jordanian villages, advised the Arab inhabitants that they would be wiser to stay in Israeli occupied territory, rather than crowding overcrowded refugee camps. But the exodus from Jordan's west bank appeared to have taken place already.

As the long Council meeting proceeded, conflicting reports flowed in from the two opponents and from news services. The most authoritative evidence appeared to be Gen-

★ Please turn to Page 2

Red China chaos?

While world attention has been focused on the Mideast, Communist China's behind-scenes upheaval has reached a new low in chaos and disorder.

The Peking government consequently has embarked on a new campaign to put down lawlessness and violence. It has forbidden illegal search or illegal entry into party and state premises, as well as private dwellings.

Although some reports reaching Hong Kong observers may prove to be exaggerated, the latest trouble inside China is regarded as very close to a term experts so far have avoided —namely, civil war.

Further details: Page 2

House debate

GOP fights to remold anticrime program

By Lyn Shepard
Staff correspondent of The Christian Science Monitor

Washington

Republicans are waging a fierce struggle behind the great walnut doors of the House Judiciary Committee to reshape the President's anticrime program.

After two closed sessions of debate on the $1.35 billion safe-streets and crime-control bill, one major issue remains unsettled.

It is by now a familiar question to the 90th Congress: What ties should exist between Washington and the states in carrying out a grant-in-aid program to aid the cities?

This question strikes at the heart of the argument posed by Democrats as a defense of "creative federalism." It asks what role state governors should play in this concept, if any.

Fight renewed

The White House bill would authorize grants to help finance research, fight certain crime problems, and extend police facilities.

"It will improve the quality of life everywhere in our nation," Rep. Peter Rodino (D) of New Jersey told House members, "in every hamlet, in every suburb, on every Main Street."

Mr. Rodino, a ranking member of the subcommittee which studied the bill, called it an "historic strategy . . . for an expanding partnership between federal, state, and local governments."

Yet neither the New Jersey lawmaker nor his Democratic colleagues explained the intended state role. Republicans find their omission distressing.

Some GOP members sought to spell out an advisory function for the governors. They lost the fight at the subcommittee level, but are renewing it in the 35-member Judiciary Committee.

"The Democrats have resisted all our efforts," admitted Rep. Clark MacGregor (R) of Minnesota. "We've only tried to introduce the concept of creative federalism so often espoused by Lyndon Johnson."

The tall, husky Minneapolis lawyer said the GOP amendments would grant the governors a means to express their views on the priorities which should be accorded program applications from cities in their states.

"I was frankly surprised," Mr. MacGregor said, "to see committee Democrats beat down every attempt to give the governor this role."

But another Judiciary Committee member, Rep. Charles McC. Mathias Jr. (R) of Maryland, found the Democratic moves predictable.

Opposition explained

"The word is obviously out," Mr. Mathias mused. "The administration wants to keep amendments to the bill down to an absolute minimum."

Like other GOP members, Mr. Mathias expects a fierce fight to erupt on the House floor if the effort to amend fails in committee.

Democrats explain their opposition to the state House advisory role this way: the governor may submit a state plan to improve law enforcement under the bill which would actually compete with plans presented by cities within his state. Thus his advice would be biased in favor of his own plan.

"Take the State of Maryland," Mr. Mathias says. "Governor Agnew might submit a plan. Baltimore might. So might the City of Rockville.

Arguments noted

"Rockville and Baltimore would be considered competitors to the Maryland state plan. Therefore, the Democrats say, it isn't fair to let the governor play a determining role.

"To me this is specious reasoning," Mr. Mathias said. "I expect that an amendment short of a governor's veto will make him an integral part of the 'safe streets' concept."

Mr. Mathias holds that all city plans should flow through the governors' offices. The state executives should be given 30 days in which to comment on them—in fact, to give their judgment on the priorities of pending applications. Then the attorney general would review all plans at the federal level.

The Maryland lawmaker concedes that the Democrats raise some cogent arguments:

"They say, 'well, the governor is interested in the highway patrol. He'd give first priority to that ahead of arson and robbery in the cities.'

"But I still think the governor has a proper role to play—particularly under modern conditions where a bank robbery, let us say, is very seldom a one-town operation any more.

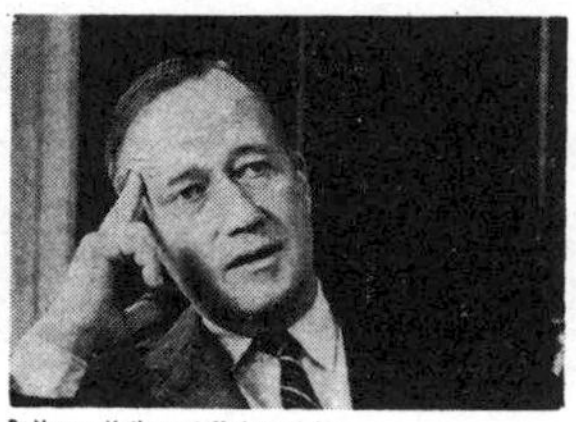

By Norman Matheny, staff photographer

Rep. Charles McC. Mathias

. . . says all city plans should flow through governors' offices.

Review sought

"You immediately begin to set up areawide if not statewide roadblocks. You begin to make it a broad search. When you're confronted with crime of this sort, it's more than a one-community effort."

A second issue will likely surface during the floor debate, which Chairman Emanuel Celler (D) of New York hopes to arrange this month. Republicans are "deeply concerned" over Attorney General Ramsey Clark's unwillingness to place checks on his own decisionmaking authority.

The bill, as drafted, empowers the attorney general to cut off funds to a law-enforcement agency without any recourse or appeal.

2nd Cl Post Pd at Boston, Mass., and add'l offices

© 1967 THE CHRISTIAN SCIENCE PUBLISHING SOCIETY All Rights Reserved

THE CHRISTIAN SCIENCE MONITOR

BOSTON, THURSDAY, JUNE 29, 1967 — *An International Daily Newspaper* — VOL. 59, NO. 182 TWO SECTIONS — EASTERN EDITION ★ 10c

FOCUS on Europe

What's ahead . . .

Another summit looms. This one a de Gaulle-Kiesinger conference.

The French President is expected to go to Bonn July 12.

Such meetings between French and German leaders are called for—at intervals of about six months—by the friendship pact that the late Chancellor Konrad Adenauer worked out with President de Gaulle. Several past meetings, however, provided only moments of tension.

But the Kiesinger government is keen for French-German friendship. It regards this as important to the better East-West relations in Europe which could prepare the way for German reunification.

Chancellor Kiesinger does not agree with the General that American troops should leave Europe. Nor does he support the Gaullist stand against British membership in the Common Market. But he has said that he sees in the French President's grand design for a "Europe from the Atlantic to the Urals" a blueprint which will promote German reunification.

⊕

This fall there'll be a big, new bank in Europe — the International Commercial Bank, with headquarters in London.

And it is really international. The Westminster Bank (Britain), the Hong Kong and Shanghai Banking Corporation, the First National Bank of Chicago, the Irving Trust Company of New York, and the Commerzbank of Düsseldorf, Germany—all have an interest in it.

The new bank will have £10 million ($28 million) capital in various currencies. In addition it is backed by long-term loans in American dollars and British sterling in the equivalent of nearly £6 million.

Trends . . .

The Soviets have their own bank in London. It's flourishing.

Moscow Narodny Bank, Ltd.—a subsidiary of the Moscow State Bank—is doing a brisk business selling dollar certificates.

They are issued against one-to-three-year dollar deposits and pay 6 percent interest as compared with the usual 4¾ to 5¼ percent on this type of deposit.

The certificates are bought widely by Middle East and Latin-American capitalists for a good reason: They represent a virtually tax-free temporary hard-currency investment.

Russia's State Bank now operates a bank in Zurich, Switzerland, also. And the Voskhod Handelsbank in Frankfurt, Germany, is Moscow's latest venture into the European international capital market.

One attraction of both banks is that they pay out deposits immediately, in contrast to the 24-hour (or longer) waiting period practiced by major Western European banks.

⊕

West Europeans in substantial numbers are emigrating beyond their own borders to settle permanently in other West European countries.

West Germans are leading this movement.

Legal barriers to resettlement no longer exist. But trying language difficulties and wartime memories sometimes hamper peaceful adjustment to new surroundings.

But on the whole, this migration of farmers, businessmen, and artisans is welcomed as a positive factor leading to better understanding, exchange of techniques, and introduction of new methods.

⊕

When Europe finally is united, will its politicians switch parliaments?

They may want to. A survey just made shows up wide variations in pay and privileges accorded members of European parliaments.

One really wouldn't be surprised to hear that a number of British MPs are learning Italian. Italy pays its lawmakers £5,500 ($15,400) plus liberal tax exemption, free rail, sea, and air travel. It even throws in cheap theater tickets.

British legislators get only £3,250, and most of that is subject to tax. What's more, they pay their own secretaries—something few European MPs have to do.

French deputies receive £4,800; West Germany's £3,400.

⊕

Moves are under way to permit architects to practice anywhere within the Common Market.

The European Economic Community has drafted three directives for consideration by the Council of Ministers:

The first makes compulsory membership by an architect in a recognized professional organization. The second covers mutual recognition by the six Common Market countries of each others' architectural diplomas and degrees. The third concerns laws and regulations affecting architects.

When the council okays these directives, architects will be able to get on with the task of building a better Europe—quite literally.

Where to look

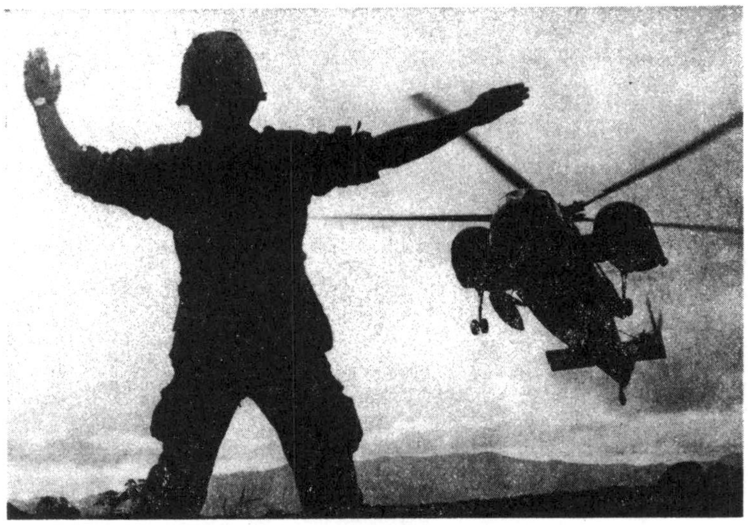

Official USMC photo

New role for marines

A United States marine guides a helicopter to a mountaintop landing zone for a food-and-water resupply. The assignment of holding hills and waiting for the enemy to move is a new one for marines more used to serving as shock forces.

In plains below lurk Viet Cong . . .

By John Hughes
Staff correspondent of The Christian Science Monitor

Cam Lo, Vietnam

It is a nameless hill, scarred and exposed, shorn of its greenery by the machinery of war.

It commands a sector of South Vietnam's sweltering coastal plain before the country tilts upward to wild and untamed mountains.

This hill is home to a battalion of United States marines. On it they live, and in more relaxed moments laugh. From it they fight. And for it, they may pay dearly.

For this hill north of Cam Lo is very close to the demilitarized zone (DMZ) which divides South Vietnam from North. In and across that zone are three, possibly four, hardened North Vietnamese divisions of sinister repute.

Since the beginning of this year, a North Vietnamese build-up across the DMZ has posed a major threat to South Vietnam and the whole allied war effort here. Savage fighting by the marines south of the zone, hasty reinforcement by American troops brought up from the southern part of the country, and a surprise sweep through the southern part of the DMZ by allied forces appear for the moment to have blunted the Communist initiative.

What will Hanoi do?

Now there is a relative lull. June is a harvesting month. But nobody knows what July will bring. Will the North Vietnamese remount their assault across the DMZ, attempting to smash the outnumbered and thinly spread marines in I Corps? Or will they hit hard, as some observers predict, in the central highlands where an American paratrooper company was cut to shreds last week? Or will they feint in one place and strike at the other?

For the allied generals these are immensely troublesome questions. The generals are short of the troops they believe they need. Whether the North Vietnamese plan their major thrust in the DMZ area or not, they have already made substantial gains there.

They have inflicted heavy casualties on the marines. They have drawn other American troops away from their assigned areas elsewhere in South Vietnam, thus halting the big spoiling operations which Gen. William C. Westmoreland had begun to launch with telling effect on long-time Viet Cong base areas.

Now the marines are assigned to detect

★ Please turn to Page 6

Social accounting

A "social accounting" bill to set up procedures not unlike those stimulating economic legislation is being studied in Congress.

A band of Senate liberals, headed by Sen. Walter F. Mondale (D) of Minnesota, proposed the "Full Opportunity and Social Accounting Act of 1967."

It would apply to social-welfare problems the same sort of machinery now operating in the economic realm.

Story: Page 12

Arab split?

Algeria and Syria nudge at Cairo

By Earl W. Foell
Staff correspondent of The Christian Science Monitor

United Nations, N.Y.

A quiet struggle over the future course and unity of the Arab world is going on behind the scenes here.

It involves the radicals, such as Algeria and Syria, in subtle rivalry with Cairo, which appears to have become at least temporarily more cautious because of its shattering experience in the war. Algeria appears, in fact, to be subtly challenging Cairo for leadership of the Arab lands.

The struggle is now in what might be called its exploratory stage. Outside the Arab sphere all four of the big powers are trying to pull strings to influence the outcome.

The role of Cairo, long the center of the pan-Arab effort, is unusually complex.

Fawzi and Rusk talk

At his own request, Egyptian Deputy Prime Minister Mahmoud Fawzi has twice seen American Secretary of State Dean Rusk during the past week. They talked for about an hour June 22 — the day before the Glassboro summit began. They met again in Mr. Rusk's suite at the Waldorf Towers June 27 for a further hour of secret talk.

Mr. Fawzi also saw British Foreign Minister George Brown last week for what was described as an amiable secret session.

These meetings were unusual inasmuch as Cairo had broken relations with both Washington and London and accused both of aiding Israel in defeating the Egyptian forces.

Specialists here note with keen interest that since these talks and the Glassboro summit, the United Arab Republic Government has instructed its press and radio to stop attacks on President Johnson and moderate its calls for a new war on Israel.

Nothing has been disclosed by either side about what was said during the talks. But some analysts here consider them to be a continuation, in sharply altered circumstances, of the bargaining that Egyptian Vice-President Zakaria Mohieddin was about to fly to Washington to undertake when the war broke out.

Mr. Mohieddin's bargaining position would have been fairly strong. He was to arrive in Washington June 7. Had the war not begun June 5 he would have come with the trump card of a blockaded Strait of Tiran to negotiate against a growing American economic squeeze on Cairo.

Diplomats can only speculate on the Fawzi-Rusk talks. But the Egyptian cards are now quite different and weaker: a

★ Please turn to Page 6

If Nixon falters, Reagan is in the wings

By John C. Waugh
Staff correspondent of The Christian Science Monitor

Los Angeles

Republicans in California look at Gov. Ronald Reagan, nod their heads, and agree he's a clear case of "condition subsequent."

That's a legal term. It means the Governor becomes a candidate to reckon with for the GOP nomination for President after something else happens first. That something else: the failure of Richard M. Nixon to grasp the prize.

One high Republican officeholder close to the Governor puts it this way:

"Reagan's position in the national picture is totally tied to a condition subsequent. If Nixon can't make it, if he fails in the primaries, then his strength would move to Reagan. A bona fide Reagan candidacy comes subsequent to that, but not before. It would then come no matter what. Reagan wouldn't have to leave the state, make a speech, or do a thing."

Primary trial awaited

This view keys all the informed California speculation now swirling around Mr. Reagan as a possible GOP nominee for President.

California Republicans see four possible GOP candidates now—former Vice-President Nixon, Michigan Gov. George Romney, Illinois Sen. Charles H. Percy, and Governor Reagan.

This is the way they look through the California lens.

Nixon:

Most top GOP political observers see him clearly in the lead at this moment. One says, "Right now, Nixon has the votes to be nominated." Another says, "If the polls show Nixon anywhere near neck and neck with President Johnson in 1968, he can have the nomination."

But it is still a long time until nomination. Mr. Nixon trails President Johnson in all the polls. And at least four key primaries lie ahead. As one Republican here says,

★ Please turn to Page 7

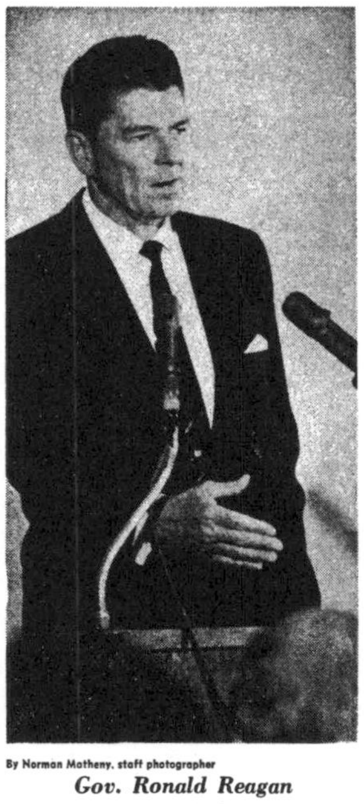

By Norman Matheny, staff photographer

Gov. Ronald Reagan

Not committed yet

Erosion check sought

Fujiyama cracking

By Charlotte Saikowski
Staff correspondent of The Christian Science Monitor

Tokyo

It seems almost heretical to say. But Mt. Fuji—that majestically serene symbol of Japan—is in need of a face-lifting.

That is, if it is to retain the magnificent, simple contours that have inspired the Japanese and travelers the world over to stand in awe of its beauty.

A deep fissure on its western side threatens to upset the mountain's symmetry. Caused by continuous landslides of volcanic ash and rock, the crack extends from near the crater at the top to about 2,800 meters (3,052 yards) down the slope. It is 125 meters (136 yards) deep and about 500 meters (545 yards) wide.

Erosion of Fujiyama has been going on for centuries, of course, and it will be centuries before the mountain loses its present comely shape. But geologists here say that in no more than 100 years the now symmetrical apex will begin to resemble the teeth of a saw. In the initial stages a V-shaped dent will divide the top into two distinct peaks.

Uniqueness crumbling?

"If we don't do anything about it," lamented a Japanese science writer, "it will be like the Matterhorn. No longer a unique symbol of Japan!"

Concern over the erosion is only partially aesthetic, however. Some 300 tons of earth and rock tumble down daily, and these landslides pose a constant threat to communities along the foot of the mountain. Precious farm land is ruined and rivers silt up.

Retaining walls have been built in the foothills to stop further sliding of the earth and the government has a five-year program to build more embankments. But villagers and local officials know from experience that it takes only a severe rain to damage or wash out such walls. They now are agitating for more drastic solutions.

The Construction Ministry says that massive construction work must be done near the peak of Fuji. One plan calls for building embankments on both sides of the sliding area, as well as retaining walls at given intervals on the slopes. But such an undertaking is estimated to cost more than $160 million and the plan already has run into opposition from the economy-minded Finance Ministry.

Meanwhile, a group of geologists, erosion-control experts and the governors of the prefectures surrounding Mt. Fuji have formed themselves into an advisory council and are devising measures to combat the landslides. They met with ministry officials this month and further talks are planned.

For some Japanese naturalists, the current debate over preserving the face of Fuji has aroused misgivings and controversy. Combating erosion to protect farmlands is one thing. But they do not see tampering with nature's plan for aesthetic reasons — though they themselves are renowned for their stylizations of nature.

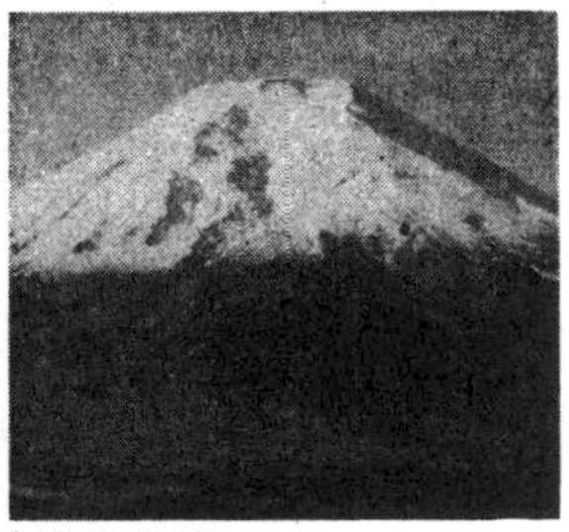

East-West from Black Star

Symmetrical symbol

A new profile for Mt. Fuji?

Photos pinpoint road defects

As the federal government announced new national standards for state highway-safety programs, an interested outsider named Joseph Linko could share some of the credit.

Mr. Linko, a TV repairman from New York's Bronx section, had built up a file of more than 3,000 color slides, illustrating potential highway perils near his home.

These were all related to "highway design, construction, and maintenance"—one of 13 headings used in the federal proclamation of safety standards.

Secretary of Transportation Alan S. Boyd announced the new benchmarks June 27. They cover essentially the same points as the draft standards made public in February by the National Highway Safety Bureau.

Details: Page 3

2nd Cl Post Pd at Boston, Mass., and add'l offices

© 1967 THE CHRISTIAN SCIENCE PUBLISHING SOCIETY
All Rights Reserved

THE CHRISTIAN SCIENCE MONITOR

BOSTON, SATURDAY, APRIL 6, 1968   *An International Daily Newspaper*   VOL. 60, NO. 113 TWO SECTIONS   NEW ENGLAND EDITION ▲ 10c

Awaken, America

The Christian Science Board of Directors has issued the following statement regarding the assassination of the Rev. Dr. Martin Luther King Jr.:

The tragic killing of Dr. Martin Luther King should awaken all Americans to the urgency of meeting hate with practical humanity and brotherhood based on a keener understanding of the one God of all men, who is infinite Love. Dullness of conscience must give way to full acknowledgment of fundamental human rights. Complacency should bow to active prayer. The divisive barriers of prejudice and exclusiveness must melt before a renewed vision of the free and just commonwealth, including all equally and with equal justice and opportunity for all, which this republic has always stood for.

Dr. King preached nonviolence. He clearly saw that no solution lies in the direction of force and extremism. There is a higher way. It is summarized in these words of the Discoverer and Founder of Christian Science, Mary Baker Eddy, who wrote many years ago:

"The history of our country, like all history, illustrates the might of Mind, and shows human power to be proportionate to its embodiment of right thinking. A few immortal sentences, breathing the omnipotence of divine justice, have been potent to break despotic fetters and abolish the whipping-post and slave market; but oppression neither went down in blood, nor did the breath of freedom come from the cannon's mouth. Love is the liberator."

Which path for civil rights?

Nonviolence was Dr. King's plea

By Geoffrey Godsell
Staff writer of The Christian Science Monitor

What remains to be seen is whether nonviolent protest as an effective weapon in the civil-rights movement was shattered by that shot which felled the man who so long had been its champion and its symbol.

The Rev. Dr. Martin Luther King Jr. symbolized in his person the civil-rights movement. And as a symbol he was unchallenged and without peer. He symbolized hope. He symbolized achievement—albeit more limited than many might yearn for. He symbolized courage. He symbolized the burden and the pain that the Negro still endures. He symbolized above all the idealism at the heart of the dream, the very American dream, of which he spoke so fervently before the Lincoln Memorial on that hot August day in 1963.

Goad to national conscience

Within the United States, for all the controversy that he sometimes stirred, he was the most respected of prominent Negroes. Abroad he was of them the best known. The seal on his international fame came with the Nobel Peace Prize in 1964.

What apparently qualified him for the prize was his dedication

★ Please turn to Page B19

'I have a dream that my four little children will one day live in a nation where they will not be judged by the color of their skin but by the content of their character. With this faith we will be able to hew out of the mountain of despair a stone of hope.'

The Rev. Dr. Martin Luther King Jr.
March on Washington
Aug. 28, 1963

By Norman Matheny, staff photographer

Dr. King in Montgomery

His movement started here in the shadow of the state capitol. He is shown here at a pause after the march from Selma to the Alabama capital in March, 1965.

'Once again the heart of America is heavy — the spirit of America weeps —for a tragedy that denies the very meaning of our land.... All men ... must stand their ground to deny violence its victory.'

President Johnson
Text of presidential statement: Page B21

'The cause for which he marched and worked will find new strength. The blight of discrimination, poverty and neglect must be erased from America, an America of full freedom, full and equal opportunity shall be his living memorial.'

Vice-President Humphrey

'Let's not burn America down. We must — we must—maintain and advocate and promote the philosophy of nonviolence.'

Hosea Williams,
one of Dr. King's close advisers

'Our greatest tribute to him will be to bear ourselves as he would want us to—with dignity and prayer.'

New York Mayor John V. Lindsay

FOCUS
on Washington

What's ahead . . .

A key factor in American cities this spring and summer will be the police.

Either they use fair and restrained tactics, if and when riots break out, or they spill over into what is called "police brutality."

In the first case, the big middle ground of public opinion in America will be with them. In the latter case, important sections of the public are expected to swing against them.

This is the sober appraisal of specialists in the race-relations field.

There is a strong wall of resistance by the public to force tactics by militants aimed at hurting society. But there is a similarly strong antagonism to police brutality which, specialists say, could be triggered by a number of unfortunate incidents.

Accurate and unbiased press coverage of any riots will be specially important, they believe. Press reports, they say, could determine which way public opinion moves.

⊕

There now is every reason to expect more "great debates" on television by presidential candidates this year.

No incumbent president would be likely to debate. He wouldn't want to give his opponent that kind of exposure.

But now Mr. Johnson has said he will not run. That leaves Messrs. Kennedy, McCarthy, and Humphrey as the most likely Democratic candidates. And all of them, particularly Senator Kennedy, are understood to be eager for debates.

So is Mr. Nixon. His aides say that despite his unhappy venture in 1960, he feels he would come out well in this kind of forum in 1968. This time the former vice-president could criticize the administration instead of having to defend it.

But before presidential debates could be arranged, congressional legislation would be needed to suspend the rule which provides equal TV time to candidates other than the debaters.

Trends . . .

The United States Supreme Court's latest one-man, one-vote decision underscores a background factor in urban racial unrest.

In a landmark 5-to-3 opinion this week, the high court extended the equal-vote rule to cover city, town, and county governments.

Three years ago two sociologists, Stanley Lieberson and Arnold R. Silverman, published the results of a study they had made of riots in American cities between 1910 and 1961.

They noted that there was a greater likelihood of riots in cities which elect officials at-large rather than from wards.

When representatives are elected at large, the sociologists said, minority groups usually are not adequately represented, if at all. As a result, they said, these groups feel deprived of a local political voice. And with no access to channels for airing their grievances, minorities are likely to resort to rioting.

Where to look

Memphis stands at crossroads

By Robert P. Hey
Staff correspondent of The Christian Science Monitor

Memphis

Precisely what the assassination of the Rev. Dr. Martin Luther King Jr. means to the future of already tense race relations in Memphis or any other American city no one can say with certainty.

But in Memphis in particular it serves to heighten immeasurably the tension and bitterness many Negroes feel. It is a great deal to expect that youthful, bitter Negroes among whom are the violence-prone now will be more inclined toward negotiation, and less toward bitterness and the violence it sometimes breeds.

Injunction obtained

Already the young are bitter toward the city administration, charging it fails to recognize the legitimate economic and human problems of the Memphis Negro. Already they are bitter against most whites, charging they live in a dream world of racial harmony, whereas Negroes believe that in fact there is racial tension in Memphis. The killing is certain to exacerbate that bitterness.

[In Washington, black power advocate Stokely Carmichael urged Negroes to arm themselves with guns and take to the streets in retaliation for the assassination of Dr. King.]

The assassination of the Rev. Dr. King as he stood on the balcony of his hotel room Thursday evening brings tragic irony to the week. Earlier the city administration had obtained an injunction to prevent Dr. King and others from organizing or leading a mass march in support of striking sanitation workers and the grievances of Memphis Negroes in general.

The city's reason: that the march, which Dr. King had billed as nonviolent, was too likely to turn into a window-smashing repetition of the previous week's violence.

And then came the week's shot of violence: Believed fired by a white man, it killed the magnetic leader who had planned yet another in more than a decade of nonviolent marches on behalf of Negroes' civil rights.

Mayor Henry Loeb called the killing a "tragedy," and imposed a nighttime curfew in an attempt to prevent widespread violence. As it was, scattered incidents—mostly vandalism — were reported in the city's Negro neighborhoods Thursday night.

Memphis fire and police director Frank Holloman promised to use "every resource" of city, county, and state law-enforcement officers to track down the killer.

Negro plight cited

Police have found a rifle which they believe to be the assassination weapon. As of this writing they are searching for a young, well-dressed white man as the murder suspect.

The parallel with the assassination of President Kennedy in November, 1963, is inescapable. In both cases the trigger of the murder weapon was pulled by only one man, yet in both cases outsiders familiar with the moods of cities insisted that the mood of Dallas, and now Memphis, was one of hatred and bigotry.

Following the Kennedy assassination, it

★ Please turn to Page 5

Different worlds

By Saville R. Davis
Staff correspondent of The Christian Science Monitor

Washington

Two different worlds within American society, one white and the other black, looked at the killing of the Rev. Dr. Martin Luther King Jr. from differing viewpoints. The divergence was the measure of the race problem in the United States today.

Whites generally, according to the conscience of the individual, mourned a great Negro leader who became a martyr to his cause, that of racial justice and the equality of man. Blacks, especially those conscious of their racial background, saw one more case in the long history of violence committed by white society

★ Please turn to Page 9

Inside today

British machine makes compost out of junk

Save that junk. A British machine is being made that promises to turn it into ready cash. It chews up old junk and garbage and turns them into cheap compost.

Story: Page B15

Brazilian students rebel at state of education

Brazilian President Costa e Silva has a new problem on his hands: student protests against the state of education which erupted throughout the country this week and led to frequent student-police clashes.

Story: Page 4

Kennedy gains among Democrats

By Godfrey Sperling Jr.
Staff correspondent of The Christian Science Monitor

©1968 The Christian Science Publishing Society
All rights reserved

Washington

Sen. Robert F. Kennedy has taken a big step up toward the Democratic presidential nomination.

Any assessment of the New York Senator's campaign must, of course, be viewed against a backdrop of imponderables, affecting 1968 politics.

Foremost, perhaps, is the civil-rights strife, now aggravated by the killing of the Rev. Dr. Martin Luther King Jr. But also there are the Vietnam war, peace maneuvers

A Monitor survey

ing, and the possibility that Vice-President Hubert H. Humphrey may enter the presidential campaign at any time.

But the latest examination of the Kennedy situation, based on reports this week from political correspondents in every state, shows that:

● Significant new party support for Senator Kennedy is found in 25 states and the District of Columbia following the withdrawal announcement of President Johnson.

● Senator Kennedy, as of now, would be the "likely winner" of the bulk of the delegates in 11 of the nonprimary states with 583 delegate votes. (1,321 needed to win the presidential nomination at the Democratic convention.)

● Two weeks ago Monitor reporters found

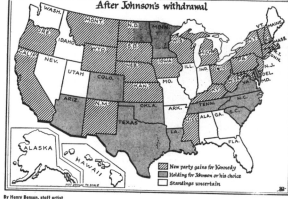

After Johnson's withdrawal

By Henry Benson, staff artist

⊟ New party gains for Kennedy
▦ Holding for Johnson or his choice
☐ Standings uncertain

that the Senator, with a long, uphill climb ahead, was the "possible winner," as of that moment, of the bulk of the delegations in only three states with 237 delegates.

● In addition, of course, the Senator is vying for delegates in a number of the primaries, including Indiana, Nebraska, Oregon, and California, where he may pick up several delegations.

● Another way of showing the move upward in the prospects of Senator Kennedy is that Monitor reporters, as of now, find only 13 states, with 575 delegate votes, where party leaders are still holding for President Johnson and for whoever his choice might be (presumably Vice-President Humphrey).

Among other findings in the Monitor's March 23 survey was that there were 28

★ Please turn to Page B19

2nd Cl Post Pd at Boston, Mass., and add'l offices

April 6, 1968

COPYRIGHT © 1968 THE CHRISTIAN SCIENCE PUBLISHING SOCIETY
All rights reserved

THE CHRISTIAN SCIENCE MONITOR

BOSTON, THURSDAY, JUNE 6, 1968 — *An International Daily Newspaper* — VOL. 60, NO. 163 TWO SECTIONS — EASTERN EDITION ★ 10c

Substantial action called for — now

The immediate reaction of shock felt by people throughout the nation that a presidential candidate could become another victim of cruel violence must now be channeled to immediate and substantial action. Those who see the self-defeating character of hate and violence now have the responsibility for holding them in check.

Men of all faiths unite in prayer for human hearts to yield to an inner awareness of God's government—to the mercy, patience, and order which flow from the divine source and guide the destiny of all mankind.

The Christian Science Board of Directors

FOCUS on Middle East

What's ahead . . .

Serious study is being given to how Arab states can rebuild their societies and economies despite Mideast unrest.

The Arab League has just allotted more than $100 million for a new Arab development fund. It will be aimed at constructive long-range projects and function much as the successful Kuwait Development Fund has operated.

At the American University of Beirut, some leading Arab and Western economists and sociologists have been quietly planning and discussing what the fund will do.

There is need, in the words of the university's Prof. Youssef Sayeghs, for "total development of a new and modern Arab society."

⊕

On the first anniversary of the June 5 Arab-Israeli war, peace feelers wiggle between King Hussein of Jordan and Israel.

Prime Minister Levi Eshkol himself heads the Israeli negotiating team. It includes several of Israel's lesser known but most expert specialists in Arab affairs.

The Arab team is headed by Palestinian Anwar al-Khatib, former Jordanian Ambassador to London.

Arab guerrilla leaders take a dim view of the secret talks.

They fear that a peace settlement restoring to King Hussein both the West Bank and Arab rights in Jerusalem would lead to joint military action by Jordan and Israel to crush the guerrillas.

This is why they are seeking to build operational bases in Iraq and elsewhere—out of reach of both Israeli and Jordanian land armies.

Trends . . .

Classic military coups are old hat now, say opponents of Syria's narrowly based military regime.

What is needed, they contend, is something like the Sudanese revolution of October, 1964, when students and workers gradually won mass support and toppled an unpopular military junta.

Senior member of the opposition front is old-style socialist politician Akram Hourani. With him is a group of pro-Nasser Syrian intellectuals and members of the clandestine Beirut-based Arab Nationalist Movement.

The front says its main goal after coming to power would be release of thousands of political prisoners.

How and why . . .

In Washington, pro-Zionist Congressmen groaned. In Amman, United States Embassy officials rejoiced.

The airlifting of American arms to Jordan last week under agreements signed back in March took some of the early summer heat off both King Hussein and the Americans in Jordan.

Many Jordanians—two-thirds of whom are Palestinian refugees — are convinced that the United States Central Intelligence Agency backed an attack on Amman's main police station May 28. Attackers were dressed like Palestinian guerrillas.

Both government officials and guerrilla leaders say they believe the incident was in fact a clumsy effort by someone to create trouble between King Hussein and the guerrillas.

If American arms and spare parts had not arrived before the June 5 war anniversary, many observers believe that anti-American and anti-Hussein pressures in Jordan might have blown their top.

Where to look

The Kennedy shooting

'Nation needs deeper disciplines'

By John C. Waugh
Staff correspondent of The Christian Science Monitor

Los Angeles

The hour had just slipped past midnight. A forest of arms lifted up in a V for victory as New York Sen. Robert F. Kennedy finished at the podium. He was winning the California Democratic primary.

Five minutes later the Senator was lying on the floor in a narrow galley passageway, shot twice. And the forest of hands uplifted in jubilant victory were suddenly, unbelievably pressed in horror against wet cheeks. And pandemonium raged from wall to wall of the Ambassador Hotel here.

Jubilation ends

The kleig-light heat in the low-ceilinged Embassy Room was oppressive. Los Angeles, like a slumbering giant just waking, was beginning to report its vote. And it was good news for Robert Kennedy — 174 delegate votes for the Chicago convention.

But the shots that suddenly rang out in the crowd that pressed in on him froze the jubilation like a sudden chill.

Hours later, following surgery, the Senator's condition was described as "extremely critical" by one of

Political scene in great confusion
Washington analysis: Page 2

his aides. A medical bulletin said the "very critical period" would extend over 24 to 36 hours.

At a secret hearing Wednesday morning a suspect in the shooting was arraigned under the name John Doe on four counts of assault with intent to murder. Bail was set at $250,000 for the suspect, who refused to identify himself or to discuss the shooting.

The arrested man was identified later as Sirhan Sirhan, 23, by a man who said he was Mr. Sirhan's brother Adel of Pasadena and who was traced through the gun. The suspect was also identified by one other person. Mayor Samuel Yorty of Los Angeles made these disclosures at a press conference at police headquarters. The Mayor said four $100 bills were found on the man, as well as a newspaper clipping not favorable to Mr. Kennedy. Mayor Yorty also said the arrested man apparently once lived in Jerusalem, but added that this was not clearly indicative of nationality.

This reporter was on his way out of the hotel when the shooting occurred. But the feeling that something was suddenly wrong literally hung on the air. As I rushed back through the crowd up the stairs, faces all around wore dazed, glazed looks.

A man sprinted past, brushing me aside. Several people shouted, "Stop that man."

The door to the press room next to the galley swung open. Out burst a sweat-drenched Jesse M. Unruh, Senator Kennedy's California campaign chairman. He was holding on to a tousel-headed youth. But nobody knew what was happening.

Inside the galley a Kennedy staff man was pounding on a stainless steel counter, crying, "Oh my God, oh my God."

Story pieced out

Senator Kennedy had just been carried out into an ambulance and sirened off to the Los Angeles Central Receiving Hospital just blocks away. Still lying on the narrow galley floor was another man—one of three besides the Senator who were shot.

Frantically, newsmen were trying to piece together what happened. A witness half sobbed out a story that finally filtered through like this:

The Senator had just stepped down from the Embassy Room podium and was moving and stopping toward the galley behind, hemmed and pressed about by jubilant backers.

He turned to say something. His tanned, orange-and-white-garbed wife, Ethel, was nearby. Then the shots slammed out — one, witnesses say, followed by several more quick ones.

Roosevelt Grier, the towering Los Angeles Rams defensive tackle and ardent Kennedy backer, boomed forward and grabbed at the man with the gun. Another famous athlete, Olympic decathlon champion Rafer Johnson, leaped for the gunner.

Paul Schrade, the Western representative of the United Automobile Workers, tall and

★ Please turn to Page 7

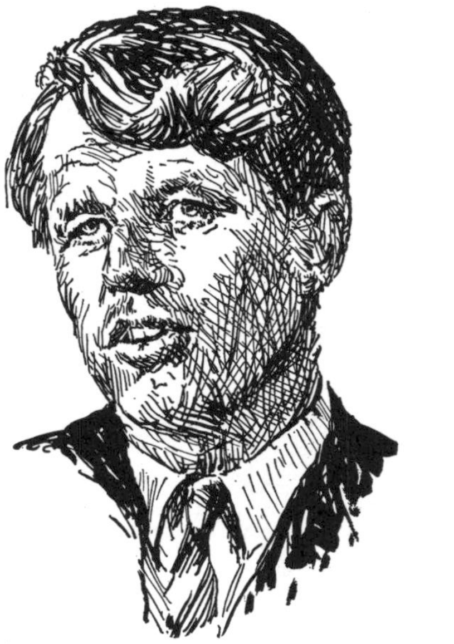

By Jim Hughes

Senator Kennedy — a tragic turn

By Erwin D. Canham
Editor in chief of The Christian Science Monitor

In the face of these years of tragedy and of sensation, people around the world — and Americans — are inevitably asking what is happening in the United States.

Seldom has a nation experienced such damaging blows to its decent respect in the thought of mankind. Seldom has the need for dedication to a better way of life been more widely recognized.

It is important to avoid exaggeration. In general, American society is being condemned. The charges are only true in part. No doubt all will agree that there is an atmosphere of violence in the United States, that it has been stimulated by many elements in national life, and that the nation needs deeper disciplines.

Undetermined motivation

Yet the three violent acts of the time — the assassinations of President Kennedy and the Rev. Dr. Martin Luther King Jr. and the shooting of Sen. Robert F. Kennedy — had specific causes and motivations, even though they have not yet been entirely clarified.

President Kennedy, according to all credible evidence, was slain by a maladjusted psychopath with general grievances against society. Evidences of conspiracy are not persuasive, still less proved.

Dr. King was murdered, it appears, by a former convict who carried out a skillful plan, both of murder and of escape. No evidence has come to light tying him with any general plot.

Whatever information is yet available on the motivation of the attack on Senator Kennedy does not suggest a relationship to the moral or social climate of the United States.

Wave of sympathy and love

It can be argued that the United States is the victim of a series of disconnected, fanatical or insane acts each of which might have been difficult if not impossible to prevent in the best-ordered society anywhere.

Whether these interpretations are in fact rational and sound, the United States faces the problem of restoring its decency and self-respect, to itself and to the world.

A great outpouring of horror has come from the entire nation. An equally intense wave of sympathy and love has gone out to the Kennedy family, so often the victim of personal tragedy.

Meantime, political campaigning has been suspended. This is entirely proper. In due course the task of nominating and electing a president will be resumed. What effect the attack on Senator Kennedy will have on that choice cannot now be estimated.

As a correspondent and editor, I have traveled with many presidents and presidential candidates. Scarcely for a moment has it been possible to prevent an assassination attempt by physical precautions alone. The United States is an open society. Candidates and presidents normally wish to move and communicate with the people freely. They have done so. They drive through the streets, push through crowded corridors, shake hands in the most open settings.

Elements of hysteria

In recent years, elements of hysteria have gripped the crowds which mill around attractive political figures, none more so than the members of the Kennedy family. Perhaps this hysteria suggests something of the problem faced by the United States: a wild, violent irrationality which induces acts not normal in a well-ordered society.

Undoubtedly shock, anger, grief, and sobriety mingle in the thoughts of the American people as they look forward. The nation must redeem itself. The therapy must go deep. Senator Kennedy himself, like other candidates for the highest office, has suggested many specific steps to foster a better climate of national life.

One obvious item is gun-control legislation. But far deeper is the acceptance of violence as a legitimate social action. It must be driven home to people that violence begets violence, and that the gains necessary in national life can only be achieved safely through normal political and social reform.

'. . . from the hearts of men . . .'

"There are no words equal to the horror of this tragedy.

"Our thoughts and prayers are with Senator Kennedy, his family, and the other victims.

"All America prays for his recovery.

"We also pray that divisiveness and violence can be driven from the hearts of men everywhere."

President Johnson

Will Congress act now on firearms controls?

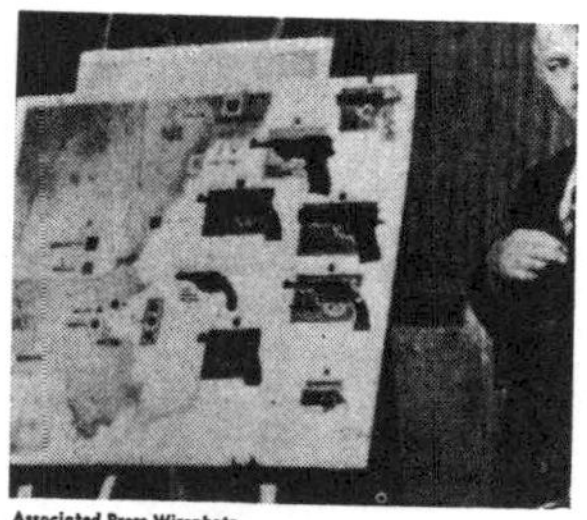

Associated Press Wirephoto

Guns, law, and shots anew

Washington hearings on firearms traffic, with exhibits such as this, have been frequent. But restraining legislation has repeatedly been watered down or rejected.

By Richard L. Strout
Staff correspondent of The Christian Science Monitor

Washington

"There is an element of violence in American society which the outsider has to learn to comprehend," wrote a British journalist in 1966. And Henry Fairlie added:

"However much I may love and admire America, its gun laws come near to ruling it out of civilized society."

On a circle in downtown Washington is the imposing $3½ million, nine-story headquarters of what is almost universally referred to as the gun lobby, although the National Rifle Association (NRA) bitterly rejects the title and does not register under the lobbying act.

It does not have to lobby in the normal sense, in view of the intense loyalty of its 850,000 members, many of them hunters and sportsmen.

With the new shooting of a presidential candidate in the United States attention once more centers on the NRA and the part it plays in blocking gun regulation.

Once more it has played a powerful role in diluting the pending firearms regulation section in the anticrime bill in Congress. This has passed in different forms in the Senate and House.

Intent obscured

In the Senate version (Title 4) the lobby helped to water down federal regulation in interstate commerce of so-called handguns (revolvers, pistols) while it eliminated control of so-called long guns (rifles, shotguns) May 16 altogether.

The Senate refused to heed the appeal of Sen. Edward M. Kennedy (D) of Massachusetts, brother of the murdered President and of Sen. Robert F. Kennedy, who was soon to be shot at Los Angeles.

Edward Kennedy declared on May 16: "Mr. President, we have it in our power to make this nation a little safer today and to keep guns out of the hands of those who should not have them . . . that 200 million Americans can sleep and walk and work and play with greater peace of mind."

The Senate would not heed his plea — the amendment to include long guns was voted down, 29-53.

The anticrime bill has become so confused in the Senate with the inclusion of amendments directed against Supreme Court decisions and wiretapping, that its original

★ Please turn to Page 7

National straw?

California GOP goes 'right'

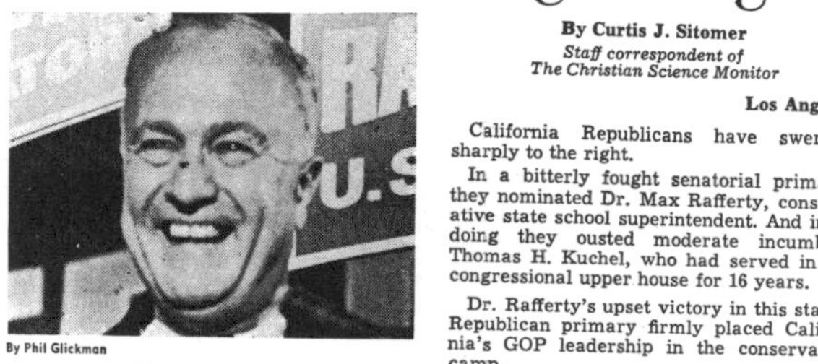

By Phil Glickman

Max Rafferty

State Superintendent of Public Instruction overturned the incumbency of assistant Senate GOP floor leader.

By Curtis J. Sitomer
Staff correspondent of The Christian Science Monitor

Los Angeles

California Republicans have swerved sharply to the right.

In a bitterly fought senatorial primary, they nominated Dr. Max Rafferty, conservative state school superintendent. And in so doing they ousted moderate incumbent Thomas H. Kuchel, who had served in the congressional upper house for 16 years.

Dr. Rafferty's upset victory in this state's Republican primary firmly placed California's GOP leadership in the conservative camp.

And some observers say this may be a national omen — perhaps one that will brighten the now somewhat flickering presi-

★ Please turn to Page 6

Inside today

Mapmakers 'bail out' the Atlantic Ocean

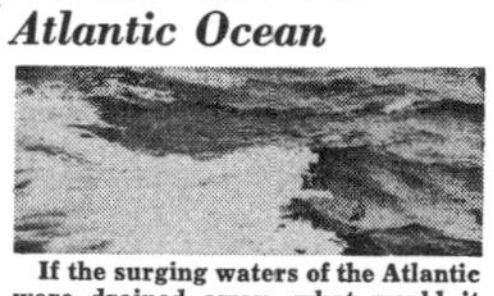

If the surging waters of the Atlantic were drained away, what would it look like? A National Geographic Society map gives the answer.

First page, second section

Boyd in cross fire over transport options

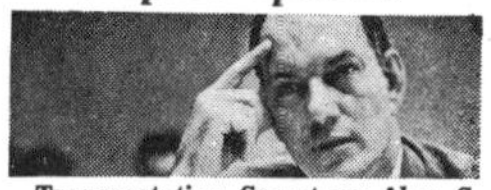

Transportation Secretary Alan S. Boyd is caught in the eye of a hurricane of dispute over America's interstate highway system. He faces protest wherever he turns.

Story: Page 15

2nd Cl Post Pd at Boston, Mass., and add'l offices

June 6, 1968

COPYRIGHT © 1968 THE CHRISTIAN SCIENCE PUBLISHING SOCIETY
All rights reserved

THE CHRISTIAN SCIENCE MONITOR

BOSTON, THURSDAY, AUGUST 22, 1968 — An International Daily Newspaper — VOL. 60, NO. 228 TWO SECTIONS — EASTERN EDITION ★ 10c

FOCUS on Africa

What's ahead . . .

There are likely to be further bumps ahead on the road of Sudan-Uganda relations.

In particular, the Sudanese Government is upset by the gift of several Soviet MIG jets to Uganda.

It is not that the Soviets are being one-sided: the Khartoum government has itself been promised Soviet military aid. What really bothers the predominantly Arab leaders in Khartoum is that the jets are going to a country which appears to be giving support to the black secessionists in southern Sudan.

Recently a "Southern Sudan provisional government" was set up in Uganda's capital, Kampala. Sudanese authorities believe this provisional regime, an offshoot of the long and bitter southern Sudanese war of secession, is getting direct backing from Uganda.

For their part, the southern Sudanese are hoping for recognition by Tanzania and the other African governments which have recognized the secessionist Biafran regime in Nigeria.

The decision by international airline pilots to cancel their planned boycott of Algerian airports was a great relief to the Algerian Government.

For Algiers is preparing for important meetings in September: African foreign ministers will be arriving there during the first week of the month to discuss plans for a three- or four-day conference of African heads of state a week or so later.

Algerian officials had been anxious that the proposed boycott by the International Federation of Airline Pilots would obstruct the visitors' travel plans. It would have made life especially difficult for those African leaders who intended to stop off in London or other European capitals en route to Algiers.

With the boycott threat removed, African diplomats now can complete their itineraries.

Trends . . .

Frelimo feels it is making an impact in southern Africa.

According to on-the-spot reports, the Mozambique Liberation Front, to give its unabbreviated name, now has an army of 8,000 in the field and controls one fifth of Mozambique.

For four years Frelimo has been fighting the Portuguese. Now it claims that South African security forces have joined Portuguese troops in Mozambique. It sees this as a sure measure of its own guerrilla warfare successes.

South African police units have been helping Ian Smith's regime in Rhodesia for about a year.

The presence of South African forces in Mozambique, if verified, would certainly indicate that Pretoria takes the Frelimo threat in neighboring Mozambique seriously.

Slimane Hoffman is a trainer—of guerrillas.

A major in the Algerian Army, he is in charge of the military training of most African "liberation" movements. He has played a leading part in organizing the teaching of guerrilla warfare to black Africans from Rhodesia, South Africa, and Portugal's African territories.

Major Hoffman's efforts are financed by the Organization of African Unity (OAU). At its September meeting in Kinshasa, Congo, the OAU voted some $2 million—two-thirds of its budget—to "freedom fighters."

This decision was backed up by the OAU's Liberation Committee in mid-July when it confirmed the allocation.

Morocco is going all out for education.

Since June King Hassan has created no less than four ministries dealing with education or cultural affairs. He wants to see more specialists at the top.

The ministries include: one for primary education; another for secondary and technical schooling; a third for higher education; and finally a new ministry of culture under Mohammed al Fassy, rector of the Moroccan University in Rabat.

How and why . . .

Zanzibar's Revolutionary Council is extending revolution to the island's legal system.

It has decided to abolish courts of law for all crimes except murder, and robbery with violence.

Henceforth minor offenders will be sent for a minimum of five years to a sort of state reform school. There they will be taught a useful trade.

The new system breaks down Zanzibar's traditional separation of powers. Branch chairmen of the island's ruling Afro-Shirazi Party now will judge minor offenses.

Western observers are reminded of the Chinese Communist system of "labor custody" or "education through labor" which also provides for a prisoner to perform useful work.

Where to look

Soviet overtures had duped Western officials. Moscow feared unchecked liberalism in Prague might doom conservative Communist regimes.

— Ellis dispatch

Realignment of the Soviet hierarchy may be in the making. Hard liners had opposed compromise, especially the Bratislava settlement.

— Wohl report

In Washington's view, Soviet police power can be very effective in the short run, but the forces of freedom are irrepressible in the long run.

— Davis analysis

Soviet jackboots tramp Czechs

But will it be a long-term victory?

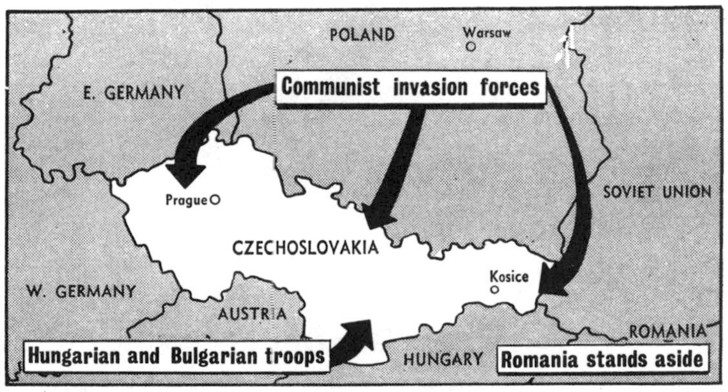

POLAND
Warsaw
E. GERMANY
Communist invasion forces
SOVIET UNION
Prague
CZECHOSLOVAKIA
Kosice
W. GERMANY
AUSTRIA
ROMANIA
Hungarian and Bulgarian troops
HUNGARY
Romania stands aside

By Joan Forbes, staff cartographer

'We hear a terrible noise . . .'

These words were spoken on Prague Radio before it played the Czechoslovak national anthem and temporarily went off the air Wednesday. People listening in hotels wept. And Czechoslovaks in the streets booed, whistled, and jeered as Soviet tanks rumbled into the center of the city.

By Saville R. Davis
Staff correspondent of The Christian Science Monitor

Washington

The question is whether the world can hold to its recent course away from the military era and toward a more civilized regime.

The alternative is for the icy blasts of cold war to sweep the earth again.

The Czechoslovak crisis struck just as the American people were painfully working their way out of the Vietnam war and

'Moscow has confessed its own weakness.'
Story by David Willis: Page 3

just as the realistic managers of the modern Soviet Union had begun to respond.

The fear in Washington, stirred by a highly emotional reaction to Soviet troops again trampling on the beginnings of Czechoslovak freedom, is that the tide now will be reversed, that a hard line in Moscow will challenge the hard line that was slowly easing here, and that the two great powers will turn back from accommodation to ideological conflict.

The corresponding hope here is that the new trend is sturdy enough to survive and that the Kremlin, once it stops the spreading force of the Czechoslovak rebellion, will not overreact and set tanks astride the satellite countries. The hope is also that the onlooking world will temper its indignation with knowledge that the Kremlin saw a vital challenge to its security only a short while after the devastation of World War II.

President Johnson, pitching his first actions on the constructive side, denounced the invasion of Czechoslovakia as tragic and contrived and appealed to the Soviet Union and other intervening nations to withdraw their troops.

The United States is steering a hairline course between its two highest desires on the world scene. Both are involved in the Czechoslovak crisis, in a highly explosive and dangerous mixture.

They are:

- To encourage freedom and national in-

UN diplomats voice despair.
Story by Earl Foell: Page 4

dependence wherever they need help—even inside the Communist world.

- To "keep the nuclear beast in its cage." The grim phrase was used by Secretary of State Dean Rusk this week to the platform committee of the Democratic National Convention.

President Johnson and his top officials are therefore using the power of ideas and rejecting the power of weapons as the instrument of policy during the crisis.

He said, "In the name of mankind's hope

★ **Please turn to Page 12**

Inside today

New poll puts Nixon ahead of Humphrey

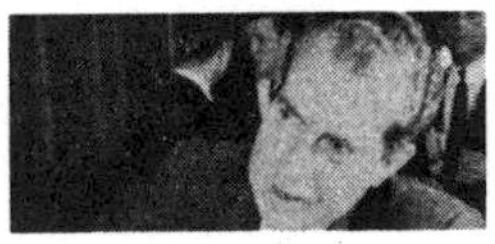

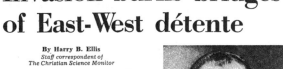

Public-opinion polls still are dominating the conventions. So far, at the coming Democratic get - together, Vice-President Hubert H. Humphrey has little to smile about pollwise.

Chicago report: Page 5

Minor novelists grasp fame but no cash

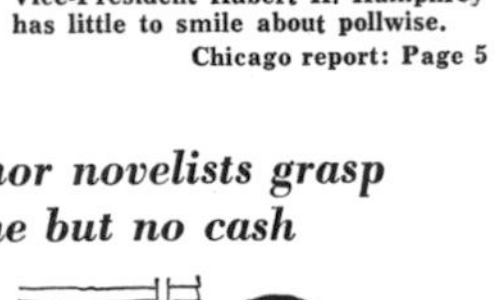

Minor novelists—are they out on a limb or in a limbo? Find out how it feels to be a writer who makes the grade but not the money.

Story: Page 11

London sees insecurity in Soviet take-over

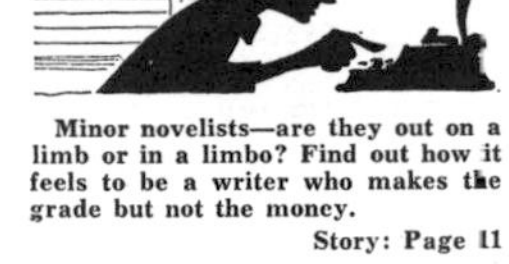

Western Europe reacted with shock and consternation to the news of the Soviet invasion of Czechoslovakia. In Britain Prime Minister Harold Wilson interrupted his vacation and recalled Parliament.

Details: Page 4

2nd Cl Post Pd at Boston, Mass., and add'l offices

Invasion burns bridges of East-West détente

By Harry B. Ellis
Staff correspondent of The Christian Science Monitor

Bonn

The Soviet-led Warsaw Pact invasion of Czechoslovakia was mounted behind a smoke screen of Communist overtures to Western governments in recent weeks.

These overtures apparently had lulled Western officials into believing that enemies of Alexander Dubcek's liberal Czech regime had been thrown on the defensive, and that the acute danger of Soviet intervention was past.

[The Czechoslovak news agency Ceteka said that Mr. Dubcek was under restriction in the party's Central Committee building.]

It was widely felt among Western diplomats that Mr. Dubcek's refusal to curb his internal Czech reforms had in itself forced Communist East Germany to adopt a more conciliatory tone toward West Germany.

East Berlin, for example, had expressed unprecedented readiness for its foreign-trade minister to confer in either part of divided Germany with his West German counterpart.

Headlines in leading West German newspapers Aug. 21—rolling off the presses just as Soviet-bloc troops were rolling into Czechoslovakia—trumpeted Bonn's approval of inter-German ministerial talks.

Planning sighted

Clearly, East German Chief of State Walter Ulbricht, in concert with Moscow, had been planning the Czech invasion, even while his foreign-trade minister was inviting West German Economics Minister Karl Schiller to confer.

Talks this reporter had with key officials only a few hours before Warsaw Pact troops began to move failed to uncover any sign that Western officials glimpsed what was about to happen.

West German Chancellor Kurt Georg Kiesinger led the rush of his ministers back from vacation to consult in early-morning hours over the drastic turn of events in neighboring Czechoslovakia.

The invasion, which burned the bridges of the budding East-West détente, testified to the deep fear in East Berlin, Warsaw, and Moscow that unchecked liberalism in Prague ultimately might doom conservative Communist governments.

In the first confused hours following the

★ **Please turn to Page 4**

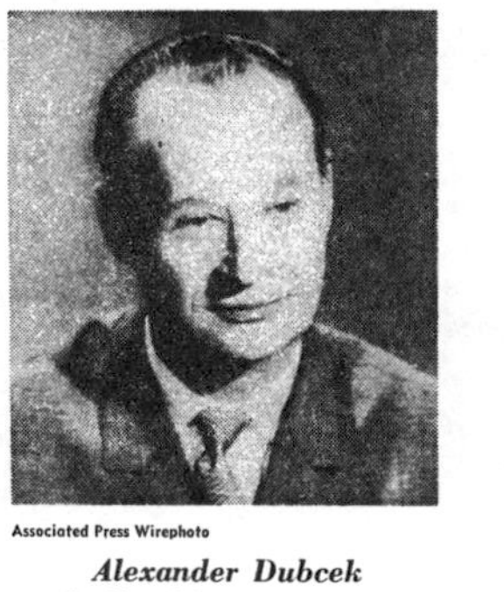

Associated Press Wirephoto

Alexander Dubcek
Swallowed by his neighbors

Kremlin hard liners prevail

By Paul Wohl
Written for The Christian Science Monitor

The carefully coordinated and secretly prepared invasion of Czechoslovakia by Warsaw Pact forces shows that the military and the hard liners in the Kremlin have won out over the compromisers.

As the Prague liberal regime goes down, the Bratislava settlement goes down with it.

The scrapping of the Bratislava settlement does not bode well for the men who sponsored it. A realignment of the Soviet leadership may be in the cards.

Criticism of Bratislava has been building up for some time. General Secretary Leonid I. Brezhnev's method of letting excitement over Czechoslovakia rise to a crescendo and then to accept, more or less, Prague's terms has been compared unfavorably with former Premier Nikita S. Khrushchev's discreet handling of the Cuban crisis during which the Soviet public virtually ignored what was being played.

Criticism of Mr. Brezhnev and several of his close colleagues came especially from the military and from Ukrainian party boss Piotr Y. Shelest, an important member of the Politburo who, according to Prague sources, took the toughest stand at the Cierna conference of the Politburo and the Czechoslovak Presidium.

The Ukraine is the one major Soviet republic where subscription to Czechoslovak periodicals is forbidden. Because the languages are similar, Czech and, even more so, Slovak broadcasts can be understood in the Ukraine. At a time when the Ukrainian leadership has its hands full with discontents at home, the

★ **Please turn to Page 6**

COPYRIGHT © 1968 THE CHRISTIAN SCIENCE PUBLISHING SOCIETY
All rights reserved

THE CHRISTIAN SCIENCE MONITOR

BOSTON, THURSDAY, NOVEMBER 7, 1968   *An International Daily Newspaper*   VOL. 60, NO. 293 TWO SECTIONS   NEW ENGLAND EDITION ▲ 10c

FOCUS
on
East Europe

What's ahead . . .

Secret reports running along the grapevines from Moscow discount theories of any significant split within the Kremlin leadership.

And for the moment at least, the ruling group which trampled over the hapless Czechoslovaks shows no sign of further aggressive sallies.

One reason may be a Soviet eagerness not to add strain to its relations with the United States, particularly because of joint efforts to fence in the spread of nuclear weapons.

Another "because" may be the Russians' anxiety about Communist China's intentions.

Peking is reported to have assured Romania (whose neutrality in the Sino-Soviet conflict has been a comfort in Peking and a thorn in Moscow) and Albania (China's open ally), that if they are "interfered with," Chinese aid will be forthcoming.

"Aid" could readily be rendered by incidents and pressures cooked up by the Chinese on Russia's eastern border.

Right now the Russians are rapidly diverting more divisions to the Soviet Far East following credible evidence that China itself already has moved up more troops.

For Russia, therefore, China remains the great, awesome imponderable.

Trends . . .

Despite their untold natural resources, the Soviets aren't taking them for granted any more.

River pollution has become a serious problem. It is said to cost the fishing industry close to $400 million a year.

Industrial plants are polluting the air. Only 14 percent have fully satisfactory exhaust-air-cleaning equipment.

And losses from soil erosion are tallied at some $3.8 billion a year.

So the Soviets are launching a big campaign to save what they have. And they've developed a new way to do it—economically.

Use of natural resources will not be free any longer. Industry will be charged a sort of rent for the resources they use.

⊕

Russia has partially rectified a major injustice of the Stalin era.

A decree of July 8, 1944, denied all unwed mothers the right to claim from the father financial support to maintain their children. On Oct. 1 that decree was amended.

Under new "Principles on Marriage and the Family," the courts now are empowered to determine the father of an illegitimate child born of a common-law marriage.

And once paternity is legally established, the father must pay a quarter of his earnings as alimony until the child has reached age 18—or 23 if still a student.

But the law contains no provision for establishing paternity of children born of casual or short-term unions. And a majority of the 10 million children born out of wedlock in the Soviet Union since 1944 are believed to be in this latter category.

Thus the new law is being severely criticized by many Russians as only a halfway measure—if that.

⊕

Tourist spending by West Europeans is giving a new lease on life to derelict and impoverished parts of East Europe.

A striking example: Yugoslavia's coastline across the Adriatic from Italy's long boot.

For years after World War II, villages along this coastal region, which is fabulously endowed by nature, went into decline. Youths fled for lack of employment.

Now a tourist boom has changed all that. It has prompted local investment in such amenities as plumbing and electricity. Young men no longer must sail west for work.

Visited by immense droves of Western Europeans, its coast accounts for millions of the dollars Yugoslavia netted from tourism this year.

The same thing is happening in other East-bloc countries. East and West Europeans are mixing on an unprecedented scale in remote, forgotten corners of Bulgaria and Romania.

This friendly invasion is bringing to East Europeans themselves bonanzas in services they otherwise would not have had for many a year.

⊕

Soviet grain crops have turned out well in spite of unfavorable weather.

Indeed, all grain yields in Russia, largest of the 15 Soviet republics, this year reached an all-time high of 1,321 pounds per acre.

This is no longer so far below the United States peak wheat yield of 1,598 pounds per acre in 1965.

However, the Soviet figure includes corn production. And in this crop the United States is still far out front with a current yield of 4,133 pounds per acre.

Where to look

By John Littlewood, staff photographer

A long seesaw night, then the dawn of victory

Electoral College severely tested

Nixon rides conservative crest

By Richard L. Strout
*Staff correspondent of
The Christian Science Monitor*

Washington

The United States has taken a strong move to the right in a seesaw presidential election.

By electing Richard M. Nixon 37th President it has picked a man critical of much of the Democratic social and economic philosophy that has obtained for all but eight of the past 36 years.

The nation has revealed its own inner doubt and uncertainty by leaving control

Nixon and foreign policy
Saville R. Davis reports
from Washington: Page 5

of Congress — both Senate and House — in the hands of Democrats.

President-Designate Nixon will take office as a minority president in the sense that he has received less than a majority of total popular vote cast, and with a relatively slight lead over Vice-President Hubert H. Humphrey.

He will be less isolated from Congress probably than the statistics indicate.

Congress will be organized by Democrats but the legislature has moved to the right, too. Prospect is that legislative power will be centered in a strengthened Republican and Southern Democratic conservative coalition.

Such a Congress might have given Mr. Humphrey even more trouble than Mr. Nixon.

Presumably it will be in sympathy with

★ Please turn to Page B18

By a staff photographer

Vice-President-Elect Agnew
Partner in a successful campaign

Senate: Seven new GOP faces,
but Democrats still in control

Page 8

House: GOP net gain four;
firmer coalition with South?

Page 8

Governors: Incumbents tumbled
on tax and spending issues

Pages 5 and B15

Wallace: Weaker than expected
but strong enough to reckon with

Page B14

Upsets dot N.E.

By Edgar M. Mills
*New England political editor of
The Christian Science Monitor*

Boston

Rhode Island's stunning upset of three-term Republican Gov. John H. Chafee by Democrat Frank Licht (above) proved to be the biggest surprise of New England's six-state elections.

Advocacy of a personal-income tax proved to be Governor Chafee's downfall as Mr. Licht, the state's first Jewish-American chief executive, made it the big issue.

The Licht victory was part of a three-way shift which returned political tradition to three of the New

★ Please turn to Page B16

Activist President

Nixon may have to deal gently and persuasively
with Democratic majority in Congress

By Godfrey Sperling Jr.
*Staff correspondent of
The Christian Science Monitor*

Washington

The shape of the new Nixon administration is visible, even as Richard M. Nixon's razor-edge victory becomes a reality.

From private conversations with the Nixon staff, together with interviews with Mr. Nixon, this can be said of the way the new President will operate:

● He will be an activist President. He believes in a strong executive. But in his dealings with Congress his approach will differ from that of President Johnson.

How to get results

Mr. Johnson has relied mainly on staff and special commissions for new ideas and for putting together new programs.

Instead, Mr. Nixon plans to look to members of Congress to come up with the fresh, helpful ideas that he as a President can put into the form of programs.

Mr. Nixon will seek a close relationship with members of Congress, hoping to get their cooperation—and their vote—by making them feel that he is always open to their advice.

Mr. Nixon has always realized that he

★ Please turn to Page 3

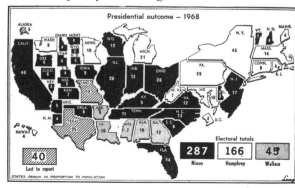

Presidential outcome – 1968

Electoral totals		
287	166	45
Nixon	Humphrey	Wallace

STATES DRAWN IN PROPORTION TO POPULATION

*Pattern
of politics*

Nixon strength combined a scattering of states: border, New England, southern, plains, and mountain. Capture of New Jersey, California, and Ohio fortified the combination as the nation waited for laggard Missouri, Texas, and Alaska votes to come in. Mr. Nixon went over the top when Illinois was declared in his corner.

2nd Cl Post Pd at Boston, Mass., and add'l offices   November 7, 1968
COPYRIGHT © 1968 THE CHRISTIAN SCIENCE PUBLISHING SOCIETY
All rights reserved

153

THE CHRISTIAN SCIENCE MONITOR

BOSTON, TUESDAY, JULY 22, 1969   *An International Daily Newspaper*   VOL. 61, NO. 200   TWO SECTIONS   NEW ENGLAND EDITION ▲ 10c

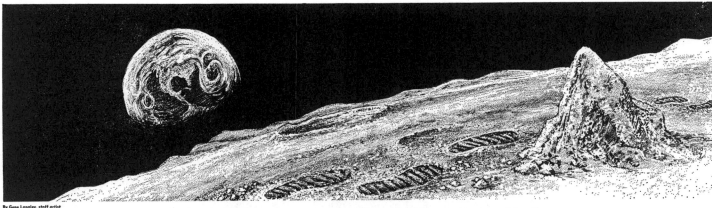

By Gene Langley, staff artist

'One small step for man, one giant leap for mankind'

Mankind embraces the moon— A milestone, not a finish line

Humanity's greatest triumphs are those that come through peace, intelligence, inspiration, not war.

Mankind's lesson: Editorial page

They scooped a priceless package of lunar rocks that may hold the secret of the origin of earth.

Neal Stanford: Page 7

The downtrodden of the world look for more than moon races and nuclear missiles.

Saville R. Davis: Page 3

Associated Press Wirephoto

They 'came in peace for all mankind'

'He fears moon no longer; man has adapted'

By Richard L. Strout
Staff correspondent of The Christian Science Monitor

Monday morning

Man walked on the moon and made it look easy. Now mankind must find something new to dream about.

There were two peaks of drama as Astronauts Neil A. Armstrong and Edwin E. Aldrin Jr. completed the first part of their great adventure, and command pilot Michael Collins, almost forgotten, circled above them.

[The astronauts successfully blasted off from the moon early Monday afternoon on the first stage of their journey back to earth. At this writing their return to lunar orbit and rendezvous with the command module remained to be executed.]

The first was as the two astronauts separated their spidery spacecraft "Eagle" from the command ship "Columbia" and made their hazardous descent. Hundreds of millions on earth heard the interchange with Houston as they neared the Sea of Tranquillity.

At the very last minute the computerized pilot aimed the fragile craft at a ridge of rocks on the projected landing site. Television viewers on earth

could only know that the countdown was in its final seconds. Neil Armstrong grabbed the control and piloted the module beyond the original landing spot. Then, clear and firm came the call:

"Houston!" Astronaut Armstrong paused and took a breath. "Tranquillity base here. The Eagle has landed."

Associated Press Wirephoto   Neil Armstrong

'It's big and bright and beautiful'

In living rooms people pinched themselves. Television announcers who had built up this big moment found themselves at a loss for words. In London's Trafalgar Square a great crowd screamed.

Man would measure time by this first landing on the moon.

The second peak of drama was even more excit-

ing. For hundreds of millions it was actually visible. It seemed almost as astounding to them that a quarter-of-a-million miles away they could see what was happening as it was actually happening.

By some freak of planning it had been scheduled that after making a successful landing on the moon the two astronauts would take a nap. The theory was that they would be better rested for the ordeal. But human nature follows man to the moon. Permission was asked and immediately given to make the first foray onto the moon's surface at once.

'Knights gird themselves'

There followed an agonizing delay. They were getting dressed. The suits they donned were $300,000 suits. They made their wearers into miniature individual space modules carrying self-contained atmosphere, pressure, oxygen, temperature, and shields from meteorites.

Half the world waited while they laboriously put on the cumbersome garments like knights girding themselves with a new style of flexible armor, doing it in space about the size of a telephone booth. Every man who had ever put on a dress suit and knew the
★ **Please turn to Page 8**

2nd Cl Post Pd at Boston, Mass., and add'l offices   July 22, 1969   COPYRIGHT © 1969 THE CHRISTIAN SCIENCE PUBLISHING SOCIETY
All rights reserved

1970-1988

THE CHRISTIAN SCIENCE MONITOR

BOSTON, WEDNESDAY, MAY 6, 1970 — *An International Daily Newspaper* — VOL. 62, NO. 136 TWO SECTIONS — EASTERN EDITION ★ 10c

FOCUS *on books* ™

Environ-meant

Now that it's happened, it seems inevitable—a book club dedicated to a great crusade of the 1970's.

Devin-Adair is launching a subsidiary, the Ecological Book Club. Its function will be to sift the flow of ecology-oriented works—those dealing with wildlife, the countryside, overpopulation, the "dying cities," soil erosion, pollution of air, land, and sea, and the threat of world famine.

Books considered especially important will then be offered to club members at reduced prices.

The first four titles are; Robert H. Boyle's "The Hudson River: a Natural History"; A. Q. Mowbray's "Road to Ruin" (about the U.S. federal highway program and the automobile); "Famine 1975!" by the Paddock brothers; and Frederick Elder's "Crisis in Eden."

The club will also issue a periodical newsletter dealing not only with books, but also with events on the ecological front — political proposals, legislation, medical testimony, and the findings of conservationists and natural scientists.

Lexicography

Due soon from World: the Second College Edition of Webster's New World Dictionary of the American Language.

It has been compiled over the past 17 years by a full-time staff and contains many changes in both information and attitude.

It is offered with an LP record which actually speaks the sounds of various phonetic symbols. The publishers say that this has never been done before; strictly for the record, this record is a record. It sounds like a resoundingly sound idea.

1,728 pages and 157,346 vocabulary entries, many not listed elsewhere. Publication date: May 15.

Southern prize

For a book, or a magazine article or series, or some other substantial study of the Appalachian South, a $500 prize is to be awarded annually.

The prize for a work published this year will be given early in 1971.

It's called the W. D. Weatherford Award, after a leader and innovator in the field of Southern racial and Appalachian problems for almost 60 years.

Inquiries to the editor of Mountain Life & Work, Council of the Southern Mountains, Inc., P.O. Box 2307, Berea, Ky., 40403.

China ware

On May 18 John Day will publish Pearl S. Buck's "China as I See It," a collection of speeches and writings dating from the 1930's to the present.

The book is optimistic about the future of the Chinese, a resourceful people who can be expected to make progressive backslidings from repressive dogmas. They will not indefinitely be held back by the Great Leap Forward.

The author deplores anti-Chinese propaganda and ignorance, and affirms that the Chinese and American peoples are, temperamentally, "extraordinarily alike."

Novel celebration

This year marks the centenary of the passing of Charles Dickens, the great English novelist.

He wrote "Oliver Twist," "David Copperfield," "Great Expectations," "A Tale of Two Cities," "Pickwick Papers" — and others equally familiar. He invented such celebrities as Mr. Micawber, Scrooge, the first Tiny Tim, Pecksniff, and Little Nell.

A memorial service in Westminster Abbey, plus lectures and special exhibitions at other places, will stress England's affection for one who was perhaps its second-greatest man of letters.

Two films based on his stories are now on circuit. A third—"A Christmas Carol"—will appear soon. Dickens serials will occupy peak time on British television.

Among new books about the great man is one from Chapman and Hall, his original publishers.

At Broadstairs, home of "Bleak House," local residents are asked to wear Victorian dress. This should be easy for young men with long hair and luxuriant whiskers, and for unbobbed girls in maxis.

It may be less easy for their parents, whose hairstyles and costumes are more modern.

Togetherness

Richard Zorza is a young Englishman, the son of the Guardian's well-known Sovietologist.

Richard was studying, etc., at Harvard during the recent tumults there.

His inside account of it, to be published by Praeger on June 15, is called "The Right to Say We: The Adventures of a Young Englishman at Harvard and in the Youth Movement."

Where to look

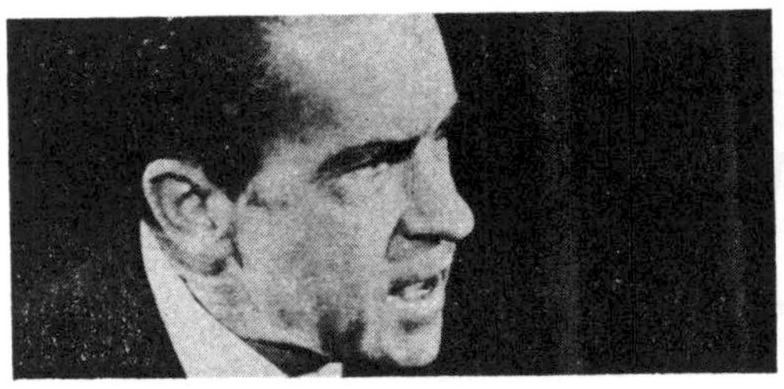

President Nixon

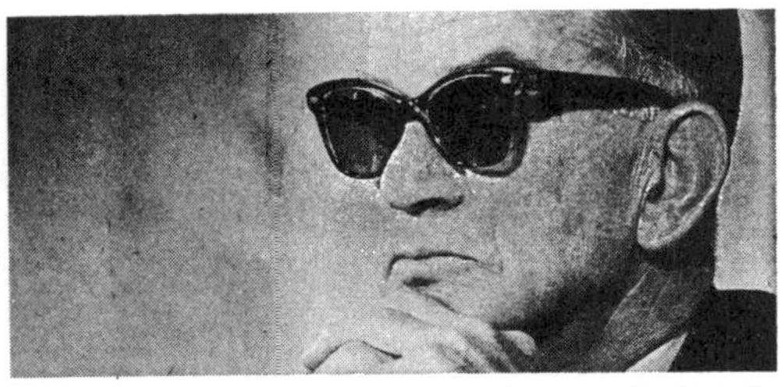

Senator Fulbright

Many senators feel they are bypassed by the Chief Executive

Nixon-Congress collision

Is Indo-China war 'constitutionally unauthorized'?

By Richard L. Strout
Staff correspondent of The Christian Science Monitor

Washington

Senators charge Mr. Nixon is waging "a constitutionally unauthorized, presidential war in Indochina" and confronted him at the White House as tension appeared to mount.

The military made a strong case for entering Cambodia but the question increasingly arises here whether Mr. Nixon can keep the lid on the domestic front.

- Congress: Antiwar senators moved their forces into position for a parliamentary showdown, while the White House stuck to its redoubts.
- Campus unrest: What appeared to be a great wave of draft-age protest gathered on campuses across the country with emotions charged by the killing of four students at Kent State University, Ohio, by national guardsmen.
- The economy: The jittery stock market, May 4, lost 19 points in the Dow-Jones Industrial Averages for reasons that partly reflected the uncertainty of the war situation.
- Foreign reaction: Premier Alexei N. Kosygin hints that U.S.-Soviet strategic arms limitation talks under way in Vienna are jeopardized by entry of U.S. troops into Cambodia.

Difficulties growing

Washington sees a difficult legislative situation developing here whose consequences are hard to appraise. A substantial number of senators are disturbed by the failure of the White House to go through the forms of advance information or consultation on a major new move in an unpopular war.

On the other hand, these senators appear to be in a minority and it remains to be seen whether the majority will go along. There are, accordingly, two points at issue, resentment by opponents of the war at what they regard as its escalation and, secondly, irritation and anxiety of a larger number of senators over being disregarded by the executive.

Observers find it difficult to explain how the Nixon administration permitted this situation to develop.

Indeed, it seems to be compounded by the administration's rejection of a direct meeting with the 15 members of the Senate Foreign Relations Committee alone. Almost as though it were a studied affront, the White House expanded its invitation to House members.

The question is raised also whether Mr. Nixon appreciates the full realities of draft-age war protest. In the quiet, middle-class rural area of Kent, Ohio, four University students were killed by National Guard gunfire and 11 others were wounded in resisting a college demonstration, and alleged sniping from a roof.

Related stories
Pages 7 and 10

In his April 30 speech Mr. Nixon denounced "mindless attacks on all the great institutions . . . great universities are being systematically destroyed."

★ Please turn to Page 2

Campus crisis of confidence

By Trudy Rubin
Staff writer of The Christian Science Monitor

Boston

The movement of American troops into Cambodia has triggered a nationwide explosion of protest on college campuses. The explosion is all the more potent because it has tapped the frustrations of both radical and moderate students alike over their inability to affect the course of the war.

The National Student Association, helping to coordinate strike information, estimates 175-200 campuses already participating at this writing. They include not only Ivy League schools like Harvard, Columbia, Brown, and the University of Pennsylvania, but small campuses like Florida Baptist College, Moravian College in Pennsylvania, and Assumption College in Worcester, Mass.

The antiwar sentiment was only given additional fuel by the deaths of four Kent State University students in Ohio when national guardsmen opened fire on antiwar demonstrators who refused to disperse and were allegedly throwing rocks at guardsmen.

★ Please turn to Page 6

May 4 in Kent, Ohio, was a day not soon forgotten

Story: Page 12

Nasser bids again for international talks

But Palestinians reject big-power role

By John K. Cooley
Staff correspondent of The Christian Science Monitor

Beirut, Lebanon

President Nasser's military tactics and those of the Palestinian commandos are drawing closer. But their political strategies differ basically.

This is a conclusion drawn here following President Nasser's policy speech May 1 and a train of military and diplomatic events immediately following it.

Despite heavy losses the commandos and the Egyptian Army have both intensified their strikes inside Israeli-occupied territory, trying to seize a military initiative.

Contradictions seen

The Egyptian Army has been able to mount major artillery bombardments and occasional air strikes on Israeli installations in Sinai. Combat patrols of company and battalion strength have been raiding the canal's east bank.

Politically, analysts here see these contradictions between President Nasser's strategy and that of the Palestinians:

- As outlined in his May 1 speech President Nasser's view is still that the United States holds the key to a just negotiated peace in the Middle East if it wants to use this key. The commandos reject United States, Soviet, or other big-power intervention.
- President Nasser wants to reinforce chances for the big-power talks. The commandos reject the big-power concept.

President Nasser's offer May 1 to Washington is seen here as the offer of a deal: If the United States will stop guaranteeing Israel, through arms deliveries, the military superiority that enables it to hold conquered Arab land, Washington can regain the lost American influence in the area.

Trade-off suggested

President Nasser's concrete proposal, as read in that speech and subsequent interpretations coming out of Cairo, is to trade an immediate cease-fire with Israel against an Israeli commitment of gradual withdrawal from the land taken in 1967.

This is, in fact, a concession to Washington's wish for a cease-fire as the first step toward peace. It would also be a way to cut the Gordian knot encountered by the Big Four in more than a year of negotiations: Arab demands for priority to Israeli evacuation; Israeli insistence on primacy of Arab security guarantees.

Cairo appears to feel that the time gap between an Arab cease-fire and the start of Israeli withdrawal could be turned to good diplomatic advantage. The Big Four could reactivate their talks on a more meaningful basis. The mission of UN emissary Gunnar V. Jarring between Arab capitals and Israel might be resumed.

[The Associated Press reports that Israeli Defense Minister Moshe Dayan told a student rally in Haifa Monday, "The government is ready to reestablish an unconditional and unlimited cease-fire, even if this will enable Egypt to reorganize and put up SAM-3 Soviet built surface-to-air missile sites."]

Israel will not agree voluntarily to withdraw. Therefore, President Nasser reasons, only Washington can oblige it to do so, through financial and other pressure of the kind President Eisenhower applied to secure Israeli withdrawal from Sinai and Gaza in 1957.

In seeking to persuade President Nixon to influence Israel, President Nasser dangles the threat of possible sanctions against U.S. economic interests and the almost inevitable growth of Soviet interests to replace them.

This is apparently the policy being explained by Mr. Nasser's envoys who set out this week for the main Arab capitals.

Aid sought

The Cairo emissaries are expected to ask each Arab Government whether or not it is really prepared to make a military contribution to a new major confrontation with Israel. Otherwise Egypt would plan its own action with whatever Soviet help is available.

One editor here describes this doctrine as "put up or shut up."

Inside today . . .

Universities turn to U.S. for aid

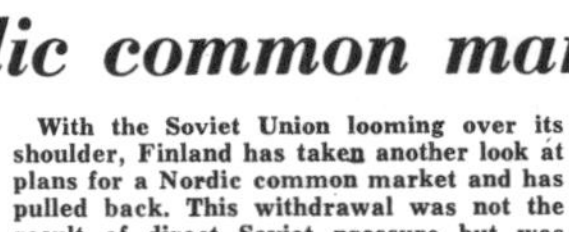

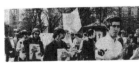

As costs zoom, colleges and universities are hard pressed to meet their bills. These students at Boston College were protesting a $500 tuition hike. But educational institutions in an age of protest are not popular with many federal officials, whose help they may need to get crucial federal assistance.

Story: Page 17

Nordic common market founders

With the Soviet Union looming over its shoulder, Finland has taken another look at plans for a Nordic common market and has pulled back. This withdrawal was not the result of direct Soviet pressure but was prompted by Finland's position of enforced neutrality. It has left the other Nordic countries disappointed and bewildered.

Report from Harry B. Ellis: Page 4

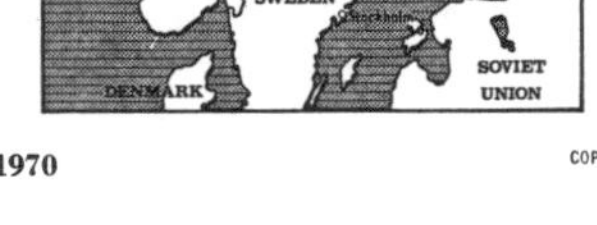

U.S. arms aid to Greece hit

By William C. Selover
Staff correspondent of The Christian Science Monitor

Washington

For three years—ever since the military junta took over the government in Greece—the United States has enforced restrictions on "heavy" arms shipments to that NATO ally.

It was done to register displeasure with the suspension of democratic freedoms ordered by the military regime.

Now, however, as the junta celebrates its third year in power, it has been learned here that the value of U.S. military equipment shipped to Greece this year will be just about double that approved by Congress.

★ Please turn to Page 10

2nd Cl Post Pd at Boston, Mass., and add'l offices

COPYRIGHT © 1970 THE CHRISTIAN SCIENCE PUBLISHING SOCIETY
All rights reserved

THE CHRISTIAN SCIENCE MONITOR

BOSTON, TUESDAY, JUNE 29, 1971 *An International Daily Newspaper* VOL. 63, NO. 181 TWO SECTIONS EASTERN EDITION ★ 15¢

New Pentagon papers

Why '62 Viet-exit plan fizzled

By David K. Willis
American news editor

and Geoffrey Godsell
Overseas news editor of The Christian Science Monitor

Boston

Highlights of the hitherto unpublished Pentagon papers made available to the Monitor:

- **Even while it was being drawn more and more into a full-scale land war in Asia, the U.S. laid plans as far back as July, 1962, to pull back almost all ground forces from Vietnam by fiscal 1968.**
- **The plan is described as good, and well programmed, but it was dropped in March, 1964 — overtaken by the rush of events, including President Diem's assassination Nov. 1, 1963, Lyndon B. Johnson's accession to the American presidency, and a steadily worsening military situation in Vietnam itself — as well as weaknesses in U.S. planning.**
- **American intelligence reporting from the field, relying heavily on Vietnamese information, was poor, and overly optimistic. It misled senior U.S. officials.**
- **Even at what the Pentagon study sees as darkest hours, U.S. intelligence, with only some exceptions, considered the fighting to be making progress.**
- **The political side of the struggle — the factional maneuvering in Saigon and other capitals, appears to have been given considerably less weight than the military side.**
- **At a critical juncture, a tough "shape-up-or-else" draft letter from President Kennedy to President Diem was scrapped in favor of a lower-key letter and conversations by Gen. Maxwell D. Taylor, then chairman of the Joint Chiefs of Staff.**
- **There is no evidence in this study to suggest that the U.S. had a hand in toppling President Diem in 1963.**

For a crucial 21 months spanning the Kennedy and Johnson administrations, the United States laid plans to pull almost all American troops out of South Vietnam over a five-year period—while being sucked inexorably deeper and deeper into the war instead.

The plan begun in July, 1962, eventually crashed to the ground in March, 1964. The story of how it crashed, detailed in hitherto unpublished Pentagon papers which have become available to this newspaper, vividly illustrates grave weaknesses in American policymaking that misled senior officials and directly contributed to the dramatic escalation of U.S. involvement in 1964-65.

Original plan outlined

The original plan was to reduce American military personnel engaged in advising, training, and support efforts from a high point of 12,000 men in fiscal 1964 to a mere 1,500 in fiscal 1968. Later, after several revisions, the plan called for a drawing down from 15,215 in fiscal 1964 to 2,610 in fiscal 1969.

Savings in the final plan in military assistance totaled about $140 million — from $180 million in fiscal 1964 to $47.8 million in fiscal 1969.

The Pentagon study implies that it was doomed almost from the beginning —by flaws and "some basic unrealities" in its conception; by serious weaknesses in intelligence reporting from the field that consistently underestimated the strength of Communist forces; by a lack of basic commitment to the idea of troop withdrawals; and by steady deterioration of the South Vietnamese political situation (culminating in the coup against President Diem in November, 1963) as well as in the military picture.

Mixed motives

The pullout plan was prompted by mixed motives, the study suggests. One was a real desire by the Kennedy administration "to extricate itself from direct military involvement" in the wake of the 14-power neutralization of Laos, signed in mid-1962, and in a period in which Soviet activities on Cuba and in Berlin dominated world headlines. Another was a strong desire to make it clear to President Diem in Saigon that the war was one the Vietnamese themselves had to win.

In other words, the plan was in part "a bargain counter with the GVN," the study says.

Again, the proposed pullout could also be seen as contingency planning, covering the possibility that the U.S. might be forced to withdraw.

And again, it was a planning technique to try and head off demands within the American Government for more and more buildups—as well as to try and counter domestic and international criticism of overall American policy.

Faulty reporting

The Pentagon study goes on to fault the plan on all counts.

While it may have "frightened" the Saigon government, it did not induce Diem to overhaul the South Vietnamese political apparatus; nor did it spur the South Vietnamese armed forces to fight harder.

It did not contain a really deep commitment to the concept of withdrawal; and based as it was on faulty reporting from the field — reporting "that cannot be explained away" — it was inadequate on other grounds as well.

It failed to give the U.S. any other contingency plans than what would ap-

Why Monitor publishes Pentagon papers

Editorial page

pear as "precipitous withdrawal"; and in the end, it may have only compounded the government's credibility gap.

Existence of the phase-out plan was carefully hinted in a public statement from the White House on Oct. 2, 1963, in which Defense Secretary Robert S. McNamara and Gen. Maxwell D. Taylor, back from a visit to Vietnam, said "the major part of the U.S. military task can be completed by the end of 1965. . . . " But the statement was also larded with restatements of the basic American commitment to "deny this country to communism. . . . "

Nor was the pullout plan wholly consistent with strong public statements being made by President Kennedy, among others. Mr. Kennedy said the U.S. was "not going to withdraw" from Vietnam (July 17, 1963); "I believe [the domino theory]; I think that the struggle is close enough. China is so large, looms up high just beyond the frontiers, that if South Vietnam went, it would not only give them an improved geographic position for a guerrilla assault on Malaya, but would also give the impression that the wave of the future in Southeast Asia was China and the Communists" (Sept. 9, 1963).

Comments the study: "One could argue that such an unequivocally strong statement of strategic importance would not be consistent with any sort of phase-out proposal short of a clear-cut victory over the Communists . . . these statements tended to reduce U.S. bargaining power because of the explicit and vital nature of the commitment."

Weaknesses scored

The study comes down hard on serious weaknesses in intelligence reporting. It quotes a report by Mr. McNamara to President Johnson after a Vietnam scouting expedition in December, 1963, which it says was "laden with gloom."

Following an extended period of optimistic intelligence reports, despite the assassination of President Diem on Nov. 1, 1963, and the Buddhist crisis which immediately preceded it in South Vietnam, Mr. McNamara said bluntly:

"The situation is very disturbing. Current trends, unless reversed in the next two-to-three months, will lead to neutralization at best and more likely to a Communist-controlled state." He said the "new government" [whose strongman was Gen. Duong Van (Big) Minh] was indecisive and drifting" and was "the greatest source of concern."

He criticized the senior council of officials at the American Embassy in Saigon (the "Country Team"). He said it "lacks leadership, and has been poorly informed."

McNamara conclusion

(Henry Cabot Lodge took over as Ambassador from Frederick E. Notling Jr. on Aug. 26.)

Mr. McNamara continued: "Vietcong progress has been great in the period since the coup, with my best guess being that the situation has in fact been deteriorating in the countryside since July to a far greater extent than we realize because of our undue dependence on distorted Vietnamese reporting."

His conclusion from this was not to send in more American troops: at the same time, he did not talk about more withdrawals. His suggestion was to hold the line — to improve "independent, U.S." intelligence reporting, but not to substantially increase U.S. resources.

Yet in his final paragraph, the Secretary admitted that his own estimate "may be overly pessimistic," since Ambassador Lodge, the commander of the Military Assistance Command, and General Minh were not discouraged, and looked for significant improvements in January, 1964.

Saigon assessments

Before the Secretary's report, assessments from Saigon had maintained that the South Vietnamese forces were improving, and that the Communist troops were having a hard time. One exception was an estimate by the State Department's Bureau of Intelligence and Research, on Oct. 22, 1963. The estimate showed a steady decline in the military balance over the preceding three months. It was greeted by a "storm of disagreement" within the government, the study says, and "in the end was disregarded"—only to be confirmed by Mr. McNamara himself a few weeks later.

So great was the pressure from Pentagon brass that Secretary of State Dean Rusk wrote Mr. McNamara a note on Nov. 8, 1963, which the study says amounted to an apology for not clearing the estimate through the Penatgon first.

Pentagon hassle

Similarly, battle was waged inside the Pentagon between the Joint Chiefs of Staff and the military mission in Saigon on the one hand, and the office of the Secretary of Defense and the International Security Affairs branch on the other. The first group wanted to spend more on military assistance and withdraw at a slower rate; the latter group wanted to spend less and withdraw faster.

★ Please turn to Page 5

Beyond the court ruling . . .

Data may refocus U.S. Viet policy

By Courtney R. Sheldon
Staff correspondent of The Christian Science Monitor

Washington

The Nixon administration is almost certain to be uncomfortably on the defensive whether it wins or loses its historic battle with the news media in the Supreme Court.

The revelations thus far of the Pentagon secret papers raise leviathan moral questions on the origins of the Vietnam war.

They could critically impair the ability of President Nixon to resist pressures to speed up his paced withdrawal from Vietnam.

While the Supreme Court took more time on June 28 for a careful assessment of the rights and responsibilities of the press under the Constitution, it was apparent that:

- Any curb by the Supreme Court on further publication of the Vietnam war papers could heighten public suspicions that the full truth is being concealed.
- A decision in favor of the newspapers could result in disclosure of more government papers which link Mr. Nixon—the vice-president under President Eisenhower, from 1952 to 1960 and a pronounced hawk at the time—with the actions of his predecessors.
- Any decision of the Supreme Court will not erase the severe mutual distrust between the news media profession and Nixon officials.

On the right of newspapers under the Constitution to publish what they wish, without prior restraint, there is almost complete unanimity among the conservatives, moderates, and radicals in the profession.

Just what Mr. Nixon will do to try to unite the country after the court ruling is not clear. He has not held a press conference in a month. He could address the nation and restate or modify priorities in Southeast Asia.

The target of war critics now is likely to be Mr. Nixon's announced intention of keeping a residual force indefinitely in Vietnam, or until the prisoners of war are released by North Vietnam.

Writing in the July issue of Foreign Affairs, retired Gen. Matthew B. Ridgway concluded:

"So long as we retain a residual force there, if only to provide logistical support for the South Vietnamese Army, our men will be mortared, shelled or otherwise attacked; and that so long as they are attacked they will counterattack with fire and movement, and the war will drag on, not end."

Ball observations

George W. Ball, undersecretary of state under Presidents Kennedy and Johnson, observed on CBS TV:

"I would say on the whole that I think the government is pulling out of Vietnam. I would hope they'll do it with an accelerated tempo . . . because it seems to me that there's been a full signal to the administration now that they haven't got a great deal more time to get American troops out of this situation without a real blowup in the United States."

Mr. Ball was among the very few who argued against escalation of the war from the start.

★ Please turn to Page 3

U.S. Supreme Court:

Parochiaid disallowed

A nearly unanimous United States Supreme Court has ruled unconstitutional almost any form of direct state aid to parochial schools or their teachers. With Associate Justice Byron R. White casting a partial dissent, the justices voided state-aid programs in Pennsylvania and Rhode Island.

Special to The Christian Science Monitor

Washington

The reasons used by Chief Justice Warren E. Burger in the 20-page parochiad opinion were so broad it appeared states would have a possible insurmountable task of justifying in court the payment of public funds to finance private education in parochial schools.

While acting against state programs, the court found—by a 5-4 vote—that there is no constitutional objection to the 1963 federal program of grants for constructing college buildings even for sectarian colleges.

The key to the court's decision appears to be the differences the justices see between schools below the college level, and colleges and universities.

In each case the court said its decision turned on whether a program of public aid would involve the government too deeply in supervising the operation of church-related institutions to make sure no public funds were used to teach religion.

Religious domination

Dealing with state-aid programs in Pennsylvania and Rhode Island, the court said the character of parochial schools below the college level was so completely dominated by religious authority that the states continually would have to check up on teachers to make sure religion was not seeping into secular-subject classrooms.

"The substantial religious character of these church-related schools gives rise to entangling church-state relationships of the kind the religion clauses (of the Constitution) sought to avoid," Chief Justice Burger declared.

Even though teachers in private schools would not consciously let religion come into their teaching of nonreligion subjects, the court declared, they would find it hard to make a "total separation between secular teaching and religious doctrine."

The Rhode Island program, which the court nullified over the lone dissent of Justice White, involved state payment of up to 15 percent of a private-school teacher's salary, provided the teacher taught secular subjects.

★ Please turn to Page 2

Where to look

Inside today

Eyewitness describes East Pakistan's plight

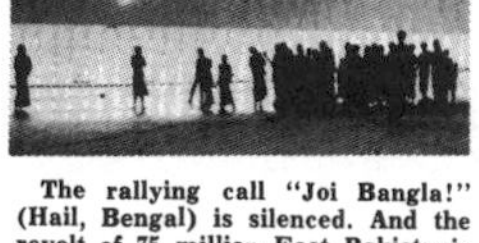

The rallying call "Joi Bangla!" (Hail, Bengal) is silenced. And the revolt of 75 million East Pakistanis is crushed. An eyewitness tells of Bengali hopes and disappointments.

First page, second section

NASA finds sincerity in Soviet space talks

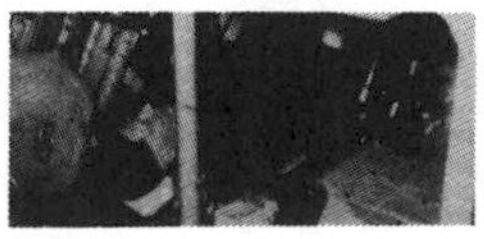

All signs are "go" for more Soviet-American exchanges of data aimed at implementing the two countries' agreement to cooperate in outer space. Experts are working out details of linking up U.S. and Russian craft in orbit.

Story: Page 3

June 29, 1971

Ellsberg surrenders, says he passed Pentagon papers

By Robin Wright
Staff writer of The Christian Science Monitor

Boston

Surrounded by the loud and visible support of antiwar demonstrators, Dr. Daniel Ellsberg turned himself in to the U.S. Attorney's office here Monday morning, June 28, just as his lawyers had announced he would two days earlier.

Upon his surrender, Dr. Ellsberg openly admitted to the press and about 150 spectators that he had indeed provided the New York Times with the top-secret Pentagon study of the Vietnam war.

He also acknowledged that his actions were "solely on his own initiative and clearly against all U.S. security regulations.

"I am prepared for all the consequences," he added.

Dr. Ellsberg, pale but calm, also claimed that "I turned over all the information contained in the Pentagon papers to the chairman [Sen. J. W. Fulbright] of the Senate Foreign Relations Committee during the fall of 1969."

Release obtained

After arraignment, he was released on $50,000 bail, without security.

Because the Senate took no action and two U.S. invasions subsequently went even deeper into Indo-China, Dr. Ellsberg said, "I can only regret that I did not release the papers to the newspapers sooner."

★ Please turn to Page 2

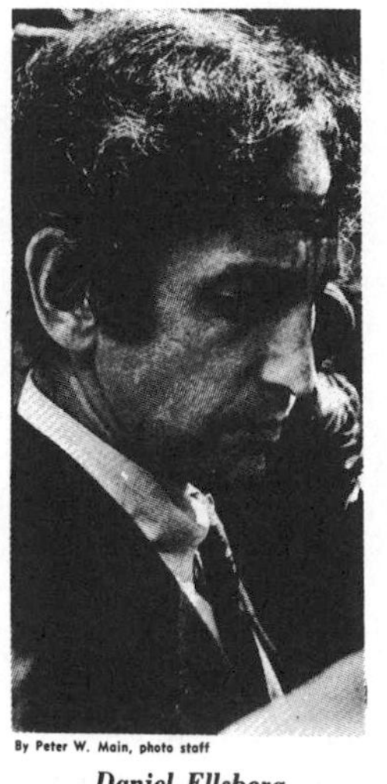

By Peter W. Main, photo staff

Daniel Ellsberg
"**. . . prepared for all consequences**"

COPYRIGHT © 1971 THE CHRISTIAN SCIENCE PUBLISHING SOCIETY
All rights reserved

THE CHRISTIAN SCIENCE MONITOR

BOSTON, FRIDAY, NOVEMBER 12, 1971 — *An International Daily Newspaper* — VOL. 63, NO. 294 TWO SECTIONS — EASTERN EDITION ★ 15c

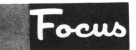

Focus

Russia's No. 1 tries harder

By Charlotte Saikowski

Moscow

"He's becoming another Khrushchev," blurted out a Russian jestingly.

No Soviet would seriously compare Leonid I. Brezhnev to the late flamboyant Kremlin leader. But people are aware that the party general secretary is receiving a public exposure here unparalleled since Khrushchev times.

The process of building up Mr. Brezhnev's image began to take clear shape at the 24th party congress last spring and so far has reached its most massive proportions in the publicity given to his recent trip to France.

Almost two weeks after that journey, which was treated here as the most significant event going on in the world at the time, Soviet news media still are profusely talking about it as occupying the "center of attention of the world public."

This week Moscow television showed a slick, hour-long documentary film about the trip which, in addition to dramatizing Moscow's vigorous European diplomacy, highlighted Mr. Brezhnev's new role as the nation's leading statesman. One effect of the film was to give Russians the impression that Mr. Brezhnev received an overwhelmingly warm welcome in France (which was not the case).

Dignity a la Russe

At the same time the documentary seemed aimed at assuring Russians, who never approved of Khrushchev's colorful antics, that Mr. Brezhnev does not play the back-slapping clown abroad but is a dignified, restrained, and fitting representative of the Soviet state.

The thick-set Politburo member was shown riding down the Champs Elysée in an open car, being enthusiastically greeted by Frenchmen, chatting genially with President Pompidou, standing alongside Mrs. Brezhnev in a reception line, talking with workers at a Renault factory, and walking down elegant, tapestry-lined corridors with dignity and self-confidence. Russians would have noticed, too, that Mr. Brezhnev looked quite dapper in his well-tailored suits and that the film was occasionally touched up to remove some of the paunchiness from his face.

Also this week, the Soviet illustrated weekly Ogonyok carries a two-page spread of the Paris visit and another page on Mr. Brezhnev's trip to East Germany. By contrast, recent travelers Premier Alexei N. Kosygin and President Podgorny have received far less public attention.

No new 'cult' seen

Though all the publicity has added a new dimension to Mr. Brezhnev's ascendancy, it has by no means reached Khrushchevian scope, and Western political observers here do not see in it the rise of a new "cult of personality." Noting that the locus of Soviet political power is in the head of the Communist Party, they deem it natural that after so many years of rather faceless collective leadership Mr. Brezhnev should have consolidated his power and emerged as the dominant figure of the collective.

It is also thought that the clear designation of one man as the top political ruler facilitates the pursuit of foreign-policy objectives. Mr. Brezhnev has, for instance, through his intimate talks with Chancellor Willy Brandt and President Pompidou, managed to secure a 1972 timetable for the much-sought-after European conference.

Some observers abroad have suggested that Mr. Brezhnev may make a bid to assume the Soviet premiership as well. Such a move is viewed unlikely by diplomatic analysts here, given the emphasis in recent party histories on the separation of the jobs of party general secretary and premier.

Where to look

News — briefly	2	Movie guide	15
Arts	12, 15	Real estate	10, 11
Business	4, 5	Sports	13
Editorials	16	Living	14

Coming soon

Editor goes from bylines to goal lines

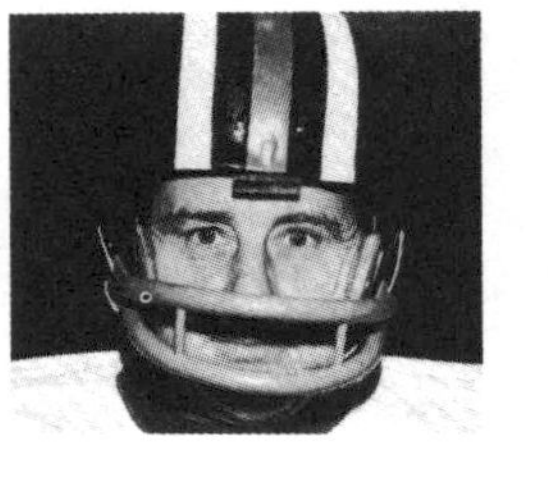

Move over George Plimpton, you've got company! The Marlboro Shamrocks, No. 2 team in the Eastern Professional Football League, are putting in a few plays Sunday for Sports Editor Phil Elderkin. His story will appear Wednesday.

Of course, this shouldn't surprise our regular readers, who are already aware of Elderkin's previous ventures into the sports world—playing basketball with the Harlem Magicians, driving in a stock race, skating in the Roller Derby, and taking the parachute-jumping course at Orange, Mass.

'Friendship for U.S. people . . .'

Chinese step into new UN era

By David Winder

Staff correspondent of The Christian Science Monitor

New York

After 22 years of exclusion from the United Nations the official delegation of the People's Republic of China made a triumphant entry into the United States on a raw and gusty Thursday afternoon.

It was not that the Chinese played to the crowd or uttered any dramatic statements that made this such a momentous event.

They were in fact relatively subdued both in their remarks and in their dress, predominantly drab gray and black topcoats and upturned peaked Mao caps. Two women members were also somberly dressed.

It was the pent-up excitement at the airport that history was in the making and that the arrival of the Chinese delegation was the final act of the Communist fight for international recognition which began in the 1949 revolution that gave this occasion such drama.

The response was extraordinary.

Hundreds of Chinese appeared from nowhere and with large Mao placards and dazzling red flags and welcoming signs.

The press were lined several feet deep and stacked up on two white mobile passenger ramps and two baggage trailers.

After the diplomats' welcome, the tall, rather stooped figure of the chairman of the delegation, Chiao Kuan-hua, in a gray topcoat and red muffler, walked up to the microphone.

Above the airport noise an unintelligible flow of Chinese followed. Then a Chinese woman said ever so softly the word everyone was waiting for:

"It is a pleasure today for the delegation of the Government of the People's Republic of China to come to New York to attend the 26th session of the General Assembly of the United Nations."

For the rest of the speech, just a brief 224 words, Mr. Chiao, Vice-Foreign Minister and close confidant of Prime Minister Chou En-lai, stressed the peaceful character of the Chinese Government.

There was no applause. The delegation melted into the awaiting limousines, and the thick wall of pressmen burst like a dam as correspondents from all over the world scattered to tell the world that a new chapter in international history had begun.

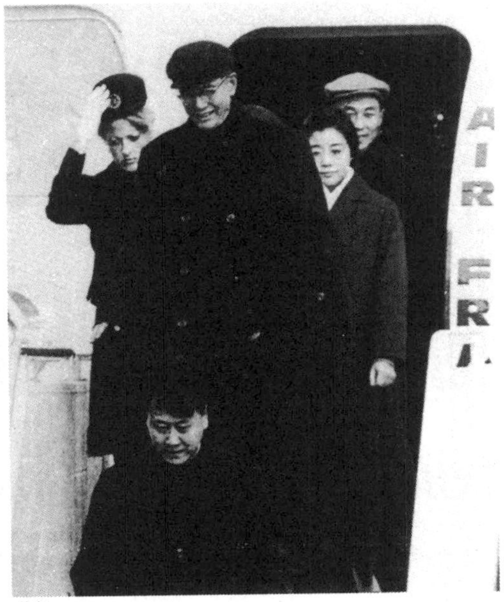

AP photo

Peking's moment of triumph

Chiao Kuan-hua (top of ramp) leads delegation off plane at New York

Europe-U.S. money men lock horns

By Richard A. Nenneman

Business and financial editor of The Christian Science Monitor

Washington

There is a European view here regarding the international monetary and trade impasse that diverges sharply from the widely held American one.

Americans have been optimistic that the mere fact of the overwhelming size of their economy and the attractiveness of their consumer market would help them get most of what the United States seeks in the way of new exchange-rate parities and reductions in trade and investment barriers.

But Europeans are rankled by the manner of the Aug. 15 actions and the follow-up demands. The sad possibility exists that Europe (along with Japan) will not cooperate in the kind of settlement the U.S. desires.

Fencing over the yen
Story: Page 6

Reacting sharply to the Japanese "cave-in" on the textile-quota agreement, one European official noted that "being conciliatory to the United States is perhaps not a very productive way to deal with it currently."

Thus, at the coming finance ministers' meeting in Rome, the issues may not be whether the United States sufficiently impresses others with the seriousness of its position. It may be, instead, he said, whether the other powers can—despite their inability to present a positive common response — get across the message that they are unable to deliver what the U.S. wants.

Said this same official, "The U.S. has no message to deliver in Rome; it has already been delivered." This was in reference to the specific details the U.S. has made in recent weeks regarding the changes it desires over and above new exchange-rate parities.

Changes outlined

These changes revolve largely around three areas:

- An easing of the Common Market's protectionist agricultural policy.
- Greater access to European markets for Japanese goods.
- Easier access by the U.S. to Japanese markets, including more direct investment.

The first two of these changes involve not just one nation but the entire Common Market area. And, said this European, "There isn't a chance in the world of [U.S. Treasury Secretary John B.] Connally getting a major change in either case from a single one of the [proposed] Ten in Europe, let alone from all of them, within the time frame he has in mind."

★ **Please turn to Page 6**

Labor's Phase 2 strategy

By Ed Townsend

Labor correspondent of The Christian Science Monitor

New York

Coming up as U.S. labor develops its opposition to the wage guidelines of Phase 2:

- A strengthening of leaders' hands in key conventions in Detroit on Saturday, Nov. 13, and in Miami next week, through blustering anger and implied threats from rank-and-file delegates under the glare of extensive TV and newspaper coverage, culminating in resolutions mandating leaders to take whatever action leaders think necessary.
- A cool political decision by labor leaders to stay inside the Pay Board machinery for the moment — though not foreclosing the option of walking out at a later date.

Walkout doubtful

Labor members will walk out only if further Pay Board majority actions provide the circumstances for a dramatic withdrawal that would not set off a strongly adverse public reaction.

Political considerations are critical to labor strategy in Phase 2. The leadership suspects that the White House would not mind, politically, a labor walkout that would lay labor open to criticism if the controls program fails, or prevent labor receiving credit if the program succeeds.

If they are convinced of that, labor members will stick fast.

George Meany, president of the AFL-CIO and leading labor member of the Pay Board, is the sharpest critic of new controls policies that, he says, "will create widespread economic instability" and that "abrogate legal collective bargaining agreements involving millions of American wage-earners."

Mr. Meany will make a full report on "the decisions and the conduct" of Pay Board sessions during the AFL-CIO's biennial convention in Bal Harbour, Fla., opening Nov. 17.

That session and a United Auto Workers convention in Detroit this Saturday will give labor's Pay Board members a strong mandate to do whatever they consider necessary to protect the interests of American workers in Phase 2—even if it means walking out.

[The Cost of Living Council has announced general guidelines for government controls in the post-freeze period, which begins Monday. Detailed, legally binding regulations are still being drafted.

★ **Please turn to Page 2**

U.S. warned on use of drug to fight heroin

By William C. Selover

Staff correspondent of The Christian Science Monitor

Washington

Now that the Nixon administration is moving toward full endorsement of methadone as a "safe and effective" drug "for combating heroin addiction," caution lights are blinking all over Washington.

Officials are warning against regarding the synthetic, addictive chemical as a cure-all for drug addicts.

But they are also rejecting the exaggerated fears that have been circulating over use of the drug when administered in proper and controlled dosages.

Dr. Jerome H. Jaffe, director of the President's Special Action Office for Drug Abuse Prevention, asserts that methadone "has no more inherent danger than other drugs when they are abused or improperly administered."

On Nov. 8, Dr. Charles C. Edwards, head of the Food and Drug Administration, indicated to a House commerce subcommittee that it appears that "the time has come" to take methadone out of the "experimental" classification and approve it for general use.

He told the subcommittee that currently there are some 380 methadone-maintenance clinics in the nation, with new sponsors filing applications at the rate of one a day.

The Bureau of Narcotics and Dangerous Drugs, until now opposed to the reclassification, backs the new move. "We are willing to accept the fact that the granting of [reclassification] for methadone maintenance is medically justified."

The FDA predicts, however, that with the change of classification for methadone, the regulations regarding its use and distribution will be considerably tightened.

★ **Please turn to Page 2**

Thin line greets Castro

A rustling in the Chilean crowd

By James Nelson Goodsell

Latin America correspondent of The Christian Science Monitor

Santiago, Chile

It had all the trappings of a gala occasion.

There was Cuban Premier Fidel Castro taking his first trip out of his island nation in seven years embracing his old friend, Chilean President Salvador Allende Gossens, on the tarmac of Santiago's modernistic Pudahuel International Airport.

The Cuban leader, nattily dressed in a new fatigue uniform very much in keeping with his style, provided a sharp contrast with the Chilean President, who was dressed more conservatively in a suit and appeared very much the typical Chilean. The Cuban Premier, apparently as a concession to the formality of the occasion, was not wearing his gun holster.

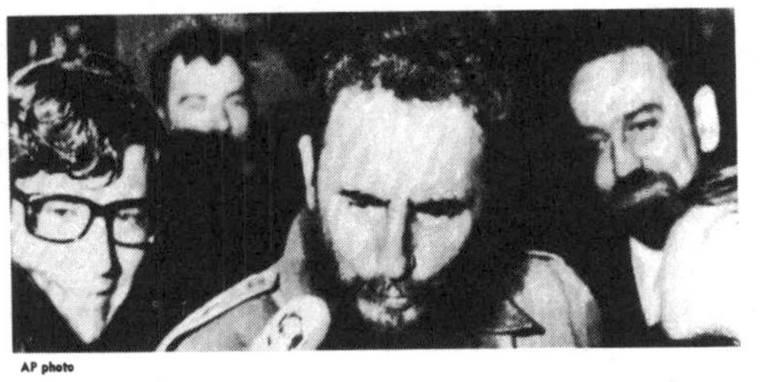

AP photo

Cuban Premier Castro greets citizens in Chile

Orderliness observed

Behind the two leaders as they embraced was the sleek Ilyushin jetliner, belonging to the Soviet airline, Aeroflot, from which Dr. Castro had just emerged. Before them were thousands of Chileans, perhaps as many as 5,000, trucked and bussed out to Pudahuel from Santiago.

The whole affair was orderly in Chilean fashion. In fact, the faithful on hand, largely representing Chile's organized and disciplined Communist Party, seemed almost more subdued than the occasion warranted.

Before the motorcade reached points en route, hundreds of Chileans lining the streets no more than one deep chatted and maintained a degree of order unique for Latin America. And as soon as the official car carrying the two leaders passed, the crowds quickly began to disperse.

In some measure, the subdued reaction was in keeping with Chilean tradition. It may also represent something of the hostility and reservations felt by many Chileans toward the visit. There were certainly fewer people on hand to greet the Cuban leader than had been expected. What this portends for the rest of Dr. Castro's voyage of discovery up and down the length of this Pacific Coast nation is difficult to assess.

He goes from here Friday to Antofagasta and the copper mine of Chuquicamata.

Dr. Castro will also visit Concepción, a southern Chilean city with strong leftist tendencies and a center of the Movimiento Izquierda Revolucionario, a far-leftist group that has also been causing Dr. Allende difficulties. The pair also go to Punta Arenas, at the tip of Chile close to the Antarctica, an area that returned Dr. Allende to office as senator a number of times.

★ **Please turn to Page 3**

COPYRIGHT © 1971 THE CHRISTIAN SCIENCE PUBLISHING SOCIETY
All rights reserved

THE CHRISTIAN SCIENCE MONITOR

BOSTON, SATURDAY, MAY 27, 1972 — *An International Daily Newspaper* — VOL. 64, NO. 155 TWO SECTIONS — EASTERN EDITION ★ 15c

Pattern of diplomacy

Winding down the cold war

By Joseph C. Harsch

President Nixon finally achieved in Moscow over the past week what his last three predecessors in the White House much wanted, and failed to get. He got to Moscow and swept aside the "cold war" pattern in Soviet-American relations.

Dwight Eisenhower wanted to go to Moscow. He never believed that the great estrangement between his country and Soviet Russia was necessary, desirable, or permanent. To the end of his eight-year presidency he greatly hoped, and always sought, a chance to go to Moscow himself and nail down by his presence there an end to the condition called the "cold war."

John F. Kennedy was less hopeful of a reconciliation and never had a real chance to approach such a project seriously. Nikita Khrushchev's adventurism got in the way. But President Kennedy would, had the times permitted, done what Mr. Nixon has just done.

Johnson's bags were packed

Lyndon Johnson dreamed seriously of the step and kept his bags packed for Moscow up to the end of his days in the White House. He much hoped to be able to go during the final days after he ended the bombing of North Vietnam. But the Russians were not interested in any visits of a "lame duck" president. They preferred to wait for the winner, Richard Nixon.

The ingredients for this trip were well understood in higher Washington levels over the whole span of those previous three presidencies. Mr. Eisenhower wanted to end the estrangement with China, well knowing that this was the necessary first step to Moscow.

But not even a president with the enormous popularity of Mr. Eisenhower dared during the '50's to end the breach with China. It would have been harder for a Democrat. Neither Mr. Kennedy nor Mr. Johnson considered such a step to be politically tolerable no matter how desirable from the national strategy point of view.

The fact is that deep currents of popular emotion through three presidencies prevented what Mr. Nixon has now been able to do. He could end the breach with China. He proved it by doing it. And this in turn gave him the leverage in Moscow which not only opened the doors but also gave him a respectable, indeed a strong, bargaining position.

To have gone to Moscow while still estranged from China would have been—foolish. The American position had no leverage while it was refusing to speak to China and also fighting in Vietnam. The men in Moscow could be careless about Washington while the bulk of American military power was deployed in Asia against China.

Position strong

The Peking trip made all the difference. It advertised the fact that the United States had room for maneuver in world affairs and could, should that become necessary, form a closer relationship with China while remaining an ally of Western Europe. Moscow faced the dreadful possibility of being truly isolated and encircled. It had no choice but to come to terms with Mr. Nixon.

The Russians' interest in receiving Mr. Nixon, and in doing all the business they possibly could with him, dates from the moment of the announcement of the Peking trip. In Moscow there was a long pause for reflection. When the debate behind the great walls of the Kremlin ended—its doors were open to Mr. Nixon. He went, in the best bargaining position any American president has enjoyed since the triumphant end of World War II.

And that moment was wasted because it came during the sudden transfer of power from Franklin Roosevelt to Harry Truman. By the time Mr. Truman learned what it was all about it was too late to take full advantage of the opportunity.

We will get the detailed measurements of the Moscow visit later. The most accurate measurement will be what happens next about Vietnam. It may be some time before that is apparent.

Inside today

The Christian Science Monitor will not be published on May 29, a legal holiday in the United States.

Historic pact limits A-missiles

U.S.-Soviet arms curb signed

By Courtney R. Sheldon
Staff correspondent of The Christian Science Monitor

Moscow

The United States and the U.S.S.R. have clamped a lid on their nuclear-missile arsenals, dramatically symbolizing their determination to live in peace.

President Nixon and General Secretary Leonid I. Brezhnev have agreed on a rough parity of offensive and defensive missiles.

Their intention is so to stabilize the arms race that neither will be vulnerable to attack by the other.

Though follow-through agreements will be necessary to keep the arms pact desirable for both countries in the long run, the Moscow accord is historic.

It starts a trend the world could follow. It unites the two competing giant superpowers in a way which seemed impossible only a few years ago.

The Moscow summit now outshadows all post World War II big-power meetings. The nuclear-missile treaty caps a wide variety of accords.

Immediately before the signing of the nuclear-missile commitment, the summit negotiators set up a joint commission to evolve a future trade agreement. This was the best they could do after efforts to resolve differences over trade during the current meeting failed.

U.S. officials said that the commission will not be responsible for settlement of the argument over how much the Soviet Union owes the U.S. for lend-lease debts, but a "satisfactory settlement is expected" of this long-raging debate.

It is expected to be tied in with an agreement to give the Soviet Union most-favored-nation treatment which the U.S. accords most nations. Congress would have to approve this action.

While the final communiqué was awaited, the unresolved question was what if anything would be agreed to concerning the supply of arms by the big powers to Vietnam and the Middle East.

Agreements in these areas were not expected at this time and their absence in the final communiqué would not seriously affect the overall success of the summit.

At this writing, only the signing of the papers on nuclear missiles is assured. The text with the full details is not available.

Even when it is, it will require close scrutiny by arms-control experts. Initial indications are that they will generally view it favorably.

As the Helsinki negotiators drafted the missile treaty before reporting to Moscow, it was in two parts. The first is a treaty, which requires Senate approval, limiting the deployment of defensive missiles to two sites and 200 launchers in each country.

One of these in each country would defend the respective political capitals, Washington and Moscow.

The second part of the accord would be in the form of a five-year executive agreement to retain current levels of offensive missiles — 1,054 for the U.S. and 1,618 for the Soviet Union.

In submarine-launched missiles, the U.S. would have 41 submarines and 656 missile launchers while the Soviets would have ultimately 42 submarines and 650 missile launchers.

★ Please turn to Page 2

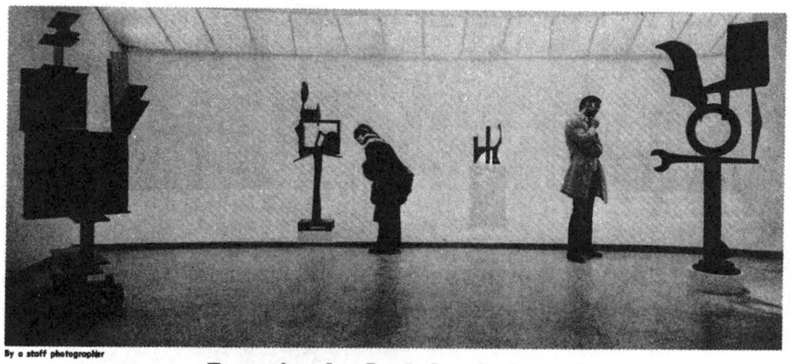

By a staff photographer

For art's sake: Look, but don't touch

Museums struggle to protect treasures

By Florence Mouckley
Staff writer of The Christian Science Monitor

Boston

A Monitor survey

How do you bring art close to the people — and still keep them at arm's length?

This is the dilemma facing museums around the country in the wake of new cases of vandalism and theft.

A Monitor survey of museum officials in the United States finds that their partial solution to the problem is to tighten security — and to rethink the whole modern, more-open approach to exhibiting art. Measures being taken by some museums include:

- Hiring more guards—some of them from professional services.
- Closer scrutiny of visitors.
- Installing sophisticated electronic equipment.
- Flooding galleries with lights, inside and out, plus parking areas.
- Erecting new barriers.
- Putting some art works behind plexiglass.
- Discouraging people from touching and handling objects.

The museums' battle against vandalism and theft was brought into sharp focus recently with the damaging of Michelangelo's sculpture of the Pietà in Rome and the theft of a Picasso, a Rembrandt, and two Gauguin paintings worth more than $1 million from the Worcester Art Museum in Massachusetts.

In question now is the whole concept of bringing art physically closer to the people.

★ Please turn to Page 2

Clashes flare on two Viet fronts

By Henry S. Hayward
Staff correspondent of The Christian Science Monitor

Saigon

Fighting has flared up on two South Vietnamese fronts. One of the flare-ups looks like the long-expected North Vietnamese assault on Kontum City.

While the tempo of conflict built up at the central-highlands city, fresh fighting also was reported 20 miles north of Hue, where a Communist regiment reportedly was beaten back from an attack that sought to skirt the My Chanh defense line.

In both instances, some observers feel the renewed Communist onslaughts are still best described as preliminary probing—rather than final all-out drives against the two cities.

Although quantities of tanks and infantry were employed in the second day of heavy fighting at Kontum on Friday, the battle had not yet taken on the proportions of an An Loc, were sharp conflict has been going on since April 7.

Thus far the opening stages of both the Kontum and Hue battles are about what was expected.

Bombing continues

Far to the north, American planes have been bombing the North Vietnamese port of Haiphong for three straight days. The objective reportedly was to isolate the key harbor city, whose waters already have been mined.

Air attacks likewise continued on North Vietnamese power plants now that most of the rail and road links are said to have been interdicted.

The scope of the Kontum battle was indicated by the total of 12 Communist tanks reported destroyed in the city and its environs. Ten were claimed by helicopters of the U.S. 1st Aviation Brigade, which are equipped with anti-tank missile systems.

Another two tanks were claimed by South Vietnamese ground troops in the Kontum area.

At this writing late Friday afternoon, more Communist tanks and troops were reported approaching the city from the north. Some of the North Vietnamese troops were said to be wearing South Vietnamese uniforms—a familiar tactic here. And some of the approaching tanks were said to be American M-41's captured from South Vietnamese units.

Kontum itself was placed under a 24-hour curfew, and late reports told of scattered North Vietnamese forces still holding on in eastern and southeastern portions of the city.

An initial thrust by North Vietnamese sappers had been turned back, although some units penetrated well into the city, and sapper remnants were still holding out south of the airfield.

Nixon plight: budget slicing or new taxes

Special to The Christian Science Monitor

Washington

A major question here now is whether in fact the Nixon administration can trim enough spending from the federal budget to avoid increasing taxes.

The White House says it can be done. Critics doubt it — and the issue is sure to play a part in the political campaigning between now and November.

Unsurprisingly in a presidential political year, the administration has rejected the notion of increasing taxes. Mr. Nixon's chief aide on domestic affairs, John D. Ehrlichman, says this is so for the "foreseeable future," though he leaves the door open for a new form of tax in place of the ailing state and local property taxes.

Three options listed

This leaves the administration with these options:

1. Ordering economies by executive order.

2. Disapproving legislation by Congress that calls for large spending.

3. Asking Congress to set a ceiling on its own spending: $246 billion.

The question now is how effective any of these options in fact can be. Mr. Ehrlichman made his latest announcements in response to a detailed book-length study by the Brookings Institution which saw no alternative to higher taxes because, it said, expenditures were now outstripping income, and new taxes would be needed even if no new federal programs were added—over and above the ones already under consideration—were approved by Congress this year.

Mr. Ehrlichman's answer, in effect, was that the study had overlooked the government's determination to economize.

★ Please turn to Page 10

Consumers to get watchdog?

By Robert P. Hey
Staff correspondent of The Christian Science Monitor

Washington

Would you like to have a powerful consumer advocate in the middle of the discussion the next time Interstate Commerce Commission officials sit down with big moving companies to discuss the way they move people like you?

Or the next time the Federal Trade Commission discusses what to do about deceptive advertising with the advertiser?

Or when the Department of Transportation and automakers argue over auto safety standards the department must set?

Loads of consumers would—and this year it appears that they might.

Consumer groups have fought to get, in effect, such a consumer ombudsman for consumers in high circles of government—and to admit him to negotiations while decisions are being made.

Now Congress appears willing to establish a broad consumer agency, able to be the consumer's ombudsman in the formal and informal dealings of government agencies that concern consumers.

After much tricky negotiation behind the scenes—not quite completed—the way seems prepared for congressional passage this year of an intensely important consumer bill. It would establish an independent consumer agency in the federal government.

★ Please turn to Page 10

Grass-roots goodwill begins to show

A few Ulster voices urge, 'End violence'

By John Allan May
Staff correspondent of The Christian Science Monitor

London

In Ulster now almost everything depends on whether goodwill at the grass roots — and a growing distaste for bombings and shootings — can break through the hard external surface of revolutionary commitment and religious and political intolerance.

Secretary of State for Northern Ireland William Whitelaw has announced the composition of the advisory commission that will advise him while direct rule of the embattled province from Westminster continues.

It comprises seven Protestants and four Roman Catholics. None of the main political leaders of the various parties and factions is included, although one Catholic, Tom Conaty, is chairman of the Catholic Central Citizens Defense Committee.

Sir Robin Kinaban, a former Unionist member of Parliament at Westminster and a former Lord Mayor of Belfast, also is included.

Other members are an economist, a farmer, a head teacher, two lawyers, two businessmen, a leading figure in local government, and a trade unionist.

As a grass-roots commission, it reflects the growing desire within both religious communities for peace, reform, and reconciliation.

A peace committee of five women from Catholic Londonderry has been talking to both the wings of the illegal Irish Republican Army and also to Mr. Whitelaw, arguing for a cease-fire.

These are very brave women. Members of the "provisional" IRA have tarred, feathered, and beaten girls suspected of opposition to the campaign of violence. They have also shot men and boys who oppose them.

Hundreds of signatures have been obtained in various churches with the aid of the Catholic clergy to a petition for peace. There is talk of a referendum in the Creggan and Bogside estates. On the Creggan a 16-man peace committee is organizing a ballot.

More and more priests also are speaking out against a type of violence which has been becoming more and more horrific.

As condemnation of the militants by the church grows, so also the split between them and the elected political leaders of the Catholic and republican community widens.

All this is encouraging. However, support for militancy on both sides, Protestant as well as Catholic, continues and is being deliberately fanned by those who still put their faith in a complete military victory.

COPYRIGHT © 1972 THE CHRISTIAN SCIENCE PUBLISHING SOCIETY
All rights reserved

THE CHRISTIAN SCIENCE MONITOR

BOSTON, THURSDAY, SEPTEMBER 7, 1972 | *An International Daily Newspaper* | VOL. 64, NO. 240 TWO SECTIONS | EASTERN EDITION ★ 15c

Olympic shock waves rock Middle East– dim recently rising prospects for peace

Sadat initiative: first casualty?

By John K. Cooley
Staff correspondent of The Christian Science Monitor

Beirut, Lebanon

The shock waves of the Munich Olympics tragedy are likely to rock the Middle East for some time and severely set back any early prospects for Arab-Israeli peace, observers here believe .

Repercussions are likely to extend beyond any immediate threat of Israeli military reprisals against Arab countries where Palestinian guerrillas are quartered, expressed Sept. 6 in Israeli newspapers and broadcasts calling for a war to eliminate the guerrillas.

Egyptian President Sadat's hopes of developing a Middle East peace initiative by enlisting Western European support may be one of the first and most severe political casualties of Munich.

Arab diplomats are speculating that the proposed West German tour of Egyptian Foreign Minister Mourad Ghaleb and any hopes of Mr. Sadat to attend the coming UN General Assembly session in New York now are canceled because of the depth and breadth of anti-Arab feeling aroused in the West.

King comments

"The Black September terrorists," said one Lebanese professional man bitterly, "have caused the Arabs to lose all the good will and sympathy they had begun to gain in one fell swoop. It means that peace is again blocked for who knows how long."

The earliest official top-level Arab reaction to the Olympics attack, before the killing of the 11 Israeli hostages was known, came from King Hussein of Jordan. He termed it a "savage, uncivilized act," the "Work of sick minds," similar terms to those he employed for the massacre of civilians at Tel Aviv airport by Japanese gunmen working for Palestinian guerrillas last May 30.

★Please turn to Page 6

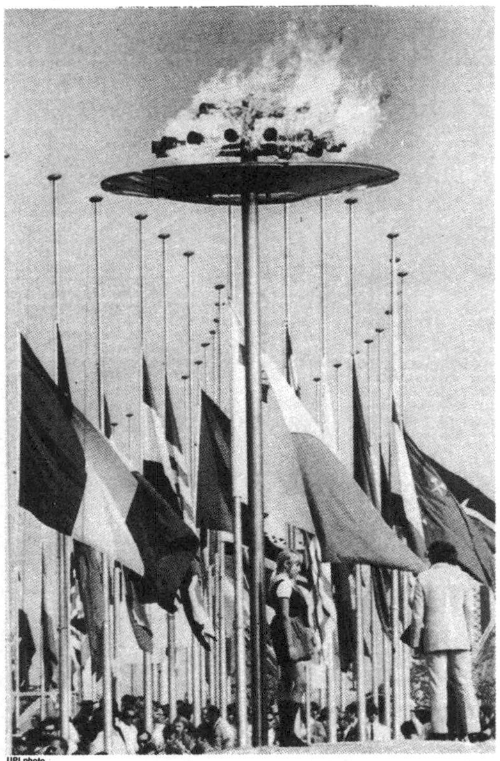

UPI photo

Olympic flags at half-staff for Israeli athletes

Israel ponders twofold reaction

By Francis Ofner
Special correspondent of The Christian Science Monitor

Tel Aviv, Israel

The Israeli Government's response to what happened in Munich is expected to be on two levels.

The first is diplomatic, the second, military.

On the diplomatic level the government will probably try to translate the sympathy received from abroad into practical measures.

"However," a senior official remarked, "all the sympathy in the world cannot console us over the loss of our people. Therefore we want to urge all governments with which we maintain relations to take such measures as will make future terror attacks more difficult."

An example of heightened diplomatic activity was seen in the fact that Foreign Minister Abba Eban brought along the director general of his ministry, Mordechai Gazit, to Wednesday's Cabinet meeting. It can also be assumed that the government will intensify its security measures for the protection of Israelis abroad. On this subject, however, the Israelis prefer not to disclose details.

Now for the military level. In general, Israelis are opposed to a merely defensive strategy. Therefore it is believed by some observers here that Israel will take hard-hitting action against the "Black September" organization and those who help or protect that group, which has accepted responsibility for the Munich killings.

Israel was deeply disappointed by the attitude of most Arab governments to West German Chancellor Willy Brandt's request to exert influence on the terrorists. A particularly serious view is taken here of the reply the Egyptian Prime Minister gave Mr. Brandt.

Israelis here have also pointed to the insensitivity of some Arab states toward the value of human life. An Israeli official recalled that this went so far that the Syrian Radio in its reports about Munich referred to the guerrillas as "martyrs." One Israeli official called King Hussein of Jordan "a laudable exception" because he had publicly condemned the Munich action.

Committee criticized

Israelis have also been dismayed by the original attitude of the International Olympic Committee. They ask why it had to take 12 hours before it became clear to the committee that the games could not go on as scheduled as long as some of the participating sportsmen were threatened with death.

In a first comment on the events of Munich, the Jerusalem Post wrote: "The terror movement has found itself forced to abandon its original purpose, namely, direct murder and sabotage, mainly because the Arabs – or Palestinians – in the areas have not been willing to continue a war in which they themselves were the worst sufferers.

★Please turn to Page 6

In shock and sorrow Olympic Games resume

Report from Munich: Page 2

Munich tragedy jolts Brandt election hopes

By David R. Francis
Staff correspondent of The Christian Science Monitor

Bonn

The tragedy at the Olympic Games is the last of a series of incidents that observers here believe could tip the scales against Chancellor Willy Brandt in the expected general election later this year.

Mr. Brandt's government had hoped that a happy and successful Olympic Games would be a feather in the cap of his government. That hope has been shattered.

What happened at the Olympics has prompted some to say that the tragic events of this week will strengthen those in Germany who advocate law and order.

The party most identified with law and order is the opposition party, the Christian Democratic Union. It holds about 50 percent of the seats in the German Bundestag, the lower house of Parliament.

Mr. Brandt's Social Democratic Party and its partners in the governing coalition, the Free Domocrats, hold the other half of the seats.

In hopes of winning a clear majority, Mr. Brandt has indicated he will call an election in late fall.

So far the opposition has not criticized the government's management of the Palestinian terrorist affair. Because the Bavarian government is a Christian Social Union government and the states in Germany are in charge of the police, it will be difficult for the opposition to attack the federal government on this score.

Public shocked by news

The morning after the tragedy the Bonn newspaper General Anzeiger said, "The world sorrows. Israeli hostages are dead."

It was a special edition handed out free in the streets of this capital city as its shocked citizens went to work.

The tragedy occurred too late for most early-sleeping Germans to have heard the news Tuesday night. They stood before the train station here with glum faces, reading the single page. The atmosphere was heavy.

"It is very bad," said a taxi driver. "But that it should happen in Germany is worse." After the first shock, the politicians here began wondering about the impact of the massacre on Germany's coming election.

"The government couldn't have done any more," said one young man, Volker Vormat. "It offered money. The Arabs refused.

"The former Mayor of Munich and the police chief there offered themselves as substitutes for the hostages," he continued. "But that was refused, too.

"The Israelis wouldn't give into the Arab demand that they free 200 terrorists. So what could the German Government do?"

'A black day'

An economist with the Commerzbank in Frankfurt, Herbert Wolf, commented: "It is a black day for all mankind and especially for the Germans. It evokes so much of the experience which we had during the Nazi Reich."

★Please turn to Page 6

Focus

'What's in a name?'

By Takashi Oka

Paris

Which means more to an adopted child, the love of his parents or the bearing of a "ridiculous" surname? The plight of Mr. and Mrs. Gerard Trognon, who have adopted a three-year-old boy and wish to give him their surname, has roused public indignation against a judge who has found them qualified in every way to be the boy's parents, except for the fact that their surname means "core" (as of an apple), "stump" (as of a cabbage), and hence, in general, a term of endearment for someone who is tiny.

Philippe B. came to the Trognons from a public orphanage in 1970, when he was a baby. Mr. Trognon works for Aerospatiale, the French national company associated with the British in producing the Concorde supersonic plane.

Mrs. Trognon is an adult-education worker. The couple live in the pleasant little suburban town of Mee-sur-Seine. They had to undergo a long, laborious process of examinations and submissions of documents before the local council of wards of the state authorized them to take in – at first for six months only – little Philippe.

Delighted, the Trognons gave Philippe his own room, filled with teddy bears and other fluffy animals, and lavished on him all their parental affection. On Feb. 26 this year, they were finally authorized to permanently adopt Philippe.

'One last formality'

One last formality remained. The couple applied to the civil court of Melun to have Philippe's surname legally changed to Trognon. The state prospecutor of Melun supported their plea.

But the judge thought otherwise. He did not doubt that "morally and materially, the full adoption of Phillipe B. by the couple Trognon would be in the child's interest."

Nevertheless, the judge continued, changing the child's surname to the "ridiculous name of Trognon" would certainly be to his disadvantage.

Thunderstruck, the parents appealed to the court of appeals in Paris and fired off letters expressing indignation to President Pompidou and to Marie-Madeleine Dienesch, Secretary of State for Public Health and Social Affairs. The mass-circulation daily France-Soir and the weeklies Express and Le Nouvel Observateur took up the Trognons' cause.

Teasing didn't hurt

"Of course my brothers, my sisters, and myself were teased at school," said Mr. Trognon. "But it wasn't bad-humor teasing. None of us were ever traumatized by it."

Letters poured in to the Trognons. No one upheld the judge, who defiantly declared, "I am proud of my intransigeance." It turned out, among other things, that the judge had 11 children and that he had gone on television to argue against a proposed law giving equal rights to children of legitimate and illegitimate birth.

The court of appeals will convene on Sept. 16, and the Ministry of Justice says that, given the public interest in the case, the Trognon affair will certainly be one of the earliest to be heard.

Meanwhile Paris-Match has dug up an Association of Handicapped Surnames, headquartered in the northern town of Lens, which dispenses advice on how legally to change unwanted names.

Some unusual examples

The association was founded by Jean-Louis Meurdesoif (die of thirst), and includes among its members people with surnames signifying goat, cows' legs, cemetery, and assassin.

But names in France, as everywhere else, are highly individual affairs, and among surnames cherished by their holders are poetic fantasies like Lafleurdespoisverts (flower of green peas).

Mr. Trognon says that if all else fails, and if changing his own surname is the only way to keep Philippe, he is willing to do so. But all of France seems to be rooting in his favor and hoping for proof from the court of appeals that, though justice may be blindfolded, it is not blind.

Inside today

Hanoi appears well stocked

By Jean Thoraval
Special to The Christian Science Monitor
© 1972 Agence France Presse

Hanoi, Vietnam

The American bombings north and south of the 17th parallel apparently have not considerably diminished the military potential of North Vietnam.

Despite the secrecy concerning all problems of defense here, officials do not hide the fact that the situation concerning the supply of military and other material "is not as bad as certain Pentagon experts state."

No statistics are available. But a high official told me, "We can say that our supplies have not dried up, and we have what is necessary to continue the war for a long time still.

"Experience has taught us that, even when we are assured of continuous supplies, we should stock reserves. This is what we have done."

Remarks confirmed

If such a statement had been made at an official ceremony, one might have been skeptical. But it was made in an off-the-record chat by an official who can be qualified as "very authoritative."

The remarks are confirmed by information from the front and by all that can be seen by foreign jounalists here, who are not confined to their hotels and who periodically go on the road to see the results of the U.S. bombings and their impact on the population.

★Please turn to Page 6

Party acceptance widens

Wallace cultivates new image as a dependable Democrat

By John Dillin
Staff correspondent of The Christian Science Monitor

Hilton Head, S.C.

Gov. George C. Wallace shows signs of shedding his old irascible image as a political maverick. His new profile: the dependable Democrat.

If the Governor's health permits, he is hoping to stump several states for local Democratic candidates.

After November, Mr. Wallace is expected to help Southern moderates and conservatives wrest control of the party in their region from "unrepresentative groups."

At a press conference at the Southern Governors' Conference here, Mr. Wallace said he thinks still about the presidency, despite his wounds. Should he run again in '76, it is increasingly doubtful that it would again be as a third-party candidate.

The Governor's move toward conventional political channels has warmed his relations with other Southern leaders – a fact apparent at this meeting with fellow governors. A year ago at a similar conference, Mr. Wallace was cold-shouldered or ignored by just about everyone except retiring Mississippi Gov. John Bell Williams.

This year Gov. John C. West of South Carolina relinquished his automatic elevation to the chairmanship of the 1973 conference in favor of Mr. Wallace. He told reporters:

"Governor Wallace has suffered emotionally and physically in the last few months. Whether or not we agree with him, this tribute from his Southern fellow governors was the least we could do."

★Please turn to Page 6

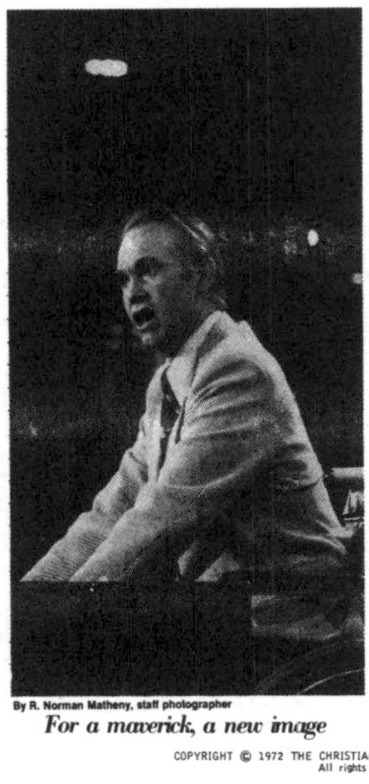

By R. Norman Matheny, staff photographer

For a maverick, a new image

Can consumer bill be pried from House?

By Robert P. Hey
Staff correspondent of The Christian Science Monitor

Washington

As Congress reconvenes, consumer interests are putting the pressure on Democratic House Speaker Carl Albert. It is a last-ditch effort to pry from the House Rules Committee a major consumer bill. This one would establish a federal Product Safety Agency to make certain that consumer products on the American marketplace are safe.

It is widely thought that if the Rules Committee would only approve it, the full House would do likewise. But at this late date in the legislative year, the only feasible way to pry the bill from the committee seems to be to have Speaker Albert insist on approval by Rules Committee Chairman Rep. William Colmer.

The consumer effort is strenuous. But the bill appears to be dying in light of last Friday's cancellation by the Rules Committee of a hearing on the bill, which had been scheduled for Sept. 6.

The cancellation came at 3:30 p.m. after most in Washington had scattered for the long Labor Day weekend. Thus there were few representatives of consumer organizations left to protest the cancellation; and fewer members of Congress to whom they could protest. Consumer interests feel sure this timing was intentional.

★Please turn to Page 2

COPYRIGHT © 1972 THE CHRISTIAN SCIENCE PUBLISHING SOCIETY
All rights reserved

THE CHRISTIAN SCIENCE MONITOR

BOSTON, WEDNESDAY, JANUARY 24, 1973 — *An International Daily Newspaper* — VOL. 65, NO. 50 TWO SECTIONS — EASTERN EDITION ★ 15c

Peace in Vietnam: Glow of hope mingles with apprehension

Reform at home, anguish abroad

Johnson: a towering figure

By Saville R. Davis

Special correspondent of The Christian Science Monitor

The towering figure of Lyndon Baines Johnson symbolized contrast and conflict in his White House years. The former President, who passed on Jan. 22, was simultaneously a reforming liberal at home, yet essentially a conservative defender of the established order abroad.

In the Johnson era, two great and convulsive changes took place in the thinking of the American people. They rebelled against social injustice and the declining quality of their domestic life, and President Johnson was in the vanguard of this change, urging it on. They also rebelled against the frustrations of the Vietnam war. President Johnson was in the rear guard of that change, resisting it.

No simple verdict can be marked down beside the name of Lyndon Johnson. Both the individual and his years in the White House were racked by storms, contradictions, and clashes of ideology. There is no agreement on these matters as the search for his place in history begins in earnest.

Acute transition

There is no consensus, even, on the question of how much he controlled events and how much events controlled him. The Johnson period was flawed by tragedy. It was a time of acute and uncertain transition when the strains of change burst into violence. The cold war had not yet ended and was grinding

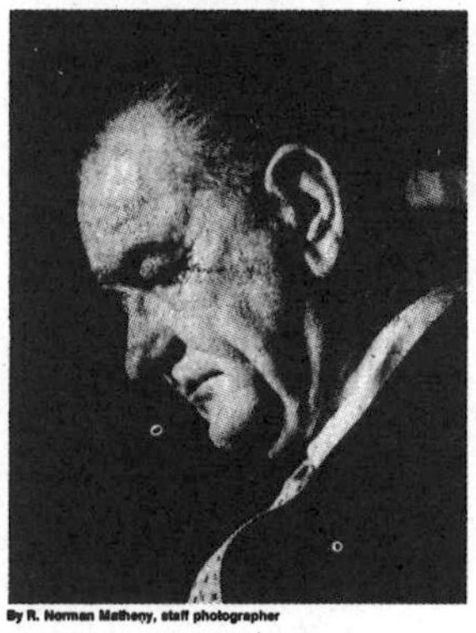

By R. Norman Matheny, staff photographer

Peace eluded friend of poor

down into rubble in Asia. At home, the political center of gravity was shifting toward the poor, the disadvantaged, and the blacks, and the smoke of riots was rising over the streets of the cities.

These events were not caused by Lyndon Johnson, but he was the presiding officer when they took place. Like the Texan that he was, activist by nature, he took strong positions and waded into trouble with all verbs — and guns — firing. And he took the consequences that often turned against him.

Chief police officer . . .

In time of violence a president has conflicting functions. Mr. Johnson was the chief police officer responsible for civil order within the United States, and the chief police officer of an anti-Communist coalition overseas. His painful but unavoidable duty, as he saw it, was to use soldiers to keep order against violence in Vietnam and in the American streets. This was a negative role considered indispensable in the world he knew.

At the same time Mr. Johnson had a constructive role as the chief political figure of his country, charged with leadership in the realm of ideas and with the task of creating the basic conditions of peace and stability.

Faced with these contradictions, he leaned on the side of advanced ideas in domestic matters, and on the side of the military in Southeast Asia.

★Please turn to Page 3

Postwar aid won't be easy

By Charlotte Saikowski

Staff correspondent of The Christian Science Monitor

Washington

Postwar aid for Indo-China will have high goals. It will also have its problems.

One stems from the fact that, in general, donor countries — the United States, Japan, West Germany, and others — want to provide the goods they produce. This often creates a gap between what a recipient country needs and what the aid giver can supply.

Where assistance is tied to the export of a donor's products, administration officials point out, there is no difficulty getting it. But, they add, it is not enough to provide beds and medical equipment for a hospital, for example; also needed are the labor and bricks to build the hospital.

Similarly, it is easy to find nations ready to supply blankets and tents for Indo-China. But it is much harder to locate Vietnamese-speaking, Lao-speaking, or even French-speaking technical personnel to run refugee resettlement projects.

Full of complexities

This is the kind of complexity with which U.S. aid planners wrestle as they await the denouement of the Paris peace talks and a go-ahead signal on postwar rehabilitation and reconstruction.

At this delicate, apparently final stage of the talks, administration officials are reluctant to comment on aid planning except to say that, once the guns are silent, time will be needed to get rolling on Indo-China's long-range economic development.

The main multilateral effort will be to build up the region's reproductive capacity and to move the people who have been uprooted by the war. But how the international community — through bilateral arrangements, multilateral efforts, and such agencies as the World Bank — will contribute to the effort remains to be sorted out.

One bottleneck, say officials, is that while the military struggle goes on, South Vietnam and other aid recipients have not had a chance to decide what they want to do.

★Please turn to Page 6

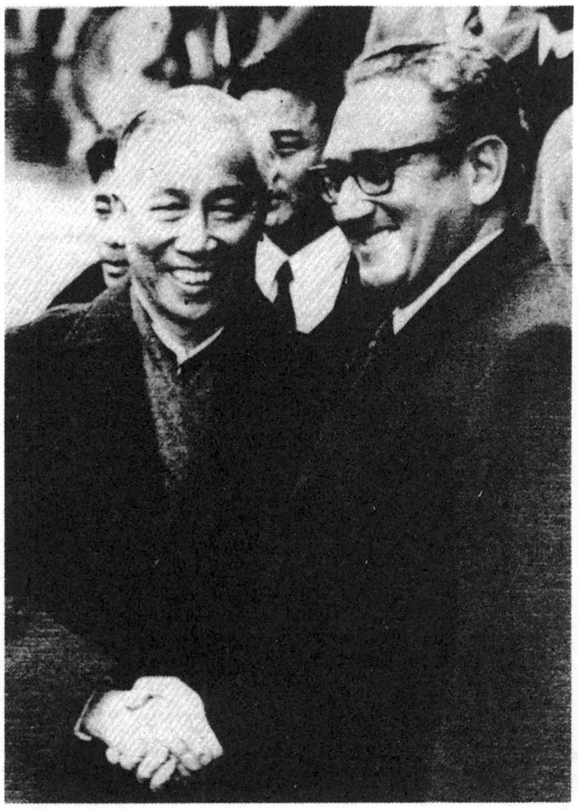

UPI photo

Le Duc Tho and Kissinger: Deal concluded

Timetable for implementation

By Takashi Oka

Staff correspondent of The Christian Science Monitor

Paris

The glow of an approaching peace in Vietnam mingles with apprehension about its implications as Henry Kissinger flew back to Washington, apparently with the completed text of an agreement "on ending the war and restoring peace in Vietnam."

At the time of writing, President Nixon was scheduled to go on television Tuesday night and was expected to announce the initialing of the agreement and give the timetable for the next few days. For the past several days the principal actors in the negotiation drama have had the air of moving in accordance with a preordained scenario, with the news-hungry public being afforded only tantalizing peeps of a process which no longer contains any surprises for its participants.

The scenario itself, as far as can be ascertained so far, calls for:

1. The initialing of the agreement. In principle this can be done by Messrs. Kissinger and Tho, and rumors are current that it may have been done already.

2. The signing of the agreement. This will be a public occasion, hosted by the French Government, and taking place probably in the old Hotel Majestic, now the official French International Conference Center.

Four should sign

Four foreign ministers should sign: Secretary of State William P. Rogers for the United States; Foreign Minister Nguyen Duy Trinh for the Democratic Republic of Vietnam (North Vietnam); Foreign Minister Tran Van Lam of the Republic of Vietnam (South Vietnam); and Foreign Minister Madame Thi Binh of the Provisional Revolutionary Government of the Republic of South Vietnam (the National Liberation Front or Viet Cong).

According to some rumors, the signing ceremony will take place in Paris Saturday. At the latest, the signature is expected to be completed by Feb. 3, the day of rebirth and renewal known to all Vietnamese, North and South, as Tet or the lunar new year.

Twenty-four hours after the signature, a cease-fire "in place" will come into effect throughout South Vietnam. Teams of international military observers from four countries — Canada, Indonesia, Poland, and Hungary — will arrive in South Vietnam to see the cease-fire is observed.

The observers will number 2,500 according to one report, 3,000 according to another. In either case they will be substantially more numerous than the 250 originally proposed by the Communists and will have their own logistics.

Timing problematical

They may not necessarily be in place by the time the cease-fire begins. This could create a brief period of confusion, last minute land-snatching, and disputes about violations by both parties.

★Please turn to Page 6

Black Muslim sects: the reason why

By Luix Overbea

Staff writer of The Christian Science Monitor

Boston

With more and more blacks in the U.S. turning to the teachings of Islam, in some 73 Muslim sects, blacks and whites alike are asking if more violence will follow recent outbreaks in Brooklyn and Washington.

Blacks generally fear that more sporadic violence might come. But they are emphatic that this will not lead to mass rioting because, many say, such riots are counterproductive.

Despite the widespread rioting of 1966-1970, inner cities have not been rebuilt, and schools, public works, and police protection for blacks have not improved, they say.

Many blacks do fear, however, that more incidents might bring a "police blacklash" — that they might encourage police to take a tougher line, to "shoot first and ask questions later," as one black minister puts it.

At the same time, membership of Muslim sects — from the nationally known Nation of Islam (Black Muslims) in Chicago with an estimated 50,000-100,000 members to tiny sects with less than 1,000 — is growing.

The seven victims of the pre-inaugural mass murder in Washington, D.C., were members of the Hanafi Madhab American Musselmans, a conservative sect. The four gunmen who held off police in a Brooklyn sports store at the weekend are said to be members of the Asanti sect.

The sects keep to themselves. They distrust outsiders, including black outsiders. Some have a minority of white members.

In perspective, total membership in all the Muslim sects is probably less than 1 percent of the nation's more than 20 million blacks.

★Please turn to Page 10

Britain's Heath prepares for Washington

By Peter Stuart

Staff correspondent of The Christian Science Monitor

London

Richard Milhous . . . Heath?

No, the name is Edward Richard George Heath.

But as the British Prime Minister packs his bags to visit the American President later this month he increasingly resembles his Washington host — in policies and personality.

Take, for example, each man's relations with his country's representative body. Both the British Parliament and the American Congress, reconvening this month after Christmas recesses, feel the sting of an executive snub.

Just about when Mr. Nixon was announcing he would deprive Congress of hearing him personally deliver the State of the Union address, Mr. Heath was depriving Parliament of hearing him announce his Phase 2 anti-inflation policy.

Shunning the stuffy chamber of the House of Commons, the Prime Minister revealed his plans last week at a press conference, slickly staged and televised nationally — a style less British than American.

There he was asked, on behalf of grumbling members of Parliament, whether "it was your duty perhaps constitutionally to consult them before you consulted (the media)." Many an unconsulted American senator moans a similar refrain.

The Heath economic controls themselves are, of course, almost pure "Nixonomics" — even down to the names of the Pay Board and Price Commission which administer the near-freeze.

★Please turn to Page 10

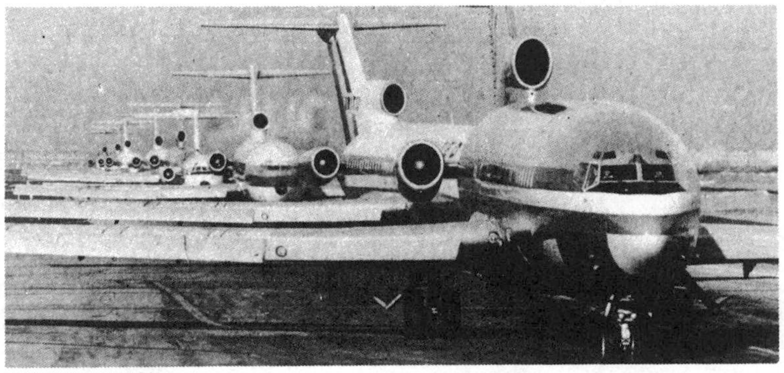

By Edward Pieratt, staff photographer

Vacation bound: Will package-tour passengers get their money's worth?

Those package tours—are they really bargains?

Some passengers are happy, but others complain about fine print in contracts

By Lucia Mouat

Staff correspondent of The Christian Science Monitor

Washington

Edwin D. Wolf and his wife thought they might just be able to make it from London to the first assigned stop on their package tour — a guest house in Dumfries, Scotland — before the stipulated time of 6 p.m.

But they did not. Their plane was late, it was noon before they climbed into their rental car for the 350-mile trip, and as Mr. Wolf says, "It takes a while to get your bearings."

To their chagrin, they were forced to forfeit the entire two-week tour. Now, with 10 others with similar experiences, they have filed a class-action court suit on behalf of themselves and thousands of other travelers accusing airline travel literature of being "wantonly misleading" and "inaccurate."

Experience like the Wolfs' — being required to travel at least 150 miles to the first night's destination by 6 p.m. on the day of arrival — and other complaints have made many U.S. travelers wonder if tour combinations are really the bargains they are supposed to be.

Airlines are fighting back. To the class-action suit (which asks for $5,000 per family and damages for the thousands of others), defendants Trans World Airlines and Flying Mercury, Inc. (the tour operator) have filed a motion for summary judgment (contending that all legal facts are on their side and that the case cannot be won).

Undiscouraged, the plaintiffs are staying in the fight.

In the past at least, stipulations on full use of such tours have generally appeared in the fine print of vouchers rather than in the advertising if they have been spelled out at all.

The vouchers are often only placed in passengers hands a few days before the flight.

Some airline personnel themselves concede that lodging arrangements are largely intended as "throwaways" and that very few travelers eligible to use them actually do so.

★Please turn to Page 10

Inside today

A rescue for Buddhist art treasure — Page 16

Can America avert '74 housing disaster? — Page 14

When violence invades school — Page 12

News — briefly	10	People	16
Books	13	Sports	7
Business	14	The Home Forum	17

COPYRIGHT © 1973 THE CHRISTIAN SCIENCE PUBLISHING SOCIETY
All rights reserved

THE CHRISTIAN SCIENCE MONITOR

BOSTON, TUESDAY, MAY 22, 1973 — *An International Daily Newspaper* — VOL. 65, NO. 150 TWO SECTIONS — NEW ENGLAND EDITION ▲ 15c

Focus

Phone fraud: many caught

By Peter Tonge

New York

A teen-ager in North Carolina, with an unwavering admiration for professional athletes recently telephoned each and every member of the Oakland Bay Bombers roller derby team in distant California; a baseball player in Baltimore, and several stars of the Pittsburg Pirates baseball team.

He made 35 calls in all, some of them costing as much as $10, but charged them to numbers that were not his own. Ultimately he wound up in court.

Three Pensacola, Fla., girls logged $950 worth of calls using the same "third number" trick. One of them even admitted to a five-hour conversation with a friend in another state.

Another way to defraud telephone companies is to quote the number of someone else's credit card when making a call. Then there are the so-called "phone phreaks," those wizards at electronics who rig intricate little gadgets to their phones that enable them to bypass the billing apparatus.

Arrests rise

But it's getting harder. Consider these figures:

Just three years ago there were 215 arrests and 207 convictions for the fraudulent use of the telephone; in 1971 there were 377 arrests and 292 convictions. Last year arrests rose to a whopping 1,050, with 844 convictions so far. Several cases still are pending.

Denis Mollura, an American Telephone & Telegraph Company spokesman whose job is to keep track of this sort of thing, now says, "Those who steal this way now stand a pretty good chance of being caught."

Five years ago, credit card and third-number fraud cost the telephone companies a relatively small $3.5 million in lost revenues. But just two years later, in 1970, that figure had climbed to $28.3 million. This did not include losses through the use of electronic gadgetry. Such losses, say telephone spokesmen, are "virtually impossible to calculate."

Fraud widespread

It became obvious that toll fraud was geographically widespread in the U.S.; that what had begun as an anti-establishment, "new Left" tactic to "beat the system" now pervaded society as a whole; that the majority of phone thieves, in fact, belonged to middle- and upper-middle-class society.

People who wouldn't take so much as a candy bar from a store apparently thought nothing of theft by wire. Many business executives, company presidents, even members of the clergy were found to be involved.

At this stage AT&T formed its Toll Fraud Control Program Task Force which devised methods to thwart and detect this type of theft. These included changes in toll office computer programming and more precise and quicker traffic-pattern analysis.

Along with the increase in the number of arrests made, toll losses have been cut by almost $11 million to $17.8 million last year.

Traffic-pattern analysis has been particularly useful in detecting "blue box" use — so named because the electronic gadgetry used to bypass the billing system in the original case investigated was contained in a fist-sized box.

The most famous of the "phone phreaks" was Captain Crunch, so named because he used the toy whistle from a Captain Crunch cereal box to duplicate the telephone system's tones and call toll free around the world.

An AT&T spokesman says many of these phone freaks do this to test their own ingenuity. "We've known of some who have used a phone in their right hand to call one in their left hand . . . by way of London."

Inside today

Congress-White House showdown on executive privilege

How much will presidential aides tell?

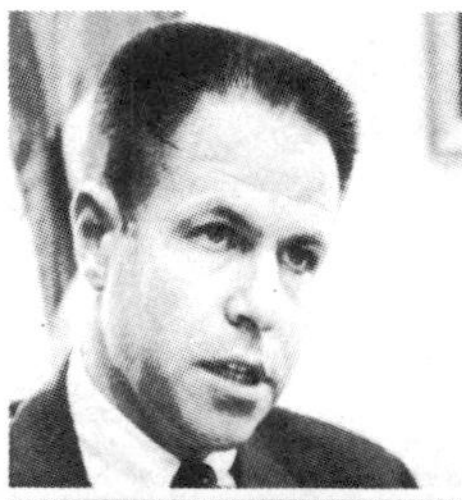

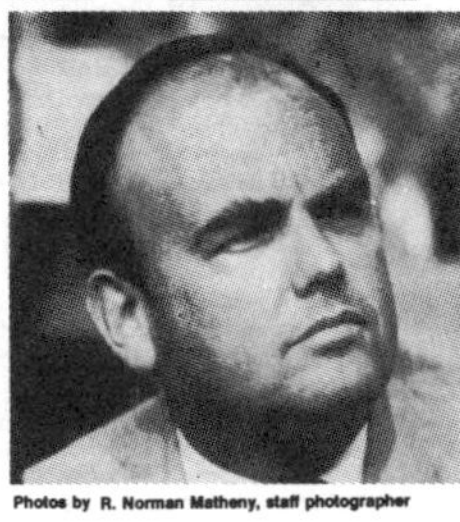

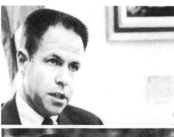

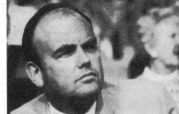

Photos by R. Norman Matheny, staff photographer

Former White House aides . . .

Haldeman [top] and Ehrlichman testimony . . .

By Courtney R. Sheldon
Staff correspondent of
The Christian Science Monitor

Washington

Congress moves swiftly toward a cataclysmic showdown with the White House over how much presidential aides should tell of their conversations with President Nixon.

The Senate Foreign Relations Committee has been told that H. R. Haldeman, former top administration aide to Mr. Nixon, informed Central Intelligence Agency officials in June, 1972, that "it is the President's wish" that the CIA help persuade the FBI to drop one phase of the Watergate investigation.

Mr. Haldeman has not yet testified to his version of what he said at a meeting with CIA officials on June 23, 1972.

Did he act on his own or was he ordered to do what he did by President Nixon? The quote from Mr. Haldeman was in a memorandum furnished the committee by Lt. Gen. Vernon Walters, former deputy director of the CIA.

New chiefs appointed

The record now given several congressional committees shows that the CIA ultimately balked at cooperating with the White House in what the CIA finally decided was an illegal request.

And within six months, the White House had appointed an entirely new upper echelon in the CIA. Richard Helms, former CIA director, now tells Congress, "Frankly, I wanted to stay as head of the agency."

The revelation before the Senate Foreign Relations Committee has more potential for incriminating Mr. Nixon than what has thus far been charged before the Ervin committee.

The White House and the Ervin committee have been sparring for weeks over whether presidential aides can report on their dealings with the President.

Showdown may come

The congressional investigations and grand-jury proceedings move so fast that the "moment of truth" on executive privilege may come at almost any hour in any number of forums.

Without detailed testimony by H. R. Haldeman and John D. Ehrlichman can the question of possible presidential involvement in Watergate and its coverup ever be resolved legally, or in the public mind?

In Senator Ervin's opinion, the refusal of Mr. Haldeman and Mr. Ehrlichman to talk fully on Watergate matters would confirm the worst suspicions about President Nixon.

As the second week of the Senate's Watergate hearings begin, Senator Ervin told a breakfast group of reporters that executive privilege

★Please turn to Page 3

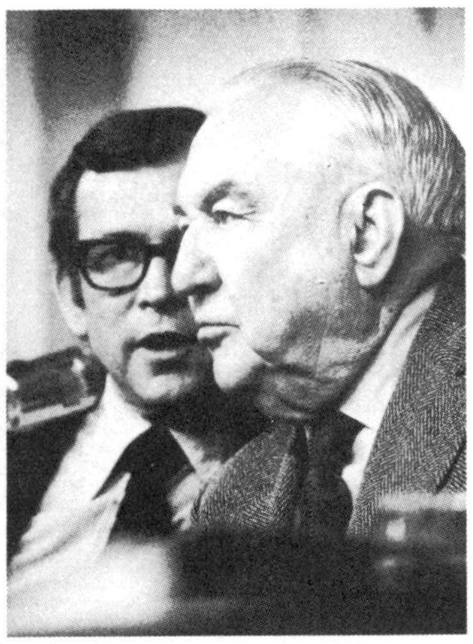

. . . vs. Senate probers

. . . before Ervin [right], Baker is in doubt

Supreme Court tie vote puts busing back in politics

By Richard L. Strout
Staff correspondent of
The Christian Science Monitor

Washington

Failure of the U.S. Supreme Court to give a clear answer on school desegregation in the Richmond case throws the emotional issue of school busing back into legal channels again, and into politics.

Because of its 4-to-4 tie vote, the Court did not give a definitive answer to constitutional questions many cities are asking on racial busing. (When the Court splits evenly, it does not announce how members voted, or deliver an opinion.)

By default, however, the court let stand a federal circuit court ruling in the particular city of Richmond, Va. — which means that white suburbs do not have to let pupils be bussed into the 90 percent black city schools there.

The result is a disappointment to civil-rights groups but is not a decisive precedent in pending cases in other cities.

Tensions heightened

Failure to rule definitively on school busing could heighten tension in this city already jittery over Watergate.

Decision on future cases will presumably turn on whether evidence exists of willful efforts by local political subdivisions to prevent school desegregation.

Justice Lewis F. Powell Jr. of Virginia, long a member of the Virginia School Board, did not participate in the case.

If Justice Powell joins the court in later cases, the ruling may well be 5-to-4 against court-imposed school busing in the interest of racial balance.

On the other hand, if clear evidence exists that local authorities are thwarting the 1954 school desegregation ruling, the court presumably would find against them.

U.S. District Court Judge Robert R. Merhige Jr. ordered a sweeping desegregation plan Jan. 11, 1972, in a 325-page opinion ruling that Virginia must merge predominantly black Richmond public schools with 90 percent white schools in suburban counties. The U.S. Circuit Court set the Merhige order aside, 5 to 1, last June.

Now the U.S. Supreme Court lets the 5-to-1 decision stand. It reserves judgment on other pending cases, including Detroit, Atlanta, and other cities.

Judge Merhige had ruled that the Richmond plan was "the only remedy promising immediate success" to ending segregation in the public schools.

"The consolidation of the respective school systems is a first, reasonable, and feasible step," Judge Merhige ruled, "toward the eradication on the effects of the past unlawful discrimination."

The decision came just as the presidential election was getting under way.

President Nixon led antibusing sentiment and promised to introduce and push through Congress legislation that would remove the issue of school busing from the federal courts, and particularly their authority to order it to achieve desegregation.

★Please turn to Page 3

Fish-'n-chips, NATO ties at stake

Cod war: Britain vs. Iceland

By Peter C. Stuart
Staff correspondent of
The Christian Science Monitor

London

The majestic strains of "Land of Hope and Glory" crackled over the radios of British fishing trawlers. The Royal Navy was steaming into waters claimed by Iceland.

Suddenly the "cod war" is no longer a West End music-hall joke — but a chillingly realistic dispute between neighbors.

It has spiraled into a virtual undeclared naval war between British frigates and Icelandic gunboats, and their armadas of trawlers.

The angry ripples wash wide — from the price of the staple British fish-'n-chips to the unity of the North Atlantic Alliance.

At issue: the productive fishing grounds on which Iceland, Britain, and West Germany rely in varying measure.

★Please turn to Page 2

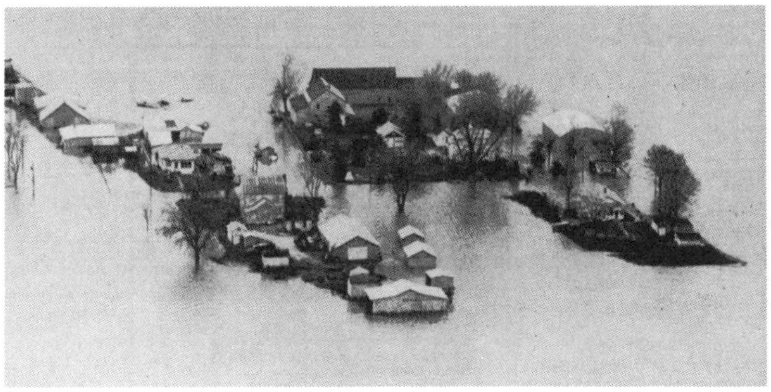

AP photo

For many, dry land is still weeks away

With this early April scene fresh in memory, people move to avoid a "next time"

Tributaries especially hard hit

More levees for Mississippi system

By John Dillin
Staff correspondent of
The Christian Science Monitor

Vicksburg, Miss.

Unprecedented Mississippi floods this spring are triggering demands from residents near the river for greatly expanded protection.

Government officials agree that the flooding has proved the need for additional levees and other control measures.

The cost will be high. But residents say that failure to act would cost the country even more in future years has come along tributary rivers—the Yazoo, the Red, the Arkansas, and others — which flow into the Mississippi. Unable to empty into the cresting Mississippi for more than two months, these tributaries have flooded thousands of homes.

The Yazoo basin near Vicksburg has been one of the hardest hit. Some 14,000 families have been forced from their homes. Property damage totals $102 million. The lower Yazoo, where the river joins the Mississippi, has become a "lake" of more than 1,100 square miles.

Channelizing causes trouble

The Yazoo flood, charges farmer James Hand Jr. of Rolling Fork, has been "created" by the federal levee system. The 3,139 miles of levees have channelized the Mississippi, he said, and pushed food waters southward at above-normal rates. This has accentuated the flooding of tributaries in the lower half of the valley.

★Please turn to Page 3

New money system — a reform package

Europeans look to 'Bretton Woods II'

By Richard Nenneman
Business and financial editor of
The Christian Science Monitor

Amsterdam

Monetary reform is in the air again.

The words conjure up images of portly or bald-headed bankers meeting in interminable sessions to discuss matters the public can never hope to understand.

But the mechanism by which companies and individuals carry on their foreign trade and their investment abroad affects the quality of life and even the pocketbook of every man and woman.

The Volkswagen agency in a small U.S. town says something about the openness of the U.S. economy to most industrial imports.

The IBM factory in France says something about the openness of Europe to U.S. investment, a fact that has aided in the prosperity of the IBM stockholder back in the United States.

The prohibition during most of the postwar period of direct American ownership in Japanese companies explains the distorted flow of goods between Japan and the United States — a flow that accounted for two-thirds of the 1972 U.S. trade deficit.

Timing pondered

Now the experts are wondering: Can the elements of a new monetary system — a "Bretton Woods II" — be put together in time for the International Monetary Fund's annual meeting this September in Nairobi?

Already the world's specialists are getting to work. Deputies of the IMF's Committee of 20 are meeting this week in Washington.

★Please turn to Page 10

After Tito— a man or team?

By Eric Bourne
Special to
The Christian Science Monitor

Belgrade

President Tito is 81 this Friday. The event and his recent absence from a major party meeting have renewed speculation about the Yugoslav "succession."

In the President's own imperturbable view it is clearly both premature and unnecessary.

Premature, because, apart from a certain slowing down of protocol and hunting but not of politics, he remains a man of remarkable vigor.

Though he was not personally present at the recent conference, his hand firmly on the tiller was very evident throughout.

★Please turn to Page 2

No U.S. denial of North Viet overflights

By Dana Adams Schmidt
Staff correspondent of
The Christian Science Monitor

Washington

The Pentagon's refusal to deny that it is flying reconnaissance missions over North Vietnam is seen here as an effort to pressure Hanoi as the Kissinger-Tho talks proceed in Paris.

The main Washington concern is to persuade Hanoi to begin respecting the Jan. 27 cease-fire by halting supplies of men and equipment to their own and Viet Cong units in South Vietnam, and to Communist forces in Cambodia.

Alleged incidents

Early this week, Hanoi alleged that after the talks between Dr. Henry A. Kissinger and Politburo member Le Duc Tho had begun in Paris, a U.S. aircraft flew over the Hon Me Island area of Thanh Hoa Province, North Vietnam. Later the same day, Hanoi claims, the U.S. again overflew coastal areas of Nghe An and Thanh Hoa provinces.

★Please turn to Page 10

COPYRIGHT © 1973 THE CHRISTIAN SCIENCE PUBLISHING SOCIETY
All rights reserved

THE CHRISTIAN SCIENCE MONITOR

BOSTON, TUESDAY, OCTOBER 9, 1973 — *An International Daily Newspaper* — VOL. 65, NO. 266 TWO SECTIONS — EASTERN EDITION ★ 15¢

Egypt's big gamble: Sadat risks third Suez defeat by Israel as he tries to push U.S., U.S.S.R. into imposing settlement

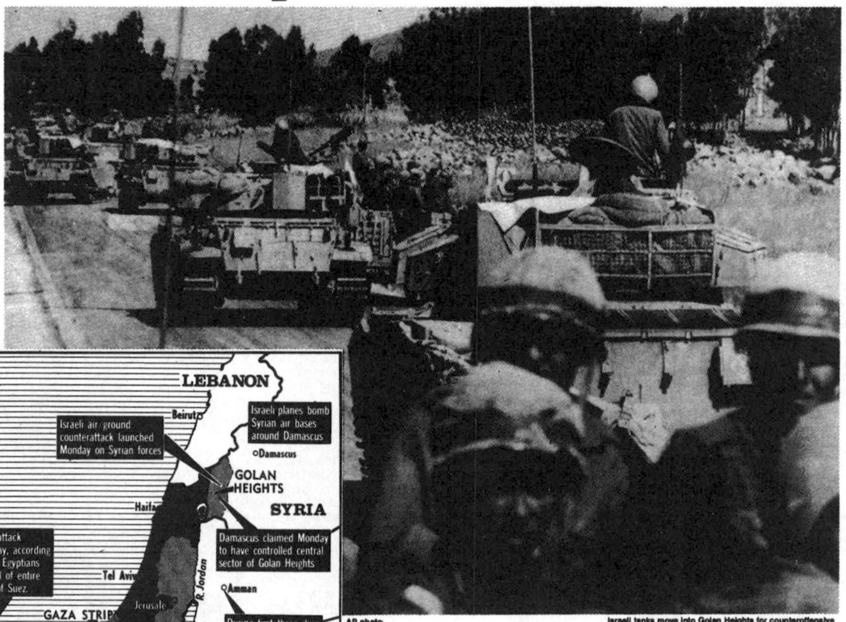

AP photo

Israeli tanks move into Golan Heights for counteroffensive

Nixon, Brezhnev confer on crisis; bargaining at UN

By Dana Adams Schmidt
Staff correspondent of The Christian Science Monitor

Washington

The one big question that keeps coming through the news of the fourth Arab-Israeli war is: Why did Egypt and Syria do it?

Out of the logic of the situation and private talks with Arab diplomats, this picture emerges: This is Anwar al-Sadat's great gamble to force the great powers to impose a settlement of the Arab-Israeli conflict that would compel the Israelis to withdraw from all of Sinai, the Syrian Golan Heights, and the Jordanian West Bank.

The Arab leaders do not care whether this is done through the United Nations or by the United States and the Soviet Union acting outside the UN. But they are convinced that it can be done only as result of agreement between the United States and the Soviet Union.

They reject direct Arab-Israeli talks because they say the Israelis, confident of their preponderant strength, would want only to dictate the terms.

Arab oil flow

The Arab leaders think the United States will come around to their view because it is so worried about the continued flow of Arab oil. Not only to Japan and Europe, but now to the U.S.

[The White House announced Monday that President Nixon had sent a personal message to Soviet party chief Leonid I. Brezhnev Sunday night, and had received a message in return.

[No details of the private messages were released. The White House also said Secretary of State Henry A. Kissinger had been in close touch with "all parties who have an interest in the area." The meetings included an unannounced meeting Saturday night with Huang Chen, head of Communist China's liaison office in Washington.]

State Department spokesman Robert J. McCloskey, asked Monday if the U.S. and the Soviet Union had a "consensus" to limit the fighting, replied, "In all fairness, I can say there is."

★Please turn to Page 10

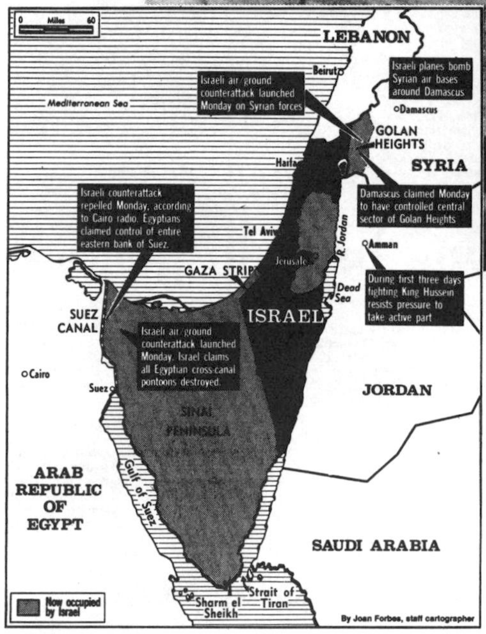

By Joan Forbes, staff cartographer

Reports from both sides

Israel sees Egyptian front as crucial

By Francis Ofner
Special correspondent of
The Christian Science Monitor

Tel Aviv, Israel

Israeli military leaders see the battle with Egypt as the key to the current war.

Although the Syrian front is much closer to Israel's population centers than the Egyptian one, the Israeli commanders are much more concerned with the fighting in the Sinai Peninsula and across the Suez Canal.

There are several reasons for this preoccupation:

First, knowledgeable military sources explain that Egypt, even without the late President Nasser's charismatic leadership, continues to be the strongest military power in the Arab world.

Israeli Defense Minister Moshe Dayan gave the strength of the Egyptian forces the Israelis are facing as a quarter-million men, 2,000 tanks, 700 airplanes, and over 1,500 artillery guns.

Armament sketched

The destruction of some 400 Egyptian tanks that entered the Sinai Peninsula, as intended by the Israelis, would reduce Cairo's armor by one-fifth.

However, the Egyptian Air Force has not joined any major battles with Israeli flyers, and Egypt's air might has remained so far virtually intact, commentators here say. The Egyptian planes have been kept back for defending Egypt, if the Israelis start sizable retaliatory operations.

★Please turn to Page 10

Cairo claims control of Suez east bank

By Joseph Fitchett
Special to
The Christian Science Monitor

Beirut, Lebanon

The Middle East fighting intensified militarily and spread politically, as the latest Arab-Israeli war went through its third day Monday.

Syria appeared to be getting the brunt of Israeli air power. Damascus radio communiques described heavy Israeli sorties starting at dawn. The Syrians say they beat off a wave of attacks on their airfields well behind the battle lines.

After this attempt to neutralize Syria's air cover, Israeli fighter planes concentrated on the Golan Heights front, where Syrian troops and Soviet-supplied T-54 tanks were trying to extend the Syrian salient in the central sector of the 20-mile front. Rain and socked-in skies provided some protection from air strikes.

Egypt claimed its forces were strengthening their grip on the eastern bank of the Suez Canal. Naming Sinai localities as held for the first time since the fighting erupted, an Egyptian military spokesman mentioned a number of villages along the southern and central part of the 90-mile waterway. Egypt is in control of the whole east bank, he added later, implying Egyptian troops had linked up with the Egyptian-held enclave near Port Fuad, where Egypt has maintained a base on mudflats since 1967.

Military observers here pointed out that Egyptian forces, even if their cross-canal supply lines remain uncut, are far from attaining the Israelis' in-depth fortifications — immense fortresses linked by mobile armor units — which have been added to the "Bar-Lev" line since the end of the war of attrition in 1970.

They believe the Israelis are more anxious to deal quickly with the Syrian threat on the Golan Heights.

★Please turn to Page 10

UN tactics of 2 sides analyzed

By David Winder
Staff correspondent of
The Christian Science Monitor

United Nations, N.Y.

The failure of diplomacy is written large on the war-ravaged lands of the Middle East.

The UN Security Council is acutely aware of this as it meets again in emergency session just as it did 21 times in 21 days, often around the clock after the six-day war in 1967.

As a prelude to Monday afternoon's Security Council session, the General Assembly heard all sides busily justifying their own points of view Monday morning. The aim seemed to be to convince their listeners that not only were they justified in their actions but also that they were winning — although the impression gained here is that the Israelis have been harder hit this time than in 1967.

Egyptian Foreign Minister Mohammud Al-Zayyat declared that "setting one's foot back on one's own home could scarcely be considered aggression."

Israeli Foreign Minister Abba Eban told the Assembly that Israel's experience now showed how right it had been to insist on negotiating with the

★Please turn to Page 2

Background to Cairo decision

By Victor Zorza
Special to
The Christian Science Monitor

Washington

The quarrels in the Egyptian leadership which preceded the decision to strike out across the canal could be discerned in the Cairo press more than a month ago. The hints in the newspapers also provided some of the reasons why the decision was taken.

When the controlled Egyptian press published early last month, for instance, an implied criticism of President Sadat for expelling Soviet troops last year, the conclusion could safely be drawn that he was under heavy pressure from some of his associates in the leadership.

The criticism appeared in an article by Mohamed Heikal, the editor of Al Ahram, and virtually a member of the top leadership himself, although he is not as close to the inner circle now as he once was.

Dr. Henry Kissinger, according to Mr. Heikal, had been puzzled by Mr. Sadat's expulsion of the Russians. Mr. Kissinger is supposed to have re-

★Please turn to Page 7

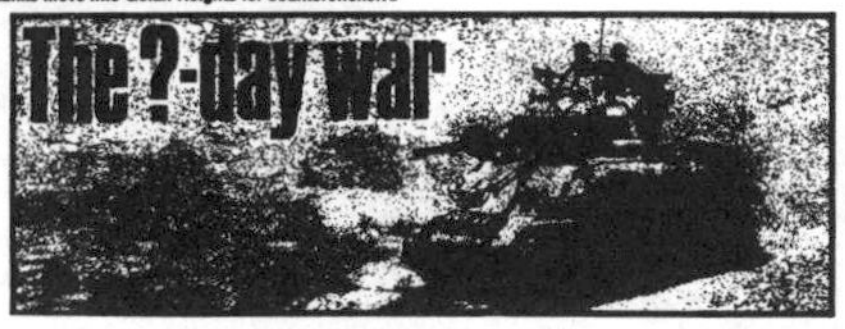

Israel, in defender role, seals off Egyptian drive; Arab debacle seen likely

By John K. Cooley
Staff correspondent of The Christian Science Monitor

The fourth Arab-Israel conflict since Israel's founding in 1948 is very different from the first three.

"This is the first time since 1948," said Israel's leading military commentator Haim Hertzog on the latest war's second day, Oct. 7, "that we are in a war of defense, where the initiative is not in our hands."

While Israeli Prime Minister Golda Meir claimed it was a "war for our survival," the minimum Egyptian war aim appeared to be to demonstrate that Egyptian troops were capable of crossing the Suez Canal and regaining territory lost in 1967, if only temporarily. By doing this, Cairo seemed to feel, a stronger negotiating position might be won for future peace talks.

In low-key statements contrasting sharply with their "destroy Israel" propaganda blasts of 1967, Cairo and Damascus this time stressed their objective was only to win back Egypt's Sinai and Syria's Golan Heights, through a combination of present military and future diplomatic action.

Arab military failure appeared virtually certain by Oct. 8, as Israel overcame what it said was the surprise effect of the Arab attack on its Yom Kippur Jewish holiday weekend, finally throwing the full force of its mobilized reserves into the battle to roll back the Egyptian and Syrian bridgeheads.

The new war thus resembled the 1967, 1956, and 1948-49 conflicts in that another major Arab military debacle appeared likely. Several Egyptian armored and infantry divisions, cut off in Sinai, faced surrender or destruction. A much smaller Syrian armored spearhead inside the Israeli-occupied Golan Heights came under equally heavy pressure from superior Israeli air and armored power.

Egyptian awareness of the probable outcome was clearly indicated by Egyptian Foreign Minister Muhammad Hassan al-Zayat. He told this and other reporters on ABC's "Issues and Answers" program Sunday that Cairo was "not sure" of military victory. Egypt's concept of the "battle" long promised by President Anwar al-Sadat "is not only military struggle. . . . There is also the political struggle," he said.

In contrast to 1948, 1956, and 1967 the big powers carefully avoided any sign that they could get directly involved or that a major Soviet-American confrontation might result.

★Please turn to Page 10

Saudi oil flow at stake for West

By Harry B. Ellis
Business -financial correspondent of
The Christian Science Monitor

Washington

"If Saudi Arabian production does not grow, there will be a world shortage of oil by 1974."

Thus a key U.S. official underlined the critical importance of King Faisal's vast desert kingdom, as the flames of Arab-Israel war spread across the Middle East.

Informed sources report the King is under pressure from Syria, Egypt, and other militant Arab countries to punish the United States by cutting off the flow of Saudi oil.

He did so for nearly three months after the 1967 Arab-Israeli war; a stoppage today would be more critical than it was in 1967 because the U.S. consumption is higher.

Many Arabs believe the most effective way to put political pressure on Israel is to strike at U.S. economic interests in the Middle East.

Iraq, for example, when it nationalized Exxon and Mobil holdings in the Basrah Petroleum Company Oct. 7, declared: "Aggression in the Arab world necessitates directing a blow at American interests in the Arab nation."

Action called symbolic

Iraq's blow was symbolic, for the nationalized American interests in the Basrah company represent about 135,000 barrels of oil per day.

Saudi Arabia, where the Arabian-American Oil Company (Aramco) pumps 8.2 million barrels daily from Arabia's oil-rich sands is an entirely different story.

What King Faisal decides to do, experts agree, will largely determine whether Americans have enough oil or must resort to painful rationing.

★Please turn to Page 7

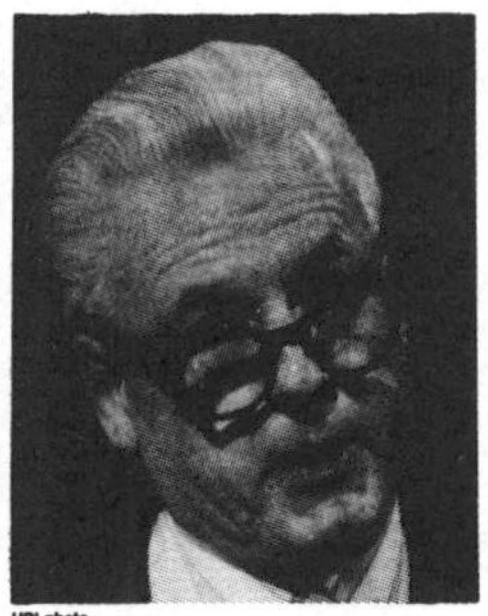

UPI photo

Brennan under fire

Target of labor. Story Page 2

Moscow aloof on war

By Leo Gruliow
Staff correspondent of The Christian Science Monitor

Moscow

All signs here indicate that Moscow is reluctant to see the Mideast flare-up turn into a major war that might create friction with the United States and endanger detente.

Although reaffirming sympathy for the Arab cause, Soviet leader Leonid I. Brezhnev has called for "a fair and lasting peace in the Middle East."

"We remain prepared to make our contribution to ensuring such a peace," he declared at a Kremlin luncheon for visiting Japanese Premier Kakuei Tanaka.

A condition of such a peace, according to a Soviet Government statement on the conflict, is the return of lands taken by Israel. The government statement seemed mild by comparison with declarations on the outbreak of the Arab-Israeli war of 1967.

Where to look

COPYRIGHT © 1973 THE CHRISTIAN SCIENCE PUBLISHING SOCIETY
All rights reserved

THE CHRISTIAN SCIENCE MONITOR

BOSTON, TUESDAY, FEBRUARY 12, 1974 | AN INTERNATIONAL DAILY NEWSPAPER | VOL. 66, NO. 55 TWO SECTIONS | EASTERN EDITION | 15¢

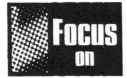

Focus on

Alaska's job rush—don't!

By Ed Townsend

New York

The American spirit of adventure still lives, and the far north has not lost its lure.

"We have a yearning to head north – to work on the frozen tundra – something an early pioneer did in our family when she homesteaded property in what we think is cold, cold Montana."

Shortly after the Monitor carried a news story in early December about employment on the trans-Alaska pipeline, a Pennsylvania housewife and mother explained her request for information on the pipeline project, expected to get under way this spring:

There had been a family conference, and "some of our sons and my husband" were interested, she said, in "the call of the wild – more than money – the excitement, adventure, and challenge, perhaps."

She was the first of literally hundreds who responded to the pipeline article, widely reprinted, citing the prospect of $1,500-a-week jobs working on the three-year construction project.

Disappointment ahead

To hundreds, jobs on the pipeline project appear to be a gold mine to be worked. The actuality will be a bitter disappointment to many of them, the jobs are there – but few of the hundreds interested in them can hope for employment.

Residents of Alaska, and particularly the large number on unemployment and welfare rolls in the state, will have first call on the jobs. Of some 6,000 jobs to be filled this spring, only those few requiring skills not available in Alaska are likely to be filled by outside workers.

Of more than 199 letters handled through the Monitor in New York and Boston, 21 were from Canada after the Montreal newspaper La Presse carried the original story in a French translation. Many of the letters were in French.

More than 30 telephone calls, again, many in French, caused problems at the Monitor's switchboard in Boston in the three hours after La Presse appeared on Montreal streets – and queries have continued.

Phone calls received

Newspapers around the country that carried the syndicated story from the Monitor received "floods of calls," largely handled through information relayed to them.

One editor said, "People are looking for windfalls, these days."

Actually, the pipeline project offers few prospects of windfalls. The expected pay will be for seven 10-hour days a week, and includes pay for the overtime being worked. Taxes will take a big bite of that income. Expenses are likely to be high.

Beyond that, the route of the pipeline will be over extremely rugged terrain, with temperatures as low as 60 degrees below zero in winter months.

According to the U.S. Department of Labor, the cost of food, clothing, housing, transportation, and other necessities could be expected to be "at least double that of the rest of the nation." The Labor Department is warning those not hired in their states: Stay away! So is the state of Alaska.

How hiring works

Hiring will be through contractors and subcontractors, so far unannounced. According to Secretary of Labor Peter J. Brennan, when job opportunities are known, they will be publicized through 2,400 federal-state employment service offices throughout the United States.

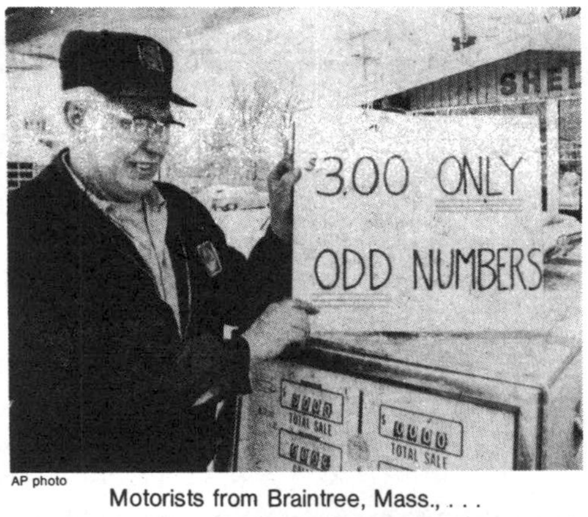

SHEL
3.00 ONLY
ODD NUMBERS

AP photo

Motorists from Braintree, Mass., . . .

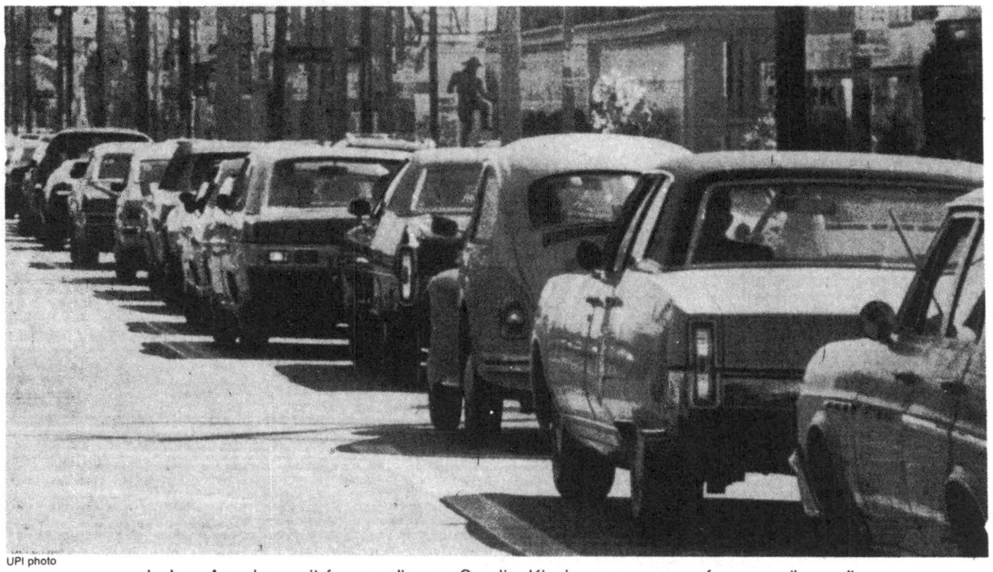

UPI photo

. . . to Los Angeles wait for gasoline as Saudis, Kissinger maneuver for new oil supplies

Saudis eye 100% take-over of giant U.S. oil combine

By Harry B. Ellis
Business-financial correspondent of
The Christian Science Monitor

Washington

Saudi Arabia will very shortly demand 100 percent operating ownership of Aramco, the American oil giant which pumps 7.1 million barrels of oil daily from Arabian sands.

If this demand is met, the largest oil producing company in the world will lose its U.S. operating ownership at one stroke and become the property of King Faisal's desert kingdom.

Details remain to be worked out, but – according to highly reliable sources – Aramco's four parent companies are resigned to a Saudi take-over in some form.

The present owners—Exxon, Texaco, Standard Oil of California, and Mobil – will seek "preferential buyer" status from Saudi Arabia, so that these U.S. majors may continue to furnish their worldwide customers with Saudi oil.

King Faisal reportedly plans to increase Saudi production to the point that Saudi Arabia can sell oil on its own, in addition to satisfying Aramco's traditional customers.

Timetable scrapped

In January, 1973, the Saudis acquired 25 percent ownership of Aramco, for a "book value" price of $500 million. The contract called for Saudi assumption of majority control of the company over a period of years.

This gradual timetable was scrapped, when Kuwait, Saudi Arabia's neighboring sheikhdom, rejected a 25 percent participation deal in the Kuwait Oil Company, owned jointly by British Petroleum and the U.S. Gulf Oil Company. Kuwait obtained 60 percent ownership, with total control to come later.

Against this background, according to reliable sources, King Faisal determined to leapfrog all the way to 100 percent ownership of Aramco. Negotiations on the transfer will begin shortly.

A likely price for the remaining 75 percent of the producing giant is $1.5 billion, to be paid by the Saudis in cash. King Faisal's Petromin or the national petroleum and minerals branch of the government, then will own all of Aramco, but none of the four American parents.

Individual Saudis own shares in the various American owner firms, according to informed sources, but Petromin owns none.

Exxon, Texaco, Standard Oil of California, and Mobil then will press to become "preferential buyers" of much of the oil which Aramco – either under its present name or a new one – will continue to pump from the desert.

★Please turn to Page 6

Oil talks: 'We must cooperate'

U.S. calls for Project Interdependence

By Charlotte Saikowski
Staff correspondent of
The Christian Science Monitor

Washington

Now: a Project Interdependence.

That was the ringing goal which the U.S. enunciated as the Washington energy conference of 13 lead oil-consuming nations opened here. The stress was on creating a dialogue, not confrontation, with the oil producers.

Secretary of State Henry A. Kissinger told assembled foreign ministers and other delegates that the U.S. stands ready to share its technology, to develop new sources of supply, and to set up a system of sharing during emergencies and periods of prolonged shortage.

He called on all nations – producers and consumers – to cooperate in solving the energy problem. Failure to do so, he warned, would threaten the world with utter chaos and depression.

Meanwhile, in Vienna, the secretary-general of the Organization of Petroleum Exporting Countries criticized the energy conference in Washington and said any grouping of advanced consuming nations will lead to "confrontation."

The official, Abderrahman Khene, stopped short of specifying the kind of retaliation his group would envisage should the consuming countries form

★Please turn to Page 4

Religious militancy in Israel

By Jason Morris
Special to
The Christian Science Monitor

Jerusalem

The militant fringe of Jerusalem's ultraorthodox Jewish community appears to have swung back into action after a six-month pause by venting its rage against Christian institutions branded as missionaries to the Jews.

In an unprecedented three-pronged assault on Christian centers based in the part of Jerusalem controlled by Israel since the 1948 Arab-Jewish war, the installations were set afire when kerosine-soaked rags were thrown inside and ignited.

It was the last thing Jerusalem Mayor Teddy Kollek's newly re-elected administration needed, considering the hypersensitive issue of Israeli control of all Jerusalem in the context of the overall Middle East dispute.

The burly Vienna-born Mayor issued an immediate apology, describing the apparent arson as "barbaric" and promising that all necessary repairs and replacement of destroyed property would be borne by the city.

★Please turn to Page 6

West Europe's gas pumps full—what oil crisis?

By Peter C. Stuart
Staff correspondent of
The Christian Science Monitor

London

Two months ago at the height of the oil crisis, Western Europeans winced at such headlines as "Petrol rationing by Christmas" and "Will Europe run dry?"

Today they might be pardoned for asking, "What oil crisis?"

Since those doomsday scares, Western Europe's shortage of fuel is fast being replaced by a shortage of fuel restrictions:

- The only two nations in the region to impose gasoline rationing, Sweden and the Netherlands, have scrapped it. Two others, Britain and Norway, have postponed rationing plans.
- Three countries (West Germany, Belgium, and Norway) have lifted Sunday driving bans – leaving only Italy and Denmark off limits on the Sabbath.
- Gasoline stations, once closed at weekends in five nations, now remain shut only in Italy, Denmark, and Portugal (with all-weekend closing hours in the latter recently cut to just half-a-day on Sunday).

"Things are much less restricted than they were a few months ago," confirms an official of one of Europe's largest motoring organizations, Britain's 4 million-member Automobile Association.

What happened? The Arab oil producers' much-publicized 25 percent cutoff to Western Europe is being offset by two developments:

1. Low fuel consumption, thanks to government-imposed conservation measures and mild winter weather.

2. Diversion of oil shipments from non-Arab suppliers, such as Nigeria and Venezuela.

In the supposedly totally boycotted Netherlands, oil deliveries in Rotterdam – an important tanker port virtually the "petrol pump of Europe" – are said to have actually increased 12.5 percent between December and January.

★Please turn to Page 6

Eating out: Fast foods boom while high style lingers

By David Anable
Staff correspondent of
The Christian Science Monitor

New York

- Sardi's, that celebrated haunt of celebrities in New York, has just dropped lobster newberg from the menu and the wine steward from the staff.
- McDonald's, that biggest hamburger dispenser of them all, opened 445 new outlets last year to reach a mammoth total of 2,717.

And therein lie two food-price tales.

On the one hand, soaring food prices are forcing some of America's restaurants into strict economies – simpler menus, reduced staff, tighter buying practices.

On the other hand, the multiple chains with already streamlined service and limited menus are expanding, largely unchecked by rising prices, capitalizing on an increasingly "eat-out" American life-style.

Rich clientele surviving

While the most exclusive establishments are usually able to retain their rich and often devoted clientele regardless – "We're out of step . . . a lovely anachronism . . . becoming more rare," says Algonquin managing director Andrew Anspach cheerfully – the middle-range restaurateur is being squeezed severely.

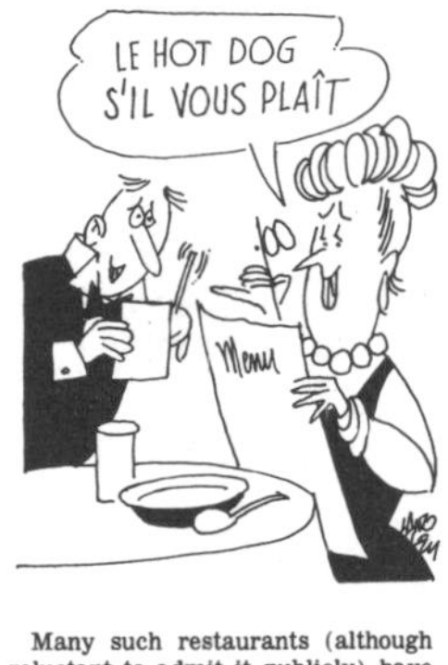

LE HOT DOG
S'IL VOUS PLAÎT
Menu

Many such restaurants (although reluctant to admit it publicly) have taken the same course as Sardi's, resorting for instance to more veal and even tripe in place of the really expensive cuts. And they are rearranging menus, in the words of one restaurateur, "so that we're merchandising lower-cost items."

Others, including Luchow's, the Steak and Brew chain, and Restaurant Associates (which owns Bras-

★Please turn to Page 6

Mortar fire always comes with lunch

South Vietnam's Highway 1 is open, safe—most of the way

By Daniel Southerland
Staff correspondent of
The Christian Science Monitor

Da Nang, Vietnam

A bus trip over South Vietnam's main north-south artery – Highway 1 – can be both educational and safe.

But a few stretches are a little less safe than others.

One of these is the stretch joining the provinces of Binh Dinh and Quang Ngai, both longtime revolutionary strongholds.

Although there is not much heavy fighting going on in either province today, minor skirmishing, assassinations, shelling, and aerial bombing seem to have become a part of life.

My trip heading north started off quietly enough. The only jarring note came from a young mini-bus driver as we rolled between Bong Son and Tam Quan.

Soldiers roamed

Guerrillas sometimes come down to the road for a few minutes and stop traffic, the driver said. If they get hold of you, they might just keep you for three or four years, he remarked, almost casually.

I stopped at Tam Quan for a noonday bowl of noodles. Heavily armed soldiers roamed in and around the town but it was quiet.

Then the mortar fire started coming in. Although I could not see where the rounds were hitting, I could hear the explosions.

Several people started to run for their sandbagged shelters, and I left my table in the noodle shop to start after them. A few soldiers grabbed their rifles, uncertain where the mortar rounds were falling. Smoke started rising a few hundred yards away.

I asked an old man with a beard why he was not running.

'For lunch every day'

"This happens every day," he said, not budging an inch from his stool. "This is what we get for lunch every day."

"No sweat, man," said a Vietnamese soldier who had obviously picked up his English from American GIs. "No sweat."

The soldier assured me that the mortar fire would stop within a few minutes. But he warned that there were "beaucoup Viet Cong" around and that they might just toss a grenade if they spotted an American. He gestured as if to hurl a grenade in my direction.

★Please turn to Page 4

COPYRIGHT © 1974 THE CHRISTIAN SCIENCE PUBLISHING SOCIETY
All rights reserved

THE CHRISTIAN SCIENCE MONITOR

BOSTON, FRIDAY, AUGUST 9, 1974 | AN INTERNATIONAL DAILY NEWSPAPER | VOL. 66, NO. 180 TWO SECTIONS | EASTERN EDITION | 15¢

Ford administration taking shape; U.S. alliances unshaken by shift

Inflation surge growing worse

By Harry B. Ellis
Staff correspondent of
The Christian Science Monitor

Washington

Soaring wholesale prices, spurred by a fresh upsurge in food costs, promise continued 10 percent-plus inflation for U.S. consumers this year.

Wholesale prices in July, reports the U.S. Department of Labor, leaped 3.7 percent — or more than 44 percent projected on an annual basis.

Since wholesale prices had been climbing at an 18.2 percent annual rate during the first six months of 1974, the July results would indicate inflation is increasing, not decreasing, as White House economists had hoped.

Consumer prices, which rose at a 12.5 percent annual clip in the first half of the year, will feel the new inflationary surge in the months ahead, especially since food prices loomed so large in the July wholesale climb.

Farm prices jumped 6.4 percent last month, as widespread drought in the Middle West cut crop estimates of wheat, corn, soybeans, and other grains.

The drought is forcing up the price of feed grains, which means in turn that fall and winter prices of meat are likely to be higher. Wholesale prices for all foods in July, lumping together raw and processed foods, rose significantly, with only a few major items, such as milk and fresh vegetables, costing less.

Equally ominous, in the view of some economists, was a July upsurge of 2.7 percent in the wholesale cost of industrial commodities — the raw materials which go into a host of consumer products. This index — embracing the cost of iron, steel, nonferrous metals, petroleum products, and other basic materials — has risen more than 2 percent monthly all year.

The latest wholesale price figures appear to make shipwreck of White House hopes that the inflation rate might shrink to 7 percent by the end of 1974.

★Please turn to Page 5

Inside today...

Nixon summitry has done its job

By Joseph C. Harsch

London

America's best friends and allies in Western Europe have been watching the collapse of Richard Nixon's presidency with some sadness, but also with composure so far as the general welfare of the Western community is concerned.

There is no detectable feeling in political or diplomatic quarters here that any harm will come to the alliance from a transfer of power in the White House from Mr. Nixon to Gerald Ford.

This would not have been the case two years ago, when Mr. Nixon himself was the prime agent in transforming American foreign policy and when the friends and allies watched with enthusiastic approval as he broke out of the straitjacket of old cold war cliches, ended the decade of hostility with China, extricated American troops from Vietnam, and changed the tone of Western relations with the Soviet Union.

All of those Nixon policies were approved and applauded here in Western Europe. Mr. Nixon was then and is still given enormous credit for them. Also he was then regarded as personally indispensable to the conclusion of the change of direction and emphasis in American foreign policy.

Innovations completed

But as the Foreign Office, the top political leaders, and the major embassies here see things, the great Nixon innovations in foreign policy have been completed. They have ceased to be controversial.

There are new problems ahead which call not for innovation but for diplomatic craftsmanship. Such problems as nailing down the cease-fire in Cyprus and keeping the Middle East on the path toward settlement rather than toward another war do not require presidential help.

There are two respects in which the experts in diplomacy think that a change from Mr. Nixon to Mr. Ford at the White House will be a definite plus.

One is that Mr. Ford, as a new president with general support from all sides in Washington, will be under no temptation to try to extract some quick foreign policy success to bolster a waning domestic position. Announcing the cease-fire in Cyprus from Washington before it happened was a case in point. The British were doing the negotiating and thought they had the right to decide when to announce success.

★Please turn to Page 5

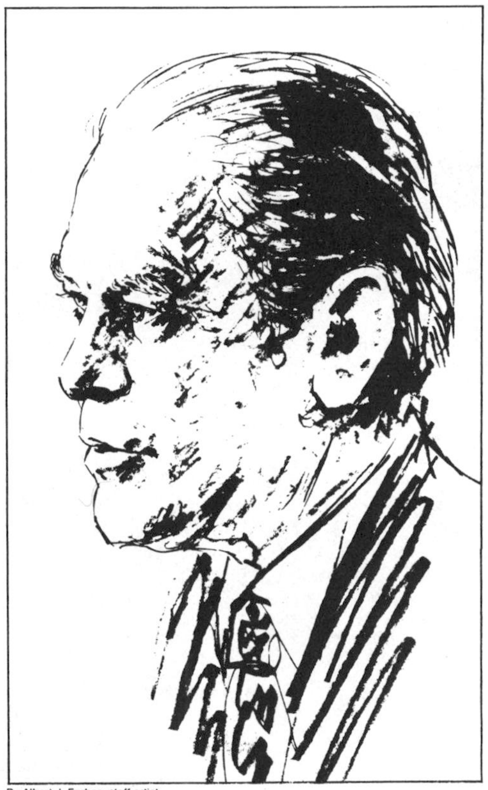

By Albert J. Forbes, staff artist

Ford: a rendezvous with history

Ford to rely on Laird, Harlow, Goodell

By Godfrey Sperling Jr.
Staff correspondent of
The Christian Science Monitor

Washington

Even before Richard Nixon spoke to the nation and the world Thursday, a Gerald Ford administration was beginning to take shape. It looked like this:

The Ford "inner circle" will include former Secretary of Defense Melvin Laird; adviser to several presidents Bryce Harlow; Wisconsin Rep. John Burns; U.S. Ambassador to NATO Donald Rumsfeld; Assistant Secretary of Defense Robert Ellsworth; and former New York Sen. Charles Goodell.

All of these men are close friends of Mr. Ford. They have been consulting with him during the last few months. They will continue to be among his closest, most-relied on consultants.

Some will be at his side in the White House or in the Cabinet. Some will remain on the outside but very close to his decisionmaking.

One, Mr. Laird, may even be the new Vice-President.

Key staff post

The White House staff: key man here is Mr. Ford's present chief of staff, Bob Hartmann, a long-time top Ford aide from days on the Hill.

Mr. Hartmann, in time, is expected to move into the spot held now by Gen. Alexander Haig and not too long ago by H. R. Haldeman. However, Mr. Hartmann is not expected to be the political power that his predecessors were. Instead, he will provide administrative leadership under the new President.

Mr. Hartmann definitely will not be the doorkeeper that Mr. Haldeman was. Instead, Mr. Ford is expected to demand that top people, in Cabinet, staff, and in Congress, have relatively easy access to him.

Mr. Ford, in a short TV address expected soon, is slated to stress a "Let-us-come-together" theme of healing. At the same time he will say that he expects the Nixon White House team to stay on for a brief period.

Slow turnover seen

Thus, the status quo in the administration will remain the same, it seems, for a few weeks.

Then some of those who are marked to go — particularly press secretary Ronald Ziegler — will leave, if he has not left earlier. General Haig is expected to depart soon, too, although Mr. Ford has a sizable appreciation of General Haig.

There is no doubt about it: Mr. Ford knows he must present a new image and part of it is to replace the men who were close around the President. But he is hoping that these men will see the point and drop out — not all at once, but at a pace which will give him a clean house within a very few months.

The replacement for Ziegler? Mr. Ford's quite competent press secretary, Paul Miltich, will stay on. But it is more likely that he will assume the role of the President's director of communications. For a press secretary spokesman, to replace Mr. Ziegler, Mr. Ford is looking for an experienced, well-respected, and highly professional newsman.

No sudden sweep

The Cabinet: again, Cabinet members will be asked to stay on. But Mr. Ford is known to feel that only one of them is indispensable — Secretary of State Henry Kissinger. Others, or at least some of the others, will go, one by one, but over a longer period of time than it will take to have a thorough house-cleaning in the White House.

High up on the list of those marked to go is William Saxbe, attorney general. No names of successors are being heard yet. But one close friend of Mr. Ford put it this way:

"If Ford is to have a fresh face as President, he must get a new attorney general. And that man must be particularly clean, particularly able. Ford has no real quarrel with Saxbe. But he will want someone else."

The vice-presidency: Mr. Laird now seems to be favored for this post. Yet he says he is not interested and is pushing Nelson Rockefeller for the spot. Elliot Richardson, former attorney general under Mr. Nixon, is also one of the contenders.

But, again, a close Ford associate makes this assessment: "Laird is in far the best position to get it. Rockefeller would be next. I think Ford would say 'no' to Mr. Richardson. He was too closely connected with the Watergate crisis. I think Jerry would feel that Richardson is too controversial. That is something he simply doesn't want."

The Vice-President's office is "floating" a list of 14 from which, it implies, Mr. Ford will make his choice for a vice-president.

This list includes the following: Messs. Laird, Rockefeller, Richardson, and Goodell; and Gov. Ronald Reagan of California; Sens. Howard H. Baker Jr., and Bill Brock of Tennessee, Charles H. Percy of Illinois, Robert A. Taft of Ohio, Mark O. Hatfield of Oregon, Robert Stafford of Vermont, Edward W. Brooke of Massachusetts, and Reps. John B. Anderson of Illinois, and Albert H. Quie of Minnesota.

Immunity for the President: Can justice and dignity be served?

By Godfrey Sperling Jr.
Staff correspondent of
The Christian Science Monitor

Washington

What is the most just and graceful way to treat a President who avoids probable impeachment and ouster by resigning?

Should he be allowed to avoid the constitutional processes designed for dealing with such questions without facing possible punishment?

The early answers to these questions are these:

- Despite urgings from Senate Majority Leader Mike Mansfield of Montana and House Speaker Carl Albert of Oklahoma that the impeachment proceedings still be carried on, the mood today in Congress would seem to be to the contrary. There is growing sentiment in favor of dropping all charges against the President in Congress.
- Sen. Edward Brooke (R) of Massachusetts has introduced a resolution that would give Mr. Nixon congressional immunity against prosecution. However, it is not at all certain that Congress is willing to pass a joint resolution giving such immunity.

Not a special case

Many congressmen think that Mr. Nixon is not entitled to be made a special case — that he must be given equal treatment under the law.

Others think that such a resolution would be unconstitutional.

And still others believe that to fully protect the President such a resolution would be virtually impossible to draft; that is, Mr. Nixon's possible court problems are so many and complex — perhaps getting into his tax difficulties and even milk fund and ITT involvement — that no resolution could be written which would guarantee foolproof immunity.

More than anything, however, the disposition of Congress is not to be vindictive against a resigning President.

- The nation is expected to welcome a stabilizing force at the helm. Interviews in recent days with politi-

★Please turn to Page 5

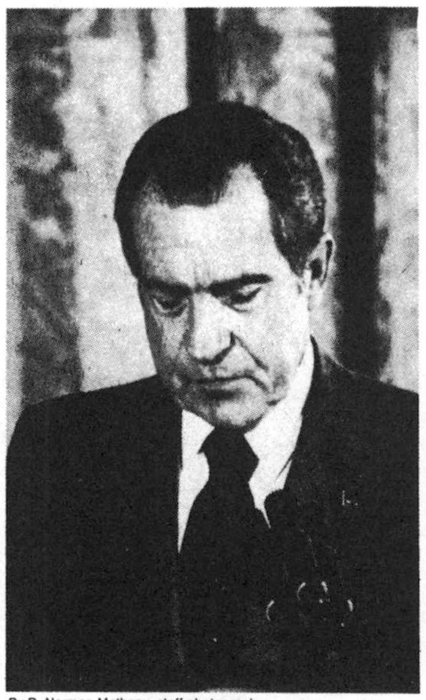

By R. Norman Matheny, staff photographer

At a time of tragedy

No. 1 economic counselor disturbs liberal senators

By Richard L. Strout
Staff correspondent for
The Christian Science Monitor

Washington

Even before a change of presidents loomed, liberal senators on the Senate Banking Committee were deeply disturbed over the conservative economic views of Wall Street consultant Alan Greenspan, chairman-designate of the president's Council of Economic Advisors.

Some call Mr. Greenspan, who has written that "protection of the consumer by regulation" is "illusory" and that capitalism is being undermined by "welfare statists," a fundamentalist mystic.

Mr. Greenspan, if confirmed, would replace Dr. Herbert Stein, who is retiring to teach, though as president, Gerald Ford may choose to withdraw his nomination. Mr. Greenspan would be only the second of nine chairmen of the CEA, starting in 1946, who does not have a doctorate in economics. His past writings indicate that he is the most conservative man ever nominated to the chairmanship in his opposition to federal intervention.

Corprations advised

Mr. Greenspan is the leading figure of the Wall Street consulting and forecasting firm of Townsend-Greenspan & Co., which has many top corporations on its advisory list. New York-born Greenspan, a summa cum laude graduate of the New York University School of Commerce, with graduate work at the University of Chicago, is a disciple of controversial Russian-born author-philosopher Ayn Rand. She has developed a philosophy, "objectivism," which elevates complete laissez-faire capitalism to a kind of cult, which she calls "rational selfishness."

★Please turn to Page 5

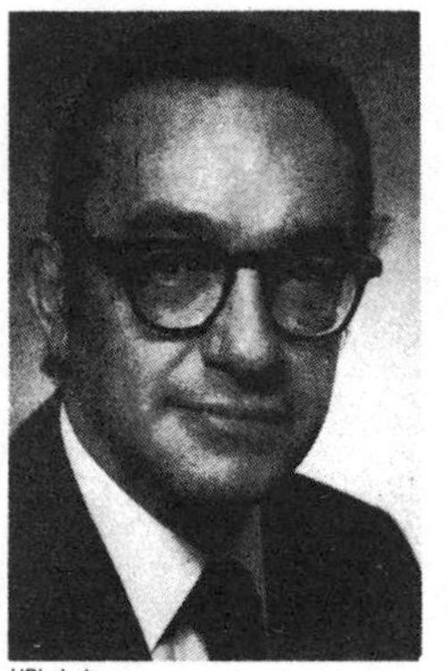

UPI photo

Greenspan: on hold?

Exotic animals and fish may find it tougher to enter U.S.

By Monty Hoyt
Staff correspondent of
The Christian Science Monitor

Washington

- Flocks of English starlings, canary-winged parakeets, and red-whiskered bulbuls are causing untold damage and nuisance to agricultural and fruit crops in the United States.
- Walking catfish, an Asiatic species introduced in Florida a decade ago for exotic fish collectors, escaped from small hatchery ponds into nearby streams and lakes by "walking" overland, using their fins and tail. Today, these voracious eaters have spread throughout Florida, Georgia, and Alabama, and are threatening to wipe out much of the local game and food fish.
- Imported monk parakeets, myna birds, monkeys, turtles, snails, and other animals have been known carriers of parasites.

What should be done about the explosion of exotic (non-native) fish and animals imported into this country — estimated at more than 100 million last year — which may pose a potential threat to native animals, agriculture, and human health?

In response to this growing risk, the U.S. Department of the Interior has proposed to limit and strictly regulate the importation of injurious wildlife.

In public hearings in four cities this week, this highly controversial proposal has brought loud applause from the nation's conservation and wildlife organizations as well as cries of "overkill" from the pet industry, zoo and aquarium officials, and medical researchers.

The Interior Department has drawn up a list of "low-risk" wildlife that may be imported freely into this country. All other wildlife would not be banned, but would require a permit for importation, and could only be used for educational, zoological, scientific, or medical purposes. It would, therefore, effectively ban their use or sale as exotic pets.

The department estimates that the pet and aquarium fish industry in the U.S. may sustain \$2.5 billion in losses as a result of the action. It is expected there would be a 50 percent reduction in imported birds, 45 percent in mammals, 15 percent in amphibians, and 3 percent in fresh water and marine fish under the proposed regulations.

"Between 1968 and 1972, almost one-half billion individual living animals

★Please turn to Page 8

COPYRIGHT © 1974 THE CHRISTIAN SCIENCE PUBLISHING SOCIETY
All rights reserved

THE CHRISTIAN SCIENCE MONITOR

BOSTON, THURSDAY, NOVEMBER 14, 1974 | AN INTERNATIONAL DAILY NEWSPAPER | VOL. 66, NO. 246 TWO SECTIONS | EASTERN EDITION | 15¢

Ford's 1975 course: liberal road rejected

President said to avoid leftward plans except for major spending for jobless

By Godfrey Sperling Jr.
Staff correspondent of
The Christian Science Monitor

Washington

President Ford has decided to reject "liberal" legislative programs for next year — despite recent election results which seemed to show U.S. voters supporting leftward-oriented candidates.

According to White House sources, the President's legislative thrust will be "moderate," with few if any "bold, new programs," simply because there will not be money for such initiatives.

One exception: There will likely be an expensive program for the unemployed. This program might take on some aspects of Franklin D. Roosevelt liberalism if the jobless indexes move well above 6 percent.

The President's Domestic Council, through its task forces, is currently studying two major social programs which would be calculated to evoke support from liberal quarters:

A welfare reform package containing elements of a guaranteed income, and national health insurance.

But they are not likely to get much presidential push this year, they are too costly.

Defense budget supported

The President also is described as "remaining tough" in his over-all support of the defense budget — although there will be some paring there.

He will make "moderate" but not "drastic" cuts in military spending — certainly not enough to evoke the support of those who are saying he should find room for social legislation by cutting way back on the military.

Also — as a concession to the conservatives — there will be further efforts by this President to return federal tax revenue to the states and localities.

Clearly, if there is to be any "boldness" in the President's legislative thrust, it will relate to the economy. Further economic decline may prompt the President to come up with new concepts and measures that will be aimed at stimulating the economy and helping those in the lower income brackets — at the expense of those in the upper income brackets.

But the election in no way is jogging the President "off-center," his aides insist. In fact, he does not read the returns as necessarily saying the voters want to move to the left.

He does think that the vote reflected disgust over Watergate and a widespread public distrust with government and politicians.

But Mr. Ford still feels that the majority of Americans are in the "center" — where he is. Thus, he is convinced that his "moderate" package is precisely what this majority wants and will welcome.

The President's own philosophy shaping his approach to legislation is that he sees himself, like Dwight Eisenhower, to be a conservative on money matters and a progressive on human problems.

As of now, this President is depicted as seeking to do all he possibly can to achieve humanitarian goals. But he is also putting great emphasis on government savings.

The outcome of these opposing views seems in most cases to be this: Programs that will not go far enough to please the liberals — and some programs that will go too far to please the conservatives. This is how Mr. Ford will translate his middle-ground position into legislation.

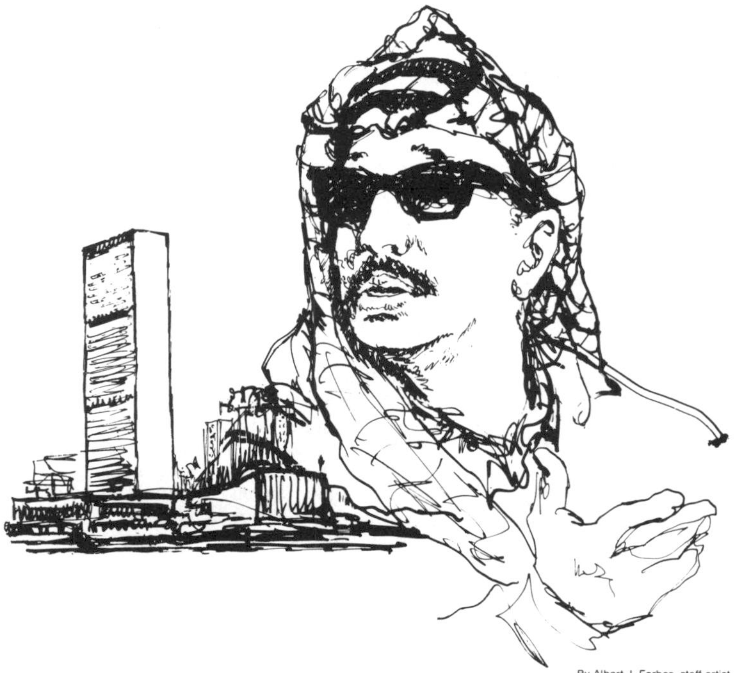

By Albert J. Forbes, staff artist

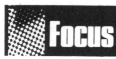

Yasser Arafat—new image for UN speech

Arafat asks UN for a 'homeland'

Little sign of compromise as PLO chief places demands before General Assembly

By David Anable
Staff correspondent of
The Christian Science Monitor

United Nations, N.Y.

It was a dramatic as well as historic moment.

Palestinian guerrilla leader Yasser Arafat, his well-known stubble-beard shaved off but still mustachioed and in his black and white check keffiya headdress — gripped the marble podium usually reserved for presidents and diplomats and spoke emotionally in Arabic to his international audience.

In coming to the United Nations to plead for the rights of the Palestinian people, he was trying to reverse a quarter century of history.

In the 1940's it was the Zionist leaders who agitated on the world diplomatic scene, and in guerrilla warfare against the British overlords in Palestine, for their rights to a Jewish homeland.

Partition approved

In 1947 it was the United Nations, then dominated by the United States, which voted for the partition of Palestine (against British wishes) and for the formation of what has become the state of Israel.

Today it is the numerous nations of the "third world" that dominate this organization. And after years of neglect as a national entity, the Palestinians have at last come in the controversial form of Mr. Arafat's Palestine Liberation Organization (PLO) to demand their own rights, apparently to the same "homeland."

Balance required

The precedent-shattering invitation to speak here was a major diplomatic victory for Mr. Arafat. His presence amid stringent land, water, and air security precautions symbolized the current attempt by the Arabs to give a new diplomatic dimension to the PLO's aggressive guerrilla stance.

Yet, in launching with such fanfare the two-week UN debate on Palestine, Mr. Arafat was compelled to balance on a thin verbal wire.

His refugee followers in camps from Lebanon to Gaza needed to be assuaged with fiery demands for Palestinian rights, which for many of them must involve the dismantling of the Jewish state of Israel.

★Please turn to Page 4

Focus

Authors publish themselves

By Jo Ann Levine

New York

Jonathan Baumbach's third novel was rejected by a number of major publishers — but today it is on the shelves of major bookstores around the U.S.

That is because a year and a half ago, Mr. Baumbach got together with his author friends whose manuscripts had also been praised — and then turned down — by publishers who said: "We haven't got the money"; "we are having to cut down on fiction"; or "we are having a paper shortage."

They started the Fiction Collective, the first such organization in this country, made up of authors who edit, copyread, design, supervise, produce, advertise, and distribute the fiction they publish.

Publicity welcome

Modeled upon Sweden's "Forfatterforlaget" (author's publishing cooperative), which now is publishing the works of 165 Swedish authors, the Fiction Collective hopes to be a model for new collectives in the United States.

Last month, the collective's first group of three novels was reviewed in the New York Times, Newsweek, and the New Republic. The reviews have been mixed — on the collective as well as the books. But the publicity has been invaluable, since the group has no advertising budget.

Publishers predict that while the Fiction Collective is not going to make money like Kentucky Fried Chicken, it will at least break even.

Manuscripts are pouring in. There are no paid personnel, so at the moment only those manuscripts that come with some kind of recommendation are being read.

Offices are located in loaned space at Brooklyn College, where Mr. Baumbach and another collective member, Peter Spielburg, are professors. The student-filled halls leading to the offices contrast markedly to the vacant carpet-lined corridors of, say, McGraw-Hill's 50-story, square-block Manhattan skyscraper.

★Please turn to Page 4

Coal agreement seems near; shutdown may end Nov. 25

By Ed Townsend
Labor correspondent of
The Christian Science Monitor

New York

Prospects for a tentative coal agreement looked good at this writing, appearing to end immediate threats of a long shutdown that would have hit the U.S. economy hard.

Even though miners will not return to jobs until an agreement can be ratified, coal now is expected to move out of the mines before critical shortages can develop.

Union and industry negotiators, in the most intensive bargaining since contract talks began three months ago, reached virtual agreement of a settlement after the industry placed a revised offer on the table late Tuesday.

Details cleared up

The parties met again Wednesday morning to clear away final details of what is certain to be the largest major labor settlement of 1974 — more than 40 percent in economic gains spread over three years with important concessions to the union in safety and other non-economic areas.

A shutdown affecting 70 percent of the coal industry costs 1.4 million tons of badly needed coal each day.

As bargaining neared a settlement, steel mills already were beginning to cut back operations to conserve coal stockpiles. Utilities were watching anxiously as reserves were drained off. Railroads were laying off crews of coal-hauling freight trains. Many of some 1,500 large coal-powered manufacturing plants were beginning to worry about the future.

Nine days required

Under the United Mine Workers new ratification procedures, it will require about nine days to get rank and file approval of a new contract — necessary before a strike can end. This would mean a resumption of coal production possibly by as early as Nov. 25, or just after Thanksgiving.

Most steel mills, utilities, and other coal-dependent industries can hold out that long — and are likely now to delay cutbacks and layoffs if they can be sure coal shipments will resume again by the end of the month.

Wealth-power image still stalks Rockefeller

'I would not behave improperly'

By Robert P. Hey
Staff correspondent of
The Christian Science Monitor

Washington

Neat and composed, Vice-President-Designate Nelson A. Rockefeller sits quietly at the witness table. As he admits, he represents the potential power of wealth. Behind a felt-topped table, eight senators are arrayed. They represent the power derived from political office.

One of the eight, Sen. Howard W. Cannon (D) of Nevada, gets to the nub of the just-renewed confirmation hearing on the Rockefeller nomination:

"The real basic concern of the citizens of this country . . . is the fear of the wedding of great economic and political power, and its potential abuse."

Mr. Rockefeller offers his own answer: "Am I the kind of man who would use his wealth improperly in public office? Or, more generally and more importantly, would my family background somehow limit and blind me, so that I would not be able to see and serve the general good of all Americans? I think the answer is no. I would not behave improperly. And I would not be limited or blinded."

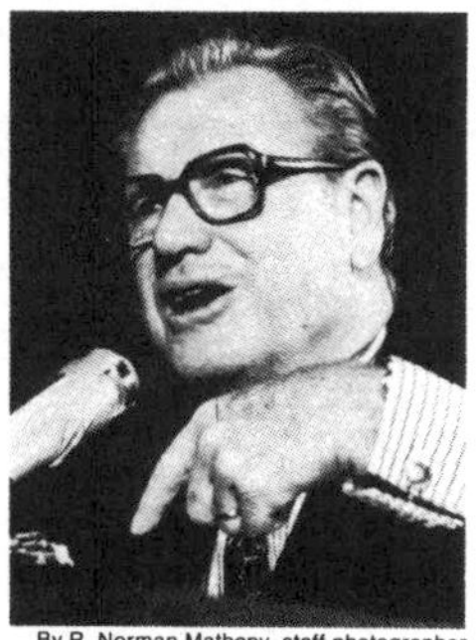

By R. Norman Matheny, staff photographer

Rockefeller questioned

Thus does long-delayed consideration of the now-troubled Rockefeller nomination resume in Congress.

★Please turn to Page 4

Governors, Ford debate offshore oil drilling plans

By Harry B. Ellis
Staff correspondent of
The Christian Science Monitor

Washington

Many governors of U.S. coastal states, in Washington to debate with President Ford the future of offshore drilling for oil, are expressing doubts and skepticism.

Concern that exploration of vast offshore tracts will lead to pollution of beaches, wetlands, and coastal waters prompts many state officials to oppose current federal leasing plans.

Mr. Ford, backed by federal energy officials, replies that only through exploitation of the outer Continental Shelf can the U.S. hope to lessen its dependence on foreign oil.

Present leasing plans, as enunciated by Interior Secretary Rogers C. B. Morton, call for six sales per year by the federal government of offshore tracts, beginning January 1975, and continuing for four years.

Target areas chosen

Areas embraced by the four-year program include waters off southern California, Cook Inlet and the Gulf of Alaska in Alaska, the Baltimore Canyon off mid-Atlantic states, and the Blake Plateau off the Georgia-Florida coast.

But, stressed a spokesman for Secretary Morton, these proposals are in the planning stage only. No leasing can be done in Atlantic waters, for example, until the Supreme Court rules on a suit brought against the U.S. by the State of Maine, supported by other Atlantic coastal states.

These states contend that, under their colonial charters, continental shelf areas beyond the three-mile limit belong to them, not to the federal government, as Washington claims.

A special master appointed by the court has found for federal government ownership. But the Supreme Court itself has yet to rule.

Of 23 states invited to the Washington conference, 15 are represented by "elected officials" — governors, governors-elect, or their lieutenant governors — and "most of the others" have sent environmental or other appointed officials, said an Interior Department spokesman. California, Washington, Oregon, Texas, and Florida, he said, are sending elected officials.

Following a meeting Wednesday with President Ford at the White House, the conferees move Thursday to an all-day session at the Interior Department, chaired by Mr. Morton, chairman of Mr. Ford's Energy Resources Council.

Potential oil spills, and damage to land and water facilities caused by onshore terminals and refineries, are among environmental concerns voiced by the governors in Washington. Some states also want a share of the royalties which the federal government will earn from offshore oil.

★Please turn to Page 4

Grass-fed beef saves Canadians 'at least 20%'

Food chain measures consumer acceptance

By Don Sellar
Special to
The Christian Science Monitor

Ottawa

It is only an experiment, but western Canadian shoppers are being offered grass-fed beef at a savings of at least 20 percent.

At a time when inflation is prodding more shoppers to buy food "on special" and when the world overall is increasingly aware that it must distribute its food reserves more fairly, a British Columbia food chain is luring its customers away from a grain-fed beef diet to something cheaper.

Last week, Vancouver residents were turned loose on a limited beef supply drawn from 300 grass-finished steers from the B.C. interior cattle country.

The food retailer, Woodward's, Ltd., says the offer was designed to measure consumer acceptance and if successful could be used at various times of the year to give producers better returns and consumers a better deal on meat.

Cattle-raisers who use increasingly expensive grain to fatten their cattle must charge higher prices — which can be avoided with grass-fattened cattle.

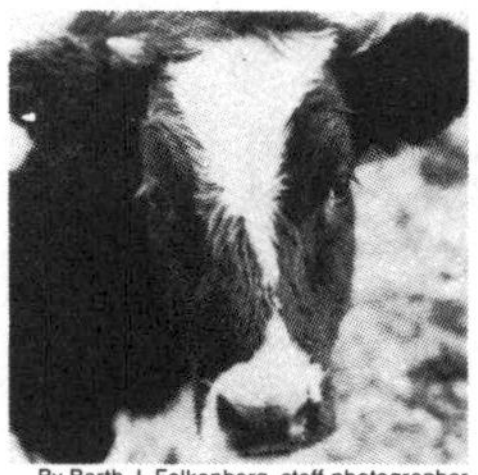

By Barth J. Falkenberg, staff photographer

Grass tastes good to me

In addition, meat is "inefficient" in terms of food value. Agricultural experts estimate that it takes about 10 pounds of grain to produce one pound of beef once the steer has gone to the feed lot. This is wasted grain, some experts say, which could be used to feed the millions in the world who have little or no food.

★Please turn to Page 4

Big gas-tax rise still under study

By Monty Hoyt
Staff correspondent of
The Christian Science Monitor

Washington

Interior Secretary Rogers C. B. Morton, the nation's latest energy chief, outlines a series of hard energy-policy decisions facing the President, Congress, and the nation.

In a breakfast discussion with reporters, the chairman of the President's newly formed Energy Resources Council, said:

- **An added gasoline tax, possibly 20-cents a gallon or higher, is still an important "option" to reduce public demand for petroleum products, he maintains, despite earlier dismissal of such an idea by President Ford and administration officials.**

However, the important question is how the billions in revenues raised by such a tax would be put back into the economy to assist people most hurt by this type of program.

★Please turn to Page 4

COPYRIGHT © 1974 THE CHRISTIAN SCIENCE PUBLISHING SOCIETY
All rights reserved

THE CHRISTIAN SCIENCE MONITOR

COPYRIGHT © 1975 THE CHRISTIAN SCIENCE PUBLISHING SOCIETY
All rights reserved   VOL. 67, NO. 109   Wednesday, April 30, 1975   25¢

Vietnamese plead for help

Americans exit Saigon in disorder

Daniel Southerland, the Monitor's correspondent in Asia, was among the last group of Americans airlifted out of Saigon. He filed this eye-witness report just before he left.

By Daniel Southerland
Staff correspondent of The Christian Science Monitor
Saigon

The United States abandoned Saigon in frenzied disorder after senior South Vietnamese officers fled from their posts and the communists continued their push on Saigon airport.

The once-immaculate U.S. Embassy compound was littered with trash, confetti-like strips of chopped up documents, luggage, and weapons, as U.S. Marines worked frantically to bring some order and help Americans and Vietnamese get out on Marine helicopters.

Saigon's new Prime Minister Vu Van Mau announced in a concession to the communists that he was asking all Americans to leave within 24 hours. Senior officials from the old Thieu regime, several Vietnamese senators, and a few police and intelligence officers who had worked with the Americans were among those awaiting evacuation from the embassy.

American officials seemed to have no idea whether the communists would try to push all the way into the city. But it appeared that with senior officers abandoning their posts, Saigon was likely to put up little resistance if the communists wanted to take the city.

Police fired over the heads of panic-stricken Vietnamese crowded around the embassy pleading to be evacuated. At about 1:30 p.m. U.S. Ambassador Graham Martin tried to drive out of an embassy side gate in a black car on an undisclosed mission. But it was felt wiser not to open the gate because so many Vietnamese were jammed against it trying to get in.

At one point earlier when the gate was opened slightly to let a few persons in, others rushed to the opening and many fell to the ground in the crush.

Among those trying to get in were a few Americans who had spent hours maneuvering to get through but were blocked by Vietnamese.

One prominent Vietnamese who did get in was rotund Gen. Dang Van Quang, a former high-level special assistant to President Nguyen Van Thieu in charge of intelligence and security under the old regime. He was dressed in a dark suit, dark tie, and wore dark glasses. "I was too long with the regime," he said, explaining why he was leaving Vietnam.

Others were not so fortunate. They thrust whatever documents they had through the gate, pleading for help. "They will shoot us all if you leave us here," said an elderly bespectacled Vietnamese, declaring that all his sons had worked for the Americans.

One Vietnamese said he had paid several hundred U.S. dollars to an American in order to get into the compound for evacuation.

Prime Minister Mau in his radio address Tuesday also announced that all political prisoners and imprisoned Vietnamese journalists would be released.

Outside U.S. embassy, Saigon   AP photo

New page for Indo-China begins

U.S. adjusts to new era in Asia—after Vietnam

By Dana Adams Schmidt
Staff correspondent of
The Christian Science Monitor
Washington

The whirling blades of U.S. helicopters carrying the last of 900 Americans and about 7,000 Vietnamese to the decks of American aircraft carriers herald a new era for the United States in Southeast Asia.

Officials here see the U.S. maneuvering in an Asian communist world with tensions not only between Moscow and Peking, but also between Peking and Hanoi, and Hanoi and Phnom Penh.

At the same time, Washington faces challenges in the noncommunist Asian world:

The State Department is concerned with the Philippines where President Marcos has announced a reassessment of relations with the Americans. The U.S. estimate is that he will be satisfied with improved terms for the operation of American bases. But the prospect of wide-spread neutralism is not dismissed lightly.

Most seriously affected by the American debacle in Vietnam and Cambodia is Thailand which has asked the Americans to close out their bases within a year. While this may yet be deferred, American analysts can see no long-term future for what was once considered the cutting edge of the American presence in Southeast Asia.

Indonesia has been affected; the anticommunist government there is now more skeptical about the United States.

South Korea is described by one American official as "very uptight," worried now about the "adventurous" North Koreans. It wonders whether the Americans would really be willing to use the troops still in the South to fight the communists.

In Japan, which until now has been considered separately from the events in Vietnam, a wave of uncertainty about the mutual security agreement with the United States can be seen. Yet, whereas elsewhere in the area the American disaster seems to have strengthened neutralist elements, among the Japanese the prevailing sentiment appears to be that the alliance with the U.S. — the country's only present source of defense — must be strengthened.

The big Chinook 'copters plucking passengers from the roof of the fortresslike American Embassy, from several private houses, and from Cantho in the Mekong Delta, ended a generation of American involvement in Indo-China. They fulfilled the last communist condition for concluding a cease-fire with the government of Duong Van Minh as head of a neutralist transitional regime.

★Please turn to Page 6

Inside today...

Archie's 'family' moves

To comply with new "family viewing" time rules, CBS moves its No. 1 show, "All in the Family," to new day and time. Page 3.

THE CHRISTIAN SCIENCE MONITOR

COPYRIGHT © 1975 THE CHRISTIAN SCIENCE PUBLISHING SOCIETY
All rights reserved   VOL. 67, NO. 117   Monday, May 12, 1975   25¢

Laos: the dignity of a woman

Cambodia: a certain venerableness

By staff photographers
Vietnam: the innocence of a child

Communists bid to add to toppling Indo-China dominoes

By a staff correspondent of The Christian Science Monitor
Hong Kong

There are signs that the Communists, after their recent victories in Cambodia and Vietnam, are trying to force the pace in Laos.

Of the three constituent parts of former French Indo-China — Vietnam, Cambodia, and Laos — only Laos is not yet under unquestioned Communist control. Until now the Communists in Laos have participated in a three-cornered government under the neutral premiership of Prince Souvanna Phouma. The other two parties in that administration, supposedly balancing Communist influence in it, have been pro-American, militarily inclined right-wingers and neutralists like the Prime Minister himself.

But the Communist Pathet Lao has in fact been able to press an advantage in that its armed force holds a large area of the countryside and has refused to let the central government's writ run there despite a cease-fire and reconciliation that went into effect in 1973 (subsequent to the cease-fire for South Vietnam negotiated in Paris by U.S. Secretary of State Henry A. Kissinger).

Ever since the early days of Ho Chi Minh's struggle against the French presence in Indo-China, the North Vietnamese Communists have treated Vietnam, Cambodia, and Laos as a whole. Many observers wondered whether victory in Vietnam and Cambodia might lead them to bring Laos more closely into line, if not under their control.

The rightist element of the coalition government in Vientiane now appears to be crumbling.

The news agency of the Pathet Lao faction reported Sunday that several right-wing leaders were "actively preparing to pack up and go abroad."

This followed an earlier announcement from Vientiane that the coalition government's defense minister and finance minister, as well as the deputy commander-in-chief of the Royal Laotian Army, were resigning. All three are key rightist leaders.

In yet another development, a group of Laotian cadet officers deserted their military camp near Vientiane Sunday and seized control of a government .technical college, declaring it a "liberation zone."

Officers belonging to the so-called neutralist faction, in the meantime, declared that all forces that supported "peace, independence, and neutrality" for Laos would be free to move through Vang Vieng Province, located north of Vientiane. A news agency report from Vientiane interpreted this to be a potential open invitation to the Pathet Lao to move into that

★Please turn to Page 17

Saigon, Phnom Penh: the contrast

By Daniel Southerland
Staff correspondent of
The Christian Science Monitor
Hong Kong

How to account for the contrast between Saigon and Phnom Penh?

In Saigon the victorious Communists allow life, temporarily at least, to continue much as it did before the take-over. But in Phnom Penh the victors swiftly emptied the capital, ordering its inhabitants to undertake a forced march into the countryside. Saigon is nearly as ·lively as ever. Phnom Penh is silent.

In Vietnam foreign newsmen have been allowed to work and travel, even if communication with the outside world is only intermittent. In Phnom Penh they had to seek refuge in an embassy compound. Although eventually allowed to leave Cambodia, they, like other foreigners, were regarded with the greatest suspicion. The new leaders in Phnom Penh seem much less sure of themselves than their counterparts in Saigon.

In Saigon, newsmen report that so far there have been no reprisals against the defeated enemy. In Phnom Penh there is no evidence of the wide-reaching "bloodbath" that American officials had predicted. But there are unconfirmed reports of executions of senior military and civilian officials.

The revolutionaries had for years vowed to kill seven leaders of the old Phnom Penh government whom they described as "traitors." Two of those leaders, Prime Minister Long Boret and former Acting Premier Sirik Matak, failed to leave Phnom Penh before it

★Please turn to Page 17

School busing inching closer in Boston

By Kristen Kelch
Staff writer of
The Christian Science Monitor
Boston

Efforts to overturn the just-announced federal district court plan here to desegregate Boston schools probably will not succeed, observers here believe.

But before the plan is put into effect, the city will witness a number of highly vocal protests and appeals, and a summer of intense preparation by a city school committee which is one of the staunchest opponents of the plan.

Reaction to the plan, issued by Judge W. Arthur Garrity Jr. here May 10, followed predictable lines.

Opponents of mandatory busing in the city repeated the criticisms they had made of an early draft of the plan on which the judge based his final design — that it infringes upon what they feel is the constitutional right of parents, black or white, to keep their children in schools in their own neighborhoods.

Advocates of "forced" busing here argue that segregated schools result in a lower, or unequal quality of education.

However, the judge is clearly determined that his plan will be carried out in September.

Similar orders in other cities have taken effect even while being appealed to higher courts. The state's highest court has supported the judge's order last June 21 which ordered Boston schools desegregated "root and branch."

★Please turn to Page 17

Inside today...

Cuba back in good graces?

After 11 years of trade and diplomatic quarantine, Cuba seems to be on the threshhold of being accepted back into the Organization of American States. U.S. eases tough position of past. Page 7.

169

THE CHRISTIAN SCIENCE MONITOR

COPYRIGHT © 1975 THE CHRISTIAN SCIENCE PUBLISHING SOCIETY
All rights reserved   VOL. 67, NO. 163

Thursday, July 17, 1975

25¢

Egypt tries pressure tactic: 'No' to UN extension

By Joseph Fitchett
Special to
The Christian Science Monitor
Beirut, Lebanon

Egypt's decision against prolonging the United Nations peacekeeping force's mandate in Sinai when it expires next week is seen here as a diplomatic pressure tactic rather than as the prelude to imminent military action.

Arab commentators said what Cairo calls "Israeli filibustering" over Mideast peace moves was threatening even the appearance of progress in the current negotiating process.

Political sources here said Egypt's fear was that Israeli delaying tactics are aimed at putting off any new accord on the theory that American leverage on Israel would diminish as the U.S. presidential election year of 1976 approached.

(U.S. Secretary of State Henry A. Kissinger said at a news conference in Milwaukee that the Egyptian move was "extremely unfortunate" and "complicates enormously" current Middle East peace efforts. He added that the U.S. was surprised by the timing of the move and was exploring whether the UN Security Council could extend the peacekeeping force's mandate without direct requests from the countries involved.)

Israel's stalling threatened to undermine Egypt's President Sadat with his domestic critics, including the military, and with both his Arab allies and critics. The latter are skeptical that his policy of relying on the United States as middleman will ever secure a negotiated Israeli withdrawal of substance.

★Please turn to Page 11

Inside today...

Mary Tyler Moore

Her MTM company will produce six (!) series on CBS this fall. The Monitor's TV critic previews the new shows being fielded by the "queen" of networks. Page 23

By Albert J. Forbes, staff artist

Space handshake staged with care

By David F. Salisbury
Staff correspondent of
The Christian Science Monitor
Johnson Space Center, Houston

"Smile, Tom and Alexei, you're on the air."
When Soviet cosmonaut Alexei Leonov and American astronaut Thomas Stafford meet in space and exchange their first historic handshake, the moment will be as well-staged as a scene in a television drama. Each minute of their joint activities has been carefully arranged.

Their meeting was planned as the world's TV spectacular of the 1970s.

Judging by comments of the largest-ever array of overseas newsmen here, interest in parts of Europe and in Japan now is as great, or even greater, as it was for the first moon landing in 1969.

More than 2,000 newsmen watched the U.S. launch at Cape Canaveral. French and Japanese newsmen here report very high interest in the joint flight.

Although at times it has required delicate negotiations, both the United States and the Soviet Union have worked diligently to play to their international audience.

A full 10 hours, or one third, of the joint activities of the spacemen will be televised. Flight television coverage was to last for 35 hours.

The handshake between spaceship commanders Stafford and Leonov originally was to take place at the hatch opening of the narrow tunnel between the two spacecraft where television cameras only would have shown the backs of the two men. But now the historic moment has been delayed a few minutes and moved back into the docking module so the international television audience can see both men's smiles.

According to Robert Shafer, NASA associate administrator for television, a number of events have been juggled around to ensure that major crew activities are televised.

This is "in keeping with the major mission objective to conduct a highly visible demonstration of international cooperation in space," he says.

Some of the most difficult negotiations involved working out the details of the first joint press conference in space. It took six months to plan. The Soviets wanted to screen reporters' questions and use their own television system to record the cosmonauts' responses.

The Americans argued that newsmen should talk directly with the two crews and that U.S. television be used. Although the Americans prevailed on the press conference the Soviet portion of a space travelog will be held in the Soyuz.

In the 24 hours following the two launches Tuesday, only one problem developed which might have interfered with the meeting. But, on a second try Astronaut Vance Brand was able to remove a docking mechanism which had blocked the passageway between the Apollo capsule and the cylindrically shaped airlock which will connect it to the Soyuz capsule. The way to the historic handshake was clear.

★Please turn to Page 6

Ford, Democrats duel on oil prices, supply dilemma

By Godfrey Sperling Jr.
Staff correspondent of
The Christian Science Monitor
Washington

The oil price battle heats up here.

President Ford fights to decontrol oil prices. On the other side, the Democrats in Congress fight doggedly to hang on to controls, warning that such decontrol may well lead to a dangerous inflationary spurt — one that might undermine recent economic gains.

• Mr. Ford's energy chief, Frank Zarb, seeks to forward the President's cause by asserting that he does not see $1-a-gallon gas "as far as I can see down the road."

This he says to a group of reporters over breakfast. Later he forecasts to Congress a 2-to-5-cent rise in price before Labor Day and then added that prices might then dip a bit if Middle East countries do not raise their prices.

• In Congress, the Democrats seek to find reasons for recent gas price rises — asking administration and oil companies.

The administration, seeking to phase out controls over a 30-month period, and the Democratic majority in Congress, both say they are trying to keep the price of gas down. But the President is putting his greatest emphasis not on a hold-down but on enabling prices to rise to stimulate production of oil in the United States.

The President's basic approach to gasoline and oil is to cut consumption by allowing prices to rise. The Democrats think they can control prices and still find ways to hold back consumption.

The Senate has passed a measure to extend control beyond Aug. 31 when the present authority ends. But the President still insists he will veto this unless it contains the elements of the phase-out decontrol which he proposes.

At the same time, the Senate is looking hard at the reasons behind declining oil inventories and the price rises they have brought about.

★Please turn to Page 11

EASTERN EDITION

THE CHRISTIAN SCIENCE MONITOR

COPYRIGHT © 1976 THE CHRISTIAN SCIENCE PUBLISHING SOCIETY
All rights reserved   VOL. 68, NO. 165

Wednesday, July 21, 1976

25¢

Viking lander safely down on Mars

Martian landscape littered with rocks, Viking lander in foreground

AP photo

On the surface of the Red Planet — man begins new effort to untangle fantasy and fact

First pictures of surface relayed to Earth

By David F. Salisbury
Staff correspondent of
The Christian Science Monitor
Pasadena, California

Finally mankind will sink steel fingers into the sands of Mars — and begin to explore the Red Planet directly.

For millennia Mars has been the object of speculation and fantasy. Now the lander from the first spacecraft has landed safely. Minutes after touchdown, the Viking lander took the first pictures of the distant planet's surface.

Two black-and-white pictures were taken: the first of the ground at the foot of the lander and the second a 340-degree panorama of the Martian landscape.

The clarity of the pictures as they appeared — line by line — astonished the scientists.

In the first picture, there are boulders six inches across. To the left side, according to camera team leader Thomas A. Mutch, is a vertical streak caused by a moving shadow. He speculates that this could be due to a moving cloud or a puff of dust.

The panoramic view shows a number of features which have excited the scientists, including sand dunes, craters on the horizon, two types of rocks — light and dark — and a sky much brighter than expected. The bright sky, say scientists, must be due to extra particles in the atmosphere, in about the amount found on earth above the oceans.

After transmitting these pictures back to earth, the spacecraft orbiter darted behind Mars — out of radio contact. However, the lander's computer had been preprogrammed to begin its work. Most of the lander's experiments are being done automatically because the spacecraft orbiter will be in radio contact with Earth only a few hours a day.

★Please turn to Page 26

British-U.S. talks seek safety for Rhodesia whites

By Geoffrey Godsell
Overseas news editor of
The Christian Science Monitor

Consultations between the British and U.S. Governments to work out a safety-net arrangement for white Rhodesians under pressure to turn their country over to black-majority rule are clearly aimed at meeting the fears of the whites.

Those fears have till now made the white Rhodesian minority dig their toes in deeper in response to every pressure — be it economic sanctions from without or mounting black guerrilla warfare within — to open the door to speedy black-majority rule.

Both the United States and Britain are committed to majority rule in Rhodesia. There blacks outnumber whites more than twenty to one, but whites have managed nevertheless to

★Please turn to Page 26

U.S. economists: higher prices, more jobs ahead

By Harry B. Ellis
Staff correspondent of
The Christian Science Monitor

Washington

Though the U.S. economy continues to grow "at a fairly strong pace," warning signs are still on the horizon for both business and consumers.

They center on inflation, which quickened a bit in the April-June quarter of 1976, and production, where growth rate slowed sharply. Also uncertainty about who will lead the nation after the fall elections adds to the economic cloud.

"However," says John W. Kendrick, chief economist of the U.S. Department of Commerce, "there is nothing in these figures to cause serious alarm" — and "signs of strength" dominate the economy.

Economists in and out of government come up with this capsule picture: higher prices but more jobs and workers filling them.

• Consumer prices are likely to rise overall about 5 percent this year, reflecting what experts call the "underlying" inflation rate built into the economy, due to the cost of labor and materials.

• Total output will climb higher than 6 percent, creating enough new jobs to absorb the increase in the U.S. labor force and put back to work some people now jobless.

• Unemployment, which peaked at 8.9 per cent in May, 1975, and now stands at 7.5 percent, is expected to hover around 7 percent at the end of this year.

Gross national product (GNP), or total output of goods and services, rose 4.4 percent in the second quarter of the year, compared to 9.2 percent in the first three months. Inflation, broadly measured, climbed at a 5 percent an-

★Please turn to Page 26

Inside today...

THE CHRISTIAN SCIENCE MONITOR

COPYRIGHT © 1976 THE CHRISTIAN SCIENCE PUBLISHING SOCIETY
All rights reserved   VOL. 68, NO. 182
Friday, August 13, 1976   25¢

Behind violence by Cape Town blacks —deep frustration

By Humphrey Tyler
Special to The Christian Science Monitor

Cape Town

The sudden flare-up of violence in the black townships around Cape Town, which up till now had remained quiet, stems from deep-rooted frustrations that are peculiar to the urban blacks of this port city at the southern tip of the African continent.

Africans in Cape Town suffer the greatest discrimination of Africans anywhere in urban areas in the whole of South Africa.

Unlike people in Soweto and other black townships outside the Western Cape they may not even buy houses on a limited 30-year leasehold plan.

They also are not allowed to do any skilled work for which there is a suitable Colored (person of mixed race) applicant, because the Western Cape has been declared a "Colored labor preferential area."

The result is that African teachers, typists, and clerks have been forced sometimes to take work as domestic servants or laborers.

Migrant workers, many from the soon to be independent black homeland of Transkei, live in squalid "bachelor quarters" and do much of the menial work, and particularly heavy laborers' work, that Coloreds and whites refuse to do.

Frequently the black migrants are followed "illegally" by their wives and children and set up home in overcrowded squatter camps.

These are often raided and the "illegal" wives are sent away if found.

The violence Aug. 11 left nearly 30 people dead, about 100 injured, and a trail of desolated buildings in the three African townships of Guguletu, Langa, and Nyanga.

Among the buildings burned out are schools, government administrative buildings, clinics, shops, beer halls, storerooms, and halls — but not houses.
★Please turn to Page 6

AP photo
Hold on a young black demonstrator in Cape Town

Momentum shifts back to Ford

Reagan backers look for a weak spot

By Godfrey Sperling Jr.
Staff correspondent of
The Christian Science Monitor

Kansas City, Missouri

The momentum apparently is moving with President Ford once again.

Ford supporters here have kept Reaganites from gaining the initiative in rules and platform meetings. And, while the Reagan challenge for the nomination remains strong, some of the wind has been taken out if its sails.

Says a key Reagan political helper here: "We still can win it. But we need a big breakthrough, a dramatic victory somewhere. We'll keep probing. When we find Ford's weak spot, we'll exploit it on the convention floor."

Item: At the first of week here many Reaganites were talking of "having the President on the run." And Ford supporters were expressing anxiety. Now the mood has shifted again, back to the Reagan appointment of Sen. Richard S. Schweiker. The Ford people are cautiously confident. Reagan workers are outwardly confident but, in private conversation, admit that they have an uphill climb.

Item: It has become clear that the problem that now faces Mr. Reagan's chief strategist, John Sears, is to find an issue he can bring to the floor and win in a way that could turn the tide in Mr. Reagan's direction.

He is said to be looking for just one particularly strong issue — one that he could feel confident of winning.

At this point, it is believed he may well push his proposal aimed at forcing Mr. Ford to select his vice-presidential running mate before the Wednesday night vote on the presidential nomination.

But will all the Reagan supporters rally behind this proposal? There are several here who indicate they might vote against this simply because such a rule would eliminate Mr. Reagan as a possible running mate for Mr. Ford.
★Please turn to Page 6

Cost of insuring a home pushing skyward

By Ward Morehouse III
Staff writer of
The Christian Science Monitor

Boston

Homeowner insurance rates are headed through the roof for millions of Americans.

"Tremendous increases in thefts," coupled with many more house and apartment fires, are driving up homeowner insurance to unprecedented levels, says Alan Fletcher, a spokesman for the Travelers Insurance Company.

Homeowners policies provide coverage for losses from thefts, fires, and personal injuries.

The Insurance Services Office (ISO), a rating bureau which represents 500 companies in rate-hike requests in 48 states, this year expects to get overall rate increases surpassing last year's average of 9 percent.

ISO is a bellwether of the homeowner insurance industry. Its member companies write from 50 to 60 percent of the nation's homeowner insurance policies.
★Please turn to Page 6

Where to look

New, super scandal may be brewing in Japan

By Daniel Southerland
Staff correspondent of
The Christian Science Monitor

Tokyo

Could a bigger scandal than the Lockheed affair be looming for Japan?

A leading adviser to Prime Minister Takeo Miki charges that some of the politicians who are pushing for the ouster of Mr. Miki are hoping, through the Prime Minister's replacement, not only to cover up disclosures emerging from the Lockheed scandal but also to conceal an equally unsavory series of payoffs involving South Korea.

"The cover-up is also aimed at a ROK [Republic of Korea] scandal," the highly placed informant told this reporter. "But in this case the money originates with the Japanese taxpayer."

He asserted that significant portions of the money given by Japan as financial and technical assistance to the Park Chung Hee regime in South Korea had found its way back into the pockets of politicians belonging to Japan's ruling Liberal Democratic Party (LDP).

Other sources are convinced that if all the financial connections between LDP politicians and governments in Southeast Asia were revealed, it would make the Lockheed affair, which involved some $12 million in bribes paid over a period of a number of years, look like chicken feed.

In the past, Japanese leaders have successfully covered up scandals such as the one involving the Lockheed Aircraft Corporation. But Prime Minister Miki, who has a reputation for being the "Mr. Clean" of the LDP, appears determined not to interfere with the prosecutors as they go about gathering evidence.

On July 27 they detained former Prime Minister Kakuei Tanaka on suspicion of having illegally received 500 million yen ($1.66 million) while in office from the Japanese agent for Lockheed. Further arrests of politicians and former officials are expected.
★Please turn to Page 6

Carter on gifts: 'Thanks but . . .'

By John Dillin
Staff correspondent of
The Christian Science Monitor

Atlanta

Gifts are pouring in — peanut jewelry, hand-made flags, lucky horseshoes, Amy dolls — and the Carter camp is befuddled.

Ever since Jimmy Carter won the Democratic presidential nomination, bags full of gifts from every state and from abroad have rained upon his national headquarters in Atlanta and his home in Plains, Georgia.

It's an outpouring of homey talent: hand-crafted dolls for young daughter Amy, home-made handbags for wife Rosalynn, hand-painted tie clasps for the candidate.
★Please turn to Page 6

THANKS, BUT NO THANKS!

THE CHRISTIAN SCIENCE MONITOR

COPYRIGHT © 1976 THE CHRISTIAN SCIENCE PUBLISHING SOCIETY
All rights reserved   VOL. 68, NO. 201   Friday, September 10, 1976   25¢

China's political future

By Merle Goldman
Special to
The Christian Science Monitor

Mrs. Goldman is professor of Chinese history at Boston University and a research associate at the East Asia Research Center at Harvard University.

What will happen in China with the passing of Mao Tse-tung?

There is no other figure in China today who has the prestige, authority, and charisma of the revered leader. Instead there are factions that, in relative terms, can be called moderates and radicals. The moderates are leaders in the Chinese Communist Party who emphasize economic and technological development. The radicals are a group who emerged in the Cultural Revolution under the guidance of Chairman Mao's wife, Chiang Ching. Their emphasis is on the need to continue the revolution and class struggle.

The party, which was decimated at the upper levels in the Cultural Revolution (1966-69), has been resurrected on the local and provincial levels, but at the top level there has been conflict between these two factions in the last 10 years.

It appeared that the moderates, led by the late Premier Chou En-lai, had the upper hand in the early 1970s. Many leaders purged in the Cultural Revolution were rehabilitated. Among them was the able administrator Teng Hsiao-ping, who became acting premier in 1974 and returned the country to the economic priorities of the pre-Cultural Revolution period. But apparently he moved too quickly to reintroduce conventional educational practices in the universities, a move that aroused the disapproval of Chairman Mao.

As a result, the radicals were able to purge Mr. Teng last spring. A relatively new leader, Hua Kuo-feng, although also in the moderate mold, apparently was acceptable to the two factions as a compromise candidate. But because he does not have the power base that Mr. Teng had in the government, party, and Army, it is unlikely that he can assert his authority as Mr. Teng might have been able to do. While the moderate faction has been weakened, with Chairman Mao's passing the radicals have lost their protector and legitimizer.

Thus, in the immediate future coalition leadership might emerge, but an uneasy coalition, fraught with rivalries and dissension. The moderates still control the political and economic apparatus, but the radicals have a potent weapon in their control of the media and propaganda apparatus. Also, the radicals' attack on the older established leadership has an appeal to the younger generation of bureaucrats, who are eager to assume greater responsibility.

China is still led by the men who made the revolution. **★Please turn to Page 26**

Heavenly Gate, Forbidden City, Peking   By John Hughes

China: no longer under the watchful eye of Mao Tse-tung

Will post-Mao leaders mend Sino-Soviet split?

By David K. Willis
Staff correspondent of
The Christian Science Monitor

Moscow
The dilemma facing Moscow in the wake of Mao Tse-tung's passing is this:

Is the way now open for a cautious Soviet signal — perhaps an offer to resume diplomatic or border talks — designed to strengthen moderate elements in Peking?

Or is this a time to sit back and watch the power struggle that Soviet leaders are certain is in progress?

Premier Hua Kuo-feng is seen here as a man without a strong independent political base, who owes his position to a compromise between radicals and moderates after the radicals had ousted former premier Teng Hsiao-ping.

Western analysts who think the Soviets will resist the temptation to strengthen the moderates cite this evidence:

Statements earlier this year by party leader Leonid I. Brezhnev and early last year in authoritative commentaries indicate Chairman Mao's departure from the scene is expected to make little difference to Chinese hostility toward Moscow, since Maoism itself is embedded in the Chinese Constitution approved by the National People's Congress in January, 1975.

Also, the radicals who fomented the Cul-

tural Revolution in China in the 1960s are still extremely strong, this view holds. They do not understand the world outside, they dislike all foreigners, and they cannot be expected to try to bridge the great chasm between Moscow and Peking, it is thought.

Mao: no other leader ever ruled so many; U.S. calls him 'a titan of our time.'

Stories p. 26

On the other hand, it is generally conceded here there has long been an intense debate within the Kremlin on how to handle China after Chairman Mao. The temptation to seek moderate elements who might be willing to draw closer to Moscow, and thus ease Moscow's fear of enemies in the East as well as the West, is strong.

Those who see Moscow tempted to issue a new signal now that Chairman Mao has gone point to an April 28 article in Pravda signed with the pseudonym "I. Alexandrov," which is said to signify approval by the Central Committee of the Communist Party. The analysts see the article, which implied Premier Hua was not responsible for the past hostility of Maoism and raised the prospect of a new round of border talks **★Please turn to Page 26**

Democrats wary of McCarthy

Threat to Carter seen from splinter vote

By Godfrey Sperling Jr.
Staff correspondent of
The Christian Science Monitor
Washington
The strongest proof that Eugene McCarthy's candidacy is threatening Jimmy Carter's lead over Gerald Ford now is available: an admission from the Democrats themselves that the former Minnesota Senator is, indeed, politically alive and kicking and drawing votes away from them.

Democratic National Chairman Robert Strauss now says that "there is no question now but what that 5 or 6 percentage thing for McCarthy is real."

Mr. Strauss then told reporters over breakfast that "the last sample I saw showed between 5 and 6 percentage points for McCarthy, with about half of that vote being taken away from Carter, 12 percent of it being taken away from the President, and the rest coming from independents."

Mr. Strauss said this came from "our own sampling within the last 10 days."

The Democratic findings conform with the latest Harris poll, which shows that in the six big Northern industrial states with a particularly large number of electoral votes Democrat Carter now holds a slim, 43 to 40 percent lead over Republican Ford — with Mr. McCarthy drawing the contestants that close together by picking up 7 percent of the vote, with the balance still undecided.

And in the 10 largest states (which includes California, New York, Illinois, Pennsylvania, Ohio, Michigan, Texas, Florida, Massachu- **★Please turn to Page 11**

Inside today...

Boston: smooth school start

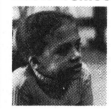

Boston's third year of busing has begun on a positive note — is the city learning to live with desegregation?

Page 4

Big business seeks
to thwart kidnappers   **3**

VP candidate Bob Dole:
conservative contradiction   **14**

Kennedy Library plans
go forward — finally   **19**

THE CHRISTIAN SCIENCE MONITOR

COPYRIGHT © 1976 THE CHRISTIAN SCIENCE PUBLISHING SOCIETY
All rights reserved   VOL. 68, NO. 238

Thursday November 4, 1976   25¢

'It's time to tap the great vitality and strength . . . and patriotism — the sense of brotherhood and sisterhood in this country — to unify the nation, to make it great once again.'

— President-Elect Carter

'I believe that we must now put the divisions of the campaign behind us and unite the country once again in the common pursuit of peace and prosperity.'

— President Ford

By Barth J. Falkenberg, staff photographer

Carter plans running start as President

First, Viet pardon, economic stimulus; then studies to streamline government and reform taxes, welfare, health care

By John Dillin
Staff correspondent of The Christian Science Monitor
Atlanta

Jimmy Carter is expected to act swiftly when he gets to the White House to put his personal stamp on the leadership of the United States.

Those who have watched Mr. Carter on his meteoric rise to the most powerful political office in the nation indicate his first actions almost will certainly include:

● An immediate pardon for draft evaders of the Vietnam war.

● Rapid moves to stimulate the economy and reduce unemployment, even if this increases the risk of inflation.

● An early gesture toward Western Europe and Japan, whose strength and friendship are seen as the linchpin of American foreign policy.

But some of the most important Carter moves in these early days will be aimed further down the road — toward long-term goals that will have heavy impact on taxes, social services, and the Washington bureaucracy.

Very quickly Mr. Carter will be expected to launch a year-long study of the federal tax structure. Loopholes, tax shelters, and other methods used by corporations and high-income persons to reduce their obligations will be subject to scrutiny with the aim of simplifying the tax system and making it more "fair."

The new President almost certainly will throw the full power of the White House behind a nationwide system of government-paid health care. If the funds to pay for it are not immediately available, the system may be instituted piecemeal.

Mr. Carter also will seek to start fulfilling his pledge that the federal bureaucracy be streamlined. Over and over during the campaign, he promised to prune away overlapping, confusing, and wasteful agencies and bureaus of government which he said make Washington ineffective.

★Please turn to Page 13

ELECTION ANALYSIS

Carter Congress support weighed

Impact on foreign policy?

The view from overseas

Gun, bottle bills win, lose

Voting wrapup across the U.S.

Women in politics

U.S. begins transition — break-in critical

By Richard L. Strout
Staff correspondent of The Christian Science Monitor
Washington

The transition period to the new Carter administration began at dawn, Nov. 3, when Mississippi tipped the Electoral College to the President-Elect — and it will last until President Ford and Jimmy Carter ride down Pennsylvania Avenue together on Jan. 20 in the traditional symbol of national unity.

In this time, Mr. Carter must name his Cabinet, prepare replacements for hundreds of top-ranking appointive jobs in executive offices, seek out and confer with leaders of his party in Congress for the legislative program of the new 95th Congress, formulate ideas for that program, get a feel for momentous decisions on foreign affairs (for example, home-made bombs went off in the potential crisis-area of Panama, even while tellers were counting U.S. ballots) and watch the crucial economic situation with absorbed attention.

The transition interval lasts approximately 11 weeks, or 79 days, and it can be critical for a new president, just as the break-in period can be critical for the engine of a new automobile.

★Please turn to Page 13

Ford will be 'catalyst' as party regroups

GOP rebuilding: new leaders sighted

By Godfrey Sperling Jr.
Staff correspondent of
The Christian Science Monitor
Washington

To come so close — and still lose — has been particularly disappointing to President Ford and Republicans everywhere.

But already GOP leaders are saying that the impressive Ford performance leaves the party strong, united, and well positioned to make a comeback.

Already party people are speaking about Republican leadership resting, at least at first, on Gerald Ford — and how they expect Mr. Ford, as a good team player, to devote himself now to strengthening and broadening of the party.

Mr. Ford probably will not be regarded as the "titular" leader of the party, simply because he is not believed to be a likely candidate for the presidency in 1980.

But he will be called upon to be the catalyst of the party as it regroups — to make speeches and meet with Republicans all around the country in the ensuing months and years.

Already, too, the stars of tomorrow for the party are being sighted. Among them:

★Please turn to Page 13

By R. Norman Matheny, staff photographer
Soon heading loyal opposition

Where to look

174

THE CHRISTIAN SCIENCE MONITOR

COPYRIGHT © 1977 THE CHRISTIAN SCIENCE PUBLISHING SOCIETY
All rights reserved   VOL. 69, NO. 163

Friday, July 15, 1977

25¢

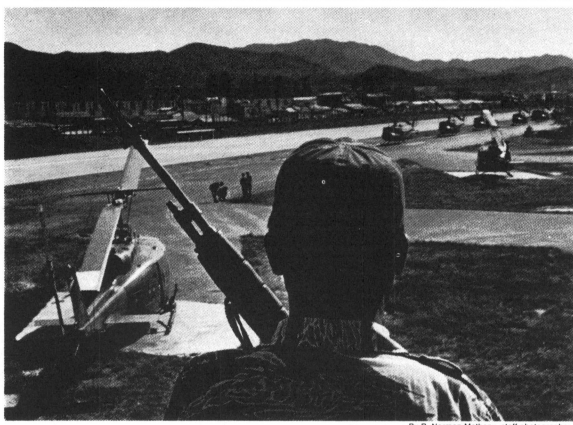

By R. Norman Matheny, staff photographer

U.S. troops in South Korea — copter incident could prolong their stay

Korea flare-up — will Carter shift?

By Peter C. Stuart
Staff correspondent of
The Christian Science Monitor

Washington

President Carter's controversial plan to withdraw American ground troops from South Korea now may come under new scrutiny.

The pullout order had drawn a surprisingly mild response in the nearly 2½ months since it was issued — apart from the dissent and subsequent transfer of the former chief of staff of U.S. forces in Korea, Maj. Gen. John K. Singlaub — but criticism is expected here to be heightened by two recent developments:

• The shooting down of an American cargo helicopter which strayed over North Korea July 13 as a result of what the President termed a "navigational mistake." Three crew members perished and one was captured.

• The disclosure by the U.S. Army's top-ranking general in congressional testimony the same day that the Joint Chiefs of Staff recommended a much smaller American withdrawal than the President ordered.

One critic of the pullout who serves on the subcommittee now studying it, Rep. David C. Treen (R) of Louisiana, says the helicopter incident will raise interest in the whole withdrawal issue — and "doubts" about the Carter approach.

The two events together may give opponents the opportunity to generate public pressure on the White House to reconsider the decision.

★Please turn to Page 26

Panama asks more money — talks slowed

Treaty hopes flicker as Congress nears recess

By Daniel Southerland
Staff correspondent of The Christian Science Monitor

Washington

A surprise Panamanian demand for "immensely large" dollar payments for continued United States management of the Panama Canal has, Carter administration officials say, left them less hopeful of swift agreement on a Panama Canal treaty.

U.S. negotiators think it important to get a new treaty to the Congress for ratification before its August recess — beginning in just three weeks — or the danger arises that approval of the treaty will be put off until next year. In that case, this highly emotional issue would get involved in congressional election year politics — something the administration would like to avoid at all costs.

As one official involved in the negotiations put it: "It would be a lot easier to get this through the Congress in a non-election year. We've got a lot of congressmen who don't really give a darn one way or the other about the canal. Some of them feel that negotiating a treaty is the right thing to do. But they don't want to go back to their constituencies in an election year and have people accusing them of giving away the canal."

But administration officials say the Panamanians recently began insisting on the payment of large sums for continued management of the canal, sums which the United States cannot agree to.

One official said the Panamanians are talking of "around $150 million to $200 million" in annual fees for the rest of this century, in addition to a "down payment" of about $1 billion. Rumors of such demands have been floating around Washington for some days now, but this appeared to be the first official confirmation that they were true.

The chief U.S. negotiators, Ambassadors Ellsworth Bunker and Sol Linowitz, have made a counteroffer to the Panamanians of $30 million to $50 million a year in annual fees. This, they believe, could be paid for at least partly by increases in the toll revenues which the U.S. collects from the canal — and would mean avoiding a situation whereby the Congress would have to authorize funds for Panama.

★Please turn to Page 26

Tracking down N.Y. blackout cause

By David Anable
Staff correspondent of
The Christian Science Monitor

New York

Why? Why? Why?

That was the question uppermost in many New Yorkers' minds as they adjusted back to comparative normality after what the city's outraged Mayor Abraham Beame called "a night of terror" — the electrical blackout July 13-14.

Despite hundreds of millions of dollars spent on equipment specifically designed to prevent any repeat of the great Northeast blackout of Nov. 9, 1965, New York City was plunged into more than 12 hours of eerie, clammy, and crime-ridden power failure July 13-14.

This time the only compensation was that engineers were able to confine the blackout to about 10 million people in the city and neighboring suburbs. In 1965 some 30 million people were affected after a switch breakdown in

New York, New York — dark Wednesday

Canada triggered a surging chain reaction through much of Northeastern United States.

Leading electrical engineers such as Allan Greenwood, director of the Center of Electric Power Engineering at Rensselaer Polytechnic Institute in Troy, New York, are very cautious about assessing causes of the disaster until the full evidence is in.

"One of the biggest changes since 1965," says Professor Greenwood "has been a terrific effort in the area of security — the ability to maintain power to customers. There's a hundred times more effort going into this kind of thing than 10 to 12 years ago."

★Please turn to Page 26

THE CHRISTIAN SCIENCE MONITOR

COPYRIGHT © 1978 THE CHRISTIAN SCIENCE PUBLISHING SOCIETY
All rights reserved   VOL. 70, NO. 102

Thursday, April 20, 1978   25¢

Carter's post-Panama momentum

I DON'T AGREE WITH YOU, SIR, BUT I'VE GOT TO ADMIRE THE WAY YOU'RE USING MY BIG STICK.

BIG STICK

TREATY

PANAMA CANAL

A. FORBES

President plans to use treaty-proven strategy in energy, tuition-tax credit, arms talks, military-spending battles

By John Dillin
Staff correspondent of
The Christian Science Monitor

Washington

President Carter's oft-rocky relations with Congress should be improved by his Panama victory, but a logjam of difficult issues remains unresolved on Capitol Hill.

White House insiders say the Panama struggle brought home an important lesson for Mr. Carter: make the tough decisions, then stand firmly until you win.

National-security adviser Zbigniew Brzezinski, chatting with reporters in the White House after the vote, observed:

"We started with 8 percent public support on this issue and only 25 senators. It shows he takes on the hard issues, sticks to it, and he prevails. We'll do that on other foreign-policy issues. Others should take note — we're going to deal with other issues the same way."

Those other issues will follow close on the heels of Panama — energy legislation, tuition-tax credits, arms talks with the Soviets, demands for added military spending, mounting concern over Soviet-Cuban activity in Africa.

"Obviously when you win in one issue it helps you in other areas," noted an administration official after the vote.

Bolstered by Panama, Mr. Carter can turn more confidently toward the deadlocked energy bill, which some officials worry could die in this session.

Panama will also encourage Mr. Carter to hang tough on "budget-busters" like tuition-tax credits and additional military spending. Already the White House budget calls for a $60.6 billion deficit in 1979, and a broad program of

Richard L. Strout assesses Panama vote consequences Page 4

tuition credits to college, elementary, and secondary-school students could add as much as $51 billion to federal spending over the next five years, according to the Senate Budget Committee.

Abroad, the Panama victory shores up the American image among third-world countries, where the United States has often been viewed as overbearing. Perhaps even more significantly, it could help Mr. Carter in his dealings with the Soviets on arms talks. The vote demonstrates that the American President can get even a two-thirds majority on a difficult issue when the chips are down.

Yet other administration officials conceded that the treaty struggle had been a close fight — so close that those around the President felt they were going to lose just 24 hours before the final Senate vote.

Monday night, Sen. Robert Byrd, the majority leader, telephoned the President, who was attending a country music concert in the White House. Mr. Byrd expressed concern about several senators who seemed to be wavering on the eve of the vote.

After the call, the President talked urgently in the usher's office of the White House with aides Hamilton Jordan and Jody Powell; then they contacted aide Frank Moore, who was at a party at the British Embassy, and Vice-Pres-

★ Please turn to Page 9

Sunset in Panama — little celebration

By James Nelson Goodsell
Staff correspondent of
The Christian Science Monitor

Balboa Heights, Canal Zone

A spectacular sunset lighted the evening sky over the Panama Canal as the United States Senate in Washington was ratifying the second of two canal treaties.

In a way, the sunset was symbolic of the approaching end of a colorful era that had witnessed the building of the waterway despite all obstacles and its smooth operation by the U.S. for 64 years.

But the symbolism was lost on most people in both the Canal Zone and neighboring Panama City. In neither place did they seem happy.

There was an atmosphere of gloom here in the zone as residents awaited the expected outcome of the Senate vote that spells joint operation of the canal for 22 years and then its

takeover by Panama in the year 2000.

"All that is left is for us to pack up our tents and then not so slowly slink away," commented a veteran of World War II who has worked on the canal for 30 years as he listened to the vote at the American Legion club here.

A woman nearby cried uncontrollably.

"I am ashamed of my country, and my senators, and everything this means," she sobbed.

For many in the zone, however, the vote was anticlimactic. Months of waiting while the Senate deliberated had in a sense drained away the outbursts of anger and bitterness, leaving most zonians, as residents here are called, certain of the outcome.

In fact, April 18 was like any other day in the zone. Thousands of workers turned up at their appointed tasks, and absenteeism was less than normal. Schools were open.

The same was true in Panama City (which lies cheek-by-jowl with the zone), where Pan-

amanians did little celebrating.

There were a number of typical Panamanian bands on the tops of trucks at the Plaza Cinco de Mayo. But the crowds were small, and the expected dancing in the streets to the music of the bands was, in the words of one guitarist, "disappointing."

Panama City simply did not appear to be in a celebrating mood. The countryside was similarly quiet. Despite the fact that Panama now is much closer than ever to controlling the waterway, most Panamanians apparently do not much care.

April 19, the day after the vote, declared a national holiday by the government, looked much like a Sunday. Thousands of Panamanians rushed to the beaches and countryside, grateful for a day off.

What fireworks there were were provided by Gen. Omar Torrijos Herrera, the chief of government, who angrily told a press conference that his patience with the U.S. was about exhausted.

Had the Senate not ratified the treaties, he commented, he was prepared to take matters "into our own hands."

Warning that if the U.S. were to intervene in Panama at some future date Panama would invade the zone, he added that the National Guard had the capacity "to destroy the canal."

Although General Torrijos's words were seen in some circles as simply so much bombast, there was anger here in the Canal Zone over what was widely described as "his poor taste."

"When you have won the round," said a Canal Zone police official, "you quit swinging."

Another zonian commented: "If he thinks he can close the canal, let him try. He would be surprised at how fast we can keep him from doing it."

France talks of own N-bomb

By Jim Browning
Special to The Christian Science Monitor

Paris

France is considering the possibility of developing its own neutron warhead, according to sources in Paris, but is not yet thought to have made a final decision.

French press reports, apparently stemming from official leaks, have said the government recently tested a miniaturization process linked to a neutron warhead at its underground testing center in French Polynesia. But expert observers think those reports may be exaggerated.

A Cabinet committee is known to be reviewing the possibility of developing the "enhanced radiation warhead," debating whether the commitment of money and resources is justified. The successful production of a neutron warhead would require several years of research and development.

The Defense Ministry has fueled speculation about a test by refusing to confirm or

★ Please turn to Page 9

Inside today...

THE CHRISTIAN SCIENCE MONITOR

COPYRIGHT ©1978 THE CHRISTIAN SCIENCE PUBLISHING SOCIETY
All rights reserved   VOL. 71, NO. 16   Monday, December 18, 1978   25¢

Rewards—and risks—of Carter's China breakthrough

By Daniel Southerland
Staff correspondent of The Christian Science Monitor

Washington

Recognition of China will enhance both the stability of Asia and the national security of the United States.

This is the simple message which the Carter administration is delivering to the world in the wake of President Carter's momentous decision to establish full relations with Peking.

The administration is taking care, however, in the way it goes about delivering this message. It does not want to provoke the Soviet Union by making it appear that the China decision, announced by President Carter Dec. 15, is directed in an aggressive way against the Soviets. The United States clearly wants good relations with both China and the Soviet Union.

But in explaining Mr. Carter's decision in meetings with reporters, senior officials have stressed that a major consideration for the President was the need to consolidate a stable balance of forces in eastern Asia, a balance which would offset the power and influence of the Soviets and thus enhance American security interests.

The main criticism of the China decision, coming mostly from conservative politicians but also from some foreign-policy experts, is that it will work in a direction precisely opposite to that envisaged by the administration.

The critics contend that America's recognition of Peking will (1) destroy the credibility of the United States with its Asian allies and (2) provoke the Soviets into an aggressive reaction, possibly causing them to move against American and Chinese interests both in Iran and Indo-China. Some also say that it is likely to undermine Israel's faith in American guarantees and protection.

Administration officials acknowledge that American credibility is being put to the test by the China decision, but they contend that Peking made a major concession by tacitly agreeing to the continuation of US weapons sales to Taiwan, even after the US-Taiwan defense treaty is

★Please turn to Page 7

Political fallout around the world

■ As Washington reverberates with shock, moderate Republican support becomes a key element in the President's attempt to "sell" his China initiative to Congress and people. But conservative hawks are circling angrily.

■ The Soviet leaders' almost obsessive anxiety about China has been given another twist by the Carter move. But the Kremlin's deeper worry is that the US (and NATO) will strengthen China's military forces.

■ Moscow's concern is reinforced by its recent failure to get Romania to join in condemning China and increasing Warsaw Pact budgets — just when NATO flatly rejects "compromise" on European force reductions.

■ In Taiwan, opposition politicians are almost more enraged than the government. The Carter move prompted the government to "postpone" the current National Assembly elections, wrecking efforts to expand limited democracy.

All stories, Page 6.

Chungking iron and steel factory   By Gordon N. Converse, chief photographer
China's industry: one beneficiary of US-China ties

How power triangle shifts: an analysis

By Geoffrey Godsell
Staff correspondent of The Christian Science Monitor

Full diplomatic relations between Peking and Washington represent the biggest and most dramatic adjustment to the triangular US-USSR-China power balance since the original Nixon breakthrough seven years ago.

Once again we are seeing that the United States tends to be the principal beneficiary of this triangular relationship — provided that administrations in Washington handle it with skill and sensitivity.

To put it another way, the deep-rooted and implacable rivalry between Moscow and Peking enables the US to have better relations with the Russians and the Chinese than the latter appear capable of having with each other.

All signs point to Peking's setting the pace in recent weeks to secure normalization of relations with Washington — with the Chinese being very much impelled by their desire to score against the Russians. For one thing, Soviet support of Vietnam against Cambodia is producing a potentially awkward situation for the Chinese on their southeastern border, and the Chinese would like something to offset this pressure.

The immediate questions now become:

Will this further rapprochement between Peking and Washington drive Moscow into being more aggressive toward either?

Or will Moscow try to ensure against Peking's and Washington's getting still closer together by turning as much charm as possible on Washington? ★Please turn to Page 7

US calculates cost of OPEC oil price hike

By Harry B. Ellis
Staff correspondent of
The Christian Science Monitor

Washington

OPEC's steeper-than-expected boost in the price of oil will add to United States inflationary woes and comes at a time when American imports of foreign oil are growing.

The 1979 price hike – 14.5 percent by the end of the year – will, by itself, add 0.5 percent to the US consumer price index, said Energy Secretary James R. Schlesinger.

What the Organization of Petroleum Exporting Countries has done, said Mr. Schlesinger Dec. 17 on the ABC television program "Issues and Answers," "could have a major impact"

on the American balance of trade, on the growth of industrialized economies, and on the strength of the US dollar.

For two reasons the oil cartel's decision to increase prices 14.5 percent by the end of 1979 will burden President Carter's ambitious effort to reduce inflation below the current 10 percent mark:

• A gallon of gasoline or heating oil may cost an additional four cents by the end of next year because of the OPEC decision, hitting American families in a direct and visible way.

Indeed, said Mr. Schlesinger, gasoline may cost five to six cents a gallon more a year from now, because the price of domestic US oil also is rising.

Some oil specialists think the combination of OPEC and domestic price factors may boost the retail price of a gallon of gasoline more than six cents next year.

• Industries that use petroleum to manufacture goods or produce electricity will push their added costs on to ultimate consumers.

All this should compel Americans to use less oil. But the normal growth of the US economy next year, even if only a modest 2 percent or so, will demand more petroleum than domestic wells, including Alaskan, can provide.

Next year's imports, oil specialists say, may average about 8.7 million barrels daily, compared with this year's 8 million daily figure.

★Please turn to Page 5

Inside today...

THE CHRISTIAN SCIENCE MONITOR

COPYRIGHT © 1979 THE CHRISTIAN SCIENCE PUBLISHING SOCIETY
All rights reserved   VOL. 71, NO. 36

Wednesday, January 17, 1979   25¢

Fall of the Shah — clues to what's next

Ayatollah Khomeini (left), Prime Minister Bakhtiar, Shah (fading from scene)

After Shah: some see threat of a vacuum

By Ned Temko
Special correspondent of The Christian Science Monitor
Beirut, Lebanon

The man who, perhaps more than anyone else, managed to unite Iran's disparate opposition forces stole a final, teary glance at Tehran Jan. 16, boarded a jet, and left.

His name: Shah Muhammad Reza Pahlavi.

With the monarch's departure, many diplomats and long-time observers of Iran feel the cement in the unlikely opposition alliance of fundamentalist Muslims and secular anti-Shah forces might weaken. The result could be internal bickering — or, worse, chaos — with damaging fallout both for the superpowers and Iran's Middle East neighbors.

For if the charismatic rallying figure for Iran's yearlong violence has been the exiled religious leader, Ayatollah Ru-

★Please turn to Page 6

As the Shah left his country, the streets of Iran erupted in jubilant demonstrations (Page 5). But his departure has shaken some of the basic assumptions of American foreign policy (Page 5) and worries Iran's Mideast neighbors (below, left).

By Geoffrey Godsell
Staff correspondent of The Christian Science Monitor
Tehran, Iran

Departure of Shah Muhammad Reza Pahlavi from Iran is the final act in a drama full of the stern moral cleansing grandeur of the Old Testament or a Greek tragedy.

Watching for it to happen over the past three weeks, like watching for a pot to boil, has tended sometimes to numb the sensitivities.

Yet what we have been seeing is the edging from his throne — and in recent days with his own cooperation — of the most personally powerful and important reigning monarch in the world.

The Shah still has not abdicated. Officially he has left Iran for a winter vacation and rest. Iran still is a monarchy, and a council of regency is standing in for him.

Some of the elite may be hoping for a reversal of fortune for him. Those who had hitched their wagons too closely to his star may even be dreaming of a replay of 1953, when the Shah was brought back in triumph from an earlier departure under political pressure.

But in the climate of today's Iran, any early return seems almost out of the question. And any attempted coup by the military or part of it to restore him would almost certainly invite strife and bloodshed far beyond that at moments of the Shah's harshest repression.

At the same time, the Shah's departure Jan. 16 does not end Iran's travail. Prime Minister Shahpour Bakhtiar still is only at the beginning of his awesome task of trying to keep constructively channeled the nationwide movement of revolt against the Shah that has forced the monarch to leave.

It remains to be seen whether that revolutionary movement will be persuaded by the Shah's departure to mark time to give Mr. Bakhtiar a period of grace — or whether its appetite will be whetted to push still harder for an immediate and even more radical overturning.

If that happened, the military — or part of it — might feel released from the pledge apparently won from it by the Shah to cooperate with

★Please turn to Page 6

FTC seeks to tame children's TV ads

By Brad Knickerbocker
Staff correspondent of The Christian Science Monitor
San Francisco

The long debate over television advertising directed toward children is coming to a head, and the results could affect millions of households across the country.

The Federal Trade Commission (FTC) this week began 10 days of public hearings in San Francisco to consider whether such advertising should be severely curtailed or banned, as consumer advocates, medical experts, and others have urged for many years. The hearings will move to Washington, D.C., in March, and the FTC is expected to rule this summer.

After conducting an investigation, the FTC staff is recommending that:

● All television advertising aimed at children under age eight be banned on the grounds that young children do not understand that they are being pressured by TV ads to buy something.

● Television advertising of highly sugared products (including presweetened cereals, snacks, and soft drinks) that is directed to children under age 12 also be banned.

● Other TV ads for sweet products shown with children's programs be balanced with mandatory nutritional and health messages.

The stakes in the complex "kidvid" battle of facts and rhetoric are extremely high, and no FTC proceeding has ever generated such controversy.

Some $600 million is spent each year on children's television advertis-

★Please turn to Page 6

Growing tug of war on natural-gas policy

By John Dillin
Staff correspondent of The Christian Science Monitor
Washington

United States energy officials, stung by criticism from Sen. Edward M. Kennedy (D) of Massachusetts, say that giving priority development to costly Alaskan gas rather than gas imports from Mexico will eventually save consumers billions of dollars.

In a study being circulated among its critics, the Energy Department says that price increases expected for Mexican gas will push the cost above Alaskan gas as early as 1985.

Energy Secretary James Schlesinger blocked a deal in late 1977 between Mexico and US firms to import 2 billion cubic feet of gas a day at a price of $2.60 per thousand cubic feet.

US officials estimate Alaskan gas, which would come down a 4,800-mile pipeline, would cost between $4.85 and $5.80 per thousand cubic feet, delivered to Illinois, when it becomes available around the mid-1980s.

But Mexican gas prices, at the insistence of officials there, would be tied to the price of No. 2 heating oil landed in New York — a price that is expected to soar in coming years.

"That Mexican gas will be very, very expensive," says one US energy official.

Congressional energy experts who agree with the Kennedy position call the Energy Department's analysis "nonsense."

The department "has a terrible record of predicting anything," says one Capitol Hill critic, who asked that he not be identified. "All Energy

★Please turn to Page 6

EASTERN EDITION
With pullout section: Page B1

THE CHRISTIAN SCIENCE MONITOR

COPYRIGHT © 1979 THE CHRISTIAN SCIENCE PUBLISHING SOCIETY
All rights reserved   VOL. 71, NO. 84

Tuesday, March 27, 1979

25¢

Penning a fresh start for the Mideast

Egypt-Israel treaty gives old adversaries time, but long-term risks remain

By Daniel Southerland
Staff correspondent of The Christian Science Monitor

Washington

With a few strokes of the pen Egypt and Israel have cut through three decades of psychological barriers, opening the way to a new era of conciliation between them.

If nothing else, the newly signed Egyptian-Israeli peace treaty stands as a monument to Egyptian President Sadat's first strong battering of those barriers through his precedent-shattering trip to Jerusalem 17 months ago.

With the signing of the treaty on the White House lawn at 2 p.m. on March 26, Mr. Sadat gave Israel much of the recognition which it has sought from the most populous and powerful of Arab nations.

It was the first peace treaty to be signed between an Arab nation and the Jewish state, and it appeared to reduce considerably the chances that any combination of Arab nations would go to war against Israel any time over the next few years.

Egypt has in the past borne the brunt of four wars against Israel, and its removal from the side of the potential combatants clearly reduces for the near future the risks of any new war. What was less clear was whether the peace treaty either increased or decreased the longer-term risks of instability in the Middle East, given the new constellation of forces arrayed against Israel, including oil-rich Iran.

It was certainly less than clear whether the claims being made for the peace treaty by President Carter, President Sadat, and Israel's Prime Minister Menachem Begin would stand the test of time.

"This peace treaty will be permanent," said President Carter two days before the signing ceremony, which was held on the front lawn of the White House under sunny skies and fleecy clouds.

"One of the greatest achievements of our time," said President Sadat, referring to Mr. Carter's successful effort to bring Egypt and Israel together for this historic moment.

"The great turning point in the Middle East," said Prime Minister Begin.

Despite all the rhetoric, however, there was a clear awareness on the part of all three parties involved that the real time of testing for the treaty may only come some months from

★Please turn to Page 9

A handshake to end four wars

UPI photo

At the White House — a far cry from 1905

By Richard L. Strout
Staff correspondent of
The Christian Science Monitor

Washington

It wasn't like this in Portsmouth, New Hampshire, in 1905 when Teddy Roosevelt forced peace on Japan and Russia. There were no loudspeakers, no helicopters, no policemen in crash helmets, no television cameras to instantly transmit the act of signing around the world; no, nor a circus tent behind the White House to hold the ceremonial banquet for 1,300 guests — with strolling violins and a menu ending with hazelnut giandja mousse.

I don't recollect the Portsmouth signing very distinctly (the last time an American president brought two nations together to sign a peace pact), although my mother always told me to remember that I was there, Aug. 25, having come by buggy from the farm at South Lee. Certainly there were no helicopters, and probably no traffic cops.

Washington does these things rather well, though, and is blasé about demonstrations and blocked-off traffic in rush hours. First, a group of police come to an intersection and halt traffic; then there is the wailing of sirens; then important foreign leaders dash through the city in limousines with flags flying, with escorts of dozens of police.

Pennsylvania Avenue this time is shut off a couple of hours before the ceremony. Right down to the last minute the reporters in the press room of the White House (suddenly invaded by swarms of Egyptian and Israeli visiting correspondents and jammed with extra equipment carrying TV operatives and big-name broadcasters) aren't sure whether the

★Please turn to Page 9

Balanced-budget battle rages

By John Dillin
Staff correspondent of The Christian Science Monitor

Washington

Surging inflation threatens to build new support in the United States for a constitutional amendment requiring a balanced federal budget.

Both friends and foes of the amendment say higher and higher inflation — latest projected annual rate, 15 percent — could become a pivotal factor supporting the amendment drive.

Already, 28 of the needed 34 states have passed petitions demanding that either Congress or a constitutional convention approve an amendment. The National Taxpayers Union, key organizer of the drive, predicts it will gain the necessary states by June.

Opponents, including the White House, are meanwhile pondering a number of possible steps that could be taken to thwart the budget-balancing tide.

A top White House aide says the amendment drive is shaping up as "the most important domestic issue of the year" — an issue that could have an impact for years to come.

Administration officials have a double dose of trouble with the amendment effort. One problem is economic. The other, political.

White House officials consider an amendment mandating a balanced budget to be an economic disaster. A tight, constitutional rule would take away a great deal of the president's flexibility to deal with the ups and downs of the economy, officials say.

Just as urgently, passage of the politically popular amendment could be a boon to the Jerry-come-lately of tax cutters, Gov. Edmund G. (Jerry) Brown Jr. of California.

Governor Brown, whose White House ambitions are much

★Please turn to Page 9

Inside today...

Soviet scientists rebuff a high party leader

By Paul Wohl
Special to The Christian Science Monitor

For the first time a prestigious Soviet institution has refused to admit into its own ranks a member of the Communist Party Central Committee.

In an unprecedented move the Soviet Academy of Sciences has refused full membership to Sergei P. Trapezhnikov, who has been a full member of the party's Central Committee since 1965, and chairman of the Science Commission of the Supreme Soviet (Legislature) since 1966.

Mr. Trapezhnikov, who also has been a corresponding member of the academy since 1976, has repeatedly asked to be admitted as a full member, but until now no formal decision had been taken.

Rejection of his request by a majority vote of 212 against 137 was possible only because the Academy of Sciences, which predates the Soviet regime, is the one institution which has retained the privilege of the secret ballot.

It is thanks to this privilege that a leading dissident, Prof. Andrei D. Sakharov, has remained a full member of the academy despite many attempts to have him ousted.

★Please turn to Page 9

THE CHRISTIAN SCIENCE MONITOR

COPYRIGHT © 1979 THE CHRISTIAN SCIENCE PUBLISHING SOCIETY
All rights reserved

VOL. 71, NO. 239

Monday, November 5, 1979

25¢

Kemeny — 'no ax' view of nuclear safety in US

By David F. Salisbury
Staff correspondent of
The Christian Science Monitor
Washington

Perhaps the greatest value of the Kemeny Commission report on the accident at Three Mile Island is that it acted as a unique surrogate for the American people as it wrestled with the complex issues surrounding nuclear power.

For the first time a group of distinguished Americans with no ax to grind

Analysis

critically reviewed the question of nuclear reactor safety.

All investigations in the past have been conducted either by technical groups like the National Academy of Sciences or by politicians. Scientists and engineers have a special perspective, and elected representatives seldom have the luxury of spending six months concentrating on a single issue, as the commission did, and must worry about re-election.

Issues like nuclear safety are too complicated to be fathomed without concentrated study and too important to be left solely in the hands of technologists. Therefore, the presidential commission was uniquely suited to the task of determining the lessons taught by Three Mile Island.

In its diversity, the commission reflected the pluralism of American society: Academic, businessman, labor leader, housewife, medical expert, nuclear engineer, environmentalist, journalist, governor, they all came together. Each brought a different background and a different set of values and concerns to the problem.

★ **Please turn to Page 6**

Attack on American Embassy: what religious hard-liners in Iran hope to gain

Radical students seek 'justice' for ousted Shah and greater Muslim control of oil-rich nation

By Geoffrey Godsell
Staff correspondent of The Christian Science Monitor

The seizure of the American Embassy in Tehran by Muslim students calling themselves "followers of the Imam" (Ayatollah Ruhollah Khomeini) should be seen against the following background:

● Short-term, the persistent vengeful desire of Iran's most ardent revolutionaries to bring the ousted Shah "to justice," and the opportunity the Shah's presence in New York for medical treatment gives them to blackmail the United States Government into surrendering him.

● Longer-term, the sharpening struggle at the top in Iran between the hard-line religious fundamentalists and the pragmatists. The fundamentalists want to establish a theocratic republic with a government run by Shia Muslim clergy. The religious pragmatists would prefer a secular government, but one sensitive and responsive to the demands of Shia Islam.

Both camps would publicly demand that pressure be put on the US Government to surrender the Shah. But the fundamentalists would be much readier to go to the ultimate in putting the squeeze on Washington — hoping thereby not only to get the Shah but also to discredit the relatively moderate pragmatists.

As night fell in Tehran Nov. 4, the students who had seized the embassy were still in control of it and were said to be holding hostage as many as 60 of the staff, most of them Americans, including at least 10 US Marines. An eyewitness said one of the students at the embassy gate had told him that unless the US surrendered the Shah, the American hostages would be tried by Islamic revolutionary tribunals.

The students claimed to have acted with the approval of Ayatollah Khomeini. An eye-

★ **Please turn to Page 13**

Ayatollah Khomeini   By Albert J. Forbes, staff artist
What lies behind US Embassy takeover?

Cambodians: pawns on the superpower chessboard

By Louis Wiznitzer
Special correspondent of The Christian Science Monitor

United Nations, New York

The people of Cambodia are being sacrificed like pawns on the global big-power chessboard.

This is the view expressed here by high-ranking, impartial officials and diplomats who are intimately familiar with Cambodia's desperate plight.

The Cambodians, they say, have become caught up in a major redistribution of the superpowers' spheres of influence. And despite all the rhetoric to the contrary, the world community is doing very little to stop the "holocaust" now occurring.

A special United Nations conference this week takes up the humanitarian problems of Cambodia, and a little later the UN General Assembly will grapple separately with the political issues involved. Funds are expected to be pledged, noble and angry words to be spoken, resolutions to be adopted. But, say these officials and diplomats, hopes of saving the ancient nation of Cambodia are dim.

The crux of the problem is that Vietnam perceives Western humanitarian aid proposals as a Trojan horse designed to weaken Hanoi's hold on the region. The West, in turn, refuses to be blackmailed

into recognizing in any fashion the Vietnam-backed Heng Samrin regime in Cambodia.

This impasse comes at a time of growing turmoil in Southeast Asia. According to these sources, the region is a powder keg where explosions are likely to occur periodically and where potential conflicts, for lack of existing constraints, could easily spread.

"In the aftermath of the successive withdrawals from Southeast Asia by Japan, France, the United States, the area has become a

Compromise saves US aid package   **Page 10**

battleground for the USSR and China by proxy," says one authoritative diplomat who has no ax to grind.

The same diplomat — with several international officials concurring — continues:

"The Chinese still play the Pol Pot card; and the United States plays the Chinese card. The Soviet Union plays the Vietnamese card; and Hanoi plays the Heng Samrin card. Both sides are ready to fight to the last Cambodian."

To complete this picture, he adds: "The present situation allows the Soviets to militarize Vietnam and transform it into a Soviet base. It

★ **Please turn to Page 13**

Saving energy suddenly seems the best way again

By Harry B. Ellis
Staff correspondent of
The Christian Science Monitor
Washington

Quietly the Carter administration has begun to dust off the word "conservation" as the nation's No. 1 energy goal.

Americans themselves, meanwhile, are reducing the amount of petroleum they burn, as the spiraling cost of gasoline and heating oil bites deeper into family pocketbooks.

Both the US Department of Energy (DOE) and the American Petroleum Institute report that higher prices, among other things, are shrinking the nation's consumption of oil.

In the four weeks ending Oct. 19, the DOE says, overall petroleum use averaged 17.0 million barrels a day, 6.7 percent below the

level for the same period of last year and well under the consumption level of 1977.

Cutting back on the use of energy, Treasury Secretary G. William Miller says, "is the surest, cheapest, cleanest way to reduce our dependence on oil."

Only in fourth place among goals — after conservation, expanded production of US conventional fuels, and development of solar and other renewable sources — does Mr. Miller list the "rigorous development" of unconventional sources, such as synthetic fuels.

This seems a far cry from President Carter's fist-pounding insistence in a nationwide TV speech July 15 that Americans should plunge into full-scale creation of a vast synthetic fuels industry.

What has happened to swing the White

House toward a fresh look at the value of conservation as the nation's top energy goal? Among other things:

● Mr. Carter's call for an $88 billion investment in synthetics ran into strong congressional opposition and, in any case, could produce commercial quantities of fuel only in the mid-1980s or later.

● The escalating price of foreign oil — an estimated $58 billion import tab this year, rising to $70 billion in 1980 — sends the US balance of trade plunging deeper into the red.

● Mr. Carter's firm pledge to hold oil imports to no more than 8.5 million barrels daily in 1980 and succeeding years could clash head-on with the nation's long-term decline in production of domestic oil.

★ **Please turn to Page 13**

Inside today...

THE CHRISTIAN SCIENCE MONITOR

COPYRIGHT © 1980 THE CHRISTIAN SCIENCE PUBLISHING SOCIETY
All rights reserved   VOL. 72, NO. 108
Monday, April 28, 1980   40¢

Iran hints US, not hostages, may be tried

The Iranian debacle has damaged US prestige, raised doubts about its military capability, and yielded an unexpected olive branch. For the first time, the Iranian militants are signaling that the Shah's return is not necessarily a quid pro quo for releasing the hostages. While Moscow responds gleefully, US allies seem determined to repair the damage by standing closer together. Events could force President Carter to abandon his 'Rose Garden' strategy. Stories, below and inside.

Tabas, Iran: US aircraft wreckage in foreground, abandoned helicopter at rear

UPI photo

Impact of foul-up: fewer US options, strained allies

By Daniel Southerland
Staff correspondent of
The Christian Science Monitor

Washington

Failure of the American rescue operation in Iran carries impact far beyond the question of the new plight of the American hostages.

The toll, in brief, appears to be this:

● Another blow to American credibility in the Middle East.

● Additional strain on US relations with West Europe and Japan.

● A further narrowing of the options available for American action against Iran.

The United States is returning for the time being to economic and diplomatic actions against Iran. At a weekend meeting in Luxembourg, the West European allies were expected, despite their misgivings over the abortive rescue operation, to reaffirm their support for such actions against Iran. But few specialists seem to think this will result in an early release of the 50 American hostages.

A senior White House official argued that the Iranians now must realize how serious the US is about securing the freedom of the hostages. This view was supported by former Secretary of State Henry A. Kissinger. But a number of independent experts on Iran think that the unsuccessful rescue effort has actually undercut the Iranian "moderates" who want to negotiate release of the hostages and strengthened the "hardliners," including Ayatollah Ruhollah Khomeini.

"There is no reason to believe that Khomeini will be any more inclined to moderate his view," said William B. Quandt, former chief specialist on the Middle East for the Carter administration and now with the Brookings Institution.

"This rescue operation was fantastic for Khomeini," said Mr. Quandt. "As far as he's concerned, it's one more humiliation for the United States."

Whether this would immediately redound to the profit of the Soviet Union was less clear. But the fear all along has been that a weakening of the Iranian moderates and a strengthening of the extremists would eventually pull Iran apart and allow the Soviets to come in.

Despite all this, it has come as no surprise to political analysts that in the immediate aftermath of the unsuccessful mission into Iran, many Americans expressed support of President Carter and his decision to make the raid. They recall that just after the abortive Bay of Pigs invasion of Cuba in 1961, President John F. Kennedy's popularity increased markedly.

A Newsweek-Gallup poll released April 26 found that 71 percent of the Americans surveyed approved of the raid. The poll also showed that 46 percent approved of President Carter's overall handling of the Iran crisis, 42 percent disapproved, and 12 percent had no opinion.

But the analysts say that there is a natural tendency to rally to the President's support in a crisis. They doubt that the support shown in the immediate aftermath of the rescue raid will translate into any lasting support for the President, particularly after it becomes apparent that the raid may have made any future rescue effort or release of the hostages by the Iranians more difficult. This appears to be all the more true in light of reports from
★ Please turn to Page 7

By Ned Temko
Staff correspondent of
The Christian Science Monitor

Tehran, Iran

President Carter's bid to free 53 captive Americans seems to have condemned them instead to weeks of fear, uncertainty, separation, and almost inevitably harsher conditions. It may even end in the very "spy trial" he strove to avoid.

If there is any silver lining in the "rescue" drama — which culminated April 27 in the macabre display of the charred remains of at least eight Americans at the captive US Embassy they had hoped to liberate — it is that the militant student captors mentioned a trial, not the execution threatened earlier in case of any US attempt to free the captives.

The militants also implied they wanted to try the United States, more than the individual hostages, and for the first time portrayed such a trial as an alternative to the return of the deposed Shah and his wealth.

But the failed American attempt to end the 25-week hostage ordeal, and its truculent aftermath, also afforded the strongest proof yet of the growing impotence of nominal "government" in a body politic dominated by militant youths and Muslim mullahs (teachers) beholden only to Ayatollah Khomeini.

"The danger," one diplomat said, "is that, given the mood in Iran, even a show trial of American policy would not necessarily mean the release of all the hostages."

Ayatollah Sadeq Khalkhali, the one-time revolutionary "hanging judge," assisted in handing over remains of the rescue-mission Americans to the militants. His involvement contradicted assurances from President Abolhassan Bani-Sadr that the bodies would
★ Please turn to Page 11

Kremlin aim: use raid to split West

By David K. Willis
Staff correspondent of
The Christian Science Monitor

Moscow

The Kremlin, handed a propaganda windfall by the failure of the US raid into Iran, is working on at least three significant fronts to try to exploit it to the hilt.

It is telling the world, especially its own allies and the third world, that the "reckless" Mr. Carter is endangering global peace. The Tass news agency April 27 picked up what it said were New York reports that the raid was actually a possible coup against Ayatollah Khomeini himself.

It is hammering at Western Europe to make NATO allies believe Mr. Carter is far too unstable to be allowed to install and control medium-range nuclear missiles in Europe.

(It is also hinting the Soviet Union might cut back huge Soviet exports of oil to Western Europe unless NATO changes policies — a threat Westerners here see as bluff, since Moscow needs the hard currency the oil earns
★ Please turn to Page 7

Hispanics — America's 'awakening giant'

The sudden influx of Cuban refugees into southern Florida is a reminder that, in addition to all the other problems it faces at home and abroad in the 1980s, the United States is challenged by the need to adjust to its fast-growing Hispanic population.

Today's Monitor begins a five-part series by staff correspondent Geoffrey Godsell on Hispanics in the US. The first article sets the scene. Following articles on Tuesday, Wednesday, and Thursday will deal with each of the three main Hispanic groups: Mexicans, Cubans, and Puerto Ricans. Finally, a summary article on Friday will analyze what lies ahead.

'Aquí se habla español.'

The questions posed include these: Can legal and illegal Hispanic immigration — or more particularly Mexican immigration, now running at an estimated rate of 1 million a year — be halted or slowed? Can the plight of the Puerto Ricans be turned in the right direction? What will be the eventual political status of the Puerto Rican homeland? What will be the long-term impact on the fabric of the US of such a massively and specifically Hispanic Roman Catholic inflow? How will US party politics be affected? How will relations develop between Hispanics and blacks? And, most portentous of all, will the growth of the Hispanic component of the population lead to an unprecedented demand for constitutional recognition for the first time of two languages and two cultures within a single US?

First of five articles: Page 3

181

THE CHRISTIAN SCIENCE MONITOR

COPYRIGHT © 1980 THE CHRISTIAN SCIENCE PUBLISHING SOCIETY   VOL. 72, NO. 242
All rights reserved

Thursday, November 6, 1980

40¢

Reagan era begins, New Deal era ebbs

Ronald Reagan's landslide spurred new hopes among Americans for solving their problems at home and abroad. Voters saw in him and his his party a chance to turn back the tide of government growth. The stock market immediately soared, backing up this 'bullish' feeling. The 40th US President says he will "hit the ground running" to implement his conservative philosophy (below). On foreign policy, he has moderated his views on defense spending and relations with Moscow and Peking (below right).

By Brad Knickerbocker
Staff correspondent of The Christian Science Monitor
San Francisco

Ronald Reagan's long odyssey from Tampico, Ill., to the White House — via Hollywood and Sacramento — now is complete. His sweeping victory forcefully culminates the nation's politically rightward (and geographically westward) movement.

There are two general objectives that the new President-elect wants to meet quickly and decisively, say the men now molding the Reagan administration. He wants to get a firm grip on the federal establishment, pulling tight a controlling cinch and redirecting it toward a narrower path. He also seeks to assure Americans, as well as allies and adversaries overseas, that he will proceed reasonably and cautiously in foreign affairs.

When Mr. Reagan first took office as governor of California in 1966, he was a political novice. But he will begin his tenure as the nation's chief executive with considerable preparation. Long before the Nov. 4 election, a team of several hundred top campaign advisers, former Republican officials, academic experts, and professional bureaucrats was drawn together.

For weeks, this "Reagan planning task force" (which numbers about 335 and includes some Democrats) has been working in groups of about 15 to prepare studies and recommendations.

"We basically have five major areas that we're working on," says Edwin Meese, Reagan staff chief for many years and the man likely to hold a similar post in Washington. These are organization and management of the White House staff and Cabinet, personnel hiring, budget development, executive actions that can be taken immediately, and proposed legislation.

Within these areas, groups soon will be reporting to Reagan on such specific topics as small business regulation, welfare reform, social security, inflation, and federal budget income. Also being studied are the findings of such private organizations as the Heritage Foundation, the National Academy of Public Administration, and Harvard University's John F. Kennedy School of Government.

Mr. Meese, who has been overseeing all of this, predicts "some very fundamental organizational differences" will result, including a strengthened Cabinet whose members firmly manage their respective bureaucracies. This has been a largely unfulfilled promise

★ Please turn to Page 11

UPI photo

Now it's the high road to Washington for President-elect and future First Lady Nancy Reagan

Will US foreign policy turn right?

By Daniel Southerland
Staff correspondent of
The Christian Science Monitor
Washington

Ronald Reagan's foreign policy will be conservative — but just how conservative will depend greatly on whom he appoints to key positions.

This seems to be the conventional wisdom in Washington as Mr. Reagan's advisers set about preparing their man for the formidable tasks of dealing with, among other things, the Soviet Union, the West European allies, the Arab-Israeli conflict, and oil supplies from the Gulf.

Some of the government's career foreign policy experts believe that

once the new President is briefed, his moves on key foreign policy issues will depart much less radically from Carter administration approaches than it might seem at first glance. Some of them believe in what might be called the

Global reaction   6

"moderating influence of the bureaucracy." Still others believe that the influence of hard realities — such as the ever-growing US dependence on Arab oil — will force Reagan at least slightly away from what appears to be a virtually unqualified pro-Israeli Middle East policy.

On the vital issues of defense spending, arms control, and relations with major nations — the Soviet Union and China in particular — Reagan already appeared during the election campaign to moderate his views. He stopped talking about nuclear superiority over the Soviets and started talking about a "margin of safety." He began emphasizing his interest in world peace.

But Reagan foreign policy advisers are widely divided into what might be called moderate, conservative, and extremely conservative groups. No one is entirely sure at this point who will come out on top. Most speculation about a future

★ Please turn to Page 15

It was one of those great turns in US history — but how far?

By Richard J. Cattani
Staff correspondent of The Christian Science Monitor
Washington

An American public that had been called indecisive and apathetic acted with firmness — if not fury — when its turn came in the voting booth.

It was a vote for optimism, historians may later observe, a drawing of the line against economic stagnation at home and humiliation abroad.

"Enough," the voters said. "America can do better."

So broadly did the sweep carry — from the Reagan landslide, to the US Senate, to the state capitals — that it must have been more than just repudiation of a sitting president, observers say.

An ideological drift may be occurring that is conservative in nature and southwestern in direction.

Looking ahead, the industrial states of New York, Ohio, Illinois, Michigan, and Pennsylvania will lose House seats and Electoral College votes starting in 1982. The gainers will be conservative states like Texas, California, Arizona, and Tennessee, as well as Florida, Oregon, and Washington.

Put another way, the "frost belt" Electoral College votes outnumbered Sunbelt votes by 41 when Democrat John Kennedy won in 1960. But for the Carter-Reagan election the Sunbelt led by 4. In the 1984 election, the Sunbelt will lead by 26, say elections experts Richard Scammon and Ben Wattenberg.

The 1980 election appears to have embedded other lasting trends as well.

The apparent success of conservative and single-issue groups that targeted liberal senators for defeat suggests

more such political citizen-posse actions in future elections. More independent committee support for presidential candidates will likely also be seen.

The limited success of John Anderson's independent effort revealed that the American electorate is still drawn to the basic Democratic and Republican poles. That may discourage more such independent attempts in the future.

In terms of party organization, the Republican National Committee under chairman Bill Brock so decisively forged a united presidential, Senate-House, and state party effort that the Democrats will have to attempt the same unified approach in the campaigns ahead. The Democrats submerged their national party machine in the President's re-election effort; the Republicans invested effectively in recruiting talent and making the best

★ Please turn to Page 15

THE CHRISTIAN SCIENCE MONITOR

COPYRIGHT © 1981 THE CHRISTIAN SCIENCE PUBLISHING SOCIETY
All rights reserved   VOL. 73, NO. 38

Tuesday, January 20, 1981   40¢

11th-hour drama: why Iran kept US waiting until Reagan inauguration

Welcome mat rolled out as hostage return delayed by temporary 'hitch'

By James Dorsey
Special correspondent of The Christian Science Monitor
Rhein Main Air Base, Frankfurt, West Germany

With excitement and relief, intermingled with anxiety over one last-minute delay, the Western world Jan. 19 awaited the final release of the 52 American hostages.

Sources in Iran, reached by telephone, insisted that the delay flowed from a minor, temporary hitch. One version — that it related to a missing Iranian signature opening an escrow bank account — was denied by Iran's hostage negotiator Behzad Nabavi.

These sources in Iran also suspected that the Iranians might prefer anyway to hand the hostages over to the incoming Reagan administration, just to make sure Ronald Reagan felt fully tied into the deal. And some observers

Other Iran stories   3,4,5

are convinced that the Iranians would be happy to upstage the pomp and ceremony of the Reagan inauguration.

Whatever the specific cause of the delay, Iranian central bankers worked late into the night, presumably to resolve the last-minute difficulties. At the same time, the Algerian doctors examining the hostages concluded their work late Jan. 19 and the team of Algerian mediators left Tehran by plane.

Meanwhile, the United States Air Force Rhein Main Air Base alongside the major European airport of Frankfurt showed tangible evidence of the anticipated arrival of the hostages.

Two US Air Force men pinned a 10-meter-long banner to one of the hangars welcoming the hostages "back to freedom." And, as more than 1,000 journalists milled around the airfield and the American military hospital in nearby Wiesbaden, US military and West German authorities stepped up their security activities.

Reporters were expected to be able to catch only a glimpse of the freed Americans as they emerged from their plane and stepped into a bus, whisking them away to the US military hospital. The top floor of the hospital has been furnished with 52 beds and 52 bedside telephones to enable the hostages to talk with their families.

★ Please turn to Page 11

Hostage William Keough's wife, Elizabeth, and daughter, Allysa, share joy   UPI photo

In a relieved and happy nation, they are among the few who were burdened most . . . and are happiest

Hostage wife: quiet talk, new tennis racquet

By Richard M. Harley
Staff writer of The Christian Science Monitor

In her suburban Virginia home, Bonnie Graves has been hard at work refurnishing her husband's study.

Now it is replete with a bed, telephone, easy chair, good reading light, and spanking new tennis racquet. "Because," she says with a glint of joy, "he's the sort of person those things interest."

But Mrs. Graves is making no further plans for her husband's return — at least, not yet.

"I don't even know what I'll wear when I meet him,

whether I'll meet him alone or with the family. That'll depend on what John himself will want when we finally have a chance to talk."

Mrs. Graves, along with the families of the other 51 American hostages, is breathing a lot easier — elated over the prospect of the return of the hostages. But the families are avoiding rigid planning. They want above all to make plenty of room for their loved ones to return to American life in ways that the hostages themselves will find easiest after their 443 days in captivity.

The 52 are individuals, they stress, and will have very

★ Please turn to Page 11

Inauguration: unprecedented twin drama

By Richard J. Cattani
Staff correspondent of The Christian Science Monitor
Washington

"This is the only time a twin star, or binary event has occurred at an inauguration. I can't think of any parallel. There is no precedent for such a blaze of drama for a departing president like Carter's. Usually all an ex-president has to do is pack up and ride to the inauguration. John Adams just quietly returned to Boston."

This is how Harvard historian Frank Friedel characterizes an inauguration that combines the drama and solemnity inherent in a change of administrations with the outpouring of national emotion over the outgoing President's resolution of a 14-month international crisis.

The hostage episode itself, after its emotional and media crest has passed, will not likely leave any lingering bitterness among the public. Although the amount of attention it consumed during the past 14 months — its domination of the news — was remark-

able, it will likely be more a "Mayaguez"-sized event, observes Everett Ladd, an opinion expert.

"Its impact will be relatively small in its bearing of the standing of the country," Mr. Ladd says, "unlike Vietnam policy or World War II China policy. After the communist victory in China, recriminations persisted."

The Reagan team is expected to take advantage of the euphoria over the hostage release to keep the transition slate clean and not antagonize the Democrats by recrimination or by prodding Republicans in Congress to demand an investigation.

"The months ahead into the summer are very precious for this administration, as for any new administration," says Friedel.

The new administration will try to keep its honeymoon period going as long as it can, husbanding its initial goodwill with Congress and the public to get its ambitious economic program enacted.

Reagan's economic challenge looks even tougher

★ Please turn to Page 11

The mantle of US leadership cloaks new shoulders for the 40th time

Colorful tour of past inaugurals: Page 12

By Richard L. Strout
Staff correspondent of The Christian Science Monitor
Washington

The crowd stills, the nation watches, the black-robed chief justice steps forward, and the former California governor and one-time Hollywood actor says, "I, Ronald Reagan, do solemnly swear . . . [to] preserve, protect, and defend the Constitution of the United States."

In Philadelphia two centuries ago John Adams wrote to his beloved Abigail that it was "the sublimest thing ever exhibited in America." The Founding Fathers wrote the words, George Washington recited them first. Mr. Reagan is the 40th president to do so.

America and the rest of the world look on the new President with awe and hope: One moment ago he was a private citizen, the next moment he is one of the most powerful men on Earth. No American soldier is fighting in a foreign war, no campus is in turmoil, and no cities are on fire.

It goes beyond this. Before the ceremony, the victorious candidate and President Carter, his defeated rival, rode in harmony together up

★ Please turn to Page 4

THE CHRISTIAN SCIENCE MONITOR

COPYRIGHT © 1981 THE CHRISTIAN SCIENCE PUBLISHING SOCIETY
All rights reserved   VOL. 73, NO. 221   Wednesday, October 7, 1981   MIDWESTERN EDITION   40¢

After Sadat, US Mideast strategy put at risk

By Geoffrey Godsell
Staff correspondent of The Christian Science Monitor

The assassination of Egyptian President Anwar Sadat puts at risk:

● The entire US plan for building a "strategic consensus" based on Egypt, Saudi Arabia, and Israel to defend the oil-rich Gulf area from any Soviet threat.

● The Camp David peace process, of which the two most outstanding steps are Israeli withdrawal, due in April, from the last remaining sector of Sinai held by Israel since the "six-day war" of 1967; and reaching agreement on a plan for "full autonomy" for the Palestinians.

● The internal stability of Egypt and the continuation of that country on the path of pro-Western moderation within the broad framework of Middle East politics and superpower rivalry in the area.

For the US, one of the consequences could be an immediate need completely to rethink its strategic planning for the defense of the Middle East and of the oil-rich Gulf in particular.

Vice-President Hosni Mubarak was handpicked by President Sadat as his No. 2 and potential successor. Under the Egyptian Constitution an election will be held

Analysis

within 60 days. Mubarak is a former Air Force chief of staff under President Sadat, and therefore should have good links with the armed services — essential for the survival of any Egyptian leader.

The fact that Mr. Mubarak and Egyptian Defense Minister Muhammad Abdul Halim Abu Ghazzala, although at Mr. Sadat's side, survived the assassins' bursts of machine-gun fire should contribute to a smoother transition

than if both or either had been incapacitated or killed.

All evidence points to Mubarak's fully supporting Sadat's policies. In announcing Sadat's death to the Egyptian people, Mubarak formally pledged that all Egypt's current international commitments will be maintained.

With Sadat no longer on the scene, Mubarak still has to prove that he can survive — just as Sadat had to prove that he could survive after the demise of the late President Nasser 11 years ago.

In the early months of his presidency, Sadat was not without jealous rivals who thought they were more rightfully Nasser's heirs than he. They also happened to be more pro-Soviet than he.

Sadat was a key figure in the strategic consensus that the US has been trying to build in the Mideast to defend the Gulf area. He was anxious to be recognized in the US

★ Please turn to Page 12

Cairo: tumult on scene, doubt on what comes next

By Louise Lief
Special to The Christian Science Monitor
Cairo

The shooting of Egyptian President Anwar Sadat by Egyptian soldiers during a military parade in Cairo throws into question the whole direction of Middle East politics and peace.

Along with other spectators this correspondent was watching an aerial acrobatic show and exhibition of heavy artillery at the Nasser City military fairgrounds here when a group of soldiers leaped from a truck in front of the grandstand where the President was sitting with high dignitaries. They tossed two grenades, and opened fire with their Kalashnikovs on the horrified crowd.

The President was whisked into a helicopter and flown away. It was learned later that he had been taken to Maadi military hospital where he died.

Vice-President Hosni Mubarak escaped uninjured, speeding away in an armored car. He subsequently took over as commander in chief of the armed forces, effectively taking some of the leading reins of power. Parliament speaker Sofi Abu Taleb assumed the formal role of president.

The scene at the fairgrounds where the military was celebrating the eighth anniversary of the October 1973 Arab-Israel war

Mubarak in Washington last weekend with US Secretary of Defense Caspar Weinberger   UPI photo
Egypt's Vice-President Hosni Mubarak, right, assumes a leading role

was pandemonium as Mirage jets screamed overhead and the panicking crowd ran or crawled from the grandstand to avoid the gunfire. Soldiers in uniform wept, crying "the President, the President."

Sadat's assassination comes about a month after he instituted a sweeping crackdown against religious fundamentalists and

political opponents. That involved the arrest of some 1,600 people, the dissolution of Christian and Muslim religious societies, and the closure of seven publications.

Although no public mention was made, informed sources reported that there had been about 50 arrests and perhaps more in the military at the time of the crackdown

★ Please turn to Page 12

US: praise for the man, doubts about the region

**By staff correspondents of
The Christian Science Monitor**

Washington

The personal impact of the assassination of Egyptian President Anwar Sadat was evident in a statement by President Reagan, who praised the late Egyptian leader as a "courageous man whose wisdom and vision brought people together. . . ."

Speaking outside the White House Tuesday, the President said that Sadat was a "humanitarian unafraid to seek peace."

"The US has lost a close friend, the world has lost a great statesman, and mankind has lost a man of peace," he added.

But along with the praise from the President and other US officials came speculation about the event's effect on Mr. Reagan's Mideast policy, especially as reflected in his controversial plan to sell AWACS surveillance aircraft to Saudi Arabia.

Early congressional reaction regarding the assassination's impact on the AWACS sale provided a mixed picture:

● Sen. Orrin G. Hatch (R) of Utah emerged from a meeting with President Reagan Tuesday afternoon saying that he would support the sale. Noting that he was one of the 50 senators initially objecting to

★ Please turn to Page 13

First non-NASA satellite may launch era of low-cost space exploration

By David F. Salisbury
Staff correspondent of The Christian Science Monitor
Boulder, Colo.

Yesterday at 5:30 in the morning, outer space came one small step closer to the common man.

In the predawn darkness a University of Colorado (UC) group became the first scientists outside of the National Aeronautics and Space Administration (NASA) to take direct control of a US satellite.

This satellite is the Solar Mesospheric Explorer (SME) which was put into a near perfect orbit Oct. 6 and will be studying the dynamics of the ozone layer which extends from 20 to 50 miles overhead and protects Earth's surface from ultraviolet radiation.

Not only is SME the first to be controlled by non-NASA personnel, but it may prove to be the prototype for the low-cost space missions required in an era of fiscal conservatism.

The atmosphere within the drab gray industrial building

where SME Mission Control is located was jubilant as the tracking stations reported their satellite had achieved a near perfect orbit and telemetry from the satellite itself showed all the instruments on board working correctly.

The control room looks a bit homely and cobbled together when compared with the sophisticated operations at the large NASA centers. Its five computer screens are set into a shallow plywood "U". Its telephone receivers sit in crudely hollowed-out plastic foam cubes. But behind this modest exterior lies some innovative control techniques which have caught the eye of NASA and the Department of Defense.

"We are the first to use color to indicate the condition of various signals," says Elaine R. Hansen, mission director. Using a sophisticated computer program, the condition of the various spacecraft systems are displayed in green if they are within normal operating limits, yellow if the readings are marginal, and red if something is wrong. "We couldn't expect students to spend hours staring intently at columns of

numbers and be so immersed in the project to know all the ranges," she explains.

The satellite will be run by a staff of 6 faculty and 14 students. For the students it is a job without academic credit like mowing lawns or working in the library. "I've had a number of nice jobs, things that look good on a resume, but I've never been involved with anything as exciting and interesting as this," says one of the undergraduate controllers, Jafar Nabkel. "For the first time I can really see where what I am learning can be put to use," continues the computer science student.

Besides being an unparalleled learning experience for the students, their presence is an example of the bare-bones approach being used by the UC space scientists. At $17 million, it is one of the least expensive scientific payloads NASA has launched in recent years. It was the most modest of the 150-odd proposals submitted to NASA for an ozone-monitoring

★ Please turn to Page 13

THE CHRISTIAN SCIENCE MONITOR

AN INTERNATIONAL DAILY NEWSPAPER

COPYRIGHT © 1981 THE CHRISTIAN SCIENCE PUBLISHING SOCIETY
All rights reserved   VOL. 74, NO. 13   Monday, December 14, 1981   MIDWESTERN EDITION   40¢

Poland cracks down on union, scuttles reforms; USSR keeps its distance from crisis next door

Moscow hangs on to détente, lets Poles impose crackdown

By Ned Temko
Staff correspondent of
The Christian Science Monitor

Moscow

The Soviet Union seems intent on portraying Poland's declaration of full military rule as a purely Polish decision, despite consistent Moscow pressure for a crackdown on the reform movement there.

The Soviets are seen as fearful that the West will brand them as masterminds of what one Washington official reportedly termed a move toward "head-cracking" in Poland.

The Warsaw television announcement early Dec. 13 of a state of emergency came as the Kremlin was bidding for improved ties with the West, particularly with Western Europe. The seriousness of this effort has been underscored by an unprecedented Soviet surrender to a protest by dissident physicist Andrei Sakharov.

The government newspaper Izvestia, in a one-paragraph item Dec. 12, confirmed that Moscow had "exceptionally" agreed to let Sakharov's daughter-in-law emigrate to the United States — the demand for which he and his wife began a hunger strike last month.

The Warsaw crackdown by Premier Wojciech Jaruzelski — including a number of arrests, a ban on strikes and demonstrations, and creation of a military "council of national salvation" — followed a renewed toughening of Soviet news media comment on the Polish situation in recent days.

But in their initial accounts of General Jaruzelski's move, the media here adopted a tone of detachment, reporting the premier's television address and subsequent developments without immediate comment.

Diplomats saw this as an indication the Soviets sought publicly to distance themselves from the Polish action and to portray it as the Poles' own decision. (The expectation is that any Western criticism of the Polish move will be roundly denounced by Moscow as "inter-

★ Please turn to Page 6

Union chief Walesa, Polish Prime Minister Jaruzelski, Soviet President Brezhnev   Sven Simon, Bandphoto, Eastfoto

Two Poles are at center of emergency; but Brezhnev watches closely

Foreign aid may be US's strongest hand in influencing Polish crisis

By Daniel Southerland
Staff correspondent of
The Christian Science Monitor

Washington

Much more than Polish freedom hangs in the balance.

If Poland's military authorities carry their crackdown to a complete suppression of the independent labor movement there, it could not only disrupt Western trade and aid relations with that country, but also derail the US-Soviet nuclear weapons talks now under way in Geneva.

According to experts on the subject here, the West could not remain indifferent to the destruction of Solidarity, the only East-bloc trade union free of communist party control.

Militarily, there is little that the West can do to influence events in Poland. American

★ Please turn to Page 12

Other Poland-related stories

Helmut Schmidt and Erich Honecker held their countries' first summit in 10 years. But events in Poland may endanger the fragile détente between Germanies. Page 12.

Poland's debts to Western nations are so large that the West as well as Moscow has a vested interest in avoiding upheaval there. But reviving the economy demands a loosening of central controls. Page 6.

What led up to the latest crisis? A blow-by-blow account. Page 6.

Biggest risk is all-out clash as workers react to new military rule

The writer is in Vienna during one of his periodic breaks from covering the Polish crisis from Warsaw.

By Eric Bourne
Special correspondent of
The Christian Science Monitor

Vienna

In one of the most severe and far-reaching internal crackdowns the Communist nations of East Europe have ever seen, Polish leader Wojciech Jaruzelski has clamped martial law on his troubled and restive country.

Clearly his move was meticulously prepared. He rolled it into place overnight Dec. 12-13 with well-oiled efficiency.

So much so that the Solidarity union movement seems to have been caught off balance. Although a number of its leaders were arrested, especially those considered "extremists" by the government, the rest of the union was slow to respond. A government spokesman said some detainees would be freed on a "case to case basis . . . possibly very soon."

With military rule imposed for the indefinite future, and with a curfew in place and a stream of regulations designed to control everything from the news media to opponents of all sorts, the three overriding issues are:

● Will the government's decision to have a showdown with the union sweep away the reforms painstakingly negotiated over the past 16 months? If the Polish Communist Party's hard-liners have their way, the nationwide hopes of last year's "Polish August" will go the way of Czechoslovakia's "Prague spring" of 1968.

There is still a chance, however, that by resorting to rule by a "Military Council of National Salvation" General Jaruzelski may be trying to curb union extremists in order to allow mutual restraint to prevail. At time of writing, for instance, Solidarity's moderate leader, Lech Walesa, was meeting with government officials in Warsaw to try to head off

★ Please turn to Page 12

Schmidt and Honecker   UPI photo

Talking again but promises and progress could be undermined by events in Poland

[See story, page 12]

A tale of 20 letters: testing the mettle of the Postal Service

By Robert Kilborn Jr.
Staff writer of
The Christian Science Monitor

Boston

Grumbling about the US Postal Service's slow delivery is almost a national pastime. Nearly everyone has woeful tales of missives sent zig-zagging around the country just to get across town.

To put the Postal Service to a test, the Monitor sent 20 letters by first-class mail from Boston to points around the United States as far away as the West Coast, Texas, and Florida and as near as this city's suburbs. Participants were asked to note the date of arrival, and then return an enclosed post card.

On arrival back in Boston, the outbound

and return-mail data were recorded. A few of the findings:

● Some of the mail traveling in both directions arrived at more distant addresses faster than did mail to nearer ones.

● In only one case — a delivery to Sandy, Utah, a suburb of Salt Lake City — did the arrival in either direction take as long as five days.

● Delivery times out and back between the same two points tended to be uneven. Some outgoing mail took longer to reach its destination than did the return mail. But the reverse was also true in some instances. The difference, however, was never more than two days.

● The type of pickup for the return post

★ Please turn to Page 8

185

THE CHRISTIAN SCIENCE MONITOR

AN INTERNATIONAL DAILY NEWSPAPER

COPYRIGHT © 1982 THE CHRISTIAN SCIENCE PUBLISHING SOCIETY
All rights reserved
VOL. 74, NO. 140
Tuesday, June 15, 1982
R
EASTERN EDITION
40¢

Falklands war ending; next step is to pay for it and rebuild Argentine-British relations

UPI photo

British Gen. Jeremy Moore sent troops into Stanley

By James Nelson Goodsell
Latin America correspondent of
The Christian Science Monitor

Buenos Aires

"It's all over," an extremely well-informed Argentine military source said here June 14.

With a cease-fire apparently in place, surrender seemed imminent and 10 weeks of Argentine military occupation of the Falkland Islands appeared to be coming to an end.

But the bitter consequences of the conflict will be around for years to come.

Moreover, the cost to both nations has been enormous and is bound to grow. As British troops pushed into Port Stanley Monday, Argentina sent its Falklands Army commander, Gen. Mario Benjamin Menéndez, to talk with Britain's Maj. Gen. Jeremy Moore. General Menéndez asked for the session shortly after noon as advanced British troops poured into Port Stanley.

At least 2,000, perhaps 3,000 Argentine soldiers, had laid down their arms Monday rather than fight a hopeless last-ditch battle for Port Stanley.

The meeting between the two generals staved off that final confrontation, ending the three weeks of savage fighting in which there have been hundreds of Argentine and British casualties, the loss of half a dozen British naval vessels, the downing of at least two-thirds of Argentina's Air Force, and untold losses in the political and diplomatic arena.

It had been a war that brought two long-time friends into a battle that neither wanted — but that neither seemed able to prevent. The beginning was April 2. But in many ways for Argentina it began 149 years ago when Britain took possession of the islands, ousting an Argentine garrison.

From that time forward, Argentina has sought the return of the islands, which it calls the Islas Malvinas. Most Argentines agreed with the seizure April 2 by the current military government in Buenos Aires, and indeed have been supportive of the 10-week-old Argentine control.

But more and more in recent weeks, questions have been raised here about the wisdom of the original takeover of the islands.

In part, this is due to the cost of the venture. Few nations have taken such an action when their own economic fortunes were at such a low point. Argentina has the world's highest inflation at 104 percent. Its gross national product fell 5.7 percent in the first four months of 1982, and it is continuing to fall. Unemployment in a nation where joblessness has traditionally been unknown is at least 12 percent. Industry is running at less than 50 percent of its capacity, and business bankruptcies and banking failures are at an all-time high.

This situation is bound to worsen as the cost of the war becomes more apparent. Already it is estimated to have reached $4 billion, increasing the nation's already back-breaking deficit.

For Britain, too, the costs have been devastating. Its defense budget, coupled with the anticipation of spending billions of dollars to replace its badly battered fleet, will mortgage the British economy for many years to come.

But even more, the cost in lost lives, wounded men, and those missing — on both sides — is enormous. At least 1,500 lives have been lost, with two-thirds of them on the Argentine side. The final tally is not yet in.

Perhaps the most long-lasting consequence of the war has been the rift between Argentina and Britain, the bitter divisions the war stirred in the Western community, and the sharp divisions in the inter-American system, which have put

★ Please turn to Page 6

Mideast reaches major turning point as US, Israelis, Arabs maneuver

Israeli noose tightens and changes Mideast landscape for PLO, Syria, West

By John Yemma
Staff correspondent of
The Christian Science Monitor

Beirut

A quick cab ride up the road and one encounters Israeli tanks, jeeps, and soldiers deployed on the hills overlooking Beirut.

Israel's coup — long predicted, but in the end coming with surprising speed — was complete.

With the Israeli Army in control of Lebanon from the southern border to Beirut International Airport and in the hills surrounding the presidential palace at Baabda, a new political dynamic has begun to operate in this long-anarchic country. The view from Lebanon on June 14 looked like this:

● The Palestine Liberation Organization (PLO) had been cornered far from Israeli borders, thus ending PLO ability to fire rockets and artillery into northern Israel. With Israeli forces so near, choking off escape routes, guerrillas have fallen back into central Beirut, some establishing themselves for a final stand, others caching weapons and trying to blend in with the populace.

● Syria had been mauled militarily, setting back several years as a military power in the Middle East and giving Syrian President Hafez Assad a political blow that could prove difficult to recover from. How much Syria hopes to recoup in lost military hardware as a result of a visit to Damascus by a top-level Soviet deputy Air Force chief is open to question.

● Israel has linked up with the Christian Phalange forces of northern Lebanon, without the Phalange appearing to be too actively involved in the week-long battle with the PLO that has just transpired.

● The Lebanese govenment has been maneuvered (willingly or unwillingly) into forming a government of "national salvation" consisting of most of Lebanon's rival factions except for the Palestinians.

● PLO leaders, who seemed to have succeeded in keeping the Israeli Army at bay, now appear to be trapped. They will either have to disarm, surrender, or face attack by any combination of the following: the Israeli Army, the Phalange, the Lebanese Army. As of June 14 it appeared the Lebanese Army was going to be deployed into west Beirut and the Palestinians were going to be delivered an ultimatum.

"Maybe now the Palestinians will give up," Israeli Col. Amos Neeman said as he looked at a Hebrew-lettered map of the country. The colonel was resting along with his armored company in the stone and tile Baabda police station June 14. Lebanese civilians and Army officers were casually fraternizing with the Israeli soldiers.

"I hope for their [the Palestinians'] sake," Colonel Neeman said, "they will come to some agreement with the Lebanese government. This must happen."

In fact, there seemed little choice, given

★ Please turn to Page 8

United States weighs options in Middle East; Israel likely to offer only limited cooperation

Analysis

By Geoffrey Godsell
Staff correspondent of
The Christian Science Monitor

Three immediate challenges face the United States in the Middle East if it seizes the present crisis as an opportunity to further long-term stability in the area.

These challenges are:

1. To contribute to some kind of political settlement in a Lebanon shattered by the Israeli invasion that will give Israel a secure northern border and open the way to Israeli withdrawal.

2. To keep open the possibility of dialogue with the Palestinians — still a national entity more than 3 million strong despite the pounding their armed men have taken from the Israelis — so that their grievances and rights can eventually be addressed in an overall Middle East settlement.

3. To restore confidence and trust in the US on the part of three all-important moderate Arab governments in the area — Saudi Arabia, Egypt, and Jordan. The three countries are dismayed by the apparent inability or unwillingness of the Reagan administration to prevent the Israelis from savaging Lebanon last week.

In the first of these tasks, Washington can count on the qualified support of Israel.

In the other two, it is likely to encounter all-out opposition not only from Israel but also from the strong pro-Israeli lobby within the US.

Israel can be expected to resist above all any suggestion of self-determination or autonomy for the Palestinians on the West Bank of the Jordan, seeing in it the thin end of the wedge for territorial compromise that could lead to dismemberment of the Israeli state.

But Israel's understandable insistence on a secure northern border (against Palestinian armed attack) is only one half of the basic equation underlying an eventual settlement. The other is meeting in some measure Palestinian grievances, as Charles Percy, chairman of the US Senate Foreign Relations Committee, indicated on CBS television June 13.

One of the problems ahead will be to find Palestinians willing to engage in dialogue on the basis of compromise. Palestine Liberation Organization (PLO) spokesman Farouk Khaddoumi, who appeared on NBC television June 13, came over as a no-compromise man, insisting that the only acceptable solution for him would be return to his home in Jaffa in a non-Jewish, secular Palestine.

But it should not be overlooked that — harsh though it be — Mr. Khaddoumi is one of thousands of Lebanon-based Palestinian refugees from the now densely Israeli-populated coastal plain whose return home is least likely of all in any compromise. The

★ Please turn to Page 8

THE CHRISTIAN SCIENCE MONITOR

AN INTERNATIONAL DAILY NEWSPAPER

COPYRIGHT © 1983 THE CHRISTIAN SCIENCE PUBLISHING SOCIETY
All rights reserved   VOL. 75, NO. 198   Friday, September 2, 1983   EASTERN EDITION   40¢ (50¢ Canadian)

Soviet downing of jetliner shocks world

Kremlin tries to counter charges

By Ned Temko
Staff correspondent of The Christian Science Monitor
Moscow

The Soviet Union, after hours of official silence, moved Thursday to counter a formal charge from the United States that it shot down a crowded civilian airliner.

But diplomats here felt the statement, if not too little, was almost surely too late to avoid a strain in Kremlin relations with the outside world.

The Soviets' long fixation with security and secrecy was seen as a major factor in the long absence of Soviet comment on the air disaster. The strict hierarchical setup of the Soviet military, meanwhile, left diplomats with little doubt any rocket attack by a Soviet pilot must almost surely have been OKed by higher authorities. This was seen as doubly likely if, as the Americans said, Soviet radar had tracked the civilian airliner for fully 2½ hours.

Moscow's brief reply, from the official Tass news agency, said a Korean Air Lines jet had twice violated Soviet airspace. The jet "did not have navigation lights," Moscow said, "did ★ Please turn to Page 8

Attitudes toward Moscow expected to harden

By Daniel Southerland
Staff correspondent of The Christian Science Monitor
Washington

Soviet destruction of a civilian South Korean jetliner has cast a pall over US relations with the Soviet Union and could harden attitudes toward Moscow around the world.

In a news conference Thursday, Secretary of State George Shultz said that a Soviet MIG fighter plane shot down the Korean Air Lines 747 jumbo jet over Soviet territory near Sakhalin Island. There were 269 people aboard, including US Rep. Lawrence McDonald (D) of Georgia. There were no known survivors.

"We can see no excuse whatsoever for this appalling act," Mr. Shultz said. He noted that the Soviet chargé d'affaires in Washington was called in to hear an American statement of "strong concern" and a demand for an explanation from the Soviet Union. President Reagan was described as deeply disturbed and concerned.

The secretary of state said the Soviet attack — which occurred early Thursday local Asian time, or 2:26 p.m. Wednesday EDT — came after Soviet MIGs had tracked the commercial plane for 2½ hours and had made visual contact with it. Some defense experts said the attack immediately raised questions as to how well controlled the Soviet armed forces are. The Soviets are normally thought to operate under rigid control.

The seriousness of the incident will almost certainly lead to some countermeasures from both the US and Japan, and to a further cooling of relations between those two nations and Moscow. Korean Air Lines officials said 81 Koreans, 22 Japanese, 34 Taiwanese, and 103 others, including an undetermined number of Americans, were aboard the plane besides the crew.

In Japan, the incident could contribute to pressures for increased defense spending and greater military preparedness.

The attack came at a time when US relations with the Soviet Union were improving slightly and at a time when a US-Soviet summit meeting was viewed as a possibility for next year. The Soviets had recently shown greater flexibility, at least on secondary issues, in the strategic arms reduction talks (START) in Geneva.

★ Please turn to Page 8

Antimissile demonstrators blockade the US military depot at Mutlangen, West Germany, on first day of Sept. 1-3 protests   UPI photo

NATO missiles damaging W. German democracy?

By Elizabeth Pond
Staff correspondent of
The Christian Science Monitor
Bonn

The government sees it as a test of resolve and loyalty to the West.

The antinuclear demonstrators see it as a test of moral conscience — one the Germans failed under Hitler and must not fail now.

The government will win, observers agree, and the new NATO Euromissiles will be deployed here starting in December.

But, as the expected "hot fall" of protests gets under way with the Sept. 1-3 blockade of potential Euromissile and other sites, the question is:

What will be the cost of the government victory?

For those celebrities joining in the blockade — like Nobel prize novelist Heinrich Boell, futurologist Robert Jungk ("The Atom State"), and various Greens and Social Democrats — the answer is clear: a diminishing of democracy.

They view the 70 percent of the public that polls show as opposing the new missile deployment as a clear voice of West German citizens that should not be overridden by the government.

They fear an erosion of civil rights as the conservative government introduces new legislation holding a person's mere presence at a demonstration where there is violence as participation in that violence unless the person can prove that he tried to stop the violence.

And, most fundamentally, they view the introduction of the new NATO missiles into West Germany as ★ Please turn to Page 16

Scowcroft: US needs consensus on arms if it wants pact with USSR

By Brad Knickerbocker
Staff correspondent of The Christian Science Monitor
Washington

Without a bipartisan political consensus on nuclear arms and arms control, it is unlikely that the controversial MX missile will ever be built, Brent Scowcroft warned this week. It's equally unlikely the United States and the Soviet Union will reach an accommodation on strategic weapons, he said.

Mr. Scowcroft, who heads the presidential commission on strategic forces and is a key figure in the Washington arms control debate, will be taking a more visibly active role in coming weeks. Acting as a liaison between the administration and Congress, his group will suggest ways to accelerate what until now has been a relatively slow pace in strategic arms negotiations at Geneva.

"If all hands in the government put their minds to it, it is conceivable that substantial progress can be made," Scowcroft told reporters at the Pentagon Thursday.

While the MX has survived years of criticism, congressional approval of the large intercontinental ballistic missile (ICBM) has never been more than

Brent Scowcroft

half-hearted and tentative. Just as the missile is seen by the administration as a lever to pry the Soviets away from their reliance on very large land-based rockets, so is it viewed by many supporters on Capitol Hill as a bargaining chip to urge the White House toward greater efforts at Geneva.

Before they left town last month, House and Senate budget conferees approved production of the first 21 MX missiles, six fewer than the administration had wanted for the coming fiscal year. Pro-MX Democrats, led by Rep. Les Aspin of Wisconsin, also won approval of an authorization amendment linking MX production to design, development, and testing of the smaller, single-warhead missile dubbed "Midgetman."

Representative Aspin has been one of many participants and observers noting the need for a clearer domestic political consensus on strategic arms and arms control before headway can be made at Geneva.

The first indication of the possibility of consensus came last spring with the recommendations of the Scowcroft Commission. In essence, the panel of experts, appointed to find a ★ Please turn to Page 17

THE CHRISTIAN SCIENCE MONITOR

COPYRIGHT © 1983 THE CHRISTIAN SCIENCE PUBLISHING SOCIETY
All rights reserved   VOL. 75, NO. 232   AN INTERNATIONAL DAILY NEWSPAPER   MONDAY, OCTOBER 24, 1983   A TWO SECTION PAPER   40¢ (50¢ Canadian)

Stouthearted shoppers pay bottom dollar at Boston basement store

By Hilary DeVries
Staff writer of The Christian Science Monitor

Boston

"Famous-Maker Animal Slippers — $10.99," reads the orange cardboard sign. It is tacked to a wooden stick and stuck in a bin of what are indeed famous-maker animal slippers at $10.99 — and are being pawed over by curious would-be buyers.

You know right off that this is not Saks Fifth Avenue. There is no bouncy carpeting underneath. No hushed "May I help you?" from tastefully dressed sales personnel. No clever display of Italian silk sport jackets gently spotlighted from above like fine art objects. Instead, there is linoleum underfoot, fluorescent lights overhead, and a wealth of humanity at your elbow.

Is this any way to shop?

You bet it is, say the customers of Filene's Basement, the oldest and best-known bargain-basement store in the country. And they've got the numbers to prove it — not the least of which is the 75th anniversary which "the basement," as the locals call it, has just celebrated, cake and all.

Filling the bottom two floors of Filene's department store in the heart of Boston, the basement offers top-quality goods at discount prices. However rough and tumble, the basement is, in fact, a miniature department store.

There are no dressing rooms. Clothing hangs on

Please see SHOPPERS back page

Beirut bombings lend urgency to search for a settlement in Lebanon

As White House officials weigh options for policy in Lebanon, there are signs that growing pressure from the American public and from Congress will force President Reagan to redouble efforts toward a negotiated end to the Lebanese crisis. One immediate need: avoiding the appearance of siding with any of the factions in Lebanon. But foremost, protecting the marines.

UPI

Somber President denounces attack on marines

By Charlotte Saikowski and Daniel Southerland
Staff writers of The Christian Science Monitor

Washington

President Reagan now faces in Lebanon the greatest crisis of his presidency.

In the short run, he appears to lean toward reinforcing the American commitment in Lebanon following the Beirut bombings that took the lives of at least 135 United States marines and 27 French soldiers.

But most analysts predict that in the long run, strong pressure from the public and Congress will force the President to focus more intensively than ever before on a negotiated way out of the Lebanon crisis. This will require a skillful use of both force and diplomacy.

Reagan's response to the crisis could determine whether he is reelected or not, if he decides to run for a second term.

A recent poll showed that half of all Americans oppose the involvement of US marines in Lebanon and that even

Please see BEIRUT back page

Attacks jolt Lebanese hopes for reconciliation and point up vulnerability of peacekeepers

By Robin Wright
Special to The Christian Science Monitor

Beirut

The dawn bomb attacks on United States and French peacekeeping forces in Beirut have badly shaken the Lebanese — and the few remaining hopes that eight years of violence and bloodshed in Lebanon will ever end.

Coming on the eve of scheduled reconciliation talks, the simultaneous kamikaze-style attacks by trucks laden with some 2,000 pounds of explosives also emphasize the vulnerability of the US, French, British, and Italian contingents who are serving on a peacekeeping mandate in Lebanon.

All four of the forces have come under attack since the new civil strife began in Lebanon in mid-August.

But because of US and French decisions to counterattack by land, sea, or air, both countries have recently been labeled partisan by Muslim dissidents. The dissidents are demanding greater power from the government led by minority Christians.

There were no assaults Sunday against the Italian or British contingents, which have so far not become involved in returning fire.

It was not known at time of writing whether the attacks would affect the long-anticipated summit of Lebanon's leading warlords. The summit is scheduled to convene in

Please see ATTACKS page 32

European peace protesters, buoyed by weekend marches, aim to keep momentum

UPI

Protesters in Stuttgart clog traffic in march against deployment of NATO missiles

By Wellington Long
Special to The Christian Science Monitor

Bonn

Buoyed by the success of their weekend demonstrations, leaders of West Germany's self-styled "peace movement" plan to maintain the momentum of their antimissile protests until at least the middle of December.

The leaders admit that a majority of the Bundestag, the lower house of parliament, probably will support the deployment of United States Pershing II and cruise missiles when the assembly votes on the issue on Nov. 21.

But protest leaders want to make it impossible for the 497 deputies to claim they had to submit to party discipline. Instead, they plan to hold each "personally responsible" for his or her vote.

They called for another "national day of protest" on Nov. 21, and for the picketing of the offices of deputies until then. Protests will continue, they said, even after deployment begins, and they suggested that Dec. 12, the anniversary of the 1979 NATO decision to deploy, be treated as "a day of national resistance."

The antimissile movement both lost and gained points during the last week. It lost points when attempts to blockade

Please see MARCH page 12

THE CHRISTIAN SCIENCE MONITOR

COPYRIGHT © 1983 THE CHRISTIAN SCIENCE PUBLISHING SOCIETY
All rights reserved   VOL. 75, NO. 236   AN INTERNATIONAL DAILY NEWSPAPER   FRIDAY, OCTOBER 28, 1983   A TWO SECTION PAPER   40¢ (50¢ Canadian)

ON PUMPKINS
Barth Falkenberg discovers some extraordinary jack-o'-lanterns
27

DISCOVERY
Daniel J. Boorstin on the discoverers from Marco Polo to Marx
21

Building 'wings for the common man' is a turbulent business

By David Clark Scott
Staff writer of The Christian Science Monitor

Turners Falls, Mass.

For Bernt Petterssen, soaring over an oxbow in the Connecticut River at 200 feet is a dream come true. It's the kind of open-cockpit dream he'd like to share — for a moderate price. But his fledgling ultralight-aircraft company is tossing in turbulent economic winds.

Ultralight aircraft have been disparagingly described as rickety lawn chairs with wings. They've also been heralded as the common man's wings: Anyone with $5,000 (no license required) can join the ranks of those with "the right stuff."

"There are hundreds of thousands, perhaps millions, of people who have dreamed of being able to fly, and suddenly there is a machine that doesn't cost more than a motorcycle that will allow you to do it," the president of Aerodyne Systems Inc. says at his rented airport hangar here. "The potential size of the market is so enormous."

But for the industry and Mr. Petterssen, that optimism is being sapped by some dream-tempering business realities. Sales are even with last year, competition is heating up, and the industry is still long on wide-eyed enthusiasts and short on experienced manufacturers.

"An ultralight looks very simple, Petterssen says. "It looks like just some tubes. You bolt it together and you take off." But, he says with a sigh, "the reality of it

Please see WINGS page 6

Caliste, Grenada, Thursday: students and US soldiers wait by helicopters as smoke rises from burning building in the town

AP

US in Grenada: the political costs

Fighting eases on the island, but now Reagan finds himself engaged in a number of public-relations battles

By Daniel Southerland
Staff writer of The Christian Science Monitor

Washington

As the combat diminished on Grenada, the Reagan administration found itself fighting public-relations battles on several other fronts — both domestic and foreign.

The administration was taking a beating on the foreign front from a number of nations, including allies who criticized the Grenada invasion. But the President was picking up some points on the home front, thanks to American students evacuated from Grenada who said they had felt they were in danger and needed rescuing.

At the same time, the administration was criticized by major American news organizations, which complained that their access to the invasion was unnecessarily restricted. Some congressmen complained that the notification letter President Reagan sent to Congress Tuesday evening concerning the invasion of Grenada did not meet the requirements of the 1972 War Powers Resolution. Others questioned whether the administration had made a serious effort to negotiate an orderly evacuation of Americans from the island before moving to invade.

Please see BATTLES back page

Invasion gives Moscow a windfall, as the world moves its gaze from the Korean jet downing to the US assault

By Ned Temko
Staff writer of The Christian Science Monitor

Moscow

The United States invasion of Grenada is shaping up as a political windfall for Moscow, which had been thrown on the political defensive in recent weeks.

The crisis is bound to be particularly welcome in the Kremlin at a time when senior officials have been voicing increasing bitterness over the Reagan administration and, privately, increasing concern that they would likely be dealing with Mr. Reagan for another term.

The Caribbean crisis could also strengthen the Soviet Union's hand in its public bid to forestall deployment of new US missiles in Western Europe.

But most diplomats here feel it is premature to speak of any major Soviet gain on that front — and doubly premature to speak of "good news" over Mr. Reagan's reelection prospects.

In practical terms, the importance of Grenada to Soviet security interests is seen by foreign envoys here as considerably less than the US administration has suggested. The pin-dot island is also much less important to

Please see MOSCOW back page

'Build-down' and 'bipartisanship': buzzwords at strategic arms talks in Geneva

Cutting the missile count

	SALT II agreement	US build-down proposal	Soviet START proposal
Ballistic missile warheads	14,600	5,000	11,400
ICBM warheads (land-based)	820	throwweight limit or Soviet offer	680 (MIRVed)
Bombers	120 (11 ALCMs* each)	400 (20 ALCMs each)	120 (10 ALCMs each)

*Air-launched cruise missiles

By Elizabeth Pond
Staff writer of The Christian Science Monitor

Bonn

Bipartisanship is the new American buzzword at the strategic arms reduction talks (START) in Geneva.

The Republican-Democratic togetherness is producing a yeomanlike plowing ahead in the START talks that is noteworthy in this time of embittered Soviet-American relations.

It is not yet producing any positive response from Moscow, however, according to information reaching NATO countries from the Geneva negotiations.

By now the United States has spelled out its basic "build-down" proposal in this fall's fifth round of talks, with the last segment — bombers — having been presented Oct. 25. The two delegations have also drafted annexes on counting rules and definitions and have begun discussing a verification annex.

The build-down is a bipartisan idea that was initially advanced on the MX intercontinental missile and related strategic issues. It is described by a proponent as "a good basis for whatever party gets elected" in fall of 1984.

To ensure that the build-down is pur-

sued seriously by the Reagan administration, congressional arms control advocates like Wisconsin Democrat Les Aspin are essentially holding hostage biennial funding of the MX to support for the build-down. They adopted this tactic last summer after concluding that only bipartisanship could protect arms control against some future veto by an opposition party that could always muster the minimum of Senate seats needed to block two-thirds' ratification of any treaty.

As it is being presented to the Soviets in the October-November negotiating ses-

Please see TALKS back page

189

COPYRIGHT © 1984 THE CHRISTIAN SCIENCE PUBLISHING SOCIETY
All rights reserved VOL. 76, NO. 56   AN INTERNATIONAL DAILY NEWSPAPER   TUESDAY, FEBRUARY 14, 1984   40¢ (50¢ Canadian)

THRILLS ON ICE
Carruthers duo
ended US medal
drought in stylish
fashion **20**

TEN STORIES
deep, sunlight
fills these
underground
offices **21**

Chernenko as leader: Is orthodoxy enough?

By Gary Thatcher
Staff writer of The Christian Science Monitor

Moscow

The winds of change may one day blow through Russia, gusting right down Gorky Street, one of Moscow's main avenues leading to Red Square.

But that day appears still some way off.

Instead, the selection of Konstantin Chernenko to succeed Yuri Andropov is widely seen here as an embrace of a familiar past — and a postponement of an inevitable reckoning with an unpleasant future.

Chernenko, now in his 70s, is closely identified with Leonid Brezhnev. He seemed always at Brezhnev's side as Andropov's burly predecessor held sway over the Soviet Union for 18 years.

It was a period notable for the buildup of military power, neglect of the consumer economy, and inertia within the party bureaucracy.

It is, of course, impossible to predict whether Chernenko will follow the same policies as his mentor.

If past pronouncements are any guide, his view of the world is shaped by orthodox communist ideology. Indeed, ideology and propaganda have been his special field during the last two years of his six-year tenure on the ruling Communist Party Politburo.

As far as is known, however, he has never demonstrated any substantial expertise in economics. He never worked in industrial management, and his published speeches contain only vague references to economic matters.

Yet no one in the Communist Party leadership can ignore this country's economic straits.

Chernenko, in his first speech as general secretary, told the party's Central Committee, "The system of economic management, the whole of our economic machinery, needs a serious restructuring. Work in this direction has only been started."

If Chernenko took a stroll outside his office in the Kremlin, stopping in the shops along Gorky Street, he would find abundant evidence of the need to speed up the process.

He would find plenty of bread, at absurdly low prices (as low as 9 cents a loaf). But he wouldn't find

Views from US, East and West Europe
Pages 3, 12, 13

Please see **CHERNENKO** back page

NOGES/SYGMA

Chernenko: reviving the economy will be his biggest challenge

Applications are sifted through fine screen at Bates College, Maine

By Jim Bencivenga
Staff writer of The Christian Science Monitor

Lewiston, Maine

OUTSIDE, the snow falls gently on the wooded New England campus. Inside, seven pairs of hands rise decisively. Each hand has only one or two fingers extended. No clenched fist. It is a low score. Applicant admitted.

Blackball session for an undergraduate fraternity or sorority? Not at Bates College, a private coeducational school of some 1,430 students. The school has not allowed fraternities or sororities since it opened its doors in 1855.

The raised hands belong to the seven members of the admissions committee. They have just approved the application of a high school senior.

In the next three months the committee members will raise their hands some 2,300 to 2,500 times. That is the expected number of applications they must winnow down to fill the 425 seats reserved for the class of 1988. (The hand and finger count works this way: Left hand rates academic record, right hand rates nonacademic record. One finger is tops; five is worst. A score of five or less from each committee member is usually the cutoff. A closed fist "flags" the application as a risk but worth further consideration.)

In the highly competitive world of college admissions at prestigious colleges, Bates is singled out as having one of the most refined acceptance procedures in the country. The director of admissions at one Ivy League campus acknowledges Bates as a standard-setter

Please see **BATES** page 6

Allies agree to 'speak softly' to Moscow

By Elizabeth Pond
Staff writer of The Christian Science Monitor

Bonn

The timing is bad. The margins of outside influence are slim. But both Europe and the United States think the West should now offer a new beginning in East-West relations to Soviet General Secretary Konstantin Chernenko.

Alliance harmony on this point is striking as US Vice-President George Bush, British Prime Minister Margaret Thatcher, and West German Chancellor Helmut Kohl all pay their respects at Yuri Andropov's funeral in Moscow. It contrasts sharply with internal Western strains as Mr. Andropov succeeded Leonid Brezhnev 15 months ago.

In the analysis of American and European diplomats two developments account for this welcome difference:

● NATO's success in proceeding as planned with deployment of new NATO nuclear missiles in West Europe (and Moscow's conspicuous failure to block them).

● President Reagan's election-year move away from ideological confrontation toward foreign-policy pragmatism.

A senior European diplomat in Bonn summarized the first point crisply: "Magnanimity in victory is a good diplomatic and even a good power political principle. We should not now seek to rub Soviet faces in this Soviet failure but should offer them dialogue with both hands."

This European attitude is hardly surprising. For some months the European maxim has been to speak

Please see **ALLIES** back page

Hussein, Mubarak seek US aid against radical states

Hussein (r), Mubarak, and Hussein's wife, Queen Noor

UPI

By Brad Knickerbocker
Staff writer of The Christian Science Monitor

Cairo

Against the backdrop of US troop withdrawal and continued factional violence in Lebanon, two key Arab leaders brought strong messages to President Reagan this week.

Egyptian President Hosni Mubarak and Jordan's King Hussein want two things from the United States:

● More financial aid — especially military — to offset the growing power of aggressive Mideast states.

● A more active US effort to help settle the region's underlying causes of discontent — mainly the Palestinian question.

Their requests are highlighted by Mr. Hussein's meeting with Mr. Mubarak on Sunday in Washington, a step that helps bring Egypt back into the Islamic fold.

Egyptian officials — and other moderate Arab leaders

Please see **AID** page 14

THE CHRISTIAN SCIENCE MONITOR

/RIGHT © 1984 THE CHRISTIAN SCIENCE PUBLISHING SOCIETY
All rights reserved   VOL. 76, NO. 238   AN INTERNATIONAL DAILY NEWSPAPER   THURSDAY, NOVEMBER 1, 1984   A THREE SECTION PAPER   R   50¢ (60¢ Canadian)

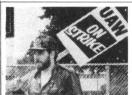

AUTOMAKERS
emerge with wage position best in 40 years **21**

HIGH COURT
The case against 'court packing' by presidents **23**

OL' MAN RIVER
Traveling the Mississippi by car, and pen **18**

After assassination, India turns to Rajiv

By Mary Anne Weaver
Special to The Christian Science Monitor

New Delhi

India has rushed to try to fill the tremendous leadership vacuum caused by the assassination of its formidable prime minister, Indira Gandhi.

Mrs. Gandhi was gunned down early Wednesday by a fusillade of bullets from members of her own security guard in the lush gardens of the prime minister's residence.

Within hours, her only surviving son, Rajiv, was sworn in as successor to the world's longest-serving, democratically-elected premier. His selection as the country's seventh prime minister apparently continues the extraordinary Nehru-Gandhi dynasty which has ruled this vast and complex land, except for two brief periods, throughout its 37 years of independence.

Despite outbreaks of rioting here in the capital and in at least six other Indian states, initial signs were that, politically, the abrupt transfer of power would proceed smoothly as in the past. All of the nation's most distinguished leaders — Mohandas Gandhi (no relation), Jawaharlal Nehru (Mrs. Gandhi's father), Lal Bahadur Shastri, and now Mrs. Gandhi herself — have died at the zenith of power; and the democratic fabric of the world's largest democracy has always held.

But Rajiv Gandhi faces challenges of daunting proportions, both in holding on to power and in keeping this disparate nation together. Though he was widely considered Mrs. Gandhi's chosen successor, his prompt installation came as something of a surprise. Only three weeks ago he told this correspondent that he was not yet ready to even think of following in his mother's controversial and charismatic footsteps. The 40-year-old former airline pilot and junior member of Parliament readily acknowledged that he was inexperienced and young.

His mother, on the other hand, behind the soft exte-

Please see **INDIRA** back page

India's leadership stays in the family
- **Rajiv Gandhi, new prime minister** —
- **Political career of Indira Gandhi** —

UPI

Indira Gandhi walking with her son, Rajiv, in the garden of her residence earlier this month

Does swing to GOP extend beyond Reagan popularity?

By Charlotte Saikowski
Staff writer of The Christian Science Monitor

Washington

Exuding good cheer and feeling that he's on a roll, President Reagan is forecasting a "historic electoral realignment" of political parties, as millions of Democrats abandon their traditional base to vote Republican in 1984.

Is such a realignment in the wind? Or are the Republicans simply whipping up campaign momentum?

As Mr. Reagan embarks today on a final five-day, 10-state campaign blitz across the United States, surveys do show that the Republicans are edging closer to the Democrats, who still remain the majority party. But election experts caution that the apparent voter shifts could be due more to support for the President and to the Reagan coattail effect than to a basic and enduring change in political attitudes. That is something that will have to be

ELECTIONS '84

analyzed carefully after election day and will not become evident until the elections of 1986 and beyond.

"The parties are closer than we've seen in a long time, closer than in the rout of 1972," says Andrew Kohut, president of the Gallup Organization. "But I do not see a fundamental ideological shift in the climate of the country. It's more a case of 'If nothing's broke, don't fix it.' On many issues people disagree with Reagan, yet they support him."

Political analysts suggest that GOP talk about realignment is designed primarily to make American voters believe that the race is over. They see Reagan not as a Franklin Roosevelt, who did lead a party realignment, but as a Dwight Eisenhower, who won a second term as a popular president. After the election, a fierce struggle is expected among the different wings of the Republican Party for control

Please see **REAGAN** back page

Poles keep calm despite crisis

Outrage over priest's murder has brought authorities, church, and Solidarity together rather than dividing them

By Eric Bourne
Special to The Christian Science Monitor

Vienna

In a strange paradox, even as a stunned Poland awaits the funeral of the Rev. Jerzy Popieluszko, there is now an atmosphere of greater hope for social peace than at perhaps any previous moment in the turbulent years of crisis since 1980.

In March 1981 — only six months after the formation of the now-banned trade union Solidarity — violent action by the Bydgoszcz police against Rural Solidarity came dangerously near to provoking nationwide civil strife.

But this time, something most Poles would perceive as vastly more sinister — the murder of a priest who had continued to speak out for union rights and other civil liberties — has had the opposite effect. The killing has brought the communist authorities, the Roman Catholic Church, and the still-powerful Solidarity movement to a common sense of outrage

and national purpose.

Poles at large reacted similarly. Tuesday evening, thousands at a mass at Fr. Popieluszko's parish church in Warsaw were told of the retrieval of his body from a water reservoir on the Vistula River, 90 miles from the capital. They wept, lit votive candles, and sang a favorite hymn about freedom. Then they went quietly home. And Warsaw remained calm with no unusual police presence and no hint of the disorders that even minor incidents had provoked hitherto.

Popieluszko's fate has brought Solidarity back into the picture in the most meaningful way since the lifting of martial law and the subsequent political amnesty.

The union's former chairman, Lech Walesa, has spoken out openly and forthrightly since the priest's abduction Oct. 19 without any effort by the authorities to decry his words or to prevent him from exercising his old role as a national figure.

Mr. Walesa alluded to the implication

Please see **PRIEST** page 13

THE CHRISTIAN SCIENCE MONITOR

COPYRIGHT © 1984 THE CHRISTIAN SCIENCE PUBLISHING SOCIETY
All rights reserved   VOL. 76, NO. 243   AN INTERNATIONAL DAILY NEWSPAPER   THURSDAY, NOVEMBER 8, 1984   A TWO SECTION PAPER   R   50¢ (60¢ Canadian)

SOVIET VIEW
Chernenko asks for deeds in Reagan's new term **9**

COSMIC
Astronomers disagree on the universe's age and size **25**

POLITE
Miss Manners on the art of rearing 'perfect children' **31**

Airlift to Ethiopia: a view from the cockpit

By David K. Willis
Staff writer of The Christian Science Monitor

Addis Ababa, Ethiopia

WE are 17,000 feet above dry, red, Grand Canyon-like terrain as no-nonsense Flt. Lt. Nigel Watson eases himself out of the pilot's seat of his Royal Air Force Hercules C-130 transport plane.

He takes off his headset, glances at a pad sewn into the knee of his flight suit, and remarks: "We've flown 2,100 miles today, and carried 87,000 pounds of grain. Not bad. . . .".

He, his copilot, and his cheerful crew, a long way from their home base in southern England, ply this correspondent in the cockpit with soft drinks and questions about how the drought-affected people below will prepare the emergency food.

In a grueling day, they had flown from Addis Ababa to Makele, capital of Tigre Province, on to the port of Assab to pick up grain, then across to the city of Aksum to unload, back to Assab, back to Makele. and now, with two US and several British correspondents hitching a ride, back to base at the bustling Addis Ababa airport.

This thundering plane, with its camouflage paint, its circular red-white-and-blue Royal Air Force markings, and its yawning 20-ton hold, is part of Operation International Airlift carrying relief supplies to the starving in Ethiopia.

Droning ahead of us in the late afternoon sky, also en route to Addis Ababa, is the huge shape of a Soviet Antonov-22 transport, its extra-heavy metal frame requiring the thrust of four engines — each

Please see **AIRLIFT** page 34

'We are going to continue...and, if need be, take our case to the people'

Vote sweep for Reagan with limits

By Charlotte Saikowski
Staff writer of The Christian Science Monitor

Washington

Pluralism persists in the American body politic.

Exulting in his 49-state election victory, Ronald Reagan is poised to continue the basic conservative approach to government he launched four years ago.

But he does not have a mandate for a move further to the right in his second term. The American people, while electing a Republican President for the fourth time in the last five elections, stopped short of giving Mr. Reagan the strength he needs in the US Congress to enact his conservative agenda. The Republicans only partly recovered the losses they sustained in the House of Representatives in 1982. And their majority in the Senate was reduced by two seats.

This bifurcated public mood will act as a brake on any rightward ideological swing, political experts say. Divided government will continue to pose a challenge to resolving controversies in such urgent areas as nuclear arms control, budget deficits, and immigration reform.

Moreover, Reagan will be a lame-duck president in his second term as the next election cycle looms and the political battle for leadership succession begins in both the Democratic and Republican Parties.

"This is no mandate to the far right," says presidential scholar Robert Murray of Pennsylvania State University. "The country as a whole is fairly satisfied with

Please see **VOTE** back page

As election dust settles, tests of policy return to center stage

This week's election results confirm the elements of existing administration policy. But as circumstances shift in the economy, in foreign policy, and on Capitol Hill, priorities may need to be adjusted. In reports below, staff writers John Yemma, Julia Malone, and Brad Knickerbocker examine the implications of the 1984 elections for these important areas.

THE ECONOMY

If one factor alone carried President Reagan to his landslide victory, it was probably the widespread sense of economic well-being throughout the United States on election day.

The biggest component of the pocketbook factor: lower inflation, thus more buying power.

True, interest rates were still high. But only borrowers are affected by these, and borrowing has never been universally regarded as wholesome in America.

The budget deficit was a big worry — but this problem seemed intangible to many voters. And although unemployment was still considerable, thousands of new jobs had been created in Mr. Reagan's first term.

The pocketbook was not the only factor in the Reagan win. A month before the election, a Citicorp analysis of the "misery index" (unemployment plus in-

Please see **POCKET** page 6

THE CONGRESS

The President's smashing personal victory has left Congress almost untouched.

Even as he made his 49-state sweep through the nation, the enormously popular incumbent failed to pull along enough Republicans to give him a working majority in the House of Representatives. In the Senate, the Republican ranks will be reduced by two, for a total of 53.

The result is that any hopes for a second wave of the Reagan revolution similar to the budget-cutting and tax-reduction blitz of 1981 have now been doused. President Reagan will have to deal with a feisty, Democratic-controlled House and a cautious Republican Senate in 1985.

Although the GOP expected to retake the 26 House seats it lost two years ago and thus regain the clout it enjoyed during the first two years of the Reagan

Please see **CONGRESS** page 6

DEFENSE & DIPLOMACY

Ronald Reagan's political triumph does not diminish the national security and diplomatic problems he faces. Nor does it offer the likely prospect of being able to solve those problems with significantly greater ease.

The President says the top priorities of his second term are "peace and disarmament," backed up by a continued strengthening of US military might. Yet he must deal with the same wary and sometimes truculent Kremlin leaders on arms control, men who themselves are sorting out succession difficulties.

Mr. Reagan's push to "rearm America" will continue to be modified by lawmakers, just as it was in the second half of his first term.

Controversial military items — the MX missile, antisatellite weapons, and space-based systems to defend against attacking warheads — will be fought over as hard as ever.

Please see **DEFENSE** page 4

THE CHRISTIAN SCIENCE MONITOR

COPYRIGHT © 1985 THE CHRISTIAN SCIENCE PUBLISHING SOCIETY
All rights reserved   VOL. 77, NO. 75   AN INTERNATIONAL DAILY NEWSPAPER   TUESDAY, MARCH 12, 1985   50¢ (60¢ Canadian)

MIDEAST
Violence rises
as Egypt's leader
calls for greater
US role   **9**

INTERVIEW
Education chief
William Bennett
comes on strong,
stirs critics   **3**

SHELTER
A visit to
Anne Frank's
hideaway in
Amsterdam   **25**

SWELTER
Why Earth
was a hothouse
100 million
years ago   **23**

THE KREMLIN IN TRANSITION

Soviet leadership passes to a new generation

View from Moscow

Smooth transfer of power marks historic changeover for USSR

By Gary Thatcher
Staff writer of The Christian Science Monitor

Moscow

The Soviet Union seems set to leave a lot of its past behind.

Moving with unprecedented speed, it has installed 54-year-old Mikhail Gorbachev as the youngest leader in its 68-year history.

The decision was made public within five hours of yesterday's announcement that Konstantin Chernenko had passed away Sunday evening.

The rapidity of the succession convinced many Western analysts that the changeover was worked out well in advance, suggesting that the Kremlin has established a mechanism for transferring power smoothly. Most analysts expect it will be years before Mr. Gorbachev consolidates his grip on power.

The selection of Gorbachev also marks a generational change in the Soviet leadership. He is a full 18 years younger than his predecessor was upon taking power, and was only a teen-ager during World War II. He did not see combat duty, and he was not involved in the excesses of Soviet dictator Joseph Stalin.

He appears to be more self-confident than many previous Soviet leaders, and seems somewhat more forthcoming and open. Although he is expected to engineer some policy changes, one key Western Kremlin-watcher cautions, "It's a mistake to cast him as a liberal."

He is, the analyst continues, "very much in the mold of [former Soviet leader Yuri] Andropov" — a tough dis-

Please see **MOSCOW** page 18

Gorbachev: Moscow's man of the hour

Profile of the new leader

A self-assured Gorbachev rockets to top

By Gary Thatcher
Staff writer of The Christian Science Monitor

Moscow

A political biography of Mikhail Sergeevich Gorbachev might borrow its title from a work by Charles Dickens.

"Great expectations" have been pinned to Mr. Gorbachev throughout his rise in the Soviet hierarchy which, by Soviet standards, was lightning fast. Now the agriculture specialist from southern Russia is the leader of the Soviet Union.

At age 54, Gorbachev becomes the youngest man to take power in the Soviet state. This shift of power to a younger generation has been inevitable since the passing of Leonid Brezhnev in 1982.

Western diplomats who have met him say that he is self-assured, well-spoken, and impressive in his grasp of facts. Moreover, he seems to exhibit little of the lack of self-confidence that, in some Soviet officials, is masked by brusqueness or even rudeness.

Please see **GORBACHEV** back page

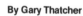

Funeral flags in Moscow

View from Washington

US analysts look at Gorbachev and see shifts in style, but not substance

By Charlotte Saikowski
Staff writer of The Christian Science Monitor

Washington

There will be more zip in the Kremlin now. There may be a more polished style. But don't look for any changes of substance in relations between the two superpowers.

So say Kremlinologists in and out of government as the United States prepares to deal with new Soviet party leader Mikhail S. Gorbachev.

"Most of the indications are that he is a clone [of the older leaders]," says one administration analyst. "Gorbachev is not a revolutionary, because he wouldn't have gotten there. You may not have change but only more vigor on policies already agreed upon and worked out by consensus."

Despite urgings from some quarters, President Reagan has decided not to travel to Moscow for the funeral of Soviet President Konstantin U. Chernenko on Wednesday. Vice-President George Bush, Secretary of State George P. Shultz, and US Ambassador to Moscow Arthur A. Hartman will represent the US.

Diplomatic experts and congressional leaders are divided on the President's decision. Some say that Mr. Reagan is missing an opportunity to give an impetus to US-Soviet relations by meeting General Secretary Gorbachev. Others argue that a presidential pilgrimage would simply have been grandstanding.

"It would just be exhibitionist," says Malcolm Toon, former US ambassador to Moscow. "He never met Chernenko, so it would have been a mistake to go."

"Just as we're starting arms negotiations, it would have been a good opportunity for Reagan to explain to the new Soviet leadership his vision of the future and hear directly from them that they share his long-term vision, but [I believe] that his short-term plans will make it impossible to get there," says Mark Garrison, director of the Center for Foreign Policy at Brown University and a former US diplomat.

Please see **WASHINGTON** page 19

View from Geneva

US-Soviet talks opening today mark a crucial shift in arms control philosophy

By Elizabeth Pond
Staff writer of The Christian Science Monitor

Geneva

The superpower negotiations opening here are perhaps the most ambitious arms control talks ever attempted. The first session is proceeding as scheduled, despite the death of Soviet General Secretary Konstantin Chernenko.

The negotiations will explore nothing less — say the Americans — than the possibility of shifting the whole basis of nuclear deterrence from an offensive to a defensive balance.

The talks will focus on stability. The Soviets agreed to this goal for the first time in the joint statement made by US Secretary of State George P. Shultz and Soviet Foreign Minister Andrei Gromyko at their January meeting here. At this point, the change in the Soviet leadership is not expected to alter the basic arms talks equation.

The joker in the pack is the US Strategic Defense Initiative — which is called SDI in Pentagonese, and "star wars" by the man in the street. No one yet knows just where this

antimissile defense research initiative will lead or how it might transform the nuclear balance.

These talks are said to be very different from the pragmatic horse-trading of previous arms control talks. They represent a revolutionary effort to reach a common Soviet-American "philosophy" on the nuclear threat, as Mr. Shultz has repeatedly stressed — and an effort to work out mutually agreed force structures on the basis of this philosophy.

The old arms control philosophy can be

Please see **ARMS** back page

PALESTINIANS
As PLO fights to survive, Israel considers talking peace with Palestinians   **9**

PIANO CONTEST
Does the prestigious Van Cliburn competition really serve music?   **29**

Court blocks silent prayer in school

Major 6-to-3 ruling is setback to Reagan and religious fundamentalists

By Curtis J. Sitomer
Staff writer of The Christian Science Monitor

Boston

Prescribed moments of silence in the public schools for the purposes of prayer are inconsistent with First Amendment guarantees of church-state separation.

So declared the US Supreme Court by a 6-to-3 margin on Tuesday in a long-awaited, perhaps landmark, ruling.

This decision in an Alabama case will affect moment-of-silence laws in more than 20 states. Some such statutes will undoubtedly be invalidated unless they are rewritten to exclude the specific mention of prayer.

The school-prayer ruling also has major implications

for what has lately become a hotly contested political battle in the United States over religion in the public arena.

President Reagan has been a strong supporter of prayer in the schools. And he joins fundamentalist church groups, among others, who staunchly back the adoption of a constitutional amendment to, as Mr. Reagan has put it, "restore God to the classroom." The US Justice Department, also in support of the Alabama law that was just struck down, held that such state statutes enhanced the opportunity of students to bolster their religious convictions without intruding on those of others.

On the other hand, civil rights groups such as the

Please see **SILENCE** page 5

Sorting out Walker spy-case damage

By Warren Richey
Staff writer of The Christian Science Monitor

Washington

Bit by bit, pieces of the puzzle known as the Walker espionage ring are falling into place.

Already, in comparison with other publicly disclosed US espionage cases, the case involving former naval officer John A. Walker Jr. and several alleged associates qualifies in terms of longevity and manpower as one of the most extensive Soviet spy efforts on record in the US.

What remains to be established — and what is very worrisome to US officials — is how badly the spy efforts may have damaged US national security. With each new revelation about what is

now described as at least a four-man conspiracy to gather, transport, and sell sensitive US Navy documents to the Soviets, another question looms larger: How could such an operation continue undetected for so long?

While US officials are reluctant to declare a new surge in Soviet espionage activity, Justice Department officials note that records have been set over the past year for prosecutions of alleged spies. According to the Federal Bureau of Investigation (FBI), 16 individuals (including suspects in the Walker case) were charged with espionage or related activities for the Soviet Union or other East-bloc countries.

Please see **SPIES** page 7

CLAYTON JONES

Soviet sub in Leningrad: At sea, would it now be easier to hide from US?

Key figures in alleged spy ring:

The FBI charges that John A. Walker Jr. and some of his accomplices have been spying for the Soviets since 1965.

John A. Walker Jr.
Alleged ringleader who was under FBI scrutiny for the last six months.

Arthur J. Walker
John's brother, who worked for a Navy contractor and held a 'secret' clearance.

Michael L. Walker
John's son. Arrested while serving as operations clerk on the USS Nimitz.

Jerry Alfred Whitworth
Retired from Navy in 1983 as a senior enlisted radioman.

Jackson thunders pulpit politics to Democrats

By Lucia Mouat
Staff writer of The Christian Science Monitor

Chicago

"WE came on slave ships, and we're now fighting for the championship," thunders the Rev. Jesse Jackson to his largely black audience.

It is a Saturday morning, and the charismatic Baptist minister, master of the colorful, rhythmic phrase, is giving his all, as usual, to the weekly meeting of the Chicago-based Operation PUSH (People United to Serve Humanity).

What takes place is part inspirational worship service, part political convention, part pep rally, as the crowd chants, "I am somebody." The band, chorus, and audience frequently interrupt the dialogue with music, standing ovations, and shouts of "tell it like it is."

To the delight of this former Democratic candidate for president, his audience is increasingly a mixed one. Besides the usual

Please see **JACKSON** back page

Welfare reforms spark debate in Britain

KENNETH H. McKELVIE

As Britain prepares to overhaul its welfare system, many citizens are pondering how the proposed changes might affect them

By David Winder
Staff writer of
The Christian Science Monitor

London

The Conservative Party's long-awaited proposal for an overhaul of the welfare state is expected to set the tone for Britain's next general election.

The ruling Conservative Party and the opposition Labour Party have different views of the Britain of the future. Few issues dramatize more clearly that difference than the question of whither the welfare state.

The Labour Party regards the complex and about-to-be-reformed social-welfare system as the cornerstone of a

compassionate and caring society, particularly in these times of high unemployment.

Prime Minister Margaret Thatcher, however, and her ruling Conservatives partly blame Britain's economic malaise of the 1960s and '70s on the state's excessively protective role in providing cradle-to-grave security.

The Thatcher government says Britain's costly welfare system has "lost its way." When all costs are tallied, Britain spends over 42 percent of its total annual budget on social welfare. Social security alone soaks up £40 billion (about $51 billion), or almost

Please see **WELFARE** back page

THE CHRISTIAN SCIENCE MONITOR

COPYRIGHT © 1985 THE CHRISTIAN SCIENCE PUBLISHING SOCIETY
All rights reserved   VOL. 77, NO. 253   AN INTERNATIONAL DAILY NEWSPAPER   FRIDAY, NOVEMBER 22, 1985   50¢ (60¢ Canadian)

EDUCATION
Mixed reviews for personal computers on campus **27**

THE GAMBIA
'Roots' fame has brought change to life in Juffure **35**

CURBS ON ESPIONAGE
Pentagon panel says informants, lie detectors will deter spies in US **3**

Though less visible in media, S. Africa's unrest rumbles on

By Patrick Laurence
Special to The Christian Science Monitor

Johannesburg

Any impression that violence in South Africa has subsided, perhaps created partly by restrictions on media coverage, was shattered this past week.

At least 19 people have died since last Sunday — a jolting reminder that the violence that has racked South Africa for 14 months and claimed more than 850 lives has not gone away.

The South African government imposed media restrictions Nov. 2, requiring journalists to receive police permission to cover unrest in areas under a state of emergency. This permission is often denied, and journalists must rely solely on police accounts of events. Thus it has been difficult to independently verify the level of violence recently. But events of the past several days tell an unmistakable tale of continuing unrest.

Please see **S. AFRICA** back page

From Vietnam foxhole to the Army's highest post

By Peter Grier
Staff writer of The Christian Science Monitor

Washington

EARLY on an October morning 18 years ago, a North Vietnamese rocket exploded in John A. Wickham Jr.'s tent.

General Wickham — at the time commander of a United States infantry battalion in Quang Ngai Province — rolled into a foxhole, gravely wounded by shrapnel. Seconds later he was sprayed with bullets from an enemy's AK-47 rifle. He lay in the hole for three hours, using a radio to direct American return fire until the attackers were driven off.

At the aid station a Roman Catholic chaplain administered last rites. Today Wickham is the highest-ranking general officer in the US Army, its four-star chief of staff.

"Having gone through that, I learned eternal humility," he says. "For some reason I may have been given another chance. I am reminded of that every day."

Please see **WICK** page 6

A new start for superpowers

AP

Geneva concludes with handshakes all around: (l. to r.) Shevardnadze, Gorbachev, translator, Reagan, and Shultz

The ice has been broken. The leaders of the superpowers say they have achieved a working relationship. The vigorous exchanges of the 'fireside summit' are to be followed by further Reagan-Gorbachev get-togethers in the US and Soviet Union. But Geneva's actual agreements were few and peripheral. And much hard work lies ahead if conflicting arms control positions, especially on 'star wars,' are to be resolved. Meanwhile, the rest of the world tried Thursday to assess what it all added up to — as the two leaders flew out of Geneva to brief their respective allies and peoples.

By Gary Thatcher
Staff writer of The Christian Science Monitor

Geneva

The superpower dialogue has been resumed after six years of virtual silence, but very tough bargaining lies ahead before any agreement can be reached on the main issue of arms control.

At their Geneva summit Nov. 19-21, President Reagan and Soviet leader Mikhail Gorbachev agreed to hold another summit in the United States next year and to "accelerate" their arms control talks.

But they did not hammer out any guidelines for their negotiators, and the joint statement concluding the summit acknowledged that "serious differences remain on a number of critical issues." The most serious differences concern the US program of research into space-based defense.

The only agreements that were announced were on such lesser issues as cultural and sports exchanges, consulates, and air safety in the Pacific. In a briefing, however, a senior US official hinted that he now expects quiet moves by the Soviet side on human-rights issues.

Both sides stressed the working relationship that developed between the two leaders in what Mr. Reagan called the "fireside summit." Mr. Gorbachev spoke of "both sides' determination to improve relations." He said the world was a somewhat

Please see **SUMMIT** back page

Global reactions

US hopeful
Qualified praise for Reagan's performance in Geneva, even though major issues are yet to be resolved. . .Page 22

Europe relieved
West Europe welcomes lessening of East-West tension. East Europe looks forward to increased contacts with West. . .Page 22

Soviet press
Gorbachev's cue on how official media will play summit: pick out positive elements, but say progress depends on US. . .Page 23

195

THE CHRISTIAN SCIENCE MONITOR

COPYRIGHT © 1986 THE CHRISTIAN SCIENCE PUBLISHING SOCIETY
All rights reserved   VOL. 78, NO. 44   AN INTERNATIONAL DAILY NEWSPAPER   WEDNESDAY, JANUARY 29, 1986   R   50¢ (60¢ Canadian)

EMBASSIES
Terrorism is hampering US diplomacy overseas **14**

PEACE FILMS
Documentaries from 24 countries on TV series **21**

SIN
Philippine cardinal warns against election fraud **7**

Shuttle tragedy stuns US, highlights dangers

Loss of Challenger and its crew underscores fact that spaceflight remains a pioneering endeavor, using cutting-edge technology

By Robert C. Cowen
Staff writer of The Christian Science Monitor

Boston

Tuesday's tragic loss of the shuttle Challenger and its crew has shocked the nation and the world.

It has also underscored the fact that manned spaceflight still is a pioneering venture.

Christa McAuliffe and her astronaut companions were not just travelers on a routine trip. Spaceflight is the cutting edge of humanity's continuing development. And like the great outreaching explorations of the past, there is significant risk involved.

President Reagan recognized this when he said that, in spite of the great sadness he feels at this tragic loss, he would tell schoolchildren, "You have to be out there on the frontier taking risks."

Seventy-five seconds into Tuesday's launch, the shuttle Challenger exploded, killing the seven-member crew. It was the first fatal in-flight accident in the history of the US space program. It also was the first launch from a new shuttle pad at Kennedy Space Center, and Mrs. McAuliffe was the first teacher scheduled to fly into space.

Sen. Jake Garn (R) of Utah, the first nonastronaut to fly on board a shuttle, said that the cause of the tragedy must be determined, but the spaceflight program has to go ahead. And former astronaut Sen. John Glenn (D) of Ohio declared, "After the investigations, we should proceed with the [shuttle] program and that would include the civilian-in-space program as well."

It is in this spirit that officials of the National Aeronautics and Space Administration (NASA) are preparing their investigation.

At this writing, neither the cause of the accident nor the exact fate of Challenger was yet known. The flight began with an apparently perfect liftoff after being delayed because of concern over icicles that had formed. Challenger's early ascent proceeded smoothly. The astronauts had

Please see **SHUTTLE** back page

AP PHOTOS

Challenger's crew

Challenger's crew, from left to right — Front row: Michael J. Smith, Francis R. Scobee, and Ronald E. McNair. Back row: Ellison S. Onizuka, Sharon Christa McAuliffe, Gregory B. Jarvis, and Judith A. Resnik. The crew was to have studied Halley's comet, and Mrs. McAuliffe, a high school teacher from New Hampshire, was to have conducted two classes from space. Their flight was tragically cut short by an explosion soon after launch (left).

Sentiment for tax increase of some kind grows as Congress reopens reform debate

By David T. Cook
Staff writer of The Christian Science Monitor

Washington

Act II of the nation's tax-overhaul drama is about to begin amid growing talk of a tax increase.

The Senate Finance Committee begins a series of hearings today on the economic impact of the tax-reform bill that the House of Representatives passed in December. After the hearings, the panel will draft the Senate version of tax "reform," President Reagan's top domestic priority.

Senior Reagan administration members are now saying that the Senate will probably need to impose some form of new consumption tax, like a tax on energy use, as well as limit the deduction of some state and local taxes.

Those steps will be needed to make the

> ● How Washington may dull Gramm-Rudman ax Page 3
> ● Coping with IRS changes in US tax forms Page 17

changes Mr. Reagan wants in the House bill and still produce a revenue-neutral bill, an unidentified senior administration official told the Washington Post. Mr. Reagan has insisted that the tax overhaul raise the same amount of revenue for the government as the current tax law.

Not only may new taxes be needed to keep the tax-overhaul process on track, but there is also growing sentiment in Congress and the country that a tax hike will be needed to cope with the deficit targets set by the balanced-budget law Congress passed last month.

White House officials said a major theme of President Reagan's delayed State of the Union address would be continued opposition to new taxes, on the ground that a higher federal income-tax bite would impose an additional burden

Please see **TAX** page 5

President insists space program go forward, delays State of Union address

By Charlotte Saikowski
Staff writer of The Christian Science Monitor

Washington

Sharing a nation's shock over the explosion of the Challenger, President Reagan has voiced his deep sorrow to the families of those who were aboard the space shuttle. But he also stressed the importance of going forward with space exploration.

Because of the tragic event yesterday, the President after consulting with leaders of Congress postponed his State of the Union address until next Tuesday. He also sent Vice-President George Bush to Cape Canaveral's Kennedy Space Center to convey his concern for the families of

those aboard the space shuttle.

Mr. Reagan instructed acting NASA director Bill Graham to fly to Cape Canaveral with the Vice President to begin probing the cause of the explosion and and then to proceed with the space program. "These people were dedicated to the exploration of space," the President stated. "We could do no more to honor them, these courageous Americans, than to go forward with the program."

The President was having an Oval Office meeting with top aides when he learned that the shuttle had blown up. He stood in "stunned silence" as he watched a televised replay of the disaster, said

Please see **REAGAN** back page

196

COPYRIGHT © 1986 THE CHRISTIAN SCIENCE PUBLISHING SOCIETY
All rights reserved   VOL. 78, NO. 63   AN INTERNATIONAL DAILY NEWSPAPER   WEDNESDAY, FEBRUARY 26, 1986   R   50¢ (60¢ Canadian)

Popular revolt sweeps Marcos out, Aquino in

With Marcos gone, US must rethink Philippine policy, starting with issue of asylum

By Peter Grier and George D. Moffett III
Staff writers of The Christian Science Monitor

Washington

Secretary of State George Shultz is not a dramatic man. But when he stood up in the White House briefing room Tuesday and announced that the rule of Philippine leader Ferdinand Marcos had finally ended, the event was all the more gripping for the flatness of Mr. Shultz's voice.

"The new government has been produced by one of the most stirring and courageous examples of the democratic process in modern history," he said. "We honor the Filipino people."

As Secretary Shultz left the room, cries of "Where is Marcos going now?" hung in the air. For the United States, that question is a crucial part of a larger issue — what is US policy toward the Philippines now going to be? "Events have unfolded so fast," a congressional source says. "There's just been no focus on what happens next."

Much of Washington's attention has been focused on what was seen as the tricky, inevitable slide of Mr. Marcos from power. That transition, in what some see as a minor diplomatic miracle, has apparently been accomplished without significant bloodshed or rise in anti-US feeling.

As the reporters' shouts indicated, Marcos himself is the first post-Marcos Philippine question. As of this writing, it was not clear whether the deposed autocrat was heading for the US, or using US transportation to go to another destination.

Shultz said that Marcos was welcome in the US, if that was where he wanted to come. Sen. Paul Laxalt (R) of Nevada, who has served as a personal messenger to Marcos for President Reagan, said that the former Philippine leader called him on Monday and sought assurance he would not be

Please see **MARCOS** *back page*

President Aquino beams after taking oath of office yesterday

Filipinos' last look at Marcos

Hours after taking the presidential oath for the fourth time, Marcos and his family left the opulent Malacañang Palace. All afternoon, tense scenes were played out in Manila as groups of loyalist and reformist soldiers battled each other. Crowds finally broke into the palace grounds, where an eerie, surreal silence pervaded. Story, Page 7.

Marcos flees palace in largely bloodless transition; Aquino faces daunting tasks, high popular expectations

By Paul Quinn-Judge
Special to The Christian Science Monitor

Manila

The Marcos era is over, ended by a popular rebellion that swept Corazon Aquino into power.

At 9 p.m. Tuesday, Manila time, Ferdinand Marcos, his family, and entourage fled by helicopter from the presidential palace.

Only hours before, he and Mrs. Aquino had each taken separate oaths of office in different parts of the city. At press time, the Marcoses were reported to be resting at Clark Field, the US air base 40 miles north of Manila.

After the jubilation dies down, Aquino faces daunting problems: an ailing economy, growing communist insurgency, signs of some friction between her supporters and those of Vice-President Salvador Laurel, and high popular expectations.

The end for Marcos came suddenly. Helicopters were heard over the capital around 8:30 p.m. Two were seen heading for the palace, shortly after another had landed briefly at the US Embassy. A few minutes later six truckloads of troops moved away at high speed from the direction of Malacañang, the presidential palace.

"We're going home," they said. "It's all over."

Ten minutes later reporters arrived at a deserted palace. Barbed-wire barriers were open, and two armored cars were moving back into an empty barracks. Lights still burned in the buildings, armored vehicles were still parked in the grounds, and the small stage where Marcos took his oath of office was still decked with flowers.

The sound of helicopters could be heard just behind the main palace building. At 9 p.m., the first helicopter lifted off. Troops were nowhere to

Please see **AQUINO** *back page*

The Grammys: forgotten winners, remembered losers

By Christopher Swan
Staff writer of The Christian Science Monitor

Boston

Goodman honored just last night

1977 FILE PHOTO

Last night they were making new legends in the record business by conferring Grammy Awards on the music industry's artists of choice. Winners of the miniature gramophone award will join the ranks of such "old" record-industry legends as Domenico Modugno, Vaughn Meader, Christopher Cross, and Toto.

These names may not be bronzed in your own personal hall of fame. Yet they have outpointed the likes of the Rolling Stones, Little Richard, Buddy Holly in getting Grammys for their current work.

In a business known for focusing on the vanishing point and honoring the instant, the record industry has established a track record of consigning even its own fleeting stars to the dark background and thrusting forth "safe" choices that left music lovers of all breeds scratching their heads.

Enduring jazz giant John Coltrane never got recognition from

Please see **GRAMMY** *page 23*

Gorbachev casts doubt on summit

Soviet leader cool to US arms offer

By Gary Thatcher
Staff writer of The Christian Science Monitor

Moscow

Soviet leader Mikhail Gorbachev says he sees no evidence of "serious preparedness" to reduce nuclear armaments in the latest arms control proposal he received from Washington.

The proposal was contained in a letter from President Reagan that was delivered to Mr. Gorbachev over the weekend. The Soviet leader seemed to cast doubt on whether he would attend a summit meeting with Reagan later this year in the United States unless substantial progress can be made on arms control.

"There is no sense in holding empty talks," Gorbachev said yesterday in a major address to the opening session of the 27th Soviet Communist Party Congress.

He suggested that "understanding could be reached" in two areas: a cessation of nuclear testing and the removal of US and Soviet intermediate-range missiles from Europe.

"If there is readiness to seek agreement" on these two issues, he said, "the question of the time of the [summit] meeting would be resolved."

So far, however, the Kremlin has refused to set a date for the summit, which is to be held in the United States.

His address to some 5,000 congress delegates lasted more than five hours and was nationally televised. Few new themes were evident during his address. He dwelt at length on shortcomings in the Soviet economy and the Communist Party.

He did not refer to former Soviet leader Leonid Brezhnev by name, but he made it clear that the Brezhnev years had been characterized by "inertness." In so doing, Gorbachev followed a Soviet tradition of blaming the

Please see **SPEECH** *page 28*

HOMELESS
Those without homes are usually eager for jobs and a new life **16**

ALAN PATON
First look at South African author's new work in progress **30**

COPYRIGHT © 1986 THE CHRISTIAN SCIENCE PUBLISHING SOCIETY
All rights reserved   VOL. 78, NO. 98   AN INTERNATIONAL DAILY NEWSPAPER   WEDNESDAY, APRIL 16, 1986   50¢ (60¢ Canadian)

Tallying diplomatic score of US raid on Libya

Libyan antiaircraft fire streaks skyward over Tripoli during attack by US jets Tuesday

Tuesday morning's air raids are over. The reaction is pouring in. Reagan's tough line quickly gathered widespread support at home. It received active backing from Britain's Margaret Thatcher, who risked political trouble by letting US planes use British bases. But the resort to force has isolated the US abroad, alienated the Arabs, and may put new obstacles in the road to Mideast peace.

By George D. Moffett III
Staff writer of The Christian Science Monitor

Washington

In the aftermath of the United States air attacks on Libya early Tuesday morning, a balance sheet of the pluses and minuses is being drawn up.

President Reagan and top members of his administration assert that the air strikes — though they will not "bring down the curtain on Qaddafi's reign of terror," as the President acknowledged in his televised address Monday night — do demonstrate to Col. Muammar Qaddafi that sponsoring international terrorism carries a heavy price.

Judging by initial public reaction, it is also clear that many Americans are satisfied and relieved that their government has taken forceful action against Colonel Qaddafi, whom the US accuses of sponsoring terrorist attacks against American citizens.

But there is a liability side to using Air Force and Navy strikes against five Libyan targets said by the administration to be related to Qaddafi's ability to direct terrorism.

Once again, the NATO alliance is strained as most of Washington's allies reject the Reagan approach. The Soviets promptly canceled the carefully arranged meeting between Secretary of State George Shultz and Foreign Minister Eduard Shevardnadze. And some Middle East experts are deeply concerned about the impact of the Reagan action on long-term US diplomatic interests in that part of the world.

Please see **QADDAFI** *back page*

Reactions at home and abroad

Turning point in US-Arab ties?

Special to The Christian Science Monitor

Tripoli, Libya

The air attack that President Reagan ordered on Libya early Tuesday may severely damage 200 years of often constructive American relations with the Arab world.

Arabs are angrily rallying to the support of Libyan leader Muammar Qaddafi, of whom millions of Arabs, and especially their governments, are not particularly fond. There is a sense in their broadcasts and the reactions of their leaders that something basic has changed in Arab-American relations.

"There may be a way to pick up the pieces," a Western ambassador said. "A real challenge now faces the US and all of us because of what the US has done. But it is very, very late to repair the damage."

Libyan state radio said tens of civilians were killed and residential areas in both cities bombed. Several buildings in downtown Tripoli were reduced to rubble.

Government officials took foreign reporters to Tripoli's affluent Bin Ashur residential neighborhood, where five or six civilian houses and the back of the French Embassy were damaged.

The attack is not expected to end Libyan or other Arab-sponsored terrorism against the United States. On the contrary, the civilian casualties are likely to generate new terrorism. The reported death of Colonel Qaddafi's daughter and the wounding of other members of his family could give him a martyr's image.

Please see **ARAB** *back page*

US raid on Libya marks shift in war on terrorism

By Rushworth M. Kidder
Staff writer of The Christian Science Monitor

With the United States air attack on Libya, a new chapter has opened in the Western world's response to international terrorism.

"This is a milestone," says Ray Cline, an expert on terrorism at the Center for Strategic and International Studies in Washington. "I think it will make a difference," he says, in the "covert war declared upon us" by Libya.

Many analysts agree that it will not be the final chapter, and that further attacks can be expected from Libyan-backed terrorists.

But the US raid has shifted the war against terrorism in at least three ways: militarily, diplomatically, and in the use of news media.

Military response. For the first time in the West's two-decade war against terrorism, US military might has been directed against a foreign government.

ANALYSIS

In the past, military responses to terrorist incidents had tended to come from small, elite commando units. Some, like the 1977 raid by German GSG-9 troops on a hijacked Lufthansa airliner in Mogadishu, Somalia, have been spectacularly successful. Others, like last November's storming by Egyptian troops of a hijacked Egyptian airliner in Malta, have been less so. But these raids were directed not at governments but at the terrorists themselves.

A larger-scale military operation occurred in 1983, with the shelling of Lebanon by the USS New Jersey. But even that action, which followed the death of 241 marines from a bombing at their barracks in Beirut, was part of a military operation involving uniformed troops, and was not aimed at the Lebanese government.

The last six months have seen at least three incidents where sophisticated military operations were used

Please see **RAID** *back page*

THEATER
New musical 'Big Deal' brings director Bob Fosse back to Broadway

23

LEONARD BECK
Rare-cookbook curator reads between the lines of ancient recipes

25

THE CHRISTIAN SCIENCE MONITOR

COPYRIGHT © 1986 THE CHRISTIAN SCIENCE PUBLISHING SOCIETY
All rights reserved

VOL. 78, NO. 108   AN INTERNATIONAL DAILY NEWSPAPER   WEDNESDAY, APRIL 30, 1986   50¢ (60¢ Canadian)

Soviet Union hit by nuclear disaster

The apparent meltdown at Chernobyl is a blow to the world's most ambitious nuclear power program. The accident caused widespread contamination of Soviet and foreign territories. Moscow is seeking help from the West as it aids victims. Related story, Page 3.

By Gary Thatcher
Staff writer of The Christian Science Monitor

Moscow

The Soviet Union has been hit by what is believed to be the most serious accident in the history of nuclear power production.

The Chernobyl nuclear power plant apparently suffered a core meltdown, leading to widespread contamination of not only Soviet territory, but neighboring countries as well. Two deaths have been confirmed, and thousands of people have been evacuated from the area surrounding the reactor, according to the Soviet news agency Tass.

Tass has provided only scant information about the accident. It said that part of the "structural elements of the building housing the reactor" had been destroyed or damaged. Western experts here say that indicates that the radioactive core of the reactor melted down, leading to an uncontrolled nuclear reaction.

Radioactive gases escaped from the reactor, and a radioactive cloud contaminated parts of the Soviet Union and sharply increased radiation levels in neighboring Finland and Sweden.

The accident occurred at the Chernobyl nuclear plant, north of Kiev, the capital of the Ukraine. The plant has four reactors, which are cooled by light water, nuclear experts say. They use graphite in the core as a moderator to help sustain the reaction.

Tass said medical aid was being administered at the site. Radio Moscow referred to "victims" of the "disaster," but provided no further details.

Although Tass said the "radiation situation" at the plant had "stabilized," Soviet officials asked West German and Swedish experts for technical advice on fighting fires in the plant. [An official of the West German atomic energy lobbying group said a Soviet diplomat had asked that antiradiation experts and medicine be made available, the Associated Press reported.]

The United States offered technical and humanitarian assistance.

Meanwhile, the Kremlin is refusing to provide details of what is actually taking place at the reactor site.

"We've heard nothing from the Soviets yet," a Western diplomat said.

The official silence is "unsatisfactory," said another, since the accident has already affected nearby countries.

In Dublin, Stanley Clinton Davies,

Please see **NUCLEAR** back page

Control panel at Chernobyl power station, before accident

There's Tex-Mex and Texarkana; now there's Tex-Taiwan

By Howard LaFranchi
Staff writer of The Christian Science Monitor

Missouri City, Texas

IT was no doubt the first appearance by Chinese dragons in Missouri City, but it probably won't be the last. Heralded by snaking "dragons," young men swinging martial-arts staffs, and a bilingual ribbon-cutting ceremony, the initial phase of what is being called the nation's first master-planned Chinatown opened over the weekend in this small city on the far southwest side of Houston.

To its Chinese-American developers, the project, called Tang City, represents the first fruits of a dream to bring a modern example of Chinese enterprise to the United States. For Houston in general, the 200-acre development, dominated at its entrance by a 65-foot-high, green-tile-roofed archway, symbolizes the tremendous growth the city has witnessed in its various Asian communities over the past decade. [**Efforts to lessen prejudice against Asian refugees in the US. See story, Page 3.**]

"Tang City will have a very strong Oriental flavor, but it will be different from what you normally see in a Chinatown," says Calvin Leung, the southern California developer who is Tang City's major investor. "I think it's something the Orientals here can be proud of, yet some-

Please see **CHINESE** page 28

Washington's 'revolving door' dilemma

By Charlotte Saikowski
Staff writer of The Christian Science Monitor

Washington

Michael Deaver is in hot water.

But the embarrassments of one former top White House aide, whose lobbying activities have spawned investigations and hearings, are only a symbol of the growing ethical problem of the selling of influence in Washington. Political observers voice concern that:

• During the Reagan administration, with its heavy stress on the marketplace and profit-taking and its constant downgrading of government, the trend toward "revolving door" influence peddling has intensified.

• The American people seem increasingly indifferent to and cynical about the federal government and the questionable ethical behavior of high officials.

As the Senate Judiciary Committee held hearings Tuesday on lobbying by former government employees, political analysts pointed out that influence peddling by those who have left public service is nothing new — either in Democratic or Republican administrations. But the practice has reached a grander scale.

"It's the magnitude of it," says John W. Gardner, founder of the private interest group Independent Sector, and a former Cabinet secretary. "In this administra-

Please see **DEAVER** back page

BANDPHOTO

Suharto has big plans for Indonesia as a regional power

Reagan in Bali: focus on Vietnam

By Clayton Jones
Staff writer of The Christian Science Monitor

Manila

President Reagan's talks this week with Southeast Asian allies — especially Indonesia — are expected to help Washington decide what to do next about improving ties with Vietnam.

Those ties are currently strained over the slow progress on the issue of American soldiers unaccounted for since the Vietnam war. They could become warmer or cooler, depending on how Mr. Reagan reads the mood of the United States' partners in the Association of Southeast Asian Nations (ASEAN) this week on the paradise isle of Bali.

Indonesia has been courting Hanoi, much to the displeasure of fellow-ASEAN member Thailand, which faces the threat of some 160,000 Vietnamese troops along its border with Cambodia. That's why Reagan's pri-

Please see **BALI** page 10

COPYRIGHT © 1986 THE CHRISTIAN SCIENCE PUBLISHING SOCIETY   VOL. 79, NO. 5   AN INTERNATIONAL DAILY NEWSPAPER   TUESDAY, DECEMBER 2, 1986   R   50¢ (60¢ Canadian)

All rights reserved

PLO resurgence in Lebanon

Entrenched presence in face of Shiite onslaught poses embarrassing dilemma, challenge for Syria

By Jim Muir
Special to The Christian Science Monitor

Nicosia, Cyprus

More than two months of fierce but unresolved battles between Palestinians and Shiite Muslim militiamen have left a resurgent Palestinian armed presence entrenched in Lebanon.

This presence is a major challenge to both Israel and Syria, as well as their local allies. Local political observers see it as a particular embarrassment and dilemma for Syria, whose efforts to sponsor a settlement were spurned by the Palestine Liberation Organization's leader, Yasser Arafat.

As with most developments in Lebanon, the observers see wider political issues and regional strategies tied up in the Palestinian resurgence.

The PLO, and Mr. Arafat in particular, are widely seen as trying to regain their lost foothold in Lebanon – both to keep alive their struggle against Israel and to irk the Syrians. If any peace agreement leaves

armed Palestinians in independent control of the refugee camps in Lebanon, this will be a major thorn in Syria's side, the observers say.

But if Damascus encourages its allies and proxies in Lebanon to go all out and overrun the camps, it would face condemnation and pressure not only from mainstream Arab states, but also from its allies, Libya and Iran.

Since the so-called "camps war" first erupted between the Shiite Amal militia and Palestinian fighters in Beirut refugee camps in May 1985, all of Amal's efforts to stifle a regrowth of Palestinian armed power in Lebanon have failed.

Syria, which has close political and military ties to Amal and is deeply and directly involved in Lebanon, has also tried to prevent a comeback by Arafat's men.

Arafat and some 10,000 PLO men were forced to evacuate Beirut in 1982 as a result of Israel's siege of the city. Since then, particularly in the past year, hun-

Please see **PLO** back page

As S. Africa rulers dig in, prospects for reform dim

By Ned Temko
Staff writer of The Christian Science Monitor

Johannesburg

Signs are increasing that the South African government has put off any major new retreat from the apartheid system of race segregation for at least five months – and probably for closer to a year.

Escalating Western sanctions, the likelihood of an early white-South African referendum or election, and the government's primary concern with quelling political unrest are all keeping political reform squarely on the back burner.

This, at least, is the private view of a variety of political analysts here, including members of President Pieter W. Botha's governing National Party, academics, and foreign diplomats.

"I think it is clear that reform is on hold at least through April," comments a politically moderate professor at Stellenbosch University, the academic mecca of South Africa's dominant Afrikaans-speaking whites. "The open question is what will happen after April." The professor says his personal view is that the moratorium on the repeal of

Please see **S. AFRICA** back page

Where Raisa goes, KGB follows

By Paul Quinn-Judge
Special to The Christian Science Monitor

New Delhi

THE men of the KGB's ninth directorate were taking no chances.

As the four bulletproof Zil limousines swung into the yard of the handicraft shop, bodyguards of the Soviet secret police (KGB) were already jumping out of the rear cars, closing the high gates of the compound, and surrounding Raisa Gorbachev's car. Other Indian and Soviet security men, more than 100 in all, had already sealed the building.

Raisa's shopping trip to the Indian Handicrafts Emporium – a rambling building just outside New Delhi filled with silks, handmade carpets, ivory, and jewelry – provided the press with a useful opportunity to see her up close. It also offered a chance to see the Gorbachevs' personal bodyguards in action. Both the bodyguards and Mrs. Gorbachev proved very good at their job; their objectives, however, were not always compatible.

The KGB's ninth directorate handles VIP protection. The Gorbachev family's body-

Please see **RAISA** page 20

Reagan is being urged by Republicans as well as Democrats to act decisively to restore trust in his presidency on the Iran-contra affair. His actions could make a difference for the GOP in who runs for the White House in 1988 – and who wins.

Iran crisis tests Reagan leadership

By Charlotte Saikowski
Staff writer of The Christian Science Monitor

Washington

This is Ronald Reagan's hour of decision.

As the crisis over the Iranian and Nicaraguan arms operations deepens, the President faces the imperative of restoring his credibility and showing that he – not his aides – is in charge. If he acts quickly and decisively, at the least changing the guard at the White House, he may still be able to put the present crisis behind him.

But if Mr. Reagan decides to ride out the storm without some bold action, say political friends as well as foes, he is likely to find himself in increasingly hot water. Even if it emerges that he did not personally know the details of the Iranian and Nicaraguan capers, he will be held responsible for not ensuring good management in his own shop.

Calls for a shake-up at the White House, appointment of an independent counsel to take over the Justice Department investigation of the Iranian arms sales, and a special session of Congress to initiate a Watergate-style probe continue to be heard among GOP lawmakers. It is felt that Congress has to be

Please see **CONTRAS** back page

If President Reagan tries to ride out the storm without bold action, say friends and foes, he is increasingly likely to find himself in hot water.

Being a good team player could hurt Bush in 1988

By John Dillin
Staff writer of The Christian Science Monitor

Washington

This week, Vice-President George Bush makes his first major speech since the secret funding for contra rebels hit the headlines. Political experts say he must put on a sterling performance.

It is widely agreed here that the current crisis puts Mr. Bush's political future in jeopardy.

"Bush has been hurt very badly," says political analyst Norman Ornstein of the American Enterprise Institute.

John Deardourff, a top GOP consultant, observes: "This has the potential for a devastatingly negative impact on Bush for 1988. He's the most seriously threatened. . . . From the purely political standpoint, the Republican Party has to reconsider how it approaches the 1988 election."

Bush has consistently led every poll as the party favorite for the 1988 presidential nomination. That strong position has been based on two things:

● Closeness to President Reagan.
● Loyalty to President Reagan.

Vice-President George Bush, with an apparent inside track to '88 GOP presidential nomination, could be derailed by the contra funding crisis.

Please see **BUSH** page 6

COPYRIGHT © 1987 THE CHRISTIAN SCIENCE PUBLISHING SOCIETY
All rights reserved   VOL. 79, NO. 120   AN INTERNATIONAL DAILY NEWSPAPER   TUESDAY, MAY 19, 1987   50¢ (60¢ Canadian)

US plays down attack on ship

Stark's reaction points up issue of fleet vulnerability

By Peter Grier
Staff writer of The Christian Science Monitor

Washington

United States officials are doing their best to play down the political significance of the May 17 Iraqi missile attack on a US Navy frigate in the Persian Gulf.

Both White House and Pentagon spokesmen on Monday affirmed their belief that the attack had been inadvertent, but they promised a full investigation.

"This tragic incident underscores the need to bring the Iran-Iraq war to the promptest possible end," President Reagan said in brief remarks at a White House ceremony.

The ship was hit just above the waterline, forward of its superstructure. Of the 28 confirmed dead, 25 were probably asleep in a forward berthing area.

Though the exact circumstances of the attack were still unclear as of this writing, serious questions as to the state of military readiness of the crippled frigate, the USS Stark, are beginning to emerge. The ship apparently used none of its defensive systems in an effort to shoot down or electronically confuse the missile that struck it.

"Why it did not, we don't know," said Vice-Adm. Henry Mustin, a deputy chief of naval operations, who briefed reporters on the incident.

Pentagon officials said that late Sunday evening, local time, radar picked up one or possibly two Iraqi F-1 Mirage jet fighters crossing out of Iraq and flying south, hugging the Persian Gulf coast. Sources with military experience in the area said the radar referred to was likely to be that of an airborne warning and control system plane flown out of Saudi Arabia. An AWACS craft is

Please see **STARK** back page

USS Stark: after being 'inadvertently' fired on, it didn't try to stop missile

Strike highlights risks to superpowers in Gulf
Arabs worry about US's next moves

By Jim Muir
Special to The Christian Science Monitor

Nicosia, Cyprus

The Iraqi air strike on the USS Stark is being seen in the Middle East as the first major test for Washington's post-Irangate policy of buttressing the Arab states of the Gulf region against any Iranian threat.

The incident, following hot on the heels of damage to two Soviet vessels in the Persian Gulf in the space of 10 days, also highlights the unpredictable dangers raised by the recent intensification of superpower involvement in the region.

Following a spate of Iranian attacks on ships bound to or from Kuwait, both Washington and Moscow responded to Kuwait's requests for help in protecting its shipping. Washington is close to completing an agreement whereby half of Kuwait's 22-

Please see **GULF** back page

'Reality' shapes Vietnam artist's style

By Clayton Jones
Staff writer of The Christian Science Monitor

Hanoi

ON the apartment wall of Vietnam's most famous living painter hangs a primitive wood sculpture of Buddhist fairies, slightly damaged in 1972 by an American bomb attack. "I picked it up from the ruins of a house up north," says Tran Van Can, sitting on a low bamboo chair in his Hanoi home. "I find it inspiring for the whimsical faces, carved by Vietnamese peasants."

The simple art and life of people are his favorite subjects, says Mr. Can. After five decades of working as an artist, he finds art styles just come and go – including his own. He began his painting career as a star pupil of French art teachers in colonial Hanoi during the 1930s. Today he is chairman of Vietnam's Fine Arts Association, which works closely with the Communist Party to create "constructive" art.

The evolution of his style, from classical European to what he calls "artist-cum-soldier," reflects not only his own life's work, but Vietnam's long transition from French colony to a communist-run nation.

"My style is based on reality, and reality starts from the people," he says, surrounded by a dozen of his works, mostly portraits. Two cats dart through the tall, shuttered windows of his small room as the sound of bicycle bells comes up from the street.

Please see **ARTIST** page 8

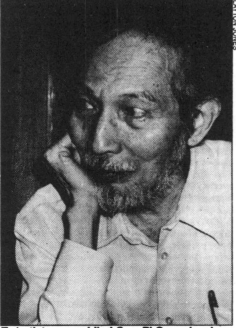

To 'artist-cum-soldier' Can, El Greco is a hero

Con artists move in on alien amnesty program

By Scott Armstrong
Staff writer of The Christian Science Monitor

Los Angeles

Authorities are gearing up for a boom in bogus documents as unethical elements try to take advantage of the new United States immigration law.

Since passage last year of the Immigration Reform and Control Act, officials of the Immigration and Naturalization Service (INS) have expected to see a plethora of fake rent receipts, utility bills, and other papers tailored to the requirements of the law.

And, as expected, there have been reports of unscrupulous consultants, notaries public, and others trying to take advantage of aliens as they seek to become legal residents.

Two weeks ago, INS agents seized more than 150 counterfeit documents and arrested two major suppliers of bogus papers in Los Angeles. The seized files included ID cards and other counterfeit papers that were backdated in an apparent attempt to establish the five-year residency required for amnesty under the new law.

In March, federal authorities arrested an immigration consultant from Chula Vista, near San Diego, for allegedly selling forged rent receipts to illegal aliens applying for legal status.

At the state and local levels a number of task forces are preparing to probe consumer complaints of illegal, unethical, or misleading practices carried out by immigration consultants, lawyers, and others.

"The vultures who prey on frightened and confused immigrants are already in business," says John Van de Kamp, California's attorney general, who has

Please see **BOGUS** back page

North's show is over, but key questions remain

Contra leaders amazed to find star witness's stunning appearance has helped their cause

By Marshall Ingwerson
Staff writer of The Christian Science Monitor

Miami

Nicaraguans opposed to the Sandinista regime have watched Lt. Col. Oliver North testify on Capitol Hill with a welcome wonder and some mixed emotions.

"Frankly," says Arturo Cruz, a former contra director, who resigned this spring from the United Nicaraguan Opposition, "I think he's the best thing that has happened for the contra movement."

Alvaro Jerez, a political party leader in the contra movement, has been astonished at what Colonel North hath wrought. He sat on a Miami beach with his family this weekend as an airplane towed the message: "We love Ollie North, America."

North has done what the Reagan administration has not been able to do in recent months, Mr. Jerez says, "and that is to turn public opinion."

After watching the leftist Sandinista government of Nicaragua consistently score public relations victories in the United States, notes Mr. Cruz, North's riveting testimony has turned the tables.

"This could be the first time the contra movement has had its day in court, so to speak, in this country," Cruz says.

Ironically, though, it was partly the strategy of North that favored the conservative faction of the contra movement, led by Adolfo Calero, and froze out the center-left leadership, such as Cruz and

Please see **CONTRA** *back page*

The Marine officer who captivated a nation
Ramrod straight and defiant to the end, Oliver North made a strong impression; but testimony may mean trouble for superiors. **Page 32**

A convicted drug smuggler is expected to testify on contra ties

By Dennis Volman
Staff writer of The Christian Science Monitor

Miami

While the Iran-contra hearings dominate American TV screens, some members of the Senate today will be listening with almost equal intensity to what is expected to be the startling testimony of a jailed Colombian drug smuggler.

Jorge Morales, who until his ar-

rest last year was a high-level drug operator in the Miami area, is expected to charge that top leaders of the contras' southern-front forces that formerly operated under Edén Pastora in Costa Rica cooperated in drug-smuggling ventures.

Mr. Morales's accusation will be made to a subcommittee of the Senate Foreign Relations Committee

Please see **DRUGS** *page 4*

His testimony under immunity makes it hard for Walsh to prosecute

By Nicholas C. McBride
Staff writer of The Christian Science Monitor

Washington

Mounting a successful prosecution against Lt. Col. Oliver North, following his performance in congressional hearings, will be extremely difficult, says former Watergate special prosecutor Charles Ruff.

The question, Mr. Ruff says, is whether the Iran-contra special prosecutor, Lawrence Walsh, has facts other than those disclosed by Colonel North under questioning in the joint House-Senate hearings.

Prosecutor Walsh is saddled with the inability to use testimony by North, compelled under a grant of "use immunity" by the congressional committees. Mr. Walsh and his staff cannot even develop leads from that testimony.

"The issue is not, can he prosecute," says Ruff, "but can he convince a court that the case he puts on hasn't been tainted by North's testimony."

North has acknowledged lying to Congress to help maintain the contra war in Nicaragua. In addition, he admitted to accepting a home security system worth $13,800, which was paid for with government funds, then writing fake letters to cover up that fact. North testified that he prepared false chronologies of events and admitted to shredding documents right under the noses of

Please see **WALSH** *page 6*

> ### Iran-contra hearings
>
> Future of contra funding is at stake, but so too is America's democratic process.
>
> **Opinion, Editorial Pages 14, 15**

AIDS: anguish in the clergy

Seeking a compassionate and moral stand, churches face Solomon-like choices

By David Winder
Staff writer of The Christian Science Monitor

London

THE problem of AIDS is confronting the world's religious communities with some of their most acute moral and ethical challenges since the permissive society dawned back in the 1960s.

An anguished debate in all the major faiths in Britain over the implications and consequences of acquired immune deficiency syndrome mirrors the wider international concern.

Writing in "AIDS, meeting the community challenge" (a compilation of articles by religious

leaders), the chief rabbi of Britain, Sir Immanuel Jakobowits, contends that the provision of condoms, which he feels condone and encourage sexual irresponsibility, is hardly the answer to AIDS. "What has to be carefully weighed is individual safety against the erosion of public standards," he writes.

To the chief rabbi, there's too much talk about the need for clean needles for intravenous drug users, who are among the known carriers of the AIDS virus, and not enough emphasis on clean speech, clean lives, and clean conduct.

Continued on Page 16

Strong US action would deter Iran, Gulf analysts say

By Warren Richey
Staff writer of The Christian Science Monitor

Manama, Bahrain

A direct US-Iranian military confrontation may be the fastest way to end the Gulf war, some observers here say.

Arab and Western analysts, who spoke on the condition they not be named, maintain that if the United States is to restore stability in the region, Washington must send a clear message to the government in Tehran – by force, if necessary.

"I think a showdown is long overdue," says a veteran Western diplomat. "With someone so fanatical, sometimes the only thing that will wake them up is a slap in the face."

"Something has to happen," adds a well-placed Arab analyst. He says that a growing number of Gulf Arabs are hoping that the American military will teach Iran a lesson in the weeks ahead. "It will put Iran in its place and make them think a million times before doing anything," he says.

Please see **GULF** *page 10*

US VS. JAPAN
Transpacific race to create superconductor markets

7

TELLURIS
Theoria
Sacra

BOOKS
Stephen Jay Gould and the meaning of history

21

THE CHRISTIAN SCIENCE MONITOR

COPYRIGHT © 1988 THE CHRISTIAN SCIENCE PUBLISHING SOCIETY
All rights reserved   VOL. 80, NO. 129   AN INTERNATIONAL DAILY NEWSPAPER   TUESDAY, MAY 31, 1988   50¢ (60¢ Canadian)

Arms control takes center stage in Moscow

MOSCOW SUMMIT

Soviet leaders wish the US President would ease off on human rights talk, but both sides are clearly willing to tolerate differences for a successful summit.

By Charlotte Saikowski
Staff writer of The Christian Science Monitor

Moscow

Despite dissonant notes on human rights, the superpower leaders appear to be making modest progress on strategic arms control.

As the second day of the United States-Soviet summit meeting drew to a close yesterday, Soviet spokesman Gennady Gerasimov said some progress had been made on the sticky issues of ground-based mobile missiles and air-launched cruise missiles (ALCMs).

But, Mr. Gerasimov indicated, there was no movement on the most difficult problems – sea-launched cruise missiles (SLCMs) and the question of space-based defense. It remains clear these are the principal stumbling blocks to completion of a strategic arms limitation (START) agreement before the end of the Reagan administration.

A senior US official, however, took issue with Gerasimov. He said there is no agreement on a verification scheme for mobile missiles, and that he was not quite as optimistic about the progress made on ALCMs.

Arms control aside, President Reagan yesterday experienced a series of extraordinary and in many ways moving events.

The American President who once called the Soviet Union an "evil empire" stood in Moscow's white-walled Danilov Monastery and gave a ringing call for religious liberty.

"We in our country share this hope for a new age of religious freedom in the Soviet Union,"

Please see SUMMIT back page

Soviet leader Gorbachev and President Reagan begin second day of summit conference

---

Heart of the church

A monastery President Reagan missed in Moscow symbolizes the spiritual core of the church.
Page 32

Soviet Jews in Israel

After battling Soviet system, émigrés face some readjustments in Israel. But sense of unity gets them through.
Page 9

Harnessing star power

Scientists from East and West look to the heavens and fusion energy to supply needs of a crowded world.
Page 20

The new détente

History offers some sobering lessons on how to view the changes under way in US-Soviet relations.
Page 9

Meanwhile, Soviet struggle goes on behind the scene

By Paul Quinn-Judge
Staff writer of The Christian Science Monitor

Moscow

For both supporters and opponents of reform in the Soviet Union, the summit is a sideshow.

Watching journalists set up their computers and cameras in the 1,000-capacity summit press center, a Soviet Communist Party official talked of the "real political struggle" that is pitting reformers against conservative party leaders. The struggle has intensified in recent months, with the approach of the nationwide party conference scheduled for the end of June.

The party official, a staff member of the Central Committee, noted that an attempt to derail the reforms in April had been beaten back. But, he predicted, opponents of the policies would probably try to strike again.

Some of the officials who have accompanied President Reagan to Moscow say that Mikhail Gorbachev is in firm command of the situation. Many Soviet observers see a precarious balance of power between Mr. Gorbachev and more-conservative leaders, headed by Yegor Ligachev, the official No. 2 man in the Soviet leadership. President Reagan will be meeting some of the most outspoken supporters of *perestroika* (restructuring) in two meetings today.

In the morning, he addresses a group of writers and intellectuals, many of whom have been in the forefront of change. In the afternoon, he is due to talk to students and faculty of the Moscow State University, the alma mater of Gorbachev and a number of other reform-minded leaders.

One United States official commented that Gorbachev's failure so far to move against conservative leaders was simply an effort

Please see STRUGGLE back page

N.H. MOUNTAINS
Presidential Range map project took 200 volunteers and 10 years **19**

CURIOUS GEORGE
50 years of monkey business delights young and old **23**

ART WORLD
Joyce Treiman, nonconformist painter, still wins considerable acclaim **21**

Bush tries to step from Reagan's shadow
Vice-president sets out own agenda on taxes, education, ethics, drugs

By John Dillin
Staff writer of The Christian Science Monitor

Washington

George Bush, who brags about his loyalty to the Reagan administration, has gradually begun to define some of his key differences with the Reagan White House.

The variations from Reagan policies aren't huge. But they encompass a range of vital issues, from the war on drugs to the education of America's youth.

In the drug war, Mr. Bush declares that he would intensify efforts to destroy drug laboratories and illicit crops in other nations. Mr. Reagan has put prime emphasis on interdiction at the United States border.

Politically, Bush's efforts to step out on his own carry risks. Some Bush advisers worry that if the vice-president appears to differ too sharply with Mr. Reagan, he could alienate his somewhat shaky political base among Republicans and independents.

Chip Nielsen, a Republican attorney and activist in San Francisco, puts it this way: "If you criticize Ronald Reagan in his own state [California], you are dead. He's still a god here."

Furthermore, Bush's close ties to Reagan have political advantages – and the vice-president wants to hold onto those. Peter Teeley, a Bush adviser, notes that the Reagan-Bush team can claim credit for lower inflation and interest rates, millions of new jobs, higher industrial productivity, progress on arms talks, and improved relations with the Soviet Union.

"There are a lot of benefits to being tied to this administration," Mr. Teeley says.

Yet it has become politically imperative for Bush to become his own man, analysts say. His standing in the polls tumbled drastically during the past 60 days. Voters express widespread unhappiness with him as a strong, decisive leader.

The newest Washington Post poll shows that voters consider Democrat

Please see BUSH page 4

COPYRIGHT © 1988 THE CHRISTIAN SCIENCE PUBLISHING SOCIETY
All rights reserved   VOL. 80, NO. 153   AN INTERNATIONAL DAILY NEWSPAPER   TUESDAY, JULY 5, 1988   50¢ (60¢ Canadian)

Mexicans go to the polls tomorrow in the most hotly contested presidential election ever. Despite opposition inroads, the ruling party is a sure winner – partly because it appeals to voters' basic conservatism.

Candidate Salinas: his party's grip is weakening

Mexico vote: it's the contest, not the winner, that counts

By Brook Larmer
Staff writer of The Christian Science Monitor

Mexico City
On the eve of the most competitive presidential election in Mexican history, the three main candidates are fighting over the same turf: the political center.

Despite widespread discontent with the country's authoritarian political system, the battle for the center shows a recognition of the basic conservatism that still pervades Mexican society, according to leading politicians and analysts here.

"Everybody in Mexico criticizes the system," says social scientist Ignacio Marvan.

"We despise corruption, ineptitude, and arbitrary decisions. But we don't want to invent a new country."

In a society seemingly obsessed with its violent past, memories of the bloody 1910-20 revolution and the 1968 student massacre loom as tangible warnings of extremism – and reminders of the value of stability. **(Candidate's adviser shot dead, Page 2.)**

In many ways, historical conservatism benefits the ruling Institutional Revolutionary Party (PRI), which has won every presidential, gubernatorial, and senatorial election since it emerged from the rubble of

Please see **MEXICO** page 13

Mexicans' shrinking purchasing power
Since last presidential election in July 1982*

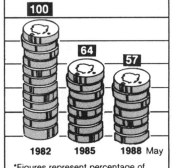

1982	1985	1988 May
100	64	57

*Figures represent percentage of 1982 buying power

Source: Bank of Mexico; Natl. Minimum Wage Commission

Searching for secrets in the stars
A look at astrology's ancient roots and modern practice in America

Recent revelations about astrology in high places are nothing new. This ancient belief has had its ups and downs for some 4,000 years. Its hold on modern thought – in America and around the world – has deep roots in history and culture. Here is the first of a two-part series that looks at astrology's influence and where it comes from.

By Alan Bunce
Staff writer of The Christian Science Monitor

SWINGING his hand toward a nearby rack, a busy Boston newsstand operator says, "Astrology magazines are selling like hotcakes. We carry six different kinds of them, and they go in no time."

A Florida professor reports: "The pendulum is swinging back! We're definitely seeing a resurgence of student interest in astrology and other aspects of

the occult."

In Buffalo, N.Y., a group of academics awaits replies to a letter sent to every major US newspaper, asking that disclaimers be run next to the growing number of horoscopes.

Religions condemn it. Scientists scoff at it. Comedians have a heyday with it. But astrology – the ancient belief linking events on earth to the movement of heavenly bodies – is on a roll.

Please see **ASTROLOGY** page 4

❛ **. . . the fault, dear Brutus, is not in our stars but in ourselves that we are underlings.** ❜

– Shakespeare, 'Julius Caesar'

US stands by its policy in the Gulf

Despite accident, officials see Navy role as effective

By E. A. Wayne
Staff writer of The Christian Science Monitor

Washington
Washington policymakers and lawmakers agree that the downing of an Iran Air jet on Sunday was "a terrible human tragedy," in President Reagan's words, and a blow to America's image.

But the incident has not generated pressure to change fundamental United States policy in the Gulf. Nor, US officials say, has it chilled an imminent warming in US-Iran relations, as some reports suggested. In fact, they say, there is nothing brewing.

Confusion about downing – and Iran's war aims.
Pages 9, 36

"This is a tragedy, but it doesn't do anything to change the basic outlines of what has been a relatively successful policy," says a well-placed official, "nor does it change the facts of the situation that led to that policy."

President Reagan said US warships will remain in the Gulf in the wake of the US missile attack on the Iranian jetliner with 290 people

Please see **GULF** back page

SOVIET CONFERENCE

Gorbachev gets support – and a taste of Soviets' deep concerns

By Paul Quinn-Judge
Staff writer of The Christian Science Monitor

Moscow
The just-completed Communist Party conference marks a watershed in the history of Soviet reform.

By sleight of hand and force of personality Mikhail Gorbachev has shifted the center of attention to the reshaping of political institutions. A clear timetable has been laid out for the changes **(see Page 5)**.

But the conference, which ended Friday, also revealed the remarkable diversity of political views within the Soviet Communist Party.

The conference was a personal victory for Gorbachev – and arguably a more discreet victory for the architect of radical reform, Alexander Yakovlev. Gorbachev proved wrong pessimistic predictions that the debate would get bogged down in wrangling and recriminations.

It was, however, a paradoxical victory. He

Please see **SOVIET** page 5

AIRBUS
European jetmaker sees no end to subsidies **18**

BIOBRICKS
Recycling sludge into high-quality, energy-efficient bricks **21**

DANCE
Mark Morris bids US farewell, as he moves his troupe to Belgium **24**

COPYRIGHT © 1988 THE CHRISTIAN SCIENCE PUBLISHING SOCIETY
All rights reserved   VOL. 80, NO. 186   AN INTERNATIONAL DAILY NEWSPAPER   FRIDAY, AUGUST 19, 1988   R   50¢ (60¢ Canadian)

GULF CEASE-FIRE

MELANIE STETSON FREEMAN - STAFF

Ramadi, Iraq: Iranian prisoners of war are to be repatriated under terms of the UN cease-fire resolution

Eight years and a war later . . .

Iranian revolution can now turn its attention inward

By Robin Wright
Special to The Christian Science Monitor

Washington

For Iran, the formal implementation tomorrow of the United Nations cease-fire is just the first step of a broader strategy to initiate a new phase in its revolution.

The goal is to ensure the Islamic revolution's survival, which has become more urgent because of Ayatollah Ruhollah Khomeini's failing health. Ending the costly conflict now opens the way for Tehran to address political and economic problems that had begun to undermine the ruling mullahs, and to set a framework for the future before the imam's passing.

The new agenda taking shape involves several significant and related changes:

● Finally addressing economic issues, specifically the role of the state in creating what the theocrats

Please see **IRAN** *page 6*

Iraq faces host of challenges on diplomatic, economic fronts

By Jim Muir
Special to The Christian Science Monitor

Nicosia, Cyprus

Iraq's President Saddam Hussein has been behaving as though he had won the war with Iran, declaring a three-day national holiday in honor of Iraq's "victory." But the belief is gaining ground among observers in the region that he may lose the peace.

Iran's acceptance of a UN cease-fire, scheduled to take effect Saturday (11 p.m. Friday EDT), opens the way for a rush of outside interest in restoring ties with Tehran. At home, Mr. Hussein could face severe economic problems as resources poured in from wartime supporters are curtailed. And there is speculation that he may face challenges to his ruthless rule once his Army is no longer fully engaged in battle.

Members of a UN force have arrived in Iran and Iraq to monitor the cease-fire. Direct peace talks are

Please see **IRAQ** *page 6*

SPUTTERING START

Bush, Quayle launch race with clouds looming

By John Dillin
Staff writer of The Christian Science Monitor

New Orleans

THE race for the White House officially begins today, but Republicans are off to a stumbling start.

George Bush and Dan Quayle fly to Indiana to launch their campaign in Senator Quayle's home state, but in this convention city, Republican insiders are asking: Did Mr. Bush make a mistake?

Mr. Quayle, untested on the national scene, finds himself besieged with questions about his background after Mr. Bush picked him for the No. 2 spot.

Potentially the most damaging incertitude was summed up in a banner headline in the Times-Picayune of New Orleans: "Draft-dodger questions dog Quayle."

Former Treasury Secretary James Baker III, who takes over today as director of the Bush campaign, says Quayle may have obtained family help in getting into the National Guard in 1969 – at a time when draftees were being sent to Vietnam.

If the "draft dodger" label sticks, it could not only damage Quayle's reputation, but it could undercut Republican strategy to use the defense issue against Democrat Michael Dukakis.

Ed Rollins, a Republican consultant who managed President Reagan's 1984 race, says the Bush-Quayle ticket can still recover. On Thursday many observers continued to say that an effective acceptance speech by Bush would be a large stride in that direction (Bush spoke after the Monitor's deadline).

Please see **GOP** *back page*

Other coverage inside

■ For Bush campaign, it's Jim Baker to the rescue. **Page 14**

■ Republicans admit Dukakis will be tough opponent. **Page 15**

■ 'Youth vote' a quirk, not a constant in elections. **Page 28**

FLASH: America is losing its cool!

By Mark Clayton
Staff writer of The Christian Science Monitor

Boston

THIS year's Great Heat Wave has gradually turned into the Great Air Conditioner Shortage of 1988.

In a Boston appliance store, Marcos Bigil gazes at a display of room air conditioners. He twists the knobs and looks longingly at the exposed and gleaming cooling coils. All of these models, he knows, are already sold out, and have been for about two weeks. No new shipments are expected.

Still, hope springs eternal.

"I thought I would look now – for next year," says Mr. Bigil, who is no stranger to hot weather. Bigil and his family moved from El Salvador to the United States eight years ago.

Now, however, he lives in a small apartment in Cambridge, Mass. The apartment has been so hot this year that Bigil has found himself lugging his family's lone air conditioner (a small window unit) from room to room.

"In San Salvador it is hot," Bigil says. "You get used to it. But the

weather here in Boston was terrible last week, and it is beautiful today. Tomorrow, who knows?"

Room air conditioners lately have become nearly as endangered as the snail darter. Bigil's plight is mirrored a thousandfold across the nation's heat belt, as air conditioner manufacturers and appliance dealers concede there is indeed a nationwide shortage.

"There are virtually no air conditioners in the marketplace," says Michael Piraino, a Whirlpool merchandising manager in charge

Please see **COOL** *page 11*

INNER-CITY ENTREPRENEURS
Teacher explains basics and teens in South Bronx start businesses of their own

17

THEATER
Original cast gathers again to stage prizewinning musical 'Ain't Misbehavin' '

20